HANDBOOK
OF EDUCATIONAL
PSYCHOLOGY

HANDBOOK
OF EDUCATIONAL
PSYCHOLOGY

SECOND EDITION

EDITED BY

PATRICIA A. ALEXANDER

PHILIP H. WINNE

LEA
LAWRENCE ERLBAUM ASSOCIATES, PUBLISHERS
2006 Mahwah, New Jersey   London

Editorial Director:	Lane Akers
Assistant Editor:	Karin Willig-Bates
Cover Design:	Tomai Maridoy
Full-Service Composition:	TechBooks
Text and Cover Printer:	Hamilton Printing Company

This book was typeset in 10/12 pt. ITC Garamond Roman, Bold, and Italic.
The heads were typeset in Novarese, Novarese Medium, and Novarese Bold Italic.

Lawrence Erlbaum Associates, Inc., Publishers
10 Industrial Avenue
Mahwah, New Jersey 07430
www.erlbaum.com

Library of Congress Cataloging-in-Publication Data

Handbook of educational psychology / edited by Patricia Alexander, Philip Winne.—2nd ed.
   p. cm.
  1st ed. edited by: David C. Berliner and Robert C. Calfee.
  Includes bibliographical references and indexes.
  ISBN 0-8058-4937-8 (clothbound : alk. paper)—ISBN 0-8058-5971-3 (pbk. : alk. paper)
  1. Educational psychology—Handbooks, manuals, etc.
  I. Alexander, Patricia A.   II. Winne, Philip H.
  LB1051.H2354   2006
  370.15—dc22   2005035459

CONTENTS

Part
I
FOUNDATIONS OF THE DISCIPLINE   1

v

Part
IV
MOTIVATION 325

Part
V
EDUCATIONAL CONTENT 425

Part
VIII
ASSESSMENT OF LEARNING, DEVELOPMENT, AND TEACHING 823

FOREWORD

Philip H. Winne
Simon Fraser University

Patricia A. Alexander
University of Maryland

Handbooks are becoming practically ubiquitous. There are handbooks of and for jazz, nuclear properties, the modern world, tennis, comets, flags, acoustic ecology, experimental economics, ballet accompanists, African languages, flavor ingredients... and more. When the term appeared in the English language circa 900 A.D., according to the Oxford English Dictionary, a handbook was—surprise!—a book that could be held in the hand, often intended to provide guidance for completing a task—a manual. Nine hundred years later, circa 1800, the meaning of *handbook* was elaborated to refer to volumes that collected articles in succinct form about a wide variety of topics.

A decade ago, David C. Berliner and Robert C. Calfee compiled the *The Handbook of Educational Psychology*. This first edition of the Handbook had an elegant and seminal architecture. In the contemporary sense of a handbook, to quote from its book jacket, Berliner and Calfee's *Handbook*

for the first time in the history of the field, gathered in one definitive reference work the theories, research, and methodologies of leading educational psychologists throughout the world. It [was] designed for a professional audience as a source of background information, but also as a tutorial. [Authors were charged] to prepare chapters that build on the history of a particular domain, lay out seminal issues and questions, and survey the major results and puzzlements, illuminating each with in-depth descriptions of particular findings, and connecting the domain with important questions that warrant further investigation, as well as with implications for practice and policy.

The first *Handbook of Educational Psychology* was not a manual in the literal sense—holding a 1,071-page tome in the hand is a challenge few of us can meet! Notwithstanding, it unequivocally was designed to help a diverse audience advance their respective engagements in education by enlarging and updating their work with state-of-the-art facts and properly validated scientific interpretations. It was specifically written to guide graduate students, teachers, researchers, and policymakers in their respective pursuits to shape and understand effective and rewarding education at all levels in all subjects.

Production of this second edition of the *Handbook* was initiated by Patricia A. Alexander and Paul R. Pintrich following approval in August 2002 to develop a plan for the project under the aegis of Division 15—Educational Psychology of the American Psychological Association. Alexander and Pintrich sought and received informed and thoughtful input on a preliminary plan from a board of advisors, whom we acknowledge for their contribution on p. xii of this volume. On July 12, 2003, Paul Pintrich died just as the project was taking final shape and preparing to launch. Alexander approached Philip H. Winne to take up the role of coeditor and, with heavy heart, he agreed.

This second edition of the Handbook had been designed to achieve the same goals as its predecessor and, in light of changes since that monumental work, to take on several new challenges. Key features of our plan for this new edition build on the superlative platform established in the first edition. But the field and its context have changed since the first volume was developed. In particular, even though the time scale is short for as robust and wide a field as educational psychology, diversity of views has increased. Major policies have come into force. And, the occasional skirmish of paradigms has flared.

Our response in designing this Handbook was to celebrate diversity, to highlight roles for educational psychology in meaningful and policy-laden situations, and bring forward for close and critical inspection—diplomatically, we hope—paradigmatic issues. The major sections of this new edition reflect an attempt to coalesce without constraining the major facets of educational psychology. In re-examining this framework and the informative chapters in each of the volume's major sections, we perceive the field of educational psychology is approaching a cusp, a metaphor we adopt for its beautiful imagery of paths traveled along several arcs that will and ultimately do intersect. The source for our speculation reaches back to the roots of empirical work in our field.

Nearly a century ago, E. L. Thorndike mentored the field of educational psychology about how to pursue elegant and cumulative empirical investigations of theory with a balanced dedication to what we today label *technology transfer*—making applications of theory to practice that "add value" to what was done before. Although he and others of the field's progenitors recognized and researched the nature and bounds of generalization and transfer, they adopted either explicitly or implicitly a stance that the human mind they studied in the laboratory setting and with contrived tasks such as paired associates of nonsense syllables was the same kind of mind that crafted complex essays, learned to speak a foreign language, comprehended and used arithmetic, and made choices about how to solve problems in school and in life. Although properties of prior knowledge, features of a particular situation, and other variables matter—indeed, transfer remains a central challenge for the field—the ontological stance of their research entailed that principles in theory necessarily have practical application.

It is this commonplace that leads us to offer the metaphor of a cusp. Notwithstanding what is said pejoratively about theory, we believe it does have practical implication. What we suggest as one source of problems in building bridges from theory to practice is the all too large challenge of language: How might theory be described so that its applications become more apparent?

With this question, we set a stage for you, our reader, from which to survey this state-of-the-art compendium of educational psychology. We invite you to challenge each author or team of authors and, in so doing, to travel the arcs toward the potential of this cusp. It remains to you and the editors of this volume's successor to assess whether and, possibly, to what degree our speculation holds.

ACKNOWLEDGMENTS

We are immeasurably in the debt of our Board of Advisors for their sage counsel and genuinely constructive critique:

David C. Berliner, University of Arizona
Robert C. Calfee, University of California, Riverside
James Greeno, University of Pittsburgh
Richard E. Mayer, University of California, Santa Barbara
Gary Phye, Iowa State University
Daniel H. Robinson, University of Texas at Austin
Paul Schutz, University of Georgia
Richard J. Shavelson, Stanford University
Allan Wigfield, University of Maryland
Philip H. Winne, Simon Fraser University (Canada)
Barry J. Zimmerman, City University of New York Graduate Center

We thank Lane Akers of Lawrence Erlbaum Associates for his contagious enthusiasm, unfailing support, and savvy mentoring in bringing this volume to press.

Authors and the reviewers of their chapters set an extraordinary standard for superb scholarship and collegiality in making this *Handbook* a significant resource for the field and a stimulus for its continued evolution.

LIST OF CONTRIBUTORS

Phillip L. Ackerman
School of Psychology
Georgia Institute of Technology
Atlanta, GA 30332-0170

Patricia A. Alexander
Department of Human Development
College of Education
University of Maryland
College Park, MD 20742-1131

Donna E. Alvermann
Department of Language & Literacy Education
309 Aderhold Hall
University of Georgia
Athens, GA 30602-7123

Eric M. Anderman
Department of Educational and Counseling
   Psychology
University of Kentucky
Lexington, KY 40506-0001

Roger Azevedo
University of Maryland
Department of Human Development
3304 Benjamin Building
College Park, MD 20742

Brigid Barron
School of Education
485 Lausen Mall
Stanford University
Stanford, CA 94305-3096

Philip Bell
Cognitive Studies in Education
College of Education
University of Washington
312 Miller Hall, Box 353600
Seattle, WA 98195-3600

Carl Bereiter
Institute for Knowledge Innovation and
   Technology and Ontario Institute for
   Studies in Education
University of Toronto
252 Bloor St. W.
Toronto, Ontario M5s 1V6
Canada

David C. Berliner
Educational Leadership and Policy Studies
College of Education
Arizona State University
PO Box 870211
Tempe, AZ 85287-0211

John Bransford
College of Education
University of Washington
210 Miller Hall, Box 353600
Seattle, WA 98195-3600

Eric Bredo
Department of Leadership, Foundations
   and Policy
University of Virginia
Charlottesville, VA 22903

Jere Brophy
Department of Teacher Education
Michigan State University
East Lansing, MI 48824

Deborah L Butler
Department of Educational Counselling
Psychology, and Special Education
University of British Columbia
Vancouver, BC V6T 1Z4
Canada

James P. Byrnes
Department of Psychological Studies
College of Education
Temple University
1301 Cecil B. Moore Ave.
Philadelphia, PA 19122

Robert Calfee
School of Education,
Stanford University,
Stanford CA 94305-3096

Harris Cooper
Program in Education
Box 30739
Duke University
Durham, NC 27707-0739

Heather A. Davis
College of Education
The Ohio State University
Ramseyer Hall 165A
29 West Woodruff Ave.
Columbus, OH 43210

Jacquelynne S. Eccles
Gender and Achievement Research Program
Institute for Research on Women and Gender
University of Michigan
204 S. State St.
1251 Lane Hall
Ann Arbor, MI 48109-1290

Kadriye Ercikan
Educational and Counselling Psychology and Special
   Education
Faculty of Education
2125 Main Mall
University of British Columbia
Vancouver, BC, V6S 1Z4

Bat-Sheva Eylon
Department of Science Teaching
Weizmann Institute of Science
Rehovot 76100
Israel

Jill Fitzgerald
School of Education
Peabody Hall CB 3500
The University of North Carolina at Chapel Hill
Chapel Hill, NC 27599-3500

Douglas H. Fuchs
313 MRL Building
Box 328 Peabody College
Department of Special Education
Nashville, TN 37203

Steve Graham
Vanderbilt University
Box 328 Peabody College
Department of Special Education
Nashville, TN 37203

Patricia M. Greenfield
Department of Psychology
University of California, Los Angeles
1285 Franz Hall
Box 951563
Los Angeles, CA 90095-1563

Allyson F. Hadwin
Department of Educational Psychology & Leadership
   Studies
University of Victoria
Victoria, BC, V8W 3N4
Canada

Diane F. Halpern
Psychology Department
Claremont McKenna College
850 Columbia Avenue
Claremont, CA 91711

Karen Harris
Vanderbilt University
Box 328 Peabody College
Department of Special Education
Nashville, TN 37203

Anita Woolfolk Hoy
College of Education
The Ohio State University
Ramseyer Hall 159A
29 West Woodruff Ave.
Columbus, OH 43210

Ton de Jong
Faculty of Behavioral Sciences
University of Twente
PO BOX 217
7500AE Enschede, The Netherlands

Janna Juvonen
Department of Psychology
University of California, Los Angeles
Los Angeles, CA 90095

Heidi Keller
Department of Culture and Development
University of Osnabrueck
Seminarstrasse 20
49069 Osnabrueck
Germany

Patricia K. Kuhl
Institute for Learning and Brain Sciences
University of Washington
Box 357920
Seattle, WA 98195-7920

Susanne P. Lajoie
Department of Educational and Counselling
    Psychology
3700 McTavish St
McGill University
Montreal Quebec H3A 1Y2

Margarita Limón
Departmento de Psicologia Básica
Facultad de Psicologia
Universidad Autónoma de Madrid
Cantoblanco, 28049
Madrid, Spain

Marcia C. Linn
4523 Tolman Hall #1670
Graduate School of Education
University of California at Berkeley
Berkeley, CA 94720-1670

David F. Lohman
Psychological & Quantitative
    Foundations
College of Education
The University of Iowa
Iowa City, IA 52242

Lucia Mason
Department of Developmental and
    Socialisation Psychology (DPSS)
University of Padova
Via Venezia, 8
35131 Padova, Italy

Gerald Matthews
Department of Psychology
University of Cincinnati
Cincinnati, OH 45221

Richard E. Mayer
Department of Psychology
University of California
Santa Barbara, CA 93106-9660

Andrew N. Meltzoff
Institute for Learning and Brain
    Sciences
University of Washington
Box 357920
Seattle, WA 98195-7920

Debra K. Meyer
Faculty of Education
Elmhurst College
190 Prospect Avenue
Elmhurst, IL 60126

Kevin F. Miller
Combined Program in Education and Psychology
610 E. University Avenue
Ann Arbor, MI 48109

Frederick J. Morrison
Department of Psychology
530 Church St.
University of Michigan
Ann Arbor, MI 48109-1043

P. Karen Murphy
Educational Psychology
229 CEDAR Building
The Pennsylvania State University
University Park, PA 16802-3109

Nailah Nasir
Psychological Studies in Education
School of Education
Stanford University
Stanford, CA 94305-3096

John C. Nesbit
Faculty of Education
Simon Fraser University
Burnaby, BC, V5A 1S6
Canada

Angela M. O'Donnell
Department of Educational Psychology
Rutgers, The State University of New Jersey,
GSE, 10 Seminary Place,
New Brunswick, NJ 08901-1183

Lynn Okagaki
Department of Child Development and Family
    Studies
Purdue University
West Lafayette, IN 47907-2020

Amado M. Padilla
School of Education
Stanford University
Stanford, CA 94305-3084

Stephen J. Pape
College of Education
The Ohio State University
Arps Hall 333
1945 N High Street
Columbus, OH 43210

Scott G. Paris
Department of Psychology
530 Church Street
University of Michigan
Ann Arbor, MI 48109-1043

Roy Pea
School of Education
Stanford University
Stanford, CA 94305-3096

Stephen C. Peck
Institute for Research on Women and Gender
University of Michigan
Ann Arbor, MI 48109-1290

Nancy E. Perry
Department of Educational and Counselling Psychology
    and Special Education
University of British Columbia
2125 Main Mall
Vancouver, BC V6T 1Z4
Canada

Jules M. Pieters
Faculty of Behavioral Sciences
University of Twente
PO BOX 217
7500AE Enschede, The Netherlands

Michael Pressley
College of Education
Michigan State University
East Lansing, MI 48824

Blanca Quiroz
Department of Teaching, Learning and Culture
College of Education and Human Development
MS 4232,
Texas A&M University
College Station, Texas 77843-4232

Byron Reeves
Wallenberg Hall, Room 229
Stanford University
Stanford, CA 94305

Thomas G. Reio, Jr.
Department of Leadership, Foundations and Human
    Resource Education
University of Louisville
Louisville, KY 40292

Richard D. Roberts
ETS (Center for New Constructs)
Rosedale Road MS 16-R
Princeton, NJ 08541

Robert W. Roeser
Department of Applied Psychology
Steinhardt School of Education
New York University
New York, NY 10011

Jeremy Roschelle
Center for Technology in Learning
SRI International
333 Ravenswood Ave.
Menlo Park, CA 94025

Carrie Rothstein-Fisch
Department of Educational Psychology and Counseling
Michael D. Eisner College of Education
California State University, Northridge
18111 Nordhoff Street
Northridge, CA 91330-8265

Nora H. Sabelli
Center for Technology and Learning
SRI International
BN 316
333 Ravenswood
Menlo Park, CA 94025

Marlene Scardamalia
Institute for Knowledge Innovation and Technology
    and Ontario Institute for Studies in Education/
    University of Toronto
252 Bloor St. W.
Toronto, Ontario M5s 1V6
Canada

Alan H. Schoenfeld
Education, EMST
Tolman Hall # 1670
University of California
Berkeley, CA 94720-1670

Gregory Schraw
Department of Educational Psychology
University of Nevada, Las Vegas
PO Box 453003
Las Vegas, NV 19154

Dale H. Schunk
329 Curry, University of North Carolina at Greensboro
1000 Spring Garden Street
Greensboro, NC 27402

Dan Schwartz
School of Education
Stanford University
Stanford, CA 94305-3096

Michele L. Simpson
Institute of Higher Education
University of Georgia
Athens, GA 30602

M Cecil Smith
Department of Leadership, Educational Psychology &
    Foundations
Northern Illinois University
DeKalb, IL 60115-2854

Reed Stevens
Cognitive Studies in Education
College of Education
University of Washington
406A Miller Hall, Box 353600
Seattle, WA 98195-3600

Lalita K. Suzuki
HopeLab
101 University Avenue, Suite 220
Palo Alto, CA 94301

Carol Kehr Tittle
Ph.D. Program in Educational
    Psychology
Graduate School and University Center
The City University of New York
365 Fifth Avenue
New York, NY 10016

Elisa Trumbull
6363 Longcroft Drive
Oakland, CA 94611

Julianne C. Turner
Department of Psychology
University of Notre Dame
Notre Dame, IN 46556

Bruce A. VanSledright
Department of Curriculum and Instruction
University of Maryland
College Park, MD 20742

Nancy Vye
College of Education
University of Washington
210 Miller Hall, Box 353600
Seattle, WA 98195-3600

Allan Wigfield
Department of Human Development
University of Maryland
College Park MD 20742

Philip H. Winne
Faculty of Education
Simon Fraser University
Burnaby, British Columbia V5A 1S6 Canada

Christopher A. Wolters
Department of Educational Psychology
University of Houston
Houston, TX 77204-5029

Daniel B. Wright
Psychology Department
University of Sussex
Falmer, Drighton
BN1 9QH United Kingdom

Moshe Zeidner
Center for Interdisciplinary Research of Emotions
University of Haifa
Mt. Carmel, 31905, Israel

Barry J. Zimmerman
Graduate Center, City University of New York
365 5th Avenue
New York, NY 10016

HANDBOOK REVIEWERS

Peter Afflerbach
University of Maryland

Richard Allington
University of Tennessee

Mark Aulls
McGill University

Keith Barton
University of Cincinnati

Camilla Benbow
Vanderbilt University

Phyllis Blumenfeld
University of Michigan

Mimi Bong
Ewha Womans University

Roger Bruning
University of Nebraska

Michelle Buehl
University of Memphis

Joseph Campione
University of California, Berkeley

Jerry Carlson
University of California, Riverside

Alice Corkill
University of Las Vegas, Neveda

Lyn Corno
Teachers College, Columbia University

Ann Cunningham
University of California, Berkeley

Richard De Lisi
Rutgers, The State University of New Jersey

Andre diSessa
University of California, Berkeley

Carol Dwyer
Educational Testing Service

Barry J. Fishman
University of Michigan

Helenrose Fives
Texas Tech University

Nathaniel L. Gage
Stanford University

Mark Gierl
University of Alberta

Shawn Glynn
University of Georgia

Sandra Graham
University of California, Los Angeles

Susan Harter
University of Denver

Cindy Hmelo-Silver
Rutgers, The State University of New Jersey

Shelley Hymel
University of British Columbia

Janis Jacobs
Pennsylvania State University

David Jonassen
University of Missouri

Daniel Keating
University of Michigan

Jonna Kulikowich
Pennsylvania State University

Virginia Kwan
Princeton University

Peter Lee
University of London

Xiaodong Lin
Teachers College, Columbia

Kathryn Lindholm-Leary
San Jose State University

Joost Lowyck
Catholic University Leuven

David Lubinsky
Vanderbilt University

Charles MacArthur
University of Delaware

Ellen Mandinach
Center for Children and Technology

Herbert Marsh
University of Western Sydney

Michael Martinez
University of California, Irvine

Dennis McInerney
University of Western Australia

Judith Meece
University of North Carolina, Chapel Hill

David Moore
Arizona State University West

Richard Newman
University of California, Riverside

Martin Packer
Duquesne University

P. David Pearson
University of California, Berkeley

Denis Phillips
Stanford University

Barbara Plake
University of Nebraska, Lincoln

Richard Prawat
Michigan State University

Ralph Putman
Michigan State University

Jonmarshall Reeve
University of Iowa

Alexander Renkl
University of Freiburg

Ralph Reynolds
University of Nevada, Las Vegas

Dan Robinson
University of Texas, Austin

Todd Rogers
University of Alberta

Don Saklofske
University of Saskatchewan

R. Keith Sawyer
Washington University in St. Louis

Ulrich Schiefele
University of Bielefeld

Val Shute
Educational Testing Service

Gale Sinatra
University of Nevada, Las Vegas

Jan Sinott
Towson University

Robert Slavin
Success for All

Nancy Songer
University of Michigan

Robert Stevens
Pennsylvania State University

Deborah Stipek
Stanford University

Lee Swanson
University of California, Riverside

Bruce Thompson
Texas A&M University

Dennis Thompson
Georgia State University

Lisa Towne
National Research Council

Gary Troia
University of Washington

Megan Tsannen-Moran
College of William and Mary

Tim Urdan
University of Santa Clara

Peggy Van Meter
Pennsylvania State University

Simone Volet
Murdoch University

RoseMary Webb
Vanderbilt University

Noreen Webb
University of California, Los Angeles

HANDBOOK
OF EDUCATIONAL
PSYCHOLOGY

FOUNDATIONS
OF THE DISCIPLINE

EDUCATIONAL PSYCHOLOGY: SEARCHING FOR ESSENCE THROUGHOUT A CENTURY OF INFLUENCE

David C. Berliner
Arizona State University

We start the 21st century with ideas that had not gained widespread attention until after the middle, or near the end, of the 20th century. In the study of learning, new ideas include situated cognition, constructivism, social constructivism, cultural-historical perspectives, and various other cognitive and Vygotsky-inspired approaches to learning, to name but a few. We weave into our studies of learning concerns about metacognition and self-efficacy, topics that were not found to be of great interest until closer to the end of the past century, though such topics were easily found in nascent form in James's *Principles of Psychology* and Dewey's *How We Think* (Pajares, 2000). In our new century the perspectives of other social and behavioral sciences are now more common. We see this in the development of concern for the idiographic as well as the nomothetic in our research, in employment of design experiments, and in our increased understanding of the sensibility of using multimethod forms of inquiry. We now know that Pasteur's quadrant (Stokes, 1997) is a proper place for educational psychology to do much of its work, as exemplified by the distinguished research careers of Ann Brown (Palincsar, 2003) and Lauren Resnick (see, for example, Learning Research Development Center, 2001). As we start this new century we also note that the ubiquity of the computer and the creativity of our scholars now provide us with powerful new methods of data analysis, such as hierarchical linear modeling, and powerful ways to visualize the data we obtain

from any of our analyses. The computer may also allow brain researchers of this century to finally realize Lashley's early 20th-century ambitions for the direct physical study of learning.

Perhaps these contemporary ideas, perspectives, and methods will stay with us for a century. But if history is our guide it is more likely that by the end of the 21st century many of these ideas will have been replaced with newer ways of thinking to guide the 10th generation of educational psychologists. (We begin as a discipline around the start of the 20th century. Thus, with about 20 years per generation, those near the end of their careers, like me, are only the fourth generation of educational psychologists. Those who were trained and started their careers around 1980, and holding leadership roles today, are the fifth generation. Our history is quite short!)

Our newest scholars are likely to move past the current ideas and topics that are of interest, as we moved past the behaviorism of Watson, Thorndike, and Skinner; moved beyond simple animal models of motivation based on drive reduction theory; and have finally downgraded the importance of significance testing (Kline, 2004). There is now less interest in many topics that were, in their day, vitally important: creativity, process-product research, nonsense syllables and verbal learning studies devoid of real contexts, concept learning, taxonomic work on academic and affective objectives, mastery learning, programmed instruction, and many others.

Clearly educational psychology changed over the 20th century, and it is likely to do so again in this new century. In writing this introduction to our history, I hope to help us understand what was stable amidst the change: to look at what makes us educational psychologists and not some other kind of social scientist or professional educator. I seek in this chapter to understand the essence of educational psychology by looking first at our roots in ancient history, and then at some of the people and research trends that affected us over the past century, particularly focusing on the founders of our field.

Excellent history has been written by professionals such as Joncich (1962, 1968) and Lagemann (2000), but their focus was not always educational psychology, per se. Nonhistorians among our colleagues in educational psychology have done that job admirably, for example, the contributors to Glover and Ronning's (1987) edited book on *Historical Foundations of Educational Psychology* and those contributing to Zimmerman and Schunk's edited book on *Educational Psychology: A Century of Contributions* (2003). As an amateur historian I relied heavily on these secondary sources. A more insightful history of our field will occur when we can attract professional historians to look at our discipline with professionals' eyes. Until then, amateurs like myself will try to make sense of our past for those who use this volume to build our future.

THE ORIGINS OF EDUCATIONAL PSYCHOLOGY

The emergence of the modern discipline of educational psychology can be traced to the same year in which Granville Stanley Hall called 26 colleagues to his study to organize the American Psychological Association (APA). Although we are not sure that Hall's summer meeting ever really took place (Hothersall, 1984), something motivated people between July and December 1892 to attend the founding meeting of the APA, hosted by the University of Pennsylvania. From the very beginning of the APA, psycho-educational issues were important to its leaders, and those issues influenced the growth of modern academic and scientific psychology. But our origins predate the start of academic and scientific psychology.

The Distant Past

Our field probably started unnoticed and undistinguished, as part of the folk traditions of people trying to educate their young. For example, the ancient Jewish ritual of Passover precedes the work of Cronbach and Snow (1977) by hundreds if not thousands of years, yet fully

anticipates their inquiries into aptitude–treatment interactions. The leader of the Passover service is commanded to tell the story of Passover each year but is ordered to tell it *differently* to each of his sons, according to their individual differences. To the wise son he teaches the entire story, with all its details and complexity. To the contrary son he teaches in a way that emphasizes belonging to a community. To his simple son the leader responds in still different ways. It is likely that even before these times, from the emergence of *Homo sapiens*, whoever reflected on teaching probably had thoughts that we would now label as mainstream educational psychology. It could not have been otherwise. To reflect on *any* act of teaching and learning demands thinking about individual differences, development, the nature of the subject matter being taught, problem solving, assessment, and transfer. These psychological topics are central to education, and therefore are central to human social life. Thus many of our current interests have been the subject of discussion down through the millennia. These foci are part of what is essence in educational psychology, but it is clear these topics are not ours alone.

In the fifth century B.C., Democritus wrote about the advantages conferred by schooling and the influence of the home on learning (R. Watson, 1961). A century later, Plato and Aristotle discussed the following educational psychology topics (Adler, 1952; R. Watson, 1961): The kinds of education appropriate to different kinds of people; the training of the body and the cultivation of psychomotor skills; the formation of good character; the possibilities and limits of moral education; the effects of music, poetry, and the other arts on the development of the individual; the role of the teacher; the relations between teacher and student; the means and methods of teaching; the nature of learning; the order of learning; affect and learning; and learning apart from a teacher. What we think of as essence in educational psychology has a long history in philosophy and education.

During Roman times, Quintilian (35–100 A.D.) argued in favor of public rather than private education to preserve democratic ideals—a battle still being fought today. He condemned physical force as a method of discipline, commenting that good teaching and an attractive curriculum take care of most behavior problems—advice that is as appropriate today as it was 2000 years ago. He urged that teachers take into account individual differences, suggesting that they take time to study the unique characteristics of their students, pre-dating the child study movement of the early 20th century. Quintilian also set forth criteria for teacher selection (Quintilian's *Institutio Oratoria*, translated by Butler, 1953; *Quintilian on education*, translated by Smail, 1966; Wilds & Lottich, 1964). Quintilian's arguments, though archaic in form, are still functional educational psychology today. For example, in Book 1 of the *Oratoria* he writes:

As soon as the child has begun to know the shapes of the various letters, it will be useful to have them cut out on a board, in as beautiful script as possible, so that the pen may be guided along the grooves. Thus mistakes such as occur with wax tablets will be impossible to make for the pen will be confined between the edges of the letters and will always be prevented from going astray. (Adapted from the Butler and the Smail translations)

Similar advice might be given by some educational psychologists and psychologically trained special educators. But now it would be B. F. Skinner's work on error reduction that would be cited, rather than a 2000-year-old reference by a nonacademic!

The Renaissance

Comenius (1592–1671), a humanist writing at the beginning of the modern era, also influenced both educational and psychoeducational thought (1657; and Broudy, 1963). He wrote texts based on a developmental theory, and in them inaugurated the use of visual aids in instruction. Media and instructional research, a vibrant part of contemporary educational psychology, has its origins in the writing and textbook design of Comenius. He recommended that instruction start with the general and then move to the particular, and that nothing in books be accepted unless checked by a demonstration to the senses (Broudy, 1963). He taught that understanding, not memory, is the goal of instruction; that we learn best that which we have an opportunity to teach; and that parents had a role to play in the schooling of their children. Every topic of 350 years ago that was addressed by Comenius is still with us today, especially concerns about how development and information technologies influence instruction.

The contributions of one of our many ancestors, Juan Luis Vives (1492–1540), are often overlooked, yet he wrote very much as a contemporary educational psychologist might. In the first part of the 16th century (Charles, 1987; Vives, 1531/1913), he taught teachers and others with educational responsibilities, such as those in government and commerce, that there should be an orderly presentation of the facts to be learned. In this way Vives anticipated Herbart and the 19th-century psychologists, perhaps even anticipating the standards movement in modern America. Vives noted that what is to be learned must be practiced, and in this way anticipated Thorndike's law of exercise. He wrote on practical knowledge and the need to engage student interest, anticipating Dewey. He

wrote about individual differences and the need to adjust instruction for all students, but especially for the feeble-minded, the deaf, and the blind, anticipating the work of educational psychologists in special education and the area of aptitude–treatment interaction. He discussed the schools' role in moral growth, anticipating the work of Dewey, Piaget, Kohlberg, and Gilligan. He wrote about learning being dependent on self-activity, a precursor to contemporary research on metacognition, where the ways in which one monitors one's own cognitions are studied. Finally, Vives wrote about the need for students to be evaluated on the basis of their own past accomplishments, and not in comparison to other students, anticipating both the contemporary motivational theorists who eschew social comparisons and those researchers who find the pernicious elements of norm-referenced testing to outweigh their advantages. Thus, long before we claimed our professional identity, there were individuals thinking thoughtfully about what we would eventually call educational psychology. Our roots are seen to be deep within the corpus of work that makes up Western intellectual history. If we choose to claim these scholars as our ancestors, then parts of what is essence in educational psychology are made manifest: individual differences in learning, especially for those with disabilities; motivation, especially learning guided by interest and a need for concern about social comparisons; ordering of learning through objectives, hierarchies, structures, advance organizers, curriculum standards, and the like, so that learning promotes transfer; project methods of learning for learning by doing; evaluation that is mastery oriented as well as comparative; and so forth.

What Is Educational Psychology?

In looking at the past it seems clear that it is not learning theories such as constructivism or behaviorism that unite or divide us. Nor is it method of inquiry such as ethnography or randomized clinical field studies that unites or divides us. Neither theory nor method is essence for educational psychology. Our essential concern is a set of related fundamental topics about human teaching and learning, with particular emphasis on the empirical study of those phenomena. Philosophical, political, and other analytic work on these issues is not unrelated to what is essence in educational psychology, nor is work from sociological, anthropological, economic, or other social science viewpoints. But if we look at our origins we see that the fundamental nature of our enterprise is about using psychological concepts and methods for understanding the four commonplaces of education that philosopher Joseph Scwhab (1973) first made popular:

someone (a teacher, parent, or technological device) teaches *something* (how to fix a bicycle, two-column addition with regrouping, the periodic table) to *someone else* (a student, novice, worker) in *some setting* (classroom, garden, assembly line).

The teaching and learning that we study almost always takes place inside the intersection of *teachers* × *students* × *task* × *setting*. The complexity mounts for educational psychologists because it is not merely teachers that we study, but all the attributes associated with teachers such as their training, intelligence, ethnicity, sociability, actions, and myriad other characteristics that are our concern, along with attributes of nonhuman teachers such as instruction by means of print, television, and computers. The complexity of the teacher facet is matched by the complexity associated with the learner or student facet as we study students' attributes such as their sociocultural history, intellectual ability, social class status, motivation, and parental educational level. Curriculum complexity is manifest in the diverse subject areas we encounter or try to understand, including mathematics, history, physical education, art, music, and vocational preparation. And within each of those areas we often must choose subtopics to study, such as the teaching and learning of percent, fractions, or word problems in mathematics, or an appropriate instructional design for fostering learning how to repair a carburetor. The setting facet is not any less complex because learning differs in the classroom, playground, assembly line, or at home, and it differs whether learning is taking place in group or individual settings, as well.

Essence for educational psychologists is the study of these phenomena, often in interaction, and our reward occurs when we detect a signal amid the noise created through the interactions of, literally, hundreds of variables. It is complex enough an enterprise to make some educational psychologists and social scientists despair (e.g., Cronbach, 1975, 1982; Gergen, 1973), although others remain optimistic (Gage, 1996; Shavelson & Towne, 2002).

It is certainly true that educational research is hard-to-do social science research (Berliner, 2002). And because of the immense complexity of what we study, we do not always design our research to explore the full four-way interaction that lies at the heart of the educational psychologists' interest. We do what scientists often do: we simplify in order to understand. One way we simplify is to retreat from the real world of practice. We also simplify by studying one or two of the four commonplaces with little regard to the other two or three. But Schwab (1973) noted that these commonplaces must not just be present in our research, they must be equal in rank in terms of our interests: "coordination, not superordination–subordination is the proper relation of these four commonplaces" (p. 509). By adopting the reasonable scientific strategy of simplification in experimentation, we may sometimes appear irrelevant to educators needing to be successful in environments of greater complexity than the psychological laboratory. Irrelevance, sadly, may also be essence for educational psychology, a problem that has been noted often throughout the brief history of our field.

The irrelevance I talk about throughout this paper is from the viewpoint of the practitioner and is not a charge that comes from many of our own educational psychologists, though some certainly do make that claim (e.g., Jackson, 1981). Educational psychologists clearly have made important contributions to the study of transfer, memory, learning via technology, control of the behavior of special students, classroom management, bullying, group work, teacher thinking, the teaching of various subject matters, assessment, and dozens of other areas. But the scientific work for which we are justifiably proud seems not to translate easily into practice. For whatever reasons, we do not affect the lives of teachers in the ways we had hoped. Our scientific work often has implications for classroom practice, but does not end up often *changing* practice. Irrelevance is a charge that we live with, perhaps because scientists and practitioners have different perspectives on what constitutes useful research, and the complexity of classrooms makes implementing laboratory findings so difficult. When I discuss irrelevance as essence in this paper, I am only pointing out a long-standing problem of our discipline, not asking readers to accept the truth of this claim.

HERBART AND THE BEGINNING OF MODERN EDUCATIONAL PSYCHOLOGY

In this brief reminder of our roots we must note also the mid-19th century philosopher and psychologist Johann Friedrich Herbart (1776–1841). He not only may be considered the first voice of the modern era of psychoeducational thought, but his disciples, the Herbartians, played a crucial role in preparing the way for the scientific study of education and therefore for educational psychology. Herbartians wrote about what we now call *schema theory*, advocating a cognitive psychology featuring the role of past experience and schemata in learning and retention. Herbartians promoted teaching by means of a logical progression of learning, a revolutionary idea at the end of the last century. They promoted the five formal steps for teaching virtually any subject matter: (1) *preparation* (of the mind of the student, which today we would call bringing forth the relevant schema for learning and finding ways to engage students' interest), (2) *presentation* (of the material to be learned, in some sensible sequence), (3) *comparison* (the teacher shows how new learning is related to old learning), (4) *generalization*, and (5) *application* (the latter two stages were about teaching for transfer and making sure that the learning had concrete referents). Clearly American Herbartians of the 19th century were quite modern sounding. It was the Herbartians, also, who first made pedagogical technique the focus of scientific study, and thus pointed the way, eventually, to the field of research on teaching.

Although the Herbartians oversold their ideas, and claimed a scientific base that they did not have, the educational psychologists emerging at the end of the 19th century owed them a monumental debt. It was the Herbartians who played a crucial role in convincing the teachers and school administrators of America that education was a field that could be studied scientifically. Just before the turn of the 20th century the National Herbart Society for the Scientific Study of Education founded a yearbook series under that name. The yearbooks of that organization and its successor (the National Society for the Study of Education [NSSE]), featured chapters on the emerging science of pedagogy written by prominent educational psychologists. Current yearbooks do the same.

Science and Education

In this 21st century it is easy to forget how remarkable the work of Wundt, Ebbinghaus, and James was at the end of the 19th century. In their laboratories they each developed experimental methods to study mind. This was a breakthrough of enormous magnitude because until then mind had been the domain of philosophers, and thus outside the purview of science. Thus, as the 20th century dawned, their influence allowed for something quite new, namely, the use of experimental methods for the study of teaching, learning, curriculum, and the like. Empirical investigations in these areas were not easily accepted by most educators of those times.

Opposition to experimentation in education was thus based, in part, on the strong belief that education is a philosophical and moral endeavor, and therefore, its problems could not be subjected to scientific study. Such beliefs permeated education because its leaders often came from religious backgrounds and training (Tyack & Hansot, 1982), rather than from either the liberal arts or the then-emerging sciences. Breaking down the resistance to science as a means for the study of education, and the acceptance of scientific findings as a guide to educational policy, was one of the most important events in the history of our field. Currently, precisely *what* it is that we mean when

we claim to do science in education is the subject of intense debate (Berliner, 2002; Ericson & Guiterrez, 2002; Gage, 1994; Shavelson & Towne, 2002), but challenges to scientific approaches to the study of education are simply no longer an issue. Those whose scholarship is not ordinarily classified as scientific, such as educational researchers doing narrative, critical, or arts-based research, do not regard the scientific research of educational psychologists as wrong or inappropriate. Their concerns are much more about the dominance of scientific approaches to research at the expense of other ways of doing serious, rigorous, and informative educational inquiry. The interchange between educational psychologist Richard Mayer (2000, 2001) and arts-based researcher Thomas Barone (2001) is a good example of this debate.

The pendulum has swung: a hundred years earlier it was science that was struggling for legitimation against a discourse that was overwhelmingly philosophical and moral. Now it is the hegemony of that scientific approach that is under attack by others. And it was educational psychology, more than any other organized community of scholars, that helped to win the battle for using scientific methods to understand and improve education. Thus, when we speak of educational psychology historically, we see a focus on the "scientific" (and thus the empirical) study of education. And to promote inquiry of that kind, many of our colleagues have been involved in measurement and statistics over the years. This was a common way for educational psychologists to become "scientific," for to many in our field, *scientific* meant "quantitative," revealing a confusion about science that still exists today.

Paving the Way for Thorndike

It is customary to attribute the paternity of educational psychology to E. L. Thorndike, whose contributions I will note later. He was bright, brash, and amazingly productive, and as he proceeded to organize the field, he revealed an unshakable faith that psychological science could solve many of the ills of society. But others set the stage for him, and they need to be remembered as well.

One of those who set the stage for Thorndike was the great muckraker and classroom observer Joseph Mayer Rice (1912), the father of research on teaching. Rice endured great difficulties for his beliefs just a few years before the experimental psychology of E. L. Thorndike was deemed acceptable. In 1897, at Atlantic City, New Jersey, Rice was asked to present his empirical classroom-based research on the futility of the spelling grind to the annual meeting of school superintendents. He used achievement test data in ways unique for his time. His audience was not as polite as today's administrators, since they attacked the speaker, yelling the equivalent of "Give him the hook." Leonard P. Ayres (1912) reports on the meeting as follows:

The presentation of these data threw that assemblage into consternation, dismay, and indignant protest. But the resulting storm of vigorously voiced opposition was directed, not against the methods and results of the investigation, but against the investigator who had pretended to measure the results of teaching spelling by testing the ability of the children to spell.

In terms of scathing denunciation the educators there present, and the pedagogical experts who reported the deliberations of the meeting to the educational press, characterized as silly, dangerous, and from every viewpoint reprehensible the attempt to test the efficiency of the teacher by finding out what the pupils could do. With striking unanimity they voiced the conviction that any attempt to evaluate the teaching of spelling in terms of the ability of the pupils to spell was essentially impossible and based on a profound misconception of the function of education. (p. 300)

The school administrators would not hear Rice's research because faculty psychology was still dominant, and thus it was clear to them that the spelling faculty needed exercise; besides, it was good for children to work hard and memorize, learning obedience, diligence, and habits of concentration along the way. At that late 19th–century meeting it was the process, not the outcome, that determined "good teaching." Good teaching, a normative judgment, was more valued than efficient, effective, or successful teaching, terms that derive their meaning from empirical data. Educational leaders could not imagine deciding educational issues on the basis of scientific work. Decisions about what was best for children, they thought, were best made by those with a religious background or philosophic training, called to the profession to take responsibility for educating the young. These pervasive views had to be overcome before Thorndike could establish the dominance of empirical/scientific studies of education, as spread so thoroughly by the educational psychology community that followed Thorndike.

By 1912, however, the climate had undergone a change. At that year's meeting of the superintendents, 48 addresses and discussions were devoted to tests and measurement of educational "efficiency." Underlying the addresses and discussions was the proposition "that the effectiveness of the school, the methods, and the teachers must be measured in terms of the results secured" (Ayres, 1912, p. 305). In 1915 the antiscience forces had their last chance to challenge the new science, and they lost. Charles Judd (1925) remarked about that superintendent's meeting:

There can be no doubt as we look back on that council meeting that one of the revolutions in American education was accomplished by that discussion. Since that day tests and measures have gone quietly on their way, as conquerors should. Tests and measures are to be found in every progressive school in the land. The victory of 1915 slowly prepared during the preceding twenty years was decisive. (pp. 806–807)

The Grandfather and Granduncles of Educational Psychology

Three individuals who prepared the way to that victory over the antiscience forces were William James, his student G. Stanley Hall, and his student John Dewey. These three men—whom I think of as our grandfather and granduncles—distinguished themselves in general psychology as well as in educational psychology, fields that overlapped considerably at the end of the last century. The science that these three men promoted, however, was not the science that was ultimately adopted by our field. Instead, Thorndike's views were predominant for most of a century. But I will argue that Thorndike's version of science and his vision of educational psychology led us to a narrower conception of our field than would have been true had the views of the others among our ancestors gained more prominence.

William James (1842–1910)

The central figure in the establishment of psychology and educational psychology in America was William James. Compared to his contemporary the great Wilhelm Wundt (1832–1920), the German founder of experimental psychology, James was said to have had "the courage to be incomplete" (Boring, 1957, p. 516). His was a psychology of humility, humor, and tolerance, particularly when it is compared to the psychology of Wundt or later, that espoused by James' very serious student E. L. Thorndike. James' *Principles of Psychology* (1890), published after 12 years of labor, was the preeminent event in American psychology (Barzun, 1983), though Professor James did not think so at the time. When he finally sent the manuscript to his publisher, Henry Holt, he wrote (H. James, 1920):

No one could be more disgusted than I at the sight of the book. *No* subject is worth being treated of in 1000 pages! Had I ten years more, I could rewrite it in 500; but as it stands it is this or nothing—a loathsome, distended, tumefied, bloated, dropsical mass, testifying to nothing but two facts: 1*st*, that there is no such thing as a *science* of psychology, and 2*nd*, that W. J. is an incapable. (p. 294)

James' version of psychological science argued against the elementism of the Europeans, giving us instead the notion that consciousness was continuous, a stream, and not easily divisible. Moreover, and still more startling, he said consciousness chooses, it controls its own attention. Thus, built into James' views of experimental psychology were cognitive and teleological conceptions of individuals. These were precisely the conceptions the nascent behaviorists chose to ignore, and in doing so, sowed the seeds of their own eventual demise. Self-regulation is clearly rooted in James' psychology (Pajares, 2003), but was shunted aside as an object of study for almost a century.

What James wanted was for psychologists to remember that there were other legitimate ways to conduct inquiries about human consciousness and behavior than those that became favored by the behaviorists. He might well have joined Barone (2001) in his argument with Mayer (2000, 2001) over the role of science in educational research. James was quite catholic in his views of science, whereas Thorndike, his student, was not. Certainly James would have found nothing wrong with a rigorous scientific and strongly behavioral psychology if it helped the field make progress (he was, after all, a founder of pragmatism, a philosophy where the utility of an idea is the way of determining its truth). But if James had commented on the scientific and behavioral psychology that emerged more strongly just after his death, he might have scolded that it could not provide a complete picture of humans, that it afforded merely a glimpse of those complex beings.

The *Principles* also made much of the role of nurture by emphasizing the plasticity of the nervous system, at least among the young. Thus James saw education as a crucial element of society, with the school a place for habits to be acquired by design, not willy-nilly. In his emphasis on habit he provided the intellectual environment for his student E. L. Thorndike, who would more thoroughly explore habit formation in school and out. Sadly for psychologists, the *Principles* marked the point at which philosophy rather than psychology was to dominate James' life. But in that philosophy he gave us another set of uniquely American views, pragmatism, in which the test for truth was whether or not ideas worked for the individual. As a result, James took away the eternal verities of Aristotle and the revealed truths of religion and gave us social criteria for determining truth. Pragmatism and James made clear that "Truth" would forever after be written with a small "t." Testing whether ideas work, whether they were functional for the individual or for an animal (the distinction between human and animal disappeared after Darwin), led to psychology's

development of functionalism. This set of beliefs (see Angell, 1907) became the theoretical underpinning for growth in many areas of psychology, particularly applied psychology, where the search for functional relationships rather than for grand theory was honored. Functionalism, known as the criterion-of-effectiveness paradigm in educational and industrial research (Gage, 1963), gave educational psychology its early character.

In 1891 Harvard's administrators asked James to provide some lectures on the new psychology to the teachers of Cambridge, Massachusetts. These talks were polished and expanded over the years and published in 1899 as the now famous *Talks to Teachers on Psychology* (W. James, 1899/1983). With that book we have our field's first popular educational psychology text, reporting speeches first delivered in 1892 (see p. 3, W. James, 1899/1983).[1] The lectures of 1892 mark the beginning of a vigorous educational psychology presence in America because a scholar of international renown had become associated with our field and provided intellectual grounding for its growth. And it was also in this year that APA, with William James as one of its leaders, was founded. Both psychological science and one of its major subdisciplines, educational psychology, may be said to begin their modern forms in 1892. (See the *William James* Web site for more about the accomplishments of this great American thinker: http://www.emory.edu/EDUCATION/mfp/james.html#talks. The full texts of both the 1899 *Talks to Teachers* and the *Principles* are available there.)

Although James may be thought of as our grandfather, he did not have much respect for the teachers to whom he spoke. On teachers' comprehension of his lectures, he said: "A teacher wrings his very soul out to understand you, and if he ever does understand anything you say, he lies down on it with his whole weight like a cow on a doorstep so that you can neither get out nor in with him. He never forgets it or can reconcile anything else you say with it, and carries it to the grave like a scar" (W. James, 1899/1983, p. 241).

And during his 1898 lecture tour to California he wrote to his brother Henry that it ended in a blaze of glory,

with many thanks for having emancipated the school teachers' souls. Poor things they are so servile in their natures as to furnish the most promising of all preys for systematic mystification and pedantification on the part of the paedogogic authorities who write books for them, and when one talks plain common sense

---

[1]In the preface to *Talks to Teachers,* James wrote, "In 1892 I was asked by the Harvard Corporation to give a few public lectures on psychology to the Cambridge teachers." But in the history and the letters covering the origins of that series of lectures (p. 234, W. James, 1899/1983), it appears that James began them in the fall of 1891 and finished them in the winter of 1892. He appears to have forgotten some of the background to the origins of the lecture series when he wrote the preface, which was approximately seven or so years later. He regarded the enterprise as forced labor and lamentable work (p. 234), so it is not surprising if some error of memory occurred.

with no technical terms, they regard it as a sort of revelation. (W. James, 1899/1983, p. 241)

James' science was an eclectic one, and this he communicated in his talks to teachers. In one of his *most* quoted and *least* influential statements, conspicuously ignored by educational psychologists over the years, we find James saying:

You make a great, a very great mistake, if you think that psychology, being the science of the mind's laws, is something from which you can deduce definite programmes and schemes and methods of instruction for immediate school-room use. Psychology is a science, and teaching is an art; and sciences never generate arts directly out of themselves. An intermediate inventive mind must make that application, by using its originality. (W. James, 1899/1983, p. 15)

James recognized that psychologists could not tell educators precisely what to do:

A science only lays down lines within which the rules of the art must fall, laws which the follower of the art must not transgress; but what particular thing he shall positively do within those lines is left exclusively to his own genius.... To know psychology, therefore, is absolutely no guarantee that we shall be good teachers. To advance that result we must have an additional endowment altogether, a happy tact and ingenuity to tell us what definite things to say and do when that pupil is before us. That ingenuity in meeting... the pupil, that tact for the concrete situation, ... are things to which psychology cannot help us in the least. (W. James 1899/1983, pp. 15–16)

James did not espouse the psychology or the science that Thorndike would soon promote, and James' science was not the kind called for by the U.S. Department of Education in its No Child Left Behind Act of 2001. While essence of educational psychology can be found in experimental work, James further understood that such work was needed in the field, not the laboratory. He might well have applauded the move to design experiments (Brown, 1992; Schoenfeld, in press), and been leery of the federal government's reliance on randomized clinical trials which must simplify in order to control the variables of primary interest. In a slap at our contemporary high-stakes testing environment, which Thorndike might have applauded, as he had helped to start it, James notes:

Man is too complex a being for light to be thrown on his real efficiency by measuring any one mental faculty taken apart from its consensus in the working whole.... No elementary measurement, capable of being performed in a laboratory, can throw any light on the actual efficiency of the subject; for the vital thing about him, his emotional and moral energy and doggednesss can be measured by no single experiment, and becomes known only by the total results in the long run.... [T]he total impression

which a perceptive teacher will get of the pupil's condition, as indicated by his general temper and manner, by the listlessness or alertness, by the ease or painfulness with which his school work is done, will be of much more value than those unreal experimental tests, those pedantic elementary measurements of fatigue, memory, association, and attention, etc., which are urged upon us as the only basis of a genuinely scientific paedagogy. Such measurements can give us useful information only when we combine them with observations made without brass instruments, upon the total demeanor of the measured individual, by teachers with eyes in their heads and common sense, and some feeling for the concrete facts of human nature in their hearts. (W. James, 1899/1983, pp. 82–84)

It is James who makes the point repeatedly that too heavy a reliance on a particular notion of science makes irrelevance a likely part of essence in educational psychology. Because of his concerns James would not have approved the high-stakes assessment movement of our times, but he would likely have supported the ways in which Howard Gardner (1983) and Robert Sternberg (Sternberg & Wagner, 1986) broadened our conceptions of intelligence. James consistently held a holistic view of human beings, and he understood the important distinction between the real world on the one hand and both laboratory and school tasks on the other hand. Despite his private comments about the pedestrian minds of teachers, he put faith in the classroom teacher to guide the young to acquire proper habits. In so doing he rejected those who saw the mission of the school as curriculum bound, with the teacher there merely to impart facts (Bowen, 1981). The moral dimension of teaching would have been emphasized by him, as well. Since he believed that science could not provide much advice to teachers about what to do in concrete situations, he probably would have applauded cognitivist Donald Schoen's (1983) work on reflection "in" and reflection "on" practice that has influenced our understanding of how professionals in such complex environments make decisions and learn to succeed. Pajares (2003) also makes the case for James being the originator of the ideas embodied in the conceptual change literature, most of what we today call the study of self, and what we now call situated cognition. Had James rather than Thorndike molded educational psychology, says Pajares (2003), we would have been in constant dialog with other social sciences, with the arts and humanities, and developed a much more interdisciplinary social science.

G. Stanley Hall (1844–1924)

Hall was APA's organizer and its first president, the founder of the child-study movement that James worried about, and a promoter of a psychology that James must have found distasteful. Hall was as much an educational psychologist as anything else we might label him, and that came to him naturally. Hall's mother was a major influence on him, a school teacher who did something quite unusual for her time, or for any time. She kept detailed records of her students' developmental progress. Hall, in becoming our first developmental psychologist, eventually followed the paths that she had originally laid out. Hall's father had for a time also been a school teacher. Thus it should come as no surprise that Hall also taught school upon completion of his precollege education. After additional studies, some for the ministry, some in Europe, Hall eventually received the first American doctoral degree in psychology. The granting institution was Harvard, the year was 1878, and Hall's major advisor was William James. Hall promptly returned to study in Europe for 2 years, returning home without funds. This is when the famous president of Harvard Charles W. Eliot made the first of the two requests by the administration of Harvard that markedly influenced educational psychology. In 1880 Eliot rode by Hall's house, and while still astride his horse asked the impoverished Hall to deliver a series of public lectures on education, under the auspices of the University (see Joncich, 1968). The delivery of that Saturday morning series of talks on psychology and education *preceded* James' by about a decade! It was such a smashing success that the president of the newly founded Johns Hopkins University asked Hall to visit his institution and repeat them. Once again the lectures on psychoeducational issues were a great success, and the ebullient Hall was offered a job as a professor of psychology *and of pedagogy*. Interestingly, E. G. Boring never mentioned the latter part of Hall's title in his classic *History of Experimental Psychology* (1957).

The research laboratory Hall founded at Johns Hopkins, as opposed to the one James had half-heartedly developed, was the first formal laboratory for the study of psychology in the United States. The laboratory also introduced, by courtesy of the university president, something unique in America: fellowships for graduate students. It was a fellowship that attracted John Dewey to Hall's laboratory.

While Hall was at Hopkins he founded the first English language psychology journal, the *American Journal of Psychology*. But Hall also founded the second English-language psychological journal in America, and it was a journal of educational psychology. That came

about after Hall went to Clark University as its first president in 1888. There he founded first a pedagogical seminary, or workshop, for the scientific study of education. Then he provided it with a journal titled the *Pedagogical Seminary*, which is still published today under a different name, the *Journal of Genetic Psychology* (Boring, 1957).

Hall placed the pedagogy department at Clark University in the hands of W. H. Burnham, a psychologist he brought with him from Hopkins. Burnham stayed at Clark 36 years, making it one of the first universities to have a genuine and continuous department of educational psychology, though it was not originally known by that name.[2]

With his study of the contents of children's minds, begun in 1883 among Boston kindergarten children, Hall is credited with starting American developmental psychology in general, and the child study movement in particular. Like Piaget 50 years later, Hall inquired into children's conceptions of nature, including animals, plants, and the solar system. And like Robert Coles 100 years later, he questioned what children knew about number, religion, death, fear, sex, and their own bodies. By 1915 Hall, with his students and co-workers, had developed 194 questionnaires to determine what youngsters and adolescents knew.

Hall's influential views on science are of primary interest. His was a science that was open to common people, not removed from daily life and definitely not conducted in a laboratory. Hall (1897) wrote that the laboratory was not a place to learn about the real feelings and beliefs of individuals. The natural environment, using ordinary people as data collectors, was necessary to establish his new science of child study. Essence for Hall was empirical work, but not in the laboratory, and not necessarily even by trained scientists. The Boston study of children's knowledge that launched Hall's career was a brilliant educational psychology investigation, and since there had never been any studies like it in America, it may qualify as the first empirical educational psychology study that was widely disseminated.

The teachers who collected the data learned that 80 percent of the children knew where milk came from, but only 6 percent knew that leather came from animals. They learned that 94 percent of the children knew where their stomachs were, but only 10 percent knew where their ribs were. Actually, although the United States was still a rural country, 20 percent of those youngsters had never

---

[2]A great deal of the subject matter of educational psychology had been taught, from 1863 on, at the normal school in Oswego, New York, in a child study course. That course probably was the model for the child study courses that spread to other normal schools after the Civil War (Watson, 1961) And those courses are the immediate predecessors of the courses on educational psychology that we see today in programs of teacher preparation. Courses explicitly titled Educational Psychology generally began just prior to the end of the 19th century (Charles, 1987). The first of these was apparently taught at the University of Buffalo in 1895, followed by one at the Normal school at Greeley, Colorado, in 1896. The third course in the country with that particular title was taught by E. L. Thorndike at Teachers College, beginning in 1902 (Joncich, 1968).

seen a cow or a hen, 50 percent had never seen a pig or a frog, and 80 percent had never seen a crow or a beehive. Boring (1957, p. 568) informs us of the important moral that was derived from this research: "Show children objects, explain relationships to them, do not trust them to know meanings or referents of common words; they must be taught." This advice to urban educators dealing with children from many different language groups and cultures is as compelling today as it was when it was first given 100 years ago.

Hall was a great organizer, popularizer and teacher of psychology. By 1915 Hall's students numbered well over half of all PhDs in American psychology, a group that included Lewis Terman and Arnold Gesell, both of whom profoundly influenced general, developmental, school, and educational psychology.[3] So Hall was arguably the most influential psychologist in the United States in the years just before and after 1900. But Hall's very popular science actually became more unscientific with each passing year. The samples he obtained were poorly described or unknown, the questionnaires he developed were not psychometrically sound, the data collectors were untrained, and the data were poorly analyzed.

Though E. L. Thorndike (1898b) was remarkably tolerant of the amateurish quality of the child study movement, he still called their movement "very poor psychology, inaccurate, inconsistent and misguided." He believed that little verification of their findings would occur. Here again is essence in our field, verification, the same goal as in all the experimental sciences. Ultimately, the child study movement failed. It was not good science and Hall, who held it together, had developed strange views of education and childrearing. The legacy of the child study movement, however, was enormous. These terribly imperfect, naturalistic studies that relied upon teachers and parents as researchers, formed "the beginnings of a host of new areas focusing on the child, such as experimental child psychology, educational psychology, school psychology, physical education, social work, mental retardation, mental hygiene, and early education" (Davidson & Benjamin, 1987, p. 56).

So we had a popular movement that accomplished at least three things. First, it presented a view that science could guide educational thought, paving the way for Thorndike, who would soon follow. (Thorndike's second book, it should be noted, was entitled *Notes on Child Study* [Davidson & Benjamin, 1987; Joncich, 1986]). Second, the movement promoted the belief that anyone could be a scientist, that is, that reliable data could be gathered by minimally trained individuals. This is still contested ground, but the teacher-researcher movement has

not gone away, and in many ways is thriving (Cochran-Smith & Donnell, in press; Zeichner & Noffke, 2001). Finally, the child study movement promoted the idea that data from the natural environment are superior to those of the laboratory. This too is a contemporary issue in educational research. So although Hall's science was eventually not good science, it prepared a lot of people for better science and for different views of what scientific work might look like.

John Dewey (1859–1952)

Dewey's contributions, like James', were in all three intertwined fields of study; philosophy, psychology, and pedagogy. In the earliest days of the 20th century the lines between these fields were indistinct.

Dewey obtained his doctorate at Hopkins in 1884 with Hall as his advisor. They appear not to have liked each other. Dewey wrote a psychology text in 1886, four years before James' *Principles* came out. Although well received, it was not a major intellectual event in the field. It was decidedly philosophical, which was perfectly natural for its time (Dewey, 1886). One of Dewey's few empirical papers was published in 1894, the year he went to the then newly created University of Chicago. It was a paper on the relative frequency of word use by young children, probably his own (Dewey, 1894). His first major paper in psychology came out in 1896. It was on the relations between stimuli and responses, and it had a particular American flavor to it (Dewey, 1896). As with the work of James, before him, it was against elementism and in defense of a more holistic view of stimuli and their associated responses, including the context in which they occur. He noted that stimuli and responses occur as part of previous and future chains, because that is the nature of experience. Therefore, we should really think of the stimulus and response as unseparable entities. Experience, as James had noted, and about which Dewey concurred, is a stream. Dewey argued that what held together stimuli and their responses were the interpretations given to both, thus putting consciousness, attribution, and constructivist views squarely before emerging S-R psychologists who rejected these ideas about psychology. Dewey would have been at home with contemporary attribution theory and constructivist perspectives on learning. And he would have agreed, I think, with Messick (1989) that validity is more about interpretations and argumentation than about correlations.

But Dewey's important psychological paper had immediate educational implications. If it was the whole act that

---

[3]It appears that the first person in the nation to hold the license of school psychologist was Hall's student Arnold Gesell (Kramer, 1987).

constituted the basis for learning, then the prevalent form of instruction at that time had to be inappropriate. Reciting lessons to students, where teachers acted like they were pouring knowledge into students' heads, had to be a mistake. Lessons of that type were, at best, emphasizing only one part of a system. Where was the emphasis on having children respond, on having them be active in some way? What was to be done about will, volition, and motivation? And where was time allotted during teaching for interpretation, to the making-of-meaning out of what was presented? These concerns are as relevant today as they were 100 years ago when they were forcefully brought to the attention of educators. And lest we forget how radical these ideas were and are, we should note that powerful forces lined up against Dewey when he was introducing the "new" education in the first yearbook of the Herbartians (Dewey, 1895). For example, two years later in the third yearbook of that series, United States Commissioner of Education William T. Harris (1897) was still advocating traditional methods. Harris stated the four cardinal rules for efficient instruction: "The child must be regular [in attendance] and punctual [in assignments], silent and industrious (p. 59)." It is this which "builds character" (p. 65). For Harris then, and for many educators today, obedience to authority was considered necessary for developing the child's personal sense of responsibility and duty (Monroe, 1952).

Dewey and his colleagues at the University of Chicago founded the functionalist school of psychology, a way of thinking about psychology strongly influenced by Darwin. Functionalists promoted a psychology interested in the purpose of behavior, or, put slightly differently, the function of mind. That is, instead of just describing some event, say a rat's pursuit of food or a child's acquisition of fear, psychologists should ask what would that behavior accomplish? What purpose will it serve? What is the behavior's function? Functionalism promoted the study of both animal psychology (for Darwin linked us to the animal world) and educational psychology (for social Darwinism suggested that societies evolve, hence one of the most important means to accomplish that seemed to be education). Educational psychology has its roots deep in the functional school of psychology that emerged at the turn of the century, and that point of view continues to have contemporary followers (Berliner, 1990).

Before obtaining his doctorate with a thesis on the psychology of Kant, Dewey had been a high school teacher. Thus, more than most, he could fulfill the duties expected of him when he moved to Chicago to the Department of Philosophy, Psychology and Pedagogy (the title of the department emphasizes again the intertwining of the three fields). In fact, soon after his arrival he founded an elementary school as a place to learn more philosophy, more

social theory, and more psychology. His laboratory school began as a place to study how children learn, not as a site for teacher education, as some laboratory schools became later. Dewey, the pedagogue, was against imparting mere knowledge, which he believed was either wrong or would soon be outdated. He was against rote learning and approaches that used drill and practice. He was for what we would call today the development of thinking skills, and against the attainment of decontextualized, inert forms of knowledge. In the fullest functionalist tradition he said that knowledge was a tool, not an end in itself (Dewey, 1910). He would have easily aligned with and participated in the Cognition and Technology Group of Vanderbilt University (1997), as educational psychologists John Bransford, Susan Goldman, and others developed the *Adventures of Jasper Woodbury* series. The videotapes in this series were designed to help students to think in context, that is, to think functionally. Dewey could also happily have joined the community of learners using the Computer Supported Intentional Learning Environment (CSILE), built primarily by educational psychologists Marlene Scardamalia and Carl Bereiter at the Ontario Institute for the Study of Education (Scardamalia, Bereiter, & Lamon, 1994). Dewey's reading list for his students would no doubt have featured works by Jerome Bruner and Ann Brown, both of whom had influences on the Jasper Woodbury and CSILE projects and both of whom choose for some of their work to "mess around" in Pasteur's quadrant.

Dewey also favored allowing students to participate in the educational process because it was their personal needs that were the starting place of the educative process. This was as progressive at the start of the 20th century as it is today at the start of the 21st century. Reading the modern and authoritative *How People Learn* (Bransford, Brown, & Cocking, 1999) is a reminder of how far we went wrong in educational and general psychology, and how we are now recovering the psychology of Dewey and leaving behind the psychology of Thorndike.

Although the principles of effort and interest were the guiding psychological principles of the early part of the 19th century, to Dewey neither was appropriate because they were conceptualized as external factors, under the direction and control of the teacher. Dewey felt that the individual's internal process must be understood. Most important were the urgent needs, impulses, and habits that each child possessed (Dewey, 1895, 1910). It was when the teacher found these and created an environment to free these qualities that the greatest and most meaningful learning took place. Dewey, therefore, believed in a personal and idiosyncratic curriculum for each child. The Individualized Educational Plan (IEP) required by federal law for all special education students today is what Dewey might have wanted for all students. Thus the project method was advocated by the progressive educators who tried to put Dewey's ideas into practice, since it allowed for the individualization of learning based on a child's own interests. Dewey's project method has been updated and elaborated by educational psychologist Phyllis Blumenfeld and her colleagues (1991). It is still persuasive, and still little used.

It is also likely that Dewey would have been strongly against the contemporary standardized achievement tests that are based on the assumption of a common set of standards for all students to master. He was not a fan of having every child learn the same things to the same extent. His advocacy of the recognition of individual talents among students was not just to ensure their personal growth but to provide for the maintenance of our democracy. He was an enemy of all forms of education that homogenize what is to be learned, and he celebrated individual differences.

Dewey further recognized the uniqueness of the teacher's role as a fellow human being in what we today would call a community of learners. In his presidential address before the APA, in 1899, John Dewey (1900) chose to discuss educational issues, particularly psychology, and social practice. He pointed out the failure likely to occur should educational psychology not recognize that the teacher

lives in a social sphere—he is a member and an organ of a social life. His aims are social aims; . . . Whatever he as a teacher effectively does, he does as a person; and he does with and towards persons. His methods, like his aims, . . . are practical, are social, are ethical, are anything you please—save merely psychical. In comparison with this, the material and the data, the standpoint and the methods of psychology, are abstract. . . . I do not think there is danger of going too far in asserting the social and the teleological nature of the work of the teacher; or in asserting the abstract and partial character of the mechanism into which the psychologist . . . transmutes the play of vital values. (p. 117)

In that speech, in which he reminded psychologists about the nature of classroom teaching, Dewey asked also whether it was possible to have the educational psychologist on the one side, acting as a legislator, and classroom teachers on the other as a class of obedient subjects. He wondered: "Can the teacher ever receive 'obligatory prescriptions'? Can he receive from another a statement of the means by which he is to reach his ends, and not become hopelessly servile in his attitude?" (p. 110).

Dewey's answer, of course, was that the pronouncements of psychologists with regard to classroom practice had to be tempered. Today Dewey might add that the U.S. federal government, with its concern about "evidence based education," ought to be equally careful in what it demands of our teachers and how that is communicated.

In addition to his basic democratic concern for building relationships between the educational psychologist and classroom teacher based on equality, Dewey would add another factor, particularly if the results to be disseminated were based primarily upon laboratory work. That factor was tentativeness:

The great advantage of the psychophysical laboratory is paid for by certain obvious defects. The completer control of conditions, with resulting greater accuracy of determination, demand an isolation, a ruling out of the usual [means] of thought and action, which leads to a certain remoteness, and easily to a certain artificiality. When the result of laboratory experiments informs us, for example, that repetition is the chief factor influencing recall, we must bear in mind the result is obtained with nonsense material—i.e., by excluding the conditions of ordinary memory. The result is pertinent if we state it thus: The more we exclude the usual environmental adaptations of memory, the greater importance attaches to sheer repetition. It is dubious (and probably perverse) if we say: Repetition is the prime influence in memory.

Now this illustrates a general principle. Unless our laboratory results are to give us artificiality's, mere scientific curiosities, they must be subjected to interpretation by gradual re-approximation to conditions of life. . . . [T]he school, for psychological purposes, stands in many respects midway between the extreme simplifications of the laboratory and the confused complexities of ordinary life. Its conditions are those of life at large; they are social; and practical. But it approaches the laboratory in [that it is simpler.] . . . While the psychological theory [c]ould guide and illuminate the practice, acting upon the theory would immediately test it, and thus criticize it, bringing about its revision and growth. In the large and open sense of the words psychology becomes a working hypothesis, instruction is the experimental test and demonstration of the hypothesis; the result is both greater practical control and continued growth in theory. (pp. 119–120)

So Dewey had a concern for the social life of teachers, a deep respect for them, and a distrust of laboratory studies as influences on practice. In our present climate he would be a dissenter to the policies of the U.S. Department of Education that show a profound disrespect for teachers, and he would dissent also to the federal Institute for Educational Sciences that gives priorities in funding only to "experimental" work.

Summary of the Views of the Founders before Thorndike

William James taught that psychology did not have the whole picture of human beings, and that science probably never would. He saw such things as mental testing and the like as pieces of the individual, and would have protested vehemently about their use as the only source of data used to make decisions about individuals. There is little doubt that he would have fought against today's high-stakes testing programs. Although he held private beliefs about the pedestrian intellects of teachers and their docile nature, he saw school people as having practical wisdom. Teaching was an art that could not in any direct way be much touched by psychology. Laboratory findings could not lead to statements about what teachers ought to do. Teachers, James noted, were ethical and concrete, psychologists were abstract and analytic, and their relationship was necessarily fraught with difficulty. These beliefs might have led James to argue against the belief that only a single method of inquiry defines the nature of "good" science.

In Hall and Dewey we have former classroom teachers who respected teachers and the complexity of teaching more than did James. Hall's science had a common sense to it, it trusted teachers to be good observers and data collectors, and it defended passion, sentiment, and love as elements in the making of a good science of child and educational study. Although generally poorly carried out, his was a science more naturalistic than laboratory based, more clinical than experimental, and more qualitative than quantitative. Dewey held to a holistic psychology, understood the teacher as a social being, and thought that if psychology tried to present its findings as truths to be applied it would necessarily put teachers in a position of servitude. This was an unacceptable position in a democratic community of learners, which is what he wanted for teachers and their students. He saw laboratory psychology as inapplicable unless it was reworked to fit school settings, and even then he saw that psychological findings could only be tentative, a working hypothesis for teachers to test.

Despite their many personal and professional differences, these three founders of general and educational psychology had no problem agreeing that psychology had to take a major interest in education and that it was destined to be the "master science" for pedagogy. There was still a question, however, about which view of science was to dominate. This was the context for the emergence of the father of our field, Edward Lee Thorndike, whose views differed from these individuals in important ways.

THE PROGENITOR: EDWARD LEE THORNDIKE (1874–1949)

Our discipline has prospered enormously because of Thorndike's contributions, whose number and quality is remarkable (Mayer, 2003). It is difficult, therefore, to also

say, "Thanks, Ned, but you took too narrow a path." But Thorndike's views resulted in a major shift in psychology. From a field genuinely interested in issues of schooling, psychology changed to become disdainful of school practice. Thorndike's influence promoted an arrogance on the part of educational psychologists, a closed-mindedness to the complexities of the life of the teacher and the power of the social and political influences on the process of schooling. It was fated, however, because Thorndike was a product of a time when an unbounded faith in what science could accomplish seemed completely justified. He was a product of his age as we are of ours, and we are as obligated to look differently at his contributions as he was obliged to break with his mentors and peers.

Thorndike was a bright New England minister's son, who with his brothers, needed to get high grades to receive scholarship help for college. Eventually three Thorndikes became professors at Columbia University, attesting to the powerful values of that family.[4] As an undergraduate at Wesleyan, in 1895, Thorndike provided some intimation about what was to come when he wrote about the criteria for judging a novel. He commented that a proper novel was one designed to transmit information, to influence the intellect through its truth. The novel was definitely not to be judged on its ability to excite the emotions (Joncich, 1968). Permeating Thorndike's formative years, and influencing the work of his lifetime, was a strong belief about how truth, coming from science, was the way to perfect mankind. The mind and science, not emotion, were to be trusted. Soon after being awarded his PhD, he was to express his worship of science and his detachment from feelings as a rebuke of sentimentality in science teaching. Thorndike wrote: "One can readily show that the emotionally indifferent attitude of the scientific observer is ethically a far higher attitude than the loving interest of the poet" (E. L. Thorndike, 1899, p. 61).

While at Wesleyan, Thorndike (and his fellow undergraduate Charles Judd, an often overlooked founding figure of our field) studied psychology out of James Sully's (1889) *Outlines of Psychology*, the first edition of which was published in 1884, six years before James' *Principles*. Sully's book had a subtitle that is often overlooked, namely, "*With Special Reference to the Theory of Education.*" Sully wrote that his goal was "to establish the proposition that mental science is capable of supplying those truths which are needed for an intelligent and reflective carrying out of the educational work." Psychology's interest in education was clearly a part of the times. Thorndike may have been influenced by this general and educational psychology text before he read James' *Principles*. In his autobiography, however, he noted that it was James who

---

[4]The tradition continued, as two of E. L. Thorndike's sons acquired doctorates in physics, his daughter earned a doctorate in mathematics, and son Robert went on to a distinguished career as a professor of psychology and education at his father's institution, Teachers College, Columbia University.

so interested him that he bought the two volumes of the *Principles*, the only text he purchased while an undergraduate (E. Thorndike, 1936).

After graduating from Wesleyan Thorndike went to Harvard for two years (1895–1897), where he came under the influence of the brilliant and eclectic William James. There he took up experimental psychology, first with children, then with animals as subjects, housing his chickens in James' basement after his landlady refused to let him keep them in her house. Dissatisfied, in part, with James' increasing distance from psychology, Thorndike moved to Columbia for a year of study with the well-respected James McKeen Cattell, a student of Wundt, Galton, and Hall. Cattell was the first person in the world to hold the title professor of psychology and ranked second only to James as the most influential psychologist of his time. With a life devoted to the study of individual differences and mental measurement, this founder of the Psychological Corporation was certainly as much an educational as he was a general psychologist.

Cattell allowed Thorndike to bring his chickens from James' basement to the attic of the new facilities at Columbia University. In this setting Thorndike wrote his classic thesis, *Animal intelligence* (1898a), and gained his first notice as a psychologist of considerable talent. His first job after graduation was as a professor of pedagogy and director of the practice school at Western Reserve University. His disdain for most of what had been written about education is palpable in Thorndike's claim that he read everything of use in pedagogy in the six weeks before the semester began!

His teaching was not a problem, but his experience in the schools was not a happy one: "The bane of my life is the practice school they stuck me with. It takes a whole day every week and is a failure at that." Instead of promoting the practice school he tried to open an educational laboratory (Joncich, 1968, p. 163). How different from Dewey at Chicago, who saw the school as the laboratory!

A year later, in 1899, Thorndike was brought to Teachers College as an instructor in psychology, where he remained a dominant force in psychology for 43 years, writing 50 books and many hundreds of articles, all done without a typewriter or a calculator (R. L. Thorndike, 1985). In comparison to the brilliant Dewey, whose students said he was at his best when he forgot to come to class, Thorndike rated quite favorably as a teacher. But he did not handle practical concerns very well. He was not unkind when such issues arose, but when a school superintendent asked him what he might do about a particular real-world dilemma, he responded "Do? Why, I'd resign!" (Joncich, 1968, p. 217).

Thorndike fought with his dean over the usefulness of the real-world experience for training teachers, with Thorndike against it. In fact, by 1914, he advised his graduate students, the future leaders of our discipline, to read all they could about education in order to learn what was happening in the schools but not to bother spending their precious hours visiting the classroom (Joncich, 1968, p. 231). Arthur Gates, a student of Thorndike's at about that time, and soon to be a nationally recognized educational psychologist on the faculty of Teachers College, had "never heard of him going into the schools" (Joncich, 1968, p. 231). Under Thorndike's sway, graduate students in educational psychology found essence in the avoidance of praxis.

Educational psychologists always celebrate the successes of Thorndike in banishing mental discipline with his transfer studies, the many editions of his *Educational Psychology* textbooks that gave our field prominence in schools of education, and his ground-breaking work on mental and social measurement. He also wrote influential books on the psychology of school subjects, such as arithmetic and reading. He gave us the first standardized achievement test (Watson, 1961), developed intelligence tests, and compiled dictionaries, as well. He was named president of APA in 1912, very early in his career. The written works and attitudes of this enormously influential teacher of educational psychology promoted and directed our field for the first half of the 20th century.

The Written Record

Thorndike was one of the first American psychologists to see the potential of educational measurement as a cornerstone for psychology's empirical work. And, of course, he believed that only empirical work should guide education. His faith in experimental science and statistics was unshakable. In his *Introduction to Teaching* he says (E. Thorndike, 1906, reprinted in Joncich, 1962):

The sciences of biology, especially human physiology and hygiene, give the laws of changes in bodily nature. The science of psychology gives the laws of changes in intellect and character. The teacher studies and learns to apply psychology to teaching for the same reason that the progressive farmer studies and learns to apply botany; the architect, mechanics; or the physician, physiology and pathology. (p. 60)

There was a mechanical model underlying Thorndike's ideas about the application of psychology to schooling. Although he often noted that schools were complex sites, he managed to ignore the difficulties inherent in applying psychological science to school problems. He didn't seem to recognize the need for the "intermediate inventive mind" that James did, nor did he feel the need to reapproximate psychological findings into school, as Dewey did. He not only ignored the unscientific musings of educators, he ridiculed them. For example, in his introduction to his first educational psychology text he stated (E. Thorndike, 1903); "This book attempts to apply to a number of educational problems the methods of exact science. I have therefore paid no attention to speculative opinions and very little attention to the conclusions of students who present data in so rough and incomplete a form that accurate quantitative treatment is impossible" (p. v).

The reason educational psychology was so caught up in the paradigm wars between qualitative and quantitative approaches to understanding educational phenomena toward the end of the 20th century (Gage, 1989) now seem clearer: Thorndike would never have approved of investigations that were neither quantitative nor experimental. In part, educational psychology's participation in the paradigm wars, particularly our stubbornness in accepting other forms of scholarship, were Thorndike's legacy.

Thorndike showed his unbridled faith in science once again, in the introduction to the inaugural issue of the *Journal of Educational Psychology* (E. Thorndike, 1910):

A complete science of psychology would tell every fact about every one's intellect and character and behavior, would tell the cause of every change in human nature, would tell the result which every educational force . . . would have. It would aid us to use human beings for the world's welfare with the same surety of the result that we now have when we use falling bodies or chemical elements. In proportion as we get such a science we shall become masters of our own souls as we now are masters of heat and light. Progress toward such a science is being made. (p. 6)

Thorndike, unlike his mentor James, did not have the courage to defend an incomplete science. It is unlikely, for example, that James or Dewey could have ever thought what Thorndike (1909, reprinted in Joncich, 1962) wrote with fervor; "Man is free only in a world whose every event he can understand and foresee . . . We are captains of our own souls only in so far as . . . we can understand and foresee every response which we will make to every situation" (p. 45).

We can contrast this attitude with the one expressed by E. C. Tolman in his presidential address to the APA in 1937. There Tolman wondered if psychology was ready to guide any kind of human behavior, since it still could not predict which way a rat would turn in a maze (Joncich, 1968). Thorndike had no such discomfort with psychology. He had absolute certainty about the potential of a rational, scientific approach to education. For example, when

he applied his connectionist psychology to the learning of school subjects, as in his *Psychology of Arithmetic* (1922), he derived his practices from logic and laboratory, not from the teaching of arithmetic in the field. He then claimed that this new pedagogy differed from the old because "The newer pedagogy of arithmetic . . . scrutinizes every element of knowledge, every connection made in the mind of the learner, so as to choose those which provide the most instructive experiences, those which will grow together into an orderly, rational system of thinking about numbers and quantitative facts" (p. 74).

No tentativeness here! Every connection is analyzable and then analyzed. Today we would call this body of work commonsensical, systematic, and organized according to reasonable principles of instruction. We probably would be less inclined to call the work scientific because Thorndike apparently never field-tested the ideas and materials he promoted in the different subject matter areas. He was so sure of his scientific footing that field-testing his texts and educational materials in the various school subjects seemed absurd! Thorndike seems to have fallen into the same trap that the school administrators had fallen into when they would not accept Joseph Mayer Rice's work on spelling. The administrators with their moral philosophy, and Thorndike with his science, both believed strongly that they knew what was proper. Their beliefs were so powerful that empirical data from real-world settings were not seen as relevant (Travers, 1985).

Thorndike's surety about science carried over into his work on quantitative methods, where he wrote eloquently about the power of educational measurement (E. Thorndike, 1918):

Whatever exists at all exists in some amount. To know it thoroughly involves knowing its quantity as well as its quality. Education is concerned with changes in human beings; a change is a difference between two conditions; each of these conditions is known to us only by the products produced by it—things made, words spoken, acts performed, and the like. To measure any of these products means to define its amount in some way so that competent persons will know how large it is, better than they would without measurement. . . . We have faith that whatever people now measure crudely . . . can be measured more precisely. (p. 18)

There is more of this throughout Thorndike's writings and those of his graduate students. Psychology need not go into the classroom, it can derive its laws from the laboratory and hand them down to teachers, thus creating the very condition that Dewey in a nearby office had decried. Thorndike promoted the belief that science and only science would save education. Indeed, he believed it would save all of society. His belief was that quantitative experiments were to be preferred over qualitative, clinical, or naturalistic observation.

By the time World War II was near, at many institutions, these beliefs had resulted in the perception by many inside the field of education that the discipline of educational psychology had become irrelevant. It had, in general, oversold what it could deliver. For example, Frank N. Freeman wrote the conclusion to the 1938 yearbook of the National Society for the Study of Education, a publication summarizing the achievements of the scientific movement in education. Freeman (1938) remarked that what had been accomplished appeared to be superficial, addressing the husk, not the kernel of the educational process. He speculated that the scientific movement that Thorndike headed had gone as far as it could in improving education. Hilgard (1996), reviewing the 37 chapters of that yearbook, believed that it provided ample testimony that wrong directions had been taken by the field. Church (1971) reviewed the first 10 volumes of our *Journal of Educational Psychology* and found "a surprising lack of concern for education's social role and a dearth of programmatic statements about what social service education was to perform and what ends it was to serve" (p. 391). As V. Hall (2003) notes, sadly, one could come to the same conclusion reading current issues of our journal.

Thorndike's legacy was an educational psychology that refused to take seriously the world of schooling and the importance of the social lives of the students, teachers, and others who spend considerable amounts of time in that setting. Disdain for practice was the prevailing attitude: it was the scientific not the professional side of the field that dominated (see Berliner, 2003a, 2003b). Thorndike's contributions were remarkable and his contributions were many, important, and enduring (Mayer, 2003). But it appears to me to be equally true that Ned and his followers took too narrow a view of the field and thus, by mid-20th century, our field had begun to show its weaknesses.

The Nether Side of Thorndike's Influence

McDonald (1964) called that period before the war the nadir of the profession. Educational psychology had clearly gone astray. But the debacle could not be addressed properly until after the war, a time that was one of opportunity and progress for our discipline. Psychologists and educational psychologists found meaningful work to perform in World War II since they, better than others, could advise on how to take a farmer or a store clerk and 8 weeks later provide an electronics repairman or a bombardier. They tested, evaluated, and designed instruction. The theoretical debates about the status of constructs within different learning theories, which had dominated psychology in the 1930s, seemed to end with the war, though it was another decade or so until it was generally agreed that this was the case. Such issues never again interested the field of psychology as they had. In part, that was because the practical concerns of education during the War made it clear that there was little hope of finding a single, all-purpose learning theory. Learning theories provided guidance for thinking about different kinds of instructional problems, but as James had noted long before, intermediate inventive minds were needed to solve the real problems of education. The war did not require theoretical elegance from its psychologists. It required solving not laboratory problems, but practical problems, such as the problem of rapidly teaching masses of men to reach acceptable levels of competency in hundreds of specialty areas (see Allport, 1947; Skinner, 1947; and McKeachie, 1974, for discussions of these issues). With the help of psychologists, the task was accomplished. Some of the people that came to a better understanding of educational problems during that time period, and who later influenced our field, include Walter Borg, Lee J. Cronbach, John Flanagan, N. L. Gage, Robert Gagné, Robert Glaser, J. R. Guilford, and B. F. Skinner. The roots of some of the changes that were to come in educational psychology had their origin in the Second World War, but those changes were still quite slow to come.

Every few years from the end of the war on, committees were formed to deal with educational psychology's increasingly obvious problems (Grinder, 1978). A 1948 committee of Division 15 concerned with our irrelevance noted that educational psychology had disavowed responsibility for the directions in which education would go. Educational psychologists seemed to be interested in the laws of learning, not issues of schooling and teaching. Worse, this committee noted that educational psychologists could neither understand nor be understood by educators—the ultimate irony for a field that once accepted the homage of educators as practitioners of the "master science" (Cubberley, 1919; Grinder, 1989).

Another report issued in 1954 (Grinder, 1978) pointed out that the most influential theorists were abandoning educational psychology and retreating to the field of experimental psychology. In the 1970s yet another report noted our failures and tried to define the discipline and chart its future (Scandura et al., 1978).

Each report, it seems to me, was still burdened by the "middle-man" notion, articulated well by Robert Grinder, the official historian of Division 15 (1978). Grinder wrote that we should take again the middle ground once envisioned for our discipline, a position between psychology with its disciplinary rigor on the one hand, and education with its messy problems on the other. But I think history teaches us that this is not wise. That position is looked down upon by psychology because it is applied and practical, and it is looked down upon by teachers and teacher educators because it is scientific and irrelevant to their problems. Something a bit different from just a middle position may be needed for educational psychology in the 21st century, a point to be discussed at the end of this chapter.

Some of the problems of our field were due to the overall success of psychology in the United States. Over a half century ago Woodruff (1950) noted that educational psychology had no domain that was really its own to any greater extent than it belonged to others. Unfortunately, essence for educational psychology could not be patented by us, but was the concern of other disciplines as well. The APA divisions of Evaluation and Measurement, Childhood and Adolescence, Personality and Social Psychology, School Psychology, and Maturity and Old Age appeared to have as much claim as we did on the study of such psychological functions as learning, adjustment, individual differences, tests and measurements, statistics, and growth and development. Moreover, it was not just psychology that explored the domains we often thought of as ours. By the end of the 20th century, for example, teaching and learning in classrooms were explored by ever-growing numbers of anthropologists, sociologists, and social linguists. And subject matter learning (science, history, literature, mathematics, and reading) came to be explored by subject matter specialists often trained by educational psychologists to use the methods of educational science, whose status we had secured. Our success in training subject matter researchers resulted in a reduction of the territory that our field once claimed as its own, though the methods-of-teaching texts in the various subject matter areas are filled with studies conducted by educational psychologists.

The perception of Woodruff (1950) and others in the last half of the 20th century was that we had no particular mission other than to apply general psychology to education. With few exceptions, textbook writers in educational psychology, from Thorndike's time to the 1960s, usually presented versions of Thorndike's S-R associationism and general psychology, with the students required to do all the work to figure out how that material applied to education (Grinder, 1989). Although educational psychology had established itself as the "master science" in teacher education, the texts we produced were found to be terribly wanting according to studies of educational psychology texts conducted in 1915 (Hall-Quest, 1915), 1922 (Remmers & Knight, 1922), 1927 (Worcester, 1927) and 1949 (Blair, 1949). Wolfle (1947), writing

about psychology textbooks a half century ago, gave a formula for writing textbooks in educational and child psychology:

If you wish to write an educational psychology text, start with a good average introductory text. Remove the chapters which deal with the nervous system and sense organs and write three new chapters to use up the space. These three new chapters will have such titles as Learning in the Schoolroom, Measuring Student Progress, and Social Psychology of the Schoolroom. . . . While you are collecting royalties on your text in educational psychology you will want to write a child psychology text. The rules are easy to follow. Start again with the good average elementary text . . . [etc]. (p. 441)

Wolfle added that for the educational psychology texts you had to delete all references to "subjects" and insert the term "pupil," whereas if you were writing a child psychology text you had to use the term "children" instead of "subject." His final advice to authors of educational and child psychology texts was to rearrange the order of the chapters that were found in the general psychology text. Even as late as 1968, when Ausubel (1968) wondered if there was such a thing as a discipline of educational psychology, he noted that the texts in use were "a superficial, ill-digested, and typically disjointed and watered-down miscellany of general psychology, learning theory, developmental psychology, social psychology, psychological measurement, psychology of adjustment, mental hygiene, client-centered counseling and child-centered education" (p. 1).

In the same year in which the distinguished educational psychologist John B. Carroll published his model of school learning (Carroll, 1963a), he also wrote about the discipline of educational psychology. The creator of one of our discipline's most elegant, parsimonious, and influential theories of learning, one derived from a *practical* problem of instruction, noted that the potential of educational psychology remained untapped because it seemed not to be concerned with genuine educational problems. Carroll said that until educational psychology provided evidence that it dealt with the real problems of schooling, "we shall continue to teach educational psychology to teachers with a mixture of pious optimism and subdued embarrassment" (Carroll, 1963b, p. 119).

The distinguished educational psychologist Philip Jackson (1981) laid the problems of our field squarely at Thorndike's feet. He cited four ways in which the introduction to the maiden issue of the *Journal of Educational Psychology* set the stage for the difficulties that would follow. In that introduction Thorndike first failed to distinguish between the goals and the methods used in the physical and the social sciences. To Thorndike, people were as easy to study as stones and toads. The methods of psychology, geology, and biology were not different, and the validity of the inferences to be made were seen to be equivalent. Second, Thorndike did not pay enough attention to the social and historical contexts in which people live and in which schools operate. Third, Thorndike had a blind faith that all of the achievements of science were desirable. He seemed to believe this even after Hiroshima and the Nazi extermination camps, events that caused many people to question their faith in science. Finally, Thorndike overlooked the aesthetic dimension of science. The art of educational psychology surfaces occasionally, as it does in every other branch of science. Ironically, although completely unaware of it, E. L. Thorndike displayed that artistic quality a number of times, a quality that helped make him such a towering figure in our field.

As Jackson (1981) also noted, the final blow to Thorndikian conceptions of educational science came from another one of our most respected educational psychologists, Lee J. Cronbach (1975). At the APA convention in 1974, on the occasion of his receipt of the award for distinguished contributions to psychological science, Cronbach made it clear that inconsistent findings hindered certain kinds of progress in our field. Once we attend to the interactions in our data, he said, "we enter a hall of mirrors that extends to infinity" (p. 119). He noted that many social science findings do not hold for long. Educational psychologists can demonstrate decade × treatment interactions, an occurrence almost unfathomable to most physical scientists. Thorndike would not know what to do with Cronbach's advice to social scientists, namely, to join with humanistic scholars and artists in trying to pin down the contemporary facts. For to understand individuals in their contexts, Cronbach said, is no mean aspiration. But Cronbach's negativism about the limitations on generalization in the social sciences, and thus in educational psychology, did not go unchallenged. N. L. Gage (1996) took the opposite position, making a strong case that the negativism about the usefulness of the social sciences was unwarranted, a position that was comfortable to many educational psychologists who see themselves more as Thorndike's disciples than Cronbach's heirs.

In sum, Thorndike's contributions were both monumental and misleading. While he brought rigor to educational research and gained a respected place for educational psychology in the colleges of education of the last century, he led us to irrelevance as well. His influence hardened the lines of separation between those who sought general principles of teaching and learning, or valued quantification of their findings, and those who valued local understandings and chose qualitative ways

to study phenomena. We certainly must thank Ned, and we must also move on. [For more on the period of educational psychology from 1890 to 1920, see V. Hall, 2003. The individual contributions to our field by William James (Pajares, 2003), John Dewey (Bredo, 2003), E. L. Thorndike (Mayer, 2003), and others are provided in Zimmerman and Schunk, 2003].

OTHER EARLY INFLUENCES ON OUR FIELD

There were of course others who contributed to the founding of the field and gave us our domains of interest and sense of mission. Space limitations prevent mentioning them all. But among the woman there was Leta Hollingworth, studying what today would be regarded as feminist issues, and who made the study of exceptional children essence for educational psychology. Maria Montessori influenced our field too, bringing to America proof (her *Case dei Bambinos*) that psychological thinking can overcome the negative effects of poverty. Although lauded by some educational psychologists, she was rejected by more powerful others, and her influence on our field was only short-lived (V. Hall, 2003).

Left out in discussions of the founders of our field was Charles Judd, whose cognitive approaches to psychology were ahead of his time, which was, in most ways, Thorndike's time. It was Judd who fought against Thorndike's atomistic views of transfer, but to little avail. And it was Judd, not Thorndike, who understood the psychology of school subjects, resurrected for our field by Lee Shulman and others near the end of the 20th century (e.g., Shulman & Quinlan, 1996, and the section on this topic in the first *Handbook of Educational Psychology*, edited by Berliner & Calfee, 1996). History is funny. Judd may even have out-written Thorndike, 685 articles and books versus 507 (V. Hall, 2003; Mayer, 2003), and been closer in his thinking to the cognitive psychology of today. However, Thorndike was an integral part of and a contributor to the zeitgeist, whereas Judd was something of an outsider.

Left out of this history is the immense role that assessment and methodology played in defining who we are (Spearman, Binet, Terman, and Cronbach are just a few of the scholars who influenced our field enormously). Left out of this history also are those who in the last century developed learning theories that spoke to teachers, not just psychologists (Gagné, Ausubel, and Skinner, among others). I have also slighted those who influenced developmental psychology and instruction (e.g., Piaget, Vygotsky, and Bruner, among others) and those who contributed to research on teaching (e.g., Gage, Bloom). The contributions of many of these fascinating and productive figures in our field are described in Zimmerman and Schunk (2003) by contemporary educational psychologists who often knew and worked with some of the most distinguished educational psychologists of the second and third generation. In addition, essays on the trends in our field over the time period 1920–1960 (Asher, 2003) and 1960–2000 (Pressley & Roehrig, 2003) are also included in that volume. This chapter was not meant to be a complete history of educational psychology, but a look at our roots to find our essence. And that now seems possible.

HISTORY AND THE SEARCH FOR ESSENCE IN EDUCATIONAL PSYCHOLOGY

Pressley and Roehrig (2003) looked at the topics covered in both the first *Handbook of Educational Psychology* (Berliner & Calfee, 1996) and the second edition of the *International Encyclopedia of Developmental and Instructional Psychology* (DeCorte & Weinert, 1996). They found the following 11 topics to encompass much of what educational psychologists studied in Europe and the United States: cognition, behavioral learning, sociocultural perspectives, social relations and education, development, motivation, individual differences, psychological foundations of the curriculum, teaching and instruction, educational media, and research methods and assessments. These were, of course, not mutually exclusive categories. Nevertheless, reliable judgments were made for classifying these chapters into these categories. Pressley and Roehrig also examined contemporary issues of the *Journal of Educational Psychology* and found that two-thirds of the articles were accounted for by the categories cognition, motivation, and individual differences. The largest change from earlier in the 20th century until the end of the 20th century was a considerable reduction in articles classified as "behavioral learning," with a concomitant increase in articles falling into the category "cognition." But learning of all types, across the decades, represent about one-quarter of what gets published in our field's venerable journal. Another noticeable change was that articles on motivation are more frequent among the topics appearing today.

What is most interesting in these analyses is that we see how well Democritus, Quintilian, Comenius, Vives, and others defined the domains we now call our own. It may be humbling, but after 2,500 years of Western thought there is nothing very new here. There have been shifts in emphasis over time, and new insights occasionally take us to the far reaches of the domains that we claim as ours, blurring lines between educational psychology and other disciplines. For example, the educational psychologists doing research on cooperative learning, distributed cognition, situated learning, and school reform share common interests in these domains with anthropologists, sociologists, and policy analysts, all of whom study the same set of problems. Our concepts and methods are changed by these interactions with others, and like so many contemporary scientific fields of study we seem inexorably moving from disciplinary, to interdisciplinary, to transdisciplinary research in which we are the specialists in the study of a particular set of variables that have been the object of inquiry for millennia. These 11 topics about learning and instruction, and the four commonplaces of instruction to which we attend, may be essence for us, but they are not our exclusive property.

The prevailing views at any one time in the growth of our discipline change our preferences and styles of research much more than they change the objects of our study. For example, with the burgeoning work on the sociology and anthropology of education, with critical theorists making themselves heard, and with emphasis on the poor performance of particular groups of students in schools, educational psychologists in the latter part of the 20th century came to understand the power of interpersonal, social, institutional, and economic contexts to shape cognition, volition, and performance. As we learned that contexts moderated aptitudes, context came to the foreground of our research. The boundaries of educational psychology, therefore, had to blur with those of anthropology and sociology (among others), so that the powerful effects of social and cultural contexts could be understood and built into our research, neither pushed to the background nor controlled away through experimental design.

Studies of sociocultural influences on cognition are now well established. Abetted no doubt by the enormous increase in the diversity in America's students and the voices of critical theorists raising issues of race, class, and gender, sociocultural thinking in educational psychology has become more prevalent. History thus informs us that the more obvious shift of paradigms in educational psychology, from behavioral to cognitive psychology, was accompanied by another, much less obvious, shift in paradigms. The latter shift was from the study of the individual to the study of the individual situated *in* and bringing a sociocultural history *to* a context that exerts powerful influences on the thoughts and actions of all those in that context. So although learning and instruction is still our focus, it is more likely to be a situated learning theory that we end up supporting. This seems more sensible than continuing the quest of our forebears for learning and instructional theories that were broadly general in nature.

Method is definitely not essence. That is why the design experiments of one scholar and the laboratory research of another can both be exemplars of educational psychology. What does distinguish educational psychologists from other educational researchers is an emphasis (though not an exclusive one) on empirical methods, and the desire that our studies be judged by the usual standards of science: rigor, competence, public availability of the data, a strong warrant for assertions, and so forth (see Phillips & Burbules, 2000; Shavelson & Towne, 2002).

With a preference for empirical work in our field goes a preference for quantitative studies, but neither Piaget nor Vygotsky relied much on numbers, and they are treated in our textbooks as important educational psychologists. Moreover, the qualitative work of some of our most prestigious quantitative researchers does not change them from members of the educational psychology community to anthropologists. Furthermore, a great deal of the work on cognitive psychology is often more qualitative in its nature than quantitative, and yet remains mainstream educational psychology. So method is not essence.

What was argued, above, was that irrelevance for the world of practice seemed also to be essence for our discipline. That is an historic theme, certainly debatable, but argued more recently in two of our own disciplinary journals, the *Educational Psychologist* (Fenstermacher & Richardson, 1994) and *Educational Psychology Review* (Salomon, 1996). Pessimistic views about our field are echoed across the Atlantic by two of Europe's leading educational scholars (Weinert and De Corte, 1996):

After 100 years of systematic research in the fields of education and educational psychology, there is, in the early 1990s, still no agreement about whether, how, and under what conditions research can improve educational practice. Although research and educational practice have changed substantially since the beginning of the twentieth century, the question of how science can actually contribute to the solution of real educational problems continues to be controversial.

1981: The Year Educational Psychology Glimpsed the 21st Century

When it comes to influencing practice our cheerless history is hard to deny. Yet the seeds of change were planted toward the end of the last century. Slowly there seemed to be a little less reverence for Thorndike and his very disciplinary view of educational psychology, and a little more reverence for James and Dewey. Slowly, educational psychology appeared to be outgrowing the charge of irrelevance as a part of its essence. The changes actually began in the 1960s, but by the time that Lauren

Resnick (1981) wrote in the *Annual Review of Psychology*, the movement away from irrelevance was occurring. Resnick noted that the problems of real world instruction were beginning to guide the development of instructional psychology:

An interesting thing has happened to instructional psychology. It has become part of the mainstream of research on human cognition, learning and development. For about 20 years the number of psychologists devoting attention to instructionally relevant questions has been gradually increasing. In the past 5 years this increase has accelerated so that it is now difficult to draw a clear line between instructional psychology and the main body of basic research on complex cognitive processes. Instructional psychology is no longer basic psychology *applied* to education. It is fundamental research *on* the processes of instruction and learning. (p. 660)

Resnick in her writing and her own work immersed in school settings makes clear that the kinds of psychoeducational problems that influenced the discipline of psychology at the end of the 19th century were finally doing so again as the 21st century loomed. With a return to the problems of practice by psychologists has come a more positive attitude about the complexity of the problems faced by teachers and administrators, and a valuing of their practice and social lives, as Dewey reminded us to do 100 years ago. But it is not just respect for practice that makes this turn of our field so exciting. It is the understanding that theory building in situ, in the real world, constitutes our greatest scientific challenge and the most exciting opportunity to affect practice. As Greeno, Collins, and Resnick (1996) note, "by embedding research in the activities of practical reform, the theoretical principles that are developed will have greater scientific validity than those that have been developed primarily in laboratory work and in disinterested observations of practice, because they will have to address deeper questions of how practices function and develop." (p. 41)

If we are to sustain the change in our field that has been occurring slowly since the 1960s, the visions we hold of educational psychology will have to be modified. Many writers, particularly Wittrock (1967, 1992) and Berliner (1992), have remarked that we should stop thinking of ourselves as a subdiscipline, or merely an applied discipline, carrying psychology to education. In fact, the evidence is quite clear that the gifts to general psychology from educational psychology have been many and profound (Berliner, 1992), so that it clearly is not a one-way thoroughfare for the passing on of knowledge.

There was something wrong with the middle-man perspective that seemed to be part of our self-image for

100 years, but there did not seem to be an alternative until Richard Snow (1981) provided a slight modification that solves the problem for us. Snow was writing in the same year that Resnick (1981) was writing about changes in instructional psychology, and in the same year that Calfee (1981) was explaining the history of, and changes wrought by a cognitive educational psychology. This was also the year in which Lee Shulman (1981) suggested that educational psychology was beginning to go back to school. Shulman both recognized that our field was beginning to see its role differently, and he promoted that change though his own research program. This was also the same year that a model for our future work was set forth by another distinguished social scientist, the Nobel laureate Herbert Simon (1981). Simon offered educational psychology a design role: more engineering than laboratory scientist, more Dewey and James than Thorndike, more field and practice oriented than a good deal of educational psychology had been.

In 1981 the shape of the 21st century was visible. All five writers expressed new ways for us to view ourselves and our work, with Snow, in my estimation, saying it best. Snow wrote that the job of the educational psychologist is to psychologize about authentic educational problems and issues, and not simply to bring psychology to education, as if we were missionaries carrying out the Lord's work. The latter approach somehow breeds arrogance and disdain, characteristics that got us into trouble in colleges of education throughout the nation. The designation of our field as the "master science," by Cubberley (1919), though flattering, proved not to be conducive to building equality among the members of the interdisciplinary teams of social scientists and practitioners with whom we work.

To see ourselves, instead, as psychologizing about the problems and issues of education is different in subtle but important ways from simply being a middle-man. It is the difference between having a hammer and seeing the world in terms of nails that we might put in, versus understanding the goals of the architect, the function the structure is to serve, and the behavior of the people who will inhabit the structure. It is the difference between bringing behavioral psychology or self-efficacy theory or mastery learning to teachers having trouble getting high levels of achievement from some students, versus trying to understand what it is about this mix of teacher, student, curriculum, and setting that might be better understood through a strong grounding in psychology.

The psychologizing role requires that we bring our considerable talents, our rich disciplinary perspective, our concepts and methods and habits of mind to bear on the genuine problems of administrators, teachers, students, curriculum and instruction, teacher education, and so forth. Interactions among the four commonplaces and work on the 11 topics will likely be our focus for some time, and the chapters of this handbook, like those of the last one, reflect that. But the change that started to be noticed in the last decades of the 20th century and that is slowly being recognized is that for many in our field there has been *a change in the origin of the problems that we study*. When more of the problems educational psychologists choose to study are located in the world of teachers and schools, we will go a long way to casting off the label of irrelevance that has plagued our field for a century. Both the mathematics-education and science-education research communities, in Europe and the United States, seem to be leading the general educational psychology community in recognizing this problem and designing their way out of it (see, for example, Cobb, Confrey, diSessa, Lehrer, & Schauble, 2003, and related articles in a special issue of the *Educational Researcher*; and De Corte, Verschaffel, Entwhistle, & Van Merriënboer, 2003). Many of our nation's most outstanding researchers, some of whom are educational psychologists, have also pointed the way for us to counter the charge that the work of the educational psychologist is not relevant for practice. In a book infused with this new turn toward practice (Lagemann & Shulman, 1999), Bruner (1999) says:

Education research, if it is to be effective in the broader society, must extend its concern, as it is now doing, beyond the classroom and beyond pedagogy narrowly defined. It needs also to participate in the task of discerning the consequences of such culturally constituted ends as a society prescribes for its education system. Education research, under the circumstances, becomes a cultural science, however much it may rely on methods developed in the natural sciences.

Going to practice as a source of the problems we wish to study is a subtle but crucial difference in the way educational psychology has been thought about since Thorndike conquered the field. This formulation recognizes both the importance of understanding the problems that are faced by the individuals struggling to make schooling successful *and* the importance of our disciplinary perspective. This way of defining our field lends dignity to the work of the educators, since *their* work rather than our discipline becomes the basis for our inquiries. Implicit in recognizing the primacy of the problems of practice is that we have license to explore more deeply the social, moral, political, and economic forces that impinge on the psychological processes we have a preference for exploring. A closer relationship to practice will give us theories that are surely more complex and more interesting, though probably less generalizable, than those that emerge from our laboratory work. It would be nice, I think, if this growing trend in our discipline were to be nurtured.

CONCLUSION

Psychologizing the problems of practice, that is, making them more often the source of our inquiries, could eliminate the characteristic of irrelevance that history shows is as much essence in educational psychology as are our achievements in assessment or motivation. This approach was never better expressed than by that giant of the third generation of educational psychologists, Lee J. Cronbach. In a discussion with him about portfolio assessment I commented that although they were so useful, their unreliability seemed to preclude our using them for any important decisions about individuals, or in large-scale evaluations.

Cronbach remarked that the job of the psychometrician was not to impede educational progress, or hold back educators from designing assessments that better met their values. Rather, he said, the job of the psychometrician was to help educators do better what they wanted to do. The educator, not the psychometrician must be the one to pose the problem.

If this advice were taken to heart by more of the educational psychology community we would lose what is arguably our discipline's most negative quality. It would be satisfying (in the Thorndikian sense of the term) if, over the next few decades, the perception by educational practitioners that educational psychologists are irrelevant becomes more difficult to defend. A paraphrase of another Cronbach statement should increase the likelihood that our discipline will be influential in the coming years: "It would be no mean achievement to know educators as they are, in the contexts in which they work, through the eyes of an educational psychologist."

References

Adler, M. (Ed.). (1952). *The great ideas: a syntopicon of the great books of the Western world*. Chicago: Encyclopedia Britannica.

Allport, G. W. (1947). Scientific models and human morals. *Psychological Review, 54*, 182–192.

Angell, J. R. (1907). The province of functional psychology. *Psychological Review, 14*, 61–91.

Asher, J. W. (2003). The rise to prominence: educational psychology 1920–1960. In B. Zimmerman and D. Schunk (Eds.), *Educational psychology: A century of progress*. Mahwah, NJ: Lawrence Erlbaum Associates.

Ausubel, D. P. (1968). Is there a discipline of educational psychology? *Educational Psychologist, 5*(1), 4, 9.

Ayres, L. P. (1912). Measuring educational processes through educational results. *School Review, 20*, 300-309.

Barone, T. (2001). Science, art, and the predispositions of educational researchers. *Educational Researcher, 30*(7), 24–28. Retrieved March 5, 2005, from http://www.aera.net/uploadedFiles/Journals_and_Publications/Journals/Educational_Researcher/3007/AERA3007_RNC_Barone.pdf

Barzun, J. (1983). *A stroll with William James*. New York: Harper & Row.

Berliner, D. C. (1990). The place of process-product research in developing the agenda for research on teacher thinking. *Educational Psychologist, 24*, 325–344.

Berliner, D. C. (1992). Telling the stories of educational psychology. *Educational Psychologist, 27*, 143–161.

Berliner, D. C. (2002). Educational research: The hardest science of all. *Educational Researcher, 31*(8), 18–20. Retrieved March 1, 2005, from http://www.aera.net/uploadedFiles/Journals_and_Publications/Journals/Educational_Researcher/3108/3108_CommentBerliner.pdf

Berliner, D. C. (2003a). Educational psychology as a policy science, including some thoughts on the distinction between a discipline and a profession. *Canadian Journal of Educational Administration and Policy, 26*. Retrieved March 1, 2005, from http://www.umanitoba.ca/publications/cjeap/articles/miscellaneousArticles/berliner.html

Berliner, D. C. (2006). Toward a future as rich as our past. In C. Golde and G. Walker (Eds.), *Envisioning the future of doctoral education: Preparing students of the discipline* (pp. 268–289). San Francisco, CA: Jossey-Bass.

Berliner, D. C., & Calfee, R. C. (Eds.). (1996). *Handbook of educational psychology*. New York: Macmillan.

Blair, G. M. (1949). The content of educational psychology. In *Educational psychology in the education of teachers*. Reprints of The National Society of College Teachers of Education. Baltimore, MD: Warwick and York.

Blumenfeld, P., Soloway, E., Marx, R., Krajcik, J., Guzdial, M., & Palincsar, A. (1991). Motivating project-based learning: Sustaining the doing, supporting the learning. *Educational Psychologist, 26*(3 & 4), 369–398.

Boring, E. G. (1957). *A history of experimental psychology*. New York: Appleton-Century-Crofts.

Bowen, J. (1981). *A history of western education*: Vol. 3. New York: St. Martin's Press.

Bransford, J. D., Brown, A. L., & Cocking, R. R. (Eds.). (1999). *How people learn: Brain, mind, experience, and school*. Committee on Developments in the Science of Learning, Commission on Behavioral and Social Sciences and Education, National Research Council. Washington, DC: National Academy Press.

Bredo, E. (2003). The development of John Dewey's psychology (pp. 81–111). In B. Zimmerman and D. Schunk (Eds.), *Educational psychology: A century of progress*. Mahwah, NJ: Lawrence Erlbaum Associates.

Broudy, H. S. (1963). Historic exemplars of teaching method. In N. L. Gage (Ed.), *Handbook of research on teaching*. Chicago, IL: Rand McNally.

Brown, A. L. (1992). Design experiments: Theoretical and methodological challenges in creating complex interventions in classrooms settings. *The Journal of the Learning Sciences, 2*(2), 141–178.

Bruner, J. (1999). Postscript: Some reflections on educational research. In E. C. Lagemann and L. S. Shulman (Eds.), *Issues in education research: problems and possibilities*. San Francisco: Jossey-Bass.

Calfee, R. C. (1981). Cognitive psychology and educational practice. In D. C. Berliner (Ed.), *Review of research in education*, 1981. Washington, DC: American Educational Research Association.

Carroll, J. B. (1963a). A model of school learning. *Teachers College Record, 64*, 723–733.

Carroll, J. B. (1963b). The place of educational psychology in the study of education. In J. Walton and J. L. Kuethe (Eds.), *The discipline of education*. Madison, WI: University of Wisconsin Press.

Charles, D. C. (1987). The emergence of educational psychology. In J. A. Glover and R. R. Ronning (Eds.), *Historical foundations of educational psychology*. New York: Plenum.

Church, R. L. (1971). Educational psychology and social reform in the progressive era. *History of Education Quarterly*, 390–403.

Cobb, P., Confrey, J., diSessa, A., Lehrer, R., & Schauble, L. (2003). Design experiments in educational research. *Educational Researcher, 32*(1), 9–13.

Cochran-Smith, M., & Donnell, K. (in press). Practitioner inquiry: blurring the boundaries of research and practice. In J. L. Green, G. Camilli, G. and P. B. Elmore (Eds.), *Complementary methods for research in education* (3rd ed). Washington, DC: American Educational Research Association.

Cognition and Technology Group at Vanderbilt (1997). The Jasper project: Lessons in curriculum, instruction, assessment, and professional development. Mahwah, NJ: Lawrence Erlbaum Associates.

Comenius, J. A. (1657). *Didacta magna*. Amsterdam: D. Laurentii de Geer.

Cronbach, L. J. (1975). Beyond the two disciplines of scientific psychology. *American Psychologist, 30*, 116–127.

Cronbach, L. J. (With the assistance of K. Shapiro)(1982). *Designing evaluations of educational and social programs*. San Francisco: Jossey-Bass.

Cronbach, L. J., & Snow, R. E. (1977). *Aptitudes and instructional methods: A handbook on interactions*. New York: Irvington.

Cubberley, E. P. (1919). *Public education in the United States*. Boston: Houghton Mifflin.

Davidson, E. S., and Benjamin, L. T., Jr. (1987). In J. A. Glover and R. R. Ronning (Eds.), *Historical foundations of educational psychology*. New York: Plenum.

De Corte, E., Verschaffel, L., Entwhistle, N., & van Merriënboer, J. (Eds.). (2003). *Powerful learning environments*. Oxford, UK: Pergamon.

De Corte, E., & Weinert, F. E. (Eds.). (1996). *International encyclopedia of developmental and instructional psychology*. Oxford, UK: Elsevier.

Dewey, J. (1886). *Psychology*. New York: Harper and Brothers.

Dewey, J. (1894). The psychology of infant language. *Psychological Review, 1*, 63–66.

Dewey, J. (1895). Interest as related to will. In *Yearbook of the National Herbart Society for the Scientific Study of Education*. Chicago, IL: University of Chicago Press.

Dewey, J. (1896) The reflex arc concept in psychology. *Psychological Review, 3*, 357–370.

Dewey, J. (1900). Psychology and social practice. *Psychological Review, 7*, 105–124.

Dewey, J. (1910). *How we think*. Boston: D. C. Heath.

Ericson, F. & Guiterrez, K. (2002). Culture, rigor, and science in educational research. *Educational Researcher, 31*(8), 21–24. Retrieved [September 2, 2005] from http://www.aera.net/uploadedFiles/Journals_and_Publications/Journals/Educational_Researcher/3108/3108_CommentErikson.pdf

Fenstermacher, G. D., & Richardson, V. (1994). Promoting confusion in educational psychology: How is it done? *Educational Psychologist, 29*, 49–55.

Freeman, F. N. (Ed.). (1938). *The scientific movement in education*. Thirty-seventh yearbook of the National Society for the Study of Education, Part 2. Bloomington, IL: Public School Publishing.

Gage, N. L. (1963). Paradigms for research on teaching. In N. L. Gage (Ed.), *Handbook of research on teaching*. Chicago: Rand McNally.

Gage, N. L. (1989). The paradigm wars and their aftermath: a "historical" sketch of research on teaching since 1989. *Educational Researcher, 18*(7), 4–10.

Gage, N. L. (1994). The scientific status of the behavioral sciences. *Teaching and Teacher Education, 10*, 565–577.

Gage, N. L. (1996). Confronting counsels of despair for the behavioral sciences. *Educational Researcher, 22*, 5–15.

Gardner, H. (1983). *Frames of Mind*. New York: Basic Books.

Gergen, K. J. (1973). Social psychology as history. *Journal of Personality and Social Psychology, 26*, 309–320.

Glover, J. A. & Ronning. R. R. (Eds.) (1987). *Historical foundations of educational psychology*. New York: Plenum.

Greeno, J. G., Collins, A. M., & Resnick, L. (1996). Cognition and learning. In D. C. Berliner and R. C. Calfee (Eds.), *The handbook of educational psychology* (pp. 2–46). New York: Macmillan.

Grinder, R. E. (1978). What 200 years tells us about professional priorities in educational psychology. *Educational Psychologist, 12*, 284–289.

Grinder, R. E. (1989). Educational psychology: The master science. In M. C. Wittrock and F. Farley (Eds.), *The future of educational psychology*. Hillsdale NJ: Lawrence Erlbaum Associates.

Hall, G. S. (1897). A study of fears. *American Journal of Psychology, 8*, 147–249.

Hall, V. C. (2003). Educational psychology from 1890 to 1920. In B. Zimmerman and D. Schunk (Eds.), *Educational psychology: A century of progress.* Mahwah, NJ: Lawrence Erlbaum Associates.

Hall-Quest, A. L. (1915). Present tendencies in educational psychology. *Journal of Educational Psychology, 6,* 601–614.

Harris, W. T. (1897). In *Yearbook of the National Herbart Society for the Scientific Study of Education.* Chicago: University of Chicago Press.

Hilgard, E. R. (1996). History of educational psychology. In D. C. Berliner and Robert C. Calfee (Eds.), *Handbook of educational psychology.* New York: Macmillan.

Hothersall, D. (1984). *History of psychology.* Philadelphia: Temple University Press.

Jackson, P. W. (1981). The promise of educational psychology. In F. H. Farley and N. J. Gordon (Eds.), *Psychology and education: The state of the union.* Berkeley, CA: McCutchan.

James, H. (Ed.). (1920). *The letters of William James:* Vol. 1. Boston: The Atlantic Monthly Press.

James, W. (1890). *Principles of psychology.* 2 Vols. New York: Henry Holt.

James, W. (1899/1983). *Talks to teachers on psychology and to students on some of life's ideals.* Cambridge, MA: Harvard University Press.

Joncich, G. (Ed.). (1962). *Psychology and the science of education. Selected writings of Edward L. Thorndike.* New York: Bureau of Publications, Teachers College Press.

Joncich, G. (1968). *The sane positivist: A biography of Edward L. Thorndike.* Middletown, CT: Wesleyan University Press.

Judd, C. H. (1925). The curriculum: A paramount issue. *Addresses and proceedings* (pp. 806–807). Washington, D C: National Education Association.

Kline, L. B. (2004). *Beyond significance testing: Reforming data analysis methods in behavioral research.* St. Paul, MN: Assessment Systems Corporation.

Kramer, J. J. (1987). School psychology. In J. A. Glover and R. R. Ronning (Eds.), *Historical foundations of educational psychology.* New York: Plenum.

Lagemann, E. C. (2000). *An elusive science: The troubling history of educational research.* Chicago: University of Chicago Press.

Lagemann, E. C., & Shulman, L S. (Eds.). (1999). *Issues in education research: problems and possibilities.* San Francisco: Jossey-Bass

Learning Research and Development Center (2001). Final Report. *High performance learning communities Project.* September 15, 2001. Retrieved February 24, 2005, from: http://www.lrdc.pitt.edu/hplc/Publications/HPLC_FinalReport_Sept2001.pdf

Mayer, R. E. (2000). What is the place of science in educational research? *Educational Researcher, 29,* 38–39.

Mayer, R. E. (2001). Resisting the assault on science: The case for evidence-based reasoning in educational research. *Educational Researcher, 30*(7), 29–30. Retrieved March 5, 2005, from http://www.aera.net/uploadedFiles/Journals_and_Publications/Journals/Educational_Researcher/3007/AERA3007_Mayer.pdf

Mayer, R. E. (2003). E. L. Thorndike's enduring contributions to educational psychology. In B. Zimmerman and D. Schunk (Eds.), *Educational psychology: A century of progress* (pp.113–154). Mahwah, NJ: Lawrence Erlbaum Associates.

McDonald, F. J. (1964). The influence of learning theories on education (1900–1950). In E. R. Hilgard (ed.), *Theories of learning and instruction.* Sixty-third yearbook of the National Society for the Study of Education, Part 1. Chicago; University of Chicago Press.

McKeachie, W. J. (1974). The decline and fall of the laws of learning. *Educational Researcher, 3*(3), 7–11.

Messick, S. (1989). Validity. In R. L. Linn (Ed.), *Educational measurement* (3rd ed., pp. 13–103). New York: Macmillan.

Monroe, W. S. (1952). *Teaching-learning theory and teacher education, 1890 to 1950.* Urbana, IL: University of Illinois Press.

Pajares, F. (2000, January) *Schooling in America: Myths, mixed messages, and good intentions.* Paper presented at the Great Lecture Series, Emory University, Atlanta, GA. Retrieved January 10, 2005, from http://www.emory.edu/EDUCATION/mfp/pajaresgtl.html

Pajares, F. (2003). William James: Our father who begat us. In B. Zimmerman and D. Schunk (Eds.), *Educational psychology: A century of progress.* Mahwah, NJ: Lawrence Erlbaum Associates.

Palincsar, A. S. (2003). Ann L. Brown: Advancing a theoretical model of learning and instruction. In B. Zimmerman and D. Schunk (Eds.), *Educational psychology: A century of progress* (pp. 459–476). Mahwah, NJ: Lawrence Erlbaum Associates.

Phillips, D. C., & Burbules, N. C. (2000). *Postpositivism and educational research.* Lanham, MD: Roman and Littlefield.

Pressley, M., & Roehrig, A, (2003). Educational psychology in the modern era: 1960 to the present. In B. Zimmerman and D. Schunk (Eds.), *Educational psychology: A century of progress.* Mahwah, NJ: Lawrence Erlbaum Associates.

Quintilian, F. B. (1953). *Institutio oratoria.* 4 Vols. (H. E. Butler, Trans). Cambridge, MA: Harvard University Press.

Remmers, H. H., & Knight, F. B. (1922). The teaching of educational psychology in the United States. *Journal of Educational Psychology, 13,* 399–407.

Resnick, L. B. (1981). Instructional psychology. In M. R. Rosenzweig and L. W. Porter (Eds.), *Annual review of psychology* (Vol. 32). Palo Alto, CA: Annual Reviews.

Rice, J. M. (1912). *Scientific management in education.* New York: Hinds, Noble, and Eldredge.

Salomon, G. (1996). Unorthodox thoughts on the nature and mission of contemporary educational psychology. *Educational Psychology Review, 8,* 397–417.

Scandura J. M., Frase, L. T., Gagné, R. M., Stolurow, K., Stolurow, L. T., & Gruen, G. (1978). Current status and future directions of educational psychology as a discipline. *Educational Psychologist, 13,* 43–56.

Scardamalia, M., Bereiter, C., & Lamon, M. (1994). The CSILE project: Trying to bring the classroom into World 3. In K. McGilley (Ed.), *Classroom lessons: Integrating cognitive theory and classroom practice* (pp. 201–228). Cambridge, MA: MIT Press.

Schoen, D. (1983). *The reflective practitioner.* New York: Basic Books.

Schoenfeld, A. (in press). Design experiements. In J. L. Green, G. Camilli, and P. B. Elmore (Eds.), *Complementary methods for research in education* (3rd ed). Washington, DC: American Educational Research Association.

Schwab, J. J. (1973). The Practical 3: Translation into curriculum. *School Review, 81,* 501–522.

Shavelson, R. J., & Towne, L. (Eds.) (2002). *Scientific research in education.* National Research Council, Committee on scientific principles for education research. Division of Behavioral and Social Sciences and Education. Washington DC: National Academy Press. Retrieved March 5, 2005, from http://books.nap.edu/books/0309082919/html/index.html

Shulman, L. S. (1981). Educational psychology returns to school. In A. G. Kraut (Ed.), *G. Stanley Hall lecture series: Vol. 2.* Washington, DC: American Psychological Association.

Shulman, L. S., and Quinlan, K. M. (1996). The comparative psychology of school subjects. In D. C. Berliner and R. Calfee (Eds.). *The handbook of educational psychology.* New York: Macmillan.

Simon, H. A. (1981). *The sciences of the artificial* (2nd ed.). Cambridge, MA: The MIT Press.

Skinner, B. F. (1947). Experimental psychology. In W. Dennis et al. (Eds.). *Current trends in psychological theory* (pp. 16–49). Pittsburgh: University of Pittsburgh Press.

Smail, W. M. (Trans.) (1966). *Quintilian on education.* New York: Teachers College Press.

Snow, R. E. (1981). On the future of educational psychology, *Newsletter for Educational Psychologists* (Division 15, American Psychological Association), 5(1), 1.

Sternberg, R. J., & Wagner, R. K. (eds.). (1986). *Practical intelligence: Nature and origins of intelligence in the everyday world.* New York: Cambridge Univesity Press.

Stokes, D. (1997). *Pasteur's quadrant: basic scientific and technological innovation* Washington, DC: Brookings Institute Press.

Sully, J. (1889). *Outlines of psychology with special reference to the theory of education. A textbook for colleges.* New York: Appleton.

Thorndike, E. L. (1898a). Animal intelligence. *Psychological Review,* Monograph Supplement II, No. 2, Whole No. 8. (Also New York: Macmillan, 1911).

Thorndike, E. L. (1898b). What is a psychical fact? *Psychological Review, 5,* 645–650.

Thorndike, E. L. (1899). Sentimentality in science teaching. *Educational Review, 17,* 56–64.

Thorndike, E. L. (1903). *Educational psychology.* New York: The Science Press.

Thorndike, E. L. (1906). *The principles of teaching based on psychology.* New York: A. G. Seiler.

Thorndike, E. L. (1909). Darwin's contribution to psychology. *University of California Chronicle, 12,* 65–80.

Thorndike, E. L. (1910). The contribution of psychology to education. *Journal of Educational Psychology, 1,* 5–12.

Thorndike, E. L. (1918). The nature, purposes, and general methods of measurements of educational products. *The measurement of educational products.* Seventeenth Yearbook of the National Society for the Study of Education. Bloomington, IL: Public School Publishing.

Thorndike, E. L. (1922). *The psychology of arithmetic.* New York: Macmillan.

Thorndike, E. L. (1936). Edward L. Thorndike. In C. Murchison (Ed.), *History of psychology in autobiography: Vol. 3.* Worcester, MA: Clark University Press.

Thorndike, R. L. (1985, April). *E. L. Thorndike—A personal and professional appreciation.* Paper given at the meetings of the American Educational Research Association, Chicago, IL.

Travers, R. M. W. (1985, April). *Thorndike's scientific empiricism and the pragmatic approach.* Paper presented at the meetings of the American Educational Research Association, Chicago, IL.

Tyack, D., & Hansot, E. (1982). *Managers of virtue: Public school leadership in America, 1820-1980.* New York: Basic Books.

Vives, J. L. (1531/1913). De tradendis disciplinis. In *Vives on education* (F. Watson, Trans.) Cambridge, UK: Cambridge University Press.

Watson, R. I. (1961). A brief history of educational psychology. *The Psychological Record, 11,* 209–242.

Weinert, F. E., & De Corte, E. (1996). Translating research into practice. In E. De Corte and F. E. Weinert (Eds). *International encyclopedia of developmental and instructional psychology.* Oxford, UK: Elsevier.

Wilds, E. H., & Lottich, K. V. (1964). *The foundations of modern education.* New York: Holt, Rinehart and Winston.

Wittrock, M. C. (1967). Focus on educational psychology. *Educational Psychologist, 4,* 7–20.

Wittrock, M. C. (1992). An empowering conception of educational psychology. *Educational Psychologist, 27,* 129–141.

Wolfle, D. (1947) The sensible organization of courses in psychology. *American Psychologist, 2,* 437–445.

Woodruff, A. D. (1950, February). Functional structure needed. *Newsletter of Division 15, American Psychological Association, 5.*

Worcester, D. A. (1927). The wide diversities of practice in first-courses in educational psychology. *Journal of Educational Psychology, 18,* 11–17.

Zeichner, K. M., & Noffke, S. E. (2001). Practitioner research. In V. Richardson (Ed.), *Handbook of research on teaching* (4th ed., pp. 298-330). Washington, DC: American Educational Research Association.

Zimmerman, B., & Schunk, D. (Eds.). (2003). *Educational psychology: A century of progress.* Mahwah, NJ: Lawrence Erlbaum Associates.

· 2 ·

EDUCATIONAL PSYCHOLOGY
IN THE 21ST CENTURY

Robert Calfee
Graduate School of Education, University of California Riverside

My assignment for this chapter was "to review changes in the field since the first edition, and to project future trends." The story will start in 1986 (my memory of when Berliner and I first discussed the first Handbook, HBEPI), and move through time to 2025, the likely time frame for the influence of the second edition (HBEPII). The conceptual framework for this voyage will be both historical and normative: where have we been since the first edition, where might we be in 2025, and where should we be in 2025? In particular, what might we expect in HBEPIII?

Along the way three lenses will serve to define the discipline: psychology, education, and research:

Psychology: Almost everything in the parent discipline has potential bearing on educational psychology, from classical conditioning to fMRIs. My intention, however, is not to survey the entire domain of psychology, but to consider how selected developments in this area relate to and influence educational psychology. Berliner (this volume) describes historical trends in educational psychology, including the rollercoaster relation with psychology. Pintrich (2000) offers a succinct definition of psychology as the "study of the individual in context" (p. 223), which he sees as particularly critical for educational psychology because education is the context. Sarason (2001; Plucker & Dow, 2003) presents a view of the relation between psychology and the schools that is notable (and useful) for its disregard of trends in educational psychology.

Education: An enormous challenge! In preparing for HBEPI, I asked Ralph Tyler, "What is education?" "Rather simple," he responded. "Education consists of the institu-

tions and activities that a society uses to continue its traditions" (personal communication, 1987). But whose traditions, and what is the proper balance between the past and the future? Richardson (2003; also Berliner, 2003a) suggests that the domain is partly a profession, partly a discipline, but most generally what we refer to as *schooling*. The range of possibilities is broad and complex, the source of enormous discussion and debate.

Research: This facet may seem redundant to many readers, but is included for two reasons. First, much about who educational psychologists are and what they do does not fall under this heading, but reflects our roles in practice and policy. Second, our hegemony as educational researchers no longer exists, as other disciplines have entered the arena with their concepts and methods. Indeed, the methodological arena is presently cacophonous— randomized field trials, design experiments, hierarchical linear models, ethnographies and case studies, and action research, among others. Graduate programs in education no longer rely solely on educational psychologists to teach research methods, and even the meaning of *research* seems at times uncertain in an age of postmodern critiques (Phillips & Burbules, 2000).

The challenge in preparing this chapter has been whether to write a review or an essay, to predict or prognosticate. Several colleagues have offered advice and reactions, and the stack of sources is substantial (Ausubel, 1968; Corno, 1998; Gage, 1996; Glover & Ronning, 1987; Salomon, 1996; also cf. Calfee, 1981, 1991, 1992, for previous thoughts). My decision finally was to consult a crystal ball, taking care to include citations where appropriate. Today's times are turbulent, but during my career I have seen several storms come and go. As Chauncey Gardner put it in *Being There* (Kosinski, 1970), "After the winter comes the spring," and so on. The chapter conveys an optimistic tone, for the most part. The record of our field thus far is one of steady progress—with a few bumps along the way. Conceptualizations, methods, and applications springing from the work of educational psychologists during the past quarter century are rather spectacular, when gauged against the previous quarter century (cf. Berliner, 1992; also Fenstermacher & Richardson, 1994, who try to explain the Rashomon-like accounts of the discipline, and Corno, 1998, who provides a personal account). This comment does not mean to belittle our predecessors; Berliner's stories in the present volume are marvelous! Rather, the field should celebrate its successes, and anticipate future accomplishments.

SNAPSHOTS: 1985 TO 2005

Snapshots are brief. Editors and authors in the present volume, especially my colleague, David Berliner, provide more detailed accounts of this territory. The remarks in this section set the stage for reviewing longer term trends, based largely on comparisons between the first and second editions.

In Woolfolk Hoy's (1998; also cf. Wise, 1997) review of HBEPI, she remarks on how different the volume might have been if begun in 1970! At that time, educational psychology had reached a high-water mark by any of a number of indicators, including prestige, funding, and influence. The field had established a sense of assurance, theoretically, methodologically, and practically. Federally funded research and development centers established in the mid-1960s at major universities, along with the regional educational laboratories, were for the most part managed and staffed by educational psychologists. By the mid-1980s, the situation had changed rather dramatically (cf. Good & Levin, 2001, for several jeremiads along with more optimistic assessments). Information-processing models, our primary paradigm, were being challenged on several fronts, qualitative methods stood as a complement (if not the more desirable alternative) to statistical techniques, and the generalizability of field experimentation was being seriously questioned.

The creation of HBEPI, as Woolfolk Hoy (1998) notes, was a work *de novo*, starting from scratch, "a compendium of what was, not a map of what could be" (p. 448). Berliner and I began with our predilections, which were then shaped by board members of APA Division 15, Educational Psychology. Three features of our original proposal evoked significant discussion and debate: (a) an emphasis on practice (e.g., substantial attention to curriculum matters), (b) a review of the work of teachers, including the preparation of professionals, and (c) the substance and placement in the volume of material on foundational areas, especially methodologies. The third matter proved unexpectedly problematic. Strong arguments were advanced for placing methods up front, leading from presumed strength. For a variety of reasons, we decided instead to begin with cognition and motivation, and to end with foundations. Authors of the methodology chapters did yeoman service in capturing the essential elements of these areas, but appeared less successful in corralling the chaos of the 1980s and 1990s (cf. Woolfolk Hoy, 1998, p. 449).

The table of contents for HBEPII reveals several shifts in organization and emphasis. Historical and philosophical foundations are separated from methodology and moved to the front of the volume, with new entries on sociocultural topics and neuroscience. Cognition and motivation appear in the middle of the volume, but are substantially altered from HBEPI. Methodology again concludes the volume, with serious attention to design experiments.

The new edition incorporates other recent developments noted by many observers. First, cognition remains the discipline's predominant paradigm, but both substance and style have changed significantly, with much more attention to metacognitive elements grounded in Vygotskian analyses. In general, interest in "the self in social context" has increased over the past two decades. Not only has motivation emerged as a significant growth area, both conceptually and empirically, but development of the concept of self-regulation has become a major field of study in understanding academic motivations. To be sure, gauging and influencing the impact of this work on practice remain challenging. Also back on the table are questions about the relations among performance, learning, and motivation (echoes of Hull and Spence). Finally, methodology remains a somewhat chaotic and contentious mix of extraordinary accomplishments and heated debates, with encouraging advances in technical areas such as hierarchical linear modeling, emerging potential in the design experiment arena, and a revisiting of controlled experiments as the gold standard (Pearson, 2004).

To set the stage for the rest of the chapter, let me venture a few thoughts about these trends. First, educational psychology continues to struggle with the most appropriate relation to practice. On the one hand, many of us deal daily with practical matters—the preparation of teachers, development and implementation of programs and program evaluations, and consultations with educators and educational policy makers. On the other hand, as revealed in the Handbooks (and many textbooks), the field can easily come across as highly theoretical and detached from the day-to-day business of schooling (e.g., Good & Levin, 2001).

Second, the position of adults in educational psychology remains a puzzlement. Educational psychologists were key players in the field of human engineering during World War II, but that linkage seems to have disappeared for the most part. Teachers are adults, but exploration of teacher preparation, professional development, and workplace environments has fallen to ethnographers and sociologists. "Teacher" generally refers to the K-12 spectrum, but instructors of community college students are a significant part of the picture, along with professional development in fields like medicine (e.g., the preparation of residents and interns). Psychological studies of educational leaders in the K-12 system are relatively rare.

Third, neither HBEPI nor HBEPII include "Learning" in a chapter title! To be sure, there is the remarkable report on *How People Learn*, which demonstrates the power of cognitive analyses of teaching and learning (Bransford, Brown, & Cocking, 2000; also Phillips & Soltis, 2004). Unfortunately, public policy relies on fairly simplistic portrayals. For instance, program evaluations typically assess pre-post performance on a standardized test. Schools are judged on whether annual test scores go up or down. The real challenge is to capture complex patterns such as "learning to read" or "acquiring algebra" across years of instruction and study. A promising candidate for this task is the expert-novice distinction (Alexander, 2003a). Although much is known about differences between experts and novices, the critical missing piece is understanding how novices attain expertise (but cf. Bereiter & Scardamalia, 1992; Bloom & Sozniak, 1984). LaJoie (2003) proposed the investigation of novice-expert trajectories, which seems the right language, but could only conclude that the area needs fundamental work, conceptually and empirically. Schools offer excellent environments for such investigations, but aside from occasional ethnographies, long-term learning of significant accomplishments (e.g., becoming a reader) has been difficult to track in classroom settings. Indicators tend to be rather thin (e.g., standardized tests, Running Records or DIBELS, cf. www.dibels.org; Airasian, 2004; Popham, 2004), and documentation of instructional programs (both general and student-specific) presents a serious challenge. Learning is a function of time—opportunities to practice with feedback. But much depends on what happens during the time. The editorial team for the next Handbook can build on a solid foundation, but will hopefully find new tales to tell.

A fourth and final set of issues centers around methodology. The problem is not that our field lacks a richness of methods; to the contrary. Rather, the challenge is, for a particular problem, how to assemble an appropriate design and associated analytic-interpretive techniques. Although exemplary models of this strategy can be found, these seem rather rare. The tendency is to assign a method—quantitative or qualitative, survey or experiment—rather than analyzing the structure of the research question. This simple-minded strategy has been aggravated by federal mandates calling for randomized field trials as the "gold standard" (Towne, Wise, & Winters, 2004). Fortunately, federal resources have also supported reports describing problem-based methods for investigating specific educational issues (e.g., Shavelson & Towne, 2002). Second, it can be really hard to conceptualize and construct an integrated design for a given problem; Berliner (2002) suggests that "Educational science may be the hardest of the social sciences to do." The task requires broad preparation and the capacity for collaborative work, both of which pose challenges to graduate programs. Third is the lack of textbooks adequate for these tasks. Today's methods texts encompass a broader array of techniques than a decade or so ago (e.g., Creswell, 2002; Gall, Gall, & Borg, 2005; Johnson & Christensen, 2003; Krathwohl, 1998), often promising an integrated approach. The reality seems closer to parallel play.

AN EYE TO THE FUTURE

So much for the past 20 years. The remainder of the chapter, prognosticative and normative, is organized in four chunks: First, starting from this moment in time, who are "we" likely to be? Then, over the next two decades, what are we likely to be doing; what should we be doing; and how should we prepare our progeny for these tasks?

Who Are We?

The centerpiece for all four questions in this section is "we." A recurring theme for more than a century has been the struggle by educational psychologists to define and defend their identity (Berliner, this volume). If you are a member of Division 15 of the American Psychological Association, you know that your affiliation with educational psychology "provides a collegial environment for psychologists with interests in research, teaching, or [sic] practice in educational settings at all levels to present and publish papers about their work in the theory, methodology, and applications to a broad spectrum of teaching, training, and learning issues" (APA, 2000, p. 7, *Membership Dues Statement*). This description includes several significant parameters—theory, methodology, practice, and application in teaching, training, and learning.

Additional tensions surface during discussions of our *Weltanschauung*. For instance, Richardson (2003) raises the perennial question of whether the field should advance psychology through the study of education, or advance the practice of education through the application of psychological principles. Stokes (1997) placed this tension in a two-dimensional framework, suggesting that research and development activities can be judged by contributions to fundamental knowledge or to practical utility. He represents the two dimensions as a 2 × 2 matrix, with pure basic research in one quadrant (Neils Bohr), pure applied research in a second cell (Thomas Edison), and a mix of the two in a third, which he labeled "Pasteur's Quadrant." (Stokes did not offer a name for the remaining quadrant, research that is of limited value for either knowledge or application, but the cell is surely not empty.) It is tempting to place educational psychology in Pasteur's quadrant, but the reality is that the discipline ranges over much of the matrix, depending on the times, the contexts (including paradigms and funding opportunities), and individual (or group) interests and inclinations.

The suggestion that the discipline as a whole should find a comfortable resting place might have appeal at first glance, but it is probably neither possible nor desirable to limit the activities of individuals, nor for that matter to "fix" the discipline for time everlasting. The main point about "us" is the enormous variability among individuals who view themselves as educational psychologists, whatever the center (Berliner, 2003a). At one point in my career, many of us thought we were on the verge of fundamental discoveries about the nature of the learning process, locating us solidly in the "Bohrian" quadrant. Those aspirations have largely exceeded our grasp, but who knows what the future may bring. Some colleagues bristle at the view of educational psychology as a kind of "social engineering," but others are quite comfortable with this idea. For example, Glass (Robinson, 2004) has proposed that "educational research would do well to regard itself not as a science seeking theory to explain such phenomena as classroom learning, teaching, aptitude, and the like, but as a technology designing and evaluating lessons, programs, and systems" (p. 29).

"Who we are" partly reflects the substance of the field—education, teaching, training, learning, and so on. It also reflects various perspectives on these issues, which emerge in the form of theories or *schools*. For instance, *cognition* has served as the dominant paradigm for the past few decades (e.g., Mayer, 2001; Pressley & Roehrig, 2003). This label encompasses several scenarios, ranging from computer-based information-processing machineries to socio-constructivist models. Over time, the paradigm has moved from a focus on internal mental activities of individual thinkers to examination of the socio-cultural discourse of collectives. The preeminence of cognition has not gone unchallenged. Indeed, Roediger (2004) has claimed victory for *behaviorism*, offering evidence that (a) all psychological researchers depend on observable behaviors as the source of data, and (b) behavioral methods have proven effective in dealing with a range of educational challenges, ranging from classroom management to the treatment of autism. Whatever the case, doctoral programs in education seem less likely at the moment to provide courses on schools than was typical a few decades ago. We spend less time on epistemology and are less inclined to reflect on how we think about what we think. More generally, philosophical and historical foundations receive rather short shrift. For instance, philosophy of science, once a required course for doctoral students, seems to have fallen through the cracks (but cf. Alexander, 2003a; Murphy, 2003).

One might think that "who we are" for the individual might center around a specific educational domain—early education, motivation, assessment, or one or another of the chapter titles in the Handbook. My experience suggests that *methodology* may actually come in second to school in defining variations among individual views. The tension among educational methodologies that has emerged in recent decades includes both inter- and intradisciplinary elements. On the one hand, fields such as anthropology, sociology, and the humanities have materialized as significant players in educational research and scholarship. On the other hand, a substantial proportion of today's educational psychologists identify themselves with methods that would have been considered nontraditional only a few decades ago (but cf. earlier path-breaking studies of Cole and his colleagues; e.g., Cole & Scribner, 1974; Newman, Cole, & Griffin, 1990, inter alia). As noted earlier, individuals vary in their commitment to pure versus applied investigations and their position in "Pasteur's quadrant," which often carries implications for methodological preferences and convictions, and for epistemological positions.

Context matters greatly in determining individual identity. The editors and authors of the Handbooks reside mostly in research universities, focusing on research and the preparation of graduate students. Their progeny, however, are more likely to deal with the preparation of teachers (and, as a corollary, writing textbooks), and with evaluation and assessment for school districts and in state settings. Subtle differences among Piagetian, Vygotskian, and Bahktian views of classroom discourse can be fascinating in a graduate seminar, but for the working professional seeking a doctorate to support her promotion to Director of Research and Evaluation in a large urban district, the more immediate task centers around constructing a design for an evaluation project that is valid and meets federal regulations. Ideally, our graduates have learned how to bridge these worlds; in the previous example, the student has read the regulations, but has also internalized principles and pragmatics developed by Cronbach's extraordinary team (1982) as it wrestled with similar tasks not that long ago. Indeed, Cronbach's legacy demonstrates the possibilities of moving around in Pasteur's quadrant. During his career, he wrestled in turn with the intricacies of generalizability theory, the messiness of aptitude-treatment interactions, and the complexities of evaluation projects—a compelling example of who "we" can be. Zimmerman and Schunk (2003) tell the stories of several other individuals whose prominence in educational psychology illustrates the breadth of our endeavors (e.g., Benjamin Bloom, Nathaniel Gage, Jerome Bruner, Albert Bruner, and Ann Brown).

Finally, "we" depend on organizations for our identification as a discipline and a profession. Within the American Psychological Association (APA), Division 15 offers the primary affiliation. APA, the parent organization, has struggled for decades over the balance between a focus on scientific activities and the task of providing service to its members. Partly reflecting these tensions, science-focused organizations such as the Psychonomic Society and the American Psychological Society have spun away from the mother ship, with separate conventions and journals. Interestingly, the *Journal of Educational Psychology*, the profession's flagship, appears remarkably healthy as part of the APA publication network.

For many educational psychologists, the American Educational Research Association (AERA) is preferred for meeting and networking. Division C, *Learning and Instruction*, is heavily populated by educational psychologists, who also congregate in several of the numerous Special Interest Groups (SIGs). Although disciplinary identification is not antithetical to AERA principles (e.g., *History and Historiography*, *Philosophical Studies*), educational psychologists are not identified as such within the organization.

In academic environments, educational psychologists occupy a variety of settings. Education units are probably most typical, followed by psychology departments. At research universities, schools and colleges of education can be viewed with skepticism by other academics as lacking in high standards of scholarship, even while teacher preparation programs serve as "cash cows" for the campus. Educational psychologists offer courses in foundations and methodology, neither of which garner particular praise by the candidates. The ed psych

course lacks practical value, and statistics is too hard. In Psychology departments, our work is viewed as too practical!

What then may be our image as educational psychologists in 2025—a brief two decades hence? Inertia suggests that the picture will remain about the same, unless the profession takes steps to change it. Division 15 offers an institutional locus for any repositioning; it has the right title, provides a meeting place, supports the *Journal of Educational Psychology* and sponsors *Educational Psychologist*, and has developed the *Handbook* series. Schools of education are another natural base, but they are under attack from several directions. One might think that educators in the school community would have positive things to say about our contributions to research. Unfortunately, anecdotes serve more often for policy decisions than does systematic evidence; class size, retention in grade, teacher preparation, and testing all illustrate how policy and practice can fly in the face of solid research (cf. Berliner & Biddle, 1995; Bracey, 2003, for other examples). The profession, or discipline, or collective—however we characterize ourselves—clearly needs to continue the work of defining itself. The question is not whether we are doing important work; the evidence seems clear that we are. The challenge—partly substance and partly public relations—is to assemble the diverse accomplishments into a coherent and convincing portrait. The Handbooks might undergird such an effort as a resource base for the discipline and other audiences.

What Are We Likely to Be Doing?

As noted earlier, inertia is a powerful force, and the best guess about future directions generally comes from past trajectories. To be sure, educational psychology has seen significant shifts during the past few decades. Some observers worry whether the discipline will survive—my prediction is that it surely will. Will it look different—probably. What will it look like—the answer to this question requires educated guesses. This section presents several such guesses, relying for guidance on handbooks, journals, textbooks, conventions, and jobs.

The Handbook aimed from the beginning to serve the discipline as a touchstone, a rallying point, a standard. Reviewers generally saw HBEPI as making progress toward this goal (Wise, 1997; Woolfolk Hoy 1998), and HBEPII promises further advances. Of critical importance are issues of utility and use. Does the Handbook model allow broad access? How likely are colleagues to incorporate the series into their professional activities, including teaching and graduate preparation? It was rewarding to read Woolfolk Hoy's (1998; Woolfolk Hoy, 2000) account of how she included HBEPI in her teacher preparation courses: "In educating prospective teachers about learning, we face a significant challenge—helping our students distinguish between learning and teaching" (p. 264). On the other hand, the volumes are expensive (and heavy). How many colleagues have a copy in their professional library? Do they assign *Handbook* readings in graduate courses? Can we also assume familiarity with the multiple editions of the *Handbook of Research in Teaching*, the *Manual of Child Psychology*, and *Educational Measurement*, among others (e.g., Olson & Torrance, 1996), as foundational experiences? To the degree that these assumptions hold, then the field will be partly shaped by these works.

Journals can also exert considerable influence on the shaping of a discipline. Life was simpler a few decades ago. In our field, the *Journal of Educational Psychology* (*JedP*) was clearly required, along with *Child Development* and perhaps the *Journal of Genetic Psychology* and *American Journal of Psychology*. The first two journals were associated with professional organizations and conventions, a package deal. Today, the array of journals for our discipline—print and online—is overwhelming; in addition to *JedP*, my collection includes *Educational Psychologist* and *Educational Psychology Review*, along with *Educational Researcher, American Educational Research Journal*, and *Review of Educational Research* (all from AERA), and *Cognition and Instruction.* I have skipped several on the shelf, including various specializations (for me, *Reading Research Quarterly*).

Numbers are only part of the picture. Costs have risen considerably. Many are private publications, and not connected with professional groups. The outlets differ in audience, character, quality, and recognition. The explosion in technical and scientific publications is widespread, of course, meaning that libraries have to make hard choices, so that readers cannot rely on the local campus library for comprehensive coverage. Joining a professional society provides only partial relief, and reprint requests may not evoke responses. Technology promises some help, but be careful what you ask for. Google plans to scan the libraries in the next decade, probably a mixed blessing. The ERIC (Educational Resources Information Center) system demonstrates the power and vulnerability of federalized efforts to collect and organize a literature. ERIC clearinghouses have made valiant efforts to provide comprehensive coverage of the literature on educational research, while also dealing with the GIGO (garbage in, garbage out) effect. The question is how to effectively and efficiently introduce today's novices to the literature of the discipline. Answers to this challenge—including the emergence of open-access

journals—will do much to determine the future of the discipline.

Professional organizations sponsor journals, and they also conduct conferences, sometimes in great variety. APA and AERA convene annually and regionally in gatherings that offer opportunities for presentations, networking, and job searches. Participation in these meetings can do much to shape professional identity, and to support variations in this identity. The growth in SIGs speaks to the importance of such variations, which further the vitality of the discipline. The leadership of APA Division 15 has made stalwart efforts during the past few decades to encourage and enthuse our profession, partly through publications, but also through workshops at national and regional conventions. AERA is the other gathering place, but with an emphasis on "educational" rather than "psychological." My crystal ball is quite fuzzy about the resolution of this institutional tension, but it appears that both groups will continue to provide gathering places for educational psychologists.

Textbooks, especially those designed for introductory courses, play a substantial role in educational psychology for the clientele of classroom teachers, both for better and for worse. Like the handbooks, these volumes attempt a comprehensive portrayal of the field, with the primary purpose of demonstrating the application of psychological principles and research findings to the practice of classroom teaching. As Berliner notes (this volume), the record is somewhat mixed and has been for some time.

For a final look at what we will be doing, consider the range of jobs held by educational psychologists, those with doctorates but also master's degrees. A relatively small number occupy positions in research universities, think tanks (e.g., the Rand Corporation), regional educational laboratories, and federal agencies, where they conduct investigations, prepare graduate students, and consult on policy. Many more are employed in teacher preparation programs, where research is typically a lower priority. This stratification is likely to persist during the foreseeable future. The largest professional group, some doctorates but more with master's degrees, work for school districts, publishing companies, and governmental organizations. These individuals handle a smorgasbord of tasks, including testing (increasingly critical under No Child Left Behind), curriculum design and project evaluation, and management of categorical programs spawned by federal and state regulations. The impact of these individuals on the business of schooling is substantial, but they are almost invisible at present. My "wish list" for the future would include more attention to these on-site "engineers" responsible for the daily application of educational psychology to local problems in local situations.

What Should We Be Doing?

This question, clearly normative, warrants particular attention during times of political turmoil. Especially since the dire pronouncements of *A Nation at Risk* (Gardner, 1983), education and educators in the United States have indeed been placed at risk. Criticisms have come from all quarters, ranging from the failures of classroom teachers to the incompetence of education faculty and questions about the validity of educational research. Legislative mandates presently dictate methodology for funded research and restrict federal funds to the purchase of materials certified by such methodology (Towne et al., 2004).

Normative statements mean that someone has to take a stance, and in this section I take on this responsibility. My first recommendation is that, as a profession, we should *profess*: We should speak out, based on warrants available from our concepts and theories, from scholarly analysis and empirical findings, on behalf of ourselves and our clients. One example of such action mentioned earlier is the thoughtful response to federal mandates regarding research methods by Shavelson and his colleagues (Shavelson & Towne, 2002). Also mentioned previously is the contrarian volume by Berliner and Biddle (1995) on the discrepancy between the evidence about the remarkable performance of the educational system in the United States versus claims of widespread inadequacy and outright failures. These and similar translations of research into practice—by individuals and organizations—are critically important professional activities.

A second task has both normative and methodological aspects—to observe or to intervene. Lee Shulman tells the story of a researcher observing a stream of dead bodies flowing down a large river, carefully documenting size, sex, appearance, apparent age, and so on. A visitor asks the researcher, "Have you thought about walking upstream to see what you can do about this disaster!" Not to stretch the metaphor—observations and surveys are important for exploring an unknown situation, but often the real challenge is to fix the problem. Fundamental understandings can also emerge from experimentation and evaluation, when conducted to high standards. Standards for program evaluation have been promulgated (Sanders, 1994), but have yet to become part of the *lingua franca* of most researchers and evaluators.

A third challenge centers around identifying the "really important problems"—RIPs—that are confronting today's public schools, mindful of Tyler's advice about the function of education, and considering the continuing turmoil around values and traditions. One prime candidate for RIP status is undoubtedly the *achievement gap*, defined as the correlation of school success with demographic factors such as race, social class, and gender (Haycock, 2001; Williams, 2004). Practically speaking, most standardized testing is unnecessary; individual student scores can be predicted virtually within the margin of error by combining demographic factors. The persistent fact is that, in the world's wealthiest nation, educational inequities span the continuum from other wealthy nations to those at the bottom of socioeconomic ladder. Despite the *War on Poverty* and its successors, the gap persists, with some narrowing in the 1960s and '70s, but little change during the past three decades. Unpacking this RIP reveals several topics that have been studied by educational psychologists, including testing and assessment (to what degree do the typical measures serve as valid indicators of achievement); genetic and environmental components of individual differences (the well-worn nature-nurture contrast); the nature of intelligence in relation to schooling (Martinez, 2000; Sternberg, 1997); and the *Matthew* effect (Stanovich, 1986; as students progress through the grades, the gap increases).

A second RIP centers around how best to provide *effective and efficient teaching and learning* for all children (e.g., Pressley, 2002). A corollary topic inquires into the role of *technology in schooling*, reflecting the incredible impact of new technologies elsewhere in society. Other than electrification, today's classroom is remarkably unchanged from the end of the 19th century. The cast of characters and the activities remain virtually unchanged, along with the length of the school day and year and several other parameters. Schools have thwarted numerous innovations, radio, television, and even telephones have minimal presence in today's classrooms. Systems that we take for granted outside the school walls—computers, the Internet, cell phones, PDAs, handhelds—are either somnolent or prohibited. How often can you spot a plasma display or a PDA in a classroom? To be sure, one can find selected exceptions to this generalization, mostly in schools serving more affluent families and in secondary classrooms directed by math and science teachers.

The third RIP is a new kid on the block—*brain studies*. Inquiry into the relation between neurophysiology and learning has a long history, of course. But the arrival of innovative techniques has sparked interests, hopes, and claims (Brown, Donovan, & Cocking, 2000; Solso, 1997). Some findings appear salutary: discoveries about the biochemistry of the synapse, and the remarkable connectivity of the human cortex. New phrenologies and rediscovery of neurological plasticities have encouraged educators to rethink human intellectual potential. PET scans and fMRI techniques provide spectacular images of cortical activity during performance and—more incredibly—learning. But let me offer two caveats. One is recurring confusion around cause and effect. For instance, imaging studies of poor readers have led some observers to attribute these problems to cortical patterns, when one might equally well argue that instructional experiences have produced the brain variations. The second caution centers around individual differences. Educational psychologists have certainly proven their expertise in the exploration of individual differences in the quantitative arena, including the analysis of complex multivariate structures. But brain images pose a challenge akin to qualitative analysis. The typical strategy today is to present pictures of imaged patterns—"look at that!" The resemblance to analyses of anecdotal reports and verbal portraits is uncanny. Later in the chapter I will suggest a strategy for bridging quantitative and qualitative data bases; the application there aims toward verbal protocols, but a similar strategy seems applicable to "brain data." As things now stand, many of these reports have a decidedly anecdotal flavor.

My final RIP is admittedly idiosyncratic—the study of *leadership and school organization*. While this territory clearly falls within the province of psychologists (cf. the contributions of John Gardner, 1993), I cannot recall a single manuscript on this essential topic during my several years as editor of *JedP*, nor subsequent years as a reviewer. But much might be learned from sociocognitive analyses of the work of teacher leaders, school principals, and superintendents, as well as mid-management participants, many of whom are educational psychologists.

The one certainty about RIPs—and the preceding list is only a start—is that they call for responses of the magnitude of the Manhattan project or the response to September 11. Educational psychology, even during the Lab and Center years, when the federal government made earnest efforts to encourage collaboration, remains a largely entrepreneurial enterprise, hampering the capacity to deal with big issues. And so, to conclude this section, let me offer two recommendations: (a) "we," however we choose to constitute ourselves, should consider setting an ambitious agenda for the decade ahead, and (b) we should explore the development of professional networks to work on that agenda. If the nation really is at risk because of shortcomings in the public schools, and if *No Child Left Behind* is a serious national goal, then educational psychology should act more vigorously to become a serious player in the enterprise. Division 15 would seem an obvious starting point for such action.

How Should We Prepare the Next Generation of Professionals?

Much of my professional life has been devoted to the education of young people for positions in the wide vari-

ety of tasks that are available to graduates of educational psychology programs. The parade of talented individuals applying for these programs has been rather amazing, a spectrum ranging from new baccalaureates fresh from camp counseling to experienced practitioners far wiser than I. Their postgraduate careers encompass a grand variety. Some have replicated their mentors in academic research settings, but many have found positions in business, government, the military, and public service institutions.

The combination of psychology and education provides an extraordinary breadth of knowledge and a remarkable range of tools for graduates. We need to continue to prepare authorities in educational psychology across the broad spectrum reflected in the Handbook series, striving to sustain the best features of earlier programs—a comprehensive view of psychology and education, rigorous methods, and flexibility. We also need to consider establishing vigorous recruitment strategies for the pipeline, with particular attention to underrepresented groups (Dickson et al., 2004).

A continuing challenge is to define and defend the discipline's core, while also recognizing our subspecializations. Berliner (2003b) has suggested an agenda for revitalizing the discipline, which includes (a) rethinking methods courses; (b) introducing the content through "big ideas" rather than schools; (c) requiring a year-long practicum, much like that required for certification problems such as school psychology; (d) providing a research internship in a complex environment; and (e) ensuring experience in the policy arena. This agenda is consonant with other recommendations (e.g., Richardson, 2003; Robinson 2004), but as always the devil is in the details. Later I will say more about internships and methods preparation. Perhaps the area of least certainty is the identification of the "big ideas"; presently there seem to be too many of them, and they come in distinctively different flavors.

As to practicum experiences, we could definitely do a better job of familiarizing our graduates with life in the world of practice. Clinical and school psychologists typically engage in internships as part of their professional preparation, understanding that their careers will engage them in practice, with research as a secondary task. The image of the educational psychologist—for reasons eloquently spelled out by Berliner—is more often that of the scientist. The reality is that many educational psychologists devote considerable time and effort to the "field," to the preparation of teachers, in project evaluation, consulting on program development, advising on various mandates (especially those related to testing), and so on. Many of us "talk with teachers," a demanding task, one that probably merits as much preparation as learning to compute a *t*-test. Better preparation might enhance the establishment of professional networks with other members of our profession, and might foster better communication with our clientele—students, teachers, educational leaders, and beyond.

In considering the preparation of the next generation, however, an area of particular importance is research competence. It was something of a shock, several years ago, when the Spencer Foundation launched an initiative to study deficiencies in the preparation of educational researchers (Lagemann, 2000; Spencer Foundation, 1997), and to propose recommendations for improving the situation. The evidence supporting the Spencer initiative seemed rather convincing—proposals from researchers affiliated with educational institutions appeared less competitive than those from the basic disciplines. Several top-ranked schools of education were invited to participate in a nationwide project, reviewing their preparatory programs and studying their graduates—a work still in progress (cf. Richardson, 2003, for one report; also www.spencer.org, Annual Reports 1997 and 2004).

Beyond the Spencer project, it makes sense for many reasons to reflect on our present and future role in the preparation of educational researchers. The methodology arena seems to offer substantial opportunities for our discipline to provide students with a more coherent foundation for carrying out their work, whether basic research or program evaluation, whether conceptual or pragmatic. Educational psychologists typically teach quantitative methods at the graduate level, including "stats" classes, design and analysis, multivariate methods, tests, and measurements, among others. As noted earlier, these courses can be centerpieces of delight or objects of dread. Beyond our heritage as quantitative experts, it seems to me that we have a broader responsibility to participate in today's debates about valid research strategies, which range from the tension between quantitative and qualitative methods to the positioning of randomized field trials as a "gold standard." Social science methodology in general, and educational research in particular, are in a time of turmoil, vulnerability, and excitement (Green, Camilli, & Elmore, 2005; Sandoval & Bell, 2004). The earlier hegemony of educational psychology and quantitative methods is no longer a sure thing, and today's students expect and need to acquire a broad array of tools during their preparation.

The challenges to methodological preparation come from two directions. First is the substantial growth in the array of tools required for tomorrow's educational researchers to claim competence. The difficulty here is that additional courses and practica are unlikely to be well received by students, given the already high opportunity costs in the education professions. Second is the continu-ing tension between the two primary methodological arenas, generally labeled as quantitative and qualitative. The tensions arise in part because of associated epistemological differences, which are separable from the question about how to conduct research. Practical problems arise because of the sharp contrasts between the two domains, with the consequence that students have to learn two different languages, as well as two different conceptual systems.

Both issues—acquiring two methodological domains and learning how they relate to one another—suggest that it might be worthwhile to explore integration of the two paradigms. The tension has a long history in psychology (e.g., Cronbach, 1975), and similar strains appear in other sciences. Some disciplines—sociology comes to mind—seem to have managed accommodations, as has psychology. Education, perhaps reflecting its practical focus, has emerged as a more contentious battleground.

Resolution may be a matter of translation. Integration requires more than placing all the techniques between the covers of a single book. It means identifying and connecting similar constructs, highlighting parallels, and working through the differences. Later I offer a few illustrations of this strategy as an entree for the next edition. My background as a quantitativist may suggest a bias, but so be it.

The examples spring from the classical areas of design and analysis, the wellsprings of my preparation as an experimental psychologist. Fisher introduced the concepts of factorial design – factors and levels, and plans for combining these elements into a thematically coherent arrangement (Chambliss & Calfee, 2002; Fisher, 1951). Educational psychologists possess technical expertise in the implementation of these ideas—they can diagram a $2 \times 3 \times 2$ design, providing specifications for crossed and nested factors, fixed and random elements, taking scarcely a breath along the way. Where they might need help is in the "thematically coherent" aspect, where the challenge is creating a conceptual framework that offers a rationale for the design. Educational psychologists still tend toward a "what works" Thorndikian empiricism (cf. www.whatworks.ed.gov).

Analysis must be considered as well as design. On the one hand, numbers are numbers, and conform easily to numerical operations and procedures. They can be added and subtracted, averaged and squared. Words and portraits are qualitatively different, beings from another world. Quantitative data can be encapsulated by constructs such as average, standard deviation, correlation, main effect, and interaction. The quantitative researcher can enter an array of numbers into a spreadsheet, and in the twinkling of an eye obtain indicators of these constructs, along with graphic portrayals of (literally) significant patterns. The qualitative researcher meanwhile struggles with notebooks of protocols festooned with post-its and highlighter codes. The activity may provide a compelling and entertaining case study, but where is the generalizability? Where are the *p*-values and variance components?

Following are a few thoughts about the shape of a possible resolution, and the suggestion that educational psychologists are well positioned to take the initiative in this regard (Phillips & Burbules, 2000). First a brief comment on the role of technology in fostering the integration of methodologies. During the past quarter century, we have come to take for granted the power of the personal computer to handle the analysis of quantitative information in ways that, before 1960, were virtually inaccessible to most scholars, and from 1960 through 1980 required worshiping at the altar of the campus computer center. Today's laptop has far greater capacity than the IBM 360 that I relied on to complete my dissertation in the 1960s.

Less often noticed, several programs have emerged during the past decade offering similar analytic power for handling qualitative data sets, including words along with a broad range of other artifacts, including graphics and video segments (Weitzman & Miles, 1995). These programs allow the researcher to catalogue and classify information, to tally patterns and profiles, and to construct graphic representations. The potential of these developments is emerging rather slowly; notebooks, highlighters, and Post-Its are still favored by qualitative researchers, judging from conference presentations. The most interesting examples that I have seen have appeared in evaluation studies, perhaps reflecting the practical bent in this area, the importance of employing genuinely mixed methods, and the need to link claims to defensible evidence rather relying on anecdotal excerpts. My prediction is that, two decades hence, this application will have become much more commonplace.

A second issue around the integration of methods centers around terminology. In the quantitative area, a relatively small number of constructs and labels go a long way: average, standard deviation, and correlation, for instance. In the design field, researchers talk about main effects, interactions, and confounding. Let me suggest that each term has a parallel in qualitative data. For instance, it often makes sense to talk about the typicality of a particular pattern, and to describe variations around this pattern. The IRE (Interrogate-Respond-Evaluate) sequence apparent in teacher-student discourse in the early grades illustrates the idea (Cazden, 2001). Although one can count IRE sequences, counting is not the only or necessarily the best way to characterize the data. Similarly, qualitative analyses can report co-occurrence of events without resorting to the Pearson product–moment correlation. When a qualitative study reports different patterns for boys versus girls,

or distinguishes classrooms of more or less experienced teachers, the parallel with main effects is direct. A slipperier challenge is the characterization of interactions, in the technical sense that the effect of one factor is moderated by variation in a second factor. The interpretive task is not unique to qualitative work, however; one encounters rather strange discussions of this construct in quantitative reports as well. To be sure, qualitative methods do not presently have the well established machineries of *significance*, *confidence intervals*, or *effect size*, which quantitative researchers routinely employ to warrant their claims; to be sure, these machineries are presently the subject of considerable debate (Harlow, Muliak, & Steiger, 1997). The point is that correspondences might be drawn to good advantage between the constructs and tools that have emerged during the development of the two major methodologies now employed in educational research, permitting more genuine integration of the methods, and fostering more authentic discussions among researchers.

Pursuing an integration offers conceptual as well as practical benefits. Thorndike (1918) claimed that "Whatever exists at all exists in some amount" (p. 18), setting the stage for his view of scientific research as essentially quantitative. The phrase has a nice ring to it, but is probably wrong. The fact that one can devise a way of attaching numbers to a collection of objects does not ensure that the numbers have captured the essence of the objects; construct validity is not so easily established. Many sciences have gained status by resort to qualitative strategies, or, more promisingly, by combining methods in ways that mesh conceptually and empirically with the problem under investigation. Today's graduate students are often advised to chose a methodology that suits a particular problem. They are also often counseled to identify one particular methodology as their specialization. My suggestion is that the field might benefit from serious efforts to construct bridges that promote better communication among researchers, and that support the preparation of a new generation of graduates with a broader array of methodological tools.

What If. . . .

Formal educational institutions are huge and possess enormous inertia, and K-12 schools weigh in heavily in this mix. Identify yourself as an educational psychologist, and most people assume you have something to do with teachers and teaching. Berliner mentions Schwab's (1973) four commonplaces of schooling—*someone* teaching *something* to *someone else* in *some setting*—which resonate with many audiences. It is difficult to imagine that the world of schooling 20 years hence will differ much from today. Today's schools continue do a lot of things remarkably well. They situate "somebody else's children" for 13 or more years in a relatively secure and supportive environment (Delpit, 1996; also Ladson-Billings, 2001). Most children acquire significant skill and knowledge through these experiences, and along the way also learn how to get along with others—an element in the informal curriculum. To be sure, much depends on the particulars. Not all schools are pleasant places, and many youngsters learn at an early age that they are destined for failure (Kozol, 1992). Nonetheless, most teachers carry out difficult work under demanding conditions; many are truly extraordinary.

The plain fact, however, is that most children (and their parents) have limited say in what they study, or in where and how they study it, when it comes to formal education. Consider life for a typical teenager in school and at home. School is divided into 50-minute slices of time during which the modal activity is listening to a grownup talk about a topic of marginal interest, while the tweener sits silently surrounded by fellow "prisoners," forbidden to talk, play, text-message, mess around, or do anything else. Most of the action takes place in the brief hurry-scurry between classes. In contrast, bedroom at home has become a multimedia event, where "doing homework" is likely to be a group event with MTV on the plasma, Internet exchanges on the desktop computer, cell phone jingling with calls from other friends, no adults in sight (Rideout, 2005).

What would Schwab (much less Thorndike!) make of the latter environment as a "learning situation?" How could a youngster possibly acquire anything of importance under these circumstances? Actually, stories from the dot.com era portray work environments remarkably like the tweener bedroom, settings that actually foster the creation of inventive products. Managing education under these conditions would be quite different than today's controlled classroom environment, and the concept of "student-centered learning" would take on an entirely new meaning.

My reason for mulling about tweener "home rooms" arises from involvement with a project on *pentop computers*, a new technology with smart pens and smart paper. To illustrate the concept, imagine a time several years hence. You have called a meeting with several colleagues to discuss a research proposal. As the session moves ahead, you and the group scribble key ideas and sketch images on note pads. You require access to background material from time to time—research notes, telephone numbers, URLs—you jot a request, tap an icon, the pen hums briefly and your PDA buzzes displaying the information on the screen. You have also entered email

addresses for other participants; the information automatically appears on their PDAs. By the end of the discussion, you have filled several pages with "stuff," as have your partners. Each of you taps an icon on the face sheet, and the pen transmits images of each page to his or her PDA, with copies to everyone on the list.

The topic of the meeting was a proposal to transform the middle school learning environment to take advantage of pentop computers by providing teachers and students with a seamless technology stretching from paper through PDAs to personal computers. At this future time, virtually all middle school students carry smart pens, which they use continuously in and out of school. Unlike old-fashioned cell phones and pagers, smart pens are cheap and handy, difficult to detect and impossible to prohibit, promoting widespread networking and collaboration.

This scenario is not science fiction; at least one version of a smart pen will be in stores before this volume appears. How will schools and teachers respond when anything that a student writes can be instantly and silently accessible to every other student in the classroom? When students can communicate almost anything anytime, is the result an opportunity for widespread collaboration or uncontrolled cheating? Previous technologies have been bulky, noisy, and expensive: easy to control and hard to introduce. Pentop computers will be quite the opposite.

As noted earlier, schools have proven amazingly resistant to technological change. But imagine that, through some new technology, a genuine revolution begins to emerge. What role will educational psychology play in this scenario? How will our progeny respond to these events? How can constructs and traditions developed over the past century accommodate these opportunities? We should feel encouraged, in my judgment. Educational psychologists have led the way in technology-oriented program developments, going back to MACOS (Man: A Course of Study, in Bruner, 1960, 1986) and extending forward to Jasper (Cognition and Technology Group at Vanderbilt, 1997). To be sure, classroom constraints have limited the "scaling up" of innovative programs. But design experiments (Sandoval & Bell, 2004) provide integrated methodologies that connect directly with practice, typical of how engineers operate, from architecture and agriculture and on through the alphabet. More important than technology, however, are the concepts and findings from the past half-century of endeavors, so capably captured in *How People Learn* and its offspring (Bransford, Pelligrino, & Donovan, 1999). The next 20 years will pass in the blink of an eye. Barriers to fundamental change appear substantial, but the potential is intriguing. Technology brings the sparkle of innovation and opportunity, but more significant are the social dimensions—the RIPs mentioned earlier are grounded in the quest for equity and social justice, ethical dimensions perhaps voiced infrequently but fundamental to the discipline (Oakes & Lipton, 2002). Perhaps HBEPIII will contain an entry on the topic.

References

Airasian, P. W. (2004). *Classroom assessment: Concepts and applications*. New York: McGraw-Hill.

Alexander, P. A. (2003a). Coming home: Educational psychology's philosophical pilgrimage. Special Issue, *Educational Psychologist, 38*(3), 129–186.

Alexander, P. A. (2003b). Expertise: Can we get to there from here? *Educational Researcher, 32*(8), 3–29.

American Psychological Association (APA). (2000). *Membership dues statement*. Washington, DC: Author.

Ausubel, D. P. (1968). Is there a discipline of educational psychology? *Educational Psychologist, 5(1)*, 4, 9.

Bereiter, C., & Scardamalia, M. (1992). *Surpassing ourselves: An inquiry into the nature and implications of expertise*. Peru IL: Open Court.

Berliner, D. C. (1992). The science of psychology and the practice of schooling: The one hundred year journey of educational psychology from interest, to disdain, to respect for practice. In T. K. Fagan & G. R. VandenBos (Eds.), *Exploring applied psychology: Origins and critical analysis*. Washington, DC: APA.

Berliner, D. C. (2002). Educational research: The hardest science of all. *Educational Researcher, 31*(8), 18–20.

Berliner, D. C. (2003a). Educational psychology as a policy science: Thoughts on the distinction between a discipline and a profession. *Canadian Journal of Educational Administration and Policy, 26*.

Berliner, D. P. (2003b). *Toward a future as rich as our past*. Carnegie Initiative on the Doctorate, Carnegie Foundation for the Advancement of Teaching, Stanford CA.

Berliner, D. C., & Biddle, B. J. (1995). *The manufactured crisis: Myth, fraud, and the attack on America's public schools*. New York: Longman.

Bloom, B. S., & Sozniak, L. A. (1984). *Developing talent in young people*. New York: Random House.

Bracey, G. W. (2003). *On the death of childhood and the destruction of public schools*. Portsmouth NH: Heinemann.

Bransford, J. D., Brown, A. L., & Cocking, R. R. (Eds.). (1999). *How people learn: brain, mind, experience, and school*. Washington, DC: National Academy Press.

Bransford, J. D., Pellegrino, J. W., & Donovan, M. S. (1999). *How people learn: Bridging research and practice*. Washington, DC: National Academy Press.

Brown, A. L., Donovan, M. S., & Cocking, R. R. (2000). *How people learn: Brain, mind, experience, and school* (Expanded Edition). Washington DC: National Academy Press.

Bruner, J. (1960). *The process of education*. Cambridge MA: Harvard University Press.

Bruner, J. (1986). *Actual minds, possible worlds*. Cambridge MA: Harvard University Press.

Calfee, R. C. (1981). Cognitive psychology and educational practice. In D. C. Berliner (Ed.), *Review of research in education* (pp. 3–74). Washington, DC: American Educational Research Association.

Calfee, R. C. (1991). Educational psychology: Past, present, and future? [Review of Wittrock and Farley (Eds.), *The future of educational psychology.*] *Contemporary Psychology, 36*, 5–6.

Calfee, R. C. (1992). Refining educational psychology: The case of the missing links. *Educational Psychologist, 27*, 163–175.

Cazden, C. B. (2001). *Classroom discourse: The language of teaching and learning*. Portsmouth NH: Heinemann.

Chambliss, M. C., & Calfee, R. C. (2002). The design of empirical research. In J. Flood, J. M. Jensen, D. Lapp, & J. R. Squire (Eds.), *Handbook of research on teaching the English language arts* (2nd ed., pp. 152–170). Mahwah NJ: Lawrence Erlbaum Associates.

Cognition and Technology Group at Vanderbilt. (1997). *The Jasper Project: Lessons in curriculum, instruction, assessment, and professional development*. Mahwah NJ: Lawrence Erlbaum Associates.

Cole, M., & Scribner, S. (Eds.). (1974). *Culture and thought: A psychological introduction*. New York: Wiley.

Corno, L. (Ed.). (1998). Topics for the new educational psychology [Special issue]. *Teachers College Record, 100*(2).

Creswell, J. W. (2002). *Research design: Qualitative, quantitative, and mixed methods* (2nd ed.). Thousand Oaks CA: Sage.

Cronbach, L. J. (1975). Beyond the two disciplines of scientific psychology. *American Psychologist, 30*, 116–127.

Cronbach, L. J. (With the assistance of K. Shapiro). (1982). *Designing evaluations of educational and social programs*. San Francisco: Jossey-Bass.

Delpit, L. D. (1996). *Other people's children: Cultural conflict in the classroom*. New York: New Press.

Dickson, W. P., Bouck, E., Collins, B., Kiwai, K., Phillips, M., & Yadav, A. (2004, April). Top twelve educational psychology doctoral programs: What their web sites say about themselves. Presentation to American Educational Research Association, San Diego, CA.

Fenstermacher, G., & Richardson, V. (1994). Promoting confusion in educational psychology: How is it done? *Educational Psychologist, 29(1)*, 49–55.

Fisher, R. A. (1951). *The design of experiments*. Edinburgh: Oliver and Boyd.

Gage, N. L. (1996). Confronting counsels of despair for the behavioral sciences. *Educational Researcher, 22*, 5–15.

Gall, J. P., Gall, M. D., & Borg, W. R. (2005). *Applying educational research* (5th ed.). New York: Allyn & Bacon.

Gardner, D. P. (1983). *A nation at risk*. Washington, DC: U.S. Department of Education.

Gardner, J. W. (1993). *On leadership*. New York: Simon and Schuster.

Glover, J. A., & Ronning. R. R. (Eds.). (1987). *Historical foundations of educational psychology*. New York: Plenum.

Good, T. L., & Levin, J. R. (2001). Educational psychology: Yesterday, today, and tomorrow [Special issue]. *Educational Psychologist, 36*(2).

Green, J. L., Camilli, G., & Elmore, P. B. (Eds.). (2005). *Complementary methods for research in education (3rd ed)*. Washington, DC: American Educational Research Association.

Harlow, L., Muliak, S., & Steiger, J. (Eds.). (1997). *What if there were no significance tests?* Mahwah NJ: Lawrence Erlbaum Associates.

Haycock, K. (2001). Closing the achievement gap. *Educational Leadership, 58*(6), 6–11.

Johnson, B., & Christensen, L. B. (2003). *Educational research: Quantitative, qualitative, and mixed approaches* (2nd ed.). New York: Allyn & Bacon.

Kosinski, K. (1970). *Being there*. New York: Harcourt, Brace, Jovanovich.

Kozol, J. (1992). *Savage inequalities: Children in American schools*. New York: Harper Collins.

Krathwohl, D. R. (1998). *Methods of educational and social science research: An integrated approach*. (2nd ed.). New York: Longman.

Ladson-Billings, G. (2001). *Crossing over to Canaan: The journal of new teachers in diverse classrooms*. New York: Wiley.

Lagemann, E. C. (2000). *An elusive science: The troubling history of educational research*. Chicago: University of Chicago Press.

Lajoie, S. P. (2003). Transitions and trajectories for studies of expertise. *Educational Researcher, 32*(8), 21–25.

Martinez, M. E. (2000). *Education as the cultivation of intelligence*. Mahwah, NJ: Lawrence Erlbaum Associates.

Mayer, R. E. (2001). Resisting the assault on science: The case for evidence-based reasoning in educational research. *Educational Researcher, 30*(7), 29–30.

Murphy, P. K. (2003). Rediscovering the philosophical roots of educational psychology [Special issue]. *Educational Psychologist, 38*(3).

Newman, D., Cole, M., & Griffin, P. (1990). *The construction zone: Working for cognitive change in school*. Cambridge, UK: Cambridge University Press.

Oakes, J., & Lipton, M. (2002). *Teaching to change the world*. New York: McGraw-Hill.

Olson, D. R., & Torrance, N. (1996). *Handbook of education and human development: New models of learning, teaching, and schooling*. Cambridge, MA: Blackwell.

Pearson, P. D. (2004). The reading wars: The politics of reading research and policy—1988 through 2003. *Educational Policy, 18*(1), 216–252.

Phillips, D. C., & Burbules, N. C. (2000). *Postpositivism and educational research*. Lanham, MD: Roman and Littlefield.

Phillips, D. C., & Soltis, J. F. (2004). *Perspectives on learning*. New York: Teachers College Press.

Pintrich, P. R. (2000). Educational psychology at the millennium: A look back and a look forward. *Educational Psychologist, 35*(4), 221–226.

Plucker, J. A., & Dow, G. T. (2003). What type of role should psychologists play in education? [Review of S. B. Sarason, *American psychology and schools: A critique*.] *Contemporary Psychology, 48*, 604–606.

Popham, W. J. (2004). *Classroom assessment: What teachers need to know* (4th Ed.). New York: Allyn & Bacon.

Pressley, M. (2002). *Reading instruction that works: The case for balanced teaching* (2nd Ed.). New York: Guilford.

Pressley, M., & Roehrig, A. (2003). Educational psychology in the modern era: 1960 to the present. In B. Zimmerman and D. Schunk (Eds.), *Educational psychology: A century of progress* (pp. 333–366). Mahwah, NJ: Lawrence Erlbaum Associates.

Richardson, V. (2003). *The Ph.D. in education*. Carnegie Initiative on the Doctorate, Carnegie Foundation for the Advancement of Teaching, Stanford CA.

Rideout, V. (2005). *Generation M: Media in the lives of 8–18 year-olds*. Technical Reports 7250/7251. Menlo Park CA: Kaiser Family Foundation.

Robinson, D. H. (2004). An interview with Gene Glass. *Educational Researcher, 33*(3), 26–30.

Roediger, R. (March, 2004). What happened to behaviorism? *Newspaper of the American Psychological Society, 17*(3), 5, 40–42.

Royer, J. (2003). The best of times. *Newsletter for Educational Psychologists, 26*(3), 1, 8.

Salomon, G. (1996). Unorthodox thoughts on the nature and mission of contemporary educational psychology. *Educational Psychology Review, 8*, 397–417.

Sanders, J. R. (1994). *The program evaluation standards*. Thousand Oaks, CA: Sage.

Sandoval, W. A., & Bell, P. (2004). Design-based research methods for studying learning in context. *Educational Psychologist, 39*(4), 199–203. Whole issue (4).

Sarason, S. B. (2001). *American psychology and schools: A critique*. New York: Teachers College Press.

Schwab, J. J. (1973). The Practical 3: Translation into curriculum. *School Review, 81*, 501–522.

Shavelson, R. J., & Towne, L. (Eds.) (2002). *Scientific research in education*. Washington, DC: National Academy Press.

Solso, R. L. (1997), *Mind and brain sciences in the 21st century*. Cambridge, MA: MIT Press.

Spencer Foundation. (1997). *Annual Report*. Chicago: Author.

Stanovich, K. E. (1986). Matthew effects in reading: Some consequences of individual differences in the acquisition of reading. *Reading Research Quarterly, 21*, 360–406.

Sternberg, R. J. (1997). *Successful intelligence*. New York: Plume.

Stokes, D. (1997). *Pasteur's quadrant: Basic scientific and technological innovation*. Washington, DC: Brookings Institute Press.

Thorndike, E. L. (1918). The nature, purposes, and general methods of measurements of educational products. *The measurement of educational products. Seventeenth Yearbook of the*

National Society for the Study of Education. Bloomington, IL: Public School Publishing Company.

Towne, L., Wise, L. L., & Winters, T. M. (Eds). (2004). *Advancing scientific research in education.* Washington, DC: National Research Council.

Weitzman, E., & Miles, M. (1995). *Computer programs for qualitative data analysis: An expanded sourcebook* (2nd ed.). Thousand Oaks, CA: Sage.

Williams, B. (Ed.). (2004). *Closing the achievement gap: A vision for changing beliefs and practices.* Arlington, VA: Association for Supervision and Curriculum Development.

Wise, P. S. (1997). A difficult book to pick up or put down. [Review of *Handbook of Educational Psychology.*] *Contemporary Psychology, 42,* 983–985.

Woolfolk Hoy, A. (1998). Complexity and coherence. *Teachers College Record, 100*(2), 437–452.

Woolfolk Hoy, A. (2000). Educational psychology in teacher education. *Educational Psychologist, 35,* 257–270.

Zimmerman, B., & Schunk, D. (Eds.). (2003). *Educational psychology: A century of progress.* Mahwah, NJ: Lawrence Erlbaum Associates.

·3·

CONCEPTUAL CONFUSION AND EDUCATIONAL PSYCHOLOGY[1]

Eric Bredo
University of Virginia

Emerson began one of his essays with the story of how "Man," once whole, was divided by the gods into "men," and separated from one another in a division of labor. As Emerson noted:

The old fable covers a doctrine ever new and sublime; that there is One Man,—present to all particular men only partially . . . and that you must take the whole society to find the whole man. . . . But, unfortunately, this original unit . . . has been so distributed to multitudes, has been so minutely subdivided and peddled out, that it has spilled into drops, and cannot be gathered. The status of society is one in which the members have suffered amputation from the trunk, and strut about so many walking monsters,—a good finger, a neck, a stomach, an elbow, but never a man. (Emerson 1946, p. 52)

This fable relates to fields like psychology that are dedicated to studying human behavior because such fields all too often chop behavior into pieces in a way that makes it is difficult to recompose a whole from the fragments. As Gordon Allport wrote, "psychological science partakes of the same general dismemberment" as the rest of modern culture (Allport, 1968a, p. 103).

While there are excellent reasons for utilizing a division of labor, the way a field is defined in relation to everyday life, distinguished from others, and further subdivided internally can be a source of some of its deepest difficul-ties. As the Danish mathematician/poet Piet Hein (1969) put it:

> Our choicest plans are fallen through,
> Our airiest castles tumbled over,
> Because of lines we neatly drew
> And later neatly stumbled over.

Sometimes the "lines," or conceptual distinctions, are drawn in the wrong places. At other times they adopted too rigidly or generalized beyond their proper sphere. For all of these reasons the basic distinctions utilized in a field may trip its practitioners up in subtle ways.

CONCEPTUAL CONFUSION AND PHILOSOPHICAL REFLECTION

One of philosophy's primary functions is to help identify and correct conceptual confusion. The working educational psychologist may well be skeptical that philosophy has much to contribute to his or her field. When one is engaged in an activity that seems to be going well the focus is on the activity at hand. Reflecting on whether the task is a good one, or whether it is being approached in the right way, seems an unwanted distraction from the business at hand. Adopting a "philosophical" attitude

---

[1] I want to thank Ben Paxton, Denis Phillips, Ralph Reynolds and Phil Winne for many helpful comments and criticisms.

towards psychological concepts is not intended to be wantonly disruptive, however. Its aim is, rather, to assist in avoiding self-defeating patterns of thinking, valuing, and acting.

As the community psychologist, Edward Seidman, argued some years ago, psychologists pay a great deal of attention to type I and type II errors, but tend to ignore "type III" errors (Seidman, 1978).[2] A "type III error," in Seidman's terms, is an "error of conceptualization." He illustrated this using the example of a puzzle that cannot be solved when approached in a conventional manner. In a familiar matchstick puzzle, for example, one is directed to take six matchsticks, and without bending or breaking them, or letting any matchstick cross over another, make four identical equilateral triangles. Most people attempt to solve the problem by laying the matchsticks flat on a table and trying various patterns with them, but the problem turns out to be impossible when approached in this way. It is easily solved, however, when one uses the matchsticks to build a three-dimensional pyramid with three matchsticks forming a triangle on the table and the other three going from each of its vertices to a common apex above them. In this case, the usual two-dimensional approach can be considered "wrong" or "erroneous" because thinking of the problem in that way makes it impossible to solve, while the three-dimensional conceptualization is "right" or "correct" because it makes the problem easily solvable.

"Type III" errors are related to familiar type I or type II errors, but are not the same thing. Saying that one has made a conceptual error is equivalent to saying that the propositions being considered are of the wrong class. It is not so much that they are false, although they may be, as that they are irrelevant, cumbersome, misleading, or otherwise inappropriate for the task at hand. As Carl Becker wrote of the medieval thinker, Thomas Aquinas, we can understand his work and perhaps wonder at it, nonetheless "Its conclusions seem to us neither true nor false, but only irrelevant" (Becker, 1932, pp. 11–12). Aquinas's thought is irrelevant because his way of thinking is virtually incomprehensible to us and of little or no assistance for the issues we care about. In conceptual error, then, one's propositions are composed of the wrong terms, like sentences using the wrong vocabulary.

Books on research methods commonly overlook type III errors because they take it for granted that one has the proper conceptualization of a problem, the only issue being how to proceed within that framework. Nevertheless,

it is not uncommon for the initial conceptualization to be a poor one. Seidman cited the case of community psychologists who suggested that problems of structural unemployment could be addressed by retraining the unemployed. This involves a "conceptual error," he argued, because if the initial difficulty really is *structural* unemployment (too many people seeking too few jobs), then *individual* retraining will never solve it. At best, it will only alter which individuals are employed or unemployed. Approaching a structural problem in individualistic terms is an example of a "type III" error because it makes the original problem impossible to solve, resulting in policies that only reproduce or exacerbate the original difficulty (Watzlawick, Beavin, & Jackson, 1967; Watzlawick, 1974).

While philosophy has been greatly concerned with issues of truth and falsity, it has also been centrally concerned with conceptual confusion. All of the classical "great" philosophers can be viewed as attempting to reframe the problems of their times in less self-defeating ways. Wittgenstein's metaphor of helping the fly buzzing against the side of an open flybottle is apt here. With proper redirection the "fly's" difficulty is easily resolved; without it, its problem remains unsolvable. Even the logical positivists who focused narrowly on truth and logic were greatly concerned with eliminating conceptual confusion, such as confusion between descriptive and normative statements, or descriptive and metaphysical statements (Carnap, 1935/1966). While philosophy should not be reduced to any single task, redirecting the way people think about the issues of their times has been a central part of its mission historically. Or, as Ambrose Beirce wrote, "All are lunatics, but he who can analyze his delusion is called a philosopher."

Philosophers are, nevertheless, not the only ones addressing conceptual confusion. As Denis Phillips argued in a previous edition of this *Handbook*, there is no reason to think that only philosophers engage in critical reflection on the adequacy of the assumptions, models, or metaphors informing a field (Philips, 1996). Some of the best "philosophical" work on psychology has been done by psychologists, just as some of the most influential philosophies of education have been developed by non-philosophers. The issue is primarily one of attitude or orientation, not job title. Thinking that questions deep and pervasive assumptions in a field and attempts to gain the most general possible perspective tends to be considered "philosophical" no matter who does it. As John Searle

---

[2]One commits a type I error when accepting a claim as true that is really false. This tends to be treated as a cardinal sin in science because it results in directly stating a falsehood. A type II error, rejecting a claim as false that is really true, seems to be less frowned upon, perhaps because it does not lead to direct assertion of a falsehood. Nevertheless losing a truth may be as or harmful as asserting a falsehood if the truth is vital and the falsehood trivial.

notes, "recent philosophical discussions about quantum mechanics, or about the significance of Bell's theorem within quantum mechanics, reveal that it is now impossible to say exactly where the problem in physics ends and the problem in philosophy begins. There is a steady interaction and collaboration between philosophy and science on such philosophically puzzling questions" (Searle, 2003, p. 11).

DIFFICULTY RECOGNIZING CONCEPTUAL CONFUSION

One reason that conceptual confusion is worthy of attention is that it is so difficult to recognize. Without attempting to review the vast literature on the subject one can suggest several reasons for this. The first derives from the invisibility of familiar habits or conventions. As Wittgenstein put it:

The aspects of things that are most important to us are hidden because of their simplicity and familiarity. (One is unable to notice something because it is always before one's eyes). The real foundations of his enquiry do not strike a man at all. Unless *that* fact has at some time struck him.—And this means: we fail to be struck by what, once seen, is most striking and most powerful. (Wittgenstein, 1958, p. 50)

Einstein suggested, similarly, that:

... the scientist makes use of a whole arsenal of concepts which he has imbibed practically with his mother's milk; and seldom if ever is he aware of the eternally problematic character of those concepts. He uses this conceptual material, or, speaking more exactly, these conceptual tools of thought, as something obviously, immutably given; something having an objective value of truth that is hardly ever, and in any case not seriously, to be doubted. How could he do otherwise? How would the ascent of a mountain be possible, if the use of hands, legs, and tools had to be sanctioned step by step on the basis of the science of mechanics? And yet in the interests of science it is necessary over and over again to engage in the critique of these fundamental concepts, in order that we may not be unconsciously ruled by them. (Einstein & Jammer, 1953/1969, pp. xi–xii)

Conceptual confusion can also be difficult to recognize or acknowledge because it is emotionally gratifying. Concepts that are fashionable, politically acceptable, or useful for gaining status may be accepted despite their other limitations. Paradigm changes in education and the social sciences often seem to be driven more by changing political climates, for example, than by internal scientific considerations (Karabel & Halsey, 1976). Much the same may be true in psychology as successive waves of thought are over-generalized and viewed as *the* way things are. Behaviorism promised to put psychology on a sound, scientific basis at a time when physics was the preeminent science and logical positivism the dominant philosophy. Its neglect of mind led to cognitivism at a time when the computer was a high status novelty and educating the expert society a priority. Overgeneralization of the computational model led, in turn, to the rise of sociocultural theories at a time when educating across cultural differences was becoming a priority. Now genetics and brain scans are novelties, leading to a shift toward biological and brain based theories. Each of these changes could be viewed as a scientific advance, and something has certainly been learned from them, but their overgeneralization may well have been driven by extra-scientific considerations.

Enthusiasm for an approach may also lead to selective attention to data confirming its usefulness. Behaviorists and gestaltists often looked only at data that each approach could most easily explain, neglecting other phenomena (Hilgard & Bower, 1966). Research conditions may also be arranged that are particularly favorable to a given conception, much as a physicist convinced that light is a wave might arrange for only the wave-like aspects of light to become evident. Even educational psychology as a whole may be blinded if psychological concepts are institutionalized in schools in ways that make them real in their consequence, and educational psychologists look primarily at behavior in schools. If schooling is in important respects an institutionalization of psychological theory and then becomes the primary site for studying that theory, then educational psychologists may lose perspective on the wider limitations of their ways of conceiving things (McDermott & Hood, 1982).

Even when not driven by fads or emotions, conceptual overshoot can be difficult to correct because there is no way to get outside of one's conceptual universe to see how it relates to reality itself. Concepts are the beginnings, the points of conception, of an inquiry that provide the framework within which that inquiry takes place. Since the only way we consciously know about the world is through inquiry, we never have an articulate experience independent of some way of approaching or studying a phenomenon. As a result, the researcher is in a position analogous to that of a small businessman who has no idea whether to try harder with the current business model or give up and try another since the only way to test the model is to try it. For much the same reason, one of the principal ways to find the limits of a conceptualization is to push it beyond these limits. That is why judgments about the goodness or badness of a conceptualization tend to be a posteriori and relative, rather than a priori and absolute. Accumulating anomalies and lack of progress relative to its competitors indicate that trouble is brewing, while "going from success to success" tends to indicate the opposite (Lakatos & Musgrave, 1970).

These introductory remarks are meant to suggest that reflection on the concepts used in educational psychology may be of considerable theoretical and practical relevance. Before marching off to correct conceptual confusion, however, it is important to consider some caveats that emerge from this discussion. If conceptual confusion is so hard to detect then it may be unclear whether one way of thinking about an issue is more "confused" than another. Since many conceptual disputes are tacit political struggles involving competing aims or values (Bruner, 1985), judgments about a given conceptualization may also be biased by partisan interests. For these reasons I will use the term conceptual confusion in what follows, instead of Seidman's conceptual error. I will continue to suggest that some ideas are more confused than others, but acknowledge that such claims depend on other assumptions that may not be shared.

CONCEPTUAL CONFUSION IN PSYCHOLOGY

While all of the human sciences can be accused of harboring considerable conceptual confusion, psychology has at times come in for specific criticism. As Ludwig Wittgenstein wrote:

The confusion and barrenness of psychology is not to be explained by calling it a "young science"; its state is not comparable with that of physics, for instance, in its beginnings.... For in psychology, there are experimental methods and conceptual confusion. The existence of the experimental method makes us think that we have the means of solving the problems which trouble us; though problem and method pass one another by. (Wittgenstein, 1958, p. 232)

Wittgenstein's point seems to have been that psychology is confused because psychologists often think that they can study mental phenomena directly or nakedly, without bias or interpretation, whereas in fact many of the phenomena being studied are constituted by the very linguistic distinctions and practices used to understand them (Searle, 2003, p. 9). In other words, confusion results from thinking (wrongly) that one has escaped the circle of language or culture, giving one's claims a specious certainty and universality.[3]

William James described a very similar form of conceptual confusion that he believed occurred so commonly in psychology that he called it "the psychologist's fallacy." As he noted: "The great snare of the psychologist is the confusion of his own standpoint with that of the mental fact about which he is making his report. I shall hereafter call this the 'psychologist's fallacy' par excellence" (James, 1890/1950, p. 196).

In this form of conceptual confusion the psychologist believes that the concepts he or she uses to explain an organism's behavior are used by the organism itself. If behavior can be described as consistent with a certain rule, for example, then it is thought that the person is actually following that rule. This is like believing that if a person speaks grammatical English they must be using the rules of grammar to construct their sentences. This is conceivable, but it is more likely that most people most of the time use habit and example. Be that as it may, projecting rules describing behavior onto those one is studying tends to lead to considering people's behavior in overly intellectualistic terms, as in current talk about babies having "theories" of other persons. This is an understandable shorthand way of talking about the logic *implicit* in a child's behavior, but once this way of talking becomes familiar, invalid projection of the psychologist's concepts onto the child can become easy to overlook.

It is then only a small step from projecting concepts *onto* a subject to projecting them *into* the subject. Psychological concepts such as "mind," "intelligence," "schemata," and the like, being nouns, are often confused with concrete entities and considered to be inside of people. In this case not only is the standpoint of the observer confused with that of the observed, but, in addition, a concept is confused with a tangible thing. As John Stuart Mill wrote of such reification or misplaced concreteness,

The tendency has always been strong to believe that whatever received a name must be an entity or being, having an independent existence of its own. And if no real entity answering to the name could be found, men did not for that reason suppose that none existed, but imagined that it was something particularly abstruse and mysterious. (quoted in Gould, 1994)

Despite this tendency the one thing we can be sure of is that no such entities will ever be found among the neurons, blood-vessels, and other matter in a person's skull (Phillips, 1987). This is because they are concepts, not concrete things.[4] Confusing the two is like confusing the

---

[3] Physical phenomena are, of course, also affected by the scientist's instruments and procedures, resulting in similar indeterminacy. However, physics tends to take this point into account, whereas psychology has often ignored it.

[4] To avoid confusion I should note that some concepts obviously *refer* to entities. The *concept* of an "atom," once hypothetical, refers to a class of material things that can now be observed. Nonetheless, the concept an "atom" is not itself a tangible thing.

map with the territory or attempting to eat the restaurant menu instead of the food (Bateson, 1972a).

Treating psychological concepts as reified inner entities is a problem because it results in "metaphysical explanation" that explains nothing (Comte, 1856/1957). One takes a pattern of behavior, gives that pattern a name, takes this named "thing" to be a physical entity or as having some of the properties of a physical entity, and then views the person's behavior as caused by having this entity inside of them. As John Dewey noted,

. . . such logic only abstracts some aspect of the existing course of events in order to reduplicate it in a petrified eternal principle by which to explain the very changes of which it is the formalization. (Dewey, 1910/1997, p. 14)

An example would be claiming that a volcano erupts because it has "eruptability" inside of it or that a student performs well because they have a high IQ.

Confusing psychological concepts or functions with entities not only results in mystified explanations, but also leads to inappropriate localization of causes. If one thinks of the "mind" as a thing, one is likely to view "it" as located somewhere, like a physical thing. But locating "mind" turns out to be difficult for the same reason that locating "health" in one's body or "driving" in one's car are difficult. Your "health" is not located in any particular organ because it has to do with the way your organs work together enabling you to thrive and survive in your environment. "Driving" is not located anywhere in your car, because it has to do with what you do with the car. Similarly, "mind" may be better viewed as a function or adaptive way of acting in or responding to the environment, than as an entity in one's skull.

These are clearly not the only forms of conceptual confusion in psychology or educational psychology. Other confusions frequently result when the same term is used with different meanings. The term "learning," for example, has been used for so many different kinds of change that some have proposed doing away with it entirely (Newman, Griffin, & Cole, 1989).[5] Similar confusion occurs when words, like "intelligence" are used in a technical sense one moment and an everyday sense the next (see, e.g., Murray & Herrnstein, 1994). My focus in what follows will be primarily on the psychologist's fallacy, however, and on difficulties resulting from conceiving of psychological functions as entities. I will do so by considering three influential traditions in educational psychology: behaviorism, personality psychology, and cognitive

psychology. While these are not the only traditions of interest today, showing how a form of conceptual confusion recurs in all of them will hopefully indicate that there is a persisting problem that needs attention if it is to be avoided in the future.

STIMULUS AND RESPONSE

A first example of an approach falling into the psychologist's fallacy comes from behavioristic psychology. Many behaviorists, like the early promoter of this approach, John Watson, reacted against the notion that mind is some kind of mysterious inner entity, like the soul or transcendental ego. Seeking to put psychology on a sound scientific footing, they focused on objectively observable physical events, such as changes in an organism's physical environment (stimuli) or changes in its behavior (responses). As Watson wrote:

I believe we can write a psychology . . . and . . . never use the terms consciousness, mental states, mind, content, introspectively verifiable imagery, and the like. . . . It can be done in terms of stimulus and response, in terms of habit formation, habit integrations and the like. . . . In a system of psychology completely worked out, given the response the stimuli can be predicted; given the stimuli the response can be predicted. (Watson, 1913, pp. 511-512, 514)

If "stimulus" and "response" could be defined as externally observable, objectively defined, physical events, and universal laws relating these events discovered, then a (positivistic) science of psychology might be developed analogous to Newtonian physics.

This was in many ways a commendable approach. A psychology aspiring to be a science should certainly be based largely on externally observable behavior (although a role for introspection may remain). It should also refuse to take mind to be a mystified inner thing or entity. Later behaviorists, B. F. Skinner in particular, criticized appeal to inner mental entities in a devastating way, correctly pointing out that it resulted in metaphysical explanations that explain nothing and offer no practical way of changing things (Skinner, 1953). To say that a person's nervous behavior is caused by an inner "neurosis," for example, merely repeats the observation that they tend to behave in a nervous way. Once one cleared the ground of such metaphysical claptrap it seemed possible to build a real science of psychology based on what was essentially an

---

[5]Does it mean receipt of an item of information, such as "learning" that it is now 12 o'clock? Is it change in a *pattern* of response, such as "learning" to eat lunch at noon every day? Or, maybe it means "learning" a pattern common to a broad class of tasks, such as becoming familiar with tasks having an instrumental pattern of contingency? See (Bateson, 1972b) for a discussion of relations between these different forms of "learning."

input-output model of the organism. It also seemed as though a positivistic psychology might make it possible to mechanize education and perhaps even create a scientifically managed social utopia (Skinner, 1976; Skinner and Epstein, 1982). Yet something went wrong with this attempt to develop a positivistic science of behavior based on relations between externally observed physical events.[6] And this "something" is directly related to the psychologist's fallacy.

John Dewey criticized this kind of input-output psychology prior to Watson's writing (Dewey, 1896; Bredo, 1998). In his critique of what he termed the "reflex arc concept" in psychology, Dewey argued that if a person really behaved in this way the result would be only "a series of jerks" rather than a coordinated, purposeful *act*. If a "stimulus" is just an external event that is unrelated to what the organism is already doing, in one way or another, then it may cause another independent event, such as startling the organism, but these separate events will not result in well-coordinated behavior. For that to happen, stimulus and response must be constructed in parallel, helping shape one another during their development, much as one might alter the way one shapes a question in response to dawning evidence of the way it is being received by another. In the conventional way of thinking evident at the time a "stimulus" was viewed as a sensory input, and a "response" as a motor output. The stimulus is then a prod to the organism's sensory nerves, creating the motor response (the word "stimulus" comes from the name of a short Roman sword).

Dewey argued that this was all wrong, at least when one is observing routine, well-habituated behavior. "Stimulus" and "response" should both be viewed as acts, or "sensori-motor coordinations," rather than as sensory or motor events. Viewed properly, a "stimulus" is an *act* of perception and not the mere bombardment of a nerve by external stimulation. Similarly, a "response" is a manipulatory act rather than a mere motor jerk. Seeing something involves turning one's head, focusing one's eyes, and so forth, until an object can be properly resolved. Reaching out for something similarly involves physical activity guided by sensory input. Viewing behavior as a sequence of acts gives a more active interpretation of the organism's role in it, since in an act the organism moves in order to change its stimulation, rather than being merely prodded by it. In other words, Dewey adopted something like a cybernetic interpretation of behavior in which it is governed by feedback.

Once one views stimuli and responses as acts rather than as sensory and motor events, respectively, then it becomes clear that they cannot be defined in interpretation-free, external physical terms. One cannot draw a line between organism and environment, taking stimuli as external (stimulating) events and responses as organismic responses since in the new conception stimulus and response involve both organism and environment. The organism has a role in making itself sensitive to different events, just as the environment has a role in guiding and regulating its response. As Dewey put it:

The fact is that stimulus and response are not distinctions of existence, but teleological distinctions, that is, distinctions of function, or part played, with reference to reaching or maintaining an end. (W)e may say, positively, that it is only the assumed common reference to an inclusive end which marks each member off as stimulus and response, that apart from such reference we have only antecedent and consequent; in other words, the distinction is one of interpretation. (Dewey, 1896, p. 365)

In other words, in the normal (well-habituated) case, both "stimulus" and "response" are acts which are themselves parts of a larger act, just as the act of looking for a cup and the act of reaching out to grab it are parts of the larger act of "taking a sip of coffee." Approached in this way a "stimulus" is an act that serves to prepare the situation so that a later act, a "response" can complete the action for which the stimulus prepared the way. Given a sequence of such developmentally-related acts, it becomes somewhat arbitrary whether a given one is viewed as a "stimulus" or a "response," because it will generally play both roles, having had its own preconditions prepared by earlier acts and preparing the way for further acts. Which sub-act is a beginning and which an ending depends on how you parse the sequence.

Dewey argued that the mechanistic (i.e., linear, deterministic) S-R model of his day was in error because it succumbed to the psychologist's fallacy:

The fallacy that arises when this is done is virtually the psychological or historical fallacy. A set of considerations which hold good only because of a completed process, is read into the content of the process which conditions this completed result. A state of things characterizing an outcome is regarded as a true description of the events which led up to this outcome; when, as a matter of fact, if this outcome had already been in existence, there would have been no necessity for the process (Dewey, 1896, p. 367).

---

[6]I use the term "positivistic" to refer to a specific family of approaches to philosophy of science. It is neither an epithet nor as a description of quantitative research or scientifically oriented research in general. For an excellent discussion of the assumptions implicit in positivism and its post-positivistic successors see Phillips & Burbules (2000).

Or, as Ward and Throop suggest, the psychologist who thinks that prior events cause later events without the activity of the organism helping to co-construct these sequences is like one who looks through a crack at a series of cats walking by and concludes that "whiskers cause tails" (Ward & Throop, 1997).

The implication of Dewey's analysis was that a positivistic science of psychology modeled on 18th century physics, is impossible. It is impossible because in order to understand how an event functions in an organism's behavior one needs to observe how it is perceived. Similarly, in order to understand the function of a response one needs to observe what it is apparently organized to accomplish. In effect, the psychologist faces the equivalent of a hermeneutic circle, using an interpretation of what the organism is trying to do to figure out what the relevant "stimuli" and "responses" are, and a guess as to these sub-functions to figure out the activity of which they are a part. Such a psychology can still focus entirely on publicly observable behavior, but in cases where it is uncertain how to interpret a given behavior the psychologist must look at subtler aspects of behavior, such as the *way* a stimulus is sought or the *way* a response is enacted.

B. F. Skinner attempted to remedy some of these problems with earlier behaviorism (see Bredo, 1997). He recognized that "stimulus" and "response" have to be defined functionally and not merely as independent physical events. In his revised view, a discriminating stimulus is an environmental event that alters the probability of a response, while a response is a behavior whose probability is altered by a stimulus. A reinforcing stimulus was then defined as a stimulus that makes a response emitted in the presence of a (discriminating) stimulus more probable (or intense). Each term was defined, as it must be, in terms of its functional relationship to the others (Skinner, 1935). This raises difficulties, however, since a set of terms defined circularly in terms of one another does not give any of them a concrete interpretation. Skinner avoided this problem by imposing a set of contingencies whose relation to one another and the animal's needs, he controlled. By starving an animal to 80% of its initial body weight, for example, he could be sure that food pellets would be "reinforcing." By setting up a set of conditions in which reinforcement only occurs in the presence of an event he controlled, he could effectively define what counted as a "discriminating stimulus." This approach recognized implicit the meaning, purpose, or "function" of the different events in the organism's behavior, while maintaining the objectivity of a purely external description of it. In effect, the psychologist's fallacy was maintained by so controlling the environment that the organism has to come around to the psychologist's definition of things. In addition, behavior not oriented to these meanings could be ignored and interpreted as merely "random."

This approach saved a positivistic, interpretation-free psychology but at the cost of making it testable only under highly controlled conditions. As Noam Chomsky argued, in a well-known critique of Skinner's work on verbal behavior, this puts the behaviorist in a very awkward dilemma:

If he (a behaviorist) accepts the broad definitions, characterizing any physical event impinging on the organism as a stimulus and any part of the organism's behavior as a response, he must conclude that most behavior has not been demonstrated to be lawful. . . . If we accept the narrower definitions, then behavior is lawful by definition (if it consists of responses); but this fact is of limited significance, since most of what the animal does will simply not be considered behavior. Hence the psychologist either must admit that behavior is not lawful, or must restrict his attention to those highly limited arenas in which it is lawful . . . Skinner does not consistently adopt either course. (Chomsky, 1959, p. 30)

In effect, the doctrinaire behaviorist has to choose between being "scientific" in a narrow, positivistic sense only under highly controlled conditions, or generalizing to less controlled conditions in a merely metaphorical or interpretive way. Chomsky argued that Skinner could not have it both ways.

If this analysis is correct then this set of conceptual confusions has important implications for educational research and practice. Its implication for research is that a positivistic science of behavior, modeled on a narrow interpretation of physics, is impossible. Psychologists can dispense with the need for interpreting the implicit meaning or function of behavior only under highly controlled conditions. If they do so they blind themselves to the processes by which the organism itself parses events, making its activity seem simpler than it is. They also limit severely their ability to generalize to less controlled settings. Psychologists studying behavior in less controlled situations may have more to say of practical relevance, but at the cost of greater interpretive ambiguity or unreliability. Valuable things may be learned in both ways, but neither should be regarded as *the* way things are.

The practical implication of this critique is that educators must be sensitive to what students are trying to do and how they interpret and respond to their experiences. This typically means they must be sensitive to the social relationships implied in the manner or style in which something is done, and not merely in their brute accomplishment. This is because an interpretation of the relationship is generally used to frame or interpret the actions of others (Bateson, 1972b). A supposed "reward" offered in a patronizing manner will have different value than one offered sympathetically, for example, and may have still another value if offered in a humorous manner. Student responses will similarly have different meanings indicated by their form or style. Whether work is done just to get it over with, or is taken seriously in itself, can be empirically evident in the manner or style in which a student does it. Interpreting such signals may be difficult but is nonetheless necessary in order to know what is rewarding or punishing to a student in the first place. Although any successful educator recognizes this and attempts to act on such cues, a reductive theory based on confusing the observer's and agent's points of view tends to make one insensitive to them.

TRAIT AND TREATMENT

A second example of conceptual confusion occurs in traditional personality psychology. This branch of psychology, sometimes termed differential psychology, attempts to identify differences between individuals in personality "traits" or "aptitudes" which are viewed as inner causes of outwardly observable behavior. The trait or aptitude most commonly considered in education and elsewhere has, of course, been the traditional psychometric conception of intelligence, or "IQ." This concept has frequently been treated as a kind of reified inner entity causing individual differences in school performance. As Richard Snow wrote,

In yesterday's theoretical writing, the interpretation of aptitude differences typically relied on one or another kind of entity theory. Aptitudes were reified as things in the head of the person. They were not things actually—the old phrenology and faculty psychology had been soundly rejected....—but they were the products of things genetic and physiological, and they were described metaphorically as things in the head (e.g., mental energy, mental engines, functional unities, instinctive responses, and stimulus-response bonds) that the person possesses. (Snow, 1992, p. 7)

As Snow went on to note, "the picture of aptitude most psychologists and educators carried around with them was an entity theory of a fixed, single rank order, general-purpose cognitive trait called *intelligence*" (p. 8).

The defense of trait psychology relied on the fact that people's behavior can sometimes be predicted by personality factors across a wide variety of environments (Allport, 1968b). A person who behaves in a relatively "defensive" manner in one environment may tend to behave similarly in others, for example. As a result a measure of relative "defensiveness" might predict much of the difference between people in certain aspects of behavior across a variety of environments, while environmental factors might predict little of this variance. Such predictive evidence was used to bolster the suggestion that behavior is *caused* by inner traits or aptitudes.

Problems with this type of explanation have already been noted. "Defensiveness" is a description of an observed pattern of behavior. To take this word describing a type of behavior and think that it is a cause of a person's behavior is a form of self-befuddlement: Why does a person behave defensively? Because they are "defensive" or have lots of "defensiveness" inside! This is exactly like explaining a volcano's eruption by saying it has a great deal of "eruptability" inside. Such "metaphysical" explanations explain nothing because the explanation merely repeats a description of the initial behavior, adding nothing to what one knows. The same point applies to the notion that IQ *causes* school performance. If IQ is measured by determining a person's performance relative to others on a set of school-like tasks, then it should be no mystery that this measure predicts relative school performance: those who do relatively well on school like tasks are, indeed, likely to do relatively well on other school-like tasks. The vacuousness of the explanation is concealed by pointing to a mystified inner entity, IQ or "g," as the cause of the performance.

Thinking of aptitudes as entities also tends to lead to mislocating causes, as suggested earlier. If aptitudes are taken as concrete things then they must *be* somewhere. Because they characterize individual behavior they are apparently inside of the person. Therefore the causes of the form of behavior named by the aptitude must be inside of, or intrinsic to, the person. For example, if a personality variable such as IQ predicts more variance in performance than a set of environmental variables, then it is thought that IQ is the stronger cause of these outcomes. The error of this line of thinking has been pointed out by many scholars (Corno et. al., 2002; Cronbach, 1957, 1975; Lewontin, 1976; Snow, 1992, 1974). A personality variable might predict more variance in a particular population because there is little variation in the relevant environmental variables within that population. But whichever set of variables works best, this should not be mistaken for a proper understanding of how individual or environmental factors cause behavior (See Lewontin, 1976). As the statistics books say, prediction should not be confused with causation.

A second point is that personality and environmental factors may interact, rather than having merely additive effects. A person of a given personality type may be relatively more defensive in one kind of environment, but relatively less defensive in another. If

3. CONCEPTUAL CONFUSION AND EDUCATIONAL PSYCHOLOGY • 51

the relative "effects" of individual differences depend on the character of environments, and the relative "effects" of environmental differences depend on the character of individuals, then aptitudes and treatments need to be identified in terms of one another, rather than independently (much like stimulus and response in the preceding discussion).

Such thinking has led to reconceptualizing the concept of "aptitude." Terming the older view "a stultifying misconstrual," Snow noted that "in the (newer) line of research that has developed . . . thinking skills reside in the person-situation interaction, and not solely in the mind of the person" (Snow, 1992, p. 7, pp. 19–20). In this newer conception, aptitude is viewed as describing a behavioral tendency resulting from a particular relationship between person and environment, rather than a property of the person or environment alone. As Snow notes, an aptitude might be thought of as the relative "readiness" of a person to take advantage of certain environments in a certain way. Approached in this manner, it is illegitimate to talk of a person's aptitude without specifying the environment in which it functions or is relevant. Adopting this approach, one might reinterpret the traditional psychometric conception of IQ as a measure of relative readiness to perform well in schools as we know them. This interpretation is supported by the fact that what IQ tests predict best, other than other IQ tests, is school performance. Admittedly, some aptitude differences might be relevant to differences in performance over a wide range of environments, while others might be specific to a narrow range, but determining the degree of generality becomes an empirical matter rather than something presupposed at the start.

The traditional model of aptitude can be viewed as an example of the psychologist's fallacy because it projects the psychologist's explanatory concepts into the person whose behavior is being explained. It confuses the psychologist's viewpoint with that of the subject and, in addition, confuses a concept with a concrete thing. The newer approach based on aptitude x treatment interactions, undermines the older certainty about finding the causes of behavior in *either* the person *or* the environment, suggesting that both are always necessary to produce behavior. Once again, an attempt to cut up the problem into isolated parts, such as those inside versus outside of the skin, has failed with important implications for research and practice.

Wider implications for research came from subsequent investigation of aptitude x treatment interactions which found some relatively stable interaction "effects," but also many interactions that vary, apparently with changing social and cultural conditions. The complexity of this situation in which interaction effects appear to interact with

other conditions, leading to an "endless hall of mirrors," resulted in Cronbach's concluding that the whole attempt to find universal laws of behavior analogous to Newtonian laws in physics might be in error:

Too narrow an identification with science . . . has fixed our eyes upon an inappropriate goal. The goal of our work, as I have argued here, is not to amass generalizations atop which a theoretical tower can someday be erected . . . The special task of the social scientist in each generation is to pin down the contemporary facts. Beyond that, he shares with the humanistic scholar and the artist an effort to gain insight into contemporary relationships, and to realign the culture's view of man with present realities. To know man is no mean aspiration. (Cronbach, 1975)

In other words, a positivistic psychology modeled on physics may be an unrealistic aspiration.

One of the practical implications of this shift in thinking is that there may be no "best practice" that is good for everyone. Different ways of teaching may have to be tailored to fit different types of students, rather than applied in a "one size fits all" manner. It also suggests that students should not be viewed as having general propensities to do well or badly, since their behavior may depend on the environments in which they are placed. Some may learn relatively well in one environment, but not in another, and so forth. Viewed in this way it becomes more difficult to blame the student's inherent nature for failure because they might do well in a different environment. Both partners in the teaching/learning relationship are likely to bear some responsibility for its outcomes, although the generality of an aptitude's implications for performance across a variety of treatment environments, or a treatment's implications across a range of aptitudes remains an empirical matter.

Even the newer aptitude x treatment interaction approach may face further conceptual difficulties, however. The problem is that the statistical interaction effects on which it is based focus on the average performance of different types of people in different types of environments. This leads one to think that the solution to educational difficulties involves matching *types* of students with *types* of treatments. But if people are unique- when considered as a whole, then no student is a "type." As Dewey put it, "each individual constitutes his own class" (Dewey, 1916, p. 90). The statistically knowledgeable know this, but it is all too easy to turn a student into a type when using generalizations about learning styles, cultural differences, and the like that appeal to interaction effects based on average differences. The problem is that statistical differences between groups cannot be validly projected onto the behavior of a given individual, who may well behave in a distinctive way.[7] If nothing else, this reminds us that teaching is an art and not a science. Teachers may use psychological generalizations to inform their practice, but must ultimately practice their art using their own judgment regarding the particular situation at hand. As William James put it:

I say moreover that you make a great, a very great mistake, if you think that psychology, being the science of the mind's laws, is something from which you can deduce definite programmes and schemes and methods of instruction for immediate schoolroom use. Psychology is a science, and teaching is an art; and sciences never generate arts directly out of themselves. An intermediary inventive mind must make the application, by using its originality. (James, 1899/1992, pp. 7–8)

The point may seem obvious but judging by the frequency with which "definite programs and schemes of instruction" are proposed it has apparently not been absorbed.

MIND AND MATTER

A third example of conceptual confusion in psychology comes from the adoption of the computational theory of mind. The leaders of the cognitive revolution that began in the late 1950s rejected both behaviorism and trait psychology. As Herbert Simon described the situation,

from the time of William James almost down to World War II. American psychology was dominated by behaviorism, the stimulus-response connection, . . . the nonsense syllable, and the rat. Cognitive processes—what went on between the ears after the stimulus was received and before the response was given–were hardly mentioned, and the word *mind* was reserved for philosophers, not to be uttered by respectable psychologists. (Simon 1991, p. 190)

Those, like Simon, who sought to "bring mind back in" tended to view it more dynamically than trait psycholo-

gists, suggesting that "mind" is not a thing or quantity, but a process or function. Rather than measuring its size one needed to understand how it does its job. For this purpose the development of the computer provided a helpful (and high status) metaphor.

One of the great philosophical advantages of the computational metaphor is that it offers a promising approach to the mind/body problem, a problem that goes back to Descartes (1637/1969), if not earlier. Descartes viewed the body as a physical entity or machine, while the soul or mind, was a meta-physical entity. This created all the familiar problems of mind/body dualism: How is the mind related to the body? How can the two interact given that they are entirely different kinds of "substances"? How can the mind know the external world? The whole issue seems to derive from the fact that we have developed two incompatible ways of explaining things. A materialistic account, drawn from the natural sciences, explains the behavior of things in terms of the interaction of material entities in accord with physical laws. Everyday moral accounts, on the other hand, explain behavior in terms of beliefs and desires, hopes and fears, wishes and intentions. As long as these two types of explanation are applied to different types of objects there is no problem. We can explain the movement of the planets in one way and the actions of our neighbors in another. But once these two kinds of things interact, as it seems they do in human behavior, we face the Cartesian problem of explaining how such different kinds of entities can possibly affect one another.

One approach to a dualism is to try to eliminate one of the sides, viewing it as unreal or as a side effect of the operation of the other side. Behaviorists tended to deny that "inner" mental phenomena are real, or even if existent, that they have any explanatory use, because they cannot be directly manipulated (Skinner 1953).[8] A second approach admits that mental experiences exist, but equates them with physiological events in the brain. In this "identity theory" of mind, if one feels a pain, that's simply a

---

[7]This point has been forcibly made by Borsboom, Mellenbergh & van Heerden (2003), who argue that the usual interpretation of latent variables, like IQ, as causes of individual performance rests on the "fallacy of division" (p. 212). This amounts to confusing a between-subjects and within-subjects account. In other words it is forgotten that such traits are measured by comparing the relative performance of individuals within a population (a between-subjects account). They note, "such misinterpretations are very common in the interpretation of results obtained in latent variables analysis. However, they can all be considered to be specific violations of the general statistical maxim that between-subjects conclusions should not be interpreted in a within-subjects sense" (p. 214). Something like this reasoning seems to have led Snow to begin to describe aptitudes in terms of affordances that a *unique* set of environmental features offer a person with a *unique* set of habits or tendencies, with each sampling from among elements in the other (Snow, 1992).

[8]To be more precise, there are different forms of behaviorism. An "eliminative behaviorist," such as Watson, would claim that there are no such things as mental states or events, only behavioral responses to stimuli. An "analytical behaviorist" claims that ascriptions of mental states or events simply mean certain kinds of responses to certain environmental events, hence that the mental language adds nothing to a proper scientific account. Finally, a "reductive behaviorist" claims that mental ascriptions are ultimately made true by behavioral responses to environmental events (Lycan, 2003, p. 175). Thus, in the latter version, the behavioral description is seen as the basic or fundamental one, while the mental description is viewed as derivative.

certain set of nerves firing. This helps account for the possibility that two people may have different subjective experiences yet show the same outward behavior, which the behavioristic account cannot deal with.. On the other hand it may relate subjective experiences too concretely to the operation of a specific physical substrate. Suppose that another species exists with a sensory apparatus materially different from but functionally identical to ours. Wouldn't members of such a species also feel" pain." The apparent plausibility of this suggestion is one thing that has tended to lead to rejection of the identity theory (Lycan, 2003, p. 178).

But if mind and matter, or mind and brain, really are different in some way that cannot be so easily swept aside, and yet are not different entities, one physical, the other metaphysical, then how can their relationship be understood? Here is where the computational model offers a solution. It views the "mind" as equivalent to the *functioning* of a computer running certain software, while the "brain" is equivalent to the computer's hardware. In other words, "thinking" is like running an inner computer simulation of the behavior of outer objects using inner symbolic representations of the external world (see, e.g., Newell & Simon (1972)). This *function* is different from the material entity allowing it to be performed. The core of this theory, termed the "physical symbol system hypothesis," was stated as follows:

The study of logic and computers has revealed to us that intelligence resides in physical symbol systems. This is computer science's most basic law of qualitative structure. Symbol systems are collections of patterns and processes, the latter being capable of producing, destroying and modifying the former. The most important properties of patterns is that they can designate objects, processes, or other patterns, and that, when they designate processes, they can be interpreted. Interpretation means carrying out the designated process. The two most significant classes of symbol systems with which we are acquainted are human beings and computers. (Newell & Simon 1976, p. 125)

In other words, any physical "system" (person or machine) that can store a structured pattern, alter such patterns under the control of another pattern, and "interpret" these patterns so that they control the behavior of the system, can, in principle, be "intelligent." It does not matter what the machine is made of, if it can do these things it can exhibit "intelligent" behavior.

This view of "mind" does not deny that mental phenomena exist or are useful in explaining behavior, in contrast to radical behaviorism. It also does not reduce mental phenomena to brain events, like the identity theory. Rather, it views mind as the *functioning* of a computa-

tional system instantiated in a material system, the brain. Since the computational approach treats "mind" as a function rather than a thing the Cartesian problem dissolves. The mind is not a strange metaphysical entity, but a particular kind of useful process. The problem of how to relate mental functioning to the operation of the material brain remains, of course, but it becomes clear that these are just two different descriptions of what goes on when an information-processing "system" performs a task rather than two different things.

This approach, which is in some ways similar to that adopted by the earlier functional psychologists, appears more rigorous and "tough-minded" than the earlier work since it allows mental phenomena to be understood in terms of the operation of a well-understood machine, the computer. Nonetheless, many have concluded that something has gone seriously wrong with the computational model of mind, (Dreyfus, 1979/1972; Winograd & Flores, 1986).

The basic problem is, again, that it frequently falls into the "psychologist's fallacy." As Bill Clancey put it,

...in AI research we look at the structures of our models and we say, "This is the knowledge; this program is an expert; this is what the student knows...." In so doing, we have claimed an isomorphism. We have said that what is in the student's head and these representations are functionally identical. But if people literally followed such grammatical patterns or shuffled them about grammatically the way our learning programs do, they would not be very intelligent. We have confused our representations with the phenomenon we are modeling. The map is not the territory. (Clancey, 1991, p. 6)

In other words, things that are meaningful to the observer, such as a problem represented in familiar mathematical symbols, are viewed as equally meaningful to the computer "solving" the problem. We project our sense of meaning onto the computer. But, unlike us, the computer solves the problem in an entirely formal or syntactic way that is insensitive to the meaning of the patterns it alters (Winograd & Flores, 1986). Thus the computer may appear "smart" in a certain sense, but only because we falsely attribute meaningful activity to it.

The roboticist Rodney Brooks argues that the computational theory of mind got things confused in this way because the field of artificial intelligence developed in a fragmented manner. Those modeling reasoning and problem-solving processes tended to work separately from those modeling perceptual and motor processes (Brooks, 1991). As a result, thinking was modeled independently of the process of functioning in the world, giving an overly formal or intellectualist view of mind.

Brooks and others like Clark (1997), have suggested that this perspective needs to be reversed by starting with activity in the world, and asking how thinking is stimulated by experienced problems of coordination and control. In this revised view, thinking is a process that reorganizes conflicting habits in context rather than a removed spectator on a world "out there." Such criticisms suggest that mind is better viewed in terms of organism/environment relations than as something "inside" of the organism or "between the ears," as Simon referred to "it."

Another criticism of the computational model of mind comes from asking for whom the symbols being used are meaningful. In the computational model, the "meaning" of "2 + 2" is a particular "interpretation" of this pattern in terms of lower-level machine instructions. But in what sense is this what the marks "2 + 2" mean? Saying "2 + 2" could have many meanings in everyday life. It might even be an oblique marriage proposal, suggesting that two adults, each with a child already, consider forming a blended family. As Wittgenstein argued, symbols may "mean" many different things depending on the occasions and social activities in which they are used (Wittgenstein, 1958). Words gain shared meaning because they are used in similar ways in mutually understood conjoint activities (Dewey, 1916). In this view, linguistic or symbolically represented "meaning" is not just the performance of a certain set of concrete operations. It is, rather, a signal from one person to another of a desired or intended line of conduct in a mutually understood "game" or social activity in which the participants are involved.

Summarizing these two points, the computational model of mind has tended to confuse a narrow view of function and meaning located inside of the "system" with a wider, interactive one. The limitations resulting from this view have often been hidden by studying problem-solving in well-defined or well-controlled task situations (Newman, et al., 1989). In such situations people are, in effect, made to function like computers. But this makes generalization to less well-defined or controlled settings difficult. Among other things, in "everyday" settings, tasks tend to be socially distributed in varying ways and meanings socially negotiated (Newman, et al., 1989). A model that does not take these processes into account is likely to be a model of an agent that is literally "out of it" (Bredo, 1994).

Criticisms of this sort, combined with changing practical interests, have led to the computational model being supplanted, in many circles, by socio-cultural or socio-historical approaches based on Vygotsky's theories, or on situative theories of cognition and learning with similar and other origins (Brown, Collins & Duguid, 1989; Greeno & Moore, 1993; Lave, 1988; Lave & Wenger, 1991). In these accounts, the focus is on person/environment dynamics in a context that is itself constructed at least in part by the interactants.

The practical ramifications of this shift from a computational to a practice-based, socially-collaborative model are substantial. The computational metaphor is consistent with the notion that thinking or learning involves working alone, sitting still, while solving abstract problems in one's head. In contrast, a view of mind that sees it as an interactive activity situated in the world, using symbols whose meaning is shared and negotiated with others, is more consistent with an active and collaborative view of learning based on "authentic" problems. At the very least, an education based on the latter model would seem more consistent with two important ways that people contrast with computers, their tendency to physically manipulate things and communicate with one another (Dewey, 1956/1900; Vygotsky, 1934). Whether these latter day models will eventually fall prey to similar confusions, such as reifying the notion of community (Ortiz, 1999), remains to be seen. What seems clear is that any attempt to claim that one has mind in a box will fall prey to the same fallacy.

CONCLUSIONS

In the foregoing I have attempted to trace certain forms of conceptual confusion through a variety of movements in psychological and educational theory. I have suggested that psychology gets into theoretical and practical difficulties whenever it attempts to enclose human psychic life in a watertight conceptual box. Attempting to capture psychic life in a closed system cannot be done because there is no place to stand from which it can be accomplished. It might be seen as analogous to trying to swallow oneself or catch the self that is observing oneself. Everything suggests that we are too close to our own behavior, too much a product our own linguistic and cultural practices, too narrowly interested, to get the necessary distance. As a result our conceptualizations are partial "in both senses of the word," as James put it.

Nonetheless, there always seems to be a new effort on the horizon to identify *the* right conceptual level to capture thinking or learning in a scientific net. Although each new model or metaphor, or each new level of analysis—genetic, individual, socio-cultural, or some other—adds something to our understanding, each is limited. Problems arise when a given approach is confused with *the* way things are, as in the psychologist's fallacy. In effect, there is a confusion of map and territory, of representation and thing represented. If the world just naturally and inherently *is* one's model, if nature speaks one's language, then that model or expression seems much more real and secure because it is founded in nature itself. But, as a former student of mine likes to say, "Don't paint yourself into your own picture."

Such confusion starts harmlessly by drawing a conceptual line around the "system" being studied, dividing it neatly into an inside and an outside. Having done this one can study the system by seeing how its inputs are transformed into outputs. This is what the behaviorists tended to do when they discriminated between stimulus and response, viewing the stimulus as coming from the environment and the response as coming from the organism. It is also what trait psychologists did when they drew a neat line between person and environment and then studied the "inner" causes of a person's behavior. It is, finally, what cognitive psychologists have done when they drew a line between brain and body and placed the mind in the cranium, viewing it as analogous to a computer. Each of these sets of "lines" might have remained harmless had they been treated as helping to constitute the phenomena being observed. If one recognizes that one's model helps create the data, not by creating it of whole cloth, but by altering the way one interacts with one's environment, then one takes responsibility for the effects of one's approach. But the tendency is strong to forget that one is using a model or metaphor, especially when it becomes familiar, transparent and, ultimately, literal. In the case of the computational model of mind, for example, what began as a metaphor tended to end up with the claim that people *are* computers. Adopting the latest metaphor, particularly a high status mechanical one, may seem tough-minded and scientific, but over-enthusiasm can also lead to overgeneralizing the approach, confusing the model with the world. Such overgeneralization can be disguised by limiting research to well-controlled settings in which people behave in a way that is consistent with the model, but this tends to break down when extrapolated to less controlled settings.

The attempt to reduce human behavior to a particular model may also lead to practical harm. It leads, primarily, to treating people as though they were limited in the ways in which the model is limited. If the model is one of behavioral conditioning, this may lead to ignoring people's aims and interpretations. But a "reward" offered in a patronizing fashion is likely to have a different effect than one offered humorously, making the issue more complicated than presupposed. Potentially harmful side effects of use of the trait model are also quite evident, principally the ease with which it shifts all responsibility to the character of the person being described (This is not to say that they do not bear some of the causal responsibility. Their degree of moral culpability is another issue.) Finally, the computational model may lend support to a passive and socially isolated model of thinking and learning. It may also tend to lead to confusing artificial or inauthentic "problems" and feigned thought with genuine thinking arising from uncertainty about how to act (see, e.g., James, 1896/1956), resulting in teaching superficiality and irresponsibility in thinking (Dewey, 1910).

One remedy for these difficulties would seem to be to adopt a situated view of educational psychology itself. In this view, educational psychology is a partial effort, based on a variety of untested and unrecognized assumptions, to understand the way things work for certain purposes. Conceived in this way, there is no one way the world is, for the world *is* many ways (Goodman, 1972). As William James put it,

...the truth is too great for any one actual mind....The facts and worths of life need many cognizers to take them in. There is no point of view absolutely public and universal, Private and uncommunicable perceptions always remain over, and the worst of it is that those who look for them from the outside never know *where*. (James, 1899/1992, p. 708)

The way to keep from losing the "whole man," then, is to acknowledge the partiality of one's view rather than confusing it with *the* way things are. Approached in this way, scientific and everyday points of view inform and correct one another, as do psychological perspectives focusing on different functions or different levels of analysis. No view should have the last word, because each represents a partial attitude or orientation, good for limited purposes.

References

Allport, G. W. (1968a). Imagination in psychology: Some needed steps. In G. W. Allport (Ed.), *The person in psychology*. Boston: Beacon Press.

Allport, G. W. (1968b). Traits revisited. In G. W. Allport (Ed.), *The person in psychology*. Boston: Beacon Press.

Bateson, G. (1972a). *Steps to an ecology of mind*. New York: Ballentine.

Bateson, G. (1972b). The logical categories of learning and communication. In *Steps to an ecology of mind*. New York: Ballantine.

Becker, C. (1932). *The heavenly city of the eighteenth century philosophers*. New Haven, CT: Yale University Press.

Borsboom, D., Mellenbergh, G. J. & van Heerden, J. (2003). The theoretical status of latent variables. *Psychological Review, 110*(2):203-219.

Bredo, E. (1994). Reconstructing educational psychology: Situated cognition and Deweyian pragmatism. *Educational Psychologist, 29*(1):23-35.

Bredo, E. (1997). The social construction of learning. In G. Phye (Ed.), *Handbook of academic learning: the construction of knowledge*. New York: Academic Press.

Bredo, E. (1998). Evolution, psychology, and John Dewey's critique of the reflex arc concept. *The Elementary School Journal, 98*(5): 447-466.

Brooks, R. A. (1991). New approaches to robotics. *Science, 253*:1227-1232.

Brown, J. S., Collins, A. & Duguid, P. (1989). Situated cognition and the culture of learning. *Educational Researcher, 18*(1):32-42.

Bruner, J. (1985). Models of the learner. *Educational Researcher* (June/July), 5-8.

Carnap, R. (1935/1966). The Rejection of Metaphysics. In M. Weitz (Ed.), *20th-Century Philosophy: The Analytic Tradition*. New York: Free Press.

Chomsky, N. (1959). A review of B. F. Skinner's *Verbal Behavior*. *Language, 35*(1).

Clancey, W. J. (1991). A Boy scout, Toto, and a bird: How situated cognition is different from situated robotics. Paper presented at NATO Workshop on Emergence, Situatedness, Subsumption, and Symbol Grounding.

Clark, A. (1997). *Being there: Putting brain, body and world together again*. Cambridge, Mass.: MIT Press.

Comte, A. (1856/1957). *A general view of positivism* (J. H. Bridges, trans.) Robert Speller and Sons.

Corno, L., & et al. (2002). *Remaking the concept of aptitude: extending the legacy of Richard E. Snow*. Mahwah, NJ: Lawrence, Erlbaum.

Cronbach, L. J. (1957). The two disciplines of scientific psychology. *American Psychologist* (12):671-684.

Cronbach, L. J. (1975). Beyond the two disciplines of scientific psychology. *American Psychologist* (February):116-127.

Descartes, R. (1637/1969). Discourse on the method of rightly conducting one's reason and seeking truth in the sciences. In M. D. Wilson (Ed.), *The essential Descartes*. New York: Mentor.

Dewey, J. (1896). The reflex arc concept in psychology. *The Psychological Review*:356-370.

Dewey, J. (1910). *How we think*. Boston, MA: D. C. Heath.

Dewey, J. (1910/1997). The influence of Darwinism on philosophy. In J. Dewey (Ed.), *The influence of Darwin on philosophy and other essays*. Amherst, New York: Prometheus.

Dewey, J. (1916). *Democracy and education*. New York: Macmillan.

Dewey, J. (1956/1900). *The school and society*. Chicago, IL: University of Chicago Press.

Dreyfus, H. L. (1979/1972). *What computers can't do*. New York: Harper and Row.

Einstein, A, & Jammer, M. (1953/1969). *Concepts of space*. Cambridge, MA: Harvard University Press.

Emerson, R. W. (1946). The American scholar. In C. Bode (Ed.), *The portable Emerson*. New York: Viking Penguin. Original edition 1837.

Goodman, N. (1972). The way the world is. In N. Goodman (Ed.), *Problems and Projects*. Indianapolis, IN: Hackett.

Gould, S. J. (1994). (November, 28) *The New Yorker*: 149.

Greeno, J. G, & Moore, J. L. (1993). Situativity and symbols: Response to Vera and Simon. *Cognitive Science, 17*(1): 49-59.

Hein, P. (1969). *Grooks*: Vol. 1. Garden City, NY: Doubleday.

Hilgard, E. R., & Bower, G. H. (1966). *Theories of learning*. NY: Appleton-Century-Crofts.

James, W. (1890/1950). *The principles of psychology:* Vols. I and II. New York: Dover.

James, W. (1896/1956). *The will to believe and other essays in popular philosophy*. New York: Dover.

James, W. (1899/1992). Talks to teachers. In G. E. Myers (Ed.), *William James: Writings 1878-1899*. New York: Library of America.

Karabel, J. & Halsey, A. H. (Eds.) (1976). *Power and Ideology in Education*. New York: Oxford University Press.

Lakatos, I. & Musgrave, A. (1970). *Criticism and the growth of knowledge*. Cambridge, UK: Cambridge University Press.

Lave, J, & Wenger, E. (1991). Situated learning: Legitimate peripheral participation. Cambridge, UK: Cambridge University Press.

Lave, J. (1988). *Cognition in Practice: Mind, Mathematics and Culture in Everyday Life*. Cambridge, UK: Cambridge University Press.

Lewontin, R C. (1976). The analysis of variance and the analysis of causes. In N. J. Block and G. Dworkin (Eds.), *The IQ Controversy*. New York: Random House.

Lycan, W. G. (2003). Philosophy of mind. In N. Bunnin and E. P. Tsui-James (Eds.), *The Blackwell companion to philosophy*. Oxford, UK: Blackwell.

McDermott, R. P. & Hood, L. (1982). Institutionalized psychology and the ethnography of schooling. In P. Gilmore and A. Gladthorn, *Children in and out of school*. Washington, D. C.: Center for Applied Linguistics.

Murray, C, & Herrnstein. R. (1994). *The Bell Curve*. New York: Free Press.

Newell, A, & Simon, H. A. (1972). *Human problem solving*. Engelwood Cliffs, NJ: Prentice-Hall.

Newell, A. & Simon, H. A. (1976). Computer science as empirical inquiry: Symbols and search. *Communications of the ACM, 19*(3 (March)):113-126.

Newman, D., Griffin, P. & Cole, M. (1989). *The construction zone: Working for cognitive change in schools*. Cambridge, UK: Cambridge University Press.

Ortiz, D. (1999). Categorical community. *Stanford Law Review*, v. 51 (April): 769-806.

Phillips, D. C. & Burbules, N. C. (2000). *Post-positivism and educational research*. Lanham, MD: Rowman and Littlefield.

Phillips, D. C. (1996). Philosophical perspectives. In R. C. Calfee (Ed.), *Handbook of educational psychology*. New York: MacMillan.

Phillips, D. C. (1987). *Philosophy, science, and social inquiry*. Elmsford, New York: Pergamon.

Searle, J. R. (2003). Contemporary philosophy in the United States. In N. Bunnin & E. P. Tsui-James (Eds.), *The Blackwell companion to philosophy*. Oxford, UK: Blackwell.

Seidman, E. (1978). Justice, values and social science: unexamined premises. In R. J. Simon (Ed.), *Research in law and sociology*. Greenwich, CN: JAI Press.

Simon, H. A., ed. 1979. *Models of Thought*. New Haven: Yale University Press.

Simon, H. (1991). *Models of my life*. New York: Basic Books.

Skinner, B. F. (1935). The generic nature of the concepts of stimulus and response. *The Journal of General Psychology, XII*(1):40-65.

Skinner, B. F. (1953). *Science and human behavior*. New York: Free Press.

Skinner, B. F. (1976). *Walden two*. New York: MacMillan.

Skinner, B. F. & Epstein, R. (1982). *Skinner for the classroom*. Champaign, IL: Research Press.

Snow, R. E. (1974). Research on aptitude for learning: A progress report. *Review of Research in* Education.

Snow, R. E. (1992). Aptitude Theory: Yesterday, Today, and Tomorrow. *Educational Psychologist, 27*(1):5-32.

Vygotsky, L.S. (1934). *Thought and Language*. (E. Hanfmann and G. Vakar, Trans. 1986). Cambridge: MIT Press.

Ward, L. G. & Throop, R. (1997). Editor's notes: The reflex arc concept in psychology. http://paradigm.soci.brocku.ca/pclt/meand/sup/title_00x.htm. St. Catherine's, Canada: Dept. of Sociology, Brock University.

Watson, J. B. (1913). Psychology as the behaviorist views It. In E. H. Madden (Ed.), *A source book in the history of psychology*. New York: Russell and Russell.

Watzlawick, P. (1974). *Change: principles of problem formation and problem resolution*. New York: W. W. Norton.

Watzlawick, P., Beavin, J. H. & Jackson, D. D. (1967). *Pragmatics of human communication*. New York: W. W. Norton.

Winograd, T., & Flores, F. (1986). *Understanding Computers and Cognition*. Reading, MA: Addison-Wesley.

Wittgenstein, L. (1958). *Philosophical investigations*. New York: Macmillan.

DEVELOPMENT AND INDIVIDUAL DIFFERENCES

ACADEMIC PATHWAYS FROM PRESCHOOL
THROUGH ELEMENTARY SCHOOL

Scott G. Paris
Fred J. Morrison
Kevin F. Miller
University of Michigan

In the first edition of the *Handbook of Educational Psychology* Paris and Cunningham (1996) summarized young children's enculturation into education according to the theme of children becoming students. The experiences involved in "becoming" capture the myriad developmental changes of childhood and emphasize the emerging identities of children as students (Roeser, Eccles, & Sameroff, 2000). The theme also confirms the close connections between developmental and educational psychology for understanding children's emerging lives as students in academic worlds. The child-centered theme of becoming is still relevant for understanding how children progress from home to preschool to formal school, especially between the ages of 3 and 10 years that is the focus in this chapter, but we have added a theme of "pathways" to illustrate how children follow different routes through educational experiences. Children's opportunities for learning vary widely in American homes, schools, and communities, and they contribute to large ranges of skill levels at every grade level. These diverse and developing skill trajectories, especially for literacy and numeracy, help to establish different pathways, as well as different identities, for children into and through formal schooling.

The chapter begins with identification of important educational research and policies since the mid-1990s that affects children beginning their education in the 21st century. Next, we review family and preschool supports for learning and how children make the transition to formal schooling. Then we review recent research and policies on early reading and examine what children learn and how they are instructed and assessed in K-5 grades. The chapter then turns to a review of children's mathematical development. We trace their emerging knowledge and experiences that prepare them for classroom mathematics instruction. Next, we review policies of accountability, such as the No Child Left Behind Act of 2001, and how accountability and assessment influence the academic pathways of American school children.

RESEARCH TRENDS IN EDUCATIONAL PSYCHOLOGY

Skeptics of a second *Handbook* 10 years after the first edition might ask, "Has the field of educational psychology changed significantly, and has the fund of knowledge about children's beginning education grown substantially?" The answer to the first question is "No" because the field of educational psychology has not changed dramatically during the past 10 years. The same trends evident in 1990 have continued with perhaps more emphasis on discipline-based learning and assessment and less emphasis on motivation and teaching. However, the answer to the second question about the fund of knowledge generated in educational psychology is "Yes" because research has advanced knowledge about children's education substantially. Our answers are based on the kinds of research published in educational journals as well as the changes in federal policies regarding curriculum, instruction, and assessment.

Several researchers have surveyed the history of publications in the *Journal of Educational Psychology* to identify trends in the field. Paris and Cunningham (1996) reviewed the articles in the lead issues published in 1910, 1930, 1950, 1970, and 1990 and noted several trends. First, the numbers of published papers increased each decade and nonempirical papers practically disappeared. Second, the age group most frequently studied was elementary students followed by college students and adults. Surprisingly, there were relatively fewer papers on preschool and high school students. Third, research on learning, cognition, motivation, and attitudes dominated the journal between 1970 and 1990. Overall, research on children's education at the end of the 20th century examined children's learning as embedded in conceptual development and sociocultural contexts. Research revealed shifts toward integrated and interdisciplinary curricula connected to children's interest and backgrounds. Research on classroom instruction changed from didactic to scaffolded and from teacher-directed to inquirydriven.

These trends have continued in the past 10 years. O'Donnell and Levin (2001) used similar methods to survey the articles in the *Journal of Educational Psychology* in each decade plus the 1999 issue. In 1999, 60% of the topics reported in the *Journal* were about learning compared to 13% in 1910. In contrast, only 10% of the topics were related to intelligence tests and measurement in 1999 compared to 37% in 1910. Research on motivation and attitudes accounted for a combined 24% of the total in 1999, 34% in 1990, and less in each preceding decade. These general trends were confirmed by M. Smith et al. (1998), who analyzed publications in other educational psychology journals between 1991 and 1996. They concluded that "Reading, learning, achievement, assessment of student learning, human development, motivation, mathematics education, and issues related to the identity of the field of educational psychology represent the most frequently published topics" (p.178). The popularity of these topics remains strong. Our analysis of all the articles in the *Journal of Educational Psychology* during 2003 revealed a total of 66 empirical papers, and 37 (56%) described students' learning. Among these 37 articles on learning, there were 18 (27%) on literacy, 4 (6%) on mathematics, 2 (3%) on self-regulated learning, and 13 on miscellaneous topics such as science and problem-solving. Motivation was popular with 14 articles (21%), but social relationships only had 4 (6%) articles. It is safe to conclude that research on students' learning, especially reading, continues to be the most popular research subject for educational psychologists.

Three general conclusions appear warranted from the historical changes in articles published in the *Journal of Educational Psychology*, and each will be elaborated in the remaining sections. First, researchers have provided new and more scientifically rigorous information about children's academic skills such as literacy and numeracy, and this knowledge has been used to establish educational policies that directly influence classroom practices. Second, research has shown that skills and concepts acquired in preschool and primary grades are crucial for continued academic success because they enable faster and higher trajectories of skill achievement. Thus, early identification and intervention are important for facilitating positive pathways through school. Third, accountability through assessment has permeated educational research at every grade level, and testing is used to validate educational materials, methods, curricula, and instruction more than ever before. These three historical changes and their ramifications underlie (a) the kinds of research funded and conducted by educational psychologists, (b) the types of curricula, instruction, and assessments that are regarded as effective and substantiated by scientifically based research, and (c) the public perception of educational quality and effectiveness in local schools.

The historical changes are most evident in the fields of reading and mathematics education, perhaps because they are the central focus of elementary education and the largest disciplines within federal and state educational budgets. There are more reading educators and teachers in professional organizations devoted to reading than any other discipline and more reading journals than other disciplines, followed closely by mathematics educators and publications. Reading and language arts consume the greatest instructional time in the school day and the most resources in the elementary school budget, followed closely by mathematics. Furthermore, the two disciplines tested most often for achievement from primary grades to college admission are reading and mathematics. Part of the impetus for increased research on literacy and numeracy during the past 10–20 years has been the recognition of their developmental importance for establishing successful pathways into formal schooling and sustained educational success. The roots of literacy and numeracy begin to grow in preschool, though, so we begin our analysis there.

TRANSITIONS FROM PRESCHOOL TO FORMAL SCHOOLING

Efforts to understand and improve the academic skills of children continue to be central foci of educational psychologists. Research in the past 15 years has revealed several important factors that influence children's pathways into school. First, it has become clear that meaningful individual differences in language, literacy, and foundational skills for learning emerge before children begin formal schooling in kindergarten (Morrison, Bachman, & Connor, 2005; Shonkoff & Phillips, 2000). Second, early variability is shaped by many factors in the child, family, preschool, and larger socio-cultural context (NICHD-ECCRN, 2005a). Third, these sources of influence interact and shape children's variable trajectories beginning before school entrance (Storch & Whitehurst, 2002). Fourth, the early schooling experiences of American children are highly variable, in some cases exacerbating the differences established prior to school entry (NICHD-ECCRN, 2002b, 2005b; Pianta, Paro, Payne, Cox, & Bradley, 2002). The cumulative impact of these factors means that children begin formal education with vastly different preparation for academic learning, and their pathways for early academic success have already begun to diverge. In this section we describe the major factors contributing to school readiness and the different paths charted by children before they begin formal education.

Socioeconomic Factors

A substantial body of research has established clear connections between socioeconomic factors (SES) and academic achievement. Likewise, strong links between race/ethnicity and school success have been documented, particularly the persistently poorer performance of African-American students compared to their European-American and Asian-American peers. SES is highly correlated with other variables that may place young children at risk including minority status, modest educational levels of parents, and limited or nonexistent English language in the home. Thus, factors such as race/ethnicity may be associated with less preparation for schooling among young children, but other factors, especially, poverty, may mediate the effects (Berliner, 2005). Recently, scientists have attempted to disentangle the independent and combined influences of social, economic, linguistic, and racial/ethnic influences on academic development.

The National Assessment of Educational Progress or NAEP reports (NAEP, 2003; National Center for Education Statistics, 1999) show that 9-, 13-, and 17-year-old students from families with less than high school education scored lower on tests of reading, math, and science than did children whose parents completed some education after high school. More significantly, children from low-SES families begin school behind their more affluent peers and progress more slowly through the early years of elementary school (Alexander & Entwisle, 1988; Stipek & Ryan, 1997). Longitudinal studies reveal that children from low-SES families lose more ground during summer vacation, probably because their families engage in fewer academic activities, so these children show a cumulative summer loss in achievement that leads to a lower trajectory through school (Entwisle, Alexander, & Olson, 1977). In a pioneering study, Hart and Risley (1995) found that preschool children from welfare families had smaller vocabularies compared to children from working-class and professional families as early as 3 years of age. Moreover, their rates of vocabulary acquisition were much slower.

Despite the strong association of socioeconomic disadvantage and poor school performance, it is not obvious how SES factors operate to shape children's academic trajectories, especially in the preschool years. In their efforts to probe more deeply into the mechanisms underlying the SES–performance connection, scientists have distinguished between direct and mediated pathways of influence. Direct pathways reflect influences that operate directly on the child to affect academic performance. For example, poor children are more likely to have experienced negative perinatal events, such as prematurity (Saigal, Szatmari, Rosenbaum, Campbell, & King, 1991) or low birth weight, in addition to poorer nutrition and health care in early childhood (Korenman & Miller, 1997), all of which can directly limit a child's cognitive growth and potential. Yet, increasingly, scientists are describing the contribution of SES as operating indirectly through more immediate influences in the child's environment. For instance, mothers living in poverty are less likely to receive adequate prenatal care and may not provide adequate diets for infants and toddlers (Morrison, Bachman, & Connor, 2005). The effects of SES are mediated through proximal factors, such as parenting. Parents living in poverty are less likely to talk to their preschool children. They communicate with a more limited vocabulary, offer fewer questions or descriptive statements to them, and are more repetitive (Hart & Risley, 1995; Hoff-Ginsberg, 1991). In general, parents with fewer economic and/or educational resources are less likely to provide the stimulating home environments children require to be prepared for school.

Early Child Care and Preschool

A majority of the almost 20 million preschoolers in this country will spend some amount of time in alternate care (K. Smith, 2002). Hence, scientists have become increasingly interested in the psychological consequences of caregiving for preschool children as well as its impact on school transition and later school functioning (NICHD-ECCRN, 2002a, 2005a). In addition, for children most at risk for school failure, intensive interventions during the preschool years have attempted to help children at risk for academic failure (e.g., children living in poverty) catch up to their peers and be equally ready for school (Barnett, 1995). In this section we will first review the evidence on the impact of childcare on children's cognitive and social development. Next we will summarize the evidence on the outcome of early interventions for at-risk children.

What effect does day care have on children? The NICHD Study of Early Childcare (NICHD-ECCRN) investigated the nature and consequences of early child care beginning in the late 1980s. The cumulative evidence points to both the quality and quantity of care as crucial factors. In broad terms, higher quality childcare produces positive effects on children's cognitive, language, and literacy skills (NICHD-ECCRN, 2002a), whereas high quantities of care (defined as more than 30 hours per week) have been associated with poorer social outcomes (Brooks-Gunn, Han, & Waldfogel, 2002). However, these generalizations do not capture the complexity of the role of child care. Parents are active agents in choosing alternate care for their child; more educated mothers have been shown to be more sensitive and responsive to their children than mothers with less education (NICHD-ECCRN, 2002a, 2002b). The more educated and responsive mothers likely chose higher quality child care, monitored it more closely, and could afford to pay for it. In fact, when direct comparisons were made between parenting and child care environments, the impact of the quality of parenting was three to four times greater than that of child-care on children's language and social skills (NICHD-ECCRN, 2004, 2005b). Nevertheless, there is evidence that, independent of quality, children who spend more than 30 hours per week in center-based care may be less socially competent and somewhat more disruptive to other children and teachers (NICHD-ECCRN, 2003).

Do intervention programs for at-risk students work? Again, the issue of program quality is central to answering this question. High-quality interventions enhance development, whereas poor-quality programs can impede children's progress (Barnett, 1995). High-quality preschool interventions significantly improve children's prospects for academic success (Barnett, 1995), promote stronger language and literacy development (Dickinson & Tabors, 2001), and demonstrate significant return on investment over children's lifetimes (Reynolds, Temple, Robertson, & Mann, 2003).

There are a number of interventions that have been implemented for at-risk children. Some of the more prominent and successful model programs include the Perry Preschool Project (Barnett, 1995), the Abecedarian Project (Campbell & Ramey, 1994), the School Development Program (Haynes, Comer, & Hamilton-Lee, 1988), and the Chicago Title 1 Child-Parent Centers (Reynolds

et al., 2003). In every instance, children receiving these interventions showed significantly stronger academic and social skill development compared to equally at-risk children not enrolled in the programs.

The mounting weight of evidence demonstrates that high-quality child care and high-quality interventions for at-risk children, in moderation and coupled with high-quality parental care, can improve the psychological well-being of preschool children, enhance their school readiness, and improve their chances for successful school transition. But what defines high quality for both child care and interventions? Examination of the characteristics of programs that work yielded five crucial elements.

1. Parental involvement. Successful programs coupled intensive intervention with home visits, parent education, and parent involvement.
2. Intensity. Programs that were more available to children all day, 5 days a week, like the Abecedarian project, tended to produce stronger, more durable outcomes for children.
3. Starting early. Programs that yielded greater cost-benefit ratios (e.g., Abecedarian and Chicago Title 1) began their interventions when participants were infants.
4. Well-qualified teachers. Programs with more teachers who were certified produced more consistently positive effects than those with fewer who were certified.
5. Rich linguistic and literacy environments. Successful programs emphasized language and literacy skills such as vocabulary, syntax, phonology, alphabet knowledge, and word decoding.

In summary, the nature of a child's experience in alternate forms of care outside the home can have a measurable effect on subsequent psychological development and preparation for school. Although not as crucial as parenting, to which we will turn next, high-quality experiences in a child-care environment can improve cognitive functioning among children at risk. Alternatively, some children who spend more than 30 hours per week in child care, particularly prior to 1 year of age, may endure some short-term risks (Brooks-Gunn et al., 2003).

Family Learning Environments

The learning experiences and teaching provided at home have direct influences on children's academic achievement. Measures of "cognitive stimulation" or "home learning" have predicted preschoolers' IQ and receptive vocabulary (Bradley et al., 1994) as well as reading, math, and vocabulary skills in elementary school (J. Smith, Brooks-Gunn, & Klebanov, 1997). Recent work has revealed a high degree of specificity in the impact of the learning environment. Parental behaviors, such as book reading, promote language development but do little for specific literacy skills such as letter knowledge and word decoding. In contrast, deliberate efforts by parents to teach these emerging literacy skills to their children help to promote their alphabet knowledge and word decoding skills but do little to enrich vocabulary (Senechal & LeFevre, 2001).

The quality of parental communication also has direct influences on children's language and cognitive development. Parents who label and describe objects in the environment promote language development in their children (Hart & Risley, 1995; Hoff-Ginsburg, 1991). The overall amount and complexity of parental speech to children predicts their vocabulary and complex grammar acquisition (Huttenlocher, Haight, Bryk, Seltzer, & Lyons, 1991; Huttenlocher, Vasilyeva, Cymerman, & Levine, 2002). Beyond size and content, the manner of speaking and interacting with children contributes to oral language growth. Children who received a greater proportion of commands and prohibitions from their parents developed relatively limited vocabularies in the study by Hart and Risley (1995). In related work, Tomasello and Todd (1983) showed that parents who maintained longer periods of joint attention on an object had children with larger vocabularies. Joint conversations that provide rich vocabulary, descriptions, and explanations are evidence of a supportive family learning environment.

Shared book-reading has been demonstrated to be a powerful tool, for some children, to enhance vocabulary development (Haden, Reese, & Fivush, 1996; Lonigan & Whitehurst, 1998; Reese & Cox, 1999). In randomized experiments, book reading styles that involved active labeling and describing illustrations or encouraging and assisting children's storytelling significantly enhanced vocabulary development (Lonigan & Whitehurst, 1998; Whitehurst et al., 1988). Literacy-promoting activities by parents may require more direct instruction than those that nurture oral language growth. When parents explicitly teach their children how to name and print letters and words, children's print knowledge improves (Senechal et al., 1998) as does later word decoding and comprehension skills in school (Senechal & LeFevre, 2002). However, Scarborough and Dobrich (1994) reviewed studies of parental book reading with children and noted that the studies accounted for no more than 8% of the variance in literacy-related abilities. They suggested that the effects of parental assistance on children's achievement may not be linear and could depend on a minimum threshold. All children may need a certain threshold amount of parental book reading activities in order to develop vocabulary and reading skills, but more interactions beyond the threshold may not improve literacy or achievement directly.

Parenting

Parenting is a critical mediator of the effects of sociocultural factors, including the influences of caregiving. One way to gauge the power of parenting is through intervention studies to see if they improve parenting skills measurably and, subsequently, if they lead to corresponding increases in children's academic skills. Two strategies have been adopted: (a) family-focused early childhood education (ECE) coupled with home-based services; and (b) exclusively parent-focused home visiting programs. Recent reviews (e.g., Brooks-Gunn, in press) concluded that home-based interventions alone, without a center-based child-intervention component, were surprisingly ineffective for improving children's cognitive skills. Many of these adult-based efforts did not increase parental outcomes, such as educational attainment, which may explain why their children's cognitive performance did not improve (Magnusson & Duncan, in press).

If parenting is so important to a child's development, then why haven't the interventions been more powerful? Actually, there are several reasons these efforts may have fallen short. First, as the authors themselves noted, case managers in these studies quickly found that they needed to deal with a number of family crises and chronic adversities, such as inadequate housing, lack of food, and heat and legal problems, that made it difficult to move beyond crisis intervention (St. Pierre & Layzer, 1999). In addition, there were sizable differences across families in the uptake of services or the "dosage" effect. Because participation in these interventions was voluntary, parental participation varied widely, with about half the scheduled visits actually taking place (Gomby, Culross, & Behrman, 1999). Significantly, when eligible families were split by their participation level, children in families with greater involvement made greater gains than did their peers whose families participated less (Brooks-Gunn, Burchinal, & Lopez, 2001). Finally, it should be noted that focused interventions (e.g., around book reading) have yielded measurable gains in children's oral language skills (Lonigan & Whitehurst, 1998; Payne, Whitehurst, & Angell, 1994; Reese & Cox, 1999; Senechal & LeFevre, 2001). Thus, interventions directed at specific skills that are prerequisite for schooling may be more productive than general parenting interventions.

Dimensions of Parenting

Most of the intervention efforts to improve parenting have been limited in time and scope. For example, in the Comprehensive Child Development Program (St. Pierre & Layzer, 1999), parents received training from a home visitor for a maximum of 13 hours, which may be insufficient to promote and maintain lasting change over time in parental habits. Further, interventions that focus primarily on one aspect of parenting may necessarily be limiting their impact. Research over the past 20 years has clearly demonstrated that parenting for literacy involves more than reading to children and even more than providing a rich literacy environment (Morrison & Cooney, 2002).

It has become useful to think of parenting as varying along a number of dimensions (Morrison, Bachman, & Connor, 2005; Morrison & Cooney, 2002), with three proximal dimensions being most salient for shaping academic skills. These are (a) the family learning environment, (b) parental warmth/responsivity, and (c) parental control/discipline. A separate distal dimension of parental knowledge and beliefs operates primarily through the other three proximal sources. These dimensions are considered to exert independent influences on different aspects of a child's behavior and to be independent of one another (although correlated in most instances). For example, parents who provide a rich learning environment for their child might not necessarily also give the child the high degree of emotional warmth needed for emotional security, or the rules, standards, and limits needed to develop cognitive or moral self-regulation.

Parental Warmth/Responsivity. The degree to which parents display open affection to their children and show sensitivity to their feelings and wishes has been linked to preschoolers' literacy and language skills as well as their later school achievement (Berlin & Brooks-Gunn, 1995). Mothers' sensitivity to children's developmental progress during the first 2 years of life has been shown to predict cognitive and language skills later in preschool (NICHD-ECCRN, 1998; Tamis-Lemonda, Bornstein, & Baumwell, 2001) as well as kindergarten and first grade (Coates & Lewis, 1984; Kelly, Morisset, Barnartd, Hammond, & Booth, 1996). More responsive mothers are more likely to reduce the length of their utterances to their infants so that the child can comprehend them better (Murray, Johnson, & Peters, 1990). At-risk children can make substantial progress when mothers interact with them in a highly responsive manner. The combination of cognitive and affective stimulation is evident in joint book reading when it is interactive, responsive, and warm. In addition to increasing cognitive and language skills, shared book reading promotes emotional closeness. Affection provides the child with the undivided attention of a loving parent. Such interchanges may nurture self-regulation and emotional well-being.

Parental Control/Discipline. Though less well researched, the degree to which parents establish rules, standards, and limits on a child's behavior creates a structured and supportive context for literacy development (Chase-Lansdale & Pittman, 2002; Hartup, 1989). In book reading, for example, this interaction affords parents the opportunity to resist children's fidgeting and squirming and to sustain their attention until the story is finished. In one study, Cooney (1998) found that parents' use of disciplinary practices did not directly predict literacy outcomes, but they did reliably predict self-regulation measures (e.g., cooperation, independence, and responsibility), which in turn contributed positively to literacy skill levels at kindergarten entry. In summary, the evidence supports a clear role for parenting in shaping children's pathways for academic development, albeit in complex ways.

The Effect of Schooling and the Specificity of Learning

A major challenge to researchers has been to demonstrate the unique impact of schooling, over and above the influence of background factors (Coleman et al., 1966; Rutter & Maughan, 2002). One set of studies has attempted to demonstrate causal effects of schooling on children's literacy skill growth (Morrison & Connor, 2002) by exploiting a natural experiment stemming from the rather arbitrary birth date that school districts mandate for school entry. Children who just make or just miss this cut off birth date are essentially the same age chronologically, but those whose birthdays fall after the cutoff date start first grade while those whose birthdays fall just before the cutoff go to kindergarten. Consequently, schooling and maturational effects on children's development can be examined separately. If both groups demonstrate similar rates of growth in a particular skill, then that skill is most likely a product of maturation. Alternatively, if children who are the same age demonstrate rates of skill growth that are greater than those of their age peers who are a grade behind them, then there is a schooling effect.

Kindergarten schooling effects are evident for alphabet recognition, word decoding, phonemic (individual sounds within words) awareness, general knowledge, addition, short-term memory, sentence memory, and visual-spatial memory. Yet there are no kindergarten schooling effects for receptive vocabulary, rhyming, conservation of number and quantity, addition strategies, and narrative coherence (Morrison, Bachman, & Connor, 2005; Morrison, Smith, & Dow-Ehrensberger, 1995). One interpretation of these results is that schooling effects reflect the content of classroom instruction. First-grade teachers usually provide frequent and explicit instruction on the alphabet, word decoding, phonemic awareness, and addition, so attending school may provide specific advantages for these skills. These skills are also content-specific, constrained, rule-bound, and learned relatively rapidly with practice so they are "teachable" to 6- to 7-year-olds. However, the schooling effects for memory and general knowledge variables suggests that some general cognitive skills benefit from school experiences as well. The lack of schooling effects in kindergarten may reflect a lack of specific instruction on each of the variables or an inability of kindergarten children to benefit from the instruction because they did not have the prerequisite knowledge or were not in the "zone of proximal development" for these skills (e.g., conservation).

Specific schooling effects are evident in a closer examination of the results from three phonological awareness tasks. The tasks differed only in the level of segmentation the child was asked to complete—syllabic, subsyllabic, and phonemic. For the syllabic segmentation task, children were asked to identify the number of syllables in a word. For example, *cucumber* has three syllables, *cu-cum-ber*. In the subsyllabic task, children were asked to say the first sound in each word. For example, /t/ is the first sound in the word *toy*. For the phonemic task, children were asked to count the number of sounds in a word. For example, *rest* has four sounds, /r-e-s-t/. The study revealed that there were schooling effects but only for specific skills. For syllabic segmentation, neither first-grade nor kindergarten instruction had an effect on growth in these skills. For subyllabic segmentation, only age effects were found. In contrast, for phonemic segmentation, strong schooling effects were observed for first grade but not for kindergarten. The pattern of findings from this study, as well as others, demonstrated that the impact of instruction was quite specific to the amount and type of instruction devoted to particular literacy skills. Later, we describe why some reading skills more than others may exhibit accelerated growth in response to school or special instruction.

LEARNING TO READ

Research conducted in the 1980s and 1990s showed that children begin to acquire literacy before formal schooling. Most 3- and 4-year-olds listen to stories that are read or told by adults, and "dialogic reading" (Whitehurst, Arnold, Epstein, & Angell, 1994) between parent and child allows reciprocal questioning and interactive construction of meaning from books. Children recognize environmental print in texts, begin to scribble and write, rhyme words, play language games, and recognize familiar words such as their own name—all by 4–5 years of age (Sulzby, 1986). These precursors to literacy can be regarded as cognitive concepts and skills or emergent literacy activities that approximate conventional reading and writing, but they are rarely taught directly to preschoolers. Instead, children's early approaches to literacy are embedded in parent–child interactions that are mainly social and affective experiences.

It is the frequency and quality of literate interactions that establish different pathways for preschoolers. When children begin kindergarten, there is remarkable diversity in their skills and experiences. Thus, some children begin kindergarten knowing the alphabet, writing familiar words, and reciting the text of well-known books, whereas other children struggle to catch up. Adams' (1990) seminal book described the developing skills, concepts, and experiences that children need in order to begin reading, and she showed the importance of children's phonological and orthographic awareness for learning to read. The research on developmental precursors of literacy was the foundation for recent advances in reading education.

Two special groups were commissioned in the 1990s to examine the state of literacy research and education, and their reports have had a huge impact on researchers and educators. The first group was a large committee of reading experts convened under the auspices of the National Academy of Sciences and directed to examine ways to prevent reading problems among young children. The report by Snow, Burns, and Griffin (1998), *Preventing Reading Difficulties in Young Children* (PRD), was a comprehensive review of a large body of research on skills and experiences that influence beginning reading. The authors identified the main factors that shape the development of reading and provided recommendations to help children who have persistent difficulties learning to read. They identified three obstacles to skilled reading that influence young children: difficulty using and understanding the alphabetic principle, failure to transfer comprehension skills of spoken language to reading, and lack of motivation for reading. In addition, Snow, Burns, and Griffin (1998) provided recommendations for identifying struggling readers, delivering appropriate instruction to them, and training educators to help struggling readers.

The second group was the National Reading Panel (NRP, 2000) commissioned by Congress and convened by the Director of the National Institute of Child Health and Human Development (NICHD) and the Secretary of Education. The NRP used the PRD as a springboard to review scientific research on reading in an effort to identify rigorous research that supports effective instructional practices to help children learn to read. The NRP report in 2000 was organized around the following topics: alphabetics, fluency, comprehension, teacher education, and computer technology. Although there was some controversy over the membership of the panel, the specific studies included and omitted in the reviews, and the interpretations of the findings, both national reports influenced the educational policies included in the Reading First part of the No Child Left Behind (NCLB) Act of 2001. This federal legislation is the most sweeping reform ever in literacy education, and perhaps K-12 education, and it has affected how reading is taught and assessed throughout the United States. The key element in both the NRP report and the NCLB legislation was the identification in reading research of five essential components of reading: the alphabetic principle, phonemic awareness, oral reading fluency, vocabulary, and comprehension. We describe each briefly because they are the foundation for reforms in elementary educational practices in curriculum, instruction, and assessment.

Knowledge of Letter Names and Sounds

Children learn to identify the names and sounds of some letters before they begin formal schooling, and most children know the entire alphabet by the middle of first grade. For example, Morris, Bloodgood, Lomax, and Perney (2003) used a task of identifying 15 letters in upper and lower cases and reported that children knew about half of them at the beginning of kindergarten and all of them by the end of kindergarten. They learn various skills such as visual discrimination of symbols, remembering letter names and sounds, and coordinating visual–auditory relations (Lorusso, 1994). These skills are incorporated into "the alphabetic principle" noted by Snow, Burns, and Griffin (1998) as a foundation for beginning reading. The alphabetic principle also includes the skills of segmenting and blending sounds associated with letters and what is generally referred to as phonics knowledge. One reason for the importance of alphabet knowledge is that children's knowledge about letters and letter-sound relations predicts subsequent reading. Lonigan, Burgess, and Anthony (2000) said, "Knowledge of the alphabet (i.e., knowing the names of letters and the sounds they represent) at entry into school is one of the strongest single predictors of short- and long-term success in learning to read" (p. 597).

Phonemic Awareness

Phonemic awareness involves the ability to recognize and manipulate phonemes in *spoken* syllables and words. Understanding the relations among sounds and letters in *print* is phonics and clearly depends on phonemic awareness. Knowing the sounds associated with letters helps children to identify the distinct phonemes associated with printed text. For example, by age 5, most children can identify onset-rime patterns—such as *c-at*, *b-at*, and *f-at*—that are the bases for initial rhyming. Later, they develop the ability to segment words into phonemes and to blend separate sounds into words. The same skills can be applied to printed or spoken words. These are the basic analytic and synthetic aspects of decoding that follow from phonemic awareness. Many research studies have found significant concurrent and predictive correlations between phonemic awareness and literacy (e.g., Bradley & Bryant, 1983; Juel, Griffith, & Gough, 1986; Rayner, Foorman, Perfetti, Pesetsky, & Seidenberg, 2001). However, there have been recent challenges to the direct causal role of phonemic awareness for improving reading.

Some researchers suggest that the link is mediated by letter knowledge (Blaiklock, 2004), whereas others maintain that no causal link has been demonstrated in previous research (Castles & Coltheart, 2004). The NRP found nearly 2,000 citations to phonemic awareness but conducted their meta-analysis on only 52 studies that met their criteria. Those studies showed that training in phonemic awareness improved children's reading and spelling. Furthermore, the NRP concluded that all varieties of systematic phonics training, including analogy phonics, analytic phonics, embedded phonics, phonics through spelling, and synthetic phonics, produce significant benefits for elementary students who have difficulty reading. The NRP advocated the integration of phonics instruction in a total reading program that also emphasizes the other four essential components.

Oral Reading Fluency

Fluent oral reading is the coordination of several automated decoding skills through practice. Fluency includes reading text quickly, accurately, and with intonation (Kuhn & Stahl, 2003). Measuring children's oral reading accuracy has a long history of practical use in informal reading inventories that collect miscues or running records of children's oral reading (e.g., Clay, 1991; Paris & Carpenter, 2003). Reading rate is an indicator of automatic decoding, so children who can read faster often identify words more accurately and have more cognitive resources left over for reading with expression and comprehension (Rasinski & Hoffman, 2003). That may be why reading rate is a popular measure in primary grades.

For example, the use of reading rate as a measure of fluency has a long tradition in special education under the name of curriculum-based measurement (Deno, Mirkin, & Chiang, 1982; Fuchs & Fuchs, 1999). The central measure in curriculum-based measurement (CBM) is oral reading fluency (ORF), defined as the number of words read correctly in 1-minute samples of text drawn from the student's curriculum. The purposes of CBM are to use text from the regular curriculum, to embed ORF assessments in everyday activities, and to provide general outcome measures of reading achievement that can be monitored over time for both diagnostic and accountability functions. ORF is also a main feature of the Dynamic Indicators of Basic Early Literacy Skills (DIBELS), a popular and quick battery of early reading assessments (Good & Kaminski, 2002). It is easy to assess how many words children read correctly in a minute and compare the rates to grade-level norms, but the data need to be interpreted cautiously because speed is only one index of reading proficiency.

Vocabulary

Vocabulary includes understanding words in either oral or written form, and it is obvious that knowledge in both modalities improves reading comprehension. Vocabulary is related developmentally to both intelligence and oral language skills, so vocabulary growth during preschool years helps establish a pathway for literacy during schooling (Hart & Risley, 1995). Vocabulary, both receptive and expressive, predicts early reading skill (Storch & Whitehurst, 2002). The number of different words that children understand, as well as the number they speak, helps with word decoding efforts and may facilitate growth of phonological awareness (Dickinson et al., 2003). The NRP reviewed 50 studies drawn from a potential pool of 20,000 citations on vocabulary, and they concluded that direct instruction in vocabulary facilitates reading comprehension. Repetition, multiple exposures to words, computer technology, and learning in rich contexts all enhance vocabulary acquisition. Initial instruction on vocabulary and related conceptual content can facilitate children's subsequent reading comprehension (Beck, McKeown, & Kucan, 2002). Likewise, instruction based on word study can increase children's understanding of orthography, spelling, and vocabulary (Bear, Invernizzi, Templeton, & Johnston, 2004).

Comprehension

Comprehension involves many different levels of understanding, and it is difficult to define and measure (Kintsch, 1998). The NRP concluded that reading comprehension is a complex process that is influenced by (among other things) vocabulary knowledge and instruction, the thoughtful interaction between reader and text, and the abilities of teachers to equip students with appropriate reading strategies. The effective use of reading strategies

becomes more important as texts become more complex and children's goals for reading expand. Instruction in primary grades helps children learn to read mostly by decoding words in print, but by grade 2, they are taught to read to learn for a variety of purposes (Chall, 1967). The NRP report identified seven types of instruction that foster reading comprehension, especially if taught in combinations as multiple-strategy approaches: comprehension monitoring, cooperative learning, use of graphic and semantic organizers, question answering, question generation, story structure, and summarization. When children use these strategies and skills, they can understand and remember better the meaning of texts that they read.

CRITIQUE OF THE FIVE ESSENTIAL COMPONENTS OF READING

The five essential components in the NRP report and NCLB legislation are consistent with many theories of reading development that emphasize assembly and integration of skills. They portray the acquisition of multiple skills in a series of steps or stages that focus on (a) acquisition and initial use followed by a period of (b) practice and automatic use that permits (c) amalgamation and coordination with additional reading skills. These traditional models of componential assembly and automatic use fail to address the differences among the components. Paris (2005) has suggested that the differences are substantial and warrant reexamination of the developmental trajectories of each component. For example, the alphabetic principle is acquired relatively quickly and completely compared to vocabulary and comprehension. Learning the names and sounds associated with letters in the English alphabet is a small set of knowledge compared to learning new vocabulary words throughout one's life. Phonemic awareness includes a larger set of knowledge, but the essential features of phonemic rhyming, segmenting, and blending are learned in primary grades by most children. Thus, the component skills vary in the scope of knowledge acquired and the duration of learning.

Paris (2005) differentiated "constrained" from "unconstrained" skills to call attention to the differences in developmental acquisition. Skills such as letter knowledge and phonemic awareness are "constrained" because they are learned to an asymptotic level by nearly all children compared to vocabulary and comprehension, which are much less constrained in their developmental trajectories. Constrained skills reflect the same knowledge that is mastered by all children learning to read, so they are more universal and similar among readers than comprehension and vocabulary, which can be considered unconstrained in their developmental trajectories over time and across individuals. Oral reading fluency is less constrained than alphabet knowledge but more constrained than vocabulary development because most children reach their asymptotic rate of accurate oral reading by fourth or fifth grade (Fuchs & Fuchs, 1999).

Differences in Developmental Trajectories

The general critique of the five essential reading components is that they have vastly different developmental trajectories. This has several important implications. First, skills and knowledge develop at different times and rates so the distributions of variables change considerably with age. Alphabet knowledge is at floor levels for 4-year-olds and ceiling levels for 7-year-olds so it changes rapidly. Alphabet knowledge is not a normally distributed variable except in special samples of children who exhibit partial mastery, usually kindergarteners. That is why claims about the predictive power of letter name knowledge are constrained to a small period of time with most research focusing only on preschool and kindergarten children (e.g., Scanlon & Vellutino, 1996).

This leads directly to a second implication, namely, that correlations with constrained skills are unstable and transitory. For example, results from Scarborough's (1998) review of 61 emergent literacy studies indicated that the strongest individual difference predictor of reading ability in first through third grade was letter name identification in kindergarten, with a mean correlation with decoding measures of $r = 0.52$ ($SD = 0.14$) across all 24 research samples measuring this variable. However, by first grade, letter name knowledge is no longer the strongest predictor of later reading ability, most often eclipsed by phonological processing skills such as letter sound knowledge and phoneme synthesis and analysis tasks (e.g., Mann & Foy, 2003; McBride-Chang, 1996).

In general, researchers are aware of changing patterns of stability in individual differences. Pennington and Lefly (2001) highlight the methodological foundation of this, noting that greater variance within measures produces stronger correlations. Because of this developmental change in growth and variance, Walsh, Price, and Gillingham (1988) suggested that letter knowledge is related to reading achievement in a transitory fashion. Thus, constrained skills such as alphabet knowledge yield skewed distributions early and late in mastery learning that make correlations unstable longitudinally.

The third implication of constrained skills concerns interpretations of the unstable correlations. Even though letter knowledge in kindergarten is a significant predictor of later reading, the restricted developmental window is often neglected when interpreting predictive correlations. They are regarded as enduring individual differences when they are not. Among skilled decoders, perhaps after 10 years of age, who have mastered the alphabetic principle, have learned most phonological-orthographic patterns, and have attained a stable oral reading rate, these constrained skills exhibit reduced correlational strength with other variables. So interpretations of correlations, especially predictive validity correlations, must be restricted to the rapidly changing period of the developmental trajectories of specific skills and knowledge.

There is another problem with interpretations of correlations with constrained skills: proxy effects. The strong predictive correlation between letter knowledge in kindergarten and reading achievement 2 years later does not imply a causal relation. Since nearly all children learn the alphabet to nearly the same levels eventually, the differences in developmental trajectories in kindergarten reflect transitory skill differences, but they might reflect enduring environmental differences. For example, it is plausible that kindergarten children who know most of the alphabet ahead of their peers may have had more frequent and richer literacy experiences with adults as preschoolers. Their temporary advantage in alphabet knowledge during kindergarten may predict their later reading achievement because their environments remain more supportive with more opportunities for learning compared to their peers with less alphabet knowledge. Thus, early and rapid learning of the alphabet, concepts about print, word recognition, and phonemic awareness may all be proxy measures of other social-contextual conditions that foster better reading achievement (Paris, Carpenter, Paris, & Hamilton, 2005).

The fourth implication of constrained skills is that traditional methods of testing validity with concurrent and predictive correlations are inappropriate because the correlational patterns change dramatically with skill development (Carpenter & Paris, 2005). It is not just floor and ceiling effects that influence the correlations; it is the characteristics of any specific sample, because each group includes children at different levels of mastery so the strength of the correlations depend on the sample's expertise. This is a consequence of the developmental window of rapid growth and the temporary rather than enduring differences between individuals in degree of mastery. Skills that are most constrained, such as alphabet knowledge, will exhibit a narrower developmental window and more unstable correlations than less constrained skills such as phonemic awareness and oral reading fluency, but the important point is that constraints influence validity correlations according to the developmental trajectories of the skills. These fluctuations are less likely in unconstrained skills such as vocabulary and comprehension.

Low-Hanging Fruit and Intervention Research

The criticism of correlational evidence is that they yield transitory relations that may serve as proxy variables for many associated changes in children's development and literacy learning. It could be argued that experimental evidence has established the construct validity of the five essential components for reading development. For example, studies have shown that when children are taught letter knowledge or phonemic awareness, they show increases in the instructed skills that are sustained (e.g., Adams, Treiman, & Pressley, 1998). Such studies have been cited as "scientifically based reading research" by which to judge claims about the importance of reading skills or the effectiveness of interventions. However, interventions that teach children universally mastered skills and knowledge may be open to alternative interpretations.

The first problem is that intervention studies can reveal sufficient conditions for enhanced skills but not necessary conditions. Many interventions might boost children's learning temporarily, but they may not be necessary. The rate of learning or level of skill proficiency of mastered skills such as letter knowledge can be accelerated through interventions, and even sustained over months, but other children usually catch up later. Of course there are some children who do not catch up or whose rates of mastery are much lower than those of their peers, and special interventions are needed for them. These are the children identified in research as struggling readers or dyslexic readers. Children who struggle to read early and persistently exhibit developmental skill trajectories that diverge from their peers more with time, evidence of the "Matthew effects" (Stanovich, 1986). The diverging trajectories may be due to early mastery of constrained skills, enduring individual differences, or other supportive environmental conditions that persist for these children, such as differences in time spent reading or the sheer volume of reading during childhood (Cunningham & Stanovich, 1997). Regardless of the reason, the demonstration of an effective intervention for some children does not imply that all need it or would benefit from it.

The second problem is that interventions that target mastered skills will show only temporary advantages until the peers in the control conditions acquire the same knowledge and skills through other means. If interventions create temporary boosts in children's skills and knowledge, the correlations may also reveal temporary and enhanced relations with other measures of reading,

but the interpretations are subject to the same proxy effects as other mastered skills. Usually, the significance of the treatment is reported with tempered claims about the persistence of the advantage, so it may be more prudent to interpret temporary gains on universally mastered skills and knowledge as transitory effects. For example, brief interventions that increase children's letter knowledge in kindergarten or phonemic awareness in first grade relative to their peers may not provide any long-term advantage for children's reading development. Constrained skills allow highly specific interventions and easily quantified results, but both may reveal ephemeral effects on children during a narrow window of skill acquisition.

The third problem is the developmental timing of the intervention for constrained skills. It makes little sense to intervene with a treatment that is far beyond children's abilities, such as teaching phonemic awareness to 2-year-olds. It is also unreasonable to provide interventions for children who have already acquired most of the skills. That is exactly why researchers arrange interventions on constrained skills and knowledge for children who are "ripe" for learning the target skills. Although these practices are common, they suggest metaphors such as "picking low-hanging fruit" or "catching fish in a barrel" because they are obvious. Said differently, the interventions have developmental validity only for children who have the prerequisite knowledge and skills to take advantage of the treatment or who are in the "zone of proximal development" (ZPD) so they have a proclivity for the skills (Vygotsky, 1978). Moreover, these skills can be acquired through many means and will be acquired in time by nearly all children.

The fourth problem is the lack of transfer of interventions. Consider one well-known study as an example. Foorman, Francis, Fletcher, Schatschneider, and Mehta (1998) provided three kinds of instruction to first and second graders in Title I programs; direct code instruction (DC) in letter–sound correspondences with decodable text, embedded code (EC) instruction of sound–spelling patterns in connected text, and indirect code instruction (IC) with connected text. Growth in reading skills was assessed four times during the year with multiple measures, and the data were analyzed with sophisticated growth curve analyses. The data revealed significant growth in phonological processing, but the first graders were at floor levels of the four-point factor score and they improved during the year to midrange on the assessment. Second graders started the year at about 1.5 and moved to midrange scores by the end of the year. Thus, the DC condition accelerated the rate of growth more than other conditions in phonological processing from near floor levels to midrange levels. The greater rate of growth seems due to the close correspondence between the DC instruction on phoneme blending and segmentation and the phonological assessment tasks of the same skills.

Growth analyses of word reading revealed similar advantages of the DC instruction in slope and intercept measures, again because initial levels were near floor. The authors analyzed the relation between growth in phonological processing and word reading and concluded from regression analyses that "the generally flatter line for the DC group is precisely what one would expect if phonological processing is a determinant of growth in word reading and DC is effective in improving phonological processing" (Foorman et al., 1998; p. 48). Granted that phonological processing is necessary for decoding unknown words, the data could also be interpreted as floor effects in initial phonological awareness and word reading for all groups, and the DC condition accelerated the rates of change of both skills more than other conditions. Temporary acceleration of growth curves based on "teaching to the test" is a more conservative interpretation than a causal attribution that a specific commercial reading program facilitated reading development.

A key issue in this discussion is whether the temporary effects generalized to other skills. All children were tested at the end of the year with the Woodcock–Johnson Revised (WJ-R) tests of letter–word identification, pseudoword decoding, and passage comprehension. They were also assessed for comprehension on a different reading inventory and for spelling. The DC condition revealed significantly higher scores only on WJ-R tests of letter-word identification and pseudo-word decoding. There was no transfer to comprehension or spelling. Attitudes toward reading were also significantly worse in the DC condition than one of the IC groups.

The authors noted the lack of generalization and the lack of measures of sustained effects. Nevertheless, this widely cited study of instructional intervention has been used to support the authors' claim that "it may well be possible to prevent reading failure for large numbers of children if beginning reading instruction explicitly teaches the alphabetic principle" (p. 52). This claim is dubious because (a) the code-based interventions in the study did not compare interventions based on provision of the alphabetic principle versus no provision of the principle, (b) the advantages of the intervention were only temporary among children who exhibited floor levels of performance on those skills, and (c) there was no generalization of the narrow instructed skills to warrant the claim that reading failure had been prevented. The fact that children in the DC condition had more negative attitudes about reading also seems noteworthy.

A general problem with interventions on constrained reading skills is the failure to treat constrained and unconstrained variables differently in experimental designs.

This error confuses temporary differences in levels of knowledge and proficiency during periods of partial mastery with enduring and stable individual differences that persist over time. It has led to experimental demonstrations that the rates of acquisition of some skills can be accelerated by special interventions in brief time periods. However, the effects are transitory; they fail to generalize to other reading skills and knowledge, and they fail to lead to any long-term advantages in reading achievement.

Experimental research in reading has provided a strong foundation for educators and policymakers because it has identified important skills and knowledge that children need to become successful students. The five essential components of reading were distilled from voluminous research on reading, and they are all necessary for children to become skilled readers. This critique does not diminish their importance or the need to teach children the components early and thoroughly. However, it is useful to recognize the limitations of correlational data and experimental research in reading. Correlations with nonlinear, constrained skills require careful interpretation because of the unstable patterns of correlations longitudinally. The demonstrated benefit of an intervention A does not mean that other interventions have no value, that intervention A works equally well for all students of various ages and abilities, that intervention A is needed by all students, nor that intervention A alone is sufficient to prevent reading failures. A successful pathway to literacy includes a wide variety of experiences with print and explicit instruction that enable children to decode fluently and comprehend meaning within and beyond the explicit text. Early reading success allows children more opportunities to learn, and it cultivates confidence and competence that leads to continued academic achievement.

CHILDREN'S DEVELOPING KNOWLEDGE OF MATHEMATICS

As is the case with literacy, the development of mathematical competence begins during the preschool period, and school learning builds on and presumes a base of understanding that not all children bring with them to school. The research base for understanding children's developing mathematical understanding differs in two important ways from that of literacy, reflecting the nature of subject matter. First, because American children on average engage in far less activity related to mathematics outside of school, research has focused on the nature of mathematics instruction and the kind of teacher knowledge and activities that promote successful mathematics learning. Second, because much of the conceptual content of mathematics and even the symbolic representations used are universal, mathematics has been a key focus of international comparative research on school achievement.

Although still controversial (Berliner & Biddle, 1995), a consistent pattern across more than 30 years of research on mathematics achievement has been the finding that American children perform significantly below their peers in a number of other countries, particularly those in East Asia (Beaton & Robitaille, 1999; Husén, 1967; Peak, 1997; Travers & Weinzweig, 1999). These differences are substantial. On the Third International Mathematics and Science Study (TIMSS), U.S. fourth graders at the 95th percentile did not perform significantly better than the average student in Singapore (Peak, 1997). These findings are not limited to the TIMSS and its predecessor studies. In a long series of studies comparing U.S. children with those in Taiwan, Japan, and mainland China, Stevenson and Lee (1998) found equally large differences that increased with age, and the differences were mainly in mathematics as opposed to science or literacy. For example, a comparison of the average math achievement scores for schools revealed that only one sample in Chicago at the fifth grade performed as well as the lowest-performing school in Beijing (Stevenson et al., 1990).

What Children Bring To School: Two Components of Early Numeracy

As with literacy, children's mathematical development begins long before their formal instruction begins. There is evidence that infants are sensitive to numerosity from an early age, possibly from birth (Antell & Keating, 1983), although the relative influence of numerical and other features remains a matter of some dispute (Feigenson, Carey, & Spelke, 2002; Simon, 1997). During the preschool years, children develop a counting-based understanding of number, which provides them with a powerful but limited tool for learning about addition and subtraction and developing a familiarity with larger numbers (Ginsburg, Klein, & Starkey, 1998).

It is useful to distinguish between two components of early numeracy. The first involves a set of insights into number, which are universal in nature. The second involves mastery of symbol systems used to represent number, which can vary across languages and over time. This division corresponds to some extent to Geary's (1995) distinction between *biologically primary* abilities, presumed to have extensive biological support, and *biologically secondary* abilities, which require the scaffolding of culture and schooling to develop. Even as rudimentary a task as counting, however, contains some components that are universal and others that are dependent on lan-

guage and cultural practices, which suggests that it may be more productive to think of a continuum of abilities and tasks in terms of the extent to which their acquisition is dependent on environmental and cultural support.

Universal Features of Number. Many aspects of counting are inherent in the underlying definition of enumeration and therefore should be universal. Gelman and Gallistel (1978) described these as a set of counting principles, the first three of which correspond to an operational definition of counting systems, specifying that (1) there be exactly one tag (such as a number name) per element when counting, (2) the tags be used in a consistent order, and (3) the last tag corresponds to the numerosity of the entire set. Other features of number, such as the fact that $N + 1$ is consistently larger than N (and by exactly 1); are inherent in children's experiences with numbers. This experience with counting provides an early and natural basis for understanding the effects of addition and subtraction (Baroody & Dowker, 2003; Huttenlocher, Jordan, & Levine, 1994). Evidence from school-cutoff studies (Bisanz, Morrison, & Dunn, 1995) shows that age rather than schooling is associated with development of early strategies for adding small numbers and for the development of a basic understanding of number as measured by the Piagetian number conservation task. Cross-cultural research (e.g., Miller, Smith, Zhu, & Zhang, 1995) has shown relatively little variation in children's developing mastery of these universal features of number.

Language-Dependent Aspects of Numerical Symbols. In addition to the universal components of numbers, there are features that reflect the nature of the symbols used to represent them. Cross-language comparisons show that children are quite sensitive to the structure of number-naming systems, with difficulties and delays in learning to count in their native language that reflect the complexity of number name morphology in that language. For example, Chinese number names reflect a consistent base-10 structure (i.e., the name for "11" corresponds to "ten-one") in contrast to the more complex and varying morphology of English number names (Miller & Paredes, 1996). Differences in the nature of errors and the speed of learning different parts of the number-naming sequence correspond precisely to these variations in the complexity of what children must learn (Miller et al., 1995). A similar pattern of specific and limited effects of the structure of symbol systems has been found for ordinal numbers (Miller, Major, & Shu, 2000), and rational numbers (Miura, Okamoto, Vlahovic-Stetic, Kim, & Han, 1999).

The relative importance of universal and language-dependent factors can vary by concept and with development. With development, children's interaction with mathematics increasingly is mediated by symbol systems, so developing facility with mathematical symbols is a critical aspect of mathematical development. That interaction increasingly involves Arabic numerals, which are a completely consistent base-10 system. Speakers of languages such as Chinese that map more consistently onto Arabic numerals have an advantage in learning them. Once Arabic numerals are mastered, an abstract representation based on them may become the canonical representation of number (McCloskey, Sokol, Goodman-Schulman, & Caramazza, 1990), with consequent diminution of effects of the characteristics of the spoken names for numbers (Miller & Zhu, 1991).

Environmental Influences on Early Mathematical Development

Most U.S. children enter school with mathematical abilities that provide a strong base for formal mathematical instruction. These abilities include an understanding of the magnitudes of small numbers, an ability to count and to use counting to solve simple mathematical problems, and an understanding of many of the basic concepts underlying measurement. For example, a large survey by the National Center for Education Statistics (NCES, 2000), reported that 94% of first-time kindergartners passed their Level 1 test (they could count to 10 and recognize numerals and shapes), and 58% passed their Level 2 test (they could read numerals and count beyond 10, sequence patterns, and use nonstandard units of length to compare objects).

However, a number of children, particularly those from low socioeconomic groups, enter school with some specific gaps in their mathematical competence. For example, the NCES report found that 79% of children whose mothers had a bachelor's degree passed the Level 2 test just described, but only 32% of children whose mothers had less than a high school degree could do so. The NCES report found large differences between different ethnic groups on their more difficult tests (but not on the Level 1 tasks), with 70% of Asian and 66% of non-Hispanic white children passing the Level 2 tasks, whereas only 42% of African-Americans and 44% of Hispanics, 48% of Hawaiian Native/Pacific Islanders, and 34% of American Indian/Alaska Native participants passed. Because ethnicity and SES are often correlated, they broke their samples down using maternal education (high school or equivalency degree or beyond, vs. less than high school). A consistent finding within ethnic groups was that an additional 15–25% of children whose mothers graduated from high school passed the Level 2 tasks (e.g., 49% of Hispanic children whose mothers had graduated from high school

passed vs. 27% of those whose mothers did not have a high school education). Other research has shown that children from lower SES backgrounds are substantially more likely to have difficulties that involve understanding the relative magnitudes of single-digit cardinal numbers (Griffin, Case, & Siegler, 1994).

Several promising approaches to deal with these early gaps in mathematical knowledge have been developed. For example, the "Rightstart" (Griffin, Case, & Siegler, 1994) program consists of a set of games and number-line activities aimed at providing children with an understanding of the relative magnitudes of numbers. Results showed that 20 minutes a day over a 3- to 4-month period in kindergarten was successful in bringing children's mathematical knowledge up to a level commensurate with their peers, gains that persisted through the end of first grade. Starkey, Klein, and Wakeley (2004) described a substantial reduction in the difference across SES groups in mathematical competence following a pre-kindergarten intervention that coupled a school curriculum with a home component consisting of activities for parents to do with their children. Sophian (2004) also reported significant effects of an intervention focused on teaching children the importance of units and of part–whole relations in early mathematics. Fuson, Smith, and Lo Cicero (1997) reported striking results from an intervention aimed at ensuring that Latino children understand the base-10 structure of number names, something that many U.S. children find confusing. Performance at the end of the year-long intervention was at levels comparable to those reported for Asian children, and substantially above those typically reported for nonminority children. Taken together, these results suggest that relatively simple interventions may yield important payoffs in ensuring that all children enter first grade ready to profit from school mathematics instruction.

Value Placed on Mathematics Achievement

Parents prepare their children in many different ways for the transition to school. For example, surveys of parents of preschool children in China and the United States (Kelly, 2002; Stevenson et al., 1990) found that parents report teaching their children explicitly for school entry. Two differences were noteworthy. First, Stevenson et al. (1990) found that mothers of first-graders in Taiwan significantly increased their educational involvement as their children began first grade, but this did not occur with the American sample. Kelly (2002) also found an important difference in the distribution of activities in the two countries. American mothers showed a clear emphasis on literacy over mathematics both in the time they reported spending in teaching their children and in the importance they placed on the domain. Chinese mothers were much more balanced in their emphases on the importance of literacy and mathematical skills, as well as in the effort they reported spending in preparing their children in each area. This suggests that cross-national differences in achievement may also reflect differences in the relative value of different areas of achievement (Hatano, 1990) that emerge early in children's lives.

A more detailed picture of possible mechanisms behind parental influences on cross-national differences in achievement emerges from research by Huntsinger, Jose, Larson, Balsink, and Shaligram (2000) comparing Chinese-American and European-American parents' socialization of mathematics. Chinese-American parents spent more time teaching, used more formal teaching methods, and expected their children to do much more homework. Indeed, they often assigned their own additional homework. Chinese-American parents had higher expectations for their children, and their children performed better at school than the comparison group.

The ultimate source of these differences in emphasis and effort expended on the teaching of mathematics between the U.S. and East Asian countries is not clear (Hatano, 1990), and there is some evidence that it may be a recent phenomenon (Cohen, 1982; Geary, Salthouse, Chen, & Fan, 1996). However, differences in values and effort may account for much of the large cross-national differences in mathematics achievement.

The Nature of Mathematical Proficiency

Controversies in mathematical education in the United States have tended to involve arguments about whether particular aspects of mathematics, such as computational skills, are as important as others, such as conceptual understanding. The Mathematics Learning Study of the National Research Council (Kilpatrick, Swafford, & Findell, 2001) summarized the state of mathematics education in the United States and suggested that mathematical competence can be conceived of as a rope woven from five strands that comprise a complex whole. The five strands are:

Conceptual understanding: comprehension of mathematical concepts, operations, and relations
Procedural fluency: skill in carrying out procedures flexibly, accurately, efficiently, and appropriately
Strategic competence: ability to formulate, represent, and solve mathematical problems
Adaptive reasoning: capacity for logical thought, reflection, explanation, and justification

Productive disposition: habitual inclination to see mathematics as sensible, useful, and worthwhile, coupled with a belief in diligence and one's own efficacy.

Reviewing existing research, Kilpatrick et al. (2001) argued that these are in fact mutually reinforcing components of competence, and that shortcomings in any one can cause difficulties in development of the others. There is a parallel approach between the rope analogy in mathematics and the five essential components identified for reading development. Both approaches are distilled from voluminous research; both identify the key concepts and skills acquired in early childhood; both include some skills that are acquired universally and some that are dependent on specific teaching; both emphasize fluency and automaticity in the component skills; and both describe the components as interdependent during development. The result of both approaches is a characterization of the different trajectories of early skills in literacy and numeracy that, by the age of 8–10 years, set children on different pathways through formal education.

Mathematical Development in Grades K-5

Three generalizations can be made from the studies of children's understanding of fundamental arithmetic operations during elementary school. Each one shows that children approach mathematics in multiple ways, using their prior knowledge to construct meaning in mathematical problems and relations. First, children's representations of problems are tied more closely than adults' representations to the semantic rather than mathematical features of the problem (Briars & Larkin, 1984). Consider the following problems (Carpenter, Fennema, Franke, Empson, & Levi, 1999):

(a) *Connie has 5 marbles. How many more does she need to have 13 marbles altogether?*
(b) *Connie had 13 marbles. She gave some to Juan. Now she has 5 marbles left. How many marbles did Connie give to Juan?*

The solutions to both problems can be represented as $13 - 5 = N$, but children tend to think of them in terms of different underlying schemas (termed "join" and "separate" by Carpenter et al., 1999). These different schemas lead children to analyze the quantitative relations in different ways. At least within the U.S. instructional context, the move from concrete situations to more abstract mathematical representations is a key difficulty in early school mathematics.

A second generalization is that, compared to older children and adults, younger children show a greater diversity of strategies in response to the same problem. In performing simple addition problems (such as adding "3 + 5"), children commonly use a large set of strategies that include:

(a) Retrieval—remembering a known sum ("8")

(b) Counting all—counting the total sum (e.g., putting up three fingers and five fingers and then counting "1, 2, 3, . . . 4, 6, 7, 8")

(c) Counting up from one of the addends ("3, . . . 4, 5, 6, 7, 8")

(d) Min counting—finding the larger of two addends and counting up from there ("5, . . . 6, 7, 8")

(e) Decomposition—decomposing the problem into a related and known problem ("3 + 5 is like 4 + 4, so it's 8")

(f) Guessing

Kindergartners use all of these strategies, and second-graders use all of them except for counting all (Bisanz et al., 1995; Jordan, Huttenlocher, & Levine, 1992; Siegler & Shrager, 1984). Variability in children's performance is quite pervasive; individual children typically show multiple strategies even on repetition of the same problem, and they will continue to use a strategy even after they have begun to use one that appears to be more efficient. Siegler (1994) has argued that this variability in strategy plays a critical role in promoting cognitive change. Children are most likely to show such variability before discovering new strategies, and children who show varied ways of thinking in pretests are more likely to profit from instruction (Graham & Perry, 1993).

The third generalization is that conceptual understanding and procedural fluency play a mutually reinforcing role in learning. Conflicts over the relative importance of conceptual understanding of mathematics and fluency at calculation have been at the heart of popular controversies in mathematics instruction (the so-called math wars, e.g., Marshall, 2003). Kilpatrick et al. (2001) argued that the dichotomy between conceptual understanding and procedural fluency is a false one, because procedures developed without conceptual understanding are likely to become isolated bits of knowledge (e.g., Nunes, 1992), whereas much of later mathematics depends on fluent mastery of earlier procedures. An elegant set of studies by Rittle-Johnson, Siegler, and Alibali (2001) provide empirical support for the mutually reinforcing nature of conceptual understanding and procedural fluency. They studied fifth- and sixth-grade children who were learning about decimal fractions and found that children's initial conceptual knowledge predicted gains in procedural knowledge, whereas gains in procedural knowledge predicted improvements in conceptual knowledge. In a second experiment, support for correct problem representation was experimentally manipulated, and these conceptual manipulations led to gains in procedural knowledge. They concluded that conceptual and procedural knowledge develop iteratively, and that improved representation of the problems is an important mechanism underlying this improvement. These studies suggest that the popular dichotomy between conceptual understanding of mathematics and fluent performance of mathematical procedures is a false one, although much remains to be learned about the optimal timing of the relation between them in particular areas of mathematics education.

The parallel argument has been made in the "reading wars" between conceptually-driven versus decoding-driven models of reading development (Chall, 1967). Stanovich (1980) described an interactive-compensatory view of reading that postulates that children approach the task of reading using one or the other, i.e., top-down or bottom-up approaches to reading, and they continue to use the approach until it breaks down and then they revert to the other one. As children read, they use both conceptual and decoding processes, and, like the progress in mathematical development, they mutually reinforce each other as children build fluency.

DIVERGING PATHWAYS THROUGH SCHOOL

Research on children's early development of reading and mathematical competence has shown that family environments, values, and practices influence their pathways into school. As a consequence, American children begin kindergarten and first grade with widely different abilities that are often traced to environmental differences in SES, parental levels of education and support, and measures of preschool vocabulary and number knowledge. Compensatory education, preschool, and child-care programs are often designed to ameliorate these differences, but elementary education is not a level playing field. Public schools serve a growing number of immigrant children who must overcome economic, cultural, and linguistic obstacles. Children with learning disabilities and special needs are mainstreamed in regular classes. These various factors within the child and family contribute to differences in educational access and achievement, and they often restrict the advancement of students who face multiple risks. In contrast, children who exhibit early mastery of literacy and numeracy build on success to gain access to more and better educational resources.

The diverging pathways in elementary grades are amplified by "summer loss" of academic skills among disadvantaged students. Heyns (1978) examined the effects of summer learning programs and found that Caucasian students in sixth grade gained about 2.5 months (using grade norm scores) on achievement tests, regardless of whether they attended summer programs or not. However, African-American students who attended summer programs gained .3 months, whereas Africa-American students who did not attend summer programs lost an average of 1.8 months. Cooper, Charlton, Valentine, and Muhlenbruck (2000) found that math achievement for middle-class and disadvantaged students declined equally over the summer, but reading achievement increased for middle-class students and declined for disadvantaged students.

Entwisle et al. (1997) found that students from disadvantaged schools showed greater summer achievement losses than students from middle-class schools. However, they had equal learning rates during the school year, so the diverging achievement levels reflect a cumulative summer loss throughout elementary school. Summer school programs provide modest help. According to a meta-analysis of summer programs, successful reading and math programs had average effect sizes of 0.20–0.25 (Cooper et al., 2000). Thus, the widening achievement differences, or Matthew effects, between successful and struggling students are not simply due to instructional differences during the school year.

Cross-cultural studies reveal that parents provide different supports for young children through their expectations, teaching, and home learning environments. East Asian families, in general, provide more effective support for children's transition to formal school. This may contribute to the lower level of achievement in grade 1 of American children compared to children in East Asian schools (Stevenson et al., 1990). Unequal starting points for American first graders create a classroom problem for American elementary teachers, who are often confronted with huge differences among their students in skill levels, language, motivation, and home support.

The documentation of early differences in academic skills, coupled with research that shows the importance of early skill trajectories (e.g., Adams, 1990; Snow et al., 1998), has led to greater emphases on teaching children literacy and numeracy in K-3 grades. The emphases are apparent in educational research, instruction, and policies. Parents and teachers, especially in some families and some countries, provide explicit teaching and multiple supports for learning, but teachers and schools cannot compensate for the cumulative lack of home support that some disadvantaged children endure. Individual differences in opportunities and abilities to learn are amplified,

not minimized, as children progress through elementary school.

ASSESSMENT AND ACCOUNTABILITY IN ELEMENTARY SCHOOL

The most visible manifestation of policies designed to improve student achievement in the past 20 years is the greater emphasis on standards and testing in reading and mathematics at primary grades. Until the 1990s, curricula, instruction, and assessment for reading and math in grades K-3 were largely left to teachers, but the poor performance on achievement tests at grade 4 indicated that better instruction was required in primary grades. One salient indication of the new policy was the introduction of new reading assessment batteries in many states, including Texas, Virginia, Michigan, and Illinois. These assessment batteries were based on the five essential components of reading and were designed for 5- to 8-year-old children.

A concomitant effort has occurred in the domain of mathematics, although the meaning and utility of the mathematics results remains somewhat unclear. Taking the case of Texas, which was a pioneer in the accountability movement, Klein, Hamilton, McCaffrey, and Stecher (2000) found that improvement on the state mathematics assessment was substantially greater than that found on the National Assessment of Educational Progress exams, and that reductions in the achievement gap across ethnic groups could be attributed to ceiling effects, reflecting a relatively easy set of items on the state test.

Early assessments of academic skills fit well within the educational accountability movement of the 1990s, and they were incorporated in new policies for instruction and assessment under the NCLB Act of 2001. The Reading First part of the NCLB legislation emphasized teaching and testing the five essential components in K-3, whereas the other parts of the legislation implemented annual achievement testing in reading, math, and science. The end result is greater emphases on early achievement in reading and mathematics and greater accountability from students, teachers, and schools to meet explicit standards.

Consequences of Accountability

The most evident consequence of the trend for earlier academic accountability is the increase in the number of early assessments available to teachers as well as the increasing pressure to use them often (Rathvon, 2004). Paris and Hoffman (2004) reported the results of several research projects in the Center for the Improvement of

Early Reading Achievement (CIERA) that showed dramatic increases in the number of reading assessments, both commercial and noncommercial, used by teachers in K-3. The primary use of the assessments is diagnostic so that children who have inadequate basic skills can be identified by early first grade and then provided with extra instruction to bolster their skills. This is consistent with the model of Reading Recovery advocated by Clay (1991), but newer approaches emphasize better assessment and more rigorous training on decoding skills, especially phonological awareness. Thus, most early reading assessments are administered individually, include a diagnostic battery that includes the five essential components, and are connected to remedial instruction or interventions that include explicit teaching about basic skills. These are all positive features of renewed emphases on early reading assessment.

However, there are also some unintended but negative consequences of increased assessments. Teachers are concerned that the focus on basic skills narrows the curriculum and may decrease children's motivation for reading, especially for children who struggle to read (Hoffman, Paris, Patterson, Salas, & Assaf, 2003). If children fail to perform well on standardized tests in elementary grades, they may develop self-handicapping motivational and test-taking strategies in order to rationalize less effort and diminished value of the tests (Paris, 2000). When children become disillusioned about their prospects for academic success based on test results, they may exhibit less engagement in the classroom and more passive orientations to learning (Wigfield & Guthrie, 1997). These potential negative effects are more likely on standardized tests given to groups of older students. Murphy, Shannon, Johnston, and Hansen (1998) reviewed both external and internal validity of popular reading tests and concluded that they often do not meet acceptable psychometric standards and are insensitive to broader notions of assessment validity.

The increased assessment of children's early literacy and numeracy in K-3 offers promise of early diagnoses and intervention for children who start school less prepared than their peers. Yet careful attention is required to assure that increased assessment does not reduce the quality of early instruction. Among children in upper elementary grades, the goal of assessment must include remedial help and rich opportunities for learning that go beyond accountability. Sacks (1999) called standardized testing the "crooked measure of meritocracy" and described how such tests penalize women, minorities, and students with disabilities from elementary school through college. Heubert and Hauser (1999) also described the increased use of standardized tests used to certify retention and promotion, and they expressed caution about

the long-term risks to students who experience failure. Haney (2000) described how increases in state achievement test scores obscure hidden problems such as the increased dropout rates of minorities.

Three conclusions are relevant here. First, students' pathways through school become more influenced by specific classroom curriculum, instruction, and assessment as they progress through elementary grades. When these meet high quality standards, academic success is more likely. Second, when struggling students encounter repeated failure on achievement tests, they are at risk for developing low self-efficacy and negative orientations to school that exacerbate their original difficulties. Third, children's academic pathways may diverge more as they progress through K-12 grades based on their mastery of early skills and responsiveness to instruction. The net effect of these developmental patterns is often an "achievement gap" between groups of students.

The Black–White Test Score Gap

In general, African-American children do not perform as well on academic achievement tests as their European-American peers (National Assessment of Educational Progress, 2000). The most common explanations for "the gap" have focused on socioeconomic and sociocultural factors. In particular, the higher rate of poverty among African-American families has been offered as an explanation for poorer performance of African-American children. Likewise, the legacy of racial discrimination, which limits opportunities for African-American children, may contribute to lower academic attainment. However, two recent findings have caused scientists to reassess the nature and sources of the discrepancies. First, it has become clear that the test-score gap is not limited to lower SES groups (Phillips, Crouse, & Ralph, 1998). Black middle-class children are performing more poorly than their White middle-class peers. Second, the gap in academic performance emerges before children begin school (Phillips et al., 1998). Both findings have caused researchers to look more deeply into the environments of African-American families for a more comprehensive understanding of the achievement gap.

A salient and controversial factor implicated in the Black–White test score gap is differences in parenting. Growing evidence has pointed to differences across racial groups in the quality of the home learning experiences provided to children (Phillips et al., 1998) and other aspects of the literacy environment (Morrison, Bachman, & Connor, 2005). These differences also seem to extend to middle-class parenting practices (Bachman, 1999). Although the reasons for these differences in parenting are not clearly understood, the focus on literacy experiences at home is yielding a more comprehensive picture of the complex forces contributing to the achievement gap.

Spencer, Noll, Stoltzfus, and Harpalani (2001) suggest that the focus on an "achievement gap" perpetuates stereotypes of uniform White and Black groups of students and stereotypical group differences. They disagree with the claim that African-American students learn to "act White" by adopting European-American values and attitudes in order to succeed in school. Spencer et al. (2001) report a study of African-American adolescents in which high academic achievement was correlated with strong, coherent proactive identities as African-Americans. The researchers argue that academic success is more difficult for minority students who need to negotiate multiple identities at the same time they negotiate other developmental problems of adolescence. Becker and Luthar (2002) identified four critical factors for academic success: academic/school attachment, teacher support, peer values, and mental health. They suggest that minority students are at risk for each factor to a greater extent than White students, and they argue that any school reform effort aimed at reducing the achievement gap must address all four factors.

CONCLUSIONS

This chapter reviews recent evidence on children's preschool and early school experiences that help to establish their developmental pathways through formal education. As children progress from toddlers to children and from home to school, they become increasingly independent as they assume roles as students in a larger world. This transition helps define their identities and social relationships during childhood as well as shape their perceptions about self-competence and self-efficacy. By 10 years of age, students begin to develop distinct views of their competence in different domains (Marsh, Craven, & Debus, 1998), and these in turn influence their interests and expenditures of time and effort. Most 5-year-olds are wide-eyed, optimistic children who go to school with vague ideas about what they will do or learn, but by the age of 10, they have become savvy students who know the rules and procedures in school, understand the scope and sequence of formal education, and begin to identify their own likelihood of academic success based on the evidence provided by peers, teachers, parents, and external reports of their achievement.

Research has shown that some children begin school more prepared than others. Parenting practices and opportunities to learn at home vary widely and contribute to initial differences that often become more divergent pathways if the discrepant experiences continue. The best predictor of a successful pathway is early mastery of essential skills involved in literacy and numeracy, because so much of elementary education depends on fluent application of these skills. We know that poverty and poor home environments place children at risk for early and sustained failure in school. Rich language experiences, parental scaffolding of learning, and competent peers and siblings set preschoolers on the right track. Primary grade teachers who diagnose and correct early learning difficulties, as well as provide challenging curricula to students, also help steer children on successful pathways. As children move through upper elementary grades, they must remain engaged in academic tasks and withstand the pressures of standardized tests so they can create positive views of their own abilities, efforts, and efficacy. This is the high road to academic success, and it is a long road that begins early, so parents and teachers must provide explicit teaching and motivation to young children to ensure they can reach their potential.

References

Adams, M. J. (1990). *Beginning to read: Thinking and learning about print*. Cambridge, MA: MIT Press.

Adams, M. J., Treiman, R., & Pressley, M. (1998). Reading, writing, and literacy. In I. E. Sigel & K. A. Renninger (Eds.), *Handbook of child psychology: Vol. 4. Child psychology in practice* (pp. 275–355). New York: Wiley.

Alexander, K., & Entwisle, D. (1988). Achievement in the first 2 years of school: Patterns and processes. *Monographs of the Society for Research in Child Development, 53*(2).

Antell, S. R., & Keating, D. (1983). Perception of numerical invariance by neonates. *Child Development, 54*, 695–701.

Bachman, H. (1999). *How did we get here? Examining the sources of White–Black differences in academic achievement. In F. Morrison (Chair), Racial differences in academic achievement: When and why?* Symposium conducted at the biennial meeting of the Society for Research in Child Development, Albuquerque, NM.

Barnett, S. (1995). Long-term effects of early childhood programs on cognitive and school outcomes. *Future of Children, 5*(3), 25–50.

Baroody, A. J., & Dowker, A. (Eds.). (2003). *The development of arithmetic concepts and skills: Recent research and theory*. Mahwah, NJ: Lawrence Erlbaum Associates.

Bear, D. R., Invernizzi, M., Templeton, S., & Johnston, F. (2004). *Words their way.* Upper Saddle River, NJ: Pearson.

Beaton, A. E., & Robitaille, D. F. (1999). An overview of the Third International Mathematics and Science Study. In E. L. G. Kaiser, E. Luna, & I. Huntley (Ed.), *International comparisons in mathematics education* (pp. 30–47). London: Falmer Press.

Beck, I. L., McKeown, M. G., & Kucan, L. (2002). *Bringing words to life: Robust vocabulary instruction.* New York: Guilford Press.

Becker, B. E., & Luthar, S. S. (2002). Social-emotional factors affecting achievement outcomes among disadvantaged students: Closing the achievement gap. *Educational Psychologist, 37*(4), 197–214.

Berlin, L. J., & Brooks-Gunn, J. (1995). Examining observational measures of emotional suport and cognitive stimulation in Black and White mothers of preschoolers. *Journal of Family Issues, 16.*

Berliner, D. (2005). Our impoverished view of educational reform. *Teachers College Record,* August 2, 2005 http://www.trecord.org

Berliner, D. C., & Biddle, B. J. (1995). *The manufactured crisis: Myths, fraud, and the attack on America's public schools.* Reading, MA: Addison-Wesley.

Bisanz, J., Morrison, F. J., & Dunn, M. (1995). Effects of age and schooling on the acquisition of elementary quantitative skills. *Developmental Psychology, 31,* 221–236.

Blaiklock, K. E. (2004). The importance of letter knowledge in the relationship between phonological awareness and reading. *Journal of Research in Reading, 27*(1), 36–57.

Bradley, L., & Bryant, P. E. (1983). Categorizing sounds and learning to read: A causal connection. *Nature, 301*(3), 419–421.

Bradley, R., Whiteside, L., Mundform, D., Casey, P., Kelleher, K., & Pope, S. (1994). Early indications of resilience and their relation to experiences in the home environments of low birthweight, premature children in poverty. *Child Development, 65,* 346–360.

Briars, D. J., & Larkin, J. H. (1984). An integrated model of skill in solving elementary problems. *Cognition and Instruction, 1,* 245–296.

Brooks-Gunn, J. (in press). What do we know about children's development from theory, intervention, and policy? In P. L. Chase-Lansdale, K. E. Kiernan & R. J. Friedman (Eds.), *Human development across lives and generations: The potential for change.* New York: Cambridge University Press.

Brooks-Gunn, J., Burchinal, M., & Lopez, M. (2001). *Enhancing the cognitive and social development of young children via parent education in the Comprehensive Child Development Program.* Manuscript submitted for publication.

Brooks-Gunn, J., Han, W., & Waldfogel, J. (2002). Maternal employment and child cognitive outcomes in the first three years of life: NICHD study of early child care. *Child Development, 73*(4), 1052–1072.

Brooks-Gunn, J., Klebanov, P. K., & Smith, J. (2003). The black-white test score gap in young children: Contributions of test and family characteristics. *Applied Developmental Science, 7*(4), 239–252.

Campbell, F., & Ramey, C. (1994). Effects of early intervention on intellectual and academic achievement: A follow-up study of children from low income families. *Child Development, 65,* 684–698.

Carpenter, R. D., & Paris, S. G. (2005). Issues of validity and reliability in early reading assessments. In S. G. Paris & S. A. Stahl (Eds.), *Children's reading comprehension and assessment* (pp. 279–304). Mahwah, NJ: Lawrence Erlbaum Associates.

Carpenter, T. P., Fennema, E., Franke, M. L., Empson, S. B., & Levi, L. W. (1999). *Children's mathematics: Cognitively guided instruction.* Portsmouth, NJ: Heinemann.

Castles, A., & Coltheart, M. (2004). Is there a causal link from phonological awareness to success in learning to read? *Cognition, 91,* 77–111.

Chall, J. (1967). *Learning to read: the great debate.* New York: McGraw-Hill.

Chase-Lansdale, P., & Pittman, L. (2002). Welfare reform and parenting: Reasonable Expectations. In M. K. Shields (Ed.), *Children and welfare reform* (Vol. 12, pp. 167–183). Los Altos, CA: The David and Lucile Packard Foundation.

Clay, M. M. (1991). *Becoming literate: The construction of inner control.* Auckland, NZ: Heinemann.

Coates, D., & Lewis, M. (1984). Early mother–infant interaction and infant cognitive status as predictors of school performance and cognitive behavior in six-year-olds. *Child Development, 55,* 1219–1230.

Cohen, P. C. (1982). *A calculating people: The spread of numeracy in early America.* Chicago: Chicago.

Coleman, J., Campbell, E., Hobson, C., McPartland, J., Mood, A., Weinfeld, F., et al. (1966). *Equality of educational opportunity.* Washington, DC: U.S. Government Printing Office.

Collins, W. A., Maccoby, E., Steinberg, L., Hetherington, E. M., & Bornstein, M. H. (2000). Contemporary research on parenting: The case for nature and nurture. *American Psychologist, 55,* 218–232.

Cooney, R. (1998). *Relations among aspects of parental control, children's work-related skills and academic achievement.* Paper presented at the Conference on Human Development, Mobile, AL.

Cooper, H., Charlton, K., Valentine, J. C., & Muhlenbruck, L. (2000). Making the most of summer school: A meta-analytic and narrative review. *Monographs of the Society for Research in Child Development, 65*(1, Serial No. 260).

Cunningham, A. E., & Stanovich, K. E. (1997). Early reading acquisition and its relation to reading experience and ability ten years later. *Developmental Psychology, 33*(6), 934–945.

Deno, S. L., Mirkin, P., & Chiang, B. (1982). Identifying valid measures of reading. *Exceptional Children, 49,* 36–45.

Dickinson, D. K., McCabe, A., & Anastasopoulos, L. (2003). The comprehensive language approach to early literacy: The interrelationships among vocabulary, phonological sensitivity, and print knowledge among preschool-aged children. *Journal of Educational Psychology, 95*(3), 465–481.

Dickinson, D. K., & Tabors, P. O. (2001). *Beginning literacy with language.* Baltimore: Paul H. Brookes.

Entwisle, D. R., Alexander, K. L., & Olson, L. S. (1997). *Children, schools, and inequality.* Boulder, CO: Westview.

Feigenson, L., Carey, S., & Spelke, E. (2002). Infants' discrimination of number vs. continuous extent. *Cognitive Psychology, 44*, 33–66.

Foorman, B. R., Francis, D. J., Fletcher, J. M., Schatschneider, C., & Mehta, P. (1998). The role of instruction in learning to read: Preventing reading failure in at risk children. *Journal of Educational Psychology, 90*, 37–55.

Fuchs, L. S., & Fuchs, D. (1999). Monitoring student progress toward the development of reading competence: A review of three forms of classroom-based assessment. *School Psychology Review, 28*, 659–671.

Fuson, K. C., Smith, S. T., & Lo Cicero, A. M. (1997). Supporting Latino first graders' ten-structured thinking in urban classrooms. *Journal for Research in Mathematics Education, 28*, 738–766.

Geary, D. C. (1995). Reflections of evolution and culture in children's cognition: Implications for mathematical development and instruction. *American Psychologist, 50*, 24–37.

Geary, D. C., Salthouse, T. A., Chen, G. P., & Fan, L. (1996). Are East Asian versus American differences in arithmetical ability a recent phenomenon? *Developmental Psychology, 32*, 254–262.

Gelman, R., & Gallistel, C. R. (1978). *The child's understanding of number.* Cambridge, MA: Harvard University Press.

Ginsburg, H. P., Klein, A., & Starkey, P. (1998). The development of children's mathematical thinking: Connecting research with practice. In I. Sigel & A. Renninger (Eds.), *Handbook of child psychology: Child psychology and practice* (5th ed., Vol. 4, pp. 401–476). New York: Wiley.

Gomby, D. S., Culross, P. L., & Behrman, R. E. (1999). Home visiting: Recent program evaluations—analysis and recommendations. *Future of Children, 9*(4–26).

Good, R. H., & Kaminski, R. A. (Eds.). (2002). *Dynamic indicators of basic early literacy skills* (6th ed.). Eugene, OR: Institute for the Development of Educational Achievement.

Graham, T., & Perry, M. (1993). Indexing transitional knowledge. *Developmental Psychology, 29*, 779–778.

Griffin, S., Case, R., & Siegler, R. S. (1994). Rightstart: Providing the central conceptual prerequisites for first formal learning of arithmetic to students at risk for school failure. In K. McGilly (Ed.), *Classroom lessons: Integrating cognitive theory and classroom practice* (pp. 25–49). Cambridge, MA: MIT Press.

Haden, C. A., Reese, E., & Fivush, R. (1996). Mothers' extratextural comments during storybook reading: Stylistic differences over time and across text. *Discourse Processes, 21*, 135–169.

Haney, W. (2000, April). *The myth of the Texas miracle in education.* Paper presented at the annual meeting of the American Educational Research Association, New Orleans, LA.

Hart, B., & Risley, T. R. (1995). *Meaningful differences in the everyday experience of young American children.* Baltimore: Paul H. Brookes.

Hartup, W. (1989). Social relationships and their developmental significance. *American Psychologist, 44*, 120–126.

Hatano, G. (1990). Toward the cultural psychology of mathematical cognition. Comment on Stevenson, H. W., Lee, S-Y. (1990). *Contexts of achievement. Monographs of the Society for Research in Child Development, 55* (1-2, Serial No. 221), 108–115.

Haynes, N. M., Comer, J., & Hamilton-Lee, M. (1988). The School Development Program: A model for school improvement. *Journal of Negro Education, 57*(1), 11–21.

Heubert, J. P., & Hauser, R. M. (1999). *High stakes: Testing for tracking, promotion, and graduation.* Washington, DC: National Academy Press.

Heyns, B. (1978). *Summer learning and the effects of schooling.* New York: Academic Press.

Hoff-Ginsberg, E. (1991). Mother–child conversation in different social classes and communicative settings. *Child Development, 62*, 782–796.

Hoffman, J. V., Paris, S. G., Patterson, E., Salas, R., & Assaf, L. (2003). High stakes assessment in the language arts: The piper plays, the players dance, but who pays the price? In J. Flood & D. Lapp (Eds.), *Handbook of research on teaching the English language arts* (2nd ed., pp. 619–630). Mahwah, NJ: Lawrence Erlbaum Associates.

Husén, T. (1967). *International study of achievement in mathematics.* New York: Wiley.

Huntsinger, C. S., Jose, P. E., Larson, S. L., Balsink, K. D., & Shaligram, C. (2000). Mathematics, vocabulary, and reading development in Chinese-American and European-American children over the primary school years. *Journal of Educational Psychology, 92*(4), 745–760.

Huttenlocher, J., Haight, W., Bryk, A., Seltzer, M., & Lyons, T. (1991). Early vocabulary growth: Relation to language input and gender. *Developmental Psychology, 27*(2), 236–248.

Huttenlocher, J., Jordan, N., & Levine, S. (1994). A mental model for early arithmetic. *Journal of Experimental Psychology: General, 123*(3), 284–296.

Huttenlocher, J., Vasilyeva, M., Cymerman, E., & Levine, S. (2002). Language input and syntax. *Cognitive Psychology, 45*, 337–374.

Jencks, C., & Phillips, M. (1998a). *The Black–White test score gap.* Washington, DC: Brookings Institute.

Jordan, N. C., Huttenlocher, J., & Levine, S. C. (1992). Differential calculation abilities in young children from middle- and low-income families. *Developmental Psychology, 28*, 644–653.

Juel, C., Griffith, P., & Gough, P. (1986). Acquisition of literacy: A longitudinal study of children in first and second grade. *Journal of Educational Psychology, 78*, 243–255.

Kelly, J., Morisset, C., Barnartd, K., Hammond, M., & Booth, C. (1996). The influence of early mother–child interaction on preschool cognitive/linguistic outcomes in a high-social-risk group. *Infant Mental Health Journal, 17*, 310–321.

Kelly, M. K. (2002). Getting ready for school: A cross-cultural comparison of parent and child beliefs about and preparations for entry into first grade in China and the United States. *Dissertation Abstracts International, 63(11-B),* 5550 (UMI No. 3070347).

Kilpatrick, J., Swafford, J., & Findell, B, (2001). *Adding it up: Helping children learn mathematics.* Washington, DC: National Academy Press.

Kintsch, W. (1998). *Comprehension: A paradigm for cognition.* New York: Cambridge University Press.

Klein, S., Hamilton, L., McCaffrey, D., & Stecher, B. (2000) *What do test scores in Texas tell us?* Santa Monica, CA: Rand.

Korenman, S., & Miller, J. (1997). Effects of long-term poverty on physical health of children in the national longitudinal survey of youth. In G. Duncan & J. Brooks-Gunn (Eds.), *Consequences of growing up poor*. New York: Russell Sage.

Kuhn, M. R., & Stahl, S. A. (2003). Fluency: A review of developmental and remedial practices. *Journal of Educational Psychology, 95*(1), 3–21.

Lonigan, C., Burgess, S., & Anthony, J. (2000). Development of emergent literacy and early reading skills in preschool: Evidence from a latent-variable longitudinal study. *Developmental Psychology, 36*, 596–613.

Lonigan, C. J., & Whitehurst, G. J. (1998). Relative efficacy of parent and teacher involvement in a shared book-reading intervention for preschool children from low income backgrounds. *Early Childhood Research Quarterly, 13*(2), 263–290.

Lorusso, M. (1994). A critical review of Bakker's balance model of dyslexia. In R. Licht, & G. Spyer (Eds.), *The balance model of dyslexia* (pp. 1–22). The Netherlands: Van Gorcum, Assen.

Magnusson, K., & Duncan, G. (in press). Parent- vs child-based intervention strategies for promoting children's well-being. In A. Kalil & T. DeLeire (Eds.), *Family investments in children's potential*. Mahwah, NJ: Lawrence Erlbaum Associates.

Mann, V., & Foy, J. (2003). Phonological awareness, speech development and letter knowledge in preschool children. *Annals of Dyslexia, 53*, 149–173.

Marsh, H. W., Craven, R. G., & Debus, R. (1998) Structure, stability, and development of young children's self-concepts: A multicohort-multioccasion study, *Child Development, 69*(4), 1030–1053.

Marshall, J. (2003). Math wars: Taking sides. *Phi Delta Kappan, 85*(3), 193–200.

McBride-Chang, C. (1996). Models of speech perception and phonological processing in reading. *Child Development, 67*, 1836–1856.

McCloskey, M., Sokol, S. M., Goodman-Schulman, R. A. & Caramazza, A. (1990). Cognitive representations and processes in number production: Evidence from cases of acquired dyscalculia.In A. Caramazza (Ed.), *Advances in cognitive neuropsychology and neurolinguistics* (pp. 1–32). Hillsdale, NJ: Lawrence Erlbaum Associates.

Miller, K. F., Kelly, M. K., & Zhou, X. (in press). Learning mathematics in China and the United States: Cross-cultural insights into the nature and course of mathematical development. In J. I. D. Campbell (Ed.), *Handbook of mathematical cognition*. New York: Psychology Press.

Miller, K. F., Major, S. M., & Shu, H. (2000). Ordinal knowledge: Number names and number concepts in Chinese and English. *Canadian Journal of Experimental Psychology, 54*(2), 129–139.

Miller, K. F., & Paredes, D. R. (1996). On the shoulders of giants: Cultural tools and mathematical development In R. Sternberg & T. Ben-Zeev (Eds.), *The nature of mathematical thinking* (pp. 83–117). Hillsdale, NJ: Erlbaum.

Miller, K. F., Smith, C. M., Zhu, J., & Zhang, H. (1995). Preschool origins of cross-national differences in mathematical competence: The role of number naming systems. *Psychological Science, 6*, 56–60.

Miller, K. F., & Zhu, J. (1991). The trouble with teens: Accessing the structure of number names. *Journal of Memory and Language, 30*, 48–68.

Miura, I. T., Okamoto, Y., & Vlahovic-Stetic, V. (1999). Language supports for children's understanding of numerical fractions: Cross-national comparisons. *Journal of Experimental Child Psychology, 74*(4), 356–365.

Miura, I. T., Okamoto, Y., Vlahovic-Stetic, V., Kim, C. C, & Han, J. H. (1999). Language supports for children's understanding of numerical fractions: Cross-national comparisons. *Journal of Experimental Child Psychology, 74*(4), 356–365.

Morris, D., Bloodgood, J. W., Lomax, R. G., & Perney, J. (2003). Developmental steps in learning to read: A longitudinal study in kindergarten and first grade. *Reading Research Quarterly, 38*(3), 302–328.

Morrison, F. J., Bachman, H. J., & Connor, C. M. (2005). *Improving literacy in America: Guidelines from research*. Yale University Press.

Morrison, F. J., & Connor, C. M. (2002). Understanding schooling effects on early literacy. *Journal of School Psychology, 40*(6), 493–500.

Morrison, F. J., & Cooney, R. (2002). Parenting and academic achievement: multiple paths to early literacy. In J. G. Borkowski, S. L. Ramey & M. Bristol-Power (Eds.), *Parenting and the child's world: Influences on academic, intellectual, and social-emotional development*. Mahwah, NJ: Lawrence Erlbaum Associates.

Morrison, F. J., Smith, L., & Dow-Ehrensberger, M. (1995). Education and cognitive development: A natural experiment. *Developmental Psychology, 31*(5), 789–799.

Murphy, S., Shannon, P., Johnston, P., & Hansen, J. (1998). *Fragile evidence: A critique of reading assessment*. Mahwah, NJ: Lawrence Erlbaum Associates.

Murray, A., Johnson, J., & Peters, J. (1990). Fine-tuning of utterance length to preverbal infants: Effects on later language development. *Journal of Child Language, 17*, 511–525.

National Assessment of Educational Progress. (2003). *The nation's report card: Reading highlights* (No. NCES 2004–452). Washington, DC: NCES.

National Center for Education Statistics. (1999). *NAEP 1999 trends in academic progress: Three decades of student performance (NCES Statistical Analysis Report No. 2000-469)*. Jessup, MD: U.S. Department of Education.

National Center for Education Statistics. (2000). *America's kindergartners* (NCES 2000-070). Jessup, MD: U.S. Department of Education.

National Reading Panel (NRP). (2000). *Teaching children to read: An evidence-based assessment of the scientific research literature on reading and its implications for reading instruction: Reports of the subgroups*. Bethesda, MD: NICHD.

NICHD-ECCRN. (1998). Relations between family predictors and child outcomes: Are they weaker for children in child care? *Developmental Psychology, 34,* 1119-1128.

NICHD-ECCRN. (2002a). Child-care structure-process-outcome: Direct and indirect effects of child-care quality on young children's development. *Psychological Science, 13*(2), 199-206.

NICHD-ECCRN. (2002b). The relation of first grade classroom environment to structural classroom features, teacher, and student behaviors. *The Elementary School Journal, 102*(5), 367-387.

NICHD-ECCRN. (2003). Does amount of time spent in child care predict socioemotional adjustment during the transition to kindergarten? *Child Development, 74*(4), 969-1226.

NICHD-ECCRN. (2004). Multiple pathways to academic achievement. *Harvard Educational Review, 74*(1), 1-29.

NICHD-ECCRN. (2005a). Predicting individual differences in attention, memory, and planning in first graders from experiences at home, child care, and school. *Developmental Psychology, 4*(1), 99-114.

NICHD-ECCRN. (2005b). Pathways to reading: The role of oral language in the transition to reading. *Developmental Psychology, 41*(2), 428-442.

NICHD-ECCRN. (2005c). A day in third grade: A large-scale study of classroom quality and teacher and student behavior. *Elementary School Journal, 105*(3), 305-323.

No Child Left Behind Act of 2001. (2001). Pub. L. No. 107-110, paragraph 115 Stat, 1425. Nunes, T. (1992). Ethnomathematics and everyday cognition. In D. A. Grouws (Ed.), *Handbook of research on mathematics teaching and learning* (pp 557-574). New York: Macmillan.

O'Donnell, A. M., & Levin, J. R. (2001). Educational psychology's healthy growing pains. *Educational Psychologist, 36*(2), 73-82.

Paris, S. G. (2000). Trojan horse in the schoolyard: The hidden threats in high-stakes testing. *Issues in Education, 6*(1, 2), 1-16.

Paris, S. G. (2005). Re-interpreting the development of reading skills. *Reading Research Quarterly, 40*(2), 184-202.

Paris, S. G., & Carpenter, R. D. (2003). FAQs about IRIs. *The Reading Teacher, 56*(6), 578-580.

Paris, S. G., & Carpenter, R. D. (2004). Children's motivation to read. In J. Hoffman & D. Schallert (Eds.), *The texts in elementary classrooms* (pp. 61-82). Mahwah, NJ: Lawrence Erlbaum Associates.

Paris, S. G., Carpenter, R. D., Paris, A. H., & Hamilton, E. E. (2005). Spurious and genuine correlates of children's reading comprehension. In S. G. Paris & S. A. Stahl (Eds.), *Children's reading comprehension and assessment* (pp. 131-160). Mahwah, NJ: Lawrence Erlbaum Associates.

Paris, S. G., & Cunningham, A. (1996). Children becoming students. In D. Berliner & R. Calfee (Eds.) *Handbook of educational psychology* (pp.117-147). New York: Macmillan.

Paris, S. G., & Hoffman, J. V. (2004). Early reading assessments in kindergarten through third grade: Findings from the Center for the Improvement of Early Reading Achievement. *Elementary School Journal, 105*(2), 199-217.

Payne, A. C., Whitehurst, G. J., & Angell, A. L. (1994). The role of home literacy environment in the development of language ability in preschool children from low-income families. *Early Childhood Research Quarterly, 9,* 427-440.

Peak, L. (1997). *Pursuing excellence: A study of U.S. fourth-grade mathematics and science achievement in international context.* Washington, DC: U.S. Government Printing Office.

Pennington, B. F., & Lefly, D. L. (2001). Early reading development in children at family risk for dyslexia. *Child Development, 72*(3), 816-833.

Phillips, M., Crouse, J., & Ralph, J. (1998). Does the black-white test score gap widen after children enter school? In C. Jencks & M. Phillips (Eds.), *The Black-White test score gap* (pp. 229-272). Washington, DC: Brookings Institution.

Pianta, R., Paro, L., Payne, K., Cox, C., & Bradley, R. H. (2002). The relation of kindergarten classroom environment to teacher, family and school characteristics and child outcomes. *Elementary School Journal, 102*(3), 225-238.

Rasinski, T. V., & Hoffman, J. V. (2003). Theory and research into practice: Oral reading in the school literacy curriculum. *Reading Research Quarterly, 38*(4), 510-523.

Rathvon, N. (2004). *Early reading assessment: A practitioner's handbook.* New York: Guilford Press.

Rayner, K., Foorman, B. R., Perfetti, C. A., Pesetsky, D., & Seidenberg, M. S. (2001). How psychological science informs the teaching of reading. *Psychological Science in the Public Interest, 2*(2), 31-74.

Reese, E., & Cox, A. (1999). Quality of adult book reading affects children's emergent literacy. *Developmental Psychology, 35,* 20-28.

Reynolds, A. J., Temple, J. A., Robertson, D. L., & Mann, E. A. (2003). Age 21 cost-benefit analysis of the Title I Chicago child-parent centers. *Educational Evaluation and Policy Analysis, 24*(4), 267-303.

Rittle-Johnson, B., Siegler, R. S., & Alibali, M. W. (2001). Developing conceptual understanding and procedural skill in mathematics: An iterative process. *Journal of Educational Psychology, 93,* 346-362.

Roeser, R. W., Eccles, J. S., & Sameroff, A. J. (2000). School as a context of early adolescents' academic and social-emotional development: A summary of research findings. *Elementary School Journal, 100*(5), 443-471.

Rutter, M., & Maughan, B. (2002). School effectiveness findings 1979-2002. *Journal of School Psychology, 40*(6), 451-475.

Sacks, P. (1999). *Standardized minds.* Cambridge, MA: Perseus Books.

Saigal, S., Szatmari, P., Rosenbaum, P., Campbell, D., & King, S. (1991). Cognitive abilities and school performance of extremely low birth weight children and matched term control children at age 8 years: A regional study. *The Journal of Pediatrics, 118,* 751-760.

Scanlon, D. M., & Vellutino, F. R. (1996). Prerequisite skills, early instruction, and success in first-grade reading: Selected results from a longitudinal study. *Mental Retardation & Developmental Disabilities Research Reviews, 2*(1), 54-63.

Scarborough, H. S. (1998). Early identification of children at risk for reading disabilities: Phonological awareness and some other promising predictors. In P. Accardo, A. Capute, & B. Shapiro (Eds.), *Specific reading disability: A view of the spectrum.* Timonium, MD: York Press.

Scarborough, H. S., & Dobrich, W. (1994). On the efficacy of reading to preschoolers. *Developmental Review, 14,* 245-302.

Schatschneider, C., Fletcher, J. M., Francis, D. J., Carlson, C. D., & Foorman, B. R. (2004). Kindergarten prediction of reading skills: A longitudinal comparative analysis. *Journal of Educational Psychology, 96*(2), 265-282.

Senechal, M., LeFevre, J., Thomas, E., & Daley, K. (1998). Differential effects of home literacy experiences on the development of oral and written language. *Reading Research Quarterly, 33*(1), 96-116.

Senechal, M., & LeFevre, J. (2001). Storybook reading and parent teaching: Links to language and literacy development. In P. R. Britto & J. Brooks-Gunn (Eds.), *New directions in child development: No. 92. The role of family literacy environments in promoting young children's emerging literacy* (pp. 39-52). San Francisco: Jossey-Bass.

Senechal, M., & LeFevre, J. (2002).

Shonkoff, J. P., & Phillips, D. A. (Eds.). (2000). *From neurons to neighborhoods: The science of early childhood development.* Washington, DC: National Academy Press.

Siegler, R. S. (1994). Cognitive variability: A key to understanding cognitive development. *Current Directions in Psychological Science, 3,* 1-5.

Siegler, R. S., & Shrager, J. (1984). Strategy choices in addition and subtraction: How do children know what to do? In C. Sophian (Ed.), *Origins of cognitive skill* (pp. 229-294). Hillsdale, NJ: Lawrence Erlbaum Associates.

Simon, T. J. (1997). Reconceptualizing the origins of number knowledge: A "non-numerical" account. *Cognitive Development, 12,* 349-372.

Smith, J., Brooks-Gunn, J., & Klebanov, P. (1997). Consequences of living in poverty for young children's cognitive and verbal ability and early school achievement. In G. J. Duncan & J. Brooks-Gunn (Eds.), *Consequences of growing up poor* (pp. 132-189). New York: Russell Sage.

Smith, K. (2002). *Who's minding the kids? Child care arrangements: Spring 1997.* Washington DC: U.S. Census Bureau.

Smith, M. C., Locke, S. G., Boissee, S. J., Gallagher, P. A., Krengel, L. E., Kuczek, J. E., McFarland, J. E., Rapoo, B., & Wertheim, C. (1998). Productivity of educational psychologists in educational psychology journals, 1991-1996. *Contemporary Educational Psychology, 23,* 171-181.

Snow, C. E., Burns, M. S., & Griffin, P. (1998). *Preventing reading difficulties in young children.* Washington, DC: National Academy Press.

Sophian, C. (2004). Mathematics for the future: Developing a Head Start curriculum to support mathematics learning. *Early Childhood Research Quarterly, 19,* 59-81.

Spencer, M. B., Noll, E., Stoltzfus, J., & Harpalani, V. (2001). Identity and school adjustment: Revisiting the "acting white" assumption. *Educational Psychologist, 36*(1), 21-30.

Stanovich, K. E. (1980). Toward an interactive-compensatory model of individual differences in the development of reading fluency. *Reading Research Quarterly, 16,* 32-71.

Stanovich, K. E. (1986). Matthew effects in reading: Some consequences of individual differences in the acquisition of literacy." *Reading Research Quarterly, 21,* 360-407.

Starkey, P., Klein, A., & Wakeley, A. (2004). Enhancing young children's mathematical knowledge through a pre-kindergarten mathematics intervention. *Early Childhood Research Quarterly, 19,* 99-120.

Stevenson, H. W., & Lee, S. (1998). An examination of American student achievement from an international perspective. In D. Ravitch (Ed.), *The state of student performance in American schools* (pp. 7-52). Washington, DC: Brookings.

Stevenson, H. W., Lee, S.-Y., Chen, C., Stigler, J. W., Hsu, C. C., & Kitamura, S. (1990). Contexts of achievement: A study of American, Chinese, and Japanese children. *Monographs of the Society for Research in Child Development, 55* (Serial No. 221).

St. Pierre, R. G., & Layzer, J. I. (1999). Using home visits for multiple purposes: The Comprehensive Child Development Program. *Future of Children, 9,* 134-151.

Stipek, D., & Ryan, R. (1997). Economically disadvantaged preschoolers: Ready to learn but further to go. *Developmental Psychology, 33*(4), 711-723.

Storch, S. A., & Whitehurst, G. (2002). Oral language and code-related precursors to reading: Evidence from a longitudinal structural model. *Developmental Psychology, 38*(6), 934-947.

Sulzby, E. (1986). Writing and reading: Signs of oral and written language organization in the young child. In W. H. Teale & E. Sulzby (Eds.), *Emergent literacy: Reading and writing* (pp. 50-87). Norwood, NJ: Ablex.

Tamis-Lemonda, C., Bornstein, M., & Baumwell, L. (2001). Maternal responsiveness and children's achievement of language milestones. *Child Development, 72,* 748-767.

Tomasello, M., & Todd, J. (1983). Joint attention and lexical acquisition style. *First Language, 4,* 197-212.

Torgesen, J. K. (2000). Individual differences in response to early intervention in reading: The lingering problem of treatment resisters. *Learning Disablities Research and Practice, 15,* 55-64.

Torgesen, J. K., Alexander, A. W., Wagner, R. K., Rashotte, C. A., Voelier, K. K. S., & Conway, T. (2001). Intensive remedial instruction for children with severe reading disabilities: Immediate and long-term outcomes from two instructional approaches. *Journal of Learning Disabilities, 34*(1), 33-58.

Torgesen, J. K., Wagner, R. K., Rashotte, C. A., Rose, E., Lindamood, P., Conway, T., et al. (1999). Preventing reading failure in young children with phonological processing disabilities: Group and individual responses to instruction. *Journal of Educational Psychology, 91,* 579-593.

Travers, K., J., & Weinzweig, A. I. (1999). The Second International Mathematics Study. In E. L. G. Kaiser, & I. Huntley (Ed.), *International comparisons in mathematics education* (pp. 19-29). London: Falmer Press.

Vygotsky, L. S. (1978). *Mind in society*. Cambridge, MA: Harvard University Press.

Wagner, R., Rashotte, C., Hecht, S., Barker, T., Burgess, S., & Donohue, J. (1997). Changing relations between phonological processing abilities and word level reading as children develop from beginning to skilled readers: A 5-year longitudinal study. *Developmental Psychology, 33*, 468–479.

Walsh, D. J., Price, G. G., & Gillingham, M. G. (1988). The critical but transitory importance of letter naming. *Reading Research Quarterly, 23*(1), 108–122.

Whitehurst, G. J., Arnold, D. S., Epstein, J. N., & Angell, A. L. (1994). A picture book reading intervention in day care and home for children from low-income families. *Developmental Psychology, 30*(5), 679–689.

Whitehurst, G. J., Falco, F. L., Lonigan, C. J., Fischel, J. E., DeBaryshe, B. D., Valdez-Menchaca, M. C. et al. (1988). Accelerating language development through picture book reading. *Developmental Psychology, 24*(4), 552–559.

Wigfield, A., & Guthrie, J. T. (1997). Relations of children's motivation for reading to the amount and breadth of their reading. *Journal of Educational Psychology, 89*(3), 420–432.

· 5 ·

DEVELOPMENT DURING EARLY AND MIDDLE ADOLESCENCE

Allan Wigfield
James P. Byrnes[1]
University of Maryland

Jacquelynne S. Eccles
University of Michigan

In this chapter we discuss development during the early and middle adolescent years (approximately ages 10 to 20), updating the chapter on this topic from the first edition of this *Handbook* (Wigfield, Eccles, & Pintrich, 1996).[2] The adolescent time period is one in which individuals experience many changes, including the biological changes associated with puberty, cognitive changes, and numerous changes in social relations. In addition, adolescents make many major life transitions, from elementary to middle school, middle school to high school, and high school to college or the work force. Many early adolescents deal with these changes well. However, as discussed in the previous edition of this Handbook and elsewhere, the early adolescent years mark the beginning for some individuals of a downward spiral in achievement and motivation that can lead to academic disengagement, failure and school dropout, and sometimes delinquency and other serious social problems (Eccles, 2004; Eccles et al., 1993; Lerner & Steinberg, 2004; NRC, 2004; Wigfield & Eccles, 2002a). As a result a substantial portion of America's adolescents are not succeeding as

well as might be hoped for. Depending on ethnic group, between 15 and 50 percent drop out of school before completing high school; adolescents as a group have the highest arrest rate of any age group; and increasing numbers of adolescents consume alcohol and other drugs on regular basis (NRC, 2004). Thus this developmental period clearly is a turning point for many of our youth.

Because this Handbook is for the educational psychology audience, we focus primarily on changes in adolescents' cognition and motivation, and how these changes influence adolescents' achievement. We also consider briefly the important biological changes that occur at adolescence. We take an interactionist approach in this chapter, as we believe adolescent development reflects changes within the individual, as well as changes in the environments and relationships adolescents experience (Bronfenbrenner & Morris, 1998). Thus we discuss changes in the major contexts and relationships in adolescents' lives, including the peer group, the family, and school. Within many of the sections we discuss gender and ethnic differences in the psychological

---

[1] James P. Byrnes is now at Temple University.
[2] We dedicate this chapter to Paul R. Pintrich, who coauthored with Wigfield and Eccles the chapter on adolescent development for the first edition of this *Handbook*. Paul passed away on July 12, 2003.

constructs and contexts discussed. It is important to acknowledge at the outset that adolescence is very much a cultural phenomenon, and the experiences adolescents have vary greatly across different cultures. We focus in this chapter primarily on adolescent development in the United States.

BIOLOGICAL, COGNITIVE, AND MOTIVATIONAL CHANGES DURING ADOLESCENCE

Biological Changes During Adolescence

The biological changes associated with puberty are among the most dramatic ones that individuals experience during their lifetimes. In part because of these dramatic biological changes, different theorists portrayed the early adolescent period as a period of "storm and stress," where there is a great deal of conflict between children, parents, and teachers (e.g., Blos, 1979; Hall, 1904). Although major physical changes occur during early adolescence, many researchers now believe that the characterization of this time period as one of storm and stress is an overstatement (see for example Arnett, 1999; Dornbusch, Petersen, & Hetherington, 1991). Whether or not adolescents are in crisis, the biological changes they go through do have many influences on their thinking and behavior (Arnett, 1999; Buchanan, Eccles, & Becker, 1992).

A complete review of the biological changes that occur during puberty is beyond the scope of this chapter (see Buchanan et al., 1992; Graber, Petersen, & Brooks-Gunn, 1996; Susman & Rogol, 2004). Briefly, during early adolescence children undergo a growth spurt and develop secondary sex characteristics, as a result of the activation of the hormones controlling these physical developments. The processes by which the hormones become activated are still not well understood, but their effects are quite clear. Most researchers think the effects of hormones on behavior are mediated through psychological processes and also are influenced by the contexts adolescents are in, rather than having direct effects on behavior (Buchanan et al., 1992; Susman & Rogol, 2004).

Two issues with respect to pubertal development are particularly germane to children's development in school. First, puberty is occurring earlier for many children in this country, beginning as early as age 8 for some girls, particularly African-American girls (Herman-Giddens, Slora, Wasserman, Bourdony, Bhapkor, & Koch, 1997). Relations between children and teachers, and among children themselves, change as children enter puberty, and this is happening earlier. Second, the timing of puberty is quite different for girls and boys. Girls enter puberty approximately 18 months before boys do, which means

that during early adolescence girls and boys of the same chronological age are at quite different points in their physical development, a fact that is readily apparent to anyone observing in middle grade classrooms. There now is a large literature on the effects of early versus late maturity for boys and girls. There is some evidence that early maturity is advantageous for boys, particularly with respect to their participation in sports activities and social standing in school (Malina, 1990; Petersen, 1985), although the findings for boys are not always consistent and change over time. For instance, Ge et al. (2003) reported that fifth-grade early-maturing boys report more depressive symptoms than do later maturing or on time boys, but by seventh grade this no longer is the case. For girls the evidence is more consistent and shows that early maturity is especially problematic. Early-maturing girls are the first to experience pubertal changes and so can feel out of sync with their age mates, thus experiencing greater depression and other adjustment issues (e.g., Angold, Costello, & Worthman, 1998; Ge, Conger, & Elder, 2001; Ge et al., 2003). The challenges for early-maturing girls continue over time, particularly if they face other life stressors (Ge et al., 2001). Further, Simmons and her colleagues reported that early-maturing girls have the most difficulty adjusting to school transitions, particularly the transition from elementary to junior high school (Simmons & Blyth, 1987; Simmons, Blyth, VanCleave, & Bush, 1979).

One important educational implication of the work on pubertal changes and their effects concerns the issue of timing for the transition from elementary to secondary school. Many researchers and educational policy analysts urged that middle school should begin earlier, so that students make the school transition before they enter puberty. The concern is that dealing both with puberty and school changes make both transitions more complex (Wigfield & Eccles, 2002a; Wigfield et al., 1996). Many school districts have followed this advice. Middle school now often encompasses sixth through eighth grade, rather than seventh through ninth grade. Others have argued that a K-8 organizational structure may be most beneficial to early adolescents. The issue of timing this transition is complicated by the fact that boys and girls go through puberty at different times, making it very difficult to time the school transition to avoid the pubertal transition for one gender group or the other.

Another important area of research on biological development, and one that has grown markedly since the publication of the first edition of this *Handbook*, is research on brain development during adolescence (Byrnes, 2001b and Keating, 2004, provide reviews of this work). Imaging techniques such as fMRI (functional magnetic resonance imaging) allow researchers to study brain functioning and development, and they have found that the brain indeed does change in important ways during adolescence. The changes include a reorganization of synaptic connections, and changes in the levels of different neurotransmitters in the areas of the brain that control emotional functioning. The first of these changes may relate to more efficient information processing, and the second to greater emotional activity. The prefrontal cortex (which controls executive functioning) becomes fully mature during late adolescence (Keating, 2004), which could relate to the changes in cognition that occur at adolescence (we describe these changes in the next section). Researchers are beginning to connect changes in brain structure and functioning to cognition and behavior, with decision-making being one area of particular interest (Byrnes, 1998; Keating, 2004). The specific ways in which brain structure relates to cognition and behavior remain elusive at this point (Byrnes, 2001b), although research over the next 10 years likely will enhance greatly our understanding of the relations of brain structure and function to adolescents' cognition and behavior.

These physical changes are not the only changes early adolescents face. They also undergo school transitions and important cognitive and social changes as well, as we will discuss. Researchers adopting a "cumulative effects" model argue that it is the combination of changes occurring at early adolescence that can be problematic for some early adolescents (e.g., Sameroff, Gutman, & Peck, 2003; Simmons, Burgeson, Carleton-Ford, & Blyth, 1987). Biological changes, school transitions, social changes such as dating, and possibly family changes all can occur at this time; if several of those changes are negative, children can be at risk for developmental problems such as lowered self-esteem, depression, and early sexual activity. Again, because girls enter puberty earlier than boys do, they are more likely than boys to be coping with pubertal changes at the same time they make the middle grade school transition, and thus are more likely to face multiple transitions simultaneously.

Changes in Cognition and Achievement During Adolescence

Important cognitive changes during this period of life include the increasing ability to think abstractly, consider the hypothetical as well as the real, engage in more sophisticated and elaborate information processing strategies, consider multiple dimensions of a problem at once, and reflect on oneself and on complicated problems (see Byrnes, 1988; Keating, 2004; Moshman, 1998). Historically, these developments were attributed to the emergence of formal operational thinking as defined by Piaget

(e.g., Piaget & Inhelder, 1973). Whereas it is clearly the case that older adolescents and adults are more likely to demonstrate such higher order cognitive processes than younger adolescents and children, the evidence as a whole fails to support the strong form of the Piagetian account (i.e., that children younger than 11 are incapable of abstract thinking, that most children older than 11 are capable of it, and there are global, domain-general increases in performance). In addition, a further problem is that adolescents are also more likely to demonstrate other kinds of skills and tendencies as well, and these skills and tendencies are not captured by the original model of formal operations proposed by Piaget. For a growing number of scholars, the key shift that occurs in adolescence is not so much the emergence of an abstract logical ability as much as the capacity to organize, coordinate, and reflect on formal operational constructs and other abilities and tendencies (Keating, 2004; Moshman, 1998). This executive function aspect of cognition is thought to be subtended by a neural network that involves the frontal lobes and important subcortical structures related to emotional processing and inter-hemispheric communication.

Enhancement of the executive function aspect of cognition clearly affects learning and problem solving skills in adolescents, along with other aspects of adolescent psychology such as adolescents' self-concepts, thoughts about their future, and understanding of others, which we discuss later. In this section, we consider answers to the following questions with respect to cognitive development during adolescence: Are there age changes in the structural and functional aspects of cognition, and do these age-related trajectories in cognitive skills differ across gender and ethnic groups? We consider such issues briefly (see Byrnes, 2001a, 2001b, and Bjorklund, 1999, for fuller discussion).

Changes in Structural Aspects. Structural aspects of cognition include the knowledge possessed by an individual, as well as the information-processing capacity of that individual. Structuralist researchers often focus on the following two questions: (a) what changes occur in children's knowledge as they progress through the adolescent period? and (b) what changes occur in the information processing capacities of adolescents? In what follows, we provide answers to these questions in turn.

The term *knowledge* refers to three kinds of information structures that are stored in long-term memory: declarative knowledge (i.e., "knowing that"), procedural knowledge ("knowing how"), and conceptual knowledge. The third kind of knowledge, *conceptual knowledge*, is the representation of adolescents' understanding of their declarative and procedural knowledge. Byrnes (2001a, 200b) describes conceptual knowledge as "knowing why" (e.g., knowing why one should use the least common denominator method to add fractions), and as knowledge that reflects insight into abstract commonalities and principles.

Various sources in the literature suggest that these three forms of knowledge increase with age during the adolescent period (Byrnes, 2001a). The clearest evidence of such changes can be found in the National Assessments of Educational Progress (NAEPs) conducted by the U.S. Department of Education every few years. NAEPs measure the declarative, procedural, and conceptual knowledge of 4th, 8th, and 12th graders ($N > 17,000$) in seven domains: reading, writing, mathematics, science, history, geography, and civics. In mathematics, for example, NAEP results show that children progress from knowing arithmetic facts and being able to solve simple word problems in Grade 4 to being able to perform algebraic manipulations, create tables, and reason about geometric shapes by Grade 12 (Reese, Miller, Mazzeo, & Dossey, 1997). Although similar gains are evident for each of the other six domains (Beatty, Reese, Perksy, & Carr, 1996), in no case can it be said that a majority of 12th graders demonstrate a deep conceptual understanding in any of the domains assessed (Byrnes, 2001a, 2001b). One reason for the low level of conceptual understanding in 12th graders is the abstract, multidimensional, and counterintuitive nature of the most advanced questions in each domain. Even in the best of circumstances, concepts such as *scarcity*, *civil rights*, *diffusion*, *limit*, and *conservation of energy* are difficult to grasp and illustrate. Moreover, the scientific definitions of such concepts are often counter to students' preexisting ideas. As a result, there are numerous studies showing misconceptions and faulty information possessed by adolescents and adults (see Byrnes 2001a, 2001b).

In sum, then, one can summarize the results on knowledge as follows:

- In most school-related subject areas, there are modest, monotonic increases in declarative, procedural, and conceptual knowledge between the 4th grade and college years.
- Misconceptions abound in most school subjects and are evident even in 12th graders and college students.
- The most appropriate answer to the question "Does knowledge increase during adolescence?" is the following: It depends on the domain (e.g., mathematics versus interpersonal relationships) and type of knowledge (e.g., declarative vs. conceptual).
- Although there is little evidence of dramatic and across-domain increases in understanding (as Piaget proposed), there is consistent evidence of within-domain, incremental increases in understanding as children move into and through adolescence. To abandon their misconceptions, children sometimes need to experience within-domain qualitative shifts in their thinking as well.

Do these kinds of changes in knowledge influence behavior? For example, do older adolescents make better life decisions because they know more? Are they better employees? Parents? College students? Life-long learners? Do they solve problems better in their coursework or personal lives? At some level, the answer to these questions has to be yes. Certainly expanded domain-specific knowledge makes it easier to solve problems and perform complex tasks in activities very closely linked to the same knowledge domain (e.g., Ericsson, 1996). But does expanded knowledge on its own increase the wisdom of more general life decisions? The answer to this question is less clear because such decisions depend on many other aspects of cognitive as well as motivational and emotional processes that influence the likelihood of accessing and effectively using one's stored knowledge. For example, younger adolescents may have the knowledge needed to make decisions or solve problems (on achievement tests or in social situations), but they may lack the processing space needed to consider and combine multiple pieces of information. We turn to these other aspects of cognition next.

Processing space or capacity is analogous to RAM memory on a computer. A very good software package may not be able to work properly if the RAM memory on a PC is too small. One key index of processing capacity in humans is *working memory*—the ability to temporarily hold something in memory (e.g., a phone number). Not too long ago, it was assumed that working memory capacity changes very little after childhood. Several recent studies, however, suggest that this assumption is wrong. For example, Zald and Iacono (1998) charted the development of spatial working memory in 14- and 20-year-olds by asking them to remember the location of objects that were presented briefly on a computer screen and then removed. Zald and Iacono found that the introduction of delays and various forms of cognitive interference produced sharper drops in the performance of the younger than the older participants. Similarly, Swanson (1999) found monotonic increases in both verbal and spatial working memory between the ages of 6 and 35 in a large normative sample. Such increases should make it easier for older adolescents and adults to solve complex problems in school and also consider multiple pieces of information simultaneously when making important decisions.

Changes in Functional Aspects of Cognition. Functionalist aspects of cognition include any mental processes that alter, operate on, or extend incoming or existing information. Examples include learning (getting new information into memory), retrieval (getting information out of memory), reasoning (drawing inferences from single or multiple items of information), and decision making (generating, evaluating, and selecting courses of action). As noted earlier, both structural and functional aspects of cognition are critical to all aspects of learning, decision-making, and cognitive activities. For example, experts in a particular domain learn new, domain-relevant items of information better than novices. Also, people are more likely to make appropriate inferences and make good decisions when they have relevant knowledge than when they do not have relevant knowledge (Byrnes, 1998; Ericsson, 1996). With this connection in mind, we can consider the findings sampled from three core areas of research to get a sense of age changes in functional aspects: (a) deductive reasoning, (b) decision-making, and (c) other forms of reasoning.

People engage in deductive reasoning whenever they combine premises and derive a logically sound conclusion from these premises (Ward & Overton, 1990). Adolescents are likely to engage in deductive reasoning as they try to make sense of what is going on in a context and what they are allowed to do in that context. Moreover, deductive reasoning is used when they write argumentative essays, test hypotheses, set up algebra and geometry proofs, and engage in debates and other intellectual discussions. It is also critical to decision making and problem solving of all kinds.

Although the issue of age differences in deduction skills is somewhat controversial, most researchers believe that there are identifiable developmental increases in deductive reasoning skills that occur between childhood and early adulthood. Competence is first manifested around age 5 or 6 in the ability to draw some types of conclusions from "if-then" (conditional) premises, especially when these premises refer to fantasy or make-believe content (e.g., Dias & Harris, 1988). Several years later, children begin to understand the difference between conclusions that follow from conditional premises and conclusions that do not (Byrnes & Overton, 1986; Girotto, Gilly, Blaye, & Light, 1989; Haars & Mason, 1986; Janveau-Brennan & Markovits, 1999), especially when the premises refer to familiar content about taxonomic or causal relations. Next, there are monotonic increases during adolescence in the ability to draw appropriate conclusions, explain one's reasoning, and test hypotheses even when premises refer to unfamiliar, abstract, or contrary-to-fact propositions (Klaczynski, 1993; Markovits & Vachon, 1990; Moshman & Franks, 1986; Ward & Overton, 1990). But again, performance is maximized on familiar content about legal or causal relations (Klaczynski & Narasimham, 1998). However, when the experimental content runs contrary to what is true (e.g., All elephants are small animals. This is an elephant. Is it small?) or has

no meaningful referent (e.g., If there is a D on one side of a card, there is a 7 on the other), less than half of older adolescents or adults do well.

Performance on the latter tasks, however, can be improved in older participants if the abstract problems are presented after exposure to similar but more meaningful problems or if the logic of the task is adequately explained (Klaczynski, 1993; Markovits & Vachon, 1990; Ward, Byrnes, & Overton, 1990). Even so, such interventions generally have only a weak effect. These findings imply that most of the development after age 10 in deductive reasoning competence is in the ability to suspend one's own beliefs and think objectively about the structure of an argument (e.g., "Let's assume for the moment that this implausible argument is true...", Moshman, 1998) and the ability to retrieve appropriate information from memory while reasoning (Markovits & Barrouillet, 2002). Little evidence exists for an abstract, domain-general ability that is spontaneously applied to new and different content.

Turning next to decision making, surprisingly few studies have been conducted to determine whether there are age changes during adolescence. Nevertheless, these findings suggest that there may be age changes in the following aspects of decision making: (a) the ability to understand the difference between options likely to satisfy multiple goals and options likely to satisfy only a single goal (Byrnes & McClenny, 1994; Byrnes, Miller, & Reynolds, 1999), (b) the tendency to anticipate a wide range of consequences of their actions (Halpern-Felsher & Cauffman, 2001; Lewis, 1981), and (c) the ability to learn from their decision-making successes and failures with age (Byrnes & McClenny, 1994; Byrnes, Miller, & Reynolds, 1999). There is also some suggestion that adolescents are more likely to make good decisions when they have metacognitive insight into the factors that affect the quality of decision-making (Miller & Byrnes, 2001; Ormond, Luszcz, Mann, & Beswick, 1991). However, additional studies are needed to verify these initial findings.

In contrast to the dearth of studies on decision making in adolescents, there are quite a number of developmental studies in a related area of research: risk taking (Byrnes, 1998). If a decision involves options that could lead to negative or harmful consequences (i.e., anything ranging from mild embarrassment to serious injury or death), adolescents who pursue such options are said to have engaged in risk-taking (Byrnes, Miller, & Schafer, 1999). Although all kinds of risk taking are of interest from scientific standpoint, most studies have focused on age changes in physically harmful behaviors such as smoking, drinking, and unprotected sex. Regrettably, these studies reveal the opposite of what one would expect if decision skills were improving during adolescence; that is, these studies show that older adolescents are more likely to engage in these behaviors than younger adolescents or preadolescents (DiClemente, Hansen, & Ponton, 1995). Repeatedly, studies have shown that those who take such risks do not differ in their knowledge of possible negative consequences. Given that risk takers and risk avoiders do not differ in their knowledge of options and consequences, it is likely that the difference lies in other aspects of competent decision making (e.g., self-regulatory strategies; ability to coordinate health-promoting and social goals; the ability to regulate emotions) or in the fact that opportunities to take risks usually increase throughout the adolescent period. These hypotheses remain to be tested.

In addition to finding age-related increases in deductive reasoning and decision-making skills, researchers have also found increases in mathematical reasoning ability, certain kinds of memory-related processes, the ability to perform spatial reasoning tasks quickly, and certain aspects of scientific reasoning (Byrnes, 2001a). The variables that seem to affect the size of age increases in these areas include (a) whether students have to learn information during the experiment or retrieve something known already, and (b) the length of the delay between stimulus presentation and being asked to retrieve information. In the case of scientific reasoning, the ability to consciously construct one's own hypotheses across a wide range of contents, test these hypotheses in controlled experiments, and draw appropriate inferences from evidence also increases (e.g., Klaczynski & Narasimham, 1998; Kuhn, Garcia-Mila, Zohar, & Andersen, 1995).

Summary. The literature suggests that there are changes in the intellectual competencies of children as they progress through the adolescent period. However, there are many ways in which the thinking of young adolescents is similar to that of older adolescents and adults. Thus, before one can predict whether an age difference will manifest itself on any particular measure of intellectual competence or achievement, one needs to ask questions such as: "Does exposure to the content of the task (e.g., mathematics) continue through adolescence?", "How many issues have to be held in mind and considered simultaneously?", "Are the ideas consistent with naïve conceptions?", and "Does success on the task require one to suspend one's beliefs?" If the answers to these questions are "No," then younger adolescents, older adolescents and adults should all perform about the same. However, if one or more "Yes" answers are given, then one would expect older adolescents and adults to demonstrate more intellectual competence than younger adolescents. Educators can use such questions as guides when they design curricula appropriate for younger and older adolescents.

Group Differences in Achievement

Given that gender and ethnic differences are considered in other chapters in this *Handbook* we provide only a thumbnail sketch here (see Byrnes, 2001a, 2001b, for a more complete summary). With respect to gender differences, male and female adolescents perform comparably on measures of mathematics, science, and social studies knowledge (e.g., NAEPs) and also obtain nearly identical scores on measures of intelligence, deductive reasoning, decision making, and working memory. Three areas in which gender differences have been found to occur are risk taking, SAT-math performance, and performance on standardized tests of writing skill (e.g., NAEP). With regard to risk taking, the pattern of gender differences is mixed. Whereas males are more likely than females to take such risks as driving recklessly or taking intellectual risks on standardized exams, females are more likely than males to take such health risks as smoking. The size of such gender differences, however, varies by age (Byrnes, Miller, & Schoefer, 1999). These findings seem to reflect differences in males' and females' expectations, values, and self-regulatory tendencies. For example, females might believe that accidents are more likely than males and would therefore drive more carefully. The former may be more likely to regulate their impatience and anger in traffic situations as well.

With regard to gender differences on the SAT math test, the average score for males is routinely found to be higher than that for females (De Lisi & McGillicuddy-De Lisi, 2002). It is still not clear why this difference obtains, given the fact that gender differences are typically not found on measures of math knowledge, the NAEP for math, or other kinds of reasoning. Researchers have shown, however, that part of this difference reflects gender differences in test-taking strategies, confidence in one's math ability, ability and motivation to use unconventional problem-solution strategies, mental rotation skills, and anxiety about one's math ability particularly when one's gender is made salient (see De Lisi & McGillicuddy-De Lisi, 2002, for review).

In the case of standardized writing assessments, females perform substantially better than males in both elementary school and high school. Thus, there is something unique about mathematics problem solving that contributes to the emergence of gender differences only during adolescence. As was the case for math, however, the reasons for the gender difference in writing are not entirely clear, but there is reason to suspect factors such as different levels of interest in writing and different levels of practice (Byrnes, 2001a).

With respect to ethnic differences, European-American and Asian-American students perform substantially better than African-American, Hispanic, and Native

American students on standardized achievement tests, the SAT, and most of the NAEP tests. In contrast, no ethnic differences are found in studies of deductive reasoning, decision making, or working memory. Moreover, ethnic differences on tests such as the SAT and NAEP are considerably reduced once variables such as parent education and prior course work are controlled (Byrnes, 2001a).

Changes in Motivation During Adolescence

Research on motivation has continued to flourish since the first edition of this *Handbook* was published. Much of this research has focused on children's and adolescents' beliefs, values, and goals as the major determinants of motivation (Eccles & Wigfield, 2002; Pintrich & Schunk, 2002; Wigfield, Eccles, Schiefele, Roeser, & Davis-Kean, in press; the separate motivation chapters in this volume provide extended review of this literature). We focus here on the development of adolescents' competence-related beliefs, valuing of achievement, intrinsic and extrinsic motivation, and achievement goals, as these have been prominent in the recent research on motivation.

Adolescence is a time in which these motivational beliefs, values, and goals change in important ways. It is also a time in which many more choices and options become available to adolescents, which means that their motivational beliefs and values for different activities could have more substantial effects on their behavior. During the early school years and even in middle school, students have little choice about which subjects to take. So, even if they believe they lack competence for a particular subject and do not like it much, they still have to take it. During high school students begin to make choices about which courses to take and whether to continue taking classes in areas such as mathematics and science. The interplay of cognitive and motivational processes in this decision making is an area that needs more investigation.

Change in Competence and Efficacy Beliefs. Competence-related beliefs (including self-efficacy) are individuals' beliefs about their ability to accomplish different activities, and how much they believe they control what happens to them. There are theoretical and methodological discussions about how similar or different constructs are such as competence beliefs, expectancies, for success, and self-efficacy beliefs (Bandura, 1997; Wigfield & Eccles, 2000; Zimmerman, 2000). However, for our purposes here we group them together. As we will see, these kinds of beliefs relate in important ways to children's performance on different activities, and to their choices of which activities to pursue.

There are three main ways these kinds of beliefs change over time. First, they become increasingly differentiated so that children have quite specific competence beliefs for different achievement domains and even activities within these domains (Bandura, 1997; Eccles, Wigfield, Harold, & Blumenfeld, 1993; Marsh & Ayotte 2003). Indeed, this differentiation starts quite early during the elementary school years (Eccles, Wigfield, & Schiefele, 1998; Wigfield et al., in press)). Second, these beliefs become increasingly stable, when stability is assessed by correlating these beliefs over time. In some domains, those correlations reach as high as .75 across a one-year period by the end of elementary school (Eccles et al., 1989; Wigfield et al., 1997).

Third, children and adolescents' competence-related beliefs generally decline across the entire elementary and secondary school period (see Wigfield & Eccles, 2002a). Three recent longitudinal studies are illustrative. Jacobs, Lanza, Osgood, Eccles, & Wigfield (2002) and Fredericks and Eccles (2002), utilizing the same dataset, examined change over the elementary and secondary school years in U.S. children's competence beliefs in mathematics, language arts, and sports, and Watt (2004) did so for math and English beliefs and values of middle and high school Australian students. Jacobs et al. (2002) found that children's perceptions in each area were strongly positive early on. However, the overall pattern of change was a decline in each domain. Fredericks and Eccles and Watt also found declines over time in competence beliefs, although the specific trends were somewhat different across their investigations, perhaps reflecting contextual differences in secondary schools in the United States and Australia. Because these studies were done in schools, they include only adolescents who are at least engaged enough in school to still be there; the academic competence beliefs of adolescents who drop out may become even more negative at earlier ages.

Age differences in self-efficacy beliefs show a different pattern, with older children having more positive beliefs about their efficacy to do different activities than younger children. Shell, Colvin, and Bruning (1995) found that 4th graders had lower self-efficacy beliefs for reading and writing than did 7th and 10th graders, and the 7th graders' efficacy beliefs were lower than 10th graders' beliefs (see Zimmerman & Martinez-Pons, 1990, for similar findings). The inconsistency of these findings with those on children's competence beliefs just discussed likely reflects the self-efficacy measure used by Shell et al. Their instrument measured children's estimates of their efficacy on specific reading and writing skills rather than more general reading and writing, which should be higher among older children. Also, efficacy beliefs usually are not measured comparatively, whereas many measures of competence beliefs include comparisons of one's ability with that of others. The latter kind of measure may be more likely to show declines over age.

Change in Children's Valuing of Achievement and Intrinsic and Extrinsic Motivation. Children's valuing of achievement refers to reasons or incentives children have for doing different activities. Eccles, Wigfield, and their colleagues defined different aspects of achievement task values: interest value, or doing an activity for its own sake; importance value, or the salience of the activity to the individual; and utility value, or how useful the activity may be to the individual (see Eccles, 1984a, 1984b; Eccles et al., 1983; Wigfield & Eccles, 1992, 2000). As with competence-related beliefs, researchers have determined that children's valuing for different activities are differentiated early on and become more stable over time, although the stability correlations are not as high as those for competence beliefs (Eccles & Wigfield, 1995; Eccles, Wigfield, Harold, & Blumenfeld, 1993; Eccles et al., 1989; Wigfield et al., 1997).

Jacobs et al. (2002) found that children's valuing of the domains of mathematics, language arts, and sports declined. As was the case for competence beliefs, children's valuing of language arts declined most during elementary school and then leveled off. By contrast, children's valuing of mathematics declined the most during high school (see also Fredericks & Eccles, 2002; Watt, 2004).

Intrinsic motivation refers to doing an activity for its own sake or because it is pleasurable to the individual, whereas extrinsic motivation involves doing an activity to receive a reward (Ryan & Deci, 2000). Intrinsic motivation thus is somewhat similar to interest value, and extrinsic motivation to utility value, although it should be noted that these constructs come from different theoretical traditions. Research done with both American and European children (e.g., Gottfried, Fleming, & Gottfried, 2001; Harter, 1981; Hedelin & Sjoberg, 1989; Helmke, 1993) has shown that that intrinsic motivation in different subject areas school declines across the school years. This is especially true for the natural sciences and mathematics (e.g., Oldfather & McLaughlin, 1993) and particularly during the early adolescent years. Pekrun (1993) found that intrinsic motivation stabilized after 8th grade, and Gottfried et al. (2001) reported surprisingly high stability coefficients for intrinsic motivation measured across a 1-year period for children ages 13 and above.

The negative changes in children's competence-related beliefs, achievement values, and intrinsic motivation have been explained in two ways: (a) Because children become much better at understanding, interpreting, and integrating the evaluative feedback they receive, and engage in more social comparison with their peers, children become more accurate or realistic in their self-assessments, leading some to become relatively more negative and also to devalue achievement (see Dweck, 2002; Stipek & Mac Iver, 1989; Wigfield et al., 1996); (b) because school environment changes in ways that make evaluation more salient and competition between students more likely, some children's self-assessments and valuing of achievement will decline as they get older (e.g., Eccles & Midgley, 1989; Wigfield, Eccles, & Rodriguez, 1998).

Change in Achievement Goal Orientations and Achievement Goals. Work on achievement goal orientations has burgeoned over the last 15 years. Initially researchers distinguished two broad orientations to achievement that students can have, a mastery or task-involved orientation, and a performance or ego orientation (Anderman, Austin, & Johnson, 2002; Pintrich, 2000a). With mastery orientation, individuals focus on mastering tasks and increasing competence at different tasks. Performance-oriented children and adolescents focus on demonstrating their competence and outperforming others. Mastery-oriented children and adolescents choose challenging tasks and are more concerned with their own progress than with outperforming others. Researchers studying goal orientations generally believe that having a mastery orientation is more facilitative to long-term motivation and learning than is a performance orientation. Different researchers defining these goal orientations used somewhat different labels for them (Thorkildsen & Nicholls, 1998); however, in our view, the similarities outweigh the differences between the conceptualizations of these orientations (see also Harackiewicz, Barron, Pintrich, Elliot, & Thrash, 2002).

Recently, researchers distinguished approach and avoidance components of each of these goal orientations, with the approach component generally seen as more positive (e.g., Elliot, 1999; Elliot & McGregor, 2000; Pintrich, 2000b; Skaalvik, 1997). However, there has been debate among goal orientation researchers about the relative merits of performance approach goals in particular, with an interesting series of articles appearing on this topic in the *Journal of Educational Psychology* (see Harackiewicz et al., 2002; Kaplan & Middleton, 2002; Midgley, Kaplan, & Middleton, 2001). Harackiewicz et al. (2002) argue that performance-approach goals are beneficial for some educational outcomes, whereas Midgley et al. (2001) and Kaplan and Middleton (2002) continue to believe that mastery goals hold the most promise for long-term engagement in learning.

Increasingly, goal orientation researchers discuss how children have multiple goals that can influence outcomes in multiple ways (Meece & Holt, 1993; Pintrich, 2000a, 2000b; Wolters, 2004). For instance, Wolters (2004) found that middle school aged students endorsed both mastery and performance approach and avoided goals, although they endorsed mastery goal to a greater extent. Students' mastery and performance approach goals showed differential relations to engagement, learning strategies, and school performance, with the former predicting engagement and use of learning strategies, and the latter predicting school achievement.

There is a growing body of work on the development of achievement goal orientations. Anderman, Maehr, Midgley, Turner, and their colleagues conducted a number of studies looking at how classroom instructional practices relate to children's goal orientations and how these relations may change over time. Turner et al. (2002) found that sixth-grade students are more likely to adopt mastery-oriented goals in classrooms that emphasize learning, the importance of effort, and the enjoyment inherent in learning. Anderman and Anderman (1999) reported that adolescents endorse performance goals more than mastery goals. A major reason for this likely is that schools increasingly emphasize performance goals as children get older. One clear example of this is how evaluations of different kinds proliferate and have stronger consequences for adolescents' futures. Midgley, Anderman, and their colleagues have done a number of studies showing two major things: (a) elementary-school teachers focus on mastery-oriented goals to a greater extent than do middle-school teachers, and (b) middle-school students perceive school as more performance oriented than do elementary school students (see Anderman et al., 2002, for review).

Other researchers have looked at the content of children's goals rather than children's goal orientations. Wentzel (1989, 1994, 1996) studied children's social and academic goals in school, finding that high-achieving children have positive academic and social goals, and lower achieving children emphasize social goals at the expense of academic goals (Wentzel, 2002b). To date, there has been little developmental work on how the content of children's goals may change over time. Based in part on Wentzel's work, it seems that adolescents doing poorly in school may be especially likely to seek goals other than academic ones in school, or reject school altogether (Finn, 1989; Rumberger, 1987). How individuals choose among these different goals should have a lot to do with their engagement in school (Fredericks, Blumenfeld, & Paris, 2004).

Relations of Achievement Beliefs, Values, and Goals to Academic Performance and Choice

Researchers have examined how adolescents' specific achievement beliefs relate to their academic achievement and choice of activities. For instance, they have shown that self-efficacy beliefs relate to individuals' goals, performance, persistence, and choice of different activities

(e.g., Bandura, Barbaranelli, Caprara, & Pastorelli, 1996, 2001). Researchers have looked at how adolescents' competence-related beliefs and values relate to their performance and choice of different academic and nonacademic activities (Bong, 2001; Eccles et al., 1983; Meece, Wigfield, & Eccles, 1990; Pintrich & De Groot, 1990). Two fundamental findings emerge from this work. First, children's perceptions of ability and expectancies for success are the strongest predictors of subsequent grades in mathematics and English, predicting those outcomes more strongly than either previous grades or achievement values. Second, children's achievement values such as liking of tasks, importance attached to them, and their usefulness are the strongest predictors of children's intentions to keep taking mathematics and actual decisions to do so (Wigfield, 1994; Wigfield & Eccles, 2002b) As we discussed, given the increasing opportunities for choice among different academic courses during middle adolescence, the finding that adolescents' achievement values relate most strongly to their choices is particularly important.

In the self-concept literature (where self-concept often is measured as perceived competence in different areas), there was debate for many years about the causal direction of relations between self-concept and achievement, with some researchers proposing that change in self-concept produced change in achievement, and others arguing just the opposite (Marsh & Yeung, 1997; Wigfield & Karpathian, 1991). A myriad of studies were done on this issue with no clear resolution of the debate emerging in large part due to methodological problems with the research (see Marsh, 1990; Marsh & Yeung, 1997). Researchers have argued more recently for a reciprocal effects model of these relations, rather than the more simplistic "which causes which" approach (Guay, Marsh, & Boivin, 2003; Marsh & Yeung, 1997; Wigfield & Karpathian, 1991). In such models, achievement and self-concept are posited to exert causal influences on each other, rather than one variable having causal predominance. Guay et al. (2003) and Marsh and Yeung (1997), both utilizing multiwave designs incorporating multiple measures of self-concept and achievement, found support for the reciprocal effects model in children and adolescents. Valentine, DuBois, and Cooper (2004) recently provided a meta-analysis that supports the contention that self-perceptions of ability predict subsequent performance even when previous performance is controlled.

Along with performance motivational beliefs, values, and goals relate to cognitive strategy use and self-regulation. For instance, students' efficacy beliefs relate to their use of cognitive strategies and to the regulation of their achievement behavior (Meece, Blumenfeld, & Hoyle, 1988; Pintrich & De Groot, 1990; Pintrich &

Zusho, 2002; Schunk, 1994). Students with mastery goal orientations and performance approach goals appear to be more self-regulated in their approach to learning, whereas students with performance avoid goals are not (Pintrich, 2000a, 2000b; Wolters, Yu, & Pintrich, 1996). Turning these relations around, Wolters (2003) discussed the importance of students regulating their motivation during different learning activities.

We now need more studies of the processes involved in these relations, and studies of different developmental trajectories in both these achievement-related characteristics, and their relation to school performance and choice. Pintrich (2003) discussed the complex interplay of motivation, cognition, and self-regulation in relation to achievement outcomes, providing important guidance for the direction this work might take.

Group Differences in Motivation During Adolescence

Gender Differences. Although sex-typing itself occurs in the preschool years (Ruble & Martin, 1998), several researchers have suggested that engaging in gender-role appropriate activities may become important to early adolescents, as they try to conform more to gender-role stereotypes once they enter puberty (Eccles, 1987; Hill & Lynch, 1983). Hill and Lynch (1983) labeled this phenomenon gender-role intensification. This phenomenon may lead early adolescents to have less positive beliefs and be less involved in activities that they see as less appropriate to their own gender. However, recent research on children's competence-related beliefs and values in different areas does not show increasing gender differences at adolescence, casting doubt on the gender intensification hypothesis. Nonetheless, girls' involvement in different activities remains relatively strongly sex-typed during adolescence (McHale, Shananan, Updegraff, Crouter, & Booth, 2004).

Despite evidence that performance differences in skill areas such as mathematics and English decreased over the past 30 years (Ruble & Martin, 1998), there are many gender differences in children's competence beliefs for activities in different domains. These gender differences appear particularly in gender-role stereotyped domains and on novel tasks. For example, boys hold higher competence beliefs than girls for mathematics and sports, even after all relevant skill-level differences are controlled; in contrast, girls have higher competence beliefs than boys for reading and English, music and arts, and social studies (see Wigfield et al., in press, for review). Recent work done in the United States shows that the gender differences in competence beliefs in math narrow during adolescence, but those in English remain (Jacobs et al., 2002). Further, the extent to which children endorse the cultural stereotypes regarding which sex is likely to be most talented in each domain predicts the extent to which girls and boys distort their ability self-concepts and expectations in the gender stereotypic direction (Early, Belansky & Eccles, 1992; Eccles & Harold, 1991). However, these sex differences are generally quite small (Marsh, 1989).

Earlier work showed gender differences in mathematics value favoring boys emerging during adolescence (Eccles, 1984a, 1984b), but more recent studies show that boys and girls value mathematics equally during adolescence (Jacobs et al., 2002). Although boys and girls now appear to value mathematics equally, girls are less interested in science (with the exception of biology) and engineering than are boys and enroll much less frequently in these majors in college (Wigfield, Battle, Keller, & Eccles, 2002).

Differences for Minority Adolescents. In 1996, Wigfield et al. reported that there is much less information on differences in self-beliefs and values between minority and majority adolescents. This picture has changed greatly over the past 10 years, although more work on this topic still is needed. Much of this work has focused on the academic problems and prospects of African American (see Meece & Kurtz-Costes, 2000; Slaughter-Defoe, Nakagawa, Takanishi, & Johnson, 1990); Mexican-American (e.g., Padilla & Gonzalez, 2001); and Asian-American youth (Fuligni & Tseng, 1999; Lee, 1994). Recent work has also focused on immigrant populations within the United States, some of whom are doing much better in school than both white middle class children and third and fourth generation members of their same national heritage (e.g., Chen & Stevenson, 1995; Kao & Tienda 1995; Slaughter-Defoe et al., 1990).

Graham (1994) reviewed the literature on differences between African- American and European-American students on such motivational constructs as need for achievement, locus of control, achievement attributions, and ability beliefs and expectancies. She concluded that, in general, the differences are not very large. Further, she argued that many existing studies have not adequately distinguished between race and socioeconomic status, making it very difficult to interpret any differences that emerge.

Graham and her colleagues have studied differences in the valuing of achievement across different minority groups. They (Graham & Taylor, 2002; Graham, Taylor, & Hudley, 1998) used a peer nomination technique to assess group differences in achievement values. Participants indicated which children in their class they admired, respected, and wanted to be like, and Graham and her colleagues argued that this is one way to gauge what children value. Results showed that White, Latino, and African-American girls chose high-achieving girls as those whom they admired, respected, and wanted to be like. For boys, this was only true for White boys; the other two groups of boys admired low achievers more. In a third study, Graham and her colleagues looked at this issue developmentally and found that in 2nd and 4th grades, all children were more likely to nominate higher achievers. In 7th grade the sex-differentiated pattern for the different groups emerged. This intriguing work needs to be followed up to examine what it is about entering adolescent and puberty that seems to cause many African-American and Mexican-American youth to endorse values and role models that exclude school achievement (e.g., Tatum, 1997).

Researchers interested in ethnic and racial differences in achievement have proposed models linking social roles, competence-related beliefs and values. For example, Steele (1992, 1997) proposed stereotype vulnerability and disidentification to help explain the underachievement of African-American students (see also Aronson, 2002). Confronted throughout their school careers with mixed messages about their competence and their potential and with the widespread negative cultural stereotypes about their academic potential and motivation, African American students should find it difficult to concentrate fully on their schoolwork because of the anxiety induced by their stereotype vulnerability (Steele & Aronson, 1995). In turn, to protect their self-esteem, they should disidentify with academic achievement, leading to both a lowering of the value they attach to academic achievement and a detachment of their self-esteem from both positive and negative academic experiences. In support, researchers have found that academic self-concept of ability is less predictive of general self-esteem for some African-American children (Winston, Eccles, Senior, & Vida, 1997)).

In considering performance and motivational differences across different ethnic and minority groups, it is essential to point out that such differences must be considered in light of larger contextual issues that influence development. Indeed, several researchers have pointed out the importance of taking a contextual view of minority achievement and motivation. For example, Spencer and Markstrom-Adams (1990) discussed identity formation during childhood and adolescence in different groups of minority children (see also Wigfield & Wagner, 2005, for discussion of recent models of multiethnic identity formation). Spencer and Markstrom-Adams argued that in forming their identities minority children have to deal with

several difficult issues that majority adolescents do not face, such as the often negative view of their group held by many members of the majority society, conflict between the values of their group and those of larger society, and lack of "identity achieved" adults in their group who can serve as models for them. These difficulties sometimes impede identity formation in these adolescents, leading to identity diffusion or possibly an inadequate exploration of different possible identities that the adolescent could take on.

Identity Development During Adolescence

Erikson (1968) proposed that identity formation is a major task of adolescence. This Handbook has a chapter on self-processes and identity, so we touch on identity development only briefly here. Identity is a term broader than either self-concept or self-esteem, referring to individuals' general sense of themselves and their psychological reality that includes many different beliefs and attitudes about the self (Spencer & Markstrom-Adams, 1990; Wigfield & Wagner, 2005). Identity formation involves the successful negotiation of a variety of activities during adolescence, including school achievement, social relations with others, and development of career interests and choices, along with a great deal of exploration of different activities and roles (Cantor & Kihlstrom, 1987). One's gender, ethnicity, and sexual orientation all are important to the adolescent's developing identity, and work on ethnic identity and its role in adolescents' overall identity development has flourished of late (Oyserman, Harrison, & Bybee, 2001; Phinney, 1996). Integrating these experiences and characteristics into a coherent sense of self is fundamental to identity formation, and researchers have proposed different phases of the identity development process (Marcia, 1980, 2002; Waterman, 1982, 1999).

Development of identity as student is an especially important topic for this chapter. Roeser and Lau (2002) describe adolescents with *positive student identities* as having histories of positive academic performance and relationships with classmates, positive emotions related to academic goals, high academic efficacy, positive conceptions of themselves as students, and a commitment to learning. Adolescents with *negative student identities* have histories of academic failure and difficulties with peers, negative emotions associated with academic goals, poor academic efficacy, frustration with themselves as students, and diminishing aspirations for educational attainment. Roeser and Lau argue that school environments play an important role in the development of students' identities.

FRIENDSHIPS AND THE PEER GROUP AT ADOLESCENCE

During the childhood years, children become more and more involved in social activities, sports activities, and a variety of other extracurricular activities. At adolescence, these trends become even more pronounced. Indeed, involvement in sport and social activities with peers, peer acceptance, and appearance can take precedence over school activities at this time period, often to the chagrin of parents and teachers. Friendships are important to adolescents for many reasons. In terms of the issues discussed in this chapter, a major reason is that friends help each other through major life transitions, such as the school transitions that adolescents experience (Rubin, Coplan, Chen, Buskirk, & Wojslawowicz, 2005). Children lacking friends are at risk for a variety of negative developmental outcomes (Rubin, Bukowski, & Parker, 1998).

By contrast, social acceptance has been shown to relate to a variety of positive mental health outcomes, both before and during adolescence (Rubin et al., 1998). For instance, Perry (1987) found that adolescents who were satisfied with their friendships report higher self-esteem. Unfortunately, school transitions often disrupt children's friendships, perhaps causing some difficulties in these important psychological outcomes. In our study of how the transition to junior high school influenced children's perceptions of social ability, we found a dramatic decrease in those beliefs immediately after the transition. Fortunately, this effect moderated during the 7th-grade year, although children's perceptions of their social ability at the end of 7th grade still were lower than they were at the end of 6th grade, before the transition (Wigfield, Eccles, Mac Iver, Reuman, & Midgley, 1991).

Children's friendships undergo some important changes during adolescence (Berndt & Perry, 1990; Rubin et al., 1998; Rubin et al., 2005). Sullivan (1953) suggested that adolescent friendships are characterized more by fulfilling intimacy needs than are earlier friendships, and indeed most research shows that children state that friends are those with whom one can share intimate thoughts. This depiction may be somewhat truer for girls (Rubin et al., 2005). In addition, adolescents state that their friends share similar psychological characteristics, interests, and values, and that friends should be loyal to one another (Berndt & Perry, 1990; Savin-Williams & Berndt, 1990). Many of these changes in adolescents' conceptions of friendships can be linked to changes in their growing cognitive skills, increased perspective-taking ability, and more varied social experiences (Rubin et al., 2005). Yet, Elkind (1967, 1985) proposed that many adolescents become more egocentric and

self-focused, thinking the world revolves around them (see Lapsley & Murphy, 1985, for an alternative view). Such egocentrism might reflect adolescents' struggles with their newly developed thinking skills (Keating, 1990, 2004).

Perhaps because of the importance of social acceptance during adolescence, friendships during this time period often are characterized by their organization into cliques and groups (see Brown, 1990; 2004; NRC, 2004). Adolescents often form different groups based on interests and participation in different activities, and these groups often differ in their overall status in the school. For instance, Perry (1987) found that more popular children tended to have friends who also were more popular, whereas less popular children's friends also were less popular. One reason for the existence of these cliques is to help adolescents establish a sense of identity; belonging to a group is one way to solve the problem of "who am I?" A second and related phenomenon is that children's conformity to their peers peaks during early adolescence; children are most likely to go along with others' wishes at this time (Rubin et al., 1998). This also has been related to the overwhelming importance of social acceptance to adolescents, as well as to children's developing identity. Individuals less certain of their own identities may be more likely to conform to others. The identity of these groups remains relatively constant during adolescence (e.g., jocks, brains, band members), but adolescents drift in and out of these groups as they go through middle and high school (Brown, 2004).

In the popular literature, much has been written about how conformity to peers can create many problems for adolescents, and that "good" children often are corrupted by the negative influences of peers. However, although pressure from peers to engage in misconduct does increase during adolescence (Brown, 1990, 2004), many researchers disagree with the simplistic view that peer groups mostly have a bad influence on adolescents. Brown (1990) reviewed studies showing that it is poor parenting that sometimes leads children to get in with a "bad" peer group, rather than the peer group pulling the child into difficulties. He also argued that adolescents usually seek out similar peers; this means that those involved in sports will have other athletes as friends, those serious about school will seek those kinds of friends, and those less involved in school may form groups. Thus, for many adolescents, the peer group acts more to reinforce predispositions, rather than to change adolescents' characteristics in a major way (Kindermann, 1993). Ryan (2001) provided further evidence for this view with respect to student groups and their impact on students' motivation and achievement, finding that students with similar levels of achievement tend to be friends.

One particular type of conformity to a group, gang membership, has received increasing attention and concern. Gang membership is increasing in many areas, particularly but not exclusively large urban areas, and it is extending into the suburbs as well. Although membership in a gang provides adolescents with some social support (Padilla, 1992), research indicates that gangs promote a variety of antisocial behaviors, including delinquency and various criminal activities, drug use, and poor school achievement (Battin-Pearson, Thornberry, Hawkins, & Krohn, 1998; NRC, 2004). As discussed by the National Research Council, adolescents who join gangs most often are low achievers who are marginalized in school, and often have various academic as well as social problems. Interventions to discourage gang membership have had some success, but much more needs to be done to combat the growing problem of gang membership (NRC, 2004).

Another concern with respect to social relations at adolescence receiving increasing attention is bullying and peer violence, and broader issues of school safety. Fighting increases during the middle school years, and more students are bullied in middle school than in either elementary or high school (Juvonen, Le, Kaganoff, Augustine, & Constant, 2004). Being bullied is associated with many negative developmental outcomes, including loneliness, depression, and social anxiety, as well as lower school performance (Juvonen & Graham, 2001; Juvonen, Nishina, & Graham, 2001). Increasing percentages of both middle and high school students report concerns about their safety in school, which of course distracts them from their school learning (Brand, Felner, Shim, Seitsinger, & Dumas, 2003). Victimization occurs at the individual level but also can include groups of children; some low-status groups of children (e.g., those who other adolescents perceive as "nerds") are at risk for being rejected and victimized at school. Creating safer school environments where bullying and other forms of violence are less likely clearly is an important priority.

How do children's friendships relate to their school achievement? The work just reviewed suggests that students who fear for their safety in school achieve less well. From Brown's (1990, 2004) and Ryan's (2001) reviews, it appears that friends potentially can have both positive and negative effects on school achievement. High-achieving children who seek out other high achievers as friends could end up performing better as a result of their interactions with these other children, although Ryan (2001) found that such groups' achievement declines less in comparison to other groups, rather than increasing. In contrast, low achievers whose friends are primarily other low achievers do even worse in school (Dishion, Andrews, & Crosby, 1995). In a similar vein, Altermatt and Pomerantz (2003) found in a study of early adolescents that best friends' report card grades were similar, as were their beliefs about their competence in different subject areas. In addition, friends had significant (but modest) influence on each others' grades and motivational beliefs across the two school years studied.

In sum, peers play increasingly important roles in children's development during the adolescent period. Peers have many positive influences on one another, and also can have some negative influences as well. Fostering positive relations among adolescents in classrooms can have many benefits for both the adolescents and teachers.

CHANGES IN FAMILY RELATIONS DURING ADOLESCENCE

Relations between parents and children change as children enter adolescence, although the stereotypical view often presented in the popular media that adolescence means an inevitably stormy period for these relations is not supported in much of the psychological research on parent–child relations at adolescence (Collins & Laursen, 2004; Steinberg & Silk, 2002). Some of the major changes that do occur are (a) adolescents and parents spend less time together, in large part because adolescents are away from home more, spending more time with their peers and with various kinds of media and other activities; (b) a psychological "distancing" in parent-adolescent relations, because many adolescents desire more autonomy and often share less with their parents; and (c) some increase in conflict, or if not conflict, debate and bickering over a variety of things as adolescents assert their independence. This increase in conflict and discussion of parental rules likely emerges in part due to some of the cognitive and social changes in adolescents that were discussed earlier in this chapter. Finally, (d) there is a waning of parental influence as adolescents become more independent and also are more influenced by their peers. Parents' influence remains strong in many areas of adolescents' lives, however, and positive relations between parents and their adolescents have many beneficial outcomes to both parents and adolescents (Steinberg & Silk, 2002).

Since the last edition of this handbook, there has been a major debate within the field of developmental psychology about how much influence parents indeed do have on their children. Harris (1995, 1998) argued that genetics, peers, and the broader culture have a much stronger role in children's development than do parents. Similar arguments have been raised by some behavioral geneticists (see Rowe, 1994). Researchers who study children's socialization have responded in effective ways to these arguments, documenting ways in which parents indeed do have important influences in a variety of aspects of their children's lives, including their overall psychological adjustment and various educational outcomes (e.g., Collins, Maccoby, Steinberg, Hetherington, & Bornstein, 2000; Steinberg & Silk, 2002). This debate served an important role in sharpening socialization research designs and interpretations of research bearing on the issue of the degree of parental influence, and specifying more clearly the kinds of influence parents do have on different adolescent outcomes.

As discussed in the previous edition of this *Handbook* and by many others, parenting styles have long been a major topic in the parent socialization literature. Baumrind (1971, 1978) identified four major parenting styles (i.e., authoritative, authoritarian, permissive or indulgent, and indifferent), and she and others have discussed their implications for children and adolescents' development. As Steinberg and Silk (2002) noted, these styles vary on dimensions of control and emotional warmth, with the authoritative style having the best blend of adequate control over children along with support of their autonomy, and provision of emotional warmth. In studies done in the United States, authoritative parenting style has been associated with many positive psychological and educational outcomes, including school achievement (Steinberg & Silk, 2002). This also appears to be the case in other countries and cultures, although there is evidence that the nature of these parenting styles differ across culture and relate in different ways to important child outcomes such as achievement (Chao & Tseng, 2002). For instance, in Asia authoritative parenting does not relate as clearly to children's educational achievement.

Work on parenting in different groups within our country and in different cultures has increased greatly over the past 10 years (e.g., Chao & Tseng, 2002; Garcia Coll & Pachter, 2002; Harwood, Leyendecker, Carlson, Ascencic, & Miller, 2002; McAdoo, 2002), as has work on family structural variables and parenting. There are similarities across these groups in practices and styles, but many important differences as well, both within and across ethnic groups. Because of space limitations, we can only mention a few examples.

Authoritative parenting is more common among European-American parents than among parents in some other ethnic groups, likely reflecting differences in cultural beliefs and values about appropriate parenting (Garcia Coll & Pachter, 2002; Harkness & Super, 2002). Latino children appear to be more family oriented than European American children, and more likely to live with members of their extended families (Harwood et al., 2002). Many Asian parents focus strongly on family interdependence, and also appear to be more controlling in interactions with their children and adolescents (Chao & Tseng, 2002). More broadly, ethnic minority parents also have to decide how to teach their children about race, and prepare them for instances of racism and discrimination they likely will encounter, experiences that can profoundly affect these children's motivation and achievement (McAdoo, 2002).

Researchers also have examined more closely the impact of poverty on parental effectiveness, finding that poverty adds stress to lives in families that can change parent–child relations in important ways (Magnuson & Duncan, 2002; McLoyd, 1990). In addition, with the number of single-parent families in this country increasing dramatically, researchers also have looked at how living in single-parent homes influences adolescents. The stress of divorce and separation often disrupts parent–child relations and other child outcomes at least initially. Yet, these disruptions can be overcome (Hetherington & Stanley-Hagan, 2002).

During adolescence parents continue to be concerned about and influence adolescents' school performance in different ways, and we close this section by noting several of these influences. First, parents of children from many different ethnic groups and backgrounds continue to see schooling as the primary way for their children to achieve success in this society, and hope and expect that their children will go to college. Second, parents' specific beliefs about their adolescents' abilities, skills, and characteristics influences adolescents' own self-beliefs, performance, and choice of which activities to pursue (Bleeker & Jacobs, 2004; Eccles, Adler, & Kaczala, 1982; Heller & Ziegler, 1996; Jacobs, 1991). Bleeker and Jacobs found that mothers' predictions about their seventh-grade children's success in a mathematics-oriented career predicted their math ability beliefs in tenth grade, and math/science career efficacy during their middle twenties (although this relationship was mediated by adolescents' own beliefs). Mothers' beliefs about children's ability were an especially strong predictor of their daughters' choices of a math or science career.

Third, we noted earlier that relations between parents and adolescents become more distant at adolescence, and that this is in many ways a natural progression as most adolescents do desire more autonomy in their lives. One area in which this can be problematic is parents' involvement in adolescents' schooling. Most studies of parental involvement in schooling show that it is highest in elementary school, and drops off after that (Eccles & Harold, 1993; Sanders & Epstein, 2002). Although adolescents must learn to control their own achievement behaviors and often want their parents to be less involved in their schooling, parents' continuing involvement in their children's education helps to ensure their success in school, and school improvement programs often include parent involvement as a major component (Comer, 1988; NRC, 2004). Parents' decreasing involvement in school likely reflects their adolescents' wishes to a degree, but also may reflect the characteristics of secondary schools themselves. As will be discussed, the larger and more bureaucratic secondary schools that parents encounter may be more difficult to become involved in than neighborhood-based elementary schools. However, many successful secondary schools encourage continued parent involvement in a variety of ways, with benefits for students (Sanders & Epstein, 2002).

In summary, relations between parents and adolescents change in important ways relative to relations of parents to their younger children. These changes, often portrayed as routinely negative in the media, pose challenges for both parents and adolescents, but in many cases are handled well by both groups. Further, parents continue to have a strong influence on adolescents' development both in and out of school, and parents who provide their adolescents with structure, autonomy support, and emotional support help the adolescents negotiate the challenges of this time period successfully.

SCHOOL TRANSITIONS AND ADOLESCENT DEVELOPMENT

As we hope is clear from our review to this point, very few developmental periods are characterized by so many changes at so many different levels as adolescence—changes due to pubertal development, cognitive development, social role redefinitions, and changes in peer and parent relations. We discussed that children facing multiple transitions and stressors are at greater risk for these negative outcomes. Here, we consider two major school transitions that most adolescents experience, from elementary to middle school and middle school to high school. The middle school transition has received most of the attention, and researchers (e.g., Eccles, 2004; Eccles & Midgley, 1989; Midgley & Edelin, 1998) have stated that there is a mismatch between the developmental needs of early adolescents and the school environments that many early adolescents experience (see also Eccles et al., 1993, and Wigfield et al., 1996, 1998).

The Middle School Transition

Traditional junior high schools and middle schools differ structurally in important ways from elementary schools. Most junior high schools are substantially larger than elementary schools, because they draw students from several elementary schools. As a result, students' friendship networks often are disrupted as they attend classes with students from several different schools. Students also are likely to feel more anonymous because of the large size of many middle schools. Instruction is likely to be organized and taught departmentally. Thus, middle school teachers typically teach several different groups of students each day and are unlikely to teach any particular students for more than 1 year. This departmental structure can create a number of difficulties for students. One is that the curriculum often is not integrated across different subjects. A second is that students typically have several teachers each day with little opportunity to interact with any one teacher on any dimension except the academic content of what is being taught and disciplinary issues. It is becoming increasingly clear that caring relations with teachers are very important to adolescent development (Wentzel, 2002a). Finally, as mentioned, family involvement in school often declines during the middle school years.

Researchers also have discussed how in traditional junior high schools and middle schools, classroom and school environments emphasize mastery goals and intrinsic motivation less and performance goals more (Anderman & Maehr, 1994; Eccles, 2004; Maehr & Midgley, 1996; Midgley, 2002). Such shifts also can contribute to the decline in students' academic competence beliefs, interest, and intrinsic motivation discussed earlier. The major kinds of changes that have been discussed include changing authority relationships between teachers and students with authority issues becoming more salient, use of whole-class instruction and between-classroom ability grouping, decreases in teachers' sense of efficacy to reach all students, and stricter grading criterion (Eccles et al., 1998; Roeser, Eccles, & Sameroff, 1998; Wigfield & Eccles, 2002a). Finally, as noted peer networks are disrupted when children change schools. Many times friends are separated from one another, and it takes some time for children to reestablish social networks. Such disruptions could influence children's academic motivation as well (Ryan, 2001).

In summary, traditional junior high schools and middle schools have a variety of organizational characteristics and classroom practices that can have negative effects on students' competence beliefs, mastery goals, and intrinsic motivation for learning. Eccles and Midgley (1989) argued that a main reason these practices have a negative impact is that they are developmentally inappropriate for early adolescents. At a time when the children are growing cognitively and emotionally, desiring greater freedom and autonomy, and focusing on social relations, they experience teaching practices like those described, which do not fit well with the developmental characteristics of early adolescents. Therefore, for many early adolescents, these practices contribute to the negative change in students' motivation and achievement-related beliefs.

Middle School Reform Efforts and Student Motivation

Based in part on the research showing declining student motivation and achievement during middle school, there have been a variety of proposals for reorganizing middle schools, and schools across the country are implementing these changes (Carnegie Council on Adolescent Development, 1989; Clark & Clark, 1993; Irvin, 1992; Mac Iver, Young, & Washburn, 2002; Midgley & Edelin, 1998). There is growing consensus about what kinds of changes should be made in middle grade schools (Lipsitz, Mizell, Jackson, & Austin, 1997). One structural change adopted in many school districts has been to move the transition to middle school from after to before sixth grade. This change on its own accomplishes little; what is more important is changing school organization and instructional practices in systematic ways (Mac Iver & Epstein, 1993). Both the Carnegie Council on Adolescent Development and the National Middle Schools Association have made recommendations for how middle schools should be changed. The broadest goal of these recommendations is to provide developmentally appropriate education for early adolescents (Wigfield & Eccles, 2002a).

There are a number of important ways in which these recommendations have been implemented in different middle schools. One is replacing department structures with teams of teachers working with the same group of students. This practice allows groups of teachers to spend more time with the same group of adolescents, thus getting to know them better. It also allows for greater integration across the curriculum. Teachers serving as advisors and counselors have become more prevalent, so that adolescents can develop relationships with adults other than their parents. To create smaller learning communities in often-large middle schools, "schools within schools" have been created, in part through the teaming approach just discussed. This is particularly likely to occur for the youngest group in a middle school, be they 5th graders, 6th graders, or 7th graders. Cooperative learning practices are used more frequently, in part to reduce the use of ability grouping or tracking.

Felner, Jackson, Kasak, Mulhall, Brand and Flowers (1997) reported systematic evaluations of schools implementing fully the recommendations from the Carnegie Council, comparing them with schools implementing the recommendations to a degree and not at all. Felner et al. obtained measures of students' achievement, school

attitudes, and behavior problems. Preliminary analyses indicate that schools in which the implementation has been fullest have higher achieving students. Students in these schools report higher self-esteem and fewer worries about bad things happening to them in schools, and teachers report fewer behavior problems. These results provide encouraging support for the efficacy of the reform efforts. One crucial point made by Felner et al. is that comprehensive reform is what is needed. Schools in which one or two of the recommendations have been implemented, or schools in which the implementation of several recommendations has proceeded slowly, have not been as successful.

In summarizing middle school reform efforts, Midgley and Edelin (1998) argued that many middle schools have improved the climate of their school, particularly relations between teachers and students, but fewer have changed their instructional practices. They argued for the need for both kinds of changes to occur in order for reform to occur more completely and therefore, for adolescents' achievement and motivation to improve.

The High School Transition

Work on the transition to high school is increasing, and the existing evidence suggests quite similar problems as occur in traditional middle schools (Lee & Smith, 2001; Mac Iver, Reuman, & Main, 1995; NRC, 2004). For example, traditional high schools are typically even larger and more bureaucratic than junior high schools and middle schools. There is little opportunity for students and teachers to get to know each other and, likely as a consequence, there is distrust between them and little attachment to a common set of goals and values. There is also little opportunity for the students to form mentor-like relationships with a nonfamilial adult, and little effort is made to make instruction relevant to the students. Such environments are likely to further undermine the motivation and involvement of many students, especially those not doing particularly well academically, those not enrolled in the favored classes, and those who are alienated from the values of the adults in the high school (NRC, 2004).

Many adolescents begin doing more poorly academically in high school, which has a strong impact on their engagement in school. Roderick and Camburn (1999) documented the increases in failure rates among Chicago public high school students (particularly minority students), and how early failures in high school strongly predict later poor performance. Other studies of ethnic minority youth document the negative impact of alienating and noninclusive high school practices on school engagement and achievement of students of color (e.g., Darling-Hammond, 1997; Ferguson, 1998).

Most large public high schools also organize instruction around curricular tracks that sort students into different groups, although this appears to be changing at least to a degree (NRC, 2004). As a result, there is even greater diversity in the educational experiences of high school students than of middle grade students. Unfortunately, this diversity is often associated more with the students' social class and ethnic group than with differences in the students' talents and interests (Lee & Bryk, 1989; Lee & Smith, 2001). Curricular tracking has served to reinforce social stratification rather than foster optimal education for all students, particularly in large schools (Lee & Bryk, 1989; Lee & Smith, 2001). Both Lee and Bryk (1989) and Lee and Smith (2001) documented that average school achievement levels do not benefit from this curricular tracking. Quite the contrary, evidence comparing Catholic high schools, which track less, with public high schools suggests that average school achievement levels are increased when all students are required to take the same challenging curriculum. This conclusion is true even after one has controlled for student selectivity factors.

High School Reform Efforts. As at the middle-school level, there are efforts across the country aimed at reforming high schools to promote student engagement and achievement (see NRC, 2004, for summaries of a number of these efforts). These reform efforts vary, but many are guided by principles such as (a) having high and consistent standards and expectations for all students; (b) creating learning communities within schools and stronger personal relations between teachers and students so that adolescents feel connected to their schools; (c) creating curricula that students find meaningful and engaging; and (d) promoting family and community involvement in the schools. The NRC (2004) provided a set of recommendations for further high school reform that includes many of the suggestions just listed, and others, including the strong suggestion to do away with tracking and ability grouping to the largest extent possible. Unfortunately to date there is not extensive research evaluating the effectiveness of these reform efforts with respect to student learning, engagement, and adjustment, but studies are underway to provide these evaluations, and preliminary evidence is promising (NRC, 2004). As successful reform efforts are validated, the next challenge will be "scaling up" successful reforms to larger settings. The process of scaling up is very complex, however, and much remains to be learned about how to do so effectively.

Leaving High School Early: The Problem of Dropping Out

We reviewed the research on decision making that shows that adolescents' developing cognitive skills do not necessarily translate into better decision making in different areas in their lives. One major difference between middle school and high school is that there are many more social and educational choices available to high school students, choices that can have both positive and negative consequences. The educational choices students face include the kinds of classes they will continue to take in high school: for example, whether to focus on academically oriented or vocationally oriented courses. Such choices have the potential to increase student engagement and learning, as students choose areas of study in which they are interested and have the competencies to succeed.

A more fundamental educational decision is whether or not to stay in school at all. In middle or junior high school students can disengage from school by not trying, acting out, or being truant. However, they still are required to be in school. At age 16, students can make the decision to leave school, and unfortunately, many choose to do so. Nationally, approximately 75% of adolescents graduate from high school. This overall number masks huge differences across different groups of adolescents, however. About 56% of African-American students graduate and 54% of Latino students do so. Within these two groups there are striking variations depending on where the adolescents live and which schools they attend, with graduation rates dropping below 40% for students in some big cities (NRC, 2004).

Entwisle (1990) reviewed the work that has examined the characteristics of students more likely to drop out of high school (see also Rumberger, 1987). These characteristics include students with lower ability, those who achieve less well, those from poverty backgrounds, those who begin working too early and work too many hours while trying to go to school, and girls who become pregnant. Entwisle pointed out that there are inadequate prospective studies that can be used to identify which children will be most likely to drop out. Work that is available, however, suggests that students doing poorly when they are in elementary school, exhibiting serious behavior problems in school, and being truant on a frequent basis will be more likely to drop out of high school. Finn (1989) discussed how these problems often are interrelated. Understanding the factors related to dropping out certainly is important. However, Rumberger (1987) argued for the need to understand the processes related to dropping out better, rather than just listing factors associated with the problem. In beginning to address that issue, Finn (1989) argued for a participation-identification model of the drop out process, stating that students who participate less in academic and nonacademic activities in school (beginning in elementary school) will identify less with the educational process, and ultimately be more likely to drop out of school.

As part of participation-identification processes, Finn pointed to the importance of valuing of school, a construct we have discussed extensively in this chapter and elsewhere (e.g., Wigfield & Eccles, 1992, 2002b). From our research, we know that students who do not value mathematics will be more likely to opt out of math when they no longer have to take it. Do adolescents' specific achievement values relate to their bigger decision about dropping out or staying in school? Assessing students' particular subjective values and other aspects of motivation over the school years may help predict which students will become disengaged from school, and could provide a better model for how students' achievement-related beliefs influence their decisions to stay in or leave school (Vallerand, Fortier, & Guay, 1997). Most researchers examining how students' beliefs relate to dropping out of school have focused on students' general self-esteem, a construct that may be too broad to have much predictive utility in explaining specific decisions such as dropping out of school.

We have been discussing dropping out of school as a decision; however, many students likely drift into dropping out of school rather than consciously deciding to do so. That is, the circumstances of their lives might be such that continuing to go to school would be very difficult. These circumstances include the economic pressure many poor students face, discrimination, and poor schools, to name just a few. These circumstances likely play a major role in influencing some students to drop out (Finn, 1989, Rumberger, 1987).

Of course, one of the major outcomes of dropping out of school is that it seriously limits the adolescent's chances of obtaining a well-paying job (NRC, 2004). Not only do individuals who drop out lose potential earnings, but society often has to provide more extensive social services for dropouts, because they often are more likely to engage in some or all of the problem behaviors that McCord (1990) discussed. Although receiving a high school diploma may alleviate some of these problems, unfortunately in today's society a high school degree no longer ensures reasonable job prospects. When our society was an industrial society a high school diploma often was enough to guarantee access to reasonably well-paying and secure jobs. As we move further into a postindustrial society that no longer is the case; indeed, some students now may be dropping out of high school because they realize a high school diploma will not mean much to them in terms of job prospects.

CONCLUSION

In their chapter for the first addition of this *Handbook* Wigfield et al. (1996) concluded that although much had been learned about different aspects of adolescents' biological, cognitive, and motivational development, much remained to be done. They noted in particular the need to do more research on adolescent development in the different cultural and ethnic groups in our society. They also called for more work on the high school transition and its impact, to complement the larger body of work on the middle school transition. There now is a growing literature on these topics.

Perhaps we can now say that research on adolescent development is entering its own adolescence. We have learned much since 1996 about biological, cognitive, and motivational development during this critical developmental period (see Lerner & Steinberg, 2004). Theoretical models of adolescent development in different areas emphasize even more clearly both psychological processes and the influence of contexts in which adolescents develop. As we hope is evident in this chapter, much has been learned about adolescent development in different cultural and ethnic groups in our society, an accomplishment that is particularly noteworthy. Clearly there is much more to be done in this area, but the progress has been substantial. Studies of adolescents from different groups have provided and will continue to provide important tests of the generalizability of our theoretical models of different cognitive and motivational processes, helping to refine and sharpen these models.

We are encouraged that there have been important methodological and statistical advances that allow us to study adolescent development in richer and more meaningful ways. A number of the studies discussed in this chapter are using these methodologies. The growing focus on multiple methods in studies, particularly studies combining qualitative and quantitative methods are providing a richer understanding of adolescent development (e.g., Turner et al., 2002). Analyses of long-term change in the growth curves of different characteristics also help us understand the total picture of development across childhood and adolescence (e.g., Jacobs et al., 2002; Watt, 2004). HLM is allowing researchers to address carefully influences of different sources of variation in the outcomes of educational and intervention studies, which should lead to a better understanding of the effects of these interventions as well as improvements in them (Mac Iver et al., 2002). Structural equation modeling techniques also continue to advance (Guay et al., 2003). These new and evolving methodologies provide powerful tools for the next generation of research on adolescent development.

With respect to school reform efforts, progress has been made in middle school reform, but it remains spotty. As evidenced by the volume published by the National Research Council (2004), suggestions for high school reform increasingly are on the national agenda. Like others (Deci & Ryan, 2002) we are concerned that the recommendations for reform coming from researchers doing the important work on changes in cognition, learning, and motivation (and summarized in places like the NRC book) often are at odds with policies adopted at the national level, particularly those policies emphasizing assessment as the driving force in education. We researchers need to find ways to communicate our findings more effectively,

to inform better educational policy to optimize adolescents' learning and development.

We characterize research on adolescence as being in the phase of adolescent development itself because a major task of adolescence is to integrate multiple possible selves into a coherent whole. In the case of research on adolescence, this means integrations across different areas that historically have remained distinct, such as research on how cognition and motivation interact to affect learning, or research on the interface of biological processes and cognitive development. Theorists and researchers now are making important connections across these areas. For example, Pintrich (2003) discussed cogently links between motivation and cognition, and Byrnes (2001b) provided an overview of the relevance of what we know about brain development in relation to educational outcomes. We think such integrations should be a major focus of the work of the next decade.

References

Altermatt, E. R., & Pomerantz, E. M. (2003). The development of competence-related and motivational beliefs: An investigation of similarity and influence among friends. *Journal of Educational Psychology, 95,*111–123.

Arnett, J. J. (1999). Adolescent storm and stress reconsidered. *American Psychologist, 54,* 317–326.

Anderman, E. M., Austin, C. C., & Johnson, D. M. (2002). The development of goal orientation. In A. Wigfield & J. S. Eccles (Eds.), *Development of achievement motivation* (pp. 197–220). San Diego, CA: Academic Press.

Anderman, E. M., & Maehr, M. L. (1994). Motivation and schooling during the middle grades. *Review of Educational Research, 64,* 287–309.

Anderman, L. H., & Anderman, E. M. (1999). Social predictors of changes in students' achievement goal orientations. *Contemporary Educational Psychology, 25,* 21–37.

Angold, A., Costello, E. J., & Worthman, C. (1998). Puberty and depression: The role of age, pubertal status, and pubertal timing. *Psychological Medicine, 28,* 51–61.

Aronson, J. (2002). Stereotype threat: contending and coping with unnerving expectations. In J. Aronson (Ed.). *Improving academic achievement: Impact of psychological factors on education* (pp. 279–301). San Diego, CA: Academic Press.

Baltes, P. B., Linderberger, U., & Staudinger, U. M. (1998). Lifespan theory in developmental psychology. In W. Damon (Series Ed.) and R. M. Lerner (Volume Ed.), *Handbook of child psychology* (5th ed., Vol. 1., pp. 1029–1145). New York: Wiley.

Bandura, A. (1997). *Self-efficacy: The exercise of control.* San Francisco: W. H. Freeman.

Bandura, A., Barbaranelli, C., Caprara, G. V., & Pastorelli, C. (1996). Multifaceted impact of self-efficacy beliefs on academic functioning. *Child Development, 67,* 1206–1222.

Bandura, A., Bandura, A., Barbaranelli, C., Caprara, G. V., & Pastorelli, C. (2001). Self-efficacy beliefs as shapers of children's aspirations and career trajectories. *Child Development, 72,* 187–206.

Battin-Pearson, S. R., Thornberry, T. P., Hawkins, J. D., & Krohn, M. D. (1998). *Gang membership, delinquent peers, and delinquent behavior* (Rep. No. 1-11). Washington, DC: U.S. Department of Justice

Baumrind, D. (1971). Current patterns of parent authority. *Developmental Psychology Monographs, 4* (1, Part 2, 1–103).

Baumrind, D. (1978). Parental disciplinary patterns and social competence in children. *Youth and Society, 9,* 239–276.

Beatty, A. S., Reese, C. M., Perksy, H. R., & Carr, P. (1996). *The NAEP 1994 U.S. History Report Card for the nation and the states.* Washington, DC: U.S. Department of Education, Office of Educational Research and Improvement, National Center for Education Statistics.

Berndt, T. J., & Perry, T. B. (1990). Distinctive features of early adolescent friendships. In R Montemayor, G. R. Adams, & T. P. Gullotta (Eds.), *From childhood to adolescence: A transitional period?* (pp. 269–287). Newbury Park, CA: Sage.

Bjorklund, D. F. (1999). *Children's thinking: Developmental function and individual differences.* Belmont, CA: Wadsworth.

Bleeker, M. M., & Jacobs, J. E. (2004). Achievement in math and science: Do mothers' beliefs matter 12 years later? *Journal of Educational Psychology, 96,* 97–109.

Blos, P. (1979). *The adolescent passage.* New York: International Universities Press.

Bong, M. (2001). Role of self-efficacy and task-value in predicting college students' course performance and future enrollment intentions. *Contemporary Educational Psychology, 26,* 553–570.

Brand, S., Felner, R., Shim, M., Seitsinger, A., & Dumas, T. (2003). Middle school improvement and reform: Development and validation of a school-level assessment of climate, cultural pluralism, and school safety. *Journal of Educational Psychology, 95,* 570–588.

Bronfenbrenner, U., & Morris, R. A. (1998). The ecology of developmental processes. In W. Damon (Series Ed.) & R. M. Lerner (Vol. Ed.), *Handbook of child psychology* (5th ed., Vol. 1, pp. 993–1028). New York: Wiley.

Brown, B. B. (1990). Peer groups and peer cultures. In S. S. Feldman & G. R. Elliott (Eds.), *At the threshold: The developing adolescent* (pp. 171–196). Cambridge, MA: Harvard University Press.

Brown, B. B. (2004). Adolescents' relationships with peers. In R. M. Lerner & L. D. Steinberg (Eds.), *Handbook of adolescent psychology* (2nd ed., pp. 363–394). New York: Wiley.

Buchanan, C. M., Eccles, J. S., & Becker, J. B. (1992). Are adolescents the victims of raging hormones? Evidence for activational effects of hormones on moods and behaviors at adolescence. *Psychological Bulletin, 111,* 62–107.

Byrnes, J. P. (1988). Formal operations: A systematic reformulation. *Developmental Review, 8,* 66–87.

Byrnes, J. P. (1998). *The nature and development of decision-making: A self-regulation perspective.* Mahwah, NJ: Lawrence Erlbaum Associates.

Byrnes. J. P. (2001a). *Cognitive development and learning in instructional contexts* (2nd ed.). Needham Heights, MA: Allyn & Bacon.

Byrnes, J. P. (2001b). *Minds, brains, and education*: Understanding the psychological and educational relevance of neuroscientific research. New York: Guilford.

Byrnes, J. P., & McClenny, B. (1994). Decision-making in young adolescents and adults. *Journal of Experimental Child Psychology, 58,* 359–388.

Byrnes, J. P., Miller, D. C., & Reynolds, M. (1999). Learning to make good decisions: A self-regulation perspective. *Child Development, 70,* 1121–1140.

Byrnes, J. P., Miller, D. C., & Schaefer, W. D. (1999). Sex-differences in risk-taking: A meta-analysis. *Psychological Bulletin, 125,* 367–383.

Byrnes, J. P., & Overton, W. F. (1986). Reasoning about certainty and uncertainty in concrete, causal, and propositional contexts. *Developmental Psychology, 22,* 793–799.

Cantor, N., & Kihlstrom, J. (1987). *Personality and social intelligence.* Englewood Cliffs, NJ: Prentice-Hall.

Cantor, N., & Norem, J. (1989). Defensive pessimism and stress and coping. *Social Cognition, 7,* 92–112.

Carnegie Council on Adolescent Development. (1989). *Turning points: Preparing American youth for the 21st century.* New York: Carnegie Corporation.

Chao, R., & Tseng, V. (2002). Parenting of Asians. In M. Bornstein (Ed.), *Handbook of parenting* (2nd ed., Vol. 4, pp. 59–94). Mahwah, NJ: Lawrence Erlbaum Associates.

Chen, C., & Stevenson, H. W. (1995). Motivation and mathematics achievement: A comparative study of Asian-American, Caucasian-American, and East Asian high school students. *Child Development, 66,* 1215–1234.

Clark, S. N., & Clark, D. C. (1993). Middle level school reform: The rhetoric and the reality. *Elementary School Journal, 93,* 447–460.

Collins, W. A., & Laursen, B. (2004). Parent–adolescent relationships and influences. In R. M. Lerner & L. D. Steinberg (Eds.), *Handbook of adolescent psychology* (2nd ed., pp. 331–364). New York: Wiley.

Collins, W. A., Maccoby, E. E., Steinberg, L., Hetherington, E. M., & Bornstein, M. H. (2000). Contemporary research on parenting: The case for nature and nurture. *American Psychologist, 55,* 218–233.

Comer, J. P. (1988). Educating poor minority children. *Scientific American, 259*(5), 42–48.

Darling-Hammond, L. (1997). *The right to learn.* San Francisco: Jossey-Bass.

Deci, E. L., & Ryan, R. M. (2002). The paradox of achievement: The harder you push, the worse it gets. In J. Aronson (Ed.), *Improving academic achievement: Impact of psychological factors on education* (pp. 61–87). San Diego, CA: Academic Press.

De Lisi, R., & McGillicuddy-De Lisi, A. (2002). Sex differences in mathematical ability and achievement, In A. McGillicuddy-De Lisi & R. De Lisi (Eds.), *Biology, society, and behavior: The development of sex differences in cognition* (pp.155–182). Westport, CT: Ablex.

Dias, M. G., & Harris, P. L. (1988). The effect of make-believe play on deductive reasoning. *British Journal of Developmental Psychology, 6,* 207–221.

DiClemente, R. J., Hansen, W. B., & Ponton, L. E. (1995). *Handbook of adolescent health risk behavior.* New York: Plenum.

Dishion, T. J., Andrews, D. W., & Crosby, L. (1995). Antisocial boys and their friends in early adolescence. *Child Development, 66,* 1139–1151.

Dornbusch, S. M., Petersen, A. C., & Hetherington, E. M. (1991). Projecting the future of research on adolescence. *Journal of Research on Adolescence, 1,* 7–18.

Duncan, G. J., Brooks-Gunn, J., & Klevbanov, P. K. (1994). Economic deprivation and early childhood development. *Child Development, 65,* 296–318.

Dweck, C. S. (2002). The development of ability conceptions. In A. Wigfield & J. S. Eccles (Eds.), *Development of achievement motivation* (pp. 57–88). San Diego, CA: Academic Press.

Early, D. M., Belansky, E., & Eccles, J. S. (1992, March). *The impact of gender stereotypes on perceived ability and attributions for success.* Poster presented at the Biennial Meeting of the Society for Research on Adolescence, Washington DC.

Eccles, J. S. (1984a). Sex differences in achievement patterns. In T. Sonderegger (Ed.), *Nebraska Symposium on Motivation* (Vol. 32, pp. 97–132). Lincoln, NE: University of Nebraska Press.

Eccles (Parsons), J. S. (1984b). Sex differences in mathematics participation. In M. Steinkamp and M. L. Maehr (Eds.), *Advances in motivation and achievement* (Vol. 2, pp. 93–137). Greenwich, CT: JAI Press.

Eccles, J. S. (1987). Gender roles and women's achievement-related decisions. *Psychology of Women Quarterly, 11*, 135-172.

Eccles, J. S. (2004). Schools, academic motivation, and stage-environment fit. In R. M. Lerner & L. D. Steinberg (Eds.), *Handbook of adolescent psychology* (2nd Ed., pp. 125-153). New York: Wiley.

Eccles, J. S., Adler, T. F., Futterman, R., Goff, S. B., Kaczala, C. M., Meece, J., & Midgley, C. (1983). Expectancies, values and academic behaviors. In J. T. Spence (Ed.), *Achievement and achievement motives* (pp. 75-146). San Francisco: W. H. Freeman.

Eccles, J. S., Adler, T. F., & Kaczala, C. M. (1982). Socialization of achievement attitudes and beliefs: Parental influences. *Child Development, 53*, 322-339.

Eccles, J. S., Adler, T., & Meece, J. L. (1984). Sex differences in achievement: A test of alternate theories. *Journal of Personality and Social Psychology, 46*, 26-43.

Eccles, J. S. & Harold, R. D. (1991). Gender differences in sport involvement: Applying the Eccles' expectancy-value model. *Journal of Applied Sport Psychology, 3*, 7-35.

Eccles, J. S., & Harold, R. D. (1993). Parent-school involvement during the early adolescent years. *Teachers' College Record, 94*, 568-587.

Eccles, J. S., & Midgley, C. (1989). Stage-environment fit: Developmentally appropriate classrooms for young adolescents. In C. Ames & R. Ames (Eds.), *Research on motivation in education* (Vol. 3, pp. 139-186). San Diego Academic Press.

Eccles, J., Midgley, C., & Adler, T. (1984). Grade-related changes in the school environment: Effects on achievement motivation. In J. G. Nicholls (Ed.), *The development of achievement motivation* (pp. 283-331). Greenwich, CT: JAI Press.

Eccles, J., & Wigfield, A. (1995). In the mind of the achiever: The structure of adolescents' achievement task values and expectancy-related beliefs. *Personality and Social Psychology Bulletin, 21*, 215-225.

Eccles, J. S., & Wigfield, A. (2002). Motivational beliefs, values, and goals. *Annual Review of Psychology, 53*, 109-132.

Eccles, J. S., Wigfield, A., Flanagan, C., Miller, C., Reuman, D., & Yee, D. (1989). Self-concepts, domain values, and self-esteem: Relations and changes at early adolescence. *Journal of Personality, 57*, 283-310.

Eccles, J. S., Wigfield, A., Harold, R.D., & Blumenfeld, P. B. (1993). Age and gender differences in children's achievement self-perceptions during the elementary school years. *Child Development, 64*, 830-847.

Eccles, J. S., Wigfield, A., Midgley, C., Reuman, D., Mac Iver, D., & Feldlaufer, H. (1993). Negative effects of traditional middle schools on students' motivation. *Elementary School Journal, 93*, 553-574.

Eccles, J. S., Wigfield, A., & Schiefele, U. (1998). Motivation to succeed. In W. Damon (Series Ed.) & N. Eisenberg (Volume Ed.), *Handbook of child psychology* (5th ed., Vol. III, pp. 1017-1095). New York: Wiley.

Eisenberg, N., Martin, C. L., & Fabes, R. (1996). Gender development and gender effects. In D. C. Berliner & R. C. Calfee (Eds.), *Handbook of educational psychology*. New York: Macmillan.

Elkind, D (1967). Egocentrism in adolescence. *Child Development, 38*, 1025-1034.

Elkind, D. (1985). Egocentrism redux. *Developmental Review, 5*, 218-226.

Elliot, A. J. (1999). Approach and avoidance motivation and achievement. *Educational Psychologist, 34*, 169-189.

Elliot, A. J., & McGregor, H. A. (2001). A 2 × 2 achievement goal framework. *Journal of Personality and Social Psychology, 80*, 501-519.

Entwisle, D. R. (1990). Schools and the adolescent. In S. S. Feldman & G. R. Elliott (Eds.), *At the threshold: The developing adolescent* (pp. 197-224). Cambridge, MA: Harvard University Press.

Ericsson, K. A. (1996). *The road to excellence: The acquisition of expert performance in the arts, science, sports, and games.* Mahwah, NJ: Lawrence Erlbaum Associates.

Erikson, E. H. (1968). *Identity: Youth and crisis.* New York: W. W. Norton.

Felner, R. D., Jackson, A. W., Kasak, D., Mulhall, P., Brand, S., & Flowers, N. (1997). The impact of school reform for the middle years: Longitudinal study of a network engaged in Turning Points-based comprehensive school transformation. *Phi Delta Kappan, 78*, 528-532; 541-550.

Ferguson, R. (1998). Can schools narrow the achievement gap? In C. Jencks & M. Phillips (Eds.), *The black-white test score gap* (pp. 318-374). Washington, DC: The Brookings Institution.

Finn, J. D. (1989). Withdrawing from school. *Review of Educational Research, 59*, 117-142.

Fredericks, J. A., Blumenfeld, P. B., & Paris, A. H. (2004). School engagement: Potential of the concept, state of the evidence. *Review of Educational Research, 74*, 59-109.

Fredericks, J. A., & Eccles, J. S. (2002). Children's competence beliefs and value beliefs from childhood through adolescence: Growth trajectories in two male sex-typed domains. *Developmental Psychology, 38*, 519-533.

Fuligni, A. J., & Tseng, V. (1999). Family obligation and the academic motivation of adolescents from immigrant and American-born families. In T. Urdan (Ed.), *Advances in motivation and achievement, Volume 11: The role of context* (pp. 159-183). Stamford, CT: JAI Press.

Galper, A., Wigfield, A., & Seefeldt, C. (1997). Head Start parents' beliefs about their children's abilities, task values, and performance on different activities. *Child Development, 68*, 897-907.

Garcia Coll, C., & Pachter, L. M.(2002). Ethnic minority parenting. In M. Bornstein (Ed.), *Handbook of parenting* (2nd ed., Vol. 4, pp. 1-20). Mahwah, NJ: Lawrence Erlbaum Associates.

Ge, X., Conger, R. D., & Elder, H. H. (2001). Pubertal transition, stressful life events, and the emergence of gender differences in adolescent depressive symptoms. *Developmental Psychology, 37*, 404-417.

Ge, X., Kim, I. J., Brody, G., Conger, R. D., Simons, R. L., Gibbons, F. X., et al. (2003). It's about timing and change: Pubertal transition effects on symptoms of major depression among

African American youths. *Developmental Psychology, 39*, 430–439.

Gerard, J. M., & Buehler, C. (in press). Cumulative environmental risk and youth maladjustment: The role of youth attributes. *Child Development.*

Girotto, V., Gilly, M., Blaye, A., & Light, P. (1989). Children's performance in the selection task: Plausibility and familiarity. *British Journal of Psychology, 80*, 79–95.

Gottfried, A. E., Fleming, J. S., & Gottfried, A. W. (2001). Continuity of academic intrinsic motivation from childhood through late adolescence: A longitudinal study. *Journal of Educational Psychology, 93*, 3–13.

Graber, J. A., Petersen, A., & Brooks-Gunn, J. (1996). Pubertal processes: Methods, measures, and models. In A. Graber, J. Brooks-Gunn, & A. Petersen (Eds.), *Transitions through adolescence: Interpersonal domains and contexts* (pp. 23–53). Mahwah, NJ: Lawrence Erlbaum Associates.

Graham, S. (1994). Motivation in African Americans. *Review of Educational Research, 64*, 55–118.

Graham, S., & Taylor, A. Z. (2002). Ethnicity, gender, and the development of achievement values. In A. Wigfield & J. S. Eccles (Eds.), *Development of achievement motivation* (pp. 121–146). San Diego, CA: Academic Press.

Graham, S., Taylor, A. Z., & Hudley, C. (1998). Exploring achievement values among ethnic minority early adolescents. *Journal of Educational Psychology, 90*, 606–620.

Guay, F., Marsh, H. W., & Boivin, M. (2003). Academic self-concept and academic achievement: Developmental perspectives on their causal ordering. *Journal of Educational Psychology, 95*, 124–135.

Haars, V. J., & Mason, E. J. (1986). Children's understanding of class inclusion and their ability to reason with implication. *International Journal of Behavioral Development, 9*, 45–63.

Hall, G. S. (1904). *Adolescence: Its psychology and its relations to anthropology, sex, crime, religion, and education.* New York: Appleton.

Halpern-Felsher, B. L., & Cauffman, E. (2001). Costs and benefits of a decision: Decision-making competence in adolescents and adults. *Journal of Applied Developmental Psychology, 22*, 257–276.

Harackiewicz, J. M., Barron, K. E., Pintrich, P. R., Elliot, A. J., & Thrash, T. M. (2002). Revision of achievement goal theory: Necessary and illuminating. *Journal of Educational Psychology, 94*, 638–645.

Harkness, S., & Super, C. M. (2002). Culture and parenting. In M. Bornstein (Ed.), *Handbook of parenting* (2nd ed., Vol. 2, pp. 253–280). Mahwah, NJ: Lawrence Erlbaum Associates.

Harris, J. R. (1995). Where is the child's environment? A group socialization theory of development. *Psychological Review, 102*, 458–489.

Harris, J. R. (1998). *The nurture assumption: Why children turn out the way they do.* New York: Free Press.

Harter, S. (1981). A new self-report scale of intrinsic versus extrinsic orientation in the classroom: Motivational and informational components. *Developmental Psychology, 17*, 300–312.

Harter, S., Whitesell, N., & Kowalski, P. (1992). Individual differences in the effects of educational transitions on children's perceptions of competence and motivational orientation. *American Educational Research Journal, 29*, 777–808.

Harwood, R., Leyendecker, Carlson, V., Asencio, M., & Miller, A. (2002). Parenting among Latino families in the U. S. In M. Bornstein (Ed.), *Handbook of parenting* (2nd ed., Vol. 4, pp. 21–46). Mahwah NJ: Lawrence Erlbaum Associates.

Hedelin, L. & Sjoberg, L. (1989). The development of interests in the Swedish comprehensive school. *European Journal of Psychology of Education, 4*, 17–35.

Heller, K. A., & Ziegler, A. (1996). Gender differences in mathematics and the sciences: Can attributional retraining improve the performance of gifted females? *Gifted Child Quarterly, 40*, 200–210.

Helmke, A. (1993). The development of learning from kindergarten to fifth grade. *German Journal of Educational Psychology, 7*, 77–86.

Herman-Giddens, M., Slora, E., Wasserman, R., Bourdony, C., Bhapkar, M., Koch, G., & Hasemeier, C. (1997). Secondary sexual characteristics and menses in young girls seen in office practice: A study from the Pediatric Research in Office Settings Network. *Pediatrics, 88*, 505–512.

Hetherington, E. M., & Stanley-Hagan, M. (2002). Parenting in divorced and remarried families. In M. Bornstein (Ed.), *Handbook of parenting* (2nd ed., Vol. 3, pp. 287–316). Mahwah, NJ: Lawrence Erlbaum Associates.

Higgins, E. T., & Parsons, J. E. (1983). Social cognition and the social life of the child: Stages as subcultures. In E. T. Higgins, D. W. Ruble, & W. W. Hartup (Eds.). *Social cognition and social behavior: Developmental issues.* New York: Cambridge University Press.

Hill, J. P., & Lynch, M. E. (1983). The intensification of gender-related role expectations during early adolescence. In J. Brooks-Gunn & A. C. Petersen (Eds.), *Girls at puberty* (pp. 201–228). New York: Plenum.

Huston, A. C., McLoyd, V., & Coll, C. G. (1994). Children and poverty: Issues in contemporary research. *Child Development, 65*, 275–282.

Irvin, J. L. (Ed.). (1992). *Transforming middle level education: Perspectives and possibilities.* Boston: Allyn and Bacon.

Jacobs, J. E. (1991). Influence of gender stereotypes on parent and child mathematics attitude. *Journal of Educational Psychology, 83*, 518–527.

Jacobs, J. E., Lanza, S., Osgood, D. W., Eccles, J. S., & Wigfield, A. (2002). Ontogeny of children's self-beliefs: Gender and domain differences across grades one through 12. *Child Development, 73*, 509–527.

Janveau-Brennan, G., & Markovits, H. (1999). The development of reasoning with causal conditionals. *Developmental Psychology, 35*, 904–911.

Johnson, B., & Onwuegbuzie, A. J. (2004). Mixed methods research: A research paradigm whose time has come. *Educational Researcher, 33*, 14–26.

Juvonen, J., & Graham, S. (Eds.). (2001). *Peer harassment in school: The plight of the vulnerable and victimized.* New York: Guilford Press.

Juvonen, J., Le, V. N., Kaganoff, T., Augustine, C., & Constant, L. (2004). *Focus on the wonder years: Challenges facing the American middle school.* Santa Monica, CA: Rand Corporation.

Juvonen, J., Nishina, A., & Graham, S. (2001). Self-views and peer perceptions of victim status among early adolescents. In J. Juvonen & S. Graham (Eds.), *Peer harassment in school: The plight of the vulnerable and victimized* (pp. 105–124). New York: Guilford Press.

Kao, G., & Tienda, M. (1995). Optimism and achievement: The educational performance of immigrant youth. *Social Science Quarterly, 76,* 1–19.

Kaplan, A., & Middleton, M. J. (2002). Should childhood be a journey or a race? Response to Harackiewicz et al. (2002). *Journal of Educational Psychology, 94,* 646–648.

Keating, D. P. (1990). Adolescent thinking. In S. S. Feldman & G. R. Elliott (Eds.), *At the threshold: The developing adolescent* (pp. 54–89). Cambridge, MA: Harvard University Press.

Keating, D. P. (2004). Cognitive and brain development. In R. M. Lerner & L. D. Steinberg (Eds.), *Handbook of adolescent psychology* (2nd ed., pp. 45–84). New York: Wiley.

Kindermann, T. A. (1993). Natural peer groups as contexts for individual development: The case of children's motivation in school. *Developmental Psychology, 29,* 970–977.

Klaczynski, P. A. (1993). Reasoning schema effects on adolescent rule acquisition and transfer. *Journal of Educational Psychology, 85,* 679–692.

Klaczynski, P. A., Byrnes, J. E., & Jacobs, J. E. (2001). Introduction to the special issue on the development of decision-making. *Journal of Applied Developmental Psychology, 22,* 225–236.

Klaczynski, P. A., & Narasimham, G. (1998). Representations as mediators of adolescent deductive reasoning. *Developmental Psychology, 34,* 865–881.

Kuhn, D., Garcia-Mila, M., Zohar, A., & Andersen, C. (1995). Strategies of knowledge acquisition. *Monographs of the Society for Research in Child Development, 60,* v–128.

Lapsley, D., & Murphy, M. (1985). Another look at the theoretical assumptions of adolescent egocentrism. *Developmental Review, 5,* 201–217.

Lee, S. J. (1994). Beyond the model-minority stereotype: Voices of high- and low-achieving Asian American students. *Anthropology & Education Quarterly, 25,* 413–429.

Lee, V. E., & Bryk, A. S. (1989). A multilevel model of the social distribution of high school achievement. *Sociology of Education, 62,* 172–192.

Lee, V., & Smith, J. B. (2001). *Restructuring high schools for equity and excellence: What works. Sociology of education series.* New York: Teachers' College Press.

Lerner, R. (1986). *Concepts and theories of human development.* New York: Random House.

Lerner, R. M., & Steinberg, L. (Eds.). (2004). *Handbook of adolescent psychology* (2nd ed.). New York: Wiley.

Lewis, C. (1981). How do adolescents approach decisions: Changes over grades seven to twelve and policy implications. *Child Development, 52,* 538–544.

Lipsitz, J., Mizell, M. H., Jackson, A. W., & Austin, L. M. (1997). Speaking with one voice: A manifesto for middle-grades reform. *Phi Delta Kappan,* 533–540.

Lounsbury, J. H., Marani, J. V., & Compton, M. F. (1980). *The middle school in profile: A day in the seventh grade.* Fairborn, OH: National Middle School Association.

Mac Iver, D. J., & Epstein, J. L. (1993). Middle grades research: Not yet mature, but no longer a child. *Elementary School Journal, 93,* 519–533.

Mac Iver, D. J., & Plank, J. B. (1997). Improving urban schools: Developing the talents of students placed at risk. In J. L. Irvin (Ed.), *What current research says to the middle level practitioner* (pp. 243–256). Columbus, OH: National Middle School Association.

Mac Iver, D. J., Reuman, D. A., & Main, S. R. (1995). Social structuring of school: Studying what is, illuminating what could be. In M. R. Rosenzweig & L. W. Porter (Eds.), *Annual Review of Psychology, 46,* 375–400.

Mac Iver, D. J., Young, E. M., & Washburn, B. (2002). Instructional practices and motivation during middle school (with special attention to science). In A. Wigfield & J. S. Eccles (Eds.), *Development of achievement motivation* (pp. 333–351). San Diego, CA: Academic Press.

Maehr, M. L., & Midgley, C. 1996). *Transforming school cultures.* Boulder, CO: Westview Press.

Magnuson, K. A., & Duncan, G. (2002). Parents in poverty. In M. Bornstein (Ed.), *Handbook of parenting* (2nd Ed., Vol. 4, pp. 95–122). Mahwah, NJ: Lawrence Erlbaum Associates.

Malina, R. M. (1990). Physical growth and performance during the transitional years (9–16). In R. Montemayor, G. R. Adams, & T. P. Gullotta (Eds.), *From childhood to adolescence: A transitional period* (pp. 41–62). Newbury Park, CA: Sage.

Marcia, J. E. (1980). Ego identity development. In J. Adelson (Ed.), *Handbook of adolescent psychology* (pp. 159–187). New York: Wiley.

Marcia, J. E. (2002). Identity and psychosocial development in adulthood: *Identity: An International Journal of Theory and Research, 2,* 7–28.

Markovits, H., & Barrouillet, P. (2002). The development of conditional reasoning: A mental model account. *Developmental Review, 22,* 5–36.

Markovits, H., & Vachon, R. (1990). Conditional reasoning, representation, and abstraction. *Developmental Psychology, 26,* 942–951.

Marsh, H. W. (1989). Age and sex effects in multiple dimensions of self-concept: Preadolescence to early adulthood. *Journal of Educational Psychology, 81,* 417–430.

Marsh, H. W. (1990). Causal ordering of academic self-concept and academic achievement: A multivariate, longitudinal panel analysis. *Journal of Educational Psychology, 82,* 646–656.

Marsh, H. W., & Ayotte, V. (2003). Do multiple dimensions of self-concept become more differentiated with age: The differential distinctiveness hypothesis. *Journal of Educational Psychology, 95,* 687–706.

Marsh, H. W., & Yeung, A. S. (1997). Causal ordering of academic self-concept on academic achievement: Structural equation models of longitudinal data. *Journal of Educational Psychology, 89,* 41-54.

McAdoo, H. P. (2002). African American parenting. In M. Bornstein (Ed.), *Handbook of parenting* (2nd ed., Vol. 4, pp. 47-58). Mahwah, NJ: Lawrence Erlbaum Associates.

McHale, S. M., Shanahan, L., Updegraff, K. A., Crouter, A. C., & Booth, A. (2004). Developmental and individual differences in girls' sex-typed activities in middle childhood and adolescence. *Child Development, 75,* 1575-1593.

McLoyd, V. C. (1990). The impact of economic hardship on black families and children: Psychological distress, parenting, and socioemotional development. *Child Development, 61,* 311-346.

McCord, J. (1990). Problem behaviors. In S. S. Feldman & G. R. Elliott (Eds.), *At the threshold: The developing adolescent* (pp. 414-430). Cambridge, MA: Harvard University Press.

Meece, J. L., & Holt, K. H. (1993). A pattern analysis of students' achievement goals. *Journal of Educational Psychology, 85,* 582.

Meece, J. L., Blumenfeld, P. B., & Hoyle, R. H. (1988). Students' goal orientations and cognitive engagement in classroom activities. *Journal of Educational Psychology, 80,* 514-523.

Meece, J. L., & Kurtz-Costes, B. (2000). Introduction: The schooling of ethnic minority children and youth. *Educational Psychologist, 36,* 1-8.

Meece, J. L., Wigfield, A., & Eccles, J. S. (1990). Predictors of math anxiety and its consequences for young adolescents' course enrollment intentions and performances in mathematics. *Journal of Educational Psychology, 82,* 60-70.

Midgley, C. (2002). *Goals, goal structures, and patterns of adaptive learning.* Mahwah, NJ: Lawrence Erlbaum Associates.

Midgley, C., & Edelin, K. C. (1998). Middle school reform and early adolescent well-being: The good news and the bad. *Educational Psychologist, 33,* 195-206.

Midgley, C., Kaplan, A., Middleton, M. (2001). Performance approach goals: Good for what, for whom, and under what circumstances? *Journal of Educational Psychology, 93,* 77-86.

Miller, D. C., & Byrnes, J. P. (2001). Adolescents' decision-making in social situations: A self-regulation perspective. *Journal of Applied Developmental Psychology, 22,* 237-256.

Moshman, D. (1998). Cognitive development beyond childhood. In W. Damon (Series Ed.), D. Kuhn & R. S. Siegler (Volume Eds.), *Handbook of child psychology* (5th ed., Vol. 2). New York: Wiley.

Moshman, D., & Franks, B. A. (1986). Development of the concept of inferential validity. *Child Development, 57,* 153-165.

National Research Council (2004). *Engaging schools: Fostering high school students' motivation to learn.* Washington, DC: National Academies Press.

Neimark, E. D. (1983). Adolescent thought: Transition to formal operations. In B. Wolman (Ed.), *Handbook of developmental psychology* (pp. 486-502). Englewood Cliffs, NJ: Prentice-Hall.

Oldfather, P., & McLaughlin, J. (1993). Gaining and losing voice: A longitudinal study of students' continuing impulse to learn across elementary and middle school contexts. *Research in Middle Level Education, 17,* 1-25.

Ormond, C., Luszcz, M. A., Mann, L., & Beswick, G. (1991). A metacognitive analysis of decision-making in adolescence. *Journal of Adolescence, 14,* 275-291.

Oyserman, D., Harrison, K., & Bybee, D. (2001). Can racial identity be promotive of academic efficacy? *International Journal of Behavioral Development, 25,* 379-385.

Padilla, F. (1992). *The gang as an American enterprise.* New Brunswick, NJ: Rutgers University Press.

Padilla, A. M. & Gonzalez, R. (2001). Academic performance of immigrant and U.S. born Mexican-heritage students: Effects of schooling in Mexico and Bilingual/English language instruction. *American Educational Research Journal, 38,* 727-742.

Pekrun, R. H. (1993). Facets of adolescents' academic motivation: A longitudinal expectancy-value approach. In P. R. Pintrich & M. L. Maehr (Eds.), *Advances in motivation and achievement* (Vol. 8, pp. 139-189). Greenwich, CT: JAI Press.

Perry, T. B. (1987). *The relation of adolescents' self-perceptions to their social relationships.* Unpublished doctoral dissertation, University of Oklahoma.

Petersen, A. (1985). Pubertal development as a cause of disturbance: Myths, realities, and unanswered question. *Genetic, Social and General Psychology Monographs, 111,* 205-232.

Phinney, J. S. (1996). When we talk about American ethnic groups, what do we mean? *American Psychologist, 51,* 918-927.

Piaget, J., & Inhelder, B. (1973). *Memory and intelligence.* London: Routledge and Kegan Paul.

Pintrich, P. R. (2000a). An achievement goal theory perspective on issues in motivation terminology, theory, and research. *Contemporary Educational Psychology, 25,* 406-422.

Pintrich, P. R. (2000b). Multiple pathways, multiple goals: The role of goal orientation in learning and achievement. *Journal of Educational Psychology, 92,* 54-555.

Pintrich, P. R. (2003). A motivational science perspective on the role of student motivation in learning and teaching contexts. *Journal of Educational Psychology, 93,* 667-686.

Pintrich, P. R., & De Groot, E. (1990). Motivational and self-regulated learning components of classroom academic performance. *Journal of Educational Psychology, 82,* 33-40.

Pintrich, P. R., & Schunk, D. H. (2002). *Motivation in education: Theory, research, and applications* (2nd ed.). Englewood Cliffs, NJ: Prentice-Hall.

Pintrich, P. R., & Zusho, A. (2002). The development of academic self-regulation: The role of cognitive and motivational factors. In A. Wigfield & J. S. Eccles (Eds.), *Development of achievement motivation* (pp. 249-284). San Diego, CA: Academic Press.

Reese, C. M., Miller, K. E., Mazzeo, J., & Dossey, J. A. (1997). *The NAEP 1996 Mathematics Report Card for the Nation and the States.* Washington, DC: U.S. Department of Education, Office of Educational Research and Improvement, National Center for Education Statistics.

Roderick, M., & Camburn, E. (1999). Risk and recovery from course failure in the early years of high school. *American Educational Research Journal, 36,* 303–343.

Roeser, R., Eccles, J. S., & Sameroff, J. (1998). Academic and emotional functioning in early adolescence: Longitudinal relations, patterns, and prediction by experience in middle school. *Development and Psychopathology, 10,* 321–352.

Roeser, R. W., & Lau, S. (2002). On academic identity formation in middle school settings during early adolescence. In T. M. Brinthaupt & R. P. Lipka (Eds.), *Understanding early adolescent self and identity: Applications and interventions* (pp. 91–131). Albany: State University of New York Press.

Rowe, D. (1994). *The limits of family influence: Genes, experience, and behavior.* New York: Guilford Press.

Rubin, K. H., Bukowski, W., & Parker, J. G. (1998). Peer interactions, relationships, and groups. In W. Damon (Series Ed.) & N. Eisenberg (Volume Ed.), *Handbook of child psychology* (5th ed., Vol. III, pp. 619–700). New York: Wiley.

Rubin, K. H., Coplan, R., Chen, X., Buskirk, A. A., & Wojslawowicz, J. C. (2005). Peer relationships in childhood. In M. Bornstein & M. Lamb (Eds.), *Developmental science: An advanced textbook* (5th ed., pp. 469–512). Mahwah, NJ: Erlbaum.

Ruble, D. N., & Martin, C. L. (1998). Gender development. In W. Damon (Series Ed.) & N. Eisenberg (Vol. Ed.), *Handbook of child psychology* (5th ed., Vol. 3, pp. 933–1016). New York: Wiley.

Rumberger, R. W. (1987). High school dropouts: A review of issues and evidence. *Review of Educational Research, 57,* 101–122.

Ryan, A. M. (2001). The peer group as a context for the development of young adolescents' motivation and achievement. *Child Development, 72,* 1135–1150.

Ryan, R. M., & Deci, E. (2000). Self determination theory and the facilitation of intrinsic motivation, social development, and well-being. *American Psychologist, 55,* 68–78.

Sameroff, A., Gutman, L. M., & Peck S. C. (2003). Adaptation among youth facing multiple risks: Prospective research findings. In S.S. Luthar (Ed.), *Resilience and vulnerability: Adaptation in the context of childhood adversities* (pp. 364–391). Cambridge, UK: Cambridge University Press.

Sanders, M. G., & Epstein, J. L. (2002). Building school-family–community partnerships in middle and high schools. In M. G. Sanders (Ed.), *Schooling students placed at risk: Research, policy, and practice in the education of poor and minority adolescents* (pp. 339–361). Mahwah, NJ: Lawrence Erlbaum Associates.

Savin-Williams, R. C, & Berndt, T. J. (1990). Friendship and peer relations. In S. S. Feldman & G. R. Elliott (Eds.), *At the threshold: The developing adolescent* (pp. 277–307). Cambridge, MA: Harvard University Press.

Schunk, D. H. (1994). Self-regulation of self-efficacy and attributions in academic settings. In D. H. Schunk & B. J. Zimmerman (Eds.), *Self-regulation of learning and performance.* Hillsdale, NJ: Lawrence Erlabaum Associates.

Shell, D. F., Colvin, C., & Bruning, R. H. (1995). Self-efficacy, attribution, and outcome expectancy mechanisms in reading and writing achievement: Grade-level and achievement-level differences. *Journal of Educational Psychology, 87,* 386–398.

Simmons, R. G., & Blyth, D. A. (1987). *Moving into adolescence: The impact of pubertal change and school context.* Hawthorn, NY: Aldine de Gruyter.

Simmons, R. G., Blyth D. A., Van Cleave, E. F., & Bush, D. (1979). Entry into early adolescence: The impact of school structure, puberty, and early dating on self-esteem. *American Sociological Review, 44,* 948–967.

Simmons, R., G., Burgeson, R., Carlton-Ford, S., & Blyth, D. (1978). The impact of cumulative change in adolescence. *Child Development, 58,* 1220–1234.

Skaalvik, E. M. (1997). Self-enhancing and self-defeating ego orientation: Relations with task and avoidance orientation, achievement, self-perceptions, and anxiety. *Journal of Educational Psychology, 89,* 71–81.

Slaughter-Defoe, D. T., Nakagawa, K., Takanishi, R., & Johnson, D. J. (1990). Toward cultural/ecological perspectives on schooling and achievement in African- and Asian-American children. *Child Development, 61,* 363–383.

Spencer, M. B., & Markstrom-Adams, C. (1990). Identity processes among racial and ethnic minority children in America. *Child Development, 61,* 290–310.

Steele, C. (1992, April). Race and the schooling of black Americans. *Atlantic Monthly.*

Steele, C. (1997). A threat in the air: How stereotypes shape intellectual identity and performance. *American Psychologist, 52,* 613–629.

Steele, C., & Aronson, J. (1995). Stereotype threat and the intellectual test performance of African Americans. *Journal of Personality and Social Psychology, 69,* 797–811.

Steinberg, L., & Silk, J. S. (2002). Parenting adolescents. In M. H. Bornstein (Ed.), *Handbook of parenting* (2nd ed., pp. 103–133. Mahwah, NJ: Lawrence Erlbaum Associates.

Stipek, D., & Mac Iver, D. (1989). Developmental change in children's assessment of intellectual competence. *Child Development, 60,* 521–538.

Sullivan, H. S. (1953). *The interpersonal theory of psychiatry.* New York: Norton.

Susman, E. J., & Rogol, A. (2004). Puberty and psychological development. In R. M. Lerner & L. D. Steinberg (Eds.), *Handbook of adolescent psychology* (2nd Ed., pp. 15–44). New York: Wiley.

Swanson, H. L. (1999). What develops in working memory? A life span perspective. *Developmental Psychology, 35,* 986–1000.

Tatum, B. D. (1997). *"Why are all the Black kids sitting together in the cafeteria?" and other conversations about race.* New York: Basic Books.

Thorkildsen, T. A., & Nicholls, J. G. (1998). Fifth graders achievement orientations and beliefs: Individual and classroom differences. *Journal of Educational Psychology, 90,* 179–201.

Turner, J. C., Midgley, C., Meyer, D. K., Gheen, M., Anderman, E. M., Kang, Y., & Patrick, H. (2002). The classroom environment and students' reports of avoidance strategies in mathematics: A multimethod study. *Journal of Educational Psychology, 94,* 88–106.

Valentine, J. C., DuBois, D. L., & Cooper, H. (2004). The relation between self-beliefs and academic achievement: A meta-analytic review. *Educational Psychologist, 39, 111–134.*

Vallerand, R. J., Fortier, M. S., & Guay, F. (1997). Self-determination and persistence in a real-life setting: Toward a motivational model of high school dropout. *Journal of Personality & Social Psychology, 72,* 1161–1176.

Ward, S. L., Byrnes, J. P., & Overton, W. F. (1990). Organization of knowledge and conditional reasoning. *Journal of Educational Psychology, 82,* 832–837.

Ward, S. L., & Overton, W. F. (1990). Semantic familiarity, relevance, and the development of deductive reasoning. *Developmental Psychology, 26,* 488–493.

Waterman, A. (1982). Identity development from adolescence to adulthood: An extension of theory and a review of research. *Developmental Psychology, 18,* 341–358.

Waterman, A. S. (1999). Issues of identity formation revisited. *Developmental Review, 19,* 462–497.

Watt, H. M. G. (2004). Development of adolescents' self-perceptions, values, and task perceptions according to gender and domain in 7th through 11th-grade Australian students. *Child Development, 75,* 1556–1574.

Wentzel, K. R. (1989). Adolescent classroom grades, standards for performance, and academic achievement: An interactionist perspective. *Journal of Educational Psychology, 81,* 131–142.

Wentzel, K. R. (1994). Relations of social goal pursuit to social acceptance, and perceived social support. *Journal of Educational Psychology, 86,* 173–180.

Wentzel, K. R. (1996). Social goals and social relationships as motivators of school adjustment. In J. Juvonen & K. R. Wentzel (Eds.), *Social motivation: Understanding school adjustment* (pp. 226–247). New York: Cambridge University Press.

Wentzel, K. (2002a). Are effective teachers like good parents? Teaching styles and student adjustment in early adolescence. *Child Development, 73,* 287–301.

Wentzel, K. R. (2002b). The contribution of social goal setting to children's school adjustment. In A. Wigfield & J. S. Eccles (Eds.), *Development of achievement motivation* (pp. 221–246). San Diego, CA: Academic Press.

Wigfield, A. (1994). The role of children's achievement values in the regulation of their learning outcomes. In D. H. Schunk & B. J. Zimmerman (Eds.), *Self-regulation of learning and performance: Issues and educational applications.* Hillsdale, NJ: Lawrence Erlbaum Associates.

Wigfield, A., Battle, A., Keller, L., & Eccles, J. S. (2002). Sex differences in motivation, self-concept, career aspirations, and career choice: Implications for cognitive development. In A. McGillicuddy-De Lisi & R. De Lisi (Eds.), *Biology, society, and behavior: The development of sex differences in cognition* (pp. 93–124). Greenwich, CT: Ablex.

Wigfield, A., & Eccles, J. S. (1992). The development of achievement task values: A theoretical analysis. *Developmental Review, 12,* 265–310.

Wigfield, A., & Eccles, J. S. (2000). Expectancy–value theory of motivation. *Contemporary Educational Psychology, 25,* 68–81.

Wigfield, A., & Eccles, J. S. (2002a). Children's motivation during the middle school years. In J. Aronson (Ed.), *Improving academic achievement: Contributions of social psychology.* San Diego, CA: Academic Press.

Wigfield, A., & Eccles, J. S. (2002b). The development of competence beliefs and values from childhood through adolescence. In A. Wigfield & J. S. Eccles (Eds.), *Development of achievement motivation* (pp. 92–120). San Diego, CA: Academic Press.

Wigfield, A., Eccles, J., Mac Iver, D., Reuman, D., & Midgley, C. (1991). Transitions at early adolescence: Changes in children's domain-specific self-perceptions and general self-esteem across the transition to junior high school. *Developmental Psychology, 27,* 552–565.

Wigfield, A., Eccles, J. S., & Pintrich, P. (1996). Development between the ages of 11 and 25. In D. Berliner & R. Calfee (Eds.), *Handbook of educational psychology.* New York: Macmillan.

Wigfield, A., Eccles, J. S., & Rodriguez, D. (1998). The development of children's motivation in school contexts. In. A. Iran-Nejad & P. D. Pearson (Eds.), *Review of research in education* (Vol. 23, pp. 73–118). Washington, DC: American Educational Research Association.

Wigfield, A., Eccles, J. S., Schiefele, U., Roeser, R. & Davis-Kean, P. (in press). Development of achievement motivation. In W. Damon and N. Eisenberg (Eds.), *Handbook of child psychology* (6th ed.). New York: Wiley.

Wigfield, A., Eccles, J. S., Yoon, K. S., Harold, R. D., Arbreton, A., Freedman-Doan, C., & Blumenfeld, P. C. (1997). Changes in children's competence beliefs and subjective task values across the elementary school years: A three-year study. *Journal of Educational Psychology, 89,* 451–469.

Wigfield, A., Galper, A., Denton, K., & Seefeldt, C. (1999). Teachers' beliefs about former Head Start and non–Head Start first grade children's motivation, performance, and future educational prospects. J*ournal of Educational Psychology, 91,* 98–104.

Wigfield, A., & Karpathian, M. (1991). Who am I and what can I do? Children's self-concepts and motivation in achievement situations. *Educational Psychologist, 26,* 233–262.

Wigfield, A., & Wagner, A. L. (2005). Competence and motivation during adolescence. In A. Elliott and C. Dweck (Eds.), *Handbook of competence and motivation* (pp. 222–239). New York: Guilford Press.

Winston, C., Eccles, J. S., Senior, A. M., & Vida, M. (1997). The utility of an expectancy/value model of achievement for understanding academic performance and self-esteem in African-American and European-American adolescents. *Zeitschrift für Pädagogische Psychologie (German Journal of Educational Psychology), 11,* 177–186.

Wolters, C. A. (2003). Regulation of motivation: Evaluating an underemphasized aspect of self-regulated learning. *Educational Psychologist, 38,* 189–206.

Wolters, C. (2004). Advancing achievement goal theory: Using goal structures and goal orientations to predict students' motivation, cognition, and achievement. *Journal of Educational Psychology, 96,* 236–250.

Wolters, C., Yu, S., & Pintrich, P. R. (1996). The relation between goal orientation and students' motivational beliefs and self-regulated learning. *Learning and Individual Differences, 8,* 211–238.

Zald, D. H., & Iacono, W. G. (1998). The development of spatial working memory abilities. *Developmental Neuropsychology, 14,* 563–578.

Zimmerman, B. J. (2000). Attaining self-regulation: A social cognitive perspective. In M. Boekaerts, P. R. Pintrich, & M. Zeidner (Eds.), *Handbook of self-regulation* (pp. 13–39). Mahwah, NJ: Lawrence Erlbaum Associates.

Zimmerman, B. J., & Martinez-Pons, M. (2000). Student differences in self-regulated learning: Relating grade, sex, and giftedness to self-efficacy and strategy use. *Journal of Educational Psychology, 73,* 485–493.

·6·

ADULT DEVELOPMENT, SCHOOLING, AND THE TRANSITION TO WORK

M Cecil Smith
Northern Illinois University

Thomas G. Reio, Jr.
University of Louisville

PUTTING ADULT DEVELOPMENT IN CONTEXT

This chapter describes adult development from the post-high school and college years through midlife and into late adulthood. We examine the historical connections of educational psychology to the study of adult development and describe some of the theoretical and empirical work that links educational psychology and adult education. A chapter devoted to adult development is vital in the *Handbook of Educational Psychology*, and its inclusion acknowledges the historical and theoretical connections of our discipline to the study of development and learning in the adult years.

The bulk of research on adult development has examined changes in cognitive and intellectual functioning with age. Whereas studies in the first half of the 20th century depicted losses in cognitive skills with age as both inevitable and irreversible, cognitive aging research from the mid-1960s to today, which has taken into account the interactive effects of age, cohort, and time of measurement, shows that cognitive declines occur much later in life and have little functional impact until adults are well into their 70s (Schaie, 1996). Further, training studies demonstrate that cognitive declines can, in most cases, be stopped or slowed, and that some cognitive abilities can

be improved. This work has important implications for adult educators who work with older adults.

As young adults mature, they are socialized into and acquire a number of important life roles, including worker, partner, parent and caregiver, and community member. Several important theories of adult development have sought to explain the developmental tasks that adults must confront and accomplish in order to lead emotionally satisfying lives characterized by healthy relationships, productive work, a sense of ego integrity, and personal fulfillment. These theories also attempt to explain how personality evolves through adulthood. Most prominent are the writings of Erik Erikson (1968) and Daniel Levinson (e.g., Levinson, Darrow, Klein, Levinson, & McKee, 1978; Levinson & Levinson, 1996). As yet, however, no one has proposed a comprehensive theory of adult development, in large part because of the complexity and variability of adult life.

The college years are a period of profound intellectual growth, career exploration, goal setting, and planning for the future. A number of investigators have examined the effects of higher education on college students (Pascarella & Terenzini, 1991). College has traditionally been considered to be a moratorium period for youth in western societies (Erikson, 1968). In this traditional conception, the 17- to 22-year-old adult who is enrolled full time in college is considered to be free from many of the role expectations of other young adults in society (e.g., finding work, settling down, and marrying). However, society has changed dramatically in the decades since Erikson described the moratorium experience. Although many more young people are going to college than ever before, their experiences during college are not uniform. Fewer students can expect to graduate in 4 years (Arnone, 2004). Students today are much more likely to enter, leave, and return to school, with intervals of work or military service—chiefly to pay for tuition—and have other out-of-school experiences. Also, many more older and nontraditional students are enrolling in college than in past decades.

A large and growing percentage of college students are adults who are pursuing education and advanced degrees part time. In fact, students in the traditional 18- to 22-year-old age group accounted for slightly fewer than one-fourth of all postsecondary students in 2001 (U.S. Department of Education, 2002a). Postsecondary institutions have been forced to respond to these changing demographics over the past two decades. As a result, they have begun to recognize the need to understand the characteristics of adult students and of adult development in general.

Continuing or lifelong education, as it occurs within formal educational institutions and through informal, self-directed activities, is increasingly important in modern adult life. Adults returning to school are seeking new skills to remain employable in rapidly changing work environments, to expand their intellectual horizons, and simply to remain informed of and engaged in community life. Because educational psychologists are primarily concerned with learning and development in classrooms and schools, we address the significant role of schooling across the adult life span in this chapter. We also examine investigations of how effectively the population of low-literate and illiterate adults develops reading, writing, and basic mathematics skills within the variety of adult basic education programs. Although many of these programs are found in community colleges throughout the United States, others are located within local school districts, community-based organizations, libraries, public housing communities, and prisons (Morest, 2004). Literacy is assumed to contribute to adults' cognitive (West, Stanovich, & Mitchell, 1993), social, and aesthetic development (Barton & Hamilton, 1998) and is deemed to be essential for living in a rapidly changing, technological, information-rich society.

Adult learning and development also takes place within, and is influenced by the activities of, the workplace (Reio & Wiswell, 2000). Navigating the transition from high school or college to the workplace is a difficult

developmental task for older adolescents and young adults. Several avenues are possible, including vocational training programs, apprenticeships, and the military. Making the transition from the classroom to the workplace is not always smooth and uneventful. As Mortimer and Johnson (1998) note, although schooling contributes to the preparation of youth for future work roles, being a student is fundamentally different from being a worker. The task requirements of academic work differ markedly from the skills required in most jobs (Mikulecky, 1982). Youth jobs in high school and during the college years can best be understood as a bridge between education and the adult world of work. Social scientists have raised a number of questions about the effects of youth work on subsequent adult development (Mortimer, Finch, Ryu, Shanahan, & Call, 1996). Does part-time work during high school, for example, contribute to health-risk behaviors such as smoking and drinking? Does it promote engagement in delinquent behaviors such as stealing from employers? More positively, does working during high school and college help youth and young adults develop appropriate attitudes toward work and good work habits? Unfortunately, most studies of youth work are cross-sectional, so few data on outcomes in adulthood are available. We will further examine the transition from school to work later in this chapter.

Historical Foundations

The roots of educational psychology's interest in adult development can be traced as far back as World War I, when the American Psychological Association appointed a committee of prominent psychologists, led by Robert Yerkes, to create mental aptitude measures for the war effort (Anastasi, 1988). These tests, which came to be called the Army Alpha and Army Beta tests, were designed to classify young adult conscripts with regard to their intellectual abilities. Educational psychologists' interest in adult development, in fact, has a history nearly as lengthy as that of the discipline. Among others, both G. Stanley Hall and Edward L. Thorndike—pioneering founders of developmental and educational psychology, respectively—took an active interest in adult development late in their careers. This interest coincided with their own aging experiences. Hall published *Senescence: The Second Half of Life* in 1922, marking what some have called the beginning of the psychological study of aging (Birren & Schroots, 1996). Hall referred to middle life, which he defined as extending from 25 to 45 years of age, as the period when adults' abilities are at their apex. Middle adulthood—what Hall considered the prime of life—is followed by senescence, beginning in the early forties (although somewhat earlier in women), and finally, senectitude or old age proper.

Thorndike and his associates' (Thorndike, Bregman, Tilton, & Woodyard, 1928) work on adult learning was instrumental in garnering interest in the nascent field of adult education (Hiemstra, 1998), and he served as president of the American Association of Adult Education in 1934. Based on observations from a number of experiments with adults of different ages, Thorndike et al. claimed learning abilities did not decline until age 35, and only negligibly declined each year thereafter. This view was a somewhat more rosy characterization of adult cognitive development than the prevailing notion that intellectual abilities peaked in early adulthood and then began a steady deterioration throughout life (Jones & Conrad, 1933).

Although there was a modest amount of work in psychological aging taking place in the 1930s, according to Birren and Schroots (1996), scientific interest in understanding the processes of adult aging grew rapidly in the late 1940s. Coinciding with this scientific activity in the postwar years, there was also a dramatic increase in the numbers of adults enrolling in postsecondary education, in part as a result of the GI Bill (Greenberg, 1997). Participation in all forms of adult education doubled in size from 1924 to 1950 (Pressey & Kuhlen, 1957). Despite this increase in the adult population within postsecondary institutions, university and college administrators were still primarily focused on meeting the needs of traditional 18- to 22-year-old students. Well into the 1980s, educational psychologists had not yet rediscovered adults and adult students as a focus of study, having largely ignored or forgotten the work of Hall and Thorndike and a handful of others only a generation or two removed.

Adult Development and Adult Education

Important connections between research and theory in the study of adult development and aging, educational psychology research, and the principles and practices of adult education are frequently overlooked. Scientific advances in understanding age-related changes in psychomotor and perceptual abilities, cognitive and intellectual abilities, and socialization and personality over the lifespan have contributed to deeper appreciation of the variability of human development from conception to death. It is by now well accepted that adults are capable of learning throughout life and that they can remain intellectually vital, in generally good health, and actively engaged in their communities, with vibrant, satisfying relationships, even well into old age. Adults of all ages participate in formal and informal learning.

Thus, adult education is a wide-ranging field, encompassing educational programs and activities as diverse as adult basic and literacy education, continuing professional education, corporate training programs, recreation and health, museum education, and Elderhostel programs for seniors. Reflecting the diversity of these programs, the objectives, curricula, teaching methods, and assessment strategies that are employed reflect a mix of philosophies, theoretical orientations, and situational contexts. Educational psychologists' work has frequently both contributed to and bridged adult developmental research and adult education practice (Smith & Pourchot, 1998; Tennant, 1997). Many educational psychologists are trained in developmental psychology and have investigated developmental phenomena from late adolescence into the adult years (e.g., Reio & Choi, 2004). Also, theoretical work in motivation (Brophy, 1998), individual differences (Sternberg, 2000), critical thinking (Kamin, O'Sullivan, Younger, & Deterding, 2001), and literacy (Reder, 1994), among other psychological domains, has greatly contributed to adult education practice (Merriam & Caffarella, 1998).

Courtenay (1994), however, has questioned the value of developmental theory to the practice of adult education, arguing that the literature on human development has little relevance to practitioners. Taylor (1996), in response to Courtenay, argued that developmental theories help educators create appropriate learning tasks. Pourchot and Smith (2004) claim that practitioners' knowledge and application of developmental theories can have important influences on the creation of innovative curricula, the use of appropriate instructional methods and evaluation systems, and the administration of adult education programs. Thus, adult educators are well advised to understand developmental processes in adulthood to better attract, serve, and retain adult learners who are seeking education and training (Hughes & Graham, 1990).

The remainder of this chapter consists of five sections. The first section describes recent and critically important work on cognitive and intellectual development across the adult life span—in particular, the work rooted in a lifespan developmental perspective (Baltes, 1987). The second section describes some of the significant dimensions of socialization and personality development in adulthood, with a focus on the middle adult years. The third section addresses the effects of schooling and adult education on adult development. The fourth section discusses the nature of the various transitional paths from schooling (i.e., high school, vocational-technical training, or college) to the workplace. We complete the chapter by drawing some conclusions about what is understood about adult development at the outset of the millennium based on the research described in the preceding sections.

INTELLECTUAL DEVELOPMENT IN ADULTHOOD

Adult development theory and research has largely been concerned with understanding the nature and direction of cognitive and intellectual changes from late adolescence to later adulthood. The essential question of interest for educational psychologists is, are adults able to continue learning throughout the life span?

Dimensions of Adult Intellectual Development

Research on cognitive aging is largely rooted in a psychometric and quantitative orientation to understanding intellectual functioning. Intelligence, from this perspective, can be reliably measured by the application of standardized tests that tap both biologically determined and culturally moderated dimensions of intelligence. Historically, this work has found evidence of age-related declines in intellectual abilities (Bayley & Oden, 1955; Campbell, 1965; Tuddenham, Blumenkrantz, & Wilkin, 1968).

The primary theoretical model employed to interpret the findings of age-related changes in intellectual functioning is Cattell's (1963) theory of fluid and crystallized intelligence. This model suggests that intelligence consists of two sets of mental abilities. Fluid intellectual abilities (e.g., solving novel problems) are the innate, genetically determined, biological dimensions of intelligence. As such, fluid abilities are relatively impervious to environmental influences, such as education or training. The second set of abilities is referred to as crystallized intelligence (e.g., recalling the names of U.S. presidents), which is the product of knowledge acquisition through experiences within one's cultural and social context (e.g., education or everyday experiences).

Changes in intelligence are primarily attributed to declines in fluid intellectual abilities. Fluid intelligence may begin to decline by as early as the mid-40s (Schaie, 1996). Schaie's (1996) four-decade longitudinal study of more than 5,000 adults in the Pacific Northwest has shown that mental abilities improve into the late 30s and early 40s. However, even by their late 80s, only a very small percentage of adults show significant declines across all mental abilities. Generally, deficits are found within those abilities most closely tied to fluid intelligence. In contrast, crystallized intellectual abilities—those most influenced by cultural and social elements—improve over much of the life span and, thereby, largely offset any losses in fluid functioning. As knowledge becomes increasingly encapsulated (Rybash, Hoyer, & Roodin, 1986) within specific domains of skill (e.g., playing chess) or information, expertise (Charness & Bosman, 1990) and even wisdom

(Baltes, Smith, & Staudinger, 1997) result, and so functional changes in intellectual performances are unlikely until very late in life. This research suggests that adult educators should not be concerned that younger and older adult students will demonstrate meaningful differences in learning.

What accounts for declines in fluid intelligence? Salthouse (1993) has proposed the speed deficit hypothesis to account for age-related declines in mental functioning pertaining to memory. According to this model, reduced cognitive processing speed accounts for more than 80% of the age-related variance in recall measures. This loss of processing speed is likely due to physiological changes in the brain. These changes include the loss of neurons resulting in neural detours that slow processing. Also, reductions in the quantity of neurotransmitters or of synaptic receptors, or in the degree of myelinization of axons, may contribute to slower cognitive processing (Salthouse, n.d.; Salthouse, 1996).

Although age-related changes in intellectual functioning are often assumed to result from physiological changes in basic intellectual capabilities, Dittman-Kohli and Baltes (1990) suggest that observed changes may more accurately result from "the pragmatic dynamics and contexts of adult life" (p. 65). That is, changing life circumstances, personal interests, and available opportunities play a significant role in the application of, and possible declines in, intellectual abilities. As aging adults shift their concerns away from intellectually challenging, but less relevant, activities to problems that involve the resolution of more immediate developmental life tasks, they may have less need to draw upon fluid abilities. Thus, declining fluid abilities may have little real effect on cognitive functioning.

The Lifespan Developmental Perspective

As described by Baltes (1987), traditional perspectives in psychology held that cognitive growth was possible from infancy until maturity, followed by a lengthy period of stability and, eventually, gradual declines in intellectual skills. Today, life-span development offers a more optimistic perspective on adult cognitive development in an era in which people are living longer and are leading healthier and more active lives well into late life. The emergence of the life-span development perspective has coincided with a burgeoning of interest in adult education and an increasing number of opportunities for formal and informal learning.

Baltes and his associates (Baltes, 1987; Baltes, Dittmann-Kohli, & Dixon, 1984; Baltes, Lindenberger, & Staudinger, 1998 Baltes & Schaie, 1976; Baltes et al.,

1997;) as well as Schaie (1965; 1994, 1996) have been largely responsible for the growth and widespread acceptance of the lifespan developmental perspective on human development. The life-span view holds that human development is multidirectional (i.e., there are trajectories of growth and decline) and marked by considerable plasticity (i.e., many cognitive skills can be improved through practice or training). Further, multiple, overlapping factors influence individual development including normative, non-normative, and history-graded events, such as educational attainment, marriage and parenting, accidents, illnesses, natural disasters, and wars.

Given these multiple and interactive influences, Baltes & Smith (1999) view human development in terms of gains and losses in abilities. Over the life span, the ratio of intellective resources allocated to the growth and maintenance of cognitive abilities as opposed to the management of losses in cognitive skills changes. Cognitive resources are growth-directed early in life, but eventually shift to maintenance functions in the later years. Successful adaptation to changing life circumstances also requires the interplay and coordination of the processes of selection, optimization, and compensation. Age-related losses in adaptive abilities, and what Baltes et al. call "reserve intellectual potential," suggest that adults should select a few important intellectual domains in which to work. They can then optimize their performances within these selected domains by engaging in extensive practice within the activity domain.

Finally, adults can compensate for age-related losses by using strategies that enable them to support those cognitive functions that are affected by the loss of reserve capacities. Selective optimization with compensation can be applied in many domains of adult life. For example, aging distance runners might give up other physical activities, such as biking, that detract from running (selection), and then increase the quality of their training regimen by doing short, intense, workouts (optimization). They can further compensate for diminished physical abilities by reading about injury-prevention techniques, talking with a nutritionist about good dietary practices, or switching from longer (e.g., marathon) to shorter (10K) races (Baltes & Baltes, 1990). The development of expert knowledge can also offset losses in cognitive abilities.

Characteristics of Expertise. The acquisition of knowledge with age and experience contributes to the development of expertise. Expert thinking is characterized as both automatic and intuitive (Rybash et al., 1986). Experts have a well-developed, organized, and extensive base of knowledge that they have accumulated through years of experience—at least a decade of intensive preparation and practice–with certain kinds of problems (Clancy

& Hoyer, 1994; Ericsson & Charness, 1995). Experts also possess greater procedural knowledge about how to work through steps in the problem-solving process, and they rarely have to contemplate a plan of action because their knowledge is more accessible, having been efficiently organized and stored in long-term memory. Because of their better-organized knowledge base, experts' decision-making speed is much greater than that of novices (Alexander, 2004). Expertise appears to be independent of declines in general intellectual abilities. Expertise has some limits, however. Expertise is domain-specific and does not transfer to problems outside of the domain (Rybash et al., 1986). Experts are also no better than novices at solving real-world, "everyday" problems or those where only knowledge of superficial details is required (Ericsson & Charness, 1995).

Alexander (2004) has offered a new model of expertise development in academic domains—the Model of Domain Learning (MDL). According to this model, domain-specific expertise develops in three stages: acclimation, competence, and proficiency-expertise. The multidimensional, multistage MDL offers a new way to investigate the development of expertise in contrast to past approaches that emphasize generic and knowledge-rich problem solving. The MDL holds considerable research promise because it acknowledges the relevance of knowledge, interest (and curiosity), and strategic processing as contributors to the development of expertise.

Characteristics of Wisdom. Over the past two decades wisdom has become an important area of psychological research. Wisdom, defined by Clayton and Birren (1975) as the ability to grasp paradoxes, reconcile contradictions, and make and accept compromises, has been investigated from several different perspectives. One view is that wisdom is a possible outgrowth of late life personality development. Erikson (1984) held that wisdom results from the successful resolution of the final developmental task of life—accepting one's life for what it is and how it was lived. Another view holds that wisdom is a dimension of cognitive ability. This perspective has been predominant in cognitive aging research in recent years.

Baltes and his colleagues (Baltes, Mayer, Helmchen, & Steinhagen-Thiessen, 1993; Baltes & Smith, 1999) at the Max Planck Institute on Human Development in Berlin have led the way in understanding the intellective components of wisdom. Baltes et al. (1993) define wisdom as "an expert knowledge system in the fundamental pragmatics of life permitting exceptional insight, judgment, and advice involving complex and uncertain matters of the human condition (p. 76). Wisdom is considered to represent the pragmatics of intellectual ability, in Baltes et al.'s (1984) dual process theory, and it consists of five components: factual knowledge of the pragmatics or practicalities of everyday life; strategic knowledge of the pragmatics of life; knowledge of the uncertainties of life; knowledge of the relativism of values and life goals; and knowledge of the contexts of life and societal change.

Baltes and Staudinger (2000) have studied wisdom by presenting real-life scenarios to adults of different ages and in different occupations and having them describe their thinking about the scenario. They have also compared adults who have been nominated as wise persons to others deemed to have professional training and wisdom-related knowledge in regards to examining and resolving uncertain matters of life (i.e., clinical psychologists). Old wisdom nominees performed as well as clinical psychologists on the wisdom tasks, and older adults up to age 80 were found to perform as well as younger adults. Thus, although it may be possible to train people to be wise, it is most likely a combination of life experience and age that interact to produce wise thinking and problem-solving, according to Baltes and Staudinger.

Qualitative Changes in Intelligence. Other lines of work on adult intelligence, following largely on Piaget's theoretical foundation, have considered the qualitative dimensions of thinking and problem-solving abilities. This work suggests that growth in intellectual functioning is represented by transitions from one stage of cognitive development to another, more complex and advanced stage. Neo-Piagetian theorists have focused on describing qualitative changes in adult thinking leading to a hypothesized post-formal stage of cognitive development.

Piaget (1972) argued that cognitive development was largely completed by late adolescence or early adulthood with the attainment of formal operations. Generally, formal operations is said to deal with finding correct answers to specific kinds of problems that involve logical-deductive, hypothetical reasoning of the sort that is well-suited to problems in mathematics and the sciences. Neo-Piagetian, postformal theorists argue, however, that formal operations does not adequately account for adults' abilities to deal with ambiguity, subjectivity, contradictions, and relativism, which is more characteristic of the sorts of problems confronted in the everyday world. Nor does formal operational thinking satisfactorily integrate emotions with logic (Labouvie-Vief, 1992). Emotional responses play an important role in many kinds of problem-solving activities, according to Labouvie-Vief. Affect attenuates purely rational thinking and plays an essential role in everyday decision making. Contextually based, postformal thinkers create new "realities" based upon changing life circumstances, rather than searching for absolute and universal principles that apply across all situations and problems.

At least three aspects of postformal thinking have been described in the literature. One form of postformal thinking is relativistic thinking, which is based on assumptions of change, subjectivity, and novelty with regard to intellectual problems (King & Kitchener, 1994; Kramer, 1989; Perry, 1970). Relativistic thinkers understand the relative and nonabsolute nature of knowledge, and recognize that people can have different perspectives on the same problem or issue. Knowledge is seen as being influenced by the context in which it occurs, and these contexts are always in a state of flux. Thus, the understanding that life's contradictions cannot always be reconciled is central to relativism.

Perry (1970), for example, showed that, initially, undergraduate students hold a dualistic perspective in regard to the nature of knowledge. That is, they believe that the knowledge one holds is either "right" or "wrong." Over time, their views about knowledge become relative and uncertain—they see all knowledge claims as having equal validity. Finally, some students achieve contextual relativism in which they understand the relative nature of knowledge, but also become committed to a self-constructed point of view that enables them to both accept and transcend relativity. In this way, they can evaluate various knowledge claims and determine that some claims are valid and some are not.

Dialectical thinking involves the integration of contradictory ways of thinking into new and consistent ideas or models (Basseches, 1984; Riegel, 1976; Sinnott, 1998). Dialectical thinkers see contradictions as opportunities to create new and better ideas. Adults' efforts to organize and systematize knowledge lead to inherent contradictions within the cognitive system that invariably result in changes within the system of organization. Such thinking and cognitive reorganization leads to growth, according to Basseches (1984). Dialectical thinkers accept contradiction as the basis of reality, and they possess the ability to synthesize their contradictory thoughts, feelings, and experiences into a more advanced and coherent cognitive organization. Dialectical thinking is present when, for example, a person understands that it is possible to have feelings of both love and hate for another person. This knowledge leads them to a new and more complex understanding of the nature of human relationships.

Finally, Labouvie-Vief (1992) has portrayed postformal thinking as autonomous, more complex, and more flexible than formal operational thinking. It is less constrained by the "strong" logic of formal thinking, and is not driven by the need to arrive at a single solution to a problem. Advocates of postformal models have acknowledged that postformal thinking may not represent a genuine thought structure in the true Piagetian sense, but rather thinking "styles" that emerge during adulthood (Rybash et al., 1986). Like formal operations, postformal thinking has a logical quality to it that does not take into account the often irrational and illogical nature of adult thinking.

Developmental Changes in Memory. Memory performance has long been an interest of educational psychologists (Bartlett, 1932; Thorndike et al., 1928). Students having good memories generally perform well in school because they are able to efficiently encode new information, store it in long-term memory, and readily retrieve it to demonstrate their learning on both classroom and standardized tests. The human memory system is, of course, complex, and we do not yet fully comprehend exactly how it operates, although recent information processing accounts have deepened our understanding of memory functions. Tulving (1985) proposed three different memory systems. *Implicit memory* pertains to information that is learned and automatically remembered, such as how to ride a bicycle. *Semantic memory* consists of what we know, such as the capital of Illinois or how to send a document as an attachment to an e-mail message. *Episodic memory* is the ability to remember ongoing events, such as the date and time of an important meeting. Lovelace (1990) distinguished between these two forms of memory by suggesting that episodic memory is what is meant when one says "I remember," whereas semantic memory is what is meant when saying "I know."

Age-related differences in memory functioning have been demonstrated across all three types of memory (Verhaeghen, Marcoen, & Goossens, 1993), although some differences are more dramatic than are others. Memory performance is, to be sure, much more variable among the elderly than among younger adults (Weintraub, Powell, & Whitla, 1994). Older adults perform worse on implicit memory tasks than do younger adults (i.e., when exposed to information that does not involve active memorization processing), although the type of information to be remembered and the memory task itself likely play a role in findings of age differences. Sinnott (1984), for example, found age differences on incidental memory, but not on prospective memory tasks.

Semantic memory is thought to improve as an individual enters later adulthood (Wingfield & Kahana, 2002). This is due to the increase of links of associated words in older adults' semantic memory store. The amount of experience that adults gather throughout their lifetimes directly affects the complexity of their semantic networks (MacKay & Abrams, 1996). In fact, experience appears to play a compensatory role in semantic memory functioning in that aged adults with expertise in any given domain can access their procedural knowledge

automatically without draining their memory resources (Cohen, 1996).

Age-related differences are found in episodic memory (Verhaeghen et al., 1993; Woodruff-Pak, Jaeger, Gorman & Wesnes, 1999), although the range of differences depends again upon the type of memory task (Derwinger, Stigsdotter Neely, Persson, Hill, & Backman, 2003). Episodic memory is assessed in a variety of ways, but most frequently via recall and recognition measures. Declines are shown for recall measures that require active retrieval from long-term memory, but not for simple recognition tasks (Backman, Mantyla, & Herlitz, 1990; Schoenfield & Robertson, 1966). Generally, across all forms of memory and different kinds of tasks, older adults' performance is poorer in the laboratory than when tested under naturalistic, meaningful conditions (Sinnott, 1984; West, 1992). Older adults appear to benefit from the contextual cues and supports (e.g., lists and other reminders) available within familiar environments such as their homes, but not the laboratory (Morrow, Hier, Menard, & Leirer, 1998).

Even when age-related changes in memory are found in the laboratory, however, these changes often have little or no functional effect on everyday life. Adults are often quite able to adapt and compensate for either perceived or real declines in memory performance by using memory-saving techniques such as reminder lists or other environmental prompts. Memory self-efficacy (i.e., the belief that one can perform specific memory tasks) likely also plays an important role in memory performance (Cavanaugh, 1996).

Use of Memory Strategies. Adults can employ any of a variety of strategies to improve their memory performance (particularly following strategy instruction), although they do not always do so spontaneously (Pressley, Levin, & Ghatala, 1984) or without prompting. Also, there are age-related differences in the adoption and use of various memory techniques (Brigham & Pressley, 1988). Often, older adults lack knowledge about such memory techniques or strategies, having not been exposed to them in school. And, they may lack good knowledge of how memory works and have mistaken beliefs about their ability to compensate for memory declines by using strategies. Knowledge of one's memory abilities is called *metamemory*, which also includes an understanding of how memory works (Hertzog & Hultsch, 2000). Older adults have been found to have less metamemory knowledge, so they may be less able to adopt and use mnemonic strategies that would improve their memories (Hertzog, Dixon, & Hultsch, 1990). Age differences in metamemory knowledge are likely related to cohort differences in education. Generally, older adults have less education than younger ones and may be less familiar, or less practiced, with the academic memory tasks typically used in memory studies.

Memory Strategy Training. Education may be a critical factor in helping to circumvent age-related changes in cognitive functioning, including memory loss. Specifically, in memory training studies designed to improve recall, older adults who received help in devising their own mnemonic strategies were more successful than were students formally trained in mnemonics (Park, Smith, & Cavanaugh, 1990). Thus, adult educators who work with middle-aged and older adults should consider sharing information with adult learners about memory strategies.

Researchers have observed that simple practice can significantly improve memory task performance (Lachman, Bandura, Weaver, Elliott, & Lewkowicz, 1995), a finding that has led investigators to develop training programs to increase adults' memory performance and eliminate age-related declines. Training in the use of strategies such as the method of loci can significantly improve older adults' memory performance. Unfortunately, even when they see the benefits of this method, some older adults may discard these memory aids because they perceive that it requires too much effort to use them (Anschutz, Camp, Markley, & Kramer, 1987). But, simpler memory strategies such as notetaking can also be beneficial (Fitzgerald, 2000). In general, the effects of memory strategy training are long-lasting—up to 6 months or more (Verhaegen et al., 1993). Despite training, older adults typically do not achieve performance levels equivalent to that of younger adults (Baltes & Kliegl, 1992). Consequently, no type of memory strategy training seems to be better than another (Rasmussen, Rebok, Bylsma, & Brandt, 1999) with regard to improving memory or eliminating age differences.

PERSONALITY AND SOCIALIZATION IN ADULTHOOD

In addition to the important work on adult intellectual and cognitive development described earlier, the field of adult development has been influenced by theoretical work that spans several disciplines, including psychoanalytic and personality psychology, social and cognitive psychology, and gerontology. As noted by Hughes and Graham (1990), a common theme among theories of adult development is that adults exhibit predictable, stable behavioral patterns during certain age periods. Among the most well-known theories of adult development are those of Erikson (1950; 1968) and Levinson and his associates (Levinson et al., 1978; Levinson & Levinson, 1996). These theories tend to be descriptive of the ideal rather than the reality of adults' developmental changes, which are a good deal more tumultuous, irregular, and nonlinear than these and other theories suggest. Nonetheless, it is worthwhile to briefly describe these perspectives on adult psychosocial development because of their influence on developmentalists' thinking about how genetic and maturational, and socialenvironmental factors act and interact to influence personality and social development across the adult years.

Descriptive Theories of Adult Development

Erikson's Epigenetic Theory. Erik Erikson is considered a pioneer in the study of adult development. His writings in the last two decades of his life focused almost exclusively on psychological issues pertaining to aging, in which he emphasized the elder adult's need to achieve a sense of ego integrity. Erikson proposed a stage model of human development based on the epigenetic principle—that is, the sociocultural environment interacts with biogenetic factors to influence individual personality development. In contrast to Freud, Erikson believed that social factors rather than unconscious sexual drives are critical to development. Each stage of ego development in Erikson's model requires the individual to resolve, at a deeply unconscious level, conflicts between opposing intrapsychic forces (e.g., "trust" vs. "mistrust"). The elements of unresolved conflicts are carried forward and influence how the individual resolves each succeeding developmental task.

The three adult stages of Erikson's eight-stage model are viewed as struggles devoted to the accomplishment of other important psychosocial tasks. Young adults face the task of achieving intimacy with others rather than being isolated and alone. Successfully resolving the conflict of "intimacy vs. isolation" leads to love. Failure to achieve intimate relationships results in emotional, and sometimes physical, isolation from others. Middle-aged adults must demonstrate generativity through "procreation, productivity, and creativity" (Erikson, 1982, p. 67), or they risk becoming self-absorbed. Generative adults, according to Erikson, come to understand that, in some form or another, "I am what survives me" (1968, p. 141). Thus, personal meaning and individual identity are intricately tied up in strivings to achieve an enduring legacy, either through childrearing or contributing to the well-being of others and society through teaching and mentoring, community service, or creative works.

Regression to the conflicts of earlier stages may arise whenever the individual is unsuccessful at generative activities. Finally, in old age, adults struggle to achieve ego integrity, which is rooted in feelings of satisfaction with a life well lived. Ego integrity is synonymous with wisdom in Erikson's model. Erikson rarely addressed issues relating to the education of adults, except to the extent that education, as an instrument of culture, and schools as socializing institutions, can influence individual's psychosocial development positively. Erikson's theory has inspired research into identity development, generativity, and the development of wisdom during adulthood.

For example, Whitbourne and her colleagues (Whitbourne & Collins, 1998; Whitbourne, Sneed, & Skultety, 2002; Whitbourne & van Manen, 1996; Whitbourne, Zuschlag, Elliott, & Waterman, 1992) have carried out systematic studies of identity development in adulthood. Whitbourne et al. define identity somewhat more broadly than does Erikson, viewing it as the self-appraisal of various personal attributes, which include physical appearance and cognitive abilities, personality traits and motives, and social roles (Whitbourne & Connolly, 1999, p. 28). Whitbourne and van Manen (1996) examined age differences in identity from the college years into middle adulthood. Two cohorts of adults who had been undergraduates at an Eastern U.S. university in the mid-1960s and mid-1970s were compared to a contemporary cohort of students at the same university. The two earlier cohorts were participants in a longitudinal study. Members of all three cohorts were surveyed and participants completed an identity status measure, a biographical data questionnaire, and an inventory assessing psychosocial development.

The investigators hypothesized that increasingly mature resolution of identity issues would be found among the older cohorts. Also, those having made early commitments—by their early 30s—to relationships (including family) and work were hypothesized to demonstrate stronger identity commitments in midlife. Further, adults in their mid-40s (1966 cohort) would evidence stronger commitments than those in their mid-30s (1977 cohort) and early 20s (1988 cohort). The two older cohorts were found to have more mature identity development, in terms of identity commitments, than did the college student cohort. The postcollege cohorts were more likely to be identity achieved, and showed less evidence of identity diffusion (i.e., role confusion), whereas those in the younger college cohort were more likely to evidence identity moratorium (i.e., exploration) status. Changes in identity status (i.e., from moratorium to identity achievement) were in the expected direction for those in the two older cohorts.

This study and other related work by Whitbourne, Sneed, and Skultety (2002) have contributed to a proposed new model of adult identity development that integrates Erikson's and Piaget's theories (Whitbourne & Connolly, 1999). Identity process theory (Whitbourne, 2002) is a refinement of Erikson's psychosocial theory. According to identity process theory, the dual cognitive processes of assimilation and accommodation interpret the interactions between the person and their experiences through the perspective of personal identity. *Identity assimilation* occurs when individuals interpret new experiences in terms of their existing self-schemas or identities (i.e., "does this experience fit with my particular cognitive skills, personality traits, or social role?"). Identity assimilation works to preserve a positive view of the self whenever new information and experiences are contrary to one's view of the self. *Identity accommodation* occurs when the individual changes his or her view of the self based on new information and experiences that do not fit the existing self-schema. Identity formation processes, according to the theory, do not vary from early to middle adulthood, but the specific life events that initiate identity processes are different across life periods (e.g., marriage, becoming a parent, or retirement). The primary stimuli for identity processes in adult life are age-related changes in physical and cognitive functioning that upset the equilibrium between identity assimilation and identity accommodation. Thus, as individuals take notice of changes in their physical appearance and abilities, they begin to reconsider themselves in terms of being a "middle-aged," "aging," or "old" person.

Levinson's Age-Based Theory. Daniel Levinson (Levinson et al., 1978; Levinson & Levinson, 1996) understood adult development as a series of chronological stages in which specific developmental tasks must be accomplished. Levinson focused on the psychological, biological, and social aspects of individual development. Similar to Erikson, he argued that a person's life is conjointly determined by society and the self, and Levinson viewed his theory as one that builds on and contributes to Erikson's.

He considered early adulthood (ages 17–40) to be the most dramatic period of adult development in terms of biological functioning, psychological development, and social factors. All of these factors interact to shape personality development. Middle adulthood is from 40 to 60 years of age, and late adulthood from age 60 to the end of life. The individual *life structure*—defined as the basic pattern or design of a person' life at a particular point in time–is the central concept in his theory. The primary components of the life structure are shaped by the individual's relationships with others. The life structure is examined through an analysis of the choices that individuals make, in terms of career, marriage, and family. Adult development, according to Levinson et al., is the evolution of the life structure. Development occurs through alternative phases of stability (i.e., the life structure) and transitions. Transitions are 5-year periods characterized by distinct developmental tasks in which the individual evaluates and reconsiders life choices and makes new commitments, leading to a new period of stability. The early adult transition is from ages 17 to 22, the middle adult transition from ages 40 to 45, and the late adult transition from ages 60 to 65. These transitions provide the individual with a sense of continuity between the three eras of adult life—early, middle, and late adulthood.

Levinson et al. (1978) claimed that the sequence of eras and periods of development exist in all societies, and these represent the life cycle of the species. An era is a period of about 20 to 25 years in the adult life span, and each of these eras has its own distinctive, unifying qualities, which have to do with what Levinson et al. called the "character of living" (p. 18). Movement from one era to the next is a complex and lengthy process, taking 4 or 5 years to work through. Although Levinson studied men's development initially, he later conducted a study of women and found that their development was marked by similar tasks and transitions (Levinson & Levinson, 1996). A fundamental difference for women, however, was the influence of family relationships in their lives. Levinson's theory has found some support in the psychological literature on adult development. Newton and Roberts (1987) examined four dissertation studies of women's psychological development that were based on Levinson's theory. Although the studies were consistent with the theory in terms of the sequence of women's development, the developmental issues salient to women were strikingly different from those of men. In many ways, women's lives and the ways in which they negotiate family, spousal, and career roles are much more complex and challenging than are men's lives.

Like Erikson, Levinson gave little consideration to the role of education in influencing adult development, although he noted that college is "an institutional setting in which many young [people] begin the separation from family and do the developmental work of the Early Adult Transition" (p. 75). College expands and redirects individuals' outlooks on life and helps them to discover and develop new interests.

These descriptive theories of adult personality development have been enormously beneficial to psychologists and clinicians who assist and counsel adults navigating developmental transitions or wholesale life changes. It is now widely understood that change in adulthood is normative and that adults can be expected to experience alternating periods of stability and crisis as marked by identity exploration, job and career changes, dissolution of relationship bonds, and recommitments to enduring relationships.

Development in Middle Age. Middle age has been largely viewed as the most favorable period of the adult life span, and yet it is territory that has been mostly uncharted by developmental psychologists. Middle-aged adults have shed the naiveté of youth, established themselves in the world, and acquired several decades of life experience. Neugarten, Havighurst, and Tobin (1968) thought of middle adulthood as a "period of maximum capacity to handle a highly complex environment and a highly differentiated self" (p. 97). In a survey of young, middle-aged, and older adults' perceptions of the characteristics of middle age by Lachman, Lewkowicz, Marcus, and Peng (1994), all three age groups converged on the perception of middle-aged adults as better adjusted and helpful, more understanding and supportive, and more respected than others. On the other hand, some have characterized middle age as a rather static period in the life span in which the adult has essentially "settled down" to raise a family, establish a career, and acquire the trappings of contemporary life (McCrae & Costa, 1990).

Middle adulthood has been described as occurring within a broad age range—anywhere from 30 to 60 years of age—and subjective conceptions of middle age vary greatly from one cohort to another (Schaie & Willis, 1986). Because of the fluidity of age boundaries in middle adulthood, researchers have often examined this period from the perspective of middle-aged adults' responses to salient developmental tasks, such as marriage and childrearing, career consolidation and satisfaction, care for aging parents, or responses to changing physical health (Lachman, 2001). Lachman has been the leading contemporary proponent of studying development in the middle years of adulthood, arguing that research is needed to, among other things, identify the aspects of personality and self that can serve as the focus for interventions to enhance adult functioning.

SCHOOLING: COLLEGE AND ADULT CONTINUING EDUCATION

Education is a major contributor to adult development, as college provides numerous opportunities for cognitive and intellectual growth (Perry, 1970), emotional development and the confirmation of personal values (Kuh, 1995; Pascarella & Terenzini, 1991), and career preparation (Gianakos, 1996; Orndorff & Herr, 1996; Pascarella & Terenzini, 1991). Adults can participate in educational programs and courses throughout their lives, and many adults can readily be identified as "lifelong learners." According to the U.S. Department of Education (1999a), approximately 90 million adults—nearly half of all American adults—were engaged in one or more types of adult education in 1998. These adults were most likely to participate in work-related and personal development courses. Previous educational attainment plays a strong role in determining who participates in adult education. Only about 20 percent of those with a high school diploma participated in any educational activities in 1998, whereas more than 60 percent of adults having at least a bachelor's degree did so.

Pascarella and Terenzini (1991) conducted an exhaustive review of the literature on the effects of college attendance on individuals' development. They reviewed and analyzed hundreds of studies published over two decades from the 1960s to late 1980s. Among other outcomes, they analyzed the effects of college on individuals' intellectual and cognitive abilities, values and attitudes, and psychosocial and moral development. The studies they examined were limited to traditional 18- to 22-year-old, full-time students enrolled in 4-year colleges and universities. In general they found that college students experienced statistically significant and meaningful gains in knowledge and intellectual skills from their freshman to senior years in school. Effect sizes were as large as a full standard deviation. They also observed positive changes in personal values (e.g., educational and occupational values) and attitudes (e.g., altruism and civic values, attitudes regarding civil rights and religion), as well as several psychosocial and moral dimensions. However, the magnitudes of the effects of college on these outcomes were not as dramatic as for intellectual abilities. Importantly, they noted that some of the observed changes across the college years may be due simply to maturational processes rather than to college attendance and participation. The primary limitation of most studies of college effects is the lack of comparison groups; college attendance is self-determined, not a variable that can be randomly assigned.

Graham and Donaldson and their associates (Donaldson & Graham, 1999; Donaldson, Graham, Martindill, & Bradley, 2000; Graham, 1998; Graham & Donaldson, 1996, 1999) have carried out an extensive program of research investigating adult development during the college years, and the effects of the collegiate experience on adult outcomes. Graham (1998) analyzed responses to the American College Testing (ACT) College Outcomes Survey as completed by nearly 28,000 undergraduates. Two age groups were compared: those 18 to 22 years of age and those 27 years of age and older. The older adults reported slightly higher outcomes in regard to intellectual growth, problem-solving, scientific reasoning, and career development than did the younger, traditional-age students (statistical significance was not reported). These findings suggest that the ages during which adults are enrolled influences the effects of college. Perhaps older adults are better able to relate their classroom learning to their everyday lives and experiences at work, in their communities, and within their families, giving them a modest advantage over traditional students.

Emerging Adulthood and the College Years

Adolescents' transitions to adulthood are changing dramatically in the early 21st century, owing in large part to changing cultural, societal, and economic circumstances. Arnett (2000) has proposed a new conception of adult development for the period from the late teens into the early thirties, with a particular focus on the ages from 18 to 25. Arnett claims that this period, which he calls emerging adulthood, is distinct from adolescence and young adulthood in that those in this group tend to be free from social roles and normative expectations (consistent with the moratorium in Erikson's theory). Emerging adulthood is a period in which individuals may investigate many life possibilities. For many emerging adults, education plays a vital role in fostering the exploration of careers, establishing new and diverse relationships, and gaining independence from family. As increasing numbers of individuals with college degrees enter postgraduate study (U.S. Department of Education, 2001), this developmental stage will likely become more widely recognized. Arnett's theory has touched off a small explosion of research and theorizing (Arnett, 1994; Cohen, Kasen, Chen, Hartmark, & Gordon, 2003; Eccles, Templeton, Barber, & Stone, 2003).

Emerging adults adapt to developmental transitions in diverse ways, and the patterns of transitions are influenced by gender, socioeconomic status, and race. Cohen et al. (2003) found that although young men become financially independent from parents earlier than do young women, men are more likely to remain at home with their parents for a longer period of time. Adults from higher socioeconomic backgrounds are slower to attain adult roles than are those from lower SES groups. Young black adults delayed making full romantic commitments and long-term relationship plans as compared to young white adults. Participation in higher education did not mediate demographic differences in these developmental transitions.

The movement from the emerging adulthood period to adulthood proper is marked by several objective signposts of adulthood and a variety of subjective experiences that indicate to individuals that they have attained adult status. The objective markers of adulthood are socially sanctioned roles such as full-time employment, marriage, and parenthood (Hogan & Astone, 1986). Yet, it is possible to be engaged in any or all of these social roles and still not feel completely "adult" (Arnett, 1994). Thus, individuals' conceptions of themselves as having attained adulthood are also crucial. Several studies have indicated that young persons in their late teens to late twenties believe that being responsible for oneself, making one's own decisions, and having financial independence from one's parents are the three key criteria for adulthood (Arnett, 2003; Nelson, 2003).

Adult Learners in College. Increasing numbers of middle-aged adults are returning to school (U.S. Department of Education, 1999b) to obtain a college degree, earn a postgraduate degree, increase or improve their job skills and remain competitive in fluctuating and uncertain economic times, or simply improve their minds and broaden their interests (Aslanian, 2001; Kasworm, 2002a, 2002b). Adult students, older than 24 years, are often referred to as nontraditional or returning students. Some of these adults have been out of school for many years and find themselves in classrooms with traditional students who are almost the same age as their children. Many may be unprepared for the demands of academic life and lack the time necessary to devote to their studies. Despite concerns about these adults' abilities to keep up with younger students, a number of surveys of nontraditional students and their instructors have painted a very favorable picture of older adults as learners. They tend to have higher GPAs than younger, traditional students (Darkenwald & Novak, 1997), perhaps because they have more intrinsic motivation to learn and are more goal-directed than younger students (Miller, 1989).

Aslanian and Brickell (1980) described a "triggers and transitions" theory, according to which adults' decisions to return to school are rooted in developmental issues and crises that occur over the course of adulthood. Life transitions often require individuals to acquire new knowledge, develop new skills, or obtain professional credentials, which motivate them to return to college. Triggering events precipitating adults' return to school most often involve career events and family changes. Kopka and Peng (1993) found that by far the most prevalent reason adults participate in adult education is to improve their work-related skills or to advance in their jobs. Many other adults participate in education because they find it enjoyable and stimulating. They may have no particular goal in mind in terms of earning a degree or moving up the salary schedule at work. In interviews with part-time adult students at a British university, Blaxter and Tight (1995) found that half of their sample was participating in adult education out of interest and a desire for self-fulfillment. Thus, whereas life transitions motivate some adults to go back to school, others return for reasons unrelated to

dramatic changes in their lives. After about age 40, adults' participation in adult education for the sake of earning a diploma or degree declines fairly rapidly (Kopka & Peng, 1993).

Few longitudinal studies have tracked participation in education over the course of adults' lives, so it is difficult to state precisely what factors are associated with adults' participation in either formal or informal educational activities. Yang (1998), however, found, in analyzing data from the *National Longitudinal Study of the High School Class of 1972*, that socioeconomic status and prior schooling experiences, including attitudes toward education, had significant and enduring effects on this adult cohort's participation in adult education, at least until the early 30s.

Adult students also differ from traditional-age students in that they usually work full time and have life demands, such as marriage and parenting, which compete with their school work (Graham & Donaldson, 1999). Their lack of time for, and lack of interest in, collegiate activities such as campus life, student government, and sports often leaves them somewhat marginalized on traditional college campuses. Despite this, Donaldson et al. (2000) found nontraditional status to be an advantage for adult students because they are more focused on learning, can connect new information to what they already know, are able to apply what they are learning to other areas of their lives, such as work, and have a realistic view of their academic goals.

Although some higher education experts express concerns about the abilities of older, nontraditional students to fare as well academically as their younger counterparts, evidence shows that such concerns are unfounded (Richardson & King, 1998). Older students tend to be more intrinsically motivated, have better time management skills, and take a meaning-oriented approach to studying compared to traditional age college students, and they have comparable academic performance, in terms of GPA. Adult students report having higher expectations for their academic performance than do traditional students, and feel more disciplined in their approach to studying. They are also more likely to engage with and rely on the support of classmates to discuss and better understand course materials and assignments. Adult students, somewhat less restricted by peer expectations and egocentrism, may be less bothered by "looking ignorant" and thus more willing to talk with and seek help from more knowledgeable classmates. Graham (1998) found that adult students do as well or slightly better than traditional-aged students on several measures of academic and intellectual outcomes in college.

One study (Justice & Dornan, 2001) found metacognitive differences between older and younger adult students. Older students reported using higher-level study strategies, such as generating constructive information and devoting additional attention to difficult materials, compared to younger students. This difference in strategy use did not, however, result in higher academic performance compared to younger students. Nonetheless, the study suggests that developmental differences in metacognitive abilities among adult students may be significant for the design and delivery of instruction. Although instructors acknowledge that traditional and nontraditional adult students differ (Jacobs, 1989), they do not change their teaching to accommodate the needs of their older students (Gorham, 1985).

Adult Continuing Education

The U.S. Department of Education (1986) defines *adult education* as courses or educational activity taken part time and reported as adult education by respondents (ages 17 and older), although adult educators have traditionally targeted programs to those persons at least 21 years of age. The formal discipline of adult education can serve numerous roles in adults' lives. According to Courtney (1991), adult education serves a remedial function in helping adults acquire basic literacy skills that they may have failed to obtain previously. Adult education contributes to individuals' occupational development via workplace training and other forms of skill development. It has also been used to enhance personal growth by helping adults improve their interpersonal and relationship skills (cf. Merriam & Brockett, 1997). Adult education also serves important recreational purposes and has been used to develop and organize political groups and sharpen individuals' understanding of the American political system. Finally, adult education can increase individuals' involvement with their communities and society at large.

It might appear that educational psychology has had little direct influence on adult education, yet, as described in the introduction to this chapter, connections between the two disciplines can be traced to Thorndike, whose work on adult learning was very important to early adult educators. Textbooks on adult education implicitly acknowledge the educational psychologists whose work on cognitive development, sociocultural processes, motivation, student assessment, teacher knowledge, and classroom management strategies provide a theoretical foundation for the field.

Adult Learning Theories. Adult educators generally agree that adults are self-directed learners whose learning needs require facilitation more than direct instruction. Knowles' (1980, 1990) andragogical model of learning has strongly influenced adult education. Andragogy is drawn from European perspectives on adult education and refers to the art and science of helping adults learn—in contrast to pedagogy, which refers to children's learning. Andragogy is a learner-centered approach based on the assumption that adults are self-directed and possess unique personal experiences. Their accumulated life experiences provide rich resources for learning, and their desires to learn grow out of their need to accomplish developmental tasks. Thus, adults' needs, characteristics, and strengths differ from those of children, according to Knowles.

For example, adults are oriented toward solving the problems encountered in their everyday lives, and they need to apply what they have learned to these problem situations immediately. Therefore, the kinds of instruction provided to adults should differ from traditional and teacher-centered pedagogical approaches. Because adult learning is thought to be self-initiated, adult educators have tended to favor instructional approaches that capitalize on adults' independence as learners (Wilcox, 1996), rather than on instructor-controlled, didactic methods such as lectures and examinations. Several critics have suggested that the concept of andragogy is more of a descriptive model of the ideal situation rather than a valid, explanatory theory of adult learning (Brookfield, 1986; Hartree, 1984; Pratt, 1993). Other models have emerged partly in response to these critiques.

Mezirow's Transformative Learning Theory. Mezirow's (1990) theory of transformative learning is based on the idea that whenever adults engage in critical reflection on the premises, assumptions, beliefs, and values that they hold, the insights derived from such intellectual activity lead to transformative learning. Thus, transformative theory explains how adults make meaning out of their everyday experiences. Changing one's perspective is the key to transformative learning, according to Mezirow. Transformative learning is rooted in life experience and the fundamental human need to make sense of our lives. Examining the presuppositions that constrain our perceptions of the world leads to a revision of these assumptions which, in turn, results in new insights and personal meanings. Actions guided by these new meanings lead to new roles and behaviors. The primary function of adult educators, according to Mezirow, is to promote such critical reflection among adult learners.

Other Views of Adult Learning. A third theoretical perspective, which is not attributed to any one theorist, holds that adults are largely independent and self-directed learners. This perspective has derived principally from the work of pioneering adult educators such as Cyril Houle (1961) and Alan Tough (1971). Tough described self-directed learning as a form of study and argued that adults take on independent learning projects quite frequently and with largely positive outcomes. Studies of self-directed learning are numerous in the adult education literature. This theoretical orientation has received the most empirical support (Garrison, 1997; Penland, 1979; Richards, 1986; Tough, 1978).

A number of other descriptive models of adult learning also exist. Some are concerned with psychological and developmental variables in learning, such as Knox's (1980) proficiency theory, and Cross' (1981) Characteristics of Adults as Learners (CAL) model, while yet others focus on the social and cultural conditions that foster or impede adults' learning (e.g., McClusky, 1963). Still others emphasize both psychological and sociological factors in learning (e.g., Jarvis, 1987). As yet, there is no "grand" or unifying theory of adult learning that guides educators in creating optimal instructional conditions for adult learning.

Adult Basic and Literacy Education. In 2001, more than two and one-half million American adults enrolled in the adult basic and literacy education (ABLE) in the United States (U.S. Department of Education, 2002b). Most of these adults sought to obtain a GED (high school equivalency diploma) or to improve their basic literacy skills (i.e., reading, writing, mathematics) or both. About half of these adults were in English-as-a-Second-Language programs for immigrant adults who do not speak, read, or write English. ABLE and human resource development are the largest domains of adult education.

The development of literacy skills that enable one to function effectively in society is deemed to be critical in a highly technological society (Guthrie & Greaney, 1991; Hunt, 1995). The Secretary's Commission on Achieving Necessary Skills (U.S. Department of Labor, 1991) described several competencies that students must acquire in order to be well-prepared to function in the modern workforce, including the ability to acquire and use information. This competency necessitates the development of sophisticated reading, writing, and mathematic skills. Some are concerned that students graduating from high school (and those who fail to graduate) lack the necessary literacy skills to function effectively in the workplace (Smith, 2000). Also, non-English-speaking adults need to develop English literacy proficiency.

Participation in ABLE is voluntary, and adults enroll in and drop out of programs frequently (Comings, Parrella, & Sorricone, 1999). The relative instability of participation makes it exceedingly difficult for participants to improve their literacy skills rapidly. Sticht and Armstrong (1994) estimate that as many as 200 hours of classroom reading instruction may be required to gain one grade level

on standardized reading achievement tests. Most participants in ABLE average far fewer classroom hours than the 200-hour guideline (Development Associates, 1994).

Unfortunately, few studies have examined learner outcomes among adults in ABLE programs. One experimental design study has been reported in which ABLE participants were randomly assigned to different instructional programs (Friedlander & Martinson, 1996). More than 2,200 adults who were recipients of Aid to Families with Dependent Children participated in this study. Those identified as in need of basic education were required to participate in adult basic education, GED, or English-as-a-Second-Language classes as a condition of receiving their full monthly AFDC grant. Although more literacy program participants achieved a GED than did control group members who received no instruction, no statistically significant differences in literacy skills were found following participation, as measured by the Tests of Adult Literacy Skills. Other more qualitative studies have been more positive in demonstrating that adults benefit from participating in literacy education programs (Fingeret & Drennon, 1996; Purcell-Gates, 1995), in terms of increased self-esteem, self-confidence, and ability to assist their children with homework. These are important benefits, but much more difficult to assess than the literacy skills measured by paper-and-pencil tests.

THE TRANSITION FROM SCHOOL TO WORK

From High School and College to the Workplace

The transition to full-time employment from either high school or college is increasingly being investigated as an important period in the lives of young people (Castellano, Stringfield, & Stone, 2003). Economic and sociological models address the aspects of this transition at broad, societal levels, whereas psychological and educational models focus on the transition as it affects the individual (Wigfield, Eccles, & Pintrich, 1996). Economists, for instance, are demonstrating how labor-market problems, such as unemployment and job instability, affect the school-to-work transition. They are finding that this transition can be associated with joblessness, uncertainty, change, and anxiety, especially for disadvantaged, female minorities (Riphahn, 2002; Wentling & Waight, 2001).

In a longitudinal study of Hispanic high-school graduates who did not attend college, Gandertson, Santos, and Reith (2002) found that a significant number had experienced at least one period of extended unemployment. Yet they experienced greater periods of employment than unemployment. In a study of minority youth, Wentling and Waight (2001) discovered that the major barriers to successful school-to-work transition were poverty, school personnel resistance to change, and lack of communication. Mentoring, career exploration and guidance, and relevant curriculum best support the transition from school to work for minority youth.

In a comparative study in France, Germany, Japan, the Netherlands, Sweden, the United Kingdom, and the United States, Ryan (2001) found that for youth under the age of 25, unemployment rates ranged from 7% in the Netherlands to 27% in France, with an overall mean of 13%. The emergence of inactive youth (i.e., those who are neither in school or employed) is a cause of some concern, according to Ryan. Youth inactivity may reflect a preference for travel and recreation. Yet, it is more likely associated with pay inequality and lower-quality job options that reduce the motivation to seek employment. Inactivity is associated, too, with lower educational achievement, school dropout, poorer job-related skills, long-term unemployment, and even crime (Hartnagel, 1998; Riphahn, 2002). The relatively high unemployment and inactivity rates in these seven countries suggest that youth employment problems are international and most acute for socioeconomically disadvantaged minority females. It seems clear that unsuccessful transitions from school to work among youth may have important negative labor-market and societal effects (Franke, 2003; Neumark & Joyce, 2001), particularly when considering the need for a quality workforce to remain competitive in a dynamic world market (Hunt, 1995).

Recognizing the need to improve the system for preparing youth for the transition to productive work, the United States Congress and President Bill Clinton enacted the School-to-Work Opportunities Act in 1994 (STWOA; PL103-239). This Act funded an experiment that accelerated existing social and educational programs in secondary schools to improve academic skills, employ innovative pedagogies, integrate academic and vocational (i.e., career and technical) instruction and work-based learning, encourage partnerships with business and industry, foster career exploration and development activities, and help more youth move into postsecondary education (Castellano et al., 2003; Hughes, Bailey, & Karp, 2002).

Arguably due to the complexity of such a large and ambitious undertaking, research results concerning the effectiveness of school-to-work initiatives have not been consistent (Castellano et al., 2003; Spriggle, 2001). In a review of more than one hundred studies, Hughes et al. (2002) found that a preponderance of the evidence supported participation in school-to-work programs. In general, participation in such programs enhanced student academic achievement, increased the likelihood of higher wages and engagement in meaningful career paths,

provided students with a network of supportive adult mentors, and improved teachers' and employers' views about the benefits of school-to-work initiatives for both the students and themselves. Rigorous research is needed to clarify the short- and long-term results of school-to-work initiatives, particularly as they relate to improving the transition to meaningful full-time work and to adulthood for youth who are disadvantaged (Wentling & Waight, 2001), disabled (Morningstar & Kleinhammer-Tramill, 1999), or gifted (Higgins & Boone, 2003).

Whereas economic and sociological research models help us interpret disparate school-to-work transition data concerning macro-level variables (e.g., unemployment or youth inactivity) on labor markets and society in general, psychological models allow us to understand how school-to-work transition affects individuals and groups. A strength of the psychological approach is its theoretical lenses (e.g., career development, psychosocial, and sociocultural), which can guide future school-to-work transition research and practice, particularly as it relates to learning and the contextual variables associated with its optimal development (Bennert, 2002). Unfortunately, little current developmental and educational psychological research specifically addresses the school-to-work transition (Castellano et al., 2003).

Career development psychologists, however, have seen the usefulness of career development theory in interpreting and facilitating the school-to-work transition process (Lent, Hackett, & Brown, 1999). The Career Development Quarterly recently dedicated a special issue (Volume 47, Number 4) to applying career development theory as a comprehensive model for interpreting and directing the school-to-work transition for individuals. Savickas (1999) presents the developmental perspective for securing a suitable position in a preferred occupation. Savickas applies Super's (1957, 1963) theoretical model of occupational development to assist students in increasing their occupational choice awareness, information seeking, and planning to making intelligent career choices, thereby enhancing employee performance and facilitating successful school-to-work transition.

Krumboltz and Worthington (1999) present a social learning perspective in which career counselors support new learning by encouraging and developing students' curiosity and skills in order to create a satisfying life. In this model, the career counselor is a mentor, coach, and educator who facilitates both formal and informal learning in the context of continual career development. Lent et al. (1999) propose the social cognitive career perspective that emphasizes the relations among self-efficacy, outcomes expectations, and individual goals, and how each guides personal behavior. In essence, successful school-to-work transition is best predicted by strong, but realistic self-efficacy and outcome expectations where students freely identify and explore interests and career alternatives, and the ability to translate their goals into action. Finally, Swanson and Fouad (1999) offer a person-fit theoretical perspective founded on Holland's (1997) model of vocational personality types and Dawis and Lofquist's (1984) theory of work adjustment. This perspective emphasizes the importance of linking person variables to environmental variables to ensure job fit and successful school to work transition. Overall, each theory recognizes the developmental nature of the school-to-work transition, and at least implicitly acknowledges that exploration, experience, and educational activities are important dimensions of this transition.

Felsman and Blustein (1999), for instance, explored the roles of close peer relationships in facilitating exploration and commitment in career development. Late adolescents with higher levels of peer attachment and the ability to experience intimate relationships explored their environments more and made stronger commitments to their career choices. Attachment to one's mother also contributed to these developmental processes.

Erikson's (1968) psychosocial theory of development might be another useful theoretical lens though which to view the school-to-work transition. Through exploration and commitment, adolescents form secure ego identities; psychosocial achievement helps create a stable and unified sense of self. According to Erikson, developing a firm sense of identity is vital to entering the intimate relationships of young adulthood, where individuals fuse their identities with those of others. Both Marcia (1966, 1980) and Arnett (2000) have extended Erikson's notion of identity development to the healthy psychosocial development of adolescents and young adults.

With a large group of German youth, Schmitt-Rodermund and Vondracek (1999) found that exploration was a key precursor of identity achievement and healthy transition to adulthood. Individuals who engaged in a broad range of creative, technical, and cultural activities as children (i.e., those who explored more), especially with their parents, subsequently had more goal-directed interests and pursued more activities as adolescents. Exploratory activity was, in turn, related to identity status and eventual occupational choice.

In an Australian case study, Perrone and Vickers (2003) investigated transitions to work from universities. Study participants reported feelings of uncertainty, inflated expectations, "the work experience paradox," and "a low time" (p. 69). The authors called on higher education institutions to emphasize more strongly their preparation of students for this important life passage. Similarly, in an English study of trainee accountants, graduate engineers, and newly certified nurses, Eraut et al. (2003) found that new graduates in these fields had great difficulty transitioning to their jobs because they had little idea how to apply the knowledge they acquired at the university to meet the challenges of their demanding work. The authors concluded that applying learning in an individual's first professional job is best promoted by engaging in social relationships with more knowledgeable peers who can answer questions and provide informal social support.

Vaillancourt (2001) demonstrated that the postsecondary graduate job changing rate in Canada is best predicted by level of education and number of children. Those with doctoral degrees and without dependent children were most likely to change jobs within their first 2 years after graduation because they felt overqualified and dissatisfied with work conditions such as inadequate hours or pay. Vaillancourt provides compelling evidence of the considerable differences in school-to-work variations among postsecondary graduates.

Career and Technical Education

While career and technical education has been supported in the United States for more than 30 years through the secondary school system (Castellano et al., 2003), it has been backed in the community college system as well (Bragg, 2002). Two-year colleges, with their mission of access (through their open enrollment policy) and service to the lifelong educational needs of their communities, have played a significant role in preparing and developing learners for immediate employment in occupational and technical fields (Weisman & Longacre, 2000). Thirty percent of the students in community colleges are racial or ethnic minorities, one-half work full time, 15 percent work part time, and 60 percent are 21 years of age or older. In the 1990s, federal and state support allowed these colleges to extend their workforce preparation and development activities even further to both traditional and nontraditional students (Bassi & Ludwig, 2000; Hughes et al., 2002). Community colleges continue to develop alternative programs that prepare students for employment, which also includes literacy education (Reder, 1999). Mobley (2002) notes the increased emphasis on the school-to-work transition in community colleges. In 1999, in one semester alone, an estimated 2.5 million students enrolled in postsecondary career and technical education in the United States; roughly half of these students were enrolled in a vocational or technical program.

Career and technical educational programs also arise through partnerships with corporations. UPS, for example, has entered partnerships with colleges and universities to promote workforce development. In exchange for 1-year commitments to work, employees receive individual plans for personal development and educational benefits for their schooling or training. This program has been useful to both the company and young people at risk for school and work failure (Donlevey, 2001). Participants gain marketable knowledge and skills, perform at higher levels, and are more highly motivated to continue their professional development through education.

Military Service

In the early literature addressing the needs of enlisted service personnel, nearly half of the recruits described were not high school graduates. The evidence suggested that even those who had earned high school diplomas needed basic skill development (Benson, 1973). Veeman and Singer (1989) illuminate the extensive efforts of the U.S. military to meet the educational, training, and developmental needs of a modern voluntary military. In 1987, they reported that nearly 700,000 individuals were enrolled in undergraduate and graduate level college classes.

Kime and Anderson (2000) discuss how the U.S. military serves as an engine of powerful social change. Through the G.I. Bill, large numbers of service personnel have access to education for the first time. The military has contributed much to GED testing programs, off-campus programs, literacy education, and distance education as well. Notwithstanding, Smith and Murray's (2002) research suggests that previously the Air Force did not fully value training and education experiences. Although this attitude has changed in recent years because of the dire need for highly trained and competent leaders, prior emphasis was on military hardware rather than on personnel training and development. Overall, the development of more highly trained and educated soldiers has contributed significantly to a more highly skilled, competitive workforce with greater social mobility (Hunt, 1995).

CONCLUSION

We began this chapter by pointing out that several prominent educational psychologists, beginning with Edward L. Thorndike, have studied adult development. Although this work has often been overshadowed by psychology's emphasis on child and adolescent development (and how developmental processes play out in educational settings), interest in adult development is reawakening and reemerging among educational psychologists (Smith & Pourchot, 1998). This may reflect the historic emergence

of the adult population (e.g., those 25 years of age and older) as the largest group in the postsecondary education system, surpassing traditional, 18- to 22-year-olds. Adult learners bring a wealth of experience to the college classroom, and their needs as learners and their motivations and goals differ from those of younger students. Adult students present compelling, but hardly insurmountable, challenges for college and adult educators.

Because of changes in the composition of the college population, higher education administrators and faculty need to better understand adult development. Particularly of concern is the developmental trajectory of adult intelligence. Popular stereotypes to the contrary, the scientific community widely accepts that adults' intellectual skills are relatively unaffected by aging processes until quite late in life. Thus, the potential for continued development and learning throughout the adult years is quite good. Although some adult educators have been reluctant to embrace psychological models to inform and guide their practice (i.e., psychologists' emphasis on individual differences ignores social and cultural factors that influence learning), most recognize the necessity of understanding how developmental and motivational processes influence adult learning (Brookfield, 1986). Educational psychologists' research and theorizing in these domains is particularly salient to adult education practice.

Intellectual aging research within the field of life-span studies has explored the nature of changes in intelligence throughout the adult years. Different developmental trajectories have been observed for the two components of intelligence—fluid and crystallized abilities. Although fluid intelligence may begin to decline by the mid-40s, crystallized abilities improve through the accumulation of social and cultural experiences, including adult education. Much evidence shows that adults become less concerned with purely intellectual problems and puzzles and increasingly turn their attention to more pragmatic concerns as a consequence of confronting the problems of everyday living. Thus, losses in fluid performance due to aging have little practical consequence. Adults' efforts to build, elaborate, and solidify their knowledge, engage in extensive practice within specific domains, and compensate for perceived losses in abilities are crucial intellectual activities. Adult educators thus need to understand the development of expertise. And, although education may contribute to adults becoming expert in specific domains, education, in and of itself, is unlikely to make an individual wise. Experience in the world—in part, a consequence of age—appears to be the chief ingredient in wisdom.

Piaget (1972) described formal operational abilities as the apex of adult cognitive development. Yet, formal operational thinking is limited and does not seem to be fully characteristic of the ways that adults think given the different kinds of problems that they encounter in everyday and uncertain situations. Education that is limited to drawing on adults' abilities to employ logical-mathematical skills and to engage in hypothetical and scientific thinking does not fully tap into adults' intellectual capacities and does not reflect real-world reasoning. Adults must deal with uncertainty and contradictions and must create higher-order systems of thought to understand such complexities.

The middle years of the adult life span have, until quite recently, been overlooked by developmental psychologists who—if they paid attention to adult development at all—were more likely to study aged adults. However, the theoretical foundation regarding personality and social development processes and outcomes established by Erikson and, more recently, Levinson have provided fertile ground for studies of midlife development to flourish. The work of midlife researchers such as Whitbourne and Lachman has greatly contributed to our deeper knowledge of the myriad factors that influence development in the middle years of adulthood.

Increasingly, education is playing a central role in adults' lives—certainly much more so than 50 or even 30 years in the past. No longer is a high school diploma or GED sufficient to ensure reasonable long-term economic well-being. Current occupational and economic demands require adults to become lifelong learners. Higher education institutions need to adapt to the rapid influx of older, part-time, nontraditional adult learners who now make up the majority group on many college campuses. Attending college has pervasive and, in some domains of life, dramatic effects on individuals' development. Personal perspectives and beliefs are challenged, stereotypical thinking is debunked, and technical skills are improved. Although there is evidence that the transition to full-time employment is not without confusion, anxiety, and stress, the adult presumably graduates from college better prepared for work, family, and civic life.

Adult educators, who typically work with post-college-aged adults in many different kinds of educational settings, have vast experience and knowledge of adult learners' needs, motivations, and strengths. Adult education has drawn from the knowledge of learning, cognition and memory, and motivation that educational psychologists have established over the past century. University and college faculty members report that they do little to accommodate differences between their younger and older adult students. Input from adult educators could facilitate the development of methods of instruction that meet the needs of adult learners in higher education.

Adult development is a topic of great importance in a society that is becoming increasingly dominated by adults rather than youth. Developmental processes across the adult years have been studied by developmental psychologists and gerontologists who have focused on age-related changes in intellectual skills, personality psychologists interested in how social forces impinge upon and influence personality development across the life span, and educational psychologists working to improve learning and instruction for adult learners in educational settings. Greater efforts should be devoted to integrating these diverse perspectives and approaches toward building comprehensive models of adult development.

References

Alexander, P. A. (2004). A model of domain learning: Reinterpreting expertise as a multidimensional, multistage process. In D. Y. Dai & R. J. Sternberg (Eds.), *Motivation, emotion, and cognition* (pp. 273–298). Mahwah, NJ: Lawrence Erlbaum Associates.

Anastasi, A. (1988). *Psychological testing* (6th ed.). New York: Macmillan.

Anschutz, L., Camp, C. J., Markley, R. P., Kramer, J. J. (1987). Remembering mnemonics: A three-year follow-up on the effects of mnemonics training in elderly adults. *Experimental Aging Research, 13,* 141–143.

Arnett, J. J. (1994). Are college students adults? Their conceptions of the transition to adulthood. *Journal of Adult Development, 1,* 154–168.

Arnett, J. J. (2000). Emerging adulthood: A theory of development from the late teens through the twenties. *American Psychologist, 55,* 469–480.

Arnett, J. J. (2003). Conceptions of the transition to adulthood among emerging adults in American ethnic groups. *New Directions for Child and Adolescent Development, 100,* 63–75.

Arnone, M. (2004). Please leave, already: Lack of space and high costs are forcing states to push students through more quickly. *Chronicle of Higher Education, 50*(22), A20.

Aslanian, C. B. (2001). *Adult students today.* New York: College Board.

Aslanian, C. B., & Brickell, H. M. (1980). *Americans in transition: Life changes as reasons for adult learning.* New York: College Entrance Examination Board.

Backman, L., Mantyla, T., & Herlitz, A. (1990). Psychological perspectives on successful aging: The optimization of episodic remembering in old age. In P. B. Baltes & M. M. Baltes (Eds.), *Successful aging* (pp. 188–163). New York: Cambridge University Press.

Baltes, P. B. (1987). Theoretical propositions of life-span developmental psychology: On the dynamics between growth and decline. *Developmental Psychology, 23*, 611–626.

Baltes, P. B., & Baltes, M. M. (1990). Psychological perspectives on successful aging: A model of selective optimization with compensation. In P. B. Baltes & M. M. Baltes (Eds.), *Successful aging: Perspectives from the behavioral sciences* (pp. 1–34). New York: Cambridge University Press.

Baltes, P. B., Dittmann-Kohli, F., & Dixon, R. A. (1984). New perspectives on the development of intelligence in adulthood: Toward a dual-process conception and a model of selective optimization with compensation. In P. B. Baltes & O. G. Brim, Jr. (Eds.), *Lifespan development and behavior* (Vol. 6, pp. 33–76). New York: Academic Press.

Baltes, P. B., & Kliegl, R. (1992). Further testing of limits of cognitive plasticity: Negative age differences in a mnemonic skill are robust. *Developmental Psychology, 28*, 121–125.

Baltes, P. B., Lindenberger, U., & Staudinger, U. M. (1998). Life-span theory in developmental psychology. In R.M. Lerner (Ed.), *Handbook of child psychology, Vol. 1: Theoretical models of human development* (5th ed.). New York: Wiley.

Baltes, P. B., Mayer, K.U., Helmchen, H., & Steinhagen-Thiessen, E. (1993). The Berlin aging study (BASE): Overview and design. *Aging & Society, 13*, 483–515.

Baltes, P. B., & Schaie, K. W. (1976). On the plasticity of intelligence in adulthood and old age: Where Horn and Donaldson fail. *American Psychologist, 31*, 770–725.

Baltes, P. B., & Smith, J. (1999). Trends and profiles of psychological functioning in very old age. In P. B. Baltes & K. U. Mayer (Eds.), *The Berlin aging study: Aging from 70 to 100*. New York: Cambridge University Press.

Baltes, P. B., Smith, J., & Staudinger, U. M. (1997). Wisdom and successful aging. In T. Sonderegger (Ed.), *Nebraska symposium on motivation* (Vol. 39, pp. 123–167). Lincoln: University of Nebraska Press.

Baltes, P. B., & Staudinger, U. M. (2000). Wisdom: A metaheuristic (pragmatic) to orchestrate mind and virtue toward excellence. *American Psychologist, 55*, 122–136.

Bartlett, F. C. (1932). *Remembering*. Cambridge, England: Cambridge University Press. Barton, D., & Hamilton, H. (1998). *Local literacies: Reading and writing in one community*. London: Routledge.

Barton, D., & Hamilton, M. (1998). *Local literacies: Reading and writing in one community*. London: Routledge.

Basseches, M. (1984). *Dialectical thinking and adult development*. Norwood, NJ: Ablex.

Bassi, L. J., & Ludwig, J. (2000). School-to-work programs in the United States: A multi-firm case study of training, benefits, and costs. *Industrial & Labor Relations, 53*, 1–27.

Bayley, N., & Oden, M. H. (1955). The maintenance of intellectual ability in gifted adults. *Journal of Gerontology, 10*, 91–107.

Bennert, K. (2002). Formulations of participation and nonparticipation in trainee's narratives of school-to-work transitions. *Text, 22*, 369–392.

Benson, G. C. S. (1973). A great opportunity. *Education, 93*, 310–313.

Birren, J. E., & Schroots, J. J. F. (1996). History, concepts, and theory in the psychology of aging. In J. E. Birren & K. W. Schaie (Eds.), *Handbook of the psychology of aging* (pp. 3–23). San Diego. CA: Academic Press.

Blaxter, L. & Tight, M. (1995). Life transitions and educational participation by adults. *International Journal of Lifelong Education, 14*, 231–246.

Bragg, D. D. (2002). Contemporary vocational models and programs: What the research tells us. *New Directions for Community Colleges, 117*, 25–34.

Brigham, M. C., & Pressley, M. (1988). Cognitive monitoring and strategy choice in younger and older adults. *Psychology and Aging, 3*, 249–257.

Brookfield, S. (1986). *Understanding and facilitating adult learning*. San Francisco: Jossey-Bass.

Brophy, J. E. (1998). *Motivating students to learn*. New York: McGraw-Hill.

Campbell, D. P. (1965). A cross-sectional and longitudinal study of scholastic abilities over twenty-five years. *Journal of Counseling Psychology, 12*, 55–61.

Castellano, M., Stringfield, S., & Stone, J. R., III. (2003). Secondary career and technical education and comprehensive school reform: Implications for research and practice. *Review of Educational Research, 73*, 231–272.

Cattell, R. B. (1963). Theory of fluid and crystallized intelligence: A critical approach. *Journal of Educational Psychology, 54*, 1–22.

Cavanaugh, J. C. (1996). Memory self-efficacy as a key to understanding memory change. In F. Blanchard-Fields & T. M. Hess (Eds.), *Perspectives on cognitive changes in adulthood and aging* (pp. 488–507). New York: McGraw-Hill.

Charness, N., & Bosman, E. A. (1990). Expertise and aging: Life in the lab. In T. M. Hess (Ed.), *Aging and cognition: Knowledge organization and utilization* (pp. 343–385). Amsterdam: North-Holland.

Clancy, S. M., & Hoyer, W. J. (1994). Age and skill in visual search. *Developmental Psychology, 30*, 545–552.

Clayton, V. & Birren, J. E. (1975). The development of wisdom across the life span: A reexamination of an ancient topic. In P. B. Baltes & O. G. Brim, Jr. (Eds.), *Life-span development and behavior*, Vol. 3 (pp. 103–135). San Diego, CA: Academic Press.

Cohen, G. (1996). Memory and learning in normal aging: In R. T. Woods (Ed.), *Handbook of the clinical psychology of ageing* (pp. 43-58). London: Wiley.

Cohen, P., Kasen, S., Chen, H., Hartmark, C., & Gordon, K. (2003). Variations in patterns of developmental transitions in the merging adulthood period. *Developmental Psychology, 39*, 657–669.

Comings, J. P., Parrella, A. & Soricone, L. (1999). *Persistence among adult basic education students in pre-GED classes*. NCSALL Report No. 12. Cambridge, MA: National Center for the Study of Adult Learning & Literacy, Harvard University

Courtenay, B. C. (1994). Are psychological models of adult development still important for the practice of adult education? *Adult Education Quarterly, 44*, 145–153.

Courtney, S. (1991). *Why adults learn: Toward a theory of participation in adult education*. New York: Routledge.

Cross, P. K. (1981). *Adults as learners: Increasing participation and facilitating learning*. San Francisco: Jossey-Bass.

Darkenwald, G., & Novak, R. J. (1997). Classroom age composition and academic achievement in college. *Adult Education Quarterly, 47*, 108–116.

Dawis, R. V., & Lofquist, L. (1984). *A psychological theory of work adjustment*. Minneapolis: University of Minnesota Press.

Derwinger, A., Stigsdotter Neely, A., Persson, M., Hill, R. D., & Backman, L. (2003). Remembering numbers in old age: Mnemonic training versus self-generated strategy training. *Aging Neuropsychology & Cognition, 10*, 202–214.

Development Associates (1994). *National evaluation of adult education programs: Executive summary*. Washington, DC: Author.

Dittmann-Kohli, E., & Baltes, P. B. (1990). Toward a neofunctionalist conception of adult intellectual development: Wisdom as a prototypical case of intellectual growth. In C. N. Alexander & E. J. Langer (Eds.), *Higher stages of human development: Perspectives on adult growth*. Oxford: Oxford University Press.

Donaldson, J. F., & Graham, S. W. (1999). A model of college outcomes for adults. *Adult Education Quarterly, 50*, 24–40.

Donaldson, J. F., Graham, S. W., Martindill, W., & Bradley, S. (2000). Adult undergraduate students: How do they define their experiences and their success? *The Journal of Continuing Higher Education, 48*, 1–11.

Donlevey, J. (2001). Teachers, technology and training. *International Journal of Instructional Media, 28*, 329–335.

Eccles, J. S., Templeton, J., Barber, B., & Stone, M. (2003). Adolescence and emerging adulthood. In M. H. Bornstein, L. Davidson, C. L. M. Keyes, & K. A. Moore (Eds.), *Well-being: Positive development across the life course*. Mahwah, NJ: Lawrence Erlbaum Associates.

Eraut, M., Maillardet, F., Miller, C., Steadman, S., Ali, A., Blackman, C., et al. (2003, April). *Learning in the first professional job: The first full time employment after college for accountants, engineers and nurses*. Paper presented at the annual meeting of the American Educational Research Association, Chicago, IL.

Ericsson, K. A., & Charness, N. (1995). Abilities: Evidence for talent or characteristics acquired through engagement in relevant activities? *American Psychologist, 50*, 803–804.

Erikson, E. H. (1950). *Childhood and society*. New York: Norton.

Erikson, E. H. (1968). *Identity, youth, and crisis*. New York: Norton.

Erikson, E. H. (1982). *The life cycle completed: A review*. New York: Norton.

Erikson, E. H. (1984). Reflections on the last stage—and the first. *Psychoanalytic Study of the Child, 39*, 155–165.

Felsman, D. E., & Blustein, D. L. (1999). The role of peer relatedness in late adolescent career development. *The Career Development Quarterly, 54*, 279–295.

Fingeret, H. A, & Drennon, C. (1996). *Literacy for life: Adult learners, new practices*. New York: Teachers College Press.

Fitzgerald, J. M. (2000). Younger and older jurors: The influence of environmental supports on memory performance and decision making in complex trials. *Journals of Gerontology Series B: Psychological Sciences and Social Sciences, 55*, 323–331.

Franke, S. (2003). Studying and working: The busy lives of students with paid employment. *Canadian Social Trends, 11*, 22–25.

Friedlander, D., & Martinson, K. (1996). Effects of mandatory basic education for adult AFDC recipients. *Educational Evaluation and Policy Analysis, 18*, 327–337.

Ganderson, P. T., Santos, R., & Seitz, P. (2002). Employment patterns of Hispanic graduates without college experience. *School Science Journal, 39*, 301–307.

Garrison, D. R. (1997). Self-directed learning: Toward a comprehensive model. *Adult Education Quarterly, 48*, 18–33.

Gianakos, I. (1996). Career development differences between adult and traditional-aged learners. *Journal of Career Development, 22*, 211–223.

Gorham, J. (1985). Differences between teaching adults and pre-adults: A closer look. *Adult Education Quarterly, 35*, 194–209.

Graham, S. W. (1998). Looking at adult growth in college: Examining the effects of age and educational ethos. *Journal of College Student Development, 39*, 239–250.

Graham, S. W., & Donaldson, J. F. (1996). Assessing personal growth for adults enrolled in higher education. *Journal of Continuing Higher Education, 44*, 7–22.

Graham, S. W., & Donaldson, J. F. (1999). Adult students academic and intellectual development in college. *Adult Education Quarterly, 49*, 147–161.

Greenberg, M. (1997). *The GI bill: The law that changed America*. Atlanta: Lickle.

Guthrie, J. T., & Greaney, V. (1991). Literacy acts. In R. Barr, M. L. Kamil, P. Mosenthal, & P. D. Pearson (Eds.), *Handbook of reading research (Vol. II*, pp. 68–96). New York: Longman.

Hall, G. S. (1922). *Senescence: The last half of life*. New York: Appleton.

Hartnagel, T. F. (1998). Labour-market problems and rime in the transition from school to work. *Canadian Review of Sociology & Anthropology, 35*, 1–19.

Hartree, A. (1984). Malcolm Knowles' theory of andragogy: A critique. *International Journal of Lifelong Education, 3*, 203–210.

Hertzog, C., Dixon, R. A., & Hultsch, D. (1990). Relationships between metamemory, memory predictions, and memory task performances. *Psychology & Aging, 5*, 215–223.

Hertzog, C., & Hultsch, D. (2000). Metacognition in adulthood and old age. In F. I. M. Craik & T. A. Salthouse (Eds.), *The handbook of aging and cognition* (2nd ed., pp. 417–466). Mahwah, NJ: Lawrence Erlbaum Associates.

Hiemstra, R. (1998). From whence have we come: The first twenty-five years of educational gerontology. In J. C. Fisher & M. A. Wolf (Eds.). *Using learning to meet the challenges of older adulthood* (New Directions for Adult and Continuing Education, No. 77). San Francisco: Jossey-Bass.

Higgins, K., & Boone, R. (2003). Beyond the boundaries of school. *Intervention in School & Clinic, 38,* 138–144.

Hogan, D. P., & Astone, N. M. (1986). The transition to adulthood. *Annual Review of Sociology, 12,* 109–130.

Holland, J. L. (1997). *Making vocational choices: A theory of vocational personalities and work environments* (3rd ed.). Odessa, FL: Psychological Assessment Resources.

Houle, C. O. (1961). *The inquiring mind.* Madison: University of Wisconsin Press.

Hughes, J. A., & Graham, S. W. (1990). Adult life roles: A new approach to adult development. *Journal of Continuing Higher Education, 38,* 2–8.

Hughes, K. L., Bailey, T. R., & Karp, M. (2002). School-to-work: Making a difference in education. *Phi Delta Kappan, 84,* 272–279.

Hunt, E. (1995). *Will we be smart enough? A cognitive analysis of the coming workforce.* New York: Sage.

Jacobs, N. (1989). Nontraditional students: The new ecology of the classroom. *Educational Forum, 53,* 329–336.

Jarvis, P. (1987). *Adult learning in the social context.* London: Croom Helm.

Jones, H. E., & Conrad, H. S. (1933). The growth and decline of intelligence. *Genetic Psychology Monographs, 13,* 223–298.

Justice, E. M., & Dornan, T. M. (2001). Metacognitive differences between traditional-aged and nontraditional-age college students. *Adult Education Quarterly, 51,* 236–249.

Kamin, C. S., O'Sullivan, P. S., Younger, M., & Deterding, R. (2001). Measuring critical thinking in problem-based learning discourse. *Teaching and Learning in Medicine, 12,* 27–35.

Kasworm, C. E. (2002a). African American adult undergraduates: Differing cultural realities. *Journal of Continuing Higher Education, 50,* 10–29.

Kasworm, C. E. (2002b). Setting the stage: Adults in higher education. *New Directions for Student Services, 102,* 3–10.

Kime, S. F., & Anderson, C. L. (2000). Contributions of the military to adult and continuing education. In A. L. Wilson & E. R. Hayes (Eds.), *Handbook of adult and continuing education* (pp. 464–479). San Francisco: Jossey-Bass.

King, P. M., & Kitchener, K. S. (1994). *Developing reflective judgment.* San Francisco: Jossey-Bass.

Knowles, M. S. (1980). *The modern practice of adult education: From pedagogy to andragogy* (2nd ed.). New York: Cambridge.

Knowles, M. S. (1990). *The adult learner: A neglected species* (4th ed.). Houston: Gulf Publishing.

Knox, A. B. (1980). Proficiency theory of adult learning. *Contemporary Educational Psychology, 5,* 378–404.

Kopka, T. L. C., & Peng, S. S. (1993). *Adult education: Main reasons for participating.* National Center for Education Statistics Report No. 93-451. Washington, DC: U.S. Department of Education.

Kramer, D. A. (1989). Development of an awareness of contradiction across the life span and the question of postformal

operations. In M. L. Commons, J. D. Sinnott, F. A Richards, & C. Armon (Eds.), *Adult development, Vol. 1: Comparisons and applications of developmental models* (pp. 133–160). New York: Praeger.

Krumboltz, J., & Worthington, R. L. (1999). The school-to-work transition from a learning perspective. *The Career Development Quarterly, 47, 312–325.*

Kuh, G. (1995). The other curriculum: Out-of-class experiences associated with student learning and personal development. *Journal of Higher Education, 66,* 123–155.

Labouvie-Vief, G. (1992). A new Piagetian perspective on adult cognitive development. In R. J. Sternberg & C. A. Berg (Eds.), *Intellectual development.* New York: Cambridge University Press.

Lachman, M. E. (Ed.) (2001). *Handbook of midlife development.* New York: Wiley.

Lachman, M. E., Bandura, M., Weaver, S. L., & Elliott, E. (1995). Assessing memory control beliefs: The memory controllability inventory. *Aging & Cognition, 2,* 67–84.

Lachman, M. E., Lewkowicz, C., Marcus, A., & Peng, Y. (1994). Images of midlife development among young, middle-aged, and older adults. *Journal of Adult Development, 1,* 201–211.

Lent, R. W., Hackett, G., & Brown, S. D. (1999). A social cognitive view of school-to-work transition. *The Career Development Quarterly, 47,* 297–311.

Levinson, D. J., Darrow, C. N., Klein, E. B., Levinson, M. H., & McKee, B. (1978). *The seasons of a man's life.* New York: Ballantine.

Levinson, D. J., & Levinson, J. D. (1996). *The seasons of a woman's life.* New York: Ballantine Books.

Lovelace, E.A. (1990). Basic concepts in cognition and aging. In E.A. Lovelace (Ed.), *Aging and cognition: Mental processes, self awareness, and interventions* (pp. 1–28). Amsterdam: North Holland, Elsevier.

MacKay, D. G., & Abrams, L. (1996). Language, memory, and aging: Distributed deficits and the structure of new-versus-old connections. In J. E. Birren, K. W. Schaie, R. P. Abeles, M. Gatz, & T. A. Salthouse (Eds.), *Handbook of the psychology of aging* (4th ed., pp. 251–265). San Diego; CA: Academic Press.

Marcia, J. E. (1966). Development and validation of ego-identity status. *Journal of Personality and Social Psychology, 3,* 551–558.

Marcia, J. E. (1980). Identity in adolescence. In J. Adelson (Ed.). *Handbook of adolescent psychology.* New York: Wiley.

McClusky, H. Y. (1963). The course of the adult life span. In W. C. Hallenbeck (Ed.), *Psychology of adults.* Washington, DC: Adult Education Association.

McCrae, R. R., & Costa, P. T. J. (1990). *Personality in adulthood.* New York: Guilford.

Merriam, S. B., & Brockett, R. G. (1997). *The profession and practice of adult education: An introduction.* San Francisco: Jossey-Bass.

Merriam, S. B., & Caffarella, R. S. (1998). *Learning in adulthood: A comprehensive guide* (2nd ed.). San Francisco: Jossey-Bass.

Mezirow, J. (1990). *Fostering critical reflection in adulthood: A guide to transformative and emancipatory learning*. San Francisco: Jossey-Bass.

Mikulecky, L. (1982). Job literacy: The relationship between school preparation and workplace actuality. *Reading Research Quarterly, 17*, 400–419.

Miller, K. (1989). Helping faculty adapt to adult learners. *ACA Bulletin, 68*, 70–79.

Mobley, C. (2002). Community colleges and the school-to-work transition: A multilevel analysis. *Sociological Inquiry, 72*, 256–284.

Morest, V. S. (2004, April). *The role of community colleges in state adult education systems: A national analysis*. New York: Council for the Advancement of Adult Literacy. Retrieved October 14, 2004; from http://www.caalusa.org/columbiawp3.pdf.

Morningstar, M. E., & Kleinhammer-Tramill, J. P. (1999). Using successful models of student-centered transition services for adolescents with disabilities. *Focus on Exceptional Children, 31*, 1–26.

Morrow, D. G., Hier, C. M., Menard, W. E., & Leirer, V. O. (1998). Icons improve older and younger adults' comprehension of medical information. *Journal of Gerontology: Psychological Sciences and Social Sciences, 53B*, 240–254.

Mortimer, J. T., Finch, M. D., Ryu, S., Shanahan, M. J., & Call, K. T. (1996). The effects of work intensity on adolescent mental health, achievement, and behavioral adjustment: New evidence from a prospective study. *Child Development, 67*, 1243–1261.

Mortimer, J. T., & Johnson, M. K. (1998). New perspectives on adolescent work and the transition to adulthood. In R. Jessor (Ed.), *New perspectives on adolescent risk behavior* (pp. 425–496). New York: Cambridge University Press.

Nelson, L. J. (2003). Rites of passage in emerging adulthood: Perspectives of young Mormons. *New Directions for Child and Adolescent Development, 100*, 33–49.

Neugarten, B. L., Havighurst, R. J., & Tobin, S. S. (1968). Personality and patterns of aging. In B. L. Neugarten (Ed.), *Middle age and aging* (pp. 173–174). Chicago: University of Chicago Press.

Neumark, D., & Joyce, M. (2001). Evaluating school-to-work programs using the new NLSY. *Journal of Human Resources, 36*, 1–45.

Newton, P., & Roberts, P. (1987). Levinsonian studies of women's adult development. *Psychology & Aging, 2*, 154–163.

Orndorff, R. M., & Herr, E. L. (1996). A comparative study of declared and undeclared college students on career uncertainty and involvement in career development activities. *Journal of Counseling & Development, 74*, 632–639.

Park, D. C., Smith, A. D., & Cavanaugh, J. C. (1990). Metamemories of memory researchers. *Memory & Cognition, 18*, 321–327.

Pascarella, E. T., & Terenzini, P. T. (1991). *How college affects students: Finding and insights from twenty years of research*. San Francisco: Jossey-Bass.

Penland, P. R. (1979). Self-initiated learning. *Adult education, 29*, 170–179. Pittsburgh: University of Pittsburgh.

Perrone, P., & Vickers, M. H. (2003). Life after graduation as a "very uncomfortable world": An Australian case study. *Education + Training, 45*, 69–78.

Perry, W. G. (1970). *Forms of intellectual and ethical development in the college years*. Austin, TX: Holt, Rinehart & Winston.

Piaget, J. (1972). Intellectual evolution from adolescence to adulthood. *Human Development, 16*, 346–370.

Pourchot, T., & Smith, M C. (2004). Some implications of life span developmental psychology for adult education and learning. *PAACE Journal of Lifelong Learning, 13*, 69–82.

Pratt, D. D. (1993). Andragogy after twenty-five years. In S. B. Merriam (Ed.), *An update on adult learning theory*. New Directions for Adult & Continuing Education, 57. San Francisco: Jossey-Bass.

Pressey, S. L., & Kuhlen, R. G. (1957). *Psychological development through the life span*. New York: Harpers & Brothers.

Pressley, M., Levin, J. R., & Ghatala, E. S. (1984). Memory strategy monitoring in adults and children. *Journal of Verbal Learning & Verbal Behavior, 23*, 270–288.

Purcell-Gates, V. (1995). *Other people's words: The cycle of low literacy*. Cambridge, MA: Harvard University Press.

Rasmussen, D. X., Rebok, G., Bylsma, F. W., & Brandt, J. (1999). Effects of three types of memory training in normal elderly. *Aging Neuropsychology & Cognition, 6*, 56–66.

Reder, S. (1999). Adult literacy and postsecondary education students: Overlapping populations and learning trajectories. In J. Comings, B. Garner, & C. Smith (Eds.), *Annual review of adult learning and literacy*, Vol. 1. San Francisco: Jossey-Bass.

Reder, S. (1994). Practice-engagement theory: A sociocultural approach to literacy across languages and cultures. In B. M. Ferdman, R. M. Weber, & A. G. Ramirez (Eds.), *Literacy across language and cultures* (pp. 33–74). Albany, NY: SUNY Press.

Reio, T. G., Jr., & Choi, N. (2004). Novelty seeking across the lifespan: Increases accompany decline. *The Journal of Genetic Psychology, 165*, 119–133.

Reio, T. G., Jr., & Wiswell, A. K. (2000). Field investigation of the relationship between adult curiosity, workplace learning and job performance. *Human Resource Development Quarterly, 11*, 1–36.

Richards, R. K. (1986). Physicians' self-directed learning. *Mobius, 6*, 1–13.

Richardson, J. T. E., & King, E. (1998). Adult students in higher education: Burden or boon? *Journal of Higher Education, 69*, 65–88.

Riegel, K. F. (1976). The dialectics of human development. *American Psychologist, 31*, 689–700.

Riphahn, R. T. (2002). Residential location and youth unemployment: The economic geography of school-to-work transitions. *Journal of Populations Economics, 15*, 115–135.

Ryan, P. (2001). The school-to-work transition: A cross-national perspective. *Journal of Economic Literature, 33*, 34–92.

Rybash, J. M., Hoyer, W. J., & Roodin, P. A. (1986). *Developmental changes in processing, knowing and thinking*. New York: Pergamon.

Salthouse, T.A. (n.d.). *Living longer: The changing mind*. Stealing time—The new science of aging. Retrieved November 8,

2004, from http://www.pbs.org/stealingtime/living/mind.htm.

Salthouse, T. A. (1993). Speed and knowledge as determinants of adult age differences in verbal tasks. *Journal of Gerontology: Psychological Sciences, 48*, 29–36.

Salthouse, T. A. (1996). The processing-speed theory of adult age differences in cognition. *Psychological Review, 103*, 403–428.

Savickas, M. L. (1999). The transition from school to work: A development perspective. *The Career Development Quarterly, 47*, 326–336.

Schaie, K. W. (1965). A general model for the study of developmental problems. *Psychological Bulletin, 64*, 92–107.

Schaie, K. W. (1994). The course of adult intellectual development. *American Psychologist, 49*, 304–313.

Schaie, K. W. (1996). *Intellectual development in adulthood: The Seattle longitudinal study*. New York: Cambridge University Press.

Schaie, K. W., & Willis, S. L. (1986). Can decline in adult cognitive functioning be reversed? *Developmental Psychology, 22*, 223–232.

Schmitt-Rodermund, E., & Vondracek, F. W. (1999). Breadth of interests, exploration, and identity development in adolescence. *Journal of Vocational Behavior, 55*, 298–317.

Schoenfield, D., & Robertson, B. A. (1966). Memory storage and aging. *Canadian Journal of Psychology, 20*, 228–236.

Sinnott, J. (1984). *Everyday memory and solution of everyday problems*. Paper presented at the annual meeting of the American Psychological Association, Toronto.

Sinnott, J. D. (1998). *The development of logic in adulthood: Postformal thought and its applications*. New York: Plenum.

Smith, J. M., & Murray, D. J. (2002). Valuing Air Force education and training. *Air & Space Power Journal, 16*, 1–8.

Smith, M. C. (2000). What will be the demands of literacy in the workplace in the next millennium? *Reading Research Quarterly, 35*, 378–379.

Smith, M. C., & Pourchot, T. (Eds.) (1998). *Adult learning and development: Perspectives from educational psychology*. Mahwah, NJ: Lawrence Erlbaum Associates.

Spriggle, T. (2001). School-to-work: A movement in crisis. *Georgetown Journal of Poverty Law & Policy, 8*, 429–445.

Sternberg, R. J. (2000). Group and individual differences in intelligence: What can and should we do about them? In A. Kozulin & Y. Rand (Eds.), *Experience of mediated learning: An impact of Feuerstein's theory in education and psychology. Advances in learning and instruction series* (pp. 55–82). New York: Pergamon.

Sticht, T. G., & Armstrong, W. B. (1994, February). *Adult literacy in the United States: A compendium of quantitative data and interpretive comments*. San Diego: Applied Behavioral & Cognitive Sciences, Inc.

Super, D. E. (1957). *The psychology of careers*. New York: Harper.

Super, D. E. (1963). Toward making self-concept theory operational. In D. E. Super, R. Starishevsky, N. Matlin, & J. P. Jordan, *Career development: Self-concept theory*. New York: College Entrance Examination Board.

Swanson, J. L., & Fouad, N. A. (1999). Applying theories of person-environment fit to the transition from school to work. *The Career Development Quarterly, 47*, 337–347.

Taylor, K. (1996). Why psychological models of adult development are important for the practice of adult education: A response to Courtenay. *Adult Education Quarterly, 47*, 54–62.

Tennant, M. (1997). *Psychology and adult learning* (2nd ed.). London: Routledge.

Thorndike, E. L., Bregman, E. O., Tilton, J. W., & Woodyard, E. (1928). *Adult learning*. New York: Macmillan.

Tough, A. (1971). *The adult's learning projects: A fresh approach to theory and practice in adult learning* (2nd ed.). Toronto: OISE.

Tough, A. (1978). Major learning efforts: Recent research and future directions. *Adult Education, 28*, 250–263.

Tuddenham, R. D., Blumenkrantz, J., & Wilkins, W. R. (1968). Age changes in AGCT: A longitudinal study of average adults. *Journal of Counseling & Clinical Psychology, 32*, 659–663.

Tulving, E. (1985). How many memory systems are there? *American Psychologist, 40*, 385–398.

U.S. Department of Education (2002a). *Digest of education statistics*. Washington, DC: National Center for Education Statistics.

U.S. Department of Education (2002b). *The condition of education 2002*. Washington, DC: National Center for Education Statistics.

U.S. Department of Education (2001). *Integrated postsecondary education data system*. Washington, DC: National Center for Education Statistics

U.S. Department of Education (1999a). *National household education survey (NHES), adult education interview*. Washington, DC: National Center for Education Statistics.

U.S. Department of Education (1999b). *Digest of education statistics*. Washington, DC: National Center for Education Statistics.

U.S. Department of Education (1986). *Bulletin*. Washington, DC: Office of Educational Research and Improvement.

U.S. Department of Labor. (1991). *What work requires of schools*. Washington, DC: Secretary's Commission on Achieving Necessary Skills.

Vaillancourt, C. (2001). The school-to-work transition: What motivates graduates to change jobs? *Education Quarterly Review, 7*, 18–24.

Veeman, F. C., & Singer, H. (1989). Armed forces. In S. B. Merriam & P. M. Cunningham (Eds.), *Handbook of adult and continuing education* (pp. 334–355). San Francisco: Jossey-Bass.

Verhaeghen, P., Marcoen, A., & Goossens, L. (1993). Facts and fiction about memory aging: A quantitative integration of research findings. *Journal of Gerontology: Psychological Sciences, 48*, 157–171.

Weintraub, S., Powell, D. H., & Whitla, D. K. (1994). Successful cognitive aging: Individual differences among physicians on a computerized test of mental state. *Journal of Geriatric Psychiatry, 27*, 15–34.

Weisman, I. M., & Longacre, M. S. (2000). Exploring "community" in community college practice. In A. L. Wilson & E. R.

Hayes (Eds.), *Handbook of Adult and Continuing Education* (pp. 360–374). San Francisco: Jossey-Bass.

Wentling, R. M., & Waight, C. L. (2001). Initiatives that assist and barriers that hinder the successful transition of minority youth into the workplace in the USA. *Journal of Education and Work, 14,* 71–89.

West, R. L. (1992). Everyday memory and aging: A diversity of tests, tasks, and paradigms. In R. L. West & J. D. Sinnott (Eds.), *Everyday memory and aging: Current research and methodology* (pp. 3–21). New York: Springer-Verlag.

West, R. F., Stanovich, K. E., & Mitchell, H. R. (1993). Reading in the real world and its correlates. *Reading Research Quarterly, 28,* 34–50.

Whitbourne, S.K. (2002). *The aging individual: Physical and psychological perspectives* (2nd ed.). New York: Springer.

Whitbourne, S. K., & Collins, K. C. (1998). Identity and physical changes in later adulthood: Theoretical and clinical implications. *Psychotherapy, 35,* 519–530.

Whitbourne, S. K., & Connolly, L. A. (1999). The developing self in midlife. In S. L. Willis & J. D. Reid (Eds.), *Life in the middle: Psychological and social development in middle age* (pp. 25–45). San Diego, CA: Academic Press.

Whitbourne, S. K., Sneed, J. R., & Skultety, K. M. (2002). Identity processes in adulthood: Theoretical and methodological challenges. *Identity, 2,* 29–45.

Whitbourne, S. K., & van Manen, K.-J. (1996). Age differences and correlates of identity status from college through middle adulthood. *Journal of Adult Development, 3,* 59–70.

Whitbourne, S. K., Zuschlag, M. K., Elliott, L. B., & Waterman, A. S. (1992). Psychosocial development in adulthood: A 22-year sequential study. *Journal of Personality & Social Psychology, 63,* 260–271.

Wigfield, A., Eccles, J. S., & Pintrich, P. (1996). Development between the ages of 11 and 25. In D. C. Berliner and R. C. Calfee (Eds.), *Handbook of educational psychology* (pp. 148–185). New York: Simon & Schuster Macmillan.

Wilcox, S. (1996). Fostering self-directed learning in the university setting. *Studies in Higher Education, 21,* 165–176.

Wingfield, A., & Kahana, M. J. (2002). The dynamics of memory retrieval in older adulthood. *Canadian Journal of Experimental Psychology, 56,* 187–199.

Woodruff-Pak, D. S., Jaeger, M. E., Gorman, C., & Wesnes, K. A. (1999). Relationships among age, conditioned stimulus-unconditioned stimulus interval, and neuropsychological test performance. *Neuropsychology, 13,* 90–102.

Yang, B. (1998). Longitudinal study of participation in adult education: A theoretical formulation and empirical investigation. *International Journal of Lifelong Education, 17,* 247–259.

· 7 ·

INDIVIDUAL DIFFERENCES
IN COGNITIVE FUNCTIONS

Phillip L. Ackerman
Georgia Institute of Technology

David F. Lohman
University of Iowa

PREAMBLE

The study of individual differences in cognitive functioning dates back almost to the beginning of the modern psychology (e.g., Cattell, 1890; Cattell & Farrand, 1896). Intelligence testing in the service of education has been a hallmark of differential psychology since the earliest development of the Binet–Simon (1905) scales, and the English translations and adaptations by Goddard (1908), Kuhlman (1912, 1922), Terman (1916), and others. In the decades that followed these early efforts, thousands of studies have been reported on many different aspects of intellectual abilities and achievements. For example, Wright (1968) documented 6,736 articles and books concerning human intelligence. A quick survey (using Psych-Info) indicates there has been no slowing of research in the field; from 1969 to 2004, there were 36,036 articles, chapters, and books that at least mentioned "human intelligence" and another 4,567 dissertations, though there is certainly some overlap between these sets. Given this enormous literature, it is impossible to provide a comprehensive review, even if the search is limited to investigations with direct implications for educational psychology.

Thankfully, there have been several recent reviews of the field. Most notable is Carroll's (1993) reanalysis and integration of more than 460 factor-analytic studies of cognitive abilities. In addition, in the first edition of this series, Gustafsson and Undheim (1996) provided a remarkably thorough and thoughtful review of the central issues of individual differences in abilities, with special attention to educational implications and applications. More recently, Lubinski (2000) reviewed the incremental validity of ability, interest, and personality variables in the prediction of intellectual development, vocational adjustment, work performance, and other life outcomes. Jensen (1998) provided a summary of research on *g*. And McGrew and Evans (2004) summarized revisions and extensions to the Cattell–Horn–Carroll theory since the publication of Carroll's (1993) book.

Because the study of human abilities is a comparatively mature field, there is no need to reiterate the points made repeatedly in each of these reviews. Instead, our goal for this chapter is to provide an overview of a few salient areas that have evidenced either a marked increase in research activity or new substantive discussion over the past decade. For example, although cognitive psychology continues to affect in useful ways our understanding of ability constructs, most of the research in the past decade that bears this influence has focused on relationships between constructs (such as relationships among working memory, knowledge, and reasoning) rather than

139

continued, in-depth analyses of particular tasks thought to be good markers for particular abilities. Thus, we make no effort to update previous summaries of this literature (Lohman, 2000; Pellegrino, Chudowsky, & Glaser, 2001; Snow & Lohman, 1989). Instead, we focus on those research questions that have sparked widespread interest and that have the most direct implications for educators. Readers interested in broader surveys are encouraged to consult other summaries (e.g., Ackerman, Kyllonen, & Roberts, 1999; Mislevy, in press; Sternberg & Pretz, 2005). We trust that the topics reviewed in this chapter give the reader a taste of the current directions in the field, that provide a good representation of what Lakatos (1978) referred to as "progressive research programmes" and "degenerating research programmes."

RECENT DEVELOPMENTS IN THEORIES OF COGNITIVE ABILITIES

A Brief Synopsis of the Cattell–Horn–Carroll (CHC) Theory

Of the many recurring misconceptions about human abilities, one of the most harmful for educational researchers is the belief that they can adequately represent ability in their research by some measure of g. This belief is abetted in part by the fact that g is the single best predictor of many important educational and social criteria, especially those that are also averages over diverse performances. However, more specific criteria (e.g., grades in a particular class rather than GPA) are better predicted when ability constructs other than g are added to the mix (Gustafsson & Balke, 1993; Wittmann & Süß, 1999). Indeed, as behavior becomes more specific and contextualized, measures of g become less useful and measures of more specific knowledge, skills, and abilities become more useful for prediction and explanation. Educational researchers who include ability constructs in their studies need to represent abilities of different levels of breadth or generality. But to do this well requires knowledge of the abilities at different levels in the ability hierarchy and of the tests that can be used to estimate each. Therefore, we briefly summarize the key features of the major contemporary model of human abilities.

The Cattell–Horn–Carroll (CHC) theory of cognitive abilities is the best validated model of human cognitive abilities. The theory integrates Carroll's (1993) three-stratum theory with the Gf-Gc theories of Cattell (1971/1987) and Horn (1991; Horn & Noll, 1997). CHC theory posits a three-strata ability hierarchy. Stratum I contains more than 70 primary or narrow cognitive abilities (e.g., memory span, mechanical knowledge, closure speed, phonetic coding, associative memory, reading speed, speed of articulation). These are the most psychologically transparent abilities. Many are critical aptitudes for success in particular educational tasks (e.g., phonetic coding abilities for early reading). Stratum II consists of nine broad group factors: Fluid Reasoning (Gf), Comprehension-Knowledge (Gc), Short-term Memory (Gsm), Visual Processing (Gv), Auditory Processing (Ga), Long-term Retrieval (Glr), Processing Speed (Gs), Decision/Reaction Time Speed (Gt), Reading and Writing (Grw), and Quantitative Knowledge (Gq). Finally, general ability or g sits alone at stratum III.

McGrew and Evans (2004) have recently provided a review of this theory, with particular attention to changes to the theory that have occurred since the publication of Carroll's (1993) seminal book. Table 7.1 is abstracted from this review. Readers are encouraged to consult these publications for more detailed exposition of each of the factors in the model.

Recent Developments in CHC Theory

Five of the general factors in the model have been studied extensively in recent years. We briefly note some of these efforts.

Visual Processing (Gv). There has been a resurgence of interest in the utility of Gv abilities for the prediction of educational and occupational choice. For example, Shea, Lubinski, and Benbow (2001) found that spatial abilities measured in early adolescence contributed importantly to the prediction of subsequent educational and vocational preferences of academically gifted students, even after verbal and mathematic abilities had been entered in the regression models. Others have continued to explore the extent to which different spatial primary factors require different cognitive processes, particularly factors that differ in the apparent complexity of processing required (Juhel, 1991) or the involvement of executive processes in working memory (Miyake, Friedman, Rettinger, Shah, & Hegarty, 2001).

Auditory Processing (Ga). Contrary to earlier assertions by some reading researchers that phonetic coding (or phonemic awareness) involved two distinct abilities, several investigations now show that phonetic coding is a unidimensional construct (e.g., Wagner et al., 1997). Other researchers have explored relationships between phonological awareness, music perception, and early reading (Anvari, Trainor, Woodside, & Levy, 2002).

TABLE 7.1. Broad (Stratum II) and Narrow (Stratum I) Cattell–Horn–Carroll (CHC) Ability Definitions (After McGrew & Evans, 1994)

Fluid Reasoning (Gf): The use of deliberate and controlled mental operations to solve novel problems
- General Sequential (deductive) Reasoning (RG)
- Induction (I)
- Quantitative Reasoning (RQ)
- Piagetian Reasoning (RP)
- Speed of Reasoning (RE)

Crystallized Knowledge (Gc): Verbal declarative and procedural knowledge acquired during formal schooling and general life
- Language Development (LD)
- Lexical Knowledge (VL)
- Listening Ability (LS)
- General (verbal) Information (KO)
- Information about Culture (K2)
- Communication Ability (CM)
- Oral Production and Fluency (OP)
- Grammatical Sensitivity (MY)
- Foreign Language Proficiency (KL)
- Foreign Language Aptitude (LA)

General (domain-specific) Knowledge (Gkn): Breadth and depth of acquired knowledge in specialized domains
- Knowledge of English as a Second Language (KE)
- Knowledge of Signing (KF)
- Skill in Lip-reading (LP)
- Geography Achievement (A5)
- General Science Information (K1)
- Mechanical Knowledge (MK)
- Knowledge of Behavioral Content (BC)

Visual-Spatial Abilities (Gv): The ability to generate, retain, retrieve, and transform well-structured visual images
- Visualization (Vz)
- Spatial Relations (SR)
- Closure Speed (CS)
- Flexibility of Closure (CF)
- Visual Memory (MV)
- Spatial Scanning (SS)
- Serial Perceptual Integration (PI)
- Length Estimation (LE)
- Perceptual Illusions (IL)
- Perceptual Alternations (PN)
- Imagery (IM)

Auditory Processing (Ga): Abilities involved in discriminating patterns in sounds and musical structure
- Phonetic Coding (PC)
- Speech Sound Discrimination (US)
- Resistance to Auditory Stimulus Distortion (UR)
- Memory for Sound Patterns (UM)
- General Sound Discrimination (U3)
- Temporal Tracking (UK)
- Musical Discrimination and Judgment (U1 U9)
- Maintaining and Judging Rhythm (U8)
- Sound-Intensity/Duration Discrimination (U6)
- Sound-Frequency Discrimination (U5)
- Hearing and Speech Threshold factors (UA UT UU)
- Absolute Pitch (UP)
- Sound Localization (UL)

TABLE 7.1. (Continued)

Short-term Memory (Gsm): Ability to apprehend and maintain awareness of information in the immediate situation
- Memory Span (MS)
- Working Memory (MW)

Long-term Storage and Retrieval (Glr): The ability to store and consolidate new information in long-term memory and later fluently retrieve that information
- Associative Memory (MA)
- Meaningful Memory (MM)
- Free Recall Memory (M6)
- Ideational Fluency (FI)
- Associational Fluency (FA)
- Expressional Fluency (FE)
- Naming Facility (NA)
- Word Fluency (FW)
- Figural Fluency (FF)
- Figural Flexibility (FX)
- Sensitivity to Problems (SP)
- Originality/Creativity (FO)
- Learning Abilities (L1)

Cognitive Processing Speed (Gs): The ability to perform relatively easy or over-learned cognitive tasks, especially when high mental efficiency is required.
- Perceptual Speed (P)
- Rate-of-Test-Taking (R9)
- Number Facility (N)
- Speed of Reasoning (RE)
- Reading Speed (fluency) (RS)
- Writing Speed (fluency) (WS)

Decision/Reaction Time or Speed (Gt): The ability to react and/or make decisions quickly in response to simple stimuli
- Simple Reaction Time (R1)
- Choice Reaction Time (R2)
- Semantic Processing Speed (R4)
- Mental Comparison Speed (R7)
- Inspection Time (IT)

Psychomotor Speed (Gps): The ability to rapidly and fluently perform body motor movements independent of cognitive control.
- Speed of Limb Movement (R3)
- Writing Speed (fluency) (WS)
- Speed of Articulation (PT)
- Movement Time (MT)

Quantitative Knowledge (Gq): Wealth of acquired store of declarative and procedural quantitative knowledge (not reasoning with this knowledge)
- Mathematical Knowledge (KM)
- Mathematical Achievement (A3)

Reading/Writing (Grw): Declarative and procedural reading and writing skills and knowledge
- Reading Decoding (RD)
- Reading Comprehension (RC)
- Verbal (printed) Language Comprehension (V)
- Cloze Ability (CZ)
- Spelling Ability (SG)
- Writing Ability (WA)
- English Usage Knowledge (EU)
- Reading Speed (fluency) (RS)
- Writing Speed (fluency) (WS)

TABLE 7.1. (Continued)

Psychomotor Abilities (*Gp*): The ability to perform body motor movements with precision, coordination, or strength
    Static Strength (P3)
    Multi-limb Coordination (P6)
    Finger Dexterity (P2)
    Manual Dexterity (P1)
    Arm-hand Steadiness (P7)
    Control Precision (P8)
    Aiming (AI)
    Gross Body Equilibrium (P4)
Olfactory Abilities (*Go*): Abilities that depend on sensory receptors of the main olfactory system
    Olfactory Memory (OM)
    Olfactory Sensitivity (OS)
Tactile Abilities (*Gh*): Abilities that depend on sensory receptors of the tactile system for input
    Tactile Sensitivity (TS)
Kinesthetic Abilities (*Gk*): Abilities that depend on sensory receptors that detect bodily position, weight, or movement of the muscles, tendons, and joints.
    Kinesthetic Sensitivity (KS)

Short-term Memory (Gsm). Much research in recent years has focused on the construct of working memory and its overlap with measures of memory span (MS) and fluid reasoning (Gf). (We review some of this research in a subsection section.) Carroll (1993) included both primary factors for both memory span and working memory in his theory. However, McGrew & Evans (2004) concluded that more recent evidence shows that measures of working memory are invariably factorially complex, do not coincide with the primary factor called Memory Span (MS), and do not define a primary factor of their own.

Crystallized Intelligence/Knowledge (Gc). Several studies (some of which we review below) show convincingly that Gc is not to be equated with general (domain) knowledge (Gkn) (Rolfhus & Ackerman, 1999). Gc is typically assumed to estimate general (verbal) cultural knowledge, whereas Gkn represents the breadth and depth of knowledge in particular domains. Many erroneously assume that the sorts of general achievement surveys (e.g., NAEP) or tests (e.g., ITED) administered to all students sample both kinds of educational outcomes. However, most of these tests sample little domain knowledge. (In fact, tests commonly used to define factors that are labeled Gc often would load substantially on Grw.) In part, this is because students in different schools often do not study the same content or study it in different grades. However, most measures of educational achievement sample only a small part of students' domain knowledge, even in domains that all students study.

Mental Speed (Gs, Gt, and Gps). Although researchers sometimes speak of mental speed as if it were a single construct, research shows that measures of mental (and psychomotor) speed form a complex hierarchy of their own (Stankov, 2000). For example, studies by Ackerman, Beier, and Boyle (2002), O'Connor and Burns (2003), and others suggest that broad cognitive speed (Gs) may be divided into Perceptual Speed (P) and Rate of Test Taking (R9). The P factor can be further differentiated into at least four primary factors (such as Pattern Recognition; see Ackerman & Cianciolo, 2000). Similarly, the R9 factor subsumes several primaries (such as Speed of Reasoning).

Studies by Roberts and Stankov (1999) and their colleagues show that the broad decision speed factor (Gt) subsumes intermediate level Reaction Time and Movement time factors, which in turn subsume several primary factors such as Simple Reaction Time (R1) and Choice Reaction Time (2).

Finally, Broad Psychomotor Speed (Gps) subsumes at least four primary factors (including Speed of Writing [WS]). Strength and accuracy of psychomotor skills are subsumed under a separate broad group factor (Broad Psychomotor Ability [Gp]).

Extensions of CHC Theory (Gh, Gk, & Go). Primarily through the work of Stankov, Roberts, and their collaborators, CHC theory has been extended to include tactile and kinesthetic factors. Although spatial visualization accounts for much of the variance on complex tactile and kinesthetic tasks, separate Tactile (TS) and Kinesthetic (KS) elements have been identified. On the basis of several such studies, Stankov (2000) suggests that broad kinesthetic (Gk), tactile (Gt), and olfactory (Go) factors should be added to CHC theory.

Summary and Reflections on CHC Theory

In summary, the hierarchical model that Carroll (1993) proposed has been elaborated and extended several important ways in the past decade. Probably the most important message for most educational researchers in this work is that understanding how abilities moderate success in learning requires multiple measures that are chosen to represent each of multiple abilities at multiple levels in hierarchy. Deciding which abilities to measure requires knowledge of prior research, but also of the demands and affordances of the learning tasks for the study's participants. On the one hand, one need not represent the whole of the hierarchy to do this well. On the other hand, a single measure of *g* (or of some more specific ability) will not allow one to understand much about the unique demands of the task, or of the ways in which those demands may change systematically across individuals or over time.

Researchers who accept a hierarchical model continue to debate the magnitude of influence of *g* on the range of human intellectual abilities and even whether it is a psychologically meaningful construct. For example, Vernon (1950) estimated that *g* accounts for anywhere between 20 and 40 percent of the total ability variance in most test batteries. Others have argued for greater or lesser role for *g*, depending on both their theoretical orientation and the nature of the empirical samples under investigation (e.g., in an unselected sample, *g* tends to account for a greater degree of variance than in a sample with restricted range-of-talent, such as a sample of college students). Some theorists (e.g., Horn & Noll, 1997) question whether *g* is psychologically meaningful. Instead, these researchers emphasize ability factors at the primary or broad-group level (Strata III and II, respectively, in Carroll's 1993 model). For other researchers who accept *g*, the critical issue is the relative emphasis that is placed on ability factors at different levels in a hierarchical model.

A hierarchical model gives precedence to the general factor. This is not an inherent property of the model so much as the application of the principle of parsimony to interpretations the model. Parsimonious interpretation means that one does not attribute variation to lower order factors that can be "explained" by the general factor. What is left over is divided among broad group factors. Once these have had their say, then the primaries are admitted. Those interested in understanding what abilities might be have always been troubled by this. The primary factors at the base of the hierarchy are invariably psychologically more transparent than higher order factors. In fact, psychological clarity decreases as one moves up the hierarchy. There is far greater agreement on what phonemic awareness might be than what verbal ability might be; greater agreement on what verbal ability might be than on general crystallized ability (Gc); and there is least agreement on what g might be. A hierarchical model thus gives parsimony precedence over psychological clarity.

On the criterion side of the equation, a similar precedence for parsimony over educational clarity is shown when educational performance is assessed with GPA or other aggregate measures. When high levels of aggregation are adopted for both ability predictors and educational criteria, there is substantial Brunswik Symmetry (Wittmann & Süß, 1999), and a substantial degree of predictive validity for general ability measures (see, e.g., Gustafsson & Baulke, 1993).

Other, Non-CHC Theories of Abilities

In their 1996 chapter, Gustafsson and Undheim briefly reviewed two theoretical approaches that have contin-

ued to attract considerable attention from educational practitioners. These are the frameworks proposed by Gardner (1983) and Sternberg (1985), respectively. Next we provide an update on the status of these approaches to intelligence.

Gardner's Theory of Multiple Intelligences

Gardner introduced the theory of theory of multiple intelligences in a popular book in the early 1980s. The theory posited seven different intelligences: logical-mathematical, linguistic, spatial, musical, bodily-kinesthetic, interpersonal, and intrapersonal (Gardner, 1983). Since then, naturalist, spiritualist, and existential intelligences have also been proposed by Gardner (1993, 1999), although only the naturalist intelligence has survived (Gardner, 2003). In their chapter Gustafsson and Undheim (1996) pointed out that several of these intelligences are well accounted for by traditional ability constructs. For example, some abilities proposed and investigated by Cattell and Horn (e.g., Horn, 1965, 1989) map reasonably well to some intelligences proposed by Gardner; linguistic intelligence is essentially Gc; logical-mathematical intelligence maps to Gf/Gq; and spatial intelligence maps to Gv. There have also been measures developed for assessing musical abilities (e.g., Seashore, 1919; Vispoel, 1999), but the remaining abilities have eluded standardized assessment. For example, many attempts to assess social intelligence have resulted in relatively little in the way of measures that show discriminant validity with other more traditional intelligence measures (see Schneider, Ackerman, & Kanfer, 1996, for a review).

Publications in recent years have focused on many different criticisms of Gardner's theory (e.g., Brody, 1992; Klein, 1997; Lohman, 2001; Lubinski & Benbow, 1995; Messick, 1992; Willingham, 2004). These criticisms are far ranging. Some concern the implications of the theory for school curricula; others focus on the theory itself and the extent to which it has been tested empirically. Here, we limit our discussion of Gardner's theory to issues about individual differences in cognitive functioning. With respect to the traditional approaches to intellectual abilities, Gardner makes several key claims, as follows:

1. Intelligence is plural, not singular.
2. Individuals differ in their profiles of intelligences or abilities.
3. Intellectual assessment should not be limited to paper-and-pencil tests, but should include "more humane methods—ranging from self-assessment to the examination of portfolios of student work" (Gardner, 1999, p. 73).

4. "Intelligence should not be expanded to include personality, motivation, will, attention, character, creativity, and other important and significant human capabilities" (Gardner, 1999, p. 74).

There is little scientific objection to some of Gardner's objections to traditional conceptions of intelligence, but much disagreement about the alternatives he has proposed. In this context, we briefly review each of these points.

Intelligence Is Plural. This claim can be strident or prosaic. In the strident version, Gardner (1993) says that g is a methodological consequence of using short-answer, multiple-choice, paper-and-pencil tests of the sorts of linguistic and logical intelligence that are at best useful for predicting success in the narrow domain of conventionally structural schools (Gardner, 1993, p. 39). Needless to say, this view is not warmly received by those who study human abilities. The less controversial, even prosaic version of the claim is that intelligence is more than g. This allows something like g to exist, but emphasizes the importance of broad group factors. This claim is quite uncontroversial. Indeed, even the most ardent supporters of g do not claim that intelligence is wholly made up of a single general intellectual ability (see, e.g., Jensen, 1998). Carroll's (1993) comprehensive review of human cognitive abilities lists dozens of different abilities and has generated very little controversy in the field.

Individuals Differ in Their Profiles of Abilities. Again, there is little debate on this topic. Reporting of individual profiles of abilities has been a major component of ability testing in the schools and for vocational purposes for nearly as long as there has been large-scale testing (e.g., E. L. Thorndike's CAVD test, see Thorndike, Bregman, Cobb, & Woodyard, 1927; Thurstone & Thurstone's PMA test, see Thurstone, 1957). Ability profile reporting is so ubiquitous that nearly every schoolchild and parent in the United States is familiar with seeing a bar graph of multiple abilities in annual assessments. However, the use of ability profiles to describe an individual's strengths and weaknesses requires qualification, as noted by Cronbach (1960). For most multiscore tests, the several scores are often significantly correlated with one another. Because the reliability of difference scores is typically quite low when the scores are themselves substantially correlated, differences between two scores for an individual must be relatively large before it can be concluded that two scores differ dependably. In many educational contexts, however, the negative consequence of not detecting a difference (e.g., a relative weakness in reading comprehension) outweighs the negative consequences that might

attend reporting a difference where none existed. In this case, the most likely consequence would be that the student would be given additional assistance in developing reading skills. In such situations, confidence intervals that more nearly equate the probabilities of Type I and Type II errors are probably preferred over the more conservative intervals that control only for Type I errors (see Feldt, 1967).

From the perspective of a hierarchical model, however, the issue is not only whether individuals differ in their profile of abilities but whether an estimate of g (something like the overall height of the profile) also conveys useful information. Clearly, the g score is most informative when the individual scores from which it is estimated do not differ significantly and least informative when they differ markedly. Indeed, if there is considerable scatter among the scores, then a weighted average that estimates g may mislead. Importantly, even when correlations among tests are substantial and evidence for g is strong, profiles may still carry useful information for most students—and critical information for some. For example, the nine reasoning tests on the multilevel edition of the Cognitive Abilities Test (Lohman & Hagen, 2001) are grouped into Verbal, Quantitative, and Nonverbal (Figural) batteries, each with three tests. The general factor accounts for approximately 81% of the common variance in these three scores. However, only about one third of students who take the test show a profile in which the three reasoning scores do not differ significantly from each other. How can this be? Although the general factor captures most of the common variance, each battery has a substantial specific component of variance. For example, although 64% of the variance in the Verbal Battery is explained by g, 36% is not. Approximately 5% of the variance can be attributed to errors of measurement and so 31% of the variation in Verbal scores is independent of g and errors of measurement. The Quantitative and Nonverbal batteries also have substantial components of reliable but specific variance. When all three are considered simultaneously, there is substantial variability in score profiles in addition to the variability in the composite score (see also Lubinski, 2004).

Intellectual Assessment Should Not Be Limited to Paper-and-Pencil Tests. Again, there is little argument with this proposition. In fact, Binet's method of intelligence assessment (and the modern instantiations such as the Stanford–Binet and Wechsler tests) did not involve the use of paper and pencils by the examinee. Numerous examples of "performance" tests of intelligence can be found in the traditional literature (e.g., Goodenough's [1926] draw-a-person test). In addition, self-assessments of abilities tend to be relatively reasonably correlated with objective measures of intelligence (e.g., see Ackerman, Beier, & Bowen, 2002; also see Baird, 1969). However, self-assessments cannot be used effectively in applied situations, when the goals of the individual being assessed are not closely aligned with the organization's goals, for the simple reason that the individual may be motivated to give spurious responses to the questions, in order to attain his/her goals. For example, as partly evidenced by SAT prep course enrollments, many college applicants are more interested in being admitted to the college/university of their choice than they are in matching the demands of the school curriculum to their abilities. Thus, one can reasonably expect that self-assessments of abilities in a college selection context will be highly inflated by all but the most honest or the most gullible of candidates.

Gardner (1999, 2003) suggests using portfolios and other nonstandardized procedures for intellectual assessment. Portfolios and other types of performance assessment are commonly used in the measurement of educational attainment. Portfolios are often used when it is impractical to expect a student to produce a product within a limited time (such as in art), when the goal is to assemble a collection of the student's best work, or to document growth in the performance of particular tasks (e.g., writing of essays) (Nitko, 2001). However, portfolios are difficult to score reliably (Koertz, Stecher, Klein, & McCaffrey, 1994) and, like other performance assessments, may advantage students whose parents and teachers have the time and expertise to help them develop and refine their work. Further, although virtually all measurement people see value in assessments that mimic the criterion behavior (Lindquist, 1951), few would agree that standardized assessments should be abandoned altogether! Further, the assertion that performance assessments are "more humane" assumes that traditional assessments are inhumane. The claim that little children are distressed by tests, although commonly made and supported by anecdote in the popular press, actually has little empirical support. For example, in one study, Frisbie and Andrews (1990) observed the test-taking behavior of more than 600 kindergarten children in 17 schools as they took Level 5 of the ITBS. Although they note that administering a test requires more planning and care with young children than with older children, most of the kindergarten children in their study encountered no problems in taking the test. In fact, young children commonly enjoy taking these sorts of tests. What is not warranted are high-stakes decisions about children on the basis of a low test score, especially when the test is administered in a group by an inexperienced examiner, and when the test does not provide caution indices for students whose patterns of item and subtest scores depart markedly from the patterns expected under the scaling model (Lohman & Hagen, 2002, p. 62). On the other hand, not assessing children until third or fourth grade misses opportunities for intervention that could assist at least some students.

There is another, even more basic difference between traditional tests and portfolios. That difference is best articulated as the distinction between maximal and typical intellect (e.g., see Ackerman, 1994, for a discussion). Traditional tests of intelligence have focused on maximal intelligence—it was a major component of Binet's procedure to elicit the performance of the individual with maximal motivation to succeed. Binet's justification for these conditions was that he wanted to minimize, at least as far as possible, the influences of prior privilege (e.g., socioeconomic status, prior educational opportunities) from the test scores. Although portfolios often aim to collect a student's best performances, evaluating abilities by looking over a much longer time frame than the traditional intelligence test raises the influence of an individual's typical investment of intellectual effort in the particular domain. (If Gardner's goal is to eliminate "motivation" from the conceptualization of intelligence—see later discussion—the assessment of portfolios is clearly working in the opposite direction.)

"Intelligence should not be expanded to include personality, motivation, will, attention, character, creativity, and other important and significant human capabilities." Paradoxically, here Gardner parts company with many researchers, by narrowing the construct of intelligence in a major fashion. Previous researchers have taken different approaches to the integration of these constructs into their conceptualization of intelligence, albeit with different degrees of success. For example, Spearman and his students considered "Factor W" (e.g., Webb, 1915), a factor of conscientiousness or conative propensity as an integral determinant of performance on intellectual tasks, and W. Alexander (1935) identified factors X (interests) and Z (achievement) as similarly integral to an ability test performance. Guilford's (1959) framework put intelligence as only one of seven different aspects of personality. Most notably, Wechsler (1950) remarked that intelligence is much broader than simply knowing the correct answer on a reasoning test. Specifically, he stated "Actually, intelligence is an aspect of behavior; it has to do primarily with the appropriateness, effectiveness, and worthwhileness of what human beings do or want to do" (p. 135). Later, Wechsler refined his orientation, as follows: "What we measure with (intelligence) tests is not what tests measure—not information, not spatial perception, not reasoning ability. These are only a means to an end. What intelligence tests measure, what we hope they measure, is something much more

important: the capacity of an individual to understand the world about him and his resourcefulness to cope with its challenges" (Wechsler, 1975, p. 81).

The attempt to separate the cognitive from the affective and conative components of cognition runs counter from much recent work that seeks to integrate them. Corno et al. (2002) argue that it is particularly important for educational researchers to be aware of the many complex but important interactions among cognitive, affective, and conative constructs in school learning. Artificially separating cognition from, say, volition has impoverished efforts to understand both domains.

In general, the attempt by Gardner to separate intelligence from personality, motivation, attention, and the like seems to fail in an attempt to "carve nature at its joints" (Plato, in *Phaedrus*), as these constructs are integral to intellectual performance. Without motivation, for example, an individual is unlikely to accomplish any "intellectual" task. Attempting to arrive at a depiction of intelligence without motivation (or many of these other constructs) denies what is both obviously and empirically true.

Concluding Comments on Gardner. Far from standing in stark contrast with Gardner's major arguments, the preceding discussion illustrates that there is value in what he has suggested regarding the construct and measurement of intelligence. However, it would be erroneous to say that his arguments represent something new in the field of intelligence. All of these issues have been well represented in prior theoretical developments and empirical work and are present in many modern theories of intellectual abilities and several existing assessment instruments. Nonetheless, the science of intelligence research parts ways with Gardner in two ways.

First, we do not think it useful to overly restrict the construct of intelligence. Perhaps this is easier to see if one considers estimating individuals' readiness to learn or perform in a particular situation (i.e., their aptitude) rather than their intelligence. Readiness to learn algebra, for example, clearly has affective and conative components as well as cognitive components. Artificially separating the information processing from the affective and conative components of cognition (e.g., interest, motivation, anxiety) underrepresents the construct of readiness. Indeed, one of the main implications of recent research on individual differences is that understanding the joint action of constellations traits or aptitudes can significantly enhance the ability to predict and, at times, to alter outcomes for individuals (Ackerman, 2003; Corno et al., 2002; Snow, 1978).

Second, given that the foundation of science of psychology is empirical observation, until such time as there are reliable and valid measures of a construct, there must be a high level of skepticism regarding the existence of the construct. The Interpersonal, Intrapersonal, Naturalist, Spiritual, and Existential intelligences proposed by Gardner simply do not meet this criterion, and as such cannot yet be considered scientific constructs, from either verificationist (Carnap, 1987) or falsificationist (Popper, 1963) perspectives. In the final analysis, Gardner may have legitimate doubts about the feasibility of paper-and-pencil testing procedures to provide adequate measures of these proposed intelligences, but these doubts do not invalidate E. L. Thorndike's dictum that "Whatever exists at all, exists in some amount. To know it thoroughly involves knowing its quantity as well as its quality" (quoted in Joncich, 1968). Without means for measurement, the constructs are not well suited for scientific discussion.

Third, Gardner's model of parallel abilities (or "intelligences") falls short not simply because it fails to acknowledge or explain why abilities are correlated, but because it cannot explain why the observed correlational structure implies a hierarchy (Lohman, 2001). In other words, the theory does not explain why some intelligences are more intelligent than others. As Gustafsson (1988) has argued, g overlaps substantially with Gf, which in turn is virtually synonymous with the primary factor called Inductive Reasoning (IR). Although some g-theorists eschew efforts to explain psychological basis of g (Jensen, 1998), it is clear that a substantial portion of the variation in g can be attributed to individual differences in reasoning, particularly inductive reasoning. Further, as several researchers have now shown, a significant fraction of the variation in reasoning abilities is shared with measures of working memory (see later discussion). However, Gardner's extreme modular view of cognition dismisses the notion of a common working memory. Thus, one of the chief complaints cognitive psychologists have leveled against Gardner's theory (i.e., its rejection of working memory) turns out to be the basis of the differential psychologists' complaint as well (i.e., the rejection of g) (Lohman, 2001). An extreme modular view of either working memory or ability fails to explain the empirical observations in either domain.

Sternberg's Triarchic Theory of Intelligence

Sternberg (1985) introduced his triarchic theory as an attempt to expand the conceptualization of intelligence beyond the traditional construct. He argues that the first part of his framework, *analytic (or academic) intelligence*, represents the essence of the traditional view of intelligence. However, the other two parts of the framework, *creative intelligence* and *practical intelligence*, purport to go beyond the traditional conceptualization. Creative intelligence is said to be required when responding intelligently to a relatively novel task or situation. In Sternberg's (1993; 2004) yet unpublished test battery, the Sternberg Triarchic Abilities Test (STAT), creative intelligence is assessed through novel analogies, number problems with fictitious operations, and figural series items that require transformations. Practical intelligence is proposed to represent adaptation to, shaping of, and selection of real-world environments. In the STAT, practical intelligence is assessed by tests made up of "everyday reasoning," "everyday math," and "route planning" items. As operationalized on the STAT, both creative and practical intelligence appear to differ in degree rather than in kind from abilities measured by the analytic scale, and to overlap considerably with abilities measured in non-Gf branches of the hierarchical model.

The most recent version of STAT contains 45 multiple-choice items (nine scales of five items each). Each five item scale is defined by the application of a particular "intelligence" (analytic, creative, or practical) to a particular content (verbal, numerical, or figural). A recent, as yet unpublished study that uses the scale scores contains additional details (Sternberg & the Rainbow Project Collaborators, 2004). In the reported study, scores were averaged across the content facet for all three intelligences. (The content distinction was tenable only for the analytic scale.) Total score on STAT creative scale added to the prediction of undergraduate GPA after SAT scores and high school GPA were entered in the regression model. STAT analytic and practical did not. An extensive discussion of the validation of the first edition of the STAT is provided by Brody (2003a, 2003b, though see Sternberg, 2003, for a response to Brody's criticisms.)

Although we can report only modest progress in the validation of the Sternberg triarchic theory since the review provided by Gustafsson and Undheim (1996), perhaps it is as yet too early to be able to provide a critical assessment of the utility of the theory for expanding the conceptualization of intelligence to the domains of practical and creative intelligence. For example, the finding that STAT Creative (and other performance measures of creativity in Sternberg et al., 2004) predicted college GPA awaits interpretation, especially a disentangling of confounds with conventional measures of verbal reasoning, verbal fluency, and writing abilities. As noted by McNemar (1965), developing a valid measure of creativity has been a difficult task for psychometric researchers over the past century, and perhaps it will yet be another decade before significant progress is made on this front by Sternberg and his colleagues. It should be mentioned, especially in contrast to Gardner's theory of multiple intelligences, that Sternberg agrees that testing his theory requires the development of defensible ways to measure the constructs

he has proposed, and establishing their similarities and differences with measures of other constructs (though see Messick, 1992, for a contrasting view).

DEVELOPMENTS THAT FOCUS ON KNOWLEDGE

Intelligence, Learning, and Knowledge

Early theorists and modern researchers generally subscribe to the proposition that individual differences in intelligence correlate strongly with individual differences in learning (e.g., see Buckingham, 1921). Indeed, the major success of the Binet–Simon scales and subsequent omnibus tests of intelligence is based on the high predictive validities for academic success of children and adolescents. As noted in the earlier review of individual differences in cognitive functioning (Gustafson & Undheim, 1996), several decades of controversy have revolved around establishing the relationship between intellectual abilities and individual differences in learning, especially when specific learning tasks are considered (in contrast to overall academic achievement). Investigations of individual differences in learning generally find relatively small predictive validities for intellectual abilities measures, suggesting to some researchers that the relationship between intelligence and learning may be markedly overstated (e.g., see Ackerman, 2000b; Lohman, 1999, for reviews).

A critical issue in these studies is the distinction between the measurement of learning as gain or as accumulated competence (i.e., final status). Gain and final status scores show similar correlations with other variables only if the variance of individual differences in initial status is small (and thus overshadowed by the variability in final status) or is uncorrelated with final status. In most educational contexts, initial differences in performance both are substantial and are correlated with final status. In such circumstances, learning as measured by gain is unreliable and typically shows small correlations with other variables. However, if the variability in performance increases with practice, then gain scores can not only be much more reliable, but show substantial correlations with other variables as well (Lohman, 1999).

However, even when learning is measured by final status, correlations with measures of ability are often small. An approach that offers resolution to this issue is the principle of Brunswik Symmetry (see Wittmann & Süß, 1999). The basic idea is that predictor-criterion validities are maximized (a) when there is a match between predictor breadth and criterion breadth, and (b) when the mapping between predictors and criteria is direct. Generally speaking, when broad criteria are to be predicted, Brunswik Symmetry dictates that the best set of predictors will also be broad; when narrow criteria are to be predicted, narrow predictors have the potential for maximum validity. And, the mapping must be direct—such that the wrong narrow predictors may yield very low or zero validity for narrow criteria. In the context of individual differences in learning, the principle of Brunswik Symmetry would imply that one will not likely find large correlations between broad ability measures (such as IQ) and narrow learning tasks, such as those examined in laboratory studies. Instead, the prediction of individual differences in learning for narrow tasks requires a much more nuanced task analysis to determine which abilities (if any) are requisite for learning and for performance after practice or instruction. In contrast, when broad learning indicators serve as the criteria (e.g., grade point average), broad predictors such as IQ will represent an optimal match, in terms of Brunswik Symmetry, and in turn will evidence high validity coefficients. The implications of these considerations are that investigators seeking to establish the general proposition that intelligence is the ability to learn must limit their consideration to broad indicators of learning and academic achievement.

Abilities and Domain Learning

Although school serves many different purposes (e.g., see Alexander & Murphy, 1999), two major goals of educational programs are to impart general skills for problem solving and to impart domain knowledge to students. Partly because of explicit overlap between test content and criterion task content, there is relatively little controversy regarding strong relationships between intellectual abilities (such as reasoning and problem solving) and educational criteria in the areas of critical thinking (e.g., see Herrnstein, Nickerson, de Sánchez, & Swets, 1986). What is less clear is the relationship between abilities and the acquisition of domain knowledge. The main reason for this shortcoming is that traditional intellectual ability theory has focused on either general abilities or broad content abilities that are less associated with domain knowledge.

There have, of course, been exceptions to this pattern of investigations (e.g., see Vernon, 1950). In recent years, however, some researchers have turned from a focus on process and critical thinking to a focus on knowledge and the attainment of expertise (e.g. Stanovich & West, 1989). Theories proposed in this domain cover a wide range of approaches, from those that are mainly concerned with how prior knowledge and interests affect domain learning (e.g., see Alexander, Kulikowich, & Schulze, 1994) to theories that propose that individual differences in abilities

are largely irrelevant to the acquisition of expertise (e.g., Chi, Glaser, & Rees, 1982; Ericsson, Krampe, & Tesch-Römer, 1993).

In contrast, other theories such as the one proposed by Ackerman (1996) suggest an important role of individual differences in intellectual abilities in determining the direction and level of cognitive investment in the acquisition of domain knowledge. Ackerman's theoretical framework, called PPIK, for intelligence-as-Process, Personality, Interests, and intelligence-as-Knowledge, builds on the investment hypothesis of Cattell (1971/1987), but represents both a refinement and a simplification of Cattell's unified perspective. The PPIK approach takes Cattell's notion that fluid intellectual abilities (Gf) (especially those of basic processes, such as memory and abstract reasoning) are generally casually antecedent to the development of crystallized intellectual abilities (Gc).

The PPIK approach indicates that the direction and level of cognitive effort devoted to acquisition of domain knowledge are influenced by a relatively small set of trait complexes (that involve personality traits, interests, and domain self-concept). The trait complexes are generally or specifically facilitating (e.g., science/math and intellectual/cultural trait complexes) of domain knowledge acquisition, or are generally or specifically impeding of domain knowledge acquisition (e.g., clerical/conventional and social trait complexes). In this framework, both Gf and Gc are important determinants of individual differences in domain knowledge. Individual differences in Gf directly influence domain knowledge in mathematics and physical sciences, and Gc directly influences knowledge in most domains, but Gf only indirectly influences knowledge in these other domains through its influence on Gc. Consistent with Cattell's (1971) investment hypothesis, the PPIK approach is developmental, in that knowledge is acquired throughout the life span. In contrast to Cattell's investment hypothesis, and in contrast to traditional approaches to intellectual abilities, the PPIK theory specifically addresses individual differences in knowledge that is not "common" to the wider culture. (Note that in CHC theory, this knowledge would help define the Gkn factor, not the Gc factor. See Table 7.1). That is, the PPIK approach attempts to bridge Binet's approach to intelligence assessment (which attempts to focus only on processes and knowledge that are common to the dominant culture) with a perspective that gives individuals credit for knowledge that may be relatively uncommon or specific to a particular area of study or interest (e.g., current events, arts, technology, social sciences, and so on; see Ackerman, 2000a; Ackerman & Rolfhus, 1999; Beier & Ackerman, 2001, 2003). This focus on an expanded consideration of domain knowledge is especially important when one cannot expect a common school curriculum or occupational and avocational experiences, such as occurs in the study of late adolescence through adulthood. From this life-span perspective, investigations of Gf, Gc, and domain knowledge have shown that although middle-aged adults have lower Gf scores, on average, when compared to young adults, they have higher Gc scores (as expected), but also on average, have much higher levels of domain knowledge in nearly all domains assessed to date (except for knowledge in math and physical sciences, two broad domains that are most highly associated with Gf abilities; Ackerman, 2000a).

With the notable exception of advanced placement tests (see e.g., Ackerman & Rolfhus, 1999) and the subject tests of the GRE, most standardized measures of educational achievement contain relatively few items that directly sample examinees' store of declarative knowledge—at the level of either general concepts or more specific facts. For example, what students may know about the periodic table or the function on the respiratory system has, at best, an indirect impact on most measures of science achievement. In part, this is an ongoing reaction of educators to methods of instruction that emphasize the acquisition of low-level factual knowledge at the expense of more general problem-solving and thinking skills. It also reflects the lack of a common curriculum in American education. Test developers are reluctant to ask questions about the concepts that many students have not encountered in their studies. However, one of the most salient features of expertise is the attainment of vast, well-organized systems of conceptual and factual knowledge in particular domains (Glaser, 1992). Failure to assess student's progress in attaining such organized knowledge bases not only results in underrepresentation of the achievement construct (Messick, 1989), but makes it much more difficult for those who study the effects of variations in instructional methods on student learning to observe significant changes in student learning. It is generally harder to obtain improvements in the sorts of general verbal problem solving required by Gc-loaded achievement tests than improvements in domain knowledge and skills.

WORKING MEMORY

At the interface between experimental psychology and the study of individual differences, there has been considerable interest and research in the past decade on the construct of working memory (WM), especially in terms of the relationship between WM and general intelligence. A full review of this literature is beyond the scope of this chapter (see Ackerman, Beier, & Boyle, 2005). Here we provide some historical background, a brief review of the current literature, and a discussion of the implications for educational psychology.

Individual differences in immediate memory (later called short-term memory) were first investigated by Jacobs (1887), who observed that older children performed better than younger children when asked to repeat back sequences of numbers read aloud. Binet later investigated immediate memory for sentences and for unrelated words, and found similar results. Terman's (1916) introduction of the Stanford–Binet scales included both number span and sentence span tests. Terman also included a backward digit-span test, which requires examinees to repeat back the number sequence in the reverse order of presentation, which Terman claimed makes "a much heavier demand on attention" (p. 208) than the forward digit span test. Current omnibus intelligence tests, such as more recent versions of the Stanford–Binet and the Wechsler tests, have continued to incorporate span memory tests as an essential part of the overall evaluation of intellectual ability. In the most comprehensive review of the correlational literature conducted to date, Carroll (1993) identified five immediate memory factors, namely: Memory Span, Associative Memory, Free Recall Memory, Meaningful Memory [or Memory for ideas], and Visual Memory, along with one higher-order memory factor that was composed of these five lower-order group factors (see Table 7.1).

Theory and empirical research in experimental psychology have converged on a representation of immediate memory that has the characteristics of a central executive (e.g., Norman & Shallice, 1986), and two slave systems that represent a phonological loop (for "speech-based information") and a visuo-spatial sketch pad, which "is responsible for setting up and manipulating visual images" (Baddeley, 1998, p. 52). The initial attempt to bridge the construct of working memory to individual differences measures was presented by Daneman and Carpenter (1980), where they reported high correlations between a measure of WM and a measure of reading comprehension. Subsequent investigations (e.g., see Baddeley, 1986, and Daneman & Merikle, 1996) have supported a conclusion that there are indeed significant correlations between WM measures and reading comprehension, but not quite a large as initially suggested by Daneman and Carpenter.

An investigation by Kyllonen and Christal (1990) suggested a much more central role for WM ability in the larger context of intelligence. In a series of experiments, these authors suggested that reasoning ability is little more than working memory capacity, based on high correlations between latent variables of WM and a general reasoning ability. Subsequent investigators (e.g., Conway, Kane, & Engle, 1999) have taken an even more extreme view, namely that WM is "closely associated with general fluid intelligence" and "maybe isomorphic to, general intelligence and executive function" (Engle, 2002, pp. 21–22). If it would be possible to fully account for general intelligence by a small set of WM tests, there would be great potential for revolutionizing assessment methods and practice all across the educational spectrum. However, these claims have proven to be both unwarranted, and, based on a more thorough analysis of the data (e.g., Ackerman, et al., 2005), they have been largely retracted (e.g., Kane, Hambrick, & Conway, 2005). Current estimates of the overlap between WM and general intelligence are in the neighborhood of 25 percent to 50 percent of shared variance—about the same as the shared variance between other memory abilities identified by Carroll (1993) and general intelligence.

Other investigations have indicated that there are substantial correlations between more traditional span memory abilities and the more complex measures of WM, suggesting that there may not be much "value added" by WM measures above and beyond the kinds of span measures that have been used for nearly a century of intelligence testing (e.g., see Beier & Ackerman, 2004).

Beyond the issue of shared variance between WM and intelligence are other important concerns that might have relevance for understanding the components of intellectual abilities. Several investigations have been conducted that attempt to determine whether components of working memory (e.g., the phonological loop and the visuo-spatial sketchpad) represent differentiable abilities (e.g., Shah & Miyake, 1996). Other investigations have attempted to map out the developmental course of WM capacity during childhood and adolescence (Fry & Hale, 1996) and in the course of adult aging (e.g., Phillips & Hamilton, 2001). Still other investigations have attempted to separate the executive or attentional aspects of individual differences in WM from the processing and storage components of WM (for a review, see Oberauer, in press).

To date, there are too few comprehensive data and too much controversy to allow us to draw substantive conclusions from this line of investigation. The most promising domain of inquiry appears to be the narrower, but still critically important area of individual differences in reading comprehension. It may very well be that the key role played by WM abilities, beyond what can be assessed by extant measures of span memory and general intellectual abilities, lies in the specific relations between the attentional, storage, and processing aspects of WM and the underlying determinants of individual differences in reading comprehension. An answer to the question of whether individual differences in WM are a cause, consequence, or concomitant correlate of reading comprehension is currently not known.

Regardless of the outcome of these investigations, individual differences in working or short-term memory capacity will surely continue to be a fruitful area of inves-

tigation for educational researchers. Students commonly fail to learn because task demands exceed the span of information that they can maintain in an active state in working memory. For example, it is difficult to infer relationships between ideas unless both can be held in attention simultaneously. One of the most effective ways to improve performance of students who cannot do this, then, is to reduce the information processing or storage requirements of tasks, by automatizing component skills, by redesigning the tasks, or by altering instruction to offload non critical, attention-demanding processes (Merriënboer, Kirschner, & Kester, 2003). For example, even adults find it difficult to learn complex skills if they must monitor their own behavior (Kanfer & Ackerman, 1989). Learning is more efficient if the monitoring function is offloaded (to another learner, a coach, or the computer) until the student has reduced the attention demands of task performance through practice. Indeed, probably the most well documented way to improve the performance of less able, younger, or novice learners is to reduce the information processing burdens of the task (Snow, 1978). Unfortunately, this is often done by offloading problem-solving or reasoning rather than ancillary task demands. Temporary improvements in performance thus come at the expense of the development of higher-level thinking skills, thereby not developing the more critical aptitudes for academic learning (Martinez, 2000; Snow, 1996).

OTHER INFLUENCES IN COGNITIVE FUNCTIONING

Stereotype Threat and Group Differences in Intellectual Abilities

In 1995 Steele and Aronson (1995) introduced the concept of stereotype threat ("being at risk of confirming, as self-characteristic, a negative stereotype about one's group," p. 797) into the broader discussion of intellectual test performance. Specifically, these authors claimed that when African-American students at Stanford University were told that a test they were about to take was "diagnostic" of their "reading and verbal reasoning abilities" (p. 799), they performed comparatively worse than a control condition, when compared to White students in the same conditions. Steele and Aronson (1995) suggested that activating a negative stereotype (in this case, that African-Americans perform worse on intelligence-like tests) caused an "inefficiency of processing" that would lead to depressed performance scores. Although the results of their initial studies were weak (of the two reported studies, only one reached statistical significance), some distance from the original research has increased the magnitude of the reported effect. For example, the nonsignificant result ("$p < .19$") in Steele and Aronson (1995) was reported to be "strong evidence of stereotype threat; Black participants greatly underperformed White participants in the diagnostic condition but equaled them in the non diagnostic condition"; Steele, 1997, p. 620.) Steele also expanded the construct to other identifiable groups that have negative stereotypes (e.g., women and math performance). Other investigators have further expanded the construct to include a wide variety of other negative stereotypes that could presumably affect intellectual ability performance (e.g., Hispanics, low-income people [Good, Aronson, & Inzlicht, 2003], and even psychology students, in the context of a proofreading task [Seibt & Förster, 2004]). To date, there have been several empirical research studies that have purported to replicate the Steele and Aronson (1995) studies or expand the framework for stereotype threat. However, there have also been several studies that have purported to show that the results of Steele and Aronson (1995) cannot be replicated (e.g., see Cullen, Hardison, & Sackett, 2004), and there have been several articles that have outlined several methodological and statistical objections that potentially threaten the validity of the results that show negative effects of stereotype threat (e.g., Sackett, Hardison, & Cullen, 2004). It is not our aim to provide a complete review of this literature here, but there are two important issues regarding stereotype threat and intellectual abilities that merit discussion. The first issue concerns the conditions of intellectual ability testing, and the second issue is the potential of stereotype threat for understanding race, gender, and other group differences in intellectual abilities.

Conditions of Testing. In the hundred or so years of modern intellectual ability assessment, it seems to have been long forgotten (or rendered a quaint anachronism in the modern educational system where frequent testing takes place), that the mental test is essentially "an experiment" (e.g., see Terman, 1924). That is, as noted by E. G. Boring (quoted in Terman, 1924) "methodologically there is no essential difference between a mental test and a scientific psychological experiment." (p. 98). At a narrow level, this refers to the fact that each test item is a stimulus, and each answer is a response, in the classic behaviorist representation. But, at a broader level, this kind of consideration applies to the entire testing milieu as well. Several early investigators easily demonstrated that the conditions of testing (especially in terms of the rapport established between examiner and examinee) can be important determinants of performance on intelligence tests (e.g., Rothney, 1937; Sacks, 1952; and Sears, 1943). Moreover, the hypothesis that rapport was partly responsible for race differences in intelligence test scores had been reasonably well researched in the 1920s and 1930s (e.g., see Canady, 1936; Klineberg, 1928). Far from being something new and interesting, the idea that the motivation and attitude of the examinee might adversely affect intelligence test scores is as old as the Binet–Simon scales (e.g., Binet & Simon 1905; Rothney, 1937; Sears, 1943; see also Ackerman, 1996, for a more recent discussion of Binet's instructions on the conditions of intelligence testing).

As noted by many researchers over the years, what the examinee (or research participant) brings with him or her to the test can be an important determinant of test performance. Experimental research has long pointed to stressors, such as the physical environment (e.g., noise, heat/cold, vibration) as having relatively generic effects on performance—namely marked impairment of cognitive processes for tasks that are demanding or novel, and relatively little impairment for well-practiced skills (e.g., see Hancock, 1986). There is also a substantial list of psychological stressors that have been identified as having potential for impairing cognitive performance. These include general anxiety, performance evaluation apprehension, interpersonal competition, and so on. Other factors also enter into possible mediators of cognitive performance, and some have been shown to have interactive effects, such as time-of-day of testing, personality traits such as introversion/extroversion and impulsivity, and even caffeine intake (e.g., see Revelle, Humphreys, Simon, & Gilliland, 1980). Many cognitive and intellectual abilities tests are especially susceptible to these influences, because they are designed to elicit the "maximal" performance of the examinees—that is, the level of performance attained by an individual who is completely focused and optimally attentive to the task, and because such tasks have been further designed to eliminate as far as possible, any transfer of skills from outside the testing situation (Ackerman, 1994; Cronbach, 1949).

However, there are other tests that are designed to measure knowledge and skills that have been developed outside of the testing situation (e.g., some crystallized intelligence measures, such as vocabulary, general information, and domain knowledge) that should be much less susceptible to these various stressor effects because they are less dependent on limited attentional resources in the testing situation. To date, there has been virtually no research that has established whether or not the effects of stereotype threat interventions are moderated by the type of tests, but in order to understand the underlying mechanisms of such phenomena, such research is needed.

Ultimately, though, it is most certainly true that at the individual and group levels, some conditions of testing are likely to be more or less facilitating or impeding of performance on some intellectual ability tests. On the one hand, the fact that there may be interactions between these conditions of testing and group differences suggests perhaps that greater care must be taken to optimize the conditions for each group in order to maximize overall scores. On the other hand, it must be kept in mind that the primary goal of testing in admissions and employment contexts is to measure individual differences in knowledge, skills, and other characteristics required for success in school or the workplace. Equalizing the scores of identifiable groups on test scores is defensible only if these interventions also raise (or at least do not reduce) the overall test validity. For example, using nonstandard testing procedures that raise the scores of an identifiable group of examinees but do not simultaneously raise the scores on the criterion variable (such as grade point average) will not yield a psychometrically useful result. On the other hand, identification of factors that systematically moderate test–criterion relationships suggests ways in which the criterion situations might be modified better to accommodate the needs of different individuals. For example, a high correlation between spatial ability and performance in mathematics in a particular institution may reflect a general fact of nature. More likely, it reflects something about the way in which mathematics is taught at that institution.

In the final analysis, what is perhaps most surprising about the recent studies on stereotype threat is how small the effects are, in the larger context of other conditions that can depress intelligence test performance. Although there have been no studies of omnibus intelligence testing under stereotype threat, the current evidence suggests that the relatively weak results demonstrated so far would result in only a few points in overall IQ test performance under stereotype threat, at least in the laboratory and field contexts in which it has been investigated.

Gender Differences

The study of gender differences in cognitive/intellectual functioning has been a recurring theme in the past 90 or so years. The issue was first raised by Yerkes, Bridges, & Hardwick (1915), in their development of a "point scale" for measuring intelligence of children and adolescents. In their norming sample, they noticed that at some ages, girls tended to have higher average raw scores, while at other ages, boys had higher average scores. The differences in overall scores were small, but these authors concluded that separate intelligence norms should be used for girls and boys, such that each individual could be evaluated with respect to his or her own gender reference group. Terman (1916) in his development of the Stanford–Binet intelligence test also noted small gender differences, on the order of 2 or 3 points. For his test, girls tended to perform slightly better, on average, than boys up to age 13, after which boys tended to perform slightly better, on average, than girls. Terman's approach to gender differences was, however, entirely different from that adopted by Yerkes et al. That is, Terman created a single scale, which was used for both boys and girls. In later revisions of the Stanford–Binet (e.g., Terman & Merrill, 1937), the authors describe how they explicitly removed items from the test that showed large mean gender differences, in order to yield a result of no overall gender differences in intelligence test scores.

Because the specific selection of individual items and scales for an omnibus intelligence (IQ) test, such as the Stanford–Binet or the Wechsler, is somewhat arbitrary (as long as the items meet the basic properties of criterion-related validity and construct validity), few objections have been raised over the ensuing decades that the IQ test is essentially unfair to boys or girls. Whether there is a basis for arriving at a different conclusion about equivalent scores for the genders lies beyond the scope of this chapter and most likely falls into the political or public policy domain. On the one hand, Terman's decision to "make" the genders equivalent on IQ renders impossible any substantive discussion of overall intelligence differences between genders. On the other hand, when abilities that are lower in the hierarchy than general intelligence are considered, there is ample evidence for gender differences. It is these differences that we turn to for further treatment. A comprehensive review of the literature on gender differences in intellectual abilities lies beyond the scope of this chapter. Interested readers should consult some of the more extensive treatments of this research domain (e.g., Halpern, 2000; Linn & Peterson, 1986; W. Willingham & Cole, 1997).

Verbal, Spatial, and Math Content Abilities. Although hundreds of studies of gender differences in abilities have been reported in the literature, the most thoroughly researched areas of inquiry have generally proceeded along the lines of different test content, in contrast to the underlying processes of cognitive functions. The consensus opinions of researchers in the field are that, on average, girls tend to perform better than boys on a wide range of verbal tasks including fluency, reading comprehension, and vocabulary (e.g., see Halpern, 2000; Hyde & Linn, 1988). At the individual test level, the gender differences are typically small to nonexistent for reading comprehension, vocabulary, and verbal reasoning tests; intermediate for tests of grammar, syntax, or style; and largest for verbal fluency, clerical speed, and spelling tests (Cleary, 1992; Halpern, 2000). Thus, it is not so much the verbal content that generates the sex difference as the particular type of processing that is required (Lohman, 1994b). Tests that show the largest female advantage require rapid, sequential processing of arbitrary sequences of letters or phonemes. A critical requirement is keeping track of order information. For example, on a spelling test, knowing the correct letters is not enough; sequence is crucial. Anderson (1983; Anderson et al., 2004) posits that order information for such stimuli is represented in memory by a particular type of mental code (the linear order or string code). Tests that demand this sort of thinking are more likely to have their primary loading on one of the primaries that define the Ga, Gs, or Grw factors in the CHC model than the Gc factor (see Table 7.1). Indeed, one way to predict whether a task will elicit sex differences is to examine the extent to which such processing is required, especially when it must be done so fluidly and flexibly (as in tongue twisters and secret languages).

Spatial tasks often show large differences that favor males. Because of the diversity of spatial ability factors (e.g., see Lohman, 1988), and the fact that these abilities tend to be less frequently measured in standard academic testing situations, there remains some controversy about the overall magnitude of gender differences in spatial abilities, but estimates typically run in the neighborhood of about $d = .4$ to $.8$ (e.g., see Voyer, Voyer, & Bryden, 1995), which would be considered a moderate to large effect in Cohen's framework. For adolescents and adults, differences are largest on tests that require mental rotation of three-dimensional stimuli and smallest on those that can be solved by reasoning. Therefore, as with the sex difference on verbal tasks, the difference is probably best characterized not by the stimulus as by the type of mental representation that must be generated, and the nature of transformations that must be performed on that representation. High-spatial individuals evidence the ability to combine and recombine visual images at will (Lohman, 1994a).

For math abilities, boys tend to perform, on average, better than girls on several kinds of math tests, but especially in the domain of problem solving (on the order of $d = .29$; see Hyde, Fennema, & Lamon, 1990), but there are negligible differences between the genders on computational math tests (e.g., those that involve typically highly speeded basic arithmetic functions). When differences in computation skills are observed, they tend to favor girls. Differences in mathematical problem solving emerge at high school ages and persist into adulthood.

Although there is some evidence that the gender differences in these three broad content domains (especially mathematical abilities) have diminished in magnitude somewhat over the past few decades (e.g., see Feingold, 1988), there is little consensus that these differences have entirely disappeared or are likely to disappear in the near future. Further, because the interindividual differences in all of these abilities within gender groups are much larger in magnitude than the between-group differences, generalizations from group means to individual scores are not warranted. In addition, there is a well-established documentation of a divergence between gender differences in ability test scores and gender differences in academic grades, such that women tend to obtain higher grades, on average, than boys do, even when boys tend to do better on ability tests (e.g., see Willingham & Cole, 1997). Recent decisions to include measures of writing abilities on college entrance tests may alter this state of affairs, however. Girls typically outperform boys on measures of writing abilities, and so they may outperform boys both on grades and on the verbal and writing portions of the entrance tests. Nonetheless, the larger differences between gender groups on spatial abilities, some math abilities, and writing abilities have implications for selection into courses of study at the postsecondary level, especially in the physical sciences and engineering domains (Shea et al., 2001). Further, as noted by Stanley and Benbow (1982), small group differences at the mean, can result in substantial differences in the ratios of the respective group representation at the tails of the distribution of abilities.

Like all abilities, spatial abilities are amenable to training and practice. Certainly performance on particular spatial tasks can be improved substantially (e.g., Lohman, 1988; Lohman & Nichols, 1990). The extent to which improvements after small amounts of practice transfer to other spatial tasks is less clear. To the degree that training on spatial abilities may reduce the overall magnitude of individual differences, such interventions might have the effect of also reducing gender group differences. Thus, it might be possible that targeted instructional programs may ameliorate or at least diminish gender differences in spatial abilities that are critical to academic success in physical sciences and engineering. The alternative, of course, is to modify instruction in such disciplines to reduce at least some of the demands on spatial abilities.

Finally, simultaneous consideration of trait clusters or complexes often gives much more information than the examination of traits in isolation. In the case of gender differences, it is the profile of analog spatial versus sequential verbal abilities that shows the greatest relationship with both physiological variables—such as hormone levels (Bock, 1973; Nyborg, 1983)—and personality variables (Riding & Boardman, 1983). Explorations of relationships between abilities and learning styles seem more fruitful when studies attend to the spatial-sequential profile rather than to each variable separately, especially when the "verbal" domain is represented by spelling or verbal fluency rather than a more general verbal skill.

AGE DIFFERENCES

With about 25% of all students enrolled in postsecondary education in the United States over the age of 30 (*Chronicle of Higher Education Almanac*, 2004), and the proportion expected to rise in the foreseeable future, considerations of adult aging and intelligence have become more important concerns for educators than perhaps they were in the past. First, we provide a brief review of the general patterns of aging and abilities, followed by a review of the relations between abilities and learning in the context of aging. We conclude this section with a discussion of some key implications of aging, abilities, and education.

Aging and Intellectual Abilities

Cross-sectional studies generally show that intellectual ability peaks around the ages of 18–25. Cohort analyses typically reveal higher scores for each succeeding generation. Coupled with longitudinal data that reveal somewhat later peaks (in the late 20s), the general sense of adult intelligence is that declines in abilities can be expected as early as the 30s, though large differences in intelligence are not usually found until the 40s and later. Examination of general intelligence scores addresses only one salient aspect of the effects of aging on abilities. Different abilities have different patterns of growth, stability, and decline as adults enter middle age and beyond (e.g., see Schaie, 1970, 1996). From a content ability perspective, math and spatial abilities show peak levels at the youngest ages, followed by substantial declines in the 30s and 40s. Abstract reasoning and immediate memory (short-term memory and working memory) also show similar early peak performance, followed by substantial declines with increasing age. In contrast, verbal abilities tend to show a pattern of growth throughout early and middle adulthood, followed by stability well into middle age. Marked declines in verbal abilities are often not seen until age 60 or later.

The pattern of adult ability changes with age tends to be consistent with theory of fluid and crystallized intelligence outlined by Cattell (1943). That is, fluid intellectual abilities (e.g., abstract reasoning, immediate memory) tend to peak in early adulthood, followed by declines into middle and late adulthood. In contrast, crystallized abilities such as vocabulary and verbal comprehension, which are most highly associated with educational and experiential influences, show growth and stability well into the middle-adult years. The declines in fluid abilities with increasing age are typically larger than the increases in crystallized abilities, so that the overall pattern (as noted earlier) is for an overall decline in composites of general intelligence that give equal weight to the two types of abilities.

There are two important points that need to be made about this pattern of ability changes with age: First, as far as educational applications are concerned, there is no *inherent* reason why there should be an equal weighting of fluid and crystallized abilities. For domains such as physical science and mathematics, fluid intellectual abilities are more predictive of educational outcomes than crystallized abilities, especially for young children or novices of any age. For a wide range of other educational domains, crystallized abilities are more predictive of educational outcomes. (Note that in all domains, prior knowledge and skill in the domain are generally the best predictors of future success, especially when the demands of future learning are similar to those of learning to date.) Interestingly, adults have a relatively good sense of their own abilities, and of the nature of changes in fluid and crystallized kinds of abilities with increasing age (e.g., see Ackerman et al., 2002). Colleges and universities that offer programs of study specifically aimed at older, nontraditional students tend to match the content of course offerings to these changes in abilities (e.g., see Ackerman, 2000a). That is, the postsecondary courses most frequently available to older adults (in terms of night and weekend courses) are in the domains of the humanities, social sciences, and business; the courses least frequently offered are in the physical sciences and mathematics, especially at advanced levels of study.

The second point regarding age changes in fluid and crystallized abilities with age is that there are substantial interindividual differences in intraindividual change with age. That is, the average trends of growth, stability, and decline are relatively stable, but many individuals may have earlier or later peaks of ability than others, and more or less substantial declines in the various abilities with age. Prediction of these different aging patterns is a topic of keen interest in the field of life-span developmental psychology, but at present there are few, if any, diagnostic indicators for such differences (see Li et al., 2004).

The age-related changes in intellectual abilities raise important concerns for both selection programs and the design of instructional methods, especially in postsecondary education. Traditional selection programs that depend on omnibus tests (such as the SAT and GRE) have good validities for prediction of academic performance, especially for the first semester or year of college/university or graduate/professional school performance (e.g., see Lin & Humphreys, 1977). Given the age-related changes in performance on these tests, one can expect that as adults reach age 30 or 40, they will be perform at less competitive levels on these selection tests (because both cohort differences and age-related changes indicate that the older adults will perform more poorly on omnibus ability tests than younger adults). Whether these lower ability levels match the lower expected performance on academic indicators such as grade point average remains an open question. A review by Kasworm (1990) of adult undergraduates reveals just how sparse the literature is on these issues. Kasworm identified only 11 studies in this domain, and no definitive results, though several studies suggested that older adults perform at a level comparable to younger adults. Most likely, the nature of the outcome measure moderates the type of relationship observed. Adults typically perform better on essay tests and other tasks that allow them to show how well they have integrated new concepts into existing conceptual networks.

When one considers both the direction of educational interests of middle-aged and older adults (e.g., towards domains that depend more on crystallized intellectual abilities and less on fluid intellectual abilities) and the pattern of intellectual ability changes with age, it may very well be that middle-aged adults can be expected to perform at a higher level than younger adults in the programs where both are likely to be found. Selection procedures that more specifically match the ability demands of the educational program to the tests used for selection might find that higher weights for crystallized abilities might be in order in some domains. Under this scenario, middle-aged adults may find that they are much more competitive for selection, and that the selection procedure may turn out to have higher criterion-related validity than a system that uses only an omnibus intelligence or aptitude measure for selection. There is at present, though, far too little empirical research in this area to be able to provide specific recommendations.

In considering how to integrate changes in intellectual ability with the nature of instruction as far as middle-aged and older adults are concerned, Lorge and Kushner (1950) suggested that the main issue has to do with the "tempo" of instruction. That is, given that middle-aged and older adults tend to show the largest deficits (in comparison to young adults) on speeded intellectual tasks, the key toward optimizing instruction is to reduce the speed demands of the educational situation. Schaie and Willis (1978), in their review of life-span development and implications for education, agree with the conclusion of Lorge and Kushner, in that the pace of instruction should be slower for older adults than for young adults. However, Schaie and Willis also suggest that educators should consider two different approaches to education with older learners, namely "teaching to the weakness vs. teaching to the strength" (p. 131). In the former case, this could mean evaluating the patterns of cognitive decline with age, and designing educational interventions that attempt to remediate or ameliorate such declines (e.g., in terms of providing refresher courses on math and spatial tasks, or in terms of providing explicit training on memory improvement methods). In the latter case, building to strengths means that the instructional design could be tailored to that which the middle-aged or older adults bring to the learning situation that are not as well developed in young adults. Given the pattern of crystallized ability increases with age, one possibility is to structure instruction so that there is a greater dependence on transfer of knowledge, or to depend more on verbal strategies for problem solving than for nonverbal reasoning. In addition, Schaie and Willis (1978) suggest taking account of different learning strategies that appear to be better developed in older adults than younger adults (such as self-study as opposed to classroom learning), as a means toward further facilitating educational achievement.

CONCLUDING REMARKS

After 100 years of research in the field of human intelligence, and nearly 100 years of practical assessment of human intelligence in education, much is known about the structure and functions of abilities. Developments in the past decade fall into four different categories: (1) new theories that are largely reintroductions of previously investigated constructs; (2) relatively modest increments in knowledge about key abilities (what Kuhn, 1970, described as "normal science"); (3) revolutionary theoretical proposals with little or no empirical support; and (4) shifts of focus in the field, partly in reaction to the changing face of higher education. Although the study of aging and intelligence in adults is a domain that has had substantial research over the past 80 years, we believe that the last category of developments, in terms of application of intelligence theory to adult education, and in terms of aging and individual differences in domain knowledge, represents an important new area that will provide both opportunities and challenges for research and practice. Because much of what has been learned in the field depends on long-term or longitudinal research studies, this kind of research has been difficult and expensive to conduct (e.g., see Learned & Wood, 1938). Researchers have also been slow to recognize the importance of building (or using) tests that have score scales that better support interpretations of longitudinal changes than can be squeezed out of raw scores (see, e.g.,

Embretson & Hershberger, 1999; Kolen & Brennan, 2004). The paucity of longitudinal studies in the literature suggests that there are great opportunities for researchers in the future to make marked contributions to the field. We hope that, by the time the next review of the field is conducted, there will be much more to say about the interactions between intellectual abilities, other constructs, and the nature of adult intellectual development.

We also believe that intuitive theories about ability mislead not only those unfamiliar with research on abilities but, in a subtler way, the rest of us as well. Probably the most common naïve theories about ability are that (a) intelligence is unidimensional, not multidimensional, and (b) a good ability test would reveal the examinee's innate potential or capacity on this dimension. By definition, innate capacity is independent of education, culture, motivation, and other contaminants. These beliefs may explain the recurring appeal to the educators of figural reasoning tests that purport to be culture-fair measures of intelligence (e.g., Naglieri, 1997). But professionals are misled as well. If given a choice, most would choose a measure of Gf over a measure of Gc or Gkn as the better test of intelligence, even for adults. The fact that Gc and Gkn tests sample what people know and can do and are generally much better indicators of readiness for learning or performance in that domain than a measure of Gf is easily overlooked because the Gf tests (especially figural reasoning tests) appear to measure something untouched by education, culture, and the like. However, Gf-like measures are most relevant when one knows nothing about the domain (or when prediction is over much longer intervals; see Horn & Noll, 1997). Thereafter, what one knows and can do in the domain become measures of functional intelligence in the domain. These measures of acquired knowledge and skill reflect the product not only of past investments of Gf and other abilities, but also of interest, motivation, and other affective and conative variables. In such cases, Gf is more a measure of historical intelligence than of functional intelligence. It is no more the real intelligence than one's childhood home is one's current abode (except, of course, for those who never went anywhere).

Those anxious to embrace a multidimensional view of educational outcomes might attend more to the measure of Gkn—that is, the development of organized systems of conceptual and factual knowledge in domains—than to continued refinements of general measures of Gc and Grw abilities. We also believe that Gkn measures would be more sensitive to instructional interventions than tests that depend on more general thinking and problem-solving skills that define Gf. Indeed, although most educators are quite sensitive about the extent to which intelligence and other ability tests measure the direct products of schooling, few seem to care that items on many achievement tests are really better measures of general reasoning abilities (or, in the case of performance assessments, the ability to follow directions) than of achievement in the domain itself.

Lastly, abilities are, as Snow and Yalow (1982) noted, education's most important product as well as its most important raw material. Abilities are thus best viewed as both inputs and outcomes of good education. As inputs, they not only predict but moderate the success different learners experience in different instructional environments (Corno et al., 2002). As outcomes, they increase students' readiness for new learning in yet-to-be-experienced environments. More than any other construct, ability is at the heart of education. We hope that it will also continue to occupy a central role in educational psychology.

References

Ackerman, P. L. (1994). Intelligence, attention, and learning: Maximal and typical performance. In D. K. Detterman (Ed.) *Current topics in human intelligence: Vol. 4: Theories of intelligence* (pp. 1–27). Norwood, NJ: Ablex.

Ackerman, P. L. (1996). A theory of adult intellectual development: Process, personality, interests, and knowledge. *Intelligence, 22*, 229–259.

Ackerman, P. L. (2000a). Domain-specific knowledge as the "dark matter" of adult intelligence: gf/gc, personality and interest correlates. *Journal of Gerontology: Psychological Sciences, 55B(2)*, P69–P84.

Ackerman, P. L. (2000b). A reappraisal of the ability determinants of individual differences in skilled performance. *Psychologische Beiträge, 42*, 4–17.

Ackerman, P. L. (2003). Aptitude complexes and trait complexes. *Educational Psychologist, 38*, 85–93.

Ackerman, P. L., Beier, M. B., & Bowen, K. R. (2002). What we really know about our abilities and our knowledge. *Personality and Individual Differences, 34*, 587–605.

Ackerman, P. L., Beier, M. E., & Boyle, M. O. (2002). Individual differences in working memory within a nomological network of cognitive and perceptual speed abilities. *Journal of Experimental Psychology: General, 131*, 567–589.

Ackerman, P. L., Beier, M. E., & Boyle, M. O. (2005). Working memory and intelligence: The same or different constructs? *Psychological Bulletin, 131*, 30–60.

Ackerman, P. L., & Cianciolo, A. T. (2000). Cognitive, perceptual speed, and psychomotor determinants of individual differences during skill acquisition. *Journal of Experimental Psychology: Applied, 6,* 259-290.

Ackerman, P. L., Kyllonen, P. C., & Roberts, R. D. (Eds). (1999). *Learning and individual differences: process, trait, and content determinants.* Washington, DC: American Psychological Association.

Ackerman, P. L., & Rolfhus, E. L. (1999). The locus of adult intelligence: Knowledge, abilities, and non-ability traits. *Psychology and Aging, 14,* 314-330.

Alexander, P. A., Kulikowich, J. M., & Schulze, S. K. (1994). The influence of topic knowledge, domain knowledge, and interest on the comprehension of scientific exposition. *Learning and Individual Differences, 6,* 379-397.

Alexander, P. A., & Murphy, P. K. (1999). Learner profiles: Valuing individual differences within classroom communities. (pp. 413-436). In P. L. Ackerman, P. C. Kyllonen, & R. D. Roberts (Eds.), *Learning and individual differences: Process, trait, and content determinants.* Washington, DC: American Psychological Association.

Alexander, W. P. (1935). Intelligence, concrete and abstract: A study in differential traits. *British Journal of Psychology Monograph, 6*(19).

Anderson, J. R. (1983). *The architecture of cognition.* Cambridge, MA : Harvard University Press.

Anderson, J. R., Bothell, D., Byrne, M. D., Douglass, S., Lebiere, C., & Qin, Y. (2004). An integrated theory of the mind. *Psychological Review, 111,* 1036-1060.

Anvari, S. H., Trainor, L. J., Woodside, J., & Levy, B. A. (2002). Relations among musical skills, phonological processing and early reading ability in preschool children. *Journal of Experimental Child Psychology, 83,* 111-130.

Baddeley, A. (1986). *Working memory.* New York: Oxford University Press.

Baddeley, A. (1998). *Human memory: Theory and practice* (Rev. Ed.). Needham Heights, MA: Allyn & Bacon.

Baird, L. L. (1969). Prediction of accomplishment in college: A study of achievement. *Journal of Counseling Psychology, 10*(3), 246-253.

Beier, M. E., & Ackerman, P. L. (2001). Current events knowledge in adults: An investigation of age, intelligence and non-ability determinants. *Psychology and Aging, 16,* 615-628.

Beier, M. E., & Ackerman, P. L. (2003). Determinants of health knowledge: An investigation of age, gender, abilities, personality, and interests. *Journal of Personality and Social Psychology, 84*(2), 439-448.

Beier, M. E., & Ackerman, P. L. (2004). A reappraisal of the relationship between span memory and intelligence via "best evidence synthesis." *Intelligence: A Multidisciplinary Journal, 32,* 607-619.

Binet, A., & Simon, T. (1905/1973). *The development of intelligence in children.* (El. Kite, Trans.). New York: Arno Press.

Bock, R. D. (1973). Word and image: sources of the verbal and spatial factors in mental test scores. *Psychometrika, 38,* 437-457.

Brody, N. (1992). *Intelligence* (2nd ed.). San Diego, CA: Academic Press.

Brody, N. (2003a). Construct validation of the Sternberg Triarchic abilities test: Comment and reanalysis. *Intelligence, 31,* 319-329.

Brody, N. (2003b). What Sternberg should have concluded. *Intelligence, 31,* 339-342.

Buckingham, B. R. (1921). Intelligence and its measurement: A symposium. *Journal of Educational Psychology, 12,* 271-275.

Canady, H. G. (1936). The effect of "rapport" on the IQ: A new approach to the problem of racial psychology. *Journal of Negro Education, 5,* 209-219.

Carnap, R. (1987). The confirmation of laws and theories. In J. A. Kourany (Ed.), *Scientific knowledge: Basic issues in the philosophy of science* (pp. 122-138). Belmont, CA: Wadsworth.

Carroll, J. B. (1993). *Human cognitive abilities: A survey of factor-analytic studies.* New York: Cambridge University Press.

Cattell, J. McK. (1890). Mental tests and measurements. *Mind, 15,* 373-380.

Cattell, J. McK., & Farrand, L. (1896). Physical and mental measurements of the students of Columbia University. *Psychological Review, 3,* 618-648.

Cattell, R. B. (1943). The measurement of adult intelligence. *Psychological Bulletin, 40,* 153-193.

Cattell, R. B. (1971/1987). *Abilities: Their structure, growth, and action.* [Revised and reprinted as *Intelligence: Its structure, growth, and action.*] Amsterdam: North-Holland.

Chi, M. T. H., Glaser, R., & Rees, E. (1982). Expertise in problem solving. In R. J. Sternberg (Ed.), *Advances in the psychology of human intelligence* (Vol. 1, pp. 7-76). Hillsdale, NJ: Lawrence Erlbaum Associates.

Chronicle of Higher Educational Almanac, 2004-2005 (2004). Washington, DC: Author.

Cleary, A. T. (1992). Gender differences in aptitude and achievement test scores. In *Sex equity in educational opportunity, achievement, and testing: Proceedings of the 1991 ETS Invitational Conference* (pp. 51-90). Princeton, NJ: Educational Testing Service.

Cohen, J. (1988). *Statistical power analysis for the behavioral sciences.* Hillsdale, NJ: Lawrence Erlbaum Associates.

Conway, A. R. A., Kane, M. J., & Engle, R. W. (1999). Is Spearman's G determined by speed or working memory capacity? Psycoloquy: 10, #74. Deposited July 11, 2002, at http:psycprints.ecs.soton.ac.uk/archive/0000709/.

Corno, L., Cronbach, L. J., Lohman, D. F., Kupermintz, H., Mandinach, E. B., Porteus, A. & Talbert, J. E. (2002). *Remaking the concept of aptitude: Extending the legacy of Richard E. Snow.* Mohwah, NJ: Lawrence Erlbaum Associates.

Cronbach, L. J. (1949). *Essentials of psychological testing.* New York: Harper.

Cronbach, L. J. (1960). *Essentials of psychological testing* (2nd ed.). New York: Harper.

Cullen, M. J., Hardison, C. M., & Sackett, P. R. (2004). Using SAT-grade and ability-job performance relationships to test predictions derived from stereotype threat theory. *Journal of Applied Psychology, 89,* 220-230.

Daneman, M., & Carpenter, P. A. (1980). Individual differences in working memory and reading. *Journal of Verbal Learning & Verbal Behavior, 19*(4), 450-466.

Daneman, M., & Merikle, P. M. (1996). Working memory and language comprehension: A meta-analysis. *Psychonomic Bulletin & Review, 3*, 422-433.

Embretson, S. E. & Hershberger, S. L. (1999). *The new rules of measurement: What every psychologist and educator should know.* Mahwah, NJ: Lawrence Erlbaum Associates.

Engle, R. W. (2002). Working memory capacity as executive attention. *Current Directions in Psychological Science, 11*(1), 19-23.

Ericsson, K. A., Krampe, R. T., & Tesch-Römer, C. (1993). The role of deliberate practice in the acquisition of expert performance. *Psychological Review, 100*(3), 363-406.

Feingold, A. (1988). Cognitive gender differences are disappearing. *American Psychologist, 43*, 95-103.

Feldt, L. S. (1967). A note on the use of confidence bands to evaluate the reliability of a difference between two scores. *American Educational Research Journal, 4*, 139-145.

Frisbie, D. A. & Andrews, K. (1990). Kindergarten pupil and teacher behavior during standardized achievement testing. *Elementary School Journal, 90*, 435-448.

Fry, A. F., & Hale, S. (1996). Processing speed, working memory, and fluid intelligence: Evidence for a developmental cascade. *Psychological Science, 7*(4), 237-241.

Gardner, H. (1983). *Frames of mind: The theory of multiple intelligences.* New York: Basic Books.

Gardner, H. (1993). *Multiple intelligences: The theory into practice.* New York: Basic Books.

Gardner, H. (1999). Who owns intelligence? *Atlantic Monthly, 283*, 67-76.

Gardner, H. (2003, April). *Multiple intelligences after twenty years.* Paper presented at the meeting of the American Educational Research Association, Chicago. Retrieved Dec. 30, 2004 from http://www.pz.harvard.edu/PIs/HG_MI_after_20_years.pdf

Glaser, R. (1992). Expert knowledge and processes of thinking. In D. F. Halpern (Ed.), *Enhancing thinking skills in the sciences and mathematics* (pp. 63-75). Hillsdale, NJ: Laerence Erlbaum Associates.

Goddard, H. H. (1908). The Binet and Simon tests of intellectual capacity. *Training School Bulletin, 5*, 3-9.

Good, C., Aronson, J., & Inzlicht, M. (2003). Improving adolescents' standardized test performance: An intervention to reduce the effects of stereotype threat. *Journal of Applied Developmental Psychology, 24*, 645-662.

Goodenough, F. L. (1926). *Measurement of intelligence by drawings.* Yonkers-on-Hudson, NY: World Book.

Guilford, J. P. (1959). *Personality.* New York: McGraw-Hill.

Gustafsson, J.-E. (1988). Hierarchical models of individual differences in cognitive abilities. In R. J. Sternberg (Ed.), *Advances in the psychology of human intelligence,* (Vol. 4, pp. 35-71). Hillsdale, NJ: Lawrence Erlbaum Associates, Inc.

Gustafsson, J.-E. & Balke, G. (1993). General and specific abilities as predictors of school achievement. *Multivariate Behavioral Research, 28*, 407-434.

Gustafsson, J.-E., & Undheim, J. O. (1996). Individual differences in cognitive functions. Chapter in D. C. Berliner, & R. C. Calfee (Eds.) *Handbook of educational psychology* (pp. 186-242.) New York: Simon & Schuster Macmillan.

Halpern, D. F. (2000). *Sex differences in cognitive abilities* (3rd ed.). Mahwah, NJ: Lawrence Erlbaum Associates.

Hancock, P. A. (1986). Sustained attention under thermal stress. *Psychological Bulletin, 99*, 263-281.

Herrnstein, R. J., Nickerson, R. S., de Sánchez, M., & Swets, J. A. (1986). Teaching thinking skills. *American Psychologist, 41*, 1279-1289.

Horn, J. L. (1965). *Fluid and crystallized intelligence: A factor analytic study of the structure among primary mental abilities.* Ann Arbor, MI: University Microfilms International.

Horn, J. L. (1989). Cognitive diversity: A framework of learning. In P. L. Ackerman, R. J. Sternberg, & R. Glaser (Eds.). *Learning and individual differences. Advances in theory and research* (pp. 61-116). New York: W. H. Freeman.

Horn, J. L. (1991). Measurement of intellectual capabilities: A review of theory. In K. S. McGrew, J. K. Werder, & R. W. Woodcock (Eds.), *WJ-R technical manual.* Chicago: Riverside.

Horn, J. L., & Noll, J. (1997). Human cognitive capabilities: Gf-Gc theory. In D. P. Flanagan, J. L. Genshaft, & P. L. Harrison (Eds.), *Contemporary intellectual assessment: Theories, tests, and issues* (pp. 53-91). New York: Guilford.

Hyde, J. S., Fennema, E., & Lamon, S. J. (1990). Gender differences in mathematics performance: a meta-analysis. *Psychological Bulletin, 107*(2), 139-155.

Hyde, J. S., & Linn, M. C. (1988). Gender differences in verbal ability: a meta-analysis. *Psychological Bulletin, 104*(1), 53-69.

Jacobs, J. (1887). Experiments on "prehension." *Mind, 12*, 75-79.

Jensen, A. R. (1998). *The g factor.* Westport, CT: Praeger.

Joncich, G. (1968). *The sane positivist: A biography of Edward L. Thorndike.* Middletown, CT: Wesleyan University Press.

Juhel, J. (1991). Spatial abilities and individual differences in information processing. *Intelligence, 15*, 117-137.

Kane, M. J., Hambrick, D. Z., & Conway, A. R. A. (2005). Working memory capacity and fluid intelligence are strongly related constructs: Comment on Ackerman, Beier, and Boyle (2005). *Psychological Bulletin, 131*, 66-71

Kanfer, R., & Ackerman, P. L. (1989). Motivation and cognitive abilities: An integrative/aptitude-treatment interaction approach to skill acquisition. *Journal of Applied Psychology—Monograph, 74*, 657-690.

Kasworm, C. E. (1990). Adult undergraduates in higher education: A review of past research perspectives. *Review of Educational Research, 60*, 345-372.

Klein, P. D. (1997). Multiplying the problems of intelligence by eight: A critique of Gardner's theory. *Canadian Journal of Education, 22*, 377-394.

Klineberg, O. (1928). An experimental study of speed and other factors in "racial" differences. *Archives of Psychology, 15*(93), 1-109.

Kolen, M. J., & Brennan, R. L. (2004). *Test equating, scaling, and linking : Methods and practices* (2nd ed.). New York: Springer-Verlag.

Koertz, D., Stecher, B., Klein, S., & McCaffrey, D. (1994). The Vermont Portfolio assessment program: Findings and implications. *Educational Measurement Issues and Practice, 13,* 5-16.

Kuhlman, F. (1912). A revision of the Binet-Simon system for measuring the intelligence of children. *Journal of Psycho-Asthenics Monograph Supplement* (Vol. 1, No 1).

Kuhlman, F. (1922). *A handbook of mental tests.* Baltimore: Warwick & York.

Kuhn, T. S. (1970). *The structure of scientific revolutions* (2nd ed.). Chicago: University of Chicago Press.

Kyllonen, P. C., & Christal, R. E. (1990). Reasoning ability is (little more than) working-memory capacity?! *Intelligence, 14,* 389-433.

Lakatos, I. (Ed.). (1978). *The methodology of scientific research programmes: Philosophical papers* (Vol. 1). Cambridge, UK: Cambridge University Press.

Learned, W. S., & Wood, B. D. (1938). *The student and his knowledge.* New York: The Carnegie Foundation for the Advancement of Teaching.

Li, S.-C., Lindenberger, U., Hommel, B., Aschersleben, G., Prinz, W., & Baltes, P. B. (2004). Transformations in the couplings among intellectual abilities and constituent cognitive processes across the life span. *Psychological Science, 15,* 155-163.

Lin, P. C., & Humphreys, L. G. (1977). Predictions of academic performance in graduate and professional school. *Applied Psychological Measurement, 1,* 249-257.

Lindquist, E. F. (1951). Preliminary considerations in objective test construction. In E. F. Lindquist (Ed.), *Educational measurement.* Washington, DC: American Council on Education.

Linn, M.C. & Peterson, A. C. (1986). A meta-analysis of gender differences in spatial ability: Implications for mathematics and science achievement. In J. S. Hyde & M. C. Linn, (Eds.) *The psychology of gender: Advances through meta-analysis.* Baltimore: Johns Hopkins University Press.

Lohman, D. F. (1988). Spatial abilities as traits, processes, and knowledge. In R. J. Sternberg (Ed.), *Advances in the psychology of human intelligence* (Vol. 4, pp. 181-248). Hillsdale, NJ: Lawrence Erlbaum Associates.

Lohman, D. F. (1994a). Spatial ability. In R. J. Sternberg (Ed.), *Encyclopedia of intelligence* (pp. 1000-1007). New York: Macmillan.

Lohman, D. F. (1994b). Spatially gifted, verbally inconvenienced. In N. Colangelo & S. Assouline (Eds.), *Talent development: Proceedings of the Henry B. and Jocelyn Wallace National Research Symposium on Talent Development* (pp. 251-264). Dayton, OH: Ohio Psychology Press.

Lohman, D. F. (1999). Minding our p's and q's: On finding relationships between learning and intelligence. In P. L. Ackerman, P. C. Kyllonen, & R. D. Roberts (Eds), *Learning and individual differences: Process, trait, and content determinants* (pp. 55-76). Washington, DC: American Psychological Association.

Lohman, D. F. (2000). Complex information processing and intelligence. In R. J. Sternberg (Ed.) *Handbook of human intelligence* (2nd ed., pp. 285-340). Cambridge, UK: Cambridge University Press.

Lohman, D. F. (2001). Fluid intelligence, inductive reasoning, and working memory: Where the theory of Multiple Intelligences falls short. In N. Colangelo & S. Assouline (Eds.), *Talent Development IV: Proceedings from the 1998 Henry B. and Jocelyn Wallace National Research Symposium on Talent Development* (pp. 219-228). Scottsdale, AZ: Gifted Psychology Press.

Lohman, D. F., & Hagen, E. (2001). *Cognitive abilities test (Form 6).* Itasca, IL: Riverside Publishing Company.

Lohman, D. F., & Hagen, E. (2002). *Cognitive abilities test (Form 6) Research Handbook.* Itasca, IL: Riverside Publishing Company

Lohman, D. F., & Nichols, P. D. (1990). Training spatial abilities: Effects of practice on rotation and synthesis tasks. *Learning and Individual Differences, 2,* 67-93.

Lorge, I., & Kushner, R. (1950). Characteristics of adults basic to eduction. *Review of Educational Research, 20,* 171-184.

Lubinski, D. (2000). Assessing individual differences in human behavior: "Sinking shafts at a few critical points." *Annual Review of Psychology, 51,* 405-444.

Lubinski, D. (2004). Introduction to the special section on cognitive abilities 100 years after Spearman's (1904) "'General Intelligence,' Objectively determined and measured." *Journal of Personality and Social Psychology, 86,* 96-111.

Lubinski, D., & Benbow, C. P. (1995). An opportunity for empiricism [Review of H. Gardner, *Multiple intelligences: The theory in practice*]. *Contemporary Psychology, 40,* 935-938.

Martinez, M. E. (2000). *Education and the cultivation of intelligence.* Mahwah, NJ: Lawrence Erlbaum Associates.

McGrew, K. S. & Evans, J. J. (2004). Internal and external factorial extensions to the Cattell-Horn-Carroll (CHC) theory of cognitive abilities: A review of factor analytic research since Carroll's seminal 1993 treatise. Retrieved Dec. 30, 2004 from http://www.iapsych.com/CHCPP/4.CHCTheoryExtensions.html: Institute for Applied Psychometrics.

McNemar, Q. (1965). Lost: Our intelligence? Why? *American Psychologist,* 871-882.

Merriënboer, J. J. G. van, Kirschner, P. A., & Kester, L. (2003). Taking the load off a learner's mind: Instructional design for complex learning. *Educational Psychologist, 38,* 5-13.

Messick, S. (1989). Validity. In R. L. Linn (Ed)., *Educational measurement* (3rd ed.). NY: Micmillan Publishing Co.

Messick, S. (1992). Multiple intelligences or multilevel intelligence? Selective emphasis on distinctive properties of hierarchy: On Gardner's *Frames of Mind* and Sternberg's *Beyond IQ* in the context of theory and research on the structure of human abilities. *Psychological Inquiry, 3,* 365-384.

Mislevy, R. J. (in press). Cognitive psychology and educational assessment. In R. Brennan (Ed.), *Educational Measurement* (4th Ed.). Phoenix, AZ: Greenwood.

Miyake, A., Friedman, N. P., Rettinger, D. A., Shah, P., & Hegarty, P. (2001). How are visuospatial working memory, executive functioning, and spatial abilities related? A latent variable analysis. *Journal of Experimental Psychology: General, 150*, 621–640.

Naglieri, J. A. (1997). *Naglieri Nonverbal Ability Test: Multilevel technical manual.* San Antonio, TX: Harcourt Brace.

Nitko, A. J. (2001). *Educational assessment of students.* Upper Saddle River, NJ: Merrill.

Norman, D. A., & Shallice, T. (1986). Attention to action: Willed and automatic control of behavior. In R. J. Davidson, G. E. Schwartz, & D. Shapiro (Eds.), *Consciousness and self-regulation* (Vol. 4., pp. 1–18). New York: Plenum.

Nyborg, H. (1983). Spatial ability in men and women: Review and new theory. *Advances in Behavior Research & Therapy, 5*, 89–140.

Oberauer, K. (in press). The measurement of working memory capacity. To appear in O. Wilhelm & R. W. Engle (Eds.), *Handbook of understanding and measuring intelligence* (pp. 393–407). Thousand Oaks, CA Sage.

O'Connor, T. A. & Burns, N. R. (2003). Inspection time and general speed of processing. *Personality and Individual Differences, 35*, 713–724.

Pellegrino, J. W., Chudowsky, N., Glaser, R. (Eds.). (2001). *Knowing what students know: The science and design of educational assessment.* Washington, DC : National Academy Press.

Phillips, L. H., & Hamilton, C. (2001). The working memory model in adult aging research (pp. 101–125). In J. Andrade (Ed.), *Working memory in perspective.* New York: Psychology Press.

Popper, K. R. (1963). *Conjectures and refutation.* London: Routledge and Kegan Paul.

Revelle, W., Humphreys, M. S., Simon, L., & Gilliland, K. (1980). The interactive effect of personality, time of day, and caffeine: A test of the arousal model. *Journal of Experimental Psychology: General, 109*, 1–31.

Roberts, R. D., & Stankov, L. (1999). Individual differences in speed of mental processing and human cognitive abilities: Toward a taxonomic model. *Learning and Individual Differences, 11*, 1–120.

Riding, R. J., & Boardman, D. J. (1983). The relationship between sex and learning style and graphicacy in 14-year old children. *Education Review, 35*, 69–79.

Rolfhus, E. L. & Ackerman, P. L. (1999). Assessing individual differences in knowledge: Knowledge, intelligence, and related traits. *Journal of Educational Psychology, 91*, 511–526.

Rothney, J. W. M. (1937). The new Binet—A caution. *School and Society, 45*, 855–856.

Sackett, P. R., Hardison, C. M., & Cullen, M. J. (2004). On interpreting stereotype threat as accounting for African American—White differences on cognitive tests. *American Psychologist, 59*, 7–13.

Sacks, E. L. (1952). Intelligence scores as a function of experimentally established social relationships between child and examiner. *Journal of Abnormal and Social Psychology, 47*, 354–358.

Schaie, K. W. (1970). A reinterpretation of age related changes in cognitive structure and functioning. In L. R. Goulet &

P. B. Baltes (Eds.), *Life-span developmental psychology* (pp. 423–466). New York: Academic Press.

Schaie, K. W. (1996). *Intellectual development in adulthood: The Seattle longitudinal study.* New York: Cambridge University Press.

Schaie, K. W., & Willis, S. L. (1978). Life span development: Implications for education. *Review of Research in Education, 6*, 120–156.

Schneider, R. J., Ackerman, P. L., & Kanfer, R. (1996). To "act wisely in human relations": Exploring the dimensions of social competence. *Personality and Individual Differences, 21*, 469–481.

Sears, R. (1943). Motivational factors in aptitude testing. *American Journal of Orthopsychiatry, 13*, 468–493.

Seashore, C. E. (1919). *The psychology of musical talent.* Boston: Silver, Burdett, & Co.

Seibt, B., & Förster, J. (2004). Stereotype threat and performance: How self-stereotypes influence processing by inducing regulatory foci. *Journal of Personality and Social Psychology, 87*, 38–56.

Shah, P., & Miyake, A. (1996). The separability of working memory resources for spatial thinking and language processing: An individual differences approach. *Journal of Experimental Psychology: General, 125*(1), 4–27.

Shea, D. L., Lubinski, D., & Benbow, C. P. (2001). Importance of assessing spatial ability in intellectually talented young adolescents: A 20-year longitudinal study. *Journal of Educational Psychology, 93*, 604–614.

Snow, R. E. (1978). Research on aptitudes: A progress report. In L. S. Schulman (Ed.), *Review of Research in Education* (Vol. 4, pp. 50–105). Itasca, IL: Peacock.

Snow, R. E., & Lohman, D. F. (1989). Implications of cognitive psychology for educational measurement. In R. Linn (Ed.) *Educational measurement* (3rd ed.) (pp. 263–331). New York: MacMillan.

Snow, R. E., & Yalow, E. (1982). Intelligence and education. In R. J. Sternberg (Ed.), *Handbook of intelligence* (pp 493–585). New York: Cambridge University Press.

Snow, R. E., & Yalow, E. (1996). Aptitude development and education. *Psychology, Public Policy, and Law, 2*, 536–560.

Spearman, C., & Jones, L. L. W. (1950), *Human ability: A continuation of "The abilities of man."* London: Macmillan & Co., Ltd.

Stanley, J. C., & Benbow, C. P. (1982). Huge sex ratios at upper end. *American Psychologist, 27*, 972.

Stankov, L. (2000). Structural extensions of a hierarchical view on human abilities. *Learning and Individual Differences, 12*, 35–51.

Stanovich, K. E., & West, R. F. (1989). Exposure to print and orthographic processing. *Reading Research Quarterly, 24*, 403–433.

Steele, C. M. (1997). A threat in the air: How stereotypes shape intellectual identity and performance. *American Psychologist, 52*, 613–629.

Steele, C. M., & Aronson, J. (1995). Stereotype threat and the intellectual test performance of African Americans. *Journal of Personality and Social Psychology, 69*, 797–811.

Sternberg, R. J. (1985). *Beyond IQ: A triarchic theory of human intelligence.* Cambridge, UK: Cambridge University Press.

Sternberg, R. J. (1993). *The Sternberg Triarchic Abilities Test.* Unpublished test.

Sternberg, R. J. (2003). Issues in the theory and measurement of successful intelligence: A reply to Brody. *Intelligence, 31,* 319–329.

Sternberg, R. J. (2004). *The Sternberg Triarchic Abilities Test.* Unpublished test.

Sternberg, R. J., Castejón, J. L., Prieto, M. D., Hautamäki, J., & Grigorenko, E. L. (2001). Confirmatory factor analysis of the Sternberg Triarchic Abilities Test in three international samples. *European Journal of Psychological Assessment, 17,* 1–16.

Sternberg, R. J., & Pretz, J. E. (Eds.). (2005). *Cognition and intelligence: Identifying the mechanisms of the mind.* New York: Cambridge University Press.

Sternberg, R. J., & the Rainbow Project Collaborators (in press). Argumenting the SAT through assessment of analytical, practical, and creative skill. In W. Camara & E. Kimmel (Eds.), *New tools for admission to higher education.* Mahwah, NJ: Lawrence Erlbaum Associates.

Terman, L. M. (1916). *The measurement of intelligence.* Boston: Houghton Mifflin.

Terman, L. M. (1924). The mental test as a psychological method. *Psychological Review, 31,* 93–117.

Terman, L. M., & Merrill, M. A. (1937). *Measuring intelligence.* Boston: Houghton Mifflin.

Thorndike, E. L., Bregman, E. O., Cobb, M. V., & Woodyard, E. (1927). *The measurement of intelligence.* New York: Teachers College Columbia University, Bureau of Publications.

Thurstone, T. G. (1957). The tests of primary mental abilities. *Personnel and Guidance Journal, 35,* 569–578.

Vernon, P. E. (1950). *The structure of human abilities.* New York: Wiley.

Vispoel, W. P. (1999). Creating computerized adaptive tests of music aptitude: Problems, solutions, and future directions. In F. Drasgow & J. B. Olson-Buchanan (Eds), *Innovations in computerized assessment* (pp. 151–176). Mahwah, NJ: Lawrence Erlbaum Associates.

Voyer, D., Voyer, S., & Bryden, M. P. (1995). Magnitude of sex differences in spatial abilities: A meta-analysis and consideration of critical variables. *Psychological Bulletin, 117,* 250–270.

Wagner, R. K., Torgesen, J. K., Rashotte, C. A., Hecht, S. A., Barker, T. A., Burgess, S. R., Donahue, J., & Garon, T. (1997). Changing relations between phonological processing abilities and word-level reading as children develop from beginning to skilled readers: A 5-year longitudinal study. *Developmental Psychology, 33,* 468–479.

Webb, E. (1915). *Character and intelligence: An attempt at an exact study of character.* Unpublished doctoral dissertation, Cambridge University, Cambridge, UK.

Wechsler, D. (1950). Cognitive, conative, and non-intellective intelligence. *American Psychologist, 5,* 78–83.

Wechsler, D. (1975). Intelligence defined and undefined: A relativistic appraisal. *American Psychologist, 30,* 135–139.

Willingham, D. (2004). Reframing the mind. *Education Next, 3,* 18–24. Retrieved December 30, 2004, from http://www.educationnext.org/20043/18.html

Willingham, W. W., & Cole, N. S. (1997). *Gender and fair assessment.* Mahwah, NJ: Lawrence Erlbaum Associates.

Wittmann, W. W., & Süß, H.-M. (1999). Investigating the paths between working memory, intelligence, knowledge, and complex problem-solving performances via Brunswik symmetry. In P. L. Ackerman, P. C. Kyllonen, & R. D. Roberts (Eds.). *Learning and individual differences: Process, trait, and content determinants* (pp. 77–108). Washington, DC: American Psychological Association.

Wright, L. (1968). *Bibliography on human intelligence.* Washington, DC: U.S. Department of Health, Education, and Welfare.

Yerkes, R. M., Bridges, J. W., & Hardwick, R. S. (1915). *A point scale for measuring mental ability.* Baltimore: Warwick & York.

MODELS OF PERSONALITY AND AFFECT
FOR EDUCATION: A REVIEW AND SYNTHESIS

Gerald Matthews
University of Cincinnati

Moshe Zeidner
University of Haifa

Richard D. Roberts
Center for New Constructs, Educational Testing Service

Personality plays a pivotal role in students' experience of school, playing out its role in the relationships individuals share with peers and teachers, influencing classroom behavior, and contributing to academic achievement. Three educational applications of personality research may be distinguished (Braden, 1995). The first is studying the impact of normal variation in personality on outcomes such as motivation, social orientation, and learning. The second application is the study of abnormality and exceptionality. Educators need diagnostic tools for identifying individuals requiring special treatment because of dysfunctional personality, and also for recognition of the unusually gifted. The third application is facilitating educators' management of personality variation. Examples include implementing treatment programs for disturbed children, tailoring instruction methods to the individual, and training social-emotional skills (Greenberg et al., 2003).

These applications draw upon many different approaches to the study and implementation of personality models in the classroom. In this chapter, we focus primarily on the dimensional approach to personality, which describes multiple continuous traits, as opposed to typological descriptive schemes or idiographic case studies. The latter approaches are, of course, essential in understanding the individual, especially in the clinical context; to do them justice though would seemingly require an entire volume. Thus, this review will be limited to three types of psychological construct that play a pivotal role in the educational setting: (a) *dispositional constructs*, including personality traits and related stable personal qualities, (b) *mediating processes* that are influenced by traits and transmit their behavioral and experiential effects (e.g., coping with stress), and (c) *educational outcomes* such as promoting well-being, addressing problem behaviors, and improving academic achievement.

The remainder of this introduction is structured as follows. First, we review the key dispositional constructs for educational psychology. Second, we highlight the main mediating processes and outcomes to which personality traits relate and overview the applied relevance of personality assessment. Third, given that the chapter focuses also on affect, we review relations between personality and emotion. Our intention is to establish some of our assumptions and frames of reference from the outset and to provide a compelling rationale for the particular focus that we have adopted throughout this chapter.

Dimensions of Personality and Temperament

Figure 8.1 illustrates some of the key distinctions to be made between the multifarious individual difference constructs established by research on personality, motivation, and ability. Arguably, the most fundamental models describe basic traits that generalize across most areas of life, including education. Such general models often have a hierarchical structure that accommodates numerous correlated primary traits, together with a more parsimonious second-order factor structure. The Five Factor Model (FFM: Costa & McCrae, 1992) is currently the most widely used dimensional scheme of this kind. It distinguishes broad secondary factors of Extroversion (E), Neuroticism (N), Conscientiousness (C), Agreeableness (A), and Openness (O). Each one of these factors subsumes multiple primary factors; for example, anxiety, depression, and low self-esteem are some of the facets of N. Many of the standard questionnaires that assess primary and secondary traits are available in forms suitable for adolescents and older children.

Child psychology often focuses on the related construct of *temperament*, defined as biologically based behavioral tendencies that may be present from infancy (Rothbart & Bates, 1998). Measures of temperament taken in the preschool years are modestly but meaningfully predictive of personality in later childhood and early adulthood (Kagan & Snidman, 1999; Shiner & Caspi, 2003). Personality is, of course, rather less stable in childhood than it is in adults. In addition, whereas personality is typically assessed by questionnaire, temperament is most often measured using parent or teacher ratings of the child, or structured observational schedules. Three key dimensions of temperament appear to correspond to E, N, and C in the FFM (e.g., Shiner & Caspi, 2003):

Neuroticism (e.g., negative affectivity, emotional instability, worry). Temperamental qualities that appear to cohere around this construct include negative affects such as fear and sadness, distress-proneness, irritability, and behavioral inhibition.

Extroversion (e.g., sociability, liveliness and, in some accounts, positive affectivity). Cognate aspects of temperament include intensity of pleasure, activity, and a lack of social inhibition.

Conscientiousness (e.g., achievement striving, carefulness, and dutifulness). Related dimensions of temperament are inhibitory control, attentional focusing, and mastery motivation.

Shiner and Caspi (2003) also note that A (e.g., caring, trusting) and O (e.g., imaginative, intellectual) may have been unduly neglected in temperament research.

Studies of *abnormal* personality identify multiple traits that may correspond to the extremes of normal personality dimensions (Matthews, Deary, & Whiteman, 2003). For example, emotional dysregulation (e.g., anxiousness, instability) converges with N, inhibition (e.g., schizoid) converges with low E, compulsivity with high C, and dissocial traits (e.g., antisocial) converge with low A (Larstone et al., 2002). However, general traits do not fully capture variation in abnormal traits, and educational psychologists frequently use behavior checklists and self-report instruments that are geared toward childhood abnormality (see Kamphaus & Frick, 2002). A variety of *contextualized traits* appear particularly important for educational settings. The best known of these traits include those describing evaluative anxieties such as test, math, sports, and social anxiety (Zeidner & Matthews, in press). Other traits that we discuss later (e.g., academic self-concept) relate specifically to the academic context. Often such traits have greater predictive validity in context than general traits.

Other Individual Difference Constructs

Differential psychology traditionally makes a sharp distinction between personality traits as reflecting styles of behavior or preferences, from abilities, which represent individual differences in aptitude for performance. Abilities are usually represented within a hierarchical model, with general intelligence, *g*, at the apex (see Roberts, Markham, Zeidner, & Matthews, 2005, for a recent review). Studies of ability are largely beyond the scope of this chapter, but intelligence typically dwarfs personality as a predictor of academic performance (e.g., Jensen, 1998). Another important domain for assessment refers to various constructs that stand at the crossroads of personality and ability research, including learning styles and motivational factors (e.g., achievement motivation).

Of special relevance to present concerns are constructs that relate to social and emotional competence and especially emotional intelligence (EI; the person's ability to interpret and manage emotional encounters; see Mayer, Caruso, & Salovey, 1999). The nature of EI has been called into question, but its potential role in social-emotional learning will increasingly bring measures of this concept to the attention of educators (Zeidner, Roberts, & Matthews, 2002). Although EI is defined as a form of ability, it has been shown often to overlap empirically with personality. Moreover, personality traits may facilitate or impair successful emotional management. Indeed, some researchers see key components of EI (e.g., self-confidence, empathy, and resilience) as belonging more properly to the personality domain (Matthews, Zeidner, & Roberts, 2002).

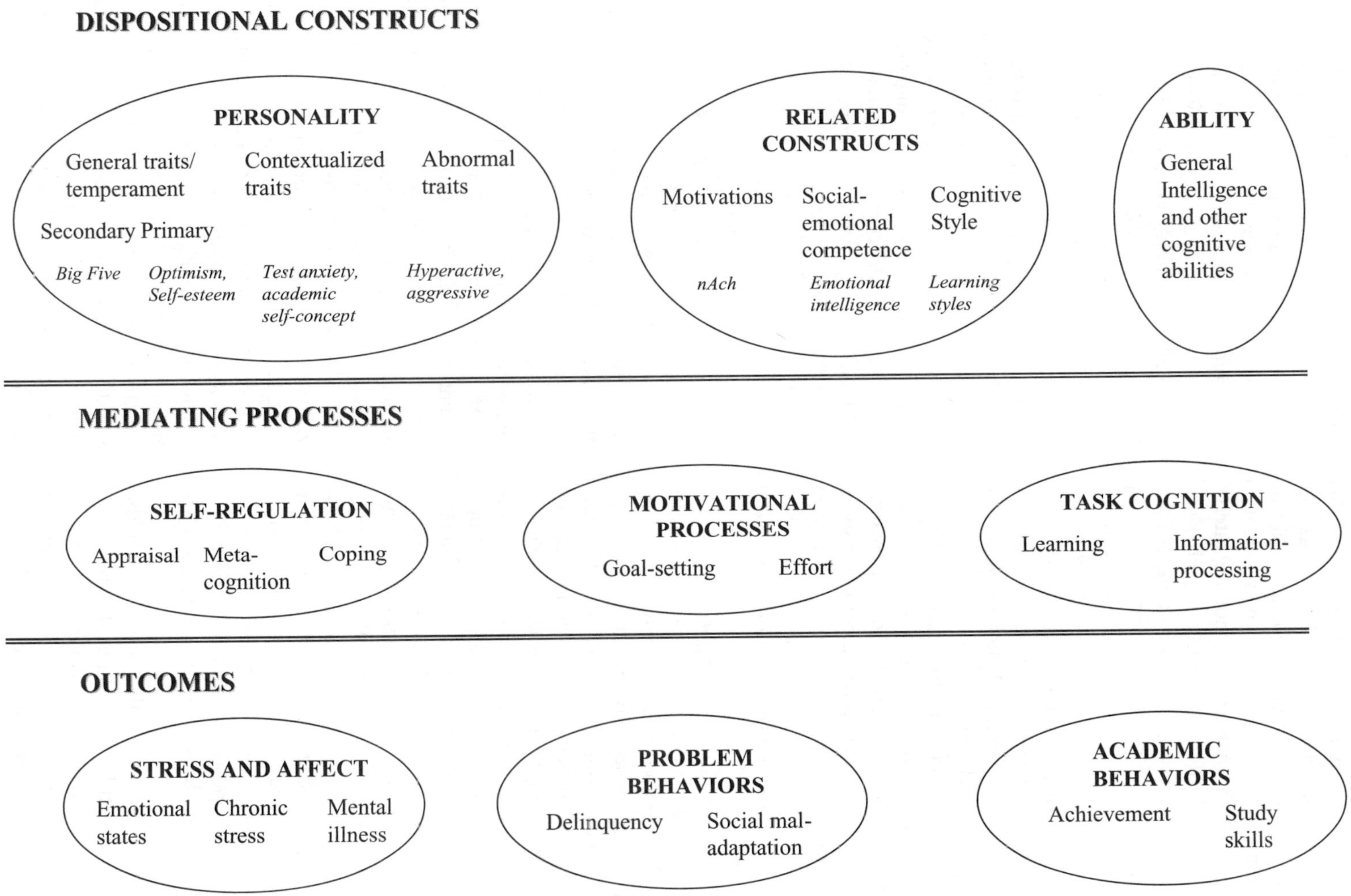

FIGURE 8.1. Some key constructs.

Outcomes and Mediating Processes

Much of the current enthusiasm for dimensional models derives from accumulating evidence for the predictive validity of the major traits in real-life settings (see Furnham & Heaven, 1999; Matthews et al., 2003, for reviews). For present purposes, we find it convenient to classify outcomes (which may or may not be interrelated) into (a) stress and affect, (b) problem behaviors, and (c) academic achievement, as shown in Fig. 8.1. Beyond establishing predictive validity, educators are concerned also with mediating processes. A process-based understanding is especially important for practical application, because it informs interventions and countermeasures, as in repairing or compensating a maladaptive process linked to a trait. One of the challenges of personality research is the various levels of mediating process to which traits may be linked, including neurophysiological processes, information processing, and high-level self-regulation (Matthews et al., 2003). In this chapter, we focus primarily on self-regulation and cognitive-social processes, which have proven to be a well-defined target for educational interventions (e.g., Schwean & Saklofske, 1999), without denying the importance of the biological bases of personality.

Boekaerts (1996) highlights the importance of self-regulation in the scholastic context. Students must apply their knowledge of their personal qualities to set appropriate learning goals and to implement and regulate strategies for goal attainment. Figure 8.1 breaks down the self-regulative process into three interrelated foci. First, there are cognitive stress processes elicited by challenging situations, including appraisal and coping, as described by Lazarus' (e.g., 1999) transactional model of emotion. Second, self-regulation depends on the interplay between cognitions and task motivations (i.e., how the person chooses goals and task strategies, regulates effort, and monitors progress; see Pintrich, 2003, for a review). Third, academic performance depends on the information-processing routines that directly control learning and comprehension of classroom material, such as focused attention, working memory, and long-term memory retrieval, processes that may be biased by personality factors, such as dispositional test anxiety (Zeidner, 1998).

In sum, students do much more than study, even in the classroom. They manage their learning goals, attempt to cope with academic and interpersonal difficulties, reflect on their own successes and failures, and are motivated to respond disparately to life events and stressors. Personality factors impinge, in varying degrees, on these mental activities that control the student's well-being, social adjustment, and academic attainment.

Personality and Affect

The role of personality in emotional response assumes particular importance in the educational context. Personality traits, as we will show, are linked to negative and positive affect, and so may color the student's entire educational experience. Personality factors also influence vulnerability to emotional disorders including anxiety, depression, and cognate personality dysfunctions (Livesley, 2001). The new field of emotional intelligence highlights the zest among educators for school-based reform that may change personality so as to enhance social and emotional functioning (e.g., Zins, Weissberg, Wang, Walberg, & Goleman, 2004).

A simple and popular model is based on the notion that there are two fundamental dimensions of affect: positive affect, referring to pleasant excited emotion, and negative affect, bringing together anxiety, sadness, and anger (Watson, 2000). Studies suggest that positive affect is substantially correlated with E, and negative affect with N. It is suggested that emotionality is at the core of these dimensions. E may index a brain reward system that generates positive emotions, whereas N is controlled by a brain punishment system producing negative emotion (Lucas & Diener, 2000). Other expressions of E and N are often a side effect of these temperamental qualities (e.g., positive emotionality produces the greater sociability of extraverts; Lucas & Diener, 2000). Positive and negative affect might also be linked to approach and avoidance motivations (Matthews et al., 2002).

Although the two-factor model is a useful working approximation, it may be too simplistic. First, two dimensions may be insufficient to capture variation in subjective states, even with respect to basic affects (e.g., Schimmack & Grob, 2000). Models of affect should be integrated with cognitive and motivational aspects of subjective state (Matthews et al., 2002); in test anxiety research, intrusive cognitions are often more damaging to performance than negative affect itself (see in particular, Zeidner, 1998). Second, personality traits cannot be reduced to brain motivation systems alone. For example, N is linked to negative affect through multiple mechanisms that also include dysfunctional cognitions of challenging events, metacognitions that heighten awareness of personal failings, and choosing ineffective coping strategies (Matthews et al., 2003; Suls, 2001). Third, like other traits, E and N have cognitive, social, and behavioral expressions that are not directly mediated by emotion. Fourth, situational factors have important moderating effects on the affective expressions of personality, in line with current interactionist perspectives (Matthews et al., 2003).

Thus, there are potentially multiple explanations, not limited to affect, for personality differences seen in the classroom. For example, in addressing excessive negative emotionality in high-N children, the educator may need to choose between restructuring negative appraisals, training more effective coping skills, training interpersonal skills to reduce conflict with others, or teaching the child to actively seek nonstressful settings and activities. A biological perspective would also suggest a role for medication in severe cases.

Overview of Chapter Structure

The remainder of this chapter is structured as follows. First, we review the contribution of research on personality and temperament to understanding individual differences in social and emotional development. The focus of much recent work is on *emotional intelligence* as an index of social-emotional maturity. Thus, we critique emotional intelligence and its measurement, discuss a developmental model of emotional competencies, and provide a brief overview of school-based programs for social-emotional learning. The next section addresses personality factors in academic achievement. We examine how the traits described by the FFM correlate with academic performance, and review some key social-cognitive and motivational constructs (e.g., academic self-concept, test anxiety). Thereafter, we discuss personality and emotional pathology, reviewing, in turn, externalizing conditions (e.g., aggressive conduct) and internalizing disorders (e.g., anxiety and depression). We conclude by summarizing the validity of personality measures in educational contexts, commenting briefly on practical applications.

Our review aims to highlight key findings and research directions, but space constraints preclude a comprehensive survey. We focus on what appear to be the typical effects of personality variables across the life span; from the outset we note that the role of personality may vary, however, with age, and within primary, secondary, and tertiary sectors of education. There may also be important moderating effects of gender and culture. For example, the unique focus of American education on raising self-esteem may generate cross-cultural differences in the relations between agency beliefs and academic attainment (Little, Oettingen, Stetsenko, & Baltes, 1995). There may also be unique features to personality in different ethnic groups within the United States and Canada (Schwean, Mykota, Robert, & Saklofske, 1999), or to low-income children in programs such as Head Start (Fantuzzo, Bulotsky, McDermott, Mosca, & Lutz, 2003). Thus, while we present a broad-brush view of personality, affect, and educational criteria in this chapter, we also underscore the need to examine personality effects in an appropriate sociocultural context.

SOCIAL AND EMOTIONAL DEVELOPMENT

The concepts of social and emotional development incorporate the related theme of EI in the educational and school context. Applications of this research extend from uses in special education (e.g., assisting children with autism, Asperger's syndrome, conduct disorders, alexithymia) to improving understanding of the source of bullying, character development, citizenship, and ways of implementing remedial and long-term community-based interventions. In the passages that follow, we first consider measures of social and emotional competence and the relations that these measures share with academic achievement and related outcomes. Next, we integrate emotional competence and temperament within a process-based model. We close with a brief discussion of recent social and emotional learning programs that have been implemented in the school system, and that represent something of a novel approach to education in the K-12 arena.

Emotional Intelligence

General intelligence provides the best single predictor of academic performance, but, even in combination with personality measures, validity coefficients for the prediction of academic criteria seldom exceed 0.60 (e.g., Jensen, 1998). It is hoped that tests of EI may predict educational criteria, such as well-being, academic achievement, and prosocial behaviors, above and beyond general (cognitive) intelligence and personality. Broadly conceived, EI represents an ability for processing emotional stimuli and managing emotional encounters adaptively (e.g., Mayer et al., 1999). Perhaps confusingly, two rather different measurement strategies have emerged, one reliant on self-report (similar to personality questionnaires), and the other on objective tests (similar to ability tests). Petrides and Furnham (2003) differentiate the two types of construct as *trait* EI and *ability* EI, respectively.

In this section, we briefly introduce relevant measures and their psychometric properties.

Self-Reported Assessment. EI assessment has often involved questionnaires eliciting self-reports of emotional competence. However, one may question whether individuals have accurate insight into their emotional functioning. A practical problem with these self-reports is the extent to which they are capable of being faked or coached, rendering problematic their application in large-scale assessments of the kind often used in education. Various tests, such as the Schutte Self-Report Inventory

(SSRI: Schutte et al., 1998) and the EQ-i (Bar-On, 1997), have been developed. Typically, these comprise multiple subtests, whose scores are summated to give an overall score for EI. However, there is substantial variation in the contents of such questionnaires. Each measure appears to represent a given proponent's view of EI. Regrettably too, many self-report measures are proprietary; that is, they have not been subject to peer-review evaluation (Matthews et al., 2002).

Despite these problems, self-report instruments show quite good criterion validity in adult samples, although there is a paucity of published studies with school-aged children. Consistent with a focus on real-world adaptation, Bar-On (1997) cites studies showing that the EQ-i relates to adjustment, well-being, and social success. The SSRI also shows reasonable criterion validity, with correlations found with optimism, impulse control, interpersonal skills, cooperative tendencies, and relationship satisfaction (e.g., Schutte et al., 1998). Unfortunately, these questionnaires are often highly correlated with existing personality traits, including low N, E, C, and A (see Mac-Cann, Matthews, Zeidner, & Roberts, 2004, for a review). Most validation studies have failed to control for personality, so that the incremental validity of EI questionnaires is in doubt (Matthews et al., 2002; Matthews, Zeidner & Roberts, 2005).

Performance-Based Assessment. The primary model for performance-based EI is the four-branch model where EI is defined as a set of hierarchically arranged competencies or abilities that cluster into four branches: (a) emotion perception, (b) emotional facilitation of thought, (c) emotional understanding, and (d) emotion management (Mayer et al., 1999). The most comprehensive instruments are the MEIS (e.g., Mayer et al., 1999) and MSCEIT (Mayer, Salovey, & Caruso, 2002), each of which includes multiple subtests.

The problem of establishing veridical scoring is one of the most serious difficulties currently plaguing the "objective" measurement of EI. *Consensus* measurement assigns scores according to the individual respondent's conformity with normative data (on the basis that optimal emotional behavior is socially defined). However, consensus may simply reflect cultural biases about emotion. Expert scoring relies on the use of psychologists with knowledge of emotion to determine correct answers. The difficulties are that it is unclear who the experts should be, since others than psychologists might have claims to expertise, and the applicability of academic knowledge of emotions to real-life adaptation is questionable. Empirical studies deliver mixed messages, although a recent study of the MSCEIT suggests good expert-consensus agreement (Mayer et al., 2002).

Despite scoring issues, performance-based measures appear psychometrically sound (Mayer et al., 2002). Expert and consensus scoring methods yield acceptable reliabilities for overall EI, even if reliabilities of some subtests are modest (see MacCann et al., 2004). With respect to predicting outcomes, Mayer et al. (1999) report correlations in the range 0.15–0.30 between overall score and life satisfaction, social skills, and parental warmth. Trinidad and Johnson (e.g., 2002) found that objective EI was low in adolescents who smoked cigarettes or consumed alcohol. Validation of the more recent MSCEIT is only just beginning, although Managing Emotions has been found to correlate significantly (i.e., 0.20–0.40) with social skills, positive relations with others, and lack of negative interaction with close friends (Lopes, Salovey, & Straus, 2003).

Izard (e.g., Fine, Izard, Mostow, Trentacosta, & Ackerman, 2003) has pioneered the use of objective tests of "emotion knowledge" in children. He has employed tasks such as identifying facial emotion from photographs, and asking children to say how characters in vignettes would feel. Although these measures are quite substantially correlated with verbal ability, they show incremental validity in longitudinal studies as predictors of social maladjustment and emotional pathology. It is unclear how children's emotion knowledge relates to adult EI, although Izard's tests appear to correspond to Emotion Perception and Emotion Understanding of the Mayer–Salovey–Caruso model.

Further Assessments. Both questionnaires and the MEIS/MSCEIT rely on explicit, declarative knowledge of appropriate emotional behavior. However, implicit, procedural skills, such as those contributing to appraising the intentions of others, may make an equally important contribution. Thus, interest is growing in assessing EI using information-processing measures, based on experimental psychological techniques. These include tests measuring the ability to recognize emotion in various stimuli and the Emotional Stroop. MacCann et al. (2003) discuss modest, but meaningful, correlations between these measures and tests of academic intelligence.

Another key process may be implicit justification, reflecting reasoning biases that operate below the level of consciousness. Recent work by James and colleagues (e.g., James, 1998) addresses a key form of "emotional illiteracy"; that is, irrational aggression and hostility toward legitimate authority. James has developed problems that appear to be basic reasoning tasks. However, the solutions to these "conditional reasoning problems" are dependent on whether reasoning is shaped by justification mechanisms for aggression. Scores on the Conditional Reasoning Test for Aggression (CRT-A) have been shown to have acceptable psychometric properties and an average, uncorrected validity of .44 against behavioral indicators of aggression (James, 1998). Thus, it may be possible to assess implicit personality dispositions, including "emotionally unintelligent" characteristics that people often attempt to deny or conceal.

Relations Among EI, Intelligence, and Achievement. Most studies of self-report EI consistently show that these measures correlate near zero with intelligence test scores (e.g., Brackett & Mayer, 2003; van Rooy & Viswesvaran, 2004). Parker et al. (2004) found that EQ-i scores were modestly associated with grade-point average in college students, but this result may plausibly reflect the confounding of the EQ-i with low anxiety and other personality factors that are known to relate to college grades. Studies have shown that the MEIS and MSCEIT correlate moderately with intelligence and academic achievement (e.g., Lopes et al., 2003), although associations are primarily driven by the Understanding Emotions branch (MacCann et al., 2003).

A Multidimensional Measurement Framework?. It is commonly assumed that, as with general intelligence, the various aspects or branches of EI may all relate to a single, general factor, an "EQ" analogous to IQ. However, this assumption may be false. For example, questionnaire measures of EI are only very modestly correlated with the MSCEIT (Brackett & Mayer, 2003; MacCann et al., 2003). Future research may require the discrimination of multiple dimensions, which are differently related to existing personality and ability constructs and which cannot be subsumed under a single general emotional aptitude. Matthews, Zeidner, and Roberts (in press) differentiated four classes of constructs that may be differentiated psychometrically, in terms of their bases in processing, and in terms of their adaptive significance:

Temperament. Dimensions of childhood temperament linked to emotionality map onto adult personality dimensions that, in turn, are highly correlated with many EI questionnaires. Various neural and cognitive processes support these dimensions. Although aspects of temperament such as distress proneness have maladaptive features, the adaptive consequences of these dimensions are not easily traced since they are intricate and multifaceted (i.e., distress also attracts the caregiver's attention and promotes risk-avoidance).

Emotional self-confidence. Recent questionnaires that explicitly target constructs distinct from standard personality traits (e.g., Petrides & Furnham, 2003) appear to assess metacognitive awareness of emotional functioning. This construct is akin to self-rated intelligence and at the process level might map onto social-cognitive constructs (e.g., self-esteem and self-efficacy) in the specific context of emotion. Thus, self-confidence may be more dependent on social learning than temperament. Like self-esteem, high emotional self-confidence may be predominantly adaptive, but with a "dark side," taking the form of narcissism, denial, and excessive self-enhancement.

Emotional processing. We have discussed how emotional competence may, in part, reside in processing of affective stimuli, as expressed in tests like the Emotional Stroop. A general factor for such abilities might correspond to fluid intelligence in the abilities domain. However, the adaptive value of emotion-processing factors remains to be explored. It is unclear that rapid processing of positive stimuli and slow processing of negative stimuli is necessarily beneficial. Even so, it is likely too that such a factor might improve over the course of schooling.

Emotional knowledge. Emotional competence may also relate to acquired, contextualized skills for handling specific encounters, such as calming a friend who is upset. We expect that such skills have similar properties to cognitive skills. Thus, although emotional self-confidence may facilitate acquisition and execution of skills, skills are numerous and specialized for specific problems. Similarly, depending on level of practice and the stimulus-response mapping (varied or consistent), skills vary on an explicit–implicit continuum. Implicit skills perhaps resemble acculturated knowledge, whereas explicit skills might correspond to declarative knowledge of emotional matters. Knowledge of this kind may play a major part in the MSCEIT, in that the instruments assesses declarative knowledge, such as "black in a painting signifies unhappiness" (emotional facilitation of thought). Generally, increased knowledge is adaptive, but it may transfer poorly across different situations or contexts. The fact that these various types of emotional components are related to knowledge suggests that they are likely to improve over the course of the school years and be susceptible to various forms of intervention.

Temperament and Social-Emotional Development

Our analysis of EI suggests that temperament, referring to styles of behavior and affective response, should be distinguished from more specific skills and self-related beliefs. Zeidner, Matthews, Roberts, and MacCann (2003) have proposed an "investment model" that seeks to explain how temperamental factors may influence emotional development (see Fig. 8.2). Akin to that proposed for traditional cognitive abilities (Ackerman, 1996), the model also indicates why there may be multiple sources of

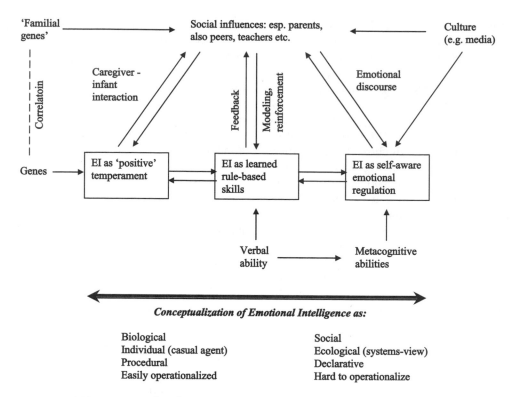

FIGURE 8.2. A developmental investment model of competencies contributing to emotional intelligence.

individual differences in emotional competence that are only weakly related to one another. As development proceeds, the range of emotion-regulative mechanisms becomes increasingly varied and differentiated. For example, Derryberry, Reed, and Pilkenton-Taylor (2003) have described how primitive behavioral strategies for emotion regulation supported by subcortical brain motivation systems are, with age, increasingly supplemented by cognitive mechanisms that allow the child to plan and anticipate.

The investment model assumes that the various dimensions of temperament provide a platform for subsequent emotional learning. Temperament interacts with situational factors to influence rule-based skills, as the preschool child learns "if-then" rules for displaying emotion, responding to the emotion of others, and simple tactics for influencing the emotions of self and others (see Denham, 1998). For example, distress proneness may disrupt the child's interactions with the caregiver, delaying emotional skill learning. Much of this learning is verbal in nature, and so verbal ability also facilitates skill acquisition. As the child enters the school-age years, further skills are required that are more dependent on insight into self and others, allowing a more flexible response to interpersonal situations: learning, for example, that crying will elicit sympathy from one adult, but annoyance from

another. Both temperament and rule-based competence may moderate insight-based learning. The adult thus possesses a varied repertoire of emotional responses, ranging from low-level emotional modulation (temperament), through simple rule-based skills, to more complex competencies based on insight and metacognition.

The investment model may also inform understanding of the relations between EI and real-world adaptation and stress management. The transactional theory of emotion and stress (Lazarus, 1999) sees adaptation to demanding situations as being shaped by multiple cognitive processes, including appraisal and coping. The process is dynamic as the person seeks to cope with changing external demands over some period of time. Other authors (e.g., Scherer, 2001) have emphasized that adaptive processes operate at multiple levels in parallel (e.g., both unconsciously and consciously). Zeidner and Matthews (2000) suggested that personality traits relate to multiple processing biases that are related functionally rather than structurally. Thus, high-N individuals are geared to anticipate and avoid threats, whereas low-N persons are more disposed to await and confront potential dangers.

Of critical importance, the developmental trajectory depends on interaction with the environment. The qualities of the distress-prone child, such as hyperawareness of threat and personal deficiencies, may lead to avoidance of feared social situations. This behavior pattern, in turn, affords fewer opportunities to develop emotion recognition skills, leading to poorer understanding of what happens in emotional situations and hence poorer management of such situations (see e.g., Wells & Matthews, 1994). The resultant skills deficits lead to further avoidance and maladaptive self-beliefs that typically lead to further withdrawal. By contrast, traits that promote engagement with challenging situations, such as sociability (corresponding to adult E), lead to greater opportunities for learning skills for handling exciting (but potentially risky) encounters. Thus, temperamental traits may influence emotional development both directly (via individual differences in emotion and attention) and indirectly (through exposure to situations for practicing and learning skills for specific emotional challenges). However, it remains unclear whether there is some specific developmental trajectory that might be linked to EI, or whether there are qualitatively different trajectories, corresponding to different personality traits that represent different styles of handling emotional encounters.

Educational Interventions Aimed at Social and Emotional Development

In the educational context, Zins et al. (2004) define Social-Emotional Learning (SEL) as teaching children to be self-aware, socially cognizant, able to make responsible decisions, and competent in self-management and relationship-management skills. These authors describe instructional techniques that promote SEL. They also emphasize that person-centered approaches are insufficient; the learning environment (including the family and community) must also be supportive of SEL. Programs instantiating these principles have a good record of success, as Greenberg et al. (2003) ascertained in their review meta-analyses suggesting beneficial outcomes on mental health, antisocial behaviors, and academic performance and learning. However, one issue of some concern is scalability; that is, can these programs be applied across the nation or in states with less infrastructure than those where these programs have been tested so far? It is also unclear what recent conceptions of EI can add to existing work. Although educational programs capitalize on enthusiasm for EI, interventions are actually directed toward specific skills (e.g., conflict resolution, impulse control) rather than some general competence (see Zeidner et al., 2002, for a review). It is unclear whether training some general competence would be more cost effective than focusing on specific skills.

Supposing general competencies exist, the practical techniques of choice depend critically on which con-

ception of competence is adopted. The different conceptions identified earlier can loosely be divided into those primarily dependent on gene–environment interaction in early childhood (e.g., temperament, information processing), and those that, although influenced by such constitutional factors, are most directly influenced by learning and socialization (e.g., emotional self-confidence, specific knowledge). In principle, temperament and basic information-processing competencies might be altered in infancy and early childhood. However, without an adaptive analysis, there is little basis for choosing to do so. It is unclear that training faster recognition of emotion in faces or insensitivity to distress would actually benefit children. An alternate strategy is investigating aptitude-by-treatment interactions that allow the individuals to make best use of their emotional dispositions.

By contrast, emotional self-confidence, declarative knowledge, and procedural skills may be trained at any stage of life, given the active cooperation of the learner. Again, an adaptive analysis is needed to tell us whether social resources should be allocated to such an enterprise. We might train emotional self-confidence by assisting the person through learning experiences that build a sense of mastery. Generally, this seems like a worthy goal, but is there a danger also of building narcissism and indifference to personal limitations? Training declarative emotional knowledge appears to be safe. Yet, as with any skill, the person also requires insight into its applicability.

These caveats notwithstanding, the Collaborative of Academic, Social, and Emotional Learning (CASEL) states that one of the main questions educators ask is how they can measure their students' social and emotional learning (SEL) skills and how they can evaluate the quality and effects of their SEL practices (Greenberg et al., 2003; Zins et al., 2004). To address this need, and across the next several years, CASEL plans to compile and create tools that (a) educators can use to assess SEL-related student outcomes and (b) schools and districts can use to assess their SEL implementation. The first phase of this work will focus on creating SEL standards and benchmarks for students in grades pre-K to 12 and compiling existing tools and procedures to assess both student outcome measures and SEL implementation. In the second phase, they plan to field-test the most promising tools and procedures in a variety of school settings. In the final phase, they plan to publish a manual of effective, scientifically sound SEL assessments and strategies for their use, including the creation of a student assessment system for SEL-related student outcomes.

In terms of educational practice, recent reviews that we conducted (Matthews et al., 2002; Zeidner et al., 2002) suggest that many intervention programs, while claiming to influence social and emotional development, were not specifically designed for that purpose. Indeed, there appear to be few systematic interventions that meet the canons of internal and external validity. Consequently, objective evidence attesting to the role of social and emotional competencies as predictors of school success and adjustment, above that predicted by traditional academic factors, is limited. These reviews, however, concluded with an agenda and guidelines for the development, implementation, and evaluation of future programs designed at inculcating social and emotional competencies:

1. Base intervention programs on a solid conceptual framework
2. Specify program goals and behavioral outcomes in a carefully constrained manner
3. Identify the sociocultural and developmental context for program implementation
4. Integrate social and emotional development programs into the school educational and instructional curriculum fully (i.e., not in a piecemeal fashion)
5. Make provisions for practice and for generalizing the domain of emotional skills across different classes of behavioral performance
6. Ensure professional development of program personnel
7. Use robust experiments and valid measures for assessing program effectiveness

These considerations suggest the need for a greater focus on multivariate approaches to program evaluation. It is important to assess social-emotional competencies using measures derived from students (e.g., emotional awareness, perceptions of classmates and teachers), teachers (e.g., teacher's backgrounds and expectations, teacher's assessment of students), and family (e.g., parental perceptions of the child, the family climate and the school). Criteria should also be multifaceted. They should extend beyond scores on state tests to include behavioral indices such as number of reprimands, frequency of absenteeism, and the like. Multivariate assessments of this kind are expensive, but may prove to be essential for testing the models and efficacy of educational interventions that are mandated, in particular, by No Child Left Behind.

PERSONALITY, MOTIVATION, AND ACADEMIC PERFORMANCE

Any attempt to understand the complete causal chain associated with school attainment must include the effects of nonintellective factors, such as personality and motivational processes, in concert with ability and social and economic factors at home and in the community (see Saklofske & Zeidner, 1995). Here we survey relations among personality, motivation, and academic achievement. We look first at personality, focusing on the FFM. Then, we review the effects of variables related to motivation, including achievement motivation, self-concept, and test anxiety. We also focus on the contribution of self-regulative theory and the possible role of social-cognitive constructs (e.g., self-efficacy) in mediating personality effects.

In addressing the personality-achievement interface, we endorse both Snow (1994) and Corno et al.'s (2002) call for educational psychologists to work toward dynamic, integrative models that include cognitive, motivational, and affective processes. Figure 8.3 depicts some of the paths through which major ability, motivational, and personality factors may influence academic performance. *Performance* pathways describe the processes through which individuals retrieve and assemble information-processing routines for accomplishing a task, and thus influence performance directly. Effects of personality may in part be mediated by transient states, such as negative affect, worry, and fatigue, that influence basic parameters of processing (Matthews, Campbell et al., 2002). *Commitment* pathways describe a parallel process, by which individuals choose strategies and invest effort in the service of guiding and regulating their behavior toward academic goals. Task engagement (i.e., *commitment*, effort, and attentional focus) is assumed to be a key mediating process. *Moderator* pathways refer to the role of personality and motivational constructs in modifying the effect of ability on cognitive attainment. For example, high C may allow the less able student to compensate for low ability by studying extensively or taking extra–credit assignments.

In this model, cognitive, affective, and motivational determinants of performance and outcomes are viewed as a dynamic process unfolding over time (Corno et al., 2002). Feedback loops are not shown in Fig. 8.3, but achievement and nonintellective factors (motivation and personality) are assumed to be reciprocally related and to act in mutually reinforcing ways. For example, emotional stability (low N) and high self-efficacy may positively affect a student's scholastic performance, which then cycles back to strengthen emotional stability and self-agency, which, in turn, triggers further positive educational achievement.

Personality and Achievement

Many different personality traits have been linked to individual differences in academic performance. Increasingly,

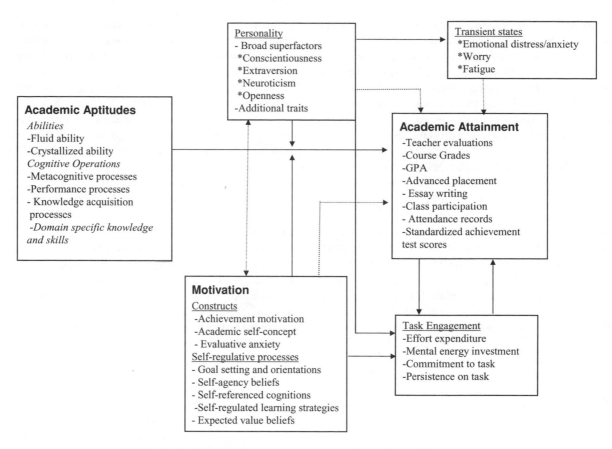

FIGURE 8.3. Some paths for expressions of individual differences in academic attainment.

research is structured around the FFM: the traits most commonly linked to better academic performance are Openness, Conscientiousness, and Emotional Stability (see Chamorro-Premuzic & Furnham, 2003, for a review). Next, we review the evidence relating to the Big Five traits, and indicate some possible mechanisms.

Openness (O). Ackerman and Heggestad's (1997) meta-analysis revealed a positive relation between O and standardized measures of knowledge and achievement. This review suggested that crystallized intelligence (i.e., acquired cognitive skills) may be one potential mediating factor in the relationship between O and scholastic ability. However, O is only modestly correlated with intelligence; correlations typically range between 0.20 and 0.30. O has been positively associated with final grades, even when controlling for intelligence (Farsides & Woodfield, 2003). Others have suggested that O may facilitate the use of efficient learning strategies (e.g., critical evaluation) that, in turn, affects academic success (Mumford & Gustafson, 1988). Notwithstanding, recent studies of college students have failed to replicate significant relations between O and academic achievement (e.g., Busato, Prins, Elshout,

& Hamaker, 2000). Indeed, the creative and imaginative nature of open individuals may be sometimes a disadvantage in academic settings, particularly when individuals are required to reproduce curricular content rather than produce novel response or creative problem solving (De Fruyt & Mervielde, 1996).

Conscientiousness (C). C has been consistently found to predict academic achievement from childhood to adulthood (De Fruyt & Mervielde, 1996; Shiner, Masten, & Roberts, 2003). High C may be associated with personal attributes necessary for learning and academic pursuits such as being organized, dependable, efficient, striving for success, and exercising self-control (Matthews, Deary, & Whiteman, 2003). In the Project Competence longitudinal study, the trait of academic conscientiousness (i.e., a contextualized measure) measured in schoolchildren became a strong predictor of academic achievement at age 20 and eventual academic attainment at age 30 (Shiner & Masten, 2002). The effects of C on academic performance may be mediated by motivational processes such as expenditure of effort and persistence (Boekaerts, 1996). However, not all studies have found significant correlations between C and academic success at the high school level, and Ackerman and Heggestad's (1997) meta-analysis includes one study showing a significant *negative* correlation between C and "knowledge and achievement" among college students. Some authors have speculated that C may affect academic performance beyond ability, and even compensate for poor intellectual ability (Chamorro-Premuzic & Furnham, 2003).

Neuroticism (N). In early studies, N was shown to predict poorer academic performance among school-aged children. For example, Entwisle and Cunningham (1968) used data from an almost complete age group of 3,000 13-year-olds and reported that emotional stability was related to academic success. Shiner and Masten (2002) reported results for a longitudinal study of 205 children who were assessed around ages 10, 20, and 30. Negative emotionality at age 20 was correlated with poor adaptation concurrently and 10 years previously. Meta-analyses have suggested a correlation of around −0.2 between N and academic achievement measures (e.g., Seipp, 1991). However, some studies of both school children (Heaven, Mak, Barry, & Ciarrochi, 2002) and university students (Busato et al., 2000) failed to find any significant correlations between N and attainment. Such inconsistencies may reflect the role of moderator factors. For example, McKenzie and Tindell (1993) showed that N was related to lower achievement only in students with weak superegos. Self-control and focusing of motivation may compensate for negative emotionality.

Extraversion (E). The effect of E on academic success appears age dependent. Whereas before the age of 11–12 years extraverted children seem superior to introverted children (Entwisle & Entwisle, 1970), among adolescents and adults introverts show higher achievement than extraverts (e.g., Chamorro-Premuzic & Furnham, 2003). This change in the direction of the correlation has been attributed to the move from the sociable, less competitive atmosphere of primary school to the rather formal atmospheres of secondary school and higher education in which introverted behaviors such as avoidance of intensive socializing become advantageous. Extraverts and introverts also differ in parameters of information processing such as speech production, attention, and reflective problem solving (Zeidner & Matthews, 2000), with performance varying along meaningful dimensions. For example, extraverts have been shown to be better at oral contributions to seminars but poorer at essay writing than introverts (Furnham & Medhurst, 1995).

Agreeableness (A). Although the temperamental precursors of A, such as prosocial orientation, relate to better so-cial adjustment, relations between this trait and academic attainment are consistently nonsignificant (Shiner, Masten, & Roberts, 2003). However, antisocial personality traits associated with low A may have detrimental effects.

In sum, generalized personality traits constitute one of several nonintellective factors that may affect classroom learning and academic performance. Personality assessment may also be informative about a student's strengths and weaknesses at the process level. For example, high-N students may need help with stress management, low-C students with maintaining interest, and high-E students with managing social distractions. Indeed, studies of anxiety-by-treatment interaction in education imply that educators may attempt to design personalized learning environments matched with key personality factors (Snow, Corno, & Jackson, 1997). For example, students high in trait anxiety may benefit more from structured learning-teaching environments, whereas students low on trait anxiety (as well as those higher on E or O) may benefit from unstructured learning-teaching environments (Zeidner, 1998).

Cognitive-Motivational Influences on Achievement

Current cognitive-social theory views academic learning and performance as goal oriented and intentional activities, thus situating academic learning squarely in the center of motivational research (Lens, Simons, & Dewitte, 2002). Traditionally, research of this kind has focused on achievement motivation (McClelland, 1987), representing the balance between approach (i.e., striving for success) and avoidance (i.e., avoiding failure). Certainly, achievement motivation relates to effort and task engagement, with meta-analyses confirming a robust positive association with indices of academic achievement (Robbins, Lauver, Le-Huy, Langley & Carlstrom, 2004). However, contemporary research tends to differentiate multiple constructs and processes that govern motivations to learn and perform effectively (Heggestad & Kanfer, 2000). We illustrate this research by discussing two key constructs: academic self-concept and evaluative (test) anxiety. We then review key self-regulative *processes*, focusing on self-agency, goal setting, and goal orientation.

Academic Self-concept. This construct refers to the content of the self-related academic information that the person processes, stores, and organizes systematically (Schwarzer & Jerusalem, 1989). Children acquire their academic self-concepts through direct interactions with their environments, as well as from the direct and indirect feedback they receive from others in their environment, such as teachers, peers, and parents (Bracken & Howell, 1991). In the school context, academic self-concept is shaped langely by social comparison processes. An impressive body of empirical research suggests that it is better for academic self-concept to be, as it were, a big fish in a little pond than to be a small fish in a big pond (Marsh & Hua, 2003).

Academic self-concept is consistently related to higher academic attainment (e.g., Zeidner & Schleyer, 1999). A substantial correlation ($r=0.56$) has been observed between academic selfconcepts and school grades (Byrne & Shavelson, 1986). It appears to be specifically academic rather than general self-concept that relates to educational criteria (Marsh & Hua, 2003). However, there is still some debate as to whether academic performance influences academic self-concept more than the reverse; that is, the causal dynamics of the relations between scholastic attainment and self-concept are ambiguous. Given conflicting findings, it seems plausible that the relation between academic self-concept and performance is reciprocal (see Trzesniewski, Donnellan, & Robins, 2003). Thus, educators should be cautious in specifying the development and maintenance of a positive self-concept in the absence of related achievement as an important goal for education.

Evaluative (Test) Anxiety. The term *test anxiety* refers to the negative affect, worry, physiological arousal, and behavioral responses that accompany concern about failure or lack of competence on an exam or similar evaluative situation (Zeidner, 1998). Hundreds of studies have investigated the complex pattern of relations between anxiety and a wide array of conventional measures of school performance at elementary, high school, and college levels. Meta-analysis of available data reveals the correlation between anxiety and achievement to be around -0.2 across these disparate years of education (e.g., Hembree, 1988; Seipp, 1991).

Academic deficits are more strongly related to the Worry rather than Emotionality component of test anxiety. Hembree (1988) reports higher effect sizes for low-than for high-ability students and for difficult tasks relative to those perceived as easy. Hence, detrimental effects of anxiety in the real world may represent more than just distraction from performance by the person's immediate worries about the test situation, which relates to state rather than to trait anxiety. Nonetheless, meta-analysis also shows that state and trait anxiety measures serve equally well as predictors of educational performance.

There is a large literature on test anxiety as a predictor of information processing that overlaps with studies of general anxiety in laboratory studies (Zeidner & Matthews, in press). The information-processing components sensitive to test anxiety relate to input (e.g., encoding), central processing (e.g., memory, conceptual organization), and output (e.g., response selection and execution). These various performance deficits are often attributed to high levels of worry and cognitive interference. Test anxiety may also relate to selective attention to threat, producing vulnerability to distraction (Eysenck, 1997).

Behavioral avoidance also plays a key role in maintenance of evaluative anxiety and concomitant skill degradation. Procrastination, including failure to study or to complete homework, leads to failure acquiring requisite knowledge. In turn, this lack of preparation leads to poor performance and anxiety under test conditions (Naveh-Benjamin, 1991), increasing subsequent anxiety and avoidance of study. However, the nature of the task plays an important moderating role. Generally, test anxiety is more detrimental to demanding tasks and may even facilitate performance on easy tasks.

Like the relation between self-concept and performance, the anxiety-competence relation appears best viewed as reciprocal. Thus, high levels of test anxiety, with elevated levels of worry and cognitive interference, absorb part of the capacity needed for attention, problem-solving, or other cognitive processes required for successful completion of exams. Test anxiety also produces certain aversive patterns of motivation, coping, and task strategies that interfere with learning and performance. The result is that competence and self-efficacy suffers, thus leading to further anxiety over time, and generating a vicious circle of increasing anxiety and degrading competence.

Motivational Processes. Figure 8.3 represents the intercorrelation often found between motivational dispositions and personality traits (e.g., Heggestad & Kanfer, 2003). However, recent research has focused especially on the role of self-regulative processes as mediators of the effects of motivational and affective constructs. This perspective shifts the focus from relatively fixed cognitive abilities, personal dispositions, and environmental features to the student's personally initiated strategies for improving learning outcomes and the study environment. Reviews suggest that the effective exercise of self-regulatory skills enhances performance, confidence, and insight (e.g., Zimmerman & Bandura, 1994).

Cognitive-social theories of self-regulation (e.g., Carver & Scheier, 1991; Wells & Matthews, 1994) focus on the interplay among affect, motivation, and cognition. Individuals' comparisons of their actual and desired status generate emotions that signal functional status of the system, and motivations directed toward aligning actual and ideal self-states (e.g., choosing whether to engage in an activity, and what level of effort to expend).

Self-regulative theories aim to differentiate various subprocesses that support system function. Space constraints preclude a detailed account, but we will illustrate the potential of this approach by reviewing two important classes of process, relating to (a) self-agency beliefs and (b) goal-setting/orientation.

Self-agency Beliefs. According to social cognitive theory, people's beliefs and expectancies about their own competence and effectiveness influence present performance as well as future learning and personal development (e.g., Bandura, 1997). In the academic setting, self-efficacy beliefs refer to students' beliefs in their capabilities to master challenging academic demands by organizing and executing the courses of action (i.e., cognitive, behavioral, or social skills) necessary for successful academic performance (Bandura, 1977). Such efficacy or agency beliefs are distinct from general outcome expectancies, beliefs about causality and controllability (investigated in studies of causal attributions), and self-esteem. Perceived self-efficacy may directly affect academic performance by enhancing efficient use of acquired skill, and indirectly, by heightening persistence, goal setting, management of work time, and flexibility in testing problemsolving strategies (Schunk, 1984; Zimmerman & Bandura, 1994).

Multon, Brown, and Lent (1991) summarized the findings of a large number of studies showing that efficacy beliefs contribute to scholastic performance in both children and adults. Furthermore, level of student achievement proven to be an important moderator variable, with students' self-efficacy beliefs more highly related to academic outcomes for low (than for high) achievers. Academic self-efficacy also appears more predictive of achievement than outcome expectancies, positive self-concept, and perceived control (Zimmerman, 2000). A meta-analysis of 109 studies relating psychosocial factors to college achievement found that academic self-efficacy was among the most predictive factors, correlating around 0.5 with GPA (Robbins et al., 2004).

Although Bandura (e.g., 1997) has preferred to see self-efficacy beliefs as dynamic and context-specific, self-efficacy may also be conceptualized as a stable personality trait. It may refer either to self-agency in general, or to specific contexts including academic performance. Low self-efficacy, along with other negative self-perceptions, may play an important role in mediating the effects of N (e.g., Judge & Ilies, 2002; Matthews, Schwean et al., 2000). High self-efficacy has also been linked to E and to C (Matthews et al., 2003).

Goal Setting and Orientation. A major component of self-regulatory learning is the specification of personal salient goals. A review of the literature suggests that high achievers use goal setting significantly more frequently and more consistently across academic tasks than low achievers (Zimmerman & Risemberg, 1997). Several parameters of goal setting appear related to academic achievement. Proximal goals, relative to distal goals, are viewed as more conducive to scholastic achievement. Self-motivation and regulation are best served by combining long-range goals, which set the overall direction of one's endeavor, with a series of explicit short-term, self-set, and attainable subgoals, which guide and sustain one's efforts along the way (Bandura, 1997). Goal difficulty is also important. Research on achievement motivation reveals that students with low achievement motivation tend to set goals that are either too easy or too difficult to be helpful (McClelland, 1987). By contrast, self-regulated learners are better able to set personally attainable goals.

Goal orientation is currently viewed as a relatively stable motivational variable that assumes two forms—learning (or mastery) outcomes, or performance (or ego-oriented) outcomes (Ames, 1992). The focus of learning goal orientation is increasing competence by developing new skills and promoting mastery-oriented responses to failure. Learning goals focus on students' attention on processes and strategies that help students master the study materials or acquire competencies. Performance goals, in contrast, orient students to a concern for their ability and performance relative to others. The distinction also corresponds, at least approximately, to the familiar distinction between intrinsic and extrinsic motivation. Students are intrinsically motivated to the extent that learning is an end in itself, and extrinsically motivated when those activities are done for the sake of material or other rewards, not intrinsically related to school learning. Educational psychologists have generally seen intrinsic motivation as more advantageous (Lens et al., 2002).

Performance goals are generally seen as less adaptive in terms of subsequent motivation, affect, strategy use, and performance (Pintrich & Schunk, 1996). As normative goal theory acknowledges, students who are concerned mainly with besting others and with no concern for mastery are likely to follow a fairly maladaptive pathway in terms of motivation and affect in the classroom. Furthermore, performance-oriented students seeking to gain favorable judgment of their competence or avoid negative judgments from others are predicted to experience more learned helplessness when encountering obstacles. By contrast, if a student approaches the learning task with a focus on mastery and learning goals, the student will seek to increase competence, and consequently goals foster success. Studies have generally confirmed the theoretical prediction that learning goals relate to various adaptive outcomes, including performance, interest, and positive affect, whereas performance goals have been linked to less adaptive outcomes (Pintrich, 2000).

In the recently revised goal theory perspective, several researchers (e.g., Elliot & Thrash, 2001) have made an important distinction between two categories of performance goals: (a) approach performance goals, in which students approach tasks in terms of demonstrating their ability and competence by trying to best or outperform others and (b) avoidance performance goals, where students are attempting to avoid looking stupid or incompetent, which leads them to avoid the task. Performance-approach goals are clearly positively related to a number of positive outcomes, such as effort, performance attainment, and self-efficacy (Elliot & Moller, in press).

Studies provide support for both normative and the revised goal theory, with mastery goals linked to adaptive (and performance goals to less adaptive) outcomes. Thus, Pintrich (2000) collected data over three waves from eighth and ninth graders ($N = 150$) in their math classrooms using both self-report questionnaires and actual math grades. In line with normative goal theory, mastery goals were adaptive, but also in line with the revised goal theory perspective, approach performance goals, when coupled with mastery goals, were just as adaptive. The pathways to learning were similar for both performance- and mastery-oriented students, and they seemed to end up at the same level of achievement as well. Both types of goals may foster more positive values for task performance and studying (Vansteenkiste, Simons, Lens, Soenens, & Matos, 2003).

Various personality traits relate to motivational constructs and processes. The beneficial effects of C on performance may be attributable to goal setting and goal commitment (Barrick, Mount, & Strauss, 1993) and to mastery goals (Heggestad & Kanfer, 2000). Test anxiety correlates with adoption of performance-avoidance goals, which may mediate some of its detrimental effects on affect and behavior (McGregor & Elliot, 2002). High A is negatively related to motivations toward competitive excellence (Heggestad & Kanfer, 2000). Personality may also affect goals qualitatively, with, for example, social affiliation goals relating to A and dominance goals to E (Matthews et al., 2003).

PERSONALITY AND PSYCHOPATHOLOGY

Psychodiagnostic Issues

Children may be referred to an educational psychologist because of concerns about personality traits such as aggressiveness or anxiety. It is not unusual for such problems to be clinically significant. In the United States, 12% of all children aged under the age of 18 have a diagnosed mental disorder, and there are many additional children with undiagnosed or subclinical problems in need of professional services (House, 2002). The school psychologist is increasingly called on to use the psychiatric DSM-IV classification system in evaluating children. In this section, we look at how personality trait models may inform the intersecting concerns of educational and clinical psychologists in diagnosing, understanding, and treating children with behavioral or emotional problems.

Traditionally, pathological conditions are treated as categorical, as in DSM-IV. However, recent work on the Axis II personality disorders made a strong case that abnormal personality may be described in terms of several separate dimensions, which converge, to some extent, with the extremes of the normal traits of the FFM (Livesley, 2001). N relates to traits associated with emotional dysregulation, low E to social avoidant traits, low A to both emotional dysregulative and antisocial traits, and C to obsessive-compulsive personality (Larstone et al., 2002). The outcome variables representing behavioral and emotional disorder (or subclinical disturbance) on rating scales such as the Child Behavior Check List (CBCL) are also represented multidimensionally. The dimensional approach accommodates the frequent comorbidities of both types of disorder.

Diagnosis and assessment raise some special problems in children. DSM-IV does not make any formal distinction between childhood and adult disorders (House, 2002). Disorders including Conduct, Separation Anxiety, Autistic, and Attention-Deficit/Hyperactivity Disorders (ADHD) are characteristic of childhood, but are defined only as showing first onset or symptoms during childhood, and could, in principle, be diagnosed in adults. At the same time, educators are understandably wary of the view that children are simply mini-adults in their pathologies, and it is important to recognize that symptoms may vary with age. It is also often difficult to establish the causal basis for associations between personality and mental illness, given that personality is more plastic in children than in adults, and the use of behavior ratings to assess child behavior may cause difficulties in separating personality as a latent factor from observed behavior.

With these cautions in mind, we will review the associations between personality and behavioral and clinical problems. We will suggest that the cognitive-social perspective links personality traits to the mediating processes that generate pathology (while also accepting the importance of biological perspectives). Our brief review is organized around the distinction between *externalizing* problems, referring, for example, to aggression, conduct problems, and poor behavioral control, and *internalizing* problems such as inhibition and negative affect. The distinction is not rigid: Externalizing and internalizing problems are frequently comorbid. Negative emotions may be a driver of problem behaviors, and the social disapprobation that attaches to conduct problems may be a source of unhappiness for the child.

Externalizing Problems. The most parsimonious view of conduct problems, including delinquency, substance use, and risky sexual behaviors, is that they reflect a single underlying syndrome (Cooper, Wood, Orcutt, & Albino, 2003), corresponding to broad traits such as dissocial behavior or psychopathy (see Larstone et al., 2002). Other studies show that 60–75% of children referred to clinics with ADHD show significant problems relating to conduct and aggression (Kamphaus & Frick, 2002). However, it is important also to discriminate between different externalizing conditions, as defined by the CBCL, for example, and also to differentiate different subtypes within conditions. For example, ADHD is often broken down into inattentive and overactive subtypes, whereas children with conduct problems include both callous and unemotional children, as well as those that show emotional hyperresponsivity to provocations and frustrations (Kamphaus & Frick, 2002).

Thus, personality research may be directed toward behavior problems studied at different levels of granularity (see Livesley, 2001). In a study of 1,978 adolescents that used structural equation modeling, Cooper et al. (2003) confirmed the existence of a general factor of problem behavior, related to impulsive personality. However, they also found more fine-grained associations between specific aspects of personality and behavior. For example, thrill seeking was significantly related to alcohol use, tobacco use, and violent acts. The prediction of impulsive behaviors may be enhanced by breaking down global impulsivity into more narrowly defined subtraits such as lack of premeditation and sensation-seeking (Miller, Flory, Lynam, & Leukefeld, 2003).

Research on younger children identifies behaviorally disinhibited temperament as a precursor to a variety of disruptive behavioral conditions including ADHD, oppositional defiant disorder, and aggression (Hirshfeld-Becker et al., 2004). Disinhibition also relates to indices of school problems and academic dysfunction such as being placed in special classes and repeating grades (Hirshfeld-Becker et al., 2004).Temperament influences problem behaviors in interaction with important situational factors, including the family environment, teachers' behavior management skills, and demographic factors (Stormont, 2002). For this analysis, we will adopt a midlevel grain size, reviewing studies of personality and, first, ADHD, and second, aggression and delinquency.

ADHD. Most research on personality and ADHD has been conducted within a biosocial framework that recognizes the roles of both genetic predisposition and situational factors such as family cohesion in shaping vulnerability to the condition. Key brain systems may include those regulating executive control of attention, arousal, and reward signals. White's (1999) review of personality studies points toward traits relating to impulsivity, thrill-seeking, disinhibition, and N as playing a central role. Another review, focusing more on early childhood, identifies lack of effortful control as the key temperamental factor in the etiology of ADHD (Nigg, Goldsmith, & Sacek, 2004). Negative affectivity may also increase vulnerability, but Nigg et al. (2004) suggest that this aspect of temperament may be most salient in children who also exhibit oppositional (or aggressive) tendencies. These authors also emphasize the heterogeneity of ADHD, such that different subtypes may be differently related to personality and emotion. For example, they identify a group of children in whom ADHD is secondary to unsocialized conduct disorder. This group is characterized by low anxiety and arousal and may be at risk for later psychopathy.

In a study on the FFM, Nigg et al. (2002) collected data from an adult sample of 1,620 participants. They determined that prevalence of ADHD symptoms is nearly as prevalent in college-student as community populations, indicating a problem for educators of adults. On the Achenbach scales for adult symptoms, the major FFM correlates of ADHD were A ($r = -0.44$), C ($r = -0.33$) and N ($r = 0.37$). Data based on (a) other rating scales, (b) reported childhood symptoms, and (c) spouses' ratings of the participants showed similar findings. The study also showed that different FFM factors related to different symptom types. Low C related especially to attention problems, low A to conduct problems and impulsive behavior, and high N to negative affect, and more weakly, to attention problems. Although E has sometimes been linked to ADHD (White, 1999), this hypothesis was not supported. Nigg et al. speculate that ADHD may relate positively to some facets of E (e.g., activity level, thrill seeking), but negatively to others (e.g., warmth, social competence). Another study of adults obtained similar findings, using a single rating scale for ADHD symptoms (Parker, Majeski, & Collin, 2004). For total ADHD symptoms, the FFM accounted for 41 percent of the variability, with low C, N, and low A emerging as the strongest predictors.

Given the heterogeneity of children presenting with ADHD symptoms, it is likely that multiple pathways link temperamental and personality traits to behavioral disorders. Nigg et al. (2004) build on temperament models in discriminating two major pathways that may be implicated in the preschool years. Low levels of effortful control (relating to low C) may make it difficult for the child to focus attention and to inhibit impulses and affective responses. Other pathways relate to both positive and negative emotional reactivity, but their role in symptomatology may vary with ADHD subtype. To the extent that children are overreactive to reward signals and underreactive to punishment, they may be prone to engage in risky behaviors. Traits linked to underarousal such as thrill seeking may operate similarly. Moreover, children characterized by N and reactivity in negative affect may show ADHD symptoms including inattention because anxiety interferes with cognitive control (Nigg et al., 2004). The role of low A in ADHD points to the importance of social-cognitive processes similar to those implicated in aggressive behaviors.

Aggression and Delinquency. Many cross-sectional studies show that personality traits including impulsivity, psychoticism, hostility, and low self-esteem are associated with various indices of aggression, delinquency, and illegal acts, in both children and adults (Furnham & Heaven, 1999). A meta-analysis has shown that the traits associated with antisocial behavior typically relate to low A or to low C, with traits associated with N showing a smaller but significant relation also (Miller & Lynam 2001). Comparable findings are obtained in school settings, using criteria such as violence, vandalism, and theft (e.g., Heaven, 1996). It may also be important to distinguish personality facets beyond the FFM. Miller, Lynam, and Leukefeld (2003) found that angry hostility and impulsiveness, measured as facets of N, correlated with antisocial behavior, but other facets, such as anxiety and stress vulnerability, did not.

Various longitudinal studies in the United States and Europe have confirmed that childhood temperament measures related to aggressiveness and misconduct are predictive of criminal behaviors later in life. The Dunedin study in New Zealand (Roberts, Caspi, & Moffitt, 2000), has tracked personality and antisocial behaviors in a representative community sample from birth through to age 21. At age 3, children were classified as being undercontrolled, inhibited, or well-adjusted. Undercontrolled children tended, at age 21, to score as aggressive and unconscientious in personality, and they were more likely to report antisocial behaviors, to have a criminal conviction, and to be diagnosed with antisocial personality disorder. However, effect sizes associated with personality were modest: temperament at age 3 is not destiny. Situational factors such as parenting style and deprivation also play major roles as influences on antisocial behavior; these factors may moderate the impact of temperamental factors. For example, parental discipline may be more effective in building conscience in fearful, as opposed to nonfearful, children (Shiner & Caspi, 2003).

Aggression is often divided into cold-blooded proactive aggression, employed as a means to an end, and reactive aggression, involving angry outbursts to perceived provocation (Coie & Dodge, 1998). Although aggressive children often display both forms of behavior, measures of the two traits show discriminant validity. Compared with proactive aggressors, reactively aggressive children show more difficulties in interpersonal interaction, more internalizing problems, less self-efficacy, and less delinquency (Vitaro, Gendreau, Tremblay, & Oligny, 1998). Bullying children tend to be high on both aspects of aggression, but their victims are marked by reactive aggression only (Camodeca, Goossens, Terwogt, & Schuengel, 2002). Caprara, Barbaranelli, and Zimbardo (1996) distinguished dimensions of Positive Attitudes Toward Violence (e.g., tolerance of violence, moral disengagement) and High Emotional Responsivity (e.g., irritability, proneness to anger). Trait friendliness (similar to A in the FFM) was negatively correlated with both dimensions, whereas emotional instability (N) was strongly correlated with Emotional Responsivity.

It is likely that multiple mechanisms link personality and temperament factors to antisocial behaviors. Frick and Morris (2004) articulate an account of multiple temperamental factors contributing to conduct problems, which picks up on the distinction between reactive/overemotional and proactive/callous-unemotional subtypes of antisocial youth. As with ADHD, the key dimensions of temperament appear to be emotional reactivity (both high and low), and effortful control. Both overreactivity and poor effortful control appear to contribute directly to conduct problems (e.g., Eisenberg, Fabes, Guthrie, & Reiser, 2000), so that, in part, the reactively aggressive child is one who is both easily angered, and also reacts impulsively when feeling anger.

Frick and Morris (2004) also identify indirect pathways for reactive aggression. Children who show intense, unregulated emotion may be rejected by their peers. They may also generate dysfunctional cycles of interaction with caregivers in which both adult and child try to control the other through increasingly aversive behavior. By contrast, callous-unemotional children do not show a primary deficit in emotion regulation. Instead, their temperament is characterized by low levels of autonomic reactivity, few fearful inhibitions, and deficits in conscience development. Effortful control may also be implicated, in that fearfulness in young children relates positively to this aspect of temperament (Kochanska & Knaack, 2003). Frick and Morris (2004) see lack of fearful inhibition as directly influencing risk-taking behaviors, including aggressive acts.

Several authors have implicated self-regulative processes, including coping, in disorders of conduct (Kendall, 2000). Cooper et al. (2003) suggest that avoidance coping, in the forms of denial of problems or engagement in risk-taking behavior as a form of mood elevation, may play a key role. Effortful control may facilitate the development of coping strategies that allow the child to resist immediate impulses according to his or her moral values and beliefs about personal control. Matthews, Schwean et al. (2000) argue that aggressive personality traits appear related to functionally coherent cognitive biases. In general, aggressive children are prone to appraise others as hostile, to evaluate aggressive or confrontive behaviors as successful coping options, and to access rapidly specific aggressive responses (Coie & Dodge, 1998). In addition, reactive-aggressive children are especially prone to attribute hostility to their peers, whereas proactive-aggressive children are especially likely to perceive aggression as an effective means for achieving personal goals.

Internalizing Problems

The major emotional disorders of adults, including depression, generalized anxiety, phobias, post-traumatic stress disorder, and obsessive-compulsive disorder, are seen in children also, with broadly similar symptoms (Coleman & Hoyle, 1999; Kendall, 2000). One of the DSM-IV disorders linked to childhood is Separation Anxiety, in which the child shows intense anxiety when separated from the primary caregiver. In around 75 percent of cases, school avoidance or refusal appears as a symptom (House, 2002). In fact, "school phobia" is not recognized as a diagnostic category, because of its multiple sources, also including social anxiety and specific fears (e.g., evaluative anxiety). Anxiety disorders may be difficult to diagnose in younger children, because of children's limited capacity to verbalize their mental states. Thus, prevalence of internalizing disorders has proven difficult to estimate, but they may approach up to 5 percent for depression and 9 percent for anxiety disorders, tending to increase in adolescence and adulthood (Kamphaus & Frick, 2002).

House (2002) draws attention to the high levels of comorbidity for the different anxiety disorders, which call into question their distinctiveness. In general, it seems that temperamental factors linked to effect, including behavioral inhibition, act as general risk factors for the spectrum of emotional disorders (Kagan & Snidman, 1999; Rothbart & Bates, 1998). Low positive affectivity may also contribute to risk of depression, but not anxiety, especially in adolescents (Johnston & Murray, 2003). As in the case of externalizing disorders, environmental factors including life events, deprivation, and family interaction patterns are also critical (Kendall, 2000).

It appears that many of the distinctive social-cognitive characteristics of anxiety in adults are also apparent in children. These include negative self-beliefs and self-concept, bias in attention toward threat stimuli, and dysfunctional coping (e.g., Daleiden & Vasey, 1997; Derryberry et al., 2003). Southam-Gerow and Kendall (2002) highlight the importance of dysfunctional emotion regulation in childhood pathology. Inhibition of emotional expression, poor control of expression, and unusual expression may all occur. Pathology also relates to lack of understanding of emotion, and to a reduced range of strategies for managing emotion.

Thus, process models of internalizing disorders resemble those developed for adults (e.g., Wells & Matthews, 1994) in conceptualizing clinical anxiety and depression as the outcome of dysfunctional patterns of adaptation to perceived threats and loss. Disordered self-regulation is expressed through biases and deficits in multiple cognitive processes, although limited by cognitive development. For example, metacognitions, such as excessive concerns about internal thoughts and images, play an important role in adult pathology (Wells & Matthews, 1994), but younger children do not have the facility to reflect on their own thought processes. Interestingly, one metacognitive factor, anxiety sensitivity (i.e., beliefs that anxiety symptoms are harmful) is predictive of pathology over and above negative affectivity (Johnston & Murray, 2003).

Daleiden and Vasey (1997) set out an information-processing model of childhood anxiety that reflects numerous correspondences between abnormalities of cognition in children and adults. These include selectively attending to threat, interpreting ambiguous information as threatening, expecting negative outcomes, preferring escape/avoidant coping strategies, and deficits in enacting behavioral coping. Cognitive models have also addressed more specific anxiety conditions, such as social anxiety, in which negative cognitions are especially directed toward social concerns.

CONCLUSIONS

In this chapter, we have surveyed the pervasive influence of personality traits and allied constructs on students' well-being, emotional states, vulnerability to psychopathology, and academic performance. Many traits play significant roles in shaping the educational experience of the learner. Each one of the Big Five is important: N in stress vulnerability, C in task commitment, E and A in social adjustment, and O in intellectual engagement. Furthermore, high N, low A, and low C are risk factors for conduct problems. Beyond the FFM, contextualized traits including test anxiety, self-concept, self-efficacy, and self-esteem relate to both subjective and objective outcomes. We have also highlighted the new construct of EI as an umbrella term for a variety of factors linked to emotional functioning and competence that may be pivotal for social-emotional learning.

The range and variety of educational issues raised by studies of personality and affect is taxing for the reviewer of the field, and we emphasize that our coverage here has been selective. However, we consider that cognitive-social approaches to personality have provided a family of theories that provides a powerful explanatory framework. Under the general heading of self-regulation, we have referred to the transactional theory of stress (e.g., Lazarus, 1999), investment theories of ability and personality development (e.g., Zeidner et al., 2003), self-efficacy theory (e.g., Bandura, 1997), the cognitive-attentional theory of emotional disorder (e.g., Wells & Matthews, 1994), and various other accounts of motivation and task engagement (e.g., Pintrich, 2003). Although there are important differences in scope and content of these theories, there are sufficient conceptual similarities to hold out the promise of an integrated theory of personality functioning. We identify five key themes of the emerging cognitive-social theory of personality and affect:

1. Neurobiology provides the platform for cognitive and affective development, but biological accounts of personality have limited explanatory power; the cognitive-social perspective is essential.

2. Personality traits are distributed across multiple cognitive processes, including both basic components of information processing such as selective attention and working memory, and the high-level processes that support self-regulation. The many facets of traits possess a functional unity that reflects the adaptive relevance of the trait, for example toward anticipation of danger (N) or maintaining systematic, focused effort (C).

3. Goals and motivations play a key role in the self-regulative process. High levels of motivation and mastery goals promote a process of selective optimization in the educational domain, maintaining effort, persistence and exposure to a variety of challenging task situations. Conversely, avoidance motivations and undue pessimism disrupt both learning and perceptions of self-efficacy.

4. Personality, ability, motivation, affect, and educational outcomes participate in a dynamic, reciprocal and developmental process, as delineated by previous commentators (Snow et al., 1997). Personality influences academic achievement, but appraisals of achievement feed back into changes in motivations, self-referent beliefs, and activity preferences. The nature of the feedback process varies with stage of development; with personal insights and self-awareness, acquired through social learning, becoming increasingly important with increasing age.

5. Situational factors play an essential role in moderating the influence of personality factors, over both shorter and longer time spans. Person-situation takes various forms (Shiner & Caspi, 2003), but we have highlighted the interplay between personality traits and situational exposure. Traits that are adaptive within the educational context promote engagement with environments that are supportive for further learning. For example, high O promotes intellectually challenging encounters, and high A increases contact with supportive others. By contrast low C (and low A) may encourage the child to seek out "bad company," and high N attracts social situations characterized by interpersonal strife.

Contemporary personality research lends weight to the rapidly growing support among educators for assessing noncognitive constructs beyond those currently covered by traditional academic assessments, both at the K-12, community college, and 4-year college level. We conclude by summarizing some of the main areas of application for the research reviewed.

Selection. In a recent article in the *New York Times* (January 18, 2004), Wayne Camara of the College Board stated, "To better predict college readiness, we need to look at non-cognitive factors—personality, temperament, flexibility, proclivity to learn, ability to adjust, to get along with a roommate, to make appropriate decisions about studying." In higher education, a suitable goal may be to develop a standardized test (or set of procedures) that might supplement the SAT. Everson (e.g., 2003) outlines a "palette" of dimensions along which humans differ, including aptitudes (traditional admissions variables), achievement, personality (and other noncognitive variables), and developing abilities that might form the basis for college admissions.

Full-Spectrum Assessment of the Strengths and Weaknesses of the Student. There is a growing realization that the criterion space for assessing the worthiness of education and scholastic achievement has been much restricted. In addition to GPA, it may be important to look at criteria such as mental health, citizenship, and prosocial behavior (despite the measurement challenges involved). Focus on a wider spectrum of criteria may improve the advice given to individual students, alerting them to strengths and weaknesses that are not necessarily of an academic kind, such as dealing with difficult instructors or interacting with people from diverse cultural groups.

Matching the Educational Environment to the Student. We have already discussed the principle of ATI (Snow, 1994), the principle of matching instruction techniques to personality. In addition, counseling may be geared toward the personality of the student, in capitalizing on the student's strengths and developing strategies to compensate for his or her weaknesses.

Educating Teachers. Carey (1998) points out that teachers appear ill-informed about contemporary research on personality and temperament. Teachers have much to learn about (a) handling normal variations in temperament, (b) managing negative feelings elicited by 'difficult' children, (c) modifying teaching style to avoid 'personality clashes' with students, and (d) developing professional skills for dealing with children of variable temperamental qualities (see also Stormont, 2002).

Personality Change. The extent to which fundamental personality attributes could (or should) be changed in students free from clinical disorder is controversial. However, recent work on SEL as developed by CASEL at least implicitly suggests the value of personality change that elevates EI and cognate qualities (Greenberg et al., 2003). We have questioned whether such a goal is preferable to training specific skills. Yet, at the least, any such attempt should be based on a scientific understanding of affect.

Clinical Applications. Treatments for internalizing and externalizing problems are beyond the scope of this review, but we note that personality assessment may have much to offer the clinician, in terms of supporting diagnosis, choosing a suitable therapy, and anticipating treatment problems (e.g., Harkness & Lilienfeld, 1997).

References

Ackerman, P. L. (1996). A theory of adult intellectual development: Process, personality, interests, and knowledge. *Intelligence, 22*, 227–257.

Ackerman, P. L., & Heggestad, E. D. (1997). Intelligence, personality, and interests: Evidence for overlapping traits. *Psychological Bulletin, 121*, 219–245.

Ames, C. (1992). *Achievement goals, motivational climate and motivational processes.* Champaign, IL: Human Kinetics.

Bandura, A. (1977). Self-efficacy: Toward a unifying theory of behavioral change. *Psychological Review, 84*, 191–215.

Bandura, A. (1997). *Self-efficacy: The exercise of self-control.* New York: W. H. Freeman.

Bar-On, R. (1997). *Bar-on Emotional Quotient Inventory (EQ-i): Technical Manual.* Toronto: Multi-Health Systems.

Barrick, M. R., Mount, M. K., & Strauss, J. P. (1993). Conscientiousness and performance of sales representatives: Test of the mediating effects of goal setting. *Journal of Applied Psychology, 78*, 715–722.

Boekaerts, M. (1996). Personality and the psychology of learning. *European Journal of Personality, 10*, 377–404.

Bracken, B. A., & Howell, K. K. (1991). Multidimensional self concept validation: A three-instrument investigation. *Journal of Psychoeducational Assessment, 9*, 319–328.

Brackett, M. A., & Mayer, J. D. (2003). Convergent, discriminant, and incremental validity of competing measures of emotional intelligence. *Personality and Social Psychology Bulletin, 29*, 1147–1158.

Braden, J. P. (1995). Intelligence and personality in school and educational psychology. In D. H. Saklofske & M. Zeidner (Eds.), *International handbook of personality and intelligence* (pp. 621–650). New York: Plenum.

Byrne, B. M., & Shavelson, R. J. (1986). On the structure of adolescent self-concept. *Journal of Educational Psychology, 78*, 474–481.

Busato, V. V., Prins, F. J., Elshout, J. J., & Hamaker, C. (2000). Intellectual ability, learning style, personality, achievement motivation and academic success of psychology students in higher education. *Personality and Individual Differences, 29*, 1057–1068.

Camodeca, M., Goossens, F. A., Terwogt, M. M., & Schuengel, C. (2002). Bullying and victimization among school-age children: Stability and links to proactive and reactive aggression. *Social Development, 11*, 332–345.

Caprara, G. V., Barbaranelli, C., & Zimbardo, P. G. (1996). Understanding the complexity of human aggression: Affective, cognitive, and social dimensions of individual differences in propensity toward aggression. *European Journal of Personality, 10*, 133–155.

Carey, W. B. (1998). Temperament and behavior problems in the classroom. *School Psychology Review, 27*, 522–533.

Carver, C. S., & Scheier, M. F. (1991). A control-process perspective on anxiety. In R. Schwarzer & R. A. Wickland (Eds.), *Anxiety and self-focused attention* (pp. 3–8). London: Harwood.

Chamorro-Premuzic, T., & Furnham, A. (2003). Personality traits and academic examination performance. *European Journal of Personality, 17*, 237–250.

Coie, J. D., & Dodge, K. A. (1998). Aggression and antisocial behavior. In N. Eisenberg & W. Damon (Eds.), *Handbook of child psychology, Vol. 3: Social, emotional, and personality development* (5th ed., pp. 779–862). New York: Wiley.

Coleman, M. C., & Hoyle, J. C. (1999). Internalizing disorders of childhood and adolescence. In V.L. Schwean, & D.H. Saklofske (Eds.), *Handbook of psychosocial characteristics of exceptional children* (pp. 171–218). New York: Kluwer/Plenum.

Cooper, M. L., Wood, P. K., Orcutt, H. K., & Albino, A. (2003). Personality and the predisposition to engage in risky or problem behaviors during adolescence. *Journal of Personality & Social Psychology, 84*, 390–410.

Corno, L., Cronbach, L., Kupermintz, H., Lohman, D., Mandinach, E., Porteus, A., & Talbert, J. (2002). *Remaking the concept of aptitude: Extending the legacy of Richard E. Snow.* Mahwah, NJ: Lawrence Erlbaum Associates.

Costa, P. T., Jr., & McCrae, R. R. (1992). Four ways five factors are basic. *Personality and Individual Differences, 135*, 653-65.

Daleiden, E., & Vasey, M. W. (1997). An information-processing perspective on childhood anxiety. *Clinical Psychology Review, 17*, 407-429.

De Fruyt, F., & Mervielde, I. (1996). Personality and interests as predictors of educational streaming and achievement. *European Journal of Personality, 10*, 405-425.

Denham, S. A. (1998). *Emotional development in young children*. New York: Guilford Press.

Derryberry, D., Reed, M. A., & Pilkenton-Taylor, C. (2003). Temperament and coping: Advantages of an individual differences perspective. *Development and Psychopathology, 15*, 1049-1066.

Eisenberg, N., Fabes, R. A., Guthrie, I. K., & Reiser, M. (2000). Dispositional emotionality and regulation: Their role in predicting quality of social functioning. *Journal of Personality and Social Psychology, 78*, 136-157.

Elliot, A. J., & Moller, A. (in press). Performance-approach goals: Good or bad forms of regulation? *International Journal of Educational Research*.

Elliot, A. J., & Thrash, T. M. (2001). Achievement goals and the hierarchical model of achievement motivation. *Educational Psychology Review, 13*, 139-156.

Entwisle, N. J., & Cunningham, S. (1968). Neuroticism and school attainment: A linear relationship? *British Journal of Educational Psychology, 38*, 123-132.

Entwisle, N. J., & Entwisle, D. (1970). The relationship between personality, study methods and academic performance. *British Journal of Educational Psychology, 40*, 132-43.

Everson, H. T. (2003). *Innovation and change in the SAT: A design framework for future college admissions tests*. The College Board and Teachers College, Columbia University, College Entrance Examination Board.

Eysenck, M. W. (1997). *Anxiety and cognition: A unified theory*. Hove, England: Psychology Press.

Fantuzzo, J., Bulotsky, R., McDermott, P., Mosca, S., & Lutz, M. N. (2003). A multivariate analysis of emotional and behavioral adjustment and preschool educational outcomes. *School Psychology Review, 32*, 185-203.

Farsides, T., & Woodfield, R. (2003). Individual differences and undergraduate academic success: The roles of personality, intelligence, and application. *Personality and Individual Differences, 34*, 1225-1243.

Fine, S. E., Izard, C. E., Mostow, A. J., Trentacosta, C. J., & Ackerman, B. P. (2003). First grade emotion knowledge as a predictor of fifth grade self-reported internalizing behaviors in children from economically disadvantaged families. *Development & Psychopathology, 15*, 331-342.

Frick, P. J., & Morris, A. S. (2004). Temperament and developmental pathways to conduct problems. *Journal of Clinical Child and Adolescent Psychology, 33*, pp. 54-68.

Furnham, A., & Heaven, P. (1999). *Personality and social behavior*. London: Arnold.

Furnham, A., & Medhurst, S. (1995). Personality correlates of academic seminar behavior: A study of four instruments. *Personality and Individual Differences, 19*, 197-208.

Greenberg, M. T., Weissberg, R. P., O'Brien, M.U., Zins, J. E., Fredericks, L., Resnik, H., & Elias, M. J. (2003). Enhancing school-based prevention and youth development through coordinated social, emotional, and academic learning. *American Psychologist, 58*, 466-474.

Harkness, A. R., & Lilienfeld, S. O. (1997). Individual differences science for treatment planning: Personality traits. *Psychological Assessment, 9*, 349-360.

Heaven, P. C. L. (1996). Personality and self-reported delinquency: A longitudinal analysis. *Journal of Child Psychology and Psychiatry and Allied Disciplines, 37*, 747-751.

Heaven, P., Mak, A., Barry, J., & Ciarrochi, J. (2002). Personality and family influences on adolescent attitudes to school and academic performance. *Personality and Individual Differences, 32*, 453-462.

Heggestad, E. D., & Kanfer, R. (2000). Individual differences in trait motivation: Development of the Motivational Trait Questionnaire. *International Journal of Educational Research, 33*, 751-776.

Hembree, R. (1988). Correlates, causes, effects, and treatment of test anxiety. *Review of Educational Research, 58*, 7-77.

Hirshfeld-Becker, D. R., Biederman, J., Faraone, S. V., Segool, N., Buchwald, J., & Rosenbaum, J. R. (2004). Lack of association between behavioral inhibition and psychosocial adversity factors in children at risk for anxiety. *American Journal of Psychiatry, 161*, 547-555.

House, A. E. (2002). *DSM-IV diagnosis in the schools*. New York: Guilford Press.

James, L. R. (1988). Measurement of personality via conditional reasoning. *Organizational Research Methods, 1*, 131-163.

Jensen, A. R. (1998). The g factor: The science of mental ability. Westport, CT: Praeger.

Johnston, C., & Murray, C. (2003). Incremental validity in the psychological assessment of children and adolescents. *Psychological Assessment, 15*, 496-507.

Judge, T. A., & Ilies, R. (2002). Relationship of personality to performance motivation: A meta-analytic review. *Journal of Applied Psychology, 87*, 797-807.

Kagan, J., & Snidman, N. (1999). Early childhood predictors of adult anxiety disorders. *Biological Psychiatry, 46*, 1536-1541.

Kamphaus, R. W., & Frick, P. J. (2002). *Clinical assessment of child and adolescent personality and behavior* (2nd ed.). Needham Heights, MA: Allyn & Bacon.

Kendall, P. C. (2000). *Childhood disorders*. Hove, England: Psychology Press.

Kochanska, G., & Knaack, A. (2003). Effortful control as a personality characteristic of young children: Antecedents, correlates, and consequences. *Journal of Personality, 71*, 1087-1112.

Larstone, R. M., Jang, K. L., Livesley, W.J., Vernon, P. A., & Wolf, H. (2002). The relationship between Eysenck's P-E-N model of personality, the five-factor model of personality, and traits delineating personality disorder. *Personality and Individual Differences, 33*, 25-37.

Lazarus, R. S. (1999). *Stress and emotion: A new synthesis*. New York: Springer.

Lens, W., Simons, J., & Dewitte, D. (2002). From duty to desire: The role of students' future time perspective and instrumentality perceptions for study motivation and self-regulation. In F. Pajares & T. Urdan (Eds.), *Academic motivation of adolescents* (pp. 221–245). Greenwich, CT: Information Age Publishing.

Little, T. D., Oettingen, G., Stetsenko, A., & Baltes, P. B. (1995). Children's action-control beliefs about school performance: How do American children compare with German and Russian children? *Journal of Personality & Social Psychology, 69*, 686–700.

Livesley, W. J. (2001). A framework for an integrated approach to treatment. In W. J. Livesley (Ed.), *Handbook of personality disorders: Theory, research, and treatment* (pp. 570–600). New York: Guilford.

Lopes, P. N., Salovey, P., & Straus, R. (2003). Emotional intelligence, personality, and the perceived quality of social relationships. *Personality and Individual Differences, 3*, 641–659.

Lucas, R. E., & Diener, E. (2000). Personality and subjective well-being across the life span. In V. J. Molfese & D. L. Molfese (Eds.), *Temperament and personality development across the life-span* (pp. 211–234). Hillsdale, NJ: Lawrence Erlbaum Associates.

MacCann, C., Matthews, G., Zeidner, M., & Roberts, R. D. (2003). Psychological assessment of emotional intelligence: A review of self-report and performance-based testing. *International Journal of Organizational Assessment, 11*, 247–274.

Marsh, H. W., & Hua, K-T. (2003). Big-Fish–Little-Pond effect on academic self-concept: A cross-cultural (26-country) test of the negative effects of academically selective schools. *American Psychologist, 58*, 364–376.

Matthews, G., Campbell, S. E., Falconer, S., Joyner, L. A., Huggins, J. G. K., Grier, R., & Warm, J. S. (2002). Fundamental dimensions of subjective state in performance settings: Task engagement, distress, and worry. *Emotion, 2*, 315–340.

Matthews, G., Deary, I. J., & Whiteman, M. C. (2003). *Personality traits* (2nd edition). Cambridge, England: Cambridge University Press.

Matthews, G., Schwean, V. L., Campbell, S. E., Saklofske, D. H., & Mohamed, A. R. (2000). Personality, self-regulation, and adaptation: A cognitive-social framework. In M. Boekaerts & P. R. Pintrich (Eds.), *Handbook of self-regulation* (pp. 171–207). San Diego, CA: Academic Press.

Matthews, G., Zeidner, M., & Roberts, R. D. (2002). *Emotional intelligence: Science and myth*. Cambridge, MA: MIT Press.

Matthews, G., Zeidner, M., & Roberts, R. D. (2005). Emotional intelligence: An elusive ability. In O. Wilhelm & R. Engle (Eds.), *Handbook of understanding and measuring intelligence* (pp. 79–100). Thousand Oaks, CA: Sage.

Matthews, G., Zeidner, M., & Roberts, R. D. (in press) Measuring emotional intelligence: Promises, pitfalls, solutions? In A. D. Ong & M. Van Dulmen (Eds.), *Handbook of methods in positive psychology*. Oxford, UK: Oxford University Press.

Mayer, J. D., Caruso, D. R., & Salovey, P. (1999). Emotional intelligence meets traditional standards for an intelligence. *Intelligence, 27*, 267–298.

Mayer, J. D., Salovey, P., & Caruso, D. R. (2002). Mayer-Salovey-Caruso Emotional Intelligence Test (MSCEIT) User's Manual. Toronto, Canada: MHS Publishers.

McClelland, D. C. (1987). *Human motivation*. New York: Cambridge University Press.

McGregor, H. A., & Elliot, A. J. (2002). Achievement goals as predictors of achievement -relevant processes prior to task engagement. *Journal of Educational Psychology, 94*, 381–395.

McKenzie, J., & Tindell, G. (1993). Anxiety and academic achievement: Further Furneaux factor findings. *Personality and Individual Differences, 15*, 609–617.

Miller, J. D., Flory, K., Lynam, D. R., & Leukefeld, C. (2003). A test of the four-factor model of impulsivity-related traits. *Personality and Individual Differences, 34*, 1403–1418.

Miller, J. D., & Lynam, D. (2001). Structural models of personality and their relation to antisocial behavior: A meta-analytical review. *Criminology, 39*, 765–798.

Miller, J. D., Lynam, D., & Leukefeld, C. (2003). Examining antisocial behavior through the lens of the Five Factor Model of personality. *Aggressive Behavior, 29*, 497–514.

Multon, K. D., Brown, S. D., Lent, R. W. (1991). Relation of self-efficacy beliefs to academic outcomes: A meta-analytic investigation. *Journal of Counseling Psychology, 38*, 30–38.

Mumford, M. D., & Gustafson, S. B. (1988). Creativity syndrome: Integration, application, and innovation. *Psychological Bulletin, 103*, 27–43.

Naveh-Benjamin, M. (1991). A comparison of training programs intended for different types of test-anxious students: Further support for an information-processing model. *Journal of Educational Psychology, 83*, 134–139.

Nigg, J. T., John, O. P., Blaskey, L. G., Huang-Pollock, C. L., Willicut, E. G., Hinshaw, S. P., et al. (2002). Big Five dimensions and ADHD symptoms: Links between personality traits and clinical symptoms. *Journal of Personality & Social Psychology, 83*, 451–469.

Nigg, J. T., Goldsmith, H. H., & Sachek, J. (2004). Temperament and Attention Deficit Hyperactivity Disorder: The development of a multiple pathway model. *Journal of Clinical Child and Adolescent Psychology, 33*, 42–53.

Parker, J. D. A., Majeski, S. A., & Collin, V. T. (2004). ADHD symptoms and personality: Relationships with the five-factor model. *Personality & Individual Differences, 36*, 977–987.

Parker, J. D. A., Summerfeldt, L. J., Hogan, M. J., & Majeski, S. A. (2004). Emotional intelligence and academic success: examining the transition from high school to university. *Personality & Individual Differences, 36*, 163–172.

Petrides, K. V., & Furnham, A. (2003). Trait emotional intelligence: Behavioral validation in two studies of emotion recognition and reactivity to mood induction. *European Journal of Personality, 17*, 39–57.

Pintrich, P. R. (2000). Multiple goals, multiple pathways: The role of orientation in learning and achievement. *Journal of Educational Psychology, 92,* 544-555.

Pintrich, P. R. (2003). A motivational science perspective on the role of student motivation in learning and teaching contexts. *Journal of Educational Psychology, 95,* 667-686.

Pintrich, P. R., & Schunk, D. (1996). *Motivation in education: Theory, research, and application.* Columbus, OH: Merrill/Prentice Hall.

Robbins, S. B., Lauver, K., Le-Huy, D. D., Langley, R., & Carlstrom, A. (2004). Do psychosocial and study skill factors predict college outcomes? A meta-analysis. *Psychological Bulletin, 130,* 261-288.

Roberts, B. W., Caspi, A, & Moffitt, T. (2001). The kids are alright: Growth and stability in personality development from adolescence to adulthood. *Journal of Personality and Social Psychology, 81,* 670-683.

Roberts, R. D., Markham, P. M., Zeidner, M., & Matthews, G. (2005). Assessing intelligence: Past, present, and future. In O. Wilhelm & R. Engle (Eds.), *Handbook of understanding and measuring intelligence* (pp. 333-360). Thousand Oaks, CA: Sage.

Rothbart, M. K., & Bates, J. E. (1998). Temperament. In W. Damon & N. Eisenberg (Eds.), *Handbook of child psychology: Vol. 3. Social, emotional, and personality development* (5th ed.) (pp. 105-176). New York: Wiley.

Saklofske, D. H., & Zeidner, M. (Eds.), *International handbook of personality and intelligence.* New York: Plenum.

Scherer, K. R. (2001). Appraisal considered as a process of multilevel sequential checking. In K. Scherer, A. Schorr & T. Johnstone (Eds.), *Appraisal processes in emotion: Theory, methods, research* (pp. 92-120). New York: Oxford University Press.

Schimmack, U., & Grob, A. (2000). Dimensional models of core affect: A quantitative comparison by means of structural equation modeling. *European Journal of Personality, 14,* 325-345.

Schunk D. H. (1984). Self-efficacy perspective on achievement behaviour. *Educational Psychologist, 19,* 48-58.

Schutte, N. S., Malouff, J. M., Hall, L. E., Haggerty, D. J., Cooper, J. T., Golden, C. J., & Dornheim, L. (1998). Development and validation of a measure of emotional intelligence. *Personality and Individual Differences, 25,* 167-177.

Schwarzer, R., & Jerusalem, M. (1989). Development of test anxiety in high school students. In I. G. Sarason & C. D. Spielberger (Eds.), *Stress and anxiety* (Vol. 12, pp. 65-79). Washington, DC: Hemisphere.

Schwean, V. L., Mykota, D., Robert, L., & Saklofske, D. H. (1999). Determinants of psychosocial disorders in cultural minority children. In V.L. Schwean, & D. H. Saklofske, (Eds.) *Handbook of psychosocial characteristics of exceptional children.* New York: Kluwer/Plenum.

Schwean, V. L., & Saklofske, D. H. (Eds.). (1999). *Handbook of psychosocial characteristics of exceptional children.* New York: Kluwer/Plenum.

Seipp, B. (1991). Anxiety and academic performance: A meta-analysis of findings. *Anxiety Research, 4,* 27-41.

Shiner, R. L., & Caspi, A. (2003). Personality differences in childhood and adolescence: Measurement, development, and consequences. *Journal of Child Psychology and Psychiatry, 44,* 2-32.

Shiner, R. L., & Masten, A. S. (2002). Self-efficacy, attribution, and outcome expectancy mechanisms in reading and writing achievement: Grade level and achievement level differences. *Journal of Educational Psychology, 87,* 386-398.

Shiner, R. L., Masten, A. S., & Roberts, J. M. (2003). Childhood personality foreshadows adult personality and life outcomes two decades later. *Journal of Personality, 71,* 1145-1170.

Snow, R. E. (1994). Abilities in academic tasks. In R. J. Sternberg & R. K. Wagner (Eds.), *Mind in context: Interactionist perspectives on human intelligence* (pp. 3-37). Cambridge, MA: Cambridge University Press.

Snow, R. E, Corno, L., & Jackson, D. N., III. (1997). Individual differences in affective and conative functions. In D. C. Berliner & R. C. Calfee (Eds.), *Handbook of Educational Psychology* (pp. 243-308). New York: Simon & Schuster.

Southam-Gerow, M. A., & Kendall, P. C. (2002). Emotion regulation and understanding: Implications for child psychopathology and therapy. *Clinical Psychology Review, 22,* 189-222.

Stormont, M. (2002). Externalizing behavior problems in young children: Contributing factors and early intervention. *Psychology in the Schools, 39,* 127-138.

Suls, J. (2001). Affect, stress and personality. In J. P. Forgas (Ed.), *Handbook of affect and social cognition* (pp. 392-409). Mahwah, NJ: Lawrence Erlbaum Associates.

Trinidad, D. R., & Johnson, C. A. (2002). The association between emotional intelligence and early adolescent tobacco and alcohol use. *Personality and Individual Differences, 32,* 95-105.

Trzesniewski, K. H., Donnellan, M. B., & Robins, R. W. (2003). *Integrating self-esteem into a process model of academic achievement.* Paper presented at the Biennial meeting of the Society for Research on Child Development, Tampa, Florida.

van Rooy, D. L. & Viswesvaran, C. (2004). Emotional intelligence: A meta-analytic investigation of predictive validity and nomological net. *Journal of Vocational Behavior, 65,* 71-95.

Vansteenkiste, M., Simons, J., Lens, W., Soenens, B., & Matos, L. (2003). Less is something more: Goal content matters. Unpublished manuscript, University of Leuven.

Vitaro, F., Gendreau, P. L., Tremblay, R. E., & Oligny, P. (1998). Reactive and proactive aggression differentially predict later conduct problems. *Journal of Child Psychology and Psychiatry, 39,* 377-385.

Watson, D. (2000). *Mood and temperament.* New York: Guilford Press.

Wells, A., & Matthews, G. (1994). *Attention and emotion: A clinical perspective.* Hillsdale, NJ: Lawrence Erlbaum Associates.

White, J. D. (1999). Personality, temperament, and ADHD: A review of literature. *Personality and Individual Differences, 27,* 589-598.

Zeidner, M. (1998). *Test anxiety: The state of the art.* New York: Plenum.

Zeidner, M., & Matthews, G. (2000). Intelligence and personality. In R. J. Sternberg (Ed.), *Handbook of intelligence* (pp. 581–610). New York: Cambridge University Press.

Zeidner, M., & Matthews, G. (in press). Evaluative anxiety: Current theory and research. In A. Elliot & C. Dweck (Eds.), *Handbook of competence and motivation.* New York: Guilford.

Zeidner, M., Matthews, G., Roberts, R. D., & MacCann, C. (2003). Development of emotional intelligence: Towards a multi-level investment model. *Human Development, 46,* 69–96.

Zeidner, M., Roberts, R. D., & Matthews (2002). Can emotional intelligence be schooled? A critical review. *Educational Psychologist, 37,* 215–231.

Zeidner, M., & Schleyer, E. (1999). The big-fish-little-pond effect for academic self-concept, test anxiety, and school grades in gifted children. *Contemporary Educational Psychology, 24,* 305–329.

Zimmerman, B. J. (2000). Self-efficacy: An essential motive to learn. *Contemporary Educational Psychology, 25,* 82–91.

Zimmerman, B. J., & Bandura, A. (1994) Impact of self-regulatory influences on writing course attainment. *American Educational Research Journal, 31,* 845–862.

Zimmerman, B. J., & Risemberg, R. (1997). Self-regulatory dimensions of academic learning and motivation. In G. D. Phye (Ed.), *Handbook of academic learning* (pp. 105–125). San Diego, CA: Academic Press.

Zins, J. E., Weissberg, R. P., Wang, M. C., Walberg, H. J., & Goleman, D. (Eds.). (2004). *Building school success through social and emotional learning: What does the research say?* New York: Teachers College Press.

COGNITIVE PROFILING OF CHILDREN WITH GENETIC DISORDERS AND THE SEARCH FOR A SCIENTIFIC BASIS OF DIFFERENTIATED EDUCATION

Douglas Fuchs

Peabody College of Vanderbilt University

THE NEED FOR DIFFERENTIATED EDUCATION

What Is Differentiated Education and Why Is It Important?

Some terminally ill patients with lung cancer live months and years longer than expected when given the new drug Iressa, developed to block epidermal growth factor receptor (EGER), which the cancer produces in excessive amounts (Neergard, 2004). However, only 10 percent of patients respond to Iressa, and doctors have been incapable of predicting for whom it will work. Thus, they have felt obligated to offer it to all of their most advanced-stage patients to find the small fraction it helps. However, recently published studies in *Science* and the *New England Journal of Medicine* show that responsiveness to Iressa depends on whether the patient has a mutated gene that makes a pocket into which the drug fits exactly, thereby blocking a certain molecule from getting in and promoting runaway cell growth. The search is now on for a test to determine for whom Iressa will be effective. Dr. David Johnson, president of the American Society of Clinical Oncology, characterized the discovery of how the drug works selectively in patients as "incredibly important." He predicted, "This is just the beginning of personalized medicine" (Neergard, p. 5).

Dr. Johnson's characterization notwithstanding, Iressa does not represent personalized medicine. It was not developed and validated for individual patients. Rather, it is emerging as a drug of choice for a group of cancer patients who share similar and important genetic characteristics. Thus, it is more accurate to say Iressa exemplifies "differentiated" medicine, or medicine differentiated at the group level. Which prompts this question: Is there an educational equivalent of differentiated medicine? The answer is "yes" and "no."

Envision a first-grade teacher, Ms. Smith, who teaches a class of 24 children of color in a high-poverty Title I school. Ms. Smith's reading curriculum is Open Court. She monitors her children's oral reading fluency (number of words read correctly in 1 minute) biweekly to identify those whose growth rate is too slow. By October, 16 of 24 children are making adequate or better-than-adequate progress; 8 are not. She trains 8 third graders to use a strategy that promotes beginning decoding skills and, under her supervision, they begin one-to-one tutoring with her 8 at-risk students three times per week. Ms. Smith also trains a classroom aide whom she shares with the other first-grade teachers in the building in a modified version of Reading Mastery. After 2 months of peer tutoring and continued Open-Court instruction, the oral reading fluency data indicate that 3 of 8 children's growth rate is now adequate. The 5 nonresponsive children remain in Open Court, continue with their respective tutors three times per week, and begin working with the classroom aide in a group of 5 for 2 additional days per week in Reading Mastery.

Clearly, the fictional Ms. Smith provides differentiated education to her charges: Some get X; others get X and Y; and still others get X, Y, and Z. Put differently, Ms. Smith uses repeated measures of oral reading fluency to determine for whom her instruction is effective and ineffective; for those not benefiting, she intensifies her approach by adding additional instructional components, while she continues her evaluation of their progress. Yet, there is an important difference between this example of differentiated education and the previous illustration of differentiated medicine. Research on the cancer drug, Iressa, was theory driven and deductive in nature. It provided a biochemical explanation for why the drug works. By contrast, there is no theory-guided research to explain why a combination of Open Court and small-group instruction on early decoding skills works for some children but not for others. Ms. Smith's differentiated education is not just a-theoretical; it procedes inductively through trial and error. Such an approach can indeed help some students. Maybe it can help many. But if our goal is to educate virtually all children, trial and error and intensifying instruction by themselves is insufficient. Educating virtually all children will require an understanding of individual differences and what kinds of instruction address these differences.

Research attempting to sort this out has been chronically underfunded and sporadic; its quality has been uneven; its results, unclear. Moreover, applications of this type of research to practice have often been unsuccessful, sometimes disastrously so. Partly for these reasons—but only partly so—there are very few attempts in schools to differentiate instruction by learner characteristics. Most everywhere, there is a one-size-fits-all approach, reflecting an assumption that all children will do well if only teachers select the right instruction and faithfully implement it. If the science and practice of differentiated medicine is in its infancy, its educational equivalent is in utero.

Describing and Explaining the Absence of Differentiated Education in Classrooms

There is persuasive evidence that most classrooms are bereft of any type of differentiated instruction. Baker and Zigmond (1990) conducted interviews and observations in reading and math classes in an elementary school to explore whether teachers implement *routine* adaptations (e.g., differentiating instruction by creating multiple reading groups to accommodate weak-to-strong readers at the start of the school year). Baker and Zigmond found no evidence of routine adaptations. Rather, they reported that teachers typically taught to large groups, using lessons incorporating little or no differentiation based on student needs. McIntosh, Vaughn, Schumm, Haager, and Lee (1994) described similar results from their observations of 60 social studies and science classrooms across grades 3 to 12.

L. Fuchs, Fuchs, and Bishop (1992) explored whether general and special educators used *specialized*, not routinized, adaptations (i.e., instruction deliberately customized in response to an individual student's difficulty). They administered a Teacher Planning Questionnaire to 25 general educators and 37 special educators whose responses reflected a view that individualized instruction and small-group instruction were not important to their students' academic success—a result also found through various means by Baker and Zigmond (1990), D. Fuchs, Fuchs, and Fernstrom (1993), D. Fuchs, Roberts, Fuchs, and Bowers (1996), Peterson and Clark (1978), and Zigmond and Baker (1994).

Others have expressed a different take on why educators often fail to differentiate instruction. Explanations of this perspective sometimes begin with the fact that many classroom teachers, especially those in large urban school districts, are faced with a considerable diversity of languages and cultures and a very broad range of academic performance (see Hodgkinson, 1995; Jenkins, Jewell, Leicester, Jenkins, & Troutner, 1990; Natriello, McDill, & Pallas, 1990; Puma, Jones, Rock, & Fernandez, 1993). Peterson and Clark (1978), Brown and Saks (1981, 1987), and Gerber and Semmel (1984) have written that teachers typically react to this student heterogeneity by ignoring it; that is, by monitoring student performance in selective fashion, and by teaching to the more academically accomplished students. According to Schumm and Vaughn and their colleagues, teachers in grades 3 through 12 whom they interviewed in focus groups and observed in classrooms are unresponsive to this student diversity because they believe themselves lacking in necessary knowledge and skills (e.g., Schumm & Vaughn, 1992; Schumm, Vaughn, Gordon, & Rothlein, 1994; Vaughn & Schumm, 1994). Moreover, say their teachers, even if they were more knowledgable and skillful, providing differentiated instruction would be nearly impossible because of inadequate resources for the necessary comprehensive and systematic monitoring of student performance.

Irrespective of why teachers typically do not provide differentiated instruction, its absence clearly contributes to the school failure of many at-risk children. Findings from numerous studies document that many low-achieving children, including those with special needs, not only fail to obtain differentiated instruction but receive less *undifferentiated* instruction and practice than their more accomplished classmates (e.g., Delquadri, Greenwood, Whorton, Carta, & Hall, 1986; Hall, Delquadri, Greenwood, & Thurston, 1982; Lesgold & Resnick, 1982; McDermott & Aron, 1978; O'Sullivan, Ysseldyke, Christenson, & Thurlow, 1990).

Evidence-Based Classroom Instruction: Advances and Limitations

Thanks in good measure to federally sponsored research programs in the U.S. Department of Education, National Institutes of Health, and National Science Foundation, researchers and practitioners have become much more knowledgeable about and skilled in improving general classroom instruction. So-called best practices developed during the past 20 years have included cooperative learning (e.g., Johnson & Johnson, 1994); Success For All, (e.g., Slavin & Madden, 2000, 2003); Direct Instruction (e.g., Carnine, Silbert, Kame'enui, & Tarver, 2004); peer tutoring programs such as Peer-Assisted Learning Strategies (e.g., D. Fuchs & Fuchs, 2005) and Class-wide Peer Tutoring (e.g., Delquadri et al., 1986; Greenwood, Delquadri, & Hall, 1989); self-regulated strategy instruction (e.g., De La Paz, Owen, Harris, & Graham, 2000; Deshler et al., 2001); and curriculum-based measurement (e.g., Deno, 1985). No Child Left Behind (NCLB) codifies the importance of developing and using evidence-based curricula and instructional programs and procedures, and they seem to be paying off in improved national student achievement. Further, NCLB has helped establish the What Works Clearinghouse in the U.S. Department of Education to help practitioners select and implement best practices in the schools.

Without attempting to diminish these important accomplishments, it is noteworthy that best practices typically represent only modest attempts to differentiate instruction. Few developers of best practices recognize (a) that some children will not benefit from them even when they are implemented faithfully, and (b) what these children require is a validated variant of the practice or a research-backed supplement to it. Thus, it should not be surprising that, whereas a majority of students benefit from best practices, many do not. Cooperative learning is a case in point.

Cooperative learning makes use of small, heterogeneous groups of students who work together to achieve common learning goals (Johnson & Johnson, 1992). The oft-repeated recommendation to use it with students with

disabilities is based largely on hundreds of studies of students in the general population. Positive academic and social outcomes have been reported for students in every major subject area, at all grade levels, and in many types of schools worldwide. Nevertheless, researchers have reported mixed results in studies in which it was used to improve the academic achievement of students with disabilities. In a recent review of this literature, McMaster and Fuchs (2002) found that, among the 15 studies meeting their inclusion criteria, only six studies reported cooperative learning to reliably promote special-needs students' achievement beyond controls' achievement (see their Table 1, pp. 109–110). This finding does not discredit the importance of cooperative learning to children with and without disabilities. Rather, it underscores a truism known to educators for centuries: There are no silver bullet solutions. Irrespective of the general effectiveness of a given curriculum, or instructional program or procedure, there will inevitably be nonresponders.

Nonresponders

Nonresponders, or children whose skills do not improve despite their participation in generally effective instruction, have been the focus of intermittent research over the past two decades. In the mid-1980s, the Office of Special Education Programs encouraged research into "pre-referral intervention" as a means of providing support to classroom teachers who may or may not have been using evidence-based instruction and curricula. The aim of pre-referral intervention was to help the teachers deal with their most difficult-to-teach student because of learning or behavior problems in hopes of strengthening the teachers' pedagogic skills and precluding the formal referral of these students for testing and possible special education placement. This research led to the development of various school-based consultative models such as Teacher Assistance Teams (e.g., Chalfant, Pysh, & Moultrie, 1979), Instructional Consultation Teams (e.g., Rosenfield & Gravois, 1996), and Mainstream Assistance Teams (e.g., D. Fuchs, Fuchs, Bahr, Fernstrom, & Stecker, 1990). These models, or models like them, were adopted, usually in modified form, by educational leaders in Pennsylvania (Instructional Support Teams; e.g., Conway & Kovaleski, 1998), Ohio (Intervention Based Assessment teams; e.g., Telzrow, McNamara, & Hollinger, 2000), and Iowa (Building Assistance Teams; e.g., Ikeda & Gustafson, 2002), and implemented statewide. (See D. Fuchs, Mock, Morgan, and Young, 2003, for a review of the effectiveness of these efforts.)

More recently, nonresponders are again the focus of intense research activity. The current work differs from the earlier work on pre-referral intervention in an important respect. In the 1980s research, the consultative process was often explicitly defined, whereas the intervention was not. In the current work on nonresponders, instruction is explicitly defined and the process often is not. In the 1980s, nonresponders may have been "nonresponsive" to what in fact was a poorly designed, poorly implemented, or poorly designed and executed pre-referral intervention. Nonresponders in the current research, however, are usually unresponsive to a well-described and generally effective treatment protocol (e.g., McMaster, Fuchs, Fuchs, & Compton, in press; Torgesen et al., 1999; Vaughn, Linan-Thompson, & Hickman, 2003; Vellutino et al., 1996), most often addressing early reading. This research typically explores instructional modifications necessary to make responders out of nonresponders (e.g., McMaster et al., in press; O'Connor, 2000; Vaughn et al., 2003). Such modifications typically increase the frequency or duration of instruction, increase the expertise of the person delivering it, or involve explicit and systematic instruction, often within the context of what is currently described as a "multi-tier" approach to instruction. More complex variants of this research also explore learner characteristics predictive of children's nonresponsiveness to treatment to identify such students more quickly for intervention, and to guide development of more effective intervention (e.g., Al Otaiba & Fuchs, in press; L. Fuchs et al., 2005; McMaster et al., in press; Speece & Case, 2001; Speece, Case, & Molloy, 2003; Torgesen et al., 1999; Vellutino et al., 1996).

Torgesen (2000) estimates that such multi-tier programs help all but 2 to 7 percent of kindergarten and first-grade children. This probably underestimates the proportion of nonresponders in the general population because researchers implemented these programs with a degree of treatment fidelity that no doubt exceeds the fidelity with which practitioners are capable given their comparatively meager resources. Nevertheless, if we use a conservative 5 percent rate of nonresponsiveness, 2.5 million children (5 percent of 50 million school-age students) will be nonresponders to state-of-the-art instruction. In other words, if schools faithfully implement a cutting-edge, evidence-based curriculum in the classroom, and follow up with an empirically validated standard treatment protocol for small groups of nonresponders, large numbers of children will still be expected to fail. These students will need more than intensified instruction. They will require truly differentiated education on the order of the new drug, Iressa, described earlier. How do we develop such education?

ATI: THEORY AND PAST PRACTICE

Lee Cronbach had twin purposes in his widely read 1957 paper in the *American Psychologist*. The first was to bring the two traditions of applied *experimental* and *correlational* psychology together. The second was to promote an Aptitude X Treatment Interaction (ATI) approach to instruction. "The experimental method brings situational variables under tight control," Cronbach wrote, "permitting rigorous tests of hypotheses and confident statements about causation" (p. 672). Its purpose "is to modify treatments so as to obtain the highest performance when all persons are treated alike—a search, that is, for the 'one best way'" (p. 678). For the experimenter, "individual differences [are] an annoyance.... Variation within treatments is cast into that outer darkness knows as 'error variance... to be reduced by any possible device" (p. 674). By contrast, "[t]he correlational method can study what man has not learned to control or can never hope to control" (p. 672). Its purpose "is to raise average performance by treating persons differently—different job assignments, different therapies, different disciplinary methods. The correlationist is utterly antagonistic to a doctrine of the one best way'" (p. 678), and "is in love with just those variables that the experimenter left home to forget" (p. 674).

Cronbach declared it was time for a merger of the experimental and correlational traditions. "If kept independent," he warned, "they can give only wrong answers or no answers at all regarding certain important problems" (p. 673). He proposed that "the manipulating and correlating schools of research... crossbreed, to bring forth a science of [ATI]" (Cronbach, 1975, p. 116). Cronbach (1957) stated:

Applied psychologists should deal with treatments and persons simultaneously. Treatments are characterized by many dimensions; so are persons. The two sets of dimensions together determine a payoff surface. For any practical problem, there is some best group of treatments to use and some best allocation of persons to treatments. Ultimately, we should *design* treatments, not to fit the average person, but to fit groups of students with particular aptitude patterns. (pp. 680–681)

Here then was an idea at midcentury—theory driven and based on a medical model requiring practitioners to understand individuals before prescribing treatments for them—for moving beyond the conventional, one-size-fits-all approach to differentiated classroom instruction. ATI has been described by many as one of the most attractive ideas in all of basic and applied psychology (e.g., Reschly & Ysseldyke, 1995). It generated excitement in the academy and launched hundreds of studies in the 1960s and 1970s. Some proved productive; others, not.

In this same time frame, there were several infamous applications of ATI. One of the more memorable involved the "abilities training, movement." Beginning in the early to mid-1960s, practitioners, encouraged by many academics, began using the Illinois Test of Psycholinguistic Abilities (ITPA) and similar tests to identify "weak information-processing "abilities" presumed responsible for children's poor academic performance and special-education status. Such putative abilities included "visual decoding," "kinesthetic associations," and "auditory encoding." The ITPA was understood to identify weak abilities in need of training and the test was valued for its recommendations about specific training regimens necessary for strengthening them. Many children were removed from reading and math programs for 1 year or more for this training. Arter and Jenkins (1979) and others finally documented that, in the vast majority of instances, these training programs failed to strengthen the targeted abilities or improve academic performance.

By the early 1980s, the abilities training movement was completely discredited in the academy. Because of its close association with this movement, ATI was seen by many (in and beyond special education) as an interesting idea with little practical payoff. Some behaviorists were particularly emphatic in their rejection of ATI, never having liked its medical-model orientation. Reschly and Ysseldyke (1995), for example, describe ATI as an unfortunate, if well-intentioned, mistake; a dead end. According to Reschly and Ysseldyke, Cronbach, too, finally repudiated the idea. They write, "In less than two decades, Cronbach's frustration with ATI . . . was palpable in [his 1975 *American Psychologist* article—the companion piece to his 1957 paper in which he] abandoned ATI as the basis for applied psychology" (p. 18).

Cronbach, of course, did no such thing. In the 1975 article, he refers to the experimentalist-correlationist "hybrid discipline" (p. 116) as now "flourishing." He briefly mentions ATI studies in social behavior, in response to drugs and therapy, in learning and motivation, and finally, in work on instruction. About instruction, he says the research programs conducted by McKeachie, Atkinson, Kropp and King, Stern, Hunt, Bunderson, and Dunham, and Snow "have brought us a long way" (p. 116). He writes, "Important as ATIs are proving to be [however], the line of investigation I advocated in 1957 no longer seems sufficient" (p. 116). In the remainder of the article, he encourages a more complex view of, and humble stance toward, ATIs in particular and theory building in general. Generalizations in the best of circumstances, he argues, accrue by testing them in many situations and over time. What may work in location A may not work in B; what works in 2005 may not work in 2010.

Exciting work continues on ATIs in language development (e.g., Yoder & Stone, 2005), classroom instruction (e.g., Connor, Morrison, & Petrella, 2004), and other areas. Equally true, however, is that there is much less work conducted today on ATIs than during their heyday; fewer networks of scholars are exploring how ATIs can help them understand theoretical and practical educational problems. At least one important exception to this statement may be the work on the cognitive profiling of children with genetic disorders. There is considerable enthusiasm among the clinical and developmental psychologists and medical researchers working in this area. In the next several sections, I first describe and then critique the cognitive profiling research on Down syndrome (DS) and neurofibromatosis (NF-1). Next, I discuss what future cognitive profiling and ATI research might look like. Last, I consider the importance of cognitive profiling and ATI research in the context of special education service delivery.

My aims are general and specific. Generally, I hope this chapter will contribute to others' efforts to resurrect interest in research that explores meaningful interactions between aptitudes and treatments. Without sustained ATI study, researchers and practitioners will not develop a much-needed science of differentiated education. My more specific aim is that, by discussing strengths and weaknesses of the cognitive profiling literature, I wish to suggest additional or alternate ways of conducting such studies in hopes of increasing the likelihood that stronger, more productive ATI studies will be implemented in the future. In short, the stance I take here is that of a "critical friend."

Finally, a couple of caveats. My discussion of and judgments about the cognitive profiling literature may have been very different had I selected additional or different genetic syndromes to review. My colleague, Bob Hodapp (personal communication, March 31, 2005), has argued to me that this chapter would have been better served on various grounds had I chosen Williams syndrome instead of NF-1. Additionally, although I worked hard to collect appropriate research papers, my review of the literature on DS and NF-1 was unsystematic and, I'm guessing, incomplete. Had I conducted a more comprehensive review, my discussion and conclusions may have changed.

CURRENT COGNITIVE PROFILING STUDIES OF CHILDREN WITH GENETIC DISORDERS

Cognitive Profiling and Social Justice

Who are children with genetic disorders? What is cognitive profiling? Why is there interest in discovering cognitive profiles among such children? And, why am I pursuing such questions in this chapter? Children with genetic disorders include (but are not limited to) those with Down syndrome (DS), fragile X, neurofibromatosis (NF-1), Prader-Willi, and Williams. Many have mild to severe mental retardation. Since the late 1970s, and with increasing frequency during the 1990s, researchers have tried to describe one or more of these groups in terms of their behavior or cognitive-linguistic performance and development. The goal has been to determine whether these disorders are associated with unique learner characteristics, or "phenotypes," with the understanding that a given group's phenotype would be an expression of its unique genotype (e.g., Hodapp & Freeman, 2003). Typically, cognitive-linguistic profiling has been explored in terms of cognitive styles (e.g., simultaneous vs. sequential processing); modalities (e.g., auditory vs. visual processing); and functional domains (e.g., language vs. visuospatial).

To understand the interest in the cognitive profiles of genetically disordered children, one first needs to appreciate that there have been at least two well-known lines of behavioral research on children with mental retardation. The first, and arguably more important, was to try to identify a core "deficit," or "defect," of mental retardation: a single explanation, if you will, of the disability (Hodapp, personal communication, March 31, 2005). In the face of strong and longstanding sentiment that etiologies and syndromes were unimportant to understanding mental retardation, researchers in the late 1970s began exploring whether children with syndromes such as DS, NF-1, and fragile X demonstrated etiology-specific profiles, personalities, or maladaptive behaviors (Hodapp, personal communication, March 31, 2005).

A second, unrelated line of inquiry contrasted children with and without mental retardation. Its primary purpose was to improve the classification and labeling of children with mental retardation. Snart, O'Grady, and Das (1982) write:

Psychodiagnostic efforts with the mentally retarded have been concerned with the classification of children in terms of their various intellectual acquisitions or possessions. In this way one was able to classify the child as trainable or educable, or even, as pseudo-retarded. [These assessments] offered few cues for educational planning or remediation . . . [which] can be attributed to the fact that intelligence has been considered largely in quantitative terms. (p. 78)

The reason for the decades-long fixation on quantitative analyses and issues of classification and labeling was quite simple: Few researchers or educators believed children with mental retardation were capable of learning anything but functional life skills; they had little need of serious, sustained academic instruction. This perspective began changing in the 1980s, with a quickening pace in the 1990s—a decade of new, "inclusive" school policies that emerged from a context in which there was a heightened sense of social justice. Today, parents and profes-

sional advocates expect that many children with mental retardation will be taught in public schools to read and write, as well as to participate fully in all other aspects of schooling. Evidence that policymakers share these expectations is the Office of Special Education Program's (U.S. Department of Education) Summer 2004 Request for Applications for national research centers to determine how to accelerate the reading development of children with mental retardation.

Cognitive-profiling research, therefore, represents a major shift from traditional testing of children with mental retardation for classification and labeling purposes, and toward the use of testing for instructional purposes. It also reflects a belief that children with mental retardation (like children without retardation) have cognitive strengths and weaknesses, which may be uniquely associated with the various genetic syndromes responsible for the mental retardation. That is, students with DS may have a qualitatively different cognitive profile than children with Williams syndrome, and these differences may require different types of instruction. Hodapp and Freeman (2003) write, "Using information on profiles . . . we may now be able to construct interventions that are targeted to the child's specific type of developmental disorder" (p. 1). The rationale for a search of possible signature cognitive profiles and ATIs would appear strengthened by the apparent, relative homogeneity of the children sharing the same genetic syndrome.

All this notwithstanding, many important questions must be asked of this promising line of inquiry. What is the validity of the specific putative strengths and weakness of children of a given syndrome? What is the uniqueness of a given profile relative to children without disabilities? What is its uniqueness in comparison to children with other genetic syndromes? What is the educational importance of the profile? Following is extended discussion of the cognitive profiling literature on two syndromes, DS and NF-1, chosen because of the relatively large number of children affected and the relatively high level of research activity associated with them.

Cognitive Profiling and Down Syndrome (DS)

What is DS? At present, approximately half of all individuals with mental retardation show a clear organic cause for their mental retardation with many having a genetic disorder (Hodapp, 1996). DS is "the most common genetic cause of mental retardation. [It] occurs in 1 of every 800–1,000 live births. Most cases—up to 95% are caused by a trisomy, or third chromosome, at the 21st pair. DS is common in other ways. It is represented in almost as many behavioral studies as the remaining several hundred genetic causes of retardation considered to-gether" (Hodapp, 1996, p. 881).

"Down Syndrome may be particularly interesting [with regard to cognitive profiling] because children with this disorder show relative weaknesses in grammar, articulation, and [expressive] language; [and] . . . relative strengths in visual and short-term memory" (Hodapp & Freeman, 2003, p. 1). Which leads to the question: "What empirical evidence exists for the view that children with DS have common strengths and weaknesses, and that this "profile" is unique among children with genetic disorders? There have been two pertinent and related lines of research addressing this issue: one exploring sequential versus simultaneous processing; the other, auditory versus visual processing.

Sequential Versus Simultaneous Processing. Snart, O'Grady, and Das's (1982) research was influenced by information integration theory, reflecting the idea that the brain uses two mutually dependent ways of coding information. Simultaneous coding involves the synthesis of various separate elements into groups with spatial overtones. Successive synthesis involves the integration of separate elements into a series or groups that are related temporally rather than spatially. Snart et al.'s objective was to examine coding and planning in three distinct subgroups of persons with moderate mental retardation. Participants were 62 students from a special school for students with moderate mental retardation in Edmonton, Canada. Group 1 consisted of 15 persons with medically documented brain damage (mean IQ = 50.77). Group 2 was 18 students with DS (mean IQ = 47.23). Group 3 was 31 subjects with mental retardation of unknown causes (mean IQ = 53.20). The ages of the three groups ranged from 9 to 22 with a mean of 16 (see pp. 466–467). There was no description of the children's educational instruction.

The three groups were tested on figure copying; memory for designs; auditory serial recall of lists of acoustically similar and unrelated words; digit span; trail making; and visual search (see Snart et al., 1982, p. 467, for details). Those with documented brain damage and the group with mental retardation of unknown causes performed statistically significantly better in the area of successive processing than the DS group. The DS group's greatest deficit was in the area of auditory sequential memory, which, according to Das, Kirby, and Jarman (1979), underlies much of language production. "[F]indings suggest," write Snart et al., "[that] information may be best presented to Down syndrome children emphasizing the visual modality and that remedial programs for both simultaneous and successive strategies may be beneficial" (p. 471). "In a more general sense," they continue, "the exact manner in which

education can be structured for groups with differential processing strengths will lie within the framework of an 'Aptitude × Treatment' interaction" (p. 471).

Pueschel, Gallagher, Zartler, and Pezzullo (1987) asked whether they would see similar differential cognitive performance for children with DS "using a recently developed instrument, the Kaufman Assessment Battery for Children [K-ABC]" (p. 21). The K-ABC is an intelligence test divided into three domains. The first is sequential processing, which assesses the ability to recall stimuli presented in temporal, or serial order. Its three subtests are hand movements, number recall, and word order. The second domain is simultaneous processing. It assesses the integration of stimuli in a spatial, gestalt-like manner, and includes magic window, face recognition, gestalt closure, triangles, matrix analogies, spatial memory, and photo series subtests. The third domain is academic achievement.

Pueschel et al.'s (1987) subjects were 20 children with DS (chronological age: 8 to 12.5 years); 20 younger brothers and sisters of the DS children; and 20 children without mental retardation referred to a clinic for school, developmental, or medical concerns. None had specific neurologic deficits. They were matched to the children with DS on mental age. The children with DS performed significantly less well than both the sibling and MA-matched non–mentally retarded groups on sequential processing and simultaneous processing tasks. But, in contrast to Snart et al.'s (1982) findings, there was no statistically significant difference between simultaneous and sequential processing for any group. To test whether children with DS performed better in visual processing than in auditory processing, means and standard deviations of scaled scores were calculated for number recall (auditory-vocal channels), word-order (auditory-motor channels), gestalt closure (visual-vocal channels), and hand movement (visual-motor channel; see their Table 3, p. 30). The group with DS had more difficulties in their auditory-vocal and auditory-motor channels of communication when compared to visual-vocal and visual-motor channels.

Like Pueschel et al. (1987), *Hodapp, Leckman, Dykens, Sparrow, Zelinsky, and Ort (1992)* explored the cognitive performance of children with mental retardation on the K-ABC. Unlike Pueschel et al., Hodapp and colleagues tested the cognitive functioning of three groups with genetic disorders within the same study design. They involved children with fragile X, DS, and nonspecific mental retardation. To minimize effects of chronological age, level of impairment, and gender, children across the groups were males of similar chronological and mental age. Each group comprised 10 children. The chronological ages (and mental ages in parentheses) of the fragile X, DS, and nonspecific groups were 8.7 (4.1), 9.0 (4.5); and 8.7 (4.8), respectively (see Hodapp et al.,

p. 41). There was no information about the children's educational backgrounds, except that none appeared to be institutionalized.

Hodapp et al. (1992) did not find reliable main effects for domain (sequential vs. simultaneous processing) or for group (fragile X vs. DS vs. non specific). The authors also looked for interactions between study groups and subtests of the sequential and simultaneous processing domains. In comparison to DS and nonspecific groups, the fragile X children tended to perform poorly on all sequential processing subtests. Hand movements was a statistically significant strength for the children with DS, whereas it was the weakest subtests (although not significantly so) for the fragile X children. For the simultaneous processing subtests, gestalt closure was a significant strength across the groups (see Hodapp et al., p. 43).

Apparently referring to an absence of main effects for domain (sequential vs. simultaneous processing) and group (fragile X vs. DS vs. nonspecific), Hodapp et al. (1992) write that their findings provide "limited support" (p. 44) for both the level of impairment and etiology-specific approaches to mental retardation. At the same time, they state:

There were several patterns that appear to be etiology-specific and that have implications for intervention with particular mentally retarded groups. [T]his study and that of Pueschel et al. (1987) revealed that Down syndrome children appear especially proficient at imitating sequences of hand movements . . . [a possible] advantage in acquiring manual signs as opposed to spoken words in early communicative development. In contrast, boys with fragile X syndrome appear to be unable to imitate a series of hand movements; therefore, they may be poor candidates for sign language training. (p. 45)

Auditory Versus Visual Processing. Bilovsky and Share's (1965) purpose was to describe the "cognitive patterns" (p. 79) of 24 children and young adults with DS. Their chronological age ranged from 6 yrs., 11 mos. to 23 yrs., 6 mos. (mean = 13 yrs., 11 mos.); their IQs ranged from 41 to 86 (mean = 46.6); and they were in public schools. Bilovsky and Share do not provide information on study methods, other than to say that they tested their study participants on the ITPA.

The authors used the language age norms of the ITPA. The sum of the raw scores on the nine subtests determined participants' overall, or mean, language age. Their scores on each of the nine subtests were then compared to their mean score. So, reported strengths and weaknesses were relative to their own mean language performance (p. 80). The auditory channel showed the greatest relative deficit. A distribution of rank orders of the 24 participants on the nine ITPA subtests showed that 14

performed best (ranked first) on motor encoding (i.e., expressing ideas in gestures or a manual manner rather than vocally); for 15, the auditory-vocal channel was ranked eighth or ninth. Primary deficits were in the auditory-vocal channels on the automatic-sequential levels. Primary strengths were motor encoding and visual decoding channels at the representational level. (Visual decoding represents understanding pictures with little or no vocal demands.)

Marcell and Armstrong (1982) write:

Mentally retarded people are widely recognized as having special difficulties in the realms of language and memory. [T]o isolate causes of these information-processing difficulties, several investigators have reported that retarded persons show a short-term memory deficit for information presented auditorially. This conclusion is based on performance differences found between the auditory and visual subtests of the [ITPA]. The auditory-visual memory difference appears to be strongest on those subtests that assess ordered recall for sequences of information. (p. 86)

However, "an analysis of the two most pertinent ITPA subtests, auditory sequential memory and visual sequential memory suggests that this conclusion is premature" (Marcell & Armstrong, 1982, p. 86). The two subtests differ in several ways other than sensory modalities. First, the instructions for the Visual task are more involved than those for the auditory task. Second, the stimuli to be remembered are abstract designs in one case and digits in the other. Third, the rates of presentation are different: Visual stimuli are presented for a greater duration. Fourth, the manner of stimulus presentation is simultaneous in one task and sequential in the other. Fifth, the mode of required response is manual in the visual task; oral in the auditory task. Any or all of these task-related differences, say Marcell and Armstrong, could be responsible for the finding that children with mental retardation display average performance on the visual subtest and poor performance on the auditory subtest.

The authors conducted three interrelated studies to determine whether this auditory over visual preference held when auditory and visual tasks were very carefully equated on complexity of instructions, nature of stimulus items, rate of stimulus presentation, manner of stimulus presentation, and mode of subject response. Results across the studies indicated an absence of modality preference for the children with DS.

Summarizing Research on Sequential Versus Simultaneous and Auditory Versus Visual. Across the just-described studies, it is difficult to discern a pattern among children with DS in regard to sequential versus simultaneous processing. Snart et al. (1982) found that children with DS had poor sequential processing relative to children with brain injury and typically developing children. Pueschel et al. (1987) found that children with DS did less well than siblings and MA-matched children on sequential and simultaneous processing, but did not demonstrate a preference for one kind of processing over the other. The children with DS in Hodapp et al.'s (1992) study did equally well on sequential and simultaneous processing and, further, their performance was no different from those with fragile X or with nonspecific mental retardation.

With respect to modality preferences, Snart et al. (1982), Pueschel et al. (1987), and Bilovsky and Share (1965) all reported a visual-over-auditory preference for children with DS. And, to the extent that the hand movements subtest in the sequential processing domain on the K-ABC may be viewed as a visual task, Hodapp et al., too, reported a visual modality preference for the DS group. However, Marcell and Armstrong (1982) questioned the meaningfulness of this preference. Whereas their three interrelated studies take aim at the ITPA, their findings raise questions about task comparability across studies of modality preference in children with mental retardation. Such concerns notwithstanding, there seems to be evidence for a modality preference among children with DS—more of a suggestion than a conclusion. Despite an apparent need for caution, there is a strong belief in the literature that the visual modality is indeed the strongest processing channel among children with DS, and many educators and researchers have based recommendations for educational programming on this putative fact. In other words, they have promoted the notion that there may be an important ATI with regard to children with DS.

Logographics Versus Phonics: Implications of Cognitive Profiling for Reading Instruction.

Arguments for a Logographic Approach. Partly on the basis of investigations like those of Snart et al. (1982), Pueschel et al. (1987), and Bilovsky and Share (1965), which suggest a visual-over-auditory modality preference, Byrne, Buckley, MacDonald, and Bird (1995) have proposed that children with DS are logographic, or sight-word, readers. Most nondisabled readers, they say, "will at first recognize words by sight only. They will then go on to an alphabetic stage when words can be sounded out letter by letter and then on to an orthographic stage of morpheme recognition" (p. 53). However, Buckley (cited in Byrne et al.) has suggested that children with DS do not translate print to speech to retrieve the meaning of words; rather, they go straight from the visual form of the word to its meaning. Several reading studies seem to provide evidence of this.

Cossu, Rossini, and Marshall (1993a), for example, studied the phonological awareness of 10 Italian children with DS who ranged in age from 8 to 15 years and who could read single words and nonwords aloud as well as typically developing 7-year-olds. Surprisingly, however, these 10 children did less well on tests of phoneme blending, oral spelling, phoneme counting, and phoneme deletion than the 7-year-old, reading-matched controls. Cossu and Marshall (1990) and Evans (1994) have also described children with DS who have learned to read despite their apparent "inability to perform phonological awareness tasks" (Byrne et al., p. 54).

In an attempt to provide further documentation of this apparent phenomenon, Byrne et al. (1995) recruited three groups of children: 24 with DS (8 yrs., 2 mos.); 42 average readers (7 yrs., 3 mos.) in the same class as the DS children; and 31 reading-matched children without DS (7 yrs., 1 mo.). The children in each group were tested at one point in time on tests of intelligence, reading, and language. Results indicated that the children with DS, in comparison to the reading-matched group and the average readers, were poorer on memory, language, and number. Byrne et al. concluded that the DS children "have advanced reading ability compared to their other cognitive abilities" (p. 57). On this basis, and influenced by previously cited research, they offered the "controversial proposal" (Snowling, Hulme, & Mercer, 2002, p. 471) that, for these children, phonological awareness is not a prerequisite of learning to read.

Arguments for a Phonics Approach. Snowling, Hulme, and Mercer (2002) are dismissive of Cossu and colleagues' research, claiming it suffers from "significant limitations" (p. 472). Snowling et al. conducted a series of studies to test the proposition that phonological awareness may be less important to children with DS than to typically developing children. In their first investigation, they recruited 29 children with DS (mean chronological age: 13 yrs., 2 mos.) and 31 primary-grade children as controls (mean chronological age: 5 yrs., 3 mos.). The two groups were matched on reading ability (p. 475), and their phonological awareness performance is displayed in Snowling et al.'s Table 2 (p. 478). The DS group showed similar knowledge of nursery rhymes as controls, "but performed significantly less well in syllable segmentation, rhyme detection, and phoneme detection" (p. 478).

About these unexpected findings, the authors say, "Superficially, [our] results . . . are similar to the findings of Cossu et al. (1993a)." They continue, "[I]t is possible [however] that group differences in syllable and phoneme awareness were the result of uncontrolled differences in general cognitive ability, affecting the ability to understand the task demands of the tests" (pp. 478–479). So,

Snowling et al. (2002) selected subgroups from each of their two initial groups who were matched pairwise for verbal mental age. This produced 17 matched pairs of children with and without DS (34 children of an original sample of 60). The reading performance of each member of a pair was then compared to that of the other. In this reanalysis, the children with DS were slightly superior in their knowledge of nursery rhymes, but scored "marginally less well on syllable segmentation" (i.e., $M = 15.18$ v. $M = 18.03$, $p = .09$, Table 3, p. 479) and on phoneme identification ($M = 10.41$ vs. $M = 11.06$). Statistically significant differences were again obtained on rhyme detection ($M = 2.00$ vs. $M = 4.76$, $p < .05$). Therefore, Snowling and her colleagues' reanalysis did not change the original findings: Children with DS continued to perform generally worse on phonological awareness while reading as well as reading-matched controls.

Nevertheless, Snowling et al. (2002) write, "Our findings lead us to reject the proposal of Cossu and his colleagues that phonological awareness is not a necessary prerequisite of learning to read" (p. 489). They allow that, in some respects, the development of reading and phonological awareness skills in children with DS follows "a qualitatively different path" (p. 489); specifically, their apparent capacity to identify phonemes (at least in syllable initial positions) despite their seeming difficulty in making judgments about rime units of spoken words. In comparison to typically developing children, this so-called rime deficit suggests a different order of acquisition of phonological awareness.

One more point about the Snowling et al. (2002) study: A majority of students with DS came from special schools, and it is likely they did not get the same reading instruction as those without special needs. It appears the authors do not know whether and, if so, what reading instruction was offered to the two study groups. In this regard, the Snowling et al. study is like that of many others described in this review (e.g., Byrne et al., 1995; Snart et al., 1982). Little effort was made to determine the nature and extent of the prior educational experience of study participants with mental retardation.

Cupples and Iacano (2002), like Snowling and her associates (2002), explored the importance of phonological awareness for children with DS. Cupples and Iacano state that students with DS are typically taught to read using a sight-word approach, partly because of a literature, described earlier, suggesting a "visual over auditory" modality preference among children with DS and because of Buckley's advocacy in the mid-1980s of a sight word approach. Like Snowling et al., Cupples and Iacano take Cossu and colleagues (1993a, 1993b) to task for their use of weak research methods. Cossu and associates, they say, used phonological awareness tasks poorly designed

to accommodate the cognitive limitations of their study participants (e.g., despite that the children with DS had digit spans ranging from 2 to 4, they were given four to six individual phonemes to blend on each trial).

Cupples and Iacano's (2002) subjects were seven English-speaking children with DS (8 yrs., 6 mos. to 11 yrs., 1 mo.) who, we are told, demonstrated little or no nonword reading ability prior to instruction. Nevertheless, their levels of reading instruction varied considerably, ranging from 5 yrs., 5 mos. to 1 yr., 2 mos. (see their Table 1, p. 556). The children were instructed in either onset-rime (phonetic) instruction ($n = 4$) or whole word instruction ($n = 3$), once per week for 6 weeks, totaling six individual training sessions, 45–60 min. in duration (p. 559). Two of the three children in the whole-word group appear to have been the very best readers among the study participants by a considerable margin (see Table 2, p. 557). There was no control group. Oral reading was assessed at pretreatment and post-treatment on 30 trained words (regularly spelled monosyllabic words) and 30 nontrained words (generalization nonsense words).

Six of seven children with DS read more training words correctly at post-treatment than at pre-treatment. More importantly, reading of untrained generalization words improved significantly for only the three children who received phonetic training (see Cupples & Iacano's Fig. 2). Also, phonological awareness (nonword blending skills) improved from pretreatment to post-treatment only for those getting phonetic training (see their Table 5, p. 567). The authors conclude that their participants' characteristically weak auditory memory (digit spans of between 2 and 3) "did *not* prevent them from benefiting from an analytical approach to reading instruction. Quite the opposite" (italics in the original; p. 570).

Summarizing the Evidence for Logographics Versus Phonics. Cossu and Marshall (1990), Cossu et al. (1993a), Evans (1994), and Byrne et al. (1995) all provide evidence that children with DS learn to read sight words, and possibly nonsense words, despite poor phonological awareness. This led Byrne et al. to claim provocatively that phonological awareness is unnecessary for DS students' reading development. Snowling et al. (2002) expressed skepticism of this proposition, but their research does little to weaken it. Cupples and Iacano's (2002) investigation provides stronger evidence for the importance of phonological awareness training, but their work is limited in part by a very heterogeneous group of just seven children. If pressed for an answer to the question, Logographics or phonics for children with DS?, I would have to say that logographics should not yet be ruled out, as improbable as this may sound to some. I base this partly on the evidence, and partly because, across investigations of best ways to teach reading to children with DS—that is, including the studies claiming to find for and against a logographic approach—most are descriptive (e.g., one-point-in-time testing of one or more groups); are not intervention oriented—and the very few that are do not include controls; use inadequately described reading treatments; and use a small number of study participants diverse in performance or behavior. There is obvious need for more rigorous research. As Snowling et al. write, "An important and powerful technique for uncovering causal relationships is that of a training study [that controls for materials, procedures, instructors, etc.]," a point to which I will return.

Cognitive Profiling and Neurofibromatosis (NF-1)

NF-1 is one of the most common genetic disorders of childhood, occurring in 1 infant per 3,000 live births. It is an autosomal dominant disorder, although new mutations are responsible for as many as 50 percent of cases. Manifestations of NF-1 are variable. Cafe-au-lait spots are found in 90 percent of affected children. NF-1 rarely develops until late childhood or early adolescence (Eliason, 1986). The NF-1 population has a slightly skewed incidence of mental retardation: 4 to 8 percent. IQ scores vary from 87 to 100 on the WISC, with some evidence of a bimodal pattern with respect to general cognitive functioning (Rosser & Packer, 2003). Specific cognitive difficulties and learning disabilities of varying severity have been noted in 30 to 65 percent of children across prevalence studies (see North et al., 1997).

Early research on the neuropsychological profiles of children with NF-1 proposed that nonverbal learning problems (e.g., difficulty with written work, poor organizational skills, impulsivity, and a decreased ability to perceive social cues) were predominant in the population. The principal basis for this nonverbal learning disability was a discrepancy between verbal and performance (VIQ>PIQ) found in two studies (cf. North et al., 1997), poor performance on tests of spatial memory (cf. North et al.), and consistent deficits in the Judgment of Line Orientation (cf. North et al.), a test of visuospatial function. More recent studies have shown that language-based learning problems (e.g., reading and spelling) are at least as common as nonverbal learning deficits in NF-1 children.

Visuospatial Impairment: The "Hallmark" Cognitive Deficit of NF-1? Cutting, Clements, Lightman, Yerby-Hammack, and Denckla (2004) make this last point, citing weaknesses among children with NF-1 in motor, visuomotor, visuospatial, reading, and language domains.

"These cognitive differences," they write, "are very common not only among children with NF-1 but also among children with learning disabilities in the general population. Therefore while NF-1 is a genetic disorder, the cognitive weaknesses are strikingly similar to the most common spectrum of learning disabilities in school systems" (p. 157). However, they add that, "The one notable difference between children with NF-1 and children with learning disabilities from the general population is the presence of significant visuospatial impairment, which is commonly present in NF-1" (p. 157). Cutting et al. call this impairment the hallmark of the cognitive profile of NF-1 children. North et al. (1997) concur: "The [Judgment of Line Orientation] is consistently abnormal in all studies to date, and…is a robust indicator of NF1[sic]-related neuropsychological deficits" (p. 4).

Eliason (1986). Eliason was first to suggest that visuospatial processing may be a hallmark weakness. The 23 children with NF-1 in her study sample had been referred to a Pediatric Learning Disorders Clinic for evaluation of school learning and/or behavior problems. IQ scores came from archival records and ranged from 62 to 114, a 3-standard-deviation spread (see her Table 2, p. 177). Using the language and visual-perceptual-motor scores of her study participants, Eliason arbitrarily created three subtypes: language disability (1 or more SDs below the mean on three of four tests of language functioning); visual-perceptual disability (deficits on three of four visual perceptual-motor tasks but performing at least average on the language measures); and mixed cognitive disability (deficits on two or more tests in both areas).

Eleven children (48%) displayed a verbal IQ that was 15 points or more greater than their performance IQ. Two children showed the opposite pattern with performance IQ 15 points greater than verbal IQ. Eliason (1986) claims that verbal–performance splits of 15 points or more (in either direction) occur in only 25 percent of children in the general population; splits of 25 points or more occur in only 5 percent of the general population (p. 176). In Eliason's NF-1 sample, 56 percent had more than a 15 point split; 18 percent had splits greater than 25 points. (Two questions: Is an NF-1 vs. general population comparison appropriate given the fact that Eliason's NF-1 sample is an unrepresentative clinically referred subgroup? A better question: What is the clinical NF-1 group to non-clinical NF-1 group comparison like? Or, what part of the difference is NF-1 and what part is due to referred status?)

Eliason (1986) then compared her sample of 23 clinic-referred NF-1 children to 297 children referred to a learning disabilities clinic at a tertiary care center. The children with learning disabilities met the federal definition of the disorder. The two samples were contrasted on proportions meeting the foregoing criteria for the three subtypes: visual-perceptual disability, language disability, mixed cognitive disability. Eliason writes:

It is apparent that the distribution of cognitive subtypes is different in the NF sample than in a clinic sample of LD children from the same geographical area. Language disability was [the] most common subtype of LD . . . whereas visual-perceptual deficits were more common in the NF sample. The most striking . . . finding was that 20 of 23 children with NF had a visual perceptual disability (with or without a language deficit)." (pp. 177–178)

Cutting, Koth, and Dencla (2000). Cutting and her colleagues conducted a partial replication of Eliason's (1986) study by comparing an NF-1 group ($n = 20$; 17 boys, $M = 9.65$ yrs.) to clinic-referred students with learning disabilities ($n = 13$, $M = 8$ boys, $M = 8.08$ yrs.) to typically developing controls ($n = 16$, 8 boys, $M = 10.21$ yrs.) on neuropsychological measures (Judgment of Line Orientation and the Boston Naming Test) and reading-related measures (phoneme segmentation, RAN, and Digit Span). The groups of children with NF-1 and learning disabilities had reading-related deficits when compared to controls. However, in comparison to the learning disabilities group, the NF-1 children were more globally language impaired. They also did not score as well as the learning disabilities group on the visuospatial measures. Surprisingly, however, the NF-1 group scored as well as controls. Equally unexpected was that the NF-1 versus learning disabilities difference on visuospatial measures disappeared when IQ was controlled (see Cutting et al., p. 38, and the note in their Table 3, p. 40). Hence, Cutting and her associates' findings do not seem to support Eliason's. However, their results are difficult to interpret because of initial differences between their study groups. The learning disabilities group, for example, seems to have had higher IQ, vocabulary, and block design scores than their NF-1 group (see Cutting et al., Table 1, p. 39).

Judgment of Line Orientation Test. Finally, Cutting et al. (2000), like many other researchers "worldwide" (see Paquier et al., 1999, p. 243) used the Judgment of Line Orientation test to determine the visuospatial performance of children with NF-1 and with other genetic disorders. Arthur Benton, the test's developer, has claimed that the Judgment of Line Orientation is "as pure a measure of one aspect of spatial thinking as could be conceived" (Benton et al., 1983, cited in Riccio & Hynd, 1992, p. 210). Many seem to agree. It has become a kind of litmus test for visuospatial abnormality. To wit: "The [Judgment of Line Orientation test] is consistently abnormal in all studies [of NF-1 children] to date, and thus, at some level,

is a robust indicator of NF-1-related neuropsychological deficits" (North et al., 1997, p. 4). And, "The JLO [Judgment of Line Orientation] test stands out among studies as being consistently abnormal. Thus, [it] is believed to be an important indicator of neurocognitive dysfunction in NF1" (Rosser & Packer, 2003, p. 130). Yet, there is reason to question the test's validity.

Paquier et al. (1999) conducted a retrospective analysis of the extant files of 32 right-handed children with left or right hemisphere damage and admitted to the hospitals in the Netherlands and one in Belgium. The Judgment of Line Orientation had been given in all three places as part of a routine neuropsychological assessment. The three groups were similar in age. Paquier et al. found that the Judgment of Line Orientation discriminated only 15.6 percent of the pathologic cases, and that it and age together predicted only 34 percent of the pathologic cases. The proportion of misses was reported to be extremely high (see p. 245).

Riccio and Hynd (1992) asked whether the Judgment of Line Orientation differentiates between clinic populations and a control group, as well as among specific groups within the clinic population. Subjects were 73 students ranging in age from 85 to 175 months ($M = 123$ months). Their full-scale IQ on the WISC-R ranged from 65 to 145 ($M = 104$). They were consecutive clients at the Center for Clinical and Developmental Neuropsychology at University of Georgia. Those with known neurological disorders (e.g., epilepsy and traumatic brain injury) were excluded from study. There were three groups: A clinic-referred group identified as learning disabilities (reading, math, or both, $n = 27$); a clinic-referred non-learning disabilities group ($n = 32$); and a normal control group ($n = 14$). The Judgment of Line Orientation correlated moderately with math and reading, but not with spelling. On this basis, Riccio and Hynd say that there is evidence of "sufficient construct and criterion-related validity with this population" (p. 217). However, when controlling for cognitive ability, the Judgment of Line Orientation did not discriminate effectively among the three different groups (see their Table 5, p. 216).

Is Visuospatial Weakness a Hallmark Cognitive Deficit? A Summary. According to Cutting et al. (2000) and others, Eliason (1986) was first to advance the idea that visuospatial weaknesses were defining phenotypic markers of NF-1 children. She based her claim on a study of 23 such children who were more likely to show large verbal–performance discrepancies on IQ tests than nondisabled children in the general population and who were also more likely than a large sample of students with LD to demonstrate a visual-perceptual disability, using her own definition of the disability. Cutting et al. (2000) attempted to replicate Eliason's findings by comparing test performance of children with NF-1 to children with LD and to typically developing children. As in Eliason's study, the NF-1 group performed less well than the LD group on visuospatial tasks. But they performed as well as controls on these measures. Thus, visuospatial performance did not distinguish NF-1 children from nondisabled children. Moreover, Paquier et al. (1999) and Riccio and Hynd (1992) have raised serious questions about the discriminative validity of the Judgment of Line Orientation. Hence, there appears to be inconsistent evidence for the claim that poor visuospatial is a valid marker of NF-1 children. Finally, in contrast to the literature on children with DS, there has been little effort in the NF-1-related research to explore instructional implications of the cognitive profiling. Perhaps this is because of the smaller group of researchers interested in NF-1 and that educational research in NF-1 is a relatively recent phenomenon.

Critique of Cognitive Profiling Studies on DS and NF-1 Children

Conceptual Concerns

Relative to Whom? Frequently used phrases in the cognitive profiling literature are "relative weaknesses" and "relative strengths" as in, "Children with [DS] show relative weaknesses in grammar, articulation, and receptive language [and] . . . relative strengths in visual short-term memory" (Hodapp & Freeman, 2003, p. 1). But what exactly does *relative* and *strength* mean? With respect to "relative," relative to whom? In reading the literature on children with DS and NF-1, I counted 10 different comparison groups. Children's performance was compared to themselves (e.g., Cupples & Iacano, 2002; Dykens, Hodapp, & Leckman, 1987); to a test's normative population (e.g., Bilovsky & Share, 1965); to nondisabled siblings (e.g., Pueschel et al., 1987); to nondisabled children of similar chronological age (e.g., Marcell & Armstrong, 1982; McDade & Adler, 1980); to typically developing (usually younger) children of similar mental age (e.g., Fidler, Hepburn, & Rogers, 2003; Pueschel et al., 1987); to typically developing (usually younger) children with similar reading skills (e.g., Byrne et al., 1995; Snowling et al., 2002); to children with different genetic syndromes (e.g., Hodapp et al., 1992; Snart et al., 1982); to children with similar or different genetic syndromes in a different study (e.g., Dykens et al., 1987); and to children with mental retardation of "mixed" (e.g., Fidler et al., 2003) or "nonspecific" (e.g., Hodapp et al., 1992) etiologies. "Mixed-etiology" and "nonspecific-etiology" groups are often seen as one and the same. But Hodapp and Dykens (2001) explain that children in a mixed group show different causes as well as no clear cause for mental retardation. In a nonspecific group, all individuals show no obvious cause.

In drawing attention to these many different comparisons, my intention is not to criticize, but to encourage discussion about whether all are equally valid; whether some may be valid for some purposes but not for others; and whether one or more are invalid regardless of the question at hand.

What Are "Strengths" and "Weaknesses"? Hodapp and Dykens (2001) suggest that a relative strength would be observed when a group performed significantly above mental age but below chronological age. This seems reasonable enough. Yet, I wonder about the theoretical or empirical justification for describing the performance of an individual or a group as a strength or weakness. Are there theoretically derived benchmarks against which performance may be evaluated for strengths and weaknesses? Are there empirically derived guidelines in determining how much of a standard score or grade equivalence difference is necessary between, say, verbal working memory and visuospatial performance to call the former a strength and the latter a weakness? What does it mean when a child's, or a group's, performance is described as a strength, and yet it is dramatically below the performance of typically developing peers? *Strength* and *weakness* are words sometimes used rather cavalierly in the literature.

In a different vein, strengths and weaknesses of different etiological groups are rarely discussed in connection with treatment selection. Yet such a discussion is critically important for productive ATI research. A group's strength, for example, may be defined in terms of the level of skill (expressed in raw scores or age equivalents) determined empirically to be a threshold, or a requisite level, for a given treatment to be effective. As Yoder (personal communication, April 2, 2005) writes, "To justify an etiology-specific treament, we [would] want to know the degree to which a particular etiological group . . . [does or does not] posses this level of skill." To reflect an ATI, the requisite skill level should be unique to both group and treatment.

Similar issues involve the popular terms *distinct profile* and *spared domain*. Fidler (in press) writes, "Over the past few decades, research has begun to converge on a specific behavior phenotype, or a distinct profile of behavior outcomes" (p. 4). "Distinct" in what sense? As in differentiating the phenotypic profile of children with DS from that of children with different genetic disorders, or as in a "clear" and "explicit" profile, apart from how unique it may be? "Spared domain" refers to an area of functioning (e.g., visual perceptual) that is normal, or nearly so. Hodapp and Dykens (2001) write that performance in a spared domain would be at or near a standard score of 100. What about 95? Is 95 "near" 100? If so, how about 93? Again, I failed to find theoretical or empirical support for these proposed cut-points in the distribution.

An Overemphasis on Traits?

Much of the cognitive profiling literature consists of psychometric studies in which researchers explore *traits*: that is, child characteristics implicitly or otherwise believed to be fixed and unresponsive to instruction. There seems to be insufficient curiosity in this literature about how children with DS and NF-1 learn, and how educators may accelerate their learning. There are several indications of this overly strong emphasis on traits and correspondingly inadequate concern about learning. First, most researchers use one-point-in-time testing. Few measure performance across time, which would permit exploration of whether, why, and how learner characteristics change. Second, there seems to be widespread uninterest among researchers in the educational histories of their study participants with DS and NF-1 (see, as examples, Byrne et al., 1995; Snart et al., 1982; Snowling et al., 2002); and infrequent attempts to link observed psychometric performance with prior learning histories and instruction. Third, a very small number of research teams conduct experimental or quasi-experimental studies to explore relationships between cognitive profiles of DS and NF-1 children and instruction, such as the teaching of reading. This is surprising and disappointing given that there is some evidence of a visual-over-auditory modality preference among children with DS. All of this may help explain the virtual absence of ATI studies. Cupples and Iacano's (2002) modest study is an exception.

How Homogeneous are DS and NF-1 Groups?

There seems to be a not unreasonable belief that children with DS are as similar phenotypically as they are genetically; that "DS behavior" is more uniform than not. Similar assumptions are made about NF-1 children. And yet I did not find one study in the DS or NF-1 literature that explored the truthfulness of these beliefs. I did find studies of children with the same genetic deficit in which they varied markedly along one or more dimensions of performance. For example, some of Byrne et al.'s (1995) children with DS (mean chronological age = 8 yrs., 2 mos.) did not respond to any of their reading measures, whereas other children with DS in their study sample read like average 8-year-olds and 9-year-olds on the same measures (see Byrne et al., Table 1, p. 56). The apparent heterogeneity of behavior among groups of children with the same genetic deficit raises important questions about how they might be studied in an ATI framework.

Methodological Concerns. In several studies, researchers used incorrect statistical analyses or pursued intragroup contrasts of a given etiology when they might have more profitably focused on intergroup comparisons across etiologies. A greater number of researchers failed to describe the educational histories of study participants, which may have interacted with study treatments (cf. Byrne et al., 1995; Snart et al., 1982; Snowling et al., 2002). Most researchers were able to recruit only a very small number of subjects who, nevertheless, often represented very great heterogeneity.

Probably the most frequent, obvious, and serious methodological concern is that researchers have tended to rely on tests without documented validity for the purposes to which they were put. In earlier studies, use of the ITPA undercut the importance of many researchers' efforts (cf. Bilovsky & Share, 1965). More recently, researchers (e.g., Eliason, 1986) have explored visuospatial performance among children with NF-1 with the Judgment of Line Orientation, a test with questionable validity (Paquier et al., 1999; Riccio & Hynd, 1992).

In a similar vein, across the studies of children with DS and NF-1, there is the strong likelihood that the sensitivity and usefulness of many researchers' tests were limited by floor effects. Most were conventional, norm-referenced, and commercially published—measures that Spector (1992) and others have derogated as "static." Generally, these tests were originally developed for nondisabled children and, partly as a result, contain few items to which many children with DS and NF-1 can respond. That is, the tests' sampling of behavior for such children is often thin and inadequate. Moreover, as explained by Spector, most conventional tests assess only two states: unaided success and failure. The child either answers a question correctly without prompts or cues or she is viewed as failing the item. Such tests do not explore the possibility that, with minimal instruction, the child with DS or NF-1 might do considerably better. (More about this later.)

Summary of Conceptual and Methodological Concerns. Contributors to the cognitive profiling literature are pursuing how we might someday differentiate education for children with (and without) disabilities. I cannot think of a more important question for public education. I applaud their focus and wish them nothing but success. But success will require reconceptualizing the task.

Currently, researchers are exploring different etiologies (e.g., DS and NF-1), and different traitlike characteristics within a given etiology (e.g., sequential vs.

simultaneous processing or auditory vs. visual processing of children with DS), in different domains (e.g., general cognitive functioning vs. reading), using different measures. Moreover, the researchers compare the children with DS or NF-1 to themselves; to children with different genetic syndromes; to younger nondisabled siblings; to typically developing children of similar chronological age but higher mental age; to nondisabled children of similar mental age but higher chronological age; and so forth. Such variability in focus, subjects, and methods makes it difficult to find coherent patterns or generalizations. Add to this the fact that many researchers develop descriptions of their study samples by using tests of questionable validity, and that few researchers are pursuing instructional implications of various cognitive profiles, and one is left with an impression that much work must still be accomplished before cognitive profiling may be seen as a legitimate and desirable road to ATI.

Future Directions in Cognitive Profiling and ATI Research

Dynamic Assessment and Responsiveness-to-Instruction. There is demonstrable need to rethink how to explore the phenotypic behavior of children with genetic deficits. The strategic approach reflected in prior work is insufficient if researchers wish to achieve more accurate and comprehensive cognitive profiling and ATIs that improve the education and lives of children with disabilities.

From Static to Dynamic. I suggest researchers consider alternative assessments: that is, supplementing their traditional, one-point-in-time testing with more frequent testing of children as the children are learning academically relevant tasks. There are at least two ways of structuring the learning context to understand more about children with DS and NF-1. The first is dynamic assessment, which is often defined procedurally as a series of carefully graded prompts or cues or hints. Typically, the first prompt provides minimal help; the last, much greater help.

Lynn Fuchs, Don Compton, and I recently developed a five-level sequence of prompts to determine how much support is necessary for at-risk kindergartners to read consonant-vowel-consonant words. After each level of prompt, or support, the child is asked to read the same six nonsense words. If the child reads all six words correctly, the assessment ends and the examiner records the level of support that was necessary for the child's error-free performance. If the child reads one or more of these words incorrectly, the examiner engages the child at the next

higher level prompt, or level of support—again followed by the six-word assessment.

Next are the verbatim protocols for a level 2 prompt (providing relatively little support) and a level 5 prompt (providing maximal support). The level 2 prompt teaches "onsets" (e.g., the "c" in "cat"). The level 5 prompt, by contrast, teaches onset and "rime" (i.e., the /c/ and the /at/ in "cat"), and how to blend the two. Words below in bold are spoken by an examiner. Words in parentheses are directives to the examiner. First, is our level 2 prompt.

"These words (zod, bod, zon, bon, zok, bok, and zom) **are nonsense words. I'm going to read them and put them into two piles. I'll put the words that start with the letter "z" here** (point). **The letter "z" says /z/. Here** (point), **I'll put the words that begin with the letter "b," /b/. Watch me.** (First, read the cards one by one. Then place them correctly into one of the two piles. When you've completed the sorting, reshuffle them and place the deck in front of the child and say,) **Now you make two piles. One pile is for words that begin with "z." The other pile is for words that begin with "b."**

Our level 5 prompt: **This letter is "b." It says /b/. These two letters** ("o-m") **say /om/. Together the sounds say /bom/.** (Repeat with "z" and "o-d.") **Now you be the teacher. You teach me how to read the word "bom." I'll show you how to be my teacher. First, point to the "b" and say, "This says /b/. What does it say? Say that to me.** (Wait for the child to repeat the directive and help as necessary. Afterwards, respond as if you're the student. Point to the "o-m," and say,) **"These letters say /om/. What do they say?" Your turn.** (Wait for the child to repeat the question. Help as necessary, and then respond as if you're the student.) **Now say to me, these sounds say /bom/.** (Repeat with the nonsense word, "lod.")

(Give the child a card with "zod," "bod," "mod," and "zom" on it. Say,) **Now, let's play a game called Guess My Word. I am going to say a word and you point to that word on this card.** (Play the game using all of the words. Then, you and the child switch roles. The child says a word, you point to it, and you say it.) **Now you say one of these words and I'll point to it.**

Children's performance on this consonant-vowel-consonant task is indexed by how independent of prompts, or dependent on prompts, they are. Put differently, What level of prompting is necessary before they read consonant-vowel-consonant nonsense words to criterion? This assessment is different from the traditional assessments used by many researchers who have contributed to the cognitive profiling literature. As indicated previously, examiners using traditional tests usually assess only two states: unaided success and failure. The child either answers a question correctly without prompts from the tester or the child is considered to have failed the item. From a Vygotskian perspective, however, the child may be somewhere between these two states: unable to perform the task independently but able to achieve success with minimum help. Hence, it would seem there is a need for use of more dynamic measures in cognitive profiling research. Dynamic measures like the one just illustrated may improve prediction over traditional tests because they can identify children who failed the task at a level 1 prompt but who are ready to improve (as indicated by their success on a higher level prompt) versus those who failed and are not as ready to improve. Research suggests that such an approach is more sensitive to performance at the lower end of the distribution; more discriminating among the children there (e.g., Spector, 1992).

How does the dynamic nature of such assessment relate to ATIs? Because of its comparative sensitivity and accuracy, dynamic assessment may be more likely than traditional assessment to lead to the discovery of the child construct(s) requisite for the selection of one treatment over another, or the specific areas of need that treatment A, but not treatment B, can provide.

A second way to structure the learning context to understand more about children with DS and NF-1—and other children with and without disabilities—is responsiveness-to-intervention. *Responsiveness-to-intervention* refers to a process by which children unresponsive to classroom instruction are given more intensive instruction (e.g., more frequent instruction, small-group instruction, more expert instruction) as their performance is monitored frequently. Children who remain unresponsive are given even more intensive attention (e.g., individualized instruction) while their performance is monitored. The purposes of a responsiveness-to-intervention approach are remedial and diagnostic: As instructors attempt remediation, they explore the adaptations necessary to make responders of nonresponders. Whereas dynamic assessment may take only one session, or several sessions, responsiveness-to-intervention usually occurs over a 10-week period (see L. Fuchs, 1995; L. Fuchs, Fuchs, & Speece, 2002; D. Fuchs et al., 2003). A presumption is that, at some point, level of treatment intensity becomes a qualitative, not just quantitative, change that children with certain constructs (etiologies) will require, whereas others will not.

From Distal to Proximal. In comparison to the traditional approach to cognitive profiling, dynamic assessment and responsiveness-to-intervention alternatives represent a move from distal to proximal as well as change from static to dynamic. By the phrase "distal to proximal," I mean that these alternative assessments represent a focus on domain-*specific*, academically relevant tasks, rather

than a focus on domain-*general* and general tasks such as general cognitive-linguistic tests. Spector's (1992) work suggests that tasks that predict future academic success need to be both dynamic and proximal; one without the other is insufficient.

Proposed Sequence of ATI Research: Importance of Theory and Experimentation in Identifying the "Proximal Behaviors" Responsible for Differential Responsiveness to Instruction. Following is the outline of a strategy—an ordering of research activity—for exploring ATIs. It highlights the importance of what my colleague Paul Yoder refers to as "proximal behaviors"; behaviors or characteristics likely to facilitate or impede desired academic performance. It also highlights the importance of both strong theory and empirical research.

The first step in such a strategy is to identify the nature of the task (e.g., reading), and level of the task (e.g., letter-sound correspondence). The second step is to ask, What specific knowledge (e.g., print conventions) and skills (e.g., segmenting/blending printed words) are required for successful task performance? Third, which cognitive (e.g., rapid naming) and linguistic (e.g., vocabulary) abilities associated with "knowledge" and "skills" facilitate successful task performance? How do we validly measure them? On the basis of empirical evidence, can we prioritize their importance to task performance, and does this rank ordering pertain to all children or are different orderings (i.e., cognitive profiles) necessary for different groups of children?

To validate the relative importance of the cognitive abilities to successful task performance, researchers should determine whether they influence interventions selectively. They might choose, say, two demonstrably effective interventions to accelerate word recognition. Based partly on theory, they might anticipate that one intervention would be more effective than the other for children with a certain cognitive-linguistic profile. A heterogeneous group of children ($N = 50$–100) might be assigned randomly and in equal proportions to the two treatments and to a control group. Testing for ATIs at this stage is not really "ATI research." Rather, it represents critical planning for such research. It helps identify the proximal behaviors explaining the "mechanism" of differential responsiveness to instruction.

After identifying the relevant variable by which treatment effects vary, researchers can look for more homogeneous samples of children who represent an "oversampling" of the cognitive-linguistic abilities shown previously to be key in explaining differential responsivity. Perhaps children with DS (or a group of children with a different genetic disorders; or children with LD; or a group of demographically, racially, or economically unique children) are likely to have this cognitive-linguistic profile. For this group, then, specific ATI hypotheses may be pursued. And if found, then relatively distal (as opposed to proximal) variables (e.g., DS, learning disabilities, low SES) become validated predictors of which instruction will be more effective.

FINAL THOUGHTS ON DISTINGUISHING ATIS FROM SPECIAL EDUCATION AND "A LONG HARD SLOG"

ATIs Versus Special Education

Many incorrectly view ATI as a means of individualizing instruction. My friend and mentor, Stan Deno (1990), for example, wrote of three problems "inherent" in an ATI approach to individualized instruction: First, an overemphasis on the importance of predicting and prescribing programs from diagnostic testing procedures prior to program implementation; second, an assumption that probabilistic predictions reasonable for groups will apply to individuals; third, an underemphasis of the importance of formative evaluation for determining student progress and adjusting operational predictions that prove inaccurate. Together, wrote Deno, these problems make ATI instructional technology insufficiently responsive to individual differences (p. 164).

Others, too, have expressed one or more of these concerns. And yet, the concerns do not connect to what Cronbach originally wrote about ATI. "Ultimately," he wrote, "we should design treatments, not to fit the average person, but to fit groups of students with particular aptitude patterns" (Cronbach, 1957, pp. 680–681). ATI, for Cronbach, was less about individual differences than it was about differences between discrete groups. It was not about particular truths, but about universal truths—albeit universal truths with narrow parameters. Hence, Cronbach did not conceive ATIs to compete with, or to be considered synonymous with, a special-education-like focus on individualized instruction.

By incorrectly understanding that ATI was meant to serve individualized instruction, Deno and others cannot see a service delivery model in which ATI activity might fit productively between the (nomothetic) regular classroom level and the (idiographic) special education level. As explained, the search for generally effective instruction in the regular classroom is probabilistic; some students (hopefully just a few) will fail to respond appropriately. Currently, certain educators (e.g., Ikeda & Gustafson, 2002) claim that nonresponders deserve individualized attention in general education, and that there are evidence-based approaches to accomplish this. Such claims notwithstanding, general education is not currently providing individualized instruction to nonresponders and it is not likely to do so. What general educators needs is a second-level probabilistic instructional response based on sound knowledge about nonresponders. In principal, this is where ATIs come in. Choosing curricula, materials, and instructional procedures based on what is known about the cognitive-linguistic profiles of *groups* of nonresponders, and engaging children with all this in small groups, will increase the likelihood that many—not all—will become responsive learners. Truly individualized instruction, including iterative, or continuous, progress monitoring, should be reserved for chronic nonresponders. And special educators should be the ones with the responsibility, training, and work conditions to deliver it. In short, there is strong need for both ATI-guided instruction and special education. They are supplementary approaches; they are not synonymous, or in competition, with each other.

"Hard Slog"

In mid-August, 2004, with the Presidential campaign entering the homestretch, *the New York Times* ran an editorial critical of President Bush's underfunding of stem cell research. It described a recent speech by Laura Bush in which she emphasized the preliminary nature of the research and deplored the implication that cures were just around the corner. The editorial countered with the following: "Mrs. Bush is surely right that some advocates of stem cell research leave the impression that cures may be just around the corner, whereas virtually all experts agree it will be a long, hard slog with success by no means guaranteed. Yet there seems little doubt that the slog will be all the harder if the federal government, traditionally the main driving force in basic medical research, hangs back from the field."

"A long, hard slog" is also the right description of what's in store for those who intend to seriously pursue cognitive profiling and ATIs. On the other hand, the potential payoffs to children with and without disabilities and their parents and teachers are great. To find ATIs, and to produce validated differentiated instructional programs, researchers must rethink strategies and methods. The federal government should encourage this effort by creating appropriate funding mechanisms that reward ambitious, programmatic, and rigorous work.

ACKNOWLEDGMENTS

To Bob Hodapp and Paul Yoder, thanks for your generous and helpful feedback. To Patricia Alexander, thanks for your patience and encouragement. Any errors of omission or commission are mine alone.

References

Al Otaiba, S., & Fuchs, D. (in press). Who are the young children for whom best practices in reading are ineffective? An experimental and longitudinal study. *Journal of Learning Disabilities*.

Arter, J. A., & Jenkins, J. R. (1979). Differential diagnosis—prescriptive teaching: A critical appraisal. *Review of Educational Research, 49*(4), 517-555.

Baker, J. M., & Zigmond, N. (1990). Are regular education classes equipped to accommodate students with learning disabilities? *Exceptional Children, 56*, 515-526.

Bilovsky, D., & Share, J. (1965). The ITPA and Down's Syndrome: An exploratory study. *American Journal of Mental Deficiency, 70*(1), 78-82.

Brown, B. W., & Saks, D. H. (1981). The microeconomics of schooling. In D. C. Berliner (Ed.), *Review of research in education* (Vol. 9, pp. 217-254). Washington, DC: American Educational Research Association.

Brown, B. W., & Saks, D. H. (1987). The microeconomics of the allocation of teachers' time and student learning. *Economics of Education Review, 6*, 319-332.

Byrne, A., Buckley, S., MacDonald, J., & Bird, G. (1995). Investigating the literacy, language and memory skills of children with Down's syndrome. *Down's Syndrome: Research and Practice, 3*(2), 53-58.

Carnine, D. W., Silbert, J., Kame'enui, E. J., & Tarver, S. G. (2004). *Direct instruction reading* (4th edition). Upper Saddle River, NJ: Prentice-Hall.

Chalfant, J. C., Pysh, M. V., & Moultrie, R. (1979). Teacher assistance teams: A model for within-building problem solving. *Learning Disability Quarterly, 2*, 85-96.

Connor, C. M., Morrison, F. J., & Petrella, J. N. (2004). Effective reading comprehension instruction: Examining child × instruction interactions. *Journal of Educational Psychology, 96*(4), 682-698.

Conway, S. J., & Kovaleski, J. F. (1998). A model for statewide special education reform: Pennsylvania's Instructional Support Teams. *International Journal of Educational Reform, 7*, 345-351.

Cossu, G., & Marshall, J. C. (1990). Are cognitive skills a prerequisite for learning to read and write? *Cognitive Neuropsychology, 7*(1), 21-40.

Cossu, G., Rossini, F., & Marshall, J. C. (1993a). When reading is acquired but phonemic awareness is not: A study of literacy in Down's syndrome. *Cognition, 46*(2), 129-138.

Cossu, G., Rossini, F., & Marshall, J. C. (1993b). Reading is reading is reading. *Cognition, 48*(3), 297-303.

Cronbach, L. J. (1957). The two disciplines of scientific psychology. *The American Psychologist, 12*, 671-684.

Cronbach, L. J. (1975). Beyond the two disciplines of scientific psychology. *American Psychologist, 30*(2), 116-127.

Cupples, L., & Iacono, T. (2002). The efficacy of "whole word' versus 'analytic' reading instruction for children with Down syndrome. *Reading and Writing, 15*(5-6), 549-574.

Cutting, L. E., Koth, C. W., & Denckla, M. B. (2000). How children with neurofibromatosis Type 1 differ from "typical" learning disabled clinic attenders: Nonverbal learning disabilities revisited. *Developmental Neuropsychology, 17*(1), 29-47.

Cutting, L. E., Clements, A. M., Lightman, A. D., Yerby-Hammack, P. D., & Denckla, M. B. (2004). Cognitive profile of neurofibromatosis type I: Rethinking nonverbal learning disabilities. *Learning Disabilities Research and Practice, 19*(3), 155-165.

Das, J. P., Kirby, J., & Jarman, R. F. (1979). *Simultaneous and successive cognitive processes*. New York: Academic Press.

De La Paz, S., Owen, B., Harris, K., & Graham, S. (2000). Riding Elvis' motorcyle: Using self-regulated strategy development to PLAN and WRITE for a state writing exam. *Learning Disabilities Research and Practice, 15*, 101-109.

Delquadri, J. C., Greenwood, C. R., Whorton, D., Carta, J. J., & Hall, R. V. (1986). Classwide peer tutoring. *Exceptional Children, 52*(6), 535-561.

Deno, S. L. (1985). Curriculum-based measurement: The emerging alternative. *Exceptional Children, 52*, 219-232.

Deno, S. L. (1990). Individual differences and individual difference: The essential difference of special education. *Journal of Special Education, 24*(2), 160-173.

Deshler, D. D., Schumaker, J. B., Lenz, B. K., Bulgren, J. A., Hock, M. F., Knight, J., & Ehren, B. J. (2001). Ensuring content-area learning by secondary students with learning disabilities. *Learning Disabilities Research and Practice, 16*, 96-108.

Dykens, E. M., & Hodapp, R. M. (1997). Treatment issues in genetic mental retardation syndromes. *Professional Psychology: Research and Practice, 28*, 263-270.

Dykens, E. M., Hodapp, R. M., & Leckman, J. F. (1987). Strengths and weaknesses in the intellectual functioning of males with fragile X syndrome. *American Journal of Mental Deficiency, 92*(2), 234-236.

Eliason, M. J. (1986). Neurofibromatosis: Implications for learning and behavior. *Journal of Developmental and Behavioral Pediatrics, 7*(3), 175-179.

Evans, R. (1994). Phonological awareness in children with Down's syndrome. *Down Syndrome: Research and Practice, 2*(3), 102-105.

Fidler, D. J. (2005). The emerging Down Syndrome behavior phenotype in early childhood: Implications for practice. *Infants and Young Children, 18*, 86-103.

Fidler, D. J., Hepburn, S., & Rogers, S. (in press). Early learning and adaptive behavior in toddlers with Down syndrome: Evidence for an emerging behavioral phenotype? *Down syndrome: Research of Practice*.

Fuchs, L. S. (1995). *Incorporating curriculum-based measurement into the eligibility decision-making process: A focus on treatment validity and student growth*. Paper presented at the Workshop on IQ Testing and Educational Decision

Making, National Research Council, National Academy of Science, Washington, DC.

Fuchs, D., & Fuchs, L. S. (2005). Peer-Assisted Learning Strategies: Promoting word recognition, fluency, and reading comprehension in young children. *Journal of Special Education, 39*(1), 34–44.

Fuchs, D., Fuchs, L. S., Bahr, M. W., Fernstrom, P., & Stecker, P. M. (1990). Prereferral intervention: A prescriptive approach. *Exceptional Children, 56*(6), 493–513.

Fuchs, D., Fuchs, L. S. & Fernstrom, P. (1993). A conservative approach to special education reform: Mainstreaming through transenvironmental programming and curriculum-based measurement. *American Educational Research Journal, 30*, 149–177.

Fuchs, D., Mock, D., Morgan, P. L., & Young, C. L. (2003). Responsiveness-to-intervention: Definitions, evidence, and implications for the learning disabilities construct. *Learning Disabilities Research & Practice, 18*(3), 157–171.

Fuchs, D., Roberts, P. H., Fuchs, L. S., & Bowers, J. (1996). Reintegrating students with learning disabilities into the mainstream: A two-year study. *Learning Disabilities Research & Practice, 11*(4), 214–229.

Fuchs, L. S., Compton, D. L., Fuchs, D., Paulsen, K., Bryant, J., & Hamlett, C. L. (2005). Responsiveness to intervention: Preventing and identifying mathematics disability. *Teaching Exceptional Children, 37*, 60–63.

Fuchs, L. S., Fuchs, D. & Bishop, N. (1992). Teacher planning for students with learning disabilities: Differences between general and special educators. *Learning Disabilities Research & Practice, 7*, 120–128.

Fuchs, L. S., Fuchs, D., & Speece, D. L. (2002). Treatment validity as a unifying construct for identifying learning disabilities. *Learning Disability Quarterly, 25*(1), 33–45.

Gerber, M. M., & Semmel, M. I. (1984). Teacher as imperfect test: Reconceptualizing the referral process. *Educational Psychologist, 19*(3), 137–148.

Graham, S., & Harris, K. (in press). Improving the writing performance of young struggling writers: Theoretical and programmatic research from the Center on Accelerating Student Learning. *Journal of Special Education, 39*(1), 19–33.

Greenwood, C. R., Delquadri, J. C., & Hall, R. V. (1989). Longitudinal effects of classwide peer tutoring. *Journal of Educational Psychology, 81*(3), 371–383.

Hall, R. V., Delquadri, J. C., Greenwood, C. R., & Thurston, L. (1982). The importance of opportunity to respond in children's academic success. In E. Edgar, N. Haring, J. Jenkins & C. Pious (Eds.), *Mentally handicapped children: Education and training* (pp. 107–140). Baltimore: University Park Press.

Hodapp, R. M. (1996). Down syndrome: Developmental, psycheatric, and management issues. *Mental Retardation, 5*(4), 881–894.

Hodapp, R. M., & Dykens, E. M. (2001). Strengthening behavioral research on genetic mental retardation syndromes. *American Journal on Mental Retardation, 106*(1), 4–15.

Hodapp, R. M., & Freeman, S. F. N. (2003). Advances in educational strategies for children with Down syndrome. *Current Opinion in Psychiatry, 16*(5), 511–516.

Hodapp, R. M., Leckman, J. F., Dykens, E. M., Sparrow, S. S. Zelinsky, D. G., & Ort, S. I. (1992). K-ABC profiles in children with fragile X syndrome, Down syndrome, and nonspecific mental retardation. *American Journal on Mental Retardation, 97*(1), 39–46.

Hodgkinson, H. L. (1995). What should we call people?: Race, class, and the census for 2000. *Phi Delta Kappan, 77*, 173–179.

Ikeda, M. J., & Gustafson, J. K. (2002). *Heartland AEA 11's problem solving process: Impact on issues related to special education.* (Research Report No. 2002-01). Available from authors at Heartland Area Education Agency 11, 6500 Corporate Dr., Johnston, IA, 50131.

Jenkins, J. R., Jewell, M., Leicester, N., Jenkins, L., & Troutner, N. (1990, April). *Development of a school building model for education handicapped and at-risk students in general education classrooms.* Paper presented at the Annual Meeting of the American Educational Research Association, Boston.

Johnson, R. T., & Johnson, R. T. (1992). Implementing cooperative learning. *Contemporary Education, 63*, 173–180.

Johnson, R. T., & Johnson, R. T. (1994). *Learning together and alone.* Boston, MA: Allyn and Bacon.

Lesgold, A. M., & Resnick, L. (1982). How reading difficulties develop: Perspectives from a longitudinal study. In J. Das, R. Mulcahy & A. Wall (Eds.), *Theory and research in learning disabilities.* New York: Plenum.

Marcell, M. M., & Armstrong, V. (1982). Auditory and visual sequential memory of Down syndrome and nonretarded children. *American Journal of Mental Deficiency, 87*(1), 86–95.

McDade, H. L., & Adler, S. (1980). Down syndrome and short-term memory impairment: A storage or retrieval deficit? *American Journal of Mental Deficiency, 84*, 561–567.

McDermott, R. P., & Aron, J. (1978). Pirandello in the classroom: On the possibility of equal educational opportunity in American culture. In M. C. Reynolds (Ed.), *Futures of education for exceptional students* (pp. 41–64). Reston, VA: Council for Exceptional Children.

McIntosh, R., Vaughn, S., Schumm, J. S., Haager, D., & Lee, O. (1994). Observations of students with learning disabilities in general education classrooms. *Exceptional Children, 60*(3), 249–261.

McMaster, K. N., & Fuchs, D. (2002). Effects of cooperative learning on the academic achievement of students with learning disabilities: An update of Tateyama-Sniezek's review. *Learning Disabilities Research and Practice, 17*(2), 107–117.

McMaster, K. L., Fuchs, D., Fuchs, L. S., & Compton, D. L. (2005). Responding to nonresponders: An experimental field trial of identification and intervention methods. *Exceptional Children, 71*(4), 445–463.

Natriello, G., McDill, E. L., & Pallas, A. M. (1990). *Schooling disadvantaged children: Racing against catastrophe.* New York: Teachers College Press.

Neergard, L. (2004, April 30). *Working wonders on a few patients, lung cancer drug points way to tailored therapy.* The Tennessean, p. 5A.

North, K. N., Riccardi, V., Samango Sprouse, C., & Ferner, R., Moore, B., Legius, E., Ratner, N., & Denekla, M. B. (1997). Cognitive function and academic performance in neurofibromatosis 1: Consensus statement from the NF1 cognitive disorders task force. *Neurology, 48*(4), 1121-1127.

O'Connor, R. E. (2000). Increasing the intensity of intervention in kindergarten and first grade. *Learning Disabilities Research and Practice, 15,* 43-54.

O'Sullivan, P. J., Ysseldyke, J. E., Christenson, S. L., & Thurlow, M. L. (1990). Mildly handicapped elementary students' opportunity to learn during reading instruction in mainstream and special education settings. *Reading Research Quarterly, 25,* 131-146.

Paquier, P. F., van Mourik, M., Van Dongen, H. R., Catsman Berrevoets, C. E., Creten, W. L., & Stronks, D. L. (1999). Clinical utility of the Judgment of Line Orientation Test and Facial Recognition Test in children with acquired unilateral cerebral lesions. *Journal of Child Neurology, 14*(4), 243-248.

Peterson, P. L., & Clark, C. M. (1978). Teachers' reports of their cognitive process during teaching. *American Educational Research Journal, 15,* 555-565.

Pueschel, S. M., Gallagher, P. L., Zartler, A. S., & Pezzullo, J. C. (1987). Cognitive and learning processes in children with Down syndrome. *Research in Developmental Disabilities, 8,* 21-37.

Puma, M. J., Jones, C. C., Rock, D., & Fernandez, R. (1993). *Prospects: The congressionally mandated study of educational growth and opportunity: The interim report.* Washington, DC: U.S. Department of Education, Planning and Evaluation Service. (ERIC Document Reproduction Service No. ED 361 466)

Reschly, D. J., & Ysseldyke, J. E. (1995). School psychology paradigm shift. In A. Thomas & J. Grimes (Eds.), *Best practices in school psychology* (pp. 17-31). Washington. DC: National Association of School Psychology.

Riccio, C. A., & Hynd, G. W. (1992). Validity of Benton's Judgment of Line Orientation test. *Journal of Psychoeducational Assessment, 10*(3), 210-218.

Rosenfield, S., & Gravois, T. (1996). *Instructional consultation teams: Collaborating for change.* New York: Guilford.

Rosser, T. L., MD, & Packer, R. J., MD. (2003). Neurocognitive dysfunction in children with neurofibromatosis Type 1. *Current Neurology and Neuroscience Reports, 3,* 129-136.

Schumm, J. S., & Vaughn, S. (1992). Planning for mainstreamed special education students: Perceptions of general classroom teachers. *Exceptionality, 3*(2), 81-98.

Schumm, J. S., Vaughn, S., Gordon, J., & Rothlein, L. (1994). General education teachers' beliefs, skills, and practices in planning for mainstreamed students with learning disabilities. *Teacher Education and Special Education, 17,* 22-37.

Slavin, R. E., & Madden, N. A. (2000, September). Research on achievement outcomes of success for all: A summary and response to critics. *Phi Delta Kappan,* 38-40, 59-66.

Slavin, R. E., & Madden, N. A. (2003). *Success For All/Roots & Wings: Summary of research on achievement outcomes.* Center for Research on Education of Students Placed At Risk: Baltimore, MD.

Snart, F., O'Grady, M., & Das, J. P. (1982). Cognitive processing by subgroups of moderately mentally retarded children. *American Journal of Mental Deficiency, 86*(5), 465-472.

Snowling, M. J., Hulme, C., & Mercer, R. C. (2002). A deficit in rime awareness in children with Down syndrome. *Reading and Writing, 15*(5-6), 471-495.

Spector, J. E. (1992). Predicting progress in beginning reading: Dynamic assessment of phonemic awareness. *Journal of Educational Psychology, 84*(3), 353-363.

Speece, D. L., & Case, L. P. (2001). Classification in context: An alternative approach to identifying early reading disability. *Journal of Educational Psychology, 93,* 735-749.

Speece, D. L., Case, L. P., & Molloy, D. E. (2003). Responsiveness to general education instruction as the first gate to learning disabilities identification. *Learning Disabilities Research & Practice, 18,* 147-156.

Telzrow, C. F., McNamara, K., & Hollinger, C. L. (2000). Fidelity of problem-solving implementation and relationship to student performance. *School Psychology Review, 29*(3), 443-461.

Torgesen, J. K. (2000). Individual differences in response to early interventions in reading: The lingering problem of treatment resisters. *Learning Disabilities Research and Practice, 15*(1), 55-64.

Torgesen, J. K., Wagner, R. K., Rashotte, C. A., Rose, E., Lindamood, P., Conway, T., et al. (1999). Preventing reading failure in young children with phonological processing disabilities: Group and individual responses to instruction. *Journal of Educational Psychology, 91,* 579-593.

Vaughn, S., Linan-Thompson, S., & Hickman, P. (2003). Response to instruction as a means of identifying students with reading/learning disabilities. *Exceptional Children, 69,* 391-409.

Vaughn, S., & Schumm, J. S. (1994). Middle school teachers' planning for students with learning disabilities. *Remedial and Special Education, 15,* 152-161.

Vellutino, F. R., Scanlon, D. M., Sipay, E. R., Small, S. G., Chen, R., Pratt, A., et al. (1996). Cognitive profiles of difficult-to-remediate and readily remediated poor readers: Early intervention as a vehicle for distinguishing between cognitive and experiential deficits as basic causes of specific reading disability. *Journal of Educational Psychology, 88,* 601-638.

Yoder, P., & Stone, W. (2005). *Randomized comparison of two communication interventions for preschoolers with autism spectrum disorders.* Submitted for publication.

Zigmond, N., & Baker, J. (1994). Is the mainstream a more appropriate educational setting for Randy? A case study of one student with learning disabilities. *Learning Disabilities Research & Practice, 9*(2), 108-117.

Part
·III·

COGNITION AND COGNITIVE PROCESS

·10·

LEARNING THEORIES AND EDUCATION: TOWARD A DECADE OF SYNERGY

John Bransford
Reed Stevens
Dan Schwartz
Andy Meltzoff
Roy Pea
Jeremy Roschelle

Nancy Vye
Pat Kuhl
Philip Bell
Brigid Barron
Byron Reeves
Nora Sabelli

The LIFE Center: The University of Washington, Stanford University, & SRI, Inc.

LEARNING THEORIES AND EDUCATION:
TOWARD A DECADE OF SYNERGY

Our goal is to provide an overview of important aspects of human learning that are particularly relevant to educators. Doing so represents an exciting but difficult challenge because human learning is a highly complex topic. Different theories have emerged as researchers have focused on different kinds of learning. Some have focused on the acquisition of skills such as learning to type, write and read (e.g., Anderson, 1981; Bryan & Harter, 1897; LaBerge & Samuels, 1974; National Research Council [NRC], 2000). Others have focused on learning with understanding and its effects on schema formation and transfer (e.g., Anderson & Pearson, 1984, Judd, 1908; NRC, 2000; Wertheimer, 1959). Still others study the emergence of new ideas through interactions with other people and through "bumping up against the world" (e.g., Carey, 2000; Gopnik, Meltzoff, & Kuhl, 1999; Karmiloff-Smith & Inhelder, 1974; Papert, 1980; Vygotsky, 1978).

Learning theorists have also explored different settings for learning—including preschool, school, experimental laboratory, informal gathering spots, and everyday home and workplace settings—and they have used a variety of measurements of learning (e.g., neurobiological, behavioral, ethnographic). Furthermore, learning theorists work at time scales that range from milliseconds of processing time to life-span and even intergenerational learning (e.g., Lemke, 2001; Newell, Liu, & Mayer-Kress, 2001). Making sense of these different perspectives, and giving each their just due, is a challenging task.

In addressing this challenge, we have the good fortune of being able to build on the previous edition of the *Handbook of Educational Psychology* (Calfee & Berliner, 1996). For example, Calfee and Berliner (Chapter 1) provide an excellent introduction to the origins and goals of educational psychology. Mayer and Wittrock (Chapter 3) discuss research on transfer—a key concept for educators. Greeno, Collins, and Resnick (Chapter 2) examine important traditions of thought that have been used to analyze the processes of human learning—traditions such as the rationalist, empiricist, and sociohistorical. Greeno et al. contrast the different ways in which these traditions have viewed cognition and learning, and how each tradition has contributed to the design of educational

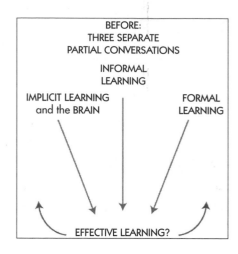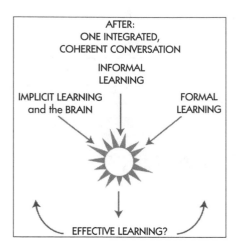

FIGURE 10.1. Toward an integrated sciences of learning.

practices. Greeno et al. also discuss major changes in how learning research has been conducted during the past 30 years—changes that involve moving from "laboratory only" studies to research conducted in complex environments such as classrooms, schools and districts (e.g., Brown, 1992; Cognition and Technology Group at Vanderbilt [CTGV], 2000; Collins, 1992; Design-Basel Research Collective [DBRC], 2003; Linn, Davis, & Bell, 2004; Resnick, 1987), plus learning "in the wild" in everyday settings (e.g., see Bransford & Heldmeyer, 1983; Lave, 1988; Resnick, 1987; Stevens, 2000a). These changes are fundamental to the discussion that appears later.

As indicated by the title of this chapter, our goal is to write with an eye toward the coming decade, which we believe will be a "decade for synergy." We do not attempt an exhaustive review of all learning research that is potentially relevant to education. Instead, we build on discussions by Greeno et al. and focus on several key traditions of thinking and research that have the potential to mutually influence one another in ways that can transform how we think about the sciences of learning, and how future educators and scientists are trained. We believe that the timing is right for targeted efforts toward synergy to become an explicit goal of educational researchers.

The three major areas of research that we explore include (1) implicit learning and the brain, (2) informal learning, and (3) designs for formal learning and beyond. As illustrated in Fig. 10.1A, these three areas have tended to operate relatively independently of one another. Researchers in each of these areas have attempted to apply their thinking and findings directly to education, and often the links between theory and "well grounded implications for practice" have been tenuous at best.

The goal of integrating insights from these strands in order to create transformative theories of learning is illustrated in Fig. 10.1B. The fundamental reason for pursuing this goal rests on the assumption that successful efforts to understand and propel human learning require a simultaneous emphasis on informal and formal learning environments, and on the implicit ways in which people learn in whatever situations they find themselves.

In the remainder of this chapter we explore examples of research from each of the three strands depicted in Fig. 10.1. We then suggest ways in which learning theorists of the future might draw on these traditions in order to create a more robust understanding of learning that can inform the design of learning environments that allow all students to succeed in the fast changing world of the 21st century (e.g., Darling-Hammond & Bransford, 2005; Vaill, 1996).

IMPLICIT LEARNING AND THE BRAIN

The first strand illustrated in Fig. 10.1 is implicit learning and the brain. *Implicit learning* refers to information that is acquired effortlessly and sometimes without conscious recollection of the learned information or having acquired it (Berry, 1997; Graf & Schacter, 1985; Reber, 1967; Seger, 1994; Stadler & Frensch, 1998). There are many types of implicit learning, but a common process may underlie all forms—the rapid, effortless, and untutored detection of patterns of covariation among events in the world in the absence of conscious, reflective strategies to learn (Reber, 1993). Our interest in implicit learning reflects the view that (a) it is implicated in many types of learning that take place in both informal and formal educational settings, (b) it encompasses skill learning, which plays a vital role in many other types of learning, and (c) it plays a substantive role in learning about language and people across the life span.

Implicit learning occurs in many domains. For example, it influences social attitudes and stereotypes regarding gender and race (Greenwald et al., 2002), visual pattern learning (DeSchepper & Treisman, 1996), motor response time tasks (Nissen & Bullemer, 1987), syntactic language learning (Reber, 1976), early speech learning (Goodsitt, Morgan, & Kuhl, 1993; Kuhl, 2004; Saffran, 2002), and young children's imitative learning of the tools/artifacts behaviors, customs, and rituals of their culture (Meltzoff, 1988b; Rogoff, Paradise, Mejía Arauz, Correa-Chávez, & Angelillo, 2003; Tomasello, 1999).

Moreover, a substantial portion of learning from media and technology is implicit. Only a minority of research about the effects of media and technology test purposive effects of messages, for example, formal classroom learning from instructional media (Mayer, Fennell, Lindsay, & Cambell, 2004) or the ability of television news to teach citizens about how candidates stand on political issues (Krosnick & Branon, 1993; Schleuder, McCombs, & Wanta, 1991). More commonly, media research examines effects that are indirect, involve automatic attentional processes, and are often beyond the conscious awareness of those processing the information. This includes the ability of media to determine the perceived importance of political issues (Iyengar & Kinder, 1987; Spiro & McCombs, 2004); learning about the appropriateness of social behavior in interpersonal relationships (Glascock, 2001; Larson, 2001); the influence of media on perceptions of social reality, for example, what people learn about the prevalence of crime (Shanahan & Morgan, 1999; Sparks & Ogles, 1990); learning from persuasive consumer messages that occurs subliminally (Petty, Priester, & Briñol, 2002; Trappey, 1996) or through frequent and implicit associations between people, places, and appeals (Chang, 2002; Invernizzi, Falomir, Manuel, Muñoz, & Mugny, 2003); learning about the personal qualities of prominent figures in politics and government based on how messages are framed (Benoit & Hansen, 2004; Iyengar & Simon, 1993) and on the visual structure (e.g., cuts, camera angles, use of motion sequences) used to present information (Mutz & Reeves, in press); and learning to control complex media such as computer games (Berry & Broadbent, 1988).

Across both live, face-to-face interactions and mediated interactions, the common conclusion is that people can learn patterned regularities without intending to do so and sometimes without being able to describe the patterns they have learned (though this is not always the case; see Buchner, Erdfelder, Steffens, & Martensen, 1997). In some instances, it can be shown that "trying to learn" patterns of covariation through explicit instruction actually impedes learning, underscoring the idea that implicit and explicit forms of learning are different (Howard & Howard, 2001). Studies also suggest that it may not be the material per se that distinguishes implicit from explicit learning, but how the material is presented to learners and encoded (Poldrack et al., 2001). Implicit learning has educational and even evolutionary value inasmuch as it enables organisms to adapt to new environments simply by being in them and observing and interacting with the people and objects encountered there (Howard & Howard, 2001). (We explore the idea of what it means to "be in an environment" in more detail in a later section, "Looking Toward the Future.")

The label *implicit learning* that we are using in this chapter is not meant to be an operationally defined category with necessary and sufficient conditions for inclusion and exclusion. We focus on two domains that are prototypical cases of implicit learning and which provide much food for thought—language learning (Kuhl, 2004; Kuhl, Tsao, & Liu, 2003; Saffran, 2003; Newport & Aslin, 2004) and learning about people, sometimes called "social cognition" (e.g., Flavell & Miller, 1998; Meltzoff & Decety, 2003; Ochsner & Lieberman, 2001; Taylor, 1996), with heavy emphasis on the former case. Our lifelong learning about language and people begins before kindergarten, and in some cases important foundations are established in the first year of life. In these domains parents are the first "teachers" and much is absorbed through spontaneous and unstructured play (Meltzoff, 2005).

For purposes of this chapter we explore three key hypotheses: (a) implicit learning plays an important role across the life span, starting very early in life; (b) research on language has discovered principles of learning that emphasize the importance of patterned variation and the brain's coding of these patterns, and these findings may illuminate other cognitive and social domains; and (c) principles uncovered through research in language and social learning raise questions about K-12 education and "oversimplified" curriculum design. We say more about this later. First we explore whether, how, and why studies of the brain and early learning inform broader issues in the science of learning and are important for educators to know.

What Does Brain Science Add to the Study of Learning?

Research that attempts to find correlations between brain and behavior has a long history, but work in this area has skyrocketed in the past several decades. The 1990s were dubbed "The Decade of the Brain" and produced advances in neuroscience techniques. Modern neuroscience can reveal learning in an alive, awake brain, detecting the impact of experiential learning *before it can be observed in behavior.* This is a change from studies in the 70s and 80s in which most knowledge of the brain came from the study of brains at autopsy. The study of a live brain "at work" is new, and is now being done in infants and children as well as adults.

The potential of new neural measures of mental activity were quickly noted by educators and policymakers. In 1996, the Education Commission of the States and the Dana Foundation held a conference entitled *Bridging the Gap Between Neuroscience and Education,* which brought together leaders in the two fields (Denver, Colorado, July 26–28, 1996). The conference sparked a heated debate. The gap between the neuron and the chalkboard was acknowledged as substantial— many agreed it was perhaps a "bridge too far" at that point in time—and scholarly articles and books resulted (e.g., Bruer, 1997, 1999; NRC, 2000; Gopnik et al., 1999).

Although excitement about advances in brain research is evident, it is useful for educators to pose a probing question: What, precisely, are the advantages of knowing which brain regions are activated over time and how they are associated with behavioral changes? Will brain studies *really* alter what we do in our schools?

The answer to that question is not straightforward (Bruer, 1997, 1999; NRC, 2000). Brain studies link neural underpinnings to behavioral function; they will help us understand learning. Altering what we do in classrooms is a step beyond this and will take much more than brain science. However, there are new research topics, for example, the effects of bilingual exposure on language, cognition, and mathematical learning, that should affect educational policy. That said, it is also important to understand limitations. Few, if any, neuroscientists think that brain science will, for example, generate a new science curriculum or tell us how to structure a high school student's day to optimize learning. Research in the future needs to combine educators and neuroscientists to study learning across settings—and this will take a great deal of collaborative work. We discuss this more in the section on the future.

Neurobiological studies do, however, provide crucial knowledge that cannot be obtained through behavioral studies, and this provides at least three justifications for adding cognitive neuroscience to our arsenal of tools for developing a new science of learning. First, a mature science of learning will involve understanding not only *when* learning occurs, but also understanding *how* and *why* it occurs. The how and why of learning are exposed if we discover its neural underpinnings and identify the internal mechanisms that govern learning across ages and settings. Second, neural learning often precedes behav-

ior (Tremblay, Kraus, & McGee, 1998), offering a chance for scientists and educators to reflect on what it means to "know" and "learn." Third, behaviors that appear similar may involve different neural mechanisms that have different causes and consequences. Better categorization of behaviors, according to neural function instead of the appearance of behavioral similarity, should allow the educational strategies and policies that affect learning to be usefully grouped in ways not obvious absent the study of brain function.

Learning theories of the future will embody both neural and behavioral aspects of learning, and both behavioral and brain-imaging methods are used by researchers engaged in Strand 1 research ("Implicit learning and the brain"). It is the premise of Strand 1 research that neither brain nor behavior trumps the other; the approaches are thoroughly complementary and not competitive. In the following discussion, we provide a few targeted examples that illustrate research on brain that raises important questions about understanding and optimizing learning.

Learning to Interpret Brain Data

Introducing neuroscience to learning science is challenging because, for some, biological constraints on common behaviors must be studied at an unfamiliar level of analysis. That's not where the complexity stops, however. Practically, researchers must also learn new methods that go with the new theories. There are a number of ways to measure brain activities. Examples include event-related potentials (ERPs), which track changes in the electrically evoked potentials measured on the surface of the scalp; fMRI (which tracks hemodynamic changes in the brain); and MEG (which tracks magnetic field changes in the brain over time). Each of these measures can be used to study learning.

It is especially important to note that valid inferences about brain processes often require a series of converging experiments rather than only one or two. In the language domain, learning of the basic building blocks—the consonants and vowels that make up words—is of interest because it develops early in infancy, it is resistant to change in adulthood (for example, people find it difficult to rid themselves of accents), and it reflects a "critical period" for learning. A thorough understanding of this process requires a programmatic research effort. In the case of speech perception, for example, the literature has progressed rapidly over the last 10 years (see Kuhl, 2000, for review). Learning induced changes in the brain involve biological processes that have many complicated and interacting pathways of regulation just like other biological processes. This is another reason why the "bridge" from neuroscience to education is difficult to build. Nevertheless, there are important conjectures from brain research that are relevant to educators' thinking, and selected examples are provided later.

Some Key Brain Findings and Their Importance

The Brain at Birth. It is a common misconception that each individual's brain is entirely formed at birth. This is not the case. Instead, experiences during development have powerful effects on the physical development of the brain itself (e.g., Greenough, Juraska, &Volkmar, 1979). One intriguing aspect of the human brain's development is the process of "pruning." In young children, the brain "overproduces" synapses that are then either maintained or removed as a result of experience. The process of synaptic overproduction takes place at different rates in different parts of the brain (Huttenlocher & Dabholkar, 1997). For example, in the primary visual cortex, the peak in synaptic density occurs early in life, whereas the process is more protracted in brain regions associated with higher cognitive functions. Neuroscientists speculate that pruning may provide an explanation for a range of developmental changes that occur in people; for example, in the area of language development, it has been found that very young children have the capacity to discriminate among more phonemes than they do as adults (Kuhl, 2004; Werker and Tees, 1984). It is tempting to think that synaptic overproduction accounts for children's early precocities, and that experience with a specific language— where some phonemes are not used—results in the maintenance of connections for those phonemes represented in the language, and loss of connections for those not represented. However, we are far from a conclusion on this claim; the underlying physiological mechanisms that account for our changing abilities to discriminate phonemes outside our native language are not well understood, although proposals do exist for future investigations (McClelland, 2001; McClelland, et al., 2002; Zhang, Kuhl, Imada, Kotani, & Tokura 2005).

Although synaptic development and subsequent "pruning" have received much attention in the press (perhaps because the reduction of synapses over time is counterintuitive), it is only one example among many that demonstrate changes in the brain during development. The next decade of research in neuroscience will focus on the relationship between behavioral development and brain development, further expanding the field of cognitive neuroscience. One thing has been established without a doubt—experiences helps sculpt an individual's brain. Brain development is not a product of nature or nurture exclusively, but is a complex interaction of both.

Assumptions About Critical Periods for Learning. For educators, the idea of rapid brain organization during the early years of life is important but can also lead to serious misconceptions (Bruer, 1999). For example, people often question whether children who spend their early years in understimulating environments will have fewer chances for future learning and development. The popular literature is filled with discussions of "critical periods" for learning, and the assumption persists that the ability to learn certain kinds of information shuts down if the critical period is missed, with detrimental effects on learning forever. Assumptions such as these sometimes cause teachers and parents to underestimate the abilities of students whose early years seemed less rich and more chaotic than others who come to school.

Brain research shows that the timing of critical periods differs significantly depending on whether one is discussing the visual, auditory, or language systems. Even within different systems, there is emerging evidence that the brain is much more plastic than heretofore assumed, and that the idea of rigid "critical periods" does not hold.

New studies by Kuhl and colleagues explored potential mechanisms underlying critical periods in early language development (e.g., Kuhl, 2004; Kuhl, Conboy, Padden, Nelson, & Pruitt, 2005). She introduced the concept of a *neural commitment* for learning language patterns. These recent neuropsychological and brain imaging studies suggest that language acquisition involves the development of attentional networks that focus on and code specific properties of the speech signals heard in early infancy, resulting in neural tissue that is dedicated to the analysis of these learned patterns. Early in development, learners commit the brain's neural networks to patterns that reflect natural language input. Kuhl's claim is that early learning both supports and constrains future learning. Early neural commitment to the phonetic units of a specific language supports the learning of more complex patterns, such as words, of that language. However, neural commitment to learned patterns also constrains future learning because neural networks dedicated to native-language patterns are incompatible with non-native patterns, and in fact may interfere with their analysis (Iverson et al., 2003). The concept of neural commitment is linked to the long-standing issue of a "critical" or "sensitive" period for language acquisition. If the initial coding of native-language patterns interferes with the learning of new patterns (such as those of a foreign language), because they do not conform to the established "mental filter," then early learning can limit later learning. The "critical period" thus depends on experience as much as time and is a *process.* Thus both maturation and learning determine the critical period. Maturation may "open" the period during which learning can occur, but learning itself may play a powerful role in "closing" the period (Gopnik et al., 1999; Kuhl, 2004).

The general point is that learning can produce neural commitment to the properties of the stimuli we see and hear. Exposure to a specific data set alters the brain by establishing neural connections that "commit" the brain to processing information in an ideal way for that particular input (e.g., one's first language but not for subsequent languages). Neural commitment functions as a "filter" that affects future processing (Kuhl, 1991; Kuhl, Williams, Lacerda, Stevens, & Lindblom, 1992; Näätänen et al., 1997). This results in highly efficient processing of learned material (Zhang et al., 2005). The most well studied example concerning the development of neural commitment is language, but it is only one of many.

Broadening this discussion, the neural commitment concept can be thought of as a neural instantiation of important dimensions of "expertise" in any domain. Expertise in many areas may reflect these kinds of filters on experience—filters that focus attention, and structure perception, thought, and emotions so that we work more efficiently. This focused efficiency simultaneously frees up our attention and energies to think creatively in other domains, and may also, in certain circumstances, limit our ability to think in novel ways within the area of expertise (e.g., Gopnik & Meltzoff, 1997). For example, learning algebraic principles or mastering the scientific method changes our filters (our concepts and theories), leading us to perceive the world in a new way. This learning alters the brain's future processing of information. A fundamental question is how the brain can form neural commitments while also maximizing our ability to stay open for adaptive change. This is an issue that receives more attention later when we discuss adaptive expertise.

New Learning and Existing Neural Commitments: Neuroplasticity.
In adulthood, second language learners have to work with committed brains to develop new networks. As years of research attest, babies are better at learning new languages than we are! Infants' systems are not yet thoroughly committed and are therefore capable of developing more than one "mental filter." For example, in a recent study, Kuhl and colleagues tested whether American 9-month-old infants who had never before heard Mandarin Chinese could learn the phonemes of Mandarin by listening to Chinese graduate students play and read to them in Mandarin Chinese (Kuhl, Tsao, & Liu, 2003). The study was designed to test whether infants can learn from short-term exposure to a natural foreign language.

In the experiment, 9-month-old American infants listened to four native speakers of Mandarin during 12 sessions in which they read books and played with toys. After the sessions, infants were tested with a Mandarin phonetic contrast that does not occur in English to see whether exposure to the foreign language had reversed the usual decline in infants' foreign-language speech perception. The results showed that infants learned during these targeted, live sessions, compared with a control group that heard only English. Indeed the American infants performed at a level that was statistically equivalent to infants tested in Taiwan who had been listening to Mandarin for 11 months. The study shows how readily young infants learn from natural language exposure at this age, apparently running computational algorithms on natural language that they hear delivered in a playful and social way (Kuhl et al., 2003).

Kuhl et al. (2003) designed a test to examine the degree to which infant language learning depends on live human interaction. A new group of infants saw and heard the same Mandarin speakers on a television screen (or heard them over loudspeakers). The auditory cues available to the infants were identical in the televised and live settings, as was the use of "motherese." If simple auditory exposure to language prompts learning, the presence of a live human being would not be essential. However, the infants' Mandarin discrimination scores after exposure to televised or audio-taped speakers were no greater than those of the control infants who had heard only English. These infants simply did not learn language in the TV or auditory-alone conditions. Further experiments clearly are needed to determine the factors contributing to the advantage provided by live/social interaction versus television or audiotapes. It may be due to the young age of the children, the domain of learning (language), or the limitations of the television display used in this experiment (e.g., it was not interactive TV). The strong interpretation of the findings is that infants may need a social tutor to learn natural language (and evolution may have prepared this), but clearly more work is needed before this strong claim can be accepted (Kuhl, 2003).

One reason social environments may enhance learning is that real social interactions provide more complex and variable training that highlights the critical parameters necessary in mastering a task. In this sense, the "complexities" of live interactions may be good for young infants, at least in certain circumstances. There are hints from other literature as well that initial learning that takes into account the full complexity of situations may make initial learning a little more difficult but ultimately improve transfer and generalization (e.g., Bransford & Nitsch, 1978; Simon & Bjork, 2002). There is also some fledgling evidence in the cognitive literature that "hybrid models" of instruction might enhance initial learning and subsequent transfer (e.g., Bransford & Nitsch, 1978). Appropriate social interactions may provide hybrid conditions because they present complexity in manageable proportions. There is much work to be done to understand these processes in more detail.

Even with social interaction, adults do not learn everything with ease, and language again provides a well-worked-out example. For instance, classic experiments show that even with extensive training, adults often do not learn foreign-language contrasts (see Strange, 1995, for review). Recent experiments, however, show that mimicking the features of infant-directed speech may help adult learners and those with language impairments. In studies of Japanese adults, McClelland and his colleagues (McClelland, 2001; McClelland et al., 2002), showed that learning increased when the /r/ and /l/ sounds were acoustically "stretched" to highlight the differences between the two instances. Tallal et al. (1996) and Merzenich et al. (1996) showed the same advantage when "stretched" acoustic instances were used to teach children with dyslexia to discriminate speech sounds. What is interesting about these cases is that infant-directed speech also exaggerates, literally "stretches," the acoustic features of native language when addressing infants; this is a universal feature of "motherese" across cultures (Kuhl et al., 1997). And infants whose mothers stretch the acoustic features of speech show better speech discrimination abilities (Liu, Kuhl, & Tsao, 2003). In other words, both first and second language learners are assisted by acoustically exaggerated speech. Kuhl (2000) hypothesized that the early highlighting of the acoustic features of speech helps establish the brain's initial mapping for speech; in adulthood, this stretching may also assist adults in going beyond their first language's neural maps (McClelland et al., 2002; Kuhl, 2000 for discussion). This is a key example where work concerning first learning in infancy can be extrapolated and used to inform formal learning and instruction in adults. The importance of understanding how to help people move beyond their current "comfort zones" of efficiency is also emphasized in a later section ("Designs for Formal Learning and Beyond").

Other features are also proving important to adult "retraining" with foreign-language stimuli. Early experiments on training utilized one talker's speech sounds. Training was highly successful, but there was virtually no generalization to novel cases by new talkers or new speech contexts (McClelland, 2001; McClelland, et al., 2002). Others have shown that learners do best with more complexity, and that optimal learning is produced when many talkers' sounds are presented during training (Pisoni et al., 1994). The newer research with adults again takes a lesson from infant learning; adults addressing infants and children vary speech to resemble multiple talkers, which appears to be helpful to language learning (Burnham et al., 2002; Kuhl et al., 1997; Liu et al., 2003).

Children's Implicit Learning From Other People: The Case of Imitative Learning

Other studies by brain and developmental scientists are also relevant to sciences of learning. One example that has increasingly attracted the attention of developmental psychologists, neuroscientists, evolutionary biologists, and those interested in robotics comes from children's learning from watching other people. This is a skill that is important both for the transmission of culture from parents to children and in peer-group learning. The topic of imitative learning has undergone a revolution in the past decade, as studies have revealed the ubiquitous nature of imitation among humans across the life span (e.g., Meltzoff, 2005; Meltzoff & Prinz, 2002). Research now shows that human beings are the most imitative creatures on the planet. Humans imitate from birth (Meltzoff & Moore, 1977), and the young child's capacity to learn from imitation outstrips that found in other primates such as chimpanzees and gorillas (Povinelli, Reaux, Theall, & Giambrone, 2000; Tomasello & Call, 1997; Whiten, 2002).

Recently, the importance of imitative learning has been given a boost by the discovery of "mirror neurons" that are activated whether a subject sees an action performed by another or performs the action themselves (e.g., Hurley & Chater, 2005; Meltzoff & Prinz, 2002). There are mirror neurons in the premotor cortex of the monkey (e.g., Rizzolatti, Fadiga, Fogassi, & Gallese, 2002; Rizzolatti, Fadiga, Gallese, & Fogassi, 1996), but monkeys do not imitate. So imitative learning involves more than the presence of mirror neurons, and neuroscientists are trying to determine the special, perhaps uniquely human abilities that support our proclivity for learning by observing others in the culture (see Meltzoff & Decety, 2003, for a review).

One possibility is that even a simple act of imitation is connected with perspective-taking and therefore is more of a social and collaborative activity than it first appears (Meltzoff, 2005). Consider that the model or teacher and child rarely see the world from the same perspective. The child sees her own body and own actions from a "first person" perspective; but we see others from a "third-person" perspective. Imitation requires that the child watch the adult and be able to "transform" what the adult does across differences in points of view, size, and sensory modality. Even a simple act of imitation requires facility in identifying with others and being able to "take their perspective."

This capacity for perspective taking may be fundamental to humans and important to a wide range of learning activities. Indeed, some have argued that the close neural coupling of self and other that undergirds imitation may also be implicated in such other distinctively human traits as social collaboration (Rogoff, 2003), the preservation of cultural practices involving implicit teaching and learning across generations (Meltzoff, 1988b, 2005; Tomasello, 1999), and empathy for others, where empathy is viewed as a kind of emotional perspective taking that requires us to stand in another's shoes (e.g., Jackson, Meltzoff, & Decety, 2005).

Regardless of these theoretical views, ample research shows that young children learn a great deal about people and cultural artifacts through imitation, and children are influenced not just by their parents, but also by their peers and what they see on television. For example, one study showed that toddlers learn from and imitate their peers in day-care centers (Hanna & Meltzoff, 1993). Another showed that preschoolers learn and remember novel actions they see on television (Meltzoff, 1988a). In that study, 2-year-olds watched an adult perform a novel action on TV. The children were not allowed to play with the object, but returned to the lab after a 1-day delay, and then were presented with the novel object for the first time. The results showed they duplicated from memory the specific act that they had seen on TV one day earlier.

Current research is exploring the conditions under which infants and young children can or cannot learn from TV. Recall that the Kuhl experiments (noted earlier) suggested that infants under 1 year old did not learn foreign speech sounds purely from watching TV. We want to know whether the difference between the Kuhl (no learning from TV) and Meltzoff (learning from TV) findings are due to a difference in age of the subjects (10-month-olds vs. 2-year-olds), the type of material being learned (speech vs. human actions on objects), or motivational/interactive factors—to name just a few possible variables. The outcome of this line of research is likely to be informative not only for theory, but for the booming market of media toys and educational materials for infants and preschoolers.

INFORMAL LEARNING

The second strand of research illustrated in Fig. 10.1 involves a focus on informal learning. The term *informal learning* has been used to refer to at least two distinct but overlapping areas of study, and we draw an initial distinction to make clear our use of the phrase within this chapter. Some researchers use the phrase to refer to learning that happens in designed, nonschool public settings such as museums, zoos, and after-school clubs. Others use the phrase *informal learning* to focus attention on the largely emergent occasions of learning that occur in homes, on playgrounds, among peers, and in other situations where a designed and planned educational agenda is not authoritatively sustained over time. For our current purposes, we will focus on the latter sense of informal learning, but later in the section we will revisit the general issue of how to define the domain of interest for informal learning research.

If we begin by looking outside of traditional schooling and focus our attention on children rather than adults, we note that 79 percent of a child's waking activities, during the school-age years, are spent in nonschool pursuits—interacting with family and friends, playing games, consuming commercial media, and so on (NRC, 2000). If we extend this calculation to the human life span, the portion of time spent outside of school, and therefore a potential source of informal learning, would be over 90 percent. Turning to adults specifically, we note that a great deal of what an adult learns in a lifetime is not "covered" in school (e.g., raising a child, saving and investing money wisely). And even with regard to what is "covered," it remains an open question to ask in what ways school-based learning substantively transfers to nonschool life in both occupational and every day contexts.

Informal learning is understudied when compared with learning in schools. Nevertheless, it is noteworthy that even the limited research that exists shows a strong divergence of views concerning the nature, effects, and value of informal learning (e.g., Smith, diSessa, & Roschelle, 1993). On one hand, informal learning has been championed as a romantic alternative to schools, where productive proto-forms of disciplinary knowledge and other forms of productive knowledge develop with minimal effort. A contrasting perspective argues that informal learning leads people to form naïve and misconceived ideas at odds with disciplinary knowledge (e.g., Driver, Guesne, & Tiberghien; 1985; McCloskey, 1983), and that these everyday "naïve" ideas need to be overcome to allow normative knowledge to develop. Another pair of contrasting perspectives on informal learning concerns the quality of the thinking and practices in which informal situations engage people. On one hand, some view informal learning situations as wellsprings of new knowledge and cultural production, especially among young people (e.g., Gee, 2003a, 2003b). On the other hand, some view informal situations as characterized by a lack of thinking and the consumption of a degraded popular culture (Healy, 1991). These diverging views, along with the sheer amount of time spent at informal learning, argue for more research to clarify these questions.

Despite these differences in views about informal learning, we feel that the learning tradition described in this section is essential to "the decade of synthesis" that was discussed earlier (see Fig. 10.1). With this goal in mind, we must remind ourselves that achieving a genuine synthesis of distinct traditions on learning is a formidable challenge that may be facilitated by articulating the history and principles that animate each tradition (see Astuti, Solomon, & Carey, 2004). With this in place, we will be in a better position to unearth conceptual collisions that can sharpen, challenge, and extend the respective traditions, as we do in the final section. Articulating these principles also creates opportunities to forge new transdisciplinary connections, in terms of new approaches both to research on learning and to new educational projects informed by such a synthesis.[1]

History of Informal Learning and Everyday Cognition Research

In this section we offer a thumbnail sketch of important researchers, projects, and institutions where informal learning research has been conducted. As we noted, the research tradition on informal learning has its origins mostly outside of mainstream educational psychology. Ethnographic work in anthropology established the perspective in the first half of the 20th century, by showing that while many non-Western societies lack formal schooling they do not lack meaningful, everyday learning. This poses the problem of how people learn without teaching, curricula, and schooling as conventionally understood in Western industrialized societies. As recently argued by McDermott (2001), an informal learning perspective is clearly present in Margaret Mead's *Coming of Age in Samoa (1928)* and is developed further in Mead's continuing work with Gregory Bateson. As McDermott (2001) notes,

Mead did not write much about learning theory, at least not directly; but it would be easy to reshape her ethnographies into accounts of what the people studied were learning from each other about how to behave, be it about adolescence in Samoa; gender among the Arapesh, awayness among the Balinese. Her version of the social actor, that is, the unit of analysis in her ethnographies, was in constant need for guidance from others. (p. 855)

A second line of work that provides theoretical roots for an informal learning perspective comes out of the sociological ethnography of Howard Becker and his colleagues. Beginning in the late 1950s and finding full expression in the 1960s and early 1970s, Becker and colleagues explored questions of how and what people learned, mostly in occupations, but also in clearly informal situations for which no curricula or schooling exists. Characteristic of the latter was Becker's influential article *Becoming a Marihuana User* (1953). Becker argued against an exclusively skill-based notion of learning that has been characteristic of both behaviorism (physical skills) and cognitivism (mental skills). Becker's critical addition was to show that learning also involved the development of particular *meanings* for a skill, which were learned among other community members:

Marihuana-produced sensations are not automatically or necessarily pleasurable. The taste for such experience is a socially acquired one, not different in kind from acquired tastes for oysters or dry martinis. The user feels dizzy, thirsty; his scalp tingles; he misjudges time and distances; and so on. Are these things pleasurable? He isn't sure. (p. 239)

Becker argues that becoming a marihuana user requires that one learn to experience the sensations of smoking as pleasurable, through the appropriation of a set of socially transmitted *meanings* of experience. What's important about this argument is that it focused on a type of learning that is often understood in terms of biophysical effects and the skills needed to produce these effects. Becker's analysis clearly shows that these skills are necessary but hardly sufficient; equally critical are the socially transmitted, gradually appropriated meanings for the experience.[2] Becker's view of how people acquire these meanings foreshadows the view that has come to be known as *guided participation* (Rogoff, Matusov, & White, 1996) and resonates with the focus on guidance in Margaret Mead's early anthropological studies, thus tracing a pair of interrelated concepts—*guiding* and *participating*—across nearly a century of studies of informal learning.

Becker and colleagues' studies of how people learn in occupations—what has been described as "the becoming a..." genre (Katz, 2001, p. 457)—have also been important for a number of reasons. First, these studies also brought significant attention to the peer-maintained informal cultures that arose among students in formal institutions—what might be called the informal properties of formal settings. Second, these were among the

---

[1] An alternative approach is when one tradition seeks to co-opt or swallow another whole. A good example of this approach, which we do not recommend, is well represented by Vera and Simon's (1993) claim that studies of situated action can be easily subsumed by a cognitivist symbol system approach.

[2] Bruner suggests that attention to the appropriation of meaning was intended to be part of the original agenda for the "cognitive revolution" but was shelved in the pursuit of a pure machine cognitivist paradigm (Bruner, 1990).

earliest studies to locate the development of identity as a dimension of learning (e.g., Becker & Carper, 1956). As we will describe later, the concept of identity has become central to understanding informal learning. When one is learning outside of school, it is as much about who one wants *to be* as what one demonstrably comes *to know*. Becker's studies of how people learned outside of formal schooling also led Becker to be among the first to explicitly seek to compare the different conditions under which learning in and out of schools takes place. Becker's provocation was that school, despite its labeled purpose, is often a "lousy place to learn anything in." Becker argued that it was the specific structural properties of how school is *typically* organized (cf. Tyack & Tobin, 1984, on the "grammar of schooling") when compared to other learning situations, such as on-the-job training, that made it lousy.

At about the same time Becker and his colleagues were conducting their studies on informal learning, a movement among some psychologists began to establish a "comparative psychology of cognition" (Cole & Bruner, 1971). In practice, this programmatic goal led to many studies of informal learning, both within non-Western cultures and within nonschooled activities in Western societies. The two most prominent contributors to this line of work at the time were collaborators Michael Cole and Sylvia Scribner.[3] For these psychologists, suspicions about the limited validity of psychological tests for understanding people's thinking led them to pursue a culturally sensitive methodology for studying cognition and learning (Cole, 1996). Because Anglo-American psychology confined itself rather rigidly to testing-based laboratory approaches at the time, Scribner and Cole looked to the work of Russian scientists on human learning and cognition for inspiration (Leont'ev, 1978; Luria, 1976; Vygotsky, 1962, 1978, 1987).

One foundational study that influenced the comparative tradition was *The Logic of Nonstandard English* by sociolinguist William Labov (1969). This study sought to challenge what Labov called a deprivation view and what has come to known as *the deficit hypothesis*: "[This view] rests on the assumption that a community under conditions of poverty [e.g., most ethnic minority communities] . . . is a disorganized community, and this disorganization expresses itself in various forms of deficit" (Cole & Bruner, 1971, p. 867).

Labov's specific focus was a purported deficit in speech practices of African-Americans attributed to them by prominent educational psychologists of the time.[4] What Labov's study showed was two-fold: (1) that although different, African-American speech practices obeyed just as strict a "logic" as middle-class European-American speech, and (2) that seemingly small changes in the context of eliciting speech, used to make research generalization about categories of people, can have a decisive impact on the kinds of performances displayed by research subjects *to research scientists*. To make this point, Labov presented the case of an African-American boy named Leon who when interviewed at school by a skilled African-American interviewer was taciturn and "nonverbal" in response to questions. Upon review of the recordings made, Labov and his colleagues decided to use this data as "a test of [their] own knowledge of the sociolinguistic factors which control speech" (Labov, 1972, p. 160). When the same interviewer spoke again with Leon, the interview was held in Leon's room at home, with Leon's best friend and a bag of potato chips as part of the conversational scene. In comparison with the first interview at school, there was a "striking difference in the volume and style of speech" (Labov, 1969). In this situation, Leon had a lot to say, competed for the floor, and spoke as much to his friend as to the interviewer—all strong contrasts with the first interview situation.

What links all of the studies that form a foundation of an informal learning tradition is an insistence on including *fieldwork* to document naturally occurring activities among its data collection strategies. A well-elaborated program of research that combined fieldwork and experimentation was led by Sylvia Scribner and is exemplified in Scribner's studies of learning and cognition among dairy workers (Scribner, 1997a, 1997b; Scribner & Fahrmeir, 1982). A number of important features of Scribner's work are relevant to our discussion here. First, Scribner substantially challenged the limited role that mainstream psychology gave to fieldwork. For mainstream psychologists, the only role that the field held for studies of cognition and learning was the generation of hypotheses that would then be tested in the laboratory.[5] Scribner argued that controlled experimentation—in the form of posed simulation tasks closely based on field observations—was valuable in exploring specific hypotheses about human cognition and activity, but that these claims still needed to be tested *again* in various fields of naturally occurring activity. A second feature of Scribner's studies was that she showed how physical and mental labor were both elements of what people learned as part of everyday work

---

[3]For a partial history of the LCHD (1972–1984) from Cole's perspective, see http://lchc.ucsd.edu/Histarch/lchc.history.html.
[4]Labov quotes representative passages from Deutsch, Jensen, and Bereiter.
[5]This conceptualization of the role of fieldwork remains common in contemporary accounts of research methods.

and that demands of the work environment substantially explained the distribution of these types of labor in daily work practice. Finally, Scribner showed the limited relevance of certain school-based mathematical learning to mathematical tasks that arose in dairy work, thus presenting an early challenge to the view that "formal" learning transferred to "informal" tasks.

In addition to the research on informal learning associated with Cole & Scribner's research laboratories (see Cole, Engeström, & Vasquez, 1997, for an overview; also, Tobach, Falmagne, Parlee, Martin, & Kapelman, 1997), the early 1980s brought work by anthropologists, sociolinguists, and a small subset of psychologists into closer conversation, both theoretically and methodologically. Jean Lave, whose research in the 1970s involved an explicit comparison of formal and informal mathematics among Liberian apprentice tailors, went on to lead a project (The Adult Math Project) in the 1980s studying how adults in everyday situations used mathematics. This project culminated in her influential 1988 book *Cognition in Practice*. Lave's research took aim at the cognitivist concept of transfer and argued against the view of everyday cognition as degraded or lesser form of cognition when compared with its formal counterparts. This is a move Scribner also made in her studies of dairy workers and has been made forcefully by Mike Rose in a series of recent studies looking at the complex learning and cognition involved in blue-collar work (Rose, 2004).

Among the other important researchers taking up questions of informal learning in the early 1980s were Geoffrey Saxe (1982), Catherine Snow (1982), Shirley Brice Heath (1983), Barbara Rogoff (Rogoff & Lave, 1984), and Carraher, Carraher, and Schliemann (1985). Regardless of disciplinary background, studies by all of these scholars employed fieldwork methods, often along with posed tasks, to explore the relations between informal learning and learning in schools.

Though this is just a thumbnail sketch, unforgivably partial, of informal learning research, it should serve to orient readers to some relevant landmarks in this terrain. And, although the number of studies of informal learning pale in comparison to those of formal learning, a range of insights and principles nonetheless distinguish informal learning research. These we describe next.

Principles and Basic Contributions of an Informal Learning Perspective

In this section, we describe some of the animating principles and contributions that have been made by studies of informal learning as they have sought to provide an account of the distinctive processes, conditions and outcomes of learning in human activities outside of formally prepared educational designs.

Clarification of the Role and Meaning of Context *in Learning.* Two related senses of *context* have been important in informal learning and everyday cognition research. The first sense of *context* has been a setting-based one, with settings such as "work," "play," "school," and "street" forming the bases for comparative analysis. A second sense of context is more analytically fine-grained and is often embedded within the first, with comparisons being made across activities, forms of participation, and types of interaction in the respective settings. Many researchers have explored, for example, how learning in homes and learning at school compare. Findings from these studies sort out in two basic ways, depending on the forms of knowledge and practice under consideration and depending on the research participants. On one hand, researchers sometimes find alignments between different activity contexts being compared. This is the case in Ochs, Taylor, Rudolph, & Smith's (1992) well-known study, which found that the dinner-table conversations of middle-class families served as settings for children to develop theory-making discourse practices common in some arenas of academic discourse practice. More typically, however, informal learning studies have found that the practices and knowledge of compared settings differ in important and consequential ways, thus leading to the view that what is important or necessary to learn in each setting differs accordingly.

An early influential study of this kind was Philips' (1983) study that compared the participation structures and speech practices of Native American children in school and in their cultural community contexts. Philips found that the adults in the respective contexts—the elders of the community and the teachers at school—differed in their expectations for children's speech and that these differences manifested themselves at the level of how turns at talk were allocated. This had the effect of leading the children's teachers, of a different cultural background, to misunderstand their abilities. Other informal learning studies that have compared contexts for learning include Saxe (1982), Carraher, Carraher, and Schliemann (1985), Heath (1983, 2001), deAbreu (1995), Hall and Stevens (1995), and Stevens (2000a).

Although studies of informal learning have been used to cast a critical eye on the traditional practices of schooling and to provide ideas for formulating alternative educational practices, the focal attention to context as a theoretical construct among informal learning researchers has led to a more general reinterpretation of school as a context, namely that *it is one*. As one interpreter of Lave's argument put it, many view school as "a neutral ground *apart from* the real world, in which things learned are later *applied in* the real world. . . . Lave's argument is rather that all learning is learning in situ, and that schools constitute a very specific situation for learning with their own cultural, historical, political, and economic interests; interests obscured by the premise that schools are asituational" (Suchman, 1995, p. 72; for related views, see Eckert, 1989; Willis, 1981).

New Ways to Understand **How** ***People Learn.*** Nearly all studies of informal learning highlight that learning happens without most of the apparatus of schooling such as intentional teaching, designed and sequenced curricula, and regular individualized knowledge assessments. This leads researchers to try to describe the means, pathways, and practices by which learning happens in nonschool settings. Many of the alternative formulations of how people learn play off concepts of apprenticeship (Lave & Wenger, 1991; Rogoff et al., 1996). Specific constructs include Lave & Wenger's idea of *legitimate peripheral participation*, which highlights the practices by which newcomers are gradually enculturated into participation in existing "communities of practice" and Rogoff et al.'s related notion of *intent participation*, in which learning is described as happening "through keen observation and listening, in anticipation of participation . . . [children] observe and listen with intent concentration and initiative, and their collaborative participation is expected when they are ready to help in shared endeavors" (Rogoff, 2003, p. 176). Understanding learning in this way attends to how individuals can learn without explicit teaching but through participation in a community's ongoing activities.

New Theoretical Constructs for **What Changes When** ***People Learn.*** In the machine cognitive era, psychologists typically viewed learning changes in terms of individual mental contents (e.g., concepts) or mental processes (e.g., reasoning strategies). Informal learning researchers have described other, though not necessarily incompatible, dimensions of change when people learn. For example, a number of informal learning researchers have described learning in terms of changing forms of *participation* in ongoing cultural activities (Engeström, Brown, Christopher & Gregory, 1997; Lave & Wenger, 1991; Rogoff et al., 1996). We noted earlier that other researchers have highlighted that learning involves changes in people's *identities*—who they understand themselves to be and who others position them to be (Becker, 1953; Holland, Lachicotte, Skinner, & Cain, 1998; Lave & Wenger, 1991; Nasir, 2002; Wenger, 1999). Others have highlighted that learning, even in activities typically understood as academic or theoretical, involves changes in *tool-mediated, embodied skills* (Goodwin,

2000; Rose, 2004; Stevens & Hall, 1997, 1998; Wertsch, 1998). Though no single definition of learning unites studies of informal learning, Hutchins' definition of learning as "adaptive reorganization in a complex system" (Hutchins, 1995) is a reasonable placeholder for a working consensus view and one that links it to other contemporary views on "adaptive expertise" described in the next section.

Promising Directions for Informal Learning Research

As documented in the previous sections, research on informal learning and everyday cognition has progressed in fits and starts. Yet, just as the past two decades of research on learning in school environments have reshaped our understanding of human cognition and influenced educational practice (NRC, 2000, 2005), there is reason to hope that sustained research focused on *learning in informal settings* can be similarly transformative in the coming decades. In the remainder of this section we describe some general contemporary issues worth pursuing.

Within-Context Studies. A good proportion of research in the everyday cognition and informal learning traditions documents adult activities within specific settings. In terms of settings where this research has been conducted, these studies range from what is conventionally viewed as "lowbrow" work (Beach, 1993; Rose, 2004; Scribner, 1997b) to "highbrow" professional work (Hall & Stevens, 1995; Hall, Stevens, and Torralba, 2002; Hutchins, 1995; Jacoby & Gonzales, 1991; Latour, 1995; Ochs et al., 1992; Stevens & Hall, 1998). Taken together, these studies expose the limitations of assumed hierarchies (i.e., low to high or concrete to abstract) and entrenched binary distinctions such as "mind/body," "expert/novice," and "theoretical/practical." A similarly extensive program of research on children's informal activities may hold the possibility of additional theoretical reframings of how we understand the basic categories of children's activities and development, such as, for example, the unexamined distinction between "play" and "work." At a more basic level, these studies can help us understand how the demands, problems, constraints, and affordances of particular contexts organize stable forms of learning and development within these contexts for children and how children organize their own learning in contexts. Even in anthropology, ethnographic description "of children and their agency" has been "sparse" (Das, 1998).

We have just described the ways that within-context studies have challenged a variety of common distinctions. Perhaps the most limiting distinction of all, and one in need of reformulation, is the distinction between "informal" and "formal." As we described earlier, this distinction serves as an entry point into our discussion of different traditions for studying learning and marks some rough differences between self-organized, emergent learning and learning occasioned by organized instruction and designed curricula. Nevertheless, the distinction is limiting because, as argued from many perspectives, a setting-based notion of context makes too many assumptions about the homogeneity of settings (i.e., that all activities in places called "schools" or "homes" are similar) and the homogeneity of experience within these settings for individual learners (Becker, 1972; Rogoff, Paradise, Mejía Arauz; Correa-Chávez, & Angelillo, 2003; Schegloff, 1992). For example, emergent learning may be as present in some school contexts as in out-of-school ones (Stevens, 2000a, 2000b). If we set aside the firm distinction between "informal" and "formal," the foundational issue becomes *the structuring properties of contexts for learning and development*, with the very nature of what constitutes a "context" remaining an open theoretical question (Goodwin, 1992).

One particular direction for further research is to identify and study *exceptional informal contexts* in which young people are in control of advancing their own learning, with the goal of understanding *how people advance their own learning* by assembling and coordinating heterogeneous resources (Barron, 2004, in review; Becker, 1972; Crowley & Jacobs, 2002; Lave & Wenger, 1991). As with any field-based scientific discipline, we need to better understand the distribution of "ecological niches" in which children are most actively engaged, and study how the problems that emerge in these nonschool settings make new knowledge necessary and certain kinds of thinking and action adaptive. We also have strong reason to believe that descriptions of mean tendencies are insufficient, because distributions of resources and practices vary widely by gender, ethnicity, and socioeconomic status, an issue of importance for translating findings from basic research to the educational goal of developing more equitable learning environments.

Across-Context Studies. Reframing the core theoretical issue in terms of contexts for learning and development, rather than in terms of an "informal/formal" distinction, points to one of the most understudied topics in this area, namely, *how people learn and develop as they make transitions across contexts.* Questions about transitions need to be studied along temporal dimensions that are both synchronic (i.e., as children move from school to home on a particular day[6]) and diachronic (i.e., as people move from postsecondary "training" to occupational work) dimensions. For example, research following this

perspective would include how children and their families manage transitions across home, school, and peer activities. A suggestive finding taking on this perspective comes from Gutierrez, who challenges a mismatch view of why children of poor backgrounds fare less well in school than their peers of middle-class backgrounds. The mismatch view holds that there is a close match between what children learn in middle-class homes and what they are asked to learn in schools, and a mismatch between what poor children learn at home and what they are asked to learn in schools. An alternative view comes from studying children moving across the contexts of school and home. This is the view that school reorganizes home life for *all* families, but that middle-class homes have greater resources (e.g., to hire tutors or parents with time to "help" with homework)[7] to respond to how school reorganizes home life (Gutierrez, 2005).

A better understanding of what people bring to, take from, and adapt across different contexts may also have important implications for how educators design the next generation of designed learning environments. To understand and facilitate extended meaningful subject-matter learning, we need to better understand the specific resources that young people bring to school from their informal activities as well as how school-based knowledge is utilized to further informal learning. One fruitful model for how to do this is represented in studies and educational initiatives organized around the concept of young people's "funds of knowledge" (González, Moll, & Amanti, 2005; see also Heath, 1983; Lee, 1995).

DESIGNS FOR FORMAL LEARNING AND BEYOND

The third strand of research illustrated in Fig. 10.1 involves the use of knowledge about learning to create designs for formal learning and beyond (where "beyond" includes ideas for school redesign and connections to informal learning activities), and to study the effects of these designs to further inform theoretical development. Most research in educational psychology falls within this strand of research. Several chapters in the original *Handbook of Educational Psychology* (Calfee & Berliner, 1996) provide particularly relevant information about designs for formal education (see especially Greeno, Collins, & Resnick, 1996; Mayer & Wittrock, 1996). Since publication of the *Handbook*, several additional research summaries have become available. These include *Being Fluent with Information Technology*

---

[6]A similar perspective may be fruitful for studying children's learning within school across the different subjects that they experience during the school day (Stevens, Wineburg, Herrenkohl, & Bell, in press).
[7]See McDermott, Goldman & Varenne (1984).

(1999), *How People Learn* (NRC, 2000), *Knowing What Students Know* (NRC, 2001), *Learning and Understanding* (NRC, 2002), *Learning and Instruction: A SERP Research* Agenda (NRC, 2003), *Internet Environments for Science Education* (Linn, Davis, & Bell, 2004), *How Students Learn* (NRC, 2005), and *Preparing Teachers for a Changing World* (Darling-Hammond & Bransford, 2005).

It is impossible to do justice to all the work in this area. We organize discussion around three design questions for creating effective learning environments (e.g., Wiggins & McTighe, 1997):

1. What do we want students to know and be able to do (and what configurations of attitudes, skills, and knowledge structures support these goals)?
2. How will we know if we are successful? For example, what kinds of assessments do we need?
3. What is known about the processes involved in helping students meet our learning goals?

Clarifying Learning Goals and the Processes That Support Them

During the past decade, progress has been made in defining standards for proficiency in areas such as reading, science, mathematics, and history. A number of publications and Web sites are available to help educators translate general national standards into particular ones at the state or local level, and to also link standards to curricula (e.g., National Council of Teachers of Mathematics [NCTM], 1989, 1995, 2000; NRC, 1996; Project Achieve at www.achieve.org).

Efforts to define standards represent an important advance in U.S. and international education. From a learning perspective, it is also important to understand the social and cognitive processes that support the kinds of competencies that we want students to develop. Studies of expertise provide valuable information about these competencies.

Lessons from Studies of Expertise

Researchers have explored the nature of the skills and knowledge that underlie expert performance (e.g., Ackerman, 2003; Alexander, 2003; Chi, Glaser, & Farr, 1988; Hatano & Osuro, 2003; Lajoie, 2003; NRC, 2000; Sternberg, 2003). This research is relevant to education *not* because we need to make everyone a world-class expert in some field. Instead, the research is important for understanding ways that knowledge, skills, attitudes, and thinking strategies combine to support effective

performances in a wide variety of domains. For example, Rose's *The Mind at Work* (2004) illustrates characteristics of everyday expertise that fit closely with characteristics of "academic" expertise.

Expertise and Noticing. One important finding from the expertise literature is that experts notice features of problems and situations that may escape the attention of novices (e.g., see Chase & Simon, 1973; Chi, Glaser & Rees, 1982; deGroot, 1965). They therefore "start problem solving at a higher place" than novices (deGroot, 1965).

The fact that expertise affects noticing has a number of important educational implications. One is that merely showing novice students videos of experts doing things does not guarantee that the novices notice all the relevant features (e.g., Michael, Klee, Bransford, & Warren, 1993). Second, the idea that what we learn depends in part on what we notice highlights the need to clarify what it means to "be in" a situation. For example, peoples' sensitivity to noticing can affect their "sense of disequilibrium" (Feuerstein, Rand & Hoffman, 1979; Piaget, 1964), which in turn can trigger "fault driven" learning strategies (e.g., Van Lehn, 1990). If people fail to notice subtle examples that create disequilibria, they do not experience the need to attempt to change their views.

Expertise and Knowledge Organization. Research on expertise also provides important information about knowledge organization. Experts' knowledge is much more than a list of disconnected facts about their disciplines. Instead, their knowledge is connected and organized around important ideas of their disciplines, and it includes information about conditions of applicability of key concepts and procedures. The latter information helps experts know when, why, and how aspects of their vast repertoire of knowledge and skills are relevant in any particular situation (see Chi et al., 1988; NRC, 2000, Chapter 2).

Courses are often organized in ways that fail to develop the kinds of organized knowledge structures that support activities such as effective reasoning and problem solving. For example, texts often present lists of topics and facts in a manner that has been described as "a mile wide and an inch deep" (e.g., NRC, 2000). This is very different from focusing on the "enduring ideas of a discipline" (Bruner, 1960). Wiggins and McTighe (1997) argue that the knowledge to be taught should be prioritized into categories that range from "enduring ideas of the discipline" to "important things to know and be able to do" to "ideas worth mentioning." Thinking through these issues and coming up with a set of "enduring connected ideas" is an extremely important aspect of educational design (e.g., Bransford, Vye, Bateman, Brophy, & Roselli, 2004; Diller, Roselli, & Martin, 2004; Harris, Bransford & Brophy, 2002).

Expertise and Teaching. Information about relationships between expert knowledge and teaching abilities is especially important for thinking about instruction. Teachers need considerable content knowledge in order to answer a wide range of content questions that arise from the problems that students confront. Teachers who don't understand their subject matter will often have difficulty answering these questions. A potential downside to a great deal of knowledge about subject matter is that this information has beome so tacit and intuitive that experts lose sight of what it was like to be a novice. Nathan, Koedinger, and Alibali (2001) use the term *expert blind spots* to indicate that experts are often blind to the fact that much of their subject matter knowledge has moved from explicit to tacit and hence can easily be skipped over in instruction (Brophy, 2001). Shulman (1987) explains that effective teachers need to develop "pedagogical content knowledge" that goes well beyond the content knowledge of a discipline (see also Hestenes, 1987). It includes an understanding of how novices typically struggle as they attempt to master a domain and an understanding of strategies for helping them learn (see Grossman, Schoenfeld, & Lee, 2005).

Adaptive Expertise

Many researchers suggest that it is important to differentiate "routine expertise" from "adaptive expertise" (e.g., Alexander, 2003; Hatano & Inagaki, 1986; Hatano & Osuro, 2003). Both routine experts and adaptive experts continue to learn throughout their lifetimes. Routine expertise involves the development of a core set of competencies that can be applied throughout one's life with greater and greater efficiency. In contrast, adaptive expertise involves the willingness and ability to change core competencies and continually expand the breadth and depth of one's expertise. This often requires people to leave their current " comfort zones" and venture into areas where they must function as "intelligent novices" who often struggle initially in order to learn new things (e.g., Brown, Bransford, Ferrara, & Campione, 1983; Bruer, 1993). It seems likely that most people function as routine experts in some parts of their lives and as adaptive experts in others.

This restructuring of core ideas, beliefs, and competencies can be a highly emotional experience (e.g., Gopnik

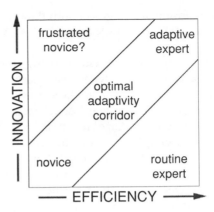

FIGURE 10.2. Two dimensions of adaptive expertise.

& Meltzoff, 1997) and may reduce people's efficiency in the short run but make them more flexible in the long run. For example, a tennis player may take lessons and be told that he is gripping the racket incorrectly. In order to reach a new level of performance, he will have to unlearn that behavior and take the time to learn a new one. In short, he'll have to get worse in order to get better in the long run, what some psychologists have called "regression in the service of development" (Bever, 1982). In the leadership literature, similar regressions are often referred to as the "implementation dip" that frequently accompanies attempts to move away from old efficiencies and try something new (Fullan, 2001, 2003). Issues of learning at the level of company strategies for product development also require such adaptive expertise for survival, as Christensen (1997) writes about in *The Innovators' Dilemma*[8] for the hard-disk storage industry, which has repeatedly been reborn with the inventions of new approaches rather than by making previous approaches more efficient.

Two Dimensions of Adaptive Expertise. Recently, some have suggested that the concept of adaptive expertise involves at least two major dimensions: namely, processes that lead to *innovation* or invention and those that lead to *efficiency* through well-practiced routines (e.g., Schwartz, Bransford, & Sears, 2005). These two dimensions are illustrated in Fig. 10.2.

The horizontal dimension in Fig. 10.2 emphasizes efficiency; the vertical dimension emphasizes innovation. Sometimes these two dimensions are characterized as mutually exclusive ends of a continuum (e.g., high and low road transfer, Salomon & Perkins, 1989). However, because there are different processes involved, they are not necessarily exclusive of one another. Adaptive experts, for

---

[8]http://www.businessweek.com/chapter/christensen.htm

example, are presumably high on both dimensions (e.g., Gentner et al., 1997; Hatano & Inagaki, 1986; Wineburg, 1998).

It is noteworthy that different theorists and theoretical traditions can be represented by particular dimensions of Fig. 10.2. For example, Thorndike's classic studies, as well as the work of modern-day "direct instruction" advocates (e.g., Bereiter & Engelmann, 1966; Engelmann, 1992), provide examples of work on the efficiency dimension of expertise. The theories of Dewey, Piaget, and Vygotsky include principles that move one closer to the innovation dimension, although not necessarily. For example, Vygotsky's "zone of proximal development" could be applied to goals of either efficiency or innovation. Figure 10.2 reminds us that different dimensions of learning may exist.

Some educators, in contrasting theorists such as Dewey versus Thorndike, have asked, "Who is right?" The representation of adaptive expertise in Fig. 10.2 suggests that it may be more fruitful to ask instead how these different theorists and traditions can help us learn how people can become *both* efficient and innovative so that they can continually adapt to change.

Exploring What Success Looks Like

Central to the goal of helping students achieve important learning outcomes is to clarify what success looks like (e.g., Wiggins & McTighe, 1997). This is important both for issues of summative assessment (seeing how students perform at the end of some course or program of study) and formative assessment (creating measures that provide feedback to students and teachers plus opportunities for revision that speed learning progress over time; for example, see NRC, 2001; Darling-Hammond & Bransford, 2005). Vygotsky provides an excellent example of the need for both summative and formative assessments of progress:

Like a gardener who in appraising species for yield would proceed incorrectly if he considered only the ripe fruit in the orchard and did not know how to evaluate the condition of the trees that had not yet produced mature fruit, the psychologist who is limited to ascertaining what has matured, leaving what is maturing aside, will never be able to obtain any kind of true and complete representation of the internal state of the whole development. (1934/1987, p. 200)

As noted earlier, design theorists such as Wiggins and McTighe (1997) emphasize the importance of aligning formative and summative assessments with one's learning goals. This might sound obvious, but it is much trickier to accomplish than first meets the eye—especially if the idea of "adaptive expertise" becomes an important goal for education in the 21st century.

Assessments of Efficiencies Versus Innovation

A number of researchers suggest that typically used assessments provide useful yet incomplete pictures of the kinds of skills, knowledge, and attitudes needed for success in the 21st century. In particular, if we return to the adaptive expertise dimensions shown in Fig. 10.2, there is a concern that most of today's assessments tend to be "efficiency" assessments. They are sensitive to well-learned routines and schema-driven processing but typically fail to capture the issues of flexibility that are important components of current thinking about the nature of adaptive expertise.

Efficiency assessments fit with (tacit or explicit) theories of transfer that focus on people's abilities to directly apply the procedures and schemas learned in the past to new problems and settings (e.g., Bereiter & Scardamalia, 1989, 1993; Bransford & Schwartz, 1999; Schwartz, Bransford & Sears, 2005). The expertise literature shows very clearly that well-established routines and schemas are an important characteristic of expertise. These allow people to free attentional resources that enable them to notice and deal with information that would overwhelm novices (e.g., beginning readers often have such problems with decoding fluency that they cannot attend to the meaning of what they read). Direct application theories of transfer typically involve tests of "sequestered problem solving" where people have access to what is currently "in their heads" (Bransford & Schwartz, 1999). The ability to directly and efficiently apply previously acquired skills and knowledge is important in many circumstances. If students have been trained to drive a car or fly a plane, for example, we want them to transfer directly from training to action. If they have to stop to read a driver's manual, or keep practicing parking by bumping other cars and learning from the experience, that's not a good outcome.

Nearly all summative measures such as standardized tests are "direct application" and "sequestered problem solving assessments." Many new variations on standardized testing such as "performance assessments" and "free response" items" (designed to go beyond multiple choice questions) are still mainly sequestered problem solving (SPS) assessments. Some argue (Bransford & Schwartz, 1999; Schwartz, Bransford & Sears, 2005) that SPS conceptualizations of transfer and assessment are responsible for much of the pessimism about evidence for transfer (e.g., Detterman & Sternberg, 1993). Equally if not more importantly, when instructional programs are assessed by traditional assessments, they tend to get reduced to a "teach for efficiency" profile because this is an effective way to ensure good outcomes on typical tests. This is often true even for "thinking skills," "problem solving," and "creativity" courses, where SPS assessments often provide an impetus to teach in ways that prepare people for fixed sets of problem types that appear on subsequent tests (e.g., Bransford, Arbitman-Smith, Stein, & Vye, 1985; Schoenfeld, 1985).

Beyond Efficiency Measures. Research conducted during the past 5 years has spawned a wide variety of new ways to think about transfer (e.g., Mestre, 1994; Mestre, Thaden-Koch, Dufresne & Gerace, in press). One alternative to a "direct application view of learning and transfer" emphasizes people's "preparation for future learning" (PFL). Here the focus shifts to assessments of people's abilities to *learn* in knowledge-rich environments. When organizations hire new employees, they don't expect them to have learned everything they need for successful adaptation. They want people who can learn, and they expect them to make use of resources (e.g., texts, computer programs, social networks of friends, and new colleagues) to facilitate this learning. The better prepared people are for future learning, the greater the transfer (in terms of speed and/or quality of new learning). Examples of ways to "prepare students for future learning" are explored in Schwartz and Bransford (1998), Bransford and Schwartz (1999), Schwartz and Martin (2004), Martin and Schwartz (2005), and Spiro, Vispoel, Schmitz, Samarapungavan, and Boeger (1987).

The PFL perspective is different from the older (but still important) learning-to-learn literature because the PFL's primary focus is not on the existence of a set of general learning and memory skills (e.g. uses of mnemomic techniques) that are content free. The expertise literature (Chi et al., 1988; NRC, 2000) shows clearly how strategies and knowledge are highly interdependent. Broudy (1977) provides an example: "The concept of bacterial infection as learned in biology can operate even if only a skeletal notion of the theory and the facts supporting it can be recalled. Yet, we are told of cultures in which such a concept would not be part of the interpretive schemata" (p. 12). The absence of an idea of bacterial infection should have a strong effect on the nature of the hypotheses that people entertain in order to explain various illnesses, and hence would affect their abilities to learn more about causes of illness through further research and study, and the strategies one uses in order to solve new problems.

One of the implications of a switch from SPS to PFL thinking links to Norman's (1993) work on designs that

"make us look smart" versus the opposite. Many SPS assessments of learning may make people look much less smart than is actually the case. For example, televised interviews with recent Harvard graduates revealed serious misconceptions about the cause of the seasons. Some believed that the cause of the seasons was dependent on how close the earth was to the sun, and others thought that clouds caused the seasons. By this assessment, their Ivy League education seemed useless. But this would be a severe misdiagnosis. If these students cared to learn about the cause of the seasons, there is little doubt they would be more prepared to do so than most young adults who never went to college. Ideally, preparation for future learning (PFL) assessments include opportunities for people to try out hunches, receive feedback, and attempt to revise based on the feedback. In contrast, typical tests provide few opportunities for feedback and revision— the only option is to provide one's initial thoughts with no opportunities to test them and revise.

The idea that people may look better on PFL than SPS assessments does not imply that educators should use PFL assessments so they can be more satisfied with the quality of education. Rather, the implication is that SPS assessments can lead people to make incorrect decisions about the quality of educational experiences. Schwartz, Bransford, and Sears (2005) provide a number of examples of how PFL assessments reveal the effects of educational experiences whose benefits are invisible when standard SPS measures of assessment are used. A number of different research groups are currently exploring innovative ways to measure adaptive expertise (Crawford, Riel, & Schlager, 2005; Hatano, 2005; Hodge & Brophy, 2005; Martin, 2005; Petrosino, 2005; Schwartz, Blair, Davis, Chang, & Hartman, 2005; Walker, 2005).

Research on Instructional Strategies for Achieving Important Goals

Principles of learning have largely emphasized the development of routine expertise, where people become faster and more accurate at solving recurrent problems. For example, a great deal of current learning research is based on cognitive theories that emphasize procedures, scripts, and schemas (for definitions and examples see Anderson & Pearson, 1984; J. Anderson, 1976; Black and Bower, 1980; Bransford & Johnson, 1972; Schank & Abelson, 1977). These are very important for allowing people to solve particular sets of problems more efficiently. A great deal of the instruction in schools attempts to help students acquire schemas of particular problem types in order to increase problem solving efficiency by turning non-routine problems into routine problems. An example involves problem types that take the form: *"Jim's parents live 60 miles away. He drove to their house at 60 mph and returned at 40 mph due to fog. What was his average speed?"* Most people simply say 50 mph—not realizing that Jim spends a longer amount of time going the slower speed so the average must be less than 50. There are a variety of problems of this type. When people are helped to acquire schemas that allow them to identify particular problem types, they are much less likely to get tripped up when later encountering similar examples.

Studies by Gick and Holyoak (1980, 1983) and others (e.g., Adams et al., 1988; Lockhart, Lamon, & Gick, 1988; NRC, 2000, Chapter 3) provide important information about learning conditions required to make "schema transfer" work (e.g., sufficient degrees of initial learning, applications of abstract concepts in a variety of different contexts, transfer appropriate processing). The acquisition of well-organized and fluently accessed procedures, scripts, and schemas is extremely important for effective performance—otherwise people are overwhelmed by attentional demands (e.g., see Bereiter & Scardamalia, 1993; NRC, 2000, Chapters 2 and 3). Learning these procedures and concepts "with understanding" typically provides better guidance for future actions than simply learning them by rote (e.g., NRC, 2000, 2005).

Beyond Schema-Based Applications. We argued earlier that an emphasis on innovation often includes the need to "let go" of previously acquired knowledge and skills and that this can have emotional consequences. This suggests that efficiency-oriented instruction that turns nonroutine into routine problems may need to be supplemented with different kinds of instruction that allow students to actively engage in inquiry and accept the emotional consequences of ambiguity and disconfirmation.

The conceptual change literature provides valuable information about the importance (and difficulties) of helping people resist over assimilation and change how they think (e.g., Carey, 2000; Gopnik et al., 1999; NRC, 2005). An emphasis on adaptive expertise reminds us that conceptual change is often needed in all areas of life. Indeed, failures to restructure our approaches to everyday social situations may frequently have more personal consequences than failures to restructure aspects of our scientific thinking (unless we are scientists dealing with a particular area of inquiry). For example, a person can live with the misconception that "the earth is hotter in the summer because it is closer to the sun." For most people this will not be life threatening or ruin their careers. However, failures to restructure our thinking in social settings often result in problematic actions. In the business literature, failures to change strategies in new contexts are often described as being due to "the tyranny of success"

(Robinson & Stern, 1997). People try the same thing that worked last time, but because the context is changed the old strategies no longer work. A simple example is a relatively new employee who gets along with others well and loves to engage in "around the water fountain" chats that provide important information about ways to improve the company. Then the employee is promoted to manager and all his colleagues treat him differently; his casual "around the water cooler" conversations no longer work for getting relevant information. Unless the new manager reinvents his way of gathering information, he will have a difficult time staying up to date.

Examples of ways to increase students responsive to innovation include metcognitively rich activities that engage them in (a) "knowledge building" rather than merely "knowledge telling" (Scardamalia & Bereiter, 1991), and (b) systematic inquiry with an emphasis on theory building and disconfirmation (e.g., Karmiloff-Smith & Inhelder, 1974/1975) rather than simply "following procedures for how to find some result" (e.g., NRC, 2005).

Some argue that innovation and change are facilitated by beginning instruction with "advance disorganizers" (e.g., Roediger, see Shaughnessy, 2002) rather than "advance organizers" (e.g., Ausubel, 1960). For example, students may first be asked to grapple with issues and try to solve them, which sets the stage for learning from and appreciating the kinds of insights developed over decades and centuries by experts in various disciplines. As an example, researchers have demonstrated the value of providing problem-solving and analysis experiences that create "times for telling" and help people resist overassimilation (e.g., Schwartz & Bransford, 1998; Schwartz & Martin, 2004; Schwartz, Bransford & Sears, 2005). This reverses the typical efficiency paradigm, which provides explicit problem-solving instruction followed by application problems at the end of the lecture or book chapter.

Being Innovative in Order to Increase Efficiency. Some researchers have attempted to design "working smart" environments that promote innovation in order to increase efficiency (Vye et al., 1998). Students learn about the general goal of efficiently solving a future set of *recurring* (quasi-repetitive) problems. In preparation for meeting this goal, they are encouraged to adopt, adapt, and invent "smart tools" that can help them work efficiently. Graphs, charts, spreadsheets, computer simulations, social networks, norms for distributed expertise, and a host of other resources are candidates for "working smart" (e.g., Bransford et al., 2000; Vye et al., 1998; Zech et al., 1998) by leveraging "distributed intelligence" (Pea, 1993). Working smart assessments combine the dimensions of innovation and efficiency shown in Fig. 10.2

LOOKING TOWARD THE FUTURE

How can work in the three research strands discussed earlier (see Fig. 10.1) be leveraged to move the field toward "a decade of synthesis"? By *synthesis*, we do not mean that all three of the research strands discussed previously will merge into one grand "melting pot" theory that eliminates the unique perspectives of each of them. Instead, we think that these strands can inform one another and, in the process, create more coherent and useful theories that better illuminate how, when, where, and why people learn. Examples of ways to accelerate collaboration are provided later.

Sharing Methodologies

One important area of connection among strands involves cases where their respective methodological strengths can be leveraged to increase the quality of research that is conducted. We discuss two examples—many more are possible as well (see Astuti, Solomon, & Carey, 2004).

Combining Experimental and Control Designs with Ethnographic Analyses. An example of sharing methodologies involves efforts by several researchers to combine the neuroscience, linguistic, and social-cognitive expertise of Strand 1 (implicit learning and the brain) with the use of fine-grained ethnographic analysis of social interactions that is characteristic of research in Strand 2 (the informal learning tradition).

As noted in Section 2, work by Kuhl and colleagues found that exposing American infants to play situations involving Chinese speakers enabled the American children to maintain their abilities to differentiate Chinese sounds, instead of losing this ability as is normally the case. However, this worked only under conditions where there was interactive play between the children and live Chinese speakers. This maintenance did not occur when the Chinese speakers were shown via television, despite the fact that the media could be considered to present "supernormal" stimuli with beautiful records of the facial expressions and lip movements by the mentors as they talked in Chinese.

Work in progress will replicate the previous study (this time with Spanish as the new language) and add researchers from the informal learning with expertise in social interaction analysis. The goal is to provide information about the relationships between the quality of child–mentor interactions and the quality of learning. Interestingly, issues about the kinds of video records needed for this kind of analysis had to be addressed in order to develop this research collaboration. This is a good example of ways that implicit learning and informal learning researchers can both benefit from collaborative work.

Exploring Reasoning in Everyday Versus Laboratory Settings. A second example of potential benefits of studying the same or similar topic from the perspective of between different research strands involves the conjecture that children often seem to employ sophisticated arguments in everyday, informal settings, yet may have difficulty constructing scientific arguments in the classroom and in the laboratory (e.g., Bell, 2004; Bell & Linn, 2000). Can in-depth understanding of children's out-of-school linguistic competencies with argument directly inform the design of formal science instruction where students learn through scientific argumentation and debate? Do laboratory studies of children's knowledge of reasoning mispredict their everyday argumentation and thinking? And if so, why? These kinds of questions can be most directly explored through a coordination of ethnographic, lab-based, and classroom intervention research. An exploration of these kinds of questions seems important and fruitful to explore in order to better understand the everyday competencies with argument that children develop in different contexts, to refine lab-based protocols for gauging children's theory of mind, and to improve the design of learning environments for scaffolding argumentation.

Perspectives on People Knowledge and the Social Brain

Researchers from all three of the strands discussed earlier are beginning to explore implications of the idea that people—from infancy to adulthood—seem to naturally pay attention to other people and to learn from them. For example, Strand 1 researchers note that human children are socially attuned from birth—infants are particularly interested in human faces and voices and learn a great deal through observing and imitating the behaviors, customs, and use of technologies in their culture (e.g., Gopnik et al., 1999; Meltzoff, 2005). Similarly neuroscientists are beginning to tackle higher-order questions, such as the brain bases of empathy in adults (Jackson et al., 2005) and cooperative learning versus competition (Decety, Jackson, Sommerville, Chaminade, & Meltzoff, 2004).

Informal learning researchers note how groups where people know one another function differently from groups of relative strangers. Experimental research has shown that collaboration can lead to better problem solving and learning than individual work (Barron, 2000; Johnson & Johnson, 1981; Stevens & Slavin, 1995).

Cognitive researchers have also been concerned with explaining why groups outperform individuals, and several cognitive mechanisms have been proposed and empirically documented. These include opportunities to share original insights (Bos, 1937), resolve differing perspectives through argument (Amigues, 1988; Phelps & Damon, 1989), explain one's thinking about a phenomenon (King, 1990; Webb, Troper, & Fall, 1995), provide critique (Bos, 1937), observe the strategies of others (Azmitia & Montgomery, 1993), and listen to explanations (Coleman, 1988; Hatano & Inagaki, 1991; Webb, 1989).

Detailed video analysis of interactions has revealed that in group learning situations, capitalizing on collective knowledge is both a social and a cognitive endeavor, and that the quality of the conversations and nature of shared engagement mediates how much is learned (Barron, 2003). Other experimental research has demonstrated that friends have better conversations during problem-solving activities than acquaintances, and this translates into more learning for individuals. (e.g., Azmitia & Montgomery, 1993; Miell & McDonald, 2000). Friends are more likely to elaborate and extend the ideas of their partners. They also talk more and offer more ideas to one another. Past experiences with one another allow for this kind of exchange as well as motivation to nurture the relationship. These findings are relevant for understanding how schools can promote better collaborative skills—an area of research that is just beginning. Comparative studies suggest that some schools prepare students to work together more than others (Matusov, Bell, & Rogoff, 2002).

Strand 3 researchers have explored how knowledge of the personal backgrounds of other people can produce powerful changes in opinions about them (Lin & Bransford, 2005), and how knowledge of people with whom one is talking can lead to a number of shortcuts for effective communication (Bransford, Derry, Berliner, Hammerness, & Beckett, 2005). Lin and Bransford (2005) also note that experts' knowledge seem to be organized around people in their field as well as around abstract concepts, yet few studies of expertise have explored this idea (for an exception see Loftus & Loftus, 1974). Overall, there may be considerable potential to increase student learning by using technologies that humanize instruction in ways that let students learn about content while also learning about the people who have developed that content. Initial work by Magnusson & Palincsar (2005), Hong & Lin (2005), and Vye, Bransford, Davis, and Lee (in preparation) support this point of view.

Our understanding of people knowledge and its role in learning can be enhanced by comparing methods from different research traditions. For example, imagine that you are communicating via e-mail with someone you know well versus a stranger. Are there unique neural patterns and arousal patterns associated with these different conditions? Similarly, is it easier to learn new information from well-known people because of increased abilities to (implicitly) elaborate based on knowing the background of the people and being able to identify affectively with their struggles and questions (e.g., Lin & Bransford, 2005; Magnusson & Palincsar, 2005; Hong & Lin, 2005). Questions such as these could have a dramatic impact on new ways to create more "people centered" curricula in formal education. The issue of "people knowledge" and its benefits for learning seems ripe for collaboration across all three of the research strands illustrated in Fig. 10.1.

Sharing Research Tools

A second way to accelerate synthesis across research strands is to share research tools that make it easier to study learning and which can help promulgate affiliated theory and methodologies. The Pittsburgh Science of Learning Center (www.learnlab.org) provides an interesting model for how this might be accomplished. The Center has developed an innovative paradigm for experimentation on learning that they call LearnLab. The LearnLab environment consists of seven "highly instrumented courses" in mathematics, science, and language at the high school and college levels. Each course is available for use in "real" classrooms and incorporates state-of-the-art design features to promote learning; including, for example, intelligent tutors and peer dialog capabilities. An especially exciting aspect of this vision is that LearnLab includes advanced technology for researchers across the country to use to design and conduct studies in the context of courses—an *in vivo* lab. This is facilitated by the availability of authoring tools, student interaction data collection tools, and tools for data analysis built into the technology-based courseware.

Members of the Pittsburgh Center argue—as others have too—that learning science research is currently (1) either rigorous or realistic, but rarely both, (b) fine grain or long duration, but rarely both, and (c) mostly inadequate from the standpoint of measuring learning in a robust way. LearnLab was developed to address each of these issues and to promote a widespread research initiative for the field that is high quality and can produce important findings that can be effectively and rapidly implemented in classrooms.

Needless to say, any set of tools provides both opportunities and constraints. In the context of the present chapter, it will be useful to see whether and how researchers from different strands view the LearnLab tools from their unique perspectives. Will they seek to redesign the tools, or can they work with them to create a variety of unique applications? Whatever the conclusions, the Learnlab concepts seems like a powerful way to help the field increase its ability to communicate and advance.

Many other tools are being developed and shared by members of the broader learning research communities. For example, a number of different groups are using technology tools for helping make students' thinking more visible (e.g., Minstrell, 2005; Penuel & Yarnall, 2005). Members of these different groups are beginning to collaborate in order to find what works well (e.g., the nature of the questions that are asked) and what needs improving. SRI's Web site provides a number of powerful examples of lessons learned (www.SRI.com); so does the "Just in Time Teaching" Web site (www.JITT.org).

Other tools are being developed and shared that permit the research community to capture information that otherwise would be difficult to capture. Examples include sophisticated video analysis and collaboration tools such as *VideoTraces* (Stevens, Cherry & Fournier, 2001; Stevens & Hall, 1997; Stevens & Toro-Martell, in press; Stevens, in press) and *DIVER* (Pea et al., 2004; Pea, in press), which enables collaborative video analysis and the functions of a "digital video collaboratory" for cumulative knowledge building from video datasets. New generations of learning management systems are also making it possible to study the effects of a variety of challenge-based approaches to instruction and capture data from individual students as they proceed through these (e.g., see the CAPE system at www.VaNTH.org). Other groups are using shared data sets as anchoring points for uncovering multiple perspectives on common issues (e.g., MacWhinney et al., 2004). Overall, the shared use of shared tools provides a common ground for communication that increases the probability for meaningful across-strand conversations.

Searching for "Conceptual Collisions"

In addition to sharing methods and tools is the broader strategy of actively attempting to identify fruitful "conceptual collisions" among different research traditions. Because of different ways of talking about phenomena and doing research, it is easy for members of different strands to talk past one another rather than effectively communicate (e.g., Kuhn, 1962). Attempts to look at similar phenomena from multiple perspectives (what some have called *anchored collaboration*, CTGV, 1997) can help surface (often tacit) assumptions that can then be compared. There are at least two approaches one might take toward conceptual collisions. One anchors the collision around important principles that guide thinking about learning. The other anchors the collision around common phenomena.

Conceptual Collisions Around Important Claims

Several reports from the National Academy of Sciences (NRC, 2000, 2005) have identified three principles of learning that are important for helping students move along a pathway to develop expertise (including adaptive expertise). We can use these principles to give examples of how conceptual collisions play out. The three principles are:

1. Students come to the classroom with preconceptions about how the world works. If their initial understanding is not engaged, they may fail to grasp the new concepts and information, or they may learn them for purposes of a test but revert to their preconceptions outside the classroom.
2. To develop competence in an area of inquiry, students must (a) have a deep foundation of factual knowledge, (b) understand facts and ideas in the context of a conceptual framework, and (c) organize knowledge in ways that facilitate retrieval and application.
3. A "metacognitive" approach to instruction can help students learn to take control of their own learning by defining learning goals and actively monitoring their progress in achieving them.

Preconceptions. The three traditions of research add complementary perspectives to understanding the role of preconceptions. Strand 3 points to the efficiency × innovation characterization of adaptive expertise illustrated in Fig. 10.2. The idea that all learners begin with preconceptions can be represented by assuming that they all start from their existing "efficiencies"—their habitual ways of thinking about and doing things. This efficient knowledge is critically important. People need prior knowledge to make sense of new situations, and they need fluent access to this knowledge so that they can "reinvest" their attentional resources in other matters (e.g., Bereiter & Scardamalia, 1993). Often, however, efficient access to knowledge and skills results in the overassimilation of new ideas to existing schemas as described in the language cases of Strand 1 and also by Strand 3 researchers in other domains (e.g., Schwartz & Bransford, 1998; Wineburg, 1998). One might hypothesize that—at least for some concepts and procedures—the more automatized (and tacit) one's current scripts and schemas (characterized by moving to the right on the efficiency dimension), the harder it may be to resist the urge to overassimilate. This would correspond to the Strand 1 argument that implicit learning leads to neural commitment and ways of thinking that become highly efficient, but sometimes at the expense of learning new ways of thinking.

As discussed in the first section, Strand 1 researchers emphasize both the advantages and the disadvantages of neural commitment in areas of expertise. Disadvantages are illustrated in second language learning, which is made more difficult if the second language is learned late in life when the brain is already committed to the way of listening and processing language that is embodied in one's "mother tongue." In this case an implication of Strand 1 theorizing is that new learning will require exposure to patterns of covariance that fall outside the normal pattern—experience that does not support the initial "mental filter" or preconception. The exposure to new instances may need to have a frequency that can outweigh the huge number of original instances that led to the neural commitment (or preconception) to begin with.

Work from Strand 2 draws our attention to instances outside of language learning where it may not be maximally adaptive or desirable to sidestep preconceptions rather than replace them. For example, they might argue that it is important to develop patterns of social participation and mediation that help people transition back and forth between everyday preconceptions and the more formal treatments characteristic of school. Overall, the three strands provide different perspectives on a fundamental principle, and each strand can help nuance one another's claims.

Learning with Understanding. A number of studies show that novices often focus on surface features of concepts (e.g., Chi, Feltovich, & Glaser, 1981) and that learning with understanding can increase the flexibility of transfer (e.g., Judd, 1908; NRC, 2000; Wertheimer, 1959). Learning with understanding involves developing a recognition of the deep structure of an idea or situation, including the "why." Strand 2 proposes that this recognition arises from the significance and meaning provided by a matrix of social practices. For example, other people model the value and identity attached to particular interpretations. Strand 1 agrees with Strand 2 on the significance of social interaction, with a special emphasis on learning through observing the behaviors and customs of other people. To explain why learning with understanding transfers better than "brute learning," Strand 1 might argue that "understanding" usually means that people have seen enough instances that they can infer (albeit sometimes through an "unconscious inference") the causal structure beneath a variety of instances (e.g., Gopnik et al., 1999).

Strand 3 is more likely to focus on the structural characteristics of knowledge that support understanding, which includes knowledge of assumptions about when a particular body of knowledge applies and the implications that knowledge yields. It examines the types of designed environments that help people explicitly understand why and how particular aspects of their knowledge (including skills) are relevant.

Metacognition. The third learning principle noted earlier involves helping students learn to take a metacognitive stance to their own learning—complete with habits of mind for self-generated inquiry and self-assessment. There is a strong body of evidence showing the value of being reflective about learning. For example, students who were directed to engage in self-explanation as they solved mathematics problems developed deeper conceptual understanding than students who solved those same problems but did not engage in self-explanation (Chi, Bassok, Lewis, Reimann, & Glaser, 1989). This was true even though a common time limitation on both groups meant that the self-explaining students solved fewer problems in total.

Similar findings about the value of metacognitive processing have been found in science learning (e.g., Dufresne, Gerace, Leonard, Mestre, & Wenk, 1996; Lin & Lehman, 1999; NRC, 2000; Vye et al., 1998; White & Frederiksen, 1998), mathematics (Shoenfeld, 1992) and reading comprehension (e.g., Brown & Campione, 1994, 1996; Palincsar & Brown, 1989; Pressley, 1995).

Donovan and Bransford (2005) emphasize that metacognition is not a "knowledge free skill" that works independently of content knowledge. To be optimally effective, metacognitive strategies need to be taught in the context of the individual subject areas (e.g., Vye et al., 1998). Many of the questions one asks in the monitoring process change to some extent with the subject, though there is certainly a great deal of overlap. In history, for example, we want students to ask from what perspective the author writes, and about the purpose of his or her writing—questions that are often less relevant in mathematics. In mathematics, on the other hand, we want students to monitor their progress toward a solution to a problem, and reflect on whether that solution is within expectation. In writing, we want students to reflect on the audience, what they will understand, and what more they need to know. In the sciences and in history, the question "What is the evidence?" is especially important, as is the mind-set of looking for disconfirming as well as confirming evidence. *How Students Learn* (2005) provides rich examples of metacognitive monitoring as students learn about mathematics, science, and history.

Many researchers across the three traditions view the development of metacognition as the result of social processes. For example, the notion of "cognitive apprenticeship" emphasized in Strand 2 (Brown, Collins, & Duguid, 1989) can provide learners a chance to internalize the reflective practices of an expert. Here, the focus is on the social and cultural context that supports the development of metacognition for recurrent situations. Strand 1 also emphasizes the developmental aspects of metacognition, examining it as emergent from simpler beginnings that at first did not include the "meta" component. In this regard, Strand 1's emphasis on the "social brain" (e.g., Kuhl, 2004; Meltzoff & Decety, 2003) and the young child's natural attunement to other people may provide a foundation from which children can bootstrap to more conscious and metacognitive ways of understanding their own thoughts and the thoughts of others (Meltzoff, 2005). Metacognition itself may not emerge through a maturational process, but as a downstream development outcome of a human brain (and child) cared for by other people (Gopnik & Meltzoff, 1997; Gopnik et al., 1999).

Strand 3 is particularly concerned with the types of activities that promote the kinds of metacognitive activities that support adaptation and innovation. So, rather than only entraining on a set of metacognitive routines or skills that improve the efficiency at a recurrent set of tasks, an additional question is how to help people develop characteristics of adaptive expertise that include the habits of mind of reflecting on situations and actions with the goal of trying out new ideas, moving away from existing comfort zones, and actively seeking feedback in order to test new ideas.

For metacognition, as with preconceptions and learning with understanding, there are areas of substantial overlap between the traditions. It is useful to explore the overlaps and determine if there is a larger theoretical framework that can organize the commonalities. However, there are also significant differences in the particular phenomena of interest, the types of explanations that are satisfying, and the language for expressing explanations.

Overall, multiple perspectives anchored around key principles of learning are a fruitful approach to the identification of conceptual collisions, but they also represent a difficult approach because of the need for different strands to learn to talk with one another at relatively abstract levels of discourse. An alternative (complementary) approach to exploring conceptual collisions is to collect multiple perspectives on relatively concrete anchoring phenomenon. An example is provided next.

Anchoring Collaborations Around Phenomena

Members of the LIFE Center (www.LIFE-slc.org) have begun to use anchored collaborations around specific phenomena as a way to surface interesting conceptual collisions across research traditions. One way to do this is to create vignettes that people from different strands are asked to comment on. To illustrate, consider a vignette of novices going in a boat with an expert fisherman who takes them to a good spot on the lake, helps them select the right bait and set the hook at the right depth, shows them how to set the hook, and so forth. Some of the novices catch several fish and feel good about their efforts. A month later they come back to the lake by themselves. They return to the spot and repeat the previous behaviors because they were successful earlier. The challenge asks people to respond from the perspective of implicit learning, informal learning, and designs for formal learning. Several "collisions of ideas" emerged from this simple exercise that were surprising to the LIFE members and raised important questions about learning.

Issue 1: What Do We Really Mean by "Learning from Experience"?. The people who created the fishing challenge were from Strand 3 (formal learning and beyond) and were interested in whether researchers from Strand 1 (implicit learning and brain) and Strand 2 (informal learning) would bring up differences between "learning by rote" versus "learning with understanding" (e.g., Judd, 1908). Differences on a "rote-understanding" dimension of the fishing vignette could presumably have a large effect on transfer. For example, if one understands the reasons for the mentor's fishing decisions and activities (including linking them to changing needs of fish and their life in a lake that also changes), coming to the lake 1 month later and slavishly repeating the previous behaviors without variation and adaptation to the current situation may be undesirable. These ideas suggest the need to clarify what "learning from experience" (be it implicit, informal or formal learning) might mean.

Issue 2: Multiple Levels of Simultaneous Learning. Comments on the challenge from Strand 1 researchers (implicit learning and brain) suggested that multiple levels of learning could be occurring simultaneously. These comments were a surprise to the people who had developed the vignette (Strand 3 researchers). The latter had focused solely on the "intended curriculum" of learning to fish and ignored all the other possible lessons embedded in this general scenario. Several possible examples of learning that were suggested by Strand 1 researchers appear in Table 10.1.

The idea that multiple lessons may be learned in any slice of life is a very important potential insight. As noted earlier, the developers of the vignette had focused solely on the "intended curriculum" of learning to fish. Similarly, in schools we often talk about students who do and do not learn the intended curriculum, but we often ignore the many things that they are learning. Examples might include "I am good (or not good) at X (reading, mathematics, science, art, music, etc.)" or "I am (or am not) liked

TABLE 10.1.

1. **Learning About Morality**—The fisherman may or may not have a license. The fisherman may catch only his limit or "assume no one will know" and overfish. The child will implicitly learn from this. The fisherman may catch more than he can eat for the thrill of the hunt, or only take from the environment what he needs.
2. **Learning About Philosophy**—When the fish aren't biting on the lures, Joe Hunter threads live worms to his hook, because they are "best for catching fish." But another parent goes out on a boat with his child and refuses to fish even with lures. Without saying a word, the child learns different lessons about human kinship and distance from other living things, different lessons about whether humans can or should use other animate beings as "a means" to the child's own ends.
3. **Learning About People (Motives and Attitudes)**—When going fishing, one person may want to talk a lot about the day's problems ("complaining about folks back home") and another may want to "be in the moment, at one with nature." The child will absorb this implicit attitude towards people and the environment. When the child grows up, this pattern may even be repeated, because it is deeply engrained with what it means to "fish on weekends."
4. **Learning About Stereotypes**—The Challenge shows a male fisherman. This is a gender stereotype. One child may learn that fishing is a time for father–son bonding. Another child may learn that it's a great time for "father–daughter" or "mother–daughter" or "whole-family" bonding. Children implicitly learn from what we do. The information is there, and they learn a "way of life" from it.
5. **Learning of Physics**—When the novice gets in the canoe it rocks. After a full summer of canoeing the lesson learned may be that "getting low" in the boat prevents rocking. This in turn may give an intuitive grounding for later learning about "center of gravity." The child knows nothing about "center of gravity" or center of buoyancy as yet, but the child does learn that it helps to "get low" and may be able to draw on this experience later in life. When the physics professor explains the center of gravity concept in class, the child has the potential to relate it to previously learned physical intuitions. Of course, as noted earlier, everyday experiences (e.g., related to physics) can create misconceptions as well, especially in the cases where advanced scientific explanations are not in line with our everyday intuitive "felt experience."

by my peers or my teacher." As noted earlier, Holt (1964) argued that the key issue of learning, is never *whether* students are learning, but *what* they learn.

Do people really learn multiple lessons in various "slices of life"? Doesn't this clash with the idea that attention has to be explicitly focused on particular events in order to learn? Or is there indeed a great deal of "non-focused" background learning that functions as a kind of "hidden curriculum?" If the latter, what kinds of data exist, or could be collected, to support the "multiple dimensions of (often implicit) learning" point of view? The discussion of media research and its emphasis on subtle but powerful effects on behavior (discussed in the first section) provides important clues about exploring this question. So does the literature on implicit learning (Reber, 1993) and implicit memory (Shaughnessy, 2002).

The issue of "multiple levels of learning" raises possibilities that might help us rethink the design of informal and formal educational environments. For example, consider phonics taught in a stripped-down worksheet-centered context. This may end up depriving students of many opportunities for implicit learning compared to contexts where a great deal of language-rich interactions accompany a focus on phonics (e.g., Valdes, Bunch, Snow, Lee, & Matos, 2005). The language-rich experiences may not show up on tests of phonics knowledge, but they may well provide crucial support for later learning of vocabulary and content-specific reading abilities. The same is true of science lessons, mathematics lessons, etc. Possibilities such as this are too potentially important for researchers to ignore.

Issue 3: Multiple Avenues for Participation. Responses to the fishing scenario from Strand 2 researchers surfaced another important issue: namely, questions about the units of analysis for what counts as success. A typical unit of analysis in school is individual students—and they are typically compared to other students on the same criteria. In informal settings the unit is often the group and different people may contribute in very different ways (see Section 2).

On a fishing trip, the fishing party as a whole may have success at catching fish even though a few people do not. But even the non-fish-catchers can share in the success *if* they have been able to do things that helped everyone else. For example, one person may be good at using a trolling motor, another may be great at helping others land their fish with a net, another at cleaning fish, another at telling stories that keep the group motivated during "dry" spells, and so forth. There are many possible roles for participation, and success is often a function of the distributed expertise of the group (e.g., see Hutchins, 1993). Note that the issue here goes beyond the idea of group versus individual learning opportunities. In school, group assignments still often end by assessing all students on the same criteria.

In addition, school assignments often do not provide genuine opportunities for a wide range of distributed expertise. In many nonschool environments, it is the diversity of expertise that makes for success and is celebrated. Is it possible to create "diversity of expertise" curricula in science, mathematics, etc., so that people can each bring particular subsets of skills to an overall project (e.g., where some excel at the visual representation of mathematical ideas, some have great proficiency with proportional reasoning, some are wonderful at formulating formal proofs, etc.)? For examples, see Brown and Campione (1994) and CTGV (2000).

Multiple pathways toward success should be able to increase motivation because each person is likely to be able to contribute while also learning new skills and concepts (e.g., each person is a [relative] expert as well as a novice). This is a very different experience from being in the bottom quartile in some particular class (for example) and never having a chance to also be good (and appreciated) at other things in that class.

Issue 4: Multiple Cycles That Encourage "Working Smarter". Issues of multiple types and levels of participation are also related to another issues that LIFE researchers highlighted in the context of the fishing vignette: namely, that learning to fish is not typically a "one chance only" activity. Instead, most people fish many times and, between trips, have opportunities to think about what worked and find ideas, tools, and strategies for doing better the next time. In short, fishing involves what we earlier (Section 3) called "quasi-repetitive activity cycles" (QRACS) that provide opportunities for feedback, reflection, and revision—in part by learning to "work smarter" the next time around.

"Working smart" can involve practicing isolated skills such as learning to cast by putting up a target in the back yard or learning to tie knots that hold on lures. Nevertheless, people get to practice while also having the big picture of why they are practicing, and they have multiple opportunities to try the "big task" (i.e., catching fish).

A way to introduce people to fishing that is more similar to school might be to learn to tie knots, then to tie on hooks, then to bait hooks, then to cast, etc. In this model, people do not get to try their hand at fishing until they master each of the building blocks. If fishing were taught this way, it is likely that many would lose interest; others would learn more slowly because they don't know why they are practicing. In a previous section we discussed "working smart" curricula that utilize some of the QRAC structures that seem characteristic of many activities in the workplace and everyday life.

Issue 5: Assessments of Progress. Related to ideas about different kinds of participation opportunities over time is the fundamental issue of assessment. Do we hold all people accountable for catching a certain amount of fish at each age level, for example, or do we celebrate multiple avenues of individual progress? There appear to be many reasons for preferring the latter. One person might have great trouble tying hooks but be excellent at setting the hook once the fish bite. Or as noted earlier the person may be skilled at running a boat, keeping others entertained during "dry spots," etc. People on a fishing trip would probably make note of these individual contributions— and would probably also be patient as each learns to do things that are hard for him or her (e.g., tie or bait hooks).

Academic environments often fail to celebrate unique strengths and tend to look at placements within a class (e.g., bottom 10 percent) rather than progress over time. In addition, assessments often fail to fully consider a wide range of possible skills that can make people successful. In fishing, for example, one could imagine an arthritic grandfather who can no longer cast and catch fish but knows where to fish and knows whom to invite to have a great outing. He could be considered a great fisherman because he knows how to create distributed expertise environments. The pursuit of new ways of thinking about assessment is a fundamental issue that we believe will receive more and more attention in the next 10 years.

SUMMARY

Our goal in this chapter has been to argue for the benefits of treating the next decade as a decade for synergy among different traditions of learning theorists. We built on previous work in this area (e.g., Greeno et al., 1996) and discussed three areas of research that seem well-positioned to inform one another: (1) Implicit Learning and Brain; (2) Informal Learning; (3) Designs for Formal Learning and Beyond.

Discussion in the first three sections provided samples of research and theorizing from each of these areas. Our reviews of these areas was far from exhaustive, but we hope the discussions provided sufficient information to motivate readers to explore each of these areas in more detail.

In the last section of this chapter we discussed some initial strategies for accelerating the movement toward synergy among different learning traditions. These included sharing methods, sharing research tools, and actively searching for "conceptual collisions" that can, we hope, uncover new ways of thinking about learning and educational design. One set of conceptual collisions that we discussed was anchored around basic principles of learning that have been discussed most explicitly in the context of research in Strand 3 settings (e.g., Darling-Hammond & Bransford, 2005; NRC, 2000, 2005). A second set was anchored around a simple vignette of learning to fish. This fishing exercise was conducted by members of the LIFE Center, and everyone who participated learned something fundamental from seeing others' points of view.

This chapter is being written at the beginning of what we are calling a decade for synthesis. There is a great deal of work to be accomplished. We realize that our discussion of the potentially relevant research literature barely scratches the surface of what has actually been accomplished by learning research. Furthermore, our discussion of strategies for synthesis across strands represents only a subset of what we can do as a field. However, we hope that this chapter provides a rationale for the value of pulling different research traditions together—and searching for and celebrating collisions among them—in order to address the formidable but exciting challenges of helping all learners succeed.

ACKNOWLEDGMENTS

This work was supported by a grant from the National Science Foundation (NSF#0354453). Any opinions, findings and conclusions expressed in the paper are those of the authors and do not necessarily reflect the views of the National Science Foundation. The authors thank the following individuals for their contributions to the chapter: Leah Bricker, Hank Clark, Barbara Conboy, Joan Davis, Katie Hardin, Toshi Imada, Beth Koemans, Tiffany Lee, Laurie McCarthy, Maisy McGaughey, Raj Raizada, Suzanne Reeve, Maritza Rivera-Gaxiola, Tom Satwicz, Yang Zhang, and Heather Toomey Zimmmerman.

References

Ackerman, P. (2003). Cognitive ability and non-ability trait determinants of expertise. *Educational Researcher, 32*, 15–20.

Adams, L., Kasserman, J., Yearwood, A., Perfetto, G., Bransford, J., & Franks, J. (1988). The effects of facts versus problem-oriented acquisition. *Memory & Cognition, 16*, 167–175.

Adamson, L. B., & Bakeman, R. (1991). The development of shared attention during infancy. In R. Vasta (Ed.), *Annals of child development, 8*, 1–41.

Alexander, P., (2003). The development of expertise: The journey from acclimation to proficiency. *Educational Researcher, 32*, 10–14.

Amigues, R. (1988). Peer interaction in solving physics problems: Sociocognitive confrontation and metacognitive aspects. *Journal of Experimental Child Psychology, 45*(1), 141–158.

Anderson, J. R. (1976). *Language, memory and thought*. Hillsdale, NJ: Lawrence Erlbaum Associates.

Anderson, J. R. (Ed.) (1981). *Cognitive skills and their acquisition*. Hillsdale, NJ: Lawrence Erlbaum Associates.

Anderson, D. R., & Lorch, E. P. (1983). Looking at television: Action or reaction? In J. Bryant & D. R. Anderson (Eds.), *Children's understanding of television: Research on attention and comprehension* (pp. 1–33). New York: Academic Press.

Anderson, R. C., & Pearson, P. D. (1984). A schema-theoretic view of basic processes in reading comprehension. In P. D. Pearson (Ed.), *Handbook of reading research* (pp. 255–291). New York: Longman.

Astuti, R., Solomon, G., & Carey, S. (2004). Constraints on conceptual development: A case study of the acquisition of folk-biological and folksociological knowledge in Madagascar. *Monographs of the Society for Research in Child Development, 69*(3), 1–163.

Ausubel, D.P. (1960). The use of advance organizers in the learning and retention of meaningful verbal material. *Journal of Educational Psychology, 51*, 267–272.

Azmitia, M., & Montgomery, R. (1993). Friendship, transactive dialogues, and the development of scientific reasoning. *Social Development, 2*(3), 202–221.

Barron, B. (2000). Problem solving in video-based microworlds: Collaborative and individual outcomes of high achieving sixth grade students. *Journal of Educational Psychology, 92*, 391–398.

Barron, B. (2003). When smart groups fail. *The Journal of the Learning Sciences, 12,* 307–359

Barron, B. (2004). Learning ecologies for technological fluency: Gender and experience differences. *Journal of Educational Computing Research, 31*(1), 1–36.

Barron, B. Processes of knowledge growth across contexts: A learning ecologies perspective. Submitted for publication.

Beach, K. D. (1993). Becoming a bartender: The role of external memory cues in a work-directed educational activity. *Journal of Applied Cognitive Psychology, 7*, 191–204.

Becker, H. S. (1953). Becoming a marihuana user. *American Journal of Sociology, 59*, 235–242.

Becker, H. S. (1972). A school is a lousy place to learn anything in. *American Behavioral Scientist, 16*, 85–105.

Becker, H. S. (1996). The epistemology of qualitative research. In R. Jessor, A. Colby & R. Schweder (Eds.), *Essays on ethnography and human development* (pp. 53–71). Chicago: University of Chicago Press.

Becker, H. S., & Carper, J. (1956). The elements of identification with an occupation. *American Sociological Review, 21*(3), 341–348.

Bell, P. (2004). Promoting students' argument construction and collaborative debate in the science classroom. In M. C. Linn & E. A. Davis & P. Bell (Eds.), *Internet environments for science education* (pp. 115–143). Mahwah, NJ: Lawrence Erlbaum Associates.

Bell, P., & Linn, M. C. (2000). Scientific arguments as learning artifacts: Designing for learning from the web with KIE. *International Journal of Science Education, 22*(8), 797–817.

Benoit, W. L., & Hansen, G. J. (2004). Presidential debate watching, issue knowledge, character evaluation, and vote choice. *Human Communication Research, 30*(1), 121–144.

Bereiter, C., & Scardamalia, M. (1989). Intentional learning as a goal of instruction. In L.B. Resnick (Ed.), *Knowing, learning, and instruction: Essays in honor of Robert Glaser* (pp. 361–392). Hillsdale, NJ: Lawrence Erlbaum Associates.

Bereiter, C., & Engelmann, S. (1966). *Teaching disadvantaged children in the preschool.* Englewood Cliffs, NJ: Prentice-Hall.

Bereiter, C., & Scardamalia, M. (1993). *Surpassing ourselves: An inquiry into the nature and implications of expertise.* Chicago: Open Court.

Berliner, D. C. (1991). Educational psychology and pedagogical expertise: New findings and new opportunities for thinking about training. *Educational Psychologist, 26*(2), 145–155.

Berliner, D. C. (2001). Learning about and learning from expert teachers. International *Journal of Educational Research, 35*(5), 463–468.

Berry, D., & Broadbent, D. (1988). Interactive tasks and the implicit-explicit distinction. *British Journal of Psychology, 79,* 251–272.

Berry, D. C. (Ed.). (1997). *How implicit is implicit learning.* New York: Oxford University Press.

Bever, T. G. (1982). Regression in the service of development. In Bever et al. (Eds.), *Regression in child development* (pp. 153–188). Hillsdale, NJ: Lawrence Erlbaum Associates.

Black, J., & Bower, G. (1980). Story understanding as problem-solving. *Poetics, 9,* 223–250.

Bos, M.C. (1937). Experimental study of productive collaboration. *Acta Psychologica, 3,* 315–426.

Bransford, J.D., Arbitman-Smith, R., Stein, B.S., Vye, N.J. (1985). Three approaches to improving thinking and learning skills. In R. Segal, S. Chipman, & R. Glaser (Eds.), *Thinking and learning skills: Relating instruction to basic research* (Vol. 1, pp. 133–206). Hillsdale, NJ: Lawrence Erlbaum Associates.

Bransford, J., Derry, S., Berliner, D., Hammerness, K., & Beckett, K. (2005). Theories of learning and their roles in teaching. In L. Darling-Hammond & J. Bransford (Eds.), *Preparing teachers for a changing world* (pp. 40–87). San Francisco: Jossey-Bass.

Bransford, J. D., & Heldmeyer, K. (1983). Learning from children learning. In J. Bisanz, G. Bisanz, & R. Kail (Eds.), *Learning in children: Progress in cognitive development research* (pp. 171–190). New York: Springer.

Bransford, J. D., & Johnson, M. K. (1972). Contextual prerequisites for understanding: Some investigations of comprehension and recall. *Journal of Verbal Learning and Verbal Behavior, 11,* 717–726.

Bransford, J. D., & Nitsch, K. E. (1978). Coming to understand things we could not previously understand. In J. F. Kavanagh & W. Strange (Eds.), *Speech and language in the laboratory, school, and clinic* (pp. 267–301). Cambridge, MA: MIT Press.

Bransford, J. D., & Schwartz, D. (1999). Rethinking transfer: A simple proposal with multiple implications. In A. Iran-Nejad & P. D. Pearson (Eds.), *Review of research in education* (Vol. 24, pp. 61–100). Washington, DC: American Educational Research Association.

Bransford, J. D., Vye, N., Bateman, H., Brophy, S. & Roselli, R. (2004). Vanderbilt's Amigo[3] project: Knowledge of how people learn enters cyberspace. In T. Duffy & J. Kirkley (Eds.),

Learner-centered theory and practice in distance education. Mahwah, NJ: Lawrence Erlbaum Associates.

Bransford, J. D., Zech, L., Schwartz, D. L., Barron B. J., Vye, N. J., & Cognition and Technology Group at Vanderbilt (2000). Design environments that invite and sustain mathematical thinking. In P. Cobb (Ed.), *Symbolizing, communicating and mathematizing: Perspectives on discourse, tools, and instructional design* (pp. 275–324). Mahwah, NJ: Lawrence Erlbaum Associates.

Bronfenbrenner, U. (1977). Toward an experimental ecology of human development. *American Psychologist, 32,* 513–531.

Brophy, S. P. (2001). *Exploring the implication of an expert blind spot on learning.* Unpublished manuscript, Vanderbilt University, Nashville, TN.

Broudy, H. S. (1977). Types of knowledge and purposes of education. In R. C. Anderson, R. J. Spiro, & W. E. Montague (Eds.), *Schooling and the acquisition of knowledge* (pp. 1–17). Hillsdale, NJ: Lawrence Erlbaum Associates.

Brown, A. L. (1992). Design experiments: Theoretical and methodological challenges in creating complex interventions in classroom settings. *Journal of the Learning Sciences, 2*(2), 141–178.

Brown, A. L., Bransford, J. D., Ferrara, R. A., & Campione, J. C. (1983). Learning, remembering, and understanding. In J. H. Flavell & E. M. Markman (Eds.), *Handbook of child psychology: Cognitive development* (Vol. 3, pp. 77–166). New York: Wiley.

Brown, A. L., & Campione, J. C. (1994). Guided discovery in a community of learners. In K. McGilly (Ed.), *Classroom lessons: Integrating cognitive theory and classroom practice* (pp. 229–272). Cambridge, MA: MIT Press.

Brown, A. L., & Campione, J. C. (1996). Psychological theory and the design of innovative learning environments: On procedures, principles, and systems. In L. Schauble & R. Glaser (Eds.), *Innovations in learning: New environments for education* (pp. 289–325). Mahwah, NJ: Lawrence Erlbaum Associates

Brown, J. S., Collins, A. & Duguid, P. (1989). Situated cognition and the culture of learning. *Educational Researcher, 18,* 32–42.

Bruer, J. T. (1993). *Schools for thought: A science of learning in the classroom.* Cambridge, MA: MIT Press

Bruer, J. T. (1997). Education and the brain: A bridge too far. *Educational Researcher, 26,* 4–16.

Bruer, J. T. (1999). *The myth of the first three years: A new understanding of early brain development and lifelong learning.* New York: The Free Press.

Bruner, J. (1960). *The process of education.* Cambridge, MA: Harvard University Press.

Bruner, J. (1990). *Acts of meaning.* Cambridge, MA: Harvard University Press.

Bryan, W. L., & Harter, N. (1897). Studies in the physiology and psychology of the telegraphic language. *Psychological Review, 4,* 27–53.

Burnham, D., Kitamura, C., & Vollmer-Conna, U. (2002). What's new, pussycat? On talking to babies and animals. *Science, 296,* 1435.

Buchner, A., Erdfelder, E., Steffens, M. C., & Martensen, H. (1997). The nature of memory processes underlying recognition judgments in the process dissociation procedure. *Memory & Cognition, 25*, 508–517.

Cadiz, J.J., Balachandran, A., Sanocki, E., Gupta, A., Grudin, J., & Jancke, G. (2000). *Distance learning through distributed collaborative video viewing.* Proceedings of the 2000 ACM conference on Computer Supported Cooperative Work (CSCW) (pp. 135–144). Philadelphia, PA.

Calfee, R., & Berliner, D. (1996). Introduction to a dynamic and relevant psychology. In R. Calfee & D. Berliner (Eds.) *Handbook of educational psychology* (pp. 1–11). New York: MacMillan.

Callan, D. E., Jones, J. A., Callan, A. M., & Akahane-Yamada, R. (2004). Phonetic perceptual identification by native- and second-language speakers differentially activates brain regions involved with acoustic phonetic processing and those involved with articulatory-auditory/orosensory internal models. *NeuroImage, 22*, 1182–1194.

Carey, S. (2000). Science education as conceptual change. *Journal of Applied Developmental Psychology, 21*, 13–19.

Carraher, T. N., Carraher, D. W., & Schliemann, A. D. (1985). Mathematics in the streets and in schools. *British Journal of Developmental Psychology, 3*, 21–29.

Carraher, D.W. & Schliemann, A.D. (2002). The transfer dilemma. *Journal of the Learning Sciences, 11*, 1–24.

Chang, C. (2002). Self-congruency as a cue in different advertising-processing contexts. *Communication Research, 29*(5), 503–536.

Chase, W. G., & Simon, H. A. (1973). Perception in chess. *Cognitive Psychology, 1*, 33–81.

Chi, M. T. H., Bassok, M., Lewis, M., Reimann, M., & Glaser, R. (1989). Self-explanations: How students study and use examples in learning to solve problems. *Cognitive Science, 13*, 145–182.

Chi, M. T. H., Feltovich, P. & Glaser, R. (1981). Categorization and representation of physics problems by experts and novices. *Cognitive Science, 5*, 121–152.

Chi, M. T. H., Glaser, R., & Farr, M. (1988). *The nature of expertise.* Hillsdale, NJ: Lawrence Erlbaum Associates.

Chi, M. T. H., Glaser, R., & Rees, E. (1982). Expertise in problem solving. In R. J. Sternberg (Ed.), *Advances in the psychology of human intelligence*, (Vol. 1, pp. 1–75). Hillsdale, NJ: Lawrence Erlbaum Associates.

Christensen, C.M. (1997). *The innovator's dilemma: When new technologies cause great firms to fail.* Cambridge, MA: Harvard Business School Press.

Cognition and Technology Group at Vanderbilt. (1997). *The Jasper Project: Lessons in curriculum, instruction, assessment, and professional development.* Mahwah, NJ: Lawrence Erlbaum Associates.

Cognition and Technology Group at Vanderbilt (2000). Adventures in anchored instruction: Lessons from beyond the ivory tower. In R. Glaser (Ed*.), Advances in instructional psychology: Educational design and cognitive science*, (Vol. 5, pp. 35-100). Mahwah, NJ: Lawrence Erlbaum Associates.

Cole, M. (1996). *Cultural psychology: A once and future discipline.* Cambridge, MA: Harvard University Press.

Cole, M., & Bruner, J. S. (1971). Cultural differences and inferences about psychological processes. *American Psychologist, 26*, 867–876.

Cole, M., Engeström, Y., & Vasquez, O (1997). Introduction. In M. Cole, Y. Engeström, & O. Vasquez (Eds.), *Mind, culture and activity.* Cambridge: Cambridge University Press.

Cole, M., Hood, L., & McDermott, R. (1978). *Ecological niche picking: Ecological invalidity as an axiom of experimental cognitive psychology.* New York: Rockefeller University, Laboratory of Comparative Human Cognition and Institute for Comparative Human Development.

Cole, M., Hood, L., & McDermott, R. (1997). Concepts of ecological validity: Their differing implications for comparative cognitive research. In M. Cole, Y. Engeström & O. Vasquez (Eds.), *Mind, culture, and activity: Seminal papers from the Laboratory of Comparative Human Cognition* (pp. 49–56). New York: Cambridge University Press.

Coleman, E. (1998). Using explanatory knowledge during collaborative problem solving in science. *Journal of Learning Sciences, 7*, 387–427.

Collins, A. (1992). Toward a design science of education. In E. Scanlon and T. O'Shea (Eds.), *New directions in educational technology* (pp. 15–22). New York: Springer-Verlag.

Crawford, V., Riel, M., & Schlager, M. (2005). *Characterizing adaptive expertise in biology teachers' reasoning.* Paper presented at the American Educational Research Association Annual Meeting, Montreal, Canada.

Cronbach, L. J. (1975). Beyond the two disciplines of scientific psychology. *American Psychologist, 30*, 116–127.

Cronbach, L. J., & Meehl, P.E. (1955). Construct validity in psychological tests. *Psychological Bulletin, 52*, 281–302.

Crowley, K., & Jacobs, M. (2002). Building islands of expertise in everyday family activity. In G. Leinhardt, K. Crowley & K. Knutson (Eds.), *Learning conversations in museums* (pp. 333–356). Mahwah, NJ: Lawrence Erlbaum Associates.

Darling-Hammond, L., & Bransford, J. (Eds.). (2005). *Preparing teachers for a changing world.* San Francisco: Jossey-Bass.

Das, V. (1998). Wittgenstein and Anthropology. *Annual Review of Anthropology, 27*, 171–195.

deAbreu, G. (1995). Understanding how children experience the relationship between home and school mathematics. *Mind, Culture, and Activity, 2*(3), 119–142.

deGroot, A. D. (1965). *Thought and choice in chess.* The Hague, the Netherlands: Mouton.

Decety, J., Jackson, P. L., Sommerville, J., Chaminade, T., & Meltzoff, A. N., (2004). The neural bases of cooperation and competition: an fMRI investigation. *NeuroImage, 23*, 744–751.

Dehaene, S., & Changeux, J.-P. (1997). A hierarchical neuronal network for planning behavior. *Proceedings of the National Academy of Sciences, 94*, 13293–13296.

DeSchepper, B., & Treisman, A. 1996. Visual memory for novel shapes: Implicit coding without attention. Journal of *Experimental Psychology: Learning, Memory, and Cognition, 22*, 27–47.

Design-Based Research Collective (DBRC). (2003). Design-based research: An emerging paradigm for educational inquiry. *Educational Researcher, 32*(1), 5-8.

Detterman, D. K., & Sternberg, R. J. (1993). *Transfer on trial: Intelligence, cognition and instruction*. Norwood, NJ: Ablex.

Diller, K. R., Roselli, R., & Martin, T. (2004). *Teaching biotransport based on "How People Learn" motivated methodology*. Proceedings of 2004 American Society of Mechanical Engineers International Mechanical Engineering Congress, Anaheim, CA.

diSessa, A. A.(1982). Unlearning Aristotelian physics: A study of knowledge-based learning. *Cognitive Science, 6*, 37-75.

Donovan, M. S. & Bransford, J. D. (2005). Introduction. In National Research Council, *How students learn* (pp. 1-28). Washington, DC: National Academy Press.

Driver, R., Guesne, E., & Tiberghien, A. (Eds.). (1985). *Children's ideas in science*. Philadephia: Open University Press.

Dufresne, R. J., Gerace, W. J., Leonard, W. J., Mestre, J. P., & Wenk, L. (1996). Classtalk: A classroom communication system for active learning. *Journal of Computing in Higher Education, 7*, 3-47.

Eckert, P. (1989). *Jocks and burnouts: Social categories and identity in the high school*. New York: Teachers College Press.

Elkind, D. (2001). *The hurried child: Growing up too fast too soon* (3rd ed.). Cambridge, MA: Perseus.

Emerson, R. (2001). *Contemporary field research: Perspectives and formulations*. Prospect Heights: Waveland Press.

Engelmann, S. (1992). *War against the school's academic child abuse*. Portland, OR: Halcyon, House.

Engeström, Y., Brown, K., Christopher, L., & Gregory, J. (1997). Coordination, cooperation, and communication in the courts: Expansive transitions in legal work. In M. Cole, Y. Engeström & O. Vasquez (Eds.), *Mind, culture, and activity: Seminal papers from the Laboratory of Comparative Human Cognition* (pp. 369-385). New York: Cambridge University Press.

Erickson, F. (1986). Qualitative methods in research on teaching. In M. Wittrock (Ed.), *Handbook of research on teaching*. New York: MacMillan.

Feuerstein, R., Rand, Y., & Hoffman, M. (1979). *The dynamic assessment of retarded performers: The learning potential assessment device, theory, instruments, and techniques*. Baltimore, MD: University Park Press.

Flavell, J. H., & Miller, P. H. (1998). Social cognition. In W. Damon (Series Ed.) D. Kuhn & R. Siegler (Eds.), *Handbook of child psychology: Vol. 2. Cognition, perception, and language* (5th ed., pp. 851-898). New York: Wiley.

Fromkin, V., Krashen, S., Curtis, S., Rigler, D., & Rigler, M. (1974). The development of language in Genie: A case of language acquisition beyond the "critical period." *Brain & Language, 1*, 81-107.

Fullan, M. (2001). *Leading in a culture of change*. San Francisco: Wiley.

Fullan, M. (2003). *Change forces with a vengeance*. London: RoutledgeFalmer.

Gee, J. P. (2003a). *What video games have to teach us about learning and literacy*. New York: Palgrave.

Gee, J. P. (2003b). *Learning about learning from a video game: Rise of nations*. University of Wisconsin-Madison.

Gentner, D., Brem, S., Ferguson, R. W., Markman, A. B., Levidow, B. B., Wolff, P., et al. (1997). Analogical reasoning and conceptual change: A case study of Johannes Kepler. *Journal of the Learning Sciences, 6*(1), 3-40.

Gibbons, J. F., Kincheloe, W. R., & Down, K. S. (1977, March). Tutored videotape instruction: a new use of electronics media in education. *Science*, 1139-1146.

Gick, M. L., & Holyoak, K. J. (1980). Analogical problem solving. *Cognitive Psychology, 12*, 306-365.

Gick, M. L., & Holyoak, K. J. (1983). Schema induction and analogical transfer. *Cognitive Psychology, 15*, 1-38.

Glascock, J. (2001). Gender roles on prime-time network television: Demographics and behaviors. *Journal of Broadcasting & Electronic Media, 45*(4), 665-669.

Golestani, N., & Zatorre, R. J. (2004). Learning new sounds of speech: reallocation of neural substrates. *NeuroImage, 21*, 494-506.

González, N., Moll, L. C., & Amanti, C. (2005). *Theorizing education practice: Funds of knowledge in households*. Mahwah, NJ: Lawrence Erlbaum Associates.

Goodsitt, J., Morgan, J., & Kuhl, P. (1993). Perceptual strategies in prelingual speech segmentation. *Journal of Child Language, 20*, 229-252.

Goodwin, C. (1992). Rethinking context: an introduction. In A. Duranti & C. Goodwin (Eds.), *Rethinking context: Language as an interactive phenomenon*. Cambridge: Cambridge University Press.

Goodwin, C. (2000). Action and embodiment within situated human interaction. *Journal of Pragmatics, 32*, 1489-1522.

Gopnik, A., & Meltzoff, A. N. (1997). *Words, thoughts, and theories*. Cambridge, MA: MIT Press.

Gopnik, A., Meltzoff, A. N., & Kuhl, P. K. (1999). *The scientist in the crib: Minds, brains, and how children learn*. New York: William Morrow.

Graf, P., & Schacter, D. L. (1985). Implicit and explicit memory for new associations in normal and amnesic subjects. *Journal of Experimental Psychology: Learning, Memory, and Cognition, 11*, 501-518.

Greeno, J., Collins, A., & Resnick, L. (1996). Cognition and learning. In R. Calfee & D. Berliner (Eds.), *Handbook of educational psychology* (pp. 15-46). New York: MacMillan.

Greenough, W. T., Black, J. E., & Wallace, C. S. (1987). Experience and brain development. *Child Development, 58*, 539-559.

Greenough, W. T., Juraska, J. M., & Volkmar, F. (1979). Maze training effects on dendritic branching in occipital cortex of adult rats. *Behavioral and Neural Biology, 26*, 287-297.

Greenwald, A. G., & Banaji, M. R. (1995). Implicit social cognition: Attitudes, self-esteem, and stereotypes. *Psychological Review, 102*, 4-27.

Greenwald, A. G., Banaji, M. R., Rudman, L. A., Farnham, S. D., Nosek, B. A., & Mellott, D. S. (2002). A unified theory of implicit attitudes, stereotypes, self-esteem, and self-concept. *Psychological Review, 109*, 3-25.

Grossman, P., Schoenfeld, A., & Lee, C. (2005). Teaching subject matter. In L. Darling-Hammond & J. Bransford (Eds.), *Preparing teachers for a changing world* (pp. 201-231). San Francisco: Jossey-Bass.

Guenther, F. H., Nieto-Castanon, A., Ghosh, S. S., & Tourville, J. A. (2004). Representation of sound categories in auditory cortical maps. *Journal of Speech, Language, and Hearing Research, 47*, 46-57.

Gutierrez, K. (2005). *Revisiting the continuity/discontinuity narrative: How schools reorganize the everyday routines of middleclass working families*, Working Paper. Center for the Everyday Lives of working Families, UCLA.

Hall, R., & Stevens, R. (1995). Making space: A comparison of mathematical work at school and in professional design practice. In S. L. Star (Ed.), *Cultures of computing* (pp. 118-145). London: Basil Blackwell.

Hall, R., Stevens, R., & Torralba, A. (2002). Disrupting representational infrastructure in conversations across disciplines. *Mind, Culture, and Activity, 9*(3), 179-210.

Hanna, E., & Meltzoff, A. N. (1993). Peer imitation by toddlers in laboratory, home, and day-care contexts: Implications for social learning and memory. *Developmental Psychology, 29*, 701-710.

Harris, T. R., Bransford, J. D., and Brophy, S. P. (2002). Roles for learning sciences and learning technologies in biomedical engineering education: A review of recent advances. *Annual Review of Biomedical Engineering 4*, 29-48.

Hatano, G. (2005). *Adaptive expertise*. Paper presented at the American Educational Research Association Annual Meeting, Montreal, Canada.

Hatano, G., & Inagaki, K. (1986). Two courses of expertise. In H. Stevenson, H. Azuma, & K. Hakuta (Eds.), *Child development and education in Japan* (pp. 262-272). New York: Freeman.

Hatano, G. & Inagaki, K. (1991). Sharing cognition through collective comprehension activity. In L. B. Resnick, J. Levine, & S. Teasley (Eds.), *Perspectives on socially shared cognition* (pp. 331-348). Washington, DC: American Psychological Association.

Hatano, G. & Osuro, Y. (2003). Commentary: Reconceptualizing school learning using insight from expertise research. *Educational Researcher, 32*, 26-29.

Healy, J. M. (1991). *Endangered minds: Why children don't think and what we can do about it*. New York: Simon & Schuster.

Heath, S. B. (1983). *Ways with words: Language, life, and work in communities and classrooms*. New York: Cambridge University Press.

Heath, S. B. (2001). Three's not a crowd: Plans, roles, and focus in the arts. *Educational Researcher, 30*(7), 10-17.

Hendrickson, G. & Schroder, W.H. (1941). Transfer of training in learning to hit a submerged target. *Journal of Educational Psychology, 32*, 205-213.

Hestenes, D. (1987). Toward a modeling theory of physics instruction. *American Journal of Physics, 55*, 440-454.

Hodge, L., & Brophy, S. (2005). *How is identify relevant to the notion of adaptive expertise?* Paper presented at the American Educational Research Association Annual Meeting, Montreal, Canada.

Holland, D., Lachicotte, W., Skinner, D., & Cain, C. (1998). *Identity and agency in cultural worlds*. Cambridge, MA: Harvard University Press.

Holt, J. (1964). *How children fail*. New York, NY: Dell.

Hong, H., & Lin, X. D. (2005). *Effect of people knowledge on science learning*. Paper presented at the meeting of the American Educational Research Association, Montreal, Canada.

Howard, D. V., & Howard, J. H., Jr. (2001). When it does hurt to try: Adult age differences in the effects of instructions on sequential pattern learning. *Psychonomic Bulletin and Review, 8*(4), 798-805.

Hurley, S., & Chater, N. (Eds.). (2005). *Perspectives on imitation: From cognitive neuroscience to social science* (Vols. 1 & 2). Cambridge, MA: MIT Press.

Hutchins, E. (1993). Learning to navigate. In S. Chaiklin & J. Lave (Eds.), *Understanding practice: Perspectives on activity and context* (pp. 35-63). Cambridge: Cambridge University Press.

Hutchins, E. (1995). *Cognition in the wild*. Cambridge, MA: MIT Press.

Huttenlocher, P. R., & Dabholkar, A. S. (1997). Regional differences in synaptogenesis in human cerebral cortex. *Journal of Comparative Neurology, 387*, 167-178.

Iverson, P., Kuhl, P. K., Akahane-Yamasa, R., Diesch, E., Tohkura, Y., Kettermann, A., & Siebert, C. (2003). A perceptual interference account of acquisition difficulties for non-native phonemes. *Cognition 87*, B47-B57.

Invernizzi, F., Falomir, P., Manuel, J., Muñoz, R. D., & Mugny, G. (2003). Social influence in personally relevant contexts: The respect attributed to the source as a factor increasing smokers' intention to quit smoking. *Journal of Applied Social Psychology, 33*(9), 1818-1836.

Iyengar, S., & Kinder, D. R. (1987). *News that matters: Television and American opinion*. Chicago: University of Chicago Press.

Iyengar, S., & Simon, A. F. (1993). News coverage of the Gulf War and public opinion: A study of agenda-setting, priming, and framing. *Communication Research, 20*, 365-383.

Jackson, P. L., Meltzoff, A. N., & Decety, J. (2005). How do we perceive the pain of others? A window into the neural processes involved in empathy. *NeuroImage, 24*, 771-779.

Jacoby, S., & Gonzales, P. (1991). The constitution of expert-novice in scientific discourse. *Issues in Applied Linguistics, 2*, 150-181.

Jessor, R., Colby, A., & Shweder, R. A. (Eds.) (1996). *Ethnography and human development*. Chicago: University of Chicago Press.

Johnson, D. & Johnson, R. (1981). Effects of cooperative, competitive, and individualistic goal structures on achievement: A meta-analysis. *Psychological Bulletin, 89*(1), 47-62.

Judd, C. H. (1908). The relation of special training to general intelligence. *Educational Review, 36*, 28-42.

Karmiloff-Smith, A., & Inhelder, B. (1974). "If you want to get ahead, get a theory," *Cognition, 3*(3), 195-212.

Katz, J. (2001). From how to why: On luminous description and causal inference in ethnography (Part I). *Ethnography, 2*(4), 1466-1381.

King, A. (1990). Facilitating elaborative learning in the classroom through reciprocal questioning. *American Educational Research Journal, 27*, 664-687.

Krosnick, J. A., & Branon, L. A. (1993). The impact of the Gulf War on the ingredients of presidential evaluations: Multidimensional effects of political involvement. *American Political Science Review, 87*, 963-978.

Kuhl, P. K. (1991). Human adults and human infants show a "perceptual magnet effect" for the prototypes of speech categories, monkeys do not. *Perception & Psychophysics, 50*, 93-107.

Kuhl, P. K. (2000). A new view of language acquisition. *Proc National Academy of Science, USA, 97*, 11850-11857.

Kuhl, P. K. (2003). Human speech and birdsong: Communication and the social brain. *Proceedings of the National Academy of Sciences, 100*, 9645-9646.

Kuhl, P. K. (2004). Early language acquisition: Cracking the speech code. *Nature Reviews Neuroscience, 5*, 831-843.

Kuhl, P. K., Andruski, J. E., Chistovich, I. A., Chistovich, L. A., Kozhevnikova, E. V., Ryskina, V. L., et al. (1997). Cross-language analysis of phonetic units in language addressed to infants. *Science, 277*, 684-686.

Kuhl, P. K., Conboy, B. T., Padden, D., Nelson, T. and Pruitt, J. (2005). Early speech perception and later language development: Implications for the "critical period." *Language Learning and Development, 1*, 237-264.

Kuhl, P. K., & Meltzoff, A. N. (1982). The bimodal perception of speech in infancy. *Science, 218*, 1138-1141.

Kuhl, P. K., Tsao, F.-M., & Liu, H.-M. (2003). Foreign-language experience in infancy: Effects of short-term exposure and social interaction on phonetic learning. *Proceedings of the National Academy of Sciences, 100*, 9096-9101.

Kuhl, P. K., Williams, K. A., Lacerda, F., Stevens, K. N., & Lindblom, B. (1992). Linguistic experience alters phonetic perception in infants by 6 months of age. *Science, 255*, 606-608.

Kuhn, T. S. (1962). *The structure of scientific revolutions*. Chicago: University of Chicago Press.

LaBerge, D. & Samuels, S. J. (1974). Toward a theory of automatic information processing in reading. *Cognitive Psychology, 6*, 293-323.

Labov, W. (1969). The logic of nonstandard English. *Georgetown Monographs on Language and Linguistics, 22*, 1-31.

Labov, W. (1972). *Language in the inner city: Studies in the Black English vernacular*. Philadelphia: University of Pennsylvania Press.

Lajoie, S. (2003). Transitions and trajectories for studies of expertise. *Educational Researcher, 32*, 21-25.

Larson, M. S. (2001). Sibling interaction in situation comedies over the years. In Bryant, Jennings & J. A. Bryant (Eds.), *Television and the American family* (pp. 163-176). Mahwah, NJ: Lawrence Erlbaum Associates.

Latour, B. (1995). The "pedofil" of Boa Vista: A photo-philosophical montage. *Common Knowledge, 4*(1), 144-187.

Lave, J. (1988). *Cognition in practice: Mind, mathematics and culture in everyday life*. New York: Cambridge University Press.

Lave, J., & Wenger, E. (1991). *Situated learning: Legitimate peripheral participation*. New York: Cambridge University Press.

Lee, C. D. (1995). A culturally based cognitive apprenticeship: Teaching African American high school students skills in literary interpretation. *Reading Research Quarterly, 30*(4), 608-631.

Lemke, J. L. (2001). The long and the short of it: Comments on multiple time-scale studies of human activity. *The Journal of the Learning Sciences, 10*, 17-26.

Leont'ev, A. N. (1978). *Activity, consciousness, and personality*. Englewood Cliffs, NJ: Prentice-Hall.

Lin, X. D., & Bransford, J. (2005). *People knowledge: A useful ingredient for bridging cultural differences between teachers and students*. Paper presented at the American Educational Research Association Annual Meeting, Montreal, Canada.

Lin, X. D., & Lehman, J. (1999). Supporting learning of variable control in a computer-based biology environment: Effects of prompting college students to reflect on their own thinking. *Journal of Research in Science Teaching, 36*(7), 837-858.

Linn, M. C., Davis, E. A., & Bell, P. (2004). *Internet environments for science education*. Mahwah, NJ: Lawrence Erlbaum Associates.

Liu, H.-M., Kuhl, P. K., & Tsao, F.-M. (2003). An association between mothers' speech clarity and infants' speech discrimination skills. *Developmental Science, 6*, F1-F10.

Lockhart, R. S., Lamon, M., & Gick, M. L. (1988). Conceptual transfer in simple insight problems. *Memory and Cognition, 16*, 36-44.

Loftus, E. F., & Loftus, G. R. (1974). Changes in memory structure and retrieval over the course of instruction. *Journal of Educational Psychology. 66*(3), 315-318.

Luria, A. R. (1976). *Cognitive development: Its cultural and social foundations*. Cambridge, MA: Harvard University Press.

MacWhinney, B., Bird, S., Cieri, C., & Martell, C. (2004). *TalkBank: Building an open unified multimodal database of communicative interaction*. LREC 2004, Lisbon.

Magnusson, S., & Palinscar, A. (2005). Teaching to promote the development of scientific knowledge and reasoning about light at the elementary level. In National Research Council, *How students learn: History, science, mathematics and science in the classroom* (pp. 421-459). Washington, DC: National Academy Press.

Martin, T. (2005). *Measuring preparation for future learning in children's mathematics: Instructional implications*. Paper presented at the American Educational Research Association Annual Meeting, Montreal, Canada.

Martin, T., & Schwartz, D. L. (2005). Physically distributed learning: Adapting and reinterpreting physical environments in the development of fraction concepts. *Cognitive Science, 29*, 587-625.

Matusov, E., Bell, N. & Rogoff, B. (2002). Schooling as a cultural process: Shared thinking and guidance by children from schools differing in collaborative practices. In R. Kail & H. Reese, (Eds.) *Advances in Child Development and Behavior, 29*. San Diego, CA: Academic Press, Inc.

Mayer, R., & Wittrock, M. (1996). Problem-solving transfer. In R. Calfee, & D. Berliner (Eds.) *Handbook of educational psychology* (pp. 47-62). New York: MacMillan.

Mayer, R. E., Fennell, S., Lindsay, F., & Campbell, J. (2004). A personalization effect in multimedia learning: Students learn better when words are in conversational style rather than formal style. *Journal of Educational Psychology, 96*(2), 389-395.

McCandliss, B. D., Fiez, J. A., Protopapas, A., Conway, M., & McClelland, J. (2002). Success and failure in teaching the [r]-[l] contrast to Japanese adults: tests of a Hebbian model of plasticity and stabilization in spoken language perception. *Cognitive, Affective, and Behavioral Neuroscience, 2*, 89-108.

McClelland, J. L. (2001). Failures to learn and their remediation: A Hebbian account. In J. L. McClelland and R. S. Siegler (Eds.), *Mechanisms of cognitive development: Behavioral and neural perspectives*, (pp. 97-121). Mahwah, NJ: Lawrence Erlbaum Associates.

McClelland, J. L., Fiez, J. A., & McCandliss, B. D. (2002). Teaching the /r/-/l/ discrimination to Japanese adults: Behavioral and neural aspects. *Physiology & Behavior, 77*, 657-662.

McCloskey, M. (1983). Intuitive physics. *Scientific American, 284*(4).

McDermott, R. (2001). A century of Margaret Mead. *Teacher's College Record, 103*(5), 843-867.

McDermott, R. P., Goldman, S. V., & Varenne, H. (1984). When school goes home: Some problems in the organization of homework. *Teachers College Record, 85*, 391-409.

Mead, M. (1928). *Coming of age in Samoa: A psychological study of primitive youth for western civilization*. New York: William Morrow.

Meltzoff, A. N. (1988a). Imitation of televised models by infants. *Child Development, 59*, 1221-1229.

Meltzoff, A. N. (1988b). Imitation, objects, tools, and the rudiments of language in human ontogeny. *Human Evolution, 3*, 45-64.

Meltzoff, A. N. (1995). Understanding the intentions of others: Re-enactment of intended acts by 18-month-old children. *Developmental Psychology, 31*, 838-850.

Meltzoff, A. N. (2005). Imitation and other minds: The "like me" hypothesis. In S. Hurley & N. Chater (Eds.), *Perspectives on imitation: From neuroscience to social science* (Vol. 2, pp. 55-77). Cambridge, MA: MIT Press.

Meltzoff, A. N., & Decety, J. (2003). What imitation tells us about social cognition: A rapprochement between developmental psychology and cognitive neuroscience. *Philosophical Transactions of the Royal Society of London: Biological Sciences, 358*, 491-500.

Meltzoff, A. N., & Moore, M. K. (1977). Imitation of facial and manual gestures by human neonates. *Science, 198*, 75-78.

Meltzoff, A. N., & Prinz, W. (Eds.). (2002). *The imitative mind: Development, evolution and brain bases*. Cambridge: Cambridge University Press.

Merzenich, M. M., Jenkins, W. M., Johnston, P., Schreiner, C., Miller, S. L., & Tallal, P. (1996). Temporal processing deficits of language-learning impaired children ameliorated by training. *Science, 271*, 77-81.

Mestre, J.P. (1994, February). Cognitive aspects of learning and teaching science. In S.J. Fitzsimmons & L.C. Kerpelman (Eds.), *Teacher Enhancement for Elementary and Secondary Science and Mathematics: Status, Issues and Problems* (pp. 31-53). Washington, DC: National Science Foundation (NSF 94-80).

Mestre, J. P., Thaden-Koch, T. C., Dufresne, R. J., & Gerace, W. J. (in press). The dependence of knowledge deployment on context among physics novices. In E. Redish & M. Vicentini (Eds.), *Proceedings of the International School of Physics "Enrico Fermi", Course CLVI, Research on Physics Education*. Amsterdam: IOS Press.

Michael, A. L., Klee, T., Bransford, J. D., & Warren, S. (1993). The transition from theory to therapy: Test of two instructional methods. *Applied Cognitive Psychology, 7*, 139-154.

Miell, D. & MacDonald, R.A.R. (2000). Children's creative collaborations: The importance of friendship when working together on a musical composition. *Social Development, 9*, 348-369.

Minstrell, J. (2005). *Facets of student thinking: A classroom assessment framework*. Paper presented at the American Educational Research Association Annual Meeting, Montreal, Canada.

Miyawaki, K., Strange, W., Verbrugge, R., Liberman, A. M., Jenkins, J. J., & Fujimura, O. (1975). An effect of linguistic experience: The discrimination of [r] and [l] by native speakers of Japanese and English. *Perception & Psychophysics, 18*, 331-340.

Mutz, D. C., & Reeves, B. (in press). Exposure to mediated political conflict: Effects of civility of interaction on arousal and memory. *American Political Science Quarterly*.

Näätänen, R., Lehtokoski, A., Lennes, M., Cheour, M., Huotilainen, M., Iivonen, A., et al. (1997). Language-specific phoneme representations revealed by electric and magnetic brain responses. *Nature, 385*, 432-434.

Nasir, N. S. (2002). Identity, goals, and learning: mathematics in cultural practice. *Mathematical Thinking and Learning, 4*(2 & 3), 213-247.

Nathan, M. J., Koedinger, K. R., & Alibali, M. W. (2001). "Expert blind spot: when content knowledge eclipses pedagogical content knowledge." In L. Chen et al. (Eds.), *Proceeding of the Third International Conference on Cognitive Science*. (pp. 644-648). Beijing, China: USTC Press.

National Council of Teachers of Mathematics. (1989). *Curriculum and evaluation standards for school mathematics*. Reston, VA: Author.

National Council of Teachers of Mathematics (1995). *Assessment standards for school mathematics*. Reston, VA: NCTM.

National Council of Teachers of Mathematics (2000). *Principles and standards for school mathematics.* Reston, VA: NCTM.

National Research Council (1996). *National science education standards.* Washington, DC: National Academy Press.

National Research Council (1999). *Being fluent with information technology.* Washington, DC: National Academy Press.

National Research Council (2000). *How people learn: Brain, mind, experience, and school* (Expanded Edition). Washington, DC: National Academy Press. [On-line]. Available: http://www.nap.edu/html/howpeople1/

National Research Council (2001). *Knowing what students know: The science and design of educational assessment.* Washington, DC: National Academy Press.

National Research Council (2002). *Learning and understanding: Improving advanced study of mathematics and science in U.S. high schools.* Washington, DC: National Academy Press.

National Research Council (2003). *Learning and instruction: A SERP research agenda.* Washington, DC: National Academy Press.

National Research Council (2005). *How students learn: History, math, and science in the classroom.* Washington, DC: National Academies Press.

Newell, K., Liu, Y., & Mayer-Kress, G. (2001). Time scales in motor learning and development. *Psychological Review, 108,* 57–82.

Nielsen, A. C. (1987). *Annual Nielsen report on television: 1987.* Nielsen Media Research, New York.

Neisser, U. (1976). *Cognition and reality.* San Francisco: Freeman.

Newport, E.L. and Aslin, R.N. (2004). Learning at a distance I. Statistical learning of non-adjacent dependencies. *Cognitive Psychology, 48,* 127–162.

Nissen, M. J., & Bullemer, P. T. (1987). Attentional requirements for learning: Evidence from performance measures. *Cognitive Psychology, 19,* 1–32.

Norman, D. A. (1993). *Things that make us smart: Defending human attributes in the age of the machine.* New York: Addison-Wesley.

Ochs, E., Taylor, C., Rudolph, D., & Smith, R. (1992). Storytelling as a theory-building activity. *Discourse Processes, 15*(1), 37–17.

Ochsner, K. N., & Lieberman, M. D. (2001). The emergence of social cognitive neuroscience. *American Psychologist, 56,* 717–734.

Palincsar, A. S. & Brown, A. L. (1989). Instruction for self-regulated reading. In L. B. Resnick & L. E. Klopfer (Eds.), *Toward the thinking curriculum: Current cognitive research* (pp. 19–39). Alexandria, VA: ASCD.

Papert, S. (1980). *Mindstorms: Children, computers, and powerful ideas.* New York: Basic Books.

Pea, R. D. (1987). Socializing the knowledge transfer problem. *International Journal of Educational Research, 11,* 639–663.

Pea, R. D. (1993). Practices of distributed intelligence and designs for education. In G. Salomon (Ed.). *Distributed cognitions.* New York: Cambridge University Press, pp. 47–87.

Pea, R. D. (in press). Video-as-data and digital video manipulation techniques for transforming learning sciences research, education and other cultural practices. To appear in J. Weiss, J. Nolan & P. Trifonas (Eds.), *International Handbook of Virtual Learning Environments.* Dordrecht: Kluwer Academic Publishing.

Pea, R., Mills, M., Rosen, J., Dauber, K., Effelsberg, W., & Hoffert. E. (2004, Jan–March). The DIVER™Project: Interactive Digital Video Repurposing. *IEEE Multimedia, 11*(1), 54–61.

Penuel, W. R., & Yarnall, L. (2005). Designing handheld software to support classroom assessment: An analysis of conditions for teacher adoption. *Journal of Technology, Learning, and Assessment, 3*(5), Available from http://www.jtla.org.

Petrosino, A. (2005). *Measures of adaptive expertise in bioengineering.* Paper presented at the American Educational Research Association Annual Meeting, Montreal, Canada.

Petty, R. E., Priester, J. R., & Briñol, P. (2002). Mass media attitude change: Implications of the elaboration likelihood model of persuasion. In Bryant, J. & D. Zillman (Eds.), *Media effects: Advances in theory and research* (pp. 155–198). Mahwah, NJ: Lawrence Erlbaum Associates.

Phelps, E., & Damon, W. (1989). Problem solving with equals: Peer collaboration as a context for learning mathematics and spatial concepts. *Journal of Educational Psychology, 81*(4), 639–646.

Philips, S. (1983). *The invisible culture: Communication in classroom and community on the Warm Springs Indian Reservation.* Prospect Heights, IL: Waveland Press, Inc.

Piaget, J. (1952). *The origins of intelligence in children.* (M. Cook, Trans) New York: International Universities Press.

Piaget, J. (1964). Development and learning. In R. E. Ripple & V. N. Rockcastle. (Eds.). *Piaget rediscovered.* New York: Cornell University Press.

Pisoni, D. B. (1993). Long-term memory in speech perception: Some new findings on talker variability, speaking rate and perceptual learning. *Speech Communication, 13,* 109–125.

Pisoni, D., Aslin, R., Perey, A., & Hennessy, B. (1994). Perceptual learning of normative speech contrasts: Implications for theories of speech perception. In J. Goodman & H. Nusbaum (Eds.), *The development of speech perception: The transition from speech sounds to spoken words* (pp. 121–166). Cambridge, MA, USA: The MIT Press.

Polanyi, M. (1958). *Personal knowledge: Towards a post-critical philosophy.* London: Routledge.

Polanyi, M. (1967). *The tacit dimension.* New York: Anchor Books.

Poldrack, R. A. (2000). Imaging brain plasticity: Conceptual and methodological issues. *NeuroImage, 12,* 1–13.

Poldrack, R. A., Clark, J., Pare-Blagoev, J., Shohamy, D., Creso Moyano, J., Myers, C., et al. (2001). Interactive memory systems in the human brain. *Nature, 414,* 546–550.

Povinelli, D. J., Reaux, J. E., Theall, L. A., & Giambrone, S. (2000). *Folk physics for apes: The chimpanzee's theory of how the world works.* New York: Oxford University Press.

Pressley, M. (1995). More about the development of self-regulation: Complex, long-term, and thoroughly social. *Educational Psychologist, 30*(4), 207–212.

Reber, A. S. (1967). Implicit learning of artifical grammars. *Journal of Verbal Learning and Verbal Behavior, 6,* 855-863.

Reber, A. S. (1976). Implicit learning of synthetic languages: The role of instructional set. *Journal of Experimental Psychology: Human Learning and Memory, 2,* 88-94.

Reber, A. S. (1993). *Implicit learning and tacit knowledge: An essay on the cognitive unconscious.* New York: Oxford University Press.

Resnick, L. (1987). Learning in school and out. *Educational Researcher, 16*(9), 13-20.

Rideout, V. J., Vandewater, E., & Wartella, E. A. (2003, Fall). *Zero to six: Electronic media in the lives of infants, toddlers and preschoolers.* Kaiser Family Foundation Report.

Rizzolatti, G., Fadiga, L., Fogassi, L., & Gallese, V. (2002). From mirror neurons to imitation, facts, and speculations. In A. N. Meltzoff & W. Prinz (Eds.), *The imitative mind: Development, evolution, and brain bases* (pp. 247-266). Cambridge: Cambridge University Press.

Rizzolatti, G., Fadiga, L., Gallese, V., & Fogassi, L. (1996). Premotor cortex and the recognition of motor actions. *Cognitive Brain Research, 3,* 131-141.

Robinson, A., & Stern, S. (1997). Corporate creativity: How innovation and improvement actually happen. San Francisco: Berrett-Koehler.

Rogoff, B. (1990). *Apprenticeship in thinking: Cognitive development in social context.* New York: Oxford University Press.

Rogoff, B. (1995). Observing sociocultural activity on three planes: participatory appropriation, guided participation, and apprenticeship. In J. Wertsch, P. del Río, & A. Alvarez. (Eds.) *Sociocultural studies of mind.* New York: Cambridge University Press.

Rogoff, B. (2003). *The cultural nature of human development.* New York: Oxford University Press.

Rogoff, B., & Lave, J. (1984). *Everyday cognition: Its development in social context.* Cambridge, MA: Harvard University Press.

Rogoff, B., Matusov, E., & White, C. (1996). Models of teaching and learning: Participation in a community of learners. In D. Olson & N. Torrance (Eds.), *Handbook of education and human development: New models of learning, teaching, and schooling* (pp. 388-414). London: Basil Blackwell.

Rogoff, B., Paradise, R., Mejía Arauz, R., Correa-Chávez, M., & Angelillo, C. (2003). Firsthand learning by intent participation. *Annual Review of Psychology,* 54.

Rose, M. (2004). *The mind at work: Valuing the intelligence of the American worker.* New York: Viking.

Saffran, J. R. (2002). Constraints on statistical language learning. *Journal of Memory and Language, 47,* 172-196.

Saffran, J. R. (2003). Statistical language learning: Mechanisms and constraints. *Current Directions in Psychological Science. 12,* 110-114.

Salomon, G., & Perkins, D. (1989). Rocky road to transfer: Rethinking mechanisms of a neglected phenomenon. *Educational Psychologist, 24,* 113-142.

Saxe, G. B. (1982). Developing forms of arithmetic operations among the Oksapmin of Papua New Guinea. *Developmental Psychology, 18*(4), 583-594.

Schacter, D. L. (1987). Implicit memory: History and current status. *Journal of Experimental Psychology: Learning, Memory, and Cognition, 13*(3), 501-518.

Schank R., & Abelson R. (1977). *Scripts, plans, goals and understanding: An inquiry into human knowledge structures.* Hillsdale, NJ: Lawrence Erlbaum Associates.

Schegloff, E. A. (1992). On talk and its institutional occasions. In P. Drew & J. Heritage (Eds.), *Talk at work* (pp. 101-134). New York: Cambridge University Press.

Schleuder, J., McCombs, M., & Wanta, W. (1991). Inside the agenda-setting process: How political advertising and TV news prime viewers to think about issues and candidates. In F. Biocca (Ed.), *Television and political advertising 1: Psychological processes* (pp. 263-310). Hillsdale, NJ: Lawrence Erlbaum Associates.

Schliemann, A. D., & Acioly, N. M. (1989). Mathematical knowledge developed at work: The contribution of practice versus the contribution of schooling. *Cognition & Instruction, 6,* 185-222.

Schmuckler, M. A. (2001). What is ecological validity? A dimensional analysis. *Infancy, 2*(4), 419-436.

Schoenfeld, A. H. (1985). *Mathematical problem solving.* New York: Academic Press.

Schoenfeld, A. H. (1992). Learning to think mathematically: Problem solving, metacognition and sense-making in mathematics. In D. Grouws (Ed.),*Handbook for research on mathematics teaching and learning.* New York: Macmillan.

Schwartz, D. L., & Bransford, J. D. (1998). A time for telling. *Cognition & Instruction, 16*(4), 475-522.

Schwartz, D. L., & Martin, T. (2004) Inventing to prepare for learning: The hidden efficiency of original student production in statistics instruction. *Cognition & Instruction, 22,* 129-184.

Schwartz, D., Bransford, J., & Sears, D. (2005). Efficiency and innovation in transfer. In J. Mestre (Ed.), *Transfer of learning: from a modern multidisciplinary perspective* (pp. 1-51). Greenwich, CT: Information Age Publishing.

Schwartz, D., Blair, K., Davis, J., Chang, J., & Hartman, K. (2005). *Iterative dynamic assessments with feedback to students.* Paper presented at the American Educational Research Association Annual Meeting, Montreal, Canada.

Scribner, S. (1997a). Knowledge at work. In E. Tobach, R. J. Falmagne, M. B. Parlee, L. M. W. Martin & A. S. Kapelman (Eds.), *Mind & social practice: Selected writings of Sylvia Scribner* (pp. 308-318). Cambridge: Cambridge University Press.

Scribner, S. (1997b). Studying working intelligence. In E. Tobach, R. J. Falmagne, M. B. Parlee, L. M. W. Martin, & A. S. Kapelman (Eds.), *Mind and social practice: Selected writings of Sylvia Scribner* (pp. 338-366). Cambridge: Cambridge University Press.

Scribner, S., & Fahrmeir, E. (1982). *Practical and theoretical arithmetic: Some preliminary findings, industrial literacy project* (Working Paper No. 3). New York: City University of New York, Graduate Center.

Seger, C. A. (1994). Implicit Learning. *Psychological Bulletin, 115,* 163–196.

Shanahan, J., & Morgan, M. (1999). *Television and its viewers: Cultivation theory and research.* Cambridge: Cambridge University Press.

Shaughnessy, M. F. (2002, December). An Interview with Henry L. Roediger III. *Educational Psychology Review, 14*(4), 395–411.

Shulman, L. (1987). Knowledge and teaching: Foundations of the new reform. *Harvard Educational Review, 57,* 1–22.

Simon, D. A., & Bjork, R. A. (2002). Models of performance in learning multisegment movement tasks: Consequences for acquisition, retention, and judgments of learning. *Journal of Experimental Psychology: Applied, 8,* 222–232.

Singer, J. L., & Singer, D. G. (1981). *Television, imagination, and aggression: A study of preschoolers.* Hillsdale, NJ: Lawrence Erlbaum Associates.

Smith, J. P., diSessa, A. A., & Roschelle, J. (1993). Misconceptions reconceived: A constructivist analysis of knowledge in transition. *The Journal of the Learning Sciences, 3*(2), 115–163.

Snow, C. E. (1981). The uses of imitation. *Journal of Child Language, 8,* 205–212.

Snow, C. E. (1982). Are parents language teachers? In K. Borman (Ed.), *The social life of children in a changing society* (pp. 81–95). Hillsdale, NJ: Lawrence Erlbaum Associates.

Snow, C. E. (1983). Saying it again: The role of expanded and deferred imitations in language acquisition. In K. E. Nelson (Ed.), *Children's language* (Vol. 4, pp. 29–58). New York: Gardner Press.

Sparks, G. G., & Ogles, R. M. (1990). The difference between fear of victimization and the probability of being victimized: Implications for cultivation. *Journal of Broadcasting & Electronic Media, 34*(3), 351–358.

Spiro, K., & McCombs, M. (2004). Agenda-setting effects and attitude strength: Political figures during the 1996 presidential election. *Communication Research, 31*(1), 36–57.

Spiro, R. J., Vispoel, W. L., Schmitz, J., Samarapungavan, A., & Boeger, A. (1987). Knowledge acquisition for application: Cognitive flexibility and transfer in complex content domains. In B. C. Britton & S. Glynn (Eds.), *Executive control processes in reading* (pp. 177–199). Hillsdale, NJ: Lawrence Erlbaum Associates.

Stadler, M. A., & Frensch, P. A. (1998). *Handbook of implicit learning.* Thousand Oaks, CA: SAGE.

Stephenson (2000). *Language use in mathematics classrooms.* Unpublished doctoral dissertation, Stanford University.

Sternberg, R. (2003). What is an "expert student"?. *Educational Researcher, 32,* 5–9.

Stevens, R. J., & Slavin, R.E. (1995). The cooperative elementary school: Effects on students' achievement, attitudes, and social relations. *American Educational Research Journal, 32,* 321–351.

Stevens, R. (2000a). Divisions of labor in school and in the workplace: Comparing computer and paper-supported activities across settings. *The Journal of the Learning Sciences, 9*(4), 373–401.

Stevens, R. (2000b). Who counts what as math: Emergent and assigned mathematical problems in a project-based classroom. In J. Boaler (Ed.), *Multiple perspectives on mathematics education* (pp. 105–144). New York: Elsevier.

Stevens, R. (in press). Capturing ideas in digital things: A new twist on the old problem of inert knowledge. In Goldman, R., Pea, R. D., Barron, B. & Derry, S. (Eds.). *Video research in the learning sciences.* Mahwah, NJ: Lawrence Erlbaum Associates.

Stevens, R., Cherry, G., & Fournier, J. (2001). Video Traces: Rich media annotations for teaching and learning. In G. Stahl (Ed). *Proceedings of the Computer Supported Collaborative Learning Conference.* Mahwah, NJ: Lawrence Erlbaum Associates.

Stevens, R., & Hall, R. (1997). Seeing Tornado: How *Video Traces* mediate visitor understandings of (natural?) spectacles in a science museum, *Science Education, 18*(6), 735–748.

Stevens, R., & Hall, R. (1998). Disciplined perception: Learning to see in technoscience. In M. Lampert & M. L. Blunk (Eds.),*Talking mathematics in school: Studies of teaching and learning* (pp. 107–149). Cambridge: Cambridge University Press.

Stevens, R., & Toro-Martell, S. (in press). Leaving a trace: Digital Meta-exhibits for supporting visitors to represent and exchange their ideas about museum exhibits. *Journal of Museum Education.*

Stevens, R., Wineburg, S., Herrenkohl, L. & Bell, P. (in press). The comparative understanding of school subjects: Past, present and future. *Review of Educational Research.*

Strange, W. (1995). *Speech perception and linguistic experience: Issues in cross-language research.* Timonium, MD: York.

Suchman, L. (1995). Making work visible. *Communications of the ACM, 38*(9), 57–64.

Tallal, P., Miller, S. L., Bedi, G., Byma, G., Wang, X. Q., Nagarajan, S. S., et al. (1996). Language comprehension in language-learning impaired children improved with acoustically modified speech. *Science, 271,* 81–84.

Taylor, M. (1996). A theory of mind perspective on social cognitive development. In E. C. Carterette & M. P. Friedman (Series Eds.) R. Gelman & T. Au (Eds.), *Handbook of perception and cognition: Vol. 13. Perceptual and cognitive development* (pp. 283–329). New York: Academic Press.

Tobach, E., Falmagne, R., J., Parlee, M. B., Martin, L. M. W., Kapelman, A. S. (Eds.) (1997). *Mind and social practice: Selected writings of Sylvia Scribner.* New York: Cambridge University Press.

Tremblay, K., Kraus, N., & McGee, T. (1998). The time course of auditory perceptual learning: neurophysiological changes during speech-sound training. *NeuroReport, 9,* 3557–3560.

Tomasello, M. (1999). *The cultural origins of human cognition.* Cambridge, MA: Harvard University Press.

Tomasello, M., & Call, J. (1997). *Primate cognition.* New York: Oxford University Press.

Trappey C. (1996). A meta-analysis of consumer choice and sub-liminal advertising. *Psychology & Marketing, 13*(5), 517-530.

Tsao, F.-M., Liu, H.-M., & Kuhl, P. K. (2004). Speech perception in infancy predicts language development in the second year of life: A longitudinal study. *Child Development, 75,* 1067-1084.

Tyack, D., & Tobin, W. (1984). The grammar of schooling: Why has it been so hard to change? *American Educational Research Journal, 31*(3), 453-479.

Vaill, P. B. (1996). *Learning as a way of being: Strategies for survival in a world of permanent white water.* San Francisco: Jossey-Bass.

Valdes, G., Bunch, G., Snow, C., Lee, C., & Matos, L. (2005). Enhancing the development of students' language. In L. Darling-Hammond & J. Bransford (Eds.), *Preparing teachers for a changing world* (pp. 126-168). San Francisco: Jossey-Bass.

Van Lehn, K. (1990). *Mind bugs: The origins of procedural misconceptions.* Cambridge, MA: MIT Press.

Vera, A. H., & Simon, H. A. (1993). Situated action: A symbolic interpretation. *Cognitive Science, 17,* 7-48.

Vye, N. J., Schwartz, D. L., Bransford, J. D., Barron, B. J., Zech, L., & Cognition and Technology Group at Vanderbilt. (1998). SMART environments that support monitoring, reflection, and revision. In D. Hacker, J. Dunlosky, & A. C. Graesser (Eds.), *Metacognition in educational theory and practice* (pp. 305-346). Mahwah, NJ: Lawrence Erlbaum Associates.

Vygotsky, L. S. (1962). *Thought and language.* Cambridge, MA: MIT Press.

Vygotsky, L. S. (1978). *Mind in society: The development of higher psychological processes.* Cambridge, MA: Harvard University Press.

Vygotsky, L. S. (1987). Thinking and speech (N. Minick, Trans.). In R. W. Rieber & A. S. Carton (Eds.), *The collected works of L. S. Vygotsky: Vol.* (pp. 37-285). New York: Plenum Press.

Walker, J. (2005). *Design scenarios as a measure of adaptive understanding.* Paper presented at the American Educational Research Association Annual Meeting, Montreal, Canada.

Webb, N. M. (1989). Peer interaction and learning in small groups. *International Journal of Educational Research, 13,* 21-39.

Webb, N. M., Troper, J. D., & Fall, R. (1995). Constructive activity and learning in collaborative small groups. *Journal of Educational Psychology, 87,* 406-423.

Wenger, E. (1999) *Communities of practice: Learning, meaning and identity.* Cambridge: Cambridge University Press.

Werker, J. F., & Tees, R. C. (1984). Cross-language speech perception: Evidence for perceptual reorganization during the first year of life. *Infant Behavior & Development, 7,* 49-63.

Wertheimer M. (1959). *Productive thinking.* New York: Harper and Row.

Wertsch, J. V. (1998). *Mind as action.* New York: Oxford University Press.

White, B. C., & Frederiksen, J. (1998). Inquiry, modeling, and metacognition: Making science accessible to all students. *Cognition & Instruction, 16*(1), 39-66.

Whiten, A. (2002). The imitator's representation of the imitated: Ape and child. In A. N. Meltzoff & W. Prinz (Eds.), *The imitative mind: Development, evolution, and brain bases* (pp. 98-121). Cambridge: Cambridge University Press.

Wiggins, G. & McTighe, J. (1997). *Understanding by design.* Association for Supervision and Curriculum Development, VA.

Willis, P. (1981). *Learning to labor.* New York: Columbia University Press.

Wineburg, S. (1998). Reading Abraham Lincoln: An expert/expert study in the interpretation of historical texts. *Cognitive Science.*

Zech, L., Vye, N. J., Bransford, J. D., Goldman, S. R., Barron, B. J., Schwartz, D. L., et al. (1998). An introduction to geometry through anchored instruction. In R. Lehrer & D. Chazan (Eds.), *New directions for teaching and learning geometry* (pp. 439-463). Mahwah, NJ: Laweence Erlbaum Associates.

Zhang, Y., Kuhl, P. K., Imada, T., Kotani, M., & Tohkura, Y. (2005). Effects of language experience: Neural commitment to language-specific auditory patterns. *NeuroImage 26,* 703-720.

·11·

KNOWLEDGE: STRUCTURES AND PROCESSES

Gregory Schraw
Department of Educational Psychology,
University of Nevada, Las Vegas

This chapter addresses the role of knowledge in learning. To do so, it is necessary to examine how knowledge is represented in memory, what kinds of knowledge we hold in memory, and how we use that knowledge to think, solve problems, and self-regulate our learning. This chapter is divided into five sections. The first section briefly discusses historical perspectives on knowledge acquisition and representation, and how these views have changed over the past century. The second section considers how knowledge is represented in memory and provides a taxonomy of different kinds of knowledge. The third section focuses on the acquisition of knowledge as the learner moves from novice to expert. This section reviews characteristics of experts, stages in skill acquisition, and different models of the development of expertise. The fourth section discusses four emergent themes and implications for education, and the fifth provides a summary and three main conclusions.

EVOLVING VIEWS OF KNOWLEDGE

What is knowledge, where does it come from, and how does it change? These questions have sparked debates for centuries among philosophers, educators, and psychologists. The study of knowledge acquisition and representation (i.e., epistemology) has become a branch of philosophy all its own. Many theories have come and gone over the past three centuries, and lively debate continues today (Fitzgerald & Cunningham, 2002; Guba & Lincoln, 1994; Murphy, 2003; Prawat & Floden, 1994; Reynolds, Sinatra, & Jetton, 1996). This section briefly addresses

how theories of knowledge have changed over the past three centuries. Understanding these differences is important because different theories make different assumptions about the acquisition, structure, and development of knowledge.

Chronicling evolving views of knowledge is a huge undertaking (Hofer, 2002). Table 11.1 classifies different epistemological theories into three perspectives I refer to as positivist, postpositivist, and postmodern. A number of authors have compared these three perspectives on multiple dimensions. Table 11.1 summarizes each perspective's stance on four of these dimensions and provides representative schools of thought and key intellectual proponents.

Positivism is characterized by a belief in learning through experience (Philips & Burbules, 2000). Knowledge is viewed as stable in that it is constant over time from person to person. It is objective in nature rather than subjective; thus, knowledge is not amenable to personal interpretation by the knower. Knowledge acquisition occurs through experience and is imparted to others through their experiences and by transmission through books, lectures, and other varieties of formal schooling. Key historical figures include Locke, the British Empiricists such as John Stuart Mill, and more recently, American behaviorists such as B. F. Skinner and connectionists such as David Rumelhart, who argue that it is primarily experience that enables us to acquire, represent, and reorganize knowledge.

Postpositivist views of knowledge reflect a shift from objectivist views of knowing to consensual understanding, which is situated in everyday experience (Peters &

TABLE 11.1. Three Epistemological Perspectives

	Positivist	Postpositivist	Postmodern
Stability of knowledge	Stable	Slowly changing	Ever changing
Objectivity of knowledge	Objective	Consensual	Subjective
Mode of knowledge acquisition	Discovered through sensory experience	Constructed through social interactions and experience	Constructed through personal experience
How knowledge is imparted to others	Transmission	Transaction with others	Transaction with self
Historical examples	Behaviorism (Skinner); connectionism (Rumelhart & McClelland) (Rumelhart)	Structuralism (Piaget, Chomsky); modernism (Freud)	Poststructuralism (Foucault); postmodernism (Lyotard)

Burbules, 2004). Postpositivists view knowledge as changeable via rational analysis, rather than static. Knowledge does not possess inherent meaning, but must be interpreted within the context in which one encounters and uses it. In addition, there is a belief that knowledge is negotiated among a number of individuals to reach an agreed-on consensus. For example, laws and constitutional principles represent approximations to an ideal, rather than an objective ideal. Learning is based on experiences with others within real-world contexts and is consensual in nature rather than individualistic. Historically, postpositive views of knowledge are based on grand narratives (i.e., comprehensive explanatory theories) that attempt to impose an overarching structure on complex processes and date back to early rationalist philosophers such as Descartes and Kant, who argued that rational thought is the primary means for understanding and testing the validity of knowledge. More recent examples include Noam Chomsky, who developed his theory of transformational grammar to explain all linguistic aspects of communication. Similarly, Jean Piaget proposed a comparable structural model of development, which involved four discrete stages and key mechanisms such as equilibration.

Postmodern theories of knowledge often question the grand narrative and structural models of postpositivists (Kelly, 1997; Prawat, 1996). Knowledge is seen as highly subjective and derived chiefly through the individual experience of each person. Knowledge is not transmitted or transacted on with others, but is self-constructed to create personal meaning for the individual that may differ substantially from others' interpretation of the same information. Historical examples include the work of Foucault and Lyotard, who emphasized the deconstruction of grand narratives and denied that knowledge has a basis in external, objective being.

The three perspectives summarized in Table 11.1 represent three very different perspectives on knowledge. In essence, the positivist perspective claims that knowledge exists independent of the knower, and that the knower does not change knowledge, but simply consumes and uses it as an intellectual means to an end. Another key assumption is that knowledge is more or less universal for all people. Postpositivists propose that knowledge changes in a consensual manner, and that although there is a grand order to things, our understanding of that grand order grows and changes as we gain more knowledge about it. Postmodern perspectives believe that objective knowledge does not exist, but rather, that we are all knowledgeable in highly subjective and idiosyncratic ways based on our personal experiences and interpretative biases.

Perhaps the most important distinction among these three perspectives is their position on *constructivism*, which refers to the belief that meaning is constructed actively by the learner, rather than simply assimilated in a passive manner. Positivists do not fully endorse constructivism because knowledge is assumed to be objective and stable. Postpositivists endorse a constructivism based on consensual understanding based on shared social meanings. Postmodernists endorse a subjective constructivism based largely on individual experience. Most contemporary educators would support a constructivist view of learning in some way, shape, or form. A highly readable discussion of different types of constructivism may be found in Prawat (1996).

The present chapter is situated primarily within the postpositivist perspective. It assumes that there is an overarching structure to how knowledge is organized and represented in memory, even though there is disagreement about how these processes occur. This chapter also presumes that knowledge is not completely subjective and unique to the individual. Indeed, research suggests that people within a common culture share similar schemata and scripts that guide shared communication and understanding (Anderson, 2000; Reynolds et al., 1996). Much of the research cited in this chapter also implicitly assumes that whereas it is impossible for researchers to know the true state of mental structures and processes, it is possible to generate an empirically supported approximation of them through systematic theory, testing, and revision.

I encourage you to critically examine the information and theories presented here. All theories are fallible and only as good as the data that supports them. This chapter presents the more plausible and defensible theories available at this time. These theories undoubtedly will change and may become obsolete as more evidence emerges. Ultimately, theories improve due to careful analysis and revision. I also hope you consider and discuss your own epistemological beliefs and conclusions about the information presented here.

KNOWLEDGE STRUCTURES

The word *knowledge* is deceptive because it suggests that knowledge constitutes a single category in which all knowledge is the same. This section focuses on two main issues, which refute this view. The first issue is what types of knowledge are represented in memory. We consider three generic types, commonly referred to as declarative, procedural, and self-regulatory knowledge. The second issue is how knowledge is represented in memory. Three general types of representational models have been proposed over the past 50 years, including hierarchical network models, nonhierarchical production system models, and nonhierarchical connectionist models.

A Taxonomy of Knowledge

People store many different types of knowledge in memory. Different types of knowledge serve different purposes, yet all are important and necessary for daily intellectual success. This section focuses on three main types of knowledge and subtypes within each of the three main categories shown in Fig. 11.1. Declarative knowledge refers to the facts and concepts we know. Procedural knowledge refers to how we do things. Self-regulatory knowledge refers to knowledge we have about ourselves as learners, what we know, and how to control our learning. All three types of knowledge are important. However, even large amount of declarative and procedural knowledge, without self-regulatory knowledge to support it, do little to help us survive and adapt (Zeidner, Boekaerts, & Pintrich, 2000; Zimmerman, 2000).

Declarative Knowledge. *Declarative knowledge* is a broad category that includes facts, concepts, and the relationships among concepts that lead to an integrated conceptual understanding of a domain of knowledge. Declarative knowledge includes thousands of facts such as the names of colors, numbers, coins, and trees. Concepts represent categories such as automobiles or rock music. Often concepts are phenomena we can describe abstractly, such as love or self-efficacy. Declarative knowledge also includes integrated conceptual knowledge that is sometimes referred to as *structural knowledge* (Jonassen, Beissner & Yacci, 1993) or *mental models* (Halpern, 2003). The information in Fig. 11.1 provides an example of structural knowledge in which facts and concepts are interrelated into a single conceptual model. If Fig. 11.1 existed only in memory rather than on paper, one might refer to it as a mental model.

Declarative knowledge usually is subdivided into two categories called semantic and episodic knowledge. *Semantic knowledge* refers to abstract knowledge that is acquired without particular reference to a place or time. *Episodic knowledge* is information about specific episodes or events that are remembered as separate entries in memory. Each of these categories can be subdivided further.

Semantic Knowledge. Semantic knowledge consists of facts, concepts, and abstract principles in memory. Most adults have an enormous amount of semantic knowledge in memory that ranges from knowledge about letters in the alphabet to understandings of concepts such as perjury, infinity, and nonexistence. Not all semantic information is at the same level of specificity. Much of our semantic knowledge is factual in nature, which refers to a specific object or piece of information such as *oak tree*. Another huge segment of semantic knowledge is

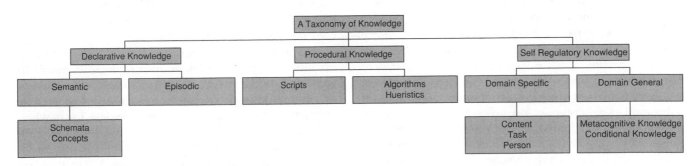

FIGURE 11.1 A taxonomy of knowledge.

conceptual, which refers to general categories such as mammals, cars, or sports.

There is so much semantic information in memory that we need some way to organize it. Imagine for a moment that you memorized every telephone number in metropolitan New York City, which includes approximately 8 million residential telephone numbers. Now imagine trying to search your memory for any one of those numbers if they were arranged randomly. It is unlikely that you would be able to do so successfully. Now imagine that you decide to organize these numbers to save yourself time and effort. Although there are many ways to do so, one of the most effective is to order all the numbers by the last name of the individual holding that number. Any number could be found quite easily using this system.

Information in memory is cross-listed using several organization systems, which enables us to optimize retrieval of that information (Neath, 1998; Zacks, Hasher, & Li, 2000). Like any good filing system, memory works best when we have access to information from a number of different retrieval points.

One on the most important organizational units in memory is the *schema*, which refers to an organized body of information about some distinct domain of knowledge. For example, every adult has a "car schema" in which information about different types of cars is organized. A schema (pl., *schemata*) provides a mental framework that guides perception and understanding. Schemata enable us to construct meaning based on what we already know and what we expect to happen given our knowledge about the world. Schemata also affect how we reconstruct events and understanding at a later time.

A schema is essential to learning for several reasons. One reason is that it enables us to organize a large amount of information into an integrated body of knowledge in an efficient manner. In essence, a schema can be likened to a file drawer in a file cabinet. The file cabinet might contain many drawers, which each contains different types of information. When we need to find a particular type of information, we go to the drawer it is filed in. A second reason is that a schema reduces the effort needed to encode and retrieve information due to organizational efficiency (Sweller, van Merrienboer, & Pass, 1998). Each schema contains *slots* for specific types of information. For example, if you told me that you drive a Volkswagen Beetle, I could quickly file that information in a slot subsumed under compact foreign cars in my car schema. Remembering that information at a later time would be facilitated by going directly to the slot in memory where it is stored. A third reason is that a schema can be activated to

support thinking and problem solving. Skilled readers, for instance, use organized knowledge in a schema to make predictions when they read, to fill in missing information in a text, to form plausible hypotheses, and to interpret events in a story (Wagner & Stanovich, 1996).

How is information in a schema arranged? One characteristic is that information is organized hierarchically. For example, in Fig. 11.1, the concept *schema* is subsumed under semantic knowledge, which is subsumed under declarative knowledge. A schema can be entered at whatever level of specificity is needed, which facilitates access to information. A second characteristic is that a schema can be connected to other schemata; thus, searching memory to find one particular piece of information may make it easier to find another piece of related information.

There are probably thousands of schemata in most adults' memory. We simply could not organize all that we know effectively without something like an integrated collection of schemata. Unfortunately, schemata also may create problems because they enable us to generate inferences consistent with what we already know, even though that inference may not be justified in every case. For example, people may remember events that never happened because those events are consistent with information in memory. A large number of studies have demonstrated that people make constructive and reconstructive errors when remembering events because they generate inferences consistent with their knowledge about the world (Neath, 1998; Schacter, 2001).

Episodic Knowledge. Episodic knowledge consists of memories for specific time-stamped events and episodes in our life. Everyone has memories of particular events such as a high school prom, weddings, births, or other highly memorable events in our lives. Episodic memories differ from semantic memories on a number of dimensions, including content, where they are represented physically in the brain, and even how they are remembered. Whereas semantic knowledge is factual and conceptual in nature, episodic knowledge is autobiographical in nature (Greene, 1992). Serious injuries to the head may affect semantic memory without affecting episodic memory, or the reverse.

Researchers have studied one type of episodic memory known as *flashbulb memories* in detail. A flashbulb memory is one in which there is a detailed recollection of a highly specific event, which often is unexpected or traumatic in nature. I still remember where I was when I heard that John F. Kennedy was shot. I was in fifth-grade music class. I also remember the song our music teacher was teaching the class at the time and many other particulars of the episode as we listened to the news over the school intercom. Oddly, flashbulb memories are no more accurate than other memories, even though people are much more confident in the veracity of those memories (Neath, 1998). The risk of potential memory errors and their consequences is especially important for courtroom testimony. People may feel sure they remember an event accurately when they do not.

Episodic memories need not be only for specific events, but may include a sequence of events such as the ebb and flow of a basketball game. Kintsch (1998) has postulated what he refers to as a *situation model*, which is an integrated, conceptual representation for a situation. Situation models are common, or even necessary, when we read a novel or watch a movie. We also construct situation models of sporting events, or to a certain extent, of our lives as we live them. Zwann and Radvansky (1998) proposed that people construct different types of situational models as a means to help them remember the temporal (i.e., time sequence), causal, or spatial events in a sequence. Situation models serve as a means for encoding and remembering large amounts of information, and also help us organize and retrieve information later.

Procedural Knowledge. *Procedural knowledge* is knowledge about how to do things, ranging from simple action sequences such as buttering toast, to complex actions such as writing a dissertation or flying an airplane. Most adults possess an enormous amount of procedural knowledge, which enables them to perform complex activities such as driving a car easily because those procedures are automated though practice. Although there are many different types of action sequences, there are three sequences of special importance, including complex scripted actions, algorithms, and heuristics. *Scripts* are extended action sequences stored as single entities in memory. *Algorithms* are rules for performing an activity that rarely change and are guaranteed to achieve the desired goal. *Heuristics* are "rules of thumb" that may help us achieve a goal, but do not guarantee success.

Scripts. Scripts refer to extended action sequences and plans that are stored in memory as single units of knowledge (Ashcraft, 1994). Each person possess thousands of scripts for getting dressed, driving a car, dining at restaurants, and social interactions that save us enormous amounts of time because we can activate the script intact from memory. Scripts are analogous to schemata. Whereas schemata help us organize declarative knowledge about a topic or domain, scripts help us organize procedural knowledge and remember steps in a complicated action sequence.

There are several important advantages regarding scripts. One is that a large repertoire of scripts in memory enables us to perform many of our daily activities in a straightforward, automated manner without expending a great deal of thought or effort to do so. For example, most of us wake up, shower, eat, brush our teeth, and drive to work without ever giving any of these activities much thought. Instead, as we perform these scripted activities automatically, we plan other nonroutine daily activities such as when to schedule a doctor's appointment, service the car, and arrange our schedules to accommodate family needs, travel, and other pressing business. In a nutshell, scripts save us an incredible amount of time and effort.

A second advantage of scripted behavior is that it allows us eventually to perform activities that initially appear to be beyond the normal range of performance for most people. For example, with extended practice, chess experts can play several games simultaneously while blindfolded, doctors perform complicated surgeries, and performing artists reach amazing levels of technical proficiency.

A third advantage of scripts is that they enable us to predict what is likely to happen in the future. For example, an experienced salesperson possesses a "closing the deal" deal script that enables her to sequence her sales pitch, monitor whether the pitch is working, and steer her client toward accepting the deal. Or consider an "argument script" you may have with a sibling, spouse, or parent. Sometimes key words or events in the script occur that trigger ensuing events, such as an outburst or verbal threat, that you wish to avoid. Scripts may be very useful in helping us negotiate interpersonal communications.

Scripts have their downside too. Because so much of what we do in life is scripted, it is possible that we make choices and decisions in a scripted manner that leads to a state of mindlessness at times (Langer, 1989). Perhaps you have had the experience of meeting a casual acquaintance in public and engaging in a highly scripted conversation, only to realize later how empty the conversation was. Scripts can also lead to biased reactions to people or automated responses rather than critical evaluation of arguments.

Scripts frequently work to our advantage. They enable us to perform complicated activities with relative ease. Adults possess a wide variety of scripts. One type of script that is especially important in learning is a general problem-solving script, shown in Fig. 11.2. This script suggests that there is a general logical sequence to follow when solving a problem, which includes identifying the nature of the problem, developing an internal or external representation of the problem, selecting the most

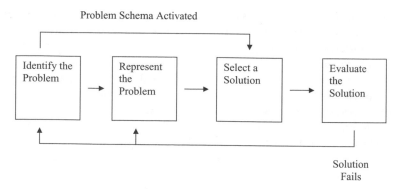

FIGURE 11.2 A general problem solving script.

appropriate solution strategy, and evaluating the solution (Pretz, Naples, & Sternberg, 2003). Figure 11.2 also reveals the role that expert schemata play in problem solving by eliminating the problem representation stage because experts have solved similar problems many times before. Research indicates that experts construct a schema in memory, which enables them to categorize different types of problems and solution strategies, and in turn, quickly match an appropriate strategy to the problem (Halpern, 2003).

Algorithms. An algorithm is a rule for solving a problem that always works. All of us learned a variety of algorithms in mathematics classes as high school students. One example is computing the hypotenuse of a right triangle. In words, one squares the values for the opposite and adjacent sides, sums their squares, and takes the square root of the sum to find the length of the hypotenuse. This algorithm always works. In general, algorithms are an effective way to solve well-defined problems, which refer to problems with one clear solution that can be broken down into smaller steps (Pretz et al., 2003).

Heuristics. A heuristic is a rule of thumb for solving a problem that often works, but not always. Heuristics are useful ways to solve ill-defined problems, which have no clear solution or a number of solutions. One example of a heuristic is a selecting a route when we drive to work. If you live in a large city and are faced with a long commute, you may have developed a variety of routes depending on the time of day and traffic conditions. I usually take one of three general routes to work, but there are many subtle variations within each of the three main routes. In the parlance of this chapter, one could say that I have a general "driving to work" script in procedural memory with three main subscripts, which are subject to minor variations depending on the conditions. This knowledge is approximate rather than exact. Some days I choose the best route and some days I do not. Typically I choose wisely based on my knowledge of the routes I have to choose from.

Self-regulatory Knowledge. *Self-regulatory knowledge* is knowledge about how to regulate our memory, thought, and learning. Declarative and procedural knowledge alone are not sufficient to be an adaptive learner. In addition, we must possess knowledge about ourselves as learners and about the skills we need to learn effectively. Self-regulatory knowledge can be divided into two types, including domain-specific knowledge and domain-general knowledge (Alexander, 2003). The former is knowledge we possess about ourselves with regard to a domain such as mathematics or a subdomain such as algebra. In contrast, the latter includes general knowledge such as learning strategies that enable us to adapt and self-regulate across all domains.

Domain-Specific Knowledge. *Domain-specific knowledge* refers to knowledge that is encapsulated within a particular domain of learning such as mathematics, history, or literature. Sometimes domain specific knowledge is referred to as *topic knowledge*, although this term suggests knowledge about a specific topic such as geometry within a broader domain such as mathematics. Domain-specific knowledge is extremely important in the development of expertise and skilled problem solving (Ericsson, 2003). Cognitive psychologists once believed that it was possible to capture the knowledge of experts through interviews and observation, and in turn, help novices become experts quickly. Instead, researchers discovered that experts become experts slowly through years of hard work, deliberate practice, and guidance from other experts. Most experts have deep knowledge in one domain, yet shallow knowledge in other domains, due in large part to the amount of time (e.g., 50,000 hours) they invest in developing expertise in their chosen domain. Expertise in one domain usually does not transfer spontaneously to other domains, although it can be facilitated through direct instruction and analogical cues that help the learner understand the relationship between two different problems (Bassock, 2003).

Domain-General Knowledge. Domain-general knowledge refers to knowledge that is equally useful to learners across domains and topics. Domain-general knowledge often is referred to as *metacognitive knowledge.* There are two main types of metacognitive knowledge, including knowledge of cognition and regulation of cognition (Kuhn, 1999; Schraw, 2001). The former includes strategy knowledge and conditional knowledge, whereas the latter includes knowledge of regulatory skills such as planning, monitoring, and evaluation of learning.

Knowledge of learning strategies is essential for effective self regulation (Butler & Winne, 1995; Pressley & Wharton-McDonald, 1997). Skilled learners possess a wide variety of strategies, but research suggests that self-regulated learners rely in large part on a relatively small repertoire of general strategies used in a flexible way. These include identifying main ideas, drawing plausible inferences, slowing down for important information, skipping unimportant information, and summarizing in words or by creating graphic organizers (Duffy, 2002). Reviews by Hattie, Biggs, and Purdie (1996) and Rosenshine, Meister, and Chapman (1996) support the following four claims regarding strategy instruction:

1. Strategy instruction typically is moderately to highly successful.
2. Strategy instruction appears to be most helpful for younger and underachieving students.
3. Programs that combine several interrelated strategies are more effective than those that include only one strategy. An interrelated repertoire of four or five strategies seems optimal.
4. Strategy interventions are more effective when they teach conditional knowledge. *Conditional knowledge* refers to knowing why, when, and where to use a particular strategy. Individuals with a high degree of conditional knowledge are better able to identify the demands of a specific learning situation and, in turn, select strategies that are most appropriate for that situation (Schraw, 2001).

Regulation of cognition refers to knowledge about how to self-regulate one's learning. Three essential skills include planning, monitoring, and evaluating one's learning. Planning involves the selection of appropriate strategies and the allocation of resources. Planning includes goal setting, activating relevant background knowledge, and budgeting time. Previous research suggests that experts are more self-regulated compared to novices largely due to effective planning, particularly global planning that occurs prior to beginning a task (Bruning, Schraw, Norby, & Ronning, 2004). Monitoring includes self-testing skills necessary to control learning. Research indicates that adults monitor at both the local (i.e., an individual test item) and global levels (i.e., all items on a test). Research also suggests that even skilled adult learners are poor monitors under certain conditions (Kuhn, 1999). Evaluation refers to appraising the products and regulatory processes of learning. Typical examples include reevaluating one's goals, revising predictions, and consolidating intellectual gains.

Research suggests that domain general knowledge is late developing and often implicit in nature (Alexander, Carr, & Schwanenflugel, 1995). Adults tend to have more knowledge about their own cognition and are better able to describe that knowledge than children and adolescents. However, many adults cannot explain their expert knowledge and performance and often fail to spontaneously transfer domain-specific knowledge to a new setting. Indeed, much of the domain-general knowledge that learners possess may be tacit in nature and acquired implicitly without conscious awareness (Schraw & Moshman, 1995).

Summary

Knowledge is multifaceted. There are at least three types of knowledge, including declarative knowledge about facts and concepts, procedural knowledge about how to do things, and self-regulatory knowledge about how to manage our learning. Although knowledge differs from person to person, there is agreement among experts that learners within a common culture share many of the same scripts and schema, and that while there are differences among learners, there are important similarities. These conclusions seem to be most consistent with the postpositivist view of knowledge described earlier.

MODELS OF KNOWLEDGE REPRESENTATION IN LTM

The previous section summarized different types of knowledge. This section addresses how knowledge is represented in memory. Views and models of knowledge representation have changed dramatically over the

TABLE 11.2. Three Models of Knowledge Representation in Long Term-Memory

	Network	Production System	Connectionist
Type of architecture	Hierarchical	Nonhierarchical production rules	Nonhierarchical distributed neural networks
Important components	Nodes, properties, relational links	Production rules and systems of rules	Units (explicit and hidden); weighted connections; neural networks
Important processes	Spreading activation	Spreading activation	Activation; forward and back propagation
Strengths	Simple; does good job of modeling hierarchical relationship of declarative knowledge	Models procedural knowledge. Explains development of expertise.	Modeled after brain physiology. Can be tested using computer simulations. Generalizes to other life forms.
Weaknesses	Does not explain procedural, conceptual, or self-regulatory knowledge	Mechanistic. Places strong role on experience and practice rather than reflection.	Very data-driven. Removes "mind" from learning.

past 50 years. One model that continues to be useful as a metaphor for memory and information processing is the *modal model* (Greene, 1992; Neath, 1998). The original modal model postulated three main memory subsystems, including sensory, short-term, and long-term components of memory. Sensory memory consisted of very brief storage and initial processing of incoming stimuli such as visual and auditory information. The assumption was that limited amounts of information were processed and forwarded to short-term memory or were lost from the system. Information advanced to short-term memory was processed for meaning within 10 to 15 seconds or was lost through decay. Based on its importance, information in short-term memory was advanced to long-term memory, where it was stored indefinitely.

The modal model has undergone considerable changes since its inception. For example, the concept of a unitary short-term memory has been replaced by more complicated models such as Baddeley's three-component model of working memory, which includes a decision-making executive system, a verbal storage subsystem referred to as the articulatory loop, and a computation subsystem referred to as the visuo-spatial sketch pad (Baddeley, 1998, 2001). Both experimental and brain scanning data support this model. Working memory is assumed to play an essential role in human cognition because it is the fundamental bottleneck through which sensory information must pass to reach permanent storage in long-term memory. Nevertheless, despite agreement that working memory has psychological reality and is of utmost importance in cognition, a number of different models of working memory have been proposed that differ in important ways from each other (Shah & Miyake, 1999). For example, Baddeley (1998) describes a three-component model of short-term working memory that differs from the model described by Ericsson and Delaney (1999), which suggests that many of the regulatory activities of working memory are relegated to long-term working memory.

Even more changes have occurred in our understanding of knowledge representation in long term memory. As described earlier, Tulving (1972) subdivided declarative knowledge into semantic and episodic types of knowledge, where the former refers to memory for abstract concepts, and the latter refers to memory for specific episodes or events. Another important additional is the distinction between schemata and scripts (Bruning et al., 2004; Rumelhart, 1984).

Researchers have proposed three general types of knowledge representation models we refer to as network, production systems, and connectionist models. Each of these systems proposes a radically different *cognitive architecture:* that is, rules by which knowledge is stored and organized in the brain. Table 11.2 summarizes some of the key differences among the three models. A more detailed comparison can be found in Bruning et al. (2004, Chapter 3).

Network Models

Network models of knowledge representation became popular in the 1960s. Early models focused on the hierarchical representation of declarative knowledge in memory and the relationship among different knowledge units (Collins & Quillian, 1969; Quillian, 1968). Network models possess three major components, including *nodes* in which a specific unit of information is stored, *properties* of information within nodes, and *relational links* among nodes. For example, consider the domain of animals. Subsumed within this domain are different types of animals such as birds, fish, and mammals. Network models envisioned each of these categories as nodes, where each node possessed a number of essential properties. The "animal" node included properties such as breathes, eats, has skin. The "bird" node included properties such as has wings, has feathers, and flies; whereas the "fish" node included different properties such as has fins, has gills, and swims. Network models emphasized parsimony in mental representation; thus, properties included in a superordinate node were not replicated at a subordinate node. Because birds and fish are both animals, it was not necessary to include the property "has skin" because this property was included already in the "animal" node.

Quillian (1968) proposed five different kinds of relational links between nodes, including superordinate and subordinate, modifier, disjunctive, conjunctive, and residual links. These links specified whether properties of one node were shared with another node. For example, the fact that all animals have skin is a superordinate link that is true of all other links subsumed beneath it unless otherwise noted as a disjunctive link. Network models based on the notion of nodes, properties, and links helped explain how people remember information in an efficient manner and why it is relatively easy to search memory and make simple judgments such as whether a canary eats and has skin.

The search process of memory was explained by the concept of *spreading activation* of attention among nodes. Some concepts activated particular nodes and activation would spread to adjacent nodes. For example, the word *camel* would activate the "mammal" node and all properties of mammals would be activated, whereas properties of distance nodes such as fish would not be activated. Thus, activation spreads through memory both vertically and horizontally. Activation spreads vertically in upward (i.e., camel to mammal) or downward (i.e., camel to dromedary). Activation also spreads horizontally (i.e., camel to horse, camel to mule). Activation typically spreads further in a horizontal than a vertical direction, although activation is constrained in part by the situational demands of learning.

The idea that memory is organized into nodes of specific information that are interrelated to other nodes has been a lasting idea. Almost all other models of knowledge representation incorporate the idea of node, although what a node includes varies from model to model (Anderson, 2000). The assumption that nodes have properties and are linked in a manner that indicates the type of relationship between nodes has not fared as well. Early network models provided a useful description of how declarative knowledge was represented in long-term memory, but they failed to explain the construction and representation of procedural and self-regulatory knowledge.

Network models also paved the way for the development of schema theory in the 1970s (Rumelhart & Ortony, 1977), which spawned hundreds of practical experiments about the effect of schemata on learning and memory.

Production Systems Models

Production models of knowledge representation and learning were first developed in the 1970s. One goal of these models was to explain a broader array of memory phenomena such as procedural learning, in addition to the representation of declarative knowledge. The most comprehensive production model is the ACT-R model (Adaptive Character of Thought, Revised) by John Anderson (1996, 2000). Anderson's model developed from the human associative learning (HAM) model proposed by Anderson and Bower (1973).

ACT-R proposes three interactive memory systems that support adaptive thinking, including declarative knowledge, procedural knowledge, and working memory. The declarative knowledge component consists of schemata and chunks within schemata that encode specific declarative knowledge units. The procedural knowledge component consists of *production rules* that break down complex action sequences into a number of if-then steps, which enable the learner to perform complex actions using a series of simple steps. Declarative and procedural components are connected to each other, as well as a working memory system where activated declarative and procedural units are used to solve problems, make decisions, and adapt to environmental conditions.

ACT-R differs from earlier network models in that it proposes production rules, which are combined into production systems, which enable the brain to represent complex actions. A production rule specifies the action to be taken to achieve a specific goal and the conditions under which each action is taken. For example, imagine you have a ring of five keys and need to open an office door. This scenario can be represented as a simple production as follows:

IF you must open a door
THEN insert key one and open door
IF key one fails to open door
THEN insert key two. . .

This production rule could be subdivided further into more finely grained production rules that specify how to use each key until the correct key is identified, or none of the keys opens the door. In addition, conditions could be added to each substep in the production sequence to assist the learner. For instance, one might add a condition statement such as *do not attempt to use long, narrow keys with square heads* because these keys often open car doors rather than office doors.

Anderson states that complex cognitive activity can be understood and explained in terms of small productions, based on simple units of declarative and procedural knowledge. According to Anderson (1996, p. 356), all human learning and performance, as well as the more abstract construct of human intelligence, can be described as "the simple accrual and tuning of many small units of knowledge that in total produce complex cognition. The whole is no more than the sum of its part."

This statement reveals clearly that Anderson views learning as a systematic process of acquiring declarative and procedural knowledge through experience and using this knowledge under specific conditions to execute complex actions, which themselves are made up of many small productions. The theory of ACT-R also discusses how individuals construct and infer new knowledge based on past experiences. Thus, the theory is not entirely experience driven as the foregoing quote suggests. Nevertheless, ACT-R views learning as a systematic process of acquiring the right knowledge and using that knowledge under the right conditions. Using knowledge repeatedly (i.e., practicing) increases the speed and accuracy of productions. Tuning productions to varying conditions also increases the efficiency of learning and performance.

Like network models, ACT-R postulates a process of spreading activation among declarative and procedural knowledge units during the execution of production sequences. Anderson (1996) proposed weighting systems, which determine which production rules apply under particular conditions. Activation spreads among production rules as a function of conditions and weights, which highlight some rules and downplay others. Activation is not necessarily hierarchical from superordinate to subordinate nodes, as is often the case in network models. Thus, production systems tend to be less hierarchical than networks.

Production system models have two clear advantages over earlier network models. First, they incorporate procedural knowledge into the model and explain how procedural and declarative knowledge are interrelated through working memory. Second, they do an excellent job of explaining incremental skill acquisition and the development of expertise. Production systems have been used to create and model intelligent tutoring systems that might take the place of human tutors. One potential criticism is that production systems are highly mechanistic; that is, they postulate that learning and performance is the sum and nothing more than the sum of a sequence of discrete productions. Related to this criticism is the fact that production systems highlight the role of experience and direct leaning and downplay rational reflection and the role of discovery and creativity.

Connectionist Models

Connectionist models of knowledge representation and learning became popular in the 1980s and sometimes are referred to as neural networks or parallel distributed processing (PDP) models (Anderson, 1995). Connectionist models represent an important paradigm shift from network and production system models because they deemphasize the intentional role of the learner, while emphasizing the role of experience in building neural pathways and connections, as well as assumptions about cognitive architecture (Bechtel & Abrahamsen, 2002). Although a great deal of attention has been devoted to connectionist models in the past 20 years, especially the seminal work of Rumelhart and McClelland (1986), their origin can be traced to earlier researchers such as Selfridge (1959).

Connectionist models differ from network and production models in two important ways. The first difference is that previous cognitive models used a computer metaphor to describe human cognition. In this view, information passes through an initial sensory system, is acted on in working memory, and is represented in permanent store in long-term memory. Connectionist models replaced the computer metaphor with a neural pathway metaphor modeled on the human brain. In this view, information is represented as patterns of activation across a variety of units, which correspond to neurons in the human brain.

A second difference is that network and production models focus on the representation of discrete units of information within a node in memory (e.g., a fact or a simple production rule), whereas connectionist models view knowledge representation as continuous across a number of interconnected units in memory. Thus, information such as facts, concepts, and production rules is not represented within single nodes, but distributed across nodes.

Connectionist models propose a rather simple architecture based on *units*, which maintain elementary information, typically simpler than corresponding nodes in network and production models. Multiple units are connected to create information that one might label as facts or concepts. The *connectivity pattern* among these units is of utmost importance. Any given unit may be connected to many other units, using a number of different connectivity patterns. Thus, one unit may be part of different knowledge representations, much as a single light in a theatre marquee may be used to spell different words. Connectionist theories have proposed different types of units. The most important of these are input units, output units, and hidden units, which are mediating connections between inputs and outputs.

Each unit has an activation value assigned to it under different processing conditions. Activation spreads throughout the system, but depends in part on the connectivity pattern among units, as well as connection weights, which determine whether one unit contributes more activation than another unit. There are a variety of activation algorithms; however, the two most important are forward (i.e., input to output units) and backward propagation (i.e., output to input units). Training (i.e., learning) in a connectionist network occurs as units are activated and deactivated, and connection weights change due to environmental conditions and feedback to the connectionist network through back propagation.

Connectionist models have several strengths and weaknesses. Strengths include its close physiological analogy to the human brain, the fact that its major claims can be tested using computer simulations, and that it provides a general theory of learning that is not unique to humans, but explains how learning may occur in other mammalian and nonmammalian life forms. Possible weaknesses, depending upon one's theoretical point of view, are that connectionist models are too bottom-up (i.e., learning occurs exclusively through experience and data-based feedback), and the mind is removed from models of learning (i.e., the role of rational reflection and inference construction is downplayed).

Summary

Differences remain regarding the representation of knowledge in long-term memory. Network models described how declarative knowledge might be represented. Production models extended this approach in two ways: first, by describing the representation of procedural knowledge, and second, by describing how declarative and procedural knowledge are related. Connectionist models postulate a radically different cognitive architecture modeled on the human brain, rather than a computer. Each of the three models has strengths and weaknesses, although it is premature at this point to determine whether one is superior to another.

KNOWLEDGE PROCESSES: SKILL ACQUISITION AND EXPERTISE

Knowledge has two important roles in human cognition: We use it as an organizational and retrieval structure in memory, and we use it as a tool to think and solve problems. This section examines how individuals use knowledge to engage in learning processes more effectively. To do so, learners progress from novices to experts and acquire a variety of skills that evolve through several different stages. This section addresses four aspects of the relationship between knowledge and expert performance. One aspect concerns salient characteristics of expertise and constraints on its development. A second aspect considers three stages in the development of expertise and skill acquisition. A third aspect focuses on the role of deliberate practice in the development of expertise, and compares several competing models of developing expertise. A fourth aspect addresses the role of talent in expertise and skilled learning.

Dimensions of Expertise

Experts are made, not born. This is not to say that intellectual ability and talent do not exist, or are unimportant, but that effort, deliberate practice, and feedback from experts are essential to the development of high-level expertise (Ericsson, 1996; Glaser & Chi, 1988). It is clear that intellectual ability and talent are important; however, it is less clear whether intellectual ability or talent are sufficient for the development of expertise (Sternberg, 1996, 2001). Many highly intelligent and talented students drop out of schools each year. It also is unclear whether high levels of intellectual ability and talent are necessary for skilled expertise. A number of studies suggest that even average students can acquire exceptional memory skills through extended training and practice (Ericsson, 1996), and that experts use cognitive resources such as working memory in different, more adaptive ways than novices with equivalent levels of ability (Ericsson & Delaney, 1999). Overall, 30 years of research suggests that intelligence and talent provide initial advantages, but that high levels of expertise are due primarily to sustained, systematic effort on the part of the learner. Ability alone is not sufficient for high levels of expertise. Ability and sustained practice are ideal. Sustained practice even without pronounced native ability may be sufficient for very high levels of skill development (Ericsson, 2003).

Much has been written about the characteristics of experts. Sternberg (2001) provides one of the most cogent summaries, including the following attributes: large, organized schematic networks within a particular domain of expertise; choosing efficiently from a large repertoire of useful strategies; quickly constructing detailed integrated mental models of a problem; performing skills in a highly automated fashion; and carefully monitoring the difficulty of problems and one's ability to solve problems. That is, experts possess a large knowledge base, which they use

TABLE 11.3. Stages of Skill Acquisition

Stage	Activities	Example: Writing a Research Paper
Knowledge accumulation	Acquire facts and concepts related to skill	Acquire knowledge about educational research, including content knowledge, research methods, data analysis, and drawing valid conclusions
Knowledge integration	Organize information into schemata, procedural routines, and scripts	Integrate this knowledge into an explicit script. Use this script to plan, execute, and evaluate one's performance of the skill.
Automation and tuning	Practice routines until they are fully automated; refine automated procedures as necessary	Practice the skill until it becomes routine and automated, with the understanding that some skills never become fully automated

to self-regulate their learning. There is general agreement that deep expertise develops slowly, usually requiring 5 to 10 years and more than 50,000 hours of practice to reach very high levels of performance. The 10-year rule applies equally to all domains (Ericsson, 1996) and even occurs in the development of creativity (Simonton, 1996).

Stages of Skill Acquisition

Earlier in this chapter, we considered the distinction between declarative and procedural knowledge. These two elements are the building blocks in the development of cognitive skills and expertise. A *skill* is a particular procedural routine we use to accomplish a goal. Some skills are simple, whereas other skills are more complex. Experts develop a large repertoire of skills needed to be successful in their domain. These skills develop in a systematic sequence. Different researchers use different names for the steps in skill development, but there is general agreement that three stages are essential. For descriptive reasons, I refer to these three stages as the knowledge accumulation stage, knowledge integration stage, and the automation and tuning stage (Ackerman, 1996, 2003; Alexander, 2003; Anderson, 2000; Glaser, 1996; Zimmerman & Kisantas, 1999). Table 11.3 lists these three stages and some characteristics of each stage.

The knowledge acquisition stage consists of accumulating declarative knowledge needed to understand and perform a skill (Ericsson, 1996). For example, imagine that you enroll in a graduate educational research class, which requires you to conduct research and write a professional research paper. This skill requires you accumulate a wide range of knowledge about the content of the research question, research methods, data analysis, and how to interpret data and draw valid conclusions. Typically, the acquisition of a sophisticated skill such as professional publication would require a number of graduate-level courses and intensive mentoring. Some skills such

as tying a shoe or making a pot of coffee are much simpler and require less knowledge and practice.

The knowledge construction stage marks the transition from accumulating isolated segments of knowledge to integrating that knowledge into larger conceptual chunks such as schemata and scripts, or still larger chunks such as explicit conceptual models of a complex process. Some simple skills include only a few steps and therefore are easy to integrate into a meaningful sequence. Other skills require years to integrate. For example, many graduate students and university professors never fully master the process of conducting and writing professional research reports. My own experience has taught me that very few graduate students ever develop an explicit model of what a professional paper should include. This has led me to develop a writing rubric I use to make the steps in writing a paper explicit and easier to understand and integrate into a seamless whole.

The point of using the rubric is twofold. First, it provides an integrated, systematic approach to the writing process for novice writers. Second, it encourages students to plan and evaluate their research explicitly in a manner that promotes self-regulation. The automation and tuning stage occurs as a skill is performed faster and more efficiently due to extended practice, often coupled with feedback from experts (Anderson, 2000). Complex skills require thousands of hours of practice to automate. Even high-level performance is never fully automated, in part, because most skills are performed in novel situations or under slightly different circumstances (Ericsson, 2003). For example, world-class tennis players may have hit tens of thousands of serves in their careers, yet still vary their serve depending on their opponent, court conditions, score of the game, and other factors. Highly automated skills are tuned continuously and to optimize performance as a function of local conditions.

It is important to bear in mind that not all novices become experts and that there are multiple paths to expertise (Alexander, 2003; Lajoie, 2003). The three stages shown in Table 11.3 provide a general framework. The road to expertise is long and difficult, requiring a great deal of support, as well as frequent assessment and feedback (Lajoie, 2003). Schools can facilitate skill acquisition and the development of expertise by providing distributed support using expert teachers, technology, and peers. In addition, schools can facilitate expertise by situating learning in real-life contexts as much as possible.

Deliberate Practice and Skilled Performance

Ericsson (1996, 2003) has developed a theory of skill acquisition and expertise based on *deliberate practice*. Deliberate practice differs from ordinary practice or haphazard skill acquisition in four ways. First, deliberate practice is intentional and highly goal directed. Individuals select specific skills they wish to improve and practice those skills repeatedly before moving to different skills. Second, practice is very systematic. Ericsson (1996) reports that most experts practice 2 to 3 hours a day, usually in the morning, taking periodic short breaks to relieve fatigue. Third, effective deliberate practice is situated in an authentic setting. Individuals practice in the environment where they will use their skills under real-world conditions as much as possible. For example, to the greatest extent possible, baseball players will practice their batting skills against real pitchers under simulated game conditions rather than in a batting cage. Fourth, individuals utilize at least three different types of feedback, all of which are essential. One is feedback from expert coaches and mentors. A second type is self-generated feedback, including mental visualization. A third is textbooks and strategy guides. For example, Charness, Krampe, and Mayr (1996) found that the number of chess books in the library of skilled players was one of the best predictors of long-term expertise in chess.

Ericsson (1996, 2003) argues that deliberate practice is the primary determinant of developing expertise. This claim has been hotly debated because Ericsson (1996) appears to dismiss the role of native ability and talent in the development of expertise. Sternberg (1996, 2001), for example, suggests that very high levels of expertise require native ability, talent, and deliberate practice, rather than only deliberate practice.

Figure 11.3 presents three different schematic models of the relationship among ability/talent, deliberate practice, and expertise. For present purposes, no distinction is made between ability and talent, even though the difference between the two is important and has been discussed elsewhere (Bloom, 1985; Feldman, 1999; Freeman, 2000; Winner, 1996).

Model 1: The Deliberate Practice Model

Deliberate practice → Ability/Talent → Expertise

Model 2: The Talent Model

Ability/Talent → Deliberate practice → Expertise

Model 3: The Interactive Model

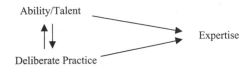

FIGURE 11.3 Three models of ability, deliberate practice, and talent.

Model 1 illustrates the deliberate practice model, which assumes that deliberate practice over an extended period of time increases the ability, skills, and talents that lead to expertise. This model is consistent with Ericsson (1996, 2003), Charness et al. (1996), and Bloom's theory of talent development (Bloom, 1985). The core assumption of this model is that expertise is 90 percent perspiration and 10 percent inspiration. Of course, hard work alone is not sufficient. Pretz et al. (2003) remind us that practice must be systematic and that expertise is constrained by the amount of knowledge one possesses, the sophistication of one's strategy repertoire, native abilities, and social support.

Winner (1996, 2000) has proposed a framework for understanding giftedness consistent with model 2, which I refer to as the *talent model*. The core assumption of the talent model is that native abilities and talent give rise to deliberate practice, which in turn, leads to expertise. Thus, Winner does not discount the role of deliberate practice, but suggests that deliberate practice is a consequence of talent rather than a cause, and is insufficient to create high levels of expertise when ability and talent are absent. Winner (1996) lists four characteristics of highly talented individuals that distinguish them from less talented individuals: (a) They learn more rapidly in their domain of talent even when deliberate practice is equal, (b) they are more motivated to acquire necessary skills, and in fact, often are characterized by a near-obsessive "rage to master," (c) they make discoveries easily without the help of others, and (d) they reach levels of achievement that others never reach. Although beyond the scope of this chapter, Winner (2000) reviews physiological (e.g., bilateral language representation and immune system disorders) and social (e.g., introversion) correlates of talent that support the four characteristics of talent just described.

The deliberate practice and talent models make incommensurable assumptions about ability, practice, and expertise. There is a middle ground, however, that is illustrated in model 3, which I refer to as the *interactive model*. This model is consistent with the research of Sternberg (2001) and Feldman (1999). The core assumption of the interactive model is that ability, talent, and deliberate practice are necessary and collectively sufficient for high levels of expertise, but that the absence of ability and talent, or deliberate practice, precludes expertise. One of the more interesting questions raised by the interactive model is the relationship between ability and talent versus deliberate practice. It is reasonable to assume that talent positively affects deliberate practice (Winner, 2000) and that deliberate practice may increase talent (Ericsson, 1996). One issue of special importance is whether a compensatory relationship exists between these components: that is, whether high levels of talent reduce the need for deliberate practice, and whether extended deliberate practice mitigates the role of ability and talent. Some type of compensatory relationship is reasonable, although currently, there is little empirical research to address the extent to which a compensatory relationship exists.

Debate continues as to the trainability of talent and expertise. Most scholars who study expertise agree that deliberate practice enables average students to reach high levels of expertise. Whether deliberate practice alone is enough to lead to very high levels of expertise is unclear. By the same token, native ability and talent are important precursors to the development of expertise. However, as Bloom (1985) and Ericsson (1996) suggest, even highly talented individuals often fail to achieve their potential because of low motivation, poor training, injuries, or the pressure of training and incessant practice.

Development of Talent

Most people agree that talent exists and is a significant contributor to expertise. Several researchers have addressed how talent develops over time (Bloom, 1985; Feldman, 1999; Glaser, 1996; Winner, 2000). Bloom (1985) described three stages of talent development he referred to as the early, middle, and late years. In the early years, a child is identified as having a particularly high level of ability in a domain, which is characterized by rapid skill development. These children usually are rewarded and given special attention by family and coaches. During these years, teaching and learning are geared toward play and recreation rather than serious professional development.

The transition to middle years occurs when the child makes a decision to devote special attention to the development of a particular talent. Usually a professional coach is sought out to accelerate talent development. The talented child is exposed to other children with similar or even higher levels of talent. Talented children often are highly motivated and receive a great deal of motivational support from parents, teachers, and other talented youth. Highly talented children also receive special treatment within the family. Full commitment to skill development occurs during this stage.

The later years emphasize the development of talent to its highest level. Often, individuals leave home to study with world-class experts or participate in special training programs with other highly talented students. Individuals work intensively with master teachers who place great demands on the student. Some form of competition is often involved. Motivation becomes increasingly internalized.

Bloom (1985) conducted a longitudinal study with 120 talented youth. The full developmental sequence typically took 10 to 15 years to complete. Initial level of talent was not a good predictor of subsequent expertise, whereas motivational factors such as passion for the activity and dedication to practice were better predictors (Freeman, 2000). Four qualities stood out as being especially important, including a strong interest and emotional commitment, a desire to reach a high level of attainment, willingness to devote a great deal of time to training and practice, and an ability to learn skills rapidly and well.

Several variables seem especially important to the development of talent. One is the opportunity for deep immersion within a specific program rather than general enrichment (Freeman, 2000). Attending special sport camps or master classes in music or mathematics is common. A second important factor is exposure to outstanding coaches who provide constructive model skills at a very high level of expertise and provide constant feedback. A third factor is the ability to set and achieve specific goals through continuous deliberate practice, utilizing the principles summarized by Ericsson (1996).

Although there has been little research on the development of talent, the available research supports the interactive model in Fig. 11.3 in two ways. First, talented children possess skills that ordinary children do not possess, and typically are highly motivated to engage in the activity for leisure and parental praise. This finding is consistent with the talent model proposed by Winner (1996). Second, given even high levels of talent, a 5- to 10-year period of deliberate practice is necessary to bring talents to fruition. This finding is consistent with the deliberate practice model proposed by Ericsson (1996).

Some Limitations of Expertise

Much has been written about the benefits of expertise. These include the ability to perform at remarkably high levels of achievement, as well as financial and personal benefits that accrue from mastering a highly difficult task. However, there are at least three potential costs related to expertise. One is that the amount of time invested in the development of expertise precludes developing expertise in other domains, as well as other casual activities. For this reason, many people view the time necessary to become an expert as too great a personal sacrifice.

A second and far more serious cost of expertise is conceptual rigidity, in which the expert finds it difficult to consider other points of view. Sternberg (1996) suggests that expert scientists may be at risk for confirmation bias because they expect certain outcomes to occur and often have invested years of research and effort in trying to document these outcomes. Stanovich (2003) refers to this phenomenon as *knowledge projection*, in which faulty heuristics are used to reach inadvertently faulty conclusions. Experts may be at greater risk in certain situations because they possess more heuristics than novices.

Yet a third problem related to expertise is what Nathan and Petrosino (2003) refer to as the *expert blind spot effect*, in which experts view student problem solving from an expert's perspective rather than a novice student's perspective. The expert blind spot effect may lead expert teachers to overlook the developmental needs of novice students and to select curriculum that is too advanced for novices because it requires students to utilize organizing principles and expert heuristics they do not possess.

One Final Caveat

Expertise requires years of hard work. To become an expert, individuals need to be highly motivated and self-regulated (Alexander, 2000; Zimmerman, 2003). A discussion of motivation is beyond the scope of this chapter; however, factors such as intrinsic motivation, self-efficacy, mastery goals, and a broad repertoire of self-regulated learning strategies are essential. Only highly motivated students engage in difficult tasks and persist long enough to become experts. In addition, hard work alone is not sufficient. An individual must work in a planful, self-regulated manner to achieve high levels of expertise. Fortunately, many of these skills and motivational attributes develop as individuals interact with motivated peers and experts who provide feedback.

Summary

This section reviewed principles of expertise and skill acquisition. Expertise develops slowly and is characterized by a large, integrated knowledge base; sophisticated mental models of a domain that guide problem solving and critical thinking; highly automated procedural skills; and excellent monitoring skills within the domain. Skills are learned gradually in three stages. Expertise is acquired primarily through extended deliberate practice that may require up to 10 years to reach the highest levels of performance. Deliberate practice is systematic, regular, and occurs under the watchful eye of teachers or other experts. It is unclear currently whether deliberate practice is sufficient to cause high levels of expertise. Three competing models were discussed and special emphasis was given to the interactive model, which suggests that both talent and deliberate practice are necessary and sufficient for expert performance.

EMERGENT THEMES AND EDUCATIONAL IMPLICATIONS

This chapter addressed how knowledge is acquired and represented in memory. Fig. 11.1 provided a taxonomy of different types of knowledge, and Table 11.2 summarized three different perspectives on knowledge representation. I also reviewed recent literature related to expertise, skill acquisition, and the development of talent via deliberate practice. This section discusses four emergent themes about knowledge, and discusses ways in which knowledge and beliefs about knowledge affect learning, problem solving, and critical thinking (Halpern, 2004; Kuhn, 1999).

The most important theme of this chapter is that knowledge affects learning by providing an integrated conceptual network that links declarative, procedural, and self-regulatory information in memory. Knowledge in isolation (i.e., inert knowledge) is of little value. Knowledge is powerful to us because it is highly organized and easily accessible. Research shows that knowledge is organized into schemata and scripts, which are interconnected to other schemata and scripts. Organized knowledge enables us to sort and store information in memory, predict and judge, and evaluate our learning accurately. Knowledge also provides an interpretative context for understanding (Hofer, 2002), which enables us to make plausible inferences based on what we already know, and to construct situational models of phenomena and events (Kintsch, 1998; Zwann & Radvansky, 1998). In addition, knowledge enables us to use process information more efficiently (Sweller et al., 1998). Without an extensive knowledge base to assist us, even highly capable learners find a task exceptionally difficult. Thus, to succeed academically, students need a large, interconnected knowledge base (Alexander, 2003). Students also need to interact with other expert students and teachers to understand how experts construct mental models within a domain and regulate their learning.

A second theme is that knowledge and expertise are acquired very slowly. The 10-year rule applies in every domain of learning. Skills are built up slowly over time, automated over hundreds of hours of practice, and often honed under the watchful eye of mentors and master teachers. Ericsson's (1996) theory of deliberate practice suggests that expertise is acquired systematically through hard work, feedback, and gradual mastery of a domain. Whether high levels of talent and native ability are necessary for high levels of expertise is still being debated. Winner (1996, 2000) provides a compelling argument in support of the role of talent as an essential component. From an educational perspective, it seems naïve to expect students to become highly knowledgeable within a domain without many years of exposure and practice within that domain. One implication is whether the school curriculum should be deep or wide. If we wish students to possess broad knowledge, then a wide curriculum seems prudent. However, if we wish students to acquire deep knowledge in at least one domain, than more depth should be offered, and opportunities for deeper learning with other skilled students and expert teachers should be put in place as well.

A third theme is that expertise is strongly encapsulated within a domain and does not transfer to other domains (Sternberg, 2001). Currently, there is debate as to how many skills acquired during the development of expertise might transfer to new domains. Schraw (2001) suggested that domain-general self-regulatory skills such as planning and monitoring may transfer more readily than lower level domain-specific skills such as solving equations in mathematics. There is evidence that self-regulatory skills acquired during the acquisition of expertise transfer to some extent to other domains, provided that instruction occurs across the curriculum, and that teachers teach specifically for transfer (Randi & Corno, 2000). One implication is that students often do not use the knowledge and skills acquired in one domain in a different domain. Teachers who want to promote self-regulation should make special effort to encourage the use of skills across the curriculum by highlighting similarities across the two domains (Bassock, 2003).

A fourth theme is that beliefs about knowledge affect engagement and deeper processing. The first section of this chapter summarized three different epistemological perspectives. Researchers know that beliefs change over time, moving from positivist to postpositivist, especially among those who attend college (Baxter-Malgoda, 2002; King & Kitchener, 2002). Endorsing a positivist, postpositivist, or postmodern world view also affects the way that students learn (Hofer, 2002) and teachers teach (Schraw & Olafson, 2002). Oddly, little is known about the personal epistemological beliefs of experts compared to novices, nor is it known whether years of deliberate practice cause a change in one's epistemological perspective. Positivist beliefs, especially a belief in fixed ability, appear to interfere with engagement, persistence, and learning, whereas nonpositivist beliefs lead to better problem solving and critical thinking (Halpern, 2004; Kuhn & Weinstock, 2002). More research is needed in this area to better understand the effect that personal beliefs have on learning and the development of expertise.

SUMMARY AND CONCLUSIONS

This chapter addressed the role of knowledge structures and processes. Regarding structures, I reviewed different types of knowledge in memory and recent perspectives about the architecture of representation. A distinction was made among declarative, procedural, and self-regulatory knowledge. All three are essential to human learning, problem solving, and critical thinking. I compared network, production, and connectionist models of knowledge representation. Currently, there is debate as to the relative pros and cons of these models, although most experts would agree that production and connectionist models are more comprehensive than network models. It is likely that hybrid models based on production systems and connectionist models will develop in the future. Regarding processes, I reviewed characteristics of expertise and skill acquisition, and compared the relative roles of deliberate practice and talent. The most reasonable conjecture at this point is that both deliberate practice and talent are necessary to reach the highest levels of performance, whereas deliberate practice alone may be sufficient for improving problem solving to nonexpert levels of performance.

Three main conclusions seem warranted. The first is that knowledge is essential to human learning. To be an expert, each individual must possess extensive knowledge, organize that knowledge into interconnected schemata and scripts, and use that knowledge to construct conceptual mental models of a domain, which are used to solve problems and think critically. The second conclusion is that knowledge acquisition and organization is a slow process that takes years to complete, requiring extensive practice and help from others. The more support a novice receives in terms of modeling and feedback, as well as motivational scaffolding, the more likely it is that the novice will develop into an expert. The third conclusion is that deliberate practice makes perfect. Those with more talent may succeed faster and go further, but there is no substitute for hard work inside or outside the classroom. It is indisputable that systematic deliberate practice transforms students from novices to highly skilled learners. Research indicates that deliber-

ate practice coupled with interest and motivation leads to academic success (Ackerman, 2003; Alexander, 2003). Deliberate practice works because it helps the individual become automated and construct broad conceptual understanding within a domain.

ACKNOWLEDGMENTS

The author thanks Roger Bruning, Bob Hoffman, Matt McCrudden, and Anne Poliquin for their comments on this chapter.

References

Ackerman, P. L. (1996). A theory of adult intellectual development: Process, personality, interests, and knowledge. *Intelligence, 22*, 229–259.

Ackerman, P. L. (2003). Cognitive ability and non-ability trait determinants of expertise. *Educational Researcher, 32*, 15–20.

Alexander, P. A. (2003). The development of expertise: The journey from acclimation to proficiency. *Educational Researcher, 32*, 10–14.

Alexander, J. M., Carr, M., & Schwanenflugel, P. J. (1995). Development of metacognition in gifted children: Directions for future research. *Developmental Review, 15*, 1–37.

Anderson, J. A. (1995). *An introduction to neural networks.* Cambridge, MA: MIT Press.

Anderson, J. R. (1996). ACT: A simple theory of complex cognition. *American Psychologist, 51*, 255–365.

Anderson, J. R. (2000). *Cognitive psychology and its implication (5th ed.).* New York: Worth.

Anderson, J. R., & Bower, G. H. (1973). *Human associative memory.* Washington, DC: Winston.

Ashcraft, M. H. (1994). *Human memory and cognition (2nd ed.).* New York: HarperCollins.

Baddeley, A. D. (1998). *Human memory: Theory and practice.* Boston: Allyn and Bacon.

Baddeley, A. D. (2001). Is working memory still working? *American Psychologist, 56*, 851–864.

Bassock, M. (2003). Analogical transfer in problem solving. In J. E. Davidson & R. J. Sternberg (Eds.), *The psychology of problem solving* (pp. 343–369). Cambridge, England: Cambridge University Press.

Baxter-Magolda, M. B. (2002). Epistemological reflection: The evolution of epistemological assumptions from age 18 to 30. In B. Hofer & P. R. Pintrich (Eds.), *Personal epistemology: The psychology of beliefs about knowledge and knowing* (pp. 89–102). Mahwah, NJ: Lawrence Erlbaum Associates.

Bechtel, W., & Abrahamsen, A. (2002). *Connectionism and the mind: Parallel processing, dynamics, and evolution in networks (2nd ed.).* London: Blackwell.

Bloom, B. S. (1985). Generalizations about talent development. In B. S. Bloom (Ed.), *Developing talent in young people* (pp. 507–549). New York: Ballantine Books.

Bruning, R. H., Schraw, G., J., Norby, M. M., & Ronning, R. R. (2004). *Cognitive psychology and instruction (4th ed.).* Upper Saddle River, NJ: Pearson Education.

Butler, D. L., and Winne, P. H. (1995). Feedback and self-regulated learning: A theoretical synthesis. *Review of Educational Research, 65*, 245–281.

Charness, N., Krampe, R., & Mayr, U. (1996). The role of practice and coaching in entrepreneurial skill domains: An international comparison of life-span chess skill acquisition. In K. A. Ericsson (Ed.), *The road to excellence: The acquisition of expert performance in the arts and sciences, sports, and games* (pp. 51–80). Mahwah, NJ: Lawrence Erlbaum Associates.

Collins, A. M., & Quillian, M. R. (1969). Retrieval time from semantic memory. *Journal of Verbal Learning and Verbal Behavior, 8*, 240–248.

Duffy, G. (2002). The case for direct explanation of strategies. In C. C. Block and M. Pressley (Eds.), *Comprehension instruction: Research-based best practices* (pp. 28–41). New York: Guilford.

Ericsson, K. A. (1996). The acquisition of expert performance: An introduction to some of the issues. In K. A. Ericsson (Ed.), *The road to excellence: The acquisition of expert performance in the arts and sciences, sports, and games* (pp. 1–50). Mahwah, NJ: Lawrence Erlbaum Associates.

Ericsson, K. A. (2003). The acquisition of expert performance as problem solving: Construction and modification of mediating mechanisms through deliberate practice. In J. E. Davidson and R. J. Sternberg (Eds.), *The psychology of problem solving* (pp. 31–83). Cambridge, England: Cambridge University Press.

Ericsson, K. A., & Delaney, P. F. (1999). Long-term working memory as an alternative to capacity models of working memory in everyday skilled performance. In A. Miyake & P. Shah (Eds.), *Models of working memory: Mechanisms of active maintenance and executive control* (pp. 257-297). Cambridge, England: Cambridge University Press.

Feldman, D. (1999). The development of creativity. In R. J. Sternberg (Ed.), *The handbook of creativity* (pp. 169-186). Cambridge, England: Cambridge University Press.

Fitzgerald, J., & Cunningham, J. W. (2002). Mapping basic issues for identifying epistemological outlooks. In B. K. Hofer & P. R. Pintrich (Eds.), *Personal epistemology: The psychology of beliefs about knowledge and knowing* (pp. 209-228). Mahwah, NJ: Erlbaum.

Freeman, J. (2000). Teaching for talent: Lessons from research. In C. F. van Lieshout & P. G. Heymans (Eds.), *Developing talent across the life span* (pp. 231-248). Philadelphia: Psychology Press.

Glaser, R. (1996). Changing the agency for learning: Acquiring expert performance. In K. A. Ericsson (Ed.), *The road to excellence: The acquisition of expert performance in the arts and sciences, sports, and games* (pp. 303-311). Mahwah, NJ: Lawrence Erlbaum Associates.

Glaser, R., & Chi, M. T. (1988). Overview. In M. Chi, R. Glaser, & M. Farr (Eds.), *The nature of expertise* (pp. 15-28). Mahwah, NJ: Lawrence Erlbaum Associates.

Greene, R. L. (1992). *Human memory: Paradigms and paradoxes.* Mahwah, NJ: Erlbaum.

Guba, E. G., & Lincoln, Y. S. (1994). Competing paradigms in qualitative research. In N. K. Denzin & Y. S. Lincoln (Eds.), *Handbook of qualitative research* (pp. 105-117). Thousand Oaks, CA: Sage.

Halpern, D. F. (2003). *Thought and knowledge: An introduction to critical thinking (4th ed.).* Mahwah, NJ: Lawrence Erlbaum Associates.

Hattie, J., Biggs, J., & Purdie, N. (1996). Effects of learning skills interventions on student learning: A meta-analysis. *Review of Educational Research, 66,* 99-136.

Hofer, B. (2002). Personal epistemology as a psychological and educational construct. In B. K. Hoer & P. R. Pintrich (Eds.), *Personal epistemology: The psychology of beliefs about knowledge and knowing* (pp. 3-14). Mahwah, NJ: Lawrence Erlbaum Associates.

Jonassen, D. H., Beissner, K., & Yacci, M. (1993). *Structural knowledge: Techniques for representing, conveying, and acquiring structural knowledge.* Hillsdale, NJ: Lawrence Erlbaum Associates.

Kelly, U. A. (1997). *Schooling desire: Literacy, cultural politics, and pedagogy.* New York, NY: Routledge.

King, P. M., & Kitchener, K. S. (2002). The reflective judgment model: Twenty years of research on epistemic cognition. In B. K. Hofer & P. R. Pintrich (Eds.), *Personal epistemology: The psychology of beliefs about knowledge and knowing* (pp. 37-62). Mahwah, NJ: Lawrence Erlbaum Associates.

Kintsch, W. (1998). *Comprehension: A paradigm for cognition.* Cambridge, England: Cambridge University Press.

Kuhn, D. (1999). A developmental model of critical thinking. *Educational Researcher, 28,* 16-25.

Kuhn, D., & Weinstock, M. (2002). What is epistemological thinking and why does it matter? In B. K. Hofer & P. R. Pintrich (Eds.), *Personal epistemology: The psychology of beliefs about knowledge and knowing* (pp. 121-144). Mahwah, NJ: Lawrence Erlbaum Associates.

Langer, E. L. (1989). *Mindfulness.* Reading, MA: Addison-Wesley.

Lajoie, S. P. (2003). Transitions and trajectories for studies of expertise. *Educational Researcher, 32,* 21-25.

Murphy, P. K. (2003). The philosophy in thee: Tracing philosophical influences in educational psychology. *Educational Psychologist, 38,* 137-145.

Nathan, M. J., & Petrosino, A. (2003). Expert blind spot among preservice teachers. *American Educational Research Journal, 40,* 905-928.

Neath, I. (1998). *Human memory: An introduction to research, data, and theory.* Pacific Grove, CA: Brooks/Cole.

Peters, M. A., & Burbules, N. C. (2004). *Poststructuralism and educational research.* Lanham, MD: Rowman and Littlefield.

Phillips, D. C., & Burbules, N. C. (2000). *Postpositivism and educational research.* Lanham, MD: Rowman and Littlefield.

Prawat, R. S. (1996). Constructivisms: Modern and postmodern. *Educational Psychologist, 31,* 215-225.

Prawat, R. S., & Floden, R. E. (1994). Philosophical perspectives on constructivist views of learning. *Educational Psychologist, 31,* 37-48.

Pressley, M., & Wharton-McDonald, R. (1997). Skilled comprehension and its development through instruction. *School Psychology Review, 26,* 448-466.

Pretz, J. E., Naples, A. J., & Sternberg, R. J. (2003). Recognizing, defining, and representing problems. In J. E. Davidson and R. J. Sternberg (Eds.), *The psychology of problem solving* (pp. 3-30). Cambridge, England: Cambridge University Press.

Quillian, M. R. (1968). Semantic memory. In M. Minsky (Ed.), *Semantic information processing* (pp. 21-56). Cambridge, MA: MIT Press.

Randi, J., & Corno, L. (2000). Teacher innovations in self-regulated learning. In M. Boekaerts, P. R. Pintrich, & M. Zeidner (Eds.), *Handbook of self-regulation* (pp. 651-686). San Diego, CA: Academic Press.

Reynolds, R. E., Sinatra, G. M., & Jetton, T. L. (1996). Views of knowledge acquisition and representation: Continuum from experience centered to mind centered. *Educational psychologist, 31,* 93-104.

Rosenshine, B., Meister, C., & Chapman, S. (1996). Teaching students to generate questions: A review of the intervention studies. *Review of Educational Research, 66,* 181-221.

Rumelhart, D. E., McClelland, J. L., and the PDP Research Group. (1986). *Parallel distributed processing: Explorations in the microstructure of cognition, Vol. 1: Foundations.* Cambridge, MA: MIT Press.

Rumelhart, D. E., & Ortony, A. (1977). The representation of knowledge in memory. In R. C. Anderson, R. J. Spiro, &

W. E. Montague (Eds.), *Schooling and the acquisition of knowledge* (pp. 99–135). Mahwah, NJ: Lawrence Erlbaum Associates.

Rumelhart, D. E. (1984). Schemata and the cognitive system. In R. S. Wyer & T. K. Srull (Eds.), *Handbook of social cognition* (Vol. 1, pp. 161–188). Mahwah, NJ: Lawrence Erlbaum Associates.

Schacter, D. L. (2001). *The seven sins of memory: How the mind forgets and remembers.* Boston: Houghton Mifflin.

Schraw, G., & Moshman, D. (1995). Metacognitive theories. *Educational Psychology Review, 7,* 351–371.

Schraw, G. (2001). Promoting general metacognitive awareness. In H. J. Hartman (Ed.), *Metacognition in learning and instruction: Theory, research and practice* (pp. 3–16). London, England: Kluwer Academic.

Schraw, G., & Olafson, L. (2002). Teacher's epistemological world views and educational practices. *Issues in Education, 8,* 99–148.

Selfridge, O. G. (1959). Pandemonium: A paradigm for learning. In *The mechanization of thought processes.* London: H. M. Stationery Office.

Shah, P., & Miyake, A. (1999). Models of working memory. In A. Miyake & P. Shah (Eds.), *Models of working memory: Mechanisms of active maintenance and executive control* (pp. 1–25). Cambridge, England: Cambridge University Press.

Simonton, D. K. (1996). Creative expertise: A life-span developmental perspective. In K. A. Ericsson (Ed.), *The road to excellence: The acquisition of expert performance in the arts and sciences, sports, and games* (pp. 227–254). Mahwah, NJ: Lawrence Erlbaum Associates.

Stanovich, K. E. (2003). The fundamental computational biases of human cognition: Heuristics that (sometimes) impair decision making and problem solving. In J. E. Davidson & R. J. Sternberg (Eds.), *The psychology of problem solving* (pp. 291–342). Cambridge, England: Cambridge University Press.

Sternberg, R. J. (1996). Costs of expertise. In K. A. Ericsson (Ed.), *The road to excellence: The acquisition of expert performance in the arts and sciences, sports, and games* (pp. 347–354). Mahwah, NJ: Lawrence Erlbaum Associates.

Sternberg, R. J. (2001). Metacognition, abilities, and developing expertise: What makes an expert student? In H. J. Hartman (Ed.), *Metacognition in learning and instruction: Theory, research, and practice* (pp. 247–260). Dordrecht, The Netherlands: Kluwer Academic Publishers.

Sweller, J., van Merrienboer, J. J. G., & Pass, F. (1998). Cognitive architecture and instructional design. *Educational Psychology Review, 10,* 251–296.

Tulving, E. T. (1972). Episodic and semantic memory. In E. Tulving & W. Donaldson (Eds.), *Organization of memory* (pp. 381–403). San Diego, CA: Academic Press.

Wagner, R. K., & Stanovich, K. E. (1996). Expertise in reading. In K. A. Ericsson (Ed.), *The road to excellence: The acquisition of expert performance in the arts and sciences, sports, and games* (pp. 189–226). Mahwah, NJ: Lawrence Erlbaum Associates.

Winner, E. (1996). The rage to master: The decisive role of talent in the visual arts. In K. A. Ericsson (Ed.), *The road to excellence: The acquisition of expert performance in the arts and sciences, sports, and games* (pp. 271–302). Mahwah, NJ: Lawrence Erlbaum Associates.

Winner, E. (2000). The origins and ends of giftedness. *American Psychologist, 55,* 159–169.

Zacks, R. T., Hasher, L., & Li, K. Z. (2000). In C. I. M. Craik & T. A. Salthouse (Eds.), *The handbook of aging and cognition (2nd ed.,* pp. 293–357). Mahwah, NJ: Lawrence Erlbaum Associates.

Zeidner, M., Boekaerts, M., & Pintrich, P. R. (2000). Self-regulation: Directions and challenges for future research. In M. Boekaerts, P. R. Pintrich, & M. Zeidner (Eds.), *Handbook of self-regulation* (pp. 13–39). San Diego, CA: Academic Press.

Zimmerman, B. J. (2000). Attaining self-regulation: A social cognitive perspective. In M. Boekaerts, P. R. Pintrich, & M. Zeidner (Eds.), *Handbook of self-regulation* (pp. 13–39). San Diego, CA: Academic Press.

Zimmerman, B. J., & Kisantas, A. (1999). Acquiring writing revision skill: Shifting from process to outcome self-regulatory goals. *Journal of Educational Psychology, 89,* 1–10.

Zwann, R., & Radvansky, G. (1998). Situation models in language comprehension and memory. *Psychological Bulletin, 123,* 162–185.

·12·

COGNITIVE STRATEGIES INSTRUCTION: FROM BASIC RESEARCH TO CLASSROOM INSTRUCTION

Michael Pressley
Michigan State University

Karen R. Harris
Vanderbilt University

Successful major league baseball managers are effectively strategic during games. They make decisions about who to put in the lineup based, in part, on their perception of which players are most likely to perform well against today's opposing pitcher. During the game, they make pitching changes when they feel their starting pitcher is no longer effective or seems to be getting tired, attempting to replace the starter with a relief pitcher likely to retire the next few batters. Their strategies are not static, but subject to change depending on their effectiveness. Individual strategies are often embedded in a network of strategies, with the baseball manager's strategy for getting the most out of his pitcher complemented by strategies for increasing run productivity and reducing the chances that a recovering player will be reinjured.

There are many, many problems that human beings attempt, with some strategies more likely to result in success than others. Understanding effective performance requires understanding the psychology of strategies; promoting human effectiveness at a task requires understanding of the strategies that can accomplish the task and how to develop such strategies among learners. Strategies development has deservedly received much study by cognitive psychologists, with educational psychologists doing much work to detail how affective, behavioral, and cognitive strategies develop, and can be developed, to increase student performance with respect to important academic tasks.

In this chapter, we begin with a definition of a "strategy" and a brief discussion of constructs related to research in this area, including procedural and declarative knowledge, long- and short-term memory, metacognition, and good information processing. We then turn to important findings from the earliest research on human strategies use, as these are both critical to understanding current research and to the development of further research. What we have learned about strategies use and strategies instruction in academic areas among students in the elementary through secondary grades then becomes the focus of this chapter.

STRATEGIES: DEFINITION AND RELATED CONSTRUCTS

The modern conception of strategies emerged in the 1950s, 1960s, and 1970s in the context of human information processing theory, rooted in strictly theoretical conceptions of information processing (e.g., Miller, Gallanter, & Pribram, 1960) and in models intended to promote learning of traditional school content, such as mathematical problem solving (e.g., Polya, 1957). Indeed, during this time there was much reflection and debate about what defines a strategy (Pressley & Harris, 2001).

Strategy Defined

As definitions of *strategy* evolved, one issue proved more debatable than any other. Must a strategy be used intentionally? Certainly, when people are first learning to use a strategy, they are very intentional, deliberately planning every move and monitoring its execution. With increasing expertise, however, what was once consciously deliberate becomes much more automatic, requiring much less conscious attention and reflection. That potential for conscious control is a critical part of the definition of strategy proposed by Pressley, Forrest-Pressley, Elliot-Faust, and Miller (1985, p. 4), a definition that has endured: "A strategy is composed of cognitive operations over and above the processes that are natural consequences of carrying out the task, ranging from one such operation to a sequence of interdependent operations. Strategies achieve cognitive purposes (e.g., comprehending, memorizing) and are potentially conscious and controllable activities."

Procedural and Declarative Knowledge

Strategies are knowledge of procedures, knowledge about how to do something—how to decode a word, comprehend a story better, compose more completely and coherently, play first base better, and so on. Such knowledge contrasts with declarative knowledge, the knowledge of facts (Mandler, 1998). Of course, procedural and declarative knowledge are not unrelated, with declarative knowledge potentially affecting execution of even an overlearned procedure (Rabinowitz, 2002). Indeed, there is growing realization that interventions promoting procedural learning include aspects that increase learning of declarative information that can interactively support and complement the procedural knowledge. Thus, when students are required to explain their problem-solving strategies as they do geometry problems, their understanding and transfer of strategies increases. Such an increase is probably because self-explanation promotes development of both declarative and procedural knowledge about problem-solving situations (Burkell, Schneider, & Pressley, 1990). Further, more sophisticated strategies use often results in increases in declarative knowledge (Kuhn & Udell, 2003).

Throughout the discussion that follows, there will be many instances where declarative and procedural knowledge intermingle. For example, word decoding strategies make use of factual knowledge of letter–sound associations. Comprehension strategies such as predicting ideas in text require prior knowledge about the topic of the text. Written composition depends on strategies to organize content the writer already knows or has found through research.

Long- and Short-Term Memory

Both procedural and declarative knowledge reside in long-term memory, most of which is out of consciousness most of the time, retrieved and activated only when the knowledge is needed. Much of human intelligence is such knowledge, referred to as crystallized knowledge in Horn and Cattell's theory (1967). Active thinking, however, takes place more in working memory, the part of intelligence that permits active reflection on and manipulation of information (Baddeley, 2003). That is, when the contents of long-term memory are activated, they are activated into this working memory system, where the contents are thought about with respect to a current task demand (e.g., understanding a story, writing a text, solving a problem). One of working memory's most salient characteristics is that it is limited. There is only so much that a person can consciously think about at any given time. Another salient characteristic is that some people's working memories seem to be greater in capacity, with smaller working memory associated with a variety of learning and language disorders (e.g., Swanson & Sáez, 2003).

So, how does information get activated into working memory? Some activation is automatic and associative, not much under the thinker's control. Other activation is quite controlled, with the thinker very deliberately activating that knowledge. Thus, on hearing a rate–distance problem, an effective algebra student immediately activates the strategies known for solving such problems. A less effective student might not do so, but would be able to apply such strategies if someone reminded her or him that these are the strategies to apply to this type of problem. The difference between effective and less effective performance is often related in part to metacognitive understanding of when and where to apply known strategies.

Metacognition

Metacognition is knowledge of cognition, including knowledge about the value of cognitive strategies. People are much more likely to continue using a strategy they have learned if they understand that the strategy does have a positive impact on performance (Pressley, Borkowski, & O'Sullivan, 1985). A related and equally important form of metacognition is knowing when and where particular cognitive strategies should be used, sometimes referred to as *conditional knowledge* (Paris, Lipson, & Wixson, 1983). Such conditional knowledge is essential for broad and appropriate use of cognitive strategies (Borkowski, Carr, Rellinger, & Pressley, 1990; O'Sullivan & Pressley, 1984). Deciding to use strategies requires effort, which explains why strategy utility knowledge is so important. As a general rule, people do not expend effort unless they expect payoff. Knowing that a strategy will produce impact can motivate the use of strategies, if the impact matters to the thinker (Borkowski et al., 1990).

Good Information Processing

In the late 1980s and early 1990s, Pressley, Borkowski, Schneider, and their associates conceived of effective strategies use as good information processing (e.g., Pressley, Borkowski, & Schneider, 1987; Schneider & Pressley, 1997). Such thinking depends on intact working memory capacity and long-term memory. The long-term memory of the good information processor includes well-developed procedural and declarative knowledge as well as extensive metacognition, especially conditional and strategy utility knowledge. The good information processor is also motivated to use her or his strategies and knowledge, recognizing that good performance depends more on effort expended on task-appropriate strategies, rather than on factors out of her or his control, such as native ability, ease of the task, or luck (Borkowski et al., 1990). All of the main tenets of this perspective remain intact in more contemporary elaborations of effective information processing (e.g., Alexander, 2003).

The good information processing perspective proved to be remarkably uncontroversial, perhaps reflecting that it was constructed in light of a great amount of data on strategy development, including through instruction, that were generated in the 1960s, 1970s, and 1980s. Understanding the main findings from this literature on strategy development is essential to understand current research and theory regarding strategies. Thus, before turning to the literature on strategies instruction in educational arenas, we turn to basic research on cognitive strategies instruction and cognitive development.

THE DEVELOPMENT OF STRATEGIC COMPETENCE: UNDERSTANDINGS FROM BASIC RESEARCH

Without a doubt, the most complete study of strategic competence has been conducted in the area of children's memory (Schneider & Pressley, 1997). Thus, much of what follows in this section is about memory development. Basic research studies of other aspects of thinking and learning, including elementary problem solving, scientific thinking, and critical thinking, have been conducted and also inform this summary of basic understandings about strategic competence.

Initial Research: Elementary Grade Children

Interest in strategies development increased dramatically with the publication of a study by Flavell, Beach, and Chinsky (1966). The investigators presented children with a list of pictures to memorize in order. The participants in the study were between 5 and 10 years of age. Flavell and his associates were especially interested in what the children did to memorize the pictures and if developmental differences in what children did to memorize might account for differences in memory performance. The outcomes of the study were clear. With advancing age, recall improved as did use of a particular memory strategy. With increasing age, children were more likely to rehearse the names of the objects depicted.

Keeney, Cannizzo, and Flavell (1967) extended the Flavell et al. (1966) study. They investigated what happened if young children, who did not rehearse on their own when presented a list to learn, were taught to do so. Primary-grades students easily learned how to verbally rehearse pictures lists, with the result increased recall of the pictures on the list. Children could be taught a memory strategy that they did not think of on their own. Rehearsal was established as a causal mechanism in children's memory, a mechanism that kindergarten students used much less than students in the middle elementary grades.

Flavell's early work stimulated a number of investigations of children's use of rehearsal strategies, both when children were left to their own devices to memorize and when they were instructed to use rehearsal strategies (e.g., Cuvo, 1975; Gruenenfelder & Borkowski, 1975; Hagen, Hargrave, & Ross, 1973; Kingsley & Hagen, 1969; Naus, Ornstein, & Aivano, 1977; Ornstein, Naus, & Liberty, 1975). There was great convergence across these studies. First of all, the last items on the picture list tended to be better recalled than items in the middle of the list, reflecting that the last few items continued to be active in working memory, and, hence, were easily remembered. Better recall of the last items on a list came to be known as the *recency effect*. The first few items on the list tended to be remembered better than items in the middle of the list, referred to as a *primacy effect*. Primacy effects, in particular, were developmentally sensitive, with children in the middle elementary grades more likely than younger children to remember the initial items on a list, reflecting that older children rehearsed the list items more than younger children.

Across studies, it was quite clear that when nonrehearsing children were taught to rehearse list items, a primacy effect would occur, strengthening causal conclusions: That is, instruction to rehearse increased previously nonrehearsing children's visible rehearsal of the items on lists, with memory increased especially for the items that were most rehearsed, the beginning of the list items. Young children's failure to use rehearsal strategies on their own came to be known as a *production deficiency* (Flavell, 1970), a deficiency that could be overcome with instruction. As will become clear as this chapter proceeds, researchers have discovered many production deficiencies as they have studied children's cognition, occasions when students fail to produce a strategy that could help them do a task, although they can be taught to use the strategy in that situation (Pressley & Hilden, in press-a).

We emphasize at this juncture that Flavell's early work would set the stage for the study of memory strategy development, including strategy discovery and acquisition through instruction, during the preschool years, the years of elementary schooling, and beyond through middle school and high school. More generally, Flavell's (1970) work would go far to encourage the perspective that children can be taught to use strategies that they often do not produce on their own.

Preschool and Primary-Grades Years: New Understandings

One conclusion in the work just reviewed was that preschoolers did not use rehearsal strategies for learning lists of items. Does that mean preschoolers are never strategic? One possibility was that picture list learning was just a very strange situation for kindergarten-age children, that young children might perform more competently if given tasks more consistent with ones they encountered in their everyday lives. To find out, researchers studied memory situations more familiar to young children.

Strategies Production. DeLoache, Cassidy, and Brown (1985) reported one of the most important studies of strategies use by preschoolers. The study took place in a living room, with an experimenter hiding a Big Bird doll under a pillow on a couch. When the experimenter asked children 18 months to 2 years of age to remember where the doll was hidden, the children looked at the hiding place until it was time to retrieve the doll. Even when the experimenter tried to distract the preschoolers, they kept looking back at the pillow on the couch. In one condition of the study, rather than putting Big Bird under the pillow, the experimenter put the doll on the pillow, in full view of the participant. In this situation, there is no memory requirement. Accordingly, the children did not look back at the doll. That is, only when there was a memory requirement (i.e., the doll was hidden under a pillow) did the children evidence any strategies to remember where the doll was. This was the first of several studies making clear that even 2- to 3-year-old children can be strategic when confronted with a familiar task (see also Haake, Sommerville, & Wellman, 1980).

Other demonstrations of preschool use of memory strategies were generated in the 1980s. Thus, Baker-Ward, Ornstein, and Holden (1984) showed that preschoolers were much more strategic when they were asked to remember a group of toys than when they were instructed to play with the toys. When asked to remember the toys, they tend to say the names of the toys more often than when directed to play with the toys. Preschoolers certainly understood, at least in some situations, that remembering calls for different processing than playing.

Utilization Deficiencies. Something that was quite interesting in the Baker-Ward et al. (1984) study was that, often, even if 4- and 5-year-olds tried to remember a group of toys by saying and repeating the names of the toys, their efforts did not increase their memory. When children execute a strategy and it does not increase memory, the phenomenon is known as a *utilization deficiency* (Miller & Seier, 1994). Such utilization deficiencies were observed in several very well controlled studies of preschoolers' memory strategy use (e.g., Lange, MacKinnon, & Nida, 1989; Newman, 1990). Why utilization deficiencies occur still is not well understood, although there is some evidence that such deficiencies are linked to working memory capacity limitations during preschool and the early elementary years (Woody-Dorning & Miller, 2001).

Mediation Deficiencies. Sometimes when young children are asked to use a memory strategy, the problem is that they cannot execute the strategy, cannot construct the mediator they are being asked to construct, a difficulty referred to in the literature as a *mediation deficiency* (Reese, 1962). This seems to be the case when 4- to 7-year-old children are asked to generate mental images, for example, representing ideas expressed in a text they read or hear (see Pressley, 1977, for a review of the data). The likely culprit is limited working memory capacity in young children (see analyses by Cariglia–Bull & Pressley, 1990; Pressley, Cariglia-Bull, Deane, & Schneider, 1987), a problem perhaps accentuated by the fact that internal cognitive operations are performed more slowly by younger compared to older children, with slower operations consuming more working memory capacity to execute.

Retrieval Deficiencies. Finally, even if children construct a mediator, sometimes they will fail to use it later when they are required to remember what they studied, a failure known as a *retrieval deficiency* (Kobasigawa, 1977). That is, even if students construct mental images that have the potential to increase their later memory of material, it does little good if they do not think to use their previously constructed images at test time. More positively, at least on some occasions, a reminder to think back to strategies used at study and the mediators constructed at study is all that is required to get students to search their memories and use the mediators they constructed previously, thus, increasing memory performance on a test (e.g., Pressley & MacFadyen, 1983).

These historical findings should be understood better by many educational psychologists, for they make clear that strategies use by young children is more complicated than many practitioners believe. Indeed, some prominent recommendations regarding strategies use in the practitioner literature may, in fact, be wrong. For example, there are many suggestions in the practitioner literature that it makes sense to teach early primary grades children to construct mental images representing the ideas expressed in stories (see Miller, 2002). This recommendation flies in the face of voluminous basic research data that such children experience great difficulties in generating images representing the ideas in stories (Pressley, 1977), even when given strong support for doing so (e.g., partial pictures that strongly suggest the parts of the picture that could be imagined by the child; Guttmann, Levin, & Pressley, 1977). More careful study of the substantial basic research literature could result in a more informed applied science with respect to strategies instruction as well as more complex study of strategies development and instruction.

Strategies Development: Discovery, Direction or Instruction?

As a general rule of thumb, across many domains, there is evidence of greater strategy use with increasing age/grade level, proceeding through middle and late elementary grades, middle school, high school, and college (see Pressley & Hilden, in press-a, for a review). Questions of enduring significance are whether, when, and how young children discover strategies for performing academic tasks. There can be no doubt that even 2- and 3-year-olds discover some strategies, for example, keeping their eyes on a hidden toy in order to remember where it is. Other strategies are learned later, as a function of new task demands on children. Nonetheless, often children and adults do not discover and use the most potent strategies possible as they confront academic tasks.

For example, Kuhn and her colleagues (Kuhn et al., 1988) studied whether children and adults use a controlled comparison strategy as they tried to decide which characteristics of a set of balls (e.g., size, rough or smooth) determined whether a ball could be reliably served in a paddle game. The most efficient strategy was to compare balls that differed with respect to only one characteristic (e.g., large or small), repeating such trials until all of the dimensions of difference were assessed. Although there was improvement from childhood to adulthood in use of the controlled comparison strategy, even college students often failed to be maximally systematic as they evaluated characteristics of balls that could affect bounce.

Kuhn (1991) extended her work on strategy use by evaluating the social scientific reasoning strategies of children and adults as they constructed arguments about important social problems, such as the causes of criminal recidivism, school failure, and unemployment. Both children and adults had difficulties reasoning on several sides of these issues, difficulty in generating counterarguments to the arguments of others. In short, there was not much evidence that either children or adults used sophisticated critical thinking skills (see Baron & Sternberg, 1987; Perkins, Lochhead, & Bishop, 1987).

More positively, there is evidence that children sometimes do discover strategies as they do tasks, although some situations make that more likely than others. For example, Kuhn and Udell (2003) studied argument skills in inner city students in grades 7 and 8. Students who favored and opposed capital punishment prepared for a showdown debate on capital punishment. The control participants experienced some dyadic practice in arguing about capital punishment, working with peers (but supported by teacher scaffolding) to generate and refine arguments in favor of their position on capital punishment. Participants in the experimental condition received the same dyadic practice as controls but also participated in scaffolded, dyadic practice that led them to generate counterarguments to criticisms of their position, focusing on rebuttals of opposing positions. The experimental condition also provided opportunities to think and reason about mixed evidence. The most important finding was that the experimental participants evidenced more growth in argument strategies from pretest to posttest than control participants. In particular, they improved in making counterarguments with respect to the position on capital punishment that they opposed. The experimental participants also increased their knowledge of the topic of capital punishment as a function of the dyadic experiences in generating counterarguments. That is, consistent with other evidence reviewed later, more sophisticated strategies use often results in increases in declarative knowledge.

Although there is improvement in performance in reasoning and argumentative skills with practice and reflection, there is also a great deal of variability from trial to trial and task to task, with children and adults normally using a mix of strategies, some more effective than others (e.g., Kuhn, 1995; Kuhn, Garcia-Mila, Zohar, & Andersen, 1995). Such variability in strategies use is apparent even in some more basic task situations, ones simple enough that there are single strategies that can effectively mediate performance (cf. Pressley & Levin, 1977). More positively, there is evidence that some later-elementary and middle school age children mix effective and ineffective strategies but shift to more exclusive use of effective strategies with practice (Schlagmueller & Schneider, 2002). Moreover, some high ability child learners do use effective memory strategies very consistently (Coyle, Read, Gaultney, & Bjorklund, 1998).

In short, although there is increased use of more effective strategies with advancing age, we have encountered little evidence in any task domain that children certainly discover and consistently use the most effective strategies that can be used to accomplish tasks. Of course, this finding is in synchrony with a generally poor record for discovery learning (Mayer, 2004). Even when people discover effective strategies, they then tend to use them variably. Still, we know little about the defining characteristics of such situations. More positively, however, there is one approach that works better than any other for ensuring that learners actually learn strategies: strategies instruction. Some important, analytical work in strategies instruction first occurred with respect to very basic memory strategies.

Strategies Instruction: Early Issues of Maintenance and Generalization

There was incredible consistency in the basic research literature with respect to the issue of instruction: For many basic memory tasks, from learning lists of pictures to recalling main ideas and details from texts, children can learn effective strategies when they are taught them, with clear benefits in learning and memory. By the early 1980s, this conclusion held for normally achieving children, students with learning disabilities, and children with mental retardation (Pressley, Heisel, McCormick, & Nakamura, 1982). Moreover, by the early 1980s, it was apparent that a variety of strategies increased performance in basic memory and learning tasks (Pressley et al., 1982).

One troubling finding in the early strategies instruction literature was that students often did not continue to use strategies they were taught, both failing to maintain the strategies (i.e., using them with materials similar to the materials they experienced during strategies instruction) and failing to transfer them (i.e., use taught strategies in new situations where they could be deployed profitably). One of the most important analyses of how to increase continued use of strategies was produced by Belmont, Butterfield, and Ferretti (1982). They were particularly interested in the potential of strategies functioning for students with mental retardation, analyzing about 100 studies of strategies instruction with people afflicted by retardation. They discovered an important regularity: Students with mental retardation did evidence transfer of strategies taught when instruction was rich in encouraging metacognitive understanding of strategies. Thus, when strategies transfer occurred, learning goals were definitely emphasized, as was the necessity of planning as part of tackling academic tasks. Students were encouraged to monitor whether using the strategy was improving performance (e.g., asking themselves, "Did the plan work?"). Maintenance and transfer also were more likely if students were taught to cope if they experienced some failure or frustration, taught to consider making and trying a new strategy.

Belmont et al.'s (1982) analysis made very clear that strategies instruction could be very potent even with students at risk for academic failure (i.e., students with retardation). This complemented work with normal and less disabled children, research establishing that children in general were more likely to continue to use and transfer strategies if strategies instruction and practice included opportunities to learn when and where the strategies worked, the benefits produced, and how the strategy might be adapted to new situations (O'Sullivan & Pressley, 1984; Pressley, Borkowski, & O'Sullivan, 1985). That is, children proved more likely to maintain and transfer strategies they learned if instruction was metacognitively rich.

STRATEGIES USE AND INSTRUCTION
IN ACADEMIC AREAS

Strategies use and instruction has been more prominent in some academic areas than in others. In this section, we discuss work in four areas where there has been extensive consideration of the role of strategies in academic cognition: reading, writing, foreign language learning, and mathematical problem solving. Issues and commonalities across these areas are then noted in the final section of this chapter.

Reading

Researchers have learned a great deal about skilled reading. One method, verbal protocol analyses, has been particularly useful in understanding skilled, and less skilled, reading (Pressley & Afflerbach, 1995). Skilled readers are actively predictive as they read, developing expectations about upcoming text in reaction to the title, section headers, pictures, and other clues, basing their predictions in part on prior knowledge they possess about the topic of the text. Throughout reading, good readers connect ideas in a current text to their general and specific understandings of and opinions about the world. They ask questions as they read and look for answers. Good readers create envisionments of the settings, characters, and events portrayed in text. They also consciously reflect on what the big ideas are in text and construct personal interpretations of what they read. Often, reading is anything but linear, with readers jumping back and forth in text. Moreover, good readers recognize that not all parts of text deserve equal attention, with them adjusting their reading rate and analytic set as they go through the text, reading some sections more carefully than others (Anderson, 1992; Brown, Pressley, Van Meter, & Schuder, 1996; Collins, 1991).

In contrast, weaker readers are much more likely to read word by word, reading less actively, a strategy that certainly produces some understanding, often enough to do well on simple, multiple-choice comprehension tests. Weaker readers face a number of problems as they seek meaning from text.

Two problems have consumed researchers interested in reading more than other problems: The first is how children can be taught to read words, and the second is how children and adults can be taught to process text so as to increase comprehension. Both are tasks that can be accomplished strategically, and researchers have invested considerable effort to identify strategies that can be taught

to promote both word recognition and comprehension as well as to identify how such strategies can be taught so that students, in fact, use the strategies and use them appropriately.

Word Recognition

Good readers recognize most words automatically but are capable of consciously sounding out unfamiliar words; this is possible because of their understanding of the letter–sound associations in English. The goal in teaching children to read words is to get them to that point at which they automatically recognize most words and sound out words they do not recognize.

Most children arriving at the kindergarten door cannot read many words if they can read any at all. More positively, an important finding in 20th century educational science is that many children can make great progress in learning how to read words by teaching them phonics strategies. That is, children can be taught the letter–sound associations in English and taught to make the sounds represented by the letters in a word, blending those sounds to pronounce the word. That this approach works much of the time was one of the most important conclusions in the National Reading Panel (2000) report. Awareness of the power of teaching young children sounding-out strategies has had broad impact. The most recent federal elementary and secondary school act (107th Congress, 2002), the *No Child Left Behind (NCLB)* legislation, mandates teaching primary-grades students phonics strategies in those elementary schools receiving *NCLB* funds.

That said, phonics instruction's impact on beginning reading is not large, with a moderate-sized effect in meta-analytic terms (Cohen, 1988). One reason that the impact is modest is that teaching phonics strategies does not work all of the time. Consider a couple of recent studies. Morris, Tyner, and Perney (2000) provided tutorial reading instruction to grade 1 students in the lowest 20 percent of their classes (i.e., with respect to reading achievement). The tutoring included a great deal of explicit, systematic phonics instruction, with most participants who received the tutoring experiencing great growth, especially relative to control participants. However, about 7 percent of the participants made little to no progress. Similarly, Fuchs et al. (2001) provided intense phonics instruction to kindergarten students in intact classes for about 20 weeks. It worked for most students, but for a few there were no gains.

What bothers us is that so little is known about why phonics instruction does not work when it does not work. We think it would make sense to study such children's performance carefully, considering the possibility that some of the deficiencies noted in basic strategies research might have counterparts with respect to phonics strategies. Thus, are there children who simply cannot sound out words no matter how hard they try, a phonics mediational deficiency? Or perhaps they can sound out words but somehow the sounding out does not click as a word–that is, the student sees *ball* and sounds out /b/ followed by /a/ followed by /l/, but does not make the connection that this sounded-out word is the same as that word in their oral vocabulary, *ball*, that refers to a round, bouncy thing. This would be a utilization deficiency. Alternatively, what if the child learns how to sound out phonetically and yet does not transfer the approach to new situations, such as reading on a standardized test? In short, there are a number of possible ways that phonics may not work.

We suspect that skilled reading clinicians might be able to think of interventions for dealing with mediation deficiencies, utilization deficiencies, or transfer failures. For example, failure to transfer phonics might be addressed by providing meaningful metacognitive embellishment to phonics instruction, making clear that phonics can and should be used whenever unfamiliar words are encountered. Phonics can and should be studied as basic strategies have been studied, and failures of phonics should be examined as potentially similar to other strategy failures.

The most popular strategies-oriented hypothesis with respect to phonics is that some students respond better to some forms of phonics instruction than others, although this hypothesis is not so well developed that there has been a true test of the suggested aptitude by treatment interaction. Nonetheless, Lovett and her colleagues have examined the relative efficacy of two popular forms of phonics instruction, their impact alone and in combination. Since Chall's (1967) analysis, synthetic phonics has been the most prevalent phonics strategy taught. This involves teaching students the letter–sound associations and then teaching them to blend sounds to recognize words. An alternative is to teach students to focus on larger word parts, making maximum use of the many word families in English (e.g., focus on the *-ight* in *might, sight, light*, and so on; focus on the *-aid* in *raid, laid*, and *paid*) as well as the common prefixes and suffixes, teaching students to decode new words through analogy to known words (e.g., to read a new word, *fade*, by analogy with a known word, *made*).

The participants in Lovett et al. (2000) were 6- to 13-year-olds who experienced severe problems learning to read. These students were provided 70 hours of intervention in the study. In one condition, students received only synthetic phonics instruction. In a second condition, they received instruction emphasizing decoding by analogy with known words. In a third condition, students were taught both synthetic phonics and decoding by analogy. Students in a control condition were taught math skills and classroom survival skills. The results were very clear. After instruction, students taught the decoding strategies could read words better than control participants, with reading in the combined synthetic phonics and analogy condition exceeding reading in either the synthetic phonics alone or analogy alone condition, with performances in those conditions not varying.

It is also apparent that one type of decoding instruction does not work with all learners. Moreover, it seems likely that the effectiveness of the various decoding strategies will vary with word characteristics: Words having salient parts that are common to other words are likely susceptible to recognition through analogy (e.g., recognizing *spat* as analogous to *sat, fat, pat*, and so on). In contrast, more morphologically unique words may be better sounded out by blending the component sounds as represented by the individual letters and letter clusters (e.g., digraphs) in the words.

Lovett, Barron, and Benson (2003) are currently evaluating an intervention that involves teaching struggling beginning readers to use five strategies as a repertoire: (a) sounding out words by blending individual sound; (b) decoding by analogy to known words, focusing on whether an unknown word might rhyme with a known word; (c) peeling off prefixes and suffixes and isolating a smaller root word; (d) trying each of the sounds a word's vowels could make; and (e) looking for smaller, known words in a longer unknown word. Lovett et al. (2003) have been very much influenced by researchers who emphasize teaching students to self-regulate their use of strategies, who emphasize metacognitively embellishing strategies instruction (e.g., Harris, 1982; Harris & Graham, 1992; Meichenbaum & Biemiller, 1998).

For example, while trying to decode the word *unstacking*, students would self-regulate strategy use through four steps (Lovett et al., 2003, p. 285, Table 17.1): (a) They would choose a strategy, saying to themselves something like the following: "My game plan is first to use peeling off. Then I am going to use the rhyming strategy and look for the spelling patterns I know." (b) The students would use these strategies, self-verbalizing as they do so: "I am peeling off *un* and *ing*. My next game plan is rhyming. I see the spelling pattern *-ack*. The key word is *pack*. If I know *pack*, then I know *stack*." (c) The reader would then check: "I have to stop and think about whether I am using the strategies properly. Is it working? Yes, I'll keep on going. I will put all the parts together— *un-stack-ing*." (d) The student self-reinforces by declaring she or he "scored," if the word seems correct. If not, the student would start the sequence again, choosing, using, and checking strategy use: "The word is *unstacking*. I scored. I used peeling off and rhyming to help me figure out this word and that worked." Evaluations of this self-instructional approach are now underway, with our expectation that there will be increased study of how to increase beginning readers' self-regulated use of a variety of strategies that can be used to decode unfamiliar words, with the goal of developing beginning readers who continue and generalize use of effective word recognition strategies.

Comprehension. In the 1970s and early 1980s, the study of comprehension was largely the evaluation of individual comprehension strategies (e.g., prediction, question asking, imagery generation, monitoring and seeking clarification when confused, summarization). In a typical study, one group of young readers would be taught to use a particular strategy and a control group would be left to their own devices to read and understand text. In general, a variety of individual strategies proved effective in promoting reading comprehension, often assessed by answering questions about a text just read or simply retelling the text just read (e.g., Pearson & Fielding, 1991; Pressley, 2000; Pressley, Johnson, Symons, McGoldrick, & Kurita, 1989).

Good readers do not rely on individual strategies, however, as they read text, but rather articulate a repertoire of strategies, flexibly applying and adapting individual comprehension strategies before they read a text, while they are reading, and after they conclude a first reading of a document (Pressley & Afflerbach, 1995). In the 1980s, researchers turned their attention to teaching elementary and middle school students repertoires of comprehension strategies, with improved comprehension generally following such instruction (e.g., Bereiter & Bird, 1985). The best known of such instructional interventions was reciprocal teaching (Palincsar & Brown, 1984; Rosenshine & Meister, 1994), which involved teaching students to make predictions, ask questions, seek clarification when confused, and summarize. When deployed in classrooms, however, there often was departure from the version of reciprocal teaching developed and studied by Palincsar and Brown, with students using the strategies very flexibly (and not necessarily in the originally proposed order). In addition, Palincsar and Brown advocated strategies development in the context of small-group reading, with students in the group taking turns leading the group as it applied strategies to reading. In classrooms, however, teachers who employ reciprocal teaching as a way to begin strategies instruction eventually use a variety of instructional tactics to encourage their students to make predictions, generate questions, seek clarifications,

and construct summaries (Hacker & Tenent, 2002; Marks et al., 1993).

Indeed, many educators came to teach comprehension strategies in a more flexible manner than reciprocal teaching. Pressley, El-Dinary et al.(1992) coined the term *transactional comprehension strategies instruction* to emphasize that teachers and students often flexibly interacted as students practiced applying strategies as they read. Students in transactional strategies instruction are encouraged to use the comprehension strategies that seem appropriate to them at any point during a reading. There is dynamic construction of understanding of text when small groups of children make predictions together, ask questions of one another during a reading, signal when they are confused, seek help to reduce confusion, and make interpretive and selective summaries throughout a reading and as a reading concludes.

There are several very good evaluations of transactional strategies instruction (e.g., Anderson, 1992; Collins, 1991). Brown et al. (1996) studied grade 2 students, who received transactional comprehension strategies instruction over the course of the grade 2 school year or who experienced conventional reading instruction that year. The strategies were taught directly in small reading groups, through teacher modeling and explanations, followed every day by application of the strategies to stories being read in reading group. Although at the beginning of the school year the two groups did not differ on any measures of reading achievement, by the end of the school year, the group taught comprehension strategies using the transactional approach outperformed control participants on a wide variety of measures, from standardized test performance to remembering more content from stories read during reading group. In general, consistent with Anderson (1992) and Collins (1991), the effects of a year of comprehension strategies instruction were large in Brown et al. (1996) and apparent in many ways (i.e., not just on standardized tests but on other measures, both quantitative and qualitative).

During the past half dozen years, there has been increasing awareness of how difficult it is for teachers to learn how to teach comprehension strategies (Pressley & El-Dinary, 1997). As this chapter is being written, Hilden, Moxley, and Pressley are collecting data on the many challenges to effective comprehension strategies instruction in elementary and middle schools. The problems range from teachers not understanding the approach because they do not read using consciously controlled comprehension strategies to lack of school resources to provide in-class coaching to teachers about comprehension strategies instruction. Just as was the case a generation ago (Durkin, 1978-79), there is still too little comprehension instruction occurring in schools (Pressley,

Wharton-McDonald, Mistretta, & Echevarria, 1998; Taylor, Pearson, Clark, & Walpole, 2000).

Writing

Learning to write is difficult and demanding, as writing is a highly complex process. The good writer must not only negotiate the rules and mechanics of writing, but also must maintain a focus on important aspects of writing, including organization, form and features, purposes and goals, audience needs and perspectives, and evaluation of the communication between author and reader (Applebee, Langer, Mullis, Latham, & Gentile, 1994; Bereiter & Scardamalia, 1982; Hayes, 2004; Hayes & Flower, 1980). In addition, writing requires extensive self-regulation, persistence, and attention control (Graham & Harris, 1994, 2000). In its report, *The Neglected "R,"* the National Commission on Writing in America's Schools and Colleges (2003) expressed strong concern with the narrative, expository, and persuasive writing of students in the United States. Scardamalia and Bereiter (1986) identified five areas of writing competence particularly difficult for most students: (a) generating content, (b) creating an organized structure for compositions, (c) formulating goals and higher level plans, (d) quickly and efficiently executing the mechanical aspects of writing, and (e) revising text and reformulating goals.

Good writers, in contrast, engage in purposeful and active self-direction of the processes and skills underlying writing, and like good readers, use a repertoire of strategies. Seminal research by Hayes and Flower (1980), involving analysis of "think aloud" protocols, provided a window into the cognitive processes of good writers and led to the development of an influential model of skilled writing. For skilled writers, the process of writing is goal directed; they organize and execute their goals flexibly, switching from simple to complex goals while drawing on a rich store of cognitive processes and strategies for planning, text production, and revision. Good writers also have knowledge of the organizations typifying different genres; can develop novel or modified organizations as needed; are sensitive to the functions of their writing; and attend to the needs and perspectives of their audience (Harris & Graham, 1992).

Study of good writers and the development of expertise in writing, combined with recognition of the difficulties many children face in learning to write, fueled interest in instruction in writing from cognitive theoretical perspectives in the 1980s (Scardamalia & Bereiter, 1986). The largest body of research in the area of writing performance, however, has evolved in the area of strategies instruction.

Writing Strategies Instruction. Most writing strategies instructional research has primarily involved either participants with learning disabilities or students who struggle with writing, typically defined as scoring in the lower quartile on norm-referenced measures (Harris & Graham, 1992). An important by-product of writing instructional research with students with learning disabilities is that what works for these students also improves performance of average and good writers (Englert et al., 1991; Graham, in press; Graham & Harris, 2003; Wong, Harris, Graham, & Butler, 2003). A number of researchers have carried out important studies of writing strategies instruction (for a complete list, see Graham, in press). Three major lines of research are especially notable, however, having had broad impact.

Englert and her colleagues published two influential studies involving elementary students with learning disabilities, using their Cognitive Strategies Instruction in Writing (CSIW) program (Englert, Raphael, & Anderson, 1992; Englert et al., 1991). "Think sheets" are used in CSIW to prompt students to carry out specific activities during writing processes, including planning, organizing information, writing, editing, and revising. A number of features common to strategies instruction models are used to aid students in coming to own and internalize the strategies and framework represented on the think sheets, including teacher modeling, self-instructions, gradually faded support, and helping students understand what they are learning, why it is important, and when it can be used.

In the Englert et al. studies, students with and without learning disabilities improved their knowledge of the writing process and their writing abilities. Most impressive, students with learning disabilities performed similarly to normally achieving peers on all five posttest variables after CSIW instruction. Consistent with the good information processor perspective, metacognitive knowledge was positively related to measures of performance, both for writing and for reading.

Wong and her colleagues are among the few researchers who have conducted writing strategies research among secondary students, validating genre-specific strategies (personal narrative, opinion essays, and compare and contrast essays) in a series of three studies involving students with learning disabilities (Wong, Butler, Ficzere, & Kuperis, 1996, 1997; Wong, Wong, Darlington, & Jones, 1991). They considered several critical principles in designing their strategies instruction, including the need to develop among these students procedural and declarative knowledge of the writing process, understanding of the recursive nature of the writing process and the importance of planning and revising, and important knowledge about good writing (being clear for the reader, good word choice, importance of powerful introductions and conclusions, cadence, and so on). Heeding the call for addressing affective needs and characteristics of learners in good strategy instruction, Wong and her colleagues included development of self-efficacy for writing and positive attitudes about writing in their instructional approach.

Writing strategies instruction was effective for the secondary students in these studies, with instruction increasing both the quality and quantity of what students wrote across the three genres. Students with learning disabilities, however, needed more instruction and opportunities to write in order to reach a satisfactory level of performance in each genre than did their normally achieving peers. Far more research in secondary writing strategies instruction is needed.

Harris and Graham have provided detailed discussions of the multiple, integrated theoretical and research roots of the Self-Regulated Strategy Development (SRSD) model (Harris, 1982; Harris & Graham, 1992; Harris et al., 2003). Since 1985, more than 30 studies have been reported using the SRSD model of instruction in the area of writing), involving students in the second through eighth grades (Graham, in press; Graham & Harris, 2003; Graham et al., in press; Wong et al., 2003), including randomized classroom trials (Graham, Harris, & Zito, in press; Harris, Graham, & Mason, in press), and strategies instruction conducted by both regular and special education teachers (Graham, in press; Harris, Graham, & Adkins, 2004).

The major goals of SRSD are threefold: (a) assist students in developing knowledge about writing and powerful skills and strategies involved in the writing process, including planning, writing, revising, and editing; (b) support students in the ongoing development of the abilities needed to monitor and manage their own writing; and (c) promote children's development of positive attitudes and motivation about writing and themselves as writers. Whereas current models of strategies instruction have converged in many ways (Pressley & Harris, 2001), in the early years SRSD differed from other strategies instruction models in at least three important ways.

First, based in part on the research on expertise in writing and research on children's self-regulation (cf. Harris & Graham, 1992), explicit instruction in and supported development of self-regulation were integrated throughout the stages of instruction in the SRSD model. Second, progression through SRSD instructional stages is criterion-based rather than time-based, so that students have the time they need to attain important outcomes. Third, struggling learners often face additional challenges related to reciprocal relations among academic failure,

self-doubts, learned helplessness, low self-efficacy, maladaptive attributions, unrealistic pretask expectancies, and low motivation and engagement in academic areas. Thus, children's attitudes and beliefs about themselves as writers and the strategies instruction they participate in became critical targets for intervention as well as assessment during and after strategies instruction. Throughout SRSD instruction, students are supported in the development of attributions for effort and the use of powerful writing strategies, knowledge of writing genres, self-efficacy, and high levels of engagement (Harris & Graham, 1992).

There has been SRSD research with respect to a variety of genres, including personal narratives, story writing, persuasive essays, report writing, expository essays, and state writing tests. SRSD produces significant and meaningful improvements in children's development of planning and revising strategies, including brainstorming, self-monitoring, reading for information and semantic webbing, generating and organizing writing content, advanced planning and dictation, revising with peers, and revising for both substance and mechanics (Graham & Harris, 2003).

SRSD has resulted in improvements in four main aspects of students' performance: quality of writing; knowledge of writing; approach to writing; and self-efficacy, effort, or motivation (Graham, in press; Graham & Harris, 2003). Across a variety of strategies and genres, the quality, length, and structure of students' compositions have improved. Depending on the strategy taught, improvements have been documented in planning, revising, content, and mechanics. These improvements have been consistently maintained for the majority of students over time, with some students needing booster sessions for long-term maintenance. SRSD students have generalized writing strategies across settings, persons, and writing media. That SRSD improves the writing of both normally achieving students as well as students with LD makes it a good fit for inclusive classrooms.

Meta-analyses of Strategies Instruction in Writing. Recently, two meta-analyses of research in writing strategies instruction have been reported. The first focused on the SRSD model (Graham & Harris, 2003). The second encompassed all empirical research in writing strategies instruction that met established criteria, including both group comparisons (including experiments involving random assignment to treatments and quasi-experimental designs) and single subject design studies from grades 1–12 (Graham, in press).

Thirty-nine studies are included in Graham's (in press) meta-analysis: 20 involving group comparisons and 19 using single subject design. Writing strategy instruction proved effective across diverse measures of writing performance. The mean effect size immediately following strategy instruction in 20 group comparison studies was 1.15, with effect sizes at posttest for key measures (writing quality, elements, length, and revisions) of 1.21, 1.89, 0.95, and 0.90, respectively. The effect size for mechanics was relatively weak, 0.30, at posttest. The effect sizes calculated for the single subject design studies were similar. Graham placed these effect sizes in perspective by noting that the most successful intervention (the environmental model) in Hillock's (1984) meta-analysis of different methods for teaching writing has an average effect size of 0.44. SRSD is clearly powerful relative to alternatives.

Graham (in press) also found that while maintenance was assessed in only 54 percent of the studies reviewed and generalization in only 38 percent of studies, effect sizes were large here as well. For example, in the group comparison studies, maintenance, generalization to genre, and generalization to setting/person effect sizes were 1.32, 1.13, and 0.93, respectively. These were not related to the type of student receiving instruction, grade level, strategy taught, or genre. Finally, although it has been suggested that teachers may not be able to realize effects as strong as those obtained by researchers and research assistants delivering interventions, there was no statistically significant difference between type of teacher in the group comparison studies, and teachers obtained larger effects than graduate assistants/researchers in the single subject design studies reviewed.

Finally, Graham (in press) noted that studies using the SRSD model accounted for 45 percent of the group comparison studies and 68 percent of the single subject design studies. The average effect size for SRSD studies was almost twice that of the other studies. The three characteristics of SRSD noted previously might explain this: There is explicit development of self-regulation strategies in tandem with writing strategies; instruction is criterion based rather than time based; and such instruction explicitly targets attitudes, beliefs, and motivation.

Much more remains to be learned about writing strategies instruction and the SRSD model. SRSD continues to evolve. Mason (2004) is now studying the effects of SRSD on multiple measures of both expository reading comprehension and expository writing among fifth-grade students who struggle with reading and writing. The instruction is being studied with both special education and general education teachers, with the reading and writing part of science and social studies instruction (i.e., there are strong cross-curricular connections).

Foreign Language Learning[1]

There has been considerable advance in understanding the nature of second language acquisition in the past half century, with much of the work carried out and interpreted within information processing theory (McLaughlin & Heredia, 1996). Teaching second languages in school is challenging. Contrary to some early hypotheses that children are especially adept at second language acquisition, in fact, the younger the child, the greater the challenge in learning a second language. Acquiring a second language is definitely a long-term developmental process.

Well before educational psychologists conceived of good information processors, foreign language educators advanced the idea of good language learners (Rubin, 1979), with this conception of language learning definitely consistent with most aspects of the good information processing perspective. Good second language learners are very strategic. For example, they habitually make informed guesses about the meanings of words and phrases they encounter, making inferences about possible meanings based on context clues. When good language learners do not know exactly how to say something in the second language, they creatively use what they do know about the language to attempt to express meaning, often adapting the rules of the language. They learn strategies for keeping conversations going and approaches that work to keep them in a conversation even if they cannot quite say what they mean. Good language learners use a variety of memory strategies to remember the meanings of words encountered, including mnemonic systems, such as the keyword method, discussed previously in this chapter. They learn "chunks" of language and pay attention to idioms and proverbs, which can be learned as wholes. The good language learner pays attention to meaning, habitually making the most of context clues (e.g., speaker gestures) to guess at the meaning of a word or phrase.

Such attention to context clues permits the development of sophisticated metacognitive competence, with the good language learner aware of when and where to use particular aspects of the language being learned (e.g., when and how to speak formally versus informally). Indeed, the good language learner actively and consciously monitors her or his language and the effects it has, gaining insights about the language by doing so. Further, the good language learner is motivated to learn the second language, wanting to learn how to communicate well in the second language. In short, good language learning is self-motivated and self-regulated. The good language learner

---

[1] The authors are grateful to Professor Anna U. Chamot of George Washington University who provided conceptual guidance to us about contemporary second language education research as this chapter was being developed.

knows and uses a variety of strategies, improving as a result of practice and reflection on the language during attempts to understand and communicate with the language. Thus, good language learners develop ever greater strategic, metacognitive, and other knowledge about language (e.g., vocabulary).

Considerable evidence supports the major tenet that good second language learners are considerably more strategic than weaker second language learners (O'Malley & Chamot, 1990). There is growing evidence that among K-12 students, good second language learners are more sophisticated in their use of strategies than weaker second language learners, with some of the most compelling work consisting of analyses of verbal protocols of language learning (i.e., think-alouds as students attempt foreign language tasks; e.g., Vandergrift, 2003). Thus, employing verbal protocol analyses to document strategy use, Chamot and El-Dinary (1999) found that better child language learners used more of some strategies than weaker learners when they read in the second language. Stronger students made more predictions, inferences, and elaborations based on background knowledge, whereas the weaker students expended more effort on sounding-out strategies (i.e., stronger students attempted to process the text meaningfully, whereas weaker students were still struggling with simply reading the words).

Research supports the remaining tenets as well. Good language learners monitor their learning and use of language more than weaker learners (Chamot, 1999; Chamot & El-Dinary, 1999). Better students also are more likely to relate aspects of the second language to prior knowledge than weaker students, for example, using cognates to make inferences about the meanings of words in the second language (O'Malley, Chamot, & Küpper, 1989). Even when good and poor learners use the same number of strategies, the good learners are more likely to use task-appropriate strategies, probably caused by greater metacognitive understandings about when and where particular strategies should be used (e.g., Chamot, Dale, O'Malley, & Spanos, 1993; Chamot & El-Dinary, 1999; Vann & Abraham, 1990). Better second-language learners do more cognitive and metacognitive processing—much of it strategic processing—than do less skilled second-language learners (Vandergrift; 2003).

Are good language learners good at language learning because they use strategies? An answer to that question could only follow from experimental studies. The most complete experimentally evaluated foreign language learning strategy is the keyword method, which generally improves learning of associations between second language vocabulary items and their definitions (Pressley, Levin, & Delaney, 1982, for a review). The keyword method involves identifying part of the foreign word that sounds like a familiar word in the first language (e.g., for the Spanish word *pato*, *pot* might serve as a keyword). Then, learners either construct (i.e., make a mental image) or look at a picture depicting the keyword and definition referent in interaction (e.g., an image of a *duck* with a *pot* on its head). Work on the keyword method for learning foreign vocabulary is continuing (Zhang & Schumm, 2002), stimulated in part by concerns that the method does not facilitate learning of the foreign word as completely and reliably as other approaches and concerns that the keyword method produces only short-term memory advantage for foreign word–definition associations (Carney & Levin, 1998; Gruneberg, 1998; Lawson & Hogben, 1998; Nikol, Levin, & Woodward, 2003; Wang & Thomas, 1995, 1999). In general, however, there is at best mixed support for these points of concern, although we anticipate that research will continue to document the boundary conditions on keyword method efficacy.

Although other single second-language learning strategies have not been validated in true experiments as extensively as the keyword method, in a few studies (Cohen, 1998; Thompson & Rubin, 1996), second-language education researchers have evaluated the effects of teaching students a large repertoire of strategies appropriate for a range of second language goals (e.g., learning second-language vocabulary, comprehending text in a second language, composing in the second language). The results in these studies have been mixed, although at least slightly more positive than negative. Even so, we expect more such work in the future, with Chamot and O'Malley (e.g., 1996) offering powerful justification for providing broadly applicable strategies instruction to students learning a second language for use in school (i.e., instruction in how to tackle academic content and tasks as well as strategies for second-language acquisition). Although research on the consequences of teaching such strategies is not as far along as in other academic arenas, there has been enough evidence of improved second-language learning following strategies instruction to encourage continued research on this topic.

Mathematical Problem Solving

Mathematical problem solving is being intensely researched at present, by a wide variety of investigators, from basic cognitive scientists to educational psychologists to mathematics educators and curriculum developers. Much has been learned about how children solve mathematical problems and how they can learn to solve them through instruction, with strategies instruction proving a potent contributor to advancing children's mathematical competencies.

Researchers interested in basic cognitive development have devoted considerable attention in the past two decades to determining whether young children (i.e., preschoolers to children in the primary grades) use strategies when they solve simple problems, most prominently simple arithmetic fact problems (e.g., $5 + 4 = ?$). By carefully observing young children attempting to solve such problems, studying their reaction times (i.e., how long it takes to produce answers to such problems), and studying their patterns of errors, researchers have come to understand that even preschoolers and kindergarten children are sometimes strategic (e.g., counting on their fingers to solve a math fact problem, counting up from the larger addend). With advancing age and practice with particular problems, children come to know the answer without having to do the computation, so that with advancing age/grade basic fact problem-solving is less mediated by strategic computation and more simply retrieval of information from long-term memory (Barrouillet & Fayol, 1998; Siegler, 1996). Even some adults, however, occasionally rely on mathematical computation over fact retrieval for simple arithmetic (Hecht, 2002).

Many cognitive developmentalists believe that children discover the strategies they use to solve such simple math problems, including discovering that after a while they do not have to do the computation but can rely on the answer they know from previous problem-solving trials, although some children will do the computation just to make certain (see Siegler, 1996, for a review). That young children use strategies to do math fact problems with developmental shifts in strategies use is consistent with a great deal of research establishing that, with increasing age and education, students exhibit more use of strategies and more use of powerful strategies increasingly better matched to the problems being tackled, with this holding for a wide variety of problem types (e.g., Carpenter, Franke, Jacobs, Fennema, & Empson, 1998; Christou & Phillipou, 1998; Dixon & Moore, 1996). How much of such development represents strategy discovery and how much is due to instruction, however, is impossible to discern in these studies.

Although children do discover strategies some of the time, problem-solving strategies instruction is often needed. Indeed, there is a long history of strategy instruction being at the heart of developing mathematical problem solving skills. One of the most famous books in the field of mathematics education is Polya's (1957) *How to Solve It*. Polya advocated that students attack problems using four general strategies: (a) The problem solver first should attempt to understand the problem as completely as possible. This can be accomplished by identifying and reflecting on information in the problem. This is decidedly reflective activity. Rather than starting to compute

an answer when first encountering a number in a problem, the good problem solver reads the entire problem and reflects on the meanings of the numbers in it and the other relationships specified in the problem. (b) The problem solver devices a plan for solving the problem, relying somewhat on prior knowledge to do so. For example, good problem solvers try to determine whether this problem is similar to previous problems encountered and whether solutions that worked with previous problems might be applied here. (c) The problem solver attempts to carry out the problem-solving plan. (d) The problem solver checks the solution and reflects on the solution plan, perhaps trying to get the same result using a different approach. As part of such reflection, the good problem solver notes the key features of the problem and the solution plan, recognizing that similar problems might occur in the future.

In general, there has been good empirical support for Polya's position. When Burkell, Schneider, and Pressley (1990) analyzed successful problem-solving instruction with children, they found that such instruction included steps to increase understanding of problems, careful planning of solutions, carrying out solutions, and monitoring problem-solving attempts. When Hembree (1992) examined the full range of studies that evaluated Polya's approach, he found that the impact of such instruction varied with age/grade. Such teaching tended to have a small impact in the elementary grades but a large impact during high school, with the impact in college students moderately sized. That said, there are prominent research demonstrations that long-term, thorough mathematical problem-solving strategies instruction produces clear improvements in performance by the late elementary grades, even among struggling math students (e.g., Charles & Lester, 1984; Mastropieri, Scruggs, & Shiah, 1991; Montague & Bos, 1986).

More recently, there has been successful problem-solving strategies instruction in the early elementary grades, documented in well-designed studies. In Fuchs et al. (2003a, 2003b; see also Fuchs & Fuchs, 2003, for a review), grade 3 students were provided strategies to solve particular types of problems. Fuchs and Fuchs embellished such instruction with metacognitive information, specifically teaching the students that the strategies they were learning could transfer and giving them information about how superficially different problems can have the same underlying structure. The students had opportunities to practice the strategies they learned with a variety of such superficially transformed problems. In their most extensive treatment condition, the grade-3 students were also taught to use the strategies in a self-regulated fashion. Thus, they were instructed to check to see if their answers made sense and always to recheck their computations. In checking problems, there was emphasis both on getting the answer correct and on using the strategies taught appropriately and completely. Students engaged in such reflection when doing problems both in class and as homework. The bottom line in their work is that grade 3 students, even average and weaker problem solvers, in fact, learned the strategies and transferred them appropriately, with each strategy taught and practiced over 1 to 2 weeks. Nonetheless, there was room for additional transfer in their studies; the type of elaborated problem-solving strategies instruction that Fuchs and Fuchs studied deserves broader research attention.

In general, Polya's approach is consistent with the good information processing perspective, although subsequent models of mathematical cognition and problem solving were more comprehensively consistent. Thus, Schoenfeld (1992) and Pressley (1986) both dealt with the role of prior knowledge and motivation in problem solving much more explicitly than did Polya. An important development in the past decade and a half has been K-12 mathematical curricula that stress student understanding of mathematics, the development of strategic competence, and instruction that is motivating because it encourages student exploration and reflection—that is, curricula that are broadly consistent with Polya's framework. An important characteristic of recently developed curricula emphasizing understanding is that they are engaging curricula (Henningsen & Stein, 1997). Problems are presented in interesting ways, and connections between the math they are learning and the worlds they experience and care about are made clear to students. Efforts are made to provide tasks that are challenging but not so far beyond students' current understandings to be impossible. Teachers scaffold student attempts at problem-solving, providing hints and supports as needed for the student to make progress in problem solving. Students are given enough time to explore, understand, and solve problems. These are environments that emphasize learning rather than grading and competition for grades (e.g., Anderman et al., 2001).

A number of such curricula have been studied in well-designed comparative studies (i.e., the curricula emphasizing understanding have been compared with more conventional curricula, which involve more direct teaching of formula and routines). In general, such curricula have fared very well in such comparisons, with student mathematical achievement generally higher when understanding, reflection, and teacher-assisted discovery of strategies is emphasized (e.g., Boalar, 1998; Carroll, 1997; Cramer, Post, & delMas, 2002; Fuson, Carroll, & Drueck, 2000; Hollar & Norwood, 1999; Huntley, 2000; McCaffrey, Hamilton, Stecher, Klein, & Robyn, 2001; Reys, Reys, Lapan, Holliday, & Wasman, 2003; Riordan & Noyce, 2001; Thompson & Senk, 2001).

Although there is evidence that children can and do invent basic arithmetic problem-solving strategies, there is substantial evidence that teaching problem-solving strategies improves math achievement. Successful math instruction targets the development of strategies for understanding problems, strategies for solving problems, metacognitive understandings about when and where to use particular strategies, and how much strategies can be appropriately adapted and transferred, as well as motivation to do mathematics. We expect work on cognitive strategies instruction in math to continue, but probably more as part of multicomponent instructional packages attempting to develop the strategies, knowledge, and understanding that excellent problem solvers use. Far more analytical research on these packages is needed, for these packages are at the center of contemporary mathematics reform efforts.

DISCUSSION

The focus in this chapter has been on students in K-12, for most work on strategies instruction has occurred with those students. There is now great interest, however, in studying strategies instruction in postsecondary education. We refer interested readers to Butler (e.g., Butler, Elaschuk, & Poole, 2000; Wong et al., 2003), an emerging leader in the application of strategies instruction in postsecondary settings. Thus, academic strategies instruction has the potential to affect a variety of content areas and diverse students. Butler's work and the work of many others studying cognitive strategies instruction in academic domains was informed by the basic research reviewed early in this chapter. We believe that cognitive strategies instruction research and practice is most likely to thrive if there is high awareness of the historic work and substantial reflection on why academic strategies instruction works well when it works well; models such as transactional strategies instruction and SRSD were clearly designed to include components with proven potency in the basic strategies instructional literature.

Basic theory and research on strategies instruction, mostly carried out in the 1960s through the 1980s, set the stage for researchers interested in curricular issues to begin teaching strategies in reading, writing, second-language learning, and mathematical problem solving. This basic research was very analytical, which was possible because it was conducted with relatively simple tasks (as compared to all that is involved in reading, writing, second-language acquisition, and math problem solving) and simple strategies, often ones that could be taught in a few minutes. Far more analytical research is needed addressing the multicomponent strategies instruction models evolving now. One explanation for the lack of a correspondingly analytical literature with respect to strategies instruction in the curriculum is the huge difference in the complexities of the situations studied by the basic scientists interested in strategies and the applied researchers interested in moving strategies instruction into school settings.

One of the most important concepts emerging from the basic strategies instructional literature was that of production deficiency: People can often be taught to use strategies they do not use on their own. There were many examples of production deficiencies covered in this chapter. Young learners who do not use reading, writing, second language, and math problem-solving strategies often can be taught to use them with benefit, although the instruction can be complex and long-term.

A second important insight emerging from the basic strategies instruction literature was that maintenance and transfer of learned strategies requires instruction that includes metacognitive information and self-regulated use of the strategies being taught. Two bodies of research covered in this chapter have established that state-of-the-art/science strategy instruction is metacognitively rich and does demand self-regulated student use. The first is contemporary comprehension strategies instruction, as conceptualized in the transactional strategies instruction model. Extensive qualitative data documenting what goes on in such classrooms (e.g., Pressley, El-Dinary, et al., 1992) has documented the characteristics of this approach. The second is SRSD for writing (Graham & Harris, 2003) where the model has been presented in detail and studies have included assessment of whether the instructional model was followed as intended. Although such complete instruction probably occurs at least some of the time with respect to word recognition strategies instruction, second-language strategies instruction, and mathematical problem-solving strategies teaching, the literature we reviewed did not include complete enough analyses to be certain. For example, although there have been many experimental studies of phonics instruction (i.e., teaching students to use phonics strategies), we cannot locate any analyses of all that goes on during effective phonics instruction. The National Reading Panel (2000) applauded the many experimental evaluations of phonics instruction, but we point out here that phonics researchers have not provided research that makes clear just how phonics should be taught—that is, how students can be motivated to do phonics, how critical metacognitive information can be highlighted, and how such instruction mixes with other aspects of the language arts morning. Thus, we urge both more experimental evaluations

of most forms of strategies instruction but also qualitative analyses that make clear how such instruction can be done well.

Basic researchers were also interested in determining who could learn strategies and who could not. Thus, one hypothesis was that learning some capacity-demanding strategies requires substantial short-term/working memory, with at least some evidence generated to support that perspective (Cariglia-Bull & Pressley, 1990; Pressley et al., 1987). There has not been corresponding attention to short-term/working memory constraints in analyzing applied strategies instruction, with many of the curricular strategies reviewed in this chapter highly demanding of short-term capacity, or so it seems to us as we reflect on what learners must do to execute them. We think that there should be attention to the issue of whether working memory capacity differences make a difference in whether students can learn a variety of strategies, noting that such work would be consistent with indications in the literature that short-term/working memory differences matter in academic learning (e.g., for reading, see Cain, Oakhill, & Bryant, 2004; for writing, see Butterfield, Hacker, & Albertson, 1996; Hoskyn & Swanson, 2003).

A more general point is that the basic strategies researchers were much more attentive to when participants could not learn or would not use strategies. There has been much less attention to this in the applied strategies instructional arena. We urge applied strategies instructional researchers to study carefully concepts such as mediational and utilization deficiencies to determine whether such processes might be helpful in understanding when some students do not benefit as much from strategies instruction as others.

Are we anywhere near to understanding academic strategies use the way that we seem to understand strategies use by skilled baseball managers? The answer is that we are getting there. Future research is needed to address the complexities and subtleties inherent in such understanding. We note that one methodology has been more illuminating than any other with respect to the complex strategies used by the academically competent versus those who struggle with learning—verbal protocol analysis (Ericsson & Simon, 1993). We encountered many verbal protocol analyses as we reviewed this literature. This methodology allows documenting use of conscious cognitive processing (Pressley & Hilden, in press-b); documenting the complex orchestration of strategies by skilled learners and the less complete orchestration of processing by less skilled learners.

Such work is decidedly qualitative rather than experimental, and we note that far more qualitative research is needed to further our understandings of strategies and strategies instruction. Excellent programs of research on strategies instruction have been, and will continue to be, characterized by qualitative studies to generate descriptive understandings of students' use of strategies, as well as by experimentation to validate that the cognitive strategies reported by effective learners can be successfully taught to those who experience difficulties. We are confident that there will be much more programmatic study of strategies use and strategies instruction in the years and decades ahead.

It is clear that successful academic performance in each of the domains we have addressed requires specific strategies for the many different types of tasks and challenges encountered from preschool through high school. As there are numerous specific strategies for students to learn, the development of strategic competence must be conceived as a long-term venture. Developmental research is clearly needed. Finally, such development through instruction cannot occur unless teachers receive the support needed to move strategies instruction from research to practice. We hope the research community will rise to the challenge of developing and investigating professional development approaches that will make this possible.

References

Alexander, P. A. (2003). Profiling the developing reader: The interplay of knowledge, interest, and strategic processing. In C. M. Fairbanks, J. Worthy, B. Maloch, J. V. Hoffman, D. L. Schallert (Eds.), *The fifty-first yearbook of the National Reading Conference* (pp. 47–65). Oak Creek, WI: National Reading Conference.

Anderman, E. M., Eccles, J. S., Yoon, K. S., Roeseer, R., Wigfield, A., Blumenfeld, P. (2001). Learning to value mathematics and reading: Relations to mastery and performance-oriented instructional practices. *Journal for Research in Mathematics Education, 26*, 76–95.

Anderson, V. (1992). A teacher development project in transactional strategy instruction for teachers of severely reading disabled adolescents. *Teaching & Teacher Education, 8*, 391–403.

Applebee, A., Langer, J., Mullis, I., Latham, A., & Gentile, C. (1994). *NAEP 1992: Writing report card.* Washington, DC: U.S. Government Printing Office.

Armstrong, B., & Larson, C. N. (1995). Students' use of part-whole and direct comparison strategies for comparing partitioned triangles. *Journal for Research in Mathematics Education, 26*, 2–19.

Baddeley, A. (2003). Working memory and language: An overview. *Journal of Communicative Disorders, 36*, 189–208.

Baker-Ward, L., Ornstein, P. A., & Holden, D. J. (1984). The expression of memorization in early childhood. *Journal of Experimental Child Psychology, 37*, 555–575.

Baron, J. B., & Sternberg, R. J. (1987). *Teaching thinking skills: Theory and practice.* New York: Henry Holt.

Barrouillet, P., & Fayol, M. (1998). From algorithmic computing to direct retrieval: Evidence from number and alphabetic arithmetic in children and adults. *Memory and Cognition, 26*, 355–368.

Belmont, J. C., & Butterfield, E. C. (1977). The instructional approach to developmental cognitive research. In R. V. Kail & J. W. Hagen (Eds.), *Perspectives on the development of memory and cognition* (pp. 437–481). Hillsdale NJ: Lawrence Erlbaum Associates.

Belmont, J. M., Butterfield, E. C., & Ferretti, R. P. (1982). To secure transfer of training: Instruct self-management skills. In D. K. Detterman, & R. J. Sternberg (Eds.), *How and how much can intelligence be increased?* (pp. 147–154). Norwood, NJ: Ablex.

Bereiter, C., & Bird, M. (1985). Use of thinking aloud in identification and teaching of reading comprehension strategies. *Cognition and Instruction, 2*, 131–156.

Bereiter, C., & Scardamalia, M. (1982). From conversation to composition: The role of instruction in a developmental process. In R. Glaser (Ed.), *Advances in instructional psychology* (Vol. 2, pp. 1–64). Hillsdale, NJ: Lawrence Erlbaum Associates.

Bjorklund, D. F. (Ed.) (1990). *Children's strategies: Contemporary views of cognitive development.* Hillsdale, NJ: Lawrence Erlbaum Associates.

Boalar, J. (1998). Open and closed mathematics: Student experiences and understanding. *Journal for Research in Mathematics Education, 29*, 42–62.

Borkowski, J. G., Carr, M., Rellinger, E. A., & Pressley, M. (1990). Self-regulated strategy use: Interdependence of metacognition, attributions, and self-esteem. In B. F. Jones (Ed.), *Dimensions of thinking: Review of research* (pp. 53–92). Hillsdale, NJ: Lawrence Erlbaum Associates.

Brown, R., Pressley, M., Van Meter, P., & Schuder, T. (1996). A quasi-experimental validation of transactional strategies instruction with low-achieving second grade readers. *Journal of Educational Psychology, 88*, 18–37.

Burkell, J., Schneider, B., & Pressley, M. (1990). Mathematics. In M. Pressley & Associates (Eds.), *Cognitive strategy instruction that really improves children's academic performance* (pp. 147–177). Cambridge, MA: Brookline Books.

Butler, D. L., Elaschuk, C. L., & Poole, S. (2000). Promoting strategic writing by postsecondary students with learning disabilities: A report of three case studies. *Learning Disability Quarterly, 23*, 196–213.

Butterfield, E. C., Hacker, D. J., & Albertson, L. R. (1996). Environmental, cognitive, and metacognitive influences on text revision: Assessing the evidence. *Educational Psychology Review, 8*, 239–297.

Cain, K., Oakhill, J., & Bryant, P. (2003). Children's reading comprehension ability: Concurrent prediction by working memory, verbal ability, and component skills. *Journal of Educational Psychology, 96*, 31–42.

Cariglia-Bull, T., & Pressley, M. (1990). Short-term memory differences between children predict imagery effects when sentences are read. *Journal of Experimental Child Psychology, 49*, 384–398.

Carney, R. N., & Levin, J. R. (1998). Do mnemonic memories fade as time goes by? Here's looking anew! *Contemporary Educational Psychology, 23*, 276–297.

Carney, R. N., & Levin, J. R. (2003). Promoting higher-order learning benefits by building lower-order mnemonic connections. *Applied Cognitive Psychology, 17*, 563–575.

Carpenter, T. P., Franke, M. L., Jacobs, V. R., Fennema, E., & Empson, S. B. (1998). A longitudinal study of invention and understanding in children's multidigit addition and subtraction. *Journal for Research in Mathematics Education, 29*, 3–20.

Carroll, W. M. (1997). Results of third-grade students in reform curriculum on the Illinois state mathematics test. *Journal for Research in Mathematics Education, 28*, 237–242.

Chall, J. S. (1967). *Learning to read: The great debate*. New York: McGraw-Hill.

Chamot, A. U. (1999). How children in language immersion programs use learning strategies. In M. A. Kassen (Ed.), *Language learners of tomorrow: Process and Promise!* Lincolnwood, IL: National Textbook Company.

Chamot, A. U., Dale, M., O'Malley, J. M., Spanos, G. A. (1993). Learning and problem solving strategies of ESL students. *Bilingual Research Quarterly, 16*, 1–38.

Chamot, A. U. & El-Dinary, P. B. (1999). Children's learning strategies in immersion classrooms. *The Modern Language Journal, 83*, 319–341.

Chamot, A. U., & O'Malley, J. M. (1996). The Cognitive Academic Language Learning Approach: A model for linguistically diverse classrooms. *Elementary School Journal, 96*, 259–273.

Charles, R. I., & Lester, F. K., Jr. (1984). An evaluation of a process-oriented instructional program in mathematical problem solving in grades 5 and 7. *Journal for Research in Mathematics Education, 15*, 15–34.

Christou, C., & Phillippou, G. (1998). The developmental nature of the ability to solve one-step word problems. *Journal for Research in Mathematics Education, 29*, 436–442.

Cohen, A. D. (1998). *Strategies in learning and using a second language*. London: Longman.

Collins, C. (1991). Reading instruction that increases thinking abilities. *Journal of Reading, 34*, 510–516.

Coyle, T. R., Read, L. E., Gaultney, J. F., & Bjorklund, D. F. (1998). Giftedness and variability in strategic processing on a multitrial memory task: Evidence for stability in gifted cognition. *Learning and Individual Differences, 10*, 273–290.

Cramer, K. A., Post, T. R., & delMas, R. C. (2002). Initial fraction learning by fourth- and fifth-grade students: A comparison of the effects of using the rational number project curriculum. *Journal for Research in Mathematics Education, 33*, 111–144.

Cuvo, A. J. (1975). Developmental differences in rehearsal and free recall. *Journal of Experimental Child Psychology, 19*, 265–278.

DeLoache, J. S., Cassidy, D. J., & Brown, A. L. (1985). Precursors of mnemonic strategies in very young children's memory. *Child Development, 56*, 125–137.

Dixon, J. A., & Moore, C. F. (1996). The developmental role of intuitive principles in choosing mathematical strategies. *Developmental Psychology, 32*, 241–253.

Durkin, D. (1978–79). What classroom observations reveal about reading comprehension instruction. *Reading Research Quarterly, 14*, 481–533.

Englert, C., Raphael, T., & Anderson, L. (1992). Socially mediated instruction: Improving students' knowledge and talk about writing. *Elementary School Journal, 92*, 411–445.

Englert, C., Raphael, T., Anderson, L., Anthony, H., Steven, D., & Fear, K. (1991). Making writing and self-talk visible: Cognitive strategy instruction writing in regular and special education classrooms. *American Educational Research Journal, 28*, 337–373.

Ericsson, A., & Simon, H. A. (Eds.) (1993). *Protocol analysis, Revised edition: Verbal protocols as data*. Cambridge, MA: MIT Press.

Flavell, J. H. (1970). Developmental studies of mediated memory. In H. W. Reese & L. P. Lipsitt (Eds.), *Advances in child development and behavior: Vol. 5* (pp. 181–211). New York: Academic Press.

Flavell, J. H., Beach, D. H., & Chinsky, J. M. (1966). Spontaneous verbal rehearsal in a memory task as a function of age. *Child Development, 37*, 283–299.

Fuchs, D., Fuchs, L. S., Thompson, A., Otaiba, S. A., Yen, Y., Yang, N. J., et al. (2001). Is reading important in reading-readiness programs? A randomized field trial with teachers as program implementers. *Journal of Educational Psychology, 93*, 251–267.

Fuchs, L. S., & Fuchs, D. (2003). Enhancing the mathematical problem solving of students. In H. L. Swanson, K. R. Harris, & S. Graham (Eds.), *Handbook of learning disabilities* (pp. 306–322). New York: Guilford.

Fuchs, L. S., Fuchs, D., Prentice, K., Burch, M., Hamlett, C. L., Owen, R., & Schroeter, K. (2003a). Enhancing third-grade students' mathematical problem solving with self-regulated learning strategies. *Journal of Educational Psychology, 95*, 306–315.

Fuchs, L. S., Fuchs, D., Prentice, K., Burch, M., Hamlett, C. L., Owen, R., Hosp, M., & Jancek, D. (2003b). Explicitly teaching for transfer: Effects on third-grade students' mathematical problem solving. *Journal of Educational Psychology, 95*, 293–305.

Fuson, K. C., Carroll, W. M., & Drueck, J. V. (2000). Achievement results for second and third graders using the standards-based curriculum *Everyday Mathematics*. *Journal for Research in Mathematics Education, 31*, 277–295.

Graham, S. (in press). Strategy instruction and the teaching of writing: A meta-analysis. In C. MacArthur, S. Graham, & J. Fitzgerald (Eds.), *Handbook of writing research*. New York: Guilford.

Graham, S., & Harris, K. R. (1994). The role and development of self-regulation in the writing process. In D. Schunk & B. Zimmerman (Eds.), *Self-regulation of learning and performance: Issues and educational applications* (pp. 203–228). Hillsdale, NJ: Lawrence Erlbaum Associates.

Graham, S., & Harris, K. R. (2000). The role of self-regulation and transcription skills in writing and writing development. *Educational Psychologist, 35*, 3–12.

Graham, S., & Harris, K. R. (2003). Students with learning disabilities and the process of writing: A meta-analysis of SRSD studies. L. Swanson, K. R. Harris, & S. Graham (Eds.), *Handbook of research on learning disabilities* (pp. 323–344). New York: Guilford.

Graham, S., & Harris K. R., & Zito, J. (in press). Promoting internal and external validity: A synergism of laboratory experiments and classroom based research. In G. Phye, D. Robinson, & J. Levin (Eds.), *Experimental methods for educational intervention*. San Diego, CA: Elsevier.

Gruenenfelder, T. M., & Borkowski, J. G. (1975). Transfer of cumulative-rehearsal strategies in children's short-term memory. *Child Development, 46*, 1019–1024.

Gruneberg, M. M. (1998). A commentary on criticism of the keyword method of learning foreign languages. *Applied Cognitive Psychology, 12*, 529–532.

Guttman, J., Levin, J. R., & Pressley, M. (1977). Pictures, partial pictures, and children's oral prose learning. *Journal of Educational Psychology, 69*, 473–480.

Haake, R. J., Sommerville, S. C., & Wellman, H. M. (1980). Logical ability of young children in searching a large-scale environment. *Child Development, 51*, 1299–1302.

Hacker, D. J., & Tenent, A. (2002). Implementing reciprocal teaching in the classroom: Overcoming difficulties and making accommodations. *Journal of Educational Psychology, 94*, 699–718.

Hagen, J. W., Hargrave, S., & Ross, W. (1973). Prompting and rehearsal in short-term memory. *Child Development, 44*, 201–204.

Harris, K. R. (1982). Cognitive-behavior modification: Application with exceptional students. *Focus on Exceptional Children, 15*, 1–16.

Harris, K. R., & Graham, S. (1992). Self-regulated strategy development: A part of the writing process. In M. Pressley, K. R. Harris, & J. T. Guthrie (Eds.), *Promoting academic competence and literacy in school* (pp. 277–309). New York: Academic Press.

Harris, K. R., Graham, S., & Adkins, M. (2004). *The effects of teacher-led SRSD instruction on the writing and motivation of young struggling writers*. Manuscript in preparation.

Harris, K. R., Graham, S., & Mason, L. (2003). Self-regulated strategy development in classroom: Part of a balanced approach to writting instruction for students with disabilities. Focus on Exceptional Children, *35*(7), 1–16.

Harris, K. R., Graham, S., & Mason, L. (in press). *Improving the writing performance, knowledge, and motivation of struggling writers in second grade: The effects of self-regulated strategy development. American Educational Research Journal*.

Hayes, J. (2004). What triggers revision? In Allal, L. Chanquoy, & P. Largy (Eds.), *Revision: Cognitive and instructional processes* (pp. 9–20). Boston: Kluwer.

Hayes, J., & Flower, L. (1980). Identifying the organization of writing processes. In L. Gregg & E. Steinberg (Eds.), *Cognitive processes in writing* (pp. 3–30). Hillsdale, NJ: Lawrence Erlbaum Associates.

Hecht, S. A. (2002). Counting on working memory in simple arithmetic when counting is used for problem solving. *Memory & Cognition, 30*, 447–455.

Hembree, R. (1992). Experiments and relational studies in problem solving: A meta-analysis. *Journal for Research in Mathematics Education, 23*, 242–273.

Henningsen, M., & Stein, M. K. (1997). Mathematical tasks and student cognition: Classroom-based factors that support and inhibit high-level mathematical thinking and reasoning. *Journal for Research in Mathematics Education, 28*, 524–549.

Hillocks, G. (1984). What works in teaching composition: A meta-analysis of experimental treatment studies. *American Journal of Education, 93*, 133–170.

Hollar, J. C., & Norwood, K. (1999). The effects of a graphing-approach intermediate algebra curriculum on students' understanding of function. *Journal for Research in Mathematics Education, 30*, 220–226.

Horn, J. L., & Cattell, R. B. (1967). Age differences in fluid and crystallized intelligence. *Acta Psychologica, 26*, 107–129.

Hoskyn, M., & Swanson, H. L. (2003). The relationship between working memory and writing in younger and older adults. *Reading and Writing, 16*, 759–784.

Huntley, M. A. (2000). Effects of standards-based mathematics education: A study of the core-plus mathematics project algebra and functions strand. *Journal for Research in Mathematics Education, 31*, 328–361.

Keeney, F. J., Cannizzo, S. R., & Flavell, J. H. (1967). Spontaneous and induced verbal rehearsal in a recall task. *Child Development, 38*, 953–966.

Kingsley, P. R., & Hagen, J. W. (1969). Induced versus spontaneous rehearsal in short-term memory in nursery school children. *Developmental Psychology, 1*, 4–46.

Kobasigawa, A. (1977). Retrieval strategies in the development of memory. In R. V. Kail & J. W. Hagen (Eds.), *Perspectives on the development of memory and cognition* (pp. 177–201). Hillsdale, NJ: Lawrence Erlbaum Associates.

Kuhn, D. (1991). *The skills of argument*. Cambridge, England: Cambridge University Press.

Kuhn, D. (1995). Microgenetic study of change: What has it told us? *Psychological Science, 6*, 133–139.

Kuhn, D., Amsel, E., O'Loughlin, M., Schauble, L., Leadbeater, B., & Yotive, W. (1988). *The development of scientific thinking skills*. San Diego, CA: Academic Press.

Kuhn, D., Garcia-Mila, M., Zohar, A., & Andersen, C. (1995). Strategies of knowledge acquisition. *Monographs of the Society for Research in Child Development, 60* (Vol. 128).

Kuhn, D., & Udell, W. (2003). The development of argument skills. *Child Development, 74,* 1245–1260.

Lampert, M. (2001). *Teaching problems and the problems of teaching.* New Haven CT: Yale University Press.

Lange, G., MacKinnon, C. E., & Nida, R. E. (1989). Knowledge, strategy, and motivational contributions to preschool childrens' object recall. *Developmental Psychology, 25,* 772–779.

Lawson, M. J., & Hogben, D. (1998). Learning and recall of foreign-language vocabulary: Effects of a keyword strategy for immediate and delayed recall. *Learning and Instruction, 8,* 179–194.

Lovett, M. W., Barron, R. W., & Benson, N. J. (2003). Effective remediation of word identification and decoding difficulties in school-age children with reading disabilities. In H. L. Swanson, K. R. Harris, & S. Graham (Eds.), *Handbook of learning disabilities* (pp. 273–292). New York: Guilford.

Lovett, M. W., Lacerenza, L., Borden, S. L., Frijters, J. C., Steinbach, K. A., & De Palma, M. (2000). Components of effective remediation for developmental reading disabilities: Combining phonological and strategy-based instruction to improve outcomes. *Journal of Educational Psychology, 92,* 263–283.

Mandler, J. M. (1998). Representation. In W. Damon (Editor-in-chief) & D. Kuhn & R. S. Siegler (Volume eds.), *Handbook of child psychology*: Vol. 2. *Cognition, perception, and language* (5th ed., pp. 255–308). New York: Wiley.

Marks, M., Pressley, M., in collaboration with Coley, J. D., Craig, S., Gardner, R., Rose, W., & DePinto, T. (1993). Teachers' adaptations of reciprocal teaching: Progress toward a classroom-compatible version of reciprocal teaching. *Elementary School Journal, 94,* 267–283.

Mason, L. H. (2004). *A multi-component self-regulated strategy approach for expository reading comprehension and writing for students with and without disabilities who struggle with reading and writing: Examination of effects in reading and content classrooms.* Field Initiate Research Grant, funded by the Office of Special Education Programs, U.S. Department of Education.

Mastropieri, M. A., Scruggs, T. E., & Shiah, S. (1991). Mathematics instruction for learning disabled students: A review of research. *Learning Disabilities Research and Practice, 6,* 89–98.

Mayer, R. E. (2004). Should there be a three-strikes rule against pure discovery learning? *American Psychologist, 59,* 14–19.

McCaffrey D. F., Hamilton, L. S., Stecher, B. M., Klein, S. P., & Robyn, A. E. (2001). Interactions among instructional practices, curriculum, and student achievement: The case of standards-based high school mathematics. *Journal for Research in Mathematics Education, 32,* 493–517.

McLaughlin, B., & Heredia, R. (1996). Information-processing approaches to research on second language acquisition and use. In W. C. Ritchie & T. K. Bhatia (Eds.), *Handbook of*

second language acquisition (pp. 213–228). San Diego; CA: Academic Press.

Meichenbaum, D., & Biemiller, A. (1998). *Nurturing independent learners: Helping students take charge of their learning.* Cambridge, MA: Brookline Books.

Miller, D. (2002). *Reading with meaning: Teaching comprehension in the primary grades.* Portsmouth, NH: Heinemann.

Miller, G. A., Gallanter, E., & Pribram, K. H. (1960). *Plans and the structure of behavior.* New York: Holt, Rinehart, & Winston.

Miller, P. H., & Seier, W. L. (1994). Strategy utlization deficiencies in children: When, where, and why. In H. W. Reese (Ed.), *Advances in child development and behavior*: Vol. 25 (pp. 107–156). New York: Academic Press.

Montague, M., & Bos, C. S. (1986). The effect of cognitive strategy training on verbal math problem solving performance of learning disabled students. *Journal of Learning Disabilities, 19,* 26–33.

Morris, D. Tyner, B., & Perney, J. (2000). Early steps: Replicating the effects of a first-grade reading intervention program. *Journal of Educational Psychology, 92,* 681–693.

National Commission on Writing (2003). *The neglected "R."* New York: College Entrance Examination Board.

National Reading Panel (2000). *Teaching children to read: An evidence-based assessment of the scientific research literature on reading and its implications for reading instruction.* Washington, DC: National Institute of Child Health and Development.

Naus, M. J., Ornstein, P. A., & Aivano, S. (1977). Developmental changes in memory: The effects of processing time and rehearsal instructions. *Journal of Experimental Child Psychology, 23,* 237–251.

Newman, L. S. (1990). Intentional and unintentional memory in young children. *Journal of Experimental Child Psychology, 50,* 243–258.

Nikol, R., Levin, J. R., & Woodward, M. M. (2003). Do pictorial mnemonic text-learning aids give students something worth writing about? *Journal of Educational Psychology, 95,* 327–334.

O'Malley, J. M., & Chamot, A. U. (1990). *Learning strategies in second language acquisition.* Cambridge, England: Cambridge University Press.

O'Malley, J. M., Chamot, A. U., & Küpper, L. (1989). Listening comprehension strategies in second language acquisition. *Applied Linguistics, 10,* 418–437.

107th U.S. Congress (2002). *Public Law 107–110: The No Child Left Behind act of 2001.* Washington, DC: Goverrment Printing Office.

Ornstein, P. A., Naus, M. J., & Liberty, C. (1975). Rehearsal and organizational processes in children's memory. *Child Development, 46,* 818–830.

O'Sullivan, J. T., & Pressley, M. (1984). Completeness of instruction and strategy transfer. *Journal of Experimental Child Psychology, 38,* 275–288.

Palincsar, A. S., & Brown, A. L. (1984). Reciprocal teaching of comprehension- fostering and monitoring activities. *Cognition and Instruction, 1,* 117–175.

Paris, S. G., Lipson, M. Y., & Wixson, K. K. (1983). Becoming a strategic reader. *Contemporary Educational Psychology, 8,* 293–316.

Pearson, P. D., & Fielding, L. (1991). Comprehension instruction. In R. Barr, M. L. Kamil, P. B. Mosenthal, & P. D. Pearson (Eds.), *Handbook of reading research: Vol. II* (pp. 815–860). New York: Longman.

Perkins, D. N., Lochhead, J., & Bishop, J. (Eds.) (1987). *Thinking: The Second International Conference.* Hillsdale, NJ: Lawrence Erlbaum Associates.

Polya, G. (1957). *How to solve it.* New York: Doubleday.

Pressley, M. (1977). Imagery and children's learning: Putting the picture in developmental perspective. *Review of Educational Research, 47,* 586–622.

Pressley, M. (1986). The relevance of the good strategy user model to the teaching of mathematics. *Educational Psychologist, 21,* 139–161.

Pressley, M. (2000). What should comprehension instruction be the instruction of? In M. L. Kamil, P. B. Mosenthal, P. D. Pearson, & R. Barr (Eds.), *Handbook of reading research, Vol. III* (pp. 545–561). Mahwah, NJ: Lawrence Erlbaum Associates.

Pressley, M., & Afflerbach, P. (1995). *Verbal protocols of reading: The nature of constructively responsive reading.* Hillsdale, NJ: Lawrence Erlbaum Associates.

Pressley, M., Borkowski, J. G., & O'Sullivan, J. T. (1985). Children's metamemory and the teaching of strategies. In D. L. Forrest-Pressley, G. E. MacKinnon, & T. G. Waller (Eds.), *Metacognition, cognition, and human performance* (pp. 111–153). Orlando, FL: Academic Press.

Pressley, M., Borkowski, J. G., & Schneider, W. (1987). Cognitive strategies: Good strategy users coordinate meta-cognition and knowledge. In R. Vasta & G. Whitehurst (Eds.), *Annals of child development, Vol. 4* (pp. 89–129). Greenwich, CT: JAI Press.

Pressley, M., Cariglia-Bull, T., Deane, S., & Schneider, W. (1987). Short-term memory, verbal competence, and age as predictors of imagery instructional effectiveness. *Journal of Experimental Child Psychology, 43,* 194–211.

Pressley, M., El-Dinary, P. B., Gaskins, I., Schuder, T., Bergman, J. L., Almasi, J., et al. (1992). Beyond direct explanation: Transactional instruction of reading comprehension strategies. *Elementary School Journal, 92,* 511–554.

Pressley, M., Forrest-Pressley, D., Elliott-Faust, D. L., & Miller, G. E. (1985). Children's use of cognitive strategies, how to teach strategies, and what to do if they can't be taught. In M. Pressley & C. J. Brainerd (Eds.), *Cognitive learning and memory in children* (pp. 1–47). New York: Springer-Verlag.

Pressley, M., & Harris, K. R. (2001). Cognitive strategies instruction. In A. L. Costa (Ed.), *Developing minds: A resource book for teaching thinking (3rd ed.).* Alexandria, VA: Association for Supervision and Curriculum Development.

Pressley, M., Heisel, B. E., McCormick, C. G., & Nakamura, G. V. (1982). Memory strategy instruction with children. In C. J. Brainerd & M. Pressley (Eds.), *Progress in cognitive development research: Vol. 2. Verbal processes in children* (pp. 125–159). New York: Springer-Verlag.

Pressley, M., & Hilden, K. R. (in press-a). Cognitive strategies: Production deficiencies and successful strategy instruction everywhere. In D. Kuhn & R. Siegler (Eds.), W. Damon & R. Lerner (Series Eds.), *Handbook of child psychology, Vol. 2: Cognition, perception, and language* (6th edition). Hoboken, NJ: Wiley.

Pressley, M., & Hilden, K. A. (in press-b). Verbal protocols of reading. In N. K. Duke & M. H. Mallette (Eds.), *Literacy research methodologies,* New York: Guilford.

Pressley, M., Johnson, C. J., Symons, S., McGoldrick, J. A., & Kurita, J. A. (1989). Strategies that improve memory and comprehension of what is read. *Elementary School Journal, 90,* 3–32.

Pressley, M., & Levin, J. R. (1977). Developmental differences in subjects' associative learning strategies and performance: Assessing a hypothesis. *Journal of Experimental Child Psychology, 24,* 431–439.

Pressley, M., Levin, J. R., & Delaney, H. D. (1982). The mnemonic keyword method. *Review of Educational Research, 52,* 61–91.

Pressley, M., & MacFadyen, J. (1983). The development of mnemonic mediator usage at testing. *Child Development, 54,* 474–479.

Pressley, M., Wharton-McDonald, R., Mistretta, J., & Echevarria, M. (1998). The nature of literacy instruction in ten grade-4/5 classrooms in upstate New York. *Scientific Studies of Reading, 2,* 159–191.

Rabinowitz, M. (2002). The procedural-procedural knowledge distinction. In N. L. Stein, P. J. Bauer, & M. Rabinowtiz (Eds.) (2002). *Representation, memory, and development: Essays in honor of Jean Mandler* (pp. 185–198). Mahwah, NJ: Lawrence Erlbaum Associates.

Reese, H. W. (1962). Verbal mediation as a function of age level. *Psychological Bulletin, 59,* 502–509.

Reys, R., Reys, B., Lapan, R., Holliday, G., & Wasman, D. (2003). Assessing the impact of standards-based middle grades mathematics curriculum materials on student achievement. *Journal for Research in Mathematics Education, 34,* 74–95.

Riordan, J. E., & Noyce, P. E. (2001). The impact of two standards-based mathematics curricula on student achievement in Massachusetts. *Journal for Research in Mathematics Education, 32,* 368–398.

Rosenshine, B., & Meister, C. (1994). Reciprocal teaching: A review of nineteen experimental studies. *Review of Educational Research, 64,* 479–530.

Rubin, J. (1979). What a "good language learner" can teach us. In J. B. Pride (Ed.), *Sociolinguistic aspects of language learning and teaching* (pp. 17–26). London: Oxford University Press.

Ruddell, R. B., & Unrau, N. J. (2004). *Theoretical models and processes of reading* (5th ed.) Newark, DE: International Reading Association.

Scardamalia, M., & Bereiter, C. (1986). Written composition. In M. Wittrock (Ed.), *Handbook of research on teaching* (3rd ed., pp. 778–803). New York: MacMillan.

Schlagmueller, M., & Schneider, W. (2002). The development of organizational strategies in children: Evidence from a microgenetic longitudinal study. *Journal of Experimental Child Psychology, 81*, 298-319.

Schneider, W., & Pressley, M. (1997). *Memory development between two and twenty* (2nd ed.), Hillsdale, NJ: Lawrence Erlbaum Associates.

Schoenfeld, A. (1992). Learning to think mathematically: Problem solving, metacognition, and sense making in mathematics. In D. A. Grouws (Ed.), *Handbook of research on mathematics teaching and learning* (pp. 334-370). New York: MacMillan.

Siegler, R. S. (1996). *Emerging minds: The process of change in children's thinking.* New York: Oxford University Press.

Swanson, H. L., & Sáez, L. (2003). Memory difficulties in children and adults with learning disabilities. In H. L. Swanson, K. R. Harris, & S. Graham (Eds.), *Handbook of learning disabilities* (pp. 182-198). New York: Guilford.

Taylor, B. M., Pearson, P. D., Clark, K., & Walpole, S. (2000). Effective schools and accomplished teachers: Lessons about primary-grade reading instruction in low-income schools. *Elementary School Journal, 101*, 121-165.

Thompson, D. R., & Senk, S. L. (2001). The effects of curriculum on achievement in second-year algebra: The example of the University of Chicago Mathematics Project. *Journal for Research in Mathematics Education, 32*, 58-84.

Thompson, I., & Rubin, J. (1996). Can strategy instruction improve listening comprehension? *Foreign Language Annals, 29*, 331-342.

Vandergrift, L. (2003). Orchestrating strategy use: Toward a model of the skilled second language listener. *Language Learning, 53*, 463-496.

Vann, R. J. & Abraham, R. G. (1990). Strategies of unsuccessful language learners. *TESOL Quarterly, 24*, 177-198.

Wang, A. Y., & Thomas, M. H. (1995). The effect of keywords on long-term retention: Help or hindrance? *Journal of Educational Psychology, 87*, 468-475.

Wang, A. Y., & Thomas, M. H. (1999). In defence of keyword experiments: A reply to Gruneberg's commentary. *Applied Cognitive Psychology, 13*, 283-287.

Weinstein, C. E. (1994). Students at risk for academic failure: Learning to learn classes. In K. W. Prichard & R. M. Sawyer (Eds.), *Handbook of college teaching: Theory and applications*. Westport, CT: Greenwood.

Weinstein, C. E., Husman, J., & Dierking, D. R. (2000). Self-regulation interventions with a focus on learning strategies. In M. Boekaerts & P. R. Pintrich (Eds.), *Handbook of self-regulation*. San Diego, CA: Academic Press.

Wong, B. Y. L., Butler, D. L., Ficzere, S. A., & Kuperis, S. (1996). Teaching adolescents with learning disabilities and low achievers to plan, write, and revise opinion essays. *Journal of Learning Disabilities, 29*, 197-212.

Wong, B. Y. L., Butler, D. L., Ficzere, S. A., & Kuperis, S. (1997). Teaching adolescents with learning disabilities and low achievers to plan, write, and revise compare-and-contrast essays. *Learning Disabilities Research & Practice, 12*, 2-15.

Wong, B. Y. L., Butler, D. L., Ficzere, S. A., Kuperis, S., & Corden, M. (1994). Teaching problem learners revision skills and sensitivity to audience through two instructional modes: Student-teacher versus student-student interactive dialogues. *Learning Disabilities Research & Practice, 9*, 78-90.

Wong, B. Y. L., Harris, K. R., Graham, S., & Butler, D. L. (2003). Cognitive strategies instruction research in learning disabilities. In H. L. Swanson, K. R. Harris, & S. Graham (Eds.), *Handbook of learning disabilities* (pp. 383-402). New York: Guilford.

Wong, B. Y. L., Wong, R., Darlington, D., & Jones, W. (1991). Interactive teaching: An effective way to teach revision skills to adolescents with learning disabilities. *Learning Disabilities Research and Practice, 6*, 117-127.

Woody-Dorning, J., & Miller, P. (2001). Children's individual differences in capacity: Effects on strategy production and utilization. *British Journal of Developmental Psychology, 19*, 543-557.

Zhang, Z., & Schumm, J. S. (2000). Exploring effects of the keyword method on limited English proficient students' vocabulary recall and comprehension. *Reading Research and Instruction, 39*, 202-221.

·13·

PROBLEM SOLVING

Richard E. Mayer
University of California, Santa Barbara

Merlin C. Wittrock
University of California, Los Angeles

A major challenge of education is improving students' minds—a goal that is reflected in people being able to solve novel problems they encounter. This is the premise underlying much of the interest in problem solving, including how to teach in ways that enable students to apply what they have learned to new situations and how to teach thinking skills. In this chapter, after defining key terms and providing a historical overview, we examine research on teaching for problem-solving transfer and research on teaching of thinking skills.

WHAT IS PROBLEM SOLVING?

Definitions

When you are faced with a problem and you are not aware of any obvious solution method, you must engage in a form of cognitive processing called *problem solving*. Problem solving is cognitive processing directed at achieving a goal when no solution method is obvious to the problem solver (Lovett, 2002; Mayer, 1992). According to this definition, problem solving has four main characteristics. First, problem solving is *cognitive*, that is, it occurs internally in the problem solver's cognitive system, and can only be inferred indirectly from the problem solver's behavior.[1] Second, problem solving is a *process*, that is, it involves representing and manipulating knowledge in the problem solver's cognitive system. Third, problem solving is *directed*, that is, the problem solver's cognitive processing is guided by the problem solver's goals. Fourth, problem solving is *personal*, that is, the individual knowledge and skills of the problem solver help determine the difficulty or ease with which obstacles to solutions can be overcome. Thus, problem solving is cognitive processing directed at transforming a given situation into a goal situation when no obvious method of solution is available (Mayer, 1990).

Related terms such as *thinking*, *reasoning*, *creative thinking*, and *critical thinking* are sometimes used as synonyms. In this chapter, we use *problem solving*, *thinking*, and *reasoning* interchangeably, although it is possible to make finer distinctions. For example, in the strictest sense, *thinking* refers to a somewhat broader concept that includes both directed cognitive processing (i.e., problem solving) and undirected cognitive processing (e.g., day dreaming). In this chapter, we focus only on directed cognitive processing. *Reasoning*, in the strictest sense, refers to directed cognitive processing applied to a certain class of tasks—that is, reasoning tasks in which there are premises and the goal is to derive a conclusion using logical rules—and requiring a certain class of cognitive processes—that is, deduction and induction

---

[1] Although we have defined problem solving as an internal process, it can be aided and influenced by creating external representations, manipulating concrete objects, and interacting with others.

(Manktelow, 1999). In this chapter, we maintain a broader focus on all forms of directed cognitive processing. Finally, problem solving can be broken into creative thinking and critical thinking (Runco, 2003). Creative thinking involves generating ideas that could be used to solve a problem, whereas critical thinking involves evaluating ideas that could be used to solve a problem. In this chapter, we focus on both aspects of problem solving.

A problem occurs when a problem solver wants to transform a problem situation from the given state to the goal state but lacks an obvious method for accomplishing the transformation. In his classic monograph, *On Problem-Solving*, Duncker (1945, p. 1) defined a problem as follows:

A problem arises when a living creature has a goal but does not know how this goal is to be reached. Whenever one cannot go from a given situation to the desired situation simply by action, then there has to be recourse to thinking. Such thinking has the task of devising some action, which may mediate between the existing and desired situations.

In short, a problem occurs when a problem solver has a goal but lacks an obvious way of achieving the goal. This definition is broad enough to include many high-level academic tasks such as writing a persuasive essay (Kellogg, 1994), solving an unfamiliar arithmetic word problem (Reed, 1999), or determining how an electric motor works (Mayer, Dow, & Mayer, 2003). It is also broad enough to include many high-level nonacademic tasks such as determining how to get 3/4 of 2/3 of a cup of cottage cheese (Lave, 1988) or determining which is the best apartment to rent (Kahneman & Tversky, 2000).

Types of Problems

Problems can be classified as well defined or ill defined. In well-defined problems, the given state, goal state, and allowable operators are clearly specified. For example, a computation problem such as $1.27 \times 0.28 = \_$ is well defined because the given state is 1.27×0.28, the goal state is a numerical answer that is the product of 1.27 and 0.28, and the allowable operators are the procedures of decimal multiplication. Similarly, a grammar problem such as "the plural of half is $\_$" is well defined because the given state is "half," the goal state is to create a specific word that is the plural form of "half," and the allowable operators are the procedures for constructing plurals in English grammar, namely, to change f to v and add the suffix *es*. In an ill-defined problem, the given state, goal state, and/or allowable operators are not clearly specified. For example, an assignment to write an essay on whether a tax cut will stimulate the economy or to devise an advertising campaign for the campus bookstore is an ill-defined problem because the allowable operators are not clear, and to some extent, the goal state is not clear. Educational materials often emphasize well-defined problems, although most real problems are ill defined.

Problems can be classified as routine or nonroutine.[2] A routine problem is one for which the problem solver already possesses a ready-made solution procedure. For example, if a student has learned the procedure for long division of whole numbers, then a new long-division problem represents a routine problem. In contrast, a nonroutine problem is one for which the problem solver does not have a previously learned solution procedure. For example, a young student who does not yet know all the addition facts may solve the problem $3 + 5 = \_$ as follows: "Take 1 from 5 and give it to the 3, 5 minus 1 is 4, 3 plus 1 is 4, 4 plus 4 is 8, so the answer is 8." This student has invented a solution method that is new for the student. Thus, the definition of routine or nonroutine problem depends on the knowledge of the learner, whereas the definition of well-defined or ill-defined problem does not.[3] Although routine problems form the core of many educational lessons, important real-world problems are generally nonroutine.

Cognitive Processes in Problem Solving

Problem solving can be analyzed into component cognitive processes, including representing, planning/monitoring, executing, and self-regulating. Representing occurs when a problem solver converts an externally presented problem, such as a word problem in a mathematics book, into an internal mental representation, such as a *situation model* of the word problem—that is, a representation of the situation being described in the problem (Mayer, 2003; Nathan, Kintsch, & Young, 1992). In classic theories of problem solving, representing a problem involves building a problem space—a representation of the initial state, goal state, and all legal intervening states (Bruning, Schraw, Norby, & Ronning, 2004). Planning involves devising a method for solving a problem, such as breaking a problem into

---

[2] In the strictest sense, problem solving involves only non-routine problems; although in conventional usage, problem solving involves both non-routine and routine problems. We focus on non-routine problem solving in this chapter.

[3] The definition of ill-defined or well-defined problem does not depend on the problem-solver's knowledge because being ill or well defined depends on the characteristics of the problem. However, problem solvers can differ in their knowledge of the characteristics of the problems.

parts, whereas monitoring involves evaluating the appropriateness and effectiveness of the solution method. Executing occurs when a problem solver actually carries out the planned operations, such as making arithmetic calculations to solve a word problem. Self-regulating refers to instigating, modifying, or sustaining cognitive activities oriented toward the attainment of one's goals (Schunk, 2003), such as deciding to start over when having difficulty with a problem. Although executing is sometimes emphasized in classroom instruction, the major difficulties for most problem solvers involve representing, planning/monitoring, and self-regulating (Mayer, 2003).

Problem-solving processes are dependent on several different kinds of knowledge, including factual knowledge, conceptual knowledge, procedural knowledge, strategic knowledge, beliefs, and metacognitive knowledge. Factual knowledge involves knowledge of facts such as "there are 100 cents in a dollar" or "Washington is the capital of the United States." Conceptual knowledge includes knowledge of categories, principles, and models, such as the cause-and-effect explanation for why hot air rises or knowing how the Electoral College works in U.S. presidential elections. Procedural knowledge involves knowledge of specific procedures for how to do something, such as the procedure for long division or how to change nouns from singular to plural form. Strategic knowledge involves knowledge of general methods, such as how to break a problem into parts or how to summarize a passage. Metacognitive knowledge involves awareness and control of one's own cognitive processing and includes beliefs such as, "I am not good at math." Bruning et al. (2004) use the term *conditional knowledge* to refer to knowing when and why to use existing conceptual and procedural knowledge. The cognitive process of representing depends largely on facts and concepts; the cognitive process of planning/monitoring depends largely on strategies; the cognitive process of executing depends largely on procedures; the cognitive process of self-regulating depends on beliefs and related metacognitive knowledge. The types of processes and knowledge involved in problem solving are summarized in Table 13.1.

TABLE 13.1. Types of Cognitive Processes and Knowledge Involved in Problem Solving

Process	Knowledge
Representing	Facts
	Concepts
Planning/monitoring	Strategies
Executing	Procedures
Self-regulating	Beliefs/metacognitive knowledge

Problem Solving as an Educational Goal

The primary goal of education is to promote learning—that is, a change in the learner's knowledge (Mayer, 2001). However, learning can only be indirectly assessed by observing changes in the learner's behavior, such as test performance. Two classic measures of learning outcomes are retention and transfer (Anderson et al., 2001). Retention is the ability to remember what was presented and can be assessed using recall and recognition items. Transfer is the ability to use what was learned in new situations and can be assessed using a variety of problem-solving items.

For example, in assessing a student's learning of a lesson on how an electric motor works (e.g., Mayer et al., 2003), a retention item could ask the student to write definitions of each of the key components, such as "battery" and "magnet," that were defined in the lesson. In contrast, a transfer item could ask the student to figure out how to reverse the direction of the rotation of the motor, which was not directly presented in the lesson but could be determined by understanding how the motor works. A student who performs poorly on both types of assessments has a learning outcome that can be called *no learning*. A student who performs well on retention and poor on transfer has achieved a learning outcome that can be called *rote learning*. A student who performs well on both kinds of assessments has achieved a learning outcome that can be called *meaningful learning*.

In cases where the instructional objective is to promote meaningful learning rather than rote learning, it is useful to understand the nature of problem solving. Although helping students remember what was presented has been a central goal of education, there is consensus among educational psychologists that another important goal is helping students be able to apply what they learned to solve new problems (Anderson et al., 2001).

INSTRUCTIONAL METHODS THAT PROMOTE PROBLEM SOLVING

What are instructional methods that promote meaningful learning? Table 13.2 lists seven ways of promoting meaningful learning: load-reducing methods, structure-based methods, schema activation methods, generative methods, guided discovery methods, modeling methods, and teaching of thinking skills. The first six methods aim to help students learn content in ways that promote problem-solving transfer,

TABLE 13.2. Seven Ways to Promote
Problem-Solving Transfer

Instructional Method	Example
Load-reducing methods	Automaticity, constraint removal
Structure-based methods	Concrete manipulatives
Schema-based methods	Advance organizers, pre-training, cueing
Generative methods	Elaboration, note-taking, self-explanation, questioning
Guided discovery methods	Guided discovery
Modeling methods	Worked examples, apprenticeship
Teaching thinking skills	General courses, specific strategies

which can be described as promoting problem solving in a domain; the seventh method aims to teach problem-solving skills directly, which can be described as promoting general problem-solving abilities. In the remainder of this chapter, after a short historical example and theoretical discussion, we explore the seven approaches to fostering problem solving listed in Table 13.2.

Example of Instructional Methods That Promote Problem Solving

The search for methods of instruction that lead to meaningful learning—that is, learning that enables students to apply what they have learned to solving new problems—has a long, and increasingly productive history in educational psychology. For example, in his classic book *Productive Thinking*, the Gestalt psychologist Max Wertheimer (1959) described two ways of teaching children how to find the area of a parallelogram. In the rote method, summarized in the top of Fig. 13.1, students were taught to find the height (i.e., 3), find the base (i.e., 5), and then multiply height *x* base (i.e., 15), using the formula Area = Height × Base. Wertheimer calls this method senseless, blind, and arbitrary. In the meaningful method, summarized in the bottom of Fig. 13.1, students were encouraged to see that the triangle on one end of the parallelogram could be cut off and placed on the other end of parallelogram, resulting in a rectangle. As can be seen, placing 1×1 squares on the rectangle yields three rows of five squares, for a total of 15. Assuming that the problem solver already knows how to find the area of a rectangle, the solution is now apparent. Wertheimer argues that this method leads to structural insight and deep understanding. On a retention test in which students must find the area of similar parallelograms, both forms of instruction lead to good performance (Wertheimer, 1959). However, on a transfer test in which students must find the area of unusual parallelograms and other figures, the meaningful method leads to much better problem-solving

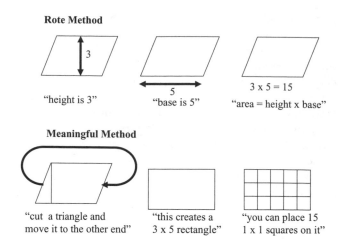

FIGURE 13.1. Two methods for teaching students how to find the area of a parallelogram.

performance than does the rote method. Thus, according to Wertheimer and other Gestalt-oriented psychologists (Katona, 1967), the distinguishing feature of meaningful methods of instruction is that they enable students to apply what they have learned to solve new problems.

Theoretical Foundations for Instructional Methods That Promote Meaningful Learning

According to the Select-Organize-Integrate (SOI) information-processing theory of meaningful learning summarized in Fig. 13.2, meaningful learning occurs when learners engage in three cognitive processes during learning: selecting relevant information, organizing the selected information, and integrating the organized information with prior knowledge (Mayer, 2001, 2003). The SOI model in Fig. 13.2 contains three memory stores indicated by boxes—sensory memory, working memory, and long-term memory—and three main cognitive processes indicated by arrows—selecting, organizing, and integrating. When material is presented to a learner, such as in a book or lecture, the pictures and printed words impinge on the learner's eyes and are represented as images in sensory memory, whereas the spoken words impinge on the learner's ears and are represented as sounds in sensory memory. If the learner pays attention, some of the incoming sounds and images in sensory memory are transferred to working memory for further processing, as indicated by the arrow labeled *selecting*. In working memory, the learner can build connections among the pieces of selected information, as indicated by the arrow labeled *organizing*, and the learner can build connections between the selected information and relevant knowledge retrieved from long-term memory,

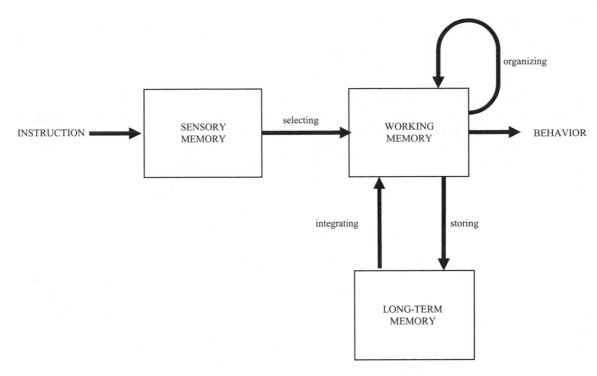

FIGURE 13.2. The SOI model of meaningful learning.

as indicated by the arrow labeled *integrating*. The result is a coherent cognitive structure that itself can be stored in long-term memory for future use, as indicated by the *storing* arrow.

A major implication of the SOI model is that three cognitive conditions must be met for meaningful learning to occur: the learner must select relevant information from the presented material, the learner must mentally organize the material into a coherent structure, and the learner must mentally integrate the organized knowledge with existing knowledge retrieved from long-term memory. Instructional methods that foster these cognitive processes—selecting, organizing, and integrating—are more likely to lead to meaningful learning—and hence, problem-solving transfer—than are methods that do not foster these processes. For example, in the parallelogram problem, the meaningful method of instruction helps learners (a) select the critical structural features of a parallelogram, namely the triangles on each end; (b) organize the parallelogram as a rectangle in disguise; and (c) integrate the rearranged parallelogram with prior knowledge about area of rectangles.

Load-Reducing Methods

The SOI model in Fig. 13.2 shows that cognitive processing takes place in working memory, but working memory capacity is limited. In problem solving, low-level processes involved in executing a solution—such as carrying out arithmetic calculations in solving a word problem—may require so much working memory capacity that the problem solver does not have capacity left for devising and monitoring a solution plan. Therefore, effective problem solving often depends on automated component skills—that is, on component skills that can be used without placing demands on the student's working memory capacity. In short, a major constraint on effective problem solving may be lack of automated component skills. Two methods for overcoming this problem are automaticity methods, in which students master component skills before moving on to higher level problem tasks, and constraint removal methods, in which problem-solving tasks are presented in ways that minimize the need for certain component skills.

Automaticity Methods. In automaticity methods, students receive drill and practice on component skills until the skills have become automatic. Automated skills require little or no conscious attention when they are applied; since attention is a limited resource, automation of low-level skills allows problem solvers to direct their attention to higher-level components of a task such as planning and monitoring the solution process. Classic work on learning hierarchies by Gagné (1968) and subsequent research on the development of problem-solving skills in children by Case (1985) and Siegler (1989) have shown how automation of low-level component skills enables the learner to build higher level problem-solving skills.

For example, reading comprehension depends on mastering lower level skills such as decoding of words. To help students become more automatic in their decoding, Samuels (1979) and LaBerge and Samuels (1974) developed the method of repeated readings, in which a student reads a short passage aloud over and over until the reading rate is fast and the error rate is low. This procedure allows students to increase their fluency, that is, to become automatic in their decoding of passages. As students automate their decoding skills, they can devote more attentional capacity to comprehending the passage. Similarly, young students who were given practice in phonological awareness—recognizing and producing the sounds in English—subsequently showed much greater performance on tests of reading comprehension than did nontrained students, and the advantage persisted for many years (Bradley & Bryant, 1983, 1985).

In mathematics, solving equations in algebra depends on component skills such as collecting all the unknowns on one side of the equation, and generating proofs in geometry depends on component skills such as recognizing when two angles are congruent. Anderson and colleagues (Singley & Anderson, 1989) have shown how the acquisition of cognitive skills progresses from effortful performance requiring conscious attention to automatic performance that does not require attention. For example, computer-based tutors for algebra, geometry, and computer programming provide systematic practice on component skills that eventually become automated and can be combined to form more powerful skills (Anderson & Schunn, 2000; Anderson, Corbett, Koedinger, & Pelletier, 1995). By performing a cognitive task analysis and providing systematic practice in the low-level component skills, "students can achieve the same level of competence in one third of the time as traditional education" (Anderson & Schunn, 2000, p. 26). Thus, the development of problem-solving expertise in algebra, geometry, and computer programming was facilitated by providing systematic practice in the lower-level component skills.

Similarly, Ericsson (2003a, 2003b) has shown that the development of expert problem-solving performance in fields such as music and sports is strongly related to the amount of *deliberate practice*—systematic and sustained practice on the elements of the task. For example, case studies of students designated as talented musicians revealed that a major difference between those who excelled and those who did not was the amount of deliberate practice accumulated during their development, with the most elite group estimated to have spent more than 10,000 hours in solitary practice by the age of 20

(Ericsson, 2003a). Thus, it appears that a prerequisite for excellence in creative performance is that basic skills have been well practiced.

Constraint Removal Methods. If automaticity methods were the only ones available, early childhood education would not provide many opportunities to engage in problem solving. An alternative method that allows novices to gain problem-solving experience, and presumably enjoyment, in a new domain is constraint removal—that is, creating problem-solving tasks that do not require attention-demanding skills. For example, in writing an essay, young writers may lack automated motor skills (such as handwriting or typing) and automated grammatical skills (such as in spelling and punctuation). To remove these motoric and grammatical constraints on effective writing, students may be asked to dictate their essays (Scardamalia, Bereiter, & Goelman, 1982) or instructed not to worry about handwriting, spelling, and punctuation as they write (Glynn, Britton, Muth, & Dugan, 1982). Such methods allow students to devote more of their attention to organizing and planning a good essay and generally result in longer and better-written essays.

In mathematics, students may be asked to solve complex word problems before they have mastered basic computational skills. To remove this computational constraint, students can be given calculators. In a meta-analysis of 88 studies, Hembree and Dessart (1992) found that mathematical problem solving was improved by the use of calculators for all ability levels and in all grade levels. In a recent review of research on calculator use, Kilpatrick, Swafford, and Findell (2001, p. 427) concluded that "a large number of empirical studies of calculator use. . . have generally shown that the use of calculators does not threaten the development of basic skills and that it can enhance conceptual understanding, strategic competence, and disposition towards mathematics." Importantly, the authors note that students who are allowed to use calculators "are better able to tackle realistic mathematics problems" (p. 427), presumably because they can allocate their limited attentional resources to high-level processes such as representing, planning, and monitoring rather than to trying to carry out low-level arithmetic procedures.

Structure-Based Methods

According to the SOI model in Fig. 13.2, meaningful learning depends on active cognitive processing during learning, including selecting, organizing, and integrating. One way to prime active cognitive processing in learners is to use structure-based methods, in which the learner is given concrete objects that can be manipulated. A primary purpose of manipulative methods is to help the learner build connections between a familiar, concrete situation and a more abstract concept or rule. For example, in mathematics instruction, concrete manipulatives such as bundles of sticks, beads on sticks, or Dienes blocks can be used to help the learner understand simple computational procedures (Brownell & Moser, 1949; Dienes, 1960; Montessori, 1964).

More recently, computer-based microworlds have been used in which students who are allowed to manipulate objects on the screen learn to solve mathematics problems better than students who do not (Moreno & Mayer, 1999; Nathan, Kintsch, & Young, 1992). For example, students who could move a bunny along a number line on the computer screen in correspondence with addition and subtraction of signed numbers learned to solve problems better than students who were not given this experience (Moreno & Mayer, 1999), and students who could construct a pictorial representation of word problems on a computer screen learned to solve word problems better than students who did not have this experience (Nathan, Kintsch, & Young, 1992).

In science instruction, hands-on activities are used in which students make predictions and then participate in an actual experiment to test the prediction (Linn & Hsi, 2000). In addition, structure-based methods have been applied successfully to computer-based learning environments, such as White's (1993; White & Frederiksen, 1998) Thinker Tools computer game for teaching Newton's laws of motion.

More than two decades ago Resnick and Ford (1981) noted that there is surprisingly little research on the effects of manipulatives on student learning. Learners may have difficulty in making connections between internal and external representations because such efforts place heavier demands on working memory, or learners may lack the metacognitive skills for self-directed manipulation of concrete objects or in microworlds (de Jong & van Joolingen, 1998). More recent studies have attempted to discriminate situations in which manipulatives are most likely to be helpful (Fuson & Briars, 1990; Hiebert et al., 1997). For example, Kilpatrick, Swafford, and Findell (2001, p. 354) note that manipulatives may overload working memory when they "become one more thing to learn" but "when used well, manipulatives can enhance student understanding." English (1997, p. 4) argues that manipulatives reflect "a move away from the traditional notion of reasoning as primarily propositional, abstract, and disembodied to the contemporary view of reasoning as embodied and imaginative." Overall, using concrete manipulatives has potential for fostering meaningful learning under appropriate conditions.

Schema-Activation Methods

In schema-activation methods, instruction either provides or activates relevant prior knowledge. Schema-activation methods encourage and enable the learner to connect new incoming material with relevant existing knowledge (as indicated by the integrating arrow in Fig. 13.2) and are especially effective for novices (Mayer, 2003). Three forms of schema-activation methods are advance organizers, pretraining, and cueing.

Advance Organizers. An advance organizer is material presented before a lesson that is intended to promote learning by helping the learner relate the new material to existing knowledge. Ausubel (1968) described how advance organizers could help learners assimilate incoming information to their existing knowledge. For example, Mayer (1983) asked students to read a passage on radar and take a problem-solving test on the material. Before reading the passage, some students received a labeled diagram showing that radar was like throwing a ball, having it hit a remote object, and measuring the time it takes to return. The purpose of the diagram was to help students think of radar in terms of their prior knowledge about bouncing objects. Students who received the diagram performed much better on the problem-solving test than students who did not receive the diagram. In a review of research on advance organizers, Corkill (1992) found consistent support for advance organizers, although concrete organizers tended to be more effective than abstract ones.

Pretraining. Another approach is to provide some pretraining that familiarizes the learner with the elements described in the lesson. For example, Mayer, Mathias, and Wetzell (2002) asked students to view a narrated animation explaining how a pump works and then take a problem-solving test. Before the lesson, some students were given a clear plastic model of a pump and told to pull the handle up and down a few times. Students who had this short pretraining performed much better on the problem-solving test than did students who had not received the pretraining. Presumably, the experience of seeing and using a concrete pump helped activate relevant prior knowledge about pistons in cylinders that was useful for making sense of the narrated animation.

Cueing. Finally, a third approach is to alter a text passage so that it cues the reader to think of relevant prior knowledge. For example, adding illustrations to a text about how pumps work greatly increased subsequent problem-solving performance (Mayer & Gallini, 1990), presumably because the concrete illustration helped people use their prior knowledge about a piston moving through a cylinder. Similarly, Beck, McKeown, Sinatra, & Loxterman (1991) rewrote a history text on the French and Indian War that was particularly difficult for students to understand. For example, they added a first sentence stating "About 250 years ago, Britain and France both claimed to own some land, here, in North America" (p. 257). This sentence was intended to "activate the conflict schema in the reader's mind" (p. 257), so students could understand that two groups wanted the same object. Consistent with predictions, the rewritten version resulted in much better performance on subsequent tests of problem solving.

Generative Methods

Generative methods require that learners generate relations between their existing knowledge and information to be learned, as indicated by the *integrating* arrow in Fig. 13.2. Four forms of generative methods are elaboration, summary note-taking, self-explaining, and questioning.

Elaborative Methods. One form of generative method involves elaboration, in which the learner is explicitly asked to explain how the new material is related to existing knowledge. For example, asking elementary school students to construct verbal and imaginal relations between printed stories and their own experiences increased comprehension substantially compared with control groups that did not engage in these elaboration activities (Linden & Wittrock, 1981). Among high school students, elaboration methods that led students to construct verbal and graphical relations between concepts in economics and their knowledge increased comprehension and transfer of economics principles (Kourilsky & Wittrock, 1987, 1992). Asking students to generate analogies as they read a text is intended to encourage them to construct connections between the new material and their existing knowledge; Wittrock and Alesandrini (1990) found that instructions to generate analogies increased comprehension.

Similarly, in a lesson on using a database programming language, some students were asked to write a short description of how each command related to a familiar situation such as sorting documents from an in-basket into two piles based on some criterion, whereas other students were not. Students who generated the descriptions relating each command to their existing knowledge about clerical work in an office performed much better on subsequent problem-solving tests in which they had to create or interpret new programs (Mayer, 1980). In elaborative interrogation, learners read a passage and answer "why" questions intended to help them make needed inferences

(Wood, Pressley, & Winne, 1990). Generative methods have also been applied to mathematics learning (Peled & Wittrock, 1990; Wittrock, 1974a) and science learning (Osborne & Wittrock, 1983, 1985). Wittrock has presented a model of generative learning (1974a, 1990) and a model of generative teaching (1991).

Note-Taking Methods. Asking students to take summary notes on a textbook lesson or classroom lecture can encourage them to select relevant information, summarize it coherently, and relate it to their past knowledge (Kiewra, 1991; Peper & Mayer, 1978). For example, Peper and Mayer (1978) found that students who were required to take notes on a videotaped statistics lecture performed better on problem-solving tests than students who were not allowed to take notes. Similarly, Doctorow, Wittrock, and Marks (1978) reported that elementary school students who were asked to generate summaries of the paragraphs in a text increased their comprehension substantially compared to students who were not allowed to generate summaries. More recently, Thiede and Anderson (2003) found that students who were asked to write summaries of a text they had read earlier displayed better metacognitive accuracy in judging how well they understood the text, when compared to students who only read the text.

Self-explanation Methods. Another form of generative learning is to engage in a process of self-explanation while learning, such as trying to explain a text to oneself while reading it (Chi, 2000). For example, as they read a passage on the human heart and circulatory system, students are asked to "read each sentence out loud and then explain what it means to you" including "how does it relate to what you've already read, does it give you new insight into your understanding of how the circulatory system works, or does it raise a question in your mind . . ." (Chi, 2000, p. 171). Chi and colleagues (Chi, 2000; Chi, Bassok, Lewis, Reimann, & Glaser, 1989; Chi, de Leeuw, Chiu, and LaVancher, 1994) have found that asking students to engage in self-explaining as they read a science text helped them understand the material and subsequently led to better problem solving performance.

Questioning Methods. Finally, as a fourth example of a generative method consider questioning methods, in which the learner is asked to generate a question for each segment of a textbook lesson or classroom lecture. Generating questions is a part of some effective reading comprehension problems (Palinscar & Brown, 1984) but is most effective when students are trained in how to ask useful questions (Pressley & Woloshyn, 1995). For example, King (1992, 1997) has shown that students learn more deeply when they are taught questions to ask and prompted to use them when learning new material.

Guided Discovery Methods

Another technique advocated for encouraging active learning is discovery. In discovery methods, a problem is presented for the student to solve. In pure discovery, no guidance is provided so learners can explore on their own. In guided discovery, the teacher provides enough guidance to ensure than the learner discovers the rule, principle, or concept that is the goal of instruction. In expository methods, the learner is simply told the correct rule, principle, or concept. According to the SOI model shown in Fig. 13.2, pure discovery methods can prime the integration process—in which the learner searches long-term memory for ideas—but may not prime the selecting and organizing processes—in which the learner comes into contact with the to-be-learned material. In expository methods, the selecting process is primed—so the learner is aware of the to-be-learned material—but the organizing and integrating processes may not be activated because the learner is not encouraged to make sense of the material. Finally, in the guided discovery method, enough guidance is provided to prime the selecting process, whereas enough freedom is allowed to prime the organizing and integrating processes, yielding a meaningful learning outcome.

One of the earliest tests of the discovery methods involved research on learning of problem-solving rules conducted through the 1960s. For example, Gagne and Brown (1961) asked students to derive formulas to solve series sum problems such as "1, 3, 5, 7, 9...". Guided discovery methods resulted in better performance on subsequent problem-solving tests than did pure discovery or expository methods. Although discovery was advocated for many large-scale curriculum development projects in the 1960s (Bruner, 1961), a review of subsequent research showed that pure discovery was not as effective as guided discovery in promoting problem-solving transfer (Shulman & Kieslar, 1966).

Through the 1970s, one avenue of research on discovery methods involved helping children discover Piagetian (1970) conservation strategies needed to solve conservation problems. For example, Gelman (1969) found that the best way to help kindergarteners learn to solve conservation problems was to provide guided practice in which the teacher directed the children's attention to relevant aspects of the task and provided feedback on their answers. In a recent review, Brainerd (2003) noted that there is a lack of evidence to support the use of pure discovery methods to help children learn conservation

strategies, whereas guided methods have been shown to be effective.

A third approach to the study of discovery methods involved research on teaching of the LOGO programming language conducted through the 1980s. Consistent with Papert's (1980) call for allowing children to learn LOGO by interacting with a computer, some early instructional programs focused on pure discovery as the method of instruction. However, Kurland and Pea (1985) found that pure discovery methods did not promote subsequent problem solving, whereas Fay and Mayer (1994) found that children learned LOGO better from a guided discovery method in which they received help in design principles for programs. In a review, Littlefield et al. (1988, p. 116) concluded that "mastery of the programming language has not been achieved when LOGO has been taught in a discovery-oriented environment," whereas guided methods have been successful.

In a recent review of these three research literatures, Mayer (2004a, p. 14) concluded that "there is sufficient research evidence to make any reasonable person skeptical about the benefits of discovery learning." Instead, consistent with the SOI model, guided discovery methods resulted in better performance on subsequent problem solving tests than did pure discovery. Mayer (2004a, p. 17) noted: "Activity may help promote meaningful learning, but instead of behavioral activity per se (e.g., hands-on activity, discussion, and free exploration), the kind of activity that really promotes meaningful learning is cognitive activity (e.g., selecting, organizing, and integrating knowledge)."

Modeling Methods

In modeling methods, an instructor demonstrates how to solve problems and, in some cases, provides an explanation of the solution steps. The goal is to help the learner make sense of the solution by mentally organizing it into meaningful chunks and relating it to relevant prior knowledge. Two forms of modeling methods are example methods, in which the learner receives worked-out examples, and apprenticeship methods, in which the learner works with others on an authentic task.

Example Methods. The goal of example methods is to show learners how to solve typical problems in a field or subject area. When confronted with a new problem (which can be called a *target problem*), the problem solver is expected to engage in three cognitive processes: *recognizing* that the target problem is like a problem the problem solver already knows how to solve (from a storehouse of *base problems* in the problem solver's long-term memory); *abstracting* a solution principle or method from the base problem; and *mapping* the principle or method back onto the target problem to aid in solving the problem (Quilici & Mayer, 1996). For example, Cooper and Sweller (1987) taught students how to solve algebra equation problems either by giving them practice in solving eight problems (learning by doing), or by giving four pairs of problems where the first one showed a step-by-step example of how to solve the problem and the second was to be solved by the learner using the same solution method (learning from examples). Students in the learning from examples group learned faster and showed better performance on solving new problems as compared to students in the learning by doing group. Paas and van Merrienboer (1994) reported similar results in teaching students to solve geometry problems.

More recent work has shown that students learn best when the worked examples clearly specify the subgoals that each set of steps accomplishes (Catrambone, 1998), when instruction is designed to fade from providing all of the steps to providing fewer and fewer of the steps and asking the learner to fill them in (Renkl & Atkinson, 2003), and when students receive structure-emphasizing training that helps focus their attention on the structural features of examples (i.e., the underlying relations among the elements) rather than the surface features (i.e., the cover story in the problem) (Quilici & Mayer, 1996). In a recent review, Renkl (2005) documents the features of effective examples based on research evidence.

Case-based learning is a more complex form of learning from examples, in which the learner is given a realistic problem scenario—that is, a case—and asked to analyze the solution method (Mayer, 2003). Although case-based learning (as well as problem-based learning) has led to some exciting development projects in professional training, there is a need for a coherent research base of scientifically rigorous evidence (Evensen & Hmelo, 2000; Lundeberg, Levin, & Harrington, 1999; Schank, 2002).

Apprenticeship Methods. Apprenticeship methods represent an extended form of learning by example in which novices work closely with more experienced performers on authentic tasks (Lave, 1988; Lave & Wenger, 1991). Collins, Brown, and Newman (1989) have shown that throughout most of human history, before schools appeared, apprenticeship was the most common method for teaching people to become experts in fields ranging from medicine to law to art. Apprenticeship includes *modeling*, in which a teacher describes her or his cognitive processes while carrying out a task; *coaching*, in which a teacher provides advice and assistance to a student who is carrying out a task; and *scaffolding*, in which

the teacher performs or removes part of the task that a student is not able to perform (Collins, Brown, & Newman, 1989). Two ways to implement aspects of the apprenticeship method in classrooms are Brown and Palinscar's (1989) reciprocal teaching and Slavin's (1990) cooperative learning.

In reciprocal teaching, a group of students and a teacher work together on an authentic academic task such as comprehending a text passage. For example, in one study (Brown & Palinscar, 1989; Palinscar & Brown, 1984), students and teacher took turns in leading a dialogue about how to carry out comprehension strategies, such as questioning (i.e., generating a relevant question that the passage answers), clarifying (i.e., identifying problematic words or phrases), summarizing (i.e., producing a concise summary), and predicting (i.e., inferring what will occur next in the passage). Students who engaged in reciprocal teaching showed a much greater improvement in their reading comprehension scores than students who learned with conventional methods.

In cooperative learning, students work in groups to learn how to perform an authentic academic task (such as how to solve arithmetic problems) in which there are incentives to help all members of the group to learn (Slavin, 1990). In a year-long study comparing cooperative learning and conventional teaching methods for teaching mathematics, students in the cooperative learning group showed much greater improvement in mathematics achievement than did students in the conventional group (Slavin & Karweit, 1984).

Although apprenticeship methods such as reciprocal teaching and cooperative learning can be effective in some situations, there are also many cases in which learning in groups is not particularly effective, so it is important to determine the conditions under which apprenticeship methods work (Johnson & Johnson, 1990). The challenge of such instruction is to encourage active cognitive processing that includes all three of the processes shown in Fig. 13.2.

Teaching Thinking Skills

Each of the preceding six methods for promoting problem solving was based on teaching content in ways that would facilitate its usability in subsequent problem solving. A somewhat different approach is to directly teach problem-solving skills to students—an approach that can be called teaching thinking skills. Teaching of thinking skills is part of the hidden curriculum, in the sense that educators expect students to be able to solve problems using the material presented in the course but rarely provide problem-solving instruction. Making such instruction part of the regular curriculum represents the seventh method for promoting meaningful learning.

Teaching Thinking Skills Courses. Many thinking skills programs and courses have been developed to teach problem-solving skills that will transfer to new problems (Adams, 1989; Chance, 1986; Martinez, 2000; Perkins & Grotzer, 1997). Mayer (1997) has proposed four issues for thinking skills programs: what to teach (e.g., thinking as a single ability or as a collection of component skills), how to teach (e.g., focusing on product or process), where to teach (e.g., in a general, domain-independent course or in an existing, specific course), and when to teach (e.g., after basic skills are mastered or before). A comparison of successful and unsuccessful programs reveals that teaching thinking skills is most effective (1) when the curriculum focuses on one or more component skills, such as how to break a problem into parts or how to evaluate hypothesis against data, rather than on improving the mind in general; (2) when the instructional method focuses on problem-solving processes, such as having experts model their problem-solving steps, rather than solely on getting the right answer; (3) when students are expected to be able to solve problems in the same domain as in the instruction rather than across domains; and (4) when skills are taught even before students have automated the underlying basic skills.

For example, in one of the first studies on teaching of thinking skills, Bloom and Broder (1950) sought to teach college students how to solve examination problems in subjects such as economics. As part of the training, students listened to successful problem solvers describe their thought processes as they solved examination problems, students described their own processes on the same problems, and students noted the differences between how they and the experts solved the problems. This training resulted in significantly higher scores on the examination than for students who did not receive training. Consistent with three of the criteria for successful instruction in thinking skills, the training focused on component skills, such as how to break a problem into parts; emphasized process, such as comparing one's own method with that of an expert; and was taught within a context that was similar to the final test. However, in terms of the fourth criterion, students already had solid knowledge of the fundamentals of economics, so in this sense the basic skills were already strong.

Perhaps the most studied thinking skills course is the Productive Thinking Program, a problem-solving course for elementary school children (Covington, Crutchfield, & Davies, 1966; Covington, Crutchfield, Davies, & Olton, 1974). The Productive Thinking Program consists of 15 cartoon-like booklets that describe various mystery or detective stories in which two children, Lila and Jim, try to solve the case. Throughout the booklet, the reader is asked to generate hypotheses, find relevant information to test the hypotheses, and engage in other problem-solving activities. Students who take the course tend to show larger pretest-to-posttest gains than control students on solving problems like those in the booklet, but "there is only limited . . .evidence of transfer to dissimilar problems" (Mansfield, Busse, & Krepelka, 1978, p. 531). Overall, this program meets the four criteria of teaching component skills (such as how to generate and evaluate hypotheses), teaching by modeling correct problem-solving processes (such as through the characters in the booklet), promoting problem-solving performance on problems like those in the booklet, and teaching high-level skills to children who had not yet automated their low-level skills.

Another well-documented attempt to teach thinking skills is Feuerstein's Instrumental Enrichment program (1980; Feuerstein, Hensen, Hoffman, & Rand, 1985). Students who were labeled as mentally retarded based on traditional tests of intelligence were given problem-solving classes several times per week over the course of several years. In a typical lesson, the teacher presented an unfamiliar problem, asked the students to work on it, and then led a class discussion in methods for solving the problem. In this way students could compare their thought processes with those of others. Evaluation studies revealed that students in the Instrumental Enrichment program showed greater pretest-to-posttest gains on tests of nonverbal intelligence than students given conventional instruction. Although the program appears to be effective, Chance (1986, p. 85) pointed out that it "requires a considerable investment of student time," and Bransford, Arbitman-Smith, Stein, and Vye (1985, p. 201) observed that the program emphasizes "training students to solve certain types of problems so they will be able to solve similar problems on their own." Again, the program meets the criteria of teaching component skills, focusing on problem-solving process, promoting performance within the same domain, and teaching young students who have not yet mastered basic skills.

Finally, Odyssey was designed as a middle-school course intended to increase students' performance on intelligence tests (Adams, 1989; Nickerson, 1994). Odyssey consists of approximately one hundred 45-minute lessons on basic problem-solving tasks such as how to solve a series completion problem—a problem sometimes found on intelligence tests. Each lesson begins with the teacher introducing the problem to the class, students work on the problem on their own, and students are asked to demonstrate and justify their solutions to the class. An evaluation of the project found that students who received Odyssey training for a year showed greater improvements than non-Odyssey students on a battery of cognitive tasks similar to those in the training. Overall, the training "enhanced the magnitude of students' intelligent behavior [on] authentic tasks at least in the short term" (Grotzer & Perkins, 2000, p. 496). The course targets component skills, focuses on modeling of appropriate problem-solving processes, improves performance mainly in the target domain, and works even when students have not fully mastered basic skills.

Overall, Mayer (2003, p. 425) has abstracted four general guidelines for the design of problem-solving programs, based on the features of successful programs: "1. Focus on a few well-defined skills. 2. Contextualize the skills within authentic tasks. 3. Personalize the skills through social interaction and language-based discussion of the process of problem solving. 4. Accelerate the skills so that students learn them along with lower-level skills." Although problem-solving courses have been popular for more than 50 years, the newer generation of thinking skills instruction focuses instead on teaching relevant cognitive skills within the context of specific subjects (Mayer, 2003). In the next sections, we explore teaching of cognitive and metacognitive skills needed for problem solving in various domains.

Teaching Domain-Specific Thinking Skills. Given the consistent evidence that thinking skills courses promote transfer mainly to similar problems within the same domain, a reasonable approach is to incorporate thinking-skills instruction within specific subjects such as mathematical, scientific, historical, and literary problem solving. In taking a domain-specific approach, the starting point is finding an authentic academic task and determining the main underlying cognitive processes through a cognitive task analysis.

For example, the academic task of writing an essay can be broken down into three major cognitive processes—planning, translating, and reviewing (Hayes, 1996; Hayes & Flower, 1980). Concerning the teaching of planning skills, students wrote better essays when they were required to spend time outlining their essay before they started writing (Kellogg, 1994). As part of a larger project, Englert, Raphael, Anderson, Anthony, & Stevens (1991) taught planning skills by asking elementary school children to fill out "plan-think-sheets" in which they answered questions such as, "Who am I writing for?", "Why am I writing this?", "What do I know?", and "How can I organize my ideas?" Filling out sheets that encouraged each of the main cognitive processes in writing resulted in increased quality of essays as compared to a group that did not receive training in planning skills and other component skills for essay writing. Similarly, Harris and Graham

(1992) devised a set of planning questions to help students learn appropriate planning skills in writing stories, such as "Who is the main character?"; "Where does the story take place?", and "What does the main character do or want to do?" Students who learned to plan using these kinds of questions showed greater improvement in the quality of their stories than students who did not receive such training. Overall, it appears that it is possible to improve students' planning skills by giving them directed practice in how to plan their writing.

As another example, the academic task of solving an arithmetic word problem can be broken down into the cognitive processes of representing, in which the problem solver builds a coherent mental model of the situation described in the problem; planning, in which the problem solver devises a solution plan; and executing, in which the problem solver carries out the plan. For example, to teach representing skills, Low and Over (1989) gave students practice with feedback in analyzing word problems; for each problem, students had to indicate if it contained enough information, not enough information (and to indicate the needed information), or too much information (and to indicate the extraneous information). Students who received this training showed greater improvements in their problem-solving performance than did students who received no instruction or practice in solving problems. Similarly, Quilici and Mayer (2002) found that students who received instruction and practice in sorting statistics word problems based on their underlying structure performed better on recognizing problem types than did untrained students. Overall, students can learn to use strategies for representing word problems.

Several reviews have shown how it is possible to analyze and teach the underlying cognitive processes required in tasks such as comprehending a passage, writing an essay, solving an arithmetic word problem, answering a scientific question, or explaining an historical event (Mayer, 2003; Pressley & Woloshyn, 1995). Teaching of domain-specific thinking skills represents one of educational psychology's greatest successes (Mayer, 2004b).

In addition to teaching specific cognitive skills, such as how to plan to write an essay, it is also possible to teach metacognitive skills, such as how to coordinate one's cognitive processes, how to adjust one's cognitive processing in light of difficulties, and how to have positive beliefs (Mayer, 1998; Zimmerman & Campillo, 2003). Knowing how to use a cognitive skill, such as how to plan in writing, must be complemented by knowing when and where to use it. For example, Pressley (1990, p. 9) noted, "Good strategy users evaluate whether the strategies they are using are producing progress towards goals they have set for themselves" and also consider "the benefits that follow from using the procedures and the amount of effort required to carry out the procedures." Becoming an effective problem solver requires the development of self-awareness about one's thinking processes and self-regulation of one's thinking processes (Pressley & Schneider, 1997; Pressley & Wharton-McDonald, 1997). Students can develop cognitive and metacognitive skills for problem solving through modeling (Butler & Winne, 1995; Duffy, 2002; Schunk, 1989).

CONCLUSION

Overall, problem solving is an important educational goal. In short, we want students to be able to apply what they learned in new situations. In this chapter, we explored seven methods for promoting learning of problem-solving skill that are supported by research evidence and consistent with cognitive theory: load-reducing methods, such as providing enough practice to build automaticity of basic skills; structure-based methods, such as using concrete manipulatives; schema-activation methods, such as advance organizers and pretraining; generative methods, such as elaborating, summarizing, self-explaining, and questioning; guided discovery methods, in which learners receive guidance while solving problems; modeling methods, such as worked-examples and apprenticeship; and teaching thinking skills in stand-alone courses or within specific subjects.

Each of the seven methods is supported by a robust and growing research base. Although exhaustive literature reviews of the evidence concerning each method are beyond the scope of this chapter, we have provided a few examples of representative research studies.

Each of the seven methods is based on a cognitive theory of learning. The first method works by reducing cognitive load in working memory, which frees up capacity to engage in active cognitive processing. The next five methods work by encouraging active cognitive processing during learning, such as encouraging learners to make connections between existing knowledge and incoming information, encouraging learners to organize incoming information into a coherent structure, and encouraging learners to pay attention to relevant incoming information for further processing. The result is meaningful learning outcomes that are encoded in ways that make them useful in solving new problems. The final method works by helping students build a repertoire of cognitive and metacognitive strategies that can be applied in specific problem-solving situations.

Overall, even since our last review (Mayer & Wittrock, 1996), much progress has been made in achieving one of educational psychology's greatest challenges: helping students become better problem solvers. In service of this goal, three educationally relevant principles that emerge from our review of research on problem solving are as follows:

Domain-specific principle: Rather than attempting to teach general problem-solving heuristics, it is better to teach problem solving skills within specific domains.
Near-transfer principle: Rather than expecting problem-solving skill to be applicable to a wide range of problems, it is better to expect that problem solving skills will be largely restricted with respect to their range of applicability.
Knowledge integration principle: Rather than focusing mainly on teaching of facts and procedures or on teaching concepts and strategies, it is better to integrate teaching of all these kinds of knowledge within guided problem solving tasks.

The study of how to improve students' problem solving performance represents a fruitful and important area of research for educational psychologists.

ACKNOWLEDGMENTS

We appreciate the helpful reviews by Patricia Alexander, Shawn Glynn, and Alexander Renkl.

References

Adams, M. J. (1989). Think skills curricula: Their promise and progress. *Educational Psychologist, 24*, 24–77.

Anderson, J. R., Corbett, A. T., Koedinger, K. R., & Pelleteir, R. (1995). Cognitive tutors: Lessons learned. *Journal of the Learning Sciences, 4*, 167–207.

Anderson, J. R., & Schunn, C. D. (2000). Implications of the ACT-R learning theory: No magic bullets. In R. Glaser (Ed.), *Advances in instructional psychology: Vol. 5* (pp. 1–34). Mahwah, NJ: Lawrence Erlbaum Associates.

Anderson, L., Krathwohl, D. R., Airasian, P. W., Cruikshank, K. A., Mayer, R. E., Pintrich, P., et al. (2001). *A taxonomy for learning, teaching, and assessing.* New York: Longman.

Ausubel, D. P. (1968). *Educational psychology: A cognitive view.* New York: Holt, Rinehart, & Winston.

Beck, I. L., McKeown, M. G., Sinatra, G. M., & Loxterman, J. A. (1991). Revising social studies text from a text-processing perspective: Evidence of improved comprehensibility. *Reading Research Quarterly, 26*, 251–276.

Bloom, B. S., & Broder, L. J. (1950). *Problem-solving processes of college students.* Chicago: University of Chicago Press.

Bradley, L., & Bryant, P. (1983). Categorizing sounds and learning to read—a causal connection. *Nature, 301,* 419-421.

Bradley, L., & Bryant, P. (1985). *Rhyme and reason in reading and spelling.* Ann Arbor, MI: University of Michigan Press.

Brainerd, C. J. (2003). Jean Piaget, learning research, and American education. In B. J. Zimmerman & D. H. Schunk (Eds.), *Educational psychology: A century of contributions* (pp. 251-287). Mahwah, NJ: Lawrence Erlbaum Associates.

Bransford, J. D., Arbitman-Smith, R., Stein, B. S., & Vye, N. J. (1985). Improving thinking and learning skills: An analysis of three approaches. In J. W. Segal, S. F. Chipman, & R. Glaser (Eds.), *Thinking and learning skills: Vol. 1. Relating instruction to research* (pp. 133-206). Hillsdale, NJ: Lawrence Erlbaum Associates.

Brown, A. L., & Palinscar, A. S. (1989). Guided, cooperative learning and individual knowledge acquisition. In L. B. Resnick (Ed.), *Knowing, learning, and instruction: Essays in honor of Robert Glaser* (pp. 393-452). Hillsdale, NJ: Lawrence Erlbaum Associates.

Brownell, W. A., & Moser, H. E. (1949). Meaningful versus mechanical learning: A study on grade 3 subtraction. In *Duke University research studies in education* (No. 8). Durham, NC: Duke University Press.

Bruner, J. S. (1961). The act of discovery. *Harvard Educational Review, 31,* 21-32.

Bruning, R. H., Schraw, G. J., Norby, M. M., & Ronning, R. R. (2004). *Cognitive psychology and instruction* (4th ed). Upper Saddle River, NJ: Merrill Prentice Hall.

Butler, D. L., & Winne, P. H. (1995). Feedback and self-regulated learning: A theoretical synthesis. *Review of Educational Research, 65,* 245-281.

Case, R. (1985). *Intellectual development: From birth to adulthood.* Orlando, FL: Academic Press.

Catrambone, R. (1998). The subgoal learning model: Creating better examples so that students can solve novel problems. *Journal of Experimental Psychology: General, 127,* 355-376.

Chance, P. (1986). *Thinking in the classroom.* New York: Teachers College Press.

Chi, M. T. H. (2000). Self-explaining expository texts: The dual processes of generating inferences and repairing mental models. In R. Glaser (Ed.), *Advances in instructional psychology, Vol. 5* (pp. 161-238). Mahwah, NJ: Lawrence Erlbaum Associates.

Chi, M. T. H., Bassok, M., Lewis, M., Reimann, P., & Glaser, R. (1989). Self-explanations: How students study and use examples in learning to solve problems. *Cognitive Science, 13,* 145-182.

Chi, M. T. H., de Leeuw, N., Chiu, M. H., & LaVancher, C. (1994). Eliciting self-explanations improves understanding. *Cognitive Science, 18,* 439-477.

Collins, A., Brown, J. S., & Newman, S. E. (1989). Cognitive apprenticeship: Teaching the crafts of reading, writing, and mathematics. In L. B. Resnick (Ed.), *Knowing, learning, and instruction: Essays in honor of Robert Glaser* (pp. 453-494). Hillsdale, NJ: Lawrence Erlbaum Associates.

Cooper, G., & Sweller, J. (1987). The effects of schema activation and rule automation on mathematical problem solving. *Journal of Educational Psychology, 79,* 347-362.

Corkill, A. J. (1992). Advance organizers: Facilitators of recall. *Educational Psychology Review, 4,* 33-68.

Covington, M. V., Crutchfield, R. S., & Davies, L. B. (1966). *The productive thinking program.* Berkeley, CA: Brazelton.

Covington, M. V., Crutchfield, R. S., Davies, L. B., & Olton, R. M. (1974). *The productive thinking program.* Columbus, OH: Merrill.

de Jong, T., & van Joolingen, W. R. (1998). Scientific discovery learning with computer simulations of conceptual domains. *Review of Educational Research, 68,* 179-202.

Dienes, Z. P. (1960). *Building up mathematics.* New York: Hutchinson Educational.

Duffy, G. (2002). The case for direct explanation of strategies. In C. Block & M. Pressley (Eds.), *Comprehension instruction: Research-based best practices* (pp. 28-41). New York: Guilford Press.

Duncker, K. (1945). On problem solving. *Psychological Monographs, 58*(5), Whole No. 270.

Doctorow, M. J., Wittrock, M. C., & Marks, C. B. (1978). Generative processes in reading comprehension. *Journal of Education Psychology, 70,* 109-118.

Englert, C. S., Raphael, T. E., Anderson, L. M., Anthony, H. M., & Stevens, D. S. (1991). Making strategies and self-talk visible: Writing instruction in regular and special education classrooms. *American Educational Research Journal, 28,* 337-372.

English, L. D (1997). *Mathematical reasoning.* Mahwah, NJ: Lawrence Erlbaum Associates.

Ericsson, A. (2003a). The search for general abilities and basic capacities: Theoretical implications for the modifiability and complexity of mechanisms mediating expert performance. In R. J. Sternberg & E. L. Grigorenko (Eds.), *The psychology of abilities, competencies, and expertise* (pp. 93-125). New York: Cambridge University Press.

Ericsson, A. (2003b). The acquisition of expert performance in problem solving: Construction and modification of mediating mechanisms through deliberate practice. In J. E. Davidson and R. J. Sternberg (Eds.), *The psychology of problem solving* (pp. 31-83). New York: Cambridge University Press.

Evensen, D. H., & Hmelo, C. E. (Eds.). (2000). *Problem-based learning.* Mahwah, NJ: Lawrence Erlbaum Associates.

Fay, A. L., & Mayer, R. E. (1994). Benefits of teaching design skills before teaching of LOGO computer programming: Evidence for syntax-independent transfer. *Journal of Educational Computing Research, 11,* 187-210.

Feuerstein, R. (1980). *Instrumental enrichment: An intervention program for cognitive modifiability.* Baltimore: University Park Press.

Feuerstein, R., Jensen, M., Hoffman, M. B., & Rand, Y. (1985). Instrumental enrichment, an intervention program for structural cognitive modifiability: Theory and practice. In J. W. Segal, S. F. Chipman, & R. Glaser (Eds.), *Thinking and learning skills: Vol. 1. Relating instruction to research* (pp. 43-82). Hillsdale, NJ: Lawrence Erlbaum Associates.

Fuson, K. C., & Briars, D. J. (1990). Using a base-ten block learning/teaching approach for first and second grade place-value and multidigit addition and subtraction. *Journal for Research in Mathematics Education, 21,* 180-206.

Gagné, R. M. (1968). Learning hierarchies. *Educational Psychologist, 6,* 1-9.

Gagné, R. M., & Brown, L. T. (1961). Some factors in the programming of conceptual learning. *Journal of Experimental Psychology, 62,* 313-321.

Gelman, R. (1969). Conservation acquisition: A problem of learning to attend to relevant attributes. *Journal of Experimental Child Psychology, 7,* 167-187.

Glynn, S. M., Britton, B. K., Muth, D., & Dogan, N. (1982). Writing and revising persuasive documents: Cognitive demands. *Journal of Educational Psychology, 74,* 557-567.

Grotzer, T. A. & Perkins, D. N. (2000). Teaching intelligence: A performance conception. In R. J. Sternberg (Ed.), *Handbook of intelligence* (pp. 492-515). New York: Cambridge University Press.

Harris, K. R., & Graham, S. (1992). *Helping young writers master the craft: Strategy instruction and self-regulation in the writing process.* Cambridge, MA: Brookline Books.

Hayes, J. R. (1996). A new framework for understanding cognition and effect in writing. In C. M. Levy & S. Ransdell (Eds.), *The science of writing* (pp. 1-28). Mahwah, NJ: Lawrence Erlbaum Associates.

Hayes, J. R., & Flower, L. S. (1980). Identifying the organization of writing processes. In L. Gregg & E. R. Steinberg (Eds.), *Cognitive processes in writing* (pp. 3-30). Hillsdale, NJ: Lawrence Erlbaum Associates.

Hembree, R., & Dessart, D. J. (1992). Research on calculators in mathematics education. In J. Fey & C. Hirsch (Eds.), *Calculators in mathematics education* (pp. 23-32). Reston, VA: National Council of Teachers of Mathematics.

Hiebert, J., Carpenter, T. P., Fennema, E., Fuson, K. C., Wearne, D., Murray, H., et al. (1997). *Making sense: Teaching and learning mathematics with understanding.* Portsmouth, NH: Heinemann.

Johnson, D. W., & Johnson, R. T. (1990). Cooperative learning and achievement. In S. Sharan (Ed.), *Cooperative learning* (pp. 23-37). New York: Praeger.

Kahneman, A., & Tversky, B. (2000). *Choices, values, and frames.* New York: Cambridge University Press.

Katona, G. (1967). *Organizing and memorizing.* New York: Hafner.

Kellogg, R. T. (1994). *The psychology of writing.* New York: Oxford University Press.

Kiewra, K. H. (1991). Aids to lecture learning. *Educational Psychologist, 26,* 37-54.

Kilpatrick, J., Swafford, J., & Findell, B. (Eds.). (2001). *Adding it up: Helping children learn mathematics.* Washington, DC: National Academy Press.

King, A. (1992). Facilitating elaborative learning through guided student-generated questioning. *Educational Psychologist, 27,* 111-126.

King, A. (1997). ASK to THINK-TEL WHY: A model of transactive peer tutoring for scaffolding higher level complex learning. *Educational Psychologist, 32,* 221-235.

Kourilsky, M., & Wittrock, M. C. (1987). Verbal and graphical strategies in teaching economics. *Teaching and Teacher Education, 3,* 1-12.

Kourilsky, M., & Wittrock, M. C. (1992). Generative teaching: An enrichment strategy for learning economics in cooperative groups. *American Educational Research Journal, 29,* 861-876.

Kurland, D. M., & Pea, R. D. (1985). Children's mental models of recursive LOGO programs. *Journal of Educational Computing Research, 1,* 235-244.

LaBerge, D., & Samuels, S. J. (1974). Toward a theory of automatic information processing in reading. *Cognitive Psychology, 6,* 293-323.

Lave, J. (1988). *Cognition into practice.* New York: Cambridge University Press.

Lave, J., & Wenger, E. (1991). *Situated learning.* New York: Cambridge University Press.

Linden, M., & Wittrock, M. C. (1981). The teaching of reading comprehension according to the model of generative learning. *Reading Research Quarterly, 17,* 44-57.

Linn, M. C., & Hsi, S. (2000). *Computers, teachers, peers.* Mahwah, NJ: Lawrence Erlbaum Associates.

Littlefield, J., Delclos, V. R., Lever, S., Clayton, K. N., Brabsford, J. D., & Franks, J. J. (1988). Learning LOGO: Method of teaching, transfer of general skills, and attitudes toward school and computers. In R. E. Mayer (Ed.), *Teaching and learning computer programming* (pp. 111-136). Hillsdale, NJ: Lawrence Erlbaum Associates.

Lovett, M. C. (2002). Problem solving. In D. Medin (Ed.), *Stevens' handbook of experimental psychology: Vol. 2. Memory and cognitive processes* (3rd ed., pp. 317-362). New York: Wiley.

Low, R., & Over, R. (1989). Detection of missing and irrelevant information in algebraic word problems. *British Journal of Educational Psychology, 59,* 296-305.

Lundeberg, M. A., Levin, B. B., & Harrington, H. L. (Eds.). (1999). *Who learns what from cases and how?* Mahwah, NJ: Lawrence Erlbaum Associates.

Manktelow, K. (1999). *Reasoning and thinking.* Hove, UK: Psychology Press.

Mansfield, R. S., Busse, T. V., & Krepelka, E. J. (1978). The effectiveness of creativity training. *Review of Educational Research, 48,* 517-536.

Martinez, M. E. (2000). *Education as the cultivation of intelligence.* Mahwah, NJ: Lawrence Erlbaum Associates.

Mayer R. E. (1980). Elaboration techniques that increase the meaningfulness of technical text: An experimental test of the learning strategy hypothesis. *Journal of Educational Psychology, 72,* 770-784.

Mayer, R. E. (1983). Can you repeat that? Qualitative effects of repetition and advance organizers on learning from science text. *Journal of Educational Psychology, 75,* 40-49.

Mayer, R. E. (1990). Problem solving. In M. W. Eysenck (Ed.), *The Blackwell dictionary of cognitive psychology* (pp. 284-288). Oxford, UK: Basil Blackwell.

Mayer, R. E. (1992). *Thinking, problem solving, cognition (2nd ed.).* New York: Freeman.

Mayer, R. E. (1997). Incorporating problem solving into secondary school curricula. In G. D. Phye (Ed.), *Handbook of academic learning* (pp. 474–492). San Diego, CA: Academic Press.

Mayer, R. E. (1998). Cognitive, metacognitive, and motivational aspects of problem solving. *Instructional Science, 26,* 49–63.

Mayer, R. E. (2001). Changing conceptions of learning: A century of progress in the scientific study of education. In L. Corno (Ed.), *Education across a century: The centennial volume, One hundredth yearbook of the National Society for the Study of Education* (pp. 34–75). Chicago: University of Chicago Press.

Mayer, R. E. (2003). *Learning and instruction.* Upper Saddle River, NJ: Merrill Prentice Hall.

Mayer, R. E. (2004a). Should there be a three-strikes rule against pure discovery learning? The case for guided methods of instruction. *American Psychologist, 59,* 14–19.

Mayer, R. E. (2004b). Teaching of subject matter. *Annual Review of Psychology, 55,* 715–744.

Mayer, R. E., Dow, G. T., & Mayer, S. (2003). Multimedia learning in an interactive self-explaining environment: What works in the design of agent-based microworlds? *Journal of Educational Psychology, 95,* 806–813.

Mayer, R. E., & Gallini, J. (1990). When is an illustration worth ten thousand words? *Journal of Educational Psychology, 82,* 715–727.

Mayer, R. E., Mathias, A., & Wetzell, K. (2002). Fostering understanding of multimedia messages through pre-training: Evidence for a two-stage theory of mental model construction. *Journal of Experimental Psychology: Applied, 8,* 147–154.

Mayer, R. E., & Wittrock, M. C. (1996). Problem solving transfer. In D. C. Berliner & R. C. Calfee (Eds.), *Handbook of educational psychology*. New York: Macmillan.

Montessori, M. (1964). *Advanced Montessori method.* Cambridge, MA: Bentley.

Moreno, R., & Mayer, R. E. (1999). Multimedia supported metaphors for meaning making in mathematics. *Cognition and Instruction, 17,* 215–248.

Nathan, M. J., Kintsch, W., & Young, E. (1992). A theory of algebra word problem comprehension and its implications for the design of learning environments. *Cognition and Instruction, 9,* 329–389.

Nickerson, R. S. (1994). Project intelligence. In R. J. Sternberg (Ed.), *Encyclopedia of human intelligence* (pp. 392–430). New York: Cambridge University Press.

Osborne, R. J., & Wittrock, M. C. (1983). Learning science: A generative process. *Science Education, 67,* 489–504.

Osborne, R. J., & Wittrock, M. C. (1985). The generative learning model and its implications for science education. *Studies in Science Education, 12,* 59–87.

Paas, F. G., & van Merrienboer, J. J. G. (1994). Variability of worked examples and transfer of geometrical problem-solving skills: A cognitive load approach. *Journal of Educational Psychology, 86,* 122–133.

Palinscar, A. M., & Brown, A. L. (1984). Reciprocal teaching of comprehension fostering and comprehension monitoring activities. *Cognition and Instruction, 1,* 117–175.

Papert, S. (1980). *Mindstorms: Children, computers, and powerful ideas.* New York: Basic Books.

Peled, Z., & Wittrock, M. C. (1990). Generative meanings in the comprehension of word problems in mathematics. *Instructional Science, 19,* 171–205.

Peper, R., J., & Mayer, R. E. (1978). Note taking as a generative activity. *Journal of Educational Psychology, 70,* 514–522.

Perkins, D. N., & Grotzer, T. A. (1997). Teaching intelligence. *American Psychologist, 52,* 1125–1133.

Piaget, J. (1970). *Science of education and psychology of the child.* New York: Oxford University Press.

Pressley, M. (1990). *Cognitive strategy instruction that really improves children's academic performance.* Cambridge, MA: Brookline.

Pressley, M., & Schneider, W. (1997). *Introduction to memory development during childhood and adolescence.* Mahwah, NJ: Lawrence Erlbaum Associates.

Pressley, M., & Wharton-McDonald, R. (1997). Skilled comprehension and its development through instruction. *School Psychology Review, 26,* 448–446.

Pressley, M., & Woloshyn, V. (1995). *Cognitive strategy instruction (2nd ed).* Cambridge, MA: Brookline Books.

Quilici, J. H., & Mayer, R. E. (1996). Role of examples in how students learn to categorize statistics word problems. *Journal of Educational Psychology, 88,* 144–161.

Quilici, J. H., & Mayer, R. E. (2002). Teaching students to recognize structural similarities between statistics word problems. *Applied Cognitive Psychology, 16,* 97–115.

Reed, S. K. (1999). *Word problems.* Mahwah, NJ: Lawrence Erlbaum Associates.

Renkl, A. (2005). Worked-out example principle. In R. Mayer (Ed.), *Cambridge handbook of multimedia learning* (pp. 229–246). New York: Cambridge University Press.

Renkl, A., & Atkinson, R. K. (2003). Structuring the transition from example study to problem solving in cognitive skills acquisition: A cognitive load perspective. *Educational Psychologist, 38,* 15–22.

Resnick. L. B., & Ford, W. (1981). *The psychology of mathematics for instruction.* Hillsdale, NJ: Lawrence Erlbaum Associates.

Runco, M. A. (2003). (Ed.) *Critical creative processes.* Cresskill, NJ: Hampton Press.

Samuels, S. J. (1979). The method of repeated readings. *The Reading Teacher, 32,* 403–408.

Scardamalia, M., Bereiter, C., & Goelman, H. (1982). The role of production factors in writing ability. In M. Nystrand (Ed.), *What writers know* (pp. 173–210). New York: Academic Press.

Schank, R. C. (2002). *Designing world-class e-learning.* New York: McGraw-Hill.

Schunk, D. (1989). Self-efficacy and achievement behaviors. *Educational Psychology Review, 1,* 173–208.

Schunk, D. (2003). Self-regulation and learning. In W. M. Reynolds and G. E. Miller (Eds.), *Handbook of Psychology* (Vol. 7, pp. 59–78). New York: Wiley.

Shulman, L. S., & Kieslar, E. R. (1966). *Learning by discovery.* Chicago: Rand McNally.

Siegler, R. J. (1989). Mechanisms of cognitive growth. *Annual Review of Psychology, 40,* 353-379.

Singley, M. K., & Anderson, J. R. (1989). *Transfer of cognitive skill.* Cambridge, MA: Harvard University Press.

Slavin, R. (1990). *Cooperative learning.* Englewood Cliffs, NJ: Prentice-Hall.

Slavin, R. E., & Karweit, N. L. (1984). Mastery learning and student teams: A factorial experiment in urban general mathematics classes. *American Educational Research Journal, 21,* 725-736.

Thiede, K. W., & Anderson, M. C. M. (2003). Summarizing can improve metacomprehension accuracy. *Contemporary Educational Psychology, 28,* 129-160.

Wertheimer. M. (1959). *Productive thinking.* New York: Harper & Row.

White, B. Y. (1993). ThinkerTools: Causal models, conceptual change, and science education. *Cognition and Instruction, 10,* 1-100.

White, B. Y., & Frederiksen, J. R. (1998). Inquiry, modeling, and metacognition: Making science accessible to all students. *Cognition and Instruction, 16,* 3-118.

Wittrock, M. C. (1974a). A generative model of mathematics learning. *Journal for Research in Mathematics Education, 5,* 181-197.

Wittrock, N. C. (1974b). Learning as a generative process. *Educational Psychologist, 11,* 87-95.

Wittrock, M. C. (1978). Developmental processes in learning from instruction. *Journal of Genetic Psychology, 132,* 37-54.

Wittrock, M. C. (1990). Generative processes of comprehension. *Educational Psychologist, 24,* 354-376.

Wittrock, M. C. (1991). Generative teaching of comprehension. *Elementary School Journal, 92,* 167-182.

Wittrock, M. C., & Alesandrini, K. (1990). Generation of summaries and analogies and analytic and holistic abilities. *American Educational Research Journal, 27,* 489-502.

Wittrock, M. C., Marks, C. B., & Doctorow, M. J. (1975). Reading as a generative process. *Journal of Educational Psychology, 67,* 484-489.

Wood, E., Pressley, M., & Winne, P. H. (1990). Elaborative interrogation effects on children's learning of factual content. *Journal of Educational Psychology, 82,* 741-748.

Zimmerman, B., & Campillo, M. (2003). Motivating self-regulated problem solvers. In J. E. Davidson & R. J. Sternberg (Eds.), *The psychology of problem solving* (pp. 233-290). New York: Cambridge University Press.

·14·

CHANGING KNOWLEDGE AND BELIEFS

P. Karen Murphy
The Pennsylvania State University

Lucia Mason
University of Padua, Italy

One of the primary foci of formal schooling is the facilitation of student learning of information that underlies core academic domains (e.g., mathematics, history, or science). Much of the learning that takes place in classrooms can be described as assimilation (Piaget, 1929) or accretion (Rumelhart & Norman, 1981). In both assimilation and accretion, students integrate new knowledge into their existing conceptual framework. In essence, students are using their existing understandings to make sense of what they are learning. For example, a 5-year-old who has grown up with a large, gentle-natured dog would likely be predisposed to acquiring new knowledge about dogs consistent with her personal experiences (e.g., dogs are mammals).

Facilitating learning, however, can become quite difficult when it requires an adaptation or abandonment of prior understandings (i.e., accommodation). If the aforementioned 5-year-old were told by a teacher that large dogs can be vicious, she would likely have difficulty believing such a proposition, and it is unlikely that she would abandon her beliefs based on one conflicting opinion. However, if all of the young girl's friends were afraid of large dogs and shared stories about large mean dogs, then there exists the potential that our 5-year-old would modify her ideas about large dogs (Rokeach, 1968). The young girl might accommodate the proposition that large dogs are vicious by restructuring her mental model of dogs. In doing so, she would likely attempt to diminish the cognitive dissonance between her new understand-

ing and her perception of her own large, gentle-natured dog (Festinger, 1957). To do so, the young girl might take on the belief that large dogs are generally vicious with the notable exception of her own dog.

Situations paralleling the aforementioned examples are pervasive in schools. Students are frequently exposed to and required to remember unfamiliar or incongruent information. In some cases, students choose to modify their current knowledge and beliefs about topics, and in other cases they do not. The questions of importance in this chapter are how, under what circumstances, and in what ways do individuals choose to modify what they know or believe? Although central to education and the learning process, studies of changes in what people know or believe have varied greatly, depending on whether researchers examined learning from the perspective of conceptual change or persuasion (Woods & Murphy, 2001). Despite the shared philosophical roots and the theoretical similarities among key constructs, researchers have historically focused on either conceptual change *or* persuasion. Consequently, we synthesize findings across these distinct bodies of literature to identify potential models for assessing and promoting change in educational settings.

To address this overarching purpose, the chapter is divided into four sections. In the first section, we briefly explore definitions of knowledge and beliefs synthesized from the philosophical and educational psychology literatures. We also offer our own working definitions of these constructs. By explicitly defining the constructs of knowledge and beliefs, we hope to bring some clarity to our discussion of change. In the second section, we overview change models pertaining to knowledge *or* beliefs. In so doing, we discuss psychological issues central to contemporary research traditions relative to conceptual change and persuasion. We then offer some recommendations for future research and educational practice. Finally, we close the chapter with a brief discussion of a model of belief change that draws on historical philosophical and psychological literature in which knowledge and beliefs have been characterized as reciprocally influential constructs.

EXPLORING RELATIONS AMONG KNOWLEDGE AND BELIEFS

The philosophical and psychological literatures are replete with varied definitions of knowledge and beliefs. Rather than attempt to overview or delineate the many definitions of knowledge and beliefs dating as far back as Plato, we urge readers to access the many thorough papers and reviews of these constructs in both philosophical (Scheffler, 1965) and psychological outlets (e.g., Alexander & Dochy, 1995). In particular, we wish to draw readers to a recent analysis of definitional variations from philosophy, science education, and psychology conducted by Southerland, Sinatra, and Mathews (2001). In summarizing their paper, Southerland and colleagues (2001) suggested that philosophers can strongly argue in favor of the distinctions between knowledge and beliefs based on reason and warrant at a theoretical level, whereas science educators have strong convictions that their job is to alter students' knowledge based on empirical, scientific evidence. By comparison, the psychologist of education must function on the empirical level of cognitive function. As a result, psychologists have, with few exceptions (Murphy & Alexander, 2004), had difficulty empirically illustrating the differential influence of knowledge and beliefs on learning. As Southerland and colleagues (2001) state: "Distinctions between knowledge and belief, complex and confusing at the theoretical level, seem to become hopelessly blurred at the empirical level" (p. 348).

Similar to Southerland et al. (2001), what we have gleaned from these vast literatures is that most educational psychology researchers seem to avoid differentiating between knowledge and beliefs by either using the terms interchangeably or by only referring to knowledge *or* beliefs. In this way, researchers avoid the issue of the relations among these constructs. Yet some distinctions are pertinent to the present discussion. One common distinction is that knowledge is true and justified, whereas beliefs can be held without necessarily having a base in evidence (Richardson, 1996). Another major distinction seems to be whether one conceptualizes knowledge as a subset of beliefs, or beliefs as a subset of knowledge.

Nisbett and Ross (1980) considered beliefs to be a type of knowledge. They described two components of generic knowledge, including a cognitive component that was schematically organized and a belief component that involved evaluation and judgment. For example, a student might have knowledge of the central limit theorem (cognitive component) but not believe that characteristics are normally distributed across a population (belief component). Rokeach (1968), by comparison, defined knowledge as a type of belief. To Rokeach (1968), belief comprised three components: (a) a cognitive component (i.e., knowledge); (b) an affective component (e.g., judgment, evaluation, emotion); and, (c) a behavioral component when action is necessary.

Rather than rely on the definitions and conceptualizations of philosophers or psychologists, Alexander and colleagues investigated how teachers and students of varying educational levels conceptualized knowledge and beliefs (e.g., Alexander & Dochy, 1995; Alexander, Murphy, Guan, & Murphy, 1998). The respondents ranged in educational experience from seventh grade through master's-level students to professors of education, and varied in cultural background from the rural, southern United States to Singapore and the Netherlands. Despite these educational and cultural differences, the respondents in these studies consistently conceptualized knowledge as factual, externally verified, or widely accepted, whereas beliefs referred to ideas or thoughts that individuals perceived as true or wanted to be true. Unlike knowledge, beliefs also included subjective claims for which truth or validity was unimportant. In spite of these conceptual distinctions, the majority of respondents perceived of knowledge and beliefs as overlapping constructs. Simply put, respondents posited that whereas some knowledge and beliefs remain independent, many ideas are both known and believed.

In this chapter, we operate from the perspective of knowledge and beliefs as overlapping constructs. Similar to James' (1911/1996) thoughts on percepts and concepts, we argue that "Neither, taken alone, knows reality in its completeness. We need them both, as we need both our legs to walk with" (p. 52). Specifically, we use the term *knowledge* to refer to all that is accepted as true that can be externally verified and can be confirmed by others on repeated interactions with the object (i.e., factual). By comparison, we use the term *belief* to refer to all that one accepts as or wants to be true. Beliefs do not require verification and often cannot be verified (e.g., opinions). A special characteristic of beliefs is that individuals attribute a valence of importance to them, and therefore, individuals are prepared to act on beliefs and to hold to them in the face of conflicting evidence. Finally, we hold that meaningful learning is most likely to occur when an individual knows and believes in the object of his or her interest.

CONCEPTUAL CHANGE

Defining Conceptual Change

Over the past four decades, research on learning and instruction has shown that individuals construct knowledge from their everyday experiences in the physical, natural, and social world. This premise was a centerpiece of the cognitive research undertaken during the 1970s, with its focus on the role of knowledge structures and processes in thinking, reasoning, and memorizing (Bobrow & Collins, 1975). The emergence of the constructivist paradigm in psychology has continued to emphasize the active role of learners who interpret, rather than passively internalize, new information on the basis of what they already know. From those early cognitive studies mainly in the domain of physics (e.g., McCloskey, 1983) to the present (Bahar, 2003), thousands of studies have documented students' unsophisticated understandings of domain-specific concepts (Duit, 2002).

As underscored by this extensive literature, when students are presented with scientific content, they do not function as "empty vessels" (i.e., *tabula rasa*). Rather, they bring the conceptions constructed from both informal and formal (i.e., schooled) experiences into the classroom. Very often these preexisting conceptions are primitive and limited: that is, in stark contrast to the scientific knowledge taught in schools (e.g., Wood-Robinson, 1994). The term *misconceptions* has been used to refer to representations that are incorrect from the point of view of established disciplinary knowledge—notions that often interfere with subsequent learning (Pines & West, 1983).

From a constructivist perspective, however, misconceptions are "fundamental and inevitable aspects of human learning" (Alexander, 1998, p. 56). Despite nuances in meaning that differentiate them, other terms such as "naïve conceptions," "alternative conceptions," "alternative frameworks," or "intuitive knowledge" are used as synonyms for misconceptions in the literature. We use the term *misconceptions* throughout this chapter, although there is some disagreement within the literature as to its suitability as a marker for students' less sophisticated understandings. When misconceptions exist, meaningful

classroom learning requires experiences that help to restructure existing knowledge. The expression *conceptual change* is used to refer to revisions in personal mental representations; revisions that are often precipitated by purposeful educational experiences. Although some scholars use the term *beliefs* when discussing conceptual change (e.g., Hynd, 2003), they are usually referring to factual understandings about a phenomenon or event; that is, knowledge.

Despite their theoretical divergences regarding the nature and labeling of conceptual change, scholars generally agree that fundamental revisions in underdeveloped knowledge structures are needed to achieve more scientific concepts. We concur with Duit (2002) that the label *conceptual change* suggests learning pathways students can follow to move from less sophisticated to more scientific conceptions. From the constructivist perspective, learning science in and of itself sometimes appeared to be conceived as conceptual change learning, since it requires revision of knowledge for the new conceptions to be successfully integrated into the existing cognitive structures (Duit, 1999).

MODELS OF CONCEPTUAL CHANGE: TWO DISTINCT TRADITIONS

Until recently, research on conceptual change has followed two relatively independent research traditions: the science education and the cognitive-developmental traditions (Duit & Treagust, 2003; Vosniadou, 1999). Each of these traditions focused on the structure of learners' existing knowledge representations and principles to be implemented in classrooms. Such research has given rise to influential models of conceptual change.

Models of Conceptual Change in Science Education Research

Science educators were among the first to widely document that misconceptions can be very resistant to change. A number of researchers turned to philosophy and history of science in order to understand the mechanisms underlying conceptual change. For example, Posner and colleagues (Posner, Strike, Hewson, & Gertzog, 1982) drew an analogy between the Piagetian concepts of assimilation and accommodation and the epistemological concepts of normal science and scientific revolution (T. Kuhn, 1970). The incorporation of new concepts into existing conceptual structures was considered as parallel to the normal growth of scientific knowledge, which is assimilated into available frameworks without modification.

Similarly, accommodating a conceptual structure to fit the new information was conceptualized as corresponding to a paradigm change in science (i.e., scientific revolution). This happens when the anomalies and limitations of the current paradigm are so evident and irreconcilable that a new paradigm must replace it to allow the examined phenomena to be reinterpreted (Thagard, 1992). Two perspectives on the nature of intuitive knowledge and conceptual change can be identified in science education literature, one proposed by science educators and philosophers of science at Cornell University, the other by di Sessa in the domain of physics.

The Conceptual Change Model (CCM). Drawing a parallel with Piagetian theory, Posner et al. (1982) at Cornell University developed perhaps the most influential conceptual change model for the domain of science, aptly called the Conceptual Change Model (CCM). The CCM incorporates four conditions for knowledge restructuring, which reflect possible sources of resistance to change. First, there must be dissatisfaction with current conceptions. Individuals must recognize that their representations are no longer appropriate to explain the events and phenomena being examined. Second, a new conception must be intelligible. Its comprehensibility allows individuals to construct a coherent representation. Also, a new conception must appear initially plausible, from a credible source, and consistent with other personally held conceptions; otherwise, it will be rejected. Finally, a new conception must be fruitful. That is, it should suggest the possibility of being useful in accounting for many events and phenomena.

In the CCM, learning is seen as the interaction between existing and new conceptions. The key concepts of the CCM are the notions of status and conceptual ecology (Hewson, 1981; Strike & Posner, 1992). The status of a conception is high when individuals understand it well and perceive it as acceptable and useful. If a new conception conflicts with an existing conception with a high status, conceptual change does not occur. Change may occur later if the status of the current conception decreases due to dissatisfaction with the representation, or if the status of the new one increases. The notion of conceptual ecology concerns three aspects (X. Toulmin, 1992). The first is that individuals' beliefs and commitments about the nature of knowledge, reality, and truth serve as the basis for establishing what counts as a valid explanation of a phenomenon. The second aspect is that conceptual ecology is characterized by an interrelated network of concepts. The third aspect is that individuals' conception may compete for the same ecological niche. The surviving ideas will be the most powerful for individuals, and most helpful in resolving conflicts and problems.

Within the science education community, the CCM has become an important guide for implementing a constructivist pedagogy in science classrooms, aimed at stimulating and supporting learners to activate, explain, test, and revise their conceptions about the phenomena being examined (Hennessey, 2003). With this regard, cognitive conflict is a pedagogical strategy that has been shown to be as effective to foster knowledge restructuring (Guzzetti, Snyder, Glass, & Gamas, 1993). This strategy involves expressly presenting students with evidence that contradicts their held conceptions. The assumption underlying the strategy is that the presentation of anomalous data will facilitate students' knowledge restructuring. The Posner et al. model was based on the assumption that learners' alternative conceptions or misconceptions are internally coherent and consistent explanatory frameworks similar to theories (Brewer & Samarapungavan, 1991; Vosniadou, 2002), although not at the level of scientific theories.

P-prims and Coordination Classes. Within the domain of physics, diSessa (1983, 1993) challenged the CCM, arguing instead for a more fragmentary nature to novices' conceptions. Specifically, novices' conceptions are conceived in terms of unstructured collections of numerous simple, intuitive elements called *p-prims* (i.e., phenomenological primitives) derived from minimal abstractions of experience with familiar events. Some examples of p-prims, often quite context-specific in their activation, include the following: things go in the direction they are pushed, more effort begets more result, or farther implies longer duration. According to this view, learning science implies the collection and systematization of some pieces of knowledge into a larger whole. P-prims go from isolated and self-explanatory entities to become part of more complex knowledge structures.

In contrast, diSessa (2002) argued for the existence of another form of mental entity, coordination classes. *Coordination classes* are large, complex systems consisting of many parts requiring a high degree of coordination across different contexts. P-prims and coordination classes are conceived in terms of knowledge types that play different roles in conceptual change and account for conceptual change phenomena. P-prims give an account of intuitive predictions and judgments of plausibility, whereas coordination classes offer a model of a whole concept. Development of a coordination class implies that pieces of knowledge, along with inferences, are put in place, integrated, and aligned to serve the learner in a range of varied contexts.

Models of Conceptual Change in Cognitive-Developmental Research

In developmental psychology, research on conceptual change is considered domain specific. Unlike Piaget, who focused on global restructuring of the logical structures of thought, the first scholar to talk about "conceptual change in childhood" took a domain-specific perspective (Carey, 1985). She argued that developmental change is the alteration of conceptual structures regarding a domain. These conceptual structures are theory-like, not fragmented or "in pieces," as argued by diSessa (1983), so they constitute, for instance, a child's naïve (or folk) biology, naïve psychology, or naïve physics. The theory-like nature of children's naïve knowledge means that it is an organized and coherent set of representations, although not necessarily aligned with scientifically held theories. Through domain-specific restructuring, the naïve theories become accepted theories as a result of children's increased knowledge of a domain.

Carey (1985) distinguished among *accretion*, weak restructuring, and radical restructuring. *Accretion* is the mere enrichment of knowledge in the cognitive structures, corresponding to the Piagetian mechanism of assimilation. The Piagetian mechanism of accommodation corresponds with both restructurings, since they imply a change in the conceptual structures of a domain. *Weak restructuring* occurs when more relations between concepts are created without changing their fundamental properties. Through the new relations, concepts can be included in more complex structures that allow new problems to be solved. *Radical restructuring* requires a substantial change in the core set of concepts, their relationships, and the range of phenomena to be explained. The shifts from impetus theory to the Newtonian theory and from the Ptolemaic to the Copernican theory are examples of radical restructuring in the history of science.

Frameworks Theories, Specific Theories, and Mental Models. The model of conceptual change proposed by Vosniadou (1994), after systematic research in the domains of elementary astronomy and mechanics, relies on the assumption that concepts are embedded in theories and that there are constraints about the behavior of physical objects that are appreciated even by infants (Spelke, 1991). This model of conceptual change distinguishes between mental models, beliefs, specific theories, and framework theories.

In problem solving situations, individuals generate *mental models* as representations with the structure of domain-specific concepts. Through mental models,

causal explanations of physical phenomena, as well as predictions, are provided. Mental models are based on *beliefs* that are generated by observation or information given in the cultural context. These beliefs constitute *specific theories* that are made up of a set of interrelated propositions describing the properties and behavior of physical objects. Specific theories are constrained by *framework theories*, of which individuals are not aware. The framework theories are made up of epistemological presuppositions about the nature of knowledge and ontological presuppositions regarding the existing entities.

To give an example of the conceptual structure that underlies a mental model, we refer to the "internal force" mental model (Vosniadou & Ioannides, 1998). This mental model is a representation of force as a property of heavy or large physical objects. The assumed belief is that some physical objects have weight, which is based on observations that some objects can push/pull other objects and cause them to change, while others do not. This information, derived from observations, constitutes a specific theory about the properties and behavior of physical objects related to force. The specific theory, in turn, is constrained by an underlying framework theory based on epistemological and ontological assumptions. Assumptions about knowledge refer to the need to explain the movement of inanimate objects, and these explanations should be causal. Assumptions about existing entities in the world refer to the distinction between animate and inanimate physical objects, which have properties, among them the property of having force.

According to Vosniadou and Brewer (1992, 1994), misconceptions or synthetic models are generated when students try to incorporate new information taught in school into their conceptual structures without changing the framework theories (i.e., making no changes at the level of epistemological and ontological assumptions). An example taken from the domain of astronomy can illustrate why radical knowledge restructuring is difficult to achieve. Children's initial mental model of the Earth is that of a flat, supported, and stable physical object, with the sky and sun located above. The synthetic mental model of the dual Earth (i.e., the flat Earth in which we live and the round Earth up in the sky that astronauts can see) is generated when children "reconcile" the flat and the spherical models of the Earth without abandoning any presupposition of their framework theory underlying the flat model. Therefore, conceptual change, as radical knowledge restructuring, requires a change in underlying beliefs (specific theories) and presuppositions (framework theories).

Since beliefs and presuppositions are derived from experience and years of confirmation, they can be particularly resistant to change. This makes the process of radical knowledge restructuring long and slow. However, Berti (1999), who studied conceptual change in the economic domain following Vosniadou's model, has argued that when students possess the necessary background knowledge and their prior conceptions are not entrenched, conceptual change may occur over a relatively shorter time.

Ontological Categories. In cognitive psychology, Chi (1992; Chi, Slotta, & de Leeuw, 1994) proposed a model that distinguishes between conceptual changes occurring *within* and *across* ontological categories. Ontological categories are conceived as a few, basic categories of the world that adults perceive as ontologically and psychologically distinct. The major ontological categories or trees are "matter" (e.g., natural kinds and artifacts), "processes" (e.g., events, constrained-based interactions) and "mental states" (e.g., emotional, intentional). Conceptual change within the same ontological category is less difficult to achieve than conceptual change across ontological categories, since the concepts can move between parallel ontological categories within a mental tree (e.g., differentiating parallel categories of living things such as plants and animals). New properties can be then added or some of them made more salient without changing their basic meaning. In contrast, conceptual change *across* ontological categories is difficult to achieve because it requires reassignment to a different category or tree.

According to this model, the misconceptions about force, heat, light, and electrical current identified in the literature are due to incorrectly assigning these concepts to the category of matter, which implies assigning to them the properties of material substances (Reiner, Chi, & Resnick, 1988). For instance, if students conceive of electricity like gas or water, they may believe that cutting an electric wire would cause electricity to leak into the room. To acquire the scientific representation of this physics concept, it must be reassigned to the correct ontological category (i.e., process). The shift from a matter-based conception to a process-based conception is a revolution within individuals' conceptual structures.

ALTERNATIVE MODELS OF CONCEPTUAL CHANGE

The two traditions of research on conceptual change contributed remarkably to our understanding of the structure of knowledge representations and the ways in which instruction can be more effective to engender their revision. However, until the early 1990s, neither tradition attended to the role of affect in cognitive change. In 1993, Pintrich, Marx, and Boyle published a highly cited article

highlighting the need to go "beyond cold conceptual change" and harness the power of affective, motivational, and contextual factors in knowledge revision. Based on the shortcomings of prior work, the two models of conceptual change proposed after that article attempted to explain the relations among a multitude of cognitive and affective factors (e.g., knowledge, beliefs, motivation, strategic processing) and text factors (e.g., text difficulty or nature of the arguments). Both are dual-process models (Stanovich, 2004) in that the cognitive architecture assumed in these models is automatic or algorithmic (i.e., low cognitive engagement), and concomitantly, intentional (i.e., high cognitive engagement). Moreover, these more recent models can offer insights into how knowledge and beliefs work together or separately to influence change during the learning process.

Cognitive Reconstruction of Knowledge Model or CRKM. Trying to take into account both cognitive and affective components, Dole and Sinatra (1998; Dole & Sinatra, 1998) have proposed a cognitive reconstruction of knowledge model (CRKM) based on issues derived from cognitive and social psychological research. Whereas developmental and cognitive psychologists have considered the process of knowledge restructuring in purely rational or cognitive terms, social psychologists have also examined affective factors underlying belief and attitude change. The Dole and Sinatra model posits that both deep cognitive information processing and affective investment are necessary for knowledge revision. Moreover, in the CRKM affect is considered to be a multidimensional construct subsuming components such as interest in the topic, investment in the outcome, and personal traits that sustain motivation (e.g., the need to be involved in effortful thinking, evaluation of argument, and analyses of problems and solutions).

When applied to changes in conceptions about phenomena of the physical world, the dual-process model predicts that if students are motivated to process information because of their interest in the topic, personal needs, or characteristics, they are able to understand the new material and are more likely to revise their knowledge representations. Enduring conceptual change is likely to occur only if individuals engage in deep metacognitive processing, elaborative strategies, and substantive reflection. Of course, the new knowledge to be acquired must be comprehensible and the learner must have sufficient background knowledge and cognitive ability to process the material. According to this model, sources of resistance to knowledge restructuring may be found in the content, which may be incomprehensible or too unfamiliar, and in the learner, who may have little interest in the topic. Students can generate a temporary change in conceptions if the social context of a group or classroom pressures them to see a phenomenon in a different way, or if reading a text that is particularly attractive because of irrelevant detail. When students' cognitive engagement is low, they will likely return to the original representations that were never entirely given up (Dole & Sinatra, 1998). Thus, intentionality to change understandings is fundamental.

Cognitive-affective Model of Conceptual Change or CAMCC. To respond to Pintrich, Marx & Boyle's (1993) view, Gregoire (2003) has proposed a dual-process model of teacher conceptual change that posits an explanation of why teachers' subject-matter beliefs are resistant to change. This model, which is reviewed extensively in the teacher belief chapter of this volume (see Woolfolk Hoy, Davis, & Pape, this volume) is intended to be "truly a *hot* model of conceptual change" (original emphasis, p. 163) because it includes more motivational factors than the CRKM, such as teachers' fears and confidence levels, which affect receptiveness to a given message. Although the model does not contribute to the conceptual clarification of the constructs, it provides useful insights into the mechanisms that influence conceptual change.

For example, the model combines the idea that automatic evaluation has a role in attitude change with the idea that cognitive processing mediates change and, in turn, motivation and ability affect cognitive processing. The model also takes into account individuals' goals and prior beliefs. As in Dole and Sinatra's (1998) model, long-lasting knowledge change cannot take place if teachers are not involved in systematic processing. However, this does not mean that systematic processing guarantees change (Gregoire, 2003). Other factors may also affect the process, such as teachers' prior knowledge and experiences; the message's characteristics, such as its intelligibility, plausibility, and fruitfulness; and whether the message processing is biased.

A Synthesis: Toward an Integrated Approach. These two models of conceptual change help us understand that such change is a process in which the interaction between emotions, appraisals, motivational aspects, and cognition can be both facilitative and inhibitory. Recent research, indeed, includes affect and motivation, beside cognition, in the study of knowledge revision, showing that it moved "beyond cold conceptual change" (Limón & Mason, 2002; Schnotz, Vosniaodu, & Carretero, 1999; Sinatra & Pintrich, 2003). In this regard, the notion of *intentionality* as a general mediator between "internal" and "external" factors implied in knowledge representations change (Vosniadou, 1999) is a further articulation of the investigation in the field. By referring to Bereiter and

Scardamalia's (1989) construct of intentional learning, Sinatra and Pintrich (2003) argued that learners should be not only active but also intentional in deliberately pursuing the goal of knowledge revision. As indicated by contemporary dual-process models, although changes can occur by chance, serendipity, or without awareness, only high levels of cognitive, metacognitive, and motivational engagement lead to deeper and longer lasting change. In addition to agency, metaconceptual awareness, volitional control, and self-regulation, intentionality in conceptual change suggests that learners initiate an activity directed toward the goal of changing their understandings. They pursue this goal by actively controlling and regulating their cognition, motivation, and affect.

PERSUASION

Defining Persuasion

A persuasive text has been described as any message—verbal or text—that is intended to shape, reinforce, or change the responses of another (Miller, 1980). This definition stresses the importance of changes in individuals' responses, as opposed to behavioral changes, and acknowledges variations in the outcome goals of persuasive messages. Among the outcome goals of persuasive activities are response shaping, response reinforcing, and response change (Miller, 1980). Response shaping occurs when the source (e.g., text) tries to form a belief where none exist and where resistance is not anticipated. Such response shaping takes place when one is exposed to new objects, people, or issues that require evaluation. Miller (1980) noted that such evaluations often take place through social learning (Bandura, 1977).

As opposed to reshaping, in response reinforcing the goal is to make beliefs less susceptible to change and strengthen previously held beliefs. A common example of this type of reinforcement would be a preacher delivering a sermon to the faithful. The most difficult outcome of persuasion deals with response change. This form of change pertains to the modification, alteration, or extreme transformation of previously held beliefs. This response is the one most frequently studied in persuasion research (Stiff, 1994). We see these varying goals mirrored in recognized models of persuasion.

Prominent Models

Learning Theory Approach or LTA. In the 1950s, programs of research dedicated to the investigation of communication, particularly persuasive communication, burgeoned. The prominent persuasive communication theory was the Learning Theory Approach (Hovland, Janis, & Kelley, 1953), which was based on the assumption that the effects of persuasion are dependent on the extent to which the message is attended to, comprehended, and accepted. Moreover, the LTA was guided by explicit conceptual definitions and the behaviorist notion that the correct or proper stimulus would prompt the desired response, which could only be maintained through schedules of reinforcement (Koballa, 1992). Basically, the relatively passive and defenseless receiver was injected with a particular message and the source of that message was seen as the symbolizing agent (e.g., Bettinghaus, 1968).

The LTA was focused on addressing Lasswell's (1948) five-part statement (i.e., *who* says *what, when*, to *whom*, and with *what effect*). The main stimulus variables of interest were (a) the source of the message; (b) the message (i.e., stimuli); (c) the audience; and (d) the responses made by the audience. Hovland et al. (1953) drew conclusions about these variables that remain the foundation of contemporary persuasion theories (e.g., Petty & Cacioppo, 1986). For instance, Hovland et al. (1953) found that the degree to which individuals responded positively to a persuasive message was heavily dependent on how credible they judged the communicator to be (i.e., degree of expertise and trustworthiness). "An individual is likely to feel that persons with status, values, interests, and needs similar to his own see things as he does and judges them from the same point of view" (p. 22).

Although few investigations by Hovland et al. (1953) manipulated the content of the message, they believed that in order to change beliefs the message had to pique the emotions of the receiver. That is, the content of effective persuasive communications had to serve as a motivating source for the receiver. Although it was recognized that rational appeals could be influential in belief change, Hovland et al. (1953) theorized that emotional appeals (e.g., threats of fear or social exile) were more convincing. It was also assumed that when audience members belonged to a particular group and valued their membership, the likelihood of opinion change toward a view that countered group norms would be greatly diminished.

Support for this perspective was found in the work of Kelley and colleagues (1952; Kelley & Volkart, 1952). For instance, Kelley (1952) found that Catholic college students were far more likely to resist persuasion toward anti-Catholic ideas than were college students from other religious groups. In addition, Kelley found that the more strongly Catholic students rated their beliefs, the more resistant they were to change. Hovland et al. (1953) also posited that the degree to which an individual would be persuaded would be affected by individual differences.

That is, just as there are between-group differences, there are also within-group differences that affect persuasion. Among those individual characteristics are variations in ability (e.g., capacity for comprehending the message of the communicator) and motive (e.g., strong desire to ignore the consequences alluded to in a message). Although Hovland et al. (1953) acknowledged that individuals differ with regard to some learner characteristics, they did not consider the intervening role of cognitive processing. The behavioral paradigm employed by Hovland and his colleagues produced some of the most salient and influential findings in the social psychology literature on persuasion. However, the dawn of the cognitive revolution in the 1960s led the way for the consideration of the thoughts of the receiver (e.g., Greenwald, 1968).

Theory of Reasoned Action. Among the models emerging during the late 1960s this time was the Theory of Reasoned Action (Fishbein & Ajzen, 1975) and its later corollary, the Theory of Planned Behavior (Ajzen, 1985). The Theory of Reasoned Action was based on Fishbein's (1967) notion that the best predictor of behavior (B) was an individual's intention (I) to perform a particular behavior. Essentially, Fishbein and Ajzen (1975) proposed that attitude change could be predicted using a series of linear equations. "Specifically, the model holds that a behavioral intention (I) is a function (f) of the importance (W_1) of an individual's attitude (A) plus the importance (W_2) of the subjective norms (SN)" (Stiff, 1994, p. 52). In this model, attitude referred to the sum of one's beliefs toward performing a particular behavior and the evaluations that those beliefs receive. The subjective norm was the sum of normative beliefs (b_i) and one's motivation to comply (m) with those beliefs. In this model, normative beliefs were differentiated from individual beliefs in that normative beliefs were the beliefs held by the reference group concerning the consequences of performing the behavior. Concomitantly, motivation referred to the probability that a person would accept influence from the reference group. Such formulae allowed for greater precision in the measurement of attitude change (Shrigley & Koballa, 1992).

Elaboration Likelihood Model or ELM. The ELM attempted to build on Greenwald's (1968) model by proposing two routes by which persuasive messages are cognitively processed—a dual process model. The central route emphasized careful processing and analysis of the information contained in the message (Petty & Cacioppo, 1986). Elaboration links any incoming arguments to issue-relevant information previously encoded within a recipients' memory. Moreover, the degree to which the message was elaborated determined the extent to which one was persuaded (Petty & Cacioppo, 1986). However, these researchers posited that the elaboration process was mediated by the receiver's motivation and ability to process. In contrast, the peripheral route involved more automatic or skillful processing. Individuals easily used contextual cues (e.g., communicator credibility) or heuristic rules (e.g., length of the article) to make decisions regarding the persuasiveness of a message. "Peripheral cues render a primary role in attitude change. Unable to contemplate deeply on all of life's issues, humankind justifiably seeks quick and simple rules for restyling attitudes and subsequent behavior" (Shrigley & Koballa, 1992, p. 35). Commonplace examples include children accepting the information they are taught in school because they perceive the teacher to be an authority, or individuals voting solely on the basis of a political party affiliation. It is important to note that although the peripheral route usually fosters short-lived belief change, the central route instills enduring belief alterations (Stiff, 1994). The ELM is very similar to the heuristic processing model (Chaiken, 1987).

Social Exchange. The Social Exchange Theory emphasized the interchange between the message source and the message recipient (Roloff, 1981). Persuasion was assumed to involve a compromise between the source and receiver in order to reach an agreement regarding the costs or benefits associated with a desired modification or alteration of beliefs (Blau, 1964). As a case in point, consider a teacher who wants her students to gain positive feelings about their homework. She might begin by stating that they must collect 16 insects for homework. As a result, the students moan and generally complain about the extensiveness of their homework. Following their complaints, the teacher might respond by decreasing the number of insects to eight. Students are quite overjoyed, and the teacher has also accomplished her goal. Cialdini (1984) has termed this form of interchange the reject-then-retreat strategy. One limitation of the strategy is that it requires the source to be somewhat deceptive when initiating the discussion. Nonetheless, the idea of social exchange possesses certain qualities that the aforementioned models lack. In particular, this model suggested that there is a dynamic interchange between source and receiver that extends beyond simplistic information processing.

ALTERNATIVE MODELS OF BELIEF CHANGE

Although the CRKM and the CAMCC address affect and intentionality, both models do so from the perspective of conceptual change or with the aim of changing students' or teachers' knowledge. Murphy (1998) has proposed a model of change that incorporates both cognitive and affective factors as independent variables and knowledge and beliefs as dependent variables, but uses research from social psychology as the basis of her theoretical framework. Murphy's model is based on the assumption that change is a multidimensional process that is influenced by individual and intraindividual differences in the learner and how they interact with varied texts (Murphy, 2001a). The model proposed has been submitted to empirical testing (e.g., Murphy, 2001b; Murphy & Alexander, 2004; Murphy, Long, Holleran, & Esterly, 2003) using compelling texts covering an array of subjects, including AIDS, human development, V-chip technology, school integration, same-sex marriages, and doctor-assisted suicide. Further, those compelling texts came from everyday sources such as newspaper editorials and magazine articles, and have been read as both traditional print media and online hypertext media. In essence, the materials were selected and presented as they would have been encountered by students in their everyday lives.

This alternative view of the change process addresses several of the shortcomings of the earlier change research. First, Murphy's (1998) model illustrates how learner and text factors interact to influence change by modeling the direct and indirect influences of each variable (e.g., knowledge, belief, or comprehensibility) in the process. Second, the model is topic specific and detailed about the nature of the constructs being modeled. Murphy suggested that learner variables including perceived topic knowledge, demonstrated topic knowledge, topic beliefs, and topic interest interact *with* textual characteristics, such as the interestingness of the text, the strength of the arguments, the comprehensibility of the text, and the persuasiveness of the text to influence knowledge and belief change.

Several relations among these variables have remained consistent across investigations. For instance, high levels of topic knowledge and interest have predicted low levels of topic beliefs before and after reading compelling texts. By contrast, high to moderate belief levels at prereading have been associated with low to moderate levels of knowledge and interest at prereading and postreading. Students with strong topic beliefs seemed not to acquire much knowledge or interest due to reading. These results suggest that students with moderate knowledge and interest appear primed for belief change. In essence, too much topic-specific knowledge can be an impediment to changes in beliefs. Finally, perceptions of knowledge may contribute significantly more to the persuasion process than actual knowledge. Such outcomes illustrate the intricacies of the persuasion process and the complex interplay of individual difference factors that shape that process.

PROMOTING CHANGE: LEARNER, TEXT, AND CONTEXT

Even in the face of effective instruction, revision of alternative conceptions is not easy. It is an effortful, intentional process that requires metacognitive awareness and a concomitant reason to exert the requisite energy. As many have suggested, students often fail to perceive a meaningful conflict or superficially combine local inconsistencies without reaching the fundamental changes that are necessary (Limón, 2001; Mason, 2000, 2001b). In the early 1990s, Chinn and Brewer (1993) identified seven possible responses to discrepant evidence in knowledge acquisition. Those responses included ignoring the anomalous data; rejecting the data or evidence; excluding the anomalous data from interpretation; holding the data in abeyance as if to evaluate it later; reinterpreting the data to fit within one's existing frame; making a peripheral change in one's existing theory; or, actually changing one's conception. In their revised taxonomy, Chinn and Brewer (1998) added an eighth response, uncertainty. In the uncertain response category, individuals are not sure whether the anomalous data are valid and believable. In this section, we overview factors related to characteristics of the learner, text, and instructional context that influence students' responses to information.

Learner

Although there are potentially innumerable learner characteristics influencing the change process, we focus on learner knowledge, metacognition, motivation, and beliefs. These factors have been found to affect text or message comprehension, and consequently, the process of knowledge and belief change (e.g., Alexander & Jetton, 1996; Manfredo & Bright, 1991).

Knowledge. One of the most consistent findings during the past three decades of text comprehension research is that prior knowledge plays a significant role in what students understand and recall from text (e.g. Alexander & Murphy, 1999; Langer, 1980). Research on conceptual change has shown the negative effects of prior knowledge. Misconceptions about a topic can be a source of resistance to change in proportion to the degree to which they are based on an entrenched theory (Chinn & Brewer, 1993; Vosniadou, 1994). The more individuals' topic knowledge is embedded in a powerful explanatory framework, the more it is resistant to revision as an effect of an instructional intervention. Further, when individuals' prior knowledge is limited, they may have difficulty

identifying contradictions between their current conceptions and scientific ones. As a consequence, individuals do not recognize the need for change in their knowledge structures (Limón, 2003).

On the other hand, research on persuasion has shown that strong arguments, those with causal explanations, are more persuasive than weak ones, especially among readers with low knowledge (Johnson, 1994; Wood, 1982). Also, individuals with high knowledge are more critical processors of arguments and are more resistant to persuasion (e.g., Johnson, 1994; Kardash & Scholes, 1995; Showers, 1995). For example, Manfredo and Bright (1991) examined the persuasiveness of informational techniques used in recreation management. Their study revealed that informational texts were more successful in influencing readers with relatively low prior knowledge. Further, participants who self-reported high knowledge generated more thoughts and were high in the acquisition of new beliefs, yet reported no significant changes in previously held beliefs. Therefore, it is essential to take into account the quantity and quality of prior knowledge in order to know what, and to what extent, preexisting information facilitates or impedes change processes.

Metacognitive Awareness. One aspect of metacognition that is pertinent to the change process is one's knowledge about their knowledge and thought processes. In their investigations into the development of scientific thinking skills, Kuhn, Amsel, and O'Loughlin (1988) pointed out that the most essential and general skills are those enabling deliberate differentiation and coordination of theory and evidence. That is, students must be able to think *about* conceptions rather than merely thinking *with* those conceptions. Metaconceptual awareness allows students to be aware of the presuppositions underlying their conceptions and the need to change them. Students are often not aware of what they know and believe, or the hypothetical nature of their knowledge and beliefs (Vosniadou, 2003).

Students should be provided with situations that help them understand that their conceptions are not necessarily facts but rather personal constructions about how the world functions, which can be falsified or verified. Students need to become aware that when they interpret an event, they are holding a personal theory. Although their current theory may not offer an adequate explanation of evidence, another theory may possess the requisite explanatory power. Science educators have developed projects to advance metacognitive awareness, such as the Project for Enhancing Effective Learning (PEEL; White & Gunstone, 1989) and the META project (Metacognitive Enhancing Teaching Activities; Hennessey, 2003). In the findings of two longitudinal studies on the implementation of META, Hennessey (2003) documented the intentional engagement of her students in more and more sophisticated reflections of their own ideas, an essential step toward conceptual change. The high-level reflections could include, for instance, drawing inferences regarding one's unobservable constructs made public by verbal discourse, considering the implications or limitations of personal knowledge claims, referring to components of one's conceptual ecology, and making comments on the status of one's conceptions. Promoting metaconceptual awareness seems to foster knowledge revision.

Motivation and Affect. Research on motivation and subsequent change of knowledge and beliefs is still rather scarce. The very limited data available indicate that a goal orientation focused on learning and understanding (mastery goal) leads to a greater conceptual progress. Lee and Anderson (1993) showed that mastery-oriented sixth graders were more advanced in their understanding of the kinetic molecular theory. The positive effects of mastery goals on intentional conceptual change about Newtonian physics have also been reported by Linnenbrink and Pintrich (2002), who carried out two studies on the relationship between undergraduate students' goal orientation and knowledge restructuring. The first study revealed that mastery goals were particularly beneficial for students who had low prior knowledge. In the second study, two factors (i.e., decrease in negative affect and an increase in elaborative strategy use) mediated the positive relation between mastery goals and an improved understanding of the physics concepts. Mastery goals were therefore found to be directly related to the development of conceptual understanding, as well as indirectly related through affective and cognitive mediators.

A few studies have also documented the effects of another motivational variable, interest, on conceptual change and persuasion. Venville and Treagust (1998) reported some contradictory evidence in a study about high school students' understanding of genetics. Some students who said they were interested in the subject reached high levels of conceptual change, but there were also a number of highly interested students who produced little knowledge restructuring. However, the authors noted that their high interest regarded human heredity and not the microscopic aspects of genetics being studied. Similarly, Murphy and Alexander (2004) found that students high in topic interest were less likely to alter their beliefs after reading. These researchers attributed the lack of change to the high correlation between knowledge and interest, and the fact that individuals high in knowledge are often resistant to change. Murphy and Alexander's (2004) contentions were supported by findings reported by Andre and Windschitl

(2003). In studying college students' learning about electricity, they found that conceptual change was influenced by interest. Both direct and indirect effects of personal interest on knowledge revision were found. The direct effect emerged after controlling two other variables, prior knowledge, and prior experience with electric circuits. The indirect effect revealed that interested students had also had more experience with the topic. This experience, associated with increased prior knowledge, predicted students' conceptual understanding at posttest. These data also revealed that personal interest may not always be beneficial to conceptual change. Instead, interest could make it more difficult to abandon prior conceptions on the topic, as pointed out by Dole and Sinatra (1998). If interest is related to greater experience that, in turn, increases prior knowledge, more preexisting knowledge would mean more resistance to change.

As mentioned, the effects of interest or personal relevance have also been investigated within persuasion research. For instance, the degree to which readers are interested in the text has been found to be an important determinant of persuasion (Chambliss & Garner, 1996; Dole & Sinatra, 1994; Petty & Cacioppo, 1986). Petty and Cacioppo (1986) found a direct relation between the relevance of the text content to the individual and the extent to which individuals elaborate, process, and recall information. Similarly, Kardash and Scholes (1995) found that undergraduates who rated a text on AIDS transmission as "very interesting" were more likely to alter their beliefs in favor of the text message. In contrast, Johnson (1994) found that individuals with high personally relevant interest were more resistant to change, and that this high personally relevant interest interacted negatively with processing.

To better understand the conflicting findings, Murphy, Holleran, Long, and Esterly (in press) conducted a study in which they tested the relative influence of four motivational constructs (i.e., need for cognition, personal relevance, topic interest, and text interestingness) in persuasion. They found that after controlling for prior beliefs and prior knowledge, the only significant predictor of belief change was students' need for cognition (Cacioppo & Petty, 1982), or the desire to effortfully process and elaborate upon problems and understandings.

Topic-Specific Beliefs. There is evidence of the influence of preexisting beliefs, such as personal positions or orientations toward a topic, on persuasion as an effect of reading a text. As Chambliss (1995) asserted, "Well-crafted persuasive text is structured to counter current beliefs of a typical reader as well as to present new ones" (p. 294). A number of studies (e.g., Allen, 1991; Kardash & Scholes, 1995; Slusher & Anderson, 1996) suggest that when individuals are presented with causal explanations concerning people, objects, or events, they are more likely to change or alter their beliefs about them. For instance, Kardash and Scholes (1995) examined how people's preexisting beliefs about AIDS transmission interacted with repeated readings of a persuasive message (i.e., one-sided) designed to influence the nature of the message encoded, the type of information recorded, and self-reported belief change. The results revealed that the causal arguments were successful in modifying students' beliefs. In fact, students whose preexisting beliefs were different from those contained in the text showed the greatest belief changes. However, participants whose beliefs were consistent with the information in the text remembered more causal explanations, as well as significantly more tangential information.

Using pretest and posttest belief listings to measure positions about a topic, Wood and colleagues (e.g., Beik, Wood, Chaiken, & Nations, 1992; Wood & Kallgren, 1988) have shown that readers who retrieve more beliefs also generate more message-relevant thoughts in response to the persuasive message than readers who retrieve fewer beliefs. Further, strong arguments are more likely than weak arguments to persuade high-retrieval readers than low-retrieval readers. Finally, regardless of argument strength, high-retrieval readers are more resistant to persuasion than low.

Johnson, Lin, Symons, Campbell, and Ekstein (1995) expanded this line of research by exploring how persuasion is related to the structural character of attitudes, including the number of beliefs, their quality, and their supportiveness. The results revealed that readers who recorded more belief statements tended to be more persuaded by strong arguments. Those with low belief retrieval were relatively unaffected by argument quality. In addition, high-retrieval participants were more persuaded than low-retrieval individuals regardless of individuals' stances. In essence, belief retrieval enhanced persuasion even when beliefs did not resonate with the message. When beliefs were initially neutral, however, the level of belief retrieval did not affect persuasion. In addition, high-belief-retrieval participants were better able to recall passage information.

Epistemic Beliefs. Epistemic beliefs are representations about the nature, organization, and sources of knowledge, its truth value and justification criteria of assertions (Hofer & Pintrich, 1997, 2002). In investigating the role of epistemic beliefs in the change process, Qian and Alvermann (1995) found that students with less sophisticated beliefs (i.e., knowledge as simple, absolute, and certain) were less likely to abandon their naïve conceptions of motion after reading a refutational text on New-

tonian theory. In contrast, students with more advanced beliefs (i.e., knowledge as complex, tentative, and continuously evolving) generated more changes in their conceptual structures. Mason (2000, 2003) documented that students who believed strongly in the changing nature of knowledge were more likely to accept evidence conflicting with prior conceptions and alter them. Mason and Boscolo (2004) also found that epistemic understanding influenced students' topic-specific belief change. Moreover, Southerland and Sinatra (2003) revealed that epistemic beliefs, as well as cognitive dispositions (e.g., engagement in effortful and open-minded thinking), were related to the understanding and acceptance of human evolution. In each of these studies, advanced beliefs about knowledge and knowing were a resource in the process of knowledge restructuring.

Text

We know that text is a primary source of information in formal education (Garner & Hansis, 1994). A large part of the new information to be learned is conveyed through expository texts. Students are required to change their conceptions or positions about a topic by learning from texts that can differ in several respects.

Characteristics. It can easily be speculated that if an instructional text is comprehensible, clear, and useful, it should facilitate the acquisition of the new knowledge it provides. Similarly, if a persuasive text offers an intelligible and credible message, which is perceived as unbiased and originating from an authoritative source, it should facilitate the acceptance of the message. A study by Garner and Hansis (1994) illustrated the importance of the perceived source of the communication. Seven different fliers (i.e., "street texts"), which shared a similar structure, designed to inform readers of some social issues (e.g., civil rights or a clothing sale) and persuade them to take action relative to those issues (e.g., attend a rally or buy clothes at the local flea market), were read by graduate students. Students described whom they perceived as the distributor of each flier and what their action would be in response to the text (i.e., throw it away, keep it for reexamination, or act immediately). When the likely distributor of a message was judged in an extremely negative way, the readers said that they would throw the flier away.

Structure and Content. Persuasion researchers have clearly indicated that the text must provide a comprehensible and credible proof or argument. Persuasion research has been substantially enhanced by the work of

S. Toulmin, a philosopher and logician. S. Toulmin (1958) proposed that rational arguments share a three-part structure (i.e., a claim, evidence, and a warrant). The claim is an assertion meant to elicit readers' attention or beliefs. Usually this claim is the position that the source is advocating. The claim, however, can also be implied by reasoning through examination of the supporting evidence (i.e., data offered to support the claim). Supporting data can include factual data originating from a source other than the speaker or author, objects or graphics, and opinions supporting a claim (McCroskey, 1969). The warrant is a propositional statement that connects the evidence to the claim. Although the warrant may be implicit or explicit, it always links the claim to the evidence.

From research on both persuasion and conceptual change there is evidence that the content of a text is important, as are its arguments. Anderson (1983) found that individuals reading vivid concrete data were persuaded more than those reading abstract data. Moreover, arguments containing causal explanations have also been referred to as strong arguments, whereas noncausal explanations have been referred to as weak arguments (e.g., Johnson, 1994; Kardash & Scholes, 1995; Petty & Cacioppo, 1986). Two broad categories of rational arguments have been discussed in the literature on persuasion. A one-sided message is one that contains only arguments that support the claim. By contrast, two-sided texts that provide arguments supporting the claim, as well as viewpoints that oppose the claim (Stiff, 1994), are nonrefutational texts in that they acknowledge, but do not refute, opposing arguments. Two-sided messages that not only recognize opposing viewpoints, but also refute one of them, are refutational texts.

Extensive research has shown that two-sided, refutational messages were more persuasive than the other two forms (Allen et al., 1990). Further, one-sided messages proved more persuasive than two-sided, nonrefutational texts. Moreover, participants who read the two-sided, refutational texts also judged the source of the message to be more credible, followed by those who read one-sided texts, and the two-sided, nonrefutational texts, respectively. A subsequent meta-analysis (Allen, 1991) confirmed the prior findings (Allen et al., 1990).

Research at the intersection between science education and reading education has also documented that refutational texts may facilitate conceptual change (e.g. Alvermann & Hague, 1989). Unlike the text in a traditional textbook, a refutational text directly states alternative conceptions about a topic, refutes them, and presents the scientific conceptions as viable alternatives. Hynd (2003) reviewed literature on refutational texts written to promote conceptual change (e.g., Alvermann, Hynd, & Qian, 1995; Hynd, Aleverman, & Qian, 1997). This type of text not only is more conducive to revising nonscientific knowledge, but also is preferred by students. When confronted with information that explicitly contradicts their existing conceptions, which are activated and challenged, students are stimulated to refine their metaconceptual awareness and are supported in engaging in deep knowledge processing by deliberately exerting cognitive effort to reach a higher level of conceptual understanding.

Interaction Between Learner and Text: Text Processing

What is evident in both conceptual change and persuasion research is that the knowledge and beliefs that learners possess play a powerful role in the change process. For example, current persuasion research suggests that higher knowledge is closely related to biased processing. Petty and Cacioppo (1986) determined that individuals with increased knowledge rely on their prior knowledge, rather than attending to arguments contained in the text. This issue highlights the interconnected nature of knowledge and beliefs in text processing, and the potential for prior knowledge to bias processing. Biased processing may also take place if the content of the persuasive text is contentious in nature. Contentious content often motivates the reader to do what is called *case building* (e.g., Buehl, Alexander, Murphy, & Sperl, 2001; Nickerson, 1991).

That is, rather than weighing the evidence and arriving at a refreshed interpretation, readers seem to pick and choose content that supports their prior knowledge and beliefs. Such biased processing was evidenced in a study by Chambliss and Garner (1996) in which students read a five-page, two-sided, nonrefutational text adapted from a recent *New Yorker* article on the extermination of the ancient forests of the Pacific Northwest. All the students in the study attended college in the Pacific Northwest, and the majority reported that they either had family members working in a mill or as loggers or they, themselves, had worked in the timber industry. As such, this study combined highly knowledgeable individuals with a two-sided, nonrefutational, contentious text. The authors determined that 71 percent of students did not change their position on the issue. A majority of reported belief changes were toward greater certainty.

These findings on persuasion are similar to the findings on conceptual change, especially regarding individuals' responses to anomalous data encountered in a written text (Chinn & Brewer, 1993; Mason, 2001b). Data conflicting with one's current theory can be simply ignored, considered irrelevant or not contradictory, or distorted to be reinterpreted within that theory, which is not abandoned. Using think-aloud methodology, Kendeou and van den Broek (2003) have shown that readers with misconceptions fail to detect the inconsistencies between their prior knowledge and the text. Participants did not slow down when reading information that contradicted their conceptions, and in their recalls they included more invalid inferences and less textual information than readers with no misconceptions (Kendeou & van den Broek, 2003). In this regard, a refutational text that activates readers' prior knowledge, contrasts it with scientific knowledge, and refutes it as limited and not viable could be an instructional resource for stimulating and sustaining conceptual change if deep processing of the text is involved.

Context

The importance of contextual aspects of the learning environment has been documented in research on conceptual change. In particular, the positive effects of collaborative reasoning and argumentation have been recognized. The cognitive potential of social interaction in school has been acknowledged relatively recently as possibly promoting higher order thinking processes. Within a Vygotskian framework, it is assumed that reasoning in children is mainly manifest in the externalized form of reasoning with others (Moll, 1990; Resnick, Levine, & Teasley, 1991).

The use of collaboration on knowledge problems during group discussions to promote high level understanding has been investigated (e.g. Mason, 2001a; Pontecorvo, 1993). Peer discussions that develop through argumentation have been considered a kind of cultural apprenticeship to scientific ways of knowing, ideas, and the discursive practice of the scientific community (Driver, Asoko, Leach, Mortimer, & Scott, 1994). To value social interaction in the classroom through collaborative reasoning and argumentation means giving students the opportunity to make claims and provide evidence, to support assertions, ask questions, reflect and talk about their conceptions with others. Researchers have developed analytic frameworks to examine the quality of discourse in peer discussions within different learning domains, capturing a variety of modes of talking in social learning contexts (e.g. Chinn & Anderson, 1998; Kumpulainen & Mutanen, 1999).

For example, Pontecorvo and Girardet (1993) showed how collaborative discourse-reasoning in classroom discussions develops through *argumentative* and *epistemic* operations. *Argumentative* operations are activated by learners to construct and support their claims and,

consequently, their thinking and reasoning (e.g., claim, justification, concession, opposition, and counteropposition). *Epistemic* operations are the cognitive processes carried out by learners while using the common methodological and discursive procedures of a particular discipline. When discussing scientific topics, for example, the following epistemic operations were identified in fifth graders' collaborative discourse-reasoning (Mason, 1996a): giving definitions, identifying significant variables, establishing connections, resolving conflicting information, applying newly learned knowledge, reflecting about one's knowledge, and appealing to shared experience, data, or counterevidence to support a claim. Evidence showed that reasoning and argumentation in small group discussions using critical opposition and co-construction can lead young students to negotiate and renegotiate meanings and ideas to understand and share more advanced explanations about the phenomenon (e.g., Mason, 1996a, 1996b). The efficacy of a conceptual change intervention, based on argumentation, for undergraduate students has also been documented (Nussbaum & Sinatra, 2003).

It can also be said that social interaction may foster metaconceptual awareness of the representations by which individuals interpret and make predictions about the world. By expressing, confronting, questioning, and criticizing ideas, students can check their plausibility and experience the need for knowledge revision in their conceptual structures (Mason & Santi, 1998). Finally, it should be added that peer discussion may amplify cognitive motivation (i.e., the desire to know more, and to understand new content better; Hatano & Inagaki, 2003).

In sum, knowledge and belief changes are the outcomes of multifaceted processes characterized by a delicate interplay of personal, cognitive, and motivational factors, text characteristics, processing strategies, and contextual aspects. To this end, intentionality acts as a general mediator between internal and external factors influential in the change process (Sinatra & Pintrich, 2003). In essence, the goal-directed and deliberate initiation and regulation of cognitive, metacognitive, and motivational processes that underlie intentionality are essential aspects of the change process.

IMPLICATIONS FOR FUTURE RESEARCH

Within this chapter we have attempted to synthesize the major research findings on changing knowledge and beliefs with the aim of identifying variables that affect the change process, as well as models of change that seem to provide mooring points for promoting and assessing change in educational contexts. Nevertheless, a great deal of work remains to be done to advance research and educational practice further. Our review of literature has highlighted several areas for future consideration. For example, it seems evident that there is ample room for improvement in definitional clarity. As we noted, it is often difficult to discern what a researcher means by *knowledge*, as compared to what another researcher means by *beliefs*. As has been done with other constructs such as motivation (e.g., Murphy & Alexander, 2000), it seems that the constructs of knowledge and beliefs, especially as they function within the change process, need to be more clearly delineated.

In conducting our review, it also became evident that the areas of conceptual change and persuasion have much in common. For instance, similar variables such as prior knowledge, self-reflection, and motivation seem to be relevant in the process of both knowledge change and beliefs change. In addition, textual factors that promote belief change (e.g., comprehensibility or strong arguments) also seem to promote knowledge change. This seems to be the case, especially when attempting to change students' knowledge and beliefs about academic topics such as earth models. It is likely that these are cases in which students' knowledge and beliefs are overlapping and students have the potential to attribute importance to their knowledge. However, the overlaps between knowledge and belief change are less evident when students' knowledge or beliefs are extremely strong. In such cases, both knowledge and belief modification is extremely difficult. Along these same lines, additional research seems to be necessary in establishing how one promotes knowledge change in ill-structured domains, and conversely, how one promotes belief change in well-structured domains.

Another area that is in need of continued investigation is that of knowledge revision and epistemic beliefs. At this point, only a few studies have investigated the role of personal epistemology in conceptual change (e.g., Mason, 2003; Qian & Alvermann, 1995). What remains unknown is the interactive dynamics between epistemological beliefs and conceptual change, assuming that the acquisition of knowledge also implies the development of representations about knowledge itself. If the change process is affected by beliefs about the nature of knowledge and knowing, can it be stimulated and supported by educational interventions implemented for the advancement of these beliefs? If the refinement of epistemic beliefs is affected by the approach to conceptual learning, can educational interventions implemented for supporting knowledge revision also be effective in fostering personal epistemologies? It seems also worth investigating the mechanism through which personal epistemology influences the change of conceptions. Do individuals' beliefs about knowledge and knowing affect the degree of intentional engagement, both cognitive and motivational, in revising knowledge?

Finally, it seems that there is much work to be done in the area of classroom interventions that will promote knowledge and belief change. Currently, text seems to be the major tool for change in educational settings. As a beginning, we propose that researchers begin to look more closely at the role and influence of talk or discourse in classroom settings. As mentioned, social interactions within peer discussion can sustain the change process by stimulating the production of explanations and meta-conceptual self-awareness. Similarly, the production of explanations also seems to increase student motivation to improve content-area understandings. Initial work in such classroom interventions can be seen in the work of Alexander and colleagues (Alexander, Fives, Buehl, & Mulhern, 2003) on teaching as a persuasive practice through the use of compelling classroom texts.

Yet, more research is needed to examine the conditions under which the sociocultural context makes it easier to be convinced to change a conception and/or position about a phenomenon. Does dialogical interaction help the revision of concepts and beliefs better than individualistic activity because it facilitates individuals to recognize the limitations and fallacies of one's knowledge and perspectives on a debated topic? Does the change depend on the quality of explanations that are produced during the social exchange? Is the change related to the compatibility of a new conception or belief with the existing ones, as it emerges from argumentation? Does the change, especially for beliefs, also involve emotional change, which is nurtured by dialogical interaction, and not only a simple shift from one valence to another? Can emotions act as an impediment to the recognition that a position conflicting with the current perspective and strongly supported by others is more evidence-based?

CODA

In considering future studies that would be conducted to address the aforementioned questions, it seems imperative that researchers think deeply about the theoretical framework undergirding such work. In our own review of relevant literature, we found that an additional factor differentiating research on knowledge emanating from science education and cognitive psychology, as well as the social and educational psychology research on beliefs, is the underlying theoretical framework. As we have suggested previously, cognitive, social, and educational psychologists are more likely to employ an information processing framework, whereas science educators usually rely on a constructivist approach. Although these frameworks have been useful in these independent lines of research, we want to close this chapter by offering a theoretical framework that we believe could help to unify and strengthen these varied lines of research. Specifically, we propose that knowledge and belief researchers return to their pragmatist roots and turn-of-the-20th-century American philosophy.

Although we cannot overview the entire theory herein, we want to offer a brief summary. Peirce (1958) conceptualized beliefs as conscious, deliberate habits of action: "Our beliefs guide our desires and shape our actions.... The feeling of believing is a more or less sure indication of there being established in our nature some habit which will determine our actions" (p. 59). Thus, beliefs cause people to act in a certain way because of the perceived consequences of their action. This is very similar to how knowledge and beliefs are characterized in alternative models of conceptual change in which one's beliefs mediate the extent to which individuals engage with the text and the subsequent knowledge gains (e.g., Dole & Sinatra, 1998).

Peirce called the consequences that you expect when you hold a belief its "practical consequences," and your belief that something is *real* consists of the sum total of such conscious habits (beliefs) of expecting practical consequences. Moreover, when acting on a belief leads to unexpected consequences, doubt arises in the individual. Peirce posited that every problem or inquiry is stimulated through the observation of some surprising phenomenon or some event that goes against one's present belief. This notion is foundational to conceptual change. Many models of conceptual change propose that individuals must be presented with discrepant information or anomalous data (Chinn & Brewer, 1993) before they will question their current conceptions, although it may not be enough to bring about change. Peirce also suggested that doubt is the single most important motive for change. We would posit that such a motive parallels Sinatra and Pintrich's (2003) conceptualization of intentionality as goal-directed and internally initiated action toward a change in understanding. Much like those researchers, Peirce proposed that engagement and processing of the doubt would lead to changes in beliefs and understandings of truth and reality (i.e., knowledge). Although Peirce described his notion of pragmatism much more fully than we can in the present work, we believe this theoretical approach holds potential as an underlying framework for research on the change process. Indeed, the beauty of Peirce's theory lies in its simplicity. That is, people will hold strongly to a belief or habit until they have a reason to change it (i.e., doubt), and such change requires motive or intentionality. Moreover, the truthfulness or veracity of a belief lies in repeated testings that can be publicly verified.

In sum, research on changing knowledge and beliefs began as a unified area of study, and we perceive that it is returning to those roots. In returning to the roots of change, however, researchers face numerous challenges, including the choice of a sufficient theoretical framework. Responses to these challenges and other questions can fruitfully extend current research and shed more light into the complex and intriguing processes of knowledge and belief change. Indeed, such research is imperative if we are going to continue to help students acquire, adapt, and abandon understandings about academic content.

References

Ajzen, I. (1985). From intentions to actions: A theory of planned behavior. In J. Kuhl & J. Breckman (Eds.), *Action-control: From cognition to behavior* (pp. 15). Heidelberg: Springer.

Alexander, P. A. (1998). Positioning conceptual change within a model of domain literacy. In B. Guzzetti & C. Hynd (Eds.), *Perspectives on conceptual change* (pp. 55–76). Mahwah, NJ: Lawrence Erlbaum Associates.

Alexander, P. A., & Dochy, F. J. R. C. (1995). Conceptions of knowledge and beliefs: A comparison across varying cultural and educational communities. *American Educational Research Journal, 32*, 413–442.

Alexander, P. A., Fives, H. R., Buehl, M. M., Mulhern, J. (2003). Teaching as persuasion. *Teaching and Teacher Education, 18*(7), 795–813.

Alexander, P. A., & Jetton, T. L. (1996). The role of importance and interest in the processing of text. *Educational Psychology Review, 8*(1), 89–121.

Alexander, P. A., & Murphy, P. K. (1999). Learner profiles: Valuing individual differences within classroom communities. In P. L. Ackerman, P. C. Kyllonen, & R. D. Roberts (Eds.), *Learning and individual differences: Processes, traits, and content determinants* (pp. 413–431). Washington, DC: American Psychological Association.

Alexander, P. A., Murphy, P. K., Guan, J., & Murphy, P. A. (1998). How students and teachers in Singapore and the United States conceptualize knowledge and beliefs: Positioning learning within epistemological frameworks. *Learning and Instruction, 8*, 97–116.

Allen, M. (1991). Meta-analysis comparing the persuasiveness of one-sided and two-sided messages. *Western Journal of Speech Communication, 55*, 390–404.

Allen, M., Hale, J., Mongeau, P., Berkowits-Stafford, S., Stafford, S., & Shanahan, W. (1990). Testing a model of message sidedness: Three replications. *Communication Monographs, 57,* 274-291.

Alvermann, D., & Hague, S. A. (1989). Comprehension of counterintuitive science text: Effects of prior knowledge and text structure. *Journal of Educational Research, 82,* 197-202.

Alvermann, D., & Hynd, C., & Qian, G. (1995). Effects of interactive discussion and text type on learning counterintuitive science concepts. *Journal of Educational Research, 88,* 146-154.

Anderson, C. A. (1983). Abstract and concrete data in the perseverance of social theories: When weak data lead to unshakable beliefs. *Journal of Experimental Social Psychology, 19,* 93-108.

Andre, T., & Windschitl, M. (2003). Interest, epistemological belief, and intentional conceptual change. In G. M. Sinatra & P. R. Pintrich (Eds.), *Intentional conceptual change* (pp. 173-197). Mahwah, NJ: Lawrence Erlbaum Associates.

Bahar, M. (2003). Misconceptions in biology education and conceptual change strategies. *Educational Sciences. Theory and Practice, 3,* 27-64.

Bandura, A. (1977). *Social learning theory.* Englewood Cliffs, NJ: Prentice-Hall.

Beik, M., Wood, W., Chaiken, S., & Nations, C. (1992). *Working knowledge, cognitive processing, and attitudes: On the inevitability of bias.* Unpublished manuscript, Texas A&M University at College Station.

Bereiter, C., & Scardamalia, M. (1989). Intentional learning as a goal of instruction. In L. B. Resnick (Ed.), *Knowing, learning, and instruction: Essays in honor of Robert Glaser* (pp. 361-392). Hillsdale, NJ: Lawrence Erlbaum Associates.

Berti, A. E. (1999). Knowledge restructuring in an economic subdomain: Banking. In W. Schnotz, S. Vosniadou, & M. Carretero (Eds.), *New perspectives on conceptual change* (pp. 113-135). Amsterdam: Pergamon/Elsevier Science.

Bettinghaus, E. P. (1968). *Persuasive communication.* New York: Holt, Rinehart, & Winston.

Blau, P. M. (1964). *Exchange and power in social life.* New York: Wiley.

Bobrow, D. G., & Collins, A. (Eds.) (1975). *Representation and understanding. Studies in cognitive science.* New York: Academic Press.

Brewer, W. F., & Samarapungavan, A. (1991). Children's theories vs. scientific theories: Differences in reasoning or differences in knowledge. In R. R. Hoffman & D. S. Palermo (Eds.), *Cognition and the symbolic processes: Applied and ecological perspectives* (pp. 209-232). Hillsdale, NJ: Lawrence Erlbaum Associates.

Buehl, M. M., Alexander, P. A., Murphy, P. K., & Sperl, C. T. (2001). Profiling persuasion: The role of beliefs, knowledge, and interest in the processing of persuasive texts that varied by argument structure. *Journal of Literacy Research, 33,* 269-301.

Cacioppo, J. T., & Petty, R. E. (1982). The need for cognition. *Journal of Personality and Social Psychology, 42*(1), 116-131.

Carey, S. (1985). *Conceptual change in childhood.* Cambridge, MA: MIT Press.

Chaiken, S. (1987). The heuristic model of persuasion. In M. P. Zanna, J. M. Olson, & C. P. Herman (Eds.), *Social influence: The Ontario Symposium* (Vol. 5, pp. 3-39). Hillsdale, NJ: Lawrence Erlbaum Associates.

Chambliss, M. J. (1995). Text cues and strategies successful readers use to construct the gist of lengthy written arguments. *Reading Research Quarterly, 30*(4), 778-807.

Chambliss, M. J., & Garner, R. (1996). Do adults change their minds after reading persuasive text? *Written Communication, 13*(3), 291-313.

Chi, M. T. H. (1992). Conceptual change within and across ontological categories: Examples from learning and discovery in science. In R. Giere (Ed.), *Cognitive models of science: Minnesota studies in the philosophy of science* (pp. 129-186). Minneapolis, MN: University of Minnesota Press.

Chi, M. T. H., Slotta, J. D., & de Leeuw, N. (1994). From things to processes: A theory of conceptual change for learning science concepts. *Learning and Instruction, 4,* 27-43.

Chinn, C. A., & Anderson, R. C. (1998). The structure of discussions that promote reasoning. *Teachers College Record, 100,* 315-368.

Chinn, C. A., & Brewer, W. F. (1993). The role of anomalous data in knowledge acquisition: A theoretical framework and implications for science education. *Review of Educational Research, 63,* 1-49.

Chinn, C. A., & Brewer, W. F. (1998). An empirical text of a taxonomy of responses to anomalous data in science. *Journal of Research in Science Teaching, 35*(6), 623-654.

Cialdini, R. B. (1984). *Influence.* New York: Harper & Row.

diSessa, A. A. (1983). Phenomenology and the evolution of intuition. In D. Gentner and A. Stevens (Eds.), *Mental models* (pp. 15 33). Mahwah, NJ: Lawrence Erlbaum.

diSessa, A. A. (1993). Toward an epistemology of physics. *Cognition and Instruction, 10,* 105-225.

diSessa, A. A. (2002). Why "conceptual ecology" is a good idea. In M. Limón & L. Mason (Eds.), *Reconsidering conceptual change. Issues in theory and practice* (pp. 29-60). Dordrecht, The Netherlands: Kluwer Academic.

Dole, J. A., & Sinatra, G. M. (1998). Reconceptualizing change in the cognitive construction of knowledge. *Educational Psychologist, 32,* 109-128.

Driver, R., Asoko, H., Leach, J., Mortimer, E., & Scott, P. (1994). Constructing scientific knowledge in the classroom, *Educational Researcher, 23,* 5-12.

Duit, R. (1999). Conceptual changes approaches in science education. In W. Schnotz, M. Carretero, & S. Vosniadou (Eds.), *New perspectives on conceptual change* (pp. 263-282). Amsterdam: Pergamon/Elsevier.

Duit, R. (2002). *Bibliography STCSE: Students' and teachers' conceptions and science education.* Kiel, Germany: IPN—Leibniz Institute for Science Education.

Duit, R., & Treagust D. F. (2003). Conceptual change: A powerful framework for improving science teaching and learning. *International Journal of Science Education, 25,* 671-688.

Festinger, L. (1957). *A theory of cognitive dissonance.* Stanford, CA: Stanford University Press.

Fishbein, M. (Ed.). (1967). *Readings in attitude theory and measurement.* New York: Wiley.

Fishbein, M., & Ajzen, I. (1975). *Belief, attitude, intention and behavior: An introduction to theory and research*. Reading, MA: Addison-Wesley.

Garner, R., & Hansis, R. (1994). Literacy practices outside of school: Adults' beliefs and their responses to "street texts." In R. Garner & P. A. Alexander (Eds.), *Beliefs about text and about instruction with text* (pp. 57–74). Hillsdale, NJ: Lawrence Erlbaum Associates.

Greenwald, A. G. (1968). Cognitive learning: Cognitive response to persuasion and attitude change. In A. G. Greenwald, T. C. Brock, & T. M. Ostrom (Eds.), *Psychological foundations of attitude change* (pp. 148–170). New York: Academic Press.

Gregoire, M. (2003). Is it a challenge or a threat? A dual-process model of teachers' cognition and appraisal processes during conceptual change. *Educational Psychology Review, 15*(2), 147–179.

Guzzetti, B. J., Snyder, T. E., Glass, G. V., & Gamas, W. S. (1993). Promoting conceptual change in science: A comparative meta-analysis of instructional interventions from reading education and science education. *Reading Research Quarterly, 28*, 117–159.

Hatano, G., & Inagaki, K. (2003). When is conceptual change intended? A cognitive-sociocultural view. In G. M. Sinatra & P. R. Pintrich (Eds.), *Intentional conceptual change* (pp. 407–427). Mahwah, NJ: Lawrence Erlbaum Associates.

Hennessey, M. G. (2003). Metacognitive aspects of students' reflective discourse: Implications for intentional conceptual change teaching and learning. In G. M. Sinatra & P. R. Pintrich (Eds.), *Intentional conceptual change* (pp. 103–132). Mahwah, NJ: Lawrence Erlbaum Associates.

Hewson, S. (1981). A conceptual change approach to learning science. *European Journal of Science Education, 3*, 383–396.

Hofer, B. K., & Pintrich, P. R. (1997). The development of epistemological theories: Beliefs about knowledge and knowing and their relation to learning. *Review of Educational Research, 67*, 88–140.

Hofer, B. K., & Pintrich, P. R. (Eds.) (2002). *Personal epistemology: The psychology of beliefs about knowledge and knowing*. Mahwah, NJ: Laurence Erlbaum Associates.

Hovland, C. I., Janis, I. L., & Kelley, H. H. (1953). *Communication and persuasion: Psychological studies of opinion change*. New Haven, CT: Yale University Press.

Hynd, C. (2003). Conceptual change in response to persuasive messages. In G. M. Sinatra & P. R. Pintrich (Eds.), *Intentional conceptual change* (pp. 291–315). Mahwah, NJ: Lawrence Erlbaum Associates.

Hynd, C., Alvermann, D., & Qian, G. (1997). Preservice elementary school teachers' conceptual change about projectile motion: Refutation text, demonstration, affective factors, and relevance. *Science Education, 81*, 1–27.

James, W. (1996). *Some problems of philosophy: A beginning of an introduction to philosophy*. Lincoln, NE: University of Nebraska Press. Original work published in 1911 in New York: Longmans, Green, and Co.

Johnson, B. T. (1994). Effects of outcome-relevant involvement and prior information on persuasion. *Journal of Experimental Social Psychology, 30*, 556–579.

Johnson, B. T., Lin, H., Symons, C. S., Campbell, L. A., & Ekstein, G. (1995). Initial beliefs and attitudinal latitudes as factors in persuasion. *Journal of Personality and Social Psychology, 21*(5), 502–511.

Kardash, C. M., & Scholes, R. J. (1995). Effects of preexisting beliefs and repeated readings on belief change, comprehension, and recall of persuasive text. *Contemporary Educational Psychology, 20*, 201–221.

Kelley, H. H. (1952). Two functions of reference group. In G. E. Swanson, T. M. Newcomb, & E. L. Hartley (Eds.), *Readings in social psychology* (pp. 410–414). New York: Holt.

Kelley, H. H., & Volkart, E. H. (1952). The resistance to change of group-anchored attitudes. *American Sociological Review, 17*, 453–465.

Kendeou, P., & van den Broek, P. (2003). *The effects of readers' misconceptions in text comprehension*. Paper presented at the American Educational Research Association annual meeting, Chicago, IL.

Koballa, T. R., Jr. (1992). Persuasion and attitude change in science education. *Journal of Research in Science Teaching, 29*, 63–80.

Kuhn, D., Amsel, E., & O' Loughlin, M. (1988). *The development of scientific thinking skills*. San Diego, CA: Academic Press.

Kuhn, T. (1970). *The structure of scientific revolutions* (2nd ed.). Chicago: Chicago University Press.

Kumpulainen, K., & Mutanen, M. (1999). The situated dynamics of peer group interaction: An introduction to an analytic framework. *Learning and Instruction, 9*(5), 449–473.

Langer, J. A. (1980). Relation between levels of prior knowledge and the organization of recall. In M. L. Kamil & A. J. Moe (Eds.), *Perspectives on reading research and instruction* (pp. 28–33). Washington, DC: National Reading Conference.

Lasswell, H. D. (1948). The structure and function of communication and society. In L. Bryson (Ed.), *The communication of ideas* (pp. 23–47). New York: Harper and Row.

Lee, O., & Anderson, C. W. (1993). Task engagement and conceptual change in middle school science classrooms. *American Educational Research Journal, 30*, 585–610.

Limón, M. (2001). On the cognitive conflict as an instructional strategy for conceptual change: A critical appraisal. *Learning and Instruction, 11*, 357–380.

Limón, M. (2003). The role of domain-specific knowledge in intentional conceptual change. In G. M. Sinatra & P. R. Pintrich (Eds.), *Intentional conceptual change* (pp. 133–170). Mahwah, NJ: Lawrence Erlbaum Associates.

Limón, M., & Mason, L. (Eds.) (2002). *Reconsidering conceptual change. Issues in theory and practice*. Dordrecht, The Netherlands: Kluwer Academic.

Linnenbrink, E. A., & Pintrich, P. R. (2002). The role of motivational beliefs in conceptual change. In M. Limón & L. Mason (Eds.), *Reconsidering conceptual change. Issues in theory and practice* (pp. 115–135). Dordrecht, The Netherlands: Kluwer Academic.

Manfredo, M. J., & Bright, A. D. (1991). A model for assessing the effects of communication on recreationists. *Journal of Leisure Research, 23*(1), 1–20.

Mason, L. (1996a). An analysis of children's construction of new knowledge through their reasoning and arguing in classroom discussions. *International Journal of Qualitative Studies in Education, 9,* 411–433.

Mason, L. (1996b). Collaborative reasoning on self-generated analogies. Conceptual growth in understanding scientific phenomena. *Educational Research and Evaluation, 2,* 309–350.

Mason, L. (2000). Role of anomalous data and epistemological beliefs in middle school students' theory change about two controversial topics. *European Journal of Psychology of Education, 15,* 329–346.

Mason, L. (2001a). Introducing talk and writing for conceptual change: A classroom study. *Learning and Instruction, 11*(4–5), 305–329.

Mason, L. (2001b). Responses to anomalous data and theory change. *Learning and Instruction, 11*(6), 453–483.

Mason, L. (2003). Personal epistemologies and intentional conceptual change. In G. M. Sinatra & P. R. Pintrich (Eds.), *Intentional conceptual change* (pp. 199–236). Mahwah, NJ: Lawrence Erlbaum Associates.

Mason, L., & Boscolo, P. (2004). Role of epistemological understanding and interest in interpreting a controversy and in topic-specific belief change. *Contemporary Educational Psychology, 29,* 103–128.

Mason, L., & Santi, M. (1998). Discussing the greenhouse effect. Children's collaborative discourse-reasoning and conceptual change. *Environmental Education Research, 4,* 67–85.

McCloskey, M. (1983). Naïve theories of motion. In D. Gentner & A. Stevens (Eds.), *Mental models* (pp. 299–313). Mahwah, NJ: Lawrence Erlbaum Associates.

McCroskey, J. C. (1969). A summary of experimental research on the effects of evidence in persuasive communication. *Quarterly Journal of Speech, 55,* 169–176.

Miller, G. R. (1980). On being persuaded: Some basic distinctions. In M. E. Roloff & G. R. Miller (Eds.), *Persuasion: New directions in theory and research* (pp. 11–28). Beverly Hills, CA: Sage.

Moll, L. C. (Ed.). (1990). *Vygotsky and education: Instructional implications and applications of sociohistorical psychology.* New York: Cambridge University Press.

Murphy, P. K. (1998). *Toward a multifaceted model of persuasion: The interaction of textual and learner variables.* Unpublished doctoral dissertation, University of Maryland, College Park, MD.

Murphy, P. K. (2001a). Teaching as persuasion: A theoretical foundation. *Theory Into Practice, 40,* 224–227.

Murphy, P. K. (2001b). What makes a text persuasive? Comparing students' and experts' conceptions of persuasiveness. *International Journal of Educational Research, 35,* 675–698.

Murphy, P. K., & Alexander, P. A. (2000). A motivated exploration of motivation terminology. *Contemporary Educational Psychology, 25,* 3–53.

Murphy, P. K., & Alexander, P. A. (2004). Persuasion as a dynamic, multidimensional process: A view of individual and intraindividual differences. *American Educational Research Journal, 41,* 337–363.

Murphy, P. K., Holleran, T., Long, J. L., & Esterly, E. (in press). *The role of motivation in the persuasion process. Contemporary Educational Psychology.*

Murphy, P. K., Long, J. L., Holleran, T., & Esterly, E. (2003). Persuasion online or on paper: A new take on an old issue. *Learning and Instruction, 13,* 51–532.

Murphy, P. K., & Woods, B. S. (1996). Situating knowledge in learning and instruction. *Educational Psychologist, 31*(2), 141–145.

Nickerson, R. S. (1991). Modes and models of informal reasoning: A commentary. In J. F. Voss, D. N. Perkins, & J. W. Segal (Eds.), *Informal reasoning and education* (pp. 291–309). Hillsdale, NJ: Lawrence Erlbaum Associates.

Nisbett, R., & Ross, L. (1980). *Human inference: Strategies and shortcomings of social judgment.* Englewood Cliffs, NJ: Prentice-Hall.

Nussbaum, E. M. & Sinatra, G. M. (2003). Argument and conceptual engagement. *Contemporary Educational Psychology, 28,* 384–395.

Peirce, C. S. (1958). The fixation of belief. In P. P. Wiener (Ed.), *Charles S. Peirce: Selected writings* (pp. 91–112). New York: Dover.

Petty, R. E., & Cacioppo, J. T. (1986). The elaboration likelihood model of persuasion. In L. Berkowitz (Ed.), *Advances in experimental social psychology* (Vol. 19, pp. 123–205). New York: Academic Press.

Piaget, J. (1929). *The child's conception of the world.* New York: Harcourt, Brace.

Pines, A. L., & West, L. (1983). A framework for conceptual change with special reference to misconceptions. In H. Helm & J. Novack (Eds.), *Proceedings of the international seminar on misconceptions in science and mathematics* (pp. 47–52). Ithaca, NY: Cornell University.

Pintrich, P. R., Marx, R. W., & Boyle, R. B. (1993). Beyond cold conceptual change: The role of motivational beliefs and classroom contextual factors in the process of conceptual change. *Review of Educational Research, 63,* 167–199.

Pontecorvo, C. (1993). Forms of discourse and shared thinking. *Cognition and Instruction, 11,* 189–196.

Pontecorvo, C., & Girardet H. (1993). Arguing and reasoning in understanding historical topics. *Cognition and Instruction, 11*(3&4), 365–395.

Posner, G. J., Strike, K. A., Hewson, P. W., & Gertzog, W. A. (1982). Accommodation of a scientific conception: Toward a theory of conceptual change. *Science Education, 66,* 211–227.

Qian, G., & Alvermann, D. (1995). Role of epistemological beliefs and learned helplessness in secondary school students' learning science concepts from text. *Journal of Educational Psychology, 87,* 282–292.

Reiner, M., Chi, M. T. H., & Resnick, L. B. (1988). Naïve materialistic belief: An underlying epistemological commitment. *Proceedings of the Tenth Annual Conference of the Cognitive Science Society* (pp. 544–551). Hillsdale, NJ: Lawrence Erlbaum Associates.

Resnick, L. B., Levine, J., & Teasley, S. D. (Eds.). (1991). *Perspectives on socially shared cognition.* Washington, DC: American Psychological Association.

Richardson, V. (1996). The role of attitudes and beliefs in learning to teach. In J. Sikula (Ed.), *Handbook of research on teacher education* (2nd ed., pp. 102–119). New York: Macmillan.

Rokeach, M. (1968). *Beliefs, attitudes, and values: A theory of organization and change.* San Francisco: Jossey-Bass.

Roloff, M. (1981). *Interpersonal communication: The social exchange approach.* Beverly Hills, CA: Sage Publishing.

Rumelhart, D. E., & Norman, D. A. (1981). Accretion, tuning, and restructuring: Three modes of learning. In J. W. Cotton & R. Klatzy (Eds.), *Semantic factors in cognition* (pp. 37–60). Hillsdale, NJ: Lawrence Erlbaum Associates.

Scheffler, I. (1965). *Conditions of knowledge.* New York: Scott, Foresman, & Co.

Schnotz, W., Vosniadou, S., & Carretero, M. (Eds.) (1999). *New perspectives on conceptual change* (pp. 3–13). Amsterdam: Pergamon/Elsevier Science.

Showers, D. E. (1995). Effects of knowledge and persuasion on high-school students' attitudes toward nuclear power plants. *Journal of Research in Science Teaching, 32*(1), 29–43.

Shrigley, R. L., & Koballa, Jr., T. R. (1992). A decade of attitude research based on Hovaland's learning theory model. *Science Education, 76*(1), 17–42.

Sinatra, G. M., & Pintrich, P. R. (Eds.) (2003). *Intentional conceptual change.* Mahwah, NJ: Lawrence Erlbaum Associates.

Slusher, M. P., & Anderson, C. A. (1996). Using causal persuasive arguments to change beliefs and teach new information: The mediating role of explanation availability and evaluation bias in the acceptance of knowledge. *Journal of Educational Psychology, 88*(1), 11–122.

Southerland, S. A., Sinatra, G. M., & Mathews, M. R. (2001). Belief, knowledge, and science education. *Educational Psychology Review, 13*(4), 325–351.

Southerland, S. A., & Sinatra, G. M. (2003). Learning about biological evolution: A special case of intentional conceptual change. In G. M. Sinatra & P. R. Pintrich (Eds.), *Intentional conceptual change* (pp. 317–345). Mahwah, NJ: Lawrence Erlbaum Associates.

Spelke, E. (1991). Physical knowledge in infancy: Reflections on Piaget's theory. In S. Carey & R. Gelman (Eds.), *Epigenesis of mind* (pp. 133–170). Hillsdale, NJ: Lawrence Erlbaum Associates.

Stanovich, K. E. (2004). *The Robot's rebellion. Finding meaning in the age of Darwin.* Chicago: Chicago University Press.

Stiff, J. B. (1994). *Persuasive communication.* New York Guilford.

Strike, K. A., & Posner, G. J. (1992). A revisionist theory of conceptual change. In R. Duschl & R. Hamilton (Eds.), *Philosophy of science, cognitive science, and educational theory and practice* (pp. 147–176). Albany, NY: Academic Press.

Thagard, P. (1992). *Conceptual revolutions.* Princeton, NJ: Princeton University Press.

Toulmin, S. E. (1958). *The uses of argument.* Cambridge, UK: Cambridge University Press.

Toulmin, X. (1992). *Human understanding: An inquiry into the aims of science.* Princeton, NJ: Princeton University Press.

Venville, G. J., & Treagust, D. F. (1998). Exploring conceptual chang in genetics using a multidimensional interpretive framework. *Journal of Research in Science Teaching, 35,* 1031–1055.

Vosniadou, S. (1994). Capturing and modeling the process of conceptual change. *Learning and Instruction, 4,* 45–69.

Vosniadou, S. (1999). Conceptual change research: State of the art and future directions. In W. Schnotz, S. Vosniadou, & M. Carretero (Eds.), *New perspectives on conceptual change* (pp. 3–13). Amsterdam: Pergamon/Elsevier Science.

Vosniadou, S. (2002). On the nature of naïve physics. In M. Limón & L. Mason (Eds.), *Reconsidering conceptual change*: *Issues in theory and practice* (pp. 61–76). Dordrecht, The Netherlands: Kluwer Academic.

Vosniadou, S. (2003). Exploring the relationships between conceptual change and intentional learning. In G. M. Sinatra & P. R. Pintrich (Eds.), *Intentional conceptual change* (pp. 377–406). Mahwah, NJ: Lawrence Erlbaum Associates.

Vosniadou, S., & Brewer, W. F. (1992). Mental models of the earth: A study of conceptual change in childhood. *Cognitive Psychology, 24,* 535–585.

Vosniadou, S., & Brewer, W. F. (1994). Mental models of the day/night cycle. *Cognitive Science, 18,* 123–183.

Vosniadou, S., & Ioannides, C. (1998). From conceptual development to science education: A psychological point of view. *International Journal of Science Education, 20,* 121–1230.

White, R. T., & Gunstone, R. F. (1989). Metalearning and conceptual change. *International Journal of Science Education, 11,* 577–586.

Wood, W. (1982). Retrieval of attitude-relevant information from memory: Effects on susceptibility to persuasion and on intrinsic motivation. *Journal of Personality and Social Psychology, 42,* 798–810.

Wood, W., & Kallgren, C. A. (1988). Communicator attributes and persuasion: Recipients' access to attitude-relevant information in memory. *Personality and Social Psychology Bulletin, 14,* 172–182.

Wood-Robinson, C. (1994). Young people's ideas about inheritance and evolution. *Science Education, 124,* 29–47.

Woods, B. S., & Murphy, P. K. (2001). Separated at birth: The shared lineage of research on conceptual change and persuasion. *International Journal of Educational Research, 35,* 633–649.

Woolfolk Hoy, A., & Murphy, P. K. (2001). Teaching educational psychology to the implicit mind. In B. Torff & R. J. Sternberg (Eds.), *Understanding and teaching the intuitive mind* (pp. 145–186). Mahwah, NJ: Lawrence Erlbaum Associates.

Part
·IV·

MOTIVATION

·15·

CLASSROOMS AS CONTEXTS FOR
MOTIVATING LEARNING

Nancy E. Perry
University of British Columbia

Julianne C. Turner
University of Notre Dame

Debra K. Meyer
Elmhurst College

In *Motivating Students to Learn*, Brophy (2004) writes:

People are born with the potential to develop a great range of motivational dispositions. A few such dispositions appear to be inborn as part of the human condition. . . . Most, however, especially higher level dispositions such as motivation to learn, are developed gradually through exposure to learning opportunities and socialization influences. (p. 17)

Our chapter focuses on classrooms as contexts for motivating students' learning. Specifically, we review research that examines the relationships among features of classroom contexts and students' motivation for and engagement in learning.

Over the past decade, more research on motivation has been conducted in classrooms, intensifying the need to contextualize theories and research methods in this field of study. Consistent with this development, three overarching questions guided our review of literature and organization of this chapter: (a) How have we studied motivation in classrooms? (b) What have we learned about motivation in classrooms from this research? (c) What should be the foci of studies of motivation in classrooms

and other teaching and learning contexts in the future? We begin by connecting research on motivation in classrooms to theories about learning and motivation that focus on the individual (e.g., behavioral and cognitive theories) and progress to theories about learning and motivation that emphasize the dynamic interplay between the individual and the social/contextual (e.g., social cognitive and sociocultural theories). Second, we describe what research conducted in classrooms reveals about student motivation. This research, which often reflects various theoretical perspectives, is related to features of classroom environments, including learning tasks, teachers' instructional practices, and how teachers and students relate to each other. Links also are made to the broader social contexts of schools. Finally, we propose an agenda for future research on motivation in classrooms and other teaching and learning contexts.

We make two major assertions about the research on motivation in classrooms to date. First, most of the research about classroom characteristics that are related to students' motivation for learning has been conducted outside of classrooms or is based solely on learners' perceptions of the classroom context. Second, much of this motivation research has isolated features of teaching and learning contexts rather than studying them in combination to learn how they support or undermine one another. Certainly progress has been made since Corno and Mandinach (1983) identified the need for an integrated theory of classroom learning and motivation more than 20 years ago, one that encompasses variables associated with learning, motivation, *and* instruction and involves research *in* rather than *about* classrooms. Contextual understandings are more integral to research on motivation today, reflecting the general shift in educational research toward situated and social perspectives on learning. However, we would argue, progress in this regard is slow, perhaps reflecting the complexity of studying motivation *in situ*, in events (Winne & Perry, 2000), and from more sociocultural points of view (Hickey & Granade, 2004).

How Do We Characterize Motivated Learning?

In the previous *Handbook of Educational Psychology*, Stipek's chapter on motivation and instruction used the terms *motivation* and *engagement* to reflect cognitive aspects of motivation (e.g., beliefs, values, expectations) and their behavioral hallmarks (e.g., persistence, avoidance, help-seeking). Specifically, she characterized students who are motivated to learn as follows:

A motivated student . . . is actively engaged in the learning process . . . approach[es] challenging tasks eagerly, exert[s] intense effort using active problem-solving strategies, and persist[s] in the face of difficulty. Motivated students focus on developing understanding and mastering skills; they are enthusiastic and optimistic; . . . they take pleasure in academic tasks and pride in their achievements. (Stipek, 1996, p. 85)

We believe this description is still accurate and compelling. However, we perceive a need to extend descriptions of motivation beyond individuals' behavior, cognition, and affect to include the contexts that are associated with their motivation and engagement. We believe more contextualized perspectives on motivation offer new ways of thinking about and studying motivation in classrooms. They seek to reveal how student characteristics (e.g., attributions, goals, expectations) are related to classroom features (e.g., activity and goal structures, instructional supportiveness) and are fused in motivational experiences. Furthermore, contextualized views recognize that no single individual characteristic or classroom feature will be sufficient for explaining motivation and, therefore, seek to identify how various combinations of

individual and classroom characteristics relate to engagement in learning.

What Do We Include as Classroom Research?

In this chapter, we give emphasis to research that takes place *in* classrooms, which reveals the progress made toward understanding the complex interplay of contextual elements that conspire to promote (or curtail) students' motivation for and engagement in classroom learning. However, we also include relevant research *about* classrooms—typically students' and teachers' reports about how they perceive what happens in classrooms—because much of what we presume to know about classrooms derives from these studies. Often, they are the basis for the conceptual categories applied to observation in classrooms and assessments of students' level of engagement in classroom work. We limit our review of classroom studies to those in kindergarten through grade 12 classrooms, and we make no claim to producing an exhaustive review of the relevant research. Rather we follow a strand of classroom research that distinguishes itself by (a) attending to both student and classroom characteristics that are related to motivation and (b) applying multiple, often qualitative, methods to address research questions.

HOW HAVE WE STUDIED MOTIVATION IN CLASSROOMS?

Historically, students' learning was the focus of educational psychology. Only since the 1970s has motivation research within educational psychology emerged in a compelling way (Ford, 1992; Weiner, 1990). Given the enormous growth in motivation research over the last three decades, it is surprising that studying learning and motivation *in classrooms* remains a relatively new endeavor in educational psychology. In this section we trace developments in research about classrooms from perspectives that focus on the individual, and perspectives that focus on the individual in context. We end this section by describing sociocultural perspectives on learning and motivation that push agendas for research in classrooms in the future.

Focus on the Individual's Behaviors and Thoughts

Behaviorist Approaches. Although behaviorists acknowledge that individuals have thoughts and motives, they view the environment as the cause of all human behaviors, which are strengthened through reinforcement. As Stipek (1996) noted, *Reinforcement Theory* is the most common behaviorist perspective associated with studies of motivation and dominated the literature until the early 1960s. According to this theory, which derives from the so-called *Law of Effect* (Thorndike, 1913), reinforcement is the primary mechanism for establishing and maintaining behavior and punishment is the primary mechanism for extinguishing it (Brophy, 2004). Therefore, from a behaviorist perspective, the increase or decrease in a behavior represents learning, and it simultaneously represents motivation because knowing individuals' histories of rewards helps us understand their actions (Mook, 1987).

Central to behaviorism's success and one of its enduring contributions is the focus on the "scientific" study of learning, requiring controlled experimentation and objective observation. Behaviorist researchers attempt to explain behavioral contingencies using the scientific method of the physical sciences. Many research designs and methods for observing motivation continue to use these mechanistic frameworks (see, for example, studies of functional assessment and positive behavior support in the special education literature, or measures of time on task in general education classrooms). Within educational psychology, Weiner (1990) contended that these methods represent "one strategy used to gain respectability for this uncertain field" (p. 617). However, most motivation researchers find purely behaviorist approaches to the study of human learning and motivation unsatisfactory and emphasize cognitive mediators of human behavior in their research, especially in achievement situations (Stipek, 1996). Also, we acknowledge the difficulty of conducting controlled studies of human learning and motivation, especially in classrooms, and their inadequacy for fully explaining purposeful behavior (Mook, 1987). However, the tension between "objective" and quantifiable methods and "interpretative" qualitative methodologies remains with us, which may be one reason that motivation researchers have been slow to enter classrooms.

In motivation research, intrinsic motivation has emerged as the more compelling "something else" that engages individuals in addition to earning a reward, avoiding a punishment, or satisfying a biological deficiency (Sansone & Harackiewicz, 2000). However, extrinsic motivation remains important in modern theories of motivation (Ryan & Deci, 2000; Sansone & Harackiewicz, 2000) because it is pervasive in human experience, especially in classrooms (e.g., competitive grading systems, rewards and reinforcement charts are still widely used), and any study of classrooms will need to involve a conceptual framework, methods, and analyses that can identify and explain its role.

Cognitive Approaches. Cognitive psychology began as situated in the individual's perceptions and information processing as behaviorism is rooted in how environments influence behaviors. In opposition to behaviorism, cognitive psychologists maintain that the human mind can be studied scientifically (Anderson, 1990) and emphasize rational processes, such as considering choices and anticipating outcomes, that lead to courses of action (Anderson, 1990; Mook, 1987). The individual mediates experiences through internal events, such as wishes, urges, expectancies, and thoughts, so within individuals is where researchers look to discover the causes of their behaviors (Mook, 1987). In motivation research, cognitive views were instantiated into the study of the decisions individuals made based on their beliefs, needs, and goals.

Cognitive models of motivation include the concept of reinforcement, but portray its effects as mediated through learners' cognitions (Brophy, 2004; Stipek, 1996), emphasizing the *how* rather than the behavioral outcome (Mook, 1987). In cognitive terms, the degree to which students can be motivated by a reinforcer depends more on their expectations of reinforcement than on whether they have been similarly reinforced in the past. Also, key in motivating behavior, from a cognitive point of view, is the extent to which learners value the reinforcer. Thus, cognitive theories of motivation privilege intrinsic sources of motivation (e.g., interest, increased knowledge and skill) more than extrinsic rewards, assuming individuals are naturally motivated to develop intellectual and other potentials and take pride in their accomplishments. Furthermore, people are expected to become more intrinsically motivated when they engage in activities that hold interest or meaning for them. Many theories of motivation have emerged from or been influenced by cognitive theory (e.g., attribution theory, expectancy-value theories, self-determination theory). These individual theories are detailed elsewhere in this volume; however, we highlight expectancy-value theories and goal orientation theories because they have generated the largest body of research about achievement motivation in classrooms (Eccles & colleagues, 1983 to the present; Pintrich & Schunk, 2002). Interestingly, the newer cognitive theories of motivation have not found their way into classroom practice in the same enduring way as the older behaviorist perspective.

Expectancy-value theories grew from collaborations between Atkinson and McClelland in the 1950s and 60s using Murray's concept of *need for achievement* (Pintrich & Schunk, 2002). In general, they explain motivation in terms of individuals' expectations that an outcome is likely in a given situation, and the extent to which they value that outcome. According to the theory, which has garnered abundant empirical support over the years, students are more motivated to engage in tasks and activities when success, not failure, is expected, and value successful outcomes when activities present a moderate degree of challenge. Also, students who are success oriented are more likely to attempt challenging tasks, for which success can reasonably be expected but is not certain, than students who fear failure. Expectancy-value theories, which originated from cognitive views of learning and motivation, have expanded over the years to incorporate social and contextual factors that are related to individuals' expectations and values (see our description of social cognitive approaches later).

Similarly, cognitive perspectives on motivation are evident in goal orientation theories because these constructs were developed by developmental, motivational, and educational psychologists wanting to study students' learning and performance on academic tasks and in classroom settings (Pintrich & Schunk, 2002). Goal orientation refers to the reasons students give for engaging in achievement-related behaviors. For example, students with a mastery goal orientation or a task focus describe their desire for deep understanding and personal progress as reasons for their achievement behaviors. According to goal theories, getting good grades and being ranked at the top of the class are not primary concerns for these students, as they are for students with performance goals or an ability focus. There is a great deal of research evidence supporting goal orientation theories; students' personal goal orientations relate to a number of important achievement-related outcomes (Anderman, Patrick, Hruda, and Linnenbrink, 2003). One strength of these theories is that they have evolved to focus on how classroom goal structures evidenced in tasks, teacher talk, and evaluation practices, are related to students' personal goal orientations. "A central tenet of goal theories is that students' adoption of personal goals is influenced, at least in part, by the goal structures present in and promoted by the classroom and broader school environment" (Anderman et al., 2003, p. 244). In this way, goal orientation theories, like expectancy-value theories, reflect both cognitive and social cognitive perspectives on learning and motivation.

A focus on individual differences influenced the methods used to study motivation (Anderson, 1990; Weiner, 1990). Self-report surveys became the primary research tool for understanding individuals' motivation-related perceptions and continue to dominate in studies of classroom motivation today. Research involving students actually engaging in learning activities has been rare and typically involves students in experiments working on "research tasks"—often short versions of school-like tasks that are designed specifically for research purposes (Corno & Mandinach, 2004, p. 302). Prior to, sometimes during,

and after completing these tasks, students respond to surveys, indicating their efficacy, attributions, goals, or other cognitions. Correlations among independent variables (e.g., students' perceptions of and beliefs about learning opportunities in their classrooms) with dependent variables (e.g., persistence, strategy use, and achievement measures) continue to be a dominant way to analyze students' motivation for learning. Over time, however, researchers have realized the limitations of these artificial situations for making inferences about how students will think and behave in naturalistic contexts (Corno & Mandinach, 2004). Researchers also recognize the susceptibility of self-report measures to threats to validity, including positive response bias, and poor calibrations between what students think they do and what they actually do. Such validity problems are especially problematic when students are asked to generalize thoughts and actions across a number of activities or settings, and when research participants are young children (Turner, 1995).

There is increasing demand for researchers to provide a context for individual differences, which may help to increase the connections between research findings and classroom practice. As Eccles and Wigfield (2002) concluded, an exclusive focus on beliefs, values, and goals "may overemphasize rational, cognitive processes in motivation, at the expense of affective and other processes" (p. 127). They argued that theories of motivation need to integrate context because "it is difficult if not impossible to understand students' motivation without understanding the contexts they are experiencing" (Eccles & Wigfield, 2002, p. 128). Therefore, motivation researchers have begun to include social and contextual constructs in studies of individuals' motivated behaviors, and are turning to social perspectives on learning to design and interpret studies of motivation in authentic learning contexts (e.g., classrooms).

What have the behaviorist and cognitive paradigms contributed to the study of motivation in classrooms? These perspectives, implicitly and explicitly, are reflected in the ways educational psychologists examine and explain relationships between individuals and the contexts in which they participate; both paradigms focus on individuals in decontextualized ways and emphasize the use of objective, quantifiable methods and analyses. Thus, both paradigms have accrued little classroom research to support their basic assumptions or to integrate relationships among contexts and individual differences. However, their collective historical importance of focusing on the individual's behavior and thoughts set the stage for more integrated theories of learning and motivation, theories that seek to articulate individuals' thoughts and actions with social/instructional settings. In sum, "metatheoretical" models of motivation have evolved from mechanistic (behaviorism) to organismic (cognitive) to interactive contextual models that examine the person in the environment (Pintrich & Schunk, 2002).

Focus on Individuals in Contexts

Social Cognitive Approaches. Social cognitive theories have been characterized as modest applications of social perspectives on learning and motivation because they continue to focus on individuals and are primarily interested in cognitive constructs (Hickey, 2003; Hickey & Granade, 2004). However, a hallmark of these theories is the view that learning involves interactions among individuals' cognitions and behavior and features of the environment (Bandura, 1986; Schunk & Pajares, 2004). Researchers who espouse social cognitive theories focus on how people acquire knowledge and experience affect as a result of interacting with and observing others (Pintrich & Schunk, 2002). Most have adopted Bandura's (1986) assumption that the interactions among individuals' thoughts and actions and the environment are reciprocal. The direction of influence among these factors is not always the same, and the factors are of equal importance in the overall model, although one or two factors may take precedence in a given event or program of research (Linnenbrink & Pintrich, 2003; Pintrich & Schunk, 2002). However, like cognitive theorists, these researchers are informed to a large extent by survey self reports (i.e., people's perceptions about contexts rather than people acting and reacting in contexts).

Social cognitive theories have historical roots in theories of imitation and social learning theory (Rotter, 1954; Pintrich & Schunk, 2002). However, social cognitive theories expand social learning theories by highlighting the reciprocity among personal, behavioral, and environmental factors, and by distinguishing learning from performance and enactive versus vicarious learning. People may not perform an action at the time they learn it, and, although learning often occurs by doing, people can learn by observing others (models) perform an action. Finally, social cognitive theories significantly expand social learning theories by including the constructs of self-efficacy and self-regulation (Pintrich & Schunk, 2002). Self-efficacy (one topic of Chapter 16, this volume) is linked to beliefs about personal agency, which is a hallmark of self-regulated learning. Scholars distinguish self-efficacy, or beliefs about what one is capable of doing, from knowing exactly what to do or having the skill/ability to do it (Schunk & Pajares, 2004). Also scholars distinguish self-efficacy, which is specific to the goals of a particular task or situation, from more global

constructs, such as self-esteem and self-concept, which reflect more general senses of well-being and ability (Linnenbrink & Pintrich, 2003).

Social cognitive theories of motivation incorporate constructs concerning individuals' expectations and values, but expand the original cognitive framework by highlighting how students reconcile the personal and social to make judgments about self, likely outcomes, and values associated with tasks and outcomes (Perry & Winne, 2004; Wigfield & Eccles, 2002). In the Wigfield and Eccles model, children's beliefs about how well they will do on a particular task, termed *competency beliefs*, derive from previous experiences with similar tasks and can vary depending on the domain of study (e.g., math, reading, sports) and whether the task environment brings out students' sense of their own competence or their competence in relation to others. Their investigations (Eccles, 1993; Eccles & Wigfield, 1995; Wigfield, 1994; Wigfield et al., 1997) consistently show that students' competency beliefs and expectations are strong predictors of future grades in domains such as English and math, even stronger than measures of ability such as prior grades. However students' interests in and beliefs about the importance and utility of tasks and subject matter (their values and society's values) are the best predictors of whether they will continue studies in these domains.

Furthermore, Wigfield and Eccles (2002) have found that students' competency beliefs and task-related values become more differentiated and, generally, decline as they advance through school. Wigfield and Eccles offer two context-related explanations for this decline. First, as children advance through the grades, they become adept at processing evaluative feedback and adjusting their approaches to classroom tasks accordingly. Also, they become more adept at making social comparisons with select peers, and information from these comparisons leads to more accurate, often lower, beliefs about competence. Second, as children advance in school, features of the context change. Evaluation becomes more salient and involves more social comparison (e.g., students are graded and grades may be publicized). When students do well, the result can be elevated competency beliefs and increased valuing of school-related activities. For students who struggle, these changes can lower beliefs about competence, depress expectations for success, and decrease valuing of school-related tasks and productive achievement-related behavior. These findings offer evidence of how features of instructional environments (e.g., classroom tasks and evaluation practices) interact with students' personal characteristics and their approaches to and engagement in learning.

In summary, social cognitive theories have advanced understandings about how personal and contextual factors are related to students' beliefs about and approaches to learning in school. However, studies that align with social cognitive theories continue to place individuals' perceptions of and responses to learning contexts at the center of their investigations. In contrast, sociocultural applications place context at the center of their investigations and, often, make activities the subject of analyses (Corno & Mandinach, 2004). This shifting emphasis is significant for studies of motivation in classrooms. Instead of conducting studies *about* classrooms via the perceptions of the students, increasingly, motivational researchers are conducting studies *in* events *in* classrooms through examining interactions.

Sociocultural Approaches. Sociocultural theories applied to motivation assert the relevance of Vygotsky's (1978) view that learning results when individuals interact in the social and material world, participate in the knowledge practices of a community, and are supported by others in a community that includes individuals more knowledgeable than them (Hickey, 2003; Lave & Wenger, 1991; McCaslin & Hickey, 2001; Serpell, 1997). Through participating in activities, learners incorporate the essential understandings, practices, and mores of particular contexts into their thinking and behavior (Corno & Mandinach, 2004, pp. 305–306). Participation and appropriation are key constructs in sociocultural theories of learning and motivation, and people are not merely products of their environments, but, through their participation, create, or co-construct, environments. Researchers applying sociocultural theories study the social and cultural practices of communities and the ways individuals use the tools available to the community. In these ways, activities—tool-mediated, goal-directed actions—that link the individual and society are fundamental units of analyses in sociocultural research (McCaslin, 2004; Wertsch, 1985). In classrooms, activity refers to what teachers and students, and students and students, say to and do with one another. Classroom tools can include discourse and participation structures, various forms of technology, teacher and peer support, and academic tasks. In contrast to cognitive perspectives that view activity as purposeful cognition and behavior on the part of individuals, activity theory, which aligns with sociocultural theory, locates and co-regulates human activity in the social realm (McCaslin, 2004). Also, in contrast to behaviorist perspectives, activity theorists believe that "human activity represents individual and collective mediation of participation in opportunities rather than as a direct effect of opportunity" (McCaslin, 2004, p. 254).

In educational psychology, perhaps the most widely recognized and applied construct from Vygotsky's sociocultural theory is the zone of proximal development (ZPD). The ZPD, which incorporates notions of participation and appropriation, refers to the space delimiting what learners can do independently and what they can do with the assistance of others. Ideally, teachers identify and work with students in their ZPDs. Brophy (1999) argued for a motivational analogue to the ZPD, advancing the idea that teachers and instructional contexts can support student motivation to engage in learning opportunities that they might not on their own. This motivational ZPD is similar to the original descriptions of *scaffolding*, in which teacher support was found to be not only cognitive, but motivational and affective (Wood, Bruner, & Ross, 1976), such as by initiating and sustaining student interest and mediating frustration. Similarly, McCaslin and colleagues (McCaslin & Good, 1996; McCaslin & Hickey, 2001) have identified an "arena of co-regulation" that exists on both social and psychological planes. It encompasses intrapsychological processes, such as motivation, enactment, and evaluation, in contexts of supportive relationships (e.g., between teachers and students and students and students), structural supports (e.g., scaffolding), and affording opportunities (e.g., tasks that challenge but don't overwhelm students cognitively, motivationally, affectively, or socially). Thus, models of co-regulated learning assume that beliefs, values, and expectations that contribute to motivation for learning are socially constructed and supported (Hickey, 2003). In sum, motivation is viewed as situated in the activity or setting, not in the person, representing a very different theoretical perspective and implicating different ways of studying motivation.

Sociocultural theories of learning and motivation are changing the ways researchers study motivation in classrooms, including the investigations of researchers that use more traditional theoretical frameworks for studying motivation. Specifically, situated and sociocultural perspectives on learning and motivation have prompted investigations of motivation and self- and co-regulation in naturalistic settings—real contexts and real time (Perry & VandeKamp, 2000; Turner, Meyer, Midgley, & Patrick, 2003; Winne & Perry, 2000; Yowell & Smylie, 1999). Researchers are using methods and measures that reveal the unique characteristics of particular teaching and learning contexts (Paris & Paris, 2001; Randi & Corno, 2000). Often, studies incorporate multiple methods and measures that support in-depth, on-line investigations of interactions among features of the social/instructional environment and students' engagement and learning. The results are deeply nuanced descriptions of classroom activity and an increasingly robust body of practical knowledge and principles about teaching and learning environments that promote (or curtail) motivation for and engagement in learning (Hickey & Granade, 2004). Much of the research described in the following section reflects this new direction.

A critical issue confronting sociocultural theorists is the extent to which individuals' intrapsychological processes are bound to the context in which they are coconstructed versus generalizable (Hickey, 2003). McCaslin (2004) argues that the formation of individual identity is fundamental in sociocultural theories of learning and motivation. In her view, learning and motivation are co-regulated at the start but, once learners internalize the structural and social supports in the environment, they are capable of relatively self-regulated learning in that domain (McCaslin & Good, 1996). In this way, co-regulated learning is the process by which socially shaped instructional environments support students toward autonomous activity in a context of relationships among teachers, peers, objects, setting, and self in the classroom.

Hickey and Granade (2004), on the other hand, argue that most applications of sociocultural theories continue to be too individually oriented. In their view, studies interested in sociocultural relationships to motivation continue to focus on how individuals internalize the standards and values of the communities in which they participate, rather than on how individuals participate in the coconstruction of the standards and values that are then internalized. Their perspectives on motivation posit beliefs, values, and expectations may be so tightly bound to the context in which they are coconstructed as to make notions of internalization and generalization, which are essential for self-regulation, irrelevant. Studies of motivation in classrooms have potential to unravel these complexities, but, to our knowledge, studies to date have yet to articulate the coconstruction of teachers' and students' motivational beliefs, values, and expectations in such precise terms.

WHAT HAVE WE LEARNED ABOUT CLASSROOMS AS CONTEXTS FOR MOTIVATING LEARNING?

In this section, we review research that examines students' motivational experiences *in* classrooms. Although this research reflects a new and growing body of work, it has roots in earlier classroom research (Corno & Mandinach, 1983; Brophy, Rohrkemper, Rashid, & Goldberger, 1983; Rohrkemper & Corno, 1988). Here we attempt an instructive rather than exhaustive review, providing detailed descriptions of a few studies to support our interpretations of what classroom research is teaching us about student motivation. We have limited the inclusion of studies that are experimental or rely

exclusively on self-report data because excellent reviews of this research already exist (Eccles, Wigfield, & Schiefele, 1998; Pintrich, 2003; Stipek, 1996). Instead, we highlight studies that use multiple and varied methods and examine constructs from cognitive, social cognitive, and sociocultural theories of motivation and learning. In an effort to achieve conceptual clarity, we divide this section into three subsections to examine how (a) classroom tasks, (b) instruction, and (c) social interactions are central to understanding student engagement in classroom learning activities. However, the research we describe in this section illustrates that no single person or classroom characteristic determines students' motivational experiences; rather, motivational experiences reflect the complex interleaving of individual and contextual characteristics (Blumenfeld et al., 1991; Blumenfeld, 1992).

Classroom Tasks That Support Student Motivation

The examination of classroom tasks and activities has a long history in studies of learning and motivation. Dewey (1916) stressed the importance of engaging children in projects that interested them, both as foundational to meaningful learning and as a way to develop responsible members of society. Motivation has long been thought to derive from the meaningfulness of activities related to daily life and society as well as to the active, rather than passive, engagement of students.

Similar to Dewey's notion of *interaction* (e.g., Glassman & Wang, 2004), researchers recently have focused on relationships among tasks, student cognition, motivation, and emotion. Working from a cognitive information processing perspective, Doyle (1983) distinguished between low-level tasks that emphasize recognition, memory skills, and algorithmic processes, and complex tasks that were more likely to elicit higher levels of thinking processes. From a social cognitive perspective, Blumenfeld, Mergendoller, and Swarthout (1987) argued that tasks socialize students' expectations about academic work. For example, tasks that are too simple and routine may induce boredom and disinterest in the content. Tasks also are related to how students interpret and experience the curriculum (McCaslin & Good, 1996). For example, students may judge reading or mathematics as interesting or important on the basis of activities they complete in each domain.

Previous research has identified many characteristics of tasks that promote students' situational interest in learning, such as variety, novelty, and diversity; meaningfulness and relevance; and fantasy embellishments (Malone & Lepper, 1987). Other task factors associated with motivation include moderate challenge;

features that stimulate interest or curiosity and enhance student control; and embedded short-term goals (Ames, 1992; Brophy, 2004; Eccles et al., 1998; Pintrich, 2003; Pintrich & Schunk, 2002; Stipek, 1996). Reflecting on a 1983 publication, Corno and Mandinach (2004, pp. 303–304), acknowledge their "thin view of the task environment... [that] gave little sense of the complexities involved when good teachers work to create experiences that fully engage their students with school." We infer that, in earlier characterizations of tasks, features of tasks, such as difficulty level or interestingness, were viewed as static; that is, tasks were challenging or interesting in some absolute sense, rather than as a consequence of how teachers design and implement them and how students interpret and manipulate them, or how they interact with other features of the classroom context.

Recent research in classrooms promotes a different conception of the most engaging tasks as having features teachers and students can manipulate to suit their teaching and learning needs. For example, Miller and Meece (1997) worked with teachers in a mostly White (15% Black) upper middle-class, high-achieving school to design complex, engaging writing assignments. Using a goal theory perspective, the authors sought to enhance students' mastery goals by designing tasks that offered students opportunities to control challenge, use complex cognitive strategies, such as planning, and collaborate with peers. Writing assignments that required at least paragraph-level writing, involved collaboration among peers, and lasted for several days were characterized as "high challenge tasks." Miller and Meece hypothesized that increasing the opportunities that students had for reading and writing assignments beyond the worksheet level would evoke more positive signs of motivation. Motivation measures included students' self-reported mastery, ego-social (e.g., self-enhancement) and task avoidance, and strategy use. Classrooms were classified as high or low implementation based both on the decrease in number of assignments and the increase in assignments requiring complex writing, peer collaboration, and student choice.

In the high-implementation classrooms, student surveys indicated that students of all achievement levels reported a significant decline in ego-social goals (e.g., students were less focused on what other students thought about their ability), whereas ego-social goals did not decline in the low-implementation group. During writing activities, teachers in high-implementation classrooms encouraged students to complete challenging assignments, provided students with clear feedback, gave adequate time to write, and gave students many opportunities to correct errors. With opportunities like these, students may have felt less anxious about evaluation and

able to concentrate on learning. Surprisingly, mastery goals remained somewhat high and stable for students in both implementation groups, possibly related to students' developmental level. The researchers reported that students' mastery goals were similar for both high-and low-challenge activities. The low achievers in the high-implementation group reported both a significant decline in work avoidance goals and the use of more high-level strategies (compared to the average achievers in their group). In interviews, students from every classroom expressed a strong preference for high-challenge tasks, with the strongest support coming from average and low-achieving students (Miller & Meece, 1999).

Although Miller and Meece (1999) premised their study on earlier research about the motivational potential of task characteristics (i.e., challenge, collaboration), they later provided further interpretation of why the tasks were motivational (personal communication, June 2004). They concluded that students were motivated because they could tailor tasks to suit their unique learning needs—high-challenge tasks became a way to differentiate instruction. In addition, the teacher support documented in high-implementation classrooms enabled students to succeed on the challenging writing assignments. Although this study began with the traditional notion of viewing motivation in the task itself, it concluded by demonstrating that the opportunities provided by complex and multiday tasks, coupled with teacher support, differentiated tasks so that they could be motivational for students of diverse ability levels, including, especially, low achievers.

This dynamic view of tasks is reflected in both Perry's (1998; Perry & VandeKamp, 2000) and Turner's (1995) research on how classroom tasks are related to primary grade students' motivation for and approaches to learning. For example, Perry (1998) observed naturally occurring writing activities in five grade 2/3 classrooms in five elementary schools on the West Coast of Canada. She characterized each class as high or low in its promotion of self-regulated learning (SRL) based on a set of conceptual categories derived from previous research on motivation and self-regulation: students' opportunities for choice, control over challenge, self-evaluation, and support from peers and teachers. Perry then observed two students in each classroom (one high and one low achiever, $N = 10$) during writing activities and interviewed them after each observation. These in-class observations were conducted over 6 months and each observation lasted for the total time allocated to writing on a particular day (up to 2 hours).

Perry observed that tasks in high-SRL classrooms were complex, addressing multiple goals and large chunks of meaning (e.g., students conducted research and wrote reports), extending over time, involving multiple cognitive and motivational processes (e.g., planning, problem solving, persistence) and resulting in the creation of varied products (e.g., children produced illustrations, diagrams, and expository text to demonstrate their learning about an animal). Compared to tasks that focused on specific information leading to predetermined products and solutions (e.g., correcting punctuation), Perry (1998) reported that complex tasks increased students' opportunities to regulate their learning by allowing them to make choices and control challenge to suit their learning needs and preferences. When students were involved in complex writing tasks, they reported feeling more in control of their learning and more motivated to write than students involved in writing tasks that limited choice and control over challenge. Moreover, low-achieving students involved in complex writing tasks demonstrated and reported less negative affect (e.g., discouragement, frustration), more constructive responses to corrective feedback, and fewer self-handicapping strategies (e.g., procrastinating or avoiding writing altogether) than low-achieving students in classrooms where undifferentiated writing tasks were the norm. In addition, Perry described how teachers supported students' engagement in complex tasks, helping them to plan ("Has anyone got a draft ready for the computer?"), solve problems ("When you have something new to do, it helps to look at something you have already done"), monitor and evaluate learning, and support one another (Perry, 1998).

Perry's study shows how classroom research can enrich understandings from earlier research that relied only on self-report data. For example, her data offer evidence of students engaging in co-regulated and self-regulated learning and making comments that reflect motivational constructs, such as task focus (a student chose a partner because he could help her "understand things") or task avoidance (a student hid her writing in her desk "so no one else would see it"). In addition, her data demonstrate the complexity of the relationships between task features and student characteristics. In one classroom, Perry observed that tasks had many characteristics associated with student motivation (e.g., they were meaningful and gave students a lot of autonomy). However, students in this class did not receive instrumental support from their teacher or from one another. In this context, students appeared frustrated and confused, their productivity was low and they engaged in a lot of off-task behavior. We acknowledge that the generalizability of Perry's (1998) findings are limited by her focus on two grades and one content area, and by the small number of classrooms studied. However, Perry's research demonstrates both how teachers design tasks and how they support tasks to enhance their motivational value for students.

Whereas Perry (1998) examined conceptual categories from previous research on motivation in naturally occurring classroom activities, other researchers have developed instructional programs based on design principles derived inductively from classrooms. Guthrie (Guthrie & Alao, 1997) collaborated with teachers and reading specialists over several years to identify and implement design principles, including collecting lessons and interviewing teachers as they viewed videotapes of their instruction. From these sources, Guthrie and Alao specified eight design principles for Concept Oriented Reading Instruction (CORI), an interdisciplinary reading/language arts and science program with a goal to increase reading engagement. Engagement was defined as evidence of motivation, strategy use, and increased conceptual knowledge during reading. A design principle states a "characteristic of the classroom context that can be controlled by the teacher and that contributes to student motivation for reading" and may include "activities, texts, teacher actions, [or] interpersonal relationships" (Guthrie & Alao, 1997, p. 95). The contextual characteristics selected as design principles in CORI instruction revolved around interdisciplinary themes, real-world experience, self-direction, interesting texts, social collaboration, self-expression, cognitive strategies, and coherent instruction. In all CORI studies, students participated in hands-on science activities, such as collecting and observing crickets, and generated questions for further research. Teachers assisted students in locating sources of information and provided strategy instruction to help students integrate their sources and present findings. Students were from a diverse (e.g., 55 percent African-American) population of low-achieving third and fifth graders in Chapter I schools.

Guthrie and his colleagues implemented these principles in several studies. In general, volunteer teachers attended summer workshops of 10 half days to plan for the year. Teachers and researchers collaboratively developed instructional goals consistent with district objectives, designed student activities and teaching strategies, and selected instructional materials to meet the goals using CORI principles. The teachers met one day per month to discuss instruction, describe their implementation of principles, and exchange instructional techniques (Guthrie, VanMeter, Hancock, & Alao, 1998; Guthrie, Wigfield, & VonSecker, 2000). In the study by Guthrie et al. (2004), teachers also viewed examples of instruction, practiced reading strategies, and used a teachers guide supplied by the project for planning their own instruction. In one study, students in the CORI program demonstrated more strategy use and text comprehension compared to students taught traditional reading and science lessons (Guthrie et al., 1998). In a subsequent study, researchers created a motivational intervention focusing on support for autonomy, competence, and collaboration, and emphasizing mastery goals and real-world interactions (Guthrie et al., 2000). CORI students reported greater curiosity and strategy use compared to students in traditional classrooms with no intervention.

The CORI research program illustrated that classroom contexts can be redesigned to support motivation and learning by integrating principles from research. These studies, like others cited (e.g., Perry, 1998; Turner, 1995), studied motivation as embedded in content areas and tasks rather than as generic behaviors, as had been common in earlier research. The science and reading task was infused with both strategy instruction and instruction known to be related to student motivation. Unfortunately, although the instructional principles are described, the researchers do not report how teachers and students interacted in the CORI classrooms, so it is not clear what was successful or problematic during the intervention. Whereas student comprehension data are derived from authentic tasks, such as posing research questions about previously unread science passages, student motivation data come from self-reports. Nevertheless, these studies are unusual among motivation studies in their attempts to design and implement interventions with teachers that integrate principles of motivation, learning, and instruction, and study their relationship to students' motivation and achievement. Finally, because the CORI intervention was implemented in schools having diverse and low-achieving student bodies, these studies provide evidence that complex, meaningful tasks can benefit all children, not just those with advantaged backgrounds.

Concerned about the proliferation of low-level tasks and the limited opportunities for cognitive engagement, especially in urban classrooms, Blumenfeld and her colleagues (Blumenfeld et al., 1991) began studies of how long-term, problem-focused, and meaningful units of instruction in project-based science (PBS) are related to students' thoughtfulness (e.g., offering justifications and critiques), self-regulation and motivation. This work was influenced by social cognitive theories of motivation and constructivist theories of learning. An outgrowth of cognitive theories, constructivism emphasizes that understanding comes from constructing and transforming knowledge rather than from simply acquiring it. This theoretical approach guided collaboration with teachers and teachers' work with students. Project implementation, including teacher development, was studied over the academic year (e.g., Blumenfeld, Krajcik, Marx, & Soloway, 1994) using student observations and interviews, videotapes of lessons and student activities, teachers' case reports, interviews with teachers, case studies of teachers, and audio- and videotapes of collaborative sessions. Teacher development was based on collaboration between teachers and researchers. The researchers grounded theory related to PBS (e.g., pose a driving question, use investigations to learn concepts) in the language of classroom practice, and these principles served as sources for iterative cycles of teachers' planning, enactment, and reflection over the year. Teachers did not simply carry out researchers' plans, but tailored PBS to fit the unique circumstances of their classrooms. In the process, researchers and teachers developed new views of instruction, improved understanding of the features of PBS, and developed a range of practices congruent with the theory. The three project design elements included (a) a focus on student interest and value, competence, strategies, and learning, (b) the development of teachers' understanding and implementation of PBS, and (c) support for teaching in a technologically rich context.

In one study, Krajcik, Blumenfeld, and their colleagues (Krajcik, Blumenfeld, Marx, Bass, & Fredricks, 1998) examined relations between task features and student learning and motivation in PBS. They constructed case studies of eight seventh-grade students (two African-Americans, one Asian, and five European-Americans, each of whom ranked at the lower middle achievement range in science) in a small urban school district. Data included videotaped observations, interviews, and examinations of students' work products and presentations over 7 months and three science units. Their data showed how students engaged in inquiry (e.g., asking questions, designing investigations) and measured levels of interest, affect, investment, and group processes. The researchers observed that the students appeared interested and curious as they designed and built equipment and carried out procedures to identify "mystery powders" and answer intriguing questions about garbage and water. Because this was their initial attempt at inquiry-based instruction, students needed teacher support to ask authentic questions (e.g., relating science to their lives), rather than merely interesting ones, to focus on substantive rather than procedural issues, and to perform simultaneous activities during the project, such as implementing complex procedures and collecting data. This study highlighted the integral roles of teacher learning, task and curriculum design, and student scaffolding, which are related to students' motivation and inquiry in PBS.

In contrast to earlier research, Krajcik et al. (1998) demonstrated that students operate differently within and across classroom activities not only as a function of personal characteristics (e.g., achievement) but also depending on the domain of study, instructional goals, familiarity with instructional processes, and even the time of year. This study's findings revealed both the time required for these students, unaccustomed to this type of instruction, to conduct inquiry, and the important role of teachers and other supports in sustaining and directing their effort.

For example, students needed scaffolding to move from their original conception of meaningful as "of personal interest" to a new construction of meaningful as "important" scientific concepts. More traditional studies about classrooms would not have followed this development or offered such thick descriptions of how the change occurred. Like the CORI studies, this research program is unique in its investigation of many relationships among learning and motivation, and its in-depth investigation of classroom instructional interactions. In addition, this study's findings demonstrate the rich knowledge about task motivation and learning, and student and teacher change that can be gained from a multimethod, qualitative approach (see also Patrick & Middleton, 2002).

Together, the studies in this section extend earlier notions of tasks as having independent and inherent characteristics that "motivate" students or promote "high-level" thinking. Although challenge, meaningfulness, and other features of activities are important for student motivation, this body of classroom research illustrates that these features are not simply in and of the task; rather, they are embedded in the interactions among student characteristics, task features, and instructional and social supports in the classroom. Two advances in our understanding of tasks and motivation emerge from these studies. First, the researchers found that tasks were dynamic not static; features, such as challenge and meaningfulness, could readily be adapted by teachers and students. Students could experience a complex or open task (see Turner, 1995) differently. Such mallcability supports students' motivation according to their interests and achievement needs (e.g., Meyer, Turner, & Spencer, 1997). Second, many of these classroom researchers found that for students to successfully complete "challenging" or "meaningful" tasks, they needed effective and multifaceted instructional support. For example, as part of instructional scaffolding (described in the next section), teachers must help students develop effective learning and problem-solving strategies so that they can successfully struggle with the demands of complex tasks. Teachers need to provide feedback that informs students about their progress and helps them make wise decisions for future learning. And together, as the next group of research studies illustrate, teachers and students need to create a classroom climate that values effort and does not penalize or embarrass students for making mistakes or learning in different ways (e.g., taking longer, needing assistance).

Instructional Practices That Support Student Engagement

Research on motivation in classrooms has provided corroborating evidence for many of the instructional practices previously associated with students' motivation for learning, including clearly communicating expectations, giving motivational messages about success and failure, providing informative feedback, displaying positive emotions, modeling and using effective strategies, and perceiving high teaching efficacy (Pintrich & Schunk, 2002; Stipek, 1996). Typically motivation has been conceptualized as the outcome of discrete instructional behaviors, rather than the result of unique combinations of practices evolving within and across contexts. In addition, much of what is known about instructional practices and their relationships to student motivation has been derived from experimental or survey research in motivation, but never studied or validated in classroom research. Therefore, in this section we highlight research that reflects a more authentic view of classroom interactions and student motivation. Often, aspects of more than one theoretical perspective (e.g., social cognitive and social constructivist theories as well as situated and sociocultural theories)—are illustrated within the same study. Given that this research has emerged from a variety of theoretical traditions, the researchers commonly conceive of motivation as arising from dynamic interactions among persons that occur across time in the context of multiple levels of classroom activity. Motivation is viewed as situated and malleable, rather than generalizable and stable, and related to other psychological experiences, such as emotions (e.g., Op't Eynde, DeCorte, & Verschaffel, 2001). Although we treat instructional and interpersonal interactions in classrooms separately here (interpersonal interactions are the topic of the next section), many of the studies we review examined both types of interactions.

One way in which teachers support student learning is by offering and adjusting support to learners depending on their needs, also called scaffolding (Wood, Bruner, & Ross, 1976). Scaffolded instruction has its origin in social perspectives on learning, such as Vygotsky's zone of proximal development (Vygotsky, 1978), as well as more recently in McCaslin's (2004) conceptualization of co-regulated learning. Although originally linked to cognitive outcomes, such as reading comprehension (e.g., Palincsar & Brown, 1984), Turner and her colleagues (Turner et al., 1998, 2002) examined how instructional scaffolding was related to student motivation. Scaffolding signals teachers' willingness to support student efforts in learning, and demonstrates their belief that students are capable of progress.

Turner and her colleagues (Turner et al., 2002) observed, audiotaped, and transcribed teachers' discourse during mathematics instruction in nine diverse (30 percent African-American) urban classrooms for 5 days each during fall and spring units. They also surveyed students about their avoidance behaviors (e.g., self-handicapping) in mathematics and their perceptions of the goal structure of the classroom. Teacher discourse was classified as providing instructional (cognitive) support or motivational support. Both types of discourse were coded as either scaffolded or nonscaffolded. Scaffolded forms of instructional discourse included helping students understand (e.g., explaining, modeling) and prompting them to explain and justify their understanding. Elsewhere, this form of prompting has been called "press" (Blumenfeld, 1992b; Kazemi & Stipek, 2001; Middleton & Midgley, 2002). In contrast, nonscaffolded forms of instructional discourse included asking for correct answers or telling students what to do, but with no explanations (i.e., Mehan's [1985] "initiation–response–evaluation" or I–R–E pattern). Scaffolded motivational discourse included a focus on learning and improvement, articulated positive emotions, and promoted collaboration, whereas nonscaffolded motivational discourse focused on students' mistakes, expressed negative affect, and fostered social comparison.

Turner et al. (2002) found that scaffolding patterns of instructional and motivational discourse were related positively to student reports of low avoidance behaviors and perceptions of mastery goals. Teachers who scaffolded wove positive affective statements into instruction as they stressed the importance of learning, made sure that all students understood, and challenged students to demonstrate their understanding, as these examples, from one sixth-grade classroom, illustrated:

Yesterday when I was done instructing you, you guys seemed to understand [the lesson]. Is there *anyone* who said. . . . I don't remember. . . . And don't look around and say to yourself, "I'm not going to raise my hand because I don't want Jennifer to think I'm dumb," [slight laughter]. If you don't remember, *please* raise your hand (Turner et al., 2002, p. 99).

This same teacher asked a student if he understood the lesson and when he responded "Yes," she countered, "You sure? You need it explained again? You come up and explain it to her. Oh yes, darling. Come on down!" (Turner et al., 2002, p. 100).

Discourse analysis afforded a detailed view of *what* teachers said and *how* they said it, and the relation of those messages to student reports of motivation. Although earlier research had noted the importance of feedback, praise, criticism, and other instructional practices, it had not demonstrated how instruction, motivation, and emotion were interwoven in everyday classroom discourse. This work demonstrated that, in practice, instruction is contextualized in rich and complex dialogues and that it is the holistic features of classroom discourse that probably account for student motivation. However, because of their focus on *teacher* discourse, Turner et al. (2002) placed student discourse and task participation in

the background, even though the authors acknowledge their importance in understanding student motivation. Although students' survey reports of avoidance behaviors and perceptions of the goal structures in their classrooms as "mastery" or "performance" oriented were reliable and theoretically consistent with patterns of teacher discourse, they were limited because students did not explain what they meant when they responded to the questionnaire items. Nonetheless, this classroom study described classroom-level interactions using teacher discourse, which highlighted the importance of *how* motivational messages are conveyed in teacher talk.

The study's findings also extended theory about the features of mastery-oriented classrooms in two ways. First, Turner et al. (2002) showed that affective aspects were important in classroom instructional interactions, in addition to cognitive ones, as premised in earlier work (e.g., Ames, 1992). For example, it was not just *that* teachers emphasized learning and improvement in their speech and actions, but also *how* such emphases got communicated. The classrooms in which teachers used the highest percentages of scaffolded motivational discourse (e.g., positive affect, feedback about improvement), in contrast to classrooms in which discourse lacked motivational discourse or was characterized by small proportions of negative motivational messages, were those perceived by students to be highest in mastery goal structures and lowest in student reports of avoidance strategies. Second, the study's findings demonstrated how combinations of instructional practices, rather than individual practices, distinguished classrooms perceived as mastery-oriented. That is, teachers in mastery-oriented classrooms helped students understand, held them accountable for their learning, encouraged them when they encountered difficulties, relieved anxiety, and provided social support. Together, these practices seemed to create affordances for student participation. In classrooms where teachers used primarily one type of practice without also scaffolding understanding or motivation, the instructional interactions appeared to limit student participation and motivation. In addition, this line of classroom research has demonstrated that such combinations of instructional practices are effective in both middle-class (e.g., Turner et al., 1998) and low-income urban classrooms (Turner et al., 2002).

Other instructional practices, such as teachers' curriculum choices and how they adapt instruction to meet student needs, also are associated with student motivation. Using multiple methods, such as interviews, observations, site records, and teacher and student survey data from Michigan and California, McLaughlin and Talbert (2001) described three types of teacher instructional behaviors in schools whose populations had shifted from middle-class to low-income. One group of teachers lowered expectations and modified the curriculum to respond to their nontraditional students' attitudes, behaviors, and backgrounds. Often teachers chose such tactics to support students and avoid high failure rates. This pattern was manifested in several ways. Some teachers taught a revised, superficial version of the curriculum at a reduced pace. One teacher described this approach as a "Cliff Notes sort of thing. I don't talk to them about the beauty of the language; I would be wasting my breath" (McLaughlin & Talbert, 2001, p. 23). Other teachers reduced the curriculum to drilling students on "prerequisite" skills. Still other teachers adopted a "relevance" approach, in which regular content was changed so that it would be "fun" and personally meaningful. McLaughlin and Talbert (2001) report that one California biology teacher devoted a third of class time to letting students play with a pet white rat or talk with friends; the objective was for them to "feel comfortable." Curriculum and expectations were changed to such an extent that students never engaged with meaningful content and, likely, would never achieve at their age-appropriate grade level. Students in these classrooms reported boredom and disengagement.

A second group of teachers continued to teach the regular curriculum with no adjustment, making it inaccessible to students with lower skill levels. Classes were teacher-centered, lecture based, and followed "the guidelines," including scope and sequence charts, daily routines, and similar work tasks on most days. Teachers located learning problems in the students, and described their students in terms of deficiencies. When his students lacked preparation, one teacher commented, "There's not much I can really do about it. Either you fall in line [with my expectations] or you get out" (McLaughlin & Talbert, 2001, p. 21). Teachers defended such positions by the need to meet their standards. As a result, they adhered to core principles of the profession in which the teacher's job is to enact the curriculum and ensure student mastery of content and skills. In these classrooms, both teachers and students became frustrated and burnt out.

A third group of teachers applied a more student-centered approach. They built on students' interests, skills, and prior knowledge while pressing them to master the high school curriculum. They emphasized depth over coverage and problem solving over routines. As one science teacher said, "What are the underlying principles? What are the commonalities? . . . You have to tap into their intellect. You'll kill their interest if you use content to teach basic skills" (McLaughlin & Talbert, 2001, p. 29). For example, one teacher discarded the textbook and used manipulatives to introduce algebraic concepts: "They can see how to represent $x^2 + 5 + 6$ and then see how to rearrange [the manipulatives] so they can actually factor it.

Today I took a group of [limited English proficient] kids who never had any algebra through squares, square roots, cubes, cube roots, and they understand what they're doing and they're having a good time" (McLaughlin & Talbert, 2001, p. 26). Teachers in these classrooms also conceived of their relationships with their students as personal and flexible. They emphasized getting to know students' strengths, experiences, knowledge, and areas for growth. As a result, one English teacher said, "Every class I plan is different . . . my approach will vary according to the needs of my students" (McLaughlin & Talbert, 2001, p. 31). She summed up her practice this way: "Forget didactic instruction! [My students] want to participate, they really want to be there, to share in the instruction and share in the learning" (p. 31). This study's findings demonstrate again that engaging teaching practices are successful across racial, ethnic, and SES groups.

Similarly, Turner and Patrick (2004) took a developmental, person-in-context perspective in the study of two students, Justin and Shanida, and their participation in mathematics instruction in sixth grade in elementary school and a year later in seventh-grade in middle school. Their goal was to investigate the joint contribution of both student characteristics and teacher instruction in the students' participation in class. Over both years, Justin (European-American) reported moderate mastery and high performance achievement goals, whereas Shanida (African-American) reported high mastery and low performance goals. The two students were in the same heterogeneous sixth-grade classroom, which they perceived as high in both performance and mastery goal structures. Patterns of teacher discourse reflected these perceptions; their sixth-grade teacher emphasized understanding as well as speed and accuracy, and sometimes became impatient if students did not understand the lesson. The emphasis on correct answers favored the high achievers, like Justin, while seeming to put lower achievers, like Shanida, at a disadvantage. The teacher called on, encouraged, and scaffolded Justin's participation, even though he volunteered infrequently. Shanida volunteered occasionally, but received little teacher support or attention, except for the time the teacher reported an error she made to the whole class.

Shanida and Justin moved into different mathematics classes in seventh grade. Justin perceived his classroom (for high-achieving students) as emphasizing high mastery and low performance goals. His seventh-grade teacher promoted student understanding, encouraged students to view errors as information about their learning, and provided support and encouragement. However, she called mostly on volunteers, and Justin did not volunteer. Two of the four times he appeared in the class transcripts were for discipline, once when the teacher admonished him as a "rude young man." Justin had been prominent in sixth-grade transcripts because the teacher had singled him out as talented and helped him achieve, but he remained in the background in seventh grade—he chose not to participate and his teacher didn't require him to participate.

Shanida perceived her seventh-grade classroom (for average-achieving students) as placing moderate emphasis on both mastery and performance goals. The teacher used supportive forms of both instructional and motivational discourse, placing more importance on justifying problem solutions than most of the teachers observed in this study. Shanida increased her volunteering and participation in seventh grade, and with teacher scaffolding, she demonstrated increasing competence. When Shanida and her partner devised a good strategy for a complex problem, the teacher called her a "clever girl." At the end of the spring semester, Shanida had taken a leadership position and persuaded the teacher to change a special project to suit the students' preferences. The seventh-grade classroom provided more affordances for Shanida, not only because she actively participated, but also because the teacher provided the kinds of instructional and motivational support that encouraged her to participate.

Turner and Patrick (2004) concluded that students' participation in both grades reflected not only their personal goals and achievement histories, but also their perceptions of the classroom goal structures *and* opportunities and constraints of the instructional interactions they experienced (e.g., their communication with the teacher and with instructional practices and support). Also, Turner and Patrick concluded that instructional practices across "mastery classrooms" were not necessarily similar. The two seventh-grade classes, though students perceived them as somewhat high in mastery goal structures, differed in whether the teachers allowed students to volunteer or whether they required most students to participate. Although both teachers supported student volunteers, those who did not volunteer did not benefit from these affordances. Therefore, the presence of certain practices, such as requiring student participation, may be related to how individual students experience the constraints and affordances of even mastery-oriented classrooms. As Turner and Patrick summarized, "This study complicates the general finding that mastery goal structures are adaptive by suggesting that certain instructional practices, such as wide calling,[1] can influence whether and how mastery-oriented classrooms promote student participation and presumably learning" (p. 1781).

Most motivation research, including studies conducted in classrooms, has focused either on how participants interpret contexts, or how particular features of contexts, such as tasks or instructional practices, are related to individuals' motivation. It is difficult to focus simultaneously on multiple aspects of contexts, even while holding the theoretical perspective that only by understanding how all features of a context work in concert can we understand motivation (e.g., Tharp, Estrada, Dalton, & Yamauchi, 2000). Järvelä (1995) attempted to capture such interactions in a study of student involvement in a problem-solving activity. Consistent with situated and sociocultural theories of learning and motivation, the unit of analysis in her study was not the individual learner, or the task, but teacher—student interactions during task completion. Her assumption was that learning and motivation are jointly constructed in a social relationship. A cognitive apprenticeship model guided the design of instruction because it is premised on joint goal-oriented problem solving between teacher and student.

Finnish comprehensive high school boys aged 13 to 14 worked in pairs over 3 days (9 hours) of instruction to investigate and model the control principles of an automatic washing machine using Logo programming language and Lego bricks. Eight students (of 22) were involved in detailed qualitative analyses. Videotapes of students during classroom activities captured students working on the task in pairs, interacting with the teacher, a view of their computer screen, and the classroom setting, for a record of events. The teacher used practices consistent with cognitive apprenticeship, including modeling his own thinking and planning processes for the group and pairs, encouraging metacognitive and reflective thinking, and fading support when it was appropriate to do so.

After each class, researchers selected video episodes that revealed teacher and student behaviors during instructional interactions. These episodes were used for stimulated recall interviews, in which students were asked about their thoughts and feelings during the observed activities. Case descriptions were constructed that included interpretations of students' behavior and verbal and nonverbal utterances, and of how the cognitive apprenticeship model functioned in the interactions. Järvelä (1995) found that in half of the 46 episodes the teachers and students interacted easily, achieving a shared understanding or similar interpretations of the situation, including seven episodes in which they did joint problem solving. These students also were relatively task focused during these interactions. In contexts where students' behavior was not task oriented, teachers and students did not interact effectively. Some students depended on the teacher for specific directions and gave up easily without teacher help. Other students preferred to address the problem in their own way and regarded teacher modeling as interference.

---

[1] *Wide calling* refers to the practice of calling on volunteers and nonvolunteers.

Järvelä's data provided detailed descriptions of classroom interactions, including student behaviors, students' responses to tasks and instruction, and students' interpretations of events. Such detailed descriptions of individuals and groups of students interacting with the teacher are rare, even in classroom research, and provide a methodological model for motivation researchers. The study's findings illustrate how combinations of classroom features relate to motivation, and may not function the same way in all interactions. Järvelä (1995) reported that "individual students interpreted the same situations and instructional episodes in different ways" (p. 254) and had different motivational and learning outcomes. Thus, even though the instruction was guided by theoretically robust principles, it was not successful in many of the teacher—student interactions.

Järvelä (1995) interpreted that differences in students' levels of motivation and engagement, task understanding, or preference for traditional teacher-directed instruction over challenging problem solving, may have resulted in differential responses to this instructional context. Such an "individual perspective" interpretation appears to be at odds with the theoretical position that motivational experiences result from social interaction, involving students, teachers, and tasks. Thus, such interpretations reflect the theoretical "growing pains" that classroom research can create; sometimes our interpretations of data do not incorporate the theoretical and methodological advances we have made. With its close analysis of instructional interactions, Järvelä's study is a convincing example of how classroom research in motivation is pushing motivation theory to truly reflect the social context for motivation.

Classroom Relationships That Support Student Motivation

Although instructional practices are obvious sources of data for understanding student motivation, interpersonal relationships, especially between students and teachers, also are drawing attention from researchers studying classroom motivation. Constructs that have been studied in the teacher-student relationship literature include teacher support, student/peer support, mutual respect, and teacher fairness. Earlier work has provided a theoretical and empirical base for the importance of relationships to motivation (see Davis, 2003, for a review). For example, self-determination theory (Deci & Ryan, 1985) posits that relating to others is a basic human need and motivation, learning, and development are dependent on affective, relational processes in the classroom (e.g., Furrer & Skinner, 2003; Ryan & Powelson, 1991; Ryan, Stiller, & Lynch, 1994; Skinner & Belmont, 1993). Similarly, Wentzel (1997, 2002) draws on theories of "belongingness" and

characterizes effective schools as "caring communities" in her studies of students' school adjustment (which includes achievement motivation and positive interpersonal relationships).

For example, in an attempt to understand how students define caring and uncaring teachers, Wentzel (1997) asked middle school students to list three things teachers do or say that show they care or do not care about students. She analyzed student responses according to the five dimensions of effective caregiving as suggested by Noddings (1992) and the family socialization literature (e.g., Baumrind, 1991): modeling, democratic communication styles, expectations for behavior, rule setting, and nurturance. Students said caring teachers made class interesting, talked and listened to students, were fair, and asked if they needed help. In contrast, uncaring teachers went off topic, did not explain when students were confused, embarrassed or yelled at students, and demeaned them by forgetting their names. Students who perceived that teachers cared about them reported positive motivational outcomes such as more prosocial and social responsibility goals, academic effort, and greater internal control beliefs. It appears that students want teachers to care for them both as learners and as people.

Teacher caring is important to students of all ages. Anthropologists Davidson and Phelan (1999) examined high school students' motivation to learn, working from the theoretical position that students draw meaning from important social and cultural contexts (e.g., family, school), and that these meanings combine in relation to students' motivation to achieve. Over two and a half years, the researchers conducted four in-depth interviews with 56 students in four large inner-city high schools in California. Many of these students were either experiencing difficulty in school or actively resisting school contexts. The researchers also observed in more than 300 classes, interacted with students informally, talked with school personnel, and examined student records. Consistent with ethnographic approaches, their goal was to gain "an insider's," in this case the students', perspective on what they thought influenced their school experiences. Most of the students in the study indicated values, beliefs, and expectations differed among their family, peer, and school worlds. Their motivation reflected the ease or difficulty encountered in "crossing the borders" among family, peer, and school worlds.

In the interviews, the students attributed increased motivation to interpersonal relationships: personal attention from adults in school, support for student input, support for diverse learning styles, and access to valued information (e.g., how to get into college). Personal attention included demonstrations of interest in students' personal lives (e.g., interest in pressing emotional issues or academic progress). For example, Diego said his math teacher "brings up the subject of life that you're doing and he pushes you to think about college math . . . he pushed me into taking math . . . like he'll call [on the telephone] and [say], 'Have you done your work?'" (p. 249). Other students said, "they [students] owe it [to do school work] to adults like these" (p. 250). In contrast, students indicated that teachers who they perceived were impatient when they asked for help, ignored their academic difficulties, or had low expectations for them left them feeling unmotivated. A Vietnamese immigrant female student commented: "The way she teaches, I know I was not going to make it" (p. 252).

In teacher–student relationships, students perceive teachers' support for autonomy as respect. Students are more willing to engage in classrooms where adults convey respect for their capabilities and perspectives. In the Davidson and Phelan (1999) study, students identified several teaching practices that communicated respect and encouraged their engagement, including encouraging classroom discussion, eliciting student perspectives, and withholding judgment. As Elvira said, "She wants to hear everyone's opinion . . . you really learn a lot" (p. 253). At the same time, students criticized adults who blatantly exerted power. Overly controlling policies, such as telling students what to think and using instructional practices that students perceive as harming their ability to learn contributed to alienation and to a sense of futility: "It just makes you not want to be there . . . you're far away from them because you don't like who they are" (p. 252). In a related study, Yowell (1999) interviewed 30 ninth-grade Latina/o students (18 girls) about their school engagement. The students attended a high school that was 98% Mexican/Mexican-American, and students ranged in achievement from high to low. Some students were interviewed while serving detention. Using possible selves theory (Markus & Nurius, 1986), the researchers asked students about their hoped-for, expected, and feared selves. In particular, they asked how relationships with teachers, administrators, and families might be related to the actualization of expected or feared selves. The interview probed three areas, including students' conceptions of their futures, their strategies for achieving hoped-for or expected selves, and how important adults might help them achieve their goals. These students reported that their possible selves were deeply embedded in their family contexts. Sadly, although the students understood the relationship between education and their future, they saw few connections between their futures and their experiences or adult relationships in the school.

Yowell (1999) reported that it was not teachers' lack of effort in providing information, nor was it students' ability to understand it that accounted for students' failure to connect school experiences to their futures. Rather, it was the negative affective quality of teacher-student relationships and the loosely structured high school environment that undermined students' perceptions of teachers as resources for their futures. Students were fairly consistent in explaining relationships as impersonal and lacking trust. This extended to teachers' pedagogical practices. One student, Juan, reported:

I just ask him [teacher] a question and he's like, he would do the problem for me, but he wouldn't explain it and that's all he does . . . he just writes the answer on the board or tells me the answer. . . . Like [I feel] kinda dumb 'cuz like, he's not explaining it to *me*. . . . And I still like, don't know what to do (Yowell, 1999, p. 16).

In contrast, when students were asked if they had a favorite teacher, all students named an elementary teacher. Students described being known to their former teachers and trusting that they would receive help if they needed it. As Rosa said,

They [elementary teachers as opposed to high school teachers] were more friendly. They, like, talked to you. They had, like, they just talked to you like friends like that. . . . He [favorite teacher] wants to know what I think . . . he would like ask me how I solved a problem . . . and then he helped me . . . like, he's like a teacher that cares about you . . . and like, helps you out whenever you need help, he's right there for you (Yowell, 1999, p. 16).

Students in Yowell's (1999) study also mentioned teachers' responsibility to hold them to standards, such as completing homework and attending class, as relevant to their future success. They appeared to interpret a structured environment as one that was designed to help them succeed, to counter their "bad habits." However, most did not see their schools performing this function. Seventy-three percent of the students mentioned school privileges as a problem and structure as a form of teacher support. As one student said, "If you miss school, they don't do nothin' about it till you're already failin' . . . [school needs to] be like pretty stricter . . . with the teachers being more strict to us" (Yowell, 1999, p. 17).

Using extensive documentation of students' understandings as coconstructed in school contexts, both Davidson and Phelan (1999) and Yowell (1999) offered a more ecological and sociocultural perspective on what motivates students to learn and engage in school, in contrast to the preponderance of motivational research that focuses on students' individual characteristics (e.g., self-efficacy, goal orientation). This perspective introduces and examines issues, such as how students navigate multiple worlds and, hence, motivational contexts (home, school, peer-social) that often are not considered in the psychological literature. In addition, the classroom research discussed in this section privileged student explanations (their words) of how teachers relate to them and how those relationships are related to their motivation for learning, rather than asking them to respond to theoretically derived constructs in a survey. The Davidson and Phelan findings convincingly delineated, in students' words, essential features of relationships, such as trust, care, and respect, which were related to their engagement. Their study also demonstrated how mutually reinforcing personal and instructional relationships are in students' engagement. When asked to describe teacher caring, students often gave examples of instructional situations. Because they are the central activity of classrooms, instructional relationships may be one of the strongest sources of students' interpretations of their relationship with their teachers. It may be the primary way that teachers demonstrate caring to students, especially to middle and high school students. Finally, their use of a sociocultural, specifically ethnographic, approach to studying motivation in classrooms offers much that can enrich or change motivational theory, emphasizing how relationships in classrooms emerge and change over time and are central to students' engagement in learning. (See also research on student coping strategies in different instructional interactions by Lehtinen, Vauras, Salonen, Okinuora, & Kinnunen, 1995; Vauras, Lehtinen, Kinnunen, & Salonen, 1992).

From Interactions to Transactions

The recent classroom studies that we have highlighted in this chapter demonstrate a shift in motivational research from a focus on individuals to a focus on the social and historical contexts in which individuals act and interact. Most recently, researchers dissatisfied with trying to interpret and analyze discrete features of classroom contexts (such as interaction between student and task, or student and teacher) are attempting to study the interplay among features and to look at multiple interactions as they constitute the larger picture, as transactions. The term *transaction,* as used by Dewey (Glassman & Wang, 2004), denotes placing importance on understanding the context as a whole, without boundaries of person, activity, or instruction:

Our own procedure is the *transactional,* in which is asserted the right to see together, extensionally and durationally, much that is talked about conventionally as if it were composed of irreconcilable separates. We do not present this procedure as being more real or generally valid than any other, but as being the one now needed in the field where we work. (Dewey & Bentley, 1949, p. 69)

Similarly, Gallimore and Tharp (1994), applying a neo-Vygotskian interpretation of this notion, used "activity setting" to denote two "essential features [of the context]: the cognitive and motoric action itself (activity); and the external, environmental, and objective features of the occasion (setting)" (p. 190). They contend that these features "cannot be unpackaged without drastically reducing the explanatory and practical utility of the concept of activity setting ... [even though] social science has always separated these features" (p. 190). Motivation is an integral process within activity settings, inseparable from learning, from person or task characteristics, or larger societal contexts, and this view is reflected in sociocultural theorists' views of cognition and motivation as participation (e.g., Greeno, Collins, & Resnick, 1996; Hickey, 2003).

Researchers have begun to capture motivation in classroom activity, analyzing, for example, how climates and norms for participation are established and supported, and struggling to describe the "whole" while examining classroom activities and their constructions over time. For example, Cobb, Yackel, and Wood (1989) analyzed how teachers and students coconstructed academic and social norms in a second-grade mathematics classroom. Brown and Campione (1994) chronicled the establishment of a *community of learners* in which expertise was distributed among all participants. Patrick and her colleagues (Patrick, Turner, Meyer, & Midgley, 2003) described how different classroom climates were established, beginning on the first day of school, and were integral to explaining student motivation later in the year.

As a group, these new lines of research illustrate how participants coconstruct and interpret the unique settings in which they learn and teach, representing how our theories and conceptualizations of motivation have begun to change in the past two decades. However, attempts to provide explanations of motivation in context may require that we construct a new language, not just translate from the old. We expect this new language to grow out of the development of motivation theories that are more compatible with our understanding of motivation in classroom contexts.

WHAT SHOULD BE THE FOCI OF STUDIES OF MOTIVATION IN CONTEXT IN THE FUTURE?

Progress has been made since Corno and Mandinach (1983) called for an integrated theory of learning and motivation in classrooms. More comprehensive and complex approaches to studying motivation in classrooms are emerging, as was evident in the research we reviewed in the previous section. Increasingly, motivation researchers are moving their investigations into classrooms and making classroom activity (e.g., teaching, learning) a primary focus of their studies. Also, social perspectives on learning and motivation are prompting researchers to use multiple and varied methods for studying motivation. Many researchers are combining methods, often qualitative and quantitative approaches, to study engagement both in and across classroom activities. These approaches have greatly elaborated our understandings of how features of teaching and learning contexts are related to traditional notions of student characteristics that enhance or undermine motivation for learning. However, we believe research along these lines is in its infancy; there is more work to do.

Here we identify four areas for future research, although we acknowledge there are many more. First, researchers need to reflect the full range of teaching and learning contexts students negotiate, including school, home, computer environments and, perhaps, a workplace. We need to consider how various contexts differ in their motivational demands on and affordances for learners, and how learners adapt accordingly. For example, there is a growing body of research comparing home and school literacy contexts and considering how children accommodate motivational messages that vary by context (Baker, Scher, & Mackler, 1997; Perry, Nordby, & VandeKamp, 2003; Serpell, 1997). In some homes there are a large number and variety of books available and a focus on reading for entertainment. Baker et al. found that contexts such as these prompted more reading and more enjoyment of reading in young children than home contexts where becoming literate was viewed as serious business and the focus was on developing specific skills in a climate that was more like work than play. McCaslin and Murdock (1991) aptly point out that researchers and educators need to consider other social and instructional environments in children's lives—other than school—if they are to understand students' beliefs and values as expressed at school.

Some of the most interesting and increasingly relevant contexts in which to study motivation and engagement involve new forms of learning activities such as those provided through computer technologies. Corno and Mandinach (2004) describe four such contexts and their affordances for academic engagement: computer games; technological innovations for teaching and learning that are implemented in schools; computer applications developed specifically for promoting motivation and self-regulation in users (see Hadwin & Winne, 2001, and Scardamalia, Bereiter, and Lamon, 1994 for good examples of this); and the Internet. Each of these contexts is rich with opportunities for studying learners' motivation and engagement, but all are mostly untapped by motivational researchers.

Second, because motivating students for learning is a complex and demanding task for teachers, we would like to see more research about how teachers can be helped to design tasks and interact with learners to foster motivation for learning (see Blumenfeld et al., 1991, and Perry & VandeKamp, 2000, for examples). Even research in classrooms has not examined how much and what kinds of expertise teachers need to have to support students' engagement positively. Furthering Brophy et al.'s (1983) line of inquiry in this regard would make a significant contribution to this field of study. For example, what are the roles of teacher competence and confidence in engaging classrooms? How are pedagogical content knowledge, teacher efficacy, and teacher motivation related to other features of the teaching and learning context known motivate students (e.g., complexity of tasks, opportunities for autonomy)? Perry, Phillips, and Dowler (2004) found a strong predictive relationship between task complexity and opportunities for students to make choices, control challenge, self-evaluate, and collaborate in the classrooms in which they observed. However, a question remains about whether and how teacher competence (i.e., subject matter knowledge, pedagogical knowledge, awareness of student differences) and confidence (i.e., efficacy for teaching a subject, comfort concerning ceding control to students) are related to teachers' task design and interactions with students. Answering questions such as these can inform researchers and teacher educators about how to prepare teachers to support student engagement intrinsically rather than extrinsically, as is common practice. In several of the studies we reviewed in the previous section, researchers both worked with and learned from teachers. We believe partnerships such as these are productive for scholarship and practice.

Third, in the past decade, research has demonstrated that young children can experience many of the motivational pitfalls that have been observed in older students (Perry, 1998; Stipek, Feiler, Daniels, & Milburn, 1995; Turner, 1995). Similarly, research indicates that when students are at the height of their motivational vulnerability (pre- and early adolescence), many are placed in environments that undermine academic achievement motivation (Juvonen, Le, Kaganoff, Augustine, & Constant, 2004). Researchers need to continue studying the developmental trajectory of motivation and its relationship to affect to better understand the features of learning contexts that are related to differences in the level and continuity of student engagement.

Finally, we believe addressing the research agenda we have just proposed requires that researchers continue studying motivation in action, in events and activities, using methods and measures that can be adapted to capture characteristics that may be unique to particular teaching and learning contexts (Paris & Paris, 2001; Randi & Corno, 2000). However, we perceive researchers have work to do to develop and enact theories and methods that truly reflect how social practices are organized to encourage and support motivation. The research we have reviewed demonstrates how data from running records of classroom activity, analyses of classroom discourse, and semistructured and retrospective interviews can clarify, elaborate, and enrich theories of motivation. We encourage researchers to use these and other tools to address questions concerning integrating context into motivation research. Specifically, researchers need to consider (a) what questions they wish to study, (b) what kinds of data can address those questions, and (c) how data can be interpreted in light of the theoretical perspectives that ground their investigations.

CONCLUSIONS

In this chapter, we have traced the historical roots of motivation research, noting that studies of motivation in classrooms are relatively recent, tracing them to the early 1980s. We considered how views about learning and motivation influenced methods for studying and interpreting classroom phenomena related to student engagement. Until recent years, most of the research about motivation in classrooms had been conducted outside of classrooms. Brophy et al. (1983), Corno & Mandinach (1983), and Blumenfeld (1982) represent a core of researchers who, since the 1980s, have been calling for studies of motivation *in* classrooms and the development of more integrated theories of motivation, learning, and instruction. Progress in this regard has been slow, but in the past decade, with the growing influence of situated and sociocultural views of

learning and motivation, researchers have begun studying motivation in situ. Social perspectives on learning, especially sociocultural perspectives, are challenging researchers to reconsider the foci of their investigations (i.e., from perceptions to interactions and activities). The new perspectives also challenge us to select methods and analyses that support in-depth, online investigations of interactions that synthesize classrooms tasks and activities, teacher and student characteristics, and learning and engagement. These investigations have resulted in detailed, deeply nuanced accounts of classroom activity and an increasingly robust body of more authentic knowledge about teaching and learning.

Research over the past 20 to 25 years has served to increase interest in how and why students engage in classroom learning. The more we learn, the more we generate complex findings that appear to have outgrown current theoretical explanations. Our review of research leaves us with at least three questions: How well can we contextualize existing theories of motivation? How well can sociocultural theories explain motivation in various contexts? Are new theories needed to advance our understanding of motivation in action? Only by generating and synthesizing this growing body of classroom research will we arrive at principles that can guide practice, develop new methodologies, and create new theoretical understanding. Certainly, some valuable insights have been discovered about motivation in classrooms. However, we look forward to findings in the next 25 years of research on students' engagement in a wide range of teaching and learning contexts and from new and more complex theoretical and methodological perspectives.

References

Ames, C. (1992). Classrooms: Goals, goal structures, and student motivation. *Journal of Educational Psychology, 84,* 261–271.

Anderman, L. H. , Patrick, H., Hruda, L. Z., & Linnenbrink, E. A. (2002). Observing classroom goal structures to clarify and expand goal theory. In C. Midgley (Ed.), *Goals, goal structures, and patterns of adaptive learning* (pp. 243-278). Mahwah, NJ: Lawrence Erlbaum Associates.

Anderson, J. R. (1990). *Cognitive psychology and its implications (3rd ed.).* New York: W.H. Freeman.

Baker, L., Scher, D., & Mackler, K. (1997). Home and family influences on motivations for reading. *Educational Psychologist, 32,* 69-82.

Bandura, A. (1986). *Social foundations of thought and action: A social cognitive theory.* Englewood Cliffs, NJ: Prentice-Hall.

Baumrind, D. (1991). Effective parenting during the early adolescent transition. In P. A. Cowan & M. Hetherington (Eds.),

Family transitions (pp. 111-164). Hillsdale, NJ: Lawrence Erlbaum Associates.

Blumenfeld, P. (1992a). Classroom learning and motivation: Clarifying and expanding goal theory. *Journal of Educational Psychology, 84,* 272-281.

Blumenfeld, P. C. (1992b). The task and the teacher: Enhancing student thoughtfulness in science. In J. Brophy (Ed.), *Advances in Research on Teaching* (Vol. 3, pp. 81-114). Greenwich, CT: JAI.

Blumenfeld, P. C., Krajcik, J. S., Marx, R. W., & Soloway, E. (1994). Lessons learned: How collaboration helped middle grade science teachers learn project-based instruction. *Elementary School Journal, 94,* 539-551.

Blumenfeld, P. C., Mergendoller, J. R., & Swarthout, D. W. (1987). Task as a heuristic for understanding student learning and motivation. *Journal of Curriculum Studies, 19,* 135-148.

Blumenfeld, P. C., Soloway, E., Marx, R. W., Krajcik, J. S., Guzdial, M., & Palincsar, A. (1991). Motivating project-based learning: Sustaining the doing, supporting the learning. *Educational Psychologist, 26*, 369-398.

Brophy, J. (1999). Research on motivation in education: Past, present, and future. In M. L. Maehr & P. R. Pintrich (Series Eds.) & T. C. Urdan (Vol. Ed.), *Advances in motivation and achievement: Vol. 11. The role of context* (pp. 1-44). Stamford, CT: JAI.

Brophy, J. (2004). *Motivating students to learn* (2nd ed.). Mahwah, NJ: Lawrence Erlbaum Associates.

Brophy, J., Rohrkemper, M., Rashid, H., & Goldberger, M. (1983). Relationships between teachers' presentations of classroom tasks and students' engagement in those tasks. *Journal of Educational Psychology, 75*, 544-552.

Brown, A. L., & Campione, J. C. (1994). Guided discovery in a community of learners. In K. McGilly (Ed.), *Classroom lessons: Integrating cognitive theory with classroom practice* (pp. 229-270). Cambridge, MA: MIT Press.

Cobb, P., Yackel, E., & Wood, T. (1989). Young children's emotional acts while engaged in mathematical problem solving. In D. B. McLeod & V. M. Adams (Eds.), *Affect and mathematical problem solving: A new perspective* (pp. 117-148). New York: Springer-Verlag.

Corno, L., & Mandinach, E. B. (1983). The role of cognitive engagement in classroom learning and motivation. *Educational Psychologist, 18*, 88-108.

Corno, L., & Mandinach, E. B. (2004). What we have learned about student engagement in the past twenty years. In D. M. McInerney & S. Van Etten (Eds.), *Big theories revisited* (pp. 299-328). Greenwich, CT: Information Age.

Davidson, A. L., & Phelan, P. (1999). Students' multiple worlds: An anthropological approach to understanding students' engagement with school. In T. Urdan (Ed.), *Advances in motivation and achievement* (Vol. 11, pp. 233-273). Stamford, CT: JAI.

Davis, H. A. (2003). Conceptualizing the role and influence of student-teacher relationships on children's social and cognitive development. *Educational Psychologist, 38*, 207-234.

Deci, E. & Ryan, R. (1985). *Intrinsic motivation and self determination in human behavior.* New York: Plenum.

Dewey, J. (1916). *Democracy and education.* New York: Macmillan.

Dewey, J., & Bentley, A. F. (1949). *Knowing and the known.* Boston: Beacon Press.

Doyle, W. (1983). Academic work. *Review of Educational Research, 53*, 159-199.

Eccles (Parsons), J., Adler, T. F., Futterman, R., Goff, S. B., et al. (1983). Expectancies, values, and academic behaviors. In J. T. Spence (Ed.), *Achievement and achievement motivation* (pp. 75-146). San Francisco: W. H. Freeman.

Eccles, J. S. (1993). School and family effects on the ontogeny of children's interests, self-perceptions, and activity choice. In J. Jacobs (Ed.), *Nebraska Symposium on Motivation, 1992; Developmental perspectives on motivation* (pp. 145-208). Lincoln: University of Nebraska Press.

Eccles, J. & Wigfield, A. (1995). In the mind of the actor: The structure of adolescents' achievement task values and expectancy related beliefs. *Personality and Social Psychology Bulletin, 21*, 215-225.

Eccles, J. S., & Wigfield, A. (2002). Motivational beliefs, values, and goals. *Annual Review of Psychology, 53*, 109-132.

Eccles, J. S., Wigfield, A., & Schiefele, U. (1998). Motivation to succeed. In W. Damon (Series Ed.) & N. Eisenberg (Vol. Ed.), *Handbook of child psychology: Vol 3. Social, emotional, and personality development* (5th ed., pp. 1017-1095). New York: Wiley.

Ford, M. E. (1992). *Motivating humans: Goals, emotions, and personal agency beliefs.* London: Sage.

Furrer, C., & Skinner, E. (2003). Sense of relatedness as a factor in children's academic engagement and performance. *Journal of Educational Psychology, 95*, 148-162.

Gallimore, R., & Tharp, R. (1990). Teaching mind in society: Teaching, schooling, and literate discourse. In L. C. Moll (Ed.), *Vygotsky and education: Teacher implications and application of sociohistorical psychology* (pp. 175-205). Cambridge, England: Cambridge University Press.

Glassman, M., & Wang, Y. (2004). On the interconnected nature of interpreting Vygotsky: Rejoinder to Gredler and Shields does no one read Vygotsky's words. *Educational Researcher, 33*, 19-22.

Greeno, J. G., Collins, A. M., & Resnick. L. B. (1996). Cognition and learning. In D. C. Berliner & R. C. Calfee (Eds.), *Handbook of Educational Psychology* (pp. 15-46). New York: Simon & Schuster Macmillan.

Guthrie, J. T., & Alao, S. (1997). Designing contexts to increase motivations for reading. *Educational Psychologist, 32*, 95-105.

Guthrie, J. T., Barbosa, P., Preencevich, K. C., Taboada, A., Davis, M. H., Scafiddi, N. T., et al. (2004). Increasing reading comprehension and engagement through concept-oriented reading instruction. *Journal of Educational Psychology, 96*, 403-423.

Guthrie, J. T., VanMeter, P., Hancock, G. R., & Alao, S. (1998). Does concept-oriented reading instruction increase strategy use and conceptual learning from text? *Journal of Educational Psychology, 90*, 261-278.

Guthrie, J. T., Wigfield, A., & VonSecker, C. (2000). Effects of integrated instruction on motivation and strategy use in reading. *Journal of Educational Psychology, 92*, 331-341.

Hadwin, A. F., & Winne, P. H. (2001). CoNoteS2: A software tool for promoting self-regulation. *Educational Research and Evaluation, 7(2-3)*, 313-334.

Hickey, D. T. (2003). Engaged participation versus marginal nonparticipation: A stridently sociocultural approach to achievement motivation. *Elementary School Journal, 103*, 401-429.

Hickey, D. T., & Granade, J. B. (2004). The influence of sociocultural theory on our theories of engagement and motivation. In D. M. McInerney & S. Van Etten (Eds.), *Sociocultural influences on motivation and learning: Vol. 4. Big theories revisited* (pp. 223-247). Greenwich, CT: Information Age.

Järvelä, S. (1995). The cognitive apprenticeship model in a technologically rich learning environment: Interpreting the learning interaction. *Learning and Instruction, 5*, 237-259.

Juvonen, J., Le, V., Kaganoff, T., Augustine, C., & Constant, L. (2004). *Focus on the wonder years: Challenges facing the American middle school.* Rand Corporation.

Kazemi, E., & Stipek, D. (2001). Promoting conceptual thinking in four upper-elementary mathematics classrooms. *Elementary School Journal, 102*, 59-79.

Krajcik, J., Blumenfeld, P. C., Marx, R. W., Bass, K. M., & Fredricks, J. (1998). Inquiry in project-based science classrooms: Initial attempts by middle school students. *Journal of the Learning Sciences, 7*, 313-350.

Lave, J. & Wenger, E. (1991). *Situated learning: Legitimate peripheral participation.* Cambridge, England: Cambridge University Press.

Lehtinen, E., Vauras, M., Salonen, P., Olkinuora, E. & Kinnunen, R. (1995). Long-term development of learning activity: Motivational, cognitive, and social interaction. *Educational Psychologist, 30*, 21-35.

Linnenbrink, E. A. & Pintrich, P. R. (2003). The role of self-efficacy beliefs in student engagement and learning in the classroom. *Reading and Writing Quarterly, 19*, 119-137.

Malone, T., & Lepper, M. R. (1987). Making learnig fun: A taxonomy of intrinsic motivations for learning. In R. Snow & M. Farr (Eds.), *Aptitude, learning and instruction* (Vol 3., pp. 223-253). Hillsdale, NJ: Lawrence Erlbaum Associates.

Markus, H. & Nurius, P. (1986). Possible selves. *American Psychologist, 41*, 954-969.

McCaslin, M. (2004). Coregulation of opportunity, activity, and identity in student motivation: Elaborations on Vygotskian themes. In D. M. McInerney & S. Van Etten (Eds.), *Sociocultural influences on motivation and learning: Vol. 4. Big theories revisited.* (pp. 249-274). Greenwich, CT: Information Age.

McCaslin, M., & Good, T. L. (1996). The informal curriculum. In D. C. Berliner & R. C. Calfee (Eds.), *Handbook of educational psychology* (pp. 622-670). New York: Simon & Schuster Macmillan.

McCaslin, M., & Hickey, D. T. (2001). Self-regulated learning and academic achievement: A Vygoskian view. In B. J. Zimmerman & D. H. Schunk (Eds.), *Self-regulated learning and academic achievement* (2nd ed., pp. 227-252). Mahwah, NJ: Lawrence Erlbaum Associates.

McCaslin, M. & Murdock, T. (1991). The emergent interaction of home and school in the development of students' adaptive learning. In M. Maehr & P. Pintrich (Eds.), *Advances in motivation and achievement* (Vol. 7, pp. 213-259). Greenwich, CT: JAI.

McLaughlin, M. W., & Talbert, J. E. (2001). *Professional communities and the work of high school teaching.* Chicago: University of Chicago Press.

Mehan, H. (1985). The structure of classroom discourse. In T. van Dijk (Ed.), *Handbook of discourse analysis* (Vol. 3, pp. 119-131). London: Academic Press.

Meyer, D. K., Turner, J. C., & Spencer, C. (1997). Challenge in a mathematics classroom: Students' motivation and strategies in project-based learning. *Elementary School Journal, 97*, 501-521.

Middleton, M. J., & Midgley, C. (2002). Beyond motivation: Middle school students' perceptions of press for understanding in math. *Contemporary Educational Psychology, 27*, 373-391.

Miller, S. D., & Meece, J. L. (1997). Enhancing elementary students' motivation to read and write: A classroom intervention study. *Journal of Educational Research, 90*, 286-300.

Miller, S. D., & Meece, J. L. (1999). Third graders' motivational preferences for reading and writing tasks. *Elementary School Journal, 100*, 19-35.

Mook, D. A. (1987). *Motivation: The organization of action.* New York: W.W. Norton.

Noddings, N. (1992). *The challenge to care in schools: An alternative approach to education.* New York: Teachers College Press.

Op't Eynde, P., DeCorte, E., & Verschaffel, L. (2001). "What to lcarn from what we feel?": The role of students' emotions in the mathematics classroom. In S. Volet & S. Järvelä (Eds.), *Motivation in learning contexts: Theoretical advances and methodological implications* (pp. 149-167). Amsterdam: Pergamon.

Palincsar, A. S., & Brown, A. L. (1984). Reciprocal teaching of comprehension-fostering and comprehension-monitoring activities. *Cognition and Instruction, 1*, 117-175.

Paris, S. G., & Paris, A. (2001). Classroom applications of research on self-regulated learning. *Educational Psychologist, 36*, 89-102.

Patrick, H., & Middleton, M. J. (2002). Turning the kaleidoscope: What we see when self-regulated learning is viewed with a qualitative lens. *Educational Psychologist, 37*, 27-39.

Patrick, H., Turner, J. C., Meyer, D. K., & Midgley, C. (2003). How teachers establish psychological environments during the first days of school: Associations with avoidance in mathematics. *Teachers College Record, 105*, 1521-1559.

Perry, N. E. (1998). Young children's self-regulated learning and the contexts that support it. *Journal of Educational Psychology, 90*, 715-729.

Perry, N., Phillips, L., & Dowler, J. (2004). Examining features of tasks and their potential to promote self-regulated learning. *Teachers College Record, 106*, 1854-1878.

Perry, N. E., Nordby, C. J., & VandeKamp, K. O. (2003). Promoting self-regulated reading and writing at home and school: A tale of two contexts. *Elementary School Journal, 103*, pp. 317-338.

Perry, N., & VandeKamp, K. O. (2000). Creating classroom contexts that support young children's development of self-regulated learning. *International Journal of Educational Research, 33*, 821-843.

Perry, N. E., & Winne, P. H. (2004). Motivational messages from home and school: How do they influence young children's engagement in learning? In D. M. McInerney & S. Van Etten (Eds.), *Sociocultural influences on motivation and learning: Vol. 4. Big theories revisited* (pp.199-222). Greenwich, CT: Information Age.

Pintrich, P. R. (2003). Motivation and classroom learning. In W. Reynolds & G. Miller (Eds.), *Handbook of psychology: Educational psychology,* (Vol. 7, pp. 103-122). New York: Wiley.

Pintrich, P. R., & Schunk, D. H. (2002). *Motivation in education: Theory, research, and applications* (2nd ed.). Upper Saddle River, NJ: Merrill Prentice Hall.

Randi, J. & Corno, L. (2000). Teacher innovations in self-regulated learning. In P. Pintrich, M. Boekaerts, & M. Zeidner (Eds.), *Handbook of self-regulation* (pp. 651–685). Orlando, FL: Academic Press.

Rohrkemper, M., & Corno, L. (1988). Success and failure on classroom tasks: Adaptive learning and classroom teaching. *Elementary School Journal, 88*, 299–312.

Rotter, J. B. (1954). *Social learning and clinical psychology.* New York: Prentice-Hall.

Ryan, R. M. & Deci, E. L., (2000). Intrinsic and extrinsic motivation: Classic definitions and new directions. *Contemporary Educational Psychology, 25*, 54–67.

Ryan, R. M., & Powelson, C. L. (1991). Autonomy and relatedness as fundamental to motivation and education. *Journal of Experimental Education, 60*, 49–66.

Ryan, R. M., Stiller, J. D., & Lynch, J. H. (1994). Representations of relationships to teachers, parents, and friends as predictors of academic motivation and self-esteem. *Journal of Early Adolescence, 14*, 226–249.

Sansone, C., & Harackiewicz, J. M. (2000). *Intrinsic and extrinsic motivation: The search for optimal motivation and performance.* San Diego, CA: Academic Press.

Scardamalia, M., Bereiter, C., & Lamon, M. (1994). The CSILE Project: Trying to bring the classroom into World 3. In K. McGilly (Ed.), *Classroom lessons: Integrating cognitive theory and classroom practice* (pp. 201–228). Cambridge, MA: MIT Press.

Schunk, D. H., & Pajares, F. (2004). Self-efficacy in education revisited: Empirical and applied evidence. In D. M. McInerney & S. Van Etten (Eds.), *Sociocultural influences on motivation and learning: Vol. 4. Big theories revisited* (pp. 115–138). Greenwich, CT: Information Age.

Serpell, R. (1997). Literacy connections between school and home: How should we evaluate them? *Journal of Literacy Research, 29*, 587–616.

Skinner, E. A., & Belmont, M. J. (1993). Motivation in the classroom: Reciprocal effects of teacher behavior and student engagement across the school year. *Journal of Educational Psychology, 85*, 571–581.

Stipek, D. J. (1996). Motivation and instruction. In D. C. Berliner & R. C. Calfee (Eds.), *Handbook of educational psychology* (pp. 85–113). New York: Macmillan.

Stipek, D. J., Feiler, R., Daniels, D., & Milburn, S. (1995). Effects of different instructional approaches on young children's achievement and motivation. *Child Development, 66*, 209–223.

Tharp, R. G., Estrada, P., Dalton, S. S., & Yamauchi, L. A. (2000). *Teaching transformed.* Boulder, CO: Westview.

Thorndike, E. L. (1913). *Educational psychology: Vol. 2. The psychology of learning.* New York: Teachers College Press.

Turner, J. C. (1995). The influence of classroom contexts on young children's motivation for literacy. *Reading Research Quarterly, 30*, 410–441.

Turner, J. C., Meyer, D. K., Cox, K. C., Logan, C., DiCintio, M., & Thomas, C. T. (1998). Creating contexts for involvement in mathematics. *Journal of Educational Psychology, 90*, 730–745.

Turner, J. C., Meyer, D. K., Midgley, C., & Patrick, H. (2003). Teacher Discourse and students' affect and achievement-related behaviors in two high mastery/high performance classrooms. *Elementary School Journal, 103*, 357–382.

Turner, J. C., Midgley, C., Meyer, D. K., Gheen, M., Anderman, E. A., Kang, J., et al. (2002). The classroom environment and students' reports of avoidance strategies in mathematics: A multi-method study. *Journal of Educational Psychology, 94*, 88–106.

Turner, J. C., & Patrick, H. (2004). Motivational influences on student participation in classroom learning activities. *Teachers College Record, 106*, 1759–1785.

Vauras, M., Lehtinen, E., Kinnunen, R., & Salonen, P. (1992). Socio-emotional coping and cognitive processes in training learning-disabled children. In B. Wong (Ed.), *Intervention research in learning disabilities: An international perspective* (pp. 163–189). New York: Springer-Verlag.

Vygotsky, L. S. (1978). *Mind in society: The development of higher-order psychological processes.* Cambridge, MA: Harvard University Press.

Weiner, B. (1990). History of motivational research in education. *Journal of Educational Psychology, 82*, 616–622.

Wentzel, K. R. (1997). Student motivation in middle school: The role of perceived pedagogical caring. *Journal of Educational Psychology, 89*, 411–419.

Wentzel, K. R. (2002). Are effective teachers like good parents? Teaching styles and student adjustment in early adolescence. *Child Development, 73*, 287–301.

Wertsch, J. V. (1985). *Vygotsky and the social formation of mind.* Cambridge, MA: Harvard University Press.

Wigfield, A. (1994). Expectancy-value theory of motivation: A developmental perspective. *Educational Psychology Review, 6*, 49–78.

Wigfield, A., & Eccles, J. S. (2002). The development of competence beliefs, expectancies for success, and achievement values from childhood through adolescence. In A. Wigfield & J. S. Eccles (Eds.), *Development of achievement motivation* (pp. 91–120). San Diego, CA: Academic Press.

Wigfield, A., Eccles, J. S., Yoon, K. S., Harold, R. D., Arbreton, A., Freedman-Doan, C., et al. (1997). Changes in children's competence beliefs and subjective task values across the elementary school years: A three-year study. *Journal of Educational Psychology, 89*, 451–469.

Winne, P. H., & Perry, N. E. (2000). Measuring self-regulated learning. In P. Pintrich, M. Boekaerts, & M. Zeidner (Eds.), *Handbook of self-regulation* (pp. 531–566). Orlando, FL: Academic Press.

Wood, D., Bruner, J. S., & Ross, G. (1976). The role of tutoring in problem solving. *Journal of Child Psychology and Psychiatry, 17*, 89–100.

Yowell, C. (1999). The role of the future in meeting the challenge of Latino school dropouts. *Educational Foundations, 13*, 5–28.

Yowell, C. M., & Smylie, M. A. (1999). Self-regulation in democratic communities. *Elementary School Journal, 99*, 469–490.

COMPETENCE AND CONTROL BELIEFS:
DISTINGUISHING THE MEANS AND ENDS

Dale H. Schunk
University of North Carolina at Greensboro

Barry J. Zimmerman
Graduate Center, City University of New York

With the paradigm shift from behaviorism to cognitive information processing that occurred between the late 1950s and mid-1960s, psychologists began to take into account individuals' cognitions to explain behavior rather than focusing only on environmental variables and events. One manifestation of this shift was an emphasis on *self-beliefs*, or beliefs people have about their thoughts, feelings, and actions, and those of others. In particular, educational psychologists have explored how self-beliefs are formulated, how they change with development and experience, and how they influence outcomes such as learning, motivation, self-regulation, and achievement.

This chapter examines two types of self-beliefs in educational contexts—competence and control—with special focus on their role in motivation and achievement. The following section defines and distinguishes competence and control beliefs and presents a model for classifying theories according to their treatment of these constructs. The next section provides a historical background on competence and control beliefs and describes some early perspectives that stressed their influence on behavior. Five theories then are examined that postulate a key role for competence and/or control beliefs in motivation and achievement: achievement motivation theory, attribution theory, social cognitive theory, goal theory, and self-determination theory. The relevance of these beliefs to the related processes of self-regulation, metacognition, and volition is discussed. The chapter concludes with recommendations for future research and implications for educational practice.

DEFINITIONS AND DISTINCTIONS

There is debate among educational researchers about the precise nature of competence and control beliefs, and the boundaries between the two are not always clearly demarcated. In this chapter *competence beliefs* are defined as students' perceptions about their means, processes, and capabilities to accomplish certain tasks. These beliefs are self-evaluative because learners must weigh their knowledge, skills, and strategies, against the demands of the task to determine perceptions of competence. Competence beliefs are reflected in the following statements: "I am very sure that I can solve these math problems," "I am certain that I can learn the material in this section of the book," and "I know that I can high jump over that bar."

Control beliefs are students' perceptions about the likelihood of accomplishing desired ends or outcomes under certain conditions. Control beliefs refer to the outcomes of actions, not to the actions themselves. Simply feeling competent does not guarantee the perception of control, because the conditions to learn or perform often are unfavorable. Control beliefs are reflected in

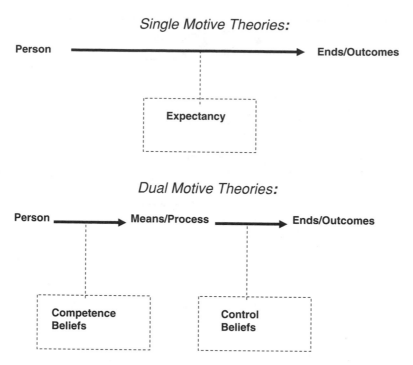

FIGURE 16.1. Model for distinguishing competence and control beliefs in psychological theories.

statements such as: "If I study the material diligently I know I can perform well on the test," "I know that I will have enough time to solve these problems," and "If I try my best I know that I can run a fast time."

Both competence and control beliefs are types of *expectancies,* or perceptions about future events. Competence beliefs are expectancies about one's capabilities to learn or perform actions; control beliefs are expectancies about the consequences of actions.

Older theories of motivation and achievement typically did not distinguish competence from control beliefs and included only one type of expectancy. This expectancy construct may have reflected primarily competence beliefs or primarily control beliefs or some of both. In contrast, contemporary theories often distinguish these two types of beliefs. The educational implication of this distinction is that a perceived lack of competence should be addressed differently than a perceived lack of control. Students who lack perceived competence may require educational interventions that help them develop skills, whereas those with low perceived control may need opportunities to use the skills they possess to accomplish desired ends.

This theoretical distinction is portrayed in Fig. 16.1 and is patterned after the process-outcome distinction model of self-regulation proposed by Zimmerman and Schunk (2004). Single motive theories postulate that expectancy beliefs mediate the relation between the person and the outcome, but they do not differentiate these beliefs. In contrast, dual motive theories postulate separate competence and control beliefs. Competence beliefs come into play when students select means and processes to use to learn or perform actions. Control beliefs are important in helping to link those actions with desired outcomes.

Contextual factors are seen as key influences on students' control beliefs. Theories that give strong emphasis to these factors also predict that although competence and control beliefs often are consistent, they need not be. Thus, students who feel competent about learning generally expect positive outcomes for their efforts. Learners who feel competent in mathematics expect to perform well in courses and receive high grades. Students who feel competent about learning might not expect positive outcomes if they perceived little control over outcomes, such as classes in which the teachers give good grades to the students they like regardless of how well the students perform. Under the latter conditions, motivation and learning suffer.

HISTORICAL BACKGROUND

Understanding how competence and control beliefs were treated in earlier theories helps to clarify the processes portrayed in Fig. 16.1 and illuminates the evolution from single to dual motive theories. This section does not cover historical theories in depth because these are not the focus of this chapter. Readers who desire more historical background—especially on how earlier theories treated self-beliefs—are referred to other sources (Pajares, 2003; Pajares & Schunk, 2002; Zimmerman & Schunk, 2003).

Competence and control beliefs enjoyed no position of prominence until the paradigm shift (mentioned earlier) occurred because behaviorism was dominant in psychology. The basic tenet of behaviorism was that for psychology to be a meaningful discipline it had to emphasize what other scientific disciplines did—observable events, such as behavior. Self-perceptions and other internal (mental) states could play no meaningful role. Although behaviorists did not deny the existence of mental states (they did, after all, have to think about their theories and experiments), they believed that mental states added nothing to explanations of behavior. Rather, one looked to the conditions in the environment (see also Perry, Turner, & Meyer, Chapter 15 of this volume).

The remainder of this section describes three theoretical perspectives that challenged the assumptions of behaviorism and included competence or control beliefs as influences on behavior: humanistic theories, locus of control, and self-concept.

Humanistic Theories

Humanistic theories discuss individuals' capabilities and potentialities as they make choices and seek control over their lives. Unlike behaviorism, which attempted to reduce behavior to discrete acts, humanistic theories are holistic and contend that to understand why people act as they do requires understanding their behaviors, thoughts, and feelings. The notions of competence and control are central to these views.

Although there were several participants in the humanistic movement, two of the most influential were Carl Rogers and Abraham Maslow. Rogers (1963) believed that life represented an ongoing process of growth and achieving wholeness, and that this *actualizing tendency* was an innate fundamental human motive. Rogers described the actualizing tendency as "a tendency toward fulfillment, toward actualization, toward the maintenance and enhancement of the organism" (Rogers, 1963, p. 6).

According to Rogers, people's perceptions about themselves played the critical roles in their development and adjustment. The development of self-awareness produced a need for *positive regard,* or feelings such as respect, liking, warmth, sympathy, and acceptance. People also have the need for *positive self-regard,* or positive

regard that derives from personal experiences. The actualizing tendency develops when people accept all of their experiences, and their self-perceptions are consistent with the feedback they receive from others.

Maslow (1954) promulgated a theory postulating that people are motivated by needs that are hierarchically organized. Basic needs (e.g., survival, safety) must be satisfied before higher order needs (e.g., belonging, esteem) can be fulfilled. The ultimate goal—although few people ever may attain it—is the final level of *self-actualization,* defined as the developing of one's full potential as evidenced by self-fulfillment and contentment.

For Maslow, as with Rogers, a general sense of self was the central construct of the human personality. One's perceptions of oneself—including competence beliefs—and desire to influence control over the fulfillment of needs were primary motivators of behavior. Humanistic ideas are useful for a general understanding of human behavior and for counseling, but the generality of their central constructs (actualizing tendency, control of need satisfaction) limits empirical investigations that could specify their role in an overall theory of human functioning.

Locus of Control

Rotter (1966) advanced a social learning theory that included *locus of control*—a motivational construct that refers to generalized control over outcomes. People differ in where they believe this control lies. Individuals may believe that outcomes occur independently of how they act (external control) or that outcomes are highly contingent on their actions (internal control).

Rotter (1966) assumed that generalized perceptions of control could affect outcomes across domains; however, other investigators have noted that locus of control can vary depending on the situation (Phares, 1976). Regardless of whether locus of control is generalized or situationally specific, its educational importance stems from its motivational effects. Students who believe they can control outcomes are more likely to choose to engage in those situations, expend effort, and persist. Those who believe that their behaviors have little impact on outcomes would not be expected to demonstrate the same level of motivation because they will believe that factors outside of their control will be primarily responsible for success or failure.

Locus of control is a type of *outcome expectation,* or belief about the anticipated outcomes of actions. Although research supported the operation and effects of locus of control (Rotter, 1966), general constructs often do not predict behaviors in specific situations (Bandura, 1986). Further, as a type of outcome expectation, locus of control alone is insufficient to predict achievement behavior. Students with a strong sense of internal control who believe that they can write an excellent essay may nevertheless not put forth the effort if they believe that no matter how good their work is the instructor will not reward it. Conversely, students who believe that the instructor will reward them may not work hard if they doubt their capability to put forth the requisite effort. Clearly other types of beliefs are needed to adequately explain achievement behavior.

Self-Concept

Although not a theory as such, self-concept is germane to the topic of competence and control beliefs. Self-concept has been defined in various ways, but it typically is construed as a general construct that reflects one's collective self-perceptions formed through experiences with the environment and interpretations of those experiences and influenced by interactions with significant other persons (Shavelson & Bolus, 1982). Researchers exploring the structure of self-concept have identified its critical features: organized, multifaceted, hierarchical, stable, developmental, evaluative, and differentiable (Marsh & Shavelson, 1985).

The hierarchical feature refers to the notion that one's self-perceptions in specific situations give rise to more general self-concepts. These general self-concepts contribute to a global self-concept. With respect to academics, self-perceptions in specific domains lead to self-concepts in various subject areas such as mathematics and science. These in turn contribute to an academic self-concept.

Much research has explored the relation of self-concept to learning and achievement. Wylie (1979) reviewed self-concept research and obtained a correlation of $r = +0.30$ between global self-concept and academic achievement. This moderate relation suggests that other factors are important. Hansford and Hattie (1982) analyzed several studies and found positive, negative, and no correlation between self-concept and achievement.

More specific measures of self-concept typically bear a stronger relation to achievement (Pajares & Schunk, 2001, 2002). Wylie (1979) found limited evidence for stronger associations between self-concepts of ability and achievement than between overall self-concept and achievement.

Competence beliefs are inherent in the definition and measurement of self-concept, but self-concept typically does not address control beliefs. Another issue is that as self-concept becomes defined more specifically, it resembles other constructs discussed in this chapter (e.g.,

self-efficacy). Although self-concept is an active research area, it does not provide the type of unified treatment of competence and control beliefs needed to understand their operation in educational contexts.

CONTEMPORARY PERSPECTIVES ON COMPETENCE AND CONTROL BELIEFS

This section discusses five contemporary psychological theories that assign a prominent role to competence and/or control beliefs: achievement motivation theory, attribution theory, social cognitive theory, goal theory, and self-determination theory. Their treatment of competence and control beliefs and some key research findings are described. Table 16.1 summarizes each theory's major points regarding these beliefs.

Achievement Motivation Theory

Classical theory. *Achievement motivation*, or the desire to display competence in activities (Elliot & Church, 1997), has been the subject of scientific study for many years (see also Anderman & Wolters, Chapter 17 of this volume; Perry et al., Chapter 15 of this volume). Murray (1938) included the achievement motive among the psychological needs that affected personality development. Motivation resulted from the desire to satisfy needs. Murray (1936) also devised the *Thematic Apperception Test (TAT)*, a projective technique comprising a series of ambiguous pictures shown to participants who then made up stories or answered a set of questions. McClelland, Atkinson, Clark, and Lowell (1953) adapted the TAT to assess the achievement motive.

A breakthrough in the study of achievement motivation was *expectancy-value theory*, developed by Atkinson and his colleagues (Atkinson, 1957; Atkinson & Feather, 1966; Atkinson & Raynor, 1974). Atkinson drew on work by Lewin and others on the *level of aspiration* or goal that people set in a task (Lewin, Dembo, Festinger, & Sears, 1944). Their research showed that successes raised level of aspiration and that failures lowered it. People generally felt more successful when they met the goals they had set for themselves than when they attained objective standards. Level of aspiration is a type of competence belief that is affected by individual and group experiences.

In Atkinson's theory, achievement behavior was a function of one's (a) expectancy of attaining a given outcome contingent on performing certain behaviors, and (b) value that one placed on that outcome. Motivation resulted from the belief that a valued outcome was attainable.

TABLE 16.1. Psychological Theories Emphasizing Competence and Control Beliefs

Theories	Competence Beliefs	Control Beliefs
Achievement motivation theory	Atkinson's theory did not address competence beliefs, but Eccles and Wigfield's theory states that task-specific judgments of ability or competence influence one's expectancies for success.	Atkinson's construct of expectancy is a form of control belief because it reflects the idea that certain actions lead to successful outcomes.
Attribution theory	Competence beliefs are not addressed directly in this theory, but attributions can give rise to perceptions of competence or incompetence that have motivational effects.	Attribution theory emphasizes the role of control beliefs in motivating students to persist in their efforts to learn and perform academically. Students perceive optimal control when outcomes are attributed to internal, stable, and controllable causes.
Social cognitive theory	The key competence belief in Bandura's theory is self-efficacy, which refers to expectancies about one's capabilities to learn or perform at designated levels. The attainment of self-efficacy is a key source of academic motivation.	Outcome expectancy is a control variable because it reflects personal confidence that certain outcomes will result from given actions. Both outcome and self-efficacy expectancies are necessary to be optimally motivated.
Goal orientation theory	A mastery or learning goal orientation focuses one's attention on processes and strategies that can improve one's competence.	Performance goals focus on controlling one's success and failure experiences via selective exposure to socially competitive events.
Self-determination theory	The need for competence refers to a generalized need to master one's environment.	The need for autonomy refers to one's desire to experience a sense of control, agency, or autonomy in environmental interactions (i.e., an internal locus of causality).

Achievement behavior represented a conflict between approach (*hope for success*) and avoidance (*fear of failure*). The conflict resulted because any achievement action could result in success or failure. Individuals gauge the probability of success and failure. *Resultant achievement motivation*—expressed mathematically—was the tendency to approach an achievement goal decreased by the tendency to avoid failure. Thus, having a high hope for success did not automatically lead to achievement behavior because the strength of the motive to avoid failure also had to be taken into account. Achievement behavior was strongest when a high hope for success was combined with a low fear of failure.

The theory predicts that students high in resultant achievement motivation will select tasks of intermediate difficulty, or those they believe are attainable and whose outcomes are valued. Difficult tasks—for which success is unlikely—are apt to be avoided, as are easy tasks whose accomplishment holds little value. Conversely, students low in resultant achievement motivation should be more likely to select either easy or difficult tasks. The former require little effort, whereas the latter—because they are virtually unattainable—provide one with reasons for not expending effort because effort is unlikely to produce success.

Research on Atkinson's theory has yielded mixed results (Cooper, 1983; Ray, 1982). The prediction that high achievement motivation leads to a preference for tasks of intermediate difficulty is problematic. Kuhl and Blankenship (1979), for example, found that with repeated task success, students tended to choose more difficult tasks; this outcome did not vary as a function of the individual's motive to attain success or motive to avoid failure. It also seems likely that task success builds perceived competence, which leads people to select tasks of greater difficulty. Atkinson's theory did not address competence beliefs and likely overestimated the importance of the achievement motive.

Research also has addressed the development of the achievement motive. Rosen and D'Andrade (1959) studied parents' interactions with their sons. Parents of boys with high achievement motivation interacted more with them, gave more rewards and punishments, and held higher expectations for them, compared with parents of boys with low achievement motivation. It is difficult, however, to isolate parental behaviors that help develop children's achievement motivation because parents display many behaviors with their children.

As shown in Table 16.1, Atkinson's expectancy for attaining a given outcome as a result of performing certain actions is a type of control belief because it reflects the idea that certain actions lead to given outcomes. The theory does not directly address the issue of perceived competence. Another issue with this theory is that a global achievement motive rarely manifests itself uniformly across different achievement domains. Because the achievement motive varies with the domain—perhaps partly because of differences in control beliefs—how well a general trait predicts behavior in specific situations is questionable. Contemporary views of achievement motivation have addressed these issues.

Contemporary Theory. Researchers have built on the original expectancy-value theoretical foundation by incorporating constructs to give the theory better explanatory power. The theory of Eccles and Wigfield (Eccles, 1983, 1993; Wigfield, 1994; Wigfield & Eccles, 2000; see also Chapters 15 and 17 of this volume), which is complex and has many predictors of achievement behavior, postulates that two important influences are expectancy and task value. Unlike Atkinson's theory, this theory does not highlight a general motive to achieve.

The *expectancy* construct refers to the issue of whether one can accomplish the task (Pintrich & Schunk, 2002). The expectancy variable is actually a type of expectancy for success: for example, students' beliefs about how well they will do on a future test.

The *value* component addresses the question, "Why should I do this task?" (Pintrich & Schunk, 2002). "Value" is multifaceted and includes attainment value (importance of doing well on a task), intrinsic value (interest and enjoyment experienced while performing the task), utility value (perceived usefulness of the task in terms of future goals), and cost belief (perceived negatives of doing the task in terms of what cannot be done instead).

Individuals' judgments of ability or competence influence their expectancies for success. Ability judgments are domain specific self-beliefs and pertain to the subject area or task at hand. There are other cognitive and affective variables in the theory, but there is no specific control variable. Perceptions of control may be assumed (i.e., expectancies for given outcomes) but they are not made explicit.

Research on this model has yielded a great deal of support for the predicted effects of variables and relations among them. Studies have employed both cross-sectional and longitudinal designs that assess beliefs and achievement of students at different developmental levels. Higher expectancies for success have been shown to relate positively to task choice, persistence, and achievement (Eccles, 1983; Wigfield, 1994). Expectancies and task-specific self-concepts (perceptions of ability or competence) are mediators between environmental events and achievement actions. Values have been shown to be positively related to achievement, although when both expectancies and values are used as predictors expectancies are typically stronger (Pintrich & Schunk, 2002). In contrast, values—especially attainment, intrinsic, and utility value beliefs—are excellent predictors of intentions to take courses and enrollment in them. Values seem more important for achievement choices, whereas expectancies bear a stronger relation to achievement.

There also has been considerable research on the development of children's achievement beliefs and values (Wigfield & Eccles, 2002). Children have reported a decrease in self-perceptions of competence as they move into adolescence, with the sharpest decline occurring when they make the transition from elementary to middle or junior high school. In addition, elementary children (third and fourth graders) displayed low levels of congruence between their self-perceptions of competence and more-objective measures (e.g., teacher grades), whereas middle/high school children (eighth and ninth graders) reported higher levels of congruence in these measures. Both of these findings may be due to high self-perceptions of competence reported by students in the early elementary grades. These younger students' overestimates may in turn be due to their tendency to use an absolute standard to judge their academic competence instead of the social comparative standard, which is used by older students (Blumenfeld, Pintrich, & Hamilton, 1987).

Regarding developmental changes in children's task values, Wigfield and Eccles (1992) found that children in the early elementary school grades do not distinguish reliably among three key forms of task values—interest, utility, and importance—but can do so by the time they reach the fifth grade. Paralleling developmental changes in competence ratings, children's value ratings for interest, importance, and utility of school subjects generally decrease with age, especially during the transition from elementary to middle or junior high school. This decline in academic values may be due to students' efforts to protect their self-esteem. For example, if students perceive themselves as declining in mathematical competence, they would not experience a corresponding decline in self-esteem if mathematics were devalued.

The achievement motivation theory advanced by Eccles and Wigfield includes different types of competence beliefs (Table 16.1). There is a question about how well they are empirically differentiated and whether in making judgments they are clearly differentiated in students' minds (Pintrich & Schunk, 2002). The notion of control does not appear as a separate variable. More research clearly is needed on the variables specified in the theory, especially on the causal ordering of expectancies and values. For example, do higher expectancies for success lead students to value tasks more, does value develop first and then as students experience success they gain expectancies for success, or do values and expectancies influence one another?

Attribution Theory

Attributions are perceived causes of outcomes. Attribution theory explains how people perceive the causes of their actions and those of others (Weiner, 1985). The assumption is that people are motivated to seek information to form attributions. In turn, attributions have motivational consequences. The process of assigning attributions is governed by principles. Attribution researchers have sought to determine those principles and have investigated how people's attributions (and therefore their achievement behaviors) can be changed.

Rotter's (1966) *locus of control* (discussed earlier) incorporates attributional concepts. Another historical influence on contemporary attribution was Heider's *naive analysis of action*. Heider (1958) examined what ordinary people believe are the causes of events in their lives (*naive* means that the average person is unaware of the objective influences). According to Heider, people attribute causes to internal (effective personal force) or external (effective environmental force) factors. The personal force comprises two factors: power (abilities) and motivation (trying). Together power and environment constitute the *can* factor, which when combined with the *try* factor is used to explain outcomes. One's power is relative to the environment, because the environment may aid or restrict what one can accomplish. Assuming that ability is sufficient to overcome environmental forces, then trying (effort) influences outcomes.

Heider's framework was general and provided few testable hypotheses. Other researchers have drawn from his work and formulated more explicit theories. Weiner's attribution theory is described next.

Attribution Theory of Achievement. A series of studies by Weiner and his colleagues provided the basis for an attributional theory of achievement (Weiner, 1979, 1985; Weiner et al., 1971; see also Chapter 17 of this volume). These investigators postulated that achievement successes and failures are largely attributed to such general factors as ability, effort, task difficulty/ease, and luck. There are other attributions (e.g., illness, physical appearance), but these four are common in achievement contexts.

Drawing on the work by Rotter and Heider, Weiner et al. (1971) classified causes along two dimensions: locus (internal/external to the person), and stability(relatively stable/unstable over time). Ability is internal and relatively stable; effort is internal and unstable; task difficulty/ease is external and relatively stable; luck is external and unstable. Weiner (1979) added a third dimension of controllability (controllable/uncontrollable by the person) to create a 2 × 2 × 2 classification. Effort is a controllable factor, whereas task difficulty is uncontrollable. Immediate effort is internal and unstable, but there also may be a general effort factor (typical effort) that is more stable. Although this classification has proven to be useful in research, how attributions are classified (and therefore their

consequences) may vary across individuals and cultures. Thus, "help from others" presumably is controllable, but some students may believe that they can exert little control over the help they receive—perhaps because they have unresponsive teachers.

In forming attributions people use situational cues. Cues for ability attributions are the ease, speed, or frequency of success; cues for effort attributions are physical or mental exertion; cues for task difficulty/ease are social norms (how others do) and task features; and cues for luck are randomness of outcomes and lack of relation of outcomes to effort.

Attributions are important because they have motivational consequences. The stability dimension is postulated to influence expectancy of success. Assuming that task conditions remain stable, attributions of success to stable causes should lead to higher expectations of future success than attributions to unstable causes. The locus dimension is hypothesized to influence affective responses. People experience greater pride/shame after succeeding/failing when outcomes are attributed to internal/external causes. Controllability has diverse effects. Feelings of control promote choice of academic tasks, effort, and persistence. Students who believe they have little control over academic outcomes have low expectations for success and motivation to succeed.

Attributional researchers have examined the process whereby individuals form attributions and attributional consequences (Pintrich & Schunk, 2002). In general this research has provided support for the theory and its predictions, although there are further issues to be addressed such as whether there are two distinct types of effort and whether external factors can be controlled.

Another type of research is attributional change, in which researchers attempt to improve students' motivation by altering their attributions for success and failure. For example, some students attribute difficulty in learning to low ability. This is dysfunctional for motivation because it can lead to lack of trying and skill improvement. Change programs that stress the value of effort try to alter students' attributions of low ability to insufficient effort.

Dweck (1975) compared children who always succeeded on tasks with those who occasionally failed and were given feedback stressing effort (need to work harder). On a subsequent test where all children were given insolvable problems, the attribution retraining children showed less performance impairment than those who always had succeeded. Research shows that dysfunctional attributions can be altered and that stressing effort can lead to improved performance (Pintrich & Schunk, 2002).

Developmental research shows that young children do not have clearly differentiated conceptions of ability and effort, but that these begin to differentiate by the later elementary years (Nicholls, 1983). After that, children may value ability more than effort, which presents a paradox because teachers tend to emphasize effort. The credibility of effort feedback also is critical. Effort feedback on easy tasks can signal that the person providing the feedback doubts the student's ability to learn. Thus, effort feedback seems most credible in the early stages of learning when students must expend effort to succeed. As students develop competencies, switching to ability feedback can have better motivational effects (Schunk, 1984).

Attribution theory emphasizes the role of control beliefs in motivating students to persist in their efforts to learn and perform well academically. From this theoretical perspective, students perceive optimal control when outcomes are attributed to internal, stable, and controllable causes. Competence beliefs, on the other hand, are not addressed directly, but attributions can give rise to perceptions of competence or incompetence that have motivational effects.

Social Cognitive Theory

Social cognitive theory counts various perspectives as its predecessors including the social learning theories of Miller and Dollard (1941) and Rotter (1954). Beginning in the 1960s, Bandura and his colleagues conducted a series of research studies on observational learning (Bandura & Walters, 1963). This work set the stage for Bandura's (1986) social cognitive theory of human behavior. Competence perceptions and control beliefs are integral components of the theory.

Bandura (1986) discussed human behavior within a framework of *triadic reciprocality*, or reciprocal interactions among behaviors, environmental variables, and personal factors (e.g., cognitions). Thus, one's actions can change the environment and affect how one thinks about oneself; the environment can affect what we do and think; and how we think can affect what we do and how we view the environment.

In this model of reciprocal causation, people are both producers and receivers of environmental influence. Self-referential processes allow people to go beyond immediate environmental stimuli and exert a large measure of control over their lives through planning, organizing, and self-regulation (Zimmerman, 2000).

The central variable representing competence beliefs is *self-efficacy*, defined as people's beliefs about their capabilities to learn or perform actions at designated levels (Bandura, 1997). In gauging self-efficacy, people assess their skills and capabilities to translate those skills into actions. Self-efficacy is a key to promoting a sense of *agency*

in individuals that they can influence their lives (Bandura, 1997, 2001; see also Chapter 15 of this volume).

Self-efficacy is contrasted with another social-cognitive variable—*outcome expectations*, or beliefs about the expected consequences of actions. Outcome expectations are types of control beliefs. Self-efficacy and outcome expectations often are related; for example, self-efficacious students expect to perform well and receive positive outcomes for their efforts (e.g., high grades). But there is no automatic connection between self-efficacy and outcome expectations. Students may expect positive outcomes if they perform well on a test (e.g., teacher praise, A grade), but may doubt their capabilities to study diligently enough to perform well.

Self-efficacy is primarily a domain-specific construct. It is contrasted with self-concept (discussed earlier), or one's collective self-perceptions (Pajares & Schunk, 2002). Although self-efficacy is influenced by one's abilities, it is not synonymous in meaning with them. Research shows that students of different ability levels differ in their self-efficacy (Collins, 1982).

Self-efficacy has diverse effects in achievement settings (Bandura, 1997; Pajares, 1996; Schunk, 1995). Self-efficacy can influence choice of activities. Students with low self-efficacy for learning may avoid tasks, whereas those who feel efficacious should participate more eagerly. Self-efficacy also affects effort expenditure, persistence, and learning. Students who feel efficacious about learning generally expend more effort and persist longer than those who doubt their capabilities, especially when they encounter difficulty. In turn, these behaviors promote learning.

People acquire information to gauge their self-efficacy in a given domain from various sources: actual performances, vicarious experiences (e.g., social models), persuasive information, and physiological symptoms (e.g., sweating, heart rate) (Bandura, 1997). Information acquired from these sources does not automatically influence self-efficacy but rather is cognitively appraised. Self-efficacy appraisal is an inferential process in which individuals weigh and combine the contributions of personal, behavioral, and environmental factors. Persons consider factors such as perceptions of their ability, effort expended, task difficulty, teacher assistance, and number and pattern of successes and failures (Bandura, 1997; Schunk, 1995).

Research on developmental changes in academic self-efficacy has revealed a complex pattern of outcomes. Shell, Colvin, and Bruning (1995) studied self-efficacy for reading and writing *tasks* (e.g., writing a letter to a friend) and self-efficacy for reading and writing *skills* (e.g., use the correct part of speech in your writing). They found a developmental increase in self-efficacy for reading and writing tasks across fourth, seventh, and tenth graders, but not in self-efficacy for reading or writing skills. Zimmerman and Martinez-Pons (1990) studied students' self-efficacy beliefs for solving specific mathematical problems or defining specific words across fifth, eighth, and eleventh graders and found significant developmental increases in self-efficacy on both tasks. Both studies revealed increases in self-efficacy to manage specific academic tasks as students' progress through the grades.

Recently Pajares, Valiante, and Cheong (in press) studied self-efficacy beliefs using items that also focused on writing skills, such as "write a strong paragraph that has a good topic sentence or main idea," with students from the fourth through eleventh grades. These researchers found that these self-efficacy beliefs declined as students moved from elementary to middle school but then remained stable through high school. Thus, although self-efficacy for completing specific academic tasks may increase developmentally, self-efficacy for academic skills may decline during elementary school but stabilize during middle and high school. It is possible that students' completion of specific tasks, such as writing to a friend or what one did on summer vacation, are judged in terms of absolute standards of success or failure, whereas academic skills, which are emphasized by teachers, are evaluated using peer comparison standards.

Research has shown that self-efficacy is a key variable predicting learning, motivation, and achievement, and that self-efficacy is a stronger and more consistent predictor of motivation and performance than are general constructs (e.g., self-concept) (Pajares, 1996; Schunk, 1995; Schunk & Pajares, 2004). Research also shows that educational interventions can enhance self-efficacy, motivation, and achievement. Positive effects on self-efficacy have been obtained by teaching students to set proximal goals and assess progress, providing them with opportunities to evaluate their progress in learning, giving them feedback linking their successes to effort and ability, having them work on progress goals that involve skill acquisition, having them self-monitor and record their progress, and linking rewards to the level of their performance (Schunk, 1995; Schunk & Ertmer, 2000).

Social cognitive theory addresses the notion of personal agency over important aspects of one's life, which involves perceptions of competence and control. Both positive self-efficacy and outcome expectations are necessary to optimally motivate: Students with a strong sense of agency expect to perform well and receive positive outcomes for their efforts (e.g., praise). A sense of agency also depends on one's *self-regulatory skill*, or the processes whereby students activate and sustain behaviors, cognitions, and affects, which are systematically oriented toward the attainment of learning goals (Zimmerman,

2000). Individuals can gain greater self-regulatory competence by developing effective learning strategies, practicing time management, arranging an environment conducive to learning, setting goals and assessing progress, maintaining a sense of self-efficacy for learning, and rewarding themselves for progress (Zimmerman, 2000). The literature on self-regulation underscores its relevance to developing the belief that one can control many important events in one's life (self-regulation is discussed later in this chapter).

Goal Theory

Goal theory postulates that important relations exist among individuals' goals, goal orientations, expectations, attributions, conceptions of ability, social and self-comparisons, and achievement behaviors (Linnenbrink & Pintrich, 2002; Pintrich, 2000). Goal theory incorporates many constructs shown to be important for motivation and learning, and it attempts to relate them in systematic fashion. The theory addresses a wide array of variables in explaining achievement behavior, some of which do not directly involve goals. This is a key difference between goal theory and goal-setting theory (Locke & Latham, 1990), which is more concerned with how goals are established and altered and with the roles of their properties (e.g., specificity, difficulty, proximity).

A key construct in goal theory is *goal orientation*—the purpose and focus of an individual's engagement in achievement activities or the reasons for engaging in academic tasks (Anderman, Austin, & Johnson, 2002; Pintrich, 2000; see also Chapter 17 of this volume). Goal orientation also bears directly on perceptions of competence and control beliefs, as discussed later. A central feature of goal theory is its emphasis on how different types of goal orientations can influence achievement actions.

One distinction is between mastery and performance goals (Dweck, 1999, 2002; see also Chapter 15 of this volume). A *mastery goal* reflects a focus on the acquisition of knowledge, skill, and competence, relative to one's prior performance; a *performance goal* involves a focus on striving to demonstrate competence by outperforming others (Elliot & Harackiewicz, 1996; Pintrich, 2000). Other types of goals that are conceptually similar to mastery goals are learning, task-involved, and task-focused goals; those similar to performance goals include ego-involved and ability-focused goals.

Goal orientations are distinguished because they are hypothesized to have different effects on achievement behaviors. Although there is ongoing debate about the benefits of different goal orientations, most researchers stress the desirability of mastery goals (Dweck, 1999; Pintrich,

2000). A mastery goal orientation focuses students' attention on processes and strategies that help them acquire skills and improve their competencies. The task focus presumably motivates behavior and directs and sustains attention on task features critical for learning. Students who pursue a mastery goal are apt to feel self-efficacious for attaining it and be motivated to engage in activities that assist their learning (e.g., expend effort, persist, handle distractions). Self-efficacy is substantiated as they work on the task and note their progress. The perception of progress sustains motivation and furthers skill acquisition (Schunk, 1995).

In contrast, because a performance goal orientation focuses attention on outperforming others, it does not highlight the importance of the processes and strategies needed to learn or raise self-efficacy for learning. Students may not compare their present and past performances to determine progress. Performance goals typically lead to social comparisons with others to determine progress, which can result in low perceptions of competence among students who do not perform as well as their peers. Lower perceived competence can reduce motivation for learning. Thus, performance goals focus on controlling success and failure experiences via selective exposure to socially competitive events.

Pintrich and others (Elliot, 1999; Linnenbrink & Pintrich, 2002; Pintrich, 2000, 2003) adopted a multiple-goals perspective on motivation. They crossed this mastery–performance dimension with an approach–avoid dimension according to whether students were attempting to approach or avoid the goals. Mastery-approach goals involve working on tasks to develop skills; mastery–avoid goals might involve avoiding the possibility of not meeting high standards; performance–approach goals entail a focus on outperforming others; and performance–avoid goals entail a concern with avoiding the demonstration of low ability. In any given context it is possible to hold more than one goal simultaneously. Thus, students may desire to improve their skills (mastery–approach) and outperform others to earn high grades (performance–approach).

Several investigators have suggested that goal orientation is closely related to one's theory about the nature of intelligence or ability (Dweck, 1999; Dweck & Leggett, 1988; Nicholls, 1983). Dweck proposed two theories of intelligence. Students who hold an *entity theory* believe that intelligence is relatively fixed and stable over time. Effort can help one to reach one's limit but not able to push one far beyond it. Difficulties are obstacles that can lower self-efficacy, lead to use of ineffective strategies, and cause one to quit or work halfheartedly.

In contrast, students who hold an *incremental theory* roughly equate intelligence with learning. They believe that ability can increase over time with learning and effort. If there is an upper limit on ability it is very high and should not prevent one from working harder to improve. Difficulties are challenges and can raise self-efficacy if students mobilize effort, persist, and use effective strategies.

Although there are exceptions, students holding an incremental theory of intelligence are likely to believe that learning will raise their ability and to adopt mastery goals. Students holding an entity theory may not adopt mastery goals because they believe that learning cannot raise ability much, if at all (i.e., they believe that they do not control their ability).

Research evidence offers good support for many of the predictions of goal theory (Pintrich, 2000). Students with a mastery goal orientation demonstrate better cognitive monitoring and use of learning strategies. Mastery-approach goals also relate positively to use of better (deeper) cognitive processing strategies during learning and to many motivational variables such as high self-efficacy and positive attributions. Students who adopt mastery-approach goals are able to maintain self-efficacy and perceptions of competence, even when confronted with difficult tasks (Dweck & Leggett, 1988).

To date there is little research on mastery-avoid goals, an area clearly in need of exploration. Research also is needed on how mastery goals affect perceptions of control. Support for the idea that mastery goals relate positively to perceptions of control is mainly indirect. Students who adopt mastery goals are more likely to monitor their cognition, seek ways to become aware of their learning, check their level of understanding, and use various learning strategies including those that promote learning at a deeper (rather than superficial) level (Pintrich, 2000). These and other effective learning techniques should promote control beliefs about outcomes, but research is needed.

Existing research presents mixed evidence on the relation of performance goals to motivation and self-regulated learning. Wolters, Yu, and Pintrich (1996) found that adolescents' performance-approach goals related positively to self-efficacy and use of cognitive and self-regulatory strategies; however, Kaplan and Midgley (1997) obtained no correlation between adolescents' performance-approach goals and adaptive learning strategies. Wolters (2004) showed that performance-approach goals did not relate to use of cognitive strategies. Middleton and Midgley (1997) found no relation between either performance-approach or performance-avoid goals and cognitive self-regulation. Given these conflicting findings, researchers should continue to explore the conditions under which performance-approach goals relate to achievement outcomes. Research also is needed on performance-avoid goals.

There is little developmental research on changes in goal orientations (Eccles, Wigfield, & Schiefele, 1998). Dweck's (1999) theory predicts an increase in performance goals with development, given an increasing emphasis on entity theories. Also, as children progress in school classrooms become more norm-referenced and competitive, especially with the transition from elementary to middle school or junior high. This change in contextual conditions further strengthens the prevalence of performance goals. The general decline with development in children's competence beliefs mirrors this change in goal orientation (Eccles et al., 1998).

Goal theory postulates key relations among goal orientations, theories of intelligence, perceptions of competence, and achievement outcomes. Pintrich (2000) showed how goal orientations are central components of self-regulated learning. In general, since a mastery orientation focuses on learning, students holding this goal orientation should feel a sense of control over outcomes because they adopt their strategies to help them learn and gauge their progress, which sustains motivation. Students holding a performance goal, conversely, should experience a lower sense of control over learning because their focus is outperforming others. Thus, goal theory includes both competence (e.g., self-efficacy) and control beliefs and distinguishes their effects.

Self-Determination Theory

Deci, Ryan, and colleagues developed a self-determination model of intrinsic motivation (Deci, 1980; Grolnick, Gurland, Jacob, & Decourcey, 2002; Ryan, Connell, & Deci, 1985). *Self-determination* is the process of using one's capacity to choose how to satisfy one's needs (Deci, 1980). Self-determination requires that people decide how to act on their environment.

Earlier writings by other investigators capture many of self-determination theory's central ideas. For example, de Charms (1968) discussed *personal causation*, or an individual's initiation of behavior intended to alter the environment. People strive to be causal agents and are motivated to produce changes in their environment. He distinguished origins from pawns. *Origins* are people who perceive their behaviors to be self-determined; *pawns* are those who believe their behaviors are determined by causes beyond their control. Personal causation training programs seek to engender in students a greater sense of responsibility for their actions, and thus help them become more like origins than pawns (Alderman, 1999).

Also relevant is White's (1959) *effectance motivation,* or the inner need to deal effectively with the environment. This motive is undifferentiated in infants and young children and is seen in actions such as grasping and crawling. With development the motive becomes specialized and may be seen in achievement behaviors in given school subjects.

Harter (1978) developed a model of *mastery motivation*. Whereas effectance motivation focused on success, Harter also took failure into account. Harter's model described the process whereby children internalize mastery goals and develop a self-reward system. Harter also stressed the role of socializing agents who reinforce independent mastery attempts and help children develop a sense of control and perceived competence. When socializing agents do not reinforce or openly discourage independent mastery attempts, children develop a sense of dependency, which does not facilitate perceptions of control or competence.

Self-determination theory postulates that there are three basic innate psychological needs: competence, autonomy, and relatedness. The need for competence is akin to White's (1959) general need for mastering the environment. The need for autonomy refers to the desire to experience a sense of control, agency, or autonomy in environmental interactions (i.e., an internal locus of causality). The need for relatedness (or belongingness) denotes the desire to belong to a group or groups.

Self-determination theory emphasizes the internalization of social values. Society contains many extrinsic rewards and controls that may not fit with children's desire for self-determination but which lead to desired behaviors. With development these external motivators can become part of an internalized self-regulatory system.

The self-determination view puts great emphasis on *intrinsic motivation*, or "the human need to be competent and self-determining in relation to the environment" (Deci, 1980, p. 27). Intrinsic motivation is the desire to do things for their own sake; it is distinguished from *extrinsic motivation,* or the motivation to engage in actions that lead to desired results (see also Chapter 15 of this volume). Intrinsic motivation leads people to seek and master challenges, which satisfies their needs to be competent and self-determining (Pintrich & Schunk, 2002). Intrinsic motivation decreases when people cannot be self-determining: that is, when they are not free to make choices or take responsibility for their actions. Intrinsic motivation suffers when people believe their actions are extrinsically determined, such as when they perceive their actions as means to an end (e.g., to a desired reward).

The theory postulates that intrinsic motivation is an innate human need and originates in infants as an undifferentiated need for competence and self-determination. With development the need differentiates into specific areas (e.g., academics, sports) and interactions with the environment influence its direction.

Intrinsic and extrinsic motivation may be thought of as two ends of a continuum. In the middle are behaviors that originally were extrinsically motivated but have become internalized and now are self-determined. Thus, students may want to avoid some academic activities but work on them to obtain rewards and avoid punishment. As skills develop and students believe they are becoming more competent, they perceive a sense of control and self-determination over learning. The activities become more intrinsically motivating.

Self-determination theory distinguishes competence from control beliefs. Skinner, Wellborn, and Connell (1990) identified three types of beliefs that contribute to perceived control. *Capacity beliefs* refer to beliefs about perceived capabilities with respect to ability, effort, other persons, and luck. *Strategy beliefs* are perceptions about factors that influence success in school and how what one does influences outcomes. *Control beliefs* are expectations about one's likelihood of doing well without regard to specific means.

Research has explored the relation of self-determination to intrinsic motivation (Ryan, 1993). Studies have shown that choice affects intrinsic motivation and that when persons believe they have control over their environments, they perform higher and tolerate aversive stimuli better.

Research also has explored the relations among intrinsic motivation and environmental conditions. When individuals are offered rewards for performance and view the rewards as controlling their behaviors, their intrinsic motivation for the task suffers. Other factors shown to be detrimental for intrinsic motivation are threats, deadlines, surveillance, and evaluations. Unfortunately, these factors occur commonly in schooling.

Intrinsic motivation can be enhanced by providing students with feedback indicating that they are becoming more competent and that they are developing skills. Allowing students more choices of activities also can raise intrinsic motivation. Although points in the theory need greater specification (e.g., influences on and consequences of the need to be self-determining), the literature supports many predictions of self-determination theory, especially that perceptions of competence and control are essential for intrinsic motivation.

RELEVANCE TO OTHER PROCESSES

The preceding discussion focuses on the roles of competence and control beliefs in achievement behaviors such as motivation and learning. Perceptions of competence and control also are relevant to other achievement processes. This section discusses their roles in self-regulation, metacognition, and volition.

Self-regulation

Self-regulation is a critical process in many theories of learning and achievement (Zimmerman, 2000). Self-regulation originally was studied in therapeutic contexts as a means of helping persons control dysfunctional behaviors. In recent years self-regulation has been increasingly applied to academic contexts to improve students' motivation and learning.

Various theories of self-regulation include competence judgments and control beliefs as key variables (Zimmerman & Schunk, 2001). According to Zimmerman (2000, 2001), self-regulation comprises forethought, performance/volitional control, and self-reflection phases. Self-efficacy is a key competence belief that is linked to self-regulatory control processes, such as goal setting and strategy selection. During forethought that precedes actual performance, learners assess their self-efficacy for learning. During the performance/volitional control phase, they monitor their performance and adjust strategies as needed; self-efficacy helps keep them focused and motivated. During periods of self-reflection, learners evaluate their goal progress, make causal attributions of personal control regarding that progress, and adjust their perceptions of self-efficacy accordingly. Perceived control involves not only self-efficacy beliefs but also judgments of personal effectiveness of one's self-regulatory processes. Pintrich's (2000) model of self-regulation also includes phases (forethought, planning, and activation; monitoring; control; reaction and reflection) and postulates that self-efficacy is critical throughout. Effective self-regulation requires that learners believe they can exert control over contextual factors and their cognitions, motivational processes, and behaviors.

Competence and control beliefs are integral to many theories of self-regulation, but the latter is broad in scope and includes many other processes. Most models of self-regulation include use of strategies (cognitive, motivational, behavioral), time management, self-observation and self-evaluation, environmental structuring, help seeking, and goal setting. Although perceived competence and control are important, they will not produce effective self-regulation in the absence of other self-regulatory processes.

Metacognition

Metacognition refers to the deliberate conscious control of cognitive activity (Flavell, 1985). Metacognition requires that one understands what skills, strategies, and resources are required to complete a task, as well as how and when to use those skills and strategies.

Metacognition is influenced by variables associated with learners, tasks, and strategies. Level of development is a key learner variable; with development, children are better able to understand task demands and are more cognizant of their capabilities for accomplishing them (Alexander, Carr, & Schwanenflugel, 1995). Features of the task affect learners' beliefs about what skills and strategies are required; for example, a lengthy passage with difficult words signals a different type of comprehension strategy than does a short passage with easy words. Learners' skills and knowledge of strategies and beliefs about which are useful in a given situation also affect what skills and strategies they actually employ.

As with self-regulation, competence and control beliefs come into play during metacognitive activities, but metacognition includes other processes. Learners who feel more self-efficacious about learning generally do so because they believe that they possess the skills and strategies needed to learn. Likewise, the belief that one can exercise control over one's cognitive activity is critical, but simply possessing that belief will not produce effective metacognition without the requisite knowledge, skills, and strategies.

Volition

Volition has interested psychologists for a long time. James (1890) believed that volition was the process of translating intentions into actions and had its greatest effect when different intentions competed for action. Volition executed actions by activating mental representations of them, which served as behavioral guides. Current thinking views volition as the process that mediates the relation between goals and actions and implements actions to attain goals (Corno, 1993; Kuhl, 1984). Volition helps to protect goals from being altered or discarded by applying self-regulatory activities to direct them.

Unlike theories of self-regulation that include activities that occur before, during, and after tasks, volition separates predecisional activities (e.g., goal setting, assessment of task demands) from postdecisional ones (e.g., application of strategies to attain goals). Volition comprises a set of psychological control processes that protect one's concentration and direct effort in the face of obstacles and distractions (Corno, 1993).

Competence and control beliefs are germane to volition, because to exert volitional control students must believe that they can control their focus and activities and feel competent about doing so. More research is needed in this area, because volitional researchers have focused on types of strategies to use for volitional control rather than the roles of perceived competence and control in the process (Corno, 1993, 1994; Kuhl, 1984). It seems clear,

however, that like self-regulation and metacognition, volition includes a set of skills and strategies that extend beyond competence and control beliefs.

FUTURE RESEARCH AND IMPLICATIONS FOR PRACTICE

Theory and research evidence support the idea that competence and control beliefs are important achievement constructs and contribute in critical ways to learners' motivation and learning. This section suggests future research directions and discusses some implications for educational practice.

Future Research Directions

Competence and control beliefs offer many possibilities for research. Some areas that deserve further research attention are described next.

Construct Refinement and Differentiation. The preceding theories address competence or control beliefs or both. Theories that include both (e.g., social cognitive, self-determination) distinguish them, while noting that these beliefs often are related. Bandura (1997), for example, differentiates outcome expectations (control beliefs) from self-efficacy (competence beliefs) but explains how they commonly relate to one another. Efficacious people experience a greater sense of personal control over situations; people with lower self-efficacy typically believe they have less control.

It is possible, of course, to feel competent without feeling in control or vice versa. Some students, for example, may feel highly competent about learning mathematics but believe they have little control over their grades because of the teachers' capricious grading practices. Yet because the two constructs often are related, this raises the issue that they share common variance with one or more other factors (e.g., ability).

More research is needed on the structure of these constructs to include the conditions under which they show the greatest relation. Developmental research also can address the issue of whether control is a basic human need (as postulated by self-determination theory) or rather a characteristic that develops in conjunction with one's goals and societal norms. Cross-cultural research suggests that individual competence and the emphasis on personal ability are stronger in Western cultures (Fletcher & Ward, 1988; McInerney, Hinkley, Dowson, & Van Etten, 1998). Cross-cultural research should address the issue of the generality of perceived control and the cultural influences on it.

Importance of Competence and Control Beliefs. A general theme in this chapter is that competence and control beliefs make key contributions to the prediction of achievement beyond the effects of other variables. At the same time, one might question whether these beliefs really are important in school. Students typically have little control over classroom activities, teaching, assignments, and assessments. Most activities in K-12 schooling are regulated by teachers and curricula. Given the current emphasis on state and national assessments (with the rewards and sanctions that accompany them), one might ask whether it makes any difference if students feel competent or in control, so long as they can pass and ideally score high on standardized tests. Feelings of competence and control may become more important with fewer external constraints in place: for example, when students are out of school and pursuing careers.

Although research has shown motivational benefits of competence and control beliefs (Pintrich, 2000; Schunk, 1995), further research is needed to investigate the desirability of different types of beliefs. For example, are some types of competence beliefs "better" than others? What serves adolescents better in high school—competence and control beliefs for school achievement or for social interactions? It is tempting to say the former, but a case can be made that students with higher perceived social competence and control are happier, less anxious, and more motivated to perform well in school to maintain their social standing among their peers. A related research issue concerns the desirability of individual versus collective competence and control beliefs. Since much success in life after school depends on collective competence and control, researchers might address how these beliefs develop and relate to school success relative to individual beliefs.

Another issue involves the assumption that higher competence and control beliefs are desirable. We might ask whether there are conditions under which lower competence and control beliefs are more functional. Intuitively it seems important to recognize situations where one lacks competence and control. These can signal that one needs to develop skills, or perhaps abandon the situation (e.g., drop a college major when one lacks the perceived competence and control for learning and being successful). Research is needed on the conditions in which lower competence and control beliefs are more desirable than are higher beliefs.

Differentiating Activities. There is a clear need for classroom research investigating how teachers can best differentiate instruction and activities to address the various levels of ability and achievement that typically are represented in their classrooms. Even in more homogenous classrooms (e.g., honors classes) different levels of student ability and achievement will be represented. Given this diversity, how can teachers address the competence and control beliefs of the lower achievers, who may well experience lower perceptions of competence and control than others?

Conversely, the *big fish—little pond effect* postulates that students compare their abilities with those of their peers and use this social comparative information in gauging their academic self-concept (Marsh & Craven, 2002). Thus, higher achievers may actually form lower academic self-concepts when grouped with other high achievers than when most of their peers are of lower ability. This raises the research question of how teachers can strengthen the competence and control beliefs of students in honors and advanced placement classes.

It would be valuable for investigators to conduct classroom-based studies that mapped students' competence and control beliefs onto prevailing classroom norms and followed these over time to determine how students' beliefs changed as a function of changes in classroom conditions. For example, it is not unusual for high school students to be in some honors or advanced placement classes and some regular or college preparatory classes. Are students' competence and control beliefs differentiated according to class placement? Do learners feel more efficacious and in control in the regular classes than in the honors classes, or do their competence and control beliefs depend on the subject matter and other contextual factors (e.g., instructional format)? Research will help to clarify how changing conditions affect students' beliefs.

Generality/Specificity. Another important research issue concerns specificity versus generality. Domain-specific measures of competence and control beliefs predict achievement behaviors better than general measures, but we might ask to what extent competence and control beliefs developed in one context generalize to others.

Although older students often display some consistency in competence beliefs across different subject areas (Bong, 1997), we should expect less generality between school subject areas (e.g., history to math) and between teachers (e.g., one teacher who allows choices to another who generally does not) than between different levels of the same subject area (e.g., algebra 1 to algebra 2) and among similar content covered in different courses (e.g., reading comprehension in English and history). Generality might be improved when students perceive the value, or different uses for the learning. Thus, learning strategies such as organizing, outlining, and rehearsing are apt to aid learning across many domains. Students who believe they are skillful in these activities should hold higher perceptions of competence and control for learning than students who feel less confident about using strategies effectively. More research also is needed on interventions designed to promote transfer of skills and strategies.

Diverse Student Populations. There is a need to test the influence of competence and control beliefs with diverse student populations. Much of the extant research has been conducted using predominantly White Americans. The rapidly changing demographics of many schools—especially the influx of Hispanic and Asian-American students—has resulted in changed school cultures. It is important to determine whether competence and control beliefs are central to motivation and learning for diverse populations.

Although the theories covered in this chapter postulate that competence and control are universally important, there may be differences in how they can be developed in students from different ethnic backgrounds. Some cultures value individual achievement, whereas others stress group achievement. For theoretical clarification, as well as for instructional planning, it is important to determine how competence and control beliefs can be enhanced in all students.

Instructional Technology. The rapid advent of instructional technology offers new instructional possibilities that did not exist even a few years ago. Teachers and students today have available such technologies as the Internet, Web-based learning, two-way videoconferencing, video streaming, DVDs, e-mail, chat rooms, and instant messaging.

It seems important to investigate how competence and control beliefs for learning from technology can be developed. Some students who feel competent about writing a term paper using print resources may feel less confident about using Web-based resources. They may perceive that they have less control over the process and outcome. But instructional technology also may help build students' competence and control beliefs. Students who use the Internet to complete class projects may experience a sense of control over academic learning as they navigate sites, devise effective search strategies, and decide which information to retain and which to discard.

As with other forms of learning, teachers may need to teach students how to use technology for learning: for example, by teaching Internet search and navigation skills. Such research would be relevant to the issue of transfer of competence and control beliefs to different instructional formats.

Implications for Practice

A central idea is that the development of skills, knowledge, and strategies is critical, but students also must believe that they have become more competent. Thus, most theories stress the perception of progress as central to developing competence beliefs.

There are various ways to convey progress to students. Theories that include goals as a motivational mechanism postulate that evaluating progress toward goals helps students form perceptions of competence. If a learner's goal is to develop skill (rather than to outperform others) then the student should be able to perceive progress by comparing present with prior performance. Other ways of conveying progress are through teacher feedback (e.g., "You've gotten so much better at this"), having students monitor their performances and periodically assess their progress, and giving periodic review exercises that allow students to witness how much they have learned.

Competence beliefs also can be enhanced by exposing students to social models. Although different models can teach skills, the literature suggests that perceived similarity to models is critical to building perceptions of competence (Schunk, 1995). Students who observe similar peers succeed are apt to believe that they can as well. This vicarious increase needs to be substantiated by subsequent performance success. Persuasive feedback (e.g., "You can do this") also needs performance substantiation for the enhanced perception of competence to endure.

Perceptions of competence can be increased through good curricular structuring. Ideally skill development will be sequenced such that later learning builds on prior learning. Thus, many students take a course in algebra followed by a course in geometry. If the geometry curriculum is properly structured, it will include activities that require algebraic operations, and the curriculum should include sections showing the integration with algebra. As students use their algebraic skills in geometry, their perceptions of competence in algebra are further strengthened.

Control beliefs may seem somewhat harder to address, given that in school students often have little control over the curriculum, assignments, grouping, grading, and the like. How can educators help students develop the belief that they can assess and overcome conditions that can thwart successful performance even when students perceive themselves as competent? This may require a type of instruction not often provided in schools—teaching metacognitive awareness and self-regulatory strategies. Some teachers believe that their job is to impart knowledge but not teach students how to learn. Greater success may be attained when school administrators take the lead and meet with teachers within and across departments to structure learner activities that help to foster the belief that successful actions will lead to positive outcomes.

Another way to build control beliefs is to show students how learning certain skills and strategies can help them in multiple ways. While teaching students a reading comprehension strategy, it is useful to show how the strategy can be used with different types of reading, such as newspapers, magazines, books, and Internet sources. In mathematics, the study of ratios and proportions can be linked to scale drawings; students can determine the proportions and make the drawings.

Control beliefs can be engendered when teachers build in some unplanned class periods. Students can be allowed to lead discussions on topics relevant to the subject area and can be given opportunities to ask teachers to review topics that they are having difficulty understanding. During group projects, students can be responsible for planning the project and setting their work schedules. The key is not to have a lock-step curriculum or rigid structure for every class period.

Classroom contextual factors affect student motivation (Pintrich, 2000, 2003; see also Chapter 15 of this volume). A motivational scheme for classifying these factors is *TARGET*—task, authority, recognition, grouping, evaluation, time (Ames, 1992; Epstein, 1989). The *task* dimension involves the design of learning activities and assignments. *Authority* refers to whether students can display leadership and develop control over learning activities. *Recognition* involves the formal and informal use of praise, rewards, and incentives. The *grouping* dimension addresses student groupings for instruction and activities. *Evaluation* involves methods for monitoring and assessing student learning and for providing feedback. *Time* comprises time allotted for completing work, pace of instruction, and appropriateness of workload. Teachers who address these dimensions can help build students' competence and control beliefs: for example, by recognizing individual student progress, teaching students organizational and time management strategies, and giving students some choices in assignments.

CONCLUSION

Competence and control beliefs have been of interest in educational psychology for many years. Competence beliefs will not motivate unless students also perceive themselves in control of the learning context. Many contemporary theories distinguish these two types of self-beliefs, and research has substantiated that these beliefs are predictive of diverse outcomes such as learning, motivation, self-regulation, metacognition, and volition. Future research will further clarify their operation and suggest effective ways to develop these beliefs in students. This pedagogical goal is important because positive perceptions of competence and control are essential for learners to maximize their talents for succeeding in a changing world.

References

Alderman, M. K. (1999). *Motivation for achievement: Possibilities for teaching and learning*. Mahwah, NJ: Lawrence Erlbaum Associates.

Alexander, J. E., Carr, M., & Schwanenflugel, P. J. (1995). Development of metacognition in gifted children: Directions for future research. *Developmental Review, 15*, 1-37.

Ames, C. (1992). Classrooms: Goals, structures, and student motivation. *Journal of Educational Psychology, 84*, 261-271.

Anderman, E. M., Austin, C. C., & Johnson, D. M. (2002). The development of goal orientation. In A. Wigfield & J. S. Eccles (Eds.), *Development of achievement motivation* (pp. 197-220). San Diego, CA: Academic Press.

Atkinson, J. W. (1957). Motivational determinants of risk-taking behavior. *Psychological Review, 64*, 359-372.

Atkinson, J. W., & Feather, N. T. (1966). *A theory of achievement motivation*. New York: Wiley.

Atkinson, J. W., & Raynor, J. O. (1974). *Motivation and achievement*. Washington, DC: Hemisphere.

Bandura, A. (1986). *Social foundations of thought and action: A social cognitive theory*. Englewood Cliffs, NJ: Prentice-Hall.

Bandura, A. (1997). *Self-efficacy: The exercise of control*. New York: Freeman.

Bandura, A. (2001). Social cognitive theory: An agentic perspective. *Annual Review of Psychology, 52*, 1-26.

Bandura, A., & Walters, R. H. (1963). *Social learning and personality development*. New York: Holt, Rinehart & Winston.

Blumenfeld, P., Pintrich, P. R., & Hamilton, V. L. (1987). Teacher talk and students' reasoning about morals, conventions, and achievement. *Child Development, 58*, 1389-1401.

Bong, M. (1997). Generality of academic self-efficacy judgments: Evidence of hierarchical relations. *Journal of Educational Psychology, 89*, 696-709.

Collins, J. L. (1982, March). *Self-efficacy and ability in achievement behavior*. Paper presented at the annual meeting of the American Educational Research Association, New York.

Cooper, W. H. (1983). An achievement motivation nomological network. *Journal of Personality and Social Psychology, 44*, 841-861.

Corno, L. (1993). The best-laid plans: Modern conceptions of volition and educational research. *Educational Researcher, 22*(2), 14-22.

Corno, L. (1994). Student volition and education: Outcomes, influences, and practices. In D. H. Schunk & B. J. Zimmerman (Eds.), *Self-regulation of learning and performance: Issues and educational applications* (pp. 229–251). Hillsdale, NJ: Lawrence Erlbaum Associates.

de Charms, R. (1968). *Personal causation: The internal affective determinants of behavior.* New York: Academic Press.

Deci, E. L. (1980). *The psychology of self-determination.* Lexington, MA: D.C. Heath.

Dweck, C. S. (1975). The role of expectations and attributions in the alleviation of learned helplessness. *Journal of Personality and Social Psychology, 31,* 674–685.

Dweck, C. S. (1999). *Self-theories: Their role in motivation, personality, and development.* Philadelphia: Taylor & Francis.

Dweck, C. S. (2002). The development of ability conceptions. In A. Wigfield & J. S. Eccles (Eds.), *Development of achievement motivation* (pp. 57–88). San Diego, CA: Academic Press.

Dweck, C. S., & Leggett, E. L. (1988). A social-cognitive approach to motivation and personality. *Psychological Review, 95,* 256–273.

Eccles, J. S. (1983). Expectancies, values, and academic behaviors. In J. T. Spence (Ed.), *Achievement and achievement motivation* (pp. 75–146). San Francisco: Freeman.

Eccles, J. S. (1993). School and family effects on the ontogeny of children's interests, self-perceptions, and activity choice. In J. Jacobs (Ed.), *Nebraska Symposium on Motivation* (Vol. 40, pp. 145–208). Lincoln, NE: University of Nebraska Press.

Eccles, J. S., Wigfield, A., & Schiefele, U. (1998). Motivation to succeed. In N. Eisenberg (Ed.), *Handbook of child psychology* (Vol. 3, pp. 1017–1095). New York: Wiley.

Elliot, A. J. (1999). Approach and avoidance motivation and achievement goals. *Educational Psychologist, 34,* 169–189.

Elliot, A. J., & Church, M. (1997). A hierarchical model of approach and avoidance achievement motivation. *Journal of Personality and Social Psychology, 72,* 218–232.

Elliot, A. J., & Harackiewicz, J. M. (1996). Approach and avoidance achievement goals and intrinsic motivation: A mediational analysis. *Journal of Personality and Social Psychology, 70,* 461–475.

Epstein, J. L. (1989). Family structures and student motivation: A developmental perspective. In C. Ames & R. Ames (Eds.), *Research on motivation in education* (Vol. 3, pp. 259–295). San Diego, CA: Academic Press.

Flavell, J. H. (1985). *Cognitive development* (2nd ed.). Englewood Cliffs, NJ: Prentice-Hall.

Fletcher, G., & Ward, C. (1988). Attribution theory and processes: A cross-cultural perspective. In M. H. Bond (Ed.), *The cross-cultural challenge to social psychology* (pp. 230–244). Newbury Park, CA: Sage.

Grolnick, W. S., Gurland, S. T., Jacob, K. F., & Decourcey, W. (2002). The development of self-determination in middle childhood and adolescence. In A. Wigfield & J. S. Eccles (Eds.), *Development of achievement motivation* (pp. 147–171). San Diegos, CA: Academic Press.

Hansford, B. C., & Hattie, J. A. (1982). The relationship between self and achievement/performance measures. *Review of Educational Research, 52,* 123–142.

Harter, S. (1978). Effectance motivation reconsidered: Toward a developmental model. *Human Development, 21,* 34–64.

Heider, F. (1958). *The psychology of interpersonal relations.* New York: Wiley.

James, W. (1890). *The principles of psychology* (Vols. I & II). New York: Henry Holt.

Kaplan, A., & Midgley, C. (1997). The effect of achievement goals: Does level of perceived academic competence make a difference? *Contemporary Educational Psychology, 22,* 415–435.

Kuhl, J. (1984). Volitional aspects of achievement motivation and learned helplessness: Toward a comprehensive theory of action control. In B. A. Maher (Ed.), *Progress in experimental personality research* (Vol. 13, pp. 99–171). New York: Academic Press.

Kuhl, J., & Blankenship, V. (1979). Behavioral change in a constant environment: Shift to more difficult tasks with constant probability of success. *Journal of Personality and Social Psychology, 37,* 549–561.

Lewin, K., Dembo, T., Festinger, L., & Sears, P. (1944). Level of aspiration. In J. McV. Hunt (Ed.), *Personality and the behavior disorders* (Vol. 1, pp. 333–378). New York: Ronald Press.

Linnenbrink, E. A., & Pintrich, P. R. (2002). Achievement goal theory and affect: An asymmetrical bi-directional model. *Educational Psychologist, 37,* 69–78.

Locke, E. A., & Latham, G. P. (1990). *A theory of goal setting and task performance.* Englewood Cliffs, NJ: Prentice-Hall.

Marsh, H. W., & Craven, R. G. (2002). The pivotal role of frames of reference in academic self-concept formation: The "big fish—little pond" effect. In F. Pajares & T. Urdan (Eds.), *Academic motivation of adolescents* (pp. 83–123). Greenwich, CT: Information Age.

Marsh, H. W., & Shavelson, R. (1985). Self-concept: Its multifaceted, hierarchical structure. *Educational Psychologist, 20,* 107–123.

Maslow, A. H. (1954), *Motivation and personality.* New York: Harper & Row.

McClelland, D. C., Atkinson, J. W., Clark, R. A., & Lowell, E. I. (1953). *The achievement motive.* New York: Appleton-Century-Crofts.

McInerney, D. M., Hinkley, J., Dowson, M., & Van Etten, S. (1998). Aboriginal, Anglo, and immigrant Australian students' motivational beliefs about personal academic success: Are there cultural differences? *Journal of Educational Psychology, 90,* 621–629.

Middleton, M., & Midgley, C. (1997). Avoiding the demonstration of lack of ability: An underexplored aspect of goal theory. *Journal of Educational Psychology, 89,* 710–718.

Miller, N. E., & Dollard, J. (1941). *Social learning and imitation.* New Haven, CT: Yale University Press.

Murray, H. A. (1936). Techniques for a systematic investigation of fantasy. *Journal of Psychology, 3,* 115–143.

Murray, H. A. (1938). *Explorations in personality.* New York: Oxford University Press.

Nicholls, J. (1983). Conceptions of ability and achievement motivation: A theory and its implications for education. In

S. G. Paris, G. M. Olson, & H. W. Stevenson (Eds.), *Learning and motivation in the classroom* (pp. 211–237). Hillsdale, NJ: Lawrence Erlbaum Associates.

Pajares, F. (1996). Self-efficacy beliefs in achievement settings. *Review of Educational Research, 66,* 543–578.

Pajares, F. (2003). William James: Our father who begat us. In B. J. Zimmerman & D. H. Schunk (Eds.), *Educational psychology: A century of contributions* (pp. 41–64). Mahwah, NJ: Lawrence Erlbaum Associates.

Pajares, F., & Schunk, D. H. (2001). Self-beliefs and school success: Self-efficacy, self-concept, and school achievement. In R. J. Riding & S. G. Rayner (Eds.), *Self perception: International perspectives on individual differences* (Vol. 2, pp. 239–265). Westport, CT: Ablex.

Pajares, F., & Schunk, D. H. (2002). Self and self-belief in psychology and education: A historical perspective. In J. Aronson (Ed.), *Improving academic achievement: Impact of psychological factors of education* (pp. 3–21). San Diego, CA: Academic Press.

Pajares, F., Valiante, G., & Cheong, Y. F. (in press). Writing self-efficacy and its relation to gender, writing motivation, and writing competence: A developmental perspective. In S. Hidi & P. Noscolo (Eds.), *Motivation and writing: Research and school practice.* Dordrecht, The Netherlands: Kluwer.

Phares, E. J. (1976). *Locus of control in personality.* Morristown, NJ: General Learning Press.

Pintrich, P. R. (2000). The role of goal orientation in self-regulated learning. In M. Boekaerts, P. R. Pintrich, & M. Zeidner (Eds.), *Handbook of self-regulation* (pp. 451–502). San Diego: Academic Press.

Pintrich, P. R. (2003). A motivational science perspective on the role of student motivation in learning and teaching contexts. *Journal of Educational Psychology, 95,* 667–686.

Pintrich, P. R., & Schunk, D. H. (2002). *Motivation in education: Theory, research, and applications* (2nd ed.). Upper Saddle River, NJ: Prentice-Hall.

Ray, J. J. (1982). Achievement motivation and preferred probability of success. *Journal of Social Psychology, 116,* 255–261.

Rogers, C. R. (1963). The actualizing tendency in relation to "motives" and to consciousness. In M. R. Jones (Ed.), *Nebraska Symposium on Motivation* (Vol. 11, pp. 1–24). Lincoln, NE: University of Nebraska Press.

Rosen, B., & D'Andrade, R. C. (1959). The psychosocial origins of achievement motivation. *Sociometry, 22,* 185–218.

Rotter, J. B. (1954). *Social learning and clinical psychology.* New York: Prentice-Hall.

Rotter, J. B. (1966). Generalized expectancies for internal versus external control of reinforcement. *Psychological Monographs, 80*(1, Whole No. 609).

Ryan, R. M. (1993). Agency and organization: Intrinsic motivation, autonomy, and the self in psychological development. In J. E. Jacobs (Ed.), *Nebraska Symposium on Motivation* (Vol. 40, pp. 1–56). Lincoln, NE: University of Nebraska Press.

Ryan, R. M., Connell, J. P., & Deci, E. L. (1985). A motivational analysis of self-determination and self-regulation in education. In C. Ames & R. Ames (Eds.), *Research on motivation in education* (Vol. 2, pp. 13–51). Orlando, FL: Academic Press.

Schunk, D. H. (1984). Sequential attributional feedback and children's achievement behaviors. *Journal of Educational Psychology, 76,* 1159–1169.

Schunk, D. H. (1995). Self-efficacy and education and instruction. In J. E. Maddux (Ed.), *Self-efficacy, adaptation, and adjustment: Theory, research, and applications* (pp. 281–303). New York: Plenum.

Schunk, D. H., & Ertmer, P. A. (2000). Self-regulation and academic learning: Self-efficacy enhancing interventions. In M. Boekaerts, P. R. Pintrich, & M. Zeidner (Eds.), *Handbook of self-regulation* (pp. 631–649). San Diego, CA: Academic Press.

Schunk, D. H., & Pajares, F. (2004). Self-efficacy in education revisited: Empirical and applied evidence. In D. M. McInerney & S. Van Etten (Eds.), *Big theories revisited* (pp. 115–138). Greenwich, CT: Information Age.

Shavelson, R. J., & Bolus, R. (1982). Self-concept: The interplay of theory and methods. *Journal of Educational Psychology, 74,* 3–17.

Shell, D. F., Colvin, C., & Bruning, R. H. (1995). Self-efficacy, attribution, and outcome expectancy mechanisms in reading and writing achievement: Grade-level and achievement-level differences. *Journal of Educational Psychology, 87,* 386–398.

Skinner, E. A., Wellborn, J. G., & Connell, J. P. (1990). What it takes to do well in school and whether I've got it: A process model of perceived control and children's engagement and achievement in school. *Journal of Educational Psychology, 82,* 22–32.

Weiner, B. (1979). A theory of motivation for some classroom experiences. *Journal of Educational Psychology, 71,* 3–25.

Weiner, B. (1985). An attributional theory of achievement motivation and emotion. *Psychological Review, 92,* 548–573.

Weiner, B., Frieze, I. H., Kukla, A., Reed, L., Rest, S., & Rosenbaum, R. M. (1971). *Perceiving the causes of success and failure.* Morristown, NJ: General Learning Press.

White, R. W. (1959). Motivation reconsidered: The concept of competence. *Psychological Review, 66,* 297–333.

Wigfield, A. (1994). The role of children's achievement values in the self-regulation of their learning outcomes. In D. H. Schunk & B. J. Zimmerman (Eds.), *Self-regulation of learning and performance: Issues and educational applications* (pp. 101–124). Hillsdale, NJ: Lawrence Erlbaum Associates.

Wigfield, A., & Eccles, J. S. (1992). The development of achievement values: A theoretical analysis. *Developmental Review, 12,* 265–310.

Wigfield, A., & Eccles, J. S. (2000). Expectancy-value theory of motivation. *Contemporary Educational Psychology, 25,* 68–81.

Wigfield, A., & Eccles, J. S. (2002). The development of competence beliefs, expectancies for success, and achievement values from childhood through adolescence. In A. Wigfield & J. S. Eccles (Eds.), *Development of achievement motivation* (pp. 91–120). San Diego, CA: Academic Press.

Wolters, C. A. (2004). Advancing achievement goal theory: Using goal structures and goal orientations to predict students' motivation, cognition, and achievement. *Journal of Educational Psychology, 96,* 236–250.

Wolters, C. A., Yu, S. L., & Pintrich, P. R. (1996). The relation between goal orientation and students' motivational beliefs and self-regulated learning. *Learning and Individual Differences, 8*, 211–238.

Wylie, R. C. (1979). *The self-concept* (Vol. 2). Lincoln, NE: University of Nebraska Press.

Zimmerman, B. J. (2000). Attaining self-regulation: A social cognitive perspective. In M. Boekaerts, P. R. Pintrich, & M. Zeidner (Eds.), *Handbook of self-regulation* (pp. 13–39). San Diego, CA: Academic Press.

Zimmerman, B. J. (2001). Theories of self-regulated learning and academic achievement: An overview and analysis. In B. J. Zimmerman & D. H. Schunk (Eds.), *Self-regulated learning and academic achievement: Theoretical perspectives* (2nd ed., pp. 1–38). Mahwah, NJ: Lawrence Erlbaum Associates.

Zimmerman, B. J., & Martinez-Pons, M. (1990). Student differences in self-regulated learning: Relating grade, sex, and giftedness to self-efficacy and strategy use. *Journal of Educational Psychology, 82*, 51–59.

Zimmerman, B. J., & Schunk, D. H. (Eds.) (2001). *Self-regulated learning and academic achievement: Theoretical perspectives* (2nd ed.). Mahwah, NJ: Lawrence Erlbaum Associates.

Zimmerman, B. J., & Schunk, D. H. (2003) (Eds.). *Educational psychology: A century of contributions.* Mahwah, NJ: Lawrence Erlbaum Associates.

Zimmerman, B. J., & Schunk, D. H. (2004). Self-regulating intellectual processes and outcomes: A social cognitive perspective. In D. Y. Dai & R. J. Sternberg (Eds.), *Motivation, emotion, and cognition: Integrative perspectives on intellectual functioning and development* (pp. 323–349). Mahwah, NJ: Lawrence Erlbaum Associates.

·17·

GOALS, VALUES, AND AFFECT: INFLUENCES ON STUDENT MOTIVATION

Eric M. Anderman
University of Kentucky

Christopher A. Wolters
University of Houston

In the first *Handbook of Educational Psychology*, two chapters were devoted exclusively to motivation. The chapter by S. Graham and B. Weiner (1996) provided a discussion of several key historical and contemporary theoretical models used to understand achievement motivation. The chapter by D. Stipek (1996) provided a comprehensive review of the instructional applications of these different theories. In addition to these two chapters, motivation was a key concern in several other chapters, including those on development, individual differences, cognition, ethnicity, and gender. Since the publication of the first *Handbook*, the significance of achievement motivation as an area of study within educational psychology has continued to flourish. In this chapter we draw on recent developments in the motivation literature to discuss theoretical and empirical research concerning students' goals, values, and affect.

Despite its pivotal role within educational psychology, a simple and commonly understood definition of motivation is difficult to identify. In their chapter, Graham and Weiner (1996) stated that motivational psychologists attempt to explain behavioral choices, persistence at tasks, and both cognitive and affective experiences during task engagement. Similar arguments about the behavioral outcomes of motivation have been made by others (e.g., Maehr, 1976; Pintrich & Schunk, 2002; Wolters, 2004).

Other definitions have focused less on what motivation *does* and more on what motivation *is*. From this perspective, motivation can be characterized as either a product or a process (Winne & Marx, 1989). When viewed as a product or state, motivation refers to a willingness, desire, or condition of arousal or activation. At any particular time, students have a level of motivation that they experience phenomenologically, that influences their initial and ongoing engagement with regard to a particular activity. Motivation can also describe the cognitive and affective processes through which students' level of motivation or goal-directed behavior is determined (Pintrich & Schunk, 2002). From this perspective, motivation refers not just to an end state, but also to the cognitive processes that govern how that end state is achieved (Winne & Marx, 1989).

This understanding contradicts a naïve assumption among many that equates motivation with achievement or performance. As an influence on students' choice and engagement, motivation would clearly have an influence on learning, achievement, and performance. However, these outcomes are often poor indicators of motivation because they are each affected substantially by nonmotivational factors, such as ability level and prior knowledge. It is quite possible for some students to achieve at high levels yet not be highly motivated. Such students perform well based due to superior ability, not superior effort.

Historically, efforts to understand and explain motivation have relied on factors that include instincts, internal drives or traits, behavioral associations, and psychoanalytic forces; in contrast, contemporary models of motivation emphasize cognitive processes (Graham & Weiner, 1996; Pintrich & Schunk, 2002). Even within the more cognitive tradition, there are a wide variety of constructs that have been used to understand, to predict, and to influence motivation within academic contexts. In this chapter we focus on three related constructs: goals, values, and affect. A second key area from within cognitive views of motivation is addressed in the chapter by Schunk and Zimmerman (Chapter 16 of this volume). For a broader and more elaborate explanation of these many constructs and theories readers are directed to one of the many excellent textbooks now available on this topic (e.g., Pintrich & Schunk, 2002).

The overall purpose of this chapter is to review and provide evidence for the importance of goals, values, and affect to achievement motivation. To achieve this objective, the chapter is organized into four sections. In the first section, we provide brief historical perspectives and examine important distinctions within each area. In the second section, we review empirical research examining each, to document the relations between these constructs and indicators of students' choice, effort, and performance. In the third section, we examine studies that have attempted to examine the interrelations between and among goals, values, and affect. Finally, in the concluding portion of the chapter, we highlight important directions for future research.

DEFINITIONS AND DISTINCTIONS WITHIN GOALS, VALUES, AND AFFECT

In this section we provide brief histories of goals, values and affect within the field of educational psychology. As well, we provide conceptual explanations of these constructs, and outline the major dimensions or distinctions that are made within each area.

Goals

The term *goal* has a long history in the field of motivation. Goals have been defined in a variety of different ways, by a number of researchers (e.g., Austin & Vancouver, 1996; Urdan, 1997). Today, motivation researchers discuss a variety of different goal-related constructs and theories, including goal-setting, proximal and distal goals, goal orientations, and goal structures. However, other researchers have examined related constructs, using different terminologies (e.g., Cantor & Langston, 1989).

In their review of goal constructs in the field of psychology, Austin and Vancouver (1996) describe a number of dimensions of goals. These include the perceived importance of the goal, the perceived difficulty level of the goal, the specificity of the goal, the temporal range of the goal (i.e., an immediate goal vs. a longer term goal), the level of consciousness of the goal (i.e., some goals are conscious, whereas other are unconscious in nature), and the complexity of the goal. Although this list is not comprehensive, it does describe the multifaceted nature of goals in psychology.

The study of goals within the field of motivation has a long history. Goals emerged as a predominant motivation construct after several other constructs waned in popularity. For example, as noted by Pintrich and Schunk (2002), "needs" models of academic motivation proliferated in the literature in the early 20th century. Nevertheless, the concept of "needs" fell out of favor, because needs theories (e.g., Maslow, 1954; Murray, 1938) did not provide adequate explanations for many types of motivated behaviors. Instead, *needs* were recharacterized as *motives*, and then later as *goals* in many contemporary social-cognitive theories of academic motivation. However, it is important to note that motives and needs still remain important components of some theoretical perspectives, such as self-determination theory (Deci & Ryan, 1985).

When the difference between an individual's goal and the individual's self-perceived performance on a task is large, the individual becomes motivated to reduce this incongruity. More specifically, research suggests that when individuals are assigned relatively challenging goals, they tend to perform better at tasks than individuals who are assigned easy or vague goals (Tubbs, 1986).

In recent years, the study of goals has predominated the field of achievement motivation. In the present review, we focus on a few of the more prominent research programs involving goals. These include achievement goal theory (including both personal goals and perceived goal structures), proximal and distal goals, and social goals.

Achievement Goal Theory. The most prominent and highly researched current area in the study of goals is *goal orientation theory*. Goal orientation theory has emerged as a prominent explanatory theory within the motivation literature over the past 25 years. Whereas some theories explain perceptions of competence at tasks (e.g., self-efficacy theory), and other theories explain task engagement in terms of values and self-perceptions of ability (e.g., expectancy-value theory), goal orientation theorists are concerned with the reasons why students choose to engage with particular tasks. A plethora of researchers have examined goal orientations throughout the years (e.g., Ames & Archer, 1988; Anderman & Maehr, 1994; Dweck & Leggett, 1988; Elliot & Harackiewicz, 1996; Harackiewicz, Barron, & Elliot, 1998; Kaplan & Midgley, 1997; Maehr & Anderman, 1993; Meece, Blumenfeld, & Hoyle, 1988; Meece & Miller, 2001; Midgley et al., 1998; Nicholls, 1989; Nolen, 1988; Pintrich, 2000a, 2000b; Urdan, 1997; Wolters, Yu, & Pintrich, 1996). These and numerous other researchers have examined and defined goal orientations in a variety of ways.

It is difficult to exactly determine the specific origins of goal orientation theory. A number of different researchers were examining goal orientation constructs during the 1980s, including Carole Ames, John Nicholls, Martin Maehr, and Carol Dweck. These researchers all made important contributions to the development of current conceptions of goal orientation theory. Moreover, as noted by Elliot and Thrash (2001), achievement goal constructs have been characterized in two distinct ways. Some researchers define achievement goals in terms of the purposes for which individuals engage with specific tasks, whereas others describe achievement goals as a compilation of variables that foster either a mastery or performance orientation toward learning.

Another important distinction within achievement goal theory is between personal goal orientations and classroom goal structures. Personal goal orientations are the types of goals that individuals adopt in various learning situations, whereas classroom goal structures represent perceptions of the types of goals that are stressed in a classroom setting (Ames, 1992; Midgley, 2002).

Classification of Goal Orientations. As the work on achievement goal theory has evolved, researchers have identified several different types of goal orientations. Whereas many of these differences are small, they represent important distinctions in individuals' motives for learning, and in researchers' approaches to the study of goal orientations. For example, some goal orientation theorists have focused on students' *reasons* for engaging in academic tasks (e.g., Ames & Archer, 1988; Dweck & Leggett, 1988; Midgley et al., 1998). In comparison, other models have emphasized students' feelings of success at tasks (Nicholls, Cobb, Wood, Yackel, & Patashnick, 1990).

In the present chapter, we define goal orientations in terms of the purposes that individuals have for engaging in specific behaviors. Our definition draws on the work of others who have tried to synthesize work across various scholars' goal orientation research (e.g., Pintrich & Schunk, 2002; Urdan, 1997). Our definition assumes that individuals use standards to judge their performance in relation to the attainment of goals (Elliot, 1997; Pintrich, 2000a; Pintrich & Schunk, 2002).

Recently, research on personal goal orientations has begun to focus on two important distinctions with regard to goal orientations. One distinction is between mastery and performance goals. The second more recently emphasized distinction is between approach and avoidance goals.

Mastery and Performance Goals. Although this array of constructs is referred to by various names in the literature (e.g., mastery goals, task goals, learning goals), in the present chapter we have chosen to use the term *mastery goal*. Broadly defined, a student who is mastery-goal oriented is interested in truly mastering an academic task. Mastery-oriented students make self-comparisons and are interested in exerting effort and working toward self-improvement at tasks. Students who are mastery oriented use themselves and their past performances as a standard for judging success at a task.

The other major goal that has been identified in the literature has been referred to by a variety of names as well (e.g., performance goal, ability goal, relative ability goal, competitive goal). In the present chapter, we have chosen to use the term *performance goal* to refer to this broad array of goals. A student who is performance oriented is interested in demonstrating his or her ability at a task. Such students are interested in appearing more competent than others. Students who are performance oriented use other students as standards of comparison.

Approach and Avoidance Goals. Drawing from early work by researchers such as Atkinson (1957) and McClelland (McClelland et al., 1953), goal theorists have begun to differentiate between goals that focus on approach versus avoidance tendencies. Recently a number of researchers have distinguished between two types of performance goals: *performance-approach* and *performance-avoid* goals (e.g., Elliot & Church, 1997; Middleton & Midgley, 1997). This distinction emerged because early studies using a goal orientation theory perspective often confounded two types of performance goals. A *performance-approach* goal is the goal of demonstrating one's ability, or outperforming others; in contrast, a *performance-avoid* goal is the goal of avoiding appearing incompetent. Although there is much debate concerning the effects of performance-approach goals, there is general consensus that performance-avoid goals are maladaptive and related negatively to many valued educational outcomes.

Recently, Pintrich (2000b) argued that mastery goals can be broken down into mastery-approach goals and mastery-avoid goals, similar to the system now used to describe performance goals. When students are mastery-approach oriented, they are focused on mastering, learning, and truly understanding the task at hand; in contrast, when students are mastery-avoid oriented, they are focused on avoiding misunderstanding or not being able to learn from the specific task.

Several other types of goals also have been examined within a goal orientation theory framework. For example, several researchers have identified an *extrinsic* goal orientation as a unique achievement goal (Anderman, Maehr, & Midgley, 1999; Maehr & Midgley, 1996; Pintrich, Smith, Garcia, & McKeachie, 1993; Wolters et al., 1996). Students who are extrinsically goal oriented engage in an academic task to achieve some type of reward (e.g., a grade, money, praise, a gold star).

Classroom Goal Structures: Contextual Determinants of Personal Goal Orientations.

Although personal goal orientations are the primary constructs of interest for goal orientation researchers, it is important to distinguish another related albeit somewhat different construct: classroom goal structures. Classroom goal structures are "goal-related messages that are made salient in the achievement setting (i.e., the laboratory, classrooms, schools) that are related to, and most likely influence, the personal goals that individuals pursue in those settings" (Kaplan, Middleton, Urdan, & Midgley, 2002, p. 24). For many students, the perceived classroom goal structure serves as a source for adopting personal goal orientations.

Ames first identified goal structures as distinct entities (e.g., Ames, 1992). Later, Midgley, Maehr, and their colleagues built on Ames' earlier work to clarify and expand the study of goal structures in classroom settings (e.g., Roeser, Midgley, & Urdan, 1996; Urdan, Midgley, & Anderman, 1998). Specifically, Midgley, Maehr, and their colleagues demonstrated that the policies and practices emphasized by classroom teachers are perceived by their students as a constellation of behaviors that emphasize particular goals to students. An example of one such behavior would be a teacher who persistently talks about and emphasizes the importance of grades; students who experience a variety of these practices simultaneously are likely to report that they perceive a performance-oriented goal structure. When students experience these types of environments, they are likely to behave in ways that will enhance perceptions of their ability, or decrease perceptions of their inability (Covington, 1992). In contrast, when teachers truly focus on the intrinsic value of tasks and do not encourage ability comparisons, students are likely to report that they perceive a mastery-oriented goal structure (Maehr & Anderman, 1993; Maehr & Midgley, 1996).

Maehr and his colleagues also have identified school-level goal structures, which they refer to as "school cultures" (Maehr & Anderman, 1993; Maehr & Midgley, 1996). Just as classrooms can be classified as being perceived as mastery- or performance-oriented, entire schools also can be perceived via these dimensions. Research indicates that the school-level goal structures are more strongly related to student outcomes during the higher grades (Maehr, 1991).

Other Motivational Perspectives on Goals.

Although goal orientation theory holds a prominent place in current and recent research, a variety of other discussions of goals have emerged and influenced the thinking of motivation researchers. Although these other perspectives are not the focus of this chapter, they are reviewed, as they represent important considerations when examining the role of goal orientations in motivation research.

Social Goals.

The study of students' social goals is often considered as part of goal orientation theory. Whereas "classic" goal orientation theory examines mastery and performance goals, researchers have acknowledged that students' social goals also are related in important ways to academic outcomes. Indeed, researchers now agree that most students pursue multiple goals simultaneously (Wentzel, 1993).

A number of researchers have examined students' social goals in recent years (L. H. Anderman, 1999; Murdock, Hale, & Weber, 2001; Patrick, Anderman, & Ryan, 2002; Urdan & Maehr, 1995; Wentzel, 1993, 1999). Social goals include a variety of goals, including the goals of seeking approval from others, being responsible, and making friends (Wentzel, 1993, 1994, 1999). In addition, some students may pursue various academic goals to also meet social goals (Urdan & Maehr, 1995).

Thus students' academic goals (e.g., mastery and performance goals) and social goals should not be viewed as mutually exclusive. Indeed, students pursue a variety of goals at the same time (Wentzel, 1993). In addition, the pursuit of social goals is related to academic variables. For example, research indicates that the pursuit of social responsibility goals is related to effort in achievement settings (Wentzel, 1996).

Motivational Systems Theory.

Ford's Motivational Systems Theory (Ford, 1992) incorporates goals somewhat differently than does goal orientation theory. Ford argues that most motivation theories fall short in terms of the incorporation of goals. Indeed, many goal-focused theories of motivation either do not consider the content of individuals' goals, or only focus on one or two goals, as opposed to a broader variety of goals.

Ford's theory is more comprehensive than goal orientation theory, in that Ford's theory attempts to explain all aspects of human motivated behavior. Ford argues that motivation is a function of three components: goals, emotions, and personal agency beliefs. Ford distinguishes between goal content and goal processes. *Goal content* describes "the desired or undesired consequence represented by a particular goal" (Ford, 1992, p. 83), whereas *goal processes* represent the ways that individuals set up and carry out the goals represented by the goal content.

Distal and Proximal Goals. Additional research in motivation distinguishes between "proximal goals", which are reachable, short-term goals, and "distal goals", which are longer-term goals. An example of a proximal goal would be the goal of *finishing 10 mathematics problems for homework on Monday night*; an example of a distal goal would be the goal of *learning algebra*. Long-term goals such as "learning algebra" often can be broken down into several shorter-term proximal goals. Proximal goals may be particularly helpful for students who experience difficulties with learning. Teachers can encourage proximal goals, distal goals, or both types of goals during instruction.

Bandura and Schunk have examined the effects of these goals on a variety of academic outcomes and have demonstrated that adopting proximal goals is related to enhanced learning and motivation (Bandura & Schunk, 1981; Schunk, 1983). Other researchers (Manderlink & Harackiewicz, 1984) also have obtained similar results.

Values

A number of researchers have approached the study of academic motivation through an examination of students' achievement values. At a general level, these various perspectives on achievement values are similar in that they all are concerned with the benefits, rewards, or advantages that individuals believe may accrue as a result of participation within a domain, subject area, task, or activity. The perceived value of a task is a strong determinant of why an individual would want to become or stay engaged in an academic activity or task. One discernible perspective examines both students' expectancies for success at academic tasks and their valuing of those tasks. Most of these theoretical perspectives are referred to more broadly as *expectancy-value* theories of motivation. In the present chapter, we focus on the *value* component of these theories, particularly because previously, greater attention has been given to expectancies than to values (Brophy, 1999). Readers interested in expectancy beliefs are directed to the chapter in this volume by Zimmerman and Schunk. In addition, we address a second line of research related to achievement values by examining interest as another source or type of achievement value.

Expectancy-Value

A number of researchers have examined expectancies and values throughout the past 70 years. In the 1930s and 1940s, Kurt Lewin discussed expectancies and values in his early models of human motivation. For example, Lewin used the term *valence* to refer to the value that individuals attach to objects (Lewin, 1935). Later, Atkinson (1957, 1964) developed a comprehensive model in which he argued that an individual values an academic task when he or she experiences pride after having accomplished the task. In Atkinson's original model, he posited that expectancies and values were related inversely: As a student's expectations for success at a particular task rise, the student's valuing of the task would decline. The logic in this initial model was that an individual would not experience as much pride at accomplishing a simple task as the individual would at completing a more complex task (Atkinson, 1957, 1964). However, Eccles and her colleagues later demonstrated that the inverse relation between expectancies and values was not valid (Eccles, 1983; Wigfield & Eccles, 1992). Other researchers (Battle, 1965; V. C. Crandall, 1969; V. J. Crandall, Katkovsky, & Preston, 1962; Feather, 1992) also examined the roles of expectancies and values in achievement motivation. In addition, a number of researchers have examined a broader range of values than just academic achievement values (e.g., Rokeach, 1973; Schwartz, 1992). For example, Rokeach distinguished between terminal and instrumental values. Whereas terminal values represent lifelong goals (e.g., success), instrumental values represent styles of behavior that will help individuals to attain their terminal values (e.g., capable) (Rokeach, 1979). Although expectancies are important components of this model, values in particular have not been examined as extensively in research (Brophy, 1999; Wigfield & Eccles, 1992).

A Contemporary Expectancy-Value Model of Motivation. Eccles, Wigfield, and several of their colleagues have developed and tested a comprehensive expectancy-value framework of achievement motivation (Eccles, 1983; Eccles, Arberton et al., 1993; Eccles, Barber, Jozefowicz, Malenchuk, & Vida, 1999; Wigfield & Eccles, 1992, 2000, 2002). Building on earlier expectancy-value models, this research originally focused on adolescents' motivation toward mathematics. Based on large samples of adolescents, Eccles and Wigfield have identified four psychometrically distinguishable components of achievement values that include *attainment value, intrinsic value, utility value,* and *cost*.

One of these components is *attainment value* (i.e., the importance of doing well on a particular academic task). Eccles et al.'s definition of attainment value builds on earlier work on this construct by Battle (1966). The attainment value that an individual attaches to a particular task can help to validate various self-beliefs. For example, if a student believes that being a good writer is an important part of her self-schema, and an important aspiration for the future, then the student is likely to hold writing tasks high in attainment value, since such tasks will help the student to confirm this self-belief (Wigfield & Eccles, 1992).

Intrinsic value refers to how much the student likes doing the task. Students who have high intrinsic value for a task will be more likely to choose to engage with the task. Thus a student who truly enjoys doing science experiments might be more likely to ask his or her parents for a home chemistry set.

Utility value pertains to the perceived usefulness of an academic task. Usually the perceived utility value of a task is related to the perceived utility of the task toward the students' future goals (e.g., career goals). Wigfield and Eccles (1992) note that students may choose to engage in academic tasks that are of high perceived utility value, even though the students may not have high intrinsic value for the task. For example, a student might choose to take Spanish throughout high school, even though the student hates learning foreign languages, because the student knows that taking a foreign language will help the student get admitted to college. Whereas the intrinsic value component represents *intrinsic* reasons for learning, utility value is more extrinsic in nature, since the valuing of a task for utilitarian purposes should lead to other desired outcomes (Deci, Koestner, & Ryan, 1999, 2001; Deci & Ryan, 1985).

Cost (i.e., a consideration of what the student must give up to engage in the task, or the negative aspects of engaging in a task) is the final component in Eccles and Wigfield's model of achievement values. When a student engages in an academic task, the student must examine what she might *not* be able to experience, as a result of having engaged with the task. Thus an adolescent might consider attending a summer program to learn about computers, but ultimately might decide not to attend the program, because the student might then be unable to play baseball. The student must decide if the cost of attending the summer program is worth the price that must be paid by forfeiting baseball. The perceived costs of engaging in a task include emotional costs (e.g., anxiety) and the perceived cost in terms of effort for a task (Wigfield & Eccles, 1992).

Recently, Anderman and his colleagues (Anderman, Noar, Zimmerman, & Donohew, 2004) expanded on Eccles' and Wigfield's model to suggest a fifth possible dimension of achievement values: *sensation value*.

This proposed dimension is based on an information-processing perspective. Specifically, individuals must initially pay attention to a specific task to activate the information processing system (Byrnes, 2001). However, research from personality psychology indicates that some individuals demonstrate the personality characteristic of *need for sensation*. Such individuals demonstrate the need for sensation, novelty, complexity, or physical stimulation (Zuckerman, 1979). Academic tasks that are designed to meet this need may encourage high sensation-seeking students to engage with tasks that they otherwise might not consider.

The Components Taken Together. Students evaluate academic tasks in terms of all four components of Eccles and Wigfield's model. For example, a given task may be perceived as important, useful, but not interesting, and not worth the time (i.e., cost). Another task might be perceived as useful and worth the time (cost), but not very interesting or important. Thus all four components of achievement values contribute to students' involvement with various academic tasks.

Research indicates that the various subcomponents of task value are empirically distinguishable. For example, Eccles and Wigfield (1995) used confirmatory factor analysis to demonstrate that attainment value, intrinsic value, and utility value are distinct constructs. The distinctions between the different subcomponents of values (i.e., attainment value, utility value, intrinsic value, and cost) emerge during adolescence (Eccles, Wigfield, Harold, & Blumenfeld, 1993; Wigfield & Eccles, 2002). Younger students do not think about the valuing of academic tasks using the same cognitive complexity as do older students. Research also indicates that children and adolescents do reliably distinguish between expectancies and values. In addition, research indicates that elementary school-aged children can distinguish between achievement values across a variety of domains (Eccles, Wigfield et al., 1993). In related work, Gottfried found that elementary-school-aged children could distinguish between intrinsic motivation for reading, mathematics, and general intrinsic motivation (Gottfried, 1990).

Interest. A somewhat different perspective on *values* comes from the research examining *interest*. Researchers who study interest distinguish between two types of interest: *personal (individual) interest* and *situational interest* (Renninger, 2000; Schraw & Lehman, 2001). The first, *personal interest*, represents a person's ongoing affinity, attraction, or liking for a domain, subject area, topic or activity. This type of interest is viewed as an individual difference variable because it is relatively stable and does not vary greatly across time and situations (Krapp, Hidi, & Renninger, 1992; Renninger, 1992; Schiefele, Krapp, & Winteler, 1992). One reason for this stability is that a well-developed level of relevant content knowledge is a prerequisite for having a true personal interest (Renninger, 2000; Tobias, 1994). Personal interest, therefore, includes an underlying value as well as an elaborated understanding of a particular domain.

A second type of interest, *situational interest,* represents a person's current enjoyment, pleasure, or satisfaction as produced by the immediate context (Schraw & Lehman, 2001). Situational interest is ephemeral and can change quickly as dictated by cues within the existing environment. Situational interest is not construed as a personality characteristic, in contrast to personal interest (Hidi, 1990). Unlike personal interest, which relies on a preexisting level of background knowledge, researchers argue that educational contexts can be structured to *elicit* situational interest among learners (Schraw, Flowerday, & Lehman, 2001; Schraw & Lehman, 2001).

In addition to the critical distinction between personal and situational interest, researchers have differentiated these types of interest from the actual *state of being interested* (Krapp et al., 1992). This distinction highlights the idea that a person may or may not be in the phenomonological state of being interested at any particular time. When individuals are in this state of interest, it may represent the activation of some ongoing personal interest, or it may be the result of a situationally interesting context, or some confluence of both influences. For instance, a person may be in a state of interest while watching a televised sports show because his personal interest in basketball has been activated, as well as because the show includes highlights of specific plays that are situationally interesting. Ainley and her colleagues make a similar point when they describe *topic interest* as something elicited by a text that both activates a person's personal interest and has strong situationally interesting characteristics (Ainley, Hidi, & Berndorff, 2002). Csikszentmihalyi's (1990) concept of flow represents an extreme and perhaps longer lasting version of this phenomenological state.

Affect

History of Affect in Educational Psychology. As noted by Meyer and Turner (2002), it is nearly impossible to study student motivation without also considering affect. Efforts to understand and study affect stretch back to the earliest roots of psychology. The ancient Greeks, for instance, developed an explanation for individual differences in temperament based on the relative balance of four core substances within the body (Kagan, 1994). As well, individuals' affective experience was a prominent concern of many of the earliest efforts within the formal study of psychology (e.g., James, 1890).

One consistent issue within this research has been the relative primacy of biology and cognition in the explanation of affect. One side of this debate argues that a biologically based physiological response precedes any cognitive interpretation of stimuli; hence, emotions are driven by innate biological processes that are subsequently interpreted by the cognitive system. The contrasting view is that physiological and emotional experiences are initiated by some cognitive appraisal or interpretation of the experienced stimuli (Zajonc, 1980).

Within this history of psychological research, affect has at times been integrated with explanations of motivation, or why people engage in particular behaviors. Freud, for example, viewed the unconscious influence of emotions derived from fear and lust as important for understanding people's actions and decisions (Freud, 1966). From a behavioral perspective, the positive and negative emotions experienced as a consequence of actions were viewed as important forms of reinforcement or punishment (Thorndike, 1913). Thus the idea that affect is related to motivation certainly is not new to the field of psychology.

The ascendance of cognitive psychology led to a greater disconnect between the work on affect and motivation. Hence, affect has not been consistently and extensively studied within the cognitive research in educational psychology generally, or the more recent research on achievement motivation more specifically (Linnenbrink & Pintrich, 2002; Pekrun, 1992; Schutz & DeCuir, 2002). One explanation for this decline is that affect, along with cognition and conation (will), have been viewed as the three primary aspects of human psychological functioning. This distinction has led to the reductionist view that each area could be studied and understood more or less in isolation from the others (Snow, Corno & Jackson, 1996). Motivation typically has been viewed as falling within the realm of conation, and therefore has been considered as distinct or separable from affect.

There were, of course, notable exceptions to this relative paucity of cognitive research integrating affect and motivation. Two significant exceptions were the research on attribution theory (Weiner, 1985, 1986) and test anxiety (Zeidner, 1998). Attribution theory has been used to explain both students' emotional experiences and their motivation for academic tasks. In line with Lazarus and others (e.g., Lazarus, 1991; Schacter & Singer, 1962), Weiner (1985, 1986) has argued that the attributional process was a form of cognitive appraisal, and that the attributions that individuals made about the events in their lives affected their emotional responses to those events. For instance, a student who attributes a failure to an internal, stable, uncontrollable cause (e.g., low ability) may subsequently feel a sense of shame or hopelessness. The anticipated emotions formed through prior experiences also have a motivational influence in that they affect a person's choice of activities. A student who experiences repeated episodes of shame and hopelessness in one math course will be likely to anticipate and shy away from similar experiences by declining to enroll in future math courses.

Test anxiety also has been considered an affective construct within educational psychology. Research on test anxiety has included both cognitive and affective variables. Individuals who experience test anxiety think about the implications of testing situations, and also experience emotional arousal when taking tests (Johnson, Maruyama, Johnson, Nelson, & Skon, 1981; Liebert & Morris, 1967; Wigfield & Eccles, 1989; Zeidner, 1998).

Although never absent, the call to incorporate students' affective functioning into the theories and research on achievement motivation has been growing (e.g., Meyer & Turner, 2002; Pekrun, 1992). As a major context within their lives, school is clearly a setting within which students can experience a range of affective responses. In fact, students do report experiencing a variety of emotions when involved in academic tasks (Do & Schallert, 2004; Pekrun, Goetz, Titz, & Perry, 2002). The intensity and variety of affective experiences that are commonplace occurrences for students in school may range from anxiety, frustration, shame, and guilt to more positive emotions such as pride, joy, and relief. School also provides the context for more social and interpersonal activities that can lead to other emotions not tied to learning or achievement. For example, school-based social interactions provide the context for developing peer friendships (e.g., cliques) as well as romantic relationships that drive a host of other emotional experiences (Juvonen & Wentzel, 1996).

Distinctions within Affect. *Affect* is a broad term that is used to describe many different psychological phenomena. Rosenberg (1998) identifies three levels at which affect might be evaluated. At the most stable level are personality-like characteristics or *traits* that make up a person's temperament (Kagan, 1994). These traits, styles, or personality characteristics reflect stable differences in how basic emotions are experienced across individuals. Rosenberg (1998) cites hostility, or a person's threshold for experiencing anger, as an example of these traits. Hence, a person's affective condition is driven partly by

this type of enduring individual difference (Snow et al., 1996). Less stable than these are *moods*, which can be viewed as more diffuse, longer lasting yet transitory periods, characterized by a particular affective state (Forgas, 2001; Linnenbrink & Pintrich, 2002; Rosenberg, 1998). Finally, *emotions* can be described as more situationally driven, short-lived, but more potent psychological states (Forgas, 2001; Linnenbrink & Pintrich, 2002; Schutz & DeCuir, 2002).

Pekrun (1992; Pekrun et al., 2002) has described a taxonomy specifically for the emotions experienced in academic settings. Pekrun et al. (2002) postulate that academic emotions can be categorized as to whether they are positive activating emotions, positive deactivating emotions, negative activating emotions, and negative deactivating emotions. Positive emotions pertain to those that are generally experienced as pleasant, sought after, or appreciated. Negative emotions are typically unpleasant, avoided, and not actively pursued. Activating emotions are those that energize the individual to action or push the individual to approach or engage in some task or action. Examples of this type of emotion include enjoyment of learning and hope for success. Deactivating emotions, in contrast, are those that facilitate rest, disengagement, or avoidance of action. Examples of this type of emotion include boredom and hopelessness.

In addition, Pekrun et al. (2002) contend that certain affective states are derived from the self or the task. For instance, emotions such as hope and anxiety can occur when one contemplates engaging in a particular task. Process-related emotions are those that result from the actual completion of the task (e.g., boredom or enjoyment). Finally, retrospective emotions occur after task engagement, when the individual reflects on the task; examples would include shame and pride (Pekrun et al., 2002). In contrast to self- or task-based emotions, social emotions describe feelings that stem from interactions with others (e.g., envy, admiration), or that are directed at others (e.g., anger, gratitude) (Pekrun, 1992).

Summary of Definition/Distinction Section. In this section we have identified and reviewed the historical roots and major contemporary distinctions within the motivational research on goals, values, and affect. The brief history of these different areas illustrates the common ancestry of many of these constructs.

Goals, values, and affect all have been studied in a variety of manners. Nevertheless, some of these constructs (e.g., goals) have been related to academic motivation more than have others (e.g., affect). Next, we turn to a discussion of the relations of these constructs to other indices of motivation and achievement.

GOAL ORIENTATIONS, VALUES AND AFFECT: RELATIONS TO ENGAGEMENT, LEARNING AND ACHIEVEMENT

In this second section we review empirical research that documents the relations between goal orientations, values, and affect on the one hand, and students' engagement and achievement on the other. The intent of this section is not to serve as an exhaustive review of empirical research documenting these relations; rather, our purpose is to provide support for the critical role these motivational constructs play in students' learning and achievement within academic contexts. In this review, we touch specifically on how goal orientations, values, and affect have been associated with indicators of students' choice or persistence, their effort or quality of engagement, and their performance or achievement level.

Goal Orientations

Mastery and Performance Goal Orientations. Within achievement goal theory, critical differentiations among students are characteristically based on the type of goal orientation that students adopt. Goal theory leads to different predictions depending on whether students are focused on one goal orientation or another. Much research, therefore, has examined the ways in which personal goal orientations are related to indicators of students' engagement and performance. Although there is much debate regarding the effects of some goal orientations, some consistent patterns have emerged (Harackiewicz, Barron, Pintrich, Elliot, & Thrash, 2002; Midgley, Kaplan, & Middleton, 2001)

Mastery Goals. The general consensus in this research is that adopting mastery goals is related to adaptive outcomes (for reviews, see Anderman & Maehr, 1994; Urdan, 1997; Harackiewicz et al., 2002; Midgley et al., 2001; Pintrich, 2000b). Several studies have found that a mastery goal orientation is associated with choice and persistence (Archer, 1994; Elliott & Harackiewicz, 1996; Harackiewicz, Baron, Tauer, Carter, & Elliot (2000); Ryan, Koestner, & Deci, 1991). For instance, Harackiewicz and her colleagues (2000) found that college students with a greater focus on mastery goals tended to enroll in additional psychology courses more often than other students. Among secondary students, mastery goal orientation was associated positively with self-reported effort and persistence at academic tasks (Miller, Greene, Montalvo, Ravindran, & Nichols,

1996). Additional evidence for the utility of mastery goals comes from the many studies linking mastery goals to effort or engagement, in both experimental and academic tasks. For instance, greater endorsement of mastery goals has been associated with more frequent reported use of deep, metacognitive and self-regulatory strategies (Archer, 1994; Elliot & McGregor, 2001; Elliot, McGregor & Gable, 1999; Greene & Miller, 1996; Meece et al., 1988; Meece, Herman, & McCombs, 2003; Meece & Miller, 2001; Middleton & Midgley, 1997; Nolen, 1988; Pintrich, 2000b; Pintrich & De Groot, 1990; Schraw, Horn, Thorndine-Christ, & Bruning; 1995; Wolters, 2004; Wolters et al., 1996). Converging evidence for the adaptiveness of mastery goals for students' engagement also emanates from studies showing that mastery-oriented students tend to report lower levels of self-handicapping (Midgley & Urdan, 2001; Pintrich, 2000).

One notable caveat to the position that mastery goals are adaptive, however, is that few researchers have been able to document direct positive relations between adopting mastery goals and academic performance (Harackiewicz et al., 2002). In most studies the expected positive association between mastery goals and performance or instructor-assigned grades has failed to occur (Ames & Archer, 1988; Barron & Harackiewicz, 2001; Elliott & Church, 1997; Elliot & McGregor, 2001; Elliot, 1999; Harackiewicz Barron Carter, Lehto, & Elliot, 1997; Harackiewicz, Baron, Tauer, Carter, & Elliot, 2000; McWhaw & Abrami, 2001; Miller et al., 1996; Pintrich, 2000; Skaalvik, 1997). A clear and accepted explanation for this apparent contradiction has yet to emerge and remains an important consideration for research (Harackiewicz et al., 2000).

Performance Goals. The empirical results linking a performance goal orientation to students' engagement and achievement are less straightforward. A critical reason for this ambiguity is that performance–approach and –avoid constructs often were confounded in early goal theory research. This confounding of approach and avoidance performance goals within the same measures has been used in retrospect to explain the inconsistent results found with regard to performance goals in some earlier studies (Archer, 1994; Bouffard, Boisvert, Vezeau, & Larouche, 1995; Greene & Miller, 1996; Miller et al., 1996; Nolen, 1988; Pintrich & Garcia, 1991; Schraw et al., 1995).

Researchers now regularly distinguish between performance–approach and performance–avoid goals with separate measures. In addition, research now distinguishes between the unique correlates of performance–approach and –avoid goal orientations. Although the evidence is still accruing, there is little indication that performance avoid goals are related to adaptive educational outcomes (e.g., cognitive engagement) (Elliot et al., 1999; Middleton & Midgley, 1997; Wolters, 2004). In contrast, there is general consensus that adopting performance-avoid goals is related to maladaptive forms of engagement and lower performance (e.g., Elliot & Church, 1997; Elliot & Covington, 2001; Elliot & Harackiewicz, 1996; Kaplan, Middleton; Urdan & Midgley, 2002; Middleton & Midgley, 1997; Midgley & Urdan, 2001; Skaalvik, 1997). For example, Midgley and Urdan (2001) found that students who adopted personal performance-avoid goals were more likely to report engaging in self-handicapping behaviors. In a review of the research on the effects of performance-avoid goal orientations on avoidance behaviors (e.g., self-handicapping, avoidance of help-seeking, and avoidance of challenge), Urdan and his colleagues suggest that although both performance-avoid and approach goals are related to avoidant behaviors, performance-avoid goals are related to such behaviors more strongly (Urdan, Ryan, Anderman, & Gheen, 2002). Some research has also found that students' who adopt performance-avoid goals tend to get lower grades than their peers (Elliott & Church, 1997; Elliot & McGregor, 2001; Skaalvik, 1997). The overall pattern for performance-avoid goals, therefore, suggests that they are detrimental to learning.

The pattern of findings for performance-approach goals continues to be ambiguous. For example, Elliot and his colleagues reported that in college students, performance-approach goals are positive predictors of persistence (Elliot et al., 1999). Other studies, however, have failed to link performance-approach goals to greater choice and persistence (Wolters, 2004). As well, a consistent pattern between performance-approach goals and students' use of learning strategies has failed to emerge. In some studies, performance-approach goals have been related to the more frequent use of some cognitive and metacognitive strategies (e.g., Pintrich, 2000b; Wolters et al., 1996). In other studies evidence for the adaptive nature of performance-approach goals has not been found (e.g., Middleton & Midgley, 1997; Wolters, 2004).

In contrast, other researchers have found that adopting performance-approach goals is related to maladaptive educational outcomes. For example, Ryan and her colleagues (Ryan, Hicks, & Midgley, 1997; Ryan & Pintrich, 1997) found that students were more likely to report that they avoided help-seeking when they also reported that they adopted performance-approach goals. In another study, students' self-reported avoidance of challenge was related positively to performance-approach goals (Middleton & Midgley, 1997). A clear link between maladaptive educational outcomes and performance-approach

goals has not, however, been found in all studies (Midgley & Urdan, 2001; Wolters, 2003, 2004).

Findings often have indicated a positive relation between course achievement and college students' performance-approach goal orientation (Church et al., 2001; Elliot & Church, 1997; Elliot & McGregor, 1999, 2001; Elliot et al., 1999; Harackiewicz et al., 1997, 2000. A similar pattern has emerged in some (Skaalvik, 1997; Wolters, 2004), but not all (McWhaw & Abrami, 2001; Pintrich, 2000; Wolters et al., 1996) studies with younger students. Untangling the uncertainty over when and why performance-approach goals are adaptive, maladaptive, or have no relation to students' engagement and performance remains an important objective for future research.

Goal structures. It is important to consider goal structures when discussing the relations of personal goal orientations to various educational outcomes. The goal structures that are perceived in a classroom or school are predictive of the types of personal goal orientations that students adopt (Ames & Ames, 1984; Wolters, 2004). When students perceive a mastery-oriented goal structure, they are likely to adopt personal mastery goal orientations; when student perceive a performance-oriented goal structure, they are likely to adopt performance goals (Anderman & Maehr, 1994; Anderman et al., 1999; Maehr & Anderman, 1993; Maehr & Midgley, 1996; Midgley, 2002; Wolters, 2004). Research generally indicates that perceptions of a mastery-oriented classroom goal structure are related to adaptive educational outcomes, whereas perceptions of performance-oriented goal structures are related to maladaptive outcomes. (Ames & Archer, 1988; L. H. Anderman, 1999; Midgley, 2002; Turner et al., 2002; Wolters, 2004). These findings may in part be due to the fact that perceptions of classroom goal structures influence the adoption of personal goal orientations. Consequently, goal structures may act on various educational outcomes indirectly, via personal goals.

Interestingly, when it comes to academic achievement, results are not as consistent. Most studies indicate that perceptions of a mastery goal structure are unrelated to students' grades, and that perceptions of a performance goal structure are related negatively to grades (e.g., Anderman & Midgley, 1997; Anderman & Anderman, 1999; Urdan, Midgley, & Anderman, 1998b). Nevertheless, some researchers have reported different findings for goal structures. For example, Midgley and Urdan (2001) found positive relations between perceptions of a mastery-goal structure and grades in mathematics (Midgley & Urdan, 2001).

It is important to note that most researchers to date have not distinguished between the approach and avoid aspects of classroom goal structures. In a recent study,

Wolters (2004) adapted Midgley et al.'s *Patterns of Adaptive Learning Survey* items and tried to develop measures of performance–approach and– avoid classroom goal structures. The measure of performance–avoid goal structure proved to be unreliable (Wolters, 2004).

Values

As with achievement goal theory, models of achievement values and interest include internal distinctions between different types of values or interest. For the most part (cf., Harp & Mayer, 1998; Mayer, Heiser, & Lonn, 2001), higher levels of all types of value and interest are assumed to be associated with more adaptive academic outcomes. Hence, the research on value and interest has been directed at establishing the expected positive association between higher levels of value and interest and students' engagement and performance.

Expectancy-Value Theories. Research by Eccles and her colleagues clearly indicates that when students value an academic task, they are more likely to choose to engage in the task in the future. Specifically, values predict outcomes such as future enrollment in courses, whereas expectancies predict achievement in courses (Eccles, 1983; Meece, Wigfield, & Eccles, 1990; Wigfield & Eccles, 1992). In addition, some research suggests that the different subcomponents of task values may predict outcomes differently. For example, Wigfield and Eccles (1992) have found in some of their work that attainment value in mathematics predicted middle school students' intentions to keep taking math, whereas both attainment value and utility value predict older adolescents' intentions to continue taking mathematics courses.

Research using the *Motivated Strategies for Learning Questionnaire* (MSLQ) has produced similar results. The MSLQ was developed by Pintrich and his colleagues (Pintrich & de Groot, 1990; Pintrich et al., 1993) to examine a variety of motivational constructs and related cognitive and motivational strategies. The measure has been used widely, and has been translated to other languages, such as Chinese (Rao & Sachs, 1999). One of the scales included in the MSLQ taps into a form of value that is similar to the attainment/importance and interest components of Eccles' and Wigfield's model.

Research utilizing the MSLQ supports the positive link between high value and positive academic outcomes (Pintrich & de Groot, 1990; Wolters & Pintrich, 1998). Pintrich and de Groot (1990), for instance, found that intrinsic value was related positively to both cognitive strategy use and self-regulation. They also found that intrinsic value was correlated positively, albeit weakly, with a number of indices of academic performance, including semester grades, exams, essays, and seat-work. However, when self-regulation or cognitive strategy use were included in regression models predicting performance, intrinsic value was no longer related to performance. This is similar to Eccles' (1983) findings concerning the direct relation of value to choice, but not to achievement. Other research (e.g., Murdock, Anderman, & Hodge, 2000) has documented similar positive relations between achievement values and adaptive educational outcomes.

Interest. Research also indicates that both personal and situational interest are related to beneficial outcomes (Hidi, 1990; Krapp et al., 1992; Renninger, 1992; Schiefele et al., 1992). Students who are personally interested in a task tend to be cognitively engaged, to persist longer at tasks, and to enjoy tasks; additionally, situational interest may be particularly beneficial for low-achieving students, who may lack personal interest in many tasks (Hidi & Harackiewicz, 2000).

Some forms of situational interest, unlike personal interest, have also been associated with less adaptive learning outcomes. Most notably, Mayer and colleagues' research on seductive details indicates that some methods of creating situational interest may detract from more productive cognitive processing in some circumstances. For instance, Harp and Mayer (1998) found that students who read passages that included interesting but irrelevant information displayed poorer recall and were less able to transfer information than students who read passages without this additional information. Thus in some circumstances, situational interest may reduce students' focus on the cognitive engagement necessary for the deeper understanding or learning.

Affect

Affect has a complex reciprocal relation with cognitive processing, learning, and achievement. In this section, we focus on the ways in which affect may influence individuals' processing within academic settings. In line with our previous discussion, we consider students' levels of affect, as well as types of affect, and how each may influence cognitive processing. Indeed, affect may serve as a context, precursor, or antecedent of cognitive processing and engagement in learning. There are at least four different mediational pathways leading from students' affective conditions to their cognitive processing (Pekrun, 1992; Pekrun et al., 2002).

One route, identified as *mood congruent effects*, concerns the content or outcome of students' thinking and recall of information. Prior research indicates that individuals are more likely to recall information that is congruent with their mood at the time of encoding than material that is incongruent (Bower, 1981). The proposed explanation for this effect is that mood-related information is stored, and academic material consistent with this mood will be encoded more effectively, and later recalled more easily. A corollary to this effect is that information is also recalled better when students are in a similar mood at the time of recall (Forgas, 2000).

Reflecting a second pathway, affect is also thought to influence the quality of students' cognitive engagement. Mood and emotion related thoughts may require cognitive resources that might otherwise be devoted to attention, problem solving, or other task-directed cognitive processing. An important caveat to this pathway is evidence indicating that certain types of moods require greater cognitive resources than do others. For instance, Pekrun (1992) argues that negative moods require more cognitive resources than do positive moods, leaving fewer resources available for task-directed activities, and therefore leading to less efficient cognitive processing. This pathway is consistent with much of the research exploring the effects of evaluation anxiety on students' academic performance (Zeidner, 1998). The rumination, worry, and thoughts of self-doubt associated with test anxiety, it is argued, disrupt students' efficient processing directed at successfully completing the evaluation task.

A third pathway concerns the nature of students' cognitive engagement in a task, albeit through the types of strategies selected or used (Forgas, 2000, 2001; Pekrun, 1992). This pathway represents the view that affective states have an impact on the cognitive resources available to a learner at any given time. For example, positive mood has been associated with the use of holistic, creative forms of engagement that are adaptive for learning. For instance, Isen (1999) noted that positive mood can increase divergent and creative flexible thinking. In contrast, negative emotional states have been associated more with analytical and detail-focused forms of cognitive engagement. These negative emotions, furthermore, may trigger the use of rigid or less adaptive, or more surface-level, cognitive strategies.

In addition to this more automatic influence, affect might be tied to students' choice of cognitive and metacognitive strategies in a less direct fashion. Students' affective state may be interpreted as a signal regarding the effectiveness of the strategies used to accomplish a particular task. For instance, if a student does poorly and feels disappointed, this emotional response may be self-observed and interpreted as a sign that the strategy used to complete the task is inefficient. This is consistent with Zimmerman's perspectives on self-regulated learning (Zimmerman, 1989) as well as attribution the-

ory (Weiner, 1986). When this reflection and influence on strategy use is completed as part of an ongoing task, it could influence students' overall persistence with the task. Hence, emotional reactions can be used as information that helps to determine the usefulness of different learning strategies.

Finally, Pekrun (1992) suggests that a fourth potential pathway involves emotions affecting educational outcomes indirectly, via their effects on intrinsic and extrinsic motivation. Specifically, the experience of pleasant emotions may lead to enhanced intrinsic motivation toward a particular academic task; the enhanced perceptions of intrinsic motivation may then lead to changes in learning, cognition, and task involvement (see also Linnenbrink & Pintrich, 2000).

Summary of Relations to Engagement, Learning, and Achievement

As noted by Maehr (1976), there are a variety of outcomes to consider in the study of achievement motivation. From this brief review, it is clear that goal orientations, values, and affect are related in important ways to many of the most critical outcomes associated with learning and achievement. This review also emphasizes the need to distinguish between the types and levels of these constructs when looking at their relations to other outcomes. Goal orientations, values, and affect all are related to learning and achievement in important albeit different ways. As well, certain dimensions of these construct are related to particular educational outcomes (e.g., holding mastery goals is related to a host of positive outcomes, whereas holding performance-avoid goals is not related to many positive outcomes). In addition, goal orientations, values, and affect do not necessarily predict achievement in similar manners. Some of the effects on achievement are direct, some are indirect, and some constructs simply do not relate directly to achievement. Thus it is important to consider a broad array of outcomes when examining the effects of goals, values, and affect.

SYNTHESIZING GOALS, VALUES, AND AFFECT

Thus far we have described the definitions of goals, values and affect, and the important distinctions within the research. In addition, we have reviewed research documenting the relations of these constructs to engagement and performance. In short, we have argued and demonstrated that goals, values, and affect all are unique entities that play important roles in the general motivation equation.

From this review, one might logically inquire about the relations between and among these different constructs, and the relative utility and practicality of the research in each area. In this section, we address this issue by examining research that links students' goals, values, and affect.

Relations Among Constructs

Some theoretical models have been presented that demonstrate that various motivation constructs do overlap. Indeed, some of the more comprehensive motivation theories do incorporate aspects of goals, values, and/or affect. For example, Eccles' and Wigfield's expectancy-value of motivation includes goals, affective memories, and values within the overall model (Wigfield & Eccles, 2000). In their model, goals are determined by a number of variables, including attitudes, gender roles, and activity stereotypes. Affective memories are determined by other variables, including causal attributions, aptitude, and previous achievement-related experiences. Values ultimately are determined by a host of variables, including affective memories and goals. In their model, expectancies and values ultimately predict achievement-related choices.

In addition, Weiner's attribution model, although not a focus of the present chapter, does provide another example of a motivation model that incorporates a variety of these constructs. Specifically, Weiner's model includes affect and expectancy as immediate predecessors to behavioral outcomes (i.e., achievement, persistence, etc.) (Weiner, 1986, 1992). Students experience affect and expectancy for success after having made an attribution (e.g., to ability or luck).

Although comprehensive models of goals and affect are not plentiful, there is ample evidence suggesting that goals and affect are related. For example, Linnenbrink, Ryan, and Pintrich (1999) suggest that affect may mediate the effects of goal orientations on working memory. Others have suggested that negative affect may be particularly salient when students hold performance goals, because in such situations students may feel that they have less control over outcomes, which consequently may lead to negative affect (Dweck, 1985).

Relations Between Goals and Values

As noted by Hidi and Harackiewicz (2000), both goals and values play important roles, particularly in the potential improvement of educational practices for unmotivated students. A few studies have examined relations among students' goals, goal structures, and achievement values. In general, results indicate that mastery goals and

perceptions of mastery goal structures are related to greater valuing of academic material.

In one study, Bergin (1995) examined the relations between mastery and performance goals, and interest. Participants were assigned randomly to either a mastery or "competitive" situation and were asked to read a passage. Results indicated that participants assigned to the mastery situation reported greater enjoyment of the reading passage than did students in the competitive situation.

In a study directly applying tenets of both goal orientation theory and expectancy-value theory, Anderman, Eccles, and their colleagues examined the longitudinal effects of teachers' instructional practices on achievement values in mathematics and reading. Results indicated that the use of performance-oriented instructional practices by teachers (e.g., hanging up the "best" work as examples for others) was related to declines in students' reported valuing of mathematics and reading over time (Anderman et al., 2001).

Pintrich and his colleagues examined the relations between goals and values in several studies (Pintrich & Garcia, 1991; Pintrich et al., 1993; Wolters et al., 1996). In a study examining the reliability and predictive validity of the MSLQ, Pintrich et al. (1993) reported strong positive correlations between intrinsic goal orientation and task value, and weak positive correlations between an extrinsic goal orientation and task value. In another study, Pintrich and Garcia (1991) examined the relations between task value and intrinsic and extrinsic goal orientations in college students. Results indicated that the valuing of academic tasks was correlated positively with an intrinsic (mastery) goal orientation, but was virtually unrelated to an extrinsic goal orientation. In contrast, Wolters et al. (1996) found that mastery and relative ability orientations predicted students' task value positively, whereas an extrinsic orientation was associated with lower levels of task value in three different subject areas.

Relations Between Goals and Affect

Emotional responses can also be viewed as a consequence of goal setting and goal orientation. Target goals drive affective reactions by serving as standards or objectives that students use to evaluate their progress (Schunk, 2001). Students appraisals of whether they have achieved or made sufficient progress toward their target goals have emotional implications (Linnenbrink & Pintrich, 2000). Students may feel joy, relief, or pride in accomplishment for the goals they have reached or are progressing toward at a reasonable rate. Alternatively, when students are focused on avoiding certain outcomes, the ability to move away from or create distance from these unwanted outcomes can also produce positive emotional reactions (Linnenbrink & Pintrich, 2002). In a similar way, negative emotional responses follow when progress toward goals is judged to be slow, insufficient, or absent altogether. In this way, having target or behavioral goals sets the stage for experiencing emotions within academic settings.

The types of achievement goals that students adopt may also have implications for their emotional experiences in school. Linnenbrink and Pintrich (2000, 2002) argue that the emotional implications of success and failure may be quite different depending on whether students are oriented toward mastery or performance goals. Specifically, when students are mastery oriented, any lack of progress or failure to meet expectations may be viewed as an opportunity for learning. In contrast, when students are performance–approach oriented, this lack of progress may be viewed as more of a threat to the ego. Hence, the particular emotional consequences of success or failure may be mediated by the type of goal orientation that students adopt.

By contributing to the value perceived in particular behaviors, activities, or domains, students' affective experiences would also influence the target goals they adopt. Some outcomes would be sought after and pursued more frequently and more actively because they are valued, and they may be valued because they have been associated with more positive emotional experiences in the past. This view of affect as an influence on goals and choice fits with attribution theory (Weiner, 1985). In this view of motivation, the emotions students experience are based on the types of attributions they make. These recollected emotional reactions, furthermore, are conceptualized as influencing students' subsequent choices about whether to engage in or avoid similar activities.

In addition to their association with adopting particular target goals, affective conditions can also be viewed as goal states in and of themselves. Most individuals want to experience and sustain positive emotions, and avoid or reduce negative emotional states. From this perspective, the desire to be in a positive mood or to avoid being in a negative mood can be adopted as a goal, and thus can drive students' choices, effort, and persistence at different tasks. For example, a student engaged in a particular activity and in a negative mood may decide to change activities because the change is viewed as a means of avoiding or eliminating the negative mood. Similarly, a student engaged in a task and experiencing more positive emotions may persist longer in an attempt to continue experiencing the positive emotions associated with the task (see also Csikszentmihalyi, 1990, 1996).

Achievement Goal Orientations and Affect. Along with its relation to the target goals that students pursue, affect may also help to determine the types of achievement goals students adopt. Linnenbrink and Pintrich (2000) contend that some aspects of affect (e.g., mood) influence the types of personal goal orientations that students adopt. A few studies have examined relations between students' goal orientations and affect. Results indicate that mastery goals are related to more positive indices of affect, whereas performance goals are related to more negative indices of affect.

Roeser et al. (1996) examined the relations among personal goal orientations, perceived school goal structures, and affect in middle school students. Personal mastery goals were related positively to positive school affect, whereas personal performance goals were unrelated to affect. A school mastery goal structure also was related positively to affect, whereas perceptions of a school performance goal structure were related negatively to affect.

L. Anderman (1999) examined the relations between affect in school and perceived classroom goal structures. Perceptions of a classroom mastery goal structure were related positively to positive affect, and negatively to negative affect. In contrast, perceptions of a classroom performance goal structure were related negatively to positive affect, and positively to negative affect. Increases in positive affect over time were related to perceptions of a classroom mastery goal structure, whereas increases in negative affect over time were predicted by perceptions of a performance goal structure.

Smith, Sinclair, and Chapman (2002) examined the relations between goal orientations and several measures of affect, including depression, anxiety, and stress. A mastery orientation was unrelated to the affective variables, whereas performance–approach and –avoid orientations were related positively to stress. Other studies examining relations between students' goal orientations and various indicators of affect also suggest that mastery goals are related to positive affect (e.g., Meece et al., 1988).

Relations Between Values and Affect

Achievement values also play a role in understanding students' emotional reactions to their academic experiences. Students who highly value a task may experience more intense emotional reactions. Success at a task that is highly valued will presumably instill a stronger and perhaps qualitatively different emotional response than success within a domain that is not as highly valued. The type of value that one has for an activity, task, or domain may also modify the form of emotional response. As noted earlier, some domains, activities, or tasks are valued because they are closely tied to the self or to an individual's self-concept. It stands to reason that affective reaction to outcomes within this domain will be felt more intensely than will reactions to tasks that are merely valued because they are expected to lead to more immediate extrinsic rewards.

Students' affective experiences can lead to the valuing of particular tasks, activities, or behaviors. This process may initiate with the emotions experienced during the completion of various school-related activities or tasks. Students engaged in the behavioral or cognitive activities necessary to finish an activity may feel positive emotions ranging from excitement, enjoyment, and pride to more negative emotions such as boredom, apathy, or anger as they work on academic tasks. Pekrun et al. (2002) categorized these online, in-the-moment affective experiences as *process-related emotions*. These emotional experiences also have been examined within the research on situational interest. In line with the work on situational interest, these process-related emotions repeatedly experienced over time represent one way through which value, interest, or other intrinsic forms of motivation may develop. That is, students initially experience the activities within a domain as enjoyable, and then over time transform these short-lived emotions into a more sustained value or interest for similar tasks. Over time and with repeated exposure to a domain, students develop more enduring values.

Eccles and Wigfield's model also indicates that task values are predicted by a host of variables. Many of these variables are affective in nature. One of the variables that is hypothesized as being causally related to task values is the individual's perceptions of socialization agents' attitudes and expectations (Wigfield & Eccles, 1992). For example, if a student perceived that his mother had a very negative attitude toward mathematics, then this could lead to negative affect, which ultimately may influence the development of negative achievement values toward mathematics.

Specific studies examining relations between achievement values and affect are not plentiful. Results tend to indicate that increased valuing of academic tasks is related to positive affect, whereas decreased valuing of tasks is related to negative affect. For example, in their validation study of the MSLQ, Pintrich et al. (1993) examined the relations between task value and affect, using text anxiety as an indicator of affect. Results suggested that the valuing of academic tasks is related negatively and weakly to text anxiety.

Summary of Relation of Goal, Values, and Affect Section

As a whole the review of research in this section substantiated the key role that motivational beliefs, and specifically students' goals, values, and affect, have in determining individuals' engagement and learning within academic contexts. Although research examining the relations between and among these motivational variables is scarce, some general patterns do emerge. The clearest finding is that mastery goals are for the most part related to positive affect and to the valuing of academic tasks. Future research examining the interrelations of all three constructs is needed.

In addition, there have been few efforts to examine the interrelations of these constructs within a more comprehensive theoretical model of achievement motivation. Although some theoretical models do incorporate multiple constructs (e.g., expectancy-value theory and attribution theory), combined theoretical models are still not the norm. Finally, factor analytic studies that examine the uniqueness of various indicators of students' goals, values, and affect are warranted. For example, there is a need to examine whether goal orientations (e.g., mastery goals) and achievement values (e.g., intrinsic value) are truly unique constructs.

CONCLUSIONS AND IMPLICATIONS

In the present chapter, we have reviewed the history and theoretical definitions, as well as research on the correlates of goal orientations, values, and affect, as they relate to academic motivation. All three of these motivational constructs have rich histories in both the educational and psychological literatures. In addition, all three are related to a host of valued educational outcomes.

As we have indicated, a number of researchers have attempted to synthesize these and other constructs into comprehensive models. Future research efforts should examine both the utility and reliability of such models. In addition, future research also should continue to examine the roles of other motivation constructs in these models (e.g., attributions and self-efficacy).

Perhaps the area that is most lacking in this domain of research is the implementation of comprehensive intervention programs, aimed at improving the motivation of students in schools. Whereas some comprehensive interventions aimed at motivational and affective variables have been attempted (Battistich, Solomon, Watson, & Schaps, 1997; Maehr & Midgley, 1996; Weinstein et al., 1991), such interventions are rare and are sorely needed. Given national and international discussions of the need for school reform, and the ramifications of reform legislation such as *No Child Left Behind* in the United States, comprehensive motivational interventions represent an important and underexplored area for researchers, educators, and policymakers.

Another area that is particularly ripe for exploration involves the relations of these motivational variables to specific aspects of information processing. Initial work in this area suggests that different motivational orientations yield different types of cognitive outcomes (e.g., Huber, Beckmann, & Herrmann, 2004). For example, results of some studies suggest that performance goals may adversely affect information processing (e.g., Graham & Golan, 1991). Still other research suggests that the inclusion of irrelevant but interesting material within academic tasks may hinder cognitive functioning (Harp & Mayer, 1998; Mayer et al., 2001). Future studies examining the relations of motivation constructs to specific aspects of cognition will help to clarify some of these initial findings.

Finally, researchers will need to continue to examine the effects of social contexts on student motivation. Motivational variables do not operate in a vacuum; rather, students experience motivation within the contexts of their classrooms, their peers, their families, and their

communities (E. Anderman & L. Anderman, 2000; Eccles, Arberton et al., 1993; Eccles, Midgley et al., 1993; Turner & Meyer, 2000). The motivational contexts of schools and classrooms also influence students' mental health and overall psychological well-being (Roeser & Eccles, 2000; Roeser, Eccles, & Freedman-Doan, 1999; Roeser, Eccles, & Sameroff, 2000). Studies that utilize multiple methodologies (Turner et al., 2002) may be particularly useful, as they help to disentangle the multiple contextual and individual influences on student motivation.

In conclusion, goals, values, and affect all are related to important educational outcomes. Although there is debate as to the causal ordering of these constructs, there is little debate as to the importance of these constructs in determining students' motivation toward learning in school settings.

References

Ainley, M., Hidi, S., & Berndorff, D. (2002). Interest, learning, and the psychological processes that mediate their relationship. *Journal of Educational Psychology, 94,* 545–561.

Ames, C. (1992). Classrooms: Goals, structures, and student motivation. *Journal of Educational Psychology, 84,* 261–271.

Ames, C., & Ames, R. (1984a). Systems of student and teacher motivation: Toward a qualitative definition. *Journal of Educational Psychology, 76,* 535–556.

Ames, C., & Ames, R. (1984b). Goal structures and motivation. *Elementary School Journal, 85*(1), 39–52.

Ames, C., & Archer, J. (1988). Achievement goals in the classroom: Students' learning strategies and motivation processes. *Journal of Educational Psychology, 80,* 260–267.

Anderman, E. M., & Anderman, L. H. (2000). The role of social context in educational psychology: Substantive and methodological issues. *Educational Psychologist, 35,* 67–68.

Anderman, E. M., Eccles, J. S., Yoon, K. S., Roeser, R. W., Wigfield, A., & Blumenfeld, P. (2001). Learning to value math and reading: Individual differences and classroom effects. *Contemporary Educational Psychology, 26,* 76–95.

Anderman, E. M., & Maehr, M. L. (1994). Motivation and schooling in the middle grades. *Review of Educational Research, 64,* 287–309.

Anderman, E. M., Maehr, M. L., & Midgley, C. (1999). Declining motivation after the transition to middle school: Schools can make a difference. *Journal of Research and Development in Education, 32,* 131–147.

Anderman, E. M., & Midgley, C. (1997). Changes in achievement goal orientations, perceived academic competence, and grades across the transition to middle-level schools. *Contemporary Educational Psychology, 22,* 269–298.

Anderman, E. M., Noar, S., Zimmerman, R. S., & Donohew, L. (2004). The need for sensation as a prerequisite for motivation to engage in academic tasks. In M. L. Maehr & P. Pintrich (Eds.), *Advances in motivation and achievement: Motivating students, improving schools: The legacy of Carol Midgley* (Vol. 13). Greenwich: JAI Press.

Anderman, L. H. (1999). Classroom goal orientation, school belonging and social goals as predictors of students' positive and negative affect following the transition to middle school. *Journal of Research and Development in Education, 32,* 89–103.

Anderman, L. H., & Anderman, E. M. (1999). Social predictors of changes in students' achievement goal orientations. *Contemporary Educational Psychology, 25,* 21–37.

Archer, J. (1994). Achievement goals as a measure of motivation in university students. *Contemporary Educational Psychology, 19,* 430–446.

Atkinson, J. W. (1957). Motivational determinants of risk taking behavior. *Psychological Review, 64,* 359–372.

Atkinson, J. W. (1964). *An introduction to motivation.* Princeton: Van Nostrand.

Austin, J. T., & Vancouver, J. B. (1996). Goal constructs in psychology: Structure, process, and content. *Psycholgical Bulletin, 120,* 338–375.

Bandura, A., & Schunk, D. (1981). Cultivating competence, self-efficacy, and intrinsic interest through proximal self-motivation. *Journal of Personality and Social Psychology, 41,* 586–598.

Barron, K. E., & Harackiewicz, J. M. (2001). Achievement goals and optimal motivation: Testing multiple goal models. *Journal of Personality and Social Psychology, 80,* 706–722.

Battistich, V., Solomon, D., Watson, M., & Schaps, E. (1997). Caring school communities. *Educational Psychologist, 32,* 137–151.

Battle, E. (1965). Motivational determinants of academic task persistence. *Journal of Personality and Social Psychology, 2,* 209–218.

Battle, E. (1966). Motivational determinants of academic competence. *Journal of Personality and Social Psychology, 4*, 634-642.

Bergin, D. A. (1995). Effects of a mastery versus competitive motivation situation on learning. *Journal of Experimental Education, 63*(4), 303-314.

Bouffard, T., Boisvert, J., Vezeau, C., & Larouche, C. (1995). The impact of goal orientation on self-regulation and performance among college students. *British Journal of Educational Psychology, 65*, 317-329.

Bower, G. H. (1981). Mood and memory. *American Psychologist, 36*, 129-148.

Brophy, J. (1999). Toward a model of the value aspects of motivation in education: Developing appreciation for particular learning domains and activities. *Educational Psychologist, 34*, 75-85.

Byrnes, J. P. (2001). *Cognitive development in instructional contexts* (2nd ed.). Needham Heights; MA: Allyn & Bacon.

Cantor, N., & Langston, C. A. (1989). Ups and downs of life tasks in a life transition. In L. A. Pervin (Ed.), *Goal concepts in personality and social psychology* (pp. 87-126). Hillsdale, NJ: Lawrence Erlbaum Associates.

Church, M. A., Elliot, A. J., & Gable, S. L. (2001). Perceptions of classroom environment, achievement goals, and achievement outcomes. *Journal of Educational Psychology, 93*, 43-54.

Covington, M. V. (1992). *Making the grade: A self-worth perspective on motivation and school reform*. New York: Cambridge University Press.

Crandall, V. C. (1969). Sex differences in expectancy of intellectual and academic reinforcement. In C. P. Smith (Ed.), *Achievement-related motives in children* (pp. 11-45). New York: Russell Sage Foundation.

Crandall, V. J., Katkovsky, W., & Preston, A. (1962). Motivational and ability determinants of young children's intellectual achievement behavior. *Child Development, 33*, 643-661.

Csikszentmihalyi, M. (1990). *Flow*. New York: Harper & Row.

Csikszentmihalyi, M. (1996). *Creativity: Flow and the psychology of discovery and invention*. New York: HarperCollins.

Deci, E. L., Koestner, R., & Ryan, R. M. (1999). A meta-analytic review of experiments examining the effects of extrinsic rewards on intrinsic motivation. *Psychological Bulletin, 125*, 627-668.

Deci, E. L., Koestner, R., & Ryan, R. M. (2001). Extrinsic rewards and intrinsic motivation in education: Reconsidered once again. *Review of Educational Research, 71*, 1-27.

Deci, E., & Ryan, R. M. (1985). *Intrinsic motivation and self-determination in human behavior*. New York: Plenum.

Do, S. L., & Schallert, D. L. (2004). Emotions and classroom talk: Toward a model of the role of affect in students' experiences of classroom discussions. *Journal of Educational Psychology, 96*, 619-634.

Dweck, C. S. (1985). Intrinsic motivation, perceived control, and self-evaluation maintenance: An achievement goal analysis. *Research on Motivation in Education, 2*, 289-305.

Dweck, C. S., & Leggett, E. L. (1988). A social-cognitive approach to motivation and personality. *Psychological Review, 95*, 256-273.

Eccles, J. S. (1983). Expectancies, values and academic behaviors. In J. T. Spence (Ed.), *Achievement and achievement motives* (pp. 75-146). San Francisco: Freeman.

Eccles, J. S., Arberton, A., Buchanan, C. M., Janis, J., Flanagan, C., Harold, R., et al. (1993). School and family effects on the ontogeny of children's interests, self-perceptions, and activity choices. In J. E. Jacobs (Ed.), *Nebraska Symposium on Motivation, 1992: Developmental perspectives on motivation. Current theory and research in motivation* (Vol. 40; pp. 145-208). Lincoln, NE: University of Nebraska Press.

Eccles, J. S., Barber, B., Jozefowicz, D., Malenchuk, O., & Vida, M. (1999). Self-evaluations of competence, task values, and self-esteem. In N. G. Johnson (Ed.), *Beyond appearance: A new look at adolescent girls* (pp. 53-83). Washington, DC: American Psychological Association.

Eccles, J. S., Midgley, C., Wigfield, A., Miller-Buchanan, C. M., Reuman, D., Flanagan, C., et al. (1993). Development during adolescence: The impact of stage-environment fit on young adolescents' experiences in schools and in families. *American Psychologist, 48*, 90-101.

Eccles, J. S., & Wigfield, A. (1995). In the mind of the actor: The structure of adolescents' achievement task values and expectancy-related beliefs. *Personality and Social Psychology Bulletin, 21*, 215-225.

Eccles, J. S., Wigfield, A., Harold, R. D., & Blumenfeld, P. (1993). Age and gender differences in children's self- and task perceptions during elementary school. *Child Development, 64*, 830-847.

Elliot, A. J. (1997). Integrating the "classic" and "contemporary" approaches to achievement motivation: A hierarchical model of approach and avoidance achievement motivation. In M. L. Maehr & Pintrich (Eds.), *Advances in motivation and achievement* (Vol. 10, pp. 243-279). Greenwich: JAI Press.

Elliot, A. J., & Church, M. A. (1997). A hierarchical model of approach and avoidance achievement motivation. *Journal of Personality and Social Psychology, 72*, 218-232.

Elliot, A. J., & Covington, M. V. (2001). Approach and avoidance motivation. *Educational Psychology Review, 13*, 73-92.

Elliot, A. J., & Harackiewicz, J. M. (1996). Approach and avoidance achievement goals and intrinsic motivation: A mediational analysis. *Journal of Personality and Social Psychology, 70*, 461-475.

Elliot, A. J., & Mcgregor, H. A. (1999). Test anxiety and the hierarchical model of approach and avoidance achievement motivation. *Journal of Personality and Social Psychology, 76*(4), 628-644.

Elliot, A. J., & McGregor, H. A. (2001). A 2 * 2 achievement goal framework. *Journal of Personality and Social Psychology, 80*, 501-519.

Elliot, A. J., McGregor, H. A., & Gable, S. (1999). Achievement goals, study strategies, and exam performance: A mediational analysis. *Journal of Educational Psychology, 91*, 549-563.

Elliot, A. J., & Thrash, T. M. (2001). Achievement goals and the hierarchical model of achievement motivation. *Educational Psychology Review, 13*, 139-156.

Feather, N. T. (1992). Values, valences, expectations, and actions. *Journal of Social Issues, 48*, 109-124.

Ford, M. E. (1992). *Motivating humans: Goals, emotions, and personal agency beliefs*. Newbury Park; CA: Sage.

Forgas, J. (2000). The role of affect in social cognition. In J. Forgas (Ed.), *Feeling and thinking: The role of affect in social cognition* (pp. 1-28). New York: Cambridge University Press.

Forgas, J. (2001). Introduction: Affect and social cognition. In J. Forgas (Ed.), *Handbook of affect and social cognition* (pp. 1-24). Mahwah, NJ: Lawrence Erlbaum Associates.

Freud, S. (1966). *The complete introductory lectures on psychoanalysis* (J. Strachey, Trans.). New York: Norton.

Gottfried, A. E. (1990). Academic intrinsic motivation in young elementary school children. *Journal of Educational Psychology, 82*, 525-538.

Graham, S., & Golan, S. (1991). Motivational influences on cognition: Task involvement, ego involvement, and depth of information processing. *Journal of Educational Psychology, 83*, 187-194.

Graham, S., & Weiner, B. (1996). Theories and principles of motivation. In D. C. Berliner & R. C. Calfee (Eds.), *Handbook of educational psychology* (pp. 63-84). New York: Macmillan.

Greene, B. A., & Miller, R. B. (1996). Influences on achievement: Goals, perceived ability, and cognitive engagement. *Contemporary Educational Psychology, 21*, 181-192.

Harackiewicz, J. M., Barron, K. E., Carter, S. M., Lehto, A. T., & Elliot, A. J. (1997). Predictors and consequences of achievement goals in the college classroom: Maintaining interest and making the grade. *Journal of Personality and Social Psychology, 73*, 1284-1295.

Harackiewicz, J. M., Barron, K. E., Tauer, J. M., Carter, S. M., & Elliot, A. J. (2000). Short-term and long-term consequences of achievement goals: Predicting interest and performance over time. *Journal of Educational Psychology, 92,* 316-330.

Harackiewicz, J. M., Barron, K. E., & Elliot, A. J. (1998). Rethinking achievement goals: When are they adaptive for college students and why? *Educational Psychologist, 33*, 1-21.

Harackiewicz, J. M., Barron, K. E., Pintrich, P. R., Elliot, A. J., & Thrash, T. M. (2002). Revision of achievement goal theory: Necessary and illuminating. *Journal of Educational Psychology, 94*, 638-645.

Harackiewicz, J. M., Barron, K. E., Tauer, J. M., Carter, S. M., & Elliot, A. J. (2000). Short-term and long-term consequences of achievement goals: Predicting interest and performance over time. *Journal of Educational Psychology, 92*, 316-330.

Harp, S. F., & Mayer, R. E. (1998). How seductive details do their damage: A theory of cognitive interest in science learning. *Journal of Educational Psychology, 90*, 414-434.

Hidi, S. (1990). Interest and its contribution as a mental resource for learning. *Review of Educational Research, 60*, 549-571.

Hidi, S., & Harackiewicz, J. M. (2000). Motivating the academically unmotivated: A critical issue for the 21st century. *Review of Educational Research, 70*, 151-179.

Huber, F., Beckmann, S. C., & Herrmann, A. (2004). Means-end analysis: Does the affective state influence information processing style? *Psychology and Marketing, 21*(9), 715-737.

Isen, A. (1999). Positive affect. In T. Dalgleish and M. Power (Eds.), *Handbook of cognition and emotion* (pp. 521-539). New York: Wiley.

James, W. (1890). *The principles of psychology* (Vol. 1). New York: Henry Holt.

Johnson, D. W., Maruyama, G., Johnson, R., Nelson, D., & Skon, L. (1981). Effects of cooperative, competitive, and individualistic goal structures on achievement: A meta-analysis. *Psychological Bulletin, 89*, 47-62.

Juvonen, J., & Wentzel, K. R. (1996). *Social motivation: Understanding children's school adjustment*. New York: Cambridge University Press.

Kagan, J. (1984). On the nature of emotion. In N. Fox (Ed.), The development of emotion regulation: Biological and behavioral considerations (pp. 7-24). *Monographs of the Society for Research in Child Development, 59*(2-3, Serial No. 240).

Kagan, J. (1994). On the nature of emotion. *Monographs of the Society for Research in Child Development, 59* (2-3), 7-24, 250-283.

Kaplan, A., Middleton, M. J., Urdan, T., & Midgley, C. (2002). Achievement goals and goal structures. In C. Midgley (Ed.), *Goals, goal structures, and patterns of adaptive learning* (pp. 21-53). Mahwah, NJ: Lawrence Erlbaum Associates.

Kaplan, A., & Midgley, C. (1997). The effect of achievement goals: Does level of perceived academic-competence make a difference? *Contemporary Educational Psychology, 22*, 415-435.

Krapp, A., Hidi, S., & Renninger, K. A. (1992). Interest, learning, and development. In K. A. Renninger, S. Hidi & A. Krapp (Eds.), *The role of interest in learning and development* (pp. 3-25). Hillsdale, NJ: Lawrence Erlbaum Associates.

Lazarus, R. (1991). *Emotion and adaptation*. Oxford: Oxford University Press.

Lewin, K. (1935). *A dynamic theory of personality: Selected papers* (D. K. Adams & K. E. Zener, Trans.). New York: McGraw-Hill.

Liebert, R., & Morris, L. (1967). Cognitive and emotional components of test anxiety: A distinction and some initial data. *Psychological Reports, 20*, 975-978.

Linnenbrink, E. A., & Pintrich, P. R. (2000). Multiple pathways to learning and achievement: The role of goal orientation in fostering adaptive motivation, affect, and cognition. In C. Sansone & J. M. Harackiewicz (Eds.), *Intrinsic and extrinsic motivation: The search for optimal motivation and performance* (pp. 195-227). San Diego, CA: Academic Press.

Linnenbrink, E. A., & Pintrich, P. R. (2002). Achievement goal theory and affect: An asymmetrical bidirectional model. *Educational Psychologist, 37*, 69-78.

Linnenbrink, E. A., Ryan, A. M., & Pintrich, P. R. (1999). The role of goals and affect in working memory functioning. *Learning and Individual Differences, 11*, 213-230.

Maehr, M. L., (1976). Continuing motivation: An analysis of a seldom considered educational outcome. *Review of Educational Research, 46*, 443-462.

Maehr, M. L. (1991). The "psychological environment" of the school: A focus for school leadership. In P. Thurston & P. Zodhiates (Eds.), *Advances in educational administration* (pp. 51–81). Greenwich: JAI.

Maehr, M. L., & Anderman, E. M. (1993). Reinventing schools for early adolescents: Emphasizing task goals. *Elementary School Journal, 93*(5), 593–610.

Maehr, M. L., & Midgley, C. (1996). *Transforming school cultures*. Boulder, CO: Westview Press.

Manderlink, G., & Harackiewicz, J. M. (1984). Proximal versus distal goal setting and intrinsic motivation. *Journal of Personality and Social Psychology, 47*, 918–928.

Maslow, A. (1954). *Motivation and personality*. New York: Harper.

Mayer, R. E., Heiser, J., & Lonn, S. (2001). Cognitive constraints on multimedia learning: When presenting more material results in less understanding. *Journal of Educational Psychology, 93*, 187–198.

McClelland, D., Atkinson, J., Clark, R., & Lowell, E. (1953). *The achievement motive*. New York: Appleton-Century-Crofts.

McWhaw, K, & Abrami, P. (2001). Student goal orientation and interest: Effects on students' use of self-regulated learning strategies. *Contemporary Educational Psychology, 26*, 311–329.

Meece, J. L., Blumenfeld, P. C., & Hoyle, R. H. (1988). Students' goal orientations and cognitive engagement in classroom activities. *Journal of Educational Psychology, 80*, 514–523.

Meece, J. L., Herman, P., & McCombs, B. (2003). Relations of learner-centered teaching practices to adolescents' achievement goals. *International Journal of Educational Research* [Special Issue on Achievement Goal Orientations], *39*, 457–476.

Meece, J. L., & Miller, S. D. (2001). A longitudinal analysis of elementary school students' achievement goals in literacy activities. *Contemporary Educational Psychology, 26*, 454–480.

Meece, J. L., Wigfield, A., & Eccles, J. S. (1990). Predictors of math anxiety and its influence on young adolescents' course enrollment intentions and performance in mathematics. *Journal of Educational Psychology, 82*, 60–70.

Meyer, D. K., & Turner, J. C. (2002). Discovering emotion in classroom motivation research. *Educational Psychologist, 37*, 107–114.

Middleton, M. J., & Midgley, C. (1997). Avoiding the demonstration of lack of ability: An underexplored aspect of goal theory. *Journal of Educational Psychology, 89*, 710–718.

Midgley, C. (Ed.). (2002). *Goals, goal structures, and patterns of adaptive learning*. Mahwah, NJ: Lawrence Erlbaum Associates.

Midgley, C., Kaplan, A., & Middleton, M. (2001). Performance-approach goals: Good for what, for whom, under what circumstances, and at what cost? *Journal of Educational Psychology, 93*, 77–86.

Midgley, C., Kaplan, A., Middleton, M. J., Maehr, M. L., Urdan, T., Anderman, L. H., et al. (1998). The development and validation of scales assessing students' achievement goal orientations. *Contemporary Educational Psychology, 23*, 113–131.

Midgley, C., & Urdan, T. (2001). Academic self-handicapping and achievement goals: A further examination. *Contemporary Educational Psychology, 26*, 61–75.

Miller, R. B., Greene, B. A., Montalvo, G. P., Ravindran, B., & Nichols, J. D. (1996). Engagement in academic work: The role of learning goals, future consequences, pleasing others, and perceived ability. *Contemporary Educational Psychology, 21*, 388–422.

Murdock, T. B., Anderman, L. H., & Hodge, S. A. (2000). Middle-grade predictors of students' motivation and behavior in high school. *Journal of Adolescent Research, 15*, 327–351.

Murdock, T. B., Hale, N. M., & Weber, M. J. (2001). Predictors of cheating among early adolescents: Academic and social motivations. *Contemporary Educational Psychology, 26*, 96–115.

Murray, H. A. (1938). *Explorations in personality*. New York: Oxford University Press.

Nicholls, J. G. (1989). *The competitive ethos and democratic education*. Cambridge, MA: Harvard University Press.

Nicholls, J. G., Cobb, P., Wood, T., Yackel, E., & Patashnick, M. (1990). Assessing students' theories of success in mathematics: Individual and classroom differences. *Journal for Research in Mathematics Education, 21*, 109–122.

Nolen, S. B. (1988). Reasons for studying: Motivational orientations and study strategies. *Cognition and Instruction, 5*, 269–287.

Patrick, H., Anderman, L. H., & Ryan, A. M. (2002). Social motivation and the classroom social environment. In C. Midgley (Ed.), *Goals, goal structures, and patterns of adaptive learning* (pp. 85–108). Mahwah, NJ: Lawrence Erlbaum Associates.

Pekrun, R. (1992). The impact of emotions on learning and achievement: Towards a theory of cognitive/motivational mediators. *Applied Psychology: An International Review, 41*, 359–376.

Pekrun, R., Goetz, T., Titz, W., & Perry, R. (2002). Academic emotions in students' self-regulated learning and achievement: A program of qualitative and quantitative research. *Educational Psychologist, 37*, 91–105.

Pintrich, P. R. (2000a). An achievement goal theory perspective on issues in motivation terminology, theory, and research. *Contemporary Educational Psychology, 25*, 92–104.

Pintrich, P. R. (2000b). Multiple goals, multiple pathways: The role of goal orientation in learning and achievement. *Journal of Educational Psychology, 92*, 544–555.

Pintrich, P. R., & de Groot, E. V. (1990). Motivational and self-regulated learning components of classroom academic performance. *Journal of Educational Psychology, 82*, 33–40.

Pintrich, P. R., & Garcia, T. (1991). Student goal orientation and self-regulation in the college classroom. In M. L. Maehr & Pintrich (Eds.), *Advances in motivation and achievement* (Vol. 7, pp. 371–402). Greenwich; CT: JAI Press.

Pintrich, P. R., & Schunk, D. (2002). *Motivation in education: Theory, research, and applications* (2nd ed.). Upper Saddle River; NJ: Merrill Prentice Hall.

Pintrich, P. R., Smith, D. A. F., Garcia, T., & McKeachie, W. J. (1993). Reliability and predictive validity of the Motivated

Strategies Learning Questionnaire (MSLQ). *Educational and Psychological Measurement, 53*, 801–813.

Rao, N., & Sachs, J. (1999). Confirmatory factor analysis of the Chinese version of the Motivated Strategies for Learning Questionnaire. *Educational and Psychological Measurement, 59*, 1016–1029.

Renninger, K. A. (1992). Individual interest and development: Implications for theory and practice. In K. A. Renninger, S. Hidi & A. Krapp (Eds.), *The role of interest in learning and development* (pp. 361–395). Hillsdale; NJ: Lawrence Erlbaum Associates.

Renninger, K. A. (2000). Individual interest and its implications for understanding intrinsic motivation. In J. M. Harackiewicz & C. Sansone (Eds.), *Intrinsic and extrinsic motivation: The search for optimal motivation and performance* (pp. 373–404). San Diego; CA: Academic Press.

Roeser, R. W., & Eccles, J. S. (2000). Schooling and mental health. In A. J. Sameroff (Ed.), *Handbook of developmental psychopathology* (2nd ed., pp. 135–156). Dordrecht, The Netherlands: Kluwer Academic.

Roeser, R. W., Eccles, J. S., & Freedman-Doan, C. (1999). Academic functioning and mental health in adolescence: Patterns, progressions, and routes from childhood. *Journal of Adolescent Research, 14*, 135–174.

Roeser, R. W., Eccles, J. S., & Sameroff, A. J. (2000). School as a context of early adolescents' academic and social-emotional development: A summary of research findings. *Elementary School Journal, 100*(5), 443–471.

Roeser, R. W., Midgley, C., & Urdan, T. (1996). Perceptions of the school psychological environment and early adolescents' psychological and behavioral functioning in school: The mediating role of goals and belonging. *Journal of Educational Psychology, 88*, 408–422.

Rokeach, M. (1973). *The nature of human values*. New York: Free Press.

Rokeach, M. (1979). From individual to institutional values with special reference to the values of science. In M. Rokeach (Ed.), *Understanding human values* (pp. 47–70). New York: Free Press.

Rosenberg, E. (1998). Levels of analysis and the organization of affect. *Review of General Psychology, 2*, 247–270.

Ryan, A. M., Hicks, L., & Midgley, C. (1997). Social goals, academic goals, and avoiding seeking help in the classroom. *Journal of Early Adolescence, 17*, 152–171.

Ryan, R. M., Koestner, R., & Deci, E. L. (1991). Ego-involved persistence: When free-choice behavior is not intrinsically motivated. *Motivation and Emotion, 15*, 185–205.

Ryan, A. M., & Pintrich, P. R. (1997). Should I ask for help?: The role of motivation and attitude in adolescents' help-seeking in math class. *Journal of Educational Psychology, 89*, 329–341.

Schacter, S., & Singer, J. E. (1962). Cognitive, social, and physiological determinants of emotional state. *Psychological Review, 69*, 379–399.

Schiefele, U., Krapp, A., & Winteler, A. (1992). Interest as a predictor of academic achievement: A meta-analysis of research. In K. A. Renninger, S. Hidi & A. Krapp (Eds.), *The role of interest in learning and development* (pp. 183–212). Hillsdale; NJ: Lawrence Erlbaum Associates.

Schraw, G., Flowerday, T., & Lehman, S. (2001). Increasing situational interest in the classroom. *Educational Psychology Review, 13*, 211–224.

Schraw, G., Horn, C., Thorndike-Christ, T., & Bruning, R. (1995). Academic goal orientations and student classroom achievement. *Contemporary Educational Psychology, 20*, 359–368.

Schraw, G., & Lehman, S. (2001). Situational interest: A review of the literature and directions for future research. *Educational Psychology Review, 13*, 23–52.

Schunk, D. (1983). Developing children's self-efficacy and skills: The roles of social comparative information and goal setting. *Contemporary Educational Psychology, 8*, 76–86.

Schunk, D. (2001). Social-cognitive theory and self-regulated learning. In B. Zimmerman & D. Schunk (Eds.), *Self-regulated learning and academic achievement: Theoretical perspectives* (2nd ed., pp. 125–151). Mahwah, NJ: Lawrence Erlbaum Associates.

Schutz, P., & DeCuir, J. (2002). Inquiry on emotions in education. *Educational Psychologist, 37*, 125–134.

Schwartz, S. H. (1992). Universals in the content and structure of values: Theoretical advances in empirical tests n 20 countries. In M. P. Zanna (Ed.), *Advances in experimental social psychology* (Vol. 24, pp. 1–65). San Diego, CA: Academic Press.

Skaalvik, E. M. (1997). Self-enhancing and self-defeating ego orientation: Relations with task and avoidance orientation, achievement, self-perceptions, and anxiety. *Journal of Educational Psychology, 89*, 71–81.

Smith, L., Sinclair, K. E., & Chapman, E. S. (2002). Students' goals, self-efficacy, self-handicapping, and negative affective responses: An Australian senior school student study. *Contemporary Educational Psychology, 27*, 471–485.

Snow, R. E., Corno, L., & Jackson, D. (1996). Individual differences in affective and conative functions. In D. C. Berliner & R. C. Calfee (Eds.), *Handbook of educational psychology* (pp. 243–310). New York: Macmillan.

Stipek, D. J. (1996). Motivation and instruction. In D. C. Berliner & R. C. Calfee (Eds.), *Handbook of educational psychology* (pp. 85–113). New York: Macmillan.

Thorkildsen, T. A., & Nicholls, J. G. (1998). Fifth graders' achievement orientations and beliefs: Individual and classroom differences. *Journal of Educational Psychology, 90*, 179–201.

Thorndike, E. L. (1913). *Educational psychology: Vol. 2. The psychology of learning*. New York: Teachers College.

Tobias, S. (1994). Interest, prior knowledge, and learning. *Review of Educational Research, 64*, 37–54.

Tubbs, M. (1986). Goal setting: A meta-analytic examination of the empirical evidence. *Journal of Applied Psychology, 71*, 474–483.

Turner, J. C., & Meyer, D. K. (2000). Studying and understanding the instructional contexts of classrooms: Using our past to forge our future. *Educational Psychologist, 35*, 69–85.

Turner, J. C., Midgley, C., Meyer, D. K., Gheen, M., Anderman, E. M., Kang, Y., et al. (2002). The classroom environment and students' reports of avoidance strategies in mathematics: A multimethod study. *Journal of Educational Psychology, 94*, 88-106.

Urdan, T. (1997). Achievement goal theory: Past results, future directions. In M. L. Maehr & Pintrich (Eds.), *Advances in motivation and achievement* (Vol. 10, pp. 99-141). Greenwich: JAI Press.

Urdan, T., & Maehr, M. L. (1995). Beyond a two-goal theory of motivation and achievement: A case for social goals. *Review of Educational Research, 65*, 213-243.

Urdan, T., Midgley, C., & Anderman, E. M. (1998). The role of classroom goal structure in students' use of self-handicapping strategies. *American Educational Research Journal, 35*, 101-122.

Urdan, T., Ryan, A. M., Anderman, E. M., & Gheen, M. (2002). Goals, goal structures, and avoidance behaviors. In C. Midgley (Ed.), *Goals, goal structures, and patterns of adaptive learning* (pp. 55-83). Mahwah, NJ: Lawrence Erlbaum Associates.

Weiner, B. (1985). An attribution theory of achievement motivation and emotion. *Psychological Review, 92*, 548-573.

Weiner, B. (1986). *An attributional theory of motivation and emotion.* New York: Springer-Verlag.

Weiner, B. (1992). *Human motivation: Metaphors, theories, and research.* Newbury Park, CA: Sage.

Weinstein, R. S., Soule, C. R., Collins, F., Cone, J., Mehlorn, M., & Stimmonacchi, K. (1991). Expectations and high school change: Teacher-researcher collaboration to prevent school failure. *American Journal of Community Psychology, 19*, 333-363.

Wentzel, K. R. (1993). Social and academic goals at school: Motivation and achievement in early adolescence. *Journal of Early Adolescence, 13*, 4-20.

Wentzel, K. R. (1994). Relations of social goal pursuit to social acceptance, classroom behavior, and perceived social support. *Journal of Educational Psychology, 86*, 173-182.

Wentzel, K. R. (1996). Social goals and social relationships as motivators of school adjustment. In K. R. Wentzel (Ed.), *Social motivation: Understanding children's school adjustment* (pp. 226-247). Cambridge, England: Cambridge University Press.

Wentzel, K. R. (1999). Social-motivational processes and interpersonal relationships: Implications for understanding

students' academic success. *Journal of Educational Psychology, 91*, 76-97.

Wigfield, A., & Eccles, J. S. (1989). Test anxiety in elementary and secondary school students. *Educational Psychologist, 24*, 159-183.

Wigfield, A., & Eccles, J. S. (1992). The development of achievement task values: A theoretical analysis. *Developmental Review, 12*, 265-310.

Wigfield, A., & Eccles, J. S. (2000). Expectancy-value theory of achievement motivation. *Contemporary Educational Psychology, 25*, 68-81.

Wigfield, A., & Eccles, J. S. (2002). The development of competence beliefs, expectancies for success, and achievement values from childhood through adolescence. In A. Wigfield & J. S. Eccles (Eds.), *Development of achievement motivation. A volume in the educational psychology series* (pp. 91-120). San Diego, CA: Academic Press.

Winne, P., & Marx, R. (1989). A cognitive-processing analysis of motivation with classroom tasks. In C. Ames & R. Ames (Eds.), *Research on motivation in education* (Vol. 3, pp. 223-257). Orlando, FL: Academic Press.

Wolters, C. A. (2003). Regulation of motivation: Evaluating an underemphasized aspect of self-regulated learning. *Educational Psychologist, 38*, 189-205.

Wolters, C. A. (2004). Advancing achievement goal theory: Using goal structures and goal orientations to predict students' motivation, cognition, and achievement. *Journal of Educational Psychology, 96*, 236-250.

Wolters, C. A., & Pintrich, P. R. (1998). Contextual differences in student motivation and self-regulated learning in mathematics, English, and social studies classrooms. *Instructional Science, 26*, 27-47.

Wolters, C. A., Yu, S. L., & Pintrich, P. R. (1996). The relation between goal orientation and students' motivational beliefs and self-regulated learning. *Learning and Individual Differences, 8*, 211-238.

Zajonc, R. B. (1980). Feeling and thinking: Preferences need no inferences. *American Psychologist, 35*, 151-175.

Zeidner, M. (1998). *Test anxiety: The state of the art.* New York: Plenum.

Zimmerman, B. J. (1989). A social cognitive view of self-regulated academic learning. *Journal of Educational Psychology, 81*, 329-339.

Zuckerman, M. (1979). *Sensation seeking: Beyond the optimal level of arousal.* Hillsdale; NJ: Lawrence Erlbaum Associates.

SELF AND IDENTITY PROCESSES IN SCHOOL MOTIVATION, LEARNING, AND ACHIEVEMENT

Robert W. Roeser
New York University

Stephen C. Peck
University of Michigan

Nailah Suad Nasir
Stanford University

All day long I think about it, then at night I finally say it,
Who am I, and what am I supposed to be doing?
I have no idea ...

—Rumi, 13th century CE, Turkey

The purpose of this chapter is to present ideas and research findings on self and identity processes that are relevant to the study of students' motivation, learning, and achievement in school. Towards the pragmatic end of initiating intellectual dialogue concerning self and identity processes in education, we pursue five basic aims. First, we discuss differing approaches to the study of *self* and *identity* in social science. Second, we clarify the meaning of the terms *self* and *identity* as used historically in the works of William James and Erik Erikson. Third, we update our understanding of these bodies of work in relation to developments in social-personality psychology and the learning, developmental, and brain-behavioral sciences. Fourth, we provide an integrative framework that may be useful to educational researchers who wish to

study self and identity processes in educational settings. Fifth, we discuss the implications of these first four aims for contemporary educational research and practice.

APPROACHING SELF AND IDENTITY IN EDUCATION

For over a century, there have been debates in the social sciences about how best to conceptualize the phenomena variably called *self* and *identity* (cf. Côté & Levine, 2002). Such debates continue. On the one hand, many contemporary psychologists continue in the tradition of William James (1890) by viewing self/identity in terms of (a) *psychological contents* such as self-categorizations, beliefs, and goals; (b) *psychological processes* associated with awareness such as self-appraisal, self-definition, and self-reflection; and (c) the personal project of self-development in which individuals construct a

---

[1]On behalf of the authors, this chapter is dedicated to Richard E. Snow and Robbie Case—mentors and colleagues remembered in knowledge, friendship, and spirit.

representational self-system out of their unique history of social experiences in local and more distal social and physical worlds. Aspects of this *psychological conceptualization of self/identity* are found in many subdisciplines of psychology, including developmental, social-personality, educational, and cultural psychology. On the other hand, social scientists across various disciplines continue in the traditions of Baldwin (1895), Cooley (1902), and Mead (1934) by viewing self/identity in terms of (a) *social and cultural structures* that assign to individuals various consequential group labels (social categorizations), statuses, and roles; (b) *interpersonal processes* associated with the appraisals of, and social positioning by, other people; and (c) the sociocultural project of self-envelopment by which individuals, based on their array of group memberships, develop multiple *identities* through patterns of participation in shared activities. Aspects of these *social and cultural conceptualizations of self/identity* are found in sociology and sociological social psychology, cultural psychology, educational anthropology, and sociocultural theory.

These two general characterizations of *self* and *identity* research traditions are convenient introductory organizing devices because they give the appearance of relatively clear conceptual distinctions in approaches (e.g., the first is about the construction of the *psychological self*, the second is about the construction of *social identity*). The actual state of self/identity research, however, suggests otherwise with conceptions, definitions, and terms spilling over these neat characterizations into an oftentimes confusing body of scholarship. Given the diversity of scholarship in this area, the approach we adopt in this chapter is an eclectic one. We highlight selected ideas and research from both of these broadly defined traditions of scholarship on self and identity. For, in a basic sense, individuals are embedded across their lifespans in social structures, social groups, and shared systems of meaning, as suggested in *social and cultural conceptualizations of self/identity*. As such, individuals' selves/identities are continuously being shaped by social others and negotiated within sociocultural spaces and activities. At the same time, individuals experience the sociocultural conditions of their lives *through* their awareness and their psychological representations of those conditions as suggested in various *psychological conceptualizations of self/identity*. Thus, individuals are constantly, and sometimes creatively, constructing their views of self and world. These psychological dimensions of self/identity make possible *not freedom from external conditions*, as Victor Frankl (1962) put it, *but freedom in*

attitude towards conditions; not just *adaptation to cultural environments*, as Abraham Maslow (1968) put it, but *transcendence of these environments*. Any theory of self/identity needs to address itself to both enculturation and its prospects for social participation as well as individuals' awareness and representations, and their potentials for self-determination.

Education, in its optimal form, also addresses enculturation and self-determination. The education of young members of democratic societies is not only about socializing them in cultural ways of thinking and feeling about themselves as learners and citizens (what we call *me-self education*), nor is it only about scaffolding their development of knowledge and disciplined ways of knowing (i.e., subject-matter education). Education is also about assisting young people in becoming aware of and extricating themselves from habitual (automatic) ways of attending, perceiving, feeling, thinking, and doing by cultivating more *mindful* approaches to these basic self processes and ways of being in the world (what we call *I-self education*). Whereas the first two educational aims are essential for sociocultural participation, I-self education is a precondition for creativity, freedom of thought, and myriad forms of personal and social renewal.

SELF AND IDENTITY IN THE HISTORY OF PSYCHOLOGY

In this section, we trace the history of the self and identity concepts through the work of William James (1890) and Erik and Joan Erikson (1950).[2] We use these works to establish the historical grounds for the idea that *self* consists of multiple aspects—including the "*knower*" (I-self), the "*known*" (me-self), and individuals' phenomenological *sense of identity* at any given moment. Before elaborating on these views, we describe two fallacies that typify research on self and identity and that perpetuate terminological confusion and theoretical fragmentation.

Two Fallacies in Self and Identity Research

The *jingle fallacy* is defined as a situation where "two things that are quite different may be labeled equivalently, and thus the unwary may consider them interchangeable" (Block, 1995, p. 209, on Thorndike, 1904). Using the same word to describe two different things invites confusion. For example, some scholars use the term *identity* to refer to symbolic beliefs about oneself as represented

---

[2]See Friedman (1999) for a description of the mutual collaboration between Erik and Joan Erikson on the 1950 classic *Childhood and Society*. For ease of presentation, we continue to attribute this work to Erik Erikson, although the historical record shows it was a collaboration.

in memory (i.e., self-categorizations or self-concept), whereas others use it to denote the experience of oneself that fluctuates from moment-to-moment (i.e., phenomenological awareness). Given conceptual and operational definitions corresponding separately to self-representations (i.e., the me-self) and the phenomenological experience of those representations (i.e., I experiencing me), a jingle fallacy is perpetuated by using the bare term *identity* where referring to both of these distinct phenomena.

In contrast, the *jangle fallacy* is defined as a situation where two things that are the same, or almost the same, are labeled differently (Block, 1995, on Kelley, 1927). Using two different words to describe the same thing also invites confusion. For example, researchers commit a jangle fallacy where using the two terms *self* and *identity* to refer to a single phenomenon, such as self-concept (e.g., beliefs about being good at math). This particular jangle fallacy abides to the extent that we fail to specify the ways in which the terms *self* and *identity* denote distinct phenomena.

We do not intend to resolve in this chapter the many jingle and jangle fallacies that plague self and identity research. Although we introduce concepts and language that can be used for this purpose, we nevertheless continue to use the terms *self* and *identity* interchangeably throughout the chapter. Doing otherwise would be simple enough, but might also give an impression of false consensus concerning the distinct meaning of these terms and would be unlikely to contribute to any long-term solution to the problem. For example, we could use the term *identity* where referring to socially assigned group memberships or to the conscious experience of self-sameness, and use the term *self* where referring to relatively enduring beliefs, values, and identifications stored in long-term memory. Such decisions are arbitrary, however, given the different ways that different theorists now use these terms. Consequently, we would likely exacerbate the growing confusion surrounding these terms. Instead, we focus on some of the key biological, psychological, and social phenomena that these terms have been used to describe, and attempt to place these phenomena into an integrative framework that may be useful to researchers who study issues of school motivation, learning, and achievement.

James on Self and Identity

James (1890) developed a comprehensive view of self and related it to the notion of a *sense of personal identity* in ways that continue to inform psychology today (Markus, 1990). James described two fundamentally different aspects of *self*: the empirical "me-selves" described as that which is known about me, and the "I-self" (or "Thought"), described as the "knower of me." Summarizing his discussion of self, James (1890) made the following proposal: "Hereafter let us use the words 'me' and 'I' for the empirical person and the judging Thought" (p. 371).

James and the Me-Self. For James (1890), the "empirical me" consists of what is known about oneself. He described the content of me-selves in terms of material, social, and spiritual (i.e., psychological) characteristics. James' "material self" referred to the body and one's possessions; the "social self" to the recognition or condemnation that we receive from others; and the "spiritual self" as our "inner or subjective being, psychic faculties or dispositions, taken concretely" (p. 296). James' concept of me-selves corresponds to what contemporary psychologists refer to collectively as the *self-concept, self-theory,* or *self-schemas*. For instance, researchers continue to focus on the content of individuals' *psychological* selves in terms of their values, goals, and beliefs (Harter, 1999); on the content of their *social selves* in terms of central and salient group memberships, roles and reputations, and internalized images of self as seen through the eyes of significant social others (Ashmore, Deaux, & McLaughlin-Volpe, 2004; Stets & Burke, 2000); and on their *body selves* in terms of their perceived body image, physical appearance, romantic appeal, and athletic competence (Harter, 1999).

James and the I-self. After a lengthy review of various philosophical positions on the substantive nature of the I-self as *knower*, James (1890) concluded that "I" is synonymous with "Thought" and that "it is enough to know that it exists; and that in everyone, at an early age, the distinction between thought as such, and what it [Thought] is of or about, has become familiar to the mind" (pp. 296–297). He maintained that "the reality of such pulses of thought, with their function of knowing, [are] the ultimate kind of fact that the psychologist must admit to exist" (p. 338) and that "if the passing thought be the directly verifiable existent which no school has hitherto doubted it to be, then that thought is itself the thinker, and psychology need not look beyond" (p. 401). James relegated any further conclusions about the substantive nature of the I-self to either metaphysical speculation or future scientific discoveries, though he did go on to describe how the I-self or Thought is experienced within the stream of consciousness. Specifically, he described the I-self as "the present mental state [that] binds the individual past facts with each other and with itself" (p. 338). He maintained that "Thought is a perishing and not an immortal or incorruptible thing" (345) and that despite its moment-to-moment, pulsating quality, the I-self fulfills several essential psychological functions for the individual. These included the "subjective synthesis" and the "appropriating and disowning" of experience. For James, the experience of particular me-selves was dependent on distinguishing what was me from what was not me; therefore, there must be an agent of the "appropriating and disowning.... It is the Thought to whom the various Constituents are known. That Thought is a vehicle of choice as well as of cognition" (p. 340). In short, James viewed the I-self as synonymous with *phenomenal awareness* and assigned to this awareness the capacity for self-regulatory and agentic functions.

James and Personal Identity. James went on to describe how it was possible to have a phenomenological experience of being the same person over time despite the fact that experience was constantly changing. He considered the conscious experience, or *sense of*, personal continuity and selfsameness over time within the context of his theory of the self and referred to it as the *sense of personal identity*. He argued that this *sense* arose from the relation between the I-self and me-self. Although the I-self functions of subjective synthesis, appropriation, and disowning were enough to signify the *facts* of one's existence (I am), they could not provide what James understood as the *sense* of personal identity without having as their "objects" the past and present me-selves that denoted *what* I am (and am not). In sum, James suggested that it is the subjective *relation* between I-as-subject and me-as-object that provides the basis for the phenomenological experience that we call the *sense of personal identity*.

Erikson on Psychosocial Identity

In contrast to James' focus on selfsameness, Erikson was more interested in the objective relationships between the person (ego) and their social and cultural environments (ethos), or what he termed *psychosocial identity* (Erikson, 1968). Erikson wanted to develop a conceptual language that would move beyond what he referred to as the "pseudo biology" typical of the traditional psychoanalytic perspective of his day and towards a view of human development *in cultural context*. He drew upon the concept of the "average expectable environment" to capture what he meant by the term *psychosocial*. In this view, humans are born "preadapted" to an average expectable environment and are dependent upon a continual series of these environments for healthy development.

Erikson (1970) depicted this persistent endeavor of social others to incorporate individuals into an "on-going cultural concern" in terms of an epigenetic series of stages

of psychosocial identity development, stages defined by particular life tasks, ideologies, and social contexts encountered across the life span. According to this view, promising or problematic forms of psychosocial identity development are a product of:

an intricate relation between inner (cognitive and emotional) development and a stimulating and encouraging environment [that] exists from the beginning of life, so that no stage and no crisis could be formulated without a characterization of the mutual fit of the individual's capacity to relate to an ever expanding life-space of people and institutions, on the one hand, and on the other, the readiness of people and institutions to make him [*sic*] part of an ongoing cultural concern. (Erikson, 1970, p. 754)

Erikson's epigenetic stage theory portrays development during childhood in terms of transactions between children and their environments, and the resultant favorable or unfavorable resolution of tasks associated with basic self needs. These needs include (a) relatedness in attachment relationships during infancy (trust vs. mistrust), (b) autonomy in the exploration of the environment and in the mastery of the body, moral rules, and social roles during early childhood (autonomy and initiative vs. shame, doubt, and guilt), and (c) competence in academic and social endeavors during middle and late childhood (industry vs. inferiority).

In childhood, the average expectable environment consists of predictable, warm, and consistent caregiving, moral socialization that is neither overly harsh nor overly lenient, peers who expand the child's social world through mutual and cooperative interpersonal relationships with equals, and teachers who afford all children the opportunity to develop their competence in a setting free of social prejudice. Concerning this last point, Erikson (1959) discussed the critical role played by children's experience of school and developing sense of competence for their emerging sense of belonging and participation in an ongoing cultural concern:

Since industry involves doing things beside and with others, a first sense of *division of labor* and *equality of opportunity* develops at this time. When a child begins to feel that it is the color of his [*sic*] skin, the background of his parents, or the cost of his clothes rather than his wish and his will to learn which will decide his social worth, lasting harm may ensue for the sense of identity. (p. 93)

After the triggering event of puberty, Erikson (1968) posited that relatedness, autonomy, and competence needs are renegotiated in terms of the increasingly diverse range of experiences and people that typify adolescents' social worlds. Specifically, earlier orientations toward interpersonal trust are renegotiated in terms of new friends, romantic partners, role models, cultural ideals, and social institutions in which youth can have *faith*; earlier orientations toward personal autonomy are renegotiated in terms of self-images, activities, and ideologies to which youth can *freely chose to commit*; and earlier orientations toward competence and achievement are renegotiated in terms of social and occupational roles in which youth might expect to *excel*. Renegotiating these needs in culturally appropriate ways was viewed as the basis for developing a mature psychosocial identity.

Erikson and the I-Self. Erikson's focus on the *objective relationships* between the person and the environment, as opposed to the subjective relationship between I and me, brought needed attention to the cultural and intergenerational nature of psychosocial identity development. Nevertheless, Erikson also discussed the concept of the *I-self*, although, in contrast to James, he never provided an explicit definition. Erikson tended to think about the I-self in process terms, having referred to it as "an observing center of awareness and of volition" (1968, p. 135) and as "a center so numinous that it amounts to a sense of being alive" (1981/1996, p. 284).

JAMES AND ERIKSON IN MODERN TIMES

James' Me-Selves in Modern Perspective

Psychological research on self/identity, personality, and motivation took a profound turn in the 1970s when it began to explore the concept of mental representations and when it was considered

legitimate—in fact, necessary—to posit a separate level of analysis which can be called the "level of representation." When working at this level, a scientist traffics in such representational entities as symbols, rules, images—the stuff of representation which is found between input and output—and in addition, explores the ways in which these representational entities are joined, transformed or contrasted with one another. (Gardner, 1985, p. 38)

In a classic article, Markus (1977) proposed that self be viewed in representational terms: as "cognitive generalizations about the self, derived from past experience, that organize and guide the processing of self-related information contained in the individual's social experiences" (p. 64). Researchers interested in self and motivation began exploring how cognitive processes (e.g., activation) and representations (e.g., beliefs) serve basic motivational and self-regulatory functions such as directing attention to, and speeding the processing of,

particular features and domains of self-relevant experience, people, and situations. Eventually, the notion of self-representations provided a way of understanding how, despite limits on information-processing capacity, humans efficiently and often automatically motivate and regulate their experience and behavior (Bargh, 1999). It also provided a view of self (with its motivational and regulatory functions) that was consistent with James' (1890) description of the content-rich "empirical me-selves" and is the basis for what are today referred to as self-schemas, self-theories, self-concepts of ability, self-efficacy beliefs, possible selves, beliefs about intelligence, educational aspirations, school values, achievement goals, and so on.

Multiple Forms of Mental Representations. Conceptualizing the me-self (and "motivation") in terms of mental representations lead scholars interested in self/identity to encounter an issue that was debated at the outset of cognitive science: namely, what are

the best ways of conceptualizing mental representations. Some investigators favor the view that there is but a single form of representation (usually, one that features propositions or statements); some believe in at least two forms of mental representations—one more like a picture (or image); the other closer to propositions; still others believe that it is possible to posit multiple forms of mental representations and it is impossible to determine which is the correct one. (Gardner, 1985, p. 40)

The idea that humans have more than one way of constructing mental representations of their physical and social worlds is the subject of an increasing amount of research in the social sciences under the rubric of "dual processes."

The notion of dual processes in psychological functioning attracted much attention during the first 100 years or so of psychology. For example, Freud (1911/1953) postulated that we have both a "primary process" mode of functioning characterized by emotion, unconscious drives, and iconic imagery, and a "secondary process" mode characterized by reason, conscious thoughts, and symbolic language. The former system has been hypothesized to underlie relatively rapid and "hot" modes of information processing and behavioral regulation, whereas the latter system has been hypothesized to mediate slower and "cool" modes of processing and regulation (Goleman, 1995, 2003; Metcalfe & Mischel, 1999).

The idea of qualitatively different psychological systems attuned to different forms of meaning making and social interaction has received increasing research attention and support across many subdisciplines of psychology (Goleman, 1995; Greenwald & Banaji, 1995;

TABLE 18.1. Dual Psychological Systems Across the History and Disciplines of Psychology

Dual Systems	Source	Discipline
Impulsive—Voluntary	Wundt (1897)	Experimental
Primary—Secondary process	Freud (1953/1911)	Clinical
Holistic (eros)—Analytic (logos)	Jung (1923)	Clinical
Need—Quasi-need	Lewin (1935)	Personality
Inferred self—Self-in-awareness	Hilgard (1949)	Motivation
Spatial—Linear	Sperry (1961)	Neuroscience
Iconic—Symbolic	Bruner (1964)	Cognition
Implicit—Explicit	Reber (1967)	Learning
Appositional—Propositional	Bogen (1969)	Neuroscience
Intuitive—Reasoned	Kahneman & Tverskey (1973)	Cognition
Automatic—Controlled	Shiffrin & Schneider (1977)	Cognition
Heuristic—Systematic	Chaiken (1980)	Social
Concrete—Abstract	Martindale (1981)	Cognition
Procedural—Declarative	Anderson (1982)	Learning
Slow to change—Quick to change	Conley (1984)	Personality
Syncretic—Analytic	Buck (1985)	Cognition
Operant—Respondent	McClelland (1985)	Motivation
Implicit—Explicit	Schacter (1987)	Memory
Direct perception—Re-cognition	Neisser (1988)	Perception
Implicit—Self-attributed	McClelland et al. (1989)	Motivation
Algorithmic—Rational	Anderson (1990)	Cognition
Experiential—Rational	Epstein (1990)	Personality
Unconscious—Preconscious	Lazarus (1991)	Clinical
Slow learning—Fast learning	J. McClelland, McNaughton, & O'Reilly (1995)	Neuroscience
Associative—Rule-based	Sloman (1996)	Cognition
Context—Text	Ornstein (1997)	Education
Fast processing—Slow processing	O'Reilly & Munakata (2000)	Neuroscience
Experiential—Verbal-symbolic	Schultheiss (2001)	Personality
Reflexive—Reflective	Lieberman et al. (2002)	Neuroscience

Metcalfe & Mischel, 1999; Ornstein, 1997; Shiffrin & Schneider, 1977). In Table 18.1, we present a selection of concepts from investigators who have posited the existence of at least two different psychological systems that are relevant to research on self/identity: those related to perception (e.g., Bruner, 1964), emotion (e.g., Lazarus, 1991; Zajonc, 1980), social cognition (e.g., Chaiken, 1980; Kihlstrom, 1990); learning (e.g., Bruner, 1960; Reber, 1967); motivation (e.g., McClelland, 1985; Murray, 1938) personality (e.g., Allport, 1961; Epstein, 1990) and neuropsychology (e.g., Lieberman, Gaunt, Gilbert, & Trope, 2002; Sperry, 1961). The diversity of such "dual process" theories and research traditions indicate "not so much claims about how many processes there *are*, but claims about how many processes there *aren't*. And the claim is this: There aren't one" (Gilbert, 1999, p. 4).

The postulate of dual processes has important implications for the qualitatively different kinds of (me-) self-representations individuals construct from their social and physical experience. Early in life, infants relate to the world through attention, sensation, emotion, and motor acts that are nested within a network of close physical and social relationships (Meltzoff, 1999; Stern, 2000). Between the first and second years of life, children gradually acquire the capacity to relate to self and world through language as well (Stern, 2000). Developmentally, these primary and secondary modes of knowing and social interaction are hypothesized to correspond to (at least) two different kinds of me-self representations: the iconic and the symbolic (Case, 1991).

Two Examples: Dual Systems Perspectives on the Me-Self and on Motivation

Epstein (1990) has provided theory and evidence regarding these two levels of the me-self—what he terms the "experiential" (i.e., iconic) and the "rational" (i.e., symbolic) self-systems (i.e., me-selves). In his view, both of these systems function to assimilate experience and maintain the organism's health, social relations, self-esteem, and pleasure–pain balance. The *experiential self-system* is a rapid-response, holistic, emotion-mediated information processing system that develops slowly (over the course of many directly experienced occasions) from the encoding of sensory, affective, and motor experience into representational images, feelings, and metaphors. Epistemically, this system is predicated on the notion that "experiencing is believing." Structurally, this system is hypothesized to be derived from emotionally significant experiences that are organized as "emotional complexes" (i.e., iconic schemas). Functionally, this system maintains the person's health, well-being, and social relations by guiding behavior through use of these emotion complexes. For instance, the experiential self-system provides evaluative information in the form of "good and bad vibes" in instances of decision-making (cf. Kahneman, 2003) and "hot" emotional arousal in certain situations—an experience often described as suddenly being "seized by our emotions." Epstein (1990) suggested that, phenomenologically, we experience self-regulation via the "experiential self-system" passively or preconsciously—its activation does not require our conscious attention (cf., Bargh, 1999).

Epstein (1990) described the *rational self-system* as a fast-learning, analytic, reason-mediated information-processing system that encodes experience in terms of verbal, mathematical, and other kinds of symbolic representations. Epistemically, this system is predicated on the notion that logic and evidence undergird belief. Structurally, this system is hypothesized to be differentiated into specific domains (e.g., school, sports, social) and dimensions (e.g., self-concepts of ability, values) as well as integrated into hierarchically organized *belief systems* (e.g., self-as-student-at-school). Functionally, this system guides behavior through such belief systems and direct, conscious (and relatively slow) appraisals of events prior to action (cf. Metcalfe & Mischel, 1999). Phenomenologically, the rational self-system is readily available to our awareness and thus is intimately known by people in the form of explicit beliefs about themselves and the world.

Epstein (1990) posited that integration between the two systems is necessary for overall effective functioning. Whereas the experiential self-system provides strong energy and a rapid, holistic approach to problem solving, the rational system provides strong measured appraisals and an analytic approach to problem solving. The experiential and rational systems interact in a number of ways. For example, the experiential system provides the rational system with evaluative "vibes" and feelings that can summate with beliefs in motivating courses of action. These systems can also provide conflictual inputs to behavior as in the common experience of feeling dissonance between what our "hearts" feel and what our "heads" think about a given decision, person, or situation (Epstein, 1990). Both the experiential and the rational self systems operate largely below the level of conscious awareness in shaping behavior because, according to Epstein, "that is the natural mode of operation of the human mind, as it is more efficient for behavior to be directed automatically than to require conscious reflection" (p. 190; cf. Bargh, 1999).

Similarly, McClelland and his colleagues have described two different motivational systems in terms of "implicit motives" (i.e., iconic me-self) and "self-attributed motives" (i.e., symbolic me-self; McClelland, 1985; McClelland, Koestner, & Weinberger, 1989). Implicit motives (derived from natural incentives and emotions) and self-attributed motives (derived from social incentives and language) differ both *substantively* (in terms of psychological representation) and *functionally* (in terms of the ways they affect behavior). McClelland (1985) defined implicit motives as learned, affectively charged, anticipatory goal states (aroused by specific cues) whose functions are to attain pleasure or avoid pain. Implicit motives such as the need for achievement (*n*Ach) are defined as situationally evaluative, affectively energizing, anticipatory schemas that function to motivate individuals to approach an end state that is rewarding or to avoid an end state that is punishing. In the case of *n*Ach, that desired end state is the desire to do something better compared to a standard of excellence (McClelland, 1985). These motives are hypothesized to be relatively nonconscious, preverbal, and predictive of long-term behavioral trends, habits, and decisions.

In contrast, self-attributed motives are preconscious, evaluative, and related most strongly to choices made within immediate contexts. In contemporary terms familiar to educational psychologists, self-attributed motives refer to constructs such as goals, values, and competence-related beliefs (Eccles, Wigfield, & Schiefele, 1998). McClelland (1985) posited that goals and values (symbols) often direct the affective energy of implicit motives (icons) toward responses in particular situations. Despite the evidence that shows distinct correlates of iconic and symbolic forms of motivation with, respectively, long-term behavioral *habits* over the life span and short-term behavioral *choices* in specific situations, McClelland et al. (1989) noted that both forms of motivation serve similar functions: the energization and direction of behavior.

McClelland (1985) reviewed a range of studies showing that symbolic motives (e.g., the goal of performing well on an achievement task) play their most obvious role in directing behavior where the affectively charged iconic motive (e.g., need for achievement) has been activated in the self-system. For example, students high in *n*Ach performed better than those low in *n*Ach only when these high levels of *n*Ach were accompanied by high levels of a symbolic desire (i.e., a goal) to perform well. McClelland et al. (1989) extended these ideas by describing how the two motive systems interact differentially with distinct aspects of the environment. For example, *explicit* content-specific social expectations (e.g., to complete your homework) are more closely related to the activation of content-specific symbolic motives than to the activation of content-related iconic motives (e.g., the need for achievement). Alternatively, *implicit* task demands (e.g., difficulty level) are more likely to activate iconic rather than symbolic motives. For example, McClelland et al. described research showing that people who score high on *n*Ach measures perform better at moderately challenging cognitive tasks (and often worse on easy tasks) than people who score low on *n*Ach because, *implicitly*, "such tasks provide the maximum incentive of feeling good from doing something better" (p. 693).

In cases where both iconic and symbolic motives are activated by situational cues, McClelland et al. (1989) argued that these different kinds of motivation can *summate* to facilitate performance or *conflict* to undermine performance. For example, they described a study in which social interaction (i.e., talking to other people) was predicted best by including information about individuals' implicit (iconic) and self-attributed (symbolic) affiliative motivation. Specifically, those who were high on both forms of affiliative motivation were found to talk to other people the most. They also described conflict in these systems by showing how different motivational configurations can predict different forms of behavior expression. For example, people with strong iconic *and* symbolic affiliation motives were more often observed talking with other people, whereas those with strong iconic affiliation motives but weak symbolic affiliation motives were more often observed writing letters to other people.

In sum, the existence of "dual processes" in psychological functioning is related to the contemporary postulate of *at least* two kinds of representations in the construction of "empirical me-selves" across development: the iconic and the symbolic (Case, 1991). Thus, we define James' (1890) me-self in modern perspective, in part, in terms of these two levels of representation: the iconic (affective–experiential) and the symbolic (evaluative–rational) me-self systems. These two levels develop over time, are stored in long-term memory, and serve motivational and regulatory functions when activated by acts of volition or (automatically) by environmental stimuli (see later discussion).

James' I-Self in Modern Perspective

Based on developments in contemporary neuroscience and ancient insights into the nature of consciousness, we find it pragmatically useful and theoretically viable to define James' (1890) I-self as *awareness* and relate it to the concepts of *passive observation* and *willful attention*. We view this as consistent with Erikson's (1968) conceptualization of the "I" as "an observing center of awareness and of volition" (p. 135) and James' view of the I-self as the "vehicle of cognition" and as "pulses of thought, with their function of knowing" (p. 338).

Neuroscientists have described a mode of awareness that is present at or very near birth (e.g., Damasio, 1999). Damasio calls this "core consciousness." He describes it as a simple biological phenomena that is stable across the lifespan; independent of memory, reasoning, and language; and lasting only during the present moment (*here and now*). This mode of awareness can be described in terms of *alert* but *passive observation* and forms the ground of *conscious, subjective experience*. There is a growing body of research that distinguishes a second mode of awareness that can be described in terms of *agentic regulation of conscious experience through attention* (Lieberman et al., 2002; Shiffrin & Schneider, 1977). This second mode is characterized by the I-self functions described by James (1890) as appropriation, synthesis, and choice. Specifically, it is characterized by the capacity for the *willful direction of attention*. The willful and conscious shifting of attentional focus allows for the monitoring and discrimination, and therefore the "appropriation and disowning," of conscious experience. Another capacity of this second mode of awareness is the *willful sustaining of attention*. The willful and conscious maintenance of attentional focus on specific contents of experience allows for both discrimination and "subjective synthesis" of these contents. The directing and sustaining of attention also afford choice insofar as individuals can use their awareness to *volitionally* activate psychological resources, focus on particular aspects of the inner and external environments rather than others, and hold particular contents in working memory to accomplish specific ends (e.g., remaining aware of an intention until it comes to fruition in action).

Studies have documented that young children who can shift their attention away from negative sensory stimuli, concepts, and response tendencies (and sustain focus on more positive stimuli, concepts, and responses) also do better in school and enjoy better mental health across development compared to young children who do not manifest these potentials (Derryberry, 2002; Posner & Rothbart, 2000; Shoda, Mischel, & Peake, 1990). More generally, these modes of awareness are the foundation of all educational efforts, and in particular, self-regulated learning (Brown, 1997; Langer, 1989; Winne, 1996).

In sum, the I-self can be defined as a center of alert but passive observation and a vehicle for the willful directing and sustaining of attention. As such, it can be distinguished from the me-self and its automatic directing of attention through various processes (e.g., orienting reflex, sensory-affective-motor schemas; Bargh, 1999). The

I-self can be considered a master regulatory mechanism by which attentional, cognitive, and affective resources can be *consciously and willfully* deployed (Derryberry, 2002; Posner & Rothbart, 2000). Given developments in our scientific understanding of the I-self and its functions, we believe that ignoring the I-self in research on self/identity can lead to the commission of a jingle fallacy (i.e., where I-self functions are mistakenly attributed to me-self functions).

Moving the Legacy of James and Erikson Forward

In this section, we move the legacy of James and Erikson forward by using their work to clarify the widespread use of the terms *implicit* and *explicit* in contemporary self/identity research. The complex nature of the psychological and social phenomena to which these terms are assigned requires more precise terminology than is commonly used today. Consequently, we distinguish among and interrelate three ways of thinking about the concepts of implicit and explicit: the phenomenological (I-self), the representational (me-self), and the developmental.

Phenomenological Meaning. The terms *implicit* and *explicit* are most often used to indicate whether or not psychological contents or processes are *outside of* or *within* conscious awareness, respectively. This usage reflects Murray's (1938) *double-aspect hypothesis:* namely, that every conscious experience reflects some underlying psychological process but that "not every regnant process has a conscious correlate" (p. 49). For example, research on implicit perception, implicit memory, and implicit learning examines environmental stimuli that are processed by the brain and affect subsequent behavior in ways that do not involve conscious awareness (Kihlstrom, 1987). Perceptual and semantic priming studies, in which individuals are exposed to a perceptual or language stimulus below the threshold of their phenomenal awareness, have demonstrated that such "mere exposure" affects subsequent recall of the priming stimulus even though participants do not consciously remember learning it. This provides one way of understanding how students can learn from *tacit* (i.e., implicit) dimensions of classroom contexts. In contrast, perception, memory, and learning are considered *explicit* when there are relevant correlates of these processes within phenomenological awareness *and* behavior. For example, someone tells you a phone number, you consciously attend to the information by hearing and rehearsing the phone number, and you later recall and use the phone number. We urge readers to use the terms *implicit* and *explicit* only where referring to psychological contents and processes that are *noncon-*

scious or *conscious*, respectively. This understanding of the implicit–explicit distinction is consistent with our definition of the I-self as *awareness*.

Representational Meaning. The fact that psychological contents and processes exist whether or not we are aware of them tells us little about their substantive nature. For example, where researchers refer to attitudes, stereotypes, and cognitive abilities as being *implicit*, it is often unclear whether they mean something about the substantive nature of these contents or processes, how they were measured, or the extent to which they exist outside of phenomenal awareness (Fazio & Olsen, 2003). For example, some theorists refer to self-theories as *implicit* and mean only that these theories exist outside of awareness (Dweck, 1999). However, other theorists have used the term *implicit* where referring to the substantive nature of the constructs in question (e.g., "implicit motives;" McClelland et al., 1989).

As noted earlier, one of the dominant themes in the literature summarized in Table 18.1 is that self/identity can be characterized by at least two qualitatively distinct kinds of psychological representations (e.g., Bruner, 1964; Peirce, 1955). The first, which we refer to as *iconic*, can be described in terms of sensory-affective-motor schemas. A contemporary developmental postulate is that infants (perhaps even before birth) construct iconic representations from their rich web of sensory, affective, and motor experiences (Case, 1991; Meltzoff, 1999). The second, which we refer to as *symbolic*, can be described in terms of valenced (e.g., good–bad) beliefs and belief systems (e.g., expectations, attitudes, goals, and plans). Language is the prototypic example of such a symbolic system, and it obviously plays an enormous role in self-development (Harter, 1999; Stern, 2000). From this perspective, energy (e.g., affect, valence) and direction (e.g., content, structure) are fundamental properties of both iconic and symbolic (me-self) representations. We urge researchers to use terms other than *implicit* and *explicit* (e.g., *iconic* and *symbolic*) where referring to the *substantive* nature of representational contents and processes. Such distinctions allow for the possibility of discussing *iconic content* that operates *explicitly* (although this is relatively uncommon) and *symbolic content* that operates *implicitly* (which is common).

Developmental Meaning. Scholars who study motivation, self, and personality sometimes fuse these phenomenological and representational meanings together into a third meaning—that of *development*. For example, McClelland et al. (1989) posited that implicit (iconic) motives begin to develop during infancy, before language, and operate largely outside of awareness, whereas self-attributed (symbolic) motives develop after the acquisition of language and are largely available to conscious awareness. This suggests a normative developmental progression of experience and behavior dominated by implicit iconic content and processes early in life (Case, 1991; Lewis & Brooks-Gunn, 1979); explicit, basic symbolic contents and processes during childhood (Case, 1991; Harter, 1999); self-reflective symbolic contents and processes during adolescence (Keating, 1990); and complex "reflective judgments" involving abstract symbolic systems in adulthood (Fischer & Bidell, 1998). This developmental progression depends in large measure on whether or not social environments scaffold the unfolding of these I-self potentials and the construction of these me-self contents (Keating, 1990). Thus, the *developmental meaning* of the implicit–explicit distinction refers to the intertwining of the contextualized *I* and *me* over time. In the next section, we draw these ideas together into a heuristic framework for studying self/identity processes in relation to school learning and achievement.

BASIC ASPECTS OF SELF IN CONTEXT (BASIC) MODEL

A holistic-interactionistic perspective on human development (Magnusson, 2003), applied to over a century of empirical research related to self/identity, draws attention to several key features of the person-in-context system (Peck, 2004, 2005). First are the contents and processes that have been described as identity, self, and personality and that implicate multiple levels of representation (contents) and dynamics (processes) within the person. Second are the contents and processes that have been described as context, culture, and geography and that implicate multiple levels of organization and dynamics within the environmental context. Third are the dynamic interrelations among the contents and processes that exist within and between these various personal (intraindividual) and contextual (interindividual) levels. These features can be summarized by a person-in-context model (see Fig. 18.1) that includes several "focal" levels within both the person and the context (Peck, 2004, 2005). We call this the Basic Aspects of Self in Context (BASIC) model. It highlights the extent to which understanding self/identity in relation to learning and achievement depends on research and theory related to multiple levels of representation (i.e., within the person) and organization (i.e., between whole individuals and various social contexts).

Research in psychology, biology, and neuroscience has revealed how the intraindividual aspects of self/identity

can be described in terms of the contents, structures, and functions of the brain, mind, and experience. From this perspective, self/identity is encoded in memory, activated (e.g., in awareness) when personally or contextually invoked, and enacted as verbal or nonverbal behavior. Research in psychology, sociology, anthropology, and education has revealed how the interindividual aspects of self/identity can be described in terms of social actors' group labels (e.g., American), roles (e.g., student), and statuses (e.g., poor), as well as by participation in cultural practices (in settings such as the family, classroom, or mall). From these perspectives, identities are afforded, assigned, and recognized by other people, places, and things in the environment. In the next sections, we describe each of the BASIC levels and the implications they have for understanding self and identity processes in school learning and achievement.

Basic Levels of Self (BLOS) Model

Educational research on school motivation at the intraindividual levels has focused heavily on how symbolic (me-self) representations such as competency beliefs, task values, achievement goals, and learning strategies relate to variations in school engagement and achievement (Eccles et al., 1998). Other work has taken a more "self-regulatory" perspective in terms of meta-cognitive and meta-motivational processes. These processes directly implicate the role of the I-self in relation to me-self contents, emotions, and so on (Pintrich, 2003; Winne, 1996). In general, motivation researchers treat basic forms of symbolic me-self representations as core directive constructs that shape students' actions in the classroom by addressing such questions as "Why do I want (or not want) to do this task?" (values), "What goal am I trying to accomplish by doing (or not doing) this task?" (goals), "Can I do this task?" (self-perceived competence and efficacy), and "How do I go about trying to accomplish this task?" (strategies; Eccles et al., 1998). This exclusive focus on symbolic representations has been repeatedly criticized for not addressing the issue of the energization of behavior. Needs have often been postulated as serving such energizing functions (Deci & Ryan, 1985; Thrash & Elliot, 2002). More recently, researchers have begun to study the relatively neglected topic of how different emotions energize (and eventuate from) learning episodes in school (see Schutz & Lanehart, 2002). This work on emotions is consistent with broader trends in research in developmental and social-personality psychology on self. For instance, the idea that the energy of moods and aroused emotions "color" iconic and symbolic self-representations that are constructed from social experience is at the

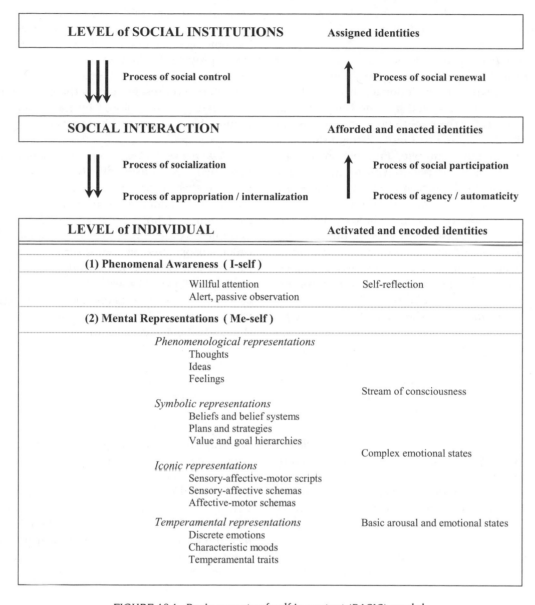

FIGURE 18.1. Basic aspects of self in context (BASIC) model.

heart of contemporary research in neo-Piagetian theory (Case, 1991; Harter, 1999), cognitive-experiential self theory (Epstein, 1990), cognitive-affective personality systems theory (Mischel & Shoda, 1995), and the theory of possible selves (Markus & Nurius, 1986). Thus, in the next sections, we highlight the relatively neglected topics of mood and emotion in relation to self and identity processes in school motivation, learning, and achievement.

BLOS Overview. We describe the intraindividual levels of representation (e.g., temperamental, iconic, symbolic, and phenomenological) that function to motivate (ener-

gize) and regulate (direct) learning and achievement behavior in school by reference to the Basic Levels of Self (BLOS) heuristic model (Fig. 18.1). This model assumes the foundational role of temperamental traits, moods, and emotions in shaping "higher order" levels of me-self representation from birth onward (Case, 1991; Damasio, 1999; Stern, 2000). This synchronic (single moment in time) simplification allows for clear explication of several qualitatively different kinds of encoded me-self representations that play critical roles in the diachronic (across time) whole-person processes that are called *sense of identity*, *cognition*, *emotion*, and *behavior*. The BLOS model also situates the me-self in specific relation to both the I-self and the wider social and physical contexts in which individuals (as I/Me) function as unified wholes.

Temperamental Representation. Self/identity, as either phenomenological experience or representational content, depends heavily on evolutionary history (Buss, 2004), without which we would have no body or brain to provide the basis for the experiences or contents we call self/identity. The feature that most distinguishes temperamental from iconic, symbolic, and phenomenological representations is their species-typical content; that is, all members of the human species share the same basic anatomy (e.g., the central and peripheral nervous systems). These common elements include the inherited biopsychological mechanisms that provide our most basic arousal and response dispositions, including a set of core emotions and response tendencies first described by Darwin (Lazarus, 1991). Although these dispositions are well rooted in the biochemistry and physiology of the evolved brain and body, their manifestations (e.g., states of emotional arousal) vary across developmental time and place (e.g., due to variations in diet, exercise, cultural socialization factors, life events, and other self-representations; Kitayama & Markus, 1994; Lewis, 1998; Thayer, 1989).

Four key dimensions of temperament relevant to learning and achievement are activity level, reactivity, emotionality, and sociability (see Snow, Corno, & Jackson, 1996). Activity level refers to the intensity and speed of movement; reactivity refers to approach and avoidance response thresholds; emotionality refers to the quality, intensity, and frequency of emotional responses; and sociability refers to the preference for social interaction. These factors influence students' sensitivity to environmental stimulation and hence, their preference for particular kinds of teaching styles and learning tasks. For example, individuals with high activity and emotionality levels can become overstimulated during learning and need frequent breaks to allow "particular mental functions rest" (Snow et al., 1996, p. 256). Further, such individuals tend to prefer well-defined learning tasks that require algorithmic problem-solving strategies. In contrast, students who are less reactive and emotional seek out more novelty and complexity and prefer abstract tasks requiring heuristic problem-solving strategies.

Whereas moods reflect enduring baseline states of physiological arousal (which can be characterized by two independent dimensions: energetic–tired and tense–calm), emotions reflect transient states of arousal (Lazarus, 1991; Thayer, 1989). Theorists have proposed that all humans are born with a core set of basic emotions (e.g., anger, fear, love) that are responsive to particular classes of environmental opportunities and threats

(Ekman, 1992; see Table 18.2). Given this temperamental foundation, ongoing experience is always characterized by some blend of mood and emotion, and these arousal states provide the immediate intrapersonal context for most forms of learning (Damasio, 1999). In these terms, any internal representation of the external environment is at least partially colored by the quality of emotional arousal that was present during its formation.

Iconic Representation. Iconic representations have been described as sensory-affective and affective-motor schemas that become increasingly differentiated and integrated into higher order sensory-affective-motor scripts as a function of direct experience with the immediate environment (Case, 1991; Fischer & Bidell, 1998). Higher order sensory-affective-motor scripts have been conceptualized as motives (McClelland, 1985) and attachment styles (Bowlby, 1988; Case, 1995). Iconic representations, as schemas that have been "emotionally charged" with various blends of the core emotions, provide the basis for the gradual emergence of more complex states of emotional arousal (see Table 18.2).

Whereas the capacity for iconic representation is a species-typical characteristic, the content and structure of iconic representations vary considerably across individuals and developmental time based on experience. Although the iconic representational system as a whole is highly impressionable (i.e., with old and new content continuing to be elaborated), the domain-specific contents and structures encoded in this system (i.e., sensory-affective-motor schemas and scripts) are nevertheless relatively stable over time (Case, 1991, 1995; Rothbard & Shaver, 1994; Waters, Hamilton, & Weinfield, 2000). This has implications for school-aged learning and achievement as the iconic system, through repeated experiences early in development, settles into what appear to be relatively stable attachment styles and motive complexes that can promote or inhibit subsequent readiness and motivation to learn in school (McClelland, 1985). For example, two key features of iconic me-self development involve (a) physical and emotional bonding with caregivers and (b) the use of these bonds to support the exploration of novel features of the physical and social world (Case, 1995). The qualities of the schemas and scripts that result from these bonding experiences promote more or less security and trust, hence, more or less initiative and autonomy in exploration during the subsequent stage, with implications for competence development in the following stage (Erikson, 1950).

Symbolic Representation. In contrast to iconic representations, symbolic representations have been described as relatively enduring, valenced psychological structures

TABLE 18.2. A Descriptive Taxonomy of Positive and Negative Emotions

	Positive Emotions		Negative Emotions	
Types	(Approach)	Theme	(Avoidance)	Theme
Complex emotions				
Epistemic	Cognitive interest	Task relevance or challenge	Boredom	Lack of task relevance or challenge
Social	Belonging	Participation in social activity	Jealousy	Resenting third party for loss
	Empathy	Attunement to others' distress with goal of assistance	Envy	Wanting what someone else has
Self-conscious	Pride	Ego enhancement by taking credit for valued object or achievement	Shame	Ego depletion due to failure to live up to an ideal
	Hope	Yearning for better	Guilt	Transgression of moral imperative
Basic emotions				
Epistemic	Interest-surprise	Moderate novelty and deviations from expectancy	Fear	Imminent harm, large deviations from expectancy
	Excitement	Having impact	Disgust	Too close to or the taking in of unpleasant sensations, ideas, etc.
Social	Love	Participation in affection	Sadness	Irrevocable loss
	Joy-delight	Progress toward goals	Anger	Harm to me and mine
	Comfort-relief	Distress gone away	Distress	Lack of consistency with expectation

consisting of declarative (e.g., beliefs about things) and procedural (e.g., beliefs about how to do things) knowledge (primarily verbal in nature) that becomes increasingly differentiated into dimensions and domains and integrated into higher order belief systems as a function of both direct and vicarious experience over time (e.g., Damon & Hart, 1988; Harter, 1999). For example, beliefs in the existence of a thing become connected to beliefs about the attributes of that thing (Fishbein & Raven, 1962), which, together, form increasingly complex belief systems (Rokeach, 1968) such as values (i.e., beliefs about the goodness of things), goals (e.g., beliefs about desired end states), and plans (e.g., beliefs about the sequence of subgoals necessary to achieve desired end states). These beliefs, along with all of the previously discussed self/identity contents and processes, serve to energize and direct behavior.

Similar to iconic representations, the capacity to form symbolic representations is a species-typical characteristic; however, the content and structure of symbolic belief systems is even more variable across individuals and developmental time than iconic representations.

This relative plasticity allows for high degrees of flexibility in adapting to environmental conditions (e.g., allowing humans to quickly learn complex information and do so without having to rely on trial and error), yet beliefs also tend to be relatively stable over development time. Beliefs also differ from temperamental and iconic representations in that their content is more accessible to awareness. As a result of this accessibility, individuals can more easily describe this content verbally; hence, there is a massive body of empirical research documenting the content, structure, and functions of individuals' symbolic representations. For example, expectancy-value and goal theories have been used extensively by educational researchers to understand the beliefs students have about their current state (e.g., self-concept of ability), future state (e.g., educational goals), and learning environments (e.g., instructional style preferences) as well as how these beliefs relate to achievement behavior (Eccles et al., 1998). Finally, the symbolic me-self system also appears to provide a necessary but not sufficient condition (without the I) for experiencing the *self* as an object of awareness (Lewis & Brooks-Gunn, 1979).

For example, activating some of our relatively detailed symbolic knowledge about the self and the world can produce a complex phenomenological *stream of consciousness* reflecting, for example, me-in-relation-to-my-past-and-future. This phenomenological stream of conscious contents, in turn, can be used for a wide variety of self-regulatory purposes (e.g., making choices about goals or behavior).

The ability to represent the *self* as an object of awareness has implications for the continuing enrichment of emotional arousal states in the form of complex emotions (Harter, 1999). These higher order states of arousal represent a blending of core emotions with increasingly sophisticated iconic and symbolic representations of self and others. For instance, complex self-conscious emotions such as pride or shame are predicated on a linguistic I-self (i.e., symbolic self-awareness) that allows the causes of actions to be explicitly attributed to one's self (e.g., Lewis, 1998). As shown in Table 18.2, complex emotions that develop over time include those associated with anticipatory hopes for success and fears of failure; feelings of pride in a job well done when behaviors meet personal or social standards or feelings of shame and guilt when they do not; feelings of empathy and belonging; and so on. These complex emotions "color" (i.e., *affectively valence*) individuals' emerging beliefs about their goodness or badness and their behavioral competence or incompetence in various life domains. Thus, from about 18 months onward, affectively valenced symbolic representations are (a) coupled to prior iconic representations associated with relational security, mastery, and exploration, (b) form an important basis for subsequent symbolic representations associated with moral, school, and peer competence, and thus (c) play a fundamental role in energizing and directing moral, social, and achievement-related behavior outside and within schools.

Whereas many educational psychologists study the self-representations of students who are motivated to learn, it is students who display negative moods and emotions in the classroom who occupy the greatest amount of teachers' time and contribute to teachers' feelings of burden and lack of teaching efficacy (Bandura, 1993; Roeser & Midgley, 1997). The "reasons" for withdrawn, resistant, or aggressive behaviors in classrooms are not simply beliefs and schemas related to academic and peer incompetence (though these are important) but basic and complex negative emotions (e.g., anger, shame, guilt) and enduring negative moods (e.g., depression; Roeser, Eccles, & Strobel, 1998). Similarly, the complex emotions of boredom and interest, not only students' beliefs regarding the *utility* and *importance* of learning tasks, are key "reasons" for variations in their engagement in class-

room learning activities (Eccles, 1983). A complete understanding of self/identity processes in education necessarily includes how various emotions and moods (as much as competence- and task-related beliefs and goals), energize and direct behavior in learning settings (Becker & Luthar, 2002; Snow et al., 1996).

Phenomenological Representation. *Phenomenological representation* refers to all of the currently activated contents and processes, characteristic of the other levels just described coming together in the stream of consciousness. Phenomenological representation has been the object of empirical investigation since the advent of Wundt's 1879 experimental psychology laboratory. James' (1890) *Principles* and subsequent "radical empiricism" built nicely on this work by describing in detail the kinds of psychological contents that fill the "stream of consciousness" and the functions of the I-self within this stream. For example, regardless of the complexity of the information represented, this content is experienced holistically, at each moment, as a single *object of awareness*.

Although phenomenological representations arise from the contents of the other levels, they are not isomorphic with this information. Rather, they exist only as long as they remain activated in what has been described as "working memory." For example, conscious thoughts about our self/identity are constructed (implicitly and explicitly) from temperamental, iconic, and symbolic content (and their associated moods and emotions) and can be described in terms of the *subjective relationship* between the observing I-self and these activated contents. It is from the vantage point of the phenomenal center of awareness that the mechanistic automaticity of these other subsystems can, potentially, be volitionally regulated. Individuals can work from the phenomenal center with the contents of their conscious experience and thereby regulate behavioral choices, reorganize contents of the symbolic me-self, and regulate emotions, moods, and cognitive resources.

Basic Levels of School Context (BLOSC) Model

Just as the accumulated body of research and theory associated with the *psychological conceptualization of self/identity* implicates the basic levels of self presented in the BLOS framework, a body of research and theory associated with the *social and cultural dimensions of human development* implicates some basic levels of context (Peck, 2004, 2005). These levels are conceived of as a series of proximal and progressively more distal levels of sociocultural organization that inform and regulate individuals' development from birth to old age. These levels include families, peer groups, schools, neighborhoods, communities and broader cultural institutions, ideologies, and societal structures (Bronfenbrenner, 1993; Erikson, 1950; Sameroff, 1983). The sociocultural structures and processes that characterize these levels of context influence individuals' self/identity development by (a) assigning to individuals various consequential group labels, statuses, roles, and related opportunities; (b) providing appraisals and feedback that position individuals into particular kinds of selves/identities; and (c) affording or constraining pathways to competence, autonomous functioning, and social belonging and thereby patterns of participation and associated selves/identities. We focus here on how Basic Levels of School Contexts (BLOSC) can influence young people's self/identity development in relation to school learning and achievement.

The BLOSC model is a description of a set of concentric contexts that radiate inward from the macro-levels of society and culture, in which *schools* as institutions are embedded, to the micro-level of *classrooms,* in which teachers and students interact (Cole, 1996). These two levels correspond to those described in the BASIC model in Fig. 18.1: the level of social institutions (e.g., the macro-level) and the level of social interaction (e.g., the micro-level).

Macro Levels: Schools as Social Institutions and Organizations.

Schools are social institutions that exist within broader contextual, cultural, and societal structures. At the local level, these include neighborhoods, communities, and school districts—with their particular characteristics (e.g., social class), values, resources , and administrative procedures. At more distal levels, schools and their local contexts exist within state governance structures, cultural ideologies, and the problems and promises of the wider society (e.g., poverty, cultural diversity). These broad sociocultural structures and processes influence students indirectly through micro-settings such as the classroom. Schools also exist as social organizations that provide an administrative context and organizational culture (Sarason, 1990) within which the social-interactional spaces of the school (e.g., classrooms) are embedded. At the level of the school, administrative and organizational structures and processes relevant to social interactions in classrooms include the characteristics of school leaders and teaching staffs; the grade span, school size and sector; the school culture; and the school's level of resources and infrastructure. In general, organizational structures and processes have direct influences on teachers (and their teaching practices) and indirect influences on students' self/identity in classrooms through teachers and their pedagogical practice (see later discus-

sion). A significant body of research exists on how school-level factors directly and indirectly influence teachers and students, respectively (Lee, Bryk & Smith, 1993; Talbert & McLaughlin, 1999).

Micro Levels: Classrooms as Spaces of Social Interaction.

Classrooms and various noninstructional places such as the playground represent basic micro-settings in schools within which individuals act and interact (Bronfenbrenner, 1993). Studies at these micro-levels focus on teacher and peer characteristics (e.g., social class, race/ethnicity), and relationships and discourse patterns among and between teachers and students; teaching practices (e.g., mode of instruction, grouping arrangements, discipline style); academic tasks, resources, and artifacts (e.g., curriculum, availability of books, displays of student work), climate (e.g., norms, rules, roles, and goals), and the nature of the physical room (e.g., noise level). Noninstructional spaces such as bathrooms, hallways, lunch rooms, stages, sports fields, and geographical areas around the school are also important micro-settings that can influence dimensions of students' self/identity in school (Astor, Meyer, & Behre, 1999; Nasir, 2000).

The processes by which school micro-settings influence students' self/identity development are described in similar ways by theorists with differing perspectives (e.g., Bronfenbrenner, 1993; Erikson, 1950; Rogoff, 2003; Ryan & Deci, 2000; Vygotsky, 1978; Wenger, 1998). Social environments such as classrooms are catalysts for self/identity development insofar as these settings invite, permit, or inhibit movement from more peripheral to more central forms of participation in activities and responsibilities over time. The different forms of participation that contexts afford to different individuals provide the *stuff* (i.e., the experiences) from which they encode and elaborate their situation-specific self-representations and emotional experiences (e.g., competence-as-student, felt belonging in school, educational aspirations).

Bronfenbrenner (1993) differentiated "constructive" from "destructive" environments according to their developmental consequences. Constructive environments are characterized by people, practices, tasks, and resources that foster individuals' sense of safety and belonging, encourage their autonomous (but safe) exploration of the environment, scaffold their competence development, and invite them into increasingly more central forms of participation. Such environments foster the construction, elaboration, and internalization of positive context-related self-representations and values (Ryan & Deci, 2000). Destructive environments undermine individuals' sense of belonging and safety, overly restrict their autonomous exploration, forestall their competence development, and inhibit more central forms of participation.

Such environments foster the construction, elaboration, and internalization of apathetic, resistant, or oppositional context-related self-representations and values.

Examples of Macro and Micro-Level Influences on Students' Self/Identity

The Student Role. One example of how macro- and micro-level processes can combine to influence young people's school-related selves/identities concerns the nature of the student role as defined and communicated in American schools. American cultural ideologies in which competition, individualism, and success and failure are focal concerns (Spindler & Spindler, 1985); school policies and practices that promote competition and relative ability as the purpose of learning (Maehr & Midgley, 1996); and school-organizational structures that assign students to age-graded classrooms all combine to shape teachers' affordances of particular kinds of competence-related role identities in the classroom. Role identities can be defined as the meanings and expectations imparted to individuals by others who "position" them within a set of shared social roles and "counter-roles" (Stryker, 1980). Role identities promote forms of "interconnected uniqueness" in which one's statuses vis-à-vis others are salient (Stets & Burke, 2000). Higgins and Parsons-Eccles (1983) have described the student role in American schools as

a task-oriented role in which performance is systematically evaluated with regard to pre-set performance standards of excellence, normative progress, and acceptable style. As such, students will vary in their status within that role depending on their performance. Further, segregating the children into grades based primarily on age, as is done in most North American schools, focuses attention of both the teacher and the students on these status variations, making competition and social comparison probable events. (p. 21)

Based on this (tacit) definition of the student role at the macro-levels, teachers often create affordances and communicate expectations to students in the classroom (micro-level) that position them into these particular role identities—that of the successful student or that of a school failure (Goldman & McDermott, 1987). That students internalize these messages about their relative success or failure in school and encode such experiences into their me-selves is the inescapable conclusion of over 30 years of work in educational psychology (Covington, 2000). Creating classroom and school cultures that reframe student role identities in terms of cooperation, multiple intelligences, effort, and improvement toward attaining standards rather than in terms of competition and relative ability has been an important approach of

school reform movements whose aim is to achieve equity *and* excellence in learning outcomes (e.g., Brown, 1997; Maehr & Midgley, 1996).

Tacit definitions of the student role and academic success in American schools and classrooms can engender challenges not only for students who are not "the best" but also for students who belong to nonmainstream ethnic and cultural groups whose values, linguistic styles, and modes of behavior may not conform to those inherent in the institutionally-defined student role (Ogbu, 1995). The student role can be said to reflect what Markus and her colleagues have called an independent cultural frame / construal of self in which assertiveness, autonomy, competitiveness and personal distinction are defining features (Adams & Markus, 2004; Markus & Kitayama, 1991). Thus, individuals from cultures characterized by more interdependent cultural frames / construals of self in which modesty, conformity to in-group behavior, cooperation, and social harmony are defining features may have more difficulty navigating the pathways to success as instantiated in the student role in American schools (Davidson & Phelan, 1999).

Resources and Qualified Teachers. A second example of how macro- and micro-level structures and processes in school can affect young peoples' school-related selves/identities can be seen in the complex chains of relationships between community/school resources, the characteristics of teaching staffs and student populations, and classroom teaching practices. Low-income schools have disproportionately low numbers of well-qualified teachers compared to affluent schools often because school leaders do not have the resources to attract and hire qualified teachers (Evans, 2004). In addition to lower qualifications in their content areas, teachers in low-income schools are more likely to exercise strong control over students and limit their use of constructivist teaching practices in part because they believe poor children lack the inner control necessary to play a responsible role in their own learning (Solomon, Battistich, & Hom, 1996). Furthermore, because a substantial minority of low-income students often arrive to school with social-emotional and behavioral problems that compromise their readiness to learn (Adelman & Taylor, 1998), their teachers are more likely to experience feelings of burden in relation to their students' emotional needs (Roeser & Midgley, 1997); to feel a need to distance themselves from their students emotionally (Solomon et al., 1996); and to see themselves as less efficacious as a teacher (Bandura, 1993). These environments are not conducive to the success of teachers or their students. Given the lack of opportunities for student initiative, for competence development in terms of good teaching, and for belonging in terms of supportive classroom relationships, an alarmingly high percentage of students in such schools develop and internalize an image of themselves as failures and drop-out of school (Fine, 1991).

Beyond the Classroom. Other studies have documented how young people who are not very successful in school can nonetheless acquire complex knowledge and skills that engender competence, belonging, and participation in prosocial activities outside of the classroom (Nasir, 2000) and outside of school altogether (McLaughlin, Irby, & Langman, 1994; Rose, 2004). This work not only reveals how schools can operate as destructive settings for certain students, but also gives indications of what more motivating activity structures might look like. For example, in settings such as sports, work, and community-based organizations, structured apprenticeships and rewarding collaborative relationships afford young people experiences of competence, belonging, and productive forms of participation. Such experiences provide young people the opportunity to elaborate existing and construct new me-self representations that are positive (Lave & Wenger, 1991; Nasir & Saxe, 2003).

Summary of the BASIC Model

The BASIC model describes multiple levels within the person (BLOS) and the social and physical environments surrounding schools (BLOSC) that are the bases for understanding self/identity-in-context. The BASIC model highlights how self/identity is defined differently by researchers working from different disciplinary perspectives. There are fundamental and oft-neglected distinctions between definitions of self/identity as (a) individuals' iconic, symbolic, and phenomenological representations of phenomena such as social group memberships and roles (e.g., Case, 1991); (b) the negotiation of social and physical affordances through behavioral enactments (e.g., Moje, 2004) and patterns of participation (e.g., Lave & Wenger, 1991); or (c) social categories, statuses, or roles assigned to individuals by macro-level social structures and institutions (e.g., Stryker, 1980). No one type of self/identity definition is more accurate or appropriate than the others; each refers to a distinct part of the multilevel BASIC system. Unfortunately, researchers from diverse disciplinary perspectives have been using both the same words to describe different parts (a jingle fallacy) and different words to describe the same parts (a jangle fallacy) of this BASIC system. Although we have made no serious attempt here to resolve this terminological confusion, we have outlined several conceptual frameworks that can be put to work towards this end. In

the final two sections, we describe the implications of the BASIC, BLOS, and BLOSC heuristic models for educational research and practice.

IMPLICATIONS FOR EDUCATIONAL RESEARCH

Early Attachment Relations and Readiness to Learn in School

The BASIC perspective provides a means of understanding how early parent–child relationships, their representation as relational *schemas* within the iconic system, and related dimensions of I-self functioning can influence a child's "readiness to learn." For instance, Sroufe, Fox, and Pancake (1983) reported that children who were classified as having avoidant and resistant attachment relationships with parents were subsequently found to be highly dependent on preschool teachers for physical contact, guidance, discipline, and security. In contrast, children classified as securely attached were less dependent on teachers and sought interpersonal attention in age-appropriate and positive ways. The authors concluded that the roots of overdependence in preschool lie in the quality of the early infant–caregiver relationship.

Teo, Carlson, Mathieu, Egeland, and Sroufe (1996) found that the quality of children's attachments with primary caregivers and movement toward autonomous self-regulation during the first 3 years of life correlated positively with the quality of their social competence (as rated by teachers) and their standardized test achievement in reading and math during the 1st, 3rd, 6th, and 11th grades. Using this same sample, Jimerson, Egeland, Sroufe and Carlson (2000) showed that these same factors were related to reduced rates of school dropout over a decade later. They concluded that the quality of children's psychosocial development prior to school entry was a major factor in predicting academic success.

Similar to these studies, research on maltreated children (i.e., those who have been physically or sexually abused and/or neglected) has revealed the importance of parenting styles and early attachment relationships for self-development and subsequent school adaptation and achievement (see Cicchetti, Toth, & Hennessey, 1993; Harter, 1999). Maltreated children tend to have parents who are authoritarian (Baumrind, 1968). Such parents hold high expectations for their children without providing them with the requisite level of autonomy support and unconditional love that scaffolds the child's ability to meet parental expectations. The probable consequences of this parenting style are that infants and toddlers learn that they cannot rely on their caregivers to provide the necessary social support and emotional heightening and dampening necessary to build self-confidence and cope with anxiety during early exploratory behaviors (Case, 1995). These "style" factors alone can promote insecure attachment styles and a lack of initiative that can subsequently develop into a child's "insecure readiness to learn" during pre- and primary school (Cicchetti et al., 1993). The addition of physical abuse and neglect eventuates in maltreated children being (a) overly concerned with relational security and threats to their physical well-being and (b) fearful of exploration and mastery at home and then in school. Physically abused children, for instance, tend to show aggressive classroom behavior and are retained and referred to special education at rates higher than other children. Sexually abused children tend to show social isolation or "clinginess," marked by passivity or anxiety, and an inability to internalize rules of conduct at school. Neglected children tend to show the poorest performance on cognitive tests and the highest rates of retention and special education referrals. Characteristic emotions and behaviors of these children include high levels of anxiety and inattention, clinginess, a general lack of empathy in social relationships at school, and a lack of initiative in approaching schoolwork (Erickson, Egeland, & Pianta, 1989).

The implication of these studies is that the early and ongoing quality of parent–child relationships are carried into elementary school learning situations via children's relational schemas, exploration-related schemas (e.g., felt competence, mastery orientations), and collaborative problem-solving skills developed within these relationships (Erikson, 1950; Sroufe, 1996). Under average-expectable conditions, parents provide opportunities conducive to infants' development of secure attachments and the construction of relational self-schemas imbued with a sense of love. Secure attachment schemas and the ongoing presence of a supportive caregiver during early exploratory behavior provides the young child with both psychological (secure attachment schema) and social (actual parental support) buffers against the inevitable fears that occur during exploration. The result is the construction of iconic schemas associated with interest in the world, the felt experience that exploration and mastery have social worth, and competence in mastering physical and social tasks (Case, 1991; Deci & Ryan, 1985; Erikson, 1950). In contrast, in childrearing situations of abuse and neglect, the relational supports for security and exploratory behavior are absent interpersonally and psychologically. In such situations, the child is more likely to develop relational schemas imbued with emotions of anger, sadness, and distress. In these ways, ongoing relational difficulties, maladaptive self-schemas, and an (I-self) attentional focus on threats all serve to inhibit exploratory behavior and the development of initiative (Erickson

et al., 1989; Sroufe et al., 1983; Harter, 1999). Ongoing abuse and neglect can lead to emerging symbolic beliefs of "moral badness" in the next stage (Harter, 1999), and all of these factors together provide the basis for subsequent forms of academic helplessness, social difficulties, and emotional-behavioral problems during the elementary school period (Roeser & Eccles, 2000). Of course, the possibility of resilience among maltreated children (e.g., in terms of academic readiness and success) is important to acknowledge given the importance of *discontinuities,* as well as *continuities,* in development (Kagan, 1996).

The Study of Educational Resilience

Thus, another research topic worthy of more attention is that of *educational resilience* and the self and social contextual factors that promote it. We define *educational resilience* as *better than expected* classroom participation and learning, school achievement, and educational attainments across development among children and adolescents who, based on their pattern of psychological and social risk conditions, are more likely to disengage from, fail at, and/or drop out of school before graduation. The focus of resilience research is on documenting the psychological, family, school, peer, and neighborhood factors that (a) compensate or buffer vulnerable (risk-exposed) children and adolescents from academic failure and (b) promote the academic success of these individuals despite the odds. Factors that forecast difficulties and failure in school include (a) a psychological profile marked by frequent and severe feelings of anxiety, depression, fear, or anger (Kessler, Foster, Saunders & Stang, 1995); (b) a life situation marked by the *presence* of multiple physical, psychosocial, and socioeconomic risk factors including parental abuse and neglect (Evans, 2004); and (c) a life situation marked by the *absence* of average expectable opportunities for cultivating mastery motivation, social and problem-solving skills, and well-being (Roeser & Peck, 2003; Sameroff, Seifer, & Bartko, 1997).

Although it is often true that as risk loads increase, young people's ability to extend themselves in learning activities in school is diminished with predictable declines in their achievement and increases in their absences and acts of misconduct (Gutman, Sameroff, & Eccles, 2003), it is not always true. As just one example, using pattern-centered prodigal analyses, Roeser and Peck (2003) examined unexpected processes of academic resilience (defined as enrollment in college after completion of high school) among young people who in early and middle adolescence faced significant psychological and environmental risks in their families and schools. They found that participation in positive extracurricular activities was a key factor associated with vulnerable youths' manifestation of academic resilience despite an otherwise pervasive portrait of psychological and contextual risks. These findings and others highlight how academic resilience can emerge from nonschool environments (McLaughlin et al., 1994).

The study of educational resilience is of particular relevance in relation to *specific* groups of academically successful ethnic minority students (e.g., African-, Mexican-, and Native Americans; Ogbu, 1995) and immigrant students (e.g., those from Mexico and Central America; Portes & Rumbaut, 2001) who face an accumulation of risk conditions that members of the majority culture and members of other ethnic minority and immigrant groups do not. These include impoverished living conditions, failing schools, exposure to violence and racial prejudice, a scarcity of high-achieving adult role models in their community and group, and the task of managing ethnic identities in mainstream institutions such as school (Graham, Taylor, & Hudley, 1998; Ogbu, 1995; Spencer & Markstrom-Adams, 1990). Perhaps the most pernicious risk factor facing members of these ethnic groups (and others) in relation to their educational prospects is their experience of racial discrimination and the impugning of their intellectual capacity to be successful in school (Steele, 1997). For example, Wong, Eccles, and Sameroff (2003) found that perceived discrimination perpetrated by teachers, school staff, and classmates at middle school was associated with declines in African-American adolescents' academic self-concept and grades and increases in their psychological distress across middle school. Other studies have corroborated the negative correlation of perceived discrimination and the mental health of immigrant high school students (Portes and Rumbaut, 2001) and Puerto Rican middle school students (Szalacha et al., 2003). It is the stressful and often emotionally distressing consequences of dealing with discriminatory experiences within and beyond the school context that makes the study of academic success among members of these groups the study of *educational resilience*.

From a BASIC perspective, we hypothesize that positive social relationships and opportunities to learn in just one consequential life context are able to buffer or compensate for other risk conditions by providing an "average expectable environment" that meets basic self needs for competence, autonomy, and social relationships (Ryan & Deci, 2000). These environments may promote the construction of positive relational and mastery-related self-schemas that counterbalance other negative self-schemas or ascribed identities. For example, African-American adolescents whose parents cultivate their sense of ethnic group membership and teach them strategies for dealing with racial discrimination are more resilient emotionally

when exposed to racism than youth who lack these family supports (Eccles, 2004; Wong et al., 2003). Such studies of academic resilience (and the self and social processes that underlie and promote it) represent an important direction for future research, especially with regard to those ethnic minority youth who experience multiple life stressors yet nonetheless succeed in school.

Patterns of School Motivation and Educational Lifepaths

Elsewhere we have discussed the utility of a holistic, person-in-context view of learning, achievement, and educational attainments across development (Roeser & Galloway, 2002; Roeser & Peck, 2003). Such a perspective is predicated on the capacity for self-organization, defined here in relation to two organizing principles of the self (Case, 1991; Deci & Ryan, 1985; Fischer & Bidell, 1998). These include differentiation, in which novel experiences result in the construction of iconic and symbolic representations that are used to guide behavior, and integration, in which such representations are hierarchically organized into more complex, unified forms. These self-organizing tendencies form a theoretical justification for holistic, pattern-centered approaches to studying self/identity processes in education. Specifically, they highlight a need to examine how variations in learning and achievement are associated with differing organized patterns of psychological contents and processes that get activated in particular kinds of achievement situations for different individuals (Snow et al., 1996).

Tracing the educational consequences of such situated *patterns* of self/identity processes in school achievement across time results in the study of *educational lifepaths*. A basic assumption behind this approach is that, for any particular educational outcome, there exists a diverse yet finite set of patterns of self/identity contents and processes that lead to that outcome—a concept called *equifinality* (to the same outcome, many paths). A second assumption is that, for any particular self/identity content or process among a population of individuals within an achievement situation, there exists a diverse yet finite set of other self/identity contents and processes that interact with the first and thereby condition its relation to educational outcomes. This concept is called *multifinality* (from the same starting point, many outcomes; Richters, 1998).

The existence of equifinality in relation to patterns of school motivation and achievement has been demonstrated in a series of studies by Dweck (1999) and others (Haydel & Roeser, 2002; Roeser, Strobel, & Quihuis, 2002). Two different profiles of motivational goals and beliefs associated with positive engagement and achievement among students in elementary, middle, and high school classrooms have been identified. The first is the *ego-oriented pattern of motivation*. This pattern characterizes children who orient towards performance goals in achievement situations, have high self-confidence in their academic ability, and believe that their intelligence is fixed.[3] The second is the *mastery-oriented pattern*, which characterizes children who orient towards mastery goals and view their intelligence as malleable.

Two patterns have also been identified in relation to poor academic persistence and achievement—each associated with the *helpless pattern* (Dweck, 1986). The helpless pattern characterizes children who orient towards performance goals in achievement situations, have low perceived self-confidence in their academic ability, and believe that their intelligence is fixed. Two variations of the "helpless" pattern have been documented among elementary and middle school students (Roeser, Strobel, et al., 2002). Some students manifest a form of academic helplessness coupled with internalizing distress in the form of sadness, anxiety, and withdrawn classroom behavior; others manifest a form of academic helplessness coupled with externalizing distress in the form of anger, aggression, and disruptive classroom behavior. Collectively, these studies illustrate the concept of equifinality by documenting two patterns associated with positive school achievement, and two patterns associated with poor achievement. These two sets of patterns can be viewed as variations on what Erikson (1950) called *industry* and *inferiority*, and they probabilistically forecast groups of students moving along educational lifepaths towards high school graduation and school withdrawal prior to graduation, respectively (Ollendick, Greene, Weist, & Oswald, 1990).

The concept of *multifinality* was exemplified in a recent debate among goal theorists concerning the adaptive versus maladaptive educational consequences of students' pursuit of performance approach goals (in which the focus is on demonstrating superior ability relative to others; Harackiewicz et al., 2002; Midgley, Kaplan, & Middleton 2001). From a pattern-centered perspective, understanding the adaptive versus maladaptive nature of performance–approach goals necessitates attention to the conditionalities between individuals' pursuit of such goals and (a) their developmental stage and social statuses, (b) the patterning of these goals with other iconic and symbolic representations within the person,

and (c) the demands and affordances of the person's learning environment.

For example, evidence suggests that for early adolescents who are in a stage of heightened self-consciousness (Midgley, 1993), and for those who are members of ethnic or racial groups that are targeted by stereotypes of intellectual inferiority (Aronson & Steele, 2004), the pursuit of performance goals may not be adaptive in terms of performance. By making relative ability salient to the individual, such goal pursuits can activate anxiety, debilitating self-beliefs, and/or concerns about stereotype confirmation that impair performance (Aronson & Steele, 2004; Roeser & Rodriguez, 2004). Age and race/ethnicity condition the relation of performance–approach goals to academic performance. Second, as research on academic helplessness shows, performance–approach goals are not adaptive if the individuals pursuing them also have low confidence in their ability and a belief that their intelligence is fixed (Dweck, 1986) or if their pursuit of such goals is based upon the iconic motive called fear of failure (Elliot, 1997). Finally, it appears that for (a) primary and secondary students with high confidence in their abilities (Dweck, 1999; Haydel & Roeser, 2002; Roeser, Stroebel, et al., 2002); (b) secondary school students who pursue both performance approach and mastery goals simultaneously (Pintrich, 2000); (c) college students with a strong iconic need for achievement (Elliot & Thrash, 2001); and (d) college students who are attending selective universities in which the learning environment presses for relative ability and social comparison (Harackiewicz et al., 2002), the pursuit of such goals is in fact associated with better achievement. These examples illustrate the phenomenon of multifinality: From a single starting variable (e.g., performance goals), diverse educational outcomes can result depending upon the patterning of that variable with other self representations and dimensions of the social context.

Advancing research on the diversity of motivational patterns associated with promising and problematic educational lifepaths among different students in different kinds of learning environments seems particularly important at this juncture in history. The school-aged population (ages 5–18 years) in the United States consists of about 54 million individuals and is as large and ethnically diverse as it has ever been. As of 2002, approximately 40 percent of the entire school-aged population were members of an ethnic group other than European-American (U.S. Department of Education, 2002), and about 20 percent were "New Americans"

---

[3]Although many goal theorists now differentiate the pursuit of performance approach and avoidance goals, there are critiques of this differentiation (see Roeser, 2004). Furthermore, the studies by Roeser and colleagues referenced here show that middle and high school students characterized by either an ego-oriented or helpless pattern, more so than those characterized by a mastery-oriented pattern, tend to report orienting toward *both* performance approach and avoidance goals as Dweck (1986) originally proposed.

growing up in immigrant families (Suarez-Orozco & Saurez-Orozco, 2001).

Thus, another application of the concept of equifinality relates to the diverse kinds of self-processes that do and do not motivate achievement among members of different cultural and ethnic groups (Maehr & Braskamp, 1986). Research has begun to document, for example, how students from immigrant backgrounds are sometimes motivated by obligations to parents to do well in school given their parents' sacrifices in emigrating to the United States (Fuligni & Tseng, 1999; Roeser & Rodriquez, 2004). Instrumental goals such as getting into a good college, getting a good job, and avoiding poverty may also be differentially important for motivating achievement among students from immigrant/nonimmigrant and poor/wealthy backgrounds (Roeser & Rodriquez, 2004).

A second application of the patterns and pathways concepts relates to how members of immigrant and ethnic minority groups manage their ethnic identities in relation to schooling and achievement. Beginning in adolescence, ethnic minority youth often have to find ways to navigate between different social worlds because their ethnic-based identities at home and with friends are in some ways different from their mainstream identities in institutions such as school (Davidson & Phelan, 1999; Tatum, 1997). Several authors have described the different ways that youth do this as well as the kinds of identity conflicts that can complicate such efforts, perhaps especially for males (Cross, 1991; Fordham, 1988; Fordham & Ogbu, 1986; Graham et al., 1998; Lafromboise, Coleman, & Gerton, 1993; Nasir & Saxe, 2003; Phinney & Devich-Navarro, 1997). Specifically, individuals can (a) reject or deemphasize their ethnicity/culture and assimilate to the mainstream culture (assimilation or racelessness); (b) reject or deemphasize mainstream culture and identify with their own ethnicity/culture (separation or opposition); (c) reject both (marginalization or alienation); or (d) develop a bicultural outlook in which both ethnic-cultural and mainstream identities are part of their overall self (biculturalism or code switching). Some research has documented positive educational and mental health outcomes among those adopting a bicultural approach and the significant risks associated with marginalization (Phinney & Devich-Navarro, 1997), whereas evidence regarding the opposition status remains controversial (see Portes & Rumbaut, 2001; Wigfield, Eccles, Schiefele, Roeser, & Davis-Kean, in press).

From a BASIC perspective, both the increasing diversity of the school-aged population and an understanding of the role of organization in human learning and development highlight the need for complementing variable-centered approaches to studying self and identity processes in learning and achievement with pattern-centered

approaches. Such methods are useful for addressing issues of equifinality and multifinality in relation to educational lifepaths. Pattern-centered methodologies are also useful if scholars wish to move beyond group comparisons based on social categories that are assumed to be static features of individuals over time (e.g., race) toward group comparisons based on theoretically derived self/identity contents and processes that are relevant to achievement in particular kinds of contexts. Ascribed demographic characteristics of individuals can then be examined in relation to the composition of process-measure derived subgroups (e.g., Roeser & Peck, 2003).

Hierarchical Models of Achievement Motivation

Elliot and his colleagues have integrated "classic" models of achievement motivation—in which the need for achievement and fear of failure were of focal concern (Atkinson, 1957; McClelland, 1985; Murray, 1938)—with "contemporary" goal theory approaches to motivation, in which symbolic achievement-related goals (e.g., mastery, demonstration of superior competence, and avoidance of demonstrating inferior competence) are of central concern (Elliot, 1997; Elliot & Church, 1997). According to Elliot & Thrash (2001), "achievement goals are viewed as the concrete aims through which individuals pursue their more abstract desires, concerns, needs, and motives (i.e., reasons)" (p. 147). They proposed a variety of needs as providing the energy for the pursuit of such goals, including the need for achievement and the fear of failure, self-esteem and self-validation needs, and the need for affiliation and the fear of rejection. Consistent with McClelland's (1985) theory, they argued that intrapsychic or environmental stimuli activate "underlying reasons" (i.e., iconic motives) that then activate goals that direct this energy toward particular behaviors. Although viewed as independent constructs, Elliot and Thrash (2001) nonetheless see needs and goals as integrated into what they call "goal complexes" that regulate achievement behavior.

From a BASIC perspective, the dual motivational (me-self) systems these authors implicate suggest that a "goal complex" is a configuration of domain-relevant (e.g., social, achievement-related) iconic and symbolic content that serves motivational and regulatory functions (Thrash & Elliot, 2001). There is no absolute separation of the energizing and directive functions between *needs* and *goals*, across levels, however. Iconic content, as Elliot and Church (1997) note, energize goal pursuits *and* provide broad direction to behavior. These energizing and directive tendencies are rooted in the basic emotions that give iconic motives their "charge" (McClelland, 1985).

Similarly, goals not only direct iconic content toward specific ends, but they are represented psychologically in cognitive-affective patterns related to certain contexts and experiences (e.g., Ford, 1992; Mischel & Shoda, 1995). One view of such patterns is that they have energy derived from complex emotions (e.g., valences) that also energize behavior independent of, and sometimes in direct conflict with, that of motives (see Nucci, 2001). For example, consider a prototypic moral situation where an aroused basic motive to approach a desired end (e.g., take the tasty candy) is overridden by an aroused social value to approach a different desired end (e.g., be an honest person).

Elliot and colleagues have demonstrated that the differentiation of these two motivational systems allows researchers to address complex motivational dynamics. For example, Thrash & Elliot (2002) examined the multimethod correlations of (a) self-attributed (survey-based) measures of nAch and fear of failure; (b) TAT (projective) measures of nAch and fear of failure; and (c) self-reported achievement goals. The two methods of assessing these constructs yielded moderate, positive correlations for both nAch ($r = 0.22$) and fear of failure ($r = 0.29$), comporting with the results of two meta-analyses (Spangler, 1992). Furthermore, replicating an earlier study (Elliot & McGregor, 1999), they found that students' pursuit of performance–approach goals was positively associated with the survey and TAT measures of nAch and fear of failure their pursuit of mastery goals was positively associated with survey and TAT measures of nAch, and their pursuit of performance–avoidance goals was positively associated with the survey and TAT measures of fear of failure. These findings, generated with variable-centered analyses, indicate summative iconic and symbolic forms of motivation and reflect "average" motivational dynamics *across* all individuals in their sample.

Future studies could complement these analyses with pattern-centered analyses aimed at distinguishing individuals who show different goal complexes (e.g., Thrash & Elliot, 2002). For instance, in the findings discussed earlier, pattern-centered analyses could be used to differentiate two different subgroups of performance-oriented individuals—those who try to outperform others in the college classroom because of fears of failure and those who pursue such goals out of a need for achievement. Both patterns may be associated with the same level of achievement, but the first one seems more fragile and perhaps reflects a hypercompetitive style that has hidden mental health costs, whereas the latter seems more like a healthy form of competitive striving (see Roeser, 2004). More importantly, pattern-centered analyses could also reveal "off-diagonal" individuals—those whose goal complexes are simply not captured by the average statis-

tical trends. What might be learned, for example, from individuals who are characterized by a goal complex in which strong iconic fears of failure are coupled with the pursuit of mastery goals in the classroom? The study of such off-diagonal cases is at the heart of studies of resilience in education and human development more generally.

The hierarchical model of motivation is one of the few contemporary research traditions that is actively addressing education-relevant constructs across the levels described in the BASIC framework. This model not only provides a way of modeling motivational dynamics of the person but of the person-in-context. For instance, consider that we know that (a) activated (iconic) fear of failure predicts the pursuit of (symbolic) performance–avoidance goals (Elliot, 1997); (b) performance–avoidance goals in turn are associated with the avoidance of help seeking, especially in classrooms where students perceive the teacher as nonsupportive (e.g., Ryan, Pintrich, & Midgley, 2001); and (c) such goals are also associated with self-handicapping strategies as a means of protecting self-worth against failure, especially in classrooms that students perceive as emphasizing social comparison and competition (e.g., Urdan, Midgley, & Anderman, 1998). These findings, in the aggregate, provide insight into levers for change at the classroom level of analysis. Specifically, they suggest that by increasing social support and deemphasizing competition in classrooms, educators may be able to reduce motivational problems associated with fears of failure (Midgley, 1993).

Stereotype Threat

Whereas hierarchical models of motivation have generally focused on summative motivational dynamics, conflictual motivational dynamics, as in the case of stereotype threat, are also important to understand (Aronson & Steele, 2005; Steele, 1997). Stereotype threat effects refer to performance decrements in particular achievement situations among academically committed students who are members of groups that are targeted with stereotypes of intellectual inferiority. These effects involve tacit features of achievement situations (e.g., those where race is made salient and/or those that emphasize relative ability/social comparison) that *implicitly* (below the level of phenomenal awareness) activate certain psychological contents and processes that lead to performance decrements. Such contents include physiological arousal (e.g., nonverbal anxiety), symbolic representations (e.g., of stereotypes, group membership identities, and of oneself confirming a negative self-relevant stereotype), and iconic representations (e.g., fears of failure).

The fact that certain achievement situations activate not only relevant aptitude resources for individuals who are the targets of competence-related stereotypes but additional self contents may produce a "cognitive load" that leads to performance decrements ("cognitive load explanation"). From a BASIC perspective, however, it is the fact that the activated self-contents across levels represent conflicting motivational energies for the individual under a threat condition that is most significant. On the one hand, there is activated approach motivation associated with the individuals' conscious (explicit) symbolic goal to do well and the related affective valence of this goal. On the other hand, there is the activated avoidance motivation associated with their nonconscious (implicit) temperamental (physiological stress), iconic (fear of failure), and symbolic representations (i.e., about confirming a negative stereotype, with the affective valence of these beliefs). Unlike the summative motivational dynamics described earlier, these activated contents motivate in opposite (conflicted) ways and thereby reduce the total resources available for learning ("motivational conflict explanation"). Finally, activated me-self contents with conflicting valences can be distracting and undermine performance if these contents alternate in I-self awareness ("divided attention explanation"). Intervention research has shown that (a) inculcating a belief in the malleability of intelligence and (b) raising individuals' awareness about the existence of stereotype threat reduces such effects (Aronson & Steele, 2004). From a BASIC perspective, these interventions work because they address the underlying self-conflict by (a) providing individuals with new me-self content that can be activated in relevant achievement situations and thereby produce summative rather than conflictual motivational inputs, and (b) raising this conflict to the level of I-self awareness such that individuals can recognize and choicefully cope with it (see later discussion).

In sum, we view research that addresses the dynamic relations between iconic and symbolic me-self contents, and between implicit and explicit forms of symbolic representation *in context* as an exciting new area of research. We believe this work can reveal how motivational dynamics within and across different levels of self summate, conflict, or operate independently. In our view, this work will prove most fruitful if it attends to how different configurations of self-processes relate to the educational outcomes of particular students (e.g., helpless or mastery-oriented), in particular settings (elementary, secondary, postsecondary), with respect to particular kinds of outcomes (e.g., choice, performance, mental health) using both variable and pattern-centered analytic approaches (see Roeser & Peck, 2003).

The "Problem" of Student Motivation to Learn: Dewey's "Three Evils"

The BASIC framework also provides a unique perspective on the educational "problem" of motivating students to learn in school—one that is commensurate with Dewey's (1902) classic essay, *The Child and the Curriculum*, in which he addressed this and related educational problems. Dewey advocated a view of pedagogy that synthesized two apparently contradictory views of education. The first view placed the curriculum, decided on by adults, at the center of pedagogy and efforts to motivate students (a curriculum-centered view). The second placed children and their developmental interests at the center (a child-centered view). Dewey exhorted educators to locate what they were trying to teach within the capacities, interests, and everyday experiences of students at different ages (Phillips, 1998). He called this pedagogical process by which teachers brought the *logical* ordering of the subject matters (e.g., science, history) into the *psychological* world of the developing child as the *psychologizing of the curriculum* and viewed this as the solution to the *problem* of students' motivation to learn in school.

Unfortunately, Dewey (1902) did not see educators psychologizing the curriculum in his time, creating what he described as the "three evils of modern schooling." The first evil was the failure of educators to teach the curriculum in a way that took into account children's emotional and relational experiences of self and world: "In the first place, the lack of any organic connection with what the child has already seen and felt and loved makes the material purely formal and symbolic" (p. 24). This eventuated in a second evil—the undermining of students' intrinsic motivation to learn in school:

> The second evil in this external presentation is lack of motivation.... When the subject-matter has been psychologized, that is, viewed as an outgrowth of present tendencies and activities (of the child), it is easy to locate in the present some obstacle, intellectual, practical, or ethical, which can be handled more adequately if the truth in question be mastered. This need supplies motive for the learning. An end which is the child's own carries him [*sic*] on to possess the means of its accomplishment. But when material is directly supplied in the form of a lesson to be learned as a lesson, the connecting links of need and aim are conspicuous for their absence. (p. 25)

The inevitable outcome of educators' failure to psychologize the curriculum and thereby cultivate students' intrinsic motivation to learn was a resort to the use of external pressures and rewards to supply the need and aim (e.g., the extrinsic motivation) for learning: "The externally presented material, conceived and generated in standpoints and attitudes remote from the child, and developed in motives alien to him [sic], has no such place of its own [in the life of the child]. Hence the recourse to adventitious leverage to push it in, to factitious drill to drive it in, to artificial bribe to lure it in" (p. 27).

Research on students' school motivation, and on the motivational practices used by elementary and secondary school teachers, provides evidence that these "evils" are still present today. Cross-sectional and longitudinal studies in Europe and the United States have documented linear declines from elementary through high school in school-aged students' intrinsic motivation to learn (conceived of variously as curiosity, preference for challenge, independent attempts at mastery, goal of mastery, and interest or valuing of specific subject matter; see Eccles et al., 1998). Coupled with these declines, there is a general increase in students' orientations toward extrinsic goals (e.g., getting good grades and trying to outperforming others) as they progress through school (Anderman & Anderman, 1999).

Such changes in students' school motivation over time are related to changes in context factors (Wigfield et al., in press). Declines in intrinsic motivation to learn, for instance, are associated with a lack of curricular meaningfulness and declining social-emotional bonds between teachers and students as students grow older and move into bigger schools (Eccles & Roeser, 1999). At the same time, shifts toward more extrinsic motivational orientations are paralleled by educators' increasing use of extrinsic motivational strategies as students progress from elementary to secondary school (Roeser, Marachi, & Gehlbach, 2002).

From a BASIC perspective, and consistent with Dewey's analysis, it appears that schools continue to create the problem of student motivation. They do this by failing to provide students with opportunities for challenging and authentic work and close relationships with teachers that would engage students' iconic motives for learning. Failing to do this, educators resort to motivational practices that stress symbolic grades and outperforming others, despite the fact that such practices can provide only weak (extrinsic) symbolic motives "alien to the child" for learning. Research on best practices in education, however, shows that this need not be the case. In schools that provide opportunities for students and teachers to get to know one another, and for students to cooperate with each other around projects that connect their learning to meaningful life issues, intrinsic motivation and learning are enhanced for students of all races and socioeconomic classes (NRC, 2000; Slavin & Fashola, 1998). Furthermore, affordances for multicultural curricula, flexible approaches to students' use of different languages and di-

alects, and supportive teacher–student relationships appear to be particularly important for enhancing the intrinsic motivation, felt belonging, learning, and achievement of immigrant and ethnic minority group members (especially those who come from groups targeted with stereotypes of intellectual inferiority; Lee, 1995; Lucas, Henze, & Donato, 1990; Martin, 2000).

IMPLICATIONS FOR EDUCATIONAL PRACTICE

Interventions Along the Educational Life Course

Normative life changes, particularly school transitions, are associated with changes in young people's self-representations and feelings of self-worth. This is due, in part, to changes in the nature of the academic and social environment and related changes in the roles and responsibilities that young people encounter as they make these transitions (cf. Eccles & Roeser, 1999). Transition programs assist students' self-development and related motivation to learn by helping them (re)achieve a sense of trust, initiative, and competence in their new school environments. These factors, in turn, make it possible for them to meet new demands and successfully adopt new social roles. Such programs are especially important for students who are immigrants or who are vulnerable to educational failure due to poverty or other adverse life conditions (Jason, Danner, & Kurasaki, 1993; Olsen, 1997; Slavin & Fashola, 1998).

Restoring Relationships to the Heart of Learning

The power of good relationships for enhancing students' motivation, learning, and well-being seems hard to overestimate (e.g., Becker & Luthar, 2002). Supportive relationships between teachers and students are the crucible in which values, information, and feedback are transmitted and, thereby, the internalization of healthy images of self and principled forms of knowledge are facilitated. Many of the most important innovations in educational practices today have emphasized the importance of relationships for reinvigorating education and reengaging disenfranchised students (Brown, 1997; Commission for At-Risk Children, 2003; Slavin & Fashola, 1998). This consensus makes sense given our explication of self/identity processes in this chapter. A sense of belonging and membership in a learning community is an important precursor to extending oneself in learning, perhaps especially for young people who must traverse significant ethnic and racial, socioeconomic, and sociolinguistic borders to feel fully part of a school in which middle-class, majority cultural norms often predominate (Becker & Luthar, 2002; Davidson & Phelan, 1999; Lucas et al., 1990).

Factors that enable schools to become caring communities in which students experience a sense of belonging include the creation of smaller organizational units within large schools (e.g., schools-within-schools) and increases in the personalization of instruction through various means (e.g., use of homerooms, advisory periods, team-teaching; Midgley, 1993). Equally important are practices that directly engage students in cooperative and community-building activities at school. These include the use of cooperative learning techniques in classrooms, classroom management strategies that rely on student participation in norm setting and decision making, teaching of conflict resolution skills, and curricula that focus students on themes of care. Research and intervention studies have shown that such practices foster a "community of care" that positively influences students' self-understanding, beliefs and feelings, and in-school behavior (Greenberg, Kusche, Cook, & Quamma, 1995; Schaps, 2003).

The Enlightened Educator

Another implication for educational practice that arises from the BLOS framework is that the truly enlightened educator is one who relates to students by being wholly present in the classroom and by giving of himself or her*self* to students in appropriate, respectful, and mutually uplifting ways. Such healthy and appropriate extensions of self occur in relation to the teachers' body (nonverbal gestures and physical presence), heart (emotions), and mind (speech, thought, and awareness). Furthermore, because role modeling is one of the most powerful ways in which human beings learn, educators' ability to be authentic in their roles as teachers can have deep and often implicit influences on students' self development. How can educators use their power as role models to positively influence students' self development?

We believe that the most basic answer to this question lies in educators' efforts to continue to develop themselves as whole, healthy, and knowledgeable people. We should strive to stay or become healthy in body, mind, and spirit. Good diet, adequate sleep and exercise, and good personal hygiene are the kinds of basic habits children need to develop to avoid a life of health difficulties. Educators (and adults in general) can cultivate these habits in the young by examining and working with their own health-related behaviors. Educators can also role model what it means to live a moral life through their speech, principled forms of classroom management, and a demon-

strated commitment to social causes. For instance, teachers can role model a willingness to discuss and critically examine what are often painful and silenced issues around oppression and prejudice (Tatum, 1997). Educators can also practice "mindful and life-long learning" by being inquisitive in their classroom about many topics, including "youth culture" and students' lives outside of school. Finally, educators can explore the benefits of exercise, being in nature, hatha yoga (postures), meditation, and other free-time activities that reduce stress and tension (Benson, 1983). By practicing healthy habits and a commitment to compassionate and just causes, by being a lifelong learner, and by managing stress effectively, educators can offer young people values and behaviors for imitation that support their healthy self-development and social responsibility. As the saying goes, values are more "caught" by example than "taught" by direct instruction.

I-Self and Me-Self Education

We see education as not only about socializing young people in cultural ways of thinking and feeling about themselves as learners and members of society (me-self education), nor only about scaffolding their development of disciplined ways of knowing (subject-matter education), but also as a process that can assist them in moving from habitual (automatic) ways of attending, perceiving, feeling, thinking, and doing toward more *mindful* approaches to these basic self-related and learning processes (i.e., I-self education). Because the processes of cultivating healthy self-beliefs and relationships with others (me-self education) and becoming more disciplined in thought in relation to the subject matters (subject-matter education) require a degree of self-awareness, all me-self and subject-matter education occur in the context of I-self education.

In relation to what we are calling me-self education, educational psychological research has consistently demonstrated how teachers can reengage or more strategically engage students in the process of learning in school by offering them particular motivational and self-regulatory tools (Pintrich, 2003). Through direct instruction and role modeling, teachers can assist students in learning how to (a) take up goals associated with mastery and self-improvement, (b) break down tasks into proximal subgoals, (c) attribute difficulties to effort and inadequate problem-solving strategies, (d) seek help when needed, and (e) employ various learning strategies. The most effective way that educators can cultivate students' willingness to take up such motivational and strategic tools is by building good relationships with them. Relationships foster the internalization of psychological resources by engaging positive emotions and activating what is called a "broaden and build" orientation (Fredrickson, 2001).

In relation to the I-self, educators can assist their students in participating more mindfully in their lives and in their school learning by helping them to develop their capacities to direct and sustain their attention in ways that yield tangible benefits (see Langer, 1989). For instance, teachers can provide students with experiences that demonstrate to them that "the ability to focus awareness volitionally sets the stage for the use of our talents" (Tart, 1986, p. 12). Here we highlight four things teachers can do in this regard with their students.

Insightful Awareness. One way that educators can work with their students with respect to their awareness concerns granting them insight into psychological beliefs that are debilitating in learning situations. For instance, both anxiety intervention and attributional training programs have demonstrated how assisting individuals to become aware of, and then willfully replace, debilitating self-beliefs can help them to boost their performance. During the first stage, this involves helping students to become aware of ego-focused, self-deprecating thoughts and maladaptive attributional processes in the face of difficulties during learning ("I will never be able to do this right. I will always be dumb"). In the second stage, it involves providing students with new task-relevant, problem-focused thoughts and attributions ("Let me see what the task requires me to do—maybe I wasn't able to solve the problem because I don't have an effective problem-solving strategy") that they can invoke in the face of challenges during learning. In this way, educators can assist students in lowering their achievement-related "worries" and improving their learning and performance (e.g., Meichenbaum & Butler, 1980). Cultivating students' insight with respect to their naïve subject-matter theories is another application of this idea (NRC, 2000). Cultivating insightful awareness is closely related to cultivating choiceful awareness.

Choiceful Awareness. Choiceful awareness (in terms of shifting and sustaining the focus of attention) represents the underlying basis for what Kelly (1955) referred to as *constructive alternativism.* This refers to our capacity to change our personal experience of our selves and the world by choosing what to believe or what beliefs to activate in regard to a particular setting or life situation. The practice of constructive alternativism relies on the effortful control of attention. In part, effortful attention refers to our ability to shift attention away from threatening stimulus cues and debilitating habitual thoughts as well as our ability to inhibit dominant response tendencies that may engender short-term gains and long-term costs

(Derryberry, 2002). These manifestations of effortful control set the stage for individuals' abilities to exercise choiceful awareness with respect to volitional focus on specific stimulus cues and volitional activation of particular beliefs and response sets.

Some of the most impressive evidence for the benefits derived from the use of these capacities has been generated by over three decades of research associated with Mischel's "delay of gratification" paradigm (e.g., Metcalfe & Mischel, 1999). In this work, children's ability to shift attention away from desired objects and sustain focus on less interesting objects (e.g., in order to gain larger rewards) is generally associated with less impulsivity and negative affect. Over time, this type of self-regulatory competence translates into both social (e.g., better stress management) and academic (e.g., higher SAT scores) competencies. Teaching students how to work with their attention in this regard requires patience and personalization, things that, unfortunately, are often not supported in the current environments of teaching. Nonetheless, teachers can begin to cultivate choiceful awareness in their students by teaching them this simple lesson derived from the experience of a Jewish psychiatrist who survived the Nazi death camps: Although we do not always or even often have freedom over our external conditions, we do have freedom over what we attend to and our attitude towards these external conditions (Frankl, 1962).

Mindfulness. In contrast to helping students gain insight into how they habitually think or feel around learning (insightful awareness), or helping them to realize that they have a choice over what kinds of beliefs, feelings, stimuli and so forth that they attend to (choiceful awareness), teachers can also instruct their students in *mindfulness*—the process of becoming more fully aware of what *is* rather than what one wishes, judges, or automatically assumes *is.* Mindful learning, in essence, requires individuals (including both teachers and their students) to willfully extricate their awareness from previously developed and automatically activated habits, emotional patterns, beliefs, and knowledge such that they can perceive, feel, and think *freshly.* This is what it means to "raise one's awareness"—to step over habitual ways of perceiving, feeling, and thinking and gain new insights into self, others, and life from the vantage point of the observing I. In essence, the representational me-self contents of our minds both assist and constrain us. Throughout this chapter we have discussed how they assist us, but it would be an incomplete story if we did not also mention how they also constrain us. They do this insofar as they cause us to enter unique moments of learning, loving, and living with old concepts that may inhibit inquisitiveness and openness to new experiences. We are constantly, as Freud noted, *making the present past* through our representational mental constructs. To accomplish mindfulness education with students, teachers might simply draw students' attention to the definition of mindfulness offered by Langer (1989) and use it as a metacognitive tool before, during, and after lessons. She described mindful learning as (a) continually creating new categories of experience as one progressively masters new tasks, skills, and domains of knowing; (b) being open to new information and experience; (c) being open to perspectives other than one's own; and (d) exercising choiceful attention to the process rather than the outcome of learning. Teachers can simply ask their students to try these *habits of mind* during classroom learning activities and thereby cultivate the *habit of mindfulness*.

One-Pointed Attention. One final aspect of I-self education we want to highlight concerns whether or not educators can assist students in developing their ability to sustain their attention over longer and longer periods of time. The cross-situational value of cultivating this potential of the I-self, if it were possible, would be enormous given the fact that almost everything worthwhile in life requires devoted and one-pointed attention for sustained periods of time. As James (1890) wrote of such a capacity, "The faculty of voluntarily bringing back a wandering attention, over and over again, is the very root of judgment, character, and will.... An education which should improve this faculty would be *the* education *par excellence*. But it is easier to define this ideal than to give practical directions for bringing it about" (p. 424).

This situation is now changing. The traditions of India and their instantiation in classical Brahmanical and Buddhist modes of contemplative education have always had the training of one-pointed attention in young people as a central aim (Mookerji, 1947; Scharfe, 2002). Modern neuroscience has now documented how contemplative-educational practices that train attention can positively influence individuals' psychological well-being (Goleman, 2003; Lutz, Greischar, Rawlings, Ricard, & Davidson, 2004). Studies are also beginning to examine how attentional training can enhance concentration and cognitive performance among children with attention-deficit disorder (see Posner & Rothbart, 2000). How can educators cultivate one-pointed awareness in students in school settings? This remains an open question. Practices such as physical martial arts, various forms of hatha yoga (e.g., body postures), mental memorization, and meditation are the traditional means of cultivating one-pointed awareness. More than 15 centuries of educational practice in India suggest the viability of such practices with young people in this regard, but the effects of using such practices in nonsectarian ways with students in modern public school settings awaits both practical innovations and their scientific validation.

CONCLUSION

The purpose of this chapter was to present ideas and research findings on self and identity processes that are relevant to the study of students' motivation, learning, and achievement in school. The concepts of *self* and *identity* have a long history in psychology and other branches of the social sciences, and interest in these topics is growing rapidly. As a colleague once quipped, "Identity is a disease in the social sciences, and it seems to be spreading."

We began with some overarching themes in self and identity research, including two broad characterizations of scholarship in these areas. The first was a psychological conceptualization of self/identity, and the second a more sociocultural one. We then presented the twin problems of the jingle and jangle fallacies in the rather voluminous body of scholarship on *self* and *identity*. Next, we traced the *self* and *identity* concepts through the work of James and Erikson and updated their concepts in relation to new developments in the social-personality, learning, developmental, and brain-behavioral sciences. In these sections of the chapter, we attempted to bring some coherence to the widespread use of the implicit–explicit distinction in psychological research by differentiating the phenomenological (I-self), representational (me-self), and developmental meanings of these terms as used in the literature today. We believe that greater attention needs to be paid to self-processes associated with school motivation, learning, and achievement that exist below the threshold of phenomenal awareness (e.g., those that are implicit), and that the time is right for exploring in greater depth the I-self and its master functions: the shifting and focusing of attention. Further, we discussed how the study of various kinds of self-representations that function to motivate and regulate school learning and achievement, particularly those that are iconic and symbolic in nature, were both an historical and exciting new direction in educational and social-personality research.

The BASIC model of self-in-context was presented and used to organize the various scholarly traditions that study self and identity processes in education today at the level of the individual, the level of social interaction, and the level of social institutions. Within this context, we presented the BLOS model, in which we posited that self consists of various levels of representation, including the temperamental, iconic, symbolic, and phenomenological. We proposed that each set of these contents provides both energy and direction to behavior. In doing so, we explicitly suggested that *motivation* (i.e., the energization of behavior) is a key *function* of self at each of these levels and their associated contents. Similarly, we suggested that *regulation* (i.e., the direction of behavior) is also a key *function* of self at all of these levels and ranges from reactive and relatively automatic forms at the me-self levels to volitional and effortful forms at the I-self level. We also highlighted the importance of bringing emotions and mood back into the motivational picture in educational psychology.

Next, we expanded our outlook and presented the BLOSC model, in which we described the macro- and micro-levels of school environments that affect students' self/identity development. Because of space limitations, we were only able to make suggestive remarks about how structures, processes, people, practices, activities, and things at each of these levels affect students' self/identity. We highlighted the notions of constructive and destructive environments and discussed how constructive environments are those that invite young people into increasingly central forms of participation in their learning communities at school.

Finally, we applied these "BASIC" concepts to contemporary areas of educational research and related areas of educational practice. Specifically, we discussed the relation between early childrearing, self-development, and children's *readiness to learn in school*, and emphasized the importance of iconic relational schemas for healthy self-development as students move into and through different schools. We examined the issue of *educational resilience* among those who face significant barriers that threaten educational attainments and described how extra-school contexts can promote such resilience. We proposed that focusing on patterns of self/identity processes and educational lifepaths (using pattern-centered methods and holistic-interactionist views of learning and human development) represents a fruitful direction for future scholarship, especially given the increasing ethnic and cultural diversity of the school population. We extended the BASIC framework to discuss current research on hierarchical models of motivation, stereotype threat, and the problem of declining intrinsic motivation to learn among students as they progress in school. Because of space limitations, we were unable to provide a nuanced developmental and social-contextual view of self and identity processes in school settings during and across particular stages in the lifespan. Nonetheless, we covered much ground. We hope to have stimulated thought and contemplation among researchers interested in issues of self and identity processes in education.

ACKNOWLEDGMENT

The first author thanks the J. William Fulbright Program, the William T. Grant Foundation, and the Department of Applied Psychology, School of Education, New York University, for their support in completing this work. Thanks also to Drs. Jan Jacobs, Johnmarshall Reeve, and Phil Winne for comments on an earlier draft.

References

Adams, G., & Markus, H. R. (2004). Toward a conception of culture suitable for a social psychology of culture. In M. Schaller & C. S. Crandall (Eds.), *Psychological foundations of culture* (pp. 335–360). Mahwah, NJ: Lawrence Erlbaum Associates.

Adelman, H. S., & Taylor, L. (1998). Reframing mental health in schools and expanding school reform. *Educational Psychologist, 33*, 135–152.

Allport, G. W. (1961). *Pattern and growth in personality*. New York: Holt, Rinehart, & Winston.

Anderman, L. H., & Anderman, E. M. (1999). Social predictors of changes in students' achievement goal orientations. *Contemporary Educational Psychology, 25*, 21–37.

Anderson, J. R. (1982). Acquisition of cognitive skill. *Psychological Review, 89*, 369–406.

Anderson, J. R. (1990). *The adaptive character of thought*. Hillsdale, NJ, England: Lawrence Erlbaum Associates, Inc.

Aronson, J., & Steele, C. M. (2005). Stereotypes and the fragility of academic competence, motivation, and self-concept. In A. J. Elliot & C. S. Dweck (Eds.), *Handbook of competence and motivation* (pp. 436–456). New York: Guilford.

Ashmore, R. D., Deaux, K., & McLaughlin-Volpe, T. (2004). An organizing framework for collective identity: Articulation and significance of multidimensionality. *Psychological Bulletin, 130*, 80–114.

Astor, R. A., Meyer, H. A., & Behre, W. J. (1999). Unowned places and times: Maps and interviews about violence in high schools. *American Educational Research Journal, 36*, 3–42.

Atkinson, J. W. (1957). Motivational determinants of risk taking behavior. *Psychological Review, 64*, 359–372.

Baldwin, J. M. (1895). *Mental development of the child and the race*. New York: MacMillan.

Bandura, A. (1993). Perceived self-efficacy in cognitive development and functioning. *Educational Psychologist, 28*, 117–148.

Bargh, J. A. (1999). The cognitive monster: The case against the controllability of automatic stereotype effects. In S. Chaiken

& Y. Trope (Eds.), *Dual-process theories in social psychology* (pp. 361–382). New York: Guilford.

Baumrind, D. (1968). Authoritarian vs. authoritative parental control. *Adolescence, 31*, 255–272.

Becker, B. E., & Luthar, S. S. (2002). Social-emotional factors affecting achievement outcomes among disadvantaged students: Closing the achievement gap. *Educational Psychologist, 37*, 197–214.

Benson, H. (1983). The relaxation response: Its subjective and objective historical precedents and physiology. *Trends in Neuroscience, 6*, 281–284.

Block, J. (1995). A contrarian view of the five-factor approach to personality description. *Psychological Bulletin, 117*, 187–215.

Bogen, J. E. (1969). The other side of the brain: II. An appositional mind. *Bulletin of the Los Angeles Neurological Society, 34*, 135–162.

Bowlby, J. (1988). *A secure base: Parent-child attachment and healthy human development*. New York: Basic Books.

Bronfenbrenner, U. (1993). The ecology of cognitive development: Research models and fugitive findings. In R. H. Wozniak and K. W. Fischer (Eds.), *Development in context: Acting and thinking in specific environments: The Jean Piaget symposium series* (3–44). Hillsdale, NJ: Lawrence Erlbaum Associates.

Brown, A. L. (1997). Transforming schools into communities of thinking and learning about serious matters. *American Psychologist, 52*, 399–413.

Bruner, J. S. (1960). *The process of education*. New York, Vintage Books.

Bruner, J. S. (1964). The course of cognitive growth. *American Psychologist, 19*, 1–15.

Buck, R. (1985). Prime theory: An integrated view of motivation and emotion. *Psychological Review, 92*, 389–413.

Buss, D. M. (2004). *Evolutionary psychology: The new science of the mind* (2nd ed.). Boston: Allyn and Bacon.

Case, R. (1991). Stages in the development of the young child's first sense of self. *Developmental Review, 11*, 210–230.

Case, R. (1995). The role of psychological defenses in the representation and regulation of close personal relationships across the lifespan. In G. Noam & K. Fischer (Eds.), *Development and vulnerability in close personal relationships* (pp. 59–88). Hillsdale, NJ: Lawrence Erlbaum Associates.

Chaiken, S. (1980). Heuristic versus systematic information processing and the use of source versus message cues in persuasion. *Journal of Personality & Social Psychology, 39*, 752–766.

Cicchetti, D., Toth, S. L, & Hennessy, K. (1993). Child maltreatment and school adaptation: Problems and promises. In D. Cicchetti & S. L. Toth (Eds.), *Child abuse, child development, and social policy* (pp. 301–330). Norwood, NJ: Ablex.

Cole, M. (1996). *Cultural psychology: A once and future discipline*. Cambridge, MA: Harvard University Press.

Commission for At-risk Children (2003). *Hardwired to connect: The new scientific case for authoritative communities*. New York: Institute for American Values.

Conley, J. J. (1984). The hierarchy of consistency: A review and model of longitudinal findings on adult individual differences in intelligence, personality and self-opinion. *Personality and Individual Differences, 5*, 11–25.

Cooley, C. H. (1902). *Human nature and the social order*. New York: Scribner.

Corno, L., Cronbach, L. J., Kupermintz, H., Lohman, D. F., Mandinach, E. B., Porteus, A. W., and Talbert, J. E. (2002). *Remaking the concept of aptitude: Extending the legacy of Richard E. Snow*. Mahwah, NJ: Lawrence Erlbaum Associates.

Côté, J. E., & Levine, C. G. (2002). *Identity formation, agency, and culture: A social psychological synthesis*. Mahwah, NJ: Lawrence Erlbaum Associates.

Covington, M. V. (2000). Goal theory, motivation, and school achievement: An integrative review. *Annual Review of Psychology, 51*, 171–200.

Cross, W. E. (1991). *Shades of black: Diversity in African-American identity*. Philadelphia: Temple University Press.

Damasio, A. (1999). *The feeling of what happens*. New York: Basic Books.

Damon, W., & Hart, D. (1988). *Self-understanding in childhood and adolescence*. Worcester, MA: Cambridge University Press.

Darling-Hammond, L. (1997). *The right to learn: A blueprint for creating schools that work*. San Francisco: Jossey-Bass.

Davidson, A. L., & Phelan, P. (1999). Students' multiple worlds: An anthropological approach to understanding students' engagement with school. In Urdan, T. C. (Ed.) *Advances in motivation: The role of context* (Vol. 11, pp. 233–273). Stamford, CT: JAI.

Deci, E., & Ryan, R. (1985). *Intrinsic motivation and self-determination in human behavior*. New York: Academic Press.

Derryberry, D. (2002). Attention and voluntary control. *Self and Identity, 1*, 105–111.

Dewey, J. (1902/1990). *The child and the curriculum*. Chicago: The University of Chicago Press.

Dweck, C. S. (1986). Motivational processes affecting learning. *American Psychologist, 40*, 1040–1048.

Dweck, C. S. (1999). *Self-theories: Their role in motivation, personality, and development*. Philadelphia: Taylor & Francis.

Eccles, J. S. (1983). Expectancies, values and academic behaviors. In J. T. Spence (Ed.), *The development of achievement motivation* (pp. 283–331). Greenwich, CT: JAI Press.

Eccles, J. S. (2004, March). *Race and racial identity as developmental contexts for African-American adolescents*. Presidential address, Biennial meeting of the Society for Research on Adolescence, Baltimore.

Eccles. J. S., & Roeser, R. W. (1999). School and community influences on human development. In M. H. Boorstein & M. E. Lamb (Eds.), *Developmental psychology: An advanced textbook* (2nd ed. pp. 503–554). Hillsdale, NJ: Lawrence Erlbaum Associates.

Eccles, J. S., Wigfield, A., & Schiefele, U. (1998). Motivation to succeed. In W. Damon (Series Ed.) & N. Eisenberg (Volume Ed.), *Handbook of child psychology (5th ed.): Vol. 3 Social,*

Emotional, and Personality Development (pp. 1017–1095). New York: Wiley.

Ekman, P. (1992). An argument for basic emotions. *Cognition and Emotion, 6*, 169–200.

Elliot, A. (1997). Integrating the "classic" and the "contemporary" approaches to achievement motivation. A hierarchical model of approach and avoidance motivation. In M. L. Maehr & P. R. Pintrich (Eds.), *Advances in motivation and achievement* (Vol. 10, pp. 143–179). Greenwich, CT: JAI Press.

Elliot, A., & Church, M. (1997). A hierarchical model of approach and avoidance achievement motivation. *Journal of Personality and Social Psychology, 70*, 461–475.

Elliot, A., & McGregor, H. A. (1999). Test anxiety and the hierarchical model of approach and avoidance achievement motivation. *Journal of Personality and Social Psychology, 76*, 628–644.

Elliot, A. J., & Thrash, T. M (2001). Achievement goals and the hierarchical model of achievement motivation. *Educational Psychology Review, 13*, 139–156.

Epstein, S. (1990). Cognitive-experiential self-theory. In L. A. Pervin (Ed.), *Handbook of personality: Theory and research* (pp. 165–192). New York: Guilford Press.

Erickson, M. F., Egeland, B., & Pianta, R. (1989). The effects of maltreatment on the development of young children. In D. Cicchetti & V. Carlson (Eds.), *Child maltreatment: Theory and research on the causes and consequences of child abuse and neglect* (pp. 647–684). New York: Cambridge University Press.

Erikson, E. H. (1950). *Childhood and society*. New York: Norton.

Erikson, E. H. (1959). Identity and the life cycle: Selected papers by Erik H. Erikson. *Psychological Issues, 1*(1, Monograph 1).

Erikson, E. H. (1968). *Identity: Youth and crisis*. New York: Norton.

Erikson, E. H. (1970). Autobiographic notes on the identity crisis. *Daedalus, 99*, 730–759.

Erikson, E. H. (1996). The Galilean sayings and the sense of "I." *Psychoanalysis & Contemporary Thought, 19*, 291–337. (Original work published 1981.)

Evans, G.W. (2004). The environment of childhood poverty. *American Psychologist, 59*, 77–92.

Fazio, R. H., & Olson, M. A. (2003). Implicit measures in social cognition research: Their meaning and use. *Annual Review of Psychology, 54*, 297–327.

Fine, M. (1991). *Framing dropouts: Notes on the politics of an urban public high school*. Albany: State University of New York Press.

Fischer, K. W., & Bidell, T. R. (1998). Dynamic development of psychological structures in action and thought. In W. Damon (Ed.) & R. M. Lerner (Vol. Ed.), *Handbook of child psychology, (5th ed.): Vol. 1. Theoretical Models of Human Development* (pp. 467–561). New York: Wiley.

Fishbein, M., & Raven, B. H. (1962). The AB scales: An operational definition of belief and attitude. *Human Relations, 15*, 35–44.

Ford, M. E. (1992). *Motivating humans: Goals, emotions, and personal agency beliefs*. Newbury Park, CA: Sage.

Fordham, S. (1988). Racelessness as a factor in Black students' school success: Pragmatic strategy or pyrrhic victory. *Harvard Educational Review, 58*, 54–84.

Fordham, S., & Ogbu, J. U. (1986). Black students and school success: "Coping with the burden of 'acting white'." *The Urban Review, 18*, 176–206.

Frankl, V. (1962). *Man's search for meaning: An introduction to logotherapy*. Boston: Beacon Press.

Fredrickson, B. L. (2001). The role of positive emotions in positive psychology: The broaden-and-build theory of positive emotions. *American Psychologist, 56*, 218–226.

Freud, S. (1953). Formulations on the two principles of mental functioning. *Standard edition of the complete psychological works of Sigmund Freud* (XII, 218–226) (J. Strachey, Trans.). London: Hogarth. (Original work published in 1911.)

Friedman, L. J. (1999). *Identity's architect: A biography of Erik H. Erikson*. New York: Scribner.

Fuligni, A., & Tseng, V. (1999). Family obligation and the academic motivation of adolescents from immigrant and American-born families. In T. Urdan (Ed.), *Advances in motivation and achievement: Vol. 11. The role of context* (pp. 159–183). Stamford, CT: JAI.

Gardner, H. (1985). *The mind's new science*. New York: Basic Books.

Gilbert, D. T. (1999). What the mind's not. In S. Chaiken & Y. Trope (Eds.), *Dual-process theories in social psychology* (pp. 3–11). New York: Guilford.

Goldman, S. V., & McDermott, R. (1987). The culture of competition in American schools. In G. D. Spindler (Ed.), *Education and cultural process: Anthropological approaches* (2nd ed. pp. 282–299). Prospect Heights, IL: Waveland.

Goleman, D. (1995). *Emotional intelligence*. New York: Bantam.

Goleman, D. (2003). *Destructive emotions: How can we overcome them?* New York: Bantam Books.

Graham, S., Taylor, A. Z., & Hudley, C. (1998). Exploring achievement values among ethnic minority early adolescents. *Journal of Educational Psychology, 90*, 606–620.

Greenberg, T. M., Kusche, A. C., Cook, T. E., & Quamma, P. J. (1995). Promoting emotional competence in school-aged children: The effects of the PATHS curriculum. *Development & Psychopathology, 7*, 117–136.

Greenwald, A. G., & Banaji, M. R. (1995). Implicit social cognition: Attitudes, self-esteem, and stereotypes. *Psychological Review, 102*, 4–27.

Gutman, L. M., Sameroff, A. S., & Eccles, J. S. (2002). The academic achievement of African American students during early adolescence: An examination of risk, promotive, and protective factors. *American Journal of Community Psychology, 30*, 376–399.

Harackiewicz, J. M., Barron, K. E., Pintrich, P. R., Elliot, A. J., & Thrash, T. M. (2002). Revision of achievement goal theory: Necessary and illuminating. *Journal of Educational Psychology, 94*, 638–645.

Harter, S. (1999). *The construction of self: A developmental perspective*. New York: Guilford.

Haydel, A. & Roeser, R. W. (2002). On motivation, ability, and the perceived situation in science test performance: A person-centered approach with high school students. *Educational Assessment, 8,* 163–189.

Higgins, E. T., & Parsons-Eccles, J. (1983). Social cognition and the social life of the child: Stages as subcultures. In E. T. Higgins, D. N. Ruble, & W. W. Hartup (Eds.). *Social cognition and social development* (pp. 15–62). Cambridge, MA: Cambridge University Press.

Hilgard, E. R. (1949). Human motives and the concept of the self. *American Psychologist, 4,* 374–382.

James, W. (1890). *The principles of psychology.* New York: Holt.

Jason, L. A., Danner, K. E., & Kurasaki, K. S. (1993). *Prevention and school transitions.* New York: Haworth Press.

Jimerson, S. R., Egeland, B., Sroufe, A. L., & Carlson, B. (2000). A prospective longitudinal study of high school dropouts: Examining multiple predictors across development. *Journal of School Psychology, 38,* 525–549.

Jung, C. G. (1923). *Psychological types or the psychology of individuation.* (H. G. Baynes, Trans.); Oxford, England: Harcourt Brace.

Kagan, J. (1996). Three pleasing ideas. *American Psychologist, 51,* 901–908.

Kahneman, D. (2003). A perspective on judgment and choice: Mapping bounded rationality. *American Psychologist, 58,* 697–720.

Kahneman, D., & Tversky, A. (1973). On the psychology of prediction. *Psychological Review, 80,* 237–251.

Keating, D. P. (1990). Adolescent thinking. In S. S. Feldman & G. R. Elliott (Eds.), *At the threshold: The developing adolescent* (pp. 54–89). Cambridge, MA: Harvard University Press.

Kelley, E. L. (1927). *Interpretation of educational measurements.* Yonkers, NY: World.

Kelly, G. A. (1955). *The psychology of personal constructs.* New York: Norton.

Kessler, R. C., Foster, C. L., Saunders, W. B., & Stang, P. E. (1995). Social consequences of psychiatric disorders, I: Educational attainment. *American Journal of Psychiatry, 152,* 1026–1032.

Kihlstrom, J. F. (1987). The cognitive unconscious. *Science, 237,* 1445–1452.

Kitayama, S., & Markus, H. R. (Vol. Eds.). (1994) *Emotion and culture: Empirical studies of mutual influence.* Washington, DC: American Psychological Association.

Lafromboise, T., Coleman, H. L. K., & Gerton, J. (1993). Psychological impact of biculturalism. Evidence and theory. *Psychological Bulletin, 114,* 395–412.

Langer, E. (1989). *Mindfulness.* Reading, MA: Addison-Wesley.

Lave, J., & Wenger, E. (1991). *Situated learning: Legitimate peripheral participation.* Cambridge, England: Cambridge University Press.

Lazarus, R. S. (1991). *Emotion and adaptation.* New York: Oxford University Press.

Lee, C. D. (1995). A culturally based cognitive apprenticeship: Teaching African American high school students skills in literary interpretation. *Reading Research Quarterly, 30,* 608–630.

Lee, S. J. (1994). Beyond the model-minority stereotype: Voices of high- and low-achieving Asian American students. *Anthropology & Education Quarterly, 25,* 413–429.

Lee, V. E., Bryk, A. S., & Smith, J. B. (1993). The organization of effective secondary schools. In L. Darling-Hammond (Ed.), *Review of Research in Education* (Vol. 19, pp. 171–267). Washington DC: American Educational Research Association.

Lewin, K. (1935). *A dynamic theory of personality: Selected papers by Kurt Lewin* (D. K. Adams & K. E. Zener, Trans.). New York: McGraw-Hill.

Lewis, M. (1998). The development and structure of emotions. In M. Mascolo & S. Griffin (Eds.), *What develops in emotional development?* (pp. 29–50). New York: Plenum.

Lewis, M., & Brooks-Gunn, J. (1979). *Social cognition and the acquisition of self.* New York: Plenum.

Lieberman, M. D., Gaunt, R., Gilbert, D. T., & Trope, Y. (2002). Reflection and reflexion: A social cognitive neuroscience approach to attributional inference. In M. Zanna (Ed.), *Advances in experimental social psychology* (pp. 199–249).New York: Academic Press.

Lucas, T., Henze, R., Donato, R. (1990). Promoting the success of Latino language-minority students: An exploratory study of six high schools. *Harvard Educational Review, 60,* 315–340.

Lutz, A., Greischar, L. L., Rawlings, N. B., Ricard, M., & Davidson, R. J., (2004). Long-term meditators self-induce high amplitude gamma synchrony during mental practice. *Proceedings of the National Academy of Sciences, 101,* 16369–16373.

Maehr, M. L., & Braskamp, L. (1986). *The motivation factor: Towards a theory of personal investment.* Lexington, MA: Lexington Books.

Maehr, M. L., & Midgley, C. (1996). *Transforming school cultures to enhance student motivation and learning.* Boulder, CO: Westview.

Magnusson, D. (2003). The person approach: Concepts, measurement models, and research strategy. In W. Damon (Series Ed.) & S. C. Peck & R. W. Roeser (Vol. Eds.), *New directions for child and adolescent development: Vol. 101. Person-centered approaches to studying human development in context* (pp. 3–23). San Francisco: Jossey-Bass.

Markus, H. (1977). Self-schemata and processing of information about the self. *Journal of Personality and Social Psychology, 35,* 63–78.

Markus, H. (1990). On splitting the universe. *Psychological Science, 1,* 181–185.

Markus, H., & Kitayama, S. (1991). Culture and the self: Implications for cognition, emotion, and motivation. *Psychological Review, 98,* 224–253.

Markus, H., & Nurius, P. (1986). Possible Selves. *American Psychologist, 41,* 954–969.

Martin, D. (2000). Mathematics success and failure among African-American youth: The roles of sociohistorical context, community forces, school influence, and individual agency. Mahwah, NJ: Lawrence Erlbaum Associates.

Martindale, C. (1981). *Cognition and consciousness.* Homewood, IL: Dorsey Press.

Maslow, A. H. (1968). *Toward a psychology of being* (2nd ed.). New York: Van Nostrand Reinhold.

McClelland, D. C. (1985). *Human motivation.* Glenview, IL: Scott, Foresman.

McClelland, D. C., Koestner, R., & Weinberger, J. (1989). How do self-attributed and implicit motives differ? *Psychological Review, 96,* 690–702.

McClelland, J. L., McNaughton, B. L., & O'Reilly, R. C. (1995). Why there are complementary learning systems in the hippocampus and neocortex: Insights from the successes and failures of connectionist models of learning and memory. *Psychological Review, 102,* 419–457.

McLaughlin, M. W., Irby, M. A., & Langman, J. (1994). *Urban sanctuaries: Neighborhood organizations in the lives and futures of inner-city youth.* San Francisco, CA: Jossey-Bass, 1994.

Mead, G. H. (1934). *Mind, self, and society.* Chicago: University of Chicago Press.

Meichenbaum, D., & Butler, L. (1980). Toward a conceptual model of the treatment of test anxiety: Implications for research and treatment. In I. G. Sarason (Ed.), *Test anxiety: Theory, research, and applications.* Hillsdale, NJ: Lawrence Erlbaum Associates.

Meltzoff, A. N. (1999). Origins of theory of mind, cognition, and communication. *Journal of Communications Disorders, 32,* 251–269.

Metcalfe, J., & Mischel, W. (1999). A hot/cool system analysis of delay of gratification: Dynamics of willpower. *Psychological Review, 106,* 3–19.

Midgley, C. (1993). Motivation and middle level schools. In M. L. Maehr and P. Pintrich (Eds.) *Advances in motivation and achievement: Vol. 8. Motivation and adolescent development* (pp. 217–274). Greenwich, CT: JAI Press.

Midgley, C. M., Kaplan, A., & Middleton, M. (2001). Performance-approach goals: Good for what, for whom, under what circumstances, and at what cost? *Journal of Educational Psychology, 93,* 77–86.

Mischel, W., & Shoda, Y. (1995). A cognitive-affective system theory of personality: Reconceptualizing situations, dispositions, dynamics, and invariance in personality structure. *Psychological Review, 102,* 246–268.

Moje, E. B. (2004). Powerful spaces: Tracing the out-of-school literacy spaces of Latino/a youth. In K. Leander & M. Sheehy (Eds.), *Space matters: Assertions of space in literacy practice and research.* New York: Peter Lang.

Mookerji, R. K. (2003). *Ancient Indian education: Brahmanical and Buddhist.* Delhi, India: Motilal Banarsi Dass. (Original work published in 1947.)

Murray, H. A. (1938). *Explorations in personality: A clinical and experimental study of fifty men of college age.* Oxford, England: Oxford.

Nasir, N. (2000). Points ain't everything: Emergent goals and average and percent understandings in the play of basketball among African-American students. *Anthropology and Education Quarterly, 31,* 283–305.

Nasir, N., & Saxe, G. (2003). Ethnic and academic identities: A cultural practice perspective on emerging tensions and their management in the lives of minority students. *Educational Researcher, 32,* 14–18.

National Research Council (2000). *How people learn: Brain, mind, experience and school.* Washington, DC: National Academy Press.

Neisser, U. (1988). Five kinds of self knowledge. *Philosophical Psychology, 1,* 35–59.

Nucci, L. P. (2001). *Education in the moral domain.* Cambridge: Cambridge University Press.

Ogbu, J. U. (1995). Cultural mode, identity, and literacy. In J. W. Stigler, R. A. Schweder, & G. Herdt (Eds.), *Cultural psychology: Essays on comparative human development* (pp. 520–541). New York: Cambridge University Press.

Ollendick, T. H., Greene, R. W., Weist, M. D., & Oswald, D. P. (1990). The predictive validity of teacher nominations: A five year follow-up of at-risk youth. *Journal of Abnormal Child Psychology, 18,* 699–713.

Olsen. L. (1997). *Made in America: Immigrant students in our public schools.* New York: New Press.

O'Reilly, R. C., & Munakata, Y. (2000). *Computational explorations in cognitive neuroscience: Understanding the mind by simulating the brain.* Cambridge, MA, US: The MIT Press.

Ornstein, R. E. (1997). *The right mind: Making sense of the hemispheres.* New York: Harcourt Brace.

Peck, S. C. (2004). *The jingle-jangle jungle of identity: Historical perspective and future directions.* Unpublished manuscript, University of Michigan at Ann Arbor.

Peck, S. C. (2005, January). TEMPEST in a gallimaufry: Applying hierarchical systems theory to person-in-context research. In B. W. Roberts (Chair), *Contextualized identities: Integrating self-in-context to traditional issues in personality psychology.* Symposium conducted at the Society for Personality and Social Psychology conference, New Orleans, LA.

Peirce, C. S. (1955). Logic as semiotic: The theory of signs. In J. Buchler (Ed.), *The philosophical writings of Peirce* (pp. 98–110). New York: Dover Books.

Phillips, D. C. (1998). John Dewey's The Child and the Curriculum: A century later. *Elementary School Journal, 98,* 403–414.

Phinney, J. S., & Devich-Navarro, M. (1997). Variations in bicultural identification among African-American and Mexican-American adolescents. *Journal of Research on Adolescence, 7,* 3–32.

Pintrich, P. R. (2000). Multiple pathways, multiple goals: The role of goal orientation in learning and achievement. *Journal of Educational Psychology, 92,* 544–555.

Pintrich, P. R. (2003). A motivational science perspective on the role of student motivation in learning and teaching contexts. *Journal of Educational Psychology, 95,* 667–686.

Portes, A., & Rumbaut, R. G. (2001). *Legacies: The story of the immigrant second generation.* Berkeley: University of California Press.

Posner, M. I., & Rothbart, M. K. (2000). Developing mechanisms of self-regulation. *Development and Psychopathology, 12,* 427–441.

Reber, A. S. (1967). Implicit learning of artificial grammars. *Journal of Verbal Learning and Verbal Behavior, 6,* 855–863.

Richters, J. E. (1998). The Hubble hypothesis and the developmentalist's dilemma. *Development and Psychopathology, 9,* 193–229.

Roeser, R. W. (2004). Competing schools of thought in achievement goal theory? In M. L. Maehr & P. R. Pintrich (Eds.), *Advances in Motivation and Achievement: Vol. 13. Motivating students, improving schools* (pp. 265–299). New York: Elsevier.

Roeser, R. W., & Eccles, J. S. (2000). Schooling and mental health. In A. J. Sameroff, M. Lewis, & S. M. Miller (Eds.), *Handbook of developmental psychopathology* (2nd ed., pp. 135–156). New York: Plenum.

Roeser, R. W., Eccles, J. S., & Strobel, K. R. (1998). Linking the study of schooling and mental health: Selected issues and empirical illustrations at the level of the individual. *Educational Psychologist, 33,* 153–176.

Roeser, R. W., & Galloway, M. G. (2002). Studying motivation to learn in early adolescence: A holistic perspective. In F. Pajares & T. Urdan (Eds.), *Academic motivation of adolescents: Adolescence and education (Vol. II,* pp. 331–372). Greenwich, CT: Information Age.

Roeser, R. W., Marachi, R., & Gelhbach, H. (2002). A goal theory perspective on teachers' professional identities and the contexts of teaching. In C. M. Midgley (Ed.), *Goals, goal structures, and patterns of adaptive learning* (pp. 205–241). New Jersey: Lawrence Erlbaum Associates.

Roeser, R. W., & Midgley, C. M. (1997). Teachers' views of aspects of student mental health. *Elementary School Journal, 98,* 115–133.

Roeser, R. W., & Peck, S. C. (2003). Patterns and pathways of educational achievement across adolescence: A holistic-developmental perspective. In W. Damon (Series Ed.) & S. C. Peck & R. W. Roeser (Vol. Eds.), *New directions for child and adolescent development: Vol. 101. Person-centered approaches to studying human development in context* (pp. 39–62). San Francisco: Jossey-Bass.

Roeser, R. W., & Rodriquez, R. (2004, April). *On academic motivation, achievement, and the diversity of selfways in school during early adolescence.* Paper presented at the annual meeting of American Educational Research Association, San Diego, CA.

Roeser, R. W., Strobel, K. R., & Quihuis, G. (2002). Studying early adolescents' academic motivation, social-emotional functioning, and engagement in learning: Variable- and person-centered approaches. *Anxiety, Stress, and Coping, 15,* 345–368.

Rogoff, B. (2003). *The cultural nature of human development.* Oxford: Oxford University Press.

Rokeach, M. (1968). *Beliefs, attitudes, and values: A theory of organization and change.* San Francisco: Jossey-Bass.

Rose, M. (2004). The *mind at work: Valuing the intelligence of the American worker.* New York: Viking.

Rothbard, J. C., & Shaver, P. R. (1994). Continuity of attachment across the life span. In M. B. Sperling & W. H. Berman (Eds.), *Attachment in adults: Clinical and developmental perspectives* (pp. 31–71). New York: Guilford.

Ryan, A. M., Pintrich, P. R., & Midgley, C. (2001). Avoiding seeking help in the classroom: Who and why? *Educational Psychology Review, 13,* 93–114.

Ryan, R. M., & Deci, E. L. (2000). Self-determination theory and the facilitation of intrinsic motivation, social development, and well-being. *American Psychologist, 55,* 68–78.

Sameroff, A. J. (1983). Developmental systems: Contexts and evolution. In W. Kessen (Ed.), P. H. Mussen (Series Ed.), *Handbook of child psychology: Vol. 1. History, theory, and methods* (pp. 237–294). New York: Wiley.

Sameroff, A. J., Seifer, R., & Bartko, W. T. (1997). Environmental perspectives on adaptation during childhood and adolescence. In S. S. Luthar, J. A. Burack, D. Cicchetti, & J. R. Weisz (Eds.), *Developmental psychopathology: Perspectives on adjustment, risk, and disorder* (pp. 507–526). New York: Cambridge University Press.

Sarason, S. B. (1990). *The predictable failure of school reform.* San Francisco: Jossey-Bass.

Schacter, D. L. (1987). Implicit memory: History and current status. *Journal of Experimental Psychology: Learning, Memory, & Cognition, 13,* 501–518.

Schaps, E. (2003). The heart of a caring school. *Educational Leadership, 60,* 31–33.

Scharfe, H. (2002). *Education in ancient India.* Boston: Brill.

Schultheiss, O. C. (2001). An information processing account of implicit motive arousal. In M. L. Maehr & P. Pintrich (Eds.), *Advances in motivation and achievement* (pp. 1–41). Greenwich, CT: JAI Press.

Schutz, P. À., & Lanehart, S. L. (2002). Introduction: Emotions in education. *Educational Psychologist, 37,* 67–68.

Shiffrin, R. M., & Schneider, W. (1977). Control and automatic human information processing: II. Perceptual learning, automatic attending, and a general theory. *Psychological Review, 84,* 127–190.

Shoda, Y., Mischel, W., & Peake, P. (1990). Predicting adolescent cognitive and self-regulatory competencies from preschool delay of gratification: Identifying diagnostic conditions. *Developmental Psychology, 26,* 978–986.

Slavin, R. E., & Fashola, O. S. (1998). *Show me the evidence! Proven and promising programs for America's schools.* Thousand Oaks, CA: Corwin Press.

Sloman, S. A. (1996). The empirical case for two systems of reasoning. *Psychological Bulletin, 119,* 3–22.

Snow, R. E., Corno, L., & Jackson, D. (1996). Individual differences in affective and conative functions. In D. C. Berliner & R. C. Calfee (Eds.), *Handbook of educational psychology* (pp. 243–310). New York: Simon & Schuster Macmillan.

Solomon, D., Battistich, V., & Hom, A. (1996). Teacher beliefs and practices in schools serving communities that differ in socioeconomic level. *Journal of Experimental Education, 64,* 327–347.

Spangler, W. D. (1992). Validity of questionnaire and TAT measures of need for achievement: Two meta-analyses. *Psychological Bulletin, 112,* 140–154.

Speece, D. L., & Keogh, B. K. (1996). *Research on classroom ecologies: Implications for inclusion of children with learning disabilities*. Mahwah, NJ: Lawrence Erlbaum Associates.

Spencer, M. B., & Markstrom-Adams, C. (1990). Identity processes among racial and ethnic minority children in America. *Child Development, 61*, 290-310.

Sperry, R. W. (1961). Cerebral organization and behavior. *Science, 133*, 1749-1757.

Spindler, G., & Spindler, L. (1985). Ethnography: An anthropological view. *Educational Horizons, 63*, 154-157.

Sroufe, L. A. (1996). *Emotional development: The organization of emotional life in the early years*. New York: Cambridge University Press.

Sroufe, L. A., Fox, N. E., & Pancake, V. R. (1983). Attachment and dependency in developmental perspective. *Child Development, 54*, 1615-1627.

Steele, C. M. (1997). A threat in the air: How stereotypes shape intellectual identity and performance. *American Psychologist, 52*, 613-629.

Stern, D. N. (2000). *The interpersonal world of the infant: A view from psychoanalysis and developmental psychology*. New York: Basic Books.

Stets, J. E., & Burke, P. J. (2000). Identity theory and social identity theory. *Social Psychological Quarterly, 63*, 224-237.

Stryker, S. (1980). *Symbolic interactionism: A social structural version*. Menlo Park, CA: Benjamin Cummings.

Suarez-Orozco, C., & Suarez-Orozco, M. (2001). *Children of Immigration*. Cambridge, MA: Harvard University Press.

Szalacha, L. A., Erkut, S., Garcia Coll, C., Alarcon, O., Fields, J. P., & Ceder, I. (2003). Discrimination and Puerto Rican children's and adolescents' mental health. *Cultural Diversity and Ethnic Minority Psychology, 9*, 141-155.

Talbert. J. E., & McLaughlin, M. W. (1999). Assessing the school environment: Embedded contexts and bottom-up research strategies. In American Psychological Association (Ed.), *Measuring environment across the life span: Emerging methods and concepts* (pp. 197-227). Washington DC: APA.

Tart, C. T. (1986). *Waking up: Overcoming the obstacles to human potential*. Boston: New Science Library.

Tatum, B. D. (1997). *"Why are all the Black kids sitting together in the cafeteria?" and other conversations about race*. New York: Basic Books.

Teo, A., Carlson, E., Mathieu, P. J., Egeland, B., & Sroufe, L. A. (1996). A prospective longitudinal study of psychosocial predictors of achievement. *Journal of School Psychology, 34*, 285-306.

Thayer, R. (1989). *The biopsychology of mood and arousal*. New York: Oxford.

Thorndike, E. L. (1904). *An introduction to the theory of mental and social measurements*. New York: Teachers College, Columbia University.

Thrash, T. M., & Elliot, A. J. (2001). Delimiting and integrating achievement motive and goal constructs. In A. Efklides, J. Kuhl, & R. Sorrentino (Eds.), *Trends and prospects in motivational research* (pp. 3-21). Dordrecht, The Netherlands: Kluwer.

Thrash, T. M., & Elliot, A. J. (2002). Implicit and self-attributed achievement motives. Concordance and predictive validity. *Journal of Personality, 70*, 729-756.

U.S. Department of Education, National Center for Education Statistics. (2002). *The Condition of Education 2002* (NCES 2002-025), Section 1.

Urdan, T., Midgley, C., & Anderman, E. (1998). The role of classroom goal structure in students' use of self-handicapping strategies. *American Educational Research Journal, 35*, 101-122.

Vygotsky, L. S. (1978). *Mind in society* (Cole, M., John-Steiner, V., Scribner, S., & Souberman, E., Eds.). Cambridge: Harvard University Press.

Waters, E., Hamilton, C. E., & Weinfield, N. S. (2000). The stability of attachment security from infancy to adolescence and early adulthood: General introduction. *Child Development, 71*, 678-683.

Wenger, E. (1998). *Communities of practice: Learning, meaning, and identity*. New York: Cambridge University Press.

Wigfield, A., Eccles, J. S., Schiefele, U., Roeser, R. W. & Davis-Kean, P. (in press). Development of achievement motivation. To appear in W. Damon (Series Ed.) & N. Eisenberg (Volume Ed.), *Handbook of child psychology (6th ed.): Vol. 3. Social, emotional, and personality development*. New York: Wiley.

Winne, P. H. (1996). A metacognitive view of individual differences in self-regulated learning. *Learning & Individual Differences, 8*, 327-353.

Wong, C. A., Eccles, J. S., & Sameroff, A. J. (2003). The influence of ethnic discrimination and ethnic identitifcation on African-Americans adolescents' school and socioemotional adjustment. *Journal of Personality, 71*, 1197-1232.

Wundt, W. M. (1897). *Outlines of psychology* [Electronic version]. (C. H. Judd, Trans.).

Zajonc, R. B. (1980). Feeling and thinking: Preferences need no inferences. *American Psychologist, 35*, 151-175.

EDUCATIONAL CONTENT

·19·

TEACHING AND LEARNING IN READING

Donna E. Alvermann
University of Georgia

Jill Fitzgerald
University of North Carolina-Chapel Hill

Michele Simpson
University of Georgia

Our goal in writing this chapter for the second edition of the *Handbook of Educational Psychology* has been to document, interpret, and critique the research on teaching and learning in reading published between January1996 and February 2004 in refereed journals. Prior to beginning our search for suitable articles, we agreed on a set of common search procedures (keywords, databases) and developed criteria that would provide guidance when we had to make decisions about which articles to include or exclude. Those criteria can be found in Table 19.1. Briefly, they allude to our intention to limit our review to research reported in peer-refereed journal articles (not books, chapters, literature reviews, or tech reports) on reading instruction that took place in "regular" classrooms spanning kindergarten through college. The "regular classroom" stipulation was on the setting and not the participants. For instance, if a study reported on students with learning disabilities taught in a mainstream classroom, the study was included; but if a study reported on students with learning disabilities taught in a resource room or pullout program, the study was not included. Further, because we sought to differentiate our chapter from one being developed on a similar topic and coauthored by Michael Pressley and Karen Harris (see Chapter 12 of this volume), we defined reading instruction as that which focuses on teacher action or teacher–student interaction during a classroom reading instruction.

Another stipulation was that instruction had to be provided by actual classroom teachers rather than researchers. Finally, the intervention could not consist of "scripted" commercial programs or computer-assisted interventions in which teachers played secondary or nonessential roles. A major reason for focusing on teacher action or teacher–student interaction within regular classrooms where instruction consisted of more than "scripted" programs was our desire to steer clear of evaluation studies that tend to be directed more toward market research than theory development. In electing to report on studies having interventions that were teacher administered rather than researcher administered, we attempted to avoid problems associated with classroom validity and low-transfer effects.

The chapter is divided into six major sections. In the first section, 28 reading instructional studies conducted in kindergarten through fifth grade met our criteria for inclusion. In the second section, 13 reading instructional studies conducted in 6th through 12th grade (the middle and high school level) met our inclusion criteria. In the third section, 10 reading instructional studies at the college level met our inclusion criteria. In the fourth section, we provide separate critiques and recommendations for

TABLE 19.1. Criteria for Inclusion/Exclusion of Studies

Include	Exclude
Journal articles only	Tech reports, dissertations, theses, ERIC docs, books, book chapters, monographs, evaluation studies
Publication dates between January 1996 and February 2004	
Span of grade/age levels is kindergarten through adult	Preschool
Focus is on *regular* classroom reading instruction. The stipulation here is upon the setting, not the participants. For instance, students with learning disabilities being taught in a mainstream classroom are included here.	Supplementary reading instruction efforts—not including: "tutoring," Reading Recovery or similar supplementary interventions Reading instruction that takes place in "special education" setting. For instance, students with learning disabilities taught in Resource room setting are not included.
Focus is on classroom *teacher* reading instruction. The stipulation here is that the research focuses on teacher action or teacher–pupil interaction, not upon a "packaged" program Re "whole language" or "dual language" programs, include if researchers report a teacher using either of these as her instruction.	Studies of "pre-packaged programs"
Focus is on classroom teacher reading *instruction*. The stipulation here again is that the research focuses on teacher action or teacher-pupil interaction, not *solely* on student learning. For experiments or quasi-experiments, the study has to have a control or comparison group or normative data. Where comparison groups are used, need to be more than four subjects. For quasi-experiments, must be pretesting of outcomes of interest (with the exception of regression discontinuity designs). For correlational studies, samples have to have 20 subjects or more Criteria for rigor in qualitative work is dependent upon the particular paradigm used. However, in general, reports of qualitative research should contain all of the following: • Detail how the study was done (e.g., an audit trail); reveal multiple perspectives and/or other forms of complexity • Show researcher reflectivity; address alternative explanations (how this is done varies greatly by genre) • Present primary data, quotes, stories, scenes, and so on • State conclusions about what has been learned, that is, show evidence of learning from the study rather than the study validating the author's original beliefs • Point to how the "learnings" relate to a wider discourse (G. Noblit, personal communication, January 18, 2004).	Studies of student learning in reading where no teacher instruction is studied. Studies of reading assessment where no teacher instruction is studied.

research and theory development at each of the three grade-level categories. Implications for classroom practice follow in the fifth section, again by grade levels. The final section pulls together the grade-level categorical information by looking at cross-grade trends and issues.

In the first three sections, divided by grade level, we use the following organizational structure: First, we state the number of studies in a particular category along with a brief description of the researchers' purpose; second, we summarize the theoretical bases for the studies; third, we synthesize across studies to the extent we were able to do so; and fourth, we provide a brief annotation for each study, relating selected features of study design, nature of assessments used in the study—whether they were teacher/researcher-made or published, the extent to which reliabilities were reported, and if reported, the type of reliability estimate given—such as "interrater" or

"split-half," the range of reliability estimates; and a brief statement of the main finding(s).

KINDERGARTEN THROUGH GRADE FIVE STUDIES

A total of 107 kindergarten through fifth-grade research reports on reading–instruction research was retrieved. Twenty-eight reports met our inclusion criteria. The issues addressed in the 28 reports coalesced into five broad categories, with four studies addressing characteristics of exemplary early reading instruction, eight having a focus on word- or sound-level instruction, eight having a comprehension, fluency, or affective instructional focus, seven examining overarching reading instruction in relation to student reading, and one addressing how reading instruction is the same or different for children with learning disabilities.

Characteristics of Exemplary Early Reading Instruction

Four sets of researchers examined characteristics of first-through fifth-grade teachers' reading instruction in an effort to delineate most effective instructional practices for student reading achievement (Pressley et al., 2001; Taylor, Pearson, Clark, & Walpole, 2000; Taylor, Pearson, Peterson, & Rodriguez, 2003; Wharton-McDonald, Pressley, & Hampston, 1998). All four designs were observational and were supplemented with other data sources, such as teacher interviews.

As for theoretical bases for the studies, Taylor and colleagues (Taylor et al., 2003) suggested a set of teacher behavior variables that might theoretically be related to different student literacy outcomes. However, rather than providing explicit theory about such teacher and student characteristics, investigators in the remaining studies in this group tended to ground their rationales in findings from effective teaching or effective schooling research.

Summarizing a single set of "most effective practices" from these four studies is difficult, in large part because only Taylor and colleagues used the same or similar observational systems across two studies. That is, in these four studies, there were three different means of coding or creating categories for what was observed. Since decisions about coding or categorization set boundaries on findings, subtle and not-so-subtle differences in these analytical decisions affected how findings were stated. However, collectively the findings from the four studies suggest that classroom teachers considered "effective" in their reading instruction practices teach using a wide array of practices, perhaps most notably teaching in a "balanced" way so that students may develop a wide array of reading subprocesses, dispositions, and attitudes toward reading; teaching a wide range of ways of "getting" words; encouraging self-regulation; integrating reading and writing; doing high-density instruction; doing small-group instruction, enabling independent reading; having strong home connections; coaching; and using higher level questions.

Fifteen "most-effective-for-locale" first-grade teachers versus 15 "least-effective-for-locale" teachers were each observed between 15 and 30 hours, and they were also interviewed (Pressley et al., 2001). The investigators labeled the study "qualitative" and provided detailed description of the analytical procedures, citing "methodological triangulation" and construction of "grounded theory." No student assessments were given. The "most-effective-for-locale" teachers were distinguished by exhibiting excellent classroom management; creating a positive, reinforcing, cooperative environment; balancing skills instruction with "whole language"; at the word level, teaching students to attend to a variety of cues, such as letter/sound cues, pictures and semantic content, and syntax; matching accelerating demands to student competence, with a lot of scaffolding; encouraging self-regulation; making strong connections across the curriculum; and emphasizing process writing.

Nine first-grade teachers nominated by language arts coordinators as either "outstanding" or "typical" were observed approximately twice a month during language arts lessons for 7 months, and they were also interviewed (Wharton-McDonald et al., 1998). No student assessments were given. Constant-comparison analysis was used. Characteristics of the three teachers whose students demonstrated the highest levels of achievement were that they exhibited coherent and thorough integration of skills with high-quality reading and writing experiences; high density of instruction (integration of multiple goals in a single lesson); extensive use of scaffolding; encouragement of student self-regulation; thorough integration of reading and writing activities; high expectations for all students; masterful classroom management; and awareness of their practices and the goals underlying them.

Seventy first- through third-grade teachers in 14 schools across the United States were rated on degree of accomplishment and were observed teaching reading, each for an hour five times across 5 months (Taylor et al., 2000). Teachers also completed a written survey and a weekly log of reading/language arts activities for two nonconsecutive weeks in the spring. In addition, principals completed a questionnaire, and there were several student reading assessments, some of which were research-constructed. Reliabilities (ranging from 80 percent to 100 percent interrater agreement) were given for some, but not all, of the child-, classroom-, and school-level variables that were created. Teachers determined to be "more accomplished" were distinguished by spending more time in small-group reading instruction, allowing more independent reading, establishing high levels of on-task student behavior, having strong home communication, supplementing explicit phonics instruction with coaching for strategic thinking during reading of connected text, using higher-level questions, and requiring considerable writing in response to reading.

Taylor and colleagues (Taylor et al., 2003) examined the effect of 88 first- through fifth-grade teachers' instruction on 792 students' reading and writing growth. The teachers, who were in nine high-poverty schools across the United States, were interviewed and observed three times across the school year during reading lessons. Children were assessed in the fall and spring on several standardized and research-made literacy measures. Interrater reliabilities were provided for variables created from coded observations and for a child writing assessment (all were at least 80 percent agreement). Key findings were as follows: higher-level questioning was positively related to student growth on many literacy outcomes; explicit phonics skills instruction in grades 2 through 5 was associated with lower reading achievement growth; routine practice-oriented comprehension instruction was associated with slower growth in comprehension; passive student responding was negatively related, and high engagement was positively related, to comprehension growth; coaching and involving students in active reading enhanced fluency growth; and teacher telling was negatively related to writing growth, whereas modeling was positively related to writing growth.

Word- or Sound-Level Instruction

Eight studies focused on word- or sound-level instruction. Five were quasi-experimental/experimental, and three sets of researchers classified teachers' behaviors in order to examine those behaviors in relation to children's reading behaviors. As for theoretical grounding of the investigations in this section, two studies stood out as offering explicit discussion of theoretical bases, both psycholinguistic in outlook—Juel and Minden-Cupp (2000) and Jiménez and Guzmán (2003). Each suggested possible linkages between key teacher behaviors and child psycholinguistic processes. Juel and Minden-Cupp hypothesized about particular child reading processes that might be promoted by phonics instruction, and Jiménez and Guzmán theorized about how words would be recognized in a transparent orthography (Spanish) and what instruction would best influence those psycholinguistic processes. The remaining researchers tended to build rationales for their investigations based on prior research, though in some cases, theoretical relationships among key variables of interest were inferable. For instance, one might infer an implicit theory in the reports by Mathes and colleagues (Mathes & Babyak, 2001; Mathes, Torgesen, & Allor, 2001)—phonological processing is a necessary antecedent to comprehension processing, "explicit" instruction can "implant" phonological processing in children's minds, and once that is accomplished, word recognition will be enhanced.

Phonological Awareness and Phonics Instruction. Five studies investigating effects of phonological awareness and phonics instruction in kindergarten and first grade revealed that overall, that there was a strong tendency for such instruction to be associated with enhanced phonological awareness and word-level reading and spelling abilities, as well as, in at least one case, comprehension. In two studies, children with lower literacy levels at first-grade entry received particular benefit from early and heavy exposure to phonics, but in one of the two studies, once they could read independently, other types of instruction were beneficial.

A total of 128 kindergarten children participated in an 11-week phoneme–awareness program followed by a first-grade reading program (extended to second grade for a subsample of children) that emphasized explicit, systematic instruction in the alphabetic code (Blachman, Tangel, Ball, Black, & McGraw, 1999). Several child assessments were given, both published and experimenter-designed. Reliabilities were reported for all except one, and they ranged from .91 to .99. There were 41 15- to 20-minute lessons conducted in small heterogeneous groups of four or five children. The format for the lessons was a phoneme-segmentation activity in which children moved disks to represent the sounds in one- to three-phoneme words spoken by the teacher; a segmentation activity, such as grouping words on the basis of shared sounds; and one of a variety of activities to teach letter names and sounds of eight letters. The experimental children outperformed control group children on measures of phonological awareness, letter name, and letter sound knowledge, three measures of word recognition, and two measures of spelling. On average, the subset of children who had extended experimental instruction in second grade outperformed control group children at the end of second grade on four measures of word recognition.

Juel and Minden-Cupp (2000) observed four first-grade teachers and 72 students and then classified teachers' reading-instruction behaviors and examined their relationships to repeated child literacy outcomes. Some assessments were published, and some were experimenter designed. Either interrater or statistical reliabilities were reported for coding observations and all but two outcomes, and the range was .78 to .98. Children with lower literacy levels at first-grade entry benefited from early and heavy exposure to phonics, but once they could read independently, they profited from other types of instruction.

Two sets of researchers examined first-grade Peer-Assisted Literacy Strategies instruction focusing on phonological elements and reading of connected text (Mathes & Babyak, 2001; Mathes et al., 2001). There were 28 and 36 teachers, respectively, and 130 and 183 students, respectively. A wide array of assessments was given, nearly of all of which were published, with the few remaining assessments experimenter designed. Authors either provided reliabilities (that ranged from .68 to .98) or gave citations for "strong psychometiric properties." Peer-Assisted Literacy Strategies instruction was done in 30-minute sessions, three times a week, for 14 weeks. Across the two studies, in relation to comparison groups, Peer-Assisted Literacy Strategies instruction enhanced students' reading performance, but not equally for all learners, with a tendency for lower-achieving students to benefit more. Significant effects for lower- and average-achieving students were found for word identification, word attack, basic skills, and passage comprehension subtests of a standardized reading test, and for low-achieving students relatively consistently across time for curriculum-based measurement for selected indicators of fluency (Mathes & Babyak, 2001). Moreover, computer-assisted instruction added to peer-assisted learning strategies did not affect student performance beyond that achieved by peer-assisted learning strategies alone (Mathes et al., 2001).

As part of a larger study of 186 kindergarten teachers, Baker and Smith (1999) reported that children who had teachers focusing on phonemic awareness and alphabetic understanding outperformed a control group during a "sustainability" year on a standardized test of phonemic segmentation (no reliability cited) (Baker & Smith, 1999).

Other. Two sets of researchers found for first- and second-grade children in Spain and in the United States that word- and/or letter-sound oriented instruction, on average, benefited students' word recognition processes and attainment, and in one case, that more isolated word work was more beneficial than word work accomplished in predictable texts (Jimenéz & Guzmán, 2003; Johnston, 2000). A third set of researchers, however, found few effects of instructional approach ("whole language" versus "phonics/skills-based") on third-graders' word reading abilities (Wilson & Norman, 1998).

Specifically, in a cross-sectional design, Jiménez and Guzmán (2003), working in Spain, used researcher-designed lexical-decision and naming tasks to analyze first- and second-graders' reaction times and error performance. They also used a questionnaire and a structured interview to categorize teachers regarding their reading-instruction orientation. Agreement for teacher classification was "over 90%," and no reliabilities were given for other variables in the study. Students who had teachers who used a meaning-oriented approach had difficulty naming words in conditions that required "extensive phonological computation" (Jiménez & Guzmán, 2003, p. 75), and as well, when teachers emphasized letter-sound correspondences, children showed rapid development of "the alphabetic route" (Jiménez & Guzmán, 2003, p. 75).

Using predictable books, Johnston (2000) compared the effectiveness of three reading treatments that reflected different components of a whole-to-part instructional model. Three first-grade teachers taught 56 students in three conditions involving repeated readings, sentence contexts, or word banks. Tasks appeared to be both publisher and experimenter designed, and no relia-

bilities were given. Children who had teachers who provided word work in a modified word bank activity learned more words than students of teachers who had children work with sentence strips. Students using sentence strips learned more words than students in instructional conditions where they simply read and reread books. In short, "beginning readers learn[ed] more words when those words . . . [were] removed from the supportive context offered by predictable texts" (Johnston, 2000, p. 248).

Finally, comparing two groups of 54 second-grade students whose teachers differed in reading-instruction approach, Wilson and Norman (1998) explored potential differences on various word recognition tasks. Teachers were categorized as "whole language" or "phonics/skills-based" instructors, based on a word-completion-in-a-cloze procedure. Tasks were both standardized and experimenter designed, and no reliabilities were given. On a cloze procedure, students who had teachers categorized as "whole language" teachers outscored those who had teachers categorized as "phonics/skills-based." There were no other significant effects between the two groups of students, including for assessments of word identification, grapheme substitution, or comprehension. In short, teacher's instructional approach, as defined in this study, had little effect on word recognition strategies.

Comprehension, Fluency, or Affective Instruction

The eight studies in this category could be described in three categories—studies addressing the question, "Does comprehension strategy instruction affect children's reading outcomes" (three studies), "How do teachers and students learn to do literature discussions or classroom theatre and what are the effects on children's thinking and reading" (two reports), and "How do teachers and students together construct literacy activity, and how does that affect students' motivations" (one study). There was quite a bit of variation in study methodology in this category, with three quasi-experimental/experimental studies; two studies using observation, interview, and constant-comparison analyses; one using teacher observation during an intervention and then conducting statistical analyses; another labeled "ethnographic" by the author; and one in which a qualitative method was well detailed. Three sets of investigators (Chinn, Anderson, & Waggoner; 2001; Nolen, 2001; Wolf, 1998) specifically referenced sociocognitive, social constructivist, or social constructionist theoretical grounding for their work, delineating the importance of social understandings to literacy teaching and learning. Two sets of investigators (Brown, Pressley, Van Meter, & Schuder, 1996; Wolf, 1998) referred to Rosenblatt's (1991) reader response theory or her term *transactional*, with Brown and colleagues suggesting that *transactional* refers to readers' construction of meaning by using strategies to link text to prior knowledge and to represent codetermination of meaning. Wolf (1998) also grounded her study in theories of nonverbal communication, referencing Stanislavski (1961), stating that "interpretation depends not only on an analysis of the inner life of a text, but on the external physical action that accompanies the words and demonstrates meaning to others" (p. 386). The remaining four investigators (Bogner, Raphael, & Pressley, 2002; Dolezal, Welsh, Pressley, & Vincent, 2003; Janzen, 2003; Vaughn et al., 2000) developed rationales for the research based on findings from prior research.

Three sets of investigators examined *comprehension strategy instruction*. The overall results of the three studies suggest that strategy instruction enhanced students' awareness of such strategies (Brown et al., 1996; Janzen, 2003, Vaughn et al., 2000). However, there were mixed effects of such instruction on reading abilities. One set of researchers (Brown et al., 1996) found significant impact on comprehension and word study skills, and one (Vaughn et al., 2000) found an effect for rate of reading, but in two cases (Janzen, 2003; Vaughn et al., 2000) there were no significant effects on comprehension and/or word identification.

Specifically, Brown and colleagues (Brown et al., 1996) studied 10 second-grade teachers and 60 low-achieving students. Five experimental groups of six low achievers were matched to five control groups of six low achievers. The experimental students received "transactional strategies instruction" which had multiple facets such as instruction in prediction, alteration of expectations according to unfolding text, questioning, visualizing, and summarizing. Control students received "more conventional second-grade reading instruction," described as "eclectic." Teachers completed a survey and a questionnaire and were classified as to theoretical orientation to reading. Students completed researcher-constructed tasks and published assessments. Reliabilities (statistical and interrater) for all assessments were provided, and they ranged from .85 to .94. Students receiving strategy instruction exhibited greater awareness of strategies by year-end than did the other students (Brown et al., 1996). As compared to the other group, strategy-instruction students also learned more information, both literal and interpretive, from stories read during their reading groups, and evidenced richer, more personalized understanding of the stories.

Janzen (2003) examined effects of strategy instruction in a Navajo setting for two teachers and 39 third graders. A treatment class was compared to a control class. A standardized reading assessment was given, students completed think-alouds, and a researcher-made questionnaire about strategy use was done. No reliabilities were reported. Experimental students were taught to predict, preview, ask questions, identify purpose for reading, and think about what was already known. Students' instruction in the control group focused on "decoding" and word meaning. Strategy instruction resulted in enhanced awareness of strategic thinking and demonstrated increases in the size of the repertoire of reading behaviors (although the experimental students did not display some of the strategies they were taught).

With eight teachers and 111 third-grade students, Vaughn and colleagues (Vaughn et al., 2000) conducted an experiment to compare the effectiveness of Collaborative Strategic Reading (CSR) instruction, designed to affect students' comprehension, to Partner Reading, designed to affect students' fluency. CSR focused on teaching students to preview, read chunks of text, and then use fix-up strategies to figure out word meanings, gist-making, and summarizing. In Partner Reading, students took turns reading aloud and using word-correction procedures on one another. Both interventions were done two to three times per week for 12 weeks during the spring. Published assessments were given to the children for fluency and comprehension, with references cited for reliability for fluency (but no reliability figures stated), and statistical reliabilities for the remaining variables ranging from .88 to .91. Both 12-week-long Partner Reading and Collaborative Strategic Reading enhanced fluency.

We turn now to the question, "How do teachers and students learn to do *literature discussions or Readers' Theater* and what are the effects on children's thinking and reading?" In a 7-week-long intervention, four grade 4 teachers and their 84 students (Chinn et al., 2001) were generally able to learn about and implement Collaborative Reasoning, an instructional frame designed to transfer much control over discourse in reading lessons to students. Four key parameters defined differences between Collaborative Reasoning and recitation-type lessons: the stance to be taken; who holds interpretive authority; who controls turn-taking; and who controls the topic of the discourse. Videotapes of discussions were coded for several features, including cognitive processes involved in the instruction and student and teacher questions. Reliabilities for coding ranged from 91 percent to 94 percent agreement. Descriptive and statistical analyses were done. Compared to recitation-type lessons, Collaborative Reasoning discussions were associated with greater engagement and enhanced use of higher-level cognitive thinking.

In a year-long effort (Wolf, 1998), a teacher of 17 third- and fourth-grade remedial readers used classroom theater as means of encouraging interpretation of text and to enable children to "negotiate among texts, their own ideas, and other players' interpretations as well" (p. 385). Wolf collected data twice a week for a full academic year, using participant observation along with audio- and videotape recordings, site documents, and informal interviews. Using qualitative analyses, Wolf analyzed the teacher's instruction and children's reading over time, and she created interpretive categories and patterns from the data. She documented instructional shifts away from round-robin reading toward more intensive use of classroom theater as well as shifts in children learning to see themselves as characters, actors, and readers.

Finally, regarding the question, *"How do teachers and students together construct literacy activity, and how does that affect students' motivations?"* four teachers and their 20 at-risk kindergarten children (five "target" children per teacher for the study) together constructed literacy activity that framed the children's motivation (Nolen, 2001). The investigator took field notes during six to eight observations per classroom over 1 year, along with teacher and student interviews. Using coding and analysis of patterns in the data, the researcher concluded that in classrooms where reading and writing were used for multiple purposes, children's initial motivations and interests were maintained and positively shaped throughout the year, but where reading and writing were more narrowly defined, children saw school literacy tasks as different from real-life literacy.

Overarching Reading Instruction and Overarching Instruction in Relation to Student Reading

The seven studies in this cluster addressed, in various ways, either descriptions of overarching classroom reading instruction or whether overall classroom reading instructional approach was related to students' reading. The studies in this cluster also reflect a wide methodological range within the kindergarten through fifth-grade group, with one study using observation and questionnaire methodology, another using factor analysis, cluster analysis, and analysis of variance to reanalyze data from a large database, three others using "qualitative" methods, and two being quasi-experimental/experimental studies.

As for theoretical bases for this category of studies, two sets of researchers (Asselin, 1997; Scanlon & Vellutino, 1997) rooted their investigations in theories of how instructional "code emphasis," "meaning emphasis" (or whole language), or "strategic thinking" emphasis would be related to student reading outcomes. Three other sets of investigators (Fitzgerald & Noblit, 1999, 2000; Neufeld & Fitzgerald, 2001) studying English-language learners tended to refer to the lack of explicit theories or models of young second-language learners' reading develop-

ment and its relation to instruction as well as constructivist and sociocognitive outlooks such as a sociocognitive model of reading that accounts for instruction. Another set of researchers, Koskinen and colleagues (2000), referenced three "models": "expert theory," suggesting that teachers who create learning environments where students read with understanding and are motivated (among other features) will be better readers; the teacher creates a classroom culture that fosters reading motivation by being a reading model, having lots of books, and providing student choices; and home reading experiences influence English-language learners' English reading development. Finally, Roehrig and colleagues (Roehrig, Pressley, & Sloup, 2001) built a rationale for their study based on outcomes of prior research.

It is difficult to summarize results across the seven studies, at least in part because the seven studies straddled a wide array of topics. Findings from two studies using qualitative methodology suggested that first-grade balanced reading instruction, consisting of attention to word-level, comprehension, and affective processes, tended to be associated with students taking on a balanced understanding of reading, including for English-language learners (Fitzgerald & Noblit, 1999, 2000). In a third qualitative study, a first-grade teacher's writing instruction appeared to influence two English-language learners' writing development, and lack of explicit instruction in sounds and patterns in words in reading may have been related to the children's lack of manifestation of such knowledge in reading development (Neufeld & Fitzgerald, 2001). A fourth set of researchers found that book-rich classrooms enhanced students' comprehension and that audio models provided particular benefits to English-language learners (Koskinen et al., 2000). On the other hand, a reanalysis of data from the Reading Literacy Study of the International Association for the Evaluation of Educational Achievement suggested no relationships between instructional approach and student reading (Asselin, 1997). Also, in another study of kindergarten children determined to be at risk for later reading achievement, cognitive abilities accounted for a greater proportion of variance in their end-of-first-grade word-level abilities than did the kindergarten instructional program (Scanlon & Vellutino, 1997). However, those who were better achievers on the word-level tasks at the end of first grade had kindergarten teachers who spent a greater proportion of instructional time analyzing the structure of spoken words. Last, one set of researchers found that regular classroom teachers trained in Reading Recovery did use Reading-Recovery-type instructional practices (Roehrig et al., 2001).

Specifically, in an I-witnessing, confessional narrative research genre (Geertz, 1988; Van Maanen, 1988), Fitzgerald and Noblit (1999) used observations, field notes, the teacher's journal, and other data sources such as audio- and videotapes to examine two English-language-learner first-grade children's cognitive literacy development over the course of a year in relation to the first investigator's balanced reading approach. The balanced reading approach entailed four central components: word study, writing workshops, reading good literature, and "putting it all together." Numerous child data sources in English were collected, including published and researcher-designed assessments of sight words, oral reading of graded passages to understand instructional reading level and reading strategies, writing vocabulary, number of sounds heard in spoken words and knowledge of correct letter/sound relations (from writing dictation), receptive vocabulary, oral English fluency, decontextualized descriptive oral language, and decontextualized formal and informal oral definition ability. Additionally, the latter three indicators were also obtained in Spanish oral language. Reliabilities, some interrater and some publisher-provided, were reported for all measures, and they ranged from .72 to 1.00. The teacher's balanced reading approach appeared to be associated with the literacy cognitive development of two English-language learners, and their development appeared highly similar to that portrayed in prior research and theory for native-English speaking young children.

In another study involving that same teacher's classroom, a participant-observer and the teacher as co-researchers asked what first-grade children could learn about reading within a balanced approach to emergent reading instruction and whether a balanced approach to emergent reading instruction could be used successfully in first-grade classrooms with high proportions of low-income or minority children, including English-language learners (Fitzgerald & Noblit, 2000). Data sources were the same as those used in the previous Fitzgerald and Noblit (1999) study, labeled as a "naturalistic study." They used qualitative constant-comparison analysis to examine patterns and themes in the data. The authors concluded that the teacher's year-long balanced reading approach was associated with children's constructions of a balanced view of reading processes and purposes, regardless of ethnicity or language status (Fitzgerald & Noblit, 2000).

One first-grade teacher's instruction over the course of a year appeared to be influential in three English-language learners' reading and writing development across the year (Neufeld & Fitzgerald, 2001). The three boys were in the teacher's "low" reading group. Observations, interviews, and field notes were done, and then case analyses were conducted. Coding categories were created, and themes were drawn. Triangulating procedures were used. Student assessments across the year were the same as those used in studies reported by Fitzgerald and Noblit (1999,

2000). A central feature of the teacher's instruction was whole-class work during writing instruction on sound-to-letter matches. Also, during that writing instruction, products were emphasized over processes and rote learning over strategic thinking. Over the year, the three boys tended to grow in writing ability, particularly in manifesting more understanding of the sound-to-letter match-ups and correct spellings that the teacher emphasized. However, the teacher provided the boys with very little reading instruction, and instead, the boys were assigned the teacher assistant who did homework checks with them, used flash cards to memorize sight words, and attempted oral round-robin reading. The boys' reading development over the year was modest, and the knowledge of letter–sound match-ups that they displayed in their writing was not manifested in their reading. In short, the boys learned well what they were taught, but failed to learn what they were not taught.

Koskinen and colleagues (Koskinen et al., 2000) randomly assigned 16 first-grade classrooms to one of four treatment conditions—a book-rich classroom environment, a book-rich environment and daily rereading of books at home, a book-rich environment and daily rereading of books with audiotapes at home, and unmodified reading instruction at school. In the book-rich conditions, 154 multilevel books supplemented the classroom library, and teachers regularly conducted small-group shared reading using those books. The shared reading sessions involved a 5-minute mini-lesson, book introduction, requests for predictions, connections to background knowledge, purpose-setting for reading, the teacher reading aloud, and rereading by both the teacher and students. The rereading at home part of the intervention involved rereading two or three times the same multilevel books that were used in the small-group sessions. The audiotape part of the intervention involved the same home rereading component as just described, but in addition, students were given prerecorded tapes of the stories and tape recorders, and they listened to the books on tape. Student assessments included publisher- and researcher-made: oral reading, writing vocabulary, oral story retelling, a Likert-indicator assessment of motivation and literacy behavior, a teacher survey of child behavior, child interviews, a parent survey, and a teacher questionnaire and interview. Interrater and statistical reliabilities were reported for all assessments except the child interview and teacher questionnaire and interview, and they ranged from .64 to .94. Students who had teachers who established book-rich classrooms had enhanced comprehension, both with and without the home component. Home-based rereading increased children's reading motivation and prompted parental involvement. Also, use of audio models provided particular benefit to English-language learners.

A British Columbian reanalysis of data from the 1990–1991 Reading Literacy Study of the International Association for the Evaluation of Educational Achievement (IEA) was done. In the IEA study, 154 schools, 154 teachers, and 2,813 third-grade students were sampled. There were teacher and student questionnaires and a student reading achievement. Sources and reliabilities for IEA measures were not cited, but readers were referred to the IEA manual for further detail. For the reanalysis, items were selected from the original data sources, and factor analyses, cluster analyses, and analyses of variance were done. Statistical reliabilities were provided for student achievement variables that were created for the reanalysis study, and they ranged from .21 to .95. Two approaches to reading instruction were identified—teaching comprehension strategies in communicative contexts, and teacher-centered instruction of hierarchical skills. Eighty percent of the teachers used "eclectic" approaches, and there were no relationships between instructional approach and teacher background, student background, and student achievement (Asselin, 1997).

One study result suggested that children's cognitive abilities might play a greater role in first-grade reading success than would the type of kindergarten reading instruction (Scanlon & Vellutino, 2000). During the school year, Scanlon and Vellutino (2000) observed each of 38 kindergarten classrooms with "approximately 1,000 children," five or six times, for a full day each time. A subsample was drawn of 151 children defined as at-risk on the basis of letter-name knowledge at the beginning of kindergarten. A battery of published and researcher-made child assessments was given to the kindergarten children, measuring world knowledge, semantic development, syntactic comprehension, letter identification, phoneme segmentation, rapid automatized naming, sentence memory, word memory, visual-auditory learning, visual memory, block design, matching familiar figures, target search, print awareness, and print conventions. Reliabilities for coding from observations were at or above 85 percent agreement. No other reliabilities were reported, but a prior publication was cited as providing further details about the measures. Children who were more successful in reading, as defined by "skill in word identification and phonetic decoding," at the end of first grade had kindergarten teachers who spent more instructional time on sound and spelling aspects of words and on writing. Also, reading-related cognitive abilities accounted for more variance in end-of-first-grade word-reading achievement than kindergarten instructional emphasis, although both were influential.

Roehrig and colleagues (2001) observed 10 kindergarten through second-grade classrooms in which teachers had been trained in Reading Recovery. Teachers were observed during language arts instruction from one to seven times for approximately 45 minutes each time. Teachers also completed a questionnaire about integration of Reading Recovery techniques into their regular classroom instruction. No student assessments were given. Observations were coded using a "grounded theory approach." Interrater agreement was 73 percent for instructional practices and 92 percent for assignment of strategies to particular teachers. No reliability was provided for variables that resulted from the questionnaire. All 10 teachers used instructional practices and teaching strategies typical of Reading Recovery.

Children With Learning Disabilities

Only one study examined the extent to which regular classroom reading instruction tends to be the same or different for children with learning disabilities. The researchers rooted the investigation in a rationale based on prior research and writing that documented a trend to inclusive, heterogeneous grouping for children with special needs. Three times across the school year, for 90 minutes each time, Schumm and colleagues (Schumm, Moody, & Vaughn, 2000) observed language arts instruction of 29 regular third-grade teachers in classrooms with 147 children. They also took field notes, did interviews, and obtained teacher self-reports about grouping practices. Student assessments were publisher- and researcher-made: reading achievement, self-concept, and attitude. Interrater reliabilities of .80 or higher were reported for observations. Statistical reliabilities were provided for some, but not all, of the remaining assessments, with the reported ones ranging from .42 to .96. Students with learning disabilities and their peers received the same reading instruction because their teachers tended to use whole-class reading instruction.

Summary of Kindergarten Through Fifth-Grade Findings

On the whole, the findings from the research and the implications for teachers do not tend to move in directions that are remarkably "new" or "different" from those of prior years. Rather, they push toward a balanced instructional outlook in which teachers engage children's cognitive mechanisms and self-regulation as well as affective dispositions. Main findings from the 28 studies of kindergarten through fifth-grade studies of classroom reading instruction may be summarized as follows: (a) Classroom teachers considered "effective" in their reading instruction practices teach using a wide array of practices, perhaps most notably teaching in a "balanced" way so that students may develop a wide array of reading subprocesses, dispositions, and attitudes toward reading;

teaching a wide range of ways of "getting" words; encouraging self-regulation; integrating reading and writing; doing high-density instruction; doing small-group instruction; enabling independent reading; having strong home connections; coaching; and using higher-level questions. Among the various findings in this category, we might highlight one in particular—because of its timeliness in relation to a general contemporary emphasis on early phonological awareness and phonics instruction and because it may shed light on findings from studies in our second category of issues. That is, across 88 first-through fifth-grade teachers' instruction with 792 students, explicit phonics instruction *in grades 2 through 5* was associated with *lower* reading achievement growth. (b) In general, in kindergarten and first grade, sound-, letter-, and word-level instruction, such as phonological awareness and phonics instruction, were associated with students' enhanced phonological awareness, word-level reading and spelling abilities, and in one case, comprehension. In two studies, such instruction was particularly beneficial for children with lower literacy levels at first-grade entry, but in one of those two studies, once the children could read independently, other types of instruction were beneficial. But in a study involving third graders, few effects were found on word-reading abilities when a "whole language" versus a "phonics/skills-based" approach were compared. (c) Comprehension strategy instruction enhanced students' awareness of strategies, but effects of such instruction on reading abilities were unclear. (d) In one study, teachers and students were able to learn about and implement an instructional frame for student control over discourse in reading lessons, and such discussions were associated with greater engagement and enhanced use of higher level cognitive thinking. (e) Classroom theater enhanced children's ability to see themselves as readers, and in classrooms where reading and writing were broadly defined, children's motivations and interests in reading were positively shaped. (f) From studies of overarching reading instruction: first-grade balanced reading instruction tended to be associated with students, including multilingual learners, taking on a balanced understanding of reading; book-rich classrooms enhanced comprehension, and audio models were especially beneficial for English-language learners; a first-grade teacher's lack of reading instruction may have been related to three English-language learners' lack of progress in reading; no relationships were found between instructional approach and students' reading in one study, and in another, cognitive abilities in kindergarten accounted for a greater proportion of variance in end-of-first-grade word-level abilities than did the kindergarten instructional program; and in one study, Reading-Recovery-trained teachers used Reading-Recovery-type instructional practices in their regular classrooms. (g) In one study, third-grade students with learning disabilities and their peers received the same reading instruction because their teachers tended to use whole-class reading instruction.

MIDDLE AND HIGH SCHOOL (GRADES 6–12) STUDIES

Adolescent literacy is a topic of increasing interest as evidenced by the number of position papers commissioned in the last few years by professional organizations, such as the International Reading Association (Moore, Bean, Birdyshaw, & Rycik, 1999), the National Reading Conference (Alvermann, 2002), and policy groups in the private sector, such as the Alliance for Excellent Education (see Kamil, 2003, available at http://www.all4ed.org) and the RAND Reading Study Group (2002). There is a growing consensus in the United States that early-intervention reading programs, although necessary, are not sufficient to the task of ensuring that students at the middle and high school levels are able to comprehend a wide range of texts (print, visual, and digital) required by the various states' curriculum standards; yet the number of published research reports has not kept pace. This is especially the case for studies that report instructional effects on adolescents' reading achievement.

Of the 44 secondary school studies that matched the focus of the chapter, only 13 met our inclusion criteria. Most were disqualified on the basis of having someone other than the teacher in charge of instruction. Hand searches of the *Journal of Educational Psychology*, the *American Educational Research Journal*, the *Journal of Literacy Research*, and *Reading Research Quarterly* turned up several additional studies whose titles did not contain the keywords we had initially defined as setting the parameters for our search, but only three fit our criteria. Among the final 13 studies included here, 1 fit into the category of characteristics of exemplary literacy instruction, 5 in the category of comprehension and conceptual/strategic instruction, 5 in the category of discipline-specific reading instruction, and 2 in the category of instruction for students with reading disabilities.

Characteristics of Exemplary Literacy Instruction

The single study (Langer, 2001) included in this category focused on 88 English/language arts classrooms in 25 schools that had been trying to increase student achievement in reading, writing, and English. Its purpose was to investigate the characteristics of literacy instruction in demographically comparable schools, some of which had made more progress than others toward their goal of higher student performance. Langer (2001) anchored her work in Bakhtin's (1981) concept of dialogic thinking and Vygotsky's (1986) sociocognitive framework as a way of offering insight into the reciprocal nature of teaching and learning. She also used Gee's (1996) conceptual framing of primary and secondary discourse communities to interpret what counts as appropriate knowledge and how it gets taught and learned. Constant comparison analysis of multicase qualitative data (both within and across cases) identified six instructional features that distinctively separated higher performing ("beat the odds") schools from more typically performing schools. These features included (a) systematic skills instruction; (b) test preparation integrated into ongoing goals, curriculum, and lessons; (c) knowledge and skills overtly connected across classes and grades, and connected between in- and out-of-school applications; (d) overt teaching of strategies for planning, organizing, completing, and reflecting on content and activities; (e) teachers moving students to deeper understanding of content once a learning goal was met; and (f) teachers encouraging students to work together to develop deeper understanding of content.

Comprehension and Conceptual/Strategic Instruction

The five studies that made up this category were known from previous research on instructional strategies to be effective in improving students' comprehension and vocabulary in pull-out programs and content area classes where researchers or specially trained assistants taught them. Used either singly or in combination, these strategies included Reciprocal Teaching (Alfassi, 1998); teacher-posed questions (Lapkin & Swain, 1996); explicit instruction in prior knowledge activation and main idea (Spires & Donley, 1998); guided discovery using class discussion (Echevarria, 2003); and a combination of structured strategy instruction (Schorzman & Cheek, 2004) that included the Directed Reading/Thinking Activity (Stauffer, 1975), the Pre-reading Plan (Langer, 1981), and graphic organizers (Barron & Earle, 1973). Although the literature on the effectiveness of these instructional strategies is fairly abundant (Dole, Duffy, Roehler, & Pearson, 1991; National Reading Panel, 2000; Palincsar & Brown, 1984; Pearson & Gallagher, 1983; Pressley & McDonald, 1997), there have been relatively few studies conducted in middle and high school content area classrooms where regular teachers actually provided instruction in the use of such strategies. Thus, the group of five studies presented here are somewhat unusual in their focus.

Three of the five studies could be said to draw most heavily on social constructivism, a theory of learning as opposed to a theory of teaching. In its most general sense, social constructivism can be defined as learning that is both social and constructed through participation in the cultural and linguistic practices of any given community (e.g., a school). The theory's relation to teaching can best be discerned in its central metaphor—a *scaffold* that supports a building under construction, until such time that the building is finished and can stand by itself. Teachers (as well as students' more capable peers) can provide instructional scaffolding when socially interacting to develop new knowledge structures (Wood, Bruner, & Ross, 1976). A point worth noting about this metaphor is that it encourages generalizing about social constructivism in ways that are often contradictory (Hruby, 2002). This seemed to be the case with the present group of studies. For example, Echevarria (2003) and Spires and Donley (1998) relied on social constructivist theory as a rationale for investigating socially oriented inquiry learning and guided practice, whereas Lapkin and Swain (1996) used the same theoretical construct to study a more didactic form of content-oriented instruction. The other two studies (Alfassi, 1998; Schorzman & Cheek, 2004) drew from theories of comprehension that suggest the need for actively monitoring one's understanding while reading (Brown, 1980; Cross & Paris, 1988).

The researchers in all five of the studies reported that strategy instruction was effective. The three experimentally designed studies found evidence supporting the superiority of the intervention group over the control group on a variety of comprehension measures. For example, Alfassi (1998) reported that Reciprocal Teaching strategy instruction (using 350 to 500-word expository passages with 53 students of average ability who were experiencing comprehension problems) produced superior results on experimenter-designed tests when compared to traditional remedial reading instruction with 22 students who served as the controls. Consistent with previous research on Reciprocal Teaching, however, no differences were found between the two groups on standardized measures of reading.

Spires and Donley (1998) conducted a true experiment in which equal numbers of high-, average-, and low-achieving readers (as determined by their scores on a standardized achievement test) were assigned to each of four treatment groups using random stratified sampling; teachers were also randomly assigned to treatment groups. After 6 days of explicit instruction in prior knowledge activation (PKA) and main idea (MI) strategies, students in the PKA and the MI-PKA combination groups statistically significantly outperformed the MI and control groups on application-level comprehension questions. All three experimental treatment groups outperformed the control group on the delayed measure of literal level comprehension questions. All comprehension questions were based on three social studies passages (natural texts reduced to about 1,200 words each), plus one literary text (a short story).

In Schorzman and Cheek's (2004) examination of structured strategy instruction, three sixth-grade teachers instructed their students ($n = 103$) in the use of directed reading/thinking activities, a prereading plan, and graphic organizers over a period of 7 weeks. Results of this pretest/posttest study revealed that compared to the control group, structured strategy instruction produced a statistically significant difference ($p < .05$) on an informal measure of reading comprehension; however, no statistically significant difference was found between the experimental and control groups on a formal measure of reading comprehension.

In a mixed-methods study involving a comparison of two seventh-grade science classrooms, Echevarria (2003) used content analysis and nonparametric statistics to measure the effectiveness of instruction that involved guided discovery and class discussion. The specific purpose of the study was to examine students' knowledge construction and scientific reasoning when presented with anomalies found in simulation software on Mendelian genetics. The science teacher, selected for her expertise in inquiry-oriented instruction, made use of guided discovery and class discussion to develop students' mental models of dominant trait transmission. Qualitative and quantitative data analyses showed a significant shift in students' mental models of dominant trait transmission at the end of the 3-week inquiry unit. Findings were discussed in light of earlier work on conceptual change instruction (Posner, Strike, Hewson, & Gertzog, 1982).

Lapkin and Swain's (1996) descriptive case study of a French immersion class in Toronto, Canada, analyzed the teacher's question-posing strategy for instructing eighth-grade students in the use of passive and pronominal verbs. This instruction took place in the context of teaching students to take notes on the greenhouse effect. Although the study's design did not permit the researchers to draw any conclusions about the teacher's instruction relative to students' expanded lexicon, they did note instances of mastery in certain vocabulary items and associated structures that elude many beginning-level immersion students.

Discipline-Specific Reading Instruction

The five studies in this category are representative of a larger literature on reform-minded efforts directed at curriculum change through the implementation of instructional models based on previously validated reading approaches. Factors that made these particular studies interesting were the scope of their efforts, the variation in their design features, and their outcomes.

Theoretically speaking, the five studies were grounded quite differently in this category. Applebee and his colleagues (Applebee, Langer, Nystrand, & Gamoran, 2003) situated their work in a long line of studies that borrowed from the sociocognitive tradition and that were, in turn, informed by literary theory (Scholes, 1985) and the work of linguists, such as Cazden (1988) and Gee (1996). In developing their Reading Apprenticeship framework, Greenleaf, Schoenbach, Cziko, & Mueller (2001) also relied on the sociocognitive tradition, and especially on the research on metacognition (Brown, 1980; Palincsar, 1986; Palincsar & Brown, 1984). Stevens (2003) drew from Slavin's (1990) work on collaborative learning that takes into account early adolescents' orientation toward peer-socialization practices. The National Reading Panel (2000) found instruction that took advantage of collaborative learning activities resulted in improved student comprehension. Hobbs and Frost (2003) looked to a cultural studies perspective (Luke, 1997; Masterman, 1985) for theoretical support in terms of expanding the concept of literacy to include the comprehension of media messages and authentic learning in student-centered environments.

The researchers in all of the five studies in this category reported findings that favored student-centered instruction and/or collaborative learning. Agee's (2000) in-depth study of how five high school English teachers defined and gauged effective literature instruction used data from classroom observations, videotaped lessons, and audiotaped interviews with the teachers to triangulate her findings. The profiles of the five experienced teachers were mini-case studies and reflected the researcher's decision to seek participants who represented a range of pedagogical perspectives and identity markers, such as ethnic and racial backgrounds. The schools varied by locale (two states) and size (both large and small high schools). Agee used Strauss and Corbin's (1990) open coding system as the first level of analysis; this was followed by an examination of the relations between each teacher's definition of effective literature instruction and the characteristics of the students he or she taught. A third level of analysis, which consisted of viewing videotaped lessons, involved the teachers in reflecting on their instruction and answering questions about the typicality of such instruction. Analyses of the five profiles suggested that teachers who were flexible and defined effective literature instruction within a student-centered model were able to address student differences and needs more effectively than were teachers who were inflexible and favored a teacher-centered model of literature instruction.

Applebee and colleagues (2003) conducted a year-long naturalistic, classroom observation study of 64 middle and high school English classes in 19 schools spread across five states. The classes represented roughly one honors, one remedial, and two regular classes per school. Principal components analyses and a series of hierarchical linear models revealed that discussion-based approaches were effective (controlling for fall performance and other background variables) across a range of teaching situations for both low- and high-achieving students. Overall, the results suggest that discussion-based approaches in the context of high academic demands benefit students by enabling them to internalize the knowledge and skills needed for engaging in challenging literacy tasks on their own.

Like Applebee and colleagues, Greenleaf and her colleagues (2001) were interested in studying the effects of academic literacy instruction in natural settings. Their year-long study focused on an urban, low-SES high school in which the entire ninth-grade class was enrolled in a required academic literacy course that made use of the Reading Apprenticeship framework. Explicit instruction in Reciprocal Teaching (Palincsar & Brown, 1984), think-alouds (Baumann, Jones, & Kessell, 1993), sustained silent reading (SSR), notetaking strategies, graphic organizing, identifying text structure, and vocabulary strategies took place in two 90-minute blocks each week, plus one 50-minute period per week for 7 months. Using a pre/post design that included analyzing normative data on a standardized test, Greenleaf et al. found that the students enrolled in the academic literacy course caught up to the national norm on that test for ninth graders. They started the year scoring at late seventh grade and finished at late ninth grade (a gain of 2 years in reading proficiency in only 7 months). Illustrative case studies showed how low-performing readers can develop metacognitive monitoring and strategic control of their reading processes.

In the other two studies in this category, quantitative analyses of overarching literacy reform efforts produced statistically significant differences that favored the instructional intervention group over the control group in both instances. Stevens (2003) used a quasi-experimental (pre/post) design to study the effects of implementing Student Team Reading and Writing (STRW) in two middle schools located in a large urban district. Three comparison schools were matched to the intervention schools on ethnicity, SES, and scores on a widely used standardized achievement test. STRW, which is a cooperative learning approach that uses literature-related activities and direct instruction in comprehension and writing related to the literature selections, was compared to a more traditional approach that uses basal reading materials and literature anthologies. Following 4 months of implementation and coaching teachers in the use of STRW, the

researchers observed each of the intervention teachers on three randomly selected days to assess the fidelity of the treatment. A class-level MANCOVA (nesting class within treatment) revealed that STRW classes scored statistically significantly higher on measures of reading vocabulary, comprehension, and language expression. For three statistically significant main effects, effect sizes ranged from +.25 to +.38.

Hobbs and Frost (2003) used a nonequivalent groups design to study the effects of a media literacy curriculum on 293 11th-grade students' comprehension, critical thinking, and writing. The entire junior class was enrolled in a year-long English/media/communication course taught by seven regular classroom teachers who integrated critical analysis of print, audio, and visual texts into their instruction. A comparison group was matched on demographic variables and randomly selected from a group of students who had not been exposed to instruction in critically analyzing media messages. Content validity for the course was established by using a five-critical-questions model that supported student-centered instruction and routine learning tasks in the teachers' English language arts classrooms. A series of ANCOVAs revealed statistically significant differences that favored the intervention group over the control group on researcher-developed measures that evaluated students' ability to comprehend media messages, think critically, and write about what they had learned.

Instruction for Students With Reading Disabilities

Although a primary assumption of early intervention research is that the number of students experiencing reading difficulty later on should decrease significantly as a result of such intervention, in reality, there are currently large numbers of middle and high school students needing assistance because of reading disabilities and inadequate instruction (Deshler et al., 2001; Strickland & Alvermann, 2004). The two studies included in this category are part of the larger literature on learning disabilities associated with reading difficulties among adolescents.

Researchers in only one of the two studies included here provided a discussion of the theoretical perspective that informed the study. Bulgren and her colleagues (Bulgren, Deshler, Schumaker, & Lenz, 2000) acknowledged their debt to Ausubel (1963) and other learning theorists whose work informed their own and led to the development of certain instructional procedures thought to be effective with students who have reading disabilities. Although the researchers in the second study (Fuchs, Fuchs, Mathes, & Simmons, 1997) did not refer to a specific theoretical perspective, they appeared to draw from earlier research on peer tutoring (Cohen, Kulik, & Kulik, 1982) and instruction in reading comprehension (Dole, Duffy, Roehler, & Pearson, 1991).

Both studies employed quantitative methodologies, but only one (Fuchs et al., 1997) was quasi-experimental in design. The other study (Bulgren et al., 2000) used an ABAB reversal design. In the Fuchs et al. study of 120 middle and upper elementary students from 40 classrooms in 12 schools, the researchers investigated the effectiveness of Peer-Assisted Learning Strategies (PALS) on three types of readers' (LD, low-performing, and average-achieving) comprehension. Teachers trained in PALS provided instruction in 35-minute blocks per day, 3 days per week for 15 weeks. The PALS intervention consisted of partner reading with retell, paragraph summary, and prediction relay. The materials that students read were primarily narratives (400-word folk tales) taken from basals, supplemented by some content-area texts and Weekly Readers. A series of ANOVAs on each of three researcher-developed tests revealed that LD, low-performing, and average-achieving students in PALS classrooms made statistically significantly greater progress than students in the control group (No-PALS classrooms).

In the Bulgren et al. study (2000), a general science teacher trained in the use the Concept Anchoring Routine (cue, do, and review with analogical instruction of known/new concepts) taught 18 seventh-grade students in a heterogeneous-grouped classroom that included students with learning disabilities. Four parallel, equivalent forms of a nine-item open-ended test were created by the researchers to measure student recall of information related to four targeted science concepts. T-tests were used to assess mean test performance differences between Concept Anchoring Routine instruction and nonenhanced instruction. Statistically significant differences were found that favored the anchoring routine.

Summary of Middle and High School (Grades 6–12) Findings

Thirteen instructional studies at the middle and high school level were grouped into four categories: characteristics of exemplary literacy instruction, comprehension and conceptual/strategic instruction, discipline-specific reading instruction, and instruction for students with reading disabilities. Findings from these studies can be summarized as follows. First, adolescents' comprehension of content area reading materials was enhanced when teachers overtly and systematically taught them strategies that required organizing, integrating, and reflecting on informational and/or narrative texts. However, it should be noted that statistically significant differences between experimental and control groups' performance on comprehension tasks as a result of strategy intervention were more frequently associated with researcher-designed assessments than with standardized reading measures. Second, teachers who were student centered in their instructional approaches (e.g., encouraged class discussion and student inquiry) maintained high expectations for student performance on outcome measures. This included teachers who taught students with learning disabilities in regular content area classrooms. Third, teachers who were experienced in using Reciprocal Teaching (Palincsar & Brown, 1984) and prior knowledge activation strategies were equally effective in teaching high-, average-, and low-achieving readers. Students in these teachers' classrooms outperformed their control-group peers on a variety of comprehension measures. It is worth noting, too, that Reciprocal Teaching combined with instruction in think alouds, notetaking strategies, graphic organizing, text structure, and vocabulary produced a gain of 2 years in reading in only 7 months in one of the studies reported here. Finally, exemplary literacy instruction at the middle and high school level included much more than the explicit, systematic teaching of reading strategies. These strategies were often embedded in larger efforts aimed at establishing and maintaining collaborative learning environments, teaching for conceptual learning, and connecting youth's knowledge and experiences across time and space. In keeping with the findings from Langer's (2001) large-scale study of the characteristics of exemplary literacy instruction, effective middle and high school teachers encouraged students to work together to develop a deep conceptual understanding of content and to make real-world connections between old and new knowledge across the curriculum.

COLLEGE-LEVEL STUDIES

Although the improvement of students' reading comprehension remains an important issue at the college level, the number of instructional studies focusing on this issue is quite limited. Initially, more than 70 studies were identified that tackled this topic in some manner, but only 10 met our inclusion criteria. Most were disqualified because they were descriptive (e.g., college students are not monitoring what they read) or because the researchers chose to compare one comprehension technique to another (e.g., mapping vs. summarizing) without providing any direct instruction on the technique. These 10 studies fell into three basic categories, with 7 studies focusing on the improvement of recall and basic comprehension, the first category. The second category, the improvement of students' metacognition and self-regulatory processes (e.g., planning, reflecting, calibrating, and evaluating), included two studies. One study was in the third category, instructional studies focusing on students' critical thinking about single texts and multiple sources.

Instruction to Improve Recall and Basic Comprehension

In the seven instructional studies included in this category, the researchers/instructors focused on teaching students the strategies or techniques of summarization, organizing, self-explanation, and reciprocal teaching. Each of the studies provided a theoretical rationale pertinent to the particular strategy being investigated (e.g., summarization based on the theories of Van Dijk and Kintsch, 1983). Although not stated explicitly, most of the studies in this category were embedded within a constructivist perspective. In general, the findings from these experimental or quasi-experimental studies indicated that instruction in the targeted strategy or technique improved the students' recall or assisted the students in performing better than a control group that received no instruction. When other dependent variables were included in the studies, the findings were not as robust (i.e., De Simone, Oka, & Tischer, 1998; O'Reilly, Symons, and MacLatchy-Gaudet, 1998). For instance, in the study conducted by De Simone and colleagues, the experimental group who constructed networks performed significantly better than the control group on the free recall measure, but no significant differences between the groups appeared on multiple-choice measure.

Summarization. In a study of summarization as a means to improving recall and comprehension, Friend (1999) employed a direct instruction model to teach college students how to form generalizations or argument repetitions or how to self-reflect on what they had read. Once the instruction was completed, the subjects read a short expository passage and wrote their summaries. Using five indicators, two independent raters scored the summaries. If the raters' agreement in scoring fell below 80 percent, they met to discuss and resolve differences. The generalization group's summaries were judged to be significantly better in terms of thesis statements. In terms of an overall summarization skill, the two experimental groups produced summaries significantly better than the self-reflection group's. Friend notes that the scores for all treatment conditions certainly did not indicate that students had attained summarization mastery. Sanchez, Lorch, and Lorch (2000) also examined the impact of teaching students to summarize, but they added the variable of having students read text with headings or texts without headings. Students read an expository passage about energy and participated in a free recall. These free recalls were scored using four indicators, yielding an interrater reliability of .95. The participants with training and/or headings tended to have higher recall than the students who received no training or read a text without headings.

Organization. Three instructional studies focused on organizational strategies of teaching students how to create their own spatial displays using specific nodes and links (i.e., maps, networks). Using the early work of Diekhoff, Brown, and Dansereau (1982) on networking, Chmielewski and Dansereau (1998) sought to determine, in two different experimentally oriented studies, whether knowledge mapping implicitly improves the manner in which students interact with expository text. In their first experiment one group of students was trained to construct and evaluate maps while the control group completed a variety of assessment measures. During the last day of training both groups also completed a self-report questionnaire to determine how they read the expository texts. Five days later the two groups took a free recall test that was scored using a propositional analysis. The interrater reliability for the second scorer ranged from .93 to .94. Although the free recalls were low for both groups, the trained participants recalled significantly more macro-level information. No differences, however, occurred between the groups on how they responded to the questionnaire. The second study was similar to the first except that one question about students' level of motivation was added to the questionnaire. In Experiment 2 the trained group recalled significantly more macro and micro-level information, but no differences appeared on the self-report questionnaire.

De Simone, Oka, and Tischer's (1998) study, a pretest/posttest nonequivalent control group design, tackled the question of whether students who mentally construct networks can satisfactorily recall and recognize information from what they have read. Unlike the studies discussed thus far, these researchers administered prior knowledge tests on the targeted passages and a baseline measure of the students' abilities to network. After participating in 10 hours of training, the subjects read a short expository text and completed a researcher-constructed multiple-choice test and a free recall. Using idea units as the criteria, two coders scored the free recalls and produced an interrater reliability ranging from .85 to .95. The results indicated that the participants recalled significantly more key ideas from the pre- to posttest, but the trained participants made significantly greater gains on the recall measure and were more time efficient. No differences were discernible on the multiple-choice measure.

Verbal, Interactive. In contrast to the previous strategies that have emphasized written artifacts, O'Reilly, Symons, and MacLatchy-Gaudet (1998) examined the impact of elaborative interrogation (Stein & Bransford, 1979) and self-explanations (Chi & Van Lehn, 1991), two strategies capitalizing on verbal rehearsal. With the elaborative interrogation strategy students answered "why" questions (e.g., "Why is this fact true of . . . and not of . . . ?") on what they had read in order to make new connections between their prior knowledge and novel information. With the self-explanation strategy students were asked to explain or summarize information (e.g., "Explain what it means to you" or "Does it raise a question in your mind?"). After the practice phase subjects read a biology text containing 22 factual sentences that were presented to them on a computer screen. They then took a fill-in-the-blank and matching test, predicted their score, and completed a questionnaire that assessed their subjective opinions of the strategies they had been trained to use. The 2×3 ANOVA indicated that the self-explanation participants performed statistically significantly better than the elaborative interrogation and control group on both comprehension measures. No differences occurred across the groups in terms of prediction accuracy, but the self-explanation participants rated their strategy as significantly more effective and attractive in terms of future use.

The last study in this category focused on reciprocal teaching (Palincsar & Brown, 1984), a strategy or heuristic that embodies many of the reading processes studied in the previous six studies in this category (i.e., summarizing, clarifying). Using a quasi-experimental nonequivalent group design, Hart and Speece (1998) investigated the impact of training college students, enrolled in two different required assistance courses, to engage in reciprocal teaching or a control condition they dubbed *cooperative discussion* (i.e., interactions but no explicit emphasis on reading comprehension processes). The instruction in the former was characterized by intensive modeling and guided practice. The participants completed a standardized reading test, a learning strategy self-report inventory, and a task asking them to apply the four processes embedded in reciprocal teaching to two different brief passages. Two independent raters scored the transfer task, yielding an interrater reliability of .80. The results indicated that the reciprocal teaching participants performed better on the standardized reading test and the strategy application task, but there were no statistically significant differences on the self-report strategies inventory.

Instruction to Improve Metacognition and Self-regulation

Research in the area of metacognition and self-regulation is not as prevalent as research conducted with specific comprehension strategies such as summarization. Perhaps this is due, in part, to the difficulties researchers have in identifying measures that are valid, reliable, and practical to use in a classroom setting. We located two studies for this review, one a quasi-experimental study and one a descriptive case study. Both appeared to be working from a constructivist perspective. As with the previous studies, these two studies also provided theoretical rationales for the strategies and techniques they were investigating. Although the studies were conducted in two different content areas, psychology and history, it is noteworthy that both of them concluded that students who were more successful on their content area exams were also the ones who improved their metacognition or self-regulation.

Hacker, Bol, Horgan, and Rakow's (2000) quasi-experimental study capitalized on the previous work of researchers such as Glenberg and Epstein (1985) and Maki and Berry (1984) who have investigated students' metacognitive judgments. Specifically, Hacker et al. sought to determine if students enrolled in educational psychology courses could improve, over a semester period of time, their metacomprehension judgments or test prediction accuracy. The 99 students made pre and postdictions estimating their performance and reported the amount of time they spent studying for three different researcher-constructed, multiple-choice unit exams. Throughout the course the students also received instruction on the importance of reflection and accurate self-assessment and participated in this reflection after each exam. The findings indicated that the higher performing students increased their accuracy in pre/postdictions, but the low-performing students did not and continued their overpredictive tendencies. In addition, the results suggested that study time was not related to students' test performance.

Hubbard and Simpson (2003) focused their descriptive case study in a history course to document the changes students made over a semester in terms of the strategies they chose to employ, their accuracy in knowledge monitoring, and the type of calibrations they made as they evaluated their performance. Using a model of instruction embedded in self-regulation theory, the researchers also wanted to characterize the students' practices to see if any patterns existed across performance levels. Over a 16-week period of time, the 24 students in the study were taught task-appropriate strategies and techniques designed to generate self-reflection and internal feedback. To document possible changes, the participants reflected on their performance after each exam and made grade postdictions, described the strategies they employed, and recounted the time spent studying. Findings indicated that the most successful students calibrated global planning processes and the type and level of self-selected, task-appropriate strategies sooner than the less successful students. Except for the A students, knowledge monitoring did not improve, but students' explanations did shift from external to internal ones.

Instruction to Improve Critical Thinking

The one study representing this last category was a descriptive study conducted by Manuel (2002). Although Manuel does not explicitly identify a guiding theoretical perspective, it appears from the article's introduction that the study was influenced and guided by a media literacy perspective. In the study 63 students enrolled in an information literacy course were taught how to identify and evaluate types of information and use appropriate search strategies. After an 11-week period, they were randomly assigned to read articles from *Popular Science* and to complete a one-page paper that discussed the nature of the information, the documentation, the article's purpose and intended audience, and the author's credentials. Manuel's analysis indicated that the participants had difficulties identifying problems with the sources (e.g., biases, lack of credentials, lack of documentation). More specifically, 57 percent could not identify the article's thesis, 61 percent could not pinpoint the evidence the author used to support the thesis, and 68 percent could not make any connection between the author's credentials and areas of possible personal interest in their topics. In her conclusions, Manuel suggests that students need numerous opportunities for close reading, modeling, and feedback if they are to improve their critical thinking skills.

Summary of College-Level Findings

Ten studies were identified that focused on reading comprehension instruction for college students. In general, the four main findings from these studies were as follows. First, the five classroom instructional studies that focused on teaching college students how to summarize or organize what they have read determined that these students outperformed others who received no instruction or who employed alternative techniques. However, it should be noted that the scores on the dependent measures were low, indicating that more instructional time was necessary for students to master the skills of summarizing and organizing. Second, the two classroom studies that focused on verbal rehearsal (i.e., self-explanation) and interactive heuristics that embody several reading processes (i.e., reciprocal teaching) found that students trained in these strategies performed better than their

counterparts on employing alternative strategies. Third, the two studies on metacognition and self-regulation (i.e., planning, reflection, strategy calibration) determined that students who were more successful on content-area exams were the ones who improved their metacognitive judgments and calibrated global planning processes and strategy choices sooner than the less successful students. Finally, the one study that trained students to think critically about information determined that more than half of the students continued to have difficulties in identifying and evaluating the authors' viewpoints, credentials, and arguments. Again, the importance of sustained instructional time was noted, as was the necessity for students to receive numerous opportunities for modeling and feedback on their work.

CRITIQUES AND RECOMMENDATIONS FOR RESEARCH AND THEORY DEVELOPMENT

In this section, we provide separate critiques and recommendations for research and theory development at each of the three grade-level categories. Implications for classroom practice follow in the next section of this chapter.

Kindergarten Through Grade Five

We begin our critique of the kindergarten through fifth-grade studies by attending to theory. Fewer than half of the reports provided explicit discussion of theoretical bases for the studies. For research on classroom early reading instruction to make a difference, it is likely that greater reliance on theory building or theory grounding is needed. When researchers specifically focus on the theoretical relationships that might occur between particular instructional variables or constructs and specific student outcomes, the studies are most likely to be clearly focused on the hypothesized relationships in ways that enable greater precision in design and methodology. "Tight" research, across the range of possibilities of kinds of research, is most likely to lead to dependable outcomes that in turn can have greater potential for affecting classroom practices. In the ideal, some "grand" theory detailing a host of instructional variables as they relate to a wide array of particular child reading outcomes and processes would be useful for guiding a program of research on classroom reading instruction. Collective sets of studies conducted around hypotheses entailed in such a "grand" theory could lead to theory refinement as well as to enhanced practices. Ruddell and Unrau's (1994) sociocognitive model of reading comes to mind as one example of such a "grand" theory effort. In that model, classroom reading instruction is featured as a construct that affects children's reading. Short of relying on a "grand" theory, some of the researchers among those in the lower grade category did provide their underlying hypothetical theoretical relationships between constructs of interest in their studies. Among the several possible exemplars of researchers who explicitly provided such underlying theory in our report, here we reference just a few: Taylor and colleagues (Taylor et al., 2003), who carefully laid out a set of teacher behavior variables that might hypothetically be related to different student literacy outcomes; Juel and Minden-Cupp (2000) and Jiménez and Guzmán (2003), both of whom explicitly hypothesized which child reading processes might be promoted by particular kinds of instruction; and Wolf (1998), who thoughtfully led the reader through ways in which teachers, students, and texts might coconstruct meanings through social interaction.

A second noteworthy point about theory in the early-grade studies is that, among those researchers who did provide explicit theoretical undergirding, a wide array of constructs was represented, ranging from explicit teaching behaviors such as asking higher-level questions or coaching in relation to a child's internal mental representations, to particular forms of nonverbal communication, including external physical actions that accompany words, in relation to ways in which children demonstrate meanings.

Next, we move to an overall critique of the methodologies used in the K-5 studies. Notably, there were quite a few qualitative studies relative to the total number, and it is interesting that such work is appearing in some journals, such as the *Journal of Educational Psychology* and *Cognition and Instruction*, that traditionally have singularly published quantitative work.

For researchers investigating effective teacher practices, greater use of a common coding scheme across studies would enable better comparison across samples and reports and also would facilitate meaningful aggregation of results across studies. Further, echoing our earlier point about the need for more theory-based methods, it would be helpful if more observational coding schemes were built in relation to explicit theoretical underpinnings about the relationships between particular teacher behaviors and particular student outcomes.

What topics and groups of children need further exploration in the future? Perhaps it is not surprising to find in our early-grades section more studies of word- or sound-level instruction than other areas of instruction and not surprising to find that such studies tended to be concentrated at the kindergarten and first-grade levels. Juel and Minden-Cupp (2000, p. 458) have said, "In preparing

the grant proposal for the Center for the Improvement of Early Reading Achievement . . . , we asked teachers and administrators what research questions they most needed answered in order to improve primary-grade reading instruction. They raised more questions about how to teach children to read words than any other area in early reading." At the same time, reviews such as Adams' (1990) landmark review of research on reading acquisition and the *Report of the National Reading Panel* (National Reading Panel, 2000) have emphasized the central role of phonological awareness and word recognition in early reading development.

However, the studies of word-level instruction since 1996 that we examined were about phonology. Few studies since 1996 have examined the impact of instruction that emphasizes semantics and syntax in word recognition strategies, such as teaching students how to use context clues for word recognition. It is useful to know that phonological understandings play a critical role in early word learning. At the same time, the utility of instruction in other psycholinguistic understandings, such as deployment of syntactic and semantic knowledge in contextual guessing, continues to be debated (cf. Juel & Minden-Cupp, 2000). More research—and theory—that explores the interplay of instruction in more than one linguistic system (phonological, syntactic, and semantic) for word recognition might reveal more about the relative importance of each system and/or about their combinatory impact.

There were few studies in the comprehension, fluency, and affective instruction category, and the six that were found were also scattered across instruction related to the three areas. Perhaps recent public focus on phonology at the lower grade levels has led to lesser effort to understand instruction in other areas? In any case, more concerted study of instruction in such areas at the lower grade levels would perhaps inform the extent to which such instruction is beneficial and warranted. Further, it might be useful to study these instructional emphases in relation to word- and sound-level instructional emphases, so as to better ascertain the benefits and detriments of each, affording a larger picture of instructional needs.

Turning to the category of "overarching reading instruction," some recent researchers have suggested that elementary classroom teachers' reading instruction is not easily categorized as emphasizing one domain of reading processes over another (such as word or code emphasis vs. meaning emphasis). Rather, more often than not, their instruction tends to perhaps equally emphasize many different reading process, and as well, it tends to reflect an understanding of the connectedness of those processes. Over the past decade, the term *balanced reading instruction* has been perhaps one of the most popular labels for such overarching instructional frames. To some degree, when we researchers decontextualize selected reading instruction of particular reading processes in order to study them, we simplify in ways that have potential for distorting what actual classroom teachers do. Studying the "whole" of instruction, with all of its complexity, is appealing at least in part because it means studying what teachers actually do within the messiness of their classrooms. From this standpoint, the investigations in the "overarching reading instruction" category hit a necessary target in their effort to understand reading instruction in its broader, more layered, frame.

At the same time, investigations of broader instructional frames are perhaps among the most difficult to accomplish, because of what they are—messy, complicated, multifaceted, and layered. Descriptions of those more complex instructional frames and how they interplay with student reading development are often studied through various forms of qualitative research methods. In these cases, one result is clearer delineation of the broader instructional frames, such as when a teacher's "balanced reading instruction" is detailed and defined through careful description of its components and their interrelationships. Such delineation may be quite useful to teachers who want to implement similar reading instruction. Inferences about linkages between grand instructional frames and student reading growth might also provide valuable hypotheses for further study. One tentative inference from a subset of the investigations on overarching reading instruction with a small number of students is that what teachers emphasize in instruction tends to be reflected in student understandings about reading, and what teachers fail to emphasize may likewise fail to be learned by students. In short, what you teach matters in relation to what children learn. Although there is ample research at least as far back as the now-famous First Grade Studies (Bond & Dykstra, 1997) to suggest that children's reading *achievement* is not dependent on a particular *reading instruction method*, the body of research reviewed in this category provides a further and unique contribution indicating that nuances of *what* children learn *are* related to *what* teachers teach.

Still, correlational, quasi-experimental, and experimental research, done with an eye toward permitting firmer causal inferences between the broader instructional frame and development of student knowledge about reading, is downright problematic. First, the parameters of the overall instructional frame must be very clearly defined, and it is sometimes very difficult to do that. Second, in most of this research, even if significant results are obtained, what we learn is that something about the overarching instruction mattered. What we generally do not know is whether some particular component(s) in the package might have accounted for the significant results. What might be productive in future research are quasi-experimental and experimental studies that build in controls for the various components so that effects of particular features of the overarching instructional package, and even interactions among them, may be assessed. Additionally, examining shifts in student learning over time in relation to the instructional frame would lend a better sense of whether particular instructional components ought to be emphasized more at different times in a student's reading development. In other words, "grand" repeated measures designs, controlling for, and comparing different components of an overarching reading instructional frame might hold promise for further informing classroom teachers about nuances of their already complex reading instruction. But what would it take to accomplish such research? Most likely, it would require teams of researchers, with considerable funding, and considerable time.

Notably absent were studies of teachers using technology to enhance children's reading, studies of vocabulary meaning instruction, and of metacognition instruction. One exception was the study by Mathes and colleagues (2001) in which there was a computer-assisted-instruction condition. There were but a few studies involving English-language learners or children with disabilities, and no studies of bilingual reading instruction. All of these areas would be fruitful future venues.

Middle and High School Level

As with the early-grade studies, we begin our critique of the research on middle and high school reading instruction by attending to theory development. Although we applaud the relatively well-grounded theoretical work that undergirds the qualitative studies reported in this section, we are hard pressed to find the same depth of theorizing in the quantitative studies. Further, regarding the research on instruction for students with reading disabilities, we were disappointed to find that only one of the two studies that met our criteria for inclusion had an explicitly stated theoretical frame. To underscore the need for greater understanding of why a particular intervention works for which students under what conditions, it is essential that researchers move beyond a simple "what works" frame of thinking. We support full disclosure of the theory (or theories) underlying a particular intervention. In addition, we suggest that researchers provide a relatively detailed analysis of the assumptions inherent in a particular theory and describe why those assumptions could be expected to have an impact on how an intervention is implemented.

Methodologically speaking, it was somewhat rare to find a study at the middle and high school level that included open-ended dependent measures or tasks that required students to think critically or to defend their answers in writing. This, despite the fact that nearly a decade ago, the National Educational Longitudinal Survey (NELS) report (Gamoran, Nystrand, Berends, & LePore, 1995) pointed out that reading instruction that emphasized understanding and analytical writing (as contrasted with instruction that emphasized grammar and lower level processing) was associated with higher achievement gains. On a more positive note, a good number of studies at the secondary level did include natural texts of sufficient length to merit the use of reading strategies. Given these observations, we commend researchers' use of natural texts and call for greater attention to reading-thinking-writing connections in the design of future reading instruction research at the secondary level.

The research on teaching and learning in content area reading classrooms at the middle and high school level varied considerably on several dimensions. Researchers choosing experimental or quasi-experimental designs presented ample evidence in support of their conclusions. Those choosing purely descriptive studies (from either a quantitative or qualitative perspective) were not as convincing in the data they presented. However, researchers who used naturalistic and case study designs tended on the whole to include exceedingly rich and complex data sets. Ethnographic studies of teachers providing content-area reading instruction at the secondary level (and that were published between 1996 and 2004) were difficult to find. Although several qualitative studies used ethnographic methods, we did not find a single ethnography that met our criteria for inclusion. This would not have been the case had we considered studies published earlier than 1996 or in books. Thus, our inclination is to call for more rigorously designed and analyzed descriptive studies, as well as a renewed interest in ethnographic work at the secondary level.

Overall, we were not surprised to find that between 1996 and 2004 relatively few researchers have focused on reading instruction at the middle and secondary levels. This may change in the near future, however, with the growing emphasis on adolescent literacy. But for the present, even an expanded literature search that included keywords such as *content area*, *subject matter*, *comprehension*, *analogical reasoning*, *textbooks*, *struggling readers*, *teaching strategies*, and *vocabulary* (in addition to the agreed-on terms) produced a very limited data set. In addition, those found were focused largely on English/language arts classrooms. Thus, we recommend that researchers focus increasingly more on instruction that occurs in a broad array of content area classrooms (e.g., social studies, mathematics, science, and foreign language).

We were also not surprised to find only two studies that incorporated media literacy in their design. For the most part, the studies that met our criteria for teaching and learning in reading at the middle and high school levels focused on traditional print materials and depended on paper-and-pencil tasks to measure the effectiveness of an intervention. This seems a bit out of synch with the growing literature on integrating literacy and technology in the curriculum (International Reading Association, 2001). To overcome this limitation in the research literature, we recommend that future research take into account the impact of newer information communication technologies (e.g., multimedia/hypermedia, e-mail, instant messaging) on reading instruction at the secondary level. Doing so may more adequately reflect the multiliteracies youth have available (and make use of) in out-of-school settings.

Although one study focused on foreign language instruction and learning in Canada, we did not find a single study that investigated reading instruction for students who are learning English as a second language in the United States at the middle and high school level. The closest we came to locating such a study was Jiménez and Gersten's (1999) investigation of the instructional practices of two Latina/o elementary school teachers who provided quality instruction aimed at preparing their students "to benefit from all-English instruction in middle school" (p. 274). This seemed a bit incongruous given the growing number of linguistically and culturally different students in our schools. Taking into account Langer's (2001) work with "beat the odds" schools, it would seem exceedingly important that researchers design studies that take into consideration the reading needs of English language learners in subject matter classrooms at the middle and high school level.

Another underrepresented area of research was that dealing with preservice or beginning-level teachers' professional development needs. We did not find a single study that met our inclusion criteria and that also examined how preservice or early induction-year teachers instruct students in content-area reading. This seemed telling to us because it marked a serious gap in the research knowledge base, especially given the grave concerns surrounding the retention issue in the early years of teaching. Highlighting these concerns was a Capitol Hill briefing on June 23, 2004, by the Alliance for Excellent Education, a bipartisan policy group located in Washington, DC. Among other things, the briefing pointed out that "American schools spend more than $2.6 billion annually replacing teachers who have dropped out of the teaching profession." This report, which is available at http://www.all4ed.org/ also pointed out that comprehensive induction, especially in a teacher's first 2 years on the job, is the single most effective strategy for stemming a rapidly increasing teacher attrition rate. Strickland's (2002) work on the importance of studying professional development and its impact on content literacy instruction would seem to support the Alliance's findings. Given the situation just described, we recommend developing a line of research that examines the specific needs of preservice and induction-year teachers who are expected to assume instructional responsibilities for middle and high school students' reading growth in content-area classes.

In contrast to the notable absence of research on beginning teachers' professional development needs, special educators seem particularly active in the area of researching effective reading instruction at the secondary level. To us, this makes sense given that adolescents who struggle with their school reading assignments are often those who have been identified previously as having learning disabilities. One particularly interesting finding was that special education researchers are becoming increasingly focused on studying the instructional needs of students with reading disabilities in general education classrooms. The rationale they give is that teachers in these general education classrooms are often reluctant to implement an intervention that will benefit only a subset of the class. Considering this possibility, we have to wonder why much of the research to date has not been designed to examine the effectiveness of instructional interventions for students of all ability levels in general education classrooms.

College Level

As with the other studies, we begin our critique of the college-level studies by focusing on theory. On a consistent basis theoretical rationales and explanations were provided for the strategies and techniques (e.g., summarization, networking) that students were trained to employ. However, what was missing in many of the studies was an overarching or encompassing theory that detailed a rationale, a set of assumptions, or an explanation as to how the targeted strategy or technique related to other variables having an impact on students' comprehension. To illustrate, an encompassing theory such as self-regulated learning could have been used to explain the possible relationship between students' metacognitive judgments, their self-evaluations, and their subsequent reading comprehension.

The research studies on comprehension instruction at the college level have been limited in scope in two basic ways. First, most of the studies included in this review employed either experimental or quasi-experimental designs. Although we applaud the rigor and quality of

these studies, we urge future researchers to consider the use of descriptive case studies, ethnographic studies, and multidesign studies that incorporate both qualitative and quantitative data sources. Second, an overwhelming majority of the studies in this review focused on strategies or heuristics that have been researched extensively. Rather than conducting another study on summarization, we think it would be advantageous to investigate planning, calibrating, or evaluating, higher level cognitive processes critical to college students' reading and learning from (and with) text. Such research endeavors would be unique and a contribution to the field.

Turning to methodology, we were concerned that so many of the studies we read and reviewed were still using free recall measures as a means to measure students' reading comprehension. Because free recall measures are not typical tasks for college students, they lack ecological validity. If we really want to know whether students have improved their reading comprehension, it would be advantageous to incorporate into our studies dependent measures that encourage students to think on higher levels and to apply the techniques they have learned. For example, in the Hynd-Shanahan, Holschuh, and Hubbard (2004) study on critical thinking about multiple sources, one of the dependent measures, an essay exam, asked students to answer a question that required them to construct a generalization about what they had read during the training period. To investigate transfer in even more depth, Hynd-Shanahan and colleagues also required students to read and incorporate another text (an excerpt they had been given during the exam) into their essay answer.

If dependent measures need to be more representative and challenging, so do the texts that students read during training sessions and testing periods. In most of the studies we reviewed, participants were reading short (i.e., 200–1,400 words) expository passages taken from psychology or humanities textbooks. Admittedly, some of the studies (e.g., Hacker et al., 2000) used lengthy text pieces, but that was the exception. One wonders why a student would need to try out a new comprehension strategy technique with such short passages. Given these trends, we recommend that researchers design studies using authentic texts from a variety of academic disciplines (e.g., chemistry, biology) and to consider the use of alternative texts such as magazines and newspapers, as Manuel (2002) did in her study.

In a similar vein, it would be refreshing to see more studies that assessed students' progress and improvement after a sufficient period of time, allowing for numerous samples of their behaviors and skills before, during, and after the targeted instruction. Measuring students' progress after instruction certainly implies a time frame sufficient to measure their control and transfer of a strategy or technique. In fact, most studies would benefit from multiple data collection methods that converge and provide triangulation for the findings. To illustrate, in Butler's study (1998) of learning-disabled students tutored in a clinical situation (and thus not included in our review), the students completed a variety of quantitative and qualitative measures throughout the study to measure their metacognition, reading performance, motivation, and strategy transfer.

Methodologically speaking, it was a bit disconcerting to note that most of the studies did not include an effort to trace or validate whether students had mastered the targeted technique or whether they had actually used the technique during the criterion-testing period. In the one study that did address the issue of how students were actually reading the targeted passages, they were asked to complete a self-report questionnaire at the end of the study. Admittedly, it is difficult to conceive and operationalize a method to trace students' internal processing, strategy transfer, and improvement, but it is an important challenge the field needs to address. Some researchers (Butler, 1998; Nist, Simpson, Olejnik, & Mealey, 1991) have sought a compromise by collecting students' actual work and coding it to reveal patterns of progress, but these tasks are extremely time consuming.

IMPLICATIONS FOR CLASSROOM PRACTICE

In this section, we discuss implications for classroom practice based on the main findings reported in the summaries following each of the three grade-level categories (K-5, middle/high school level, and college level). Taking each of the main findings, one at a time, we draw corresponding implications for classroom practice.

Kindergarten Through Grade Five

First, effective teachers in kindergarten through fifth grade tend to teach in particular ways. Teachers might aim to internalize the cluster of behaviors that were noted in the findings and in the previous summary of main findings. On the whole, the portrait of the effective teacher is of someone who has a "balanced" outlook about teaching students to learn about various internal processes and mechanisms and who teaches students in ways that encourage self-regulation and positive dispositions toward reading.

Second, the findings about explicit instruction in phonics were interesting in that they represent a refinement of some past conclusions. They suggest that, on average, for kindergarten and first grade, explicit phonics instruction is very helpful, and it is particularly helpful for children who enter school at lower literacy levels. However, on average, from second grade onward, such instruction tends to be associated with lower reading achievement growth or is no more effective than another approach. Taken together, the implication of these findings is that, on the whole, teachers might emphasize phonics more in kindergarten and first grade, and then, from second grade onward, increase emphasis on other kinds of word recognition strategies as well as on other subprocesses of reading while simultaneously decreasing emphasis on phonics. Of course, there would be exceptions when individual children in second grade and above are reading on lower grade levels and may need instructional emphasis on phonics.

Third, although explicit comprehension strategy instruction has not been clearly shown to enhance reading level or reading achievement, it seems prudent at the present time to suggest that teachers do such instruction as it is likely to broaden children's repertoire of strategic thinking for meaning making.

Fourth, only one study was found in which student discussion about text was enhanced, and thus, the finding here is quite tentative. However, the results of this study lead to the belief that when teachers learn how to structure lessons so as to encourage student dialog, enriched understandings are more likely to be created and learned.

Fifth, one study pointed to the affective impact of joining drama with reading instruction. Here again, we see an implied benefit of teachers' understanding of reading processes as more than just internal cognitive mechanisms involving mental routines and strategies. Wanting to read and liking to read are equally as important as having the cognitive strategies and skills to do it, and classroom theater may be one useful instructional means of engagement.

Sixth, when we think of overarching reading instruction, we again see benefits of teachers targeting a wide array of goals for their students learning. At least at the lower grade levels, instruction that balances the cognitive with the affective, the child-centered with the teacher-centered, may be associated with students, including multilingual learners, assuming similarly balanced understandings of reading and what it means to be a reader. And to learn to read, children need to do it. Books on tape appear to be particularly beneficial for English-language learners. At the same time, only one study compared the effectiveness of whole reading programs, and so it is difficult to make inferences about the effectiveness of balanced approaches to reading instruction as compared to other approaches.

Seventh, the finding in one study, that cognitive abilities in kindergarten mattered more than instructional program for later word-reading abilities, may have more implications for how teachers think about their instruction relative to student individual differences than for what instruction to use. That is, teachers might well consider a student's reading developmental level and adjust and modulate instruction in relation to that level.

Eighth, and here we echo the sentiment just expressed, the one study involving third-grade children with learning disabilities suggests that teachers did not modulate instruction for those children. Given that some of the research on effective reading instruction practices suggests that small-group instruction is related to children's reading progress, it seems likely that students with learning disabilities might benefit from lessons that are modulated to address the critical features of learning associated with their particular reading levels.

Middle and High School Grades

First, explicit and systematic instruction in the use of a wide range of reading strategies can support students' comprehension of content area texts—whether in print, visual, or digital media forms. This support appears to come from teachers' attention to the importance of helping students organize or summarize information in meaningful ways. Such organizational skills also enhance students' chances of remembering content long enough to integrate it with other subject matter learning.

Second, here it is abundantly clear that teachers who invite students to take an active role in content-area reading and learning base their instruction on students' needs and interests as much as possible. Whether this is done through choosing relevant reading materials, keeping students apprised of the progress they are making toward short- and long-term goals, or simply providing an open forum for discussion, teachers who are student centered in their approaches to instruction can expect increased student performance on a variety of outcome measures.

Third, teachers at the middle and high school level can be assured that instructional techniques developed for students with learning disabilities to increase their sense of self-competency will benefit students from a wide range of ability levels. This is especially important for inclusion classroom teachers to know. In short, effective instructional interventions such as Reciprocal Teaching and prior knowledge activation are procedures for

enabling all students to internalize the knowledge and skills necessary for engaging in challenging literacy tasks on their own.

Fourth, instruction that encourages students to make connections between what they know already and what they are expected to learn that is new from reading a variety of text types will build self-efficacy and a sense of accomplishment. Toward a related end, teachers can capitalize on adolescents' interests in socializing with their peers by building into the school day opportunities for collaborative reading and writing activities. Such activities are likely to foster student engagement by helping them make connections between literacies they value out of school and those they are expected to apply in their content area classes.

College Level

First, the trends from the literature indicated that college instructors can improve their students' comprehension and retention of expository text if they teach them how to summarize and organize information. When students are summarizing information using their own words and forging relationships between ideas into a format or organizational schema, they are actively engaged in their reading.

Second, explicit instruction in how to conduct verbal rehearsals or self-explanations and how to participate in reciprocal teaching can enhance students' comprehension, especially those students who profit from verbal, interactive opportunities. These findings echo the ones from the studies conducted with middle school and high school students.

Third, two studies suggested that students benefit from being taught how to make accurate metacognitive judgments about their understanding and how to calibrate their planning processes and strategy choices. However, college instructors should remember that initially it will be the higher performing students (i.e., the ones scoring better on content area exams) who will understand and embrace these metacognitive and self-regulatory processes.

Finally, college instructors hoping to improve their students' critical thinking skills should know that it is a difficult, but not impossible teaching task. As determined in Manuel's (2002) study, some students may quickly master the skill of evaluating documents, but others will need a sustained period of time. In fact, it should be noted for each of the strategies, heuristics, and skills outlined in this section that it is important for college instructors to plan their interventions over a sustained time frame and to provide numerous opportunities for modeling, guided practice, and feedback. Moreover, it is important for instructors to stress, sometimes in a recursive fashion, the advantages and costs of each targeted strategy or technique.

CROSS-GRADE TRENDS AND ISSUES

Findings from the 51 studies on reading instruction that met our criteria for inclusion in this chapter share some common attributes, namely, the cross-grade trends and issues that we focus on next. Before we do so, however, we make two prefatory comments. First, on the whole, although our inclusion/exclusion criteria may have narrowed the number of studies considerably, we believe that those criteria resulted in a set of studies that were at least reasonably well conducted, and some were clearly representations of research done at its finest. The quality of the research suggests that we may, with some justification, place good faith in the findings. At the same time, a fair number of researchers did not provide complete details about measures and/or about reliabilities for measures, practices that should become standard in the future—at least for the purposes of informing readers so that they can judge the extent to which findings might be considered reliable and valid.

Second, it is important to point out that despite concerted efforts by researchers, school-based educators, and policymakers across the past decade, reading achievement gaps between and among groups of students stubbornly persist (Alliance for Excellent Education, 2004; Kamil, 2003; RAND Reading Study Group, 2002; Strickland & Alvermann, 2004). It is with these gaps in mind that we wrote the chapter's final section.

A Need for Multiple Frames and Methodologies

The wide array of theoretical constructs in evidence across the studies represented in this chapter might be construed to be a healthy sign. That is, one might argue that diverse theoretical frameworks represent researchers' efforts to work amid a universe of diverse epistemologies. For example, in the early grades this diversity of effort could reflect researchers' interests in gaining knowledge about (and knowing how) to teach reading in relation to young children's cognitive and social development. Spelled out, this developmental interest might be oriented toward studies of children's internal and mental states (such as their strategic thinking or knowledge about phonology); alternatively, it might be situated between and among teachers' and children's minds and texts, or in some complementary combinations of internal and external representations and actions. At the middle and high school level, a proclivity for diverse theorizing might reflect researchers' attempts to frame their studies in ways that account for teachers' epistemological beliefs about adolescents' multiple ways of knowing. Or, it might reflect researchers' attempts to cast a broad net in looking for answers (partial at best) to complex issues surrounding the acknowledged decline in adolescents' motivations for reading, especially school-related reading. At the college level, the tendency to theorize a variety of specific strategies and techniques (while simultaneously overlooking opportunities to understand the more encompassing relationships among variables of interest) might reflect the field's current views of what counts as college-level reading. It seems to us that exploring the fullest array of possible theoretical frameworks holds the greatest potential for furthering understandings about classroom reading instruction and students' reading development.

Just as we suggest that the wide array of theoretical frameworks represented in the 51 studies included here is a healthy sign, we also suggest that diversity in methodologies is welcomed and needed. Different research questions beg different methodologies; thus, one's question(s) and choice of methodology are inextricably linked. In the early grades, researchers have attended to this linkage by choosing methodologies that enable them to examine a wide-reaching range of issues, stretching from the instructional impact on children's phonological awareness to the ways in which reader's theater enhances children's understandings of what it means to be literate. Equally diverse is the span of methodologies chosen by researchers who conduct their studies at the secondary level. However, we would maintain that the methodologies used in studying adolescent reading instruction reflect a more restricted range of research questions. This might be due to the greater focus during the middle and high school years on "fixing" reading difficulties—a concept that is increasingly shot full of critiques of the notion that teachers should be changing *students* rather than re/mediating the *conditions* in which students learn (Alvermann & Rush; 2004; Flood & Lapp, 1995; Luke & Elkins, 2000). A similar concern for "fixing" students' reading comprehension occurs at the college level. All too often mandated reading strategy courses focus their goals, almost exclusively, on raising students' scores on standardized reading tests. Unfortunately, courses such as these are myopic in that they do not address the academic tasks that students must confront once they score at the specified level on the reading test and exit the mandated course.

A Need for Studies of Content-Area Reading Instruction

At the elementary level, no studies specifically involving content-area reading instruction and learning were located for this review. Broadening the scope of research into reading in the content areas would likely better inform our understandings of instruction as it relates to helping young children read to learn. It is in the content areas that we most typically find informational texts, and such reading texts can require ways of thinking and knowing that are different from those used when reading narrative texts. Research on elementary-grades reading instruction and learning in the content areas could help us to better gauge the extent to which such instruction has transformative power for shaping students' abilities to ways of considering reading for learning as well as the extent to which such instruction affects students' breadth and depth of content knowledge.

Studies of reading instruction conducted at the middle and high school level have tended to focus overwhelmingly on the English language arts curriculum, if not specifically on the teaching and learning that goes on in English classes. This bias toward the English language arts is perhaps understandable given some rather long-standing beliefs that reading is the primary "subject matter" of elementary teachers and that students should be prepared to read grade-level texts by the time they enter the middle grades. The fact that neither of these beliefs (or assumptions, as some might claim) is accurate is even more reason for designing studies of content-area reading instruction that encompass more than the English language arts. A further reason for broadening the disciplinary areas in which content reading instruction is studied lies in the increased number of students who speak a language other than English as their first language. Teaching additional languages is a form of instruction that has important implications for content learning at the secondary level, yet it has been largely ignored in the current research.

Because most of the studies conducted at the college level focus on the familiar or comfortable settings of a psychology or literature course, we know very little about reading and learning from (and with) texts in the other academic disciplines such as chemistry, biology, or physics. Moreover, because the research has focused almost exclusively on training students to read single pieces of expository text, we cannot recommend research-validated techniques or suggestions that would assist students as they read alternative texts or as they struggle to reconcile multiple, conflicting sources on the same topic. Shortcomings such as these suggest the need for studies that cut across disciplines and text types.

A Need for Finer Grained Analyses

With few exceptions, the middle grades and high school studies included in this chapter reflect the research community's continued reliance on global means of assessment. Without more fine-grained analyses of the influence of individual differences in the research on reading instruction in kindergarten through the postsecondary level, the field is left with partial, at best, understandings of which interventions work and why, as well as which students benefit more or less from such interventions and why.

Middle and high school researchers of reading instruction studies that met our criteria for inclusion tended to be satisfied with global measures of comprehension and vocabulary development. This would come as no surprise had we limited our review to include only quantitative or large-scale descriptive studies. However, such was not the case. With few notable exceptions, assessments of student outcomes were mostly limited to standardized reading achievement tests or researcher-constructed measures of comprehension and vocabulary development. Even adolescents' interests in (and attitudes toward) a particular instructional intervention were captured by means of survey instruments that measured only the most surface-level features of the intervention. Finer grained analyses, especially the kind associated with ethnographies and descriptive case studies of classroom-based content-area reading instruction, are needed if we are to understand the nuances of such instruction. Practically speaking, however, this is a tall order inasmuch as ethnographies take a long time to do and their findings do not generalize.

As with the studies conducted with elementary, middle school, and high school students, the studies conducted at the college level rely on global measures of comprehension. Because these studies have not included designs and instruments that invite finer grained analyses, we never are sure whether college students are actually employing a particular strategy or technique and, if so, why. Descriptive case studies with multiple, overlapping data sources could be conducted in order to trace students' behaviors over a period of time and provide researchers with insights into what type of students benefit and what type of students may need a longer period of time to master a targeted skill or strategy.

References

Adams M. J. (1990). *Beginning to read: Thinking and learning about print*. Cambridge, MA: MIT Press.

Agee, J. (2000). What is effective literature instruction? A study of experienced high school English teachers in differing grade- and ability-level classes. *Journal of Literacy Research, 32*, 303–348.

Alexander, P. A., & Jetton, T. L. (2000) Learning from text: A multidimensional and developmental perspective. In M. L. Kamil, P. B. Mosenthal, P. D. Pearson, & R. Barr (Eds.), *Handbook of reading research* (Vol. III, pp. 285–310). Mahwah, NJ: Lawrence Erlbaum Associates.

Alfassi, M. (1998). Reading for meaning: The efficacy of reciprocal teaching in fostering reading comprehension in high school students in remedial reading classes. *American Educational Research Journal, 35*, 309–332.

Alliance for Excellent Education. (2004). Issue Brief: *Adolescent literacy policy update*, n. p. Retrieved February 9, 2004, from http://www.all4ed.org/publications/Adolescent%20Literacy%20Policy%20Update.pdf

Alvermann, D. E. (2002). Effective literacy instruction for adolescents. *Journal of Literacy Research, 34*, 189–208.

Alvermann, D. E., & Moore, D. W. (1991). Secondary school reading. In R. Barr, M. L. Kamil, P. Mosenthal, & P. D. Pearson (Eds.), *Handbook of reading research* (Vol. II, pp. 951–983). White Plains, NY: Longman.

Alvermann, D. E., & Rush, L. S. (2004). Literacy intervention programs at the middle and high school levels. In T. L. Jetton & J. A. Dole (Eds.), *Adolescent literacy research and practice* (pp. 210–227). New York: Guilford.

Applebee, A. N., Langer, J. A., Nystrand, M., & Gamoran, A. (2003). Discussion-based approaches to developing understanding: Classroom instruction and student performance in middle and high school English. *American Educational Research Journal, 40*, 685–730.

Asselin, M. M. (1997). Teachers' knowledge of reading instruction: A description and investigation of effects. *Alberta Journal of Educational Research, 43*, 235–252.

Ausubel, D. P. (1963). *The psychology of meaningful verbal learning*. New York: Grune & Stratton.

Baker, S., & Smith, S. (1999). Starting off on the right foot: The influence of four principles of professional development in improving literacy instruction in two kindergarten programs. *Learning Disabilities Research & Practice, 14*, 239–253.

Bakhtin, M. M. (1981). *The dialogic imagination: Four essays* [C. Emerson & M. Holquist, Trans.]. Austin: University of Texas Press.

Barron, R. F., & Earle, R. A. (1973). An approach for vocabulary instruction. In H. L. Herber and R. F. Barron (Eds.), *Research in reading in the content areas: Second year report* (pp. 84–100). Syracuse, NY: Syracuse University Reading and Language Arts Center.

Baumann, J. F., Jones, L. A., & Kessell, N. S. (1993). Using think alouds to enhance children's comprehension monitoring abilities. *The Reading Teacher, 47*, 184–193.

Blachman, B. A., Tangel, D. M., Ball, E. W., Black, R., & McGraw, C. K. (1999). Developing phonological awareness and word recognition skills: A two-year intervention with low-income, inner-city children. *Reading and Writing: An Interdisciplinary Journal, 11*, 239–273.

Bogner, K., Raphael, L., & Pressley, M. (2002). How grade 1 teachers motivate literate activity by their students. *Scientific Studies of Reading, 6*, 135–165.

Bond, G. L., & Dykstra, R. (1997). The cooperative research program in first-grade reading instruction. *Reading Research Quarterly, 32*, 348–427.

Brown, A. L. (1980). Metacognitive development in reading. In R. Spiro, B. Bruce, & W. Brewer (Eds.), *Theoretical issues in reading comprehension* (pp. 453–481). Hillsdale, NJ: Lawrence Erlbaum Associates.

Brown, R., Pressley, M., Van Meter, P., & Schuder, T. (1996). A quasi-experimental validation of transactional strategies instruction with low-achieving second-grader readers. *Journal of Educational Psychology, 88*, 18–37.

Bulgren, J. A., Deshler, D. D., Schumaker, J. B., & Lenz, B. K. (2000). The use and effectiveness of analogical instruction in diverse secondary content classrooms. *Journal of Educational Psychology, 92*, 426–441.

Butler, D. L. (1998). The strategic content learning approach to promoting self-regulated learning: A report of three studies. *Journal of Educational Psychology, 90*, 682–697.

Cazden, C. B. (1988). *Classroom discourse: The language of teaching and learning*. Portsmouth, NH: Heinemann.

Chi, M., & Van Lehn, K. (1991). The content of physics self-explanations. *The Journal of the Learning Sciences, 1*, 69–105.

Chinn, C. A., Anderson, R. C., & Waggoner, M. A. (2001). Patterns of discourse in two kinds of literature discussion. *Reading Research Quarterly, 36*, 378–411.

Chmielewski, T. L., & Dansereau, D.F. (1998). Enhancing the recall of text: Knowledge mapping training promotes implicit transfer. *Journal of Educational Psychology, 90*, 407–413.

Cohen, P. A., Kulik, J. A., & Kulik, C. (1982). Educational outcomes of tutoring: A meta-analysis of findings. *American Educational Research Journal, 19*, 237–248.

Cross, D. R., & Paris, S. J. (1988). Developmental and instructional analyses of children's metacognition and reading comprehension. *Journal of Educational Psychology, 80*, 131–142.

Deshler, D. D., Schumaker, J. B., Lenz, B. K., Bulgren, J. A., Hock, M. F., Knight, J., & Ehren, B. J. (2001). Ensuring content-area learning by secondary students with learning disabilities. *Learning Disabilities Research & Practice, 16*, 96–109.

De Simone, C., Oka, E. R., & Tischer, S. (1998). Making connections efficiently: A comparison of two approaches used by college students to construct networks. *Contemporary Educational Psychology, 24*, 55–69.

Diekhoff, G. M., Brown, P. J., & Dansereau, D. F. (1982). A prose learning strategy training program based on network and depth-of-processing models. *Journal of Experimental Education, 50,* 180–184.

Dole, J. A., Duffy, G. G., Roehler, L. R., & Pearson, P. D. (1991). Moving from the old to the new: Research on reading comprehension instruction. *Review of Educational Research, 61,* 239–264.

Dolezal, S. E., Welsh, L. M., Pressley, M., & Vincent, M. M. (2003). How nine third-grade teachers motivate student academic engagement. *The Elementary School Journal, 103,* 239–267.

Echevarria, M. (2003). Anomalies as a catalyst for middle school students' knowledge construction and scientific reasoning during science inquiry. *Journal of Educational Psychology, 95,* 357–374.

Fitzgerald, J., & Noblit, G. W. (1999). About hopes, aspirations, and uncertainty: First-grade English language learners' emergent reading. *Journal of Literacy Research, 31,* 133–182.

Fitzgerald, J., & Noblit, G. W. (2000). Balance in the making: Learning to read in an ethnically diverse first-grade classroom. *Journal of Educational Psychology, 92,* 3–22.

Flood, J., Heath, S. B., & Lapp, D. (1997). *Handbook of research on teaching literacy through the communicative and visual arts.* New York: Macmillan.

Flood, J., & Lapp, D. (1995). Broadening the lens: Toward an expanded conceptualization of literacy. In K. A. Hinchman, D. J. Leu, & C. K. Kinzer (Eds.), *Perspectives on literacy research and practice* (Forty-fourth Yearbook of the National Reading Conference, pp. 1–16). Chicago: National Reading Conference.

Friend, R. (1999). Effects of strategy instruction on summary writing of college students. *Contemporary Educational Psychology, 26,* 3–24.

Fuchs, D., Fuchs, L. S., Mathes, P. G., & Simmons, D. C. (1997). Peer-assisted learning strategies: Making classrooms more responsive to diversity. *American Educational Research Journal, 34,* 174–206.

Gamoran, A., Nystrand, M., Berends, M., and LePore, P. C. (1995). An organizational analysis of the effects of ability grouping. *American Educational Research Journal, 32,* 687–715.

Gee, J. P. (1996). *Social linguistics and literacies: Ideology in discourses* (2nd ed.). London: Taylor & Francis.

Geertz, C. (1988). *Works and lives.* Stanford, CA: Stanford University Press.

Gersten, R., Fuchs, L. S., Williams J. P., & Baker, S. (2001). Teaching reading comprehension strategies to students with learning disabilities: A review of research. *Review of Educational Research, 71,* 279–320.

Glenberg, A. M., & Epstein, W. (1985). Calibration of comprehension. *Journal of Experimental Psychology: Learning, Memory, and Cognition, 11,* 702–718.

Glynn, S. M., & Takahashi, T. (1998). Learning from analogy-enhanced science text. *Journal of Research in Science Teaching, 35,* 1129–1149.

Greenleaf, C. L., Schoenbach, R., Cziko, C., & Mueller, F. L. (2001). Apprenticing adolescent readers to academic literacy. *Harvard Educational Review, 71,* 79–130.

Gruenewald, D. A. (2003). Foundations of place: A multidisciplinary framework for place-conscious education. *American Educational Research Journal, 40,* 619–654.

Hacker, D. J., Bol, L., Horgan, D. D., & Rakow, E. A. (2000). Test prediction and performance in a classroom context. *Journal of Educational Psychology, 92,* 160–170.

Hart, E. R., & Speece, D. L. (1998). Reciprocal teaching goes to college: Effects for postsecondary students at risk for academic failure. *Journal of Educational Psychology, 90,* 670–681.

Herber, H. L. (1970). *Teaching reading in content areas.* Englewood Cliffs, NJ: Prentice-Hall.

Hobbs, R., & Frost, R. (2003). Measuring the acquisition of media-literacy skills. *Reading Research Quarterly, 38,* 330–355.

Hruby, G. G. (2002). Social constructivism. In B. J. Guzzetti (Ed.), *Literacy in America: An encyclopedia of history, theory, and practice* (pp. 584–588). Santa Barbara, CA: ABC-CLIO.

Hubbard, B. P., & Simpson, M. L. (2003). Developing self-regulated learners: Putting theory into practice. *Reading Research and Instruction, 42,* 62–89.

Hynd-Shanahan, C., Holschuh, J. P., & Hubbard, B. P. (2004). Thinking like a historian: College students' reading of multiple historical documents. *Journal of Literacy Research, 4,* 238–250.

International Reading Association (2001). *Integrating literacy and technology in the curriculum.* Retrieved January 3, 2004, from http://www.reading.org/positions/technology.html

Janzen, J. (2003). Developing strategic readers in elementary school. *Reading Psychology, 24,* 25–55.

Jimenéz, J. E., & Guzmán, R. (2003). The influence of code-oriented versus meaning-oriented approaches to reading instruction on word recognition in the Spanish language. *International Journal of Psychology, 38,* 65–78.

Jimenéz, R. T., & Gersten, R. (1999). Lessons and dilemmas derived from the literacy instruction of two Latina/o teachers. *American Educational Research Journal, 36,* 265–301.

Johnston, F. R. (2000). Word learning in predictable text. *Journal of Educational Psychology, 92,* 248–255.

Juel, C., & Minden-Cupp, C. (2000). Learning to read words: Linguistic units and instructional strategies. *Reading Research Quarterly, 35,* 458–492.

Kamil, M. L. (2003). *Adolescents and literacy: Reading for the 21st century.* Washington, DC: Alliance for Excellent Education.

Koskinen, P. S., Blum, I. H., Bisson, S. A., Phillips, S. M., Creamer, T. S., & Baker, T. K. (2000). Book access, shared reading, and audio models: The effects of supporting the literacy learning of linguistically diverse students in school and at home. *Journal of Educational Psychology, 92,* 23–36

Langer, J. A. (1981). From theory to practice: A pre-reading plan. *Journal of Reading, 25,* 152–156.

Langer, J. A. (2001). Beating the odds: Teaching middle and high school students to read and write well. *American Educational Research Journal, 38,* 837–880.

Lapkin, S., & Swain, M. (1996). Vocabulary teaching in a grade 8 French immersion classroom: *Canadian Modern Language Review, 53*, 242–256. Retrieved June 28, 2004, from http://vnweb.hwwilsonweb.com

Luke, A., & Elkins, J. (2000). Re/mediating adolescent literacies. *Journal of Adolescent & Adult Literacy, 43*, 396–398.

Luke, C. (1997). Media literacy and cultural studies. In S. Muspratt, A. Luke, & P. Freebody (Eds.), *Constructing critical literacies: Teaching and learning textual practices* (pp. 19–49). Cresskill, NJ: Hampton Press.

Maki, R. H., & Berry, S. (1984). Metacomprehension of text material. *Journal of Experimental Psychology: Learning, Memory, and Cognition, 10*, 663–679.

Manuel, K. (2002). How first-year college students read *Popular Science*: An experiment in teaching media literacy skills. *Simile*, May, n.p.

Masterman, L. (1985). *Teaching the media*. London: Routledge.

Mathes, P. G., & Babyak, A. E. (2001). The effects of peer-assisted literacy strategies for first-grade readers with and without additional mini-skills lessons. *Learning Disabilities: Research & Practice, 16*, 28–44.

Mathes, P. G., Torgesen, J. K., & Allor J. H. (2001). The effects of peer-assisted literacy strategies for first-grade readers with and without additional computer-assisted instruction in phonological awareness. *American Educational Research Journal, 38*, 371–410.

Moje, E. B., & O'Brien, D. G. (Eds.). (2001). *Constructions of literacy: Studies of teaching and learning in secondary schools*. Mahwah, NJ: Lawrence Erlbaum Associates.

Moore, D. W. (1996). Contexts for literacy in secondary schools. In D. J. Leu, C. K. Kinzer, & K. A. Hinchman (Eds.), *Literacies for the twenty-first century: Research and practice* (pp. 15–46). Chicago: National Reading Conference.

Moore, D. W., Bean, T. W., Birdyshaw, D., & Rycik, J. A. (1999). Adolescent literacy: A position statement. *Journal of Adolescent & Adult Literacy, 43*, 97–112.

National Reading Panel. (2000). *Report of the National Reading Panel*. Washington, DC: National Institute of Child Health and Human Development.

Neufeld, P., & Fitzgerald, J. (2001). Early English reading development: Latino English learners in the "low" reading group. *Research in the Teaching of English, 36*, 64–109.

Nist, S. L., Simpson, M. L., Olejnik, S. & Mealey, D. (1991). The relation between self-selected study processes and performance. *American Educational Research Journal, 28*, 84–874.

No Child Left Behind Act of 2001, Public Law No. 107–110, 115 Stat. 1425 (2002).

Nolen, S. B. (2001). Constructing literacy in the kindergarten: Task structure, collaboration, and motivation. *Cognition & Instruction, 19*, 95–142.

O'Reilly, T., Symons, S., & MacLatchy-Gaudet, H. (1998). A comparison of self-explanation and elaborative interrogation. *Contemporary Educational Psychology, 23*, 434–445.

Palincsar, A. S. (1986). The role of dialogue in providing scaffolded instruction. *Educational Psychologist, 21*(1 & 2), 73–98.

Palincsar, A. S., & Brown, A. L. (1984). Reciprocal teaching of comprehension-fostering and comprehension-monitoring activities. *Cognition and Instruction, 1*, 117–175.

Pearson, P. D., & Gallagher, M. (1983). The instruction of reading comprehension. *Contemporary Educational Psychology, 8*, 317–344.

Pintrich, P. R. (2003). A motivational science perspective on the role of student motivation in learning and teaching contexts. *Journal of Educational Psychology, 95*, 667–686.

Posner, G. J., Strike, K. A., Hewson, P. W., & Gertzog, W. A. (1982). Accommodation of a scientific conception: Toward a theory of conceptual change. *Science Education, 66*, 211–227.

Pressley, M., & McDonald, R. (1997). Skilled comprehension and its development through instruction. *School Psychology Today, 26*, 448–466.

Pressley, M., Wharton-McDonald, R., Allington, R., Block, C. C., Morrow, L., Tracey, D., et al. (2001). A study of effective grade-1 literacy instruction. *Scientific Studies of Reading, 5*, 35–58.

Pressley, M., Wharton-Macdonald, R., Mistretta-Hampston, J., & Echevarria, M. (1998). Literacy instruction in 10 fourth- and fifth-grade classrooms in upstate New York. *Scientific Studies of Reading, 2*, 159–194.

RAND Reading Study Group. (2002). *Reading for understanding: Toward an R&D program in reading comprehension*. Santa Monica, CA: Science & Technology Policy Institute, RAND Education.

Roehrig, A. D., Pressley, M., & Sloup, M. (2001). Reading strategy instruction in regular primary-level classrooms by teachers trained in Reading Recovery. *Reading & Writing Quarterly, 17*, 323–348.

Rosenblatt, L. M. (1978). *The reader, the text, the poem: The transactional theory of literary work*. Carbondale: Southern Illinois University Press.

Rosenblatt, L. M. (1991). Literary theory. In J. Flood, J. M. Jensen, D. Lapp, & J. R. Squire (Eds.), *Handbook of research on teaching the English language arts* (pp. 57–62). New York: Macmillan.

Ruddell, R. B., & Unrau, N. J. (1994). Reading as a meaning-construction process: The reader, the text, and the teacher. In R. B. Ruddell, M. R. Ruddell, & H. Singer (Eds.), *Theoretical models and processes of reading* (pp. 996–1056). Newark, DE: International Reading Association.

Sanchez, R. P., Lorch, E. P., & Lorch, R. F. (2000). Effects of headings on text processing strategies. *Contemporary Educational Psychology, 26*, 418–428.

Scanlon, D. M., & Vellutino, F. R. (1997). A comparison of the instructional backgrounds and cognitive profiles of poor, average, and good readers who were initially identified as at risk for reading failure. *Scientific Studies of Reading, 1*, 191–215.

Scholes, R. (1985). *Textual power: Literary theory and the teaching of English*. New Haven, CT: Yale University Press.

Schorzman, E. M., & Cheek, E. H. (2004). Structured strategy instruction: Investigating an intervention for improving sixth-graders' reading comprehension. *Reading Psychology, 25,* 37–60.

Schumm, J. S., Moody, S. W., & Vaughn, S. (2000). Grouping for reading instruction: Does one size fit all? *Journal of Learning Disabilities, 33,* 477–488.

Slavin, R. E. (1990). *Cooperative learning: Theory, research, and practice.* Englewood Cliffs, NJ: Prentice-Hall.

Snow, C. E., Burns M. S., & Griffin, P. (1998). *Preventing reading difficulties in young children.* Washington, DC: National Academy Press.

Spires, H. A., & Donley, J. (1998). Prior knowledge activation: Inducing engagement with informational texts. *Journal of Educational Psychology, 90,* 249–260.

Stanislavski, C. (1961). *Creating a role.* New York: Theatre Arts Books.

Stauffer, R.G. (1975). *Directing the reading-thinking process.* New York: Harper & Row.

Stein, B., & Bransford, J. (1979). Constraints on effective elaboration: Effects of precision and subject generation. *Journal of Verbal Learning and Verbal Behavior, 18,* 769–777.

Stevens, R. J. (2003). Student team reading and writing: A cooperative learning approach to middle school literacy instruction. *Educational Research and Evaluation, 9*(2), 137–160.

Strauss, A., & Corbin, J. (1990). *Basics of qualitative research: Grounded theory procedures and techniques.* Newbury Park, CA: Sage.

Strickland, D. S. (2002). Improving reading achievement through professional development. In M. L. Kamil, J. B. Manning, & H. J. Walberg (Eds.), *Successful reading instruction* (pp. 103–117). Greenwich, CT: Information Age.

Strickland, D. S., & Alvermann, D. E. (Eds.). (2004). Learning and teaching literacy in grades 4–12: Issues and challenges. In D. S. Strickland & D. E. Alvermann (Eds.), *Bridging the literacy achievement gap, grades 4–12* (pp. 1–13). New York: Teachers College Press.

Taylor, B. M., Pearson, P. D., Clark, K., & Walpole, S. (2000). Effective schools and accomplished teachers: lessons about primary-grade reading instruction in low-income schools. *The Elementary School Journal, 101,* 121–165.

Taylor, B. M., Pearson, P. D., Peterson, D. S., & Rodriguez, M. C. (2003). Reading growth in high-poverty classrooms: The influence of teacher practices that encourage cognitive engagement in literacy learning. *The Elementary School Journal, 104,* 3–28.

Van Dijk, T. A., & Kintsch, W. (1983). *Strategies of discourse comprehension.* New York: Academic Press.

Van Maanen, J. (1988). *Tales of the field.* Chicago: University of Chicago Press.

Vaughn, S., Chard, D. J., Bryant, D. P., Coleman, M., Tyler, B-J., Linan-Thompson, S., et al. (2000). Fluency and comprehension interventions for third-grade students. *Remedial and Special Education, 21,* 325–335.

Vygotsky, L. S. (1986). *Thought and language.* Cambridge, MA: The MIT Press.

Wade, S. E., & Moje, E. B. (2000). The role of text in classroom learning. In M. L. Kamil, P. B. Mosenthal, P. D. Pearson, & R. Barr (Eds.), *Handbook of reading research Vol. III,* pp. 609–627). Mahwah, NJ: Lawrence Erlbaum Associates.

Wharton-McDonald, R., Pressley, M., & Hampston, J. M. (1998). Literacy instruction in nine first-grade classrooms: Teacher characteristics and student achievement. *The Elementary School Journal, 99,* 101–128.

Wilson, K., & Norman, C. A. (1998). Differences in word recognition based on approach to reading instruction. *Alberta Journal of Educational Research, 44,* 221–230.

Wolf, S. A. (1998). The flight of reading: Shifts in instruction, orchestration, and attitudes through classroom theatre. *Reading Research Quarterly, 33,* 382–415.

Wood, D., Bruner, J., & Ross, G. (1976). The role of tutoring in problem solving. *Journal of Child Psychology, 17,* 89–100.

·20·

WRITING

Steve Graham
Vanderbilt University

Every story has a beginning. With writing, this beginning took place more than 5,000 years ago when Sumerians invented cuneiform to record goods using a wedge-shaped reed stylus and a moist clay tablet. From this simple beginning, writing has undergone an incredible metamorphosis. The hardware of writing moved from marks on clay to marks on paper to marks on computer screens. The software of writing evolved from cuneiform to a wide array of scripts, including syllabries, logographic forms, and the many variants of the alphabet (Cook, 2003).

As writing tools and systems developed, so did its purposes. It is no longer just a tool for representing the number of animals or commodities; it now provides a tool for communication and learning as well as artistic, political, spiritual, and self-expression (Graham & Harris, 2000a). In terms of communication, writing allows us to maintain personal links with family, friends, and colleagues even when we are unable to be with them. It connects more than just our circle of associates and loved ones, however. Writing can foster a sense of heritage and purpose among larger groups of people. In China, for instance, the adoption of a standard system of writing 2,300 years ago promoted national unity (Swedlow, 1999).

Writing is an indispensable tool for learning. It makes it possible to gather, preserve, and transmit information, with great detail and accuracy (Diamond, 1999). The permanence of writing makes ideas readily available for review and evaluation; its explicitness encourages the establishment of connections between ideas; and its active nature may foster the exploration of unexamined assumptions (Applebee, 1984). E. M. Forster's observation, "How can I know what I think until I see what I say" (Brodie, 1997, p. 135), captures the potential of writing as a tool

for refining and extending one's knowledge about a particular topic (average effect size of writing on learning in school, however, is modest, 0.26; Bangert-Drowns, Hurley, & Wilkinson, 2004).

Another purpose of modern writing is captured in Stephen King's admission that he writes "such gross stuff [horror books]" because "I have the heart of a small boy—and I keep it in a jar on my desk" (Brodie, 1997, p 137). For Mr. King, writing not only is artistic, but also provides a personal means for self-expression. People have used writing to explore who they are, to combat loneliness, and to chronicle their experiences. Furthermore, writing about one's feelings and experiences can be beneficial psychologically and physiologically (Smyth, 1998, found that the average effect size for these variables was 0.42 when healthy participants were asked to write about a traumatic experience).

Writing also provides a powerful tool for persuading others. Chairman Mao's *Little Red Book* introduced millions to the ideology of communism, and Thomas Paine's pamphlet, *Common Sense*, inflamed revolutionary sentiment in colonial America. The persuasive power of writing is so great that some governments ban "subversive" documents and jail authors.

Writing has become so important today that more than 85 percent of the world's population now write (Swedlow, 1999). People who do not write are at a disadvantage. They lose a valuable tool for communication, learning, and self-expression. Failure to acquire adequate writing skills restricts opportunities for employment and education (Graham, 1982). In terms of education, writing is the major means by which students demonstrate their knowledge. They use it to gather, remember, and share subject-matter knowledge as well as to explore, organize, and refine their ideas about a topic (Durst & Newell, 1989). Students who do not write well cannot fully draw on its power to support and extend learning. Their grades are also likely to suffer, especially in classes where writing is the primary means for assessing progress. If their writing problems persist, they are unlikely to realize their educational, occupational, or personal potential.

Writing has a long and rich history, but the scientific study of writing totals no more than 100 years. Although it is not possible to review all available research in this chapter, I did not limit myself just to literature published since 1996, the publication date for the first *Handbook of Educational Psychology*. Because writing was not included as a separate topic in the first edition, it was necessary to cover some earlier work here. The material that is covered, however, is not comprehensive, as the lenses for this review are psychological and educational. Scholarship involving the social, historical, and political contexts of writing (e.g., rhetorical criticism, cultural studies, critical theory, and so forth) is not included, and I do not draw heavily on research involving the sociocultural orientation to the study of writing (see Prior, in press, for a discussion of this research and its impact).

MODELS OF THE WRITING PROCESS

Professional writers delight in complaining about the demanding nature of their work. The novelist Red Smith quipped: "Writing is easy. All you have to do is sit down at a typewriter and open a vein" (Phillips, 1993, p. 338). Even the venerable Dr. Seuss concurred, noting, "Every sentence is like a pang of birth. The *Cat In The Hat* ended up taking well over a year" (Brodie, 1997, p. 78). These authors' complaints are well founded, as the scientific study of writing supports their observations.

Hayes and Flower (1980) Model

The complexity and difficulty of writing is illustrated in what is arguably the most influential study of writing in the last 25 years. Hayes and Flower (1980) asked adults to "think aloud" while composing. Analysis of the resulting protocols provided them with a window into the cognitive and psychological processes involved in writing, allowing them to construct a model of skilled writing that included three basic components. One component, *task environment*, involved factors that were external to the writer, but influenced the writing task. These included attributes of the writing assignment (e.g., topic, audience, and motivating cues) as well as the text produced so far.

Another component, *cognitive processes*, provided a description of the mental operations employed during writing. This included planning what to say and how to say it, translating plans into written text, and reviewing to improve existing text. Planning, in turn, involved three ingredients—setting goals, generating ideas, and organizing ideas into a writing plan—whereas reviewing included reading and editing text. Hayes and Flower indicated that the execution of these cognitive processes was under the writer's direct control, and proposed that virtually any subprocess could interrupt or incorporate any other subprocess. For example, planning might interrupt translation, if a writer identified the need to develop additional writing goals while producing a first draft. The final component, *writer's long-term memory*, included the author's knowledge about the topic, the intended audience, and general plans or formulas for accomplishing various writing tasks.

Hayes and Flower's analysis of the verbal protocols also showed that composing is a goal-directed process, as skilled writers typically establish their main writing goals (e.g., be convincing and succinct) early in the process, and establish subgoals for meeting these goals (e.g., use strong arguments and refute counterarguments). These subgoals may in turn have their own subgoals, as the writer expands each main goal into a hierarchical structure of subgoals.

The Hayes and Flower model emphasized that skilled writing is demanding in three ways. One, it is a conscious and self-directed activity that involves the intelligent use of a variety of mental operations in order to satisfy the writer's goals. Two, the deployment of these mental operations does not necessarily proceed in a linear fashion from planning to translating to revising, but generally involves a complex interplay where they are interwoven or nested one within the other. Three, the writer must deal with many demands at once. In fact, Hayes and Flower (1980) suggested that skilled writers caught in the act looked very much like busy switchboard operators, trying to juggle a number of demands on their attention simultaneously (e.g., making plans, drawing ideas from memory, developing concepts or creating an image of the reader). As Kellogg (1993) later noted, writing does "not simply unfold automatically and effortlessly in the manner of a well learned motor skill . . . writing anything but the most routine and brief pieces is the mental equivalent of digging ditches" (p.17).

The Hayes and Flower model not only fixed much of the vocabulary that people use when talking about the composing process (Scardamalia & Bereiter, 1986), it served as a catalyst for much of the subsequent research on the cognitive nature of writing and the architecture of the writing process (Alamargot & Chanquoy, 2001). For example, Kellogg (1986) indexed the cognitive effort involved in each of the three major cognitive processes in the Hayes and Flower model by measuring interference from a secondary task. College students were asked to detect a randomly presented tone (the secondary task) while engaged in the process of composing a text (the primary task). It is assumed that spare capacity not directed to the primary task is available for the secondary task. Thus, the longer it takes the writer to identify the signal, the more demanding the primary task. He found that the writing operations of planning ideas, translating ideas into text, and reviewing ideas and text required far more cognitive effort than a variety of other tasks, including incidental learning, playing chess (at the novice level), and reading simple and complex texts. In fact, the cognitive effort consumed by these three writing processes approached the level of effort expended by expert chess players involved in move selection. In a series of three studies, Kellogg (1987, 1993a) examined the pattern of attentional allocation by college students as they wrote. As they composed, they spent one-half of their time engaged in translating, devoting the rest of the time to planning and reviewing. Time devoted to planning decreased from the start to the end of the writing process, whereas reviewing increased. Translating, however, required less cognitive effort than either planning or reviewing.

Rijlaarsdam and colleagues (Breetvelt, Van den Bergh, & Rijlaarsdam, 1994, 1996; Van den Bergh & Rijlaarsdam, 1996, in press) have extended Kellogg's work by doing an even more detailed analysis of how writers employ the mental operations identified by Hayes and Flower (1980). They examined the occurrence and timing of 11 cognitive activities (e.g., reading the assignment, generating information, and revising) with students about 15 years old. Their findings provide considerable support for Hayes and Flower model, as 87 percent of the variance in the quality of students' writing was accounted for by these 11 categories. However, this was only the case when the time at which the activity took place was included in the prediction. Consequently, no cognitive activity appeared to be beneficial during the whole writing process (divided into thirds). Instead, some contributed positively or negatively during one or two phases, whereas the relationship reversed for others across phases (e.g., reading the assignment was positively related to text quality at the start of writing, but negatively correlated with text quality at the end).

Like Kellogg (1987, 1993a), Van den Bergh and Rijlaarsdam (in press) also found that writers are more likely to use some mental operations than others depending on where they are in the composing process. For example, reading the assignment is more likely to occur at the beginning of the composing process than toward the end,

whereas generating information occurs less frequently in the beginning, but gradually increases before decreasing toward the end. Furthermore, the function of an activity may change depending on when it occurs. For instance, revising plays a different function when a writer is experiencing startup trouble (i.e., beginning over and over), than it does when a writer is revising a fluently produced first draft.

Some combinations of cognitive activities have a higher probability of occurring at certain times in the composing process, and a specific combination may have positive or negative consequences depending on when it occurs. To illustrate, reading text already produced to generate new ideas has a negative relation with text quality during the first half of the composing process, but the relation is reversed during the second half. Finally, in the verbal protocols from the think-alouds, writers appear to tell themselves what to do from time to time, suggesting that the choice of which cognitive activity to employ is partly under their control and requires attention (Breetvelt et al., 1994). This is consistent with Hayes and Flower's (1980) contention that the cognitive processes involved in writing are under the writer's control.

It should be noted that Hayes (1996) made some modifications to the terminology of the 1980 model (to reflect more current usage). This included changing the labels translation to text generation and reviewing to revising. Because this model is often used as a touchstone by researchers working with children, Berninger, Fuller, and Whitaker (1996) recommended that translation be divided into two components: text generation (turning ideas into language) and text transcription (turning language into written symbols on the page). Participants in Hayes and Flower's (1980) study did not often mention text transcription skills in their verbal protocols, probably because they required little conscious attention for these adult writers.

Bereiter and Scardamalia (1987) Model

One of the advantages of the Hayes and Flower (1980) model is that individual differences among writers can be explained by different specifications of the model. Bereiter and Scardamalia (1987) developed a model of novice writing, referred to as *knowledge telling*, that is a radically reduced version of the Hayes and Flower model. They proposed that novice writers use a greatly simplified version of the idea generation process proposed in the earlier 1980 model. They convert the writing task into simply telling what is known about the topic.

The architecture of the knowledge telling model included three components. One component, *mental representation of the assignment*, involves understanding the assignment by defining the topic and function of the text to be produced. A second component, *long-term memory*, includes two types of knowledge the writer can draw on to complete the assignment: content knowledge (what the writer knows about the assigned topic) and discourse knowledge (writer's linguistic knowledge and knowledge about the type of text to be produced). The third component, *knowledge-telling process*, consists of seven operations. The first two operations are constrained by the writer's *mental representation of the assignment* and involve making a decision on the actual topic of the text (locate topic identifiers) and type of text (locate genre identifiers) to be produced. This serves to guides the writer's search (construct memory probes) and retrieval (retrieve content from memory using probes) in *long-term memory* of relevant content and discourse knowledge. The retrieved information is tested (run tests of appropriateness) to determine if it is appropriate with the nature and topic of the text. If it is appropriate, the retrieved knowledge is transcribed into written text (write). The text produced so far, including what was just transcribed, serves as a stimulus for conducting the next search of *long-term memory* (update mental representation of text).

Although observations of how immature and struggling writers compose are generally consistent with the knowledge telling model (e.g., Graham, 1990), it is important to realize that even adults who are good writers employ this approach at times. For instance, knowledge-telling typically works well when the information for the writing task can be easily retrieved from memory, such as leaving a note for a spouse about something that happened earlier. The knowledge telling approach may also serve an adaptive function for young writers. As noted earlier, translation requires considerable cognitive effort (Kellogg, 1987, 1993a), and this is likely amplified for beginning writers who have not yet mastered text transcription skills, such as handwriting and spelling. McCutchen (1988) proposed that young children use the knowledge approach because it minimizes their use of other cognitive processes, such as planning and revising, which exert considerable processing demands as well (Kellogg, 1993b).

Bereiter and Scardamalia (1987) also proposed a more expert model of writing referred to as *knowledge transforming*. This approach to writing involves planning text content in accordance with rhetorical, communicative, and pragmatic constraints. Similar to the knowledge telling model, the writer's starting point is to develop a *mental representation of the assignment*. Based on this understanding, the writer then engages in *problem analysis and goal setting* to determine what to say (content

planning), as well as how to say it and whom to say it to (rhetorical process planning). This is done by analyzing the task, setting content and rhetorical goals, and deciding on the necessary means to obtain these objectives. These two types of planning are carried out in their own space: *content problem space* and *rhetorical problem space*. Within these spaces, the writer retrieves and transforms knowledge about what they plan to say (*content knowledge*), as well as knowledge about their audience and how to say it (*discourse knowledge*).

These processes are guided by the goals and constraints established during *problem analysis and goal setting*. Planning in these two spaces operate in a close interaction through a *problem translation* component, which transfers goals and constraints from one space to the other. Thus, topic knowledge can be transformed by taking into account content goals as well as theoretical and pragmatic constraints. Likewise, rhetorical and pragmatic dimensions can be transformed by content constraints. The resulting plans are then elaborated in writing through the *knowledge-telling process* (described earlier). As the writer transcribes text using the *knowledge-telling process*, the text is analyzed and the resulting information is fed back into the *problem analysis and goal-setting* component, providing additional opportunities to engage in content and rhetorical planning based on the fit between intentions and the resulting written product.

As Alamargot and Chanquoy (2001) note, it is probably best to think of the knowledge telling and knowledge transforming models as representing two extremes of the writing continuum. According to Bereiter, Burtis, and Scardamalia (1988), the development of writing expertise does not move from knowledge telling to knowledge transformation, but evolves through a series of intermediate stages. Although the knowledge-telling model appears to provide a reasonably sound description of how novice and inexperienced writers compose and has served as a focal point for much instructional research, especially with struggling writers (Graham & Harris, 2003), the impact of the knowledge transforming model is more limited. There is also little evidence to validate that it provides an accurate description of skilled writing.

Hayes (1996) Model

In 1996, Hayes revised the 1980 model developed in conjunction with Flower. He reorganized, expanded, and modified the 1980 framework so that it captured the ensuing 16 years of writing research and advances in cognitive psychology. In the new model, *task environment* was expanded to include a social component (e.g., the audience, other texts read while writing, and collaborators) and physical component (e.g., text read so far and the writing medium, such as a word processor). Hayes did not limit his overhaul to just contextual factors, as he also reconceptualized the internal factors involved in writing (in the original model this included *cognitive processes, long-term memory*, and the *monitor*). First, he included the *motivation/affect* component and indicated that affective factors such as goals, predispositions, beliefs, and attitudes influence the writing process. Second, the *long-term memory component* was upgraded to include not only the writer's knowledge of the audience and writing topic (included in the 1980 model), but also linguistic and genre knowledge as well as task schemas that specify how to carry out specific writing tasks, such as revising, writing business letters, and reading text to obtain information. These schemas are typically activated by environmental cues or through reflection and include information about the goals of the task, the procedures for accomplishing the goals, the sequencing of these procedures, and criteria for evaluating success.

Cognitive processes were also overhauled. Planning was now subsumed under a more general category, reflection, which encompassed problem solving, decision making, and inferencing. In the new model, the writer relies on general problem-solving (including planning) and decision-making skills to devise a sequence of steps to reach one or more writing goals. These reflective processes are abetted by inferencing, as writers make judgements or draw conclusions about their audience, possible writing content, and so forth.

Like planning, translation was included under a more general category, referred to as *text production*. Cues from the writing plan or text produced so far act to guide the retrieval of semantic information, which is then held in working memory. This information is expressed as sentence parts that are produced vocally or subvocally and evaluated by the writer. The resulting production may be deleted, modified, or transcribed depending on the writer's evaluation.

The process of reviewing was replaced by text interpretation. Reading plays a central role in text interpretation, as the writer may read and evaluate text when revising, read source texts to obtain writing content, and read to define the writing task. With each of these tasks, the writer forms an internal representation of the text that can then be acted upon. Interestingly, revising is viewed as a composite of the three *cognitive processes*: text interpretation (critically reading text produced so far to make it better), reflection (problem solving to determine how to fix a problem in text), and translation (implementing the change).

Finally, *working memory* was added to the model (see Kellogg, 1996, for an alternative model of working memory in writing). This component provides a limited place for holding information and ideas for writing as well as carrying out cognitive activities that require the writer's conscious attention. It is also assumed that working memory serves as an interface between *cognitive processes, motivation/affect*, and *long-term memory*, making it central to the act of writing. Working memory contains three registers for maintaining and processing information: phonological memory, visuo/spatial sketchpad (visual and spatial information), and semantic memory (particularly used to store semantic information during text production).

Although Hayes's (1996) new model provides a needed update to the 1980 version, it is too early to tell if it will have the same impact. It seems unlikely that the new model will fix the vocabulary of writing as the earlier model did, but it is possible that the inclusion of motivation and working memory as part of the equation may prove to have the most enduring influence, as these topics are receiving increased attention in the writing literature (e.g., Bruning & Horn, 2000; McCutchen, 2000; Pajares & Valiante, in press).

Zimmerman and Risemberg (1997) Model

In the models reviewed so far, little attention was directed at explaining how writers acquire the cognitive and noncognitive skills underlying writing performance. Instead, the models serve as a snapshot of the composing process at a particular developmental level. A model developed by Zimmerman and Risemberg (1997) partially addressed this issue. Based on a theory of social cognitive learning (Zimmerman, 1989), the model describes the "self-initiated thoughts, feelings, and actions that writers use to attain various literary goals, including improving their writing skills as well as enhancing the quality of the text they create" (Zimmerman & Risemberg, 1997, p. 4). According to this model, self-regulation occurs when writers use personal processes to strategically regulate their writing behavior or the environment.

Zimmerman and Risemberg proposed that writers manage the composing process by bringing into play self-regulatory strategies for controlling their actions, the writing environment, and their internal thoughts. Writers employ these strategies when composing and monitor, evaluate, and react to their use. This allows them to learn from the consequences of their actions. Self-regulatory strategies that are viewed as successful are more likely to be retained, whereas those that are viewed as unsuccessful are more likely to be abandoned. Moreover, a writer's sense of efficacy may be enhanced or diminished depending on the perceived success of the employed strategies. Self-efficacy, in turn, influences intrinsic motivation for writing, the use of self-regulatory processes during writing, and eventual literary attainment.

Learning in this model is determined by interactions between personal processes, as well as behavioral and environmental events. For example, a student's success on a writing assignment is determined not only by personal perceptions of competency, but also by environmental factors such as help from the teacher as well as behavioral events such as the use of a self-evaluation strategy to monitor whether the writing assignment is completed as intended. Similarly, the environmental tactic of arranging a quiet place to write involves intervening behavioral actions, such as closing the door. The continued use of this environmental structuring strategy, however, depends on the writer's perceptions of its effectiveness in facilitating writing.

Although Zimmerman and Risemberg's (1997) model is limited, as it does not address the interaction between self-regulation and other processes involved in writing, such as working memory or text transcription skills, it provides an important contribution to descriptions of the composing process for three reasons. One, it offers an explicit explanation of how writers exert deliberate control over the act of writing. Even though writing is commonly viewed as a difficult and demanding task, requiring extensive self-regulation and attentional control (Kellogg, 1993a; McCutchen, 2000), the details of how writers manage the composing process received only cursory attention in previous models (Graham & Harris, 1997a). Two, it provides a description of how writers' beliefs about competence influences and are influenced by their self-regulatory actions and subsequent performance. This interplay was not examined in previous models. Three, the model not only describes what writers do, but also addresses the process of change, by introducing mechanisms through which writers acquire new self-regulatory behaviors.

Comments on Models of the Writing Process

Since the advent of the Hayes and Flower model in 1980, increasingly sophisticated descriptions of the composing process have emerged. Using a metaphor developed by Hayes (1996), these models are best described as incomplete paintings, where some parts have taken definite shape, other parts are still sketchy, and still other parts of the canvas are blank. For example, while motivational influences are included in more recent models of composing (Hayes, 1996; Zimmerman & Risemberg, 1997), they are not completely drawn, as they do not capture aspects of motivation such as topic interest, nor do they take full advantage of the increasingly sophisticated

body of motivational theory and research (see Pintrich, 2000).

Descriptions of the broader contextual, cultural, and social influences on writing remain relatively untouched in the cognitive models of writing reviewed in this chapter. There is, however, an impressive body of research on the social, historical, and political context of writing (see Prior, in press). Schultz and Fecho (2000) argue that this literature shows that writing is influenced by the social and historical contexts in which it occurs, tied to the writer's social identity, varies across different contexts, reflects classroom pedagogy and curriculum, and is shaped by social interactions (Schultz & Fecho, 2000). Unfortunately, there has been little synthesis of this contextual stance with the cognitive/motivational paradigm typically embraced by educational psychologists. Such a synthesis will provide a richer, but clearly more complicated, understanding of writing and its development.

Last, there is a need to create models that capture what the writing process looks like at different levels of development, extending the work of Bereiter and Scardamalia (1987). Models also need to address how writing development occurs, building on Zimmerman and Risemberberg's (1997) work. Such models would be especially useful in designing writing interventions, as they would provide both developmental and theoretical guidelines.

WRITING DEVELOPMENT

Our understanding of how writing develops is also like an incomplete painting, with some parts of the canvas more completely realized than others. Although writing development is not fully understood, the road from novice to competent to expert writer is likely paved by changes in a writer's self-regulatory or strategic behaviors, basic writing skills, knowledge, and motivation (Alexander, 1997; Alexander, Graham, & Harris, 1998). In this section, I examine whether each of these forces contribute to writing development. I do not examine every possible aspect of strategies, skills, knowledge, and will, but focus on those aspects of each that are best understood and most likely to contribute to shaping writers' capabilities. For example, I do not examine punctuation and capitalization skills, even though much is known about their progression (e.g., Ferreiro & Pontecorvo, 1999). The acquisition of theses skills probably has little impact on overall writing development. The text transcription skills of handwriting and spelling, however, are addressed, as difficulty acquiring these skills may interfere with other writing processes and impede writing development (Berninger, Mizokawa, & Bragg, 1991; Graham & Harris, 2000b).

Self-Regulation

A common point of agreement in the models described earlier is that skilled writing is a self-directed process. Even professional writers employ strategies to help them regulate the composing process. R. L. Stine, creator of the popular *Goosebumps* series, relied heavily on advanced planning: "I do a very complicated and detailed chapter-by-chapter outline of every book first. . . . So when I actually sit down to do the book, I know everything that's going to happen . . . then I can write and just enjoy the writing part of it" (Associated Press, 1995, p. B1). Truman Capote, author of *In Cold Blood*, in contrast, placed considerable emphasis on repeatedly revising text. After writing a first draft in longhand, he completely revised it in longhand. Then he did a second revision typed on yellow paper. After the manuscript was set aside for a while, he revised it again on white paper (Cowley, 1958). Perhaps the most extravagant self-regulating writing strategy of all time was used by George Cohen, who rented a Pullman car drawing room, traveling in it until his book was finished (Hendrickson, 1994).

Theorists have identified a variety of self-regulation strategies that writers use to manage the process of writing (Scardamalia & Bereiter, 1985; Zimmerman & Risemberg, 1997). These include goal setting and planning (e.g., establishing rhetorical goals and tactics to achieve them), seeking information (e.g., gathering information pertinent to the writing topic), record keeping (e.g. making notes), organizing (e.g., ordering notes or text), transforming (e.g., visualizing a character to facilitate written description), self-monitoring (e.g., checking to see if writing goals are met), reviewing records (e.g., reviewing notes or the text produced so far), self-evaluating (e.g., assessing the quality of text or proposed plans), revising (e.g., modifying text or plans for writing), self-verbalizing (e.g., saying dialogue aloud while writing or personal articulations about what needs to be done), rehearsing (e.g., trying out a scene before writing it), environmental structuring (e.g., finding a quiet place to write), time planning (e.g., estimating and budgeting time for writing), self-consequating (e.g., going to a movie as a reward for completing a writing task), seeking social assistance (e.g., asking another person to edit the paper), and self-selecting models (e.g., emulating the writing style of a more gifted author).

Graham and Harris (2000b) indicated that if self-regulation strategies play an important role in shaping writing development, it is reasonable to expect that (a) skilled writers are more self-regulated than less skilled writers, (b) developing writers become increasingly self-regulated with age and schooling, (c) individual differences in self-regulation predict writing performance, and (d) teaching self-regulation strategies improves the writing performance of developing writers. Although there is not enough research to examine each of these assumptions with all of the self-regulations strategies identified earlier, this can be done with planning and revising.

Planning. The available evidence supports the position that planning is an important ingredient in writing development (Graham & Harris, 2000b). First, skilled writers are more planful than less skilled writers. Hayes and Flower (1980) found that 80 percent of content statements produced by skilled writers early in the process of composing focus on planning. Gould (1980) reported that business executives spend about two-thirds of their time planning, whereas Kellogg (1987) found that college students spend about one-fourth of their time planning.

Although all writers engage in some planning, novice or less skilled writers typically do little explicit planning, especially in advance of writing (McCutchen, 1995, in press). For instance, the average amount of time that sixth-grade writers spend planning in advance is 2 minutes (Cameron & Moshenko); struggling writers of the same age spend less than one-half minute (MacArthur & Graham, 1987). In contrast, Bereiter and Scardamalia (1987) reported that more skilled, undergraduate students planned their entire composition in advance, generating multiple and abbreviated lists of ideas that were connected by lines or arrows. Conceptual planning notes, evaluative statements, and structural markers were also quite common. The planning notes produced by less skilled writers (children in grades 4, 6, and 8) primarily involved generating content (i.e., complete sentences that were edited into a final draft during writing), with little attention devoted to developing other types of goals.

Second, the planning of developing writers becomes increasingly sophisticated with age. In the Bereiter and Scardamalia (1987) study cited earlier, the number of planning notes produced between fourth and sixth grade doubled, whereas conceptual planning increased slightly from fourth to eighth grade. In addition, Boscolo (1990) reported that most of the planning notes produced by second and fourth graders were sentences that were repeated with minor changes when writing, but about 35 percent of the notes generated by sixth and eighth graders were reminders to recall a certain item when writing or superordinate titles that synthesized information.

Third, the available data generally support the assumption that individual differences in planning behavior predict writing performance. In their review, Hayes and Nash (1996) reported that the correlations between writing quality and amount of planning ranged from .11 to .66

for adults, whereas correlations between writing quality and quality of plans ranged from .23 to .87 for students in grades 6 through college. Hayes and Nash cautioned, however, that these correlations may be due to a confounding variable, namely time-on-task. Previously significant correlations between writing quality and planning became nonsignificant in several of the studies they reviewed once time-on-task was held constant via partial correlations. Nevertheless, time-on-task was not a confounding variable in other studies not reviewed by Hayes and Nash (Berninger, Whitaker, Feng, Swanson, & Abbott, 1996; Troia & Graham, 2002).

Fourth, teaching novice and struggling writers how to plan improves how well they write. In a recent meta-analysis of the strategy instructional literature (Graham, in press), I found that teaching developing writers strategies for planning had a strong impact on their writing performance. The average effect size at posttest was 1.53, and it was 1.38 at maintenance.

Revising. Revising also plays an important role in writing development (Graham & Harris, 2000b). First, skilled writers are better at revising than less skilled writers. Although revising may not be as prominent as planning, Kellogg (1987) found that college students spend 20 percent of their time revising, whereas Hayes and Flower (1980) reported that 10 to 15 percent of content statements made by skilled writers involved revising. Novice or less skilled writers, in contrast, typically devote little attention to revising, and the nature of their revising differs from that of skilled writers, as the changes they make are mostly superficial, aimed at correcting errors and making small changes in wording (Fitzgerald, 1987; MacArthur, Graham, & Harris, 2004).

Second, the revising of developing writers becomes increasingly sophisticated with age. Although there is considerable individual variation (see for example Chanquoy, 2001), revising behavior changes with age, as older writers revise more often, revise larger units of text, and make more meaning-based revisions (Fitzgerald, 1987; MacArthur et al., 2004).

Third, the weakest link in the assumption that revising plays an important role in writing development involves the predictive validity of revising. Until high school, revising behavior is generally unrelated to overall writing performance, probably because young children do not revise much and limit much of their revising efforts to proofreading and minor word changes (Fitzgerald, 1987; Graham & Harris, 2000b). Nevertheless, teaching novice and struggling writers how to revise does have a positive impact on their writing. When school-age children are taught strategies for revising text, the average effect size on writing was .74 (Graham, in press).

Although it is not possible to conduct this same kind of analysis with the other self-regulatory strategies identified earlier, it is unlikely that all of them are as important in shaping writing development as are planning and revising. The cumulative effects of multiple self-regulation strategies, however, are likely greater than any single strategy.

Writing Skills

The distinction between a skill and a strategy is not always straightforward, as both involve a series of operations designed to accomplish a particular task (Alexander et al., 1998). Two important distinctions between skills and strategies involve effort and volition. Strategies are effortful and intentional processes that writers use to accomplish their goals, whereas skills are efficient and relatively automatic operations. Nevertheless, even a basic skill such as handwriting can be executed in an unconscious, automatic mode or a conscious, effortful mode (Willingham, 1998). For adult writers, handwriting is mostly an automatic task, unless the writer sets a goal, such as "write as neatly as possible." For young writers, handwriting is a more effortful activity, as the processes for producing letters still require conscious attention (Graham & Weintraub, 1996).

Until writing skills become efficient and relatively automatic, they may exact a toll on writing and its development. As noted earlier, the skills involved in translating ideas into text require considerable cognitive effort, even for adults (Kellogg, 1986, 1987, 1993a). Two text skills that may play an important role in shaping writers' capabilities are handwriting and spelling (Graham & Harris, 2000b). Difficulty mastering these skills can result in three unwanted consequences. One, illegibilities and misspellings make it more difficult to read the written text. As the novelist Lily Tuck complained, such mistakes can "stop the reader cold on the page" (2003, p. 10). Two, having to devote conscious attention to handwriting and spelling can interfere with other writing processes (Graham, 1990). For example, having to switch attention during composing to how to spell a word may lead writers to forget ideas or plans held in working memory as well as restrict their vocabulary selection. Three, difficulties with handwriting and spelling may constrain writing development. McCutchen (1988) proposed that such skills are so demanding for beginning writers that they minimize the use of other writing processes, such as planning and revising, because they exert considerable processing demands too. Furthermore, Berninger et al. (1991) reported that difficulties with handwriting and spelling led children that they worked with to avoid writing and develop a mind set that they cannot write.

Handwriting and Spelling. With one addition, the same criteria used to assess the relationship between self-regulation and writing development were applied to handwriting and spelling. The added criteria examined if the elimination of handwriting and spelling via dictation enhances writing performance.

Overall, the available evidence supports the proposition that handwriting and spelling play an important role in writing development (Graham & Harris, 2000b). First, the process of transcribing ideas onto paper (which is dominated by handwriting and spelling) is more demanding for children than adults. Bourdin and Fayol (1993, 1994) found that transcription processes imposed higher costs on the writing of children than it did for adults. In their experiments, adults were equally adept at recalling information and generating sentences when responding orally or in writing, but children's performance was poorer when writing.

The handwriting and spelling skills of children who experience writing difficulties are also less well developed than those of their normally developing peers (Deno, Marsten, & Mirkin, 1982; Graham & Weintraub, 1996). This was illustrated in a longitudinal study by Juel (1988), where 14 of 21 fourth-grade children classified as poor writers scored one standard deviation below the mean on a standardized test of spelling.

There is a considerable body of research showing that handwriting and spelling improves with age (Farr, Hughes, Robbins, & Greene, 1990; Graham & Weintraub, 1996; Treiman, 1993). The developmental aspects of spelling are particularly evident in young children (Gentry, 1982), as they move through the following stages from preschool to the early elementary years: precommunicative (symbols bear no relationship to the sounds in a word), semiphonetic (letters represent some but not all of the sounds in a word), phonetic (complete phonological structure of a word is represented, but often with unconventional orthography), transitional (more conventional orthographic conventions are applied), and correct (grade-level words spelled correctly). Beyond these early grades, spelling continues to improve, as the percentage of words spelled correctly in students' papers increases from one grade to the next, at least through grade 9 (Farr et al., 1990). Likewise, children's fluency with handwriting increases by 10 letters or more per minute, leveling off at the start of high school (Graham, Berninger, Weintraub, & Schaefer, 1998).

Individual differences in handwriting and spelling predict writing achievement. In a review of 13 studies, Graham, Berninger, Abbott, Abbott, and Whitaker (1997) indicated that both handwriting fluency and spelling were moderately correlated with measures of writing achievement. In an empirical study presented in the same paper, handwriting and spelling skills together accounted for a sizable proportion of the variance in the writing skills of 600 first- through sixth-grade children. Transcription skills accounted for 25 percent and 42 percent of the variance in writing quality at the primary and intermediate grades, and 66 percent and 41 percent of the variance in writing output at these same grade levels, respectively.

Even though the research base is thin, teaching handwriting and spelling to young writers can improve writing performance. Three studies found that handwriting instruction improved first-grade students' handwriting as well as one or more aspects of their writing performance, including sentence construction skills, writing output, or writing quality (Berninger et al., 1997; Graham, Harris, & Fink, 2000; Jones & Christensen, 1999). Likewise, two spelling studies found that spelling instruction improved second-grade students' spelling as well as writing output or sentence construction skills (Berninger et al., 1998; Graham, Harris, & Fink-Chorzempa, 2002).

Finally, eliminating handwriting and spelling through dictation has a positive impact on the writing of specific groups of writers. In a review of literature, De La Paz and Graham (1995) found that young and old writers usually produced more text when they dictated versus wrote their compositions. Dictation also resulted in qualitatively better text for young children just learning to write and older elementary-age children with poorly developed handwriting and spelling skills. It is possible that the De La Paz and Graham paper underestimated the impact of dictation, because participants in the studies reviewed probably had little access to text as it was being dictated and may have viewed dictation as a request to speak extemporaneously. In a series of studies with fifth- and sixth-grade children, Reece and Cumming (1996) addressed these weaknesses. Dictated text was made accessible by having it appear on a computer screen, and it was emphasized that dictation was not telling a story, but composing it. Text dictated under these conditions were qualitatively better than those that were handwritten.

Other Writing Skills. Translation skills not only involve handwriting and spelling, but include transforming ideas into the words and syntactic structures that convey the author's intended meanings. This includes constructing sentences, as well as using appropriate grammar, punctuation, and capitalization. Although grammar and correct usage make the text more readable, it is unlikely that they have the same impact on writing development as self-regulation or handwriting and spelling. For instance, teaching grammar has little to no effect on students' writing (Hillocks, 1986; Smith, Cheville, & Hillocks, in press).

The development of sentence construction skills, however, may play a role in shaping writing development. I offer this as a tentative proposition, as there are caveats for each of the criteria subsequently examined. First, there is some evidence that the sentences of better writers are more complex than those of less skilled writers (Hunt, 1965; Raiser, 1981) and low language-ability students (Gilliam & Johnston, 1992), but these findings do not appear to hold for poor readers (e.g., Houck & Billingsley, 1989). Second, the sentences that students craft become increasingly complex with age, although this finding varies by task and genre (Hunt, 1965; Scott, 1999; Scott & Windsor, 2000). Third, individual differences in sentence skills are correlated with writing performance in some studies (Hillocks, 1986; Quinlan, 2004), but this may vary by genre (Crowhurst, 1980), and there are a number of studies where this was not the case (see Hillocks, 1986). Fourth, efforts to improve sentence skills have been successful, at least in the case of sentence combining instruction (Hillocks, 1986), but the impact of such instruction on other writing measures such as writing quality has been mixed (Saddler & Graham, 2005; Smith et al., in press).

Knowledge

In the models of writing described earlier, writers access different kinds of knowledge from memory. The types of knowledge identified in these models were knowledge about writing topic, intended audience, genre, task schemas, and linguistic awareness (this was addressed as grammar, sentence construction, and spelling in the previous section). Although the empirical literature on knowledge and writing is relatively thin, the accumulated evidence supports the position that writing development is shaped by changes in writing knowledge.

First, skilled writers are more knowledgeable about writing than less skilled writers. Good writers have a more sophisticated conceptualization of writing than poor writers (Graham, Schwartz, & MacArthur, 1993), and they possess greater knowledge about the attributes and structure of different genres (C. Englert & Thomas, 1987), strategies for carrying out the processes of writing (S. Englert, Raphael, Fear, & Anderson, 1988), the role of audience in writing (Wong, Wong, & Blenkinsop, 1989), and the purpose of writing (Saddler & Graham, in press). It is not clear, however, if stronger writers possess more knowledge than weaker writers about the topics they write about; I was unable to locate any research that examined this issue.

Second, developing writers become increasingly knowledgeable about writing with age. There is considerable evidence that knowledge of the attributes and structures of different genres develops early and becomes more complex with age (Donovan & Smolkin, in press). In addition, older writers have a more sophisticated conceptualization of writing than younger writers (Graham et al., 1993) as well as greater knowledge about the role of audience in writing (Holliway & McCutchen, 2004). Although it seems likely that students' knowledge about potential writing topics increases with age, a study by McCutchen, Francis, and Kerr (1997) suggested that this may not always be the case. They found no differences in seventh-grade and college students' knowledge about the two writing topics (i.e., Christopher Columbus and Margaret Mead) they asked participants to write about in their study.

Third, the level of knowledge that writers' bring to the composing task is related to their writing performance. For example, S. Englert et al. (1988) asked fourth- and fifth-grade students a series of questions designed to assess their knowledge of strategies for carrying out different writing processes. The researchers made this task more concrete by tying the questions to vignettes of children who were experiencing difficulty on a specific writing task, and asking the respondent to give these students advice. Correlations between performance on expository writing tasks and knowledge of 10 different strategies ranged from 0.25 to 0.70. Knowledge for all but two of the strategies, sources of information and revising, were significantly related to writing achievement. Furthermore, Bonk, Middleton, Reynold, and West (1990) reported that knowledge of writing strategies was significantly related to the overall quality of papers produced by students in grades 6 through 8 (correlations ranged from .35 to .45).

Writers' familiarity with the writing topic is also related to writing performance. Albin, Benton, and Khramtsova (1996) found that undergraduate students' baseball knowledge accounted for unique variance in the prediction of the thematic maturity of a paper about baseball and number of game actions included in the story, after variance due to gender and English usage skills was controlled. Similar effects for topic knowledge were reported with undergraduates by Voss, Vesonder, and Spilich (1980) and fourth-grade students by Mosenthall, Conley, Colella, and Davidson-Mosenthall (1985). Although Kellogg (1987) found that topic knowledge was not related to how often college students engaged in various writing processes, students with lower topic knowledge expended more cognitive effort when writing than more knowledgeable peers. Other researchers reported that topic knowledge is related to children's and adults' revising behavior (Butterfield, Hacker, & Plumb, 1994; McCutchen et al., 1997).

There are several lines of evidence showing that instruction aimed at increasing writers' knowledge improves writing performance. Fitzgerald and her colleagues found that teaching fourth-grade students about the parts of a story improved the organization and quality of their story writing (Fitzgerald & Teasley, 1986), whereas instruction designed to increase knowledge about revising had a positive impact on sixth-grade students' revising behavior and writing quality (Fitzgerald & Markham, 1987). Still other research demonstrates that brief instruction can reorient the schemas used by both adults and children when they revise (Graham, MacArthur, & Schwartz, 1995; Wallace et al., 1996). In addition, providing writers with firsthand experience with the types of difficulties an audience might experience with their text improved the descriptions generated by both children and college students (Holliway & McCutchen, 2004; Traxler & Gernsbacher, 1993). Last, acquiring knowledge by observing a competent writer compose can have a positive impact on writing performance (Couzijn, 1999).

Motivation

"Ah, to have your name in print! There are certain people who commit a crime for that pleasure alone" (Brodie, 1997, p. 134). This observation by the novelist Gustave Flaubert captures how motivating writing can be. Other writers use motivational strategies to help them gain dominion over this challenging task. The novelist Sophy Burnham (1994), for example, rewards herself with a prize such as ice cream when she meets a writing goal.

Although motivation has been more fully incorporated in recent models of writing (see Hayes, 1996; Zimmerman & Risemberg, 1997), research on writing and motivation has been limited mostly to the study of attitudes about writing, self-efficacy, interest, writing apprehension, and attributions for writing success (Bruning & Horn, 2000; Hidi & Boscolo, in press; Pajares, 2003). Theoretically, it is reasonable to expect that motivational factors such as these play an important role in writing development. For instance, students who develop an "I can do" attitude are more likely to set challenging writing goals, plan a course of action for achieving them, exert needed effort, persevere in the face of difficulty, and believe that they will be successful (Bandura, 1995). Although current research generally supports the contention that motivation helps shape writing developing, this assertion is more tenuous than the claims made for the forces of self-regulation, skills, and knowledge. There are limited data for at least two of the assumptions that I have used to guide my analysis and conflicting data for a third assumption.

There are few data on the motivational differences between more skilled and less skilled writers. Graham et al. (1993) reported that average writers were more positive about their desire to write than weaker writers, but there was no difference between the two groups in their self-efficacy for writing. In contrast, Shell, Colvin, and Bruning (1995) found that stronger writers had higher self-efficacy than less skilled writers and that attributions for writing success were related to writing ability. In addition, the perceived self-efficacy of more advanced writers in a study by Vrugt, Oort, and Zeeberg (2002) was related to pursued writing goals, and these goals contributed to course grades. The relation between these variables was stronger for advanced writers than it was for beginners. Although few in number, these investigations support the assumption that motivational differences exist between more and less skilled writers.

Not only are data on whether developing writers become more motivated over time mixed, but on some variables there is a decline in motivation. Knudson (1991, 1992) found that attitude toward writing declined with age. Graham et al. (1993), however, found no difference in the writing attitudes of younger and older students. In his comprehensive review, Pajares (2003) indicated that self-efficacy for writing declined with age in some studies and increased in others. Shell et al. (1995) found that younger students were more likely than older ones to give higher ratings for effort and luck as a cause of success in writing. Finally, several studies show that interest in writing develops over time (Lipstein & Renninger, in press; Nolen, 2003).

Despite the mixed data on the development of writing motivation over time, the available evidence is consistent with the assumption that individual differences in motivation predict writing. For example, Knudson (1995) found that even after variance due to grade level was controlled, attitudes toward writing predicted writing achievement. Pajares (2003) indicated that self-efficacy beliefs were positively related to writing performance in his review of the literature. Although Hidi and McLaren (1991) did not find a relation between the writing interest and performance of sixth graders, Albin et al. (1996) found that interest predicts the writing performance of older students. In addition, writing apprehension typically correlates negatively with measures of writing performance (Madigan, Linton, & Johnston, 1996).

Although there are a number of recommendations for how to enhance writing motivation in the literature (Walker, 2003), there are virtually no data on the impact of motivation instruction on writing performance. Although procedures for enhancing motivation are included in many interventions, researchers rarely separate the effects of the motivational components from other aspects of instruction. An exception is a series of studies conducted by Schunk and Swartz (1993a, 1993b) with fourth- and fifth-grade students. In two studies (Schunk & Swartz, 1993a), they provided students with feedback on their learning progress in order to enhance self-efficacy. All of the participating students were taught a strategy for writing a paragraph. Students were also given a process-goal to learn the strategy, a product goal of writing paragraphs, or a general goal of working productively. Half of the process-goal students received feedback on their progress in learning the strategy. In both experiments, the process goal plus feedback resulted in stronger gains in self-efficacy and writing performance than the product and general goal conditions. However, any claims about the effects of feedback must be tempered by the fact that there were no statistically significant differences between students with a learning goal who received or did not receive feedback. Nevertheless, in a study with gifted fourth-grade students (Schunk & Swartz, 1993b), children in the learning goal condition receiving feedback had higher self-efficacy for improvement scores, writing performance at maintenance, and strategy use than learning goal students who did not receive feedback.

Correlates of Writing Performance

Strategies, skills, knowledge, and motivation are not the only factors that influence writing development. How well children write is related to environmental variables, such as literacy learning in family contexts (Senechal, LeFevre, Thomas, & Daley, 1998) and the setting in which education occurs (Walberg & Ethington, 1991).

Personal factors such as reading and oral language competence also are thought to play a role in writing development. In a review of literature, Shanahan (in press) reported that writing achievement is related to both oral language and reading, but that reading shares more variance with writing than oral language. The relation between these domains are further highlighted by findings showing that children with language or reading problems experience difficulties learning to write (Juel, 1989; Scott & Windsor, 2000). Although oral language and writing are connected, and writing appears to draw on earlier growth in oral language, it is difficult to determine if oral language instruction influences writing development, as there is little research on this issue (Shanahan, in press). Early research (Beidler, 1969; Wiggins, 1968) found that language training did not enhance writing, but there is some evidence that oral activities, such as orally combining sentence kernels into more complex sentences, can

affect writing skills (Miller & Ney, 1968). In contrast, there is considerable research showing that reading instruction has a positive impact on writing (Fitzgerald & Shanahan, 2000; Graham, 2000; Shanahan, in press).

Gender, disability, and socioeconomic status are also related to writing achievement. Girls tend to be better writers than boys (Berninger & Fuller, 1992; Walberg & Ethington, 1991). Students with disabilities—including those with learning disabilities (Graham & Harris, 2003), speech and language difficulties (Scott & Windsor, 2000), and attention deficit disorders (Ross, Poidevant, & Miner, 1995)—typically experience difficulty learning to write. Children from poorer families tend to be weaker writers than their more affluent peers (Mavrogenes & Bezruczko, 1993; Walberg & Ethington, 1991). I draw special attention to these three variables because they provide information about a child's risk for developing writing problems.

TEACHING WRITING

Although writing development is a complex and somewhat uncertain process, the evidence just examined is consistent with the view that growth in writing is shaped by changes in knowledge, skill, will, and self-regulation. Even though there is more support for some of these forces than for others in terms of writing development, evidence from other academic domains show that these same variables play a vital role in transforming learner's capabilities (Alexander, 1997). Changes in a learner's knowledge, skill, will, and self-regulation in one academic domain, however, does not affect development in all other domains. Nevertheless, there may be some transfer from domains that share a common body of declarative and procedural knowledge, such as writing and reading (Fitzgerald & Shanahan, 2000).

These conclusions have several implications for the teaching of writing. One, writing programs should be designed so that they promote the development of the skills, knowledge, and self-regulation strategies needed to write effectively, as well as enhance writers' motivation. Two, it should be possible to teach reading so that it promotes writing development and vice versa (Shanahan, in press). Because the correlations between writing and reading are far from perfect, it is necessary to provide separate instruction and experiences in each domain, while taking advantage of how they can be mutually supportive (Fitzgerald & Shanahan, 2000).

Another implication from the literature just reviewed is that a "one size fits all" model of instruction is not appropriate. Writers' instructional needs vary depending on their knowledge, skills, will, and self-regulation, and some groups of writers, such as students with disabilities, may need extra help to maximize writing development. If a recent national survey is representative, however, a sizable proportion of teachers do little to adapt their writing programs to students' needs. Graham, Harris, MacArthur, and Fink-Chorzempa (2003) reported that 20 percent of the primary-grade teachers they contacted made no adaptations for struggling writers, whereas another 24 percent made only one or two adaptations.

A final implication is that writing development takes place over a long period of time, and whereas many people become competent writers, few become experts. Thus, the effective teaching of writing cannot be limited to a single teacher or year, but requires a coherent, coordinated, and extended effort by schools. At the present time, the scientific data on writing instruction are not rich enough to allow us to draw a roadmap that fully addresses each of these implications. Just like writing development and the models reviewed earlier, the painting is incomplete. It is possible, however, to provide some evidence-based principles to guide writing instruction. For each principle, I provide research-supported examples of how teachers can facilitate the development of writing strategies, skills, knowledge, and motivation. These examples are illustrative and not exhaustive, and many are drawn from my own research.

Although the proposed principles focus on the instructional moves that teachers can bring to bear in the classroom, it is important to realize that what teachers do is influenced by societal, institutional, and personal factors. For instance, statewide policies on writing influence school practices (Bridge, Compton-Hall, & Cantrell, 1997). A school's shared vision of writing instruction, in turn, affects teacher practices (Stahl, Suttles, & Pagnucco, 1996), whereas the beliefs of teachers shape what they do in the classroom (Graham, Harris, Fink, & MacArthur, 2001, 2002). Also, because the proposed principles are limited to the classroom, they are incomplete, as they do not consider the impact a student's family has on writing development.

Principle 1: Directly Teach Writing Strategies, Skills, and Knowledge

Louis L'Amour (1990), a popular writer of Western novels, observed that "A writer's brain is like a magician's hat. If you're going to get anything out of it, you have to put something in first." This advice captures the first principle: Directly teach writing strategies, skills, and knowledge that enhance writing development. The aim of such instruction is to improve the tools that students bring to the task of writing.

There is a notable body of experimental research that shows that students can be taught self-regulations strategies for planning and revising (Graham, in press; Graham & Harris, 2003) and writing skills such as handwriting, spelling, and sentence construction (Graham, 1983; Graham & Weintraub, 1996; Hillocks, 1986; Saddler & Graham, in press b). There is a smaller body of work that demonstrates that knowledge about writing can be enhanced through instruction (e.g., Fitzgerald & Markham, 1987; Fitzgerald & Teasley, 1986). In addition, self-regulation writing strategies can be taught in such a way that both knowledge and motivation are enhanced too (Harris, Graham, & Mason, in press).

Teaching Strategies for Regulating the Writing Process. One of the most powerful ways of improving school-age students' writing is to directly teach them strategies for planning and revising. In a recent meta-analysis of 20 group comparison studies (Graham, in press), the average effect size across all measures immediately following strategy instruction was 1.15. When key aspects of writing, such as writing quality, schematic structure of the text, length, and revisions, were considered separately, the effect sizes were still large: 1.21, 1.89, 0.95, and 0.90, respectively. To provide a benchmark for interpreting these effect sizes, the most successful intervention, the environmental mode in Hillock's (1986) meta-analysis of different methods for teaching writing had an average effect size of 0.44.

A frequently voiced concern about strategy instruction is that students may not continue to use what they learn over time or they may not be able to use this knowledge flexibly (Graham & Harris, 2003). The results of the Graham (in press) meta-analysis do not support these contentions, as the average effect size of strategy instruction across all writing variables at maintenance was 1.32. Likewise, this instruction resulted in improvements in genres where students had not been taught to apply the target planning and revising strategies, as the average effect size for transfer to an uninstructed genre was 1.13.

The impact of teaching planning and revising strategies for school-age students was robust, as average effect size for group comparison studies was not related to type of student who received instruction (good, average, or poor writers as well as students with learning disabilities), their grade-level placement (elementary versus secondary), type of cognitive process or strategy taught (planning, revising, or both), or genre (narrative versus expository) that served as the focal point for instruction. However, the Self-Regulated Strategy Development model (SRSD; Harris & Graham, 1996, 1999), a specific approach for teaching strategies, yielded a mean effect size at posttest of 1.57; this was almost double the average effect size for all of the non-SRSD studies combined (effect size 0.89).

Because SRSD instruction had such large average effect sizes, I use a study from this literature to illustrate how self-regulation strategies can be directly taught (Harris, Graham, & Mason, in press). Although instruction in this investigation centered primarily around teaching students strategies for planning text, students also learned how to apply other self-regulatory strategies such as self-monitoring and goal setting. This study further illustrates how strategy instruction in writing can be designed to enhance students' knowledge about writing as well as their motivation.

In the Harris et al. (in press) study, second-grade students who were experiencing difficulty learning to write were taught a general planning strategy that reminded them to carry out three processes: select a topic to write about, organize possible ideas into a writing plan, and use and upgrade their plan as they wrote. They first learned to use this general strategy in conjunction with a genre-specific strategy for story writing that helped them generate ideas for their papers. This involved thinking about each element of a story in advance of writing and developing possible writing ideas (as notes) for each one. Students were also taught how to brainstorm "million dollar" words to use in their story to enhance story vocabulary and ideation.

After learning to use these strategies with stories, students practiced applying them to persuasive writing. At this point, students continued to use the general strategy, but the genre-specific strategy shifted to generating notes about the basic elements of persuasive essays, and the brainstorming of "million dollar" words was upgraded to include transition words, too. For both stories and persuasive essays, teachers first described the strategy and discussed with students their benefits. Strategy use was then modeled and students practiced using the strategies, with help from the teacher and peers, until they could use them effectively.

Part of teaching students to use these strategies included learning about the basic parts of a story and persuasive essay, the importance of using words that make a paper more interesting, and self-talk that facilitates performance (this was introduced when teachers modeled how to use the strategies). This provided students with knowledge essential to using the aforementioned strategies. They also learned about the purpose of stories and persuasive writing, including the characteristics of a well-constructed paper in each genre. This was accomplished through discussion and by reading model stories and essays. Students were further taught how to set goals to write complete papers (e.g., ones that included all of the basic elements as well as million-dollar words), monitor and graph their success in achieving these goals, compare their preinstructional performance with their performance during instruction, and credit their success to effort and the use of the inculcated strategies. Goal-setting, self-reflective, and attributional practices such as these can enhance students' effort and motivation (Schunk & Zimmerman, 1998). Finally, peers were paired together to discuss when and where they could use what they were learning, help each other apply the strategies in other settings, and discuss their successes and difficulties in doing these.

Students who received this instruction not only spent more time planning in advance of writing than control students, but there was also a general improvement in their overall writing. This occurred both for stories and persuasive essays, as well as for personal narratives and informational papers. These children were also more knowledgeable than controls about planning, as well as the attributes of both a good story and persuasive paper.

Teaching Skills. Instructional research in both handwriting and spelling spans almost a century of time. Research in both of these areas shows that handwriting and spelling skills can be improved through direct instruction (see Graham, 1983, 2000; Graham & Weintraub, 1996). Although space does not permit a thorough review of this research, I provide an example of research-based methods for directly teaching each of these skills.

Graham et al. (2000) provided first-grade children (who had slow handwriting and generally poor writing skills) with 7 hours of instruction that focused on learning to recognize and write the lowercase letters of the alphabet and to increase handwriting fluency. Three times a week, each child received 15 minutes of instruction. Each lesson included four activities. One, students learned to name and identify the letters of the alphabet. Two, letters that shared common formational characteristics (e.g., *l*, *i*, and *t*) were introduced and practiced. The instructor modeled how to form the letters, followed by the student practicing each letter by tracing it three times, writing it three times inside an outline of the letter, copying it three times, and circling the best formed letter. Three lessons were devoted to mastering each letter set, with the second and third lessons focusing on practicing the letters in the context of single words (e.g., *lit*) or hinky-pinks (rhyming words such as itty-bitty). Three, students copied a short sentence quickly and accurately for a period of 3 minutes. The sentence contained multiple instances of the letters emphasized during that lesson (e.g., **Little** kids **li**ke **t**o ge**t** le**tt**ers.). The number of letters written was recorded on a chart, and during the next two lessons, students tried to beat their previous score. Four, the instructor showed students how to use a target letter in a fun way (e.g., turning an *i* into a butterfly or an *s* into a snake). Students who received this handwriting instruction became quicker and better handwriters than peers in the control condition. They also evidenced greater gains in their ability to craft sentences and generate text when writing a story.

Second-grade children who were poor spellers and writers were provided with 12 hours of instruction by Graham et al. (2002). Instruction involved six units with five lessons each, and each unit was structured in a similar way. During the first lesson of each unit, children completed a word-sorting activity that introduced them to the spelling patterns taught in that unit (these primarily focused on long or short vowel patterns). Students sorted word cards into two or three spelling pattern categories. Each category was represented by a master word (e.g., the words "ma**de**," "ma**id**," and m**ay** for the long /*a*/ sound). Once all words were placed, the instructor helped students discover rules for the patterns emphasized in that word sort. Students were encouraged to "hunt" as they later wrote and read for words that fit the emphasized patterns.

During the next four lessons, students studied eight new spelling words that matched one of the spelling patterns emphasized in that unit. Students used two basic procedures to study these words. One procedure, "Graph Busters," involved students recording the number of times they correctly practiced the words during a lesson using a traditional study strategy. The second procedure involved studying words while playing a game with a peer. Pairs of students also practiced identifying sound-letter associations for consonants, blends, digraphs, and short vowels, as well as building words by combining these combinations with rimes that fit the spelling patterns emphasized in the unit (e.g., "ay").

Students who received this spelling instruction not only learned and maintained almost all of the words taught, but their performance on two standardized tests of spelling improved dramatically, too. Furthermore, there was a corresponding improvement immediately following instruction in their sentence construction skills and reading word attack skills.

Like handwriting and spelling, sentence construction skills can also be improved through instructional procedures such as sentence combining. With this approach, students are taught how to construct more complex and sophisticated sentences by combining two or more basic (i.e., "kernel") sentences into a single sentence (Strong, 1976). The goal of such instruction is to teach students how to craft more syntactically complex sentences as well as produce better sentences, ones that more closely convey the writer's message. Sentence-combining instruction often involves the teacher modeling how to combine two

or more kernel structures ("Ralph was in Ryan's pocket: "Ralph looked around;" and "Ralph did not know where he was") into a more complex one ("Ralph, who was in Ryan's pocket, did not know where he was, but stuck his head out and looked around."). This is followed by students practicing this process with other kernel sentences. The practice can be oral, written, or both. In Hillocks' (1986) meta-analysis, the effects of sentence combining instruction were positive, but modest (average effect size 0.35).

Teaching Knowledge. In the Harris et al. (in press) study described earlier, part of instruction included teaching students about the characteristics of good stories and persuasive essays. Similarly, Fitzgerald and Teasley (1986) directly taught fourth-grade students story parts and their interrelations by defining each part and its relationship to other parts, identifying each part in a story, generating parts orally, distinguishing between examples and nonexamples of each part, predicting which part would come next when reading stories, and using their knowledge in activities such as reordering a scrambled story. This instruction enhanced both the structure and quality of students' stories.

Another approach for teaching writing knowledge involves the study of models thought to exemplify specific properties of good writing. With this method, students study and analyze model pieces of writing and then try to imitate the forms embodied in the model compositions. Although luminaries such as Benjamin Franklin used this approach (Isaacson, 2003), its impact in scientific studies has been positive, but small (effect size of 0.22 in Hillocks' 1986 review).

Principle 2: Structure the Writing Environment to Maximize Students' Success and Learning

In addition to directly teaching writing strategies, skills, and knowledge, teachers can put into place procedures and activities designed to help students be more successful when they write. This includes developing a writing environment in which they are likely to flourish (Graham & Harris, 1997b), as well as providing substantive and facilitative assistance in carrying out writing processes (Scardamalia & Bereiter, 1986). Substantive facilitation involves collaborating with students on what they wrote or plan to write (e.g., teacher comments on student compositions or conferences where teachers ask leading questions about what the student plans to do next), whereas procedural facilitation does not focus on the text per se, but involves help in carrying out specific writing process (e.g., the editing capabilities of a word processor or the use of cues to remind writers to carry out certain processes). In many ways, these procedures are analogous to a heart pacer, as they do some of the work for the student, prodding, orienting, or supporting them. It is typically assumed that some learning occurs as a result of repeated use of these procedures, but developing writers may apply these external supports in unpredictable ways (Scardamalia & Bereiter, 1986).

There is good reason to believe that instructional Principles 1 and 2 work together to promote writing development. For example, students may be less likely to use the writing strategies they are taught if writing assignments are viewed as boring or confusing, the classroom is seen as an unfriendly or punitive place, or there are few opportunities to apply the inculcated strategies (Graham & Harris, 1997a). Furthermore, learning in writing is not solely dependent on instruction. For instance, students' fluency with handwriting primarily develops after formal handwriting instruction stops and is mainly a consequence of experience generating text (Graham & Weintraub, 1996). Similarly, school-age students are typically taught how to spell somewhere around 3,000 to 3,600 words. Most adults can spell three to four times more words than this. They learn many of these other words as a result of writing and reading (Graham, 2000).

Motivation. How can teachers structure the writing environment to heighten motivation? A series of studies that examines the teaching practices of effective teachers of literacy provides some examples (Pressley, Rankin, & Yokoi, 1996; Pressley, Yokoi, Rankin, Wharton-McDonald, & Hampston, 1997; Wray, Medwell, Fox, & Poulson, 2000). The teachers in these studies undertook a variety of actions and activities to make writing more motivating, including modeling their own love for writing, conveying the importance of writing in life, connecting writing to reading and other subjects, creating a writing environment where students felt comfortable taking risks, developing a sense of community in the classroom, setting an exciting mood, reinforcing children's accomplishments, displaying students' writing on the walls and other prominent places, allowing students to select some of their own writing topics and work at their own pace, specifying the goals for each lesson, promoting an "I can do" attitude, allowing peers to work together on writing projects, and publishing completed papers.

Self-regulation. The effective literacy teachers in the aforementioned studies also put into place structures to promote more strategic writing behavior. These included stressing students' ownership of their writing and establishing a predictable routine where students were encouraged to plan, draft, and revise.

How students compose can be prodded, oriented, or supported in a number of other ways too. One, teachers can provide students with writing goals that direct how they allocate their attention. For instance, Graham, MacArthur, and Schwartz (1995) asked fifth- and sixth-grade struggling writers to add three things to their paper to make them better. This goal helped students shift their attention during revising from an almost exclusive focus on form to more emphasis on substance, resulting in improvements in text quality. Two, electronic technologies can be used to support the composing process. Although the impact of word processing on planning and revising behavior is uncertain (MacArthur, in press), a recent meta-analysis supports the power of word processing over traditional composing by hand (Goldberg, Russell, & Cook, 2003), as the average effect size for both quality (0.41) and length (0.50) favored word processing. Three, students can be provided with procedural support to carry out specific writing processes. For example, De La Paz, Swanson, and Graham (1998) asked eighth-grade struggling writers to revise a composition by reading their first draft and picking evaluation cards (e.g., "Too few ideas") that best described the paper. For each evaluation card selected they chose a tactic card (e.g., "Add") and made the desired revision. Next, they reread their paper and used a highlighter to mark additional problems. Finally, they used evaluation and tactic cards to help them decide what to do about each marked area. The use of this routine resulted in more revisions and more meaning-changing revisions that improved text, as well as better overall text quality.

Skills. As noted earlier, the development of some writing skills, such as handwriting and spelling, is facilitated by the act of writing and reading (Graham, 2000). Thus, an important aspect of developing an educational environment where the learning of writing skills is maximized is to ensure that students write and read frequently. It is important to realize, however, that the amount of incidental learning that occurs is likely tied to students' existing level of competence. In reviewing the spelling literature, for example, Graham (2000) found that poor spellers and readers gain much less from reading and writing than their counterparts who are good spellers and readers.

Knowledge. It is commonly assumed that students acquire some knowledge about writing through reading. A study by Bereiter and Scardamalia (1984) suggests that it is possible to acquire some knowledge about writing just from a single reading. For example, they found that writers from third grade to graduate school acquired rhetorical knowledge about restaurant reviews, even though it was of limited complexity, as a result of a single exposure to this type of writing. The cumulative effects of daily reading on writing knowledge, however, are unknown. To maximize such development, Bos (1988) recommended that teachers play an active role in guiding the process of acquiring knowledge through reading. As students read a particular book, the teacher can encourage discussion, focusing attention on important features of text, such as the use of dialogue, plot development, and foreshadowing. Students should then be asked to apply what they have learned in their own writing.

Principle 3: Facilitate Writing Development Through Peer Interactions

Students' classmates can also play an important role in facilitating writing development. For example, they can serve as a resource during planning, drafting, and revising; reinforce the mastery of skills or strategies taught by the classroom teacher; and enhance motivation by serving as a collaborator, an audience, or both. Thus, Principle 3 emphasizes strategically using peers to enhance writing knowledge, strategies, skills, and will. This can be illustrated with several examples from the research literature. For instance, Kuhn, Shaw, and Felton (1997) found that adolescents' knowledge and beliefs about an assigned writing topic, capital punishment, changed as a result of planned discussions with peers. Yarrow and Topping (2001) reported that a paired writing approach, where a peer (tutor) helped another child (tutee) carry out the processes of planning, drafting, and revising compositions, had a positive impact on the writing and self-efficacy of 10- and 11-year-olds. Saddler and Graham (2004) indicated that fourth-grade students improved their sentence combining skills, revising, and overall quality of text as a result of sentence combining instruction that included peer-supported practice. In this study, the instructor first explained and modeled how to apply a specific sentence combining strategy. Student pairs then practiced applying the procedure under the instructor's guidance. This was followed by the student pair alternatively acting as tutor and tutee, as they independently applied the sentence combining strategy.

A FINAL COMMENT

In 2002, the National Commission on Writing in America's Schools and Colleges released a report, *The Neglected "R,"* highlighting the need to make writing improvement a national goal. The report implied that we already have the technology needed to teach writing effectively. Although much is known about writing and effective writing instruction, it is misleading to suggest that the science of writing has advanced this far. It may even be harmful to make such a claim, as funding agencies may see no reason to fund additional research in this area. Additional research is needed, however, to complete our incomplete portraits of writing, writing development, and writing instruction.

References

Alamargot, D., & Chanquoy, L. (2001). *Through the models of writing*. Dordrecht: Kluwer.

Albin, M., Benton, S., & Khramtsova, I. (1996). Individual differences in interest and narrative writing. *Contemporary Educational Psychology, 21*, 305–324.

Alexander, P. A. (1997). Mapping the multidimensional nature of domain learning: The interplay of cognitive, motivational, and strategic forces. In M. L. Maehr & P. R. Pintrich (Eds.), *Advances in motivation and achievement* (Vol. 10, pp. 213–250). Greenwich, CT: JAI Press.

Alexander, P., Graham, S., & Harris, K.R. (1998). A perspective on strategy research: Progress and prospects. *Educational Psychology Review, 10*, 129–154.

Applebee, A. (1984). Writing and reasoning. *Review of Educational Research, 54*, 577–596.

Associated Press. (1995, December 27). This man gives children 'Goosebumps' and 'Fear Street.' *Valdosta Daily Times*, p. B1.

Bandura, A. (1995). Exercise of personal and collective efficacy in changing societies. In A Bandura (Ed.), *Self-efficacy in changing societies* (pp. 1–45). Cambridge, England: Cambridge University Press.

Bangert-Drowns, R., Hurley, M., & Wilkinson, B. (2004). The effects of school-based writing-to-learn interventions on academic achievement: A meta-analysis. *Review of Educational Research, 74*, 29–58.

Beidler, A. (1969). *The effects of the Peabody Language Development Kit on the intelligence, reading, listening, and writing of disadvantaged children in the primary grades.* Unpublished doctoral dissertation, Lehigh University.

Bereiter, C., Burtis, P., & Scardamalia, M. (1988). Cognitive operations in constructing main point in written composition. *Journal of Memory and Language, 27*, 261–278.

Bereiter, C., & Scardamalia, S. (1984). Learning about writing from reading. *Written Communication, 1*, 163–188.

Bereiter, C., & Scardamalia, M. (1987). *The psychology of written composition.* Hillsdale, NJ: Lawrence Erlbaum Associates.

Berninger, V., & Fuller, F. (1992). Gender differences in orthographic, verbal, and compositional fluency: Implications for assessing writing disabilities in primary grade children. *Journal of School Psychology, 30*, 363–382.

Berninger, V., Fuller, F., & Whitaker, D. (1996). A process model of writing development across the life span. *Educational Psychology Review, 8*, 193–218.

Berninger, V., Mizokawa, D., & Bragg, R. (1991). Theory-based diagnosis and remediation of writing disabilities. *Journal of School Psychology, 29*, 57–79.

Berninger, V., Vaughn, K., Abbott, R., Abbott, S., Rogan, L., Brooks, A., et al. (1997). Treatment of handwriting problems in beginning writers: Transfer from handwriting to composition. *Journal of Educational Psychology, 89*, 652–666.

Berninger, V., Vaughn, K., Abbott, R., Brooks, A., Abbott, S., Rogan, L., et al. (1998). Early intervention for spelling problems: Teaching functional spelling units of varying size with a multiple-connections framework. *Journal of Educational Psychology, 90*, 587–605.

Berninger, V., Whitaker, D., Feng, Y., Swanson, L., & Abbott, R. (1996). Assessment of planning, translating, and revising in junior high writers. *Journal of School Psychology, 34*, 23–32.

Bonk, C., Middleton, J., Reynolds, T., & Stead, L. (1990). *The index of writing awareness: One tool for measuring early adolescent metacognition in writing.* Paper presented at the Annual Meeting of the American Educational Research Association, Washington, DC.

Bos, C. (1988). Process-oriented writing: Instructional implications for mildly handicapped students. *Exceptional Children, 54*, 521–527.

Boscolo, P. (1990). The construction of expository text. *First Language, 10*, 217–230.

Bourdin, B., & Fayol, M. (1993). *Comparing speaking span and writing span: A working memory approach.* Paper presented at the Meeting of the European Association for Research in Learning and Instruction, Aix-en-Provence, France.

Bourdin, B., & Fayol, M. (1994). Is written language production more difficult than oral language production? A working memory approach. *International Journal of Psychology, 29*, 591–620.

Breetvelt, I., Van den Bergh, H., & Rijlaarsdam, G. (1994). Relations between writing processes and text quality: When and how. *Cognition and Instruction, 12*, 103–123.

Breetvelt, I., Van den Bergh, H., & Rijlaarsdam, G. (1996). Rereading and generating and their relation to text quality: An application of mutilevel analysis on writing process data. In G. Rijlaarsdam, H. Van den Bergh, M. Couzjin (Eds.), *Theories, models and methodologies on writing research* (pp. 10–21). Amsterdam: Amsterdam University Press.

Bridge, C., Compton-Hall, B., & Cantrell, S. (1997). Classroom writing practices revisited: The effects of statewide reform on writing instruction. *Elementary School Journal, 98*, 151–170.

Brodie, D. (1997). *Writing changes everything: The 627 best things anyone ever said about writing.* New York: St. Martin.

Bruning, R., & Horn, C. (2000). Developing motivation to write. *Educational Psychologist, 35*, 25–38.

Burnham, S. (1994). *For writers only.* New York: Ballantine Books.

Butterfield, E., Hacker, D., & Plumb, C. (1994). Topic knowledge, linguistic knowledge, and revision skill as determinants of text revision. In E. Butterfield (Ed.), *Children's writing: Toward a process theory of the development of skilled writing* (pp. 83–141). Greenwich, CT: JAI.

Cameron, C., & Moshenko, B. (1996). Elicitations of knowledge transformational reports while children write narratives. *Canadian Journal of Behavioural Science, 28*, 271–280.

Chanquoy, L. (2001). How to make it easier for children to revise their writing: A study of text revision from 3rd to 5th grades. *British Journal of Educational Psychology, 71*, 15–41.

Cook, M. (2003). *A brief history of the human race.* New York: Norton.

Couzijn, M. (1999). Learning to write by observation of writing and reading processes: Effects on learning and transfer. *Learning and Instruction, 9*, 109–142.

Cowley, M. (1958). *Writers at work: The Paris Review interviews.* New York: Viking.

Crowhurst, M. (1980). Syntactic complexity and teachers' quality ratings of narrations and arguments. *Research and the Teaching of English, 14*, 223–231.

De La Paz, S., & Graham, S. (1995). Dictation: Applications to writing for students with learning disabilities. In T. Scruggs & M. Mastropieri (Eds.), *Advances in Learning and Behavioral Disabilities* (Vol. 9, pp. 227–247). Greenwich, CT: JAI Press.

De La Paz, S., Swanson, P., & Graham, S. (1998). The contribution to executive control to the revising by students with learning and writing difficulties. *Journal of Educational Psychology, 90*, 448–460.

Deno, S., Marston, D., & Mirkin, P. (1982). Valid measurement procedures for continuous evaluation of written expression. *Exceptional Children, 48*, 368–371.

Diamond, J. (1999). *Guns, germs, and steel: The fates of human societies.* New York: Norton.

Donovan, C., & Smolkin, L. (in press). Children's understanding of genre and writing development. In C. MacArthur, S. Graham, & J. Fitzgerald (Eds.), *Handbook of writing research.* New York: Guilford.

Durst, R., & Newell, G. (1989). The uses of function: James Britton's category system and research on writing. *Review of Educational Research, 59*, 375–394.

Englert, C., & Thomas, C. (1987). Sensitivity to text structure in reading and writing: A comparison between learning disabled and non-learning disabled students. *Learning Disability Quarterly, 10*, 93–105.

Englert, S., Raphael, T., Fear, K., & Anderson, L. (1988). Students' metacognitive knowledge about how to write informational texts. *Learning Disability Quarterly, 11*, 18–46.

Farr, R., Hughes, C., Robbins, B., & Greene, B. (1990). *What students' writing reveals about their spelling.* Bloomington, IN: Center for Reading and Language Studies.

Ferreiro, E., & Pontecorvo, C. (1999). Managing the written text: The beginning of punctuation in children's writing. *Learning and Instruction, 9,* 343–364.

Fitzgerald, J. (1987). Research on revision in writing. *Review of Educational Research, 57,* 481–506.

Fitzgerald, J., & Markham, L. (1987). Teaching children about revision in writing. *Cognition and Instruction, 4,* 3–24.

Fitzgerald, J., & Shanahan, T. (2000). Reading and writing relations and their development. *Educational Psychologist, 35,* 39–50.

Fitzgerald, J., & Teasley, A. (1986). Effects of instruction in narrative structure on children's writing. *Journal of Educational Psychology, 78,* 424–432.

Gentry, R. (1982). An analysis of development spelling in GYNS AT WRK. *Reading Teacher, 36,* 192–200.

Gilliam, R., & Johnston, J. (1992). Spoken and written language relationships in language/learning children. *Journal of Speech and Hearing Research, 35,* 1303–1315.

Goldberg, A., Russell, M., & Cook, A. (2003). The effects of computers on student writing: A metaanalysis of studies from 1992 to 2002. *Journal of Technology, Learning, and Assessment, 2,* 1–51.

Gould, J. (1980). Experiments on composing letters: Some facts, some myths, and some observations. In L. Gregg & E. Steinberg (Eds.), *Cognitive processes in writing* (pp. 97–127). Hillsdale, NJ: Lawrence Erlbaum Associates.

Graham, S. (1982). Composition research and practice: A unified approach. *Focus on Exceptional Children, 14,* 1–16.

Graham, S. (1983). Effective spelling instruction. *Elementary School Journal, 83,* 560–568.

Graham, S. (1990). The role of production factors in learning disabled students' compositions. *Journal of Educational Psychology, 82,* 781–791.

Graham, S. (2000). Should the natural learning approach replace spelling instruction? *Journal of Educational Psychology, 92,* 235–247.

Graham, S. (in press). Strategy instruction and the teaching of writing: A meta-analysis. In C. MacArthur, S. Graham, & J. Fitzgerald (Eds.), *Handbook of writing research.* New York: Guilford.

Graham, S., Berninger, V., Abbott, R., Abbott, S., & Whitaker, D. (1997). The role of mechanics in composing of elementary school students: A new methodological approach. *Journal of Educational Psychology, 89,* 170–182.

Graham, S., Berninger, V., Weintraub, N., & Schafer, W. (1998). Development of handwriting speed and legibility. *Journal of Educational Research, 92,* 42–51.

Graham, S., & Harris, K. R. (1997a). Self-regulation and writing: Where do we go from here? *Contemporary Educational Psychology, 22,* 102–114.

Graham, S., & Harris, K. R. (1997b). It can be taught, but it does not develop naturally: Myths and realities in writing instruction. *School Psychology Review, 26,* 414–424.

Graham, S., & Harris, K. (2000a). Writing development: Introduction to the special issue. *Educational Psychologist, 35,* 2.

Graham, S., & Harris, K. (2000b). The role of self-regulation and transcription skills in writing and writing development. *Educational Psychologist, 35,* 3–12.

Graham. S., & Harris, K. R. (2003). Students with learning disabilities and the process of writing: A meta-analysis of SRSD studies. In L. Swanson, K. R. Harris, & S. Graham (Eds.). *Handbook of research on learning disabilities* (pp. 383–402). New York: Guilford.

Graham, S., & Harris, K. R. (in press). *Writing better: Teaching writing processes and self-regulation to students with learning problems.* Baltimore, MD: Brookes.

Graham, S., Harris, K. R., & Fink, B. (2000). Is handwriting causally related to learning to write? Treatment of handwriting problems in beginning writers. *Journal of Educational Psychology, 92,* 620–633.

Graham, S., Harris, K. R., & Fink-Chorzempa, B. (2002). Contributions of spelling instruction to the spelling, writing, and reading of poor spellers. *Journal of Educational Psychology, 94,* 669–686.

Graham, S., Harris, K. R., Fink, B., & MacArthur, C. (2001). Teacher efficacy in writing: A construct validation with primary grade teachers. *Scientific Study of Reading, 5,* 177–202.

Graham, S., Harris, K. R., Fink, B., & MacArthur, C. (2002). Primary grade teachers= theoretical orientations concerning writing instruction. Construct validation and a nationwide survey. *Contemporary Educational Psychology, 27,* 147–166.

Graham, S., Harris, K. R., MacArthur, C., & Fink-Chorzempa, B. (2003). Primary grade teachers' instructional adaptations for weaker writers: A national survey. *Journal of Educational Psychology, 95,* 279–293.

Graham, S., MacArthur, C., & Schwartz, S. (1995). The effects of goal setting and procedural facilitation on the revising behavior and writing performance of students with writing and learning problems. *Journal of Educational Psychology, 87,* 230–240.

Graham, S., Schwartz, S., & MacArthur, C. (1993). Knowledge of writing and the composing process, attitude toward writing, and the self-efficacy for students with and without learning disabilities. *Journal of Learning Disabilities, 26,* 237–249.

Graham, S., & Weintraub, N. (1996). A review of handwriting research: Progress and prospects from 1980 to 1994. *Educational Psychology Review, 8,* 7–87.

Harris, K. R., & Graham, S. (1999). Programmatic intervention research: Illustrations from the evolution of self-regulated strategy development. *Learning Disability Quarterly, 22,* 251–262.

Harris, K. R., Graham, S., & Mason, L. (in press). Improving the writing performance, knowledge, and self-efficacy of young struggling writers: The effects of Self-Regulated Strategy Development. *American Educational Research Journal.*

Hayes, J. (1996). A new framework for understanding cognition and affect in writing. In M.. Levy & S. Ransdell (Eds.), *The science of writing: Theories, methods, individual differences, and applications* (pp. 1–27). Mahwah, NJ: Lawrence Erlbaum Associates.

Hayes, J., & Flower, L. (1980). Identifying the organization of writing processes. In L. Gregg & E. Steinberg (Eds.), *Cognitive processes in writing* (pp. 3–30). Hillsdale, NJ: Lawrence Erlbaum Associates.

Hayes, J., & Nash, J. (1996). On the nature of planning in writing. In M. Levy & S. Ransdell (Eds.), *The science of writing: Theories, methods, individual differences, and applications* (pp. 29–55). Mahwah, NJ: Lawrence Erlbaum Associates.

Hendrickson, R. (1994). *The literary life and other curiosities*. San Diego, CA: Harcourt Brace.

Hidi, S., & Boscolo, P. (in press). Motivation and writing. In C. MacArthur, S. Graham, & J. Fitzgerald (Eds.), *Handbook of Writing Research*. New York: Guilford.

Hidi, S., & McLaren, J. (1991). Motivational factors in writing: The role of topic interestingness. *European Journal of Psychology of Education, 6*, 187–197.

Hillocks, G. (1986). *Research on written composition: New directions for teaching*. Urbana, IL: National Council of Teachers of English.

Holliway, D., & McCutchen, D. (2004). Audience perspective in young writers' composing and revising. In L. Allal, L. Chanquoy, & P. Largy (Eds), *Revision: Cognitive and instructional processes* (pp. 87–101). Boston: Kluwer.

Houck, C., & Billingsley, B. (1989). Written expression of students with and without learning disabilities: Differences across grades. *Journal of Learning Disabilities, 22*, 561–565.

Hunt, K. (1965). *Grammatical structures written at three grade levels*. Champaign, IL: National Council of Teachers of English.

Isaacson, W. (2003). *Benjamin Franklin: An American life*. New York: Simon & Schuster.

Jones, D., & Christensen, C. (1999). The relationship between automaticity in handwriting and students' ability to generate written text. *Journal of Educational Psychology, 91*, 44–49.

Juel, C. (1988). Learning to read and write: A longitudinal study of 54 children from first through fourth grade. *Journal of Educational Psychology, 80*, 437–447.

Kellogg, R. (1986). Designing idea processors for document composition. *Behavior Research, Methods, Instruments, and Computers, 18*, 118–128.

Kellogg, R. (1987). Effects of topic knowledge on the allocation of processing time and cognitive effort to writing processes. *Memory & Cognition, 15*, 256–266.

Kellogg, R. (1993a). Observations on the psychology of thinking and writing. *Composition Studies, 21*, 3–41.

Kellogg, R. (1993b). *The psychology of writing*. New York: Oxford University Press.

Kellogg, R. (1996). A model of working memory in writing. In M. Levy & S. Ransdell (Eds.), *The science of writing: Theories, methods, individual differences, and applications* (pp. 57–72). Mahwah, NJ: Lawrence Erlbaum Associates.

Knudson, R. (1991). Development and use of a writing attitude survey in grades 4 to 8. *Psychological Reports, 68*, 807–816.

Knudson, R. (1992). Development and application of a writing attitude survey for grades 1 to 3. *Psychological Reports, 70*, 711–720.

Knudson, R. (1995). Writing experiences, attitudes, and achievement of first to sixth graders. *Journal of Educational Research, 89*, 90–97.

Kuhn, D., Shaw, V., & Felton, M. (1997). Effects of dyadic interaction on argumentative reasoning. *Cognition & Instruction, 15*, 287–315.

L'Amour, L. (1990). *The education of a wandering man*. New York: Bantam.

Lipstein, R., & Renninger, K. (in press). "Putting things into words": 12–15 year-old students' interest for writing. In S. Hidi & P. Boscolo (Eds.), *Motivation and writing: Research and school practice*. Dordrecht: Kluwer.

MacArthur, C. (in press). The effects of new technologies on writing and writing processes. In C. MacArthur, S. Graham, & J. Fitzgerald (Eds.), *Handbook of writing research*. New York: Guilford.

MacArthur, C., & Graham, S. (1987). Learning disabled students' composing under three methods of text production: Handwriting, word processing, and dictation. *Journal of Special Education, 21*, 22–42.

MacArthur, C., Graham, S., & Harris, K. R. (2004). Insights from instructional research on revision with struggling writers. In L. Allal, L. Chanquoy, & P. Largy (Eds), *Revision: Cognitive and instructional processes* (pp. 125–138). Boston: Kluwer.

Madigan, R., Linton, P., & Johnston, S. (1996). The paradox of writing apprehension. In M. Levy & S. Ransdell (Eds.), *The science of writing: Theories, methods, individual differences, and applications* (pp. 295–307). Mahwah, NJ: Erlbaum.

Mavrogenes, N., & Bezruczko, N. (1993). Influences on writing development. *Journal of Educational Research, 86*, 237–245.

McCutchen, D. (1988). "Functional automaticity" in children's writing: A problem of metacognitive control. *Written Communication, 5*, 306–324.

McCutchen, D. (1995). Cognitive processes in children's writing: Developmental and individual differences. *Issues in Education: Contributions from Educational Psychology, 1*, 123–160.

McCutchen, D. (2000). Knowledge, processing, and working memory in writing and writing development. *Educational Psychologists, 35*, 13–24.

McCutchen, D. (in press). Cognitive factors in the development of children's writing. In C. MacArthur, S. Graham, & J. Fitzgerald (Eds.), *Handbook of writing research*. New York: Guilford.

McCutchen, D., Francis, M., & Kerr, S. (1997). Revising for meaning: Effects of knowledge and strategy. *Journal of Educational Psychology, 89*, 667–676.

Miller, B., & Ney, J. (1968). The effect of systematic oral exercises on the writing of fourth grade students. *Research in the Teaching of English, 2*, 44–61.

Mosenthall, P., Conley, M., Colella, A., & Davidson-Mosenthall, R. (1985). The influence of prior knowledge and teacher lesson structure on children's production of narratives. *Elementary School Journal, 85*, 621–634.

National Commission on Writing (2003). *The neglected "R."* College Entrance Examination Board.

Nolen, S. (2003, August). *The development of interest and motivation to read and write.* Paper presented at the 10th biannual meeting of the European Association for Research on Learning and Instruction, Padova, Italy.

Pajares, F. (2003). Self-efficacy beliefs, motivation, and achievement in writing: A review of the literature. *Reading & Writing Quarterly, 19*, 139–158.

Pajares, F., & Valiante C., (in press). Self-efficacy beliefs and motivation in writing development. In L. Swanson, K. R. Harris, & S. Graham (Eds.). *Handbook of research on learning disabilities* (pp. 383–402). New York: Guilford.

Phillips, B. (1993). *Phillip's book of great thoughts and funny sayings.* Wheaton, IL: Tyndal House.

Pintrich, P. (2000). An achievement goal theory perspective on issues in motivation terminology, theory, and research. *Contemporary Educational Psychology, 25*, 92–104.

Pressley, M., Rankin, J., & Yokoi, L. (1996). A survey of instructional practices of primary teachers nominated as effective in promoting literacy. *Elementary School Journal, 96*, 363–384.

Pressley, M., Yokoi, L., Rankin, J., Wharton-McDonald, R., & Hampston, J. (1997). A survey of instructional practices of grade-5 teachers nominated as effective in promoting literacy. *Scientific Studies of Reading, 1*, 145–160.

Prior, P. (in press). A sociocultural theory of writing. In C. MacArthur, S. Graham, & J. Fitzgerald (Eds.), *Handbook of writing research.* New York: Guilford.

Quinlan, T. (2004). Speech recognition technology and students with writing difficulties: Improving fluency. *Journal of Educational Psychology, 96*, 337–346.

Raiser, V. (1981). Syntactic maturity, vocabulary diversity, mode of discourse and theme selection in the free writing of learning disabled adolescents. *Dissertation Abstracts International, 42*, 2544A.

Reece, J., & Cumming, G. (1996). Evaluating speech-based composition methods: Planning, dictation, and the listening word processor. In M. Levy & S. Ransdell (Eds.), *The science of writing: Theories, methods, individual differences, and applications* (pp. 361–380). Mahwah, NJ: Lawrence Erlbaum Associates.

Ross, P., Poidevant, J., & Miner, C. (1995). Curriculum-based assessment of writing fluency in children with attention-deficit hyperactivity disorder and normal children. *Reading & Writing Quarterly, 11*, 201–208.

Saddler, B., & Graham, S. (in press). Knowledge about writing and writing performance: Differences between students who are more or less skilled writers. *Reading & Writing Quarterly.*

Saddler, B., & Graham, S. (2005). The effects of peer-assisted sentence combining on the writing performance of more or less skilled young writers. *Journal of Educational Psychology, 97*, 43–54.

Scardamalia, M., & Bereiter, C. (1985). Fostering the development of self-regulation in children's knowledge processing. In S. Chipman, J. Segal, & R. Glaser (Eds.), *Thinking and learning skills: Current research and open questions* (Vol. 2, pp. 563–577). Hillsdale, NJ: Lawrence Erlbaum Associates.

Scardamalia, M., & Bereiter, C. (1986). Written composition. In M. Wittrock (Ed.). *Handbook of research on teaching* (3rd ed., pp. 778–803). New York: MacMillan.

Schultz, K., & Fecho, B. (2000). Society's child: Social context and writing development. *Educational Psychologist, 35*, 51–62.

Schunk, D., & Swartz, C. (1993a). Goals and progress feedback: Effects on self-efficacy and writing achievement. *Contemporary Educational Psychology, 18*, 337–354.

Schunk, D., & Swartz, C. (1993b). Writing strategy instruction with gifted students: Effects of goals and feedback on self-efficacy and skills. *Roeper Review, 15*, 225–230.

Schunk, D., & Zimmerman, B. (1998). *Self-regulated learning: From teaching to self-reflective practices.* New York: Guilford.

Scott, C. (1999). Learning to write. In H. Catts & A. Kamhi (Eds.), *Language and reading disorders* (pp. 224–258). Boston: Allyn & Bacon.

Scott, C., & Windsor, J. (2000). General language performance measures in spoken and written narrative and expository discourse of school-age children with language learning disabilities. *Journal of Speech, Language, and Hearing Research, 43*, 324–339.

Senechal, M., LeFevre, J., Thomas, E., & Daley, K. (1998). Differential effects of home literacy experiences on the development of oral and written language. *Reading Research Quarterly, 33*, 96–116.

Shanahan, T. (in press). Relations among oral language, reading, and writing development. In C. MacArthur, S. Graham, & J. Fitzgerald (Eds.), *Handbook of writing research.* New York: Guilford.

Shell, D., Colvin, C., & Brunning, R. (1995). Self-efficacy, attribution, and outcome expectancy mechanisms in reading and writing achievement: Grade-level and achievement-level differences. *Journal of Educational Psychology, 87*, 386–398.

Smith M., Cheville, J., & Hillocks, G. (in press). "I guess I'd better watch my Englis": Grammars and the teaching of the English language arts. In C. MacArthur, S. Graham, & J. Fitzgerald (Eds.), *Handbook of Writing Research.* New York: Guilford.

Smyth, J. (1998). Written emotional expression: Effect sizes, outcome types, and moderating variables. *Journal of Consulting and Clinical Psychology, 66*, 174–184.

Stahl, S., Suttles, W., & Pagnucco, J. (1996). First graders' reading and writing instruction in traditional and process-oriented classes. *Journal of Educational Research, 89*, 131–144.

Strong, W. (1976). *Creative approaches to sentence combining.* Urbana, IL: ERIC Clearinghouse on Reading and Communication Skills and the National Council of Teachers of English.

Swedlow, J. (1999). The power of writing. *National Geographic, 196*, 110–132.

Traxler, M. & Gernsbacher, M. (1993). Improving written communication through perspective-taking. *Language and Cognitive Processes, 8*, 311–344.

Treiman, R. (1993). *Beginning to spell*. New York: Oxford University Press.

Troia, G., & Graham, S. (2002). The effectiveness of a highly explicit, teacher-directed strategy instruction routine: Changing the writing performance of students with learning disabilities. *Journal of Learning Disabilities, 35,* 290-305.

Tuck, L. (2003, July 2). The writing life. *Washington Post Book World,* p. 10.

Van den Bergh, H. & Rijlaarsdam, G. (1996). The dynamics of composing: Modeling writing process data. In C. Levy & S. Ransdell (Eds.), *The science of writing* (pp. 207-232). Mahwah, NJ: Lawrence Erlbaum Associates.

Van den Bergh, H., & Rijlaarsdam, G. (in press). Writing process theory: A functional dynamic approach. In C. MacArthur, S. Graham, & J. Fitzgerald (Eds.), *Handbook of writing research*. New York: Guilford.

Voss, J., Vesonder, G., & Spilich, G. (1980). Text generation and recall by high-knowledge and low-knowledge individuals. *Journal of Verbal Learning and Verbal Behavior, 19,* 651-667.

Vrugt, A., Oort, F., & Zeeberg, C. (2002). Goal orientations, perceived self-efficacy and study results among beginner and advanced students. *British Journal of Educational Psychology, 72,* 385-397.

Walberg, H., & Ethington, C. (1991). Correlates of writing performance and interest: A U.S, National assessment study. *Journal of Educational Research, 84,* 198-203.

Walker, B. (2003). The cultivation of student self-efficacy in reading and writing. *Reading and Writing Quarterly, 19,* 173-187.

Wallace, D., Hayes, J., Hatch, J., Miller, W., Moser, G., & Silk, C. (1996). Better revision in eight minutes? Prompting first-year college writers to revise globally. *Journal of Educational Psychology, 88,* 682-688.

Wiggins, R. (1968). *A study of the influence of oral instruction on students' ability in written sentence structure.* Unpublished doctoral dissertation, University of South Carolina.

Willingham, D. (1998). A neuropsychological theory of motor skill learning. *Psychological Review, 105,* 558-584.

Wong, B., Wong, R., & Blenkinsop, J. (1989). Cognitive and metacognitive aspects of learning disabled adolescents' composing problems. *Learning Disability Quarterly, 12,* 300-322.

Wray, D., Medwell, J., Fox, R., & Poulson, L. (2000). The teaching practices of effective teachers of literacy. *Educational Review, 52,* 75-84.

Yarrow F., & Topping (2001). Collaborative writing: The effects of metacognitive prompting and structured peer interaction. *British Journal of Educational Psychology, 71,* 261-282.

Zimmerman, B. (1989). A social cognitive view of self-regulated learning. *Journal of Educational Psychology, 81,* 329-339.

Zimmerman, B., & Risemberg, R. (1997). Becoming a self-regulated writer: A social cognitive perspective. *Contemporary Educational Psychology, 22,* 73-101.

MATHEMATICS TEACHING AND LEARNING

Alan H. Schoenfeld
Graduate School of Education, University of California, Berkeley

It was the best of times, it was the worst of times,
it was the age of wisdom, it was the age of foolishness,
it was the epoch of belief, it was the epoch of doubt,
it was the season of Light, it was the season of Darkness,
it was the spring of hope, it was the winter of despair,
we had everything before us, we had nothing before us.

Charles Dickens, *A Tale of Two Cities*

OVERVIEW

This chapter focuses on advances in the study of mathematics teaching and learning since the publication of the first edition of the *Handbook of Educational Psychology* (Berliner & Calfee, editors) in 1996. Because of the scope of the review, comprehensive coverage is not possible. In what follows I have chosen to focus thematically on major areas in which progress has been made or where issues at the boundaries of theory and practice are controversial.[1] These areas include research focusing on issues of teacher knowledge and aspects of professional development; issues of curriculum development, implementation, and assessment; issues of equity and diversity; and issues of learning in context(s). The chapter concludes with a discussion of the state of the field and its contextual surround.

TEACHER KNOWLEDGE

Significant progress has been made over the past decade in understanding mathematics teachers' knowledge, how it plays out in practice, and how it can be developed. The field can boast of two major books and two additional programmatic bodies of work, all of which add significantly to our understanding. Over the past decade, two major works have emerged that expand the field's conception of the nature and complexity of the knowledge that teachers bring to the classroom. Liping Ma's 1999 book *Knowing and Teaching Elementary Mathematics* demonstrated the unique character of highly accomplished mathematics teachers' knowledge—a knowledge clearly different from knowledge of the mathematics alone. Magdalene Lampert's 2001 book *Teaching Problems and the Problem of Teaching* offers a remarkably detailed empirical and theoretical examination of the multiple levels of knowledge, planning, and decision making entailed in a year's teaching. Next, I briefly describe Deborah Ball, Hyman Bass, and their colleagues' studies of the mathematical knowledge that supports effective teaching, and the work of Miriam Sherin in describing teachers' *professional vision*. Like the work described before it, this work sheds light on the character of knowledge

---

[1] This approach, like any approach to mapping out a huge territory, results in some unfortunate omissions. Many fine pieces of work, specifically, many studies that focus on learning and conceptual growth in particular mathematical topic areas, are not discussed here. Nor is the role of technology in mathematics learning. Readers with specific interests in these topics will want to consult the forthcoming *Second Handbook of Research on Mathematics Teaching and Learning* (Lester, in preparation). The previous editions of that *handbook* (Grouws, 1992) and this one (Berliner & Calfee, 1996) provide relevant background and context for this article.

that enables teachers to interact effectively with students over substantial mathematics.

This work is followed by a description of the work by the Teacher Model Group at Berkeley, which has worked to characterize both the nature of teacher knowledge and the ways that it works in practice. Like the work of Ball, Bass, and colleagues, this work characterizes teaching as problem-solving. It contributes to the problem-solving and teaching literatures by describing, at a theoretical level of mechanism, the kinds of decision making in which teachers engage as they work to solve the problems of teaching.

Pedagogical Content Knowledge

The study of teacher knowledge was revitalized in the mid-1980s when Lee Shulman (1986, 1987) introduced the notion of *pedagogical content knowledge.* Although the term was not clearly defined at the beginning, the very notion of *specialized content-related knowledge for teaching* caught the field's imagination and opened up significant new arenas for both research and practice. We shall begin by exemplifying the concept and indicating its practical implications, after which we turn to contemporary research.

Here is an example familiar to any algebra teacher. Relatively early in the course, one may use the distributive property to show that $(a + b)^2 = a^2 + 2ab + b^2$. One may also suggest the truth of the formula with an "area model." But, one also knows (after having taught the course once) that, later in the course, when students do their homework or one writes the expression $(x + y)^2$ on the blackboard, a significant proportion of the students will complete the expression by writing, incorrectly, $(x + y)^2 = x^2 + y^2$. The first time this happens, a beginning teacher may be taken aback. But with a little experience, the teacher knows to anticipate this, and to be ready with either examples or explanations. For example, the question "Why don't you try your formula with $x = 3$ and $y = 4$?" can lead the student to see the mistake. It exemplifies yet another valuable strategy (testing formulas with examples if one is unsure), and can set the stage for a more meaningful reprise of the reasons that the formula works the way it does.

This kind of knowledge—knowing to anticipate specific student understandings and misunderstandings in specific instructional contexts, and having strategies ready to employ when students demonstrate those (mis)understandings—is an example of pedagogical content knowledge (PCK). PCK differs from general pedagogical knowledge, in that it is tied to content. A general suggestion such as "generate examples and nonexamples of important concepts" may seem close, but it hardly arms the teacher with the knowledge for this particular situation (or thousands of others like it). There is a critical aspect of fine-grained domain specificity here: in *this* situation, this kind of example is likely to prove necessary and useful. PCK also differs from "straight" content knowledge: one can understand the correct ways to derive the algebraic relationship under discussion without knowing to anticipate student errors.

The concept is critically important because it points to a form of knowledge that is now understood to be a central aspect of competent teaching—and, one that is at variance with simple notions of teacher "training." Some policymakers and others have a strongly held belief that what is needed for competent teaching in any domain is a combination of subject matter knowledge and either "common sense" or general pedagogical training. This belief is part of the support structure for a wide range of programs aimed at taking professionals in various mathematical and scientific fields and getting them into the classroom rapidly—the expectation being that a bit of pedagogical training and/or common sense will suffice to prepare those who have solid subject matter backgrounds for the classroom. An understanding of the true bases of pedagogical competency is essential as an antidote to such "quick fixes," and as a precondition for bolstering teacher preparation programs in ways that allow them to prepare prospective teachers more adequately. (For more extended discussions of this issue, see National Academy of Education, 2005.)

Liping Ma's Discussion of "Profound Understanding of Fundamental Mathematics"

In simplest terms, Liping Ma's 1999 book *Knowing and Teaching Elementary Mathematics* is a comparison of the knowledge possessed by a relatively small sample of elementary school mathematics teachers in the United States and Mainland China. Ma studied 23 "above average" teachers in the United States and 72 teachers from a range of schools in China. Her finding was that the most accomplished teachers in China (approximately 10 percent of those interviewed) had a form of pedagogical content knowledge she calls "profound understanding of fundamental mathematics" or PUFM—a richly connected web of understandings that gave them a deep understanding of the domain and of ways to help students learn it. Broadly speaking, such knowledge was not present in the U.S. teachers Ma interviewed.

In four substantive chapters, Ma studies teachers' understandings of approaches to teaching subtraction with regrouping; student mistakes in multidigit multiplication;

the generation of meaningful contexts and representations to help students understand division by fractions; and explorations of the relationships between perimeters and areas of rectangular figures. Here I shall describe the third of these, division by fractions, and use it as a vehicle for discussing PUFM in general.

Ma offered her interviewees the following scenario:

People seem to have different approaches to solving problems involving division with fractions. How do you solve a problem like this one?

$$1\frac{3}{4} \div \frac{1}{2} =$$

Imagine that you are teaching division with fractions. To make this meaningful for kids, something that many teachers try to do is relate mathematics to other things. Sometimes they try to come up with real-world situations or story-problems to show the application of some particular piece of content. What would you say would be a good story or model for $1\frac{3}{4} \div \frac{1}{2}$? (Ma, 1999, p. 55)

Only 9 of the 21 U.S. teachers who worked the problem produced the correct numerical answer to the division problem. This clearly points to a problem with the teachers' algorithmic competency. In contrast, all 72 Chinese teachers performed the computation correctly. Some teachers made formal arguments, in effect justifying the algorithm by either explaining why one inverts $\frac{1}{2}$ and multiplies by its reciprocal, 2. Some converted to decimals. Of much greater interest, however, are the ways in which teachers offered different story representations for the divisions. In trying to produce stories that could motivate and represent the division, 10 of the U.S. teachers confounded division by $\frac{1}{2}$ with division by 2— they discussed two people sharing $1\frac{3}{4}$ pies, or other objects, equally between them. Six more confounded division by $\frac{1}{2}$ with multiplication by $\frac{1}{2}$. Only one of the U.S. teachers generated a story that corresponded correctly to the given division. In contrast, 90 percent of the Chinese teachers generated appropriate stories for the division.

Many of the teachers worked through their stories, giving meaning to the mathematical processes thereby. They demonstrated a wide range of ways to think through, and give meaning to, what it means to divide by one half.

Ma proceeds from her empirical description of the Chinese teachers' knowledge to a theoretical description. She characterizes their understandings of various mathematical topics (for teaching) as "knowledge packages"— tightly bound collections of information that include the meaning of a given concept and related mathematical concepts, representations of the concept and related mathematical concepts, skills (algorithms) and their concep-

tual underpinnings, and relationships between all of the above. She argues that a *profound understanding of fundamental mathematics* (PUFM) is built up of a well-organized collection of such knowledge packages, and she goes on to suggest ways in which teachers develop such understandings.

PUFM is fundamentally mathematical—the core ideas are about mathematical structure. But it is also fundamentally pedagogical, with an organization aimed at meaning-making and deep understanding. In this sense, the knowledge possessed by an accomplished teacher overlaps with, but is different from, that of an accomplished mathematician. There are likely to be aspects of elementary mathematics such as rational number (fractions) that any mathematician knows, and that a highly accomplished teacher does not know—for example, the formal definition of the rational numbers as equivalence classes of ordered pairs of integers. But, there are also aspects of elementary mathematics that teachers with PUFM possess, and professional mathematicians do not. These include having a substantial number of ways of giving meaning to mathematical operations and concepts, and seeing and fostering connections among them. PUFM represents a deeper, more connected understanding of elementary mathematical sense-making than mathematicians are likely to know. It is a different (though related) form of knowledge.

Magdalene Lampert's "Teaching Problems and the Problem of Teaching"

In *Teaching Problems and the Problem of Teaching*, Lampert (2001) takes on the extraordinarily difficult challenge of unraveling the complexities of teaching—of portraying the complex knowledge, planning, and decision making in which she engaged, over the course of a year, as she taught a class in fifth-grade mathematics. This book is an eloquent and elegant antidote to simplistic views of the teaching process. Lampert writes:

One reason teaching is a complex practice is that many of the problems a teacher must address to get students to learn occur simultaneously, not one after another. Because of this simultaneity, several different problems must be addressed by a single action. And a teacher's actions are not taken independently; there are inter-actions with students, individually and as a group....

When I am teaching fifth-grade mathematics, for example, I teach a mathematical idea or procedure to a student while also teaching that student to be civil to classmates and to me, to complete the tasks assigned, and to think of herself or himself and everyone else in the class as capable of learning, no matter what their gender, race, or parents' income. As I work to get students to learn something like "improper fractions," I know

I will also need to be teaching them the meaning of division, how division relates to other operations, and the nature of our number system. (Lampert, 2001, p. 2).

Lampert views and portrays her teaching through multiple lenses. She begins close up, with a view of a specific lesson. Lampert describes individual students in the class, and how they began to work on a problem she assigned. She zooms in on one particular interaction, which occurred when a student wrote something on the board that she did not understand. She asked the class if others could explain where that answer might have come from. The student she called on asked instead if she could explain her own solution. This raised a series of dilemmas for Lampert. Which train of reasoning should be followed? Whom does she run the risk of enfranchising or disenfranchising with her choice, and what implications will this have for the power relationships developing in the classroom? Which aspects of the mathematics will be publicly aired, helping other students to connect not only to the "correct" answer but to think through the various ways of understanding the problem? As she wrestles with these issues, the first student asks to change what he has written. He does, and the number he places on the board is close to the right answer. Now Lampert faces yet another choice. How can she "unpack" this student's thinking, so the class can see how and why he arrived at it, and orchestrate a classroom conversation that will result in the student and the class figuring out the right answer? How can she do so in a way that teaches meta-lessons about reviewing and verifying one's work, that connects to as many of the students' understandings as possible, and that reinforces the classroom's norms of respectful and substantive mathematical interactions?

All this and more happens in one segment of one lesson. And, a lesson is a very small part of a year (which, it should be noted, is 10 percent of a fifth-grader's life to date, so personal as well as intellectual development is a very big issue!). The art of Lampert's book is that she presents the incidents in enough detail to allow one to experience them, at least vicariously; then she steps back, providing an analytic commentary on what took place. Over the course of the book, Lampert displays and reflects on multiple aspects of her teaching, at various levels of grain size. In an early chapter, she presents her reflections and notes on how to get the year started. She identifies her major goals. She compiles a list of productive activities. She views the year through a content lens—students will need to learn the concept of *fraction*, *long division* and *multiplication*, and more. She considers issues related to "learning the practice of mathematics, things like: revision; hypothesizing; giving evidence, explanation; representation." There are issues of physical environment. These are planned in some detail, and then revised in response to ongoing reality—who the students are, and how things seem to be working. Here too, Lampert presents a substantial amount of detail. If, for example, you want students to learn how to make conjectures public, and then to work through those conjectures respectfully (including challenging others' ideas and/or retracting one's own when it turns out not to be right), one must pick problems that will support rich interactions, and work on establishing the right classroom norms.

As noted above, classroom considerations for a fifth-grade teacher go far beyond issues of content. A chapter of Lampert's book is devoted to "teaching students to be people who study in school." How does one realize goals such as "teaching intellectual courage, intellectual honesty, and wise restraint"—having students learn to be willing to take considered risks, be ready to change their position with regard to an issue on the basis of new evidence, but weighing evidence carefully before taking or revising a position? How does one define accomplishment, and establish classroom norms consistent with that definition? Here too, Lampert stakes out a particular kind of territory and then explains how she works toward the goals she has defined.

In a final theoretical chapter, Lampert presents an elaborated model of teaching practice. There she reframes the problems of teaching multiple students at the same time, and the social complexities of practice; the problems of teaching over time; the complexities of teaching content with a curriculum that is largely problem-based; and the complexities of teaching in an environment where all the actors—students as well as the teacher—are taken seriously as contributors to a goal-oriented, emergent agenda. This model, and the book, raise far more questions than they resolve. But that is as it should be. Lampert has taken an ill-understood domain and portrayed its complexity. She has done so in a structured and theoretical way, which makes that complexity accessible and identifies key dimensions of teaching performance and goals. Now that the framework exists, further work by others should move toward the elaboration of the model and toward practical research questions of teacher development toward the kinds of competencies described in it.

Ball, Bass, and Colleagues' Study of Mathematical Knowledge for Teaching

Deborah Ball, Hyman Bass, and colleagues have embarked on a number of projects aimed at understanding the mathematical competencies that underlie teaching. Like the work described earlier, this growing body of work is predicated on the assumption that mathematics teaching is a deeply mathematical act that is built on a base of mathematical understanding and that also calls for different types of knowledge.

The group's research agenda, writ large, is to understand the mathematical underpinnings for a broad range of pedagogical undertakings, to understand how the teachers' knowledge shapes their classroom practices, and how those practices ultimately affect student learning in mathematics. Papers that describe this agenda and document some progress toward its achievement, include Ball and Bass (2000, 2003b); Cohen, Raudenbush, and Ball (2003); Hill and Ball (2004); Hill, Rowan, and Ball, (in press); the RAND Mathematics Study Panel report (2002); and the Study of Instructional Improvement (2002).

A central component of this enterprise is the creation of a series of measures that serve to document teacher knowledge and its impact (see http://www.sii.soe.umich.edu/instruments.html, and Study of Instructional Improvement, 2002). For example, one of the project's released assessment items shows three hypothetical students' work on multiplying multidigit numbers:

Student A	Student B	Student C
35	35	35
×25	×25	×25
125	175	25
+75	+700	150
875	875	100
		+600
		875

The item asks teachers to identify which of the students might be using a method that could be used in general. Answering the item correctly involves inferring the procedure used by the student in each case, and judging whether it will always produce a correct answer. This involves substantial mathematical problem solving, and extends far beyond knowing and being able to demonstrate the standard procedure. Other items under development examine key aspects of competency in central areas of the elementary mathematics curriculum. Ball and colleagues are beginning to use such measures to document the impact of professional development interventions in mathematics: see Hill and Ball (2004).

Sherin's Studies of Teachers' Professional Vision. A body of studies that sits squarely at the intersection of teacher knowledge and teacher learning has been conducted for some years by Miriam Sherin (Sherin, 2001, 2002, 2004; Sherin & Han, 2004). A key construct employed by Sherin, reflecting an important part of accomplished teachers' knowledge, is an adaptation of Charles Goodwin's (1994) notion of *professional vision.* Sherin argues that teachers, like other professionals, develop a particular type of perception common to their profession. Archaeologists recognize the remnants of structures where others see piles of rocks. Doctors recognize clusters of symptoms where laypeople may note individual symptoms or none at all. Similarly, mechanics see and hear functions and malfunctions in mechanical devices; architects note structural stability and other characteristics of buildings; and so on. In the case of teaching, Sherin argues that one form of professional vision is a shift from a focus on pedagogy (examining the moves teachers make in particular circumstances) to a perspective that includes a more intense and critical focus on students' thinking. Sherin & Han (2004) document the use of *video clubs* (meetings in which one or more teachers, in collaboration with university researchers, examine videotapes of the participating teachers' classrooms) as a powerful form of professional development, which can serve as a catalyst for this kind of change. In these video clubs, initial conversations about stimulus videotapes typically involved teachers commenting on pedagogy and researchers focusing on student thinking. Over time, the balance changed. Toward the end of the yearlong series of conversations, the bulk of teacher-initiated comments focused on student thinking—and, teachers' comments both explored the meanings of students' statements and synthesized student ideas. This feeds into pedagogy, of course—but into a diagnostic, student-based pedagogy, which is more typical of accomplished teachers.

The Berkeley Teacher Model Group's Modeling of the Teaching Process. The next research discussed lies at the intersection of research on problem solving and on teaching. Although it overlaps substantially with other work described in this section, it also differs substantially in style.

A major goal of the Teacher Model Group at Berkeley has been to move toward the modeling of increasingly complex behavior—first problem solving in the laboratory (see, e.g., Schoenfeld, 1985), then in tutoring, and finally in teaching. There are at least two dimensions of complexity here. The first is the complexity of the task. Problem solvers in the laboratory had essentially one goal: solve the given problem. Tutors' goals are more complex, as they hope to facilitate learning and must take many other factors related to their students' knowledge into account. And, as Lampert's book makes abundantly clear, teachers are working toward many goals at once: among them having students learn the content under discussion, connect it to other content, learn to become good students, learn to interact productively with others, and develop productively as people. The task of teaching is far more multidimensional than the task of solving mathematics problems. Second, mathematics problems (at least in the laboratory) are static. In contrast, the problems one encounters while teaching are highly interactive and contingent: New issues arise constantly and must be dealt with.

A second major goal has been to address the one major theoretical problem remaining in research on problem solving. Research through the 1980s produced a *framework* for the analysis of mathematical problem solving—one that included aspects of the knowledge base (knowledge and strategies), of decision making (including monitoring and self-regulation), and of beliefs (which shape the problem solver's choice of actions). What was lacking was a *theory*—a specification of how all this fit together, and explained how and why individuals made the problem solving choices they did, on a moment-to-moment basis.

The Teacher Model Group (TMG) has worked to address these issues by building a theory of teaching that produces analytic models of teachers' classroom behavior. These models have the specificity typical of cognitive modeling. They seek to capture how and why, on a moment-by-moment basis, teachers make the decisions they do in the midst of their teaching.

In a series of papers, Schoenfeld and the teacher model group (Arcavi & Schoenfeld, 1992; Schoenfeld, 1998a, 1999, 2000, 2002a, 2005; Schoenfeld et al., 1992; Schoenfeld, Minstrell; & van Zee, 2000) used a theory-based approach to model an increasingly complex and widely varying set of tutoring and teaching episodes.

The basic idea is that a teacher's decision making can be represented by a goal-driven architecture, in which ongoing decision making (problem solving) is a function of that teachers' knowledge, goals, and beliefs. The teacher enters the classroom with a particular set of goals in mind, and some plans for achieving them. At any given time, activated goals may include short-term goals (having students learn the particular content intended for this lesson), medium-term goals (creating and maintaining a supportive climate in which students feel that they can take risks and interact in substantial ways over subject matter), and long-term goals (having students come to see the discipline as a form of sense-making; aiding in their intellectual and personal development). Plans are chosen by the teacher on the basis of his or her beliefs and values. That is, if a teacher believes that skills are crucially important, the plan may include a fair amount of drill. If the teacher wants to foster a certain kind of conceptual understanding, then the activities chosen for the class will reflect that. The teacher then sets things in motion and monitors lesson progress. If there are no untoward or unusual events, various goals are satisfied and other goals and activities take their place as planned. If something unusual does take place, then a decision is called for—the teacher will decide whether to set a new goal on the basis of what he or she believes is important at the moment. If a new high-priority goal is established, the teacher will search through his or her knowledge base for actions to meet that goal (and perhaps other high-priority goals as well). This results in a change of direction, with a new top-level goal. When that goal is satisfied, there may be a return to the previously suspended goal, or a reprioritization.

The analyses of teaching conducted by TMG work at a line-by-line level. Space allows for just one example. In an introductory lesson, Jim Minstrell's class has been discussing ways of computing the "best number" to represent a collection of data. Students have discussed whether outliers should be included in the data set; they have begun to discuss representing the data with a single number—by the average, by the mode. At that point a student raises her hand and says

This is a little complicated but I mean it might work. If you see that 107 shows up four times, you give it a coefficient of 4, and then 107.5 only shows up one time, you give it a coefficient of 1, you add all those up and then you divide by the number of coefficients you have.

Note that a teacher in this kind of situation has many options, ranging from sticking to his lesson plan, telling the student they'll discuss the issue after class, to clearing up the issue with a "mini-lecture," to putting his lesson plan on hold to pursue the issue raised by the student. The question: is enough known about Minstrell, in a principled way, to explain what he does (or even to predict what he is likely to do)?

TMG's model of Minstrell includes his goals and beliefs, which include having students experience physics as a sense-making activity; creating a classroom climate in which students feel free to (and rewarded for) pursuing content-related ideas in sensible ways; and having students learn to sort such things out. Minstrell also believes in minimizing teacher "telling," and has developed a technique he calls "reflective tosses" in which he often answers questions with questions, clarifying things but leaving responsibility for generating (at least partial) answers to them with the students. Thus, confronted with the question from the student, the model acts as follows. The question is germane and substantive. It reflects serious engagement on the part of the student, and its clarification will be a clear act of sense-making. Addressing it will provide an opportunity to instantiate the sense-making values Minstrell espouses. So he will address it—now, and in full. How? Via reflective tosses. He will ask the student to clarify what she means, and ask her and the class how her proposed formula relates to the simple version of average ("add up all the numbers and divide by the number of numbers you have") that the class had already discussed.

Evidence from the range of cases that have been modeled suggests that the underlying architecture of TMG's model, and the theory it instantiates—that teachers' decision making and problem solving are a function of the teachers' knowledge, goals, and beliefs—are robust. This in turn suggests a series of practical applications. First, the better one understands how something is done, the better one can diagnose it and assist others in their professional growth. Second, it may be possible to delineate typical "developmental trajectories" of teaching skill, aiding in professional development. Third, close analysis has revealed some surprising similarities and common teaching routines in what, on the surface, seem to be the very different classroom action by teachers such as Deborah Ball, Jim Minstrell, and myself. These routines may be things that novice teachers can learn. (See, e.g., Schoenfeld, 2002a.)

TEACHER LEARNING: ISSUES OF PROFESSIONAL DEVELOPMENT

The content of the preceding section on teacher knowledge leads naturally to the issue of the growth and change of teacher knowledge—and hence to issues of teacher learning and professional development. In this regard, it is important to recall injunction found in *How People Learn* (National Research Council, 2002a, expanded edition) that learning is learning, whether the learner is child or adult (or, specifically, a teacher). That is, the mechanisms by which adults and children learn are the same— as are issues of identity, engagement, conceptual understanding, and the development of productive practices. Some of the most interesting approaches to professional development are those that take the notion of teacher learning seriously.

In various ways, a focus on student thinking is a hallmark of the most noted approaches to professional development. We discuss three such approaches. Discussions of the professional development workshops are largely pragmatic, but the efforts are grounded in research.

Developing Mathematical Ideas (DMI)

The DMI program (Cohen, 2004; Schifter, 1993, 1998; Schifter, Bastable, & Russell, 1999; Schifter & Fosnot, 1993; Schifter, Russell, & Bastable, 1990) is a professional development seminar for elementary school teachers of mathematics. In a section of Schifter (2001) entitled "What mathematical skills do teachers need?" Schifter identifies and exemplifies four critical skills that, she says, are often absent:

Skill 1: Attending to the mathematics in what one's students are saying and doing. This may sound obvious, but, as Sherin's work indicates, focusing on student thinking is actually a learned skill—and not necessarily one that teachers have when they emerge from their teacher preparation programs.

Skill 2: Assessing the mathematical validity of students' ideas. Recall the example from the Study of Instructional Improvement (2002), given earlier, which showed three different ways that students might find the product (35×25) The issue is: even if the work looks nonstandard, is the mathematics correct?

Skill 3: Listening for the sense in students' mathematical thinking—even when something is amiss. Once one is alert to the mathematical possibilities in student thinking, one can often find the core of a correct mathematical approach in something that produces an incorrect answer. This gives something to build on.

Skill 4: Identifying the conceptual issues the students are working on. Schifter provides an example of a student responding to a problem with a strange combination of arithmetic operations. Upon closer examination, the student's work is seen to represent an incorrect generalization of a strategy that was useful in a different context. This provided the basis for an interesting mathematical conversation with the student.

The DMI program attempts to provide a series of experiences that help teachers develop these skills. Cohen (2004) provides a detailed description of one of the DMI seminars and its impact on the participants. There is much to learn from the close and sympathetic examination of adult learners.

Cognitively Guided Instruction

Focusing on student thinking lies at the core of one of the most widely known programs of professional development, Cognitively Guided Instruction, or CGI (Carpenter, Fennema, and Franke, 1996). CGI is based on an extensive body of developmental research on students' understanding of elementary mathematical situations—for example, the mathematically isomorphic *change* situation in "join" form:

> Connie had 5 marbles. Jim gave her 8 more marbles. How many marbles does Connie have altogether?

and in "separate" form:

> Connie had 13 marbles. She gave 5 marbles to Jim. How many marbles does she have left?

Research summarized in Carpenter (1985) documented the kinds of models children construct to represent such situations and a developmental trajectory of the growth in the children's models and their linkages to arithmetic operations. This knowledge base provides a solid grounding with which teachers can interact with students. When a student faces a particular situation, the teacher (guided by a knowledge of developmental trajectories in general, and possessing a repertoire of situation models and ways to formalize them) can determine which understanding the student has, and help the student (a) solve problems based on those understandings, and (b) conceptualize and formalize what he or she knows, thus expanding the student's knowledge base. CGI does not offer a prescriptive pedagogy; rather, it provides the knowledge by which teachers can respond flexibly to and build on their students' current understandings. A large body of research (see, e.g., Carpenter et al., 1996; Carpenter, Fennema, Franke, Empson, & Levi, 1999; Carpenter, Franke, Jacobs, Fennema, & Empson, 1998; Carpenter & Lehrer, 1999; Franke, Levi, Carpenter, & Fennema, 2001) indicates that as teachers become more familiar with student understanding, they become more flexible in their teaching—and that the effects of the professional development support "generative growth" in teachers' understanding over time (Franke et al., 2001).

A difference between CGI and DMI identified by Carpenter, Fennema, and Franke (1996) is that CGI explicitly uses an understanding of student work to help teachers develop deeper understandings of the mathematics itself, whereas DMI uses the study of mathematics to sensitize teachers to a wide range of students' mathematical thought processes. It would seem that these two emphases are part of a productive dialectic in teachers' professional growth. Awareness of student cognition provides an opportunity to think more deeply about mathematics and student conceptions of mathematics. These, in turn, can shape instructional practices, and reflection on those can provide deeper awareness of student cognition.

Lesson Study

Lesson study, an aspect of teacher professionalism in Japan, has the potential to either become the next large-scale educational fad in the United States or a powerful form of professional development. The practice has received widespread attention in the West largely as a result of a book entitled *The Teaching Gap* (Stigler & Hiebert, 1999). Stigler and Hiebert explored possible explanations of mathematics performance data revealed by the Third International Mathematics and Science Study, or TIMSS. A wide range of performance reports (see, e.g., Beaton et al., 1997; Kelley, Mullis, & Martin, 2000; Mullis et al., 1998, 2000) indicated that the mathematics performance of U.S. students was roughly at the median internationally (and toward the bottom of scores for highly industrialized nations), whereas Singapore, Korea, and Japan scored consistently at the top. TIMSS video studies (see, e.g., Hiebert et al., 2003; Stigler, Gonzales, Kawanaka, Knoll, & Serrano, 1999) provided compelling evidence that Japanese mathematics lessons were far more coherent than parallel mathematics lessons in the United States.

Stigler and Hiebert (1999) argue that teaching is a *cultural activity*—that there is relatively little within-country variation in teaching practices compared to between-country variation. That is, the teaching styles in the United States and in Japan are relatively consistent, and different. So are forms of professional development. A key component of instructional improvement is lesson study—the design, implementation, testing, and improvement, *by teachers,* of "research lessons."

The most detailed examination to date of the principles and practices of lesson study can be found in Fernandez and Yoshida (2004). Fernandez and Yoshida provide extensive detail regarding the ways in which a collective of Japanese schoolteachers select a topic of curricular importance, identify the focus of the intended research lesson or lessons, and begin to design the lesson(s). The level of specificity in these deliberations is extraordinary. A typical lesson plan in the United States consists of the description of a sequence of intended teacher actions. In contrast, lesson plans developed as part of lesson study include descriptions of the sequence of intended learning activities; the ways in which students are expected to react to each of these activities; a planned teacher response to each of the likely student reactions; and intellectual foci for the evaluation of the progress of the lesson. Extensively detailed lesson plans are developed and refined by a teacher planning group over a sequence of meetings, as a truly collaborative effort. A group member then volunteers to teach the research lesson, for the collective. The lesson is not seen as the individual teacher's "property."

Instead, the teacher is seen as the means of implementation of the group's design. The other teachers observe the trial lesson closely, looking to see what seems to be effective and what is not. The collective then "debriefs" in an elaborate process that leads to the refinement and reteaching of the lesson by someone else. Ultimately, the tangible product is a shared lesson that is extremely well designed and documented, so that all the participants (and others) can use it. A somewhat intangible but equally important product is the professional growth of those who contribute to the design process. The sequence of lesson design activities consists of thinking hard about the desired content and learning outcomes; about activities intended to promote those outcomes; about student thinking (including anticipating student reactions to activities, and what those reactions mean in terms of student understanding); and about principled revisions to the materials on the basis of careful assessments of student learning. Beginning teachers undertake these activities in the company of more experienced and accomplished colleagues, so there is a natural apprenticeship into the community of skilled practitioners.

There is significant potential for appropriate adaptations of aspects of lesson study to powerful mechanisms for professional development in school systems outside of Japan. At the same time, there is significant potential for the practices of lesson study to be trivialized in ways that render the process superficial and of little or no value. As summarized briefly earlier, a major component of lesson study involves focusing on student understanding, and then evaluating the pedagogy on the basis of the impact of the designed activities. The lesson design practices described by Fernandez and Yoshida (2004) take place at a very fine level of detail, much more fine-grained than those typically conceptualized by American teachers. As Sherin (2001, 2002) and others have shown, focusing on student work does not necessarily come naturally; one has to learn how to do it. In this author's experience, and that of others who have observed attempts to implement lesson study in the United States, teachers need to learn how to judge lesson effectiveness. Teachers' first judgments about lesson effectiveness are often global and not grounded in data. One hears statements like "the timing felt pretty good" or "they were engaged most of the time" much more frequently than one hears commentary on the actual content of what students said and did. The question, then, is whether teachers will be provided the support structures (including time, and perhaps external resources until teachers have developed the relevant skills and understandings) that will enable them to bootstrap the skills needed to implement lesson study effectively. Absent such support, the prognosis is not good.

CURRICULUM DEVELOPMENT, IMPLEMENTATION, CONTROVERSY, AND ASSESSMENT

The 1990s were (in the United States and in places around the globe that are influenced by U.S. curricula) the time of the greatest curricular change and controversy since the "new math" of the 1960s. Research over the latter part of the 20th century produced new understandings about the nature of mathematical thinking and learning—ideas that would result in the reconsideration of the foci and contents of mathematics curricula. New goals for curricula were codified in the National Council of Teachers of Mathematics' 1989 *Curriculum and Evaluation Standards for School Mathematics.* Concurrently, perceptions of national economic crises provided an impetus for the revision of mathematics curricula. With a significant infusion of funding from the National Science Foundation, a number of "standards-based" curricula were developed. Many of these curricula, produced in the 1990s, differed substantially in look, feel, and classroom implementation from "traditional" curricula. Many turned out to be controversial—so much so that the term *math wars* was coined to describe the public controversies that followed. Resolving such controversies depends, or course, on the evidence available. This raises issues of assessment: What should be assessed regarding mathematical thinking and learning, and how does one assess such things? What should be examined when one examines the impact of various curricula? How does one examine curricular impact in rigorous and informative ways? Those are the issues explored in this section.

Context

By the mid-1980s, scholars in mathematics education had reconceived the epistemological foundations of mathematics learning. Broadly speaking, the view of mathematics learning as the "acquisition of knowledge" had been superseded by the perspective that being competent at mathematics meant understanding and being able to use mathematical concepts and procedures—and that in addition, strategic competence, metacognitive ability (including monitoring and self-regulation), and productive beliefs and affect (or disposition) were important aspects of mathematical competence.

In the 1980s, the United States was also feeling threatened economically. *A Nation at Risk* (1983) issued a clarion call for the reform of U.S. mathematics and science education. In 1989 the National Council of Teachers of Mathematics (NCTM), a professional organization of mathematics teachers, produced the *Curriculum and Evaluation Standards for School Mathematics* (subsequently known as the *Standards*). The *Standards* were a philosophical as well as a curricular document. The goal of the writers was to "create a coherent vision of what it means to be mathematically literate" in a rapidly changing world, and to "create a set of standards to guide the revision of the school mathematics curriculum." (p. 1). The authors defined "standard" as follows: "*Standard*. A standard is a statement that can be used to judge the quality of a mathematics curriculum or methods of evaluation. Thus, standards are statements about what is valued" (p. 2).

That is, the *Standards* were intended to be a statement of "what matters" in mathematics instruction or testing. They were not intended to be a blueprint for curriculum development. Philosophically, they focused on new goals for students and society: "New social goals for education include (1) mathematically literate workers, (2) lifelong learning, (3) opportunity for all, and (4) an informed electorate" (p. 3). The *Standards* were oriented toward "five general goals for all students: (1) that they learn to value mathematics, (2) that they become confident in their ability to do mathematics, (3) that they become mathematical problem solvers, (4) that they learn to communicate mathematically, and (5) that they learn to reason mathematically" (p. 5).

Here I focus on the curricular descriptions found in the *Standards*—the first three sections, which discuss curricular desiderata in kindergarten through grade 4, grades 5–8, and grades 9–12, respectively. Each of the three grade band sections contained 13 or 14 Standards. For the first time in curricular history, a major curriculum document gave as much attention to the *process* aspects of mathematical performance as it did to the mathematical content to be covered in the curriculum. At each of the grade bands, the first four standards were the same: Mathematics as Problem Solving, Mathematics as Communication, Mathematics as Reasoning, and (making) Mathematical Connections. The remaining standards described content—but again, in a very broad way, covering four or five grades at a time. As a result, there was no single model curriculum that "fit" or "met" the *Standards;* one could imagine a wide range of very different curricula that had the same content and process emphases, and that achieved the same broad goals.

In 1989 no commercial publisher would undertake the creation and production of "standards-based" mathematics curricula, because doing so was too risky in financial terms. Mathematics curricula were typically sold in K-

8 series, which were produced by large writing teams. This was done in something like production-line fashion, to meet the textbook adoption deadlines of major states such as California, Texas, and New York. In order not to lose huge chunks of the market, publishers made sure their books met the adoption criteria of those three states. Publishers claimed the cost of developing and marketing a K-8 series was on the order of $25 million—far too much to risk on an untried product.

In sum, the national context in 1989 looked like this. There was a perceived need for an upgrading of mathematics curricula. The NCTM *Standards* offered a set of criteria by which a new curriculum could be judged—but commercial publishers would not make the investment. The U.S. National Science Foundation (NSF) addressed this dilemma by serving as a catalyst for curriculum development. NSF began issuing requests for proposals (RFPs) for Standards-based curricula in the early 1990s.[2] A list of NSF-supported curriculum projects can be found at http://forum.swarthmore.edu/mathed/nsf.curric.html. The NSF provided support for the development and implementation of standards-based curricula in a variety of ways.

For example, NSF sponsored a series of annual "Gateway" conferences from 1992 through 1998 at which curriculum developers came together to discuss issues of common concern. Later NSF established four national centers devoted to the support of standards-based curricula: the K-12 mathematics curriculum center, whose web site is http://www.edc.org/mcc; an elementary grades curriculum center at http://www.arccenter.comap.com; a middle grades center at http://showmecenter.missouri. edu; and a high school center at http://www.ithaca.edu/ compass. In parallel, NCTM worked steadily to maintain support for standards-based instruction. NCTM's annual meetings focused on *Standards*-related activities, and NCTM produced a number of publications aimed at helping teachers to implement *Standards*-based instruction in their classrooms.

When the previous version of this Handbook was published in 1996, there was scant evidence—either positive or negative—regarding the effectiveness of the new curricula. This stands to reason. The NSF curriculum RFPs were first issued in 1991, so in 1996 the various curriculum projects were just completing their first (alpha) round of development. Indeed, it was not until the turn of the 21st century that cohorts of students had worked through the full beta versions of many of these curricula. The current situation with regard to data evaluating curricular effectiveness is not much better. The

---

[2]It should be noted that a small number of "reform" efforts had begun (also with grant funding, independent of the major publishers) prior to the NSF call for proposals. For example, the University of Chicago School Mathematics Project (UCSMP) and the Interactive Mathematics Project (IMP) predated the NSF curriculum RFPs.

current state is discussed later. First, however, it is important to discuss the largest social confrontation over mathematics curricula since the controversies over the "new math."

Math Wars

Although the "math wars" in the United States (and now in parts of the world as far distant as Israel) are in a sense outside the realm of educational psychology (though not social psychology!) and research in mathematics education, they are a critically important phenomenon that needs to be discussed. Researchers need to understand the contexts within which their work is done.

For a detailed history of the math wars in California (where they began), see Rosen (2000); see also Jackson (1997a, 1997b) and Schoenfeld (2004). The 1985 California Mathematics *Framework* was considered a mathematically solid and progressive document. State Superintendent of Education Bill Honig supported educational reform, and the California Mathematics Council (the state affiliate of NCTM) actively supported *Standards*-based practices after the *Standards* were published. The 1992 California Mathematics *Framework* represented a next step in the change agenda. Publishers created texts in line with their view of *Standards*- and *Frameworks*-based mathematics. In 1994 the California State Board of Education approved instructional materials consistent with the Mathematics *Framework*.

The *Framework,* like the *Standards,* was a vision statement regarding the desired substance and character of instruction rather than a blueprint for them. Such documents invite curriculum designers to create innovative materials. But, there is a downside to opening the door to such creativity. Rosen (2000, p. 61) notes:

The new textbooks were radically different from the traditional texts' orderly, sequential presentation of formulas and pages of practice problems familiar to parents. New texts featured colorful illustrations, assignments with lively, fun names and sidebars discussing topics from the environment to Yoruba mathematics (prompting critics to dub new programs with names such as "Rainforest Algebra" and "MTV Math").

Sometimes frenetic in appearance, sometimes different in content, many of the new texts could be easily caricatured. Once the rhetorical battles heated up, they were.

In addition, many "reformers" and reform curricula called for new teaching practices, urging less dependence on teacher exposition and whole-class recitations, and increased dependence on small group work. Maintaining a focus on substantial mathematics while also fostering communication and collaboration in group work is quite

difficult. Teachers who had themselves been taught in traditional ways were now being asked to teach in new ways. Many were not up to the task (see, e.g., Ferrini-Mundy & Schram, 1997).

These new materials and practices raised concerns among some parents, some of whom viewed them as a repetition of the mistakes of the "new math." Parent groups organized, established websites hostile to "reform," and created a very effective antireform movement. Local oppositional movements soon coalesced into a statewide (and then nationwide) movement, supported by prominent conservatives such as California Governor Pete Wilson. The state legislature held highly contentious public hearings on the *Frameworks* in 1995 and 1996. Conservatives prevailed, and a new mathematics *Frameworks* writing team was convened ahead of schedule. The state legislature enacted AB 170, which "requires the State Board of Education to ensure that the basic instructional materials it adopts for reading and mathematics in grades 1 to 8, inclusive, are based on the fundamental skills required by these subjects, including ... basic computational skills." (See http://www.cde.ca.gov/board/readingfirst/exhibit-i.pdf.)

The next major skirmish took place over the California Mathematics Standards. In line with traditional California practice, a draft had been developed by a committee and submitted to the State Board of Education. The orientation of the draft, which had been put together over a year and a half and had undergone a substantial amount of public review, was generally consistent with that of the NCTM *Standards*. The State Board summarily rejected the draft. Over a period of just a few weeks, the Board rewrote much of the elementary grades section itself. It commissioned a small number of mathematics faculty (who had negligible experience with K-12 classrooms or curricula) to rewrite the standards for the secondary grades. These acts elicited protests from highly visible scholars such as Hyman Bass, research mathematician and Director of the National Research Council's Mathematical Sciences Education Board, and William Schmidt, who had conducted curriculum content analyses for the Third International Mathematics and Science Study. The Board ignored the protests.

How one views these events depends on one's perspective. Here is how antireform activist David Klein described them:

Question: What would happen if California adopted the best, grade-by-grade mathematics achievement standards in the nation for its public schools?
Answer: The education establishment would do everything in its power to make them disappear.

In December 1997, the State Board of Education surprised the world by not accepting extremely bad, "fuzzy" math standards written by one of its advisory committees, the Academic Standards Commission. Instead, in a few short weeks and with the help of four Stanford University math professors, the state board developed and adopted a set of world-class mathematics standards of unprecedented quality for California's public schools.

Klein's rhetoric suggests the level of vitriol spewed in the math wars—for example, Maureen DiMarco, California State Secretary of Child Development and Education, referred to the new curricula as "fuzzy crap." Acrimony reached the point where U.S. Secretary of Education Richard Riley felt compelled in January 1998 to address the annual Joint Mathematics Meetings,[3] urging civility and respectful exchange in battles over mathematics curricula. His words went unheeded, and Riley soon found himself immersed in the math wars: antireform forces orchestrated the signature-gathering for an open letter to Riley, published in major newspapers nationwide, protesting the U.S. Department of Education's listing of "exemplary" and "promising" instructional programs in mathematics education. In California, those who had power exercised it without restraint. For example, members of the State's Curriculum Framework and Criteria Committee were barred from introducing research into the record or into the group's deliberations. Interested readers should see Becker and Jacob (2000), Jacob (1999, 2001), and Jacob and Akers (2003) for details.

The point here is that when educational/psychological issues enter the political arena, scholarly discourse and well-grounded research findings are often marginalized. The research community needs to think about how to deal responsibly with such issues. Research does little good if it can be ignored for purposes of political expediency.

We now return to research issues and the question of evidence. Just what evidence was there, at the time of the math wars, of the efficacy of traditional or reform curricula? What evidence is there now?

Evidence, Then and Now: Issues of Assessment

Simply put, the math wars were fought in an informational vacuum. As noted a few standards-based instructional programs were under development when NSF issued its curricular RFPs in the 1991. Preliminary development of most of the NSF-supported curricula took four or five years, and refinements (to the "beta level") took another few years. It was not until the late 1990s that full cohorts of students had worked their way through any of the new curricula. Perhaps surprisingly, there are even fewer detailed evaluations of "traditional" curricula than of the more recent standards-based curricula.[4] The traditional curriculum has existed for many years in various forms—over the years, mainstream textbook series came to resemble each other closely in content coverage. However, until recently—specifically, until the passage of the No Child Left Behind legislation (see http://www.ed.gov/offices/OESE/esea/)—textbook publishers had little or no incentive to gather data regarding student performance. Textbook marketing depends on focus groups (what do the consumers want?) and testimonial in advertising rather than on data. This stands in sharp contrast to the marketing of consumer items such as cellular phones, washing machines, and cars, where marketing depends of necessity on focus groups, testimonials, *and* data. If one wants to buy a new car or washing machine, there are specialist magazines (e.g., *Car and Driver* or *Motor Trend*) and general consumer magazines (e.g., *Consumer Reports*) that evaluate the features of various models on their own or in comparison with others. If a product has a specific design flaw, a bad performance record, or some other problem, that problem will be made public and will need to be addressed. In contrast, until recently, there was no mechanism for curricular performance evaluations in education.[5] Since such assessments are costly, there was no reason for publishers to undertake them.

Second and equally important, there is the question of just what a test "covers." The standardized tests available until recently, including NAEP, were designed under the standard psychometric assumptions of trait and/or behaviorist psychology (see Glaser, Linn, & Bohrnsteat 1997; Greeno, Pearson, & Schoenfeld, 1997). They focused largely on content mastery. In contrast, the more fine-grained analyses of proficiency developed over the past decade or so (for example the *New Standards* and *Balanced Assessment* tests) tend to be aligned with the content and process delineations found in NCTM's (2000) *Principles and Standards for School Mathematics*.

---

[3] The meetings are sponsored by the American Mathematical Society, Mathematical Association of America, Association for Symbolic Logic, Association for Women in Mathematics, National Association of Mathematicians, and Society for Industrial and Applied Mathematics.

[4] There have been, of course, many studies of the impact of traditional curricula. The issue here is whether there have been evaluations along dimensions now considered appropriate for assessing students' mathematical competency.

[5] That mechanism is the What Works Clearinghouse, which is discussed later.

Let us consider a topic such as "understanding fractions" to see why test coverage is a critically important issue. A traditional assessment would look for students' ability to perform standard algorithms, for example

Task 1. Find $(1/2)(3/5) + (1/2)(1/5)$.

More contemporary assessments might seek to understand students' abilities to work with different representations of fractions, for example:

Task 2. Write a fraction for the shaded part of the region below.

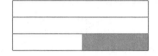

or

Task 3. Write a fraction for point A.

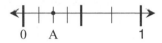

Each of Tasks 2 and 3 calls for understanding a particular representation of fractions. Many students will respond "1/4" to Task 2, neglecting the criterion that the four ostensible "fourths" of the figure must all have equal area. Similarly, many students will respond "2/6" to Task 3. Interestingly, students may answer correctly to one of those two tasks and not the other. Responding correctly depends on some familiarity with the representation.

Different tasks may probe for conceptual understanding:

Task 4. Explain what happens to the value of a fraction when its denominator is doubled.

Or, they may call for a combination of representational use and problem solving. Consider the following problem, for example.

Task 5. Write a fraction for the shaded part of the region below.

There are various ways to solve this problem, but here is one:

Each of the boxes is 1/5 of the whole region. The diagonal line on the left-hand side of the figure divides the first three boxes in half, so the shaded area on the left is $(1/2)(3/5) = (3/10)$ of the region; the shaded area on the right is $(1/2)(1/5) = (1/10)$ of the region; so the area of the two shaded regions combined is $(3/10) + (1/10) = (4/10) = 2/5$ of the region.

Note that this solution calls for problem solving in making use of a nonstandard representation, "seeing" the rectangle formed by the first three boxes, knowing that the diagonal divides a rectangle in half, obtaining the areas of each of the shaded regions, and performing the numerical computations given above. It stands to reason that many students who could obtain the correct answer to Task 1 would fail to obtain the correct answer to task 5—which includes the computation in Task 1 as a subproblem.

These few examples are just the tip of the proverbial iceberg. The point is that what one assesses matters. A student who does well on a test composed of items like Task 1 might do poorly on a test that included Tasks 2 through 5; hence a test composed of items like Task 1 might yield a "false positive" for the student, indicating more competency than was actually there. Or, consider two curricula, with Curriculum A focusing on procedural skills and Curriculum B giving attention to skills, conceptual understanding, and problem solving. If a test composed of items like Tasks 1 through 5 was used to assess learning outcomes, Curriculum B would most likely outperform Curriculum A. But if a test using only items like Task 1 was used, it is possible that both groups would perform comparably—an assessment "false negative," because the test did not capture a range of understandings possessed by students of Curriculum B.

This example is not hypothetical. Ridgway et al. (2000) compared students' performance at grades 3, 5, and 7 on a standardized high-stakes, skills-oriented test (the California STAR test, primarily the SAT-9 examination) with their performance on a much broader standards-based test (the Balanced Assessment tests produced by the Mathematics Assessment Resource Service, or MARS). For purposes of simplicity, scores reported here are collapsed into two simple categories. A student is reported as being either "proficient" or "not proficient" as indicated by his or her scores on each of the examinations. The data are given in Table 21.1.

These data suggest that more than 20 percent of the student population, who passed the SAT-9 but failed the MARS test, were actually "false positives." With this as context, I examine data that provide comparative evaluations of standards-based and more "traditional" curricula. I first

TABLE 21.1

Grade 3 (N = 6,136):

		SAT-9	
		Not Proficient	Proficient
MARS	Not Proficient	27%	21%
	Proficient	6%	46%

Grade 5 (N = 5, 247):

		SAT-9	
		Not Proficient	Proficient
MARS	Not Proficient	28%	18%
	Proficient	5%	49%

Grade 7 (N = 5, 037):

		SAT-9	
		Not Proficient	Proficient
MARS	Not Proficient	32%	28%
	Proficient	2%	38%

describe the general knowledge base, then findings from the What Works Clearinghouse.

As noted earlier, there exist sparse data regarding the effectiveness of the newer curricula, and even less evidence regarding traditional curricula. This is partly a matter of timing, partly a matter of incentives. Because the first cohorts of students emerged from standards-based curricula just about the turn of the 21st century, there has not been time for extensive studies of those curricula. Most of the newer curricula have been examined, however—as proposed alternatives to the status quo, they had to prove themselves. In contrast, the mainstream texts, which dominated the marketplace, had little incentive to prove themselves until the passage of the No Child Left Behind act, known as NCLB. (See http://www.ed.gov/nclb/landing.jhtml?src=pb for the U. S. Department of Education's website devoted to NCLB.) The accountability procedures specified in NCLB mandate the gathering of testing data, though they do not specify the content of the tests. Hence the issues discussed above remain central.

The most complete record of evaluations of standards-based curricula to date can be found in Senk and Thompson (2003). Putnam (2003) summarized the results of four elementary curriculum evaluations as follows:

[These four curricula] . . . all focus in various ways on helping students develop conceptually powerful and useful knowledge of mathematics while avoiding the learning of computational procedures as rote symbolic manipulations. . . . Students in these new curricula generally perform as well as other students on traditional measures of mathematical achievement, including

computational skill, and generally do better on formal and informal assessments of conceptual understanding and ability to use mathematics to solve problems. These chapters demonstrate that "reform-based" mathematics curricula can work. (Putnam, 2003, p. 161).

Putnam notes common assumptions underlying the four programs: that there should be a focus on important mathematics, that instruction should build on students' current understanding, that learning should be grounded in settings that are meaningful to students, that curricula should build on students' informal knowledge and help them formalize what they learn; and that the curricula call for teachers' guiding students through learning experiences to achieve curricular goals. He also notes the difficulties of using widely available standardized measures: "A disadvantage in using standardized measures is that they often do not shed much light on the more complex mathematical understanding, reasoning, and problem solving emphasized in the new curricula." This is the "curricular false negative" problem mentioned earlier. Putnam observes that the authors of the curricula used a range of measures to get at competencies not revealed by standardized measures, including "evaluator-developed measures, with their concomitant strengths and weaknesses" (Putnam, 2003, p. 166).

The story was much the same at the middle school level.Like the elementary curricula, the NSF-supported middle school curricula discussed are grounded in NCTM's 1989 Standards; they too focus on meaningful and engaging problem-based mathematics. There are differences in emphases and style, but the similarities in character and outcomes outweigh the differences. Chappell (2003) summarizes the results as follows:

Collectively, the evaluation results provide converging evidence that Standards-based curricula may positively affect middle-school students' mathematical achievement, both in conceptual and procedural understanding. . . .They reveal that the curricula can indeed push students beyond the 'basics' to more in-depth problem-oriented mathematical thinking without jeopardizing their thinking in either area (Chappell, 2003, pp. 290–291).

One sees similar results at the high school level. On standardized tests such as the CTBS or PSAT, there were no significant differences between student performance on three reform curricula; on two other reform curricula students "performed as well, if not better, than students from a traditional curriculum on standardized or state assessments" (Swafford, 2003, p. 459). When one turns to evaluator-developed measures of conceptual understanding or problem solving, students in all of these curricula outperformed students from traditional curricula. In sum: "Taken as a group, these studies offer overwhelming evidence that the reform curricula can have a positive impact on high school mathematics achievement. It is not that students in these curricul[a] learn traditional content better but that they develop other skills and understandings while not falling behind on traditional content" (Swafford, 2003, p. 468).

A series of studies in Pittsburgh, PA (see Briars, 2001; Briars & Resnick, 2000; Schoenfeld, 2002b) documents what may be the most positive "local" implementation of a standards-based curriculum. Diane Briars, mathematics specialist for the Pittsburgh schools, had been conducting *Standards*-based professional development activities for some years when the *Everyday Mathematics* curriculum became available. Uneven implementation of the new curriculum in Pittsburgh provided the opportunity for a natural experiment—a comparison of student performance in "strong implementation schools" where teachers implemented the curricula with strong fidelity with student performance in demographically matched schools where the new curricula were essentially ignored, and teachers implemented the prior, "traditional" curriculum. The Pittsburgh data document an across-the-boards improvement in test scores for the new curriculum on tests on subscores of skills, conceptual understanding, and problem solving. Indeed, some "racial performance gaps" were overcome with the new curricula.

Because of the context, this is a somewhat idealized case—but it indicates that when:

- A district's mathematics program is grounded in a rich, connected set of standards;
- The mathematics curricula used are consistent with the standards;
- Assessments are consistent with the standards;
- Teachers' professional development is consistent with the standards; and
- There is enough systemic stability for sustained growth and change,

there is the potential for substantial improvement in student performance, and for the reduction of racial performance gaps.

Riordan and Noyce (2001) report on a series of comparison studies in Massachusetts. These studies, which used the statewide assessment (the MCAS) as the measure of performance, show that fourth and eighth graders using standards-based texts "outperformed matched comparison groups who were using a range of textbooks commonly used in Massachusetts. . . .These performance gains . . . remained consistent for different groups of students, across mathematical topics and different types of

questions on the state test" (Riordan & Noyce, 2001, pp. 392–393).

Reys, Reys, Lappan, Holliday, and Wasman (2003) examined the impact of standards-based curricula on the performance of more than 2,000 eighth-grade students in three matched pairs of school districts in Missouri. The assessment used for the comparison was the state-mandated mathematics portion of the Missouri Assessment Program (MAP), which is administered annually to all Missouri eighth graders. The MAP assesses mathematical skills, concepts, and problem-solving abilities as delineated in the State Mathematics Framework for. Students who had used standards-based materials for at least 2 years scored significantly higher than students from the districts that used non-NSF curricular materials.

In the largest study conducted to date, the ARC Center (see http://www.comap.com/elementary/projects/arc/), an NSF-funded project, examined reform mathematics programs in elementary schools in Massachusetts, Illinois, and Washington. The study included more than 100,000 students. It compared the mathematics performance of students from schools implementing *Standards*-based curricula with a matched sample of comparison schools that used more "traditional" curricula. (Criteria for matching included reading level and socioeconomic status.)

Results show that the average scores of students in the reform schools are significantly higher than the average scores of students in the matched comparison schools. These results hold across all racial and income subgroups. The results also hold across the different state-mandated tests, including the Iowa Test of Basic Skills, and across topics ranging from computation, measurement, and geometry to algebra, problem solving, and making connections. The study compared the scores on all the topics tested at all the grade levels tested (Grades 3–5) in each of the three states. Of 34 comparisons across five state–grade combinations, 28 favor the reform students, six show no statistically significant difference, and none favor the comparison students. (See http://www.comap.com/elementary/projects/arc/tri-state%20achievement.htm.)

There are a few additional studies comparing standards-based and "traditional" curricula, which will be considered in the discussion of the What Works Clearinghouse. But let us take stock at this point. Overall, there are a quite small number of studies that compare the two kinds of curricula. It is the case that the "score sheet" is uniformly in favor of the Standards-based curricula: Virtually every study in the literature shows either no significant differences or an advantage to the standards-based curricula on measures of skills, and most show significant advantages to the standards-based curricula on measures of conceptual understanding and problem solving. However, the evidence base is embarrassingly weak. The vast majority of studies, like the majority of those reported in Senk and Thompson (2003), employed evaluator-developed measures of conceptual understanding and problem solving. These could be considered biased toward the curricula they evaluated. Little was said about the comparative conditions of implementation. Because beta versions of the standards-based curricula were generally being tested, one can assume that there was some implementation fidelity in the case of those curricula. In contrast, one knows little about implementation fidelity, or the overall quality of instruction, in the comparison classrooms. Hence the comparative studies can best be considered existence proofs about what the newer curricula can do rather than definitive comparative evidence. This point is made in very clear terms by a recent report of the National Research Council (2005).

The What Works Clearinghouse

Let us now turn to the evaluation effort conducted by the What Works Clearinghouse (WWC, at http://www.whatworks.ed.gov/). To quote from the front page of the WWC website:

On an ongoing basis, the What Works Clearinghouse (WWC) collects, screens, and identifies studies of the effectiveness of educational interventions (programs, products, practices, and policies). We review the studies that have the strongest design, and report on the strengths and weaknesses of those studies against the WWC Evidence Standards so that you know what the best scientific evidence has to say.

WWC was established to address the kinds of issues discussed earlier—the fact that there is a paucity of rigorous studies assessing the effectiveness of various kinds of interventions, ranging from mathematics and reading curricula to programs for dropout prevention. WWC's efforts are largely modeled on the Cochrane Collaboration's efforts to develop "evidence-based health care." (See http://www.cochrane.org/index0.htm.) The idea is not for WWC to conduct new studies, but to comb the literature for studies that meet its very stringent methodological criteria, to report on those studies, and ultimately to conduct meta-analyses regarding the effects of educational (and other) interventions.

The WWC does not endorse any interventions nor does it conduct field studies. The WWC releases study, intervention, and topic reports. A study report rates individual studies and designs to give you a sense of how much you can rely on research findings for that individual study. An intervention report provides all findings that meet WWC Evidence Standards for a particular intervention. Each topic report briefly describes the topic and each intervention that the WWC reviewed. (http://www.whatworks.ed.gov/)

WWC considers for review only studies that employ randomized controlled trials, regression discontinuity designs, and quasi-experimental designs with equating. If a study is of one of those types, it is then examined for possible flaws such as lack of implementation fidelity, differential dropout rates between groups, and such. (See http://www.whatworks.ed.gov/reviewprocess/standards.html for a list of criteria.) One can, legitimately, complain that the paradigmatic choices made by WWC are far too narrow: There are many ways to conduct informative studies of mathematics curricula, and the three kinds of studies potentially acceptable to WWC represent only a small part of that universe. (See the framework developed by the National Research Council, 2004, discussed later). That critique notwithstanding, one can take the comparison studies on their own terms. The question is, what kinds of information does WWC, which is intended as a sort of "consumer's guide to curricula," actually provide?

The first topic report produced by WWC, concerning middle school mathematics curricula, was produced in December 2004. Here is WWC's summary of the evidence base.

From a systematic search of published and unpublished research, the What Works Clearinghouse (WWC) identified 10 studies of 5 curriculum-based interventions for improving mathematics achievement for middle school students. These include all studies conducted in the past 20 years that met WWC standards for evidence. . . .The WWC identified 66 other studies that included evaluations of 15 additional interventions. Because none meets the WWC standards for evidence, we cannot draw any conclusions about the effectiveness of these other 15 interventions. The WWC also identified an additional 24 interventions that did not appear to have any evaluations. (What Works Clearinghouse, 2004a)

These are indeed slim pickings. Moreover, they are controversial, and for good reason. As noted earlier, there are a wide range of studies other than randomized controlled trials, regression discontinuity designs, and quasi-experimental designs with equating that can provide valuable information about curricular effectiveness. Thus WWC can be accused of being far too narrow in its criteria for what counts as documented evidence of effectiveness. But even if one restricts one's attention to just the types of studies examined by WWC, the way in which WWC has chosen to report the studies that do meet its methodological criteria raises serious issues. Viadero (2004) described the controversy over one of those studies (What Works Clearinghouse, 2004b), as follows:

James J. Baker, the developer of a middle school mathematics program known as Expert Mathematician, is also dismayed at the way his research on the program is reported. His study—the only one that fully met the criteria for this topic—used a random assignment strategy to test whether students could learn as much with this student-driven, computer-based program as they could from a traditional teacher-directed curriculum known as Transition Mathematics. The problem, he argues, is that the [WWC] web site said his program had no effect without explaining that students made learning gains in both groups. (p. 32)

This issue is important in applied terms, for a study that says there were "no significant differences" due to the use of a particular curriculum may be taken by readers to mean that the curriculum in question had no beneficial impact. This problem can, of course, be resolved in a straightforward way. The summaries provided by WWC can be rewritten to indicate the size of the gains made through the use of each curriculum.

Another study report, however, WWC's (2004c) detailed study report of C. Kerstyn's (2001) evaluation of the I CAN LEARN Mathematics Classroom, demonstrates what may be a fatal flaw in the nature of current WWC reports. Kerstyn's study employed a quasi-experimental design with matching. It met the WWC standards "with reservations"; there were concerns regarding the implementation fidelity of the curriculum, some sampling issues, and issues regarding which subgroups of students were tested. However, the statistical reporting in the study fully meets WWC criteria. In discussing the measures used, the WWC report says:

The fifth outcome is the Florida Comprehensive Assessment Test (FCAT), which was administered in February 2001. The author does not present the reliability information for this test; however, this information is available in a technical report written by the Florida Department of Education (2002). This WWC Study Report focuses only on the FCAT measures, because this assessment was taken by all students and is the only assessment with independently documented reliability and validity information.

This is deeply problematic. Reliability and validity scores represent psychometric properties of the FCAT; they say *nothing* about the actual mathematical content of the examination. In other words, the report provides no information about the mathematics actually covered by the measure. As a result, the report cannot be interpreted in meaningful ways—and it could be seriously misinterpreted. Consider the data given earlier in this section regarding students' differential performance on the

SAT-9 and the MARS examinations. Is the FCAT more like the former or the latter? What content does it emphasize? Does it focus on procedural knowledge, or does it demand some relatively sophisticated problem solving skills? Unless WWC provides an independent auditing of the examination's contents, it is impossible to say what students actually learned. This raises the possibility of individual "false positives" and curricular "false negatives," as described earlier in this section. Moreover, not knowing what the outcome measures actually test makes it impossible to conduct meaningful meta-analyses of studies of the same curriculum. The author has urged WWC to redo its analyses and to include content analyses of all assessment measures in its mathematics studies, so that readers of its study reports can determine what students actually learned. Unless and until the reports are redone, the value of the entire enterprise is in question.

How Should One Study Curricular Effectiveness?

Determining whether and in what ways something as complex as a curriculum "works" is a complex matter. One view of the subject, rather different from that put forth by WWC, is offered by the National Research Council's (2004) committee for the review of the evaluation data of the effectiveness of NSF-supported and commercially generated mathematics curriculum materials. The committee's report, which urges methodological pluralism, presents a broad-based framework for evaluating curricular effectiveness.

The NRC framework is bipartite. First, it articulates a *program theory*—in essence, a description of what needs to be examined in the evaluation of an instructional program. Foci for examination include program components (including the mathematical content of the program and curricular design elements), implementation components (including resources, processes, and contextual influences), and student outcomes (including multiple assessment, enrollment patterns, and attitudes).

The second part of the framework elaborates the kinds of decision-making to be made by program evaluators. In any evaluation, there are methodological choices: What does one decide to look at, and how? The NRC panel points to three intellectually robust ways to examine curricula: content analyses, comparative studies, and case studies. It notes that there is a wide range of things to look at, and a wide range of rigorous ways in which such evaluations can be conducted. It points to the ways in which all of these kinds of studies can contribute to the field's collective understanding of curricular impact. The methodological pluralism of the NRC report stands in sharp contrast to the narrowly defined criteria employed by the What Works Clearinghouse.

A proposal by Burkhardt and Schoenfeld (2003) stakes out a middle ground in terms of breadth and focus. The authors argue that consumers of educational materials would profit from having access to reports that describe the conditions under which curricula can be successfully implemented, and on the kinds of results one might expect under those conditions; they should also be warned about conditions that make it unlikely for a particular curriculum to succeed. Thus, both comparative studies and benchmarking studies (using a stable and rigorous set of standards and outcome measures) would help inform those who are faced with curricular choices.

Burkhardt and Schoenfeld argue that the leap to experimental studies in education is premature. In both engineering and medical studies, research proceeds in stages. The first sets of studies typically include the design of prototypes (whether products or treatments) and the close observation of their effects under very controlled (and narrow) circumstances. This corresponds to design experiments (see, e.g., Brown, 1992; Cobb, Confrey, diSessa, Lehrer, & Schauble, 2003; Collins, 1992; Schoenfeld, in press) or "alpha testing" of curricula. The goals of such work are to understand what is happening: to develop theory and instruction in dialectic with each other, under "greenhouse" conditions. Once the phenomena are understood, it is time to broaden the range of conditions of implementation. Here the issue becomes: In what conditions does the "treatment" function, in what ways? Which factors shape the implementation, with what results? One engineering analogy among many is that some equipment is appropriate for rough terrain, while other equipment will function well on smooth but not rough terrain. Obviously, it is important to know this. Medical analogies are that one needs to discover how a medicine will be affected if it is taken with or without food, and whether the medicine interacts with other medicines or with particular conditions. Presumably there are factors that can affect the success of a curriculum in similar ways. What degree and kind of teacher professional development is necessary? How well is the curriculum suited for second language learners, and how can it be modified to make it more accessible if need be? What kinds of prerequisites are necessary? And more. The "beta stage" of curriculum study would consist of a planned series of observational evaluations of curricula in a carefully chosen range of contexts: urban, suburban, and rural schools with a range of demographic factors, including the competency of the teacher corps, the amount of curriculum-specific professional development obtained by the teachers, the demographics of the student body, the availability and character of backup support for students, and so on.

When these conditions are met—that is, when one is in a position to say "in a school or school district that looks like *this,* you should expect to provide *these* specific curricular supports, and then you can expect the following spectrum of results"—then one is ready to proceed to the most informative kinds of widespread experimental or comparative ("gamma stage") testing.

To sum up, the state of the art is still somewhat primitive. Much needs to be done along the lines of instrumentation (the development of robust outcome measures covering a wide range of expected mathematical content and processes), the creation of observational protocols, and the conduct of the wide range of studies described in *On Evaluating Curricular Effectiveness* (National Research Council, 2004). The challenges are not necessarily theoretical, although some theoretical work will need to be done; rather, this is in large measure a challenge of instrumentation, incentives, and implementation (Burkhardt & Schoenfeld, 2003).

EQUITY AND DIVERSITY IN MATHEMATICS EDUCATION

This topic area and the next, "Learning in Context(s)," are deeply intertwined, in that they both cross borders of classroom and culture. The division between the two is thus somewhat arbitrary. The same is the case for any separation between mathematics education and education writ large concerning these issues. For example, while the conditions of poverty described in Kozol (1992) unquestionably contribute to racial performance gaps in mathematics (see, e.g., J. Lee, 2002; Schoenfeld, 2002b; Tate, 1997), they contribute to performance differences in other fields as well. Hence, in this section and the next, I sketch the larger surround and then point to particular pieces within mathematics education.

The issues here are especially complex, because they cross traditional disciplinary boundaries as well. Many fields have *something* to say that informs our collective understanding of, for example, why different ethnic, racial, socioeconomic, linguistic, and gender subgroups of the population perform differently on a wide range of measures. However, although each casts some light on the phenomena, the illumination is partial and the underlying theoretical perspectives are often different.

For example, Willis (1977/1981) makes it clear that issues of identity are central to one's participation (or not) in school practices. The students Willis examined defined their personal affiliations along class lines. Those affiliations shaped their interactions with schooling—and thus, in large measure, the outcomes. Nothing in Willis's book is specific to mathematics classrooms. Yet, it clearly applies, at least in broad-brush terms: the students' *identities* shape their participation in all classrooms, including mathematics. Consider as well the econometric analyses of the contributions of schooling and parental economic status to people's economic success found in Bowles and Gintis' classic (1976) volume *Schooling in Capitalist America: Educational Reform and the Contradictions of Economic Life*. This says *something*, at least in correlational terms, about mathematical performance. The grand theoretical issue is how to meld such theoretical perspectives, and other powerful perspectives, into or with the sociocultural and cognitive perspectives that now predominate in discipline-oriented fields such as mathematics education. This is not merely a matter of one perspective subsuming another, or of foregrounding and backgrounding. The challenge is to build a theoretical and empirical program that provides leverage for the examination and explanation of the phenomena that are considered central to each of the constituent perspectives.

This section begins with a brief reprise of data indicating the reasons that "equity" and "diversity" have been, and remain, major concerns. It then discusses a series of efforts within mathematics education to redress some of the inequities documented by the literature. It concludes with a discussion of a theoretical reconceptualization of these issues offered by Cobb and Hodge.

Statistics on what have come to be known as "racial performance gaps" can be found in J. Lee (2002), National Science Foundation (2000), and Tate (1997). As is well known, when data on in mathematics course-taking, course grades, high school graduation rates, scores on national examinations such as the SAT, and college enrollments are disaggregated by racial or ethnic groups or by socioeconomic status, one sees persistent and substantial differences—to the disadvantage of Latinos, African-Americans, Native Americans, and poor children. The differences are consequential. These are the words of noted civil rights leader Robert Moses:

Today . . . the most urgent social issue affecting poor people and people of color is economic access. In today's world, economic access and full citizenship depend crucially on math and science literacy. I believe that the absence of math literacy in urban and rural communities throughout this country is an issue as urgent as the lack of Black voters in Mississippi was in 1961. (Moses & Cobb, 2001, p. 5)

In brief, Moses' argument is that a lack of mathematical and scientific literacy leads to economic disenfranchisement. Moses' approach to the problem, called the "Algebra Project" and described in Moses & Cobb (2001), is focused on providing mechanisms of mathematical en-

franchisement for students. The project began by providing students with a set of empirical experiences that served as a basis for internalizing certain mathematical notions—for making them personally meaningful, so that mathematical formalization (via a process called the "regimentation of ordinary discourse" motivated by the ideas of the philosopher and mathematician Willard Van Orman Quine) became the codification of personally meaningful experiences rather than a set of instructions for operating on abstract symbolic structures. This idea of rooting mathematics in personally meaningful experiences lies at the core of work done in the Algebra Project. But, the project goes far beyond that. Moses' goals are ultimately those of the civil rights movement.

It was when sharecroppers, day laborers, and domestic workers found their voice, stood up and demanded change, that the Mississippi political game was really over. When these folk, people for whom others had traditionally spoken and advocated, stood up and said, "We demand the right to vote," refuting by their voices and actions the idea that they were uninterested in doing so, they could not be refused. . . . To understand the Algebra Project you must begin with the idea of our targeted young people finding their voice as sharecroppers, day laborers, maids, farmers, and workers of all sorts found theirs in the 1960s. (Moses, 2001, p. 20)

Thus, in Moses' view (but in this author's interpretation and phrasing), issues of voice, issues of entitlement, issues of responsibility, and issues of identity are all central concerns when considering enfranchisement in mathematics. This perspective is shared in various ways by a number of authors who view mathematics through a social justice lens. Martin (2000, in press), for example, identifies an aspect of identity that he calls *mathematics identity*.

Mathematics identity refers to the dispositions and deeply held beliefs that individuals develop about their ability to participate and perform effectively in mathematical contexts (i.e., perceived self-efficacy in mathematical contexts) and to use mathematics to change the conditions of their lives. A mathematics identity therefore encompasses how a person sees himself or herself in the context of doing mathematics (i.e. usually a choice between a competent performer who is able to do mathematics or as incompetent and unable to do mathematics). (Martin, in press, p. 10)

Martin (2000) presents case studies of underrepresented minority students who succeed in mathematics at school while the vast majority of their peers do not. His work indicates that those students tend to have a sense of personal agency (closely related to their mathematical identities) that has them act in ways that, at times, defy the norms and expectations of their peers and others. Martin's research also indicates, in the same ways that Shirley Brice Heath's (1983) study of literacy patterns does, that membership in different subpopulations (or perhaps subcultures) of the population at large tends to provide very different affordances for participation in school practices. Martin (in press) expands on these ideas by considering, in the case of African-Americans, the potential conflicts between one's mathematics identity and one's racial identity: "for [the subject of his study] and other African Americans like him, there is often a struggle to maintain and merge positive identities in the contexts of being African American and being a learner of mathematics. This struggle is brought on by a number of forces that racialize the life and mathematical experiences of African Americans."

Martin's language, although somewhat different from Wenger's (Wenger, 1998), is entirely consistent in theoretical terms. Wenger writes in terms of an individual's (unitary) identity—a "work in progress," shaped by both individual and collective efforts "to create a coherence in time that threads together successive forms of participation in the definition of a person" (p. 158). Wenger stresses that:

We all belong to many communities of practice, some past, some current; some in more peripheral ways. Some may be central to our identities while others are more incidental. Whatever their nature, all these various forms of participation contribute in some way to the production of our identities. As a consequence, the very notion of identity entails

1) an experience of multimembership
2) the work of reconciliation necessary to maintain one identity across boundaries. (Wenger, 1998, p. 158)

If one reads Martin's "mathematics identity" and "racial identity" as aspects of one larger identity, then one sees Martin's case studies as cases in point for Wenger's theoretical claims. And, to be explicit: just as participation in communities of practice has ramifications for one's construction of identity, one's identity shapes patterns of participation. Hence the issue of "multimembership" in different communities of practices and the affordances each community offers for the individual are central. Are the practices that constitute or signal membership in one community (say the mathematics classroom) consistent with those of another community that is central to one's identity (say one's home life, or peer group)? Do they build on one's perceived strengths, or do they negate or undermine them?

Some of the most promising empirical and theoretical work is grounded in these underlying perspectives. There is, for example, the idea that students have "funds of knowledge" (González, Andrade, Civil, & Moll, 2001;

Moll, Amanti, Neff, & González, 1992; Moll & González, 2004) on which school knowledge can be built and expanded, rather than having "deficits" that need to be remediated. This perspective is also powerfully demonstrated in work by Carol Lee (C. Lee, 1995) and explicated by K. Gutiérrez and Rogoff (2003). There is the related idea that culturally responsive pedagogy (Ladson-Billings, 1994, 1995) meets the "whole child" and creates a classroom community of students who feel and are empowered to learn. In various ways, these underlying perspectives are represented in analyses by Brenner (1994; Brenner & Moschkovich, 2002), R. Gutierrez (1996, 2002), Khisty (1995, 2002), and Moschkovich (1999, 2002, in press). Empirically, they are embodied in a number of powerful attempts at teaching mathematics or science for social justice. One of the longest established and best-known programs is Chèche Konnen. The project (see, e.g., Rosebery, Warren, & Conant, 1992; Rosebery, Warren, Ogonowski & Ballenger, 2005; Warren, Ballenger, Ogonowski, Rosebery, & Hudicourt-Barnes, 2001; Warren & Rosebery, 1995) emphasizes the sense-making resources that children from ethnically and linguistically diverse backgrounds bring to the study of science, and how instruction can build on them.

A second series of papers with a social justice focus in mathematics comes from Gutstein and colleagues (Gutstein, 2003, 2005; Gutstein, Lipman, Hernández, & de los Reyes, 1997). Gutstein takes direct aim at issues of social justice and at empowering students as advocates for themselves and their communities by assigning projects that use mathematics to address social injustices. For example, Gutstein asks his students to consider the cost of a B-2 bomber and asks his students to compute how many students could be given fellowships to a major university if the money were used for that purpose instead.

Gutstein and others teaching for social justice recognize that they, like anyone teaching a somewhat nonstandard mathematics class, are the servants of at least two masters. They will be held accountable for their students' performance on standard mathematical content, and then for whatever additional goals they have for instruction. Thus, Gutstein (2003) provides evidence of his students' mathematics learning according to traditional, standardized measures. He also provides evidence of his students' empowerment—of their eagerness after his course to use their mathematical knowledge to address issues of social justice.

A third example, "Railside School," is discussed in the next section. But, it is worth noting here as an exemplar of a coherent attempt on the part of a high school mathematics department to create a culture, both for staff and for students, that supports a strong equity agenda. Boaler (in press) documents the disappearance of racial performance gaps in mathematics scores at Railside. The claim is that such results were possible because of a department-wide effort that focused on a curriculum that allowed all students to engage with meaningful mathematics; a pedagogy grounded in the assumption that all students are capable of grappling meaningfully with mathematically rich problems, and have something to contribute to their solution; as part of that pedagogy, a set of classroom accountability structures that hold students accountable to each other and to the teacher for very high standards of mathematics; and a number of mechanisms for supporting the teachers in implementing the pedagogy just described (Boaler, in press; Horn, 2003).

Each of the efforts described in this section, in different ways, considers individual learners as members of a number of different communities and as participants in different Discourses (in the sense of Gee, 1996) associated with each of those communities; each is concerned with continuities and discontinuities between those communities and the Discourses in them. In various ways, the educational efforts try to bridge the discontinuities. This interpretation of these efforts is consistent with a reframing of the issues of diversity and equity put forth by Paul Cobb and Linn Liao Hodge in a seminal piece entitled "A relational perspective on issues of cultural diversity and equity as they play out in the mathematics classroom" (Cobb & Hodge, 2002).

One version of the standard notion of diversity might be as follows: The diversity of a group is related to the number of members of the group who come from different ethnic/racial/socioeconomic/gender/sexually oriented/other subgroups of the general population. Cobb and Hodge offer the following alternative framing:

We propose to conceptualize diversity relatively broadly in terms of students' participation in the practices of either local, home communities or broader groups or communities within wider society. . . . Equity as we view it is concerned with how continuities and discontinuities between out-of-school and classroom practices play out in terms of access (Cobb & Hodge, 2002, p. 252).

Cobb and Hodge's perspective and the standard notion can result in different views of the diversity of a particular group. A recent example of the difference in the two characterizations and their entailments came in series of news articles about the town of Cupertino, a wealthy enclave in Silicon Valley that has very high-performing schools—and real-estate values to match. The town was characterized in the media as "diverse." It is diverse, in the standard sense: the town is populated by Whites and a wide range of (mostly Asian) ethnic minorities. Cobb and Hodge's characterization provides an alternative view. Part of the

reason Cupertino's schools do as well as they do is that parents with particular sets of values and practices (and the incomes to back them up) comprise a huge majority of the town's inhabitants. In that sense there are relatively few discontinuities between some important in-school and out-of school practices for the children who attend school in the district—i.e., not tremendously much diversity along some of the main dimensions that "count" in this context.

A shift to Cobb and Hodge's characterization of diversity has some slight drawbacks but also some potentially significant advantages. One disadvantage of the definition is that it obscures the traditional focus on the differential treatment of different subgroups of the general population—e.g., the data on racial performance gaps that make so tangibly clear the inequities of our educational system. On the flip side, however, this kind of definition takes a significant step away from the stereotyping and essentializing that often come as an entailment of classification—the idea that members of any particular ethnic, racial, socioeconomic, gender, or other group all share important attributes by virtue of their membership in that group, and therefore can be "pigeonholed" and treated in ways appropriate for members of those groups.

The main advantage of the shift in perspective, however, may be its shift in focus. Learning is a concomitant of the practices in which we engage. Hence a focus on the opportunities that various contexts provide to individuals to engage in particular kinds of practices provides a central lens on learning. The opportunities available to each individual are clearly a function of the continuities and discontinuities between the practices of the different communities in which that individual is a member. This framing, thus, is a potentially useful lens with which to view all of learning. It leads us to the next section of this chapter.

LEARNING IN CONTEXT(S)

This section focuses directly on the issue of learning. Somewhat more than a quarter century ago, the field of cognitive science began to coalesce. Its emergence as an interdisciplinary enterprise was motivated in large part because its varied constituent disciplines—among them anthropology, artificial intelligence, education, linguistics, neurobiology, philosophy, and psychology—all offered partial views of a phenomenon (cognition) that was too big for any one of them to grasp individually. As a result of that coming together, tremendous progress has been made over the past few decades. That progress can be seen in the flowering of understandings and results described in the two editions of this Handbook. The outlines of individual pieces of the puzzle of learning are beginning to become clear. But, how they fit together is still at issue. This section describes some of those pieces, and some of what remains before they can be put together. It begins with some brief additional commentary on the character of the puzzle, and then works its way down from the big picture to more fine-grained issues of mechanism, and an evaluation of the state of the art.

The issue is how to put things together—how to see everything connected to an individual (both "internally" in the sense of knowledge, identity, etc., and "externally" in terms of that person's relationship to various communities) and the communities to which the individual belongs as a coherent whole. Ideally, one would like to be able to understand the evolution of individuals and communities as well. Obviously, there are issues of grain size: some phenomena are "macro" and some "micro," and different explanatory lenses (local theories) will be appropriate for focusing in on different levels. But, the linkages should be smooth, in the same sense that (for example) a "big picture" theory of ecosystems should frame the discussion of the ecology or a particular region, establishing the context for a discussion of the evolving state of classes of organisms in that region. A more micro view of a specific class of organisms in that region describes how they live in interaction with that region, and yet more micro analyses describe the anatomy and physiology of individual organisms (and so on).

I consider one broad metaphor before returning to mathematics education. It is in the tradition of an early paper by Greeno (1991), which compared learning in a content domain (and the affordances of various symbolic and physical tools therein) with learning to make one's way comfortably around a physical environment.

Learning the domain . . . is analogous to learning to live in an environment: learning your way around, learning what resources are available, and learning how to use those resources in conducting your activities productively and enjoyably. . . . In [pursuing] the metaphor of an environment such as a kitchen or a workshop, this section is about knowing how to make things with materials that are in the environment. . . . (pp. 175–177)

Motivated by Greeno's metaphor and a passion for food, the author (Schoenfeld, 1998b) pursued some parallels between learning to cook and learning mathematics, such as the development of skills and the ability to perceive and take advantage of affordances in the environment, and the character of memory and representation in the two domains. Here I would like to pick up the metaphor, in terms of the big themes introduced in this chapter—for example, the relationships between identity, knowledge, and community, and how each can be foregrounded and explored in ways that lead continuously from one to the other. To put things simply: being a "foodie," like being a mathematician and being an educational researcher, is part of the author's identity. Manifestations of that aspect of the author's identity are easy to spot, both materially and personally: materially in his well-equipped kitchen and in a large collection of cookbooks and of restaurant guidebooks, personally in his ongoing practices (taking pains to prepare meals, stopping off at specialty stores to buy provisions for dinner, using food metaphors in his research group, and occasionally mixing his food and work identities by writing about both). If one were interested in understanding these aspects of the author's identity, his personal history would be clearly important; so would membership in various (sometimes distributed, but clearly defined) communities and the role they played not only in the development of identity but in the development of skills and understandings. Deeply intertwined with identity is a body of skills and knowledge—his knowledge that particular dishes are best made in particular kinds of pans, that a particular preparation calls for a blazingly hot pan while another calls for gentle heat; his knowing (by sight, or "feel," or other input) when a particular stage in the cooking process is done; and more. Call this a "knowledge inventory" if you will; the fact is that no description of the author as cook is complete without a thorough categorization of the set of skills, practices, and understandings he possesses (cf. Hillman, 1981; McGee, 2004). This can be done, more or less in standard cognitive science tradition. What is called for in theoretical terms is specifying the linkage between the author's identity and knowledge base. One can imagine ways to specify the linkage: narrative stories of the protagonist's enjoyment of food; descriptions of familial and other practices that enhanced that enjoyment; a characterization of the support he had in developing various culinary practices, on his own and in interaction with others; and the details of that support structure and those interactions, which gave rise to the entries in the knowledge inventory and the coherence among them. This set of issues—explaining and linking aspects of identity, participation, and knowledge—is by analogy the set of issues one confronts when trying to paint the big picture in (mathematics) learning as well.

A recent paper by Saxe and Esmonde (in press) takes on some of the large-scale issues related to the dialectic shaping, over time, of relationships between individual and community. In a distillation of research that includes field studies conducted in 1978, 1980, and 2001 and a historical analysis that covers 1938 to the present, Saxe and Esmonde examine the micro and macro changes in the counting systems used by inhabitants of the Oksapmin valleys in the highlands of central New Guinea. In the mid-20th century, the Oksapmin people used a body part counting system, counting digits and pointing to different places on their bodies. By the time of Saxe's first visit in 1978, commercial incursions from the West had put pressure on the indigenous people to switch (at least in some interactions) from a trade-based economy to a cash-based economy involving Western currency such as pounds and shillings. The effects of those changes were recorded in Saxe's early work. When he returned in 2001, he saw further changes in the body count system. Saxe and Esmonde (in press) present an analytic framework to guide their analyses of the interplay between the social history of the Oksapmin and the development, over time, of new forms of mathematical representation and thought. The framework is fundamentally *cultural;* it is also fundamentally *developmental.* The authors present intertwined arguments at three levels: microgenetic, sociogenetic, and ontogenetic. Microgenetic analyses show the ways in which individuals "turn cultural forms like the body system into means for accomplishing representational and strategic goals" (p. 65). Sociogenetic analyses focus on the ways in which such changes become part of a community. The argument is that (as with some theories of language development) at first the new developments are synchronic, developing locally in a variety of locations (in this case, in trade stores, where the Western currency began to displace the body count system). Later the process of change is diachronic (taking place over a longer time interval), as interlocutors from different sites encounter each other and need to negotiate shared meanings. Finally, there is the issue of ontogenesis, used here to mean changes in the organization of cognition over the course of an individual's life span. Interviews with individuals at least suggested a longitudinal progression of conceptual growth.

The work by Saxe and Esmonde addresses some of the same issues, though from a somewhat different perspective, that are addressed by Engeström (1987, 1993, 1999). Engeström's activity-theoretic framing of the issues situates individual activities amid a nexus of complex social structures, highlighting the tensions negotiated by individuals and communities over time. This theoretical structure was used by K. Gutiérrez, Baquedano-Lopez, & Tejeda (1999) to explore what they call "third spaces," zones of development that can open up within classrooms to accommodate productive activities by diverse sets of learners. As noted in the previous section, Wenger (1998) provides a theoretical framework that focuses on issues of practice(s) and (aspects of) identity, and the dialectic relationships between them.

Issues of identity are explored in interesting ways by Nasir and Saxe (Nasir, 2002; Nasir & Saxe, 2003). Drawing on Wenger's (1998) and Saxe's (1999) frameworks, Nasir (2002) illustrates the ways in which individuals change as they engage in the practices of playing dominos and basketball. Her analyses indicate that as individuals become more accomplished, their goals change; their relationships to the communities of practice (domino and basketball players) change; and their own definitions of self relative to the practices change. Nasir illustrates the bidirectional character of relations between identity, learning, and goals. (Learning creates identity, and identity creates learning; and so on.) Nasir & Saxe (2003) examine different facets of identity—ethnic identity and academic identity—and point to circumstances in which the two may be in conflict.

As noted in the previous section, Cobb and Hodge (2002) offer a theoretical framing of issues related to the continuities and discontinuities between practices in which individuals engage, inside the classroom and outside, that serves as a useful lens with which to examine all learning. Much of the work in the previous section of this paper is grounded in, or at least consistent with, this perspective. Let us now focus more directly on the mathematics classroom.

At the broad level of linking practices to outcomes, Boaler (2002; in press; Boaler & Greeno, 2000) has identified the characteristics of different communities of classroom mathematical practice and their impact both on student performance and on aspects of identity. In her book *Experiencing School Mathematics,* Boaler (2002) describes two very different environments. "Amber Hill" was the very embodiment of exemplary "traditional" mathematics instruction. It had hard-working and professional teachers, a clearly specified curriculum (the English National Curriculum), and a straightforward, department-wide approach to instruction. There was a very high rate of "time on task" as Amber Hill students watched teachers model the solutions to problems at the blackboard, and then worked collections of problems on worksheets.

"Phoenix Park" school had a population similar to Amber Hill in terms of demographics, but a radically different approach to mathematics instruction. The curriculum was "problem-based," with little emphasis on drill. One problem, for example, was for students to find as many shapes as they could whose volume was 216. Once the problem was assigned, teachers then worked with individual students, tailoring the problem to the students' needs and skills. Students had a great deal of autonomy, and time on task was very low at times.

Boaler used multiple measures to determine the outcomes, in the aggregate and by way of individual descriptions. In the aggregate, there were few differences on skills-oriented tasks between students at the two schools—but there were differences in perspective. Students at Amber Hill felt qualified only to solve problems that were nearly identical to problems they had worked, and they were uncomfortable at times even with that.

Similar patterns were found in American schools studied by Boaler and Greeno (2000). In the "ecologies of didactic teaching," students view their roles vis-à-vis mathematics as passive memorizers; in the "ecologies of discussion-based teaching," students are active collaborators and co-constructors of knowledge:

J: The teacher gives us something and has us work on a work sheet, because if I understand something, then I can explain it to the group members or if I don't understand it the group members may explain it to me. Whereas if she teaches the lesson and sends us home with it, I'm not really that confident because I haven't put like things together (Boaler & Greeno, 2000, p. 178).

Boaler (in press) pursues this issue in more fine-grained detail, examining the accountability structures by which the teachers at "Railside School" hold students, and the students hold each other, accountable for producing clear and cogent explanations of the mathematics under consideration. In a lesson described by Boaler (in press), one member of a group is asked a question by the teacher. When the student does not produce a viable explanation, the teacher simply says "I'll be back." The group knows the teacher will return to ask the same student the same question again. One member of the group gives the student a quick tutorial, saying "answer it this way." But the student resists. She argues that the teacher will not be satisfied with a pat answer—that the teacher will probe until the student produces an explanation that is mathematically correct and stands up to robust questioning. It is the group's responsibility to make sure every member of the group understands and can explain the material. The group takes on that responsibility, with the result that the student does come to understand the material—and, after demonstrating her understanding of it (withstanding tough questioning from the teacher), she is clearly more self-assured as well. In the classroom videotapes from Railside one sees, at a micro-level, the ways in which classroom practices interact with issues of individual identity and knowledge.

The examples just given are cases in point for an argument by Engle and Conant (2002), that there tend to be the following substantial consistencies in some of the most productive learning environments for students:

• *Problematizing*: Students are encouraged to take on intellectual problems

• *Authority*: Students are given authority in addressing such problems
• *Accountability*: Students' intellectual work is made accountable to others and to disciplinary norms
• *Resources*: Students are provided with sufficient resources to do all of the above. (Engle and Conant (2002, pp. 400–401).

The discussion of the Railside example also brings us explicitly to the issue of mechanism—the means by which the dialectic between individual and collective is worked out, with each being shaped as a result. Central to the study of classroom practices, of course, is the study of patterns of classroom discourse.

There are at least two useful theoretical notions involved in the discussion of the Railside classroom. The first is *sociomathematical norms*. Erna Yackel and Paul Cobb (Cobb & Yackel, 1996; Yackel & Cobb, 1996) adapted the concept of general social norms to describe situations that specifically involve patterns of *taken-as-shared mathematical behavior*: "Normative understandings of what counts as mathematically different, mathematically sophisticated, mathematically efficient, and mathematically elegant are sociomathematical norms. Similarly, what counts as an acceptable mathematical explanation and justification is a sociomathematical norm" (Cobb & Yackel, 1996, p. 461).

The second closely related notion is that of *accountability structures*. In the Railside classroom studied by Boaler, the students are accountable to the teacher, to each other (in that the group is responsible for making sure that all of its members understand the mathematics), and to the mathematics—their discussions and explanations are expected to be rigorous and to meet high mathematical standards. Ball and Bass (2003b) provide examples of ways in which a third-grade class, over the course of the school year, comes to grapple with such issues. Horn (in preparation) provides a fine-grained analysis of the accountability structures in Deborah Ball's well-known January 19, 1990, class. Some of the critical aspects of what Horn calls *accountable argumentation* are that it uses terms from the mathematical and academic registers (e.g. "proof," "conjecture"); discussions have a slow and measured pace; and, disagreements are important and may not (and need not) be resolved. Horn argues:

In this classroom, accountable argumentation brings the often hidden practices of mathematical reasoning into the visible world of classroom interactions. . . . During the class session, these thinking activities are focused on a particular set of ideas. Accountable argumentation supports engagement with specific ideas, particularly through the expectations that (a) students attend to whole class discussions and (b) students take a justified position in a discussion which they will act on or defend. In addition, once they are engaged in a disagreement, the stakes for engagement increase. Dissenters are obliged to ask questions or otherwise substantiate their position to their peers. Principals, on the other hand, must articulate their thinking to the whole class.

Effectively, these thinking activities and the engagement in particular ideas support both the learning and creation of mathematics. (Horn, 2005, p. 25)

At an equally fine level of grain size, and also focusing on issues of mechanism, are studies of teachers' discourse moves such as those conducted by O'Connor (1998) and O'Connor and Michaels (1993, 1996). O'Connor and Michaels characterize a teacher move they call *revoicing*. In revoicing, a teacher picks up on a comment made by a student and draws attention to it—sometimes paraphrasing, sometimes clarifying, sometimes commenting on its relevance or importance. This act can legitimate and give status to a student; it can bring his or her ideas to center stage; it can position the student as author of the comment and place the student at the center of a dialogue, in which other students are expected to participate. All of these moves can contribute to the creation of a classroom discourse community in which students are given authority to work on consequential problems, positioned as knowledgeable members of the community, and attributed ownership of important ideas. This kind of discourse move on the part of teachers stands in stark contrast to traditional classroom discourse communities in which the teacher typically initiates discussion with a "short answer" question, a student responds, and the teachers evaluates the response ("IRE sequences"; see Mehan, 1979).

Also at the level of mechanism, there is the question of what actually takes place in extended (and not always productive) interactions between students. Sfard and Kieran (2001) present a detailed analysis of a series of interactions between two 13-year-old boys learning algebra over a 2-month period. They introduce the notions of *focal* and *preoccupational* analyses as analytical tools—the former for giving direct attention to the mathematical content contained in students' interactions, and focusing on communication and miscommunication between the two students, the latter focusing on metamessages and engagement, providing tentative explanations for some of the students' communication failures. The authors note their conclusions as follows:

We realized that the merits of learning-by-talking cannot be taken for granted. Because of the ineffectiveness of the students' communication, the collaboration we had a chance to observe seemed unhelpful and lacking the expected synergetic quality.

Second, on the meta-level, we concluded that research which tries to isolate cognitive processes from all the other kinds of communicative activities is simply wrongheaded.... For us, thinking became an act of communication in itself. This reconceptualization led to the disappearance of several traditional dichotomies that initially barred our insights: the dichotomy between "contents of mind" and the things people say or do; the split between cognition and affect, and the distinction between individual and social research perspectives. (Sfard & Kieran, 2001, p. 42)

This latter issue is also pursued in Sfard (2001).

Finally, there is a need to understand classroom discourse practices and the use of artifacts—and the development of shared meanings over both. A fascinating exercise in multiple interpretation was carried out in Sfard & McLain (2003), in which a series of authors with related but different theoretical perspectives examine the same set of video-recorded classroom data from an experiment in teaching statistics. The juxtaposition of theoretical perspectives in the issue shows the progress the field has made in untangling social-cognitive phenomena. See also Sfard (2000), which provides a detailed examination of how symbols come to take on meanings.

To sum up, all of the studies referenced in this section offer advances over the perspectives and tools available to the field when the previous edition of the *Handbook of Educational Psychology* was published. As the field has matured, it has begun to grapple with complex issues of learning in context(s). The studies referenced here represent points of light in territory that, not long ago, was largely uncharted. As such, there is progress. There is not enough light to illuminate the terrain; but there may be enough points of light to allow one to get a sense of the landscape.

THE STATE OF THE FIELD

The main substance of this chapter has delineated thematic progress in a number of domains central to mathematics teaching and learning: research focusing on issues of teacher knowledge and aspects of professional development; issues of curriculum development, implementation, and assessment; issues of equity and diversity; and issues of learning in context(s). This brief concluding section takes a step back from the details to examine the contextual surround within which researchers in mathematics education do their work.

As this chapter indicates, there has been a fair amount of theoretical progress—with the theory being grounded in, and tested by, empirical findings. However, this steady progress has not been met with recognition or support outside the field, and research has not had nearly the impact on practice that it might. Moreover, the external context (including the funding environment) for high-quality research in mathematics education is as hostile as it has been for at least a quarter century. Some of this is undoubtedly outside the control of the field, but (mathematics) educators may have contributed to some of it them/ourselves.

The Political Context

Educational research as a whole in the United States is under attack. Consider, for example, the following language from the U.S. Department of Education's Strategic Plan for 2002–2007:

> Unlike medicine, agriculture and industrial production, the field of education operates largely on the basis of ideology and professional consensus. As such, it is subject to fads and is incapable of the cumulative progress that follows from the application of the scientific method and from the systematic collection and use of objective information in policy making. We will change education to make it an evidence-based field. (http://www.ed.gov/pubs/stratplan2002-07/index.html, p. 48)

That language does not represent an empty threat. "Evidence-based" has been taken to mean "quantitative," and a narrow band of quantitative at that; sources of funding for anything other than a narrow, quantitative research agenda are drying up (see later discussion).

Funding

Funding for educational research has always been ridiculously low. In 1998 the U.S. House Committee on Science wrote, "Currently, the U.S. spends approximately $300 billion a year on education and less than $30 million, 0.01 percent of the overall education budget, on education research. . . . This minuscule investment suggests a feeble long-term commitment to improving our educational system" (p. 46).

The vast majority of funding for research in science and mathematics education in the United States in recent years has come from the Education and Human Resources (EHR) Directorate of the National Science Foundation, with the lion's share of funding for basic research coming from EHR's Division of Research, Evaluation, and Communication (REC). The March 25, 2005, issue of *Science* magazine contains the following information on a new $120 million funding initiative focusing on the use of randomized controlled trials to test the effectiveness of mathematics curricula:

> The initiative comes at the same time the Administration has requested a $107 million cut in NSF's $840 million Education and Human Resources (EHR) directorate. The cuts include . . . a 43% decrease for the foundation's division that assesses the impact of education reform efforts (*Science*, 11 February, p. 832). [Assistant secretary for vocational and adult education at the Department of Education Susan] Sclafani says this "reallocation of education dollars" reflects the Administration's eagerness for clear answers on how to improve math and science learning across the country. That's OK with NSF Director Arden Bement, who says ED is in a better position than NSF to implement reforms nationwide. (Bhattacharjee, 2005, p. 1863)

The Division of EHR sustaining the 43% budget cut identified by Bhattacharjee is the Division of Research, Evaluation, and Communication. Given that the REC has ongoing funding obligations, the proposed cuts essentially bring to a halt the funding for new research projects within the Division. Of course, it remains to be seen what the value of the new project at the Department of Education will be. But, given the track record of the What Works Clearinghouse to date (see the earlier discussion), there is some reason for concern.

Impact on Practice

As discussed in the section on curriculum, the educational R&D community lacks robust mechanisms for taking ideas from the laboratory into "engineering design" and then large-scale implementation. This is partly for fiscal reasons. (The design refinement process outlined in this chapter is costly. As long as publishers can sell books based on the results of focus groups and avoid the expenses of that design refinement process, they will.) It is also partly a result of academic value systems. In promotion and tenure committees, theory and new academic papers tend to be valued over applications; new ideas tend to be valued over replications, extensions, and refinements; single authored work is valued more than work in teams (shares of "credit" are notoriously difficult to assign). Those who would systematize the R&D process thus face an incentive system that devalues teamwork, applications, and iterative design. Here, too, some changes would help the field to have greater impact.

It should be noted that a focus on the engineering model described here does not represent an endorsement of the "linear model" of research-into-practice. A substantial proportion of the work done under this aegis can and should be done in "Pasteur's Quadrant" (Stokes, 1997), contributing both to theory and to the solution of practical problems. Both design experiments (the initial phases of design) and contextual studies (explorations of the ways in which instructional interventions work) can and should contribute as much to theory development as they do to the creation of improved instructional materials and practices.

Some Final Words

These are, in Dickens' words, the best of times and the worst of times; an age of wisdom and an age of foolishness. This chapter documents substantial progress in research on mathematical teaching and learning over the decade since the publication of the first *Handbook of Educational Psychology*. There have been significant theoretical advances in many areas, and practical advances as well (although the data in substantiation of those advances are less robust than one would like). There is, in sum, good reason for optimism on the intellectual front. At the same time, the larger climate is remarkably hostile to the scholarly enterprise, and there appears to be little prospect of improvement in the short run. A short-term view of the situation would be pessimistic. However a sense of history suggests that support for and hostility to the research enterprise seem to come in cycles and that in the long run, intellectual progress is sustained. It will be interesting to see what progress is reflected in the next edition of this Handbook.

ACKNOWLEDGMENT

I am indebted to Jim Greeno and Lani Horn, Abraham Arcavi, Hugh Burkhardt, Mari Campbell, Charles Hammond, Vicki Hand, Markku Hannula, Manya Raman, Miriam Sherin, and Natasha Speer for their incisive comments on a draft version of this manuscript. This chapter is much improved for their help. The flaws that remain are all my responsibility. I would also like to express my thanks to Patricia Alexander and Lane Akers for their graciousness and support from the beginning to the end of the process of producing the chapter.

References

Arcavi, A. A., & Schoenfeld, A. H. (1992). Mathematics tutoring through a constructivist lens: The challenges of sense-making. *Journal of Mathematical Behavior, 11*(4), 321–336.

Ball, D. L., & Bass, H. (2000). Interweaving content and pedagogy in teaching and learning to teach: Knowing and using mathematics In J. Boaler (Ed.), *Multiple perspectives on the teaching and learning of mathematics* (pp. 83–104). Westport, CT: Ablex.

Ball, D. L., & Bass, H. (2003a). Making mathematics reasonable in school. In J. Kilpatrick, W. G. Martin, & D. Schifter, D. (Eds.). *A research companion to Principles and Standards for School Mathematics* (pp. 27–44).Reston, VA: National Council of Teachers of Mathematics.

Ball, D. L., & Bass, H. (2003b). Toward a practice-based theory of mathematical knowledge for teaching. In B. Davis & E. Simmt (Eds.), *Proceedings of the 2002 Annual Meeting of the Canadian Mathematics Education Study Group* (pp. 3–14). Edmonton, AB: CMESG/GCEDM.

Beaton, A., Mullis, I., Martin, M., Gonzalez, E., Kelly, D., & Smith, T. (1997). *Mathematics Achievement in the Middle School Years: IEA's Third International Mathematics and Science Report*. Boston: The International Association for the Evaluation of Educational Achievement, at Boston College.

Becker, J., & Jacob, B. (2000). The politics of California school mathematics: The anti-reform of 1997-99. *Phi Delta Kappan, 81*, 529-37.

Berliner, D., & Calfee, R. (Eds.) (1996). *Handbook of educational psychology*. New York: MacMillan.

Bhattacharjee, Y. (2005). Can randomized trials answer the question of what works? *Science, 307,* 1861-1863.

Boaler, J. (2002). *Experiencing school mathematics* (Revised and expanded edition). Mahwah, NJ: Lawrence Erlbaum Associate.

Boaler, J. (in press). Promoting relational equity in mathematics classrooms—Important teaching practices and their impact on student learning. "Regular lecture" given at the 10th International Congress of Mathematics Education (ICME X), 2004, Copenhagen. To appear in the ICME X *Proceedings*.

Boaler, J., & Greeno, J. (2000). Identity, agency and knowing in mathematical worlds. In J. Boaler (Ed.), *Multiple perspectives on mathematics teaching and learning* (pp. 171–200).Westport, CT: Ablex.

Bowles, S., & Gintis, H. (1976). *Schooling in capitalist America: Educational reform and the contradictions of economic life*. New York: Basic Books.

Brenner, M. (1994). A communication framework for mathematics: Exemplary instruction for culturally and linguistically diverse students. In B. McLeod (Ed.), *Language and learning: Educating linguistically diverse students* (pp. 233-268). Albany, NY: SUNY Press.

Brenner, M., & Moschkovich, J. (Eds.), (2002). *Everyday and academic mathematics in the classroom. JRME* Monograph Number 11. Reston, VA: NCTM.

Briars, D. (2001, March). *Mathematics performance in the Pittsburgh public schools*. Presentation at a Mathematics Assessment Resource Service conference on tools for systemic improvement, San Diego, CA.

Briars, D., & Resnick, L. (2000). *Standards, assessments—and what else? The essential elements of standards-based school improvement.* Unpublished manuscript.

Brown, A. L. (1992). Design experiments: Theoretical and methodological challenges in creating complex interventions in classroom settings. *Journal of the Learning Sciences, 2*(2), 141–178.

Burkhardt, G. H., & Schoenfeld, A. H. (2003). Improving educational research: toward a more useful, more influential, and better funded enterprise. *Educational Researcher 32*(9), 3–14.

Carpenter, T. P. (1985). Learning to add and subtract: An exercise in problem solving. In E. A. Silver (Ed.), *Teaching and learning mathematical problem solving: Multiple research perspectives,* (pp. 17–40). Hillsdale, NJ: Lawrence Erlbaum Associates.

Carpenter, T. P., Fennema, E., Franke, M. L., Empson, S. B., & Levi, L. W. (1999). *Children's mathematics: Cognitively guided instruction.* Portsmouth, NH: Heinemann.

Carpenter, T. P., Franke, M. L., Jacobs, V. R., Fennema, E., & Empson, S. B. (1998). A longitudinal study of invention and understanding in children's multidigit addition and subtraction. *Journal for Research in Mathematics Education, 29,* 3–20.

Carpenter, T. P., & Lehrer, R. (1999). Teaching and learning mathematics with understanding. In E.Fennema & T. A. Romberg (Eds.), *Mathematics classrooms that promote understanding* (pp. 19–32). Mahway, NJ: Erlbaum.

Carpenter, T. P., Fennema, E., & Franke, M. L. (1996). Cognitively Guided Instruction: A knowledge base for reform in primary mathematics instruction. *Elementary School Journal, 97*(1), 1–20.

Chappell, M. (2003). Keeping mathematics front and center: Reaction to middle-grades curriculum projects research. In S. Senk & D. Thompson (Eds.), *Standards-based school mathematics curricula: What are they? What do students learn?* (pp. 285–298). Mahwah, NJ: Erlbaum.

Cobb, P., Confrey, J. diSessa, A., Lehrer, R., & Schauble, L. (2003). Design experiments in educational research. *Educational Researcher, 32*(1), 9–13.

Cobb, P., & Hodge, L. L. (2002). A relational perspective on issues of cultural diversity and equity as they play out in the mathematics classroom. *Mathematical Thinking and Learning, 4*(2&3), 249–284.

Cobb, P., & Yackel, E. (1996). Constructivist, emergent, and sociocultural perspectives in the context of developmental research. *Educational Psychologist, 31*(3–4), 175–190.

Cohen, D., Raudenbush, S., & Ball, D. (2003). *Resources, instruction, and research.* Educational Evaluation and Policy Analysis, *25*(2), 1–24.

Cohen, S. (2004). *Teachers' professional development and the elementary mathematics classroom.* Mahwah, NJ: Lawrence Erlbaum Associates.

Collins, A. (1992). Toward a design science of education. In E. Scanlon & T. O'Shea (Eds.), *New directions in educational technology* (pp. 15–22). Berlin: Springer.

DeCorte, E., Greer, B., & Verschaffel, L. (1996). Mathematics teaching and learning. In D. Berliner & R. Calfee (Eds.), *Handbook of educational psychology,* (pp. 491–549). New York: MacMillan.

Educational Researcher (2002, November). *Theme issue on scientific research and education, 31*(8).

Engeström, Y. (1987). *Learning by expanding.* Helsinki, Finland: Orienta-Konsultit Oy.

Engeström, Y. (1993). Developmental studies of work as a test bench of activity theory: The case of primary care medical practice. In S. Chaiklin & J. Lave (Eds.), *Understanding practice: Perspective on activity and context* (pp. 64 DH103). Cambridge, England: Cambridge University Press.

Engeström, Y. (1999). Activity theory and individual and social transformation In Y. Engeström, R. Miettinen, & R. Punamaki (Eds.), *Perspectives on activity theory* (pp. 19–38). Cambridge, England: Cambridge University Press.

Engle, R., & Conant, F. (2002). Guiding principles for fostering productive disciplinary engagement: Explaining emerging argument in a community of learners classroom. *Cognition and Instruction, 20*(4), 399–483.

Fernandez, C., & Yoshida, M. (2004). *Lesson study: A Japanese approach to improving mathematics teaching and learning.* Mahwah, NJ: Lawrence Erlbaum Associates.

Ferrini-Mundy, J., & Schram, T. (Eds.). (1997). The recognizing and recording reform in mathematics education project: Insights, issues, and implications. *Journal for Research in Mathematics Education, Monograph Number 8.* Reston, VA: National Council of Teachers of Mathematics.

Franke, M., Carpenter, T. P., Levi, L., & Fennema, E. (2001). Capturing teachers' generative change: A follow-up study of professional development in mathematics. *American Educational Research Journal, 38*(3), 653–689.

Gee, J. (1996). *Social linguistics and literacies: Ideology in discourses (2nd ed.).* Philadelphia: Routledge/Falmer.

Glaser, R., Linn, R., & Bohrnstedt, G. (1997). *Assessment in Transition: Monitoring the Nation's Educational Progress.* New York: National Academy of Education, 1997.

Goodwin, C. (1994). Professional vision. *American Anthropologist, 96,* 606–633.

González, N., Andrade, R., Civil, M., & Moll, L. (2001). Bridging funds of distributed knowledge: Creating zones of practices in mathematics. *Journal of Education for Students Placed at Risk (JESPAR), 6(1–2),* 115–132.

Greeno, J. G. (1991). Number sense as situated knowing in a conceptual domain. *Journal for research in mathematics education, 22(3),* 170–218.

Greeno, J.G., Collins, A., & Resnick, L. (1996). Cognition and learning. In D. Berliner & R. Calfee (Eds.), *Handbook of Educational Psychology,* (pp. 15–46) New York: Macmillan.

Greeno, J. G., Pearson, P. D., & Schoenfeld, A. H. (1997). Implications for the National Assessment of Educational Progress of Research on Learning and Cognition. In: *Assessment in transition: Monitoring the nation's educational progress, background studies* (pp. 152–215). Stanford, CA: National Academy of Education.

Grouws, D. (Ed.), (1992). *Handbook of Research on Mathematics Teaching and Learning*. New York: MacMillan.

Gutiérrez, K., Baquedano-Lopez, P., & Tejeda, C. (1999). Rethinking diversity: Hybridity and hybrid language practices in the third space. *Mind, Culture, & Activity*, 6, 286–303.

Gutiérrez, K., & Rogoff, B. (2003). Cultural ways of learning: Individual traits or repertoires of practice. *Educational Researcher, 32*(5), 19–25.

Gutierrez, R. (1996). Practices, beliefs, and cultures of high school mathematics departments: Understanding their influences on student advancement. *Journal of Curriculum Studies, 28*, 495–466.

Gutierrez, R. (2002). Beyond essentialism: The complexity of language in teaching mathematics to Latina/o students. *American Educational Research Journal, 39*(4), 1047–1088.

Gutstein, E. (2003). Teaching and learning mathematics for social justice in an urban, Latino school. *Journal for Research in Mathematics Education, 34*, 37–73.

Gutstein, E. (2005). "And that's just how it starts": Teaching mathematics and developing student agency. In N. S. Nasir & P. Cobb (Eds.), *Diversity, equity, and access to mathematical ideas.* New York: Teachers College Press.

Gutstein, E., Lipman, P., Hernández, P., & de los Reyes, R. (1997). Culturally relevant mathematics teaching in a Mexican American context. *Journal for Research in Mathematics Education, 28*, 709–737.

Heath, S. B. (1983). *Ways with words: Language, life and work in communities and classrooms.* Cambridge, England: Cambridge University Press.

Hiebert. J., Gallimore, R., Garnier, H., Givvin, K., Hollingsworth, H., Jacobs, J., et al. (2003). *Teaching mathematics in seven countries: Results from the TIMSS 1999 Video Study.* Washington, DC: National Center for Education Statistics.

Hill, H. C., and Ball, D. L. (2004). Learning mathematics for teaching: Results from California's mathematics professional development institutes. *Journal for Research in Mathematics Education, 35*(5), 330–351.

Hill, H. C., Rowan, B., & Ball, D. (in press). *Effects of teachers' mathematical knowledge for teaching on student achievement.* American Educational Research Journal.

Hillman, H. (1981). *Kitchen science.* Boston: Houghton Mifflin.

Horn, I. (2003). *Learning on the job: Mathematics teachers' professional development in the contexts of high school reform.* Doctoral dissertation, University of California, Berkeley.

Horn, I. (2005). Accountable argumentation as a participant structure to support learning through disagreement. Manuscript submitted for publication.

Jacob, B. & Akers, J. (2003). Research-Based mathematics education policy: The case of California 1995-1998. *International Journal for Mathematics Teaching and Learning.* Retrieved on June 27, 2003 from the website of the Centre for Innovation in Mathematics Teaching, University of Exeter, U.K., http://www.intermep.org.

Jacob, B. (1999). Instructional materials for K-8 mathematics classrooms: The California adoption, 1997. In E. Gavosto, S. Krantz, and W. McCallum (Eds.), *Contemporary Issues in Mathematics Education* pp. 109–22. Mathematical Sciences Research Institute Publications 36. Cambridge: Cambridge University Press.

Jacob, B. (2001). Implementing Standards: The California Mathematics Textbook Debacle. *Phi Delta Kappan* 83(3), 264–272.

Kelley, D., Mullis, I., & Martin, M. (2000). *Profiles of student achievement in mathematics at the TIMSS International Benchmarks: U.S. performance and standards in an international context.* Boston: The International Association for the Evaluation of Educational Achievement, at Boston College.

Kerstyn, C. (2001). *Evaluation of the I CAN Learn® mathematics classroom: First year of implementation (2000-2001 school year).* (Available from the Division of Instruction, Hillsborough Country Public Schools, 901 East Kennedy Blvd., Tampa, FL 33602)

Khisty, L. L. (1995). Making inequality: Issues of language and meanings in mathematics teaching with Hispanic students. In W. G. Secada, E. Fennema, & L. B. Adajian (Eds.), *New directions for equity in mathematics education* (pp. 279–297). New York: Cambridge University Press.

Khisty, L. L. (2002). Mathematics learning and the Latino student: Suggestions from research for classroom practice. *Teaching Children Mathematics*, 9(1), 32–35.

Kirshner, D., & Whitson, J. A. (Eds.). (1997). *Situated cognition.* Mahwah, NJ: Lawrence Erlbaum Associates.

Klein, D. (2003). A brief history of American K-12 mathematics education in the 20th century. Retrieved July 1, 2003, from http://www.csun.edu/~vcmth00m/AHistory.html

Kozol, J. (1992). *Savage inequalities.* New York: Harper Perennial.

Ladson-Billings, G. (1994). *The dreamkeepers.* San Francisco: Jossey-Bass.

Ladson-Billings, G. (1995). But that's just good teaching! The case for culturally relevant pedagogy. *Theory Into Practice, 34*(3), 159–165.

Lampert, M. (2001). *Teaching problems and the problem of teaching.* New Haven, CT: Yale University Press.

Lee, C. D. (1995). Signifying as a scaffold for literary interpretation. *Journal of Black Psychology, 21*(4), 357–381.

Lee, J. (2002). Racial and ethnic achievement gap trends: Reversing the progress toward equity? *Educational Researcher, 31*(1), 3–12.

Ma, L. (1999). *Knowing and teaching elementary mathematics.* Mahwah, NJ: Lawrence Erlbaum Associates.

Martin, D. (2000). Mathematics success and failure among African-American youth: The roles of sociohistorical context, community forces, school influence, and individual agency. Mahwah, NJ: Lawrence Erlbaum Associates.

Martin, D. (in press). Mathematics learning and participation in African American context: The co-construction of identity in two intersecting realms of experience. In N. S. Nasir & P. Cobb (Eds.), *Diversity, equity, and access to mathematical ideas.* New York: Teachers College Press.

McGee, H. (2004). *On food and cooking: The science and lore of the kitchen.* New York: Scribner.

Mehan, H. (1979). *Learning lessons: Social organization in the classroom.* Cambridge, MA: Harvard University Press.

Moll, L. C., Amanti, C., Neff, D., & González, N. (1992). Funds of knowledge for teaching: Using a qualitative approach to connect homes and classrooms. *Theory Into Practice, 31*(2), 132–141.

Moll, L., & González, N. (2004). Engaging life: A funds-of-knowledge approach to multicultural education. In James Banks & Cherry Banks (Eds.), *Handbook of research on multicultural education* (pp. 699–715). San Francisco: Jossey-Bass.

Moschkovich, J. N. (1999). Supporting the participation of English language learners in mathematical discussions. *For the Learning of Mathematics, 19*(1), 11–19.

Moschkovich, J. N. (2002). A situated and sociocultural perspective on bilingual mathematics learners. *Mathematical Thinking and Learning, 4*(2&3), 189–212.

Moses, R. P. (2001). *Radical equations: Math literacy and civil rights.* Boston MA: Beacon Press.

Moschkovich, J. N. (in press). Bilingual mathematics learners: How views of language, bilingual learners, and mathematical communication impact instruction. In N. S. Nasir & P. Cobb (Eds.), *Diversity, equity, and access to mathematical ideas.* New York: Teachers College Press.

Moses, R. P., & Cobb, C. E. (2001). *Radical equations: Math literacy and civil rights.* Boston: Beacon Press.

Mullis, I. Martin, M., Beaton, A., Gonzalez E., ,Kelly, D., & Smith, T. (1998). *Mathematics and science achievement in the final year of secondary school.* Boston: The International Association for the Evaluation of Educational Achievement, at Boston College.

Mullis, I., Martin, M., Gonzalez, E., Gregory, K., Garden, R., O'Connor, K., et al. (2000). TIMSS 1999. *Findings from IEA's repeat of the Third International Mathematics and Science Study at the Eighth Grade (International Mathematics Report). Boston:* The International Association for the Evaluation of Educational Achievement, at Boston College.

Nasir, N. S. (2002). Identity, goals, and learning: Mathematics in cultural practice.*Mathematical Thinking and Learning, 4*(2&3), 213–248.

Nasir N. S., & Saxe, G. (2003). Ethnic and academic identities: A cultural practice perspective on emerging tensions and their management in the lives of minority students. *Educational Researcher, 32*(5), 14–18.

National Academy of Education, Committee on Teacher Education. (2005). *Preparing teachers for a changing world.* San Francisco, CA: Jossey-Bass.

National Commission on Excellence in Education. (1983). *A nation at risk: The imperative for educational reform.* Washington, DC: U.S. Government Printing Office.

National Council of Teachers of Mathematics. (1989). *Curriculum and evaluation standards for school mathematics.* Reston, VA: Author.

National Council of Teachers of Mathematics. (2000). *Principles and standards for school mathematics.* Reston, VA: Author.

National Research Council. (1998). *Preventing reading difficulties in young children.* Washington, DC: National Academy Press.

National Research Council. (1989). *Everybody counts: A report to the nation on the future of mathematics education.* Washington, DC: National Academy Press.

National Research Council. (2002a). *How people learn (Expanded edition).* Washington, DC: National Academy Press.

National Research Council. (2002b). *Scientific research in education.* Washington, DC: National Academy Press.

National Research Council. (2004). *On Evaluating Curricular Effectiveness: Judging the Quality of K-12 Mathematics Evaluations.* Committee for a Review of the Evaluation Data on the Effectiveness of NSF-Supported and Commercially Generated Mathematics Curriculum Materials. Mathematical Sciences Education Board, Center for Education, Division of Behavioral and Social Sciences and Education. Washington, DC: The National Academies Press.

National Research Council. (2005). *On evaluating curricular effectiveness: Judging the quality of K-12 mathematics evaluations.* Washington, DC: National Academy Press.

National Science Foundation. (2000). *Science and engineering indicators.* Washington, DC: National Science Foundation.

O'Connor, M. C. (1998). Language socialization in the mathematics classroom: Discourse practices and mathematical thinking. In M. Lampert & M. Blunk (Eds.), *Talking mathematics: Studies of teaching and learning in school* (pp. 17–55). New York: Cambridge University Press.

O'Connor. M. C., & Michaels, S. (1993). Aligning academic task and participation status through revoicing: Analysis of a classroom discourse strategy. *Anthropology and Education Quarterly, 24,* 318–335.

O'Connor. M. C., & Michaels, S. (1996). Shifting participant frameworks: Orchestrating thinking practices in group discussion. In D. Hicks (Ed.), *Discourse, learning, and schooling* (pp. 63–103). New York: Cambridge University Press.

Pólya, G. (1945). *How to solve it.* Princeton, NJ: Princeton University Press.

Putnam, R. (2003). Commentary on Four elementary mathematics curricula. In S. Senk & D. Thompson (Eds.), *Standards-oriented school mathematics curricula: What does the research say about student outcomes?* (pp. 161–178). Mahwah, NJ: Lawrence Erlbaum Associates.

RAND Mathematics Study Panel. (2002). *Mathematical proficiency for all students: Toward a strategic research and development program in mathematics education.* Santa Monica, CA: RAND Foundation.

Reys, R. E., Reys, B. J., Lappan, R., Holliday, G., & Wasman, D. (2003). Assessing the impact of standards-based middle grades mathematics curriculum materials on student achievement. *Journal for Research in Mathematics Education, 34*(1), 74–95.

Ridgway, J., Crust, R., Burkhardt, H., Wilcox, S., Fisher, L., and Foster, D. (2000). *MARS Report on the 2000 Tests* (p. 120). San Jose, CA: Mathematics Assessment Collaborative.

Ridgway, J, Zawojewski, J., Hoover, M., and Lambdin, D. (2003). Student attainment in the connected mathematics curriculum. In Sharon Senk & Denisse Thompson (Eds.), *Standards-oriented school mathematics curricula: What does the research say about student outcomes?* (pp. 193–224). Mahwah, NJ: Lawrence Erlbaum Associates.

Riordan, J., & Noyce, P. (2001). The impact of two standards-based mathematics curricula on student achievement in Massachusetts. *Journal for Research in Mathematics Education, 32*(4), 368–398.

Rosebery, A., Warren, B., & Conant, F. (1992). Appropriating scientific discourse: Findings from language minority classrooms. *Journal of the Learning Sciences, 2*, 61–94.

Rosebery, A., Warren, B., Ogonowski, M. & Ballenger, C. (2005). The generative potential of students' everyday knowledge in learning science. In T. Carpenter and T. Romberg (Eds.), *Understanding matters: Improving student learning in mathematics and science* (pp. 55–80). Mahwah, NJ: Lawrence Erlbaum Associates.

Rosen, L. (2000). Calculating concerns: The politics or representation in California's "Math Wars." Unpublished doctoral dissertation, University of California, San Diego.

Saxe, G. (1999). Cognition, development, and cultural practices. In E. Turiel (Ed.), *Development and cultural change: Reciprocal processes* (pp. 19–35). San Francisco: Jossey-Bass.

Saxe, G. B., & Esmonde, I. (In preparation). Studying cognition in flux: A historical treatment of 'fu' in the shifting structure of Oksapmin mathematics.

Schifter, D. (Eds.). *A research companion to Principles and Standards for School Mathematics* (pp. 333–352).Reston, VA: National Council of Teachers of Mathematics.

Schifter, D. (1993). Mathematics process as mathematics content: A course for teachers. *The Journal of Mathematical Behavior, 12(3)*, 271–283.

Schifter, D. (1998). Learning mathematics for teaching: From the teachers' seminar to the classroom. *Journal for Mathematics Teacher Education, 1*, 55–87.

Schifter, D. (2001). Learning to See the Invisible: What skills and knowledge are needed to engage with students' mathematical ideas? In T. Wood, B. S. Nelson, & J. Warfield (Eds.), *Beyond classical pedagogy: Teaching elementary school mathematics* (pp. 109–134). Mahwah, NJ: Lawrence Erlbaum Associates.

Schifter, D., Bastable, V., & Russell, S. J. (1999). *Developing mathematical ideas.* Parsippany, NJ: Dale Seymour.

Schifter, D. & Fosnot, C.T. (1993). *Reconstructing mathematics education: Stories of teachers meeting the challenge of reform.* New York: Teachers College Press.

Schifter, D., Russell, S.J., & Bastable, V. (1999). *Teaching to the big ideas. In M. Solomon (Ed.), The diagnostic teacher* (pp. 22–47). New York: Teachers College Press.

Schoenfeld, A. H. (1985). *Mathematical problem solving.* Orlando, FL: Academic Press.

Schoenfeld, A. H. (1992). Learning to think mathematically: Problem solving, metacognition, and sense-making in mathematics. In D. Grouws (Ed.), *Handbook of research on mathematics teaching and learning* (pp. 334–370). New York: MacMillan.

Schoenfeld, A. H. (1998a). Toward a theory of teaching-in-context. *Issues in Education, 4*(1), 1–94.

Schoenfeld, A. H. (1998b). Making mathematics and making pasta: From cookbook procedures to really cooking. In J. G. Greeno & S. V. Goldman (Eds.), *Thinking practices in mathematics and science learning* (pp. 299–319). Mahwah, NJ: Lawrence Erlbaum Associates.

Schoenfeld, A. H. (Special Issue Editor). (1999). *Examining the complexity of teaching* [Special issue]. *Journal of Mathematical Behavior, 18*(3).

Schoenfeld, A. H. (2000). Models of the teaching process. *Journal of Mathematical Behavior, 18*(3), 243–261.

Schoenfeld, A. H. (2002a). A highly interactive discourse structure. In J. Brophy (Ed.), *Advances in Research on Teaching: vol. 9. Social constructivist teaching: Its affordances and constraints* (pp. 131–170). New York: Elsevier.

Schoenfeld, A. H. (2002b). Making mathematics work for all children: Issues of standards, testing, and equity. *Educational researcher, 31*(1), 13–25.

Schoenfeld, A. H. (2004). The math wars. *Educational Policy, 18(1)*, 253–286.

Schoenfeld, A. H. (2005). Dilemmas/decisions: Can we model teachers' on-line decision-making? Manuscript submitted for publication.

Schoenfeld, A. H. (in press.) Design experiments. In P. B. Elmore, G. Camilli, & J. Green (Eds.), *Complementary methods for research in education.* Washington, DC: American Educational Research Association.

Schoenfeld, A. H. (in preparation). *Educational research and practice.*

Schoenfeld, A. H., Gamoran, M., Kessel, C., Leonard, M., Orbach, R., & Arcavi, A. (1992). Toward a comprehensive model of human tutoring in complex subject matter domains. *Journal of Mathematical Behavior, 11*(4), 293–320.

Schoenfeld, A. H., Minstrell, J., & van Zee, E. (2000).The detailed analysis of an established teacher carrying out a non-traditional lesson. *Journal of Mathematical Behavior, 18*(3), 281–325.

Senk, S., & Thompson, D. (Eds.). (2003). *Standards-oriented school mathematics curricula: What does the research say about student outcomes?* Mahwah, NJ: Lawrence Erlbaum Associates.

Sfard, A. (2000). Symbolizing mathematical reality into being: How mathematical discourse and mathematical objects create each other. In P. Cobb, E. Yackel, & K. McClain (Eds.), *Symbolizing and communicating: Perspectives on mathematical discourse, tools, and instructional design* (pp. 37–98). Mahwah, NJ: Lawrence Erlbaum Associates.

Sfard, A. (2001e). There is more to discourse than meets the ears: Learning from mathematical communication things that we have not known before. *Educational Studies in Mathematics, 46*(1/3), 13–57.

Sfard, A., & Kieran, C. (2001). Cognition as communication: Rethinking learning-by-talking through multi-faceted analysis of students' mathematical interactions. *Mind, Culture, and Activity, 8*(1), 42–76.

Sfard, A., & McLain, K. (2003). *Analyzing tools: Perspectives on the role of designed artifacts in mathematics learning* [Special issue]. *Journal of the learning Sciences, 11*(2&3).

Sherin, M. G. (2001). Developing a professional vision of classroom events. In T. Wood, B. S. Nelson, & J. Warfield (Eds.), *Beyond classical pedagogy: Teaching elementary school mathematics* (pp. 75–93). Mahwoh, NJ: Lawrence Erlbaum Associates.

Sherin, M. G. (2002). When teaching becomes learning. *Cognition and Instruction, 20*(2), 119–150.

Sherin, M. G. (2004). New perspectives on the role of video in teacher education. In J. Brophy (Ed.), *Using video in teacher education* (pp. 1–27). New York: Elsevier Science.

Sherin, M. G., & Han, S. Y. (2004). Teacher learning in the context of a video club. *Teaching and Teacher Education 20*, 163–183.

Shulman, Lee S. (1986). Those who understand: Knowledge growth in teaching. *Educational Researcher, 17*(1), 4–14.

Shulman, L. (1987). Knowledge and teaching: Foundations of the new reform. *Harvard Educational Review, 57*, 1–22.

Stigler, J.W., Gonzales, P., Kawanaka, T., Knoll, S., and Serrano, A. (1999). *The TIMSS videotape classroom study: Methods and findings from an exploratory research project on eighth-grade mathematics instruction in Germany, Japan, and the United States. (NCES 1999-074*, U.S. Department of Education). Washington, DC: National Center for Education Statistics.

Stigler, J., & Hiebert, J. (1999). *The teaching gap*. New York: Free Press.

Stokes, D. E. (1997). *Pasteur's quadrant: Basic science and technical innovation*. Washington, DC: Brookings.

Study of Instructional Improvement. (2002). *Measuring teachers' content knowledge for teaching: Elementary mathematics release items*. Ann Arbor: University of Michigan. Retrieved February 6, 2005, from http://www.sii.soe.umich.edu/instruments.html

Swafford, J. (2003). Reaction to high school curriculum projects' research. In Sharon Senk & Denisse Thompson (Eds.), *Standards-oriented school mathematics curricula: What does the research say about student outcomes?* (pp. 457–468). Mahwah, NJ: Lawrence Erlbaum Associates.

Tate, W. (1997). Race-ethnicity, SES, gender, and language proficiency trends in mathematics achievement: an update. *Journal for Research in Mathematics Education, 28*(6), 652–679.

Thorndike, E. L. (1931). *Human learning*. New York: Century.

U.S. House Committee on Science. (1998). *Unlocking our future: Toward a new national science policy. A report to Congress by the House Committee on Science*. Washington, DC: Author. See also http://www.house.gov/science/science_policy_report.htm

Viadero, D. (2004, August 11). Researchers question clearinghouse choices. *Education Week,* pp. 30–32.

Warren, B., Ballenger, C., Ogonowski, M., Rosebery, A., & Hudicourt-Barnes, J. (2001). Rethinking diversity in learning science: The logic of everyday sense-making. *Journal of Research in Science Teaching 38*: 1–24.

Warren, B., & Rosebery, A. (1995). Equity in the future tense: Redefining relationships among teachers, students, and science in linguistic minority classrooms. In W. Secada, E. Fennema & L. Adajian (Eds.), *New directions for equity in mathematics education* (pp. 298–328). New York: Cambridge University Press.

Wenger, E. (1998). *Communities of practice: Learning, meaning, and identity*. Cambridge: Cambridge University Press.

What Works Clearinghouse (2004a). Curriculum-based interventions for improving K-12 mathematics achievement—middle school. Retrieved February 27, 2005, from http://www.whatworks. ed.gov/

What Works Clearinghouse (2004b). Detailed study report: Baker, J. J. (1997). Effects of a generative instructional design strategy on learning mathematics and on attitudes towards achievement. Unpublished doctoral dissertation, University of Minnesota. Retrieved February 27, 2005, from http://www.whatworks.ed.gov/

What Works Clearinghouse (2004c). Detailed study report: Kerstyn, C. (2001). Evaluation of the I CAN LEARN Mathematics Classroom. First year of implementation (2000–2001 school year). Unpublished manuscript. Retrieved February 27, 2005, from http://www.whatworks.ed.gov/

Willis, P. (1977/1981). *Learning to labour. How working class kids get working class jobs*. Farnborough, Hants: Saxon House, 1977; New York: University Press, 1981

Yackel, E., & Cobb, P. (1996). Sociomathematical norms, argumentation, and autonomy in mathematics. *Journal for Research in Mathematics Education, 27*(4), 458–477.

SCIENCE EDUCATION: INTEGRATING VIEWS
OF LEARNING AND INSTRUCTION

Marcia C. Linn
University of California at Berkeley

Bat-Sheva Eylon
Weizmann Institute of Science

INTRODUCTION

Science education research has undergone a series of shifts and convergences in leadership and focus as described in the last handbook (Linn, Songer, & Eylon, 1996). Leadership in science education has shifted among discipline specialists, classroom teachers, curriculum designers, policymakers, and cognitive scientists. In the past decade, these shifts have stimulated a convergence on research partnerships that implement a system of shared leadership and respect the experiences and commitments of each stakeholder. These broader partnerships carry out investigations that underscore the systemic, interconnected nature of science education and address the full range of policy issues including curriculum standards, science topic sequences, assessment practices, equitable access to instruction, and the role of technology in science courses. Current partnerships offer more and more integrated views of learning and instruction.

The broader partnerships include members with expertise in fields such as technology, policy, sociology, anthropology, neuroscience, and the psychology of learning. These comprehensive partnerships study diverse sets of learners, multiple learning contexts, and a stunning array of issues. They examine science learning at schools, museums, zoos, aquariums, sports events, research laboratories, cultural environments, online chat rooms, and after school programs. Researchers investigate scientific thinking among teachers, students, athletic team members, home-schooled students, families, cultural groups, and every age group. Researchers explore connections among intuitions about scientific phenomena, beliefs about the nature of science, and perceptions of scientists, as well as notions of how to learn science. They study varied forms of instruction and methods of presenting material including computer simulations, models, collaboration, and debate. They use a broadening array of research methods suited to the complexity of the problem, including case studies, design studies, longitudinal investigations, and comparisons of promising alternatives.

The emerging research from these partnerships draws attention to the multiple ideas about science that learners amass, the tendency of students to localize their learning in specific contexts rather than integrating all the ideas they have about science, and the value of this variation for design of instruction. By stimulating fruitful grappling with multiple ideas and encouraging students to consider ideas linked to social, cultural, educational, or personal experiences, science instruction can set in motion a lifelong process of formulating, connecting, distinguishing, and investigating scientific conjectures. When varied scientific ideas bump up against each other, students have the potential of crafting criteria for distinguishing among them; instructional activities can encourage learners to build coherent criteria about scientific investigations, the nature of science, and science learning; and activities can focus students on creating cohesive views of science informed by these criteria.

Partnerships today place emphasis on lifelong learning, equitable opportunities to learn, and the fruitfulness of instruction for science-related decisions at home, at work, or in daily life. They have extended the goals for science education to include language literacy and technology literacy (American Association for the Advancement of Science, 1994; Bybee, 1997; National Research Council, 2000). They highlight elements of language learning relevant to science such as the challenges of learning from science texts, distinguishing the specialized meanings of science terminology, engaging in the discourse practices of science, appreciating the epistemological basis for scientific argumentation, and interpreting persuasive messages about such topics as genetically modified foods. They explore the role of technology in scientific advance and the impact of modern technologies such as computer programs, visualization tools, and probeware on learning (Snyder et al., 1999).

The diverse members of partnerships bring together a plethora of perspectives, frameworks, lenses or theories of science learning. This proliferation has motivated commentators to liken educational theories to toothbrushes—useful to their owner, but rarely shared. In this chapter we connect the emerging view of the learner to the developmental, sociocultural, cognitive, and constructivist lenses on the learner and note signs of a convergence that emphasizes the way students take advantage of the varied ideas they formulate. We refer to this as a knowledge integration perspective.

This convergence on a knowledge integration perspective stems from research practices that capture the interplay of multiple factors in learning contexts, emphasizes iterative refinement of instruction, and documents the trajectories of students and teachers. Partnerships conduct studies at varied levels of analyses and draw on emerging research methods such as brain imaging. Partnerships compare varied learning contexts, such as classrooms, museums, and psychology laboratories. Studies take advantage of technology-enhanced learning environments to compare well-controlled alternative forms of instruction. They study innovations such as modeling, collaborative learning, inquiry instruction, or real-time data collection in these learning environments. The environments offer embedded assessments to document student progress and provide day-to-day feedback to teachers.

These research practices enable more and more precise study of science learning and instruction.

Policy Issues

International assessment studies in science document the systemic, interconnected nature of education, while also signaling the importance of three policy issues: curriculum coverage, classroom activity structures, and assessment designs. The Third International Mathematics and Science Study suggests that mandating coverage of numerous topics each year might do more harm than good (Schmidt, Raizer, Britton, Bianchi, & Wolfe, 1997). Countries such as the United States, with standards calling for as many as 65 topics such as electricity, thermodynamics, mitosis, and the rock cycle in one year, generally have lower performing students than countries such as Japan that call for eight topics to be covered in the same time span (Linn, Tsuchida, Lewis, & Songer, 2000).

Classroom observation studies show that countries use distinctive activity structures that impact learning (Schmidt et al., 1997; Stigler & Hiebert, 1999). For example, Japanese classrooms emphasize reconciling the views of all students and negotiating a common view warranted by classroom experiments (C. Lewis, 1995; C. Lewis & Tsuchida, 1998).

Innovative curriculum materials call for the same activity structures that Japanese classrooms emphasize. However, observations in America show that most classrooms focus on reinforcing normative ideas by following an instructional pattern that involves motivating students with an attention-grabbing event, informing students about normative ideas, and assessing whether students recall the normative ideas, a pattern that could be called *motivate*, *inform*, and *assess* (Stigler & Hiebert, 1999). Analyses of high-stakes assessments, including the assessments used in international studies, reveal limits to their sensitivity to instruction that calls for understanding of the discipline and problems with the message they send to textbook publishers and teachers (Heubert & Hauser, 1998). Multiple-choice items that appear to require recall of facts turn out to be much less sensitive to instruction emphasizing understanding than assessments that require generation of short answers (Clark & Linn, 2003). These recall items also reinforce the idea that science instruction should focus on the learning of vocabulary and facts. In contrast, cognitive research shows that such instruction misleads students and their teachers into thinking that they have learned and understood the material, when actually it is rapidly forgotten (Bjork, 1999). Instruction that requires students to make predictions, generate arguments, critique experiments, or design solutions leads to far more desirable learning (Bjork, 1994, 1999).

Researchers are beginning to develop more sensitive assessments that detect the impact of curriculum materials, preparation of teachers, technology-enhanced instruction, standards, and sequences of topics in the knowledge integration of students and teachers. These new assessments clarify which activity structures promote understanding. When used in longitudinal research, they document the limits of the traditional instructional pattern (motivate, inform, and assess).

Chapter Focus

In summary, results from the partnerships that have emerged in the past decade offer a fresh view of science learning and instruction that emphasizes knowledge integration. This chapter documents the emerging view of the learner, illustrates the varieties of ideas about science that students formulate, and shows how these ideas provide fertile ground for science instruction. We synthesize instructional research that often includes iterative refinement studies carried out in complex settings where the systemic character of education can be explored. We capture instructional findings in design patterns that emphasize ways to encourage students to explore, connect, and sort out their varied ideas about scientific phenomena. We define *design patterns* as tested sequences of learning activities, such as discussing, modeling, or reading, that take advantage of the variety of student ideas and promote integrated understanding. We argue that design patterns represent a form of research synthesis that can help the field capture partnership research and affect educational policies. These research findings have important implications for educational policy.

This chapter synthesizes findings in science education to inform the view of the learner and the design of instruction. This review is selective rather than exhaustive. We select studies from research programs and comprehensive investigations that look at education as a systemic process. We highlight case studies of learners, longitudinal studies of the trajectories of students, and design studies that investigate comprehensive curriculum innovations.

We primarily rely on work reported in the past decade. We seek research conducted in varied countries and with diverse students. We emphasize research on middle and high school students. We mention studies of higher education as they become relevant and especially when they include preservice teachers. We also draw on elementary education research that seeks to affect lifelong learning. We emphasize research that takes advantage of emerging research methods, including technology-enhanced approaches. We connect to issues covered in other chapters such as professional development, teacher learning, diversity, assessment, educational administration, policy, and research methods, but do not have space to review the research in these areas.

VIEW OF THE LEARNER

The broadening of partnerships, appreciation for the systemic nature of education, and emerging research methods have shifted research on the science learner toward two related themes. First, case studies and surveys of student views of science topics reveal the rich *repertoire* of ideas students formulate about each topic and challenge instructors to help students sort out their ideas. We use the term *idea* to refer to each view held by the learner. We include descriptive, complex, mathematical, visual, and analogical views. The repertoire includes ideas that arise in distinct contexts, ideas at varied levels of analyses, ideas that many students hold, and unique ideas often tied to a specific context. We highlight four central varieties of ideas—ideas about the discipline, the nature of investigation, the nature of science and scientists, and the nature of science learning.

Second, research on origins of the ideas in the repertoire underscores the multiple perspectives on science learning in the field. We highlight developmental, sociocultural, cognitive, and constructivist research and discuss how current findings are converging on a view of learners as grappling with varied ideas and as benefiting from sorting out the alternatives they encounter. We argue that, by merging these perspectives, we gain a more comprehensive understanding of science learning.

Case Studies Illustrating the Repertoire of Ideas

Inspired by Piaget (Inhelder & Piaget, 1958), researchers have documented the wide range of ideas students articulate in every aspect of science (Eylon & Linn, 1988; Pfundt & Duit, 1991). In the past decade, researchers have studied learners of varied ages (e.g., Howe, 1998; McDermott, 2001; Metz, 2000), teachers (Davis, 2003a; Shepard, 2000; Van Zee, 1998), participants in science laboratories (Dunbar, 1995; Holyoak & Thagard, 1995; Latour, 1998), museum visitors (Leinhardt, Crowley, & Knutson, 2002), families (Ochs & Capps, 2000), online chat users (Barron, 2000), and students in classrooms (Linn & Hsi, 2000).

They show that learners gain ideas in multiple contexts and often keep ideas isolated in their context of origin.

The broadening leadership of research partnerships to include philosophers of science, historians of science, anthropologists, and social psychologists has drawn attention to the multiple origins of ideas about science (Bell & Linn, 2000; diSessa, Elby, & Hammer, 2002; Knorr Cetina, 1995; Latour, 1998; Lin, 2001; Palinscar, Magnusson, & Cutter, 2001; Rosebery & Warren, 1998). Research on diverse cultural groups reveals contextually derived ideas based on language, beliefs, navigation techniques, cooking methods, and agricultural practices (Calabrese Barton, 2003; Fadiman, 1997; C. Lee, 1997; O. Lee & Fradd, 1998; Moschkovich, 1999). These studies underscore the importance of eliciting and respecting student ideas and taking advantage of the variation in ideas.

Recent case studies of learners track how ideas emerge. Researchers have conducted microgenic analyses of learning (diSessa, 2000; Metz, 2000), analyzed video case studies of students and teachers (Ball, 1996; Davis, 2003b; Minstrell & Van Zee, 2000; Van Zee, 2000), and used interviews to document how ideas develop over time (Carey, 1992; Clark & Linn, 2003; diSessa, 2000; E. Lewis & Linn, 1994; Linn & Hsi, 2000; Tabak, 2004). These researchers emphasize the efforts of the learner to make sense of their varied views and illustrate the complexities of this process (Bransford, Brown, & Cocking, 1999).

Howe emphasizes that students formulate multiple unique views. Howe (C. Howe, Tolmie, Duchak-Tanner, & Rattray, 2000; C. Howe & Tolmie, 2003) interviewed students age 6 to 15 about scientific phenomena such as buoyancy, heat transfer, motion, and force. As a group, the students hold an impressive array of views. For example, she reports that students age 8 to 12 generated more than 200 unique ideas relevant to buoyancy. Individual students mentioned between 5 and 15 ideas about buoyancy. Students form separate ideas about the shape of the object, the orientation of the object [balanced, stuck to the top], the surface of the object [smooth, prickly], the constitution of the object [metal, wood], the contents [holes, points], the temperature [of object and liquid], the movement [of objects and liquid], and other idiosyncrasies [glass cannot be seen so cannot push it down; icebergs float because they have been here a long time]. She found that students separate ideas by context and also link ideas when they bump up against each other.

Metz reports a similar plethora of ideas about science investigations and science topics among young children participating in an inquiry-oriented curriculum. Metz studied second, fourth, and fifth graders as they conducted structured and independent investigations about the behavior of organisms such as crickets. In the structured investigations, one group of three students postu-

lated that temperature, light, and the proximity of kids could explain the frequency of chirping. Others, trying to explain where crickets would go if released, identified location (natural habitat, asphalt, sand, shade), proximity to others (crickets, kids, insects), and weather (heat, cold, dampness) as possible factors. In the individually initiated investigations, students compared ideas about the behavior of organisms. They held numerous ideas about how to find out more about organisms. Students speculated that the answer would be different depending on the context (playground, terrarium, classroom) and the nature of the investigation, mentioning imprecise measurement, artificial lab conditions, order effects, range of conditions, or idiosyncratic behavior. Metz points out that student ideas are similar across the different age groups but vary by understanding of the context.

diSessa (1988) argues that scientific knowledge held by students is fragile and fragmented. He supports this point in analysis of case studies of undergraduate physics students. An analysis of seven interviews with a student called J shows that she provides multiple interpretations of the same events in the same interview and seems to accept all these views as reasonable explanations for the scientific events (diSessa et al., 2002). For example, J is asked to explain the forces on a ball tossed in the air and caught. She twice argues that after the hand released the ball, there would be only one force on the ball—gravity. When asked about what happens at the peak of the toss she argues that the force pulling the ball up and the gravity pulling the ball down are equal. She also says that the upward force can only last so long. When prompted to think about acceleration, J articulates the view she learned in physics class—that there is only one force and it is gravity. However, another prompt recalling an earlier drawing leads J to return to the two-force explanation. The authors note that the surprising aspect of this rapid change of explanations is that J does not see this as changing her mind—rather she sees it as changing her language. The varied explanations articulated in all these studies resonate with research identifying the repertoire of ideas students formulate about heat and temperature (Clark & Linn, 2003; Linn & Hsi, 2000). Clark used Minstrell's (1992) notion of facets to track student ideas over a span of 5 years. He shows that students typically report anywhere from 10 to 25 views of heat at each interview. Students report that heat flows, that cold flows, that heat is absorbed, that air is a barrier that prevents heat flow, that heat only flows through air, that objects have their own temperature, and numerous other ideas. During instruction, students add normative ideas, including ideas about how to investigate thermal phenomena and ideas about how to learn science. By the end of instruction, students have connected many of their normative ideas in cohesive accounts and often neglect their more idiosyncratic ideas. The longitudinal interviews document a process of building more cohesive ideas about thermal phenomena, connecting ideas about methods of investigation to ideas about thermal phenomena, and continuing to sort out ideas into coherent views of aspects of investigative methods, the nature of science, and science learning.

Many additional researchers report on the varied ideas held by students in science and other disciplines. Siegler (1996) analyzes research from mathematics, biology, reading, memory, and physics to show the wide variability in student ideas for complex tasks as well as for simple arithmetic problems. Siegler reports on students who give alternative answers to the same question within minutes of each other—and do not see this as problematic. Siegler argues for the value of variability in student ideas and advocates instruction that takes advantage of the efforts individuals devote to dealing with their diverse ideas.

We discuss four emerging and established varieties of ideas that deserve attention in science learning. Students benefit when they develop cohesive ideas about, for example, scientific investigation, but they also need to connect these ideas to the varied problems that scientists research. Methods for studying the rock cycle need to be distinguished from methods for studying the factors influencing the movement of a train.

Ideas About Disciplinary Phenomena. Student ideas about the disciplines have been studied extensively. Researchers have compiled lists of alternative views (Driver, Newton, & Osborne, 1996; Pfundt & Duit, 1991). Students build varied views of concepts and processes such as force, atoms, DNA, the rock cycle, power generation, evolution, phase change, or mitosis. Students may hold descriptive perspectives, such as *to see the eye emits light*, as well as scientifically normative perspectives, such as *objects need to be illuminated for the eye to detect them* (Bell, 2004b; Langley, Ronen, & Eylon, 1997).

To illustrate, students learning about electricity often have colloquial, schoolish, and intuitive ideas about concepts such as current, voltage, and batteries (Grayson, 1996). For batteries, students report that bulbs use up all the current, that charging a battery adds electrons, and that batteries store charge so it can flow in wires. For electrical circuits, most people think of electricity as flowing from the wall to the wires, often believing that electricity is a substance, possibly made up of electrons (Slotta, Chi, & Joram, 1995). Students may also think that the two wires going from battery to bulb supply positive and negative charges that combine to fuel the bulb, a view often referred to as "clashing currents" (Driver, Leach, Millar, & Scott, 1996). Dave Barry (2001) captures popular views

by remarking, "We know from our junior high school science training that electricity is actually a fast-moving herd of electrons, which are tiny one-celled animals that can survive in almost any environment except inside a AA battery, where they die within minutes." These rich and contradictory ideas include both fleeting and enduring views. They include ideas that generate useful predictions and help with household trouble-shooting as well as ideas that stand in the way of future learning. Sorting out these ideas strengthens scientific understanding.

Ideas About Scientific Investigation. Students link conceptions about science investigations to their views of scientific phenomena. They acquire ideas about how to research a conjecture, distinguish evidence and hypotheses, form an argument, communicate to an audience, interpret findings, or identify a research question (Klahr, 2000; Krajcik, Blumenfeld, Marx, & Soloway, 1999; Redish, 2003). They often connect strategies such as controlling variables, repeating demonstrations, seeking evidence, or testing ideas to the scientific topic (Dunbar & Fugelsang, 2004; Feldman, Konold, & Coulter, 2000; Polman, 2000; Ranney & Schank, 1995). Students generally agree about how to create a fair footrace or determine which cake tastes best. Many students report that controlled experiments have their place, as do other techniques for establishing scientific validity. Students may argue that you need to control the surface of the ramp to find out which car will go faster down an inclined plane, but ignore evidence that plants were grown in different locations in the garden when determining which fertilizer is best. Students may also argue that problems involving inspection of the scientific record, such as dinosaur extinction or earthquake prediction, are not amenable to scientific study because conditions cannot be varied.

By connecting ideas about investigations and the scientific discipline students create a wealth of possibilities. For example, in the topic of electricity, students' varied ideas about how electricity works connect to multiple ideas about investigative activities (Vreman de-Olde & de Jong, 2004; Wallace, Hand, & Yang, 2004). Effective instruction should help students sort out these ideas. Many teachers give up on student-initiated investigations because of this variety in ideas. They find it difficult to respond to the numerous questions students ask and become frustrated when students copy each other's experiments. Rather than encouraging students to make sense of their varied ideas, many texts provide step-by-step recipes. As a result, students may not gather any evidence to help them understand science. Design of effective, consequential, and manageable experiments is very difficult. For example, in exploring batteries, bulbs, and wires, students who believe in clashing currents may connect three bulbs in series and conclude that the other two bulbs light slightly faster, whereas those who support the idea that electricity flows in one direction may look at the same experiment and conclude that the bulbs light sequentially (Chinn & Brewer, 1993; Gauld, 1989). These groups need new models of electricity and more effective experimental materials to resolve the dilemma. These dilemmas do, however, resonate with difficulties faced by scientists historically (Holyoak & Thagard, 1995).

Ideas About the Nature of Science and Scientists. Students develop varied ideas about how science progresses, how scientists establish valid results, how scientists select topics for study, and how laboratories work— *epistemological* ideas (Hammer & Elby, 2003; Hofer & Pintrich, 2002; Latour, 1998). These ideas about the nature of scientific advance, the role of theories, and behavior of scientists often connect to scientific methods and disciplines and shape reasoning (e.g., Bell & Linn, 2000). Students' ideas about scientists' notebooks reveal their varied ideas about planning and executing experiments (e.g., de Carvalho, 2004; Kafai & Resnick, 1996; Palinscar et al., 2001; Webb & Palinscar, 1996). Researchers who initially thought that views of the nature of science were enduring traits are now recognizing that these views are linked to specific science topics or contexts (e.g., Hofer & Pintrich, 2002).

Impoverished and fragmented views of the nature of scientific research—assuming that science unfolds, that scientists disagree most of the time, that disagreements cannot be resolved, that all disputes are resolved by empirical experiments, or that results from investigations lack errors—can thwart reasoning. Students may link beliefs about how scientists interpret results to their own ideas about interpreting scientific phenomena. Students who build cohesive ideas about the nature of science— reporting that findings are tenuous and could be refuted by a future experiment—are more likely to sort out their own ideas (Linn & Eylon, 2000; Songer & Linn, 1992).

Many students hold impoverished views of the nature of science, yet these ideas are essential today. For example, the cacophony of advertisements for new drugs requires deep understanding of the nature of science. In electricity, Vreman de-Olde and de Jong (2004) report that when students were required to design investigations for other students learning electricity, they represented the work of exploring new topics as involving recall or computation, rather than experimentation, 61 percent of the time. Helping students build cohesive ideas about science that bridge specific disciplines and apply in new contexts has both educational and practical benefits.

Ideas About the Nature of Science Learning. Students develop ideas about their own science learning, about how to monitor progress, about the value of memorizing, or about how to deploy personal resources. Recent research reveals that students have varied and discipline-specific ideas about how to interpret their progress, often relying on superficial indicators such as ease of understanding (Bjork, 1999; Hammer & Elby, 2003; Langley & Eylon, in press; Lin, 2001; Linn & Hsi, 2000; Redish, 2003; Sternberg, 2004). Students also develop ideas about who can learn science and about the difficulty of each discipline. For example, some students view physics less favorably than biology (Spall, Stanisstreet, Dickson, & Boyes, 2004) or assert that women are less likely to succeed than men in science (AAUW, 2000; Seymour & Hewitt, 1994). Students have views of the role of the social context, often reporting that their success or satisfaction depends on the teacher, peer group, opportunity to collaborate, or opportunity to engage in debate (Margolis & Fisher, 2001).

In learning a topic such as electricity, students often prefer to add conflicting ideas rather than monitoring their progress or resolving inconsistencies. Students may lack understanding of the role of analysis. In a case study of students learning about electric currents, the instructor makes links between each aspect of a water system and experiments on parallel circuits (Paatz, Ryder, Schwedes, & Scott, 2004). The student relies solely on the water analogy, rather than make links.

Blurring the Boundaries and Linking Ideas. Studies in multiple contexts blur the boundaries between varieties of ideas and show the importance of focusing knowledge integration so students can generalize ideas. Controversy has arisen about the boundaries between, for example, science concepts and investigation strategies. Some see the contextualized nature of learning as predominating— linking methods of investigation primarily to the learning context (Greeno, Collins, & Resnick, 1996)—whereas others argue that students can learn strategies that generalize (Klahr & Nigam, 2004). Both views deserve respect. Students have a variety of ideas about investigation— some linked to the context and some connected to a view of the scientific method. The authentic, messy examples from student experience capture important details about the natural world (Linn & Hsi, 2000). The parsimonious principles and decontextualized examples that are often called the scientific method often lack the nuances students need to make sense of research in new domains, but can help sort out conflicting examples. To promote effective investigations in new contexts, instruction needs to take advantage of the variation in ideas and help learners create a robust, integrated understanding of scientific evidence, strategies, and investigations. Students are then poised to connect this rich view to new scientific questions.

Origins and Trajectories of Student Ideas

Research programs on the origins and trajectories of student ideas about science come from developmental, sociocultural, cognitive, and constructivist perspectives. The disparate commitments, methods, and terminologies have impeded collaboration across perspectives (Eylon & Linn, 1988). In the past decade we note a convergence on a view that respects the diversity of ideas learners formulate, sees value in enabling these ideas to bump up against each other, and recognizes the importance of designing instruction so students integrate their ideas.

Developmental Perspective. Piaget (Inhelder & Piaget, 1958) pioneered in characterizing the origins of student ideas and describing rapid developmental transitions. Piaget described an equilibrium in student reasoning at concrete operations for much of the early school years, a rapid transition, and an equilibrium at formal operations in adolescence. Piaget (1970) argued that only at formal operations do students become capable of questioning their ideas, making conjectures, appreciating the methods of natural science, identifying contradictions, and reasoning abstractly, consistent with the practices in natural science.

Recent research revisits the issues of developmental transitions. Klahr and his collaborators (Klahr & Nigam, 2004; Masnick & Klahr, 2003) show that elementary school students can add a controlling variables strategy to their repertoire and generalize it across contexts. Students can see parallels in manipulating variables influencing how fast cars descend ramps or boats travel in water. These results resonate with historical findings of Case (1985) and others that cast doubt on a strict interpretation of the Piagetian view.

The *theory-theory* perspective, inspired by T. Kuhn's (1970) depiction of scientific revolutions, focuses on transitions, consistent with the Piagetian view. Researchers argue that students exploring complex concepts such as the shape of the earth, electricity, or thermodynamics protect their intuitive views (Carey, 1992; Gopnik & Wellman, 1994; Vosniadou, 2002; Vosniadou & Brewer, 1992). For example, Vosniadou argues that students develop coherent explanations that interfere with appreciation of alternatives. They view students who defend their views that the earth is round like a pancake as requiring a scientific revolution to abandon this view.

Researchers reanalyzing and replicating these studies see a more responsive sense-making process. diSessa (diSessa, Gillespie, & Esterly, in press) reanalyzes some of Vosniadou's results and provides evidence that students have fragmented knowledge, rather than strong theories. Analyses that identify a single view that best describes the ideas of a student obscure the variation in ideas. Many studies show that learners' ideas are less coherent than scientists' ideas. Although students do hold on to some ideas in the repertoire more strongly than others, they also appear to hold contradictory ideas about the same phenomena.

Similarly, researchers studying concepts that depend on emergent properties such as heat and electricity argue that a non-normative ontological category, viewing heat and electricity as substances, impedes learning in these domains (Chi & Roscoe, 2002). Chi documents the substance-based views of heat and electricity that many students hold and argues that this view prevents transition to the scientifically normative view that heat and electricity are constraint-based systems.

Others studying scientific phenomena, such as traffic jams, that also have emergent properties argue that learners have a centralized mind-set but respond well to instruction offering alternatives (Resnick, 1994). Resnick shows how students—and experts—frequently interpret emergent processes, such as the behavior of ants in ant colonies or birds in flocks, as governed by a centralized plan rather than a set of constraints. Resnick creates simulations to show that these processes emerge as each ant or bird follows a straightforward rule (such as *fly behind the bird you can see*). Traffic jams can emerge when a driver enters the highway and maintains a different velocity from the group while each driver follows the rule that they should remain 10 car lengths behind the car in front of them. These simulations help learners sort out centralized and emergent processes.

In summary, Piaget's developmental perspective stresses an equilibrium at concrete and formal operations and rapid transitions between stages. Followers of this perspective have gleaned important insights from studies of specific transitions. The constructivist perspective revisits these issues but emphasizes the intentions of the learner rather than the constraints of development.

Sociocultural Perspective. Vygotsky (1978) spurred science educators to recognize the sociocultural perspective, as reflected in the impact of families, peers, and popular culture on learning. This view resonates with Dewey's (1901) position that all learning is social. Many research scientists privilege the empirical bases of scientific advance and question the idea that knowledge is socially constructed (Keller, 1993). This tension has ramifications for design of instruction and understanding of student learning. Recently, partnerships have begun to research the sociocultural basis of science learning and to identify ways to resolve the tension.

Vygotsky described the *zone of proximal development* as the progress a learner could make with the help of other learners. Researchers have refined this notion, showing how peers shape ideas of others, demonstrating how learners can specialize to advance each other's understanding, and explaining how even unsophisticated collaborators can help learners consider alternatives (Brown & Campione, 1994; Greeno et al., 1996; Lee & Songer, 2003; Palinscar et al., 2001; Rosebery & Warren, 1998).

The sociocultural perspective clarifies the origins of ideas students add to their repertoire and also highlights the mechanisms that can enable knowledge integration. Students gain rich, compelling, and generative scientific ideas in their everyday lives, but the culture of the science class may stifle these ideas and lead learners to distinguish school and out-of-school learning (Hofer & Pintrich, 2002). Thus, students report that memorizing is better than understanding science and that everything in the science textbook is true, consistent with texts and assessment practices in their schools (Bell & Linn, 2000; Hammer & Elby, 2003). Students often view scientific experiments as uncovering knowledge rather than part of a process aimed at interpreting anomalies. Many classroom experiments that involve following a procedure confirm this view (Hammer, 2000). Students report either that science is everywhere or that science is not relevant to their lives, often pointing out that they have never used the material they learned in science (Hofer & Pintrich, 2002; Linn & Hsi, 2000).

Including a rich variety of scientific ideas can improve learners' ability to interpret media coverage of science, including advertisements. Citizens have become more and more aware that advances in health care might be essential for the treatment of their disease while at the same time encountering a bewildering array of carefully worded persuasive messages that may confuse rather than inform (Bell, 2004b). Media depictions of science may deter students from analyzing scientific claims if neglected in science learning.

Researchers show that when instruction privileges specific cultural perspectives, students who do not share these views can feel excluded and even alienated from science. In contrast, instruction that respects and builds on these ideas can help many more students succeed (AAUW, 2000; Linn & Hsi, 2000; Rosebery & Warren, 1998).

The tension between sociocultural perspectives on the learner and traditional instructional practice plays out dramatically when students formulate ideas based on colloquial usage of language (Mason, 2001). Designing instruction to take advantage of the variety of ideas captured in diverse forms of language can promote understanding (Linn & Hsi, 2000; Moschkovich, 1999; Rosebery & Warren, 1998) or cloud reasoning (Linn & Burbules, 1993). Students' everyday usage of terms such as *force, model, evolution, reproduction, catalyst,* and *bond* confuse scientific discussions. Students may say that heat and temperature are the same because the terms can be used interchangeably. They may assert that streams and fires are alive because they grow, die, or move. They may conflate current, voltage, and electricity because these terms are often used interchangeably in everyday discourse. Students may mimic experts and use scientific-sounding terms to enhance their sophistication, even when they are fully aware that they have no clear understanding of the meaning of the word (Grayson, 1996). When students try out scientific terms such as *force, acceleration, velocity, genetics, energy,* or *evolution* without a clear sense of their meaning, they can engage in a rich sociocultural process of negotiating understanding or they could reinforce non-normative practices.

The sociocultural perspective draws attention to power relationships and their role in establishing stereotypes about who can succeed in science. Those in power tend to prefer collaboration with others who resemble them. Media depictions strengthen bias, often emphasizing differences between males and females or between underrepresented and overrepresented groups. Research shows that these stereotypes, when activated, can affect performance of students from underrepresented groups on high-stakes tests such as the SAT, influence judgments of essays, and affect hiring decisions (Bargh, 2001; Crouch & Mazur, 2001; Steele, 1999).

In summary, the sociocultural perspective helps explain the sources of ideas that students formulate about science. By encouraging students to consider these ideas along with instructed ideas, science classes can help the classroom community build accounts of science that apply to situations they encounter regularly. By respecting the ideas students bring to science class, instructors communicate their respect for each student and reach out to cultural groups who might feel marginalized by traditional instruction. This respect is also a feature of the constructivist perspective.

Cognitive Perspective. The cognitive perspective on the learner contributes a long history of research on remembering and forgetting that helps explain how students form their repertoire and select ideas to apply in different contexts. Starting with short-term laboratory studies using word lists or nonsense syllables, research has progressed to include longer retention intervals and more complex material.

Recently, Lagemann (2000) analyzed the impact of early cognitive research led by Thorndike. Lagemann argues that this research led to educational practices such as the traditional science education pattern described as *motivate*, *inform*, and *assess* in the introduction. Texts that articulate expert ideas and emphasize scientific vocabulary reflect this research tradition. Recent partnerships between cognitive researchers and science educators have explored the role of analogies, desirable difficulties, and visualizations in complex settings. These studies show that recall is not sufficient for solving complex problems and illustrate mechanisms important for instructional design.

Research on analogies offers a mechanism to explain how students add ideas to their repertoire. Students make productive analogies, applying scientific principles such as conservation of energy from one setting to another or comparing electricity to heat. They also make unproductive analogies, between heat and temperature, trajectories of released and thrown balls, or intentional behavior of humans and physical properties of objects (Cooke & Breedin, 1994; diSessa, 2000; Linn & Hsi, 2000; McDermott, 2001). Research comparing forms of analogies shows benefit from animated and visual representations (Pedone, Hummel, & Holyoak, 2001). These studies distinguish the roles of specific parts of the brain and underscore the importance of activating the right pathways for certain forms of learning (Baddeley & Longman, 1978; Bilkey, 2004; Shonkoff & Phillips, 2000). Advances in cognitive neuroscience help explain how animated and visual representations can spur learners to form more coherent ideas (Holyoak & Thagard, 1995; Koedinger & Anderson, 1998; Linn, 2005).

Research on analogies points to the importance of selecting the right analogies to add to the repertoire and encouraging analyses of analogies. Holyoak and Hummel (2001) report that teachers in the United States and other countries regularly use analogies to explain mathematical and scientific phenomena, but find that students rarely comprehend the analogies. Research on the characteristics of ideal analogies suggest criteria for selecting generative analogies (Linn, 2005; Pedone, Hummel, & Holyoak, 2001). Research also suggests the value of encouraging students to generate and test analogies. Linn and Eylon (1996) report that students can productively generate and reformulate their own analogies. In their case study a student makes analogies between the size of holes in sweaters, blankets, or shawls and the ability of the material to insulate. Initially, the student makes an analogy between the hole and a door, assuming that a hole would let heat flow out. Later, this student adds a new analogy between a hole and a bubble and develops a more normative idea of the hole as potentially creating a bubble of still air. Research in cognitive neuroscience has drawn attention to multiple interacting systems in the brain.

Cognitive research on remembering and forgetting helps explain how students select and retain ideas in their repertoire. The well-established advantages of spaced over massed practice clarify why students remember everyday science ideas that they encounter regularly over classroom ideas covered in a single week of instruction. The research on advantages of interleaving topics rather than studying topics sequentially raises complex issues. If students fail to understand material before the next topic is initiated, interleaving does not help. Both spacing and interleaving point to the problems with fleeting coverage of science topics and the advantages of cumulative testing (Bjork, 1999).

Cognitive research on generation effects help clarify how students develop ideas about their own science learning. When students are asked to generate ideas during learning, by giving predictions, explanations, short answers to test items, or arguments, they make more errors than when they are only required to read or repeat material. These generation activities slow learning. They often mislead students into thinking that the course is too difficult and lead instructors to question their teaching methods. Generation activities slow learning but improve long-term retention (Bjork, 1994, 1999; Kintsch, 1998; Linn & Hsi, 2000). This research highlights the role of generation in helping students recognize the material that they do not understand and in sorting out their ideas. When students need to process jumbled text (Kintsch, 1998) or deal with interleaved sequences of topics, they have the opportunity to organize the information and recognize gaps (Richland, Bjork, Finley, & Linn, 2005). Students who succeed learn to monitor their progress and develop insights into their own learning.

In summary, cognitive research initially studied memory, reinforcing the idea that learners absorb information. Today, partnerships explore memory, reinforcing the idea that students build a repertoire of ideas and need opportunities such as generation to sort out their diverse views and ideas from well-constructed analogies to improve understanding.

Constructivist Perspective. The constructivist perspective explains how the intentional efforts of learners to make sense of complex social, disciplinary, and cultural settings contribute to scientific understanding. Researchers emphasize that learners draw on epistemic, evidentiary, and interpersonal aspects of these settings. Students formulate ideas about how they learn, how to learn from peers, and what counts as evidence in science.

The constructivist perspective merges Piaget's (1970) account of structuralism and Vygotsky's (1978) analysis of the role of the social context in interpreting the natural world. Researchers following this perspective focus on how learners' own activities enable them to handle complex science disciplines, rich social contexts, and sustained investigations.

The constructivist perspective focuses on the compelling connections students make between their ideas about the natural world, the nature of science, science methods, and their own learning. Many explorations of the natural world reinforce alternatives to normative scientific views. Students observe that metals feel cold to the touch at room temperature and conclude that metal might have the property of imparting cold (Lewis, 1996). Students observe that plants generally need soil to grow and conclude that plants eat dirt (Williams, Linn, Ammon, & Gearhart, 2004). In studying electricity, students plug in appliances and see that what appears to be a single wire delivering power. They toss a coin and observe that the coin continues in the direction it was tossed, assuming that it retains a force in that direction. Constructivist researchers design learning so students refine these observations, encounter alternate interpretations, and become more sophisticated about gathering evidence to distinguish ideas.

Constructivist research emphasizes that students grapple with multiple ideas and often contextualize their views, interpreting their experiences as more localized or more general than the normative view. Many have shown that students distinguish science class ideas from ideas developed outside of class (e.g., Gilbert & Boulter, 2000). Some students describe heat as flowing at a macroscopic level and think that this same process extends to the microscopic level (Lewis & Linn, 1994). Others hold a descriptive heat flow model along with a constraint-based microscopic model (Linn & Muilenburg, 1996). Students may contextualize ovens and freezers as separate environments rather than concluding that thermal equilibrium applies to each. Harnessing these efforts to construct understanding is the focus of the constructivist research program.

Constructivism has motivated a series of frameworks that draw attention to the intentional activities of learners as they construct meaning and to the promising links and connections students can make among the varieties of ideas about science, including disciplinary, epistemological, metacognitive, and investigative views. *Intentional learning* (Bereiter & Scardamalia, 1989) focuses on the commitments of the learner in the context of a social group. Successful learners intentionally guide their own learning. Instruction supporting intentional learning scaffolds students by prompting them to consider epistemic,

evidentiary, and metacognitive ideas. *Cognitive apprenticeship* (Collins, Brown, & Holum, 1988) draws on successful instructional programs to explain why students benefit from working on complex, authentic problems, succeed when they are scaffolded in performing complex tasks until they can perform the whole task on their own, profit from investigating meaning in collaboration with others, and sustain their understanding when they develop metacognitive abilities. This research illustrates the complexity of science learning and draws attention to the need for research methods aligned with the complexity of the tasks. *Situated cognition* (Greeno et al., 1996) stresses that student ideas become entwined in the context of learning and emphasizes the importance of drawing on realistic, appropriately complex tasks and activities to understand how students make sense of novel contexts. This research helps explain why learners have difficulty applying knowledge to new problems, disciplines, or topics. The *fostering communities of learners* research program (Brown & Campione, 1994) shows how individuals can help each other learn, building on Vygotsky's zone of proximal development notion discussed earlier. By encouraging students to specialize in one aspect of a problem, individuals can help each other make sense of complex situations. In addition, peers can help learners monitor progress, critique accounts of science, and sustain the process of considering alternatives. *Conceptual change* researchers focus on the times when students abandon one idea for another (Strike & Posner, 1985). Consistent with the theory-theory view, researchers argue that when students recognize the limitations of their existing ideas, learn an alternative, and understand the strength of the alternative idea, they prefer the new idea. This view suggests that cognitive conflict can motivate students to endorse new ideas. Research supporting conceptual change draws on evidence that students frequently develop the same non-normative ideas. In the Children's Learning in Science program, Driver (Driver et al., 1996) shows that when students learn that circuits can explain phenomena that the clashing current or source-receiver view does not elucidate, they recognize the value of the new idea and embrace it. Many research investigations, however, show that students are fickle—changing their ideas more rapidly than this theory suggests and retaining both old and new ideas (diSessa & Sherin, 1998). diSessa offers an alternative to conceptual change for explaining the ideas that students construct. diSessa synthesizes studies of the ideas held by many high school and college students to show that student ideas have multiple origins, can be brittle, and lack coordination. He describes learners (such as J, discussed previously) as having *knowledge in pieces*. diSessa defines phenomenological primitives ("p-prims" for short) as descriptive accounts of the natural world. Often, these ideas lead to reasonable predictions in everyday situations, even though they do not accurately depict underlying scientific concepts. diSessa has shown that these ideas are contextually grounded and loosely connected to other ideas. Some p-prims have similar characteristics, such as *light dies out* or *sound dies out*. Frequently, p-prims reflect specific experiences. Students often conclude that light dies out because they cannot see it as they go farther from the source. Minstrell (Minstrell & Van Zee, 2000), inspired by the knowledge in pieces view, has identified *facets*, a taxonomy of student ideas, for many domains of physics. He describes facets as emergent ideas that are often weakly held. He shows how these facets can be organized by their proximity to normative ideas. Stavy and Tirosh (2000) take a similar position, proposing that intuitive logical rules such as *everything can be divided endlessly* are often overgeneralized and lead to misconceptions about such things as elementary particles. These rules explain why learners react in similar ways to unrelated situations and predict students' responses to scientific and mathematical problem-solving tasks.

Scaffolded knowledge integration (Linn, 1995; Linn & Hsi, 2000) emphasizes that students generate multiple ideas about scientific phenomena, scientific methods, their own learning, and the nature of science. Learners link and connect these ideas in response to the context, comments of peers, and instructional demands. Effective instruction encourages learners to use evidence to test and reformulate their ideas and to monitor their own progress.

In summary, the constructivist perspective stresses the effort that students expend to make sense of the natural world. It resonates with research showing that the intuitive ideas students formulate tend to remain in the repertoire even when normative ideas are added (Clark & Linn, 2003; diSessa & Sherin, 1998; Linn & Hsi, 2000). It is consistent with reports that students often seem unperturbed when shown that their ideas do not converge or align with scientific principles.

Constructivism attests to the complexity of students' ideas and to the multiple alternatives for dealing with this complexity. When students value coherence, they will look for contradictions. When they value connections, they often create boundaries between contexts or experiences to preserve links. When they value intuition, they dismiss some connections to promote others. The rich variety in student ideas, as well as the multiple ways that students combine ideas to advance their understanding, points to the importance of creating conditions that enable these ideas to get sorted out. The intentional learning, situated cognition, cognitive apprenticeship, fostering communities of learners, and knowledge integration research programs suggest that enabling students to monitor and evaluate their learning contributes to productive construction of understanding.

Emerging Perspective on the Learner

Perspectives on the learner are converging on the idea that student reasoning is nuanced and complex, yet aimed toward the goal of making sense of experiences in scientific contexts. Investigators have formulated multiple explanations for both the variety of student ideas and for the popularity of certain non-normative ideas about science. Some explain the popularity and persistence of ideas as due to developmental stages, ontological categories, or theories. Others explain these regularities as based on colloquial uses of language, everyday experience, or cultural practices. Still others argue that regularities are illusive and that students formulate idiosyncratic ideas that provide opportunities for refinement. Each perspective has arrived at a role for the variation of student ideas.

The constructivist and sociocultural perspectives stress the importance of student-formulated ideas and call on instructional designers to shape the processes that lead to these ideas. The cognitive and developmental perspectives place emphasis on the learners' limitations or constraints and call on instructional designers to attend to these obstacles. Conceptual change researchers stress the coherence of the ideas students construct and focus on creating conditions where students will replace one idea with another. The knowledge in pieces and knowledge integration interpretations of constructivism pay attention to how students interpret the natural world. Knowledge in pieces emphasizes the consistency in the ideas that students formulate to explain their experiences. Knowledge integration emphasizes the contextualization of ideas and the advantage of capitalizing on variation in ideas.

The rich variety of ideas held by students, both individually and collectively, provides fertile ground for making sense of science. When ideas bump up against each other, students have many options. They can resolve contradictions by contextualizing—assuming that each idea applies in a different context. They can embrace seemingly conflicting ideas, relying on views of the nature of science to buttress their approach. They can behave like cognitive economists, making judicious choices about when to pay attention to alternatives (Linn & Hsi, 2000). They can also resolve conflicts, identify synergies, and seek ways to achieve coherence.

The way learners take advantage of variation is supported by the work of Rosch (1978) on the representation and development of natural categories. Rosch shows how learners develop prototypes for categories, along with a spectrum of objects that can serve as exemplars of each natural category. These exemplars, reinforced by the community, capture emerging criteria. Natural categories enable learners to test community norms on new exemplars. For example, using an exemplar of a table to interpret the meaning of the *chair* concept enables the learner to extend understanding of both the concepts. The way scientists respond to variation in ideas in many ways parallels the responses of students. Evolutionary advance thrives on variation. Groups negotiate criteria or expectations over time, influenced by status, power, logic, and availability of new evidence (Keller, 1993; Latour, 1998; Longino, 1994). In emerging fields, scientists have ideas at multiple levels of analysis that do not necessarily cohere.

In conclusion, for all learners, happenstance, serendipity, unanticipated consequences, efforts to interrogate the natural world, and careful analysis contribute ideas that can help advance understanding. The emerging view of the learner describes the process that students use to integrate their ideas and form a more coherent view of science.

In the next section, we address ways that instruction can activate the full repertoire of ideas, introduce new and powerful ideas, enable ideas to bump up against each other, and allow learners to develop criteria that help them sort out their ideas. Emerging understanding of knowledge integration can help by articulating the optimal repertoire and characterizing processing links between levels of analysis for scientific problems. Attention to the broader ideas of students and teachers about the nature of science and of learning will enhance the knowledge integration process.

VIEW OF INSTRUCTION

Partnerships investigating science instruction often incorporate a view of the learner as integrating ideas, use design studies to orchestrate the process of knowledge integration, and employ assessments that tap the variation in student views. Design patterns and design principles offer promising ways to synthesize this research.

Design studies test innovative instructional materials in realistic learning contexts and capture the systemic character of science education (Bell, Hoadley, & Linn, 2004; Brown, 1992; Collins, Joseph, & Bielaczyc, 2004). Guided by a theoretical framework, these studies use a process of iterative refinement to explore contextual factors such as prior instruction; investigate ways to teach specific topics such as evolution, mechanics, or water quality; incorporate novel technologies such as handhelds

or probeware; deal with learning contexts such as large classes, computer laboratories, after-school programs, or informal environments; and respond to science standards. Comparison studies of instruction cannot always isolate the factors contributing to learning, but they can distinguish design patterns that promote or inhibit knowledge integration.

Design studies often contrast assessments that measure knowledge integration with state or national high-stakes tests. Many high-stakes tests lack sensitivity to gains in knowledge integration (Clark & Linn, 2003). These assessments can lead instructors to reject materials that have benefits. Recent research calls into question short-term gains as indicators of lifelong learning. These studies show that evidence of progress during learning is often a poor indicator of long-term retention (Bjork, 1994, 1999). Research on training, tutoring, and lecturing suggests that skills are more successfully developed and maintained when they become part of coherent understanding of the domain (Aleven & Koedinger, 2003; Crouch & Mazur, 2001, Koedinger & Anderson, 1998; Scherz, Spektor-Levy, & Eylon, in press). Students may respond successfully to multiple choice tests given during instruction but perform poorly on cumulative tests and embarrass their instructors when they take subsequent physical science courses (Sokoloff & Thornton, 2004).

Technology-enhanced learning environments increase the power of design studies. These environments can represent activity structures precisely and orchestrate comparisons (Krajcik, Czerniak, & Berger, 2003; Reiser, 2004). They increase the precision of instructional research by gathering results from embedded assessments. Technology-enhanced learning environments often break activities down into steps represented in an inquiry map or cycle (see Fig. 22.1). These maps guide students to conduct experiments, make decisions, engage in discussion, respond to embedded questions, and create artifacts (Brown & Campione, 1994; Edelson, Gordin, & Pea, 1999; Linn & Clancy, 1992; Scardamalia & Bereiter, 1999). Using these maps, we can identify patterns of activities. Sequences of activities form the basis for the design patterns described later. Research programs using these environments enable comparison studies that document alternative forms of instruction in the same classroom (Aleven & Koedinger, 2002; Davis, 2003a; Quintana et al., 2004), as well as tests of the same materials in diverse contexts (e.g., Richland et al., 2005).

Researchers have captured findings from design studies in *design patterns* and *design principles* (Bell et al., 2004; Collins et al., 2004; diSessa et al., 2002; Edelson, 2001; Eylon, 2000; Linn & Hsi, 2000; Linn, Davis, & Bell, 2004; Reiser et al., 2001). Design patterns can be represented as a sequence of activities followed by teachers and students in a classroom. The activities that make

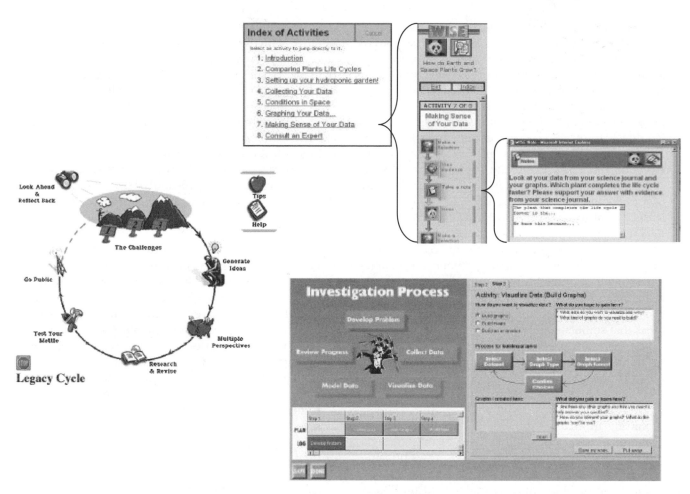

FIGURE 22.1. Examples of inquiry environments. Clockwise from top: Web-based Inquiry Science Environment inquiry map (http:// wise.berkeley.edu/), Symphony Inquiry Wheel (http://hi-ce.org/teacherworkroom/software/symphony), Legacy Inquiry Cycle (http:// peabody.vanderbilt.edu/ctrs/1tc/brophys/legacy.html).

up the patterns, such as discussion, evidence gathering, prompts for reflection, hands-on experiments, or diagnosis of ideas, can also occur in unproductive patterns. Patterns orchestrate the mechanisms of knowledge integration by combining the contributions of curriculum materials, instructors, and peers. For example, in the *collaborate* pattern the curriculum may add ideas, the instructor may contribute new ideas, and peers may also add ideas. These representations offer promising starting points for instructional design and new forms of synthesis for researchers.

Processes Embedded in Design Patterns

Design patterns take advantage of the process of knowledge integration to achieve instructional goals such as reflection, collaboration, and experimentation. Researchers have compared the traditional pattern described in the introduction (motivate, inform, and assess), to patterns such as *predict, observe, explain*, that reflect the emerging view of the learner. In this chapter, we capture the sequences of activities. Patterns are implemented in a discipline and require decisions about the examples introduced, and the content of the activities students perform. We leave the important topic of how to tailor patterns to specific disciplines to a subsequent contribution.

The research on instruction points to four interrelated processes of knowledge integration that form the bases for each design pattern: eliciting current ideas, adding new ideas, developing criteria for evaluating ideas, and sorting out ideas. Instruction typically interleaves the four processes, moving among them rather than following a linear sequence. These processes underlie all the patterns described in this chapter (see Fig. 22.2).

Elicit ideas. First, researchers agree that to promote knowledge integration, instruction must *elicit existing student ideas* about the scientific phenomena either to contradict these ideas (Inhelder & Piaget, 1969; Strike & Posner, 1985) or to forge new connections to these ideas (Bransford et al., 1999; Collins et al., 1988; Linn & Hsi, 2000). Research shows the benefit of eliciting ideas to ensure that students integrate across the full range of ideas rather than ignoring contexts and isolating new learning (Brown & Campione, 1994).

Introduce new ideas. Second, historically, science instruction has emphasized the *introduction of new, normative ideas*, usually in lectures or text accounts of a phenomenon often emphasizing a model of the learner as absorbing information (Thorndike, 1963). Recently, research on analogies and other examples has demonstrated the benefit of careful design of the ideas that are added to the mix held by students. Encouraging designers to select the appropriate level of analysis rather than using only the most sophisticated ideas improves outcomes (Feynman, Leighton, & Sands, 1995). Ideas that stimulate knowledge integration have been called *bridging analogies* (Clement, 1993), *benchmark lessons* (diSessa & Minstrell, 1998), *didactic objects* (Thompson, 2002), *prototypes* (Songer & Linn, 1992), and *pivotal cases* (Linn, 2005).

Promising approaches for adding ideas share the goal of generating connections and helping establish criteria for normative ideas. Clement (1993) describes bridging analogies, such as considering a book on a spring, pillow, and table to help students understand the forces between the book and the table. Minstrell (diSessa & Minstrell, 1998) describes benchmark lessons that provide compelling animations and engage the whole class in making comparisons between possible outcomes for an experiment. Thompson (2002) describes didactic objects that stimulate reflective mathematical discourse. Songer and Linn (1992) describe prototypes as promising additions to the repertoire of ideas. Prototypes are examples where students can accurately predict the outcome of an experiment but do not necessarily understand the mechanism. For example, students can predict that wooden spoons are better than metal spoons for stirring boiling water because the wooden spoon will be cooler to the touch. This idea, when added to the view that metals can impart cold, may cause the student to reorganize their ideas about the behavior of metals in hot and cold environments.

Linn (2005; Linn et al., 2004) describes pivotal cases as more comprehensive than prototypes. Research on thermal equilibrium revealed the impact of two pivotal cases. In one, students use an interactive animation to explore the rate of heat flow in different materials, learning that heat flows faster in wood than metal. In the other,

students compare the feel of wood and metal at room temperature with the feel of these materials at the beach on a sunny day. Both examples stimulate learners to reconsider their ideas (Linn & Hsi, 2000). Research suggests that successful pivotal cases (a) make a compelling, scientifically valid comparison between two situations, (b) draw on accessible, culturally relevant contexts, such as everyday experiences, (c) provide feedback that supports students' efforts to develop criteria and monitor their progress, and (d) encourage students to create narrative accounts of their ideas using precise vocabulary so they can discuss them with others. The thermal equilibrium cases meet all these criteria.

Develop criteria. Third, instruction needs to help learners develop coherent ways to *evaluate the scientific ideas they encounter*. Students encounter many questionable scientific domains, such as advertisements for new drugs, persuasive accounts of research findings, and compelling personal anecdotes. Students rarely explore the controversies that led to scientific advance or learn that research methods have limitations (Bell & Linn, 2000). Often, the scientific method is exalted rather than explained as a social construction open to negotiation (Keller, 1993; Longino, 1994). As a result students may accept bogus results—often available on the Internet or in popular publications— because they are cloaked in scientific jargon. Alternatively, students may discredit all of science when they learn that some drugs approved by federal agencies turn out to be harmful (Angell, 2004) or that some procedures intended to save lives actually do the opposite (Esanu & Uhlir, 2003). To become lifelong learners, students need to integrate their ideas about criteria for evaluating scientific information. This process includes negotiating criteria with others and jointly evaluating class ideas. To negotiate criteria, communities of learners need to integrate scientific ideas about the fallibility of methods in specific disciplines, the epistemology of the discipline (such as earthquakes, cloning, design of new drugs, and environmental conservation), and the nature of scientific advance.

Sort out ideas. Fourth, instruction needs to help students *sort out new and current ideas*. Students need to apply their criteria to evidence, sort out potential contradictions, and identify situations where more information is needed (Bagno, Eylon & Ganiel, 2000; Bransford et al., 1999; Collins et al., 1988; Linn & Hsi, 2000; Scardamalia & Bereiter, 1999). To succeed, students need to allocate their limited energy to the most central confusions and to monitor their progress so they can gain the information they need (Bielaczyc, Pirolli, & Brown, 1995; Lin & Schwartz, 2003). Many students instead respond to the barrage of information in science courses by memorizing information they expect on tests (Songer & Linn, 1992) and forgetting what they memorized (Bjork, 1994). In the course of sorting out ideas, students reformulate both their criteria and their accounts of scientific phenomena. By encouraging ideas to bump up against each other, instruction can promote a lifelong process of refining ideas.

Design Patterns

We describe 10 design patterns (see Fig. 22.2) that capture the most compelling findings in current research and illustrate how these knowledge integration processes work in each of them. Each pattern involves all the processes, but typically has a primary focus that is shaded in the figure. We represent the processes in separate boxes but in practice learners go back and forth among the processes. The figure marks common cyclic relationships by connecting boxes with **bold** lines. For example, students often generate ideas, consider ideas from a lecture or demonstration, and generate more ideas. When the patterns are combined, overlapping processes may be handled by one of the patterns. For example, interactive lectures combine *orient, diagnose,* and *guide* with *collaborate* and take advantage of the shaded processes for each pattern (Crouch & Mazur, 1997). Similarly, the inquiry combination pattern of *predict, observe, explain + experiment + construct an argument* takes advantage of shaded processes for each pattern.

To achieve goals such as inquiry or autonomy, to take advantage of varied learning contexts such as computer labs, lecture halls, or after-school programs, and to teach specific topics such as evolution or mechanics, instruction combines patterns targeting the same knowledge integration processes: eliciting ideas, adding new ideas, generating criteria to distinguish ideas, and sorting out ideas. Combinations of patterns may repeat processes to strengthen knowledge integration. For example, in inquiry learning, students may benefit from multiple methods for adding ideas such as experiments, models, and demonstrations. Combinations of patterns may vary learning activities to appeal to diverse learners, to connect to multiple contexts, or to activate verbal, visual, and social modes of learning.

To characterize the 10 patterns that best represent current research on instruction, we describe each pattern, show how it utilizes the knowledge integration processes, discuss how instructors, curriculum, and peers might enact the pattern, highlight research comparing alternative versions, report on studies showing pitfalls in implementing the pattern, and illustrate how the pattern works in combination with other patterns. We introduce the patterns in the order found in Fig. 22.2, starting with patterns that focus on eliciting ideas.

Orient, Diagnose, and Guide. The *orient, diagnose, and guide* pattern enables students to articulate their full range of ideas and get new information about a topic. In this pattern, curriculum materials or instructors orient students to a topic by connecting it to personally relevant, varied contexts. Students generate ideas and instructors respond to student ideas by determining new ideas to add to the mix of student ideas to stimulate knowledge integration. For example, Bransford (Bransford et al., 1999) introduced anchored instruction as a way to orient students to a topic, often using video clips to bring the challenges to life. In anchored instruction, students generate multiple ideas and select one or more to explain. Instructors guide the process by providing additional ideas, asking probing questions, and helping groups develop criteria for evaluating their techniques for addressing the challenge.

This pattern sets in motion an iterative process. Students refine their ideas, instructors may narrow or broaden the scope of the topic, students respond, and instructors may add normative or non-normative ideas to stimulate students. Ultimately, the full range of students' ideas should be elicited. This pattern contrasts with a pattern based on the conceptual change perspective that could be described as *elicit ideas + replace non-normative ideas + practice* (Abraham, 1998). In a longitudinal study of students' learning about the particulate nature of matter, Margel, Eylon, and Scherz (2001) show the benefit of this pattern. Following the pattern, students generate ideas and discuss their views with peers, leading them to add more ideas. The instructor then introduces opportunities to test ideas against evidence and revisit them in more complex contexts (e.g., learning about polymers). These students developed a more robust understanding of the particulate model than a comparison group who learned the model and applied it in varied contexts but did not test ideas against evidence or struggle with more complex contexts.

The pattern helps instructors customize instruction. Instructors are often surprised by student ideas, especially based on what they think students studied in prior courses (McDermott, 2001). Teachers can pose questions and use class survey technologies, a show of hands, or other indicators to determine the range of ideas held by students. Research on this pattern in higher education shows that short (5- to 10-minute) orienting lectures combined with opportunities for learners to respond to questions succeed better than traditional lectures (Beichner, 2000; Light, 1990). In this pattern, instructors

Pattern \ Process	Elicit or generate ideas from repertoire of ideas.	Add new ideas to help distinguish or link ideas.	Evaluate ideas and identify criteria.	Sort out ideas by promoting, demoting, merging, and reorganizing.
Orient, diagnose, & guide	Generate alternative ideas about a topic or phenomena.	Orient learners to a topic with a mini-lecture, video, or demonstration.	Diagnose weaknesses and offer analogies, pivotal cases, or examples.	Reconsider ideas based on alternatives, evidence, and criteria.
Predict, observe, explain (POE)	Generate predicted outcomes for a phenomenon.	Observe the situation and distinguish new ideas from predictions.	Evaluate the connection between the prediction and the observation.	Explain the connection between predicted and actual outcome.
Illustrate ideas	Elicit the repertoire of ideas for a topic.	Model the process of considering alternatives for a complex problem.	Identify emergent or established criteria to distinguish alternatives.	Enable learners to sort out their ideas based on model and criteria.
Experiment	Elicit questions and frame the investigation	Generate or use methods to gather evidence.	Evaluate results using criteria consistent with the methods.	Connect results of experiment to repertoire of ideas.
Explore a simulation	Frame an activity, game, or question and elicit ideas about activities.	Test conjectures using the simulation or game and analyze feedback.	Evaluate resulting ideas using criteria supplied by the simulation.	Revise ideas based on interactions with the simulation or game.
Create an artifact (model, simulation, physical object, or illustration)	Elicit ideas and frame a design question.	Generate an artifact using technological or other resources.	Evaluate and explore the artifact using personal or group criteria and revise.	Use results to revise views of phenomena and of role of artifacts.
Construct an argument	Identify evidence and ideas about a phenomenon.	Construct a perspective by warranting views with evidence.	Evaluate the perspective using individual or group criteria.	Revise perspective based on new evidence or criteria.
Critique	Elicit ideas and criteria about a phenomenon.	Seek and review new perspectives.	Use criteria to evaluate new perspectives.	Use results to revise ideas and criteria.
Collaborate	Generate ideas for a class or on-line discussion.	Review the ideas of other contributors.	Evaluate ideas using personal or group criteria.	Create group consensus about connections.
Reflect	Identify question or conundrum.	Generate, read, listen, or observe ideas.	Identify personally valid, uncertain, or invalid ideas.	Revise ideas and seek needed information.

FIGURE 22.2. Each pattern involves all four processes of knowledge integration. The primary contribution of each pattern is shaded. When patterns are combined, the shaded processes of the pattern predominate while other processes may be supplied by a different pattern. Rather than following a linear order, most patterns interleave the processes; commonly interleaved processes are indicated by **bolded** lines around the boxes.

modify the instruction based on student responses. Instructors who customize instruction to student ideas can substantially improve student outcomes (Crouch & Mazur, 2001).

Recently, researchers have shown how driving questions (Krajcik et al., 1999), personally relevant problems (Linn & Hsi, 2000), and topics that evoke passion (Collins et al., 2004) help students appreciate the scope of the topic by connecting the topic to relevant aspects of everyday life, to the fallibility of methods, or to common

alternative interpretations. Designers need to select orienting events to capture the scope of the ideas students connect to the scientific phenomena and to guide students so they question intuitions (Krajcik et al., 1994). By delimiting the scope of a topic, this pattern also makes the task of integrating ideas manageable.

Finding the best bridging analogy, pivotal case, or benchmark lesson to add to the mix held by the student often involves trial and refinement. Many unhelpful examples in textbooks illustrate this challenge (Linn,

2005). Some analogies or models, such as the image of electricity as water flowing, foster unproductive connections (Gentner, Rattermann, & Forbus, 1993). Ben-Zvi, Eylon, and Silberstein (1987) show how models of single particles can convince students that individual atoms or molecules have the properties of the collection such as color or viscosity. Research on criteria for good examples, discussed in conjunction with the general pattern, informs this process.

Tutoring software often employs this pattern. Tutors orient learners, elicit ideas, and offer useful ways to represent ideas. When students express their ideas in words, systems such as latent semantic analysis can interpret the comments and match student views to responses designed by the teacher (Graesser, VanLehn, Rose, Jordan, & Harter, 2001). Cognitive researchers in mathematics and science have studied tutoring and built technology-enhanced tutoring environments (Corbett, Koedinger, & Hadley, 2001). Tutors add innovative representations of topics such as geometry, mechanics, or algebra word problems. Cognitive tutors work best when the scope of the potential responses is constrained, which explains why tutors work better for topics such as mechanics or Mendelian genetics than they do for topics such as evolution or global warming. Tutors track student solutions to problems and quickly intervene when students start down a wrong path, consistent with research suggesting that errors reduce learning efficiency (Aleven & Koedinger, 2002; Koedinger & Anderson, 1998). Classroom observations suggest that some students come to believe that the tutor only accepts a subset of the total correct paths, allowing learners to retain non-normative views.

This pattern resonates with the constructivist perspective on the learner and forms the first step in several pattern combinations including most forms of inquiry instruction. This pattern captures the goal of the *engage* step in the Science Education National Standards (NRC, 2000). The *exploration* step in Karplus's learning cycle for the Science Curriculum Improvement Study (Karplus & Thier, 1967) elicits student ideas using hands-on laboratory or field experiences. The *motivate* step in the Learning for Use model (Edelson, 2001) arouses curiosity by revealing gaps in student ideas. The *make science accessible* tenet in the Scaffolded Knowledge Integration framework (Linn & Hsi, 2000), the *driving question* in the Model-It inquiry system (Metcalf, Krajcik, & Soloway, 2000), and the *acquire* step in Thinker Tools (B. White & Frederiksen, 1998) all implement this pattern. This pattern is part of the pattern combination used for Just in Time Teaching (Novak & Wandersee, 1990), and in the SCALE-UP project (Beichner, 2000).

To promote inquiry in Japanese classrooms, teachers combine this pattern with *predict, observe, explain*, and *collaborate* (Hatano & Inagaki, 1991; C. Lewis & Tsuchida, 1998). Called the Ikatura method, this combination starts with a compelling problem and asks students to predict the outcomes. In one example, students predict how much a vat of water weighs before and after adding a wooden raft weighing 300 grams or a metal bench weighing 300 grams. Students make predictions and justify their guesses. They then describe the discrepancies between predictions and outcomes, generate criteria, and sort out ideas in small groups and later with the whole class.

Predict, Observe, Explain. The *predict, observe, explain* pattern involves introducing a demonstration of a scientific phenomenon, eliciting predictions, running the demonstrations, and asking the student to reconcile contradictions (McClelland, 1994; R. White & Gunstone, 1992). To contribute to knowledge integration, the *predict, observe, explain* pattern strips away some of the complexities of a scientific phenomenon and engages students in testing conjectures.

This pattern focuses students on effective aspects of what some call active learning. Observing a demonstration is much less effective than trying to determine whether the demonstration supports a prediction (Crouch & Mazur, 2001). This pattern helps students test their alternative ideas and offers evidence that distinguishes among ideas. The observation part of the pattern can induce conflict (Caravita & Halldén, 1994), but could reinforce non-normative views by enabling students to explain the observation in creative ways. The *explain* step in the pattern encourages learners to reconcile any discrepancies between their prediction and the outcome. Some students often respond to a contradiction about, for example, conservation of mass by generating a new explanation to support their original view (Inhelder & Piaget, 1958). This pattern has the greatest benefit when students use evidence to analyze their predictions.

Many research groups have incorporated the *predict, observe, explain* pattern into technology-enhanced instruction. For example, in the Model-It software, students build a model of how they believe the variables in a water quality situation will interact, gather data, run the model, and compare their prediction to the outcome (Krajcik, Blumenfeld, Marx, & Soloway, 1994). In a genetics modeling project, Gobert and Pallant (2004) ask students to make predictions about the genotypes of individuals with particular phenotypes. The Biologica simulation provides data on the outcomes and asks learners to revise their predictions based on this information. Learners interact with the *predict, observe, explain* pattern until they have enough evidence to document the genotype. These researchers demonstrate that students need scaffolding to use the pattern productively. When students engage in trial and error without guidance, they are less successful than when they have hints and structures to support predictions (Krajcik et al., 1999).

To promote inquiry, the *predict, observe, explain* pattern frequently occurs in combination with the *experiment, collaborate*, and *construct an argument* patterns described later. The Interactive Lab Demonstration incorporates *predict, observe, explain* as a part of a pattern combination to improve the effectiveness of lecture demonstrations. In this method, the lecturer describes the demonstration, asks students to make individual written predictions, then asks them to discuss their predictions in small groups and to form group predictions. The lecturer then carries out the demonstration and the students record the results. A final class discussion relates the result to the various predictions and asks students to explain why their responses were or were not supported. Studies of this method show a significant improvement in students' learning compared to demonstration alone (Sokoloff & Thornton, 2004).

Illustrate Ideas. The *illustrate ideas* pattern enables students to showcase their reasoning and instructors to model authentic reasoning about a complex topic. The pattern promotes knowledge integration by showcasing the process of generating alternatives and selecting among ideas and by supporting learners as they emulate the model. Too often instructors describe only the normative or expert solution to a problem—providing an inaccessible and inaccurate model of how individuals solve novel problems. Using the *illustrate ideas* pattern, instructors contrast various perspectives—including those held by their audience—and discuss how a learner could use criteria to distinguish among them. Case studies, historical notebooks, and accounts of wrong paths can illustrate how scientists frame questions and select methods for exploring important phenomena (Clancy, Titterton, Ryan, Slotta, & Linn, 2003; Palinscar et al., 2001; Schofield, 1995).

Clancy (Clancy & Linn, 1999) describes how he designs interactive case studies of programming problems to illustrate ideas. He assigns a complex problem, examines the solutions students generate, identifies how students get stuck, identifies perplexing decisions, interviews students to hear how they conceptualized the problem, revises the problem, and repeats the process with a new class. From this evidence he designs a case study to model how students could distinguish the ideas they typically generate. Research comparing lectures on the solutions, case studies with solutions but not commentary, and interactive case studies demonstrates that interactive cases with commentary have the most impact on learners (Linn & Clancy, 1992; Clancy et al., 2003).

Some technology environments support a variation on this pattern where an electronic agent illustrates ideas. Inquiry Island (B. White, Shimoda, & Frederiksen, 1999) enables students to interact with software advisors (investigator, collaborator, reflector, and reviser) who play roles based on what Collins calls *epistemic games* (Collins et al., 1988) that encourage learners to develop criteria for distinguishing ideas. Studies conducted with 10- to 11-year-olds suggest that students who ask the advisors to illustrate ideas improve their understanding and their ability to monitor their own learning (White et al., 1999).

In literacy, reciprocal teaching (Palinscar & Brown, 1984) takes advantage of when teachers model how they interpret text and then guide students to follow the model. The instructor gradually increases the complexity of the task and reduces the supports for students. Students start with sentences, then advance to paragraphs and to longer activities. To implement the pattern, teachers initially offer considerable guidance in following the model and gradually turn more of the guidance over to pairs of students working together. Reif and Scott (1997) show how the benefit of this approach for tutoring physics students. The *illustrate ideas* pattern occurs regularly in combinations that promote inquiry such as *predict, observe, explain + illustrate ideas + collaborate*. In this combination, learners generate their own ideas and test whether they explain a phenomenon. Then they compare their explanations to those of the model. Next, they collaboratively consider group ideas, negotiate criteria, and reach consensus. Clark and Jorde (2004) show how this combination improves understanding of thermal equilibrium.

Experiment. The *experiment* pattern helps students frame a manageable question, enables students to gather evidence, and enables instructors to manage the investigation. This pattern involves a recursive process of refining a question, connecting the question to methods of investigation, carrying out an investigation, evaluating the results, and using the findings to sort out the repertoire of ideas. The *experiment* pattern supports knowledge integration because ideas about scientific phenomena bump up against ideas about how to conduct an investigation. The pattern helps teachers and students focus on a manageable scope for the experiment, while at the same time connecting to personally relevant problems.

Researchers debate the importance of autonomous versus guided investigation. The constructivist perspective stresses the importance of independent inquiry, but teachers often avoid this pattern because they lack time and resources to provide guidance to a class full of independent learners. Many researchers report that students cannot narrow ideas or fail to complete projects (Edelson et al., 1999). Feldman et al. (2000) studied more than 20 schools where teachers used online databases to support student investigations. He reported that most teachers struggled to help students in narrowing and refining their questions. Koslowski (1996) discusses the difficulties students face in designing effective experimental conditions. He argues that the interpretations students place on data depend on whether they can imagine an underlying mechanism that might account for the patterns observed.

Polman (2000) describes how a skilled teacher created a set of milestones and guidelines to enable students to conduct projects. The students spent 6 weeks refining their questions and developing a feasible plan. Many teachers lack the time in the curriculum to provide the guidance and support their students need (Linn & Hsi, 2000).

Ultimately, learners need the ability to carry out their own investigations. Practice of the complete process of experimentation in supportive environments may enable learners to develop a manageable set of investigative practices and know when to consult experts or peers to become more successful. Technology-enhanced learning environments can provide guidance, as well as free teachers to interact with small groups and respond to student ideas (Barab, Hay, Barnett, & Keating, 2000; Kafai & Resnick, 1996; Linn, Clark, & Slotta, 2003; Linn et al., 2004). The BioKIDS CyberTracker uses "taxonomic common sense" to allow students to categorize animals with accurate but understandable intuitive classification schemes (Lee & Songer, 2003). WISE enables interactions with handheld devices and guides students to explore the spread of malaria (Slotta & Aleahmad, 2002).

Reiser (2004) calls for problematizing and structuring experimentation so that students can explore a manageable set of questions. He problematizes the BGuILE curriculum by challenging students to perform experiments using a database of Darwin's studies in the Galapagos to explain the adaptation of finches (Reiser et al., 2001). He structures their experiments by using a table to capture conjectures about such variables as beak shape and size. The software structures experimentation by asking students to give a rationale for their question, interpret their results, and identify their criteria. The structure constrains investigation by preventing learners from changing more than one variable at a time (Tabak, 2004).

Masnick and Klahr (2003) structure experimentation for young children using both easily manipulated materials and clear guidelines. They found that 16 percent in second grade and 40 percent in fourth grade could suggest possible sources of error and conduct controlled experiments. They show that young students have a rich but unsystematic and poorly integrated conception of experimental error and its possible sources and benefit from the right structure. Structuring can go too far, making an investigation like following a recipe (Hofstein & Lunetta, 2004)

Kanari and Millar (2004) argue that the *experiment* pattern can help students learn about the nature of science. They distinguish scientific reasoning from logical reasoning. Logical reasoning involves reasoning from given propositions, whereas scientific reasoning requires dealing with the error and uncertainty in primary data. They say, "Reasoning from primary data is a step that students find particularly demanding in situations where error matters, such as those that involve interpretation of small differences" (p. 767). They asked 10-, 12-, and 14-year-olds to investigate the motion of a pendulum and the force required to move boxes of varied surface area. Students had much greater difficulty with interpreting data (e.g., deciding whether a variable had increased, decreased or stayed the same), in experiments in which the variables did not covary than in interpreting experiments involving covariation.

To teach for inquiry, designers often combine the *experiment* pattern with the *orient*, *diagnose and guide*, *construct an argument*, or *reflect* patterns. Students integrate their findings by discussing how the experiment supports the conceptual framework or how it leads to a new family of experiments. The *experiment* pattern differs from the *predict, observe, explain* pattern in that students are identifying their own question and planning an experiment rather than observing an experiment designed for them. Teachers using the *predict, observe, explain* pattern capture some of the elements of the *experiment* pattern, but give students less experience in the challenges of guiding their own inquiry. Teachers can create *inquiry* combination patterns to balance experiments with observations.

Explore a Simulation. The *explore a simulation* pattern enables students to try out their ideas using simulations, virtual worlds, or scientific models. Simulations elicit ideas, support the testing of ideas with feedback, enable learners to develop roles of guidelines, and encourage students to monitor their performance, often in relationship to their peers or an ideal performer. Gamelike activities fit this pattern, including some powerful video games (Gee, 2003).

Technology-enhanced learning environments offer access to powerful simulations and models. The *explore a simulation* pattern is a key element in the WorldWatcher software that provides access to weather analysis tools (Edelson et al., 1999). WorldWatcher (Edelson, 2001) uses energy balance diagrams to help students understand the weather. The WorldWatcher team represents geographic data in the form of interactive color maps that users can customize by adjusting the color scheme, magnification, and spatial resolution. To ensure that these tools help learners, they advocate principles of learner-centered design (Soloway, Guzdial, & Hay, 1994), consistent with the call for structuring use of the *experiment* pattern. Supports for using Geological Information Systems (GIS) have required such refinements (Kali & Orion, 1996; Liben, Kastens, & Stevenson, 2002). Similarly, Model-It replaces quantitative expressions with qualitative language when students are building relationships between variables in a model (Metcalf et al., 2000). Thinker Tools conveys the notion of acceleration to objects by having moving objects in a simulation leave a visual trace of equally timed marks (B. White & Frederiksen, 1998).

Many simulations are embedded in learning environments that offer supports that free teachers to respond to disciplinary questions and tutor individuals. Krajcik et al. (1999) stress the importance of designing good driving questions to organize interactions with simulations. They spell out some key features of effective simulations: feasibility (students should be able to design and perform the investigations), worth (they should deal with rich science content and match local curriculum standards), relevance (simulations should be anchored in lives of learners and deal with important and real-world questions), meaning (projects should be interesting and exciting), and sustainability (projects should sustain student interest over time).

Combinations of *create an artifact* and *explore a simulation* are part of many instructional programs. Virtual reality environments (Barab et al., 2000), molecular dynamics (Pallant & Tinker, 2004), and electrical circuit instruction (White & Frederiksen, 2000) show the advantage of these combinations.

Create an Artifact. Instructors use the *create an artifact* pattern to enable students to test their ideas by designing a complex representation of a scientific phenomena such as electricity, the weather, planetary motion, heat flow, or oxygenation of blood. The *create an artifact* pattern enables students to use scientific ideas to design solutions to scientific problems such as creating an energy-efficient house, a robot, or a container that keeps an egg from breaking. The pattern involves refining a question, selecting or using methods for creating an artifact, identifying scientific principles to guide the design, creating a draft artifact, evaluating the results, using the findings to improve the artifact, and connecting the results to views of the topic.

The opportunities for creating artifacts have expanded with new media and creative use of everyday materials (Kozma, 2003). Learners can use animation software to illustrate a process, drawings to highlight complex ideas, constructions to implement a solution, models to capture the movement of electrons or molecules, and graphs to capture processes or comparisons. Students can represent complex ideas such as the movement of the elbow using familiar materials such as paper rolls (Penner, Giles, Lehrer, & Schauble, 1997). Students may design a representation to clarify, test, communicate, or consolidate their ideas. Like the *experiment* pattern, this pattern merges ideas about scientific phenomena with ideas about how to design, test, and refine alternatives. This creates an often daunting array of alternatives and can perplex learners.

Students often need guidance to get started. Curriculum materials can constrain creative activities by reducing them to recipes or step-by-step procedures or overwhelm teachers when every student clamors for guidance. To make the *create an artifact* pattern succeed, Linn and Hsi (2000) described ways to constrain the options while still encouraging students to explore personally relevant problems. In longitudinal studies of insulation and conduction, students were asked to determine which material to use for a container to keep a picnic cool. Many students envisioned a layered container. They discussed topics such as whether to include a layer of wool, concerned that wool would warm up the picnic just like wool sweaters warm up humans. Their experiments often compared the best and worst design, rather than determining the best materials.

Constructing an artifact may spark ideas not elicited by verbalizations, taking advantage of multiple interacting brain functions (Bilkey, 2004). Technology-enhanced modeling environments, such as StarLogo, allow learners to create models of emergent phenomena, including transport of materials in an ant colony (Colella, Klopfer, & Resnick, 2001; Resnick, Berg, & Eisenberg, 2000). Redish (2003) devised computer tools for introductory physics courses so students can create models of topics in astronomy and physics.

When students engage in designing artifacts such as representational systems for complex phenomena, they develop the general skills of technological literacy (Snyder et al., 1999) along with an important aspect of scientific literacy that diSessa (2004) calls *meta-representational competence*.

Combinations of patterns that resonate with constructivism and support inquiry often include iteration between *create an artifact* and *critique*. The Learning by Design research program shows the benefits of combining *create an artifact*, *critique*, and *collaborate* to teach complex emerging topics in the context of inquiry (Kolodner et al., 2003). diSessa (2000) reports on a classroom community that jointly developed representations to capture the information when a ball was bounced and allowed to continue to bounce until it came to rest. Students generated potential representations, critiqued each other, and collaborated to create a representation that resembled graphing. The students generated creative alternatives and the teacher masterfully guided the creative process.

Construct an Argument. Instructors use the *construct an argument* pattern to stimulate students to link their ideas and warrant their views with evidence. The pattern involves responding to questions, generating ideas, identifying evidence, articulating a viewpoint, responding to counterarguments, and revising the viewpoint based on feedback or new evidence. This pattern supports knowledge integration by helping students contrast varied forms of evidence, link evidence to methods, explore the criteria for selecting evidence, and reflect on the nature of scientific investigation.

Millar and Osborne (1998) report that when argumentation is a central element in science learning, it engages learners in the coordination of conceptual and epistemic goals, motivates students to articulate their scientific thinking, enables students to get feedback on their knowledge integration, and entwines ideas about validity, feasibility, and interpretation of investigations with ideas about outcomes. They argue that epistemic goals are not additional extraneous aspects of science but instead represent an essential element of science teaching and learning. Hogan and Maglienti (2001) compared argument construction for scientists, students, and nonscientists. As expected, scientists outperformed the other groups, but in addition, students and nonscientists performed similarly.

To encourage argument construction, teachers shift the authority structure toward the students, stress epistemological issues, and use pedagogical strategies that encourage argumentation. Scott (1998) reviewed the literature on classroom discourse and showed that authoritative discourse, where the teacher asks questions and the students respond, predominates over dialogue discourse, where students generate complex conjectures and need to resolve uncertainties.

Teachers often feel unprepared to deal with controversy in science because textbooks rarely acknowledge historical debates, and epistemological issues, such as the validity of methods, are neglected in the curriculum. Research shows that debates, where students emulate the techniques used by practicing scientists to defend competing hypotheses about dinosaur extinction, the causes of frog deformities, or other topics, provide a window on science in-the-making (Bell, 2004a; Driver et al., 2000; Duschl & Osborne, 2002). Argument construction tools embedded in technology-enhanced learning environments can scaffold this pattern by helping learners organize and warrant their ideas. These tools enable teachers and peers to inspect arguments. They reveal how students support arguments and often show that different students use the same evidence to support opposing ideas (Bell, 2004a). These tools incorporate decisions about what to represent as an idea, how to separate ideas and evidence, and how to communicate to others. Argument representation tools such as concept mapper (Baumgartner, 2004), Belvedere (Cavalli-Sforza, Weiner, & Lesgold, 1994), SenseMaker (Bell, 2004a), Camile (Guzdial & Turns, 2000), and Explanation Constructor (Sandoval & Reiser, 2004) illustrate opportunities but also showcase the difficulties students face in using complex or cumbersome interfaces.

Research shows the lifelong benefits of argument construction activities (Novak & Wandersee, 1990). Comparison studies show that when students identify arguments for and against a scientific idea they gain more understanding than when they only look at one side of the argument (Bell, 2004b). Students who make concept maps develop more detailed understanding of water quality than those who do not (Baumgartner, 2004). Zohar and Nemet (2002) explore the guidance students need to develop arguments and extend the skill to new topics. One group of ninth graders studying dilemmas in human genetics learned how to develop arguments from multiple perspectives. This group gained in both biological understanding and argument construction skills. Students who spent the same amount of time on only the relevant biological content did not make progress in argumentation. In addition to being able to support their arguments with specific biological evidence, the students who studied argument construction formed higher quality arguments and were able to transfer the skills to dilemmas from everyday life. Importantly, the program benefited the full range of students.

Osborne (Newton, Driver, & Osborne, 1999) shows that supporting argumentation about the scientific context is harder than supporting argumentation about the socioscientific context. Research demonstrates that strategies for supporting argumentation, including writing frames (*My idea is that...*, *My reasons are that...*, *Arguments against my idea might be that...*, *I would convince somebody who does not believe me by...*, *The evidence I would use to convince them is that...*), role-plays, and group presentations improve outcomes (Newton et al., 1999). They report that, in the context of socioscientific issues, pupils can draw on knowledge developed informally through their own life-world experience, their sense of ethical values, and economic considerations. For scientific arguments, students need specific knowledge of the relevant phenomena. Making the relevant evidence available and helping students link disciplinary and epistemological ideas depends on both effective teacher guidance and a carefully refined learning environment.

The *construct an argument* pattern frequently occurs in combination with patterns that enable learners to gather evidence such as *experiment*, *explore a simulation*, *create an artifact*, or *predict, observe, explain*. Wellington (1998) reports advantages when students explore controversies regarding physical or biological concepts, use empirical procedures for resolving these controversies, and then construct arguments to incorporate the empirical activity. Bell (2004b) shows that *construct an argument* is much more effective when combined with *collaborate* to reach consensus. Researchers report that learners who generate a repertoire of ideas about a phenomenon construct better arguments (Driver et al., 2000; Monk & Osborne, 1997), suggesting the benefit of the *orient, diagnose, and guide* and *construct an argument* combination. In addition, teachers gain appreciation of student ideas from the *construct an argument* pattern and make better use of the *orient, diagnose, and guide* pattern (Markow & Lonning, 1998; Shepardson, 1997; Wallace & Mintzes, 1990).

Critique. Instructors use the *critique* design pattern to help students evaluate scientific information. The *critique* design pattern asks learners to evaluate both established and potentially invalid, misleading, persuasive, or confusing information presented in Internet resources, textbooks, articles, models, experiments, arguments, or peer reports. Students recursively review ideas about a scientific phenomenon, generate or identify criteria for evaluating the material, apply the criteria, and raise questions, concerns, or issues about the material. The pattern helps learners integrate their ideas about criteria for arguments, experiments, and artifacts.

The *critique* pattern encourages students to question scientific claims and explore the epistemological underpinnings of scientific knowledge. Students tend to trust scientific information, rather than questioning Web sites

or persuasive messages (Millar & Osborne, 1998; Monk & Osborne, 1997; Newton et al., 1999). Hammer advocates *critique* to activate epistemological resources that students already possess but rarely apply. In the How To Learn Physics program (Hammer, 2000), students are prompted to generate potentially compelling, but inaccurate, answers, to say why they are inadequate, and to compare them to more normative ideas. Critique, although neglected in science courses, is often easier than argument construction, experimentation, or creating artifacts and can help students begin to formulate criteria.

Consistent with Piagetian developmental views, Kuhn (1993) argues that many respondents do not consider the possibility that their theory might be false or that alternative theories might exist. Kuhn (1993) asked students to determine whether new data supported or conflicted with a particular theory and to explain their reasoning. Kuhn found that many children and adults have difficulty coordinating evidence (data) and theory (claim), distinguishing causal and correlational relationships, and determining the validity of information.

Technology enhanced learning environments can scaffold critique (Bell, 2004a; Davis & Linn, 2000; Lee & Songer, 2003). Cuthbert and Slotta (2004) found that when students learn to evaluate Web pages in a critique project they are more successful in spontaneously evaluating new material than when they have equal amounts of practice but no direct instruction in the establishment of criteria. The *critique* pattern encourages learners to establish criteria for evaluating new information and to pay attention to alternatives.

When the *critique* pattern often occurs in combination with *illustrate ideas*, teachers model the process of critiquing ideas and enable learners to emulate them. In addition, *critique* can enhance patterns where individuals or groups conduct experiments, create artifacts, or construct arguments. Research shows that when *critique* is combined with *collaborate*, learners develop more cohesive ideas (Cuthbert & Slotta, 2004; Kolodner et al., 2003; Linn & Hsi, 2000).

Collaborate. Instructors use the *collaborate* design pattern to help learners generate their own ideas, learn of the ideas of others, respond to group ideas, determine methods for distinguishing ideas, articulate warrants for their views, and reach consensus. The *collaborate* pattern promotes knowledge integration by taking advantage of the variation in student ideas and helping groups negotiate criteria for valid inferences.

Many students and observers of science believe that scientists work in isolation (Dunbar and Fugelsang,

2004). Thoughtful use of this pattern helps students gain realistic images of the field. Studies of science laboratories (e.g., Dunbar and Fugelsang, 2004; Holyoak & Thagard, 1995; Latour, 1998) and historical analyses of discoveries (Nersessian, 1999) emphasize the role of political, social, and personal commitments in scientific discourses.

Group work is abundant in classrooms and science museums (Leinhardt et al., 2002). For example, a survey of British primary schools shows that about one-third of the teaching of science is carried out by groups attempting to develop a group product (Blatchford, Kutnick, & Baines, 1999), but often groups fail to integrate ideas and could instead reinforce non-normative ideas. To establish multiple zones of proximal development in a classroom, Brown and Campione (1994) advocate using *collaborate* to enable learners to specialize in specific topics. In the jigsaw approach, groups of students specialize in a particular aspect, and then mixed groups are formed to learn from each other through collaboration (Aronson, 1978). Songer (1996) encourages students to negotiate understanding of weather patterns. In the CSILE environment students use sentence starters that encourage them to warrant critiques with evidence as they contribute to a communal database about a topic (Scardamalia & Bereiter, 1999). Hoadley (Hoadley & Linn, 2000) experimented with design of collaborative spaces in a technology-enhanced environment and found that adding ideas attributed to experts, especially well-known experts such as Newton and Kepler, enabled students to integrate ideas after participating in discussion alone. In the Kids as Global Scientists program, groups distributed around the world specialize in wind, landforms, bodies of water, and precipitation.

This pattern reflects the sociocultural perspective and engages learners in revealing their cultural commitments. Students often express amazement that peers hold views that differ from their own (Clark & Jorde, 2004; Linn & Hsi, 2000). Instructors need to monitor progress and help students learn to respect the ideas of others to implement this pattern (Cohen, 1994). Factors such as status, gender, and cultural background can endanger collaboration and reinforce stereotypes about who can participate in science (e.g., Bagno & Eylon, 1997; Burbules & Linn, 1991; Howe & Tolmie, 2003).

The *collaborate* pattern promotes inquiry in combination with *critique*, *experiment*, and *reflect*. When used in conjunction with the *reflect* pattern or the *orient, diagnose, and guide* pattern, students generate ideas and then compare their ideas with those of others. Students can collaborate to generate burning questions and then use the *experiment* pattern to gather evidence and the *collaborate* pattern to develop criteria for distinguishing among their ideas.

Technology-enhanced learning environments can orchestrate combinations of patterns featuring collaboration. Clark and Jorde (2004) combined *create an argument + make thinking visible + critique + collaborate*. They designed instruction that enabled students to review evidence, form a principle to describe their perspective, and enter their principle into a discussion. Students then critiqued each other's principles. Groups revised their principles based on the criticism. As students support their own principles and distinguish them from principles generated by other groups, they learn to weigh evidence, but they also realize that peers disagree about which ideas are compelling. Research shows the benefit of *orient, diagnose, and guide* in combination with the *collaborate* pattern (Dunbar & Fugelsang, 2004).

Reflect. When instructors use the *reflect* design pattern, they encourage learners to analyze the connections they are making and consider their prior ideas. Consistent with research on desirable difficulties, reflection stimulates metacognition, encouraging learners to evaluate ideas, identify gaps in their reasoning, and seek ways to fill the gaps (Bjork, 1994; Chi & Van Lehn, in press; Schoenfeld, 1987).

Chi and her collaborators find that students who spontaneously reflect—even when their explanations are incomplete or incorrect—learn more than those who do not provide what they call self-explanations (Chi & Van Lehn, in press). Chi views the process of self explanations as involving generation of inferences between ideas that fill gaps in text accounts of science and also as involving repair of connections among ideas. Studies of programming and science text comprehension reveal that students who are asked to reflect often distinguish among their ideas and learn more than those who use typical methods of learning (Bielaczyc et al., 1995; Chi & Van Lehn, in press). Instruction that stresses generating explanations improves performance even after the prompts are discontinued (Bielaczyc et al., 1995).

Reflection has a long history in education. Tutors ask reflection questions, encouraging learners to go over their work and look for places where they might have gone wrong (Koedinger & Anderson, 1998; Lepper, 1985). Tutors can time their questions, direct students to specific information, and ensure that students consider their questions when they are asked. Textbooks, case studies, and worksheets have reflection questions, but these materials are often used differently from the intentions of the authors—students skip the questions or skip the reading and just answer the questions.

Today, many technology-enhanced environments guide learners to reflect at appropriate times (Thinker-Tools, B. White & Frederiksen, 1998; CSILE, Scardamalia & Bereiter, 1999; WISE, Linn et al., 2003; and KIE, Davis & Linn, 2000). Comparison studies that vary the conditions of reflection show that too much guidance can lull students into complacency, that some students are unaware of their weaknesses, and that some prompts derail rather than promote knowledge integration (Davis, 2003b; Davis & Linn, 2000; Kintsch, 1998; Koedinger & Anderson, 1998). For example, Davis and Linn (2000) show that explicit reflection prompts can convince students to focus on completing all the steps in a project without connecting their ideas. Davis (2003b) reports that, when asked to reflect, some students take the opportunity to report that they understand the material perfectly, rather than identifying gaps in their reasoning.

Explicit direction to reflect can benefit students who are struggling with the content. Zohar and Dori (2003) report that students who have difficulty with experimental design benefit from explicit reflection prompts in carrying out inquiry projects. Using the ThinkerTools Inquiry Curriculum, B. White and Frederiksen (2000) report that assessments asking students to reflect on their progress especially helped the students who were struggling to improve their performance. Kruger and Dunning (1999) show that often the least successful students are unaware of their lack of understanding.

Reflection occurs in combination with *experiment*, *create an artifact*, *construct an argument*, or *critique* to promote inquiry. In these combinations, students generate new evidence and reflect on the validity and limitations of the material. In the Create a World project (Edelson, 2001), students use the progress portfolio tools (Loh et al., 1998) for reflection. They annotate, organize, monitor their progress, and create presentations of their work.

Design Principles. Many researchers formulate design principles to make the field more cumulative (Kali, Bos, Linn, Underwood, & Hewitt 2002; Linn et al., 2004; Quintana et al., 2004; Redish, 2003). We define design principles as abstractions backed by theoretical and experimental evidence that can guide future designers. Brown (1992), in her call for design-based research, argued that principles might be the best way to capture the results of these experiments. Researchers on knowledge integration (Kali, Orion, & Eylon, 2003; Linn et al., 2004; Linn & Hsi, 2000) describe principles at three progressively more detailed levels of analysis: meta-principles, pragmatic principles, and specific principles. Kali synthesizes these in the Design Principles Database

(Kali et al., 2002, http://www.design-principles.org/dp/index.php). Quintana et al. (2004) focus on scaffolding and offer seven guidelines organized around four steps of the inquiry process: sense making, process management, articulation, and reflection. Reiser (2004) describes principles for authentic inquiry. These approaches connect to theoretical formulations such as constructivism and incorporate results from design studies where principles are typically tested. Design principles help the community communicate about research findings and suggest directions for future studies. They can increase the cumulative nature of the field.

Implications of Design Patterns and Principles

The design patterns and principles synthesize recent research consistent with the emerging perspective on the learner that values the variation in student ideas. They benefit from studies using technology-enhanced curriculum materials that give more precise information about alternative forms of instruction and more detailed accounts of student trajectories. Design principles clarify abstract ideas about instruction such as active learning, or promoting autonomy by acknowledging the role of the learner in developing understanding. Design patterns capture promising classroom activity structures.

The traditional pattern (motivate, inform, assess) is consistent with the work of Thorndike, envisions the learner as absorbing information, and occurs over and over again as students read chapters in science texts that start with startling events such as depictions of man eating plants, articulate normative ideas, and take classroom tests. Many defend the traditional pattern as essential for development of skills such as learning the multiplication tables, the periodic table, formulas, or science vocabulary. At the policy level, to meet the numerous state standards, many districts reinforce reliance on this pattern, requiring coverage of several chapters on topics such as electricity and thermodynamics each week.

The traditional pattern, under the best of circumstances, stimulates students to expand their repertoire but fails to tighten the connections among ideas. Students retain normative, non-normative, idiosyncratic, and superficial ideas, rather than promoting ideas that have potential for explaining complex phenomena and that meet criteria for scientific sophistication. The 10 patterns in Fig. 22.2, explored in recent research, clarify what has been called meaningful, active, intentional, or autonomous learning. These patterns offer approaches that implement the knowledge integration processes and can meet the needs of all learners. By varying patterns in classroom instruction, teachers accomplish three important goals. First, the variety maintains student motivation and interest because students encounter multiple personally relevant contexts and are more likely to identify with one of them. Second, variety in classroom activities can meet the needs of learners who might benefit more from one type of activity such as modeling than another such as collaborating. Third, variety ensures that students participate in some activities that require them to develop new abilities and improve weak abilities. Courses that feature a broad range of knowledge integration strategies prepare learners to deal with novel situations where their preferred mode of learning might be unavailable or inappropriate.

The design patterns leave many questions unanswered. Most importantly, the patterns are silent on the issue of which aspects of the discipline to emphasize, as well as which examples to use to promote student understanding. In addition, selecting the scope of a topic to maximally engage the repertoire of ideas students bring to science class contributes to learning outcomes (diSessa, 2000; Holyoak & Hummel, 2001; Linn et al., 2004; Vosniadou & Brewer, 1992). We need research combining design patterns with alternative perspectives on disciplinary topics to advance science instruction. Efforts to refine design patterns based on evidence from classroom trials leads to better patterns and benefits from advances in the design study methodology.

Efforts to refine and customize patterns yield promising design principles. Principles can emerge when instructors routinely customize instruction for the available curriculum time, classroom resources, and current students, based on classroom evidence. Instructors leave out aspects of instruction when time is short and take advantage of computer laboratories or handheld devices when those are available. Customization studies gather evidence on the value of various technologies such as handheld computers, data collection with probes, graphs to represent results, classroom laboratories, animations, inquiry maps, GIS systems, CAD systems, and other curricular variations. They also provide insight into the capabilities of cultural groups including gender groups and immigrant populations. Complex decisions including which example to use to illustrate a problem, how much time to spend on each of the aspects of a basic design pattern, or how to order design patterns in a given topic are areas where synthesis of customization findings could greatly improve learning outcomes. Often, findings of customization studies become more like anecdotes than evidence. Documenting these studies and adding the insights to a design principles database can guide others making customization decisions. By synthesizing research in design patterns and design principles, we hope to stimulate the field to find representations for research findings that advance our understanding and offer promising guidelines for design.

To summarize, preliminary evidence suggests that capitalizing on the variety of ideas held by individual students and implementing an assortment of design patterns to support knowledge integration can enhance student learning. The patterns and principles suggest ways to make science instruction more efficient and durable by constructing activities that continue to foster knowledge integration after courses end.

CONCLUSIONS

The complex, systemic nature of science education calls for new ways to conduct research and new forms of research synthesis. Research enterprises have expanded to include partnerships composed of teachers, curriculum, technology, learners, policymakers, and cultural advocates. This paper draws on new research methodologies including *design studies*, *case studies*, and *longitudinal studies*. It characterizes the repertoire of ideas held by learners, synthesizes promising instructional sequences in *design patterns*, and describes how emerging *design principles* can guide customization of patterns in unique contexts.

Case studies of science learning reveal that learners develop a rich repertoire of ideas about scientific phenomena. Because ideas emerge in unique contexts, settings, or experiences, the resulting repertoire is often mutually contradictory. Rather than confronting these contradictions, learners, often isolate their ideas, drawing on them depending on the circumstances.

Over the past decade, researchers, in seeking to make sense of the repertoire of ideas, have identified the varieties of ideas that students have about scientific phenomena. Underappreciated varieties of ideas, such as ideas about the nature of science, about science methods, and about one's own science learning, have been shown to influence the process of knowledge integration and the kinds of understandings that students develop about science. Ideas about the nature of science shape how students interpret controversies in science—when students think that science unfolds, they see less need to make sense of their repertoire. Students' views of their own science learning, as well as expectations held by family and peers, play a role in equity arenas, shaping expectations about who should succeed in science and about career choices.

Developmental, sociocultural, cognitive, and constructivist perspectives on the learner help clarify the sources of student ideas and illustrate the value of variety in student views. These perspectives reveal the many paths that learners follow as they build understanding.

The repertoire of ideas provides fertile ground for making sense of science. Research points to four main processes that work together to promote knowledge integration: eliciting ideas, adding ideas, developing criteria, and sorting out ideas. Instruction often neglects the processes of developing criteria and sorting out ideas.

Study of these processes draws attention to the complexities involved in design of classroom instruction. If a discipline is presented so abstractly that students cannot connect it to their everyday experiences or other ideas, then the chance for knowledge integration is lost. Students often isolate classroom experience with science and settle for less than complete knowledge integration. Such experiences dissuade many students from believing that integrating their ideas about science is even worthwhile. Creating a more and more unified perspective on science, including merging information from different disciplines, is a lifelong goal. To accomplish this, we need to enable learners to compare ideas, distinguish them, and forge new connections.

Over the past decade, research groups have conducted sophisticated instructional studies aimed at knowledge integration. The activity sequences making up the design patterns represent essential elements in successful instruction. Design patterns transcend disciplinary knowledge, but raise questions about which design patterns are successful for which disciplinary topics. This area of research remains an open and exciting arena for further exploration.

Research on design patterns benefits from technology-enhanced learning environments that feature embedded assessments and can deliver instruction systematically, using the full range of learning activities. Embedded assessments record how students go about connecting, linking, sorting out, and making sense of scientific phenomena. They stand in contrast to typical standardized multiple-choice assessments that are often insensitive to knowledge integration instruction. Designing assessments aligned with inquiry instruction remains a contentious area of research.

As researchers conduct studies on design patterns, they begin to identify criteria to characterize the nature of knowledge integration and assessments to measure progress. These assessments help determine: What makes a learner a successful science reasoner? How do we identify learners who have gained a firm foundation for continuing knowledge integration throughout their lives?

Study of design patterns and fine tuning of instruction in classrooms requires attention, not only to the immediate accomplishments of learners, but also to their ability to use their knowledge in the future. This is an active research area.

Over the past decade, science education researchers have generated an impressive repertoire of ideas about science learning, science instruction, learning in specific disciplines, learning in different contexts, learning of different individuals, and learning of the same individual under different circumstances. This exciting, powerful, inspiring, creative, and stimulating set of ideas illustrates the value of variety we champion for science learners. The emerging repertoire of ideas in science education draws attention to the challenge of reforming science instruction. Researchers disagree about specific recommendations for teaching complex topics such as electricity or evolution, label the ideas that students generate as misconceptions, alternative conceptions, and insights, and advocate varied remedies. Design patterns and principles are an effort to capture recommendations that have the potential to influence and improve designs or instruction in new disciplines and settings. We call on those concerned about science education to integrate the varied ideas in the field, to respond to the proposed design patterns, and to empirically test emerging ideas.

ACKNOWLEDGMENTS

This material is based on work supported by the National Science Foundation under Grant Nos. 9873180, 9805420, 0087832, 9720384 and 0334199. Eylon's contribution was supported in part by the Chief Justice Bora Laskin Chair of Science Teaching. Any opinions, findings, and conclusions or recommendations expressed in this material are those of the authors and do not necessarily reflect the views of the National Science Foundation.

The authors gratefully acknowledge helpful discussions of these ideas with members of the Web-based Inquiry Science Environment (WISE) group, the Technology Enhanced Learning in Science (TELS) group, and the memory group at the Center for Advanced Study in the Behavioral Sciences. Special thanks go to Philip Bell, Robert Bjork, Jennie Chiu, Douglas Clark, Allan Collins, Elizabeth Davis, Andy diSessa, Rick Duschl, John Gilbert, Sherry Hsi, Hee-Sun Lee, Jabari Mahiri, Kevin McElhaney, and Jim Slotta for stimulating discussions and comments on earlier drafts.

The authors appreciate help in production of this manuscript from David Crowell and Jonathan Breitbart.

References

AAUW. (2000). *Tech-savvy: Educating girls in the new computer age*. Washington, DC: AAUW.

Abraham, M. R. (1998). The learning cycle approach as a strategy for instruction in science. In B. J. Fraser & K. G. Tobin (Eds.), *International handbook of science education* (pp. 513–524). Dordrecht, The Netherlands: Kluwer.

Aleven, V. A., & Koedinger, K. R. (2002). An effective metacognitive strategy: Learning by doing and explaining with a computer-based cognitive tutor. *Cognitive Science, 26*, 147–179.

American Association for the Advancement of Science. (1994). *Benchmarks for science literacy: Project 2061*. New York: Oxford University Press.

Angell, M. (2004). *The truth about the drug companies: How they deceive us and what to do about it*. New York: Random House.

Aronson, E. (1978). *The jigsaw classroom*. Beverly Hills, CA: Sage.

Baddeley, A. D., & Longman, D. J. A. (1978). The influence of length and frequency of training session on the rate of learning to type. *Ergonomics, 21*, 627–635.

Bagno, E., & Eylon, B.-S. (1997). From problem-solving to a knowledge structure: An example from the domain of electromagnetism. *American Journal of Physics, 65*(8), 726–736.

Bagno, E., Eylon, B.-S., & Ganiel, U. (2000). From fragmented knowledge to a knowledge structure: Linking the domains of mechanics and electromagnetism. *American Journal of Physics, 68*(7), S16–S26.

Ball, D. L. (1996). Teacher learning and the mathematics reforms: What we think we know and what we need to learn. *Phi Delta Kappan*, 500–508.

Barab, S. A., Hay, K. E., Barnett, M., & Keating, T. (2000). Virtual solar system project: Building understanding through model building. *Journal of Research in Science Teaching, 37*(7), 719–756.

Bargh, J. A. (2001). The psychology of the mere. In J. A. Bargh & D. K. Apsley, (Eds), *Unraveling the complexities of social life* (pp. 25–37). Washington, DC: American Psychology Association.

Barron, B. (2000). Achieving coordination in collaborative problem solving groups. *Journal of the Learning Sciences, 9*(4), 403–436.

Barry, D. (2001, February 4). Ben Franklin could solve California's electricity problem. *Holland Sentinel*. Available online at: www.thehollandsentinel.net/stories/020401/fea_Franklin.shtml.

Baumgartner, E. (2004). Synergy research and knowledge integration: Customizing activities around stream ecology. In M. C. Linn, E. A. Davis, & P. Bell (Eds.), *Internet environments for science education* (pp. 261–288). Mahwah, NJ: Lawrence Erlbaum Associates.

Beichner, R. (2000). Student-Centered Activities for Large Enrollment University Physics (SCALE-UP). In *Proceedings of the Sigma Xi forum "Reshaping undergraduate science and engineering education: Tools for better learning"* (pp. 43–52). Sigma Xi: Minneapolis, MN.

Bell, P. (2004a). Promoting students' argument construction and collaborative debate in the science classroom. In M. C. Linn, E. A. Davis, & P. Bell (Eds.), *Internet environments for science education* (pp. 115–144). Mahwah, NJ: Lawrence Erlbaum Associates.

Bell, P. (2004b). The educational opportunities of contemporary controversies in science. In M. C. Linn, E. A. Davis & P. Bell (Eds.), *Internet environments for science education* (pp. 233–260). Mahwah, NJ: Lawrence Erlbaum Associates.

Bell, P., Hoadley, C., & Linn, M. (2004). Design-based research in education. In M. C. Linn, E. A. Davis, & P. Bell (Eds.), *Internet environments for science education*. Mahwah, NJ: Lawrence Erlbaum Associates.

Bell, P., & Linn, M. C. (2000). Scientific arguments as learning artifacts: Designing for learning from the Web with KIE. *International Journal of Science Education, 22*(8), 797–817.

Ben-Zvi, R., Eylon, B. S., & Silberstein, J. (1987). Students' visualisation of a chemical reaction. *Education in Chemistry, 24*(4), 117–120.

Bereiter, C., & Scardamalia, M. (1989). Intentional learning as a goal of instruction. In L. B. Resnick (Ed.), *Knowing, learning, and instruction: Essays in honor of Robert Glaser* (pp. 361–392). Hillsdale, NJ: Lawrence Erlbaum Associates.

Bielaczyc, K., Pirolli, P., & Brown, A. L. (1995). Training in self-explanation and self-regulation strategies: Investigating the effects of knowledge acquisition activities on problem solving. *Cognition and Instruction, 13*(2), 221–252.

Bilkey, D. K. (2004). In the place space. *Science, 305*, 1245–1246.

Bjork, R. A. (1994). Memory and metamemory considerations in the training of human beings. In J. Metcalfe & A. Shimamura (Eds.), *Metacognition: Knowing about knowing* (pp. 185–205). Cambridge, MA: MIT Press.

Bjork, R. A. (1999). Assessing our own competence: Heuristics and illusions. In D. Gopher & A. Koriat (Eds.), *Attention and performance XVII. Cognitive regulation of performance: Interaction of theory and application* (pp. 435–459). Cambridge, MA: MIT Press.

Blatchford, P., Kutnick, P., & Baines, E. (1999). *The nature and use of classroom groups in primary schools* (final report to the Economic and Social Research Council, ref: R000237255).

Bransford, J. D., Brown, A. L., & Cocking, R. R. (Eds.). (1999). *How people learn: Brain, mind, experience, and school*. Washington, DC: National Research Council.

Brown, A. (1992). Design experiments: Theoretical and methodological challenges in creating complex interventions in classroom settings. *Journal of the Learning Sciences, 2*(2), 141–178.

Brown, A. L., & Campione, J. C. (1994). Guided discovery in a community of learners. In K. McGilly (Ed.),

Classroom lessons: Integrating cognitive theory and classroom practice (pp. 229-270). Cambridge, MA: MIT Press/Bradford Books.

Burbules, N. C., & Linn, M. C. (1991). Science education and the philosophy of science: Congruence or contradiction? *International Journal of Science Education, 13*(3), 227-241.

Bybee, R. (1997). *Achieving science literacy: From purposes to practice.* Portsmouth, NH: Heinemann Books.

Calabrese Barton, A. (2003). Kobe's story: Doing science as contested terrain. *Qualitative Studies in Education, 16*(4), 533-552.

Caravita, S., & Halldén, O. (1994). Re-framing the problem of conceptual change. *Learning and Instruction, 4,* 89-111.

Carey, S. (1992). The origin and evolution of everyday concepts. In R. N. Giere (Ed.), *Cognitive models of science* (Vol. XV, pp. 89-128). Minneapolis, MN: University of Minnesota Press.

Case, R. (1985). *Intellectual development: Birth to adulthood.* Orlando, Fl: Academic Press.

Cavalli-Sforza, V., Weiner, A., & Lesgold, A. (1994). Software support for students engaging in scientific activity and scientific controversy. *Science Education, 78*(6), 577-599.

Chi, M. T. H., & Roscoe, R. D. (2002). The process and challenges of conceptual change. In M. Limon & L. Mason (Eds.), *Reconsidering conceptual change: Issues in theory and practice* (pp. 3-27). Dordrechts, The Netherlands: Kluwer Academic.

Chi, M. T. H., & Van Lehn, K. A. (in press). The content of physics self-explanations. *Journal of the Learning Sciences.*

Chinn, C. A., & Brewer, W. F. (1993). The role of anomalous data in knowledge acquisition: A theoretical framework and implications for science instruction. *Review of Educational Research, 63*(1), 1-49.

Clancy, M. J., & Linn, M. C. (1999). Patterns and pedagogy. *SIGCSE Bulletin, 31*(1), 37-42.

Clancy, M., Titterton, N., Ryan, C., Slotta, J., & Linn, M. C. (2003). New roles for students, instructors, and computers in a lab-based introductory programming course. *ACM SIGCSE Bulletin, 35*(1), 132-136.

Clark, D. B., & Linn, M. C. (2003). Scaffolding knowledge integration through curricular depth. *Journal of The Learning Sciences, 12*(4), 451-494.

Clark, D., & Jorde, D. (2004). Helping students revise disruptive experientially supported ideas about thermodynamics: Computer visualizations and tactile models. *Journal of Research in Science Teaching, 41*(1), 1-3.

Clement, J. (1993). Using bridging analogies and anchoring intuitions to deal with students' preconceptions in physics. *Journal of Research in Science Teaching, 30*(10), 1241-1257.

Cohen, E. G. (1994). Restructuring the classroom: Conditions for productive small groups. *Review of Educational Research, 64*(1), 1-35.

Colella, V. S., Klopfer, E., & Resnick, M. (2001). *Adventures in modeling: Exploring complex, dynamic systems with Star-Logo.* New York: Teachers College Press.

Collins, A., Brown, J. S., & Holum, A. (1988). The computer as a tool for learning through reflection. In H. Mandl & A. M. Lesgold (Eds.), *Learning issues for intelligent tutoring systems* (pp. 1-18). Chicago: Springer-Verlag.

Collins, A., Joseph, D., & Bielaczyc, K. (2004). Design research: Theoretical and methodological issues. *Journal of the Learning Sciences, 13*(1), 15-42.

Cooke, N. J., & Breedin, S. D. (1994). Constructing naive theories of motion on the fly. *Memory and Cognition, 22,* 474-493.

Corbett, A. T., Koedinger, K. R., & Hadley, W. H. (2001). Cognitive tutors: From the research classroom to all classrooms. In P. S. Goodman (Ed.), *Technology enhanced learning: Opportunities for change* (pp. 235-263). Mahwah, NJ: Lawrence Erlbaum Associates.

Crouch, C. H., & Mazur, E. (2001). Peer instruction: Ten years of experience and results. *American Journal of Physics, 69,* 970-977.

Cuthbert, A., & Slotta, J. (2004). Designing a Web-based design curriculum for middle school science: The WISE Houses in the Desert project. *International Journal of Science Education, 24*(7), 821-844.

Davis, E. (2003a). Knowledge integration in science teaching: Analyzing teachers' knowledge development. *Research in Science Education, 34*(1), 21-53.

Davis, E. A. (2003b). Prompting middle school science students for productive reflection: Generic and directed prompts. *Journal of the Learning Sciences, 12*(1), 91-142.

Davis, E. A., & Linn, M. C. (2000). Scaffolding students' knowledge integration: Prompts for reflection in KIE. *International Journal of Science Education, 22*(8), 819-837.

de Carvalho, A. M. P. (2004). Building up explanations in physics teaching. *International Journal of Science Education, 26*(2), 225-238.

Dewey, J. (1901). *Psychology and social practice* (Vol. 11). Chicago: University of Chicago Press.

diSessa, A. (1988). Knowledge in pieces. In G. Forman & P. Pufall (Eds.), *Constructivism in the computer age* (pp. 49-70). Hillsdale, NJ: Lawrence Erlbaum Associates.

diSessa, A. A. (2000). *Changing minds: Computers, learning and literacy.* Cambridge, MA: MIT Press.

diSessa, A. A. (2004). Metarepresentation: Native competence and targets for instruction. *Cognition and Instruction, 22*(3), 293-331.

diSessa, A., Elby, A., & Hammer, D. (2002). J's epistemological stance and strategies. In G. M. Sinatra & P. R. Pintrich (Eds.), *Intentional conceptual change* (pp. 237-290). Mahwah, NJ: Lawrence Erlbaum Associates.

diSessa, A. A., Gillespie, N. M., & Esterly, J. B. (in press). Coherence versus fragmentation in the development of the concept of force. *Cognitive Science.*

diSessa, A. A., & Minstrell, J. (1998). Cultivating conceptual change with benchmark lessons. In J. G. Greeno & S. Goldman (Eds.), *Thinking practices* (pp. 155-187). Mahwah, NJ: Lawrence Erlbaum Associates.

diSessa, A. A., & Sherin, B. L. (1998). What changes in conceptual change? *International Journal of Science Education, 20*(10), 1155-1191.

Driver, R., Leach, J., Millar, R., & Scott, P. (1996). *Young people's images of science.* Buckingham, UK: Open University Press.

Driver, R., Newton, P., & Osborne, J. (2000). Establishing the norms of scientific argumentation in classrooms. *Science Education, 84,* 287–312.

Dunbar, K. (1995). How scientists really reason: Scientific reasoning in real-world laboratories. In J. D. R.J. Sternberg (Ed.), *Mechanisms of insight* (pp. 365–395). Cambridge, MA: MIT Press.

Dunbar, K., & Fugelsang, J. (2004). Scientific thinking and reasoning. In K. J. Holyoak & R. Morrison (Eds.), *Cambridge handbook of thinking and reasoning.* Cambridge, MA: Cambridge University Press.

Duschl, R. A., & Osborne, J. (2002). Supporting and promoting argumentation discourse in science education. *Studies in Science Education, 38,* 39–72.

Edelson, D. C. (2001). Learning-for-Use: A framework for the design of technology-supported inquiry activities. *Journal of Research in Science Teaching, 38*(3), 355–385.

Edelson, D. C., Gordin, D. N., & Pea, R. D. (1999). Addressing the challenges of inquiry-based learning through technology and curriculum design. *Journal of the Learning Sciences, 8*(3/4), 391–450.

Esanu, J. M., & Uhlir, P. F. (Eds.). (2003). *The role of scientific and technical data and information in the public domain: Proceedings of a symposium.* Washington, DC: The National Academies Press.

Eylon, B. S. (2000). Designing powerful learning environments and practical theories: The knowledge integration environment. *International Journal of Science Education, 22*(8), 885–890.

Eylon, B. S., & Linn, M. C. (1988). Learning and instruction: An examination of four research perspectives in science education. *Review of Educational Research, 58*(3), 251–301.

Eylon, B.-S., Ronen, M., & Ganiel, U. (1996). Computer simulations as tools for teaching and learning: Using a simulation environment in optics. *Journal of Science Education and Technology, 5*(2), 93–110.

Fadiman, A. (1997). *The spirit catches you and you fall down: A Hmong child, her American doctors, and the collision of two cultures.* New York: Farrar, Straus & Giroux.

Feldman, A., Konold, C., & Coulter, B. (2000). *Network science, a decade later: The internet and classroom learning.* Mahwah, NJ: Lawrence Erlbaum Associates.

Feynman, R. P., Leighton, R. B., & Sands, M. L. (1995). *Six easy pieces : Essentials of physics, explained by its most brilliant teacher.* Reading, MA.: Addison-Wesley.

Gauld, J. A. (1989). A study of pupils' responses to empirical evidences. In R. Millar (Ed.), *Images of science in science education* (pp. 62–82). London: Falmer Press.

Gee, J. P. (2003). *What video games have to teach us about learning and literacy.* New York: Palgrave Macmillan.

Gentner, D., Rattermann, M. J., & Forbus, K. D. (1993). The roles of similarity in transfer: Separating retrievability from inferential soundness. *Cognitive Psychology, 25,* 525–575.

Gilbert, J. K., & Boulter, C.J. (2000). *Developing models in science education.* Dordrecht, The Netherlands: Kluwer.

Gobert, J. D., & Pallant, A. (2004). Fostering students' epistemologies of models via authentic model-based tasks. *Journal of science education and technology, 13*(1), 7–22.

Gopnik, A., & Wellman, H. M. (1994). The theory theory. In L. A. Hirschfeld & S. A. Gelman (Eds.), *Mapping the mind: Domain specificity in cognition and culture* (pp. 257–293). New York: Cambridge University Press.

Graesser, A., VanLehn, K., Rose, C., Jordan, P., & Harter, D. (2001). Intelligent tutoring systems with conversational dialogue. *AI Magazine, 22*(3), 39–51.

Grayson, D. (1996). Improving science and mathematics learning by concept substitution. In D. Treagust, R. Duit & B. Fraser (Eds.), *Improving teaching and learning in science and mathematics* (pp. 152–161). New York: Teachers College Press.

Greeno, J., Collins, A, and Resnick, L. (1996). Cognition and Learning. In D. B. a. R. Calfee (Ed.), *Handbook of educational psychology* (pp. 15–46). New York: Macmillan.

Guzdial, M., & Turns, J. (2000). Effective discussion through a computer-mediated anchored forum. *Journal of the Learning Sciences, 9,* 437–470.

Hammer, D. (2000). Student resources for learning introductory physics. *American Journal of Physics, 68*(S1), S52–S59.

Hammer, D., & Elby, A. (2003). Tapping students' epistemological resources. *Journal of the Learning Sciences, 12*(1), 53–91.

Hatano, G., & Inagaki, K. (Eds.). (1991). *Sharing cognition through collective comprehension activity.* Washington DC: American Psychological Association.

Heubert, J. P., & Hauser, R. M. (1998). *High stakes: Testing for tracking, promotion, and graduation.* Washington, DC: National Academy Press.

Hoadley, C. M., & Linn, M. C. (2000). Teaching science through on-line, peer discussions: SpeakEasy in the Knowledge Integration Environment. *International Journal of Science Education, 22*(8), 839–857.

Hofer, B. K., & Pintrich, P. R. (Eds.). (2002). *Personal epistemology as a psychological and educational construct: An introduction.* Mahwah, NJ: Lawrence Erlbaum Associates.

Hofstein, A., & Lunetta, V. N. (2004). The laboratory in science education: Foundations for the twenty-first century. *Science Education, 88,* 28–54.

Hogan, K., & Maglienti, M. (2001). Comparing the epistemological underpinnings of students' and scientists' reasoning about conclusions. *Journal of Research in Science Teaching, 38,* 663–687.

Holyoak, K. J., & Thagard, P. (1995). *Mental leaps: Analogy in creative thought.* Cambridge, MA: MIT Press.

Holyoak, K. J., & Hummel, J. E. (2001). Toward an understanding of analogy within a biological symbol system. In D. Gentner, K. J. Holyoak, & B. N. Kokinov (Eds.), *The analogical mind: Perspectives from cognitive science* (pp. 161–195). Cambridge, MA: MIT Press.

Howe, C., & Tolmie, A. (2003). Group work in primary school science: discussion, consensus and guidance from experts. *International Journal of Educational Research, 39,* 51–72.

Howe, C., Tolmie, A., Duchak-Tanner, V., & Rattray, C. (2000). Hypothesis testing in science: group consensus and the acquisition of conceptual and procedural knowledge. *Learning and Instruction, 10,* 361–391.

Howe, K. (1998). The interpretive turn and the new debate in education. *Educational Researcher, 27*(8), 13–21.

Hunt, E., & Minstrell, J. (1994). A cognitive approach to the teaching of physics. In K. McGilly (Ed.), *Classroom lessons: Integrating cognitive theory and classroom practice* (pp. 51–74). Cambridge, MA: MIT Press.

Inhelder, B., & Piaget, J. (1958). *The growth of logical thinking from childhood to adolescence; An essay on the construction of formal operational structures.* New York: Basic Books.

Inhelder, B., & Piaget, J. (1969). *The early growth of logic in the child.* New York: Norton.

Kafai, Y. B., & Resnick, M. (Eds.). (1996). *Constructionism in practice: Designing, thinking, and learning in a digital world.* Mahwah, NJ: Lawrence Erlbaum Associates.

Kali, Y., Bos, N., Linn, M. C., Underwood, J., & Hewitt, J. (2002). Design principles for educational software. In G. Stahl (Ed.), *Computer support for collaborative learning: Foundations for a CSCL community* (Proceedings of CSCL 2002). Hillsdale, NJ: Lawrence Erlbaum Associates.

Kali, Y., & Orion, N. (1996). Spatial abilities of high-school students in the perception of geologic structures. *Journal of Research in Science Teaching, 33,* 369–391.

Kali, Y., Orion, N., & Eylon, B. (2003). The effect of knowledge integration activities on students' perception of the earth's crust as a cyclic system. *Journal of Research in Science Teaching, 40*(6), 415–442.

Kanari, Z., & Millar, R. (2004). Reasoning from data: How students collect and interpret data in scientific investigations. *Journal of Research in Science Teaching, 41*(7), 748–769.

Karplus, R., & Thier, H. D. (1967). *A new look at elementary school science: Science Curriculum Improvement Study.* Chicago: Rand McNally.

Keller, E. F. (1993). *A feeling for the organism: The life and work of Barbara McClintock* (10th anniversary ed.). New York: W.H. Freeman.

Kintsch, W. (1998). *Comprehension: A paradigm for cognition.* Cambridge, MA: MIT Press.

Klahr, D. (2000). *Exploring science: The cognition and development of discovery processes.* Cambridge, MA: MIT Press.

Klahr, D., & Nigam, M. (2004). The equivalence of learning paths in early science instruction. *Psychological Science, 15*(10), 661–667.

Knorr Cetina, K. (1995). Laboratory studies: The cultural approach to the study of science. In S. Jasanoff, G. E. Markle, J. C. Petersen & T. Pinch (Eds.), *Handbook of science and technology studies* (pp. 140–166). Thousand Oaks, CA: Sage.

Koedinger, K. R., & Anderson, J. R. (1998). Illustrating principled design: The early evolution of a cognitive tutor for algebra symbolization. *Interactive Learning Environments, 5,* 161–180.

Kolodner, J. L., Crismond, D., Fasse, B., Gray, J., Holbrook, J., & Puntembakar, S. (2003). Putting a student-centered learning by design curriculum into practice: lessons learned. *Journal of the Learning Sciences, 12,* 495–548.

Koslowski, B. (1996). *Theory and evidence: The development of scientific reasoning.* Cambridge, MA: MIT Press.

Kozma, R. (Ed.). (2003). *Technology, innovation, and educational change: A global perspective.* Eugene, OR: International Society for Educational Technology.

Krajcik, J. S., Blumenfeld, P. C., Marx, R. W., & Soloway, E. (1994). A collaborative model for helping middle grade science teachers learn project-based instruction. *Elementary School Journal, 94*(5), 483–497.

Krajcik, J., Blumenfeld, P., Marx, R., & Soloway, E. (1999). Instructional, curricular, and technological supports for inquiry in science classrooms. In J. Minstrell & E. V. Zee (Eds.), *Inquiry into inquiry: Science learning and teaching* (pp. 283–315). Washington, DC: AAAS Press.

Krajcik, J., Czerniak, C., & Berger, C. (2003). *Teaching children science in elementary and middle school classrooms: A project-based approach (2nd ed.).* Boston: McGraw-Hill.

Kruger, J., & Dunning, D. (1999). Unskilled and unaware of it: How difficulties in recognizing one's own incompetence lead to inflated self-assessments. *Journal of Personality and Social Psychology, 77*(6), 1121–1134.

Kuhn, D. (1993). Science as argument: Implications for teaching and learning scientific thinking. *Science Education, 77*(3), 319–337.

Kuhn, T. S. (1970). *The structure of scientific revolutions* (2nd ed.). Chicago: University of Chicago Press.

Lagemann, E. C. (2000). *An elusive science: The troubling history of education research.* Chicago: University of Chicago Press.

Langley, D., & Eylon, B.-S. (in press). Probing high school physics students' views and concerns about learning activities. *International Journal of Science and Mathematics Education.*

Langley, D., Ronen, M., & Eylon, B.-S. (1997). Light propagation and visual patterns: Pre-instruction learners' conceptions. *Journal of Research in Science Teaching, 34*(4), 399–424.

Latour, B. (1998). From the world of science to the world of research. *Science, 280,* 208–209.

Lee, C. D. (1997). Bridging home and school literacies: Models for culturally responsive teaching, a case for African American English. In J. Flood, S. B. Heath, & D. Lapp (Eds.), *A handbook for literacy educators: Research on teaching the communicative and visual arts* (pp. 334–345). New York: Macmillan.

Lee, H.-S., & Songer, N. (2003). Making authentic science accessible to students. *International Journal of Science Education, 25*(8), 923–948.

Lee, O., & Fradd, S. H. (1998). Science for all, including students from non-English language backgrounds. *Educational Researcher, 27*(3), 12–21.

Leinhardt, G., Crowley, K., & Knutson, K. (2002). Learning conversations in museums. Mahwah, NJ: Lawrence Erlbaum Associates.

Lepper, M. R. (1985). Microcomputers in education: Motivational and social issues. *American Psychologist, 40,* 1–18.

Lewis, C. (1995). *Educating hearts and minds: Reflections on Japanese preschool and elementary education.* New York: Cambridge University Press.

Lewis, C., & Tsuchida, I. (1998, Winter). A lesson is like a swiftly flowing river: Research lessons and the improvement of Japanese education. *American Educator,* 14–17, 50–52.

Lewis, E. (1996). Conceptual change among middle school students studying elementary thermodynamics. *Journal of Science Education and Technology, 5*(1), 3–31.

Lewis, E. L., & Linn, M. C. (1994). Heat energy and temperature concepts of adolescents, adults, and experts: Implications for curricular improvements. *Journal of Research in Science Teaching, 31*(6), 657–677.

Liben, L. S., Kastens, K. A., & Stevenson, L. M. (2002). Real-world knowledge through real-world maps: A developmental guide for navigating the educational terrain. *Developmental Review, 22*, 267–322.

Light, R. J. (1990). *Explorations with students and faculty about teaching, learning, and student life.* Cambridge, MA: Harvard University Press.

Lin, X. (2001). Reflective adaptation of a technology artifact: A case study of classroom change. *Cognition and Instruction, 19*(4), 395–440.

Lin, X. D., & Schwartz, D. (2003). Reflection at the crossroad of cultures. *Mind, Culture & Activities, 10*(1), 9–25.

Linn, M. C. (1995). Designing computer learning environments for engineering and computer science: The Scaffolded Knowledge Integration framework. *Journal of Science Education and Technology, 4*(2), 103–126.

Linn, M. C., & Eylon, B. S. (1996). Lifelong science learning: a longitudinal case study. In *Proceedings of Cognitive Science Society, 1996* (pp. 597–602). Mahwah, NJ: Lawrence Erlbaum Associates.

Linn, M. C. (2005). WISE design for lifelong learning—Pivotal cases. In P. Gärdenfors & P. Johannsson (Eds.), *Cognition, education and communication technology.* Mahwah, NJ: Lawrence Erlbaum Associates.

Linn, M. C., & Burbules, N. C. (1993). Construction of knowledge and group learning. In K. Tobin (Ed.), *The practice of constructivism in science education* (pp. 91–119). Washington, DC: American Association for the Advancement of Science (AAAS).

Linn, M. C., & Clancy, M. J. (1992). The case for case studies of programming problems. *Communications of the ACM, 35*(3), 121–132.

Linn, M. C., Clark, D., & Slotta, J. D. (2003). WISE design for knowledge integration. *Science Education, 87,* 517–538.

Linn, M. C., Davis, E. A., & Bell, P. (Eds.). (2004). *Internet environments for science education.* Mahwah, NJ: Lawrence Erlbaum Associates.

Linn, M. C., & Eylon, B. S. (2000). Knowledge integration and displaced volume. *Journal of Science, Education, and Technology, 9,* 287–310.

Linn, M. C., & Hsi, S. (2000). *Computers, teachers, peers: Science learning partners.* Mahwah, NJ: Lawrence Erlbaum Associates.

Linn, M. C., & Muilenburg, L. (1996). Creating lifelong science learners: What models form a firm foundation? *Educational Researcher, 25*(5), 18–24.

Linn, M. C., Songer, N. B., & Eylon, B. S. (1996). Shifts and convergences in science learning and instruction. In R. Calfee & D. Berliner (Eds.), Handbook of Educational Psychology (pp. 438–490). Riverside, NJ: Macmillan.

Linn, M. C., Tsuchida, I., Lewis, C., & Songer, N. B. (2000). Beyond fourth-grade science: Why do U.S. and Japanese students diverge? *Educational Researcher, 29*(3), 4–14.

Loh, B., Radinsky, J., Russell, E., Gomez, L. M., Reiser, B. J., & Edelson, D. C. (1998, April). *The Progress Portfolio: Designing reflective tools for a classroom context.* Paper presented at the CHI (Computer-Human interactions) '98: Conference on Human Factors in Computing, Los Angeles.

Longino, H. (1994). The fate of knowledge in social theories of science. In F. F. Schmitt (Ed.), *Socializing epistemology: The social dimensions of knowledge* (pp. 135–158). Lanham, MD: Rowan and Littlefield.

Margel, H., Eylon, B., & Scherz, Z. (2001). A longitudinal study of high school students' conceptions of the structure of materials. In N. Valanides, *The First IOSTE Symposium in Southern Europe: Science and Technology Education, Preparing Future Citizens* (pp. 21–30). Paralimni, Cyprus: University of Cyprus.

Margolis, J., & Fisher, A. (2001). *Unlocking the clubhouse: Women in computing.* Cambridge, MA: MIT Press.

Markow, P. G., & Lonning, R. A. (1998). Usefulness of concept maps in college chemistry laboratories: Students' perceptions and effects on achievement. *Journal of Research in Science Teaching, 35*(9), 1015–1029.

Masnick, A. M., & Klahr, D. (2003). Error matters: An initial exploration of elementary school children's understanding of experimental error. *Journal of Cognition and Development, 4,* 67–98.

Mason, L. (2001). Introduction: Special issue "Instructional practices for conceptual change in science domains." *Learning and Instruction, 11,* 259–263.

McClelland, D. C. (1994). The knowledge-testing educational complex strikes back. *American Psychologist, 49,* 66–69.

McDermott, L. C. (2001). Oersted Medal Lecture 2001: Physics education research—The key to student learning. *American Journal of Physics, 69*(11), 1127–1137.

Metcalf, S. J., Krajcik, J., & Soloway, E. (2000). Model-It: A design retrospective. In J. M. Jacobson & R. B. Kozma (Eds.), *Innovations in science and mathematics education: Advanced design for technologies of learning* (pp. 77–115). Mahwah, NJ: Lawrence Erlbaum Associates.

Metz, K. (2000). Young children's inquiry in biology. Building the knowledge bases to empower independent inquiry. In J. Minstrell & E. Van Zee (Eds.), *Inquiring into inquiry learning and teaching in science.* Washington, DC: American Association for the Advancement of Science.

Millar, R., & Osborne, J. (Eds.). (1998). *Beyond 2000: Science education for the future.* London: King's College.

Minstrell, J. (1992). Facets of students' knowledge and relevant instruction. In R. Duit, F. Goldberg, & H. Niedderer (Eds.), *Research in physics learning: Theoretical issues and empirical studies* (pp. 110–128). Kiel, Germany: IPN.

Minstrell, J., & Van Zee, E. (Eds.). (2000). *Teaching in the inquiry-based science classroom.* Washington, DC: American Association for the Advancement of Science.

Monk, M., & Osborne, J. (1997). Placing the history and philosophy of science on the curriculum: a model for the development of pedagogy. *Science Education, 81,* 405–424.

Moschkovich, J. N. (1999). Supporting the participation of English language learners in mathematical discussions. *For the Learning of Mathematics, 19*(1), 11–19.

National Research Council (NRC). (2000). *National science education standards.* Washington, DC: National Academy Press.

Nersessian, N. J. (1999). Model-based reasoning in conceptual change. In L. Magnani, N. J. Nersessian & P. Thagard (Eds.), *Model-based reasoning in scientific discovery* (pp. 5–22). New York: Kluwer Academic/Plenum.

Newton, P., Driver, R., & Osborne, J. (1999). The place of argumentation in the pedagogy of school science. *International Journal of Science Education, 21*(5), 553–576.

Novak, J. D., & Wandersee, J. H. (1990). Perspectives on concept mapping. *Journal of Research in Science Teaching, 27,* 921–1079.

Ochs, E., & Capps, L. (2000). *Living narrative.* Cambridge: Harvard University Press.

Paatz, R., Ryder, J., Schwedes, H., & Scott, P. (2004). A case study analyzing the process of analogy-based learning in a teaching unit about simple electric circuits. *International Journal of Science Education, 26*(9), 1065–1085.

Palinscar, A. S., & Brown, A. L. (1984). Reciprocal teaching of comprehension-fostering and comprehension-monitoring activities. *Cognition and Instruction, 1,* 117–175.

Palinscar, A. S., Magnusson, S., & Cutter, J. (2001). Making science accessible to all: Results of a design experiment in inclusive classrooms. *Learning Disability Quarterly, 24,* 15–32.

Pallant, A., & Tinker, R. (2004). Reasoning with atomic-scale molecular dynamic models. *Journal of Science Education and Technology, 13*(1), 51–66.

Pedone, R., Hummel, J. E., & Holyoak, K. J. (2001). The use of diagrams in analogical problem solving. *Memory and Cognition, 29,* 214–221.

Penner, D. E., Giles, N. D., Lehrer, R., & Schauble, L. (1997). Building functional models: Designing an elbow. *Journal of Research in Science Teaching, 34,* 1–20.

Pfundt, H., & Duit, R. (1991). *Students' alternative frameworks* (3rd ed.). Federal Republic of Germany: Institute for Science Education at the University of Kiel/Institut für die Pädagogik der Naturwissenschaften.

Piaget, J. (1970). *Structuralism.* New York: Basic Books.

Polman, J. L. (2000). *Designing project-based science: Connecting learners through guided inquiry.* New York: Teachers College Press.

Quintana, C., Reiser, B. J., Davis, E. A., Krajcik, J., Fretz, E., Golan, R. D., et al. (2004). A scaffolding design framework for software to support science inquiry. *Journal of the Learning Sciences, 13*(3), 337–386.

Ranney, M., & Schank, P. (1995). Protocol modeling, textual analysis, the bifurcation/bootstrapping method, and convince me: Computer-based techniques for studying beliefs and their revision. *Behavior Research Methods, Instruments, and Computers, 27,* 239–243.

Redish, E. F. (2003). *Teaching physics with the Physics Suite.* New York: Wiley.

Reif, F., & Scott, L. A. (1999). Teaching scientific thinking skills: Students and computers coaching each other. *American Journal of Physics, 67,* 819–831.

Reiser, B. (2004). Scaffolding complex learning: The mechanisms of structuring and problematizing student work. *Journal of the Learning Sciences, 13,* 273–304.

Reiser, B. J., Tabak, I., Sandoval, W. A., Smith, B. K., Steinmuller, F., & Leone, A. J. (2001). BGuILE: Strategic and conceptual scaffolds for scientific inquiry in biology classrooms. In S. M. Carver & D. Klahr (Eds.), *Cognition and instruction: Twenty five years of progress* (pp. 263–305). Mahwah, NJ: Lawrence Erlbaum Associates.

Resnick, M. (1994). *Turtles, termites, and traffic jams: Explorations in massively parallel microworlds.* Cambridge, MA: MIT Press.

Resnick, M., Berg, R., & Eisenberg, M. (2000). Beyond black boxes: Bringing transparency and aesthetics back to scientific investigation. *Journal of the Learning Sciences, 9*(1), 7–30.

Richland, L. E., Bjork, R. A., Finley, J. R., & Linn, M. C. (2005). Linking cognitive science to education: Generation and interleaving effects. In B. G. Bara, L. Barsalou, & M. Bucciarelli (Eds.), *Proceedings of the Twenty-Seventh Annual Conference of the Cognitive Science Society.* Mahwah, NJ: Lawrence Erlbaum Associates.

Rosch, E. (1978). Principles of categorization. In E. Rosch & B. Lloyd (Eds.), *Cognition and categorization.* Hillsdale, NJ: Lawrence Erlbaum Associates.

Rosebery, A. S., & Warren, B. (Eds.). (1998). *Boats, balloons and classroom video: Science teaching as inquiry.* Portsmouth: Heinemann.

Sandoval, W. A., & Reiser, B. J. (2004). Explanation-driven inquiry: Integrating conceptual and epistemic scaffolds for scientific inquiry. *Science Education, 88,* 345–372.

Scardamalia, M., & Bereiter, C. (1999). Schools as knowledge-building organizations. In D. Keating & C. Hertzman (Eds.), *Today's children tomorrow's society: The developmental health and wealth of nations* (pp. 274–289). New York: Guildford.

Scherz, Z., Spektor-Levy, O., & Eylon, B.-S. (in press). Scientific communication: A program for explicit instruction of high order learning skills. In *Research and the Quality of Science Education, selected papers from the 4th ESERA conference.* Kluwer Academic.

Schmidt, W. H., Raizen, S. A., Britton, E. D., Bianchi, L. J., & Wolfe, R. G. (1997). *Many visions, many aims: A cross-national investigation of curricular intentions in school science.* Dordrecht, The Netherlands: Kluwer Academic.

Schoenfeld, A. H. (1987). What's all the fuss about metacognition? In A. H. Schoenfeld (Ed.), *Cognitive science and mathematics education* (pp. 189–215). Hillsdale, NJ: Lawrence Erlbaum Associates.

Schofield, J. W. (1995). *Computers and classroom culture.* New York: Cambridge University Press.

Scott, P. (1998). Teacher talk and meaning making in science classrooms: A Vygotskian analysis and review. *Studies in Science Education, 32,* 45–80.

Seymour, E., & Hewitt, N. (1994). *Talking about leaving: Factors contributing to high attrition rates among science, mathematics, and engineering undergraduate majors* (Report on an ethnographic inquiry at seven institutions). New York: Alfred P. Sloan.

Shepard, L. A. (2000). The role of assessment in a learning culture. *Educational Researcher, 29*(7), 4–14.

Shepardson, D. P. (1997). The nature of student thinking in life science laboratories. *School Science & Mathematics, 97,* 37–44.

Shonkoff, J. P., & Phillips, D. A. (Eds.). (2000). *From neurons to neighborhoods: The science of early childhood development.* Washington, DC: National Academy Press.

Siegler, R. S. (1996). *Emerging minds: The process of change in children's thinking.* New York: Oxford University Press.

Slotta, J. D., Chi, M. T. H., & Joram, E. (1995). Assessing the ontological nature of conceptual physics: A contrast of experts and novices. *Cognition and Instruction, 13,* 373–400.

Slotta, J., & Aleahmad, T. (2002). Integrating handheld technology and Web-based science activities. *World Conference on Educational Multimedia, Hypermedia and Telecommunications 2002, 1,* 25–30.

Snyder, L., Aho, A. V., Linn, M. C., Packer, A., Tucker, A., Ullman, J., et al. (1999). *Be FIT! Being fluent with information technology.* Washington, DC: National Academy Press.

Sokoloff, D. R., & Thornton, R. K. (2004). *Interactive lecture demonstrations in introductory physics.* New York: Wiley.

Soloway, E., Guzdial, M., & Hay, K. E. (1994). Learner-centered design: The challenge for HCI in the 21st century. *ACM Interactions, 1*(2), 36–48.

Songer, N. (1996). Exploring learning opportunities in coordinated network-enhanced classrooms—A case of kids as global scientists. *Journal of the Learning Sciences, 5*(N4), 297–327.

Songer, N. B., & Linn, M. C. (1992). How do students' views of science influence knowledge integration? In M. K. Pearsall (Ed.), *Scope, sequence and coordination of secondary school science: Vol. I. Relevant research* (pp. 197–219). Washington, DC: National Science Teachers Association.

Spall, K., Stanisstreet, M., Dickson, D., & Boyes, E. (2004). Development of school students' constructions of biology and physics. *International Journal of Science Education, 26,* 787–803.

Stavy, R., & Tirosh, D. (2000). *How students (mis-)understand science and mathematics: Intuitive rules.* New York: Teachers College Press.

Steele, C. M. (1999). Thin ice: "Stereotype threat" and Black college students. *Atlantic Monthly, 284*(2), 44–54.

Sternberg, R. J. (2004). Culture and intelligence. *American Psychologist, 59*(5), 325–338.

Stigler, J. W., & Hiebert, J. (1999). *The teaching gap: Best ideas from the world's teachers for improving education in the classroom.* New York: Free Press.

Strike, K. A., & Posner, G. J. (1985). A conceptual change view of learning and understanding. In L. H. West & A. L. Pines (Eds.), *Cognitive structure and conceptual change.* Orlando, FL: Academic Press.

Tabak, I. (2004). Synergy: A complement to emerging patterns of distributed scaffolding. *Journal of the Learning Sciences, 13*(3), 305–335.

Thompson, P. W. (2002). Didactic objects and didactic models in radical constructivism. In K. Gravemeijer, R. Lehrer, B. v. Oers, & L. Verschaffel (Eds.), *Symbolizing and modeling in mathematics education.* Dordrecht, The Netherlands: Kluwer.

Thorndike, R. L. (1963). *The concepts of over- and under-achievement.* New York: Bureau of Publications, Teachers College, Columbia University.

Van Zee, E. H. (1998). Fostering elementary teachers' research on their science teaching practices. *Journal of Teacher Education, 49*(245–254).

Van Zee, E. H. (2000). Ways to foster teachers' inquiries into science learning and teaching. In J. M. E. H. v. Zee (Ed.), *Inquiring into inquiry learning and teaching in science* (pp. 100–119). Washington, DC: American Association for the Advancement of Science.

Vosniadou, S. (2002). On the nature of naïve physics. In M. Limón & L. Mason (Eds.), *Reconsidering conceptual change: Issues in theory and practice* (pp. 61–76). Dordrecht, The Netherlands: Kluwer Academic.

Vosniadou, S., & Brewer, W. (1992). Mental models of the earth: A study of conceptual change in childhood. *Cognitive Psychology, 24,* 535–558.

Vreman de-Olde, C., & de Jong, T. (2004). Student-generated assignments about electrical circuits in a computer simulation. *International Journal of Science Education, 26*(7), 859–874.

Vygotsky, L. S. (1978). *Mind in society: The development of higher psychological processes.* Cambridge, MA: Harvard University Press.

Wallace, J. D., & Mintzes, J. J. (1990). The concept map as a research tool: Exploring conceptual change in biology. *Journal of Research in Science Teaching, 27*(10), 1033–1052.

Wallace, C. S., Hand, B., & Yang, E. (2004). The science writing heuristic: Using writing as a tool for learning in the laboratory. In E. W. Saul (Ed.), *Crossing borders in literacy and science instruction: Perspectives on theory and practice* (pp. 355–367). Newark, DE: International Reading Association.

Webb, N. M., & Palinscar, A. M. (Eds.). (1996). *Group processes in the classroom.* New York: Macmillan Library Reference USA.

Wellington, J. (1998). *Practical work in science: Which way now?* London: Rutledge.

White, B. Y., & Frederiksen, J. R. (1998). Inquiry, modeling, and metacognition: Making science accessible to all students. *Cognition and Instruction, 16*(1), 3–118.

White, B. Y., & Frederiksen, J. R. (2000). Technological tools and instructional approaches for making scientific inquiry accessible to all. In M. J. Jacobson & R. B. Kozma (Eds.), *Innovations in science and mathematics education* (pp. 321–359). Mahwah, NJ: Lawrence Erlbaum Associates.

White, B. Y., Shimoda, T. A., & Frederiksen, J. R. (1999). Enabling students to construct theories of collaborative inquiry and reflective learning: Computer support for metacognitive development. *International Journal of Artificial Intelligence in Education, 10*(2), 1–33.

White, R., & Gunstone, R. (1992). *Probing understanding.* New York: Falmer Press.

Williams, M., Linn, M., Ammon, P., & Gearhart, M. (2004). Learning to teach inquiry science in a technology-based environment: A case study. *Journal of Science Education and Technology, 13*(2), 189–206.

Zohar, A., & Dori, Y. J. (2003). Higher order thinking skills and low achieving students: Are they mutually exclusive? *Journal of the Learning Sciences, 12*(2), 145–181.

Zohar, A., & Nemet, F. (2002). Fostering students' knowledge and argumentation skills through dilemmas in human genetics. *Journal of Research in Science Teaching, 39*(1), 35–62.

LEARNING AND TEACHING SOCIAL STUDIES: A REVIEW OF COGNITIVE RESEARCH IN HISTORY AND GEOGRAPHY

Bruce VanSledright
University of Maryland

Margarita Limón
Universidad Autónoma de Madrid

Social studies is a very broad field. To many, it means the study of virtually all the academic disciplines one might name for the purpose of preparing active, thoughtful citizens (National Council for the Social Studies, 1993). The educational process often entails an interdisciplinary or integrated effort that draws from the humanities and social sciences to inquire into social problems and the nature of the social world. Such study, say proponents, creates good democratic citizens who engage and participate in the affairs of their communities and pursue social justice agendas. To survey all the research work done under the social studies umbrella in a single chapter would be a daunting task. As a result, we circumscribed our review task. We extend on the work of reviewing the research literature on learning and teaching history undertaken in 1996. We add to that effort by examining some of the literature on learning and teaching geography. We specifically examine research done in the cognitive vein.

Our rationale for these boundary settings hinges on several related matters. First, this is a handbook on research in educational psychology with a focus on the psychology of what it means to learn and to teach. To the extent that there has been what some call a cognitive revolution in the field over the last several decades, we find it useful to review work that explores the cognitive aspects of learning and teaching of the school subjects history and geography. A look at these two subject areas—from the larger array of possible social studies—yields a reasonably rich portrait of cognitive research work done to date. Other social studies subjects lag behind for reasons that we speculate about at chapter end.

Second, following the cognitive revolution, educational psychologists (and other researchers as well) became increasingly interested in subject-specific research programs. Although this interest is not new—it has ebbed and flowed among educational psychologists for more than 100 years—this recent, renewed interest in part can be traced to Shulman's (1987) call for research that examined subject matter as an important contextual factor in teaching and learning. Schwab's (1978) work can be understood as an important precursor to Shulman's call. Schwab noted that there were four commonplaces of education: teachers/teaching, learners/learning, the educational milieu in which teachers and learners interacted, and subject matter. Process-outcome research in the United States, for example, prior to about 1985 focused more generally on global learning-teaching variables without much regard to the subject matter being studied (e.g., motivation, teacher behaviors such as wait time, student on-task behavior). In other words, that research typically left unexamined what teachers and learners knew or believed about the subject matter and its influence on how they engaged the learning and teaching process. In this line of research, Schwab's subject matter commonplace seemed uncommon. Beginning in the late 1980s and since, this has changed, and in the case of history education research, quite dramatically. Geography education research in the cognitive vein has also changed, but to a lesser degree.

Third, a more specific rationale for limiting our review to cognitive studies in these two particular social studies subject areas involves our attempt to draw from the work being done to begin shedding light on a progression of thought processes required to move from being a beginning learner in a social studies domain to the development of greater expertise. If cognitive research can point in a direction of what learning looks like as growth in, say, thinking historically or geographically, it has the potential to speak to the psychology of teaching these school subjects (although some would argue that we are some distance from that accomplishment). Understanding a relationship between learning and teaching in this way has the potential of bearing fruit for constructing theories of domain-specific cognitive development (Alexander, 2000).

HISTORY EDUCATION RESEARCH

History as a Knowledge Domain

A domain can be roughly defined as a category of specialized knowledge in which those who produce that knowledge employ particular methods for doing do. The knowledge and methods are distinct from other domains; however, overlap is common. For example, historians share methods and tools for producing knowledge with humanities disciplines (e.g., textual analysis) and with some social sciences (e.g., analyzing population and migration patterns). Nonetheless, there remain peculiar practices and types of knowledge that mark the history domain and its culture of practitioners off from these others.

Many historians and philosophers (e.g., Carr, 1986; Collingwood, 1946/1993; Koselleck, 2002; Mink, 1987; Nora, 1996; Rusen, 1993; White, 1978) have written about the nature of history as a knowledge domain. There is some agreement among these theorists, but the landscape remains contested. For our purposes here, we assume a more cognitive psychological and educational perspective and talk about domain knowledge in terms of its substantive and procedural (or strategic) elements. Portions of this vocabulary appeared first in the British history education tradition (see Shemilt, 1980). We also draw, in part, on studies of expertise in historical thinking and understanding conducted in the 1990s and reviewed in the first edition of the *Handbook of Educational Psychology* (Wineburg, 1996). We use this categorization of domain knowledge as a theoretical touchstone for reviewing the studies that follow. However, we also should caution that the categories of knowledge we describe have been debated and remain open to debate, and that they are closely interconnected to the point of depending on one another to the degree that the boundaries separating their subdivisions are porous. We also are aware that they represent a sociocultural position that we stake out in an effort to make a number of points about the scholarship we review. To this end, our distinctions serve useful analytic and organizational purposes.

In the substantive knowledge portion of the domain, types of knowledge can be said to fall under two frames, first order and second order. The products of investigative work in the domain constitute what we are calling *first-order substantive knowledge*. These products turn on accounts that make up the *what of the past*: descriptions and explanations about what occurred, who was involved, when things happened, in what larger historical context, and what it means when taken together. Ideas such as the French Revolution, American capitalism, Chinese communism, Roman Catholicism, and the like play defining roles. Most histories that appear in print form can be said to put on display first-order knowledge. Standardized tests, at least in the United States, almost exclusively sample students' recall or recognition of first-order ideas.

Second-order substantive knowledge includes concepts and ideas that historical investigators impose on the past to bring some order to its temporally broad and often complex scope. These impositions occur as investigators wrestle with the traces of the past and use them to build first-order knowledge, the latter frequently drawn in narrative representations. For example, change over time, causation, and progress/decline are especially critical second-order organizing concepts that historical investigators deploy as they attempt to temporally connect disparate historical events. Other examples that bridge from procedural forms of knowledge include empathy, evidence, significance, agency, and account status. Experts use these types of second-order conceptual ideas as tools to help them make sense of and organize the residua of the past (artifacts, testimonies, second-hand accounts). It is important to stress that second-order concepts and ideas are not inherent property of the past; rather they are the historian's linchpin, connecting her procedural

Substantive Knowledge Types

---

(1) First-Order Conceptual and Narrative Ideas and Knowledge

- Knowledge of the substance of the past that come from who, what, where, when, and how questions.

- Examples: Stories of nation building, change over time capitalism, socialism, economic production, military exploits, democracy, chronology, political parties, names, dates, etc.

---

(2) Second-Order Conceptual Ideas and Knowledge

- Knowledge of concepts and ideas that investigators impose on the past in the practice of interpreting and making sense of the it.

- Examples: Causation, progress, decline, evidence, primary and secondary sources, historical context, author perspectives, source reliability, etc.

Procedural Knowledge Type

Strategic Knowledge

- Knowledge of how to research and interpret the past.

- This knowledge is rule bound and criteria laden. It is subject to decisions about its proper practice from within the community of historical inquirers, but also remains open to debate.

- Examples of procedures:

  —Assessing status of sources:
         Identifying and attributing sources, assessing perspective,
         and judging reliability.
  —Building cognitive maps or models.
  —Interpreting within historical context.
  —Constructing evidence-based arguments.
  —Writing an account.

FIGURE 23.1. A characterization of history domain knowledge.

investigative practices and questions to the substantive first-order ideas and knowledge she seeks to construct and produce.

Procedural (or *strategic*) *knowledge*[1] refers to understandings and applications of the specific practices (sometimes called historical thinking or reasoning) investigators engage in when researching the past and building interpretations that result in first-order types of knowledge. Historical investigators spend considerable time engaged in, for example, reading and intertextual analysis. They attempt to assess the status of accounts. Accounts of what occurred in the past form a principal evidentiary basis in historical study. Seasoned investigators use a variety of heuristics—source attribution and identification, author perspective assessments and reliability judgments,

the latter involving the reading of subtexts and evidence corroboration—to establish the ways in which they can use accounts as evidence (see Ashby & Lee, 1998; Wineburg, 1991). In an integrated, interactive manner, investigators apply their knowledge of procedures and second-order concepts to construct first-order knowledge, drawing to the extent that they can in the process from prior first-order knowledge they possess. Figure 23.1 displays the three types of specialized knowledge in the domain.

Studies of learning in history often locate themselves by staking out which type or types of knowledge and ideas they are exploring among the informants they study. Much of the British work has explored students' (ages 7 to 14) understandings of second-order concepts and ideas such as evidence and account status, empathy, and

---

[1] The British tradition does not include procedural knowledge as a distinct category, lumping it instead in with second-order knowledge. Based on the research done on expertise in history, we think distinguishing procedural knowledge from second-order ideas makes reasonable sense.

causation. Some studies in the United States have looked at learners' capacities to understand and deploy history's procedural knowledge. Other U.S. studies have examined students' conceptualization of the second-order concept *historical significance*. Still other studies have examined what students can recall of the first-order substantive knowledge they study in school.

STUDIES IN HISTORICAL COGNITION AND LEARNING

Frequently underpinned by a constructivist view of learning, much of the current research on history learning has focused on students' prior knowledge and on the strategies needed to gain greater expertise in history, and therefore to promote a deep understanding of first-order historical ideas. As in non–social studies domains, some researchers have explored learners' misconceptions, their beliefs and/or naive understandings of historical concepts, and how they may be changed to more sophisticated ideas indicative of attaining a greater level of expertise. However, for learners to develop deep understandings of first-order ideas, the study of second-order concepts, thinking capabilities, and domain-specific procedural knowledge appears to be required. This makes sense; studies of expertise in the domain indicate that historical investigators draw heavily (but not exclusively) from their procedural knowledge and knowledge of second-order ideas to construct deep first-order understandings (see such studies in volumes by Carretero &Voss, 1998; Stearns, Seixas, & Wineburg, 2000; Wineburg, 2001). Applied to cognitive research in school history education, this work suggests, as we will show, that, for children and adolescents to build deep first-order ideas and understandings, possessing reasonably sophisticated procedural and second-order ideas would be a necessary condition (whether it is sufficient remains an open question). Consequently, researchers have been asking: How and under what circumstances does this knowledge and idea construction occur for learners?

As a result of this work on historical cognition, it is possible to classify research done in the area of K-12 learning history into three general categories: (1) research on learning first-order historical ideas and understandings, (2) research on learning second-order ideas, and (3) research on learning about history's knowledge-producing procedures (or strategies). However, reflecting the necessarily interconnected nature of the types of domain knowledge, some research designs combine study of different categories. For example, a design might involve examining how learners engage in reading historical

sources (procedural) as a means of constructing first-order understandings regarding a particular event, or it might study how learners make decisions about historical significance (second-order) as they come to understand how selection appears in a history textbook account (first-order) they study in history class. We locate these types of combined-category studies according to our sense of which of the types of knowledge the researchers were primarily attempting to examine among the learners they studied.

Studies of Learning About First-order Historical Ideas

Questions of Meaning. It has been pointed out in several studies that substantive historical concepts and ideas can be characterized in four different ways: (a) as abstract and theoretical, (b) as embedded in narratives, (c) as multiple in meaning, and (d) as representing ill-defined, fuzzy categories (e.g,. Carretero, Jacott, Limon, Lopez-Manjon, & Leon, 1994; Lee, Dickinson, & Ashby, 1997; Limón, 2002; van Drie & van Boxtel, 2003). Researchers contend that these characteristics can make substantive historical concepts and ideas in themselves difficult to learn.

First-order concepts and ideas are (a) abstract and theoretical when they do not refer or apply to concrete objects that can be manipulated (e.g., a revolution), and when they are not typically presented in an isolated way, as is often the case in other domains (e.g., concepts from physics, such as energy or force). Rather, they often appear (b) embedded in narrative accounts. As a consequence, the concept's or idea's meaning has to be inferred by learners if it is not explicitly explained in the text or by a teacher. To illustrate, the Roman Empire is a period commonly taught in schools. Maps illustrating the territories under control of the Roman Empire or references to personalities such as Trajan, Caesar or Nero are often mentioned, but it is rare that an explanation of the concept of *empire* appears as well. Also, references to revolutions are typically embedded in history curricula and textbooks (e.g. French Revolution, Industrial Revolution), but usually, an understanding of the concept of revolution has to be inferred from those examples. As the revolution concept example illustrates, (c) historical concepts change their meaning over time and often are polysemic. They may have a different meaning depending on the historical context in which they are applied. Other such first-order concepts and ideas include *democracy, power*, or *nation*. Van Drie and van Boxtel's (2003) work has shown that some first-order concepts' meanings can be used only to describe a particular event or period, and, as a result, it is difficult for learners to understand the unique usage if it is not explained explicitly.

Additionally, researchers in the line of research cited earlier have observed that some first-order concepts and ideas can represent ill-defined and fuzzy categories. Many such ideas are not defined in the same way by historians who work from different historiographical standpoints (Limón, 2002). From a disciplinary point of view, the meanings of some concepts remain contested. For example, the frontier defining the difference between *revolution* and *revolt* is far from clear, and historical writers can exacerbate the problem by using the terms in different ways while invoking roughly the same idea. The complexity of such usages and their changes over time often makes learning about the ideas and concepts difficult for school-age students.

Jim Crow and Civil Rights. In an effort to understand how a group of black ($n = 18$) and white ($n = 37$) elementary ($n = 18$), middle ($n = 15$), and high school ($n = 23$) students in the U.S. South differed in their understanding of the history of the U.S. Jim Crow period and the Civil Rights Movement, Foster, Hoge, and Rosch (1999) showed the students a cluster of photographs. The photographs ranged in dates of origin from the late 1890s to1968. All depicted something about life among African-Americans (e.g., women riding in a car; doctors in a Harlem, New York hospital; Dr. Martin Luther King standing on the balcony of the Lorraine Motel in Memphis). The researchers asked the students to (a) date the photographs as best they could, (b) speculate about why the photographs were taken, and (c) talk about what inferences they could draw from what the photographs showed. Foster et al. used the concepts of chronology (dating the photos), the nature of accounts (why the photos were taken), and empathy (inferences about people's lives) to sort through the knowledge the students held about the periods in question and what second-order cognitive tools the students had at their disposal to organize that knowledge.

Regarding chronology, the younger students (third graders) had difficulty dating the photos. However, the older students were more adept at using context clues within the photos to organize them in a defensible chronological sequence, suggesting that they had access to a more robust understanding of the concepts of dating and chronology in history and why they are important to historical understanding. In making sense of the photographs as accounts and speculating about why they were taken, the younger students offered highly personalized reasons (e.g., it was a "special occasion" or a "celebration") often connected to the types of circumstances at home in which they see photographing done. The middle-grades students knew that someone had a specific purpose for taking a photograph, but reasons offered seldom moved beyond documenting the event to help in remembering it. The significance of the depiction or the nature of its larger historical context was not something about which these students had much knowledge. By high school, the students could talk about a willful photographer, and some speculated about the photographer's purpose and perspective. Historical context and the significance of events in American history were occasionally noted by these older students. However, references appeared more incidental than deliberative.

Making inferences about people's lives during Jim Crow and the Civil Rights Movement and efforts at being empathetic with those depicted followed similar patterns (Foster et al., 1999). The older the student, the more sophisticated she was in working with drawing inferences and empathic regard. Most notable here was that the black students in the sample, and the older ones in particular, more readily displayed empathy and attempts to historically understand a photographer's intent, the photographs themselves, and the people depicted in them. Age and the cognitive development that proceeds with it along with personal connections to the depictions for the African-American students helped with the photograph-analysis task. However, even the older students appeared generally unaware of using second-order concepts (assigning historical significance, engaging in empathic understanding to historically contextualize the images) and historical thinking strategies (assessing the status of images as accounts) to make better sense of photographs as historical artifacts. This constrained the first-order understandings the students could develop from them.

Learning About Native Americans. VanSledright and Frankes (2000) explored what two groups of U.S. fourth graders learned about Eastern Woodlands Native American tribes as part of a unit of study on Maryland state history. The two groups were taught by two different veteran teachers in different schools (one more urban, the other more exurban), but within the same school system. The researchers were interested in what knowledge the students constructed around first-order concepts and ideas such as hunting and gathering, tribal customs, warfare, and shelter as they read and did comparative research on Chesapeake tidewater natives. The researchers observed in both classrooms every day for the duration of the unit and interviewed six students from each class concerning what they knew about the native tribes before they studied them and about what they thought they had learned upon completing the unit. Comparing pre- and post-unit interview data indicated that most of students in the two subsamples had difficulty understanding the concepts and applying them in a comparative way across the tribes they studied.

The researchers contended that the mixed results appeared as a consequence of several instruction-related issues. First, the students appeared overwhelmed by attempting to learn about such a variety of different tribes (approximately 10 in one class; and a smaller number in the other class; however in the latter, non–Eastern Woodlands customs and cultural practices were also included by the teacher as illustrations of general native culture). Second, because the students were asked to do research on the tribes, they encountered problems wrestling with how to engage history's procedural knowledge. Observation data indicated that the students in one class did not receive much explicit help from the teacher regarding issues of source perspective and testimony corroboration. For example, when conflicts among source testimony arose, students had little capacity to adjudicate them. In the other class, students received no assistance with the research process other than from the generic directions printed on the worksheets they used to record the results of examining sources. Under the circumstances, students simply tried their best to ignore testimonial conflicts as they encountered them. Third, students were not aware of the processes associated with working from history's second-order concepts such as assigning historical significance, constructing causal relations, attributing agency, and working from historical empathy. As a result they lacked the conceptual tools to bring order to the disparate accounts they explored and organization to the interpretations of native life they were asked to craft. On related results among students at this age regarding their historical understandings of individuals and institutions, see Barton (1997). He noted that little knowledge of second-order concepts (e.g., historical agency) caused the young students he studied to overendow individuals with power to shape past events.

Terrorism, Images of America, Andrew Jackson, and Abraham Lincoln.

First-order ideas among high school and college students and historians have been explored in other studies as well. In Canada, Levesque (2003) studied secondary students' understandings of terrorism in the wake of the attacks on the World Trade Center towers and the Pentagon in the United States. Cornbleth (2002) examined images 25 high school students held of America in an interview study. VanSledright and Afflerbach (2000) asked two undergraduate prospective elementary teachers to read and think out loud about two revisionist history accounts of Andrew Jackson in order to understand how their prior narratives of Jackson were influenced by the revisionist accounts. And in a larger program involving research on the nature of expertise in history, Wineburg

(1998, 2000, 2001) invited gifted high school students, prospective teachers (one in history, another in science), and historians (both experts and nonexperts on the subject) to read, think aloud about, and construct interpretations from sources by or concerning Abraham Lincoln. Each of these studies suggests that depth of knowledge (or the lack thereof) about the historical context surrounding the topics, understandings of second-order ideas, and the possession of rich strategic knowledge capacities were influential in how the participants in the studies addressed the questions they were asked and analytic tasks they undertook.

Studies of Learning About Second-order Ideas

Metaconcepts. Distinguishing second-order concepts from first-order knowledge and ideas in history provides researchers with a connecting hinge that links the first-order ideas with procedural knowledge in history. Lee, Dickinson, and Ashby (1997) observe, "Second-order means something more than a higher-order group of substantive concepts within a field; the higher order to which reference is being made is a meta-level, in terms of which the discipline is given epistemological shape" (p. 228). In a research program in Spain, Limón (2002), adopting this distinction, referred to second-order concepts as *metaconcepts*. She noted that metaconcepts can be thought of as axes around which students organize their first-order substantive knowledge about history. Metaconcepts are related to the epistemological beliefs individuals have about history and to their beliefs about what learning and teaching history is.

Metaconceptual knowledge is related to the development of procedural (strategic) knowledge that is considered part of historical thinking and reasoning, such as in the use of the heuristics sourcing, corroboration and contextualization (Wineburg, 1991). For instance, if an individual sustains a rather naive idea of the two second-order concepts *evidence* and *source status*, one that does not allow him the capacity to assess the status of sources he accumulates in order to address historical questions he is asking, he likely will encounter difficulties in evaluating and interpreting those sources as he reasons toward an explanation of what happened in a particular historical situation being studied. He may conclude that one source is as good as any other because he lacks second-order understandings of source status and evidence to know better. As a result, his explanation likely will be less sophisticated and weaker than one built by an individual with a more developed notion of evidence and source status and who possesses the heuristics necessary to deploy them.

Given the relevance of these second-order concepts and their importance in historical thinking, research during the period since 1996 has focused on these issues perhaps more than on researching individuals' ideas and beliefs (prior knowledge) about substantive first-order concepts. This does not mean first-order substantive concepts are unimportant. However, given that second-order concepts appear to work as axes around which first-order ideas are frequently organized, research about them and their close relation to reasoning and cognition in history on one hand, and to epistemological beliefs and ideas on the other, have become important issues in the study of history education. Limón's work is illustrative here as well.

Epistemologies and Beliefs About History. In an exploration of students' understandings of epistemology in the history domain and epistemological beliefs, Limón (2000) presented to 669 seventh and 10th graders the opposite arguments introduced by two supposed textbooks about the so-called discovery of America. One seventh grade student said, when she was asked if it was possible to reconcile the two views, "No, it is impossible to reconcile these views. Nothing is the same! They're totally different. If these are real textbooks, what a mess the world is in!" When another student was asked if students in Latin America would study the same ideas as she had in Spain about the "discovery of America," she noted, "Yes, because although the years pass, history is always the same."

These answers point to beliefs these students hold about what they think history is and what textbooks seem to communicate about it. In the first case, the student thinks the textbooks are problematic because they say different things. So, for her, textbooks must say the same things; that is, there is one true unchangeable knowledge of the past. Such ideas have been referred to in recent literature as subject-specific epistemological beliefs (Hofer & Pintrich, 2002; Murphy & Mason, Chapter 14 of this volume). Epistemological beliefs are defined as beliefs about knowledge and knowing. The first student just quoted understands historical knowledge as fixed and stabile. There are no options for alternative perspectives or interpretations about what happened in the past; the past and history are one and the same.

It is possible to imagine that the student just described would not reach a more sophisticated level of understanding in history because she evaluates evidence about what occurred in the past as either consonant with her perceived idea or not. She lacks a conceptual understanding of how perspective in accounts influences the ways in which it can be considered as evidence in addressing

historical questions she might want to ask. In other words, her epistemological beliefs help characterize her understanding of the second-order concept of *evidence*. Metaconcepts such as evidence mediate students' understanding of substantive first-order ideas (Limón, 2002). As Lee and Shemilt (2003) point out, making sense of the reliability of sources is cognitively weak in students at lower levels of progression in historical thinking. Therefore, for students to understand differences among sources and why sources are useful in providing supporting or disconfirming evidence, they also would need to consider that historical knowledge is open to different understandings depending on the questions an investigator asks. As a result, it also must remain, in part, uncertain. If a history teacher sought to change this young female's historical understanding, likely he would have to (a) influence her epistemological beliefs, those that seem to be at the core of more specific beliefs she may have about history, and (b) work on her understanding of the relationship between history metaconcepts (e.g., evidence) and the nature and origin of historical knowledge.

Individuals' epistemological beliefs may also be linked to particular standpoints of history. For instance, the two aforementioned students may be closer to a more naïve realist view of history (naïve in the sense that history is simply that which is recorded, rather than to the realist view of history characterizing some French historians of the School of Annales or School of Mentalities). Connections among individuals' epistemological beliefs, individuals' beliefs about history (as a particular domain), and individuals' beliefs about learning and teaching history are of rather recent import in this line of research (Buehl, Alexander, & Murphy, 2002; Limón, Massa, & Serrano, 2004). Further exploration is needed to clarify the connections and their implications for learning and teaching history.

On Defining History. Some studies have explored students' ideas and understanding of what history is and its connections to second-order understandings. We review several of the studies conducted since 1996. We begin with a brief review of the Youth and History project results (Angvik & von Borries, 1997). The Youth and History project involved a survey in which 27 European countries were involved and approximately 31,000 secondary students participated. In each country, students were asked to fill in a questionnaire that sampled their historical consciousness. Some of the questions on the questionnaire referred to their view of history. We note as examples some results from three of the 48 questions on the questionnaire.[2]

---

[2]The original questionnaire can be found in Angvik and von Borries (1997).

In responding to the question "What does history mean to you?" participants rated eight subitems by means of a Likert scale (from "least like me" = 1 to "most like me" = 5) to answer the question. The subitems students agreed were most like them included "history means a chance for myself to learn from failures and successes of others" (mean = 3.37, SD = 1.16, N = 30,722); "history means a number of instructive examples of what is right or wrong, good or bad" (mean = 3.37, SD = 1.07, N = 30,578); and "history shows the background of the present day and explains today's problems" (mean = 3.60, SD = 1.10, N = 30,604).

Another question asked about the importance the three aims presented had for history. Subitems again were rated using a Likert scale (least important = 1 and most important = 5). Aim 1 was "knowledge of the past;" aim 2 was "understanding of the present;" and aim 3 was "orientation for the future." Results showed that students' considered aims 1 (mean = 3.88, SD = 0.97, N = 30,843) and 2 (mean = 3.56, SD = 1.06, N = 30,780) as the more important for history.

In a third question that sampled beliefs about the second-order ideas of progress and decline, students were asked to choose from five possibilities presented that they considered to be the best representation of historical development over time. The five items from which students had to choose were (a) things generally get better, (b) things generally do not really change, (c) things generally get worse, (d) things generally repeat themselves, and (e) things generally go from one extreme to another. Thirty-one percent of students chose option (e) and 30.5 percent of students chose option (d). Of the remaining options, only 8.4 percent chose (b), 8.8 percent selected (c), and approximately 24 percent chose option (a).

Angvik and von Borries (1997) and the national coordinators of the project in each country analyzed the results in considerable detail. They concluded that European adolescents have a generalized idea of history as a disciplinary practice that engages in studying the past, but that it also may be useful in explaining the present and helping us understand what happens in the world currently. Implicit in this belief is the idea that we can use the study of history to learn from past mistakes and thus avoid repeating them, something VanSledright (1997) also found among students he studied in the United States. Approximately a third of the students held a rather firm belief that history is a story about progress. Slightly fewer than that thought history involved both extremes of significant progress and unfortunate decline, a result also encountered by Barton (2001), who studied grade school student's ideas about historical development comparatively in Ireland and the United States. Temporality (e.g., progress and decline,

change over time) is a second-order metaconcept that continues to receive some attention from researchers. These studies show that temporality—and in these cases just reviewed, how the historical-development perception is conceived—may also be linked to individuals' historical epistemologies.

In other studies of learners' views of history and their underlying epistemological structures and second-order ideas, researchers have noted three tendencies in how the more novice learners conceptualize the nature of first-order historical knowledge: they personify, simplify, or objectify it. *Personification* refers to students' maximization of the role of human action and minimization of the role of institutional structures as causal factors in the explanation of historical events (Jacott, López-Manjón, & Carretero, 1998). *Simplification* refers to what Gardner (1991) calls a "fact, script and personality" conception of history and the use of stereotypes. It suggests that novices in history tend to cognitively simplify the analysis of the situations that happened in the past (see also Barton, 1996). *Objectification* refers to novices' understanding of historical knowledge as something objective, fixed, and stabilized, rather than unsettled and open to reinterpretation.

Voss, Wiley, and Kennet (1998) presented college students (non–history majors) with a list of statements that focused categories of second-order ideas (e.g., nature of facts, nature of causality). One category turned on the nature of accounts and explanation and was designed to explore whether participants viewed history as explanation or as narration and how they viewed the role of the historian. Another category statement sought to explore participants' ideas about historical change and the role of agency in it. Statements were presented in three different contexts: an abstract one as in the case of the first study (e.g., "historical events are produced by a single cause"), a concrete one (e.g., "the collapse of the Soviet Union was produced by a single cause"), or an "everyday" one (e.g., "everyday events are produced by a single cause"). Statements were rated on a 1–7 Likert scale (1 = not true, 7 = true). Two conditions were established. One group received the 50 "abstract" statements plus the 50 statements about the collapse of the Soviet Union. The other group received the 50 "abstract" statements plus 50 "everyday" ones. A 20-item prior-knowledge test (measuring first-order historical knowledge) was used, and participants in each group were divided into "low" and "high" knowledge groups via a median split.

We summarize the results as follows. First, there were no differences in how statements were rated in the three contexts (abstract, Soviet Union, everyday statements). Second, data did not support participants' adherence to a particular historiographical standpoint; their epistemological and theoretical frameworks in history appeared mixed. Third, participants rejected historical events as single causes and strongly agreed with multiple-cause explanations. Fourth, historians were viewed as detectives, especially in the case of subjects with a lower level of knowledge. Finally, participants generally tended to question the nature of historical facts, suggesting that historical sources needed to be interpreted and evaluated. Voss et al.'s (1998) results indicate that, by college, some students may have learned sophisticated ideas about history, theories of history, and second-order ideas. Where that knowledge comes from, particularly given what we know about how history is typically taught in grade school in the United States (e.g., Cuban, 1991), remains an open question. This implies that studies interested in mapping cognitive development in thinking and understanding history need to carefully account (as much as is possible) for the learning biographies of those they study.

Comparative Sociocultural Contexts and Purposes for Studying History.

Learning history, as the foregoing studies make clear, always takes place within a sociocultural context. This context matters in terms of what learners have opportunities to learn, how they go about it, what they take away, and the purposes they deem for studying the subject. In one of the few cross-national comparative studies, Barton (2001) explored these ideas—especially the issue of purposes—among groups of young students in Northern Ireland and in the United States. In the United States, students described how the purpose for studying history involved them in better understanding who they are as Americans in the sense of a collective memory (Seixas, 2000) that helps define their identities as Americans. In Northern Ireland, where participating in such a univocal collective memory is highly contested, if not impossible, as a result of decades of civil and religious strife, students there conceptualized the purposes of learning history to be about coming to understand people who are different than themselves. Barton argued that such differing sociocultural contexts shape student's initial and subsequent understandings of history as a domain and as a school subject. Barton noted that learning about the nature and purposes of history in both contexts is contested, but in different ways. As a result, this creates unique challenges to teaching history because context can so vividly mold the out-of-school understandings and dispositions children develop about history and its purposes.

Sources, Accounts, and Evidence.

Other studies of second-order ideas have specifically attempted to map out development and progression regarding the relationship between evidence accounts and sources; the nature of historical significance; and change over time in history.

We begin by considering several representative studies on learners' understandings of evidence and sources. Much of the sustained developmentally oriented work on these second-order ideas comes from England. Several additional studies have been conducted by researchers in the United States.

Ashby and Lee (1987) outlined a model of progression on children's ideas about historical evidence based on extensive studies of how English children ages 7 to 14 understand it. Project Chata, developed by a group of U. K. researchers, has provided further empirical support to refine the model previously constructed (see for example, Lee & Ashby, 2000). This model of progression includes six stages, adapted here from Lee and Shemilt (2003). Cognitive sophistication is weakest at the lower levels, becoming more complex at the upper end. Lee and Shemilt highlight that, even though second-order historical concepts often can be counterintuitive to children, progression models are useful for mapping students' ideas about history as a discipline and making sense of students' prior conceptions. However, as they also stressed, progression models should not be "cages." They are not a sequence of ladder-like steps that every student must move through sequentially. Such models are valid for groups, not individuals. Researchers in the United States also have explored how students there understand and work with accounts and sources as forms of historical evidence. However, they have been less likely to categorize students' ideas into developmental progressions. Despite this, the results in the United States tend to parallel those that have emerged from the British studies.

Barton (1997) examined fourth and fifth graders' ideas about evidence across a school year. He interviewed both fourth and fifth graders. When students were asked at the beginning of the year about sources as evidence—that is, how it was possible anyone could know what happened in the past—students said that information passed orally from one generation to another, constituting how people knew about the past. Even if students showed this personalized understanding of historical sources, they later were able to realize that individual bias could influence accounts and explanations. Students also came to make some sense of the idea that direct sources can provide different hints and evidence than indirect ones, and that, therefore, some sources were more reliable than others. Barton's results are similar to those found by other U.S. researchers (VanSledright & Frankes, 2000; VanSledright & Kelly, 1998). VanSledright and Kelly's results also indicated that some of the fifth graders participating in their study were capable of assessing varying perspectives in history texts and were beginning to build cognitive models to understand a particular event when they were presented with a variety of conflicting source testimonies.

- *1st stage: Pictures of the past.* The past is viewed as if it was the present. Basis of statements are not questioned.

- *2nd stage: Information.* The past is seen as fixed and known by some authority. Potential evidence is treated as information that is seen as correct or incorrect. No methodology is attributed to historians to find out what happened in the past.

- *3rd stage: Testimony.* The past can be known thanks to what people who lived in the past reported. Therefore, those evidences that provide direct eyewitness are considered best. Biases, exaggeration, and losses of information become a supplement to the dichotomy—truth versus telling lies. Evaluation of evidence involves making a decision on the best reports. Yet knowledge about the past is seen basically as true or false. However, students begin to understand that historians use a methodology to know about the past.

- *4th stage: Scissors and paste.* The past can be probed even if there is no direct witness. A version of what happened can be built by cutting and pasting the best pieces of the reports available. It is also considered important to know if the reporter was a reliable source in order to consider report.

- *5th stage: Evidence in isolation.* The past can be inferred from sources of evidence. Historians may "know" historical facts even if no testimony is available. Reliability is not a fixed property of sources.

- *6th stage: Evidence in context.* Sources only produce evidence when they are understood in their historical context. Contexts change across time and space.

FIGURE 23.2. Stages in a progression model of understanding sources as evidence.

Both Barton and VanSledright and Frankes noted improvements in students' understandings of sources and evidence when teaching activities provided them explicit practice in using, discussing, and applying those second-order concepts. None of the studies assessed students' understanding of the notion of evidence according to a progression model such as Lee and Shemilt's (2003; Fig. 23.2).

Based on these studies, we can say, though, that the U.S. fourth and fifth graders' understanding of sources and evidence seemed to situate them around stage 3. However, variability was common, something Lee and Shemilt (2003) noted as being also prevalent among British children. One thing is clear: On the whole, British students at the same age appear better able to manage sources and accounts as forms of historical evidence than their American counterparts (compare results from, for example, the U.S. studies just noted with Foster & Yeager, 1999, and Lee & Ashby, 2000). This is largely the consequence of the many opportunities children have in England to learn about second-order concepts such as sources and evidence in the classroom. In the United States the preoccupation is with familiarizing students with a progress-oriented, nation-building story. In England, for many years now, the emphasis has been on developing in students an understanding of history as a disciplinary practice. Again, sociocultural context matters, and especially so in terms of the context of teaching and learning history.

As the results obtained by Barton (1997), Foster and Yeager (1999), Lee and Ashby (2000), VanSledright and Kelly (1998), and VanSledright and Frankes (2000) suggest, teaching approaches play an important role in promoting progress (or not) in students' understanding of the second-order concepts, source and evidence. In this regard, Paxton (1999) points out that textbooks in the United States often silence authorial voices, contributing to the fact that students seldom perceive authorship of texts as an important element in understanding historical narratives and conceptualizing them as sources that can be used as evidence in addressing questions. Students' beliefs about teaching and learning history compiled through their experience focusing almost exclusively on studying first-order substantive knowledge in "authorless" textbook narratives—in the United States especially—appears to play a significant role in the slower development of their understandings of second-order concepts compared to students in England.

In an examination of older learners, Rouet, Marron, Perfetti, and Favart (1998) studied undergraduate college students' understanding of historical sources in the United States. Twenty-four undergraduates studied four controversies related to the history of the Panama Canal. Half of the students were presented with two original sources, plus two historians' essays, two participants' testimonies (written after the fact), and one textbook excerpt using a hypertext interface. The other half did not read the two original sources because they were replaced by two additional accounts. The remaining documents were the same. After studying the documents, all students ranked the sources' usefulness and trustworthiness.

Both groups ranked the textbook excerpt as the more trustworthy source. The group that read original sources ranked them as more trustworthy and useful than the historians' essays and *ex post facto* participants' accounts. Despite the fact that the undergraduates were not experts in history, they appreciated the value of original sources. Also, the undergraduates referred to sourcing processes such as author's identity, type of document (official or private), date of the document, or role of the document. They showed some awareness that documents can be evaluated according to some criteria, independently of their content. For more on the nature of sourcing processes, see Lee and Ashby (2000), VanSledright (2004), and Wineburg (1998).

As the study by Rouet et al. (1998) points up, individuals' understanding of sources become more pronounced when they are explicitly asked to solve controversies and to take into account the reliability and usefulness of the documents presented. Rouet et al.'s (1998) results also suggest that the difference between undergraduates and history experts may be more qualitative in nature than quantitative. Both may be able to interpret and evaluate documents, but they may differ on what knowledge and understanding they hold about the historical period the documents describe or in which they are situated (contextualization) and how they employ this knowledge during a task. Put a different way, the differences between college undergraduates and historians, for example, may be attributable to the more sophisticated levels of understanding the experts possess about decision-making criteria (e.g., judging significance of an event in question with respect to knowing the larger historical context, understanding how reliability judgments depend on the questions an investigator is asking) they can employ as they engage in source work and work with evidence. What distinguishes those with greater expertise in the domain is not only that they possess more first-order knowledge about a period under study (context), but that they also have greater knowledge of second-order ideas and concepts, and the strategic capacity (criteria applied in making assessments) to manage and deepen their first-order understandings. Lee and Shemilt's (2003) conceptualization of progression in learners' ideas about evidence (see Fig. 23.2) is a case in point. Notice the differences in cognitive sophistication (decision-making criteria employable, second-order concept understandings) between each level and particularly between the first two levels and the last two.

The foregoing studies make clear that being able to recall a large number of first-order historical ideas alone does not necessarily mean that a learner can manage those ideas well, make defensible decisions about how to read and assess their significance, or use them to organize deeper understandings. Such ideas are necessary but insufficient; second-order ideas and procedural forms of knowledge appear to be additional cognitive requirements if deep historical understandings are to be obtained, ones that contribute to the capacity of learners to be active, participatory, and engaged citizens in the societies in which they live.

Historical Significance. Another second-order idea—historical significance—has received some attention, particularly in the United States. The idea of historical significance is a complex one that students and historians can wrestle with alike (Seixas, 1996), although, as with many second-order historical ideas and concepts, it is rarely discussed directly in grade school, at least in the United States. The past, as we have mentioned, is a broad, seemingly endless landscape. From it, we tell many stories or generate many histories. But it is virtually impossible to tell every story. Selections about which stories to tell and about whom and what to mark as important form the landscape on which historical significance plays out. It is a selection process that defies tidy efforts, and it remains open to much debate. Nonetheless, choosing is necessary. How this selection process works for learners has been the subject of research on historical significance.

Epstein (1998) explored this idea with 19 high school students (10 African-Americans and 9 European-Americans) in an urban working-class community in Michigan using interviews and a task that included sorting events (e.g., Dr. Martin Luther King's assassination, Twentieth Century wars), themes (e.g., nation building, African-American equality), and names of famous Americans (e.g., George Washington, Harriet Tubman) from most significant to least. In the interviews, Epstein asked students to offer rationales about how they made their selections.

The African-American students' most important person was Martin Luther King, Jr. (33 percent put him at the top of their lists), most important event was the Civil Rights movement (25 percent), and most important theme was African-American equality (66 percent). The European-American students selected, respectively, George Washington (22 percent), the Civil War (18 percent), and nation building (56 percent). Overall, the African-American students consistently selected events, people, and themes that represented what they described as about their history of efforts to achieve equality, whereas the European-American students selected events, people, and themes that typically drive U.S. history textbook treatments. When Epstein asked them about their selections, the European-American students said their ideas came from teachers (32 percent of the students) and the textbook (38 percent) and that they trusted these two sources most when it came to understanding what was significant in American history. The African-American students noted their families (34 percent), teachers (21 percent) and television/film/video (21 percent) as influential sources for determining historical significance. Epstein observed that African-American students thought of standard textbook treatment as "white people's history" and that, as such, it tended to downplay the nature of their experiences and struggles as marginalized Americans, suggesting that they were suspicious about why they were not more adequately represented in United States history books.

In another comparative study, Yeager, Foster, and Greer (2002) examined how 44 adolescents in England (n = 21; ages 11 to 18; all were white) and the United States (n = 23; ages 13 to 14; 4 African-American, 1 Hispanic, 1 Asian, 17 European-American) assigned historical significance to events. Students were asked first to list up to 10 of the most significant twentieth century events from memory. They were then given a list of 47 events from the twentieth century that were considered "officially important" in England and the United States. They were asked to select 10 that were most important on their view and rank order them.

At the top of the English students' self-identified lists were World Wars I and II and the death of Princess Diana. Eleven students included other events on their lists that were drawn from personal or family experiences. Students identified the same most significant events from the "official list" as they had originally selected. The rationale they provided about their selection of Princess Diana's death turned on the enormous international media coverage the event spawned. Most of the events the English students selected were tied rather closely to English history and events with significant impact on the country's citizens. At the top of the American students self-generated lists were World War II, the Great Depression, and World War I in that order. From the "official list" presented, the American students selected in order World War II, World War I, and the Great Depression as being most important. Similar to their English counterparts, the American students rationalized their choices by relating the importance of these events for their impact on Americans and for U. S. history as a whole. Both groups of students' ideas about historical significance were related to what gets commemorated and/or dealt with most in school (and the media in some cases). Differences were attributed to the different cultural assignments concerning what is most worth remembering in the two countries. One difference was linked directly to school teaching-learning practice. The English students were more quick to note that assigning significance is related to how one thinks about evidence, and "evidence" (see Lee & Shemilt's 2003 characterization) arises as a result of what gets studied most by historical investigators. Reflecting the fact the evidence is rarely a second-order concept that is treated in U.S. classrooms, as we have observed, none of the 23 American students offered a similar idea.

These studies and others like them (see Barton & Levstik, 1998; Cercadillo, 2001; Levstik, 2000; Seixas, 1997) indicate that students of various ages hold views of historical significance that can be related to their own personal histories and connected to what gets commemorated as significant in school. Depending on the culture and/or subculture, the two may not necessarily align (e.g., Epstein's 1998 results), indicating how important a second-order idea historical significance can be as matter for pedagogical consideration.

Change Over Time. In the U.S., Levstik and Barton (1996) invited 58 students from seven grade levels (kindergarten through sixth grade) to chronologically order nine historical images (from 1772 through 1993) in order to understand how the students worked with the concept of change over time. The images contained a variety of historical markers that the researchers assumed most adults would recognize and thus be able to order the images chronologically. Their question turned on how young children would handle the task. To that end, Levstik and Barton taught the students how to think aloud as they arranged the images. The younger children readily noted changes in material culture and patterns of everyday life depicted in the images. They used the changes they observed as a guide to order the images. The researchers linked much of this practice and knowledge to the children's out-of-school contact with historical material (e.g., trips with family to historic sites). They also noted that the younger children's comments provided evidence that learning about history in school influenced their ordering decisions and enhanced their capabilities in successfully arranging the images.

The older students (e.g., fifth graders) had begun to learn the second-order conceptual structure of periodization (e.g., the colonial period, the American Revolution era). They used what they knew about that structure to order the images and make more discipline-related interpretations of details in the images, although at times in a shaky, novice manner, reflecting their recent exposure. However, the researchers noted that these older students' new-found capacity to use the periodization scheme helped them provide deeper insights into the images, suggesting to them that images coupled with periodization structures can be a powerful source for helping students build ideas about chronology and change over time. Whether children's understanding of change over time in the United States is a story about progress and/or decline (two other important second-order ideas in history) has been studied, for example, by Barton (1996). For a work on the role of human agency and causation in relation to change over time, see den Heyer (2003) and Voss (1998), respectively.

Studies of Learners' Development and Deployment of Strategic Knowledge

Some researchers have looked specifically at how students of various ages develop strategic knowledge and use it in conjunction with second-order ideas to construct deeper understandings of the past. By strategic knowledge we mean those understandings of specific procedural practices, reasoning orientations, and heuristics that historical investigators employ to make sense of the residua of the past (see Fig. 23.1). This involves engaging in source work, conjecturing about the past and interpreting it via mental models that turn on applying second-order concepts, and ultimately writing. Strategic knowledge so defined is equivalent to a type of domain-specific reasoning that enables deeper understandings of the past. As Lee and Ashby (2000) and Wineburg (2001) have noted, there is little about this form of reasoning that is likely to appear on its own among learners (particularly novices to the domain), unaided by assistance from more knowledgeable others such as teachers.

Understanding how novices come to learn about this way of reasoning in history has been an ongoing preoccupation of the Chata Project in England (see Lee & Ashby, 2000). Because Chata Project researchers seldom distinguish, as we noted, between second-order ideas and strategic knowledge in history, they have studied how these forms of knowledge develop together. This makes sense because to engage, for example, in source work involves the use of both strategic activity and second-order concepts as a means of making sense of the past. We reviewed in the previous section how some of the Chata Project research has developed. Perhaps most importantly, the benefit of this work has been to show how children progress in the ways in which they come to know about second-order ideas and strategies for deploying them. In other words, the fruit of these efforts has given those interested a sense of the ways in which such reasoning develops academically (e.g., see the progression levels in Fig. 23.2).

Other studies have attempted to more specifically take apart the process of how young learners, for example, come to acquire knowledge about working with sources and assessing their status (e.g., VanSledright & Afflerbach, 2005). Part of what guides this work is an attempt to understand the academic developmental process of acquiring domain-specific strategic knowledge. Fourth graders in the United States, for instance, can learn rather quickly some of the rudiments of doing source work when provided with scaffolded learning opportunities. Assessing the status of sources is a complex process that involves at a minimum (a) identifying what a source is, (b) attributing a historically positioned author (or artist) to the source, (b) understanding the historicized positionality of that author, and (d) making some judgments about the reliability of a source with respect to the questions being investigated and other comparable sources. Fourth graders with no prior experience assessing the status of historical sources quickly took to the practice of identifying and attributing accounts from early colonial American history with help from the teacher (VanSledright & Afflerbach, 2005). They also were able to understand that accounts have authors—that accounts do not simply fall out of the sky already formed. Learning to make judgments about the reliability of accounts turned out to be a much trickier process because the fourth graders had a tendency to get caught up in making binary distinctions, such as whether an author was telling the truth or lying, something difficult for them to resolve definitively.

Such results also have appeared among young students in Chata Project research (Lee & Ashby, 2000; Lee and Shemilt, 2003). However, students in England, as noted, generally move father along, and one could argue more quickly in general, on progression in historical reasoning than students in the United States, if we compare the advanced high school students in Wineburg's (1991) study to many of the 10- to 12-year-olds study by Chata Project researchers (Lee & Ashby, 2000).

RESEARCH ON THE TEACHING OF HISTORY

Research that has examined history teaching has not been as prolific as that which has focused on student learning. In the United States, this is arguably a consequence of the remarkable resilience of common practice in history teaching (see Cuban, 1991; Smith & Niemi, 2001).

Teaching typically turns on efforts to cover the vast expanse of U.S. history and all the potentially significant stories and details it contains. The stories and details typically hold an Anglocentric, nationalist cast with more multicultural stories residing on the sidebars and margins, usually included only because they point toward the central nationalist story in some way. Survey courses predominate because that is what history curricula specify. In order to achieve this coverage, teachers must be efficient. Efficiency is commonly operationalized in lecturing, storytelling, and showing videotape histories that reinforce the standard textbook treatment students are asked to read. Teacher talk dominates. Assessments often take the form of multiple-choice tests that ask students to "exhibit" the details and bits of the stories and lectures they have heard and the material the textbook contains (see Barton & Levstik, 2004). Of course, there are variations on this practice, but they are relatively rare. The view appears to be that if teachers lecture and tell stories about the events and details and students read the textbook, then learning history will occur. However, the results of the periodic National Assessments of Educational Progress in history in the United States (e.g., Beatty, Reese, Persky, & Carr, 1996) indicate that these typical approaches to teaching produce relatively poor performances on students' capacity to recall what they were taught. With this portrait in mind, we surmise that researchers find little that is edifying about studying such history courses short of trying to understand why typical practices produce such relatively poor results.

We would argue that part of what explains the penchant in the United States for wide survey studies, broad coverage, and bit-like multiple-choice assessments is the preoccupation with telling a detailed nation-building story and getting learners to commit this story to memory. If the standard U.S. history textbook is the repository of this tale, then it is largely a commemorative, Whiggish account of increasing freedom and an ever-widening franchise (see Wertsch, 2000). Seixas (2000) refers to this an effort to build "collective memory" in students around a common nationalist story that helps fashion their identities as Americans. Lowenthal (1996) calls it an exercise in heritage celebration (as distinct from historical study).

In Great Britain, the culture of history teaching has followed a different path. There, although what history teaching is to look like remains contested, history teachers are more engaged in teaching their students about how to think historically and use second-order ideas to reason about the subject matter and construct first-order understandings (e.g., Husbands, Kitson, & Pendry, 2003). These developments are largely a consequence of the Schools Council History Project (Shemilt, 1980), in which researchers examined the benefits and limits of teaching

students to think historically, relying on history domain knowledge. Lee and Ashby (2000) observe:

> While politicians, journalists, and some professional historians argued about the ideological implications of particular stories [collective memories], for many [British] teachers, textbook writers, and researchers the central concern was the development of students' ideas about the discipline of history itself. The changes in English history education can therefore be described as a shift from the assumption that school history was only a matter of acquiring substantive [first-order] history to a concern with students' second-order ideas. Many stories are told, and they may contradict, compete with, or complement one another, but this means that students should be equipped to deal with such relationships, not that any old story will do. (pp. 199– 200)

Seixas (2000) refers to this approach to teaching history as an effort to inculcate disciplinary understandings in students, where students learn to investigate the past and build first-order historical knowledge using second-order ideas and procedural practices derived from the discipline. Lowenthal (1996) simply calls this the study of history (as distinct from heritage commemoration).

What these observations make clear is that research concerning teaching history occurs on highly contested and politicized terrain. Much of the debate turns on what learners are to do with all the different "hi-stories" that can be told and what history teaching should look like as a result. Competing visions about what history is and how it ought to be taught frame the political contest in the United States and to a lesser extent in Great Britain, the two countries in which most of the history education research has been conducted (for an account of similar contests in Australia, see Clark, 2004, and in continental Europe, see Dickinson, Gordon, Lee, & Slater, 1995). Politics and contest may also influence the desire researchers have to conduct studies in the disputed classroom spaces; it may be less problematic and anxiety-provoking to study learners and learning in sites that approximate laboratory settings. Researchers are implicated in these politics to be sure, and they do not necessarily agree among themselves what good practice should consist of (see Wilson, 2001). We explore a handful of studies of teaching with this note about controversy and questions about definition in view. We use a type of matrix in which we examine studies for what sense of history (e.g., collective memory, disciplinary) researchers had in mind in their analyses of teachers' practices and cross it with the history domain framework we used in the foregoing (first-order, second-order, procedural). We also comment on how what the teachers appeared to be doing in these accounts aligns with various visions of what history could look like in the classroom. We begin with studies done in the United States.

History Teaching in the United States

In a comparative case study of two New York secondary history teachers who each taught a unit on the American Civil Rights era, Grant (2003) explored both how the teachers taught the unit and how they responded to the state's standards and Regent's Exam expectations. For George Blair, a self-proclaimed traditionalist, the emphasis was on committing the details of the textbook to memory. To augment the textbook, Blair lectured about the events and details covered in each chapter and occasionally showed a videotape. His approach was deeply rooted in collective memory that was underwritten by the textbook he used.

Linda Strait taught history by drawing regularly from different accounts, videotapes, and occasionally primary sources, but still relied primarily on the standard textbook. Effectively, she pluralized the idea of collective memory in order to make it look more like collective memories in the spirit of multiculturalizing the American history curriculum. She told Grant (2003) that she used additional sources because she was interested in motivating her students and "wanted to appeal to them on an emotional level" (p. 26). In this latter sense, Strait sought to teach her students, for example, about empathy, a second-order historical concept, although she appeared to be more interested in it as a motivational tool and taught a form of everyday empathy rather than context-based historical empathy. Even though Strait varied her practices, employed a multicultural purview, and worked with the concept of (everyday) empathy, both teachers' approaches could be characterized as representing differing images of collective memory. Blair's was more traditional and singular and Strait's was more plural and nuanced, and about multicultural collective memories. Whereas Strait's practices opened up the interpretive landscape of the Civil Rights Movement, which Grant argues translated into greater benefits for her students, it was unclear how she helped her students deal with the interpretive conflicts that they may have encountered as a result of meeting collective *memories*.

Grant (2003) noted that the influence of the New York State Regents' Exam and its document-based questions (DBQs) on the teachers was uneven and of limited consequence. Rather, the teachers' personal commitments and visions about what history teaching should look like and their individual repertoires of first-order historical knowledge most influenced their practices. However, readers could conclude from reading the study that the Regents Exam was asking students to put on display their understanding of American collective memories (bits and pieces of several of them residing uncomfortably together) and that the teachers in different ways were helping students to do just that. In this sense, the teacher's visions of history could be understood as more closely aligned with and influenced by the Exam than it would seem.

Several recent studies have explored how beginning history teachers navigate the transition from their teacher education programs to the history classroom. What appears to motivate the research is the desire to document how teachers' knowledge of engaging their students in historical thinking practices common to the disciplinary approaches learned in teacher education programs is applied once the teachers leave the program and are inducted into the classroom. These studies are revealing. Effectively, the studies show how history teachers become primarily lecturers and storytellers (e.g., Strait, and particularly Blair), despite being taught in teacher preparation courses to engage their students more frequently in historical inquiry activities that forefront story analysis and interpretation. We summarize one such study here and refer to several others.

Hartzler-Miller (2001) studied a newly inducted history teacher, David, during his third year of teaching. David was a history major who chose to become licensed and teach high school students. As a student of history, he excelled. In both his history coursework and his teacher education program, David was immersed in coming to understand the nature of historical inquiry, learning that history was a consequence of the historian's effort to research, study, and interpret the past, and that such practices produced different interpretations that were disputed in the discipline. In interviews about how he understood what he was doing in the classroom, he talked about how important it was for his students to question the stories and narrative accounts of the past that historians construct. In the classroom, Hartzler-Miller's observation data showed that most of the time was spent with David talking (lecturing and storytelling) and students listening. Students were not asked "to interpret evidence [or] build their own interpretations" (p. 685). Hartzler-Miller referred to instruction as recitation style (see common practice descriptions in Cuban, 1991).

In attempting to understand the discrepancies between David's convictions about the importance of teaching historical inquiry to his students and his noninquiry, recitation-style classroom practice, Hartzler-Miller (2001) attributed it to his belief that first students should come to understand the enduring themes of a changing historical scholarship. It was his job to instill in students an understanding of those themes. Inquiry practices would be reserved for later in the students' history education careers, perhaps in college. For now, inquiry practices were best left to the trained professionals in history departments. David's beliefs appear to be relatively common among history teachers: Grade-school students are incapable of engaging in historical inquiry until they have mastered the "enduring narratives" produced by historians (collected in progressive, nation-building format in the textbook). What such beliefs ignore is that these narratives come about—in the first place—as a consequence of deep historical thinking and inquiry. As the research on the development of knowledge surrounding historical thinking strategies and use of second-order ideas makes clear, strategic and second-order understandings enable the production of stories that constitute first-order historical knowledge. Historical thinking and inquiry appear to be the *sine qua non* of deep historical understanding of the first-order type, a connection David seems not to have made—yet. However, the data Hartzler-Miller displays suggest that he could be very close to making it. For a similar study, that documented much the same results in the case of a second-year teacher, Angela, see van Hover and Yeager (2003). And for additional work on influences on history teaching practices in this vein, see Bohan and Davis (1998), Leinhardt (2000), McDiarmid & Vinten-Johansen (2000), Slekar (1998), and Yeager and Davis (1996).

Using a multifaceted survey, Hicks, Doolittle, and Lee (2004) asked 158 high school history teachers to indicate their purposes for teaching history, why they thought students should learn history in school, their purposes for using source materials in the history classroom, what sorts of actions students engaged in using such sources, and their frequency in using both print and Web-based source material. The most common rationales teachers provided for teaching the subject were to encourage individual student growth in a general sense and to help them understand common historical knowledge. The two most prevalent beliefs about why students should study history included the importance of making connections between the past and present and coming to understand "the story of America." Most of the teachers (67 percent) thought that the most important factor in using original source material involved providing students with a sense of conditions relevant to a historical period being studied. Sixty percent also thought that it was very important to use original source material as a context for developing "historical thinking skills." However, when Hicks et al. (2004) asked the teachers what types of actions they engaged their students in when analyzing the sources, 82 percent of the teachers indicated that much or most of the time students, at their request, were scouring sources looking for key individuals, events, and ideas. Evaluating the nature of the sources, engaging in identification and attribution, and judging their credibility in building historical arguments (i.e., source work) were practices most of the teachers said that they pursued only occasionally. Print and Web-based documents and sources appeared to be used as alternatives to the textbook account (the latter less so), but in the end the principal purpose for using them—despite indicating otherwise—remained the same: Acquiring those key names, events, and ideas that frame the collective memory of the American nation-building story covered by the standard textbook, history curricula, and common assessments.

These studies point to the conserving influences teachers' traditional beliefs about history and history teaching have on their practice. They also show the power of broad, coverage-based curricula and simplistic assessments to push teachers toward opting for the perceived efficiencies of lecturing and textbook study concerning a nationalist collective memory over relying on other teaching approaches. Searching to test alternative practices, some teachers-turned-researchers with dispositions toward disciplinary approaches have taken to reporting studies of their own teaching efforts. These studies describe some of the psychological and cognitive dimensions of teaching by using disciplinary approaches, and note their promises and limitations.

Bain (2000), for example, reported on the nature of how he taught history to high school students. He described teaching history as fundamentally an epistemic act. By that he meant that it involved understanding how historical knowledge is constructed, how the constructors work with traces of the past to shape the understandings that later appear in history books, and with what warrants for counting it as knowledge. He found that his students initially had difficulty with such ideas, preferring to think of history as ready made and authorless. Using a series of discussions and a variety of writing activities, Bain taught his students how to analyze historical accounts and build interpretations based on how varying accounts could be understood as forms of evidence in building arguments about what the past means. Using some preliminary analysis of student journal writing and data gleaned from classroom discussions of curricular topics studied, Bain noted that there was emerging evidence that the students' cognitive ideas and thinking capacities changed, and in some cases deepened. Bain appeared to have some success in showing students how analytic strategies (e.g., reading texts) and working with second-order concepts (e.g., accounts as evidence) influenced the nature of their first-order ideas in ways that focusing almost exclusively on the products of historical thinking (e.g., a textbook account) would not.

In a related study, VanSledright (2002) worked in a fifth-grade classroom for a semester to teach students American history (the colonial and the American Revolution periods). The students in the class were significantly diverse racially and ethnically, but less so socioeconomically in that most were working and/or middle class. VanSledright's goal, much like Bain's (2000), was to see if he could teach the fifth graders about the epistemic acts necessary to construct their own interpretations of the American past. This involved them in learning to read and analyze a variety of history texts as sources. On a path toward helping the students build their own understandings, he taught them, among other things, to think of recent synthetic historical accounts such as textbooks as fashioned from the artefacts and *residua* of the past and from what others have said those things mean when assembled together. The classroom culture became an investigative milieu in which groups of students worked from documents and accounts on curricular topics to construct interpretations that were later discussed and often vigorously debated by the whole class.

In an effort to document the consequences of his teaching practices, VanSledright (2002) collected specific data on what students learned from the experience. For example, in a pretest/post-test design using a group of eight students from the larger class of 23, he had them read a number of documents and images (on the Boston Massacre and the battle at Lexington Green) and think aloud about them while a tape recorder was running. In comparing the verbal protocol results from the pre and post assessments, he observed that seven of the eight had became more sophisticated in their capacity to read, analyze, and build interpretations from the texts, and that their interpretations grew more probing and finely nuanced. Several students noted that historical analysis can be difficult and sometimes leads to places where multiple interpretations must be maintained because perspective and sociocultural positions matter in history, both for those in the past and for us in the present. Despite cognitive and epistemic growth for some, other students clung tenaciously to the belief that if investigators dig deeply enough into the past, the one correct answer will appear. Researchers on Project Chata have also found similar patterns among the young students they studied (e.g., Lee & Ashby, 2000). Both of these self-studies provide insight into the complex nature of the cognitive, epistemic, and curricular thought and decision making that history teachers must engage in to teach their students from a disciplinary perspective. In this sense, they begin to answer the question: What do teachers need to know in order to teach history using a disciplinary approach?

The foregoing studies of history teaching suggest that there often is a mismatch between the disciplinary approaches (learning history by doing it; see, for example, Levstik & Barton, 1997) that researchers, teacher educators, and some reformers appear to advocate and the curricular, standards, accountability, and assessment policies (e.g., learning history by committing a commemorative story to memory and then recalling it later) currently in force particularly in the United States. The latter bring with them visions of history teaching that attempt to drive classroom practice by holding teachers accountable through assessments of their students. However, these visions of what history teaching should entail vary also. For example, in the state of Virginia, a look at the assessment practices that provide test score results on how well students master the state's Standards of Learning indicate that the vision of what history teaching should be is organized around the coverage of names and dates and events that policymakers there think important. Teachers focus on helping students commit that myriad of historical data to memory for the purpose of recalling it on the state's history assessment. Attention is paid almost exclusively to history's first-order knowledge terrain. The vision seems deeply committed to the collective memory (or heritage) approach. Students taking the history examination typically score at the lowest level of the smattering of subject-area tests the state administers every year.[3] For more on the influence of Virginia's test on teachers, see VanSledright and James (2002).

As Grant's (2003) study noted, in New York state, assessment officials include document-based questions (DBQs) in the history portion of Regents' Exam (in addition to an array of questions that more directly sample students' recall of first-order conceptual and narrative knowledge). Such DBQ items ask students to read, analyze, and write an interpretive essay based on a handful of source documents arranged around a particular historical event. Document-based questions can tap students' capacity to engage in a form of reasoning that may require some of the expertise disciplinary professionals use in the practice of doing history (Grant, 2003). If the items demand more than reading comprehension, they can require that teachers know how to engage in the process in order to teach their students how. New York's assessment and standards approach represents a somewhat different vision of what teaching history means than Virginia's, for example, one that borrows from both the collective memory (first-order knowledge recall items) and disciplinary approaches (DBQs). For an additional study of assessment policy and practice in New York state, see Grant et al. (2002).

---

[3]For more on the test score results, see Virginia's State Department of Education Web site, www.pen.k12.va.us/.

As this research work indicates, to the extent that testing and standards practices vary from state to state and country to country and shape history teaching, researchers studying history teachers in situ would expect to witness somewhat different teaching practices and visions. However, the most common approach observed and assessed, as we have noted, continues to be rooted in the capacity to teach elements of a nation-building collective memory represented in textbook treatments, at least in the United States and in other countries where historical study is principally used to promote a shared and official sense of national identity (Barton & Levstik, 2004; Dickinson et al., 1995; Wertsch, 2000). However, the results from these assessments, as we noted, are historically less than salutary, which, by extension, can serve to indict textbooks, traditional coverage-based curricula, and the types of common practices used to teach them. Nonetheless, it is important to note that the assessments themselves are not without serious flaws. For essays on the significant limits of such history assessments in general and for how they impact history teaching practices and with what consequences, see Segall (2003) and Wineburg (2004). Disputes over what history teaching should look like, what students should know, and what the overall purpose for studying history in school should be recently prompted Rothstein (2004) to declare that education policymakers in the United States are in no position to be using high-stakes assessments in history education until these matters are better resolved.

History Teaching in England

Although the British experience similar contestations over what history teaching should entail (e.g., Lee, 1995), there has been considerably more agreement that the approach teachers take should center on the disciplinary method. This has enabled British researchers over three decades to study how children's ideas of procedural (strategic) and second-order knowledge progress as they learn more about them. This obviously requires that teachers know about these concepts and ideas if they are to be able to teach them. As in the United States, history teaching in England has not been researched as heavily as has student learning. However, there has been no shortage of recommendations for teaching arising from the work on student learning (e.g., Arthur & Phillips, 2000; Haydyn, Arthur, & Hunt, 1997; Husbands, 1996; Lomas, 1990). Recently, a school-based study indicative of British scholarship emerged.

Husbands et al. (2003) worked closely with four teachers at four different grade levels and in four different schools in Great Britain. Their principal concern was to understand the types of knowledge teachers described themselves using as they planned to teach and actually taught history lessons. The researchers documented how the teachers drew from different types of knowledge to develop lesson goals, then plan and teach them. Husbands et al. noted that the teachers held deep domain knowledge, of both first-order and second order ideas and procedures for doing history (strategic knowledge). They also knew about a variety of resources (documentary evidence, activities, videotapes) that they drew from in planning and teaching history. Attempts to use lessons to move students' historical-thinking capacities on a progression from less to more sophisticated required that the teachers also know much about their students. Teachers were astute at describing their knowledge of students' learning processes. They were able to anticipate the problems and catch points students would encounter and map strategies for dealing with them because they understood progression in historical cognition (e.g., Fig. 23.2). The researchers provided a variety of excerpts of the teachers talking about their practice, knowledge, and decision making. In this study, the researchers claimed to let the teachers tell them what they knew and believed about teaching history, rather than impose their own preconceived categories. However, it is clear that the researchers were interested in the full complement of types of domain knowledge (along with how this knowledge intersected with their students' cognitive capabilities) and used them as categories to describe how the teachers negotiated their practices.

Being able to articulate historical thinking and understanding and its application to the classroom from a disciplinary perspective is characteristic of the British tradition in history education research since about 1975. Finding teachers who can articulate these ideas cogently, so that researchers avoid imposing them, is another characteristic more common to what occurs in England than in other places, most notably the United States. Because such teachers teach second-order ideas and strategic-reasoning capabilities, this enables researchers studying student learning in the United Kingdom to develop progression models that describe how students' historical thinking develops in classroom contexts (Fig. 23.2). As the Husbands et al. (2003) study points up, being able to chart progression among students studying history in the classroom can assist teachers in making pedagogical decisions that in turn help students become more powerful thinkers and, therefore, move along the path toward deeper historical understandings.

By contrast, progression models, for example, on understanding and working with accounts, thinking about what constitutes historical evidence, or developing a sense of empathy that makes historical context more intelligible, are of little use in classrooms where accounts, evidence, and empathy are seldom seriously considered. As research in the United States suggests, the preoccupation with focusing almost exclusively on the products (first-order knowledge) of historical thinking makes such progression models seem of little pedagogical value to teachers because the models focus on ideas and practices they seldom teach. This is unfortunate, particularly in view of the fact that historical understanding—making sense of the past—depends on being able to become more sophisticated in reasoning with and about the past.

Work in history education continues apace. A recent volume edited by Seixas (2004) has appeared that attempts to theorize about the nature of historical consciousness. It draws on work by a variety of authors, hailing from countries such as Canada, Germany, and Great Britain. The book is divided into three sections, the middle one of which trains its sights on the relationship of theorizations about historical consciousness to history education, both in and out of school.

Cognitive research in history education, perhaps in a nod to Shulman's call for more subject-specific research, tends to draw from the discipline of history and the types of substantive and procedural knowledge comprising it. This work has begun to provide valuable insights into how students at various ages learn to think historically as they come to make better and deeper sense of the past. It remains early yet, but the progression models constructed by British researchers may emerge as particularly useful in thinking about a theory of academic development in the domain that, in turn, may provide valuable tools for thinking about psychologies of teaching the subject in school. However, a note of caution and one of concern are in order.

Developmental models often promise more than they can deliver in that they suggest ways of thinking about learners that can imply rigid, lock-step movement across a progression in cognitive change. We witnessed such applications of Piagetian ideas in history education in England in the 1960s and 1970s with gloomy predictions about children's capacities to understand the subject that turned out to be deceptive. Avoiding the act of turning progression models into developmental cages is the focus of the caveats described in detail by Lee and Shemilt (2003). Their observations about progressive cognitive development in history education are tempered by concerns that children's ideas are constructed directionally (from less to more cognitively sophisticated), but that this development does not occur at the same pace for every student and that cognitive backsliding, if you will, can and does occur, often in new learning situations. The nature of sociocultural contexts in which children have opportunities to study history remain important to consider.

This brings us to our note of concern. It is difficult to understate the powerful sociopolitical purposes to which history education can be put. We have observed that, in some countries (notably the United States), historical study appears to serve the primary purpose of nationalist identity building. In this sense, the typical school contexts in which children study history submerge it largely under the banner of collective memory and heritage commemoration (Seixas, 2000; Lowenthal, 1996). To the extent that this primary purpose continues to drive history education policy, broad history curriculum coverage routines, correct commemorative story reproductions, and traditional teaching practices will predominate. If accountability projects continue to rely on inexpensive, standardized assessments rooted in the efficiencies of psychometrics (Wineburg, 2004) that willfully, or not, align with this celebratory nationalist purpose, they will only reinforce practices and policies that are already in place and have been for decades. The result may be that, despite the power of the cognitive research to point a constructive path toward what it means to learn about and deeply understand the past, there will be quite little impact on history education as a whole.

GEOGRAPHY EDUCATION RESEARCH

Cognitive research in geography education has focused largely on spatial reasoning. Spatial reasoning is important in geography because cartographic practices (map making) and map reading remain pivotal activities in the domain. Geography explores the relationships of the Earth's many different surface features with how human populations interact with them. Geographers represent these relationships primarily through maps. In many ways, maps (as spatial representations) are to geography what texts (as linguistic representations) are to history.

Mapping involves generating external representations of the Earth. Doing research on understanding those representations has been a preoccupation of cognitive researchers working in the domain. Part of this has to do with charting academic developmental paths in children's spatial reasoning in geography. Some researchers have been asking how spatial-reasoning capacity develops, when, and in what teaching contexts. Unlike the research in history education where much of the literature has accumulated in mainstream educational research journals, geography education research appears most frequently in disciplinary journals such as the *Journal of Geography* and the *Annals of the Association of American Geographers*. Although a variety work appears there, space limitations prevent us from sampling more than a small number of studies that fall in the cognitive realm.

It is important to observe, that, although there is a body of work in geography education, only a relatively small portion of it is cognitive in orientation; much of the rest concerns itself with advocacy for different geographic education policies, curriculum designs, and teaching approaches; and it lags behind the cottage industry research in history education. For a look at a fuller spectrum of studies, see Gregg and Leinhardt (1994).

Spatial Reasoning in Geography with Implications for Teaching

Experts in geography who construct maps use them as means to represent the ways in which they address questions stemming from land-to-hand relationships. That is, they investigate how humans interact with the Earth's surfaces and use spatial reasoning and cartographic illustrations to depict these relationships. Symbol systems such as coordinates (longitude and latitude), scale and proportion, and directionals (north, south, east, west) predominate. Because maps often appear as proportional two-dimensional projections of a three-dimensional Earth (sphere), distortion is a common by-product. Understanding symbol systems and distortions and methods for controlling the latter create demanding cognitive requirements for learners.

Downs and Liben (1990, 1991) have extensively studied the development of ideas and understandings of spatial reasoning regarding maps and map making (see also Downs, 1985, and Liben & Downs, 1989). Theirs is likely the most extensive program in the field from a cognitive developmental standpoint. In one study, Downs and Liben (1991) used data from their research program to compare the spatial-reasoning expertise of cartographers with that of the college students they teach. Cartographers, who are deeply knowledgeable about the process of rendering three-dimensional space into two-dimensional projections, work with relatively precise correspondences that dictate map form. Through correspondences, experts attempt to control and limit the inevitable distortions that occur. How correspondences work and what clues a map provides to understanding them is the task of learning to read, think geographically about, and ultimately understand a map. Correspondences have complex geometric properties that function through map projections and their coordinate systems. Downs and Liben argue that understanding these relationships is central to developing geographic and spatial-reasoning expertise.

Downs and Liben (1991) studied how college students in their sample understood projection. They used a Piagetian task in which the students imagined how shadows of various three-dimensional objects (triangles, circles,

pentagons; some thin, others thick) would appear projected onto a two-dimensional screen at various angles to the eye (90 degrees to either side of zero at 30-degree increments). The college students had some difficulty identifying the correct projections at all degrees but zero, especially for the thicker forms. Extrapolating from other Piagetian studies of Euclidian spatial concepts, they argued that children in general and adults without specific geographic domain knowledge would have difficulty understanding the system by which cartographers transform (using coordinates) a three-dimensional space to a two-dimensional one. They pointed out that this transformation is bounded by a coordinate system of some sort (variety is possible) that is linked to a map's purpose. Once a system is chosen, however, it remains rule-bound. Unless learners were able to quickly make sense of a map's purpose and intent, they would have difficulty recognizing the coordinate system and how it functions. Experts (e.g., academic geographers), they noted, take such knowledge for granted because it served an automaticity function. Assuming that college students held it as well makes teaching them difficult, they observed. They used the observations gleaned from the data to suggest a cognitive-developmental approach to geographic education. They recommended the shadow task and efforts to relate coordinate systems and two-dimensional projections directly to actual three-dimensional physical spaces as strategies for making geographic thinking more transparent in the classroom. They also acknowledged how much more work researchers in the field needed to accomplish in order to make geographic thinking clear. They proposed additional expert-novice studies as a centerpiece of such a research program.

On the release of the United States National Geography Standards in 1994, Downs (1994) published a paper in which he laid out a more full agenda for geographic education research. First, he underscored the lack of a substantive empirical research literature that could be used to address questions about what it means to become more expert in geographical thinking and to make scope and sequence decisions about a K-12 geography curriculum. (Although Downs shows no such concern, it might be considered ironic that K-12 Standards, which at least imply a developmental progression, were constructed largely in the absence of a solid body of research work.) Downs reaffirmed the importance of expert-novice studies as a means of understanding development in what he called a life-span approach to geographic education. He described how he understood expertise in the domain and then noted as exemplary the type of research work Vosniadou and Brewer (1992) were doing to understand U.S. elementary children's developing knowledge of the shape of the Earth. Vosniadou and Brewer's research pointed up a progression in students' thinking as they moved from personal, experiential understandings to more scientific, geographical constructions. He also noted an empirical study on what types of cartographic skills readers needed to possess to navigate the *New York Times*, undertaken by Gregg, Stainton, and Leinhardt (1997) at the University of Pittsburgh, as a second example of the type of research needed in the field. Finally, he described a set of questions that he believed should frame the cognitive and developmental research agenda he was imagining.

Although Downs was calling principally on his fellow geographers to mount this research program, the response often has come from educational psychologists, such as Leinhardt and her students (current and former) and colleagues at the Learning and Research Development Center (LRDC) in Pittsburgh (e.g., Bausmith & Leinhardt, 1998; Gregg, Stainton, & Leinhardt, 1997; Leinhardt, Stainton, and Bausmith, 1998). One recent study by these LRDC researchers may further exemplify what Downs (1994) had in mind. Anderson and Leinhardt (2002) constructed a novice-expert map-projection task in which they asked expert geographers (n = 7) and three groups of novices (seven college students enrolled in their first cartography class, seven undergraduate geography majors, and nine preservice secondary social studies teachers) to estimate how they would plot a flight path between pairs of cities around the world (e.g., New York to Moscow, Santiago to Singapore, New York to Cape Town). They were interested in charting the differences among the groups on how they identified (successfully or not) and then reasoned about most efficient flight routes. The tasks involved thinking aloud about spatial reasoning regarding plotting the course of the flights on two-dimensional Mercator projections of the Earth's three-dimensional surface. Such studies, they argued, help us understand the nature of the cognitive moves separating novices from experts and begin the process of charting the progression from one to the other.

Anderson and Leinhardt (2002) coded successful responses of each of the four groups using three codes: impasse (success prompted by devising a strategy following a task obstruction), rule (success by invoking a rule learned for such tasks), retrieval (success following the use of a set of domain-specific strategies retrieved from memory and applied to the problem). The experts solved almost 70 percent the flight-path problem tasks using primarily impasse-driven strategies. However, the experts also were able to draw on rules and retrieval strategies for almost half of the tasks. Advanced novices (the geography majors) solved 60 percent of the tasks correctly drawing most on map-projection rules and impasse-driven strategies. By contrast with the experts, they used retrieval strategies to solve fewer than 5 percent of the tasks. Both undergraduate non-geography students and preservice teachers drew only from impasse-driven strategies and rules and possessed no retrieval strategies that worked for them successfully. The preservice teachers scored lowest in solving the tasks correctly, doing so on fewer than 15 percent of the occasions. The researchers described the spatial reasoning efforts of each group, comparing and contrasting the ways in which they thought about the problem spaces. They also examined and described the cognitive processes the groups engaged in that failed to produce success (e.g., rigidly invoking the rule that the shortest distance between two points is a straight line).

Anderson and Leinhardt (2002) noted that differences in performance were tied to the amount of formal education each group had in geography, and specifically, what geographical thinking capabilities they could draw on in understanding how map projections distort the Earth's surface (see also Rossano & Morrison, 1996). Success as expressed in the ability to use rules and criteria about distortion in map projections following an impasse in task solution was associated with greater expertise. The researchers pointed out that the preservice teachers, in most cases, were "unaware even that the [flight path] would be a curve" and that they had "no mechanism for figuring out the relation between the curvature of the Earth and a flat map" (p. 313). They used the data from the study to highlight the relationship between map-projection reasoning and capacity to solve map-related problems. In turn, they linked this to what was needed in improvement of the preparation of preservice teachers and to how that improvement might help deepen their students' map-reasoning capabilities and understandings.

Teaching About Maps and Projection in Schools

We were unable to locate recent studies of teachers teaching geography to students in classrooms in the United States or elsewhere that approached it from a cognitive or psychological perspective. Anecdotal reports about geography teaching (see Downs, 1994) indicate that much time in the United States anyway is spent drilling students on map characteristics and concepts (e.g., compass rose, longitude, latitude) without much effort devoted to teaching students how to reason with or about maps or understand how the concepts are deployed to construct maps. Another common practice, or so the reports go, involves asking students to memorize place names and locations and reproduce them later on assessments. Very little time is spent working with pivotal ideas such as how all maps involve some distortion and distortion is something cartographers take pains to control with regulatory systems that must be imposed, remain rule-bound, and operate relative to map purpose.

National standardized test results such as those produced by the National Assessment of Educational Progress (e.g., Persky et al., 1996) in the United States indicate that students develop some general understandings about maps and the concept of projection, but that they lack understandings of how projection works and are influenced by the structure and rule-boundedness of the representational system (e.g., Mercator projection), and how cartographers make such decisions based on defining map function. In many ways, the situation in history education in the United States is paralleled by that in geography: Students are taught to focus on relatively narrow elements of the much larger, richer array of domain concepts and ideas with relatively poor retention. Instead of participating in and coming to understand map construction and function as a means of becoming spatially literate, students appear to be taught to acquire map concepts and ideas without knowing what they are for or for what purpose they might be used. Spatial reasoning often is sacrificed to term, place, and type recognition, but without significant retention successes (Anderson & Leinhardt, 2002, p. 315).

RESEARCH IN OTHER DOMAINS

Like history and geography, the domains of economics and political science also serve as referents for social studies school subjects. However, sustained cognitive research in these areas has lagged behind. There are research studies in these domains scattered across the child development literature undertaken often by developmental psychologists, but long-term focused work has been limited. We note a few exceptions here.

In economics, the exception has been cognitive research accomplished by Berti (and sometimes with Bombi) in Italy (e.g., Berti, 1995; Berti & Bombi, 1988, 1989) on children's understandings of banking, production and distribution systems, the nature of work, and how workplace environments are structured and influence economic exchange. Carreterro and Voss (1994) also have made contributions to this field, drawing from international studies. Recently, Berti and other colleagues have begun examining children's understandings of political concepts and ideas such as the nature of law, nation-state, and the workings of governmental and judicial systems (Berti, 2004, Berti & Andriolo, 2001; Berti & Benesso, 1998; Berti & Ugolini, 1998).

Political socialization research has typically characterized much of the more sustained work in the domain of political science. Arguably the most notable of this work has been done by Torney-Purta (1990). Most recently, Torney-Purta and colleagues (Amadeo, Torney-Purta, Lehmann, Husfeldt, & Nikolova, 2002) have been engaged in an international study of political attitudes, ideas, and understandings of students at a variety of ages. This work tries to make sense of how students learn about political ideas and concepts, in what contexts both in and out of school, and how what they learn influences the types of political actions they may or do engage in.

At the early elementary school level in the United States, economics and political science as domain referents for social studies tend to be vague. However, many students do study about transportation systems; governmental structures; the production, function, and distribution of clothing, food, shelter; and other topics that Brophy and Alleman (2005) refer to as "cultural universals." Since about the middle 1990s, Brophy and Alleman have undertaken a sustained study of what children in grades K through 3 understand about these ideas and concepts before and after they are taught about them. They have been particularly interested in charting how these young students' ideas change as a consequence of different types of pedagogies. Portions of this body work have appeared in individual publications over the past decade, but are collected in full in Brophy and Alleman (2005).

LOOKING FORWARD

In the domains that constitute social studies, much empirical work in the cognitive vein remains to be undertaken in order to plot pathways toward academic development. This is particularly the case with regard to geographic, economic, and political forms of cognition. The work in history has begun to yield some encouraging results, as the foregoing review implies. However, even in this domain, despite the development of models of progression in history, work lags behind that in mathematics education, for example. We hope that researchers and graduate students read this review to find openings in which they can pursue new lines of work that will bring us closer to understanding academic growth in the social studies domains. In turn, and with concerns for possible misuses of developmental theories in mind, we would like to envision a day when this corpus of research enables a more robust psychology of teaching in the field.

ACKNOWLEDGMENT

The authors collectively thank Patricia Alexander, Keith Barton, and Peter Lee for constructive criticism on early versions of this chapter. The second author thanks the Comunidad Autonoma de Madrid (Grant No. 06/0114/2003) and the Spanish Ministry of Education (Grant No. PR2003-0026 and SEJ20043-01879/EDUC) for their support.

References

Alexander, P. (2000). Toward a model of academic development: Schooling and the acquisition of knowledge. *Educational Researcher, 29*, 28-33, 44.

Amadeo, J., Torney-Purta, J., Lehmann, R., Husfeldt, V., & Nikolova, R. (2002). *Civic knowledge and engagement: An IEA study of upper secondary students in sixteen countries*. Amsterdam: International Association for the Evaluation of Educational Achievement.

Anderson, K., & Leinhardt, G. (2002). Maps as representations: Expert novice comparison of projection understanding. *Cognition and Instruction, 20*, 283-321.

Angvik, M., & von Borries, B. (1997). *Youth and history: A comparative European survey on historical consciousness and political attitudes among adolescents*. Hamburg: Korber-Stiftung.

Arthur, J., & Phillips, R. (2000). *Issues in history teaching*. London: Routledge.

Ashby. R., & Lee, P. J. (1987). Discussing the evidence. *Teaching History, 48*, 13-17.

Ashby, R., & Lee, P. J. (1998, April). *Information, opinion, and beyond*. Paper presented at the annual meeting of the American Educational Research Association, San Diego, CA.

Bain, R. (2000). Into the breach: Using theory and research to shape history instruction. In P. Stearns, P. Seixas, & S. Wineburg (Eds.), *Knowing, teaching, and learning history: National and international perspectives* (pp. 331-352). New York: New York University Press.

Banks & McGee-Banks, C. (Eds.) (2001). *Handbook of research on multicultural education*. New York: Macmillan.

Barton, K. (1996). Narrative simplifications in elementary students' historical thinking. In J. Brophy (Ed.), *Advances in research on teaching: Vol. 6. Teaching and learning history* (pp. 51-84). Greenwich, CT: JAI.

Barton, K. (1997). "I just kinda know": Elementary students' ideas about historical evidence. *Theory and Research in Social Education, 24*, 407-430.

Barton, K. (2001). "You'd be wanting to know about the past": Social contexts of children's understanding in Northern Ireland and the USA. *Comparative Education, 37*, 89-106.

Barton, K., & Levstik, L. (1996). "Back when God was around and everything": Elementary students' understanding of historical time. *American Educational Research Journal, 33*, 419-454.

Barton, K., & Levstik, L. (1998). "It wasn't a good part of our history": National identity and students' explanations of historical significance. *Teachers College Record, 99*, 478-513.

Barton, K., & Levstik, L. (2004). *Teaching history for the common good*. Mahweh, NJ: Lawrence Erlbaum Associates.

Bausmith, J., & Leinhardt, G. (1998). Middle-school students' map construction: Understanding complex spatial displays. *Journal of Geography, 97*, 93-107.

Beatty, A., Reese, C., Persky, H., & Carr, P. (1996). *NAEP 1994 U.S. history report card*. Washington, D.C.: U.S. Department of Education, Office of Research and Improvement.

Berliner, D., & Calfee, R. (Eds.) (1996). *Handbook of educational psychology*. New York: Macmillan.

Berti, A. (1995). Knowledge restructuring in an economic subdomain: Banking. In W. Schnotz, S. Vosniadou, & M. Carrertero (Eds.), *New perspectives on conceptual change* (pp. 113-133). New York: Pergamon.

Berti, A. (2002). Children's understanding of society: Psychological studies and their educational implications. In E. Nasman & A. Ross (Eds.), *Children's understanding in the new Europe* (pp. 89-107). Stoke on Trent, UK: Trentham.

Berti, A. (2004). Children's understanding of politics. In M. Barrett & E. Buchanan-Barrow (Eds.), *Children's understanding of society*. Hove, England: Psychology Press.

Berti, A., & Andriolo, A. (2001). Third graders' understanding of core political concepts (law, nation-state, government) before and after teaching. *Genetic, Social, and General Psychology Monographs, 127*, 346-377.

Berti, A., & Benesso, C. (1998). The concept of nation-state in Italian elementary school children: Spontaneous concepts and effects of teaching. *Genetic, Social, and General Psychology Monographs, 124*, 185-209.

Berti, A., & Bombi, A. (1988). *The child's construction of economics*. Cambridge, UK: Cambridge University Press.

Berti, A., & Bombi, A. (1989). Environmental differences in understanding production and distribution. In J. Valsiner (Ed.), *Child development in cultural context* (pp. 247-272). Toronto: Hogrefe & Huber.

Berti, A., & Ugolini, E. (1998). Developing knowledge of the judicial system: A domain-specific approach. *Journal of Genetic Psychology, 159*, 221-236.

Bodnar, J. (1992). *Remaking America: Public memory, commemoration, and patriotism in the twentieth century*. Princeton, NJ: Princeton University Press.

Bohan, C., & Davis, O. L. (1998). Historical constructions: How social studies student teachers' historical thinking is reflected in their writing of history. *Theory and Research in Social Education, 26*, 173-197.

Brophy J., & Alleman, J. (2005). *Children's thinking about cultural universals*. Mahwah, NJ: Lawrence Erlbaum Associates.

Brophy, J., & VanSledright, B. (1997). *Teaching and learning history in elementary schools*. New York: Teachers College Press.

Buehl, M., Alexander, P., & Murphy, P. (2002). Beliefs about schooled knowledge: Domain specific or domain general. *Contemporary Educational Psychology, 27*, 415-449.

Carr, D. (1986). *Time, narrative and history*. Bloomington: Indiana University Press.

Carretero, M., Jacott, L., Limon, M., Lopez-Manjon, A., & Leon, J. (1994). Historical knowledge: Cognitive and instructional implications. In M. Carretero & J. Voss (Eds.), *Cognitive and instructinal processes in history and the social sciences* (pp. 357-376). Hillsdale, NJ: Lawrence Erlbaum Associates.

Carretero, M., L., Limon, M., Lopez-Manjon, A., & Leon, J. (1994). Historical knowledge: Cognitive and instructional implications. In M. Carretero & J. Voss (Eds.), *Cognitive and instructional processes in history and the social sciences* (pp. 357-376). Hillsdale, NJ: Lawrence Erlbaum Associates.

Carretero, M., & Voss, J. (1994). *Cognitive and instructional processes in history and the social sciences*. Hillsdale, NJ: Lawrence Erlbaum Associates.

Cercadillo, L. (2001). Significance in history: Students ideas in England and Spain. In A. Dickinson, P. Gordon, & P. Lee (Eds.), *International review of history education* (pp. 116–145). London: Woburn.

Clark, A. (2004). History, historiography, and the politics of pedagogy in Australia. *Theory and Research in Social Education, 32*, 379–396.

Collingwood R. (1946/1994). *The idea of history*. Oxford: Oxford University Press.

Cornbleth, C. (2002). Images of America: What youth *do* know about the United States. *American Educational Research Journal, 39*, 519–552.

Cuban, L. (1991). History of teaching in social studies. In J. Shaver (Ed.), *Handbook of research on social studies teaching and learning* (pp. 197—209). New York: Macmillan.

den Heyer, K. (2003). Between every 'now' and 'then': A role for the study of historical agency in history and social studies education. *Theory and Research in Social Education, 31*, 411–434.

Dickinson, A., Gordon, P., Lee, P., & Slater, J. (Eds.) (1995). *International yearbook of history education, vol. 1*. London: Woburn.

Downs, R. (1985). The representation of space; Its development in children and in cartography. In R. Cohen (Ed.), *The development of spatial cognition* (pp. 323–345). Hilldale, NJ: Lawwrence Erlbaum Associates.

Downs, R. (1994). Being and becoming a geographer: An agenda for geography education. *Annals of the Association of American Geographers, 84*, 175–191.

Downs, R., & Liben, L. (1990). The role of projective spatial concepts in map understanding by children. *Children's Environments Quarterly, 7*, 17–27.

Downs, R., & Liben, L. (1991). The development of expertise in geography: A cognitive-developmental approach to geographic education. *Annals of the Association of American Geographers, 81*, 304–327.

Epstein, T. (1998). Deconstructing differences in African American and European American adolescents' perspectives on United States history. *Curriculum Inquiry, 28*, 397–423.

Foster, S., Hoge. J., & Rosch, R. (1999). Thinking aloud about history: Children and adolescents' responses to historical photographs. *Theory and Research in Social Education, 27*, 179–214.

Foster, S., & Yeager, E. (1999). "You've got to put together the pieces": English 12-year-olds encounter and learn from historical evidence. *Journal of Curriculum and Supervision, 14*, 286–317.

Gardner, H. (1991). *The unschooled mind*. New York: Basic Books.

Grant, S. G. (2003). *History lessons: Teaching, learning, and testing in U. S. high school history classrooms*. Mahwah, NJ: Lawrence Erlbaum Associates.

Grant, S. G., Gradwell, J., Lauricella, A., Derme-Insinna, A., Pullano, L., and Tzetzo, K. (2002). When increasing stakes need not mean increasing standards: The case of the New York state global history and geography exam. *Theory and Research in Social Education, 30*, 488–515.

Gregg, M., & Leinhardt, G. (1994). Mapping out geography: An example of epistemology and education. *Review of Educational Research, 64*, 311–361.

Gregg, M., Stainton, C., & Leinhardt, G. (1997). Strategies for geographic memory: Oh, what a state we're in! *International Research in Geographical and Environmental Education, 6*, 41–59.

Hartzler-Miller, C. (2001). Making sense of "best practice" in teaching history. *Theory and Research in Social Education, 29*, 672–695.

Haydn, T., Arthur, J., & Hunt, M. (1997). *Learning to teach history in the secondary school*. London: Routledge.

Hicks, D., Doolittle, P., & Lee, J. (2004). Social studies teachers' use of classroom-based and web-based historical primary sources. *Theory and Research in Social Education, 32*, 213–247.

Hofer, B. K., & Pintrich, P. (2002). *Personal epistemology: The psychology of beliefs about knowledge and knowing*. Mahwah, NJ: Lawrence Erlbaum Associates.

Husbands, C. (1996). *What is history teaching? Language, ideas, and meaning in learning about the past*. Buckingham; UK: Open University Press.

Husbands, C., Kitson, A., & Pendry, A. (2003). *Understanding history teaching*. Philadelphia: Open University Press.

Jacott, L., López-Manjón, A., & Carretero, M. (1998). Generating explanations in history. In J. F. Voss, & M. Carretero (Eds.), *Learning and reasoning in history* (pp. 307–330). London: Woburn.

Koselleck, R. (2002). *The practice of conceptual history: Timing history, spacing concepts*. Stanfords, CA: Stanford University Press.

Lee, P. J. (1995). History and the national curriculum in England. In A. Dickinson, P. Gordon, P. Lee, & J. Slater, *International yearbook of history education, vol. 1* (pp. 73–123). London: Woburn.

Lee, P. J., & Ashby, R. (2000). Progression in historical understanding among students ages 7–14. In P. Stearns, P. Seixas, & S. Wineburg (Eds.), *Knowing, teaching, and learning history* (pp. 199–222). New York: New York University Press.

Lee, P. J., Dickinson, A., & Ashby, R. (1997). Just another emporer: Understanding action in the past. *International Journal of Educational Research, 27*, 233–244.

Lee, P. J., & Shemilt, D. (2003). A scaffold not a cage: Progression and progression models in history. *Teaching History, 113*, 13–24.

Leinhardt, G. (2000). Lessons on teaching and learning in history from Paul's pen. In P. Stearns, S. Wineburg, & P. Seixas (Eds.), *Knowing, teaching, and learning history* (pp. 223–245). New York: New York University Press.

Leinhardt, G., Stainton, C., & Bausmith, J. (1998). Constructing maps collaboratively. *Journal of Geography, 97*, 19–30.

Levesque, S. (2003). "Bin Laden is responsible; it was shown on the tape": Canadian high school students' historical understanding of terrorism. *Theory and Research in Social Education, 31*, 174–202.

Levstik, L. (2000). Articulating the silences: Teachers' and adolescents' conceptions of historical significance. In P. Stearns, S. Wineburg, & P. Seixas (Eds.), *Knowing, teaching, and learning history* (pp. 284-305). New York: New York University Press.

Levstik, L., & Barton, K. (1996). They still use some of their past: Historical salience in elementary children's chronological thinking. *Journal of Curriculum Studies, 28*, 531-576.

Levstik, L., & Barton, K. (1997). *Doing history: Investigating with children in elementary and middle schools*. Mahwah, NJ: Lawrence Erlbaum Associates.

Liben, L., & Downs, R. (1989). Understanding maps as symbols: The development of map concepts in children. In H. Reese (Ed.), *Advances in child development and behavior* (pp. 145-201). New York: Academic Press.

Limón, M. (2000). Motivación y cambio conceptual: implicaciones para el aprendizaje y la enseñanza de las Ciencias Naturales, la Historia y la Etica en la E. S. O. [Motivation and conceptual change: implications for science, history and ethics learning and teaching]. Madrid: CIDE.

Limón, M. (2002). Conceptual change in history. In M. Limón & L. Mason (Eds.), *Reconsidering conceptual change: Issues in theory and practice* (pp. 259-289). Dordrecht, Netherlands: Kluwer.

Limón, M., Massa, L., & Serrano, M. (2004, May). Influence of prior knowledge and interest in the evaluation of epistemological beliefs. Paper presented at the European Symposium on Conceptual Change, Athens, Greece.

Lomas, T. (1990). *Teaching and assessing historical understanding*. London: Historical Association.

Lowenthal, D. (1996). *The heritage crusade and the spoils of history*. Cambridge; UK: Cambridge University Press.

McDiarmid, W., & Vinten-Johansen, P. (2000). A catwalk across the great divide: Redesigning the history teaching methods course. In P. Stearns, P. Seixas, and S. Wineburg, (Eds.), *Knowing, teaching, and learning history* (pp. 156-117). New York: New York University Press.

Mink, L. (1987). Philosophical analysis and historical understanding. In B. Fay, E. Golob, & R. Vann (Eds.), *Historical understanding* (pp. 130-149). Ithaca; NY: Cornell University Press.

National Council for the Social Studies (1993). Defining the social studies. *The Social Studies Professional, 114*, 7.

Nora, P. (1996). *Realms of memory: The construction of the French past*. New York: Columbia University Press.

Paxton, R. (1999). A deafening silence: History textbooks and the students who read them. *Review of Educational Research, 69*, 315-339.

Perfetti, C., Britt, M. A., Rouet, J., Georgi, M., & Mason, R. (1994). How students use texts to reason about historical uncertainty. In M. Carretero & J. Voss (Eds.), *Cognitive and instructional processes in history and the social sciences* (pp. 257-284). Hillsdale, NJ: Lawrence Erlbaum Associattes.

Persky, H., Reese, C., O'Sullivan, C., Lazer, S., Moore, J., & Shakrani, S. (1996). *NAEP 1994 geography report card*. Washington, DC: U. S. Government Printing Office.

Rossano, M., & Morrison, T. (1996). Learning from maps: General processes and map-structure influences. *Cognition and Instruction, 14*, 109-137.

Rothstein, R. (2004). We are not ready to assess history performance. *Journal of American History, 90*, 1381-1391.

Rouet, J. F., Marron, M. A., Perfetti, Ch. A.; & Favart, M. (1998). Understanding historical controversies: Students' evaluation and use of documentary evidence. In J. F. Voss & M. Carretero (Eds.), *Learning and reasoning in history* (pp. 95-116). London: Woburn.

Rusen, J. (1993). *Studies in metahistory*. Pretoria: Human Sciences Research Council.

Schwab, J. (1978). The practical: Translation into curriculum. In I. Westbury & N. Wilkop (Eds.), *Science, curriculum, and liberal education: Selected essays* (pp. 365-383). Chicago: University of Chicago Press.

Segall, A. (2003). The impact of state-mandated testing according to social studies teachers: The Michigan Educational Assessment Program (MEAP) as a case study of consequences. *Theory and Research in Social Education, 31*, 287-325.

Seixas, P. (1996). Conceptualizing the growth of historical understanding. In D. Olson & N. Torrance (Eds.), *The handbook of psychology in education*. Oxford, UK: Blackwell.

Seixas, P. (1997). Mapping the terrain of historical significance. *Social Education, 61*, 28-31.

Seixas, P. (2000). Schweigen! die Kinder! or, does postmodern history have a place in the schools? In P. Stearns, P. Seixas, & S. Wineburg, (Eds.), *Knowing, teaching, and learning history* (pp. 15-37). New York: New York University Press.

Seixas, P. (Ed.) (2004). *Theorizing historical consciousness*. Toronto: University of Toronto Press.

Shemilt, D. (1980). *History 13-16 evaluation study*. Edinburgh: Holmes McDougall.

Shemilt, D. (1987). Adolescent ideas about evidence and methodology in history. In C. Portal (Ed.), *The history curriculum for teachers* (pp. 62-99). London: Falmer.

Shulman, L. (1987). Knowledge and teaching: Foundations of a new reform. *Harvard Educational Review, 57*, 1-22.

Slekar, T. (1998). Epistemological entanglements: Preservice elementary teachers' "apprenticeship of observation" and the teaching of history. *Theory and Research in Social Education, 26*, 485-507.

Smith, J., & Niemi, R. (2001). Learning history in school: The impact of course work and instructional practices on achievement. *Theory and Research in Social Education, 29*, 18-42.

Stanford, M. (1986). *The nature of historical knowledge*. Oxford: Blackwell.

Stearns, P., Seixas, P., & Wineburg, S. (2000). *Knowing, teaching, and learning history: National and international perspectives*. New York: New York University Press.

Torney-Purta, J. (1990). From attitudes and knowledge to schemata: Expanding the outcomes of political socialization research. In O. Ichilov (Ed.), *Political socialization, citizenship education, and democracy* (pp. 98-115). New York: Teachers College Press.

van Drie & van Boxtel (2003). Developing conceptual understanding through talk and mapping. *Teaching History, 110*, 27-31.

van Hover, S., & Yeager, E. (2003). "'Making' students better people?': A case study of a beginning history teacher. *International Social Studies Forum, 3*, 219-232.

VanSledright, B. (1997). And Santayana lives on: Students' views on the purposes for studying American history. *Journal of Curriculum Studies, 29*, 529-557.

VanSledright, B. (2002). *In search of America's past: Learning to read history in elementary school.* New York: Teachers College Press.

VanSledright, B. (2004). What does it mean to think historically and how do you teach it? *Social Education, 68*, 230-233.

VanSledright, B., & Afflerbach, P. (2000). Reconstructing Andrew Jackson: Elementary teachers' readings of revisionist history texts. *Theory and Research in Social Education, 28*, 411-444.

VanSledright, B. & Afflerbach, P. (2005). Assessing the status of historical sources: An exploratory study of eight elementary students reading documents. In P. Lee. (Ed.), *International Research in History Education, Vol. 4. Children and teachers' ideas about history,* London: Routledge/Falmer.

VanSledright, B., & James, J. H. (2002). Constructing ideas about history in the classroom: The influence of competing forces on pedagogical decision making. In J. Brophy (Ed.), *Advances in research on teaching, Vol. 9* (pp. 263-299). Stamford; CT: JAI.

VanSledright, B. A., & Frankes, L. (2000). Concept- and strategic-knowledge development in historical study: A comparative exploration in two fourth-grade classroom. *Cognition and Instruction, 18*, 239-283.

VanSledright, B., & Kelly, C. (1998). Reading American history: The influence of using multiple sources on six fifth graders. *The Elementary School Journal, 98*, 239-265.

Vosniadou, S., & Brewer, W. (1992). Mental models of the earth: A study of conceptual change in childhood. *Cognitive Psychology, 24*, 535-585.

Voss, J. (1998). Issues in the learning of history. *Issues in Education: Contributions from Educational Psychology, 4*, 163-209.

Voss, J. F., Wiley, J. & Kennet, J. (1998). Students' perceptions of history and historical concepts. In J. F. Voss & M. Carretero (Eds.), *Learning and reasoning in history* (pp. 307-330). London: Woburn.

Wertsch, J. (2000). Is it possible to teach beliefs, as well as knowledge about history? In Stearns, P., Seixas, P. and Wineburg, S. (Eds). *Knowing, teaching & learning history* (pp. 38-50). New York: University Press.

White, H. (1978). *Tropics of discourse: essays in cultural criticism.* Baltimore: Johns Hopkins University Press.

Wilson, S. (2001). Research on history teaching. In V. Richardson (Ed.), *Handbook of research on teaching,* 4th ed. (pp. 526-544). New York: Macmillan.

Wineburg, S. (1991). On the reading of historical texts: Notes on the breach between school and academy. *American Educational Research Journal, 28*, 495-519.

Wineburg, S. (1996). The psychology of teaching and learning history. In R. Calfee & D. Berliner (Eds.), *Handbook of Educational Psychology* (pp. 423-437). New York: Macmillan.

Wineburg, S. (1998). Reading Abraham Lincoln: An expert/expert study in historical cognition. *Cognitive Science, 22*, 319-346.

Wineburg, S. (2000). Making historical sense. In P. Stearns, P. Seixas, & S. Wineburg, (Eds.), *Knowing, teaching, and learning history (pp. 306-325).* New York: New York University Press.

Wineburg, S. (2001). *Historical thinking and other unnatural acts: Charting the future of teaching the past.* Philadelphia: Temple University Press.

Wineburg, S. (2004). Crazy for history. *Journal of American History, 90*, 1401-1414.

Yeager, E., & Davis, O. L. (1996). Classroom teachers thinking about historical texts. *Theory and Research in Social Education, 24*, 146-166.

Yeager, E., Foster, S., & Greer, J. (2002). How eighth graders in England and the United States view historical significance. *The Elementary School Journal, 103*, 199-219.

SECOND LANGUAGE LEARNING: ISSUES IN RESEARCH AND TEACHING

Amado M. Padilla
Stanford University

Although a very large proportion of the world's population speaks two (or more) languages, the psychological study of language has mostly been confined to monolinguals. Typically, courses in second language learning are offered in applied linguistics programs, and few psychology students ever have the opportunity to avail themselves of such classes. This lack of knowledge of the psychological implications of second language learning also runs deep among faculty members who teach and conduct research in the area of educational psychology. Interestingly, most of us have studied a second language either in high school or as undergraduates, but few have developed a specialized interest in the intricacies of learning a second language, much less doing research in second language learning. Thus, researchers who work on the margins of psychology, linguistics, psycholinguistics, and education (Hakuta, 1986; Hamers & Blanc, 2000; McLaughlin, 1984, 1985; Rivers, 1964) produce most second language learning research of a psychological nature. It is possible to examine this research from a variety of disciplinary perspectives and to extrapolate its relevance to practitioners in teaching English as a second language, bilingual education, and foreign language education.

In this chapter I begin by highlighting the major issues in second language learning. The goal is to demonstrate why knowledge of second language learning can deepen the research agenda of educational psychologists. However, it is important to first understand how demographic shifts taking place in the United States have added to the need to focus attention on second language learning. The National Center for Education Statistics (2002)

reported that there were approximately 4.5 million English language learners in schools during the 2000–2001 school year. Also Zehler, Fleischman, Hopstock, Pendzick, and Stephenson (2003) in a nationwide study found a 72 percent increase in the number of kindergarten to 12 grade English language learners (ELLs) between 1992 and 2002. Moving to individual states, California is the state that is most impacted by the increase in the number of ELLs in our schools. In 2003–04 about one quarter of 1.6 million of California's 6.3 million students, kindergarten through the 12th grade, needed to learn English in order to succeed in school. There are more than 100 languages spoken as a first language by these students, but by far the greatest number of English learners speaks Spanish (1.36 million). In addition to California, other states with large populations of English language learners are Texas, Florida, New York, Illinois, and Arizona (Kindler, 2002).

Thus, there is a growing need for educational psychologists to be aware of the large population of English language learners in our schools. One reason for this is that by knowing about the increase in ELLs in our schools, we are in a better position to recognize the immense challenges classroom teachers face in developing curriculum for non-native speakers of English. The need to teach English language skills while also providing content instruction is difficult for the teacher with little preparation. Psychologists involved in teacher education programs need to understand that teaching ELLs poses major challenges for teachers. Further, teachers want and need their teaching methods to be guided by research. Thus, educational psychologists can play a significant role in the professional development of teachers of second language learners.

It is also important to mention that ELL students are at great risk for educational failure and special education. For instance, between 1987 and 2001 the proportion of students with disabilities who did not speak English at home increased from 3.3 percent to 14.2 pecent (U. S. Department of Education, 2002). Artiles, Trent, and Palmer (2004) provide an excellent overview of the major issues involved in the placement of ELLs in special education.

Importantly, the many pedagogical and research questions reviewed in this chapter are similar to challenges faced by teachers and researchers in many parts of the world, where multilingualism is a way of life (Arnau & Artigal, 1998; Baker, 2001; Li & Lee, 2004; Sierra & Padilla, 2003; Tabouret-Keller, 2004;). Thus, the issues of second language learning and educational psychology are as applicable in the United States as they are in many other parts of the world. The goal here is both to summarize some of the major issues in second language learning and also to stimulate educational psychologists to enrich their research programs by addressing questions that focus on how individuals of all ages learn and use a new language in and out of school.

It is also important to recognize that a sizeable proportion of English language majority students from kindergarten through college at some time in their education receive foreign language instruction either as an enrichment to their academic program or as a requirement for graduation from high school or college. Accordingly, the learning of a second language by these students, too, constitutes an important part of any discussion of second language learning.

The chapter is organized around nine questions that are frequently addressed to second language researchers by parents, educators, and policymakers. This is by no means an exhaustive list, but the inquiries do represent some of the more salient questions asked, especially in locales where ELLs are found in large numbers. The intent is to draw attention to the questions that have garnered attention and to provide a discussion around the questions drawn from diverse research traditions including applied linguistics, cognitive psychology, educational psychology, bilingual education, and second/foreign language education.

WHAT IS INVOLVED IN LEARNING A SECOND LANGUAGE?

Learning a language is a complex process whether the language is acquired in infancy as a first language or later in life as a second or third language. In either case, the learning process consists of acquiring a *language system,* rather than learning a series of disconnected components. A language system consists of not only grammatical rules and vocabulary, but also the proper way to use speech acts or pragmatic functions of language such as requesting information, inviting a friend to a social event, thanking a person for a kind act, or greeting a stranger. In addition, a language system includes discourse, whereby speakers learn what to say to whom and when.

Knowing a language involves being able to carry out a large variety of cognitive and social tasks specific to a particular language. It involves knowing and being able to produce the sounds that are used in the language, the sound sequences that make up meaningful words, and the appropriate words to form phrases and sentences. It means having a command of the linguistic system—the phonology, morphology, syntax, semantics, and pragmatics—that constitutes the essence of the language. At another level it also means knowing how to read and write in the language.

The specific elements of the language system to be learned in a second language classroom vary by language. For example, if we take the typical English as a second language (ESL) classroom, some ELLs may have to learn an entirely new orthography, whereas other learners will only have minor differences in alphabets to contend with (Akamatsu, 2002). Some languages will have very different sentence structures; others will appear to be more familiar. However, familiarity with the language system alone is not enough to enable students to engage in successful communicative activities. Learners also acquire the strategies that assist them in bridging communication gaps that result from differences of language and culture. Examples of these strategies include circumlocution (saying things in different ways), using context clues, understanding, interpreting, producing gestures effectively, asking for and providing clarification, and negotiating meaning with others.

Learning to speak any language is largely a task of learning to hear the new language in a way that allows for comprehension. This means that the quality of the language input is critical in learning a new language. No other type of language input is as easy to process as spoken language, received through listening. At the beginning stages of language learning, it is through active listening that learners can have the most direct connection to meaning in the new language. By listening, learners can develop an awareness of the interworkings of language systems at various levels and thus establish a base for more fluent production skills. As learners' vocabulary and knowledge of the language expands, they are able to comprehend more information that teachers present in greater decontextualized form. Ultimately, successful academic study in English requires a mastery of the listening demands presented to the learner in formal didactic presentations by the teacher as well as in the conversational interactive exchanges that are common in and out of the classroom.

In second language learning and teaching, much has been made of the term *comprehensible input* (Gass & Selinker, 2001; Krashen, 1985). Much of what has been studied about comprehensible input and the relationship of this to listening has been confined to the initial stages of second language learning and to informal contexts of interactive language usage. Much less attention has been given to the increasing demands of comprehensible input with succeeding grade levels and with varying types of instructional strategies in English-only classrooms. For example, ELLs may have fewer problems in elementary school when there is a heavy reliance on cooperative group work because the developing language learner may receive comprehensible input about the content of the class from the teacher as well as from English-speaking members of their work group who can reinforce the concepts that the teacher has presented (Neves, 1997). Unfortunately, there is a dearth of research on the comprehensible input side of second language learning as we move from the elementary school years, through secondary school, and even into higher education. Research on cooperative group work with second language learners has been confined largely to the elementary school years, but listening in a second language for the purpose of both developing proficiency in the language as well as comprehending the information being communicated is an ongoing process that may extend over many years.

WHAT ROLE DOES MOTIVATION PLAY IN LEARNING A SECOND LANGUAGE?

This question is not as easily answerable as it might seem. In the context of this chapter, learners of a second language can be people of any age who have immigrated to this country from a non-English-speaking country and who are attempting to acquire English in a formal (school) setting or in an informal (community) setting (e.g., such as trying to learn English from friends and/or co-workers). Gardner (1985) employed a variety of psychological and social variables in studying the role of motivation in second language learning. According to Gardner's model, anyone who seeks to learn a second language recognizes the potential value of speaking a new language and must be motivated to learn the language for one of two reasons: *instrumental* purposes (e.g., to attend an American school; or to obtain employment in order to support a family) or for *integrative* purposes (e.g., to better under-

stand American culture by reading novels in English by well known authors, or to attend films and lectures that focus on history, politics, or the arts). For learning a second language, the distinction between instrumental and integrative motivation is not always as clear-cut as originally proposed by Gardner (1985). Sung and Padilla (1998), in a study of students learning Japanese, Chinese, or Korean as either a heritage or foreign language, did not find a clear distinction between integrative and instrument reasons for learning the language. Also, in a different study with Spanish speakers in Canada, Masgoret and Gardner (1999) reported that self-rated proficiency in English depended on the learners' attitude toward assimilation or separation from Canadians and Canadian culture, which in turn mediated the individual's motivation to learn the language. Thus, it is clear that motivation is critical in second language learning, but how and why learners become motivated to learn a second language, especially in the face of the threat of losing their home language, still requires more research. Similarly, longitudinal research that examines the changing nature of motivation as a learner attains increasing proficiency in a second language is necessary to fill in the blanks in explaining the role of motivation.

WHAT ARE THE COMMON WAYS IN WHICH ENGLISH IS TAUGHT IN SCHOOL?

There are a number of formal approaches to second language learning. I discuss each of the major approaches and what the issues are from a learning, teaching, and research perspective.

Immersion Education

In this approach students are immersed in second-language-only instruction and have no recourse but to learn the new language as they go along. There are two forms of this type of instruction—one for language majority students and the other for language minority students. The first full immersion program of the latter type in the United States was established in a Culver City (West Los Angeles) elementary school in 1971 (Campbell, 1984) and was open only to English monolingual children. The Culver City immersion program was modeled after the St. Lambert French immersion program in Montreal (Lambert & Tucker, 1972); the only difference was that instruction was entirely in Spanish. Over the years this and other similar immersion type programs in Canada and the United States (for English) have demonstrated the enrichment enhancing benefits of early second language instruction in producing capable bilingual speakers (Padilla, 1998).

When second language instruction is offered in a formal context for the purposes of enrichment, this approach is called "additive" bilingualism. This type of language program has proven to be very successful with English monolingual children who are immersed in a second language instructional program for periods ranging up to 5 or 6 years. For example, Cunningham and Graham (2000) reported that students immersed in a Spanish program not only "added" Spanish to their communicative ability by becoming bilingual, but when compared to monolinguals from the same school, bilingual students performed better on a battery of linguistic and cognitive tasks in English. Cunningham and Graham (2000) conclude that their findings support the idea that Spanish immersion has English-language benefits and that positive cross-language transfer occurs from Spanish as a foreign language to English as a native language for their students.

The more common approach to immersion education is what some critics have called a "sink or swim" method. This approach has been practiced in this country with students who enter school knowing little to no English and who are enrolled in a class with no formal English language instruction whatsoever. This approach has its advocates as well as its critics. On the plus side, there is probably no faster way to acquire a new language than to be forced to learn the language by having to use it with native speakers. In other words, the expression "necessity is the mother of invention" applies here. The need to communicate in a new language—having to speak to others in their language—forces the learner to acquire a working vocabulary, some grammar, a few simplified expressions, and lots of nonverbal communicative strategies to go along with what the learner needs to communicate in the new language. Learning a new language in an informal, out-of-school context can be great fun because it requires the learner to be creative in his effort to communicate with native speakers. Often this is the type of learning situation that immigrant children experience on the playground, and adults experience in the workplace.

The difficult side of learning a new language by immersion, especially in a formal context such as school, is that if the instruction demands significant academic language—specialized vocabulary, literacy skills in the new language, and oral presentations—then the language learner is likely to have much difficulty because she not only has to learn the language (e.g., English), but also must do so in a context where it is equally important to keep up with the subject content of instruction. Although some learners are able to develop proficiency in the new language

while also learning the content of instruction, many other students encounter difficulties. One possible explanation for why some students succeed in this "sink or swim" approach is that they come from homes where parents speak English and can help their student with schoolwork. Another explanation is that some parents have the resources to provide out-of-school English language instruction through tutoring for their students. English language learners with parents with enough human capital to assist with out-of-school English acquisition are indeed fortunate. Many more students are not as fortunate and fall far behind in the class content instruction because they have not yet learned English. Further, because immersion instruction frequently does not make provision for development of proficiency in English, students fall further and further (i.e., "sink") behind their English-speaking counterparts. In recent years this "sink or swim" approach has given way to structured immersion (Ovando, Collier, & Combs, 2003).

Structured immersion is a term that refers to instruction in English that is made comprehensible to ELLs. The goal is to help ELLs acquire proficiency in English while at the same time achieving in content areas of the curriculum (Baker, 2000). The salient issue about this instructional approach is that it is not clear how English is made comprehensible to ELLs while content instruction is also being taught. Some home language support is allowed in some programs if teachers are bilingual. More often, however, it is likely that instruction proceeds at a slower pace and that important concepts are "watered down" for ELLs. In many respects this is still a "sink or swim" approach despite the label of this approach, which would make it appear that somehow it would be responsive to the English acquisition and content learning needs of ELLs.

In their exhaustive review of the educational research on various types of pedagogies for ELLs, August and Hakuta (1997) state that research on structured immersion is sorely needed. The need for research on immersion type programs is critical because California, Arizona, and other states with large ELL school-age populations have moved to immersion education for ELLs. In California, for example, this was mandated by Proposition 227, which called for 1 year of structured immersion in English, rather than bilingual education, followed by complete immersion in a mainstream English-only classroom. In the State of Arizona a similar law (Proposition 203) was passed mandating structured English immersion for ELLs.

Advocates for structured immersion argued that it was a disservice to hold students in bilingual classrooms for several years when data on the effectiveness of bilingual education were ambiguous at best (Crawford, 2004).

Advocates also put forth the argument that there were solid data from Canadian immersion programs, as well as American schools that had used such an approach, that immersing ELLs in an environment where they had no choice but to learn English was to their advantage in the long run in terms of assessed achievement gains on standardized tests in math, science, and English language arts. However, Parrish and associates (2002), in a California statewide longitudinal evaluation of immersion programs following the passage of Proposition 227, found no evidence that supported the contention of the advocates of structured immersion that the achievement gap between ELLs and English speakers would shrink with greater English language input. In a recent study Guerrero (2004) failed to find support for the assumption that 1 year of structured immersion instruction was sufficient for ELLs to succeed academically. In this study, Guerrero examined school achievement data gathered in California and Arizona following the passage of Propositions 227 (California) and 203 (Arizona). In sum, immersion education has come to mean different things to different people. Unfortunately, in recent years immersion has taken on extraneous meanings that blur its usefulness as an instructional method for use in language education.

English as a Second Language (ESL)

Another common approach is an English as a second language (ESL) program. ESL programs can be found between kindergarten and high school. In an ESL program, ELLs receive formal instruction in English from one to several hours a day or week. In elementary and secondary school, ESL can be a separate class for English language learners (ELLs) or it can be a pullout-type program where an individual student or a group of ELLs receives instruction with a teacher who specializes in ESL instruction. Depending on the age and grade level of the ELL, the instruction is generally limited to pronunciation, grammar, vocabulary building, and oral comprehension. However, depending on the needs of the learner and the availability of resources, ELLs may receive assistance in oral reading and in reading comprehension. Instruction in writing is very rare. The intent is to supplement the student's developing English with specialized instruction. The criteria may vary for determining when a student is ready to exit from an ESL program. This may be determined by a formal language assessment, by the ESL teacher's judgment that a determined proficiency level has been reached, or simply by whether there are resources (e.g., an ESL teacher) available to continue the instruction.

The goal of ESL instruction is to enable the language learner to attain interpersonal communicative skills in the language, but more importantly to acquire academic language proficiency, including literacy skills, in order to be able to succeed in different content areas. For some ESL students, their English language classes also serve as safe havens where they can practice their developing English skills in the midst of other ELLs and do so with lessened anxiety about the errors they may make in the new language (e.g., Olsen, 1997). The social dimension of ESL classrooms has not been the topic of much research and should be studied for at least two reasons. It is a commonly known fact that placement in an ESL classroom can be a negative stigma in some schools, and some ELL students may seek to exit an ESL program prior to proficiency in English in order to minimize the stigma. How early self-determined exiting from an ESL program can affect achievement in English-only classes is worthy of study. Similarly, Olsen (1997) and Igoa (1995) have noted that some ELLs prefer to remain in ESL classes because they find their ESL classrooms to be safe havens from the often ethnic and racially polarized school environment that is intolerant of ELLs.

Bilingual Instruction

Other students are enrolled in some form of bilingual education. Bilingual education is generally confined to the elementary school level. The most common form is transition bilingual education or what some call early-exit bilingual instruction. In this approach to instruction, students from the same home language background (e.g., Spanish) are grouped together and the bilingual teacher uses the home language to teach content subject material such as mathematics, science, and social studies. Another part of this instructional arrangement is to teach English with the explicit purpose of transitioning all instruction to English once the student is ready. The educational and policy question that has consumed much time is "When is the student ready for transition to an all English program?" The usual time allotment is anywhere between 1 and 3 years of bilingual instruction before the student exits and begins an all-English program (August & Hakuta, 1997).

The second form of bilingual education is late-exit, and in this case the program may run for as long as 6 or 7 years. Whereas transition to English is the explicit goal of an early-exit program, maintenance of the home language and academic language proficiency in English is the goal of a late-exit program. Another difference between early and late-exit bilingual education is that in a late-exit program, literacy skills are taught in the home language as well as in English. In other words, the goal of a late-exit program is full linguistic development in both languages.

Over the years, bilingual education has generated considerable controversy in political and educational circles (Crawford, 2004). Much of the controversy has focused on the effectiveness of bilingual programs. The purpose for discussing bilingual instruction here is not to revisit the extensive literature on this instructional approach and its effectiveness. Others have provided excellent reviews of the relevant evaluation studies and have concluded that in well-designed programs that control for confounding factors, students in bilingual programs attain higher achievement scores on measures of reading and mathematics than students in unstructured (sink-or-swim) English immersion programs (see Crawford, 2004; Hakuta & McLaughlin, 1996; Lindholm-Leary & Borsato, in press). The emphasis here is on the merits of home language instruction as a linguistic bridge while the student is mastering grade-appropriate academic English in order to transition to English-only instruction, regardless of whether this is in the third grade or in middle school. An important innovation in second language teaching that merges the best of bilingual education and foreign language education is two-way bilingual immersion.

Two-Way Bilingual Immersion Programs

A particularly popular form of elementary school second language instruction—two-way bilingual immersion—began to evolve in the mid-1970s and emerged in the 1990s as a much-sought-after instructional approach for both language minority and majority group students. Today there are more than 300 such programs (see the Web page of the Center for Applied Linguistics for a listing of these programs, http://www.cal.org/twi/directory/) in 26 states plus the District of Columbia. These programs grew out of bilingual education legislation and court-ordered mandates to provide "equal educational opportunity" for linguistic minority students. The Bilingual Education Act, or Title III, as it is more commonly called, is the instrument through which bilingual education programs are legislated and funded. Title III funding for bilingual education has provisions for supporting what at various times have been called developmental bilingual education, two-way immersion programs, and two-way bilingual education. The unique feature of this model is that linguistic majority (English monolingual kindergarten) and linguistic minority students begin together in kindergarten with the curriculum delivered in the minority language (e.g., Spanish). English, as a medium of instruction, is gradually introduced so that usually by the fourth grade, instruction is conducted about equally in Spanish and English. The outcome is "additive" bilingualism for native English speakers and for linguistic minority students since both groups achieve academic proficiency in both the minority language and in English.

The first two-way bilingual program was established by the San Diego public schools in 1975 (Crawford, 2004). This program began with a pre-kindergarten that brought together monolingual Spanish-speaking and monolingual English-speaking children. The English speakers were immersed entirely in Spanish with the exception of 20 minutes of English daily. This was extended to 30 minutes of English in kindergarten and first grade, 1 hour of English in grades 2 and 3, and half the instruction in Spanish and the other half in English from fourth through sixth grade. In a two-way program, Spanish speakers serve as language role models for the Anglophones while the Anglophones in turn serve as language models for the speakers acquiring proficiency in English.

Two-way bilingual programs have grown in popularity since the first program in San Diego. Bilingual education monies first supported this form of bilingual education in 1988 (U.S. Department of Education, 1991) when two schools received funding for programs. By the 1994–95 school year a total of 182 two-way programs were identified (Christian & Whitcher, 1995), and today the programs number more than 300. The majority of these programs are located in California and New York. However, programs can also be found in other states ranging from Alaska to Florida.

The overwhelming majority of the two-way programs involve Spanish/English instruction. Most dual-language immersion programs begin with what is known as a 90–10 model, whereby instruction is carried out in kindergarten with 90 percent of the instruction in the non-English language, and over the course of several years the percent of time spent in English gradually increases to a ratio of 50 percent English and 50 percent non-English language instruction. The goal for both groups of students (i.e., language majority students and language minority students) is bilingual academic language development. There is a second program variation that employs a 50–50 model of language instruction beginning in kindergarten and maintains this balance through the length of the program. Students in these programs also achieve well on all measures of bilingual proficiency and academic achievement.

There is considerable parental and educator support for these dual-language immersion programs. Further, the academic achievement and language proficiency data demonstrate that graduates of these programs are academically competitive on English and Spanish standardized tests when compared with their grade-level cohorts who have received instruction in English-only or in traditional bilingual education programs (e.g., Lindholm-Leary, 2001). Also, the graduates of the dual-language immersion programs are competent bilinguals, meaning that they can speak, read, and write in both languages.

There is sufficient literature documenting the educational and linguistic benefits of two-way bilingual programs (see Dolson & Lindholm, 1995; Lindholm-Leary, 2001). It is clear from evaluation studies of two-way bilingual programs that by the end of elementary school, students have acquired acceptable levels of proficiency in two languages and demonstrate grade-appropriate achievement in reading and math. Further, when this model of bilingual education is employed by a school district as a way of increasing academic achievement for working-class children, their bilingual proficiency *and* their high academic attainment in English serve the same "enrichment" function for these students as bilingualism does for linguistic majority group middle-class students.

An additional goal of two-way bilingual programs is to increase cross-cultural understanding and tolerance. This goal responds in part to efforts in schools to improve racial harmony in schools directly and in the community indirectly. The goal also has links to the belief that greater understanding of people and cultures can be facilitated through language study. Little research has been conducted to assess whether the goal of cross-cultural understanding and tolerance has been attained. In one of the few published studies, Lindholm (1994, Lindholm-Leary, 2001) developed an instrument called the Cross-Cultural Language and Attitude Scale and administered it to elementary school students who had participated in a two-way program since kindergarten. Lindholm (1994) has shown that "students held very positive attitudes toward other languages, people speaking other languages, and other students, regardless of skin or hair color" (p. 203). In a related study, Lambert and Cazabon (1994) also reported that students enrolled in a two-way program in Massachusetts held positive perceptions toward bilingualism, bilingual speakers, and their own bilingual program. More research on the long-term impact of two-way programs on intergroup relations is needed.

Foreign Language Education

A final form of second language learning (SLL) that needs to be included is foreign language education, which traditionally has been viewed as distinct from second language learning. In many respects the distinction between these two types of language learning is more imaginary than real, but the distinction is worth discussing. The social context in which the new language is learned is the deciding factor. For example, a person learning English in the United States where English is the main medium of public communication is called an English language

learner (ELL). If such learning takes place in a formal school setting this is referred to as ESL; however, in the same school and down the hall from the ESL classroom, we might find teachers instructing students in Spanish, French, Japanese, etc. Since these languages are not the primary medium of communication in this country, the students in these classes are learning a foreign language (FL). The distinction is subtle enough, but important. ELLs in this country are immersed in English and get much more English input in authentic ways than do students learning a foreign language (e.g., French) since this is not the medium of communication in this country. Thus, the source input(s) in second language learning are much more common for ELLs than they are for the FL learner, who typically only has the teacher to rely on for authentic language input. Another way of thinking about this is that ELLs have many more opportunities for authentic language input than is typically true in a foreign language class. Similarly, the student learning English in China, France, or Mexico is learning English as a foreign language (EFL). These distinctions in language learning contexts are important because they inform us of how language instruction is planned and implemented. An equally important point is whether the learner has authentic language input from native speakers of English in situations outside of the classroom as well as the opportunity to use the new language in real-life situations.

An interesting contrast between foreign language education in this country and English language instruction for immigrant students is that in a foreign language class we do not expect students to develop proficiency in 1 or 2 years of Spanish, French, or Japanese study. Even students who reach the advanced placement level in a foreign language still have considerable difficulty in showing high levels of proficiency across the board in their chosen language. This is one of the appealing features of the two-way bilingual programs, because after 6 years, graduates of these programs do appear to be adequate bilinguals for their age and grade level. However, many educators seem to be much less tolerant of the time it takes to learn a second language when the target group is ELLs. This leads naturally to the next issue in second language pedagogy.

HOW LONG DOES IT TAKE TO LEARN A SECOND LANGUAGE?

An important research question, especially in bilingual education, has to do with how long it takes to learn a second language. Usually policymakers are the group most interested in this question when trying to decide on a policy of how long students should remain in bilingual programs. Educational researchers (e.g., Cummins, 1991; Hakuta, Butler, & Witt, 2000; Snow & Hoefnagel-Hohole, 1978) have attempted to provide an empirical answer to this question, but the answer is not as simple as it might seem. It depends in part on the age of the learner and how much schooling he or she has received. If our question is simply about learning enough English, for example, to be able to interact on a social level with native English speakers, we get one answer. On the other hand, if we want to know how long it takes to be able to succeed academically with native English speakers in a classroom, the answer is quite different. Genesee (2004), in a review of the Canadian research on immersion programs, concluded that "time alone is not always the most significant predictor of L2 proficiency—the intensity of exposure and, most importantly, the nature and quality of classroom instruction are very important" (p. 560).

The learning of basic survival communication skills in a new language might only take a few months to a year or two depending on the amount of language input the learner receives from native speakers of the target language, the accuracy of second language output demanded by the context, the motivation of the learner, and the amount of practice that the learner gets in listening and speaking the new language. This depends too on the age of the learner; for example, it's one thing to know enough English for a child to interact with native English speakers on the playground, and quite a different thing for the child's parents to interact with their landlord, employer, salespersons, and even the child's teachers. Nonetheless, the time needed to master a second language for purposes of interpersonal communication is considerably less than the time required to master second language instructional competence in the second language (MacSwan & Rolstad, 2003). The reasons should be apparent. Instructional second language competence requires a high level of literacy (i.e., reading and writing) attainment in the new language as well as listening comprehension of decontextualized language and a more advanced level of oral proficiency. Again, depending on the age of the learner, the length of residence in the new country, motivation, and the amount of prior formal instruction in the home language, the attainment of second language instructional competence might take considerably longer than one or two school years. Researchers indicate that school language may take as much as 5 to 7 years (Collier, 1987, 1989; Cummins, 1991; Hakuta et al., 2000).

In sum, there is no one answer to the question of how much time is necessary to learn a second language. The answer partly depends on our expectations of what set of language skills (oral, listening, reading, or writing) and level of proficiency we expect from the ELL in each of the language skills we believe are important for the task at hand. If our expectations are fixed on basic survival communication, we get one answer; if, on the other hand, we believe that nine months of ESL or bilingual instruction should be sufficient for a student to succeed in an English-only program where the instructional language demands are high, then research informs us that we are likely doing students an injustice if we exit them from an ESL or bilingual program with no further English language assistance and expect them to succeed at a high level in an all-English classroom (Baker, 2001). Similarly, as noted earlier, research by Guerrero (2004) failed to find support for the assumption that a single year of structured English immersion education was sufficient for ELLs to develop competency in English to be successful in an English-only classroom. Interestingly, in foreign language education the question of language proficiency rarely comes up in the same way as it does in bilingual or ESL instruction. Foreign language teachers would not think of giving a high-stakes test such as an Advanced Placement test in a foreign language to a student who has completed only 1 or 2 years of language instruction. Why teachers want to mainstream ELLs into English-only classrooms is obviously more about politics than about language pedagogy and a learner's instructional language competence. This leads to our next question, which has to do with ELL proficiency.

WHEN IS A LEARNER PROFICIENT IN A SECOND LANGUAGE?

To be considered proficient in a second language, learners must exhibit a high level of accuracy in the second language. Such a level of proficiency includes being able to use the new language with increasing grammatical accuracy in ways that are contextually and culturally authentic. Accuracy pertains to the precision of the message in terms of fluency, grammar, vocabulary, pronunciation, and sociolinguistic competence. When language practice is contextualized and reflects real-world use, it forms the foundation for developing proficiency. Thus, all models of language presented to students must be grammatically correct, situationally appropriate, and culturally authentic. Such models include the language used in text materials, periodicals, and oral input from video and audiotapes. The teacher should provide direct instruction that focuses on form and structure, appropriateness to context, and cultural authenticity. The teacher should continuously monitor the language learner and provide corrective instruction as necessary. This is true regardless of age, grade level, and type of language program (e.g., bilingual, immersion, or foreign language).

The demands of accuracy in a second language, as can be seen, are high. However, there are not good classroom criteria yet for assessing accuracy in all of the ways that are demanded of students to achieve at high levels in the classroom. Let's examine this question a bit further. There are four modes of expression—listening, speaking, reading, and writing—that constitute the paths by which information and concepts are transmitted from one person to another. Listening and reading are receptive skills; speaking and writing are productive skills. Teachers need to be sure that second language learners are able to understand the language input that they receive from teachers and other students before the learners try to produce those utterances comprehensibly. Students cannot create the language they are learning without first receiving input from the teacher, peers, television, etc. At each level of proficiency, students who are literate in the language they are learning are able to better comprehend what they hear and read. They are then able to express themselves with more accuracy through speaking and writing. Proficiency in each of these modes reinforces proficiency in the other modes. All four modes of expression are important elements in second language learning, and their use is required in all formal classroom contexts.

It is important to recognize that language input provided to second language learners and the language output that is expected of them must be developmentally appropriate in two senses: (1) appropriate to the developing level of second language learning that the person has attained; and (2) appropriate to the cognitive and linguistic level of the student in his first language. Parents do not use linguistic features that are too complex—technical vocabulary, embedded grammatical structures, etc.—with their young children, and the same principle holds with second language learners. Much has been made of the strategies used by parents and other adult caretakers in talking to young children: for example, slower rate of speech, repetition, simplified vocabulary, and simplified grammar. The same strategies are useful in the early stages of second language acquisition in school. For example, ESL and bilingual teachers should be knowledgeable of developmentally appropriate ways of teaching and interacting with ELLs. To ensure this, Fillmore and Snow (2000) have provided guidance in what teachers of ELLs need to know about first and second language learning and teaching. These guidelines may also be useful to researchers preparing to conduct classroom research in settings with ELLs.

In addition, three categories of discourse describe language use on the basis of receptive and productive skills; the categories are interactive comprehension and production, receptive comprehension, and comprehensible production. In using the first category of discourse, interactive comprehension and production, ELLs communicate during many activities with peers or with adults on topics that relate to their lives. This communication can be oral, as in telephone conversations, or written, as in correspondence with friends through e-mails or instant messaging. These activities provide for an exchange of ideas. If one person does not understand the interchange, it is relatively simple to achieve understanding by seeking clarification. The interactive comprehension and production category of discourse is common in the social use of language.

The second category of discourse is receptive comprehension. Reading a book in a science class or viewing a video in a history class, activities that preclude seeking clarification from the author or narrator, exemplify this category. In such cases the reader or listener relies solely on his or her reservoir of concepts and language decoding skills for comprehension. Receptive comprehension becomes increasingly important with each grade level because students are required to do more reading and to integrate the information acquired in this fashion with new knowledge presented by the teacher. Also, a considerable amount of high-stakes testing (e.g., state mandated tests, SAT) assumes that students who do well achieve at high levels because they have acquired a storehouse of knowledge through reading on their own.

The third category is comprehensible production. Examples of activities that exemplify this category are completing a job application and delivering an oral class presentation. During such activities the writer or speaker makes a presentation that precludes any seeking or clarification of meaning by the reader or listener. Such circumstances place a responsibility on the writer or speaker to use language with clarity and accuracy. The comprehensible production category of discourse is common in the academic use of language. Further, many high-stakes tests now include a writing component that requires students to produce an essay that is scored not only for grammaticality, but for the persuasiveness of an argument buttressed by supporting facts.

Another concern that arises in assessing proficiency is how the second language learner manages to negotiate meaning with native speakers in formal and informal settings. Specifically, negotiation of meaning refers to those situations in conversation when it is important to interrupt the flow of the conversation in order for both speakers to understand what the conversation is about. In a discourse involving a native English speaker and a non-native speaker, breaks for negotiation of meaning are much more frequent than when native speakers are conversing (Gass & Selinker, 2001; Oliver, 1998, 2002). In terms of communication, the process of negotiation for meaning functions as both a means of preventing conversational trouble and a repair mechanism to overcome communication breakdown. Often the negotiations involve straightening out vocabulary or filling out background information not accessible to the language learner. Thus, learning contexts that instigate negotiations for meaning between native and non-native speakers can provide second language learners with excellent practice in authentic discourse. For example, in her study of 8- to 13-year-old children, Oliver (1998) reported that discourse that resulted in frequent instances of negotiation for meaning provided language learners with opportunities to receive comprehensible input, to produce comprehensible output, and to obtain feedback for their efforts. Oliver concluded that language teachers should find tasks that promote negotiation for meaning among same-age children—granted, of course, that there are native speakers who can fill this role, since the benefits accrue to second language learners when the discourse is between a native and non-native speaker. Thus, we cannot determine proficiency in a second language simply by a paper-and-pencil test; it is important to take into account what second language teachers know through time-worn practice. For example, listening to a conversation involving a native and non-native speaker of English can provide an enormous amount of information about the learner's developing proficiency of the language and the cultural context in which the language is embedded.

Experienced language teachers assist their students in achieving literacy in the second language by planning direct instruction based on appropriate learning strategies. According to Oxford (Hsiao & Oxford, 2002; Oxford, 1990), language learning strategies consist of focusing students' attention on learning; teaching students how to organize in advance by previewing, skimming, or reading to glean basic information; aiding students to summarize what they have just learned; and teaching students specific questioning strategies to ask for clarification or explanation. The efficacy of these and other cognitive and metacognitive strategies in assisting student learning is still not well enough understood in the teaching and learning, literature, and more is said about this later in this chapter. Major unanswered research questions still exist with regard to how students transfer their use of learning strategies for acquiring a new language to learning content material in effective ways in the new language. This is a more complicated process than simply learning academic material in a home language through the use of learning strategies. In short, attaining second language proficiency is complex and contextual. In schools, teachers need to be attentive not only to the skills of the ELL, but also to his needs and desires.

DOES CONTENT KNOWLEDGE TRANSFER ACROSS LANGUAGES?

Information learned in a home language should readily transfer to another linguistic system, provided, of course, that the person possesses the prerequisite skills to demonstrate knowledge in a second language. There is no reason why content material (e.g., biology, world history) has to be learned separately—once in the home language and again in a second language. This is the underlying assumption of bilingual and immersion education. In bilingual education the same grade-level subject matter as taught in an English-only classroom is provided to ELLs, but in the home language, while English proficiency is also being developed. Only after a language learner achieves a developmentally appropriate level of English proficiency—when she can function at high levels in interactive and receptive comprehension and is able to produce comprehensible output—should the language learner be transitioned to a mainstream English-only curriculum and classroom.

Cummins (1979) formalized the notion of cross-language transfer with his linguistic interdependence hypothesis. According to the hypothesis, the acquisition of a second language is mediated by the level of first language competence at the time the learner begins to acquire the second language. Transfer is expected for skills that are thought to be fundamental for acquisition of reading in the new language such as phonological awareness and lexical access. Thus, transfer is made possible when a learner has received instruction in the home language and has made a transition to the second language, which includes reading.

There is still much research that is necessary though to understand (1) the mechanism(s) involved in knowledge transfer across linguistic systems, (2) whether some teaching methods are better than others in the facilitation of transfer of knowledge across languages, (3) how first and second language comprehension and production facilitate transfer, and (4) the role played by age and cognitive development in knowledge transfer.

Reading in a second language is a complex task that entails an interaction between the second language and the first language. Several researchers (Hornberger, 1990; Lanauze & Snow, 1989) have concluded that academic and linguistic skills transfer relatively easily across linguistic systems. In one recent longitudinal study (Lindsey, Manis, & Bailey, 2003) of reading, Spanish-speaking students were assessed for phonological awareness, letter and word knowledge, print concepts, and sentence memory at three time periods: at the beginning of kindergarten, at the end of the kindergarten year, and then again at the end of the first grade. These authors reported that, consistent with other studies, phonological awareness was found to have a high degree of transfer from Spanish to English and to be predictive of word-identification skills. Another important finding was the relationship between Spanish oral-language measures (memory of sentences and picture vocabulary) and rapid object naming and print awareness in English reading. In addition to the information on cross-language transfer, Lindsey et al. (2003) note that the methods used in this study can be used to predict reading in English with ELLs. In a related study, Gottardo, Yan, Siegel, and Wade-Woolley (2001) reported similar results with Chinese children in British Columbia whose home language was Cantonese and who were learning to read in English. The interesting twist on this cross-language transfer study is that phonological awareness facilitated English reading, even though the children's home language was not written in an alphabetic orthography. Gottardo et al. (2001) state:

The finding that Chinese rhyme detection was predictive of English reading points to the importance of phonological-processing skill in the child's L1 for learning to decode an alphabetic orthography, even if the orthography of the child's L1 is not alphabetic. The quality of phonological representations in a child's L1 allows the child to reflect on phonology in that language.... This phonological-processing skill in a child's L1 influences reading performance in an alphabetic orthography regardless of the orthography used to represent in the child's first language. (p. 539)

In an important new direction in second language research, Tan et al. (2003) used functional magnetic resonance imaging (fMRI) to study brain activity in Chinese/English bilinguals as they read various texts in both languages, which differ markedly in phonology and orthography. MRIs showed different patterns of neural system involvement depending on which language bilinguals were reading. Further, the subjects were found to be applying their first language (Chinese) system to reading in English, and because Chinese lacks letter-to-sound conversion rules they were less capable of processing English in the same way that an English monolingual would read. Accordingly, these findings support Tan et al.'s suggestion that a first language "tunes the cortex" and this plays a role in how a second language is processed.

In a study of first and second language writing, the positive transfer of first language writing ability on the second language was shown by Schoonen et al. (2003) to be more important than linguistic and metacognitive knowledge of the second language. In this study Schoonen et al. examined the writing samples of eighth-grade students whose first language was Dutch and who were learning English as a second language. When comparisons were made of writing in the first and second language, the researchers found that proficiency of writing in English was highly correlated with writing proficiency in Dutch, and surprisingly not with English linguistic knowledge or the accessibility of this knowledge.

Thus, transfer of literacy and content knowledge across a first and second language raises important research questions of cognition and brain functioning. The question of transfer of knowledge from a first to a second language has a relatively long and complicated history in studies of the effects of bilingualism on cognitive abilities. So we turn to this question next.

WHAT ROLE DOES COGNITION PLAY IN SECOND LANGUAGE LEARNING?

Psychologists interested in intelligence testing first sought information on the relationship between bilingualism and IQ. The general consensus from this research that extended from the 1920s to 1962 was that bilingualism correlated negatively with IQ. In 1962 Peal and Lambert reported that balanced (meaning equally proficient in two languages) French–English bilingual adolescents outperformed monolingual French and English speakers on both verbal and nonverbal measures of intelligence when variables such as SES, language proficiency, gender, and age were controlled. These findings were supported by numerous subsequent studies of proficient bilingual speakers (see Lambert & Anisfeld, 1969). Peal and Lambert stated that the positive effect of bilinguality on cognition was attributable to the balanced bilingual's access to two symbolic language-based systems. The implication was that bilingualism contributed positively to cognitive ability by adding a dimension of flexibility to how bilinguals approach cognitive tasks.

As the debate about the relationship between bilinguality and intelligence ensued, Kolers (1968) took a different approach and asked whether there was a separate or shared long-term memory store for each of a bilingual's languages. According to Hamers and Blanc (2000), the interdependence or common-store hypothesis states that bilingual memory is a single system in which information is stored as a complex set of attributes or tags that enables the bilingual to store nonsemantic information such as modality, frequency, spatial and temporal aspects, and type of language (e.g., English, Korean). Language is then one of these tags through which the common store taps into two lexical systems via a "switching" mechanism. Conversely, the independence or separate-memory hypothesis holds that there are two independent language-specific memory stores in contact with each other via a "translation mechanism." Both models postulate the existence of a "mechanism" that permits the bilingual to switch from one linguistic system to the other; they differ from each other in where they locate this mechanism during processing. In the common store model, this switch is situated before semantic memory. The switching mechanism is set to whichever language is being processed and then information is sent to a common memory store. In the separate-store model, information in each language is stored separately unless it is required in the opposite language and is then translated via the translation mechanism.

Researchers (Colome, 2001; Dijkstra & Van Heuven, 2002; Hartsuiker, Pickering, & Veltkamp, 2004) continue to employ various types of experimental manipulations to test for the validity of one or the other of these two models of bilingual memory processing. Other researchers are less concerned with the question of how languages are actually stored in memory and have pursued a different set of questions having to do with information processing in second language learners and fully developed proficient bilinguals (e.g., Ellis, 1999; McLaughlin, 1987; Skehan, 1998; Tomasello, 1998). These models use the components of (1) input, (2) central processing, and (3) output. Let's examine these models in more depth from the three essential components that frame these cognitive models.

As mentioned earlier, language *input* is critical in a cognitive approach to second language learning. In fact, how well a learner of a second language does in the new language is determined by the quality of the input he or she receives in the new language. Language teachers know this and over the years have developed techniques for teaching a new language that incorporate elements such as simplified grammar and vocabulary, decreased sentence length, decreased speed of language input, offered clarifying interaction during the input process, physically highlighted important grammar points and vocabulary, and repeated communicative activities. These operations make it more likely that the learners will be able to selectively perceive or notice the input, a necessity because learners cannot take up and process all of the input they constantly receive, but they can select only certain input for attention, uptake, and processing. The learners' input processing capacity is limited.

Researchers such as Skehan (1998) and Tomasello (1998) emphasize that many second language students, especially those at lower levels of proficiency, cannot process target language input for both meaning and form at the same time. They suggest that learners have to be able to selectively perceive target forms in input before processing can take place. This is a cognitive explanation for the research finding that a purely communicative approach to language instruction for all but the youngest learners will usually not develop high levels of accuracy.

In a communicative approach to language education, the objective is to concentrate on meaning. This differs from the grammar-based approach to language instruction that demands learners attend to the new language's structure and form. In a communicative approach, effective communication is the desirable outcome, whereas in a grammar-based approach, accuracy of grammatical form is the goal. Thus, if students who are still actively engaged in the process of learning a language are able to process input for meaning only or to specific forms of the language, but not both, then teachers must decide which is more important and plan their curriculum accordingly. In the classroom both linguistic accuracy and meaning are important, which obviously complicates language instruction for teacher and student.

In a cognitive approach there are three stages for input processing: (1) the encoding stage, where existing knowledge located in long-term memory is activated and used to interpret the new input and construct meaning of it; (2) a transformation stage, where the input is transformed to meaning—this takes place in short-term or working memory; and (3) a storage stage, in which the meaning is rehearsed in working memory and transferred for storage in long-term memory.

There are two ways to envision processing of language input. The first is the bottom-up view, in which there is decoding of specific information from the input. For example, an ELL recognizes the individual sounds that make up words and the words that make up sentences (e.g., Ju & Luce, 2004). Another example would be reading in a second language, where a beginning reader recognizes the individual letters that make up words and the syntactic rules that organize the words into sentences (e.g., Lindsey et al., 2003). In the bottom-up approach, the learner decodes the input by attending to the constituent elements and then uses background knowledge to give meaning to the input.

The other approach is a top-down view. Top-down processing is necessary to understand the implications, context, and pragmatic meaning of the input. In the top-down view, the learner is "listening" for the big picture and relying extensively on background knowledge and expectancies to guess, predict, or fill in the message in order to comprehend it (Pinker, 1994). In a cognitive model, bottom-up and top-down processing of language input is occurring at the same time. The second language learner is, in other words, combining the new information from input with existing information stored in long-term memory, and as a result new knowledge is acquired from the interaction of input with prior knowledge. However, because of limited attention capacity, the second language learner finds it difficult to do both bottom-up and top-down processing. As a consequence, large chunks of the input might be lost because the learner is restricted to form or meaning and using either bottom-up or top-down processing. Monolingual speakers cannot imagine the conflicts in processing language input of the type described here for language learners, since automaticity of linguistic processing in a monolingual is set at an early age. For example, what monolinguals take for granted in a class on American history may prove to be extremely challenging for the language learner, who not only is confronted with making meaning of the teacher's input as well as ensuring learning of the form of English used in the class, but may have little prior background knowledge of American history. Thus, meaning is critical in a different way than for the monolingual, who is able to elicit some prior background knowledge. This is an important distinction and one that is not always understood or appreciated even by well-intentioned teachers of second language learners.

From the language teaching perspective, it is clear that second language learners can use top-down processing to understand the general meaning of communicative input without needing to understand all of the grammar forms or vocabulary. This is important because it suggests that teachers need to constantly reinforce the idea that language learners need to be engaged in developing accuracy in producing the target language, even though students appear to comprehend the target language reasonably well. This is especially true in the higher grade levels where comprehensible production is required for both meaning and linguistic form in, for example, an essay examination or in the writing of a term paper.

The final component of a cognitive information processing model for language learning is the *output*. An instructional program that is filled with language input, but no output, is bound to fail. Language learners may comprehend information in a second language by using top-down processing and strategies such as guessing and predicting, and through the use of their existing background knowledge, but it is in comprehensible production of the language that they demonstrate how well they truly know the new language. When the second language learner produces accurate output, whether orally or in writing that includes the use of correct grammar, rich vocabulary, and subtle meaning, we can be sure that he or she has learned the important aspects of the new language. Examples of output and proficiency are when the learner can successfully produce persuasive arguments that stir native speakers to action or when the person can successfully negotiate complex meaning with native speakers and have their point of view understood. Hamers and Blanc (2000) and Heredia and Brown (2004) have excellent state-of-the-art reviews of the research literature on the role of cognition, information processing, and memory in second language learning and bilingualism.

WHAT ROLE DOES KNOWLEDGE PLAY IN SECOND LANGUAGE LEARNING?

In answering this question, we first need to recognize that knowledge can be divided into two general types: (a) declarative or explicit knowledge, and (b) procedural or implicit knowledge. *Declarative* or *explicit knowledge* is knowledge about something. It is factual information that is conscious and consists of propositions (language-based representations) and images (perception-based representations). For example, when language learners are able to remember grammar rules, they are drawing on their explicit knowledge.

Procedural or *implicit knowledge*, on the other hand, is knowledge of a complex task that is internalized and operates seemingly unconsciously. As with any complex skill (e.g., driving a car, singing a song, or playing the piano) the ability to speak a second language fluently is a skill that is dependent on procedural knowledge used automatically. A good example of this would be the explicit knowledge that in English most verbs take "s" in the third person. However, implicit knowledge of this grammatical rule is observed when a developing English speaker uses verbs in the third person form (e.g., "he gives", "she takes") without stopping to think about the rule (DeKeyser, 1998).

These two types of knowledge exist in long-term memory as different systems. For example, it is not uncommon to determine that a second language learner has formal knowledge of the grammar rules for English indirect object placement, but lacks conversational use of the indirect object when conversing with a native speaker of English. This is because formal grammar instruction works on explicit knowledge, but frequent language input and conversational use are required for this form of knowledge to be converted to implicit (automatic) knowledge such that the learner can use the grammatical form with accuracy and without having to stop to think about the grammatical rule. I am reminded of some of the international students I have worked with in the past who have strong explicit knowledge of English language grammar because of the grammar-based approach to English as a foreign language (EFL) they received in their home country. However, these same students have low communicative ability (i.e., fluency and accuracy) in English because they lack sufficient opportunity to engage in authentic communicative interactions with native English speakers in a way that would turn their explicit knowledge of English grammar inward and thus make it automatic.

For language educators the question is how are explicit and implicit knowledge connected so that in language learning the learner manages to acquire both sets of knowledge that allow the person to make a smooth transition from a novice to fluent speaker of the second language. Language researchers (e.g., DeKeyser, 1998; Ellis, 1997; Skehan, 1998) have put forth the idea that the learner must notice and be aware of the input and output side of communication. How this works for the learner goes something like this: Once the novice language learner becomes aware of a particular grammatical feature in the language input, he continues to notice this grammatical structure in subsequent input, especially if the grammatical feature has high salience and frequency. Thus, repeated noticing and continued awareness of the language feature are important because they raise the learner's unconscious system of implicit knowledge. Once this occurs, and with conversational practice, the learner becomes more skilled and accuracy in the new language improves. Further, when this happens the learner develops new hypotheses about grammatical features and is able to move away from highly structured phrases such as "Hello, how are you today?" to a wider range of linguistic features and through feedback determine the accuracy of his communicative ability in English. Thus, explicit knowledge of the grammar of the new language becomes internalized as the learner uses the language and receives feedback about the accuracy of his usage. There is neurological evidence that supports the declarative/procedural model in first and second language usage (Ullman, 2001).

This information has useful implications for research and teaching of a second language. The important thing in instruction is to provide learning contexts where the second language learner "notices" the input and moves from explicit knowledge to implicit knowledge through guided practice. This requires that instruction first draw students' attention to linguistic elements as they occur naturally in language use, and then provide communicative activities that sharpen the learners' use of language in a way that becomes automatic and accurate. Finding effective ways to do this prompts a call for more research.

There is a controversy in second language teaching about the usefulness of focusing too much attention on teaching grammar before having the learner produce in the language. Proponents for one side hold that it is important to have a working knowledge (i.e., explicit knowledge) of grammar before it is possible to be productive in the new language. The other side, while acknowledging the importance of grammar, believes that it is impor-

tant to plan curriculum in such a way that the learner is encouraged to begin production as soon as possible regardless of errors in grammar. The proponents of this communication-based approach argue that the learner acquires grammar while using the language in authentic contexts. Both approaches are still searching for how best to teach grammar, what grammar to teach, how to sequence the grammar logically, and, when necessary, how to provide corrective feedback when errors occur (Mitchell, 2000).

Genesee (2004) states that the question of how and when language learners' grammatical errors should be corrected is an important theoretical issue in second language research and pedagogy because it addresses the central question of whether teachers focus on grammar (i.e., form) or communication (i.e., function) in their instruction. Lyster, in a study of six French immersion classrooms in Canada (Lyster, 1998; Lyster & Ranta, 1997), found that teachers' use of "recasts"—a teacher's reformulations of all or part of a student's utterance minus the grammatical error—was ineffective in eliciting from students the correct grammatical form. This may be due to the fact that recasting did not inform the students of how to correct their grammar any more than did positive feedback techniques (e.g., clarification requests, repetition, metalinguistic feedback).

Nonetheless, some guidelines generated from research are possible when grammar is taught to second language learners: (1) Grammar teaching needs to be planned and systematic; (2) the grammar taught should be developmentally appropriate and flexible enough to allow the learner some choice in the forms used in communication; (3) it is important to recognize that in the early stages of second language learning, the learner may need to switch back and forth between the home language and the new language; (4) teaching grammar should progress gradually and include lots of redundancy—frequency is a blessing in learning a new language; and (5) instruction needs to engage the learner in problem-solving tasks that get the new speaker of a language engaged in negotiating meaning in the new language.

Although we are now well aware of the workings of bottom-up and top-down processing, implicit and explicit memory, and the limitations imposed on the language learner by an attentional mechanism, there is still much research that needs to be carried out to understand how this all fits together for second language learners who differ by age, level of cognitive development, frequency of language input, and opportunities to use the language in authentic ways. We also need to understand how subject matter content (e.g., science, social studies, and math) makes differential demands on cognitive processing because of technical vocabulary and reliance on background knowledge. Also important is finding the right pedagogical style that maximizes comprehensible input without becoming monotonous for the learner.

ARE THERE STRATEGIES THAT IMPROVE SECOND LANGUAGE LEARNING?

In addition to the role of cognition in second language learning, teachers can organize their teaching around strategies that are known to facilitate learning. Several of the most cited taxonomies of language learning strategies have been proposed by Chamot, Barnhardt, El-Dinary, and Robbins (1999), O'Malley and Chamot (1990), Hsiao and Oxford (2002), and Oxford (1990). Strategies imply actual behaviors or thoughts that a learner engages in to tackle the difficult task of learning a new language. Specifically, strategies are actions that the learner uses to enhance comprehension of input and production. The strategies proposed by these language researchers are based on lists that incorporate metacognitive, cognitive, and socioaffective strategies. Metacognitive strategies involve planning, monitoring, and evaluating comprehension. Cognitive strategies are used to manipulate information. Some examples of this type of strategy are rehearsal, organization, summarization, and elaboration. Socioaffective strategies have been studied less often, but are thought to be particularly important when the listening is two-way and meaning can be negotiated between speaker and listener. Some examples of socioaffective strategies are cooperative learning, questioning for clarification, and managing one's emotions in learning situations.

Strategy use varies with proficiency and the relationship between strategy use and proficiency level. For example, more advanced language learners use a wider array of strategies than do beginning learners. Because of their more advanced stage of language acquisition, advanced learners have more strategies available to them and can employ learning strategies with greater flexibility than novice learners. I now turn to an overview of some useful strategies in second language learning that can be used by learners of any age or proficiency level (Padilla & Sung, 1992).

Organization of Information

Second language instruction and learning should be carried out in a way that maximizes the separation of the first and second language in long-term memory. There are four metacognitive strategies that can be identified as especially useful here. Two of the metacognitive strategies involve preparation for memory organization—advance organization and organizational planning. The other two are self-evaluation and self-management, which refer to learner-oriented regulation of second language performance. In advance organization, I refer to previewing the main ideas and concepts of the material in the language to be learned, often by skimming the text for the organizing principles. In organizational planning, the central notion is to plan the parts, sequences, and main ideas to be expressed orally or in writing in the second language. Self-evaluation involves the students' monitoring of how well they have performed on a second language acquisition task. In this type of monitoring, students evaluate their performances as either meeting some standard or falling below the standard. If performances fall below the standard, students need to practice the task until performance attains the standard. If attainment of the standard is too difficult, then the learners may need to reassess their or the teacher's standard and set the goal a little lower until the desired performance level can be attained. As a part of this, the student can engage in self-management of the learning environment, which entails finding opportunities for improving proficiency. This may include seeking out native speakers of the language being learned, using second language learning aids, and not avoiding challenges that demand the use of the second language.

Planning of Instruction

In addition to these metacognitive strategies, a number of cognitive strategies also can be employed in planning instruction in a second language. Students must be instructed in the use of these strategies by their language teachers, meaning that the teacher not only must plan the lesson to include language content, but must plan time devoted to learning and practicing cognitive strategies shown to be very helpful in facilitating long-term memory.

The first of these cognitive strategies is *summarizing*. In summarizing, the student is shown the power of making written summaries of the information gained through listening and reading. With practice, older students will be able to engage in mental summation. The important consideration here is the active engagement in the learning process that occurs when summarizing is going on. During appropriate opportunities, the teacher must allow time for students to engage in note taking and reviewing the notes so that the material can be rehearsed. Another useful strategy is *elaboration*, which refers specifically to the learner relating new information to what is already known. The idea is to look for ways new information is related to old knowledge already in long-term memory. To maximize the use of this strategy, teachers must be constantly on the alert to draw bridges or connections between information that is being taught and material that has already been learned. Once the learner realizes that much of what is being taught about a language can be related to what was learned earlier, or what is known in the native language, the learner understands the interconnections between what possibly had earlier seemed to be many disconnected bits of information. Through summarizing and elaboration, second language learning becomes less a series of rules to be acquired through rote memorization and more the generation of comprehensible production based on self-generated rules and connections between parts of language.

Deduction and Induction

A cognitive strategy that is not used enough in language education is deduction/induction (Norris & Ortega, 2000). *Deduction* is defined as a process that moves from the general to the specific. In language learning, a general rule is applied to particular instances of language use. Deductive instruction involves rule explanation by a teacher at the beginning of a lesson before students engage in language practice. This differs from *induction*, which is the process of moving from the specific to the general. In this situation the language learner is first exposed to instances of language use, from which emerge patterns and generalizations. In this type of instruction, learners are required to attend to particular forms and try to arrive at metalinguistic generalizations on their own. We see evidence of induction, for example, when we listen to children learning their first language when they overgeneralize the rules of regular grammatical forms to otherwise nonregular forms (e.g., *foots* for *feet* or *goed* for *went*).

In learning a second language, the learner needs to have ample opportunity to explore the rules of the new language and to apply these rules in the production of the language. However, research (Erlam, 2003) comparing learners who receive deductive (i.e., rule presentation and metalinguistic information) or inductive (i.e., focus on form with no explicit grammar) instruction shows that learners receiving deductive instruction perform better on both listening and reading comprehension and written and oral production tasks.

In sum, research has demonstrated that rule generation and deduction of rules in language production is more illuminating than rote memorization of grammatical rules in a new language without the chance to put these rules to the test in language production. Obviously, there is a large metalinguistic component inherent in the process of deducing how the new language works and how to go about acquiring it. Thus, second language acquisition is similar to other problem-solving strategies, where deduction facilitates learning.

Inferencing

Another important strategy is *inferencing*, which calls for the learner to use information in a text to guess the meaning of new information, to predict outcomes, or to complete missing parts. Again this strategy is not unique or in any way surprising. In fact, the merits of inferencing appear as mere common sense to many. However, for a learner to exercise the skill of inferencing, there needs to be an atmosphere of exploration in the classroom that permits the student to practice inferencing skills. A good example of this would be a classroom where second language instruction takes place in a nonrestrictive atmosphere and learners can play with language without sanctions or penalty. This is the type of naturalistic environment that usually exists for children learning their first language. Unfortunately, most second language learning occurs in formal classroom settings that require structure and order rather than language exploration.

Transfer of Learning

Another strategy that is easily identifiable is *transfer*, where what is already known facilitates the learning and incorporation of new information. By *transfer*, we are specifically referring to the positive transfer of knowledge that is available to us in long-term memory and which we can bring to bear in the learning of new knowledge. Positive transfer may include the categorizing of new words in the second language based on already established first language organizational structures in memory, or it may involve the extrapolation of first language concepts to new second language information. Whatever the particulars, the essential point is that prior knowledge, including linguistic knowledge, is used to shape the organization and retention of new knowledge in long-term memory.

In second language learning, one important strategy is cross-linguistic transfer of first language knowledge and skills to second language acquisition. Essentially, in second language it is not necessary to relearn all the language skills that have already been acquired in the first language, but which now must be used in the second language. For example, if a student has already learned to read in her native language and is now learning English as her new language, it is obvious that the learner does not have to start from zero, but can easily transfer the skills of reading in the native language to reading in the new language. There are numerous ways in which first language knowledge can facilitate the acquisition of a second language (see Butler & Hakuta, 2004). However, Odlin (1989) has shown that if a second language is typologically very different from the home language (e.g., English and Korean) it may take longer to learn the language than if the new language has more in common with the language of the home (e.g., English and Spanish). This is an area of research that is prime for research with the developing techniques available in the neurosciences.

Mental Imagery

Finally, a much-explored cognitive strategy that has been shown to facilitate memory involves imagery. Here the learner is encouraged and, if needed, instructed in ways to use mental imagery of information that requires storage in long-term memory. We know from research on the relationship between the use of imagery and long-term memory that some types of information (e.g., concrete words) are more readily accessible to imagery techniques than other types of material (e.g., abstract concepts). It is also known that mnemonic techniques that rely on imagery strategies are very useful in assisting in the learning process of large masses of information. Such techniques may be useful in learning vocabulary in a second language and in certain types of content areas.

In sum, the goal of this section was not to offer a shopping list of learning strategies, but rather to describe a few such strategies and discuss how teachers employ these strategies in a second language classroom. The guiding principle is that a model of second language learning that builds on cognitive information processing has great potential for the learning of a new language, as well as the added heuristic value for educational psychologists interested in second language research.

DIRECTIONS FOR FUTURE RESEARCH

Educational psychology played an especially important role in the development of theories of second language learning and in the field of second language pedagogy between the early 1940s and the late 1960s (Ausubel, 1964; Carroll, 1965; Lambert, 1963a, 1963b). However, by the mid-1960s, language educators began to look toward the emerging field of applied linguistics for intellectual leadership in the research and teaching of a second language (Byrnes, 2000; Kramsch, 2000). Among the possible reasons for this include the growing influence of Chomskian

Universal Grammar in first and second language learning and the shift in focus from the teaching of foreign languages to bilingual education by the early 1970s for the growing number of linguistic minority children in our schools (see Crawford, 2004). However, there has always been interest in second language research on the part of educational psychologists, and in recent years this interest has grown (Hakuta & McLaughlin, 1996).

Unfortunately, the learning needs of English language learners (ELLs) have long been politicized—most recently by the "No Child Left Behind Act" (see Abedi, 2004). Rather than asking questions of how to meaningfully improve instruction for ELLs, educators are now consumed with accountability and yearly progress reporting, not questions of how to ensure school success through high levels of English language attainment by linguistic minority students. From a research perspective there are still many important questions that remain unanswered about the process of second language learning and how proficiency is accomplished by learners who not only face the challenge of learning a new language, but also must learn subject area content in a second language. Accordingly, I organized my comments in this chapter around nine fundamental questions that have been addressed in different ways in the literature by graduate students, researchers, and policymakers interested in second language research and teaching. These are not new questions by any means; however, I have tried to provide a new frame to the questions and to provide current research directions taking place within the confines of each of the questions.

Language educators continue to need assistance from educational researchers in setting appropriate goals for all second language learners regardless of whether they are ELLs in a bilingual or sheltered immersion program or students learning a foreign language to fulfill a high school or college graduation requirement. Some immediate needs include:

- Teaching strategies and curriculum for instructing students with different levels of second language proficiency
- Techniques that guide teachers in the appropriate ways to use positive feedback during instruction that focuses on "form" and "meaning"
- Methods for incorporating support materials such as technology and physical activities in the learning tasks
- Assessment instruments for examining students' first and second language comprehension and comprehensible production
- Strategies that build on first language cognitive and linguistic abilities that students possess and which can facilitate second language learning

- Curriculum designed by grade level and content areas that integrates second language and content instruction
- Authentic and culturally relevant texts that combine listening, speaking, reading, and writing tasks that motivate students to learn
- Assessment techniques for determining whether the special learning needs of ELLs are due to linguistic and/or cognitive difficulties and guidance in educationally appropriate learning programs

Other research endeavors include the study of the effects of social, cultural, and affective factors on second language learners. We need to know more about the demands placed on students by formal and informal settings where the second language is required, interactive teaching that makes heavy demands on student discourse, and group work activities that are within the zone of the student's language readiness. As multimedia resources become more available in the language classroom and we come to value the role of technology in teaching, we need more research on the effects of technology (e.g., computers, videos, or the Internet) on the integration of learning a new language and subject matter. This is especially true in the teaching of ELLs, where technology use appears impoverished in comparison with foreign language education in this country.

Finally, August and Hakuta (1997), in their extensive review of the literature on improving schooling for language-minority students, call for a research agenda that extends our existing theories of first and second language learning as well as our methodologies into at least the following major areas: content area learning, second-language literacy, intergroup relations, and social context of learning.

ACKNOWLEDGMENTS

I thank Noah Borrero (Stanford University School of Education), Kathryn Lindholm-Leary (San Jose State University), and Jeff MacSwann (Arizona State University) for their many helpful comments on an earlier version of this chapter. This chapter was also supported by the California Foreign Language Project (Duarte Silva, Executive Director, Stanford University), which has provided me over the past decade with the opportunity to interact with classroom teachers who daily have the responsibility of teaching a new language to countless numbers of students.

References

Abedi, J. (2004). The No Child Left Behind Act and English language learners: Assessment and accountability issues. *Educational Researcher, 33*, 4–14.

Akamatsu, N. (2002). A similarity in word-recognition procedures among second language readers with different first language backgrounds. *Applied Psycholinguistics, 23*, 117–133.

Arnau, J., & Artigal, J. M. (Eds.) (1998). *Immersion programmes: A European perspective.* Barcelona: Universitat de Barcelona.

Artiles, A. J., Trent, S. C., & Palmer, J. D. (2004). Culturally diverse students in special education. In J. A. Banks & C. A. McGee Banks (Eds.), *Handbook of research on multicultural education* (2nd ed.). San Francisco; Jossey-Bass.

August, D., & Hakuta, K. (Eds.) (1997). *Improving schooling for language-minority children.* Washington, DC: National Academy Press.

Ausubel, D. P. (1964). Adults versus children in second language learning: Psychological considerations. *Modern Language Journal, 48*, 420–424.

Baker, C. (2000). *A parents' and teachers' guide to bilingualism* (2nd ed.).Philadelphia: Multilingual Matters.

Baker, C. (2001). *Foundations of bilingual education and bilingualism* (3rd ed). Philadelphia: Multilingual Matters.

Butler, Y. G., & Hakuta, K. (2004). Bilingualism and second language acquisition. In T. K. Bhatia & W. C. Ritchie (Eds.), *The handbook of bilingualism.* Oxford, UK: Blackwell.

Byrnes, H. (2000). Shaping the discourse of a practice: The role of linguistics and psychology in language teaching and learning. *Modern Language Journal, 84*, 472–494.

Campbell, R. N. (1984). The immersion approach to foreign language teaching. In *Studies on immersion education.* (pp. 114–143). Sacramento, CA: California State Department of Education.

Carroll, J. B. (1965). The contributions of psychological theory and educational research to the teaching of foreign languages. *Modern Language Journal, 49*, 273–281.

Chamot, A. U., Barnhardt, S., El-Dinary, P. B., & Robbins, J. (1999). *The learning strategies handbook.* White Plains, NY: Addison Wesley Longman.

Christian, D., & Whitcher, A. (1995). *Directory of two-way bilingual programs in the United States* revised 1995. Washington, DC: Center for Applied Linguistics.

Collier, V. P. (1987). Age and rate of acquisition of second language for academic purposes. *TESOL Quarterly, 21*, 617–641.

Collier, V. P. (1989). How long? A synthesis of research on academic achievement in second language. *TESOL Quarterly, 23*, 509–531.

Colome, A. (2001). Lexical activation in bilinguals' speech production: Language-specific or language independent? *Journal of Memory and Language, 45,* 721-736.

Crawford, J. (2004). *Educating English learners: Language diversity in the classroom.* Los Angeles: Bilingual Education Services.

Cummins, J. (1979). Linguistic interdependence and the educational development of bilingual children. *Review of Educational Research, 49,* 222-251.

Cummins, J. (1991). Interdependence of first- and second-language proficiency in bilingual children. In E. Bialystok (Ed.), *Language processing in bilingual children.* Cambridge, UK: Cambridge University Press.

Cunningham, T. H., & Graham, C. R. (2000). Increasing native English vocabulary recognition through Spanish immersion: Cognate transfer from foreign to first language. *Journal of Educational Psychology, 92,* 37-49.

DeKeyser, R. (1998). Beyond focus on form: Cognitive perspectives on learning and practicing second language grammar. In C. Doughty & J. Williams (Eds.), *Focus on form in classroom second language acquisition.* New York: Cambridge University Press.

Dijkstra, T., & Van Heuven, W. (2002). The architecture of the bilingual word recognition system: From identification to decision. *Bilingualism: Language and Cognition, 5,* 175-197.

Dolson, D. P., & Lindholm, K. (1995). World class education for children in California: A comparison of the two-way bilingual immersion and European school models. In T. Skutnabb-Kangas (Ed.), *Multilingualism for all.* The Netherlands: Swets & Zeitlinger.

Ellis, R. (1997). *Second language research and language teaching.* Oxford, UK: Oxford University Press.

Erlam, R. (2003). The effects of deductive and inductive instruction on the acquisition of direct object pronouns in French as a second language. *Modern Language Journal, 87,* 242-260.

Fillmore, L. W., & Snow, C. E. (August, 2000). *What teachers need to know about language: Special report.* ERIC: Clearinghouse on Languages and Linguistics.

Gardner, R. C. (1985). *Social psychology and second language learning: The role of attitudes and motivation.* London: Edward Arnold.

Gass, S. M., & Selinker, L. (2001). *Second language acquisition* (2nd Ed.). Mahwah, NJ: Lawrence Erlbaum Associates.

Genesee, F. (1987). *Learning through two languages: Studies of immersion and bilingual education.* Cambridge, MA: Newbury House.

Genesee, F. (2004). What do we know about bilingual education for majority-language students? In T. K. Bhatia & W. C. Ritchie (Eds.), *The handbook of bilingualism.* Oxford, UK: Blackwell.

Gottardo, A., Yan, B., Siegel, L. S., & Wade-Woolley, L. (2001). Factors related to English reading performance in children with Chinese as a first language: More evidence of cross-language transfer of phonological processing. *Journal of Educational Psychological, 93,* 530-542.

Guerrero, M. D. (2004). Acquiring academic English in one year: An unlikely proposition for English language learners. *Urban Education, 39,* 172-199.

Hakuta, K. (1986). *Mirror of language: The debate on bilingualism.* New York: Basic Books.

Hakuta, K., Butler, Y., & Witt, D. (2000). *How long does it take English learners to attain proficiency?* Santa Barbara: University of California Linguistic Minority Research Institute.

Hakuta, K., & McLaughlin, B. (1996). Bilingualism and second language learning: Seven tensions that define the research. In D. C. Berliner & R. C. Calfee (Eds.), *Handbook of educational psychology* (pp. 603-621). New York: Simon & Schuster Macmillan.

Hamers, J. F., & Blanc, M. H. (2000). *Bilinguality & bilingualism* (2nd ed.). Cambridge, UK: Cambridge University Press.

Hartsuiker, R. J., Pickering, M. J., & Veltkamp, E. (2004). Is syntax separate or shared between languages? *Psychological Science, 15,* 409-414.

Heredia, R. R., & J. M. Brown. (2004). Bilingual memory. In T. K. Bhatia & W. C. Ritchie (Eds.), *The handbook of bilingualism.* Oxford, UK: Blackwell.

Hornberger, N. H. (1990). Creating successful learning contexts for bilingual literacy. *Teachers College Record, 92,* 212-229.

Hsiao, T. Y., & Oxford, R. (2002). Comparing theories of language learning strategies: A confirmatory factor analysis. *Modern Language Journal, 86,* 368-383.

Igoa, C. (1995). *The inner world of the immigrant child.* New York: St. Martin's Press.

Ju, M., & Luce, P. A. (2004). Falling on sensitive ears: Constraints on bilingual lexical activation. *Psychological Science, 15,* 314-318.

Kindler, A. (2002). *Survey of the states' limited English proficient students and available educational programs, 2000-01 summary report.* Washington, DC.: National Clearinghouse for English Language Acquisition and Language Instruction Educational Programs.

Kolers, P. A. (1968, March). Bilingualism and information processing. *Scientific American,* pp. 78-86.

Kramsch, C. (2000). Second language acquisition, applied linguistics, and the teaching of foreign language. *Modern Language Journal, 84,* 311-326.

Krashen, S. (1985). *The input hypothesis: Issues and implications.* New York: Longman.

Lambert, W. E. (1963a). Psychological approaches to the study of language. Part I: On learning, thinking and human abilities. *Modern Language Journal, 47,* 51-62.

Lambert, W. E. (1963b). Psychological approaches to the study of language. Part II: On second language learning and bilingualism. *Modern Language Journal, 47,* 114-121.

Lambert, W., & Anisfeld, E. (1969). A note on the relation of bilingualism and intelligence. *Canadian Journal of Behavioral Science, 1,* 123-128.

Lambert, W.E., & Cazabon, M. (1994). *Students' view of the Amigos program* (Research Report No. 11). Santa Cruz, CA: National Center for Research on Cultural Diversity and Second Language Learning.

Lambert, W., & Tucker, G. R. (1972). *Bilingual education of children: The St. Lambert experiment.* Rowley, MA: Newbury House.

Lanauze, M., & Snow, C. (1989). The relation between first- and second-language writing skills. *Linguistics and Education, 1,* 323–339.

Li, D. C., & Lee, S. (2004). Bilingualism in East Asia. In T. K. Bhatia & W. C. Ritchie (Eds.). *The handbook of bilingualism.* Oxford, UK: Blackwell.

Lindholm, K. (1994). Promoting positive cross-cultural attitudes and perceived competence in culturally and linguistically diverse classrooms. In R. A. DeVillar, C. J. Faltis, & J. P. Cummins (Eds.), *Cultural diversity in schools: From rhetoric to practice.* Albany, NY: State University of New York Press.

Lindholm-Leary, K. (2001). *Dual language education.* Philadelphia: Multilingual Matters.

Lindholm-Leary, K., & Borsato, G. (in press). Academic achievement. In F. Genese, K. Lindholm-Leary, W. Saunders, & D. Christian, (Eds.), *Educating English language learners: A synthesis of research evidence.* New York: Cambridge University Press.

Lindsey, K. A., Manis, F. R., & Bailey, C. E. (2003). Prediction of first-grade reading in Spanish-speaking English-language learners. *Journal of Educational Psychology, 95,* 482–494.

Lyster, R. (1998). Recasts, repetition, and ambiguity in L2 classroom discourse. *Studies in Second Language Acquisition, 20,* 51–81.

Lyster, R., & Ranta, L. (1997). Corrective feedback and learner uptake: Negotiation of form in communicative classrooms. *Studies in Second Language Acquisition, 19,* 37–66.

MacSwan, J., & Rolstad, K. (2002). Linguistic diversity, schooling, and social class: Rethinking our conception of language proficiency in language minority education (pp. 329–341). In C. B. Paulston & R. Tucker (Eds.), *Sociolinguistics: The essential readings.* Oxford, UK: Blackwell.

MacSwan, J., & Rolstad, K. (2003). Linguistic diversity, schooling, and social class: Rethinking our conception of language proficiency in language minority education. In C. B. Paulston & R. Tucker (Eds.). *Sociolinguistics: The essential readings* (pp. 329–340). Oxford, UK: Blackwell.

Masgoret, A., & Gardner, R. C. (1999). A causal model of Spanish immigrant adaptation in Canada. *Journal of Multilingual and Multicultural Development, 20,* 216–236.

McLaughlin, B. (1984). *Second language acquisition in childhood: Vol. 1. Preschool children* (2nd ed.). Hillsdale, NJ: Lawrence Erlbaum Associates.

McLaughlin, B. (1985). *Second-language acquisition in childhood: Vol. 2. School-age children* (2nd ed.). Hillsdale, NJ: Lawrence Erlbaum Associates.

McLaughlin, B. (1987). *Theories of second language acquisition.* London; Edward Arnold.

McLaughlin, B., Rossman, T., & McLeod, B. (1983). Second language learning: An information-processing perspective. *Language Learning, 33,* 135–158.

Mitchell, R. (2000). Applied linguistics and evidence-based classroom practice: The case of foreign language grammar pedagogy. *Applied Linguistics, 21,* 281–303.

National Center for Education Statistics. (2002). *Public school students, staff, and graduate counts by state: School year 2000-01* (NCES Publication 2002-348). Washington, DC: Author.

Neves, H. A. (1997). The relationship of talk and status to second language acquisition of young children. In E. G. Cohen & R. A. Lotan (1997), *Working for equity in heterogeneous classrooms: Sociological theory in practice* (pp. 181–192). New York: Teachers College Press.

Norris, J., & Ortega, L. (2000). Effectiveness of L2 instruction: A research synthesis and quantitative meta-analysis. *Language Learning, 50,* 417–528.

Odlin, T. (1989). *Language transfer: Cross linguistic influences in language learning.* Cambridge, UK: Cambridge University Press.

Oliver, R. (1998). Negotiation of meaning in child interactions. *Modern Language Journal, 82,* 372–386.

Oliver, R. (2002). The patterns of negotiation for meaning in child interactions. *Modern Language Journal, 86,* 97–111.

Olsen, L. (1997). *Made in America: Immigrant Students in Our Public Schools.* New York: The New Press.

O'Malley, J. M., & Chamot, A. U. (1990). *Learning strategies in second language acquisition.* Cambridge, UK: Cambridge University Press.

Ovando, C. J., Collier, V. P., & Combs, M. C. (1998). *Bilingual and ESL classrooms: Teaching in multicultural contexts* (3rd ed.). Boston: McGraw-Hill.

Oxford, R. (1990). *Language learning strategies: What every teacher should know.* Boston: Heinle.

Padilla, A. M. (1998). Emerging policy issues in immersion education: A U.S. perspective. In J. Arnau & J. M. Artigal (1998), *Immersion programmes: A European perspective* (pp. 66–79).Barcelona: Universitat de Barcelona.

Padilla, A. M., & Sung, H. (1992). A theoretical and pedagogical framework for bilingual education based on principles from cognitive psychology. In R. V. Padilla & A. H. Benavides (Eds.), *Critical perspectives on bilingual education research* (pp. 11–41). Tempe: AZ: Bilingual Press.

Padilla, A. M., Fairchild, H., & Valadez, C. (Eds.). (1990). *Bilingual education: Issues and strategies.* Newbury Park, CA: Sage.

Parrish, T. B., Merickel, A., Linquanti, R., Perez, M., Eaton, M., & Esra, P. (2002). *Effects of Proposition 227 on the education of English learners, K-12: Year 3 report.* Palo Alto, CA: American Institutes for Research and WestEd.

Peal, E., & Lambert, W. E. (1962). The relation of bilingualism to intelligence. *Psychological Monographs: General and Applied, 76* (27, Whole No. 546), 1–23.

Pinker, S. (1994). *The language instinct: How the mind creates language.* New York: William Morrow.

Rivers, W. W. (1964). *The psychologist and the foreign language teacher.* Chicago: University of Chicago Press.

Schoonen, R., van Gelderen, A., de Glopper, K., Hulstijn, J., Simis, A., Snellings, P., et al. (2003). First language and second language writing: The role of linguistic knowledge, speed of processing, and metacognitive knowledge. *Language Learning, 53,* 165–202.

Sierra, A. M., & Padilla, A. M. (2003). United States' hegemony and purposes for learning English in Mexico. In P. M. Ryan & R. Terborg (Eds.), *Language: Issues of inequality*. Mexico, D. F.: University of Mexico Press.

Skehan, P. (1998). *A cognitive approach to language processing*. Oxford, UK: Oxford University Press.

Snow, S., & Hoefnagel-Hohole, M. (1978). The critical period for language acquisition: Evidence from second language learning. *Child Development, 49,* 1114–1128.

Sung, H., & Padilla, A. M. (1998). Student motivation, parental attitudes, and involvement in the learning of Asian languages in elementary and secondary schools. *Modern Language Journal, 82,* 205–216.

Tabouret-Keller, A. (2004). Bilingualism in Europe. In T. K. Bhatia & W. C. Ritchie (Eds.), *The handbook of bilingualism*. Oxford, UK: Blackwell.

Tan, L. H., Spinks, J. A., Feng, C., Siok, W. T., Perfetti, C. A., Xiong, J., et al. (2003). Neural systems of second language reading are shaped by native language. *Human Brain Mapping, 18,* 158–166.

Tomasello, M. (Ed.). (1998). *The new psychology of language: Cognitive and functional approaches to language structure*. Mahwah, NJ: Lawrence Erlbaum Associates.

Ullman, M. T. (2001). The neural basis of lexicon and grammar in first and second language: The declarative/procedural model. *Bilingualism: Language and Cognition, 4,* 105–122.

U.S. Department of Education. (1991). *The conditions of bilingual education in the nation: A report to the Congress and the President*. Washington, DC: Office of the Secretary.

U.S. Department of Education. (2002). *To assure the free appropriate public education of all children with disabilities: Twenty-fourth annual report to Congress on the Implementation of the Individuals with Disabilities Act*. Washington DC: Author.

Zehler, A. M., Fleischman, H. L., Hopstock, P. J., Pendzick, M. L., & Stephenson, T. G. (2003). *Descriptive study of services to LEP students and LEP students with disabilities* (report prepared for the Office of English Language Acquisition). Washington, DC: U.S. Department of Education.

SOCIETAL AND CULTURAL PERSPECTIVES

SOCIAL CULTURAL PERSPECTIVES

IN EDUCATIONAL PSYCHOLOGY

Jack Martin

Simon Fraser University

Educational psychology has traditionally been wedded to three assumptions characteristic of Enlightenment and Modern thought, which seldom are recognized explicitly in the theoretical and empirical work of educational psychologists. These assumptions concern the nature of persons, knowledge, and progress. Taken together, they are heavily implicated in the disciplinary mission of educational psychology to understand the cognitive, behavioral, affective, and motivational capacities and capabilities of learners in ways that educators can use to teach more effectively. So deep do these assumptions run that it may almost seem impossible to imagine students in classrooms as anything other than highly rational, self-conscious, and reflective purveyors of their situations and themselves. These are learners who purposefully construct knowledge of curricular content in terms of hierarchies of semantic and procedural representations amenable to various strategies of information processing and self-regulation that may be used to broaden and deepen the knowledge thus arrayed. Of course, important differences exist in the beliefs of educational psychologists who may be more or less humanistically and/or scientifically attuned. Nonetheless, common to almost all educational psychologists is an image of the independent learner standing somewhat apart from, yet strategically engaged with, the biophysical and sociocultural world of entities, events, and ideas to be understood.

But what if this image and the assumptions it reflects are mistaken? What if there is nothing especially natural about this image, and it cannot ensure the accumulation of a progressive body of knowledge about learners and

their education? Surely, it should not be surprising if such possibilities seem peculiar to many educational psychologists. Typical responses to such challenges readily admit that it is both necessary and appropriate to recognize both individual and contextual differences in learners and educational settings, at least with respect to how the expert knowledge of educational psychologists is to be applied. However, at a deeper level, the basic assumptions and image of the strategic, self-regulating learner typically remain intact. Despite surface differences in persons and contexts, the image of the learner that remains constant is that of an individual representing the world and adjusting internal knowledge stores and schemata as different tasks seem to require. Interpersonal, social, and broader cultural contexts are seen as relevant, but are treated primarily as factors that must be considered as possibly affecting the specific learning strategies employed and the manner and consequences of their employment. The core image and assumptions remain essentially unchanged, for these are taken, at least tacitly, to be universal and certain, fixed by human nature, and understood by educational psychologists as the foundation on which their scientific inquiries and professional practices are built.

Social cultural perspectives in educational psychology, despite their considerable differences, all eschew the foregoing core image and assumptions about learners, knowledge, and educational progress. For social cultural theorists and researchers, learners are not independent strategists rationally surveying knowledge domains in ways that may be improved through their own efforts, aided and abetted by the ministrations of psychological and educational experts. To social culturalists, this entire way of talking and thinking reflects deeply held convictions about the nature of persons and their worldly involvement that may be demonstrated, both logically and empirically, to be in error. All social cultural perspectives understand persons as actually constituted by sociocultural practices, not just influenced or affected by them. Processes of cultural history and sociogenesis are trumps. Yes, human learners have biophysically evolved bodies and brains, but their personhood (including their minds, selves, and agentic capabilities) are sociocultural acquisitions, not natural endowments. Both persons and the knowledge they construct are communal accomplishments within historical traditions of cultural practice that might have been, and in various parts of the world have been, different. Moreover, science and social science, including educational psychology, are themselves social and cultural practices of communities of participants that reflect the conventions and interests of these communities as much as they provide progressive knowledge that issues in societal improvement.

This chapter continues with a more formal statement of the assumptions and problems that social culturalists attribute to Enlightenment and Modern thought, both in general, and in psychology and education in particular. This opening section is followed by a clarification of different kinds of social cultural, alternative theorizing and metatheorizing with respect to persons, knowledge, and progress. A subsequent section considers the learner in historical, sociocultural, and developmental context and examines processes of teaching and learning, and the education of persons from a social cultural perspective. Selected examples of social cultural research in each of these areas are presented in considerable detail in order to give readers, many of whom may not be as familiar with social cultural work as they are with more traditional lines of psychological inquiry in education, a clear picture of the theoretical assumptions and types of questions that guide such work, and particular strategies of inquiry that embody and actualize these assumptions and questions. The adoption of this style of presentation necessitates a reasonably detailed consideration of a small number of studies and programs of inquiry to the exclusion of many equally informative investigations. On the other hand, the reader obtains a concrete sense of what was done and why it was done that is not typically available from a more inclusive, but necessarily more cursory, listing of research findings. Despite their relatively small number, the studies selected as examples of social cultural research nonetheless display a reasonably representative array of social cultural concerns and methods, as well as exhibiting work across a considerable range of curriculum areas, instructional contexts, and policy issues. The final section

of the chapter is devoted to a brief, critical consideration of the social cultural perspectives discussed.

THREE PROBLEMATIC PILLARS OF ENLIGHTENMENT AND MODERN THOUGHT

Through main contributors such as Hobbes, Descartes, Locke, and Kant, the Western history of ideas has been built around three basic assumptions. Despite huge disagreements among rationalists and empiricists with respect to the roles of reason and sense in the acquisition of knowledge, these three assumptions have been held with considerable consistency across most forms of Enlightenment and Modern thought. The first is that persons have an essential nature that is given by God and/or by Nature in advance of their worldly experience. The second is that knowledge is grounded in the nature of persons who are equipped to represent the world in ways that are not identical with it, but are nonetheless veridical to it and can be warranted through rational scrutiny and consideration, and through empirical verification. The third assumption is that the rationality and resultant knowledge of persons are necessarily progressive with respect to human betterment. In modern, scientific times, these three assumptions are reflected in the image of the elevated objectivity and rationality of scientists who seek universal, eternal truths about the world that will contribute to human progress and perfection. Not only biophysical aspects of life and world, but all human institutions and practices, are believed to be amenable to scientific inquiry and improvement.

In modern, disciplinary psychology, these core assumptions concerning persons, knowledge, and progress are enshrined in the image of a stable, coherent self—a conscious, rational, autonomous person capable of self and worldly knowledge through empirical observation and reason. This is a person who represents the world in ways amenable to its own internal operations that enable progressively more complex and effective interactions with the world and others in it. The work of Piaget is prototypic of these underlying ontological and epistemological commitments of modern psychology. In Piaget's neo-Kantian perspective, the person is understood as a biologically equipped, active knower who, during ontogenesis, constructs both knowledge of the world and new conceptual structures capable of securing such knowledge. It is true that Piaget assumes a much less rich and preexistent mental system than Kant. Nonetheless, he implies that space, time, and the objects of experience are basic a priori mental structures that differ from things and events in the world, but which allow us to infer the independent existence and nature of worldly phenomena.

Moreover, at its most basic, the individual *cogito,* as a thinking and knowing capacity, remains essentially unchanged by these processes of progressive knowledge construction (cf. Piaget, 1988).

Cognitive constructivists such as von Glasersfeld (1987) have adopted the work of Piaget as a basis for their theorizing about student learning and development. Von Glasersfeld incorporates Piagetian notions of assimilation and accommodation and uses the term *knowledge* to refer to those sensory-motor and conceptual operations that have proven viable in the knower's experience. In this approach, perturbations that the cognizing subject generates relative to a purpose or goal are viewed as powerful intellectual motivators, as the driving forces of cognitive development. The role of the teacher is to create or to facilitate productive forms of perturbation in learners. Learning itself is understood as a process by which the learner reorganizes his or her understanding and cognitive activity to eliminate perturbations. Even when learners' interactions with classroom norms and practices are considered, the burden of explanation in cognitive accounts such as von Glaserfeld's still falls on models of individual students' self-organization and on analyses of the internal processes by which these cognitively active individuals construe the classroom situation. As such, consideration of social context in contemporary cognitive theorizing in educational psychology typically is limited to immediate interactions between teachers and students that, although relevant and even influential, nonetheless give way to a prevailing primacy of the cognitive activity of the autonomously agentic learner, a central feature of a typically Modern perspective on persons, knowledge, and progress.

In education, the Enlightment and Modern tradition has assumed that persons are autonomous, rational agents in a rather strong metaphysical sense. These are fundamentally self-concerned, interested, and determining individuals capable of shaping their existence through the exercise of conscious will and purpose. Such traditional agents are able to chart their own life plans. This is true whether they are understood as transcendental subjects arrayed between angels and animals in a great chain of being, or as rational proprietors and maximizers of utility in a more worldly web of decisions and actions. These agents are, to borrow Roderick Chisholm's (1982) useful phrase, "prime movers unmoved." They are possessed of a deep core of being that remains essentially unchanged throughout the vicissitudes of history and culture. The fundamental character of these persons precedes and stands apart from those linguistic and social practices, forms of community, and interpersonal relationships in which they choose to participate. In classic liberalism, it is a condition of such persons' proper existence that they must have the liberty to make choices that affect their own lives. On this view, social institutions must be arranged so as to facilitate the free expression of the individual natures of persons thus understood. In particular, education must create a space within which persons might practice self-creation in freedom from undue interference from other persons and interests. The rights of such a person to a relatively unfettered freedom of choice and action typically override other kinds of ethical and political considerations. In general, it is assumed that if these individual rights are secured, progressive consequences for the broader society and culture will issue from such preservation.

Despite the widespread prevalence of Enlightenment and Modern conceptions of persons, knowledge, and progress in contemporary life, psychology, and education, there are several rather obvious and well-known logical and epistemological problems with them. A discussion of these problems helps both to provide a rationale for contemporary, social cultural perspectives in general, and sets the stage for distinguishing these perspectives from each other.

In modern times, the assumption that persons have an essential nature that is given prior to their worldly experience entails the belief that human nature is inherited and fixed by genetically determined biophysical structures that have evolved through natural selection. There are both historical and logical problems with such a belief. With respect to the evolutionary, biophysical determination of those human cognitive functions that we share with other mammals and primates, there has been plenty of time for biological evolution to have provided some such natural basis for mind, selfhood, and agency. However, we humans obviously employ many uniquely human cognitive functions such as those intersubjective, perspectival, and joint attentional capabilities that enable us to reproduce intentional acts, take the perspective of others, understand others as intentional beings, and express all of these and other activities in language and symbolic thought. There simply has not been sufficient time for the biological evolution of these uniquely human capabilities, even if one accepts the most generous possible time frame of approximately 6 million years (Tomasello, 1999, p. 204). Moreover, it seems clear that because such things as linguistic symbols and sociocultural, institutional practices are obviously socially constituted, the much more plausible possibility is that these uniquely human capabilities have unfolded in historical and ontogenetic time. If this indeed is the more likely scenario, it must be the case that complex human phenomena such as mind, self, and agency (all crucially important aspects of personhood) are not given a priori, in advance of wordly experience. Rather, it must be the case that personhood actually requires and is constituted by such experience, both during our collective, cultural history and during our individual, ontogenetic courses of development.

The assumption of an a priori person also creates seemingly insurmountable difficulties in understanding how knowledge is possible, given that knowledge is carried by persons. If persons pre-exist their worldly experience, and are thus separate from their biophysical environments, societies, and cultures, it must be the case that they somehow are equipped to represent the world in ways that are accurate, at least so far as human actions and understanding are concerned. The assumption of a priori personhood thus leads directly to the long-standing problems concerning relationships between mind and body, and mind and world. When the person or self is understood in a priori terms, it is understood as separate and independent from the biophysical and sociocultural body and world. So deep a gulf is created between mind and world that the question of how knowledge is possible at all becomes almost insurmountably challenging. Why? Because the only type of answer possible must invoke some form of representationalism. In other words, mind is linked to world because the pre-existent nature of mind or mental capabilities allows it to represent the world in ways that are adequate for human activity in the world.

But, all forms of representationalism (including those currently popular in the cognitive constructivist, information processing, and schema theories of educational psychologists) are beset by two highly significant logical difficulties. First, if the only access that individuals have to their world is through their representations of it, it then becomes logically impossible to explain how their represented knowledge of the world can be warranted as true, appropriate, or accurate, or how this knowledge might undergo correction and improvement. This is so because if our only access to the world is through our representations of it, then there is no way, other than through our representations, that potentially corrective feedback from our interactions with the world can be experienced. (This is as true for scientists, who must filter the outcomes of their experiments through their representations of the world, as it is for the rest of us, whose everyday interactions with the world are similarly filtered.) We thus seem to be locked inside our representations, with no other access to the world. If this is so, there is no way that our representations can count as knowledge, because knowledge (as opposed to mere belief) requires minimally that it can be warranted and potentially improved. Further, we humans seem highly responsive to corrective feedback as a consequence of our worldly involvement, indicating that we must have additional ways of interacting with, perceiving, and understanding the world, other than through our representations and conceptualizations of it.

The second difficulty with all forms of representationalism parasitic on a priori personhood concerns the matter of how knowledge might get started in the first place. If our representations are not given by our worldly experience, but pre-exist it, the only alternative explanations available are that such representations are given by Nature or God. As we already have seen, what Nature has given us through known processes of biological evolution seems inadequate to explain our uniquely human cognitive functions and capabilities. Of course, it might be argued that all representations or concepts actually are innate, despite the time-frame problem discussed earlier. But, such extreme innateness seems highly unlikely. In a strong sense, this would imply that we are born with concepts such as democracy and environmental sustainability, as well as love and death. In a weak sense, only a few "concept potentials" might be posited as innate. However, the possibility of such "conceptual seeds" developing in the absence of interactions with different things through experience in the world then seems difficult to envision. For example, imagine having a concept of fire without interactions with things such as fireplaces, or at least things such as cigarettes or heaters. Of course, divine or otherwise mysterious (e.g., transcendental) sources may be posited, but to do so moves outside of contemporary conventions concerning scientific and social scientific practices of inquiry.

Finally, the Enlightenment/Modern assumption that human rationality and knowledge practices (such as contemporary science) are necessarily progressive with respect to human betterment simply flies in the face of very obvious counter evidence. There is, of course, no doubt that many miraculous advances have been achieved through human inquiry and intervention in medicine, physical science, and other areas of human activity. However, the advent and persistence of scientifically and technologically aided warfare and oppression in many areas of recent and contemporary human activity give ample testimony to refute the "necessarily progressive" assumption.

The simple logical fact is that what we humans ought to do cannot be determined solely on the basis of what we know how to do. Enhanced knowledge alone does not ensure advances in our moral, ethical engagements with others. Even if it were established through well-conducted research in educational psychology that disruptive students are "controlled" in classrooms by threatening, potentially violent teachers, such a finding would supply no adequate warrant for how teachers ought to behave when confronted by disruptive students.

Claims concerning human betterment must attend to the obvious diversity, plurality, and legitimate contestation readily evident in many areas of contemporary societies. Interests and goals of individuals and subgroups may diverge from those of others. What is good or better for members of more dominant sociocultural groups may be directly opposed to what is good or better for members of minority groups. Moreover, reason and science are themselves not immune from the possible effects of personal and collective interests, values, and power. Human betterment and how it might be achieved and recognized are extremely complex matters that cannot be captured adequately in so simplistic an assumption as that which frequently has attended and rationalized the march of reason and science in modern times.

The foregoing arguments concerning various problems associated with the three pillars of Enlightenment and Modern thought concerning persons, knowledge, and progress should not be taken as a complete refutation of all modern projects. Because the oft-cited philosophical foundations for our rational and scientific activities are inadequate does not necessarily mean that there is no value to those activities or to the various, different perspectives and beliefs that attend them. What may be concluded is that the core philosophical bases for many modern projects, including science, social science, psychology, and education, provide inadequate, even highly misleading, bases for advancing our understanding of these important areas of human activity. It is in this context that social cultural perspectives in general, and in psychology and education in particular, can be understood as a collection of rather diverse attempts to forge a more coherent set of assumptions and practices for psychological and educational theory and inquiry. Of course, all social cultural perspectives do not react in exactly the same ways, or to the same extent, to the three pillars of Enlightenment and Modern thought. However, the ways in which they do react, and the specific alternatives that they embrace, both clarify their unique contributions and serve to distinguish them from each other.

SOCIAL CULTURAL ALTERNATIVES

Any attempt at a taxonomy of social cultural approaches is fraught with obvious difficulties of oversimplification, unduly restrictive categorization, and highly debatable placements of programs of inquiry. These difficulties are exacerbated by the understandable tendency of many social cultural proponents to adjust their theoretical and methodological "tool kits" to particular circumstances and purposes of inquiry. Nonetheless, three primary lines of development and their major subdivisions seem evident in most discussions of social cultural theory and practice in psychology and education—a Vygotskian sociocultural line, a Meadian pragmatic line, and a critical,

postmodern line. Of these three, the last may be the most contentious, in that it houses an extremely wide range of approaches that do not necessarily fit easily together. For example, many critical theorists and hermeneuts are at considerable pains to distance themselves from the extreme cultural relativism and entirely local knowledge possibilities they perceive in certain forms of postmodern social constructionism. Another obvious difficulty with the classificatory scheme employed here is that to date work in the Meadian pragmatic line has not been as frequently conducted within educational psychology per se, as in some other areas of psychology and social science. Nonetheless, despite these and other concerns, the three lines of social cultural scholarship discussed next provide an overview of the range of theoretical perspectives and inquiry orientations that describe the contemporary state of social, cultural study in psychological and educational contexts.

The Vygotskian Sociocultural Line

The first and most prominent line of development is taken to originate in the work of the Russian scholars Alexander Luria (1979) and Lev Vygotsky (1978, 1986), often as augmented and somewhat differently interpreted and developed by other Russian sociocultural psychologists and activity theorists such as Leontiev (1981) and Ilyenkov (1977). Vygotsky advanced a view of the person as socially constructed through interactions with others. For Vygotsky, the crucial step in the social formation of the person involved the acquisition of capabilities of self-expression and self-reference. The psychological tools and discursive skills required for such capabilities develop in interaction with others already skilled in speaking and acting within relevant social contexts and linguistic (and other relational) practices. In this context, whenever the infant appears to attempt some intentional act, adults or older children supplement its efforts by interpreting and reacting to the child's actions in ways that initiate the child into the social, linguistic practices and artifacts of the society. In this way, the unordered mental activity with which infants are neurophysiologically endowed evolves into the structured patterns of mature minds. Along with such socially sponsored development, the child acquires those discursive references and linguistically mediated means for responding to its own activity that permit it to experience and act in the world as an individual self. In this respect, nominal forms of self-reference (such as proper names or nicknames, and first-person pronouns) are thought to be particularly important, as they serve to index one's experience and action as an embodied person in the sociotemporal space of everyday life. For Vygotsky, language acts as an important tool by means of which individuals interpret social symbols and come to make sense of their inner processes and existence as psychological beings.

At a more general level, Luria (1979) and Vygotsky (1978, 1986) distinguished human beings from other animals in terms of the making and use of tools that have radically altered their conditions of existence and their psychological makeup. Such tools are socially spawned cultural artifacts that include not only material creations such as rakes and utensils, but more importantly, social practices and language (the "tool of tools"). Such tools mediate between the functional capacities and capabilities of tool users and their tasks and goals. In this sense, culture encompasses the pool of artifacts and practices accumulated by a social group during the course of its historical development. Human phylogeny, history, and ontogeny were understood by Luria and Vygotsky to turn respectively on the appearance of tool use amongst our primate ancestors, the emergence of labor and symbolic mediation in human history, and the acquisition of language as a transformative tool of individual development within sociocultural context.

In psychology and educational psychology, the Vygotskian line has been picked up and developed in at least two broadly different, yet highly interactive ways. Scholars such as Cole (1996), Engeström (1990), Lave and Wenger (1991), and Wertsch (1998) have advanced a conception of distributed cognition mediated by cultural artifacts that connect individuals to society and society to individuals. Others (e.g., Bruner, 1990, 1996; John-Steiner & Mahn, 1996; Newman & Holzman, 1993) have downplayed materialist and instrumental interpretations of Vygotsky and emphasized the emergent agency of the tool-using child, an agency that is both determined by, and determining of, the social and cultural context.

The Meadian Pragmatic Line

A second broad line of development in sociocultural thought flows from the work of early American pragmatists such as James, Baldwin, and Dewey, but especially George Herbert Mead (1934), sometimes as reinterpreted through sociological symbolic interactionists such as Blumer (1969). This line is most readily apparent in the work of contemporary psychologists, mathematics educators, and educational psychologists such as Bauersfeld (1988), Harré (1984), Pajares (2003), Prawat (1995), and Cobb and Yackel (1996). Mead's pragmatic social psychology merged Dewey's (1916) functionalism and theory of the act with his own unique social psychology that viewed the individual self as emergent from social interactions with others that lead the individual to behave toward herself as others do and have done. Although similar in many ways, where Vygotsky tended to view individuals as extended through sociocultural artifacts, Mead granted individuals more autonomy in their development of perspectives concerning themselves and their world. Although always related to the perspectives of others and society at large, and continuously engaged in constitutive processes of intersubjectivity, Mead's self is decidedly agentic in its ability to take perspectives that contain emergent elements not found in those other perspectives, but which unfold within activity. In Mead's view, it is the need for collective human activity in the face of problems, not abstract shared values, that builds communities and spawns individuals as social beings and agents who can, in turn, enrich their communities.

Mead, who like many pragmatists tended to avoid classic metaphysical arguments as unhelpful, did not ask if the world was a deterministic system or not. Instead, he assumed that for all practical purposes, the continuous emergence of novelty (in biological and especially in social systems populated by agents) always would exceed human predictive capabilities, even the methods of science that he elevated above all others as the epitome of human reflective intelligence. Mead understood the human physiological capacity for developing intelligence and reflective consciousness as the product of biological evolution. However, he insisted that the actual development of such agentic capability "must proceed in terms of social situations wherein it gets its expression and import; and hence it itself is a product of social evolution, the process of social experience and behavior" (Mead, 1934, p. 226). Mead accused the dualistic philosophers from Descartes onward of removing mind from the world and abandoning the task of connecting the thinker's mind with other minds and with the natural world.

To overcome dualism, Mead understood thinking as inward conversation, and traced the development of such conversation as it emerges in childhood. As children learn to talk with others, they learn to talk with themselves, sometimes constructing imaginary conversational partners. Through early use of symbols, play, role taking, and games, children's talk/thought begins to encompass a self-consciousness, initiated by adopting views of themselves from the roles of others. By adulthood, such scaffolding and full articulation fall away, leaving processes of thinking and self-consciousness that constitute the mind and self. Once again, such ontogenetic development was possible only after human beings evolved physiologically to the point where they began to use language for symbolic social interaction. Only then could mind and self emerge as private, internal conversations in the head. For Mead, self and mind were not substances, but processes in which conversations, gestures, and social practices become internalized within organic forms. Both are crucial properties of persons who emerge within, and continue to interact as dynamic parts of, social processes. Neither is presupposed as a substance out of which the social world arises. Rather, both are understood as arising within and contributing to that world.

Both the Vygotskian sociocultural and Meadian pragmatic lines of development are primarily concerned with eroding Enlightenment and Modern dualisms and theoretical perspectives that would separate persons from, and give them priority (both temporally and theoretically) over, their social cultural embeddedness. In addition, these approaches, especially pragmatism, sought to replace the foundational epistemologies favored by many Modern and Enlightenment thinkers with a picture of knowing as uncertainly and imperfectly grounded in the practical, historical, and everyday life worlds and activities of human beings. A third broad developmental line of social cultural theorizing takes a much more critical posture toward individualism, knowledge, and Enlightenment and Modern conceptions of progress.

The Critical Postmodern Line

This third line of work can be traced to Heidegger and Marx, through the contributions of numerous hermeneuts (e.g., Gadamer, 1995; Taylor, 1995), poststructuralists (e.g., Derrida, 1978; Foucault, 1980), critical theorists (Adorno, 1983; Horkheimer, 1974), postmodernists (e.g., Deleuze & Guattari, 1987; Lyotard, 1984), postcolonialists (e.g., Freire, 1972; Spivak, 1996), feminists (e.g., Butler, 1997), and neo-Marxists (e.g., Jameson, 1971). For present purposes, it currently culminates in the contemporary work of educational and psychological scholars such as Apple (1990), Gergen (1994), Giroux (1992), Lather (1991), McLaren (1998), Packer (2000), Popkewitz (1991), and Rose (1996). For these scholars and many others inspired by critical, poststructural, and postmodern thinking, the most important historical lesson with respect to disciplinary psychology in education is that it has contributed greatly to a prevailing Western way of life that is perceived as natural, essential, and progressive.

This is a lifeworld in which we see ourselves as individuals at some detachment from our societies and communities, with private motives and aspirations according to which we must be "true" if we are to live fulfilling lives. In principle, we could reject these psychologically abetted conceptions of ourselves and the good life, but such rejection is made less likely by the essentialist idea that psychology, as a science of human behavior, has succeeded in arriving at basic truths about the human condition that are ahistorical, timeless, and universal. It is such essentialism that constitutes one of the most ubiquitous examples of power/knowledge in our times. And, it is precisely this kind of essentialism that theorists active in this third line of social cultural theory and practice seek to display as erroneous and constructed through sociocultural discourses and practices, invested with the power and self-interest of dominant social and economic groups.

The hope is to clear the way for alternative discourses and practices, within psychology, education, and civic life in general, that might challenge those currently predominant in disciplinary psychology and formal education. The central issue here concerns who is allowed to call the shots. By getting everything out in the open, the stage is set for critical examination of who is talking and who is silenced, both in general and within our disciplinary practices. This third line of social cultural work is committed to creating new avenues for societal and educational development consistent with constantly evolving principles and practices of authentic engagement and participation with others, equity, diversity, and social justice that cross artificial boundaries of class, gender, race, ethnicity, and sexual orientation. By deconstructing the dualistic thinking they believe marginalizes certain groups, ideas, and practices, many advocates of the critical approach to social cultural studies hope to eradicate much discrimination and oppression. In this context, education is understood primarily as a means of liberation and empowerment. Of course, many scholars who incorporate hermeneutic, feminist, social constructionist, and critical perspectives in their work are concerned about what they regard as overly extreme forms of cultural relativism and epistemic nihilism in some forms of postmodernism (cf. Martin, Sugarman, & Hickinbottom, 2003), which they interpret as undermining positive proposals for educational reform and research. Nonetheless, as Schutz (2000) and others recently have argued, such criticisms may fail to locate resources for social action that are discernible in even the more radical postmodern proposals. Whatever the truth of such matters, if truth there may be, the various perspectives included in the critical postmodern line of work tend to share the general orientation toward educational study and inquiry just articulated.

As already indicated, there are many important differences within and across the Vygotskian, Meadian, and various critical lines of development with respect to social cultural theorizing, research, and educational practice. Nonetheless, it is possible to provide a very general characterization of how the various social cultural alternatives just considered understand the learner, the teaching and learning process, and the aims of education. Not only does consideration of these topics further clarify the nature of social cultural alternatives in educational psychology, but it also permits a reasonably clear and succinct account of social cultural conceptions of persons, knowledge, and progress in contradistinction to those problematic Enlightenment and Modern perspectives discussed earlier.

SOCIAL CULTURAL THEORY AND RESEARCH IN EDUCATIONAL PSYCHOLOGY

Against Modern and Enlightenment conceptions of a priori, detached, and essential personhood, certain knowledge and methods for attaining and anchoring it to its enduring foundations, and a steady march of progress through reason and science, social cultural thinkers have advanced a set of alternative conceptions. As evident in the work of Vygotsky, Mead, and many other social culturalists, persons are understood as constituted through their active participation within social cultural artifacts and practices, the most important of which include relational, linguistic symbols and practices. In similar fashion, learners are understood as active participants within the historically established cultural traditions of classroom practice in which they are embedded.

The social cultural perspective on knowledge understands it as socially constructed within social, cultural contexts, the most important of which include the family, the school, and other settings for play, work, and study. In fact, both knowledge and knowers are constructed and constituted in these historically established, yet constantly unfolding and evolving contexts and the traditions they sustain and develop.

Finally, like the foregoing conceptions of persons and knowledge, any acceptable conception of progress, from a social cultural perspective, must be understood as grounded in contingent human activities and practices in the world. Within any human community, social and cultural practices constitute a particular way of life. However, such traditions and practices are never monolithic, fixed, or guaranteed. They provide a basis for social interaction and activity, yet they themselves are constantly and variously interpreted, contested, and dynamically unfolding, with no Hegelian endpoint or fixed definition of progress in sight. Under such conditions, education takes on particular significance in terms of the formation of persons capable of full social engagement and participation in the ongoing reproduction and possible transformation of the very societies and cultures that constitute them.

The Learner in Social Cultural and Developmental Context

The social cultural view of learners is derived from the foregoing view of persons as constituted through participation in sociocultural artifacts and practices. Although both Vygotsky (1978, 1986) and Mead (1934, 1977) use the term *internalization* to refer to this ongoing process of personal constitution, many contemporary socioculturalists, pragmatists, and critical theorists prefer to avoid this term, and what they regard as its overly individualistic and mentalistic connotations. Tensions surrounding such matters abound in social cultural work in psychology and educational psychology. In part, this is because of the different lines of social cultural inquiry, but it also is reflected in the changing orientations of influential researchers. For example, Paul Cobb, whose work provides one of the examples of research discussed later in this chapter, describes himself as beginning as a constructivist, becoming a social constructivist, and as settling on a position that synthesizes socioculturalism and constructivism (cf. Cobb & Yackel, 1996). Such tensions are important to note because they point to important differences in the perspectives taken by social cultural researchers in education, many of which cannot be discussed here because of space limitations (see Packer & Goicoechea, 2000, for a more extended discussion of these matters). At the same time, these tensions and differences contribute significantly to the sense of excitement and creative potential that attends contemporary work in this general area. Having said this, it nonetheless is the case that almost all social cultural theorists, although emphasizing the social construction of persons, wish to maintain a perspective on human agency that is sufficient to advance their goals with respect to the educational and societal empowerment, equality, and full participation of a wide diversity of citizens. Consequently, in what follows, the sociocultural constitution of learners as self-conscious agents during ontogeny will be emphasized.

Theory. To say that persons and learners are socially constituted is to claim that human ontogenetic development can best be understood as a process in which human beings, through their activities and interactions in the sociocultural and biophysical world, take up the artifacts and practices of their culture. This intersubjectivity eventually makes possible forms of collective and individual activity capable of transforming the very cultural artifacts and practices that are available.

At birth, human infants are equipped with bodies and brains that allow them to develop within a pre-existing social and cultural world, in interaction with others whose activities and actions teach them how to participate in this world. Neonatal mimicking and protoconversation (very initial and primitive forms of orienting and reacting to others) that are unique to human infants (when compared to the newly born of all other animals) are evident very early on (perhaps from birth) (Trevarthan, 1993).

By around 9 months of age, human infants begin in minimal ways to act toward themselves as others do, and to attribute intentionality to others and themselves in early, preconceptual ways (Tomasello, 1999). Such developmental milestones can be acquired only in the context of ongoing interactions with others in social contexts. They open up more fully cultural forms of human ontogenetic development in which young children participate with others in joint attentional activities and begin to comprehend and reproduce the intentional actions of others with respect to various material and symbolic artifacts (Tomasello, 1999). With these emergent, socially enabled capabilities, language acquisition commences and extends the cultural line of development more efficiently and completely. Mastery of this one special cultural artifact transforms the capabilities and actions of the child. With language, children are able to engage intersubjectively with others and to adopt the communicative conventions of their cultures. Because linguistic symbols are both intersubjective and perspectival, when children learn to use words and linguistic forms in the manner of adults, they understand that the same objects and events can be construed variously in relation to different points of view and communicative purposes. The emergence of enhanced forms of self-consciousness and agentic understanding and capability owe much to the intersubjective, perspectival nature of language, and to the communicative exchanges and constructions it makes possible. It is important to emphasize again that all of this issues from participation with others within human societies and cultures.

By the time of formal schooling, most children have experienced an extended period of discourse and social interaction with adults and peers that has equipped them with ever more esoteric capabilities for understanding and acting intentionally. Formal schooling is replete with social interactions in which teachers comment explicitly on the children's words, actions, and "what they are thinking." In effect, teachers encourage young learners to take an outsider's perspective on their own acting and thinking in terms of what educational psychologists refer to as self-regulation, metacognition, problem solving, and so forth. All of these important and uniquely human forms of thinking do not just require, but actually are constituted by discursive interactions in school and other settings that are mediated by intersubjective and perspectival linguistic symbols and constructions. Through participation in educational contexts, the learner gains facility with these tools of thought and is immersed in widening horizons of sociocultural experience—in issues, problems, perspectives, and ways of life that might be quite distant from what has been personally experienced thus far in life. In all of this, the learner comes to understand her place within a larger historical, cultural, and contemporary world populated by ideas, debates, problems, issues, and challenges that command attention, and which encourage and enable the cultivation of increasingly complex forms of understanding and acting.

All social cultural perspectives understand the learner as a participant in educational and broader cultural contexts who gradually migrates from a "newcomer" to an "old-timer, whose changing knowledge, skill, and discourse are part of a developing identity—in short a community of practice" (Lave & Wenger, 1991, p. 122). Of equal importance, it is through the actions of learners who develop into full sociocultural participants that schools and systems of education, as communities of practice, are continuously replenished, reproduced, and even transformed.

Examples of Research. Research in support of the foregoing conceptualization of the person and learner comes from a variety of studies that have examined the ways in which sociocultural, instructional practices and content are appropriated by learners during their participation in formal and informal educational activities with others. Because much learning typically is mediated through familiar, verbal means pervasive in any social, cultural context, a great deal of informal learning goes unnoticed. One way of drawing attention to these ever-present, informal processes of appropriation through which children learn and develop as learners is to insert manufactured, novel features into the everyday contexts in which children play and interact. For example, in a study by Tomasello and Akhtar (1995), an adult introduced children to a curved pipe, down which they could throw objects. In one condition, the adult threw one novel object down the tube after another, saying "Now, modi" when she threw a particular novel object. In another condition, the adult did one thing with a novel object, then another, and eventually threw the same novel object down the pipe, saying "Now, modi." The children immediately adopted and used the term "modi," in both social, communicative situations, but in entirely different ways. In the first situation, they used "modi" when handling the particular novel object; in the second situation they used "modi" when throwing any object down the pipe.

Tomasello and Akhtar (1995) also used the expression *widgit* together with children's first names (e.g., "Widgit, Jason?"), when playing a merry-go-round game. In one condition, the adult prepared the merry-go-round for play, then held out a novel object to the child, saying "Widgit, Jason?" as she continued to alternate her gaze between the child and the merry-go-round. In another condition, the merry-go-round was not readied for play, and the adult did not alternate her gaze to the merry-go-round, but simply offered the novel object to the child, saying, "Widgit, Jason?" In the first case, the children interpreted the adult's question as a request for them to give the new toy a ride on the merry-go-round; in the second case, the children understood and used *widgit* as the name of the new toy. These results are not surprising. Their importance lies in the fact that they make readily apparent the linguistically mediated, social construction of learning and learners in social activity with others.

That such ongoing appropriation serves to construct learners as well as learning is more evident in a study by Foley and Ratner (1997) in which young children collaborated with partners in various activities, and were later asked to recall which partner performed which actions. In this context, the children frequently recalled themselves as having performed the actions that others had performed. Such results demonstrate the seeming ease with which young children appropriate the actions of others and apply them in their own present and future activities. Ratner and Hill (1991) found that kindergarten-aged children are able to reproduce the instructor's role in a teaching situation, even weeks after the original pedagogical events. Moreover, not only do children of this age apply appropriate actions to others, but they also make similar applications to themselves as a means of assisting their own learning (e.g., Goudena, 1987).

What is appropriated from active participation with others in social cultural contexts is not just words or particular actions, but entire dialogues and dialogical relations and intentions. It is perhaps the case that many learners are especially likely to appropriate content, strategies, and understandings from their active participation in instructional and other social contexts when they are experiencing difficulty in navigating particular tasks (e.g., Goodman, 1984). However, appropriating sociocultural linguistic symbols and other dialogical artifacts is both pervasive and ongoing. It is this kind of participatory activity that all social cultural perspectives recognize as constitutive of both learners and learning.

Social cultural research on children's understandings of quantitative relations further demonstrates the constitutive role played by learners' activity within sociocultural practices. In particular, such research points to the inadequacy of Piagetian models of epigenetic constructivism (the thesis that individuals generate novel intellectual structures through a reorganization of prior understandings in the face of contradictions) for conceptualizing readily apparent relations between culture and

cognition. For example, Saxe (1982, 1985) studied the development of mathematical understanding among the Oksapmin in Papua New Guinea following the introduction of a Westernized system of currency and economic exchange. With increasing participation in these new economic practices through the conduct of exchange in newly introduced trade stores, the Oksapmin became engaged with novel mathematical goals requiring addition and subtraction for which their traditional body-based system of enumeration proved inadequate. Saxe describes how the cultural form of body counting gradually shifted in function from enumeration alone to newly emergent forms in which the names of body parts gradually became differentiated from the body parts themselves. This transformation occurred through a variety of intermediate strategies such as a halved body procedure in which two quantities to be added are enumerated on opposite sides of the body, and then one body part indicative of the enumerative total on one side is imaginatively transferred to the other. Through such processes, the Oksapmin gradually created more sophisticated uses of their traditional number system to adapt to the demands of their new social, economic context.

Interestingly, Saxe (1985) also reports positive transfer of such socially emergent practices to the arithmetic learning of school-aged children who received mathematics instruction based on a Western curriculum from teachers unfamiliar with the traditional Oksapmin system of body counting. In subsequent research, Saxe (1991, 1994) studied the sociocultural dynamics of developmental changes to the mathematical understandings of candy-selling Brazilian children. Here again, he demonstrated how social, cultural contexts and practices play an indispensable role in constituting goals that children seek to achieve, and the transactional means with which they attempt to achieve them.

Such research demonstrates the extent to which learners' understandings are grounded in their practical activity in the traditional and changing practices of their societies and cultures. Of course, human learners also make use of highly specialized, biophysically evolved bodies and brains in their worldly activities, and most social, cultural theorists are fully cognizant of this fact (e.g., Packer & Goicoechea, 2000). Nonetheless, they hold that the achievement of understandings and practices constitutive of our minds and selves is accomplished through our active participation in those social cultural contexts in which we are embedded and develop. This core tenet has been repeatedly demonstrated in seminal contributions to social cultural psychology by scholars such as Michael Cole (1996), Sylvia Scribner (Scribner & Cole, 1981), Jean Lave (1988), Jacqueline Goodnow (Goodnow, Miller, & Kessel, 1995), Urie Bronfenbrenner (1979), Pierre Dasen

(1977), Robert Serpell (1976), Patricia Greenfield (1984), Jim Stigler (Stigler, Lee, & Stevenson, 1990), Charles Super (1981), Sara Harkness (Harkness & Super, 1992), Geoffrey Saxe (1991), Barbara Rogoff (2003), Dan Wagner (1993), Richard Shweder (1991), Edward Hutchins (1991), James Wertsch (1998), Yrjö Engeström (1990), Roy D'Andrade (1990), and Vera John-Steiner (1985), to list only a few of those who have made important contributions since the 1970s. (Obviously, my decision to focus in detail on only a few exemplary studies in this chapter is in no way intended as a slight to those whose important work is not mentioned explicitly on these pages.)

Processes of Teaching and Learning

In one sense, processes of teaching and learning that occur in formal educational contexts merely extend those processes of sociocultural participation that are inescapably ongoing in the lives of all human beings. However, formal education adds many additional instructional artifacts and structures that reflect the particular social and cultural histories within which educational systems and schools are situated. When young students enter schools for the first time, they become members of a class who are to behave and to be treated according to explicit and implicit rules and regulations that, for the most part, apply equally to all. Their particular interests of the moment are to give way to collective pursuits and interests of a kind that will immerse them in knowledge practices and content determined by relevant sociocultural and educational traditions. Visible and invisible cultural, social, political, moral, and psychological structures and authorities are more obviously and purposefully in play, and the interactive practices in which students are asked to participate reflect these structures and the knowledge they support.

Theory. Knowledge to be learned in schools thus reflects what a given society, through its cultural traditions of practices and values, considers necessary for its own reproduction and for the production of citizens capable of contributing to such reproduction and continuance. Processes of teaching and learning that occur in schools are constructed to ensure that children and adolescents acquire knowledge, capability, and character consistent with the exercise of civic virtue and personal responsibility. The extent to which individual freedom also is targeted varies considerably from time to time and society to society. In the context of schooling, the most basic educational challenge is somehow to merge the knowledge requirements mandated by the larger society and culture with the interests and capabilities of learners, as

these have developed during the first few years of their active participation in family and playground. This is the first manifestation of what proves to be an ongoing tension between learner interests and capabilities, and the formal curriculum content and mandated knowledge of the larger society and culture.

Dewey (1938) described this tension in a manner that broadly captures most social cultural perspectives on teaching and learning processes in an educational context. What he said was that educators must arrange conditions so that learners can participate actively in them in manners commensurate with their existing capabilities and interests. Such conditions include the actions of the teacher, the selection and use of materials and activities, and the social setting within which learning and teaching occur. Moreover, these conditions must allow learners to get the most out of their classroom experiences, and also must relate in appropriate ways to future settings in which citizenship and democratic participation are exercised. By getting the most out of educational experiences, Dewey meant "extracting at each present time the full meaning of each present experience" (p. 50) in a way that prepares learners for future participation as full members of society. Of course, such extraction is not simply a matter of the individual student inducing from her experience. It is a matter of the student working within materials, perspectives, practices, and problems provided and emergent within the educational context.

As expressed by Lave and Wenger (1991), learning is understood as "situated in the trajectories of participation in which it takes on meaning. These trajectories must themselves be situated in the social world" (p. 121). To be truly educational, processes of teaching and learning must be located in communities of practice that come increasingly to resemble those adult communities of practice that constitute the social life world of a culture. In this sense, education is an apprenticeship in the communal practices of a society and culture that serve to reproduce, transform, and change those practices in ways that make them increasingly transparent and open to newcomers and other practitioners. In Lave and Wenger's terms, Dewey's central challenge of education is to comprehend the structures and processes of the world "at the level at which it is lived" (p. 123).

Examples of Research. Reflecting the foregoing theoretical orientation, much social cultural inquiry into processes of teaching and learning focuses on participation over time in learning communities, and the developmental trajectories that run through such participation. Studies of this kind are difficult to conduct because they inevitably involve studying processes of teaching, learning, and development over reasonably lengthy periods of time in school and related contexts. For example, Yang and Cobb (1995) studied the arithmetical development of American and Taiwanese children from preschool to second grade. They found evidence of important differences in teachers' and parents' expectations for developmental trajectories and competencies to be attained.

American learning sequences appeared discontinuous in that children's initial experiences with single-digit numbers did not constitute a sufficient basis for their subsequent acquisition of place-value conceptions. American parents and teachers viewed place value as particularly challenging and chose to delay its introduction until the second grade. At the same time, they advocated direct instruction as a preferred teaching method. In contrast, Taiwanese teachers and parents regarded place-value conceptions as relatively unproblematic, introducing them in kindergarten in the context of ongoing activities and problems in the absence of direct instruction per se. In Taiwan, learning tasks and teacher actions both assumed and incorporated conceptualizations of numbers as composed of 10's and 1's. As a consequence, Taiwanese children seemed to understand and treat numbers in this way without any conceptual gap. For them, relevant place-value concepts were readily available and appropriated from their daily classroom interactions. In contrast, the American children, who had not appropriated this way of talking and thinking from the teaching and learning processes in which they had been immersed during preschool and grade one, confronted a much more formidable conceptual gap in grade 2.

Research such as that by Yang and Cobb (1995) demonstrates how learners' capabilities and experiences emerge through their participation in and appropriation of socioculturally grounded practices and processes of learning and teaching. At another level, teaching and learning processes and practices themselves reflect, and are immersed in, broader sociocultural understandings and practices concerning the nature of knowledge in particular domains such as mathematics, and how such knowledge is structured and organized. Overall, learners' participation in processes and practices of teaching and learning places them within developmental trajectories through which they build up capabilities and understandings by appropriating the forms, organizations, and strategies extant in their sociocultural and educational contexts. Some social cultural researchers have actually created entire "mini-cultures of practice" within which teaching and learning unfold in ways that permit the tracking of such developmental trajectories.

Michael Cole and his colleagues (see Cole, 1996) designed such a mini-culture that was centered around a set of computer-mediated, educational activities and games that they called the Fifth Dimension. The Fifth Dimension also was replete with its own cultural myths. For example, it was described to participants as a gift from a Wizard as a place for children to play and learn. These cultural stories sanction particular social practices such as graduation ceremonies at which participating children are elevated to the status of Wizard's Assistants. Not only is the Fifth Dimension composed of cultural artifacts (e.g., the computer system and its various games and activities), myths (e.g., the Wizard myth of origin), and practices (e.g., the ceremony to celebrate graduation as Wizard's Assistants), but it also includes particular social relations that are mediated by these artifacts, myths, and practices. Chief among these are interactions with older Wizard's Assistants (actually university undergraduate students) who are also learning to be skillful players of the many games and users of the telecommunication facilities. The presence of these more mature and experienced learners provides many levels and varieties of modeled and facilitated participation in the Fifth Dimension. In general, the interactions of the undergraduate university students with the participating children are guided by Vygotsky's (1978, 1986) notion of "the zone of proximal development." The normative rule at work is that children receive as little pedagogical guidance as possible, but as much as necessary to ensure that they enjoy the overall experience and can participate effectively in at least some aspects of it. Over time, enactment of this normative practice of participatory facilitation helps to ensure a positive learning and developmental trajectory for almost all participating children. The inhabitants of the Fifth Dimension thus consist of children (aged 6 to 12), undergraduates, and the researchers themselves, some of whom are "old timers," and some of whom are "new comers."

Some of the more interesting findings from research in the Fifth Dimension concern the ways in which participants' interactions with the artifacts evolve over time, and the way in which children's participation is mediated by more mature and experienced participants (primarily the undergraduates) to help ensure learning. With respect to participants' interactions with the computer games and other artifacts, an initial phase of orientation, during which the artifacts are treated as entities in themselves, is followed by an obviously instrumental phase, before giving way to a reflective phase. During the instrumental phase, the artifacts are used as means or mediators for the execution of various goal-directed actions. In the reflective phase, orienting and instrumental activities were subsumed within a more thoughtful consideration of the overall system of artifacts and activities, with a view to comprehending their systemic nature. In terms of enculturation, these various phases of interaction with the cultural artifacts in the Fifth Dimension may be interpreted respectively to parallel phases of knowledge acquisition, strategic activity that sometimes involves changes in roles, and the evolution of new ways of mediating interactions with, even transforming, the artifacts available.

With respect to the mediation of learners' activities through interaction with more experienced learners, it is clear that the undergraduates support the participatory learning of the children in a flexible manner. The support that is provided to the learners is based on the undergraduates' interpretations of both the Fifth Dimension and the current capabilities and levels of participation of the learners (much as Dewey, 1938, suggested). Such support typically involves the undergraduate temporarily taking over part of the task at hand, then turning the task back to the child and adopting the role of helpful spectator. The assisting activities of the undergraduates unfold in the context of ongoing joint participation in games and activities, especially when the children encounter difficulties that they cannot, after some effort, overcome or manage on their own.

The culturally constituted and supported social interactions and participatory learning described in Cole's Fifth Dimension are powerful demonstrations of the social cultural approach to teaching and learning processes. Of course, it seems clear that much of what takes place in such contexts reflects the way in which social cultural perspectives, ideas, and methods are integrated into the design of the mini-culture and activities studied. Nonetheless, it seems equally obvious that the ways in which particular processes of learning and teaching take their shape from broader cultural artifacts and social interactions are powerful confirmations of the relations between culture, social interactions, intersubjectivity, participation, and appropriation assumed in social cultural theory in general.

An example of more conventional classroom-based research on processes of teaching and learning that is conducted from a social, cultural perspective is Keith Barton's (1996, 1997, 2001) research that compares how children in different national contexts (Northern Ireland and the United States) make use of specific cultural tools when engaging in activities related to history. Barton's theoretical framework is neo-Vygotskian, drawing in particular on the work of James Wertsch (1998). He assumes that particular social cultural artifacts provide both affordances and constraints on the historical thinking of learners, and sets out to investigate this possibility in the context of primary and secondary classrooms in Northern Ireland (2001) and the United States (1996, 1997). Barton's research focuses on the ways in which particular narrative representations of history constitute cultural tools. If the same aspects of narrative were to feature equally prominently in both national locations, such features would be interpreted as general characteristics of historical thinking rather than culturally situated artifacts.

The specific focus of Barton's research concerned students' expectations of how and why life has changed over time. The research methods employed included both open-ended, semistructured interviews with students and extensive classroom observations. In addition, information collected in history-related contexts such as museums, historical parks, secondary school and university courses, and discussions with museum curators, history teachers, professors, and resource specialists provided a broader historical and social cultural context for interpreting findings.

Barton's interpretations of his findings point to several pedagogically relevant differences in the nature and manner of social cultural artifacts and students' historical thinking across the national contexts he examined. The American children employed historical narratives that featured national progress grounded in individual achievement. Despite frequently noted misunderstandings and faulty recollection, such narratives helped students to experience a sense of common identity. At the same time, they foster little in the way of appreciation for the influence of societal institutions on individual actions, and fail to acquaint students with diversity in the experiences of individuals and groups as a consequence of particular historical events and broader historical, cultural practices. On the other hand, the students in Northern Ireland were much less likely to view individuals' actions as triggers for historical change, or to regard change as equivalent to progress. In addition, a more diverse range of narrative interpretations tended to be entertained by these students. However, a casualty of this more diversified pattern of narrative thinking was the absence of a sense of shared identity.

From these and other findings and interpretations, Barton (1996, 1997, 2001) concludes that any cultural tool inevitably provides both affordances and constraints, and he suggests that this realization warrants a pedagogical strategy of encouraging student participation in multiple frameworks for understanding history that include both narrative and non-narrative tools. Of course, the nature of historical contexts and narratives, especially considered in the institutional contexts of schooling, mean that any such transformations will not be easy to achieve. Nonetheless, Barton's work illustrates several important features of a social cultural approach to educational inquiry. One aspect of the work that deserves particular attention is his refusal to embrace a strong form of social, cultural determinism. Social cultural contexts, practices, and artifacts exert affordances and constraints on collective and individual action, but stop well short of full mechanistic determination. Individual experience can differ significantly within particular historical, social, and cultural contexts, and neither societies nor cultures are monolithic.

The Aims of Education: Educating Persons

In many contemporary societies, it is through children's and adolescents' participation in formal education that human communities hope to foster forms of personhood consistent with active, full participation in social and cultural activities that advance, reproduce, and transform cultural traditions. Social cultural perspectives on human progress understand such processes of reproduction and transformation as radically contingent, in the sense that they inevitably play out in historical and developmental trajectories that are necessarily uncertain and unpredictable. We humans are literally "in our own hands," collectively and individually. There is nothing beyond our worldly activity, which interfaces our biophysically evolved bodies and brains and historically evolved cultures, that might guarantee our progressive evolution in moral, political, or psychological terms. We are members of communities of practice within our historical, sociocultural niches, and our participatory activities in these communities and niches shape both them and us. What we know and who we are both are radically contingent consequences of our worldly involvement. In such circumstances, the goals and aims of formal education are to contribute to the formation of persons capable of working collectively to achieve humanly constructed "goods."

Theory. Depending on what particular cultural traditions are at play and what social interactions are possible, such "goods" may take a wide variety of forms. However, in contemporary pluralistic, liberal and social democracies, they typically are understood as secured by rights such as equal opportunity and freedom from discrimination and oppression. Such rights are understood as conditions that enhance the possibility of broad "goods" such as individual and collective flourishing, within a polity that refuses to endorse one way to live above all others. In such a polity, a high value is placed on conversational virtues (and the conditions that foster them) as means for constantly working through differences and seeming impasses. Of paramount importance in such societies is equality of educational opportunity, and an education that aims at full sociocultural participation through the appropriation of cultural capability and conversational virtues.

The kind of education sought in most pluralistic democracies is an education of persons who can function within a wide variety of social cultural practices and traditions. These are social agents who understand their own status as persons and responsibilities as citizens, and who display conversational virtues that permit genuine engagements with others (cf. Schutz, 2000). Requisite conversational virtues typically include such things as civility, recognition of equality of others, perseverance in understanding, and openness to possibilities in others' views and positions. Importantly, such virtues and the rights and goods they support all can be seen to require an understanding of one's own personhood and its sociocultural sources, and a recognition of the personhood of others (Martin et al., 2003). With a sense of our historical, sociocultural constitution, we may be more likely to engage openly and seriously with others with different conceptions and practices of personhood.

Genuine dialogical exchange of, and reflection on, different perspectives requires a critical penetration of one's own sociocultural background at the same time that it requires an openness to possibilities contained in the backgrounds and understandings of others. Such an appreciation simultaneously provides reason to value the commitments and concerns that define one's way of life, while also understanding that such commitments and concerns, as important as they are, are not necessarily shared by others with different backgrounds and circumstances. In pluralistic social contexts, the conversational virtues and understanding of personhood associated with a social cultural perspective on persons, together with a conception of possible progress through genuine sociocultural participation and engagement with others, are precisely the conditions required for communal life. Such conditions increase the likelihood of sustained attempts to understand and cooperate with others who also may be striving to uncover better and more equitable possibilities for living together across different social and cultural backgrounds and ways of life. When stated in this way, it is clear that the critical, postmodern conception of education as the empowerment of persons aims not only at the removal of oppressive and discriminatory barriers to full social participation. It also aims at a positive social agency intended to advance the prospects of a vibrant, life-enhancing process of ongoing social transformation and greater freedom for all (Schutz, 2000).

However, it also is important not to assume too much similarity and broad consent to the foregoing portrait of educational goals and dialogical processes within liberal, democratic societies. Such societies are far from homogenous, and there exist wide differences in the organization of schooling as well as in learners' preparation for classroom participation. Many of these differences may be grounded in divergent sociocultural, economic, and political circumstances, differences that have great impact on opportunities for participation in social institutions such as schools. Such differences are of central interest to many social cultural scholars and researchers in educational psychology. In fact, many social cultural theorists and researchers would undoubtedly find some of the views expressed in the immediately preceding paragraphs to unduly infringe on the legitimate rights of local communities to determine educational aims through a process of more situated consideration, debate, and involvement—a process that should not be "short-circuited" by the adoption of perhaps overly general principles, whatever the underlying intentions of those advancing them.

Examples of Research. Packer (2000) provides an excellent example of social cultural inquiry into how schools are affected by economic and political contexts, and how schools develop people and transform the "cultures" of their internal and external communities. Packer presents a critical, narrative interpretation of how the Willow Run Community Schools in Michigan were affected by and responsive to powerful economic (the closing of the local General Motors plant) and political (new federal and state legislation mandating marketplace educational reforms—e.g., the Michigan Educational Assessment Program) occurrences. Chronicling events in the Willow Run Community Schools from 1994 to 1999, Packer examines the varied ways in which political and economic agendas of accountability and production interacted with social, relational, and cultural processes of teaching and learning.

Packer's (2000) narrative is built around his personal interpretations, detailed recordings of conversations with those involved in and affected by focal events and processes taking place in the Willow Run Schools, and his historical and theoretical analyses of school reform practices and their consequences. Through all of this, the reader is placed in close proximity to the intended and unintended ways in which accountability and assessment initiatives in education positively and negatively affect teaching, learning, school and community morale, and the motivations and interests of students, teachers, and others. Of particular interest is how school administrators and teachers at Willow Run struggled to cope with the demands of high-stakes assessments and other systemic initiatives. Their efforts to comply with state and federal mandates came at considerable cost to their typical functioning with each other and their students. Ironically, erosion of optimal modes of pedagogical functioning and relating with learners was a direct and indirect consequence of the desire of federal and state politicians and leaders outside of the school system to promote a more effective and equitable educational system. In this context, the inevitable clash between marketplace, system efficiency and more relational forms of pedagogical caring and interpersonal effectiveness looms large.

More specifically, the ways in which assessment instruments were scored and "cutoffs" established highlighted differences between students and schools. By simplistically attributing such differences to school effectiveness independent of other social and economic factors, and differentially rewarding schools and school systems on the basis of such attributions, the entire process of accountability and assessment actually seemed to further the very inequities it was intended to eradicate. Equally significant, schools as interdependent communities of care and concern for developing persons were gradually transformed into places of competitive placement and individual (versus shared) accountability. All learners now were sorted into categories of "proficient" or "not proficient" on a single overriding metric that was designed so that 50 percent of students would fall into each category. And, in further consequence, all teachers were viewed as "effective" or "not effective." Attention and concern for diversity in learners and their capabilities were understandably eroded under such conditions.

Packer's (2000) broader sociocultural interpretation of this effort to impose a single solution on every school, given that over 60 percent of student achievement typically can be attributed to non-school factors, is that "Neither systemic reform nor marketplace reform has an adequate grasp of the character of teaching and learning; neither reform effort has a satisfactory or articulated conception of the psychology of students and teachers or the sociology of school life" (p. 274). More cynically, Packer suspects that the importation to schools of marketplace practices of efficiency and accountability actually serves to shift the educational aim of producing vital persons as effective, fully participating citizens, with an actual educational process that promotes compliant, docile workers and consumers. Although Packer's judgment certainly seems harsh, it arises out his attempt to articulate how a legitimate culture of education may be inadequately served by a broader culture of individualistic consumption and corporate profit. This is a common theme of much critical, social cultural scholarship in education and educational psychology, much of which reflects a neo-Foucauldian concern with how psychology as a scholarly discipline and profession actually has promoted conceptions of personhood that are overly individualistic, internal, and removed from necessary social cultural, constitutive contexts.

My own (Martin, 2004) critical examination of conceptions of the self in educational psychology suggests just how inadequate the conceptions of personhood that animate much traditional psychological research and practice may be for communal, social cultural undertakings such as education. Under most forms of government, education has an explicit societal mandate to produce particular kinds of persons—as productive, contributing citizens capable of living lives of significance to others and for themselves. Psychology has no such official mandate, and its disciplinary "turf" typically is defined in much more individualistic terms. From a conceptual analysis of uses of the term "self" in educational psychology, I conclude that two senses of the term predominate the subdiscipline, one scientific and one humanistic. Despite the seeming surface dissimilarity of these conceptions, I argue that both are manifestations of the same underlying conception of the self as a unique center of experiencing and knowing that lies at the deep interior of each individual human being. This is a Cartesian self isolated from its surrounds, even as it is influenced by them. As an inner bastion of individual experience and existence, it surveys the exterior landscape for signs of personal affirmation and possibilities for expression on the one hand, and for strategic action on the other. Its most vital resources are available within its detached internality, and it acts as a final arbiter of the actions it promotes. Both academic tasks and social experience can be controlled by this masterful self's attention to its own basic organismic tendencies and potentials on the one hand, and to its metacognitive, strategic ruminations on the other. This is a self that already knows its business, one that requires only a facilitative grooming to become more fully socialized and intellectually engaged.

Although acknowledging that all educational psychologists do not stand united behind the foregoing conception of the self, I (Martin, 2004) express concern about the educational implications of such a self. I believe that the predominance of this conception in the works and practices of many educational psychologists contributes significantly to an overly extreme focus on individual happiness and achievement in North American schools. Moreover, this emphasis continues despite more recent widespread recognition of the shortcomings of psychological individualism with respect to the forging of communities of care, committed to the welfare of others (e.g., Noddings, 1992). I further suggest that this conception of selfhood also supports a host of psychoeducational interventions that are narrowly focused on individual self-interest and amenable to a marketplace mentality eager to package such products for profit. My conclusion is that much contemporary work in educational psychology reflects questionable assumptions concerning persons, knowledge, and progress that should be replaced by more socially and culturally grounded assumptions that emphasize collective activity, social contribution, and care for others.

A major line of critical, postmodern scholarship in education relates directly to concerns such as those voiced by Packer (2000) and Martin (2004), but attempts to locate resources in poststructuralist and critical scholarship for educating students as both persons and agents in ways that recognize adequately important social, cultural, and historical constraints and affordances, including relations of power that frequently contribute to inequality and injustice. Schutz (2000) provides a critical interpretation of the works of Spivak (1993), Giroux (1992), Lather (1991), Popkewitz (1997, 1998), Lave and Wenger (1991), MacIntyre (1984), Butler (1993), Rorty (1989), Noddings (1992), Greene (1988), Arendt (1958), Laclau (1996), Mouffe (1993), and several others, with a view to informing efforts to "teach freedom" in a postmodern age. Schutz maintains that perceptions of postmodern scholarship as eroding any rational basis from which it is possible to talk about actors (including students and teachers) as agents who can be held responsible for their actions go too far. In particular, they fail to recognize the ways in which postmodern theorists "strive to explore carefully the myriad tensions invariably involved in politics and pedagogy" (p. 215), and pay insufficient attention to the egalitarian commitments readily apparent in their various projects. Schutz concludes that although we cannot escape the tensions of empowerment and oppression (of possibilities and limitations) that attend all human activities, including teaching, we must persevere in the face of such inevitable tensions to maintain democracy as best we can "without any clear 'banisters' . . . to hold onto" (p. 245). Critical, postmodern scholarship in education and educational psychology asks us to examine the values, assumptions, and practices that constitute our pedagogical pursuits, especially in consideration of their social, cultural, and historical sources and ongoing consequences. However, such critical scrutiny should not be disconnected from an understanding of education as a promoter of persons, knowledge, and progress, even if there are no foundations, certainties, or consensual warrants to anchor education in a postmodern world.

CRITICAL CONSIDERATIONS AND CONCLUSIONS

Social cultural perspectives in educational psychology have developed alternative conceptions of learners, teaching and learning processes, and educational goals. These alternatives all resist Enlightenment and Modern conceptions of persons as prior to and detached from their sociocultural engagement with others, knowledge as founded with certainty in ahistorical and universal methods and warrants, and progress as an inevitable accompaniment to increments in human knowledge. For social cultural theorists and researchers, it is social and cultural artifacts, practices, and interactions that make persons, knowledge, and progress possible. It is the ever-changing historical, sociocultural landscape that constrains and limits what we are, what we know, and what we might become. As an influential set of human practices devoted to the transmission, reproduction, and transformation of social and cultural practices, education is an obvious site for social cultural inquiry and experimentation. It is on this basis that social culturalists advance their various proposals for changing assumptions, methods, and inquiry practices in educational psychology.

Social cultural perspectives in educational psychology do *not* understand historical, cultural, contextual, and interpersonal practices of schooling and teaching as factors that affect the cognitive and motivational strategies of learners and the instructional goals and methods of teachers. To social culturalists, these practices actually constitute both education and participants in it. Learners and teachers, like all persons, are sociocultural entities formed through their active participation in relevant historically emergent, sociocultural traditions and practices. The knowledge they attain through their participation with others in relevant sociocultural practices both inside and outside of school also is a constantly evolving product of these same practices. As a consequence, any discernable progress in knowledge and its applications with respect to human collective and individual benefit is radically contingent and inherently unpredictable, given that cultures and societies are constantly changing in exceedingly complex ways that cannot be predicted with anything like certainty.

Under such conditions, the work of educational psychologists must be reinterpreted. An applied psychology of education informed by knowledge of natural, ahistorical, and cross-cultural essentials of human development must give way to an historically and culturally sensitive examination of the in situ emergence of socially spawned activities that constitute personhood (including selfhood, identity, and moral and rational agency), knowledge practices, and warrants for improvement and progress. The guiding image of the educational psychologist must transmogrify from physicist of the mind to cultural anthropologist working with persons within local knowledge practices, perhaps combined with a bit or a lot (depending on the social cultural perspectives concerned) of social, political, and educational reformer.

Not surprisingly, most criticisms of social cultural perspectives in psychology and educational psychology are concerned that such contrasts may be too starkly drawn (e.g., Cobb & Yackel, 1996; Martin & Sugarman, 1999; von Glasersfeld, 1990). After all, persons require bodies and brains that both mature and are highly interactive with processes of sociogenesis (cf. Edelman, 1987). Knowledge is not just evolved and enshrined within the relevant social practices of scholarly, professional, and broader communities, but also in more individual processes of knowing (e.g., Archer, 2000; Smith, 1995). And

progress, although imperfectly predictable and uncertain, nonetheless displays widely accepted validation across most contemporary cultures, especially in certain areas of applied biophysical science such as programs of vaccination and power generation. It is, of course, true that persons are much more than their biophysical bodies alone, that knowledge requires social practices of validation, and that what constitutes progress catches up divergent sociocultural perspectives and valuations. But, surely it would be too strong a social culturalism that would equate persons, knowledge, and progress entirely with their undoubted sociocultural constituents. For this would amount to a kind of sociocultural reductionism that would too drastically reduce and identify the psychological agent, knowing, and progress to nothing more than sociocultural practices.

Fortunately, charges of overly strong social cultural reductionism, although perhaps applicable to some forms of postmodern social constructionism in psychology (e.g., Gergen, 1994), are not warranted by a careful consideration of the work of most social culturalists in educational psychology (cf. Packer & Goicoechea, 1996). There is a difference between regarding agents, knowledge, and progress as emergently constituted through human activity within sociocultural practices, and identifying them with social cultural practices per se. Constitution is a relation that stops well short of identity. Mountains are constituted by their various rock formations, but Mt. Everest remains Mt. Everest after a rock slide, just as the Congress of the United States remains the Congress following changes of membership and party affiliation. Learners and processes of teaching and learning are not schools or educational practices, although they are constituted within such institutions and practices. As Bandura (2001) is fond of remarking, persons are both products and producers of their societies and cultures.

Turning briefly to possible implications for the conduct of educational research that flow from the discussion of social cultural perspectives in this chapter, three suggestions seem immediately obvious. The first concerns the necessity of broadening the scope of educational research well beyond classroom walls. Not only does such an extension apply to the school as an institution (e.g., Olson, 2003) and to its surrounding community, but it also might encompass more historically established cultural practices and traditions that inform contemporary, local practices (as many hermeneuts and critical theorists encourage). Another obvious implication concerns the desire of many social cultural researchers to work closely with local communities and schools in considering and understanding problems and difficult issues as these are understood by diverse groups within those locales. Such involvement moves the researcher away from the status of an educational expert, who already has possible solutions in mind, to one participant among many, albeit with a particular interest in recording and interpreting processes of engagement and decision making that typify the particular interactions and undertakings under consideration. Finally, a major challenge for social, cultural researchers in education and educational psychology is to devise new ways of recognizing, interpreting, and understanding the "cognitive" content of social interactions and practices. This is a challenge at both theoretical and empirical levels of inquiry. For example, previously noted disagreements among social cultural researchers concerning processes of internalization and appropriation are in large part a result of failing to develop more precise and effective language and methods for describing the specific ways in which participants in social cultural practices "take up" the perspectives, strategies, and conventional means that are available to them through their activity within such practices (see Olson, 1998, 2001).

Education, given its joint commitments to sociocultural reproduction and transformation and to individual development and fulfillment, is an excellent arena for scholarly theorizing and research that focuses on mutually constitutive relations and emergent processes that best describe and explain persons, knowledge, and progress in social cultural context. Ultimately, educators and educational psychologists are concerned with the understanding and furthering of many of the most significant cultural practices through which we attempt to know ourselves and others, and in consequence to become more fully human and humane. Of course, to talk in this way is partially to endorse a Western conception of inclusive liberal education, as critical theorists such as Popkewitz (1991) are quick to point out. True enough, but this chapter and book also have their particular historical, sociocultural context, and it is a good bet that such rhetoric, although it could have been otherwise and may give way to other conceptions in the future, still captures what most educational psychologists understand to be the activity in which they are participants.

References

Adorno, T. W. (1983). *Against epistemology*. Cambridge, MA: MIT Press.

Apple, M. (1990). *Ideology and curriculum* (2nd ed). New York: Routledge.

Archer, M. (2000). *Being human: The problem of agency*. Cambridge, England: Cambridge University Press.

Arendt, H. (1958). *The human condition*. Chicago: The University of Chicago Press.

Bandura, A. (2001). Social-cognitive theory: An agentic perspective. *Annual Review of Psychology, 52*, 1–26.

Barton, K. C. (1996). Narrative simplifications in elementary children's historical understanding. In J. Brophy (Ed.), *Advances in research on teaching*, Vol. 6, pp. 51–83). Greenwich, CT: JAI.

Barton, K. C. (1997). "Bossed around by the Queen": Elementary students' understanding of individuals and institutions in history. *Journal of Curriculum and Supervision, 12*, 290–314.

Barton, K. C. (2001). A sociocultural perspective on children's understanding of historical change: Comparative findings from Northern Ireland and the United States. *American Educational Research Journal, 38*, 881–913.

Bauersfeld, H. (1988). Interaction, construction, and knowledge: Alternative perspectives for mathematics education. In D. A. Grouws, T. J. Cooney, & D. Jones (Eds.), *Perspectives on research on mathematics teaching* (Vol. 1, pp. 27–46). Hillsdale, NJ: Lawrence Erlbaum Associates.

Blumer, H. (1969). *Symbolic interactionism: Perspective and method*. Englewood Cliffs, NJ: Prentice-Hall.

Bronfenbrenner, U. (1979). *The ecology of human development*. Cambridge, MA: Harvard University Press.

Bruner, J. (1990). *Acts of meaning*. Cambridge, MA: Harvard University Press.

Bruner, J. (1996). *The culture of education*. Cambridge, MA: Harvard University Press.

Butler, J. (1993). *Bodies that matter: On the discursive limits of "sex."* New York: Routledge.

Butler, J. (1997). *The psychic life of power*. Stanford, CA: Stanford University Press.

Chisholm, R. M. (1982). Human freedom and the self. In G. Watson (Ed.), *Free will* (pp. 24–35). Oxford, England: Oxford University Press.

Cobb, P. & Yackel, E. (1996). Constructivist, emergent, and sociocultural perspectives in the context of developmental research. *Educational Psychologist, 31*, 175–190.

Cole, M. (1996). *Cultural psychology: a once and future discipline*. Cambridge, MA: Harvard University Press.

D'Andrade, R. (1990). Some propositions about the relations between culture and human cognition. In J. W. Stigler, R.A. Shweder, & G. Herdt (Eds.), *Cultural psychology* (pp. 65–129). New York: Cambridge University Press.

Dasen, P. R. (Ed.). (1977). *Piagetian psychology: Cross-cultural contributions*. New York: Gardner Press.

Deleuze, G. & Guattari, F. (1987). *A thousand plateaus*. Minneapolis: University of Minnesota Press.

Derrida. J. (1978). *Writing and difference* (A. Bass, trans.). Chicago: University of Chicago Press.

Dewey, J. (1916). *Democracy and education*. New York: Macmillan.

Dewey, J. (1938). *Experience and education*. New York: Macmillan.

Edelman, G. M. (1987). *Neural Darwinism*. New York: Basic Books.

Engeström, Y. (1990). *Learning, working and imagining: Twelve studies in activity theory*. Helsinki, Finland: Orienta-Konsultit.

Foley, M., & Ratner, H. (1997). Children's recoding in memory for collaboration: A way of learning from others. *Cognitive Development, 13*, 91–108.

Foucault, M. (1980). *Power/knowledge: Selected interviews and other writings* (C. Gordon, Trans.). New York: Pantheon.

Freire, P. (1972). *Pedagogy of the oppressed*. New York: Harper Collins.

Gadamer, H.-G. (1995). *Truth and method* (J. Weinsheimer & D. G. Marshall, Trans.) (2nd rev. ed.). New York: Continuum. (Original work published 1960.)

Gergen, K. (1994). *Realities and relationships*. Cambridge, MA: Harvard University Press.

Giroux, H. (1992). *Border crossings: Cultural workers and the politics of education*. New York: Routledge.

Goodman, S. (1984). The integration of verbal and motor behavior in preschool children. *Child Development, 52*, 280–289.

Goodnow, J. J., Miller, P., & Kessel, F. (Eds.). (1995). *Cultural practices as contexts for development*. San Francisco: Jossey-Bass.

Greene, M. (1988). *The dialectic of freedom*. New York: Teachers College Press.

Greenfield, P. M. (1984). *Mind and media: The effects of television, video games, and computers*. Cambridge, MA: Harvard University Press.

Goudena, P. P. (1987). The social nature of private speech of preschoolers during problem solving. *International Journal of Behavioral Development, 10*, 187–206.

Harkness, S., & Super, C. M. (1992). Parental ethnotheories in action. In I. E. Sigel, A. V. McGillicuddy-Delisi, & J. J. Goodnow (Eds.), *Parental belief systems* (2nd ed., pp. 373–391). Hillsdale, NJ: Lawrence Erlbaum. Associates.

Harré, R. (1984). *Personal being: A theory for individual psychology*. Cambridge, MA: Harvard University Press.

Horkheimer, M. (1974). *Eclipse of reason*. New York: Continuum.

Hutchins, E. (1991). The social organization of distributed cognition. In L. B. Resnick, J. M. Levine, & S. D. Teasley (Eds.), *Perspectives on socially shared cognition* (pp. 282–307). Washington, DC: American Psychological Association.

Ilyenkov, E. V. (1977). *Dialectical logic: Essays on its history and theory* (H. C. Creighton, Trans.). Moscow: Progress.

Jameson, F. (1971). *Marxism and form*. Princeton, NJ: Princeton University Press.

John-Steiner, V. (1985). *Notebooks of the mind: Explorations of thinking*. Albuquerque: University of New Mexico Press.

John-Steiner, V. & Mahn, H. (1996). Sociocultural approaches to learning and development: a Vygotskian framework. *Educational Psychologist, 31*, 191–206.

Laclau, E. (1996). *Emancipation(s)*. New York: Verson.

Lather, P. (1991). *Getting smart: Feminist research and pedagogy with/in the postmodern*. New York: Routledge.

Lave, J. (1988). *Cognition in practice: Mind, mathematics and culture in everyday life*. Cambridge, England: Cambridge University Press.

Lave, J., & Wenger, E. (1991). *Situated learning: Legitimate peripheral participation*. New York: Cambridge University Press.

Leontiev, A. N. (1981). *Problems of the development of mind* (M. Koplova, Trans.). Moscow: Progress.

Lyotard, J-F. (1984). *The postmodern condition*. Minneapolis: University of Minnesota Press.

Luria, A. R. (1979). *The making of mind*. Cambridge, MA: Harvard University Press.

MacIntyre, A. (1984). *After virtue: A study in moral theory*. Notre Dame, IN: University of Notre Dame Press.

McLaren, P. (1998). *Life in schools: An introduction to critical pedagogy in the foundations of education*. New York: Longman.

Martin, J. (2004). The educational inadequacy of conceptions of self in educational psychology. *Interchange: A Quarterly Review of Education, 35*, 185–208.

Martin, J., & Sugarman, J. (1999). *The psychology of human possibility and constraint*. Albany, NY: SUNY Press.

Martin, J., Sugarman, J., & Hickinbottom, S. (2003). The education of persons in multicultural Canada. In F. Pajares & T. Urdan (Eds.), *International perspectives on adolescence* (pp. 1–24). Greenwich, CT: Information Age.

Mead, G. H. (1934). *Mind, self and society from the standpoint of a social behaviorist*. Chicago: University of Chicago Press.

Mead, G. H. (1977). *George Herbert Mead on social psychology* (A. Strauss, ed.). Chicago: The University of Chicago Press.

Mouffe, C. (1993). *The return of the political*. New York: Verso.

Newman, F., & Holzman, L. (1993). *Lev Vygotsky: Revolutionary scientist*. New York: Routledge.

Noddings, N. (1992). *The challenge to care in schools: An alternative approach to education*. New York: Teachers College Press.

Olson, D. R. (1998). Institutions are real but internalization is not. *Human Development, 41*, 236–238.

Olson, D. R. (2001). Education: The bridge from culture to mind. In D. Bakhurst & S. Shanker (Eds.), *Jerome Bruner: Language, culture, self* (pp. 104–115). London: Sage.

Olson, D. R. (2003). *Psychological theory and educational reform: How school remakes mind and society*. Cambridge, England: Cambridge University Press.

Packer, M. (2000). *Changing classes: School reform and the new economy*. New York: Cambridge University Press.

Packer, M. J., & Goicoechea, J. (2000). Sociocultural and constructivist theories of learning: Ontology, not just epistemology. *Educational Psychologist, 35*, 227–241.

Pajares, F. (2003). William James: Our father who begat us. In B. J. Zimmerman & D. H. Schunk (Eds.), *Educational psychology: A century of contributions* (pp. 41–64). Mahwah, NJ: Lawrence Erlbaum Associates.

Piaget, J. (1988). *Structuralism* (C. Maschler, Trans.). New York: Harper & Row. (Original work published 1970.)

Popkewitz, T. S. (1991). *A political sociology of educational reform: Power/knowledge in teaching, teacher education, and research*. New York: Teachers College Press.

Popkewitz, T. S. (1997). A changing terrain of knowledge and power: A social epistemology of educational research. *Educational Researcher, 26*(9), 18–29.

Popkewitz, T. S. (1998). *Struggling for the soul: The politics of schooling and the construction of the teacher*. New York: Teachers college Press.

Prawat, R. S. (1995). Misreading Dewey: Reform, projects, and the language game. *Educational Researcher, 24*(7), 13–22.

Ratner, H., & Hill, L. (1991). *Regulation and representation in the development of children's memory*. Paper presented at the meeting of the Society for Research in Child Development, Seattle, WA.

Rogoff, B. (2003). *The cultural nature of human development*. Oxford, England: Oxford University Press.

Rogoff, B., & Chavajay, P. (1995). What's become of research on the cultural basis of cognitive development? *American Psychologist, 50*, 859–877.

Rorty, R. (1989). *Contingency, irony, and solicarity*. Cambridge, England: Cambridge University Press.

Rose, N. (1996). *Inventing ourselves: Psychology, power, and personhood*. Cambridge, England: Cambridge University Press.

Saxe, G. B. (1982). Developing forms of arithmetic operations among the Oksapmin of Papua New Guinea. *Developmental Psychology, 18*, 583–594.

Saxe, G. B. (1985). The effects of schooling on arithmetical understandings: Studies with Oksapmin children in Papua New Guinea. *Journal of Educational Psychology, 77*, 503–513.

Saxe, G. B. (1991). *Culture and cognitive development: Studies in mathematical understanding*. Hillsdale, NJ: Lawrence Erlbaum Associates.

Saxe, G. B. (1994). Studying cognitive development in sociocultural contexts: The development of practice-based approaches. *Mind, Culture, and Activity, 1*, 135–157.

Schutz, A. (2000). Teaching freedom? Postmodern perspectives. *Review of Educational Research, 70*, 215–251.

Scribner, S., & Cole, M. (1981). *The psychology of literacy*. Cambridge, MA: Harvard University Press.

Serpell, R. (1976). *Culture's influence on behaviour*. London: Methuen.

Shweder, R. (1991). *Thinking through cultures: Expeditions in cultural psychology*. Cambridge, MA: Harvard University Press.

Smith, E. (1995). Where is the mind? Knowing and knowledge in Cobb's constructivist and sociocultural perspectives. *Educational Researcher, 24*(6), 23–24.

Spivak, G. C. (1993). *Outside in the teaching machine*. New York: Routledge.

Spivak, G. C. (1996). *The Spivak reader: Selected works of Gayatri Chakravorty Spivak*. New York: Routledge.

Stigler, J., Lee, S., & Stevenson, H. W. (1990). *Mathematical knowledge of Japanese, Chinese, and American elementary-school children*. Reston, VA: National Council of Teachers of Mathematics.

Super, C. M. (1981). Behavioral development in infancy. In R. H. Munroe, R. L. Munroe, & B. B. Whiting (Eds.), *Handbook of cross-cultural human development* (pp. 181–270). New York: Garland.

Taylor, C. (1995). *Philosophical arguments*. Cambridge, MA: Harvard University Press.

Tomasello, M. (1999). *The cultural origins of human cognition*. Cambridge, MA: Harvard University Press.

Tomasello, M., & Akhtar, N. (1995). Two-year-olds use pragmatic cues to differentiate reference to objects and actions. *Cognitive Development, 10*, 201–224.

Trevarthan, C. (1993). The self born in intersubjectivity: The psychology of an infant communicating. In U. Neisser (Ed.), *The perceived self: Ecological and interpersonal sources of self-knowledge* (pp. 121–173). New York: Cambridge University Press.

von Glasersfeld, E. (1987). *The construction of knowledge: Contributions to conceptual semantics*. Seaside, CA: Intersystems Publications.

von Glasersfeld, E. (1990). An exposition of constructivism: Why some like it radical. *Journal for Research in Mathematics Education, 4*, 19–31.

Vygotsky, L. S. (1978). *Mind in society: The development of higher psychological processes* (M. Cole, V. John-Steiner, S. Scribner, & E. Souberman, Eds.). Cambridge, MA: Harvard University Press.

Vygotsky, L. S. (1986). *Thought and language* (A. Kozulin, Trans.). Cambridge, MA: The MIT Press. (Original work published 1934.)

Wagner, D. A. (1993). *Literacy, culture and development: Becoming literate in Morocco*. New York: Cambridge University Press.

Wertsch, J. V. (1998). *Mind in action*. New York: Oxford University Press.

Yang, M. T-L., & Cobb, P. (1995). A cross-cultural investigation into the development of place value concepts in Taiwan and the United States. *Educational Studies in Mathematics, 28*, 1–33.

· 26 ·

ETHNICITY AND LEARNING

Lynn Okagaki
Purdue University

In 2001, there were approximately 48 million students in public elementary and secondary schools in the United States, and nearly 40 percent of these students were children and adolescents of color—students whose families have lived in the United States for generations and students whose families just immigrated; students in homes where only English is spoken and students in homes where only Spanish, Vietnamese or another language other than English is spoken (U.S. Department of Education, 2004). For this chapter, I have been asked to address the roles of ethnic identification and ethnic differences in learning. I begin with four limitations to the scope of this chapter. First, although authors have defined ethnicity somewhat differently (e.g., Harwood, Handwerker, Schoelmerich, & Leyendecker, 2001; Phinney, 1996), I focus on two dimensions that are common to most discussions of ethnicity—ethnic identification and culture. Second, although ethnic group variation is associated with differential learning outcomes in many countries, the discussion in this chapter is limited to ethnicity and education in the United States. Elsewhere in this volume, Greenfield (Chapter 29) reviews research on conceptions of learning and development in other cultures and discusses non-Western cultural models of cognition, motivation, and social development. Third, I use the term *ethnic group* to refer to racial and ethnic minority groups in the United States and limit the chapter to ethnic groups of color—Black, Asian and Pacific Islander Americans, Hispanic, and American Indians.[1] I acknowledge that using the term "ethnic group" in this way is not without its prob-

lems (e.g., (Gutiérrez & Rogoff, 2003; Helms & Talleyrand, 1997). I also recognize that there is great variation and richness in the ethnic backgrounds of White Americans. Research on ethnicity and learning in the United States, however, has grown out of recognition of the differential achievement across ethnic groups and concern for the underachievement of many ethnic groups of color. Moreover, the majority of research conducted by educational psychologists in the United States has focused on White American students and is covered in other chapters in this handbook. Fourth, a comprehensive review of the research on ethnicity and learning was beyond the scope of this chapter. I have attempted to include examples of research on different ethnic groups to illustrate points.

This chapter is organized into three major sections. The first section is focused on two questions: Who are the students of color in U.S. schools, and how well are we educating them? In the second section, research on ethnic identification and education is discussed. The third section is an examination of cultural differences as they are related to learning and educational achievement. Finally, I conclude with a discussion of the relevance of research on the education of ethnic minority students to educational psychology in general.

Ethnicity and Educational Achievement

Describing the cultural diversity among U.S. students is not a simple task. Multiple factors, such as racial and

---

[1] Throughout this chapter I have adopted the racial and ethnic group terms used by the U.S. Department of Education: American Indian/Alaska Native, Asian American and Asian American/Pacific Islander, Black, Hispanic, and White. Black and White groups exclude those of Hispanic backgrounds. Where researchers have identified subgroups (e.g., Hispanic immigrants of Mexican descent, Vietnamese Americans), those subgroups are noted.

ethnic background, ancestry, immigrant or generational status, socioeconomic status, and home language, contribute to the cultural diversity of the current U.S. student population. To complicate matters, information about race, ethnicity, ancestry, and other cultural variables is not captured in a standardized format across studies. For example, the U.S. Department of Education generally reports on outcomes for non-Hispanic White, non-Hispanic Black, and Hispanic students, with some reports including data for Asian/Pacific Islander and American Indian/Native Alaskan students. These broad categories mask the variation in cultural heritage within groups. For example, in the 2000 census, 35.3 million Americans self-identified as being Hispanic (U.S. Census Bureau, 2001b). Within this broad group are those who identify as being Mexican (58.5 percent), Puerto Rican (9.6 percent), Cuban (3.5 percent), Dominican (2.2 percent), Central American (4.8 percent with the largest subgroups being Salvadorans, Guatemalans, and Hondurans); South American (3.8 percent with the largest subgroups being Colombians, Ecuadorians, and Peruvians); Spaniard (0.3 percent), and other Hispanics (17.3 percent, including those who only identified as Hispanic, Latino, or Spanish without indicating specific ancestry or nationality) (U.S. Census Bureau, 2001b). The histories, customs, economies, and political contexts of each of the countries of origin contribute to the heterogeneity of the Hispanic population (e.g., Carrasquillo, 1991; Torres, 2004). The subgroups differ on basic demographic characteristics. For instance, in 2000 the median age of Hispanics of Mexican descent was about 24 years; in contrast, the median age of Hispanics of other groups ranged from the late 20s (Puerto Ricans, Central American, Dominicans) to the 40s (Cubans) (U.S. Census Bureau, 2001a). Data from the 1990 census indicated that Hispanic groups differed in terms of nativity. Whereas two-thirds of those of Mexican descent had been born in the United States, fewer than 30 percent of the Cuban, Dominican, Central American, and South American subgroups were native born (U.S. Census Bureau, 1993a). Data from the 1992 National Adult Literacy Survey (U.S. Department of Education, 2001a) indicate that self-reported literacy varies greatly by subgroup. Among Hispanic adults of Mexican descent, 34 percent were monoliterate in English, 30 percent reported being biliterate in English and Spanish, and 29 percent were monoliterate in Spanish. Adults of Cuban and Central or South American descent were less likely to be monoliterate in English (9 percent and 14 percent, respectively) and more likely to be either biliterate (45 percent Cuban; 42 percent Central or South American) or monoliterate in Spanish (42 percent Cuban; 38 percent Central or South American).

Given the great diversity within ethnic groups, there are obvious limitations to data that are based on broadly defined racial and ethnic group classification. When available, the data reported in this chapter will include subgroups within ethnic groups. Most studies comparing student outcomes, however, are limited to data based on broad racial and ethnic categories.

School Enrollment. According to the 2000 census, the student population in the U.S. comprised 76.6 million students from preschool through college, including individuals from age 3 through older adults. Among these students, 14.9 were Black; 1.1 percent American Indians and Alaska Natives; 4.3 percent Asian; 0.2 percent Native Hawaiian and other Pacific Islander; 14.9 percent Hispanic; and 3.6 percent self-identified as two or more races (U.S. Census Bureau, 2003).

School enrollment varies across groups by age of students or level of education. In 1999, Hispanic 3-year-olds were less likely to be enrolled in center-based preschool programs than their White or Black counterparts (Hispanic 25 percent; Black, 45 percent; White 45 percent) (U.S. Department of Education, 2003a). By age 4, Hispanic children were as likely as White children to participate in a preschool or kindergarten classroom (64 percent and 69 percent, respectively); Black young children were more likely than either group to be in a preschool or kindergarten classroom (81 percent). By age 5, the vast majority of all children are enrolled in preschool or kindergarten (Black, 99 percent; Hispanic, 89 percent; White, 93 percent).

Over the past 30 years, the proportion of kindergarten through grade 12 students in public schools who are students of color has increased and generally reflected changes in the overall population. In the 2001–02 school year, approximately 17.2 percent of public elementary and secondary school students were Black; 17.1 percent were Hispanic students; 4.2 percent were Asian/Pacific Islander students; and 1.2 percent were American Indian/Alaska Native students (U.S. Department of Education, 2004). Many of these students attended schools in which they comprised at least half of the student body. Fifty-one percent of Black public school students were enrolled in schools in which Black students constituted 50 percent or more of the students; 51 percent of Hispanic students were in public schools in which they represent at least half of the student body. In contrast, only 25 percent of American Indian/Alaska Native students and 14 percent of Asian/Pacific Islander students were in public schools in which they comprised at least half of the student population. In 2001, in several areas of the country, almost half or more than half of the students were students of color. The degree to which students of color can legitimately be considered to be "minority" students varied drastically across states, from states such as California (65 percent students of color), Hawaii (79.7 percent), and New Mexico (65.7 percent) and the District of Columbia (95.4 percent) where students of color were the majority to states such as Maine (3.8 percent students of color), Vermont (4.2 percent), and West Virginia (5.5 percent) where students of color were very much in the minority. To the extent that cultural context is related to the density of the ethnic population, this demographic variation may affect the generalizability of research findings on factors influencing the learning and instruction of students of color.

The type of elementary and secondary schools students attend also varies by race and ethnicity. In 2000, 12.8 percent of White students and 10.4 percent of Asian students attended private elementary and secondary schools. In contrast, only 5.9 percent of Black students, 5.5 percent of American Indian/Alaska Native students, 6.8 percent of Native Hawaiian/Pacific Islander students, and 5.9 percent of Hispanic students were enrolled in private schools (U.S. Census Bureau, 2003). In 1999, of the 850,000 students who were homeschooled (excluding those who also enrolled in school for more than 25 hours and students who were homeschooled because of temporary medical reasons), 75.3 percent were White students; 9.9 percent were Black; 9.1 percent Hispanic; and 5.8 percent were from other ethnic groups (U.S. Department of Education, 2001b).

Whereas the proportions of students across groups in elementary and secondary schools aligns with the proportions in the general population, enrollment in college favors Asian and White students. According to the 2000 Census (U.S. Census Bureau, 2003), 9.2 million 18 to 24-year-olds were enrolled in college. A greater percentage of Asian (55.9 percent) and White (37.8 percent) young adults were enrolled in college than were young adults from other groups (Black, 26.9 percent; American Indian/Alaska Native, 20.7 percent; Native Hawaiian and other Pacific Islander, 30.1 percent; Hispanic, 14.0 percent). This difference is also reflected in educational attainment, as is discussed in the next section.

Educational Attainment and Persistence. If all students fared equally well in school, researchers might be less interested in the ways in which culture and ethnic identification are related to learning. Historically, however, most students of color have not done as well in school as their White counterparts have (Miller, 1995). Although the achievement gap has decreased, particularly for Black students, Black and Hispanic students continue to lag behind the White students (U.S. Department of Education, 2003a, 2003b).

The U.S. Census Bureau (2004) reports educational attainment for the adult population (25 years and older) in the United States. In 2003, Hispanic adults were more likely to have less than a high school education than were adults from other groups and less likely to have attended college. According to the U.S. Department of Education (2003a), high school completion rates among Hispanic young adults 18 to 24 years old has shown no consistent trend since the early 1970s; it has, however, consistently been lower than the high school completion rates of Black and White young adults. Because immigrant adults are less likely to have completed at least a high school degree than are native born adults (U.S. Census Bureau, 2004), the high proportion of immigrants among Hispanic subgroups may be one factor contributing to the lower overall educational attainment (Miller, 1995).

Dropout rates may be calculated in a number of ways. The U.S. Census Bureau, for example, reports the percentage of 16 to 19-year-olds who are not enrolled in school and are not high school graduates. In general, this dropout statistic has decreased across subgroups from 1990 to 2000 (U.S. Census Bureau, 2003). Among 16 to 19-year-olds in 2000, 11.7 percent of Black, 16.1 percent of American Indian/Alaska Native, 4.0 percent of Asian, 11.0 percent of Native Hawaiian/Pacific Islander, 21.1 percent of Hispanic, and 6.9 percent of White individuals were counted as dropouts. This rate, however, includes those individuals who, for example, immigrated to the United States as older adolescents who did not complete high school but also never enrolled in U.S. schools.

Not surprisingly, completion of postsecondary degrees varies across groups. In the 2003 Current Population Survey (U.S. Census Bureau, 2004), among adults 25 years and older, 49.8 percent of Asian, 17.3 percent of Black, 11.4 percent of Hispanic, and 30.0 percent of White adults held a bachelor's degree or higher. Among Hispanic adults, a larger proportion of native-born adults had bachelor's degrees as compared to foreign-born Hispanic adults. In contrast, for Black and White adults, a somewhat larger proportion of foreign-born adults were more likely to be college graduates.

Within racial and ethnic groups, educational attainment also varies by subgroups. For example, data from the 2000 Current Population Survey indicate that 51 percent of Hispanic adults 25 years and older of Mexican descent had attained at least a high school education; in comparison, 64 percent of Puerto Rican and Central or South American adults and 73 percent of Cuban adults 25 years and older had obtained at least a high school education (U.S. Census Bureau, 2001b). Data based on the 1990 census indicated the variation in educational attainment across American Indian nations (U.S. Census Bureau, 1993b). The proportion of adults 25 years and older who had at least a high school diploma on the 10 largest reservations ranged from 37.3 percent on the Gila River reservation to over 60 percent for the Hopi in Arizona and the Blackfeet in Montana.

Although Asian-Americans as a group have higher levels of educational attainment than other ethnic minority groups, achievement across Asian subgroups also varies greatly, and within subgroups achievement between men and women varies. According to the U.S. Census Bureau (1993c), in 1990 about 38 percent of all Asian-American adults (25 years and over) had completed at least a bachelor's degree; across subgroups, the percentages ranged from lows of less than 10 percent among Cambodian, Hmong, and Laotian adults to a high of about 66 percent for Asian Indian men. In most Asian American subgroups, the percentage of adults with college degrees was higher for men than for women.

Student Achievement. Differences across ethnic groups on measures of student learning and achievement emerge early. When children enter kindergarten, White and Asian children are more likely to have acquired emergent literacy skills (e.g., recognizing upper- and lowercase letters, knowledge of letter and sound relationships, reading common words) and beginning mathematic skills (e.g., reading numerals, counting, sequencing patterns) than are their Hispanic and Black peers (U.S. Department of Education, 2000).

On the National Assessment of Educational Progress (NAEP) 2003 fourth- and eighth-grade mathematics assessments, Asian/Pacific Islander students did better than White students, who in turn had higher scores on average than Hispanic or American Indian/Alaska Native students, who did better on average than Black students (U.S. Department of Education, 2003c). However, the mathematics scores of both Black and Hispanic fourth- and eighth-grade students steadily rose from 1990 through 2003.

Reading achievement also varies by racial and ethnic group. In general, reading achievement as measured by the NAEP reading assessment has improved for Black, Hispanic, and White fourth- and eighth-graders over the past 10 years (U.S. Department of Education, 2003d). In 2003, the average scores of White and Asian/Pacific Islander fourth- and eighth-grade students were higher than the average scores of the other groups. Among fourth graders, White students had higher average scores than Asian/Pacific Islander students; Hispanic fourth graders did better in reading on average than did their Black counterparts.

Summary. Although differences in educational attainment and achievement exist across racial and ethnic groups, the diversity within each group is also a critical consideration in understanding how students learn and in the development of programs and practices that will support the achievement of ethnic minority students. The challenge for teachers is to provide instruction that will support learning across students with diverse characteristics. To the degree that educational psychology is an applied science, that it is about discovering principles of learning, motivation, and instruction as they occur in education delivery settings, the challenge for the educational psychologist is to identify what differences among students or groups of students are critical for teachers to attend to, what general strategies or approaches can be used for understanding racial and ethnic diversity, and what strategies are useful for supporting learning among diverse groups of students. The following sections are discussions of two factors that have been related to learning among ethnic minority students—ethnic identification and cultural differences in how members of ethnic groups think about education and support learning outside of school.

ETHNIC IDENTIFICATION AND LEARNING

Social identity theorists and researchers posit that human beings define themselves in multiple ways according to the social groups to which they belong by birth (e.g., gender, ethnicity), achievement (e.g., dancer, writer), or choice (e.g., political, religious) (e.g., Bernal, Saenz, & Knight, 1991; Harwood, Leyendechers, Carlson, Asencid, & Miller, 2002; Tajfel, 1981). The salience and meaning of these social identities are not static but depend on the individual's social context. In the past decade, understanding of ethnic identity and related constructs such as cultural orientation, acculturation, and bicultural identity has developed so that current conceptualizations are multifaceted and recognize the interconnections among an individual's social identities. This section begins with a discussion of ethnic identity, then considers two ways in which ethnic identification has been related to learning among racial and ethnic minority students in the United States.

Ethnic Identity

Paralleling developments in research on self-concept in general, behavioral scientists have progressed in understandings of ethnic identity, cultural orientation, and bicultural development so that important nuances in the development of ethnic minority children and adolescents are beginning to emerge and can be related to children's approach to learning in school. For example, *cultural orientation*, which is the relation to one's ethnic culture and to the majority culture, is now considered to be multidimensional, such that an individual's acceptance or rejection of ethnic and majority cultures may vary across domains (Ying, Lee, & Tsai, 2000). An adolescent may be positively oriented toward his or her own culture when thinking about foods or what would be considered to be appropriate behavioral norms within the home. However, when it comes to music, the adolescent may be uninterested in or even reject the traditional music of his or her ethnic culture in favor of the music of the majority youth culture. Similarly, ethnic identity is considered to be multidimensional, to vary across members of an ethnic group, and to change over time within an individual. Further, the beliefs, values, and practices that are commonly shared by members of an ethnic community are not static, but evolve over time (Gutiérrez & Rogoff, 2003).

Ethnic identity has been operationalized in different ways by researchers. Broadly defined, beliefs, feelings, and behaviors contributing to one's ethnic identity include knowledge about and attitudes toward one's ethnic culture, feelings of commitment and belongingness to one's ethnic group, participation in traditional cultural activities, and attitudes toward the majority culture (Phinney, 1990). Great diversity exists within any ethnic group in terms of members' ethnic identity (e.g., Keefe & Padilla, 1987; Okagaki & Moore, 2000). Diversity comes in part because ethnic identity develops over time (e.g., Phinney, 1996), because individuals within an ethnic group differ in their exposure to the mainstream culture (e.g., consider immigrants versus native-born members of an ethnic group), because they differ in their orientation to their ethnic culture and to the mainstream culture (Buriel & De-Ment, 1997), because within a group, what is important to each group member's ethnic identity varies (Phinney, 1996), and because ethnic communities are living entities whose experiences, shared beliefs, and practices evolve over time (Gutiérrez & Rogoff, 2003). *Generation status* appears to be associated with some aspects of ethnic identity and cultural orientation more than others. In a comparison of foreign-born and U.S.-born Chinese-American adolescents, Rosenthal and Feldman (1992) found that U.S.-born Chinese-American adolescents were less likely than foreign-born adolescents to feel totally or mostly Chinese. However, there were neither differences in the degrees to which their school friends and non-school friends comprised Chinese-American and non-Chinese-American friends nor in their preference for marrying someone who was of Chinese descent. Although the foreign-born

Chinese American adolescents scored higher in their participation in culturally related behaviors (e.g., engaging in Chinese worship, speaking a Chinese language), there were no differences between groups in ratings of the importance of their ethnic identity, in their attitudes toward their Chinese backgrounds, or in their orientation toward individualism versus collectivism. Similarly, in a comparison of young adults of Mexican descent living in the Southwest and their parents (Okagaki & Moore, 2000), nearly half of the young adults described themselves as being bicultural (47 percent), with a substantial portion (42 percent) describing themselves as being mostly or very Mexican, and a small proportion (11 percent) seeing themselves as being mostly or very American. Although nearly all of the young adults (92 percent) had been born in the United States, in contrast to their parents of whom slightly more than half of the mothers (56 percent) and fathers (57 percent) had been born in the United States, the older adults were also divided in terms of identifying themselves as being mostly or very Mexican (mothers 36 percent; fathers 24 percent), bicultural (mothers: 44 percent; fathers: 60 percent), or mostly or very American (mothers: 20 percent; fathers: 16 percent). Among the young adults and the mothers (but not the fathers), those who identified more closely with being Mexican had stronger feelings about the importance of their ethnic identity than those who saw themselves as being bicultural; in turn, ethnic identity was more important to those who identified as being bicultural than to those who saw themselves as being American. In general, across the younger and older adults, those who identified more strongly with being Mexican differed from the other two groups in terms of their ability to use Spanish, ability to use English, language preference, language usage, attitudes toward the Mexican culture, and affiliation with other people of Mexican descent. Thus, even when one considers a subgroup within an ethnic group, ethnic identity can have very different meanings to the members of the subgroup and expression of their ethnicity varies widely.

In light of current emphases on the dynamic and multidimensional nature of social identities (e.g., Gutiérrez & Rogoff, 2003; Phinney, 1996), it is important to note that most of the existing research is limited to providing snapshots of ethnic identity rather than showing development and change in ethnic identity over time. In addition, although across studies, different approaches to examining ethnic identity have been utilized (e.g., interviews, questionnaires, ethnographies), very few studies have employed multiple methods to understand ethnic identity. These same limitations apply to the majority of the research discussed next on bicultural development and on stereotype threat.

Bicultural Development

Discussion of ethnic identity is relevant to school achievement in part because observations of the relations or lack of relations between academic identity and ethnic identity have led some researchers to believe that the degree to which academic achievement is compatible with their ethnic identity contributes to ethnic minority students' motivation to learn in school (e.g., Osborne, 1997; Steele & Aronson, 1995). Some have argued that positive bicultural development is necessary for ethnic minority children to be comfortable in, belong to, and achieve in both their ethnic community and in the mainstream culture (e.g., Buriel & DeMent, 1997; LaFromboise, Coleman, & Gerton, 1993; Ogbu, 1992). LaFromboise and colleagues (1993) posited that healthy bicultural development included knowledge of both cultures, positive attitudes toward both cultures, significant relationships with members of both cultures, and *bicultural efficacy*, the belief that as a member of an ethnic minority group, one can positively identify with one's ethnic group and at the same time achieve within the mainstream culture. For school achievement, this means that ethnic minority students need to develop a positive academic identity while holding onto positive ethnic identity. In a study of American Indian college students, a measure of academic identity (e.g., "Doing well in school and graduating from college are important to my view of myself") was positively correlated with a measure of bicultural efficacy (e.g., "I believe I can maintain my tribal identity and still participate in activities that are traditionally part of the White culture"; Bingham, Helling, & Okagaki, 2001). That is, the more strongly students believed that they could be a good member of their tribal community and at the same time, try to do well in school, the more positive their academic identity was. Similarly, among American Indian high school students, bicultural efficacy was found to be positively correlated with students' grades (Okagaki, Helling, & Bingham, in preparation), and among Hispanic high school students, bicultural efficacy was positively correlated with students' self-reported grades (Okagaki, Izarraraz, & Bojczyk, 2003). Thus, to the degree that school is viewed as an organization in which the purpose and norms are associated with the majority culture, it may be that for American Indian and Hispanic students, the belief that school achievement is appropriate for members of their ethnic group may contribute to their orientation to and achievement in school.

If the behavioral scientists who argue that ethnic minority students need to develop the sense that they can effectively function in both their ethnic communities and in the mainstream culture are correct (e.g., Buriel & DeMent, 1997; LaFromboise et al., 1993; Ogbu, 1992), what

factors are associated with ethnic minority students developing the perception that school is (or is not) an arena in which they can and should try to achieve? Two possibilities are considered next. First, to what degree do ethnic minority students find instrumental value in education, and how might this be related to achievement (Mickelson, 1990)? Second, to what degree are supportive school relationships associated with students' perception of school as a domain in which they can and should achieve (Wentzel, 1997)?

Instrumental Value of Education. Several behavioral scientists have suggested that the degree to which students believe that doing well in school will have direct benefits for their lives contributes to students' engagement and achievement in school. For example, to explain Asian-American students' achievement, Sue and Okazaki (1990) posited that when other avenues to upward mobility are blocked (e.g., business, politics, sports), then education becomes more important as the means to upward mobility. Belief in the instrumental importance of education, rather than a general belief in the value of education, has been related to school achievement for Black and White high school seniors (Mickelson, 1990); conversely, belief that there are barriers to one's success (e.g., job ceiling) because of discrimination against one's racial or ethnic group has been associated with a devaluing of education (Taylor, Casten, Flickinger, Roberts, & Fulmore, 1994).

What happens if students believe that working hard in school will not pay off someday? Ogbu (1992) argued that those who face barriers to their success because of discriminatory practices and policies will find alternative venues in which to achieve and will disengage themselves from trying to achieve in those domains in which discrimination keeps them from succeeding. Similarly, Steele (1997) argued that members of groups that have been stigmatized as having low ability in a particular domain will psychologically distance themselves from or "disidentify" with that domain. By not identifying with a domain, individuals' self-esteem should not suffer if they do poorly in that domain. Osborne (1997) indirectly tested the hypothesis that ethnic minority students who do not identify with academic achievement (i.e., academic disidentification) will not suffer a loss in their overall self-esteem in the face of poor school achievement with data from the National Education Longitudinal Study. White students reported higher grades than Black or Hispanic students in eighth, 10th and 12th grades and obtained higher achievement test scores in 12th grade than did students from the other two groups. At all three time points, however, Black students reported higher scores on the global measure of self-esteem. Self-esteem scores of Hispanic students were lower than those of White students in eighth grade, but higher than those of White students in 12th grade. Moreover, although grades were correlated with self-esteem for White students (albeit small but statistically significant correlations, r's ranging from 0.12 to 0.20 for White boys and from 0.12 to 0.24 for White girls), for Black boys, there was a marked decrease over time in the correlations between self-esteem and grades and between self-esteem and achievement so that only two of eight correlations between self-esteem and grades or achievement test scores were significant by 12th grade. These data are consistent with the hypothesis that over the course of adolescence there is a process of disidentification with academic achievement among Black males. However, the data for Black females and for Hispanic students were not as clear.

Along similar lines, Graham (1994; Graham, Taylor, & Hudley, 1998) proposed that underachieving ethnic minority students have aspirations other than to do well in school—that lack of motivation to achieve in school stems from having different goals and values. To examine students' values, Graham and colleagues (1998) asked Black, Hispanic, and White middle school students to identify classmates whom they admired, respected, and wanted to be like. In general, girls were more likely to identify girls of the same race and girls who were high or average achieving over those who were low achieving. The pattern of nominations for White boys paralleled those of the girls—a preference for average and high-achieving boys of the same race. In contrast, Black and Hispanic boys admired low-achieving boys of their own race. Although not testing what might lead students to not value school achievement, these data are consistent with the hypothesis that by middle school, Black and Hispanic boys may be in the process of disidentifying or disengaging with school. In accord with the hypothesis that racism leads to disengagement from school by ethnic minority students, data from a study of fourth- and fifth-grade Mexican-American students indicated that students' perception of discrimination against members of their ethnic group was negatively correlated with their school engagement, negatively correlated with intrinsic motivation for learning, and negatively correlated with their belief that school is an appropriate domain in which Mexican-American children can and should excel (Okagaki, Frensch, & Dodson, 1996). Among these elementary school students, however, perception of discrimination was not correlated with students' academic performance.

Others, however, have found that publicly distancing oneself from the appearance of working hard in school is a strategy employed by adolescents across ethnic groups, including White adolescents (e.g., Arroyo & Zigler, 1995). In studies including Black and White adolescents, Arroyo and Zigler (1995) found that academic orientation was positively correlated with feelings of alienation from peers and reported efforts to keep peers from knowing about academic success. In their study, however, Steinberg, Dornbusch, and Brown (1992) observed that for all adolescents, doing better in school was associated with having both parents and peers support academic achievement and that, in general, White and Asian-American adolescents were more likely than Hispanic or Black adolescents to have support for academic achievement from both groups.

Ethnic Group Match Between Teacher and Student. Although several aspects of schooling (e.g., resources, quality of teachers) have been posited to affect ethnic minority students' achievement and engagement in school (e.g., Miller, 1995), I have limited discussion to recent research on whether having a teacher of the same racial or ethnic group makes a difference in student learning. Do ethnic minority students identify more closely with teachers who are of the same ethnic group, and does this identification lead to stronger student engagement in learning?

The most definitive answers for causal questions are obtained through experimental studies resulting in participants being randomly assigned to condition. To examine the effect of having a teacher of the same race on student achievement, Dee (2004) analyzed data from Project STAR, the Tennessee large-scale randomized field trial to test the effects of small class size on student achievement. In Project STAR, teachers and students in kindergarten through third grade were randomly assigned to small classes, regular-size classes or regular-size classes, with teacher aides within each of the 79 schools in the study. Dee capitalized on the fact that this random assignment also resulted in students being randomly assigned to either same-race or other-race teachers. For both Black and non-Hispanic White students, assignment to a teacher of the same race resulted in a 3- to 5-percentile-point increase on math and reading achievement test scores (note, that the limited numbers of teachers and students from other ethnic groups precluded including them in Dee's analyses). The advantage of having a same-race teacher occurred primarily in regular-size classes (22 students) as opposed to small classes (15 students) and with teachers who had been teaching less than 12 years. The effect also appeared to be stronger for students from economically disadvantaged homes. Finally, having a same-race teacher for four consecutive years yielded a cumulative effect of 8 percentile points for reading and nearly 9 percentile points for math achievement test scores in the primary grades.

Dee's (2004) analysis indicated that under certain conditions having a teacher of the same race made a difference in the early grades but did not identify the underlying causal mechanisms of the effect. Existing research on possible causal mechanisms is mixed (for review, see Ferguson, 1998). One possibility is the self-fulfilling prophecy hypothesis, namely that White teachers have more negative perceptions of and expectations for Black students than Black teachers do and that students will live up (or down) to their teacher's perceptions and expectations; another hypothesis is that Black and White teachers treat Black students differently. Although a plethora of research has been conducted on teacher expectations since the late 1960s and has been reviewed by others (e.g., Ferguson, 1998; Good & Brophy, 2000; Good & Nichols, 2001), there is less research and mixed findings on whether Black and White teachers have different perceptions, expectations, and interactions with Black students. For example, in a study of preservice teachers from an urban university in the southeastern United States, White preservice teachers, as compared to Black preservice teachers, rated Black elementary school students as being more dependent than their White classmates (Kesner, 2000). On the other hand, in a study of an urban school district in the northeastern United States, Pigott and Cowen (2000) found that ratings of Black elementary school students by both Black and White teachers were more negative than were ratings of White students. To examine teachers' perceptions of students from same or other racial and ethnic groups, Dee (forthcoming) examined data from the National Education Longitudinal Study of 1988 (NELS:88), a nationally representative study of more mor than 24,000 eighth-grade students. He found that students were rated more negatively when they were rated by teachers who were not members of the same racial or ethnic group as the student. However, when the data from each region of the country (North, South, East, and West based on census classifications) were examined separately, Dee observed that the effect was only statistically significant in the South. These data suggest that conflicting findings in previous research may, at least in part, be due to cultural differences that exist across regions of the country.

Do teachers have biases that affect their perceptions of their students? In his review of the research, Ferguson (1998) concluded that when researchers considered whether a bias was evident in teachers' perceptions after controlling for prior student performance as the test for neutrality, then the weight of the evidence was that teachers were not biased in their perceptions of students. However, Ferguson asserted that on the basis of this conclusion, one could not necessarily draw inferences about teachers' expectations for students' future behaviors or about teachers' behaviors toward students. Furthermore, Ferguson and others (e.g., Casteel, 1997; Good & Nichols, 2001) have suggested that Black and White students may

differ in their responses to feedback from their teachers. In a study of middle school students (Casteel, 1997), Black students were more oriented toward pleasing their teachers; White students were focused on pleasing their parents.

Another possible mechanism is that having a same-race teacher provides a stronger role model for students and is particularly important for groups in which high-achieving academic role models are less salient. Data testing this hypothesis are thin. Although Hess and Leal (1997) found that the percentage of minority teachers in urban school districts was positively correlated with the college matriculation rates, they cautioned that increasing the proportion of minority teachers may be associated with other systemic improvements in districts. Their data could not be used in support of the role model hypothesis.

In general, the quality of students' relationships at school appears to be related to student engagement and achievement (e.g., Griffith, 2002; Wentzel, 1997). Yet, further research is needed to determine what affects ethnic minority students' identification with school and how to improve their identification with and engagement in school. Examination of what might be different for minority students when they have a teacher of the same minority group and how this affects learning might prove to be a fruitful avenue for understanding ways to improve education in all classrooms. Of course, not all racial and ethnic minority students become disengaged with school; many ethnic minority students do succeed and strongly identify with their academic achievement. Recent investigations, however, have revealed that there are also negative consequences of racism and stigmatization for those racial and ethnic minority students who are succeeding in school.

Stereotype Threat

One of the most interesting new avenues of research is at the intersection of cognitive processing and social identity research. Following the work of Claude Steele and his colleagues (e.g., Spencer, Steele, & Quinn, 1999; Steele, 1997; Steele & Aronson, 1995), a number of researchers have examined the stereotype threat phenomenon (e.g., Gonzales, Blanton, & Williams, 2002; Stangor, Carr, & Kiang, 1998). Stereotype threat is an event in which an individual's performance on a task is inhibited when a relevant negative stereotype about a group with which the individual identifies is evoked. For example, activating negative stereotypes in experimental settings has been shown to lower math performances of women (Spencer et al., 1999), to lower verbal scores of Black college students (Steele & Aronson, 1995), and to lower the math scores of Hispanic undergraduates (Gonzales et al. 2002). What makes this research particularly striking is that seemingly innocuous triggers can result in an occurrence of stereotype threat. In a typical stereotype threat experiment, high-achieving Black and White undergraduates are randomly assigned to either the stereotype threat condition or the control. All students are given the same set of problems to solve, such as items adapted from the verbal Graduate Record Examination. Just prior to taking the test, participants in the control group provide background information such as their age and major. In the stereotype threat group, the students provide the same information with one exception: They are asked to indicate their race. The result of this seemingly minor addition is that Black students in the stereotype threat group score lower than Black students in the control condition and lower than White students in the stereotype threat group. Typically scores are adjusted for prior achievement (e.g., SAT scores) and no difference in scores between Black and White students in the control condition is obtained (e.g., Steele & Aronson, 1995).

On the other hand, stereotypes have also been found to facilitate performance (Walton & Cohen, 2003) when individuals belong to a group for which there is another group (outgroup) that is negatively stereotyped as doing poorly on the task; furthermore, a given group may experience either negative or positive consequences of stereotypes depending on the reference group. In a study of Asian-American female undergraduates, priming participants on gender identity resulted in lower math scores than the scores of no-priming control group, whereas priming participants on ethnic identity produced higher math scores than the scores of the control group (Shih, Pittinsky, & Ambady, 1999).

To understand the implications of stereotype threat for learning and instruction necessitates identifying the mechanism or mechanisms through which stereotype threat operates and the conditions under which it can be evoked. Researchers have posited that stereotype threat inhibits performance through both affective and cognitive pathways. Schmader and Johns (2003), for example, demonstrated that inducing stereotype threat reduces working memory capacity and that working memory capacity mediates the effect of stereotype threat on standardized test performance. The data on stereotype threat and anxiety, however, are mixed. Some researchers have observed that stereotype threat induces higher levels of anxiety (e.g., Aronson et al., 1999; Spencer et al., 1999); others, however, have not found differences in anxiety level (e.g., Steele & Aronson, 1995). Another hypothesis is that activating stereotype threat lowers individuals' expectations for their performance, which in turn reduces actual performance. Data consistent with this hypothesis

have been obtained for performance on laboratory tasks (Stangor, Carr, & Kiang, 1998).

What conditions evoke stereotype threat? Steele (1997) argued that it is only students who strongly identify with academic achievement and are members of groups that have *not* traditionally done well in school who are vulnerable to stereotype threat. Consistent with this hypothesis, a team of Belgian researchers demonstrated that the degree to which individuals identify with a domain—that is, the degree to which they believe that the targeted skill is important to them—moderates the effect of stereotype threat (Leyens, Desert, Croizet, & Darcis, 2000). Researchers have also explored whether the phenomenon could be evoked among individuals who generally enjoy high status. That is, for an individual to be vulnerable to stereotype threat, does the individual need to identify with a stigmatized group? The answer is no; researchers have found that stereotype threat can lower math scores of White male college students (where the negative stereotype was a comparison to Asian students; Aronson et al., 1999; Smith & White, 2002) and lower the performance of White males on an affective information processing task (Leyens et al., 2000). With respect to the testing situation itself, Inzlicht and Ben-Zeev (2000, 2003) found that stereotype threat occurred when women were the minority in a math testing situation with men; women who were tested in groups in which they were the only woman with two men scored significantly lower than women who were tested in groups with two other women. Moreover, the effect held even when participants believed that the test results would be anonymous. Finally, Smith and White (2002) demonstrated that stereotype threat can be evoked implicitly by the testing situation itself without any explicit priming of the negative stereotype. That is, as long as the task is viewed as a test and negative stereotypes are commonly attributed to a group's performance on this type of test, no other manipulation is required to evoke stereotype threat.

Interventions to Reduce Stereotype Threat. Stereotype threat is perhaps most troubling because individuals appear to be most vulnerable to stereotype threat when they are high achievers in a domain. Some research has been conducted to develop and test interventions to attenuate the effects of stereotype threat. One approach to ameliorating the debilitating effects of stereotype threat is to change the way students conceptualize intelligence. Carol Dweck (2002) has established that people vary in the degree to which they believe intelligence is a fixed, innate ability—the "entity" theory of intelligence—and the degree to which intelligence is viewed as a malleable trait that can be increased as the individual tackles and masters new content and skills—the "incremental" theory of intelligence. Building on this concept, Aronson, Fried, and Good (2002) evaluated a relatively minor intervention consisting of three 1-hour sessions to reduce the impact of stereotype threat on Black college students. Black and White Stanford University students were randomly assigned to one of three conditions. In the intervention condition, as part of a pen pal mentor program, college students wrote a letter to encourage a middle school student who was struggling academically. They were told that young students often benefit from learning that intelligence is not a fixed ability but instead is more like a muscle that gets stronger with practice. To learn more about research on the malleability of intelligence, students watched a short video on brain research illustrating that responding to intellectual challenge can increase brain capacity. In addition, students were asked to include in their letter illustrations from their own life that supported this premise. As part of the intervention, students wrote letters to two middle school students and taped a short speech conveying the message that intelligence is malleable. Students in the pen pal control group engaged in the same activities, but the message they were asked to convey is that intelligence is made up of multiple abilities and that everyone has both strengths and weaknesses. A second control group only completed the pre and post-intervention measures. As a result of this brief intervention, college students in the intervention group held stronger beliefs about the malleability of intelligence and rated school as being more enjoyable. In addition, several months later, the spring quarter grades of students in the intervention group were higher than the grades of students in the control group after controlling for students' prior Scholastic Aptitude Test (SAT) scores. Despite the success of the intervention, the researchers noted that the intervention, along with controlling for prior SAT scores, did not fully ameliorate the observed difference in grades between Black and White students.

Finally, Good, Aronson, and Inzlicht (2003) evaluated an intervention designed to attenuate the effects of stereotype threat on the math performance of junior high girls by changing their beliefs about the malleability of intelligence, their attribution of academic difficulties, or a combination of both malleability and attribution of academic difficulties. Girls in all three intervention groups scored significantly higher than did girls in the control condition on end-of-year math achievement tests.

Both of these evaluations indicate that the performance of students vulnerable to stereotype threat can be improved by changing social cognitions related to academic performance. The research on stereotype threat, the disidentification of underachieving ethnic minority students with school, and bicultural development point to the role that social cognitions in general and social

identities in particular have in how ethnic minority students approach learning in school. The stereotype threat research is particularly powerful because the research has typically relied on experimental methodologies rather than observational studies. Although the effects of any one factor such as stereotype threat or the racial/ethnic match between teachers and students do not fully explain achievement differences between underachieving minority groups and White students (e.g., Aronson et al., 2002; Sackett, Hardison, & Cullen, 2004), research on stereotype threat has proved to be a fruitful avenue for understanding ethnic-group differences in achievement.

CULTURAL DIVERSITY AND EDUCATION

Both diversity and commonality exist across ethnic groups in the United States. Within the scope of this chapter, it is only possible to touch on some of the ways in which ethnic cultures (e.g., beliefs, values, traditions, customs, social norms, roles) connect to education. I focus on parents' expectations for children's learning and their involvement in children's schooling for three reasons. First, parents' expectations and parental involvement in children's education have been found to vary across racial and ethnic groups (e.g., Hao & Bonstead-Bruns, 1998) and have been correlated with student achievement (e.g., Booth & Dunn, 1996; Halle, Kurtz-Costes, & Mahoney, 1997; Hill & Craft, 2003; Jimerson, Egeland, & Teo, 1999). Second, research on ethnic minority parents' expectations and school support brings to light the importance of examining cultural models of education (Gallimore & Goldenberg, 2001; Lareau, 1996). Cultural models are widely shared "understandings of how the world works, or ought to work" (Gallimore & Goldenberg, 2001, p. 47), and there are differences and commonalities across ethnic groups in their conceptions of education, school, and learning. Cultural models of education may include the ideas that parents have about the roles of parents and teachers in children's schooling; important differences may exist, for example, in conceptualizations of what it means for parents to help their children with schoolwork (Lareau, 1996). Finally, the data in the earlier section on the educational achievement of ethnic minority students make clear that the level of education that has been attained by adults in several ethnic minority groups is lower than the educational level of most White adults. The degree to which having academic skills is important for providing effective support for one's child's education may limit the ability of some ethnic minority parents to help their children succeed in school. Research on the home–school links of ethnic minority families, however, suggests that there are alternative ways in which ethnic minority parents who have less formal education may be able to support their children's academic achievement (e.g., Arzubiaga, Rueda, & Monzo, 2002; Azmitia, Cooper, Garcia, & Dunbar, 1996; Chao & Tseng 2002).

Expectations for Academic Achievement

In general, research has shown that parents' expectations differ across racial and ethnic groups (e.g., Alexander, Entwisle, & Bedinger, 1994; Hao & Bonstead-Bruns, 1998; Okagaki & Frensch, 1998) and further, that parents' expectations are correlated with children's school performance among economically disadvantaged Black families (e.g., Gill & Reynolds, 2000; Halle, Kurtz-Costes, & Mahoney, 1997; Luster & McAdoo, 1996); Asian-American families (Hao & Bonstead-Bruns, 1998; Okagaki & Frensch, 1998), and Hispanic families (e.g., Goldenberg, Gallimore, Reese, & Garnier, 2001; Hao & Bonstead-Bruns, 1998). Current research efforts have attempted to unpack the meaning of parents' expectations and have examined whether parents' expectations influence their child's achievement or children's achievement influences their parents' expectations.

As with the research on ethnic identity, bicultural development, and stereotype threat, much of the research on ethnic minority parents' educational expectations and support for learning is limited to providing pictures of what occurs at one point in time. A notable exception is a study by Goldenberg and colleagues (2001) examining the aspirations and expectations of Hispanic immigrant parents from the time their child began kindergarten to sixth grade. Over the course of the child's elementary school years, parents' *aspirations* for school attainment—that is, how much education they wanted their child to have—remained high and were generally not correlated with the child's previous year's school performance. Parents wanted their children to go to college. Parents' *expectations* for their child's school attainment—the amount of formal education parents thought their child would obtain—were lower than parents' aspirations and fluctuated more from year to year. Path analysis was used to test whether parents' expectations predicted student achievement or student achievement predicted parents' expectations; among these Hispanic immigrant families, student performance in the previous year generally predicted parents' expectations with small to moderate correlations between student performance and subsequent expectations. Information garnered from parent interviews supported this model. For instance, when parents observed that their son's or daughter's performance and interest in school had improved, they thought their child would ultimately go further in school. When parents noted that their child was not doing well in school, their expectations were lower.

Some of the Hispanic immigrant parents also expressed a view of education in which they had less control over how their child would do and how much education their child would receive (Goldenberg et al., 2001). Over the course of study, parents were asked about their aspirations and expectations seven times. In response to the question on aspirations, rarely would a parent say that he or she had no idea; in contrast in response to the question on expectations, as many as one-fourth of the parents would not be able to say how far they expected their child to go in school. These parents believed that parents could have dreams for their child, but that the child would have to decide what he or she would do. This perspective may have grown out of a realization that they did not have much practical knowledge about education in the United States and did not have strategies for acting on their goals (Lareau, 1996). Another possibility is that their view may be based on a child-directed view of development such that the parent plays a supportive role in helping the child achieve the child's goals rather than the parent influencing the child's goals, as has been noted among many American Indian tribal communities (Harry, 1992; Joe & Malach, 1992). Alternatively it may not be that being "child-oriented" is a categorical characteristic of parenting; across (and within) cultural groups, parents' ideas about which decisions should primarily be the child's choice may vary. Comparing low-income White families and low-income Mexican immigrant families, Azmitia and colleagues (1996) observed that among Mexican immigrant parents, 11 percent thought that how much education the child would attain should be determined by the child and 25 percent thought the vocational decision should be the child's choice. Among White parents, 19 percent thought that the amount of education their child should obtain was the child's choice (not unlike the Mexican immigrant parents' responses), but 83 percent of the White parents indicated that the type of job they wanted their child to have was for the child to decide.

The causal direction and the strength of relations between parents' expectations and their children's academic achievement may in fact differ across ethnic groups depending on, for example, parents' beliefs about parenting and child development and their practical knowledge of schooling in the United States. Alexander, Entwisle, and Bedinger (1994) observed that the relation between parents' expectations and their child's subsequent performance was stronger for parents who more accurately recalled their child's prior grades. They suggested that high expectations are not particularly helpful (or in turn, predictive of subsequent child outcomes) if parents do not have an accurate perception of where their child is in terms of knowledge and skills (i.e., how far does the child have to go to achieve the goal), do not have an effective plan of action for helping the child achieve the goal, or do not have access to the resources to enact the plan of action. Second, when parents say they expect their son or daughter to go to college or to graduate from college, this does not necessarily mean that parents have an accurate conceptualization of what that means. For example, the connection between postsecondary education and careers may not be understood by the parents. In a study of low-income Hispanic families, parents had high aspirations for the types of jobs they hoped their child would have (e.g., doctors, lawyers, scientists), but it was clear from their educational aspirations (e.g., none mentioned graduate education) that they did not have an accurate understanding of the educational pathways that would lead their child toward that goal (Azmitia et al., 1996). Finally, the impact of parents' expectations on children's achievement may also be a function of the transmission of those expectations to the child. Researchers have found that there is greater agreement between parents' expectations and their young adolescents' expectations when parents and students work together on learning activities (Hao & Bonstead-Bruns, 1998). This observation is consistent with the sociocultural perspective on the importance of joint activities as a means of transmission of cultural knowledge and values (e.g., Gallimore & Goldenberg, 2001; Rogoff, 1990).

Looking across groups, Okagaki and Frensch (1998) found that Asian-American, Hispanic, and White parents of fourth and fifth graders differed in their expectations for their child's school performance. Parents were asked how happy or satisfied they would be if their child received an A, B, C, D, or F for his or her schoolwork. Everyone was happy with A's and unhappy with F's. The difference came with parents' responses to B's and C's. Asian-American parents were less satisfied with grades of B and C than the other parents were. Moreover, parents' expectations for their child's school performance obtained at the beginning of the school year were correlated with children's school achievement at the end of the year. For Hispanic and White families, parents' responses to D's predicted student performance; for Asian American families, parents' responses to B's were correlated with student performance.

Similar to the study by Goldenberg and colleagues (2001), Okagaki and Frensch (1998) also asked parents about their aspirations and expectations for their child's education, and in addition, asked what would be the *very least amount* of schooling they would allow their child to attain. Compared to other parents, Asian-American parents had higher educational aspirations and expectations

for their children. Asian-American parents ideally wanted their children to obtain a graduate or professional degree; they expected their children to graduate from college. The minimum educational attainment they set for their children was college graduation. In contrast, the ideal educational attainment level for Hispanic and White parents was for their children to graduate from college. However, Hispanic and White parents expected their children to get some college education. For White parents, the lower boundary was high school graduation; for Hispanic parents, the lower boundary was some college education. Finally, controlling for the child's grades from the previous year and parents' perceptions of their child's ability to do schoolwork, differences across groups on expected school attainment and minimum school attainment remained. In other words, differences in parents' expectations for their child's educational attainment were *not* solely a function of how well the child actually performed during the previous year or parents' perceptions of their child's abilities. In this study, the Asian-American parents described a different vision than other parents of what constituted doing well in school. They wanted their child to obtain a graduate degree; they expected their child to graduate from college. Perhaps more importantly, they were concerned when B's started to show up in schoolwork. Finally, although this particular study focused on differences across groups, other studies have found that within ethnic groups parents of high and low achievers have differed in their aspirations and expectations for their child's education (e.g., Okagaki, Frensch, & Gordon, 1995).

Cultural Models of Educational Expectations. An important advance in research on social cognitions in general, and, for this discussion, parents' social cognitions, is the recognition of the interplay among social cognitions (e.g., McGillicuddy-De Lisi & Sigel, 1995; Sigel & McGillicuddy-De Lisi, 2002). Cultural differences in educational expectations and whether expectations are antecedents to child outcomes or are informed by child performance may depend on the overall cultural model of education and learning. As discussed previously, cultural perspectives on the instrumental importance or perceived relevance of education appear to be a factor in the school achievement of ethnic minority students. Researchers have posited that in many cultural groups and for voluntary immigrants (i.e., those who choose to leave their own countries, generally to seek a better life for themselves and their families) there may be other underlying values or beliefs that elevate the importance of education. For instance, Buriel and De Ment (1997) suggested that immigrants who voluntarily choose to move to a new country for economic reasons are a self-selected group who are task oriented, willing to work hard, and willing to delay gratification to improve their lot in life. For these reasons, children of immigrants may do better in school than second- or later-generation children because there is greater press to acquire the skills needed to succeed in the newly adopted country.

In many Asian cultures, the importance of education is linked to a strong belief in human malleability and to an emphasis on the importance of bringing honor to one's family (Ho, 1994; Okagaki & Bojczyk, 2002). For example, in an ethnographic study of Punjabi high school students, Gibson (1993) observed that students were "told that those who do well in school can expect to find better marriage partners, that their accomplishments bring credit to their family, and that they set an example for other younger Punjabis to follow" (p. 121). In this context, motivation for educational attainment goes beyond the instrumental value of education but is couched in a culture that views education as a means to being virtuous (e.g., Hieshima & Schneider, 1994).

Among many Asian-American families, educational success reflects not only on the student, but also on the parent. In her work with immigrant Chinese mothers, Chao (1994, 2001) reported that one of the primary goals of the mothers was to help their children succeed in school. An essential component of Chinese parenting is "training" by which parents work to teach their children to be self-disciplined, to work hard, and to achieve in school (Chao, 2001). In a study of young Chinese-American and White elementary school students (Huntsinger, Jose, & Larson, 1998), the Chinese-American parents were more controlling and engaged in a more formal, systematic approach to teaching their children (e.g., having their child write book reports every week, using flash cards to memorize math facts). The emphasis on the parent's role in education has also been identified by Japanese-American parents (Hieshima & Schneider, 1994) and Vietnamese parents (Kibria, 1993).

The strong emphasis on school achievement among many Asian-American groups has led researchers to consider how this parental pressure might affect students' attitudes toward education and whether there is a negative emotional consequence among children and adolescents to this pressure (e.g., Chen & Stevenson, 1995; Chiu & Ring, 1998; Huntsinger et al., 1998; Lee & Ying, 2001). In a comparison of Asian-American and White adolescents (Chen & Stevenson, 1995), Asian American students' perceptions of their parents' expectations for their school performance and the importance their parents placed on getting good grades were higher than those of their White counterparts. However, there was very little evidence that the emphasis on academic achievement was associated with poor psychosocial outcomes. Similarly, even though researchers observed greater press by parents of young Chinese-American elementary school children as compared to their White counterparts (e.g., assigning book reports), there was no evidence two years later that the Chinese-American children were experiencing negative psychosocial consequences as a result of this early emphasis on learning at home (Huntsinger et al., 1998).

Eaton and Dembo (1997) compared Asian-American (including students of Chinese, Vietnamese, Korean, and Japanese descent) and non-Asian-American (primarily Caucasians, but including Mexican-Americans and Blacks) ninth-grade students on a number of dimensions to identify social cognitions and motivations that might explain differences in student achievement. The two groups of students shared similar beliefs about the degree to which they held incremental views of intellectual ability (i.e., the view that intellectual ability is modifiable and can improve as one learns to solve new problems) and, contrary to other research, similar attributions with respect to attributing achievement to effort rather than to other factors such as ability. Compared to other students, Asian-American students had a greater fear of academic failure and expressed less confidence in their ability to complete a verbal problem-solving task; yet, Asian-American students outperformed non-Asian students on an assessment of achievement behavior (persistence on a verbal problem-solving task). Fear of failure and self-efficacy predicted Asian-American students' achievement behavior; achievement attributions related to effort, incremental view of ability, and self-efficacy predicted non-Asian students' achievement behavior. These data are consistent with Lee and Ying's (2001) analysis of Asian-American adolescents' essays on being Asian-American, in which 57 percent of the adolescents expressed at least some negative attitudes toward academic achievement. The data from Asian-American students' essays alone, however, do not address the question of whether the expressed negative attitudes reflected actual maladjustment or whether these attitudes reflected, for example, normative attitudes of adolescents toward school. Eaton and Dembo's hypothesis that Asian-American students' achievement motivation may be related to their fear of failure is analogous to an observation from Steinberg, Dornbusch, and Brown (1992): The degree to which adolescents believe that there are negative consequences for school failure is a better predictor of adolescents' school performance and engagement than the belief that there are positive benefits for obtaining a good education. In their study, White and Asian-American adolescents were more likely to believe in the negative consequences of school failure than Black and Hispanic adolescents were.

From the research on expectations, it is clear that expectations for academic performance and attainment vary across ethnic groups and that whatever influence expectations may have on student learning and achievement and the mechanisms by which expectations might play a role in student learning and achievement depend on a cluster of beliefs. The cultural beliefs about education are related to students' motivation for school achievement. Ethnic minority students from some cultural backgrounds appear to benefit from cultural beliefs about education and development that seem to elevate the importance of education. Although not highlighted in this section, research on expectations also demonstrates the great variation that occurs within groups (e.g., Okagaki, Frensch, & Gordon, 1995). In the next discussion, I review research on ethnic differences in the ways in which parents provide support for learning and discuss specific examples of within-group variation in parents' approaches to supporting their children's schooling.

Parental Support for Learning

Most parents want their children to do well in school and believe that school is important. In some studies, parents from underachieving ethnic minority groups rate education as being more important than their White counterparts do (e.g., Stevenson, Chen, & Uttal, 1990). If this is true, why does parental support for education vary across ethnic (and socioeconomic) groups? One possibility is that parents may have different ideas about the appropriate roles of parents and teachers and different understandings of strategies such as "checking homework" (Lareau, 1996); another hypothesis is that some parents, especially those from some immigrant groups, may have less formal education and knowledge about working with schools (Delgado-Gaitan, 1994). What types of support for learning do parents from ethnic minority families provide?

Luster and McAdoo (1996) capitalized on the longitudinal Perry Preschool data in which preschool children were followed until they were in their late 20s to identify the characteristics and family supports that distinguished between low-income Black students who had successfully negotiated school from those who had not. In addition to finding that parental expectations were related to student achievement, they found that whether or not young adults viewed their parents as significant role models for their lives distinguished between those who had at least completed high school and those who had dropped out. Further, mothers whose young adult son or daughter described the mother as a role model could be identified from the data that had originally been collected when the son or daughter was in kindergarten. Compared to mothers who were not identified as role models, the mothers who were role models had been rated by their child's kindergarten teacher as being more cooperative and be-

ing likely to sustain positive school–parent relationships in the future.

What might constitute cooperative behaviors on the part of low-income Black parents? That is, what types of behaviors might the teachers in the Perry Preschool study have been observing that resulted in the perception of some mothers as being supportive and cooperative? In a qualitative study of Black families living in poverty, parents' strategies for supporting children's education were examined. Compared to parents of low-achieving students, parents of high-achieving low-income Black sixth graders had more specific strategies for managing their child's schoolwork (e.g., establishing homework schedules, giving extra reading and writing assignments) and were more aware of the specific difficulties their child had (Gutman & McLoyd, 2000). Parents of high achievers provided more examples of giving their child positive feedback and encouraging their child when he or she was struggling in class. They intentionally tried to bolster their child's confidence when the child was having problems in a subject. In contrast, parents of low achievers did not articulate specific strategies for helping their child with schoolwork. Although they reported spending time helping their child with homework, they did not give examples of what they did. They often focused more on their child's attitude toward school or behavior in school or on the barriers in their own lives that made helping their child difficult (e.g., time constraints). Parents of high achievers were more likely to initiate contact with their child's teacher to check on their child's progress in between marking periods and expressed a greater sense of working with the school staff to do what was best for their child. In contrast, parents of low achievers were more wary of the school staff intervening to help their child; they preferred to have the school staff tell them what the problem was but let the parents deal with it. Finally, parents of high achievers were better managers of community resources that could support their child's development (e.g., art and music classes, religious activities). The work by Gutman and McLoyd (2000) and by Luster and McAdoo (1996) is important not only because the research provides insight into how parents support their children's learning but also because these studies are good illustrations of the variation that occurs within ethnic groups.

In a comparison of Asian-American, Hispanic, and White parents (Okagaki & Frensch, 1998), no differences were observed in parents' self-reports of how frequently they engaged in activities to help their 10- and 11-year-old child with schoolwork (e.g., help study for a test, check homework) and how frequently they engaged in intellectually stimulating activities that were non-school-related (e.g., reading at home themselves, reading a non-school book with their child). Even among parents with very little formal education, researchers have found that parents report actively helping their children with their schoolwork. For example, among low-income Mexican immigrant families in which the parents on average had less than 7 years of formal education, the majority of parents indicated that they helped their child with homework— showing the child how to do problems—and checked the child's homework (Azmitia et al., 1996). Data, however, from ethnographic studies suggest that although parents may actively help their elementary school children with their schoolwork, their instrumental help is not always effective (e.g., Delgado-Gaitan, 1992). Parents who are not educated in U.S. schools do not always understand the assignments—especially when the directions for an assignment are often given verbally to the child and are not written on an assignment sheet. Moreover, other aspects of parents' cultural models of learning may lead them to approach a particular school task in ways other than how the teacher envisioned them being enacted (e.g., Gallimore & Goldenberg, 2001).

If parents are unable to provide effective instrumental assistance, does that mean that they are unable to facilitate their child's school achievement? Not necessarily. Parental encouragement and indirect help, coupled with high expectations for their adolescent's school performance, is associated with Hispanic high school students' success. In an ethnographic study of Central American immigrant adolescents, Suarez-Orozco (1993) noted that indirect help was associated with school success among the older Central American immigrant adolescents in the study. For example, instead of allowing the adolescent to work after school to contribute to the family finances, the parents would work two or three jobs. The parent's role in the adolescent's schooling was not to help the adolescent with the schoolwork. Rather, the parent's role was to ensure that the adolescent had sufficient time to study and to create a climate in which the adolescent's job was to study and do well in school. Similar indirect strategies have been reported in descriptive studies of Asian-American adolescents and their parents (for review, see Chao & Tseng, 2002).

Unpacking the cultural models of learning and education that guide the families of ethnic minority students can shed light on why parents and students do or do not engage in the types of activities that educators believe will support student learning. An elegant example comes from research on Hispanic immigrant families from Mexico and Central America (Gallimore & Goldenberg, 2001; Reese & Gallimore, 2000; Reese, Garnier, Gallimore, & Goldenberg, 2000). The parents had relatively little formal education, generally only an elementary school background, and were primarily skilled or unskilled laborers. Gallimore and his colleagues described a cultural model of literacy development in which (a) emergent literacy behaviors are not viewed as meaningful learning activities; (b) children begin to learn how to read in school; (c) the process begins with learning the letters and the sounds and putting them together to make words; and (d) success depends on repetition and practice. Further, parents believed that to prepare their children to do well in school, they needed to teach their children to know right from wrong, to be respectful, and to behave well. What are some of the implications of this view? One is that parents generally did not read to their child until they thought the child actually understood the meaning of the story, usually not until the child was about 5 years old or had entered school. The purpose of reading stories was not to help children begin to read or develop their language or encourage other aspects of cognitive development; the purpose of reading was primarily to convey moral content. It was not the case that the parents were uninterested in their child's education. In fact, they were doing what they believed was most important to help their child succeed in school, which was to put a priority on teaching the child to behave properly and giving the child a good moral foundation. Another outcome of this view came to light when teachers sent short Spanish storybooks home for the parents read with their child. The teachers intended for the parents to engage their child in reading and talking about the stories. Instead, parents used the books in the way that made sense in their model of literacy development, which was to have their child practice recognizing words. Unpacking the Hispanic immigrant parents' cultural model of literacy development provided a way for the researchers and the teachers not only to better understand why parents did what they did, but also to identify likely avenues for intervention that would allow parents to hold on to what was most important to them but modify their behaviors to better support their children's learning.

CONCLUSIONS

This chapter began with a description of the diversity across and within racial and ethnic groups. Although the variation in student outcomes (e.g., dropout rates, educational attainment, educational achievement) across groups leads educators, policymakers, and parents to be concerned about the underachievement of some ethnic minority groups, the variation within groups evokes the cautionary note that one cannot make blanket statements about any group. Not all Asian-American students are doing well in school; not all Hispanic or Black students are falling behind in school. What differences among students or groups of students, then, should teachers attend to? What does educational psychology have to say to educators who must meet the challenge of teaching students with diverse backgrounds and characteristics?

Recent research has highlighted the importance of understanding the interplay among students' social identities. In fact, Harwood and her colleagues (2002) have argued that a fundamental problem with thinking of culture as something embodied by a group is that it fosters group stereotypes and leads to conceptualizing diverse groups of people as being alike. Instead, they suggest that culture should be located "not in the group but in the contextualized individual; culture is viewed not as an entity equivalent to group membership labels but as a shifting continuum of shared commonality among individuals" (Harwood et al., 2002, p. 25). People belong to multiple groups at any given time; they have multiple social identities. It is the interplay among those social identities that directs behavior. For ethnic minority students, their ethnic, bicultural, and academic identities may work together to support, or be at odds in relation to, the student's motivation for, engagement in, and performance in school. Add to these three group memberships, for example, the student's membership in a family of immigrants, in a high-poverty neighborhood, in a church or religious group, and in a peer group of adolescents. Each one may contribute to how the student thinks about and behaves in school. Among some ethnic minority students, then, there is evidence suggesting that students may disidentify or disengage with school—they may not see school as having any pragmatic benefits in their life; they may not see any negative consequences for not succeeding in school; they may not see school as a context that is compatible with a particular social identity. Among those ethnic minority students who belong to traditionally underachieving groups but who individually have been successful in school, there is considerable evidence now that such students can be vulnerable to the effects of stereotype threat, a sort of clash between their academic identity and their racial or ethnic identity. Social identities may be one factor that may be important to attend to as educators work to make school a context in which ethnic minority students are engaged and motivated to learn.

Cultural models of education and learning may be a fruitful strategy for understanding and facilitating home—school linkages. Parents' ideas about and understandings of school may help their children's academic performance to greater or lesser degrees. Some parents have less understanding of how school "works" and may not accurately interpret teachers' feedback on students' performance or be able to instrumentally support children's efforts in an effective way. Understanding what is happening from the parents' perspective—checking their cultural model of learning—may open better avenues for interventions.

Finally, what does educational psychology gain from research on ethnic minority students? Ramsey (1998) observed that teachers often assume that parents and schools share common philosophies and practices about children and learning. This assumption can lead to misunderstanding and even conflict as cultural models about education and learning bump up against each other. The same can be said about educational psychologists observing and attempting to explain student learning. The cultural beliefs and norms that guide researchers' thinking (theories) may keep researchers from pushing harder to identify the underlying mechanisms of behaviors. We too often assume that others are acting out of the same world view that we hold and explain their behaviors in ways that are consistent with our existing theories. Research on ethnic minority students can force a second look at a phenomenon. Who would have guessed that evoking a stereotype with the most subtle of cues would actually lower student performance? Identifying stereotype threat as a phenomenon is just the beginning; stereotype threat leads to new questions about the interaction between cognition and emotion. Identifying cultural models leads to questions about how beliefs, perceptions, attitudes, and expectations interact with each other to inform behavior. Cognitive psychologists have known for a long time that experts have trouble articulating the process they engage in to solve problems. Working with people who have different cultural perspectives provides opportunities for making familiar phenomena new and different and, in so doing, challenges researchers to consider more deeply the theories and models that explain those phenomena.

References

Alexander, K. L., Entwisle, D. R., & Bedinger, S. D. (1994). When expectations work: Race and socioeconomic differences in school performance. *Social Psychology Quarterly, 57*(4), 283–299.

Aronson, J., Fried, C. B., & Good, C. (2002). Reducing the effects of stereotype threat on African American college students by shaping theories of intelligence. *Journal of Experimental Social Psychology, 38*, 113–125.

Aronson, J., Lustina, M. J., Good, C., Keough, K., Steele, C. M., & Brown, J. (1999). When White men can't do math: Necessary and sufficient factors in stereotype threat. *Journal of Experimental Social Psychology, 35*, 29–46.

Arroyo, C. G., & Zigler, E. (1995). Racial identity, academic achievement, and the psychological well-being of economically disadvantaged adolescents. *Journal of Personality and Social Psychology, 69*(5), 902–914.

Arzubiaga, A., Rueda, R., & Monzo, L. (2002). Family matters related to the reading engagement of Latino children. *Journal of Latinos and Education, 1*(4), 231–243.

Azmitia, M., Cooper, C. R., Garcia, E. E., & Dunbar, N. D. (1996). The ecology of family guidance in low-income Mexican-American and European-American families. *Social Development, 5*(1), 1–23.

Bernal, M. E., Saenz, D. S., & Knight, G. P. (1991). Ethnic identity and adaptation of Mexican American youths in school settings. *Hispanic Journal of Behavioral Sciences, 13*(2), 135–154.

Bingham, G., Helling, M. K., & Okagaki, L. (2001, April). *Ethnic identity and school achievement in Native American students.* Presented at the Biennial Meeting of the Society for Research in Child Development, Minneapolis, MN.

Booth, A., & Dunn, J. F. (1996). *Family-school links: How do they affect educational outcomes?* Mahwah, NJ: Lawrence Erlbaum Associates.

Buriel, R., & De Ment, T. (1997). Immigration and sociocultural change in Mexican, Chinese, and Vietnamese American families. In A. Booth, A. C. Crouter, & N. Landale (Eds.), *Immigration and the family* (pp. 165–200). Mahweh, NJ: Lawrence Erlbaum Associates.

Carrasquillo, A. L. (1991). *Hispanic children and youth in the United States: A resource guide.* New York: Garland.

Casteel, C. (1997). Attitudes of African-American and Caucasian eighth grade students about praises, rewards, and punishments. *Elementary School Guidance and Counseling, 31,* 262–272.

Chao, R. K. (1994). Beyond parental control and authoritarian parenting style: Understanding Chinese parenting through the cultural notion of training. *Child Development, 65,* 1111–1119.

Chao, R. K. (2001). Extending research on the consequences of parenting style for Chinese Americans and European Americans. *Child Development, 72*(6), 1832–1843.

Chao, R., & Tseng, V. (2002). Parenting of Asians. In M. H. Bornstein (Ed.), *Handbook of parenting: Vol. 4. Social conditions and applied parenting* (2nd ed.,) (pp. 59–93). Mahwah, NJ: Lawrence Erlbaum Associates.

Chen, C., & Stevenson, H. W. (1995). Motivation and mathematics achievement: A comparative study of Asian-American, Caucasian-American, and East Asian high school students. *Child Development, 66,* 1215–1234.

Chiu, Y.-W., & Ring, J. M. (1998). Chinese and Vietnamese immigrant adolescents under pressure: Identifying stressors and interventions. *Professional Psychology: Research and Practice, 29*(5), 444–449.

Dee, T. S. (2004). Teachers, race, and student achievement in a randomized experiment. *Review of Economics and Statistics, 86*(1), 195–210.

Dee, T. S. (forthcoming). A teacher like me: Does race, ethnicity or gender matter? *American Economic Review.*

Delgado-Gaitan, C. (1992). School matters in the Mexican-American home: Socializing children to education. *American Educational Research Journal, 29,* 495–513.

Delgado-Gaitan, C. (1994). Socializing young children in Mexican-American families: An intergenerational perspective. In P. M. Greenfield & R. R. Cocking (Eds.), *Cross-cultural roots of minority child development* (pp. 55–86). Hillsdale, NJ: Lawrence Erlbaum Associates.

Dweck, C. S. (2002). Messages that motivate: How praise molds students' beliefs, motivation, and performance (in surprising ways). In J. Aronson (Ed.) *Improving academic achievement: Impact of psychological factors on education* (pp. 38–60). New York: Academic Press.

Eaton, M. j., & Dembo, M. H. (1997). Differences in the motivational beliefs of Asian American and non-Asian students. *Journal of Educational Psychology, 89*(3), 433–440.

Ferguson, R. F. (1998). Teachers' perceptions and expectations and the Black–White test score gap. In C. Jencks & M. Phillips (Eds.), *The Black–White test`score gap* (pp. 273–317). Washington, DC:The Brookings Institution.

Gallimore, R., & Goldenberg, C. (2001). Analyzing cultural models and settings to connect minority achievement and school improvement research. *Educational Psychologist, 36*(1), 45–56.

Gibson, M. A. (1993). The school performance of immigrant minorities: A comparative view. In E. Jacob and C. Jordan (Eds.) *Minority education: Anthropological perspectives* (pp. 113–128). Norwood, NJ: Ablex.

Gill, S., & Reynolds, A. J. (1999). Educational expectations and school achievement of urban African American children. *Journal of School Psychology, 37*(4), 403–424.

Goldenberg, C., Gallimore, R., Reese, L., & Garnier, H. (2001). Cause or effect? A longitudinal study of immigrant Latino parents' aspirations and expectations, and their children's school performance. *American Educational Research Journal, 38*(3), 547–582.

Gonzales, P. M., Blanton, H., & Williams, K. J. (2002). The effects of stereotype threat and double-minority status on the test performance of Latino women. *Personality and Social Psychology Bulletin, 28*(5), 659–670.

Good, C., Aronson, J., & Inzlicht, M. (2003). Improving adolescents' standardized test performance: An intervention to reduce the effects of stereotype threat. *Applied Developmental Psychology, 24,* 645–662.

Good, T., & Brophy, J. (2000). *Looking in classrooms* (8th ed.). New York: Longman.

Good, T. L., & Nichols, S. L. (2001). Expectancy effects in the classroom: A special focus on improving the reading performance of minority students in first-grade classrooms. *Educational Psychologist, 36*(2), 113–126.

Graham, S. (1994). Motivation in African Americans. *Review of Educational Research, 64,* 55–118.

Graham, S., Taylor, A. Z., & Hudley, C. (1998). Exploring achievement values among ethnic minority early adolescents. *Journal of Educational Psychology, 90*(4), 605–620.

Griffith, J. (2002). A multilevel analysis of the relation of school learning and social environments to minority achievement in public elementary schools. *Elementary School Journal,* *102*(5), 349-366.

Gutiérrez, K. D., & Rogoff, B. (2003). Cultural ways of learning: Individual traits or repertoires of practice. *Educational Researcher, 32*(5), 19-25.

Gutman, L. M., & McLoyd, V. C. (2000). Parents' management of their children's education within the home, at school, and in the community: An examination of African-American families living in poverty. *Urban Review, 32*(1), 2000.

Halle, T. G., Kurtz-Costes, B., & Mahoney, J. (1997). Family influences on school achievement in low-income, African American children. *Journal of Educational Psychology, 89*(3), 527-537.

Hao, L., & Bonstead-Bruns, M. (1998). Parent–child differences in educational expectations and the academic achievement of immigrant and native students. *Sociology of Education, 71*(3), 175-198.

Harry, B. (1992). *Cultural diversity, families, and the special education system: Communication and empowerment.* New York: Teachers College Press.

Harwood, R. L., Handwerker, W. P., Schoelmerich, A., & Leyendecker, B. (2001). Ethnic category labels, parental beliefs, and the contextualized individual: An exploration of the individualism-sociocentrism debate. *Parenting: Science and Practice, 1,* 217-236.

Harwood, R. L., Leyendecker, B., Carlson, V., Asencio, M., & Miller, A. (2002). Parenting among Latino families in the U.S. In M. H. Bornstein (Ed.) *Handbook of parenting*: Vol. 4. *Social conditions and applied parenting* (2nd ed., pp. 21-46). Mahwah, NJ: Lawrence Erlbaum Associates.

Helms, J. E., & Talleyrand, R. M. (1997). Race is not ethnicity. *American Psychologist, 52*(11), 1246-1247.

Hess, F. M., & Leal, D. L. (1997). Minority teachers, minority students, and college matriculation: A new look at the role-modeling hypothesis. *Policy Study Journal, 25,* 235-48.

Hieshima, J. A., & Schneider, B. (1994). Intergenerational effects on the cultural and cognitive socialization of third- and fourth-generation Japanese Americans. *Journal of Applied Developmental Psychology, 15,* 319-327.

Hill, N. E., & Craft, S. A. (2003). Parent–school involvement and school performance: Mediated pathways among socioeconomically comparable African American and Euro-American families. *Journal of Educational Psychology, 95*(1), 74-83.

Ho, D. Y. F. (1994). Cognitive socialization in Confucian heritage cultures. In P. M. Greenfield & R. R. Cocking (Eds.) *Cross-cultural roots of minority child development* (pp. 285-313). Hillsdale, NJ: Lawrence Erlbaum Associates.

Huntsinger, C. S., Jose, P. E., & Larson, S. L. (1998). Do parent practices to encourage academic competence influence the social adjustment of young European American and Chinese American children? *Developmental Psychology, 34,* 747-756.

Inzlicht, M., & Ben-Zeev, T. (2000). A threatening intellectual environment: Why females are susceptible to experiencing problem-solving deficits in the presence of males. *Psychological Science, 11,* 365-371.

Inzlicht, M., & Ben-Zeev, T. (2003). Do high-achieving female students underperform in private? The implications of threatening environments on intellectual processing. *Journal of Educational Psychology, 95*(4), 796-805.

Jimerson, S., Egeland, B., & Teo, A. (1999). A longitudinal study of achievement trajectories: Factors associated with change. *Journal of Educational Psychology, 91*(1), 116-126.

Joe, J. R., & Malach, R. S. (1992). Families with Native American roots. In E. W. Lynch & M. J. Hanson (Eds.) *Developing cross-cultural competence: A guide for working with young children and their families* (pp. 89-119). Baltimore: Paul H. Brookes.

Keefe, S. E., & Padilla, A. M. (1987). *Chicano ethnicity.* Albuquerque: University of New Mexico Press.

Kesner, J. E. (2000). Teacher characteristics and the quality of child-teacher relationships. *Journal of School Psychology, 28*(2), 133-149.

Kibria, N. (1993). *Family tightrope: The changing lives of Vietnamese Americans.* Princeton, NJ: Princeton University Press.

LaFromboise, T., Coleman, H. L. K., & Gerton, J. (1993). Psychological impact of biculturalism: Evidence and theory. *Psychological Bulletin, 114*(3), 395-412.

Lareau, A. (1996). Assessing parent involvement in schooling: A critical analysis. In A. Booth & J. F. Dunn (Eds.) *Family-school links: How do they affect educational outcomes?* (pp. 57-64). Mahwah, NJ: Lawrence Erlbaum Associates.

Lee, P. A., & Ying, Y. (2001). Asian American adolescents' academic achievement: A look behind the model minority image. *Journal of Human Behavior in the Social Environment, 3,* 35-48.

Leyens, J.-P., Desert, M., Croizet, J.-C., & Darcis, C. (2000). Stereotype threat: Are lower status and history of stigmatization preconditions of stereotype threat? *Personality and Social Psychology Bulletin, 26*(10), 1189-1199.

Luster, T., & McAdoo, H. (1996). Family and child influences on educational attainment: A secondary analysis of the High/Scope Perry Preschool data. *Developmental Psychology, 32*(1), 26-39.

McFarland, L. A., Lev-Arey, D. M., & Ziegert, J. C. (2003). An examination of stereotype threat in a motivational context. *Human Performance, 16*(3), 181-205.

McGillicuddy-De Lisi, A. V., and Sigel, I. E. (1995). Parental beliefs. In M. H. Bornstein (Ed.), *Handbook of parenting: Vol. 3. Status and social conditions of parenting* (pp. 333-358). Mahwah, NJ: Lawrence Erlbaum Associates.

Mickelson, R. (1990). The attitude-achievement paradox among black adolescents. *Sociology of Education, 63,* 44-61.

Miller, L. S. (1995). *An American imperative: Accelerating minority educational advancement.* New Haven, CT: Yale University Press.

Ogbu, J. U. (1992). Understanding cultural diversity and learning. *Educational Researcher, 21*(8), 5-14.

Okagaki, L., & Bojczyk, K. E. (2002). Perspectives on Asian American development. In G. C. Nagayama Hall & S. Okazaki (Eds.), *Asian American psychology: The science of lives in context* (pp. 67–104). Washington, DC: American Psychological Association.

Okagaki, L., & Frensch, P. A. (1998). Parenting and children's school achievement: A multi-ethnic perspective. *American Educational Research Journal, 35*(1), 123–144.

Okagaki, L., Frensch, P. A., & Dodson, N. E. (1996). Mexican-American children's perceptions of self and school achievement. *Hispanic Journal of Behavioral Sciences, 18,* 469–484.

Okagaki, L., Frensch, P.A., & Gordon, E.W. (1995). Encouraging school achievement in Mexican-American children. *Hispanic Journal of Behavioral Sciences, 17*(2), 160–179.

Okagaki, L., Helling, M. K., & Bingham, G. E. (in preparation). American Indian students' bicultural efficacy and schooling. Purdue University.

Okagaki, L., Izarraraz, L., & Bojczyk, K. (2003, April). *Latino adolescents' ethnic beliefs, orientation to school and emotional well-being.* Presented at the Society for Research in Child Development, Tampa, FL.

Okagaki, L., & Moore, D. K. (2000). Ethnic identity beliefs of young adults and their parents in families of Mexican descent. *Hispanic Journal of Behavioral Sciences, 22*(2), 139–162.

Osborne, J. W. (1997). Race and academic disidentification. *Journal of Educational Psychology, 89*(4), 728–735.

Phinney, J. S. (1990). Ethnic identity in adolescents and adults: Review of research. *Psychological Bulletin, 108,* 499–514.

Phinney, J. S. (1996). When we talk about American ethnic groups, what do we mean? *American Psychologist, 51,* 918–927.

Pigott, R. L., & Cowen, E. L. (2000). Teacher race, child race, racial congruence, and teacher ratings of children's school adjustment. *Journal of School Psychology, 38*(2), 177–196.

Ramsey, P. (1998). *Teaching and learning in a diverse world: Multicultural education for young children* (2nd ed.). New York: Teachers College Press.

Reese, L., & Gallimore, R. (2000). Immigrant Latinos' cultural model of literacy development: An evolving perspective on home-school discontinuities. *American Journal of Education, 108,* 103–134.

Reese, L., Garnier, H., Gallimore, R., & Goldenberg, C. (2000). Longitudinal analysis of the antecedents of middle-school english reading achievement of Spanish-speaking students. *American Educational Research Journal, 37*(3), 633–662.

Rogoff, B. (1990). *Apprenticeship in thinking: Cognitive development in social context.* New York: Oxford University Press.

Rosenthal, D. A., & Feldman, S. S. (1992). The relationships between parenting behaviour and ethnic identity in Chinese-American and Chinese-Australian adolescents. *International Journal of Psychology, 27*(1), 19–31.

Sackett, P. R., Hardison, C. M., & Cullen, M. J. (2004). On interpreting stereotype threat as accounting for African American-White differences on cognitive tests. *American Psychologist, 59*(1), 7–13.

Schmader, T., & Johns, M. (2003). Converging evidence that stereotype threat reduces working memory capacity. *Journal of Personality and Social Psychology, 85*(3), 440–452.

Shih, M., Pittinsky, T. L., & Ambady, N. (1999). Stereotype susceptibility: Identity salience and shifts in quantitative performance. *Psychological Science, 10*(1), 80–83.

Sigel, I. E., & McGillicuddy-De Lisi, A. V. (2002). In M. H. Bornstein (Ed.), *Handbook of parenting: Vol. 3. Status and social conditions of parenting* (pp. 333–358). Mahwah, NJ: Lawrence Erlbaum Associates.

Smith, J. L., & White, P. H. (2002). An examination of implicitly activated, explicitly activated, and nullified stereotypes on mathematical performance: It's not just a woman's issue. *Sex Roles, 47*(3/4), 179–191.

Spencer, S. J., Steele, C. M., & Quinn, D. M. (1999). Stereotype threat and women's math performance. *Journal of Experimental Social Psychology, 35,* 4–28.

Stangor, C., Carr, C., & Kiang, L. (1998). Activating stereotypes undermines task performance expectations. *Journal of Personality and Social Psychology, 75*(5), 1191–1197.

Steele, C. M. (1997). A threat in the air: How stereotypes shape intellectual identity and performance. *American Psychologist, 52,* 613–629.

Steele, C. M., & Aronson, J. (1995). Stereotype threat and the intellectual test performance of African Americans. *Journal of Personality and Social Psychology, 69*(5), 797–811.

Steinberg, L., Dornbusch, S. M., & Brown, B. B. (1992). Ethnic differences in adolescent achievement: An ecological perspective. *American Psychologist, 47*(6), 723–729.

Stevenson, H. W., Chen, C., & Uttal, D. H. (1990). Beliefs and achievement: A study of Black, White, and Hispanic children. *Child Development, 61,* 508–523.

Suarez-Orozco, M. M. (1993). "Becoming somebody": Central American immigrants in U.S. inner-city schools. In E. Jacob and C. Jordan (Eds.). Minority Education: Anthropological Perspectives (129–143). Norwood, NJ: Ablex Publishing Corp.

Sue, S., & Okazaki, S. (1990). Asian-American educational achievement: A phenomenon in search of an explanation. *American Psychologist, 45*(8), 913–920.

Tajfel, H. (1981). *Human groups and social categories: Studies in social psychology.* Cambridge, UK: Cambridge University Press.

Taylor, R. D., Casten, R., Flickinger, S. M., Roberts, D., & Fulmore, C. D. (1994). Explaining the school performance of African-American adolescents. *Journal of Research on Adolescence, 4*(1), 21–44.

Torres, V. (2004). The diversity among us: Puerto Ricans, Cuban Americans, Caribbean Americans, and Central and South Americans. *New Directions for Student Services, 105,* 5–16.

U.S. Census Bureau (1993a). *We the American... Hispanics.* Washington, DC: Author.

U.S. Census Bureau (1993b). *We the... First Americans* Washington, DC: Author.

U.S. Census Bureau (1993c). *We the Americans: Asians.* Washington, DC: Author.

U.S. Census Bureau. (2001a). *The Hispanic population in the United States: Population characteristics,* by Melissa Therrien and Roberto R. Ramirez. U.S. Department of Commerce,

Economics and Statistics Administration. Washington, DC: Author.

U.S. Census Bureau (2001b). *The Hispanic population: Census 2000 brief* by Betsy Güzmán. U.S. Department of Commerce. Washington, DC: Author.

U.S. Census Bureau (2003). *School enrollment: 2000.* Census 2000 brief by Jennifer Cheeseman Day with Amie Jamieson. Washington, DC: Author.

U.S. Census Bureau (2004). *Educational attainment in the United States: 2003*, Current Population Reports by Nicole Stoops. Washington, DC: Author.

U.S. Department of Education, National Center for Education Statistics (2000). *America's kindergarteners*, NCES 2000-070, by Kristin Denton & Elvira Germino-Hausekn. Project Officer, Jerry West. Washington, DC: Author.

U.S. Department of Education, National Center for Education Statistics (2001a). *English literacy and language minorities in the United States*, NCES 2001-464, by Elizabeth Greenberg, Reynaldo F. Macias, David Rhodes, and Tse Chan. Washington, DC: Author.

U.S. Department of Education, National Center for Education Statistics (2001b). *Homeschooling in the United States: 1999* (NCES 2001-033) by Stacey Bielick, Kathryn Chandler, and Stephen P. Broughman. U.S. Department of Education. Washington, DC: National Center for Education Statistics.

U.S. Department of Education, National Center for Education Statistics. (2003a). *Status and trends in the education of Hispanics* (NCES 2003-008), by Charmaine Llagas. Project Officer: Thomas. D. Snyder. U.S. Department of Education. Washington, DC: National Center for Education Statistics.

U.S. Department of Education, National Center for Education Statistics. (2003b). *Status and trends in the education of Blacks* (NCES 2003-034), by Kathryn Hoffman & Charmaine Llagas. Project Officer: Thomas D. Snyder. U.S. Department of Education. Washington, DC: National Center for Education Statistics.

U.S. Department of Education, National Center for Education Statistics (2003c). *The nation's report card: Mathematics highlights 2003*. Washington, DC: Author.

U.S. Department of Education, National Center for Education Statistics (2003d). *The nation's report card: Reading highlights 2003*. Washington, DC: Author.

U.S. Department of Education, National Center for Education Statistics (2004). *Public school student, staff, and graduate counts by state: School year 2001–02*, NCES 2003-358R, by Beth Aronstamm Young. Washington, DC: Author.

Walton, G. M., & Cohen, G. L. (2003). Stereotype life. *Journal of Experimental Social Psychology, 39*(5), 456–467.

Wentzel, K. (1997). Student motivation in middle school: The role of perceived pedagogical caring. *Journal of Educational Psychology, 89*, 411–419.

Ying, Y., Lee, P. A., & Tsai, J. L. (2000). Cultural orientation and racial discrimination: Predictors of coherence in Chinese American young adults. *Journal of Community Psychology, 28*, 427–442.

ASSESSING GENDER GAPS IN LEARNING AND ACADEMIC ACHIEVEMENT

Diane F. Halpern
Claremont McKenna College

The difference between male and female is something that everybody knows and nobody knows.

— John Money (1987, p. 13)

The fact that many standardized indicators of learning from preschool through old age show average differences between boys and girls (and later, between men and women) is the proverbial "elephant in the room" in many discussions of student achievement. No one wants to acknowledge that these group differences exist because in many ways they run counter to core beliefs about equality and justice, not just in opportunity but in outcomes. Emotions run high when it is simply mentioned that many measures of academic achievement show average differences for girls and boys. In many academic circles, there is something like an educational equivalent to the United States' military policy on gays and lesbians: Don't ask and don't tell. Essentially, some psychologists and educators believe that even writing about these differences is harmful because it creates self-fulfilling prophecies as parents, teachers, and children learn about differences and then act in ways that cause them to increase. Others object to the study of educational achievement differences between boys and girls because there is considerable overlap in the distributions of scores and believe it is misleading to talk about group differences when distributions overlap (e.g., Fausto-Sterling, 1992). Of course, it is almost impossible to think of meaningful studies where distributions do not have some overlap, so this criticism seems disingenuous or naïve, but this objection is heard frequently enough that it needs to be addressed for those

who do not understand principles of distributions, statistically significant differences, practically significant differences, and so on.

Group differences in educational outcomes, and by inference in learning abilities and intelligence, are hot-button topics, and they should be, as long as the heat they are generating is also shedding light on the complex array of variables that contribute to our understanding of how people learn and helping us find ways to enhance learning. To the many critics who object to any study or discussion of sex differences in cognitive abilities or academic achievement, I ask this question: "What are the alternatives to comparing how girls and boys learn and their (average) academic achievement?" Everyone could pretend that there are no group differences, an option that will never narrow the achievement gap or advance our understanding of individual differences in learning. We (the general public and professionals together) could insist on only using tests that are written so that they never show any group differences, thereby ensuring that we are always testing at the lowest levels, or at least losing potentially important and interesting information about testing or learning or both—again, not an appealing strategy because educators and psychologists need to understand why there are group differences if we strive to raise everyone to as high a level of achievement as possible.

The question addressed in this chapter is not whether girls and boys are similar or different in their cognitive abilities or academic achievement, because we already know that they are both similar and different in many complex ways. Instead, the focus is on males and females, how they are similar and different, when similarities and differences are found, and by how much, and perhaps most importantly, why similarities and differences emerge at different times in the life span and as a function of different formats used to assess learning.

WINNERS AND LOSERS ON THE EDUCATIONAL BATTLEFIELDS

The topic of differences between boys and girls in how and how well they learn is fraught with political minefields that are impossible to avoid. The May 26, 2003, cover of *Business Week* on "The New Gender Gap" provided a long list of the ways in which boys and men are trailing girls and women in school measures of academic achievement and in leadership positions. This list outraged many who saw the gap from the other side as an unbridgeable chasm—those who still see a male advantage on most high-stakes tests that are used for admissions for college and postgraduate school and who read the statistics showing that women still earn considerably less than comparably educated men. There is a great flurry of renewed interest on the part of the general public every time the media reports what psychologists and educators already know about cognitive and academic sex differences. Comparisons about the relative successes and failures of males and females are complicated because they are uneven and difficult to understand.

In this chapter, I describe the major areas of controversy and then weigh the evidence for a variety of conclusions and their implications for education. It is likely that readers will not agree with all of the conclusions that I make, because of the hundreds of decision points that led to each conclusion and the necessity of being highly selective in my choice of references in a chapter-length review. This is a highly politicized topic, so I have tried to stay close to the data and explain my reasoning. New studies are being published at a high rate, so it is also likely that new conclusions may be warranted as new information becomes available. More complete summaries can be found in Halpern (2000, 2002, 2004).

There can be no doubt that being male or female is a central component to everyone's identity, and that it is a primary way of categorizing people into groups. Even though it may appear that girls and boys in the same family have similar life experiences, and "women's liberation" and civil rights laws put an end to differential treatment of boys and girls in the United States and many other countries decades ago (there are also many countries that still have different laws for girls and women and boys and men), data on the demand for sons in the United States

provide a profound picture of parental preferences for sons. Consider, for example, that data show that for couples who have an ultrasound test during pregnancy, those having a boy are more likely to be married at delivery. In families with at least two children, the probability of having another child is significantly higher when they are all girls than when they are all boys. Finally, parents with girls are significantly more likely to be divorced, divorced fathers are more likely to have custody of their child if it is a boy, and mothers of girls are more likely to have never been married (Dahl & Moretti, 2004). Data like these are tangible reminders that girls and boys have profoundly different meanings in family life and beyond.

Data on the preference for boys shows that boys and girls do not receive the same "treatment" as they progress through life, regardless of what we are studying. Researchers will often claim that all children were treated the same or took the same pattern of courses as a way of dismissing biasing effects caused by nuisance factors in a study, such as the possibility that boys and girls were treated differently or had different life experiences. As educators and psychologists, we can hypothesize about the ways these preferences are played out in the everyday lives of real families and children in the multiple contexts where they learn, and we can exert some control over a limited number of variables, but we cannot eliminate differential "treatment" from most research designs.

Defining Terms

Almost everything about group/individual differences/ similarities in cognition is emotional. These are polarizing and often politicized topics, so it is not surprising that the language that is used in writing and talking about this topic is scrutinized for bias. There is concern that the term *differences* is biasing and that the more neutral *comparison* should be used instead. This is a reasonable alternative, but our statistical methods only permit rejection of the null hypothesis, and it is only by multiple failures to reject the null hypothesis (with sufficient power and good research designs) that we can reach other conclusions. Similarities are the default assumption in research, so the idea that differences need to have a theoretical basis and strong data are the reasons I use the term *differences*, although often a conclusion is that there are areas where there are no differences.

Some authors prefer to use the term *gender* when referring to female and male differences that are social in origin and *sex* when referring to differences that are biological in origin. In keeping with the psychobiosocial model that is advocated in this paper and the belief that these two types of influences are interdependent and cannot be separated, only one term is used in this chapter. *Sex* is used without reference to the origin of any observed differences or similarities and is not meant to imply a preference for biological explanations. These terms are often used inconsistently in the literature.

I use the term *psychobiosocial* to refer to the mutual influences of psychological, social, and biological variables on each other. Many authors use *biopsychosocial* to emphasize that biology is primary in that human are primarily biological, or biological first in their developmental sequence. Readers should consider these to be the same term with no intended difference in meaning when I use them in this chapter, but they may or may not have nuanced differences in other contexts.

Although I will be using *cognitive abilities* and *academic achievement* together, they are closely related terms that do not have the same meaning. An ability refers to "being able" and it is measured with a test, not surprisingly called an ability test. Cognition refers to thinking, remembering, making decisions, reasoning, and other "higher thought processes." A cognitive ability test attempts to assess the likelihood of being able to succeed at certain tasks in the future, if the person received proper instruction and if she or he were motivated to learn and demonstrate the skills needed to perform the task. A low score on a mathematical ability test, for example, is meant to imply that the individual is less able to learn certain advanced concepts such as calculus or other higher mathematics than someone obtaining a higher score. It can be loosely thought of as the ability to benefit from instruction in a certain area. By contrast, an achievement test is a test of what an individual has already achieved or learned. We test mathematical ability by presenting individuals with mathematical problems to solve. Wouldn't someone who had taken more or better mathematical courses be expected to answer more questions correctly than someone with a poorer mathematical education background? In other words, aren't we also measuring achievement? To some extent, we are always measuring achievement whenever we try to measure ability. For that reason, I will usually present these terms together, and for most purposes in this chapter, the distinction is not critical, although in other contexts it can be.

COGNITIVE AREAS WHERE LARGEST DIFFERENCES ARE FOUND

There is a contemporary and acrimonious debate over who the winners and losers are in the war of the sexes. This is an unfortunate and unproductive debate because there are cognitive areas in which girls, on average, excel, and cognitive areas in which boys, on average, excel. There is no evidence for a smarter sex. Standardized intelligence tests were written to show no average overall difference between females and males, so questions that tended, on average, to be answered more often by females or males were either eliminated or balanced with questions that were answered equally more often by the other sex. So, the question of whether males or females are the smarter sex cannot be answered with traditional (multiscale) intelligence tests.

Jensen (1998), an educational psychologist who is well known for his controversial work on racial differences in intelligence, took a different approach to the question of sex differences in intelligence. He reviewed several cognitive/achievement tests that, unlike traditional tests of intelligence, were not written to yield equal scores for females and males. He concluded that there are no overall differences in intelligence, but he did find sex differences on several of the individual tests. It is important to note that there are many cognitive tests and academic indicators that show *no* difference in the academic achievement/cognitive ability of males and females, but there are also measures that show large and consistent differences favoring females and still others that show large and consistent differences favoring males. The emerging picture of sex-related cognitive abilities and academic achievement is complex, but there are consistencies across time and place that suggest that the differences are systematic and not due to random variance. One approach to understanding these differences is to think about them in terms of cognitive processes used in thinking instead of the academic areas that are tested in schools. An example should help to clarify the distinction. It is often reported that girls outperform boys on computational tasks in arithmetic, but boys outperform girls in concept/application tasks in mathematics (e.g., Seong, Bauer, & Sullivan, 1998). Thus, there are two different sorts of outcomes for different types of quantitative ability/achievement. It may be that the superior performance of girls in computational arithmetic is just another example of the usual finding that girls have better retrieval of information from memory, which includes arithmetic facts. When considered from a cognitive process model, these results are easier to interpret and fit in a meaningful framework that can advance our understanding of mathematical problem solving.

We Know What We Test

Every school curriculum includes reading, writing, arithmetic, and more advanced topics in mathematics, science, and so on. In the United States, new federal legislation known as "No Child Left Behind" requires that all students be tested in reading and mathematics in third through eighth grade. The intent is laudable—to diagnose problems in learning so they can be remediated before children fall too far behind and to provide information to teachers and schools that can be used to improve teaching and learning. One outcome relevant to the study of cognitive sex differences is the additional attention that will be created with regard to differences between boys and girls in different academic areas in different grades. The testing will not create these differences, but it will make them more visible because the additional testing, like front-page media stories about facts that we already know, will force more teachers and administrators to pay attention to these differences (Halpern, 2002).

DEVELOPMENTAL TRAJECTORIES

Human development is an uneven process, so it is not surprising that different aspects of cognition develop throughout the life span at different rates, with considerable individual variability. In the realm of physical development, there are several uneven "spurts" of height and weight that follow different trajectories for boys and girls. Cognitive development is not as easy to track and document as height and weight, but we have no reason to believe that it progresses any more smoothly.

Boys develop over a longer period of time (into their early 20s), and girls reach their full adult height at an earlier age than boys do. Girls also experience puberty at an earlier age than boys. (Over the last 100 years, the age at which girls reach menarche has been steadily declining.) Sex differences in development continue throughout the life span with women living an average of 7 years longer than men (in industrialized countries). Thus, the sexes do not develop at the same biological rate, and there is evidence that they do not develop at the same cognitive rate either, with earlier development more likely going to the girls, as evidenced by better early reading skills.

In the United States, boys often start kindergarten later than girls in the belief that boys may need an additional year before they are ready for school. The finding that boys are more likely to repeat a grade in elementary school suggests that many are not ready behaviorally for school, but we do not know if starting school a year later would have made a difference (U.S. Department of Education, 1995). Although professional opinion about the practice of having boys start school at an older age is mixed, there are data showing that boys who are born in the last 2 months of the academic year, and thus are among the youngest in their grade, are referred for learning and behavior problems more often than older boys in

their grade (De Cos, 1997; DeMeis & Stearns, 1992). The same relationship was not found for girls.

It is also misleading to think about cognitive development as a single variable that moves along anything like a lone trajectory. Different cognitive abilities develop at different rates, and there are average between-sex differences in the rates of development for many cognitive abilities. Differences also depend on the who, when, and how of measurement. The "who" is the portion of the ability spectrum that is sampled. Males are more variable in their cognitive performance than females, which means that there are more boys and men at both the low and high ends of the abilities distributions. In other words, for most people in the middle range of abilities, differences between females and males are not as great as they are for very low-ability and very high-ability individuals (De Lisi & McGillicuddy-De Lisi, 2002; Hedges & Nowell, 1995).

The "when" refers to when in the life span, but also, to a lesser extent, "when" refers to time-of-day variations caused by diurnal variations that influence performance and monthly fluctuations in hormones that are discussed briefly later. Daily and monthly variations are slight and are usually assessed with sensitive tests such as reaction time measures (Halpern & Tan, 2001). These time-of-day differences are also developmental across the life span and thus vary with timing of puberty and other markers of physical aging.

The "how" refers to the way in which learning and achievement are assessed, which turns out to be a complicated and often overlooked variable. Many reviewers concluded that the size of the female advantage in verbal abilities is small to nonexistent, but in fact, it is quite large when it is assessed with tests of writing instead of other measures (U.S. Department of Education, 1997a). Those researchers who concluded that differences in "verbal abilities" are small used a biased subset of "verbal tasks" to generalize to all verbal tasks. In fact, the most accurate conclusion would be that the differences are virtually nonexistent for many verbal tasks, moderate for some, and large to very large for some tests of verbal memory and writing. It is misleading to lump together heterogeneous tests that use words and call them "verbal" tests without any underlying theory as to how people use these tasks or why they might depend on the same brain substrate, for example. When questions require a written response instead of multiple-choice or another format, there is a group advantage for girls and women. A writing test was added to the PSAT because females score higher on writing tests, and the addition of this test has already increased the number of females who will be receiving prestigious merit scholarships. The "how" also refers to differences between grades in school and standardized assessments.

Girls and women get higher grades in school, including in those academic areas where they usually get lower average scores on aptitude-type tests but do not when the tests closely resemble material that was taught in school (Dwyer & Johnson, 1997; National Center for Education Statistics, 2004; Voyer, 1996).

Development of the Ability to Pay Attention

School success and learning in school contexts depends in part on the ability to stay focused on a task for relatively long periods of time—that is, to pay attention. Attention has "work-like" qualities and "psychic energy" costs, which are connoted with the idea that individuals "pay" for attentiveness from a limited supply of attentional resources. It is well known that the ratio of males to females diagnosed with attention deficit disorder/hyperactivity disorder ranges between 4:1 and 9:1, depending on the setting where the diagnosis is made. In a study of normal schoolchildren in grades 3, 6, and 9, researchers tested the hypothesis that boys might show more difficulty with some aspects of attention that could be responsible for some of the cognitive sex differences.

Although there is a large research literature on the sex difference in attention in attention deficit disorder, research on sex differences in attention among average or "normal" children and adults is not as well studied. In one of the few studies on the "average" population, Warrick and Naglieri (1993) assessed four different components of attention—planning, attention, simultaneous, and successive. Overall, girls were better at attending than boys, with the grade effect significant only at third grade. Girls were better than boys at planning and attention, but not on simultaneous or successive measures. The large difference in planning is especially interesting because planning processes could be improved through instruction that teaches students to be more aware of their cognitive activities. Other studies have also found sex differences in attention, all favoring girls, which suggests that this is an area that would benefit from additional research as well as additional applied work with those boys (and girls) who would benefit from instructional strategies to help them act and think more in terms of planning.

Reading and Writing

The ability to learn and use language shows a female advantage within the first 2 years of life (e.g., Huttenlocher, Haight, Bryk, Seltzer, & Lyons, 1991). There are significant sex differences in the rate of vocabulary growth during the toddler years. On average, there is a 13-word difference in vocabulary size between girls and boys at 16 months of age, which grows to a 51-word difference at 20 months and a 115-word difference at 24 months (Huttenlocher et al., 1991). These researchers found that the differential rate in vocabulary growth was unrelated to how much mothers spoke to their children—mothers spoke as much to their boy babies as to their girl babies. They concluded that "gender differences in early vocabulary growth seem to reflect early capacity differences" (p. 245). For the most part, girls maintain this advantage into adulthood, although it is likely that the size of the between-sex difference varies over the life span; however, there are not enough good data to permit comparisons of the size of the between-sex difference in language learning and usage across ages. Gleason and Ely (2002), in a review of gender differences in language development, conclude that "most sweeping claims about gender differences in the language of adults are overstated" (p. 148). Their understated conclusion pertains to adults, where admittedly there are few standardized tests of verbal memory or writing with large samples. Compare their conclusion to the meta-analytic review of the research literature by Hedges and Nowell (1995), who reported that "the large sex differences in writing . . . are alarming" (p. 41). The advantage for girls on tests of writing is large and robust.

An important, large, and real sex difference is in the frequency and severity of reading disabilities. Like all "differences" research, this is not a popular topic, and periodically studies have been highly publicized touting the message that teachers tended to recognize reading disabilities more often in boys than in girls because boys were more unruly in general, so their problems attracted more attention. Carefully controlled research now clearly shows that boys are at least twice as likely as girls to have dyslexia, a severe reading disability, and much more likely than girls to have milder forms of reading disabilities (Rutter et al., 2004).

Arithmetic and Mathematics

Some, but not all, quantitative tasks also show large and consistent sex differences. Tests of mathematical ability show advantages for girls in the early primary school years when mathematics consists of computational knowledge and speed, then usually show little or no sex difference through the rest of the primary school years, and then show a male advantage when the mathematical concepts are more spatial in nature, such as geometry and topology, which are taught in the higher secondary school grades. But these data need to be interpreted with caution, because quantity of ability/achievement is measured in early school years with tests that closely mirror what is learned in school—the type of test that usually shows female superiority (Gallagher, Levin, & Cahalan, 2002). It is when testing uses novel solutions that males pull ahead, so it is hard to separate content (arithmetic), developmental stage (early elementary school), and assessment type (assessed with materials very similar to ones used during learning).

Royer, Tronsly, Chan, Jackson, & Marchant (1999) proposed that more rapid retrieval of math facts by boys was the key to their better overall performance in higher math courses because it sped up solution times and thereby reduced the load on working memory. Because boys usually have more opportunities to practice retrieval of math facts in out-of-school contexts, perhaps in keeping score at sports or other games, their performance would be more variable than girls' performance, and this advantage would become increasingly important over time as mathematical problems required more steps and greater demands on working memory. This is an interesting hypothesis, except that many types of advanced mathematics where males excel, such as geometry, do not rely heavily on the retrieval of math facts, and it is the execution of math subroutines that becomes increasingly important as mathematics becomes progressively complex (Geary, 1999). In addition, it is girls who have superior retrieval from memory, in general and during early elementary school years. Royer and his colleagues do make an important point about automatizing lower levels of mathematics as children advance through the curriculum so that they can work more quickly, which is good advice for instructional design for all learners.

Highly publicized studies of mathematically precocious youth consistently show that the ratio of boys to girls steadily increases as the selectivity of the sample increases, with more than 12 males for every female in the upper 0.1% of the SAT-M distribution, a test that is well known to virtually every U.S. college student (Feingold, 1992). Because college-bound male and female seniors take similar patterns of math courses, this is a fact that cannot be explained by differential course-taking patterns in high school.

The Sciences

A third broad curricular area that is tested and monitored is the sciences, which are usually considered to be more variable in content than the other basic content areas. The sciences are broken into multiple subcategories of biological or life sciences and physical sciences, and then into units that correspond to courses that include biology, chemistry, physics, and sometimes psychology or ecology and others. The conclusions presented here about girls and boys and science learning come from the Third International Mathematics and Science Study (TIMSS; U.S. Department of Education, 1997b), which is based on data from students in 41 countries in fourth and eighth grades and in the final year of secondary school. The TIMSS provides a good overview of findings because it involves children in multiple grades in many countries: TIMSS data show that gender differences widen at the upper grades, and by the last year of secondary school, males have significantly higher achievement than females in both math and science in almost every country tested. Males outperform females in earth science, physics, and chemistry, but not in life science or environmental science. These are interesting findings because they favor males, especially in light of the success that girls are achieving in high school, their higher college-going rate in many of the same countries, and better grades in high school in the same subjects. How can we reconcile these two types of data? Are the standardized test scores telling us something different from the classroom assessments? It may be that at least some of the differences in the sciences and in mathematics can be understood by looking at differences in a noncurricular topic that is essential for success in math and science—visuospatial skills.

VISUOSPATIAL SKILLS

One of the largest sex differences is found on cognitive tasks that do not correspond directly to any traditional curricular topic, although many people believe that they should. These tasks are visuospatial skills and abilities (Shea, Lubinski, & Benbow, 2001). Boys have a large and consistent advantage, beginning early in life, in using spatial information. Very large sex differences favoring boys and men are found on tests that require maintaining and transforming a visuospatial image (e.g., a map or visual image of a molecular shape; Parsons et al., 2003). These differences are found in preschool, which is probably the earliest age at which they can be measured. Other tests of visuospatial ability, such as finding one figure embedded in the contours of another figure, show smaller sex differences favoring boys and men.

Because motor tasks always involve movement through space, they always have a visuospatial component. In earlier studies, the size of this effect was underestimated because most researchers failed to measure some of the larger components, such as those that involve movement and judgments about movement. In one such task, participants might be seated at a computer terminal and watch a "ball" move across the screen. As the ball approaches, midway across the screen, the ball moves "behind" a "wall." The task for the participant is to press a key at the moment the ball is expected to emerge from the other edge of the "wall," thus requiring the participant to make velocity judgments about the moving ball. This is the sort of task that shows very large effect sizes favoring males. Effects are even larger when three-dimensional displays are used (Law, Pellegrino, & Hunt, 1993; Linn & Petersen, 1985, 1986; Robert, 1990).

Males also excel at targeting tasks such as the ability to accurately hit a target with a ball or other object or to intercept a projectile. These differences do not seem to be due to differences in physique or accounted for by previous practice (although I do not understand how prior practice can ever be eliminated in tasks like these). Girls and women, on the other hand (literally), excel in fine motor tasks, such as rapidly moving pegs on a peg board in a limited amount of time. Data on gross and fine motor movement are reviewed in Kimura (1999). Although the effect sizes with visuospatial tasks are large, they are amenable to training, and most people show good improvement when they have educational interventions to improve their visuospatial skills (Newcombe, Mathason, & Terlecki, 2002).

Cognitive Components of Visuospatial Skills

Visuospatial skills are important in many kinds of mathematics, such as geometry and topology, and in the sciences, as when imagining a three-dimensional molecule or the way organs are situated in a living organism. Effect sizes favoring males are especially large for mental rotation (holding an image in working memory while rotating it) and targeting. How could cognitive processes like these be used in everyday thinking tasks, and could they be responsible for a portion of the sex differences found in math, science, reading, and writing?

In thinking about the component processes involved in visuospatial information processing, consider, for example, the many different combinations of retrieval from long-term memory, the generation, maintenance, transformation, and scanning of images, and the interplay among verbal, spatial, and pictorial cognitive codes that are needed to answer the following questions or perform the following tasks:

• Does the capital letter "t" have curved lines? The cognitive processes used in answering this question require the retrieval of information from long-term memory, the transformation of information about a letter from a verbal code to a spatial code, the generation of an image of the shape of the letter, a scan of the shape "looking for" curved lines, and then the execution of the appropriate response (e.g., answering "no").

• Does a novel, irregular shape that was just shown have five sides? The cognitive processes for this task would not require retrieval from long-term memory, but would depend instead on the ability to maintain a shape in a visuospatial working memory long enough to scan its contours, count the sides, and execute a response.

• When will a ball that is seen moving across a computer screen "collide" with a line on the screen? In order to respond to a question like this one, judgments about the speed of the ball and its distance from the line need to be made, and a response has to be timed to correspond to this calculation.

• What would a block look like when viewed from another angle? This is a perspective-taking task, which requires the ability to generate an image using knowledge about angles and "lines of sight" when objects are viewed from a different perspective.

• Draw a line to indicate where the water line will be in a tilted glass that is half full of water. This is the famous "Water Level Task" devised by the developmental psychologist Jean Piaget. In order to perform this task, knowledge that water remains horizontal regardless of the tilt of a glass must be retrieved from long-term memory, and then an approximately horizontal line must be drawn in the contours of the glass, ignoring the tilt cues that form the contours of the glass.

• Find your way to a distant location using a map or find your way back from a distant place without a map. Way-finding tasks vary depending on whether they allow the use of a map, verbal directions, or memory of routes that were previously traversed.

• If a frog can climb 2 feet every hour, but slides back down 1 foot for every 2 feet it climbs, how long will it take the frog to climb out of a well that is 5 feet deep? This word problem requires the ability to derive a visuospatial representation from text, then image the frog's progress up the well while converting progress to time. A detailed pictorial image of the frog is not useful, but a schematic representation is.

• After viewing an array of objects at various locations, other arrays are presented. Which objects were in the first array and where were they located? This task requires visuospatial memory for objects and their locations. The nature of the memory system involved depends on the length of the interval between the two arrays—visuospatial working memory if the interval is less than approximately one minute; a longer-term memory for longer intervals. (This list of tasks appears in Halpern & Collaer, in press.)

Paper-and-Pencil or Computerized Tasks That Show Sex Differences

What is surprising about this diverse set of visuospatial tasks is that when sex differences are found, they favor males. The only exception is the last example, which requires memory for objects and their location. The effect sizes for tasks that require the generation of an image vary depending on the complexity of the image to be generated and the nature of the task, and range between 0.63 and 0.77 standard deviations (Loring-Meier & Halpern, 1999). Mental rotation tasks that require the maintenance of three-dimensional figural information in working memory while simultaneously transforming information show very large sex differences, somewhere between .9 to 1.0 standard deviations (Masters, 1998; Masters & Sanders, 1993). Differences that are probably as large as these or even larger are found in spatiotemporal tasks (judgments about moving objects), but there are not enough studies with spatiotemporal tasks to allow a reliable estimate of the effect size (Law et al., 1993). By most standards, these are very large effect sizes—among the largest in psychology (not counting comparisons such as the old and the young on running speed or trivial research where huge effects are not meaningful).

GRADES, STANDARDIZED TESTING, AND HIGH-STAKES POLITICS

As psychologists and educators, our goal (as I see it) is to understand how people learn, which includes studying group and individual differences in learning and cognition, so that we can find ways to enhance teaching and learning. The purpose of our research is to help learners achieve at the highest possible level while honoring individual talents, interests, and abilities. Assessment and theory are essential to achieving these goals, but our assessments and theories are always embedded in a sociohistorical context, which guides the research questions we ask, how and whom we measure, and how we interpret results. Science is never value-free, but it is our best method for finding answers to highly politicized questions. In general, girls get higher grades in school. Women comprise a substantial majority of college enrollments in the United States and many other countries. (American women have received more college degrees than men every year since 1982, with the gap widening every year; among women between 25 and 34 years old, 33 percent have completed college compared to 29 percent of men). Despite these "successes," women score significantly lower on many (not all) standardized tests of science and mathematics when the tests are not closely related to material that has been taught in school. This discrepancy has led to calls of bias from just about every portion of the political spectrum.

Are teachers biased against boys? Are standardized tests biased against girls? How can we understand these discrepancies? What is fair assessment? These are not questions that can be answered fully in a single chapter, but here are some main points to consider before jumping on the "everything is biased" bandwagon.

Grades–Testing Disparities

On average, boys are more disruptive in school and do seem to have a more difficult time in school. Boys are more likely to repeat a grade or to show up for school unprepared, and are more likely to experience violent victimization than girls (U.S. Department of Education, 1995). Sitting still for long periods of time, turning in neatly done homework, and other stereotypes of what school is like (which may or may not correspond to what school is really like) are not as compatible with the male gender role stereotype as they are with the female gender role stereotype. In addition, the large research literature that shows a large effect size favoring girls early in elementary school in writing tasks would also suggest that girls would get better grades in school in most subjects, if writing were involved in assessing knowledge (Hedges & Nowell, 1995). If so, would the clear expression of knowledge in written prose be considered a bias?

The fact that girls are succeeding at higher rates than boys in school on objective measures makes it difficult to argue that schools are biased against girls, but some have offered exactly that argument as an explanation of the poorer results for girls on standardized examinations. These are emotional topics, and questions about qualitative aspects of classroom interactions such as whether teachers, on average, call on boys more often (perhaps because they volunteer answers more often), wait longer for boys to answer questions before moving on to someone else, offer boys more praise, or call boys by their names more often than girls have been raised as the reasons for differences in school and other academic success in the various disputes over whether "Schools Shortchange Girls" (American Association of University Women, 1992) or "Schools Shortchange Boys" (Sommers, 2000).

Stereotype Threat

Another possibility is that female performance on standardized tests is being depressed relative to what it should be, either because the test is biased against females in some way or because something else in the testing situation is operating against females. One area of research has shown the importance of the unconscious effects of stereotypes on thought and performance, called *stereotype threat*, which is the idea that if students are being assessed in an area where there is a negative stereotype about their group's ability, an unconscious "threat" will be activated and that threat will decrease performance (Steele, 1997). There is a large and old literature in psychology and education on self-fulfilling prophecies showing that experimenter or teacher expectations can unconsciously influence how people respond to situations (Rosenthal, 1992). Medical researchers are well aware of these types of effects, which is why double-blind, placebo-controlled, crossover studies are the "gold standard" for medical research.

Recent work by Steele and others has extended these principles to explain how beliefs about the cognitive abilities of different groups can cause or contribute to group differences on tests of cognitive abilities. The idea is that by making the fact that the test taker is female or male salient at the time a cognitive test is being administered, commonly held beliefs about the performance of females or males are activated. Test takers are "threatened" by these beliefs out of the concern that they will conform to their group's negative stereotype. According to this theory, stereotype threat will only affect test performance when the group membership is made salient, the test that is being taken is relevant to one's group (e.g., the stereotype that females are not as good in mathematics as males), test performance is important to the individuals taking the test, and the test is at a level of difficulty that the additional burden of defending against a perceived threat would cause a performance decrement.

In an interesting study with Asian-American women, the stereotype that Asians are good at mathematics was pitted against the stereotype that women are not good at mathematics. The Asian-American women performed relatively better on an advanced test of mathematics when the positive stereotype was salient compared with the condition when the negative stereotype was made salient (Shih, Pittinsky, & Ambady, 1999). The notion of stereotype threat has been very popular, and it has received some good confirmation in the research literature. For example, one possibility is that by priming the self-relevant negative stereotype, attentional capacity is reduced, causing working memory capacity to suffer. Schmader and Johns (2003) hypothesized that if it were necessary to keep negative thoughts suppressed (e.g., "I will not fail"), then there would be less capacity left over for other cognitive tasks, which could be the reason for the lower scores that females get in conditions of stereotype threat. As predicted, they found support for this hypothesized reduction in the capacity of working memory in a series of studies.

An interesting investigation of stereotype threat that has implications for teaching and learning involved looking at female and male performance as a function of the number and sex of the other people in the room during a high-stakes exam (Inzlicht & Ben-Zeev, 2000). Participants took difficult math or verbal tests in three-person groups in which either the other two people were the same sex as the target person, or one or both were the other sex. For females, but not males, test performance was decreased when the other people in the room were male, but only for the math test, which was the only condition that would have caused stereotype threat, according to the theory. The reason this is relevant to teaching and learning situations is that it suggests that one solution to improving scores for female test takers is to avoid having them in minority settings where they are only one of a few women, especially when taking tests in sex-stereotyped content areas. But, unfortunately, our understanding of stereotype threat is still developing and we are in need of much more research before we can understand how it applied in learning contexts.

Most people who think they understand stereotype threat are likely to be disappointed. In a review article, Sackett, Hardison, and Cullen (2004) found that even most textbook authors "got it wrong." Contrary to popular beliefs, it is *not* true that eliminating stereotype threat (e.g., saying a test is not important or failing to make one's race salient) eliminates group differences on tests that show large group differences. Without stereotype threat, group differences on these tests are what would usually be expected; it seems that the differences increase with stereotype threat, which is an important finding, but not the one that educators who want to close educational gaps were hoping to find.

There have also been several failed attempts to find evidence that stereotype threat decreases performance on high-stakes tests outside the laboratory in real-life situations. In a series of studies using real-life testing environments, researchers did not find that manipulations of the salience of one's sex or ethnicity had any effect on performance (Cullen, Hardison, & Sackett, 2004; Strickers & Beijar, 2004). Thus, there are still many unknowns about the reliability of stereotype threat and the conditions under which it operates.

Interests and Content on Exam Questions

In a study of sex differences in performance on Advanced Placement examinations (AP), Buck, Kostin, and Morgan (2002) examined the way the content of questions can bias performance on several different AP examinations. These examinations are taken by students who take college-level course work in high school. A sufficiently high score on an AP examination will usually satisfy college registrars so that students can receive college-level credit for that subject area, making the AP a "high-stakes" examination. In general, boys score higher than girls in all of the content areas in which tests are given except foreign languages, so the AP examinations have come under scrutiny given this lopsided outcome (Ackerman, Bowen, Beier, & Kanfer, 2001). As a way of developing a rubric for recognizing "female" and "male" content, Buck et al. (2002) identified 12 areas of male-oriented content and 12 areas of female-oriented content.

Male-oriented content areas: hard science; general science; applied science; business and economics; investigation and problem solving; competition and conflict; vehicles; fame and high achievement; sports; political content; dominance and authoritarian behavior; physical danger; risk taking.

Female-oriented content areas: human relationships; feelings and emotions; personality and behavior; arts and literature; domestic items and activities; personal appearance; psychology; verbal aggression; social service; health care; formal education; religion.

In a review of several AP tests using this rubric, Buck et al. (2002) found that males tended to perform better on items that related to war, armed conflict, wartime, politics, and the other topics that males are traditionally more interested in than females. Females tended to respond better to items relating to arts and literature, marginalized groups, social reform, religion, and women. This is an interesting result because it links sex differences in interests to differences that are found on standardized examinations. It provides a guide for teachers and other exam writers and for anyone who thinks critically about the meaning of sex differences on achievement tests and how they could be manipulated. Consider, for example, how a writing prompt on a high-stakes admissions test that purportedly assessed writing could appeal more to females or males depending on its topic and affect the relative balance in the next year's college freshman class.

A COGNITIVE PROCESS APPROACH

Another way of reconciling the different outcomes for males and females on standardized tests and in-class tests or, even more curiously, on tests that are closely tied to course instruction and tests that are not is to consider the cognitive processes used when answering questions instead of the actual test content. The rationale for this approach is that the differences between these two types of assessments represent two types of retrieval or problem-solving failures—one that is more typical for males and one that is more typical for females. Halpern (2000, 2004) proposed a taxonomy for understanding cognitive sex differences that is based on the underlying cognitive processes used during an assessment. A cognitive process approach offers a more fine-grained analysis of how information is retrieved from memory, the nature of the representation of meaning in memory, and what participants do when they work on a cognitive task.

Older rubrics for understanding difference between females and males grouped cognitive tasks using three categories—verbal, quantitative, and visuospatial. By contrast, a cognitive process taxonomy relies on the understanding that information is acquired, stored, selected, retrieved, and used in different contexts with different probabilities of successfully completing each component process. For example, working memory is separated into component processing subsystems—phonological and meaning subsystems—and information stored in memory has different representational codes—visuospatial and verbal. The following differences between females and males, most of which are documented early in childhood and across all industrialized societies, can be categorized according to a cognitive process model.

Women have more rapid access to phonological, semantic, and episodic information in long term memory, with higher scores on tests of verbal learning and the production and comprehension of complex prose (summarized in Halpern, 2000). As summarized earlier, females show the largest advantages in writing, retrieval from long-term memory, and other memory tasks. Girls have the advantage on quantitative tasks in the early elementary school years when math involves learning math facts and arithmetic calculations, and they perform better than males in later grades on algebra problems when the solution strategy is similar to language processing in its cognitive components (Gallagher, Levin, & Cahalan, 2002). By contrast, males have the advantage on tests of verbal analogies, a verbal task that requires mapping relationships in working memory.

Males have large advantages on tasks that require transformations in visuospatial working memory, so it is probably not coincidental that males show large advantages in their knowledge of politics and geography, which literally "map" onto spatial representations (Willingham & Cole, 1997). The data from international geography competitions (The International Geography Bee) show that these tendencies are international and effect sizes for young experts are large.

The Advantages of a Cognitive Process Taxonomy

A cognitive process taxonomy can be used to help explain the inconsistency across measures, with females achieving better grades in school and on tests in all subject areas when the material closely resembles what has been taught in school, but boys achieving higher grades on standardized tests, where the test questions are not close to the curriculum as it was taught. For some tests, these results can be partly explained by the fact that more women take advanced standardized tests like most AP tests and the Graduate Record Examinations (GREs), so their overall mean would be expected to be lower than men, but this reasoning does not apply for tests where the number of females and males is approximately equal, such as the TIMSS.

Kimball (1989) hypothesized that girls' learning is more rote than boys' learning, so girls' learning should be assessed best with familiar problems, but this theory ignores the fact that writing is a highly creative act involving novel topics, and girls perform substantially better than boys in writing. Sometimes the cooperative–competitive dimension will be mentioned as a reason for the difference, with the suggestion that standardized testing may be more like a competitive sport, which might privilege boys. Girls' preference for cooperative learning activities and boys' preferences for more competitive ones cannot explain the finding that girls and boys learn in a variety of classrooms, and that differences are found as a function of the type of test that is used to assess learning and not as a function of the learning activities. It is also difficult to understand why in-class testing would not be just as competitive. The notion that girls perform particularly well in school because their temperament is better suited for sitting for long periods of time has achieved considerable popularity, but it hard to see how the inability to sustain attention at a sedentary task would apply to students in advanced studies or how it might play out during long testing sessions for standardized tests that favor males.

In a study of the strategies used to solve mathematical problems, Gallagher et al. (2000) used the framework proposed by Halpern to see if boys and girls differed systematically in their use of mathematical strategies for different types of problems. In a series of several studies, they found that overall, the male students were more likely to use a flexible set of general strategies and more likely to solve problems that required a spatial representation, a short cut, or the maintenance of information in spatial working memory. Females were more likely to correctly solve problems with context that was familiar for females, used verbal skills, or required retrieval of a known solution or algebraic or multistep solution. In a second set of studies, Gallagher, Levin, and Cahalan (2002) examined cognitive patterns of sex differences on math problems on the Graduate Record Examination (GRE). They found the same results as predicted from the processes involved in solving the specific math problems, with differences favoring males for problems where there was an advantage to using a spatially based solution strategy (use of a spatial representation), but not when solution strategies were more verbal in nature or similar to the ones presented in popular math textbooks. Similarly, the usual male advantage was found with math problems that had multiple possible solution paths, but not on problems that had multiple steps, so the differences in the performance of males and females on GRE math problems lie in the recognition and/or selection of a solution strategy that may be novel and not in the load on working memory. They found that the usual male advantage on standardized math tests can be minimized, equated, or maximized by altering the way problems are presented and the type of cognitive processes that are optimal for their solution.

These are important findings because they advance our understanding of problem solving in general and math problem solving for all learners. These findings also suggest ways to help everyone improve at what is often the "funnel"—or sieve—in education. Everyone can be taught how to create spatial representations when they are appropriate for a specific type of mathematical problem and how to use successful strategies. This is one example where the study of sex differences can move us toward a better understanding of the cognitive processes people use and new ways to improve strategies for math problem solving.

LEARNING FROM AND ABOUT GROUP DIFFERENCES

One conclusion from this review is that on average, females and males are both similar and different in how they achieve in school subjects and various cognitive tests that are designed to tap those processes that we believe underlie academic and learning success. It is usually the differences that are more interesting, because they offer the possibility of growth; the differences show that growth is possible in a way that static similarities do not. If girls or boys are achieving at a higher level than the other group, then the other group can strive to reach the higher level also. In understanding the "why" of differences between cognitive achievement in females and males, it is impossible to ignore biological possibilities and realities. Because this is an educational handbook, only a brief section on the hormonal and brain bases of the gender differences will be included. Research into hormonal effects on brain development and learning is a fascinating area, but probably not of applied interest for most readers.

The Brain as a Sexual Organ

The same gonadal hormones that direct the shape of a developing fetus' own genitals also shape the developing brain in a male or female direction so that (when all goes right, which it usually does), the brain and genitals of every newborn are in agreement as to its sex (Hines, 2004). There are multiple sexually differentiated portions of the brain, but despite some vociferous claims, there is no direct link between brain size and weight and intelligence. The somewhat larger male brain is not indicative of greater intelligence, especially given that we have not found any meaningful overall differences in intelligence between females and males. (Other researchers strongly disagree with this conclusion, but they are using gross or overall brain measures and not accounting for multiple sex differences in the brain that render overall size and weight ineffective measures, such as differences in brain regions important in different cognitive processes, differences in rate of blood flow, and the efficiencies with smaller brains [i.e., neural pruning is a developmental process].) As I have written elsewhere, fighting over which sex has the better brain is like fighting over which sex has the better genitals.

One of the most fascinating areas of recent research has shown that testosterone and estrogen continue to play critical roles in sex-typical cognitive abilities throughout the life span in normal populations. Highly publicized studies have shown that women's cognitive abilities and fine motor skills fluctuate in a reciprocal fashion across the menstrual cycle. According to Kimura (1999), this suggests that there may be an "optimal" level of estradiol for certain spatial abilities. Women perform better on visuospatial tests when they are in the menstrual phase of their menstrual cycle, a phase in which estrogen is low, than when they are in the midluteal or follicular phase, when estrogen is much higher. Conversely, performance on verbal and fine manual skills is higher when women are in the high-estrogen phases of their cycle. A parallel finding that never attracted the same attention in the media is that males also show cyclical patterns of hormone concentrations and the correlated rise and fall of specific cognitive abilities. The spatial skills performance of normal males fluctuates in concert with daily variations in testosterone (higher testosterone concentrations in early morning than later in the day) and seasonal variations (in North America, testosterone levels are higher in autumn than in spring).

Puberty is another time in the life span when the body undergoes great biological changes and often a time of social turmoil, making it difficult to separate the effects of social events from the biological ones or to discern which is driving the other. There are numerous studies showing that menstrual cycles in women and daily and monthly fluctuations in male hormones for normal, healthy men can affect performance on several cognitive tasks, most particularly mental rotation tasks and spatial memory (Hausmann, Slabbekoorn, Van Goozen, Cohen-Kettenis, & Gunturkun, 2000; Postma, Winkel, Tuiten, & van Honk, 1999). These differences would not usually be observable except under laboratory conditions and do not need to be considered for everyday work.

Recent work has uncovered lifetime cumulative effects of estrogen on a battery of cognitive tasks. Psychologists have computed lifetime exposure to estrogen for a sample of healthy older women and found that those women who had had greater exposure to estrogen (for example, early age of menarche and late menopause) had higher scores on a battery of cognitive tasks than women with shorter exposures to estrogen. A variety of experimental techniques has shown that numerous areas of the brain that are not involved in reproduction are sexually dimorphic (e.g., hippocampus, amygdala, and thickness of portions of the cortex; see Hines, 2004, for a review). Although each of these differences has been the subject of intense disagreement among researchers, most will now agree that there are sex differences in the shape, and probably the volume, of the corpus callosum, with females in general having a larger and more bulbous structure (Allen, Richey, Chai, & Gorski, 1991; Steinmetz, Staiger, Schlaug, Huang, & Jancke, 1995). This is an important conclusion because it supports the theory that female brains are more bilaterally organized in their representation of cognitive functions (Jancke & Steinmetz, 1994). The difference in the shape of the corpus callosum, which is the largest fiber track in the brain, implies better connectivity between the two cerebral hemispheres, on average, for females (Innocenti, 1994).

Many people have suggested that the female superiority on memory tasks is related to female hormones. This is a difficult hypothesis to understand developmentally because the female advantage on many memory tasks emerges in preschool and remains through elementary school years when the gonadal hormones (sex hormones) are approximately equal and at low levels for girls and boys. In a study of the role of estradiol in memory in adult life when these levels are different, investigators compared men and women matched for age and level of estradiol (a form of estrogen—females and males have the same hormones, but usually in very different concentrations). The group of women and men were tested with a battery of memory tests that usually show large sex differences—several episodic memory tasks (memory for an event in which the memory includes when or where the event occurred or was learned). Even though they were matched on estradiol levels, females still showed an advantage on verbal memory tasks (and a correlation with estradiol on face memory tasks), suggesting that estradiol levels cannot explain why females have better verbal memories than males (Yonker, Eriksson, Nilsson, Lars, & Herlitz, 2003).

Despite much promise for hormone replacement therapy in old age as a way of maintaining cognitive functions, recent large-scale studies have been contradictory and disappointing, with most researchers concluding that there are insufficient data to recommend hormone replacement therapy for cognitive reasons (to prevent, delay, or reverse the very earliest stages of cognitive decline in older age) for men or women (Maki & Hogervorst, 2003). Random studies with nonhuman mammals show the promise of hormone use into old age for the purpose of brain maintenance, but its proven use with humans is still in the future.

MORE THAN NATURE VERSUS NURTURE

It is common to think about sex differences in cognition in terms of a dichotomy, and to ask if they are due to factors inherent in the biology of maleness or femaleness or if they are due to differential sex-related experiences and expectations. In fact, it is almost impossible to get away from some variation on the age-old question of nature and nurture. Few readers of this chapter are expecting a simple "either/or" response to this question, and most will expect an answer that is more in line with a percentage—such as a percentage of variance that can be explained with biologically oriented causes, or with "nurture," that is, with environmentally oriented causes. This view of how researchers conceptualize cause is so deeply engrained that when we report research results in journals, we are required to provide the proportion of variance explained by each independent variable and their interactions, so we expect these numbers as answers to important questions. But nature and nurture do not just interact, they mutually influence each other in cyclical ways, and there may be no real main effects. Inherent in the nature–nurture question is the idea that biology and environment/social variables can be separated into "independent variables," an assumption that is not likely to be true, and their interaction can be separated from their main effects. There is also no single number attributable to each of these sources of variance that exists in the population that clever researchers could discover. I believe

that we are better off rejecting the questions of whether it is nature or nurture that is responsible for cognitive sex differences, or what percentage of any particular cognitive sex difference is attributable to each, because they are the wrong questions. They are questions based on faulty premises about the separability of biological and environmental/social variables. The psychobiosocial model offers a better alternative to the nature-nurture dichotomy or nature–nurture continuum.

The Psychobiosocial Model in Which Cause and Effect Are Circular

The psychobiosocial model (also called biopsychosocial or similar other combinations) is based on the premise that it is not possible to separate variables into biological and psychosocial (i.e., environmental) categories. Consider, for example, the fact that there are differences and similarities in female and male brains, which are surely biological organs. The differences and similarities in brain structures could have been caused, enhanced, or decreased by environmental stimuli, because the brain changes continuously throughout life in response to experiences. Data showing that the brain is sexually dimorphic are reflective of both nature and nurture. It is now well documented that brain size and structures remain plastic throughout life. What individuals learn influences the shape of neural structures such as dendritic branching and cell size; brain architectures, in turn, support certain skills and abilities, which may lead us to select additional experiences. The interface between experience and biology is seamless. Biology and environment are as inseparable as conjoined twins who share a common heart. A psychobiosocial framework provides a more integrated way of thinking about the inextricable processes that influence brain structures and behaviors.

The psychobiosocial model consists of multiple, sequentially interacting variables that both cause and affect changes in hormone levels, brain structures and organization, the environments we select, and those that are correlated with our genetic predispositions. It recognizes the way psychological, biological, and social variables operate reciprocally on each other. The nature–nurture dichotomy is, and always has been, false. The psychobiosocial model replaces a continuum anchored at its ends by nature and nurture with a continuous feedback loop. Learning is both a biological and environmental phenomenon because individuals are differently prepared for learning and their own actions prepare them. Each individual is predisposed by his or her biology to learn some skills more readily than others, and everyone selects experiences in ways that are biased by prior learning histories

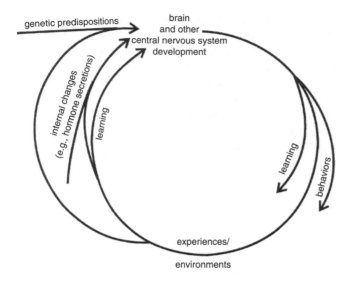

genetic predispositions

brain
and other
central nervous system
development

internal changes
(e.g., hormone secretions)

learning

learning

behaviors

experiences/

environments

FIGURE 27.1. A psychobiosocial model as a framework for understanding cognitive sex differences. It replaces the older idea of nature versus nurture with a circle that shows the way biological and psychosocial variables exert mutual influences on each other. (Reprinted from Halpern, 2000.)

and beliefs about appropriate behaviors for females and males. Similarly, many stereotypes about male and female differences reflect real group differences; by learning and endorsing them, individuals may also be selecting environments that increase or decrease these differences. A schematic diagram of the psychobiosocial model is depicted in Fig. 27.1.

Motivation and Interests

Learning and academic achievement cannot be considered apart from the motivation to learn and the motivation to demonstrate learning or perform in some way. It is generally assumed that girls have lower expectations for success and underestimate their own academic and other abilities, and that these achievement-related expectations can influence success in almost any academic context or context that depends on prior learning (Eisenberg, Martin, & Fabes, 1996). Lower expectations of success for girls and women would be a reasonable explanation for the lower numbers of women in careers in mathematics, except that girls succeed at math in the elementary school and get higher grades in math throughout school and high exam scores when the exams are "achievement" or curriculum-based or closely match what is taught in school. By some measures, girls should have higher expectations of success in math given their early experiences with success, more frequent success, and higher

aspirations for education. Girls and women are generally succeeding in school at higher rates than boys, obtaining more college degrees, and now even most master's degrees (but not more doctorates) (National Center for Education Statistics, 2004). It may be that they could be achieving even more highly than they are and the appeal to low expectations is still an accurate explanation, but it is now boys who are doing more poorly in school settings and girls who are continuing to do more poorly on standardized tests and with novel testing examples (which often have a spatial component, at least in math and science problems). The lopsided, flip-flop nature of girls' and boys' achievement patterns makes any simple theory of motivation that varies by sex more difficult to accept.

Achievement models that integrate expectancy and values have been particularly useful as a way of conceptualizing sex differences in academic achievement because they included a wider range of variables: beliefs about one's own ability, persistence, goals, other people's expectations of one's probability of success, and so on (Eccles & Wigfield, 2002). Expectancy and value theories are still valuable as the old stalwarts of psychology, but they cannot be used to explain sex differences in cognitive achievement, with girls achieving more highly on some measures and boys on others. Expectancy models can be used as the theory to guide practice with individuals even if it cannot be used to explain group-level data, because applied expectancy models can be used to boost performance by building each child's belief that the task can be accomplished with sufficient effort and then providing the needed support to ensure success.

Trait Complexes

Ackerman and his colleagues (Ackerman, Bowen, Beier, & Kanfer, 2001) have been particularly interested in the way *trait complexes*, which are combinations of interest and personality variables, combine with aptitude to determine achievement. Individuals engage in tasks that reflect their interests and their personalities, and in this way, they enhance the knowledge individuals need to achieve in a field as they develop the skills and abilities that are built on content knowledge. Interests are manifested in other ways, such as choice of major in college and career choices. Researchers in this area generally conclude that sex differences in course-taking patterns and test scores reflect differences in personalities and values and that these differences should be respected.

The idea that we have "two cultures"—a culture of science and technology and a culture of arts and humanities—was brought into public debate by C. P. Snow (1993). The idea of two cultures has important implications for education and for public policy. But, the actual division along sex-related career choices does not line up along a continuum anchored with science at one end and humanities at the other. Women tend to choose helping careers such as teaching, education, social work, and nursing. We can now add to that list veterinary medicine, where they make up a large majority of the enrollment, and women are now close to half of medical and law school classes. These are all careers that are people oriented, and some are science oriented as well. Males are overrepresented in mechanical and technical careers such as refrigerator and computer repair, accounting and business, physics and chemistry, and mechanical engineering. These choices of majors, based on this dimension, are consistent with the findings indicating that women and men differ in the relative strength of their interest on the "people versus things" dimension of individual differences scale (Lippa, 1998), with more women toward the "people" end and more men toward the "things" or mechanical end. Of course, people are influenced by many factors included their life experiences, social class, individual personalities, cognitive abilities, and education, but there are average differences that vary by sex in terms of types of interests that translate into career choices regardless of academic achievement.

USING WHAT WE KNOW

How can we use our knowledge of sex differences in cognitive abilities and academic achievement to assist learners and teachers? One immediate use comes from a longitudinal study of mathematically precocious youth, where we have the luxury of seeing if information collected from an extremely talented sample when they were in their early adolescence was predictive of their life choices and experiences in young to middle adulthood.

Tilt Data for Career Counseling

In a lifetime of studies with extremely gifted youth, Benbow and Lubinski and their students (Benbow, Lubinski, Shea, & Eftekhari-Sanjani, 2000; Lubinski, Webb, Morelock, & Benbow, 2001) have followed the career and life choices of several cohorts of young adolescents who were identified as mathematically precocious by scoring among the top 1 percent or so on the SAT-M. In a recent publication involving 1,110 participants over a 20-year period, they looked at the career choices of those who went into math and science careers and those who selected other careers. Among this elite group where all the participants were among the very most highly talented

in math, Webb, Lubinski, & Benbow (2002) found that those with "tilted cognitive profiles" often chose careers in their stronger area. For example, more women in this sample had significantly higher verbal SAT scores, and more of them chose careers in fields such as law where they could benefit from their best area of talent, despite the fact that they also had incredibly high SAT-M score as well. The researchers also found that participants' interests and values at age 13 predicted career choices 20 years later! They view the sex difference in the number of men and women who selected careers in math and science as good career choices based on interests and individual strengths, and not as a failure to convince more women to enter the math and science fields.

It seems that those precocious youth with tilted cognitive profiles (they were substantially more talented in one area than another) selected careers where they were able to use their best talent. One possible suggestion from this study is that students be provided with their own cognitive profiles and that students should be provided with career counseling about using what they do best. These "tilt advising" studies provide a philosophical perspective on sex differences in academic achievement, and especially on the number of highly talented men and women entering fields where there is de facto sex segregation. Webb et al. (2002) conclude that even if opportunities are equal, equal numbers of women and men may not choose to enter every field or achieve at the same level, especially if individuals make choices that follow their own ability patterns and interests. Of course, such reasoning is likely to be countered with the retort that individuals will not have much choice without role models in place. The idea of using individual cognitive profiles for career counseling is likely to become more popular as these studies gain more attention in education circles.

Should We Design Interventions to Reduce Gaps?

"Should" questions are always questions about values rather than data, but data can and should (another value statement, but science never was value-free) inform our decisions on a wide range of topics. The answer depends on which gaps are being reduced and why. As argued earlier, individual interests and personality attributes between males and females, on average, suggest that at least for the foreseeable future, we should not expect equal numbers of female and male scientists without strong social intervention. Few people would endorse social engineering that would force people into careers that they did not want to enter. On the other hand, if the "gap" is the achievement gap between females and males of comparable ability levels in some area that is needed for achievement, such as computer skills, then this sort of gap elimination or at least reduction seems like a much better idea. Perhaps interests and motivation would become more equal between the sexes if we made some changes that "leveled the playing field."

Consider some attempts to attract and retain more girls and women into physics, a traditionally male academic domain. A teaching Web site that is dedicated to the teaching of physics has many ideas from dedicated professors who are testing ways of making physics a more attractive subject and career for women (see http://www.physics.umd.edu/perg/). Schwedes, a physics professor in Germany, has emphasized the social context of physics as a way of making it more interesting to women. Hake, a leader in physics education, is advocating a synthesis in physics education, in which learning involves increasing communication among students, working on real problems, and emphasizing the ways in which physics is critical to problems such as world hunger and sustainability. These are common themes identified as "female" interests and should increase the number of women who are attracted to and remain in physics. Early results suggest that these changes in the way physics is being taught is having that effect, but more importantly, both men and women are showing better learning and more interest, so the result is not just a narrowing of the participation gap—it is also good learning.

What These Data Suggest

An understanding of cognitive sex differences will have to include both psychosocial and biological influences, although for most educational purposes, the biological is unlikely to find an applied use. Teachers and the larger society play an important role in developing the potential of all children and adult learners. Everyone is urged to remember that there is much variability among girls and boys, and that individual differences need to be respected because society needs many types of skills and abilities. In fact, there seems to be increased interest in understanding how individual interests and noncognitive factors influence learning and career choices, not with the goal of interfering with individual predilections, but to understand how we can use what we know in career counseling and in other ways to help individuals find careers that will fit well with their talents and interests.

There is no evidence that one sex is "smarter" than the other, and the reason is not just because standard multiscore intelligence tests were written that way. If tests had more of the content that favored females, such as questions about nutrition and child care, females on average would obtain the higher scores in these knowledge areas.

Test scores depend on what gets on the test. The more important question is who gets to decide what content is important. This is a philosophical question that is likely to be raised repeatedly in the coming decades as more women achieve positions of power and question the use of "male" content on many standardized tests. For example, it is assumed that what is important about history is the history of wars—standard "male" content. Why is it not just as legitimate to decide that the history of family life is what is important to know? If this sort of decision were made, average scores on standardized tests of history are likely to show a female advantage. Of course, I do not have data to support this predication, but there are data to show that females score higher on questions that have family content than war content, so it is not a random prediction.

There are average differences that sometimes favor males and sometimes favor females, depending on the cognitive ability or academic area that is measured, the age at which the measurement is taken, and the type of cognitive process needed to solve the problem. All children can improve in each of these ability areas with appropriate instruction. Teachers, parents, and everyone in the broader society are entrusted with the important job of ensuring that all children are given equal opportunities to develop to their fullest potential. By studying sex differences in cognitive abilities and achievement, we have discovered many ways to boost the achievement of all learners.

Changing Needs of the Workforce

The demands on the workforce have changed dramatically over the past century, with each generation needing more education than the one that came before. Jobs and opportunities for blue-collar workers are shrinking, and a college degree has become the passport to the middle class. Education is critical, so it is critical that we do all we can to help learners succeed to the best of their abilities. Computer literacy is now as critical as reading was only 150 years ago. New computer users will be relying on new types of cognitive skills, including more visuospatial information processing and more problem solving and genuine lifelong learning (De Lisi, 2002). It is time to develop and implement curricula specifically for visuospatial skill development, to make certain that opportunities for diverse learning experiences and access to emerging technologies are equally available, and to ensure that critical thinking is taught and learned so it will transfer across domains of knowledge (numerous reviews already conclude that it does—see Cohen & Thompson, 1999; Halpern, 2003).

This overview raises many exciting new areas for research that could benefit females and males. The challenges ahead of us are large, and we will need diverse sets of skills and talents to help meet them in order to stay competitive and cooperative in the shrinking global community. The cognitive sex differences listed in this chapter will probably not be the same ones listed in a follow-up chapter 10 or 20 years from now, if in fact there is such a chapter. I predict that there will be, but that it will be very different in content and structure. Today's educators help us all move ahead, even if not all of the forward movement is in the same direction.

References

Ackerman, P. L., Bowen, K. R., Beier, M. E., & Kanfer, R. (2001). Determinants of individual differences and gender differences in knowledge. *Journal of Educational Psychology, 93*, 797–825.

Allen, L. S., Richey, M. F., Chai, Y. M., & Gorski, R. A. (1991). Sex differences in the corpus callosum of the living human being. *Journal of Neuroscience, 11*, 933–942.

American Association of University Women. (1992). *How schools shortchange girls: The AAUW report*. New York: Marlowe.

Benbow, C. P., Lubinski, D., Shea, D. L., & Eftekhari-Sanjani, H. (2000). Sex differences in mathematical reasoning ability: Their status 20 years later. *Psychological Science, 11*, 474–480.

Buck, G., Kostin, I., & Morgan, R. (2002). *Examining the relationship of content to gender-based performance differences in advanced placement exams* (Research Report No. 2002-12). New York: The College Board.

Cohen, M., & Thompson, B. B. (1999). *Training teams to take initiative: Critical thinking in novel situations*. Report to the Army Research Institute. Arlington, VA: Cognitive Technologies.

Cullen, M. J., Hardison, C. M., & Sackett, P. R. (2004). Using SAT–grade and ability–job performance relationships to test predictions derived from stereotype threat theory. *Journal of Applied Psychology, 89*, 220–230.

Dahl, G., & Moretti, E. (2004, February). The demand for sons: Evidence from divorce, fertility, and shotgun marriage (NBER Web site). Retrieved October 20, 2004, from http://papers.nber.org/papers/w10281

De Cos, P. L. (1997, December).*Readiness for kindergarten: What does it mean?* Sacramento, CA: California Research Bureau.

De Lisi, R. (2002). Suggestions for educational practice, policy, and research to help manade the impending debate about sex differences in achievement test scores. *Issues in Education. Contributions from Educational Psychology, 8*, 31–38.

De Lisi, R., & McGillicuddy-De Lisi, A. (2002). Sex differences in mathematical abilities and achievement in . In A. McGillicuddy-DeLisi & R. De Lisi (Eds.), *Biology, society, and behavior: The development of sex differences* (pp. 155–181). Westport, CT: Ablex.

DeMeis, J. L., & Stearns, E. S. (1992). Relationship of school entrance age to academic and social performance. *Journal of Educational Research, 86*, 20–27.

Dwyer, C. A., & Johnson, L. M. (1997). Grades, accomplishment, and correlates. In W. W. Willingham & N. S. Cole (Eds.). *Gender and fair assessment* (pp. 127–156). Mahwah, NJ: Lawrence Erlbaum Associates.

Eccles, J. E., & Wigfield, A. (2002). Motivational beliefs, values, and goals. *Annual Review of Psychology, 53*, 135–153.

Eisenberg, N., Martin, C. L., & Fabes, R. A., (1996). Gender development and gender effects. In D. C. Berliner & R. C. Calfee (Eds.), *Handbook of educational psychology* (pp. 358–396). New York: Simon & Schuster.

Fausto-Sterling, A. (1992). *Myths of gender*. New York: Basic Books.

Feingold, A. (1992). Sex differences in variability in intellectual abilities: A new look at an old controversy. Review of Educational Research, *62*, 61–84.

Gallagher, A., Levin, J., & Cahalan, C. (2002, September). *GRE Research: Cognitive patterns of gender differences on mathematics admissions tests* (ETS Report No. 02-19). Princeton, NJ: Educational Testing Service.

Gallagher, A. M., De Lisi, R., Holst, P. C., McGillicuddy-De Lisi, A. V., Morely, M., & Cahalan, C. (2000). Gender differences in advanced mathematical problem solving. *Journal of Experimental Child Psychology, 75*, 165–190.

Geary, D. C. (1999). Sex differences in mathematical abilities: Commentary on the math-fact retrieval hypothesis. *Contemporary Educational Psychology, 24*, 267–274.

Gleason, J. B., & Ely, R. (2002). Gender differences in language development. In A. McGillicuddy-DeLisi & R. De Lisi (Eds.). *Biology, society, and behavior: The development of sex differences* (pp. 127–154). Westport, CT: Ablex.

Halpern, D. F. (2000). *Sex differences in cognitive abilities*, 3rd ed. Mahwah, NJ: Lawrence Erlbaum Associates.

Halpern, D. F. (2002). Sex differences in achievement scores: Can we design assessments that are fair, meaningful, and valid for girls and boys? *Issues in Education: Contributions from Educational Psychology, 8*, 1–19.

Halpern, D. F. (2003). *Thought and knowledge: An introduction to critical thinking* (4th ed.). Mahwah, NJ: Lawrencee Erlbaum Associates.

Halpern, D. F. (2004). A cognitive taxonomy for sex differences in cognitive abilities. *Current Directions, 13*, 15–139.

Halpern, D. F., & Collaer, M. L. (in press). Sex differences in visuospatial abilities: More than meets the eye. In P. Shah & A. Miyake (Eds.), *Higher-level visuospatial thinking and cognition*. New York: Cambridge University Press.

Halpern, D. F., & Tan, U. (2001). Stereotypes and steroids: Using a psychobiosocial model to understand cognitive sex differences. *Brain and Cognition, 45*, 392-414.

Hausmann, M., Slabbekoorn, D., Van Goozen, S. H. M., Cohen-Kettenis, P. T., & Gunturkun, O. (2000). Sex hormones affect spatial abilities during the menstrual cycles. *Behavioral Neuroscience, 114*, 1245-1250.

Hedges, L. V., & Nowell, A. (1995). Sex differences in mental test scores, variability, and numbers of high-scoring individuals. *Science, 269*, 41-45.

Hines, M. (2004). *Brain gender.* New York: Oxford University Press.

Huttenlocher, J., Haight, W., Bryk, A., Seltzer, M., & Lyons, T. (1991). Early vocabulary growth: Relation to language input and gender. *Developmental Psychology, 27*, 236-248.

Innocenti, G. M. (1994). Some new trends in the study of the corpus callosum. *Behavioral Brain Research, 64*, 1-8.

Inzlicht, M., & Ben-Zeev, T. (2000). A threatening intellectual environment: Why females are susceptible to experiencing problem-solving deficits in the presence of males. *Psychological Science, 11*, 365-371.

Jancke, L., & Steinmetz, H. (1994). Interhemispheric transfer time and corpus callosum size. *Neuroreport, 5*, 2385-2388.

Jensen, A.R. (1998). *The g factor: The science of mental ability.* Westport, CT: Praeger.

Kimball, M. M. (1989). A new perspective on women's math achievement. *Psychological Bulletin, 105*, 198-214.

Kimura, D. (1999). *Sex and cognition.* Cambridge, MA: MIT Press.

Law, D., Pellegrino, J. W., & Hunt, E. B. (1993). Comparing the tortoise and the hare: Gender differences and experience in dynamic spatial reasoning tasks. *Psychological Science, 4*, 35-41.

Linn, M. C., & Petersen, A. C. (1985). Emergence and characterization of sex differences in spatial ability: A meta-analysis. *Child Development, 56*, 1479-1498.

Linn, M. C., & Petersen, A. C. (1986). A meta-analysis of gender differences in spatial ability: Implications for mathematics and science achievement. In J. S. Hyde & M. C. Linn (Eds.), *The psychology of gender: Advances through meta-analysis* (pp. 67-101). Baltimore: Johns Hopkins University Press.

Lippa, R. (1998). Gender-related individual differences and the structure of vocational interests of the people–things dimension. *Journal of Personality and Social Psychology, 74*, 996-1009.

Loring-Meier, S., & Halpern, D.F. (1999). Sex differences in visuopatial working memory: Components of cognitive processing. *Psychonomic Bulletin & Review, 6*, 464-471.

Lubinski, D., Webb, R. M., Morelock, M. J., & Benbow, C. P. (2001). Top 1 in 10,000: A 10-year follow-up of the profoundly gifted. *Journal of Applied Psychology, 86*, 718-729.

Maki, P., & Hogervorst, E. (2003). HRT and cognitive decline. *Best Practice & Research Clinical Endocrinology & Metabolism, 17*, 105-122.

Masters, M. S. (1998). The gender difference on the mental rotations test is not due to performance factors. *Memory & Cognition, 26*, 444-448.

Masters, M. S., & Sanders, B. (1993). Is the gender difference in mental rotation disappearing? *Behavior Genetics, 23*, 337-341.

Money, J. (1987). Propaedutics of ducious G-I/R: Theoretical foundations for understanding dimorphic gender-identity/role. In J. M. Reinisch, L. A. Rosenblum, & S. A. Sanders (Eds.), *Masculinity/femininity: Basic perspectives* (pp. 13-34). New York: Oxford.

Naglieri, J. A., & Rojahn, J. (2001). Gender differences in planning, attention, simultaneous, and successive (PASS) cognitive processes and achievement. *Journal of Educational Psychology, 93*, 430-437.

National Center for Education Statistics (2004, November). *Gender differences in participation and completion of undergraduate education and how they have changed over time* (draft 5) (NCES 2004-169). Washington, DC: U.S. Department of Education Institute of Education Sciences.

Newcombe, N. S., Mathason, L., & Terlecki, M. (2002). Maximization of spatial competence: More important than finding the cause of sex differences. In A. McGillicuddy-De Lisi & R. De Lisi (Eds), *Biology, society, and behavior: The development of sex differences in cognition* (pp. 183-206). Westport, CT: Ablex.

Parsons, T. D., Larson, P., Kratz, K., Thiebaux, M., Bluestein, B., Buckalter, J. G., et al. (2003). Sex differences in mental rotation and spatial rotation in a virtual environment. *Neuropsychologia, 42*, 555-562.

Postma, A., Winkel, J., Tuiten, A., & van Honk, J. (1999). Sex differences and menstrual cycle effects in human spatial memory. *Psychoneuroendocrinology, 24*, 175-192.

Robert, M. (1990). Sex typing the water-level task: There is more than meets the eye. *International Journal of Psychology, 25*, 475-490.

Rosenthal, R. (1992). *Pygmalion in the classroom* (expanded edi). New York: Irvington.

Royer, J. M., Tronsky, L. N., Chan, Y., Jackson, S. J., & Marchant, H. III. (1999). Math-fact retrieval as the cognitive mechanism underlying gender differences in math test performance. *Contemporary Educational Psychology, 24*, 181-266.

Rutter, M., Caspi, A., Fergusson, D., Horwood, L. J., Goodman, R., Maughan, B., et al. (2004). Sex differences in developmental reading disability: new findings from 4 epidemiological studies. *Journal of the American Medical Association, 291*, 2007-2012.

Sackett, P. R., Hardison, C. M., & Cullen, M. J. (2004). On interpreting stereotype threat as accounting for African American–White differences on cognitive tests. *American Psychologist, 59*, 7-13.

Schmader, T., & Johns, M. (2003). Converging evidence: That stereotype threat reduces working memory capacity. *Journal of Personality and Social Psychology, 85*, 440-452.

Seong, H., Bauer, S. C., & Sullivan, L. M. (1998). Gender differences among top performing elementary school students in mathematical ability. *Journal of Research and Development in Education, 31*, 133-141.

Shea, D. L., Lubinski, D., & Benbow, C. P. (2001). Importance of assessing spatial ability in intellectually talented young adolescents: A 20-year longitudinal study. *Journal of Educational Psychology, 95*, 604–614.

Shih, M., Pittinsky, T. L., & Ambady, N. (1999). Stereotype susceptibility: Identity salience and shifts in quantitative performance. *Psychological Science, 10*, 80–83.

Snow, C. P. (1993). *The two cultures.* New York: Cambridge University Press.

Sommers, C. (2000). *The war against boys: How misguided feminism is harming our young men.* New York: Simon & Schuster.

Steele, C. M. (1997). A threat in the air: How stereotypes shape intellectual identity and performance. *American Psychologist, 52*, 613–629.

Steinmetz, H., Staiger, J. F., Schluag, G., Huang, Y., & Jancke, L. (1995). Corpus callosum and brain volume in women and men. *Neuroreport; 6*, 1002–1004.

Strickers, L. J., & Bejar, I. I. (2004). Test difficulty and stereotype threat on the GRE general test. *Journal of Applied Social Psychology, 34*, 563–597.

U.S. Department of Education. (1995). *The condition of education.* NCES 95-768. Washington, DC: Author.

U. S. Department of Education. (1997a). *National assessment of educational progress* (indicator 32: Writing proficiency: Prepared by the Educational Testing Service). Washington, DC: Author (http://www.ed.gov/nces).

U.S. Department of Education. (1997b). *The third international mathematics and science study.* Washington, DC: Author (http://www.ed.gov/nces).

U. S. Department of Education. (1998). *National Assessment of Educational Progress, NAEP 1996 Trends in Academic Progress.* Washington, DC: Author.

U. S. Department of Education. (2000). *National Center for education statistics.* Washington, DC: Author (http://www.ed.gov/nces).

Voyer, D. (1996). The relation between mathematical achievement and gender differences in spatial abelities: A suppression effect. *Journal of Educational Psychology, 88*, 563–571.

Warrick, P. D., & Naglieri, J. A. (1993). Gender differences in planning, attention, simultaneous, and successive (PASS) cognitive processes. *Journal of Educational Psychology, 85*, 693–701.

Willingham, W. W., & Cole, N. S. (1997). *Gender and fair assessment.* Mahwah, NJ: Lawrence Erlbaum Associates.

Webb, M. R., Lubinski, D., & Benbow, C. P. (2002). Mathematically facile adolescents with math-science aspirations: New perspectives on their educational and vocational development. *Journal of Educational Psychology, 94*, 785–794.

Yonker, J. E., Eriksson, E, Nilsson, Lars-Goran, & Herlitz, A. (2003). Sex differences in episodic memory: Minimal influence of estradiol. *Brain and Cognition, 52*, 231–238.

·28·

SENSE OF BELONGING, SOCIAL BONDS, AND SCHOOL FUNCTIONING

Jaana Juvonen
University of California, Los Angeles

Classrooms and schools are not only forums for scholarly work and learning, but also rich social arenas with constant interaction and affiliation. Some students competently interact and form relationships with their teachers and classmates, whereas others have problems getting along with their instructors or fitting into the school-based peer networks. A question addressed here is whether social success in forming and maintaining positive relationships is associated with students' school engagement and academic performance. Since the early 1990s, there has been substantial interest in the role that social relationships and sense of belonging play in motivating students to do well in school. For example, Connell and Wellborn (1991) proposed that in addition to sense of competence and autonomy, student feelings of relatedness are critical in facilitating school engagement. Educational psychologists have also attempted to integrate affiliative and achievement motivation (e.g. Juvonen & Wentzel, 1996)—domains that have traditionally been independent and separate (Weiner, 1995, 2000). Such integration involves examination of how social relationships motivate school behaviors as well as how students might deal with competing achievement and social motives. The goal of the present chapter is to review recent evidence on the links among sense of belonging, school-based social bonds, and school functioning.

It is timely to review research on social bonds in educational settings, given the impressive body of research depicting a wide range of adaptive functions of interpersonal relationships and sense of belonging in other fields of psychology since the mid-1990s. For example, we have learned that people who are socially connected tend to be mentally and physically healthier than those who are isolated (Baumeister & Leary, 1995; Leary, 2001). Even the age of mortality is higher for those who are well socially integrated compared to those who have few social connections (Berkman & Syme, 1979; House, Landis, & Umberson, 1988). Also, during conditions of distress, availability of social support ameliorates emotional pain and physical health outcomes (e.g., Bolger, Zuckerman, & Kessler, 2000; Cohen, 2004; Cohen & Wills, 1985). Research on primates and rats documents such social buffering effects of stress at physiological and neural levels (Gust, Gordon, Brodie, & McClure, 1994; Kiyokawa, Kikusui, Takeuchi, & Mori, 2004). Finally, the latest experimental studies suggest that threats to belonging impede cognitive performance (Baumeister & DeWall, 2005; Baumeister, Twenge, & Nuss, 2002). In light of these findings, it is reasonable to expect that students who are socially connected would function better in school than those who are socially disconnected or alienated, and that under stress, students would be most likely to benefit from support provided by their teachers and peers. Yet the current review will suggest that not all social bonds are equal and that sometimes sense of belonging promotes disengagement from school.

Studies published within the past decade that integrate sense of belonging or school-based social bonds with school functioning provide the main thrust of the current review. The chapter begins with the most global of the constructs: sense of belonging, which often refers to the perceived social climate of schools. After considering conditions under which sense of belonging is most critical for adaptive school functioning and when social alienation predicts school failure, research on school-based relationships is reviewed. Studies on teacher–student relationships provide insights about certain qualitative aspects of relationships and adaptive school functioning, although the general conclusions are similar to those based on research on sense of relatedness. Disconnected and alienated students are worse off than those who feel connected, and perceived support is especially helpful for youth under heightened stress.

Research on students' peer relationships with schoolmates, in turn, depicts increasingly complex associations between child and friend characteristics, dyadic relationships, and group-level processes in association with school outcomes. For example, aggressive students may be socially connected, yet their friendships do not facilitate school engagement. Such findings question the simplicity of the assumptions regarding the function of sense of relatedness in school contexts and underscore the importance of peer selection and socialization processes.

Research on social belonging versus alienation, teacher–student relationships, and peer dynamics (friendships, rejection, and harassment) remain mostly as rather separate areas of investigation. With few exceptions, multiple social relationships (e.g., teacher and peer relationships) or multiple levels of social bonds (dyadic and group-level processes) are not simultaneously considered. It is therefore important not only to review the existing empirical findings, but also to lay out some ideas on how different levels and types of relationships might interact. Hence, in contrast to the first parts of this chapter that provide reviews of the empirical findings within three bodies of research (belonging, teacher–student relationships, and peer relations), the last part of the chapter provides examples of how classroom social dynamics might interact in ways that facilitate disengagement. Relevant social psychological theories regarding social identity, self-categorization, impression management, compliance to perceived group norms, and pluralistic ignorance are applied to suggest why and how relationships with classmates might at times foster maladaptive school behaviors. A dynamic model, in which sense of belonging serves both as a motive to facilitate relationships and as an outcome of relationships, is proposed.

Terms are used broadly in this review emphasizing similarities rather than differences among related concepts. In addition to feeling included, liked, and respected as components of belongingness (Goodenow, 1993), sense of acceptance, support, and closeness are also largely overlapping. Terms such as *belongingness*, *relatedness*, and *connectedness* are used interchangeably. School

adjustment is broadly defined to include achievement motivation, engagement, and academic performance.

SOCIAL CLIMATE OF BELONGING

Research on sense of community, belongingness, and perceived support represent attempts to understand the effects of the larger social context or school climate on student behavior. The assumptions about the importance of supportive and communal school environment have guided educational practice and reform since the 1940s (Dewey, 1943) and received increased attention again in the 1990s (e.g., Bryk, Lee, & Holland, 1993; Lee & Smith, 1999; Luthar, 1997; Maehr & Midgley, 1996; Shouse, 1996). Many of the recent efforts to understand the function of social climate have specifically focused on urban schools and students from socially disadvantaged backgrounds (Battistich, Solomon, Kim, Watson, & Schaps,1995; Battistich & Hom, 1997; Becker & Luthar, 2002; Comer, 1980).

The underlying assumption is that environments characterized by caring and supportive relationships facilitate student engagement and other adaptive school behaviors (e.g., Brand, Felner, Shim, Seitsinger, & Dumas, 2003; Felner & Felner, 1989). Consequently, motivation and achievement are presumed to be undermined when students feel unsupported and disconnected from others (e.g., Becker & Luthar, 2002; Finn, 1989, 1993). Perceived support and sense of belonging appear to be important for students starting in elementary grades across diverse samples of students. Although the specific constructs, such as sense of community, belonging, and perceived supportiveness, and their operationalizations, vary across studies, the findings are consistent when measures are tapping students' subjective perceptions of their educational environments.

Examining the associations between overall sense of relatedness (e.g., perceptions of feeling accepted and valued by teachers, classmates, and parents) and school engagement among third- to sixth-grade students from predominantly White middle- and working-class families, Furrer and Skinner (2003) found that relatedness in the fall predicts spring engagement. Capitalizing on between-school variations in the socioeconomic composition of 24 elementary schools, Battistich et al. (1995) investigated the association between students' sense of school community (i.e., perceptions of caring and supportive interpersonal relationships, role in decision making) and a range of measures tapping attitudes, motivation, and achievement. By controlling for student demographics and relying on hierarchical linear modeling techniques that allow examination of students nested within schools, the findings revealed positive associations between sense of community and a range of motivational measures (e.g., enjoyment of class, liking of school, intrinsic motivation, and educational expectations) across all schools at the level of individual students. Stronger associations were obtained in schools serving most economically disadvantaged families, suggesting that students from poor homes might benefit most from a sense of belongingness.

Similar patterns of associations have been found at middle school level. Focusing on middle schools serving predominately White youth from working class families, Roeser, Midgley, and Urdan (1996) investigated associations among sense of belonging in school, teacher–student relationships, student engagement, and academic achievement. Sense of belonging mediated the association between teacher–student relationships and level of student engagement, which in turn predicted academic achievement at eighth grade. The mediational effects of sense of belonging (teacher-student relationships → sense of belonging → motivation) were robust inasmuch as other relevant motivational constructs (e.g., goal structures fostered by the school, personal achievement goal orientations) were also taken into account in the analyses.

Although none of the above-described studies found any direct associations between perceived social climate and achievement, in one large-scale investigation a direct, albeit modest, "effect" was obtained (Lee & Smith, 1999). In a study of Chicago city schools, Lee and Smith (1999) examined student perceptions of support received from teachers, parents, peers, and community. Overall sense of support predicted a modest amount of variance in mathematics and reading scores at sixth and eighth grades. The best reported achievement gains were obtained in schools in which students felt supported and in which academic goals and standards were also emphasized (i.e., schools characterised by "academic press").

Based on the empirical evidence just reviewed; the perceived social climate of schools is related to student engagement and can be predictive of academic performance. Although sense of connectedness is presumed to motivate students to do well in school, many studies do not control for student characteristics. It is therefore likely that students doing well in school experience their schools as more supportive and feel more connected than those displaying academic or behavioral problems. Hence, the causal or temporal role of supportive school climate in facilitating adaptive school behaviors is dubious based on studies presented thus far. Perhaps the most compelling evidence regarding the importance of belongingness is based on longitudinal investigations indicating the association between sense of social alienation and dropping out, which is reviewed next.

Social Alienation and Dropping Out

When interviewed about reasons for dropping out, one out of four youth say "they did not belong" at school (U.S. Department of Education, Center for Education Statistics, 1993). Focusing on the connection between sense of belonging and engagement, Finn (1989, 1993) proposed that students drop out when they do not participate in academic tasks or extracurricular activities because they do not feel a sense of belonging and identify with school. Although a number of factors contribute to students' premature school leaving, there is evidence indicating that socially disconnected students are at risk for this ultimate school failure (e.g., Hymel, Comfort, Schonert-Reichl, & McDougall, 1996).

Research on dropping out is process focused, inasmuch as premature school exit is considered as a final step in a long process of disengagement (Alexander, Entwisle, & Kabanni, 2001; Ekstrom, Goertz, Pollack, & Rock, 1986; Finn, 1993; Wehlage & Rutter, 1985). The effects of social alienation are examined among many other predictors, such as indicators of earlier academic experiences. For example, Kaplan, Peck, and Kaplan (1997) documented that, in addition to low grades and lack of motivation, social alienation from the school-based peer networks and affiliation with deviant peers during grades 8–9 independently contribute to the risk of dropping out. Although perceived rejection by teachers (perceptions of low liking and negative views by teachers) was predicted by earlier negative academic experiences, it did not predict dropping out over and above deviant peers and low motivation.

Controlling for school performance as well as students' disengagement, Alexander, Entwisle, and Kabbanni (2001) found that repeating a grade during middle school increases the probability of dropping out by sevenfold. The effects of grade retention not only accounted for low achievement but also independently predicted dropping out. The authors concluded that this independent effect is likely to reflect lack of social integration caused by off-time status. Hence, "not fitting in" factored into students' behavior to prematurely leave school.

As suggested by Finn (1989), participation in extracurricular activities also reveals students' social integration and sense of belonging. Focusing on extracurricular activities decreasing the risk of dropping out, Mahoney (2000) found that among students at high risk, participation in extracurricular activities during middle or high school decreased their chance to leave school before 11th grade (see also Eccles, Barber, Stone, & Hunt, 2003; Mahoney & Cairns, 1997). The reduced risk was even greater for those students whose peers also participated in school extracurricular activities. Taken together, these data indicate risk of dropping out is ameliorated by participation in *any* school-related activities, inasmuch as it facilitates sense of belonging. Data reviewed next also suggest that sense of connectedness might be particularly important at time of increased vulnerability or stress.

Sense of Connectedness as a Moderator of Vulnerability

As pointed out earlier, Battistich et al. (1995) found sense of community associated with positive academic attitudes, particularly among children from poor families (see also Becker & Luthar, 2002; Pianta & Walsh, 1996; Weinstein, 2002). It is possible that family economic disadvantage is associated with increased vulnerability due to limited parental support stemming from economic hardship (e.g., Dodge, Pettit, & Bates, 1994; McLoyd, 1990). Hence, sense of support and feelings of connectedness might be particularly important to maintain (or to increase) student engagement for youth who are vulnerable to stress due to their family circumstances. Hence, teacher support may compensate for lack of parent support (see Harter, 1996).

There may be times of heightened stress when sense of connection and availability of emotional support are important not only for some but most students. For example, students often experience the transition from elementary school to middle school as distressing and display declines in motivation and grades (Eccles et al., 1993; Roeser, Eccles, & Freedman-Doan, 1999; Roeser, Eccles, & Sameroff, 1998). The declines in motivation correspond to a changing school climate (e.g., less personal and more anonymous environment) typically associated with the larger size and different structure of the new middle school (Berndt, Hawkins & Jiao, 1999; Feldlaufer, Midgley, & Eccles, 1988; Midgley, Feldlaufer, & Eccles, 1989). Hence, it is presumed that negative changes in student motivation could be decreased by reducing the number of changes associated with the school transition.

Programs specifically designed to improve the social climate of middle schools offer additional support for the causal functions of sense of belonging. For example, the Turning Points model designed by the Carnegie Council on Adolescent Development (1989) strives to create a school culture that facilitates sense of community and closer relationships between students and teachers by grouping students into smaller teams and linking students with specific teachers. In their evaluation of such practices, Felner et al. (1997) find increased perceptions of teacher support and improved feelings of connectedness. Moreover, high level of fidelity to the program goals (i.e., high level of implementation) decrease behavior problems and emotional difficulties. Hence, explicit efforts to try to change the ethos of schools might indeed facilitate school adjustment.

In sum, a caring and supportive school context is particularly important when students experience distress—either chronic distress due to a history of academic problems, lack of parent support due to economic hardship, or temporary and more normative stress associated with transition from elementary to more anonymous middle school. That is, sense of connectedness and supportiveness or lack thereof can respectively promote resiliency or elevate student risk during times of increased vulnerability.

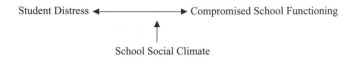

TEACHER–STUDENT RELATIONSHIPS

Of the various components of school social climate, teacher support is probably most salient. Considering the definition of belongingness by Baumeister and Leary, one can presume that "frequent, affectively pleasant interactions" with teachers "in the context of temporally stable and enduring framework of affective concern" (1995, p. 497) are important for most students. Research on teacher–student relationships is typically guided by this assumption, inasmuch as students are presumed to comply and be motivated to learn when they feel supported and respected by their teachers. When they lack a bond with a teacher or have a conflictual relationship, students are instead disengaged and possibly even disruptive (e.g., Murdock, 1999).

Research on teacher–student relationships has advanced our understanding of the role of social connectedness in school adjustment because many investigators pay attention to particular features of the relationships. Drawing on earlier research by Pianta and Steinberg (1992), Birch and Ladd (1997) demonstrated that disparate relationship provisions were associated with different school outcomes in kindergarten. In their research, teacher–student closeness correlated with better academic performance, teacher ratings of increased self-directed behavior, and school liking. In contrast, kindergarteners with dependent ("clingy") relationships with their teachers manifested negative school attitudes, disengagement, and poor academic performance. Finally, conflictual relationships with teachers were associated with lower school liking, lack of self-directed (cf. independent) behaviors, and classroom cooperation as well as increased school avoidance.

Consistent with research on kindergartners that rely on teacher ratings, research on middle school students also indicates that teacher–student relationships and adaptive school functioning are integrally related. Controlling for demographics as potential indicators of risk status, such as SES and race, Murdock (1999) showed that perceptions of negative academic and behavioral expectations by teachers predicted disengagement and disciplinary problems. Although behavioral indicators of alienation, such as teacher ratings of disengagement and disciplinary problems, were higher for low-income ethnic minority students than for others, perceptions of negative teacher views were stronger predictors of alienation than demographic status variables.

The research just reviewed relied on cross-sectional designs that do not allow temporal disentangling of antecedents and consequences. Longitudinal studies controlling for earlier academic indicators provide better evidence for the predictive power of teacher–student relationships. Controlling for both sixth-grade academic performance and level of motivation, Wentzel (1997) showed that eighth-grade student perceptions of teacher caring (teacher respect, fairness, expectations, and commitment) predicted classroom participation and willingness to put forth effort over and beyond a number of additional predictors of motivation (e.g., sense of control). Similar effects of teacher caring on student motivation at eighth grade were documented by Murdock and Miller (2003) when controlling for relationship with parents, peer socialization effects, and level of motivation at seventh grade (see also Ryan & Patrick, 2001).

Roeser, Eccles, and Sameroff (2000) also demonstrated that perceptions of positive teacher regard predicted favorable changes in academic competence, academic values, and mental health between seventh and eighth grade. In contrast, students who perceive teachers treating them disrespectfully because of their race or gender show decreased interest in school and elevated behavior problems (cf. Graham, Bellmore, & Mize, 2004). Indeed, research on perceived discrimination reveals that ethnic minority youth report experiencing unusually harsh discipline and obtaining lower-than-deserved grades (Fisher, Wallace, & Fenton, 2000; see also for review Graham & Hudley, in press). Perceived discrimination experiences, in turn, are related to negative attitudes toward school (Brand et al., 2003).

The effects of teacher–student relationships in middle school also appear to predict student engagement in high school. Following students across the transition to high school, Murdock, Anderman, and Hodge (2000) found that the quality of teacher–student relationships in seventh grade was predictive of ninth-grade level of motivation, even when controlling for earlier indicators of motivation and achievement. Hence, the prospective associations between teacher–student relationship and motivation are robust across different grade levels.

Teacher–Student Relationships as Buffers of Risk Status

The relationship quality between teachers and students in the early grades especially matters for students manifesting early behavior problems. Pianta, Steinberg, and Rollins (1995) found teacher–student conflict the most potent predictor of subsequent behavior problems among children considered at risk. Students whose kindergarten teachers reported their relationships to be close and nonconflictual received higher behavior ratings from their first-grade teachers than was expected based on behavior ratings obtained in the beginning of kindergarten. Moreover, for those deemed at high risk for grade retention, a positive teacher–student relationship reduced actual retention (Pianta et al., 1995). Hence, close, nonconflictual relations with teachers can protect students from additional risks.

Controlling for initial rate of aggression, Hughes, Cavell, and Jackson (1999) documented that both teachers' and children's reports of teacher–student relationship quality during second and third grades predicted lower teacher-rated aggression the following year. Using a longer term prospective study, Hamre and Pianta (2001) found low conflict and low dependency on teachers in kindergarten predicting fewer disciplinary problems and more positive work habits through eighth grade for children deemed at high risk based on behavior problems in kindergarten. Research on older youth also shows that perceived teacher support is positively related to indices of engagement and participation in school for eighth-grade students deemed at risk (Finn, 1993).

Temporal or "Causal" Effects

Based on the research reviewed thus far, it can be concluded that supportive relationships with teachers, particularly relationships characterized by a low level of dependency in early grades and low conflict, facilitate school functioning and might be especially critical for students who otherwise lack social support. Lack of supportive, close, and nonconflictual teacher–student relationships is particularly problematic for students at risk for school-related problems because of their disadvantaged backgrounds, low grades, and behavior problems (see also Meehan, Hughes & Cavell, 2003). Although consistent with research on social climate reviewed earlier, research on teacher–student relationships highlights student characteristics and particular circumstances (e.g., adjustment to a new school) when lack of support is especially detrimental and when supportive relationships protect students from further risks.

Similarly to research on social climate (sense of community, belongingness), most research on teacher–student relationships is guided by the assumption that positive affiliation leads to more adaptive academic functioning. Although student characteristics (e.g., demographics as well as behaviors) are taken into account when examining teacher–student relationships, the "reverse" direction of effects (i.e., academic performance predicting relationships) or reciprocal effects are rarely considered. A case in point was provided by Skinner and Bellmont (1993), who demonstrated that elementary school age (8- to 12-year-old) students more engaged in the beginning of the school year received increased teacher involvement, more optimal structure, and greater support for autonomy than did other students. It was also true, however, that students who reported teachers providing optimal structure and support for autonomy were more engaged across the entire school year. Hence, behaviorally disengaged students are also the ones most likely to lack needed support. In the following section on peer relationships, it becomes even more evident how social behaviors play a crucial role in determining the pathways by which "disconnected" students are at risk for school-related problems.

SCHOOL-BASED PEER RELATIONSHIPS

Considering the amount of student-to-student social interaction taking place in school, it is reasonable to presume that peer acceptance and friendships play a part in facilitating sense of belongingness, thereby promoting school engagement. Compared with studies on sense of connectedness and teacher–student relationships reviewed earlier, research on peer relationships and school functioning depicts increasingly complex associations among student and friend behaviors, dyadic and group processes, and developmental considerations. Starting with analyses of student friendships and peer group inclusion, and proceeding with a review of research on peer rejection, the following sections provide new insights about the link between school-based social affiliations and school functioning.

Friendships as Buffers of Distress

Friendships are dyadic, reciprocated relationships characterized by equality (Hartup, 1996). Similar to teacher–student relationships, friendships provide social support and can increase student engagement in school. This type of emotional support appears to facilitate school adaptation, particularly during periods of elevated distress, including adjustments to a new school (Ladd, 1990; Wentzel, McNamara, & Caldwell, 2004). Research on school entry as well as on middle school transition shows that students with friends fare better than students without friends as they acclimate to their new environment.

Focusing on school entry, Ladd (1990) discovered that children who formed new friendships during kindergarten performed better academically than children who did not establish friendships. In addition, children with multiple friends during entrance developed more favorable school attitudes during the first 2 months. Those maintaining these friendships also liked school more over time. These findings are particularly robust inasmuch as personal characteristics of students (e.g., mental age, preschool experience, and concurrent social status) students were taken into account. Subsequent research by Ladd and colleagues further indicates that children considering friends as sources of aid and validation are more likely to develop positive attitudes toward school (Ladd, Kochenderfer, & Coleman,1996). Hence, feelings of support, familiarity (knowing classmates in the new school), and ability to maintain old relationships as well as to make new friends are critical when young students acclimate to a new social setting of school.

Positive effects of friends and friendships also have been demonstrated with older youth as they transition to middle school. Berndt et al. (1999) demonstrated that student with stable, higher quality friendships make a more successful transition to middle school than others. Linking early middle school friendships with school outcomes, Wentzel et al. (2004) found that students with no friends in the first grade of middle school (i.e., sixth grade) were more distressed and initially received lower grades than students with friends. Both friendship status and distress also were associated with lower grades during the first grade in middle school. Hence, lack of emotional and social support provided by close friendships is particularly detrimental to adaptive school functioning for students starting in a new school, especially if students are distressed (cf., McDougall & Hymel, 1998). These findings support the earlier conclusions based on research on sense of relatedness and teacher–student relationships.

In addition to providing emotional and social support, other relationship features might explain the positive effect of friendships on school functioning. For example, friends are better than nonfriends in joint problem solving, especially when tasks are cognitively demanding (Azmitia & Montgomery, 1993). Hence, in classrooms that utilize collaborative learning activities (Slavin, 1995), ability to work with a friend might directly affect students' cognitive performance.

Peer Socialization and Selection

In spite of the positive findings of children's school-based friendships, it is imperative to keep in mind that not all friendships are equal. Not only do critical qualities (e.g., supportiveness, validation) of friendships vary, but also the desire to support one another on achievement-related tasks or work together on school assignments varies depending on the abilities and aspirations of friends (e.g., Berndt, 1999, 2002). Given that children tend to affiliate with similar others (Hallinan, 1983), academically motivated students form friendships that facilitate achievement (e.g., Mounts & Steinberg, 1995). In contrast, students who have trouble succeeding in school do not motivate their friends to excel and may instead reinforce one another's negative qualities (Dishion, Spracklen, Andrews, & Patterson, 1996). Hence, based on research on peer selection and socialization (e.g., Kandel, 1996), friends are apt to amplify students' school-related behaviors (whether positive or negative).

Perhaps the best evidence for socialization effects of peers comes not from studies of best friends, but from research on peer networks (Cairns, Cairns, & Neckerman, 1989; Kindermann, 1993; Kindermann, McCollam, & Gibson, 1996). The assumption is that it is not just children's closest friends, but also the larger group of peers, who exert influence over students. Critical in these network analyses is the characterization of the behavioral profiles of groups (Kindermann et al., 1996). The socialization hypothesis is that individual group members should become more like their group averages over time. Kindermann et al. (1996) found support for such socialization effects. When students were members of groups with high average engagement scores, their individual engagement improved over time. The opposite effect was obtained for members of groups with low engagement profiles. One of the most striking findings pertained to the stability of the motivational profiles of groups in spite of the relatively high turnover of specific group members. This finding highlights the fact that students select groups and groups welcome members based on the match between an individual's behavior and the group norm.

Quality of Friendships Versus Types of Friends

What matters more, the behaviors of peers or the qualitative aspects of the relationships (i.e., the support and validation friendships provide)? Comparing friendship qualities and friends' school-related behaviors (engagement and disruptiveness) among a sample of seventh and eight-graders, Berndt and Keefe (1995) found that both predicted changes in behaviors across the school year. Students with friendships characterized by support, intimacy, and validation increased school engagement, whereas students with friendships involving frequent conflict and rivalry or competition increased disruptive behavior during the school year. The engagement and disruptive behaviors of friends also affected changes in student behavior. Students whose friends described themselves as disruptive became more disruptive themselves by the end of the school year. Hence, it is not only the presence or absence of friendships but the relationship qualities as well as the characteristics of the friends that matter.

It is also important to consider whether relationship indicators are *directly* linked with school engagement and academic performance. It is possible that ability to get along with peers and capacity to form and maintain high-quality friendships with well-adjusted classmates reflect other competencies or social behaviors (e.g., prosocial behaviors, social competence) that predict success (Wentzel et al., 2004; Wentzel & Caldwell, 1997). The function of relationships (or lack thereof) has been tested in studies that focus on peer rejection, which is linked with a number of negative outcomes, including academic difficulties and overall school-related problems (McDougall, Hymel, Vaillancourt, & Mercer, 2001; Parker & Asher, 1987).

Peer Rejection

Peer rejection is commonly defined as peers' social avoidance of, dislike of, or reluctance to affiliate with a child. Hence, rejection by classmates threatens sense of belonging in school even more than lack of friends inasmuch as rejection affects group membership at the level of a classroom (cf. Furman & Robbins, 1985). Indeed, peer rejection assessed at an earlier point predicts lower grades in the first and second grade (O'Neil, Welsh, Parke, Wang, & Stand, 1997), less positive adjustment to kindergarten (Ladd, 1990), increased absenteeism and truancy during secondary school grades (DeRosier, Kupersmidt, & Patterson, 1994; Kupersmidt & Coie, 1990), and subsequent grade retention (Coie, Lochman, Terry, & Hyman, 1992).

Based on their review of empirical evidence, Hymel et al. (1996) conclude that peer rejection during elementary school increases the risks for subsequent dropping out of school. Although, students classified as rejected in fifth grade more frequently drop out of school than other students (Kupersmidt & Coie, 1990), there is little support suggesting that peer rejection independently contributes dropping out (see also Bierman & Wargo, 1995; Coie, Terry, Lenox, Lochman, & Hyman, 1995; Kupersmidt, Burchinal, & Patterson, 1995, for reviews on prediction of other signs of subsequent maladjustment). Cairns et al. (1989), for example, found that correlates of rejection (i.e., aggressive behavior and academic difficulties), rather than rejection per se, predicted early school leaving.

Hymel et al. (1996) contend that students prematurely leaving school are likely to (a) have experienced rejection by classmates *earlier* during their school careers, and (b) subsequently affiliate with peers who either drop out or are considered at risk of dropping out. Patterson, Capaldi, and Bank (1991) propose that childhood rejection limits aggressive children's options for healthy peer relationships, permitting them only to associate with and befriend similarly aggressive and rejected peers (see also Hektner, August, & Realmuto, 2000). Peers of aggressive-rejected youth indeed often display a wide spectrum of antisocial behaviors (French & Conrad, 2001) that are unlikely to foster connections with teachers or typical peers. Hence, although socially connected, aggressive students are alienated from the larger school community, as discussed in the earlier section of this chapter. Moreover, affiliation among antisocial peers is likely to facilitate "deviance training," thereby encouraging one another's problematic behavior (Dishion et al.,1996), including school disengagement. Deviant friends therefore partly account for the motivational and academic difficulties of aggressive students (possibly including the ultimate behavior of dropping out) who have been rejected earlier on. The temporal sequence may be depicted as:

Aggression→ Rejection→ Affiliation with Deviant Peers

→ Disengagement→ Achievement Decrements

Peer Harassment

Although aggressive and disruptive students are rejected by their classmates in elementary school (Rubin, LeMare, & Lollis, 1990), other types of behaviors and personality characteristics that deviate from peer-group norms also place students at risk for peer rejection (see for review Juvonen & Gross, 2005). For example, socially withdrawn, shy, and inhibited children (Rubin, LeMare, & Lollis, 1990) and students who are bullied or harassed (Graham & Juvonen, 1998a; Juvonen, Graham, & Schuster, 2003) are rejected by their peers, especially in middle school. Boivin and colleagues (Boivin & Hymel, 1997; Boivin, Hymel, & Bukowski, 1995) find that the

association between socially withdrawn (cf. submissive) behavior and internalizing problems can be accounted for by negative social experiences involving victimization and rejection. Moreover, peer harassment experiences and related emotional reactions are in turn associated with school adjustment problems (Graham & Juvonen, 1998b; Juvonen, Nishina, & Graham, 2000; Kochenderfer-Ladd, 2004; Nishina, Juvonen, & Witkow, 2005).

Longitudinal data on young children starting their school careers suggest that peer victimization increases lonely feelings and "colors" students' attitudes toward school. Examining changes during kindergarten, Kochenderfer and Ladd (1996) found that bullied kindergartners displayed increased loneliness and school avoidance by the end of the school year. In a similar prospective study during the first year in middle school, Nishina et al. (2005) report evidence for both direct and mediated effects of peer victimization and school functioning. Peer victimization experiences during the fall of sixth grade increased psychological maladjustment as well as health complaints during spring, which were related to end-of-the-year absences and grades. Symptoms of psychological distress (depressive symptoms, social anxiety, loneliness, and low self-worth) during fall of sixth grade also increased chances of students being victimized by spring, which was associated with worse school functioning. Hence, socially aversive peer experiences and distress are interrelated in a cyclical manner (see also Egan & Perry, 1998) and therefore likely to compromise adaptive school functioning (see also Juvonen et al., 2000).

Bullying research suggests that emotional distress (including related physical health problems) associated with aversive and exclusionary peer interactions contributes to negative school attitudes and a desire to withdraw from or avoid school. Although focusing on physical threats rather than emotional stress, analyses based on the National Household Education Survey (NHES) provide some support for this school avoidance hypothesis. In a nationwide sample of public school students, one quarter of middle and junior high school students reported deliberately staying away from certain places in the school (e.g., restrooms) to protect themselves. More importantly, about 10 percent of African American and Latino students indicated staying home from school because of worry about being targeted. The report concludes: "Students who must think about avoiding harm at school are diverting energy that should be expended on learning" (U.S. Department of Education, 1993, p. 3). The latest experimental social-psychological research indeed indicates that rejection impedes performance on cognitive tasks (Baumeister & DeWall, 2005; Baumeister et al., 2002). Hence, concerns with being cast out or ridiculed in school interfere with students' ability to fully engage and concentrate on their academic assignments.

In sum, peer relationships are related to school adjustment. However, the specific links are more complex than in the case of teacher–student relationships. The direct and indirect pathways between peer relationships and school functioning vary depending on the qualities and characteristics of friends, peer-group norms, and behaviors that evoke rejection from classmates. Although supportive friendships are generally associated with increased school adjustment, friendships with students who display antisocial tendencies increase risk of disengagement and alienation from school. Aggressive children rejected by their peers in elementary school have limited subsequent opportunities to form social bonds with adjusted peers and therefore the company they keep (i.e., deviant schoolmates) partly accounts for their school problems. In the case of socially withdrawn and submissive students, peer rejection, victimization, and distress are, in turn, predictive of increased absences from school and lower grades. Hence, different pathways can lead to compromised school functioning.

MECHANISMS AND FUNCTIONS OF SCHOOL-BASED SOCIAL BONDS

Taken together, the three bodies of research reviewed thus far (sense of belonging, teacher–student relationships, and peer relations) are consistent in demonstrating that students feeling connected and supported do better than those who are disconnected, unsupported, or socially alienated. Although frequently implicit, mechanisms can be identified that explain why and how school-based relationships might facilitate school success and why lack of support and feelings of social alienation are linked with compromised school functioning. Building on the conceptual model proposed by Connell and Wellborn (1991), Furrer and Skinner (2003) propose the association between feelings of relatedness and motivation is mediated by self-appraisals. They contend students are more likely to be involved and engaged in school when feeling valued and accepted by important others (cf. Leary, 2005). Students, who feel respected and valued, are likely to show their enthusiasm, which then leads to more opportunities to learn. Engagement in turn elicits positive feedback and thus promotes relationships between teachers and students, as depicted in the following model:

Relationships → Self-views of Worthiness → Engagement → Achievement

Although this model can also explain why students with unsupportive relationships become disengaged from school, researchers emphasize the additional role of negative emotions, such as frustration and distress. Furrer and Skinner (2003) propose that students who do not feel valued or supported in school become frustrated and distance themselves from learning activities. Wentzel (1998), in turn, finds that lack of perceived social support from peers (and also parents) is associated with emotional distress, which then decreases interest in school. Disinterest and disengagement might in turn maintain poor-quality relationships, at least with teachers.

Poor-quality school-based → Distress, → Disengagement → Achievement
relationships   frustration   problems

The findings across the domains of school social climate, teacher–student relationships, and peer relationships also indicate that positive relationships and sense of connectedness are especially critical at certain times and for particular groups of students. When students are acclimating to a new school setting, they especially benefit from sense of connectedness and support. Moreover, research on disadvantaged or "at risk" student, and specifically those displaying early behavior problems, shows that supportive relationships and sense of connectedness play critical protective functions. In other words, having alliances with trusted others buffers the negative emotional effects of either temporary or more chronic forms of stress.

Which Social Bonds Matter the Most?

Although many studies focus on peer or teacher–student relationships, there are only a handful of investigations comparing different sources or types of support as they may be differently associated with school outcomes. Comparing teacher and peer support, Marchant, Paulson, and Rothlisberg (2001) found that fifth- and sixth-grade student perceptions of teacher and school responsiveness (perceived warmth, nurturance, and safety) as well as perceptions of the achievement orientation of their peers ("My friends think it is important to do well in school") each predicted student motivation and academic competence. Furrer and Skinner (2003), in turn, demonstrated that third- to sixth-grade students' reports of relatedness to teachers, parents, and peers each contributed uniquely to subsequent engagement in school across a school year.

Wentzel's (1998) findings regarding sixth- to eighth-grade students' perceptions suggest that the effects of

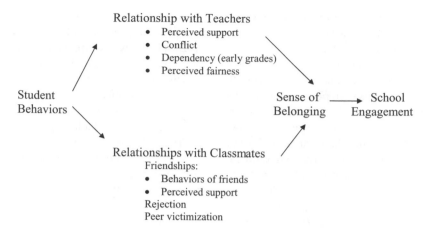

FIGURE 28.1. A model summarizing research findings regarding the associations among student behaviors, school-based relationships, sense of belonging, and school engagement.

multiple sources of support on motivation and academic performance are compensatory rather than additive. She finds teacher support most influential in facilitating classroom functioning and level of interest (cf. Malecki & Demaray, 2003). Yet in most studies comparing the predictive power of teachers versus peers, the characteristics and behaviors of the peers are not taken into account. Hence, teacher support might be a more consistent predictor of adaptive functioning because it typically promotes academic engagement and compliance to classroom rules, whereas peers can "pull" students in different directions depending on the behaviors of friends. Finally, it is important to recognize that teacher support and peer relationships might also work in a synergistic manner. For example, Ryan and Patrick (2001) found that seventh graders' perceptions of teacher encouragement of mutual respect and harmony among classmates were the best predictor of level of engagement.

Summary

Some of the main conclusions based on the current empirical research on sense of belonging and social bonds are summarized in Fig. 28.1. The review of the empirical research indicates the importance of student behaviors affecting the types of relationships they might (be able to) engage in. Consideration of maladaptive social behaviors (aggression and social withdrawal) can illustrate the sequences depicted in Fig. 28.1. For example, aggression affects whether a student forms a positive and supportive relationship with teachers. Aggression also increases the risk of the students being rejected by

classmates in elementary school and hence limits their subsequent chances of establishing and maintaining supportive friendships with classmates who do not display behavior problems. Socially withdrawn students, on the other hand, may form highly dependent or "clingy" relationships with teachers in elementary school. Moreover, they are increasingly likely to be harassed and rejected by their classmates starting in middle school. Hence, socially withdrawn and submissive students, who often are prime targets of peer harassment, might ultimately suffer most from lack of support and social isolation. In contrast, aggressive students frequently find similar others to affiliate with, but the socialization effects of these peers do not necessarily facilitate school engagement.

The proposed general model depicted in Fig. 28.1 also suggests that it is through the social relationships with teachers and peers that students develop a sense of belonging in school. Although this connection is rarely explicitly tested (see Roeser et al., 1996, for an exception), many of the measures on school climate tap onto these specific relationships. If students view their relationships with teachers as supportive, nonconflictual, and fair, they are more likely to feel they belong in school. Perceptions of unfair treatment and conflict (possibly due to discrimination), in turn, increase sense of alienation. Friendships and membership in school-based peer networks facilitate, whereas rejection and especially harassment impede, feelings of belonging in school. It should be noted, however, that rejection by classmates (e.g., because of their aggressive behavior) can be compensated by friendships with other marginalized students. Hence, some rejected students can nevertheless feel a sense of connectedness.

Although the review of the school social climate and teacher–student relationships supports the proposition that social affiliations promote school functioning, it is important to recognize that we cannot conclude from these data that social bonds always foster increased motivation and improved achievement. Rather, it is the lack of *adaptive* social bonds that places youth at greatest risk for school failure. For example, research just reviewed on aggressive students shows they are socially connected (e.g., belong to school-based peer networks and have friends), yet do not do well in school. Instead, some of the most popular or admired middle school students are not engaged and may in fact overtly display disinterest in school by acting out (e.g., Graham, Taylor, & Hudley, 1998; Juvonen & Cadigan, 2002; Juvonen, Graham, & Schuster, 2003).

Many of the negative socialization effects of peer relationships emerge not during elementary school but starting during middle grades (Juvonen & Cadigan, 2002). Given that the middle school transition is related to declining interest in school, motivation, grades, and increased behavior problems (e.g., Eccles et al., 1993), it is particularly relevant to consider how these changes might be associated with school-based peer relationships during early adolescence. Guided by relevant social-psychological theories on social identity, self-categorization, perceived group norms, impression management, compliance, and pluralistic ignorance, the last section of this chapter focuses on these relatively understudied topics in educational psychology within a developmental framework. The question is when and why peer relationships promote maladaptive rather than adaptive school behaviors in general.

WHY AND HOW SOCIAL BONDS PROMOTE DISENGAGEMENT

Tracking students from middle school to high school, Fuligni, Eccles, Barber, and Clements (2001) found that students willing to sacrifice their school performance and abidance of parent-imposed rules to facilitate their peer relationships displayed problem behaviors and poor achievement in middle school. The effect of this "extreme peer orientation" (see also Fuligni & Eccles, 1993) on school behavior was mediated by students' reported involvement in deviant peer groups. Although these findings depict the potentially detrimental "pull" of deviant peers only on a subset of students, they might be also applicable to explain more normative declines in student motivation and increased problem behaviors during middle and high school.

Redefining "Who I Am"

During early adolescence, when time spent with peers often surpasses time spent with parents and family (Larson & Richards, 1991), youth desire to become less dependent on parents (Steinberg & Silverberg, 1986; Youniss & Smollar, 1985). Young adolescents no longer use adults as their role models (Harris, 1995), but begin to define themselves in reference to their peers (Newman & Newman, 2001). Hence, the need for increased autonomy during early adolescence does not imply that young teens are striving for ultimate independence. Rather, they are simply reconfiguring their alliances to existing groups. Steinberg and Silverberg (1986) proposed that in early adolescence youth "trade" dependency on parents for increased dependency on peers. This "trade" also applies to other adult authority figures, such as teachers (Juvonen & Cadigan, 2002).

These shifting alliances to become more independent of adult authority and more like their peers have important implications on school behaviors. Not only do friends become increasingly important sources of support and validation, but concerns for peer-group approval are heightened during early adolescence (Berndt, 1979; Gavin & Furman, 1989; Harter, 1990, 1996). As youth desire to be included by their peers and be like them, it is essential to recognize which characteristics or behaviors facilitate peer approval. There is evidence suggesting that school-related attributes presumed to promote peer approval become increasingly distinct from those related to teacher liking by early adolescence.

Perceived Values of Others and Self-Categorization

In an experiment involving assessment of teacher liking and peer approval, Juvonen and Murdock (1995) asked students in grades 4, 6, and 8 to evaluate hypothetical peers who varied in terms of two main determinants of academic success: effort and ability (cf. Weiner & Kukla, 1970). The hypothetical classmates were presumed to have succeeded in an important test and they varied in terms of how hard they studied and how smart they were. Fourth through eighth graders (i.e., 10- to 14-year-olds) all believed that teachers like smart and hard-working students the most. Yet when asked to evaluate how liked these same students are among the popular group of classmates, substantial differences were documented between fourth and eighth grade. Fourth-grade students believed their peers would like the same student as teachers (i.e., the one who is smart and works hard). By eighth grade this student was rated less popular than the rest.

Instead, eighth-grade students considered students who "slack off" to be more popular (regardless of level of ability) than those who were diligent. Thus, hard work (cf. active school engagement) was not perceived to be socially rewarded by peers who have high social status.

The findings just described depict adolescents (i.e., eighth graders), as opposed to younger students, differentiating between determinants of social approval by their teachers versus classmates. These findings along with a body of ethnographic research on "oppositional" peer culture (Fordham & Ogbu, 1986; Ogbu, 1991, 1997) and resistance research (Alpert, 1991; McLaren, 1986) suggest that middle and high school students' behavior is influenced by peer culture that has contrasting values and behavioral expectations than those endorsed by adult authorities (cf. also Coleman, 1961).

The perceptions of contrasting values between peer groups and adult authority are consistent with predictions made by social psychological theories on self-categorization (Turner, 1982; Turner, Oaks, Haslam, & McGarty, 1994) and social identity (Tajfel & Turner, 1979; Tajfel, 1981), inasmuch as increased differentiation between teachers (and parents) versus peers reflects distinctions made between in-groups and out-groups (i.e., "us vs. them"). A need to become less dependent on authority figures may require that students define their new in-group (i.e., peers) in contrast to the out-group consisting of authority figures endorsing conventional values associated with academic success (cf. Hogg, Turner, & Davidson, 1990; see also Harris, 1995, for related discussion).

Personal Values Versus Perceived Values of Peers as Motivators of Behavior

Changes in student behaviors between elementary grades and subsequent grades are typically presumed to reflect changes in their values (e.g., importance of achievement), yet few age-related differences in values have been documented. Comparing age related differences in personal values and perceived values of peers among 10- to 17-year-old students, Cohen and Cohen (1996) obtained few age-related differences in personal values but substantial differences in perceptions of what peers value. Perceptions of peers valuing antisocial behaviors (being tough, defiant, fighting) increased sharply to age 15 with no significant changes thereafter, whereas perceptions of peer admiration for conventional behaviors (friendly, helpful, getting good grades) declined until age 12 and leveled thereafter. Moreover, whereas the youngest participants assumed their peers valued the same behaviors as they did, the older youth (especially 13- to 15-year-olds) presumed that their peers valued antisocial behavior more

and conventional behaviors less than they did. These perceptions of what peers value are important given that they are likely to affect how young adolescents conduct themselves in school.

Social psychological research suggests that the associations between personal attitudes (cf. values) and behaviors are weaker than expected (Eagley & Chaiken, 1993), whereas the effects of perceived norms (cf. values of relevant reference groups) might be stronger than traditionally presumed (Terry & Hogg, 1996). Specifically, constructs tapping prevalence (i.e., normativeness) of behavior and perceived attitudes among members of a reference group (i.e., agreement among group members about the importance of behavior) have been successfully used to predict action (e.g., White, Terry, & Hogg, 1994). Perceived norms of a relevant reference group predict behavior especially when individuals strongly identify with the group (Terry & Hogg, 1996).

Social psychological research on impression management or self-presentation also helps us to understand the effects of perceived peer-group norms and values. This research shows that individuals modify their public behavior so that it is consistent with the values of those they wish to please or to get along with (Baumeister, 1982; Leary & Kowalski, 1989). To be able to "fit in" within the new peer groups in middle school, students need to (a) infer what these peers value, and (b) modify their behavior in ways consistent with their values.

Recent ethnographic data reveal that middle school students are quite aware of what it takes to fit in or be popular in middle school. When asked whether students who get good grades can be popular, a sixth-grade male student replied:

"You'd still have to have your bad attitude. You have to act—it's just like a movie. You have to act. And then at home you're a regular kind of guy, you don't act mean or nothing. But when you're around your friends you have to be sharp and stuff like that, like push everybody around." (Juvonen & Cadigan, 2002, p. 282)

This example suggests that middle school students are quite aware of how this type of "acting" does not necessarily reflect their personal attitudes or values but believe it facilitates peer approval (Juvonen, 1996).

Misperceived Norms: Pluralistic Ignorance

As depicted earlier, comparisons between self-endorsed values and perceptions of peer-endorsed values show that 13- to 15-year-old students erroneously believe their peers value antisocial behaviors more and conventional behaviors less than they actually do (or report that they do; Cohen & Cohen, 1996). Although the presumed psychological contrasts between peers and adult authority can explain why youth display such biases, they are also likely to rely on behavioral observations to assess peer-group norms.

Inferences based on observations of other people's behavior are also subject to biases that can further help us understand the "direction" of error involved in estimating group norms. Miller and Prentice (1994a, 1994b) propose that although individuals are aware that they themselves modify their own behavior to facilitate social approval, they falsely assume that other people's behavior accurately reflects their personal values and attitudes. Pluralistic ignorance therefore arises when "the facades that . . . individuals present to one another are so effective that everyone is convinced of their authenticity" (Miller & Prentice, 1994b, p. 542). Thus, incoming middle school students may use the behaviors of salient high-status peers to infer group values that promote social success within their new social collective (Juvonen & Cadigan, 2002). Because of this bias, youth come to incorrectly "compute" the group norm. Hence, pluralistic ignorance may explain why inaccurate views of what peers admire or like might pull students to behave in ways that do not promote school success.

Summary and a Modified Model

Taken together, the need to fit in within a new social scene may help us understand the increased motivational and disciplinary problems associated with the transition to middle school. Developmental changes associated with the need to become less dependent on adult authority and the environmental changes associated with middle school transition are likely to prompt realignment of alliances. Simple categorization between in-groups (peers) and out-groups (teachers) may help youth master their new, much larger social world, yet it is also likely to foster a perception of peer culture that is viewed antithetical to the mission of the school. Miscalculated perceptions of peer-group norms that polarize the differences between teachers and peers then affect student behavior.

Although these social psychological explanations provide insights into negative changes in student behavior as they enter middle school, it is less clear whether their self-presentation tactics indeed compromise school success. Socially successful students appear to have learned self-presentation strategies that allow them to enjoy both social rewards and academic success. For example, Fordham and Ogbu (1996) depict examples of strategies academically successful African American students relied

on to avoid peer ridicule. Whereas some students chose to hang out with the "tough kids," others resorted to distracting tactics, such as clowning around to avoid peer ridicule. Hence, social strategies that protected their public image did not necessarily have any detrimental effects on their academic performance. Although older students indeed realize that they need to modify their *public* behavior to act consistently with their perceptions of the values of those whose company they seek, these impression management tactics nevertheless affect the climate of the learning environment in ways that does not foster engagement.

Research reviewed in this last section of the chapter points out limitations of the earlier presented models linking school-based social relationships and school functioning. Although peer relationships foster sense of belonging (see Fig. 28.1), they do not necessarily promote behaviors that increase engagement and academic functioning. From the perspective of a student who wishes to form relationships and belong, it is adaptive to infer the values of those they wish to affiliate with. Hence, public displays of behavior that are consistent with the presumed values of desirable others mediate the relation between belongingness and school behavior, as follows:

Need to → Adoption of
Belong → Valued Behaviors by Desirable Others → School Behavior

In the proposed model, belonging is considered a need or motive that prompts behavioral changes, whereas in the models proposed earlier, belonging was considered a result or outcome of relationships. It is critical to realize that although different types of social bonds indeed facilitate sense of belonging, the need to belong or the desire to be accepted by specific others is also likely to affect student behavior. If the sense of belonging is not satisfied, students must modify their behaviors in ways that help them better bond with others. For example, compliance to group norms can also be motivated by fear of exclusion or ridicule (Fordham & Ogbu, 1996). Given the aversive emotional consequences of rejection, students may wish to abide by the norms set by peers or the expectations of teachers (Juvonen & Cadigan, 2002).

Taken together, whether school-based social bonds facilitate school engagement might not be as simple as research on elementary school age students suggests. Although the links between school engagement and teacher and peer support might indeed motivate students to work hard and do well in school in lower grades, the direction of the effect might change by middle school. Research suggests that young adolescents who are increasingly concerned about peer approval (a) come to view their peer group norms inconsistent with values and expectations

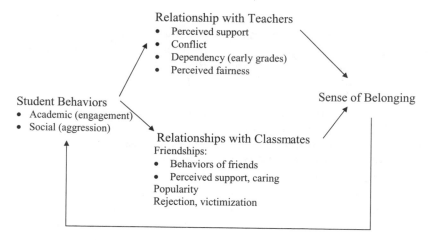

FIGURE 28.2. A proposed model depicting the associations between student behaviors, school-based relationships, and sense of belonging.

of their teachers and parents and (b) publicly behave in ways that are more consistent with their views of peer-group values. Hence, while sense of belonging might be important to all students regardless of their age, need to belong or desire to identify with peers serves as an important, developmentally relevant motive to change one's behavior when acclimating to a new social scene of middle school.

These conclusions suggest that the model depicted in Fig. 28.1 needs to be more dynamic than what the empirical research that it is based on implies. As suggested in Fig. 28.2, an added path or source of influence from sense of belonging back to student behavior is required. This effect can account for the socialization and selection influences of unsatisfied or threatened sense of belonging (Williams, 2001; Williams, Forgas, & von Hippel, 2005), which prompt behaviors that allow students to either repair their existing relationships or to form new ones. In this more parsimonious model, student behaviors refer to a range of social as well as academically related actions that affect the "social success" of students. In short, the model suggests that the need to belong affects student school behaviors in ways that in turn influence their ability to form and maintain relationships in school.

FINAL CONCLUSIONS

Based on the current review of empirical research and subsequent theorizing on school-based social bonds, sense of belonging, and school functioning, a set of conclusions can be made. The most general conclusions are summarized here.

1. School environments in which students feel disconnected, disrespected, and unfairly treated by their teachers and peers do not motivate students to work hard. Rather, *social isolation, alienation, and lack of support increase educational risks.* This conclusion applies across studies on school social climate, teacher–student relationships, and peer relationships.

2. Based on the current evidence reviewed in this chapter, *it is premature, however, to conclude that social bonds are necessary for students to be engaged in school.* Research on teacher–student relationships suggests that perceptions of teacher support might merely reflect student behavior, inasmuch as academically engaged students are most likely to get along with their instructors.

3. Although teacher support may not cause students to engage academically, *supportive, close, and non-conflictual teacher–student relationships can protect students with early behavior problems from educational risks.* Based on this buffering effect, it is therefore important to recognize that supportive teacher–student relationships are especially critical when students are unlikely to establish adaptive relationships.

4. Similar findings regarding the protective functions of school social climate were reviewed. *Caring and supportive school context appear particularly important when students experience distress* (e.g., chronic distress due to history of academic problems, or lack of parent support due to economic hardship, or temporary and more normative stress associated with transition from elementary to larger and more anonymous middle schools). Hence, the effects of belonging based

on school climate and teacher–student relationships on student engagement are likely to be mediated by distress.

5. Although relationships with classmates foster sense of belonging, they do not necessarily promote school engagement. *The effects of sense of belonging based on peer relationships vary depending on the behaviors of the company that students seek and keep.* Hence, peer selection and socialization determine whether belonging facilitates school engagement.

6. Although sense of belonging in school is psychologically important for all students regardless of their age, *the source of belonging and its effects on behaviors vary across development.* For example, the apparent declines in achievement motivation or increase in oppositional behavior associated with the transition to middle school can be explained by developmental changes in the importance of peers and the changing definition of peer groups in contrast to adult authority.

7. When considering the interplay between teacher–student relationships and social bonds with peers across development, it becomes clear that *unmet or threatened sense of belonging is not only an outcome of relationships, but also motivates changes in student behavior.* Desire to belong to a peer group that is believed to question or oppose the values of hard work and academic success fosters behaviors that do not promote engagement. These findings suggest that a conceptual model that depicts the relations among sense of belonging, school-based social bonds, and adaptive school behavior is more dynamic than what has been previously presumed.

ACKNOWLEDGMENTS

I want to thank Elisheva Gross, Sandra Graham, Shelley Hymel, Philip Winne, and Bernard Weiner for their comments on the earlier version of this chapter.

References

Alexander, K. L., Entwisle, D. R., & Kabbani, N. (2001). The drop out process in life course perspective: Early risk factors at home and school. *Teachers College Record, 103*, 760–822.

Alpert, B. (1991). Students' resistance in the classroom. *Anthropology and Education Quarterly, 22*, 350–366.

Arroyo, C. G., & Zigler, E. (1995). Racial identity, academic achievement, and the psychological well-being of economically disadvantaged adolescents. *Journal of Personality and Social Psychology, 69*, 903–914.

Azmitia, M., & Montgomery, R. (1993). Friendship, transactive dialogues, and the development of scientific reasoning. *Social Development, 2*, 202–221.

Battistich, V., & Hom, A. (1997). The relationship between students' sense of their school as a community and their involvement in problem behaviors. *American Journal of Public Health, 87*, 1997–2001.

Battistich, V., Solomon, D., Kim, D., Watson, M., & Schaps, E. (1995). Schools as communities, poverty levels of student populations, and students' attitudes, motives, and performance: A multilevel analysis. *American Educational Research Journal, 32*, 627–658.

Baumeister, R. F. (1982). A self-presentational view of social phenomena. *Psychological Bulletin, 91*, 3–26.

Baumeister, R. F., & DeWall, C. N. (2005). The inner dimension of social exclusion: Intelligent thought and self-regulation among rejected persons. In K. D. Williams, J. P. Forgas, & W. von Hippel (Eds.). *The social outcast: Ostracism, social exclusion, rejection, and bullying* (pp. 53–73). New York: Psychology Press.

Baumeister, R. F., & Leary, M. R. (1995). The need to belong: Desire for interpersonal attachments as a fundamental human motivation. *Psychological Bulletin, 117*, 497–529.

Baumeister, R. F., Twenge, J., & Nuss, C. (2002). Effects of social exclusion on cognitive processes: Anticipated aloneness reduces intelligent thought. *Journal of Personality and Social Psychology, 83*, 817–827.

Becker, B. E., & Luthar, S. S. (2002). Social-emotional factors affecting achievement outcomes among disadvantaged students: Closing the achievement gap. *Educational Psychologist, 37*, 197–214.

Berkman, L. F., & Syme, L. (1979). Social networks, host resistance, and mortality: A nine-year follow-up study of alameda county residents. *American Journal of Epidemiology, 109*, 186–203.

Berndt, T. J. (1979). Developmental changes in conformity to peers and parents. *Developmental Psychology, 15*, 608–616.

Berndt, T. J. (1999). Friends' influence on students' adjustment to school. *Educational Psychologist, 34*, 15–28.

Berndt, T. J. (2002). Friendship quality and social development. *Current Directions in Psychological Science, 11*, 7–10.

Berndt, T. J., Hawkins, J. A., & Jiao, Z. (1999). Influences of friends and friendships on adjustment to junior high school. *Merrill-Palmer Quarterly, 45*, 13–41.

Berndt, T. J., & Keefe, K. (1995). Friends' influence on adolescents' adjustment to school. *Child Development, 66*, 1312–1329.

Bierman, K. L., & Wargo, J. B. (1995). Predicting the longitudinal course associated with aggressive-rejected, aggressive (nonrejected), and rejected (nonaggressive) status. *Development and Psychopathology, 7,* 669-682.

Birch, S. H., & Ladd, G. W. (1997). The teacher-child relationship and children's early school adjustment. *Journal of School Psychology, 35,* 61-79.

Boivin, M., & Hymel, S. (1997). Peer experiences and social self-perceptions: A sequential model. *Developmental Psychology, 33,* 135-145.

Boivin, M., Hymel, S., & Bukowski, W. M. (1995). The roles of social withdrawal, peer rejection, and victimization by peers in predicting loneliness and depressed mood in childhood. *Development and Psychopathology, 7,* 765-785.

Bolger, N., Zuckerman, A., & Kessler, R. C. (2000). Invisible support and adjustment to stress. *Journal of Personality and Social Psychology, 79,* 953-961.

Brand, S., Felner, R., Shim, M. Seitsinger, A., & Dumas, T. (2003). Middle school improvement and reform: Development and validation of a school-level assessment of climate, cultural pluralism, and school safety. *Journal of Educational Psychology, 95,* 570-588.

Bryk, A. S., Lee, V. E., & Holland, P. B. (1993). *Catholic schools and the common good.* Cambridge, MA: Harvard University Press.

Cairns, R. B., Cairns, B. D. & Neckerman, H. J. (1989). Early school dropout: Configurations and determinants. *Child Development, 60,* 1437-1452.

Carnegie Council on Adolescent Development. (1989). *Turning points: Preparing American youth for the 21st century.* New York: Carnegie Corporation of New York.

Cohen, P., & Cohen, J. (1996). *Life values and adolescent mental health.* Mahwah, NJ: Lawrence Erlbaum Associates.

Cohen, S. (2004). Social relationships and health. *American Psychologist, 59,* 676-684.

Cohen, S., & Wills, T. A. (1998). Stress, social support, and the buffering hypothesis. *Psychological Bulletin, 98,* 310-357.

Coie, J. D., Lochman, J. E., Terry, R., & Hyman, C. (1992). Predicting early adolescent disorder from childhood aggression and peer rejection. *Journal of Consulting and Clinical Psychology, 60,* 783-792.

Coie, J., Terry, R., Lenox, K, Lochman, J., & Hyman, C. (1995). Childhood peer rejection and aggression as predictors of stable patterns of adolescent disorder. *Development and Psychopathology, 7,* 697-713.

Coleman, J. S. (1961). *The adolescent society.* New York: Free Press.

Comer, J. C. (1980). The influence of mood on student evaluations of teaching. *Journal of Educational Research, 73,* 229-232.

Connell, J. P., & Wellborn, J. G. (1991). Competence, autonomy, and relatedness: A motivational analysis of self-system processes. In M. R. Gunmar & L. A. Sroufe (Eds.), *Self processes and development: The Minnesota symposia on child development* (Vol. 23, pp. 43-78). Hillsdale, NJ: Lawrence Erlbaum Associates.

DeRosier, M., Kupersmidt, J. B., & Patterson, C. J. (1994). Children's academic and behavioral adjustment as a function of the chronicity and proximity of peer rejection. *Child Development, 65,* 1799-1813.

Dewey, J. (1943). The principles. *Psychological Review, 50,* 121.

Dishion, T. J., Spracklen, K. M., Andrews, D. W., & Patterson, G. R. (1996). Deviancy training in male adolescent friendships. *Behavior Therapy, 27,* 373-390.

Dodge, K. A., Pettit, G. S., Bates, J. E. (1994). Socialization mediators of the relation between socioeconomic status and child conduct problems. *Child Development, 65,* 649-665.

Eagley, A. H., & Chaiken, S. (1993). *The psychology of attitudes.* Forth Worth, TX: Harcourt Brace Jovanovich.

Eccles, J. S., Barber, B. L., Stone, M., & Hunt, J. (2003). Extracurricular activities and adolescent development. *Journal of Social Issues, 59,* 865-889.

Eccles, J. S., Midgley, C., Wigfield, A., Buchanan, C. M., Rueman, D., Flanagan, C., et al. (1993). Development during adolescence: The impact of stage environment fit on young adolescents' experiences in school and in families. *American Psychologist, 48,* 90-101.

Egan, S. K., & Perry, D. G. (1998). Does low self-regard invite victimization? *Developmental Psychology, 34,* 299-309.

Ekstrom, R. B., Goertz, M. E., Pollack, J. M., & Rock, D. A. (1986). Who drops out of high school and why? Findings from a national study. *Educational Testing Service, 87,* 356-373.

Feldlaufer, H., Midgley, C., & Eccles, J. S. (1988). Student, teacher, and observer perceptions of the classroom before and after the transition to junior high school. *Journal of Early Adolescence, 8,* 133-156.

Felner, R. D., & Felner, T. Y. (1989). Primary prevention programs in the educational context: A transactional-ecological framework and analysis. In L. A. Bond & B. E. Compas (Eds.), *Primary prevention and promotion in the schools* (pp. 13-49). Thousand Oaks, CA: Sage.

Felner, R. D., Jackson, A. W., Kasak, D., Mulhall, P, Brand, S., & Flowers, N. (1997). The impact of school reform for the middles years: Longitudinal study of a network engaged in turning points-based comprehensive school transformation. *Phi Delta Kappan, 78,* 528-550.

Finn, J. D. (1989). Withdrawing from school. *Review of Educational Research, 59,* 117-142.

Finn, J. D. (1993). School engagement and students at risk (NCES-93-470). Washington, DC: National Center for Education Statistics.

Fisher, C., Wallace, S., & Fenton, R. (2000). Discrimination distress during adolescence. *Journal of Youth and Adolescence, 29,* 679-694.

Fordham, S., & Ogbu, J. U. (1986). Black students' school success: Coping with "burden of 'acting White." *Urban Review, 18,* 176-206.

French, D. C., & Conrad, J. (2001). School dropout as predicted by peer rejection and antisocial behavior. *Journal of Research on Adolescence, 11,* 225-244.

Fuligni, A. J., & Eccles, J. S. (1993). Perceived parent-child relationships and early adolescents' orientation toward peers. *Developmental Psychology, 29,* 622-632.

Fuligni, A. J., Eccles, J. S., Barber, C. L., & Clements, P. (2001). Early adolescent peer orientation and adjustment during high school. *Developmental Psychology, 37,* 28-36.

Furman, W., & Robbins, P. (1985). What's the point? Selection of treatment objectives. In B, Schneider, K. H. Rubin, & J. E. Ledingham (Eds.), *Children's peer relations: Issues in assessment and intervention.* (pp. 41-54). New York: Springer-Verlag.

Furrer, C., & Skinner, E. (2003). Sense of relatedness as a factor in children's academic engagement and performance. *Journal of Educational Psychology, 95,* 148-163.

Gavin, L. A., & Furman, W. (1989). Age differences in adolescents' perceptions of their peer groups. *Developmental Psychology, 25,* 827-834.

Goodenow, C. (1993). Classroom belonging among early adolescent students: Relationships to motivation and achievement. *Journal of Early Adolescence, 13,* 21-43.

Graham, S., Bellmore, S., & Mize, J. (in press). *Aggression, victimization and their cooccurrence in middle school.* Journal of Abnormal Child Psychology.

Graham, S., & Hudley, C. (2005). Race and ethnicity in the study of motivation and competence. In A. Elliot & C. S. Dweck (Eds.), *The handbook of competence and motivation.* (pp. 392-413) New York: Guilford.

Graham, S., & Juvonen, J. (1998a). Self-blame and peer victimization in middle school: An attributional analysis. *Developmental Psychology, 34,* 587-599.

Graham, S., & Juvonen, J. (1998b). Social-cognitive perspective on peer aggression and victimization. *Annals of Child Development, 13,* 23-70.

Graham, S., Taylor, A. A., & Hudley, C. (1998). Exploring achievement values among ethnic minority early adolescents. *Journal of Educational Psychology, 90,* 606-620.

Gust, D. A., Gordon, T. P., Brodie, A. R., & McClure, H , M. (1994). Effect of a preferred companion in modulating stress in adult female rhesus monkeys. *Physiology & Behavior, 55,* 681-684.

Hallinan, M. T. (1983). Commentary: New directions for research on peer influence. In J. L. Epstein & N. Karweit (Eds.), *Friends in school: Patterns of selection and influence in secondary schools* (pp. 219-231). New York: Academic Press.

Hamre, B. K., & Pianta, R. C. (2001). Early teacher-child relationships and the trajectory of children's school outcomes through eighth grade. *Child Development, 72,* 625-638.

Harris, J. R. (1995). Where is the child's environment? A group socialization theory of development. *Psychological Review, 102,* 458-489.

Harter, S. (1990). Causes, correlates and the functional role of global self-worth: A life-span perspective. In J. Kolligian & R. Sternberg (Eds.), *Perceptions of competence and incompetence across the life-span* (pp. 67-98). New Haven, CT: Yale University Press.

Harter, S. (1996). Self-presentation tactics promoting teacher and peer approval: The function of excuses and other clever explanations. In J. Juvonen & K. R. Wentzel (Eds.), *Social motivation: Understanding children's school adjustment* (pp. 43-65). New York: Cambridge University Press.

Hartup, W. W. (1996). The company they keep: Friendships and their developmental significance. *Child Development, 67,* 1-13.

Hektner, J. M., August, G. J., & Realmuto, G. M. (2000). Patterns and temporal changes in peer affiliation among aggressive and nonaggressive children participating in a summer school program. *Journal of Clinical Child Psychology, 29,* 603-614.

Hogg, M A., Turner, J. C., & Davidson, B. (1990). Polarized norms and social frames of reference: A test of the self-categorization theory of group polarization. *Basic & Applied Social Psychology, 11,* 77-100.

House, J. S., Landis, K. R., & Umberson, D. (1988). Social relationships and health. *Science, 241,* 540-545.

Hughes, J. N., Cavell, T. A., & Jackson, T. (1999). Influence of the teacher-student relationship on childhood conduct problems: A prospective study. *Journal of Clinical Child Psychology, 28,* 173-184.

Hymel, S., Comfort, C., Schonert-Reichl, K., & McDougall, P. (1996). Academic failure and school dropout: The influence of peers. In J. Juvonen & K. R. Wentzel (Eds.), *Social motivation: Understanding children's school adjustment* (pp. 313-345). New York: Cambridge University Press.

Juvonen, J. (1996). Self-presentation tactics promoting teacher and peer approval: The function of excuses and other clever explanations. In J. Juvonen and K. R. Wentzel (Eds.), *Social motivation: Understanding children's school adjustment* (pp. 43-65). New York: Cambridge University Press.

Juvonen, J., & Cadigan, R. J. (2002). Social determinants of public behavior of middle school youth: Perceived peer norms and need to be accepted. In F. Pajares & T. Urdan (Eds.), *Adolescence and education, Vol. 2: Academic motivation of adolescents* (pp. 277-297).Greenwich, CT: Information Age.

Juvonen, J., Graham, S., & Schuster, M. (2003). Bullying among young adolescents: The strong, weak, and troubled. *Pediatrics, 112,* 1231-1237.

Juvonen, J., & Gross, E. F. (2005). The rejected and the bullied: Lessons about social misfits from developmental psychology. In K. D. Williams, P. P. Forgas, & W. von Hippel (Eds.), *The social outcast: Ostracism, social exclusion, rejection, and bullying* (pp. 155-170). New York: Psychology Press.

Juvonen, J., & Murdock, T. B. (1995). Grade-level differences in the social value of effort: Implications for self-presentation tactics of early adolescents. *Child Development, 66,* 1694-1705.

Juvonen, J., Nishina, A., & Graham, S. (2000). Peer harassment, psychological adjustment, and school functioning in early adolescence. *Journal of Educational Psychology, 92,* 349-359.

Juvonen, J., & Wentzel, K. R. (1996). *Social motivation: Understanding children's school adjustment.* New York: Cambridge University Press.

Kandel, D. B. (1996). The parental and peer contexts of adolescent deviance: An algebra of interpersonal influences. *Journal of Drug Issues, 26,* 289-315.

Kaplan, D. S., Peck, B. M., & Kaplan, H. B. (1997). Decomposing the academic failure-dropout relationship: A longitudinal analysis. *Journal of Educational Research, 90,* 331-344.

Kindermann, T. A. (1993). Natural peer groups as contexts for individual development: The case of children's motivation in school. *Developmental Psychology, 29,* 970-977.

Kindermann, T. A., McCollam, T. L., & Gibson, E. (1996). Peer networks and students' classroom engagement during childhood and adolescence. In J. Juvonen & K. R. Wentzel (Eds.), *Social motivation: Understanding children's school adjustment* (pp. 279-312). New York: Cambridge University Press.

Kiyokawa, Y., Kikusui, T., Takeuchi, Y., & Mori, Y. (2004). Partner's stress status influences social buffering effects in rats. *Behavioral Neuroscience, 118,* 798-804.

Kochenderfer-Ladd, B. J. (2004). Peer victimization: The role of emotions in adaptive and maladaptive coping. *Social Development, 13,* 329-349.

Kochenderfer, B. J., & Ladd, G. W. (1996). Peer victimization: Cause or consequence of school maladjustment? *Child Development, 67,* 1305-1317.

Kupersmidt, J. B., & Coie, J. D. (1990). Preadolescent peer status, aggression and school adjustment as predictors of externalizing problems in adolescence. *Child Development, 61,* 1350-1362.

Kupersmidt, J. S., Burchinal, M., & Patterson, C. J. (1995). Developmental patterns of childhood peer relations as predictors of externalizing behavior problems. *Development and Psychopathology, 7,* 825-843.

Ladd, G. W. (1990). Having friends, keeping friends, making friends, and being liked by peers in the classroom: Predictors of children's early school adjustment. *Child Development, 61,* 1081-1100.

Ladd, G. W., Kochenderfer, B. J., & Coleman, C. C. (1996). Friendship quality as a predictor of young children's early school adjustment. *Child Development, 67,* 1103-1118.

Larson, R., & Richards, M. H. (1991). Daily companionship in late childhood and early adolescence: Changing developmental contexts. *Child Development, 62,* 284-300.

Leary, M. R. (2005). Varieties of interpersonal rejection. In K. D. Williams, P. P. Forgas, & W. von Hippel (Eds.), *The Social outcast: Ostracism, social exclusion, rejection, and bullying* (pp. 35-51). New York: Psychology Press.

Leary, M. R. (Ed.). (2001). *Toward a conceptualization of interpersonal rejection.* London: Oxford University Press.

Leary, M. R., & Kowalski, R. M. (1990). Impression management: A literature review and two-component model. *Psychological Bulletin, 107,* 34-47.

Lee, V. E., & Smith, J. B. (1999). Social support and achievement for young adolescents in Chicago: The role of school academic press. *American Educational Research Journal, 36,* 907-945.

Luthar, S. S. (1997). Sociodemographic disadvantage and psychosocial adjustment: Perspectives from developmental psychopathology. In S. S. Luthar & J. A. Burack (Eds.), *Developmental psychopathology: Perspectives on adjustment and risk, and disorder* (pp. 459-485). New York: Cambridge University Press.

Maehr, M. L., & Midgley, C. (1996). *Transforming school cultures. Lives in context.* Boulder, CO: Westview Press.

Mahoney, J. L. (2000). School extracurricular activity participation as a moderator in the development of antisocial patterns. *Child Development, 71,* 502-516.

Mahoney, J. L., & Cairns, R. B. (1997). Do extracurricular activities protect against early school dropout? *Developmental Psychology, 33,* 241-253.

Malecki, C. K., & Demaray, M. K. (2003). What type of support do they need? Investigating student adjustment as related to emotional, informational, appraisal, and instrumental support. *School Psychology Quarterly, 18,* 231-252.

Marchant, G. J., Paulson, S. E., & Rothlisberg, B. A. (2001). Relations of middle school students' perceptions of family and school contexts with academic achievement. *Psychology in the Schools, 38,* 505-519.

McDougall, P., & Hymel, S. (1998). Moving into middle school: Individual differences in the transition experience. *Canadian Journal of Behavioural Science, 30,* 108-120.

McDougall, P., Hymel, S., Vaillancourt, T., & Mercer, L. (2001). The consequences of childhood peer rejection. In M. Leary (Ed.), *Interpersonal rejection* (pp. 213-247). London: Oxford University Press.

McLaren, P. (1986). *Schooling as a ritual performance: Towards a political economy of educational symbols and gestures.* London: Routledge & Kegan Paul.

McLoyd, V. C. (1990). The impact of economic hardship on black families and children: Psychological distress, parenting, and socioemotional development. *Child Development, 61,* 311-346.

Meehan, B. T., Hughes, J. N., & Cavell, T. A. (2003). Teacher-student relationships as compensatory resources for aggressive children. *Child Development, 74,* 1145-1157.

Midgley, C., Feldlaufer, H., & Eccles, J. (1989). Student/teacher relations and attitudes toward mathematics before and after the transition to junior high school. *Child Development, 60,* 981-992.

Miller, D. T., & Prentice, D. A. (1994a). The self and the collective. *Personality and Social Psychology Bulletin, 20,* 451-453.

Miller, D. T., & Prentice, D. A. (1994b). Collective errors and errors about the collective. *Personality and Social Psychology Bulletin, 20,* 541-550.

Mounts, N. S., & Steinberg, L. (1995). An ecological analysis of peer influence on adolescent grade point average and drug use. *Developmental Psychology, 31,* 915-922.

Murdock, T. B. (1999). The social context of risk: Status and motivational predictors of alienation in middle school. *Journal of Educational Psychology, 91,* 62-75.

Murdock, T. B., Anderman, L. H., & Hodge, S. A. (2000). Middle grades predictors of high school motivation and behavior. *Journal of Adolescent Research, 15,* 327-351.

Murdock, T. B., & Miller, A. (2003). Teachers as sources of middle school students' motivational identity: Variable-centered and person-centered analytic approaches. *Elementary School Journal, 103*, 383–399.

Newman, B. M., & Newman, P. R. (2001). Group identity and alienation: Giving the we its due. *Journal of Youth and Adolescence, 30*, 515–538.

Nishina, A., Juvonen, J., & Witkow, M. (2005). Sticks and stones may break my bones, but names will make me sick: The consequences of peer harassment. *Journal of Clinical Child and Adolescent Psychology, 34*, 37–38.

Ogbu, J. U. (1991). Minority responses and school experiences. *Journal of Psychohistory, 18*, 433–456.

Ogbu, J. U. (1997). Understanding the school performance of urban blacks: Some essential background knowledge. In H. Walberg, R. Reyes, & R. Weissberg (Eds.), *Children and youth: Interdisciplinary perspectives*. Thousand Oaks, CA: Sage.

O'Neil, R., Welsh, M., Parke, R. D., Wang, S., & Strand, C. (1997). A longitudinal assessment of the academic correlates of early peer acceptance and rejection. *Journal of Clinical Child Psychology, 26*, 290–303.

Parker, J. G., & Asher, S. R. (1987). Peer relations and later personal adjustment: Are low-accepted children at risk? *Psychological Bulletin, 102*, 357–389.

Patterson, G. R., Capaldi, D., & Bank, L. (1991). An early starter model for predicting delinquency. In D. J. Pepler, & K. H. Rubin (Eds.), *The development and treatment of childhood aggression* (pp. 139–168). Hillsdale, NJ: Lawrence Erlbaum Associates.

Pianta, R. C., & Steinberg, M. S. (1992). Teacher–child relationships and the process of adjusting to school. In R. C. Pianta (Ed.), *Beyond the parent: The role of other adults in children's lives. New directions for child development* (pp. 61–80). San Francisco: Jossey-Bass.

Pianta, R. C., Steinberg, M. S., & Rollins, K. B. (1995). The first two years of school: Teacher–child relationships and deflections in children's classroom adjustment. *Development and Psychopathology, 7*, 295–312.

Pianta, R. C., & Walsh, D. J. (1996). *High-risk children in schools: Constructing sustaining relationships*. New York: Routledge.

Roeser, R. W., Eccles, J. S., & Sameroff, A. J. (1998). Academic and emotional functioning in early adolescence: Longitudinal relations, patterns, and prediction by experience in middle school. *Development and Psychopathology, 10*, 321–352.

Roeser, R. W., Eccles, J. S., & Freedman-Doan, C. (1999). Academic functioning and mental health in adolescence: Patterns, progressions, and routes from childhood. *Journal of Adolescent Research, 14*, 135–174.

Roeser, R. W., Eccles, J. S., & Sameroff, A. J. (2000). School as a context of early adolescents' academic and socio-emotional development: A summary of research findings. *Elementary School Journal, 100*, 443–471.

Roeser, R. W., Midgley, C., & Urdan, T. C. (1996). Perceptions of the school psychological environment and early adolescents' psychological and behavioral functioning in school: The mediating role of goals and belonging. *Journal of Educational Psychology, 88*, 408–422.

Rubin, K. H., LeMare, L. & Lollis, S. (1990). Social withdrawal in childhood: Developmental pathways to peer rejection. In S. R. Asher & J. D. Coie (Eds.), *Peer rejection in childhood* (pp. 217–249). New York: Cambridge University Press.

Ryan, A. M., & Patrick, H. (2001). The classroom social environment and changes in adolescents' motivation and engagement during middle school. *American Educational Research Journal, 38*, 437–460.

Shouse, R. C. (1996). Academic press and sense of community: Conflict and implications for student achievement. *Social Psychology of Education, 1*, 47–68.

Skinner, E. A., & Belmont, M. J. (1993). Motivation in the classroom: Reciprocal effects of teacher behavior and student engagement across the school year. *Journal of Educational Psychology, 85*, 571–581.

Slavin, R. E. (1995). Cooperative learning and intergroup relations. In J. A. Banks (Ed.), *Handbook of research on multicultural education* (pp. 628–634). New York: Macmillan.

Steinberg, L., & Silverberg, S. B. (1986). The vicissitudes of autonomy in early adolescence. *Child Development, 57*, 841–851.

Tajfel, H. (1981). *Human groups and social categories*. Cambridge, UK: Cambridge University Press.

Tajfel, H., &Turner, J. C. (1979). An integrative theory of intergroup conflict. In W. G. Austin & S. Worchel (Eds.), *The social psychology of intergroup relations* (pp. 33–147). Pacific Grove, CA: Brooks/Cole.

Terry, D. J., & Hogg, M. A. (1996). Group norms and the attitude-behavior relationship: A role for group identification. *Personality and Social Psychology Bulletin, 8*, 776–793.

Turner, J. C. (1982). Towards a cognitive redefinition of the social group. In H. Tajfel (Ed.), *Social identity and intergroup relations* (pp. 15–40). Cambridge, UK: Cambridge University Press.

Turner, J. C., Oaks, P. J., Haslam, S. A., & McGarty, C. (1994). Self and collective: Cognition and social context. *Personality and Social Psychology Bulletin, 20*, 454–463.

U.S. Department of Education. (1993). *Dropout rates in the United States:* 1992 (NCES 93-901). Washington, DC: National Center for Education Statistics.

Wehlage, G. G., & Rutter, R. A. (1985). *Dropping out: How much do schools contribute to the problem?* Madison: Wisconsin Center for Educational Research, University of Wisconsin—Madison.

Weiner, B. (1995). *Judgments of responsibility: A foundation for a theory of social conduct*. New York: Guilford Press.

Weiner, B. (1996). Forward. In J. Juvonen & K. R. Wentzel (Eds.), *Social motivation: Understanding children's school adjustment* (pp. xiii-xv). New York: Cambridge University Press.

Weiner, B. (2000). Intrapersonal and interpersonal theories of motivation from an attributional perspective. *Educational Psychology Review, 12*, 1–14.

Weiner, B., & Kukla, A. (1970). An attributional analysis of achievement motivations. *Journal of Personality and Social Psychology, 15*, 1-20.

Weinstein, R. S. (2002). Overcoming inequality in schooling: A call to action for community psychology. *American Journal of Community Psychology, 30*, 21-40.

Wentzel, K. R. (1997). Student motivation in middle school: The role of perceived pedagogical caring. *Journal of Educational Psychology, 89*, 411-419.

Wentzel, K. R. (1998). Social relationships and motivation in middle school: The role of parents, teachers, and peers. *Journal of Educational Psychology, 90*, 202-209.

Wentzel, K. R., & Caldwell, K. (1997). Friendships, peer acceptance, and group membership: Relations to academic achievement in middle school. *Child Development, 68*, 1198-1209.

Wentzel, K. R., McNamara Barry, C., & Caldwell, K. A. (2004). Friendships in middle school: Influences on motivation and school adjustment. *Journal of Educational Psychology, 96*, 195-203.

White, K. M., Terry, D. J., & Hogg, M. A. (1994). Safer sex behavior: The role of attitudes, norms and control factors. *Journal of Applied Social Psychology, 24*, 2164-2192.

Williams, K. D. (2001). *Ostracism: The power of silence*. New York: Guilford Press.

Williams, K. D., Forgas, J. P., & von Hippel, W. (in press). *The social outcast: Ostracism, social exclusion, rejection, and bullying*. New York: Psychology Press.

Youniss, J., & Smollar, J. (1985). *Adolescents' relations with mothers, fathers, and friends*. Chicago: University of Chicago Press.

CULTURAL CONCEPTIONS OF LEARNING
AND DEVELOPMENT

Patricia M. Greenfield
FPR-UCLA Center for Culture, Brain, and Development, UCLA

Elise Trumbull
Oakland, CA

Heidi Keller
University of Osnabrueck, Germany

Carrie Rothstein-Fisch
California State University, Northridge

Lalita K. Suzuki
HopeLab, Palo Alto, CA

Blanca Quiroz
Harvard University

Appropriately, this chapter begins where the excellent chapter by Pedro Portes from the first edition of this Handbook, entitled "Ethnicity and Culture in Educational Psychology," leaves off. In his penultimate paragraph, Portes argues:

If teaching and learning are regarded as a single unitary process, then it may be argued that the process is, in fact, different for students from diverse cultures. The difference is not necessarily because of fixed, intrapersonal characteristics of students, such as so-called learning styles, but rather *learned* styles, identities, and relations. (Portes, 1996, p. 353).

In this chapter, we will consider teaching and learning to be part of a unitary cultural system. And we focus on how key differences in "*learned* styles, identities, and relations" are amalgamated into two fundamentally different cultural conceptions of learning and development. One cultural conception is termed individualistic, the other collectivistic or sociocentric. The

TABLE 29.1. Contrasting Pathways of Learning and Development

Domain	Individualistic Pathway	Collectivistic/Sociocentric Pathway
Identity	Individual identity stronger	Group, especially family identity stronger
Relations between material and social world	Ownership of property, Sharing by choice	Responsibility to share
Preferred social style	Standing out	Fitting in
Ethnotheory of development and socialization		
Ideal endpoint	Independence, Personal achievement, Individual success	Interdependence, Social responsibility, Contribution to family success
Most important relationship	External experts	Family: older generation for childrearing knowledge
Intelligence, knowledge, & apprenticeship		
Most important type of intelligence	Scientific/Academic/Cognitive	Social/Relational
Most important type of knowledge	Technical expertise	Knowledge of social roles
	Knowledge of physical world	Knowledge connected to social world
	Factual knowledge	Narrative knowledge
Valued apprenticeship processes	Independent learning	Working together
	Active participation	Observation
	Praise	Criticism
Communication		
Preferred communication style	Verbal	Nonverbal
Most important aspects of child's verbal communication	Speaking, Self-expression	Comprehending, Respect for authority
Most important type of socializing communication	Questions	Directives

Note: These contrasting aspects to learning and developmental are defined by group orientation. No society is completely individualistic or collectivistic, but definite cultural patterns and preferences exist. Cultures themselves change over time, but child-rearing values may persist over generations.

specific contrasts that will concern us in the rest of this chapter are presented in Table 29.1. These are portrayed as idealized pathways of learning and development and do not describe any specific person or even all members of a particular ethnic group. Within each group, members can be diverse with regard to socioeconomic status, levels of formal education, and rural or urban backgrounds, affecting their developmental pathway at different times. Nevertheless, child-rearing values can persist over several generations even in new contexts (Lambert, Hammers, & Frasure-Smith, 1979).

In the first part of the chapter we introduce these two contrasting cultural conceptions of learning and development. In the second part of the chapter, we draw out their implications for education in a culturally diverse society. Although both the conceptions and the educational implications draw heavily on prior writing (Greenfield et al., 2003; Greenfield & Suzuki, 1998; Greenfield, Trumbull, & Rothstein-Fisch, 2003; Trumbull, Rothstein-Fisch, Greenfield, & Quiroz, 2001), the present chapter provides a new synthesis linking cultural pathways of development to their implications for education and educational psychology in a culturally diverse society.

TWO PATHWAYS OF LEARNING AND DEVELOPMENT: THEIR IMPLICATIONS FOR EDUCATION AND EDUCATIONAL PSYCHOLOGY

In recent years, a body of evidence has cohered around a unifying and powerful way to tie together cultural conceptions of learning and development. With origins in both developmental psychology (Greenfield & Bruner, 1966) and anthropology (Whiting & Whiting, 1973), this parsimonious theory posits two idealized developmental pathways: one emphasizing individual identity, independence, self-fulfillment, and standing out; the other emphasizing group identity, interdependence, social responsibility, and fitting in (Greenfield, Keller, Fuligni, & Maynard, 2003). The first pathway is termed *individualistic*, the latter, *collectivistic* or *sociocentric*.

Each idealized pathway is part of a larger sociocultural system (Keller, 1997, 2003). The independent pathway arises as an adaptation to a large-scale, urban, rich, commercial environment featuring a highly developed system of formal education and advanced technology. The accumulation of personal goods is adaptive in this type of environment. The interdependent pathway arises as an adaptation to a small-scale face-to-face village environment with a subsistence economy and a system of informal education. Sharing goods is adaptive in this type of environment.

Immigration, conquest, and colonization all tend to incorporate people from the first kind of society into the second. When this happens, children are exposed to two contrasting and often conflicting socializing forces that are very relevant to the educational psychology of many immigrant, Native American, and Native Hawaian children in the United States, as well as the children of immigrant or conquered peoples in other industrialized countries such as Western Europe or Australia.

The first part of the chapter lays out these two developmental pathways and the value systems that generate them. The second part documents the cross-cultural value conflict and misunderstanding that ensue when children raised in a collectivistic home culture are exposed to the "mainstream" culture of individualism at school. In this situation, the home culture socializes children to follow the interdependent pathway of development, while the school culture socializes them to follow the independent pathway of development. This situation creates the need for educational intervention. "Bridging Cultures,"[1] described in the second part of the chapter, is just such an intervention; it was designed to alleviate the cross-cultural value conflict experienced by most immigrant families from Mexico and Central America when they send their children to school in the United States.

At a basic level, the independent pathway and the culture of individualism emphasize individual success, whereas the interdependent pathway and the culture of collectivism emphasize the success of the group as a whole. In collectivistic cultures, people are more likely to identify their own personal goals with those of the group—extended family, religion, or other valued group (Brislin, 1993). When asked to complete the statement, "I am..." collectivists are more likely to respond with reference to an organization, family, or religion. Individualists tend to list trait labels referring to aspects of their personalities, such as "hard-working," "intelligent," or "athletic" (Triandis, Brislin, & Hui, 1988). Not surprisingly, the United States is the most individualistic country in the world (Hofstede, 2001). However, this developmental pathway is hardly universal—70 percent of the world's cultures can be described as collectivistic (Triandis, 1989).

AN ETHNOTHEORY FOR EACH DEVELOPMENTAL PATHWAY

Whereas psychologists have explicit theories of human development, parents and other lay people have implicit ethnotheories. These implicit conceptions both reflect and instantiate cultural values. An ethnotheory of development comprises an implicit definition of the ideal child and beliefs about what socialization practices will produce this ideal (Goodnow, 1988; McGillicuddy-De Lisi & Sigel, 1995). Ethnotheories of human development are both shared and negotiated among members of cultural communities. In slow-changing, subsistence-based ecologies, ethnotheories are transmitted vertically from generation to generation within the family. This process yields continuity over historical time. In complex and fast-changing societies, in contrast, theories of parenting are negotiated horizontally within each generation. This process often utilizes resources outside the family, for example, the media and experts such as pediatricians (Hewlett & Lamb, 2002; Keller et al., 1984). These sources of ethnotheories of development and socialization yield substantial differences in child rearing practices between generations.

Relevant to our theoretical paradigm, research on ethnotheories of development has unraveled independence and interdependence as core dimensions, applicable to all developmental domains (Chao, 1994; Gutierrez & Sameroff, 1990; Yovsi & Keller, 2003). Participants from non-Western cultural communities, such as Chinese (Chao, 1994), Japanese (Rothbaum, Weisz, Pott, Miyake, & Morelli, 2000), Indians (Keller et al., 2005; Saraswathi, 1999), West Africans (Ogunnnaike & Houser, 2002, for Nigeria; and Nsamenang, 1992; Yovsi, 2001; Keller, Hentschel et al., 2004, for Cameroon), or Puerto Ricans (Harwood, Schoelmerich, Ventura–Cook, Schulze, & Wilson, 1996) hold parental ethnotheories that express the cultural ideal of interdependence. These ethnotheories stress decency (responsibility, honesty) and proper demeanor (politeness, respect for elders, loyalty to family) for social and cognitive developmental domains (Harwood, 1992).

Participants from Western industrialized cultural communities, such as Germans (Keller et al., 2005), European Americans (Harwood et al., 1996) or the Dutch (Harkness, Super, & van Tijen, 2000), hold parental ethnotheories that express the cultural ideal of independence and individualism. These ethnotheories stress

---

[1]The term "Bridging Cultures" is used to refer to both a specific project and to the approach associated with it.

personal achievement and independence (creativity, curiosity, assertiveness).

High socioeconomic status and formal education are associated with a more individualistic orientation (Keller et al., 2005; Palacios & Moreno, 1996; Tapia-Uribe, LeVine, & LeVine, 1994). Nonetheless, these cultural orientations persist across various socioeconomic and educational backgrounds (Keller et al., 2005; Harwood et al., 1996). As we describe the ethnotheories in this paper, another caution is in order. The features of each pathway refer to relative group differences. There are individual differences in every group, especially in complex, modern societies. These group differences are a matter of emphasis; they are not absolute.

Socialization practices that function to actualize a particular ethnotheory of development begin at birth or even before. In short, a parent's ethnotheory of child development generates socialization practices that move the child along a particular cultural pathway of development.

INTELLIGENCE, KNOWLEDGE, AND APPRENTICESHIP: A CONCEPTION FOR EACH CULTURAL PATHWAY

Theories and Ethnotheories of Intelligence and Knowledge

Scientific theories turn out to be more formalized derivatives of ethnotheories. In other words, scientific theories have their cultural roots, too. In developmental psychology, the classical theory of intelligence is that of Piaget. Understanding the basis for Western scientific thought was Piaget's most fundamental theoretical concern (Piaget, 1963/1977). Under Inhelder's leadership, Piaget investigated the development of scientific thought (chemistry and physics) in a set of experimental studies (Inhelder & Piaget, 1958). This body of theory and research implies the importance of scientific intelligence as a developmental goal. Conceptually, the goal of scientific intelligence belongs to the individualistic pathway because it emphasizes the person in relation to the world of objects rather than the world of people. This goal for the development of intelligence can be seen as continuous with infant caregiving practices that emphasize leaving the infant alone to manipulate technologically appealing toys.

In sharp contrast, social intelligence has been found to be the predominant ideal in Africa (e.g., Dasen, 1984; Nsamenang & Lamb, 1994; Serpell, 1993; Wober, 1974). For instance, the central feature of the Baoule concept of intelligence in Ivory Coast is willingness to help others (Dasen, 1984). Whereas the most comprehensive theory of development in Europe is Piaget's theory of cognitive development, the most comprehensive theory of development in Africa is that of Nsamenang, who outlines stages of development in terms of social roles (Nsamenang, 1992). In general, African cultures not only emphasize social intelligence, but also see the role of technical skills as means to social ends (Dasen, 1984). Such conceptions can be seen as collectivistic conceptions of intelligence (Segall, Dasen, Berry & Poortinga, 1999) and as continuous with infant caregiving practices that emphasize close bodily contact between infant and caregiver, rather than separation and independent manipulation of toys (Keller, 2003).

Closely related to the individualistic and collectivistic conceptions of intelligence are two different conceptions of knowledge. In a Maya community in Chiapas, Mexico, the word *na*, meaning "to know," emphasizes a more person-centered meaning, compared with the English word *know*. Whereas "to know" in English always involves the mind, *na* often involves the heart and soul. (According to Li, 2002, a similar concept of "heart and mind for wanting to learn" is found in China.) Whereas *knowing* connotes factual knowledge, theoretical understanding, or know-how, *na* also connotes knowledge of practice that is habitual and characteristic of a given person; it is very much akin to character (Zambrano, 1999). The former type of knowledge is more important in a culture valuing the individual's possession of technical expertise. The latter is more important in a culture placing a greater value on social character.

A similar contrast has been found between Native American and European American conceptions of giftedness (Romero, 1994). This research shows that, whereas the mainstream U.S. society focuses on identifying and meeting the needs of the "cream of the crop," an individualistic valuing of children who stand out from the group in intelligence or knowledge, Keres-speaking Pueblo Indians focus on community and inclusion. In this conception, the special qualities of a "gifted" child are supposed to contribute to the well-being and cohesiveness of the community.

Cultural Modes of Apprenticeship and Creativity

These two ethnotheories of intelligence and knowledge are supported by two different sets of apprenticeship practices and two different concepts of creativity. By apprenticeship, we simply mean informal teaching and learning, a type of transmission that has evolved from primitive roots in nonhuman primates (Boesch, 1991; Greenfield et al., 2000; Whiten, 1999). By a cultural concept of creativity, we mean simply what is considered desirable as the endpoint of a creative process. We discuss creativity along with apprenticeship because often one learns how to create something through an apprenticeship process—be it weaving out of school, writing in school, or computer programming in either situation. The first part of this section deals with apprenticeship, the second part with creativity.

Corresponding to the Keres concept of giftedness, apprenticeship processes that are valued by the Keres include cooperation, mentorship, and intergenerational modeling. "Keen observation, attentiveness, and focused listening are important methods of learning" (Romero, 1994, p. 53), while methods valued in the individualistic framework—questioning, skepticism, and curiosity—are not promoted.

Empirical study of apprenticeship documents two basic models of apprenticeship, one more independent and one more interdependent. The interdependent model is found in traditional weaving apprenticeship in one Maya community and in modes of guiding children in an experimental puzzle task in another Maya community (Chavajay & Rogoff, 2002; Greenfield, Maynard, & Childs, 2003). These modes seem adapted to subsistence economies in which learning takes place in family settings. Indeed, both studies find changes in the model with changes in the ecocultural environment.

Weaving apprenticeship moves toward a more independent mode of learning as subsistence is replaced by commerce (Greenfield, 2000, 2004; Greenfield, Maynard, & Childs, 2003). With formal education, the way in which mothers guide puzzle construction moves from shared multiparty engagement (the whole group focusing on a single aspect of the puzzle) toward division of labor where individuals or dyads work separately on different task components (Chavajay & Rogoff, 2002). Both commerce and formal schooling are associated with a more individualistic mode of apprenticeship (Greenfield, 2000; Tapia-Uribe et al., 1994).

The concept of creativity changes in parallel ways. In the same Zinacantec Maya community where weaving learners became more independent as commerce developed, the concept of creativity in textile production also changed. At the time when interdependence characterized weaving apprenticeship, woven and embroidered clothing did not differ noticeably from woman to woman or from man to man; and clothing signified, above all, membership in a particular ethnic group. However, when weaving learners became more independent, there was also a movement from a community definition of creativity to an individual one. That is, woven and embroidered designs became more highly differentiated and individuated, and creativity took on a meaning more familiar to

us—creating something that differentiates an individual by being new and innovative (Greenfield, 2000).

Cultural Modes of Communication

Communication is an essential part of both informal apprenticeship learning and formal education. Each developmental pathway is nurtured and socialized by its own preferred modes of communication. In turn, these differing modes of communication socialize the developing child to become skilled in different modes of communication.

Nonverbal Communication or Verbalization? The Cultural Role of Empathy, Observation, and Participation. Azuma (1994) notes that Japanese mothers (and nursery school teachers) rely more on empathy and nonverbal communication, whereas mothers in the United States rely more on verbal communication with their children. He sees a connection between the physical closeness of the Japanese mother–child pair (characteristic of the interdependent pathway of development; Greenfield & Suzuki, 1998) and the development of empathy as a mode of communication. He points out that verbalization is necessary when there is greater physical and psychological distance between parent and child. The development of empathy paves the way for learning by osmosis, in which the mother does not need to teach directly; she simply prepares a learning environment and makes suggestions. In turn, the child's empathy for the mother motivates learning; this tradition survives in the families of third-generation Japanese-American immigrants (Schneider, Hieshima, Lee, & Plank, 1994).

Closely related to empathy and learning by osmosis are the use of observation and participation as forms of parent-child communication and socialization. Whereas verbal instruction is particularly important in school-based learning, observation and co-participation of learner and teacher are very central to the apprentice-style learning that is common in many cultures (Rogoff, 1990). Often master and apprentice are parent and child, as in Childs & Greenfield's (1980) study of informal learning of weaving in a Maya community of highland Chiapas, Mexico.

Both learning by observation and co-participation with a parent imply a kind of closeness and empathy between parent and child. For example, in Zinacantec Maya weaving apprenticeship, the teacher would sometimes sit behind the learner, positioned so that two bodies, the learner's and the teacher's, were functioning as one at the loom (Maynard, Greenfield, & Childs, 1999). Verbal communication and instruction, in contrast, imply using words to bridge the distance through explicitness, thus reducing the need for empathetic communication.

A discourse study by Choi (1992) reveals a similar pattern of differences between Korean and Canadian mothers interacting with their young children. Comparing middle-class mothers in Korea and Canada, Choi found that Korean mothers and their children manifest a communicative pattern that is relationally attuned to one another in a "fused" state (Choi, 1992), "where the mothers freely enter their children's reality and speak for them, merging themselves with the children" (Kagitçibasi, 1996, p. 69). Canadian mothers, in contrast, "withdraw themselves from the children's reality, so that the child's reality can remain autonomous" (Choi, 1992, pp. 119–120).

Development of Comprehension Versus Self-expression. Authoritarian parenting, characteristic of socialization for interdependence, brings with it an associated style of parent-to-child communication: frequent use of directives and imperatives, with encouragement of obedience and respect (Greenfield, Brazelton, & Childs, 1989; Harkness, 1988; Kagitçibasi, 1996). This style is used where the primary goal of child communication development is comprehension rather than speaking (e.g., Harkness & Super, 1982). An important aspect of the imperative style is the fact that it elicits action, rather than verbalization from the child. This style is found in cultures such as in Africa (Harkness & Super, 1982) and in Mexico (Tapia Uribe, LeVine, & LeVine, 1994), as well as in Latino populations in the United States (Delgado-Gaitan, 1994).

The comprehension skill developed by an imperative style is particularly functional in agrarian societies in which the obedient learning of chores and household skills is a very important socializing experience (e.g., Childs & Greenfield, 1980), with the ultimate goal of developing obedient, respectful, and socially responsible children (Harkness & Super, 1982; Kagitçibasi, 1996; Keller, 2003; LeVine et al., 1994). This style of interaction is also useful for apprenticeship learning of manual skills, but it is not so functional for school where verbal expression is much more important than nonverbal action.

On the other hand, more democratic parenting brings with it a communication style in which self-expression and autonomy are encouraged from the child. This parenting style often features a high rate of questions from the parent, particularly "test questions," in which the answer is already known to the parent (Duranti & Ochs, 1986), as well as parent–child negotiation (cf., Delgado-Gaitan, 1994). Child-initiated questions are also encouraged and accepted. This style is intrinsic to the process of formal education in which the teacher, paradigmatically, asks questions to which he/she already knows the answer and tests children on their verbal expression. An important aspect of the interrogative style is the fact that it elicits verbal-

ization from the child. Such verbal expression is an important part of becoming a formally educated person and is particularly functional and common in commercial and technological societies where academic achievement, autonomy, and creativity are important child development goals. This style is the cultural norm in the U.S., Canada, Australia, and Northern Europe.

Teaching and Learning: The Role of Reinforcement. In societies that put an emphasis on commands in parental communication, there also tends to be little praise used in parent–child communication (e.g., Childs & Greenfield, 1980; Whiting & Whiting, 1975-). Where schooling comes into play, praise and positive reinforcement take on importance. Duranti and Ochs (1986) make the following observation of Samoan children who go to school:

In their primary socialization [home], they learn not to expect praises and compliments for carrying out directed tasks. Children are expected to carry out these tasks for their elders and family. In their secondary socialization [school], they learn to expect recognition and positive assessments, given successful accomplishment of a task. In their primary socialization, Samoan children learn to consider tasks as co-operatively accomplished, as social products. In their secondary socialization, they learn to consider tasks as an individual's work and accomplishment (p. 229).

Thus, there is a connection between more individualistic child development goals and the use of praise and other positive reinforcers.

Correlatively, there is a connection between a tighter primary in-group and the absence of praise and compliments. Where role-appropriate behavior is expected rather than chosen, positive reinforcement does not make sense. Miller (1995) has described how people do not say "thank you" in India; once you are part of the group, you are completely accepted and expected to fulfill your social roles and obligations. Whiting and Whiting (1975) noted the lesser need for positive reinforcement where the intrinsic worth of the work is evident, as it is in household tasks and chores. On the other hand, pointing out weaknesses that need to be improved (i.e., criticism) can be more important in a collectivistic culture, where the goal is to bring everyone up to the group norm (Greenfield, Quiroz, & Raeff, 2000).

APPLYING THE TWO CULTURAL PATHWAYS OF DEVELOPMENT TO FORMAL EDUCATION: THE BRIDGING CULTURES PROJECT

Schooling and its implications for the development of a cultural identity (i.e., self) and competence have been and still are targets of controversial debate. On the one hand, the acquisition of similar skills across cultures is being claimed as a necessary step for improving people's lives on a global scale (Kagitçibasi, 1996). On the other hand, indigenous methods and contents of schooling are strongly advocated as an alternative to the Western type of schooling to support the acquisition of locally adaptive knowledge (Nsamenang, 1992; Serpell, 1979). These discussions center on the role of culture in the process of knowledge acquisition in different cultures, including the culture of the school.

However, such discussions often leave out the multicultural reality that is a social fact in many immigrant societies, as well as in societies in which indigenous peoples have been subject to conquest by a colonial power. One major implication of this multicultural reality concerns the possibility of different cultural values among students, between students and teachers, and between home and school. Some recent educational theory and research has addressed the notion of bridging cultures of home and school by making the expectations of both explicit and supporting students to develop bicultural skills (cf., Delpit, 1995; Lipka, et al., 1998; Trumbull, Nelson-Barber, & Mitchell, 2003). It is from this perspective that the Bridging Cultures Project was conceived.

"Bridging Cultures" began with basic research documenting cross-cultural value conflict between Latino immigrant families and the schools. This research showed that immigrant parents were generally much more collectivistic in their orientation to child socialization than were their children's teachers (Greenfield, Quiroz, & Raeff, 2000; Raeff, Greenfield, & Quiroz, 2000). In the first study, Greenfield, Quiroz, and Raeff (2000) found that immigrant Latino parents of third- and fourth-grade students and their European American teacher were often in noncooperative discourse. This means that most conversations between the parents and the teacher did *not* confirm or elaborate a common theme. Instead, there were whole categories of discordance related to (1) individual versus family accomplishment, (2) praise versus criticism, (3) cognitive versus social skills, and (4) oral expression versus respect for authority. Overall, this study demonstrated the tensions between home cultures and school cultural expectations.

In the second study (Raeff et al., 2000), fifth-grade children, their mothers, and their teachers were given home-school scenarios that varied along the pathways of individualism and collectivism. In one school, where the children and parents were predominantly European American, the scenarios were solved in consistent ways by children, their parents, and their teachers. This was not the case with a different school where the families were predominantly immigrant Latino. Scenario results revealed that the parents were more concerned about their children sharing and helping, whereas the teachers generally had a greater orientation to task completion, individual choice, and personal property. The fifth-grade children were sometimes in between in their responses, demonstrating that they may have been pulled between the cultural values of their home and those of the school. For some scenarios, their responses looked more like those of their teachers than those of their parents. The school was being successful in its unwitting cultural socialization.

Based on these two studies we (Greenfield, Quiroz, Rothstein-Fisch, Trumbull, and seven elementary school teachers initially) then utilized this research to help teachers and schools understand home culture and school culture, in order to create educational "bridges" between them. Through the Bridging Cultures Project, we have been exploring with teachers the ways in which deep value orientations of cultures (including the mainstream U.S. culture) result in different expectations of children and of schooling. These orientations are less visible than the material and often superficial elements of a culture, such as the ways in which a culture celebrates holidays and heroes or creates works of art. Value orientations are more difficult to capture than the histories of groups, because cultural values are often invisible. Yet they form the basis for ways of viewing the world and vast ranges of behaviors including the way people communicate, discipline their children, and carry out everyday tasks. If schools are to succeed in promoting successful education for children and meaningful school involvement for parents, then educators need to understand how these cultural values orientations shape a whole host of beliefs, expectations, and behaviors—on the part of families on the one hand and of teachers and school personnel on the other.

We must emphasize that there are elements of both individualism and collectivism in any society and that cultures change, particularly when they come in contact with each other. As Goldenberg and Gallimore (1995) observed, "Both continuity and discontinuity across generations are part of the process of cultural evolution, a complex dynamic that contributes to change and variability within cultures" (p. 188). For example, parents' views about appropriate education for girls of the current generation of Mexican American families are different from *their own parents'* views on the same topic (Goldenberg & Gallimore, 1995). The new generation puts greater emphasis on individual educational development; the older generation put greater emphasis on family responsibility.

Intergenerational trends toward the host culture notwithstanding, there currently exists tremendous cross-cultural value conflict between Latino immigrant families and the schools. Most of these families have emigrated from rural Mexico, with a minority coming from urban

Mexico and Central America. They were generally poor in their homelands, with little opportunity for educational advancement. Hence, they are likely (as our studies show) to exhibit highly collectivistic values.

Cross-Cultural Contact and Conflict at School

Research shows the contrasting types of knowledge, intelligence, apprenticeship, and communication to be on a collision course in our multicultural schools. Whereas teachers focus on independent academic achievement, Latino parents, for example, are often more concerned about social behavior (Greenfield, Quiroz, & Raeff, 2000). These goals are crystallized in a different concept of education, *educación* (Reese, Balzano, Gallimore, & Goldenberg, 1995). This Spanish word is not an accurate translation of the English word "education." Unlike "education," *educación* refers to the inculcation of proper and respectful social behavior; like the Tzotzil *na, educación* refers to character. The connotation is that academic learning does not suffice to make a person "educated." As another example, the Native American concepts of learning by observing rather than participating and for the purpose of group rather than self (as discussed earlier) also lead to mismatches between Native children and the schools (Suina & Smolkin, 1994). In terms of communication, teachers complain that Latino students do not speak up in class and proffer their opinions. At home, however, to provide an opinion to an adult would be considered disrespectful (Delgado-Gaitan, 1994).

Ameliorating these mismatches is the foundation of the Bridging Cultures Project. Bridging Cultures began as a series of workshops for seven elementary school teachers serving Latino immigrant families in Southern California. We used our own ethnographic observations of cross-cultural value conflict in school to help make the Bridging Cultures teachers aware of the two value systems and where they might come into conflict at school. We begin with one such observation.

Example of an Individualism-Collectivism Conflict: Sharing or Personal Property?

The emphasis on social relationships rather than on the individual extends to notions of property: In collectivistic cultures, the boundaries of property ownership are more permeable. Personal items such as clothing, books, or toys are readily shared and often seen as family property rather than individual property. Through a study utilizing scenarios presented to children, parents, and the children's teachers, we found that Latino parents generally

value sharing as a child development goal, whereas their children's teachers place a greater value on personal property (Raeff et al., 2000). The following incident in school illustrates the institutional forces that make it difficult for teachers to harmonize their classroom practices with the home culture of collectivism:

The Crayons Incident (as told by the teacher)
A mentor teacher paid a visit to a kindergarten class, where she observed that the teacher had arranged the crayons by color in cups. There was a cup for the green crayons, a cup for the red crayons, and so on. Each cup of crayons was shared by the entire class. The mentor suggested to the kindergarten teacher that it would be much better if each child had his or her own cup of crayons with all the colors in it. She explained that it made children feel good to have their own property and that they needed to learn how to take care of their own property. Furthermore, those who took good care of their "property" would not have to suffer by using the "crappy" (her word) crayons of those children who did not know how to take care of their things. (Quiroz & Greenfield, 1996)

The crayons incident involves an underlying conflict between the values of sharing and personal property. The kindergarten teacher was an immigrant Latina parent herself, and her arrangement of the crayons was implicitly based on her collectivistic orientation. When she responded to the wishes of the supervising teacher by rearranging the crayons, the children, largely immigrant Latinos themselves, began to experience conflict between the sharing orientation that was familiar to them at home (and previously at school) and the new orientation to personal property. As told by the teacher, the children

did not care if their materials were misplaced, so their "personal" materials ended up having to be rearranged by the teacher every day. It was not that the children were incapable of arranging their materials in a systematic fashion because they had done so before. However, the category "personal material" simply was not important to them. (Quiroz & Greenfield, 1996, pp. 12–13)

The preceding example makes it very clear that values are in the head, not in the situation, and that they are used for the symbolic construction of social relations and social life, at school as at home. In terms of the external situation in this example, the crayons in actual fact belonged to the school. Through her actions and words, the teacher symbolically constructed them as belonging to the class as a whole, while the mentor symbolically constructed them as belonging to individual students. The mentor was clear that she wanted the children to learn a lesson about the importance of personal property; the teacher, implicitly, was communicating a message about the necessity to share. The teacher's message reflected her own socialization in Mexico; the mentor's actualized the values of the school and the mainstream society. The children's behavior indicated that the teacher's approach was more meaningful to them, undoubtedly because it harmonized with their socialization at home.

Cooperation, Competition, and Schooling: Another Arena for Conflict Between Individualism and Collectivism

The ways teachers and students interact in the classroom reflect a relative emphasis on the needs of the group or of the individual. Competition is the natural companion of a focus on the individual, whereas cooperation is the natural companion of a focus on the group. Although "cooperative learning" has been widely promoted, sometimes on the grounds that it will ensure students' later success on the job, the norm of cooperation has clearly not overridden the norm of competition. Indeed, our analysis of "cooperative learning" in schools indicates that there are two basic modes of cooperation, one more individualistic, the other more collectivistic. The more individualistic mode is characterized by division of labor; the more collectivistic by people focusing together on a common task. A comparison of more schooled and less schooled Maya mothers, guiding their children in a puzzle task, showed that formal schooling promotes the individualistic mode of cooperation (Chavajay & Rogoff, 2002). Cooperative learning, as it is practiced in schools—although it may stress "positive interdependence" (Johnson & Johnson, 1994)—also involves division of labor as a central element (e.g., Cohen, 1986; Johnson & Johnson, 1994; Aronson, Stephan, Sikes, Blaney, & Snapp, 1978); it is therefore not necessarily a comfortable mode of learning for children who have been socialized to focus together simultaneously on a common task.

The conflict between the two norms is seen most clearly in settings such as Southern California, where immigrant Latinos are introduced to U.S. schooling, or Alaska, where students from indigenous cultures meet "mainstream" teaching. Yup'ik Eskimo teacher Vicki Dull explains the situation in the village where she taught:

In the Yup'ik culture, "group" is important. There is little, if any, competition among Yup'ik people. When the Western school system entered the picture, the unity of the group slowly shattered. Children were sent hundreds and often thousands of miles away to be schooled in boarding schools where they were forced to abandon their own language for the foreign English with its accompanying foreign ways. They learned the Western value of competition. They learned to be individuals, competing against each other, instead of a group working in unity . . . There are seldom, if any times when they were allowed to help each

other, which would have been construed as "cheating." (Dull, in Nelson-Barber & Dull, 1998, p. 95)

It is difficult for educators used to U.S. "mainstream" norms to comprehend how drastic a shift this represents for students from a collectivistic culture.

Cross-Cultural Conflict in What Counts as Knowledge and Thinking at Home and at School

Cultural models not only have values attached to them—what counts as good and bad, what takes priority over what—but they also have epistemologies: what counts as knowledge. These cultural models are so basic as to normally remain implicit. So long as everyone interacting in the same social world shares the same model, the implicit quality of the models does not cause a problem. In fact, it provides an underlying set of shared assumptions that makes social life—for example, life in school—run smoothly. This next example is about what happens in a bicultural classroom when teachers and learners have different implicit understandings of what counts as knowledge.

In a pre-kindergarten class consisting of children from Latino immigrant homes, the teacher held an actual chicken egg. She asked the children to describe eggs by thinking about the times they had cooked and eaten eggs. One of the children tried three times to talk about how she cooked eggs with her grandmother, but the teacher disregarded these comments in favor of a child who explained how eggs are white and yellow when they are cracked. (Greenfield, Raeff, & Quiroz, 1996)

The two features of this incident—the first child's emphasis on a family-based story and the teacher's disregard and devaluation of the child's seemingly unscientific answer—occur frequently in classrooms with immigrant Latino students. But what is really happening here?

Our theoretical analysis rests on the following two points: What counts as knowledge for the teacher is knowledge about the physical world apart from the social world. It is the teacher's definition of scientific knowledge, and, in her mind, this is a science lesson. Her focus is on one part of her instructions, "Describe eggs." The child, in contrast, is responding more to the other part of the teacher's instructions—"Think about the times you have cooked and eaten eggs"—and, based on a different set of assumptions about what counts as knowledge, focuses on the social aspect of her experience with eggs, in particular, a family experience. This is the first aspect of the misunderstanding and cultural mismatch between teacher and learner.

The second aspect of the mismatch is that the child who was passed over is providing a narrative, also valued in her home culture, while the teacher is expecting a simple statement of fact. Implicitly, the teacher is making Bruner's distinction between narrative thought and logical-scientific thought. Bruner's analysis is very relevant here:

There appear to be two broad ways in which human beings organize and manage their knowledge of the world, indeed structure even their immediate experience: one seems more specialized for treating of physical "things," the other for treating people and their plights. These are conventionally known as *logical-scientific* thinking and *narrative* thinking (Bruner, 1996, p. 39).

The child who talks about cooking and eating eggs with her grandmother is responding in the narrative mode. But the teacher expects the logical-scientific mode: "What are the bare facts about eggs?," she wants to know. Narrative is, in the mainstream culture, associated with the humanities; logical-scientific thought is associated with the sciences. As Bruner says, the value of logical-scientific thinking "is so implicit in our highly technological culture that its inclusion in school curricula is taken for granted" (Bruner, 1996, p. 41). It is so taken for granted that the narrative mode, as the egg incident shows, becomes invisible to the teacher.

Impact of Home–School Value Conflict

Here and elsewhere we have presented examples of how these two different value orientations often collide as children from immigrant families move from home culture into U.S. schools (Greenfield & Cocking, 1994; Greenfield et al., 1998; Raeff et al., 2000). These children may be torn between the values and expectations of their native culture and those of the "mainstream." Parents and teachers (the latter representing mainstream culture) may observe the same behaviors in children but interpret them differently, because they are viewing them through very different cultural lenses. When the individualistic teacher says the child is "able to work well independently," the collectivistic parent may hear the teacher as saying the child is "too separated from the group." When the collectivistic parent asks more than once about his or her child's social development, the individualistic teacher may hear the parent as saying, "I don't really care whether she does well academically in school."

From Theory to Practice: Guiding Teachers to Bridge Cultures

To determine if knowledge of the cultural value systems of individualism and collectivism could affect teaching and

learning, we began the Bridging Cultures Project with professional development workshops for seven elementary teachers from bilingual Spanish–English classrooms in southern California. The grade level of their classes ranged from kindergarten through fifth grade. Four teachers were Latino; three were European American. Three of the four Latino teachers were immigrants to the United States (two from Mexico, one from Peru); one of the European American teachers was an immigrant (from Germany). All of the immigrant teachers had come to the United States when they were young (between 2 and 8 years of age).

These seven teachers participated in a series of three half-day workshops. In the first workshop, Greenfield and Quiroz presented the theory of individualism and collectivism, as well as the results of our research on cross-cultural value conflict between Latino immigrant families and the schools (Raeff et al., 2000).

The format was quite participatory; so, for example, we asked the teachers how they would solve certain individualism–collectivism dilemmas before showing them what our research had revealed about how Latino immigrant parents and their children's teachers resolved the same dilemmas (Raeff et al., 2000). These scenarios were also used as a pretest of teachers' beliefs. The teachers responded in a strongly individualistic manner (86 percent of the response were individualistic) despite the majority of Latino teachers in our group (Rothstein-Fisch, Trumbull, Quiroz, & Greenfield, 1997). In debriefing the scenarios, the teachers were noticeably surprised to find out that the Latino parents favored a different (i.e., collectivistic) way to resolve dilemmas that the teachers had generally solved in an individualistic mode. (In this way, we found out that the schooling process, particularly teacher training, wiped out, at least on the surface, the collectivistic values with which our Latino teachers, as they later told us, had been raised.) Starting in Workshop 1 and continuing throughout the workshops, we presented examples of cross-cultural conflict between individualism and collectivism in the schools, such as the "crayons" and "eggs" incidents described earlier.

At the end of the first workshop, we asked the teachers to observe in their schools and to bring back to the second workshop an example of conflict between individualism and collectivism that they had noticed. During the second workshop, they shared their examples, and we refined understanding of the two value systems through discussion. At the end of the second workshop, we asked the teachers to try to make one change before the next workshop that would reduce a conflict between individualism and collectivism in their classroom or school and to observe its impact. In the third workshop, they reported on what they had done and how it had worked. We discussed their interventions, and this was the beginning of a process by which teachers used the individualism–collectivism paradigm to generate new practices and learn from each others' innovations. Researchers could also record these innovations to present as important "results" of the training, for purposes of broader dissemination to the educational community.

At the end of Workshop 3, the teachers took a posttest. Again, scenarios were drawn from those used by Raeff, Greenfield, and Quiroz (2000). The posttest revealed that teachers had dramatically shifted their orientation to resolving a matched set of social dilemmas (57 percent collectivistic, 21 percent individualistic, and 21 percent both individualistic and collectivistic) (Rothstein-Fisch et al., 1997). There were now many more collectivistic solutions. However, even more important to the concept of a bridge between two cultures, the teachers' solutions were now very well distributed among both value systems.

At this point, the teachers initiated the idea and unanimously agreed that it would be worthwhile to continue to meet to explore further applications of the theory in their own classrooms and schools. We held a fourth, debriefing workshop and then arranged to keep meeting several times a year. At these meetings, teachers reported their latest Bridging Cultures innovations, researchers reported ongoing research and publications, and teacher-researcher teams practiced for upcoming outreach presentations. The meetings continued for 5 years. Workshops and meetings always included food and drink and an opportunity for socializing. These elements were extremely important to group motivation, as they made the teachers feel valued, something they told us was often lacking in their schools. The group turned into a collaborative support team, as the line between teacher and researcher became increasingly blurred.

Teachers as Researchers

A key feature of the Bridging Cultures Project is the role teachers have taken. The seven participating teachers in our original Bridging Cultures workshop are themselves acting as researchers in their own classrooms and contributing both to a deeper understanding of the theoretical framework and to the collection of examples of school-based experiences and practices that bring the framework alive. These teachers are truly "teacher-researchers" because they experiment with new ways of bridging cultures, and they report the results for others to learn from. We refer to the non-teacher researchers as "staff researchers." One of the teacher-researchers (Catherine Daley) and one of the staff researchers (Patricia Greenfield)

subsequently engaged in a formal study applying the Bridging Cultures training to parent education. We believe that teacher research is an important and unique source of knowledge about teaching and that artificial boundaries between the practice of teaching and research on teaching need to be challenged. Much can be gained from collaborations between educational psychologists and classroom teachers.

In our meetings, we discussed ways to improve home-school relationships and children's education that are based on the experimentation of the teacher-researchers in their own classrooms. This experimentation is then disseminated to the broader educational community through publications and professional workshops (Quiroz, Greenfield, & Altchech, 1998, 1999; Rothstein-Fisch, Greenfield, & Trumbull, 1999; Rothstein-Fisch & Trumbull, 2005; Rothstein-Fisch, Trumbull, Isaac, Daley, & Pérez, 2001; Trumbull, Diaz-Meza, Hasan, & Rothstein-Fisch, 2001; Trumbull, Rothstein-Fisch, & Hernandez, 2003; Trumbull, Rothstein-Fisch, Greenfield, & Quiroz, 2001). Teachers are important partners in the dissemination process. They have disseminated locally, in their schools and at the district level, regionally, and nationally, as have the staff researchers. Often we give joint presentations, including one or more teacher-researchers and one or more staff researchers.

Another aspect of teacher research that was part of the Bridging Cultures professional development process was the use of *ethnography*, a technique from anthropology that is often defined as participant observation. We encouraged teachers to get to know their individual parents and to learn more about their backgrounds— Where were they from? How old were they when they immigrated to the United States? In what country did they go to school? The last question was a good one to elicit amount of schooling in a nonthreatening manner. Parental schooling is important information for teachers to have in the population served by the Bridging Cultures teachers. Most parents of their students had had no opportunity to go beyond sixth grade in Mexico or Central America, and limited formal education then became a barrier to helping children with homework and academic skill development, a barrier that teachers needed to understand and adapt to. Ethnography was important for teachers in order to adapt to individual family differences as a function of acculturation level, economic level, educational level, and so forth. Ethnography was also important as a way to get to know about the whole family in a culture where the child is seen primarily as a family member rather than an independent individual. Whereas individualism-collectivism paradigm provided a framework by which to understand particular ethnographic details, the ethnographic approach to families prevented overgeneralization and inaccurate stereotypes.

Teachers Use the Theory to Generate New Practices

Indeed, the teachers' experimentation in their own classrooms and schools has proven the framework more generative than we ever dreamed possible. There has been no end to the applications teachers have identified and innovations they have developed. Teachers can apply the framework in ways that make sense in their classrooms and schools and which they are comfortable with. Not all innovations are of equal value or success. They need to be evaluated in light of the framework and research, as well as tested by teachers, to see how they work and what outcomes they drive. There is no recommended mix of individualism and collectivism in the classroom, although most of the innovations have, quite naturally, been in the direction of making uniformly individualistic classrooms more collectivistic. However, it is equally important to note that the teachers, in our very first workshop, decided that the basic notion is to provide a bridge from home culture to the school culture, so that students can meet the demands of mainstream schooling, which will not adapt to their home culture as they continue in school.

It is important to note that our method is nonprescriptive. We provide the paradigm; the teachers use the paradigm to generate their own innovations, which vary greatly from teacher to teacher. Here are a few examples:

In the area of home-school relations, examples include transforming parent-teacher conferences, with their traditional focus on one individual child, into a group format where the teacher meets with parents of several children (Quiroz, Greenfield, & Altchech, 1998). In the area of classroom management, helping tasks (such as cleaning the blackboard) stopped being restricted to one assigned child; children were allowed to help freely and to work together on a wide variety of classroom tasks (Greenfield, in press; Rothstein-Fisch, Trumbull, & Greenfield, in press). In the area of instruction, children were encouraged to help each other in preparing for standardized tests (while the bottom line of individual assessment was also made clear!) (Rothstein-Fisch et al., 2003). In language arts, teachers designed writing prompts and selected literature based on students' interest in the topic of "family"; they also supported students' forms of discourse that integrated academic topics with social topics (such as experiences with family) (Rothstein-Fisch, Trumbull, & Greenfield, in press).

Reason for Optimism

The outcomes of the Bridging Cultures Project are causes for optimism. Some of the most striking effects have to do with (1) the perspective teachers have gained on their own culture, their students' home culture, and school culture, (2) the degree to which this has begun to influence their thinking and their practice in ways that reduce conflicts between home and school culture, and (3) the increased confidence teachers have in their own abilities to build the kinds of relationships with families that will support student success in school and family unity at home. They know how to learn from their students' families, and they have new ways of understanding what parents are sharing with them. What they have learned will stand them in good stead whenever they encounter students from other collectivistic cultures, although the specifics may be different. We believe the project has been successful for the following reasons:

- It uses a theory- and research-based framework to guide experimentation with new educational methods.
- It offers teachers opportunities to share and analyze practice over an extended period of time, valuing their knowledge and experience.
- It allows for experimentation and has been applied to all aspects of teachers' work including staff development, classroom management, subject matter instruction, assessment, and parent–school relations.
- It has a committed group of teacher-researchers and staff researchers.
- It is not prescriptive but offers a generative framework.
- It includes meetings that incorporate both rigorous intellectual work and enjoyable interpersonal activities such as sharing meals, humor, and personal celebrations.

In the final analysis, teachers recognize that neither value system is all good or all bad. One teacher said, "I think that it is a good point to bring out about culture . . . that . . . we're not saying collectivism is right and individualism is wrong. We're just saying to recognize it. It's different."

CONCLUSIONS

A strong cultural theory of learning and development places culture at the center rather than the periphery. Culture is not simply a context for development; instead it is inside the individual, an essential component of learning, socialization, and development (Greenfield, Keller, Fuligni, & Maynard, 2003). Each cultural pathway addresses universal developmental issues. Many of these issues—for example, learning, teaching, intelligence, creativity, and knowledge—are centrally relevant to educational psychology. But each pathway addresses the issues with a different emphasis. The pathway toward independence, individuation, and innovation provides one set of developmental priorities; the pathway toward interdependence, group membership, and respect for community tradition provides another set.

Schooling intrinsically values the independent individual. In school, to help or be helped by another, especially on a test, is to commit the act of cheating (Cizek, 1999; Whiting & Whiting, 1994; Rothstein-Fisch et al., 2001). Most likely the general cultural emphasis on individualism in the United States (e.g., Hofstede, 2001) further strengthens the value schools place on the independent individual, relative to schools in some other countries.

However, it is important to realize that this individualistic value system is not part of the home culture for many, many students from immigrant or native cultures. This may also be the case, albeit to a lesser extent, in nonminority working-class homes (Lucariello, Durand, & Yarnell, 2005; Snibbe & Markus, 2005); collectivism, particularly in the form of sharing and helping, is a natural adaptation to lesser economic means. The difference between a more collectivistic home culture and a more individualistic school culture sets the stage for values conflict, with children being exposed to one set of values at home, another at school.

Although we have, in this chapter, presented examples from the elementary school years, parallel conflicts occur from early childhood through the university. At the preschool level, for example, a toddler may be hand or spoon fed by others at home (value placed on parental helpfulness and parent–child closeness), while being encouraged to self-feed in day care (value placed on child independence) (Zepeda, Gonzalez-Mena, Rothstein-Fisch, & Trumbull, in press). At the other end of the educational spectrum, when a college student is absent from a test to fulfill his/her family's request to help care for a sick relative, a common reaction on the part of the professor is that he or she is slacking from school responsibilities; it would be rare to hear the student praised for providing help at home. As another example, we have noted that the most difficult part of graduate school for some Latino students from immigrant homes is the conflict between being present for family occasions such as baptisms and birthdays and being present to fulfill tasks in the academic environment.

Part of the answer to such dilemmas is to help parents and families understand the two cultures and the conflicting demands that divergent cultural priorities place on their children. We have begun to explore this route by holding Bridging Cultures workshops for Latino immigrant parents. This was a research project initiated by one of our Bridging Cultures teachers, Catherine Daley. Our findings are that such workshops help parents understand their children's desire for more independence than the parents have wanted and also make the parents better understand their children's teachers. This latter understanding was reflected in significantly greater parent visitations with their children's teachers, relative to a control group who received the school's "standard" parent training (Esau, Greenfield, & Daley, 2004).

We also know that similar conflicts and misunderstandings occur among peers in heterogeneous classrooms or school sports teams when some members of a peer group bring a collectivistic cultural orientation and others bring a more individualistic orientation into the group situation (Greenfield & Suzuki, 1998; Greenfield, Davis, Suzuki, & Boutakidis, 2002). We have developed a Bridging-Cultures-style intervention for multiethnic high school sports teams, with some limited success (Kernan & Greenfield, in press). However, to our knowledge, no research has been done on the role of cross-cultural value conflict in peer relations in culturally diverse elementary schools. This is an area ripe for future research.

One topic that we have not touched in our research or in this chapter is whether and how teachers can adapt the Bridging Cultures approach to classrooms and schools that are ethnically heterogeneous, rather than homogenous. Our methods were developed for a situation in which the classroom population is an immigrant population from a single ethnic group with a collectivistic heritage culture. What can and should teachers do in schools and classrooms in which students come from various ethnocultural backgrounds? There are two such situations.

In one, children will be from various immigrant backgrounds, all of which share a collectivistic value system. In this situation, we believe that the Bridging Cultures approach can be used with minimal adaptation. In the second situation, children from individualistic mainstream cultural backgrounds are mixed in with children from collectivistic cultural backgrounds. Here more adaptation will surely be necessary, and research is very much needed. However, we would guess that a framework for understanding the nature of cultural differences within a classroom would have to be very helpful to a teacher and to her students. Such a framework might affect how the teacher dealt with cross-cultural misunderstandings among children coming from different cultural backgrounds. It might also affect how well the teacher understood differing concerns of parents from different cultural backgrounds. How to translate an understanding of culturally diverse value systems in a single school or classroom is an important topic for future research in educational psychology.

By using the paradigm presented in this chapter to animate their research, educational psychologists could play a major role in helping school personnel to negotiate difficult cultural waters by equipping them with detailed research-based knowledge of the two pathways and their manifestation in a multicultural school situation. Cross-cultural value conflicts can take place both externally and internally. Little is known about how they make school at every level difficult for those who experience them. It seems clear, however, that the more such cross-cultural value conflicts are understood by educational researchers and educators at all levels, the less these conflicts will interfere with processes of education and development.

ACKNOWLEDGMENTS

The first author gratefully acknowledges a fellowship at the Center for Advanced Study in the Behavioral Sciences, Stanford, CA, which provided time and space to write this chapter. Portions of this chapter have appeared in "Cultural pathways through universal development" by P. M. Greenfield, H. Keller, A. Fuligni, & A. E. Maynard (*Annual Review of Psychology*, 2003, *54*, 461–490), "Bridging Cultures" by P. M. Greenfield, E. Trumbull, & C. Rothstein-Fisch (*Cross-Cultural Psychology Bulletin*, 2003, *37*, 6–16), and "Culture and human development: Implications for parenting, education, pediatrics" by P. M. Greenfield & L. K. Suzuki (in W. Damon (General Ed.), I. E. Sigel & K. A. Renninger (Vol. Eds.), *Handbook of child psychology* (5th ed.): *Vol. 4. Child psychology in practice* (pp. 1059–1109). New York: Wiley), and "Paradigms of Cultural Thought" by P. M. Greenfield (In K. J. Holyoak & R. J. Morrison (Eds.), *Cambridge handbook of thinking and reasoning*. Cambridge, UK: Cambridge University Press, 2005). Last but not at all least, we thank Dr. Virginia Kwan of Princeton University for her incredibly perceptive and useful review, which guided and stimulated major improvements in this chapter.

Note: Blanca Quirtz is currently an Asst. Professor in the College of Education and Human Development at Texas A&M University. This work was conducted while she was at UCLA.

References

Aronson, E., Stephan, C., Sikes, J., Blaney, N., & Snapp, M. (1978). *The jigsaw classroom*. Beverly Hills, CA: Sage.

Azuma, H. (1994). Two modes of cognitive socialization in Japan and the United States. In P. M. Greenfield & R. R. Cocking (Eds.), *Cross-cultural roots of minority child development* (pp. 275-285\4). Hillsdale, NJ: Lawrence Erlbaum Associates.

Berry J. W. (1994). Ecology of individualism and collectivism. In U. Kim, H. C. Triandis, C., Kagitçibasi, S.-C. & Choi, G. Yoon (Eds.), *Individualism and collectivism: Theory, method, and applications* (pp. 77-84). Thousand Oaks, CA: Sage.

Boesch, C. (1991). Teaching among wild chimpanzees. *Animal Behavior, 41*, 530-532.

Brislin, R. (1993). *Understanding culture's influence on behavior*. Fort Worth, TX: Harcourt Brace College.

Bruner, J. S. (1996). *The culture of education*. Cambridge, MA.: Harvard University Press.

Chao, R. K. (1994). Beyond parental control and authoritarian parenting style: Understanding Chinese parenting through the cultural notion of training. *Child Development, 65*, 1111-1119.

Chavajay, P., & Rogoff, B. (2002). Schooling and traditional collaborative social organization of problem solving by Mayan mothers and children. *Developmental Psychology, 38*, 55-66.

Childs, C. P., & Greenfield, P. M. (1980). Informal modes of learning and teaching: The case of Zinacanteco weaving. In N. Warren (Ed.), *Studies in cross-cultural psychology* (Vol. 2, pp. 269-316). London: Academic Press.

Choi, S. H. (1992). Communicative socialization processes: Korea and Canada. In S. Iwawaki, Y. Kashima, & K. Leung (Eds.), *Innovations in cross-cultural psychology* (pp. 103-121). Lissez: Swets & Zeitlinger.

Cizek, G. J. (1999). *Cheating on tests; How to do it, detect it and prevent it*. Mahwah, NJ: Lawrence Erlbaum Associates.

Cohen, E. G. (1986). *Designing groupwork*. New York: Teachers College Press.

Dasen, P. R. (1984). The cross-cultural study of intelligence: Piaget and the Baoulé. *International Journal of Psychology, 19*, 407-434.

Delgado-Gaitan, C. (1994). Socializing young children in Mexican-American families: An intergenerational perspective. In P. M. Greenfield & R. R. Cocking (Eds.), *Cross-cultural roots of minority child development*. Hillsdale, NJ: Lawrence Erlbaum Associates.

Delpit, L. (1995). *Other people's children: Cultural conflict in the classroom*. New York: New Press.

Duranti, A., & Ochs, E. (1986). Literacy instruction in a Samoan village. In Schieffelin, B. B. & Gilmore, P. (Eds.), *Acquisition of literacy: Ethnographic perspectives* (pp. 213-232). Norwood, NJ: Ablex.

Esau, P. C., Greenfield, P. M., & Daley, C. (2004). Bridging Cultures Parent Workshops: Developing cross-cultural harmony in minority school communities. Paper presented at the University of California Linguistic Minority Research Institute Conference, Santa Barbara, CA.

Geary, P. (2001). *Bridging cultures with middle school counselors.* Unpublished master's thesis, California State University, Northridge.

Goldenberg, C., & Gallimore, R. (1995). Immigrant Latino parents' values and beliefs about their children's education: Continuities and discontinuities across cultures and generations. In P. Pintrich and M. Maehr (Eds.), *Advances in Achievement Motivation* (Vol. 9, pp. 183–228). Greenwich, CT: JAI Press.

Goodnow, J. J. (1988). Parents' ideas, actions, and feelings: models and methods from developmental and social psychology. *Child Development, 59*(2), 286–320.

Greenfield, P. M. (2000). Culture and universals: Integrating social and cognitive development. In L. P. Nucci, G. B. Saxe, & E. Turiel (Eds.), *Culture, thought, and development* (pp. 231–277). Mahwah, NJ: Lawrence Erlbaum Associates.

Greenfield, P. M. (in press). Applying developmental psychology to bridge cultures in the classroom. In S. I. Donaldson, D. E. Berger, & K. Rezdek (Eds.), *Applied Psychology: New Frontiers and rewarding carrers.* Mahwah, NJ: Lawrence Erlbaum Associates.

Greenfield, P. M. (2004). *Weaving generations together: Evolving creativity in the Maya of Chiapas.* Santa Fe, NM: SAR Press.

Greenfield, P. M., Brazelton, T. B., & Childs, C. (1989). From birth to maturity in Zinacantan: Ontogenesis in cultural context. In V. Bricker & G. Gossen (Eds.), *Ethnographic encounters in Southern Mesoamerica: Celebratory essays in honor of Evon Z. Vogt.* Albany: Institute of Mesoamerica, State University of New York.

Greenfield, P. M., & Bruner, J. S. (1966). Culture and cognitive growth. *International Journal of Psychology, 1,* 89–107.

Greenfield, P. M. & Cocking, R. (Eds.). (1994). *Cross-cultural roots of minority child development.* Hillsdale, NJ: Lawrence Erlbaum Associates.

Greenfield, P. M., Davis, H. Suzuki, L., & Boutakidis, I. (2002). Understanding intercultural relations on multiethnic high school sports teams. In M. Gatz, M. A. Messner, & S. Ball-Rokeach (Eds.), *Paradoxes of youth and sport* (pp. 141–157). Albany, NY: SUNY Press.

Greenfield, P. M., Keller, H., Fuligni, A., & Maynard, A. (2003). Cultural pathways through universal development. *Annual Review of Psychology, 54,* 461–490.

Greenfield P. M., Maynard, A. E., Boehm, C., & Yut, E. (2000). Cultural apprenticeship and cultural change: tool learning and imitation in chimpanzees and humans. In S. T. Parker, J. Langer, M. L. McKinney (Eds.), *Biology, brains, and behavior* (pp. 237–277). Santa Fe, NM: SAR Press.

Greenfield, P. M., Maynard, A. E., & Childs, C. P. (2003). Historical change, cultural learning, and cognitive representation in Zinacantec Maya children. *Cognitive Development, 18,* 455–487.

Greenfield, P. M., Quiroz, B., & Raeff, C. (2000). Cross-cultural conflict and harmony in the social construction of the child. In S. Harkness, C. Raeff, & C. M. Super (Eds.), Variability in the social construction of the child. *New Directions in Child Development.* (No. 87, pp. 93–108). San Fransisco: Jossey-Bass.

Greenfield, P. M., Raeff, C., & Quiroz, B. (1996). Cultural values in learning and education. In B. Williams (Ed.), *Closing the achievement gap: A vision for changing beliefs and practices* (pp. 37–55). Alexandria, VA: Association for Supervision and Curriculum Development.

Greenfield, P. M. & Suzuki, L. (1998). Culture and human development: Implications for parenting, education, pediatrics, and mental health. In I. E. Sigel, & K. A. Renninger (Eds.), *Handbook of child psychology* (5th ed.), *Vol. 4: Child psychology in practice* (pp. 1059–1109). New York: Wiley.

Greenfield, P. M., Trumbull, E., & Rothstein-Fisch, C. (2003). Bridging cultures. *Cross-Cultural Psychology Bulletin, 37*(1–2), 6–17.

Gutierrez, J., & Sameroff, A. J. (1990). Determinants of complexity in Mexican-American and Anglo-American mothers' conceptions of child development. *Child Development, 61,* 384–394.

Harkness, S. (1988). The cultural construction of semantic contingency in mother–child speech. *Language Sciences, 10*(1), 53–67.

Harkness, S. & Super, C. M. (1982). Why African children are so hard to test. In L. L. Adler (Ed.), *Cross-cultural research at issue* (pp. 145–152). New York: Academic Press.

Harkness, S., Super, C., & van Tijen, N. (2000). Individualism and the "Western Mind" reconsidered: parents' ethnotheories of the child. In S. Harkness, C. Raeff, & C. M. Super (Eds.), *Variability in the social construction of the child* (pp. 23–39), *New Directions in Child Development* (No. 87). San Fransisco: Jossey-Bass.

Harwood, R. L. (1992). The influence of culturally derived values on Anglo and Puerto Rican mothers' perceptions of attachment behavior. *Child Development, 63,* 822–839.

Harwood, R. L., Schoelmerich, A., Ventura-Cook, E., Schulze, P. A., & Wilson, S. P. (1996). Culture and class influences on Anglo and Puerto Rican mothers' beliefs regarding long-term socialization goals and child behavior. *Child Development, 67,* 2446–2461.

Hewlett, B. S., & Lamb, M. E. (2002). Integrating evolution, culture and developmental psychology: explaining caregiver infant proximity and responsiveness in Central Africa and the United States of America. In H. Keller, Y. H. Poortinga, & A. Schoelmerich (Eds.), *Between culture and biology* (pp. 241–269). Cambridge, UK: Cambridge University Press.

Hill, R. B. (1972). *The strengths of Black families.* New York: Emerson Hall.

Hobson, R. P. (1993). *Autism and the development of mind.* Hillsdale, NJ: Lawrence Erlbaum Associates.

Hofstede, G. (2001). *Culture's consequences: Comparing values, behaviors, institutions, and organization across nation.* Thousand Oaks, CA: Sage.

Inhelder, B., & Piaget, J. (1958). *The growth of logical thinking from childhood to adolescence: An essay on the construction of formal operational structures.* New York: Basic Books.

Johnson. R. T., & Johnson, D. W. (1994). An overview of cooperative learning. In J. Thousand, A. Villa, & A. Nevin (Eds.),

Creativity and collaborative learning: A practical guide to students and teachers (pp. 31–44). Baltimore: Paul H. Brookes.

Kagitçibasi, C. (1996). *Family and human development across cultures: A view from the other side.* Hillsdale, NJ: Lawrence Erlbaum Associates.

Keller H. (1997). Evolutionary approaches. In J. W. Berry, Y. H. Poortinga, & J. Pandey, (Eds.), *Handbook of cross-cultural psychology, Vol. 1: Theory and method* (pp. 215–255). Boston: Allyn & Bacon.

Keller, H. (2003). Socialization for competence: cultural models of infancy. *Human Development, 46,* 288–311.

Keller, H., Voelker, S., Yovsi, R. D., & Shastri, J. (2005). The representation of independent and interrelated conceptions of caretaking. In P. Mohite (Ed.), *Theoretical approaches to early development: Implications for interventions.* Centre of Advanced Studies in HDFS, Department of HDFS, M.S. University of Baroda, Baroda, India.

Keller, H., Hentschel, E., Yovsi, R. D., Abels, M., Lamm, B., & Haas, V. (2004). The psycho-linguistic embodiment of parental ethnotheories. A new avenue to understand cultural differences in parenting. *Culture & Psychology 10,* 293–330.

Keller, H,, Miranda, D., & Gauda, G. (1984). The naive theory of the infant and some maternal attitudes. A two-country study. *Journal of Cross-Cultural Psychology, 15,* 165–179.

Kernan, C.L. & Greenfield, P. M. (in press, 2005). Becoming a team: Individualism, collectivism, ethnicity, and group socialization in Los Angeles girls' basketball. *Ethos.*

LeVine, R. A. (1997). Mother–infant interaction in cross-cultural perspective. In N. L. Segall, G. E., Weisfeld, & C. C. Weisfeld (Eds.), *Uniting psychology and biology: Integrative perspectives on human development* (pp. 339–354). Washington, DC: American Psychological Association.

LeVine, R., Dixon, S., LeVine, S., Richman, A., Leiderman, P., Keefer, C. et al. (1994). *Child care and culture: Lessons from Africa.* Cambridge, UK: Cambridge University Press.

Lambert, W. E, Hammers, J. F., & Frasure-Smith, N. (1979). *Child rearing values: a cross-national study.* New York: Praeger.

Li, J. (2002). A cultural model of learning: Chinese "heart and mind for wanting to learn." *Journal of Cross-Cultural Psychology, 33,* 248–269.

Lipka, J., with Mohatt, G. V., & the Ciulistet Group. (1998). *Transforming the culture of schools: Yup'ik Eskimo examples.* Mahwah, NJ: Lawrence Erlbaum Associates.

Lucariello, J., Durand, T., & Yarnell, L. (2005). Social cognition in low-SES children: Erasing a cognitive gap and showing a cognitive strength. Manuscript submitted for publication.

Markus, H. R, & Kitayama, S. (1991). Culture and the self: Implications for cognition, emotion, and motivation. *Psychological Review, 98,* 224–253.

Maynard, A., Greenfield, P. M., & Childs, C. P. (1999). Culture, history, biology, and body: How Zinacantec Maya learn to weave. *Ethos, 27,* 379–402.

McCaleb, S. P. (1997). *Building communities of learners: A collaboration among teachers, students, families, and community.* Mahwah, NJ: Lawrence Erlbaum Associates.

McGillicuddy-De Lisi, A. V., & Sigel, I. E. (1995). Parental beliefs. In M. H. Bornstein (Ed.), *Handbook of parenting: Vol 3. Status and social conditions of parenting* (pp. 333–358). Hillsdale, NJ: Lawrence Erlbaum Associates.

Miller, J. G. (1995). In C. Raeff (Chair). Individualism and collectivism as cultural contexts for developing different modes of independence and interdependence. Symposium presented at the Society for Research on Child Development, Indianapolis.

Nelson-Barber, S. & Dull, V. (1998). Don't act like a teacher! Images of effective instruction in a Yup'ik Eskimo classroom. In J. Lipka (Ed.), with G. V. Mohatt in the Ciulistet Group, *Transforming the Culture of Schools: Yup'ik Eskimo examples* (pp. 91–105). Mahwah, NJ: Lawrence Erlbaum Associates.

Nsamenang, A. B. (1992). *Human development in cultural context. A third world perspective.* Newbury Park, CA: Sage.

Nsamenang, A. B., & Lamb, M. E. (1994). Socialization of Nso children in the Bamenda grassfields of Northwest Cameroon. In P. M. Greenfield & R. R. Cocking (Eds.), *Cross-cultural roots of minority child development* (pp. 133–46). Mahwah, NJ: Lawrence Erlbaum Associates.

Ogunnaike, O. A., & Houser, R. F. (2002). Yoruba toddlers' engagement in errands and cognitive performance on the Yoruba Mental Subscales. *International Journal of Behavioral Development, 26,* 145–153.

Osterman, K. F. (2000). Students' need for belonging in the school community. *Review of Educational Research, 70,* 323–367.

Palacios, J., & Moreno, M. C. (1996). Parents' and adolescents' ideas on children: origins and transmission of intracultural diversity. In S. Harkness & C. M. Super (Eds.), *Parents' cultural belief systems: Their origins, expressions and consequences* (pp. 215–253). New York: Guilford Press.

Piaget, J. (1963/1977). Intellectual operations and their development. Reprinted in H. E. Gruber & J. J. Vonèche (Eds.), *The essential Piaget: An interpretive reference and guide* (pp. 342–358). New York: Basic Books.

Portes, P. R. (1996). Ethnicity and culture in educational psychology. In D. C. Berliner & R. C. Calfee (Eds.), *Handbook of educational psychology* (pp. 331–357). New York: Simon & Schuster Macmillan.

Quiroz, B., & Greenfield, P. M. (1996). *Cross-cultural value conflict: Removing a barrier to Latino school achievement.* Unpublished manuscript, Department of Psychology, UCLA.

Quiroz, B., Greenfield, P. M., & Altchech, M. (1998). Bridging cultures between home and school: The parent–teacher conference, *Connections, 1,* 8–11.

Quiroz, B., Greenfield, P. M., & Altchech, M. (1999) Bridging cultures with a parent–teacher conference. *Educational Leadership, 56,* 68–70.

Raeff, C., Greenfield, P. M., & Quiroz, B. (2000). Conceptualizing interpersonal relationships in the cultural contexts of individualism and collectivism. In S. Harkness, C. Raeff, & C. Super (Eds.), *Variability in the social construction of the child.* (pp. 59–74). *New Directions in Child Development* (No. 87). San Fransisco: Jossey-Bass.

Reese, L, Balzano, S., Gallimore, R., & Goldenberg, C. (1995). The concept of *educacion:* Latino family values and American schooling. *International Journal of Educational Research, 23,* 57–81.

Rogoff, B. (1990). *Apprenticeship in thinking: Cognitive development in social context.* New York: Oxford.

Rogoff, B. (2003). *The cultural nature of human development.* New York: Oxford.

Romero, M. E. (1994). Identifying giftedness among Keresan Pueblo Indians: The Keres study. *Journal of American Indian Education, 34,* 35–58.

Rothbaum, F., Weisz, J., Pott, M., Miyake, K., & Morelli, G. (2000). Attachment and culture: Security in the United States and Japan. *American Psychologist, 55,* 1093–1104.

Rothstein-Fisch, C. (2004, February). *Bridging cultures in early childhood: Diverse perspectives on infant and toddler care.* Baltimore, MD: National Birth to Three Institute.

Rothstein-Fisch, C., Greenfield, P. M., & Trumbull, E. (1999). Bridging cultures with classroom strategies. *Educational Leadership, 56,* 64–67.

Rothstein-Fisch, C. & Trumbull, E. (2005, April). *Using a cultural framework to understand the variability of motivation.* Paper presented at the Society for Research in Child Development, Atlanta, GA.

Rothstein-Fisch, C., Trumbull, E., & Greenfield, P. M. (in press). *Reconceptualizing classroom management: Building on students' cultural strengths.* Alexandria, VA: Association for Supervision and Curriculum Development.

Rothstein-Fisch, C., Trumbull, E., Isaac, A., Daley, C., & Pérez, A. (2003). When "helping someone else" is the right answer. *Journal of Latinos and Education, 3, 123–140.*

Rothstein-Fisch, C., Trumbull, E., Quiroz, B., & Greenfield, P. M. (1997). *Bridging cultures in the classroom.* Poster presentation at the Jean Piaget Society, Santa Monica, CA.

Saraswathi, T. S. (1999). *Culture, socialization, and human development: Theory, research, and applications in the Indian setting.* Thousand Oaks, CA: Sage.

Schneider, B., Hieshima, J. A., Lee, S., & Plank, S. (1994). Continuities and discontinuities in the cognitive socialization of Asian-oriented children: The case of Japanese Americans. In P. M. Greenfield & R. R. Cocking (Eds.), *Cross-cultural roots of minority child development* (pp. 323–350). Hillsdale, NJ: Lawrence Erlbaum Associates.

Segall, M. H., Dasen, P. R., Berry, J. W., & Poortinga, Y. H. (1999). *Human behavior in global perspective: An introduction to cross-cultural psychology* (2nd ed.). Boston: Allyn & Bacon.

Serpell, R. (1979). How specific are perceptual skills? A cross-cultural study of pattern representation. *British Journal of Psychology, 70,* 365–380.

Serpell, R. (1993). *The significance of schooling: Life journeys in an African society.* Cambridge, UK: Cambridge University Press.

Snibbe, A. C. & Markus, H. R. (2005). You can't always get what you want: Educational attainment, agency, and choice. *Journal of Personality and Social Psychology, 88,* 703–720.

Solomon, D., Watson, M., Battistich, V., Schaps, E., & Delucchi, K. (1996). Creating classrooms that students experience as communities. *American Journal of Community Psychology, 24,* 719–748.

Suina, J., & Smolkin, L. B. (1994). From natal culture to school culture to dominant society culture: supporting transitions for Pueblo Indian students. In P. M. Greenfield & R. R. Cocking (Eds.), *Cross-cultural roots of minority child development* (pp. 115–130). Hillsdale, NJ: Lawrence Erlbaum Associates.

Tapia-Uribe, F. M., LeVine, R. A., & LeVine, S. E. (1994). Maternal behavior in a Mexican community: The changing environments of children. In P.M. Greenfield & R.R. Cocking (Eds.), *Cross-cultural roots of minority child development* (pp. 41–54). Hillsdale, NJ: Erlbaum.

Trevarthen C. (1980). The foundations of intersubjectivity: Development of interpersonal and cooperative understanding in infants. In D. Olson (Ed.), *The social foundations of language and thought* (pp. 316–342). New York: Norton.

Triandis, H. C. (1989). Cross-cultural studies of individualism and collectivism. *Nebraska Symposium on Motivation, 37, 43–133.*

Triandis, H., Brislin, R., & Hui, C. H. (1988). Cross-cultural training across the individualism-collective divide. *International Journal of Intercultural Relations, 12,* 269–289.

Trumbull, E., Diaz-Meza, R., Hasan, A. & Rothstein-Fisch, C. (2001) *Five year—Report of the Bridging Cultures Project.* San Francisco: WestEd. (www.wested.org/bridgingcultures).

Trumbull, E., Nelson-Barber, S., & Mitchell, J. (2002). Enhancing mathematics instruction for Indigenous American Students. In J. Hankes (Ed.), *Changing the faces of mathematics: Perspectives on indigenous people of North America.* Reston, VA: National Council of Teachers of Mathematics.

Trumbull, E., Rothstein-Fisch, C., and Greenfield, P. M. (2000). Bridging cultures in our schools: New approaches that work. *Knowledge Brief.* San Francisco: WestEd.

Trumbull, E., Rothstein-Fisch, C., Greenfield, P. M., & Quiroz, B. (2001). *Bridging cultures between home and school: A guide for teachers.* Mahwah, NJ: Lawrence Erlbaum Associates.

Trumbull, E., Rothstein-Fisch, C., & Hernandez, E. (2003). Parent involvement—according to whose values? *School Community Journal, 13,* 45–72.

Valdés, G. (1996). *Con respeto.* New York: Teachers College Press.

Whiten, A. (1999). Parental encouragement *in Gorilla* in comparative perspective: implications for social cognition and the evolution of teaching. In S. T. Parker, R. W. Mitchell, & H. L. Miles (Eds.), *The mentalities of gorillas and orangutans in comparative perspective* (pp. 342–366). Cambridge, UK: Cambridge University Press.

Whiting, J. W. M. & Whiting, B. B. (1973). Altruistic and egoistic behavior in six cultures. In L. Nader & T. W. Maretzki (Eds.), *Cultural illness and health: Essays in human adaptation.* Washington, DC: American Anthropological Association.

Whiting, J. W. M. & Whiting, B. B. (1994). Altruistic and egoistic behavior in six cultures. In E. H. Chasdi (Ed.), *Culture and human development.* (pp. 267–281). New York, NY: Cambridge University Prss. Reprinted from Whiting, J. W. M. & Whiting, B. B. (1973). Altruistic and egoistic behavior in six cultures. In L. Nader & T. W. Maretzki (Ed.). Cultural illness and health: Essays in human adaption* (pp. 56–66). Washington, D. C.: American Anthropological Association.

Whiting, B. B. & Whiting, J. W. M. (1975). *Children of six cultures.* Cambridge, MA: Harvard University Press.

Wober, J. M. (1974). Toward an understanding of the Kiganda concept of intelligence. In J. W. Berry, & P. R. Dasen (Eds.),*Culture and cognition* (pp. 261–80). London: Methuen.

Yovsi, R. D. (2001). Ethnotheories about breastfeeding and mother–infant interaction. The case of sedentary Nso farmers and nomadic Fulani pastorals with their infants 3–6 months of age in Mbvem subdivision of the Northwest providence of Cameroon, Africa. Unpublished doctoral dissertation, University of Osnabrück, Germany.

Yovsi, R. D., & Keller, H. (2003). Breastfeeding. An adaptive process. *Ethos, 31,* 147–171.

Zambrano, I. (1999). *From na' to know: power, epistemology and the everyday forms of state formation in Mitontik, Chiapas (Mexico).* Unpublished doctoral dissertation, Harvard University.

Zepeda, M., Gonzalez-Mena, J., Romstein-Fisch Trumbull, E. (in press). Bridging Cultures in early care and education: A training module. Mahwah, NJ: Lawrence Erlbaum & Associates.

Part

·VII·

THE EDUCATIONAL CONTEXT

EDUCATION FOR THE KNOWLEDGE AGE: DESIGN-CENTERED MODELS OF TEACHING AND INSTRUCTION

Carl Bereiter
Marlene Scardamalia
Institute for Knowledge Innovation and Technology and Ontario Institute for Studies in Education of the University of Toronto

This chapter deals with recent efforts to reshape teaching and instruction in response to perceived new needs arising from a shift from a manufacturing-based to a knowledge-based economy (Drucker, 1994). Accordingly, it does not deal with models of teaching and instruction in general (cf. Reigeluth, 1999) or with such perennial concerns as the teaching of basic academic skills and content, motivation, retention, and transfer, except insofar as changing conditions require a new look at these. Instead, the focus is on objectives and methods that are tied in some way to the rising importance of knowledge creation and knowledge work.

We begin with a necessarily cursory examination of larger economic and social trends that have implications for teaching and instruction. A key question is whether these trends have created a need for any new skills, abilities, and forms of knowledge or substantially altered traditional educational priorities. In seeking an answer to this question, we consider what is different about knowledge work from other types of skilled work. Two insights emerge from this analysis: (1) In the world of knowledge work, knowledge has acquired a thinglike or artifactual status, making it something that can be treated as a product, material, or tool. This is a radical departure from how knowledge has traditionally been treated in both episte-

mology and education. (2) Directly or indirectly, knowledge work typically serves design goals rather than "truth" goals. This puts knowledge work in diametrical contrast to school work. Together, these insights point to two educational reform objectives: (1) bringing design work into the formal or academic part of the curriculum and (2) developing in students the ability to work creatively with knowledge per se—as distinct from working creatively on tasks that *use* knowledge. Several contemporary educational approaches are examined in light of these reform objectives.

We then look more deeply into the *creativity* part of the Knowledge Age challenge. According to contemporary theories, creative ideas can only be explained as emergent results of a self-organizing, Darwinian process. The same can be said of understanding. Creating new knowledge and understanding existing knowledge are both emergent processes. We examine emergence more broadly as an educational phenomenon and note that "systems thinking" can illuminate other learning issues as well. Finally, we consider technology as support for education adapted to the Knowledge Age.

We must emphasize at the outset that, although economic changes may be driving educational changes at the policy level, it by no means follows that what happens at the classroom level need be or should be framed in terms of economic expediency. A broader and more humanistic view is suggested by A. N. Whitehead's dictum that education should enable students "to appreciate the current thought of their epoch." In our epoch, which is coming to be known as the Knowledge Age, the "current thought" is not a collection of beliefs but a dynamic process of advancing the frontiers of understanding and efficacy on all fronts. In this chapter we consider the possibility that students can participate in this process rather than only viewing it as spectators.

THE "KNOWLEDGE SOCIETY" IDEA AND ITS IMPLICATIONS FOR EDUCATION

The concept of *knowledge society* is derived from the seminal work of management scientist Peter Drucker (1968,1993). Central to Drucker's conception is the idea of *knowledge work*, which he portrayed as gaining ascendancy over manufacturing work, just as manufacturing work at an earlier time gained ascendancy over agricultural work. A difference highlighted by Drucker is that the learning required for an individual to shift from agricultural to factory work is relatively slight, whereas a shift from manufacturing to knowledge work requires extensive learning. Hence the escalating importance of education: "Education will become the center of the knowledge society, and the school its key institution" (Drucker, 1994, p. 53). This conviction was reiterated by the 30-nation Organization for Economic Co-operation and Development: "Education will be the centre of the knowledge-based economy"(OECD, 1996, p. 14). The importance of both formal ("codified") and informal ("tacit") knowledge has been recognized and even the connection between the two: "*Tacit knowledge* in the form of skills needed to handle codified knowledge is more important than ever in labour markets" (OECD, 1996, p. 13; emphasis in original).

In the hands of management specialists, the ideas of knowledge society, knowledge work, and knowledge management have become elaborated into concepts such as "intellectual capital" (Stewart, 1997) and "knowledge-creating companies" (Nonaka & Takeuchi, 1995). In economics, ideas such as "knowledge-based economy" and "knowledge capitalism" emerged, signaling a fundamental shift in the bases of wealth and productivity:

Economic historians point out that nowadays disparities in the productivity and growth of different countries have far less to do with their abundance (or lack) of natural resources than with the capacity to improve the quality of human capital and factors of production: in other words, to create new knowledge and ideas and incorporate them in equipment and people. (David & Foray, 2003, p. 21)

David and Foray added: "The 'need to innovate' is growing stronger as innovation comes closer to being the sole means to survive and prosper in highly competitive and globalised economies" (p. 22). How education can serve this "need to innovate" is the focal problem addressed in this chapter.

Education's Response to the New Economic Challenges

According to Peters (2003):

Knowledge capitalism and knowledge economy are twin terms that can be traced at the level of public policy to a series of reports that emerged in the late 1990s by the OECD...and the World Bank...before they were taken up as a policy template by world governments in the late 1990s. In terms of these reports, *education is reconfigured as a massively undervalued form of knowledge capital that will determine the future of work, the organization of knowledge institutions and the shape of society in the years to come.* (p. 364, emphasis added)

Policy template is an appropriate term for the response of education authorities to the perceived economic sea-change. Wherever we travel we are handed attractive documents that set out an official plan for shaping education to the new conditions of globalization and knowledge economy. The common elements of these plans are (1) equipping the schools with computers and Internet connectivity, (2) training teachers in the appropriate use of this technology, and (3) developing in students a set of "soft" skills, which include collaboration, learning-to-learn, self-direction, creativity, and a lifelong readiness to learn and unlearn. As judged by the allocation of funds and the spilling of ink, the first two elements have received by far the most attention. We regard this as a transitory phenomenon, however, bound to diminish as technology becomes more taken for granted in school life. It is instead the "soft" skills element that represents a major and continuing challenge and that, accordingly, we take as the focus of this chapter.

The issue here is not that the traditional "basics" are irrelevant to Knowledge Age needs. Obviously they are highly relevant. The issue is that a new and qualitatively different set of needs has arisen, and the schools are not devoting anything like the attention to those that is being lavished on schooling's traditional tasks.

The Increasing Significance of "Soft" Skills

In 1998, the University of Washington's Office of Educational Assessment surveyed about 3,000 graduates, asking them to rate the importance of various abilities in their present lives (Gillmore, 1998). Half the graduates were 5 years beyond graduation, the other half 10 years. There was little difference between the ratings of these two groups. The top-rated ability was *defining and solving problems*. Other abilities receiving an average rating of 4 or more on a 5-point scale were *locating information needed to help make decisions or solve problems, working and/or learning independently, speaking effectively,* and *working effectively with modern technology, especially computers*. These were the top-rated abilities regardless of major field of study. Abilities directly deriving from university courses varied in rating from field to field, but never made it into the top five.

These top-rated abilities are very general in nature, applying to a wide variety of activities, in contrast to job-specific skills or the more discipline-specific knowledge and skills taught in university classes. In the business skills training literature they are referred to as "soft" skills. The term "generic" skills also covers approximately the same range. (See National Centre for Vocational Education Research, 2003, for a discussion of equivalent terms used in different countries.) The terms *hard* and *soft skills*, although ubiquitous, remain vague and metaphorical, usually defined only by examples. The following contrasts, however, are frequently noted and give a general idea of what the terms imply:

Hard Skills	Soft Skills
Often job-specific	Not job-specific
Objectively testable	Assessed subjectively
Directly teachable	Not directly teachable

In an Educational Testing Service report titled *The Economic Roots of K-16 Reform*, Carnevale and Desrocher (2003) documented the rising educational requirements for Knowledge Age jobs, adding:

The kind of education and skill demanded also has changed as a result of the shift to a service and information-based economy. Skill requirements have expanded to include soft skills, such as problem-solving and interpersonal skills, that supplement the more narrow cognitive and occupational skills sought in the industrial economy. Attitudinal skills, such as a positive "cognitive style," also are growing in importance because they allow workers to cope with the accelerating pace of change in the workplace. (p. 15)

In summary, the conditions motivating an increased emphasis on soft skills include:

• Uncertainty about future job requirements, which makes teaching of vocational hard skills questionable for students not yet in the job market

• Global competitiveness, with soft skills representing a way for individuals or organizations to gain a competitive edge
• Information abundance, reducing the need for teachers to act as information providers and increasing the need for ability to locate and select task-relevant information
• Increased specialization, making critical hard skills increasingly tied to advanced specialist training
• Technical de-skilling, reducing the hard-skill requirements for use of common software and complex tools.

PROBLEMS WITH SOFT SKILLS

There has been amazingly little "problematization" of pedagogy with respect to soft skills. Yet almost every aspect of teaching soft skills is, from the standpoint of contemporary learning science, deeply problematic. Here we discuss three broad problems.

What Are They?

Is there such a thing as problem-solving skill, in anything like the sense that there is keyboarding skill or automobile-driving skill? It would seem that an answer is required before one can hope to design a program to turn students into good problem solvers. Yet there is not an obvious answer, and—what is worse—there does not seem to be much awareness among educators that there is a question here deserving of thought. Or consider the second-ranked ability in the University of Washington survey: *locating information needed to help make decisions or solve problems*. A common practice in schools, and one that teachers would surely allude to in claiming that they are teaching Knowledge Age skills, is the research project in which students gather information from the Web and other sources and compile it to produce a report—often an electronic presentation. But note that the highly ranked ability is not simply that of locating information relevant to a topic. With contemporary search engines, 10 minutes of training should suffice to enable anybody to do that. What is hard is finding information that advances understanding relevant to the solution of a problem. The typical school "research" project provides little experience in dealing with this task, yet we do not find educators bemoaning this lack and discussing what to do about it.

The "what are they?" problem reaches an extreme in expressions like the one appearing in the previously quoted statement by Carnevale and Desrocher (2003): "Attitudinal skills, such as a positive 'cognitive style.'"

What on Earth is an "attitudinal skill," and how could cognitive style be an example? It would appear that any desirable personal characteristic may count as a soft skill. This, however, raises the question whether soft skills should be regarded as skills at all. In a later section we will consider a number of alternative conceptualizations.

Learnability/Teachability

The terms *learn* and *teach* are used very loosely in the soft skills literature and in curriculum standards and guidelines referring to them. Any activity that calls for a certain soft skill is said to teach it, and students who carry out the activity are said to learn it. A bland optimism prevails in the commercial and teacher-oriented literature. For instance, one Web page, from a vendor of wall climbing equipment, proclaimed:

Through a variety of challenge activities and climbing wall initiatives, individuals and teams have:

- Learned to work cooperatively
- Gained in trust of self and others
- Increased their self confidence and willingness to take positive risks
- Developed leadership skills
- Enhanced their interpersonal communication skills (listening, speaking, and writing)
- Increased their creative problem solving skills (Everlast Climbing Utilities, n.d.)

Such ungrounded optimism is not limited to the low end of the scholarly ladder, however. For instance, in the U.S. National Research Council's guide for implementing the National Science Education Standards, we find:

The *Standards* seek to promote curriculum, instruction, and assessment models that enable teachers to build on children's natural, human inquisitiveness. In this way, teachers can help all their students understand science as a human endeavor, acquire the scientific knowledge and *thinking skills important in everyday life* and, if their students so choose, in pursuing a scientific career. (Olson & Loucks-Horsley, 2000, p. 6) (emphasis added)

Transfer

Transfer of learning is a massive and much discussed issue in education (Bransford & Schwartz, 1999; McKeough, Lupart & Marini, 1995). What is seldom recognized, however, is that transfer is largely a soft skills problem. If one has learned how to add a column of figures (a "hard" skill), one can presumably do this in any situation where it is called for. Of course, one may fail to apply the right

arithmetic operation or may apply it to the wrong figures or may draw the wrong conclusion from the result; but those are soft skill problems. They are problems of the intelligent use of arithmetic. Bereiter (1995) has argued that this is the essence of the problem of transfer: What fails to transfer from one situation to another is not the skill itself but the intelligent use of it. Situativity theorists (e.g., Lave, 1988) make a similar argument: Through continued participation in a particular sphere of action one's actions become increasingly well adapted, resourceful, and flexible—in a word, intelligent—but in a different situation one has to start over learning the ropes, mastering what constitutes intelligent action in the new context.

The problem of transferability of soft skills is so vast and intractable that the commonest approach in the Knowledge Age skills literature is simply to ignore it. There seems to be a tacit assumption of unlimited transfer. In the examples cited in the previous section, optimism about learnability and teachability carry over into optimism about transfer. The advertisement for wall climbing equipment concludes, "By learning to trust each other and by working together, you begin to develop the skills that are integral to successful team functioning. This transfer of learning moves beyond the team and has additional application at home, in school, and in the community." Possibly all of this is true. But generations of research on generalization and transfer give us reason to doubt it and to demand either evidence or at least a plausible rationale for expecting widespread benefits to come from a situation so remote from most normal spheres of action. But do we have reason to believe that the exercise of the same soft skills in a school science laboratory, for instance, will have any greater transferability? The authors of the National Research Council document on implementing science curriculum standards evidently believed so, when they wrote of students acquiring, through their science study, "thinking skills important in everyday life."

A more realistic view of the transferability of soft skills would make use of Bransford and Schwartz's (1999) concept of judging transfer by savings in future learning. Students who have learned to cooperate in carrying out school projects may not automatically be better than others at cooperating as members of a road building crew or a legal defense team. Much specialized learning of social as well as technical kinds will be required in order to cooperate effectively in these different contexts. But it is not unreasonable to suppose that prior experience in cooperative work might facilitate the new social learning, speeding up adaptation to new situations where cooperation is called for. We cannot assume that, however, nor can we assume that one kind of cooperative experience is as good as another. Once transfer of soft skills is recognized as problematic, it becomes important to analyze situations and identify learning situations that have deep similarities to situations to which transfer is intended (Greeno, Smith, & Moore, 1993).

ALTERNATIVES TO SOFT SKILLS

Some so-called soft skills, such as cooperativeness, creativity, and self-directedness, might equally well be regarded as personality traits. Soft skills also map on to Gardner's "multiple intelligences" (1983). "People" skills, for instance—which figure prominently among business-related soft skills—correspond to "interpersonal intelligence" in Gardner's scheme. Other concepts that cover all or part of the territory of soft skills are habits of mind (Costa & Kallick, 2000) and talents. In quite a different conceptual framework, soft skills may be regarded as situated practices (Lave & Wenger, 1991)—as ways of acting that come about as one moves from peripheral to full participation in a community of practice. From still another viewpoint, soft skills may be viewed as behavioral norms or rules of wide scope. These are not merely semantic variations on the same idea. They carry quite different implications as to ontology, learnability/teachability, and transfer. Table 30.1 summarizes these implications.

Table 30.1 suggests that these alternative conceptions are all over the map as regards implications for learnability, teachability, and transfer. Some of these implications

have to be wrong; the differences cannot be written off as mere differences in perspective. Thus there is a place for hypothesis-testing research to identify those conceptions that are due for elimination or revision as bases for Knowledge Age pedagogy.

A DISTINCTIVE KNOWLEDGE AGE TALENT

In their review of "Economic Fundamentals of the Knowledge Society," David and Foray (2003) asked:

Are "new skills and abilities" required for integration into today's knowledge economy? If so, what are they? Are they really as new as some might like to make out? Beyond the levels of proficiency needed for the use of information technologies, there do appear to be a number of set requirements: teamwork, communication and learning skills. But these sorts of "soft skills" can hardly be described as new. (p. 31).

It is surely true that these and other frequently mentioned soft skills are far from new and have been well recognized. But is it true that there are no new skills and abilities required for integration into today's knowledge economy? If the question is whether there are any previously unknown skills needed for contemporary knowledge work, the answer is surely no. But if the question is whether there are skills important for contemporary knowledge work that have received little attention in education, and that remain little recognized, we have an issue deserving of serious inquiry, not least by educational psychologists.

TABLE 30.1. Alternative Conceptions "Soft Skills" and Their Implicit Assumptions

Concept	What Are They?	Learnability/Teachability	Transfer
Soft skills	Learned capabilities of very wide applicability. No distinction between nominal coherence and psychological reality.	Assumed teachable like any other skills.	Sometimes acknowledged as a problem, but ignored in practice.
Traits (including multiple intelligences, cognitive styles)	Deeply ingrained characteristics. Possible genetic component. Trait coherence based on psychometric evidence.	Modifiable, but only with difficulty and over long time span. Not teachable in any normal sense.	Unavoidable. Traits condition person's response in many situations.
Situated practices	Systemically constituted appropriate and effective ways of acting within a particular community of practice.	Highly learnable in context; limited role for teaching.	Believed to be very limited.
Habits of mind	Acquired habits, like any others, except enacted at a cognitive level.	Learned through repeated enactment; can be fostered or modified but not taught.	May or may not be triggered in new situations; may or may not prove appropriate.
Talents	Things everyone can do (given required hard skills) but with greatly varying proficiency.	Improvable through practice.	Variable and easily overestimated: e.g., transfer of musical talent.
Rules	Imperative statements. No claims of psychological reality.	May be adopted by individuals or groups. Teachable through advocacy, reminding, modeling, reward structures.	Wherever the norm applies and makes sense.

To put a finer point on the question, we may ask whether there are any soft skills important in the new economy that did not already figure prominently in the early history of flight—one of the signature achievements of the Industrial Age. The Wright Brothers displayed innovativeness and creativity, a high order of collaboration, and Wilbur at least was quite good at communication. Entrepreneurship? They successfully pursued patents and patent lawsuits and were noted for aggressive business practices (Shulman, 2002). The Wright Brothers have, in fact, been used as models of the kind of thinking required in today's business environment (Eppler, 2004). But now we have instances of complete new aircraft being designed entirely on computers (Petrowski, 1996). This seems like a profound shift, but—except for the obvious need for computer skills—does it present any new intellectual or educational challenges? The present authors have argued that it does, that there is in fact one previously unrecognized ability requirement that lies at the very heart of the knowledge economy. It is the ability to work creatively with knowledge per se. To convey what this means, however, we must back off and introduce a more general concept—conceptual artifacts—and a distinction between two modes of dealing with knowledge and ideas—what we call "belief mode" and "design mode."

Conceptual Artifacts

Somewhat simplistically, *conceptual artifacts* may be defined as ideas treated as real things (Bereiter, 2002b). This is in contrast to treating ideas as mental content, as tacit knowledge, as embedded in actions or tools, or as semiotic objects—all of which are legitimate ways of dealing with ideas, but not the same as treating them as objects in their own right. Patents provide a familiar anchor for the concept of conceptual artifact. Patents are awarded for ideas, not concrete devices or verbal or other representations. But patentable ideas are not ideas in people's heads or ideas implicit in their practice. Expressing the same idea in different words does not warrant a patent; it is the idea itself, not any particular expression of it, that is protectable. Although most conceptual artifacts—such as theories, problem formulations, and interpretations—are not protectable as property, they have all the other characteristics. They are human creations, intended for some purpose. They have most of the properties of artifacts in general: They have histories; they can be described and compared, variously used and modified; importantly, they can be discovered to have attributes not known to their creators (Bereiter, 2002b, p. 65). Unlike most artifacts, however, they are immaterial and they can stand in implicative relations to one another.

When treated as real artifacts, ideas can be made objects of inquiry and development, can be adapted to novel purposes, and so on. In knowledge-based organizations, conceptual artifacts figure prominently as products and as tools. It could, in fact, be claimed that conceptual artifacts constitute the knowledge that makes a knowledge-based organization knowledge-based; for although there are other valuable kinds of knowledge (tacit, situated, personal, social, and so on), these are of such long-standing value that they cannot be taken as marks of a new era.

Inasmuch as all kinds of work depend on knowledge, identifying what is distinctive about knowledge work has not been easy. Robert Reich (1991), one-time Secretary of Labor in the United States, coined the term *symbolic analyst*. His elaboration of the term is consistent with the preceding discussion, but the term itself is unfortunate: *symbolic* is too inclusive (religious rituals, for instance, are typically symbolic), whereas *analyst* is too narrow. The idea of conceptual artifacts can be useful in delimiting the field: Not all work involves conceptual artifacts, but arguably all knowledge work does. Working with conceptual artifacts, as distinct from working primarily or exclusively with material things, might therefore serve as a defining characteristic of knowledge work. In this light other, more familiar aspects of knowledge work take on a different hue. Collaboration in knowledge work is not the same as collaboration in wall-climbing, for instance, because feedback to the collaborative process is likely to be intangible and to require analysis in its own right. "Lifelong learning" becomes increasingly problematic if the learning must include not only facts and skills but also an effective grasp of difficult ideas. Only rarely, of course, is knowledge work purely conceptual. At some point conceptual artifacts have to make contact with real people, real shoes, real money, or something of that sort, where the mapping between conceptual artifacts and physical reality has real-world consequences, and these consequences are fed back into the work with conceptual artifacts.

In the school world, however, some formidable intellectual artillery is arrayed against work with abstract knowledge objects. Dewey (1916, pp. 183–185) was wary of it. Piaget's distinction between the stages of concrete and formal logical operations has been interpreted by many as a basis for concentrating elementary education on the concretely manipulable and deferring work with abstract ideas until adolescence. More recently, situativity theory has perhaps inadvertently steered educators away from conceptual artifacts, through the idea of knowledge as constituted in practice and accordingly not to be treated apart from its constitutive practices (Lave, 1988).

All these objections can be answered. In the first place, there is no suggestion that work with conceptual artifacts should go on in isolation from concrete reality. Experimental science provides a paradigm: Experimental scientists are in the business of producing conceptual artifacts, but they carry on this business in intimate congress with some kind of concrete reality. When "hands-on" school science goes on in isolation from the production of conceptual artifacts, however, it can be argued that this is not science at all. Furthermore, it can be argued that working with conceptual artifacts *is* a variety of "learning by doing." The claim that preadolescents are incapable of and uninterested in abstract thought has come under considerable experimental attack (Goswami, 1998). And the objection from situativity theory evaporates if schooling is modeled on communities whose practice includes sustained and creative work with conceptual artifacts (Bereiter, 1997). A deep-seated anti-intellectual bias (Hofstadter, 1963; Howley, Howley, & Pendarvis, 1995) may render all such arguments inconsequential, but it is also possible that societal pressure toward innovativeness may overcome traditional tendencies to restrict schooling to the concrete, practical, and factual.

Belief Mode Versus Design Mode

Historically, the main concern of epistemology has been the bases of true or warranted belief—hence, the name *belief* mode. Activity in belief mode covers a broad expanse, from indoctrination and propaganda on one extreme to the deepest critical analysis and the most open debate on the other. Schooling practices have covered this wide range. Such different approaches as lecture/recitation, inquiry learning , conceptual change teaching (Anderson & Roth, 1989), and transformative education (O'Sullivan, Morrell, & O'Connor, 2002) may be seen from this standpoint as variations all conducted within belief mode.

In knowledge-based organizations, however, work with ideas has taken a radically different direction, signaled by terms such as *knowledge-creating companies* (Nonaka & Takeuchi, 1995). In the pursuit of innovation, concern with truth and warrant has become incidental to pragmatic concerns such as

What is this idea (concept, design, plan, problem statement, theory, interpretation) good for?
What does it do and fail to do?
How could it be improved?

Work on such questions defines activity in "design" mode.

Formal education—the "academic" part of the curriculum, dealing with conceptual content as distinct from hard skills—has historically and to this day been conducted almost exclusively in belief mode. Questions about rationale, evidence, and logical consistency may be raised (cf. Kuhn, 1993), but design-mode questions, such as those just listed, receive little if any attention in textbooks, teaching materials, and curriculum standards or in the educational research literature of past years. Design mode activity does go on in schools, of course—in practical and fine arts courses, and in extracurricular activities such as drama and fund-raising—but it is alien to the academic curriculum. This marks a deep divide between knowledge as it is treated in schools and knowledge as it is treated in Knowledge Age organizations.

Conceptual Artifacts in Design Mode: Improvable Ideas

Conceptual artifacts can figure in both belief-mode and design-mode activity. A theory, for instance, may be treated in belief mode as a tentative statement of truth, and evaluated in terms of evidence. In design mode, a theory would be treated as a human construction aimed at serving some explanatory or instrumental purpose, would be evaluated on the basis of how well it served this purpose, and could be made an object of further improvement and elaboration. *Proofs and Refutations* by Lakatos (1976) provides a paradigm of theoretical work in design mode. It presents an imaginary dialogue among a group of mathematicians, who start with an empirically based conjecture about the relation between faces and vertices in space figures, attempt to construct a proof, discover cases that are inconsistent with the conjecture, modify the conjecture to exclude the anomalous cases, and proceed through further cycles of proof, refutation, and theory revision until they arrive finally at a provable theorem that withstands criticism.

Whereas dealing critically with conceptual artifacts in belief mode is a common characteristic of the "thinking curriculum" (Resnick & Klopfer, 1989), dealing with them in design mode has typically been the work only of advanced graduate students (cf. "making a contribution to knowledge" as the criterion that traditionally distinguishes doctoral theses from lower-level dissertations). In a "knowledge creating company," however, idea improvement becomes a core activity of the whole organization. Although the end result may be a new product rather than a new theory, the cycle of work leading up to the end result is similar to that portrayed by Lakatos.

This claim leads us back to the earlier discussion of the history of flight and to the question whether solving design problems the way the Wright Brothers did is different in any educationally significant way from the way aircraft design problems are solved today, where all or most design problems may be addressed computationally. The obvious difference in medium does not in itself point to anything more profound than the need to learn how to use new tools, something that was true throughout the Industrial Age. However, there are three more significant educational implications. The first is that in solving design problems computationally one is solving them by manipulating conceptual artifacts—mathematical and theoretical abstractions—rather than tinkering directly with material things. This can have both advantages and disadvantages, but it is in any case something quite different and less "natural" than the way the pioneers of aeronautics went about it. The second implication comes from a second-order design task. Someone had to design the software that made it possible to solve aeronautic design problems computationally. The software had to embody accurate information and valid theories about flight; otherwise the end results could be disastrous. Furthermore, this knowledge had to be embodied in the software in such a way that users with less knowledge could employ it successfully. The common element in both the first- and second-order tasks is work with conceptual artifacts that map onto but are not simple representations of physical objects. The contrast between this approach and the hands-on problem solving carried out by the Wright Brothers epitomizes the fundamental change that makes the so-called Knowledge Age different from the Industrial Age. A third educational implication has to do with the kind of collaboration or teamwork required. Modern planning and design often involves hundreds of knowledge workers whose efforts must lead to a unified result. Unlike the hundreds of assembly-line workers whose efforts converge on the manufacture of an automobile, however, the knowledge workers are often engaged in nonroutine tasks and the things they are working with are often abstract objects. This represents a much more demanding kind of cooperation, for which schooling could but typically does not provide relevant experience.

On the basis of this contrast and the concepts introduced earlier, we may identify a distinctive Knowledge Age talent as follows:

A distinctive Knowledge Age talent lies in the ability to work collaboratively with conceptual artifacts in design mode.

If this definition is accepted, and if it is true that work with conceptual artifacts in design mode is virtually nonexistent in education below the advanced graduate level, this indicates a formidable and radical challenge in adapting education to needs of the Knowledge Age.

EFFORTS TO BRING DESIGN MODE ACTIVITY INTO THE ACADEMIC CURRICULUM

Terms such as "Learning by Design" (Kolodner, 2002) signal an effort, at least partly inspired by Knowledge Age priorities, to give design mode activity a more central role in education. A number of current experimental programs reflect this intent, four of which will be reviewed in this section. Our concern here is not the effectiveness of these programs in teaching scientific concepts, for instance, but rather (a) the extent to which they engage students in design work with curriculum-relevant ideas and (b) the context-limited as compared to context-general focus of student work (Bereiter & Scardamalia, 2003). Probably most creative knowledge work in the out-of-school world is context limited; it is work to design a particular product or solve a particular problem to serve the interests of a particular organization or community. The context-general end of the continuum is represented by basic research intended to advance the state of knowledge for a whole civilization. Education for the Knowledge Age would ideally prepare students in some fashion for work with knowledge and ideas across the whole spectrum. However, it should be recognized that formal education is properly concerned with knowledge of wide generality, and so a bias toward the context-general end of the continuum is appropriate. It is therefore noteworthy that most of the programs bringing design mode activity into the academic curriculum are oriented toward the context-limited end.

Learning by Design™

In Learning by Design, as described by Holbrook and Kolodner (2000, p. 221),

Science learning is achieved through addressing a major design challenge (such as building a self-powered car that can go a certain distance over a certain terrain).... To address a challenge, class members develop designs, build prototypes, gather performance data and use other resources to provide justification for refining their designs, and they iteratively investigate, redesign, test, and analyze the results of their ideas. They articulate their understanding of science concepts, first in terms of the concrete artifact which they have designed, then in transfer to similar artifacts or situations, and finally to abstract principles of science.

Although design projects are now fairly common in school science (planning a trip to Mars has been a popular one for a decade), the approach taken by Kolodner and colleagues is distinctive. The challenge for students is to design something that can actually be built and tested. Moreover, the design challenges are planned so that faulty science will lead to performance failure. An example is to maximize the distance traveled by a toy car driven by air expelled from a balloon through a straw (Kolodner, 2002). Trial-and-error design is followed up by systematic experimentation to determine how variations in the length and diameter of the straw affect performance. Note, however, that the inquiry is still very much context limited. The ultimate science-learning target is Newton's Third Law, but it is not clear how the design task and the related experimentation could lead to or raise questions leading to Newton's law. Teachers, according to Holbrook and Kolodner, wanted to teach the science first and then do the design work (thus shifting to a traditional rule–example pattern of instruction). More relevant to the present issue is an apparent shift from design mode to belief mode in order to get across the scientific idea.

Design problems can lead to engagement with deep scientific principles. In earlier work on Learning by Design, one of the problems was to design an artificial lung. Other problems in this vein would be designing a specific antibiotic and building a rain-making machine. Such design problems can only be solved by first gaining an understanding of the natural process that the design is intended to simulate or have an impact on. However, such design problems lie beyond the scope of what students could actually build and test. Consequently, Learning by Design depends on rather forced connections between the activity and basic ideas. As a result, teachers reportedly present the science separate from the design work, with basic ideas dealt with in belief mode, in parallel with, but not intrinsic to activity in design mode.

Project-Based Learning

Project-based learning covers a wide range. At one extreme is the traditional "project," which consists of choosing and narrowing a topic, collecting material, organizing and presenting it—differing from the projects of 50 years ago only in the use of digital media. At the other end are highly developed inquiry projects, mainly but not exclusively in science. As defined by Marx, Blumenfeld, Krajcik, & Soloway (1997, p. 341); "Project-based science focuses on student-designed inquiry that is organized by investigations to answer driving questions, includes collaboration among learners and others, the use of new technology, and the creation of authentic artifacts that represent student understanding." Of projects meeting these specifications, we may ask: To what extent do they engage students in design-mode as compared to belief-mode activities, and where do they lie on the context-limited to context-general continuum? Typically, the "driving question" is posed to the students: to predict the weather from real-time data (Lee & Songer, 2003), to collect and interpret observational data on schoolyard wildlife (Parr, Jones,

& Songer, 2002), to explain the increasing incidence of deformed frogs (Linn, Shear, Bell, & Slotta, 1999). These projects are highly engineered, leaving little for the students or even the teacher to design. Not only the main question but also the information sources and means of information collection, and often a step-by-step sequence leading up to the final specified product, are set out for the students. However, in the weather prediction and the wildlife projects, students are expected to produce, share, elaborate, and test theories based on the information they have obtained. This is design work of a knowledge-creating kind. In the deformed frogs project, however, the opposing theories or positions are set out for the students and their job is to gather evidence for and against, leading up to a presented argument or debate. Thus the project is framed within belief mode, reflecting the idea, as put by one of the developers, that "Science *is* Argument" (Bell, 2002).

There are instances in which students design experiments and devise explanations, but the design task common across virtually all project-based approaches is the presentation—what Marx et al. referred to earlier as "the creation of authentic artifacts that represent student understanding." The presentation may usurp so much of the students' attention (and sometimes that of the teacher) that it overwhelms cognitive goals (Anderson, Holland, & Palincsar, 1997; Moss, 2000; Yarnall & Kafai, 1996). Interestingly, similar concerns have been raised about the amount of attention business executives lavish on their PowerPoint presentations and the accompanying neglect of content (Tufte, 2003). Thus there is a danger that bringing design-mode activity into the core curriculum via Project-Based Learning may force the core curriculum off the stage.

Problem-Based Learning

Although problem-based learning is often treated as synonymous with project-based learning, there are important differences, reflecting problem-based learning's medical school origins. As originally implemented in medical education, now spreading to other kinds of professional education, PBL, as it is called, engages students in solving problems modeled as closely as possible on problems they will actually encounter in their professional practice (Barrows, 1985). Unlike project-based learning, there is little focus on a tangible end product. The end product is a problem solution—a purely conceptual artifact.

As used in professional education, PBL is quite properly context limited. Harden and Davis (1998) proposed a "continuum of problem-based learning" in medical education, with what they called "theoretical learning" lying "furthest from the problem based end of the continuum"

(p. 318). They described theoretical learning as coming about through information transmission by lectures and textbooks and tending toward rote learning, with no effort at application. A PBL approach to theoretical learning finds no place on their continuum, which is consistent with PBL's focus on professional practice. The doctor's job is not to produce a theory of pain or to devise a comprehensive approach to pain management, but to deal with the pain in a particular patient's hip joint; PBL problems are usually posed with that degree of specificity, and PBL procedures are geared to the cooperative, evidence-based solution of such problems. Extensions of PBL into general education—even elementary education—have tended to retain this context-limited specificity (Torp & Sage, 2002). Thus, the problem is likely to be to explain why the bean plant died or to develop an environmentally sound plan for school waste disposal rather than to explain photosynthesis or biodegradability.

To what extent PBL engages students in design varies considerably. In the classic medical school version, an important phase of PBL is students working on a "learning issue," in which they identify and pursue what needs to be learned in order to solve the case. This is design activity in the realm of scientific facts and ideas. In school applications of PBL that we have located, this phase seems to have been eliminated. Without it, PBL is reduced to regular guided inquiry focused on cases rather than on more central conceptual issues (Bereiter & Scardamalia, 2000).

Although case-based problems are inherently context limited, they can acquire general significance when considered in the context of a more fundamental inquiry. Deep inquiry may start with an intriguing case: In an example provided by Hunt and Minstrell (1994), inquiry starts with the problem of what happens to an object on a spring balance as the air is evacuated from around it. But attention then shifts to the students' explanatory ideas and to the testing and revision of these ideas. Experiments are chosen that broaden the inquiry to general concerns about gravity, the difference between weight and mass, and weight of the atmosphere. In this shift from context-limited to context-general, the nature of the problem itself undergoes transformation. This expansion of the problem space is something that PBL was not designed to address. The next approach we consider is also "problem-based" in a broad sense, but the problems are more context-general problems of understanding, and the students' role as designers is given much more scope.

Knowledge Building

Knowledge building differs from the other approaches by emphasizing conceptual artifacts (theories, designs, plans, histories, etc.) as products, tools, and objects of inquiry (Scardamalia & Bereiter, 2003). Activities such as model building, conducting experiments, and producing reports are carried out in the service of a broader effort to produce some innovation or advance a knowledge frontier. Knowledge building, as thus conceived, is not an activity limited to education but characterizes creative knowledge work of all kinds. In keeping with its generative character, knowledge building is not highly proceduralized. Instead, a software environment (discussed in a later section as a "Knowledge Building Environment" or KBE) provides flexible support and coordination for sustained and creative work with ideas.

In educational applications, students are engaged in design in all phases and at all levels of the knowledge-building enterprise: defining problems, advancing initial ideas, using whatever resources and inquiry possibilities are available to improve those ideas, reformulating problems as the knowledge building advances, and presenting results (Hewitt, 2002). It is not uncommon for the entire year's work in a subject to be carried out as a single knowledge-building initiative. Where the main objectives are officially mandated, these are made known to the students as part of the problem space in which they will work. Thus it could be said that instead of assimilating design-mode activity into the academic curriculum the academic curriculum is assimilated into design mode.

Educational knowledge building can be focused at any point along a context-limited to context-general continuum. However, the bias is toward the context general end. This is partly because educational standards, which are usually highly context general, contribute to the students' defining of problems (we refer here to the standards themselves, not to the recommended learning experiences, which are often quite context limited). It is also because students' "epistemic agency" drives inquiry in that direction. For instance, in one seventh-grade class an inquiry that began with the question "What is it like to stop growing?" soon evolved into the question of what causes growth to stop and what determines at what height different people's growth stops (Bereiter, Scardamalia, Cassells, & Hewitt, 1997). On a topic such as gravity, electricity, or light, students free to generate their own theories and problems of understanding naturally come up with the question, "What is it?" Although they may hold the common misconception that these things are substances (Chi, Slotta, & deLeeuw, 1994), they are likely, through their own collective efforts at idea improvement, to discover problems with this conception. As one fourth-grader put it with reference to light: "It isn't a solid or a liquid or a gas, so what is it?" This started a line of inquiry that ended with the idea that light is a kind of energy.

COMPARISONS AND POSSIBILITIES OF SYNTHESIS

If the preceding section were aimed at prospective adopters of an educational approach, we should need to consider a number of pragmatic issues that developers address in different ways—for instance, how far to go in adapting to established expectations about the lengths of units, activity structures, and even the words in which approaches are described. However, the point of this chapter is the potential of different methods and models to equip students for creative knowledge work.

The differences among approaches such as the four discussed in the preceding section are often minimized, lumping them together as constructivist. Even the brief look "under the hood" offered here should make it clear that the approaches are far from interchangeable. They all bring design-mode activity into the main academic curriculum. They all deal with ill-structured problems, which sets them apart from many thinking skills approaches. But they differ in the kind of design work students do, how central it is to curriculum objectives, and where the problems they tackle lie on a context-limited to context-general continuum.

All four of the approaches aim to bring about understanding of the big ideas that make a knowledge society possible in the first place. Knowledge Building additionally aims at the fullest possible immersion in the work by which such ideas are created and improved, which necessarily means dealing with the big ideas in design mode rather than belief mode.

All the approaches place high value on authentic activities, problems, or questions; but *authentic* means different things in the different approaches. In Learning by Design it means designing things that actually work and that appeal to students' interests in toys and games. In sophisticated versions of Project-Based Learning, it means activities and issues drawn from real-life concerns and controversies. In Problem-Based Learning it means problems closely modeled on those that will actually be encountered in practice. In Knowledge Building it means problems and questions that the students actually wonder about. These are all legitimate meanings of *authentic,* but they point in quite different directions as to the sorts of experience students will have.

A case can be made for including all four approaches in a well-rounded program of education for the Knowledge Age, on grounds that they reflect the diversity of knowledge work that actually goes on in society—from product engineering to making evidence-based policy decisions to advancing basic knowledge. This would tend to result in a grab-bag of activities, however, an all-too-common practice that we presume advocates of all the approaches would oppose. An alternative is to consider whether any of the approaches is expandable to include the full range of working with ideas in design mode. Nominally, Project-Based Learning can serve this purpose, because all the approaches involve projects of some sort. However, that would seem merely to give a name to the grab-bag.

Of the four approaches, only Knowledge Building explicitly supports design-mode work at the context-general end of the continuum—that is, design work directly aimed at creating and improving broadly significant theories, problem formulations, interpretations, and the like. So committed is knowledge building to design mode that educators frequently ask the paradigmatic belief-mode question: What is to keep the students from ending up with wrong beliefs? A dismissive answer, appealing to the research on misconceptions, is that knowledge building would have to do very badly in order to come out worse than other instructional approaches on this count. A deeper level answer is that as long as students are working seriously to improve their ideas and are making constructive use of authoritative sources in doing so, they will inevitably move beyond the naive conceptions educators are worried about.

As actually implemented in classrooms, Knowledge Building already incorporates much of the design-mode activity of the other approaches. Students have designed, built, and tested solar cookers and model airplanes, but they have done so within the context of investigations aimed at understanding light and lift. Designing experiments to test their "theories" has begun as early as first grade. They have produced multimedia presentations, dramatizations, and other such project-like displays, but these have grown out of their knowledge-building accomplishments rather than representing the endpoint toward which they are directed. Thus Knowledge Building can incorporate the strongest parts of other approaches, while avoiding contrived projects whose main purpose is to develop soft skills.

Over and above providing particular learning experiences in design mode, a coherent approach to Knowledge Age education ought to provide a means of initiating students into a knowledge-creating culture—to make them feel a part of a long-term and global effort to understand their world and gain some control over their destiny. An eclectic or mixed approach, however worthy its components may be, cannot be expected to do this. To socialize students into an emerging Knowledge Age culture, while at the same time meeting societal expectations of knowledge and skill development, would seem to demand a comprehensive design for bringing creative work with ideas into the heart of the curriculum.

THE CHALLENGE OF SUSTAINED CREATIVITY

Traditionally, creativity training has focused on idea generation, fostered through brainstorming, lateral thinking, and other techniques; that focus continues in structured programs and commercial teaching materials up to the present day (Nickerson, 1999). Both in teaching and in testing, the typical task is what we may term *single-prompt idea generation* (e.g., generating novel uses for a coat hanger). This is quite remote from the creative work called for in modern organizations, where ideas must meet multiple constraints, where there is often a surfeit of novel ideas to choose from, and where the desired outcome depends on sustaining creative input to a development process that may go on for months or years (Bereiter, 2002a; Cooper, 2003). "The Mind of Microsoft" (Microsoft Monitor Weblog, 2004, March 12) describes one large organization's disciplined approach to idea development.

Although the Internet is full of confident claims, psychologists writing on creativity have for the most part steered clear of the question of teachability. An exception is Nickerson (1999), who, after reviewing training approaches, concluded that the evidence either for or against the teachability of creativity is "less than compelling" (p. 407). (Parenthetical question: What would constitute compelling evidence that something is unteachable?) On the more positive side, researchers have shown a growing interest in career-long creativity, a topic of obvious importance in a Knowledge Society. Some high points emerging from examination of creative careers are the following:

1. The "ten year rule," first researched and enunciated by Hayes (1989). In a wide variety of fields, it is found that significant creative contributions are not made until a person has devoted 10 years or more to relevant work and study. Notably, the early years of creative careers are often devoted to imitation rather than to efforts at originality (Weisberg, 1999).

2. Evidence that creative people sustain high levels of productivity, producing more unsuccessful results as well as more successful results than less creative people (Simonton, 1999). Prolific idea production is an essential part of what appears to be the only viable theory of the creative process now going, one that treats it as a form of Darwinian evolution (Dennett, 1995).

3. Extensive and deep knowledge as a necessary and sometimes sufficient condition for creative production (Weisberg, 1999). Weisberg argued, for instance, that Watson and Crick, whatever their creative talents, were the only people who possessed the knowledge required to solve the DNA riddle. The same might be said of Darwin and Wallace, independent solvers of the speciation riddle, who had remarkably similar and unusual knowledge backgrounds (Quammen, 1996).

4. Sternberg's (2003) hypothesis that the driving force in creative careers is the decision to be creative, to pursue particular kinds of creative goals within a chosen domain, and to develop the requisite abilities.

If this career perspective is taken seriously in schools, as Sternberg (2003) urges it should, then the emphasis should shift from teaching idea generating skills to launching students on a trajectory that will result eventually in their becoming creative contributors in their chosen fields or enterprises. The career perspective elevates the importance of knowledge, contrary to folk beliefs about antagonism between knowledge and creativity (Weisberg, 1999), but at the same time it makes transfer of school learning appear increasingly problematic. The "ten year rule" applies to serious goal-oriented work within a particular field; general education and development, although they may be important, do not count as part of the ten years. Early beginnings in the arts and in some sports are characteristic of those who later excel, but these lie mainly outside ordinary schooling (Bloom, 1985).

In view of the lack of convincing outcome research (especially the lack of evidence of transfer) and the shift of emphasis toward a career perspective, it would probably be desirable to abandon all talk about "teaching" creativity in schools. Such talk only leads to false claims, illusory curriculum standards, susceptibility to fads, and an overemphasis on originality at the expense of the imitation that has been found characteristic of those who later excel. Instead of an attempt to teach creativity, material reviewed thus far suggests the following components of an approach to creative talent development:

• Shift the curriculum toward design mode, especially as regards work in core subjects. Although work in belief mode is important, virtually all the world's creative work is done in design mode.
• Strive for depth of understanding. Deep principles underlie most knowledge work and the transfer value of shallow knowledge is especially questionable.
• Create a classroom ethos that makes striving for idea improvement the norm. Sternberg (2003) offers a number of pointers for doing this.

As a framework for implementing these suggestions, knowledge building constitutes an approach in which all these elements are salient and coordinated (Scardamalia & Bereiter, 2003).

KNOWLEDGE ABOUT KNOWLEDGE

If work with knowledge is indeed becoming the leading work in developed nations, understanding knowledge itself could reasonably be set as an educational objective. In their influential book *The Knowledge-Creating Company*, Nonaka and Takeuchi (1995) criticized Western business people for their Cartesian epistemology and their neglect of implicit knowledge. Moldoveanu (2000) criticized business people for a naive and uncritical approach to matters of fact and belief.

Although the term *epistemology* was not even indexed in the 1986 *Handbook of Research on Teaching* (Wittrock, 1986), there has since been extensive research on teachers' and students' epistemological beliefs and their influence on teaching and learning (Buehl & Alexander, 2001; Hofer & Pintrich, 2002; Mason, 2003). Although epistemological beliefs are found to be multidimensional, a major dimension that turns up in all the research is one ranging from a simplistic and absolutist conception of knowledge to a conception that recognizes in some fashion the tentative and contingent character of knowledge (Mason, 2003). Noteworthy in the context of this chapter is the fact that research on students' and teachers' epistemologies pertains to what we have termed *belief mode*. To what extent these epistemological beliefs would affect functioning within design mode is unknown.

More relevant to activity in design mode has been research on teachers' and students' conceptions of inquiry (Andre & Windschitl, 2003). Here the main distinction appears to be between those who see inquiry as the enactment of routines (often under the banner of "scientific method") and those who see it in more systemic terms, as an interactive process with understanding as an emergent. Unfortunately, however, research on beliefs about inquiry typically does not distinguish between experimentation carried out in belief mode (testing whether a guess or hypothesis is correct) and experimentation carried out in design mode, where it is part of an iterative process aimed at theory or product development. One study that did differentiate (Carey, Evans, Honda, Unger, & Jay, 1989) indicated that a design-mode conception of experimentation (Level 3 in their hierarchical scheme) was relatively rare among seventh graders, even though they had undergone 6 weeks of instruction on the nature of science that was effective in other respects.

In rough summary, research on teachers' and students' conceptions shows that various kinds of instruction and experience can produce a shift from seeing knowledge as absolute ("the way things really are") to seeing it as constructed; but understanding *how* it is constructed remains as a largely unmet challenge, one quite central to creative knowledge work.

Knowledge as an Emergent

As complex systems concepts such as self-organization and emergence make their way into mainstream educational psychology, it becomes increasingly apparent that there are no simple causal explanations for anything in this field. In general, what comes out of a sociocognitive process cannot be explained or fully predicted by what goes into it. Creative works, understanding, and cognitive development are all examples of complex structures emerging from the interaction of simpler components (Sawyer, 1999, 2004). Learning itself, at both neural and knowledge levels, has emergent properties (Pribram & King, 1996). So widespread and significant is the impact of systems concepts throughout the natural and behavioral sciences, moreover, that there is also an emerging educational objective: to teach the theoretical concepts and to foster "systems thinking" in students (Jacobson & Working Group 2 Collaborators, 2003; Wilensky & Resnick, 1999). Research has begun to appear identifying and tackling the difficulties of acquiring complex systems concepts (Charles & d'Apollonia, 2004).

A good case can be made for complexity theory (Byrne, 1998) as an essential part of a Knowledge Age curriculum. Complexity theory may represent what Case and Okamoto (1996) called a "central conceptual structure" or what Ohlsson (1993) identified as an "abstract schema." Its inclusion in the curriculum can be justified on grounds of its being a schema of very wide applicability and a valuable tool for advanced study in practically any discipline and for any complex knowledge work. The problems of teaching it naturally fall within the legitimate scope of educational psychology. But the assimilation of complex systems concepts into educational psychology itself is a different matter. It remains to be demonstrated what practical value this might have.

From a complex systems standpoint, effective teaching of every kind may be characterized as *constructive intervention into an ongoing self-organizing sociocognitive process*. This is a different conception from both instructivist and "guide on the side" notions of teaching. Examples of constructive intervention into self-organizing processes may be found in holistic medicine and in agronomy (maintaining a premium vineyard, for instance); but we are not aware of any general principles to guide such intervention.

Complexity Theory as a Scientific Basis for Educational Psychology

Complexity theory promises to play an important role in educational psychology as a way of comprehending otherwise inexplicable phenomena and thereby steering a wiser course toward practical decisions. Why, for instance, does phonics work? It is easy to demonstrate that it cannot possibly work, at least not in English, with its famously irregular spellings (Smith, 1971), yet it demonstrably does work. Rule-based explanations are implausible, because they require too many rules (Simon & Simon, 1973). Yet in connectionist terms it is easy to explain how the input of a crude phoneme-by-phoneme sounding-out could produce accurate word recognition as output. This not only brings the familiar phenomenon within the scope of scientific explanation, it may also help steer instructional designers toward productive ways of eliciting and building on the sounding-out phenomenon (Harm & Seidenberg, 2004).

Another, even more puzzling phenomenon: The same scientific misconceptions appear in students of a certain age all over the world. Yet these naive conceptions are not normally taught or openly discussed (else it would not have required research to discover them), so they evidently arise spontaneously. How is this possible? To justify the misconceptions as reasonable does not answer the question, because similar reasonableness could be attributed to countless conceptions that do not arise. The problem here is to explain convergence, arrival at the same state from different initial conditions—as in the convergence of fish and aquatic mammals on a similar body shape. Such a phenomenon is easily modeled with connectionist networks, for instance.

More germane to the present topic, however, is the explanation of creativity. How do novel ideas originate? From Campbell (1960) to Simonton (1999), a growing number of theorists have maintained that creative ideas arise by chance, because there is no other way novelty could originate. But others, such as Sternberg, have found it "utterly implausible that great creators such as Mozart, Einstein, or Picasso were using nothing more than blind variation to come up with their ideas" (Sternberg, Kaufman, & Pretz, 2002, p. 112). This is the same argument used by Paley against Darwin: How could a structure as complex and beautifully designed as the eye have arisen by chance? That is the question addressed at length by Dawkins (1996) and more generally by Dennett (1995). Their answer is in what Dawkins called "cumulative selection," a process by which random variations are selectively incorporated into an emerging complex. For this to work, however, self-organization is also required. Furthermore, selection in the case of human creativity need not be limited to trial and error but may be guided by accumulated knowledge of what we have called "promisingness" (Bereiter & Scardamalia, 1993).

The larger issue here is whether educational psychology itself needs a postindustrial makeover in order to address the learning needs of the Knowledge Age. As other chapters in this volume indicate, there is no shortage of theoretical diversity in present-day educational psychology. If we move up a level, however, to *forms* of theorizing, a gap becomes evident. There is theorizing based on causal linkages, of which production system models provide impressive examples. There is theorizing based on (usually unspecified and unquantified) multivariate functions, often represented by box-and-arrow diagrams. Such theorizing is as pervasive as this familiar type of diagram. There is theorizing that relies on story lines or other literary devices to provide rich representations of ideas. Finally, there is concept-plus-example theorizing, in which concepts such as "legitimate peripheral participation" or "epistemic agency" are introduced and followed by examples that the concepts are shown to illuminate. Harder to characterize is what this varied theorizing is about. Broadly speaking, it is about individual or group processes and individual or group conditions.

Two things are notably absent from this theoretical mix:

1. Theorizing about ideas or knowledge as such. The outcome of an individual or group process is taken to be an individual or group condition (which may, however, be indexed by some objective sign such as a test score). Knowledge creation, reputedly the primary productive activity of the Knowledge Age, does not figure in educational theorizing, nor are ideas or knowledge treated as objects of inquiry.

2. Theorizing that makes substantial use of systems concepts such as self-organization or of dynamical systems methodologies. These concepts appear, of course, but they do not have the theoretical force that they are beginning to have in such fields as sociology of knowledge, memetics, child development, and cognitive psychology.

The result is that there is no theoretically grounded way for tackling the distinctive educational challenge of the Knowledge Age: developing in students a talent for creative knowledge work.

TECHNOLOGY FOR KNOWLEDGE AGE EDUCATION

As noted earlier, computers and computer use figure prominently in official plans for Knowledge Age education. Consistent with this emphasis, alumni in the University of Washington survey (Gillmore, 1998) rated *working effectively with modern technology, especially computers* as one of the abilities most important in their present lives. Note, however, that these alumni would have been in university in the 1980s or early 1990s, before computers had become a normal part of student life. It has become increasingly doubtful whether the term *computer* marks off a meaningful class of activities or abilities. In 21st-century schools, computers, we believe, are best treated as infrastructure, with educational issues being defined on more fundamental bases. There is a persisting belief, however, that a school in which high-tech resources are well integrated into the curriculum is *ipso facto* a school that is adequately preparing students for the Knowledge Age.

The main reform task for Knowledge Age education, we have argued, is to carry out more of formal education in design mode. This has several implications for educational technology:

1. Because design typically involves different groups working on different problems, technology is needed to support idea diversity and coherence-producing efforts, without micromanaging the process.
2. Because design work is frequently collaborative, technology is needed to support collaborative work.
3. Because formal education in design mode often requires working with ideas rather than with concrete objects, technology is needed that can represent and preserve ideas for sustained inquiry and development.

Developers working in the field known as Computer-Supported Collaborative Learning (CSCL) have been active since the early 1990s and sometimes before in designing software to meet these needs. As Kozma (2003) found in an international on-sites survey, however, little of this software or the thinking behind it has made its way into school use, even in schools locally identified as innovative. Instead, the software used in schools consists mainly of "productivity" applications—word processors, spreadsheets, and presentation software primarily designed for business use and frequently bundled under the name "office"—plus course delivery systems primarily designed to support traditional university instruction. The World Wide Web is used, but mainly to collect material for reports.

CSCL technology covers a wide range, from discipline-specific programs such as ChemSense (Schank & Kozma, 2002) to general-purpose course development tools based on CSCL principles (Linn, Davis, & Bell, 2004), from structured inquiry tools such as the Collaboratory Notebook (Edelson & O'Neill, 1994) to relatively open exploratory environments such as Knowledge Forum (Scardamalia, 2002, 2003) and Boxer (diSessa, 2000). A useful distinction is between *tools*, which serve particular purposes within variously structured activities, and *environments*, which constitute a system of affordances and supports within which the main work of a learning or knowledge-building community may go on.

A knowledge-building environment (KBE), as defined in the *Encyclopedia of Distributed Learning*, is:

Any environment (virtual or otherwise) that enhances collaborative efforts to create and continually improve ideas (Scardamalia, 2003).

This broad definition applies to knowledge work environments of all kinds, not limited to educational ones. Across this spectrum, however, Scardamalia identified several essential characteristics of KBEs that go beyond the more general requirements of CSCL environments. These include

Support for social organization that goes beyond division of labor

Support for collaborative creation and revision of conceptual artifacts

Shared, user-configured design spaces with supports for citing and referencing one another's work

Ways to introduce higher-order organizations of ideas (in contrast to threaded discussion that only permits downward branching)

Ways for the same idea to be worked with in varied and multiple contexts

Systems of feedback to enhance self- and group monitoring of ongoing processes

Linking of persons and groups on the basis of shared goals and problems rather than on the basis of shared topics of interest

As applied to education, Rubens et al. (2003) describe KBEs as

Sophisticated environments designed to support expert-like processing of knowledge by guiding students to work collaboratively to improve shared knowledge objects. . . . Through these kinds of environments, students may be guided to engage in productive working with knowledge objects in the same way as the scientific community is engaged with theory improvement. (p. 13)

Thus a knowledge building software environment does not merely promote Knowledge Age soft skills but embodies the essential characteristics of creative knowledge work.

CONCLUSION

A distinction between belief mode and design mode has framed the discussion in this chapter. Belief mode, we have emphasized, does not imply parroting or indoctrination; it can be critical inquiry of a high order. But it is concerned with evaluating and deciding among claims, whereas design mode—the principal mode in knowledge-based enterprises—is concerned with creating and improving ideas. Both modes are important, and creative knowledge work involves skillful movement between them. For instance, a trial lawyer's courtroom performance is conducted in belief mode insofar as it is concerned with defending or refuting truth claims. But the background work—the devising of a strategy, the construction of a case, the searching out of legal angles, and so forth—is design work of a demanding sort, design work that is continually related to the belief issues at stake in the courtroom. Parallels can be drawn to the work of a sales representative. Different forms of interaction between truth issues and design issues are to be found in investment counseling, architecture, and virtually any kind of work that calls for complex problem solving. But formal education, by being conducted almost exclusively in belief mode, fails to provide students with experience in the productive, creative side of knowledge work.

An adequate educational model for the Knowledge Age, we have argued, must rectify the imbalance by conducting more of formal education in design mode. This is not something that can be done by bringing design activities in as incidentals or homework while the main educational effort continues to be concentrated in belief mode. It will not be sufficient for students to perform experiments to satisfy themselves that Newton's laws of mechanics are valid. They also need to consider Newton's laws from a design perspective, so as to appreciate why inertia and acceleration are important ideas and why there is value in Newton's complex conceptions as opposed to the simpler everyday meanings attached to these terms. It will not be sufficient for students to learn how laws are made in their country and to consider whether the method is just and democratic. They need to see lawmaking as a human invention, to consider the difficulties it poses and the different ways that these difficulties may be surmounted.

Four approaches to bringing design mode activity into the academic curriculum were described—Learning by Design, Project-Based Learning, Problem-Based Learning, and Knowledge Building. Although all are constructivist approaches, they differ in the goals students pursue. These range along a continuum from context-limited goals, specific to a task situation, to context-general goals, concerned with advancing a knowledge frontier. Modern societies depend on sustained creativity all along this continuum. A question of balance arises, however. Most of the design-mode approaches are biased toward the context-limited end of the continuum, whereas the goals of education, as reflected in curriculum objectives, generally lean strongly toward the context-general end.

The preceding sections suggest that a design-centered model of teaching and learning for the Knowledge Age should provide for

An immersive environment in which idea improvement is a pervasive emphasis

Design experience across a context-limited to context-general continuum

Sustained as opposed to scatter-shot creative work with ideas

Flexible movement between knowledge creation and understanding of existing knowledge

Flexible movement between work with material and conceptual artifacts, with conceptual artifacts able to inform and drive interactions with material artifacts

Emergence and self-organization at various levels from individual cognition to participation in work of extended communities

Although various approaches considered in this chapter meet some of these requirements, an elaborated knowledge building model has potential to meet all of them.

ACKNOWLEDGMENTS

The authors wish to acknowledge the generous support of the Social Sciences and Humanities Research Council of Canada, along with that of students and teachers, and the global Institute for Knowledge Innovation and Technology team, who have contributed their time and talents to knowledge building.

References

Anderson, C. W., Holland, J. D., & Palincsar, A. S. (1997). Canonical and sociocultural approaches to research and reform in science education: The story of Juan and his group. *Elementary School Journal, 97*, 359–383.

Anderson, C. W., & Roth, K. J. (1989). Teaching for meaningful and self-regulated learning of science. In J. Brophy (Eds.), *Advances in research on teaching* (pp. 265–309). Greenwich, CT: JAI Press.

Andre, T., & Windschitl, M. (2003). Interest, epistemological belief, and intentional conceptual change. In G. M. Sinatra & P. R. Pintrich (Eds.), *Intentional conceptual change* (pp. 173–197). Mahwah, NJ: Lawrence Erlbaum Associates.

Barrows, H. S. (1985). *How to design a problem-based curriculum for the preclinical years.* New York: Springer.

Bell, P. (2002). Science *is* argument: Developing sociocognitive supports for disciplinary argumentation. In T. Koschmann &

R. Hall & N. Miyake (Eds.), *CSCL 2: Carrying forward the conversation* (pp. 499-505). Mahwah, NJ: Lawrence Erlbaum Associates.

Bereiter, C. (1995). A dispositional view of transfer. In A. McKeough, J. Lupart, & A. Marini (Eds.), *Teaching for transfer: Fostering generalization in learning* (pp. 21-34). Mahwah, NJ: Lawrence Erlbaum Associates.

Bereiter, C. (1997). Situated cognition and how to overcome it. In D. Kirshner & J. A. Whitson (Eds.), *Situated cognition: Social, semiotic, and psychological perspectives* (pp. 281-300). Mahwah, NJ: Lawrence Erlbaum Associates.

Bereiter, C. (2002a). Design research for sustained innovation. *Cognitive Studies: Bulletin of the Japanese Cognitive Science Society, 9*(3), 321-327.

Bereiter, C. (2002b). *Education and mind in the knowledge age*. Mahwah, NJ: Lawrence Erlbaum Associates.

Bereiter, C., & Scardamalia, M. (1993). *Surpassing ourselves: An inquiry into the nature and implications of expertise*. La Salle, IL: Open Court.

Bereiter, C., & Scardamalia, M. (2000). Process and product in problem-based (PBL) research. In D. H. Evensen & C. E. Hmelo (Eds.), *Problem-based learning: A research perspective on learning interactions* (pp. 185-195). Mahwah, NJ: Lawrence Erlbaum Associates.

Bereiter, C., & Scardamalia, M. (2003). Learning to work creatively with knowledge. In E. D. Corte, L. Verschaffel, N. Entwistle, & J. V. Merriënboer (Eds.), *Powerful learning environments: Unravelling basic components and dimensions* (pp. 73-78). Oxford: Elsevier Science.

Bereiter, C., Scardamalia, M., Cassells, C., & Hewitt, J. (1997). Postmodernism, knowledge building, and elementary science. *Elementary School Journal, 97*, 329-340.

Bloom, B. S. (Ed.). (1985). *Developing talent in young people*. New York: Ballantine Books.

Bransford, J., & Schwartz, D. (1999). Rethinking transfer: A simple proposal with multiple implications. *Review of Research in Education, 25*.

Buehl, M. M., & Alexander, P. A. (2001). Beliefs about academic knowledge. *Educational Psychology Review, 13*(4), 385-418.

Byrnc, D. (1998). *Complexity theory and the social sciences: An introduction*. London: Routledge.

Campbell, D. T. (1960). Blind variation and selective retention in creative thought as in other knowledge processes. *Psychological Review, 67*, 380-400.

Carey, S., Evans, R., Honda, M., Unger, C., & Jay, E. (1989). An experiment is when you try it and see if it works: a study of grade 7 students' understanding of the construction of scientific knowledge. *International Journal of Science Education, 11*, 514-529.

Carnevale, A. P., & Desrochers, D. M. (2003). *Standards for what? The economic roots of K-16 reform* (Educational Testing Service Leadership 2003 Series). Princeton, NJ: Educational Testing Service. Available May 2004, at http://www.ets.org/research/dload/standards_for_what.pdf

Case, R., & Okamoto, Y. (1996). The role of central conceptual structures in the development of children's thought. *Monographs of the Society for Research in Child Development, 61* (2, Serial No. 246).

Charles, E. S., & d'Apollonia, S. T. (2004). Understanding what's hard in learning about complex systems. In Y. B. Kafai, W. A. Sandoval, N. Enyedy, A. S. Nixon, & F. Herrera (Eds.), *Proceedings of the Sixth International Conference of the Learning Sciences* (p. 190). Mahwah, NJ: Lawrence Erlbaum Associates.

Chi, M. T. H., Slotta, J. D., & deLeeuw, N. (1994). From things to processes: A theory of conceptual change for learning science concepts. *Learning and Instruction, 4*, 27-43.

Cooper, R. G. (2003). *Winning at new products: Accelerating the process from idea to launch*. Cambridge, MA: Perseus Books.

Costa, A., & Kallick, B. (2000). *Habits of mind: Discovering and exploring habits of mind*. Alexandria, VA: Association for Supervision and Curriculum Development.

David, P. A., & Foray, D. (2003). Economic fundamentals of the knowledge society. *Policy Futures in Education, 1*(1), 20-49. Retrieved July 18, 2004, from http://2_David_PFIE_1_1.pdf

Dawkins, R. (1996). *The blind watchmaker: Why the evidence of evolution reveals a universe without design*. New York: W. W. Norton.

Dewey, J. (1916). *Democracy and education*. New York: Macmillan.

Dennett, D. C. (1995). *Darwin's dangerous idea: Evolution and the meanings of life*. New York: Simon & Schuster.

diSessa, A. A. (2000). *Changing mind: Computers, learning, and literacy*. Cambridge, MA: MIT Press.

Drucker, P. F. (1968). *The age of discontinuity: Guidelines to our changing society*. New York: Harper & Row.

Drucker, P. (1993). *Post-capitalist society*. New York: HarperBusiness.

Drucker, P. F. (1994, November). The age of social transformation. *Atlantic Monthly*, pp. 53-80.

Edelson, D. C., & O'Neill, D. K. (1994). The CoVis Collaboratory Notebook: Supporting collaborative scientific inquiry. In A. Best (Ed.), *Proceedings of the 1994 National Educational Computing Conference* (pp. 146-152). Eugene, OR: International Society for Technology in Education in cooperation with the National Education Computing Association.

Eppler, M. (2004). *The Wright way: 7 problem solving principles from the Wright Brothers that can make your business soar*. New York: American Management Association.

Everlast Climbing Utilities. (n.d.). *Leadership development*. Retrieved October 20, 2004, from www.traverswall.com/leadership_development.shtml

Gardner, H. (1983). *Frames of mind: The theory of multiple intelligences*. New York: Basic Books.

Gillmore, G. M. (1998, December). *Importance of specific skills five and ten years after graduation*. OEA Research Report 98-11. Seattle: University of Washington Office of Educational Assessment. Retrieved, May 12, 2004, from http://www. washington.edu/oea/9811.htm

Goswami, U. (1998). *Cognition in children*. New York: Psychology Press.

Greeno, J. G., Smith, D. R., & Moore, J. L. (1993). Transfer of situated learning. In D. K. Detterman & R. J. Sternberg (Eds.). *Transfer on trial: Intelligence, cognition, and instruction* (pp. 99–167). Norwood, NJ: Ablex.

Harden R. M., & Davis M. H. (1998). The continuum of problem-based learning. *Medical Teacher, 20*, 317–322.

Harm, M. W., & Seidenberg, M. S. (2004). Computing the meanings of words in reading: Cooperative division of labor between visual and phonological processes. *Psychological Review, 111*(3), 662–720.

Hayes, J. R. (1989). Cognitive processes in creativity. In J. A. Glover, R. R. Ronning, & C. R. Reynolds (Eds.), *Handbook of creativity* (pp. 135–146). New York: Plenum Press.

Hewitt, J. (2002). From a focus on tasks to a focus on understanding: The cultural transformation of a Toronto classroom. In T. Koschmann, R. Hall, & N. Miyake (Eds.) *Computer Supported Cooperative Learning: Vol. 2. Carrying forward the conversation* (pp. 11–41). Mahwah, NJ: Lawrence Erlbaum Associates.

Hofer, B. K., & Pintrich, P. R. (2002). *Personal epistemology: The psychology of beliefs about knowledge and knowing*. Mahwah, NJ: Lawrence Erlbaum Associates.

Hofstadter, R. (1963). *Anti-intellectualism in American life*. New York: Knopf.

Holbrook, J., & Kolodner, J. L. (2000). Scaffolding the development of an inquiry-based (science) classroom. In B. Fishman & S. O'Connor-Divelbiss (Eds.), *Fourth International Conference of the Learning Sciences* (pp. 221–227). Mahwah, NJ: Lawrence Erlbaum Associates.

Howley, C. B., Howley, A., & Pendarvis, E. D. (1995). *Out of our minds: Anti-intellectualism and talent development in American schooling*. New York: Teachers College Press.

Hunt, E., & Minstrell, J. (1994). A cognitive approach to the teaching of physics. In K. McGilley (Eds.), *Classroom lessons: Integrating cognitive theory and classroom practice* (pp. 51–74). Cambridge, MA: MIT Press.

Jacobson, M., & Working Group 2 Collaborators. (2003). *Complex systems and education: Cognitive, learning, and pedagogical perspectives*. Retrieved July 7, 2004, from http://necsi.net/events/cxedk16_2.html

Kolodner, J. L. (2002). Learning by Design: Interations of design challenges for better learning of science skills. *Cognitive Studies: Bulletin of the Japanese Cognitive Science Society, 9*(3), 338–350.

Kozma, R. B. (Ed.). (2003). *Technology, innovation, and educational change: A global perspective*. Eugene, OR: International Society for Educational Technology.

Kuhn, D. (1993). Science as argument: Implications for teaching and learning scientific thinking. *Science Education, 77*, 319–337.

Lakatos, I. (1976). *Proofs and refutations: The logic of mathematical discovery*. New York: Cambridge University Press.

Lave, J. (1988). *Cognition in practice*. Boston: Cambridge University Press.

Lave, J., & Wenger, E. (1991). *Situated learning: Legitimate peripheral participation*. Cambridge, England: Cambridge University Press.

Lee, H.-S., & Songer, N. B. (2003). Making authentic science accessible to students. *International Journal of Science Education, 25*(8), 923–948.

Linn, M. C., Davis, E. A., & Bell, P. (Eds.) (2004). *Internet environments for science education*. Mahwah, NJ: Lawrence Erlbaum Associates.

Linn, M. C., Shear, L., Bell, P., & Slotta, J. D. (1999). Organizing principles for science education partnerships: Case studies of students' learning about "rats in space" and "deformed frogs." *Educational Technology Research & Development, 47*(2), 61–84.

Marx, R. W., Blumenfeld, P. C., Krajcik, J. S., & Soloway, E. (1997). Enacting project-based science. *Elementary School Journal, 97*, 341–358.

Mason, L. (2003). Personal epistemologies and intentional conceptual change. In G. M. Sinatra & P. R. Pintrich (Eds.), *Intentional conceptual change* (pp. 199–236). Mahwah, NJ: Lawrence Erlbaum Associates.

McKeough, A., Lupart, J., & Marini, A. (Ed.). (1995). *Teaching for transfer: Fostering generalization in learning*. Mahwah, NJ: Lawrence Erlbaum Associates.

Microsoft Monitor Weblog. (2004, March 12). *The mind of Microsoft*. Retrieved July 10, 2004, from www.microsoftmonitor.com/archives/002480.html

Moldoveanu, M. (2001). Epistemology in action: A framework for understanding organizational due diligence processes. In C. W. Choo & N. Bontis (Eds.), *The strategic management of intellectual capital and organizational knowledge: A collection of readings*. New York: Oxford University Press.

Moss, D. M. (2000). Bringing together technology and students: Examining the use of technology in a project-based class. *Journal of Educational Computing Research, 22*(2), 155–169.

National Centre for Vocational Education Research. (2003). *Defining generic skills: At a glance*. Adelaide, Australia: National Centre for Vocational Education Research.

Nickerson, R. S. (1999). Enhancing creativity. In R. J. Sternberg (Eds.), *Handbook of creativity* (pp. 393–430). New York: Cambridge University Press.

Nonaka, I., & Takeuchi, H. (1995). *The knowledge creating company*. New York: Oxford University Press.

OECD. (1996). *The knowledge-based economy*. Paris: OECD.

Ohlsson, S. (1993). Abstract schemas. *Educational Psychologist, 28*(1), 51–61.

Olson, S. & Loucks-Horsley, S. (Eds.) (2000). *Inquiry and the national science standards: A guide for teaching and learning*. Washington, DC: National Academy Press.

O'Sullivan, E. V., Morrell, A., & O'Connor, M.A. (Eds.). (2002). *Expanding the boundaries of transformative learning*. New York: Palgrave.

Parr, C.S., Jones, T., & Songer, N. B. (2002). CyberTracker in BioKIDS: Customization of a PDA-based scientific data collection application for inquiry learning. In P. Bell, R. Stevens, & T. Satwicz (Eds.), *Keeping learning complex: Proceedings of the Fifth International Conference of Learning Sciences* (pp. 574–575). Mahwah, NJ: Lawrence Erlbaum Associates.

Peters, M. A. (2003). Education policy in the age of knowledge capitalism. *Policy Futures in Education, 1*(2), 361–380. Retrieved July 18, 2004, from http://12_Peters_PFIE_1_2_web.pdf

Petrowski, H. (1996). *Invention by design.* Cambridge, MA: Harvard University Press.

Pribram, K., & King, J. (Eds.). (1996). *Learning as self-organization.* Mahwah, NJ: Lawrence Erlbaum Associates.

Quammen, D. (1996). *The song of the dodo: Island biogeography in an age of extinctions.* New York: Scribner.

Reich, R. (1992). *The work of nations: Preparing ourselves for 21st century capitalism.* New York: Random House.

Reigeluth, C. (Ed.). (1999). *Instructional-design theories and models: A new paradigm of instructional theory.* Mahwah, NJ: Lawrence Erlbaum Associates.

Resnick, L. B., & Klopfer, L. E. (Ed.). (1989). *Toward the thinking curriculum: Current cognitive research.* Alexandria, VA: Association for Supervision and Curriculum Development.

Rubens, W., Dean, P., Leinonen, T., Kligyte, G., Lakkala, M., Rahikainen, M., et al. (2003). *Innovative technologies for collaborative learning.* Helsinki: ITCOLE. Available October 3, 2005, at http://www.euro-cscl.org/site/itcole/itcole_brochure.pdf

Sawyer, R. K. (1999). The emergence of creativity. *Philosophical Psychology, 12*(4), 447–469.

Sawyer, R. K. (2004). The mechanisms of emergence. *Philosophy of the Social Sciences, 34,* 260–282.

Scardamalia, M. (2002). Collective cognitive responsibility for the advancement of knowledge. In B. Smith (Ed.), *Liberal education in a knowledge society* (pp. 76–98). Chicago: Open Court.

Scardamalia, M. (2003). Knowledge building environments: Extending the limits of the possible in education and knowledge work. In A. DiStefano, K. E. Rudestam, & R. Silverman (Eds.), *Encyclopedia of distributed learning* (pp. 269–272). Thousand Oaks, CA: Sage.

Scardamalia, M. (2004). Instruction, learning, and knowledge building: Harnessing theory, design, and innovation dynamics. *EducationalTechnology, 44*(3), 30–33.

Scardamalia, M., & Bereiter, C. (2003). Knowledge building. In *Encyclopedia of education* (2nd ed. pp. 1370–1373). New York: Macmillan Reference.

Scardamalia, M., & Bereiter, C. (2003). Beyond brainstorming: Sustained creative work with ideas. *Education Canada, 43*(4), 4–7, 44. Available, at http://ikit.org/fulltext/2003BeyondBrainstorming.html

Schank, P., & Kozma, R. (2002). Learning chemistry through the use of a representation-based knowledge building environ-

ment. *Journal of Computers in Mathematics and Science Teaching, 21*(3), 253–279.

Shulman, S. (2002). The flight that tamed the skies. *Technology Review, 105*(7), 54–61.

Simon, H. A., & Simon, D. P. (1973). Alternative uses of phonemic information in spelling. *Review of Educational Research, 43,* 115–137.

Simonton, D. K. (1999). *Origins of genius: Darwinian perspectives on creativity.* New York: Oxford University Press.

Smith, F. (1971). *Understanding reading: A psycholinguistic analysis of reading and learning to read.* New York: Holt, Rinehart & Winston.

Sternberg, R. J. (2003). The development of creativity as a decision-making process. In R. K. Sawyer, V. John-Steiner, S. Moran, R. J. Sternberg, J. Nakamura, & M. Csikszentmihalyi (Eds.), *Creativity and development* (pp. 91–138). New York: Oxford University Press.

Sternberg, R. J., Kaufman, J. C., & Pretz, J. E. (2002). *The creativity conundrum: A propulsion model of kinds of creative contributions.* New York: Psychology Press.

Stewart, T. A. (1997). *Intellectual capital: The new wealth of nations.* New York: Doubleday.

Torp, L., & Sage, S. (2002). *Problems as possibilities: Problem-based learning for K-16 education* (2nd ed.). Alexandria, VA: Association for Supervision and Curriculum Development.

Tufte, E. R. (2003). *The cognitive style of PowerPoint.* Cheshire, CT: Graphics Press.

Weisberg, R. W. (1999). Creativity and knowledge: A challenge to theories. In R. J. Sternberg (Ed.), *Handbook of creativity* (pp. 226–250). New York: Cambridge University Press.

Wilensky, U., & Resnick, M. (1999). Thinking in levels: A dynamic systems approach to making sense of the world. *Journal of Science Education and Technology, 8*(1), 3–18.

Windschitl, M. (2004). Folk theories of "inquiry": How preservice teachers reproduce the discourse and practices of atheoretical scientific method. *Journal of Research in Science Teaching, 41,* 481–512.

Wittrock, M. C. (Ed). *Handbook of research on teaching* (3rd ed.). New York: Macmillan.

Yarnall, L., & Kafai, Y. (1996, April). *Issues in project-based science activities: Children's constructions of ocean software games.* Paper presented at the annual meeting of the American Educational Research Association. Available at http://www.gse.ucla.edu/kafai/Paper_Kafai%2FYarnall.html

·31·

TEACHER KNOWLEDGE AND BELIEFS

Anita Woolfolk Hoy
Heather Davis
Stephen J. Pape
The Ohio State University

For over a quarter of a century, researchers have studied the knowledge and beliefs of teachers. In 1977, Walberg first discussed "teachers' mental lives" in an article entitled, "Decision and perception: New constructs for research on teaching effects." From the 1980s to the present, consistent with the shift to cognitive perspectives in education and psychology, research has examined many aspects of teachers' mental lives including their attitudes, perceptions, implicit theories, cognitions, reasoning, images, metaphors, and epistemological beliefs (Freeman, 2002; Munby, Russell, & Martin, 2001; Pajares, 1992; Schraw & Olafson, 2001).

As research has burgeoned, so have reviews that fleshed out theoretical and conceptual issues within the domain (Pajares, 1992), synthesized findings for major areas of research (Calderhead, 1996; Woolfolk Hoy & Murphy, 2001); described and evaluated methods employed (Munby et al., 2001); and connected research questions and methods to their sociohistorical and ontological roots (Wideen, Mayer-Smith, & Moon, 1998). Researchers have investigated both explicit and implicit knowledge and beliefs of preservice, novice, and experienced teachers to identify beliefs (Gould, 2000; Levitt, 2001; Zohar, Degani, & Vaaknin, 2001) and to examine how knowledge and beliefs affect learning to teach (Anderson, 2001; Gregoire, Ashton, & Algina, 2004; Wideen et al., 1998), instruction in particular subjects (Aguirre & Speer, 2000; Stipek, Givvin, Salmon, & MacGycrs, 2001), or student outcomes (Sacks & Mergendoller, 1997; Staub & Stern, 2002).

Table 31.1 presents contributions from handbooks that include discussions of teachers' knowledge and beliefs. In the first *Handbook of Educational Psychology* (Berliner & Calfee, 1996), two chapters directly addressed teachers' knowledge and beliefs: "Learning to Teach" by Borko and Putnam and "Teachers: Beliefs and Knowledge" by Calderhead. Also, several chapters briefly mentioned knowledge and beliefs about specific school subjects, but only the chapters on mathematics (De Corte, Greer, & Verschaffel, 1996) and the informal curriculum (McCaslin & Good, 1996) discussed knowledge and beliefs more extensively. All of these chapters serve as springboards for the current review.

WHAT ARE TEACHER BELIEFS AND KNOWLEDGE, AND WHY ARE THEY IMPORTANT?

Conceptions of knowledge and beliefs have been widely debated (see Chapter 14 of this volume, by Murphy and Mason), but for much of the research on teachers' cognition (with the possible exception of the work in mathematics and science education), few clear distinctions have been made between knowledge and beliefs. Alexander and colleagues (e.g., Alexander, Murphy, & Woods, 1996) concluded that, in spite of some conceptual differences between knowledge and beliefs (knowledge was seen as more factual and verifiable whereas beliefs tended to be subjective and not require validation), the majority of

TABLE 31.1. Sources of Information on Teachers' Knowledge and Thinking From Handbooks and Empirical Reviews

Handbook Chapters	Description
Clark, C., & Peterson, P. (1986). Teachers' thought processes. In M. Wittrock (Ed.), *Handbook of research on teaching* (3rd ed.).	Review of research on teachers' thought processes, starting with Jackson's (1968) early work, *Life in Classrooms*; goal to uncover the mental processes that underlie teachers' actions.
Calderhead, J. (1996). Teachers: Beliefs and knowledge. In D. Berliner & R. Calfee (Eds.) *Handbook of educational psychology.*	How teachers make sense of their professional world; what knowledge and beliefs teachers bring to teaching; and how teachers' understandings of teaching, learning, and academic subjects inform and shape their practice. Chapter includes description and critique of methods used to study beliefs and knowledge.
Borko, H., & Putnam, R. (1996). Learning to teach. In D. Berliner & R. Calfee (Eds.), *Handbook of educational psychology.*	Describes knowledge and beliefs as the cognitive filters through which prospective and practicing teachers view information about teaching, learning, and students. Knowledge of novice and experienced teachers described as both the targets of and strong influences on change in teacher education.
Richardson, V. (1996). The role of attitudes and beliefs in learning to teach. In J. Sikula (Ed.), *Handbook of research on teacher education* (2nd ed.).	Reviews work through the mid-1990s on teacher beliefs in teacher education, including a useful consideration of the distinctions among attitudes, beliefs, and knowledge.
Munby, H., Russell, T., & Martin, A. K. (2001). Teachers' knowledge and how it develops. In V. Richardson (Ed.), *Handbook of research on teaching* (4th ed.).	Reviews teachers' knowledge from several perspectives including educational psychology; includes clear descriptions of the research paradigms used to study teacher knowledge and beliefs.
Evertson C., & Weinstein, C. S. (Eds.) (2006). *Handbook for classroom management: Research, practice, and contemporary issues.*	Reviews research on students' and teachers' perspectives and beliefs about classroom management (Woolfolk Hoy & Weinstein).

teachers and students they surveyed perceived that many ideas fall in the realm of what is both known *and* believed. In fact Kagan (1992) stated, "most of a teacher's professional knowledge can be regarded more accurately as belief" (p. 73). Thus, in keeping with precedents set by other researchers (e.g., Borko & Putnam, 1996; Fenstermacher, 1994), within this review we discuss beliefs and knowledge as generally overlapping constructs.

Richardson (1996) lists three categories of experience that influence knowledge and beliefs about teaching: personal influences, schooling, and formal knowledge. Recent research on *personal* influences examines how life experiences are encoded in images or metaphors (Gould, 2000; Jackson & Leroy, 1998; Korthagen, 2004; Korthagen, Kessels, Koster, Lagerwerf, & Wubbles, 2001). The work on teachers' stories and biographies has identified personal experiences that shape views of teaching (Bullough & Pinnegar, 2001; de Vries & Beijaard, 1999). Much has been written about the influence of *schooling* on beliefs about learning and teaching (beginning with Lortie, 1975) and this work continues today. For example, Stanford (1998) discussed the influence of remembered teachers on African American educators' knowledge and beliefs about teaching. Strauss (1996) noted that, during their precollege education, prospective teachers are in school learning situations for at least 12,000 hours; implicit models of what it means to teach, manage, and learn are inferred from these thousands of hours of schooling. Experiences with *formal knowledge* include both knowledge of academic subjects such as mathematics or history and pedagogical knowledge, as usually encountered

in formal teacher preparation programs. Because the origins of beliefs about teaching are tied to an individual's experiences, the beliefs themselves can be expected to differ (Wideen et al., 1998).

Since the 1970s, an assumption of this research was that "teachers' characteristic beliefs about children and learning have pervasive effects on their behavior, influencing the learning environment that they create for children and for themselves" (Bussis, Chittenden, & Amarel, 1976, p. 16). In a seminal paper on teachers' beliefs, Pajares (1992) noted that many college students begin their career preparation as "strangers" to the professional world they hope to join and expect to learn new knowledge, behaviors, and beliefs. Students of teaching, on the other hand, are "insiders." They need not discover the classroom or see it with new eyes because they are completely familiar with the territory. In learning to be teachers, they "simply return to places of their past, complete with memories and preconceptions of days gone by, preconceptions that often remain largely unaffected by higher education" (p. 46). Findings by other researchers also indicate that entering beliefs generally prevail, almost inoculating prospective teachers from the lessons of their training programs (Floden, 1995; Sugrue, 1996).

Researchers studying practicing teachers are also concerned about the impact of beliefs on teachers' enactments of reform. For example, researchers have examined how beliefs influenced reactions to standards such as the National Council of Teachers of Mathematics (NCTM, 2000) or the National Research Council (NRC, 1995). Because these standards encouraged teachers to adopt ways of teaching they may not have experienced as students, their beliefs became screens for interpreting the new approaches. In fact, Gregoire (2003) suggested that "understanding how teachers' beliefs relate to their practice as well as to student outcomes may be the missing link between calls for school reform and teachers' implementation of that reform" (p. 149).

As with beliefs, teacher knowledge has been conceptualized in a number of ways. Clearly teachers need knowledge of the content they teach, but this is only the beginning. Shulman and colleagues (Shulman & Quinlan, 1996) have explicated the categories of professional knowledge and highlighted the special purview for teachers, *pedagogical content knowledge*, or the transformation of content knowledge into representations, examples, and explanations that connect with the prior knowledge and dispositions of learners.

Many teacher educators have attempted to describe a propositional knowledge base for teaching derived from educational psychology research (e.g., Reynolds, 1989). For many reasons, however, such propositional knowledge does not always translate easily into classroom practice. Perhaps this is because, as Shuell (1996) noted, educational psychology is more a descriptive than prescriptive science, offering powerful ideas for analyzing classroom processes and supporting creative thinking about solutions to problems of practice without directly specifying teaching strategies.

A third type of knowledge, teachers' practical knowledge, is related to craft knowledge, or "the professional knowledge teachers use in their day-to-day classroom teaching" (Brown & McIntyre, 1993, p. 19). This contextual, situated, and often tacit knowledge may be embodied in stories, images, routines, and rhythms of classroom life (Carter, 1993; Korthagen, 2004).

The Scope of This Review

Because of the wealth of studies and reviews of teachers' beliefs and knowledge that appeared by the mid-1990s, the focus of this discussion will be on theory and investigation since 1995. We focus on research in K-12 settings; for a discussion of university teachers' beliefs, see Kane, Sandretto, and Heath (2002). Generally, we examine research within the educational psychology tradition, occasionally moving beyond those (of course fuzzy and permeable) boundaries to expand conceptual and methodological possibilities. We made difficult decisions not to address the body of work on teacher concerns (Meister & Melnick, 2003; Pigge & Marso, 1997) or teachers' craft or practical knowledge (de Vries & Beijaard, 1999) because much of this study was not conducted by

educational psychologists and has been extensively reviewed elsewhere. Our major focus is on teachers' knowledge and beliefs that undergird their practice, as conceived and examined in the psychological tradition.

Virtually every previous analysis of the research on teachers' knowledge and beliefs has ended with a comment about the complexity of the teaching process. Today teaching is more complex than ever as teachers in the United States—mostly white, female, monolingual in English, and middle class—encounter increasing numbers of students who do not share their ethnic, racial, economic, or linguistic background or who have special needs or abilities once addressed in special education classes (Wideen et al., 1998). Teachers are expected not only to align their instruction with new standards and reconceptualizations of effective teaching, but also to develop authentic tasks and tests while encouraging students' critical thinking, collaboration, and creativity (Kilpatric, Swafford, & Findell, 2001).

An Organizing Frame

We organize our review in keeping with an ecological model (Fig. 31.1; Bronfenbrenner, 1986) that suggests individuals are embedded in and significantly affected by several nested ecosystems. A teacher's knowledge and beliefs are influenced by the immediate contexts of the classroom and students, the larger contexts of the state and national policies, and the surrounding context of cultural norms and values. We begin our discussion with a consideration of cultural norms and values about childhood, adolescence, and diversity, then move to the national and state educational policy contexts of standards and accountability procedures; and finally to the immediate settings of diverse classrooms and students. We chose these because the research in these areas is recent and the issues are pressing for practicing teachers and teacher educators. Next, our discussion progresses to the teachers themselves—the research on teachers' identity and sense of efficacy. We end with thoughts about implications of this work for teacher belief change and for research methodology.

BELIEFS ABOUT CHILDHOOD, ADOLESCENCE, AND THE MEANING OF DIVERSITY

In the following sections we explore teachers' beliefs about childhood and adolescence and the nature of diversity, particularly with regard to developmental needs, function, and outcomes. We consider how culture may shape teachers' beliefs about their role as educators and

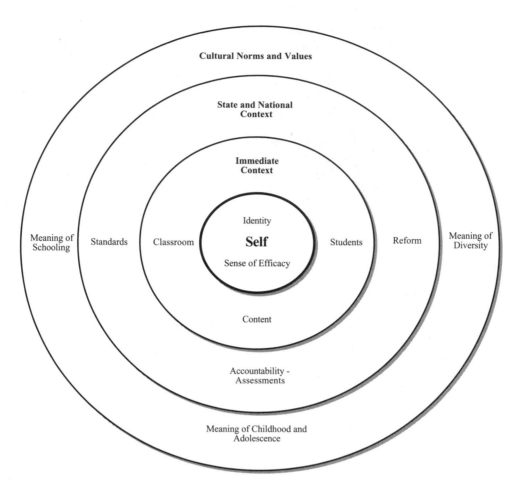

FIGURE 31.1. An ecological model of teachers' knowledge and beliefs.

the increasingly complex demands of serving diverse populations of students.

Images of Childhood

The institutionalization of childhood and adolescence in American society is a relatively new phenomenon (Arnett, 2003; Finkelstein, 2000; Kessen, 1979). We currently live in a society that views childhood as segmented into many different periods (e.g. infancy, toddlerhood, childhood, etc.; Arnett, 2003) with each group having its own set of institutions. Since the technological revolution, there has been a shift in popular culture away from the social reforms designed to protect childhood and adolescence as vulnerable periods (Finkelstein, 2000) toward initiatives designed to make the people and things in our world better, faster, and more efficient. Teachers are supposed to help children develop and learn, but instead of viewing children's current mental tools and age-appropriate skills as serving a purpose in development, teachers'

cultural beliefs about the nature of learning, schooling, and instruction may persuade them to endorse educationally counterproductive practices that push beyond age-appropriate worldviews (Bjorklund, 2005; McDevitt & Ormrod, 2002). Nowhere can the mismatch between cultural norms and findings from research be seen more clearly than in the research examining teachers' beliefs about the nature of adolescence.

Adolescence: Detachment or Connection?

Adolescents are often viewed as pushing away from parents and teachers and turning more towards peer relations for social, emotional, and academic support. Despite attempts by researchers to "debunk" these beliefs, the classic stereotype of adolescence as a time of detachment, rebellion, and conflict (with self and others) has permeated educators' thinking, particularly among novice teachers (Urdan, Midgley, & Wood, 1995). For example, Finders (1997) found that junior high teachers assumed that adolescents need adults less than younger children and began to shift their role. This appears to be consistent with other research pointing to the adolescent's growing awareness of volition and need for autonomy (Reeve, 1998). Autonomy from significant adults, however, is not a result of detachment but rather a function of attachment conceptualized as a dynamic bond allowing the expression of appropriate autonomy within the context of emotional support (Davis, 2003).

It may be that, in response to holding a stereotype of adolescence as a time of detachment, teachers engage in emotional distancing behaviors, believing themselves to be responding to adolescents' needs. But increased detachment from teachers may represent an obstacle for students in achieving emotional autonomy from adults. In fact, Oldfather and Thomas (1998) argue this stereotype is likely to undermine the quality of relationships between students and teachers. In order to stop the cycle of alienation experienced in school, "rather than maintaining the false assumptions that adolescence is a period of alienation from adults, we should acknowledge and nurture the connectedness that adolescents feel to adults" (Finders, 1997, p. 121).

On the other hand, there may be hidden consequences of holding a view of adolescence as a period of continuous emergence, one in which the adult's role is to maintain attachment and guide students towards entry into appropriate citizenship and social relationships. This is because most teachers enter the field with a set of "morality codes" that guide their interactions and pedagogical decisions (Middleton, 2002) and which outline what the appropriate, or ideal, adult outcome of adolescence should look like: a student endorsing white, female, middle-class, English-speaking, heterosexual values. This narrow set of values is likely to present opportunities for cultural conflict in the classroom.

Beliefs About the Nature of Diversity

Preservice and practicing teachers may bring to their work underlying conceptions about diversity and educational possibility. Recently four types of beliefs have been identified that present obstacles to working with increasingly diverse populations of students:

- *Optimistic individualism*—the belief that hard work and individual effort will triumph over any obstacle (Causey, Thomas, & Armento, 2000)—is related to a meritocracy orientation asserting that an individual's effort is the main determinant of success. This belief rejects the systemic social barriers and obstacles that can prevent and/or stifle success.
- *Absolute democracy*—the belief that no matter what the cultural or racial background or economic circumstance, "kids are kids" and the same good pedagogy and decision making will work for all.
- The related notion of *naïve egalitarianism* suggests that every person is created equal and equal means "same"; there is a "one pedagogy for all" orientation. But because of social, systemic, and experiential issues and differences that exist between and among teachers and students, treating students fairly does not mean treating them the same or exactly alike (Ladson-Billings, 2000).
- *Colorblindness*—this belief suggests that students' race should not be a consideration in teaching (Johnson, 2002; Lewis, 2001; Milner, 2003; Tatum, 1997). Teachers intentionally try not to recognize and build on students' race and expect success by rejecting the cultural and racial capital that students bring into the learning environment. These beliefs not only support a naïve assumption that setting and experiences do not matter in teaching, but also encourage teachers to deny their own privileged status in the society, to ignore their own racial identity (Middleton, 2002; Milner & Woolfolk Hoy, 2003), and to overlook the cultural and racial experiences of their students (Milner, 2003).

Teachers who enter economically disadvantaged rural or urban settings with any or all of these four beliefs may overlook the persistence of psychological and institutional obstacles facing students who are marginalized based on their race, socioeconomic status, or disability. Moreover, even though some preservice teachers expressed awareness of difference and privilege, they concurrently thought that they were not prejudiced or that their intelligence and consciousness about diversity could shield them from acting in oppressive ways (Middleton, 2002).

Perhaps among one of the most troubling findings is the very narrow focus assumed for the meaning of culture and diversity (for review, see Hoffman, 1996) and the degree to which these conceptions are embedded in teachers' assumptions about self and identity. For example, in a review of the research on beliefs about diversity, Pohan and Aguilar (2001) found that educators tended to most commonly associate "diversity" with the constructs of race and ethnicity, and "minority" with being African American and being "at-risk" (Gilbert, 1997); these beliefs ignored salient dimensions of self including ability, socioeconomic status, sexual orientation, religion, and gender. In a similar vein, Hoffman (1996) found that many educators tended to focus on "difference" and surface characteristics of culture/context. Moreover, preservice teachers tended to view ethnic identity as something that only people of color developed (Causey et al., 2000; Middleton, 2002; Tatum, 1997), failing to recognize and admitting a lack of knowledge about their own cultural heritages. These findings suggest educators may have a very limited conceptual (Hoffman, 1996; Middleton, 2002) and moral understanding (Gilbert, 1997) of diversity and what it means to teach a diverse population.

EDUCATIONAL POLICY CONTEXT: KNOWLEDGE AND BELIEFS ABOUT STANDARDS AND ACCOUNTABILITY

Many incoming teacher education students have personal experience with content standards and high-stakes testing, but for most experienced teachers, these procedures are new. Recent legislation such as No Child Left Behind in the United States and curricular policy mandates in England (Wood, 2004) has changed the landscape of educational practice.

Standards and Policy Reforms

The standards movement represents efforts by national organizations in the United States to identify the essential outcomes of schooling and the instruction that best supports positive outcomes. Mathematics educators were the first to publish a standards document in 1989 followed by several more specific volumes and an update (NCTM, 2000). Other fields have published similar documents. To attain these standards, teachers are called to adopt a social constructivist perspective on schooling and the academic disciplines; to take on new roles such as facilitators rather than dispensers of knowledge; and to develop classroom norms, tasks, and discourse patterns that support deep understanding. Students are expected to be constructors of knowledge, problem solvers, experimenters, and question generators. These new perspectives on teaching increase the potential impact of teacher knowledge and beliefs as mediators between curricular documents and classroom instruction.

For example, in a review of 154 research studies between 1993 and 2000, Ross, McDougall, and Hogaboam-Gray (2002) identified teachers' beliefs about mathematics teaching as the main obstacle to implementing reform. In a case study of the implementation of a standards-based mathematics textbook, Manouchehri and Goodman (2000) described the planning efforts of two teachers. "It became even more apparent that the teachers'

knowledge of mathematics, their ability and skills in directing mathematical inquiry among students in ways that were conceptual and on a meaningful mathematical continuum, and their level of pedagogical content knowledge was a crucial basis for their assessment and implementation of the innovative materials" (p. 26). Given an open-ended inquiry context, teachers need deep mathematical knowledge with well-elaborated and connected representational systems, mathematical reasoning, and appropriate dispositions to listen to children's responses to these inquiries and to foster mathematical understanding through them. In short, to fulfill the goal of the reform movement, teachers need the types of knowledge and beliefs called for by Ball and Bass (2003) and others (e.g., Kennedy, 1998).

Stritikus (2003) analyzed the reactions of one teacher to the implementation of a California English-immersion policy for English language learners and a district-mandated scripted literacy program. Initially, she readily accepted the policy changes and worked toward strict implementation of direct instruction–dominated lessons. After about a year, because her students seemed to be progressing more slowly, the teacher, also Latina, began to examine her history as a learner in English immersion classrooms, the political contexts of educational decisions, her belief in the maintenance of students' primary language, and her decreasing sense of professionalism and creativity. These reflections led her to return to a more flexible meaning-making approach to literacy development. Thus her implementation of the program changed to align with her beliefs about teaching and learning English as a second language.

Accountability Systems and High-Stakes Testing

In her review of the relationship between state-mandated high-stakes testing and teachers' beliefs and practices, Cimbricz (2002) concluded that high-stakes tests are more likely than low-stakes tests to constrain teachers' beliefs and practices. Other factors, however, influence teachers' beliefs about testing, including teachers' subject-matter knowledge, their views of teaching and learning, grade level taught, years of experience, status, building and district expectations, and school climate (see also Firestone, Mayrowetz, & Fairman, 1998; Grant, 2000; Stone & Lane, 2003). The influences of state-mandated testing seem to depend on how teachers interpret state testing policy and use it to guide their action (Cimbricz, 2002). For example, science teachers in Robinson's (2002) study reported interpreting testing programs as meaning that they must standardize the curriculum—teach the same way to everyone, even students with disabilities. In a large-scale study of state-mandated testing policy in Florida, many teachers believed that the testing movement was leading education in the wrong direction, results were inaccurate, and tests had negative effects on students and teachers. Some teachers, however, reported that increased accountability for students and teachers was a positive outcome (Jones & Egley, 2004).

Wood (2004) identified the tensions and dilemmas felt by British early-childhood educators confronting prescriptive, outcome-driven frameworks as "a new paradigm war." The power differentials between policymakers and policy implementers led to lowering teachers' sense of professional feelings. Wood reasoned that studies of teacher behaviors and cognitions provide evidence to justify reexamination of policies and their unintended negative outcomes.

Assessment Practices

It is estimated that by the 12th grade, students spend close to 1,000 hours being formally tested and many additional hours in informal assessment procedures (Oosterhof, 1999). As a result, preservice teachers enter their teacher training programs with a host of implicit and explicit notions about assessment. For example, many of the students at our institution cite the lower average test scores of minorities on the SAT and then generalize from this one example to conclude that all forms of traditional and standardized assessments are gender and racially biased. Moreover, they do not seem to be aware that poorly constructed performance assessments and portfolios can also be biased assessment measures.

Schraw (Chapter 11 of this volume; with Olafson, 2002) describes three epistemological world views, *realist*, *contextualist*, and *relativist*, that have implications for teachers' beliefs about assessment. Realist teachers (who tend to favor more traditional teaching) stress mastering a standard curriculum and being assessed over the curriculum using valid and reliable norm-referenced standardized tests. Contextualist teachers are more likely to favor criterion-referenced tests that are based on local or district curriculum standards, often including alternative procedures such as group-based projects, performance assessment, and portfolios. Relativist teachers value multiple representations of learning (oral, numerical, written, visual, dramatic, kinesthetic, technological, or performances) to match learners' multiple learning styles and abilities.

One potential impact is that some teachers' epistemological worldviews may not support the use of nontraditional assessment. In addition, portfolio assessments, performance assessments, and written responses to open-ended questions increase the role that teacher beliefs and knowledge play in the process. In the case of portfolio assessment, Schutz and Moss (2004) suggested that differential attention to details in the evidence and different evaluations constructed by different readers in portfolio assessment was unavoidable because of the filters of teachers' knowledge and beliefs. Ambiguity in these portfolio data makes it even more difficult for novice teachers or those who possess weak content knowledge to evaluate them consistently. Efforts to increase reliability (e.g., standardization or breaking portfolios into smaller pieces) contradict the very nature of alternative assessment.

In terms of assignments, prospective and practicing teachers often believe they should provide only positive feedback (e.g., Pajares & Bengston, 1995; Pajares & Graham, 1998) because positive feedback increases students' motivation, whereas specific, negative feedback decreases students' motivation. To the contrary, motivation research suggests that specific, constructive (i.e., positive and negative) feedback is the most motivating form of feedback (Stipek, 2003).

KNOWLEDGE AND BELIEFS ABOUT IMMEDIATE CONTEXTS: CLASSROOMS, STUDENTS, AND CONTENT

As noted earlier, most teachers in the United States are White, female, and middle-class (about 86 percent), monolingual, and the product of suburban or rural schools; their experiences with urban schools in low-income areas are limited (Gay & Howard, 2000).

Beliefs About Teaching and Students in Urban Schools

In a multistate survey Gilbert (1997) found that preservice teachers tended to hold a conception of typical "urban teachers" as young, middle-class, mostly females of color who were no different from other teachers in their abilities, but likely better educated and better qualified. The typical urban teacher was seen as knowledgeable about multicultural issues, caring, streetwise, and a risk taker, while at the same time vigilant and afraid of the urban context. Almost one-third of the preservice teachers felt the curriculum should be the same in every school in the state with an emphasis on basic skills. The respondents believed that curriculum resources generally were inadequate and the school context was seen as negative—older, more dangerous and crowded, dirtier, colder, uglier, and filled with locked doors, metal detectors, and armed guards. Urban teachers were seen as heroic warriors in a fight against the challenges of a dangerous urban landscape. In fact, only 23 percent of the respondents had attended urban schools; changing beliefs about environments never experienced could prove difficult.

Findings regarding teacher' confidence in their knowledge of or ability to work with diverse populations are not clear. Some preservice teachers with limited experience in diverse settings report little or no confidence (Causey et al., 2000), whereas others indicate clear confidence (Gilbert, 1997). But this optimism about abilities to serve diverse populations may not be based on an understanding of diverse students and settings (Causey et al., 2000; Easter, Shultz, Neyhart, & Reck, 1999; Taylor & Sobel, 2001). Prior experience (or shared group membership) with people of diverse backgrounds tends to increase confidence (Bakari, 2003; Causey et al., 2000; Taylor & Sobel, 2001).

Teachers' beliefs and knowledge about urban students are embedded in historical and cultural assumptions about the nature of urban life, which have grown increasingly negative as cities have been equated with economic disenfranchisement and crime (Gilbert, 1997; Finkelstein, 2001). This shift in our perceptions of urban life was accompanied by changes in our perceptions of the students. During the early part of the 20th century, immigrant and poor children living in urban centers were viewed as deficient in their cultural knowledge and social/moral behavior, in need of assimilation into mainstream culture (Finkelstein, 2000), a position sometimes characterized as a *deficit view*.

Deficit Views. Findings from across a variety of research programs suggest that preservice and practicing teachers do tend to hold a deficit view of urban students. For example, Alvidrez and Weinstein (1999) found that teachers were more likely to rate children from higher SES as having a higher IQ and capable of achieving more education. These findings remained even after controlling for children's actual IQ. Moreover, teachers may lower their expectations for student achievement, thus turning biases into actions (Causey et al., 2000; Stodolsky & Grossman, 2000; Wigfield, Galper, Denton, & Seefeldt, 1999).

Preservice teachers reported concerns about whether students in urban schools would speak the same language and would enjoy school (Easter et al., 1999). Gilbert (1997) also found that preservice teachers tended to view urban students as both *streetwise*, reflecting their ability to care for themselves, and *street-savvy*, reflecting their knowledge of drugs, promiscuity, and crime. Urban students were seen as rowdy, rude, apathetic about school,

rebellious, and dangerous. Many respondents felt that the discipline problems of urban schools prevented the successful use of teaching innovations (Gilbert, 1997). Brown (2004) cautions that this fear of urban students and urban student behavior may result in the teachers ignoring or choosing not to respond to student misconduct, thus contributing to the self-fulfilling prophecy of their initial beliefs about behavior.

Tiezzi and Cross (1997) characterized preservice teachers' norms and beliefs about parental involvement and family structures in urban population as "diverse, often conflicted, and idealized" (p. 116). "Common beliefs reflected in the data were that inner-city children couldn't learn and were poor, hostile, and unmotivated, and that their uneducated, poor parents didn't care" (Tiezzi & Cross, 1997; p. 116). Other teachers' beliefs included the "dysfunction" of urban families (Gilbert, 1997) and concerns that the parents in low-income families would not be able to support students' learning (Hauser-Cram, Sirin, & Stipek, 2003). The teachers tended to focus on the problems faced by students in urban schools and their families (Martin, 2004; Tiezzi & Cross, 1997). Urban students were seen as not well prepared for school because they lived in violent neighborhoods and/or dysfunctional homes (Gilbert, 1997).

Likewise, Tiezzi and Cross (1997) found that preservice teachers tended to characterize White children as "smartest and easiest to teach" (p. 120). Saft and Pianta (2001) found that similar teacher/student ethnic background resulted in stronger, more supportive relationships and fewer teacher referrals to special education services. Finally, only about 5 percent of the respondents in Gilbert's (1997) study connected the learning problems of urban students to the inferior facilities or resources of urban schools. Basic skills were valued for the urban schools because the students were seen as needing structure, discipline, and remediation.

These findings suggest that educators, particularly those with little urban education experience, tend to hold a deficit model of students who differ from them in race, ethnicity, SES, or family structure.

Fears of Being "Racist." Taylor and Sobel (2001) found that preservice teachers commonly listed intentionally or unintentionally offending students as a concern related to working with students of a different background. For example, Tatum (1997) found that teachers, as a defense for being called racist, characterized themselves as "colorblind," seeing no differences between children, thus silencing the dialogue on diversity and education. From this perspective, in order to promote positive instructional and interpersonal interactions with their students and parents, teachers interested in working in urban contexts must first reflect on whether they view diversity and the urban classroom as a "problem" to be managed or solved, or as a resource.

Preparing for Diversity. Teachers have lamented that their teacher preparation programs did not adequately prepare them for urban teaching, even though most teacher education programs offer at least one course in diversity. In fact, programs, particularly single courses, have not been consistently successful in preparing students for urban teaching (Pang & Sablan, 1998). Causey et al. (2000) found that the beliefs of their preservice teachers were most affected by writing autobiographical narratives and growth plans, participating in extensive field experiences in diverse settings, and having structured opportunities for reflection, self-analysis, and discourse on equity and diversity issues. Even with this careful attention to belief change, one of the two students in Causey et al.'s case study reverted to preprogram beliefs in her first 3 years of teaching.

Beliefs About Teaching in Inclusive Settings

Over the years, recommendations for educating exceptional students, including students with disabilities and gifted students, have shifted from mainstreaming (including special-needs children in a few regular education classes as convenient), to integration (fitting the special-needs child into existing class structures), to inclusion (restructuring educational settings to promote belonging for all students) (Avramidis, Bayliss, & Burden, 2000). In 1996, Scruggs and Mastropieri reviewed 28 survey studies (1958 to 1995) and concluded that about 66 percent of respondents supported integration, but not all the teachers were willing to implement integration in their classrooms and only one-third believed that they had the training, time, or resources necessary for integration. Garriott, Miller, and Snyder (2003) found that even though most of the preservice teachers surveyed had positive attitudes toward inclusion, almost half of them thought that students with mild disabilities were best served in special education classrooms. Teachers have also expressed concern regarding whether the time and attention needed for effective instruction of students with significant disabilities would be provided at the expense of other students in their classes, and if disabled students would get the individual attention they need (Downing, Eichinger, & Williams, 1997; Garriott et al., 2003).

Practicing teachers with experience in inclusion generally express support for inclusive education, and younger teachers tend to be more supportive (Avramidis et al., 2000). For example, Lieber et al. (1998) found preschool teachers believed that inclusive settings provide opportunities for social development and friendship for both nondisabled and disabled students. But the teachers may have attached different meanings to the beliefs. For example, the teachers agreed that learning to accept differences was a valuable outcome of inclusion, but "for some teachers that meant minimizing differences by ignoring them, for others it meant dealing with students' questions about differences as they arose, and for still others, differences were to be highlighted and respected" (p. 100). The differences might be explained by changing conceptions, from mainstreaming to integration to inclusion, with teachers trained at different times likely to develop different conceptions of best practices for inclusion.

Soodak and McCarthy (2006) summarized the research about instructional and classroom management practices for inclusion, including how teachers' attitudes and beliefs contribute to their use of effective strategies. They found that teachers are generally supportive of inclusive education, with training and experience in inclusive settings tending to facilitate change in teacher confidence (Avramidis et al., 2000; McLeskey & Waldron, 2002). There remains a relative dearth of research, however, concerning preservice and practicing teachers' beliefs about the students with disabilities themselves (Shechtman & Or, 1999). Even though both preservice and inservice teachers have expressed concerns about being able to meet the needs of disabled students, Hastings and Oakford (2003) found that teachers' beliefs depended on the nature of the child's needs. Teachers appeared to weigh information concerning the severity and type of disability and the age of the child when making judgments about the potential negative impact of inclusion on nondisabled students, the teacher, and the classroom environment. For example, children with less severe disabilities (Soodak, Podell, & Lehman, 1998) and/or with intellectual disabilities compared to emotional/behavioral disabilities (Hastings & Oakford, 2003) were viewed more positively as candidates for inclusion and less likely to have a negative impact on the students, teacher, and classroom environment. These findings were even stronger for teachers of young children.

Beliefs About Student Characteristics

Current trends for inclusion may intensify the importance of teachers' beliefs about the nature of intelligence (e.g., entity vs. incremental views; Dweck, 2002).

Ability. Implicit theories of ability may guide teachers' interpretations of students' competence and interactions with them. For example, Butler (2000) found that teachers who held an entity (static, set) view of intelligence were more likely to perceive students' initial outcomes on a set of tasks as indicative of higher ability. In contrast, teachers who held an incremental (changeable, malleable) view of intelligence were more likely to reserve judgment and perceive students' final outcomes on a set of tasks as indicative of their ability. Jordan, Lindsay, and Stanovich (1997) reported that teachers who assumed disability is inherent in the child tended to interact less effectively with exceptional students than did teachers who held a view that problems are the results of interactions between the child and the environment. These findings have important implications not only for the instructional decisions teachers may make, but also for their interpretations of the types of modifications needed when working with exceptional students.

Research on teachers' beliefs about student competence has investigated the extent to which teachers' perceptions of intellectual competence are independent from their beliefs/perceptions of social competence. In a study across a variety of domains (academic, behavioral, athletic, appearance, and social), Cole, Gondoli, and Peeke (1998) found teachers and parents tended to see children's competence as reflective of two higher-order domains: Well Behaved/Good Student and Athletic/Attractive/Social. Intellectual competence appeared to be somewhat confounded with the child's ability to engage in socially competent classroom behavior. However, Cole et al. (1998) also found that teachers' judgments across these domains tended be correlated more strongly with each other than parents' judgments, which suggests that teachers may overgeneralize their judgments of behavioral and academic competence to competence in other domains. The confound of social and intellectual ability may, in part, reflect the limited number of settings in which teachers actually observe their students. These findings are echoed in research by Alvidrez and Weinstein (1999), who found that teachers were more likely to rate the students they perceived as more assertive to have higher IQ. Furthermore, teachers' perceptions of IQ at preschool predicted GPA and standardized achievement at age 14.

Cole et al. (1998) found that teachers tended to rate girls as being more behaviorally competent, despite a growing body of literature to suggest that girls and boys may misbehave at similar rates but in different ways. Findings across this research suggest that teachers' beliefs about the nature of social competence, including what constituted competent classroom behavior and social interactions, may be related to biases in teachers' judgments of intellectual competence. (These findings are also echoed in the literature on students' social motiva-

tion and the role of social responsibility goals in predicting academic outcomes; see Wentzel, 1999).

Gender and Sexual Orientation. Earlier we discussed cultural stereotypes about the nature of adolescence and the role of adults in guiding them. Such cultural norms and values are likely to affect thinking about appropriate behaviors for male and female students. For example, "If teachers' culturally based expectations about levels of antisocial behaviors are lower for males than for females [lower for learning disabled students; for students of different race/ethnicity], it may be their tolerance for these behaviors in females is not a great as it is for males" (Center & Wascom, 1986).

Likewise, Talburt (2004) argued there may be a dangerous combination of beliefs teachers may hold about the nature of teaching, the nature of adolescence, and personal beliefs about the nature of being lesbian, gay, bisexual, or transgendered (LGBT). For example, teachers may hold personal beliefs that it is unnatural or wrong to be LGBT (Kumashiro, 2004). Or, teachers may hold the stereotype of the LGBT youth as being "at risk," withdrawn, having low self-esteem, and being a victim (Blackburn, 2004; Talburt, 2004), which may perpetuate teachers' beliefs that they need to help students change a part of their identity in order to fit in better with their peers and with adult society. In contrast, Blackburn (2004) argues the reality is that many LGBT youth exhibit agency behaviors, which may not conform to teachers' expectations, resulting in consequences for the teachers' instructional and interpersonal interactions. But should teachers be responsible for challenging their students' beliefs about homophobia and heterosexism (Kumashiro, 2004)? Teachers' ambivalence may reflect a conflict with being an advocate for a value they do not hold. What implication does this have for working with families and students?

"Problem" Students and "Good" Students. Earlier we reviewed literature indicating that teachers' beliefs and perceptions of students' intellectual competence may be entangled with their beliefs and perceptions of social competence. Indeed, there is a growing body of literature investigating the nature of teachers' beliefs about student behavior, including what constitutes ideal, appropriate, and inappropriate behavior as well as teachers' beliefs about relating to the students in their classrooms. Perhaps, the largest growing body of studies has explored teachers' conceptions of "problem behavior" (Bibou-Nakou, Kiosseoglou, & Stogiannidou, 2000; Brophy, 1996; Brophy & McCaslin, 1992). Using mixed methodology that enabled them to examine reported beliefs and implemented strategies in the classroom, Brophy and McCaslin (1992) were able to identify systematic differences in teachers' beliefs about 12 types of "problem students" teachers might encounter in their classroom as well as identify patterns of appraisals (e.g., locus, control, stability/generalizability) that may underlie their beliefs. For example, when teachers believed the source of problematic behavior was academic, they tended to respond to students with concern and caring; whereas when they believed the goal of students' behavior problems was to disrupt class, they tended to respond with rejection or punishment. Similarly, Bibou-Nakou et al. (2000) found that teachers were most likely to make attributions to internal student qualities when judging the source of students' behavior problems. Findings by Chang (2003) suggest these differences may reflect teachers' generalized aversions toward aggressive behaviors and empathy toward socially withdrawn behaviors.

On the one hand, these findings may reflect a bias in teachers' beliefs or perceptions that ignores their own contribution, or the contribution of contextual factors (e.g., school, classroom, peers) in perpetuating problematic behavior. However, when examining the question of accuracy versus bias, Brophy and McCaslin (1992) found that the teachers in their study tended to respond along a continuum of assuming responsibility that depended on their judgments of stability: whether the problem existed prior to the child entering their class or in their classroom. Moreover, although teachers in their study were more likely to make stable-internal attributions, they were less consistent about attributions of effort. In other words, they did not necessarily believe that students were acting intentionally inappropriately.

As we mentioned earlier, one of the challenges of increasing complexity in the classroom is that we have a history of seeing difference, be it difference in culture or difference in ability/disability, as deficit (see also Sternberg, 1996). For example, Martin (2004) found that among the teachers she observed, those who viewed difference and diversity as "opportunity" tended to experience more success understanding and managing student behavior. Findings regarding the sources of problem behavior (e.g., academic vs. disruption; stable vs. unstable; internal vs. external) suggest that some students may be systematically "at risk" for being labeled by their teachers as a "problem student."

In contrast, few studies have explored the nature of teachers' beliefs about "typical" or "good" student behavior (Chang, 2003; Davis, Ashley, & Couch, 2003a). Findings by Chang (2003) indicate that teachers tend to experience warmth toward students who evince prosocial and leadership behaviors. Brophy (1996) describes such students as "the ones who pay attention to lessons, apply themselves to their work and seem comfortable

and responsive to teachers' instructional and social initiations" (p. 1).

Beliefs About Relating to Students

A growing body of research suggests that teachers' beliefs about how to relate to their students may underlie differences in their beliefs about student behavior (Davis, in press; Davis, Ashley, et al., 2003; Delpit, 1995; Stodolsky & Grossman, 2000). For example, Brophy and McCaslin (1992) found that teachers' beliefs about problem students depended on whether they defined their role in the classroom as *instructor* or as *socializer*. These findings parallel those by Davis, Ashley, et al. (2003), who found that teachers struggled to resolve two tensions when selecting relationship partners in their classroom: Is it my responsibility to develop relationships with students, *or* are my responsibilities limited to instruction? Is it my responsibility to develop a relationship with this student, *or* are there other students in the classroom who would be better partners/need my relationship more? Using a cross-case analysis of interview data, they found that teachers tended to make instructional decisions (and in some cases referrals) depending on whether they assumed responsibility for supporting or improving lower-achieving students, or whether they saw the remediation of school underpreparedness as the responsibility of outside agents (e.g. Title/Chapter 1 teachers). Delpit (1995) argues that teachers' decisions to assume responsibility for developing rapport held important consequences for working with students of diverse backgrounds. Specifically, she found that commitment on the part of teachers to establishing and maintaining relationships with students had a transformative effect on students' attitudes and achievement patterns (Delpit, 1995). This was particularly true for negotiating conflict and helping students to regulate negative emotions in the classroom (e.g., frustration, apathy).

Beliefs About Content

Because other chapters in this handbook address the content domains, we will not repeat those specific discussions here. But a program of research by Stoldosky and Grossman looks across subjects and thus provides comparative insights. They found that teachers' perceptions of their subject area had consequences for their instructional choices regarding curriculum, such as their press for coverage, their standardization of the content, and their establishment of daily routines. For example, differential patterns of activities in elementary and secondary classrooms paralleled both teachers' and students' perceptions of the academic domain (Stodolsky & Grossman, 2000). Specifically, secondary teachers across five academic domains tended to describe their subject matter differentially in terms of status, sequence, scope, and stability (Stodolsky & Grossman, 1995). Math or science, presumably higher status domains, may claim greater sources of power within the school than lower status subjects, such as the power to "create" external motives (e.g. prerequisite for future courses). Students' and teachers' perceptions of subject matter may also act in ways that permit or constrain the types of interpersonal interactions, and consequently the interpersonal space, in the classroom. From this perspective, classroom climate dimensions of organization and rule clarity may mediate relationship quality and motivation for subject matters that tend to be narrowly defined in terms of scope, stability, and sequence, such as math or English. In contrast, there may be no effect of classroom climate or relationship quality for subject matters that tend to be broadly defined in terms of scope, stability, and sequence, such as reading, social studies or science.

TEACHERS' BELIEFS ABOUT SELF: IDENTITY AND SENSE OF EFFICACY

Research on teachers' beliefs and conceptions about themselves—their identity as teachers and their sense of efficacy for teaching—has grown in the past 15 years.

Teaching Roles and Identities

Teacher identity development is an emerging area in research on teacher knowledge and beliefs about self (for early work, see McCutcheon, 1992). As with research on teaching beliefs and knowledge, the field is conceptually "messy" (see Pajares, 1992). Research in this area remains largely qualitative, with a sampling of studies that utilized survey methodology in an instrument development/descriptive manner. This work raises both time-honored and novel questions about teachers' awareness of their own beliefs and knowledge. For example, researchers have begun to explore the development of a professional teaching identity, asking preservice and practicing teachers questions such as: Why become a teacher? (Cardelle-Elwar & Nevin, 2003; Johnson, McKeown, & McEwen, 1999; Jones Young, & Roderiguez, 1999; Schutz, Crowder, & White, 1999); What does it mean to be a teacher? (Davis, Hartshorne, Hayes, & Ring, 2003; Korthagen, 2004); What are the factors that shape the shift in identity during teacher education programs from identify-

ing as a "student of teaching" to identifying as a "teacher"? (e.g., Cardelle-Elwar & Nevin, 2003; Danielwicz, 1997; Ladson-Billings, 2001); and, How does teaching identity change throughout the life-career of a teacher? (Bullough & Baughman, 1997).

Voice. An emergent strand of research within the study of identity is a consideration of teacher voice addressing the question: How do underrepresented populations in the teaching field view their own path into teaching, their mission, and their identity (Delpit, 1988, 1995)? These questions seem critical given the declining number of African American teachers entering the field combined with an increased likelihood of leaving the field (Easter et al., 1999). Moreover, several studies (Delpit, 1995; Dixson, 2003; Stanford, 1998) suggest that African American teachers, because they bring systematically distinct prior experiences with the educational system to their careers, may hold differing conceptions of education and constructions of the teaching identity. What are the beliefs of African American teachers about the teaching profession, about working with students from dominant cultures (and serving students of diverse backgrounds)? Do certain beliefs, such as self-efficacy, serve as protective factors that might increase likelihood of resilience in the face of obstacles and the ultimate retention of teachers of diverse background in the field (Milner & Woolfolk Hoy, 2003)?

Racial Identity. Within this area of teaching identity, several studies, drawing from the rich history of research from clinical and counseling psychology, have investigated stability, change, and the consequences of preservice and practicing teachers' racial identity development including its relationship to coursework (Lawrence & Tatum, 1997; Marshall, 1999; Middleton, 2002; Tatum, 1994). Likewise, how do teachers understand themselves and their teaching tasks in terms of holding a racial identity that potentially matches/mismatches the population of students they will be teaching (Graham, 1994; Ladson-Billings, 2001; Saft & Pianta, 2001; Tatum, 1997)? In meeting the demands of increasingly diverse populations, it may also be important to consider the ways in which aspects of teachers' personal identities may act as assets or obstacles in their attempt to establish classroom routines and find meaningful ways to facilitate interactions between their students and the content, and between their students and themselves (Davis, Ashley, et al., 2003).

Facilitating Teacher Identity Development. Several studies have highlighted the importance of providing teachers with the opportunity for discourse and structured reflection (Black, Sileo, & Prater, 2000; Davis et al., 2003;

Howard & Denning del Rosario, 2000; Korthagen, 2004). However, Danielwicz (1997; see also Delpit, 2003) argues that we need to move beyond reflection on what "is" the identity of a teacher to what "can be" the identity of a teacher: "What makes someone a good teacher is not methodology or ideology. It requires engagement with identity, the very way individuals conceive of themselves so that teaching is a way of being not merely ways of acting or behaving" (Danielwicz, 1997; p. 3).

Teachers' Sense of Efficacy

One important self-referenced belief for teaching is a sense of efficacy. Tschannen-Moran, Woolfolk Hoy, and Hoy's (1998) definition emphasizes the contextual and situation specific nature of efficacy: "Teacher efficacy is the teacher's belief in her and his ability to organize and execute the courses of action required to successfully accomplish a specific teaching task in a particular context" (p. 233). Early research focused on two aspects of teacher efficacy, usually called general and personal (Gibson & Dembo, 1984). More recently, researchers have formulated other conceptions of teachers' sense of efficacy, and called for both clarification and broadening of the construct (Labone, 2004; Tschannen-Moran et al., 1998).

The model of teacher efficacy presented by Tschannen-Moran et al. (1998) suggests that teachers' efficacy judgments are the result of an interaction between (a) a personal appraisal of the factors that make accomplishing a specific teaching task easy or difficult (analysis of teaching task) and (b) a self-assessment of personal teaching capabilities and limitations specific to the task (analysis of teaching competence). The resultant efficacy judgments affect the goals teachers set for themselves, the effort they invest in reaching these goals, and their persistence when facing difficulties. These decisions and behaviors lead to outcomes that then become the basis for future efficacy judgments.

Considering the components of the model, Tschannen-Moran and Woolfolk Hoy (2001) developed the *Teachers' Sense of Efficacy Scale* (*TSES*). With in-service and preservice teachers as samples, they reported three dimensions of teaching efficacy: efficacy for student engagement, efficacy for instructional strategies, and efficacy for classroom management (see also Ho & Hau, 2004). Bandura's own scale for assessing efficacy incorporated a wider range of dimensions than instruction, including participation in decision making, affecting school climate, and working with parents and the community. Labone (2004) has encouraged researchers to expand conceptions of efficacy to include insights from interpretivist and critical theory perspectives (see Henson, 2002; Labone, 2004;

Tschannen-Moran & Woolfolk Hoy, 2001, for a complete discussion).

Effects of Efficacy Beliefs. Among practicing teachers, efficacy is one of the few teacher characteristics consistently related to student achievement (Tschannen-Moran et al., 1998). Teachers who have high efficacy expectations evince more effort and persistence in specific teaching tasks; they engage in activities that support children's learning (Ross, 1998). Teachers' efficacy is also related to commitment to teaching (Coladarci, 1992) and job satisfaction (Caprara, Barbaranelli, Borgogni, & Steca, 2003). Once established, efficacy beliefs seem resistant to change. A strong sense of efficacy can support higher motivation, greater effort, and resilience across the span of a teaching career. However, Wheatley (2002) identified a number of benefits for teacher learning that might follow from having doubts about one's efficacy. These include the possibility that doubts might foster reflection, motivation to learn, productive collaboration, and change provoking disequilibrium. A sense of efficacy may be necessary to respond to doubts in these positive ways, but the point is well taken that persistent high efficacy perceptions in the face of poor performance can produce avoidance rather than positive action.

Efficacy and Experience. The development of teacher efficacy beliefs has generated a great deal of research interest because once established, the beliefs appear to be resistant to change, even when the teachers are exposed to workshops and new teaching methods (Ross, 1994). Results are mixed, however, on the relationship between time teaching in schools and teacher efficacy. For example, in studies of science, Mulholland and Wallace (2001) found that efficacy increased with experience as the teacher in their case study grew better able to manage the students' behaviors and the science inquiry activities. But some quantitative studies found very little correlation at all between experience and teaching efficacy (Cantrell, Young, & Moore, 2003; Plourde, 2002), whereas other quantitative studies have found that efficacy decreased with time teaching (Ghaith & Yaghi, 1997). Sense of efficacy has been found to increase after student teaching then decrease during the first year of teaching (Woolfolk Hoy & Burke-Spero, 2005). One explanation for possible initial declines in efficacy with experience is that the social support available during preparation diminishes as teachers move to the public school settings (Cantrell et al., 2003; Woolfolk Hoy & Burke-Spero, 2005). Also, with experience, teachers may grow to believe that student learning is due to factors beyond their control (Ghaith & Yaghi, 1997), and so their efficacy decreases.

Sense of Efficacy for Specific Tasks

One of the fundamental notions about efficacy is that it is situation and task specific (Bandura, 1997). For example, a successful experience with the teaching of science appears to have a positive impact on science teaching efficacy (Cantrell et al., 2003; Knobloch & Whittington, 2002). Early measures of teachers' sense of efficacy such as Gibson and Dembo's (1984) *Teacher Efficacy Scale* were more global, but since the 1990s, measures have been developed that are specific to tasks such as classroom management (Emmer & Hickman, 1991), science teaching (Riggs & Enochs, 1990), and special education (Coladarci & Breton, 1997). Specific tasks of teaching likely vary across cultural context. For example, Ho and Hau (2004) found that efficacy for student guidance was a factor for their Australian and Chinese teachers, but American teachers appeared to be more concerned about efficacy for student engagement. A complete list of efficacy measures is available online (http://www.emory.edu/EDUCATION/mfp/self-efficacy.html); the site is maintained by efficacy researcher Frank Pajares. Questions for future research include understanding the sources of efficacy and tracing the ways that efficacious beliefs translate into instructional decisions, actions, and interactions with students.

Collective Efficacy

In addition to the self-referent efficacy perceptions discussed earlier, teachers have beliefs about the conjoint capability of a school faculty. These group-referent perceptions reflect an emergent organizational property known as *collective efficacy* (Bandura, 1997; Goddard, Hoy, & Woolfolk Hoy, 2004). Collective efficacy refers to the perceptions of teachers in a school that the faculty as a whole can organize and execute the courses of action required to have a positive effect on students. Teacher self-efficacy and collective efficacy are related, but they are not the same phenomenon aggregated at the group level (Caprara et al., 2003; Goddard & Goddard, 2001). In fact, perceived collective efficacy may vary a great deal more within groups than perceptions of individual efficacy (Goddard, 2001).

Several studies have documented that teachers' beliefs about the collective capability of their faculty vary greatly among schools and are strongly linked to differences in student achievement among schools (Goddard, LoGerfo, & Hoy, 2004; Hoy, Sweetland, & Smith, 2002; Tschannen-Moran & Barr, 2004). Goddard and his colleagues have shown that, even after controlling for students' prior achievement, race/ethnicity, SES and gender, collective efficacy has a stronger effect on student achievement than student race or SES. In other words, children at risk tend to be better off in schools where the culture is characterized by a robust sense of group capability. The link between collective efficacy and student achievement occurs, from a theoretical perspective, because a robust sense of group capability establishes expectations for success and norms of effort and persistence.

Ross (1995, 1998) has written extensively about the relationship between school leadership, particularly transformational leadership, and teachers' self-efficacy and collective efficacy beliefs. Ross identifies a number of principal actions that might encourage teachers' sense of efficacy including "multiple treatments that combine instructional skill development with explicit attention to teachers' beliefs about their role in guiding student learning and the creation of strong professional cultures" (Ross, 1998, p. 65).

THE POTENTIAL FOR BELIEF AND KNOWLEDGE CHANGE

Teacher learning frequently is haphazard (Richardson & Placier, 2001). Long-term, systematic learning based on local investigations of significant questions about instruction is crucial to sustained professional development. Abdal-Haqq (1995) echoed these calls and recommended professional development programs that (1) are collaborative, frequent and ongoing; (2) include training, practice, and feedback; (3) are school based and supportive of teacher inquiry; (4) incorporate constructivist approaches; and (5) recognize teachers as professionals.

Conceptual Change and Self-Regulated Learning Models

Teachers change their beliefs as they are made explicit, as they begin to doubt these beliefs, and as they are exposed to powerful alternative conceptions. There are a number of different frameworks in educational, cognitive, and social psychology used to describe the processes associated with conceptual change (Eagley & Chaikin, 1993; Gregoire, 2003; see also Chapter 14 of this volume). Many of these frameworks emphasize the social, motivational, and affective contexts of conceptual change. Gregoire (2003) argues that we need to look beyond the professional development activities to examine the perceived relevance of innovation to teachers' constructions of their teaching identities. For example, to what extent does endorsing a new belief structure, or modifying existing knowledge, threaten or align with teachers' developing understandings of who they were, are, or will be in their classrooms?

Models of Change. Preservice and practicing teachers may need multiple opportunities (both successes and failures) to reconcile contradictions with their existing beliefs and knowledge. Educational reforms and teacher education programs that attempt to change teacher beliefs may threaten teachers' existing views of themselves as teachers. These perceived external presses, combined with a lack of confidence to implement new standards-based methods or align existing pedagogy with new beliefs, may result in what Gregoire (2003) calls stress or threat appraisals. In other words, even the mere discussion of reform or innovation may inherently challenge teachers' naïve understandings of what a teacher is and how a teacher acts. Gregoire argues that in order for belief change to occur, teachers must come to see the value of an innovation as relevant to their sense of "self." Even when not threatened by reform, teachers may lack the necessary motivation for central conceptual change. Likewise, Patrick and Pintrich (2001) found that conceptual change in pre-service teachers beliefs might depend on their entering goals, interests, values, efficacy, and personal epistemologies.

Middleton (2002) analyzed changes in teachers' beliefs and attitudes blending Festinger's (1957) model of belief change with two models of ethnic identity development to understand the different cognitive approaches teachers may have toward diversity in their classroom as well as the factors that may lead to belief or attitude change. She found that among the major antecedents to belief change were creating a nonthreatening rather than coercive environment where preservice teachers could explore their own identities and beliefs, and providing enough experiences to reach the preservice teachers at both cognitive and affective levels.

CONCLUSIONS

In this review we used Bronfenbrenner's model of nested ecosystems to organize our analysis of teachers' knowledge and beliefs. We chose a few topics in each system level, selecting those that represent active research areas and are of interest to teachers and teacher educators. Thus we examined research on teachers' knowledge and beliefs about cultural norms and values (related to adolescence and to diversity), national educational policy (related to standards and accountability), immediate teaching contexts (classrooms, students, and content), and self (identity and efficacy). We did not include work on

teacher concerns, craft knowledge, propositional knowledge bases, management, or planning—because much of the research was outside educational psychology (e.g., craft knowledge), recently reviewed elsewhere (e.g., management), or lacked substantial new studies (e.g., planning, propositional knowledge bases).

The research on cultural norms raises issues about how stereotypes about adolescence or diversity might interfere with positive relationships between teachers and students—relationships that are critical for student learning. Research about standards and accountability provides some evidence for Gregoires (2003) assertion that teachers' beliefs may be the missing link between calls for school reform and teachers' implementation of that reform. Research on teachers' knowledge and beliefs about classrooms and students points to the complexity and challenge of preparing teachers for diverse settings, especially when those teachers bring possible biases born of cultural experiences that do not match those of their students. Research on teacher identity, efficacy, and change reminds us that the teacher's motivation, emotional responses, and openness to change are closely tied to beliefs about self.

Questions for the Future

We have identified three types of questions for future research on teacher knowledge and beliefs, briefly described next. The first involves beliefs that connect or intersect topics previously studied separately. The second is the question of coordinating beliefs, and the third is the perennial question of espoused versus enacted beliefs, now especially important in a time of external pressures for reform and accountability.

Crossover Studies. Two areas of previous study, planning and management, are particularly appropriate to overlay the work on beliefs about diversity. For example, questions might include: How do teachers' beliefs about student cultural, racial, language, or ability differences influence or interact with beliefs about and practices of classroom management? Do teachers have different images of what it means to comply or cooperate with class rules and procedures for different students? How are the phases of planning (preinteractive, interactive, and reflective) affected when classrooms are inclusive? Do teacher beliefs mediate the effects of high-stakes pressures on planning or management practices for diverse classroom and students?

Coordinating Beliefs at Different Levels. The nested model in Fig. 31.1 suggests possible research questions about how beliefs at one contextual level are affected by other levels. For example, how are beliefs about self influenced by students, classroom, state and national policy, or cultural factors? At many times in their careers, teachers are confronted with social pressures and challenges to their existing beliefs. For example, as they enter preparation programs, preservice teachers often are confronted with different images of teaching and learning than those they developed as students. If they undergo some conceptual change in beliefs, these same individuals may again be confronted with social and contextual pressures to accept new beliefs as they join existing school faculties in their first jobs as "real" teachers. And again, later in their careers, as reforms are either made available to them or forced on them by state or federal accountability measures, their existing beliefs may be challenged. How do teachers coordinate and reconcile these often inconsistent beliefs? Gregoire's (2003) model suggests that emotion and perceived threat play a role. Is this true? How and for whom are these inconsistencies and demands threatening?

Espoused and Enacted Beliefs. Finally, we come again to the question of when and how do teachers develop consistency between espoused and enacted beliefs, and can researchers rely on self-report if inconsistencies are common? These connections between espoused and enacted beliefs are not necessarily predictable or obvious. For example, research by Muijs and Reynolds (2001) found that having connectionist beliefs about teaching (as opposed to traditional or discovery beliefs) was the strongest predictor of both constructivist and behaviorist teaching practices. This raises a further question: What exactly constitutes a match between espoused and enacted beliefs?

Revisiting the Methods for Studying Teachers' Knowledge and Beliefs

As with our predecessors (Calderhead, 1996; Munby et al., 2001; Pajares, 1992), we also noted several methodological trends in the field. Underlying our field is the assumption that the mental lives of teachers matter for instructional decision making and ultimately for student outcomes in the classroom. Initially daunted by the complexity, limited theorizing about the nature of constructs, and challenges in how to "capture" constructs in a meaningful and consistent way, researchers in the field of educational psychology moved away from process-product approaches toward more isolated study of beliefs/knowledge (Calderhead, 1996; Pajares, 1992). The response over the past 20 years has been to parse the field into ever more discrete constructs, refining our operational definitions and establishing construct validity.

Issues of construct definition, identified by our predecessors, linger and extend into this next era of research. For example, the field will need to address what it means when we discuss teachers' beliefs about a construct such as diversity, accountability, students, or self. Do our difficulties in attempting to define the constructs of teacher beliefs and knowledge reflect the reality that different domains "care" about these constructs for different reasons and in different ways? We believe that some of the challenges we are facing with regard to construct definition also continue to reflect the interdisciplinary nature of the work being completed.

However, as our body of knowledge grows, coupled with the press to begin to address the increasingly complex task of teaching in our research, we believe that, as a field, we must move away from studying teachers' beliefs and knowledge in relative isolation and toward designs and methodologies that enable us to address the "whole" of teachers' mental lives. Emphasis over the past decade on establishing psychometric validity, both conceptual and construct, for our assessments suggests there may now be a greater selection of empirically validated, theoretically derived measures that may allow for greater flexibility in our deductive designs.

The recent explosion of empirically grounded measures (both domain general within the fields of management and efficacy, and context and domain specific), established traditions of qualitative inquiry, the implementation of mixed-methodology (Vartuli, 1999), and methods designed to analyze and compare theoretical models for their fit with empirical data and to explore the contribution of factors that operate on group/collective levels call for a renewed exploration of the utility of process-product designs in understanding complex classroom processes (Goddard & Goddard, 2001; Goddard, Hoy, & Woolfolk Hoy, 2004). For example, work by Middleton (2002; see also Gregoire et al., 2004) may be an example of how the return to process-product designs (in which we attempt to capture the effects of beliefs on behavior) can be carried out in a theoretically driven way by bounding design within theoretical guidelines, more equipped to make sense of the complexities of findings. Our emerging attempts to model data on different levels (Goddard & Goddard, 2001; Goddard, Hoy, & Woolfolk Hoy, 2004) to look at the effects of beliefs on student outcomes may also have important implications for addressing Pajares' (1992) concern about the ways in which researchers have often failed to account for how beliefs themselves may exist on different levels (some being more global/distal and some being more specific/proximal). Moreover, studies such as the one completed by Donohue, Weinstein,

Cowan, and Cowan (2000) using teachers' perceptions of student ability and potential to predict changes in parent perceptions challenge the boundaries of the traditional use of parent perceptions as predictors to explore potential novel outcomes of teacher beliefs and knowledge.

Additionally, research on teacher beliefs and knowledge may want to explore "novel," or underused, methodologies (Calderhead, 1996). For example, we came across few studies implementing cross-sectional designs to explore the presence of developmental differences in beliefs and knowledge. In one example, we were intrigued by findings from Murphy, Delli, and Edwards' (2004) cross-sectional study of beliefs about "good teachers" and "good teaching" in which they compared second-grade students' beliefs with preservice and in-service teachers' beliefs. Underlying their design were issues of how early beliefs about teaching begin to develop and how similar children's beliefs about teaching are to these of preservice and in-service teachers. Data from this study are even more interesting when examined for their implementation of novel methodology (e.g., the Kinetic School Drawing activity; a qualitative analysis of participants' drawings and subsequent descriptions of their drawings) to attempt to elicit developmentally appropriate and comparable responses across the three populations. Their findings, though preliminary and in need of further exploration, continue to push our creative thinking about how to best match our designs to answer our questions and calling us to draw on methods developed in the other fields of psychology and education. Other methodologies blossoming in the study of student beliefs, motives, and self-regulation, including the use of observational methodologies (once dominant in our field) and profiling techniques, were significantly underrepresented in the methods currently being employed.

Teacher Beliefs and Knowledge:
An Interdisciplinary Field

As Munby et al. (2001) noted, attempts to truly understand the mental lives of teachers require researchers to familiarize themselves with both "work *on* teachers' knowledge and beliefs and the work *of* teaching" (p. 878). The work of understanding teachers' mental lives is not exclusively carried out by educational psychologists. The study of belief and knowledge about teaching not only is interdisciplinary, but is one field characterized by paradigmatic tensions (see Munby et al., 2001, and Wideen et al., 1998, for review). Within the field of teacher education, there continues to be a predominate

focus on infusing teacher voice and reconciling teacher critique of theory into our frameworks. As such, we noted increasing emphasis on the use of teacher reflection and on as data utilizing the coursework of preservice teachers (e.g., analysis of their reflections/journal data, teaching portfolios, observations of their implemented behavior during student teaching and initial practicing teaching moments; see Martin, 2004; Middleton, 2001; Tiezzi & Cross, 1997). The implementation of narrative methods over time (e.g., interview or analysis of journal writing, both focused and open-ended, over time) and stimulated recall methods (e.g., reflection on videotaped teaching; Gatbonton, 1999) may help to reconcile the tensions between listening to and hearing teacher voice and the trends we've captured and the models we're developing, as well as between describing existing beliefs and our desire to understand the processes and influence of belief and conceptual change. We argue that in order to truly understand the field of teacher beliefs and knowledge, we need to draw on literatures from across a variety of fields, disciplines, methods, and potentially worldviews in order to find ways to explore, explain, and understand both the convergences and divergences of psychological theory and teacher voice.

Designs that seek to cross boundaries—both methodological and paradigmatic—may begin to synthesize, clarify, or compare the utility and transaction of constructs across theories. Moreover, interdisciplinary work that seeks to synthesize across our individual programs of research and attempts, across traditions, to ground hypotheses, models, and findings within a larger conceptual and theoretical frameworks may help to manage what could be overwhelming complexity. In doing so, we must not loose sight of Parajes' (1992) and Wideen et al.'s (1998) critique that new and revised frameworks need to outline and attempt to systematically capture the constructs we are measuring, to explicate why we are measuring them, and to delineate what we believe are the mechanisms of change lest we be left uncertain about the meaning of complex (and potentially contradictory) findings.

We began this review extending where our predecessors left off, mapping the landscape of the increasingly complex task of teaching. Historically, traditional models in educational psychology, and within the fields of teacher beliefs and knowledge, have tended to focus on intraindividual processes. However, as more distant, larger, and more complex belief structures—those socially shared within a school community or reflective of the political contexts of teaching—exert stronger presses on the teachers nested within those systems, our questions, designs and analyses must begin to explore the nature of interindividual processes in shaping teachers' beliefs and knowledge.

References

Abdal-Haqq, I. (1995). *Making time for teacher professional development (Digest 95-4)*. Washington, DC: ERIC Clearinghouse on Teaching and Teacher Education.

Aguirre, J., & Speer, N. M. (2000). Examining the relationship between beliefs and goals in teacher practice. *Journal of Mathematical Behavior, 18*, 327–356.

Alexander, P. A., Murphy, P. K., & Woods, B. S. (1996). Of squalls and fathoms: Navigating the seas of educational innovation. *Educational Researcher, 25*(3), 31–36, 39.

Alvidrez, J., & Weinstein, R. S. (1999). Early teacher perceptions and later student academic achievement. *Journal of Educational Psychology, 91*, 731–746.

Anderson, L. M. (2001). Nine prospective teachers and their experiences in teacher education: The role of entering conceptions of teaching and learning. In R. Sternberg & B. Torff (Eds.), *Understanding and teaching the implicit mind* (pp. 187–215). Mahwah, NJ: Lawrence Erlbaum Associates.

Arnett, J. J. (2004). *Adolescence and emerging adulthood: A cultural approach, 2nd Edition*. Upper Saddle River, NJ: Prentice Hall.

Avramidis, E., Bayliss, P., & Burden, R. (2000). Student teachers' attitudes toward the inclusion of children with special education needs in the ordinary school. *Teaching and Teacher Education, 16*, 277–293.

Bakari, R. (2003). Preservice teachers' attitudes toward teaching African American students: Contemporary research. *Urban Education, 38*, 640–654.

Ball, D. L., & Bass, H. (2003). Toward a practice-based theory of mathematical knowledge for teaching. In B. Davis & E. Simmt (Eds.), *Proceedings of the 2002 Annual Meeting of the Canadian Mathematics Education Study Group*, (pp. 3–14). Edmonton, AB: CMESG/GCEDM.

Bandura, A. (1993). Perceived self-efficacy in cognitive development and functioning. *Educational Psychologist, 28*, 117–148.

Bandura, A. (1997). *Self-efficacy: The exercise of control*. New York: W.H. Freeman.

Berliner, D. C., & Calfee, R. C. (Eds.). (1996). *Handbook of educational psychology*. New York: Macmillan.

Bibou-Nakou, I., Kiosseoglou, G., & Stogiannidou, A. (2000). Elementary teachers' perceptions regarding school behavior problems: Implications for school psychological services. *Psychology in the Schools, 37*, 123–425.

Bjorklund, D. F. (2005). *Children's thinking: Developmental function and individual differences, fourth edition*. Belmont, CA: Wadsworth/Thompson Learning.

Black, R. S., Sileo, T. W., & Prater, M. A. (2000). Learning journals, self-reflection, and university students' changing perceptions. *Action in Teacher Education, 21*, 71–89.

Blackburn, M. V. (2004). Understanding agency beyond school-sanctioned activities. *Theory Into Practice, 43*, 102–110.

Borko, H., & Putnam, R. (1996). Learning to teach. In D. Berliner & R. Calfee (Eds.), *Handbook of educational psychology* (pp. 673–708). New York: Macmillan.

Bronfenbrenner, U. (1986). Ecology of the family as a context for human development: Research perspectives. *Developmental Psychology, 22*, 723–742.

Brophy, J. (1996). *Teaching problem students*. New York: The Guilford Press.

Brophy, J., & McCaslin, M. (1992). Teachers' reports of how they perceive and cope with problem students. *Elementary School Journal, 93*, 3–68.

Brown, D. F. (2004). Urban teachers' professed classroom management strategies: Reflections of culturally responsive teaching. *Urban Education, 39*, 266–289.

Brown, S., & McIntyre, D, (1993). *Making sense of teaching*. Buckingham, England: Open University Press.

Bullough, R. V., & Baughman, K. (1997). *First-year teacher eight years later: An inquiry into teacher development*. New York: Teachers College Press.

Bullough, R. V. Jr., & Pinnegar, S. (2001). Guidelines for quality in autobiographical forms of self-study. *Educational Researcher, 30*(3), 13–21.

Bussis, A., Chittenden, E., & Amarel, M. (1976). *Beyond the surface curriculum: An interview study or teachers' understandings*. Boulder, CO: Westview Press.

Butler, R. (2000). Making judgments about ability: The role of implicit theories of ability in moderating interferences from temporal and social comparison information. *Journal of Personality and Social Psychology, 78*, 965–978.

Calderhead, J. (1996). Teachers: Beliefs and knowledge. In D. Berliner & R. Calfee (Eds.), *Handbook of educational psychology* (pp. 709–725). New York: Macmillan.

Cantrell, P., Young, S., & Moore, A. (2003). Factors affecting science teaching efficacy of preservice elementary teachers. *Journal of Science Teacher Education, 14*(3), 177–192.

Caprara, G. V., Barbaranelli, C., Borgogni, L., & Steca, P. (2003). Efficacy beliefs as determinants of teahcers' job satisfaction. *Journal of Educational Psychology, 95*, 821–832.

Cardelle-Elawar, M., & Nevin, A. (2003). The role of motivation in strengthening teacher identity: Emerging themes. *Action in Teacher Education, 25*, 48–58.

Carter, K. (1993). The place of story in the study of teaching and teacher education. *Educational Researcher, 22*(1), 5–12.

Causey, V. E., Thomas, C. D., & Armento, B. J. (2000). Cultural diversity is basically a foreign term to me: the challenges of diversity for preservice teacher education. *Teaching and Teacher Education, 16*, 33–45.

Center, D. B., & Wascom, A. M. (1986). Teacher perceptions of social behavior in learning disabled and socially normal children and youth. *Journal of Learning Disabilities, 19*, 420–425.

Chang, L. (2003). Variable effects of children's aggression, social withdrawal, and prosocial leadership as functions of teacher beliefs and behaviors. *Journal of Educational Psychology, 74*, 535–548.

Cimbricz, S. (2002, January 9). State-mandated testing and teachers' beliefs and practice. *Education Policy*

Analysis Archives, 10(2). Retrieved August 19, 2004, from http://epaa.asu.edu/epaa/v10n2.html

Clark, C., & Peterson, P. (1986). Teachers' thought processes. In M. Wittrock (Ed.), *Handbook of research on teaching* (3rd ed., pp. 255–296). New York: Macmillan.

Coladarci, T. (1992). Teachers' sense of efficacy and commitment to teaching. *Journal of Experimental Education, 60,* 323–337.

Coladarci, T., & Breton, W. (1997). Teacher efficacy, supervision, and the special education resource-room teacher. *Journal of Educational Research, 90,* 230–239.

Cole, D. A, Gondoli, D. M., & Peeke, L. G. (1998). Structure and validity of parent and teacher perceptions of children's competence: A multitrait-multimethod-multigroup investigation. *Psychological Assessment, 10,* 241–249.

Danielwicz, J. (1997). *Teaching selves: Identity, pedagogy, and teacher education.* Albany: State University of New York Press.

Davis, H. A. (2003). Conceptualizing the role and influence of student–teacher relationships on children's social and cognitive development. *Educational Psychologist, 38,* 207–234.

Davis, H. A. (in press). Capturing and constructing connections in middle school: Exploring the contexts of student-teacher relationship quality. *Elementary School Journal.*

Davis, H. A., Ashley, S, M., & Couch, K. N. (2003, August). *Middle school teachers' conceptions of their relationships with their students.* Paper presented at the Annual Conference of the American Psychological Association, Toronto, Canada.

Davis, H. A., Hartshorne, R., Hayes, S., & Ring, G. (2003, August). *Developing an "innovative" identity: Pre-service teachers' beliefs about technology and innovation.* Paper presented at the Annual Conference of the American Psychological Association, Toronto, Canada.

De Corte, E., Greer, B. & Verschaffel, L. (1996). Mathematic teaching and learning. In D. C. Berliner & R. C. Calfee (Eds.), *Handbook of educational psychology* (pp. 491–549). New York: Macmillan.

Delpit, L. (1988). The silenced dialogue: Power and pedagogy in educating other people's children. *Harvard Educational Review, 58,* 280–293.

Delpit, L. (1995). *Other people's children: Cultural conflict in the classroom.* New York: New Press.

Delpit, L. (2003). Educators as "seed people" growing a new future. *Educational Researcher, 7,* 14–21.

De Vries, Y., & Beijaard, D. (1999). Teachers' conceptions of education: A practical knowledge perspective on "good" teaching. *Interchange, 30,* 371–397.

Dixson, A. D. (2003). "Let's do this!" Black women teachers' politics and pedagogy. *Urban Education, 38,* 217–235.

Donohue, K. M., Weinstein, R. S., Cowan, P. A., & Cowan, C. P. (2000). Patterns of teachers' whole-class perceptions and predictive relationships between teachers' and parents' perceptions of individual child competence. *Early Childhood Research Quarterly, 15,* 279–305.

Downing, J. E., Eichinger, J., & Williams, L. J. (1997). Inclusive education for students with severe disabilities: Comparative views of principals and educators at different levels of implementation. *Remedial and Special Education, 18,* 133–142.

Dweck, C. (2002). The development of ability conceptions. In A. Wigfield & J. Eccles (Eds.), *The development of achievement motivation.* San Diego, CA: Academic Press.

Eagley, A. H., & Chaikin, S. (1993). *The psychology of attitudes.* Fort Worth, TX: Harcourt Brace Jovanovich College.

Easter, L. M., Shultz, T., Neyhart, K., & Reck, U. R. (1999). Weighty perceptions: A study of the attitudes and beliefs of preservice teacher education students regarding diversity and urban education. *Urban Review, 31,* 205–220.

Emmer, E., & Hickman, J. (1991). Teacher efficacy in classroom management. *Educational and Psychological Measurement, 51,* 755–765.

Evertson, C., & Weinstein, C. S. (Eds.) (2006). *Handbook for classroom management: Research, practice, and contemporary issues.* Mahwah, NJ: Lawrence Erlbaum.

Fenstermacher, G. (1994). The knower and the known: The nature of knowledge in research on teaching. In L. Darling-Hammond (Ed.), *Review of research in education* (Vol. 20, pp. 1–54). Washington, DC: American Educational Research Association.

Festinger, L. (1957). *A theory of cognitive dissonance.* Evanston, IL: Row, Peterson.

Finders, M. (1997). *Just girls: Hidden literacies and life in junior high.* New York: Teachers College Press.

Finkelstein, B. (2001). Is adolescence here to stay? Historical perspectives on youth and education. In T. Urdan & F. Pajares (Eds.) *Adolescence and education: General Issues in the education of adolescents, Vol. 1 (pp. 1–32).* Greenwich, CT: Information Age Publishing.

Firestone, W., Mayrowetz, D., & Fairman, J. (1998). Performance-based assessments and instructional change: The effects of testing on policy, attitudes, and achievement. *Educational Evaluation and Policy Analysis, 20*(2), 95–113.

Floden, R. E. (1995). Confrontation of teachers' entering beliefs. *ATE Newsletter 28*(6), 4.

Freeman, D. (2002). The hidden side of the work: Teacher knowledge and learning to teach. *Language Teaching, 35,* 1–13.

Gallup, G. Jr., and Proctor, W. (1984). *Forecast 2000.* New York: William Morrow.

Garriott, P. P., Miller, M., & Snyder, L. (2003). Preservice teachers' beliefs about inclusive education: What should teacher educators know? *Action in Teacher Education, 25*(1), 48–54.

Gatbonton, E. (1999). Investigating experienced ESL teachers' pedagogical knowledge. *Modern Language Journal, 83,* 35–50.

Gay, G., & Howard, T. (2000). Multicultural teacher education for the 21st century. *Teacher Educator, 36*(1), 1–16.

Ghaith, G., & Yaghi, H. (1997). Relationships among experience, teacher efficacy, and attitudes toward the implementation of instructional innovation. *Teaching and Teacher Education, 13*(4), 451–458.

Gibson, S., & Dembo, M., (1984). Teacher efficacy: A construct validation. *Journal of Educational Psychology, 76,* 569–582.

Gilbert, S. L. (1997). The "four commonplaces of teaching": Prospective teachers belief about teaching in urban schools. *Urban Education, 30*(3), 290–305.

Goddard, R. D. (2001). Collective efficacy: A neglected construct in the study of schools and student achievement. *Journal of Educational Psychology, 93*(3), 467–476.

Goddard, R. D., & Goddard, Y. L. (2001). A multilevel analysis of the relationship between teacher and collective efficacy in urban schools. *Teaching and Teacher Education, 17*, 807–818.

Goddard, R. D., Hoy, W. K. & Woolfolk Hoy, A. (2004). Collective efficacy beliefs: Theoretical developments, empirical evidence, and future directions. *Educational Researcher, 33*(3), 3–13.

Goddard, R. D., LoGerfo, L., & Hoy, W. K. (2004). High school accountability: The role of perceived collective efficacy. *Educational Policy, 18*(3), 403–435.

Gould, l. (2000). Changes in preservice teachers' schema for understanding teaching. *Action in Teacher Education, 21*(4), 90–100.

Graham, S. (1994). Motivation in African Americans. *Review of Educational Research, 64*, 55–117.

Grant, S. G. (2000, February). Teachers and tests: Exploring teachers' perceptions of changes in the New York State-mandated testing program. *Educational Policy Analysis Archives, 8*(14). [Retrieved] from: http://epaa.asu.edu/epaa/v8n14.html oct.28,2004.

Gregoire, M. (2003). Is it a challenge or a threat? A dual process model of teachers' cognition and appraisal processes during conceptual change. *Educational Psychology Review, 15*, 147–179.

Gregoire, M., Ashton, P., & Algina, J. (2004). Changing preservice teachers' beliefs about teaching and learning in mathematics: An intervention study. *Contemporary Educational Psychology, 29*, 164–186.

Hastings, R. P., & Oakford, S. (2003). Student teachers' attitudes towards the inclusion of children with special needs. *Educational Psychology, 23*, 87–94.

Hauser-Cram, P., Sirin, S. R., & Stipek, D. (2003). When teachers' and parents' values differ: Teachers' ratings of academic competence in children from low-income families. *Journal of Educational Psychology, 95*, 813–820.

Henson, R. K. (2002). From adolescent angst to adulthood: Substantive implications and measurement dilemmas in the development of teacher efficacy research. *Educational Psychologist, 37*, 137–150.

Ho, I. T., & Hau, K. T. (2004). Australian and Chinese teachers efficacy: Similarities and differences in personal instruction, discipline, guidance efficacy and beliefs in external determinants. *Teaching and Teacher Education, 20*, 313–323.

Hoffman, D. M. (1996). Culture and self in multicultural education: Reflections on discourse, text and practice. *American Educational Research Journal, 33*, 545–569.

Howard, T. C., & Denning del Rosario, C. (2000). Talking race in teacher education: The need for racial dialogue in teacher education programs. *Action in Teacher Education, 21*, 127–137.

Hoy, W. K. (2001). The Pupil Control studies: A historical, theoretical, and empirical analysis. *Journal of Educational Administration, 39*, 424–442.

Hoy, W. K., Sweetland, S. R., & Smith, P. A. (2002). Toward an organizational model of achievement in high schools: The significance of collective efficacy. *Educational Administration Quarterly, 38*, 77–93.

Jackson, P. (1968). *Life in classrooms.* New York: Holt, Rinehart, and Winston.

Jackson, R. K., & Leroy, C. A. (1998). Eminent teachers' views on teacher education and development. *Action in Teacher Education, 20*(3), 15–29.

Jarvis, S. A., Schonert-Reichl, K. A., & Krivel-Zacks, G. (2000, April). *Teachers' (mis)conceptions of early adolescence.* Paper presented at the annual meeting of the American Educational Research Association, New Orleans, LA.

Johnson, L. (2002). "My eyes have been opened": White teachers and racial awareness. *Journal of Teacher Education, 53*(2), 153–167.

Johnson, J., McKeown, E., & McEwen, A. (1999). Choosing primary teaching as a career: The perspectives of males and females in training. *Journal of Education for Teaching, 25*, 55–64.

Jones, B. D., & Egley, R. J. (2004). Voices from the frontlines: Teachers' perceptions of high-stakes testing. *Education Policy Analysis Archives, 12*(39). Retrieved August 16, 2004, from http://epaa.asu.edu/epaa/v12n39/

Jones, E. B., Young, R., & Rodriguez, J. L. (1999). Identity and career choice among Mexican American and Euro-American preservice bilingual teachers. *Hispanic Journal of Behavioral Sciences, 21*, 431–446.

Jordan, A., Lindsay, L., & Stanovich, P. (1997). Classroom teachers' instructional interactions with students who are exceptional, at risk, and typically achieving. *Remedial and Special Education, 18*(2), 82–93.

Kagan, D. (1992). Implications of research on teacher belief. *Educational Psychologist, 27*, 65–90.

Kane, R, Sandretto, S., & Heath, C. (2002). Telling half the story: A critical review of research on the teaching beliefs and practices of university academics. *Review of Educational Research, 72*, 177–228.

Kennedy, M. M. (1998). Education reform and subject matter knowledge. *Journal of Research in Science Teaching, 35*, 249–263.

Kessen, W. (1979). The American child and other cultural inventions. *American Psychologist, 34*, 815–820.

Kilpatrick, J. Swafford, J. & Findell, B. (Eds.) (2001). *Adding it up: Helping children learn mathematics.* Washington, DC: Mathematics Learning Study Committee, Center for Education, Division of Behavioral and Social Sciences and Education, National Academy Press.

Knobloch, N. A., & Whittington, M. S. (2002). Novice teachers' perceptions of support, teacher preparation quality, and student teacher experience related to teacher efficacy. *Journal of Vocational Educational Research, 27*(3), 331–341.

Korthagen, F. A. J. (2004). In search of the essence of a good teacher: Towards a more holistic approach in teacher education. *Teaching and Teacher Education, 20,* 77–97.

Korthagen, F. A. J., Kessels, J., Koster, B., Lagerwerf, B., & Wubbles, T. (2001). *Linking practice and theory: The pedagogy of realistic teacher education.* Mahwah, NJ: Lawrence Erlbaum Associates.

Kumashiro, K. (2004). Uncertain beginnings: Learning to teach paradoxically. *Theory Into Practice, 43,* 111–115.

Labone, E. (2004). Teacher efficacy: Maturing the conscrut through research in alternative paradigms. *Teaching and Teacher Education, 20,* 341–359.

Ladson-Billings, G. (2000). Fighting for our lives: Preparing teachers to teach African American students. *Journal of Teacher Education, 51*(3), 206–214.

Ladson-Billings, G. (2001). *Crossing over to Canaan: The journey of new teachers in diverse classrooms.* San Francisco: Jossey-Bass.

Lawrence, S., & Tatum, B. D. (1997). Teachers in transition: The impact of antiracist professional development on classroom practice. *Teachers College Record, 99,* 162–178.

Levitt, K. E. (2001). An analysis of elementary teachers' beliefs regarding the teaching and learning of science. *Science Education, 86,* 1–22.

Lewis, A. E. (2001). There is no "race" in the schoolyard: Colorblind ideology in an (almost) all White school. *American Educational Research Journal, 38*(4), 781–811.

Lieber, J., Capell, K., Sandall, S. R., Wolfberg, P., Horn, E., & Beckman, P. J. (1998). Inclusive preschool programs: Teachers' beliefs and practices. *Early Childhood Research Quarterly, 13*(l), 87–105.

Lortie, D. (1975). *Schoolteachers: A sociological study.* Chicago: University of Chicago Press.

Manouchehri, A, & Goodman, T. (2000). Implementing mathematics reform: The challenge within. *Educational Studies in Mathematics, 42,* 1–34.

Marshall, P. L. (1999). Teachers' racial identity and the single course in multicultural education. *Action in Teacher Education, 20,* 56–69.

Martin, S. D. (2004). Finding balance: Impact of classroom management conceptions on developing teacher practice. *Teaching and Teacher Education, 20,* 405–422.

McCaslin, M., & Good, T. L. (1996). The informal curriculum. In D. C. Berliner & R.C. Calfee (Eds.), *Handbook of educational psychology* (pp. 622–670). New York: Macmillan.

McCutcheon, G. (1992). Facilitating teacher personal theorizing. In E. W. Ross, J. W. Cornett, and G. McCutcheon (Eds.), *Teacher personal theorizing* (pp. 191–206). Albany: State University of New York Press.

McDevitt, T. M., & Ormrod, J. E. (2002). *Child development and education.* Upper Saddle River, NJ: Merrill/Prentice-Hall.

McLeskey, J. & Waldron, N. L. (2002). Inclusion and school change. Teacher perceptions regarding curricular and instructional adaptations. *Teacher Education and Special Education, 25*(1), 41–54.

Meister, D. G., & Melnick, S. A. (2003). National new teacher study: Beginning teachers' concerns. *Action in Teacher Education, 24*(4), 87–94.

Middleton, V. A. (2002). Increasing preservice teachers' diversity beliefs and commitment. *The Urban Review, 34,* 343–361.

Milner, H. R. (2003). Teacher reflection and race in cultural contexts: History, meaning, and methods in teaching. *Theory into Practice, 42*(3), 173–180.

Milner, H. R., & Woolfolk Hoy, A. (2003). A case study of an African American Teacher's self-efficacy, stereo-type threat, and persistence. *Teaching and Teacher Education 19,* 263–276.

Muijs, D., & Reynolds, D. (2001). Teacher beliefs and behavior: What really matters. *Journal of Classroom Interaction, 37,* 3–15.

Mulholland, J., & Wallace, J. (2001). Teacher induction and elementary science teaching: Enhancing self-efficacy. *Teaching and Teacher Education, 17,* 243–261.

Munby, H., Russell, T., & Martin, A. K. (2001). Teachers' knowledge and how it develops. In V. Richardson (Ed.), *Handbook of research on teaching* (4th ed., pp. 877–904). Washington, DC: American Educational Researcher.

Murphy, P. K., Delli, L. A. M., & Edwards, M. N. (2004). The good teacher and good teaching: Comparing beliefs of second grade students, pre-service teachers, and inservice teachers. *The Journal of Experimental Education, 72,* 69–92.

National Council of Teachers of Mathematics (2000). *Principles and standards for teaching school mathematics.* Reston, VA: Author.

National Research Council (1995). *National science education standards.* Washington, DC: National Academy of Sciences.

Oldfather, P., & Thomas, S. (1998). What does it mean when high school teachers participate in collaborative research with students on literacy motivations? *Teachers College Record, 99,* 617–691.

Oosterhof, A. (1999). *Developing and using classroom assessments* (2nd ed.) Columbus, OH: Merrill.

Pajares, F. (1992). Teachers' beliefs and educational research: Cleaning up a messy construct. *Review of Educational Research, 62,* 307–332.

Pajares, F., & Bengston, J. K. (1995). The psychologizing of teacher education: Formalist thinking and preservice teachers' beliefs. *Peabody Journal of Education, 70,* 83–98.

Pajares, F., & Graham, L. (1998). Formalist thinking and language arts instruction: Teachers' and students' beliefs about truth and caring in the teaching conversation. *Teaching and Teacher Education, 14,* 855–870.

Pang, V., & Sablan, V. (1998). Teacher efficacy: How do teachers feel about their abilities to teach African American students? In M. Dilworth (Ed.), *Being responsive to cultural differences: How do teachers learn?* (pp. 39–60). Thousand Oaks, CA: Corwin Press.

Patrick, H., & Pintrich, P. R. (2001). Conceptual change in teachers' intuitive conceptions of learning, motivation, and instruction: The role of motivational and epistemological beliefs. In: Torff, B., and Sternberg, R. J. (Eds.), *Understanding and teaching the intuitive mind: Student and teacher learning* (pp. 117-143). Mahwah, NJ: Lawrence Erlbaum Associates.

Pigge, F., & Marso, R. (1997). A seven-year longitudinal multi-factor assessment of teaching concerns development through preparation and early years of teaching. *Teaching and Teacher Education, 13,* 225-235.

Plourde, L. A. (2002). The influence of student teaching on pre-service elementary teachers' science self-efficacy and outcome expectancy beliefs. *Journal of Instructional Psychology, 29,* 245-253.

Pohan, C. A. & Aguilar, T. E. (2001). Measuring educators' beliefs about diversity in personal and professional contexts. *American Educational Research Association, 38,* 159-182.

Reeve, J. (1998). Autonomy support as an interpersonal motivating style: Is it teachable? *Contemporary Educational Psychology, 23,* 312-330.

Reynolds, M. (Ed.) (1989). *Knowledge base for the beginning teacher.* Washington, DC: American Association of Colleges for Teacher Education.

Richardson, V. (1996). The role of attitudes and beliefs in learning to teach. In J. Sikula (Ed.), *Handbook of research on teacher education* (2nd ed., pp. 102-119). New York: Macmillan.

Richardson, V., & Placier, P. (2001). Teacher change. In V. Richardson (Ed.), *Handbook of research on teaching* (4th ed., pp. 905-947). Washington, DC: American Educational Research Association.

Riggs, I., & Enochs, L. (1990). Toward the development of an elementary teacher's science teaching efficacy belief instrument. *Science Education, 74,* 625-638.

Robinson, S. (2002). Teaching high school students with learning and emotional disabilities in inclusion science classrooms: A case study of four teachers' beliefs and practices. *Journal of Science Teacher Education, 13*(1), 13-26.

Ross, J. A. (1994). The impact of an inservice to promote cooperative learning on the stability of teacher efficacy. *Teaching & Teacher Education, 10* (4), 381-394.

Ross, J. A. (1995). Strategies for enhancing teachers' beliefs in their effectiveness: Research on a school improvement hypothesis. *Teachers College Record, 97,* 227-252.

Ross, J. A. (1998). The antecedents and consequences of teacher efficacy. *Advances in Research on Teaching, 7,* 49-73.

Ross, J. A., McDougall, D., & Hogaboam-Gray, A. (2002). Research on reform in mathematics education, 1993-2000. *Alberta Journal of Educational Research, 48* (2), 122-138.

Sacks, C. H., & Mergendoller, J. R. (1996). The relationship between teachers' theoretical orientation toward reading and student outcomes in kindergarten children with different initial reading abilities. *American Educational Research Journal, 34,* 721-739.

Saft, E., & Pianta, R. (2001). Teachers' perceptions of their relationships with students: Effects of child age, gender, and ethnicity of teachers and children. *School Psychology Quarterly, 16,* 5-14.

Schraw, G., & Olafson L., (2002). L. J., Teachers' epistemological world views and educational practice. *Issues in Education: Contributions from Educational Psychology, 8*(2), 99-148.

Schutz, A., & Moss, P. A. (2004). Reasonable decisions in portfolio assessment: Evaluating complex evidence of teaching. *Education Policy Analysis Archives, 12*(3). Retrieved August 16, 2004 from http://epaa.asu.edu/epaa/v12n33/

Schutz, P. A., Crowder, K. C., & White, V. E. (2001). The development of a goal to become a teacher. *Journal of Educational Psychology, 93,* 299-308.

Scruggs, T. E., & Mastropieri, M. A. (1996). Teacher perceptions of mainstreaming/inclusion, 1955-1995: A research synthesis. *Exceptional Children, 63,* 59-74.

Shechtman, A., & Or, A. (1996). Applying counseling methods to challenge teacher beliefs with regard to classroom diversity and mainstreaming: An empirical study. *Teaching and Teacher Education, 12,* 137-147.

Shuell, T. J. (1996). The role of educational psychology in the preparation of teachers. *Educational Psychologist, 31,* 15-22.

Shulman, L. S., & Quinlan, K. (1996). The comparative psychology of school subjects. In D. Berliner & R. Calfee (Eds.), *Handbook of educational psychology* (pp. 399-422). New York: Macmillan.

Soodak, L. C. & McCarthy, M. R. (2006). Classroom management in inclusive settings. In C. S. Evertson & C. S Weinstein (Eds.), *Handbook for classroom management: Research, practice, and contemporary issues* (pp. 461-489). Mahwah, NJ: Lawrence Erlbaum Associates.

Soodak, L. & Podell, D. (1996). Teaching efficacy: Toward the understanding of a multi-faceted construct. *Teaching and Teacher Education, 12,* 401-412.

Soodak, L. C., Podell, D. M., & Lehman, L. R. (1998). Teacher, student, and school attributes as predictors of teachers' responses to inclusion. *Journal of Special Education, 31*(4), 480-497.

Stanford, G. C. (1998). African-American teachers' knowledge of teaching: Understanding the influence of their remembered teachers. *Urban Review, 30,* 229-243.

Staub, F. C., & Stern, E. (2002). The nature of teachers' pedagogical content beliefs matters for students' achievement gains: Quasi-experimental evidence for elementary mathematics. *Journal of Educational Psychology, 94,* 344-355.

Sternberg, R. J. (1996). *Successful intelligence.* New York: Simon & Schuster.

Stipek, D. (2003). *Motivation to learn* (4th ed). Boston: Allyn & Bacon.

Stipek, D. J., Givvin, K. B., Salmon, J. M., & MacGyvers, V. L. (2001). Teachers' beliefs and practices related to mathematics instruction. *Teaching and Teacher Education, 17,* 213-226.

Stodolsky, S. S., & Grossman, P. L. (1995). The impact of subject matter on curricular activity: An analysis of five academic subjects. *American Educational Research Journal, 32,* 227-249.

Stodolsky, S. S., & Grossman, P. L. (2000). Changing students, changing teaching. *Teachers' College Record, 102*, 125-172.

Stone, C. A., & Lane, S. (2003). Consequences of a state accountability program: Examining relationships between school performance gains and teahers, student, and school variables. *Applied Measurement in Education, 16*, 1-26.

Strauss, S. (1996). Confessions of a born-again constructivist. *Educational Psychologist, 31*, 15-22.

Stritikus, T. T. (2003). The interrelationship of beliefs, context, and learning: The case of a teacher reacting to language policy. *Journal of Language, Identity, and Education, 2*(1), 29-52.

Sugrue, C. (1996). Student teachers' lay theories: Implications for professional development. In I. F. Goodson, & A. Hargreaves (Eds.), *Teachers' professional lives* (pp. 154-177). Washington, DC: Farmer Press.

Talburt, S. (2004). Constructions of LGBT youth: Opening up subject positions. *Theory Into Practice, 43*, 116-121.

Tatum, B. D. (1994). Teaching white students about racism: The search for white allies and the restoration of hope. *Teachers College Record, 95*, 462-476.

Tatum, B. D. (1997). *"Why are all the Black kids sitting together in the cafeteria?" and other conversations about race.* New York: Basic Books.

Taylor, S. V., & Sobel, D. (2001). Addressing the discontinuity of students' and teachers' diversity: A preliminary study of preservice teachers' beliefs and perceived skills. *Teaching and Teacher Education, 17*, 487-503.

Tiezzi, L. J., & Cross, B. E. (1997). Utilizing research on prospective teacher's beliefs to inform urban field experiences. *The Urban Review, 29*, 113-125.

Tschannen-Moran, M. & Barr, M. (2004). Fostering student achievement: The relationship between collective teacher efficacy and student achievement. *Leadership and Policy in Schools, 3*, 187-207.

Tschannen-Moran, M., & Woolfolk Hoy, A. (2001). Teacher efficacy: Capturing and elusive construct. *Teaching and Teacher Education, 17*, 783-805.

Tschannen-Moran, M., Woolfolk Hoy, A., & Hoy, W. K. (1998). Teacher efficacy: Its meaning and measure. *Review of Educational Research, 68*, 202-248.

Urdan, T., Midgley, C., & Wood, S. (1995). Special issues in reforming middle level schools. *Journal of Early Adolescence, 15*, 9-37.

Vartuli, S. (1999). How early childhood teacher beliefs vary across grade level. *Early Childhood Research Quarterly, 14*, 489-514.

Walberg, H. (1977). Decision and perception: New constructs for research on teaching effects. *Cambridge Journal of Education, 7*(1), 12-20.

Wentzel, K. R. (1999). Social-motivational processes and interpersonal relationships: Implications for understanding motivation at school. *Journal of Educational Psychology, 91*, 76-97.

Wheatley, K. F. (2002). The potential benefits of teacher efficacy doubts for educational reform. *Teaching and Teacher Education, 18*, 5-22.

Wideen, M, Mayer-Smith, J., & Moon, B. (1998). A critical analysis of the research on learning to teach: Making the case for an ecological perspective on inquiry. *Review of Educational Research, 68*, 130-178.

Wigfield, A., Galper, A., Denton, K., & Seefeldt, C. (1999). Teachers' beliefs about former Head Start and non–Head Start first-grade children's motivation, performance, and future educational prospects. *Journal of Educational Psychology, 91*, 98-104.

Wood, E. (2004). A new paradigm war? The impact of national curriculum policies of early childhood teachers' thinking and classroom practices. *Teaching and Teacher Education, 20*, 361-374.

Woolfolk Hoy, A., & Burke-Spero, R. (2005). Changes in teacher efficacy during the early years of teaching: A comparison of four measures. *Teaching and Teacher Education.*

Woolfolk Hoy, A., & Murphy, P. K. (2001). Teaching educational psychology to the implicit mind. In R. Sternberg & B. Torff (Eds.), *Understanding and teaching the implicit mind* (pp. 145-185). Mahwah, NJ: Lawrence Erlbaum Associates.

Woolfolk Hoy, A., & Weinstein, C. S. (2006). Students' and teachers' perspectives about classroom management. In C. Evertson & C. S. Weinstein (Eds.), *Handbook for classroom management: Research, practice, and contemporary issues* (pp. 181-219). Mahwah, NJ: Lawrence Erlbaum Associates.

Zohar, A., Degani, A., & Vaaknin, F. (2001). Teachers' beliefs about low achieving students and higher order thinking. *Teaching and Teacher Education, 17*, 469-485.

THE DESIGN OF POWERFUL LEARNING
ENVIRONMENTS

Ton de Jong
Jules Pieters
University of Twente

In the recent past, the objectives of learning have changed quite fundamentally, from remembering to application, from factual knowledge to insight, from skills to competencies, and from algorithmic procedures to generalizable approaches. As a result, learning environments have also changed fundamentally, for example, from designer-driven drills and tutorials to self-directed, embedded, scientific discovery environments. Technology has changed the opportunities for design in such a way that new gadgets and properties such as interactivity, dynamic graphs, simulations, and games have become available (Bransford, Brown, & Cocking, 1999). Technology has also changed the roles of designers and users (teachers, trainers, and learners). All of this goes together with new theoretical insights that put an emphasis on social cognition, cognitive load, guided discovery learning, metacognition, and motivation. The consequences of these developments for educational design will be discussed in this chapter. They are the use of "powerful learning environments," changing models of instructional (educational) design, the emergence of new types of design tools, and a changing role for the designer.

CHARACTERISTICS OF POWERFUL
LEARNING ENVIRONMENTS

New types of (online) learning environments are rapidly becoming available for use in the actual classroom. Trends that nowadays dominate the field of learning and instruction are *constructivism, situationism,* and *collaborative learning* (de Jong, 2003). More specifically, we can say that the new view on learning entails that learners are encouraged to *construct their own knowledge* (instead of copying it from an authority, be it a book or a teacher), *in realistic situations* (instead of merely decontextualized, formal situations such as the classroom), *together with others* (instead of on their own). These new trends have not emerged spontaneously; they are based on changing epistemological views.

First, knowledge is no longer seen as something that is solely assessed in relation to an external objectivistic "truth," but also as possibly *individually flavored* and thus potentially different between people. Second, these individual understandings are exchanged between professionals who seek for mutual comprehension and agreement. In this respect knowledge has a strong *social character*. Third, we have started to value knowledge that is *applicable in realistic situations*, and thus is not restricted to abstract knowledge. These developments are most strongly emphasized in the social constructivist view that integrates the social and contextualized approaches on learning, and emphasizes the socially and culturally situated context of cognition (see Brown, Collins, & Duguid, 1989; Lave & Wenger, 1991).

Learning environments that incorporate the characteristics just mentioned are often called *powerful learning environments* (de Corte, Verschaffel, Entwistle, &

van Merriënboer, 2003). Powerful learning environments have been defined in many ways, and many different types of powerful learning environments exist, but as a common denominator we can say that these types of environments promote active and constructive learning and typically present opportunities for collaborative activities. In addition, powerful learning environments often offer a learning experience in the context of a real situation (van Merriënboer & Paas, 2003). In this way powerful learning environments follow the trends sketched earlier: constructive, collaborative, and situated learning.

Another important aspect of powerful learning environments is that they "stretch" the cognitive capacities of learners by adding specific types of support (called *cognitive tools* or *cognitive scaffolds*). These cognitive tools or cognitive scaffolds support learners in pivotal cognitive processes such as planning their learning process, making sense of data from an experiment, or setting up hypotheses (Linn, Bell, & Davis, 2004; Quintana et al., 2004). By using cognitive tools or scaffolds, powerful learning environments aim at extending the cognitive power of the individual learner, and can be considered as "partners in cognition" instead of "delivery systems of information" (Salomon, Perkins, & Globerson, 1991). In this view, cognitive tools or scaffolds are mechanisms or devices to promote, support, and facilitate knowledge acquisition and construction, and the practice of skill. Within powerful learning environments, these tools aim to invite, to inspire, and to encourage learners to participate in the learning challenges offered by the environment.

Though this is not necessarily the case, we see that technology can play a major role in implementing these powerful learning environments. Constructivism is supported by computer environments such as hypertexts or hypermedia (Jonassen & Mandl, 1990), concept mapping (Novak, 1998), simulation (de Jong, 2005; de Jong & van Joolingen, 1998), and modeling tools (Colella, 2000; Penner, 2001). Realistic situations can be brought into the classroom by means of video, as was, for example, done in the Jasper series (CTGV, 1997); inquiry learning is stimulated in simulation-based environments as, for example, in GenScope (Hickey, Kindfield, Horwitz, & Christie, 2003; Hickey & Zuiker, 2003), ThinkerTools (White, 1993), and SimQuest-based environments (van Joolingen & de Jong, 2003); and collaborative learning is supported in Internet-based learning environments such as Belvedere (Suthers, Weiner, Connelly, & Paolucci, 1995), Knowledge Forum (Scardamalia & Bereiter, 1993), and WISE (Linn, Davis, & Bell, 2004).

All of these environments contain cognitive tools or scaffolds that support learners in performing the required cognitive processes. SimQuest applications, for example, have several possibilities to support learners. Examples are a so-called hypothesis scratchpad, a software instrument that helps learners to state hypotheses from combinations of variables, relations, and conditions (van Joolingen & de Jong, 2003), and a "monitoring tool" that helps learners in keeping track of all experiments they have been doing (Veermans, de Jong, & van Joolingen, 2000). Elaborate overviews of cognitive tools or scaffolds specifically for inquiry learning, have recently been presented by Quintana et al. (2004) and Linn, Bell, and Davis (2004).

AN EXAMPLE OF A POWERFUL LEARNING ENVIRONMENT

An example of a powerful learning environment for collaborative inquiry learning in science domains is Co-Lab (van Joolingen, de Jong, Lazonder, Savelsbergh, & Manlove, 2005). In Co-Lab, the major characteristics of powerful learning environments are united. First, the constructive aspect is evident in the inquiry and modeling facilities of Co-Lab. Second, Co-Lab is a collaborative environment in that it offers possibilities for sharing experiences and objects (experiments, models) and presents learners with communication facilities. Third, problems within Co-Lab are presented within a real life context (e.g., water management), making Co-Lab suited for situated learning. Finally, Co-Lab offers learners a set of cognitive tools that are meant to expand the learners' cognitive capacities (e.g., the so-called process coordinator that helps learners to plan their inquiry process).

The Co-Lab environment consists of "buildings" (e.g., a "greenhouse effect" building), and each building consists of floors (e.g., a "black sphere" floor). Each floor has a similar layout and consists of a "hall," a "lab room," a "theory room," and a "meeting room." In Co-Lab, three learners work in collaboration. In the hall, learners find a general assignment (a mission statement) for the particular floor. In the lab room, learners can collect data by running simulations, operating remote laboratories, or inspecting (remote) databases. Figure 32.1 shows the Co-Lab interface with a view of the lab room. The outer edge of this figure displays the stationary part of the interface. This is the set of available tools for a specific room, a control management tool organizing and displaying the position of the learners in the building, a control tool for distributing and organizing the control over the interfaces and tools, a chat box, and a repository where learners can store states of the system (e.g., simulation states or intermediate models that they created). The upper right area displays a particular room (hall, meeting room, theory room, or

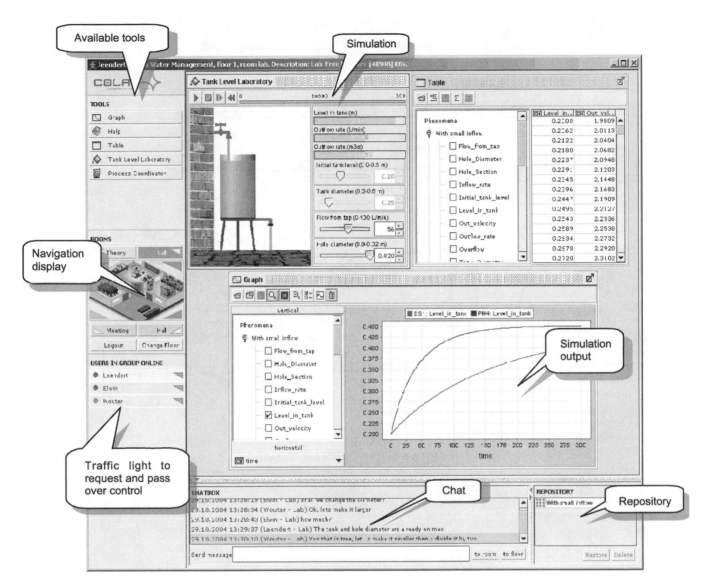

FIGURE 32.1. A Co-Lab interface, with a focus on the lab room.

lab room) at a floor in the Co-Lab building. In Fig. 32.1, an example of a lab room is depicted.

In this particular example a simulation of a water tank is shown. Learners can manipulate a number of variables such as the diameter of the tank and the initial level of water. They can also observe a number of output variables in different ways (e.g., numeric values, graphs). In the example shown, two tanks are compared and the level of water in the two tanks is depicted in the graph. The lab room can also hold databases or remote laboratories. An example of such a remote laboratory is a miniature greenhouse, with living plants. From a distance, learners can open the windows of the greenhouse, turn on a light, and collect data on the level of oxygen and carbon monoxide in the greenhouse over time. Learners use the informa-

tion from the lab room to create runnable models using a dedicated modeling tool in the theory room. From their observations learners can create a model of, in this case, the water tank in the theory room. For this they use a modeling tool that is based on system dynamics; an example of a model as created by learners is presented in Fig. 32.2. With the help of this modeling tool, learners can smoothly and gradually move from qualitative to quantitative modeling. The outcome of the self-created model can be compared with the outcomes of the experiments in the lab room.

In the meeting room, learners plan and monitor their work with the help of a so-called process coordinator. This process coordinator helps learners organize and plan their work in phases, organize their data, generate

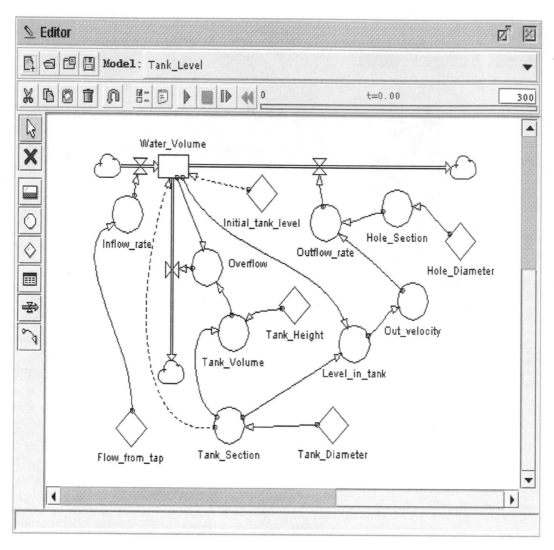

FIGURE 32.2. Example of a learner-created model in Co-Lab.

reports, and the like. Co-Lab buildings can be seen as prototypical examples of powerful learning environments. The next question is how these types of environments are designed and if the traditional design models still hold. These questions are be explored in the next sections.

MODELS OF INSTRUCTIONAL DESIGN

Instructional design models are on the verge of undergoing a substantial change. The traditional linear models based on predetermined goals, objectives, and instructional strategies will be replaced by models expressing a genuine parallel process directed by tasks, activities, and tools. This change is stimulated by the changes in learning environments, with an emphasis on powerful learning environments as discussed in the preceding section and by a changing view of the instructional design process.

A Historical Perspective on Instructional Design

Two kinds of historical developments with regard to instructional design can be discerned. The first historical line pertains to the procedures and principles of designing learning events in instructional environments, prescribed by so-called models of instructional design. These models provide the designer with theoretical and empirical devices by which a learning event can be designed and planned, given an analysis of a learning problem. These models are based on and influenced by the learning theory or approach that is embraced by the designer. Often these theories and approaches were influenced by the application of psychological learning principles. In the history of instructional design, the prevailing learning theories and their applications determined the design and development of learning events, ranging from general approaches in psychology (e.g., behaviorism, cognitivism), to comprehensive learning theories (e.g., conditioning, discovery learning), to specific approaches emphasizing different aspects of the learning process (e.g., task analysis).

The second historical line can be called the evolution of instructional systems design and development. These models provide means and methods for designers of instructional systems, by which designers follow a number of steps to come to a solution of an instructional problem. The history of educational technology from which instructional systems design models originate has been described by Anglin (1995) and recently by Reiser and Dempsey (2002). The developments within this field can be exemplified by successive types of models. The very first model of educational technology only included media selection. The emphasis was on delivery systems.

The second model of educational technology started with defining objectives in order to design instructional materials appropriately. The instructional designer only designed and constructed, without evaluation or implementation. Further task analysis was introduced in order to formulate specific goals for designing (Jonassen, Tessmer, & Hannum, 1999), with less emphasis on needs analysis and evaluation. Models like this one contained rules and algorithms that can be acquired within several weeks. Next, the standard instructional systems design model was introduced, containing needs analysis and evaluation, formative as well as summative. The ADDIE approach is an example of this type of designing. ADDIE stands for Analysis, Design, Development, Implementation, and Evaluation and is a combination of various instructional systems design models, described by researchers such as Dick and Carey (1990), Gagné, Briggs, and Wager (1992), and Smith and Ragan (1999).

The most recent model of educational technology is a systemic model with an emphasis on socially oriented systems thinking. Not only are educational theories and results of research used in this model, the designer is also aware of the social structure of the system in which the solution will be implemented. There is also a clear difference between this model and the previous models: Instruction is not always seen as the solution. During needs assessment and needs analysis it should become evident what the problem is. On the basis of the results the instructional designer and the client can collaboratively decide whether an instructional solution will be chosen or some other solution, for instance, changes in job structure or in the organization of the work.

A Changing View on the Educational Design Process

The empirical basis of instructional systems design models is limited. Usually, these models have been validated only by expert appraisal and by practical experience. According to Wilson and Jonassen (1991), empirically derived knowledge about the problem-solving heuristics of professional instructional systems designers is generally lacking, which is also confirmed by a perceived gap between theoretical models and the practical realities of instructional design (see, e.g., Gros, Elen, Kerres, van Merriënboer, & Spector, 1997; Holcomb, Wedman, & Tessmer, 1996). As a result, Perez and Emery (1995) concluded that instructional systems design models normally describe what designers should think and do rather than what designers actually think and do. A second aspect that normally is not incorporated in the classical design models is the individual differences between educational designers.

Empirical studies that were conducted in the 1990s showed that there are considerable individual differences among instructional designers, partly depending on their professional expertise (e.g., Gayeski, 1990; Greeno, Korpi, Jackson, & Michalchik, 1990; Perez & Emery, 1995; Pieters & Bergman, 1995; Rowland, 1992). These studies demonstrated that experts differ from novice designers in the way they design and deal with instructional design problems. In addition, domain expertise might also influence the way designers develop their instructional material (see, e.g., Reigeluth, 1999).

A summary of conclusions from these studies shows that, on the one hand, experts rapidly design a solution, often as a result of immediately perceiving the solution from their substantial experience. Potential solutions can also decrease the problem space for experts. On the other hand, expert knowledge is not always beneficial; it sometimes limits the designer in the number of solutions, meaning that no new and unexpected solutions will be presented. Results from a study by Rowland (1992) confirm these observations. He also noted that experts design iteratively, sometimes opportunistically, not delaying solution attempts (complete understanding is considered to be unattainable).

The main characteristic of the classic approaches to instructional systems design as presented earlier is solving instructional problems according to a general idea of problem solving in which problems are decomposed and solved following a number of consecutive stages: problem analysis, solution generation, and evaluation and implementation of the solution. However, as indicated, research on designing instruction by experts provided evidence that experts differ from novice designers in approaching instructional problems (Pieters & Bergman,

1995; Rowland, 1992). Broadbent (1973) and Goel and Pirolli (1992) concluded from reviews of the literature that designing consists of two components: a logical element, as described earlier, and a creative element. In most existent models, the logical element of the design is emphasized and the creative element of design, so characteristic of experts, is forgotten.

The awareness that the design process may not be logical and linear has the implication to consider design as an ill-defined problem. Several studies were performed to get a better view of the design process. Both novices (e.g., students) and experts (e.g., practitioners and professional designers) exhibit a pattern of designing instruction that is far more complicated than models suggest, and sometimes the process contains short-circuited paths (Holcomb et al., 1996; Perez & Emery, 1995). As a consequence, the actual design process can be characterized as being *parallel* and *nonlinear*.

A *parallel design process* means that alternative solutions are being considered simultaneously. Designers act by developing solution schemes that can be applied in different sequences and for different purposes dependent on the situation. Schön (1987) had already introduced alternative views such as the solution-driven approaches and the reflection-in-action approach, further elaborated by Schön and Wiggens (1992) and Oxman (1999). In the first approach, designers adopt a mode of problem solving that is solution driven. Designers think more in terms of solutions rather than in terms of problems. Their approach is not systematically based, but they immediately react to stimuli in the design environment. The reflection-in-action approach is far from systematically based, but is oriented toward knowing-in-action. Designers develop situative theories while acting in a world of practice. These situative theories are an integration of scientific principles, experience, and intuitions, closely connected to the situation of designing, and are developed through working in a very situated context. This design expertise is fed back into the design process. With this approach there is less emphasis on rational, problem-solving activities, but more emphasis on the situative and hence also social and relational interactions between designer and user or learner.

A second important characteristic of an expert design process is its *nonlinearity*. Many normative models have a linear structure. Even when intermediate regressions are allowed, these models basically remain linear, like, for example, the Dick and Carey (1990) design model. These approaches are characterized by the *waterfall methodology*, a top-down approach of designing: The output of the previous phase is the input of the following phase. Each phase is characterized by a couple of specific actions. The following are to be distinguished: needs assessment and needs analysis (including problem definition, and problem analysis), design, construction of a prototype, tryout, evaluation and revision, and implementation. The waterfall methodology seems powerful and logical, like the decomposition of subgoals, and is systematic, predictable, and easy to use. Instructional design practice however shows the opposite. Studies in the 1990s by, among others, Goel and Pirolli (1992) and Perez and Emery (1995) reveal that the process of designing instruction consists of consecutively or concurrently executed tasks, in which power and duration are individually and situationally determined.

With more emphasis on the prior knowledge and constructive power of the learner in recent learning theories, more emphasis on the individual expertise of designers is required by design theory (Oxman, 2004). Tessmer and Wedman (1995) suggest that to bridge the gap between theory and practice, descriptive rather than prescriptive models should be followed, taking into account the way designers actually design and the need for the design of more powerful learning environments.

The Design of Powerful Learning Environments

The instructional design process is also influenced by the product that is being designed. Instructional design aims at developing events or environments that initiate learning processes. Learning can be accomplished by different mechanisms that are implemented in instructional designs. Farnham-Diggory (1994) identified three important learning mechanisms: incrementation, perturbation, and acculturation. The first mechanism is active in the presentation and acquisition of information by the learner, leading to an increase in knowledge. The second mechanism pertains to the situation in which a learner is confronted with a challenging situation that calls for a solution. This confrontation forces the learner to reconceptualize already acquired or constructed knowledge and to apply these reconceptualizations in order to solve the designated problems. Often this process is referred to as *conceptual change*. The third learning mechanism refers to an active learner who is introduced to a new culture of practice. Actions are required to be performed by the learner. These three mechanisms are the heart of approaches for learning: the presentation approach, the exploration approach, and the action approach. These three generic approaches comprise the instructional strategies and tactics to be generally applied by instructors and by designers of learning.

The *presentation approach*, aiming at incrementation and originating from traditional instructional design and outcomes of cognitive psychological research, pertains to the presentation of information and the practice of skill. This approach is used very often in instructional design. Its effectiveness is based on the notion of phases introduced by Fitts and Posner (1969) in the acquisition of psychomotor skills and further elaborated by Anderson (1982) for the acquisition of cognitive skills. Van Merriënboer's (1997) 4C/ID model is an extension of these ideas and provides applications in instruction and training. Three phases are to be distinguished. In the first phase, the early or cognitive phase, learners try to understand the task and its demands. Instruction provides information relevant to performing the task and further conceptualizes the performance by presenting new information. During this early phase, instruction controls learning through a directive format. In the second phase, the associative or intermediate phase, learners are expected to practice the acquired skills.

Instruction can be given through several schedules of practice (e.g., massed or distributed) and determines the proper sequence in which the relevant components are practiced, either as a whole or separately. Research (van Merriënboer, 1997; van Merriënboer, Jelsma, & Paas, 1992) revealed that the schedules of practice are strongly related to the transfer of training. The third and final phase, the autonomous phase, is recognized by a compiled performance of component processes or skills. This automization, or fast proceduralization through compilation of declarative knowledge, can be postponed by well-chosen practice schedules. Postponement leads to schematization (i.e., to chunks or schemes) that will increase far transfer. Learning is taking place in a context that is separated from the eventual task execution. Tasks are to be analyzed and are taught step-by-step according to a predefined plan. The structuring of the learning process is controlled by the program, instructor, teacher or trainer and is triggered by performing (sub)tasks, not by carrying out assignments. Effective examples of this approach can be found in Merrill's contributions to instructional design theory (Merrill & ID2ResearchGroup, 1998) and in the 4C/ID model by Van Merriënboer (1997).

The *exploration approach*, which aims at perturbation and originates from cognitive psychology and constructivism, supports and guides learners toward inquiry learning and to experimentation. During exploration, hypotheses will be generated, analyzed, and tested. For instance, during a (computer) simulation learners explore the model of the process that is under study and used in the simulation. Learners generate a hypothesis and will analyze hypotheses while using their prior knowledge. The simulation is used to test the hypothesis. Successful hypothesis testing will extend the knowledge of the model. Further, generating and testing in new situations from different perspectives will lead to generalization of acquired knowledge and skills.

Some examples of this approach have already been presented in the first part of this chapter. Also, the principles of conceptual change are worth mentioning as relating to the perturbation approach. Vosniadou's (1992) research on children's conceptions of the Earth and of astronomy showed that these conceptions can be changed by reconstructing underlying mental models.

The *action approach*, aimed at acculturation and originating from research on constructivism, collaborative learning, and situationism, starts with performing in a realistic context. The acquisition of additional information is supported and learning is further amplified by articulation and reflection. Rules valid for vicarious learning and for learning-by-doing are active in these environments.

This kind of learning closely resembles (cognitive) apprenticeship learning and is based on the premise that learning knowledge or skills takes place in the context of their intended use. Brown et al. (1989) identified three essential activities: modeling, coaching, and fading. During apprenticeship training, learners perform with support (by modeling and coaching) that is gradually withdrawn (called fading). As in real apprenticeship, skills have to be mastered in order for instruction to be effective. Unlike real apprenticeship, training has to be concerned with acceleration of learning. In traditional apprenticeship, novices performed useful work; they were not primarily intended to learn specific prescribed skills. Other groups of strategies are assumed to be active: articulation and reflection—focused on making learners aware of their own cognitive and metacognitive activities; and exploration and experimentation—aiming at autonomous problem solving.

A related conception introduced by Schön (1987) is called *practicum*. A practicum is a setting designed for learning and practice. In a context that approximates a practice world, Schön assumes that learners learn by doing, although their doing usually falls short of real-world work. They learn by performing projects that simulate and simplify practice, or they work on real-world projects under close supervision. The practicum is considered by Schön a virtual world, relatively free of the pressures, distractions, and risks of the real one, to which, nevertheless, it refers.

Although the first and second approach can be full of learning power, especially in specific domains for which these approaches are very relevant, the third approach is often referenced in powerful learning environments. These environments, as explained earlier, can be defined by their constructive, situative, and collaborative character. These three characteristics are integrated in the acculturation approach. Taking powerful learning environments and the action approach as starting points means that traditional instructional design that aimed at the identification and classification of learning goals and the design and development of a delivery system that instructs learners to achieve these goals should be changed. In this traditional design approach, most of the resulting products were directive in nature, implying that the emphasis was on teaching and not on learning.

Powerful learning environments have changed this situation. Whereas in the expository mode of teaching the decisions on the context and structure of the information are fully in control of someone or something external to the learner, in powerful learning environments, learners are expected to take more initiative. An intriguing design issue concerns the balance between allowing freedom and giving direction to learners. Related to this, in models meant for expository teaching, is the role of goals and subgoals that learners are required to achieve. In powerful learning environments the (sub)goals are less clear beforehand. As in discovery learning, an emphasis is on learners' increasing responsibility for their own knowledge construction process. The designer does not need to specify in detail one path from start-state to end-state. In most existing models, however, the determination of detailed (sub)goal is central, and this influences all other activities by the designer. Giving freedom to the learner also requires goals to be defined by the learner (de Jong, 2005). Since traditional design models are not geared toward these new developments related to control for the learner, alternative design models and tools are necessary that put the (realistic) learning situation and not the learning goals in the pivot.

ALTERNATIVE DESIGN MODELS

Alternative design models only sparsely make their way into the instructional design world. New developments have found their inspiration to some degree in software engineering. De Hoog, de Jong, and de Vries (1994), for example, describe an alternative design model that is based on a model from software engineering: Boehm's spiral model (Boehm, 1988). Its main characteristics are evolutionary development and reduction of risk. In this spiral model, parallel development is possible, since different parts of the system to be developed can be in different stages of development. To start with, only the highest priority features should be recognized, defined, and implemented. After a step in the development has been taken, feedback from users can be collected (see also Quintana, Krajcik, & Soloway, 2003). With the knowledge that is fed back, designers can then return to define and implement

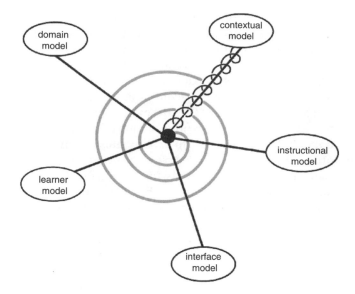

FIGURE 32.3. The web structure of a model for the design of discovery learning environments (de Hoog et al., 1994).

more features. This results in an evolutionary approach rather than an incremental one.

As a follow-up to Boehm's spiral model, de Hoog et al. (1994) described the development process as a web structure (Fig. 32.3) consisting of global and local spirals. The global development spiral represents the development state of all partial models, and thus gives a view of the total design process. Local development spirals indicate the development of a specific part of the instructional system. Designers can start with any specific part-model and at any point in time specific models can be in different stages of development. A check and control system takes care of the balance and the tuning of the different models (de Hoog et al., 1994).

In Fig. 32.3, for example, five different models are distinguished that together constitute the learning environment to be developed. The domain model describes the content of the system, the contextual model describes the situations that are used, the learner model describes the view on the learner's (developing) knowledge and skills, the instructional model contains the instructional strategy and cognitive tools, and, finally, the interface model specifies the interface (in the case of a computer program) that the learner will see. There is no specific starting point in the instructional design. A designer who has a good idea of the interface and/or the context may start with designing this and only later design the domain model that underlies it. There is evolutionary design in the way that feedback from learners who use intermediate products (or information from one of the other models being developed) may change the design of a specific model. For example, if during the design the designer finds that some required learning processes are not within the skill range of learners, new cognitive tools may be defined in the instructional model. This web-structured model of design has been made concrete in the SimQuest authoring environment (Kuyper, de Hoog, & de Jong, 2001; van Joolingen & de Jong, 2003; see also later discussion).

Another instructional systems design methodology that has its roots in software engineering is rapid prototyping. Tripp and Bichelmeyer (1990) and Moonen (1996) described this methodology as a parallel process of analysis, synthesis, and evaluation that creates prototypes that are then tested, and that may or may not evolve into a final product. The prototyping method combines the rational, problem-solving type of designing with a socially oriented approach in which designers and clients (e.g., teachers and learners) cooperate to reach agreement on the final design. In several iterative stages, these participants can negotiate on the temporary outcomes. Through the involvement of relevant participants in the design process, commitment to the final design can gradually and incrementally be achieved.

Prototyping further has the advantage that at the beginning of the design process there is no need for full and complete determination of technical specifications. These will also gradually develop during the design process by negotiating and even constructing in cooperation, as shown in several studies (see Lathi, Seitamaa-Hakkarainen, & Hakkarainen, 2004; Wilson, 1999). Participatory design in which designers and users cooperate to the extent that roles become less explicit and less mutually exclusive encompasses these characteristics, and is successful in various domains of designing. It originated as the Collective Resource Approach from design projects in Scandinavia, and found its applications in various design domains (Schuler & Namioka, 1993). It already has applications in learning and communication design as well (Fischer & Ostwald, 2003). The integration of rational and social constructive characteristics makes designing powerful learning environments an effective and productive enterprise (de Corte et al., 2003).

DESIGN TOOLS

Changing learning environments and changing instructional design processes also influence the tools that are used in instructional design (Hannafin, 1995). There are two developments that are of importance. The first is that authoring environments have changed and follow a more "spiral" approach, as described earlier, in which learning goals have a less prominent place. The second, and related, development is the use of so-called learning objects in instructional design.

There exists an abundant set of authoring tools and authoring systems, though many of the systems are not widely used and never outlasted the prototype stage (Gros & Spector, 1994). Basically, authoring tools (or AID systems, or ID tools) are meant to support the designer in the analysis, design, and production of (computerized) instructional systems. Authoring systems are used for two reasons. First, they ensure quality of the instructional systems produced by defining expert templates of instructional transactions (Merrill & ID2ResearchGroup, 1998) or instructional strategies (Ainsworth, Grimshaw, & Underwood, 1999). Second, authoring tools are also meant to accelerate the design and production process and thus make it cheaper. Overviews of authoring environments can, for example, be found in Tennyson (1992), de Jong and Sarti (1994), Tennyson and Baron (1995), van den Akker, Branch, Gustafson, Nieveen, and Plomp (1999), and Murray, Blessing, and Ainsworth (2003). Authoring systems may focus on the different aspects of the design process: the initial analysis phases, the layout of the instructional scenario, or the production of the course material. Authoring tools tend to neglect the first phases of the instructional design process (Chapman, 1995) and provide more support for the design and the production phases, with, however, some notable exceptions (McKenney & van den Akker, 2005).

Whatever the emphasis is, traditional authoring systems always take the learning objectives as their starting point, examine characteristics of learners and the domain, and from there decide on the appropriate teaching strategy (Goodyear, 1992). The resulting instructional systems always have a traditional instructive type of approach. The basic elements are presenting information (in whatever media form), asking (multiple choice) questions, providing feedback, and branching learners through the material on the basis of their responses. In this way, even the more open, simulation-based learning environments do get a step-by-step and closed character (see e.g., Merrill, 2003). In the earlier approaches just mentioned, authoring systems placed the emphasis on optimizing *design processes* (see for example, Goodyear, 1995). Although some claim that in older approaches a nonlinear way of working is also possible (Gustafson, 2002), this nonlinearity mainly means the possibility to reiterate but does not include parallel developments. New developments concentrate on flexible, parallel, sequences of design steps and on reusing structures and content, which often go hand in hand.

The idea of *reuse* is emphasized in the *learning objects* approach (Duncan, 2003). Basically, this means that authors can reuse (smaller) parts of existing learning environments or self-standing smaller parts and "glue" them together in a new learning environment. This, of course, implies that a component is *designed for reuse*, meaning that at both technical and conceptual (pedagogical and content) levels, reuse is possible. With respect to *content*, authors and teachers quite often have specific ideas about what should be included in course or lesson content, which creates a demand for adaptation. This adaptation may range from almost complete replacement of the content to the change of specific symbols or other items. Adaptation of *instructional design* components will, for example, be possible by setting parameters in the component (e.g., for a multiple choice question the number of alternatives can be set) or by even setting parameters for the complete instructional strategy as is, for example, possible in REDEEM (Ainsworth et al., 1999, 2003). Jigsawing learning objects with a specific instructional design and, possibly, a specific content also answers the need for a more spiral, open, design process.

De Jong, van Joolingen, Veermans, and van der Meij (2005) present an example in the form of the authoring language SimQuest in which object-oriented design of powerful learning environments has been put into practice. In SimQuest, both the use of learning objects and a spiral design methodology are supported. SimQuest (van Joolingen & de Jong, 2003) is an authoring system for the design of learning environments for guided discovery learning. In SimQuest the authors have libraries with building blocks at their disposal. These building blocks can be elements of a model (e.g., specific relations), an interface (e.g., a gauge), learner guidance (e.g., an assignment), and a learner model (e.g., a daemon signaling specific actions of the learner). Authors select building blocks (objects) from the libraries, fill in or adapt the content, and make connections between the building blocks (for example, to determine the sequence of presentation). This spiral, object-oriented approach is perfectly suited for the design of open, powerful learning environments, because authors do not need to start with learning goals, but can start with interesting situations (interfaces), models, or assignments and gradually link these components together.

In SimQuest, authors can indeed start at any point in the development of the learning environment, very much following the spiral approach as exemplified in Fig. 32.3. An extensive description of the authoring facilities of SimQuest, reuse of learning objects and a spiral methodology, is given in Kuyper et al. (2001). Figure 32.4 illustrates the process. In the figure to the left, a library with SimQuest learning objects is shown; the designer may select objects from here and drag them to the learning environment under construction. Then the learning object can be edited. This means that the content is filled in and parameters (e.g., the number of answer

attempts) can be set. Here also, the object (in the example, an assignment for the learner) is linked to other objects, such as simulation interfaces, underlying model, or other assignments (e.g., a designer may specify that another assignment opens when the learner fails on this one). SimQuest has specific tools for the author (e.g., graphical overviews of all of the relations between learning objects in the learning environment) that help to keep track of the overall quality of the learning environment, as is needed in a spiral approach.

THE DESIGNER

Not only do designers who design powerful learning environments use different methods and tools, but the design context also changes toward a more teamlike effort in which co-design with other designers, and even co-design with learners, plays an important role.

Collaboration in Design

Today, design is no longer an individual endeavor. Designers, differing in domain expertise, cooperate in the design of learning environments. Several studies have been carried out, not so much in instructional design, in which the process of collaboration in designing and its effects are analyzed (Lathi et al., 2004). Designing is generally considered a form of complex problem solving, and cooperation in designing can be treated in the same way as cooperation in complex problem solving (Goel, 1995; Hennessy & Murphy, 1999). Studies revealed that collaboration is not effective in every design context in which designers cooperate. It can be time-consuming and requires effective management for cooperation (Chiu, 2002). Effective communication among designers is also crucial, in particular reflective communication where designers not only share the design object, but also share the design activities (Stempfle & Badke-Schaub, 2002). Collaboration in designing is effective when designers differ in their expertise on parts of the design process and the design product but are prepared to share their expertise in carrying out the design task. Support for collaboration is crucial as well (Seitamaa-Hakkarainen, Raunio, Raami, Muukkonen, & Hakkarainen, 2001). In their study, these authors developed a system for communicative support that consisted of a knowledge-building tool and a shared discussion space. They also used shared graphic representations that were integrated in jam-sessions in which designers quickly interact and communicate and developed designs. Seitamaa-Hakkarainen et al. (2001) noticed

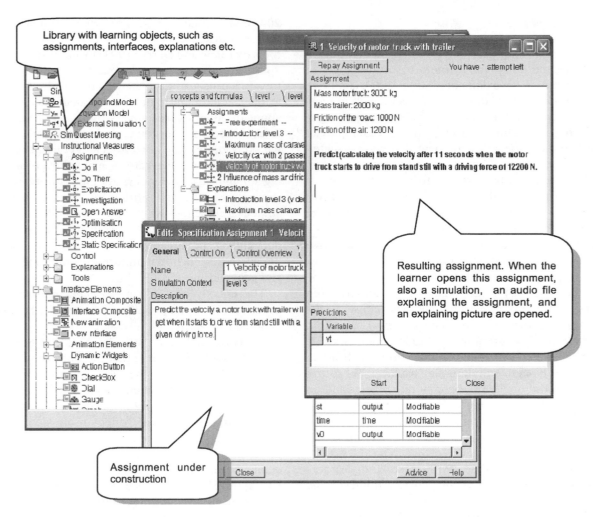

FIGURE 32.4. Example of an authoring action from the SimQuest authoring environment.

positive results as to the effectiveness of the design process and of the resulting products.

Participatory design, already outlined, is a concept referring to collaboration in design processes. It refers to the involvement of users in the process of designing, which means that not only designers are involved but also the intended users. In the domain of instructional design, this implies not only teachers or instructors as intended users but also learners. The concept of teachers as designers is very common in education. Teachers cooperating in teams in order to design a curriculum, a learning environment or learning material is less common. Hoogveld, Paas, and Jochems (2003) did a study in which working in teams was compared to individual instructional design. Results revealed that collaboration outperformed individual work regarding the designs that were made. Differences among teachers/designers were

also apparent. Low individual achievers profited more from collaborative work than high individual achievers did. High team achievers performed better in a team than as individuals. Teachers working together with designers are still rare, but with the expansion of technological opportunities for both communication and designing, collaboration will become effective.

Virtual collaboration of designers, teachers, and learners is a promising future in which authoring tools and knowledge objects can be exchanged and shared in a global learning environment. The Co-Lab example presented earlier can be illustrative for this virtual collaboration. In Co-Lab also a teacher and/or designer may take a place in the learning situation, shaping the learning environment online together with the learners. In this way role diffusion among designers, teachers, and learners is taking place.

Learners as Designers

In recent years much more emphasis has been put on the self-directed ability of learners to be designers of their own learning environments (Glaser, 2000; Liu, 1998; Nesset & Large, 2004). In particular, as a result of technological innovations, learners were able to apply cognitive tools for paving their learning paths. An example can be found in the Co-Lab environment that was presented in the section dealing with a powerful learning environment. Here learners have access to a so-called process coordinator that helps them set their own (collaborative) learning goals and lets them outline for themselves the route toward achieving these goals.

Self-direction in learning has appeared at least in two different ways. The first one pertains to the control over the learning process, transferred from the teacher to the learner. Shuell (1996) described the differences between teachers as initiators of learning and learners who take the lead in this process. The second view is quite old but has recently gained new and full attention (Kafai & Resnick, 1996; Perkins, 1996). In this approach, learners are invited to be active in designing artifacts. These artifacts may, on the one hand, be concrete objects and on the other hand, be learning artifacts, in the case of one learner designing instruction for another learner. This latter situation may eventually lead to learners designing their own learning.

In self-directed learning of the first kind, learners achieve certain learning outcomes by executing specific learning functions. These functions can be initiated by the teacher, as in traditional instruction, or by the learner, as in self-directed or self-regulative learning. Shuell (1996) recognized the major role of learning functions. He described 10 functions, from expectations to experimentation and synthesis. Each function is an essential part of the learning process and is related to cognitive, metacognitive, and affective activities a teacher or a learner may execute. The learning functions are to be compared to the instructional events or agents, referring to the various stages of the transformation of information and the regulation of this process of transformation. Shuell's functions are headed by three main functions related to cognitive, metacognitive, and affective functions.

In self-directed learning of the second kind, learners act as designers. The activities designers normally perform in developing and producing artifacts are the basics learners need to design relevant artifacts such as concrete objects: for example, making games in Logo projects (see Kafai & Resnick, 1996), designing experiments for hypothesis testing (de Jong & van Joolingen, 1998), creating flying objects (de Vries, van der Meij, Pieters, & Boersma,

2003), or learning artifacts by using thinking tools like the ones described by Perkins (1986, 1996), cognitive tools by Lajoie and Derry (1993) or mindtools (Jonassen, 2000). These *learners as designers* activities are directed toward letting learners engage in more mindful activities, leading to more meaningful and transferable knowledge about the domain that covers these activities. The self-directed activities needed to design and create are essential skills for defining objectives and content of learning, such as generating alternatives, making decisions, searching for information, understanding, classifying, and assessing, ordering, and storing information, for defining strategies and choosing resources and information, such as searching for information, collecting information, understanding, and organizing information, and for evaluating outcomes, such as monitoring, comparing, planning, and generalizing.

The effectiveness of this *learners as designers* approach has been empirically demonstrated by a number of studies by Kafai and Resnick (1996), under the heading of constructionism, and also rhetorically supported by Perkins' (1986) finding that the only people who significantly benefit from the design process and the use of tools were the designers, not the learners. Similarly, learners will benefit more from their own design activities than from those carried out by professionals or teachers as designers. Kafai and Resnick (1996) noticed that in the Game Design Project, each design had a considerable impact on the students' learning and thinking. Liu (1998) showed that learners became more intrinsically motivated and more self-confident, and their design knowledge improved. In a recent study, Vreman-de Olde and de Jong (2004) demonstrated the potential effectiveness of learners as designers of their own learning in a computer simulation environment.

SUMMARY AND CONCLUSION

In this chapter we have taken the design of powerful learning environments as our starting point. We have defined powerful learning environments as environments that have a constructivistic, collaborative, and situated character and that support the learners in their learning process by making cognitive tools or scaffolds available. Within this broad characterization, different specific views on powerful learning environments exist that emphasize aspects such as learners being active, constructive, collaborative, intentional, conversational, and reflective (Jonassen, Peck, & Wilson, 1999) or having the opportunity to make mistakes and receive feedback on these mistakes (Schank & Neaman, 2001). In all definitions, however, the learning environment is complex and contextual (Jonassen, Peck, et al., 1999).

The comprehensive nature of powerful learning environments has as a consequence that instructional design decisions normally do not follow a single theoretical approach but are based on a multitude of approaches and ideas. Hannafin and Land (1997), for example, present a broad set of characteristics of powerful learning environments (or as they call it, "technology-enhanced student-centered learning environments") together with the underlying theoretical assumptions and guidelines for design. Similar overviews can be found in CTGV (1997), Linn et al. (2004), and Quintana et al. (2004). The theoretical approach that underpins powerful learning environment is eclectic and includes elements from theories on social cognition, cognitive load, guided discovery learning, metacognition, and motivation.

Another characteristic of powerful learning environments is that they are not exclusively built around learning goals, but also start from appealing and challenging situations that are relevant for experts or practioners. These situations, problems, and issues form the anchor point for the learning environment to be designed and thus for the instructional design process (Jonassen, 1998). In the design of the Jasper series (CTGV, 1997), for example, authentic problems were taken as the pivots around which learning activities were organized. Also, for the Co-Lab environment discussed earlier, themes or topics (such as the greenhouse effect and water management) were the starting points for the design of the learning environment and not detailed specific learning goals. Co-Lab was designed in a process in which different developers designed different parts of the system concurrently, using a common platform to reach and maintain conceptual and technical integrity. During the development several intermediate versions were tested extensively with learners. Feedback from these studies was used to improve Co-lab (van Joolingen et al., 2005).

These characteristics of powerful learning environments have as an implication that traditional instructional design models that only take learning goals as the basis for further design and that strictly follow one theoretical approach are not appropriate. More flexible design models that take the specific needs of learners into account are needed. Spiral models (de Hoog et al., 1994; Kuyper et al., 2001) that allow designers to start at any point in the instructional design process and do not necessarily take learning goals as a start are clearly suited for the design of powerful learning environments. New, technology-based design tools, using learning objects, that support the spiral design approach and that focus on integrity in a complex learning environment are emerging (see, e.g., Kuyper et al., 2001). These authoring environments also support the collaborative design of learning environments by teams of authors.

For the future, further progress in authoring systems for flexible, spiral-based design methods seems necessary. In this context it is important to note that not all learning should or must take place in powerful learning environments. Traditional environments are still valid, but the type of knowledge that is acquired differs from the knowledge acquired in powerful learning environments. Nonaka and Takeuchi .(1995) have convincingly argued that there is a range of knowledge characteristics with associated instructional approaches and that an adequate curriculum combines the appropriate approaches in a balanced and timely manner. The flexibility of spiral design methods make these methods suited for the design of curricula that hold a diversity of learning and teaching approaches.

References

Ainsworth, S., Grimshaw, S., & Underwood, J. (1999). Teachers implementing pedagogy through REDEEM. *Computers & Education, 33*, 171–187.

Ainsworth, S., Major, N., Grimshaw, S. K., Hayes, M., Underwood, J. D., Williams, B., et al. (2003). REDEEM: Simple intelligent tutoring systems from usable tools. In T. Murray, S. Blessing, & S. Ainsworth (Eds.), *Authoring tools for advanced technology educational software: Toward cost-effective production of adaptive, interactive, and intelligent educational software* (pp. 205–232). Dordrecht, The Netherlands: Kluwer Academic.

Anderson, J. R. (1982). Acquisition of cognitive skill. *Psychological Review, 89*, 369–403.

Anglin, G. J. (1995). *Instructional technology: Past, present, and future* (2nd ed.). Englewood, CO: Libraries Unlimited.

Boehm, B. W. (1988). A spiral model of software development and enhancement. *IEEE Computer, 21*, 61–72.

Bransford, J. D., Brown, A. L., & Cocking, R. R. (Eds.). (1999). *How people learn: Brain, mind, experience, and school.* Washington, DC: National Academy Press.

Broadbent, G. (1973). *Design in architecture: Architecture and the human sciences.* London: Wiley.

Brown, J. S., Collins, A., & Duguid, P. (1989). Situated cognition and the culture of learning. *Educational Researcher, 18*, 32–42.

Chapman, B. L. (1995). Accelerating the design process: A tool for instructional designers. *Journal of Interactive Instructional Development, 8,* 8–15.

Chiu, M. L. (2002). An organizational view of design communication in design collaboration. *Design Studies, 23,* 187–210.

Colella, V. (2000). Participatory simulations: Building collaborative understanding through immersive dynamic modeling. *Journal of the Learning Sciences, 9,* 371–400.

CTGV. (1997). *The Jasper project; Lessons in curriculum, instruction, assessment, and professional development.* Hillsdale, NJ: Lawrence Erlbaum Associates.

de Corte, E., Verschaffel, L., Entwistle, N., & van Merriënboer, J. J. G. (Eds.). (2003). *Powerful learning environments: Unravelling basic components and dimensions.* Oxford: Elsevier Science.

de Hoog, R., de Jong, T., & de Vries, F. (1994). Constraint driven software design: An escape from the waterfall model. *Performance Improvement Quarterly, 7,* 48–63.

de Jong, T. (2003). Changing views on knowledge and knowledge acquisition and the role of technology. In J. Searle, I. Yashin-Shaw, & D. Roebuck (Eds.), *Enriching learning cultures* (pp. 147–159). Brisbane: Australian Academic Press.

de Jong, T. (2005). The guided discovery principle in multimedia learning. In R. E. Mayer (Ed.), *Cambridge handbook of multimedia learning* (pp. 215–229). Cambridge, UK: Cambridge University Press.

de Jong, T., & Sarti, L. (1994). Trends in the design and production of computer based learning material. In T. de Jong & L. Sarti (Eds.), *Design and production of multimedia and simulation based learning material* (pp. IX–XVI). Dordrecht, The Netherlands: Kluwer Academic.

de Jong, T., & van Joolingen, W. R. (1998). Scientific discovery learning with computer simulations of conceptual domains. *Review of Educational Research, 68,* 179–202.

de Jong, T., van Joolingen, W. R., Veermans, K., & van der Meij, J. (2005). Authoring discovery learning environments: In search for re-usable components. In J. M. Spector, C. Ohrazda, A. van Schaack, & D. A. Wiley (Eds.), *Innovations in Instructional Technology: Essays in Honor of M. David Merrill* (pp. 11–29). Mahwah, NJ: Erlbaum.

de Vries, B., van der Meij, H., Pieters, J. M., & Boersma, K. (2003, Sept. 16–19) *E-mail use in primary schools: Developing a tool for reflective thinking.* Paper presented at the ECER, Hamburg.

Dick, W., & Carey, L. (1990). *The systematic design of instruction* (3rd ed.). New York: Harper Collins College.

Duncan, C. (2003). Conceptions of learning objects: Social and educational issues. In A. Littlejohn (Ed.), *Reusing online resources: A sustainable approach to e-learning.* London: Kogan Page.

Farnham-Diggory, S. (1994). Paradigms of knowledge and instruction. *Review of Educational Research, 64,* 463–477.

Fischer, G., & Ostwald, J. (2003). Knowledge communication in design communities. In R. Bromme, F. Hesse & H. Spada (Eds.), *Barriers and biases in computer-mediated knowledge communication.* Dordrecht, The Netherlands: Kluwer Academic.

Fitts, P. M., & Posner, M. I. (1969). *Human performance.* Belmont, CA: Brooks/Cole.

Gagné, R. M., Briggs, L. J., & Wager, W. W. (1992). *Principles of instructional design* (4th ed.). Fort Worth, TX: Harcourt Brace Jovanovich.

Gayeski, D. M. (1990). Are you ready to automate design? *Training & Development Journal, 44,* 61–62.

Glaser, R. (2000). Cognition and instruction: Mind, development, and community. *Journal of Applied Developmental Psychology, 21,* 123–127.

Goel, V. (1995). *Sketches of thought.* Cambridge, MA: MIT Press.

Goel, V., & Pirolli, P. (1992). The structure of design problem spaces. *Cognitive Science, 16,* 395–429.

Goodyear, P. (1992). Foundations for courseware engineering. In R. D. Tennyson (Ed.), *Automating instructional design, development, and delivery* (pp. 7–29). Berlin: Springer Verlag.

Goodyear, P. (1995). Infrastructure for courseware engineering. In R. D. Tennyson & A. E. Baron (Eds.), *Automating instructional design: Computer-based development and delivery tools* (pp. 11–33). New York: Springer-Verlag.

Greeno, J. G., Korpi, M. K., Jackson, D. N. III, & Michalchik, V. S. (1990). *Processes and knowledge in designing instruction* (Tech. Rep. No. GK-3). Palo. Alto, CA: Stanford University.

Gros, B., Elen, J., Kerres, M., van Merriënboer, J., & Spector, M. (1997). Instructional design and the authoring of multimedia and hypermedia systems: Does a marriage make sense? *Educational Technology, 1,* 48–56.

Gros, B., & Spector, J. M. (1994). Evaluating automated instructional design systems: A complex problem. *Educational Technology, 34,* 37–46.

Gustafson, K. (2002). Instructional design tools: A critique and projections for the future. *Educational Technology Research and Development, 50,* 59–66.

Hannafin, M. J. (1995). Open-ended learning environments: Foundations, assumptions, and implications for automated design. In R. D. Tennyson & A. E. Baron (Eds.), *Automating instructional design: Computer-based development and delivery tools* (pp. 101–131). New York: Springer-Verlag.

Hannafin, M. J., & Land, S. M. (1997). The foundations and assumptions of technology-enhanced student-centered learning environments. *Instructional Science, 25,* 167–202.

Hennessy, S., & Murphy, P. (1999). The potential for collaborative problem solving in design and technology. *International Journal of Technology and Design Education, 9,* 1–36.

Hickey, D. T., Kindfield, A. C. H., Horwitz, P., & Christie, M. A. (2003). Integrating curriculum, instruction, assessment, and evaluation in a technology-supported genetics environment. *American Educational Research Journal, 40,* 495–538.

Hickey, D. T., & Zuiker, S. (2003). A new perspective for evaluating innovative science learning environments. *Science Education, 87,* 539–563.

Holcomb, C., Wedman, J. F., & Tessmer, M. (1996). ID activities and project success: perceptions of practitioners. *Performance Improvement Quarterly, 9,* 49–61.

Hoogveld, A. W. M., Paas, F., & Jochems, W. M. G. (2003). Application of an instructional systems design approach by teachers in higher education: Individual versus team design. *Teaching and Teacher Education, 19*, 581–590.

Jonassen, D. H. (1998). Designing constructivist learning environments. In C. M. Reigeluth (Ed.), *Instructional theories and models* (2nd ed., pp. 215–241). Mahwah, NJ: Lawrence Erlbaum Associates.

Jonassen, D. H. (2000). *Mindtools for schools*. New York: Macmillan.

Jonassen, D. H., & Mandl, H. (Eds.). (1990). *Designing hypermedia for learning*. Berlin: Springer.

Jonassen, D. H., Peck, K., & Wilson, B. G. (1999). *Learning with technology: A constructivist perspective*. Columbus, OH: Merrill/Prentice-Hall.

Jonassen, D. H., Tessmer, M., & Hannum, W. H. (1999). *Task analysis methods for instructional design*. Mahwah, NJ: Lawrence Erlbaum Associates.

Kafai, Y. B., & Resnick, M. (Eds.). (1996). *Constructionism in practice: Designing, thinking, and learning in a digital world*. Mahwah, NJ: Lawrence Erlbaum Associates.

Kuyper, M., de Hoog, R., & de Jong, T. (2001). Modeling and supporting the authoring process of multimedia simulation based educational software: A knowledge engineering approach. *Instructional Science, 29*, 337–359.

Lajoie, S. P., & Derry, S. J. (Eds.). (1993). *Computers as cognitive tools*. Hillsdale, NJ: Lawrence Erlbaum Associates.

Lathi, H., Seitamaa-Hakkarainen, P., & Hakkarainen, K. (2004). Collaboration patterns in computer supported collaborative designing. *Design Studies*, 351–371.

Lave, J., & Wenger, E. (1991). *Situated learning: Legitimate peripheral participation*. Cambridge, UK: Cambridge University Press.

Linn, M. C., Bell, P., & Davis, E. A. (2004). Specific design principles: Elaborating the scaffolded knowledge integration framework. In M. Linn, E. A. Davis, & P. Bell (Eds.), *Internet environments for science education*. Mahwah, NJ: Lawrence Erlbaum Associates.

Linn, M. C., Davis, E. A., & Bell, P. (Eds.). (2004). *Internet environments for science education*. Mahwah, NJ: Lawrence Erlbaum Associates.

Liu, M. (1998). A study of engaging high-school students as multimedia designers in a cognitive apprenticeship-style learning environment. *Computers in Human Behavior, 14*, 387–415.

McKenney, S., & van den Akker, J. (2005). Computer-based support for curriculum designers: A case of developmental research. *Educational Technology Research and Development, 53*, 41–66.

Merrill, M. D. (2003). Using knowledge objects to design instructional learning environments. In T. Murray, S. Blessing, & S. Ainsworth (Eds.), *Authoring tools for advanced technology educational software: Toward cost-effective production of adaptive, interactive, and intelligent educational software* (pp. 181–204). Dordrecht, The Netherlands: Kluwer Academic.

Merrill, M. D., & ID2ResearchGroup. (1998). ID Expert: A second generation instructional development system. *Instructional Science, 26*, 243–262.

Moonen, J. (1996). Prototyping as a design method. In T. Plomp & D. Ely (Eds.), *International encyclopedia of educational technology* (pp. 186–190). Oxford: Pergamon.

Murray, T., Blessing, S., & Ainsworth, S. (Eds.). (2003). *Authoring tools for advanced technology educational software: Toward cost-effective production of adaptive, interactive, and intelligent educational software*. Dordrecht, The Netherlands: Kluwer Academic.

Nesset, V., & Large, A. (2004). Children in the information technology design process: A review of theories and their applications. *Library & Information Science Research, 26*, 140–161.

Nonaka, I., & Takeuchi, H. (1995). *The knowledge-creating company: How Japanese companies create the dynamics of innovation*. New York: Oxford University Press.

Novak, J. D. (1998). *Learning, creating and using knowledge: Concept Map as facilitative tools in schools and corporations*. Mahwah, NJ: Lawrence Erlbaum Associates.

Oxman, R. (1999). Educating the designerly thinker. *Design Studies, 20*, 105–122.

Oxman, R. (2004). Thinks-maps: Teaching design thinking in design education. *Design Studies, 25*, 63–91.

Penner, D. E. (2001). Cognition, computers, and synthetic science: Building knowledge and meaning through modelling. *Review of Research in Education, 25*, 1–37.

Perez, R. S., & Emery, C. D. (1995). Designer thinking: How novices and experts think about instructional design. *Performance Improvement Quarterly, 8*, 80–95.

Perkins, D. N. (1986). *Knowledge as design*. Hillsdale, NJ: Lawrence Erlbaum Associates.

Perkins, D. N. (1996). Mind's in the hood. In B. G. Wilson (Ed.), *Constructivist learning environments: Case studies in instructional design* (pp. v–viii). Englewood Cliffs, NJ: Educational Technology Publications.

Pieters, J. M., & Bergman, R. (1995). The empirical basis of designing instruction: What practice can contribute to theory. *Performance Improvement Quarterly, 8*, 118–129.

Quintana, C., Krajcik, J., & Soloway, E. (2003). Issues and approaches for developing learner-centered technology. In M. Zelkowitz (Ed.), *Advances in computers* (Vol. 57, pp. 271–321). New York: Academic Press.

Quintana, C., Reiser, B. J., Davis, E. A., Krajcik, J., Fretz, E., Duncan, R. G., et al. (2004). A scaffolding design framework for software to support science inquiry. *Journal of the Learning Sciences, 13*, 337–387.

Reigeluth, C. M. (Ed.). (1999). *Instructional-design theories and models: A new paradigm of instructional theory* (Vol. II). Hillsdale, NJ: Lawrence Erlbaum Associates.

Reiser, R. A., & Dempsey, J. V. (2002). *Trends and issues in instructional design and technology*. Upper Saddle River, NJ: Merrill Prentice Hall.

Rowland, G. (1992). What do instructional designers actually do? An empirical investigation of expert practice. *Performance Improvement Quarterly, 5*, 65–86.

Salomon, G., Perkins, D., & Globerson, T. (1991). Partners in cognition: Extending human intelligence with intelligent technologies. *Educational Researcher, 20*, 2–9.

Scardamalia, M., & Bereiter, C. (1993). Technologies for knowledge-building discourse. *Communications of the ACM, 36*, 37-41.

Schank, R., & Neaman, A. (2001). Motivation and failure in educational simulation design. In K. D. Forbus & P. J. Feltovich (Eds.), *Smart machines in education* (pp. 37-71). Menlo Park, CA: AAAI Press.

Schön, D. A. (1987). *Educating the reflective practitioner*. San Francisco: Jossey Bass.

Schön, D. A., & Wiggens, C. (1992). Kinds of seeing and their functions in designing. *Design Studies, 13*, 135-153.

Schuler, D., & Namioka, A. (Eds.). (1993). *Participatory design: Principles and practices*. Hillsdale, NJ: Lawrence Erlbaum Associates.

Seitamaa-Hakkarainen, P., Raunio, A., Raami, A., Muukkonen, H., & Hakkarainen, K. (2001). Computer support for collaborative designing. *International Journal of Technology and Design Education, 11*, 181-202.

Shuell, T. J. (1996). Teaching and learning in a classroom context. In D. C. Berliner & R. C. Calfee (Eds.), *Handbook of educational psychology*. New York: Simon & Schuster MacMillan.

Smith, P. L., & Ragan, T. J. (1999). *Instructional design* (2nd ed.). New York: Macmillan.

Stempfle, J., & Badke-Schaub, P. (2002). Thinking in design teams: An analysis of team communication. *Design Studies, 23*, 473-496.

Suthers, D., Weiner, A., Connelly, J., & Paolucci, M. (1995). *Belvedere: Engaging students in critical discussion of science and public policy issues*. Paper presented at II-Ed 95, the 7th World Conference on Artificial Intelligence in Education, Washington, DC.

Tennyson, R. D. (Ed.). (1992). *Automating instructional design, development, and delivery*. New York: Springer-Verlag.

Tennyson, R. D., & Baron, A. E. (Eds.). (1995). *Automating instructional design: Computer-based development and delivery tools*. New York: Springer-Verlag.

Tessmer, M., & Wedman, J. (1995). Context-sensitive instructional design models: A response to design research, studies, and criticism. *Performance Improvement Quarterly, 8*, 38-54.

Tripp, S. T., & Bichelmeyer, B. (1990). Rapid prototyping: An alternative instructional design strategy. *Educational Technology, Research and Development, 38*, 31-44.

van den Akker, J., Branch, R. M., Gustafson, K., Nieveen, N., & Plomp, T. (Eds.). (1999). *Design approaches and tools in education and training*. Dordrecht, The Netherlands: Kluwer Academic.

van Joolingen, W. R., & de Jong, T. (2003). SimQuest: Authoring educational simulations. In T. Murray, S. Blessing, & S. Ainsworth (Eds.), *Authoring tools for advanced technology educational software: Toward cost-effective production of adaptive, interactive, and intelligent educational software* (pp. 1-31). Dordrecht, The Netherlands: Kluwer Academic.

van Joolingen, W. R., de Jong, T., Lazonder, A. W., Savelsbergh, E., & Manlove, S. (2005). Co-Lab: Research and development of an on-line learning environment for collaborative scientific discovery learning. *Computers in Human Behavior, 21*, 671-688.

van Merriënboer, J. J. G. (1997). *Training complex cognitive skills: A four-component instructional design model for technical training*. Englewood Cliffs, NJ: Educational Technology Publications.

van Merriënboer, J. J. G., Jelsma, O., & Paas, F. G. W. C. (1992). Training for reflective expertise: A four-component instructional design model for complex cognitive skills. *Educational Technology: Research & Development, 40*, 23-43.

van Merriënboer, J. J. G., & Paas, F. (2003). Powerful learning and the many faces of instructional design: Toward a framework for the design of powerful learning environments. In E. de Corte, L. Verschaffel, N. Entwistle, & J. J. G. van Merriënboer (Eds.), *Powerful learning environments: Unravelling basic components and dimensions* (pp. 3-21). Oxford: Elsevier Science.

Veermans, K. H., de Jong, T., & van Joolingen, W. R. (2000). Promoting self directed learning in simulation based discovery learning environments through intelligent support. *Interactive Learning Environments, 8*, 229-255.

Vosniadou, S. (1992). Fostering conceptual change: The role of computer-based environments. In E. D. Corte, M. Linn, H. Mandl & L. Verschaffel (Eds.), *Computer-based learning environments and problem solving* (pp. 149-162). Berlin: Springer.

Vreman-de Olde, C., & de Jong, T. (2004). Student-generated assignments about electrical circuits in a computer simulation. *International Journal of Science Education, 26*, 859-873.

White, B. Y. (1993). ThinkerTools: Causal models, conceptual change, and science education. *Cognition and Instruction, 10*, 1-100.

Wilson, B. G. (1999). Adoption of learning technologies: Toward new frameworks for understanding the link between design and use. *Educational Technology, 39*, 12-16.

Wilson, B. G., & Jonassen, D. H. (1991). Automated instructional systems design: A review of prototype systems. *Journal of Artificial Intelligence in Education, 2*, 17-30.

· 33 ·

OBSERVATIONAL RESEARCH ON GENERIC
ASPECTS OF CLASSROOM TEACHING

Jere Brophy
Michigan State University

This chapter depicts the development of observational research on classroom teaching. Along with substantive findings, it considers the data collection and analysis methods used to generate these findings, addresses certain common misconceptions and distortions in the ways that this research is sometimes portrayed, and identifies some significant aspects that have been underappreciated.

The featured lines of research received very little attention in the first *Handbook of Educational Psychology* (Berliner & Calfee, 1996). This was not surprising because even though some of the best known studies were done by educational psychologists, their work was largely applied and empirical rather than systematically rooted in educational psychology theory. Many educational psychologists have only a passing and third-hand familiarity with observational research on teaching, especially those who identify more with psychology than education and focus their work on individual learners. Because it takes place in classrooms, the work is familiar to those who identify more with education than psychology. They may not think of it as educational psychology, however, because it focuses more on teachers than learners and deals specifically with teaching in classroom settings. Consequently, even colleagues who know and value the work may think of it as work in classroom management or curriculum and instruction rather than in educational psychology.

Therefore, my primary goal for the chapter is to provide a broad historical overview of this work and develop a perspective on it for educational psychologists, not to provide detailed review and critique of individual studies. The latter can be found in many sources including previous handbook chapters, most notably in two chapters in the *Third Handbook of Research on Teaching* (Brophy & Good, 1986; Doyle, 1986) and in more recently published handbooks on research on reading, mathematics, and other school subjects.

The chapter is limited to the relatively generic aspects of research on classroom teaching (e.g., managing the classroom, developing content, scaffolding students' engagement in learning activities), because subject-specific aspects are addressed in the chapters in Section V. I begin with some methodological comments on observational research, highlighting some basic design and analysis issues that tend to be obscured by an overly exclusive focus on observer and coder reliability issues.

OBSERVATIONAL METHODOLOGIES

Broadly conceived, observational methodologies for conducting classroom research subsume a great range of tools and techniques, both for generating the basic corpus of raw data and for processing those data to develop quantitative scores or induce generalizations. The only constant is that data are collected on classroom processes as they unfold. Significant data reduction occurs on the spot when observers code or take notes. Data reduction occurs later if electronic recording methods are used to produce videos or audio transcripts for subsequent analysis. Researchers often supplement the observational data by interviewing the teacher or students or collecting lesson plans, visual aids, work samples, or other artifacts produced or used during the observation periods. Over the years, classroom observation methods have been used to describe instructional practices (depict their current status or identify problems); investigate aspects of effective teaching; document inequities in the instruction provided to students who differ in achievement level, race, gender, or other status characteristics; improve teacher education programs by including opportunities for student teachers to get feedback on their instruction; and improve in-service teachers' instruction by providing them with feedback from observers (Anderson & Burns, 1989; Good & Brophy, 2003; Hilberg, Waxman, & Tharp, 2004; Medley, 1992; Nuthall & Alton-Lee, 1990).

During the 1970s and 1980s, there was much debate about the relative merits of different observational approaches, often framed in terms of "qualitative versus quantitative methods." This construal was ultimately fruitless, for several reasons. First, it was a false dichotomy: The distinction is not easily applied to some methods, and many methods include both qualitative and quantitative aspects. Second, it suggested that one needs to choose between qualitative and quantitative methods, when most questions are probably best addressed using a combination of both. Third, the supposed differences were overstated. Qualitative advocates often depicted quantitative methods as oversimplifying or distorting classroom processes by reducing them to a few dimensions and only attending to certain events while ignoring the rest. Eventually, however, it was recognized that because qualitative researchers view classrooms through their own individual lenses, they also attend to some things but not others and project their own perspectives onto the things that they do describe. Quantitative advocates often depicted thick description as subjective and unreliable, but qualitative researchers developed painstaking procedures for maximizing the validity and reliability of their field notes and their analyses of tapes and transcripts (Bogdan & Biklen, 1982; Glaser & Strauss, 1979; Patton, 1990).

In this light, recent attempts by federal agencies and other groups to privilege certain forms of research over others can be seen as misguided, because they focus on research designs and methods (notably randomized experiments) rather than on the questions or hypotheses to be addressed. The appropriateness of research designs and the validity and reliability of research methods depend primarily on the degree to which they are well suited to the questions under study and applied knowledgeably and conscientiously by the investigators, not the degree to which they are qualitative or quantitative, experimental or correlational, and so forth. Throughout the rest of the chapter, my comments on methods will focus on their applicability and validity, assuming implicitly that the investigators took all appropriate steps to make sure that their data were reliable. For a very thorough treatment of reliability issues in classroom observation research, see Evertson and Green (1986).

Applicability and Validity of Observational Methods

Measurement reliability, indexed as percentage of agreement across independent codes made by classroom observers or transcript coders, usually is of concern to both producers and consumers of classroom research. However, much less attention has been paid to more fundamental issues affecting the applicability and validity of the observational methods used, the sampling reliability (as opposed to the measurement reliability) of the data, and the ways that scores were derived from raw codes. As a result, many studies used methods that were not well suited to the questions ostensibly being addressed, even though they featured good observer/coder reliability (e.g., studies done on novice teachers that should have been done on experienced teachers, studies that included only an hour or two of observation per classroom when 20 or 30 would have been more appropriate, or studies that aggregated across all codes instead of developing separate data sets for whole-class versus small-group settings or for managerial versus instructional discourse).

Given that the applicability of methods is rooted in their suitability to the questions under investigation, scientific research begins with clarification of these questions (or, alternatively, hypotheses), then proceeds to specification of the kinds of data that will be needed to speak to the questions, and only then proceeds to consideration of the research designs and data collection methods that will be needed to produce such data. If one starts with a commitment to particular data collection methods, rather than with generation and clarification of the questions to be addressed, one puts the cart before the horse and invites applicability and ultimately validity problems.

Research Planning and Design Issues

Using research questions to guide decisions about methods is straightforward as an abstract principle, but it becomes complicated when one begins planning operational specifics. Clarification of the research questions, for example, typically occurs within a context of intentions and assumptions that often are left implicit but ought to be made explicit, such as:

- Generalization across teacher types: Are the data intended to support inferences about teachers in general or only teachers of particular subject matter, teachers working at particular grades, and so on? This carries implications for size and scope of the sample(s).
- Generalization across time frames: Are the data intended to support inferences about teaching across an entire term or school year, an instructional unit, a lesson, or some specific teaching routine (e.g., introducing new topics, reviewing homework assignments)? This carries implications about which parts of the school year and school day need to be observed for each teacher (as do the following questions).
- Generalization across settings: Are the data intended to support inferences about teaching the whole class, small groups, or individuals?
- Relevant activity types: Which lessons, practice activities, application activities, assessments, transitions, housekeeping and management times, and so forth should be observed?
- Relevant teacher roles: Do the research questions require observing teachers introduce content, develop content, scaffold discourse (recitation, drill, brainstorming, discussion, debate, etc.), scaffold work on activities, manage classroom and students, maintain engagement in activities, or what?
- Relevant student roles: What are students supposed to be doing during these times (e.g., paying attention to teacher or peers, participating in group activities, working on assignments or tests)? Should their behavior be coded too?
- Intended use of the data: Is the intention to simply describe classroom practices, compare teachers along specified dimensions, develop grounded theory, answer specific questions or test specific hypotheses, or assess implementation of teaching models?

Clarification of the research questions and related intentions and assumptions will inform decisions about the operational specifics of the methodology. Many of these involve issues that go well beyond conventional notions of reliability and validity. Researchers need sufficient familiarity with the classroom situations under study to enable them to make good decisions about what to observe and record, how to reduce and analyze the data in ways that preserve the relevant essentials of what occurred in the classrooms, and how to interpret and generalize the findings validly. Some of these decisions have received relatively little attention in the literature (see Table 33.1).

EARLY OBSERVATIONAL RESEARCH

Very little observational research appeared during the first half of the 20th century, but it burgeoned during the second half. Although what we now call thick description is at least as old as any other observational method, most of the work published in the 1950s and 1960s featured ratings, codes, checklists, or tallies that reduced classroom processes to dimensions amenable to quantitative analysis. Most of these studies were conducted by psychologists, sociologists, or educators with interests in generic models or methods of teaching. Subsequent observational research often employed more qualitative, thick description methods, initially in studies by educational ethnographers who also had generic interests, but later, and increasingly, in studies by curriculum and instruction specialists with interests in subject-specific aspects of teaching.

Medley and Mitzel (1963) reviewed in detail the classroom observation work done through 1960. They traced the development of observation methods to supervisors' desires for more objective measures than global ratings (of general teaching effectiveness or of dimensions such as harsh vs. kindly or organized vs. disorganized). The subjectivity of such ratings had proven problematic with respect to both reliability (poor agreement across raters) and validity (poor correlation with student achievement gains) (Remmers, 1963). Consequently, researchers began using low-inference codings of specific behaviors (presence–absence checklists or running tallies of instances of prespecified events as they occurred) in addition to or instead of high-inference ratings of more general dispositions or traits.

Supervisors who developed early coding systems included Horn (1914) and Puckett (1928), who focused on pupil participation in lessons (frequencies with which students sought response opportunities and made poor vs. fair vs. good responses), and Wrightstone (1935), who coded teachers' questioning (addresses the question to the whole class vs. an individual student, provides hints) and student participation (asks questions, delivers memorized response, generates response from personal experience). Barr (1929) used a variety of low- and high-inference measures to study teachers rated as good or poor by supervisors. He reported that the "good" teachers more often smiled at their students, included interesting subject matter, connected it to students' experiences, and explained activities' purposes when introducing them. However, Barr observed the teachers for only 40 minutes each, so most of the events he coded were not recorded often enough to allow for statistical analysis.

TABLE 33.1. Decisions Involved in Aligning Observational Methods to Research Questions

- What will need to be preserved: video, audio, transcripts, field notes, or just codes?
- When to categorize: retain rich record of raw data and develop codes later, or preselect target variables and coding instruments?
- What to code: "everything" or only selected settings, activities, etc.?
- Will the coding (or even the analyses) need to preserve the sequence in which events occurred: for everything, only for certain episodes (e.g., teacher question/student answer/teacher follow-up sequences), or not at all?
- What types of observational data will be needed? Relevant dimensions go well beyond high vs. low inference or qualitative vs. quantitative, and a combination usually is preferable to just one data source.

1. Universal coding systems (to be used continuously)

   a. Time sampling (e.g., observe for 30 seconds, code for 10 seconds)
   b. Generate a running list of codes, shifting to a new code and noting the time whenever the activity shifts to a different category

2. Event sampling in real time (to be used when relevant events are occurring)

   a. Coding systems (categorize ongoing events using preselected codes)
   b. Ratings (low to high on dimensions such as teacher warmth or student engagement)
   c. Checklists (presence/absence or yes/no)
   d. Periodic counts (of off-task students, etc.)
   e. Running tallies (e.g., of attempts at humor)

3. Field notes describing events as they unfold
4. Delayed coding or analysis of tapes or transcripts

- How frequently and how long will each classroom need to be visited to allow observation of a sufficient number of relevant events to constitute a reliable enough sample to support the intended uses of the corpus of data?
- What quantitative data should be computed: frequencies (average instances of praise per hour of observation or per line of transcript), percentage scores (percentage of correct answers praised), or both?
- Will data be aggregated across all observations or segregated to allow separate analyses for different settings, activity types, or subgroups of students?
- Given the nature and intended uses of the data, how might the findings best be displayed (tables of sums, averages, or percentages; decision trees or other flow charts; verbatim transcript excerpts plus interpretations; lists of principles or steps describing each teacher's basic approach to a given situation)?
- Will the classroom observation data need to be supplemented with other kinds of data (interviews, curriculum guides, student work samples)?

STUDIES OF INFLUENCE TECHNIQUES, LEADERSHIP STYLE, AND GROUP CLIMATE

Most studies done between 1930 and 1960 focused on affective or classroom climate variables and featured ratings of teachers' general personal characteristics or leadership styles. Kounin and Gump (1961) used ratings to identify the most and least punitive of the first-grade teachers in three schools, then asked their students, "What is the worst thing you can do in school?" They found that students of punitive teachers more often mentioned aggression and were more concrete in their descriptions ("Hit George in the mouth"). In contrast, students of nonpunitive teachers more often talked about behaviors that would interfere with learning or about violations of school values and rules, using more abstract language ("Be mean to people").

Complementary findings emerged from several lines of research on leadership style and group climate. Anderson and his colleagues (Anderson, 1943; Anderson, Brewer, & Reed, 1946) used classroom observation methods in several studies comparing "dominative" teachers (unilateral, forceful) with "integrative" teachers (inviting input, working with students). They reported that domination tended to elicit either teacher dependency and rote conformity or conflict and resistance. In contrast, when teachers worked with their students, the students worked with them and their engagement in learning activities featured more spontaneity and collaboration.

Ryans (1952) and Ryans and Wandt (1952) conducted research based on ratings of students' participation in classroom activities and teachers' personal characteristics and leadership styles. In a study of 345 third- and fourth-grade classes, higher ratings of student alertness, orderliness, responsibility, constructiveness, participation, and initiative were found in classrooms taught by teachers characterized as democratic, kindly, systematic, calm, confident, mature, responsible, and consistent. Many of these findings were replicated in a study of 249 high school classes, although at this level ratings for teacher democracy and kindliness did not show significant relationships with ratings of student behavior, and a newly added rating of dull versus stimulating instruction showed the strongest relationships.

Studies of teacher leadership style, variously described as autocratic versus democratic, demanding versus permissive, dominative versus integrative, teacher-centered versus learner-centered, or direct versus indirect, continued throughout the 1950s and 1960s. Withall and Lewis (1963) noted that these studies reflected a blending of influences from educational psychology (focusing on teacher characteristics and instructional methods), the mental health movement (focusing on causes of anxiety or other blocks to learning or motivation), and social psychology (focusing on leadership style, social climate, decision-making processes, and patterns of participation). Many were conducted by investigators committed to progressive or child-centered teaching philosophies, and their proliferation was fueled by the development of reliable classroom observation systems by Flanders (1970), Withall (1960), and others. Most of the observation systems included in *Mirrors for Behavior* (Simon & Boyer, 1970), a compilation of systems developed through the late 1960s, focused on these leadership style and climate aspects of classrooms.

These studies indicated that teachers typically were more dominative and direct, for example, than integrative, indirect, and the like. Correlations with achievement gains were weak in magnitude and mixed in direction, but more positive pupil attitudes and motivational indicators typically were observed in classes taught by relatively more integrative teachers (Wallen & Travers, 1963). Reviewing these findings, Dunkin and Biddle (1974) suggested that relationships might be clearer if teacher directness and indirectness were considered separate clusters of behaviors rather than treated as poles of the same dimension, and especially if observation systems were designed to distinguish teachers' personal warmth versus coldness from the demanding versus permissive aspects of their leadership styles. These and other improvements were made in studies of teachers' general characteristics, but in the meantime, interest was shifting to other kinds of classroom research.

STUDIES OF CLASSROOM MANAGEMENT

One early and successful example was the work on classroom management begun by investigators who did ecological research analyzing environmental settings (ecologies) with an eye toward the kinds of activities they support (affordances) and prohibit (constraints) (Bronfenbrenner, 1989). Classrooms are ecologies that can be studied accordingly, with the added understand-ing that they are human inventions constructed and maintained to accomplish particular purposes.

Early ecological research focused on the characteristics of different classroom settings (e.g., whole class, small group, individual) and the activities that took place in them (e.g., more teacher–student discourse occurred in lesson settings than in seatwork settings). Studies of classroom tasks and settings continued (e.g., Bossert, 1979), but some investigators shifted attention from variations in the frequencies of types of activities to the roles of teachers in establishing and maintaining the activities. In an early study, Kounin and Gump (1958) observed in 26 kindergarten classrooms during the first 4 days of school, focusing on desist incidents in which teachers directed interventions at students who were misbehaving. Observers took running notes describing desist incidents as they unfolded, then expanded them into "specimen records" formatted for coding. Desists were coded for clarity (about how the students were misbehaving or what they should be doing instead), firmness (an "I mean it" and "right now" quality), and roughness (expression of anger or exasperation).

Kounin and Gump were interested in ripple effects on audience students who observed desists directed at peers. Analyses indicated that desist clarity was associated with greater subsequent conformity among audience students. In addition, for students coded as deviancy linked (because they were either misbehaving themselves or watching the misbehavior of the target of the desist), desist firmness was associated with subsequent conformity and desist roughness with subsequent disruptive behavior. However, these relationships were strongest on the first day and weaker on subsequent days, and later studies at higher grade levels failed to replicate them.

Kounin pursued classroom management issues in subsequent studies of elementary classrooms (Kounin, 1970; Kounin & Doyle, 1975; Kounin, Friesen, & Norton, 1966). In the process, he made three significant changes that produced original and enduringly influential findings. First, he enriched his database by shifting from specimen records developed from observers' notes to videotapes of classroom events. The opportunity to replay the videos made it possible to code more, and more subtle, aspects of both teacher and student behavior. Second, he shifted from his original narrow focus on desists to include a broader range of teacher actions. Third, he developed ratings of teachers' effectiveness as classroom managers, emphasizing their relative success at keeping students engaged in ongoing lessons and activities (these ratings were much more valid and reliable than attempts to rate overall teaching effectiveness). Kounin's work anticipated much of the design logic and methodology used later by process-product researchers (looking for teacher behavior measures that correlate consistently with measures of effectiveness) and by researchers on teaching for understanding (thick description of best practice).

Analyses of the videotapes continued to show that measures of teachers' responses to disruptive behavior (i.e., desists) were not reliably related to the teachers' overall effectiveness as classroom managers. Instead, the secret to management success was preventing students from becoming disruptive in the first place, by maintaining the momentum of learning activities and nipping potential problems in the bud before they could escalate. Several key variables emerged from subsequent analyses:

- *Withitness*. Remaining "with it" (aware of what is happening in all parts of the room at all times) by continuously scanning the classroom, even when working with small groups or individuals.
- *Overlapping*. Doing more than one thing at a time, such as using eye contact or physical proximity to restore certain students' attention while continuing the lesson without interruption.
- *Signal continuity and momentum during lessons*. Teaching well-prepared and briskly paced lessons that focus students' attention by providing them with a continuous content flow (signal) that is more compelling than the noise of competing distractions, and by sustaining the momentum of this signal throughout the lesson.
- *Group alerting and accountability during lessons*. Using presentation and questioning techniques that keep the group alert and accountable, such as waiting and looking around before calling on someone to answer a question, avoiding predictability in choice of respondent, interspersing choral responses with individual responses, requiring students to signify answers visibly, or calling on individuals to comment on or correct a peer's response.
- *Challenge and variety in assignments*. Encouraging engagement in seatwork by providing varied assignments of optimal difficulty level.

Observational measures based on Kounin's work were included in several of the process–product studies done during the 1970s. These studies extended his findings by showing that withitness, overlapping, and so on were associated not only with managerial success but also with success in eliciting student achievement gains. In addition, several investigators observed intensively at the beginning of the school year to describe the methods that effective managers used to install their management systems as they began working with a new class of students.

Moskowitz and Hayman (1976) studied 10 "best" and 11 first-year teachers in inner-city junior high schools. They found that at the beginning of the year, the "best" teachers conveyed more personal acceptance to their students, praised them more, joked more, and gave more helpful suggestions (cues, reminders, work and study tips), but they also kept close tabs on student behavior and acted quickly to nip potential problems in the bud. In contrast, new teachers were less consistent in stating and following through on expectations, often let problems develop too far before intervening, and developed less positive classroom climates.

Evertson, Emmer, and their colleagues took detailed notes about the rules and procedures that teachers introduced at the beginning of the year, the methods they used to do so, and how they followed up when they needed to enforce the rules or use the procedures. Then they related these measures to a measure of teachers' overall management success developed by scanning the room every 15 minutes to record the percentage of students who appeared to be attentive to lessons or engaged in other teacher-approved activities. Their first study, conducted in third-grade classrooms, found that on the first day and throughout the first week, successful managers gave special attention to matters of greatest concern to their students (e.g., information about the teacher and their classmates, review of the daily schedule, procedures for lunch and recess, where to put personal materials). They introduced procedures and routines gradually, so as not to overload the students with too much information at one time. Three clusters of behavior stood out as typical of the most effective managers.

Conveying purposefulness. Effective managers tried to maximize use of the available time for instruction and see that their students learned the curriculum (not just that they stayed quiet). They held students accountable for completing work on time, scheduled regular times each day to review the work, and returned completed papers promptly, with feedback.

Teaching appropriate conduct. Effective managers were clear about what they expected and what they would not tolerate. They focused on what students should be doing and, when necessary, taught them how to do it.

Maintaining attention. Effective managers continuously monitored students for signs of confusion or inattention and were sensitive to their concerns. They arranged seating so that students could easily face the point in the room where they needed to focus attention, and used variations in voice, movement, or pacing to sustain attention. Activities had clear beginnings and endings, with efficient transitions in between.

The effective managers followed up this intensive activity in the early weeks by reinforcing their expectations. They continued to give reminders and occasional remedial instruction, and they remained consistent in enforcing their rules (Emmer, Evertson, & Anderson, 1980).

A similar study of junior high school teachers revealed similar findings, as well as a few differences. These teachers did not need to spend as much time teaching their students how to follow rules and procedures, but they did have to communicate expectations concerning student responsibility for engaging in and completing assignments. They posted information describing the assignments and noting when they were due, adding any needed elaboration about the expected form or quality of the final product (Evertson and Emmer, 1982a, 1982b).

Based on narrative descriptions of events occurring in junior high English classes, Doyle (1984) observed that successful managers (a) constructed lessons that fit the schedule (50-minute classes), (b) used activities that had clear programs of action for students to follow, (c) explicitly marked the boundaries of activities and orchestrated the transitions between them, (d) demonstrated situational awareness by attending to details and commenting on events as they occurred, (e) protected activities until they became established routines by actively ushering them along, hovering over the students, focusing public attention on work, and ignoring minor misbehavior so as to avoid disrupting the rhythm and flow of events, and (f) pushing the students through the curriculum even when misbehavior was a problem. They continued this emphasis on establishing the work system in the class as a whole throughout the first month of the school year, before shifting attention to working with individual students during seatwork times. Less successful managers made this shift prematurely.

The general findings of Doyle, Evertson and Emmer, and Kounin complement one another and receive support from subsequent work done in both elementary (Freiberg, Stein, & Huang, 1995) and secondary schools (Gottfredson, Gottfredson, & Hybl, 1993). Even seeming contradictions can be resolved with careful interpretation. For example, Kounin showed that sheer frequencies of teachers' desist statements do not predict their effectiveness as managers, but Evertson and Emmer showed that it is important for teachers to nip potential disruptions in the bud. The latter finding implies that desist statements do play a role in effective management. However, the more basic principles emerging from Evertson and Emmer's work stress the importance of preparing students to follow desired protocols and providing cues to situational expectations (thus reducing the need for desist statements), as well as following up any necessary desist statements with rule reminders, additional socialization, follow-through on stated consequences, or other actions designed to prevent recurrence of the problem behavior.

Taken together, the classroom management studies constitute one of the clearest success stories of observational research in classrooms. The principles associated with them were developed mostly by working inductively from process–product findings, but with hindsight, we can see that the most basic and widely replicated findings can be understood using educational psychology concepts such as clarifying expectations, situational cueing, focusing attention, modeling, linking behavior to consequences, and supporting self-regulated learning.

EARLY STUDIES OF THE COGNITIVE ASPECTS OF TEACHING

Early observational research focused on teachers' personalities and the affective or social climate aspects of teaching, with little or no attention to its cognitive or content aspects. Getzels and Jackson (1963) noted that many of these studies failed to provide significant results and many others produced only pedestrian findings indicating "that good teachers are friendly, cheerful, sympathetic, and morally virtuous rather than cruel, depressed, unsympathetic and morally depraved" (p. 574).

Gradually, however, investigators introduced methods of coding the cognitive or content aspects of teaching, using categories such as fact questions, thought questions, providing factual information, giving explanations, using props or illustrations, and various types of activities or subject matter (Jayne, 1945; Medley & Mitzel, 1958; Morsh, 1956). Smith (Smith & Meux, 1959; Smith et al., 1967) began analyzing transcripts of secondary subject-matter teaching in terms of logical relationships between teachers' intended instructional outcomes and the content presentations and strategies they used to engage students in processing the content (questions, follow-ups to students' responses). Wright and Proctor (1961) developed a system for categorizing mathematics instruction that included attention to the mathematical rigor of content presentations and teacher–student discourse. Taba and her associates (Taba, Levine, & Elzey, 1964) developed a system for analyzing the cognitive levels of the discourse reflected in transcripts of elementary social studies lessons (e.g., classifying information, making inferences, and applying or generalizing).

Arno Bellack and his associates (Bellack, Kliebard, Hyman, & Smith, 1966) analyzed transcripts of secondary social studies lessons and identified four "pedagogical moves" that subsumed most of the discourse: (a) structuring (initiating a lesson segment by stating purposes and goals, providing advance organizers, and establishing an initial base of information), (b) soliciting (asking questions), (c) responding (to the questions), and

(d) reacting (by providing feedback, elaborating on the response, inviting additional responses, asking a new question, or following up in some other way). Ordinarily, teachers did most of the structuring, soliciting, and reacting, while students did most of the responding. Recurrent (and for the most part, logically necessary) sequences of structuring followed by rounds of solicitation, response, and reaction formed naturally occurring units of classroom discourse, so Bellack built them into his coding and analysis schemes. Subsequent process–product investigators often adopted similar formats, because this facilitated the design of coding sheets that made it easier for the coders to keep up with ongoing discourse.

Classroom observational research done through the 1960s and into the early 1970s was synthesized in two influential reviews (Dunkin & Biddle, 1974; Rosenshine & Furst, 1973). Each noted that although process–product findings were weak in magnitude and often mixed in direction, significant conceptual and methodological progress had been made and some process variables were emerging as consistent correlates of achievement outcomes. Most of these were leadership style and classroom climate variables (teacher warmth, mild rather than strong criticism of students), but classroom management variables (businesslike orientation, organization, focus on academic activities) and instructional variables (variety in materials and learning activities, clarity, enthusiasm, structuring comments, probing questions as follow-ups to initial questions) also were represented. Dunkin and Biddle organized their review within four general categories that became common parlance among investigators in the field: context variables (grade level, subject matter, student socioeconomic status, group size, type of activity, etc.), presage variables (personal characteristics and dispositions that teachers and students bring with them into the classroom), process variables (instruction, discourse, work on assignments, and other teaching and learning processes), and product variables (knowledge, skills, attitudes, or other outcomes that students acquire through their participation in the classroom processes).

THE PROCESS–PRODUCT (TEACHER EFFECTS) RESEARCH OF THE 1970S

Early attempts to link teacher behavior to learning outcomes did not yield satisfactory results because of reliability and validity problems with the (ratings) criteria of effective teaching. Many methods-comparison studies were done in the 1930s and 1940s, but these never produced coherent findings because of a variety of research design and data analysis weaknesses and because the differences

between the methods being compared usually were too small to produce significant differences in achievement outcomes (Medley, 1979). In the 1950s and 1960s, learning theorists began supplementing or replacing behavioral principles with cognitive psychology principles that were more applicable to the design of classroom teaching. Even so, the 1960s applications of these ideas focused more on development of curriculum packages than on the role of teachers in helping students to understand and respond to curricular content. At the time, many curriculum developers viewed teachers more as nuisances than as resources and, therefore, tried to make their curricula "teacher proof." In these programs, the teacher's role was downgraded from that of an instructor to that of a materials manager and test administrator.

Others depicted teachers not as harmful to student learning but as ineffectual. They noted that students display a great range of individual differences in aptitudes and motivation and suggested that these are much more powerful than anything their teacher does in determining how much they learn. This view appeared to receive support from the highly publicized Coleman report (Coleman et al., 1966), with its findings that socioeconomic status and other home background factors were more powerful predictors of academic achievement progress than measures of school characteristics were.

Such findings should have been anticipated, given that Coleman's school-level data were aggregated across teachers of varying effectiveness and no data were reported on what was happening at the individual classroom level (Good, Biddle, & Brophy, 1975). However, research by other investigators that was done at the classroom level also failed to provide much support for the commonsense belief that students learn more from some teachers than from others, let alone to produce correlations consistently linking certain processes with certain outcomes.

Within this gloomy atmosphere, and partly as a reaction to it, several groups of investigators began work designed to identify reliable relationships between classroom processes (primarily teacher behaviors) and student outcomes (primarily adjusted achievement gain). They assumed (or at least hoped) that improved research designs and measurement and analysis methods would begin to uncover replicable process–outcome relationships, and that the observed patterns would provide a basis for inducing instructional principles that then could be tested experimentally (Rosenshine & Furst, 1973). Their early work was limited to correlational studies and concentrated on basic skills instruction in the early grades. Later studies addressed a wider range of grades and subjects and included experimental verification of some of the causal hypotheses suggested by correlational findings.

Many of the best known of these studies were done within four large research programs: the Beginning Teacher Evaluation Study (Berliner, Fisher, Filby, & Marliave, 1978; Berliner & Tikunoff, 1977; Fisher, Filby, Marliave, Cahen, & Dishaw, 1980; McDonald, 1977), the Follow Through Evaluation Studies and other research done by Jane Stallings and her colleagues (Stallings, 1975, 1980; Stallings, Cory, Fairweather, & Needels, 1977, 1978; Stallings & Kaskowitz, 1974; Stallings, Needels, & Stayrook, 1979), the Missouri Math Studies (Good & Grouws, 1977, 1979; Good, Ebmeier, & Beckerman, 1978; Good, Grouws, & Beckerman, 1978; Good, Grouws, & Ebmeier, 1983), and the Texas Teacher Effectiveness Studies (Anderson, Evertson, & Brophy, 1979; Brophy, 1973; Brophy & Evertson, 1976; Evertson, Anderson, Anderson, & Brophy, 1980). These programs all involved gathering data on classroom processes and on subsequent outcomes (notably end-of-year standardized test scores adjusted using scores from the previous year, which were considered to be more valid and known to be more reliable than supervisors' or administrators' ratings), then examining relationships between process and outcome measures. This work was initially called *teacher effectiveness research*, but this term was a misnomer because it equated teacher effectiveness with success in producing achievement gains. What constitutes effectiveness is a matter of definition, and most definitions include a broader range of knowledge and skills than what is included in standardized tests, as well as success in socializing students and promoting their affective and personal development. Consequently, terms such as *process–product research*, *process–outcome research*, or *teacher effects research* are more appropriate.

Teacher effects research began as an empirical, functionalist attempt to address primarily practical concerns—identify classroom process predictors of achievement test score gains. It was not an attempt to validate any particular instructional model (and specifically, not an attempt to validate a behavioral model). I emphasize this because secondary and especially tertiary sources (i.e., authors working from reviews and purported syntheses of the work rather than from the original research reports) frequently misrepresent both the work itself and the motives and theoretical commitments of the researchers who conducted it, creating a caricature of process–product research that focuses on its accidental features rather than its fundamental ones (see Gage & Needels, 1989, on this point).

Process–product researchers were primarily concerned with craftsmanship issues involved in designing studies that would produce more stable and replicable findings than their predecessors did. My own research planning, for example, focused on identifying samples of teachers who had established track records of predictability in the levels of achievement gain they elicited (rather than studying new teachers who had not yet developed stable patterns or experienced teachers whose students' gains fluctuated unpredictably from one year to the next), developing measures of processes that seemed likely to correlate with achievement gains, and arranging to spend enough time in enough classrooms to build up reliable samples of the processes measured.

A common misconception about process–product studies is that they were limited to quantitative data based on frequency counts of low-inference codes, correlated with measures of achievement gains. In fact, they incorporated a variety of process and outcome measures. Many included student attitudes along with achievement gains as outcome measures. The Beginning Teacher Evaluation Study included a component in which ethnographers were sent to the classrooms to record field notes, and measures derived from these field notes were included in the analyses. The Texas studies included a variety of codings, ratings, and other process data, along with teacher interviews and questionnaires addressing a great range of attitudes, beliefs, and self-reported teaching practices. However, except for a cluster of questions dealing with role definitions and self-efficacy perceptions (e.g., accepting responsibility for eliciting student learning gains and expressing confidence in one's ability to do so), it was the classroom process measures, not the interview or questionnaire measures, that correlated with adjusted achievement scores.

Approaches to data collection were broadly eclectic: Recognizing that there were a great many reasonable measurement candidates (teacher behaviors or other classroom processes that might be expected to predict achievement gains) and that opportunities to conduct large, expensive studies were likely to be limited, the researchers typically cast a broad net and tried to measure as many variables as possible. Ideas about potentially significant variables were drawn from previous classroom research and from the writings of influential theorists of the time (notably David Ausubel, Jerome Bruner, Robert Gagne, and Madeline Hunter). Development of coding instruments and other measurement methods built on the work of people who had made major empirical contributions (in my case, Arno Bellack, Ned Flanders, and Jacob Kounin). To the extent that process–product investigators were guided by principles or models of teaching in designing and interpreting their studies, these tended to be commonsense or logical notions (e.g., time spent engaged in academic activities, rather than in transitions, chaos, or nonacademic activities, is important because it bounds students' opportunities to learn), the accumulated wisdom of practice as found in teacher education texts, and cognitive structuralist theories of verbally mediated learning (not behaviorist theories of operant conditioning).

Commonly Replicated Findings

Process–outcome findings developed by these four programs and by many other groups and individuals were reviewed in considerable detail by Brophy and Good (1986). Several generic findings emerged consistently from these studies:

1. *Teachers make a difference.* Some teachers reliably elicit greater gains than others, and this is because of differences in how they teach.

2. *Teacher expectations/role definitions/sense of efficacy.* Teachers who elicit strong achievement gains accept responsibility for doing so. They believe that their students are capable of learning and that they (the teachers) are capable of teaching them successfully. If students do not learn something the first time, they teach it again, and if the regular curriculum materials do not do the job, they find or develop others that will.

3. *Exposure to academic content and opportunity to learn.* Teachers who elicit greater achievement gains allocate most of the available time to activities designed to accomplish instructional goals, not activities that serve little or no curricular purpose.

4. *Classroom management and organization.* These teachers also are effective organizers and managers who minimize the time spent getting organized, making transitions, or dealing with behavior problems, and maximize the degree to which students are engaged in ongoing learning activities.

5. *Active teaching.* Teachers who elicit greater achievement gains spend a great deal of time actively instructing their students. Their classrooms feature more time spent in interactive lessons featuring teacher-student discourse and less time spent in independent seatwork. Rather than depend solely on curriculum materials as content sources, they interpret and elaborate the content for students, stimulate them to react to it through questions asked in recitation and discussion activities, and circulate during seatwork times to monitor progress and provide assistance. They are active instructors, not just materials managers and evaluators. However, most of their instruction occurs during interactive discourse with students rather than during extended lecture-presentations.

6. *A supportive learning environment.* Despite their strong academic focus, these teachers maintain pleasant, friendly classrooms and are perceived by their students as enthusiastic, supportive instructors.

In addition to these more generic findings, correlational and experimental research on teacher effects contributed knowledge about qualitative aspects of more situational instructional methods and classroom processes. For example, research on teachers' lectures and demonstrations verified the importance of delivering these presentations with enthusiasm and organizing and sequencing their content so as to maximize their clarity and "learner friendliness." Various studies showed the value of pacing, gestures, and other oral communication skills; avoiding vagueness, ambiguity, and discontinuity; beginning with advance organizers or previews that include general principles, outlines, or questions that establish a learning set; briefly describing the objectives and alerting students to new or key concepts; presenting new information with reference to what students already know about the topic; proceeding in small steps sequenced in ways that are easy to follow; eliciting student responses regularly to stimulate active learning and ensure that each step is mastered before moving to the next; finishing with a review of main points, stressing general integrative concepts; and following up with questions or assignments that require students to encode the material in their own words and apply it or extend it to new contexts (Brophy & Good, 1986; Chilcoat, 1989; Goldin-Meadow, Kim, & Singer, 1999; Luiten, Ames, & Ackerson, 1970; McCaleb & White, 1980; Patrick, Hisley, & Kempler, 2000; Rosenshine, 1970; Schuck, 1981; Smith & Land, 1981).

Similarly, research on teacher–student interaction processes identified some important dimensions of recitations and discussions. The difficulty levels of questions need to be suited to the students' levels of ability and prior knowledge. The forms and cognitive levels of the questions need to be suited to the instructional goals. Primarily closed-ended and factual questions might be appropriate when teachers are assessing prior knowledge or reviewing new learning, but most instructional goals will require sufficient emphasis on open-ended questions calling for students to apply, analyze, synthesize, or evaluate what they are learning (Brophy & Good, 1986; Dantonio & Beisenherz, 2001; Wilen, 1991).

Because questions are intended to engage students in cognitive processing and construction of knowledge about academic content, teachers ordinarily should address them to the class as a whole rather than designate an individual respondent in advance. This encourages all of the students to listen carefully and respond thoughtfully to each question. Another important dimension is wait time. After posing a question, teachers need to pause to allow students time to process the question and at least begin to formulate responses, especially if the question is complicated or high in cognitive level of response demand (Rowe, 1986; Swift, Gooding, & Swift, 1988; Tobin, 1983).

Follow-up options open to teachers who have posed a question and elicited an answer from a student include providing immediate feedback about the correctness of the answer, asking other students to comment on it, probing to elicit elaboration, praising or criticizing the answer, or accepting it and moving on (preferably in a way that uses or builds on it). When the student has answered incorrectly or is unable to respond, the teacher's options include simply repeating the question, providing negative feedback and inviting the student to try again, rephrasing the original question to make it easier for the student to answer, shifting to an easier question, giving the answer, or redirecting the question to the class. Teacher effects research has not produced findings indicating consistent relationships between these teacher reaction alternatives and student achievement gains, probably because optimal teacher behavior on these dimensions varies with the nature of the students and the goals of the instructional activities (Brophy & Good, 1986). The response options are worth considering in planning recitation and discussion activities, however, particularly in determining when and why it makes sense to terminate an interaction with the original respondent (by giving the answer or calling on someone else) rather than to sustain the interaction by repeating or rephrasing the question or giving clues. Sustaining is often desirable as a way to scaffold thinking and develop confidence, especially in reticent or self-doubting students. However, teachers often feel the need to terminate and move on because of time pressures or growing restlessness among onlooker students.

Contributions and Limitations of Process–Product Studies

Some teacher effects researchers followed up their correlational studies with experimental studies using instructional models that incorporated some of the teaching behaviors they had shown to be correlated with achievement gains (Anderson, Evertson, & Brophy, 1979; Good & Grouws, 1979). In addition, some reviewers (most notably Rosenshine & Stevens, 1986) drew from process–product findings to induce models of effective teaching that included stages such as reviewing previous homework, presenting new content, checking for understanding, supervised application, and independent application. These were legitimate uses of process–product findings, but they often are reified in ways that distort interpretation of the original correlational studies, in two respects.

First, they are not the only legitimate interpretations or uses of process–product findings. Depending on which relationships are emphasized and how they are combined with one another and with principles drawn from other sources, principles based on process–product findings can be incorporated within quite a range of instructional models (including social constructivist or sociocultural models, not just linear or transmission models).

Second, most process–product findings came from studies in which the teachers were doing whatever they usually did, without investigator attempts to influence their behavior, and specifically, without training in any particular instructional model. Consequently, the most basic and valid approach to interpreting the meanings and potential implications of process–product relationships is to consider each finding in its own right rather than treat it as if it were a component in some particular instructional model. This requires time-consuming and inexact processes of pattern finding and inductive reasoning, informed by knowledge of what typically occurred in the classrooms under study. Potential complications include the contexts in which the classroom processes occurred, the base rates of these behaviors (a 0.30 correlation with achievement gains has a different implication when the process variable occurs only rarely than when it usually occurs routinely), the possibility of inverted-U curvilinear relationships, and other factors.

For example, the Texas Teacher Effectiveness Study involved analyzing for linear and curvilinear relationships between several hundred questionnaire, interview, rating, checklist, and coding measures and measures of achievement gain on five standardized tests, replicated across two school years and analyzed separately for low and high socioeconomic status (SES) subsamples as well as for the combined sample. Factor analyses and related techniques could not be used to reduce this data corpus because there were many more measures than teachers, and it probably would not have been helpful in any case because the investigators wanted to look for context-bound and complex relationships in addition to simple generalizations.

For some measures, intended analyses could not be pursued for lack of variance (e.g., seldom-occurring classroom events, questionnaire items with which all teachers agreed). For a few other measures, analyses yielded relatively consistent patterns that held up across data sets (see Table 33.2). These findings are among the most easily interpreted from the study, both because they tend to cluster into connected sets and because they applied in both the low-SES and the high-SES subsamples.

In contrast, measures of the teacher–student discourse occurring in whole-class lessons typically did not correlate significantly with achievement gains in analyses for

TABLE 33.2. Correlates of Achievement Gain Found in the *Texas Teacher Effectiveness Study* (Brophy & Evertson, 1976)

1. Teacher perceives teaching as an interesting and worthwhile challenge (vs. just a job)
2. Teacher approaches the job with resourcefulness and dedication, assumes personal responsibility for seeing that students learn, and persists in finding ways to overcome problems (vs. discussing problems as too serious to be solvable, giving up easily, attributing failures to the number or range of ability of the students, lack of appropriate materials or sufficient help, poor attitudes on the part of the students and their parents, etc.)
3. Teacher works persistently with struggling students, seeing that they get individual reteaching and extra practice if needed (vs. accepting low achievers' consistent failure as beyond their power to change)
4. Teacher designs and maintains the general learning environment in the classroom and is continually in charge, although open to student input (vs. frequently experiencing disorder due to absence of planning, confusion about how to handle unexpected events, etc.)
5. Teacher speaks to students with a calm, normal tone of voice, mostly within curriculum-related activities (vs. either spending a lot of time cultivating personal relationships with students and discussing personal matters having nothing to do with the curriculum, or else frequently "barking" at the students, often within interactions dealing with procedural or conduct issues)
6. Teacher introduces a relatively short set of general rules dealing with attention, respect for teacher and classmates, avoiding unnecessary noise, etc., explaining these in detail at the beginning of the year and interpreting them somewhat flexibly according to the situation (vs. having either no clear rules or a large number of overly specific rules)
7. Teacher routinely monitors the whole classroom, acts quickly to nip potential disruptions in the bud, displays "withitness" and other managerial skills identified by Kounin (1970)
8. Teacher spends a lot of time actively instructing students, initially during lessons and subsequently when monitoring individual work and providing feedback (vs. teaching briefer lessons and then leaving students to work on assignments mostly on their own)
9. Lessons run smoothly with few interruptions and students work consistently on assignments
10. The teacher's questions are pitched at an optimal level of difficulty, such that 70–80% are answered correctly (vs. consistently questioning at levels that are either too easy or too difficult)
11. Length and difficulty of assignments are well matched to students (vs. students frequently finishing quickly and then having nothing to do or giving up in frustration because they are unable to do the work or get help)
12. Teacher establishes routines to enable and regulate students' opportunities to get help with assignments (e.g., writes assignment on board, establishes times for students to come for help and at other times circulates the room to check work and provide help, designates one or more students as resources to whom peers can go for help if teacher is not available)
13. Teacher establishes routines concerning what students can do when they complete assignments (read, visit learning centers, play with educational games, etc.)
14. Teacher uses symbolic rewards (gold stars, smiley faces, etc.) but does not use assignment of housekeeping chores or monitor duties as rewards
15. Teacher does not use extra assignments of normal schoolwork as punishments

the combined sample. Instead, they displayed contrasting yet interpretable patterns when analyzed separately for the two SES subsamples. High-SES classrooms were dominated by competitive students who were eager to respond. Consequently, teachers in these classrooms ordinarily had little difficulty in getting good answers to their questions, but had to work to see that everyone respected everyone else's response opportunities and that lessons did not become overly competitive. In contrast, low-SES classrooms were dominated by students who feared embarrassment or failure when put "on the spot" by being called on to make a public response. Teachers in these classes had to focus on coaxing students into responding and helping them to do so, rather than on restraining eager peers from co-opting their response opportunities.

These differences in students led to differences in patterns of correlation with achievement gains. The more successful teachers in high-SES schools conducted fast-paced lessons in which they moved around the group quickly and gave a large number of students multiple opportunities to respond. When students were unable to respond, these teachers typically gave the answer themselves rather than reinforce an already overly compet-

itive situation by calling on a peer to supply it. They also consistently suppressed call-outs, insisting that students respect peers' response opportunities and avoid waving their arms or making remarks such as, "I know, teacher!" In contrast, the more successful teachers in low-SES schools moved at a slower pace, patiently working to elicit responses. They made it clear that they expected and intended to wait for a response every time they asked a question, even if the response was, "I don't know." They also encouraged student comments, sometimes accepted relevant call-outs, and praised good efforts even when the answer was not completely correct.

The findings for motivational measures indicated that the most successful teachers in low-SES schools motivated primarily through gentle and positive encouragement and praise, whereas the most successful teachers in high-SES schools motivated through challenge and demandingness. Measures of teacher praise correlated positively with achievement gains in low-SES schools but negatively in high-SES schools. However, measures of teacher criticism of poor responses or poor work on assignments correlated positively with achievement gains in high-SES schools. Such criticism was relatively rare and typically focused on inattention or sloppy work. Thus, given its low base rates and the nature of the criticism, it appears that its positive relationships with achievement gains in high-SES schools reflected teacher projection of high expectations and demands on students, not hypercritical tendencies.

Several variables that usually correlate with achievement gains did not show such correlations consistently in this study. They included teachers' warmth and affectionateness toward students, enthusiasm when presenting content, measures related to the pattern of indirect teaching as described by Flanders (1970) (e.g., relatively less teacher talk and more student talk, stress on independent student learning, frequent praise and use of student ideas, frequent student-to-student interaction), advance organizers, clarity and sequencing of questions, the ratio of divergent to convergent questions, teacher politeness to students, and teachers' attempts to improve responses by rephrasing questions or giving hints. Most of these surprises were interpreted as related to the fact that this study focused on basic skills instruction in the early grades, whereas most of the research support for advance organizers, indirect teaching, and so on comes from studies of teaching in secondary or postsecondary settings.

In order to hypothesize about the potential instructional implications of such findings, investigators or reviewers must first look for patterns and try to determine which relationships are causal and which are merely epiphenomena that appear because the variables involved are correlated with more fundamental variables that are linked in causal relationships. Hypothesized instructional implications then can be induced from the subset of relationships that are interpreted as probably causal, although doing so typically requires lifting the level of analysis from operational definitions and correlations to instructional principles grounded in models of teaching and learning.

Skeptics might observe that no matter how elegant and ultimately accurate such interpretive reasoning might be, and even if it explicitly avoids subsuming the resultant instructional principles within a linear format, the principles it yields will be more amenable to transmission models than to constructivist models of teaching, because transmission teaching was occurring most of the time in most of the classrooms observed in these studies. This observation is accurate, and it suggests limitations on the potential generalizability of process–product findings. It is not as important a limitation as many seem to believe, however, because most of the teaching in most of today's classrooms is transmission teaching, and this pattern is likely to continue indefinitely (Cuban, 1993).

Reviews of process-outcome studies, especially if written by people developing arguments for other kinds of research, typically emphasize these studies' limitations without saying much about their accomplishments. However, these studies were important for several reasons. First, they began to move the field beyond unsupported claims about effective practices toward more scientific statements based on replicable data. Second, they validated the commonsensical but previously unsupported belief that teachers make a difference, by showing that some teachers elicit more achievement gains than others do and by identifying classroom management and instructional behaviors associated with these gains. In the process, they dampened enthusiasm for programmed instructional materials and so-called teacher-proof curricula, because they showed that achievement gains were associated with teacher–student discourse and other aspects of active teaching, not with time spent working on assignments.

Once the basic set of replicable findings had become well established and synthesized, it was time to move on, however, because the paradigm was mostly played out. New studies linking generic measures of classroom processes to adjusted gains on achievement tests would likely replicate existing findings but not produce many significant new ones. Also, because these studies typically sampled across the full range of teachers rather than focusing on best practice, and because the measures were more quantitative than qualitative, the findings were focused on important but very basic aspects of teaching. They differentiated the least effective teachers from other teachers, but did not address the subtler fine points that distinguish the most outstanding teachers from other teachers. Several theoretical and methodological advances were needed to develop detailed information about how truly outstanding teachers differ from teachers whose classrooms yield similar scores on primarily quantitative measures of opportunity to learn and active teaching.

First, the research had to become more focused on particular parts of the school day and the school year. Most process–product studies had sampled at various times during the school day at various points in the school year, coded classroom processes using generic categories that cut across school subjects and grade levels, and then correlated scores aggregated across classroom visits with year-to-year adjusted gains on standardized achievement tests. To break new ground, researchers would need to focus more intensively on particular curriculum units or even individual lessons, taking into account the teachers' instructional objectives and assessing learning using criterion-referenced measures keyed to those objectives. This required more sophistication about curriculum and instruction in the subject areas as well as thicker description of classroom processes that could be analyzed in much finer detail.

Investigators began to draw from the literature on curriculum and instruction in the subject areas, paying more attention to worthwhile instructional goals and alignment among these goals, the content selected for focus, the methods used to teach it, and the methods used to evaluate student learning. Also, now that there was no longer any question that teachers play a vital role in stimulating student learning, investigators began to focus once again on students. Influenced by advances in research on learning and cognition and by constructivist and sociocultural theories of learning, investigators began to consider the degree to which instruction connected with students' prior knowledge and supported students' attempts to construct meaningful understandings of what they were learning. Emerging theory and research, including some rooted in educational psychology, began to suggest that in addition to clear explanations, modeling, and questions about the content from their teachers, students would need opportunities to discuss or debate its meanings and implications and to apply it in inquiry, critical-thinking, problem-solving, or decision-making contexts. These activities, and especially the interactive discourse that takes place as they unfold, would provide students with opportunities to process the content actively and "make it their own" by paraphrasing it into their own words, exploring its relationships to other knowledge and to past experience, appreciating the insights it provides, and identifying potential applications to life outside of school. The process–product findings dealing with active teaching supported these views by underscoring the value of teacher-led classroom discourse. However, they did not provide much information about the strategies involved in using discourse to scaffold students' construction of subject-specific understandings.

RESEARCH ON TEACHING
FOR UNDERSTANDING

These and other insights led to the emergence of new kinds of research on instruction, which have continued to develop into the 21st century. Often called research on teaching for understanding, these studies usually focus on relatively specific aspects of teaching within particular subject areas. They typically use multiple methods of data collection and often include attention not only to classroom processes but to the curriculum (major goals and big ideas, representations, activities, instructional materials), the teacher's instructional planning, and the thinking and decision making that occur during instruction. The instruction is often considered representative of best practice, either because it is being provided by the investi-

gators themselves or by teachers whom the investigators believe to be outstanding, or because it involves implementing units or lesson plans developed to reflect state-of-the-art curriculum standards and best practice guidelines in the subject area. Such studies are reviewed in detail in the chapters in Section V, so I do not attempt to review them here. Instead, I highlight illustrative examples and then offer a perspective on how these studies developed and where they appeared to be headed.

Two Examples

A quasi-experiment by Hiebert and Wearne (1992) is an outstanding example of research on teaching for understanding. This study focused on two instructional units (one on place value and one on two-digit addition and subtraction without regrouping) taught for the same amounts of time each day during the same weeks of the school year in six first-grade classes in a school that assigned their students to classes randomly. In two of these classes, the regular classroom teachers provided the mathematics instruction, using the adopted textbook and other materials and activities within the overall approaches they had developed through prior experience. The principal investigators taught the units in the other four classes, drawing on their knowledge as mathematics educators and on guidelines published by the National Council of Teachers of Mathematics (1989) and the National Research Council (1989). The study included careful attention to curriculum, instruction, and assessment.

The experimental curriculum involved manipulating and discussing representations of the concepts and operations being taught in order to develop basic understandings before shifting to skills practice. Representations such as base-10 blocks and Unifix cubes were introduced and used as tools for demonstrating and recording quantities, acting on quantities, and communicating about quantities. Students were given opportunities to explore the properties and affordances of these representations and use them as tools for problem solving. Physical materials and verbally mediated stories were used to introduce concepts and operations, with shifting to pictures and eventually to written symbols as the students gained familiarity with the concepts, operations, and representations. Typically, stories were used to pose problems, the materials were used to represent potential solutions, and discussion focused on explanations and comparisons of proposed solutions.

To monitor the implementations of this experimental curriculum and provide a basis for comparing the instruction occurring in the experimental and comparison classes, the study included classroom observers who recorded field notes and audiotaped the discourse. Analyses based on these data identified several contrasts. First, the instructors used physical materials differently. The textbook-based teachers used them more to demonstrate while students watched, whereas the understanding-oriented instructors distributed the materials to all students and asked the students to use them for varying purposes. Their students received fewer materials but worked with them over more extended periods of time, whereas students in the textbook-based classrooms were exposed to a greater variety of materials but spent less time with each individual material and spent much of this time watching demonstrations of its use rather than using it themselves.

There was a parallel difference in time spent per problem: The understanding-oriented classes worked fewer problems but spent more time on each problem. Also, there were related contrasts in lesson coherence: The understanding-oriented classrooms spent more sustained time addressing the same topic using the same materials (but asking students to shift between the forms in which quantities or actions were represented). This approach was believed to be more effective for helping students develop networks of connected understandings than lessons that featured more breadth but less depth. Other differences included the following: The understanding-oriented instructors encouraged students to consider alternative responses and procedures, whereas the textbook-based teachers tended to guide students through a single step by step procedure; the understanding-oriented instructors tended to use connections between representations throughout the lessons, whereas the textbook-oriented teachers tended to introduce one representation and then move on to another without exploiting their connections; and the understanding-oriented instructors placed more emphasis on laying the groundwork in one lesson for developing ideas in future lessons.

The investigators anticipated most of these differences and developed hypotheses and assessment measures with them in mind. The students were given criterion-referenced written tests prior to the beginning of the first unit, between the first unit and the second unit, and following the second unit. In addition, 12 students were selected randomly from each classroom and interviewed around the same times that the tests were administered. The tests measured the students' ability to answer questions and solve problems correctly; the interviews presented the students with story problems and focused on eliciting their thinking about the problems and their explanations for the strategies they developed for solving them.

The analyses generally supported the hypotheses. Although group differences were small relative to the individual differences within groups, the data indicated that the students given understanding-oriented instruction showed higher adjusted gains scores on the tests and more indications of flexible and sophisticated strategy use in the interviews. In addition, these students were just as proficient as the textbook-based students at solving routine problems, even though they had spent more time on understanding-oriented discussion and less time working on computation problems.

Only a few classrooms were involved, and the variance of many process variables was controlled via program guidelines, so it was not possible for the investigators to explore process–product relationships for measures representing different components of their program. However, by including a well-conceived assessment component, they were able to show not only that the understanding-oriented instruction was generally more effective than the textbook-based instruction, but also that the observed profile of contrasts mostly conformed to specific predictions based on hypotheses about likely relationships between particular program features and particular aspects of mathematical learning.

A second example of noteworthy research on teaching for understanding, also focused on first-grade mathematics instruction, is the observational research reported by Fraivillig, Murphy, and Fuson (1999). It also involved instruction using a curriculum developed to emphasize understanding and implement the guidelines published by the National Council of Teachers of Mathematics (1989). In this study, the investigators did not do the teaching themselves. Instead, they observed 18 first-grade teachers who had 1 to 4 years of experience using the new curriculum, initially to develop profiles of their effectiveness in general and the fidelity of their implementation of the curriculum in particular. These observations led them to identify six of the 18 teachers as particularly skillful.

The investigators then videotaped four lessons taught by each of the six skillful teachers, with one camera focused on the teacher and another on the students. In addition, two classroom observers took detailed notes and filled out a specially designed classroom observation instrument, with one observer focusing on the teacher and the other on the students. The teachers were interviewed before and after these observations and the videos were later observed repeatedly by the investigators as they identified and discussed key aspects of the teaching.

Their analyses focused on three teaching practices considered vital to good implementation of the curriculum: eliciting students' solution methods, supporting their conceptual understanding, and extending their

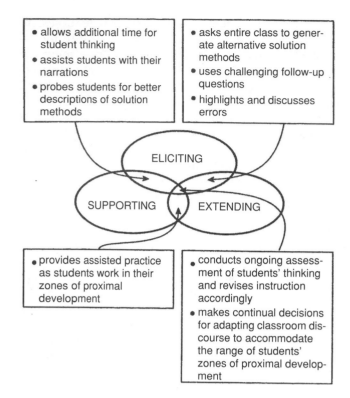

- allows additional time for student thinking
- assists students with their narrations
- probes students for better descriptions of solution methods

- asks entire class to generate alternative solution methods
- uses challenging follow-up questions
- highlights and discusses errors

ELICITING

SUPPORTING   EXTENDING

- provides assisted practice as students work in their zones of proximal development

- conducts ongoing assessment of students' thinking and revises instruction accordingly
- makes continual decisions for adapting classroom discourse to accommodate the range of students' zones of proximal development

FIGURE 33.1. Diagram of the Advancing Children's Thinking (ACT) framework and the teaching strategies that reside in the intersections between and among the instructional components of the ACT framework. *Source*: Fraivillig, Murphy, and Fuson (1999).

mathematical thinking. Initial analyses indicated that most teachers were comfortable with supporting students' thinking and did so frequently, but they were less inclined to elicit students' descriptions of their solution methods or to employ strategies for extending their mathematical thinking. However, one teacher stood out because she routinely exhibited all three of these key teaching practices.

The investigators engaged in sustained qualitative analysis of the data from this teacher's classroom, guided by the Advancing Children's Thinking (ACT) framework that they developed to focus on the instructional components of eliciting, supporting, and extending (see Fig. 33.1). Through this analysis, they identified strategies that the teacher used to implement these three components (see Table 33.3), and elaborated on the strategies in their article.

The Fraivillig, Murphy, and Fuson (1999) article is typical of much of the research on teaching for understanding because it used thick description data collection methods and qualitative data analysis methods to develop descriptions and provide examples of what teaching for understanding might look like in a particular subject taught

at a particular grade level. These studies often focus on best practice by documenting the teaching of one or a small number of teachers identified as exemplary. They sometimes include comparisons with teachers identified as less exemplary, and often include transcript excerpts, student interview excerpts, and occasionally test data to illustrate student progress toward intended outcomes. Only very rarely, however, do they include both comparison groups and formal assessment of achievement progress. Consequently, we often know little or nothing about relationships between the featured instructional strategies and gains in student achievement or other outcomes.

Warrants for claiming that the featured instructional strategies are exemplary do not lie in demonstrated process–outcome relationships, but instead in models of best practice in teaching the subject for understanding. These models are usually drawn from the standards and guidelines published by the leading professional organizations in each of the subject areas, which in turn tend to be based at least as much on theoretical models (primarily sociocultural and social constructivist) as on empirical research.

Contributions and Limitations of Research on Teaching for Understanding

The two examples drawn from first-grade mathematics teaching illustrate the many contrasts between recent research on teaching for understanding and earlier process–product research. The two kinds of research offer contrasting trade-offs. Process–product research took a broader view of teaching, subsuming its managerial and socialization aspects in addition to its subject-specific instructional aspects. The teaching strategies and behaviors that it highlighted already were known to be feasible for implementation in ordinary classrooms, because that is where the data were collected. Those that showed replicated relationships with outcome measures could be considered likely candidates for attention in teacher education programs, although follow-up studies would be needed to sort out causal relationships.

So long as such research was limited to traditional classrooms using traditional materials and methods and assessed using standardized tests, however, it would continue to develop information mostly about the more basic and generic aspects of effective teaching. In contrast, the research on teaching for understanding holds promise for expanding our knowledge of the finer points of exemplary teaching, because it focuses on such teaching, attends to both curriculum and instruction simultaneously,

TABLE 33.3. Examples of Instructional Strategies Employed to Elicit, Support, and Extend Children's Mathematical Thinking

Eliciting	Supporting	Extending
Facilitates students' responding	Supports describer's thinking	Maintains high standards and expectations for all students
Elicits many solution methods for one problem from the entire class	Reminds students of conceptually similar problem situations	Asks all students to attempt to solve difficult problems and to try various solution methods
Waits for and listens to students' descriptions of solution methods	Provides background knowledge	Encourages mathematical reflection
Encourages elaboration of students' responses	Directs group help for an individual student	Encourages students to analyze, compare, and generalize mathematical concepts
Conveys accepting attitude toward students' errors and problem-solving efforts	Assists individual students in clarifying their own solution methods	Encourages students to consider and discuss interrelationships among concepts
Promotes collaborative problem solving	Supports listeners' thinking	Lists all solution methods on the chalkboard to promote reflection
Orchestrates classroom discussions	Provides teacher-led instant replays	Goes beyond initial solution methods
Uses students' explanations for lesson's content	Demonstrates teacher-selected solution methods without endorsing the adoption of a particular method	Pushes individual students to try alternative solution methods for one problem situation
Monitors students' levels of engagement	Supports describer's and listeners' thinking	Promotes use of more efficient solution methods for all students
Decides which students need opportunities to speak publicly or which methods should be discussed	Records symbolic representation of each solution method on the chalkboard	Uses students' responses, questions, and problems as core lesson
	Asks a different student to explain a peer's method	Cultivates love of challenges
	Supports individuals in private help sessions	
	Encourages students to request assistance (only when needed)	

Source: Fraivillig, Murphy, and Fuson (1999).

generates thick data sets, analyzes them at detailed and microanalytic levels, and uses criterion-referenced assessment instruments (when it includes formal assessment). It often leaves questions, however, about the degree to which the advocated teaching methods are feasible for implementation by typical teachers working in typical circumstances, and if so, whether such teaching actually will produce the positive outcomes assumed by the investigators.

Despite the recent popularity of social constructivist and sociocultural models of teaching for understanding, these models have yet to be implemented on a broad scale. Given recent standards movements and pressures for broad coverage and preparation for high-stakes standardized tests, we are unlikely to see widespread implementation anytime soon of teaching models that favor depth of development of powerful ideas over shallow coverage of a broad curriculum. The more demanding student roles built into these models should also give pause to social constructivist educators. The image of a community of learners coconstructing understandings through sustained dialogue is very appealing, but bringing it to life in the classroom can be difficult for many teachers (e.g., a 10-grade teacher whose students mostly read at the third- or fourth-grade levels and are neither oriented toward nor accustomed to self-regulated learning). Implementing such models effectively requires careful structuring and scaffolding of learning activities by teachers who know both their subjects and their students very well.

Looking to the Future

When interpreted at the level of general principles rather than specific behaviors, most of the frequently replicated findings of both earlier process–outcome research and more recent research on teaching for understanding suggest a convergence of implications that fit well with one another and generalize across grade levels and subject areas. This bodes well for the prospects of developing an empirically grounded theory of classroom teaching to serve as a basis for teacher education. However, enthusiasm for recent findings needs to be tempered by some important qualifications and cautions.

First, the research base supporting ideas about teaching for understanding is still quite thin, especially if one looks for studies that include both comparison groups and systematic measurement of student outcomes. Inquiry and constructivist instructional models are being advocated by many leaders in the subject areas, and underlie much of what is included in the position statements published by their professional organizations. However, these models are widely acknowledged to be difficult to implement, and most have yet to be tested empirically, let alone to enjoy a rich accumulation of systematic evidence of positive effects on student outcomes.

We need empirical data that will allow us to assess the trade-offs involved in adopting these recommendations. Recent research points to several such trade-offs. One is the depth versus breadth dilemma. Commonly expressed concerns about "mile-wide but inch-deep" curricula in U.S. schools suggest the need to reduce breadth of topic coverage and shift from parades of facts and skills exercises to sustained focus on networks of connected content structured around powerful ideas. But what is the optimal balance? How much do students need to know about a topic, and how long should the teacher persist in efforts to make sure that all students master this network of knowledge? It may take weeks or even months to develop connected understandings of a topic such as photosynthesis, and even then some students will still be vague or confused. So should middle school science courses address only four or five topics across the entire school year? If not, what would be a reasonable compromise between this level of emphasis on depth and the overemphasis on breadth that we have now? Also, how would we decide which topics to retain in the curriculum and which to delete?

These questions illustrate how, even as research on teaching for understanding has generated increasing consensus around instructional method issues, it has reopened basic curricular issues: What is worth teaching to K-12 students, and why? Like the process–outcome research that preceded it, recent research has finessed these issues rather than addressed them. Process-outcome research did it by using standardized tests as the criteria for learning. Recent research does it by equating the teaching of K-12 subjects with enculturation into the academic disciplines. I believe that this leads to problematic curricular decisions.

An academic discipline is a community of inquiry that generates increasingly differentiated and elaborated knowledge about a particular content domain. The discipline focuses on expanding this specialized knowledge base, not on exploring its applications to everyday life or its connections with other forms of knowledge. In contrast, school subjects are curricula organized to prepare K-12 students for everyday living and performance of adult roles in society, not to prepare them to generate disciplinary knowledge. Therefore, decisions about what ought to be included in K-12 curricula should be informed by deliberations about what constitutes basic knowledge that all citizens need to know. This knowledge should be consistent with disciplinary knowledge, but it should be selected, organized, and taught as general education, not as induction into the academic disciplines.

When I view recent research from this perspective, I often find myself admiring the instructional methods illustrated but at the same time questioning the choice of content. In mathematics, for example, several lessons might be spent engaging students in extended reasoning about what appear to be arcane mathematical questions. From a disciplinary perspective, there is no problem here, because the students are engaged in doing mathematics, and all mathematics is more or less equally acceptable. From a general education standpoint, however, I question spending precious curriculum time on content that has little or no application potential.

Similarly, history and social studies educators with disciplinary training in history tend to advocate and develop materials and methods for K-12 history teaching that emphasize engaging students in acting as historians by examining (replicas of) multiple primary and secondary sources relating to historical events, assessing their credibility, and using them to construct defensible historical interpretations. This often leads to prolonged historiographic analyses of questions that are of interest to historians because the available source material is inconclusive and open to multiple interpretations. From a broader perspective, however, many such questions are relatively trivial and lacking in application potential, such as trying to determine who fired the first shot at Lexington Green. The available accounts are too conflicting to allow any clear answer to this question, and it is unimportant in any case, because even if the events at Lexington Green had never occurred, the American Revolution still would have begun around the same time for the same reasons. A citizen education version of school history, therefore, would devote little or no time to Lexington Green but a lot of time to learning about the issues that arose between England and the Colonies, how those affected the thinking of the framers of the Declaration of Independence and the U.S. Constitution, and what all of this might mean for decision making about contemporary constitutional issues.

I believe that educational psychologists interested in subject-matter teaching need to inform themselves about fundamental curricular issues and begin to exercise independent judgments concerning optimal K-12 curricular goals and content, rather than simply accept whatever is currently emphasized by the academic disciplines. Kliebard (1986) provides a good overview of these issues.

Sometimes I question not so much the content itself but the cost effectiveness of introducing it at a particular grade or seeking to develop it to sophisticated levels. When I read reports on conceptual change teaching in science, for example, I am impressed with the ingenuity that went into developing ways to teach complicated topics such as photosynthesis to middle school students, but I find myself questioning whether it is worth the time and trouble that it takes to do so. Perhaps the topic should be developed less completely, or even withheld until later grades.

Curricular questions such as these cannot be resolved through purely empirical methods because they involve value issues. However, they always contain implied assumptions that can be tested empirically, such as readiness assumptions (that students at a given grade level are ready to learn particular content) and transfer assumptions (that mastery of such content will enable them to handle certain life situations effectively). It is important for researchers on teaching to begin to pay attention to these curricular issues, as well as to press for clarification and testing of the empirical claims embedded in the theory-based position advocacy that typifies the public discourse about education. In summary, the school subjects and the academic disciplines are different entities with different purposes. Particular content does not necessarily belong in the K-12 curriculum just because it is currently of interest to one of the disciplines.

There also is a need for differentiated models of teaching that take into account the different conditions of learning that are presented by different school subjects and (especially) instructional situations. In this regard, many of the currently popular models of teaching and learning require qualification concerning their spheres of application. For example, models that emphasize strategy instruction, situated learning, or modeling, coaching, and scaffolding appear to be well suited to teaching basic literacy and mathematics skills and procedural knowledge in the sciences, social studies, or humanities. However, they are much less well suited to teaching propositional knowledge in the content areas.

Social constructivist and conceptual change models appear to have broader application potential, although with subject-matter differences in how feasible they are and how they are manifested in the classroom. For example, it is no accident that teaching models calling for initiating a new topic by engaging students in reasoning about problems are popular among mathematics educators. This model is most feasible when students are ready to take the next step in moving up a linear trajectory within a hierarchically organized curriculum strand, especially a strand in which relevant propositional knowledge (as opposed to procedural and conditional knowledge) is limited in scope and volume. Such strands are common in mathematics. However, science and especially social studies are much less hierarchical, subsume much broader and deeper domains of propositional knowledge, and much less often afford teaching situations in which students already possess enough prior knowledge about a new topic to allow them to move immediately into addressing topic-relevant problems or issues in an informed way.

Social constructivist and conceptual change models appear most applicable when it is possible to engage students in discussion of topics about which they have a great deal of prior knowledge, especially if this knowledge includes personal life experiences that students can reflect on as a basis for reasoning. They are less applicable when students are getting initial exposure to primarily new propositional knowledge, as when fifth graders are introduced to chronological treatment of U.S. history. It often is necessary to first establish a common base of information before attempting to engage students in forms of discourse that implicitly assume understanding of this information. I believe that some social constructivists are being unrealistic, even romantic, in suggesting that teachers should routinely avoid transmitting knowledge and instead function only as discussion facilitators.

My interest in this issue has been fueled in part by my collaboration with Janet Alleman in developing instructional units for primary-grade social studies that include a blend of transmission and social constructivist elements. As we observe the lessons being implemented, we find that social constructivist discourse often leads to lessons that have a rough rather than a smooth flow, frequently interrupted or sidetracked momentum, and a poor signal-to-noise ratio. When teachers are working with young learners or with learners whose relevant prior knowledge is very limited and poorly articulated, questions about the topic frequently fail to produce responses or elicit irrelevant or invalid responses.

Primary-grade students often use teachers' questions as occasions for launching stories that they want to tell. These stories may have little or nothing to do with the topic, in which case they distract from the focus of the lesson. In the case of lengthy anecdotes, they derail lesson momentum completely. Also, a core idea of constructivism is that each student builds his or her own unique representation of key ideas. However, students may or may not create complete and accurate reconstructions of what the teacher intended to convey, so that learning may be incomplete or distorted.

What can happen was illustrated in research by Graham Nuthall (2002), whose work is also of methodological interest because he developed unusually rich data sets that included transcripts of the utterances recorded by microphones attached to individual students. The transcripts reflect not only what the students said in whole-class settings, but also what they said when speaking to partners or fellow members of small groups and even when speaking aloud to themselves. Analyses of these utterances across time indicated that students' understandings of a term or idea often were retained in much the same form as they were encoded originally (in response to a statement by the teacher or a peer). These understandings were not necessarily improved if incorrect, transformed to more formal or generalized encodings, or connected to other understandings to form the knowledge network that the teacher wanted the students to construct.

These findings led Nuthall to recommend more teacher presentation of concepts and skills and tighter structuring and scaffolding of students' activities than most social constructivists envision. Nuthall was the most pessimistic of the contributors to an edited volume on social constructivist teaching (most of the others were much more enthusiastic and confident about its feasibility for use in a broad range of classroom situations). However, the minority whose research included assessment of the degree to which the students had acquired the intended understandings were noticeably more guarded and qualified about potential applications of social constructivist teaching than the majority who had not formally assessed learning.

GENERIC ASPECTS OF SUBJECT-SPECIFIC TEACHING

As an educational psychologist, I understand the need for subject-matter specialists to move beyond generic models of teaching and pursue subject-specific issues. However, I also retain appreciation for generic models and value them for their potential power and efficiency as teacher education tools. Consequently, I think it is worth noting that many of the findings produced by subject-matter specialists also provide support for certain generic principles, including some that go beyond those suggested in the earlier process–outcome studies.

Subject-matter specialists seldom make these connections because they usually focus on their areas of specialization. However, many connections await potential discovery by educational psychologists and others with more generic orientations. I saw this for myself when I edited a volume in which specialists representing 14 school subjects (beginning reading, content area reading and literature studies, writing, number, geometry, biology, physics, chemistry, Earth science, history, physical geography, cultural studies, citizenship education, and economics) were asked to draw on theory, research, and the wisdom of practice to synthesize statements on best practices in teaching their subjects. Inspection of these chapters revealed a great deal of subject-specific content, but also a great many commonalities that cut across subjects (Brophy, 2001). When different authors addressed similar teaching methods or learning activities, they typically emphasized the same principles for using them productively, even if they used different terminology and cited different sources. Furthermore, many of the principles developed in only a few of the chapters appeared to have much broader applicability. Noteworthy generic principles included the following.

Goals of teaching for understanding, appreciation, and life application. All authors emphasized teaching for understanding of networks of connected knowledge that would be structured around big ideas and retained in forms that made them available for life application, in contrast to disconnected knowledge learned primarily by rote and retained (if at all) only in inert forms. They also emphasized appreciation goals. Some made few distinctions between their school subject and its underlying discipline, and expressed these goals in terms of developing appreciation for the discipline. Others placed less emphasis on equipping students with disciplinary skills to use to generate knowledge, but depicted students as consumers of discipline-based subject matter who would apply this learning in their lives outside of school.

Addressing multiple goals simultaneously. Authors commonly spoke of attending in a balanced way, or even simultaneously, to multiple types of goals. They typically advocated mixtures of knowledge, skill, attitude, value, and dispositional goals, and in particular, stressed addressing content and process goals simultaneously by engaging students in authentic activities. Authors representing subjects that reflect hierarchically organized knowledge bases also emphasized processing content at several cognitive levels simultaneously.

Inquiry models. Traditional notions of instruction typically call for establishing a knowledge base before moving to application or other higher order activities. In contrast, many of the authors argued for frequent (and in some cases, primary) use of inquiry models that begin by engaging students in problem solving, decision making, and so forth. However, they also noted the need to provide sufficient orientation, structuring, and scaffolding to enable students to engage in these activities productively.

Discourse management. As part of emphasizing forms of inquiry associated with their subject area, the authors recommended teaching students to use related discourse genres, typically involving coconstruction of understandings through discussion and collaborative problem solving. Usually they added that teachers should allow students to rely primarily on their past experiences and current vocabularies before "bridging" to syntheses expressed within disciplinary structures using discipline-specific terminology.

Authentic activities. The authors typically spoke of authentic activities when discussing opportunities for students to develop and apply subject-specific learning. Those who emphasized generation of knowledge tended to depict authentic activities as activities that engage students in doing what disciplinary practitioners do, whereas those who emphasized consumption of knowledge tended to speak of activities that allow students to apply what they are learning to their lives outside of school.

Debriefing. Authors disagreed about the degree to which teachers should thoroughly orient students to an activity before allowing them to engage in it, but all emphasized the importance of postactivity debriefing to assess and reflect on what was learned.

Work with artifacts. Examples of authentic activities typically depicted students engaged in working with the field's artifacts (e.g., prose and poetry selections, geometric figures, biological specimens, chemical compounds, laboratory equipment, historical source material, maps, cultural artifacts). However, most authors expressed reservations about simulations and virtual learning, warning that these experiences can oversimplify what occurs in reality and perhaps induce misconceptions.

Fostering metacognition and self-regulated learning. Many authors emphasized teaching in ways that help students to become metacognitively aware of goals and strategies and better able to self-regulate their learning. Frequently this was part of the rationale for the recommended inquiry approaches and discourse management principles.

Trajectories, misconceptions, and representations. Authors commonly emphasized the importance of teachers being familiar with typical trajectories in the development of levels of understanding or skill in the subject area. They depicted teachers using this knowledge to select appropriate learning activities, scaffold their students' progress through the trajectories, and use (mostly informal) assessment data to keep close track of this progress. Subsumed within the notion of trajectories were notions of false starts and dead ends that occur when students develop or proceed on the basis of misconceptions, as well as ideas about using well-chosen sets of representations to ensure that students did not construct overly specific or otherwise distorted understandings. However, the authors did not have much to say about how to handle misconceptions, because as yet there is not much theory or research speaking to such issues as which misconceptions to address directly and which to ignore unless students bring them up, when and how to refer to or elicit a common misconception, or whether to correct it immediately when it comes up or to let students struggle with it for awhile.

Social aspects of learning. Most authors cited notions of learning community, social construction of knowledge, or sociocultural learning to argue that learning is most likely to be meaningful and accessible for use when it is socially negotiated through classroom discourse. Collaborative learning in small-group contexts was widely recommended, although usually with cautions that students need to be prepared for the task and for the processes involved in working together, the teacher needs to circulate to monitor and scaffold progress, and the work should culminate with whole-class debriefings.

A SYNTHESIS OF GENERIC GUIDELINES FOR GOOD TEACHING

There is broad agreement that students should learn each subject with understanding of its big ideas, appreciation of its value, and the capability and disposition to apply it in their lives outside of school. Analyses of research done in the different subjects have identified some commonalities in conclusions drawn about curricular, instructional, and assessment practices that foster this kind of learning. If phrased as general principles rather than specific behavioral rules, these emerging guidelines can be seen as mutually supportive components of a coherent model of teaching that applies across subjects. Thus, it is possible to identify generic features of good teaching, although not to outline a specific series of steps to be implemented in all situations.

Many of these generic features of good teaching are synthesized within a list of 12 principles presented in a booklet developed for the International Academy of Education (see Brophy, 1999, for elaboration and references). Much of the research support for these principles comes from studies of relationships between classroom processes and student outcomes. However, some principles are rooted in the logic of instructional design, and attention was paid to emergent theories of teaching and learning (e.g., sociocultural, social constructivist) and to the standards statements circulated by organizations representing the major school subjects. Priority was given to principles that have been shown to be applicable under ordinary classroom conditions and associated with progress toward desired student outcomes.

1. *Supportive Classroom Climate*: Students learn best within cohesive and caring learning communities.
2. *Opportunity to Learn*: Students learn more when most of the available time is allocated to curriculum-related activities and the classroom management

system emphasizes maintaining students' engagement in those activities.

3. *Curricular Alignment*: All components of the curriculum are aligned to create a cohesive program for accomplishing instructional purposes and goals.

4. *Establishing Learning Orientations*: Teachers can prepare students for learning by providing initial structuring to clarify intended outcomes and cue desired learning strategies.

5. *Coherent Content*: To facilitate meaningful learning and retention, content is explained clearly and developed with emphasis on its structure and connections.

6. *Thoughtful Discourse*: Questions are planned to engage students in sustained discourse structured around powerful ideas.

7. *Practice and Application Activities*: Students need sufficient opportunities to practice and apply what they are learning, and to receive improvement-oriented feedback.

8. *Scaffolding Students' Task Engagement*: The teacher provides whatever assistance students need to enable them to engage in learning activities productively.

9. *Strategy Teaching*: The teacher models and instructs students in learning and self-regulation strategies.

10. *Cooperative Learning*: Students often benefit from working in pairs or small groups to construct understandings or help one another master skills.

11. *Goal-oriented Assessment*: The teacher uses a variety of formal and informal assessment methods to monitor progress toward learning goals.

12. *Achievement Expectations*: The teacher establishes and follows through on appropriate expectations for learning outcomes.

CONCLUSION

A complete and well-rounded program for teaching any school subject will incorporate a considerable range of curricular and instructional elements, and the mixture of these elements will evolve as students proceed through the grades. Such programs are not likely to result from application of a few principles rooted in a single theory or model, but they can be constructed from grounded theory that respects the complexities of teaching and is informed by the accumulated knowledge base produced through classroom research.

Research on teaching for understanding has advanced the field in several respects because it incorporates a fusion of disciplinary origins and methodological approaches that needed to be synthesized to increase the power of research on teaching. In particular, it brings together the content expertise of subject-matter specialists with the research orientations and methodologies infused into education from other disciplines, including psychology. Until the 1970s and 1980s, most PhD programs for subject-matter specialists (literacy, mathematics, science, and social studies educators) did not provide much training or experience in conducting research on teaching, and relatively few graduates of such programs did much classroom research. They usually had heavy teaching loads, and even if they published frequently, their articles tended to be commentaries on current issues or suggestions about ways to teach popular topics, not research involving systematic collection and analysis of empirical data.

Meanwhile, the latter kind of research usually was being done by people trained in anthropology, ecology, psychology, or sociology. To the extent that these investigators stayed close to their disciplinary origins, their contributions to education were limited. Social psychologists who became interested in classrooms tended to focus on leadership and group dynamics, using concepts and adapting instruments originated by Bales (1950) and other social psychologists. Many of these psychology-based concepts and measures were included in subsequent process–product work done primarily by educational psychologists, whose disciplinary training oriented them toward studies of classroom management and generic aspects of teaching but not subject-specific content development.

Anthropologically trained researchers made important contributions to research on teaching by infusing and perfecting qualitative methods. However, their early substantive contributions were limited by their tendency to stick to an ethnographic perspective (treating classrooms as if they were newly discovered societies whose mores had to be painstakingly triangulated, instead of building on what was already known). For example, much early anthropologically based work went into documenting the "discovery" of what educational ethnographers came to call the initiation–reaction–evaluation (IRE) sequence in the discourse patterns typically observed in classroom lessons. However, this sequence was already so well known and recognized as basic by educators that Bellack et al. (1966) and others had incorporated it into the very structure of their observational systems. Thick description methods began to yield more substantive payoff for educators when they began to be used for purposes that were more educational than anthropological (e.g., documenting the policies and practices of outstanding teachers).

Similarly, ecologists who got interested in education contributed early studies in which commonly occurring classroom settings were identified and shown to be associated with contrasting types of activities (e.g., more teacher–student discourse occurs in lesson settings than in seatwork settings). Ecologically rooted research in classrooms began to yield findings of more value to educators, however, when investigators shifted attention from the affordances and constraints of settings to the activities that occurred during those settings, and especially, the teacher's role in structuring and scaffolding these activities (e.g., Kounin's work on classroom management).

In summary, as research on teaching developed, methods introduced from other disciplines became adapted for use in studies that were more clearly educational. In addition, PhD programs for educators in the subject areas began to train people to do classroom research, and leading universities who hired their graduates expected them to do it. Consequently, much more research on instruction is going on now than at any time previously. Much of this research focuses on subject-specific aspects of instruction and is done by subject-area specialists. However, educational psychologists are often involved as well, either because they have acquired subject-matter expertise themselves or because they collaborate with subject-area specialists. Meanwhile, research on the affective and managerial aspects of teaching continues, with most studies in these areas still being done by researchers trained in anthropology, psychology, or sociology rather than curriculum and instruction.

I believe that educational psychologists have a great deal to contribute to the improvement of schooling. However, achieving this potential will require broadening the field from its traditional focus on learners and learning to include significant attention to teachers and teaching, especially classroom teaching. Such a shift in purview is important even for the classroom management and motivational aspects of teaching, but especially for the aspects involved in helping students learn curricular content and skills.

References

Anderson, H. (1943). Domination and socially integrative behavior. In R. Barker, J. Kounin, & H. Wright (Eds.), *Child behavior and development* (pp. 459–483). New York: McGraw-Hill.

Anderson, H., Brewer, J., & Reed, M. (1946). Studies of teachers' classroom personalities. III: Follow-up studies of the effects of dominative and integrative contacts on children's behavior. *Applied Psychology Monographs, 11*.

Anderson, L., & Burns, R. (1989). *Research in classrooms: The study of teachers, teaching, and instruction*. Oxford: Pergamon.

Anderson, L., Evertson, C., & Brophy, J. (1979). An experimental study of effective teaching in first-grade reading groups. *Elementary School Journal, 79*, 193–223.

Bales, R. (1950). *Interaction process analysis*. New York: Addison-Wesley.

Barr, A. (1929). *Characteristic differences in the teaching performance of good and poor teachers of the social studies*. Bloomington, IL: Public School Publishing.

Bellack, A., Kliebard, H., Hyman, R., & Smith, F. (1966). *The language of the classroom*. New York: Teachers College Press.

Berliner, D., & Calfee, R. (Eds.). (1996). *Handbook of educational psychology*. New York: Simon & Schuster Macmillan.

Berliner, D., Fisher, C., Filby, N., & Marliave, R. (1978). *Executive summary of beginning teacher evaluation study*. San Francisco: Far West Regional Laboratory for Educational Research and Development.

Berliner, D., & Tikunoff, W. (1977). Ethnography in the classroom. In G. Borich & K. Fenton (Eds.), *The appraisal of teaching: Concepts and process*. Reading, MA: Addison-Wesley.

Bogdan, R., & Biklen, S. (1982). *Qualitative research for education: An introduction to theory and methods*. Boston: Allyn & Bacon.

Bossert, S. (1979). *Tasks and social relationships in classrooms: A study of instructional organization and its consequences*. New York: Cambridge University Press.

Bronfenbrenner, U. (1989). Ecological systems theory. In R. Vasta (Ed.), *Annals of child development* (Vol. 6, pp. 187–250). Greenwich, CT: JAI.

Brophy, J. (1973). Stability of teacher effectiveness. *American Educational Research Journal, 10*, 245–252.

Brophy, J. (1999). *Teaching* (Educational Practices Series No. 1). Geneva: International Bureau of Education.

Brophy, J. (Ed.). (2001). *Subject-specific instructional methods and activities*. New York: Elsevier Science.

Brophy, J., & Evertson, C. (1976). *Learning from teaching: A developmental perspective*. Boston: Allyn & Bacon.

Brophy, J., & Good, T. (1986). Teacher behavior and student achievement. In M. C. Wittrock (Ed.), *Handbook of research on teaching* (3rd ed., pp. 328–375). New York: Macmillan.

Chilcoat, G. (1989). Instructional behaviors for clearer presentations in the classroom. *Instructional Science, 18*, 289–314.

Coleman, J., Campbell, E., Hobson, C., McPartland, J., Mood, A., Weinfield, F., et al. (1966). *Equality of educational opportunity*. Washington, DC: U.S. Office of Health, Education, and Welfare.

Cuban, L. (1993). *How teachers taught: Constancy and change in American classrooms, 1890–1980* (2nd Ed.). New York: Longman.

Dantonio, M., & Beisenhertz, P. (2001). *Learning to question, questioning to learn: Developing effective teacher questioning practices*. Boston: Allyn & Bacon.

Doyle, W. (1984). How order is achieved in classrooms: An interim report. *Journal of Curriculum Studies, 16*, 259-277.

Doyle, W. (1986). Classroom organization and management. In M. C. Wittrock (Ed.), *Handbook of research of research on teaching* (3rd ed., pp. 392-431). New York: Macmillan.

Dunkin, M., & Biddle, B. (1974). *The study of teaching*. New York: Holt, Rinehart & Winston.

Emmer, E., Evertson, C., & Anderson, L. (1980). Effective classroom management at the beginning of the school year. *Elementary School Journal, 80*, 219-231.

Evertson, C., Anderson, C., Anderson, L., & Brophy, J. (1980). Relationships between classroom behaviors and student outcomes in junior high mathematics and English classes. *American Educational Research Journal, 17*, 43-60.

Evertson, C., & Emmer, E. (1982a). Effective management at the beginning of the school year in junior high classes. *Journal of Educational Psychology, 74*, 485-498.

Evertson, C., & Emmer, E. (1982b). Preventive classroom management. In D. Duke (Ed.), *Helping teachers manage classrooms* (pp. 2-31). Alexandria, VA: Association for Supervision and Curriculum Development.

Evertson, C., & Green, J. (1986). Observation as inquiry and method. In M. Wittrock (Ed.), *Handbook of research on teaching* (3rd ed., pp. 162-213). New York: Macmillan.

Fisher, C., Filby, N., Marliave, R., Cahen, L., & Dishaw, M. (1980). Teaching behaviors, academic learning time, and student achievement. An overview. In C. Denham & A. Lieberman (Eds.), *Time to learn*. San Francisco: Far West Laboratory for Educational Research and Development.

Flanders, N. (1970). *Analyzing teacher behavior*. Reading, MA: Addison-Wesley.

Fraivillig, J., Murphy, L., & Fuson, K. (1999). Advancing children's mathematical thinking in *Everyday Mathematics* classrooms. *Journal for Research in Mathematics Education, 30*, 148-170.

Freiberg, H., Stein, T., & Huang, S. (1995). Effects of a classroom management intervention on student achievement in inner-city elementary schools. *Educational Research and Evaluation: An International Journal on Theory and Practice, 1*, 36-66.

Gage, N., & Needels, M. (1989). Process-product research on teaching: A review of criticisms. *Elementary School Journal, 89*, 253-297.

Getzels, J., & Jackson, P. (1963). The teacher's personality and characteristics. In N. Gage (Ed), *Handbook of research on teaching* (pp. 506-582). Chicago: Rand McNally.

Glaser, B., & Strauss, A. (1979). *The discovery of grounded theory: Strategies for qualitative research*. Hawthorne, NY: Aldine.

Goldin-Meadow, S., Kim, S., & Singer, M. (1999). What the teacher's hands tell the student's mind about math. *Journal of Educational Psychology, 91*, 720-730.

Good, T., Biddle, B., & Brophy, J. (1975). *Teachers make a difference*. New York: Holt, Rinehart & Winston.

Good, T., & Brophy, J. (2003). *Looking in classrooms* (9th ed.). Boston: Allyn & Bacon.

Good, T., Ebmeier, H., & Beckerman, T. (1978). Teaching mathematics in high and low SES classrooms: An empirical comparison. *Journal of Teacher Education, 29*, 85-90.

Good, T., & Grouws, D. (1977). Teaching effects: A process-product study in fourth grade mathematics classrooms. *Journal of Teacher Education, 28*, 49-54.

Good, T., & Grouws, D. (1979). *Experimental study of mathematics instruction in elementary schools* (Final Report). Columbia, MO: Center for the Study of Social Behavior, University of Missouri (NIE-G-79-0103).

Good, T., Grouws, D., & Beckerman, T. (1978). Curriculum pacing: Some empirical data in mathematics. *Journal of Curriculum Studies, 10*, 75-81.

Good, T., Grouws, D., & Ebmeier, M. (1983). *Active mathematics teaching*. New York: Longman.

Gottfredson, D., Gottfredson, G., & Hybl, L. (1993). Managing adolescent behavior: A multiyear multi-school study. *American Educational Research Journal, 30*, 179-215.

Hiebert, J., & Wearne, D. (1992). Links between teaching and learning place value with understanding in first grade. *Journal for Research in Mathematics Education, 23*, 98-122.

Hilberg, R. S., Waxman, H., & Tharp, R. (2004). Introduction: Purposes and perspectives on classroom observation research. In H. Waxman, R. Tharp, & R. S. Hilberg (Eds.), *Observational research in U.S. classrooms: New approaches for understanding cultural and linguistic diversity* (pp. 1-20). Cambridge, UK: Cambridge University Press.

Horn, E. (1914). Distribution of opportunity for participation among various pupils in classroom recitations. *Teachers College Contributions to Education*, No. 67.

Jayne, C. (1945). A study of the relationship between teaching procedures and educational outcomes. *Journal of Experimental Education, 14*, 101-134.

Kliebard, H. (1986). *The struggle for the American curriculum, 1893-1958*. New York: Routledge.

Kounin, J. (1970). *Discipline and group management in classrooms*. New York: Holt, Rinehart & Winston.

Kounin, J., & Doyle, P. (1975). Degree of continuity of a lesson's signal system and the task involvement of children. *Journal of Educational Psychology, 67*, 159-164.

Kounin, J., Friesen, W., & Norton, A. (1966). Managing emotionally disturbed children in regular classrooms. *Journal of Educational Psychology, 57*, 1-13.

Kounin, J., & Gump, P. (1958). The ripple effect in discipline. *Elementary School Journal, 35*, 158-162.

Kounin, J., & Gump, P. (1961). The comparative influence of punitive and non-punitive teachers upon children's concepts of school misconduct. *Journal of Educational Psychology, 52*, 44-49.

Luiten, J., Ames, W., & Ackerson, G. (1970). A meta-analysis of the effects of advance organizers on learning and retention. *American Educational Research Journal, 17*, 211-218.

McCaleb, J., & White, J. (1980). Critical dimensions in evaluating teacher clarity. *Journal of Classroom Interaction, 15*, 27-30.

McDonald, F. (1977). Research on teaching: Report on Phase II of the Beginning Teacher Evaluation Study. In G. Borich & K. Fenton (Eds.), *The appraisal of teaching: Concepts and process*. Reading, MA: Addison–Wesley.

Medley, D. (1979). The effectiveness of teachers. In P. Peterson & H. Walberg (Eds.), *Research on teaching: Concepts, findings, and implications* (pp. 11–27). Berkeley, CA: McCutchan.

Medley, D. (1992). Structured observation. In M. Alkin (Ed.), *Encyclopedia of educational research* (6th ed., pp. 1310–1315). New York: Macmillan.

Medley, D., & Mitzel, H. (1958). A technique for measuring classroom behavior. *Journal of Educational Psychology, 49*, 86–92.

Medley, D., & Mitzel, H. (1963). Measuring classroom behavior by systematic observation. In N. Gage (Ed.), *Handbook of researching on teaching* (pp. 247–328). Chicago: Rand McNally.

Morsh, J. (1956). *Development report—Systematic observation of instructor behavior*. USAF Personnel Training Research Center Development Report, No. AFPTRC-TN-56-52.

Moskowitz, G., & Hayman, J. (1976). Success strategies of inner-city teachers: A year-long study. *Journal of Educational Research, 69*, 283–289.

National Council of Teachers of Mathematics. (1989). *Curriculum and evaluation standards for school mathematics*. Reston, VA: Author.

National Research Council. (1989). *Everybody counts: A report to the nation on the future of mathematics education*. Washington, DC: National Academy of Sciences.

Nuthall, G. (2002). Social constructivist teaching and the shaping of student knowledge and thinking. In J. Brophy (Ed.), *Social constructivist teaching: Affordances and constraints* (pp. 43–79). New York: Elsevier Science.

Nuthall, G., & Alton-Lee, A. (1990). Research on teaching and learning: Thirty years of change. *Elementary School Journal, 90*, 546–570.

Patrick, B., Hisley, J., & Kempler, T. (2000). "What's everybody so excited about?": The effects of teacher enthusiasm on student intrinsic motivation and vitality. *Journal of Experimental Education, 68*, 217–236,

Patton, M. (1990). *Qualitative evaluation and research methods* (2nd ed.). Newbury Park, CA: Sage.

Puckett, R. (1928). Making supervision objective. *School Review, 36*, 209–212.

Remmers, H. (1963). Rating methods in research on teaching. In N. Gage (Ed.), *Handbook of research on teaching* (pp. 329–378). Chicago: Rand McNally.

Rosenshine, B. (1970). Enthusiastic teaching: A research review. *School Review, 78*, 499–514.

Rosenshine, B., & Furst, N. (1973). The use of direct observation to study teaching. In R. Traverse (Ed.), *Second handbook of research on teaching*. Chicago: Rand McNally.

Rosenshine, B., & Stevens, R. (1986). Teaching functions. In M.C. Wittrock (Ed.), *Handbook on research on teaching* (3rd ed., pp. 376–391). New York: Macmillan.

Rowe, M. (1986). Wait time: Slowing down may be a way of speeding up! *Journal of Teacher Education, 37*, 43–50.

Ryans, D. (1952). A study of criterion data (a factor analysis of teacher behaviors in elementary school). *Educational and Psychological Measurement, 12*, 333–344.

Ryans, D., & Wandt, E. (1952). A factor analysis of observed teacher behavior in the secondary school. *Educational and Psychological Measurement, 12*, 574–586.

Schuck, R. (1981). The impact of set induction on student achievement and retention. *Journal of Educational Research, 74*, 227–232.

Simon, A., & Boyer, E.G. (Eds.). (1970). *Mirrors for behavior II: An anthology of observational instruments* (Vol. A and B). (A special edition of the *Classroom Interaction Newsletter*). Philadelphia: Research for Better Schools.

Smith, L., & Land, M. (1981). Low-inference verbal behaviors related to teacher clarity. *Journal of Classroom Interaction, 17*, 37–42.

Smith, B., & Meux, M. (1959). *A study of the logic of teaching: A report on the first phase of a five-year research project*. Washington, DC: U.S. Office of Education.

Smith, B.O., Meux, M., Coombs, J., Nuthall, G., & Precians. R. (1967). *A study of the strategies of teaching*. Urbana: University of Illinois, Bureau of Educational Research.

Stallings, J. (1975). Implementation and child effects of teaching practices in Follow Through classrooms. *Monographs of the Society for Research in Child Development, 40*(7–8, Serial No. 163).

Stallings, J. (1980). Allocated academic learning time revisited, or beyond time on task. *Educational Researcher, 8*(11), 11–16.

Stallings, J., Cory, R., Fairweather, J., & Needels, M. (1977). *Early childhood education classroom evaluation*. Menlo Park, CA: SRI International.

Stallings, J., Cory, R., Fairweather, J., & Needels, M. (1978). *A study of basic reading skills taught in secondary schools*. Menlo Park, CA: SRI International.

Stallings, J., & Kaskowitz, D. (1974). *Follow Through classroom observation evaluation, 1972–1973*. Stanford: Stanford Research Institute (SRI Project URU-7870).

Stallings, J., Needels, M., & Stayrook, N. (1979). *The teaching of basic reading skills in secondary schools, Phase II and Phase III*. Menlo Park, CA: SRI International.

Swift, J., Gooding, C., & Swift, P. (1988). Questions and wait time. In J. Dillon (Ed.), *Questioning and discussion: A multidisciplinary study* (pp. 192–212). Norwood, NJ: Ablex.

Taba, H., Levine, S., & Elzey, F. (1964). *Thinking in elementary school children*. San Francisco: San Francisco State College.

Tobin, K. (1983). The influence of wait-time on classroom learning. *European Journal of Science Education, 5*(1), 35–48.

Wallen, N., & Travers, R. (1963). Analysis and investigation of teaching methods. In N. L. Gage (Ed.), *Handbook of research on teaching* (pp. 448–505). Chicago: Rand McNally.

Wilen, W. (1991). *What research has to say to the teacher: Questioning techniques for teachers* (3rd ed.). Washington, DC: National Education Association.

Withall, J. (1960). Research tools: Observing and recording behavior. *Review of Educational Research, 30,* 496–512.

Withall, J., & Lewis, W. (1963). Social interaction in the classroom. In N. Gage (Ed.), *Handbook of research on teaching* (pp. 683–714). Chicago: Rand McNally.

Wright, E., & Proctor, V. (1961). *Systematic observation of verbal interaction as a method of comparing mathematics lessons.* St. Louis, MO: Washington University. (U.S. Office of Education Cooperative Research Project No. 816.)

Wrightstone, J. (1935). *Appraisal of newer practices in selected public schools.* New York: Bureau of Publication, Teachers College, Columbia University.

·34·

THE ROLE OF PEERS AND GROUP LEARNING

Angela M. O'Donnell
Rutgers, The State University of New Jersey

The chapter focuses on promoting a coherent and principled approach to the use of varied models of peer learning to fit the teacher's instructional goals for students. Students need to acquire a variety of different skills and knowledge in school that vary in complexity and difficulty. These varied skills and knowledge cannot all be acquired by using the same strategies, and there is no single theoretical perspective on peer learning that can explain how knowledge and skill is acquired in the widely varied tasks and demands of the classroom. This chapter describes different theoretical perspectives (both social and cognitive) on peer learning and the mechanisms by which peers promote learning. In this chapter, the terms *collaborative learning* and *cooperative learning* are used interchangeably. The kinds of classroom tasks that teachers may choose and the role of the teacher in using peer learning to accomplish those tasks are also described. Finally, the key principles that might guide teachers in selecting a peer learning method are outlined and strategies for assessing the outcomes from group learning are outlined in Table 34.1.

Peer learning is a broad umbrella term that includes cooperative and collaborative learning, peer tutoring, cross-age tutoring, and other forms of learning in which peers help one another. It is often recommended as a teaching strategy to improve students' learning and performance. The possibility of improving interaction, respect, and relations among diverse learners is thought to be a potential benefit of peer learning. Many state and national standards for curricula include recommendations for the use of groups and other forms of peer learning situations to enhance critical thinking, conceptual understanding, and other higher order skills. Too often, however, teachers do not connect specific types of peer learning to theoretical perspectives on peer learning, or goals for instruction, nor do they give due consideration to issues of assessment. There are a variety of ways in which to organize peer learning, and decisions about how to do so depend on the tasks assigned, the contingencies associated with task completion, and the size and composition of the group in which children work.

PERSPECTIVES ON PEER LEARNING: A FOCUS ON SOCIAL THEORIES

Theories of peer learning tend to give greater weight to either social or cognitive processes. Table 34.1 provides a summary of key theoretical orientations to peer learning and the implications of those orientations for practical classroom decisions. The latter part of the chapter describes a number of specific cooperative techniques that are influenced by many of these theoretical perspectives.

Many of the original theories of cooperative learning were strongly influenced by social psychological principles and had their foundation in Lewinian field theory (Deutsch, 1949). The fundamental principle underlying these theories of group learning and cooperative learning is positive interdependence among group members (Johnson & Johnson, 1991). When group members experience interdependence, the achievement of their goals depends on the other members of the group. When one individual accomplishes her goals in a competitive context, other participants cannot, a condition known as

TABLE 34.1. Implications of Theoretical Perspectives on Peer Learning

	Theoretical Perspectives					
	Social-Behavioral			Cognitive		
					Developmental	
Considerations	Motivation	Social Cohesion	Sociocultural	Elaboration	Piagetian	Vygotsky
Goals/incentives	Necessary	Not necessary	Not necessary	Not necessary	Not necessary	Not necessary
Group size	Large (4–6)	Large (4–6)	Large	Small	Small (2–4)	
Group composition	Heterogeneous	Heterogeneous	Heterogeneous	Homogeneous/heterogeneous	Homogeneous	Heterogeneous
Tasks	Rehearsal	Rehearsal/integrative	Problem solving/inquiry	Rehearsal/integrative	Exploratory	Skills
Teacher role	Director	Facilitator	Facilitator	Facilitator	Facilitator	Model/guide
Potential problems	Use of reward Group size	Poor social skills Social loafing Cognitive loafing	Unequal participation; peripheral participation	Poor help-giving; unequal participation	Inactive No cognitive conflict	Poor help-giving; providing adequate time/dialogue
Limiting problems	Improvement scores Simpler tasks Social cohesion	Team building Conflict resolutions strategies Discuss group process	Building a sense of community; valuing of contributions	Direct instruction in help-giving Modeling help-giving Scripting interactions	Structuring controversy	Direct instruction in help-giving; modeling help-giving

Adapted from O'Donnell, A. M., & O'Kelly, J. (1994). Learning from peers: Beyond the rhetoric of positive results. *Educational Psychology Review, 6,* 327.

negative interdependence. For example, when runners compete in a race, only one individual can win. In contrast, individuals in a cooperative context cannot succeed in accomplishing their goals unless everyone succeeds, a condition known as positive interdependence. The success of a cooperative group is dependent on the success of everyone in the group. A relay team is an example of a cooperatively interdependent group. No one on the team succeeds unless everyone on the team does.

Social Motivational Perspective

The use of reward to create positive interdependence among group members is characteristic of a social motivational approach to peer learning. One of the most widely researched and widely used versions of cooperative learning based on this approach is Robert Slavin's Student Teams Achievement Division (Slavin, 1986). Other techniques that are derived from this perspective include Teams-Games-Tournaments (Devries & Edwards, 1973), Team Accelerated Instruction (Slavin, Leavey, & Madden, 1986), and Cooperative Integrated Reading and Composition (Stevens, Madden, Slavin, & Farnish, 1987). The basic premise underlying these techniques is the idea that students will be motivated to work together and help one another because the group as a whole will be rewarded or receive recognition.

In STAD, cooperation among students is used to review or practice material. The teacher presents material initially to students, using his or her typical instructional manner. The cooperative task is to rehearse or practice what the teacher has already taught. The teacher makes most of the key decisions about the content to be taught, the kind of tests to be administered, and the kinds of rewards or recognition that will be used (see Table 34.1). The teacher creates heterogeneous groups of four to six students and calculates a baseline score for each student (e.g., the score on a previous quiz, last year's grade in the subject area, or some combination of scores from quizzes). The students are provided with worksheets that list questions related to the content they have been taught. Their task is to work together, asking one another questions, checking the back of the worksheets they have for the correct answers, and providing additional explanations to those who do not understand the material or get incorrect answers. Students then take individual tests over the material, thus ensuring that students are individually accountable for their performance. Students' scores are compared to their baseline scores, and improvement points are calculated. The teacher decides the range of improvement points that is necessary in order to earn specific numbers of team points. The team points generated by each individual contribute to an overall team score. Teams with high levels of performance are recognized in class. Teachers must decide on the nature of the recognition provided and how many teams should be recognized. Any reward selected must be one that is valued by students. Rewards are allocated to the team and do not involve individual grades. The goal of the teacher is to increase the motivation for academic achievement by the students.

Important features of the social-motivational approach to peer learning include the use of heterogeneous groups, individual accountability in the form of individual quizzes, the use of improvement points rather than raw scores for the calculation of overall group performance, and the use of recognition and reward in response to group performance. Interdependence is created and maintained by linking the outcomes of the team members together through the use of team points for individual performance. The key mechanism promoting interdependence is motivation.

It is difficult to maintain interdependence if students believe that they are unequal contributors to performance. Positive interdependence can be maintained if participating students believe they can contribute without risk of ridicule or pressure. A key feature of STAD that serves to maintain interdependence is that each student has the same opportunity to contribute to the team score, irrespective of the actual level of performance. The use of improvement points guarantees that each student is capable of contributing to the overall group goal. Because students use prepared answer sheets to respond to their peers' efforts to respond to questions, the cognitive levels of the cooperative tasks may remain quite low and focused more on factual recall and basic comprehension. It would be very difficult to prepare answer sheets for responses to more open-ended questions. This limitation is a weakness of the technique.

Slavin (1986) outlined a number of alternative cooperative learning techniques such as Teams-Games-Tournament, CIRC, and Team Accelerated Instruction that all rely on students' increased motivation as a result of group goals and individual accountability as the mechanism by which cooperation promotes learning. Some of these techniques were developed for specific subject matter such as mathematics (TAI: Slavin et al., 1986). The development of CIRC (Stevens et al., 1987) was based on an analysis of the research on how to teach reading and writing and reflected both social elements and cognitive strategy elements. Although particular techniques may be primarily social or cognitive, many cooperative learning techniques include both sets of elements.

Social Cohesion Perspective

Social cohesion approaches to cooperative learning also rely on positive interdependence among group members.

The source of interdependence in social cohesion approaches is the care and concern of group members for one another (see Table 34.1). There are five basic elements in structuring cooperative Learning Together (Johnson & Johnson, 1991): positive interdependence, face-to-face promotive interaction, individual accountability and personal responsibility, interpersonal and small-group skills, and group processing. The Johnsons' Learning Together technique is a good example of this approach to cooperative learning and involves a lot of attention to helping students develop the necessary social skills to work effectively together. The care and concern for others that is necessitated by a social cohesion approach may not readily be found among one's students. Teachers may have to spend considerable time in helping students to care for one another, to develop an interest in helping others, to see others' perspectives, to be respectful in response to others, and to provide encouragement and feedback.

Students are assigned to four- to six-person groups that are heterogeneous with respect to ability, gender, race, and ethnicity. Time is devoted to team building and the development of social skills. Roles are assigned to individuals (e.g., the checker is responsible for ensuring that everyone understands the material). The roles are more connected to the social management of the group and are not integrally connected to cognitive activities. Students engage in the task at hand, performing their designated roles. When the group tasks are completed, group members review the group process and identify the aspects of working together that they believed went well and those that they wish to improve. The opportunity to focus on the process of interaction prompts students to be metacognitive about their social engagement. The strengths of Learning Together include its emphasis on social skill development, the development of a caring classroom climate, and the specific involvement of the students in evaluating the way their groups work.

Students using Learning Together can work on complex tasks. They must coordinate their efforts in pursuit of a single goal, monitor progress toward that goal, and redirect their efforts if necessary. These are complex cognitive skills, and students will vary in their ability to use them. If students do not also have good social skills and know how to disagree and query the direction of the group, interpersonal difficulties may arise and escalate.

The potential weaknesses of the particular technique include the reliance on a group grade for a group product. The use of group grades is controversial (Kagan, 1995, 1996), and mechanisms for ensuring individual accountability are more often recommended. Potential conflicts can arise between the culture of the classroom and family encouragement of competitive behavior. Teachers must pay attention to creating a culture in the classroom in which children treat one another with respect and care. This may be easier to do in the elementary school, as the teacher is with the same children all, or most of the day.

Among the important features of the social-cohesion approach to peer learning are the use of heterogeneous groups, face-to-face interaction, individual accountability, and group processing of the interactions that occur. The deliberate training of students in social skills offsets potentially negative group processes that may result from the heterogeneity of the group, particularly when students work on more complex tasks. The engagement in processing by group members of the interactions that occurred enhances students' awareness of their behavior and contributes to the promotion of positive interdependence.

Effectiveness of Social Approaches

Meta-analyses of research studies that compared the effectiveness of cooperative learning methods, competitive, and individualistic learning conditions show strong support for the effects of cooperative learning (Johnson & Johnson, 1981, 1989). A great many of the studies included in these meta-analyses involved cooperative learning techniques that reflected either a social-motivational perspective or a social cohesion perspective. Slavin (1996) examined the effect sizes associated with research studies of cooperative learning methods that included group goals and individual accountability and concluded that group goals and individual accountability are necessary for successful cooperative learning. Across the 52 studies included in Slavin's analysis, the median effect size was +0.32. In 25 studies that did not include group goals and individual accountability, the median effect size for cooperative learning methods was only +0.07.

Many teachers, however, do not believe in the use of reward (Antil, Jenkins, Wayne, & Vadasy, 1998) despite the positive effects of cooperative techniques that include group goals and individual accountability. They do not use the cooperative techniques as recommended by the researchers who developed the technique and documented its effectiveness through extensive research. The published research provides evidence of the effectiveness of cooperative learning techniques when implemented as designed. When teachers deviate from this, it is unclear how effective the altered technique is.

When teachers choose not to use rewards when implementing their version of Student Teams Achievement Divisions, for example, they are eliminating a key component of the technique that contributes to student achievement and positive student interaction in heterogeneous

groups. If positive interdependence is not created by the use of group goals and rewards, other methods of promoting positive interdependence will be needed. Without positive interdependence among group members, problems in group process and productivity are highly likely. Slavin (1996) reported that the effect sizes associated with cooperative learning without individual accountability were negligible. This finding is supported by the more recent work of McMaster and Fuchs (2002).

PERSPECTIVES ON PEER LEARNING: A FOCUS ON COGNITIVE THEORIES

Social perspectives on peer learning do not ignore the cognitive processes that occur but emphasize the social processes rather than cognitive processes. The various perspectives are not mutually exclusive. Cognitive perspectives on peer learning explicitly focus on cognitive processes that may be promoted during peer learning. In this section, we describe several types of peer learning that are influenced by different cognitive or developmental theories.

Cognitive Elaboration Perspectives

Cognitive-elaboration approaches to peer learning are based on information processing theory. Peer interaction is used to amplify individual performance of basic information processing activities such as encoding, schema activation, rehearsal, metacognition, and retrieval (see Table 34.1). Information processing theory suggests that performing these activities in the presence of peers will result in deeper processing and more active engagement with the tasks at hand. The presence of a peer can help students stay on task, and the feedback provided by a peer can help students understand when they need to check their understanding of the content they are trying to explain. Scripted Cooperation (O'Donnell & Dansereau, 1992; O'Donnell, Dansereau, Hall, & Rocklin, 1987) is based on information processing theory, and pairs engage in cognitive tasks typically performed by an individual. The pair reads a section of a text. One person then summarizes the material to the other. The partner's task is to detect errors in the summary. Both partners then work on ways to elaborate on the material, finding ways to make it memorable by using imagery, generating mnemonics, and deliberately linking the material to information they already know. They then switch roles for the next section of the text and proceed in this way until they have worked through all the material. Once they have completed the activities, they work together to review the material. The technique improves text processing because it emphasizes cognitive processes known to increase learning such as rehearsal, metacognition, and elaboration.

Research has shown that Scripted Cooperation is an effective strategy (O'Donnell & Dansereau, 1992). Not only do students perform better on tests related to the material when they work together compared to comparison groups, they also perform better on subsequent tasks when they work alone (O'Donnell et al., 1987). Scripted cooperation has been used successfully by students as young as third grade (Rottman & Cross, 1990) with reading tasks, and a modified version of the script was successfully used with fifth-grade students learning to solve mathematical problems (Zuber, 1992). The technique is highly structured, and with younger children, the teacher must provide lots of opportunities for children to learn the basic component skills such as summarizing, error detection, and elaboration. The technique is focused less on what students teach one another and more on how the cooperative context provides a stimulus to deeper processing, more focused activity, and less cognitive load on an individual student.

Noreen Webb's work also stems from a cognitive elaborative approach. Much of her work has focused on students' learning of mathematics. She has explored the effects of various types of groupings (i.e., heterogeneous, homogeneous, female-dominated, male-dominated) on students' achievement. Webb's groups are more open-ended than the dyads using Scripted Cooperation. Students decide how to participate, although typically training is provided in how to do so. Students who are active participants in a group learn more than those who are passive, those who provide explanations achieve more than those who do not, and higher quality explanations are associated with higher levels of achievement (Webb, 1989, 1991, 1992). High-level explanations are expressions of deeper processing and elaboration of content and may be associated with restructuring of existing knowledge.

There are a number of possible difficulties in using the kind of approach used by Webb and colleagues. First, not all students provide good explanations or are necessarily given an opportunity to do so. Typically, the more able students provide more explanations and the less able or less experienced students seek help and look for explanations. Webb and her colleagues have made efforts to teach students how to seek appropriate help with mixed success (Webb & Farivar, 1994). There is also the risk of amplifying social status differences in a classroom. Status differences occur when students see some of their peers as more valuable and judge them as having more to contribute than others. These differences may occur because of ability or because of more diffuse status char-

acteristics such as race, ethnicity, gender, or language of origin (Meeker, 1981). Characteristics are considered *diffuse* if they have no direct bearing on task performance but are assumed to be indicators of more or less capability to perform the task (Meeker, 1981). For example, boys might be expected to perform better on certain tasks by their female peers although there may be no actual differences in performance of the task based on gender. Status differences and their implications for classrooms are described in more detail later in the chapter in the section on learning in heterogeneous groups.

Cognitive Developmental Perspectives

Both Piagetian and Vygotskian theories provide perspectives on peer learning and share a common emphasis on a constructivist approach to teaching and learning that involves both individual and social processes. The learner is an active participant in the learning process, using prior experience and knowledge to construct new understandings. The processes described by Piaget and Vygotsky may come into play when learning with peers.

Piagetian Theory. Piaget's constructivist theory of cognitive development (1985) describes how a child develops new conceptual structures as a result of interaction with the environment through adaptation involving processes of assimilation and accommodation. New objects, events, or experiences are brought into existing cognitive frameworks through assimilative processes. Modifications to existing cognitive structures occur when an existing cognitive structure is changed in some way as a result of experiencing new objects or events. The individual seeks equilibrium or balance in the cognitive system, and when this balance is disrupted, the individual seeks to restore it. Opportunities to interact with peers may provide opportunities for cognitive disequilibrium for participants. Children may come to new understandings as they work together on activities or engage in discussions.

Instructional efforts based on Piagetian theory seek to stimulate conceptual change in students by challenging students' existing conceptions in an effort to create cognitive disequilibrium on the part of students who will then attempt to restore the balance (see Table 34.1). Through a process of disequilibrium and reequilibration, students construct new cognitive structures. The teacher may elicit students' conceptions about a phenomenon, provide opportunities for students to test predictions, point toward contradictory evidence, and ask students to contrast their expectations with their experiences (Neale, Smith, & Johnson, 1990). A teacher may ask students to predict how many "heads" will appear if a coin is tossed eight times. Students are likely to suggest four. The teacher might then proceed to toss the coin eight times. One possible result is that of the eight coin tosses, six of them resulted in "heads" coming up. If the student had a belief that 50 percent of the time "heads" should come up, the actual result will be surprising. He must now reconcile the discrepancy between the expected and the actual experience. The intent of this instructional strategy is to first make students aware of their beliefs, to then create cognitive conflict on the part of the student by presenting contradictory experiences, and explicitly require the student to resolve the discrepancy.

The goal is to have the student restructure existing cognitive structures as a result, but this approach may not always be successful. Students may respond in a variety of ways to contradictory information (De Lisi & Golbeck, 1999). Students can ignore the discrepancy or come to believe that the actual event is what they anticipated. The child may not in fact experience conflict. Children often fail to change concepts because they fail to attend to key features of an experience (Chinn & Malhotra, 2002). Chinn and Brewer (1993) and De Lisi and Golbeck (1999) describe a variety of responses that children might have to information that conflicts with their current understandings.

Piaget's ideas about peer influence have important implications for cooperative and collaborative learning (De Lisi, 2002; De Lisi & Golbeck, 1999). Children are more likely to develop in contexts in which the peers have equal power and each child has the opportunity to influence one another. Children who work with adults are likely to comply with the adult because of the differential in power. Children may simply accept what the more powerful, authoritative adult says without experiencing cognitive conflicts or examining prior beliefs. The relationship is one of constraint rather than cooperation (De Lisi, 2002). Power relationships among peers may also not be equal. Certain children may have more status and power within a group as a function of perceived ability, popularity, and other characteristics such as gender or race (Cohen & Lotan, 1995). Children with high status typically have more influence over the interaction in the group. They tend to say more, offer explanations, and provide answers to the questions asked by children with lower status. Other children may simply go along with the ideas of these children with high status.

Vygotskian Theory. Vygotsky's perspective on development included both cultural/societal components but also individual components (Hogan & Tudge, 1999). There is a dialectical relationship between the child and the cultural environment: "In the process of development, the child not only masters the items of cultural experience but the habits and forms of cultural behavior, the cultural methods of reasoning" (p. 415, Vygotsky, 1929). Although the social environment provides models of performance and skill, the child must still internalize these skills and master them for himself. The features of the available environment are very important: "The presence or absence of certain types of institutions (e.g., schools) technologies, and semiotic tools (e.g., pens or computers) as well as variations in the values, beliefs, and practices of different cultural groups are interdependent with differences in ways in which children's development proceeds" (Hogan & Tudge, 1999, p. 41). Children who have had access to computers and tools such as instant messaging had opportunities to interact with others in ways that their parents never had. The characteristics of the learner are also important, as attributes such as motivation, work ethic, curiosity, and others will influence the degree to which the learner masters the skills necessary for successful participation in the community.

A key idea in Vygotsky's theory is the *zone of proximal development*, which is the level of competent performance that can be achieved by a student or learner when supported by another individual (Hogan & Tudge, 1999). A more competent child or adult can provide assistance by recognizing the current level of functioning of the learner, the kind of performance that might be possible, and is capable of providing that support to attain a better level of performance. Cognitive development occurs as the child internalizes the skills modeled or jointly constructed in interaction with a more competent other. The child's cognitive structures are reorganized, and in subsequent interactions, the child may externalize these reorganized cognitive structures by explaining her thinking or actions.

From a Vygotskian perspective, the most likely pairing to promote cognitive growth is that between an adult and a child. The adult is likely to be able recognize the current level of functioning of the child and be capable of adjusting instruction to support the child's efforts. The kind of help a learner receives must match the learner's need (Webb, 1991). Adults are likely to more effectively provide the appropriate level of help needed by a learner than a child would. The zone of proximal development is jointly constructed by the interacting participants (Hogan & Tudge, 1999) and is best accomplished when one partner is aware of the current level of functioning of the other and is able to prompt, hint, or otherwise scaffold the developing competence of the other. Adults, however, are not always effective. In a study of six experienced classroom teachers tutoring first-grade students in multicolumn addition, Putnam found that the teachers did not tailor the selection of problems to be solved to the students' understanding (Putnam, 1987). More recent work by Chi and her colleagues supports the idea that novice adult tutors do not diagnose students' flawed knowledge well (Chi, Siler, & Jeong, 2004).

Competent peers can also scaffold and support the learning of a weaker student. However, peers need substantial assistance in being able to provide the appropriate level of help to a learner. For example, naïve tutors are not very good at identifying the tutee's current level of functioning and scaffolding the tutee's efforts so that there is improved performance (Person & Graesser, 1999). It is difficult to train young students to identify or act within another learner's zone of proximal development (Webb & Farivar, 1994). With appropriate instructional support, however, peers can effectively respond to one another's efforts (King, Staffieri, & Adelgais, 1998).

Reciprocal teaching is an example of a peer learning strategy that embodies principles from Vygotskian theory (Palincsar & Brown, 1984; Palincsar & Herrenkohl, 2002) and was developed to assist poor readers with comprehension. During reciprocal teaching, a group of students generate predictions about the text. After reading a portion of the text, the discussion leader raises questions about the text and members of the group discuss these questions. Someone from the group summarizes the content read up to this point, and the group members then clarify difficult concepts and then continue to make predictions about the next portion of text. Initially, the teacher models the cognitive strategies involved and gradually transfers responsibility for the performance of the various strategies to the students as they become more capable of independently performing them. Research on reciprocal teaching and its effects on comprehension indicate that it is a very successful instructional strategy (Rosenshine & Meister, 1994).

OTHER PERSPECTIVES

Sociocultural Perspectives

Sociocultural perspectives on peer learning include both social and cognitive components. Vygotsky's theory of cognitive development (described earlier in the chapter) denotes a dialectical relationship between the individual and the social context in which the child develops. Cognitive processes are modeled in the social world before the child internalizes them (Hogan & Tudge, 1999).

A key emphasis in sociocultural theories of learning is on social participation. Learners in a sociocultural framework are social beings and develop competence through participation in valued activities from which meaning can be made (Wenger, 1998). Tasks are authentic, and all participants have legitimate roles in accomplishing the task. Identity with the group is an important element of sociocultural approaches to peer learning. When groups participate in valued activity together, group members may experience collective efficacy (Bandura, 2000). Theories of distributed cognition suggest that culturally provided tools (e.g., computers, video cameras, typical practices) can embody knowledge and can be used to distribute thinking (Lebeau, 1998). In distributed systems, a group's performance as a whole can exceed that of each individual's independent capabilities. It is not simply a division of labor that results in coacting parts but is a collaborative in which knowledge and expertise are shared: "Cognition in such instances is understood as jointly undertaken by individuals interacting with one another and with surrounding physical, social, and intellectual resources" (Lebeau, 1998, p. 3). The tools available to the group may scaffold members' performances and support their activity. For example, the availability of a calculator reduces the need for students to engage in computation when solving problems in mathematics. Examples of instructional forms that are influenced by sociocultural approaches to peer learning include Computer-Supported Intentional Learning Environments (CSILE; Scardamalia, Bereiter, & Lamon, 1994) and Communities of Learners (Brown & Campione, 1994).

Social Cognitive Theory

In many of the techniques described in this chapter (e.g., Reciprocal Teaching), modeling of cognitive activity is an important element. People can learn from observing a model perform a behavior (Bandura, 1977). Behaviors by a model are imitated if the model is reinforced. Learning involves an acquisition stage during which a person attends to the behavior and remembers it. There is also a performance stage in which the person produces the behavior. Continued practice with feedback improves the performance of the behavior. Children are more likely to select models if the models are similar to themselves and to learn from models when they have a high level of self-efficacy (Pintrich & Schunk, 2002). Cognitive apprenticeships attempt to capitalize on the power of observational learning by having the teacher model cognitive strategies and make thinking visible so that it can be appropriated (Collins, Brown, & Holum, 1991; Collins, Brown, & Newman, 1989). Feedback plays a key role in allowing the student to assume increased responsibility for the task.

The important difference among the perspectives described is in the proposed mechanism that allows peer interaction to promote learning (see Table 34.1). If teachers do not understand *how* peers promote learning, they will not make appropriate decisions about size of groups, kinds of skills needed, how to participate with groups, what kinds of tasks to assign, and other key instructional choices that will promote effective learning.

TUTORING

Tutoring is a very common practice and typically involves a more skilled student working with a less skilled student. The goal is to improve the performance of the less skilled student. Theoretical justifications for the practice of tutoring can be found in Vgotsky's theory of cognitive development (Vygotksy, 1978), information processing theory, and social cognitive theory (Bandura, 1986). The tutor's efforts to scaffold the tutee's learning by modeling targeted behaviors, providing feedback, and providing prompts to performance are often thought to be operating in the tutee's zone of proximal development. The tutee has the opportunity to observe the tutor's strategies. Some of the tutoring techniques described in this section involve whole classes of students tutoring one another.

Students who experience one-to-one tutoring gain greater understanding of targeted content, report being more motivated, and work faster (Slavin, 1987). They perform at levels that are two standard deviations above comparison students who experienced regular instruction (Bloom, 1984). An extensive empirical research base supports the benefits of tutoring (P. Cohen, Kulick, & Kulick, 1982).

Structured tutoring in particular works best to improve learning among tutees. Structuring of the tutorial interaction can take place with the use of prompt questions or question stems that the tutor and tutee can use to guide their responses. It provides individualized instruction that is consistent across many educational settings (Lindren, Meier, & Brigham, 1991; Slavin & Madden, 1989) and reduces some of the variability that occurs in outcomes as a result of the variability of the tutors. The greater the structure of a given tutoring program, the larger the post instructional increases in tutee academic achievement (Lindren et al., 1991).

Tutoring also benefits the tutor (Chi, Siler, Jeong, Yamauchi, & Hausmann, 2001). As tutors plan, prepare for, and carry out their tasks, they improve their mastery of the content they are teaching (P. Cohen et al., 1982). Tutors have opportunities to explain content to another. Providing explanations, particularly elaborated explanations, is consistently shown to promote achievement (Webb, 1991, 1992). Furthermore, tutoring may provide a tutor with metacognitive experiences about their own understanding of the content (Baker & Brown, 1984).

Processes Involved in Tutoring

Naive tutors may be inhibited by politeness rules (Person, Kreuz, Zwaan, & Graesser, 1995), and they may provide inappropriate feedback to their tutees (Person & Graesser, 1999). They are also unskilled in diagnosing flawed knowledge on the part of their tutees (Chi et al., 2004). Despite these problems, one-on-one tutoring is effective. Person and Graesser describe tutoring in terms of a five-step dialogue frame:

1. Tutor asks a question (or alternatively provides a problem for the student to solve).
2. Student answers the question.
3. Tutor gives feedback on the answer.
4. Tutor and student collaboratively improve the quality of the answers.
5. Tutor assesses student's understanding of the answer. (pp. 71–72, Person & Graesser, 1999).

These steps are illustrated in the following example from a tutoring session on the topic of factorial designs:

Step 1	1:1	Tutor	So, how many F scores would be computed?
Step 2	1:2	Student	Three
Step 3	1:3	Tutor	Three [agreeing with the student]
Step 4	1:4	Tutor	And what numbers [referring to a matrix of cell means] would you use?
	1:5	Student	You would do one for humor [one of the independent variables]
	1:6	Tutor	And what does that tell you?
	1:7	Student	I'm not sure [laughs]
	1:8	Tutor	OK, why do you do an F score? What is an F score?
	1:9	Student	To see the size, uh, significance?
	1:10	Tutor	The size of significance.
	1:11	Student	The size of significance.
	1:12	Tutor	Right, how statistically significant a variable is
	1:13	Student	Right.
	1:14	Tutor	So, you are right, you have three [F scores]; one for caffeine, one for humor, and one for…?
	1:15	Student	The scores…from caffeine and humor.
	1:16	Tutor	Interaction, the interaction of the two, right?
	1:17	Student	Um hmm.
	1:18	Tutor	[Explains independence of main effects]
Step 5	1:19	Tutor	Do you see what I am saying?
	1:20	Student	Um hmm.

Source: Person & Graesser, 1999, p. 72).

Steps 1–3 are typical of the kind of interactions that may occur between a teacher and a student in the context of whole class instruction. Steps 4 and 5 rarely occur within that context because of time constraints and the number of students in a classroom. Step 4 is the step in which the tutor is most likely to work with the tutee in the zone of proximal development. It is during this step that scaffolding is provided (Chi et al., 2001; Graesser, Person, & Magliano, 1995). Chi et al. (2001) define *scaffolding* as "any kind of guidance that is more than a confirmatory or negative feedback" (p. 473). It includes the kinds of prompts, hints, and splicing of information described by Graesser and Person (Graesser et al. 1995; Person & Graesser, 1999). In most tutoring situations, the tutor dominates the interaction (McArthur, Stasz, & Zmuidzinas, 1990). In an analysis of the activities of tutors, McArthur et al. (1990) found that 53 percent of those activities *could* have solicited constructive responses from students in which the tutees' responses would have extended the meaning of the tutors' contributions. The tutees' responses are important because the quality of those responses contributes to the effectiveness of the tutorial process (Chi et al., 2001). The efforts of students during tutoring to construct an understanding of the content in light of their prior knowledge may be at the heart of the effectiveness of tutoring. There is wide variability among tutors in their instructional efforts if they have not been trained in a highly structured training program. Because of this variability, it is unlikely that the activities of the tutor alone are responsible for the benefits of tutoring (VanLehn, Siler, Murray, & Bagget, 2003).

Chi et al. (2001) conducted two studies to examine why tutoring works. Tutors were college students who tutored eighth grade students about the circulatory system, using a prepared text consisting of 86 sentences. Each sentence was printed on a separate page. The tutor and tutee worked on each sentence one at a time. The tutors' explanations were correlated with student learning. Students' responses to scaffolding efforts by their tutors (e.g., prompts, hints, comprehension questions) were also correlated with students' learning. In a second study, tutors were trained to prompt their tutees for knowledge construction responses using a set of content free prompts. The use of prompts by tutors resulted in more episodes of deep scaffolding in which there were more extended exchanges between tutors and tutees. Students who were prompted were more constructive overall, displaying more of what they know, and putting more effort into the exchanges.

When Both the Tutor and the Tutee Are in Need

Connie Juel (1996) explored the effects of a literacy-tutoring program on two groups of students who had academic needs: 27 first-grade students at risk (the tutees) and 15 student athletes at a major university who were poor readers (the tutors). The tutors engaged in four hours of literacy-based activities each week in preparation for tutoring the first graders and in response to what happened during the tutoring sessions. They tutored the children twice a week for 45 minutes over the course of two semesters. The tutoring activities included reading children's literature, writing, creating books, keeping a journal of special words, keeping an alphabet book in which letters and pictures were kept, activities to foster phonemic awareness, and engaging in letter-sound activities.

Seventy percent of the children in the target school were African American and 30 percent were Hispanic. The children's average score on the Metropolitan Reading Readiness Test (Nurss & MacGauvran, 1995) was at the 26th percentile at the beginning of the tutoring program. The tutors' average grade equivalent score was 9.25 on the Nelson-Denny Reading Test (1981, Form E) in August and increased to 13.5 by the following May. The mean score of the tutored children on the Iowa Test of Basic Skills (1983) was the 41st percentile. Both participants in this tutoring program benefited from it. The tutors' preparation for tutoring no doubt contributed to their success. However, mere exposure to instruction in prior years through developmental education courses had not accomplished the same kinds of effects.

Some tutoring dyads were more successful than others (Juel, 1996). Two features that distinguished the successful students from less successful students were the tutors' modeling of how to read and spell unknown words and the presence of scaffolded experiences. Examples of scaffolded experiences included when the tutor enabled the child to complete a task that the child could not otherwise do (e.g., spell a word) by providing a piece of information or breaking the task down into smaller components. The children who were more successful received more frequent scaffolding from their tutors.

Tutors reported identifying with their young tutees, having experienced some of the same difficulties during their own early education. An important aspect of helping students in their zones of proximal development is being aware of what next step is possible and being able to provide the necessary assistance. The tutors in Juel's study were successful in doing so.

Tutoring and Special Needs Students

The initial conceptualization of tutoring involved having a more expert or knowledgeable student instruct a less knowledgeable student. Such an expectation is in line with one of the implications of Vygotskian theory in that a more competent other was more likely to be able to effectively provide scaffolding to support the creation of a zone of proximal development with the less competent individual. With techniques such as Classwide Peer Tutoring, Reciprocal Peer Tutoring, and Structured Tutorial Interaction, we see examples of how the interactions of same-age, same-ability peers can be supported to achieve similar outcomes.

Special needs students benefit from tutoring and from the opportunity to tutor (Cook, Scruggs, Mastropieri, & Casto, 1985–86; Osguthorpe & Scruggs, 1986; Scruggs & Mastropieri, 1998). For example, students with learning and behavioral problems tutored nonhandicapped children in reading for four 20-minute sessions per week (Top, 1984). Both tutors and tutees improved their reading skills. Scruggs and Osguthorpe (1986) reviewed 26 studies that examined the effects of tutoring on the academic performance and social development of tutors and tutees. They concluded that students with mild disabilities can serve as effective tutors for both handicapped and normally achieving peers, and their success depends on careful training and supervision. There was little effect of tutoring experiences on students' self-esteem. These results were similar to those found in a meta-analysis of studies in which students with mild disabilities served as tutors (Cook et al., 1985–86).

Classwide Peer Tutoring

Classwide Peer Tutoring (CWPT) was developed with the purpose of improving overall performance in basic academic skills (Delquadri, Greenwood, Whorton, Carta, & Hall, 1986), particularly by students who were culturally and linguistically diverse and poor. CWPT involves same-age peers and the entire class in tutoring activities. Students are paired either randomly or matched by ability or language proficiency. Students with limited English proficiency are initially paired with a student who speaks their language but whose English is better.

CWPT includes elements of both cooperation and competition and is influenced by a social-motivational perspective on peer learning. At the beginning of a week, all students are paired in tutor–tutee partnerships and assigned to one of two competing teams. One person serves as a tutor for the first 10 minutes, and the partners switch roles after the 10-minute period. The teacher presents the content to the whole class and uses the peer tutoring sessions for additional practice and rehearsal of content. The tutor asks a question of the tutee about an instructional item such as a math fact, spelling word, or other content. If the tutee answers correctly, two points are awarded. The tutor has an answer sheet so that the answer can be checked. If the answer is incorrect, the tutor engages in an error-correction procedure. The tutor provides the correct response; asks the tutee to write or say the cor-

rect answer three times, thus providing positive practice; and provides one point to the tutee for correcting the mistake. If the tutee fails to correct the answer, no points are awarded, and the tutor provides the tutee with the answer both orally and visually. The tutor and tutee are not in competition with one another, but are contributing to an overall team's score. The team is made up of numerous tutor–tutee pairs. The goal is to go through the assigned material at least twice in the allocated time. The more work that is completed correctly, the more points the pair contributes to their team. The team with the highest number of points earns recognition or rewards.

As the pairs work together, the teacher moves around the classroom and awards bonus points for appropriate tutoring behaviors such as clear presentations of material, awarding points based on performance, correct use of the error correction procedure, and providing positive comments. In this aspect of the technique, some of the elements of the Johnson's social cohesion approach are present in that positive social behaviors are also being reinforced.

Positive effects of CWPT occur on a variety of measures of academic achievement such as reading, spelling, vocabulary and mathematics (Greenwood, Carta, & Kamps, 1990; Greenwood, Maheady, & Carta, 1991; Mathes & Fuchs, 1993). A longitudinal study compared the effects of implementing CWPT with low-SES students over a 4-year period on students' achievement in grades 1 to 4. The performance of these students was compared with that of a control group of children. CWPT increased student achievement (Greenwood, Delquadri, & Hall, 1989). An additional follow-up of these students 2 years later when they were in sixth grade indicated that the advantages that accrued to the students who received Classwide Peer Tutoring were maintained although some of the effect sizes were reduced (Greenwood & Terry, 1993). In addition, fewer members of the CWPT group were placed into special education programs than students in the control group.

Peer-Assisted Learning Strategies (PALS: Fuchs, Fuchs, Mathes, & Simmons, 2003) is a technique based on Classwide Peer Tutoring (Delquadri et al., 1986). Pairs of students work on a skill with which one student experiences difficulties. The features of the structured interaction strategy include:

• Mediated verbal rehearsal in which the tutor models and gradually fades a verbal rehearsal routine delineating procedural steps for completing the problem type
• Step-by-step feedback by the tutor to confirm and praise correct responses and to provide explanations and to model strategic behavior for incorrect answers

- Frequent verbal and written interaction between tutors and tutees
- Opportunities for tutees to apply explanations in subsequent problems
- Reciprocity where both children serve in the roles of tutor and tutee within each session (Fuchs & Fuchs, 1998, p. 27)

The PALS strategy is successful with mathematics (Fuchs, Fuchs, Yazdian, & Powell, 2002) and with reading (Mathes et al., 2003). Learning-disabled students in elementary classrooms that used PALS were more socially accepted than learning-disabled students in classes that did not use PALS, and they enjoyed the same social standing as most of their nondisabled peers (Fuchs, Fuchs, Mathes, & Martinez, 2002).

Reciprocal Peer Tutoring

Reciprocal Peer Tutoring (RPT) was originally designed for pairs of low-achieving urban, elementary school children (Fantuzzo, King, & Heller, 1992). Students receive training prior to engaging in tutorial activities and are first introduced to the concepts of teamwork, partnership, and cooperation. These efforts are intended to promote a sense of social cohesion in the classrooms. Student dyads first select a team goal from among a number of available choices. The work of the peer teacher is supported by the availability of flashcards, which designate areas in which the students' mathematical performance needs improvement as identified through curriculum-based assessments. Each flashcard has a sample problem on one side and the computational steps necessary to solve it on the other. The dyad has a worksheet on which they keep track of the number of attempts made to solve the problem. One student attempts to solve the problem, and if she is successful, she is praised. If unsuccessful, the peer teacher suggests she try the problem again and records her new answer in a column of the worksheet labeled "Try 2." After the first 20 minutes, the two students complete drill sheets, and at the end of the period, they check one another's papers, computing the total number of problems that were answered correctly. The dyads compare their scores with their team's goals and determine if they have succeeded. After a predetermined number of "wins," student dyads choose rewards from a menu of choices.

Reciprocal peer tutoring combines many of the elements of both the social-motivational perspective on peer learning and the social-cohesion perspective (see Table 34.1). Students are individually accountable for their performance, and teams are rewarded based on their performance. The initial emphasis in preparing students

for teamwork and cooperation is influenced by the social cohesion perspective. The teacher must do a lot of preparation to provide flashcards and drill sheets appropriate to each dyad.

RPT involves both structured interaction and the use of rewards. In a study conducted with at-risk fourth and fifth graders in an urban elementary school, students who received both elements of RPT were most successful (Fantuzzo et al., 1992). Students who experienced structured conditions reported feeling higher levels of academic and behavioral competence. And those who were eligible to receive rewards were recognized by their teachers as behaving better than students who did not experience such contingencies. Overall, peer-assisted learning enhances students' on-task behavior during a lesson (Ginsburg-Block & Fantuzzo, 1997).

Additional studies of the effects of RPT included a parent-involvement component (Fantuzzo, Davis, & Ginsberg, 1995; Heller & Fantuzzo, 1993). The parent-involvement intervention comprised three parts: (1) co-construction of parent-involvement methods; (2) recognition of student academic effort; and (3) maintaining regular personal contacts between school and home that were exclusively positive. In comparison to students who received RPT in the classroom only or those in a wait-list control, students who experienced both RPT and parent involvement had the highest scores on accurate computations.

Both Classwide Peer Tutoring and Reciprocal Peer tutoring were developed for use with learners who are at risk for academic failure as a result of poverty or difficulty with the English language. Both have been shown to be successful in helping students succeed academically. The kinds of tasks in which students engage tend to be of a more basic level, and assessments target lower level skills. It is possible, however, for students with low levels of skills to be involved in learning tasks that require higher order thinking skills. Examples of techniques that promote such skills are Alison King's Structured Tutorial Interaction (King et al., 1998) and Elizabeth Cohen's Complex Instruction (Cohen, Lotan, Scarloss, & Arellano, 1999).

Structured Tutorial Interaction

Tutoring among same age peers can result in higher order learning outcomes. King et al. (1998) compared the performances of seventh-grade students assigned to three different mutual peer-tutoring conditions. The three different tutorial strategies involved (a) explaining material to one another; (b) asking comprehension and thought-provoking questions in addition to explaining; and

(c) asking comprehension and thought-provoking questions in a particular sequence and explaining. Every student was taught how to explain using the TEL-WHY strategy. They told their partners what they knew, explained the why and how of something, and linked the information to what their partners already knew. The second part of the strategy required them to tell why, tell how, and to use their own words. The emphasis was on elaborating ideas, explaining rather than describing, and connecting the material to what they already know. Students were also trained to ask comprehension and "thinking" questions. Students in the question sequence group learned to ask comprehension questions, following up with a probing question if the answer was not completed. If the answer was incorrect, they asked a "hint' question. Finally, they asked a thinking or knowledge-building question.

The results of the study indicated that students who asked questions, explained, and sequenced their questions and those who asked questions and explained performed better on inference and integration tasks than those who engaged in explanation alone. They had no advantage on tests of literal comprehension. Eight weeks after the initial study, students in the two tutoring groups that included inquiry maintained their advantage on tests of inference and integration. This study shows that peer tutoring need not be limited to lower level tasks or outcomes but can be used effectively for promoting higher levels of knowledge construction.

LEARNING IN HETEROGENEOUS GROUPS

Many cooperative learning techniques were designed for use with groups of between four and six students. Typically, these groups are heterogeneous with respect to academic achievement and other characteristics such as race, gender, and ethnicity. Larger groups can be used for both simple and complex tasks. Cooperative groups that are larger can also be tightly structured or more loosely structured. Techniques described in this section often combine both cognitive and social elements.

Jigsaw

One of the original cooperative learning techniques is Jigsaw (Aronson, Blaney, Stephan, Sikes, & Snapp, 1978). Students are assigned to four-person heterogeneous groups and are assigned topics on which they are to become experts. For example, if the group were learning about the rainforest, each member of the group would be responsible for becoming an expert on a subtopic (e.g., birds and animals of the rainforest, people who live in

the rainforest, plants, and the destruction of the rainforest). Students with the same "expert topic" from different teams meet in groups to discuss their topic. Their task is to become as knowledgeable as possible about their topic. They then return to their groups and teach the material to other students in their team. Each student in turn teaches other members of the group. Later, students take individual quizzes over the material and individual grades are assigned.

Each student in a group has access to materials that others in the group do not and is responsible for communicating that information to the others. Some students may experience difficulty in acquiring sufficient mastery of the target material and may be ineffective in communicating it to others in the group. From a cognitive-elaborative perspective, each student will more actively process information because of the need to "teach" the material to others. The teacher will need to ensure that students in "expert groups" ensure that all of the experts have mastered the material.

Group Investigation

Shlomo Sharan and Rachel Hertz-Lazarowitz (1980) developed this technique, in which students go through six stages during implementation. The key components of Group Investigation (Sharan & Sharan, 1992) are interaction, investigation, interpretation, and intrinsic motivation. In the first stage, the class chooses subtopics and students organize themselves into research groups, based on their interests. The teacher will most likely identify the general topic to fit with the curriculum goals. For example, an eighth-grade social studies teacher may have his students do a group investigation on the topic of "Famines." The students might organize their investigation around various countries that have experienced famines: Ethiopia, Ireland, North Korea, Somalia, Sudan, and the Ukraine. In Stage II, students plan their investigations and how they are going to gather the information necessary. In Stage III, they carry out the investigation with each student contributing to the effort. In Stage IV, the students share the information they have individually gathered and plan how they are going to make a presentation to the class. They will need to identify the key ideas that they wish to communicate and develop a strategy for effectively communicating to the other groups in the class. Each group picks a representative who works with other representatives to coordinate an overall strategy for presentation. In Stage V, the students make their presentations and finally, in Stage VI, the teacher and students work on evaluating the investigations. Students conducting a Group Investigation need to demonstrate high levels of self-regulated learning, coordination, and metacognition.

Students in Group Investigation classes typically outperform their peers in comparison classes (Lazarowitz & Karsenty, 1990; Sharan & Shachar, 1988; Sharan & Shaulov, 1990). The assessments contain different kinds of questions that require students not only to provide factual information but also to interpret information and apply it to new problems.

Structured Controversies

Students often have difficult expressing disagreement with one another. Children who are shy are unlikely to contradict the class leader. Learning to argue is a critical skill. According to Johnson and Johnson (1995), academic controversy occurs when students disagree about their ideas, information, opinions, theories, and conclusions. The controversy is resolved as students come to consensus on a position. Piagetian theory can be relevant to the analysis of what occurs during structured controversies (see Table 34.1).

Students are placed in a four-person cooperative learning group, which is then divided into two pairs. A high school class might be asked to consider whether pollution regulations for cars should be eased. Each pair of students is given the task of making the case for one side of the issue. All students will need to conduct research to support their positions. At each step of the process, the teacher plays an important role. The students may need assistance with locating appropriate resources and in distinguishing between good arguments and strong opinions. The students present their positions to one another with each pair taking turns. They then engage in an open discussion of the ideas presented, attempting to convince one another of their point of view. The pairs then reverse perspectives and present each other's positions. This shift in perspective promotes a focus on the arguments making it more possible to achieve consensus as the students consider both perspectives on the argument. The group then develops a final report that summarizes the best arguments for both perspectives and comes to a consensus judgment. Students need good social skills to engage in a structured academic controversy. It is important that students do not criticize one another personally but instead criticize the arguments made.

INFLUENCES IN HETEROGENEOUS GROUPS

Heterogeneous groups provide opportunities for students to work with others who may differ from themselves in a variety of ways and from whom they can learn. When such groups work well, students benefit both academically and socially. However, groups do not automatically work well. In the absence of explicit instruction in the cognitive skills needed for tasks or the social skills needed to coordinate complex interaction, students tend to function at the most concrete level or provide minimal support to one another (Cohen, 1994). Group interaction is influenced by the goals and incentives associated with the assigned task, the nature of the task itself, and individual differences among the participants (O'Donnell & Dansereau, 1992).

Gender and Cooperative Groups

Students who provide explanations when working in groups achieve more than those who do not (Webb, 1989, 1992). Concerns are often raised about dominance in groups because of the limited opportunities to contribute that some students might experience. Boys and girls in cooperative groups may not participate equally. The composition of a cooperative group with respect to gender influences who provides explanations (Webb, 1984). When boys in the group outnumbered girls, the boys dominated the interaction. When girls outnumbered the boys, the girls still tended to defer to the boys, even if there was only one. In groups that were balanced with respect to gender, all students tended to participate equally.

Some more recent studies have found differences between boys and girls in terms of how they interact in a group context. Underwood and Jindal (1993) found that mixed-gender pairs of students did not perform as well as same-gender pairs on a computer-based language task. Pairs of boys showed the greatest gains when directed to cooperate. The kinds of tasks on which children work also influence the extent to which gender differences in performance are found. Seven- and nine-year old children worked in same- or mixed-gender pairs on a language-based computer task and on a noncomputer task (Fitzpatrick & Hardman, 2000). Mixed-gender pairs were less collaborative than same-gender pairs. Girls in mixed-gender pairs were more assertive when collaboration broke down during the noncomputer task, whereas boys were more assertive during the computer-based task.

Similar results for mixed pairs of boys and girls were found by Tolmie and Howe (1993) with secondary students who worked on a computer-based task. Pairs of students predicted the trajectory of a falling object, came to consensus about their prediction, "drew" their prediction on screen by inserting a fixed number of points with a mouse, and were then shown the actual trajectory. They were then asked to discuss any discrepancy between their prediction and what actually happened. Boys and girls did not differ in performance but differed in interactional style. Female pairs avoided conflict, focusing instead on what problems had in common. Male pairs learned most when they discussed the feedback and referred to explanatory factors that might account for the discrepancy between predictions and events. Mixed pairs were very constrained in their interaction.

When mixed gender pairs shared a computer when doing a computer-based task there were no sex differences in performance (Light, Littleton, Bale, Joiner, & Messer, 2000). Holden (1993) examined the contributions of boys and girls to discussions on a language task and on a mathematics/technology task. When boys outnumbered girls in cooperative groups in a language task, the level of abstract talk contributed by girls was depressed in comparison to groups in which the composition of the group was more balanced. There was little abstract talk in discussion of the mathematics/technology task. Holden concluded that the kind of talk in which students engage varies as a function of the task and the group composition.

It is difficult to draw strong conclusions about the role of gender in cooperative groups based on the available research. Despite the difficulty in drawing firm conclusions about the role of gender, teachers should be sensitive to its possible influence on group interaction and consider gender when assigning students to groups.

Race, Ethnicity, and Language

Cooperative learning is often promoted as an instructional strategy that can be used to effectively integrate children from a variety of backgrounds. Slavin (1995) reviewed a number of studies that examined the effects of cooperative learning on intergroup relations. The studies included in his review were experiments of 4 weeks' duration or greater. The typical outcomes measured in the studies were sociometric peer ratings (e.g., "Who are your best friends in this class?" or observations measures. A cooperative learning technique that promotes interracial interaction in pursuit of common goals (i.e., positive interdependence) and provides roles that are of equal status to members of different groups can promote positive intergroup relationships (Slavin, 1995). The general findings from the studies reviewed indicate that children who experience cooperative learning methods of instruction report more cross-racial, cross-ethnic friendships than whole-class instruction. However, just as with the studies of the role of gender in cooperative learning environments, the research is old (from the 1970s and 1980s). The creation of positive interdependence would

seem to be crucial to the effort to promote positive intergroup relations.

A more recent study examined the effects of a cooperative learning program, Bilingual Cooperative Integrated Reading and Composition (BCIRC), on the Spanish and English reading, writing, and language achievement of limited English-proficiency second and third graders in Spanish bilingual programs (Calderon, Hertz-Lazarowitz, & Slavin, 1998). The BCIRC strategies involve a set of activities that take place before, during, and after reading. They include building background and vocabulary, making predictions, reading a selection, partner reading and silent reading, story comprehension treasure hunts, story mapping, story retelling, story-related writing, words out loud and spelling, partner checking, meaningful sentences, and tests. Three schools were included in the study that used BCIRC, and the performance of the students was compared to those of students in schools in the district with similar demographic profiles. Second graders in BCIRC classrooms performed significantly better than comparison students in writing on the Spanish Texas Assessment of Academic Skills. Third graders in BCIRC classrooms outperformed comparison students in reading but not language. If the third graders had been in BCIRC for 2 years, they outperformed comparison students on both measures. Third graders in BCIRC classrooms met the criteria for exit from bilingual classes at much higher rates than did students in comparison classes.

Special Needs and Cooperative Learning

Tateyama-Sniezek conducted a review of research studies that involved the use of cooperative learning methods to improve the academic achievement of special needs students (Tateyama-Sniezek, 1990). Only 50 percent of the studies were shown to have significantly positive effects on achievement. Studies that included individual accountability and group rewards had the strongest effects (Stevens & Slavin, 1991). Additional studies published after 1990 were reviewed by McMaster and Fuchs (2002), Their conclusions were similar to those of Stevens and Slavin (1991) and note that cooperative learning techniques that use group rewards and individual accountability are more successful.

Jenkins and O'Connor (2003) cautioned against drawing firm conclusions from the available research on the academic achievement of learning-disabled students in cooperative learning situations. They point out that more research studies of longer duration are required. In addition, they note that the available research has not paid sufficient attention to whether students retain information and/or transfer skills acquired. In a 2-year investigation of the use of Cooperative Integrated Reading and Composition (CIRC; Stevens et al., 1987), students in second through sixth grade worked in heterogeneous teams on reading and writing activities. A total of 635 students using CIRC were compared to 664 students in matched schools that did not; 72 academically handicapped students using CIRC were compared to 65 students in pullout programs at the comparison schools. The CIRC program is a blend of a social-motivational approach to peer learning and a cognitive strategy approach to literacy instruction. It combines both social and cognitive elements. The results of this extensive study were strongly in favor of CIRC for both regular students and academically handicapped students.

Some students with learning disabilities prefer not to work in groups (Elbaum, Moody, & Schumm, 1999). In mixed-ability reading groups, the difficulties experienced by students with learning disabilities are more visible to classmates. Depending on how the group is structured, the attentional demands of working with a number of others may be excessive. Students with learning disabilities may lack the necessary social skills to participate effectively in a cooperative task (Holder & Fitzpatrick, 1991; Pearl, 1992). However, cooperative learning experiences or other peer learning experiences can improve the social standing in the class of students with learning disabilities (Slavin, 1995).

Status Characteristics

Elizabeth Cohen's work focuses on the cognitive consequences of status differences in the classroom (Cohen, 1982; Cohen & Lotan, 1995, 1997; Cohen, Lotan, & Catanzarite, 1990). Students with low status typically are in the position of seeking help and are often ignored, and their contributions to groups may not be valued by their peers. The opportunity to provide explanations is associated with higher levels of achievement (Webb, 1992), but all students do not have that opportunity. Higher status students may have more opportunity when working in groups to engage in the kinds of cognitive activities that promote elaborative processing and higher achievement (Cohen, 1982). Students with high status have more opportunities to provide help and explanations, talk more, and direct more of the activity in the group, whereas those who have low status ask for help, may be ignored, and are relegated to more procedural roles rather than cognitive roles in the group. The very students who would most profit from opportunities to engage in deeper processing may not have the opportunity to do so without the intervention of the teacher.

Who has status in a group? The answer to this question depends on the culture of the classroom or school. Students who are known to be successful in school are often accorded high status in classrooms where achievement is valued. Other characteristics of students, including athletic ability, popularity, and gender, may also be associated with high status. The differential opportunity to participate effectively is very important in heterogeneous classes in which many variables, including race, ethnicity, language background, gender, and special needs, may act as status characteristics and influence interaction in a group.

Limiting Status Effects in the Classroom.. Status differences affect interaction, participation rates, and the kind of cognitive activities in which students engage (e.g., providing explanations, asking questions). Peer learning techniques that maximize the participation of all students can limit the operation of status characteristics in the classroom. A technique such as Scripted Cooperation limits inequalities of participation because of the scripted interaction each person (irrespective of ability or other characteristic) must take turns to engage in specified cognitive activities. One of the limitations of this technique, however, is that the tasks with which it can be used are relatively simple and involve more knowledge acquisition and rehearsal tasks rather than creative or knowledge construction tasks.

Elizabeth Cohen's Complex Instruction (Cohen & Lotan, 1995; Cohen et al., 1999) is a technique designed to limit the operation of status characteristics in the classroom. Key elements of this program include the use of complex and interesting tasks that are performed by heterogeneous groups and a multiple abilities treatment. In traditional classrooms, academic competence is typically understood as recognized competence in reading, mathematics, and writing—a fairly narrow range of abilities. Children who struggle with these academic tasks are often considered to be of low status. In Cohen's Complex Instruction, the teacher chooses a complex task that cannot be completed by a single student working alone and to which *all* students can contribute. The teacher begins by discussing what abilities are needed to accomplish a task. For example, the class may be asked to design a zoo. The competencies necessary to complete this task include being able to measure, write instructions, research the appropriate housing conditions and food requirements for animals in the zoo, artistic ability in creating the actual model, and many other rather specific abilities. Students come to recognize that one individual couldn't do the entire task alone and that each student has something to contribute, while also recognizing that some students contribute many skills. The focus on specific abilities needed to accomplish the task at hand allows for the inclusion of many children, whereas a narrow focus on traditional academic skills may exclude a large number of children from actively participating. In addition, the focus on what students can contribute to a task encourages students to be task oriented and to emphasize competencies rather than deficiencies.

The multiple abilities treatment includes specifying the specific abilities needed for the task. It also requires that the teacher comment positively when children contribute effectively to the task. Rather than attempting to include children by praising participation alone, the teacher must point out how particular children are contributing to the group success. It is not enough that a child measures accurately and is praised for doing so; the teacher must point out the importance of this skill to the group's task and how the particular child is contributing to other students' success. In using a strategy such as this, elements of the social cohesion and cognitive elaboration approaches are combined to change the culture of the classroom to being more inclusive and focusing on providing opportunities for students to engage in the kinds of cognitive activities that will be associated with success.

THE IMPORTANCE OF THE QUALITY OF DISCOURSE

The mere fact that children are assigned to groups does not mean that they will engage in meaningful discussions. Many factors such as the nature of task or the composition of the group will influence the quality of talk. For example, children tend to have less abstract talk on mathematics/technology tasks than they do with language-based tasks (Holden, 1993). If one adopts a Vygotskian view of peer learning, intellectual skills will be modeled externally before they can be internalized as part of the cognitive repertoire of a child. If the quality of reasoning, explanation, or questioning that is available is of a very low level, a child may acquire little practice at higher level thinking in the context of the group. Most students need support in generating the quality of discourse that is associated with learning. High levels of cognitive activity are supported by providing questions to students that vary in complexity (King, 1991, 1999; King et al., 1998). The quality of explanations that students generate while working together is associated with learning (Webb, 1992).

In a study of high-achieving sixth graders working on collaborative problem solving, Barron found that the success of various triads could not be accounted for by the quality of discussion, prior achievement, or the generation of correct ideas for solution (Barron, 2003). Less successful groups ignored or rejected correct proposals made by group members, whereas groups that were more successful discussed correct proposals or accepted them. Chinn and colleagues (Chinn, O'Donnell, & Jinks, 2000) found that fourth graders learned more when they engaged in deeper development of reasons during argumentation.

Groups can focus excessively on procedural aspects of the tasks in which they are engaged (Erkens, Prangsma, & Jasper, 2005), and even when participants list arguments, they may fail to coordinate their reasons and elaborate them sufficiently (Andriessen, 2005). Successful discourse is typically coordinated among group members with participants engaging in coconstruction of knowledge rather than generating simple lists or arguments (King, 1994, 1999).

ROLE OF THE TEACHER IN PEER LEARNING

Teachers' roles are key components of effective peer learning. These roles can be very complex. Different choices in peer learning activities require teachers to take different stances with respect to the students, tasks, and outcomes. Table 34.1 illustrates key differences among theoretical approaches to peer learning and the teacher's role within such approaches. Teachers must take into account both the social context in which learning occurs and the cognitive processes that are either supported or diminished in that specific context. Teachers will need to analyze their particular classrooms to determine whether there may be obstacles that limit the cognitive opportunities available to students or prevent them from being able to capitalize on those opportunities. Teachers can adopt many roles in the classroom in relation to the use of peer learning. The selection of these roles must be clearly linked to the promotion of student learning.

Community Builder

Students in most American classrooms are increasingly heterogeneous. The teacher as community builder develops a context in which the participants in the classroom have mutual respect, are willing to help one another, and recognize others' needs for help. Without the experience of support and community, many students may feel alienated and have low expectations. In adopting the role of community builder, a teacher may look to sociocultural theory, Vygotskian theory, or social-cohesion theory to understand the important role that *community* can contribute to promoting effective learning. Elizabeth Cohen's strategy of *assigning competence* to students is one strategy for publicly recognizing the important contributions of children with different skills to important classroom tasks.

Task Developer

Teachers in current American classrooms must be responsive to state and national standards for educational performance. The teacher will need to examine the curricular goals for the classes they teach and design tasks that are appropriate to their goals and might be facilitated by the use of some form of peer learning. Teachers will need to understand the students' initial competencies for a learning task, the desired competencies, and awareness of the kinds of tasks that will promote learning. Task design and selection will require that the teacher understand the role of practice, feedback, examples, alternative representations and many other features of instruction in order to develop effective tasks that may be accomplished by peers. The focus cannot simply be on "group performance" of a task but on the improvement of each individual student in the skills required by the task.

Teacher as Model

Techniques such as reciprocal peer tutoring place a great deal of importance on the role of the teacher as the initial model for complex cognitive activity. A skilled teacher is capable of making her or his thinking visible, allowing students to gradually practice increasingly complex skills, and eventually fading the support needed by the students.

Coordinator of Activities

Many teachers continue to teach using primarily whole-class instruction not because they necessarily believe in its instructional efficacy, but often because they are concerned about managing the learning activities of multiple groups, limiting negative social processes, and concerns about covering the curriculum.

Evaluator

The teacher can choose to evaluate many aspects of a peer-learning situation including their use of social skills, their on-task behavior, the products produced by students, how well students can perform after they have an opportunity to learn from others during collaborative

learning, and individual contributions to the group product or other individual products that might be required (Webb, 1997). Most cooperative learning techniques include individual accountability as a key feature. In using cooperative groups or other forms of peer learning, a teacher will also need to provide feedback about the adequacy and appropriateness of students' interactions. Cohen and colleagues have shown that when students are provided with the criteria for what constitutes an exemplary group product and use these criteria to evaluate their work, their interactions improve and their learning increases (Cohen, Lotan, Abram, Scarloss, & Schultz, 2002).

CLASSROOM TASKS

Teachers need to decide what are their goals for any task they assign. They may select tasks to motivate or engage students, to provide a context for social interaction with a student with particular difficulties, have students acquire knowledge of factual material, or have students engage in higher order reasoning and thinking skills. Depending on the goals of the task, the kind of peer learning selected will vary.

Not all tasks require the same level of effort, generate the same level of interest, or demand the same cognitive processes. Tasks can be classified along a number of different dimensions. The first dimension is complexity. Tasks can be simple and involve simple cognitive strategies such as rehearsal. Memorizing the names of the capitals of states requires rehearsal. *Basic knowledge acquisition tasks* are those in which content is encoded into students' memories for subsequent recall. Strategies for assisting students to master such tasks include teaching them memorization and rehearsal strategies such as the use of mnemonics, summarization, and elaboration strategies. Techniques such as STAD or Scripted Cooperation can be very useful in assisting students to perform these tasks effectively.

At the other end of a continuum of complexity, tasks can require complex cognitive skills. However, students must also master other kinds of tasks that require them to pose their own questions, explore alternative ideas, gather information, generate evidence or arguments in support of ideas, and draw conclusions. The kinds of techniques that support basic knowledge acquisition and rehearsal will be insufficient to promote these kinds of higher order thinking. Tasks that are more open-ended or require more collaborative construction of joint knowledge will require cooperative techniques that are less structured, in order to permit the kinds of interactions that will result in the desired outcomes. Consider the following. Students in a high school science class could be asked to execute a predesigned chemistry experiment by following the directions in a lab notebook. This task is much simpler, and it requires lower level cognitive skills than a task in which students are asked to design an experiment to determine whether the water from the local lake is safe to drink.

Cohen (1994) distinguishes between tasks that are inherently individual tasks and those that are group tasks. According to Cohen, "a group task is a task that requires resources (information, knowledge, heuristic problem-solving strategies, materials, and skills) that no single individual possesses so that no single individual is likely to solve the problems or accomplishes the task objectives without at least some input from others" (p. 8). Five features of such tasks are that they are open-ended and require problem solving; students can approach the task from a number of vantage points and students have multiple opportunities to demonstrate their intellectual competence; they are concerned with important discipline-based content; they require positive interdependence among group members and individual accountability of all members; and they include clear criteria for how the group's product will be evaluated. Using such tasks requires considerable time and expertise on the part of the teacher (Lotan, 2003).

It is important to note that not all students will be ready to assume complex roles and strategies immediately. Students who have not worked in cooperative groups will require some initial training and gradual experience in assuming more responsibility for their learning. Likewise, students who have not valued educational achievement will not suddenly become passionate about school learning without significant intervention in altering the class values on achievement. Techniques such as STAD can be effective in re-norming classroom values such that group success is important.

METHODOLOGICAL ISSUES IN RESEARCH ON PEER LEARNING

There are a number of methodological issues that characterize the research on peer learning. The first of these is the appropriateness of the analytical strategy being used. Many studies of collaboration are influenced by Vygotskian theory. A key idea that springs from Vygotsky's concept of the zone of proximal development is the importance of dynamic assessment of developing processes. Microgenetic methods can be used for such assessments, as they provide measures of intraindividual change as individuals are observed on numerous occasions (De Lisi,

2005). Such methods are rarely used in studies of collaborative groups. Vygotskian theory suggests that skills modeled in the external world will eventually be internalized or appropriated by the individual. However, much of the research on collaborative groups or other peer learning formats does not included delayed posttesting of accomplishment. Although students may appear to benefit from peer learning, we cannot know if those benefits are sustained and the individual's functionality enhanced.

A second methodological issue with respect to the study of peer learning is the unit of analysis used. A concern about the contribution of group learning to individual performance often leads to data analytic strategies that focus on the individual rather than on the group or pair as the unit of analysis. Limitations in sample size or number of classrooms available may make it difficult for researchers to use other strategies that take group-level variables into account.

A third methodological issue concerns the intraindividual variation in response to group composition. A particular individual may appear dominant in one group, but when working with different students, that same student may appear shy. Researchers need to be sensitive to the possibility of such variation and interpret their research findings.

CONCLUSIONS AND FUTURE RESEARCH

In the first edition of the *Handbook of Educational Psychology,* Webb and Palincsar (1996) noted the advances that had been made in understanding the complexity of peer learning and its outcomes. Research on cooperative and collaborative learning, peer tutoring, and other forms of peer interaction has resulted in a substantial research base on the topic. Changes in educational policies, particularly the passage of the No Child Left Behind Act (2002), create new demands for documenting the efficacy of peer learning strategies. Requirements to report disaggregated data for subgroups such as special needs students and limited-English-proficient students make it imperative that effective instructional strategies for these groups be identified. Future research on peer learning needs to consider how peer learning strategies can be used effectively to teach special needs students. Although research on the effectiveness of tutoring as a strategy for these students is clear, research on the use of larger groups using strategies other than tutoring is equivocal.

The influence of gender, race, and ethnicity on the effectiveness of peer learning is also not well understood and warrants additional research. There is a tendency to rely on rather dated research to make claims about the importance of such variables. Teachers vary enormously in their reported grouping practices and the actual groups they form (Webb, Baxter, & Thompson, 1997). If group composition is important to the attainment of educational outcomes, there must surely be some identifiable principles for forming groups. Research on this issue has the potential to contribute significantly to informed and principled practice.

References

Antil, L. R., Jenkins, J. R., Wayne, S. K., & Vadasy, P. F. (1998). Prevalence, conceptualizations, and the relation between research and practice. *American Educational Research Journal, 35*, 419-454.

Andriessen, J. (2005). Collaboration in computer conferencing. In A. M. O'Donnell, C. Hmelo-Silver, & G. Erkens (Eds.), *Collaborative Learning, Reasoning, and Technology* (pp. 197-132). Mahwah, NJ: Lawrence Erlbaum Assocuates.

Aronson, E., Blaney, N., Stephan, C., Sikes, J., & Snapp, M. (1978). *The jigsaw classroom*. Beverly Hills, CA: Sage.

Baker, L., & Brown, A. L. (1984). Metacognitive skills and reading. In P. D. Pearson (Ed.), *Handbook of reading research* (pp. 353-394). New York: Longman.

Bandura, A. (1977). *Social learning theory*. Englewood Cliffs, NJ: Prentice-Hall.

Bandura, A. (1986). *Social foundations of thought and action: A social cognitive theory*. Englewood Cliffs, NJ: Prentice-Hall.

Bandura, A. (2000). Exercise of human agency through collective efficacy. *Current Directions in Psychological Science, 9*, 75-78.

Barron, B. (2003). When smart groups fail. *Journal of the Learning Sciences, 12*, 307-359.

Bloom, B. S. (1984). The search for methods of group instruction as effective as one-to-one tutoring. *Educational Leadership, 41*(8), 4-17.

Brown, A. L., & Campione, J. C. (1994). Guided discovery in a community of learners. In K. McGilley (Ed.), *Classrooms lessons: Integrating cognitive theory and classroom practice* (pp. 229-272). Cambridge, MA: MIT Press.

Calderon, M., Hertz-Lazarowitz, R., & Slavin, R. E. (1998). Effects of Bilingual Cooperative Integrated Reading and Composition on students making the transition from Spanish to English reading. *Elementary School Journal, 99*(2), 153-165.

Chi, M. T. H., Siler, S. A., & Jeong, H. (2004). Can tutors monitor students' understanding accurately? *Cognition & Instruction, 22*, 363-387.

Chi, M. T. H., Siler, S. A., Jeong, H., Yamauchi, T., & Hausmann, R. G. (2001). Learning from human tutoring. *Cognitive Science, 25*, 471-533.

Chinn, C. A., & Brewer, W. F. (1993). The role of anomalous data in knowledge acquisition: A theoretical framework and implications for science instruction. *Review of Educational Research, 63*, 1-49.

Chinn, C. A., & Malhotra, B. A. (2002). Children's responses to anomalous scientific data: How is conceptual change impeded? *Journal of Educational Psychology, 94*, 327-343.

Chinn, C. A., O'Donnell, A. M., & Jinks, T. S. The structure of discourse in collaborative learning. *Journal of Experimental Education, 69*, 77-97.

Cohen, E. G. (1982). Expectation states and interracial interaction in school settings. *Annual Review of Sociology, 8*, 209-235.

Cohen, E. G. (1994). Restructuring the classroom: Conditions for productive small groups. *Review of Educational Research, 64*, 1-36.

Cohen, E. G., & Lotan, R. A. (1995). Producing equal-status interaction in the heterogeneous classroom. *American Educational Research Journal, 32*(1), 99-120.

Cohen, E. G., & Lotan, R. A. (1997). *Working for equity in heterogeneous classrooms: Sociological theory in practice*. New York: Teacher's College Press.

Cohen, E. G., Lotan, R. A., Abram, P. L., Scarloss, B. A., & Schultz, S. E. (2002). Can groups learn? *Teachers College Record, 104*(6), 1045-1068.

Cohen, E. G., Lotan, R., & Catanzarite, L. (1990). Treating status problems in the cooperative classroom. In S. Sharan (Ed.), *Cooperative learning: Theory and practice*. New York: Praeger.

Cohen, E. G., Lotan, R. A., Scarloss, B. A., & Arellano, A. R. (1999). Complex Instruction: Equity in cooperative learning classrooms. *Theory Into Practice, 38*(2), 80-86.

Cohen, P. A., Kulick, J. A., & Kulick, C. C. (1982). Educational outcomes of tutoring: A meta-analysis of findings. *American Educational Research Journal, 19*, 237-248.

Collins, A., Brown, J. S., & Holum, A. (1991). Cognitive apprenticeship: Making thinking visible. *American Educator, 15*(3), 38-39.

Collins, A., Brown, J. S., & Newman, S. E. (1989). Cognitive apprenticeship: Teaching the crafts of reading, writing, and mathematics. In L. B. Resnick (Ed.), *Knowing, learning, and instruction: Essays in honor of Robert Glazer* (pp. 453-494). Hillsdale, NJ: Lawrence Erlbaum Assiciates.

Cook, S. B., Scruggs, T. E., Mastropieri, M. A., & Casto, G. C. (1985-86). Handicapped students as tutors. *Journal of Special Education, 19*, 155-164.

De Lisi, R. (2002). From marbles to instant messenger: Implications of Piaget's ideas about peer learning. *Theory Into Practice, 41*(1), 5-12.

De Lisi, R. (2005). A developmental perspective on virtual scaffolding for learning in home and school contexts. In A. M. O'Donnell, C. E. Hmelo-Silver & G. Erkens (Eds.), *Collaboration, reasoning, and technology* (pp. 15-35). Mahwah, NJ: Lawrence Erlbaum Associates.

De Lisi, R., & Golbeck, S. L. (1999). Implications of Piagetian theory for peer learning. In A. M. O'Donnell & A. King (Eds.), *Cognitive perspectives on peer learning* (pp. 3-37). Mahwah, NJ: Lawrence Erlbaum Associates.

Delquadri, J. C., Greenwood, C. R., Whorton, D., Carta, J. J., & Hall, R. V. (1986). Classwide peer tutoring. *Exceptional Children, 52,* 535-542.

Deutsch, M. (1949). A theory of cooperation and competition. *Human Relations, 2,* 129-152.

Devries, D. L., & Edwards, K. J. (1973). Learning games and student teams: Their effects of classroom process. *American Educational Research Journal, 10,* 307-318.

Elbaum, B., Moody, S. W., & Schumm, J. S. (1999). Mixed ability grouping for reading: What students think. *Learning Disabilities Research and Practice, 14,* 61-66.

Erkens. G., Prangsma, M., & Jasper, J. (2005). Planning and coordinating activities in collaborative learning. In A. M. O' Donnell, C. Hmelo-Silver, & G. Erkens (Eds.). *Collaborative learning, reasoning, and technology* (pp. 147-170) Mahwah NJ: Lawrence Erlbaum Associates.

Fantuzzo, J. W., Davis, G. Y., & Ginsberg, M. D. (1995). Effects of parent involvement in isolation or in combination with peer tutoring on student self-concept and mathematics achievement. *Journal of Educational Psychology, 87,* 272-281.

Fantuzzo, J. W., King, J. A., & Heller, L. R. (1992). Effects of reciprocal peer tutoring on mathematics and school adjustment: A component analysis. *Journal of Educational Psychology, 84,* 331-339

Fitzpatrick, H., & Hardman, M. (2000). Mediated activity in the primary classrooms: Girls, boys, and computers. *Learning and Instruction, 10,* 431-446.

Fuchs, D., Fuchs, L. S., Mathes, P. G., & Martinez, E. A. (2002). Preliminary evidence on the social standing of students with learning disabilities in PALS and no-PALS classrooms. *Learning Disabilities Research, 17,* 205-215.

Fuchs, D., Fuchs, L. S., Mathes, P. G., & Simmons, D. C. (1997). Peer-assisted learning strategies: Making classrooms more responsive to academic diversity. *American Educational Research Journal, 34,* 174-206.

Fuchs, L. S., & Fuchs, D. (1998). General educators' instructional adaptation for students with learning disabilities. *Learning Disabilities Quarterly, 21,* 23-33.

Fuchs, L. S., Fuchs, D., Yazdian, L., & Powell, S. R. (2002). Enhancing first-grade children's mathematical development with peer-assisted learning strategies. *School Psychology Review, 31,* 569-583.

Ginsburg-Block, M., & Fantuzzo, J. W. (1997). Reciprocal peer tutoring: An analysis of "teacher" and "student" interactions as a function of training and experience. *School Psychology Quarterly, 12,* 134-149.

Graesser, A. C., Person, N. K., & Magliano, J. (1995). Collaborative dialog patterns in naturalistic one-on-one tutoring. *Applied Cognitive Psychology, 9,* 359-387.

Greenwood, C. R., Carta, J. J., & Kamps, D. (1990). Teacher versus peer-mediated instruction. In H. Foot, M. Morgan & R. Shute (Eds.), *Children helping children* (pp. 177-206). London: Wiley.

Greenwood, C. R., Delquadri, J. C., & Hall, R. V. (1989). Longitudinal effects of Classwide Peer Tutoring. *Journal of Educational Psychology, 81*(3), 371-383.

Greenwood, C. R., Maheady, L., & Carta, J. J. (1991). Peer tutoring programs in the regular classrooms. In G. Stoner, M. R. Shinn, & H. M. Walker (Eds.), *Intervention for achievement and behavior problems* (pp. 179-200). Washington, DC: National Association of School Psychologists.

Greenwood, C. R., & Terry, B. (1993). Achievement, placement, and services: Middle school benefits of Classwide Peer Tutoring used at the elementary school. *School Psychology Review, 22,* 497-516.

Heller, L. R., & Fantuzzo, J. W. (1993). Reciprocal peer tutoring and parent partnership: Does parent involvement make a difference? *School Psychology Review, 22,* 517-534.

Hogan, D. M., & Tudge, J. R. H. (1999). Implications of Vygotsky's theory of peer learning. In A. M. O'Donnell & A. King (Eds.), *Cognitive perspectives on peer learning* (pp. 39-65). Mahwah, NJ: Lawrence Erlbaum Associates.

Holden, C. (1993). Giving girls a chance: Patterns of talk in cooperative group work. *Gender and Education, 5,* 179-189.

Holder, H., & Fitzpatrick, H. (1991). Interpretation of emotion from facial expressions in children with and without learning disabilities. *Journal of Learning Disabilities, 24,* 170-177.

Jenkins, J. R., & O'Connor, R. E. (2003). Cooperative learning for students with learning disabilities. In H. L. Swanson, K. R. Harris, & S. Graham (Eds.), *Handbook of learning disabilities* (pp. 417-430). New York: Guilford.

Johnson, D. W., & Johnson, R. T. (1981). Effects of cooperative and individualistic learning experiences on interethnic interaction. *Journal of Educational Psychology, 73,* 444-449.

Johnson, D. W., & Johnson, R. T. (1989). *Cooperation and competition: Theory and research.* Edina, MN: Interaction Book Company.

Johnson, D. W., & Johnson, R. T. (1991). *Learning together and alone: Cooperative, competitive, and individualistic learning.* Englewood Cliffs, NJ:: Prentice Hall.

Johnson, D. W., & Johnson, R. T. (1995). *Creative controversy: Intellectual challenge in the classroom.* Edina, MN: Interaction Book Company.

Juel, C. (1996). What makes literacy tutoring effective? *Reading Research Quarterly, 31,* 268-289.

Kagan, S. (1995). Group grades miss the mark. *Educational Leadership, 52*(8), 68-71.

Kagan, S. (1996). Avoiding the group-grades trap. *Learning, 24,* 56-58.

King, A. (1991). Effects of training in strategic questioning on children's problem-solving performance. *Journal of Educational Psychology, 83,* 307-317.

King, A. (1994). Guiding knowledge construction in the classroom: Effects of teaching children how to question and how to explain. *American Educational Research Journal, 31,* 358-368.

King, A. (1999). Discourse patterns mediating peer learning. In A. M. O'Donnell & A. King (Eds.), *Cognitive perspectives on peer learning* (pp. 87–115). Mahwah; NJ: Lawrence Erlbaum Associates.

King, A., Staffieri, A., & Adelgais, A. (1998). Mutual peer tutoring: Effects of structured tutorial interaction to scaffold peer learning. *Journal of Educational Psychology, 90,* 134–152.

Lazarowitz, R., & Karsenty, G. (1990). Cooperative learning and students' academic achievement, process skills, learning environment, and self-esteem in 10th grade biology classroom. In S. Sharan (Ed.), *Cooperative learning: Theory and research* (pp. 123–149). New York: Praeger.

Lebeau, R. B. (1998). Cognitive tools in a clinical encounter in medicine: Supporting empathy and expertise in distributed systems. *Educational Psychology Review, 10,* 3–24.

Light, P., Littleton, K., Balc, S., Joiner, R., & Messer, D. (2000). Gender and social comparison effects in computer-based problem solving. *Learning and Instruction, 10,* 483–496.

Lindren, D. M., Meier, S. E., & Brigham, T. A. (1991). The effects of minimal and maximal peer tutoring systems on the academic performance of college students. *Psychological Record, 41,* 69–77.

Lotan, R. A. (2003). Group-worthy tasks. *Educational Leadership, 60*(6), 72–75.

Mathes, P. G., & Fuchs, L. S. (1993). Peer mediated reading instruction in special education resource rooms. *Learning Disabilities Research and Practice, 8,* 233–243.

Mathes, P. G., Torgeson, J. K., Clancy-Menchetti, J., Santi, K., Nicholas K., Robinson, C., et al. (2003). A comparison of teacer-directed versus peer-assisted instruction to struggling first-grade readers. *Elementary School Journal, 103,* 459–479.

McArthur, D., Stasz, C., & Zmuidzinas, M. (1990). Tutoring techniques in alegbra. *Cognition and Instruction, 7,* 197–244.

McMaster, K. N., & Fuchs, D. (2002). Effects of cooperative learning on the academic achievement of students with learning disabilities: An update of Tateyama-Sniezek's review. *Learning Disabilities: Research and Practice, 17,* 107–117.

Meeker, B. F. (1981). Expectation states and interpersonal behavior. In M. Rosenberg & R. H. Turner (Eds.), *Social psychology: Sociological perspectives* (pp. 290–319). New York: Basic Books.

Neale, D. C., Smith, D., & Johnson, V. G. (1990). Implcmenting conceptual change teaching in primary science. *Elementary School Journal, 91,* 109–131.

O'Donnell, A. M., & Dansereau, D. F. (1992). Scripted cooperation in student dyads: A method for analyzing and enhancing academic learning and performance. In R. Hertz-Lazarowitz & N. Miller (Eds.), *Interaction in cooperative groups: The theoretical anatomy of group learning* (pp. 120–141). New York: Cambridge University Press.

O'Donnell, A. M., Dansereau, D. F., Hall, R. H., & Rocklin, T. R. (1987). Cognitive, social/affective, and metacognitive outcomes of scripted cooperative learning. *Journal of Educational Psychology, 79,* 431–437.

Osguthorpc, R., & Scruggs, T. E. (1986). Special education students as tutors: A review and analysis. *Remedial and Special Education, 7,* 15–26.

Palincsar, A. S., & Brown, A. L. (1984). Reciprocal teaching of comprehension-fostering and comprehension-monitoring activities. *Cognition and Instruction, 1,* 117–175.

Palincsar, A. S., & Herrenkohl, L. R. (2002). Designing collaborative learning contexts. *Theory into Practice, 41,* 26–32.

Pearl, R. (1992). Psychosocial characteristics of learning disabled students. In N. Singh & I. Beale (Eds.), *Current perspectives in learning disabilities: Nature, theory, and treatment* (pp. 96–117). New York: Springer-Verlag.

Person, N. K., & Graesser, A. C. (1999). Evolution of discourse during cross-age tutoring. In A. King (Ed.), *Cognitive perspectives on peer learning* (pp. 69–86). Mahwah, NJ: Lawrence Erlbaum Associates.

Person, N. K., Kreuz, R. J., Zwaan, R., & Graesser, A. C. (1995). Pragmatics and pedagogy: Conversational rules and politeness strategies may inhibit effective tutoring. *Cognition and Instruction, 13,* 161–188.

Piaget, J. (1985). *The equilibrium of cognitive structures: The central problem of intellectual development.* Chicago: University of Chicago Press.

Pintrich, P. R., & Schunk, D. H. (2002). *Motivation in education: Theory, research, and applications* (2nd ed.). Upper Saddle River, NJ: Merrill/Prentice-Hall.

Putnam, R. T. (1987). Structuring and adjusting content for students: A study of live and simulated tutoring of addition. *American Educational Research Journal, 24,* 13–48.

Rosenshine, B., & Meister, C. (1994). Reciprocal teaching: A review of the research. *Review of Educational Research, 64*(4), 479–530.

Rottman, T. R., & Cross, D. R. (1990 April). *Scripted cooperative reading: Using student–student interaction to enhance comprehension.* Paper presented at the Annual Meeting of the American Education Research associates San Francisco.

Scardamalia, M., Bereiter, C., & Lamon, M. (1994). The CSILE project: Trying to bring the classroom into world 3. In K. McGilley (Ed.), *Classroom lessons: Integrating cognitive theory and classroom practice* (pp. 201–228). Cambridge, MA: MIT Press.

Scruggs, T. E., & Mastropieri, M. A. (1998). Tutoring and students with special needs. In K. Topping & S. Ehly (Eds.), *Peer assisted learning* (pp. 165–182). Mahwah, NJ: Lawrence Erlbaum Associates.

Scruggs, T. E., & Osguthorpe, R. (1986). Tutoring interventions within special education settings: A comparison of cross-age and peer tutoring. *Psychology in the Schools, 23*(2), 187–193.

Sharan, S., & Hertz-Lazarowitz, R. (1980). A group investigation method of cooperative learning in the classroom. In S. Sharan, P. Hare, C. Webb, & R. Hertz-Lazarowitz (Eds.), *Cooperation in education* (pp. 14–46). Provo, UT: Brigham Young University Press.

Sharan, S., & Shachar, H. (1988). *Language and learning in the cooperative classroom.* New York: Springer.

Sharan, S., & Shaulov, A. (1990). Cooperative learning, motivation to learn, and academic achievement. In S. Sharan (Ed.), *Cooperative learning: Theory and research* (pp. 173–202). New York: Praeger.

Sharan, Y., & Sharan, S. (1992). *Expanding cooperative learning through group investigation*. New York: Teachers College Press.

Slavin, R. E. (1986). *Using student team learning*. (3rd ed.). Baltimore, MD: Johns Hopkins University.

Slavin, R. E. (1987). Making Chapter 1 make a difference, *Phi Delta Kappan*, 69, 110-119.

Slavin, R. E. (1995). *Cooperative learning* (2nd ed.). Boston: Allyn & Bacon.

Slavin, R. E. (1996). Research on cooperative learning and achievement: What we know, what we need to know. *Contemporary Educational Psychology, 21*, 43-69.

Slavin, R. E., Leavey, M., & Madden, N. A. (1986). *Team accelerated instruction: Mathematics*. Waterown, MA: Charlesbridge.

Slavin, R. E., & Madden, N. A. (1989). What works for students at risk: A research synthesis. *Educational Leadership, 46*(5), 4-13.

Stevens, R. J., Madden, N. A., Slavin, R. E., & Farnish, A. M. (1987). Cooperative Integrating Reading and Composition: Two field experiments. *Reading Research Quarterly, 22*, 433-454.

Stevens, R. J., & Slavin, R. E. (1991). When cooperative learning improves the achievement of students with mild disabilities: A response to Tateyama-Sniezek. *Exceptional Children, 57*, 276-280.

Stevens, R. J., & Slavin, R. E. (1995). Effects of a cooperative approach in reading and writing on academically handicapped and non-handicapped students. *Reading Research Quarterly, 95*, 241-262.

Tateyama-Sniezek, K. M. (1990). Cooperative learning: Does it improve the academic achievement of students with handicaps? *Exceptional Children, 56*, 426-437.

Tolmie, A., & Howe, C. (1993). Gender and dialogue in secondary school physics. *Gender and Education, 5*, 191-209.

Top, B. L. (1984). *Handicapped children as tutors: The effects of cross-age, reverse-role tutoring on self-esteem and reading achievement*. Unpublished dissertation Brigham Young University, Provo, UT.

Underwood, G., & Jindal, N. (1993). Gender differences and cooperation in a computer-based language task. *Educational Research, 36*, 63-74.

VanLehn, K., Siler, S. A., Murray, C., & Bagget, W. B. (2003). Human tutoring: Why do only some events cause learning? *Cognition and Instruction, 21*, 209-249.

Vygotsky, L. S. (1929). The problem of the cultural development of the child. *Journal of Genetic Psychology 36*, 415-434.

Vygotsky, L. S. (1978). *Mind in society: The development of higher mental processes*. Cambridge, MA: Harvard University Press.

Webb, N. M. (1984). Sex differences in interaction and achievement in cooperative small groups. *Journal of Educational Psychology, 76*, 33-44.

Webb, N. M. (1989). Peer interaction and learning in small groups. *International Review of Educational Research, 13*, 21-40.

Webb, N. M. (1991). Task-related verbal interaction and mathematics learning in small groups. *Journal of Research in Mathematics Education, 22*, 366-369.

Webb, N. M. (1992). Testing a theoretical model of student interaction and learning in small groups. In R. Hertz-Lazarowitz, & N. Miller (Eds.), *Interaction in cooperative groups: The theoretical anatomy of group learning* (pp. 102-119). New York: Cambridge University Press.

Webb, N. M. (1997). Assessing students in small collaborative groups. *Theory Into Practice, 36*, 205-213.

Webb, N. M., Baxter, G. P., & Thompson, L. (1997). Teachers' grouping practices in fifth-grade science classrooms. *Elementary School Journal, 98*(2), 91-113.

Webb, N. M., & Farivar, S. (1994). Promoting helping behavior in cooperative small groups in middle school mathematics. *American Educational Research Journal, 31*, 369-395.

Webb, N. M., & Palincsar, A. S. (1996). Group processes in the classroom. In D. C. Berliner & R. C. Calfee (Eds.), *Handbook of educational psychology* (pp. 841-873). New York: Macmillan.

Wenger, E. (1998). *Communities of practice*. Cambridge, UK: Cambridge University Press.

Zuber, R. L. (1992). *Cooperative learning by fifth-grade students: The effects of scripted and unscripted cooperation*. Unpublished doctoral dissertation, Rutgers, The State University of New Jersey, New Brunswick, NJ.

TEACHING AND LEARNING IN TECHNOLOGY-RICH ENVIRONMENTS

Susanne P. Lajoie
McGill University

Roger Azevedo
University of Maryland

Research that pertains to technology in education spans decades and has been a core area of interest in several disciplines including educational psychology, cognitive science, and computer science. The focus of this paper is not to provide a comprehensive review of past research in the area, but instead, to identify relevant principles for supporting the design of technology-rich learning environments (TREs) that enhance teaching and learning. Consequently, you will not find a review of teaching machines, computer-assisted instruction, intelligent tutoring systems, multimedia environments, simulations, virtual reality, handheld devices, and so forth. Instead, we describe some of the theories of teaching and learning that can be applied to the design of effective TREs.

We broadly define a TRE as a learning environment that is designed for an instructional purpose and uses technology to support the learner in achieving the goals of instruction. The roles of the teacher and the learner will depend on both the purpose of instruction and the theory guiding the design of the TRE. Technological advances in teaching and learning environments should be designed based on a theory or model of learning and instruction. TREs should then be validated with learners and data collected to see whether or not the TREs meet the needs of learners. Having both theory and data iteratively guide the design and redesign process provides an

impetus for increasing the effectiveness of TREs as teaching and learning environments.

This chapter explores the momentum behind theory building, the design of TREs, and the assessment of learning in technology-rich environments. We provide concrete examples from our research and that of others. Finally, we would like to clarify from the onset that we are not proposing that technology-rich environments are the only way to promote effective instruction. Instead, our goal is to describe ways in which appropriate theory-driven design of TREs can be used to support both the teacher and the learner in a myriad of instructional settings.

THEORY-DRIVEN DESIGN

There are several guiding paradigms and frameworks to be reviewed in the context of learning and instruction. Theories of teaching and learning apply to all good learning environments, and hence much of what is discussed in the following sections also applies to nontechnology situations. Recent theories about learning and cognition have evolved from a pure cognitive information-processing perspective to a modified constructivist one. What we witnessed a decade ago was paradigm debates between information-processing theorists and situated learning theorists. However, the debate seems to have ended with a discussion of how theories are more alike than different (Anderson, Greeno, Reder, & Simon, 2000; Anderson, Reder, & Simon, 1998; Brown, 1994; Greeno, 1998; Mayer, 1997). We raise this to situate our discussion of a few key issues that permeate teaching and learning with technology-rich environments. These issues include describing the role of context in learning, revisiting the social context, and the role that individual differences play in the context of the social construction of knowledge. We briefly discuss the realignment of motivation and cognition considerations in teaching and learning and describe the value of understanding competencies in specific curriculum areas as a precursor to better instruction. These theoretical issues foreshadow our discussion of TREs, what they consist of now, and what they might look like in the future.

Learning in Context

Learning theories are increasingly centered on learning processes as they occur within meaningful contexts or *situations* (Brown, Collins & Duguid, 1989; Collins, Brown & Newman, 1989; CTGV, 1990, 1993; Greeno, 1989, 1998). *Situated learning theory* provides descriptions of *learning in context*, in that human thought and action are described as being responsive to the environment, occur in complex contexts that provide opportunities for integrating information from multiple sources, and often require the social construction of knowledge (Clancey,1997; Greeno, 1998; von Glaserfeld, 1995 Young & McNeese, 1995).

Early Greek philosophers, such as Socrates, may have been among the first to describe knowledge as being constructed by individuals through their interactions with their environment (Mahoney, in press). The constructivist perspective refers to the active construction of knowledge in the context of solving realistic problems where learners build knowledge and organize it in a personally meaningful form. Dewey (1938) stated that individuals learn best by doing and experiencing things as a basis for meaningful learning. Hence, *learning by doing* (Dewey, 1938) also embeds constructivist principles. It has long been said that students will lose the knowledge that they gain in school if they do not have opportunities to apply such knowledge outside of the classroom. Schooled knowledge often lies inert (Whitehead, 1929), perhaps because factual knowledge or abstract concepts are often taught independently of cognitive strategies for when and how to use such knowledge (Clancey, 1997; Resnick, 1987). Well-designed TREs can couple factual knowledge acquisition with opportunities for applying such knowl-

edge in specific problem-solving contexts. TREs can support multiple modalities creating realistic interactive environments in which learners can construct new meaning from the instructional materials provided.

The design of many effective learning environments today, be they technology-rich or technology-free, is guided by the principles of learning in context and learning by doing, and the principles of constructivism and situated learning. Examples can be found in learning environments that are case-based (Schank, 1998), problem-based (Barrows, 1996), project-based (Barron et al., 1998; Blumenfeld et al., 1991), inquiry-based (Palincsar, Magnuson, Maranol, Ford & Brown, 1998), and anchored forms of instruction (Bransford, Sherwood, Hasselbring, Kinzer, & Williams, 1990; CTGV, 1993). Each framework starts with the premise that learning in context facilitates meaningful learning. These frameworks differ in terms of how "social" the learning experience is and the role of the teacher in each activity, as well as the roles of learners, and whether the environment is technology rich or not.

Revisiting the Social Context. The social aspect of *learning in context* is a significant theme. Piaget (1926) discussed how knowledge was constructed through social arbitration, through language, values, rules, morals, symbol systems, and learning through interacting with others. Social-cultural themes are also described by Vygotsky (1978), who highlighted the role of scaffolding learners through interactions with those more competent on a particular task. According to Vygotsky, learners should be guided or scaffolded by a more capable peer to solve a problem or carry out a task that would be beyond what they could accomplish independently. We argue that a computer tutor or peer could serve as a capable peer as well and hence a TRE could also provide scaffolding (Lajoie, 2000). Alternatively, human peers can serve to assist others while working collaboratively on problems that are provided by a TRE. Traditionally, scaffolding in education has emphasized the role of dialogue and social interaction to foster (a) comprehension and monitoring activities (Palincsar & Brown, 1984), (b) student-generated self-explanations (Chi, 2000; Chi, de Leeuw, Chiu, & LaVancher, 1994), (c) instruction (e.g., telling the student a fact), (d) cognitive scaffolding that helps the student solve a problem on his or her own (e.g., hinting) (Merrill, Reiser, Merrill, & Landes, 1995), (e) motivational scaffolding (e.g., feedback on student performance) (Lepper, Drake, & O'Donnell-Johnson, 1997), and (f) tutor question-asking (Graesser, Bowers, Hacker, & Person, 1997).

Scaffolding learners often consists of modeling problem-solving strategies when an impasse occurs.

Bandura (1977) defined modeling in terms of how learning can be facilitated by observing others perform the task. He stated that:

Learning would be exceedingly laborious, not to mention hazardous, if people had to rely solely on the effects of their own actions to inform them what to do. Fortunately, most human behavior is learned observationally through modeling: from observing others one forms an idea of how new behaviors are performed, and on later occasions this coded information serves as a guide for action. (p. 22)

According to this social learning theory, human behavior is seen as an ongoing reciprocal interaction among cognitive, behavioral, and environmental factors.

The benefit of modeling is that learners do not always have to learn from mistakes but from the successful incorporation of ideas by observing others do a task efficiently (Lajoie, in press a). TREs can be designed to model human behavior or to model complex simulations that learners can attend to and learn from. In this way, learners can deliberately practice the correct skills rather than practice indiscriminately (Ericsson, 2002).

Studies of expertise have provided the foundation for developing models of what students need to know with respect to complex performance across domains (Alexander, 2003; Chi, Glaser, & Farr, 1989; Ericsson, 2002; Glaser, Lesgold, Lajoie, & 1987; Lajoie, 2003). The National Academy of Science report by Pellegrino, Chudowsky, and Glaser (2001) provides insight with regard to what to model across the K-12 curriculum. They report on a large body of scientific knowledge about the processes of thinking and learning and the development of competence in specific curriculum areas. Examining competency or proficiency within a specific context is the first step in elaborating a model of thinking that can help the less competent become more proficient in a specific domain (Lajoie, in press a; Mislevy, Steinberg & Almond, 1999; Mislevy, Steinberg, Breyer, Almond, & Johnson, in press). Scaffolding learning is dependent on assessing the learning process and providing appropriate models for extending learning. Pellegrino et al. support a curriculum-instruction assessment triad based on principles about learning and knowing that can assist learners along a learning trajectory within a specific field. They report that effective learning environments are learner centered, and instruction must therefore provide scaffolds for solving meaningful problems and supporting learning and understanding.

TREs can support the curriculum-instruction assessment triad in several ways. First, TREs can be designed to support a specific curriculum context. Instruction in this context will include scaffolding and hints that are based on theories pertaining to the nature of expertise (Chi et al., 1989; Ericsson, 2002; Glaser et al., 1989; Lajoie, 2003; Lajoie, in press b). Identifying the dimensions of expertise within domain-specific contexts can lead to improvements in instruction that will ultimately result in helping learners become more competent. Such research findings could be incorporated into TREs by making expert models of performance and competency more visible to learners in the context of problem solving. One mechanism for supporting the learning trajectories is through the dynamic assessment of learner progress within a problem-solving context.

When the computer indicates that a learner has reached an impasse, scaffolding can be automatically generated. The scaffolding could include feedback or hints that would get the learner back on track by providing either a visual or textual explanation of what an expert might do within the same context. For most ill-structured problems there is more than one way to reach a solution and hence multiple learning trajectories. Hence, support must be available to scaffold individual differences. Learning can be supported by modeling expertise, through feedback or examples that promote the active transfer of knowledge and self-monitoring (Lajoie, 2003). Expert models of problem solving promote awareness, and realistic problem-solving activities can be designed based on detailed analysis of expert performance in the field. Metacognition, or the ability to think about one's own thinking (Flavell, 1979), is a key element of expertise; however, we need to identify what experts monitor in a specific context before we can model these processes for novices. In so doing we can help learners self-regulate during the learning process (Azevedo, 2002). The domain knowledge, the structure of the knowledge, and the strategies that lead to effective problem solutions can all be modeled for the learner. However, it is not simply observation that leads to learning, but rather using such knowledge, interacting with it, and receiving specific feedback that fosters learning.

Social learning theory is based on the belief that people learn from each other in social settings by observing the behaviors and outcomes experienced by others. The social aspects of *learning in context* have continued to be examined in the literature on communities of learning (Brown, 1994) and practice (Barab & Duffy, 2000; Engstrom & Cole, 1997; Lave & Wenger, 1991; Wenger, 1999), and cognitive apprenticeship settings (Collins et al., 1989; Lajoie & Lesgold, 1989). Each of these frameworks specified how such models are established and used in instructional or real-world learning situations. Such learning communities can help broaden knowledge by providing multiple perspectives, and they might also contribute to enhancing individuals' beliefs about their own knowledge. These communities can also be supported by TREs that support community discourse and problem-solving activities. The technology itself can serve as the platform for learning, leaving teachers and experts free to observe and comment when students reach an impasse.

Where Does the Individual Fit Into the Social Context?
Although there are obvious benefits of the social learning situations discussed earlier, there are also drawbacks. The major drawback is assessing the individual within these complex settings. Anderson, Reder, & Simon (1998) purport that the social learning situation must be analyzed by studying the mind of each individual in that situation and how each individual contributes to the interaction. Design experiments are currently exploring how interactivity can be assessed as well as individual knowledge building in the context of complex social settings (Barab & Squire, 2004; Brown, 1992; Cobb, Confrey, diSessa, Lehrer, & Schauble, 2003; Cobb, Stephan, McClain, & Gravemeijer, 2001; Greeno, 1998).

The relationship between individual differences and learning is a complex one (Ackerman, Kyllonen, & Roberts, 1999; Corno et al., 2002). Corno and colleagues provide an outstanding summary of the research by Richard Snow and the Stanford Aptitude Seminar. Theories pertaining to individual differences are discussed in terms of ability, personality, and the situations in which individuals interact. In particular, people come to a situation with a repertoire of propensities, or aptitudes, and the situation makes some actions more likely or useful than others (Kyllonen & Lajoie, 2003). Individual difference research is diverse and includes studies regarding intellectual ability, aptitude, prior knowledge, interest, learner control preferences, strategic knowledge, motivation, and styles of working and learning.

Theories of individual differences can easily be incorporated into TREs since technology can be adapted to the way students learn and process information. Two people may have similar knowledge profiles but process information in different ways and have different learning preferences (Cronbach & Snow, 1977; Snow, 1989). The attraction of TREs is that they have the potential to capitalize on the notion of individual differences, having something that can attract everyone, such as visual-verbal, auditory modalities and preferences. Identifying the different strategies that successful people use within specific contexts can serve as a first step in improving instruction. For example, Mandinach and Corno (1985) examined individual differences in the types of cognitive strategies learners used to solve a computer game, Hunt the Wumpus. They found both gender and ability differences in the types of strategies learners used to solve the

problem. Students who displayed skill in self-regulated learning (SRL) performed best on the game. Successful students actively gathered information, integrated new information with prior knowledge, identified relationships among elements of the game, discriminated relevant from irrelevant stimuli, monitored their performance, and persisted even when they lost. When students received guided instruction as they played the game, performance varied by ability and gender. Lower ability students benefited from guided modeling more than higher ability students, and females benefited more than males. TREs can be designed to test assumptions regarding individual differences.

The Realignment of Motivation and Cognition

In addition to a learning context, learners, either acting alone or in a social setting, must act in that context, or, as Dewey said, they must "do" something. Perhaps even more importantly they must have the "will" to do something, to act and to learn through the application of one's actions (James, 1899). James suggests that volition on the learner's part involves substituting new responses for old ones and building systems of associations in the learner's mind. When learners act or construct new knowledge, they will more likely apply this knowledge when necessary. When teachers transmit knowledge without opportunities for students to interact with materials, it is likely that students will not know how to apply this knowledge in the future. Obvious connections between the will to act and the motivation to learn can be made, especially in terms of where the locus of control of the learning situation resides (Bandura, 1977). Intention and personal motivation of behavior has been referred to as *conation*, which plays a special role in human learning (Miller, 1991).

From the time of Plato to the present, cognitive, conative, and affective factors have been considered major determinants of learning and performance (Ackerman & Kyllonen, 1991; Shute, Lajoie, & Gluck, 2000; Snow, 1992; Thurstone, 1947). In Snow's words, "Each person's mental bank contains not only bits and pieces of knowledge and skill, but also wishes, wants, needs, intentions, interests, attitudes, etc." (1992, pp. 28–29).

Learning theories are increasingly more inclusive in that cognition, motivation, and the social context in which learning takes place are considered as interconnected (Cordova & Lepper, 1996; Lepper, 1988; Weiner, 1986). Educational research based on different theoretical positions has investigated several different types of motivation including *extrinsic*, *intrinsic*, and *engaged participation* (Greeno, Collins, & Resnick, 1997). Earlier behavioral research focused on external or extrinsic motivations as determinants of action (Lepper, Greene, & Nisbett, 1973). Cognitive research has emphasized internal or intrinsic motivation as the learner interacts with information and its organization. More recently, the situated learning perspective focuses on the engagement or motivation that maintains social relationships and the individual's place within a social organization. All of these forms of motivation may be important for learning. In addition to considering the role of cognitive abilities in learning, emotion should be considered as well, since it can contribute to learning. The role of negative emotions has been documented in the learned helplessness literature that describes how students who experience failure repeatedly come to expect failure and thus do not try to succeed (Dweck & Bempechat, 1983). Researchers are also exploring the role of positive emotions in learning (Fredericksen, 2001) to see how they influence our flexibility in adapting to new challenges and in deepening our capacities to relate to one another (Mahoney, in press).

All learning environments, including those with technology, should consider the role of motivation and affect along with cognitive abilities. Some TREs have explored this relationship directly (Cordova & Lepper, 1996) by introducing variables that can be adapted to individuals' interest in the context of a learning environment with different levels of cognitive complexity. The results indicate that learning is enhanced when TREs capitalize on student interests and when there is an optimal level of challenge for that learner. Research on the role of motivation variables which may affect students' learning with TREs would be significantly enhanced by integrating findings from contemporary research from educational research and psychology (for a recent review, see Wolters, 2003).

We have briefly addressed some of the theoretical issues that pertain to the design of learning environments. In the next section we consider specific examples of how TRE support teaching and learning.

WHAT CAN TECHNOLOGY-RICH ENVIRONMENTS SUPPORT BEYOND REGULAR TEACHING ENVIRONMENTS?

In the previous section we described the theories and frameworks that are important to teaching and learning. In this section we discuss the value added of using such frameworks with TREs. Most clearly, a TRE provides a platform for improving and studying learning. By *platform* we refer to a place to learn, to teach, and to dynamically collect data about the learning process, and often assess learning all through one medium. Such platforms can provide a standardized curriculum, or they can provide opportunities for students to explore material that they may not have opportunities to explore in the regular classroom. As stated earlier, there are many forms of TREs, and they have different theories that guide their design (Jacobson & Kozma, 2000; Jonassen & Land, 2000; Lajoie, 2000; Lajoie & Derry, 1993). TREs vary in the nature of the tasks they support, the kinds of competencies that they enhance, and the type of support that is available to learners. The types of environments discussed here all provide a meaningful context for learning new things and support the notion that the learner has some agency in interacting with the environment. They are also based on models of competency and are implicitly designed to be motivating through the tasks themselves or through social engagement in learning.

Tasks can be defined in a number of ways, and problem-solving tasks are often considered either well or ill structured. A *well-structured task* is one that has a recognized solution and a limited set of actions needed to arrive at solution. *Ill-structured tasks* do not have a clearly recognizable endpoint, and there may be more than one way to solve the problem (Lesgold, 1988; Newell & Simon, 1972). For example, an addition problem is well structured, and completing a manuscript is an ill-structured task. Designing TREs for well-structured problems is more straightforward because the goals and actions that need to be modeled or supported within the environment are limited. Ill-structured problems are more complex and need different types of environments to support flexibility in solution strategies.

TREs are designed to support different types of knowledge and competencies. The Internet search engines clearly support the search for declarative or factual knowledge, be it to find the latest "low-carb" recipe or the latest references on metacognition. It is more difficult to design environments that support procedural knowledge (Anderson, 1983) that helps individuals to "do" something, such as mechanical tasks, avionics troubleshooting (Lesgold, Lajoie, Bunzo, & Eggan, 1992) or medical hypothesis testing (Lajoie, Azevedo, & Fleiszer, 1998). When designing TREs, decisions are made about which competencies to support, be they domain dependent or independent competencies, that is, mental models, strategic knowledge, memory, schema formation, self-regulation, self-efficacy, hypothesis formation, and so on. Decisions are also made about the type of support to provide; when, where, and how much support; who or what does the supporting; and who has control over such support. Earlier we discussed the value of modeling different levels of competence to help scaffold individuals in the context of their learning. Theory-based TREs can make informed decisions about scaffolding based on learner data.

Teachers are limited in terms of their ability to monitor more than one student or group at that same time. However, the type of diagnostic feedback students need within a problemsolving context is best supported in a 1:1 tutoring situation (Bloom, 1984), regardless of whether it is human or computer supported. Diagnostic feedback is made possible via appropriate student models of performance that are dynamically monitored and updated with new evidence from assessment tasks, embedded or standalone. Bloom (1984) identified problems associated with conventional teaching methods (e.g., a teacher presenting material in front of 30 people). He asserted that this format provides one of the *least* effective techniques for teaching and learning and found that as teaching becomes more focused and individualized, learning is enhanced. TREs can support learners in several ways, as reviewed next.

Examples of TREs

Theory-driven TREs are created with the goals of (a) engaging learners in various types of cognitive processing and thereby (b) encouraging certain desirable learning outcomes. We review a few types of TREs developed by researchers, most specifically intelligent tutoring systems (ITSs) and environments designed with specific cognitive tools to support learning.

Intelligent Tutoring Systems (ITS). ITS are perhaps the most sophisticated of TREs. ITS evolved from computer-assisted instruction (CAI), which evolved from intelligent teaching machines (see Pressey, 1926; Shute & Psotka, 1996). As summarized by Shute et al. (2000), the requirements for ITS have not changed in more than two decades since Hartley & Sleeman (1973) argued that an ITS must possess (a) knowledge of the domain (expert model), (b) knowledge of the learner (student model), and (c) knowledge of teaching or training strategies (tutor) (see Lajoie & Derry, 1993; Polson & Richardson, 1988; Psotka, Massey, & Mutter, 1988; Regian & Shute, 1992; Shute & Psotka, 1996; Sleeman & Brown, 1982). Fulfilling these requirements provides ITS with the capacity for student diagnosis and the ability to change the curriculum in response to that diagnosis.

The success of these systems is largely due to the fine-grained cognitive task analyses (CTA) that underlie their design. ACT-R tutors are among the most successful ITS, having been designed and evaluated in the domains of geometry, algebra, and Lisp programming (Aleven & Koedinger, 2002; Anderson, Corbett, Koedinger, & Pelletier, 1995; Koedinger, 2001; Koedinger, Anderson, Hadley, & Mark, 1997). They attribute the success of their

cognitive tutors to the effectiveness of the task analyses that led to clear educational goals (Anderson & Schunn, 2000). ACT-R is the underlying theory of learning and cognition that drives their design principles (Anderson & Labriere, 1998). ACT-R is based on a theory of learning and cognition that has as its premise that human cognition reflects the complex composition of basic elements and principles that can be decomposed and taught to individuals through computer tutors. The outcome of a CTA includes decomposing elements of the domain so that instruction can be designed around these elements and that learners can be assessed when they interact with the instructional material. Student models are used to monitor performance and update proficiencies accordingly.

The ACT-R tutors are designed for well-structured problem-solving tasks. Sherlock is a tutoring system for real-world training problems: Specifically, it is an F-15 avionics troubleshooting tutor (Lesgold, et al., 1992). Avionics troubleshooting problems are ill structured in that there are many paths to successful solutions. Consequently, a different grain size of proficiencies must be considered in terms of knowledge decomposition. For example, specific production rules can be created for specific skills, that is, specific test measurements for tracing circuits. However, the tutor has to consider the flexibility in solution paths and provide feedback in the context of such actions. CTA is useful in establishing patterns of expert-novice difference in solution paths. The theories underlying Sherlock are based on assumptions of emerging expertise and cognitive apprenticeship (Lajoie & Lesgold, 1989). The *cognitive apprenticeship* model (Brown et al., 1989; Collins et al., 1989; Gott, 1989; Lave & Wenger, 1991) provides a template for connecting abstract and real-world knowledge by creating new forms of pedagogy based on a model of learners, the task, and the situation in which learning occurs. Participants receiving 20 hours of instruction on Sherlock were compared to a control group receiving on-the-job training over the same period of time. The average gain score, from pre to posttest, for the group using Sherlock was equivalent to almost 4 years of experience (Nichols, Pokorny, Jones, Gott, & Alley, in preparation).

Another ill-structured domain is medicine. SICUN is a computer tutor for nurses in the surgical intensive care unit (Lajoie et al., 1998). The CTA analysis led to the design of the system that encourages self-monitoring of decision-making processes. Nurses who worked with SICUN were required to post their goals before conducting patient assessments and then specify outcomes of their assessments. For example, if their goal was to check the patient's circulatory system for adequate blood supply to the heart, they might check pulse rate as well as skin condition (for swelling, edema, coloration, capillary re-fill, and temperature). Prior to moving on to a new goal or body system, the tutor would prompt them about the results of their assessment. Hence plans, goals, actions, and outcomes were all built into the system, with decision trees designed to encourage self-monitoring and comparison to expert problem solvers at various phases of problem solving. An informal evaluation of this tutor was conducted, and nurses who used SICUN and were posttested on a pencil-and-paper version of a patient case demonstrated clearer plans, goals, and actions when conducting patient assessments.

The preceding discussion provided examples of ITS where decisions were made regarding what to model for learners. Identifying robust performance models in complex domains can lead to effective instruction for those less proficient in problem solving performance. Hence knowing what to model can lead to better performance. In the next section we describe the cognitive tools approach.

Cognitive Tools. Technology is a tool, a means to an end. However, cognitive tools have come to be described as technological tools that can assist learners to accomplish cognitive tasks (Jonassen, 1996; Jonassen & Reeves, 1996; Kommers, Jonassen & Mayes, 1992; Lajoie & Derry, 1993; Lajoie, 2000; Pea, 1985; Perkins, 1985; Salomon, Perkins, & Globerson, 1991). Cognitive tools aid cognition through interactive technologies that help students during thinking, problem solving, or learning by providing them with opportunities to practice applying their knowledge in the context of complex meaningful activities.

There are many types of cognitive tools, each of which is designed for a purpose, to facilitate learning through supporting specific cognitive processes, that is, memory, lower order processes, higher order thinking, hypothesis testing (de Jong & von Joolingen, 1998; Mandinach & Cline, 2000), self-regulation, metacognition, argumentation, and reasoning. The cognitive tools and data described in BioWorld (Lajoie, Lavigne, Guerrera, & Munsie, 2001; Lajoie, in press b) provide concrete examples of how situating learning in meaningful contexts provides new opportunities for understanding the dynamic nature of learning processes.

BioWorld is a computer-based learning environment that supports students' scientific reasoning in the context of problem-based learning situations (see Fig. 35.1). It complements the biology curriculum by providing a hospital simulation where students can apply what they have learned about body systems to problems where they reason about diseases. BioWorld serves to instruct, model proficiency, and assess knowledge.

Each problem starts with a patient case history where students formulate a hypothesis about the disease. Once students select a hypothesis, they indicate how confident they are about it using the Belief Meter (percent certainty). Students collect evidence from the patient case that supports their hypothesis, and this evidence remains visible on the Evidence Palette. There is an online library where students access declarative knowledge about the disease they are researching. Information in the library includes the symptoms, diagnostic tests, and transmission routes of specific diseases, as well as a glossary of medical terminology. In order to solve problems, students must conduct diagnostic tests to confirm or disconfirm their hypotheses. They do so by ordering tests on the patient chart, where the outcomes of their tests are recorded. This chart is a procedural knowledge tool because it provides a way for actions to be conducted in the context of problem solving. A consultation tool is present and labeled as a cognitive apprenticeship tool, since learners can use it to obtain simulated feedback during the data collection process.

In line with the previous discussion, BioWorld falls under the cognitive tools approach in several ways. First, it assists students in complex problem-solving activities pertaining to scientific reasoning by engaging them in hypothesis formation and testing rather than teaching them isolated science skills such as biology vocabulary or categorizing anatomical parts. They are provided with opportunities to enter and change their hypotheses in the context of solving the realistic patient cases that they would not have opportunities to do without these tools.

Furthermore, the Belief Meter provides a trace of how student beliefs about their hypotheses change or do not change throughout the problem solving activity. These data are analyzed retrospectively to examine the relationships among hypothesis development, knowledge acquisition, and confidence in one's hypothesis. To date we have found a positive relationship between knowledge acquisition and confidence in one's beliefs. Students engage in sophisticated higher order reasoning skills while the computer environment performs lower order skills. In this example, students conduct diagnostic tests that help confirm or disconfirm their hypotheses. At the same time, BioWorld interprets these tests for students as falling into a normal or abnormal range, saving students processing time in interpreting such data.

There are several tools that scaffold the learner in the context of problem solving. One obvious tool is the online library that provides students with a mechanism to acquire new declarative or factual knowledge about diseases. Another cognitive tool is the Evidence Palette, where students post the evidence they see as relevant to the case. This tool serves two purposes: first as an external

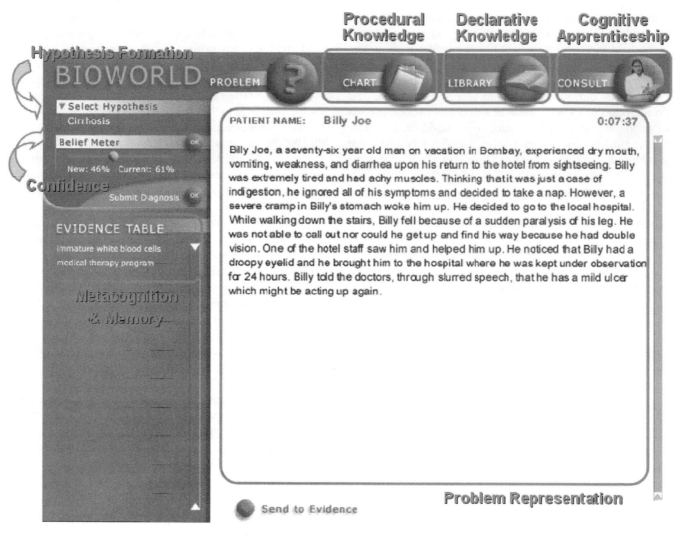

FIGURE 35.1. Annotated BioWorld case history screen.

memory device that reminds them of what they have collected; and second as a metacognitive tool, in that it helps students self-assess and monitor information that they saw as relevant to a particular problem-solving scenario. From a research perspective the evidence palette also presents an indicator of how much effort learners put into the problem-solving activity. Finally, the Consult button provides general assistance to learners when and where help is requested.

Tools that are not demonstrated in Fig. 35.1 are the Evidence Categorization and Argumentation tools. After students enter a final diagnosis, their own evidence is presented to them in a list. They are asked first to categorize the evidence by type and then to formulate a final argument that consists of a rank order of that evidence which was most relevant to their final solution. Students are then provided with a visual comparison of their fi-

nal argument with an expert argument. Finally, students select an audio button to hear an expert's oral summation of how to solve the patient case. These tools provide opportunities for students to identify relevant from irrelevant information, which is a necessary component of expertise. Furthermore, these tools help students self-assess and compare their performance with those more proficient than themselves.

Students using BioWorld become more systematic in their approach to scientific reasoning about the disease process and more expertlike in their search for evidence confirming their hypotheses (Lajoie et al., 2001). The cognitive tools approach is not really one approach but a combination of various theory-based approaches to the design of computer-based instruction (Lajoie, in press b). Every cognitive tool has an underlying purpose, and hence its design may be based on different theories. Thus, the cognitive tools themes are not restricted to one paradigm but rather are selective in choosing the model that fits the purpose of instruction or training. Hence, one must understand the context behind the tools and their design. For instance, BioWorld was designed to answer questions about specific learning processes in the context of scientific reasoning and hypothesis generation. A major strength is that through computer knowledge tracing of student actions, one can identify situations that provide the most/least opportunities for learning. For example, where do students spend the most time, or what do they do when they are in a particular situation? More specifically, when visiting the library are they examining references pertinent to their hypotheses, or are they reading material that is of general interest? Designing tools that promote the acquisition of self-monitoring skills were described earlier. These tools have the ultimate goal of promoting lifelong learning skills, or learning to learn new things. Another advantage of the tools designed for this system is that they provide a mechanism for looking at how knowledge evolves in parallel with confidence about that knowledge through the Belief Meter and Hypothesis Generation menus.

There are still unanswered questions that can be explored with BioWorld. One is a thorough plan for assessing the transfer of knowledge from one situation to another. In other words, how generalizable is this approach? Any cognitive tools approach needs to address how to assess complex reasoning patterns using technology. Although actions can be traced, there is still a need to get at the underlying reasons behind specific actions. New tools might be designed for this purpose. Although the current approach speaks to the sociology of learning or learning within a group or community, there is still a need for better articulation of assessment models for the individual learner as well as the group of learners sharing the tools. Hence, a future direction is to broaden these theories in a manner that can help refine individual and group assessments.

Metacognitive Tools. Technology-rich environments come in many forms, and hence there are questions raised about how they will foster learning (Azevedo, 2002; Mayer, 2003). According to Mayer (2003), the scientific investigation of how people learn in environments must include three basic elements—evidence, theory, and applications. The recent use of these new technologies, most of which are open-ended electronic environments such as web-based learning environments, hypermedia, and hypertext, renews our concern about the lack of theoretical and empirical evidence necessary to advance our field of educational psychology and related fields. Given the strong interest in these new technologies for teaching and learning, there is a need for extending our current theoretical frameworks, establishing a solid research base of replicated findings based on rigorous and appropriate research methods (Mayer, 2003; Shute & Towle, 2003). One extension that we see viable in this regard is to include a model of metacognition and self-regulated learning (Azevedo, in press; Graesser, McNamara, & Vanlehn, in press; White & Frederiksen, in press).

As TREs move into more open learning environments, such as self-directed online courses, students are required to regulate their learning more effectively, by sequencing their instruction, deciding on how much time to spend learning, and which of the multiple representations to attend to for their goals (Azevedo, Guthrie, & Seibert, 2004). Recent research shows that when students lack self-regulatory skills, their ability to learn from open-ended learning environments is undermined (Azevedo, Cromley, & Seibert, 2004). Hence we envision the next generation of cognitive tools to include metacognitive tools that will help learners to regulate their learning in complex situations (Katz & Lesgold, 1994; White, Shimoda, & Frederiksen, 2000).

Active learners who efficiently manage their own learning in many different ways are termed *self-regulated learners* (Boekaerts, Pintrich, & Zeidner, 2000; Butler & Winne, 1995; Paris & Paris, 2001; Schunk & Zimmerman, 1994; Winne, 2001; Winne & Perry, 2000; Zimmerman, 2001; Zimmerman & Schunk, 2001). Students are self-regulated to the degree that they are cognitively, motivationally, and behaviorally active participants in their own learning processes (Zimmerman, 1986). In other words they generate the thoughts, feelings, and actions necessary to attain their goals by actively planning, monitoring, regulating, and controlling their cognition, motivation, behavior, and context (Pintrich, 2000; Zimmerman, 2001). Models of self-regulation describe a recursive cycle of cognitive activities central to learning and knowledge construction (Pintrich, 2000; Schunk, 2001; Winne, 2001; Winne & Hadwin, 1998; Zimmerman, 2000, 2001).

SRL is a significant framework in educational and psychological research, especially in the academic achievement literature (for recent reviews refer to Boekaerts et al., 2000; Zimmerman & Schunk, 2001). SRL can also be a valuable theoretical framework with which to reframe the emerging evidence on the use of open-ended TREs. First, we provide some basic assumptions of SRL, describe a particular framework proposed by Pintrich (2000), and describe some ongoing research with TREs that shows promise in this area.

In general, models of SRL share certain basic assumptions about learning and regulation, despite the fact that each model proposes different constructs and mechanisms (see Boekaerts et al., 2000; Schunk and Zimmerman, 2001). Pintrich (2000) summarized four assumptions shared by many SRL models. One assumption, derived from the cognitive perspective of learning, is that learners are active, constructive participants in the learning process. Learners construct their own meanings, goals, and strategies from the information available from both the internal (i.e., cognitive system) and the external (i.e., context) environment. A second assumption is based on the idea that effective learners are capable of monitoring, controlling, and regulating aspects of their own cognition, motivation, behavior, and context (e.g., the learning environment). Third, biological, developmental, contextual, and individual constraints can impede or interfere with a learner's ability to monitor or control his or her cognition, motivation, behavior, or context. Fourth, many models assume that there is a goal, criterion, or standard against which the learner makes comparisons in order to assess whether the process should continue or if some type of change (e.g., in strategies) is necessary.

Pintrich (2000) presents a conceptual framework for classifying the different phases and areas of regulation based on an extensive synthesis of the literature on academic achievement. We propose to use Pintrich's model as a guiding framework for examining the complex nature of learning with open-ended learning environments (Azevedo, in press). The four phases (which make up the rows of his table) are processes that many models of regulation and self-regulation share (e.g., Zimmerman, 2000), and they portray planning, goal setting, monitoring, control, and reflection as important regulatory processes. However, it should be noted that not all academic learning follows these phases. These phases are suggested as a heuristic to organize research on SRL. Phase 1 involves planning and goal setting as well as activation of perceptions and knowledge of the task and context, and the self in relationship to the task. Phase 2 is related to various monitoring processes that represent metacognitive awareness of different aspects of the self, or task and context. Phase 3 involves efforts to control and regulate different aspects of the self, or task and context. Finally, Phase 4 represents various kinds of reactions and reflections on the self, and the task or context.

The four phases do represent a time-ordered sequence that individuals would go through as they learn or perform a task, but it should be noted that there is no strong assumption that the phases are hierarchically or linearly structured such that earlier phases always must occur before later phases. In most models of SRL, monitoring, control, and reaction can be ongoing and iterative as the learner progresses through the learning episode or task, with the goals and plans being modified or updated based on different possible sources of feedback from the monitoring, control, and reaction processes. The four columns in Pintrich's (2000) framework represent different areas for regulation that an individual learner can attempt to monitor, control, and regulate. The first three columns of cognition, motivation/affect, and behavior reflect the traditional division of different areas of psychological functioning (Bandura, 1986). These first three areas in the columns in the framework represent aspects of the individual's own cognition, motivation/affect, and behavior that he or she can attempt to control and regulate.

These attempts are termed "self-regulated" since the individual is focused on trying to control or regulate his or her own cognition, motivation, and behavior. In addition, there are usually other individuals in the learning context such as teachers, peers, parents, and/or TREs that can influence one's self-regulated learning by attempting to externally regulate an individual's cognition, motivation, or behavior, by guiding or scaffolding the individual in terms of what, how, and when to do a task. As such, other task and contextual features (e.g., task conditions, feedback systems, evaluation structures, and pedagogical resources, social agents) can facilitate or constrain an individual's attempts to regulate his or her own learning.

A closer inspection of the columns in Pintrich's (2000) framework reveals specific aspects of self-regulated learning that could inform the study learning with TREs. For example, the cognitive column involves the different cognitive strategies learners may use to learn and perform a task as well as the metacognitive strategies individuals may use to control and regulate their cognition. This would include both content knowledge (about a specific topic) and strategic knowledge (under what circumstances should that specific knowledge be used). The motivation and affect column concerns the various motivational beliefs that individuals may have about the task. For example, one's self-efficacy beliefs about one's ability to successfully accomplish the task as well as positive and negative affective reactions to the self or task would be included in this column. Finally, any strategies that individuals may use to control and regulate their motivation and affect would be included in this column. The behavior column includes an individual's effort, persistence, help-seeking, and choice behaviors. Context is included as the fourth column in the framework, and it represents the various aspects of the task environment, general classroom, or cultural context where the learning is taking place. This column deals with the external environment; thus, attempts to control or regulate it would not be considered self-regulating in some models (McCaslin & Hickey, 2001) because the context is not assumed to be part of the individual. In these models, self-regulation usually refers only to aspects of the self that are being controlled or regulated.

We demonstrated previously the effectiveness of a paradigmatic approach to theory-driven TREs, that is, the ACT-R approach to ITS taken by Anderson, Koedinger, Corbett and colleagues (Aleven & Koedinger, 2002; Anderson et al., 1995; Anderson & Labriere, 1998; Koedinger, 2001; Koedinger et al., 1997). We argue that SRL can serve as a guiding theoretical framework for developing and assessing the use of computers as metacognitive tools in openended learning environments (Azevedo, 2002, 2005). Examples are described next.

Several researchers have indicated a need for learner-controlled open-ended environments to have support for self-regulatory skills that is, to support planning, monitoring, controlling, and reflecting on their own learning (Azevedo & Cromley, 2004; Hill & Hannafin, 1997; Linn, 1992; Park, 1993). Despite the importance of self-regulatory learning with hypermedia and other openended TREs, there has been relatively little empirical research on the study of the role of SRL and the integration of various metacognitive tools designed to foster learners' self-regulated learning with such complex environments.

Recent studies on SRL in learning with hypertext/hypermedia and other open-ended learning environments have either attempted to identify what learning strategies learners use during learning from these environments (e.g., Hill & Hannafin, 1997) or identify the effectiveness of embedded strategies in these environments (e.g., Chou & Lin, 1997). The latter set of studies has attempted to identify the effectiveness of embedded learning strategies to facilitate SRL with navigation maps, note-taking, search tools, and generative cognitive strategies. Other educational researchers (e.g., Jackson, Krajcik, & Soloway, 2000; Vye et al. 1998; White et al., 2000) have designed TREs to assist certain aspects of students' metacognition. They have provided evidence regarding the effectiveness of certain features (e.g., a planning net, metacognitive awareness of the phases of the inquiry cycle). In sum, these studies have examined individual phases of SRL rather than the entire dynamic nature of SRL during learning with complex, open-ended environments. Interactions between areas and phases of SRL (based on Pintrich, 2000) need to be examined as well in the contexts in which open-ended TREs are used to enhance student learning (Azevedo, in press).

Little research has been conducted to understand the interrelatedness and dynamics of SRL variables: cognitive, motivational/affective, behavioral, and contextual during the cyclical and iterative phases of planning, monitoring, control, and reflection during learning from hypermedia environments. Recently, Winne and colleagues (Hadwin & Winne, 2001; Winne, Hadwin, McNamara, & Chu, 1998; Winne & Stockley, 1998) have designed TREs that consti-

tute authentic environments for studying as they gather trace data about SRL events during studying.

Azevedo and his colleagues have begun to examine the complex interactions between SRL and other, external regulatory agents (e.g., peers and teachers) in facilitating students' learning of complex science topics with hypermedia learning environments (e.g., the circulatory system and ecological systems) both in the lab and in learner-centered classrooms. College students learned about the circulatory system, and significant pre- and posttest learning gains were found for those students who were able to regulate their learning. These gains were indicated in the greater use of effective strategies; planning their time and effort, creating subgoals; activating prior knowledge; and monitoring their emerging understanding (Azevedo, Guthrie, & Seibert, 2004). Given that the ability to learn with hypermedia environments is enhanced when appropriate SRL mechanisms are engaged, a second study was conducted to determine whether scaffolding SRL could facilitate conceptual understanding of those who did not show learning gains earlier. Three conditions were created. The first was an *adaptive scaffolding condition*, where a human tutor provided adaptive scaffolding by deploying certain self-regulatory "moves" (e.g., activating the students' prior knowledge, assisting the student in relating prior knowledge with new knowledge, having the student construct their own representations of the topic, etc.) based on her monitoring and understanding of the learners' emerging mental model of the circulatory system.

In the second or *fixed scaffolding condition*, the students were given a list of 10 domain-specific questions designed to foster mental model development. Finally, there was a *no scaffolding condition*.

Students who were in an adaptive scaffolding condition developed more sophisticated mental models than those in a fixed or no scaffolding condition (Azevedo, Cromley, & Seibert, 2004). In a subsequent study, Azevedo and Cromley (2004) conducted an SRL training to determine whether college student could be trained to regulate their learning of the circulatory system with hypermedia. The SRL training group outperformed a control group as indicated by the quality of their mental models and conceptual understanding. This research has been extended into high school science classrooms examining SRL mechanisms and scaffolding using hypermedia to learn about water quality (Azevedo, Winters, & Moos, 2004).

Azevedo's research has begun to test and extend existing models of SRL to include research on the complex interplay between SRL processes and their role in learning complex science topics within hypermedia contexts (with and without scaffolding). This research has demonstrated the effectiveness of different types of instructional scaffolding and strategy training on students' ability to regulate their learning about complex science topics. While the use of scaffolds in TREs is not a novel concept, Azevedo's research is one of the first to provide empirical evidence regarding the effectiveness of various types of scaffolds to support students' SRL of complex topics with hypermedia environments. This research forges new directions in the design of metacognitive tools for learning (Azevedo, in press).

METHODOLOGICAL ISSUES FOR TECHNOLOGY AND ASSESSMENT

As TREs are designed to test specific theories to support teaching and learning, appropriate evaluations of these systems must follow and new forms of assessment need to be created. Design-based research methods (Bannan-Ritland, Gorard, Middleton, & Taylor, in preparation; Barab & Squire, 2004; Brown, 1992; Cobb et al., 2003; Design-Based Research Collective, 2003) provide promise in this regard since their premise is to provide robust accounts of how learning evolves in innovative contexts, documenting the interconnections between theory, design, and assessment of learning in these contexts. These new approaches suggest mechanisms for moving our theories beyond specific "designed" contexts to real-world practices by testing innovations in multiple contexts that could lead to generalizable results.

Educational researchers have been stressing the need for complex, performance-based assessments for some time (Linn, Baker, & Dunbar, 1991). Performance-based assessment contrasts strongly with more traditional types of assessment in that they are based on processes rather than products. As we begin to consider learning as a process rather than a product dynamic forms of assessment in the context of learning must co-occur (Bransford & Schwartz, 1999; Lajoie, 2003; Lajoie & Lesgold, 1992; Mislevy et al., 1999, in press; Pellegrino, Choudowsky & Glaser, 2001). It has been suggested that the true potential in a problem-solving situation is best assessed by supporting learners with hints or feedback to see what they may be capable of in the future without such support (Vygotsky, 1978).

Dynamic assessment implies that human or computer tutors can evaluate transitions in knowledge representations and performance while learners are in the process of solving problems, rather than after they have completed a problem. Consequently, the prior discussion of scaffolding is pertinent since the purpose of assessment in these situations is to improve learning. Multiple forms of evidence are needed to make decisions about what individuals know. Technology provides a platform for collecting and analyzing such evidence. One promising approach is evidence-centered assessment design (ECD), which consists of assessments linked with probability models that can be updated as evidence about the learner is collected (Mislevy, et al., in press). The ECD approach is another example of how theoretical approaches to understanding competency and proficiency can be linked to new forms of assessment with TREs.

New forms of assessment using technology show promise in providing a window on how students learn, to what they attend, and how they can self-assess in open-ended contexts. Technology can support assessment dynamically in the context of learning through computational models that indicate learners' current knowledge states in the context of learning. Technology can also support self-assessments by modeling different competencies to learners through feedback, simulations and explicit models of expert strategies. Another technology-supported assessment is to teach learners to design pedagogical agents. Usually the purpose of a pedagogical agent is to guide the learning process through different media forms, such as a talking head, a virtual reality avatar, or cartoon (Clark & Mayer, 2003). Pedagogical agents are mediators, because they have their own agency and act by scaffolding the learner when assistance is needed (Greer et al., 2001; Moreno, Mayer, Sires, & Lester, 2001; Rickel & Johnson, 2000). The design of pedagogical agents can serve as an assessment tool as well. Students can teach their agents, for example by building a concept map (Schwartz, Pilner, Biswas, Leelawong, & Davis, in press). The students can then ask their agents to answer questions. In addition to helping students self-assess, these "teachable agents" can serve as automated assessment systems. For example, the system can ask the same questions of the agent and a hidden expert map to compare results. These teachable agents are self-contained assessments that reveal what a student has learned and what that student thinks another student needs to know.

CONCLUDING REMARKS

The likelihood of technology fostering change is greatly increased when teaching and learning theories guide design. Most educational researchers have traditionally adhered to a specific theoretical framework or a pedagogical stance. This theoretical attachment has led to several healthly debates among researchers (e.g., Greeno et al., 2000) regarding the operational definitions of constructs (e.g., symbols, affordances), units of analysis (e.g., individual knowledge states vs. sociohistorical accounts of learning), methodological approaches (e.g., cognitive modeling, verbal protocols, discourse analysis) and uses of technology for learning (e.g., modelers, nonmodelers, and middle-campers; Derry & Lajoie, 1993); and, learning *from* and learning *with* technology (Salomon, et al., 1991). These debates have led to revisiting some of the recurrent themes in the literature that have evolved into more sophisticated theories of learning and instruction. It is these theories that also drive TREs.

One such theme is learning in context, which has an early history in Greek philosophy, was revisited by Dewey, and is still featured in case-based, problem-based communities of learning, cognitive apprenticeships, anchored instruction, and design experiments described today. The advantage of a TRE is that you can design an environment that can use any of the guiding principles described by these listed approaches to design an appropriate context for learning. Such contexts can vary in the nature of the problems addressed, be they well- or ill-structured, in the content and level of the subject matter or domain in question.

When learning in context, there is no unequivocal answer about who should set the context—the teacher or the learner. There should be a healthy balance between teacher and learner agency. TREs do provide opportunities for teachers to release their agency, in that they can relinquish their role as the sole dispenser of knowledge pertinent to matters in the classroom (Bracewell, LeMaistre, Lajoie & Breuleux, in press; Lin, Schwartz, & Hatano, in press). When TREs serve as a source of information, the teacher can act as a facilitator rather than as a single source of information. When the teacher becomes the sage-on-the-side, the learner has more agency, constructing knowledge through interacting in a learning context. Where the teacher is the sage, the learner often takes on a more passive role, receiving knowledge from the knowledge dispenser. This same theme is visited with TREs when deciding whether the computer is the dispenser of knowledge or a tool to assist learners in the context of their learning experience. When environments are designed to support the role of agency in the learner, more facilitating models of technology-rich design must be designed that support cognition, motivation, metacognition, and self-regulated learning.

Another recurrent theme in the literature is the social context in which learning occurs. The social aspect of learning is an important one, considering that we do learn from observing and modeling others, whether those others are human others or computer-based models of performance. Developing models of what students know is a precursor to supporting the curriculum-instruction-assessment triad described by Pellegrino and colleagues (2001). First we need to know what to model and then we need to decide how to model competence to assist individuals along a learning trajectory (Lajoie, 2003). The

issue of how others can assist in scaffolding learning is an important one that was addressed early on by Piaget, Vygotsky, Bandura, and others and is now being considered in TREs by Anderson, Azevedo, Koedinger, Graesser, Lajoie, Lesgold, Chi, Van Lehn, and others. However, just as important, individuals differ in their aptitudes, interests, motivation, and self-regulatory skills, and hence complex models of the individual must exist in tandem with how they learn within a community-of-learning model.

One could argue that TREs, when designed based on theory and evidence, could maximize opportunities for individual differences since there is more than one representation to learn from, interact with, or provide evidence of learning. Multimedia learning taps into the assumption that there are individual differences in preference of modality and that sometimes multiple representations, in particular, verbal and visual representations that are used to present an instructional message, are better than single representations (Mayer, 2003). Verbal representations are defined as text, spoken or written, and visual representations as pictures, static or dynamic. Alternative representations such as tactile graphics and text-to-speech software can provide greater access for learning-disabled students beyond the traditional verbal and visual modalities (Shute, Graf & Hansen, in press).

The roles of emotion, motivation, and conation are also recurrent themes that need to be considered in teaching and learning environments. The old adage "Where there is a will, there is a way" is simple but true. How do we help learners have the will to learn? TREs are ideal for providing flexible platforms for learning, engaging students in their various interests and different levels of challenge through fantasy or bold realism. Lepper and others have demonstrated some of the advantages to learning when motivational add-ons are a realistic part of the problem-solving endeavor. The edutainment industry seems to capitalize on these ideas as well. There is a lot of potential for research and practical application of such theories for TREs.

An argument has been made for the theory-driven design of TREs for teaching, learning, and assessment. Examples have been provided that demonstrate how different theories lead to different designs of such environments (i.e., ACT-R) leading to particular ITS designs for well-structured problems, and theories of expertise and cognitive apprenticeship have supported ill-structured domains leading to alternative designs. Further examples have been provided of specific cognitive and metacognitive tools designed and evaluated for specific complex tasks. We conclude that theories of learning, teaching, and assessment will continue to evolve and push our design of technology-rich environments. The momentum of such theories driving technology-rich environments ensures a design revision model. It is easy to be led by the seductiveness of new technology tools. It is more difficult to be driven by theories that inform the design of TREs for learning, teaching, and assessment. Pragmatic issues need to be considered as well, such as clearly meeting educational objectives and providing accessible technology. Clear partnerships among instructors, researchers, designers, and learners can serve to advance the development of TREs by serving the needs of each audience and creating a community dedicated to enhancing the quality of the educational experience.

ACKNOWLEDGMENTS

The authors thank Ellen Mandinach and Valerie Shute for their constructive review of this paper and formative feedback. We also thank Gloria Berdugo and Sonia Faremo for their assistance with the manuscript. S.P.L. gratefully acknowledges the following granting agencies: the Canadian Social Sciences and Humanities Research Council; the Quebec Ministry of Industry, Commerce, Science and Technology; Valorisation Recherche Quebec; and her research team and programmers who have contributed to the work that is reported here: Andrew Chiarella, Luy Cumyn, Sonia Faremo, Genevieve Gauthier, Susan Lu, Carlos Nakamura, Thomas Patrick, and Jeffery Wiseman. RA gratefully acknowledges the contribution of his research team: Jennifer G. Cromley, Fielding I. Winters, Daniel C. Moos, Jeffrey A. Greene, and several other members of his Cognition and Technology Lab, as well as the programmers, and the faculty, middle school, and high school teachers and their students who participated in the studies described in this chapter. The second author also acknowledges several funding agencies for supporting his research, including the National Science Foundation, the U.S. Department of Education, and the Social Science and Humanities Research Council of Canada.

References

Ackerman, P. A., & Kyllonen, P. C. (1991). Trainee characteristics. In J. E. Morrison (Ed.), *Training for performance: Principles of applied human learning* (pp. 193–230). New York: Wiley.

Ackerman, P. L., Kyllonen, P. C., & Roberts, R. D. (1999). *Learning and individual differences* (pp. 31–54). Washington, DC: American Psychological Association.

Aleven, V., & Koedinger, K. (2002). An effective metacognitive strategy: Learning by doing and explaining with a computer-based cognitive tutor. *Cognitive Science, 26*(2), 147–181.

Alexander, P. A. (2003). The development of expertise: The journey from acclimation to proficiency. *Educational Researcher, 32*(8), 10–14.

Anderson, J. R. (1983). *The architecture of cognition.* Cambridge, MA: Harvard University Press.

Anderson, J. R., Corbett, A. T., Koedinger, K. R., & Pelletier, R. (1995). Cognitive tutors: Lessons learned. *Journal of the Learning Sciences, 4*(2), 167–207.

Anderson, J., Greeno, J. G. Reder, L., & Simon, H. A. (2000). Perspectives on learning, thinking and activity. *Educational Researcher, 29*(4), 11–13.

Anderson, J., & Labriere, C. (1998). *The atomic components of thought.* Mahwah, NJ: Lawrence Erlbaum Associates.

Anderson, J., Reder, L., & Simon, H. (1998). Radical constructivism and cognitive psychology. In D. Ravitch (Ed.), *Brookings papers on education policy* (pp. 227–278). Washington, DC: Brookings Institution Press.

Anderson, J. R., & Schunn, C. D. (2000). Implications of the ACT-R learning theory: No magic bullets. In R. Glaser (Ed.), *Advances in instructional psychology: Vol. 5: Educational design and cognitive science* (pp. 1–33). Mahwah, NJ: Lawrence Erlbaum Associates.

Azevedo, R. (2002). Beyond intelligent tutoring systems: Computers as metacognitive tools to enhance learning? *Instructional Science, 30*(1), 31–45.

Azevedo, R. (2005). *Scaffolding learning with hypermedia? The role of self- and co-regulated processes during complex learning.* Paper presented at the annual meeting of the American Educational Research Association, Montréal, Canada.

Azevedo, R. (in press). The role of self-regulated learning in using technology-based learning environments as metacognitive tools. *Educational Psychologist.*

Azevedo, R., & Cromley, J. G. (2004). Does training on self-regulated learning facilitate students' learning with hypermedia? *Journal of Educational Psychology, 96*, 523–535.

Azevedo, R., Cromley, J. G., & Seibert, D. (2004). Does adaptive scaffolding facilitate students' ability to regulate their learning with hypermedia. *Contemporary Educational Psychology, 29*, 344–370.

Azevedo, R., Guthrie, J. T., & Seibert, D. (2004). The role of self-regulated learning in fostering students' conceptual understanding of complex systems with hypermedia. *Journal of Educational Computing Research, 30*(1), 87–111.

Azevedo, R., Winters, F. I., & Moos, D. C. (2004). Can students collaboratively use hypermedia to learn about science? The dynamics of self- and other-regulatory processes in an ecology classroom. *Journal of Educational Computing Research, 31*(3), 215–245.

Bandura, A. (1977). *Social learning theory.* New York: General Learning Press.

Bandura, A. (1986). *Social foundation of thought and action: A social cognitive theory*. Englewood Cliffs, NJ: Prentice-Hall.

Bannan-Ritland, B. Gorard, S., Middleton, J. A. & Taylor, C. (in preperation). The complete design experiment: From soup to nuts. To appear in E. Kelly & R. Lesh (Eds.), *Design research: Investigating and assessing complex systems in mathematics, science, and technology education*. Mahwah, NJ: Lawrence Erlbaum Associates.

Barab, S. A. & Duffy, T.M. (2000). From practice fields to communities of practice. In D. H. Jonassen & S. M. Land (Eds.), *Theoretical foundations of learning environments* (pp. 25–55). Mahwah, NJ: Lawrence Erlbaum Associates.

Barab, S. A. & Squire, K. D. (2004). Design-based research: Putting our stake in the ground. *Journal of the Learning Sciences, 13*(1), 1–14.

Barron, B. J., Schwartz, D. L., Vye, N. J., Moore, A., Petrosino, A., Zech, L., et al. (1998). Doing with understanding: Lessons from research on problem- and project-based learning. *Journal of Learning Sciences, 7*(3&4), 271–311.

Barrows, H. S. (1996) Problem-based learning in medicine and beyond: A brief overview. *New Directions for Teaching and Learning, 68*, 3–12.

Bloom, B. S. (1984). The 2-sigma problem: The search for methods of group instruction as effective as one-to-one tutoring. *Educational Researcher, 13*(6), 4–16.

Blumenfeld, P. C., Soloway, E., Marx, R. W., Krajcik, J. S., Guzdial, M., & Palincsar, A. (1991). Motivating project-based learning: Sustaining the doing, supporting the learning. *Educational Psychologist, 26*(3&4), 369–398.

Boekaerts, M., Pintrich, P., & Zeidner, M. (2000) (Eds.), *Handbook of self-regulation*. San Diego, CA: Academic Press.

Bracewell, R. J., Le Maistre, C., Lajoie, S. P. & Breuleux, A. (in press). The role of the teacher in opening worlds of inquiry driven learning with information technologies. In B. M. Shore, M. W. Aulls, M. A. B. Delcourt, & F. G. Rejskind (Eds.), *Inquiry: Where ideas come from and where they lead*. Mahwah, NJ: Lawrence Erlbaum Associates.

Bransford, J. D. & Schwartz, D. L. (1999). Rethinking transfer: A simple proposal with multiple implications. *Review of Research in Education, 24*, 61–100.

Bransford, J. D., Sherwood, R. D., Hasselbring, T. S., Kinzer, C. K., & Williams, S. M. (1990). Anchored instruction: Why we need it and how technology can help. In D. Nix & R. Spiro (Eds.), *Cognition, education and multimedia*. Hillsdale, NJ: Lawrence Erlbaum Associates.

Brown, A. L. (1992). Design experiments: Theoretical and methodological challenges in creating complex interventions in classroom settings. *Journal of the Learning Sciences, 2* (2), 141–178.

Brown, A. L. (1994). The advancement of learning. *Educational Researcher, 23*(8), 4–12.

Brown, J. S., Collins, A., &. Duguid, P. (1989). Situated cognition and the culture of learning. *Educational Researcher, 18*, 32–42.

Butler, D., & Winne, P. H. (1995). Feedback and self-regulated learning: A theoretical synthesis. *Review of Educational Research, 65*, 245–281.

Chi, M. T. H. (2000). Self-explaining: The dual processes of generating inference and repairing mental models. In R. Glaser, R. (Ed.), *Advances in instructional psychology: Educational design and cognitive science* (Vol. 5) (pp. 161–238). Mahwah, NJ: Lawrence Erlbaum Associates.

Chi, M. T. H., de Leeuw, N., Chiu, M.-H., & LaVancher, C. (1994). Eliciting self-explanations improves understanding. *Cognitive Science, 18*, 439–477.

Chi, M. T. H., Glaser, R., & Farr, M. (1988). *The nature of expertise*. Hillsdale, NJ: Lawrence Erlbaum Associates.

Chou, C., & Lin, H. (1997). *Navigation maps in a computer-networked hypertext learning system*. Paper presented at the annual meeting of the Association for Educational Communications and Technology, Albuquerque, NM.

Clancey, W. (1997). *Situated cognition: On human knowledge and computer representations*. Cambridge, MA: Cambridge University Press.

Clark, R. C., & Mayer, R. E. (2003). *E-Learning and the science of instruction: Proven guidelines for consumers and designers of multimedia*. San Francisco: JosseyBass/Pfeiffer.

Cobb, P., Confrey, J., diSessa, A., Lehrer, R., & Schauble, L. (2003). Design experiments in educational research. *Educational Researcher, 32*(1), 9–13.

Cobb, P., Stephan, M., McClain, K., & Gravemeijer, K. (2001). Participating in classroom mathematical practices. *Journal for the Learning Sciences, 10*(1&2), 113–163.

Collins, A., Brown, J. S., & Newman, S. E. (1989). Cognitive apprenticeship: Teaching the craft of reading, writing, and mathematics. In L. B. Resnick (Ed.), *Knowing, learning, and instruction: Essays in honor of Robert Glaser* (pp. 453–494). Hillsdale, NJ: Lawrence Erlbaum Associates.

Cordova, D. I., & Lepper, M. R. (1996). Intrinsic motivation and the process of learning: Beneficial effects of contextualization, personalization, and choice. *Journal of Educational Psychology, 88*(4), 715–730.

Corno, L., Cronbach, L. J., Kupermintz, H., Lohman, D. F., Mandinach, E. B., Porteus, A. W., et al. (2002). *Remaking the concept of aptitude: Extending the legacy of Richard E. Snow*. Mahwah, NJ: Lawrence Erlbaum Associates.

Cronbach, L. J., & Snow, R. E. (1977). *Aptitudes and instructional methods: A handbook for research on interactions*. New York: Irvington.

CTGV. (1990). Anchored instruction and its relationship to situated cognition. *Educational Researcher, 19*(6), 2–10.

CTGV. (1993). Anchored instruction and situated cognition revisted. *Educational Technology, 33*(3), 52–70.

de Jong, T., & van Joolingen, W. R. (1998). Scientific discovery learning with computer simulations of conceptual domains. *Review of Educational Research, 68*(2), 179–201.

Design-Based Research Collective (2003). Design-based research: An emerging paradigm for educational inquiry. *Educational Researcher, 32*(1), 5–8.

Dewey, J. (1938). *Experience and education*. New York: Collier Books.

Dweck, C., & Bempechat, J. (1983). Children's theories of intelligence. In S. G. Paris, G. M. Olson, & H. W. Stevenson (Eds.),

Learning and motivation in the classroom (pp. 239–256). Hillsdale, NJ: Lawrence Erlbaum Associates.

Engstrom, Y., & Cole, M. (1997). Situated cognition in search of an agenda. In D. Kirschner & J. A. Whitson (Eds.), *Situated cognition: Social, semiotic, and psychological perspectives* (pp. 301–309). Mahwah, NJ: Lawrence Erlbaum Associates.

Ericsson, K. A. (2002). Attaining excellence through deliberate practice: Insights from the study of expert performance. In M. Ferrari (Ed.), *The pursuit of excellence in education* (pp. 21–55). Mahwah, N J: Lawrence Erlbaum Associates.

Flavell, J. H. (1979). Metacognition and cognitive monitoring: A new area of cognitive-developmental inquiry. *American Psychologist, 34,* 906–911.

Frederickson, B. (2001). What good are positive emotions? *Review of General Psychology, 2,* 300–319.

Glaser, R., Lesgold, A., & Lajoie, S. (1987). Toward a cognitive theory for the measurement of achievement. In R. R. Ronning, J. Glover, J.C. Conoley, & J.C.Witt (Eds.), *The influence of cognitive psychology on testing,* (Vol 3, pp. 41–85). Hillsdale, NJ: Lawrence Erlbaum Associates.

Gott, S. P. (1989). Apprenticeship instruction for real world cognitive tasks. *Review of Research in Education, 15,* 97–169.

Graesser, A. C., Bowers, C. A., Hacker, D. J., & Person, N. K. (1997). An anatomy of naturalistic tutoring. In K. Hogan & M. Pressley (Eds.), *Scaffolding student learning: Instruction approaches and issues* (pp. 145–184). Cambridge, MA: Brookline Books.

Graesser, A.C., McNamara, D.S., & VanLehn, K. (in press). Scaffolding deep comprehension strategies through Point&Query, Auto Tutor, and iSTART. *Educational Psychologist.*

Greeno, J. (1989). A perspective on thinking. *American Psychologist, 44,* 134–141.

Greeno, J. (1998). The situativity of knowing, learning, and research. *American Psychologist, 53*(1), 5–26.

Greeno, J., Collins, A. M., & Resnick, L. B. (1997). Cognition and learning. In D. Berliner & R. Calfee (Eds.), *Handbook of educational psychology* (pp. 15–46). New York: Simon & Schuster McMillan.

Greer, J., McCalla, G., Vassileva, J., Deters, R., Bull, S., & Kettel, L. (2001). Lessons learned in deploying a multi-agent learning support system: The I-help experience. *Proceedings of AIED'2001* (pp. 410–421), San Antonio, TX.

Hadwin, A., & Winne, P. (2001). CoNoteS2: A software tool for promoting self-regulation. *Educational Research and Evaluation, 7*(2/3), 313–334.

Hartley, J. R. & Sleeman, D. H. (1973). Towards more intelligent teaching systems. *International Journal of Man-Machine Studies, 2,* 215–236.

Hill, J., & Hannafin, M. (1997). Cognitive strategies and learning from the World Wide Web. *Educational Technology Research & Development, 45*(4), 37–64.

Jackson, S., Krajcik, J., & Soloway, E. (2000). MODEL-IT: A design retrospective. In M. Jacobson & R. Kozma (Eds.), *Innovations in science and mathematics education: Advanced designs for technologies of learning* (pp. 77–116). Mahwah, NJ: Lawrence Erlbaum Associates.

Jacobson, M., & Kozma, R. (Eds.) (2000). *Innovations in science and mathematics: Advanced designs for technologies for learning.* Mahwah, NJ: Lawrence Erlbaum Associates.

James, W. (1958). *Talks to teachers.* New York: Norton. (Original edition, 1899).

Jonassen, D. H. (1996). *Computers in the classroom: Mindtools for critical thinking.* Columbus, OH: Prentice-Hall.

Jonassen, D. H., & Land, S. M. (Eds.) (2000). *Theoretical foundations of learning environments.* Mahwah, NJ: Lawrence Erlbaum Associates.

Jonassen, D. H., & Reeves, T. C. (1996). Learning with technology: Using computers as cognitive tools. In D. H. Jonassen (Ed.), *Handbook of research for educational communications and technology* (pp. 693–719). New York: Simon & Schuster.

Katz, S. & Lesgold, A. (1994). Implementing post-problem reflection within coached practice environments. In P. Brusilovsky, S. Dikareva, J. Greer, & V. Petrushin (Eds.), *Proceedings of the East-West International Conference on Computer Technologies in Education, Part 1* (pp. 125–130). Crimea, Ukraine.

Koedinger, K. (2001). Cognitive tutors as modeling tools and instructional models. In K. D., Forbus & P. J. Feltovich (Eds.), *Smart machines in education* (pp. 145–167). Cambridge, MA: MIT Press.

Koedinger, K. R., Anderson, J. R., Hadley, W., & Mark, M. (1997). Intelligent tutoring goes to school. *International Journal of Artificial Intelligence in Education, 8,* 30–43.

Kommers, P., Jonassen, D. H., & Mayes, T. (Eds.). (1992). *Cognitive tools for learning.* Berlin: Springer.

Kyllonen, P. C., & Lajoie, S. P. (2003). Influence of aptitude research on education and assessment. *Educational Psychologist, 38*(2), 79–83.

Lajoie, S. P. (Ed.). (2000). *Computers as cognitive tools: Vol. 2. No more walls.* Mahwah, NJ: Lawrence Erlbaum Associates.

Lajoie, S. P. (2003). Transitions and trajectories for studies of expertise. *Educational Researcher, 32*(8), 21–25.

Lajoie, S. P. (in press a). Developing computer based learning environments based on complex performance models. In W. Spaulding, & J. Poland (Eds.), *Modeling complex systems: Motivation, cognition and social processes.* Lincoln, NE: Nebraska Symposium on Motivation.

Lajoie, S. P. (in press b). Cognitive tools for the mind: The promises of technology—cognitive amplifiers or bionic prosthetics? In R. J. Sternberg & D. Preiss (Eds.), *Intelligence and technology: Impact of tools on the nature and development of human skills.* Mahwah, NJ: Lawrence Erlbaum Associates.

Lajoie, S. P., Azevedo, R., & Fleiszer, D. (1998). Cognitive tools for assessment and learning in a high information flow environment. *Journal of Educational Computing Research, 18*(3), 205–235.

Lajoie, S. P., & Derry, S. J. (Eds.). (1993). *Computers as cognitive tools.* Hillsdale, NJ: Lawrence Erlbaum Associates.

Lajoie, S. P., & Lesgold, A. (1989). Apprenticeship training in the workplace: A computer-coached practice environment as a new form of apprenticeship. *Machine-Mediated Learning, 3*(1), 7–28.

Lajoie, S. P., & Lesgold, A. (1992). Dynamic assessment of proficiency for solving procedural knowledge tasks. *Educational Psychologist, 27*(3), 365–384.

Lajoie, S. P., Lavigne, N. C., Guerrera, C., & Munsie, S. (2001). Constructing knowledge in the context of BioWorld. *Instructional Science, 29*(2), 155–186.

Lave, J., & Wenger, E. (1991). *Situated learning: Legitimate peripheral participation.* Cambridge, MA: Cambridge University Press.

Lepper, M. (1988). Motivational considerations in the study of instruction. *Cognition and Instruction, 5*(4), 289–309.

Lepper, M. R., Drake, M., & O'Donnell-Johnson, T. M. (1997). Scaffolding techniques of expert human tutors. In K. Hogan & M. Pressley (Eds), *Scaffolding student learning: Instructional approaches and issues* (pp. 108–144). New York: Brookline Books.

Lepper, M., Greene, D., & Nisbett, R. (1973). Undermining children's intrinsic interest with extrinsic rewards. *Journal of Personality and Social Psychology, 28,* 129–137.

Lesgold, A. (1988). Problem solving. In R. Sternberg & Smith, E. (Eds.), *The psychology of human thought* (pp.188–213). New York: Cambridge University Press.

Lesgold, A. (2000). What are the tools for? Revolutionary change does not follow the usual norms. In S. P. Lajoie (Ed.), *Computers as cognitive tools*; Vol. 2: *No more walls* (pp. 399–409). Mahwah, NJ: Lawrence Erlbaum Associates.

Lesgold, A., Lajoie, S. P., Bunzo, M., & Eggan, G. (1992). SHERLOCK: A coached practice environment for an electronics troubleshooting job. In J. H. Larkin & R. W. Chabay (Eds.), *Computer assisted instruction and intelligent tutoring systems: Shared goals and complementary approaches* (pp. 201–238). Hillsdale, NJ: Lawrence Erlbaum Associaes.

Lin, X., Schwartz, D., & Hatano, G. (in press). The value of adaptive metacognition for teachers. *Educational Psychologist.*

Linn, M. C. (1992). How can hypermedia tools help teach programming? *Learning and Instruction, 2*(2), 119–139.

Linn, R. L., Baker, E., & Dunbar, S. B. (1991). Complex, performance-based assessment: Expectations and validation criteria. *Educational Researcher, 20*(8), 15–21.

Mahoney, M. J. (in press). Constructive complexity and human change processes. In W. D. Spauding & J. Poland (Eds.), *Modeling complex systems: Motivation, cognition and social processes.* Lincoln: University of Nebraska Press.

Mandinach, E. & Cline, A. (2000). It won't happen soon: Practical, curricular, and methodological problems in implementing technology based constructivist approaches in classrooms. In S. P. Lajoie (Ed.), *Computers as cognitive tools II: No more walls* (pp. 377–395). Mahwah, NJ: Lawrence Erlbaum Associates.

Mandinach, E. B., & Corno, L. (1985). Cognitive engagement variations among students of different ability level and sex in a computer problem solving game. *Sex Roles, 13,* 241–251.

Mayer, R. E. (1997). Learners as information processors: Legacies and limitations of educational psychologies second metaphor. *Educational Psychologist, 31*(3/4), 151–161.

Mayer, R. (2003). Learning environments: The case for evidence-based practice and issue-driven research. *Educational Psychology Review, 15*(4), 359–373.

McCaslin, M., & Hickey, D. T. (2001). Self-regulated learning and academic achievement: A Vygotskyan View. In B. Zimmerman, & D. Schunk (Eds.), *Self-regulated learning and academic achievement: Theoretical perspectives* (pp. 227–252). Mahwah, NJ: Lawrence Erlbaum Associates.

Merrill, D. C., Reiser, B. J., Merrill, S. K., & Landes, S. (1995). Tutoring: Guided learning by doing. *Cognition and Instruction, 13*(3), 315–372.

Miller, A. (1991). Personality types, learning styles and educational goals. *Educational Psychology, 11*(3–4), 217–238.

Mislevy, R.J., Steinberg, L.S., & Almond, R.G. (1999). *Evidence-centered assessment design.* Retrieved October 5, 2004, from http:www.education.umd.edu/EDMS/ mislevy/papers/ECD_overview.html

Mislevy, R. J., Steinberg, L. S., Breyer, F. J., Almond, R. G., & Johnson, L. (in press). Making sense of data from complex assessment. *Applied Measurement in Education.*

Moreno, R. Mayer, R. E., Spires, H., & Lester, J. (2001). The case for social agency in computer-based teaching: Do students learn more deeply when they interact with animated pedagogical agents? *Cognition and Instruction, 19,* 177–214.

Newell, A., & Simon, H. A. (1972). *Human problem solving.* Englewood Cliffs, NJ: Prentice-Hall.

Nichols, P., Pokorny, R., Jones, G., Gott, S. P., & Alley, W. E. (in preparation). *Evaluation of an avionics troubleshooting tutoring system.* Technical Report, Armstrong Laboratory, Human Resources Directorate, Brooks AFB, TX.

Palincsar, A. S., & Brown, A. L. (1984). Reciprocal teaching of comprehension-fostering and comprehension-monitoring activities. *Cognition and Instruction, 1,* 117–175.

Palincsar, A. S., Magnuson, K. A., Marano, N., Ford, D., & Brown, N. (1998). Designing communities of practice: Principles and practices of the GIsML. *Teaching and Teacher Education, 14,* 5–19.

Paris, S. G., & Paris, A. H. (2001). Classroom applications of research on self-regulated learning. *Educational Psychologist, 36*(2), 89–101.

Park, O. C. (1993). Instructional conditions for using dynamic visual displays: A review. *Instructional Science, 21*(6), 427–449.

Pea, R. D. (1985). Beyond amplification: Using the computer to reorganize mental functioning. *Educational Psychologist, 20,* 167–182.

Pellegrino, J. Chudowsky, N. & Glaser, R. (2001). *Knowing what students know.* Washington, DC: National Academy Press.

Perkins, D. N. (1985). The fingertip effect: How information processing technology shapes thinking. *Educational Researcher, 14,* 11–17.

Piaget, J. (1926). *The child's conception of the world.* Paris: Alcan.

Pintrich, P.R. (2000). The role of goal orientation in self-regulated learning. In M. Boekaerts, P. Pintrich, & M. Zeidner (Eds.), *Handbook of self-regulation* (pp. 451–502). San Diego, CA: Academic Press.

Polson, M. C., & Richardson, J. J. (Eds.) (1988). *Foundations of intelligent tutoring systems.* Hillsdale, NJ: Lawrence Erlbaum Associates.

Pressey, S. L. (1926). A simple apparatus which gives tests and scores-and-teaches. *School and Society, 23,* 373–376.

Psotka, J., Massey, L. D., & Mutter, S. A. (1988). *Intelligent tutoring systems: Lessons learned.* Hillsdale, NJ: Lawrence Erlbaum Associates.

Regian, J. W., & Shute, V. J. (Eds.). (1992). *Cognitive approaches to automated instruction.* Hillsdale, NJ: Lawrence Erlbaum Associates.

Resnick, L. B. (1987). Learning in school and out. *Educational Researcher, 16,* 13–20.

Rickel, J. & Johnson, W. (2000). Task-oriented collaboration with embodied agents in virtual worlds. In J. Cassell, J. Sullivan, S. Prevost, & E. Churchill (Eds.), *Embodied conversational agents.* Boston: MIT Press.

Salomon, G., Perkins, D. N., & Globerson. T. (1991). Partners in cognition: Extending human intelligence with intelligent technologies. *Educational Researcher, 20*(3), 2–9.

Schank, R. C. (1998). *Inside multi-media case based instruction.* Mahwah, NJ: Lawrence Erlbaum Associates.

Schunk, D. (2001). Social cognitive theory of self-regulated learning. In B. Zimmerman & D. Schunk (Eds.), *Self-regulated learning and academic achievement: Theoretical perspectives* (pp. 125–152). Mahwah, NJ: Lawrence Erlbaum Associates.

Schunk, D., & Zimmerman, B. (1994). *Self-regulation of learning and performance.* Hillsdale, NJ: Lawrence Erlbaum Associates.

Schwartz, D. L, Pilner, K., Biswas, G., Leelawong, K., & Davis, J. (in press). Animations of thought: Evidence from the teachable agents paradigm. In R. Lowe & W. Schnotz (eds.), *Animation.* Boston: Cambridge University Press.

Shute, V. J., Graf, E. A., & Hansen, E. (in press). Designing adaptive, diagnostic math assessments for sighted and visually-disabled students. In L. PytlikZillig, R. Bruning, & M. Bodvarsson (Eds.), *Technology-based education: Bringing researchers and practitioners together.* Greenwich, CT: Information Age.

Shute, V.J., Lajoie, S. P., & Gluck, K. (2000). Individual and group approaches to training. In S. Tobias & H. O'Neill (Eds.), *Handbook on training* (pp. 171–207). Washington, DC: American Psychological Association.

Shute, V., & Psotka, J. (1996). Intelligent tutoring system: Past, present, and future. In D. Jonassen (Ed.), *Handbook of research for educational communications and technology* (pp. 570–600). New York: Macmillan.

Shute, V., & Towle, L. (2003). Adaptive E-learning. *Educational Psychologist, 38*(2), 105–114.

Sleeman, D. H., & Brown, J. S. (1982). *Intelligent tutoring systems.* London: Academic Press.

Snow, R. E. (1996). Individual differences, learning, and instruction. In E. De Corte, & F. E. Weinert (Eds.), *International encyclopedia of developmental and instructional psychology* (pp. 649–660). Oxford, UK: Pergamon.

Snow, R. E. (1989). Toward assessment of cognitive and conative structures in learning. *Educational Researcher, 18*(9), 8–14.

Snow, R. E. (1992). Aptitude theory: Yesterday, today, and tomorrow. *Educational Psychologist, 27*(1), 5–32.

Thurstone, L. L. (1947). *Multiple factor analysis.* Chicago: University of Chicago Press.

von Glasersfeld, E. (1995). A constructivist approach to teaching. In L. Steffe & J. Gale (Eds.), *Constructivism in education* (pp. 3–16). Hillsdale, NJ: Lawrence Erlbaum Associates.

Vye, N., Schwartz, D., Bransford, J., Barron, B., Zech, L., & CTGV. (1998). SMART environments that support monitoring, reflection, and revision. In D. Hacker, J. Dunlosky, & A. Graesser (Eds.), *Metacognition in educational theory and practice* (pp. 305–346). Mahwah, NJ: Lawrence Erlbaum Associates.

Vygotsky, L. S. (1978). *Mind in society.* Cambridge, MA: Harvard University Press.

Weiner, B. (1986). An *attributional theory of motivation and emotion.* New York: Springer-Verlag.

Wenger, E. (1999). *Communities of practice: Learning, meaning, and identity.* New York: Cambridge University Press.

White, B. Y., & Frederiksen, J. (in press). Instructional environments that foster inquiry learning and metacognitive development. *Educational Psychologist.*

White, B. Y., Shimoda, T. A., & Frederiksen, J. R. (2000). Facilitating students' inquiry learning and metacognitive development through modifiable software advisers. In S.P. Lajoie (Ed.), *Computers as cognitive tools II: No more walls* (pp. 97–132). Mahwah, NJ: Lawrence Erlbaum Associates.

Whitehead, A. N. (1929). *The aims of education.* New York: McMillan.

Winne, P. H. (2001). Self-regulated learning viewed from models of information processing. In B. J. Zimmerman & D. Schunk (Eds.), *Self-regulated learning and academic achievement: Theoretical perspectives* (p. 153–189). Mahwah, NJ: Lawrence Erlbaum Associates.

Winne, P. H., & Hadwin, A. F. (1998). Studying as self-regulated learning. In D. J. Hacker, J. Dunlosky, & A. Graesser (Eds.), *Metacognition in educational theory and practice* (pp. 277–304). Mahwah, NJ: Lawrence Erlbaum Associates.

Winne, P. H., Hadwin, A. F., McNamara, J. K., & Chu, S. T. L., (1998). *CoNoteS2: An electronic notebook with support for self-regulation and learning tactics* [Computer program]. Simon Fraser University, Burnaby, BC, Canada.

Winne, P. H., & Perry, N. E. (2000). Measuring self-regulated learning. In M. Boekaerts, P. Pintrich, & M. Zeidner (Eds.), *Handbook of self-regulation* (pp. 531–566). San Diego, CA: Academic Press.

Winne, P., & Stockley, D. (1998). Computing technologies as sites for developing self-regulated learning. In D. Schunk & B. Zimmerman (Eds.), *Self-regulated learning: From teaching to self-reflective practice* (pp. 106–136). New York: Guilford.

Wolters, C.A. (2003). Regulation of motivation: Evaluating an underemphasized aspects of self regulated learning. *Educational Psychologist, 38,* 189–205.

Young, M. F., & McNeese, M. D. (1995). A situated cognition approach to problem solving. In P. Hancock, J. Flach, J. Caird, & K. Vincente (Eds.), *Local applications of the ecological approach to human-machine systems* (pp. 359–391). Hillsdale, NJ: Lawrence Erlbaum Associates.

Zimmerman, B. (1986). Development of self-regulated learning: Which are the key subprocesses? *Contemporary Educational Psychology, 16,* 307–313.

Zimmerman, B. (2000). Attaining self-regulation: A social cognitive perspective. In M. Boekaerts, P. Pintrich, & M. Zeidner (Eds.), *Handbook of self-regulation* (pp. 13–39). San Diego, CA: Academic Press.

Zimmerman, B. (2001). Theories of self-regulated learning and academic achievement: An overview and analysis. In B. Zimmerman & D. Schunk (Eds.), *Self-regulated learning and academic achievement: Theoretical perspectives* (pp. 1–37). Mahwah, NJ: Lawrence Erlbaum Associates.

Zimmerman, B., & Schunk, D. (2001). *Self-regulated learning and academic achievement* (2nd ed.). Mahwah, NJ: Lawrence Erlbaum Associates.

ASSESSMENT OF LEARNING, DEVELOPMENT, AND TEACHING

·36·

METHODOLOGICAL ISSUES
IN EDUCATIONAL PSYCHOLOGY

John C. Nesbit
Simon Fraser University

Allyson F. Hadwin
University of Victoria

This chapter surveys a landscape of issues, trends and practices in the methods of contemporary educational psychology research. The topics selected are those we believe to have significant implications for the future of quantitatively oriented research. Of course, space limitations do not permit an exhaustive survey of this wide domain, and indeed, we were unable to include some developments that anticipate future methodological practices.

We believe that many of the methods reviewed in this chapter can contribute to new research perspectives that advance "beyond the quantitative–qualitative divide" (Butler, Chapter 39 of this Handbook). Methods continue to emerge that integrate qualitative and quantitative techniques within a single analytical procedure. Chi (1997), for example, showed how to analyze patterns of qualitatively coded verbal data with semantic networks, statistics, or other summative formalisms. Intertwining qualitative and quantitative methods even more tightly, Shaffer and Serlin (2004) described how to statistically model a grounded theory derived from qualitative data. They made the point that statistical methods can support inference from sampled observations of persons in a specific context to all potential observations of the same persons in the same context. This latter application of statistical inference is well aligned with the goals of naturalistic modes of enquiry that seek to fully describe situated phenomena.

The innovations and trends that we sample originate from a variety of sources. Some are driven by methodological advances in psychology, including methods for tracking cognitive load and the trend toward reporting effect sizes and confidence intervals. Other trends, including the use of interactive learning environments, log file analysis, and online data gathering, are driven by the availability of new technologies. Some methodological issues, such as the use of portfolios and concept maps for research assessment, are guided by developments in educational practice and other areas of educational research. Finally, methodological advances such as techniques for tracking shifts in students' interest as they read (Ainley, Hidi, & Berdorff, 2002), are originating within educational psychology as researchers strive to adapt methods to match evolving theories.

We are tempted by the observation that the methods likely to have the greatest impact are those that borrow from all the sources we have identified. That is, we believe the most powerful research strategies available today are those that exploit new technologies, situate them in educational practice, borrow from the best methods in psychology and the social sciences, and are driven by the need to test theory. As a case in point, an increasingly favored research strategy is to develop software tools functioning as cognitive tools that are theorized to facilitate learning, and will also gather and aid in the analysis of relevant data. Researchers can examine the effects of these tools in authentic settings, affording a brand of progressive naturalistic inquiry in which the tools of research are aligned with the tools for learning.

MATCHING THE METHOD TO THE MATTER: ISSUES OF GRAIN SIZE

In the past decade the question of unit of analysis or grain size has forced a rethinking of methodological and analytical techniques used to conduct research in educational psychology. Although the term *unit of analysis* is used in many research traditions to describe the type of thing being observed and analyzed (e.g., Barab, Evans, & Baek, 2004; Chi, 1997), it also has a specific technical meaning in research designs using statistical inference, where it describes the smallest unit that can be treated as statistically independent. To avoid the constraints of the more specific meaning, but retain the sense of increased resolution or observational power yielded by smaller units, we use the term *grain size*. Grain size has emerged as a concern in the measurement of self-regulated learning (SRL), metacognition, and motivation, where it has been identified by writers on methodological and assessment issues as a central theme in contemporary research (Pintrich, Wolters, & Baxter, 2000; Schraw, 2000; Winne, Jamieson-Noel, & Muis, 2001; Winne & Perry, 2000). There seems to be consensus that shifts in grain size are important because they require shifts in the methodological and analytical tools used, and "grain size affects the degree to which measurements provide a useful test of theory or interventions" (Schraw, 2000, p. 300). However, discussions about grain size often deal with quite different issues. Some suggest moving from studying aptitudes to studying situated learning events. Others stress the importance of focusing the research lens to sample multiple events occurring over time. Finally, there is discussion of shifting from the individual as the unit of analysis to sociocultural interactions. Each of these grain size shifts is discussed next.

Aptitudes Versus Events

Winne and Perry (2000) characterized aptitudes and events as information at different levels of grain size, each corresponding with specific approaches to measurement. Data about aptitudes describe global attributes of learners and can be used to predict future behavior. Aptitudes are fairly stable and consistent across time and tasks. In contrast, events are snapshots in time. Data about events describe the learner's state at a given point in time and are situated within a specific context.

When researchers examine aptitudes, they create an aggregate data set that describes a person or a set of people. For example, in the area of self-regulation, questionnaires such as the Motivated Strategies for Learning Questionnaire (Pintrich, Smith, Garcia, & McKeachie, 1991) and the Learning and Study Strategies Inventory (Weinstein, Palmer, & Schulte, 1987), and interview protocols measure self-regulated learning as an aptitude because respondents are asked to answer questions with respect to their general actions, rather than responding with a specific study episode in mind (Winne & Perry, 2000).

In contrast, when researchers shift the unit of analysis to events, they examine behavior, thinking, or motivation as the learner actually engages in a specific learning event. Data such as the think-aloud protocols described by Hofer (2004), trace methodologies (Winne, 1982), discourse analyses applied to actual learning episodes (Karasavvidis, Pieters, & Plomp, 2000; Meyer & Turner, 2002), and other observations of performance (Perry, 1998; Turner, 1995) all study learning as an event because they examine states or actions at a specific point in time and are contextualized in a particular learning episode. This type of research might examine frequency of occurrence, conditional probability of an occurrence, or patterns of occurrence (Winne & Perry, 2000).

Why is a shift in granularity from aptitudes to events important? Hadwin, Winne, Stockley, Nesbit, and Woszczyna (2001) found that student self-reports about their study tactics, goals, and use of resources varied in frequency depending on the kind of task they were completing. Correlations among items also varied as a function of context. This finding is promising because it demonstrates that students report that they strategically adapt studying to the context. However, it also demonstrates that global measures of studying behavior may not be adequate for describing or predicting context-specific behavior.

Our intent is not to suggest that self-report and interview measures focusing on larger grain sizes are unnecessary. Rather, we concur with Pintrich et al. (2000) that researchers in educational psychology need to pay closer attention to the disconnect between theories of learning and the way constructs are operationalized in research. For the most part there is an incongruity between theories that describe dynamic properties of learning and motivation, and the empirical data used to study those same phenomena.

Although theories of higher order learning processes such as motivation, metacognition, and self-regulated learning emphasize fine-grained adaptation and change, we have few instruments with satisfactory precision to capture those small-grained, dynamic events (Pintrich et al., 2000). Instead, we have an abundance of self-report instruments that capture information about enduring attributes rather than strategic adaptation and development across studying events (Winne & Perry, 2000). In later sections of this chapter on measuring psychological constructs and technology-mediated research, we take up the issues of intratask measures, but we now turn attention to the value of repeating the administration of self-report instruments over time and in different contexts.

Longitudinal Observations Are Needed to Assess Latent Variables

To identify a factor model, educational psychologists often analyze data from one administration of a questionnaire. For example, Elliot and McGregor (2001) administered the 12-item Achievement Goal Questionnaire (AGQ) to classes of psychology students and used exploratory and confirmatory factor analyses to identify four goal orientation factors: mastery–approach, performance–approach, mastery–avoidance, and performance–avoidance. The standard interpretation is that factors identified by methods of this sort are latent, mental variables that caused responses on the questionnaire. It is worth looking closely, however, at how the methods used to empirically derive such individual difference models limit their interpretation.

Borsboom, Mellenbergh, and van Heerden (2003) argued that latent variable models derived from analysis of between-subject variance are inadequate for identifying potential causal forces within the individual. That is to say, evidence that a factor model fits a population cannot be taken as evidence that the same model operates within individuals. The factor model observed in a population might result from either a mix of different individual models, or a single model that is replicated in each individual. In the case of goal orientation, the four-factor model observed in a single test administration might have resulted from a situation where some individuals vary across contexts or time only on one factor, say performance avoidance, whereas other individuals vary only on a different factor, say performance mastery. One-time testing cannot distinguish between many possible models at the level of the individual.

According to Borsboom et al. (2003), the solution is to adjust the research design to fit the level of needed explanation: "To substantiate causal conclusions at the level of the individual, one must investigate patterns of covariation at the individual level, that is, one must fit within-subject latent variable models to repeated mea-

surements" (p. 216). Because it nests repeated measures within the individual, the relatively new method of hierarchical (multilevel) linear modeling (Wright, Chapter 38 of this Handbook) is well suited to the longitudinal research agenda recommended by Borsboom et al. We predict a flurry of longitudinal studies using multilevel linear modeling to investigate theories, such as achievement motivation, in which latent variables (e.g., mastery goal orientation) vary within the individual as a product of educational intervention and other factors.

Individuals and Sociocultural Interactions as Units of Analysis

Another grain size contrast in educational psychology spans from the study of individuals and aggregates of individuals to sociocultural aspects of learning. Researchers in educational psychology strive to investigate psychological phenomena specific to individuals such as such cognition, development, behavior, and motivation, but these phenomena are conditioned by the social and educational contexts in which they unfold.

Examining learning as the interplay between individual cognition and sociocultural interaction introduces new challenges. The individual and social aspects of learning have been investigated using different analytical lenses largely determined by the theoretical perspective from which research emerges (O'Connor, 1998). Rather than viewing learning as either individual or social, research might examine the interrelationships between individual and social aspects of learning (Salomon & Perkins, 1998) and acknowledge that learning involves both individual agency and sociocultural interaction (Martin, 2004; Martin & Sugarman, 1996). We turn to one example in the area of self-regulated learning to illustrate a method for examining the interplay between social and individual aspects of learning.

Recent research has begun to uncover patterns or changes in the ownership of self-regulatory control and behavior over time. Here the shift in analytical lens has been driven by the emergence of sociocultural perspectives of learning. Specifically, sociocultural models view self-regulating as a stage occurring as children are socialized into speech patterns and practices (Gallimore & Tharpe, 1990). From this perspective self-regulating can be seen as a social process because it appears first in the social world (on an intrapsychological plane) and then becomes appropriated into a child's way of understanding, appearing on the interpsychological plane (Diaz, Neal, & Amaya-Williams, 1990; Gallimore & Tharpe, 1990).

Studying self-regulated learning from this sociocultural perspective requires that both individual aspects and social aspects of self-regulation be examined and considered in relation to one another. For example, Karasavvidis, Pieters, and Plomp (2000) examined the transition from other (teacher) to self (or student)-regulation across instructional sessions. They adopted a variation of a Vygotskian sociocultural perspective of analysis considering the dynamic interplay between student and teacher discourse as students learned to solve correlational problems. Their method of analysis focused on examining (a) frequency of utterances, (b) the sequential nature of those utterances or the way that a student's utterance shapes the teacher's and vice versa, and (c) changes in ownership or control of developing ideas. The first thing to note is that the study of the social aspects of learning also necessitated a focus on multiple events and changes across events. Second, the analysis considered shifts in who was controlling the regulatory processes—the teacher, the student, or both. By shifting the lens of focus from the individual learner to the interplay between the individual and the teacher, Karasavvidis et al. demonstrated that self-regulation appeared first in the teacher's speech and actions and was then progressively appropriated by students and reflected in their speech and actions.

Researchers studying collaborative knowledge construction and computer-supported collaborative learning have made methodological advances in diagrammatically analyzing discourse. Luckin (2003) and Hmelo-Silver (2003) use variations of "chronologically ordered representation of discourse" (CORD) to represent activities with varied grain sizes. Figure 36.1, from Hmelo-Silver (2003), shows activities of five medical students and a facilitator in a problem-based learning session. Diagrams of this type can show a single event categorized in several ways. An utterance can be categorized to identify the speaker and to indicate whether it is a question or statement, metacognitive or cognitive, novel or elaborative, task-related or conceptual, and so on. The diagram can also represent and categorize events generated by computer applications and learners' operations with tools, such as drawing on a whiteboard. CORD diagrams can be further annotated with lines linking events in different rows to show interactions or relationships between events, such as a reply made by one speaker to a question posed by another (Luckin, 2003). Figure 36.1 suggests phenomena occurring at different grain sizes. For instance, transitions between different components of the drawing task (rows 20 to 23) seem to occur at a larger grain size than metacognitive questions and statements (rows 9 and 16).

Depending on the questions being investigated, researchers could use a CORD diagram to zoom in for analysis at a finer grain size (e.g., a portion of the transcript), or zoom out to analyze macro-level phenomena. CORD diagrams can represent both the interactions of individuals with a learning environment (e.g., computer software) and collaborative interactions among learners (Luckin, 2003), and therefore may be especially suited to studying phenomena at the boundary of individual and collaborative activity.

ADVANCES IN ASSESSING PSYCHOLOGICAL CONSTRUCTS

How are educational psychology researchers extending the techniques they use to assess constructs that lie at the core of their models of learning and motivation? Self-report questionnaires will continue to play a significant role, but there is a trend toward augmenting traditional methods with techniques that are more sensitive to the dynamic manifestations of psychological constructs during complex learning activities. In this section we cite work on topic interest and cognitive load as examples of how researchers are now gathering fine-grained, intratask data. These examples also show the limitations of intratask measurement, especially how intrusive observation may alter the task to such a degree that it no longer represents a natural learning activity. Later in the section we describe innovations in the conceptualization and assessment of knowledge transfer.

Intratask Measures of Individual and Situational Interest

Educational psychologists increasingly cite interest constructs as mediators of learning and performance (McDaniel, Waddill, Finstad, & Bourg, 2000; Murphy & Alexander, 2002). According to Ainley, Hidi, and Berndorff (2002), the topic interest that learners carry through activities such as choosing and reading text passages is a composite of situational and individual factors. Whereas individual interest is a fairly stable, personal predisposition toward certain types of information and events, situational interest is an immediate affective response to properties of the situation such as novelty or ambiguity. A study by Murphy and Alexander (2002) distinguished between these two constructs by having students categorize topics in an educational psychology course as provoking individual interest ("personal interests, long-term interests, goals, or hobbies"), situational interest ("somewhat interested or intrigued"), or no interest.

Researchers have recently developed new methods for tracking situational interest, a transient construct that is

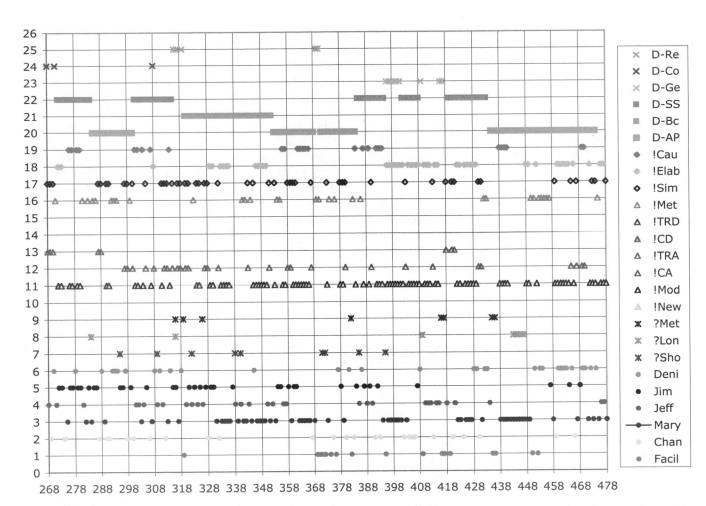

FIGURE 36.1. Chronologically ordered representation of discourse and tool-related activity from Hmelo-Silver (2003, p. 413). The horizontal axis chronologically orders conversational turns. The vertical axis represents categories of activities. Rows 1 to 6 identify the speakers. Rows 7 to 9 categorize questions. Rows 10 to 19 identify different types of statements. Rows 20 to 25 categorize drawing activities and references to the drawing. Reprinted with permission of the author.

normally difficult to measure. In addition to a self-report of topic interest before reading, Ainley et al. (2002) used a software program to measure reading choice, affect, persistence, and recall with four expository texts on scientific and popular culture topics. Each text was composed of three 250-word segments. After choosing a topic, participants were presented with the first segment of the corresponding text. At any time they could choose to switch to a different topic or continue to the next segment of the current text. The choice to continue reading a text was scored as persistence relative to the topic for that text. If participants chose to continue, before being presented with the next segment they were asked to indicate their feelings by selecting from emotions such as sad, interested, neutral, or bored. If they chose to switch to a different topic, or completed the last segment of the current topic, they were given a three-item retention test on the topic they had elected to leave. Structural modeling of

the data found that prior self-report of topic interest predicted intratask affect, affect predicted persistence, and persistence predicted learning.

The methodology used by Ainley et al. (2002) combined two fundamental research strategies for gathering intratask data. One strategy is to divide traditional self-report instruments, in this case for retention and affect, into small testlets or single items that are delivered at programmed points within the task. The researcher presents self-report probes that, one hopes, do not significantly disrupt the learner's perception of the task as a continuous activity. The second strategy is to provide a tool that both actualizes and monitors behavioral choice. By requiring a key press to execute an action that is normally covert, the researchers were able to assess quite precisely the learners' will to continue reading. A third strategy for collecting intratask data, not used in the topic interest research, is to measure physiological or cognitive side-effects of the target construct. Recent advances in assessment of cognitive load best illustrate this strategy.

Tracking Cognitive Load

Cognitive load corresponds to the amount of mental resource, primarily working memory, required to perform a task (Paas, Tuovinen, & Tabbers, 2003). Mental load and effort, the measurable aspects of this construct, are known to depend on the interaction of individuals and tasks. Cognitive load is increasingly used to explain why instructional design variations produce differing learning outcomes (e.g., Kalyuga, Ayres, Chandler, & Sweller, 2003). In 2004, a search of the PsycInfo database using the term *cognitive load* returned approximately 280 empirical studies published in peer-reviewed journals, many citing cognitive load as a mediator of learning outcomes. Instructional theorists partition load into a necessary *intrinsic* component, an unnecessary *extrinsic* component due to suboptimal task design, and a beneficial *germane* component resulting from design features such as spaced learning.

Cognitive load has been measured in several ways, each presenting the researcher with different advantages and disadvantages. According to a list of cognitive load studies given by Paas et al. (2003), subjective judgment on a difficulty rating scale is the most frequently used measure, and only a few studies have used performance on a secondary task or physiological measures such as heart rate variability and pupillary response. Ratings of task difficulty are widely used because they are easy to administer in an instructional context and have been shown to reliably detect design-induced variation in cognitive load (Paas, van Merriënboer, & Adam, 1994).

Although rarely used in educational research, subjective time estimation (STE) reported after completing a task negatively correlates with the task's cognitive complexity (Fink & Neubauer, 2001). Estimates of task duration consistently decrease, and become more accurate, as cognitive demands increase. Like difficulty ratings, STEs have been used as posttask measures that capture accumulated or average load, not the moment-by-moment variation in load as the task proceeds. To obtain an intratask measure one might interrupt the task with STE or difficulty rating probes. However, for continuous monitoring of cognitive load one must look to other methods.

Dual task methods for measuring cognitive load exploit the principle that higher cognitive demands of a primary task can produce poorer performance on a concurrent secondary task. These methods are commonly used in working memory research (Baddeley & Logie, 1999) because they can track cognitive load throughout a task

and, with appropriate selection of the secondary task, target specific cognitive components such as visuospatial and verbal memory. Instructional research using the dual task method has demonstrated that reaction time on a secondary visual monitoring task is a sensitive index of visuospatial load in multimedia learning (Brüenken, Plass & Leutner, 2003). As the visuospatial load increases, the reaction time on the secondary monitoring task also increases. A significant drawback of secondary task measures is that they may threaten ecological validity, that is, they may alter the studied learning task to an extent that it no longer represents the tasks that students experience in real life.

A potential advantage of physiological indices is that they offer fine-grained tracking of cognitive load, often without requiring any overt response. Pupil dilation has proven to be one of the most precise physiological measures. During the digit span memory task, pupil size increases with the presentation of each additional digit and recedes to a baseline size after the digits are recalled (Granholm & Steinhauer, 2004). Similarly, pupil dilation has been shown to increase as a function of the number of multiplicands in mental arithmetic and the syntactic complexity in sentence comprehension tasks. The main drawback of pupil dilation as a measure of cognitive load is that participants must be sequestered in a laboratory environment where a chin rest is used to stabilize head movements and equipment is calibrated. Another disadvantage of this method is that pupil dilation is considerably less sensitive to mental load in elderly learners (Van Gerven, Paas, Van Merrienboer, & Schmidt, 2003).

Electroencephalogram (EEG) measures are rarely used in educational research. However, neuropsychological studies have shown that EEG-based indices of cognitive load correspond with variation in subjectively experienced cognitive demand in naturalistic tasks such as mental calculation, text editing, and Web searching (Gevins & Smith, 2003; Lamberts, van den Broek, & Bener, 2000). An advantage of EEG measures is that the recording equipment can be worn by participants as they move about while performing typical school and workplace tasks (e.g., Kecklund & Akerstedt, 1993). This contrasts sharply with other neural sensing technologies, such as magnetic resonance imaging (MRI), in which data are collected under laboratory conditions that severely constrain learner activities.

Assessing Knowledge Transfer

Transfer of learning to dissimilar (far) contexts is of central importance for educational psychologists as they seek to increase the cogency of education to life beyond the classroom. There is a long-standing dispute among psychologists about the prevalence of far transfer entailing profound uncertainty about efficacy of formal education. Some reviewers have observed that demonstrations of far transfer are scarce (Perkins & Grotzer, 1997) or even nonexistent (Detterman, 1993), whereas others claim that evidence for transfer, for example from formal instruction in domains such as critical thinking, is plentiful (Halpern, 1998). Attributing the disparity in these positions to imprecise definition of the transfer construct, Barnett and Ceci (2002) developed a taxonomy in which the context of transfer tasks may vary from the original learning conditions on six dimensions: knowledge domain (e.g., science vs. history), physical context (e.g., school vs. home), temporal context (months or years later), functional context (e.g., academic vs. play), social context (e.g., individual vs. large group), modality (e.g., book learning vs. wine tasting). These dimensions clearly establish the territory over which transfer research can range, and oblige investigators to justify and contrast the transfer dimensions selected for their research designs.

Research on far transfer, as defined by Barnett and Ceci (2002), is much less common than research using near transfer to gauge the effects of instructional treatment. The near transfer measures in these studies tend to be novel tasks or problems that require learners to apply knowledge gained in prior activities. One reason to incorporate near transfer tasks in research designs is that they may be more sensitive measures of learning outcomes than simple recall and recognition tasks. In an extended research program investigating the effects of multimedia learning, Mayer and colleagues have measured both retention and transfer to demonstrate a range of multimedia effects (Mayer, 2001). In one experiment where participants learned about bicycle pumps (Mayer & Anderson, 1992), one treatment group was presented with successive animation and narration, and another was presented with concurrent animation and narration. In addition to a free recall task, participants were given redesign questions (e.g., "What could be done to make a pump more effective, that is, to move more air more rapidly?"), a troubleshooting question ("Suppose you push down and pull up the handle of a pump several times but no air comes out? What could have gone wrong?"), and a question requiring induction of underlying principles ("Why does air enter a pump? Why does air exit from a pump?"). To score the transfer questions, one point was given for each answer corresponding to a solution on a predetermined list. No statistically significant difference was found for free recall ($d = -0.35$), but the concurrent group strongly outperformed the successive group on the transfer test ($d = 1.61$). Although Mayer and Anderson's study shows

how a near transfer task can be more successful than simple recall in detecting a treatment effect, the type of analysis they used cannot pinpoint how the knowledge of the two groups differed.

To investigate conceptual change, researchers have developed more complex methods for analyzing data from near transfer tasks. This is evident in a study by Gentner, Loewenstein, and Thompson (2003) in which they qualitatively categorized participants' solutions to a near transfer negotiation problem. Two participant groups were trained on different negotiation strategies and then given a transfer problem with surface features varying markedly from the training examples. Raters classified the solutions as exhibiting either one of the strategies shown during training or a third suboptimal strategy. This resulted in a 3×3 contingency table showing the number of participants generating each kind of solution in the two treatment groups and a no-training control group. The researchers used chi-square tests to show that, compared to the no-training condition, the specific type of strategy presented during training was more likely to be used in the transfer task. The general approach used by Gentner et al., that is, analyzing frequencies of different concepts or strategies, can be applied quite broadly in learning research. For example, to investigate the conceptual change underlying the concurrent multimedia transfer effect discovered by Mayer and Anderson (1992), a researcher could examine the proportion of different solution types produced by the successive and concurrent treatment groups.

ALTERNATIVES FOR LEARNER ASSESSMENT IN EDUCATIONAL RESEARCH

Educational researchers can reap substantial benefits by gathering data from the assessments normally used in the classroom. Classroom assessments are a bountiful source of data that represent student knowledge in a way that is meaningful to teachers. Fortunately, researchers using classroom assessments are not restricted to traditional achievement tests and essays. Here we examine the utility for research of two alternative methods, concept maps and learner portfolios, that are increasingly used for assessment in schools.

Concept Maps

A persistent challenge that has given rise to extensive methodological debate is how to represent human knowledge and changes to knowledge as learning unfolds. Test scores created by summing over traditional cued-response items are suitable for normative comparisons between treatment groups, but they are limited in their ability to represent the substance of knowledge such as cognitive structure and misconceptions. Qualitative formats for representing knowledge, such as text, afford insights into a learner's understanding but are difficult to assemble into summary formats that concisely show a learner's progress or allow comparisons among learners or across groups.

Concept maps (Novak & Gowin, 1984), also known as knowledge maps or node-link maps, are increasingly used as tools for teaching, learning, and research in education. Concept maps are effective learning tools when constructed by students or presented by teachers (Horton et al., 1993; Nesbit & Adesope, 2005) and are convenient communication aids for collaborative learning (De Simone, Schmid, & McEwen, 2001; Hall, Dansereau, & Skaggs, 1992). Researchers have used concept maps to track conceptual change by comparing maps that students construct before and after a learning experience (Pearsall, Skipper, & Mintzes, 1997; Sen, 2002), or comparing maps from groups at different achievement levels (Wilson, 1998).

Concept maps may be directly constructed by individual learners, or constructed by researchers using specially developed knowledge-gathering protocols to construct map nodes and links (Gonzalvo, Cañas, & Bajo, 1994). To discover the links in cognitive structures, researchers (e.g., Schvaneveldt, 1990) have participants explicitly rate the semantic similarity of paired terms from a lexicon in a subject domain. The similarity data are transformed into matrices for individuals or groups showing the semantic distance between any two terms. The matrices are summarized or reduced by procedures such as cluster analysis, multidimensional scaling, or, in Schvaneveldt's work, a specially created software program called pathfinder. Finally, the matrices may be graphically represented as node-link maps. In a variation of this approach that was developed to discover the nodes or concepts held in common by a group, Trochim had group members sort and rate statements generated in a group brainstorming process and then used cluster analysis to assign the statements to semantic categories (Trochim, 1989; Trochim, Cook & Setze, 1994).

Scholarly interest in node-link maps extends well beyond psychology and education. In a seminal taxonomy of information visualization environments, Shneiderman (1996) identified node-link networks including concept maps as one of eight fundamental visualization types. Information scientists are developing interactive animation techniques to visualize complex and dynamic node-link networks such as the World Wide Web (Scharl, 2001) and bibliographic citation networks (Chen & Morris, 2003). We expect that some of these advanced visualization methods will be adopted by educational researchers to represent cognitive structure.

Issues have arisen about the appropriate methods for scoring concept maps constructed by learners (Ruiz-Primo & Shavelson, 1996). Following the *relational* method, a rater assigns points according to the correctness of each node-link-node proposition in the map. Following the *structural* method, in addition to crediting correct propositions, the rater assigns points for the depth of hierarchical structures, cross-links between branches in the hierarchy, and examples (Novak & Gowin, 1984). Comparative studies have found higher reliability for relational scores, but do not agree on which method provides a more valid measure of domain knowledge (McClure, Sonak & Suen, 1999: West, Park, Pomeroy & Sandoval, 2002).

Pursuant to further investigation of the validity of existing scoring methods, to support investigations of conceptual change there is a need for assessment techniques that characterize qualities of a node-link map and its component structures. The graph theory measures (Gross & Yellen, 1998) that have been extensively applied in social network analysis (Scott, 2000) and have been proposed for log file analysis (Winne, Gupta & Nesbit, 1994) are promising candidates for characterizing concept maps. For example, each node in a concept map can be described by a graph theory statistic called *centrality*, which in its simplest form is the sum of links connecting the node to other nodes in the graph. A researcher investigating conceptual change might measure shifts in the centrality of certain concepts, or identify stable differences in node centrality between novices and experts. Graph theory measures like centrality are applicable not only to maps representing one individual's cognitive structure, but also to aggregate maps formed by combining the individual maps constructed by collaborating peers or members of an experimental treatment group.

Learner Portfolios

Portfolios have gained wide acceptance as tools for (1) demonstrating achievement of specified learning outcomes, (2) authentically tracking development or growth over time, and (3) promoting metacognitive or reflective self-regulation. Here we consider the suitability of portfolios for evaluation and measurement in research, rather than their merits as an instructional intervention. Despite the popular use of portfolio assessment in elementary, vocational, and professional settings, there is considerable debate about the quality of these tools for assessment purposes. Much of the debate centers on weak findings regarding the reliability and validity of their scores (Klein, McCaffrey, Stecher & Koretz, 1995; Koretz, 1998; McBee & Barnes, 1998; Shapley & Bush, 1999; Walsh, 1999).

Koretz (1998) reviewed several large-scale portfolio assessments that articulated conceptual challenges in the measurement of portfolio performance, and evaluated the quality of performance data collected in large scale portfolio assessments in U.S. states. Koretz argued that meaningful assessment must be reasonably consistent and replicable. Portfolio assessment poses problems in this regard because there are multiple sources of measurement error including inconsistency in scoring, unreliability in the sampling of tasks, uncorrelated tasks, and small number of tasks evaluated (Koretz, 1998). Rather than being administered at a particular point in time, portfolios are collected during instruction and across time and thereby suffer from a host of confounding variables such as varied instructional support and differences in the content and level of challenge represented in the work. In other words, portfolio tasks are not standardized because what is included varies greatly from student to student and class to class. Moreover, although attempts are made to apply a set of rules or standards for scoring portfolios, research consistently demonstrates poor inter-rater correlation (Davis et al., 2001; Koretz, 1998; McBee & Barnes, 1998; Pitts, Coles, & Thomas, 1999; Shapley & Bush, 1999). When high inter-rater agreement has been reported, it is on outcome dimensions that have little variability in assigned scores (Koretz, 1998).

Koretz (1998) argued further that inconsistencies in scoring are not the largest source of unreliability in portfolio scores. Koretz, Stecher, Klein, and McCaffrey (1994) found that task sampling contributes substantially to poor score reliability, accounting for 23 percent of overall variance. This compares with 10 percent of variance accounted for by differences among raters and 48 percent accounted for by residual error. McBee and Barnes (1998) reported similar findings and suggested that the "number of tasks required to reach acceptable levels of generalizability would be prohibitively high" (p. 179).

Koretz (1998) also identified problems with the validity of portfolio scores. For example, Koretz et al. (1994) examined evidence of validity on mathematics and writing portfolio performance on Vermont's statewide portfolio assessment for mathematics. First, they examined disattenuated correlations (removing the effects of rater error) between scoring dimensions on the portfolio and the state tests of both mathematics and writing. Koretz et al. argued that ideally there should be a moderate positive correlation between math portfolios and state tests of mathematics knowledge. Neither high nor low correlations would be desirable because very high correlations

indicate that portfolios do not measure anything new, and low correlations indicate that portfolio performance has nothing to do with other kinds of mathematical knowledge. Koretz et al. found negative correlations between conceptually related tasks within mathematics measured by the portfolio versus the test. Furthermore, scores on the mathematics dimensions of the portfolio did not correlate more strongly with the mathematics test than the writing test. Although it may be argued that portfolio assessment is designed to measure different things than standardized statewide tests, the absence of any positive relationship should be a concern.

Koretz (1998) presented further evidence of poor validity by critiquing reported findings from the Pittsburg writing portfolio project (Gentile, Martin-Rehrmann, & Kennedy, 1995). Gentile et al. reported 54 percent exact agreement between portfolio writing scores and scores on an applied writing test. However, Koretz demonstrated that since scores were not well distributed across the three grading categories (low, medium, and high) on either assessment, with 79 percent of the portfolio grades falling in the medium category and 61 percent of the writing test grades falling in the medium category, one would expect 52 percent agreement based on chance alone. In other words, "the correspondence between on demand [writing test scores] and portfolio writing was generally poor" (Koretz, 1998, p. 11).

Koretz (1998) suggests that problems in validity and reliability are compounded by the fact that teachers implement the portfolio programs differently, assigning both different content and different levels of difficulty of tasks. Furthermore, there is great variance in the types and amount of support given to students as they complete these tasks both within and across classrooms.

After reviewing the efficacy of portfolio use in medical education, Roberts, Newble and O'Rourke (2002) concluded that although portfolios may be useful formative assessment tools with high face validity, there is little evidence to support their use in high-stakes testing. These points resonate across the literature examining the validity and reliability of portfolio assessment and provide a useful summary of issues researchers should consider. We found only one study reporting significant correlations between portfolio assessment scores and teacher-made tests, as well as high inter-rater reliability (Barootchi & Keshavarz, 2002). The study did not report, however, sufficient detail about the method or analysis to allow critical examination of their findings.

Present evidence does not support the use of portfolio scores as summative measures for demonstrating attainment of learning outcomes, particularly when the goal is large scale examination of interindividual differences. If portfolios are to be used instead to track development and growth over time, it is still essential that researchers carefully consider assessment issues appropriate to the qualitative or quantitative method used in scoring and analysis. Given the lack of evidence that summative portfolio scores are reliable and valid measures of performance or learning outcomes, we suggest that portfolios may be best applied as tools for qualitatively investigating individual growth, or as instructional interventions to promote learning and self-regulation.

ADVANCES IN TECHNOLOGY-MEDIATED RESEARCH

The first edition of the *Handbook of Educational Psychology* was published shortly after the birth of the Web, at a time when researchers were just beginning to explore methodologies based on Internet and digital multimedia technologies. Initially, educational researchers working with the new technologies tended to study applications such as networked learning and interactive simulations. However, as the technologies evolved from novelties to everyday tools, they were taken up by researchers addressing broader questions of learning and motivation. In this section of the chapter we highlight several of the research methods made possible by the internet and Interactive media technologies.

Web Questionnaires

Delivering questionnaires over the Web presents some obvious logistical advantages. Compared with pencil-and-paper formats, Web questionnaires reduce the expense of test administration and data entry, allow immediate scoring and feedback, and can more easily sample geographically distributed populations. It is becoming apparent that Web questionnaires are a particularly effective means to quickly gather large samples of data. Psychology researchers have exploited these advantages by setting up Web sites in which participants provide data when they take personality tests for entertainment, self-knowledge, or a few dollars. However, critics have questioned whether anonymous Web surfers respond seriously, whether self-selecting Web samples are representative, and whether the findings from Web questionnaires might diverge drastically from traditional formats (Gosling, Vazire, & Srivastava, 2004; Richman, Kiesler, Weisband, & Drasgow, 1999).

In a study addressing several of these concerns, Gosling et al. (2004) contrasted data from personality tests on a

Web site ($N = 361{,}703$) with data from all studies published in 2002 by the *Journal of Personality and Social Psychology* ($N = 102{,}959$). They found that the Web data were "more representative than traditional samples with respect to gender, socioeconomic status, geographic location, and age and . . . about as representative as traditional samples with respect to race" (p. 99). We caution that while Web samples may be more representative than the undergraduate student samples used in much social science research, self-selected Web samples are much less representative than the polling methods often needed for opinion surveys. When sampling bias is unavoidable, as is the case with both traditional undergraduate samples and self-selected Web samples, stratified analysis can be an effective means to estimate parameters or investigate structural models in subpopulations represented in the sample (Birnbaum, 2004). Stratified analysis is a method in which a sample is divided into subgroups according to variables, such as gender or nationality, that are theorized to covary with or confound other variables of interest. The diversity of Web samples with regard to demographic variables such as age, occupation, or educational status makes them more suitable for stratified analysis than traditional undergraduate samples.

It is appropriate to either recruit participants who happen on a research Web site while surfing the Web, or actively seek participants by sending e-mail to the membership lists of relevant associations who have given prior approval. Recruiting by mass e-mail distribution ("spam") is poorly regarded and likely to antagonize those who receive it. Recruiting by e-mail has advantages, but with some groups researchers should consider recruiting through the traditional postal service. Shannon and Bradshaw (2002) sent either e-mails or postal mail invitations to professional members of the Mid-South Educational Research Association. The costs for the e-mailed surveys were lower and they were returned faster, but the response rate was higher for the postal mailings.

The equivalence of Web questionnaires and traditional methods can not be assumed *a priori* and may need to be established for each instrument. Nevertheless, there is mounting evidence in the domain of personality research that Web questionnaires tend to produce the same findings as traditional methods and are not psychometrically inferior (Buchanan & Smith, 1999; Pasveer & Ellard, 1998; Smith & Leigh, 1997; Srivastava, John, Gosling, & Potter, 2003). If online participants were responding with less care and attention than traditional participants, the Web data might be expected to show lower alpha reliability. If online participants were more likely to "fake good," that is, enter socially desirable responses to obtain flattering feedback from the Web site, one might expect deviations in factor structure. Contrary to these scenarios, compared with traditionally gathered data, Web data show very similar or better alpha reliabilities and factor model fit (Buchanan & Smith, 1999; Gosling et al., 2004). It also appears that computer-administered questionnaires return results that are similar to pencil-and-paper versions. In a meta-analysis of social desirability distortion in computer-administered versus pencil-and-paper instruments, Richman, Kiesler, Weisband, and Drasgow (1999) concluded that, overall, the two modes of administration yield similar levels of social desirability distortion.

Web and Internet Experiments

In the early days of the Web, psychologists set up online laboratories capable of running full experiments in which participants were recruited, assigned to treatment conditions, and tested (Reips, 2001). There are now online psychology labs running several different experiments at one time, and attracting thousands of visitors every month (Birnbaum, 2004). A comparison of Web and laboratory versions of several studies found no major differences in results from Web and lab experiments (Krantz & Dalal, 2000). Nevertheless, the equivalence of lab and Web methods should not be assumed for every experiment. Birnbaum (2004) identified several threats to the validity of Web experiments, including participant dropout, multiple submissions, and response bias caused by the features of Web forms.

There is a higher dropout rate after assignment to treatment with Web experiments than in traditional psychology laboratories, but researchers can reduce the dropout rates by several design features such as providing pre-experimental tasks so that participants with low motivation to continue drop out before assignment to treatment groups (Knapp & Heidingsfelder, 2001). High dropout is thought to be a serious threat to validity, and it needs to be considered with special care in designing and interpreting Web-based experiments.

Although multiple submissions by the same participant have been cited as one of the ways that data gathered in online experiments can be compromised, there is an emerging consensus among online researchers that multiple submissions are too infrequent to create major problems, and when they do occur they are fairly easy to detect (Birnbaum, 2004). Birnbaum observed that researchers can take several actions to reduce the occurrence of multiple submissions. These include instructing participants not to re-enter the experiment, providing alternative incentives to repeated participation in the experiment, and

checking for the Internet protocol address that is unique to each machine.

E-mail is being used to deliver treatments and record responses of participants recruited through more traditional channels. E-mail and other asynchronous communication technologies allow an investigation to carry on outside the confines of the laboratory environment or classroom. For example, in a study of how undergraduate students cope with stressful events encountered daily, students recruited from a university participant pool were E-mailed every day as a reminder to access a Web site where they logged the events of their day, identified their coping efforts, mood, and other measures (Park, Armeli, and Tennen, 2004). In a study of verbal persuasion to enhance self-efficacy in undergraduates, Jackson (2002) showed that E-mail messages from the instructor designed to boost self-efficacy raised both self-efficacy scores and subsequent exam performance.

Interactive Learning Environments

Computer-based environments that combine multimedia presentations and navigation through hyperlinks are being increasingly used by educational psychologists to research instructional conditions that enhance self-regulated learning. These environments distribute information over a virtual space that students navigate by following hyperlinks. Students' strategies, motivations, and beliefs are exposed by their navigational activity as they seek information needed to complete the task. For example, Azevedo, Cromley and Seibert (2004) recorded students' think-aloud reports and requests for help as they navigated through a hypermedia environment about the circulatory system. The researchers transcribed and categorized the students' verbalizations as representing different self-regulatory strategies and beliefs. They showed how the relationship between instructional scaffolding and learning as measured by posttests was mediated by the regulatory processes revealed by the students' think-aloud reports.

A second important technique used to research learning in interactive environments is to provide software tools that scaffold self-regulatory action. The ways that students use these tools and the content they enter can reveal a great deal about their learning strategies, beliefs, and motivations. In BioWorld, a hospital simulation designed for high school biology, students collected evidence and formed hypotheses to diagnose virtual patients (Lajoie, Lavigne, Guerrera, & Munsie, 2001). BioWorld provided students with a belief meter that they could use to express their level of certainty in a diagnosis. It also provided an evidence palette where students recorded data they collected by navigating through the environment, and an argumentation palette where they recorded and organized the reasoning supporting their diagnoses. Among other results, Lajoie et al. showed that students were able to effectively organize evidence to support their diagnoses, and that the final level of certainty that students registered on the belief meter was highly correlated with the quality of their diagnoses.

Many metacognitive tools can be reused across a range of learning contexts and with a variety of resource materials. In principle, a tool such as Bioworld's belief meter is not limited to medical diagnosis, but could be used by learners to express their confidence in almost any assertion they might induce from resource materials. Tools for highlighting, categorizing, and linking information are other examples of widely applicable operations. gStudy (Winne, Hadwin, Nesbit, Kumar, & Beaudoin, 2005) is a learning environment incorporating a host of such software tools for researching SRL. Software tools such as gStudy are designed to overcome some of the severe limitations researchers face when trying to collect evidence or traces of learning operations with paper-and-pencil or video methods. In gStudy, learners can annotate and link text, graphics, and video resources packaged as learning kits. For example, learners can use predefined note templates with graphic sliders to numerically represent an idea's importance or how well they understand it. They can link a video segment to a learning objective, or enter an unfamiliar term into a glossary. gStudy researchers can electronically collect the package of resources after it has been annotated by a learner and analyze a log file detailing the learner's operations.

The strategy of providing tools that both scaffold and monitor learners' activities is not restricted to SRL research. Virtual School is a software program that represents a similar research strategy applied to the domain of synchronous collaboration (Carroll, Neale, Isenhour, Rosson, & McCrickard, 2003). In Virtual School, notification of edits to project management tools such as a shared Gantt chart or notebook are transmitted to all group members, and also to an event log file that can be analyzed by researchers.

Learning environments such as BioWorld, gStudy, and Virtual School can generate log files listing many events. In the case of gStudy, a single learner can generate thousands of log events in only a few sessions. Researchers who wish to identify and interpret log events as traces of learner strategies face the challenge of filtering and analyzing masses of log data. We believe that the long-term success of interactive learning environments as sites for educational psychology research will depend on the effectiveness of new methods for log file analysis.

Log File Analysis

Log file data consist of precise traces of a person's engagement with computer systems (Barab, Bowdish, & Lawless, 1997; Rouet & Passerault, 1999; Winne et al., 1994). They are believed to be more accurate than retrospective self-reports that require recall of actions and thoughts. Log file data also have advantages over concurrent think-aloud protocols, which have been found sometimes to interfere with task performance (van den Haak, De Jong, & Jan Schellens, 2003), and live researcher observations, which are constrained by human ability to attend to and record detail.

Leard and Hadwin (2000) reviewed the literature on log file analysis with the goal of creating a library of analytical techniques for analyzing and deriving meaning from log file data. They observed that log file data, also known as audit trails, event records, history transcripts, and navigation trails, are not unique to educational research. Besides the prevalence of log file analysis in library research, in the field of computer science it is used for usability testing and cybernetic modeling of user behavior (e.g., Fjeld, Schluep, & Rauterberg, 1998; Rauterberg, 1993). Unlike usability studies, which focus on the ability of computer systems to actualize user's intentions, educational researchers have analyzed log files to infer learners' characteristics, goals, or strategies as they interact with hypermedia (Horney & Anderson-Inman, 1994) or computer-supported collaborative learning (CSCL) environments (Meistad & Wasson, 2000; Nurmela, Lehtinen, & Palonen, 1999; Wasson, 1999). In contrast to traditional means of assessment, hypermedia-based log file data can document the dynamic, situated nature of learning, as well as individual event-based differences in activity (MacGregor, 1999; Marchionini, 1990; Winne et al., 1994).

Leard and Hadwin (2000) identified four major categories of log file analysis employed in the literature: frequency analysis, patterns of activity, time-based analysis, and content analysis. Frequency analysis, the most prevalent method, involves recording the frequency of specified learner actions, such as accessing a relevant Web page or entering a note. Frequencies are usually treated as continuous variables and analyzed with parametric methods (e.g., analysis of variance). For example, Fitzgerald and Semrau (1998) analyzed frequency data to compare access of hypermedia information by preservice teachers with different cognitive styles. Because they are often not normally distributed, researchers are cautioned to screen frequency data for skewness, kurtosis, and outliers before applying parametric tests.

Frequency data have been used to compare individuals and dyads on the types of information searched and the number of links searched (Kelly & O'Donnell, 1994).

Lawless and Kulikowich (1996, 1998) used cluster analysis to classify students learning from hypertext as knowledge seekers, feature explorers, or apathetic hypertext users. Variables included in the cluster analysis included the number of cards accessed for each topic, the number of resources and special features that were accessed, and the total time spent in the hypertext environment.

A limitation of frequency data is that it describes actions at one point in time but does not capture relationships across events or the time invested in those event-based actions (Guzdial et al., 1995; Misanchuk & Schwier, 1992). Patterns of activity have been examined in ways that consider contingent frequencies of specific actions or events. When activities occur in consistent proximity to one another, they may provide information about strategic actions. Transition matrixes have been used to examine patterns of activity. Types of activity events are listed in both the columns and rows of a table, and each cell represents the transition from a row action event followed to a column action event. Therefore, the frequency of paired events is analyzed, rather than the frequency of single events. Transition matrixes may be used to record finc-grained patterns that include every possible event pairing (e.g., Beasley & Waugh, 1997), or they may be collapsed to represent only key events (e.g., Marchionini, 1989).

Three important issues arise when using transition matrices for log file analysis. First, transition matrices are most commonly used to track two-event sequences. As sequences relevant to the research question increase to three, four, or more events, transition matrices become complex, multidimensional, and more challenging to interpret. Second, transition matrices can only count "traceable" steps or actions. This means that two events appearing sequentially in a log file, and counted as a pair in a transition matrix, may actually have been separated by many unrecorded user actions that are critical to the interpretation of the relationship between the two paired events. For example, the actions of entering and then correcting a single-digit answer have different interpretations depending on whether there were intervening information-seeking activities. Therefore, experimental environments should be designed to record any events that might have bearing on the research questions. Third, the size of transition matrices increases exponentially with the number of activity options. To avoid large and complex transition matrices that are difficult to analyze, researchers can collapse a group of fine-grained actions into higher order categories. Whether this shift in the analyzed grain size is appropriate depends largely on the nature of the research question.

Time-based diagrams are an alternative method for analyzing patterns of activity. Kulikowich and Young (2001) used curve-fitting techniques to graph over time a learner's fact-finding and planning activities as they solved a problem. The graphs revealed the periodic nature of the learner's activities. Horney and Anderson-Inmann (1994) developed action code charts to provide a visual overview of a learner's entire interaction with the learning environment with each event type represented by symbols graphed on a timeline. Visualizations of this type can be valuable in providing insight into activity, but can be difficult to compare or aggregate across sessions or users (Jones & Jones, 1997). A problem with both chronological event diagrams and transition matrices is that they do not represent event durations. Developing techniques for coupling patterns of activity with durations has potential to reveal important information about students' strategic interactions in these hypermedia-rich learning environments (Guzdial et al., 1995).

An invaluable but underused component of log file data is that they include a precise record of the timing of every event. This information can be used to infer the duration of time students spend on particular activities (e.g., Andris, 1996; Fitzgerald & Semrau, 1998; Schroeder & Grabowski, 1995), and total or mean time spent studying overall (e.g., Lawless & Kulikowich, 1998; Lickorish & Wright, 1994). Horney and Anderson-Inman (1994) have used time spent on particular activities to code for levels of engagement. Rouet and Passerault (1999) suggest that inferring duration from log file data is important because it cues the researcher to consider what is going on for the learner between logged events and to consider time on task as an important element of engagement. To date, techniques for incorporating duration into the graphing of activity patterns have not been adequately explored. Yet there may be great potential in examining not only the occurrence of events in sequence, but duration and overlap in those events.

To the extent that learning environments afford opportunities to add to and reshape content by highlighting, adding notes, and copying information elsewhere, it becomes important to examine the actual content students develop or work with. To our knowledge this type of analysis has rarely been conducted with computer-generated log files. Fitzgerald and Semrau (1998) coded online text entries collected in log file data. Students were able to create reports, which were written as a part of the problem-solving activities in the program. The reports were scored, and the scores were used in t-tests to find significant differences between groups of learners classified as field dependent, field dependent–mixed, field independent–mixed, or field independent. Hadwin, Boutara, Knoetze, and Thompson (in press) analyzed the depth of content appearing in students' notes and glossary entries to examine changes in depth of processing over time. New technologies such as automatic essay graders may become useful tools for coding and analyzing student-generated content recorded in log files (e.g., Shermis, Mzumara, Olson, & Harrington, 2001; Shermis, Rasmussen, Rajecki, Olson, & Marsiglio, 2001).

To date, some techniques have been developed for examining the frequency, timing, content, and patterns of activity engaged by students; however, with the exception of frequency analysis, these techniques have been successfully implemented only in very simple learning environments over fairly short periods of time. To fulfill the potential of log file analysis, powerful tools must be developed for extracting pertinent information from databases and automatically coding and scoring log data. As computer-supported learning environments develop in complexity, and studies in the field of educational psychology move toward longitudinal data collection across a series of study episodes, these kinds of tools will become necessary for sifting through large logging databases to extract key data required for specific analyses, and automatically categorizing and analyzing data. We highlight some innovative technologies and analytical techniques that have potential for assisting researchers in harnessing this type of data.

Graph theoretical methods are among the most feasible methods of examining log file data derived from complex hypermedia learning environments (Niegemann, 2000; Winne et al., 1994). Winne et al. used graph theory statistics to analyze data in transition matrices. The statistics were programmed in a log file analysis tool (Winne & Nesbit, 1995) and included *density*, a measure of sequential regularity; *structural equivalence*, a measure of the extent to which two actions are used interchangeably relative to other actions; and a measure of the similarity between two transition matrices.

New technologies such as LOGPAT (Richter, Naumann, & Noller, 2003) provide tools for reducing data from log files and conducting single-unit, sequential, and graph theoretic methods for describing user navigation. Sen and Hansen (2003) have begun experimenting with Markov models and Bayesian approaches as means for predicting user Web navigation so as to bring up or "prefetch" relevant pages based on a user's past navigation patterns.

Tools are being developed to support pattern-based sequential analysis extending beyond two-dimensional transitions matrices to more abstract representations. MacSQEAL is a computer program that allows the researcher to transform logged events into more abstract representations and segment the data into sequences (Jones & Jones, 1997). MacSQEAL queries generate a list of items specified to display matching lines and the frequency count for the queried pattern. Similar to frequencies of two-event transitions derived from transition matrices, these frequencies have potential to reveal dominant patterns for one particular participant and groups of participants by applying multidimensional scaling or graph theoretical methods.

TRENDS IN REPORTING RESEARCH OUTCOMES

The past decade has seen remarkable changes in the editorial policies of major journals toward increased reporting of effect sizes, confidence intervals, and reliability measures. Part of a broad movement in social science research, this shift is primarily a reaction to the misinterpretation and inherent limitations of null hypothesis significance testing, and common misconceptions about the reliability of test scores. The direction for these changes in reporting practice is apparently being set by the continuing success of effect-size meta-analysis (Lipsey & Wilson, 2001) and more recent innovations in reliability meta-analysis (Vacha-Haase, Henson, & Caruso, 2002).

Recognizing the Limitations of Null Hypothesis Significance Testing (NHST)

Textbooks and classes on educational research methodology continue to train researchers to define a null hypothesis and use it to frame specific research questions. The researcher is taught to set a null hypothesis that the difference in the mean performance of two populations is exactly zero. Then the researcher determines the probability of the sampled data assuming that the null hypothesis of zero difference between population means is true. If that probability is sufficiently low (e.g., $p < .05$) the null hypothesis is rejected. If the probability is not low enough to reject the null hypothesis, a researcher who is strictly following the logic of NHST is unable to claim any increment in knowledge except that the approach to the research problem must be redesigned or abandoned.

The essential objections to NHST began to appear with some frequency in the 1960s (Bakan, 1966; Lykken, 1968; Meehl, 1967; Rozeboom, 1960) and have been carried forward with little modification. These are that NHST (a) is very often misused and misinterpreted by researchers, (b) promotes unvarying application of an arbitrary probability threshold, (c) yields too little information about the data, and (d) emphasizes the direction of effects, shifting attention away from their size and practical or scientific significance.

Cohen (1994) argued that what researchers really want, and often think they are getting with NHST, is the probability of a hypothesis given the data. This is incorrect because they are actually getting the probability of the data given a hypothesis. When the null hypothesis is rejected with $p < .05$, it is misleading to claim that there is less than 5 percent chance that the null hypothesis is true. The correct interpretation is that, assuming the null hypothesis, there is less than a 5 percent chance of obtaining the observed data. In the other case, when $p > .05$, it is wrong to claim that there is a greater than 5 percent chance that the null is true or that the null can be accepted. The correct interpretation is that, assuming the null hypothesis, the chance of obtaining the observed data is greater than 5 percent. It is not unusual to find explicit commission of NHST misinterpretations in published reports and dissertations (Finch, Cumming & Thomason, 2001; Oaks, 1986). Even more frequently, though, authors allow these misconceptions to subtly condition their interpretation of findings. They may erroneously interpret failure to reject the null as evidence that the hypothesis of zero difference is more probable than the observed effect size. They often fail to recognize low statistical power as a possible reason for inability to reject the null hypothesis.

In the real world, the effects of any two treatments, or the means of large populations, are virtually never identical. As Tukey (1991) put it, "They are always different—for some decimal place." As long as one has a large enough sample size, enough statistical power, NHST almost always allows us to reject the null hypothesis. Because the p-value obtained from a significance test is highly dependent on sample size, in general it should not be used to convey the magnitude of an effect. Reporting effect sizes is a potent remedy to misinterpretations and limitations of NHST because it shifts attention to the practical significance of effect, and helps interpret the outcome of the significance test.

Reporting Effect Sizes

There is now wide agreement[1] in psychology and education that researchers should report effect sizes (Wilkinson & APA Task Force on Statistical Inference, 1999). According to the APA manual, "It is almost always necessary to include some index of effect size or strength of relationship in your Results section" (American Psychological Association, 2001, p. 25). Effect sizes can be divided into those expressed in the original units of observation and those that are generalizable across different tests measuring the same construct. The former category includes the difference between mean scores on a widely used cognitive ability test and a regression coefficient for, say, estimating income from years of formal education. The latter category includes "scale-free" effect sizes such as the correlation coefficient, the standardized mean difference[2] (Cohen, 1988), and many others (Olejnik & Algina, 2000). In an ideal world, educational psychologists might work entirely with common, raw metrics and never need to make the round trip from observation, to scale-free representation, and back to practical application. In reality the use of local, researcher-constructed measures in educational psychology often necessitates the reporting of standardized, scale-free effect sizes. Researchers should report effect sizes in forms that best accommodate replication, reanalysis, and application of findings.

Normally, standardized effect sizes should be reported regardless of statistical significance. Further, meta-analytical aggregation and comparison of effect sizes across different studies (Lipsey & Wilson, 2001) need not be restricted to large-scale literature reviews. In addition to reporting an effect size for the data in hand, empirical studies can place their results in the context of previous work by calculating a pooled effect size integrating the new data with previously published effect sizes (Thompson, 2002). For both singular and aggregated effect sizes, it is ultimately the responsibility of the consumer of research information, who is likely to be more aware of the local costs of implementation and benefits associated with an effect size, to determine whether the magnitude and certainty reported by the researcher warrants a change in policy or practice. If the cost of two alternative treatments is similar, the practitioner may justifiably use the research results to select the treatment found to be more beneficial in the sample, even if the effect is not statistically significant at the customary .05 level.

Reporting Confidence Intervals

Confidence intervals are now being widely advocated as an alternative or companion to traditional NHST. The *Publication Manual of the APA* (5th edition) states, "Because confidence intervals combine information on location and precision and can often be directly used to infer significance levels, they are, in general, the best reporting strategy. The use of confidence intervals is therefore strongly recommended" (American Psychological Association, 2001, p. 22). A confidence interval (CI) is a range of values that is likely to include a population parameter of interest. If a large number of samples are drawn from a population and each is used to construct

---

[1] Wainer and Robinson (2003) identified special situations in which effect sizes are unavailable or inappropriate. Robinson and Levin (1997) maintained that effect sizes should only be discussed after the effect has passed a test of statistical significance. Criticizing their position, Cahan (2000) advocated that effect sizes be reported with confidence intervals to prevent readers from being misled by sampling error.

[2] The standardized mean difference effect size is usually calculated as

$$d = \frac{\overline{X_1} - \overline{X_2}}{SD_{pooled}}$$

a 95 percent confidence interval, then 95 percent of the intervals will include the population mean. The width of the interval can be decreased by lowering the confidence level (e.g., from 95 to 90 percent) or increasing the sample size. Confidence intervals improve on traditional reporting practices because they emphasize the size and precision of effects.

In recent years, major journals publishing quantitative educational psychology research have modified their editorial policies to require reporting of effect sizes, and, under the influence of the fifth edition of the APA manual, many journals will likely recommend CI reporting. However, empirical studies of research reporting practices indicate that, by themselves, adjustments to editorial policy are insufficient to bring about the deeper changes to research culture that are being advocated by methodologists. In the words of Fidler, Thomason, Cumming, Finch, & Leeman (2004), "Editors can lead researchers to confidence intervals but can't make them think." In a survey of medical journals they found that compliance with new confidence interval reporting policies in those journals tended to be superficial. Authors often reported CIs in the results section but focused on statistical significance in the discussion section. CIs were most often treated as an alternate method for conducting NHST. To effect changes in the way researchers think, there must be revisions to curricula, textbooks, and statistical analysis software to facilitate the calculation, graphing, and interpretation of effect sizes and CIs.

Score Reliability Issues

Score reliability is important in educational psychology research because it affects statistical power and the precision of research outcomes. Lower reliability increases the width of CIs around direct effect sizes such as mean differences, attenuates standardized effect sizes such as d and r, and increases the p-values obtained from NHST. Psychometric reliability is dependent on measurement error from many sources in the testing process including the test form, the respondents, the setting, and the testing procedure.

With the coalescing of belief among methodologists that reliability should be regarded as a property of scores rather than tests (Joint Committee on Standards for Educational Evaluation, 1994), there has been some debate about whether it is proper to speak of "test reliability" (Sawilowsky, 2000a, 2000b; Thompson & Vacha-Haase, 2000). The core of the problem is a tendency for researchers to treat measurement error associated with the form and content of the test as the sole determinant of score reliability, neglecting error arising from other elements of the measurement process. It has been commonplace for researchers to cite a reliability coefficient published in a test manual but fail to report the reliability of their own data. The misconception that underlies this practice has been given the term *reliability induction* (Vacha-Haase, Henson, & Caruso, 2002). One possible consequence of the reliability induction misconception is a failure to recognize that a low effect size or nonsignificant NHST may be due to measurement error associated with the sample or testing procedure. The recommended remedy is for researchers to appropriately report score reliability and discuss it when interpreting their results.

Reporting Reliability

Cronbach's alpha and test-retest correlations are by far the most commonly reported reliability indices, together comprising more than 85 percent of the instances appearing in the research literatures of education, psychology, and sociology (Hogan, Benjamin, & Brezinski, 2000). Alpha is a measure of internal consistency, the degree to which a set of item scores measures the same construct. Test-retest reliability, on the other hand, shows the replicability of measurement in face of transitory, extraneous conditions. It is perhaps underappreciated that these two forms of score reliability detect different, additive sources of measurement error (Henson, 2001). Whenever practical, both internal consistency and test-retest reliability should be reported for the observed scores.

Wilkinson and the APA Task Force (1999) concluded that reporting reliability goes hand-in-hand with reporting effect sizes: "Authors should provide reliability coefficients of the scores for the data being analyzed even when the focus of their research is not psychometric. Interpreting the size of observed effects requires an assessment of the reliability of the scores" (p. 596). In interpreting results, researchers should consider low reliability as a possible explanation for poor precision evident in confidence intervals about means, lower than expected standardized effect sizes, or failure to reject the null hypothesis. Reporting confidence intervals about reliability coefficients is rare but highly recommended (Fan & Thompson, 2001).

What constitutes acceptable score reliability, or even whether such a threshold can be reasonably defined, is an enduring psychometric question. Although several somewhat different standards have been advocated (Charter, 2003), it is commonly held that for research purposes the lowest acceptable internal consistency estimate is .80, and the minimum for educational placement or treatment decisions is .90 (Nunnally & Bernstein, 1994). These thresholds are arbitrary and not produced by analysis of the prevalence and cost of wrong decisions resulting from measurement error; parameters that one presumes would vary widely across situations. An alternative is to take a normative perspective and describe reliability estimates relative to what is known about the distribution of reliabilities in education and psychology research (Charter, 2003; Hogan, Benjamin, & Brezinski, 2000). Charter found median values for the alpha and test-retest indices at .84 and .81, respectively. He showed that internal consistency varied according to the type of test, with a median of .91 for achievement scores, .85 for attitude scores, and .78 for personality scores. As an example of normative reliability reporting, a researcher gathering data with an attitude instrument might describe reliabilities below .77 as "low" and reliabilities above .90 as "high" because these approximately constitute the top and bottom quartiles in the distribution for attitude score reliabilities reported by Charter.

Reliability Generalization: A New Kind of Meta-analysis

Reliability generalization, an approach to analyzing variation in score reliability across studies, was pioneered by Vacha-Haase (1998). Reliability generalization is proving increasingly important in understanding how characteristics of a study, instrument, and respondents determine the precision with which different constructs can be measured. A reliability generalization study of Kolb's Learning Style Inventory (LSI) by Henson and Hwang (2002) illustrates the value of this method.

The Learning Style Inventory (LSI) was released in three versions between 1976 and 1985. It profiles a respondent on four subscales (concrete, reflective, active, and abstract), that are used to calculate two learning style dimensions: abstract conceptualization versus concrete experience, and active experimentation versus reflective observation. Henson and Hwang found that, of 110 studies that used the LSI, 54 percent failed to mention reliability at all, 14 percent cited prior reliability estimates from prior studies or the test manual, and only 31 percent reported reliability of the observed scores. Figure 36.2 uses box and whisker plots to show the distribution of alpha and test-retest coefficients for the each of the four LSI subscales and two dimensions. The median test-retest coefficients, shown as horizontal bars in the shaded boxes, are particularly low. Further analysis showed that test version was the greatest source of variability in internal consistency and test-retest reliability, with higher reliabilities observed for the two later versions. Also, some variability was attributable to respondent charac-

teristics. Henson and Hwang concluded that without further revision, the low reliability of the LSI makes it unsuitable for most applications. This view is consistent with other critics of the LSI who have recommended that its use as a diagnostic instrument be discontinued (Atkinson, 1991).

EMERGING THEMES

In this chapter we have reviewed research methodology issues and innovations in five broad categories: (1) match of observational grain size to research question, specifically observation of fine-grained, longitudinal, and social interaction events; (2) assessment of the psychological constructs of interest, cognitive load, and knowledge transfer; (3) assessment of learner knowledge with concept maps and portfolios; (4) data collection on the Web and in interactive learning environments; and (5) trends in reporting quantitative research results and reliability statistics. We believe that several themes emerge across and within these categories that are indicative of current directions in the research methodologies of educational psychology.

An emergent theme evident within the last section is the aggregation of data from separately published studies. Influenced by the success of formal effect size meta-analyses, researchers are now aggregating score reliabilities, and some (e.g., Thompson, 2002) are advocating a smaller-scale, localized form of meta-analysis in which authors of an empirical study combine their results (pool their effect sizes) with those of similar previous studies.

Another emergent theme is the quantitative analysis of qualitatively coded verbalizations to describe knowledge gained through learning. This approach is perhaps typified in the method explained by Chi (1997), but appears in different forms in other work reviewed in this chapter (e.g., Gentner, Loewenstein, & Thompson, 2003; Hmelo-Silver, 2003). As suggested in our introduction, this integrated methodology forms an important bridge between the cultures of quantitative and qualitative educational research.

A third theme, traversing several sections of this review, is innovation in the visual representation of cognition, behavior, and social interaction. This was evident in the CORD diagrams of Luckin (2003) and Hmelo-Silver (2003), the use of concept maps and semantic networks for representing learner knowledge, and the use of graph diagrams to interpret log file data.

After discussing the rationale for gathering intratask data in the section on grain size, we showed how intratask methods are being used to assess interest (Ainley et al., 2002) and cognitive load (Brüenken, Plass &

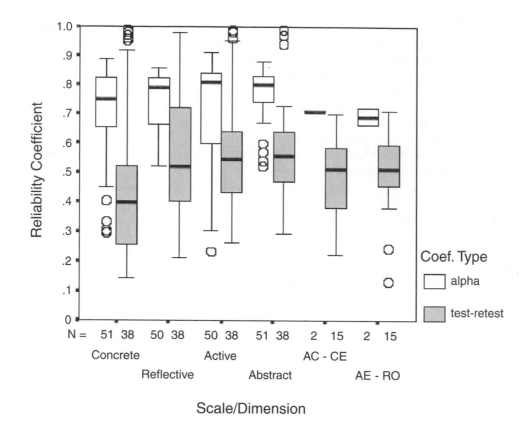

FIGURE 36.2. Distributions of alpha and test-retest coefficients for subscales and dimensions of Kolb's Learning Style Inventory from a reliability generalization study by Henson and Hwang (2002). The dimensions are AC–CE (abstract Conceptualization–concrete experience) and AE–RO (active experimentation–reflective observation). Reprinted with permission of the author.

Leutner, 2003; Van Gerven et al., 2003). The theme of intratask observation is also apparent in our review of log file analysis methods for research on problem solving (Lajoie et al., 2001) and self-regulation (Winne et al., 2003) in interactive learning environments.

Finally, in work featuring interactive learning environments (e.g., Kulikowich & Young, 2001; Lajoie et al., 2001), there is evidence of the trend toward design-based research. Sandoval and Bell (2004) defined design-based research as "theoretically framed, empirical research of

learning and teaching based on particular designs for instruction" and noted that it "simultaneously pursues the goals of developing effective learning environments and using such environments as natural laboratories to study learning and teaching" (p. 200). As a theoretically pluralistic enterprise with a focus on sustained educational innovation (Bell, 2004), we believe design-based research can serve as an excellent site for recombining and adapting many of the research methods reviewed in this chapter to create more potent research tools.

References

Ainley, M., Hidi, S., & Berndorff, D. (2002). Interest, learning, and the psychological processes that mediate their relationship. *Journal of Educational Psychology, 94*, 545–561.

American Psychological Association. (2001). *Publication manual of the American Psychological Association* (5th ed.). Washington, DC: Author.

Andris, J. F. (1996). The relationship of indices of student navigational patterns in a hypermedia geology lab simulation to two measures of learning style. *Journal of Educational Multimedia and Hypermedia, 5*, 303–315.

Atkinson, G. (1991). Kolb's Learning Style Inventory: A practitioner's perspective. *Measurement and Evaluation in Counseling and Development, 23*, 149–161.

Azevedo, R., Cromley, J. G., & Seibert, D. (2004). Does adaptive scaffolding facilitate students' ability to regulate their learning with hypermedia? *Contemporary Educational Psychology, 29*, 344-370.

Baddeley, A. D., & Logie, R. H. (1999). Working memory: The multiple-component model. In A. Miyake & P. Shah (Eds.), *Models of working memory: Mechanisms of active maintenance and executive control* (pp. 28-61). Cambridge, UK: Cambridge University Press.

Bakan, D. (1966). The test of significance in psychological research. *Psychological Bulletin, 66*, 1-29.

Barab, S. A., Bowdish, B. E., & Lawless, K. A. (1997). Hypermedia navigation: Profiles of hypermedia users. *Educational Technology Research and Development, 45*(3), 23-41.

Barab, S. A., Evans, M. A., & Back, E.-O. (2004). Activity theory as a lens for characterizing the participatory unit. In D. H. Jonassen (Ed.), *Handbook of research on educational communications and technology* (pp. 199-214). Mahwah, NJ: Lawrence Erlbaum Associates.

Barnett, S. M., & Ceci, S. J. (2002). When and where do we apply what we learn? A taxonomy for far transfer. *Psychological Bulletin, 128*, 612-637.

Barootchi, N., & Keshavarz, M. H. (2002). Assessment of achievement through portfolios and teacher-made tests. *Educational Research, 44*, 279-278.

Beasley, R. E., & Waugh, M. L. (1997). Predominant initial and review patterns of navigation in a fully constrained hypermedia hierarchy: An empirical study. *Journal of Educational Multimedia and Hypermedia, 6*, 155-172.

Bell, P. (2004). On the theoretical breadth of design-based research in education. *Educational Psychologist, 39*, 243-253.

Birnbaum, M. H. (2004). Human research and data collection via the internet. *Annual Review of Psychology, 55*, 803-832.

Borsboom, D., Mellenbergh, G. J., & van Heerden, J. (2003). The theoretical status of latent variables. *Psychological Review, 110*, 203-219.

Brüenken, R., Plass, J. L., & Leutner, D. (2003). Direct measurement of cognitive load in multimedia learning. *Educational Psychologist, 38*, 53-61.

Buchanan, T., & Smith, J. L. (1999). Using the Internet for psychological research: Personality testing on the World Wide Web. *British Journal of Psychology, 90*, 125-144.

Cahan, S. (2000). Statistical significance is not a "kosher certificate" for observed effects: A critical analysis of the two-step approach to the evaluation of empirical results. *Educational Researcher, 29*(1), 31-34.

Carroll, J. M., Neale, D. C., Isenhour, P. L., Rosson, M. B., & McCrickard, D. S. (2003). Notification and awareness: Synchronizing task-oriented collaborative activity. *International Journal of Human-Computer Studies, 58*, 605-632.

Charter, R. A. (2003). A breakdown of reliability coefficients by test type and reliability method, and the clinical implications of low reliability. *Journal of General Psychology, 130*, 290-304.

Chen, C. M. & Morris, S. (2003). Visualizing evolving networks: Minimum spanning trees versus Pathfinder networks. *IEEE Symposium on Information Visualization (InfoVis'03),* 67-74.

Chi, M. T. H. (1997). Quantifying qualitative analyses of verbal data: A practical guide. *Journal of the Learning Sciences, 6*, 271-315.

Cohen, J. (1988). *Statistical power analysis for the behavioral sciences* (2nd ed.). Hillsdale, NJ: Lawrence Erlbaum Associates.

Cohen, J. (1994). The earth is round ($p < .05$). *American Psychologist, 49*, 997-1003.

Davis, M. H., Friedman, M., Harden, R. M., Howie, P., Ker, J., McGhee, C., et al. (2001). Portfolio assessment in medical students' final examinations. *Medical Teacher, 23*, 357-366.

De Simone, C., Schmid, R. F., & McEwen, L. A. (2001). Supporting the learning process with collaborative concept mapping using computer-based communication tools and processes. *Educational Research and Evaluation, 7*, 263-283.

Detterman, D. K. (1993). The case for the prosecution: Transfer as an epiphenomenon. In D. K. Detterman & R. J. Sternberg (Eds.), *Transfer on trial: Intelligence, cognition, and instruction* (pp. 1-24). Norwood, NJ: Ablex.

Diaz, R. M., Neal, C. J., & Amaya-Williams, M. (1990). The social origins of self-regulation. In L. Moll (Ed.), *Vygotsky and education: Instructional implications and applications of sociohistorical psychology* (pp. 127-154). Cambridge, UK: Cambridge University Press.

Elliot, A. J., & McGregor, H. A. (2001). A 2 * 2 achievement goal framework. *Journal of Personality and Social Psychology, 80*, 501-519.

Fan, X., & Thompson, B. (2001). Confidence intervals about score reliability coefficients, please: An EPM guidelines editorial. *Educational and Psychological Measurement, 61*, 517-531.

Fidler, F., Thomason, N., Cumming, G., Finch, S., & Leeman, J. (2004). Editors can lead researchers to confidence intervals, but can't make them think. *Psychological Science, 15*, 119-126.

Finch, S., Cumming, G., & Thomason, N (2001). Reporting of statistical inference in the *Journal of Applied Psychology*: Little evidence of reform. *Educational and Psychological Measurement, 61*, 181-210.

Fink, A., & Neubauer, A. C. (2001). Speed of information processing, psychometric intelligence and time estimation as an index of cognitive load. *Personality and Individual Differences, 30*, 1009-1021.

Fitzgerald, G. E., & Semrau, L. P. (1998). The effects of learner differences on usage patterns and learning outcomes with hypermedia case studies. *Journal of Educational Multimedia and Hypermedia, 7*, 309-331.

Fjeld, M., Schluep, S., & Rauterberg, M. (1998). Automatic, action driven classification of user problem solving strategies by statistical and analytical methods: A comparative study. In F. E. Ritter & R. M. Young (Eds.), *Proceedings of the Second European Conference on Cognitive Modelling* (pp. 98-103). Nottingham, UK: Nottingham University Press.

Gallimore, R., & Tharpe, R. (1990). Teaching mind in society: Teaching schooling and literate discourse. In L.C. Moll (Ed.),

Vygotsky and education: Instructional implications and applications of sociohistorical psychology (pp. 175–205). Cambridge, UK: Cambridge University Press.

Gentile, C. A., Martin-Rehrmann, J., & Kennedy, J. H. (1995). *Windows into the classroom: NAEP's 1992 writing portfolio study*. Washington, DC: National Center for Education Statistics.

Gentner, D., Loewenstein, J. & Thompson, L. (2003). Learning and transfer: A general role for analogical encoding. *Journal of Educational Psychology, 95*, 393–408.

Gevins, A., & Smith, M. E. (2003). Neurophysiological measures of cognitive workload during human–computer interaction. *Theoretical Issues in Ergonomics Science, 4*, 113–131.

Gonzalvo, P., Cañas, J. J., & Bajo, M. (1994). Structural representations in knowledge acquisition. *Journal of Educational Psychology, 86*, 601–616.

Gosling, S. D., Vazire, S., & Srivastava, S. (2004). Should we trust Web-based studies? A comparative analysis of six preconceptions about internet questionnaires. *American Psychologist, 59*, 93–104.

Granholm, E., & Steinhauer, S. R. (2004). Pupillometric measures of cognitive and emotional processes. *International Journal of Psychophysiology, 52*, 1–6.

Gross, J. L., & Yellen, J. (1998). *Graph theory and its applications*. London: CRC Press.

Guzdial, M., Berger, C., Jones, T., Horney, M., Anderson–Inman, L., Winne, P. H., et al. (1995). *Analyzing student use of educational software with event recordings*. Unpublished manuscript, Georgia Institute of Technology, Atlanta.

Hadwin, A. F., Boutara, L., Knoetze, T., & Thompson, S. (in press). Cross case study of self-regulation as a series of events. *Educational Research and Evaluation.*

Hadwin, A. F., Winne, P. H., Stockley, D. B., Nesbit, J., & Woszczyna, C. (2001). Context moderates students' self-reports about how they study. *Journal of Educational Psychology, 93*, 477–487.

Hall, R. H., Dansereau, D. F., & Skaggs, L. P. (1992). Knowledge maps and the presentation of related information domains. *Journal of Experimental Education, 61*, 5–18.

Halpern, D. F. (1998). Teaching critical thinking for transfer across domains. *American Psychologist, 53*, 449–455.

Henson, R. K. (2001). Understanding internal consistency reliability estimates: A conceptual primer on coefficient alpha. *Measurement and Evaluation in Counseling and Development, 34*, 177–189.

Henson, R. K., & Hwang, D.-Y. (2002). Variability and prediction of measurement error in Kolb's learning style inventory scores: A reliability generalization study. *Educational and Psychological Measurement, 62*, 712–727.

Hmelo-Silver, C. E. (2003). Analyzing collaborative knowledge construction: Multiple methods for integrating understanding. *Computers and Education, 41*, 397–420.

Hofer, B. K. (2004). Epistemological understanding as a metacognitive process: Thinking aloud during online searching. *Educational Psychologist, 39*, 43–55.

Hogan, T. P., Benjamin, A., & Brezinski, K. L. (2000). Reliability methods: A note on the frequency of use of various types. *Educational and Psychological Measurement, 60*, 523–531.

Horney, M. A., & Anderson-Inman, L. (1994). The ElectroText project: Hypertext reading patterns of middle school students. *Journal of Educational Multimedia and Hypermedia, 3*, 71–91.

Horton, P. B., McConney, A. A., Gallo, M., Woods, A. L., Senn, G. J., & Hamelin, D. (1993). An investigation of the effectiveness of concept mapping as an instructional tool. *Science Education, 77*, 95–111.

Jackson, J. W. (2002). Enhancing self-efficacy and learning performance. *Journal of Experimental Education, 70*, 243–254.

Joint Committee on Standards for Educational Evaluation. (1994). *The program evaluation standards: How to assess evaluations of educational programs* (2nd ed.). Thousand Oaks, CA: Sage.

Jones, T., & Jones, M. (1997). MacSQEAL: A tool for exploration of hypermedia log file sequences. In T. Müldner & T. C. Reeves, *Proceedings of Ed-Media 1997* (pp. 709–716). Charlottesville, VA: AACE.

Kalyuga, S., Ayres, P., Chandler, P., & Sweller, J. (2003). The expertise reversal effect. *Educational Psychologist, 38*, 23–31.

Karasavvidis, I., Pieters, J. M., & Plomp, T. (2000). Investigating how secondary school students learn to solve correlational problems: Quantitative and qualitative discourse approaches to the development of self-regulation. *Learning and Instruction, 10*, 267–292.

Kecklund, G., & Akerstedt, T. (1993). Sleepiness in long distance truck driving: An ambulatory EEG study of night driving. *Ergonomics, 36*, 1007–1017.

Kelly, A. E., & O'Donnell, A. (1994). Hypertext and the study strategies of preservice teachers: Issues in instructional hypertext design. *Journal of Educational Computing Research, 10*, 373–387.

Klein, S. P., McCaffrey, D., Stecher, B., & Koretz, D. (1995). The reliability of mathematics portfolio scores: Lessons from the Vermont experience. *Applied Measurement in Education, 8*, 243–260.

Knapp, F., & Heidingsfelder, M. (2001). Drop-out analysis: Effects of the survey design. In U.-D. Reips & M. Bosnjak (Eds.), *Dimensions of Internet Science* (pp. 221–230). Lengerich, Germany: Pabst Science Publishers.

Koretz, D. (1998). Large-scale assessments in the U.S.: Evidence pertaining to the quality of measurement. *Assessment in Education: Principles, Policy & Practice, 5*, 309–335.

Koretz, D., Stecher, B., Klein, S., & McCaffrey, D. (1994). The Vermont portfolio assessment program: Findings and implications. *Educational Measurement: Issues and Practice, 13*(3), 5–16.

Krantz, J. H., & Dalal, R. (2000). Validity of Web-based psychological research. In M. H. Birnbaum (Ed.). *Psychological experiments on the Internet* (pp. 35–60). San Diego, CA: Academic Press.

Kulikowich, J. M., & Young, M. F. (2001). Locating an ecological psychology methodology for situated action. *Journal of the Learning Sciences, 10*, 165–202.

Lajoie, S. P., Lavigne, N. C., Guerrera, C., & Munsie, S. D. (2001). Constructing knowledge in the context of BioWorld. *Instructional Science, 29*, 155–186.

Lamberts, J., van den Broek, P. L. C., & Bener, L. (2000). Correlation dimension of the human electroencephalogram corresponds with cognitive load. *Neuropsychobiology, 41*, 149–153.

Lawless, K. A., & Kulikowich, J. M. (1996). Understanding hypertext navigation through cluster analysis. *Journal of Educational Computing Research, 14*, 385–399.

Lawless, K. A., & Kulikowich, J. M. (1998). Domain knowledge, interest, and hypertext navigation: A study of individual differences. *Journal of Educational Multimedia and Hypermedia, 7*, 51–69.

Leard, T., & Hadwin, A. F. (2001). Logfile analysis: A review of the literature. In A. F. Hadwin (organizer). *Logfile navigation profiles and analysis: Methods for tracking and examining hypermedia navigation.* Symposium presented the Annual Meeting of the American Educational Research Association: Seattle, WA.

Lickorish, A., & Wright, P. (1994). Menus and memory load: Navigation strategies in interactive search tasks. *International Journal of Human–Computer Studies, 40*, 965–1008.

Lipsey, M. W., & Wilson, D. B. (2001). *Practical meta-analysis.* Thousand Oaks, CA: Sage.

Luckin, R. (2003). Between the lines: Documenting the multiple dimensions of computer supported collaborations. *Computers and Education, 41*, 397–420.

Lykken, D. E. (1968). Statistical significance in psychological research. *Psychological Bulletin, 70*, 151–159.

MacGregor, S. K. (1999). Hypermedia navigation profiles: Cognitive characteristics and information processing strategies. *Journal of Educational Computing Research, 20*, 189–206.

Marchionini, G. (1989). Information–seeking strategies of novices using a full-text electronic encyclopedia. *Journal of the American Society for Information Science, 40*, 54–66.

Marchionini, G. (1990). Evaluating hypermedia–based learning. In D. H. Jonassen & H. Mandl (Eds.), *Designing hypermedia for learning* (pp. 355–373). Berlin: Springer-Verlag.

Martin, J. (2004). Self-regulated learning, social cognitive theory, and agency. *Educational Psychologist, 39*, 135–145.

Martin, J., & Sugarman, J. (1996). Bridging social constructionism and cognitive constructivism: A psychology of human possibility and constraint. *Journal of Mind and Behavior, 17*, 291–320.

Mayer, R. E. (2001). *Multimedia learning.* Cambridge, UK: Cambridge University Press.

Mayer, R. E., & Anderson, R. B. (1992). The instructive animation: Helping students build connections between words and pictures in multimedia learning. *Journal of Educational Psychology, 84*, 444–452.

McBee, M. M., & Barnes, L. L. B. (1998). The generalizability of a performance assessment measuring achievement in eighth grade mathematics. *Measurement in Education, 11*, 179–94.

McClure, J. R., Sonak B., & Suen H. K. (1999). Concept map assessment of classroom learning: reliability, validity, and logistical practicality. *Journal of Research in Science Teaching, 36*, 475–492.

McDaniel, M. A., Waddill, P. J., Finstad, K., & Bourg, T. (2000). The effects of text-based interest on attention and recall. *Journal of Educational Psychology, 92*, 492–502.

Meehl, P. E. (1967). Theory testing in psychology and physics: A methodological paradox. *Philosophy of Science, 34*, 103–115.

Meistad, Ø., & Wasson, B. (2000). Supporting collaborative tele-learning research using server logs. In J. Bourdeau & R. Heller (Eds.), *Proceedings of Ed–Media 2000* (pp. 679–684). Charlottesville, VA: AACE.

Meyer, D. K., & Turner, J. C. (2002). Using instructional discourse analysis to study the scaffolding of student self-regulation. *Educational Psychologist, 37*, 17–25.

Misanchuk, E. R., & Schwier, R. A. (1992). Representing interactive multimedia and hypermedia audit trails. *Journal of Educational Multimedia and Hypermedia, 1*, 355–372.

Murphy, P. K., & Alexander, P. A. (2002). What counts? The predictive powers of subject-matter knowledge, strategic processing, and interest in domain-specific performance. *Journal of Experimental Education, 70*, 197–214.

Nesbit, J. C., & Adesope, O. O. (2005). *Effects of concept and knowledge maps: A meta-analysis.* Annual meeting of the American Educational Research Association, Montreal.

Niegemann, H. M. (2000). *Analyzing processes of self-regulated hypermedia-supported learning: On the development of a log-file analysis procedure.* Paper presented at the Annual Meeting of the American Educational Research Association, New Orleans, LA.

Novak, J. D., & Gowin, D. B. (1984). *Learning how to learn.* New York, NY: Cambridge University Press.

Nunnally, J. C., & Bernstein, I. H. (1994). *Psychometric theory* (3rd ed.). New York: McGraw-Hill.

Nurmela, K., Lehtinen, E., & Palonen, T. (1999). *Evaluating CSCL log files by social network analysis.* Paper presented at the Computer Supported Collaborative Learning Conference, Stanford, CA.

O'Connor, M. C. (1998). Can we trace the efficacy of social constructivism? *Review of Research in Education, 23*, 25–72.

Oaks, M. (1986). *Statistical inference: A commentary for the social and behavioral sciences.* New York: Wiley.

Olejnik, S., & Algina, J. (2000). Measures of effect size for comparative studies: Applications, interpretations, and limitations. *Contemporary Educational Psychology, 25*, 241–286.

Paas, F., Tuovinen, J. E., & Tabbers, H. (2003). Cognitive load measurement as a means to advance cognitive load theory. *Educational Psychologist, 38*, 63–71.

Paas, F., van Merriënboer, J. J. G., & Adam, J. J. (1994). Measurement of cognitive load in instructional research. *Perceptual and Motor Skills, 79*, 419–430.

Park, C. L., Armeli, S., Tennen, H. (2004). Appraisal-coping goodness of fit: A daily internet study. *Personality and Social Psychology Bulletin, 30*, 558–569.

Pasveer, K. A. & Ellard, J. H. (1998). The making of a personality inventory: Help from the WWW. *Behavior Research Methods, Instruments, & Computers, 30*, 309–313.

Pearsall, N. R., Skipper, J., & Mintzes, J. J. (1997). Knowledge restructuring in the life sciences: A longitudinal study of conceptual change in biology. *Science Education, 81*, 193–215.

Perkins, D. N., & Grotzer, T. A. (1997). Teaching intelligence. *American Psychologist, 52*, 1125–1133.

Perry, N. E. (1998). Young children's self-regulated learning and contexts that support it. *Journal of Educational Psychology, 90*, 715–729.

Pintrich, P. R., Smith, D. A. F., Garcia, T., & McKeachie, W. (1991). *A manual for the use of the Motivated Strategies for Learning Questionnaire.* Ann Arbor, MI: University of Michigan.

Pintrich, P. R., Wolters, C. A., & Baxter, G. P. (2000). Assessing metacognition and self-regulated learning. In G. Schraw & J. C. Impara (Eds.), *Issues in the measurement of metacognition* (pp. 43–97). Lincoln, NE: Buros Institute of Mental Measurements.

Pitts, J., Coles, C., & Thomas, P. (1999). Educational portfolios in the assessment of general practice trainers: Reliability of assessors. *Medical Education, 33*, 515–520.

Rauterberg, M. (1993). AMME: An automatic mental model evaluation to analyse user behavior traced in a finite, discrete state space. *Ergonomic, 36*, 1369–1380.

Reips, U.-D. (2001). The Web experimental psychology lab: Five years of data collection on the Internet. *Behavior Research Methods, Instruments, & Computers, 33*, 201–211.

Richman, W. L., Kiesler, S., Weisband, S. & Drasgow, F. (1999). A meta-analytic study of social desirability distortion in computer-administered questionnaires, traditional questionnaires, and interviews. *Journal of Applied Psychology, 84*, 754–775.

Richter, T., Naumann, J., & Noller, S. (2003). LOGPAT: A semiautomatic way to analyze hypertext navigation behavior. *Swiss Journal of Psychology, 62*, 113–120.

Roberts, C., Newble, D. I., & O'Rourke, A. J. (2002). Commentaries: Portfolio-based assessments in medical education: Are they valid and reliable for summative purposes? *Medical Education, 36*, 899–900.

Robinson, D. H., & Levin, J. R. (1997). Reflections on statistical and substantive significance. *Educational Researcher, 26*, 21–29.

Rouet, J.-F., & Passerault, J.-M. (1999). Analyzing learner-hypermedia interaction: An overview of online methods. *Instructional Science, 27*, 201–219.

Rozeboom, W. W. (1960). The fallacy of the null hypothesis significance test. *Psychological Bulletin, 57*, 416–428.

Ruiz-Primo, M. A., & Shavelson, R. J. (1996). Problems and issues in the use of concept maps in science assessment. *Journal of Research in Science Teaching, 33*, 569–600.

Salomon, G., & Perkins, D. N. (1998). Individual and social aspects of learning? *Review of Research in Education, 23*, 1–24.

Sandoval, W. A., & Bell, P. (2004). Design-based research methods for studying learning in context: Introduction. *Educational Psychologist, 39*, 199–201.

Sawilowsky, S. S. (2000a). Psychometrics versus datametrics: Comment on Vacha-Haase's "Reliability Generalization" method and some EPM editorial policies. *Educational and Psychological Measurement, 60*, 157–173.

Sawilowsky, S. S. (2000b). Reliability: Rejoinder to Thompson and Vacha-Haase. *Educational and Psychological Measurement, 60*, 196–200.

Scharl, A. (2001). Explanation and exploration: Visualizing the topology of Web information systems. *International Journal of Human-Computer Studies, 55*, 239–258.

Schraw, G. (2000). Assessing metacognition: Implications of the Buros Institute. In G. Schraw & J. C. Impara (Eds.), *Issues in the measurement of metacognition* (pp. 297–321). Lincoln, NE: Buros Institute of Mental Measurements.

Schroeder, E. E., & Grabowski, B. L. (1995). Patterns of exploration and learning with hypermedia. *Journal of Educational Computing Research, 13*, 313–335.

Schvaneveldt, R. W. (Ed.). (1990). *Pathfinder associative networks: Studies in knowledge organization.* Norwood, NJ: Ablex.

Scott, J. P. (2000). *Social network analysis: A handbook.* London: Sage.

Sen, A. I. (2002). Concept maps as a research and evaluation tool to assess conceptual change in quantum physics. *Science Education International, 13*(4), 14–24.

Sen, R., & Hansen, M. H. (2003). Predicting Web users' next access based on log data. *Journal of Computational and Graphical Statistics, 12*, 143–156.

Shaffer, D. W., & Serlin, R. C. (2004). What good are statistics that don't generalize? *Educational Researcher, 33*(9), 14–25.

Shannon, D. M., & Bradshaw, C. C. (2002). A comparison of response rate, response time, and costs of mail and electronic surveys. *Journal of Experimental Education, 70*, 179–192.

Shapley, K. S., & Bush, M. J. (1999). Developing a valid and reliable portfolio assessment in the primary grades: Building on practical experience. *Applied Measurement in Education, 12*, 111–132.

Shermis, M. D., Mzumara, H. R., Olson, J., & Harrington, S. (2001). On-line grading of student essays: PEG goes on the World Wide Web. *Assessment and Evaluation in Higher Education, 26*, 247–259.

Shermis, M. D., Rasmussen, J. L., Rajecki, D. W., Olson, J., & Marsiglio, C. (2001). All prompts are created equal, but some prompts are more equal than others. *Journal of Applied Measurement, 2*, 154–170.

Shneiderman, B. (1996). The eyes have it: A task by data type taxonomy for information visualizations. *Proceedings IEEE Visual Languages*, 336–343.

Smith, M. A., & Leigh, B. (1997). Virtual subjects: Using the Internet as an alternative source of subjects and research environment. *Behavior Research Methods, Instruments, & Computers, 29*, 496–505.

Srivastava, S., John, O. P., Gosling, S. D., & Potter, J. (2003). Development of personality in early and middle adulthood:

Set like plaster or persistent change? *Journal of Personality and Social Psychology, 84*, 1041-1053.

Thompson, B. (2002). What future quantitative social science research could look like: Confidence intervals for effect sizes. *Educational Researcher, 31*(3), 25-32.

Thompson, B., & Vacha-Haase, T. (2000). Psychometrics is datametrics: The test is not reliable. *Educational and Psychological Measurement, 60*, 174-195.

Trochim, W. (1989). An introduction to concept mapping for planning and evaluation. *Evaluation and Program Planning, 12*, 1-16.

Trochim, W., Cook, J. A., & Setze, R. J. (1994). Using concept mapping to develop a conceptual framework of staff's views of a supported employment program for persons with severe mental illness. *Journal of Consulting and Clinical Psychology, 62*, 766-775.

Tukey, J. W. (1991). The philosophy of multiple comparisons. *Statistical Science, 6*, 100-116.

Turner, J. C. (1995). The influence of classroom contexts on young children's motivation for literacy. *Reading Research Quarterly, 30*, 410-441.

Vacha-Haase, T. (1998). Reliability generalization: Exploring variance in measurement error affecting score reliability across studies. *Educational and Psychological Measurement, 58*, 6-20.

Vacha-Haase, T., Henson, R. K., & Caruso, J. C. (2002). Reliability generalization: Moving toward improved understanding and use of score reliability. *Educational and Psychological Measurement, 62*, 562-569.

van den Haak, M., De Jong, M., & Jan Schellens, P. (2003). Retrospective vs. concurrent think-aloud protocols: testing the usability of an online library catalogue. *Behaviour and Information Technology, 22*, 339-351.

Van Gerven, P. W. M., Paas, F., Van Merrienboer, J. J. G., & Schmidt, H. G. (2003). The efficiency of multimedia learning into old age. *British Journal of Educational Psychology, 73*, 489-505.

Wainer, H., & Robinson, D. (2003). Shaping up the practice of null hypothesis testing. *Educational Researcher, 32*(7), 22-30.

Walsh, J. (1999). What is authentic about 'authentic' assessment? *Prospero, 5*(1), 28-30.

Wasson, B. (1999). *Design and evaluation of collaborative telelearning activity aimed at teacher training*. Paper presented at the Computer Supported Collaborative Learning Conference, Stanford, CA.

Weinstein, C. E., Palmer, D. R., & Schulte, A. C. (1987). *LASSI: Learning and study strategies inventory*. Clearwater, FL: H & H Publishing.

West, D. C., Park, J. K., Pomeroy, J. R., & Sandoval, J. (2002). Concept mapping assessment in medical education: A comparison of two scoring systems. *Medical Education, 36*, 820-826.

Wilkinson, L., & the APA Task Force on Statistical Inference (1999). Statistical methods in psychology journals: Guidelines and explanations. *American Psychologist, 54*, 594-604.

Wilson, J. M. (1998). Differences in knowledge networks about acids and bases of year-12, undergraduate and postgraduate chemistry students. *Research in Science Education, 28*, 429-446.

Winne, P. H. (1982). Minimizing the black box problem to enhance the validity of theories about instructional effects. *Instructional Science, 11*, 13-28.

Winne, P. H., Gupta, L., & Nesbit, J. C. (1994). Exploring individual differences in studying strategies using graph theoretic statistics. *Alberta Journal of Educational Research, 40*, 177-193.

Winne, P. H., Hadwin, A. F., Nesbit, J. C., Kumar, V., & Beaudoin, L. (2005). *gSTUDY: A toolkit for developing computer-supported tutorials and researching learning strategies and instruction* (version 2.0). Simon Fraser University, Burnaby, BC.

Winne, P. H., Jamieson-Noel, D., & Muis, K. (2001). Methodological issues and advances in researching tactics, strategies, and self-regulated learning. In P. R. Pintrich & M. L. Maehr (Eds.), *New directions in measures and methods* (Vol. 12, pp. 121-155), London: Elsevier.

Winne, P., & Nesbit, J. C. (1995). Revealing sequential relations in learners' studying actions: An application of LogMill. In M. Guzdial (Chair), *Exploring the dimensions of log file analysis*. Symposium conducted at the Annual Meeting of the American Educational Research Association, San Francisco.

Winne, P. H., & Perry, N. E. (2000). Measuring self-regulated learning. In M. Boekaerts, P. R. Pintrich & M. Zeidner (Eds.), *Handbook of self-regulation* (pp. 532-566). San Diego, CA: Academic Press.

·37·

RESEARCH QUESTIONS AND RESEARCH DESIGNS

Harris Cooper
Duke University

The toolbox analogy to research methods has grown familiar, and for good reason. It works well.

A good carpenter carries hammers and screwdrivers, among other tools of the trade. The carpenter first asks, "What do we want to build?" Based on the answer, the carpenter identifies the appropriate materials and employs different tools for different phases of the project, carefully choosing the proper tool to carry out each task. Hammers, not screwdrivers, are used to insert nails. Even the finest screwdriver wielded by a master craftsman will produce an inferior result if it is used on the head of a nail.

In analogous fashion, a good researcher "carries" an assortment of research strategies. The researcher asks, "What type of knowledge do we want to attain?" or more simply, "What is the research question?" Based on how this question is answered, the researcher determines the most appropriate type of evidence and employs multiple methods, carefully choosing the methods depending on the nature of the question at hand. Different questions will need answers at different points in the life cycle of a research problem. Answering each will call for different "tools." The most powerful method for answering one type of research question can be an inappropriate approach for answering a different question. For example, a survey, not an experiment, is needed to tell us whether the population of children with autism in schools is on the rise. An experiment, not a survey, is needed to tell us if having an aide in class for a child with autism is an effective way to increase learning or diminish classroom disruptions.

To extend the analogy further, not all carpenters are masters at all carpentry skills. A master carver may not be much better than a novice at driving a nail. Similarly, the complexity of education research requires some specialization. Both the carpenter and researcher will fail if they believe their special skill can be used to perform tasks for which it is poorly suited.

This chapter presents a broad and limited survey of the tools in the educational psychologist's research methods toolbox. As the analogy suggests, the focus will not be on the "nuts and bolts" of conducting research but rather on the process of (a) analyzing a research problem, (b) understanding what information is gained by the application of different research designs, and (c) showing how best to match research problems with research designs. I will begin by presenting a broad overview of the considerations that dictate the choice of research design. Then, I will go into more detail regarding the nature of research questions and the design options that lead to their answers. In this discussion, I will also touch on the general strengths and weaknesses of a few research design variations. This survey will be highly conceptual and very incomplete. It defines only the first and most general steps in picking the appropriate tool for a particular research undertaking. To fill in the gaps, I provide references that the reader can examine that go into much greater detail on each research tool.

One especially noteworthy effort to more fully explicate and argue for an essential set of principles to guide scientific inquiry is the volume *Scientific Research In*

Education prepared by the National Research Council's Committee on Scientific Principles in Education Research (Shavelson & Towne, 2002). This committee did not define science by delineating a preferred tool or set of tools. Rather, it set out a pluralistic definition for good science that rests on the alignment of questions, methods, theory, data, and inferences, all of which are inextricably interwoven. The operating principles set out by the committee are:

(a) Pose significant questions that can be investigated empirically

(b) Link research to relevant theory

(c) Use methods that permit direct investigation of the question

(d) Provide a coherent and explicit chain of reasoning

(e) Replicate and generalize across studies, and

(f) Disclose research to encourage professional scrutiny and critique

Although my task requires different emphases, readers of this chapter should find no inconsistencies with the recommendations in the National Research Council's volume.

CHOOSING AN APPROPRIATE RESEARCH DESIGN

A research design specifies the type of data the investigator will collect and under what conditions. In order to arrive at an appropriate research design the investigator first must answer three questions that define the broad parameters of the research problem. The three questions are:

(a) Are we seeking a description or an explanation of an event or relationship?

(b) Do we want our answers to be expressed in numbers or narrative?

(c) Are we interested in variation between people (or other units of interest) or within an individual unit over time?

Figure 37.1 depicts the three questions that relate to the choice of a research design by portraying them as three dimensions along which designs can vary. Also, the figure provides some examples of research designs associated with quantitative approaches involving groups of participants, those designs that will be the focus of this chapter.

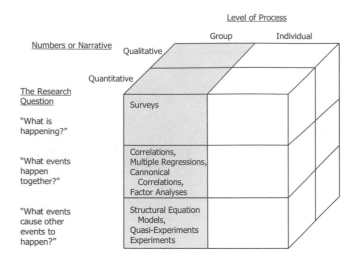

FIGURE 37.1. A three-dimensional representation of the critical aspects of research questions for choosing research designs.

Are We Seeking a Description or an Explanation of an Event or Relationship?

A research problem might be largely descriptive and take the general form "What is happening?" Here, the investigator is interested in obtaining an accurate portrayal of events or other phenomena (hereafter, for purposes of exposition, I will refer to events only, but the reader should understand this to mean not only events, but any characteristic of an event, or other delimited phenomena).

The desired description can focus on a few specific characteristics of the event and broadly sample those few aspects from multiple instances (Fowler, 2002). For example, this is the approach taken when a survey is conducted of teachers' attitudes toward placement of children with autism in regular education classrooms. Alternatively, a description can focus on a select few instances of the event but attempt to provide an in-depth picture of those, as when a descriptive case study (Yin, 2003) is conducted on the behavior of teachers who have students with autism in their class.

A second type of descriptive research problem might be "What events happen together?" Here, researchers take the descriptive approach a step further by looking across multiple instances of events and asking whether certain characteristics that vary across instances tend to co-occur, or correlate, with one another. For example, building on the survey example, a researcher might use a simple correlation to determine whether the differences in attitudes of regular classroom teachers toward students with autism are associated (happen together) with whether or not the teachers have such a student in their class. Or, the researcher might use a multiple regression analysis to examine a set of variables that could be associated with teacher attitudes.

The third research problem seeks an explanation for the event and might be phrased "What events cause other events to happen?" In this case, a study is conducted to isolate and draw a direct *productive* link between one event (the cause) and another (the effect). What constitutes evidence of causal production is a knotty philosophical question I will return to in the section titled "What Events Cause Others Events to Happen?: Problems in Drawing Causal Inferences." In practice, three types of research designs are used most often to help make causal inferences. I will call the first *modeling research*. It takes correlational research a step further by examining co-occurrence in a multivariate framework. For example, if we wish to know whether having a child with autism in class *causes* the class teacher to have better or worse attitudes toward such students, we might first establish a correlational link between the student's presence and the teacher's attitudes. Then, a structural equation model could be built that attempts to provide an exhaustive description of a network of relational linkages (Kline, 1998). This model would serve to account for other co-occurring phenomena that might explain the correlation of interest and that make it difficult to establish a productive link.

The second explanatory approach is called *quasi-experimental research*. Here, unlike the modeling approach, the researcher, or some other external agent, controls the introduction of an intervention or event but does not control precisely who may be exposed to it. For example, a school system might agree to have students with autism placed in regular classrooms, but teachers must volunteer to be in the "treated" group (Shadish, Cook, & Campbell, 2002).

Finally, in *experimental research*, both the introduction of the event (placements of children with autism) and who is exposed to it (which teachers get a student with autism) are controlled by the researcher (or other external agent), who then leaves treatment assignment to chance (Boruch, 1997). This approach minimizes average preexisting differences between classrooms with and without children with autism so that we can be most confident that any differences between the classes, after the introduction of our intervention, are caused by the intervention, rather than other potential explanations.

The National Research Council's Committee on Scientific Principles in Education Research (Shavelson & Towne, 2002) suggested that a great number of educa-

tion research questions fall into three (interrelated) types: descriptive (What is happening?), causal (Is there a systematic effect?), and process or mechanism (Why or how is it happening?). The scheme I use in this chapter is very similar, but has a few distinctions. First, I make a finer distinction among descriptive research questions. I separate out studies that seek to uncover relationships, questions that involve somewhat more than descriptions but somewhat less than causal explanations.

Second, I do not separate out process or mechanism questions. I view questions about processes or mechanisms as questions that can be addressed within the descriptive, relational, and causal types. Any of the approaches to research can shed light on the mechanisms and processes that intervene in bringing an event about.

Whether any particular relationship under study would be labeled a "How or why does it happen?" question (as opposed to a "what happens" or "what causes what" question) resides in the theoretical context of the research, rather than in the research question itself. This typically involves proposing and collecting evidence on variables that relate to mediating and moderating mechanisms (Baron & Kenny, 1986). For example, assume we have designed a study to test the hypothesis that "placement of a child with autism in regular classes causes teacher attitudes toward children with autism to be more negative." In this context, testing the related hypotheses "autistic children create distractions in regular classrooms" and "creating classroom distractions cause teachers' attitudes to be more negative" are clearly "why or how" questions. However, in the context of research meant to answer the questions "Who causes classroom distractions?" in the former case, and "What behaviors cause poorer teacher attitudes?" in the latter case, these hypotheses are no longer process or mediational in nature.

The importance of the theoretical context in defining when a research question might be labeled "process" or "mediational" serves to highlight a theme that will run throughout this chapter. Whether an investigator is in search of a simple description or the uncovering of complex causal connections, research cannot be undertaken without a theoretical underpinning. Sometimes the theory is explicit, sometimes implicit, but it is always there. Theory tells us what variables to focus on, or how to divide the world into meaningful chunks. As above, theory tells us what is process and what is product. Theory provides the context in which we can interpret the trustworthiness of findings related to our description, relation, or causal system. Throughout the chapter, I provide numerous examples of the essential role that theory plays in the interpretation of research, and return to this issue more generally in the conclusion.

Do We Want Our Answers to Be Expressed in Numbers or Narrative?

Both numbers and narrative will be important to understanding a research problem. To state this simplistically, numerical or quantitative approaches to research emphasize arriving at precise answers that are as free as possible from influence by the perspective of the researcher. Narrative or qualitative approaches to research emphasize understanding the context in which events occur, the motives and beliefs behind peoples' actions, and the meaning or interpretations participants in the events apply to them (Camic, Rhodes & Yardley, 2003; Taylor & Bogdan, 1998).

Many people tie the relative importance of numbers and narrative to the stage of the research problem in its life cycle (Camic et al., 2003). They argue that early in a problem area's development, narrative or qualitative descriptions of the event are most helpful. The narrative descriptions can best be used to discover the salient features of the problem at hand, and assist in deciding what to measure more precisely with numbers. The more open-ended, qualitative approaches to research might focus on questions such as: "What happens when an autistic child is introduced into a classroom?" and "Does the teacher change his or her style of teaching?" or "How do other students react to the child?" Quantitative surveys also can be enlightening in the early stages of problem formulation. They can answer specific questions for us across a broader array of problem instantiations. These might include: "Is the number of children with autism on the increase?" or "What is the class placement of children with autism now?"

Both qualitative and quantitative approaches to research can play a role later in a research area's development. Experiments with precisely defined numerical outcomes help us obtain clear answers to questions about an intervention's effectiveness, such as, "Does providing a trained aide for a student with autism cause classrooms to have fewer disruptions?" Still, qualitative approaches can play an important role here as well. They can help us answer questions such as: "How do the other students react to and interpret having another adult present in class?" and "Does the aide do things beyond helping the autistic child?"

In this chapter, I focus exclusively on the quantitative tools in the methodological toolbox. As my earlier description suggests, this division is not based on my relative valuing of the two approaches. The way I slice the research pie, the two approaches are neither incompatible nor contradictory. Rather, they are complementary and both are necessary to create understanding of events. Different designs have different value depending on the knowledge we seek. Qualitative research methods are described in a separate chapter written by Deborah Butler (this volume), a researcher far more expert than I in these methods.

Are We Interested in Variation Between People (or Other Units of Interest) or Within an Individual Over Time?

Some research problems make reference to changes that occur within a unit of interest over time, either naturally occurring changes or ones that happen as a function of some intervention. Other research problems relate to general tendencies across a group of units. This can include changes in the central tendency (e.g., average response) for a group, the dispersion of scores around that central tendency (group variance), or other characteristics of group statistics.

A good example of the distinction between the study of individual and group change involves the idea of *insight learning*. For example, some skills in mathematics seem to come to people as an "aha" experience, seemingly all at once, but perhaps only after repeated exposures. Once the insight occurs, the person "gets it" and a noticeable improvement in performance is evident. Different students may have "aha" experiences after different numbers of exposures. Figure 37.2a provides an example of how six people's performance on a 15 question math test might be tracked, with each of 10 tests being given after a new lesson in how to solve its constituent problems. Based on the data in this figure, the best description of how people learn the math skill would be to say, "Each person experiences a moment of 'insight' after which performance improves precipitously but the moment of insight occurs after different numbers of exposures for different people, and some people may never attain the skill." Figure 37.2b provides a graph of how the same performance scores look if they are averaged across the six people. A much different picture emerges. If we were to assume the group averages reflect what is happening to each individual person, we would say, "People appear to gradually 'catch on' but after eight exposures no additional improvement seems to take place." Clearly, this would be an incorrect characterization. The group-averaged data can be used to explain learning only at the group level, one at which the notion of "insight" has little meaning. Thus, the correct interpretation of the group-averaged data would be to say, "On average, when a group is exposed to these mathematics lessons, group performance improves in gradual increments, but there appears to be little additional increment after eight lessons." Focusing on measures of dispersion rather than

(a) Hypothetical graphs of six students' performance on a mathematics test

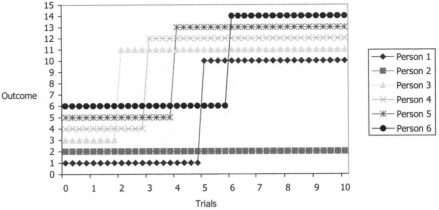

(b) Hypothetical graphs of group-averaged performance of above six students on the mathematics test

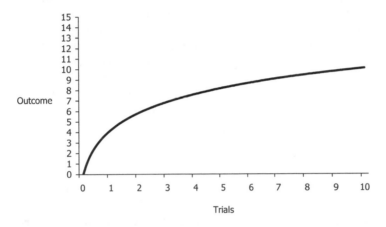

FIGURE 37.2. Hypothetical graphs of individual and group-level performance on a mathematics test.

central tendency, it could also be said, "The greatest variation in learning within the group occurs after about five lessons, with variation decreasing thereafter," and, "There was some change in the group's variability in performance due to the lessons (and this was due to a lack of performance change by one person)."

It is important to note that the designation of an individual or group effect depends upon the context in which the question is being asked. So, the group performance in this example is also a description of how one classroom might perform. Again, then, the nature of the research question becomes paramount. If our problem focuses on understanding how individuals learn, then Fig. 37.2a provides us with six replications of the phenomena of interest. Figure 37.2b is irrelevant to our question. If our focus is on how classrooms perform, Fig. 37.2b provides us with one instance of this. Figure 37.2a is irrelevant.

Summary

Figure 37.1 makes explicit the fact that any combination of answers to the three questions may motivate research. Thus, it is possible for a research question to seek a narrative description of what caused a particular event to occur. The methods used in education research associated with answering a question with these features are often drawn from the social science disciplines of history and cultural anthropology. It is also possible for a research question to seek a quantitative estimate of the frequency with which an event occurs. These designs are most often associated with political science. Finally, questions that seek quantitative estimates of the average causal influence of one event on another have found their most frequent use in psychology and sociology. I noted earlier that the remainder of this chapter focuses on quantitative research methods (those included in the shaded area of Fig. 37.1). In addition, most of the designs I introduce later relate to research questions that ask for answers that include the qualifiers "on average" or "in general" or "across people (or other units)." A notable exception occurs when I discuss time series designs. These designs can be used to answer both questions about individual change and tendencies across groups of individuals. Regression analyses can also be used to describe processes at an individual level, but this technique is predominantly used for group-level analyses.

In essence, then, the remainder of this chapter focuses on three of the twelve possible permutations on research questions created in Fig. 37.1. In addition, because of the recent emphasis in education on the search for causes, greater attention is paid to designs that help uncover causal relationships. To reiterate, these choices in focus are not meant to suggest a relative valuation of the different methods but rather the limits of this carpenter's expertise with the different tools in the social science toolbox. I now turn to a more detailed description of the research designs associated with each of the three broad classes of research questions.

WHAT IS HAPPENING?: USING SURVEYS TO DEVELOP ACCURATE DESCRIPTIONS OF EVENTS

Fowler (2002) suggests that two types of "What is happening?" questions are most appropriately answered using quantitative approaches to research. First, we may want to know *the frequency of an event's occurrence.* Pursuing the example of students with autism, we might want to know how many such students there are in schools. We might also want to know what school services are available for them and how often each type of service is used today. More specifically, we might inquire about how often students with autism are placed in regular classes and how often these placements are accompanied by the assignment of an aide to the class.

Second, quantitative surveys are also used to *collect information about attitudes and/or about opinions or perceptions about programs and policies.* Thus, we might be interested in teachers' attitudes toward regular class placement or their assessment of the value of a federal program that provides assistance to schools that have students with autism.

In education and other human services, it is often the case that the different types of evidence collected on surveys are used together to develop a *needs analysis or assessment* (McKillip, 1987). Needs assessments often col-

lect descriptive information beyond a quantitative survey by employing, for example, focus groups and public forums where more in-depth and open-ended information can be gathered to supplement the numbers. What all needs assessments have in common is a focus on a perceived need, or a discrepancy between the way things are and the way things ought to be. Needs assessments are often an important prelude to an action taken by a school district, state education agency, or federal agency. Thus, a survey that was part of an analysis assessing needs associated with educating children with autism would include questions on counts, attitudes, and evaluations. The reasoning in the needs analysis might proceed like this: "The number of students with autism being placed in regular classrooms has increased from X to Y in the past decade. Currently, Z% of these students are placed in regular classes without support services, such as the assistance of a teacher aide. A majority of teachers of students with autism feel that a dedicated aide is an effective support service to help these students function effectively in the regular class environment."

For the results of a survey to have credibility, experts in survey methodology pay special attention to two broad aspects of the research design. The first concerns how the questions are asked. The second concerns who is asked to respond.

Questions and Questionnaires

First and foremost, accurate descriptions based on survey questionnaires require precise definitions of the events of interest. For example, if the survey developer does not have a clear operational definition of *autism* (Does autism include students diagnosed with Asperger's syndrome?) and *teacher aide* (Does an untrained, part-time, parent volunteer count?), and if these definitions are not conveyed to the respondents, the survey cannot be expected to result in interpretable findings.

Surveys must be brief and, often, no one is available to answer a respondent's questions about ambiguous definitions. Therefore, survey methodologists recommend that definitions rely on common language, be operational, and remain as simple as possible (Fowler, 1995). One technique for accomplishing this is to build the definition into the question. For example, if we were surveying teachers about the number of students with autism in their classes, the question would have greater clarity, and the result would be more interpretable, if it were phrased, "How many students diagnosed with autism, including Asperger's syndrome, are in your classes?" rather than simply asking, "How many students with autism are in your classes?" For the latter question, some teachers might include students with Asperger's syndrome and some not. Some teachers might include students they suspected had autism, others not. Likewise, using the term *trained para-professionals* will lead to a clearer interpretation of results than will *classroom aide*. Of course, the survey might ask teachers separate questions about multiple types of classroom assistance provided by persons with different qualifications and skill sets and for differing amounts of time.

How a question is phrased also can make a difference in how it will be answered. For example, biases in memory become important when asking questions about the occurrences, dates, or durations of events (Tourangeau, Rips, & Rasinski, 2000). One important effect on questionnaire responses involves the interval of time the respondent is asked about. Generally speaking, more accurate responses will be obtained for the question, "How many students diagnosed with autism do you have in your current class?" than for, "How many students diagnosed with autism have you had in your classes over the past 5 years?" The latter question is open to memory biases that include *forward telescoping*, or including events that actually happened prior to the interval, or *backward telescoping*, omitting events that happened during the interval.

The order in which questions are asked can influence how they are answered (Converse & Presser, 1986). Each question provides a context for interpreting later questions. For example, asking general questions just before asking about specific instances can have profound effects on how the more specific question is answered. We can expect different responses to the question, "Do you believe students with autism should be placed in regular classrooms?" when it is preceded by the question, "Do you believe all children deserve to be educated in the least restrictive environment?" Clearly, answering yes to the general question has implications for how the second question "should" be answered.

The literature on how to best construct a questionnaire is vast. Further, different issues in the construction and asking of questions are more or less salient depending on whether the question concerns information related to frequency counts or to attitudes and evaluations (Salant & Dillman, 1994) and whether the information relates to the respondent personally (Stone et al., 1999). Adequate discussion of these topics is beyond the scope of this chapter. Most important in the context of discussing research questions and choosing appropriate designs is that constructing good questions and questionnaires is critical to all research, not only to broad surveys. The same issues arise and the same care is needed when questions and questionnaires are constructed as outcome measures of experiments, as when questions arc asked as part of national surveys. Survey methodologists have explored these issues in most depth. Researchers who construct questionnaires for other purposes can find much good advice in the survey methodology literature.

Respondents

The second central issue in survey research involves who will be asked to respond. A clear definition of respondents requires delineating the *target population* of the survey, the *accessible population,* the *sampling frame,* and the *sample* (Groves et al., 2004).

The *target population* is the set of units to be studied. The best definitions of target populations delineate them by time, place, and any critical characteristics that identify the units. In our example, although our topic refers to students with autism, our target population, those people whose experiences or attitudes are of interest to us, could be defined as "current regular classroom teachers in North America." We might further delineate the target population by deciding whether it would be restricted to elementary school teachers (we would say K-5) in public or both public and private schools.

The *accessible population* is that subset of target population members that has a chance to be selected into the sample. Ideally, the target and accessible population would be identical, but this is rarely the case. Invariably, some units in the target have little or no chance of taking part in the survey. This imperfect correspondence occurs often as a consequence of the method used to contact participants. For example, if a survey of teachers is to be conducted by phone, eligible teachers who have recently moved and changed phone numbers may be members of the target population but not be part of the accessible population. If surveys are mailed, even surveys placed in teachers' school mailboxes would mean teachers on medical leave might not appear in the accessible population.

The *sample* is selected from the *sampling frame.* Rarely is every member of a targeted or accessible population asked to take part in a survey. How the sample is chosen describes the sampling frame. Further, even when a member of a population has been chosen to be a member of a sample and is reached, there is no guarantee the person will respond. Sometimes nonresponse occurs because the sample member lacks the skill needed to complete the task. This might occur, for example, if a parent survey on autism is written in English but is sent home to parents who speak only Spanish. Nonresponse also occurs when sample members refuse to complete surveys. This might occur, for example, if some parents of children with autism feel a survey invades their privacy.

The degree of bias caused by inaccessible members of the target population and sample members who do not respond will depend on (a) the percentage of excluded sample members and (b) whether their exclusion is related to the contents of the survey. Small percentages of nonresponse will have little effect on overall conclusions. Larger percentages will always affect estimates of sample error but not necessarily bias the survey's conclusions, if it can be shown that nonresponse was a random process (for example, due to equipment failures or the weather) as opposed to nonrandom processes (for example, parents of students with the most severe autism refusing to take part).

Again, the techniques of survey sampling are vast and beyond the purview of this chapter. Most notably, I have left unmentioned the laws of probability that enable inferences about population parameters to be drawn from sample statistics (see D. B. Wright, this volume, for such an overview). Further, the issues involved in drawing accurate samples fill volumes (see Salant & Dillman, 1994, for a brief introduction and Groves et al., 2004, for greater detail).

Just as good question and questionnaire construction are issues that affect all types of research, not just research on "What is happening?" so, too, does the issue of defining target populations and describing accessible populations and samples. The issue of generalizability (that is, to whom does the result apply?) is an issue in research meant to uncover relations and causality as well as description.

WHAT EVENTS HAPPEN TOGETHER? UNCOVERING THE COVARIATION BETWEEN PHENOMENA

When the research question changes from "What is happening?" to "What events happen together?" the researcher's attention shifts from documenting the presence versus absence, frequency, and/or intensity of characteristics of events to documenting the *relationship* between characteristics of events. The focus now will be on identifying multiple event occurrences (that are members to the specified class of events) and looking for patterns of covariation in characteristics across the occurrences.

To continue our example, a researcher might want to know the answer to the question, "Are teachers' attitudes toward regular class placement for children with autism related to whether or not they have a child with autism in their class?" It is important to note that this question could be answered as part of a broad survey of teachers that also answered descriptive questions. If the survey contained questions on both of these variables (whether teachers had a student with autism in their class and what their attitude was toward regular class placement) and if

multiple teachers were asked both questions, the survey could be used to shed light on this relationship.

Just as the focus on the relationship between two variables separates this class of research questions from questions that are purely descriptive, the focus on relationships also sets these questions apart from questions about causality. The old dictum that "correlation does not imply causation" applies here. The "What events happen together?" question remains agnostic about the direction of any causal linkage. A positive teacher attitude toward teaching children with autism may cause a child with autism to be placed in that teacher's class, and/or a child with autism in a teacher's class may cause the teacher's attitude to become more positive. Indeed, relationship questions tell us nothing about whether the relationship is causal at all. The relationship may be *spurious,* that is, both (related) events may have been produced by a third event and have no causal connection between them. The placement of a child with autism in a teacher's class *and* the teacher's attitude *both* may be caused by the teacher having taken a course on teaching, children with learning difficulties in regular classrooms.

In these simplest of terms, relationship questions seem somewhat pedantic. This partly may explain why evidence that falls into the "What events happen together?" category so frequently is interpreted to imply causation. Often, when researchers explore relationships involving two variables, they do so with an implicit suggestion that a causal relationship exists between the variables. As I noted in the introduction, having such a theory is an important ingredient in the search for causes. However, having a theory that suggests causation and having demonstrated a relationship between two variables is insufficient evidence of causality.

Relational research designs extend well beyond uncovering or estimating the relationships between two variables. The techniques used to uncover relationships range from very simple to highly complex. A good way to conceptualize problems focused on uncovering and estimating relationships is to think of them as operating on data matrices with different characteristics. This helps to understand both the commonalities and differences between the research question and its associated appropriate designs.

A Matrix Approach to Conceptualizing Relational Designs

Figure 37.3 presents a visual representation of a set of data matrices. Each matrix reflects a particular relational research design and will contain data with different characteristics. The design and data differences will affect

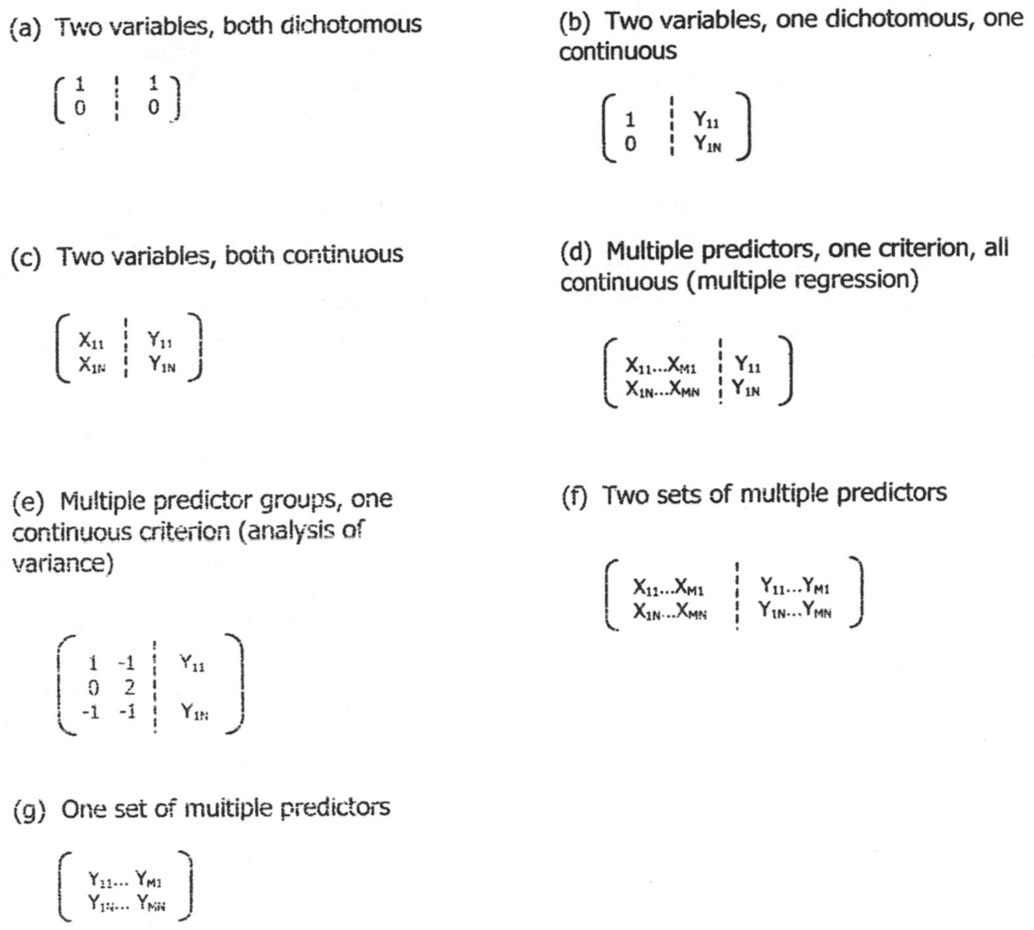

(a) Two variables, both dichotomous

$$\begin{pmatrix} 1 & \vdots & 1 \\ 0 & \vdots & 0 \end{pmatrix}$$

(b) Two variables, one dichotomous, one continuous

$$\begin{pmatrix} 1 & \vdots & Y_{11} \\ 0 & \vdots & Y_{1N} \end{pmatrix}$$

(c) Two variables, both continuous

$$\begin{pmatrix} X_{11} & \vdots & Y_{11} \\ X_{1N} & \vdots & Y_{1N} \end{pmatrix}$$

(d) Multiple predictors, one criterion, all continuous (multiple regression)

$$\begin{pmatrix} X_{11}...X_{M1} & \vdots & Y_{11} \\ X_{1N}...X_{MN} & \vdots & Y_{1N} \end{pmatrix}$$

(e) Multiple predictor groups, one continuous criterion (analysis of variance)

$$\begin{pmatrix} 1 & -1 & \vdots & Y_{11} \\ 0 & 2 & \vdots & \\ -1 & -1 & \vdots & Y_{1N} \end{pmatrix}$$

(f) Two sets of multiple predictors

$$\begin{pmatrix} X_{11}...X_{M1} & \vdots & Y_{11}...Y_{M1} \\ X_{1N}...X_{MN} & \vdots & Y_{1N}...Y_{MN} \end{pmatrix}$$

(g) One set of multiple predictors

$$\begin{pmatrix} Y_{11}...\ Y_{M1} \\ Y_{1N}...\ Y_{MN} \end{pmatrix}$$

FIGURE 37.3. Conceptualizing relational questions as various data matrices.

(a) the language that can be used in answering the research question and (b) the choice of an appropriate statistical technique for investigating relationships. The three characteristics that distinguish the matrices concern (a) whether or not the variables are partitioned into two sets, (b) the number of variables in each set, and (c) the continuous or dichotomous nature of the variables. These distinctions are important because they relate to the contents of the research question. First, does the research question indicate that we are interested in the relationships between one set of variables and the variables in a different set, or relationships among the variables in a single set? Second, does the research question indicate that the sets contain just one variable or multiple variables? Third, does one or both sets of variables contain exclusively categorical variables? This last question is somewhat less critical than the first two. It helps us identify simpler analytic options and more appropriate ways of expressing the results, although the results are also obtainable from the more general matrix. I now attempt to show briefly how the research questions relate to the matrix designs and analytic strategies, beginning with the simplest design.

Two Variables, Both Dichotomous. The simplest relational question asks whether two characteristics of events that are both dichotomous in nature tend to appear together and, if so, how strong the relationship is (Fig. 37.3a). For example, if we were interested in whether regular classroom teachers who had taken a course about students with autism were more likely to have a student with autism in their class, this would fit the simplest design data matrix. This question focuses on only two variables and each is dichotomous (yes/no) in nature.

There are several appropriate ways to analyze data in such a matrix, including using an odds ratio to express the strength of the relationship and a chi-square test to determine whether the pattern of cell frequencies defies chance (Fleiss, 1994). Alternatively, the data could be used to calculate a tetrachoric correlation (easier to calculate by hand) and its associated *t*-test. Although the metrics will be different, when applied to the same data involving truly dichotomous variables the substantive conclusions of either of these analytic approaches will be the same.

Two Variables, One Dichotomous, One Continuous. Our example involving regular class placement and teacher attitudes falls into this second class of research questions (Fig. 37.3b). Class placements are dichotomous variables and teachers' attitudes are continuous variables. Here, the chi-square test is no longer appropriate (it requires two dichotomous variables) but a point-biserial correlation and a *t*-test (for the difference between two independent group means) can be used to gauge the relationship and test the likelihood that the relationship is zero in the population.

Two Variables, Both Continuous. Providing the relationship is linear, the familiar correlation coefficient and its associated *t*-test (using Fisher's *Z* transformation) are appropriate when both variables being related are continuous (Fig. 37.3c). For example, the correlation coefficient would best express the relationship between *the number of* children with austim teachers have had in their class during the past 5 years (a continuous variable related to the dichotomous variable used above) and their attitude toward such children.

Multiple Predictors, One Criterion. This analytic strategy is referred to as *multiple regression*. Here, we have one variable, for example, teachers' attitudes toward children with autism, being related to multiple variables in the second set, for example, teachers' past experience with this type of student, the class size, and the presence of an aide (Fig. 37.3d). The single variable is often referred to as the *criterion variable* and the set of variables as the *predictor variables*. If the predictor variables have been experimentally manipulated they are often referred to as *independent variables* and the criterion as the *dependent variable* or *outcome variable*. The objective of this analysis is not only to discern what events happen together, but also to parcel out the relationships between an event of interest and multiple other events. We hope to improve our understanding of the criterion by examining multiple (predictor) variables that might covary with the criterion. It is important to remember, however, that because multiple regression partitions variation among predictor variables after controlling for other variables in the model, the results must be interpreted with caution. As Winne (1983) points out, the meaning or construct validity of residualized variables cannot be assumed to be identical to that of the "original" variables measured without residualization.

As difficult as it is to avoid making causal inferences when two variables are being related, the problem becomes more profound in the multivariate context. Part of the added problem stems from our common understandings of words. Even the terms *criterion* and *predictors* contain an implied sequencing that suggests the predictors are temporally antecedent to the criterion. But, this does not have to be the case. Predictors are often referred to as "explaining" variance in the criterion and, though not part of the word's formal definition, "explain" and "show cause" are often fused in everyday language. Further, as the prediction of the criterion becomes more complete, that is, the predictor variables become associated with larger amounts of variance in the criteria, there is an increasing tendency to view them as a causal explanation. Intuitively, we sense that because it appears a complete explanation for the criteria is contained in the prediction equation, how can they not be causal? In the next section, on drawing causal inferences, I explore the flaws, and some possible redeeming aspects, of this logic.

There are two other, more restrictive classes of matrices that contain one criterion and multiple predictors. First, the familiar analysis of variance is a variation on this matrix in which the predictor variables are categorical in nature (Fig. 37.3e). At root, the analysis of variance is a computational technique that simplifies calculations of multivariate relations, but arrives at the same substantive conclusions as when the more general multiple regression approach is used.

Returning again to the discussion of correlation and causality, the analysis of variance approach is often used to analyze data that have been collected during experimental assessments of treatments. However, the ability to draw causal inferences from experimental data derives from the conditions under which the data were collected, *not* the technique used to analyze them. Therefore, we should not interpret the results of an analysis of variance necessarily to imply causal relationships. Many researchers use analysis of variance to analyze their data because they have categorical predictors (e.g., the sex of the student and teacher, the presence of an aide), but the predictors were not introduced by the researchers. Therefore, the use of an analysis of variance should not be taken to indicate that causal relationship can be inferred from the data therein. (Of course, it is possible to mix both continuous and categorical predictors. For example, this occurs often in the analysis of covariance.)

The final variation on this matrix to mention is called a *discriminant analysis*. Here, it is the criterion variable that is dichotomous and the predictors that are either dichotomous or continuous. The label *discriminant analysis* is given to relational questions when they take the form, for example, "What weighted combination of predictors best distinguishes the criterion groups?" Concretely, we might ask, "What weighted combination of the variables (a) teacher experience, (b) class size, and (c) average class achievement best distinguishes classes that do and do not have children with autism?" Although the question has a unique phrasing, and the matrix has a dichotomous restriction on the criterion variable, these are only specifications on the more general matrix.

Again, no causality can be inferred simply because a discriminant analysis has been conducted. Indeed, in practice, discriminant analyses are frequently used in situations where theory and causality take a back seat to "brute empiricism." The predictors can be chosen because they are easy or cheaply collected. Crudely put, if we are simply interested in what predicts how well a student with autism does in classrooms with different characteristics, we might not care if the best predictor turns out to be the teacher's shoe size. Of course, such a result should lead to inductive building of a plausible (albeit, post hoc) theory. And, of course, if we used such a result to begin assigning students with autism to classrooms based on the teacher's shoe size, we would likely quickly learn that correlation does not imply causation.

Two Sets of Multiple Predictors. The next matrix configuration involves two sets of multiple continuous variables (Fig. 37.3f). The research question asks, "What weights applied to variables on both sides of the equation maximize the correlation between the resulting variable combinations?" The associated analytic strategy is referred to as a *canonical analysis* or *canonical correlation*. Note that the distinction between predictors and criteria disappears from the lexicon associated with canonical analyses. Concretely, we might ask, "What weighted combination of classroom characteristics (e.g., teacher experience, teacher attitudes, class size) correlates most strongly with what weighted combination of students with autism's achievement score in different subject areas (e.g., math, reading, science, social studies)?" By applying the weights simultaneously to both sets of variables, a canonical analysis takes into consideration the covariation between variables within each set at the same time that it examines the covariation between sets. Thus, the number of analyses conducted on (potentially) correlated variables is minimized. In the example just given, the 16 simple correlations across the two sets of variables would ignore the covariation between all variables within each set. The four multiple regressions would ignore the covariation between the test scores. Thus, in instances such as these, canonical analyses can lead to more complete understanding of the pattern of relationships in the data.

An important feature of the canonical analysis is that it can reveal more than one canonical correlation. For example, the first canonical correlation might suggest that class size and teacher experience get weighted heavily among the X variables and reading and math get weighted heavily among the Y variables. But this combination will not capture all the variance in scores on both sides of the equation. The second canonical correlation might heavily weight teacher attitudes with science and social studies achievement. Alternatively, the first canonical correlation might reveal that teacher experience is heavily weighted along with achievement in all four subject matters and no other important canonical correlations emerge. This might occur when achievement in all four domains is highly correlated.

One Set of Multiple Variables. The final matrix draws no distinctions between sets of variables. Rather, all variables are seen as "dependent on" or "expressions of" underlying constructs or *factors* (Fig. 37.3g). This might be a principal components factor analysis, one variation of many such approaches. Here, the analysis attempts to find the linear weighted combination of variables with the greatest variance and that "explains" the most variation in the original set of scores. To put this in more familiar terms, the first factor in a principal components factor analysis will be the weighted combination of variables that, if we used it as the criterion in a multiple regression, would yield the highest correlation with the variables used to provide the weights. Typically, multiple factors, or combinations of variables, emerge from such an analysis.

Factor analysis comes in numerous variations, far too many to explicate here (see Thompson, 2004). In nearly all cases, they are meant to discover an underlying structure to the data and to do so under different sets of specifications to the relationships among variables and factors. Typically, this type of analysis is conducted to help reduce the number of variables the researcher needs to consider, permit the researcher to discuss findings in broader conceptual terms, and/or construct new variables that have better measurement characteristics. So, we might use factor analysis if we had a large set of variables related to the characteristics of children with autism and we wished to reduce it to a smaller set of broader constructs with which to describe these students. Factor analysis has many other purposes as well.

Summary

I have described the relationship questions starting from the most simple and moving to the most complex. However, it should be evident from the matrices that the discussion could begin with the large, undifferentiated matrix associated with factor analysis and then move back to the simplest matrix by placing successive restrictions on the data. As noted earlier, these restrictions involve (a) whether variables are or are not partitioned into two sets, (b) the number of variables in each set, and (c) the continuous or dichotomous nature of the variables. These features of the data suggest which approach to data analysis is most appropriate. They also suggest ways to precisely express the results of these analyses.

We have also seen that nothing inherent in the relationship questions and data matrices permit inferences about causality, although language (predictor and criterion, explanation) and some research outcomes (near perfect correlation) might tempt us to do so.

WHAT EVENTS CAUSE OTHER EVENTS TO HAPPEN?: PROBLEMS IN DRAWING CAUSAL INFERENCES

Throughout the history of science, philosophers have struggled with how to define the terms *cause* and *effect*. Examining a dictionary's definitions of these two terms illustrates the problem. If you look up the word *cause* in a dictionary you might find a definition such as "the producer of an effect." If you look up *effect* you might find "something that is produced by an agency or cause." These are the actual definitions included in the *Webster's New Universal Unabridged Dictionary* (1996). This evident circularity suggests that the concept of *causality* is very abstract. Generally, people understand one another when they talk about causes and effects through repeated denotation, or the pointing out to one another of causal relationships when they are seen, rather than through connotation, or its literal meaning.

The Scottish philosopher David Hume, especially as discussed in *A Treatise on Human Nature* (1739-1740/1978), is often pointed to as having identified the conundrums associated with identifying "causes" (and is sometimes pointed to as having led social science researchers astray, see Maxwell, 2004). Briefly, Hume argued that for something to be considered a *cause*: (a) the *cause* and the *effect* had to covary, or correlate, (b) the *cause* had to occur before the *effect*, and (c) there had to be a "necessary connection" between the two events. Meeting Hume's first two conditions is relatively straightforward. We have reviewed quantitative methods for revealing covariation among events. Identifying the temporal sequence of events is sometimes problematic—as when events occur almost simultaneously or when effects are caused by anticipation of other events—but sequences are typically observable with a high degree of reliability.

The third condition, demonstrating a necessary connection between events, presents the greatest problem. Hume argued that we actually never see one event produce another. We can never know with 100 percent certainty that the event we are calling the cause was the "true" cause. A simple thought experiment might help clarify his claim. Suppose I placed my coffee cup on the edge of my desk and my elbow slid into a book that then knocked the cup to the floor. What caused the coffee cup to fall? If we were to ask a group of people who observed the event to independently identify the cause of the spill, we would be confronted with multiple nominations. Most frequently the observers would say "the book" or "my elbow." The mischievous in the group might nominate "gravity," "a sudden gust of air," or even perhaps "poltergeist."

How does this unfortunate coffee spill relate to Hume's argument? He asserted that events happen in an unending flow, and even designating where one event ends and the next begins is in many ways arbitrary or subjective (indeed, requires a theory). Therefore, whenever we identify a "cause" it remains possible to identify another event that takes place "between" the asserted cause and effect. So, if I claim my elbow caused the coffee cup to fall, you can counterclaim it was the book that was the "necessary connection." Yet another observer can claim "gravity" was the cause. Preceding events might also be viable alternate nominations—it was my writing deadline that caused me to be sitting at my desk—but these grow less persuasive the more distant they are from the effect. Further, Hume argued, causal systems are open to outside influences. That is, an outside event can enter the claimed causal system unbeknownst to us. The "gust of air" or "poltergeist" explanation for my coffee spill would be outside an "elbow-book-gravity" causal system. Could a mischievous spirit have knocked the cup just a nanosecond prior to the book hitting it? Likewise, the "elbow" or "book" explanation would be outside a "mischievous spirits" causal system.

If we accept Hume's construal, and accept that we can never know causes with certainty, then how are we to proceed to answer the question, "What events cause other events to happen?" Clearly, we must recognize that our answers to this question will always be limited, or qualified. First, causal explanations will be embedded within theoretical systems (earlier, I used the term *causal systems*), and more than one such system may provide viable explanations. Second, even within a causal system any particular explanation will always be probabilistic, not deterministic, because it may be dependent on the occurrence of preceding or subsequent events. And third, the veracity of a causal claim will rest more on the ability to demonstrate that other explanations are implausible than to demonstrate directly that the chosen cause produced the effect. This point has been made forcefully by the philosopher Karl Popper (1959), who took the stance that science cannot rule out all possible alternative explanations but must design investigations so that the most plausible alternative explanations can be convincingly ruled out. In our thought experiment, if we wish to make the case that my elbow caused the coffee spill, we could strengthen our claim through ruling out the "gust of air" explanation, by showing my office was airtight, and the "poltergeist" explanation, by showing that I routinely have a medium come to my office to rid it of mischievous spirits.

Donald Campbell and the Validity of Causal Inferences

If ruling out alternative explanations is the sine qua non of the search for causes, then a researcher whose problem calls for identifying causes must know how well different research designs accomplish this task. In education, the best-known system for evaluating the strengths and weaknesses of quantitative research designs for establishing causal links rests on the work of Donald Campbell (1957) and his colleagues (e.g., Campbell & Stanley, 1963; Cook & Campbell, 1979; Shadish et al. 2002).

In the Campbell tradition, the term *validity* refers to the strength of evidence available to support a claim about a relationship between a presumed "cause" and its supposed "effect." Different research designs (and different implementation features and patterns of data) lead to claims about causal relationships that are more or less valid, or supportable. Campbell referred to the alternative explanations that might weaken the strength of a causal claim as "threats to validity" or "plausible rival hypotheses." Over several iterations of the system, these have come to be grouped into four broad categories: *construct validity, internal validity, external validity*, and *statistical conclusion validity*.

Construct validity refers to the extent to which the operations used to represent the causes and effects in a study are intimately tied to the underlying abstract concepts for which they stand. To pursue our example regarding the effects of placing children with autism in regular classes, assessing the construct validity of the cause will focus on how carefully *regular classrooms* is defined and how well the identification of *regular classrooms* corresponds to this abstract definition. The construct validity of the effect will relate to how well a test captures the construct of academic achievement, or the academic-related knowledge possessed by the student. Of course, all definitions of constructs and their related measures are im-

TABLE 37.1. Threats to Internal Validity Outlined in Shadish, Cook, & Campbell (2002)

1. *Ambiguous temporal precedence*: Lack of clarity about which variable occurred first may yield confusion about which variable is the cause and which is the effect.
2. *Selection*: Systematic differences over conditions in respondent characteristics that could also cause the observed effect.
3. *History*: Events occurring concurrently with treatment could cause the observed effect.
4. *Maturation*: Naturally occurring changes over time could be confused with a treatment effect.
5. *Regression*: When units are selected for their extreme scores, they will often have less extreme scores on other variables, an occurrence that can be confused with a treatment effect.
6. *Attrition*: Loss of respondents to treatment or to measurement can produce artifactual effects if that loss is systematically correlated with conditions.
7. *Testing*: Exposure to a test can affect scores on subsequent exposures to that test, an occurrence that can be confused with a treatment effect.
8. *Instrumentation*: The nature of a measure may change over time or conditions in a way that could be confused with a treatment effect.
9. *Additive and interactive effects of threats to internal validity*: The impact of a threat can be added to that of another threat or may depend on the level of another threat.

perfect. The less perfect they are, the less valid will be a claim that the supposed cause produced the proffered effect.

Internal validity involves the class of validity threats that relate most closely to Hume's concern about ruling out alternative explanations. Threats to internal validity include any event that might plausibly have caused the observed effect in the absence of the offered cause. Table 37.1 presents the list of threats to internal validity outlined by Shadish et al. (2002). In our example, we know that the academic achievement of a child with autism will be influenced by many things, perhaps including the child's native ability, the skill of the teacher, and the severity of the autism condition. Any of these could be an alternative explanation (plausible rival hypothesis, threat to the validity) of the claim that class placement matters, or has a causal effect on achievement, until the alternatives are ruled out. My task now is to show how different research designs, how different methods of collecting data under different conditions, help rule out certain threats to the validity of causal inferences while leaving others plausible.

External validity refers to the generalizability of a causal claim to students, teachers, classrooms, schools, times, and outcomes. Even if we can be relatively certain that a study has good internal validity—meaning we can be relatively certain, for example, that the observed changes in achievement for students with autism was caused by their placement in a regular class—the study may have been conducted using students with mild autism placed in classes with small numbers of other students. Here, we still don't know if the results of the study will apply to students with severe autism and/or placements in large classes. And from a simple rhetorical perspective, we are more likely to accept an assertion of causality if it has been broadly demonstrated ("Regular class placement causes improved achievement for children with autism regardless of the severity of the disorder or the class size") than if it has been shown to operate in restricted circumstances only ("Regular class placement causes improved achievement for children with autism but only when the disorder is mild and the class size is small").

The issue of external validity relates to the generalizability issues of sampling discussed earlier. Indeed, studies with the strongest external validity are ones that carefully define the people, places, times, and outcomes that are relevant to the problem, then randomly sample multiple instantiations to ensure representation of each of these parameters. The ideal study also would then test to determine whether any overall findings—ones that referred to the whole sample—also held for particular subgroups. For example, after broadly sampling classrooms with students with autism and measuring achievement at multiple times using multiple measures, a study could test to see if the results held for students with mild and severe autism, for large and small classes, and so on. A study that randomly sampled from the target population and found consistent results within theoretically relevant subsamples can make a claim of stronger external validity than studies with narrow samplings not testing within subgroups.

Statistical conclusion validity refers to the validity of statistical inferences arising from a study, or the appropriate use of statistics to infer whether there is covariation between the variables in question. Simply put, descriptive statistics produce an estimate of a relationship and inferential statistics are used to tell us how likely it is that covariation exists between variables. There are multiple ways that these numerically based decisions can go wrong. Other chapters in this volume explore these issues in depth. Here, I mention one problem that is pervasive among analyses of experiments and quasi-experiments. This concerns the fact that many researchers ignore the influence that clustering (or nesting, or grouping) of individual data points within larger units has on the independence of those measurements. For example, assume we are studying the impact of a teacher aide for a student with autism on the attitudes of other students in the class. Aides are assigned to classes. The researcher then statistically tests the effect of the aide using the individual students, not the individual classrooms, as the unit of analysis. This analysis ignores the fact that the students in the same classroom will have an effect on each other and this effect will make their attitudes more similar than attitudes in other classes and will influence their reaction to the new student. This dependence of scores within classrooms is often ignored in data analyses and can lead to erroneous estimations, especially of the confidence interval around an estimate of an intervention's effect.

Summary

It is important to make a few points before beginning to discuss research designs meant to uncover causal relationships. First, as mentioned earlier, when the research problem calls for seeking causes, the focus of our evaluation of designs will be on their internal validity characteristics. This does not mean the other three classes of validity are unimportant, but rather that they are important across other research questions as well. Earlier, I noted that external validity, or generalization, was critical to the interpretation of survey research. Likewise, statistical conclusion validity clearly plays a critical role in assessing the validity of research that seeks to uncover relationships or associations. And certainly, the validity of any research project is intimately tied to how well the variables of interest are defined and their operations align with these definitions.

Second, the Campbell approach, using identified threats to validity, is a dynamic system. Over the past half century, the system has undergone revision and expansion. Campbell (1957) identified only threats to internal and external validity. In 1968, Bracht and Glass (1968) added numerous external validity threats to Campbell's list. These authors also proposed dividing external validity into separate classes of threats concerning *population* or *ecological* validity. In 1969, Campbell added *instability* to the list. He defined this as "unreliability of measures, fluctuations in sampling persons and components, autonomous instability of repeated or equivalent measures" (p. 411). Cook and Campbell (1979) made these sources of instability in numerical data part of the statistical conclusion and construct validity classes of threats and added numerous other threats to these two new classes. In the system's most recent incarnation, Shadish, Cook, and Campbell (2002) list 37 threats to validity divided into the four classes.

Finally, not only is the system dynamic in the sense that the list of threats to validity expands over time, but individual threats can move from one class to another. For example, the threat to validity called *experimenter expectancies* refers to the possibility that the behavior of the participant in an experiment might be unintentionally influenced by the characteristics or behavior of the person administering the intervention. Bracht and Glass (1968) listed this as a threat to external validity. They reasoned that if experimenter expectancies influenced the participants' behavior, it meant that the experimental effect might occur under only limited circumstances, for example, when the experimenter had certain personal qualities. Shadish et al. (2002) listed experimenter expectancy effects as a threat to construct validity. They reasoned that these effects are "part of the molar treatment package" (p. 78), but likely not the part we wish to draw causal inferences about.

Are the dynamic nature and permeable boundaries of Campbell and colleagues' system signs of weakness? I think not. Rather, these characteristics of the system point out that just as theories related to substantive issues represent our attempts to impose order on the generally disorderly state of humans in nature, so too do our theories of knowledge. I view this state of affairs not as an occasion for scorn and dismissal but as an occasion for critique, debate, and celebration. Ultimately, I take a pragmatic approach to the evaluation of theories. If they help us make sense of nature, in this case if they help us arrive at consensual, reproducible claims about causality, they are good things. The Campbell system passes this test.

APPROACHES TO REVEALING CAUSAL RELATIONS

Structural Equation Models

Over the past century several generations of social scientists have worked diligently to develop research methods that "solve" Hume's dilemma that we can never see causal production. Perhaps the most ingenious of these are the developers of methods meant to reveal the relationships between causes and effects through the estimation of structural equations.

Modern modeling procedures have their roots in a technique called *path analysis*, introduced in the 1920s by Sewell Wright (see Maruyama, 1998, for a brief history). In essence, path analysis calls for the researcher to develop a model of sequential causal relationships, culminating in the outcome of interest. The technique found its first appearance in the social sciences in the mid-1960s, used primarily by sociologists. In the 1970s, path analysis techniques were combined with improved measurement techniques to form the bases of what today is alternatively called structural equation modeling, or

latent variable models (see Hoyle, 1995, or D. Wright, this volume, for additional details).

Again to oversimplify, structural equation modelers have taken several of the techniques discussed earlier for uncovering relationships and have "packaged" them in a way meant not to reveal production between a cause and effect but to make it difficult to sustain the argument that other events explain the relationship. The modeling approach, not surprisingly, begins with the specification of a conceptual (or theoretical) model that lays out the hypothesized relationships between variables (Hoyle, 1995). These models can be quite simple, perhaps as simple as hypothesizing that in regular education classes the presence of support services causes positive change in the achievement of students with autism. Here, the quantitative calculation of the model would be a correlation coefficient.

Although this simple model has its appeal, we know that generating proof of the causal link from data collected without an experimental intervention will be difficult, if not impossible. But, suppose a researcher made three assumptions about the nonexperimental data. These were: (a) the two variables in the model were measured perfectly, that is, with no measurement error, (b) a decision on whether a classroom will have support services always precedes a change in how well children with autism will achieve in regular classes, and (c) there are no third variables correlated with both the presence of support services and student achievement that is causing them both.

Each assumption is necessary for a claim of causal relationship to be sustained. The first assumption, perfect measurement, rules out the rival hypothesis that the support-causes-achievement relationship was brought about by that part of the variance in the measured (observed) variables that was not related to the constructs we intended to measure. In terms of threats to validity, the assumption is that both measures relate perfectly to the constructs. The second assumption rules out the rival hypothesis that the achievement level of students with autism caused support services to be placed in their regular education classes. The third assumption rules out the relationship being spurious. This does not mean that the correlation between the presence of support services and achievement is perfect, that is, $r = 1$. It can be less than perfect. What it does mean is that other variables that affect achievement are completely independent of the presence of support services. They are part of separate causal systems that influences achievement.

If we object to these three assumptions because they seem untenable or implausible, we would be correct. First, asking teachers if they have support services will not produce perfectly valid measures. Achievement tests have error as well. And, it is plausible that a teacher's over- or under-reporting of available support services is systematically associated with factors other than "true" achievement that influence their students' achievement test scores. Second, assuming that the achievement level of students with autism has no effect on the level of support services in their classes certainly seems counterintuitive. Indeed, this might be the predominant direction of causal influence between these two variables. Finally, numerous plausible third variables could cause both level of support and achievement. Thus, we are correct if we object to applying this model and these assumptions to a data set and then labeling the result an estimate of a causal relationship. It does not solve Hume's dilemma. Rather than solve it, it assumes the dilemma away (see Loehlin, 2004).

If making assumptions about the data were all there was to modeling, the approach would have passed into history long ago. Instead, modelers have devised ways to express and test models that render the assumptions more plausible than in my example. First, they typically employ measurement models that do not rely on single observed variables. Rather than simply ask teachers if they have support services for their students with autism, the modeler might take multiple measures of support services, drawn from multiple sources affected by different types of random measurement error. The modeler then would combine these measures using a form of factor analysis into the single best measure of the latent variable—for example, availability of support services—that all the observed variables tap into. Although this more complex approach to developing valid measures of underlying constructs does not reduce random measurement error to zero, it certainly helps minimize it, relative to the approaches that use a single observed variable (see Borsboom, Mellenbergh, & van Heerden, 2003, for an interesting perspective on latent variable measurement, one that combines discussion of causality with the foregoing discussion on individual and group-averaged research).

This latent variable indicator is then used in the structural equation model. The structural equation model would undoubtedly contain multiple predictors of student achievement, not just the level of support services. Previously, I mentioned that when using multiple regression techniques, as the prediction of the criterion becomes more complete —that is, the predictor variables as a set become associated with larger amounts of variance in the criterion—there is an increasing tendency to view the estimates in the set as indices of the degree of causal relationship between predictors and criteria. In other words, it becomes more difficult to make the claim that important third variables that are the "real" causes are missing from the model. Structural equation models take advantage of this.

Finally, state-of-the art structural equation modeling programs can analyze data that are collected in multiple temporal waves and can provide for relationships to have bidirectional influence and feedback loops. Thus, it is possible to propose a model that permits both the level of services to cause achievement and vice versa.

These features help develop models that make it more plausible to claim that the three assumptions have been met, or to reduce the possibility that they have been violated. If I wished to claim that the path leading from availability of support services to the achievement level of students with autism expressed the degree of causal connection from the latter to the former, my case would certainly be strengthened if (a) the two variables in the model (called *endogenous variables*) were expressed as latent constructs based on multiple indicators, (b) the model included a set of predictors antecedent to support services (called *exogenous variables*) that were chosen based on theory and seemed to cover the range of plausible third variables that might explain the link, and (c) the model permitted and estimated a bidirectional relationship. Figure 37.4 presents an example of such a model.

That being said, we now need to critically examine how feasible it is to build such a model. First and foremost, it is clear that the plausibility of casual claims based on the results of a structural equation model can be no greater than the plausible completeness of the model itself. Modelers refer to this as *specification error*. This is more than a matter of looking at how much variation is explained in the outcome of interest (e.g., student achievement). It is also a function of the plausibility of the theory that led to the model's choice of variables. Returning to our coffee-spill thought experiment, if the model I am testing is based on the laws of physics it will likely generate more acceptance of its causal conclusions than a model based on poltergeist intervention, regardless of the resulting path estimates, because so much other evidence speaks to the validity of the laws of physics. For this reason, the best structural equation models begin with clearly explicated and well-specified theoretical models. In the best circumstances, these models have been tested in other related situations and proved viable.

Second, models will be more or less convincing depending on how well the indicators of latent variables measure the underlying constructs. Generally speaking, if latent variables are represented by multiple indicators that would be expected to contain different types of error variance, a stronger case can be made that the resulting path estimates are reliable. This implies that the measures were purposely chosen to represent the latent variable, not chosen because they happen to have been conveniently available.

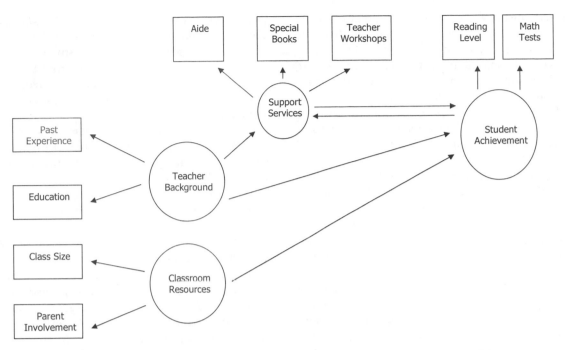

FIGURE 37.4. Hypothetical example of a simple structural equation model.

Given the caveats to the causal interpretation of structural equation models, the rhetoric surrounding the strength of causal claims derived from them has tempered greatly over the years. In fact, today, cautious methodologists even eschew using causal language when speaking of the results of models (though some would argue that the term *structural equation* implies estimating fundamental relations indistinguishable from causes). Instead, modelers will refer to their work as (a) examining the implications of different relational structures and (b) determining whether models remain plausible after empirical test. They point out that, given Hume's dilemma, even experiments never prove causality. All we can do with any method is rule out some explanations and bolster others by showing they have survived another test. This is what structural equation models do. Also, in addition to testing single models, different models can be compared to one another based on their "goodness of fit" with the data. A model that repeatedly demonstrates superior fit with the data when compared to other models grows in plausibility as an expression of underlying structural relationships.

There are other positive aspects to the evidence that emerge from structural equation models. First, because they must be based on theoretical models purported to be complete, they require the modeler to think about the entire nexus of influence on the behavior of interest. This can only have positive effects on theories of behavior. Second, because of their use of latent variables, structural equation modelers pay close attention to issues of measurement, generally more so than researchers who use other types of research designs. Ultimately, this invests their findings with a relatively high level of measurement validity and reliability.

Finally, because of the importance of obtaining stable estimates of paths, structural equation modelers typically use large data sets collected from broad samples to derive their estimates. This speaks well for the external validity or generality of their findings. A note of caution, of course, is that modelers ought not trade improved external validity for diminished construct validity and internal validity. Often, in "real-world research" these kinds of trade-offs are necessary to make, or, stated differently, it is unlikely that all threats to all kinds of validity can be addressed equally well in any given empirical investigation. Still, it is important for modelers to remember that there is a cost to choosing large data sets because they are available and not because they contain the good and varied measures or the constructions required to test a plausible and complete model.

Quasi-Experiments

All of the designs we have examined thus far, be they descriptive, relational, or model-building, typically share a common element: The events being investigated occurred naturally in the environment of those exposed to it, and began sometime in the past. Thus, in the types of data collected most often for these research designs, the researcher simply asks teachers of students with autism whether they have an aide in their classes. In the type of design we will examine next, the *quasi-experiment*, this lack of manipulation may describe the event (putative cause) but it is also possible that the event has been deliberately introduced into the environment. This can occur as part of an attempt to assess its causal impact or because the researcher is taking advantage of a planned natural introduction.

According to Shadish et al. (2002), quasi-experiments have several defining characteristics. First, they deal with manipulable causes. This is a more restricted set of causes than the types researchers might investigate using structural equation modeling. In a quasi-experiment, researchers can manipulate the presence or absence of a teacher aide, for example, but they cannot manipulate the severity of a child's autism. A structural equation can attempt to estimate the direct path of the severity of students' autism on achievement, but a quasi-experiment cannot. Because this distinction between manipulable and nonmanipulable causes is important, we will refer to the causes investigated in the designs discussed hereon as *interventions* and the effects as *outcomes*.

Second, quasi-experiments introduce the intervention before measuring outcomes. This corresponds well with Hume's criterion that causes must precede effects. However, we will see shortly that this requirement for quasi-experiments does not guarantee that the effect, or more precisely a prior instance of it, can be ruled out as the cause of the intervention.

Third, quasi-experiments *do not* employ random assignment to place participants into conditions of receiving or not receiving the intervention. Assignment occurs (a) by self-selection, for example, teachers volunteer or must request to have an aide for the students with autism in their class, or (b) by administrative selection, for example, the school principal decides which teachers who already have a student with autism will get an aide.

Random Assignment. The distinction between random assignment and self- or administrative selection into intervention and comparison conditions is critical to understanding the relative potential of different experimental and quasi-experimental designs for revealing plausible causal relationships. When teachers must apply to have an aide for students with autism or when administrators make these assignments, we are forced to entertain the possibility that teachers and classrooms receiving the intervention differ from those not receiving it in systematic ways other than the presence of the teacher aide. For example, teachers who ask for an aide may be less well trained to deal with the problems that might

arise when teaching children with autism. Classes assigned aides might get them because the administrator feels larger classes or classes with students who are not achieving well might benefit most from the extra help. These differences, existing prior to the selection into conditions, become plausible rival hypotheses to an intervention effect.

Random assignment of teacher aides to classrooms serving children with autism makes it unlikely that, on average, there are preexisting differences between the intervention and comparison classes (Boruch, 1997). There are two ways to conceptualize the difference between random assignment and self- or administrative selection into groups (see also Shadish, 2000). The first is to think of the comparison group, the group of classrooms without an aide, as representing a *counterfactual* to the intervention. That is, the comparison classrooms are used to answer the question, "What would have happened in the intervention classes had the teacher aides not been there?" If the aides are placed in classes through random assignment, then *on average* we can assume that they do not differ on characteristics that might be related to the outcome measures of choice, such as the child's prior achievement, the teacher's training, the class size, and so on. So, we can be confident, although not certain, that average group differences do not exist that predate the assignment to groups. Of course, this does not rule out differences between groups arising after random assignment has occurred. These will be discussed later when I look at the problem of attrition.

In the case of self- or administrative selection into groups, it is quite plausible, indeed likely, that the comparison group is a poor counterfactual. The primary culprit generating differences between intervention and comparison groups in quasi-experiments often is related to the motivations of people seeking the intervention. Teachers who request aides may be motivated to do so because they are teaching more poorly performing classes and therefore perceive that the child with autism will be more burdensome. Or, they are more poorly trained than teachers who pass on the opportunity, or have more students in their class.

The second way to conceive of the difference between random assignment and self- or administrative selection into groups is to construct a hypothetical *selection model* that might predict whether or not a participant is a member of the intervention or comparison group *prior* to the introduction of the intervention. Consider this an application of discriminant analysis. The criterion variable is the teachers' membership in the intervention or comparison group and the predictor variables are (a) the teachers' experience with children with autism, (b) the class achievement level, (c) the number of students in the class, and so on. When random assignment has been used to form the intervention and comparison groups, we can confidently conclude that the weight associated with each predictor in our discriminate equation is zero, roughly. More precisely, we can conclude that numerous replications of the random assignment procedure will produce weights averaged over replication that more precisely approach zero. And, because the intervention has not yet occurred, we can assume that the weight associated with the effect of the intervention is zero, prior to its implementation. Assuming that nothing else occurs after teacher assignment to make the groups different, we can also assume that all the predictors' weights should remain zero throughout the experiment (another assumption examined shortly). Then, whatever difference between the intervention and comparison group emerges during the experiment can be attributed to, that is, expressed in the weight for, the intervention.

If the intervention and comparison groups have been formed through self- or administrative selection, then we cannot assume the weights predicting group membership are zero after group assignment but before the intervention begins. The essence of quasi-experimentation is to employ some technique, other than random assignment, to reduce these weights to zero or get good estimates of them, so that the postintervention difference (or the change in difference) between the groups can, in fact, be attributed to the intervention.

The notion of selection models nicely ties the structural equation modeling approach to estimating causal effects to quasi-experimentation. That is, viewed in this context, the fundamental challenge to the modeler is to build a model that completely reflects the process through which participants were selected (nonrandomly) into intervention or comparison conditions. If the model is perfect, then the weight associated with the intervention can be a valid estimate of the intervention's effect.

Some Quasi-experimental Techniques

Shadish et al. (2002) suggest that quasi-experimental designs can be categorized into five types: (a) designs without a comparison group, (b) designs with a comparison group but no pretest, (c) designs with both a comparison group and pretest, (d) regression discontinuity designs, and, (e) time series designs. These authors catalogue more than two dozen design variations within the categories. There is neither the space nor the need to redescribe them here. Instead, I will attempt to briefly describe the general features of each design type. Figure 37.5 presents visual representations of designs from each of the first four categories.

(a) One Group, posttest only

$$X \qquad O_1$$

(b) Repeated-Treatment Design

$$O_1 \quad X \quad O_2 \quad O_3 \quad X \quad O_4$$

(c) Posttest-Only Design with Nonequivalent Groups

$$NR \quad X \quad O_1$$
$$\text{---------------}$$
$$NR \qquad O_2$$

(d) Switching Replications

$$NR \qquad O_1 \quad X \quad O_2 \qquad\qquad O_3$$
$$NR \qquad O_1 \qquad\quad O_2 \quad X \quad O_3$$

FIGURE 37.5. Some representative quasi-experimental designs.

Designs Without Comparison Groups. Designs without comparison groups involve a single group that is exposed to the intervention. There is no comparison group of separate participants who were not exposed to the intervention. Therefore, there is no counterfactual created by having the outcome measured in an untreated group at the same time it is measured in the intervention group. The problem, then, is to construct a comparison group that estimates for us the counterfactual, or how the experimental group would have performed without the intervention.

The simplest design without comparison is defined by an intervention being introduced and an outcome being measured. This design is pictured in Fig. 37.5a. In our example, a teacher aide is introduced and at some later time, long enough after for the intended effect to have occurred, the achievement of students with autism is measured. This lack of an explicit comparison group led Campbell and Stanley (1963) to suggest that this design was of "almost no scientific value" (p. 6). When the one-group, posttest-only design is used, there is typically invoked some general or implicit comparison group. So, if the outcome measure reveals that students with autism assisted by a teacher aide are performing at grade level, the inference might be that the aide caused improvement in achievement because, nationwide, children with autism perform below grade level. Obviously, there are a plethora of rival explanations for the result.

At the other extreme of inferential strength among these designs is the repeated treatment design (one variation of which is pictured in Fig. 37.5b). Here, a preintervention measurement of the outcome variable is taken, followed by the introduction of the intervention, a second measurement, removal of the intervention, another measurement, reintroduction of the intervention, and so on. If we discover that the scores on the outcome measure rise and fall in correspondence with the introduction and removal of the intervention, we grow in confidence that the intervention is the cause of the change, as it grows less plausible that other changes fortuitously occurring simultaneously with the intervention are the cause. However, these designs are not without plausible threats to validity. For example, the researcher must be careful that the timing of the introduction of the intervention is not established so that its appearance becomes tied to some extraneous event also related to the outcome measure. For example, a school principal might suggest that the teacher aides assist students with autism in October and November but not in December and January and then return for February and March. Intentionally or not, the principal has confounded the introduction and removal of the intervention with hours of instructional time, given the added vacations in December and January. Also, it will be more difficult to show intervention effects if the outcomes of interest produce more versus less stable changes. For example, changes in reading comprehension, which ought not regress when the teacher aide is removed, are more difficult to demonstrate with this design than are outcomes amenable to more transient changes. These would include behavior problems, which might be expected to diminish but reappear when the aide is no longer present, or noncumulative skills, such as successive related but largely nonoverlapping units within a social studies or science curriculum.

Designs With Comparison Groups but No Pretest. The posttest-only design with nonequivalent groups compares an intervention group's outcome scores with a comparison group not receiving the intervention. This design is open to the threats caused by self-selection and administrative selection into groups. Further, it provides us with no way to test or adjust for preexisting differences between the groups. One such design is pictured in Fig. 37.5c.

An improvement on this design is the posttest-only design using matching or stratification. *Matching* occurs when the experimenter chooses participants for the intervention and comparison group based on having similar scores on the characteristic of interest. Most often, matching occurs when a researcher begins the study after the intervention has been introduced. The researcher then accesses a pool of candidates for the comparison group to find matches for participants in the intervention group. Thus, a researcher might know that 20 third-grade students with autism in a school district had teacher aides. The researcher may want to know if this intervention influenced their score on statewide tests at year's end (that is, no pretest was available). The researcher might decide that matching the intervention and comparison students on socioeconomic status and severity of diagnosis would rule out the two most plausible rival hypotheses to the effect of the aide. For each student with an aide, the researcher would examine the records of students with autism who did not have an aide to find the closest match on the two matching variables. *Stratification* is a somewhat less precise procedure in which, rather than picking exact or close matches for each student, the researcher blocks both the intervention and comparison group based on values on important characteristics. Of course, inferences made from these designs can be threatened by using poor selection models, and poor matching, among other things.

Designs That Use Both Comparison Groups and Pretests. The existence of a pretest bestows many benefits for drawing causal inferences. Here, we can get a clearer indication of how the two groups differed before the introduction of the intervention on the variable of greatest interest. This can assist us if we wish to (a) claim little or no selection bias existed because the pretest scores for the intervention and comparison group were very similar, (b) make a statistical adjustment for differences on the pretest, a variable that likely captures much (but not all) of the selection model that makes participants in our intervention and comparison conditions different, or (c) use repeated measurements to identify data patterns consistent with a causal effect of the intervention and not many other plausible explanations.

An example of this last benefit of pretests inspires the *untreated control group* design with dependent pretest and posttest samples using switching replications" (a rather lengthy descriptor for a simple idea, one variation of which is pictured in Fig. 37.5d. Here, we would take (or have available) pretest measures of achievement from students with autism, introduce teacher aides to half of the students (nonrandomly, or know which students already have an aide), wait a length of time assumed long enough to permit the intervention to have an effect, take a second measure, switch the aides to students initially not exposed to them, and subsequently take a third measure. Then, we would inspect the resulting data to see if it conforms to our predictions concerning how the students' achievement scores would change if the aides were having a causal effect. Our prediction might be that students with teacher aides would show larger gains in achievement during both intervention phases. Inferences from this design are strengthened if the groups are similar to begin with and strategies such as matching can be used to improve their similarity.

The *switching replications* design also can be extended to include more switching phases and/or more groups. As a result this design can lead to impressive demonstrations of causal relations. For example, imagine that four schools have agreed to be part of the experiment but require that all teachers in the school either have an aide or not (they don't want to foment jealousy), making random assignment of classrooms to aides impossible. However, they have agreed that the year can be divided into six 6-week periods and understand that teachers in their schools will have the aides for only three of the six periods. They also agree that the researcher can determine which schools get aides during which periods. The researcher than randomly assigns each school to the aide or no-aide condition for each phase. From such a design, if the data pattern is consistent with predictions, we have a case for a causal effect of teacher aides that rivals, indeed may surpass, the validity of one allowed by random assignment of teachers. Importantly, this design can also be considered an experiment using random assignment at the school level. In this case, schools, rather than classrooms, would be used as the unit for analyzing results.

Regression Discontinuity. Imagine that a school district knows they have funds to hire teacher aides for only half of their students with autism (this might be the same school district that took part in the "switching replications" design experiment). Further, suppose the district has decided, perhaps because of political pressures to reach a certain percentage of students achieving at or above grade level, to provide the aides to those students with autism who are currently performing best. Thus, it appears we have a design with a known, indeed maximized, preexisting difference between the intervention and comparison group on the outcome of interest. Before the study begins, we know that every student receiving the intervention is performing better on the outcome measure than every student in the comparison condition. On the face of it, such a design seems to have little value in the search for causes. In fact, this is not so. Because the researcher knows exactly what variable was used to create the intervention and comparison groups, he or she knows, in essence, what the selection model was. So, the researcher can make an estimate of the causal effect of the intervention. This can be done by calculating separate regression equations using pre- and postintervention

(a) Regression discontinuity effect present

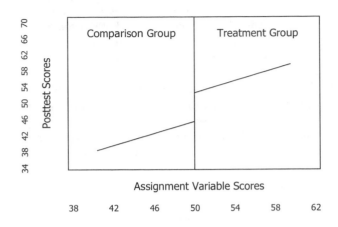

(b) Regression discontinuity effect absent

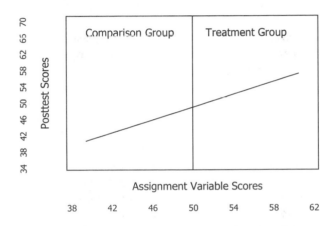

FIGURE 37.6. Hypothetical examples of results of two regression discontinuity studies.

achievement for students who do and do not receive the intervention. Then, the researcher determines whether a discontinuity occurs between regression lines at the point where they should intersect. Figure 37.6a illustrates the presence of a regression discontinuity effect, and Fig. 37.6b illustrates its absence. If a discontinuity exists, it is evidence that a causal effect of providing teacher aides may be present.

Of course, there are conditions that will compromise this causal inference. Most importantly, the assignment to conditions must be based solely on the assignment variable and the cutoff adhered to strictly. If many parents whose children fell just below the cutoff complain to the superintendent and their children are given teacher aides (while others who would have received aides don't get them), we now have the problem of self-selection into groups.

Also, the regression discontinuity design requires an assumption regarding the form of the relationship between the assignment variable and the outcome of interest. In Fig. 37.6, the assumption is made that the relationship is linear, a plausible assumption in our example given that the assignment variable and outcome are the same. In other cases the two variables may not be the same, for example, if teacher aides were assigned to students with the most severe autism and behavior problems were the outcome. In this case the relationship between the two variables might be curvilinear, that is, behavior problems increase rapidly from mild to moderate levels of autism but less rapidly from moderate to severe autism. Then, if we fit linear regression lines to the teacher-aide and no-teacher-aide halves of the data, the curvilinear effect could produce a discontinuity at the cutoff. It would also produce different slopes for the two halves of the data, giving us a clue that the form of the relationship may have been misspecified.

Time Series Designs. The final type of quasi-experimental design involves the analysis of a time series of multiple observations. When I addressed the three basic questions that determine the broad decision regarding what research designs to use, one of the questions dealt with whether an individual or group-level process was at issue. It is the time series designs that are most closely associated with individual-level processes, that is, questions asking about change in individual units over time. Also, I pointed out that the designation of an individual or group-level effect can depend on the context in which the data is being used. So, for example, if we are studying the impact of the introduction of a teacher aide on the achievement of a single student with autism, the research is certainly at the individual level. However, if we are studying the effect of this same teacher aide on the other students in the class, we can speak of the effect as "on average, for other students" (group level) or as "on this class" (individual level).

The distinguishing feature of a time series design is that it contains a series of multiple observations on the same variable taken over time. Generally, the time interval between measurements is equal. McCleary and Welsh (1992) offer three basic variations on the time series design, pictured in Fig. 37.7. The first is the *descriptive time series* (Fig. 37.7a.) As the name implies, this design is used not to uncover causal relationships but to decompose the variation in the series of measurements into (a) that which might reflect trends, that is an increase or decrease in variable values, that occurs across the entire measurement period; (b) cycles, that is, ups and downs in values that occur regularly over a consistent period of time (e.g., monthly, seasonally, yearly) but one that can be identified to occur multiple times within the series; and (c) random error.

(a) Descriptive time series (with trend and cycles present)

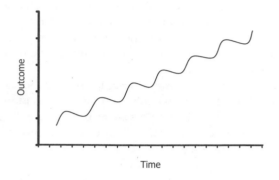

(b) Concomitant time series (with near perfect relationship)

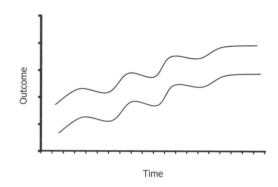

(c) Interrupted time series (with both level and slope change)

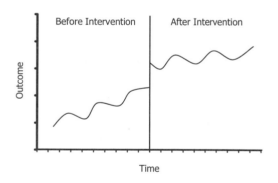

FIGURE 37.7. Hypothetical examples of three time series designs.

The second variation is the *concomitant time series* (Fig. 37.7b). In this design the covariation between two or more series of measurements is analyzed to determine whether these might be related. This design is the time series counterpart of the "relationship" designs discussed earlier. As such it has extremely limited ability to assist us in making causal inferences.

The third variation is the *interrupted time series design*. The goal here is to determine whether an intervention that occurs during the course of collecting the outcome measure had an impact on those measures' trajectory. This is the design with the most potential for establishing causes.

The simplest interrupted time series design involves a series of measures occurring both before and after the introduction of the intervention (Fig. 37.7c). As with regression discontinuity designs, the researcher looks for a change in level in scores when pre- and postintervention scores are compared. It is important to note that the outcomes in such designs need not be only class averages, but can be other group-level statistics as well. For example, placement of an autistic child in a classroom without an aide could lead to an increase in variability in achievement within the class, because middle-to low-performing students may not get the same amount of attention they received from the teacher prior to the student's arrival. An intervention effect can also appear as a change in slope between pre- and postintervention scores. This would indicate that the intervention affected the temporal trend in the scores.

Discovering discontinuities in time series designs is not a simple matter of performing separate multiple regressions on the preintervention and postintervention data. Instead, procedures developed specially for analyzing time series data need to be employed (Shumway & Stoffer, 2000). In essence, these procedures remove the "autocorrelation" between scores, the fact that scores that are closer together tend to be more similar to one another than scores that are farther apart. Any trends or cyclical patterns in the data must also be removed.

The most critical threat to validity associated with the simple interrupted time series design is that some other event might have occurred at or near the time that the intervention was implemented that is confounded with the intervention effect. A simple example would occur when a teacher aide was placed in the classroom of a student with autism at the beginning of a school year. Now, the new teacher or new classmates would be plausible rival hypotheses to claiming a causal effect of the teacher aide. Of course, for this to be a time series design, rather than a "one-group pretest-posttest design" it would need multiple pre- and postintervention measures. For example, the student's reading level might be measured each month for the year before and after the arrival of the aide.

Another important threat to the validity of simple interrupted time series designs is called the *reactive intervention*. For example, it might be the case that a particular student with autism has begun to create serious behavior problems in class. To counteract this, a teacher aide is placed in the student's class. The next month, records indicate the number of disruptions has gone down. In this case, it is plausible that the more frequent disruptions in the month before the introduction of the teacher

aide were an aberration for this child, perhaps based on a transient influence (such as a visit at home by Grandma). Much like a statistical regression effect in group research (where extreme scores can be expected to regress toward the mean on the next testing), when an intervention is implemented because the outcome variable of interest recently has attained an extreme value we must examine the long-term trend in scores to rule out the possibility that this score was an aberration and the intervention was implemented reactively.

Many of the design variations that improve the ability to infer causality from quasi-experiments also can be used in time series. These include introducing and withdrawing the intervention at different times in the series of measurements (and at random, if possible) and conducting simultaneous time series on multiple units, some of which have the intervention and others not, during any given interval. These designs, when they produce predicted patterns of results, can produce highly credible claims of causality.

Experiments

From the discussion of quasi-experiments, it is clear that the use of random assignment to place participants into conditions is an extremely valuable tool in the search for causes. Through randomization, experiments can create statistically equivalent groups. Experiments have the potential to eliminate the threat of biased selection into groups, probably the one threat that most doggedly vexes education researchers who seek to make causal claims. However, random assignment alone does not create perfect experiments that always lead to flawless inferences about causal relationships. It is important that we explore things that can happen in the course of experiments that compromise their ability to uncover causal relations.

Failure of Randomization. Efforts to place participants into conditions at random sometimes do not lead to the "on average" equivalence of groups that is its intended outcome. Why this occurs is critical to our understanding of its implications. First, randomization may fail to produce average equivalence of groups for chance reasons alone. If we use statistical significance as the benchmark for "failure," we know that if we measure 20 randomly chosen characteristics of participants who have then been randomly assigned to two groups, one of these characteristics will prove statistically significant by chance alone. One in 20 is an infrequent occurrence. And, the possibility that this chance characteristic would be an outcome of interest (or one closely related) is even smaller. Still it is the case that when researchers test the "success" of random assignment, they sometimes find the process did not result in the desired pretest equivalence of groups on outcomes of interest. This "unlucky" randomization compromises the experiment's ability to estimate the causal impact of the intervention. In such cases, it is not unusual for an experimenter to adjust the estimated impact in a fashion similar to building a selection model (often using an analysis of covariance). It is also the case that the unadjusted estimate of the intervention's impact still can be used as part of a larger array of estimates from multiple studies, for example in a meta-analysis. Here, we assume that the weights in each study's selection model will vary from zero by some degree, but we know that across the array of studies the weights, on average, will tend to zero, with greater precision than is achieved in any single study. The "unlucky" study represents an extreme case in this array, but one we can expect is counterbalanced by another "unlucky" study with weights in the opposite direction.

Randomization also may fail for more systematic reasons. For example, the experimenter may randomly assign aides to teachers of students with autism. However, the principal might then receive a phone call from the central district office telling her to give aides to three teachers initially assigned to the comparison group because the children's parents have complained. This compromised random assignment can also be adjusted using a selection model. However, unlike the "unlucky" study the unadjusted estimate of the interventions effect cannot be used as an element in a larger array of estimates. It will systematically bias the resulting overall estimate. Studies with "compromised" random assignment are best viewed as quasi-experiments; some of the participants in the intervention and comparison groups are there by random assignment but others are there due to self- or administrative selection.

Attrition. Even if randomization successfully produces intervention and comparison groups that do not differ on important characteristics prior to the introduction of the intervention, other events can occur in the period after assignment but before the outcome measures are collected that could be plausible rival explanations for what appears to be an intervention effect. Among these are problems of attrition (see Table 37.1), or participants leaving the experiment before the outcomes are measured (West & Sagarin, 2000).

There are two ways that attrition problems can manifest themselves. First, an experiment can experience *differential attrition between the intervention and comparison groups*. Simply put, differential attrition occurs when more participants leave the experiment that were slated to receive the intervention, who received part of the intervention, or who completed the intervention but then did not complete the outcome, than left from the comparison condition. Differential attrition also occurs when more participants leave the comparison than intervention group. In our example, it is most plausible to construct a scenario in which more students leave the comparison group than the teacher aide group. Here, parents of children with autism learn that their child's teacher will not have an aide and decide to take their children out of one school and put them in another, perhaps moving from public to private school. These parents tend to be wealthier than parents whose children remain in the comparison group and, therefore, also can supply their child with more ancillary private services. Now, the intervention and comparison groups differ not only because one group experiences a teacher aide in class but because, on average, the group with the teacher aide is also receiving more after-school tutoring, for example. Thus, the experiment's ability to draw causal inferences about the impact of a teacher aide is compromised. Had the wealthier families stayed in the comparison group, the experimental and comparison groups would have been roughly equal regarding how many students were receiving this extra help.

Differential attrition is a serious threat to the internal validity of experiments. By definition, the loss of participants is related to group placement. Therefore, we must assume that the differential loss is in some way related to how participants were treated, or thought they would be treated, in their respective group. Researchers can examine attriters' and nonattriters' scores on preintervention measures (for example, family wealth, severity of autism). Demonstrating (a) that no differences existed between attriters and nonattriters and (b) that the intervention and comparison groups remained equivalent even after attrition may help rule out alternative causes for differential attrition. However, it does not establish a plausible cause and does not show this cause is unrelated to the outcomes of interest.

The second form of attrition is called *severe overall attrition*. Here, the number of attriters does not differ between the intervention and comparison groups, but the total number of attriters is large. Most obviously, severe attrition is a threat to the external validity of an experiment's results (just as nonresponse is a threat to the generalizability of surveys). If the participants who leave the experiment differ systematically from those who remain, then the results of the experiment pertain only to participants with characteristics similar to those who stayed. Suppose that during the course of an experiment, 40 percent of students with autism transfer schools, regardless of whether they are in the aide or no-aide group, and their reason for leaving is unrelated to which group they are in. Perhaps they are in families with less stable, lower paying jobs, leading to higher mobility. Then, the results of the experiment based on the 60 percent who stayed are generalizable to a more limited target population, relatively wealthy families with stable jobs.

Severe attrition is also viewed as a potential threat to internal validity. As the number of participants leaving an experiment increases, it becomes more plausible that the reasons for attrition in the intervention and comparison group are different, even if the percentages of attriters appear equal. Hypothetically, if 40 percent of the students with autism leave both the intervention and comparison groups, it may be that 20 percent are leaving because they are in mobile families. The other 20 percent of attriters in the comparison group may be leaving because they want the service of a teacher aide, while 20 percent in the intervention group leave because of conflicts between the family and the teacher aide.

Crossover is a problem related to attrition. Here, students move from one condition of the experiment to another. Perhaps a conflict arises between a parent and teacher or a student moves from a school in the intervention condition to a school in the control condition.

One way to handle attrition is to carry out what is called an *intention to treat* analysis. In this case, the researcher attempts to collect outcomes measures on all participants who were originally assigned to the experimental conditions, regardless of whether they actually received the intervention (or a portion of it) or remained in the comparison group. The statistical analysis is then conducted on the complete data set. This analysis may permit causal inferences but there is a subtle and important change in the causal construct. Now, we are not asking, "What is the impact of having a teacher aide on the achievement of a child with autism?" but rather, "What is the impact of making teacher aides available on the achievement of children with autism?" This latter question can have important policy implications. For example, if the federal government is exploring whether to make funds for teacher aides available, it may be best informed by an estimate of the effect of their policy. Attrition will be a natural part of the process of delivering the new service. If this is the question under consideration, the intention to treat analysis provides the answer.

Threats to Construct, External, and Statistical Conclusion Validity in Experiments

Table 37.1 lists several different threats to internal validity in addition to severe and differential attrition. The remaining threats on the list relate to quasi-experimental, not experimental, designs. For example, statistical regression might affect scores in an experiment if all the partici-

pants were chosen because they had extreme scores on a pretest and regressed toward the mean on the posttest. However, we would not expect the regression effect to be more pronounced in the intervention or comparison group if participants were randomly assigned to conditions. Therefore, statistical regression can be ruled out as a plausible rival hypothesis to any posttest *difference* between the two groups. Likewise, maturation and testing effects may occur but ought not have different effects on the two groups if they were constituted at random. Herein lies the power of random assignment.

Random assignment assists us in disposing of threats to internal validity. The ability to randomly assign participants to conditions has no benefits per se for ruling out construct, external, and statistical threats to validity. Indeed, some would argue that certain features of experiments tend to make them more vulnerable to threats to construct and external validity relative to research designs using structural equation or quasi-experimental methods. We will examine a few of these arguments.

Construct Validity. The construct validity of an experimental intervention can be compromised because of processes set in motion by the introduction of the intervention. These processes can have no relation to the content of the intervention itself. For example, the regular class teachers who have teacher aides assigned to them might change their beliefs regarding how the student with autism will perform and change the way they treat the child in subtle ways (expectancy effects). Or, the teachers who do not receive aides might become resigned to poor performance and cut back their efforts at improving these students' achievement (resentful demoralization). Or, comparison group teachers might become energized to prove they can produce the same benefits without assistance (compensatory rivalry). Yet still, comparison group teachers might approach the teacher aides in their school and ask for tips on how to best serve students with autism (treatment diffusion). Interestingly, these threats were classified as threats to internal validity by Cook and Campbell (1979) but as threats to construct validity by Shadish et al. (2002).

The foregoing treatment contamination threats to the validity of experiments are most plausible when the participants in the intervention and comparison group are in close proximity, so one knows how the other is being treated. Thus, these threats will be minimized if the intervention is assigned at the school level rather than at the classroom level (though principals will still know). It is also important to note that these threats cannot be detected statistically. They require the experimenter to remain vigilant about how the treatment is being implemented and what its impact is on the broader social context in which the experiment is occurring. Clearly, laboratory experiments will have fewer concerns with treatment contamination than will experiments conducted in classrooms and schools. Also, identifying the broader impacts of interventions and plausible contaminations of the intervention construct is an important reason for employing mixed method designs, ones that use quantitative methods to estimate the causal impact of an intervention but embed within the experiment a collection of qualitative evidence that reveals the process of implementation and the meanings or understandings of the intervention experienced by the participants (Tashakkori & Teddie, 2003).

External Validity. Although random selection (from a target or accessible population) and random assignment (to conditions) are often confused, the two techniques have no relationship to one another. *Random selection* refers to how participants are chosen to be in a study, and *random assignment* refers to how participants are allocated to conditions once they are in the study. Thus, whether or not a study used random assignment has no necessary implication for the generalizability of its findings.

Some would argue that, in practice and on average, experiments produce less generalizable results than structural equation models or quasi-experiments. This is because experiments require participants who are willing to be allocated to conditions randomly, and not all people are. Also, the random introduction of interventions creates an artificial implementation process (teachers get picked at random) that is rarely replicated by allocation processes that occur naturally. That being said, random allocation of resources does occur in nature, and when it does it represents an excellent opportunity for studying causal effects. For example, the hypothetical school district mentioned earlier that had twice as many teachers of students with autism than teacher aides (and could have been used in a switching replications or regression discontinuity design) might have decided that the fairest way to allocate teacher aides was by lottery. This produces a natural experiment that researchers can capitalize on, even long after the intervention was implemented, if the proper data were also collected as part of the natural process.

Statistical Validity. As with external validity, knowing that a study employed an experimental design has no necessary implications for whether the data analysis has or has not been conducted properly and whether the study used data meeting the necessary mathematical assumptions. In fact, experiments generally fare well on this account because—relative to structural equation models, complex quasi-experiments (with matching, stratification, and/or switching treatments), and time series analyses—analyzing experimental data is typically straightforward.

CONCLUSION

The Role of Theory in Interpreting the Value of Research Designs

Early in this chapter, I pointed out that the National Research Council's Committee on Scientific Principles in Education Research (Shavelson & Towne, 2002) suggested that education research questions could be categorized into three types: descriptive (What is happening?), causal (Is there a systematic effect?), and process or mechanism (Why or how is it happening?). I added a third question, "What events happen together?" and I removed the question regarding processes or mechanisms. I did this because I view the process or mechanism questions as ones that transcend the different types of research designs, or more precisely that can be addressed descriptively, relationally, or causally. Within the framework I have described, uncovering processes or mechanisms is tantamount to finding moderating variables prior to and mediating variables intervening in the process that connects the events of interest. Let's briefly return to my earlier thought experiment. I made the assertion that if I claimed that my elbow caused the coffee cup to fall from my desk, then the book my elbow hit or the force of gravity could be invoked as alternative explanations. Now, I will make the claim that rather than competing with my causal explanation, these are actually intermediate or mediating events that reveal the process or mechanisms that link my cause (elbow) with the event (spill). So, if you ask why or how did the spill occur, I might respond, "Because my elbow hit the book, which pushed the cup off the edge of my desk (because two solid objects cannot occupy the same space at the same time), which then fell to the floor (because of the effect of gravity)." For Humians, then, explanations delineate the temporal flow of events that occur between the cause and its effect. The more complete the explanation is, that is, the more temporally contiguous the links are (and by implications the more links there are), the more "satisfying" the explanation will be. This "logic" plays itself out most explicitly in the construction of structural equation models because they are based on the explication or modeling of processes and propose multivariate, temporally sequenced linkages. In experiments, this reasoning can play itself out by the researcher performing (a) sequences of studies examining moderators and mediators or (b) studies that include multifactored variations in conditions (e.g.,

"What happens if I replace the coffee cup, remove the book from my desk, and then move my elbow in the same manner"?).

The primary implication of this line of reasoning is also one I return to from this chapter's beginning: *There is no explanation without theory.* In fact, it is the theory underlying the research question in conjunction with the current state of evidence (knowledge) on the question that tells us what to investigate next and what the best method will be to test it. It will also be the theory and all its tests in multiple contexts that will augment the plausibility of our proposed causal process. Do you doubt that once the coffee cup left the table, gravity caused it to fall to the floor rather than hover in the air?

The importance of theory crept into our discussion of research design in another way. This occurred when I discussed the role that different patterns of data play in interpreting causality. Our causal theory predicts how the particular intervention will operate. Let's return to our teacher aide example and our discussion of time series analyses. When the teacher aide is first introduced to the classroom, our prediction, based on theory, might suggest that we will see an immediate drop in discipline problems created by the student with autism but only a gradual improvement in the student's reading test scores. The first prediction suggests a discontinuity at the point of intervention, whereas the second suggests a gradually emerging change in slope. Suppose the revealed data pattern was the opposite, that is, reading achievement showed an immediate increase and behavior problems showed a gradual change. In this instance, we would certainly be less satisfied that it was our intervention that had caused this effect. We would be more likely to search for plausible rival explanations. Perhaps even more dramatically, suppose our theory predicted a delayed impact of the treatment, suggesting perhaps that the impact of the aide on behavior problems would not be revealed until several weeks after introduction. In the absence of such a prediction, the teacher aide might be viewed as ineffectual and the later decrease in misbehaviors attributed to some other event. In the presence of this prediction, the data pattern becomes an impressive demonstration of the effectiveness of the intervention and the theory suggested as underlying its operation.

The Interplay of Theory, Policy, and Practice in Research Questions and Designs

Although it is true that theory plays a central role in the design and construction of research, because without theory results are rarely interpretable (and most research rests on some underlying theory, explicitly or not),

it is also the case that education is an applied science. Therefore, whether education researchers are in pursuit of knowledge about basic processes or about the impact of specific interventions, it is critical that the policy and practice implications of research remain at the forefront of *what* research questions are asked and *how* answers are sought.

This issue leads us back to where we began. Fundamental to the utility of the results of any study in education is that the research design has to be appropriate for answering the question at hand. Relational designs cannot establish causality. Experiments cannot assess need. A mismatch between the research question and design renders the result of little use in the domain of policy and practice. Burkhardt and Schoenfeld (2003) provide a thorough explication of this process and the difficulties arising when it is applied in practice.

Design-Based Research Methods. Appreciation of the role of both theory and practice in the development of research design provided impetus for the development of what have come to be called *design-based research methods.* According to the Design-Based Research Collective (2003) this approach encompasses five principles. First, theory and the design of learning environments must be explicitly intertwined. Second, the design of environments and the data produced to evaluate their effects must interact in an iterative process of design, enactment, analysis, and redesign. Third, research must result in theoretical statements that are meaningful and have clear implications for education practitioners and other designers. Fourth, research must provide explanations for results that appear in authentic settings. This principle encompasses the need both for asking "why" questions and for testing designs in real-world locations. Finally, research must provide clear accounts of how interventions were carried out and how these are tied to the outcomes of interest (see also a special issue of *Educational Psychologist*, Sandoval and Bell, 2004).

The design-based research approach grows out of an engineering tradition (Collins, 1992). However, its principles are general to any approach to applied science. They call for (a) precision in definitions and documentation of how interventions are implemented (construct validity); (b) appropriate sampling of target populations, settings, and occasions, and testing of robustness within subsamples (external validity); and (c) the constant interplay of theory and data so that theory undergoes revision in light of data and data collection remains relevant to producing the next respecification of the theoretical model.

This is not a new set of dicta. The design-based research approach is refreshing, however, precisely because these principles have so rarely been applied in education research. Rather than emphasize a precise summative estimation of an intervention's effect, it emphasizes using data about effectiveness (and not necessarily from experiments) to refine both the theory and the theory-based intervention before a next testing. Further, the intervention may change in fundamental ways over the course of its development, and the use of comparison groups may be minimal until late in the development process. Because of these features, the design-based research approach cannot be neatly fit into one of the boxes depicted in Fig. 37.1. Rather, it suggests a "package" of interrelated studies, in which different research questions and designs may be more or less emphasized at different stages of development. The implementation of this approach will be critical for the development of education science, critical both in the sense that "it needs to be done" and in the sense that "it must be done without compromise regarding standards of evidence" (Shavelson, Phillips, Towne & Feuer, 2003). A similar approach to educational research and development is being developed through the Strategic Education Research Partnership (Donovan, Wigdor & Snow, 2003).

A Final Caution

In this chapter, I have attempted to provide an overview of the types of questions education researchers most frequently pose and to describe some appropriate quantitative research designs for answering them. In the course of describing research designs, I attempted to point out their strengths and weaknesses. Because I had so much to cover in limited space, descriptions invariably leave out the finer nuances of definitions and designs and many cautions.

Still, in some instances, especially in the search for causal relationships, the list of ways research can go awry, leading to improper inferences, may seem discouraging. It shouldn't be. Instead, researchers should use the list of pitfalls to ensure that they take their task seriously. No research design, in theory or practice, leads to flawless inferences, be they about descriptions, relations, or causal connections, quantitative or qualitative, about individual or group-level phenomena.

Ultimately, the veracity of scientific claims rests not on the results of a single study but on an accumulation of evidence, conducted by multiple researchers. It is best when these studies vary in their strengths and weaknesses. The task we set for ourselves in research is complex, whether it is about a theory of how nature operates or an assessment about the effects of a discrete intervention. Like any master carpenter, researchers perform their highest service when they proceed with a critical eye cast on their own work, make cautious claims regarding what their work can reveal, and humble claims about what they have achieved.

ACKNOWLEDGMENTS

Thanks are extended to Rick Hoyle, W. Todd Rogers, Lisa Towne, Jeffrey C. Valentine, Philip Winne and Angela Clinton for comments on and assistance with the preparation of this chapter.

References

Baron, R. M., & Kenny, D. A. (1986). The moderator-mediator variable distinction in social psychology research: Conceptual, strategic, and statistical considerations. Journal of Personality and Social Psychology, 51, 1173-1182.

Boruch, R. F. (1997). Randomized experiments for planning and evaluation. Thousand Oaks, CA: Sage.

Borsboom, D., Mellenbergh, G. J., & van Heerden, J. (2002). The theoretical status of latent variables. Psychological Review, 110, 203-219.

Burkhardt, H., & Schoenfeld, A. H. (2003). Improving educational research: Toward a more useful, more influencial, and better-funded enterprise. Educational Researcher, 9, 3-14.

Butler, D. (2005). Advances in qualitative methods. In P. A. Alexander & P. H. Winne (Eds.), Handbook of educational psychology (2nd ed.). Mahwah, NJ: Lawrence Erlbaum Associates.

Bracht, G. H., & Glass, G. V. (1968). The external validity of experiments. American Educational Research Journal, 5, 437-474.

Camic, P. M., Rhodes, J. E., & Yardley, L. (2003). Naming the stars: Integrating qualitative methods into psychological research. In P. M. Camic, J. E. Rhodes, & L. Yardley (Eds.), Qualitative research in psychology: Expanding perspectives in methodology and design (pp. 3-15). Washington, DC: American Psychological Association.

Campbell, D. T. (1957). Factors relevant to the validity of experiments in social settings. Psychological Bulletin, 54, 297-312.

Campbell, D. T. (1969). Reforms as experiments. American Psychologist, 24, 409-429.

Campbell, D. T., & Stanley, J. C. (1963). Experimental and quasi-experimental designs for research. Chicago, IL: Rand McNally.

Collins, A. (1992). Toward a design science of education. In E. Scanlon & T. O'Shea (Eds.), New directions in educational technology New York: Springer-Verlag.

Converse, J. M., & Presser, S. (1986). Survey questions: Handcrafting the standardized questionnaire. Thousand Oaks, CA: Sage.

Cook, T. D., & Campbell, D. T. (1979). Quasi-experimentation: Design and analysis issues for field settings. Boston, MA: Houghton Mifflin.

Design-Based Research Collective (2003). Design-based research: An emerging paradigm for educational inquiry. Educational Researcher, 32, 5–8.

Donovan, M. S., Wigdor, A. K., & Snow, C. E. (Eds.) (2003). Strategic education research partnership. Washington, DC: National Academies Press.

Fleiss, J. L. (1994). Measures of effect size for categorical data. In H. Cooper & L. V. Hedges (Eds.), *Handbook of research Synthesis*. New York: Russell Sage Foundation.

Fowler, F. J., Jr. (1995). Improving survey questions: Design and evaluation. Thousand Oaks, CA: Sage.

Fowler, F. J., Jr., (2002). Survey research methods. (3rd ed.). Thousand Oaks, CA: Sage.

Groves, R. M., Fowler, F. J., Couper, M. P., Lepkowski, J. M., Singer, E., & Tourangeau, R. (2004). Survey methodology. Hoboken, NJ: Wiley.

Hoyle, R. H. (1995). Structural equation modeling: Concepts, issues and applications. Thousand Oaks, CA: Sage.

Hume, D. (1978). A treatise on human nature. Oxford: Oxford Press. (Original work published in 1739–1740.)

Kline, R. B. (1998). Principles and practices of structural equation modeling. New York: Guilford Press.

Loehlin, J. C. (2004). Latent variable models (4th ed.). Mahwah, NJ: Lawrence Erlbaum Associates.

Maruyama, G. M. (1998). Basics of structural equation modeling. Thousand Oaks, CA: Sage.

Maxwell, J. A. (2004). Causal explanation, qualitative research, and scientific inquiry in education. Educational Researcher, 33, 3–11.

McCleary, R., & Welsh, W. N. (1992). Philosophical and statistical foundations of time series experiments. In T. R. Kratochwill & J. R. Levin (Eds.). Single-case research design and analysis (pp. 41–92). Hillsdale, NJ: Lawrence Erlbaum Associates.

McKillip, J. (1987). Need analysis: Tools for the human services and education. Thousand Oaks, CA: Sage.

Nye, B., Hedges, L.V., & Konstantopoulus, S. (2000). The effects of small classes on academic achievement: The results of the Tennessee Class Size Experiment. American Educational Research Journal, 37, 123–151.

Popper, K. (1959). The logic of scientific discovery. New York: Basic Books.

Salant, P., & Dillman, D. A. (1994). How to conduct your own survey. New York: Wiley.

Sandoval, W. A., & Bell, P. (2004). Design-based research methods for studying learning in context: Introduction. Educational Psychologist, 39(4), 199–201.

Shadish, W. R. (2000). The empirical program of quasi-experimentation. In L. Bickman (Ed.), Research design. Thousand Oaks, CA: Sage.

Shadish, W. R., Cook, T. D., & Campbell, D. T. (2002). Experimental and quasi-experimental designs for generalized causal inference. Boston, MA: Houghton Mifflin.

Shavelson, R. J., Phillips, D. C., Towne, L., & Feuer, M. J. (2003). On the science of education design studies. Educational Researcher, 32, 25–28.

Shavelson, R. J., & Towne, L. (Eds.). (2002). Scientific research in education. Washington, DC: National Academies Press.

Shumway, R. H., & Stoffer, D. S. (2000). Time series analysis and its application. Berlin: Springer.

Stone, A. A., Turkkan, J. A., Bachrach, C. A., Jobe, J. B., Kurtzman, H. S, & Cain, V. S. (1999) The science of self-report: Implications for research and practice. Mahwah, NJ: Lawrence Erlbaum Associates.

Tashakkori, A., & Teddie, C. (Eds) (2003). Handbook of mixed methods in social and behavior research. Thousand Oaks, CA: Sage.

Taylor, S. J., & Bogdan, R. (1998). Introduction to qualitative research methods (3rd ed.). New York: Wiley.

Thompson, B. (2004). Exploratory and confirmatory factor analysis: Understanding concepts and applications. Washington, DC: American Psychological Association.

Tourangeau, R., Rips, L. J., & Rasinski, K. (2000). The psychology of survey response. Cambridge, UK: Cambridge University Press.

Webster's New Universal Unabridged Dictionary. (1996). New York: Barnes & Noble Books.

West, S. G. & Sagarin, B. J. (2000). Participant selection and loss in randomized experiments. In L. Bickman (Ed.), Research design. Thousand Oaks, CA: Sage.

Winne, P. H. (1983). Distortion of construct validity in multiple regression analysis. Canadian Journal of Behavioral Science, 15, 187–202.

Yin, R. K. (2003). Case study research: Design and methods. Thousand Oaks, CA: Sage.

·38·

THE ART OF STATISTICS: A SURVEY OF MODERN TECHNIQUES

Daniel B. Wright
University of Sussex

Remember the tedium of plugging numbers into equations in your undergraduate statistics course? Statistics appeared to be solely about the computation of summary values that were used to test hypotheses. These autonomous tasks are now done by computers, leaving more interesting tasks for humans. Following Mosteller and Tukey's (1977, p. 1) lead in their classic text, *Data Analysis and Regression*, it is "the art of data analysis." It is an art. As with other arts it requires technical skills, but these technical skills must be used to fulfil the larger goals of statistics. Statistics is about revealing patterns in data, deciding how these patterns relate to theories, and communicating the results to an audience. Data must be transformed into information and this information provided to others. The communication of statistical information can be in any combination of three different modes: numeric, verbal, and graphical. As such, while the computational details in most statistics textbooks are vital for producing numeric estimates, following the writing guidelines of Strunk and White (2000) and producing graphs with the informational elegance of Tufte (2001) are also necessary skills for communicating the importance of your results to others.

The goal of this chapter is to describe some of the recent statistical techniques that are part of the educational psychologist's arsenal of statistics. As well as describing statistical techniques, there is particular emphasis on describing the data and the information embedded within. This is based on the view of most methodologists and discussed in documents for major societies and for many journals (e.g., AERA in Thompson, 1996; APA in Wilkinson et al., 1999; BPS in Wright, 2003).

It is worth asking why so many societies and journal editors felt the way that statistics are conducted is so poor that they needed to produce guidelines for conducting and reporting statistics. To answer this question, we should look at the dominant statistical approach in psychology in the 20th century and ask if there could be a better approach for the 21st century. This is covered in the first section of this chapter. The remaining sections focus on techniques that will be important tools for educational psychologists in the 21st century. The techniques are generalized linear models (GLMs), multilevel modeling, latent variables, meta-analysis, robust estimation, and small sample methods. In addition, there are brief sections on generalized additive models, longitudinal methods, structural equation models, and bootstrapping. There is a valuable statistical tool missing from this list: item response modeling. An entire chapter is devoted to this (Ercikan, Chapter 40 of this volume).

Note: Many Web pages are listed in this document. This is inevitable in the 21st century, but can be annoying because URLs change (all were active Oct., 2005). See http://www.sussex.ac.uk/Users/danw/statsisart.htm for any updates and further information about the techniques described. Many of the papers cited can be found on the Web if you have access to, for example, PSYCHLIT.

Designing a Statistical Approach

When Fisher, Gossett, Pearson, and their colleagues were laying the foundations for the method of statistical inference that dominated 20th-century psychology, they did not have the same technologies as we have today. In Karl Pearson's day, at the turn of the last century, "computers" were the people who sat in university basements conducting computations on hand-cranked calculators. Given the potentials for human error, calculations were often repeated until any two solutions matched. Indeed, some of the analyses we use today were specifically tailored to minimize the number of necessary calculations. It is ironic that we continue to use older methods developed in part to address computational issues that no longer concern us.

Further, the graphics used in those days were often painstakingly produced by hand. This has some advantages; imagine someone drawing a false third dimension onto a graph by hand and not thinking it was wasteful! But it has disadvantages. There was a reliance on just the numeric form of communication, and only in a limited way.

Statistics during the 20th century (Huberty, 1999, 2002), but especially after the 1950s (Hubbard & Ryan, 2000), was dominated by testing the significance of particular hypotheses, usually that a parameter is equal to zero (called NHST for null hypothesis significance testing, although Cohen [1994, p. 997] suggested that statistical hypothesis inference testing produced a more appropriate acronym). With this approach, a hypothesis is put forward and assumed to be correct. The researcher collects data and tests how likely it is to observe data as extreme as observed if the hypothesis were true. There are numerous problems with the way psychologists typically use NHST, but I will mention two.

The first problem is that the hypothesis assumed to be true is usually of no substantive interest, like there being no difference between a control and an intervention group. This has the consequence that as scientific instruments improve (for example, having better IQ tests) it becomes easier and easier to reject these uninteresting hypotheses (Meehl, 1967). The solution is simple: NHST should never be used unless the researcher thinks that the hypothesis being tested is worth testing. That sounds obvious, but people often test hypotheses such as the correlation between two people coding the same data being zero. This is a clear situation where the researcher should either test a more meaningful hypothesis, such as the correlation is above some minimum acceptable level, or report the confidence interval for the statistic.

The second problem is that psychologists have become too reliant on NHST as the single tool to decide whether a study is valuable or not. To understand why this happened it is necessary to look to the beginning of the last century, when NHST was in its infancy. It was not possible for each researcher to calculate the p-value associated with every set of data for a particular hypothesis. They had to rely on "computers" to produce critical points for different distributions. These were the points corresponding to $p = .10, .05, .02,$ and $.01$. In perhaps the most influential statistics book ever, Fisher (1925) provided verbal labels for different probability values:

.1 to .9	"Certainly no reason to suspect the hypothesis tested" (p. 79),
.02 to .05	"Judge significant, though barely so…these data do not, however, demonstrate the point beyond possibility of doubt" (p. 122),
Below .02	"Strongly indicated that the hypothesis fails to account for the whole of the facts" (p. 79),
Below .01	"No practical importance whether P is .01 or .000001" (p. 89).

Despite Fisher believing that different values of p should lead to different degrees of belief, his most quoted phrases are about $p = .05$: it is "convenient to take this point as a limit in judging whether a deviation is to be considered significant or not. . . . We shall not often be astray if we draw a conventional line at .05" (pp. 47, 79). People's attention focused on .05. Finding $p < .05$ became synonymous with "good" and $p > .05$ became synonymous with "bad." The problem is not that .05 became the convention ("surely, God loves the .06 nearly as much as the .05 level of significance"; Rosnow & Rosenthal, 1989, p. 1277). The problem is that people use this convention within a dichotomous decision-making procedure and rely too much on this single aspect when evaluating data.

Although NHST may have some uses (Abelson, 1997), it has become too important. Further, because it is easier to remember $p < .05$ means "good" than the statistical definition, many researchers do not understand the core of their statistical method (Oakes, 1986). This was an appalling state for the discipline. Meehl (1978) stated this most forcefully: "Sir Ronald [Fisher] has befuddled us, mesmerized us, and led us down the primrose path. The almost universal reliance on merely refuting the null hypothesis is a terrible mistake, is basically unsound, poor scientific strategy, and one of the worst things that ever happened in the history of psychology" (p. 817). He describes how psychology theories go in and out of fashion based more on "baffled boredom" (p. 807) rather than the evaluation of evidence. Others are equally as critical. Rozeboom (1997, p. 335) described NHST as "the most bone-headedly misguided procedure ever," and Schmidt and Hunter (1997, p. 37) stated that is "retards the growth of scientific knowledge." There are even Web pages (see http://biology.uark.edu/coop/Courses/thompson5.html and http://www.cnr.colostate.edu/~anderson/nester.html) listing such quotations!

Statistics became an autonomous drive (like a flow chart or a recipe) to produce a *p*-value. The main intellectual task was using those "which test" diagrams in the back cover of introductory texts. These diagrams emphasize the differences among statistical tests rather than the similarities among these tests. This makes it harder for students to generalize across procedures and it limits conceptual understanding.

During most of the 20th century, graphics were also discouraged. It was difficult to make publication-quality graphs, and publishers often discouraged their use because of costs. But the problem may be more deep-rooted. The science of displaying quantitative information has been built on two premises (Tufte, 2001): Graphs should be used to lie about your data, and your data are so uninteresting that you have to add *chartjunk* so that your audience is not bored. As Tufte pointed out: "It is hard to imagine any doctrine more likely to stifle intellectual progress in a field" (p. 53). Numerous authors have described how good graphs can help to communicate science, and computer software is improving (Wainer & Velleman, 2001; Wilkinson, 2005), but there is still much bad practice (Wainer, 1984; Wright & Williams, 2003).

The final mode of communication is verbal. In some ways the writing during the early part of the last century was better than the present day. Articles have become longer, and brevity is an important part of good writing. The interest here is in the results section. Sometimes it appears that authors try to use complex language and statistics to distance their readers from the data (or even to obscure the data). Many authors appear to believe that rules of writing style do not apply. Some argue that it does not matter if results sections are badly written because nobody reads them. It is important to break out of this self-fulfilling prophecy. If results sections were better written, more people would read them. The results section should be the most exciting part of an article. After the buildup of the introduction and methods, the findings are revealed. It is where Hercule Poirot points his finger at the guilty!

A Change in Statistics? If I had to choose a time and a place for change in statistics, they are in 1968 and at Stanford University (and then University of Chicago). Norman Nie, Hadlai Hull, and Dale Bent began writing and distributing SPSS (www.spss.com/corpinfo/history.html). They were literally giving statistics away to the users, which should be a goal of all sciences (Miller, 1969). This paved the way for nonstatisticians to conduct their own analyses. With the software revolution, further general-purpose statistics packages were created and developed for the desktop. The graphics modules improved and made it relatively easy to incorporate graphs and tables into word processing packages (Wilkinson, Rope, Carr, & Rubin, 2000). If these capabilities were around for our statistical forefathers, would NHST been developed and would it have become so dominant?

The question is whether there is some alternative that will make statistics simple. Cohen advised us not to "look for a *magic* alternative to NHST, some other objective mechanical ritual to replace it. It doesn't exist" (1994, p. 1001, emphasis added). "Objective mechanical rituals" are not usually considered part of an art, and as stated in the title of this chapter, statistics is an art. Therefore, any alternative must allow artistic freedom. Whereas "objective mechanical rituals" are not a viable alternative, Cohen may have been wrong about searching for a magical alternative. There are two general ways to improve how statistics are approached. The first is based on Abelson's MAGIC (1995) criteria for persuading people about your data. The second, based on many people's work but most notably Tukey (1977), is that we should focus on the data. Rosenthal said that you should "make friends with your data" (Wright, 2003, p. 134). Data should be turned into information, and this information used to persuade the reader about the hypotheses under consideration.

Abelson (1995) argued that the general rules of communication and persuasion should be applied to results sections. He described the MAGIC criteria for a good results section. MAGIC stands for Magnitude, Articulation, Generality, Interest, and Credibility. These labels are fairly self-explanatory:

Magnitude: report effect sizes
Articulation: focus the reader on the effects of importance
Generality: state how broadly your results should generalize
Interest: make the reader excited (which means you should be excited)
Credibility: provide good evidence for your claims

The "making friends with data" component is best exemplified by Tukey and colleagues when discussing exploratory data analysis (EDA). Hoaglin, Mosteller, and Tukey (1983) discussed the four themes, or four Rs, of EDA: resistance, residuals, re-expression, and revelation.

Resistance: statistics should not be greatly affected by a few points
Residuals: do some points appear to have arisen from different processes than the others?
Re-expression: sometimes the original variables need to be transformed
Reveal: what do your data tell you?

These four Rs should be considered whenever you are trying to extract coherent patterns from data. Abelson's MAGIC can be applied to these observed patterns to produce an accurate, convincing, and clear story.

Readings. There has been much written about the problems with the NHST. The references cited in the text are just a small selection. Harlow, Mulaik, and Steiger (1997) provide a collection of chapters discussing the problems. Two papers by Cohen (1990, 1994) and the APA task force report (Wilkinson et al., 1999) are also excellent sources.

A SURVEY OF TECHNIQUES

Broadly speaking, there are two ways that science can progress. The first is by building on the existing generally accepted techniques and theories, what Lakotos called the *core*. The second is by questioning these generally accepted beliefs. I have divided this survey into two sections: techniques that build on the existing methods, and those that question them. This division is not clear cut. All the techniques in this chapter build to some extent on previous methods, and all question some aspects of how statistics is traditionally conducted. The division is both a matter of degree and also how radical the impact of using these techniques will be on the status quo.

Building on Existing Techniques

Ordinary least squares regression is one of the most basic statistical procedures. Not only is it what people usually mean when they say they are doing a simple or a multiple regression, but ANOVAs, *t*-tests, and even calculating the mean are examples of this procedure (Cohen, 1968). Consider the following simple linear regression, where y_i is the outcome (or response or dependent) variable, x_i is the predictor (or independent or covariate) variable, $\beta 0$ and $\beta 1$ are the intercept and the slope, respectively, and the e_i are the residuals:

$$y_i = \beta 0 + \beta 1 x_i + e_i.$$

This is the same equation that is solved for a group *t*-test, just x_i is a variable that denotes the two groups (ie., $x_i = 0$ for the control group; $x_i = 1$ for the experimental group). One-way ANOVAs can be constructed by transforming the categorical variable that denotes group membership into several variables that each contrast one group to a baseline group. Suppose there are three groups (A, B,

and C). Two variables must be created. Let $x1_i$ be 1 for group A and be 0 for the other two groups. Let $x2_i$ be 1 for group B and be 0 for the other two groups. The one-way ANOVA is:

$$y_i = \beta 0 + \beta 1 x1_i + \beta 2 x2_i + e_i.$$

$\beta 1$ contrasts groups A and C, and $\beta 2$ contrasts groups B and C. This is a multiple linear regression. It is usually assumed that the e_i are normally distributed. The computation involves finding values for the estimated parameters, the βs, that minimize the sum of the squared residuals. Details can be found in most introductory textbooks.

This basic linear regression can be written more compactly as $y_i = \Sigma \beta k x k_i + e_i$, where Σ means summing all the $\Sigma \beta k x k_i$ from 0 to k (let $x0_i$ be a variable with the value 1 for every case). The $\Sigma \beta k x k_i$ is called the fixed or systematic part of the model and is denoted η_i. The e_i is called the random part of the model. Sometimes you may see these written in bold, as $\beta \mathbf{X} + \mathbf{e}$. This is matrix notation (β is a vector containing all the βk values), which can save space when writing complex equations, but for the present chapter is unnecessary.

These techniques were all in place toward the beginning of the last century. Many of the advances toward the end of the last century were helped by computations becoming much quicker and statistical advances. These are often not included in introductory courses and therefore a sample of them is described here. The procedures described in this part of the chapter advance the basic regression model. Some of the techniques are difficult computationally. Others show how statistical advances are able to bring together a large collection of techniques under a single framework, thus allowing them to be applied more generally.

Generalizing the Linear Model (GLM). One of the most important advances in statistical modeling during the past 50 years was begun by Nelder and Wedderburn (1972). They showed that linear regression could be extended to a larger set of situations including many that are frequently encountered in psychology. Requiring the model to be linearly related to the responses and requiring normally distributed residuals are not appropriate for many research problems. Different functions can be used to *link* the predicted values with a linear combination of the predictor variables, the model: η_i. Let μ_i be the predicted values and $g()$ be the link function. Thus, $g(\mu_i) = \eta_i$.

In this section three link functions are considered: the identity function, the log function, and the logit function. These link functions have different error distributions associated with them: normally distributed errors, Poisson distributed errors, and binomially distributed errors, respectively. The phrase *identity function* in mathematics means a function that maps something onto itself. For the identity function, $\mu_i = \eta_i = \Sigma \beta k x k_i$. If we assume normally distributed errors, this is simply the standard linear multiple regression that is taught to undergraduates. This is a special case of GLM.

A common situation in psychology is where the dependent variable is a frequency. For example, this might be how many times a child asks for help in a classroom. If these occurrences are independent and based only on a single mean for each person, then they may follow a Poisson distribution and the log link is appropriate: $\log(\mu_i) = \eta_i$ with error following a Poisson distribution. The Poisson distribution has high expected probabilities for low frequencies, and then the expected probabilities decline as the frequencies increase. Thus, it is expected that most children ask few questions, but that some may ask dozens. The distribution is positively skewed. The Poisson distribution has the useful mathematical property that its mean is the same as its variance. This procedure is sometimes called a *Poisson regression* or a *log-linear model*. The phrase *Poisson regression* is usually used when you have a frequency variable for an individual person. Another situation where Poisson regressions are used is when the variable is positively skewed, which makes it look like the Poisson distribution, but that researchers are not claiming that the responses actually occurred by a Poisson process. Reaction-time data are often modeled this way. The phrase *log-linear model* is used when you have categorical data and you are trying to model the number of people in a particular cell in a contingency table (Agresti, 2002). This is more common in sociology.

Another situation that often occurs in psychology is where a person's score is the number of correct responses out of some total. Kadriye Ercikan (Chapter 40 of this volume) discusses how item response models can be used in these situations to look at the individual items, but sometimes you only have the score and not the responses for the individual items on an education test. In these situations the logit link function is usually used. The logit link function is $\ln(\mu_i/[1 - \mu_i]) = \eta_i$, where "ln" means the natural logarithm. Logit stands for log-odds. It is usually assumed that error is binomially distributed. This is called a logistic regression. The predicted value, μ_i, is the probability of a correct response on an item. A special case of this is when the variable is dichotomous, for example, a pupil either passes or fails a task. The error term follows a Bernoulli distribution, which is a special case of the binomial distribution when there is only a single trial. This special case deserves mention because logistic

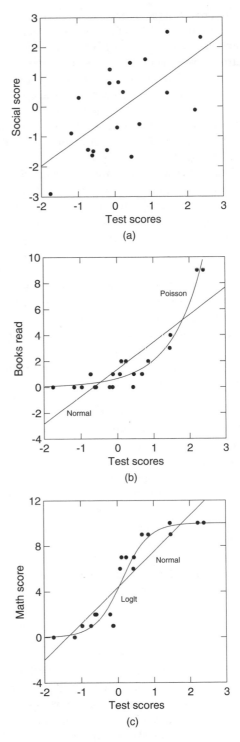

FIGURE 38.1. Data and models showing different generalized linear models. (a) Socializability with test scores with the normal linear model. (b) Books read with test scores. Both the normal linear model and the Poisson model are shown. The Poisson model is more appropriate. (c) Math scores with test scores, and the normal linear model and logit model. The logit model is more appropriate.

regressions are often used for dichotomous variables, and in fact when some people refer to logistic regression they are actually referring just to this special case.

For illustrative purposes suppose that we have data on 20 children. The data include values from some standardized intelligence test that is normally distributed with a mean of 0 and a standard deviation of 1. We want to see how these scores relate with scores from a scale of socializability, the number of books read, and number correct out of 10 on a math quiz.

The data and models are shown in Fig. 38.1a, 38.1b, and 38.1c. The first graph shows the data for socializability with the test scores and the model for the normal (linear) regression; it is well suited for the data. In the second, which compares books read with the test scores, both the normal model and the Poisson models are shown. The Poisson model fits better. If the normal model was taken at face value, it predicts that children with test scores below about −.5 (which would be about 40 percent of the population) will read a negative number of books. Similar problems exist for the normal model in the third panel, which shows the math quiz with test scores. The normal model fits less well than the binomial model and makes predictions outside the possible range of 0 to 10.

A Brief Note on Generalized Additive Models (GAMs).

A class of techniques that has a similar sounding name to GLMs is GAMs. They are a generalization of additive models. Additive models are one of several alternatives to linear models that are less restricted by assumptions (and theory) and are more data driven. In the generalized linear model, the model is the sum of predictor variables (the x_is) each multiplied by a value (the βs): $\eta_i = \Sigma \beta k x k_i$. It is assumed that each predictor variable is linearly related to the model. Sometimes it is worth relaxing this assumption and allowing the data to dictate the relationship to a greater degree.

Each of the βks of the linear model, $\Sigma \beta k x k_i$, is replaced by a function $fk()$ such that $\eta_i = \Sigma fk(x k_i)$. The fk are designed to produce a smooth line that goes through the data points. There are many different smoothing functions, but the most popular are splines. Splines are collections of simple polynomial functions joined up at what are called *knots* so that a smooth curve is fit through the data points. The degree of the polynomial and the number of knots determine how closely the curve fits the data. Figures 38.2a–c show the three different splines running through the scatterplot in Fig. 38.1a. When constructing these graphs there is a trade-off between how close the line should be to the individual points and how simple it is. These three graphs show a progression in flexibility. Although the model in Fig. 38.2c is the closest fit to the individual data points, it is too complex. Either a straight

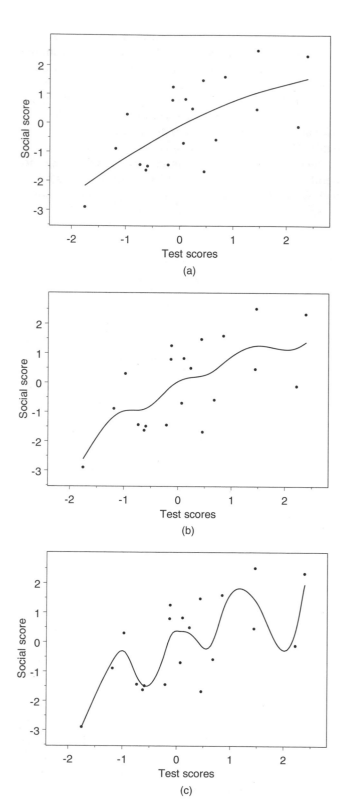

FIGURE 38.2. (a–c) Spline curves for additive models for the data from Fig. 38.1a. The figures show increasing flexibility in the models, and therefore the lines are closer to the data points. However, the lines become unrealistically complex to be useful models.

line (Fig. 38.1a) or a simple curve (Fig. 38.2a) provides the best fit.

Other smoothing functions also exist. Kernel methods, in particular, are discussed in much of the statistics literature. They fit a different function on each point of x. The function is determined by those points near x. The most popular of these is the lowess function, which fits a straight line at these points and is not strongly influenced by outliers. GAMs are most useful for exploratory analysis when producing scatterplots, identifying outliers, and when looking at just two variables. They can be more difficult to interpret when the number of predictor variables is large.

Readings. Most intermediate statistics books for psychologists include some information on GLMs. Hoffmann (2004) is an introductory book devoted to GLMs. It is well written and at the appropriate level for first-year postgraduates. The bible of GLMs is McCullagh and Nelder (1989), but this is meant for statisticians. A good, but technical, overview of GAMs and related techniques can be found in Hastie, Tibshirani, and Friedman (2001; Chapter 5 on splines, Chapter 6 on kernel methods, and Chapter 9 on GAMS); see http://www-stat.stanford.edu/gam/paper/paper.html and http://www.bioss.sari.ac.uk/smart/unix/mgam/slides/frames.htm for brief introductions.

Software. Most of the main software packages allow some GLMs to be conducted, for example logistic regression, but sometimes these are restricted to the case where the responses can only be 0 or 1. S-Plus and SAS allow more to be done (S-Plus was used here, and elsewhere in the chapter unless otherwise noted).[1] The software GLIM (Francis, Green, & Payne, 1993) was written specifically around GLMs. It is still useful for some specific applications (largely because many European statisticians write macros for it), but the increase in GLM procedures for other software (particularly S-Plus) means that its main selling point is less impressive. There are GAM procedures in S-Plus and SAS.

Multilevel (Hierarchical) Modeling. In the last section I wrote how the basic linear model assumes that the residuals are independent and normally distributed. I showed that generalized linear models (GLMs) relaxed the normality assumption. Here, the focus is on the independence assumption. In almost every undergraduate methods course students are told that their statistical models assume that

the data are independent, but they are not told what to do if the data are not independent. This is because until about 20 years ago there were neither the algorithms nor the computational power for conducting many of the statistics that can now be estimated quickly on a desktop computer. Before this, there were corrections that could be applied to nonindependent data, but these were problematic and inflexible.

A common situation is where the nonindependence is due to the data being clustered. *Multilevel modeling* (often called *hierarchical modeling*) takes into account the clustering. It allows modeling to be conducted simultaneously at the level of the cluster and at the level of the individual. It does assume that, after taking into account the clustering (and any other variables in the model), the data are independent. Further, for inference the researcher usually assumes that the units at one level are a random sample of all those from within the cluster.

Consider the following example from Barth and colleagues (Barth, Dunlap, Dane, Lochman, & Wells 2004). They looked at the peer relationships of about 600 pupils by the pupils' race and gender. The pupils were sampled from 65 different classrooms. The assumption is that the pupils sampled were representative of the pupils within these classrooms. For illustration, consider their fourth-grade sample. For the traditional single-level approach, a researcher might use a regression of the following form:

$$\text{Peer}_i = \beta0 + \beta1\,\text{Gender}_i + \beta2\,\text{Race}_i + e_i,$$

where high Peer_i values mean problematic relations, Gender_i is a dummy variable with female = 0 and male = 1, and Race_i is a dummy variable with Caucasian = 0 and non-Caucasian = 1. The standard regression assumes that the e_i are independent. They are not, because there are likely to be classroom effects: Children within the same classroom are more likely to have similar Peer_i scores than children from different classrooms. In fact, in Barth et al. about 12 percent of the total variation could be attributable to classroom-level variation. The standard errors using this traditional approach are likely to be too small, which means that you will often get a significant p-value when you should not. Because in psychology people worry more about Type 1 errors than Type 2 errors, this bias causes much concern among editors and reviewers, who now often force authors to use multilevel modeling.

For multilevel modeling, let the intercepts vary randomly for each classroom. In notation, let the intercepts

[1] A freeware version of S-Plus, called R, is available from http://cran.r-project.org/. This Web page includes many macros written by statisticians to run advanced statistics to complement Rs already impressive collection of procedures. Introductions to R include Dalgaard (2002) and Maindonald and Braun (2003), the later being more advanced.

be $\beta 0_j = \beta 0 + u_j$, where the u_j are independent and normally distributed for the schools. The subscript j is for the 65 schools. Barth et al. (2004) estimated the following model:

$$\text{Peer}_{ij} = \beta 0 + \beta 1 \, \text{Gender}_{ij} + \beta 2 \, \text{Race}_{ij} + u_j + e_{ij} \, .$$

They found a significant gender effect ($t(1325) = 4.42$) and a significant effect for race ($t(1, 325) = 5.80$) with males and non-White participants having poorer peer relations.

Multilevel modeling can be extended in many ways. First, while it is true that the pupils in Barth et al.'s study were nested within classrooms, the classrooms were nested within schools. In their paper, they looked at this using a three level model. In addition, variables that are about the classroom (such as the classroom average Peer score) and school could be included, and in their paper some of these were included. The random part of the model can also be made to incorporate more aspects of the data. It is normal to see if the slopes also vary among the classrooms. For example, to allow the gender effect to vary among schools the researchers, let $\beta 1_j = \beta 1 + v_j$, where the v_j represent the spread around the central gender effect, $\beta 1$.

A frequently asked question about multilevel modeling is what types of data can be used with it. The textbook example of pupils sampled within classrooms seems to satisfy the criterion that we can imagine pupils as a random sample of all those in the classroom. However, multilevel models are now often used for any hierarchical data set regardless of whether the lower level units can be easily thought of as a random sample of some population (see Wright, 1998, for discussion). Using a modern mathematically complex statistic cannot rectify this methodological difficulty. More caution is worthwhile when thinking whether a particular hierarchical data structure meets all the assumptions of multilevel modeling.

A Brief Note on Longitudinal Methods. There are two main questions asked by people using longitudinal methods: what is associated with change over time, and when does something happen (Singer & Willett, 2003). For the first of these questions researchers measure some variable at many different points in time and use time (and other covariates) to predict the variable. Data of this form are now often analyzed using multilevel models. The individual measurements are nested within the participant. This has many computational and conceptual advantages over traditional methods, such as the standard repeated measures analysis. For example, it is not necessary for all the people to have been measured on the same number of occasions, and the timing

of measurements need not be the same for all people. Researchers can construct trajectories for growth with time on the x-axis. Analyzing longitudinal data has been one of the major applications of multilevel modeling. Although other techniques for this type of data exist and have been used, particularly in econometrics, the flexibility of multilevel modeling has made it particularly attractive.

The other question that is often asked of longitudinal data is, When does something happen? In one sense this is the opposite question to the first question. There *time* was used to predict other variables. If you are asking when something happens such as when somebody graduates from high school, you are using other variables to predict *time*. Singer and Willett (2003) use "the whether and when test" to decide if this type of longitudinal method is necessary. If your research question is either "whether" something happens or "when" it happens, then you should probably use this approach. The main goal of this approach is to estimate functions for the probability of changing from one state to another (such as becoming a high school graduate). The analyses for this type of problem go under the names of *survival/hazard analysis, event history analysis*, and *Cox regression*. There are many issues that need to be taken into account. Singer and Willett's textbook is an excellent introduction to both types of longitudinal data analysis.

Readings. The bible of multilevel modeling is Goldstein (2003; the 1995 edition is available free on http://www.mlwin.com/publref/index.html). It is aimed at statisticians. There are several textbooks aimed at social scientists: Hox (2002), Kreft and de Leeuw (1998), and Raudenbush and Bryk (2002). Hox reads the most like a textbook for a single-term postgraduate course. Kreft and de Leeuw is probably the simplest and most clearly written of the books. Raudenbush and Bryk's book is the most detailed and is useful if you are using the package HLM. Singer and Willett's book (2003) is excellent for longitudinal data analysis. The multilevel modeling project at the University of Bristol keeps an up-to-date Web site for the topic on http://www.mlwin.com. UCLA houses many good statistical resources including http://www.ats.ucla.edu/stat/mlm/ on multilevel modelling.

Software. A few years ago there were only a few specialist packages (MLwiN and HLM being the most popular) and a few macros written for SAS and S-Plus to run multilevel models. Whereas the specialist packages have incorporated more advanced features, mainstream packages like SPSS and SYSTAT now include procedures for some simple multilevel models. Reviews of packages that can perform multilevel modeling are on http://www.mlwin.com/softrev/index.html.

Exploring What the Latent Variables Are. *Latent variables* are unobservable human constructs used to account for shared variation among several observed (or manifest) variables. A child might be given a battery of psychometric tests, each with dozens of questions. The responses to these questions are the observed variables. The psychologist uses these observations to construct latent variables. One example is where multiple tests are done to measure ability and the responses used to calculate scores on several dimensions or facets. This is what is done with item response modeling (Ercikan, Chapter 40 of this volume), which is a special case of latent variable modelling.

In the time of Galton, Spearman, and Thurstone, the introduction of these human constructs for psychological phenomena in a manner that physicists described physical constructs such as mass and distance was groundbreaking and controversial. With time, it has become part of our undergraduate curriculum and is taught in an automated manner, often without questioning either whether it is possible to create such constructs or even to ask much about the nature of these constructs. The thrust of this section is not to say that psychologists should not be dabbling with these latent variables—their value in theory construction and theory development is clear—but that researchers should now focus more on what the latent variables are. Recent statistical advances allow this. Before describing this, a brief description of structural equation modeling (SEM) is in order.

SEMs begin with a correlation or covariance matrix of observed responses. There are two main parts of a structural equation model: the measurement and the structural parts. In the measurement part of the modeling, this matrix of observed variables is transformed into a set of latent variables. In the structural part of the modeling, relationships among the latent variables are hypothesized. The researcher then tests how well these hypothesized relationships are able to re-create the original correlation or covariance matrix. If the hypothesized relations can re-create the original matrix well, then the model fits (and in some sense this supports the model, but the degree of support depends on what other models could also re-create the original matrix). If the model does not fit, it is rejected. Assessing the fit of a model is an active area of discussion (for a historical perspective, see papers in Bollen & Long, 1993; for more contemporary views, see Hu & Bentler, 1999, and Fan, Thompson, & Wang, 1999). An important aspect of SEM is that these stages are done simultaneously. Although this has some advantages, it makes the results more difficult to interpret and often focuses attention just on the structural part of the modeling. Several authors have recommended separating these stages (cf., Anderson & Gerbing, 1988). Here the focus is more on the measurement part.

The explosion of SEM meant that they rapidly found their way into the psychological literature. Being able to include lots of variables within a single model and with several caveats use the word *causal* with correlational data are attractive. There is disagreement about the value of SEM, but even advocates of the procedure agree that in many cases enthusiasm for SEM has led to reckless application. Sometimes researchers do not check the assumptions of the models, are not careful adding the appropriate caveats for their conclusions, and, more important, it seems like many authors try to awe reviewers and readers with technology rather than to communicate their findings to their audience. The biggest problem, however, is that the complexities of trying to model several variables simultaneously have sometimes made researchers not ask simple questions about the variables and their bivariate relationships. Given the problems of trying to come up with a coherent summary of the relationship even among three variables (for example, Lord's paradox, 1967; Wainer, 1991; Wright, in press), researchers should focus on simple relationships before progressing to complex ones.

Although SEM will remain popular, the trend over the next 10 years should be to focus more on questions about smaller parts of the overall model. This is good for psychology, where often the interest is in simpler relationships among a few variables, trying to learn more about those few variables, and often making some kind of causal statement about relationships among these variables. The problem with many SEMs is that their complexity makes simple interpretation difficult.[2]

In psychology we often make bold statements about complex relationships among latent variables without being able to answer simple questions about the latent variables themselves. As Thompson (2004) emphasized, only "once these measurement models are deemed satisfactory, then the researcher can explore path models (called 'structural models') that link the latent variables" (p. 110). This is because "if the specified measurement models do not fit the measured variables, then knowing the relationships among the latent/synthetic variables defined by these measurement models is essentially useless" (Thompson, 2000, p. 273). The most basic question about

---

[2]The problem is not unique to SEMs. The same arguments can be, and have been, made at multiple regression and path models without any latent variables (Simon, 1954).

a variable, whether it is something that classifies people into groups or that has values along some dimension, is seldom asked. Lenzenweger (2004) says that psychologists and sociologists usually think in dimensions or continua, so it is usually assumed that latent variables are continuous. Others, for example psychiatrists, tend to think in terms of types, and for psychiatrists this is reflected in the DSM classification. Scientists should question whether these pre-existing beliefs are valid (i.e., for theory development) and useful (i.e., for educational interventions).

In the next decade people will look more at what their latent variables are. There are two reasons. First, although there have been criticisms of path analysis (and its modern variants such as SEM) since its inception (Niles, 1922; S. Wright, 1921), the recent popularity of some latent variable techniques mean that there should be an increase in critical evaluation of its use. Second, there are more statistical procedures that address what the characteristics of the latent variables are. Two sets of these procedures, by Bartholomew and colleagues and by Meehl and colleagues, are now briefly described.

Bartholomew (Bartholomew & Knott, 1999) presented the *general linear latent variable model* (GLLVM) as a means of unifying distinct approaches that have evolved through researchers from several different disciplines modeling latent variables. The mathematics is beyond the scope of this chapter, but what they did was provide a way to solve latent variable problems that allowed the observed variables to be either continuous or discrete and the latent variables to be either continuous or discrete. When both are continuous, this is *factor analysis*. When both are discrete, this is *latent class analysis,* which is common in sociology. When the observed variables are continuous and the latent variables are categorical, they call it *latent profile analysis,* although in psychology this is sometimes called *taxometric analysis*. Finally, when the observed variables are discrete and the latent variables are continuous, it is *latent trait analysis*, which includes item response modeling. Bartholomew, Steele, Moustaki, & Galbraith (2002) provide an introduction to these techniques and links to freeware to run the analyses. Latent class models in particular are becoming more popular in psychology. They allow researchers to distinguish among particular groups of people (for example, types of drug user, market research categories). In many cases there is more value in a theory that hypothesizes different groups (or taxa) than dimensions along which people vary.

This unifying framework forces researchers to think about whether their latent variables are continuous or discrete. This is good, but Bartholomew and colleagues argue that this should primarily be done on the basis of theory, not data:

> How difficult it is to distinguish empirically between a latent trait and latent class model. The situation is even worse when we come to factor analysis and latent profile analysis. In this case, it is virtually impossible to distinguish between the two models because both models have essentially the same correlation structure. (Bartholomew et al., 2002, p. 247)

The taxometric approach, pioneered by Paul Meehl, assumes that the observed responses are related to discrete latent constructs (see Waller & Meehl, 1998). Their motto (in Waller & Meehl, 1998, on Waller's taxometric Web page, etc.) is: There are gophers, there are chipmunks, but there are no gophmunks. This is clear for biological kinds, which are clustered into species. Meehl argued that many psychological constructs are also described better by discrete latent variables than by latent dimensions. For example, Meehl (1990) has described how schizophrenia is best conceptualized as a discrete latent variable. He has provided many data to support this conceptualization, though he, like Bartholomew, often stressed how it is important to use more than just data to reach any conclusions.

Meehl's approach to statistics was inspiring (he sadly passed away in 2003). He was a true polymath. At 15 years old he told his high school counselor he would become a professor in psychology or philosophy or psychiatry or statistics (Meehl, 1989), and he made valuable contributions in each of these fields. When these skills are combined the true value of taxometrics and his writings on it are clear. His descriptions of concepts such as *latent* and *taxon*, how he embeds his statistics within his (and Faust's) meta-scientific approach to psychology, and his knowledge of how clinicians use the constructs (he described himself as 40 percent Freudian) all highlight the care that needs to be taken when doing any statistical analysis.

Many methodologists worry that typical researchers do not think in detail about what they are doing in the way that Meehl did. Too often people do not treat statistics as an art, but as a recipe that can be passively followed (perhaps because this is the easiest way to teach it). Although there are many examples that illustrate good use of latent variable modeling, it is a technique that can easily be misused. The mathematical complexities of including a large number of manifest and latent variables in a set of equations are minor compared to the conceptual complexities of having a large number of manifest and latent variables in a theory. Still, it appears that the mathematical complexities have meant that some researchers treat latent variable modeling as a black box and only interpret parts of what is output. Bartholomew, Meehl, and others provide the tools to explore a fundamental aspect of the black box, the form of the latent variables.

Readings. There is a large literature about SEM. Good introductions include Bollen (2002), Klem (2000), Miles and Shevlin (2003), and Thompson (2000, 2004). The focus here has been latent variable models where the manifest or latent variables are not continuous. The books by Bartholomew (Bartholomew & Knott, 1999; Bartholomew et al., 2002) describe how all latent variable models can be described within the same framework. The 2002 book is more introductory. Waller and Meehl's (1998) book describes both the theory of and the programs for their taxometric analyses. A recent issue of *Journal of Abnormal Psychology* (Vol. **113**, 2004) on taxometric analysis is a good introduction in relation to clinical psychological constructs.

Software. SEM is available for many of the main packages, sometimes as a supplement (for example, AMOS for SPSS), and sometimes as part of the package (for example, RAMONA for SYSTAT). The Web page for Bartholomew et al. (2002) is http://www.mlwin.com/team/aimdss.html and includes links to the freeware *LAMI* (LAtent Model Interface) that can be used for many of these models. Niel Waller's taxometrics page, http://www.psych.umn.edu/faculty/waller.edu, provides links to his work and programs for R (see footnote 1). Waller has several good Web sites that can be reached from the preceding URL. The freeware *L*EM (http:// www.uvt.nl/faculteiten/fsw/organisatie/departementen/mto/software2.html) is also useful freeware (it has been expanded into Latent Gold, which is commercial software).

Questioning Aspects of the Traditional Techniques

Three techniques are described in this section: meta-analysis, robust methods, and resampling techniques. Each is gaining in popularity and *could* be viewed as an extension of past techniques. Meta-analyses could simply be a way to combine results from studies. Robust methods could be just what you use when your data are not normally distributed. Resampling could just be an estimation procedure when you have small samples. However, each of these techniques has a deeper philosophical message. For meta-analysis, it is the belief that single studies may not be informative, and that even disparate studies can be combined to yield just a handful of summary statistics. For robust methods, it is throwing out the centuries-old

notion of minimizing least squares and in many cases focusing only on the middle of the distribution. With resampling, the often fantastic assumption that the second-year psychology students or the children at the local primary school are a random sample of anything is not made. Without that assumption, the researcher cannot make inference to the population but instead makes local causal inference.

Meta-analysis. Meta-analysis has become a hugely popular technique (Field, 2003) since its development in the 1970s (Glass, 1976; Rosenthal & Rubin, 1978). Meta-analyses can and have been used to address both substantive questions (e.g., effects of class size or of psychotherapy) and measurement (i.e., validity—Schmidt & Hunter, 1977—and reliability—Vacha-Haase, 1998). The basic idea of a meta-analysis is to gather the effect sizes (statistics such as r or the odds ratio) along with some information about the precision of the estimate (such as the standard error or the sample size) from a large number of studies and to combine these estimates into a few summary statistics (usually something like a mean effect size weighted for the precision of the study).

Meta-analyses are appearing in the top journals and are some of the most cited papers in psychology and other sciences. They offer a method to combine data from several studies and to produce a few summary numbers. Given that this procedure is now part of mainstream psychology, an obvious question is why I have included it as a challenge to traditional methods. The reason is that traditionally a single study could be used to provide evidence for or against some theory. Few theories would rest or perish on the basis of a single study, but people design their studies specifically to evaluate a hypothesis, usually in a novel way. Seldom would a study be a straight replication of another. In fact, whereas it is acceptable for the first study in a multistudy paper to be a replication (to check that the materials are adequate), it is generally frowned on if the rest of the studies are exact replications. This means that often meta-analyses are used to combine studies that were specifically designed to be different.

Imagine if to prove the existence of cold fusion, a meta-analyst simply took the mean effect size from all the studies that examined whether cold fusion exists. The result would be that cold fusion exists, but with a smaller effect than Fleischmann and Pons (1989) had originally shown. This shows two of the fundamental problems that can exist with meta-analyses. First, studies using different procedures are combined. Although it could be said that this generalizes across methods, it also dilutes the effect of any individual study. This leads to the second fundamental problem, at least for some approaches to science. If people follow the Popperian approach of making bold conjectures (such as, cold fusion does not exist in any situation) and using hypothesis testing to reject these hypotheses, then any single incident can falsify this conjecture. The example from courses in logic is that finding one black swan proves that not all swans are white. The NHST approach does not work exactly like this (Cohen, 1994), but it does rest on the importance of a single study.

The cold fusion debate can be compared with the debate about the Ganzfeld studies of extrasensory perception because of the difficulties each has had with replications. The Ganzfeld studies involve having someone mentally transmit information to another person without any sensory contact. It is argued that the results from these studies provide the best evidence for psychic ability. A meta-analysis appeared to show that there was evidence for this (Bem & Honorton, 1994), but others have been more skeptical about this and other meta-analyses (Hyman, 1996). What is agreed, even by those saying that meta-analyses show that psychic ability exist, is that substantial tests on a few individuals who appear to show high ability and further replications based on the findings of meta-analyses are needed (Hyman & Honorton, 1986).

There are situations where meta-analyses make more sense. For example, in many multicenter drug trials, results from different research groups can be combined because the centers are attempting to administer the drug in the same way. The individual participants can be treated as nested within the center, and the problem viewed as a multilevel model (Goldstein, Yang, Omar, Turner, & Thompson, 2000). To take an example of more relevance to educational psychology, Petrosino, Turpin-Petrosino, & Buehler (2002, data from Wright & Kelley, 2004) looked at seven studies of the "scared straight" program. This is where juveniles are shown prison life firsthand. Many politicians and members of the press described how these programs were successful. The studies had a similar form: Juveniles were either placed in a control group or took part in the program. The outcome variable was whether the person reoffended or not. Thus, each study could be analysed using at 2×2 χ^2 with the odds ratio as the effect size.

Meta-analyses can be conducted in several ways (see Readings). There are several freeware packages, specialist commercial packages, and procedures in general packages for meta-analysis. For these data I used syntax for SPSS for random effects binary outcome data downloaded

from http://www.spsstools.net. The data for the seven studies are input, and the package tells you that the summary odds ratio is 1.64 with a 95 percent confidence interval from 1.16 to 2.32. The direction of this effect was in the opposite direction to that claimed by politicians and the press: the reoffending rate was higher in the group that were "scared straight." It is important to stress that this shows that across samples from different populations that on average "scared straight" increases the likelihood of reoffending. But does this show that "scared straight" tends to have a negative effect? To make any strong conclusions, like this, it is necessary to assume that the populations studied are representative of some larger "super population." The inferences are about this "super population."[3] Therefore, if the studies are not a representative sample of this population, then the inference is suspect. The estimates are also open to an obvious bias. For example, if there was a particular population where the effect size was large, then to make the meta-analysis's estimates larger, simply more studies need to be done with this population (or in the particular laboratory, with the particular stimuli, etc.). How studies are sampled is called *second-order* sampling and is described in Chapter 9 of Hunter and Schmidt (2004).

It is important for any meta-analysis to look at the effects for the individual studies. A useful way to present these is to show them in ascending order of their effect sizes with their 95 percent confidence intervals:

Odds Ratio	95% Confidence Interval
1.05	(0.54, 2.07)
1.09	(0.44, 2.66)
1.48	(0.57, 3.83)
1.51	(0.61, 3.77)
2.09	(0.86, 5.09)
3.75	(1.11, 12.67)
5.08	(1.54, 16.71)

Here, all the studies have odds ratios above 1, which means that in each the reoffending rate was higher in the "scared straight" group than in the control group. For most of these the values are near 1 and their intervals overlap with 1. This means that individually none of the first four provide strong evidence for or against the "scared straight" program. The final three studies have odds ratios above 2 and provide stronger evidence against the program. It is worth noting that the final study was the only one to use boys and girls, and also Petrosino et al. (2002) discuss problems with the randomization

---

[3] The aim of many meta-analysts is to get data from all studies that have been conducted. This is the target super population, but it is often unclear if this is appropriate. A better super population might be all situations in which a particular intervention could be used.

into groups in this study (59 percent of the people in the "scared straight" group had a past conviction, compared with only 40 percent in the control condition). If this single study was excluded, the new summary odds ratio is 1.47 with a 95 percent confidence interval from 1.03 to 2.11. One fear about how people interpret meta-analyses is that it may make them less critical of aspects of the individual studies, hoping that somehow any potential biases average themselves out.

I have focused on some of the fundamental problems that there are with meta-analyses. There are also some more technical concerns. The most important of these is trying to get hold of all the data. There are two related problems: the file drawer problems and the publication bias. Researchers often do not try to publish nonsignificant findings, and journals are less likely to accept papers with nonsignificant results. This means that it is difficult to find an unbiased sample of studies, something that is necessary for inference from most meta-analyses. There is also the problem of choosing the type of meta-analysis. The main choice is between fixed and random effects models. Field (2001) describes the reasons why a random effects model should be preferred, which is why this was used earlier in this chapter.

Most of this section has concentrated on the problems with meta-analyses, which is unfair. Meta-analyses are used instead of discoursive reviews of the literature where researchers bring with them their own biases when trying to integrate research findings. One of the clearest findings in the history of psychology is that algorithmic objective integration of information is better than allowing subjective judgement (Dawes, Faust & Meehl, 1989). Therefore, meta-analysis is a welcomed addition to a researcher's toolbox, but its utility should not blind people to its limitations.

Psychology research has developed using the NHST and science, more generally, often proceeds by trying to falsify that some particular hypothesis is true in all situations. The goal then is to find one situation where this bold conjecture can be falsified. In these situations meta-analyses are less useful. In situations such as evaluating the "scared straight" program, where researchers want to know if, across some population (juvenile delinquents), the program tends to improve behavior, then meta-analyses are valuable. Given the problems discussed earlier about NHST and its underlying philosophy, the meta-analytic approach could become a framework for thinking about all research (Thompson, 2002).

Readings. For a brief introduction, see Field (2003). Details are found in Hunter and Schmidt (2004), Lipsey and Wilson (1996), and Rosenthal (1991).

Software. There are several freeware and inexpensive specialist packages. For example, see http://faculty.ucmerced.edu/wshadish/Meta-Analysis%20Links.htm. Most of the general packages (SPSS, SAS, S-Plus, etc.) have macros for meta-analysis. I used SPSS macros for the analysis in this section, downloaded from http://www.spsstools.net.

Robust Methods. In 1805 Adrien Marie Legendre introduced the idea of minimizing the square of the residuals: "it consists of making the sum of the squares of the errors a *minimum*... it prevents the extremes from dominating" (translation from Stigler, 1986, p. 13, original French manuscript printed on p. 58).[4] The ease of computing least squares, its conceptual appeal, and the fact that least squares estimation is well suited for a very particular set of situations meant that this approach has dominated statistics. Every time we calculate a mean, *t*-test, ANOVA, and so on, we are minimizing the sum of the squared residuals. The least squares approach is one of several possible *loss functions*.

The second part of the quote from Legendre deserves further scrutiny. Squaring a residual means that the impact of large residuals will be greater than if, for example, the absolute value was taken (an approach that actually predated Legendre, but is computationally difficult so was not widely used until recently). Figure 38.3 shows the impact of a residual on the fit of a model for a few different loss functions. Small values have little impact on least squares, but as the value increases the impact becomes very large. Large values are not as influential for minimizing the sum of absolute values. Another method is to trim data beyond a certain value. For example, the 20 percent trimmed mean is the mean of values excluding the extreme 20 percent from each end of the scale.[5] All three of these loss functions can be applied to estimating any quantitative parameter.

Legendre was wrong; extremes can dominate with least squares estimation. Robust alternatives lessen the

---

[4]Legendre and 1805 are generally given as the person and date for the introduction of least squares, although Gauss claimed to be using it since 1795. Soon after 1805, Gauss did publish a much extended formulation of least squares. Stigler (1999, p. 331) concluded that although Gauss may have discovered least squares, it was Legendre "who first put the method within the reach of the common man."

[5]If you are calculating the trimmed mean, do not simply exclude the extremes and conduct analyses as if the data were not trimmed. The equations to estimate the standard error (and therefore *p*-values) are different (Wilcox, 2003).

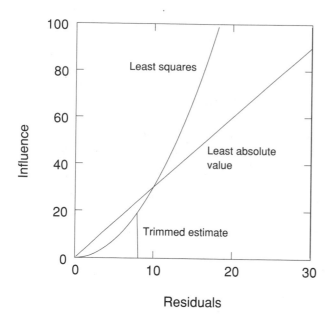

FIGURE 38.3. The impact of the size of residuals for different loss functions. As the size of the size residual increases, the impact becomes very large for least squares estimation. The increase is less for least absolute value.

impact of these extremes. Consider the following three data sets:

Set 1: 1, 2, 3, 4, 5, 6, 7, 8, 9, 10
    Mean = 5.5, 95% CI = (3.33, 7.67),
    Standard deviation = 3.03,
    $t(9) = 5.75$, $p < .001$

Set 2: 1, 2, 3, 4, 5, 6, 7, 8, 9, 100
    Mean = 14.5, 95% CI = (−7.07, 36.07),
    Standard deviation = 9.54,
    $t(9) = 1.52$, $p = .16$

Set 3: 1, 2, 3, 4, 5, 6, 7, 8, 9, 1000
    Mean = 104.5, 95% CI = (−120.59, 329.60),
    Standard deviation = 314.66,
    $t(9) = 1.05$, $p = .32$

As the most extreme point gets larger and larger, the mean goes from 5.5 to 14.5 to 104.5. This compares with minimizing the sum of least absolute values (which produces the median) and the 20 percent trimmed mean, which both remain at 5.5. The outlier has less impact with these robust estimators. Depending on your research question, you may or may not want a single point to have this much impact.

How does the outlier impact on hypothesis testing and confidence interval estimation? Suppose we wanted to

test the hypothesis that the foregoing data come from a population with a mean of 0. The standard statistic would be a t test: $t = \bar{x}\sqrt{n}/sd$ and the corresponding 95 percent confidence interval of $\bar{x} \pm t \cdot sd/\sqrt{n}$. Because the outlier affects the standard deviation even more than the mean (see earlier discussion), as the outlier moves away from the null hypothesis, it actually makes the statistic *less* significant. It makes the estimate much less precise, as is reflected in the confidence intervals. These issues are not new (see Fisher, 1925, p. 112), but only recently have alternatives have become widely available.

A recent example showing the effect of removing an outlier was published the week of the 2004 US presidential election and concerned the number of civilians deaths in Iraq since the younger George Bush's war there (Roberts, Lafta, Garfield, Khudhairi & Burnham, 2004). The most discussed statistic they report is an estimate that 98,000 more civilians died during the post-invasion occupation than expected (though the 95 percent confidence was large, from 8,000 to 194,000). This was based on a pre-invasion mortality rate of 5.0 (per 1,000 per year) with an interval from 3.7 to 6.3. They estimated the post-invasion mortality rate to be 12.3 with an interval from 1.4 to 23.2, but did not use this estimate to reach their conclusions. As the interval includes the estimated pre-invasion mortality rate, it does not provide strong evidence for an increase. Instead they removed the data from Falluja, where the fighting was most intense. This lowered the estimated morality rate to 7.9 but made the interval smaller, from 5.6 to 10.2, thereby providing better evidence for an increased mortality rate. There is an important political point raised by this paper, why were the occupying forces not doing more to keep track of the number of civilian deaths. The statistical point, that eliminating an outlier can make the confidence intervals much smaller, raises an ethical concern. Given that the researchers knew Falluja was going to be an outlier and therefore that they were going to exclude it from many of their analyses, and that Falluja was very dangerous place for their researchers to be operating, should they have been trying to gather data from there?

The three data sets just shown are clearly not normally distributed. Many people believe that: (a) psychology data sets are usually normally distributed and (b) if they are not, we would notice any discrepancy large enough to matter. Micceri (1989) surveyed a large number of psychology data sets. He found that *none* approximated the normal distribution and most were very un-normal. But would you be able to notice if a distribution was un-normal enough to matter? The main part of Fig. 38.4 shows two curves. One is normally distributed; one is not. The mixture curve (which is 90 percent a normal

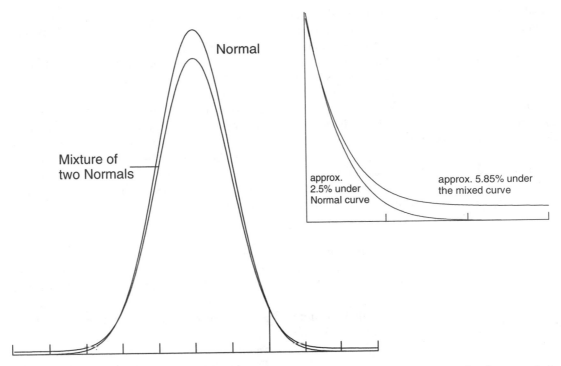

FIGURE 38.4. A normal curve and a mixture curve. The mixture curve has more area under the curve in its tails.

curve with a standard deviation of 1 and 10% a normal curve with a standard deviation of 10) looks very similar to the standard normal curve. If you observed data that looked like the mixture distribution, you would be likely to assume that the normal distribution assumption had been met. Tukey (1960) showed that these distributions are different in a very important way. The interest, particularly for NHST, is often in the tails of the distribution. The upper right-hand corner of Fig. 38.4 shows the tails of these distributions. The mixture distribution has a lot more area under the curve beyond $z = 1.96$.

Because of this area under the curve and the fact that the outliers can affect measures of precision more than location, the standard least squares procedure is often less able to identify differences. This led Rand Wilcox to ask the following question as the title of his *American Psychologist* paper: "How many discoveries have been lost by ignoring modern statistical methods?" (1998). In most situations, least squares procedures are less powerful than methods that are less influenced by outliers, despite what is said in many textbooks. This means that often you may be missing significant effects. Wilcox poignantly makes this point in the title of another paper: "ANOVA: A paradigm for low power and misleading measures of effect size?" (1995).

I have mentioned least absolute values and trimmed estimates. Trimmed statistics are fairly popular. They are

conceptually simple and have good properties. Much of the discussion in Wilcox (2003) is about trimmed estimates. Statisticians have come up with other robust loss functions. The most popular of these are M-estimators (there are also R-, L-, and W-estimators; see Wilcox, 2003, for details). The largest collection of robust procedures has been written for S-Plus (http://lib.stat.cmu.edu/S/). The procedures that come with the package allow robust GLMs (and therefore linear regressions, too), ANOVAs, correlations, principal component analysis, and so forth. Plus, many statisticians have written robust functions for S-Plus that can be downloaded from S libraries. General programs such as SPSS and SYSTAT include some M-estimators in some of their procedures.

Robust procedures increase the likelihood of finding a significant result; they are endorsed by the APA task force on statistics (Wilkinson et al., 1999) and are becoming more common in the main packages psychologists use. They will become more popular.

A Brief Note on Bootstrapping. Least squares became popular partially because it is computationally simpler than some of the robust alternatives. Part of the reason for the interest in robust methods now is that many of these more computationally demanding methods can be solved. There is a class of techniques, called *bootstrap estimation*, which can be used for estimating the precision of any statistic. One type of bootstrap procedure, called the *nonparametric bootstrap*, does not rely on assuming a particular distribution. Thus, it is well suited for robust estimation. Because of its association with robust methods, it deserves a brief mention here. The concentration in this section is on the bootstrap as a method for computing estimates and intervals, rather than as a fundamentally different approach to statistics (a more fundamentally different approach involving computationally intensive methods is discussed in the next section).

Consider the three data sets from before. The critical assumption for the nonparametric bootstrap is that the observed data are representative of the population from which they are drawn. First, take a large number of samples, say 2,000 samples, from the observed data, with replacement. You can then calculate statistics on these 2,000 samples. Histograms of the different statistics for the bootstrap samples can be made. Further, you can estimate the 95 percent confidence interval by showing the interval containing the middle 95% of these sample values. These empirical bootstrap estimates are, for the different sets:

Empirical bootstrap 95 percent confidence intervals:
    Set 1: mean = (3.70, 7.20)
        standard deviation = (1.87, 3.68)
    Set 2: mean = (3.70, 34.00)
        standard deviation = (1.89, 46.31)
    Set 3: mean = (3.90, 304.0)
        standard deviation = (1.89, 480.8)

There are other ways to calculate the confidence intervals for bootstrap samples (Diciccio & Efron, 1996). The confidence intervals that researchers often report are the "bias corrected and adjusted" or BCa intervals. These are:

BCa bootstrap 95 percent confidence intervals
    Set 1: mean = (3.53, 7.10)
        standard deviation = (2.31, 4.01)
    Set 2: mean = (4.30, 43.63)
        standard deviation = (2.22, 49.93)
    Set 3: mean = (4.40, 501.9)
        standard deviation = (2.26, 513.6)

The value of bootstrapping is most evident for statistics where calculating the confidence intervals directly is difficult. The BCa 95 percent confidence intervals for the median and 20% trimmed means (based on 2,000 replications) are:

    Set 1: median = (2.50, 8.00)
        20% trimmed mean = (3.00, 7.50)

    Set 2: median = (2.50, 8.00)
        20% trimmed mean = (3.17, 21.83)
    Set 3: median = (2.50, 7.50)
        20% trimmed mean = (3.17, 171.9)

Readings. Rand Wilcox is one of the clearest writers about robust estimation. His *American Psychologist* paper (1998) and 2003 book are good places to start. For the bootstrap, the classic introduction is Efron and Gong (1983). Despite its date, it is still worthwhile, but is more mathematical than some psychologists like. Diaconis and Efron (1983) is a less mathematical introduction. Two of the most thorough references are Davison and Hinkley (1997) and Efron and Tibshirani (1993).

Software. S-plus has a large set of functions for both robust estimation and bootstrapping (http://lib.stat.cmu.edu/S/). Both SPSS and SYSTAT allow some robust loss functions, SYSTAT allowing more. In addition, SYSTAT allows bootstrapping for many of its statistics.

Small Data Sets—Rerandomizing and Local Inference. The traditional statistical approaches are often described as *asymptotically accurate*. This means that as the sample gets large, the techniques become more accurate. Researchers have often been worried about what to do with small samples. Some researchers rely on the traditional rank-based procedures (Siegel & Castellan, 1988), but with computational advances rerandomizing approaches are becoming popular (Lunneborg, 2000). Rerandomizing is a type of resampling method, like bootstrapping. Like bootstrapping, it is computationally demanding, but can be done with modern computers. Bootstrapping was introduced earlier as a computational method to estimate standard errors and confidence intervals. Here resampling will be used in a way that leads to a fundamentally different type of inference.

Conventional statistics use data from the sample to make inferences about a population. For this inference to be valid, various assumptions about the population and the sampling are necessary, including that participants are drawn at random from some well-defined population. Often this is not the case. Instead, participants are those who respond to recruitment posters or e-mails. Researchers sometimes hand-wave and claim that the sample is representative of some undefined target population and that is what the inference is about. This is not a satisfactory solution, as the value of an inference about an undefined population is unclear. The mathematics and assumptions behind traditional statistics make this hand-waving necessary (at least implicitly), and until recently there were not viable alternatives. Rerandomizing provides an alternative.

TABLE 38.1. Several Statistical Procedures for the Luckin et al. (2003) Data

	Dependent Measures		
	Outcome	Child Acts	Adult Acts
t-test (equal variances)	$t(15) = 1.08$, $p = .30$	$t(15) = 2.18$, $p = .05$	$t(15) = 0.57$, $p = .58$
t-test (unequal variances)	$t(14.8) = 1.10$, $p = .29$	$t(10.9) = 2.11$, $p = .06$	$t(9.8) = 0.60$, $p = .56$
t-test (equal variances, w/o outliers)	$t(13) = 2.63$, $p = .02$	$t(13) = 3.62$, $p = .003$	$t(13) = 2.63$, $p = .02$
t-test (unequal variances, w/o outliers)	$t(7.1) = 2.48$, $p = .04$	$t(9.5) = 3.50$, $p = .01$	$t(13.0) = 2.66$, $p = .02$
GLM (log link, Poisson error)	$t(15) = 1.57$, $p = .14$	$t(15) = 4.01$, $p = .001$	$t(15) = 0.84$, $p = .41$
Robust M-estimator	$t(15) = 2.14$, $p = .03$	$t(15) = 2.81$, $p = .004$	$t(15) = 4.03$, $p < .001$

Notes: Positive t values correspond to the toy group being higher. The outliers removed are the data for S1 and S2 in Fig. 38.5. The t-tests were conducted with SPSS, the GLM with S-Plus, the M-estimator robust model with robust library from S-Plus. For ease of comparison, the t-value from the GLM is reported and the square root of the robust F is taken, so that it is also approximately t distributed.

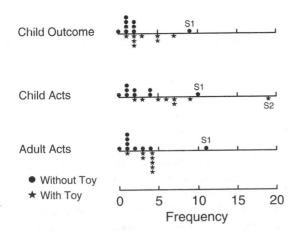

FIGURE 38.5. Comparing children's use of educational software with and without a digital toy (from Luckin et al., 2003).

Rerandomizing has traditionally been used with small samples where people have been randomly allocated into different conditions. Rather than trying to make inferences to some population, which often does not exist anyway, the researcher focuses on whether the experimental manipulation could be responsible for any differences observed in the sample. This is called *local causal inference*, whether the manipulation appears to cause a difference in that particular experiment. The critical assumption is that people are randomly allocated into their conditions.

Consider the following example from Luckin and colleagues (2003). They were interested in how an interactive digital toy (a stuffed animal with a computer inside that received wireless information from a PC computer and responded accordingly) affected children's behavior with an educational software program. Seventeen children were randomly allocated to either a "toy" or "no toy" condition (there were other conditions and other aspects of this study that are not dealt with here). Three dependent variables are considered: how often the child had a successful "help outcome," how often the child sought help, and how often the adult had to assist. The observed frequencies are shown in Fig. 38.5. There are several ways that these data can be analyzed. The results of some of these are shown in Table 38.1. The typical psychologist might try t-tests, with and without the outliers, and assuming and not assuming equal variances. Alternatively, a generalized linear model (with the log link function assuming Poisson error) or some kind of robust method (here, an M-estimator method) might be used. As can be seen, the choice of procedure influences the results. There are three problems with all these procedures. The first is that because of the small sample, the probabilities are unlikely to be accurate because the statistics are designed for larger samples. Second, it is difficult to feel certain of any assumptions about the distribution because the small sample does not provide much information about the population's distribution. Finally, and most important, all these assume that the children were randomly sampled from some population. As is true in much psychology, participants here volunteered and cannot be regarded as a random sample from a well-defined

---

[6]The confidence interval is for the particular 1,000 samples drawn. Other sets of bootstrap samples will produce intervals that should be similar, but that will not be exactly the same.

population. Further, it cannot be assumed that they are representative of some larger population of interest. All the statistical procedures covered so far assume that this is true, and this is a necessary assumption for the standard method of statistical inference.

Bootstrap methods were described in the last section. Computationally these are similar to resampling methods. The focus will be just on one variable: Outcome. The data are:

With toy:	1	2	2	2	2	3	5	5	7
Without toy:	0	1	1	1	1	2	2	9	

For calculating a (simple nonparametric) bootstrap mean for each group, you assume that the population from which these two samples are drawn is the same as the observed distribution. This means that this procedure assumes there are no 6s or 8s in the population. If 1,000 samples are taken from these distributions and the mean difference calculated for each sample, then the 95 percent confidence interval is (−0.90, 3.18).[6] Because it overlaps with 0, this is a nonsignificant finding (consistent with nonrobust procedures with outliers in Table 38.1). If the 20 percent trimmed mean is used, the 95 percent confidence interval is (−0.77, 3.55). This also overlaps with 0. The problem with bootstrapping using a sample this size is that the simple empirical bootstraps rely heavily on the distribution of the observed data. Because there are not many data points, this reliance is problematic. Alternative forms of bootstrapping can be used, but these make more assumptions about the distribution of the population data. Given the small number of data, these assumptions are difficult to justify.

Rerandomizing is better suited for this problem. It assumes there are just the 17 data points in the entire universe in which you are interested. The procedure does not make reference to them coming from any population. This is why it is called local inference. To do resampling, first assume that having a toy made no difference. Consider the observed values as simply one possible random allocation of these 17 points where there are nine with a toy and eight without. This particular randomization has certain characteristics, such as the difference in means is 1.26 and the difference in 20 percent trimmed means is 1.74. Both of these suggest that the toy may improve outcome, but this is just one randomization of thousands of possible random allocations. With this procedure a large number of rerandomizations are used, and we see how extreme the observed value is compared with the entire set of rerandomizations created when it is assumed that group membership is random. For small sam-

```
Frequency    Stem &  Leaf
    1         -2 .  &
   11         -2 .  2333
    6         -2 .  00
   23         -1 .  99999999
   54         -1 .  666666666666666667
    0         -1 .
   56         -1 .  3333333333333333333
   78         -1 .  000000000000000000000000000
    0         -0 .
   81         -0 .  7777777777777777777777777777
   78         -0 .  4444444444444444444444444444
    1         -0 .  &
  129         -0 .  000000001111111111111111111111111111111111111
   86          0 .  111111111111111111111111111111
   51          0 .  2222222222222222
   80          0 .  55555555555555555555555555555
    2          0 .  6
   74          0 .  88888888888888888888888888&
   54          1 .  111111111111111111
    0          1 .
   63          1 .  444444444444444444444
   42          1 .  7777777777777          OBSERVED VALUE
    2          1 .  &
   15          2 .  00000
    8          2 .  222
    4          2 .  4&
    1          2 .  &

Stem width:   1.000
Each leaf:       3 case(s)
& denotes fractional leaves.
```

FIGURE 38.6. A stem-and-leaf diagram of 1,000 replications of the data from Luckin et al. (2003).

ples, all possible rerandomizations can be done, but even with modern computers this is not possible when the sample gets larger. There are 24,310 ways in which 17 participants can be allocated into one group of nine and one of eight, which could be done with modern computers. Allocating 50 people into two groups of 25 requires 1.26×10^{14}, which is large enough to make computations too time consuming. In these cases the computer uses some large number, here 1,000, of randomizations. For this data set, Fig. 38.6 shows a stem-and-leaf diagram for 1,000 randomizations.

About 7 percent of the time ($42 + 2 + 15 + 8 + 4 + 1 = 72$) the rerandomization procedure produces an advantage for the toy group that is as big as the observed difference or greater. With a two-sided test this means the p-value would be approximately 14 percent, and therefore we would fail to reject the null hypothesis that the observed distribution was based on more than just randomization.[7]

While rerandomization procedures are useful because of the problems that traditional approaches have with small sample sizes, there is nothing to prevent them from being used with large samples. As said earlier, the computer would not draw all possible randomizations, but a large enough sample to produce reliable statistics. This is particularly important because often only local inference is valid, and therefore these procedures should be used much more.

---

[7]This is a conservative approach because there are several randomizations at the observed value.

Rerandomization and other computationally intensive methods have an additional advantage that should be stressed. Although computationally more time consuming for the computer, conceptually they are often simpler for teaching. It is more transparent how the inference occurs. Some universities are now teaching introductory statistics with resampling procedures. This is one way that these methods are beginning to make inroads into mainstream statistics.

Readings. Lunneborg (2000), Good (2001), and Good (2005) provide are good introductions to resampling. Berger (2000) discusses many of the important issues. David Howell has good Web pages for this and other topics. See http://www.uvm.edu/~dhowell/StatPages/Resampling/Resampling.html. He has written essays on both resampling and bootstrapping in his usual clear and insightful manner.

Software. SYSTAT and S-Plus include procedures for rerandomizing, and there are add-ons for SPSS. Good and Lunneborg provide code in R (see footnote 1). Howell's Web site includes links to software he has written and other people's software. See also http://www.resample.com/.

SUMMARY

Statistics is a lively discipline. Understanding the masses of data that we are bombarded with in everyday life, trying to grapple with the apparent chance occurrences that we face, and even understanding sports commentators, all involve statistics. Turning data into clear and compelling information for an audience requires many technical skills and much training, but at its soul it is an art. This contrasts with how students are often taught statistics, as a dry process where you simply look at a diagram and follow some mechanistic process until the computer produces a *p* value and this determines whether your study was successful or not. Cohen, Meehl, and others have shown that this approach has hindered the development of psychology.

This chapter began by describing problems with the current statistical approaches used in psychology. The emphasis was that researchers should step away from the mechanistic approaches and "make friends with their data." A theme of many methodology papers in psychology during the past decade is to point out the problems with null hypothesis significance testing (NHST). Although there are problems with NHST, for the discipline to move forward it is necessary not just to realize the limitations of NHST but to look at newer approaches. As Cohen (1994) points out, there are no saving mechanis-

tic approaches for statistics. Instead, the statistical artist must use technical skills in a more flexible and thoughtful manner.

Six modern statistical approaches were discussed, each of which increases flexibility, but also requires thought. The first was *generalized linear models* (GLMs). This class of techniques allows many different types of data to be analyzed within the same general framework. Their introduction should allow psychologists to think more about the response processes that occur to create their data, rather than just pretending they arise from some process that produces normally distributed errors.

Another extension to the standard regression model is *multilevel modeling*. This allows clustered data to be analyzed and is very popular within education and psychology. The prototypical example of a multilevel model is where pupils are nested within classrooms and these are nested within schools. The assumption is that the pupils are a random sample of those in the classroom, and that the classrooms are a random sample of those in the school. Applications of multilevel modeling have become more widespread, for example with longitudinal designs, meta-analyses, and almost anything where there is a hierarchical structure to the data. This raises the question of whether these lower level elements really are a random (or even representative) sample of all the elements in the cluster. Within psychology this was one of the criticisms of Clark's (1973) fixed-effect fallacy paper (Cohen, 1976). Clearly the mathematical sophistication and ease of estimation of multilevel modeling make it appealing, but it is important for researchers to consider whether their inference is valid. As Goldstein (2003) urges, "Multilevel models are tools to be used with care and understanding" (p. 12).

Latent variable modeling is another area that has gained much in popularity, but sometimes it is used without care and understanding. The lure of being able to take dozens of variables and combine them into a single model where the word *cause* can be used has excited psychologists (and other social scientists). And it should, but it is necessary for researchers to look more carefully at their models. People should consider what the latent variables are actually like. The work of Bartholomew, Meehl, and others allows some characteristics of these variables to be explored.

One of the hot methods today is meta-analysis. This is where data from several studies are combined. In many ways this is necessary. So many studies exist that it is often important to include data from several different studies to reach any definitive conclusions. The discursive reviews of the past were subject to the reviewers' biases, and these subjective judgments need to be replaced. Meta-analysis provides a valuable alternative. Two questions should be asked prior to conducting any meta-analysis. First, does the research question require summary statistics from a large number of studies, or is it more appropriately addressed by a specific well-designed study? Second, are the studies used representative of the population of situations in which you are interested, or are they just representative of the studies that have been done (or worse, are they not representative of any meaningful population)?

Robust methods are less influenced by extreme points than the traditional least squares approach. Sometimes you may want extreme points to have a large impact; sometimes you may not. For 100 years psychologists often did not ask whether the least squares approach was appropriate because the computations for least squares were so much simpler than the alternatives. Robust procedures are now available, so psychologists should start asking this question. It would be unfortunate if people opted for robust procedures *just* because they tend to be more powerful than least squares approaches. The two approaches are asking different research questions, but power is an extra benefit.

The final method discussed in this chapter is the most fundamentally different. In all my methods training I have been told that sample data are collected to make inference about aspects of some population. Science seemed to require inference about a well-defined population, and yet in so much psychology it is futile to try to argue that the sample is representative of some well-defined population. Rerandomizing, in some form, has been used with small samples for a long time (for example, Fisher's exact method for 2×2 tables), but usually it was used just as a means of estimation for small samples. Using these techniques was not seen as an abrupt change in philosophy of science. Now that there are fewer computational limitations, rerandomizing can be used in more situations, and therefore is something that people should consider. It has many attractive properties but is the most controversial of the topics covered here.

This has been a survey of modern techniques, not a census. Selected topics were chosen and others were not. Topics chosen were those that I think are both important and likely to become more important in the next decade. Some important topics are missing. These include those related to the design of study (e.g., sampling, experimental design, missing values, power, measurement error), estimation (e.g., maximum likelihood), Bayesian statistics, multivariate analysis (e.g., MANOVA, canonical and set correlation), graphical and exploratory methods (e.g., multidimensional scaling, cluster analysis, correspondence analysis, and dozens of new graphs that appear), classification and network models, model selection and data mining techniques, signal detection theory, and so on. The list of topics not covered is seemingly endless. That modern statistical techniques are so vast makes it clear that statistics is a lively discipline, but it makes it daunting for nonstatisticians. It is important for readers to realize that all the statistics share a common goal: to summarize the data.

This chapter began by asking if the way statistics are used in psychology would have been different if our methodological ancestors had the same computational devices that we have today. Many of the choices in statistics then were dictated by computational limitations. We can now make more informed choices. As I have tried to make clear throughout this chapter, statistics is not about telling you what to do in different situations, but about allowing you to make these informed choices.

It took decades for the uptake of statistical significance to occur (Hubbard & Ryan, 2000). It has taken almost as long for objections on rote reliance on NHST to reach critical mass, reflected in the frequencies of published demands for effect size reporting in disciplines as diverse as education, psychology, and the wildlife sciences (Anderson, Burnham & Thompson, 2000). It is impossible to estimate exactly how long the uptake of the contemporary methods discussed herein will require. However, fields do move inexorably, albeit sometimes slowly. Rather than only studying older methods, thoughtful students may wish to study methods that they will sometimes encounter today, but that they will increasingly encounter in a progressive and more enlightened future.

ACKNOWLEDGMENTS

Thanks to Lucy Lowe, Herb Marsh, Bruce Thompson. Elin Skagerberg, and Phil Winne for useful comments.

References

Abelson, R. P. (1995). *Statistics as principled argument.* Mahwah, NJ: Lawrence Erlbaum Associates.

Abelson, R. P. (1997). A retrospective on the significance test ban of 1999 (if there were no significance tests, they would be invented). In L. L. Harlow, S. A. Mulaik, and J. H. Steiger (Eds), *What if there were no significance tests?* (117–141). Mahwah, NJ: Lawrence Erlbaum Associates.

Agresti, A. (2002). *Categorical data analysis (2nd ed.).* Hoboken, NJ: John Wiley & Sons.

Anderson, D. R., Burnham, K. P., & Thompson, W. (2000). Null hypothesis testing: Problems, prevalence, and an alternative. *Journal of Wildlife Management, 64*, 912-923.

Anderson, J. C., & Gerbing, D. W. (1988). Structural equation modeling in practice: A review and recommended two-step approach. *Psychological Bulletin, 103*, 411-423.

Barth, J. M., Dunlap, S. I., Dane, H., Lochman, J. E., & Wells, K. C. (2004). Classroom environment influences on aggression, peer relations, and academic focus, *Journal of School Psychology, 42*, 115-133.

Bartholomew, D. J. & Knott, M. (1999). *Latent variable models and factor analysis (Kendall's Library of Statistics 7).* London: Arnold.

Bartholomew, D. J., Steele, F., Moustaki, I., & Galbraith, J. I. (2002). *The analysis and interpretation of multivariate data for social scientists.* Boca Raton, FL: Chapman & Hall/CRC.

Bem, D. J., & C. Honorton (1994). Does psi exist? Replicable evidence for an anomalous process of information transfer. *Psychological Bulletin, 115*, 4-18.

Berger, V. W. (2000). Pros and cons of permutation tests in clinical trials. *Statistics in Medicine, 19*, 1319-1328.

Bollen, K. A. (2002). Latent variables in psychology and the social sciences. *Annual Review of Psychology, 53*, 605-634.

Bollen, K. A. & Long, J. S. (1993) (Eds). *Testing Structural Equation Models.* Sage Publications: Newbury Park, CA: Sage Publications.

Clark, H. H. (1973). The language-as-fixed-effect fallacy: A critique of language statistics in psychological research. *Journal of Verbal Learning and Verbal Behavior, 12*, 335-359.

Cohen, J. (1968). Multiple regression as a general data-analytic system. *Psychological Bulletin, 70*, 426-443.

Cohen, J. (1976). Random means random. *Journal of Verbal Learning and Verbal Behavior, 15*, 261-262.

Cohen, J. (1990). Things I have learned (so far). *American Psychologist, 45*, 1304-1312.

Cohen, J. (1994). The Earth is round ($p < .05$). *American Psychologist, 49*, 997-1003.

Dalgaard, P. (2002). *Introductory statistics with R.* New York: Springer-Verlag.

Davison, A. C., & Hinkley, D. V. (1997). *Bootstrap methods and their application.* Cambridge, UK: Cambridge University Press.

Dawes, R. M., Faust, D., & Meehl, P. E. (1989). Clinical versus actuarial judgment. *Science, 243*, 1668-1674.

Diaconis, P., & Efron, B. (1983). Computer-intensive methods in statistics. *Scientific American, 248*(5), 116-130.

DiCiccio, T. J., and Efron, B. (1996) Bootstrap confidence intervals (with Discussion). *Statistical Science, 11*, 189-228.

Efron, B. & Gong, G. (1983). A leisurely look at the bootstrap, the jackknife, and cross-validation. *American Statistician, 37*, 36-48.

Efron, B. & Tibshirani, R. (1993). *An Introduction to the Bootstrap.* New York: Chapman and Hall.

Fan, X., Thompson, B., & Wang, L. (1999). The effects of sample size, estimation methods, and model specification on SEM fit indices. *Structural Equation Modeling, 6*, 56-83.

Field, A. P. (2001). Meta-analysis of correlation coefficients: A Monte Carlo comparison of fixed- and random-effects methods. *Psychological Methods, 6*, 161-180.

Field, A. P. (2003). Can meta-analysis be trusted? *Psychologist, 16*, 642-645.

Fisher, R. A. (1925). *Statistical methods for research workers.* London: Oliver and Boyd. (Downloaded from http://psychclassics.yorku.ca/Fisher/Methods/)

Fleischmann, M. & Pons, S. (1989). Electrochemically induced nuclear-fusion of deuterium. *Journal of Electroanalytical Chemistry, 261*, 301-308.

Francis, B., Green, M., & Payne, C. (Eds.). (1993). *The GLIM System (Release 4 Manual): Generalised linear interactive modeling.* Oxford: Oxford University Press.

Glass, G. V. (1976). Primary, secondary, and meta-analysis of research. *Educational Researcher, 51*, 3-8.

Goldstein, H. (2003). *Multilevel statistical methods (3rd ed.).* London: Edward Arnold.

Goldstein H., Yang M., Omar R., Turner, R., & Thompson, S. (2000). Meta-analysis using multilevel models with an application to the study of class size effects,. *Journal of the Royal Statistical Society: Applied (Series C), 49*, 399-412.

Good, P. I. (2001). *Resampling methods* (2nd ed.). Boston, MA: Birkhauser.

Good, P. I. (2005). *Introduction to statistics through resampling methods and R/S-Plus.* Hoboken, NJ: Wiley.

Harlow, L. L., Mulaik, S. A., & Steiger, J. H. (Eds.) (1977). *What if there were no significance tests?* London: Lawrence Erlbaum Associates.

Hastie,T., & Tibshirani, R. (1990) *Generalized additive models.* London: Chapman and Hall.

Hastie, T., Tibshirani, R., & Friedman, J. (2001). *The elements of statistical learning: Data mining, inference, and prediction.* New York: Springer.

Hoaglin, D. C., Mosteller, F., & Tukey, J. W. (Eds.) (2000). *Understanding robust and exploratory data analysis.* New York: Wiley.

Hoffman, J. P. (2004). *Generalized linear models: An applied approach.* Boston, MA: Pearson Education.

Hox, J. (2002). *Multilevel analysis: Techniques and applications.* London: Lawrence Erlbaum Associates.

Hu, L., & Bentler, P. M. (1999). Cutoff criteria for fit indexes in covariance structure analysis: Conventional criteria versus new alternatives. *Structural Equation Modeling, 6*, 1-55.

Hubbard, R., & Ryan, P. A. (2000). The historical growth of statistical significance testing in psychology—and its future prospects. *Educational and Psychological Measurement, 60*, 661-681.

Huberty, C. J. (1999). On some history regarding statistical testing. In B. Thompson (Ed.), *Advances in social science methodology* (Vol. 5, pp. 1-23). Stamford, CT: JAI Press.

Huberty, C. J. (2002). A history of effect size indices. *Educational and Psychological Measurement, 62*, 227-240.

Hunter, J. E. & Schmidt, F. L. (2004). *Methods of meta-analysis: Correcting error and bias in research findings (2nd ed.).* Thousand Oaks, CA: Sage.

Hyman, R. (1996). The evidence of psychic functioning: Claims vs. reality. *Skeptical Inquirer*, March/April. Available at http://www.csicop.org/si/9603/claims.html

Hyman, R. & Honorton, C. (1986). A joint communiqué: The psi ganzfeld controversy. *Journal of Parapsychology, 50*, 351–364.

Klem, L. (2000). Structural equation modeling. In L. G. Grimm & P. R. Yarnold (Eds.), *Reading and understanding more multivariate statistics* (pp. 227–260).Washington, DC: American Psychological Association.

Kreft, I. I., & de Leeuw, J. (1998). *Introducing multilevel modeling*. London: Sage.

Lenzenweger, M. F. (2004). Consideration of the challenges, complications, and pitfalls of taxometric analysis. *Journal of Abnormal Psychology, 113*, 10–23.

Lipsey, M.W., & Wilson, D.B. (1996). *Practical meta-analysis*. Newbury Park, CA: Sage.

Lord, F. M. (1967). A paradox in the interpretation of group comparisons. *Psychological Bulletin, 72*, 304–305.

Luckin, R., Connolly, D., Plowman, L., & Airey, S. (2003). *Out of the Box, but in the Zone? Can digital toy technology provide a more able peer for young learners?* Artificial Intelligence in Education (AIED 2003). http://www.cs.usyd.edu.au/~aied/papers.html

Lunneborg, C. E. (2000). *Data analysis by resampling: Concepts and applications*. Pacific Grove, CA: Duxbury Press.

Maindonald, J. & Braun, J. (2003). *Data analysis and graphics using R*. Cambridge, UK: Cambridge University Press.

McCullagh, P. & Nelder, J. A. (1989). *Generalized linear models* (2nd ed.). London: Chapman and Hall.

Meehl, P. (1967). Theory-testing in psychology and physics: A methodological paradox. *Philosophy of Science, 34*, 103–115.

Meehl, P. (1978). Theoretical risks and tabular asterisks: Sir Karl, Sir Ronald, and the slow progress of soft psychology. *Journal of Consulting and Clinical Psychology, 46*, 806–834.

Meehl, P. E. (1989). Autobiography. In G. Lindzey (Ed.), *History of psychology in autobiography* (Vol. VIII, pp. 337–389). Stanford, CA: Stanford University Press.

Meehl, P. E. (1990). Toward an integrated theory of schizotaxia, schizotypy, and schizophrenia. *Journal of Personality Disorders, 4*, 1–99.

Micceri, T. (1989). The unicorn, the normal curve, and other improbable creatures. *Psychological Bulletin, 105*, 156–166.

Miles, J., & Shevlin, M. (2003). Structural equation modelling: Navigating spaghetti junction. *Psychologist, 16*, 639–641.

Miller, G. A. (1969). Psychology as a means of promoting human welfare. *American Psychologist, 24*, 1063–1075.

Mosteller, F., & Tukey, J. W. (1977). *Data analysis and regression: A second course in statistics*. Reading, MA: Addison-Wesley.

Nelder, J. A., & Wedderburn, R. W. M. (1972). Generalized linear models. *Journal of the Royal Statistical Society: Series A, 135*, 370–384.

Niles, H. E. (1922). Correlation, causation, and Wright's theory of "path coefficients." *Genetics, 7*, 258–273.

Oakes, M. (1986). *Statistical inference: A commentary for the social and behavioural sciences*. Chichester, UK: Wiley.

Petrosino, A., Turpin-Petrosino, C., & Buehler, J. (2002). "Scared Straight" and other juvenile awareness programs for preventing juvenile delinquency. *Cochrane Library, 3*. Chichester, UK: Wiley.

Raudenbush, S. W. & Bryk, A. S. (2002). *Hierarchical linear models: Applications and data analysis methods* (2nd ed.). Thousand Oaks, CA: Sage.

Roberts, L., Lafta, R., Garfield, R., Khudhairi, J., & Burnham, G. (2004). Mortality before and after the 2003 invasion of Iraq: Cluster sample survey. *Lancet, 364*, 1857–1864.

Rosenthal, R. (1991). *Meta-analytic procedures for social research* (rev. ed.) Newbury Park, CA: Sage.

Rosenthal, R. & Rubin, D. B. (1978). Interpersonal expectancy effects: The first 345 studies. *Behavioral and Brain Sciences, 3*, 377–415.

Rosnow, R. L. & Rosenthal, R. (1989). Statistical procedures and the justification of knowledge in psychological science. *American Psychologist, 44*, 1276–1284.

Rozeboom, W.W. (1997). Good science is abductive, not hypothetico-deductive. In L. L. Harlow, S. A. Mulaik, & J. H. Steiger (Eds.), *What if there were no significance tests?* (pp. 335–392). Mahwah, NJ: Lawrence Erlbaum Associates.

Schmidt, F.L., & Hunter, J.E. (1977). Development of a general solution to the problem of validity generalization. *Journal of Applied Psychology, 62*, 529–540.

Schmidt, F.L., & Hunter, J.E. (1997). Eight common but false objections to the discontinuation of significance testing in the analysis of research data. In L. L. Harlow, S. A. Mulaik, & J. H. Steiger (Eds.), *What if there were no significance tests?* (pp. 37–64). Mahwah, NJ: Lawrence Erlbaum Associates.

Siegel, S. & Castellan, N. J. (1988). *Nonparametric statistics for the behavioral sciences (2nd ed.)*. McGraw-Hill Education.

Simon, H. A. (1954). Spurious correlation: A causal interpretation. *Journal of the American Statistical Association, 49*, 467–479.

Singer, J. D., & Willett, J. B. (2003). *Applied longitudinal data analysis: Modeling change and event occurrence*. Oxford, UK: Oxford University Press.

Stigler, S. M. (1986). *The history of statistics: The measurement of uncertainty before 1900*. Cambridge, MA: Harvard University Press.

Stigler, S. M. (1999). Gauss and the invention of least squares. In S. M. Stigler's *Statistics on the table: The history of statistical concepts and methods* (pp. 320–331). Cambridge, MA: Harvard University Press. Originally published in *Annals of Statistics, 9*, 465–474.

Strunk, W. Jr., & White, E. B. (1979). *The elements of style* (4th ed.). Needham Heights, MA: Allyn & Bacon.

Thompson, B. (1996). AERA Editorial policies regarding statistical significance testing: Three suggested reforms. *Educational Researcher, 25*(2), 26–30.

Thompson, B. (2000). Ten commandments of structural equation modeling. In L. G. Grimm & P. R. Yarnold (Eds.), *Reading and understanding more multivariate statistics* (pp. 261–283).Washington, DC: American Psychological Association.

Thompson, B. (2002). What future quantitative social science research could look like: Confidence intervals for effect sizes. *Educational Researcher, 31*(3), 24-31.

Thompson, B. (2004). *Exploratory and confirmatory factor analysis: Understanding concepts and applications.* Washington, DC: American Psychological Association.

Tufte, E. R. (2001). *The visual display of quantitative information* (2nd ed.). Cheshire, CT: Graphics Press.

Tukey, J. W. (1960). A survey of sampling from contaminated normal distributions. In I. Olkin, S. Ghurye, W. Hoeffding, W. Madow, and H. Mann (Eds.), *Contributions to probability and statistics* (pp. 448-485). Stanford, CA: Stanford University Press.

Tukey, J. W. (1977). *Exploratory data analysis.* Reading, MA: Addison-Wesley.

Vacha-Haase, T. (1998). Reliability generalization: Exploring variance in measurement error affecting score reliability across studies. *Educational and Psychological Measurement, 58*, 6-20.

Wainer, H. (1984). How to display data badly. *American Statistician, 38*, 137-147.

Wainer, H. (1991). Adjusting for differential base rates: Lord's paradox again. *Psychological Bulletin, 109*, 147-151.

Wainer, H., & Velleman, P. F. (2001). Statistical graphics: Mapping the pathways of science. *Annual Review of Psychology, 52*, 305-335.

Waller, N. G. & Meehl, P. E. (1998). *Multivariate taxometric procedures: Distinguishing types from continua.* Thousand Oaks, CA.: Sage.

Wilcox, R. R. (1995). ANOVA: A paradigm for low power and misleading measures of effect size? *Review of Educational Research, 65*, 51-77.

Wilcox, R. R. (1998). How many discoveries have been lost by ignoring modern statistical methods? *American Psychologist, 53*, 300-314.

Wilcox, R. R. (2003). *Applying contemporary statistical techniques.* Orlando, FL: Academic Press.

Wilkinson, L. (2005). *The grammar of graphics (2nd Ed.).* New York: Springer.

Wilkinson, L. and the Task Force on Statistical Inference, APA Board of Scientific Affairs (1999). Statistical methods in psychology journals: Guidelines and explanations. *American Psychologist, 54*, 594-604.

Wilkinson, L., Rope, D. J., Carr, C. B., & Rubin, M. A. (2000). The language of graphics. *Journal of Computational and Graphical Statistics, 9*, 530-543.

Wright, D. B. (1998). Modelling clustered data in autobiographical memory research: The multilevel approach. *Applied Cognitive Psychology, 12*, 339-357.

Wright, D. B. (2003). Making friends with your data: Improving how statistics are conducted and reported. *British Journal of Educational Psychology, 73*, 123-136.

Wright, D. B. (in press). Comparing groups in a before-after design: When *t*-test and ANCOVA produce different results.

Wright, D. B., & Kelley, K. (2004). Analysing and reporting data in health research. In S. Michie and C. Abraham (Eds.), *Health psychology in practice* (pp. 104-125). Oxford: BPS Blackwell.

Wright, D. B. & Williams, S. (2003). Producing bad results sections. *Psychologist, 16*, 644-648.

Wright, S. (1921). Correlation and causation. *Journal of Agricultural Research, 20*, 557-585.

FRAMES OF INQUIRY IN EDUCATIONAL PSYCHOLOGY: BEYOND THE QUANTITATIVE-QUALITATIVE DIVIDE

Deborah L. Butler
University of British Columbia

Educational Psychologists have a responsibility to seek broad perspectives and acquire a broad range of skills for conceptualizing and conducting research.

—Behrens and Smith, 1996

INTRODUCTION

This chapter explores the frames of inquiry on which educational psychologists might draw to investigate topics of interest to our field. In general terms, this is a chapter on research design, with the central goal of fostering discussion of how research in educational psychology can be expanded and improved. To this end, the chapter offers an integrative framework for characterizing and contrasting research designs, along with practical advice for researchers. As such, it has relevance for any academic, practitioner, graduate student, journal editor, or reviewer who reads, interprets, judges, or conducts research in the field.

A wide variety of potentially productive research designs are available to educational psychologists, springing from a variety of disciplines and reflecting a range of traditions. A central theme in this chapter is that educational psychologists could profit from considering a broad range of designs, quantitative and qualitative, when constructing research studies. But, because educational psychologists are generally well trained in designs reflecting quantitative research traditions, and because most of the research reported in major educational psychology journals is already quantitatively framed, this chapter is particularly focused on the real and potential contributions of "qualitative research" to the field of educational psychology.

Ironically, addressing this topic requires challenging the meaningfulness of a quantitative-qualitative dichotomy in capturing the very real and important differences in research methodologies. As an alternative, and as a challenge to the "quantitative" versus "qualitative" debate, this chapter presents a more nuanced analysis of the essential design features that, when combined in varying ways, form multidimensional inquiry frames. Inquiry frames encompass the logic of reasoning underlying a research study that creates coherence between theoretical frameworks, research questions, design features, and methods (Shulman, 1988). In this chapter I argue that a focus on inquiry frames allows for a more multifaceted description of any given study, and of how educational psychologists are profiting or could profit from a range of methodologies to investigate questions of importance to the field.

In the sections to follow, I start by presenting a more detailed rationale for moving beyond the quantitative-qualitative divide to a focus on frames of inquiry. I then examine the extent to which various types of inquiry frames have been employed in the past 11 years of published research in two major educational psychology journals. Finally, issues central to constructing inquiry frames are discussed, with the goal of deriving recommendations for designing, undertaking, representing, and evaluating research.

REFOCUSING ON FRAMES OF INQUIRY

In the educational research literature broadly speaking, debates raged through the 1970s and 1980s over the relative credibility of quantitative and qualitative research (e.g., Firestone, 1987; Howe, 1985; Lincoln & Guba, 1985; Smith, 1983; Smith & Heshusius, 1986). Over time, these debates have fostered productive discussion, for example, by challenging the dominance of a restricted set of inquiry frames, inviting a critical discourse about alternative modes of inquiry (Bereiter, 1994; Putney, Green, Dixon, & Kelly, 1999), and focusing attention on how research traditions delimit the knowledge that can be constructed (Behrens & Smith, 1996; Putney et al., 1999). However, it is becoming increasingly common for researchers to suggest that the quantitative–qualitative distinction is simplistic or simply not helpful (Almasi, Martin Palmer, Gambrell, & Pressley, 1994; Lather, 1992; Pintrich, 2003; Salomon, 1991; Walker, 1992).

One problem with framing design differences in quantitative or qualitative terms is that a divide is created between researchers working within different traditions. Researchers who consider themselves "qualitative" may consider quantitative work irrelevant; "quantitative" researchers may too easily dismiss methods or insights generated within qualitative research. Yet for educational psychologists to have at their disposal a sufficiently broad set of tools for answering important questions, they must be knowledgeable about a range of methodologies (Behrens & Smith, 1996). Further, all researchers face common challenges (e.g., establishing warrant for conclusions), and a multiplicity of logics for addressing them have been developed across inquiry frames (Creswell, 1998; Denzin & Lincoln, 1994, 2003; Gall, Borg, & Gall, 1996; McMillan, 2000). Increased sensitivity to design issues, as well as practical advice for improving research, can be gleaned by accessing research conducted across a range of traditions.

A second problem is that *quantitative* and *qualitative* are broad umbrella terms that at best capture design features at a very general level, and at worst serve to obscure meaningful differences between research approaches. For example, the quantitative umbrella encompasses experimental, quasi-experimental, causal-comparative, cor-

relational, and single-subject designs that use a diversity of logics and methods for collecting and interpreting data (Gall et al., 1996; McMillan, 2000). Similarly, the many research traditions classed together under the qualitative umbrella vary in fundamental ways (Denzin & Lincoln, 1994, 2003; Eisenhart, 1995; Heap, 1995). Because of the diversity of logics included within both "quantitative" and "qualitative" traditions, any kind of generalized differentiation between the two is easily dismantled. For example, it cannot be argued that quantitative designs look at aggregated data, while qualitative designs focus on individuals (Polkinghorne & Gribbons, 1999), because there are quantitative logics for interpreting individual data (e.g., time series analysis), and qualitative logics for examining patterns across people (e.g., phenomenology; grounded theory; multiple case study designs). Similarly, it is not only qualitative designs that are capable of examining complex interactions among variables in context, or experimental designs that are capable of uncovering causal relationships (Butler, 2002; Yin, 1994). Categorizing research frameworks as qualitative or quantitative is likely to lead to a stereotyped impression of essential design features rather than a real understanding of potential contributions and limitations.

A third problem is that the overarching qualitative-quantitative distinction is not useful in defining the essential features of any given study. For example, Guthrie, Weber, and Kimmerly (1993) investigated how individuals read and understand graphs, tables, and illustrations. They collected verbal protocols from 16 students who thought aloud while examining documents and answering questions. To interpret the data, Guthrie et al. divided transcripts into meaningful chunks, which they coded on three dimensions: type of process reflected, focus (statements of intentions or findings), and accuracy. In their research report, they provide a table with examples of accuracy judgments and extended excerpts from verbal protocols with associated codes.

This study has many design features typically associated with qualitative research. Not only do Guthrie et al. collect qualitative data, but they use data analytic strategies (i.e., coding) discussed extensively in the qualitative literature (e.g., Lincoln & Guba, 1985; Merriam, 1998; Miles & Huberman, 1994). When representing research, they include rich descriptions of data sequences that preserve context and meaning. But the Guthrie et al. (1993) study also has strong quantitative features. For example, the authors deliberately draw on theory in establishing their research questions and analytic strategies (e.g., their coding framework). They use language derived from quantitative traditions when describing their methodology (tasks "were administered"; "subjects were run"). Quantitative perspectives on establishing credibility are encoded in their description of analytic procedures: "the two raters had 91% agreement, indicating a satisfactory measure of objectivity for this rating scheme" (p. 196). They report results from statistical analyses used to help in drawing inferences.

A categorical judgment of the Guthrie et al. (1993) study would likely place it under the quantitative umbrella, because this work was not conducted within a design (e.g., case study, ethnography) or theoretical framework (e.g., naturalistic, interpretive, postmodern) typically associated with qualitative research. However, the point here is that such a categorization is not particularly helpful in understanding this study's methodology. Although it is critical to consider the theoretical framework and overall design underlying any given study (key features of inquiry frames), characterizing this study as quantitative would undermine recognition of the qualitative features of the work. Further, it is precisely this kind of blended work that is more and more frequently appearing in the educational psychology literature (see later discussion), and that would maximally benefit from appeal to the qualitative literature for advice on methodological issues.

If the quantitative-qualitative distinction is not helpful in capturing important differences between research designs, then what is an alternative? In this chapter I argue that it is more productive to examine the multidimensional *frames of inquiry* underlying research: an idea that is not so much original as it is integrative across other discussions (e.g., Guba & Lincoln, 1994; Howe & Eisenhart, 1990; Shank, 1994; Shulman, 1988). Frames of inquiry are "human constructions" (Guba & Lincoln, p. 108) that encompass the logic or reasoning that a researcher employs to move from theoretical frameworks to research questions, design, methods, and conclusions (Howe & Eisenhart, 1990; Putney et al., 1999; Shulman, 1988). They are multidimensional in that they comprise sets of design features that can be assembled in different combinations to construct a coherent logic of inquiry (Shulman, 1988). Figure 39.1 outlines the main features of a frame of inquiry: the theoretical frameworks underlying the research (methodological assumptions, substantive theory, researcher perspectives, and ethical stances), research questions, methodological procedures (overarching design, sampling, data collection, data reduction, data interpretation, warranting conclusions), and research representation.

Focusing on frames of inquiry provides a more nuanced approach for both carving up the research universe and describing individual studies. At a general level, prototypical inquiry frames outline coherent logics for constructing research studies. In educational research, many generalized frames of inquiry have been defined

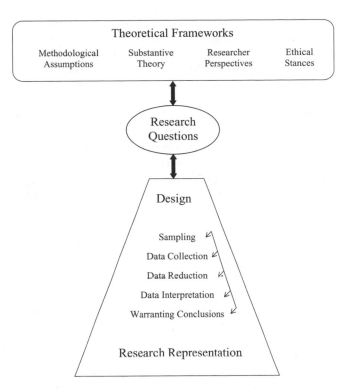

FIGURE 39.1. Essential features of inquiry frames.

(Creswell, 1998; Denzin & Lincoln, 1994; 2003; Gall et al., 1996; Jacob, 1987; Jaeger, 1988; McMillan, 2000; Shulman, 1988), such as experimental, correlational, survey, or multiple-baseline designs, narrative, naturalistic, or interpretive inquiry, historical or conceptual analysis, ethnography, case study, discourse analysis, content analysis, and phenomenology (to select just a few out of an enormous number of possibilities). Educational psychologists might draw on any of these logics to design a study, with the caveat that they should be cognizant of the "logical, philosophical, and historical foundations" of the inquiry frame selected (Behrens & Smith, 1996, p. 978).

At a more specific level, an inquiry frame can be defined within the context of a particular study (as in the Guthrie et al., 1993, example given earlier). When constructing a study, researchers establish a frame of inquiry that may diverge from the prototypical. For example, Howe and Eisenhart (1990) describe two equally excellent ethnographies that vary in terms of their logics-in-use: The first poses research questions typical to ethnography but uses innovative methods for investigation; the second employs typical ethnographic methods to answer a question not traditionally ethnographic. Howe and Eisenhart conclude that it is not whether a research design fits a mold that is important in evaluating research, but rather whether a coherent frame of inquiry is established that successfully addresses the research questions.

Further, a quick review of the history of methods articulation for any inquiry frame, qualitative (e.g., Agar, 1996; LeCompte, Preissle, & Tesch, 1993) or quantitative (e.g., Behrens & Smith, 1996), reveals that research designs are dynamic and evolving (Shank, 1994). Researchers not infrequently adapt idealized methodological procedures to better address a particular question. For example, an educational psychologist might embed multiple in-depth case studies within a quasi-experimental design to more closely trace how instructional interactions shape individual learning in context and can be associated with group differences and outcomes. Thus, a focus on frames of inquiry provides a multidimensional way of describing, not only logics of inquiry at a generalized level, but also the particularities of a given study. When conducting, interpreting, or evaluating research, it is not as valuable to classify a study (as quantitative or qualitative, as an experiment or a case study) as it is to ensure that there is an internally consistent logic of inquiry underlying the research (Shulman, 1988).

INQUIRY FRAMES IN EDUCATIONAL PSYCHOLOGY

An original motivation for writing this chapter was to examine how qualitative research is being or might be utilized within the field of educational psychology. Therefore, in preparation for writing, I enlisted the assistance of an advanced PhD candidate with considerable methodological expertise in qualitative, but not quantitative, methods in completing a literature review. Her task was to identify any "qualitative" articles published in the *Journal of Educational Psychology* (*JEP*) and *Contemporary Educational Psychology* (*CEP*) in the 11 years from 1993 to 2003 (inclusive). Examining the published articles she selected, along with her reasoning for selecting them, allowed me to observe how a qualitative researcher perceived the frames of inquiry drawn upon by educational psychologists.

Consistent with the theoretical argument provided earlier, we both found that categorizing studies as either quantitative or qualitative was both difficult and simplistic. As an alternative, we identified features of the inquiry frames within each study that seemed similar to features prevalent in the qualitative literatures (e.g., theoretical frameworks associated with qualitative research; qualitative design frameworks; methodological procedures such as purposive sampling or inductive data analysis). I then summarized each article in a large database to capture how overarching inquiry frames were assembled out of a collection of design features. This approach allowed a more multidimensional analysis of logics-in-use and of the prevalence of different kinds of methodological features. Table 39.1 presents an overview of findings from this analysis. For *JEP* and *CEP* separately, the table presents the number of articles published in the period under consideration, the number and percentage of empirical articles that included any kind of qualitative feature, and the number and percentage of articles in which a predominance of qualitative features were assembled into an inquiry frame explicitly identified as qualitative.

A first conclusion that can be drawn from these findings is that, in spite of explicit calls by editors of both the *JEP* (Pressley, 1996, personal communication) and *CEP* (Alexander & Graham, 2001; Royer, 1996) for manuscripts representing a variety of inquiry frames, educational psychologists only infrequently drew on qualitative literatures in the past 11 years to design their research studies. For example, of the 318 articles published in *CEP*, only 5 (2 percent) self-identified as employing a qualitative design (Dowson & McInerney, 2003; Driscoll, Moallem, Dick, & Kirby, 1994; Eilam & Aharon, 2003; Osana, Tucker, & Bennet, 2003; Van Etten, Freebern, & Pressley, 1997). Similarly, of the 685 articles published in *JEP*, just 16 (2 percent) explicitly used qualitative designs (Aulls, 1998, 2002; Dowson & McInerney, 2001; Evensen, Salisbury-Glennon, & Glenn, 2001; Fitzgerald & Noblit, 2000; Flowerday & Schraw, 2000; Hacker & Tenent, 2002; Johnston, Woodside-Jiron, 2001; Mamlin & Harris, 1998; Martin, Marsh, Dubus, & Williamson, 2003; McGill-Franzen, Lanford, & Adams, 2002; Perry, 1998; Schuh, 2003; Schutz, Crowder, & White, 2001; Sweet, Guthrie, & Ng, 1998; Van Meter, Yokoi, & Pressley, 1994), although another 10 used mixed methods at least in part grounded in the qualitative literature (Butler, 1998; Davis, Clarke, & Rhodes, 1994; Echevarria, 2003; Eva-Wood, 2004; Purdie, Hattie, & Douglas, 1996; Shearer, Lundeberg, & Coballes-Vega, 1997; Solmon, 1996; Thorkildsen, Nolen, & Fournier, 1994; Turner et al., 1998, 2002).

It does appear, however, that there has been an increase in the number of educational psychologists publishing studies using qualitative design frameworks in the past 5 years. For example, of the five articles using qualitative inquiry frames in *CEP*, three were published in 2003. Of the 16 qualitative designs reported in *JEP*, 11 (69 percent) were published in the 3 years between 2000 and 2003, whereas only one was published before 1998. Interestingly, seven of the 10 mixed-methods JEP articles, which explicitly drew on qualitative literatures to construct blended designs, appeared in 1998 or earlier. Perhaps researchers drawing on qualitative inquiry frames were more successful at publishing their work prior to 2000 if they used mixed designs.

TABLE 39.1. Evidence of Qualitative Features Within Inquiry Frames, 1993–2003

Journal	Total Number of Published articles Between 1993 and 2003	Number of Empirical Articles With Any Kind of "Qualitative" Feature	Number of Empirical Articles Clearly Employing a "Qualitative" Frame of Inquiry
Journal of Educational Psychology	685	99 (14%)	16 (2%)
Contemporary Educational Psychology	318	25 (8%)	5 (2%)

These findings are consistent with trends identified by others who have found an under-representation of qualitative traditions in fields of study associated with psychology (MacArthur, 2003; Polkinghorne & Gribbons, 1999; Shank, 1994). But this finding contrasts with trends observed in other educational research communities. For example, the 2000 *Handbook of Reading Research* (Kamil, Mosenthal, Pearson, & Barr, 2000) includes nine chapters focused on a diversity of inquiry frames, including historical research, teacher research, narrative approaches, critical approaches, programmatic interventions, ethnography, verbal report and protocol analysis, single-subject experiments, discourse and sociocultural studies, and research synthesis. Similarly, the 2003 *Handbook of Research on Teaching in the Language Arts* (Flood, Lapp, Squire, & Jensen, 2003) includes chapters on the design of empirical research, longitudinal research, case study research, ethnography, teacher research, teacher inquiry, synthesis research, fictive representation, and contemporary methodological issues. It is notable that in both of these handbooks differing qualitative inquiry frames (e.g., ethnography, narrative) are not subsumed under one umbrella. On the other hand, consistent with the increasing appearance of qualitative work in educational psychology journals, there does appear to be increasing recognition of multiple inquiry frames in research methods textbooks often used to train undergraduate and graduate students in the field. For example, the sixth edition of the influential text by Borg and Gall (Gall et al., 1996) has added to its comprehensive discussion of quantitative traditions an entire section on "Approaches to Qualitative Research," with separate chapters on case study research, qualitative research traditions, and historical research.

A second conclusion that can be drawn from these data is that a reasonable number of studies published in flagship journals in educational psychology contained at least one qualitative feature. These included 99 (14 percent) of the 685 articles published in *JEP*, and 25 (8 percent) of the 318 articles published in *CEP*. It appears that educational psychologists are employing inquiry design features similar to those prevalent in qualitative traditions,

more than might be assumed from a categorical analysis (e.g., a count of qualitative designs). But clearly there is also room for expansion in the range and number of design features employed. My review of the literature also suggests room for improvement in how those design features are implemented (see later discussion).

There are at least three reasons why Educational Psychologists might draw more heavily on a variety of inquiry frameworks for conducting research. First, alternative design frameworks could be profitably employed to address issues of importance to our field. For example, case study designs are useful for in-depth examination of multiple interacting variables within one or more units of analysis (e.g., a student, a classroom, a school, an event) (Merriam, 1998; Stake, 1994; 1995; Yin, 1994). Educational psychologists are starting to draw on single or multiple case study designs to investigate teaching and learning. For example, Butler (1995, 1998) used multiple case studies to examine how an innovative instructional intervention promoted self-regulated learning by adults with learning disabilities. She analyzed data from questionnaires, interviews, observations, student work, and other documents to trace dynamic interactions over time between instruction and students' metacognitive knowledge, self-efficacy, attributional beliefs, engagement in strategy development and implementation, and performance. Aulls (1998) conducted case studies of two classrooms to investigate the impact of classroom discourse on the content students learn. Driscoll et al. (1994) combined observations, questionnaires, and interviews to examine how teachers and students used textbooks in a middle school science classroom and associated effects. Johnston et al. (2001) conducted case studies of four classrooms to examine how children enter into a discourse practice, constructing knowledge about language and themselves as literate individuals. Schuh (2003) used instrumental case studies to investigate the nature of knowledge construction in classrooms that varied in learner centerdness. Clearly educational psychologists can benefit from case study methodologies to provide an "in-depth picture of the interacting influences within the instructional environment on student learning" (Driscoll et al., 1994, p. 81).

Grounded theory offers another design framework of potential value for educational psychologists (Glaser & Strauss, 1967; Strauss & Corbin, 1994). Grounded theory allows for the inductive generation of a theory to account for data collected within a complex setting. For example, Van Etten et al. (1997) were interested in university students' beliefs about exam preparation, but also recognized that there might be situational variability. They conducted interviews with students and used an inductive, grounded theory approach to generate a complex understanding of students' beliefs. Evensen Salisbury-Glenon, & Glenn (2001) provide an excellent example of a grounded theory study, with an extremely well-articulated design. They used grounded theory to develop a situated model of self-regulated learning based on a study of six medical students in a problem-based curriculum. Their goal was "to explain the development of and differences in students' strategic learning behaviours and performance outcomes" (p. 659).

Ethnographies are useful for understanding the shared understandings and practices of particular cultural groups (Agar, 1996; Creswell, 1998; LeCompte et al., 1993). Although ethnography is often associated with the cultural study of distant or foreign cultures, educational researchers in many fields have started to apply ethnography to the study of education. These applications tend to retain a central focus on culture (see Creswell, 1998), but examine how shared beliefs and/or cultural practices exist in communities, schools, and classrooms. Educational psychologists have borrowed methodological tools from ethnography when conducting studies of student learning in classrooms. For example, Van Meter et al. (1994) conducted an ethnographic interview study to build a more complete theory of self-regulated note-taking, combining previous theory and new insights gleaned from interviewing students.

Many other designs exist that could be used by educational psychologists to address important questions. For example, Dowson and McInerney (2001) conducted a content analysis of data from 114 interviews and 24 structured observation periods to expand understanding of students' social and avoidance goals as related to academic behavior, affect, and cognition. Kamann and Butler (1996) used discourse analysis to document the structure and content of teacher–student interactions within a particular intervention model. Phenomenology can be used to understand the essence of students' or teachers' experiences of a particular phenomenon (Moustakas, 1994). Marshall (2004) used narrative inquiry to examine how parents of children with autism framed and reframed their experiences as parents, and their children's experiences with the school system, using culturally specific story forms (Connelly & Clandinin, 1990).

A second reason why educational psychologists would benefit from drawing on a wider range of inquiry frames is that many are working from substantive theoretical frameworks (e.g., sociocognitive, sociocultural, constructivist, socioconstructivist, situated theories) that conceptualize individual learning as embedded in context. These researchers could draw on case studies, ethnography, discourse analysis, naturalistic, or other design frameworks to examine learning and behavior as situated in multilayered settings. For example, Nancy Perry (1998) established an inquiry frame drawing from case study research that was consonant with her sociocultural perspective. To examine relationships between classroom contexts and children's beliefs, values, expectations, and actions, she purposively selected classrooms (high or low in features that promote self-regulated learning) and students (high- and low-achieving writers), and interpreted data collected using a combination of surveys, observations, questionnaires, and interviews over a 6-month period. Similarly, educational psychologists seeking to understand how individual motivation and cognition are socially, culturally, and historically situated, or how instructors and students coconstruct meaning, need methodological tools that allow investigating individuals interacting in a dynamic context (Weade, 1992). Table 39.2 provides a sample of foci typically linked to research using qualitative methods. Scan this list to observe how many of these foci would be of great interest to researchers whose work draws on sociocognitive, sociocultural, constructivist, socioconstructivist, or situated theories.

Third, educational psychologists would benefit from drawing on a broader set of methodological tools for answering emerging research questions. Wittrock (2003) explains how changes in research questions within a field can be accompanied by a shift in methods. For example, he describes how expanding interests of teachers of English in "how individuals and students use their strategies, background knowledge and emotions to construct meaning" and "how teaching functions, how students learn, and how we might improve our own teaching and learning" (p. 273) have led to development in methods better able to examine teaching and learning processes (e.g., think-alouds, process tracing, stimulated recall). Clearly, however, the questions Wittrock outlines are also of central interest to educational psychologists, and it may be that our field would also benefit from a methods expansion. Similarly, in a literature review appearing in the *Educational Psychologist*, Almasi et al. (1994) conclude that "a wide range of methodologies will be needed to depict learning as it occurs in whole language" (p. 301).

Table 39.3 displays the links between research questions and methods within the 25 articles published in *CEP*

TABLE 39.2. Research Foci Often Associated With Use of Qualitative Research

Source	Research Foci
Behrens and Smith (1996)	⇒Understanding "qualities or essences of a phenomenon by focusing on the meanings of events to the phenomenon and the social events that transform those meanings" (p. 978). ⇒Understanding human action in context. ⇒Understanding "transactions between students and teachers in the defining of the interactions and the creation of labels and categories that occur at the local level" (p. 999). ⇒Understanding "essential features and interrelationships (how things work) and meaning/context (what to make of it)" (p. 999)
Butler (2002)	⇒Understanding complex and recursive interactions between processes as they play out in context ⇒Understanding learning as a function of teaching actions in context
MacArthur (2003)	⇒Understanding people, events, or constructs in natural settings ⇒Understanding meanings from the perspective of participants ⇒Understanding the particular in context ⇒Understanding social structures with layers of meaning
Polkinghorne and Gribbons (1999)	⇒Understanding of individual people and particular situations ⇒"A lens bringing aspects of a complex flux into focus" (p. 112) ⇒Understanding how "human actions are informed by interpretive schemes" (p. 116). ⇒Understanding how "concepts are more individually constructed and that structuring patterns are passed on to individuals through conceptual models inherent in their culture/language" (p. 116).
Putney et al. (1999)	⇒Understanding why miscommunications occur across agents ⇒Understanding "phenomena constructed in and through the everyday actions and activity of people within particular settings" (p. 374)

that contained any kind of qualitative feature. What this table shows is that educational psychologists are already asking questions (e.g., about participants' beliefs, goals, and perspectives, learning processes, teaching practices) well answered by collecting and interpreting qualitative data. Further, researchers are taking advantage of qualitative tools to help in answering these kinds of questions. For example, researchers are interpreting interview data to identify participants' perspectives and are conducting observations to capture behavior. Researchers are drawing on multiple methods, often simultaneously, to capture learning processes and knowledge about learning. These findings suggest that educational psychologists can address important, emerging questions by constructing studies with qualitative features.

EXPANDING FRAMES OF INQUIRY IN EDUCATIONAL PSYCHOLOGY

In the rest of this chapter, I describe how research in educational psychology could be extended and enhanced. To structure this discussion, I offer a more nuanced definition of inquiry frames (see Fig 39.1). As described earlier, inquiry frames comprise sets of design features that can be assembled in different combinations to construct a coherent logic of inquiry (Shulman, 1988). In the sections to follow, I identify important considerations for establishing an internally consistent inquiry frame for any research study, turning attention to each design feature

in turn. I also generate specific recommendations for research practice and training in educational psychology (see Table 39.4 for a summary of recommendations).

Theoretical Frameworks

All research is theory laden and there is no perspective-free stance (Alvermann, O'Brien, & Dillon, 1996; Behrens & Smith, 1996). In fact, research is embedded simultaneously within multiple theoretical frameworks, including methodological assumptions, substantive theories, researcher perspectives, and ethical stances. These theoretical frameworks have a collective impact on how research is conceived and conducted. They shape decisions about (1) research questions considered important, (2) methods best suited to studying phenomena, (3) criteria for establishing credibility and warranting conclusions, and (4) the form in which findings should be reported (Putney et al., 1999; Shulman, 1988). In short, theoretical frameworks delimit how research studies are framed and restrict possible findings. As a key feature of inquiry frames, theoretical frameworks are one dimension across which research approaches can be meaningfully compared. Multiple, interrelated theoretical perspectives must be made explicit when planning, interpreting, evaluating, or reporting any kind of research (Alvermann et al., 1996).

Methodological Assumptions. All researchers hold theoretical assumptions about the nature of knowledge and

TABLE 39.3. Links Between Research Questions and Qualitative Evidence in *Contemporary Educational Psychology* (1993–2003)

Authors	Research Question	Focus[a]	Obs	Int	TA	Trace	Art
Lai & Biggs (1994)	How do learners *perceive mastery learning and approach learning in context?*	Perceptions		*			
Van Etten, Freebern, & Pressley (1997)	What are university students' *beliefs about exam preparation?*	Perceptions		*			
Chan & Elliott (2002)	What are the *epistemological beliefs* of teacher education students in different cultural contexts and what might account for those differences?	Perceptions		*			
Dowson & McInerney (2003)	What are students' *motivational goals* and *how do they interact in a dynamic way?*	Perceptions and Behavior	*	*			
Ross & Cousins (1994)	What is the relationship between students' intentions to seek or give help and *what they actually do?*	Behavior	*				
Henderlong & Paris (1996)	What kinds of museum exhibits foster *motivation and engagement?*	Behavior	*				
Hrubes & Feldman (2001)	Do students who are high or low at self-monitoring evidence *nonverbal cues* when solving problems?	Behavior	*				
Moore (1995)	What are the *cognitive and metacognitive knowledge* of students when facing library search tasks in preparation for a research project?	Knowledge	*	*	*		
Guthrie, Weber, & Kimmerly (1993)	*How do students read and understand graphs, tables and illustrations*	Process			*		
Tallent-Runnels (1993)	Does participating in a problem solving course influence the *quality of students' problem solving?*	Process				*	
Schunk & Swartz (1993)	What is the impact of self-efficacy, instruction, goals, and feedback on *strategy use* and *writing quality?*	Process				*	*
Byrnes & Takahira (1994)	What is the relationship between *cognitive processing when solving math problems* and performance?	Process		*		*	
Ley & Young (1998)	Do college students differ in terms of *their self-regulated behaviors?*	Process		*			
Bornholt (2002)	How do students' *test taking strategies* impact on their scores on formal tests?	Process	*				
Ben-Zeev & Ronald (2002)	What is the origin of the *kinds of errors* that students make when solving math problems?	Process			*	*	
Eilam & Aharon (2003)	What are the *self-regulated behaviors* of average or high-ability learners in a science inquiry project?	Process	*			*	
Osana, Tucker, & Bennett (2003)	What is the *decision-making process* of adolescents asked to reason about an equity issue?	Process		*	*		
Meyer, Astor, & Behre (2002)	How do teachers from violent schools *reason about fights* between students and whether to intervene?	Process		*			
Slotte & Lonka (1999)	What is the effect of *note-taking and opportunities to review notes* on *performance?*	Process; Performance				*	*
Griffin (1995)	Is there a difference in *map skills* between students who participate in different kinds of instruction?	Performance	*				
Driscoll, Moallem, Dick, & Kirby (1994)	*How is a textbook actually used* in a middle school science classroom?	Practice	*	*			*
Shachar & Shmuelevitz (1997)	What is the relationship between teachers' *use of cooperative learning* and their collaboration with other teachers and efficacy?	Practice	*				*
Hamers, de Koning, & Sijtsma (1998)	Does students' inductive reasoning improve after participating in an intervention, and *could teachers implement the approach?*	Practice	*				

[a] Perceptions = beliefs, goals, or perceptions.
[b] Obs = observations, Int = interview, TA = think aloud, Trace = traces of processing, Art = documents, work samples, or other kinds of artifacts.

TABLE 39.4. Recommendations for Constructing a Coherent Logic of Inquiry

Design Feature	Recommendations
THEORETICAL FRAMEWORKS	⇒Make theoretical frameworks explicit when planning, interpreting, and reporting research
Methodological assumptions	⇒Be sensitive to a range of methodological assumptions that can undergird research
	⇒Recognize when and how methodological assumptions shape inquiry
	⇒ Include methodological assumptions in graduate research training
Substantive Theory	⇒Access methodological literature for guidance in how to build theory from data
	⇒Account for the influence of substantive theory on inquiry
Researcher	⇒Account for the impact of researcher perspectives on inquiry
Perspectives	⇒Recognize varied strategies for accounting for researcher perspectives
Ethical stances	⇒Recognize one's own values and biases and impact on research
	⇒Engage in a critical and progressive discourse across inquiry frames
	⇒Broaden vision of legitimate research in educational psychology
RESEARCH QUESTIONS	⇒Expand sense of complementary research questions addressed by different inquiry frames
	⇒Ensure research questions are coherent with theoretical frameworks and design
METHODS	⇒Choose all methods deliberately to establish a coherent logic-in-use
Overall design	⇒Ensure design is coherent with theoretical frameworks and questions
	⇒Consider using iterative designs to build and test findings in a study
	⇒Support students to recognize the logic of inquiry underlying designs
Sampling	⇒Choose strategies based on types of conclusions to be drawn
	⇒Avoid reverting to volunteers or convenience samples
	⇒Use purposive sampling when appropriate
	⇒Interpret findings in light of sampling strategies used
Data collection	⇒Continue to develop innovative data collection tools (e.g., traces)
	⇒Account for how and when theory impacts on the inquiry process
	⇒Triangulate data from multiple sources to corroborate findings
	⇒Use multiple data collection methods to ask complementary questions
Data reduction	⇒Explicate data reduction strategies for qualitative and quantitative data
	⇒Demonstrate that meaningfulness and completeness are maintained
	⇒Explain when and how theoretical frameworks shape data reduction
Data interpretation	⇒Articulate how data are interpreted to generate conclusions
	⇒Specify data coding methods using Constas' (1992) four dimensions
	⇒Explain when and how theoretical frameworks shape data interpretation
	⇒Draw on the full range of available strategies to select strategies for establishing credibility in data interpretation
	⇒Use displays to aid in systematic and comprehensive data analysis
	⇒Take qualitative data analysis seriously; use rigorous analyses
Warranting conclusions	⇒Ensure coherence between research questions, designs, data collection and interpretive strategies, and conclusions drawn
	⇒Judge credibility in terms of a study's logic-in-use
	⇒Explain explicitly how study design and enactment warrant conclusions
REPRESENTING RESEARCH	⇒Choose representation strategies that best present a given inquiry frame
	⇒Establish publication standards that permit different report formats
	⇒Explain individual design features but also how they fit together
	⇒Provide rationales for all design features in light of the inquiry frame
	⇒Select examples so as to show patterns, capture regularities and diversity, identify discrepant evidence, and rule out rival hypotheses

how knowledge should be constructed. In fact, much of the qualitative–quantitative debate has focused on defining essential differences between the two classes of research, not at the level of method (e.g., specific sampling techniques; collection and analysis of quantitative or qualitative data), but rather in terms of underlying philosophical and ideological assumptions about the inquiry process itself (Creswell, 1998; Guba & Lincoln, 1994). But, to return to the main theme of this chapter, it may not be so valuable to associate particular methodological assumptions with quantitative or qualitative research, broadly speaking, as it is to unearth the methodological assumptions underlying a particular frame of inquiry and as instantiated within a given study. To recognize such assumptions, educational psychologists require sensitivity to the range of theoretical assumptions that might undergird research (e.g., Alvermann et al., 1996; Bereiter, 1994, Creswell, 1998; Denzin & Lincoln, 1994; 2003; Guba & Lincoln, 1994; Lather, 1991, 1992; Salomon, 1994).

For example, Guba and Lincoln (1994) offer one influential framework for identifying assumptions underlying research. They identify four broad "inquiry paradigms" (p. 109)—positivism, post positivism, critical theory, and constructivism—that differ in terms of ontology (i.e., views about the nature of reality), epistemology (i.e., views about the relationship between the knower and what can be known), and methodology (i.e., how to go about studying a phenomenon). Taking ontological perspectives as an example, Guba and Lincoln link post postivism with a belief in a reality that is real, but only "imperfectly and probabilistically apprehendible," critical theory with "historical realism," where reality is viewed as something that is "crystallized over time," and is "shaped by social, political, cultural, economic, ethnic, and gender values," and constructivism with "relativism" and beliefs in "local and specific constructed realities" (p. 109). They suggest that ontology, epistemology, and methodology are interdependent, such that ontological perspectives (e.g., reality as socially constructed) are linked to epistemological assumptions (e.g., that generating knowledge requires a process of constructive meaning making) and methodological frameworks (e.g., a belief that "individual constructions can be elicited and refined only through interaction *between and among* investigator and respondent" (p. 111, emphasis in the original)). In short, Guba and Lincoln explicate how theoretical assumptions about the nature of reality and how it can be known are inextricably connected with a study's methodology.

For example, imagine how the assumptions identified by Guba and Lincoln (1994) might shape an investigators' approach to examining the relationship between classroom evaluation practices and student motivation. Building from a "constructivist" perspective, an investigator might assume that the meaning of classroom evaluation practices is coconstructed by students and teachers and depends on complicated, localized interactions (an ontological assumption that realities are local, situated, and coconstructed). Rather than examining cross-class patterns at an abstract level, this investigator is more likely to conduct an in-depth case study of how a teacher and his or her students, coming from unique backgrounds and perspectives, coconstruct action, perceptions, beliefs, and meaning in the context of a single classroom. Conclusions drawn would be provisional and subject to testing against relationships found in other settings.

Lincoln and Guba (1985) associate quantitative and qualitative research with incommensurable inquiry paradigms (i.e., positivism and post positivism with quantitative; critical theory and constructivism with qualitative). However, rather than reflecting mutually exclusive world views, inquiry paradigms may just be more or less relevant given different kinds of research questions. For example, consider research into the impact of special education on students with reading disabilities. Separate studies might focus, respectively, on (1) defining instructional approaches that prevent early reading failure for students with phonological processing problems (from a "postpositivist" perspective) (2) who is advantaged or disadvantaged by special education placements, considering race, socioeconomic status, school community, or other relevant factors (from a "critical" perspective); or (3) how individuals, their teachers, and/or their parents perceive and react to the labeling of individuals as "disabled" (from a "constructivist" perspective). Understanding the impact of special education on students is surely enriched if we identify effective interventions. But it is also important to understand how students experience being labeled and are advantaged or disadvantaged in school and society (MacArthur, 2003). Sensitivity to varying methodological perspectives may aid in uncovering a range of questions that should be addressed to understand an important issue.

Another approach to defining the nature of methodological assumptions in educational research, broadly speaking, is to link inquiry frames to their disciplinary origins (Darling-Hammond & Synder, 1992; Shulman, 1988; Walker, 1992). For example, Shulman (1988) explains how logics of inquiry developed within disciplines (e.g., anthropology, history, philosophy, psychology, sociology, biology) are often imported by educational researchers to address different kinds of questions. He uses the term *disciplined inquiry* when describing inquiry frames, referring not only to "the ordered, regular, or principled nature of investigation," but also to "the disciplines themselves which serve as the sources for the principles of regularity or canons of evidence employed by the investigator" (p. 5). Others have differentiated inquiry frames in education as arising from philosophic/humanistic or scientific disciplines (Darling-Hammond & Snyder, 1992; Walker, 1992), which themselves have established theoretical perspectives and methodological tools. Darling-Hammond and Snyder (1992) see both perspectives as equally valuable, but for answering different kinds of questions. For example, scientific approaches assist in understanding "how and what children learn in relation to how and what can be taught" (p. 56) whereas traditions of inquiry drawn from a philosophic/humanistic perspective (e.g., conceptual analysis, hermeneutics, critical theory) may be more useful in "illuminating the ideas and values underlying curriculum" (p. 51) and in considering what *should* be taught. Questions of value or appropriate goals (e.g., what we should value as educators in a multicultural, global society) require use of different approaches to inquiry than do questions of how things work (e.g., how students learn). Certainly educational psychologists are interested in both kinds of questions. It is difficult to judge the efficacy of instruction, for example, without considering what goals we should seek to achieve.

As a third approach to identifying theoretical perspectives underlying research, Creswell (1998) teases apart ontological, epistemological, and methodological assumptions from "ideological stances" that might be adopted in a particular study (p. 73). He highlights three stances that have had a huge impact in educational research: postmodernism, critical theory, and feminist theory (see also Bereiter, 1994; Denzin & Lincoln, 1994, 2003; Lather, 1991, 1992; Reinherz, 1992). Taken together, these (and other stances, such as poststructuralism) "challenge the notion that there is only one legitimate way to develop knowledge" (Polkinghorne & Gribbons, 1999, p. 112). Other researchers argue that these emerging theoretical stances (e.g., postmodernist, poststructuralist) are not adoptable or not in a particular study, but rather have implications for all current research in education. For example, it has been argued that all researchers now operate within a postmodern, postpositivist world (Bereiter, 1994; Howe & Eisenhart, 1990; Shank, 1994), where there is not one right way for building knowledge claims and where grand, universal theories that disregard gender, race, or researchers' influence on inquiry are simply not viable (Lather, 1992).

Educational psychologists would do well to keep abreast of the literature addressing these different perspectives, and to consider how ideological stances might shape assumptions about the nature of knowledge, knowledge construction, and/or legitimate sources of evidence for supporting knowledge claims. For example, Bereiter (1994) addresses the postmodern challenge by describing how science can function well without appealing to claims of absolute *truth* or *objectivity*. His solution is to suggest that "all theories are human constructions, designed to be replaced by better ones" (p. 4), and that progress in science "arises from continual criticism and efforts to overcome criticisms by modifying or replacing theories" (p. 5). He concludes that progress is made when both knowledge claims and the process of knowledge construction are subjected to public scrutiny, thereby feeding into a progressive discourse focused both on substantive issues and on the inquiry process itself.

In their thorough discussion of data analysis in the previous *Handbook of educational psychology*, Behrens and Smith (1996) also argue that all research is postpositivist and essentially interpretive. They explain that all data analysis is theory laden; that data, theories, and conclusions are constructed and communicated by researchers engaged in social relationships; and that words and numbers are simply symbols for representing meaning. It seems reasonable to suggest that inquiry frames simply provide a set of interpretive tools. If this is the case, then generating warranted conclusions from any given study requires understanding how findings are shaped by an inquiry frame and underlying methodological assumptions.

In sum, this discussion suggests that educational psychologists should attend to the type and source of methodological assumptions that underlie frames of inquiry (e.g., Bereiter, 1994; Creswell, 1998; Guba & Lincoln, 1994; Lather, 1992; Shulman, 1988), and that specific attention to underlying methodological assumptions should be part of graduate research training. At a minimum all researchers should be able to articulate the theoretical underpinnings of their own work (Alvermann et al., 1996; Behrens & Smith, 1996). But these examples also suggest new possibilities for educational psychologists, by expanding awareness not only of the variety of theoretical perspectives in which research might be situated, but also of the range of questions that might be asked and of methodological tools for addressing them.

Substantive Theories. The theoretical perspectives that shape an inquiry frame also derive from the substantive theories appealed to when constructing research (Alvermann et al., 1996). In the field of educational psychology, for example, researchers might work from behavioral, cognitive-behavioural, cognitive, sociocognitive, sociocultural, constructivist, socioconstructivist, and/or situated learning theories, which lend themselves to asking different kinds of questions requiring different research methods. For example, a behavioral perspective foregrounds relationships between environments and behavior and privileges observation as a methodological tool. But with the emergence of cognitive-mediational perspectives in the late 1970s and 1980s (e.g., Winne & Marx, 1982), new research tools were needed to measure students' perceptions about, not just responses to, events or stimuli in their environment. Similarly, multiple theoretical perspectives have been applied over time to the study of self-regulated learning (see Zimmerman & Schunk, 2001), with concomitant shifts in methodological tools used to study those learning processes.

The nature of the theories from which a researcher builds, coupled with theory building goals, also have implications for the logic of inquiry employed. For example, a common differentiation in the sociological literature is between nomothetic theories, which define general laws and properties, and idiographic theories, which focus on the particulars of an individual person, place, or time of study (Dooley, 1995). The "constructivist" researcher described earlier, who was interested in the relationship between classroom evaluation and student motivation, was less interested in developing or testing a generalized, nomothetic theory, and focused her investigation instead on developing an idiographic understanding of meaning in context. Yet nomothetic and idiographic perspectives are not necessarily incompatible and can actually be complementary. An educational psychologist might use a mixed design to understand the general and the particular in a single study (Aulls, 2004; personal communication).

Drawing on substantive theories when constructing a study can assist a researcher to identify and address new and important research questions, and thus to push a field of study forward. However, building on extant substantive theories can also restrict a researcher's perspective. Recognition of this problem was in large part responsible for Glaser and Strauss' (1967) original articulation of the grounded theory method. Glaser and Strauss were concerned that sociologists were too often imposing theoretical frameworks on their work, so that questions were asked, and data collected and interpreted, in terms of predetermined constructs. They saw little room in this general approach for critiquing or revising theory. As an alternative, they articulated a coherent inquiry frame that allows for constructing substantive theories "grounded" in data. Their original approach has been modified and adapted (see Strauss & Corbin, 1994) but remains influential, and many methodologists have built on their approach to define rigorous and systematic methods for analyzing and interpreting qualitative data (e.g., Guba & Lincoln, 1985; Merriam, 1998; Miles & Huberman, 1994). Educational psychologists who seek to generate new understandings from qualitative data (e.g., from interviews, observations, think-alouds, written work, traces of learning) would be well advised to refer to these well articulated logics of inquiry when constructing their own inquiry frames.

Although all inquiry frames are impacted by substantive theory, they differ in terms of when and how substantive theories enter into a study (Agar, 1996; McMillan, 2000; Merriam, 1998). In many inquiry frames (e.g., experiments), it is typically expected that the researcher will build deliberately from theory to frame research questions and hypotheses, develop instruments for measuring constructs, and provide an analytic framework for interpreting data (McMillan, 2000). But at the other end of the extreme, grounded theory methodology suggests deriving meaning from the data first, so as to avoid imposing preexisting theory on a phenomenon of interest (Glaser

& Strauss, 1967; Strauss & Corbin, 1994). Most typically, researchers operate on a continuum somewhere in between these two extremes. Either within or across studies, researchers both draw on substantive theory to provide frameworks for interpreting findings and consider findings inductively or "abductively" to revise theoretical frameworks (Agar, 1996; Polkinghorne & Gribbons, 1999; Shank, 1994). It is important for all researchers, educational psychologists included, to reflect on and articulate how and when substantive theory feeds into an investigation, not only when establishing the theoretical framework and fit of research questions with the extant literature, but also when describing the impact of theory on data collection and interpretive strategies (such as coding strategies; see later discussion).

Researcher Perspectives. All researchers bring to an inquiry "prior knowledge, capacities, intentions, and interests" (Behrens & Smith, 1996) that influence how they conduct research. They also are necessarily "gendered, multiculturally situated, and theoretically inclined to see phenomena in ways that influence question and method" (Alvermann et al., 1996, p. 116). Thus, all researchers need to account for how their own perspectives affect the design and enactment of the inquiry process (Behrens & Smith, 1996). But it is not common in research reports in educational psychology for researchers to explicitly reflect on how their own values, biases, and theoretical stances impact on research. Educational Psychologists can learn from inquiry frameworks that explicate strategies for bracketing and accounting for researcher perspectives, such as phenomenology (e.g., Moustakas, 1994).

Educational research is social (Behrens & Smith, 1996) in the sense that data collection, interpretation, and research reporting are completed in cooperation with other people (participants, an audience). Relationships are established during a study that exert influence over the findings. For example, the kind of rapport established in interviews affects the responses a participant might give (see Agar, 1996, for engaging examples). And, while inquiry frames may differ in terms of how researcher-participant relationships are constructed (e.g., trying to maintain neutrality vs. becoming engaged as a participant-observer), it is incumbent on all researchers to consider how the nature of relationships established throughout a study affects the findings that are generated. Establishing a "neutral" relationship affects findings just as much as does participant-observation, although perhaps in different ways.

Ethical Stances. Ethics, values, and politics are also features of inquiry frames (Bereiter, 1994; Creswell, 1998;

Lather, 1992; Myers, 1995). Indeed, to the three types of philosophical assumptions underlying research that Guba and Lincoln (1994) identify (ontology, epistemology, methodology), Creswell adds "axiological" assumptions regarding the role of values in research (p. 75). Educational researchers working within some research frameworks (e.g., critical or feminist) explicitly embrace certain values commitments as part of their frames of inquiry (e.g., making explicit how power and politics disadvantage some while privileging others). But it is not only these researchers whose work is affected: All researchers bring values and biases to research that must be accounted for as part of the inquiry process.

Values-based stances have an enormous impact, not only on the inquiry in a particular study, but also on how an entire field progresses. Bereiter (1994) suggests that science can move forward if a commitment is made to subjecting all beliefs to criticism, and if a critical discourse is established that is inclusive of multiple perspectives. But Mosenthal (1995) is not optimistic that such an open dialogue is possible. He suggests that deep divides in discourse about methodology are grounded in political investments and agendas, beliefs about who should act as agents of change, and perceptions of who is likely to benefit. I myself am more optimistic. Like Bereiter, I suggest that theory, research, and practice are advanced when diverse perspectives are juxtaposed. I encourage educational psychologists to engage in a critical, progressive discourse about substantive issues and methodologies (Bereiter, 1994; Putney et al., 1999).

Knowledge generation within a field of study can also be affected by politics and values when gatekeepers in government and/or in the scholarly community limit the questions addressed and/or forms of inquiry considered legitimate (Lather, 1992; Punch, 1994). For example, editors and editorial board members of key journals in a field, such as *JEP* and *CEP*, define what counts as quality research in a field of study and set standards for publication. Whether or not educational psychologists use or are exposed to a broader array of inquiry frames than is currently the case will be influenced by publication policies. Granting councils and funding agencies also define, inclusively or restrictively, what are acceptable forms of inquiry and channel resources accordingly. In this chapter I am *not* arguing that the research frames that form the traditional core of research in educational psychology should be supplanted with qualitative alternatives. But I am suggesting that journal editors, granting councils, peer reviewers, and graduate student research supervisors have a key role to play in ensuring that a full range of potentially productive designs are fairly valued and judged within our field.

Research Questions

From the preceding discussion it should be apparent that research questions and theoretical frameworks are reciprocally interdependent (Behrens & Smith, 1996; Shulman, 1988). For example, an educational psychologist working from a sociocultural learning theory (Vygotsky, 1978) might draw on that theory to question how teachers can effectively scaffold support to students during writing instruction. Conversely, an educational psychologist interested in supporting students to be more effective writers might seek out a sociocultural perspective to help in framing a research study. Either way, what is important is that the research questions posed are consonant with the theoretical framework(s) established. Ideally, all other aspects of a methodology will then be chosen to address those research questions. Note that by describing inquiry frames in a multidimensional way (i.e., theoretical frameworks, research questions, different aspects of methodology as interconnected but separable features), it is possible to tease apart and examine coherence between features within an inquiry frame.

As was described earlier, educational psychologists can draw from a variety of inquiry traditions, not only to find methods for addressing new questions, but also to surface important questions that might not otherwise be addressed. Shulman (1988) provides another excellent example of how alternative logics of inquiry both focus attention on different questions and provide methods for addressing them. Taking reading as an example, he describes how questions could focus on predicting who is at risk for reading failure (correlational design); testing the benefits of an intervention (experiment), detailing how an intervention works to effect changes (case study); canvassing how many people are illiterate in a given population (survey), defining what it even means to be illiterate (conceptual analysis), or tracing how conceptions of literacy have changed over time (historical analysis). Additional options are to examine how literacy is viewed, valued, and used as a cultural practice (ethnography), or the essence of meaning making from text as a human experience (phenomenology). Thus, like Darling-Hammond and Snyder (1992), Shulman shows how complementary forms of inquiry provide insight, not only into the learning–instruction relationships so central to the work of educational psychologists, but also into larger questions such as how literacy should be defined.

Thus, educational psychologists can draw on both emerging substantive theoretical perspectives and an expanded awareness of possible inquiry frameworks to define interesting new research questions. Although at the end of the day an inquiry frame should be selected so as to best answer a research question (rather than choosing a preferred method and finding a compatible research question), attention to different inquiry frames has the potential to increase sensitivity to the range of questions we should be asking. Note that new questions and directions for study can also emerge in the process of research. Studies that allow for inductive analysis of qualitative data can lead to new insights that form the basis for additional study.

Research Designs

In this section I focus attention on empirical frames of inquiry. These are those inquiry frames within which a researcher collects any kind of data to address one or more research questions (Pintrich, 2003). Empirical researchers may work from differing theoretical perspectives, but they face common methodological decision points when constructing a research study. Although the logics employed for doing so might differ, all empirical researchers must establish procedures for sampling, data collection, data reduction, data interpretation, and warranting conclusions. Researchers typically rely on an overarching design framework to provide a coherent and internally consistent logic for making these methodological decisions.

Overarching Design Frameworks. A key feature of an inquiry frame is the overall design. Designs provide an integrative framework within which more specific methods are assembled. For example, although all empirical research may require accessing data, it is the overall design framework that dictates when, where, and how those data should be collected.

There are many design frameworks with which educational psychologists are very familiar. For example, prototypical experiments (Gall et al., 1996; McMillan, 2000) are associated with *a priori* definition of theoretical frameworks, questions and hypotheses, development of valid and reliable measures, random sampling, use of control or comparison groups to rule out rival hypotheses, collection of pre- and posttests, and blind data analysis to prevent bias from creeping in. Data analytic strategies are generally defined in advance and linked to hypotheses, but undertaken only after all data are collected. However, instantiating this prototypical framework in practice is rarely so neat and clean. For example, in educational research it is rare that random sampling is possible, and defining control groups can be challenging. Thus, researchers typically adapt design frameworks in the context of a particular study (witness the development of quasi-experimental designs; Behrens & Smith, 1996). It

should also be noted that much work by researchers takes place in the periphery of the formal experiment. For example, researchers might pilot test procedures or collect data from interviews to guide development of measures. They also might explore their data, after the fact, to explain unexpected findings or interesting patterns, so as to generate hypotheses for future research.

Educational psychologists are often less familiar with design frameworks commonly used within disciplines outside of psychology. These frames tackle similar challenges (e.g., ruling out rival interpretations for findings), but may do so in different ways. Further, some of the work done in the periphery of other designs (e.g., learning enough about a situation to know what kinds of questions to ask) may be included within the design frame. Indeed, in quite a number of inquiry frameworks (e.g., ethnographies, grounded theory), methodological choices are less likely to be made in advance and may be more iterative and emergent (Agar, 1996; Behrens & Smith, 1996; Glaser & Strauss, 1967; Lincoln & Guba, 1985; Merriam, 1998; Miles & Huberman, 1994; Shank, 1994). For example, in a prototypical ethnography (see Agar, 1996) or grounded theory study (see Glaser & Strauss, 1967; Strauss & Corbin, 1994), a researcher might enter a new setting with orienting questions, and reserve until later definition of formal interview protocols or testable hypotheses. Informal data collection strategies (e.g., interviews, observations) might be used in early stages of inquiry, and might then become more formalized as understandings emerge that can be tested against new data. In fact, data collection and analysis would typically occur in tandem, so that analyses of data early on could inform subsequent data collection. Sampling of people or of events would also evolve planfully to aid in testing emerging understandings. Disconfirming evidence would be deliberately sought out, and rival hypotheses deliberately tested, as the study progressed.

The prototypical design frameworks just featured are stereotypical and do not capture the complexity of an actual research study. Further, they stand at two ends of a continuum on at least one dimension, from maximally prescribed to maximally emergent. Most inquiry frames fall somewhere in between. Nonetheless, educational psychologists could consider taking better advantage of iterative research designs when constructing research studies. Excellent examples can be found in educational psychology journals of studies in which researchers did just that (e.g., Dowson & McInerney, 2003, Schutz et al., 2001, Van Meter et al., 1994).

For example, Van Etten et al. (1997) conducted a grounded theory study of students' beliefs about exam preparation. They collected and analyzed data in four phases to support theory development. In the first phase, six groups of students participated in focus-group interviews. Two researchers independently coded the data and identified gaps in what they had learned. This information was then used to refine interview questions for Phase 2 of the study. In this second phase, new data were collected in additional focus group interviews and analyzed to test and refine categories that had emerged in Phase 1. Refined interview questions were used in Phase 3 to collect additional data from three final focus groups. In Phase 4, the researchers developed a 112-item questionnaire, based on the categories derived and refined in Phases 1 to 3, that was administered to a larger sample of students. The last step in theory construction involved relating categories to one another, in a step known as *axial coding*. This study provides an excellent example of how educational psychologists can use an iterative design to rigorously and systematically build, test, and extend theory within a single study.

Although overarching design frameworks might differ in substantial ways, ranging for example from totally predefined to completely emergent, researchers working within all design frameworks must address similar challenges. For example, all researchers have to define a logic for sampling persons and events, collecting meaningful data, reducing masses of data to manageable chunks, interpreting data, and warranting conclusions. In the sections to follow, I highlight ways in which researchers working within different inquiry frames might approach these various challenges.

Sampling. All researchers must make sampling decisions about which events, people, documents, time periods, etc., will be included in data collection. Researchers must choose a sampling logic based both on their research questions and on the kinds of conclusions they wish to draw. For example, experimenters wishing to find causal connections between an intervention and outcomes might select a sampling logic (e.g., random sampling) designed to minimize systematic differences between comparison groups and support generalization to populations. When less-than-idealized procedures are instantiated (e.g., random sampling is not possible), researchers must develop an alternative logic to achieve the same objectives, for example by establishing matched comparison groups or identifying a representative sample.

In other logics of inquiry (e.g., a case study; discourse analysis) researchers may be less interested in linking an intervention with outcomes or generalizing findings to populations. Instead, their goal might be to understand the values, beliefs, and practices within a given setting. As a result, they are likely to adopt purposive sampling strategies (Agar, 1996; Creswell, 1998; LeCompte et al., 1993; Merriam, 1998) so as to identify events, people,

artifacts, or documents from whom/which they can learn the most. For example, to learn about how instructional decisions are made during writing instruction, it might be maximally informative to speak with individuals privy to decision-making processes (e.g., an English department head; teachers responsible for defining the instruction) rather than sampling randomly among teachers. A number of excellent resources are available for defining different types of purposive sampling (e.g., LeCompte et al., 1993; Merriam, 1998).

In general, purposive sampling strategies are appropriate when a researcher can define the desired characteristics of people, events, artifacts, places, documents, and so forth to guide the selection of exemplars (LeCompte et al., 1993). Once selection criteria are defined, a researcher can employ a range of strategies, both early and late in a study, to select exemplars for inclusion. For example, imagine a researcher who wants to use discourse analysis to define the interaction patterns between teachers and students during a particular type of writing instruction. In this example, decisions must be made at the start of the study to select (1) a community, school district, and school within which the study will be conducted; (2) one or more teachers whose instruction follows a particular framework; (3) the class or classes within which instruction will be observed; (4) when, how often, and how long to observe instruction; (5) the students who will participate in observations; and (6) any documents or artifacts to be collected that might help in understanding interaction patterns. Sampling in any given study typically involves these kinds of multiple, layered decisions.

In this example, purposive strategies could be used to select lessons to be observed. Possibilities include comprehensive selection (e.g., all instances of writing instruction during a given time period), maximum-variation sampling (e.g., lessons that vary as widely as possible on important characteristics, such as type of writing involved), or typical case sampling (choosing writing instruction that is most like what is done on most days). To select teachers for observation, the researcher could identify individuals who are extreme on some dimension (particularly outgoing and engaging), typical (most like other teachers who use the approach), unique (use the writing approach in an innovative way), or outstanding (e.g., as recommended by a principal). Another sampling strategy is network or snowball selection, in which participants are identified by nomination from other participants who meet the selection criteria (e.g., identifying a first teacher and then asking that person for recommendations for others, and following leads until the desirable number of teachers are located for the study). Data generated using different sampling strategies yield different kinds of information. For example, comprehensive, maximum-variation, and typical sampling are more likely to warrant generalizations to similar groups or conditions. Exemplars that are extreme, unique, innovative, or outstanding can also be very useful in answering particular kinds of questions (e.g., how could this approach be used differently?; how could this approach work well?).

Another powerful strategy is sequential sampling (Glaser & Strauss, 1967; LeCompte et al., 1993; Merriam, 1998). This strategy involves adding to an initial sampling frame during a study to help in checking and extending emerging findings and/or ruling out alternative hypotheses. For example, imagine that our researcher had observed a teacher interacting differently with students from different genders or cultural backgrounds during writing instruction. The researcher might sequentially sample additional students for further observation, to check on the robustness of the first observation and to tease apart interaction patterns associated with gender and culture. When built into an iterative research design, sequential sampling supports generating and testing conclusions within a single study (Agar, 1996).

There is no one sampling logic that is the ideal across inquiry frames. Rather, what is important is that the procedures employed be best for answering a research question. To have at their disposal a fuller range of sampling logics, I recommend that educational psychologists access literature describing purposive sampling strategies (e.g., LeCompte et al., 1993; Merriam, 1998), which can be employed within a wide variety of inquiry frames. When random sampling is not possible, too many studies revert to convenience samples or volunteers, rather than formally drawing on available, well-articulated sampling strategies that would better support their research. A related recommendation is that researchers more thoroughly articulate the contributions and limitations of sampling decisions they do make (Butler, 2002). For example, a multiple case study design that purposively samples teachers adept at implementing an intervention might well illuminate what is possible, but might also be limited in its ability to identify implementation barriers. A study that purposively includes successful and unsuccessful implementers might provide greater insight for individuals struggling with implementation.

Data Collection. Many data collection strategies are available for addressing research questions. Examples are standardized, curriculum-based, or researcher-constructed tests; self-report questionnaires; unstructured, semistructured, or structured interviews or observations; retrospective or concurrent think-alouds; traces of behavior or thinking processes collected online or in learning environments; and documents, photographs, or other kinds of artifacts (Winne & Perry, 2000; Yin, 1994). As re-

search questions evolve in our field, educational psychologists should continue developing and evaluating new approaches to data collection. I support Wittrock's (2003) recommendation to focus particular attention on verbal protocols, think-alouds, retrospective and stimulated recall, and process tracing. A good example of an exciting development on the last of these is the work by Phil Winne and his colleagues (see Winne & Perry, 2000), who are developing new software that collects detailed traces of students' self-regulated learning processes as they grapple with text online.

Differences between inquiry frames arise not from the type of data collected (e.g., interviews and observations are strategies used across a broad range of inquiry frames), but rather from how these data are interpreted (see later discussion), and/or from when and how data collection fits into the inquiry process. For example, as described earlier, design frameworks can differ in whether data collection and analysis occur in tandem, or in separate, sequential steps.

Inquiry frames also differ in how researchers' roles in the inquiry process are conceived. In some logics of inquiry, researchers serve as "data collection instruments" (e.g., MacArthur, 2003; Lincoln & Guba, 1985; Merriam, 1998), a description that captures two ideas simultaneously: (1) that measurement tools need not be designed *a priori* to provide an interpretive framework, but that insights can also emerge during data collection and in the development of interpretive schemes; and (2) that it is possible to capitalize on researchers' sense-making, interpretive processes during data collection and analysis (Merriam, 1998). Critics might argue that allowing a researcher to play an interpretative role during a study is likely to introduce bias. Indeed, in the inquiry frames most commonly used in educational psychology, methodological strategies have been developed with the express purpose of protecting against researcher perspectives influencing data collection and analysis.

Yet as was explained earlier, all researchers act as interpretive instruments at some point during the inquiry process. For example, in experimental designs, researchers play a large interpretive role when reviewing a research literature to define the state of the field and identify research questions. They also have an enormous influence on data collection and analysis when operationalizing variables and constructing measurement instruments. *A priori* coding frameworks impose a particular interpretive scheme on collected data. Thus, it is not a question of if, but rather of when and how, researchers play an interpretive role in research. Thus, the common challenge to all researchers is to employ rigorous and systematic strategies to account for how research perspectives impact the inquiry process.

Educational psychologists are well versed in the strategies for controlling or accounting for researcher perspectives that have been developed within certain methodological traditions (e.g., experimental research). Examples include standardizing interview questions, blind scoring, and establishing interrater reliability. Alternative inquiry frames that capitalize on researcher interpretation in the middle of a study (i.e., during data collection and analysis) also incorporate rigorous and systematic strategies for ensuring credibility and accounting for researcher perspectives (such as bracketing, member checks, researcher triangulation, or audit trails; see later discussion). Thus, judging the credibility of a research study should be tied, not to use of certain procedures, but rather to whether and how researcher perspectives are explicated and accounted for when generating and warranting conclusions.

Some design frameworks explicitly require that multiple sources of data be collected to provide converging evidence for a finding (Lincoln & Guba, 1985; Merriam, 1998). For example, case study researchers (e.g., Merriam, 1998; Stake, 1994; Yin, 1994) argue that "triangulation" of multiple data sources is valuable for warranting conclusions (Yin, 1994, p. 92). According to Yin, "Any finding or conclusion in a case study is likely to be much more convincing and accurate if it is based on several different sources of information, following a corroboratory mode" (p. 92). Yin stresses that triangulation involves focusing converging lines of evidence on corroborating a single finding, not collecting different kinds of information to answer separate questions. For example, in a study focused on understanding how an intervention designed to promote self-regulated learning affects students' self-perceptions of competence and control over learning, triangulation would be effected if a single finding (e.g., that students' self-perceptions improved) were supported by converging sources of evidence (e.g., interviews; questionnaire data; observations of students' willingness to engage in learning) (see Butler, 1998). But it is not only in case study designs where multiple sources of information can be collected to answer research questions. Because every source of data has both strengths and limitations (Taylor & Dionne, 2000; Winne & Perry, 2000), triangulation can be used within any inquiry frame to bolster a study's findings. For example, educational psychologists could collect data using a combination of traces, observations, and concurrent verbal reports to provide converging evidence related to students' learning processes.

Multiple data sources can also be gathered in one study to address multiple questions (Yin's second alternative). For example, students' perceptions about learning processes might be gathered using both interviews and questionnaires, but what they actually do while learning could be captured using observations and traces. This combination of data sources would allow for a robust analysis of students' perceptions about learning in relation to what they do. Many educational psychologists are drawing on multiple sources of data to investigate multifaceted research questions and/or to triangulate findings (see excellent examples provided by Aulls, 1998, 2002; Butler, 1995, 1998; Graham, 1997; and Perry, 1998).

Data Reduction. All research is concerned with reducing data while at the same time preserving meaning (Behrens & Smith, 1996). For example, to reduce data in preparation for quantitative analysis, researchers map data onto a numerical scale, while paying careful attention that the numbers assigned represent important qualities in the original data (Behrens & Smith, 1996). As Behrens and Smith (1996) point out, "All quantities are measures of qualities, and the understanding of qualities is no simple matter" (p. 947). But data do not have to be reduced to numbers to assist in interpretation. Across a wide variety of inquiry frames, analytic tools have been developed to aid in interpreting visually or verbally represented data (Connelly & Clandinin, 1990; Creswell, 1998; Glaser & Strauss, 1967; Lincoln & Guba, 1985; Merriam, 1998; Miles & Huberman, 1994; Moustakas, 1994; Tesch, 1990; Weitzman & Miles, 1995; Wolcott, 1994). But these kinds of interpretive strategies also depend on data reduction. For example, a researcher facing 400 pages of transcripts from 20 interviews, 100 pages of running records from 10 classroom observations, a 50-page teacher log, and copies of 10 lesson plans must find some way of reducing those data to meaningful chunks to aid in the interpretive process (Miles & Huberman, 1994). Thus, all researchers are charged with taking complex, situated data and representing it in a simplified form. Design logics may differ in terms of how and when this simplification takes place (Constas, 1992). For example, in some designs data are essentially reduced in advance through *a priori* construction of coding frameworks, whereas in other designs coding schemes might be developed inductively during and/or after data collection. But in all empirical research, investigators must explicate how they moved from data to more simplified representations, and demonstrate how the meaning and completeness of data were maintained in the transition process. Further, as emphasized earlier, it is incumbent on all researchers to describe when and how theoretical frameworks influence data reduction.

Data Interpretation. All empirical researchers face the common challenge of developing transparent and rigorous interpretive logics for drawing trustworthy conclusions from data. It is not particularly helpful to define in broad terms the features of quantitative and qualitative data analysis, given the diversity of analytic strategies under each umbrella (see Behrens & Smith, 1996; Creswell, 1998; Denzin & Lincoln, 1994; 2003; McMillan, 2000; Miles & Huberman, 1994; Tesch, 1990). But what would be enormously helpful is for educational psychologists to draw on the wealth of interpretive tools that have been developed, quantitative and qualitative, when designing their studies. On the qualitative side, of particular relevance to educational psychologists are analytic strategies described in the literatures on case studies (Merriam, 1998; Stake, 1994, 1995; Yin, 1994), narrative inquiry (Connelly & Clandinin, 1990), ethnography (Agar, 1996; Wolcott, 1994), grounded theory (Glaser & Strauss, 1967; Strauss & Corbin, 1994), phenomenology (Moustakas, 1994), discourse analysis (MacLure, 2003), and/or critical/feminist research (Lather, 1991; 1992; Reinherz, 1992; Stewart, 1994).

These research literatures provide particularly sound advice on the subject of data coding. Empirical researchers working across inquiry frames are often similarly challenged by the task of coding or categorizing qualitative data. Common examples of coding in the educational psychology literature include assigning scores to essay tests, evaluating writing quality (e.g., Davis et al., 1994; Wright & Rosenberg, 1993), classifying participants' beliefs or perspectives (e.g., Thorkildsen et al., 1994), and cataloguing problem-solving or learning strategies (e.g., Carr & Jessup, 1997; Purdie et al., 1996). Many valuable and detailed descriptions of coding strategies are available in the literature (e.g., Glaser & Strauss, 1967; Lincoln & Guba, 1985; Miles & Huberman, 1994).

At the same time, researchers working within different inquiry frames might approach the coding challenge differently. Constas (1992) provides an excellent description of dimensions on which approaches to coding vary. Three of these are (1) *temporal*, reflecting whether categories are established *a priori*, after data collection is finished, or during the study (i.e., iteratively); (2) *origination*, reflecting whether responsibility for defining categories rests with participants, the researcher (e.g., based on research questions), prior theory or research, a program (e.g., in a program evaluation), or an interpretive framework that focuses attention on particular issues (e.g., hermeneutics); and (3) *nomination*, which reflects the source of category names, which may be linked to the origin of the categories (i.e., arising from participants, program goals, research questions, prior research or theory, or interpretive frameworks). Constas emphasizes that researchers should clarify how their coding strategies reflect these three dimensions (see also Almasi et al., 1994; Martin et al., 2003). Similarly, Alvermann et al. (1996) call for descriptions of "analytic processes and how those processes shaped the patterns generated from the data" (p. 116). Taylor and Dionne (2000) argue that "regardless of how coding categories are derived, it is imperative that researchers can articulate the theories and experiences that influence the development of a particular coding grid" (p. 416).

Constas (1992) also cautions that "categories are created, and meanings are attributed by researchers who, wittingly or unwittingly, embrace a particular configuration of analytical preferences" (p. 254). Because interpretations of data "are made, not found" (Eisenhart, 1995, p. 571), it is incumbent on researchers to ensure the trustworthiness of their analyses. Indeed, Constas (1992) offers a fourth dimension on which coding strategies vary, *verification*, to capture different methods for establishing the credibility of coding. Methods for judging codes might be external to the inquiry (e.g., a review by a panel of experts), rational (based on logic and reasoning), referential (referring to existing theory or research), empirical (if categories represent a data set well), technical (e.g., appeal to procedures such as inter-rater coding), or participative (e.g., checking meanings derived with participants). Others (e.g., Lincoln & Guba, 1985; Merriam, 1998; Yin, 1994) have also described credibility strategies such as (1) surfacing researcher perspectives and possible impacts on interpretive processes, (2) actively seeking and accounting for nonexamples or disconfirming evidence, (3) evaluating whether categorical systems are internally complete and coherent, (4) researcher triangulation, that is, having more than one person apply coding criteria and/or interpret the data in parallel, (5) member checks, which require asking participants to judge whether interpretations capture the meaning of data, and (6) external audits of the overall frame of inquiry and data-interpretation linkages.

Assigning codes or themes to chunks of data is just one part of an interpretive process. Once data are coded or categorized, broader patterns in the data must be identified. Again, multiple interpretive strategies are available to add in this larger process. For example, Miles and Huberman (1994) provide a detailed sourcebook of multiple methods for uncovering patterns in data. Among the most useful of these methods is constructing data displays (Miles & Huberman, 1994), which provide a way of systematically and comprehensively representing data (in matrices, flowcharts, graphs, etc.) and can help in identifying patterns and checking interpretations. Computer programs have also been developed to support researchers in drawing inferences from large sets of qualitative data (Tesch, 1990; Weitzman & Miles, 1995).

Based on this discussion, and my review of the educational psychology literature, I offer the general recommendation that educational psychologists should take analyses of qualitative data more seriously. There are too many studies in which qualitative analyses are perceived as a first informal part of a study or as a nice extra to flesh out findings. But often conclusions are then drawn from those data without sufficient warrant. I recommend instead that all qualitative data be subjected to rigorous analysis, and that researchers be as accountable for such analyses as they are for quantitative interpretive strategies. All interpretive processes, including coding strategies, should be very clearly articulated (Alvermann et al., 1996; Constas, 1992). Excellent examples of thorough descriptions are provided by Martin et al. (2003), Perry, et al. (1993), Shearer et al. (1997) and Turner et al. (2002). In the last, Turner et al. provide an excellent description of the origination of their coding framework and of how they tested the trustworthiness of their coding.

Warranting Conclusions. Features of empirical research frames are assembled with the explicit intention of creating an inferential bridge (Shulman, 1988) between evidence and conclusions. Thus, establishing warrant depends on both assembling design features into an internally consistent logic of inquiry and on executing individual procedures well (Howe & Eisenhart, 1990). But most important is that the design framework be appropriate for answering research questions and warranting the *kind of conclusions* drawn. For example, if a researcher wishes to draw causal inferences about the impact of an intervention, then the design framework and embedded methods should support justification of causal claims. Similarly, if researchers wish to generate findings that have applicability elsewhere (e.g., to justify generalizations), they must identify a logic of inquiry and particular methods that support that form of generalization (e.g., to a population; to a theory; case to case transfer) (Stake, 1995; Yin, 1994).

Evaluating warrant for a study's findings is not a matter of checking off that certain procedures were employed (Bereiter, 1994; Polkinghorne & Gribbons, 1999). What is required instead is a mindful judgment of whether the logic of inquiry established supports the inferences made. For example, establishing causal connections in an intervention study requires linking instruction to outcomes and ruling out rival hypotheses. The logic of an experiment meets these requirements by assigning students randomly to groups and controlling extraneous variables. Quasi-experiments support causal inferences to the extent that rival hypotheses can be dismissed. But causal conclusions might also be supported in other designs, if the same requirements can be met. For example, case study designs are particularly well suited to tracing linkages between interventions and outcomes and to uncovering and testing rival hypotheses (Butler, 2002; Yin, 1994). Imagine, for example, a study in which multiple forms of data are collected over prolonged periods to trace how student learning processes and performance evolve (or not) as an intervention is implemented (see Aulls, 1998, and Butler, 1995, 1998, for examples). Thus, it is an underlying design framework, not use of given procedures, that functions to warrant conclusions. Further, every design has strengths and weaknesses, such that using a combination may be maximally informative (Almasi et al., 1994). For example, case studies are not designed to deliberately control conditions as can be done in an experiment, but they can reveal complex embedded relationships that may be obscured within an experimental inquiry frame.

Every inquiry frame defines credibility strategies that assist in warranting conclusions. Examples of credibility strategies used within ethnographies, case studies, discourse analyses, phenomenology, grounded theory, and other "qualitative" designs include the following: (1) bracketing of researcher assumptions and positions as part of the research process, to aid the researcher and reader in judging the impact of researcher perspectives on the inquiry process; (2) data, method, researcher, or theory triangulation, which require systematic juxtaposition of data sources or perspectives to cross-check a given finding; (3) active searching for negative or discrepant cases to test findings or rule out rival hypotheses; (4) member checks, which involve checking back with participants to make sure a conclusion matches their perspectives; (5) audit trials and external audits, which require maintaining a running record of connections among research questions, data, interpretations, and conclusions, and subjecting that audit trail to scrutiny by an outsider, and (6) constructing data displays, which allow for systematic checks of conclusions against a representation of a full data set (see LeCompte et al., 1993; Lincoln & Guba, 1985; Merriam, 1998; Miles & Huberman, 1994; Moustakas, 1994; Wolcott, 1994; Yin, 1994). The credibility of any given study, regardless of inquiry frame, depends on the underlying logic used to warrant research conclusions. Again, judging the credibility of a given study should be done in relation to that study's logic-in-use (Howe & Eisenhart, 1990).

Research Representation

How a study is represented is as much a part of an inquiry frame as are other design features. And researchers are increasingly paying attention to the writing and representation process (e.g., Alvermann et al., 1996; Creswell, 1998; Polkinghorne & Gribbons, 1999; Van Manen, 1988). For example, in *Tales from the Field*, Van Manen (1988) illustrates how different ways of reporting ethnographic work are akin to alternative modes of story telling. Similarly,

Creswell focuses attention on "rhetorical" assumptions (p. 74) that underlie frames of inquiry and that reflect the language and writing conventions deemed acceptable when writing research. Thus, further discussion is clearly needed about how research should be reported. And alternative forms of representation may be necessary to best represent differing inquiry frames.

Whatever the form of representation, all empirical researchers must create a report that communicates the logic of inquiry underlying their research. This chapter has provided an overview of issues that should be addressed in any research report, for each feature of an inquiry frame (see Fig. 39.1). At some point in a research report, investigators need to describe their theoretical perspectives, research questions, overarching design, methods, and choice for research representation. But it is not sufficient to just describe each of these features separately. Researchers also must (1) explain how design features are interconnected and form a coherent logic of inquiry (e.g., how research questions were derived in relation to theoretical frameworks), (2) provide rationales for all decisions (e.g., why a particular sampling strategy was used); (3) explain how credibility was established in each step of the process (e.g., during data collection or interpretation), and (4) lead the reader to understand how conclusions are warranted given the logic of the study. Much specificity is required when describing and defending research approaches (Almasi et al., 1994; Alvermann et al., 1996; Anderson & West, 1995; Butler, 2002; Constas, 1992; Martin et al., 2003; Taylor & Dionne, 2000). For example, as described earlier, researchers should define and justify their approaches to coding along each of Constas' (1992) four dimensions (temporal, origination, nomination, and verification).

A final issue in research reporting includes the problem of selection (Butler, 2002). Researchers must choose, out of the mass of data that might be reported, what they will include. In empirical studies, researchers should present data, not just to illustrate a general finding or point, but rather to (1) show overarching patterns in the data; (2) capture regularities but also diversity (e.g., eight of 10 participants may have had some experience, but what about the other two?); (3) surface both confirming and disconfirming evidence; and (4) explain how rival hypotheses or interpretations are not as appropriate as given explanations for the data. Again, a diversity of representation forms will be required for adequately reporting research that is equal in rigor but conducted within different inquiry frameworks.

In this chapter I have offered recommendations for how educational psychologists can construct a coherent logic of inquiry. To close this section, I offer the more general recommendation that all researchers be very deliber-

ate when selecting design features for use in a study. Automatic adherence to the methodological blueprint outlined in a prototypical inquiry frame is not sufficient for instantiating in practice a given logic-in-use. Instead, researchers must carefully consider methodological options for best answering a research question, and the rationale for all decisions should be meticulously represented in a research report.

STANDARDS IN EDUCATIONAL RESEARCH

The conception of inquiry frames presented in this chapter resonates well with conclusions emerging from a prolonged debate about appropriate standards for judging educational research (e.g., Almasi et al., 1994; Anderson & West, 1995; Behrens & Smith, 1996; Eisenhart, 1995; Firestone, 1993; Heap, 1995; Howe & Eisenhart, 1990; Merriam, 1988, 1998; Mosenthal, 1995; Wolcott, 1994). Three themes appear to be endorsed in many current discussions. One is that it is the responsibility of all researchers to carefully and completely articulate logics of inquiry so as to expose them to public scrutiny (Alvermann et al., 1996; Behrens & Smith, 1996; Bereiter, 1994; Constas, 1992; Polkinghorne & Gribbons, 1999; Putney et al., 1999). As Polkinghorne and Gribbons (1999) suggest, all empirical researchers "share a commitment to the generation of knowledge propositions through a reasoned and reflective examination of empirical data and the submission of those propositions to the community of scholars for criticism and testing" (p. 130).

A second theme emerging in the literature is that common standards for evaluating research across inquiry frames can only be very abstract and general (Eisenhart, 1995; Howe & Eisenhart, 1990). Neither is it meaningful to define anything but very general standards that could apply to all varieties of qualitative (or quantitative) research (Eisenhart, 1995). But Howe and Eisenhart (1990) do offer five general standards they suggest can be applied in judging research: (1) data collection and analysis techniques fit with the research questions, (2) data collection and analysis techniques are applied effectively, (3) background assumptions are coherent and consistent with research questions and methods, (4) conclusions are warranted and credibility strategies employed (e.g., looking for confirming and disconfirming evidence), and (5) the study has value, in that it contributes understanding to the educational community and in that it has been ethically conducted. As general standards, Behrens and Smith (1996) suggest that all researchers should strive for coherence, credibility, rigor, and trustworthiness.

Finally, a third theme is that, while only general standards may be applicable across inquiry frames, specific standards can be used to evaluate a given study (see Almasi et al., 1994, for examples). But what is critical is that the standards used be appropriate to a study's frame of inquiry (Behrens & Smith, 1996; Eisenhart, 1995). It is not valid to export specific standards from one frame of inquiry and apply them to another (Behrens & Smith, 1996; Heap, 1995). Thus, how a research study should be judged depends on its logic-in use (Howe & Eisenhart, 1990). As Heap (1995) explains, "The issues of standards then becomes a question of whether we can discern for any piece of research what is required in order for its argument to be taken as justified" (p. 579). To do so, we need to "grasp the conception of inquiry that the research evidences, and the purposes served by each part of the research" (p. 579).

CONCLUSION: REFOCUSING ON FRAMES OF INQUIRY

I invested considerable space in this chapter in defining an alternative way of describing educational research that does not rely on the quantitative-qualitative distinction. I have argued that refocusing attention on frames of inquiry provides a more multidimensional and fluid perspective on the research terrain, allowing for definition both of broader, necessarily simplified inquiry prototypes and of a coherent, dynamic framework within which individual studies might be constructed. A focus on inquiry frames provides guidelines for defining key features of logics-in-use (Howe & Eisenhart, 1990) as instantiated in research.

An advantage of this shift in focus is that it provides a framework within which different frames of inquiry can be more meaningfully compared. Differences and similarities can be discerned at the level of individual design features as well as in an overall logic of inquiry. In this chapter, for example, this framework allowed for a more nuanced analysis of logics-in-use within the educational psychology literature. Further, multidimensional comparisons across inquiry frames, that make explicit commonalities as well as differences, might invite critical (Putney et al., 1999) and progressive (Bereiter, 1994) discourse about substantive topics of common concern, the range of questions we should be asking, and how inquiry frames can be adapted to answer them. Progress in developing more sophisticated, shared understandings (Bereiter, 1994) is supported, not when researchers work in separate and stereotyped "camps," but rather when different frames of inquiry are juxtaposed to surface debates and possibilities.

Numerous, specific methodological recommendations have been offered in this chapter, and are summarized in Table 39.4. These recommendations are clearly directed to educational psychologists engaged in conducting research. But implications are also clear for teaching and supervising graduate students. Students must be trained in a variety of inquiry frames to be able to select, adapt, or invent new forms of inquiry to address emerging research questions. It is also necessary, but not sufficient, for researchers-in-training to become technically proficient at using particular methods. They must also understand the theoretical assumptions underlying their work as well as the logics of inquiry foundational to any research designs they intend to use. Finally, implications are also clear for those of us who serve as editors, sit on editorial review boards, or in any way influence what counts as good research in our field. We can only enhance the contributions of educational psychology by recognizing and employing well the range of methodological tools available to advance knowledge about teaching and learning.

ACKNOWLEDGMENTS

I thank Cheryl Aman for her invaluable assistance in conducting a literature review in preparation for writing this chapter. I would also like to thank the *Handbook* editors, Phil Winne and Pat Alexander, along with the developmental reviewers for this chapter for the invaluable feedback they provided on an earlier version of this manuscript.

References

Agar, M. H. (1996). *The professional stranger: An informal introduction to ethnography* (2nd ed.). Toronto: Academic Press.

Alexander, P. A., & Graham, S. (2001). Editorial: Reflections of the incoming editors. *Contemporary Educational Psychology, 26,* 1–2.

Almasi, J. F., Martin Palmer, B., Gambrell, L. B., & Pressley, M. (1994). Toward disciplined inquiry: A methodological analysis of whole-language research. *Educational Psychologist, 29,* 193–202.

Alvermann, D. E., O'Brien, D. G., & Dillon, D. R. (1996). Conversations: On writing qualitative research. *Reading Research Quarterly, 31,* 114–120.

Anderson, T. H., & West, C. K. (1995). Commentary: An analysis of a qualitative investigation: A matter of whether to believe. *Reading Research Quarterly, 30,* 562–569.

Aulls, M. W. (1998). Contributions of classroom discourse to what content students learning during curriculum enactment. *Journal of Educational Psychology, 90,* 56-69.

Aulls, M. W. (2002). The contributions of co-occurring forms of classroom discourse and academic activities to curriculum events and instruction. *Journal of Educational Psychology, 94,* 520-538.

Behrens, J. T., & Smith, M. (1996). Data and data analysis. In D. C. Berliner & R. C. Calfee (Eds.), *Handbook of educational psychology* (pp. 945-989). New York: Simon & Schuster MacMillan.

Ben-Zeev, T., & Ronald, J. (2002). Is procedure acquisition as unstable as it seems? *Contemporary Educational Psychology, 27,* 529-550.

Bereiter, C. (1994). Implications of postmodernism for science, or science as a progressive discourse. *Educational Psychologist, 29,* 3-12.

Bornholt, L. J. (2002). An analysis of children's task strategies for a test of reading comprehension. *Contemporary Educational Psychology, 27,* 80-98.

Butler, D. L. (1995). Promoting strategic learning by post secondary students with learning disabilities. *Journal of Learning Disabilities, 28,* 170-190.

Butler, D. L. (1998). The Strategic Content Learning approach to promoting self-regulated learning: A report of three studies. *Journal of Educational Psychology, 90,* 682-697.

Butler, D. L. (2002). Qualitative approaches to investigating self-regulated learning: Contributions and caveats. *Educational Psychologist, 37,* 59-63.

Butler, D. L., Novak Lauscher, H., Jarvis-Selinger, S., & Beckingham, B. (in press). Collaboration and self-regulation in teachers' professional development. *Teaching and Teacher Education.*

Byrnes, J. P., & Takahira, S. (1994). Why some students perform well and others perform poorly on SAT math items. *Contemporary Educational Psychology, 19,* 63-78.

Carr, M., & Jessup, D. L. (1997). Gender differences in first-grade mathematics strategy use: Social and cognitive influences. *Journal of Educational Psychology, 89,* 318-328.

Chan, K., & Elliott, R. G. (2002). Exploratory study of Hong Kong teacher education students' epistemological beliefs: Cultural perspectives and implications on beliefs research. *Contemporary Educational Psychology, 27,* 392-414.

Connelly, F. M., & Clandinin, D. J. (1990). Stories of experience and narrative inquiry. *Educational Researcher, 19*(4), 2-14.

Constas, M. A. (1992). Qualitative analysis as a public event: The documentation of category development procedures. *American Educational Research Journal, 29,* 253-266.

Creswell, J. W. (1998). *Qualitative inquiry and research design: Choosing among five traditions.* Thousand Oaks, CA: Sage.

Darling-Hammond, L., & Snyder, J. (1992). Curriculum studies and the traditions of inquiry: The scientific tradition. In P. W. Jackson (Ed.), *Handbook of research on curriculum* (pp. 56-78). New York: MacMillan.

Davis, A., Clarke, M. A., & Rhodes, L. K. (1994). Extended text and the writing proficiency of students in urban elementary schools. *Journal of Educational Psychology, 86,* 556-566.

Denzin, N. K., & Lincoln, Y. S. (Eds.). (1994). *Handbook of qualitative research.* Thousand Oaks, CA: Sage.

Denzin, N. K., & Lincoln, Y. S. (Eds.) (2003) *Handbook of qualitative research: Strategies of qualitative inquiry.* Thousand Oaks, CA: Sage.

Dooley, D. (1995). *Social research methods.* Englewood Cliff, NJ: Prentice-Hall.

Dowson, M., & McInerney, D. M. (2001). Psychological parameters of students social and work avoidance goals: A qualitative investigation. *Journal of Educational Psychology, 93,* 35-42.

Dowson, M., & McInerney, D. M. (2003). What do students say about their motivational goals?: Towards a more complex and dynamic perspective on student motivation. *Contemporary Educational Psychology, 28,* 91-113.

Driscoll, M. P., Moallem, M., Dick, W., & Kirby, E. (1994). How does the textbook contribute to learning in a middle school science class? *Contemporary Education Psychology, 19,* 79-100.

Echevarria, M. (2003). Anomalies as a catalyst for middle school students' knowledge construction and scientific reasoning during science inquiry. *Journal of Educational Psychology, 95,* 357-374.

Eilam, B., & Aharon, I. (2003). Students' planning in the process of self-regulated learning. *Contemporary Educational Psychology, 28,* 304-334.

Eisenhart, M. (1995). Whither credibility in research on reading? A response to Anderson and West. *Reading Research Quarterly, 30,* 570-572.

Eva-Wood, A. L. (2004). Thinking and feeling poetry: Exploring meanings aloud. *Journal of Educational Psychology, 96,* 182-191.

Evensen, D. H., Salisbury-Glennon, J. D., & Glenn, J. (2001). A qualitative study of six medical students in a problem-based curriculum: Toward a situated model of self-regulation. *Journal of Educational Psychology, 93,* 659-676.

Evensen, D. H., Salisbury-Glenon, J. D., & Glenn, J. (2001). A qualitative study of six medical students in a problem-based curriculum: Toward a situated model of self-regulation. *Journal of Educational Psychology, 93,* 659-676.

Firestone, W. A. (1987). Meaning in method: The rhetoric of quantitative and qualitative research. *Educational Researcher, 16,* 16-21.

Firestone, W. A. (1993). Alternative arguments for generalizing from data as applied to qualitative research. *Educational Researcher, 22*(4), 16-23.

Fitzgerald, J., & Noblit, G. (2000). Balance in the making: Learning to read in an ethnically diverse first-grade classroom. *Journal of Educational Psychology, 92,* 3-22.

Flood, J., Lapp, D., Squire, J. R., & Jensen, J. M. (Eds.) (2003). *Handbook of research on teaching the English language arts.* Mahwah, NJ: Lawrence Erlbaum Associates.

Flowerday, T., & Schraw, G. (2000). Teacher beliefs about instructional choice: A phenomenological study. *Journal of Educational Psychology, 92*, 634-645.

Gall, M. D., Borg, W. R., & Gall, J. P. (1996). *Educational research: An introduction* (6th ed.). White Plains, NY: Longman.

Glaser, B., G., & Strauss, A. L. (1967). *The discovery of grounded theory: Strategies for qualitative research.* Chicago: Aldine.

Graham, S. (1997). Executive control in the revising of students with learning and writing difficulties. *Journal of Educational Psychology, 89*, 223-234.

Griffin, M. M. (1995). You can't get there from here: Situated learning, transfer, and map skills. *Contemporary Educational Psychology, 20*, 65-87.

Guba, Y. S., & Lincoln, E. G. (1994). Competing paradigms in qualitative research. In N. K. Denzin & Y. S. Lincoln (eds.), *Handbook of qualitative research* (pp. 105-117). Thousand Oaks, CA: Sage.

Guthrie, J. T., Weber, S., & Kimmerly, N. (1993). Searching documents: Cognitive processes and deficits in understanding graphs, tables, and illustrations. *Contemporary Educational Psychology, 18*, 186-221.

Hacker, D., J., & Tenent, A. (2002). Implementing reciprocal teaching in the classroom: Overcoming obstacles and making modifications. *Journal of Educational Psychology, 94*, 669-718.

Hamers, J. H. M., de Koning, E., & Sijtsma, K. (1998). Inductive reasoning in third grade: Intervention promises and constraints. *Contemporary Educational Psychology, 23*, 132-148.

Hamm, J. V., & Perry, M. (2002). Learning mathematics in first-grade classrooms: On whose authority. *Journal of Educational Psychology, 94*, 126-137.

Heap, J. L. (1995). Understanding cultural science: A response to Anderson and West. *Reading Research Quarterly, 30*, 578-580.

Henderlong, J., & Paris, S. G. (1996). Children's motivation to explore partially completed exhibits in hands-on museums. *Contemporary Educational Psychology, 21*, 111-128.

Hrubes, D., & Feldman, R. S. (2001). Nonverbal displays as indicants of task difficulty. *Contemporary Educational Psychology, 26*, 267-276.

Howe, K. R. (1985). Two dogmas of educational research. *Educational Researcher, 14*, 10-18.

Howe, K., & Eisenhart, M. (1990). Standards for qualitative (and quantitative) research: A prolegomenon. *Educational Researcher, 19*(4), 2-9.

Jacob, E. (1987). Qualitative research traditions: A review. *Review of Educational Research, 57*, 1-50.

Jaeger, R. M. (Ed.), *Complementary methods for research in education.* Washington, DC: AERA.

Johnston, P., Woodside-Jiron, H., & Day, J. (2001). Teaching and learning literate epistemologies. *Journal of Educational Psychology 93*, 223-233.

Kamann, M. P., & Butler, D. L. (1996, April). *Strategic content learning: An analysis of instructional features.* Presented at the annual meeting of the American Educational Research Association, New York.

Kamil, M. L., Mosenthal, P. B., Pearson, P. D., & Barr, R. (2000). *Handbook of reading research,* (Vol. 3). Mahwah NJ: Lawrence Erlbaum Associates.

Lai, P., & Biggs, J. (1994). Who benefits from mastery learning? *Contemporary Educational Psychology, 19*, 13-23.

Lather, P. (1991). *Getting smart: Feminist research and pedagogy with/in the postmodern.* New York: Routledge.

Lather, P. (1992). Critical frames in educational research: Feminist and post-structural perspectives. *Theory Into Practice, 31*, 87-99.

LeCompte, M. D., Preissle, J., & Tesch, R. (1993). *Ethnography and qualitative design in educational research* (2nd ed.). New York: Academic Press.

Ley, K., & Young, D. B. (1998). Self-regulation behaviors in underprepared (developmental) and regular admission college students. *Contemporary Educational Psychology, 23*, 42-64.

Lincoln, Y. S., & Guba, E. G. (1985). *Naturalistic inquiry.* Newbury Park, CA: Sage.

MacArthur, C. (2003). What have we learned about learning disabilities from qualitative research?: A review of studies. In H. L. Swanson, K. R. Harris, and S. Graham (Eds.), *Handbook of learning disabilities* (pp. 532-549). New York: Guilford.

MacLure, M. (2003). *Discourse in educational and social research.* Philadelphia: Open University.

Mamlin, N., & Harris, K. R. (1998). Elementary teachers' referral to special education in light of inclusion and prereferral: "Every child is here to learn . . . but some of these children are in real trouble." *Journal of Educational Psychology, 90*, 385-396.

Marshall, V. (2004). Coping processes revealed in the stories of mothers of children with autism. Unpublished doctoral dissertation, University of British Columbia, Vancouver.

Martin, A. J., Marsh, H. W., Debus, R. L., & Williamson, A. (2003). Self-handicapping, defensive pessimism, and goal orientation: A qualitative study of university students. *Journal of Educational Psychology, 95*, 617-628.

McGill-Franzen, A., Lanford, C., & Adams, E. (2002). Learning to be literate: A comparison of five urban early childhood education programs. *Journal of Educational Psychology, 94*, 443-464.

McMillan, J. H. (2000). *Educational research: Fundamentals for the consumer* (3rd ed.). New York: HarperCollins.

Merriam, S. B. (1988). *Case study research in education: A qualitative approach.* San Francisco: Jossey-Bass.

Merriam, S. B. (1998). *Qualitative research and case study applications in Education.* San Francisco: Jossey-Bass.

Meyer, H. A., Astor, R. A., & Behre, W. J. (2002). Teachers' reasoning about school violence: The role of gender and location. *Contemporary Educational Psychology, 27*, 499-528.

Miles, M. B., & Huberman, A. M. (1994). *Qualitative data analysis: An expanded sourcebook* (2nd ed.). Thousand Oaks, CA: Sage.

Moore, P. (1995). Information problem-solving: A wider view of library skills. *Contemporary Educational Psychology, 20*, 1-31.

Mosenthal, P. B. (1995). Why there are no dialogues among the divided: The problem of solipsistic agendas in literacy research. *Reading Research Quarterly, 30*, 574-577.

Moustakas, C. (1994). *Phenomenological research methods*. Thousand Oaks, CA: Sage.

Myers, J. (1995). The value-laden assumptions of our interpretive practices. *Reading Research Quarterly, 30*, 582-587.

Osana, H. P., Tucker, B. J., & Bennett, T. (2003). Exploring adolescent decision making about equity: Ill-structured problem solving in social studies. *Contemporary Educational Psychology, 28*, 357-383.

Paxton, R. J. (1997). "Someone with a like a life wrote it": The effects of a visible author on high school history students. *Journal of Educational Psychology, 89*, 235-250.

Perry, M., VanderStoep, S. W., & Yu, S. L. (1993). Asking questions in first-grade mathematics classes: Potential influences on mathematical thought. *Journal of Educational Psychology, 85*, 31-40.

Perry, N. E. (1998). Young children's self-regulated learning and contexts that support it. *Journal of Educational Psychology, 90*, 715-729.

Phillips, D. C. (1994). Telling it straight: Issues in assessing narrative research. *Educational Psychologist, 29*, 13-21.

Pintrich, P. R. (2003). A motivational science perspective on the role of student motivation in learning and teaching contexts. *Journal of Educational Psychology, 95*, 667-686

Polkinghorne, D. E., & Gribbons, B. C. (1999). Applications of qualitative research strategies to school psychology research problems. In C. R. Reynolds & T. B. Gutkin (Eds.), *The handbook of school psychology*, (3rd ed.) (pp. 108-136). New York: Wiley.

Punch, M. (1994). Politics and ethics in qualitative research. In N. K. Denzin & Y. S. Lincoln (eds.), *Handbook of qualitative research* (pp. 83-97). Thousand Oaks, CA: Sage.

Purdie, N., Hattie, J., & Douglas, H. (1996). Student conceptions of learning and their use of self-regulated learning stratgies: A cross-cultural comparison. *Journal of Educational Psychology, 88*, 87-100.

Putney, L. G., Green, J. L., Dixon, C. N., & Kelly, G. J. (1999). Evolution of qualitative research methodology: Looking beyond defense to possibilities. *Reading Research Quarterly, 34*, 368-377.

Reinherz, S. (1992). *Feminist methods in social research*. New York: Oxford University Press.

Royer, J. M. (1996). Editorial. *Contemporary Educational Psychology, 21*, 1-2.

Salomon, G. (1991). Transcending the qualitative-quantitative debate: The analytic and systemic approaches to educational research. *Educational Researcher, 20*(6), 10-18.

Schuh, K. L. (2003). Knowledge construction in the learner-centered classroom. *Journal of Educational Psychology, 95*, 426-442.

Schunk, D. H., & Swartz, C. W. (1993). Goals and progress feedback: Effect on self-efficacy and writing achievement. *Contemporary Educational Psychology, 18*, 337-354.

Schutz, P. A., Crowder, K. C., & White, V. E. (2001). The development of a goal to become a teacher. *Journal of Educational Psychology, 93*, 299-308.

Shank, G. (1994). Shaping qualitative research in educational psychology. *Contemporary Educational Psychology, 19*, 340-359.

Shearer, B. A., Lundeberg, M. A., & Coballes-Vega, C. (1997). Making the connection between research and reality: Strategies teachers use to read and evaluate journal articles. *Journal of Educational Psychology, 89*, 592-598.

Shulman, L. S. (1988). Disciplines of inquiry in education: An overview. In R. M. Jaeger (ed.), *Complementary methods for research in education* (pp. 3-17). Washington, DC: AERA.

Slotte, V., & Lonka, K. (1999). Review and process effects of spontaneous note-taking on text comprehension. *Contemporary Educational Psychology, 24*, 1-20.

Smith, J. K. (1983). Quantitative versus qualitative research: An attempt to clarify the issue. *Educational Researcher, 12*, 6-13.

Smith, J. K., & Heshusius, L. (1986). Closing down the conversation: The end of the quantitative-qualitative debate among educational inquirers. *Educational Researcher, 15*, 4-12.

Solmon, M. A. (1996). Impact of motivational climate on students' behaviors and perceptions in a physical education setting. *Journal of Educational Psychology, 88*, 731-738.

Stake, R. E. (1994). Case studies. In N. K. Denzin & Y. S. Lincoln (Eds.), *Handbook of qualitative research* (pp. 236-247). Thousand Oaks, CA: Sage.

Stake, R. E. (1995). *The art of case study research*. Thousand Oaks, CA: Sage.

Stewart, A. J. (1994). Toward a feminist strategy for studying women's lives. In C. E. Franz & A. J. Stewart (Eds.), *Women creating lives: Identities, resilience, and resistance* (pp. 11-35). Boulder, CO: Westview.

Strauss, A., & Corbin, J. (1994). Grounded theory methodology: An overview. In N. K. Denzin & Y. S. Lincoln (Eds.), *Handbook of qualitative research* (pp. 273-285). Thousand Oaks, CA: Sage.

Sweet, A. P., Guthrie, J. T., & Ng, M. M. (1998). Teacher perceptions and student reading motivation. *Journal of Educational Psychology, 90*, 210-223.

Tallent-Runnels, M. K. (1993). The future problem solving program: An investigation of the effects on problem-solving. *Contemporary Educational Psychology, 18*, 382-388.

Taylor, K. L., & Dionne, J. P. (2000). Accessing problem-solving strategy knowledge: The complementary use of concurrent verbal protocols and retrospective debriefing. *Journal of Educational Psychology, 92*, 413-425.

Tesch, R. (1990). *Qualitative research: Analysis types and software tools*. Briston, PA: Falmer.

Thorkildsen, T. A., Nolen, S. B., & Fournier, J. (1994). What is fair? Children's critiques of practices that influence motivation. *Journal of Educational Psychology, 86*, 475-486.

Turner, J. C., Meyer, D. K., Cox, K. E., Logan, C., DiCintio, M., & Thomas, C. T. (1998). Creating contexts for involvement in mathematics. *Journal of Educational Psychology, 90*, 730–745.

Turner, J. D., Midgley, C., Meyer, D. K., Gheen, M., Anderman, E. M., Kang, Y., et al. (2002). The classroom environment and students' reports of avoidance strategies in mathematics: A multimethod study. *Journal of Educational Psychology, 94*, 88–106.

Van Etten, S., Freebern, G., & Pressley, M. (1997). College students' beliefs about exam preparation. *Contemporary Educational Psychology, 22*, 192–212.

Van Manen, J. (1988). *Tales of the field: On writing ethnography*. London: University of Chicago Press.

Van Meter, P., Yokoi, L., & Pressley, M. (1994). College students' theory of note-taking derived from their perceptions of note-taking. *Journal of Educational Psychology, 86*, 323–338.

Vygotsky, L. S. (1978). *Mind in society*. Cambridge, MA: Harvard University Press.

Walker, D. F. (1992). Methodological issues in curriculum research. In P. W. Jackson (Ed.), *Handbook of research on curriculum* (pp. 98–118). New York: MacMillan.

Weade, G. (1992). Locating learning in the times and spaces of teaching. In Hermine Marshall (Ed.), *Redefining student learning: Roots of educational change* (pp. 87–118). Norwood, NJ: Ablex.

Weitzman, E. A., & Miles, M. B. (1995). *Computer programs for qualitative data analysis*. Thousand Oaks, CA: Sage.

Winne, P. H., & Marx, R. W. (1982). Students' and teachers' views of thinking processes for classroom learning. *Elementary School Journal, 82*, 493–518.

Winne, P. H., & Perry, N. E. (2000). Measuring self-regulated learning. In P. Pintrich, M. Boekarts, & M. Zeidner (Eds.), *Handbook of self-regulation* (pp. 531–566). Orlando, FL: Academic Press.

Wittrock, M. C. (2003). Contemporary methodological issues and future directions in research on the teaching of English. In J. Flood, D. Lapp, J. R. Squire, & J. M. Jensen (Eds.), *Handbook of research on teaching the English language Arts* (pp. 273–281). Mahwah, NJ Erlbaum.

Wolcott, H. F. (1994). *Transforming qualitative data: Description, analysis, and interpretation*. Thousand Oaks, CA: Sage.

Wright, R. E., & Rosenberg, S. (1993). Knowledge of text coherence and expository writing: A developmental study. *Journal of Educational Psychology, 85*, 152–158.

Yin, R. K. (1994). *Case study research: Design and methods* (2nd ed.). Thousand Oaks, CA: Sage.

Zimmerman, B. J., & Schunk, D. H. (Eds.) (2001). *Self-regulated learning and academic achievement: Theoretical perspectives* (2nd ed.). Mahwah, NJ: Lawrence Erlbaum Associates.

·40·

DEVELOPMENTS IN ASSESSMENT
OF STUDENT LEARNING

Kadriye Ercikan
University of British Columbia

Although educational assessment in the new century looks similar in many ways to assessment in the 1990s, some important developments are promising to make significant changes in the ways that educational psychologists and educators develop and use assessments. In particular, there are developments that are moving assessment in the direction of incorporating knowledge from educational psychology and in designing and developing assessments that serve student learning. These developments are the primary focus of this chapter.

Since the 1990s, educators have continued to deal with issues related to assessment competencies of teachers (Latham, Gitomer, & Ziomek, 1999; Melnick & Pullin, 2000; Memory, Antes, Corey, & Chaney, 2001; Mitchell & Barth, 1999; Smith & O'Day, 1997), use of performance assessments in large-scale assessments (Ercikan et al., 1998; Fitzpatrick, Ercikan, Yen, & Ferrara, 1998; Pearson, Calfee, Walker, Webb, & Fleischer, 2002), item formats (Ercikan, 1998; National Research Council, 2001), applications of new psychometric models (Junker, 1999; National Research Council, 2001), differential item functioning (Douglas, Roussos, & Stout, 1996; Roussos & Stout, 1996; Swanson, Clauser, Case, Nungester, & Featherman, 2002; Zwick, 2000) and performance standard setting (Cizek, 2001).

In recent years, however, many of these issues have received different levels of emphasis and have developed in new directions. Teacher competency assessments have gained greater levels of importance as a result of shortages of qualified teachers and an increased emphasis on

teacher quality in accountability systems. More than ever in the United States, there has been a shift to using student assessment results for high-stakes decisions. Formal accountability models associated with the No Child Left Behind (NCLB) Act of 2001, Public Law 107-110 (U.S. Department of Education, 2002) and problems associated with using assessment results in such accountability models have received a great deal of emphasis (Lee, 2004; Linn, 2003; Linn, Baker, & Betebenner, 2002; Linn & Haug, 2002). The use of performance assessment in large-scale assessments has declined with recent requirements for the testing of all students across more grades than was the practice in the 1990s. In her 2004 National Council on Measurement in Education (NCME) presidential address, Suzanne Lane (Lane, 2004) focused on the shift in assessment practices from ones that involved complex thinking to ones that ensured that accountability programs were in place. In particular, Lane focused on the effects of NCLB Act of 2001 (U.S. Department of Education, 2002) on assessment practices. As a result of NCLB, states are required to test all students from grades 3 through 8 annually in reading and mathematics and students in high school at least once by the 2005–2006 school year. As an example of how NCLB has affected state assessment programs, Lane (2004) compared the statewide assessments in Maryland prior to the NCLB and those under NCLB. From the early 1990s onwards, Maryland had developed and utilized a performance-based assessment program for grades 3, 5, and 8 to measure school performance and provide information for school accountability and improvement (Maryland State Board of Education, 1995). These assessments were designed to promote performance-based instruction and classroom assessment in an integrated manner in reading/language arts, mathematics, science, and social studies. The tasks on the assessments were interdisciplinary and required students to do hands-on activities and produce written responses. Under NCLB, Maryland has been required to provide student level-scores. As a result, Maryland has moved from an accountability system that was completely performance-based to a mostly multiple-choice, "off the shelf" assessment system that produced individual student-level scores in a timely manner.

In concert with the increasing dedication of resources over the past 10 years to the assessment of students for accountability purposes, there has been a growing awareness of the need for assessments to serve learning. The impetus for this latter trend has been a reaction not only to the increased levels of assessment for accountability purposes but also to progress in cognitive psychology. As our understanding of how students learn and the potential role of assessment in this learning process has developed, there has been a growing emphasis on designing measurement models and developing assessments that provide information about student cognitive processes, and student growth (Chudowsky & Pellegrino, 2003; National Research Council, 2001; Wilson & Adams, 1996; Wilson & Sloane, 2000).

The emphasis on assessments that support learning has been accompanied by the development of psychometric models that take interrelated set of constructs, often target outcomes in learning contexts, into account as well as those that target the assessment of student cognitive processes (Junker, 1999; National Research Council, 2001). In assessment design, tasks that can capture these constructs have gained importance. As a result, the focus on item types has shifted from one of what types of items assess which constructs best (as in the case of constructed-response items for assessing problem solving), to identifying and examining features of items and their relationship to the assessment of different levels of cognitive complexity (Baxter & Glaser, 1998; National Research Council, 2001; Pellegrino, Baxter, & Glaser, 1999).

This shift in viewing assessments as related more directly to learning and cognitive development has also affected investigations of the validity of interpretations. Methods that can be used to evaluate the cognitive complexity of tasks in both assessments and validity studies have been developed and examined. Investigations of bias and fairness issues have also been expanded to include these newer emphases on understanding student cognitive process during test taking as well as on ascertaining whether these processes are comparable for different groups.

One of the most significant developments in large-scale assessments has been in the reporting of student performance results. Increasingly, performance results are being reported in terms of a set of performance-level scores that are intended to provide information about what the students who perform at a certain score level are able to do. These scores are classifications of student performance into one of the performance level categories based on a set of cut-scores obtained from a standard setting procedure. These scores are then used for a variety of purposes, including as indicators of student learning in student report cards and for accountability purposes. With the increased importance given to performance-level scores for accountability purposes, how these scores are derived, the accuracy of such scores and validity of interpretations of such scores have been examined.

This chapter focuses on developments that are expected to continue to lead to positive changes in assessment and the development of different assessment practices and interpretations. The review of these developments is intended to inform educational psychologists in order to make informed judgments about current assessment practices, to design and develop assessments that are targeted to valued educational goals by educational psychologists, and to explain and demonstrate the importance and necessity of integrating knowledge from educational psychology and the assessment principles in order for assessment to serve learning. The first section focuses on the renewed emphasis on use of assessments that support student learning. This section considers requirements for large-scale assessments in order to guide learning and the role of classroom assessments in guiding instruction and learning. The second section of the chapter reviews assessment design models that facilitate the development of assessments for constructs related to student learning. In particular, these models can be used for developing assessments for constructs that may be considered to be too complex to be assessed by commonly used assessment design approaches. The third section describes a set of psychometric models that allow us to examine, or take into account, student cognitive processes during test taking. These models provide promise for using assessment to enhance learning in a more direct way than has been done before. The fourth section reviews and discusses research related to developments in validity research with a focus on student cognitive processes. The fifth section presents and discusses research related to the validity and accuracy of scores that are most commonly used in large-scale assessments, namely the performance level scores.

DEVELOPMENTS IN ASSESSMENTS THAT SUPPORT LEARNING

There is a growing belief among educators and educational assessment experts that better connections between assessment and curriculum and instruction can have a positive impact on learning (Black & Wiliam, 1998; Chudowsky & Pellegrino, 2003; Gipps, 1999; National Research Council, 2001; Pellegrino, Baxter, and Glaser, 1999; Shepard, 2000; Stiggins, 1997). The National Research Council (NRC) report *Knowing What Students Know: The Science and Design of Educational Assessment* (National Research Council, 2001) makes connections among curriculum, instruction, and assessment as three pillars that are critical to learning environments as well as developments of assessments that can serve learning well. Although there is overwhelming evidence to support the link between assessment and learning, to date there is little evidence to suggest that a consideration of this linkage is widespread, particularly within large-scale assessment contexts. James Popham (2003) argued that most state accountability tests fail to provide data that can be used to improve teaching and learning. Popham (2003) identified five attributes of large-scale assessments or classroom assessments that can support learning. These are: (1) the test assesses important curricular goals; (2) these goals are teachable; (3) there is a clear description of knowledge and skills assessed by the test that can be used to guide learning and instruction; (4) the test provides specific enough information to guide instruction; (5) there is minimal intrusiveness in classroom. Similarly, Chudowsky and Pellegrino (2003) addressed the question of what it will take for large-scale assessments to support learning. These authors argued that even though research on learning and thinking in substantive areas (such as mathematics, science, and social studies) provides a great deal of information about development of knowledge and competency in these areas, this information rarely gets incorporated into large-scale assessment design. They identified key elements of assessments as well as contexts that would allow for such assessments to occur. The first and foremost requirement they identified is the clarity about the underlying constructs to be assessed. One of the challenges in developing assessments that take into account the development of knowledge and competence is the limited amount of knowledge about cognitive development and how con-

siderations of cognitive development can be linked to performance on assessment tasks. The authors identify six aspects of learning models that are critical to assessment design:

1. Be based on empirical studies of learners in the domain.
2. Identify performances that differentiate competent and less competent performance in the domain.
3. Provide a developmental perspective, laying out typical progressions from novice levels toward competence and then expertise, and noting landmark performances along the way.
4. Allow for a variety of typical ways that children come to understand the subject matter.
5. Capture some, but not all, aspects of what is known about how students think and learn in the domain. Starting with a theory of how people learn the subject matter, the designers of an assessment will need to select a slice or subset of the large theory as the targets of inference.
6. Lend itself to being aggregated at different grain sizes so it can be used for different assessment purposes (e.g., to provide fine-grained diagnostic information as well as coarser-grained summary information). (p. 7)

These aspects of learning models suggest the need for close collaborations among educational psychologists, specialists in substantive areas and assessment specialists in developing assessments that can support learning. They also indicate the need for empirical research on learning models in the various substantive areas. In order for these models to guide the development of assessments, they need to describe not only the development of competency and skills in a domain but also to elaborate on the relationship between different degrees of competencies and how they correspond to performance across a wide range of tasks.

One place where assessments are expected and should be informing learning is in the classroom. Classroom assessments can be used to evaluate teaching and instructional strategies, to provide information about students' current knowledge and understanding in order to guide instruction, and to provide feedback to students in order for them to monitor their learning. Black and Wiliam (1998) conducted an extensive review of more than 250 books and articles on effects of classroom assessments. They present overwhelming evidence that ongoing assessment by teachers, combined with appropriate feedback to students, can have high impact on learning. These researchers distinguish between two types of classroom assessments, namely formative, targeted to support learning, and summative, for assigning grades. Their focus was, however, on formative assessment. From their review, the authors concluded that not all classroom assessments will have the same degree of positive impact on learning. The review identified four aspects of formative assessments that are key to effectiveness: *student self-esteem*, *student self-assessment*, *interaction in learning environments*, and *dialogue between teacher and student*. The importance of these four aspects is summarized next.

Student self-esteem. One of the first and foremost components of effective classroom assessment is identified as maintenance and promotion of student self-esteem, in particular the self-esteem of student in relation to assessment feedback. Feedback to students should focus on particular qualities of student product and should include advice on what the student can do to improve.

Student self-assessment. Students need to be trained in self-assessment so that they can understand the purposes of learning and direct their efforts and attention accordingly. This is not a simple task. Self-assessment requires a clear understanding of how each task and their performance on task is related to the targeted learning outcomes. In addition, the students need to be taught how to execute a self-assessment, how to interpret their performance on the task, and how to improve their knowledge and skills.

Interaction in learning environments. Opportunities for students to express their understandings should be part of the learning environment in order for the formative assessment to support learning. Interactions provide opportunities to teachers to respond to and orient students' thinking. This aspect of formative assessment emphasizes the ongoing and interactive nature of this type of assessment. The teacher needs to be aware of multiple learning models the students may be employing, and how students' misunderstanding may be related to the their utilization of a learning model. Further, the teacher must be able to direct students' thinking.

Dialogue between teacher and student. Dialogue between teacher and student should be thoughtful, reflective, focused to evoke and explore understanding, and conducted so that students have an opportunity to think and express ideas. This type of dialogue is different from a question-and-answer session in which the teacher engages students. For thoughtful exploratory dialogue to occur, students need to be given sufficient time to think and to reflect upon their understanding. This takes more time than that required to recall an answer to a question.

In summary, feedback on assessments should give students guidance on how to improve and each student must be given help and opportunities to work on improvement. With this type of feedback, the responsibility for learning lies with both the teacher and the student. The teacher needs to provide specific and timely feedback to the student, as well as provide support to the student in her or his improvement. The student, on the other hand, cannot be a passive receiver of information. Students must be taught how to receive and to respond to the feedback and how to use it to improve their learning.

The type of formative assessment Black and Wiliam (1998) identified as effective requires teachers to have a clear understanding of multiple learning models in a variety of substantive areas, to understand how different performance tasks may be related to these learning models, to employ effective interaction and dialogue strategies that will guide a student's thinking, to institute appropriate feedback styles, and to be able to guide students in improving their learning. Such requirements of teachers may be feasible only if teachers are provided with the relevant education and training in student learning models, assessment and instructional strategies. Chappuis and Stiggins (2002) identified characteristics of effective classroom assessment practices that also require teachers to have specialized knowledge about assessment and its relationship to learning:

1. Pretest before a unit of study and adjust instruction
2. Analyze which students need more practice
3. Adjust instruction according to the assessment results
4. Identify student strengths and weaknesses and discuss these with students
5. Model and develop group learning (p. 2)

The classroom assessment characteristics identified in the reviews conducted by Black and Wiliam (1998) and Chappuis and Stiggins (2002) highlighted the integral nature of the learning models in teaching, curriculum, and teacher training practices. They also emphasized teacher knowledge, including an understanding of multiple learning models in developing assessments that target student learning with multiple learning models in mind. One of the ways that teachers can be helped in their efforts is by providing them with assessment tools that can be integrated into their instructional practices. An example of such an embedded assessment is the Berkeley Evaluation and Assessment Research (BEAR) Assessment System (Wilson & Sloane, 2000), in which student assessment is an integral component of instruction and the instructional materials and thus indistinguishable from other classroom activities. This embedded system provides teachers with a set of tools with which to assess student performance on central concepts and skills in the curriculum, to set standards of student performance, to track student progress over time, and to provide feedback to students and others about student progress as well as the effectiveness of their teaching.

The BEAR system was designed on the basis of four principles: (1) a developmental perspective; (2) a match between instruction and assessment; (3) teacher management and principle; and (4) quality evidence. The developmental perspective is based on a student model of learning. This model guides assessment design and focuses assessment on student development rather than on current status or achievement. The match between instruction and assessment in the BEAR system is developed and maintained by assessment tasks that are embedded within classroom instruction and by the set of variables that describe progress in learning. In addition, the assessment guides instruction and informs the development of future assessment. As a result, teachers play a key role in the implementation of the BEAR system. Wilson and Sloane (2000) identified aspects of the teacher's role in assessment that are key to the success of the system. These are that teachers need to be (1) involved in collecting and selecting student work; (2) able to score and use the results immediately; (3) able to interpret results in instructional terms; (4) have a creative role in the way the assessment system is realized; and (5) play a central role in interpreting student progress and performance. All of these aspects of the BEAR Assessment System can make effective classroom assessment practices feasible for teachers.

There are four aspects of assessments that are emphasized across the research reviewed in this section. These are (1) a developmental perspective in student learning; (2) learning environments and how the assessment information is used; (3) the role of teachers; and (4) the quality of assessment. A developmental perspective that describes a typical progression of learning and development, identifies performances that differentiate between different competence levels, and notes that landmark performances for each level of competence are identified as critical for assessments to support learning. This developmental perspective needs to provide information about how students think and learn in the domain and allow for a variety of learning styles and progression models for children. The description of the progression should be specific enough to lend itself to provide fine-grained diagnostic information as well as coarser grained summary information.

Different aspects of learning environments are identified as key to the effectiveness of formative assessments. The assessment should be part of an interactive learning environment between the learner and the teacher;

the feedback based on the assessment should foster and maintain student's self-esteem, should allow and facilitate student self-assessment, and should be part of a dialogue between teacher and student.

Teachers are key to implementing an effective assessment system. In order for teachers to have an active and effective role in assessments, they need to be knowledgeable about the developmental perspective of learning in the substantive area; be involved in what's included in the assessment; be able to score and use the results immediately; be able to interpret results in instructional terms; and play a central role in interpreting student progress and performance.

The ultimate role the assessments play is providing information. The quality of this information is key to the effectiveness of all assessments. In order for assessment to serve learning well, what is assessed and the quality of the scores are critical. This means that assessments should focus on assessing important curricular goals and provide accurate and meaningful scores and information.

DEVELOPMENTS IN ASSESSMENT DESIGN

One of the key developments in assessment design that promises to facilitate the development of assessments that target the improvement of learning has been the formulation of evidence-centered assessment design (Mislevy, Steinberg, & Almond, 2002; Mislevy, Wilson, Ercikan, & Chudowky, 2002; National Research Council, 2001). Evidence Centered Design (ECD) is a framework for assessment design that specifies a clear purpose for assessment as well as clear relationships between the purpose and the components of the assessment. The framework promotes assessment that is purposeful and intentional, especially with regard to the types of evidence made available and the targeted inferences that can be made from the assessment data.

The framework has three key elements: the student model, the task model and the evidence model. The *student model* consists of aspects of cognition and learning that are the targets for the assessment. The model, which consists of constructs or construct components, specifies a progression in learning. These construct components are chosen according to reporting or instructional requirements that are tied to the purpose of the assessment. They represent latent states of knowledge that describe the progress in competency, knowledge, and skills in substantive areas. These construct components can be thought of as student variables, as shown in Fig. 40.1, with expected relationships among them, as indicated by the arrows in the diagram.

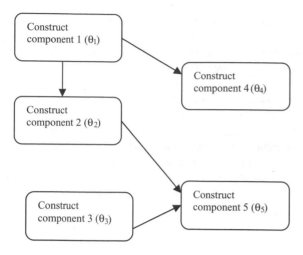

FIGURE 40.1. Student model.

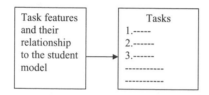

FIGURE 40.2. Task model.

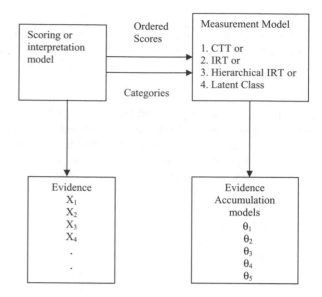

FIGURE 40.3. Evidence models.

surement models include classical test theory–based simple sum of ordered scores, or a item response theory based models among many others.

Application of Evidence Centered Design (ECD) to Assessing Historical Thinking

The three models (student, task, and evidence) provide a way of thinking about assessment design that connects what we observe, either as student performance or product, and what we would like to infer about student competence and understanding. This approach for assessment design lends itself well to conceptualizing and designing assessments that are targeted to assess constructs that have complex relationships among components. This approach can be used to systematize the way we think about and gather validity evidence in complex assessments. As an example, *historical thinking* is a target learning outcome in history education and is defined as a set of interrelated competencies and understandings that guide and shape the practice of history (Seixas & Peck, 2003). Figure 40.4 describes six elements of *historical thinking* for guiding the development of curriculum and assessment in history education (Seixas & Peck, 2003). This view of goals for history education does not represent a consensus among history educators about what history education should be and what historical thinking is. In fact, Seixas and Peck (2003) noted that the goals are radically different from those that are included in social studies curricula at present. For the purposes of this chapter, these authors' definition of historical thinking presents

The *task model* (Fig. 40.2) describes the tasks in the assessment and includes variables describing the key features of tasks or the observation contexts. This model identifies what different types of tasks require students to do and how these are related to the student model construct components. For example, cognitive requirements for completing the task are identified and how these requirements are related to the student model variables are established. This model describes how the observations we make on students' performance on tasks that are designed to elicit information about their degree of competency are related to the construct components.

The *evidence model* consists of two components, the *scoring* or *interpretation model* and the *measurement model* (Fig. 40.3). These models present rules for interpreting observations that can be used to relate observations to the latent constructs in the student model. The interpretation rules are applied to convert data and observations into evidence regarding competencies in the student model, and measurement models are used for summarizing these evidences across multiple observations. The interpretation rules identify and characterize the essential features of the student product that are relevant to the competencies in the student model and assigns student responses or products into ordered scores or categories. The measurement model accumulates evidence across student responses and products. Examples of mea-

Significance
Ability to determine what is important in the past and why, and understanding the relationship of those events and people to the present.

Epistemology and evidence
Ability to make judgments about what accounts of the past we should believe, on what grounds, and with what reservations.

Continuity and change
Understanding the distance between the past and the present, foreignness of the past and appreciation of the difficulty of knowing the past.

Progress and decline
Ability to evaluate change over time.

Empathy
Ability to see and understand the world from a perspective not our own.

Historical agency
Understanding that the active role people play in promoting, shaping, and resisting change in history.

FIGURE 40.4. Student model variables or construct components in historical thinking.

a good example of how educators may go about developing assessments for curricular goals that deviate from simpler definitions of what students should be taught in substantive areas. The elements presented by Seixas and Peck are based on empirical research, yet need not be considered as fixed. Rather, they can be regarded as a starting place from which to assess and examine this definition so that further refinements of the construct can be made. The six elements describe the processes, abilities, understandings, and awarenesses that the authors view as appropriate goals of history teaching in schools. As components of a student model, the elements could be tied to student learning outcomes or used to set benchmarks for history education. In practice, these components would be integrated with historical content. It is not meaningful to conceptualize or to assess the components devoid of such content. The complex interactions among the components and in relation to historical content make historical thinking a good example of how ECD can be used to develop assessment in a substantive area. The example may be helpful in developing assessments of similar constructs.

Using the present definition of historical thinking, the student model consists of six construct components. These components are not tied to an existing curriculum, but they can be considered, separately or jointly, as targets of instruction and learning. Although the components are expected to be related to each other, they can be considered as distinct educational student model outcomes.

Given these student model components, how might educators create an assessment of competencies, both of individuals and of groups? The cognitive theory of how people develop competence in a given domain or in each of the construct variables provides guidance about the types of tasks that will elicit evidence about competence.

Similarly, cognitive theory provides information about the types of tasks that work best for different types of competencies and is helpful in determining which features of tasks might be most appropriate for different contexts and construct components.

The task model in the historical thinking example describes tasks and features of tasks that will elicit evidence regarding students' understandings, abilities, and awarenesses regarding the six elements described above. Figure 40.5 presents a set of activities and exercises from Seixas and Peck (2003), which were designed to elicit evidence regarding competencies in each of the construct components. The bracketed suggestions are proposed to serve as examples, and they can be replaced with other topics to create similar tasks. These activities can serve as models for tasks targeted to assess elements of the student model in Fig. 40.4. Also, they can serve as the actual tasks themselves. These and other descriptions of tasks (such as how the content of the tasks should correspond to historical thinking) form the basis of the *task model*. These tasks do not necessarily need to be presented in isolation as an assessment but can be embedded in curriculum and instruction.

The next step in assessment design is to decide how to extract evidence of student competence and skills from students' responses to tasks. The interpretation model helps us to think about particular aspects of students' responses and assign the responses to specific categories. These categories may be ordered (if such an ordering is meaningful) or not, especially when the target inference is one of understanding a student's cognitive processes, which may have a multidimensional nonuniform progression. For an elaboration of growth and learning in historical thinking, we turn to different researchers in history education. Lee and Shemilt (2003) described a progression

Significance
Make a poster showing four significant events in the history of Canada. Be prepared to defend your choice of events to the class.

Epistemology and Evidence
Examine a historical artifact: What do you think this is? What makes you say so?

Continuity and change
Examine two or more photographs of the same street scene from different eras. What has changed? What has remained the same?

Progress and decline
Have things progressed (i.e. improved) since the time [pictured, written about] here? In what ways yes? In what ways no? For whom?

Empathy (historical perspective-taking) and moral judgment
What did the author of this document think about [slavery]?

Historical agency
Which groups of people [have been/are/will be] most responsible for bringing about [equal political rights/social equality/economic security]?

FIGURE 40.5. Sample tasks that are designed to elicit evidence about each of the construct components.

of ideas in historical thinking in a hierarchical form, with less developed ideas at the lower levels and more developed ideas at the higher levels. The hierarchy, however, is not meant to indicate that every student completes each of the steps of the hierarchical progression in a lockstep manner. Rather, students' progression can follow different patterns and does not need to involve each of the steps of the hierarchy. The student learning model helps us to determine which aspects of a student's responses we need to examine in order to interpret the responses as evidence in relation to the target construct we are interested in assessing. The rules that help us to extract the relevant information are called the *scoring model*. A scoring model can be a scoring rubric, which assigns scores to student responses according to the presence and degree of certain qualities in the response. These scores simply reflect ordered categories rather than scores that indicate equidistant measures of historical thinking. This is true not only in relation to the type of learning model described earlier, but also to all other scoring within the interpretation model. The scores simply reflect an increasing progression of competence or understanding. Distances between each score point in relation to the construct we are trying to assess are unknown. Within ECD, it is also possible to have interpretation models that assign responses to an unordered set of categories. This would be the case especially when the target latent construct is expected to consist of a set of unordered latent classes. In an educational context, however, we are interested typically in student learning and progress. Thus, most assessments focus on

capturing, examining, and assessing this progress. As a result, the focus here is on an example with an ordered set of scoring categories. Using the case of historical thinking as an example, Lee and Shemilt (2003) described the student learning progression (see Fig. 40.6) when the task was to explain past actions or social practices targeted to assess students' ability to make judgments about what accounts of the past we should believe, on what grounds, and with what reservations, labeled as *Epistemology and Evidence* in the student model in Fig. 40.4. In this progression model, students progressed from *Pictures of the past* to *Evidence in context*.

The next step is to link the scores or categories that emerge from the scoring or interpretation model with the expected progression in the student model. The key issue is to decide how these scores or categories provide evidence regarding the construct or the construct components. The measurement model assists us to think through how what we observe (i.e., the scores or categories we obtain using the evidence model) might be linked to the latent construct we are interested in assessing. The measurement model is typically a psychometric model that allows us to accumulate information across tasks. It can be a simple model based on classical test theory that sums the scores across tasks to create a composite score, or it can be more complex, based on item response theory, latent class models, hierarchical item response theory models, and so on. One of the key issues that the developer of an assessment needs to make a decision about is whether they would like to assess each of these student model

Type of student response	
Pictures of the past	The past is viewed as though it were the present, and students treat potential evidence as if it offers direct access to the past. Questions about the basis of statements about the past do not arise. Stories are just stories.
Information	The past is treated as fixed and known by some authority; students treat potential evidence as information. Given statements to test against evidence, students match information or count sources to solve the problem. Questions arise about whether the information offered is correct or incorrect, but no methodology is attributed to history for answering such questions beyond an appeal to books, diaries or what is dug up. These, although sometimes seen as being connected with the past, provide transparent information that is either correct or incorrect.
Testimony	The past is reported to us by people living at the time. Like eyewitnesses today, they do this either well or badly. Questions as to how we know about the past are regarded as sensible: Students begin to understand that history has a methodology for testing statements about the past. Conflicts in potential evidence are thought appropriately settled by deciding which report is best. Notions of bias, exaggeration, and loss of information in transmission supplement the simple dichotomy between truth-telling and lies. Reports are often treated as if the authors are more or less direct eyewitnesses: the more direct, the better.
Scissors and Paste	The past can be probed even when no individual reporter has told us truthfully or accurately what happened. We can put together a version by picking out the true statements from different reports and putting them together. In one student's words: "You take the true bits out of this one, and the best bits out of that one, and when you've got it up, you've got a picture." Notions of bias or lies are supplemented by questions about whether the reporter is in a position to know.
Evidence in isolation	Statements about the past can be inferred from sources of evidence. We can ask questions of sources that they were not designed to answer, so that evidence will bear questions for which it could not be testimony. Many things may serve as evidence that do not report anything . (Nineteenth-century rail timetables were not constructed for the benefit of historians.) This means that historians may "work out" historical facts even if no testimony survives. Evidence may be defective without questions of bias or lies. Reliability is not a fixed property of a source, and the weight we can rest on any piece of evidence depends on what questions we ask of it.
Evidence in context	A source only yields evidence when it is understood in its historical context: we must know what a source meant to those by and for whom it was produced. This involves the suspension of certain lines of questioning and a provisional acceptance of much historical work as established fact (a known context). We cannot question everything at once. Contexts vary across time and place and thus a sense of period is important.

FIGURE 40.6. Student progression levels in *evidence*.

variables separately or whether these variables can be meaningfully interpreted as a composite. The decision has implications for how the evidence from the evidence model are summarized by the measurement model. The decision should be based on whether a composite across construct components is meaningful as well as upon whether the decision is consistent with reporting goals.

DEVELOPMENTS IN MEASUREMENT MODELS

Developments in assessment to assess complex sets of constructs or to make advanced inferences based on a set of observations are critically dependent on psychometric models that can be used to synthesize and create meaning out of a set of observations. Psychometric models are part of the interpretation model in ECD. Meaningful interpretations and inferences from assessments are possible only if the psychometric models are consistent with the target inferences as well as with the student and task models. During the past 10 years, psychometricians have responded to the needs of educators and educational psychologists who are interested in understanding student cognitive processes. As a result, a large number of psychometric models that target this purpose have been developed. One set of models are generalizations of the basic item response theory (IRT) models, such as the one-, two-, and three-parameter models (Hambleton, 1996; Lord, 1980) for assessing multiple attributes, such as multiple aspects of knowledge and skills. IRT models are probabilistic models that define relationships between examinee ability and competence and their responses to test items. These models have allowed psychometricians to examine properties of test items and tests independent of samples they have been administered to and apply them to solve many psychometric challenges, such as equating, item banking, and computerized adaptive testing. The newer models for assessing multiple attributes are based on multivariate conceptions of knowledge and constructs. For example, the multivariate nature of knowledge in a mathematics assessment can involve mathematical content knowledge (such as geometry, algebra, and computation) and process knowledge (such as problem solving and mathematical communication). Most knowledge, skills, and educational assessment data are expected to be multidimensional in nature. Unidimensional IRT models typically provide good approximations of this multidimensional nature. The approximation may be sufficient for many purposes such as obtaining an overall estimate of mathematical competence for rank-ordering students. For a number of reasons, however, educational psychologists, educators, and researchers may be interested in separate estimates of these related competencies. One reason is that accounting for the separate nature of these competencies will lead to more accurate estimates of the construct components. A second reason is that one might be interested in estimating the correlation among these components. A third reason, more relevant for educators, is that knowledge about differential performance on these construct components may be needed for instructional purposes.

Multidimensional IRT models that assess multiple attributes or competencies can be grouped into two major categories: *compensatory* models in which different construct components combine linearly so that weakness in one construct component can be made up for by another construct component, and *noncompensatory* models in which each observable response represents the conjunction of several sub-processes that individually follow unidimensional IRT models (Junker, 1999). In compensatory models, the unidimensional latent construct θ is replaced by a linear combination of latent construct components $a_{j1}\theta_1 + a_{j2}\theta_2 + \cdots + a_{j^1k}\theta_k$, for a student model with k construct components. Each of these construct components is targeted to be assessed by one or more of the test items. A set of multidimensional compensatory models have been developed in which items are targeted to assess which construct components are assumed to be known (Adams, Wilson, & Wang, 1997; Embretson, 1991; Stegelmann, 1983). Another set of models in which no item to construct component mappings are assumed have also been developed (Fraser & MacDonald, 1988; Muraki &

Carlson, 1995; Reckase, 1985; Wilson, Wood, & Gibbons, 1983).

In the noncompensatory multidimensional IRT models, the relationship among tasks, multiple attributes, and students' ability in relation to these multiple attributes is included in the model. For example, a set of variables Y_{ijk} may be defined as

$$Y_{ijk} = \begin{cases} 1, & \text{If student } i \text{ responds correctly to the} \\ & \text{component of the task assessing} \\ & \text{attribute } k \text{ on item } j; \\ 0, & \text{otherwise.} \end{cases}$$

Each of these variables Y_{ijk} are assumed to be following an IRT model that relates examinee responses to a latent construct θ. Embretson (1985) proposed a multicomponent latent trait model (MLTM) that is an extension of the model described earlier, by adding a slip-and-guessing parameter. Slip-and-guessing parameters are intended to account for measurement error that represents examinees responding incorrectly when they had the knowledge and skills needed to respond correctly and when they responded correctly when they did not have the skills and knowledge needed, respectively. The MLTM model has been applied to free-response synonym tasks by Janssen and deBoeck (1997).

A second set of psychometric models incorporated different cognitive demands in test items or tasks. These cognitive demands include strategies and skills as well as the general competence, or ability, intended to be assessed by the item. An example of this type of model is a linear logistic test model (LLTM) (Fischer, 1995). The requirement is that overall item difficulty is the sum of difficulty based on different cognitive requirements. In the 1990s, this model and its extensions were used for examining cognitive demand components in test items (Embretson, 1995a, 1995b, 1999). Other models that incorporated cognitive demands in the psychometric models were the *rule-space* model by Tatsuoka (1990), the *unified* model by DiBello, Stout, and Roussos (1995), and the M^2 *RCMLM* by Pirolli and Wilson (1998). Tatsuoka's rule space model describes relationships between responses and a predetermined set of item cognitive requirements. Different response patterns among examinees are regarded as resulting from latent classes that differ in their approaches to item solving. Based on this, examinees are assigned to latent classes depending on their pattern of item responses. An examinee's membership in one of these classes can provide diagnostic information about their competencies. At the center of the rule-space model is a matrix called the Q matrix that identifies whether an attribute is required by an item. An attribute can be a cognitive skill

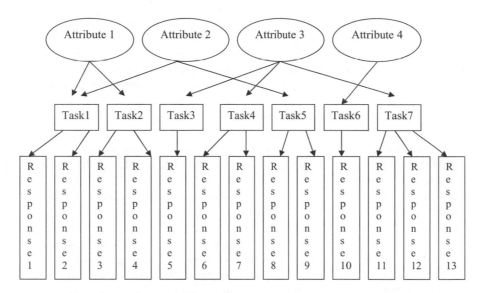

FIGURE 40.7. The relationships among attributes, tasks, and responses.

or a surface feature of an item or task. For example, in a mathematics test, item attributes can include whether they involve addition with carryover, subtraction with borrowing, or multiplication of integers. The psychometric models are defined in terms of examinee responses; therefore, these attributes are also linked to examinee responses, as well as tasks, each of which may have one or more responses. An example of the relationships among attributes, tasks, and responses is presented in Fig. 40.7.

The first step in applying the rule-space model is identifying the Q matrix: in other words, identifying all relevant attributes of items to examinees' ability to respond correctly to the test question. The second step is calculation of a measure of the fit of each examinee's pattern of right and wrong answers to the IRT model. This fit index is called the *caution index*. Each examinee gets an ability value and a caution index value. The ability by caution index plot is called the *rule-space* plot. Clustering of examinees in this two-dimensional plot is the target of interpretation regarding how different item attributes are related to response patterns (see Fig. 40.8 as an example of a rule-space plot) and how these are related to latent knowledge states. The groupings of examinees in these latent knowledge states can be useful in identifying skills and strategies examinees utilize in responding to the test questions and students who deviate from a typical pattern of such use of skills and strategies.

The rule-space model is critically dependent on the accurate and comprehensive identification of task cognitive requirements. There are some limitations in such a dependency. One is that such accuracy and compre-

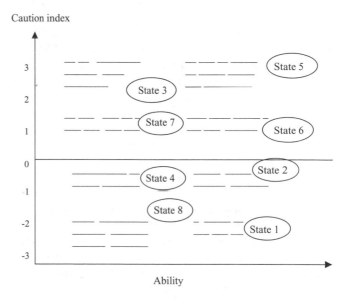

FIGURE 40.8. Example of an attribute in a rule-space model.

hensiveness may not be realized. The second is that examinees who possess certain skills required by the task may not always use these skills successfully to respond to the task correctly, leading to *slips*, or the opposite where the examinees may not possess the identified skills but respond to the task correctly by *guessing* or by using another strategy. The unified model is a generalized approach to modeling task requirements and their relationship with examinee responses. This model allows multiple strategies that may be used by students, and slips and guessing can be included in the model. Another generalized approach to modeling task attributes and student responses is the M^2RCMLM. The M^2RCMLM is a general probabilistic model in which the difficulty of test items is decomposed into attribute-specific continuous abilities, instead of discrete attributes as in the case of the rule-space model, as well as various compensatory combinations of student proficiency variables.

All of these psychometric models allow researchers to include expected cognitive requirements of test items that may include abilities and strategies in the psychometric model so that the relationship between these requirements and examinee responses can be examined systematically. The relationship between the cognitive requirements and examinee responses can provide valuable information to educational psychologists about what types of skills and knowledge the test items are assessing, the relationship between different latent knowledge states, for example hierarchical or not, reasons for poorly performing examinees, and the skills and knowledge they may be lacking.

A third set of psychometric models have been those that incorporate interrelations among variables. These include structural equation models (Jöreskog & Sörbom, 1999), and hierarchical models (Bryke & Raudenbush, 1992). The structural equation models are popularly used for examining relationships among performance on different components of tests. The hierarchical models take into account the hierarchical nature of data. These hierarchies include clustering of students in classrooms, classrooms within schools, schools within districts, and so forth. Hierarchical models account for and allow for estimation of variability of data from the various levels. Both sets of models, structural equation and hierarchical, have wide applications in educational and psychological research. For example, they have been used in capturing change in student learning over time. For these types of applications longitudinal data are needed. These new models of change are extensions of true-score approaches to the modeling of change. In true-score models, longitudinal data for each individual are grouped together and a linear or polynomial model is fitted to each individual. In contrast, these new models approximate the relationship between performance and time. One set of extensions of these models incorporates measurement error. This approach is included in the "V-known" option in the Hierarchical Linear Modeling software (Raudenbush, Bryke, & Congdon, 1999). Another approach is structural equation modeling (SEM) (Muthen & Khoo, 1998; Willett & Sayer, 1994). In the SEM approach, each time point is treated as a factor, and the relationships among the factors and the performance are estimated and examined. The LISREL and the M-Plus software packages can be used for analyzing these types of models. There are another set of IRT-based models that incorporate both the multidimensional nature of constructs and the longitudinal nature of data. These models are referred to as *multidimensional latent regression models* and can be estimated using the Conquest software (Wu, Adams, & Wilson, 1998).

DEVELOPMENTS IN VALIDITY RESEARCH

Traditionally, examinations of the validity of test score interpretations focused on test content (i.e., the degree to which the test sampled a target curricular area) and construct validity, which typically involved an analysis of test data structure using exploratory or confirmatory factor analysis. There is an increasing awareness, however, that these forms of validity evidence should be supplemented with evidence that an assessment taps the targeted cognitive processes and that aspects of test items do not create bias against some groups because of unintended cognitive requirements. A key component of validity research is a focus on fairness and bias, particularly with regard to the assessment of similar constructs with different comparison groups. This section of the chapter summarizes developments in research and validity research methods that focus on comparability of constructs assessed for different comparison groups, and methods used for examining student cognitive processes in this type of research as well as for examining cognitive requirements of assessment tasks.

Comparability of Constructs Assessed for Different Groups

Performance on assessments involves students' understanding of test items, their familiarity with the context within which the items are presented, and the students' ability to communicate their solutions, as well as the knowledge and skills required to answer test items. Differential familiarity with context and, competency in understanding test questions and in communicating solutions may lead to differences in what is assessed for different groups. One of the most commonly used methods for examining whether test items assess similar constructs for different groups is differential item functioning (DIF) detection methods. A test item is identified as *differentially functioning* if it demonstrates different psychometric properties for different groups. Absence of DIF is a requirement for items to be considered as assessing similar constructs for different groups. However, lack of DIF is not sufficient evidence that the test item is assessing similar constructs for the comparison groups, because although an item may have similar psychometric properties (such as difficulty and discrimination for similar ability levels), it may present different cognitive requirements for two groups. Differential item functioning procedures are now one of the primary methods for examining whether test items are assessing similar constructs for comparison groups such as gender and ethnic groups. During the past 10 years, DIF methods have also been applied to examining constructs assessed by different language versions of tests (Allalouf, Hambleton, & Sireci, 1999; Ercikan, 1998; 2002; 2003; Ercikan & Koh, 2005; Gierl & Khaliq, 2001; Sireci, Fitzgerald, & Xing, 1998). The findings from this research indicate that different language versions of tests cannot be assumed to be assessing similar constructs, and empirical evidence of comparability of constructs is needed for valid interpretations of test scores across different language groups.

In the 1996 edition of the *Handbook of Educational Psychology*, Ronald Hambleton (Hambleton, 1996) dedicated a long section to DIF methods, describing and discussing Mantel-Haenszel and its extensions (Holland & Thayer, 1988; Zwick, Donoghue, & Grima, 1993) and IRT-based methods (Linn & Harnisch, 1980; Lord, 1980). Some of the most commonly used DIF methods are still the Mantel-Haenszel and the IRT-based methods. Recently, however, there have been two major developments in DIF. The first, a shift in viewing DIF results from accounting for the multidimensional nature of constructs being assessed while the second is an increasing focus on identifying sources of DIF. Shealy and Stout (1993) proposed a framework for understanding how DIF occurs based on the assumption that multidimensionality produces DIF. This approach to DIF detection is called the *simultaneous item bias test* (SIBTEST). The main construct the test is intended to measure is called the *primary dimension*, and the additional dimensions that were not intended to be assessed by the test and may produce DIF are referred to as the *secondary dimensions*. When primary and secondary dimensions characterize item responses, the data are considered multidimensional. An item will exhibit DIF if the focal and reference groups that have been equated on a primary dimension differ in distribution on a secondary dimension. A further consideration is that the response function of an item must be sensitive to the secondary dimension. However, even if an item is sensitive to the secondary dimension, no DIF will occur if the conditional distributions for the two groups on the secondary dimension do not differ.

One of the challenges in using DIF methodology in examining the comparability of constructs assessed with comparison groups is identification of potential causes of DIF. Understanding causes of DIF is necessary, not only for understanding what the test items may be assessing for different groups, but also for deciding what to do with test items identified as DIF (e.g., whether to eliminate them from the test or to keep them). Several researchers have investigated potential causes of DIF for gender, ethnic, and language groups (Allalouf, Hambleton, & Sireci, 1999; Ercikan, 1998, 2002; Gierl & Khaliq, 2001; O'Neill & McPeek, 1993; Schmitt & Dorans, 1990; Scheunemann & Geritz, 1990; Sireci, Fitzgerald, & Xing, 1998). To determine potential causes of DIF, these studies combined statistical methods with reviews of items by assessment experts. Although a number of patterns of sources of DIF emerged from this line of research, the sources of DIF were not conclusive. Several statistical approaches have been proposed for identifying sources of DIF. One, based on the SIBTEST approach, was proposed by Douglas, Roussos and Stout (1996). Another, based on hierarchical linear modeling, was proposed by Swanson, Clauser, Case, Nungester, and Featherman (2002). Although both methods are promising, further research is needed for these methods to be used reliably in the identification of sources of DIF. For example, Ercikan and Mendes-Barnett (2003) examined the degree to which consistent hypothesis testing results would be found across eight test forms using the SIBTEST approach. Their study indicated inconsistencies in hypothesis testing results, thereby indicating limitations in this approach to identifying sources of DIF. Identifying sources of DIF, therefore, continues to be a challenge for educators and researchers. One method that appears to be promising in identifying sources of DIF, however, is the examination of students' thinking processes during test taking. The following section describes and discusses this approach to identifying sources of DIF.

During the past 10 years, DIF methods have also been used for investigating whether different groups of examinees with approximately the same ability appear to be using different cognitive processes to respond to test items. Investigations have focused on whether relative difficulty for different groups of examinees is a result of differences in application of cognitive processes, in language (Ercikan, 1998, 2002, 2003; Ercikan et al., 2004), in solution strategies and instructional methods (Lane, Wang, & Magone, 1996), and in the skills required by the tests that are not uniformly distributed across examinees (O'Neil & McPeek, 1993). In their study, Lane, Wang, and Magone (1996) used DIF analyses to detect differential response patterns. They also examined differences in students' solution strategies, mathematical explanations, and mathematical errors as potential sources of DIF. Ercikan (1998, 2002, 2003) used DIF methods to detect differential response patterns among language groups. Statistical detection was followed up with linguistic comparisons of test versions to determine reasons for the observed differential response patterns.

Examining Cognitive Processes Tapped by Assessment Tasks

Several researchers have described and summarized methods for examining the cognitive processes examinees use during test taking. These methods can be used to examine whether tasks within the test are tapping the intended knowledge and skills (Baxter & Glaser, 1998; Magone, Cai, Silver, & Wang, 1994; Messick, 1993). Understanding how item format, content, and context affect examinee thought processes is very important for creating tests that assess the constructs that we are interested in assessing and in avoiding unneccesary cognitive demands on student performance. Further, it is of critical importance in identifying sources of differential item functioning. There are three general types of methods that can be used for this purpose: namely, protocol analysis, analysis of reason, and analysis of error. In *protocol analysis*, students are asked to think aloud as they respond to test questions or after they have completed solving problems (Ercikan et al., 2004; Ericsson & Simon, 1984). In *analysis of reason*, students are asked to explain reasons for their responses to test questions (Lane, Wang, & Magone, 1996). *Analysis of error* involves an examination of the patterns of errors in students' responses in order to understand gaps in students' knowledge, misconceptions, and misrepresentations of concepts (National Research Council, 2001).

As part of task development and validity efforts, some researchers have considered cognitive demands of assessment tasks. Baxter and Glaser (1998), and Glaser and Baxter (2002) described techniques for examining the degree of cognitive complexity tapped by tasks in a performance assessment. Their analysis focused on the actual tasks themselves and their associated scoring rubrics. These researchers developed a framework, a content-process space of assessment tasks that described tasks according to their degree of content knowledge and the degree of complexity of process skills tapped by the tasks. Some items could be identified as rich in content knowledge requirements but poor in the level of process skills required, whereas others required complex process skills without a requirement for previous content knowledge in the substantive area. These researchers found that some tasks they analyzed indeed matched their targeted goals of content-process complexity, whereas others did not.

Other researchers explored interviews of students as a way of understanding the cognitive processes that students employ when they respond to questions. Using this approach, Hamilton, Nussbaum, and Snow (1997) iden-

TABLE 40.1. Think-Aloud Protocol

Questions Administrators Asked
What is the question asking you to do? In your own words, tell me what the question says? Interpret the question. What are you supposed to do?
Can you tell me what steps you took to actually solve the problem? (Note if student has the wrong answer and try to establish point of departure from correct problem solving track)
Why did you pick that answer? What helped you figure out the answer?
What did you find difficult about this question? Were there any hints in the question that helped you to solve it? What was helpful?

tified unexpected cognitive strategies identified by the students. In particular, these researchers identified that instructions given in test questions were very important in directing students to the kinds of strategies that they were expected to use.

Student thinking processes have been examined in an effort to identify sources of differential item functioning. Ercikan et al. (2004) demonstrated and discussed the use of think-aloud protocols to collect data about examinees' thought processes during test taking and examined the use of this information to identify sources of differential item functioning. In this study, think-aloud protocols were defined as structured interview protocols that encouraged examinees to think aloud and to talk about their interpretations of test questions and solution strategies as well as the difficulties they were having as they responded to test questions. In addition, the think-aloud protocols were used to examine student cognitive processes in an effort to understand whether similar constructs were being assessed for English and French speakers in this Canadian assessment. The methods utilized in this study can be used to examine cognitive processes in a single group, as well as to examine the cognitive processes that the items tap for other groups, such as students who have been exposed to different curricula or instruction.

The think-aloud protocol in the Ercikan et al. (2004) study consisted of a set of questions that test administrators posed to participants upon completion of each math/science item. The questions tapped four themes: (a) participants' understanding of the intent of each math/science item; (b) the steps the participants took to answer an item; (c) participants' reasons for selecting an answer; and (d) the aspects of the item that facilitated or hindered their problem-solving process. The questions asked by the administrators are presented in Table 40.1. Test administrators were instructed to ask only those questions that had not spontaneously been answered by the participants' think-aloud processes.

The data set for analysis was comprised of the transcripts of the interviews and the written notes of the interviewers. The focus of the analysis was on determining the following information for each item in the protocol: (a) whether or not the student answered the question correctly; (b) the student's understanding of the meaning of the question; (c) whether or not the student found the question difficult to answer; (d) what aspects of the question were useful for solving the problem; and (e) what aspects of the question the student found confusing or difficult to understand. Answers to these questions helped to determine the degree to which similar constructs were being assessed by the two language versions, English and French, of a set of Canadian tests.

DEVELOPMENTS IN PERFORMANCE LEVEL SCORES

A recent trend in assessment practice has been a shift to reporting assessment results in terms of a set of performance level scores. Performance level scores, which are a set of classifications based on students' performance on an assessment, are intended to provide verbal descriptors of student performance, thus facilitating the interpretation of results. To develop performance level scores, a set of scores (that may be simple sums of the number of correct scores or scores based on IRT scaling) are obtained. Next, a standard setting procedure is applied that relates these scores to a set of expected levels of competency, skills, and knowledge in order that students' results can be classified. For example, a standard setting procedure may identify the range of scores on a test deemed to indicate Basic, Proficient, or Advanced levels of competency in mathematics. Standard setting procedures are the key method for identifying cut-score points for pass/fail decisions or for classifying students into various levels of performance. In most large-scale assessments, performance level scores are used for making high-stakes decisions such as accountability. As a result, the validity of interpretations of these scores has gained heightened importance, and comprehensive investigations of the validity of such scores are important. The accuracy of performance level scores is closely related to classical notions of score reliability, but such notions of reliability are insufficient for identifying accuracy of performance-level scores or for making decisions about the number of performance level scores that may be feasible for certain levels of score accuracy. This section reviews and discusses the standard setting procedures that are the key components of methodologies used in creating performance-level scores, summarizes a comprehensive framework for validating performance level scores, and provides some guidelines regarding accuracy of performance level scores.

Standard Setting Procedures

In the 1996 edition of this volume, Hambleton (1996) described and reviewed some of the most common standard setting procedures that are used typically for multiple-choice tests as well as some methods developed for performance assessments. This description included a list of typical steps that are involved in all standard setting procedures. First, a panel (that may include parents, teachers, curriculum experts, psychometricians, and policymakers) is gathered, and the members engage in setting the standards for the assessment under consideration. Hambleton (1996) described seven steps that are followed in a typical standard setting procedure as follows:

1. Review of the purpose of the educational assessment;
2. Exposure to the assessment itself and the scoring rubrics (sometimes panelists are administered the assessment under testlike conditions);
3. Development and discussion of the performance categories: e.g., novice, apprentice, proficient, expert; or sometimes simply masters or non-masters;
4. Training and practice on the standard setting method;
5. Setting standards—panelists go through the method and set their initial standards;
6. Discussion among the panelists about their standards. Sometimes consequential information is introduced, such as the percentage of students who would be in each proficiency category if the standards were adopted. Other information panelists might receive would be difficulty levels and discriminating powers of the exercises;
7. Setting standards again—panelists repeat the process. Very often, the panelists' standards converge, remaining differences among panelists are handled by "averaging" the standards of panelists. Several rounds of discussion and standard setting are usual (that is, steps 5 and 6 may be repeated several times). (pp. 919–920)

Since 1996, several new methods have been developed for setting standards for performance assessments, most of which can also be used for multiple-choice tests. There are several reasons, however, why methods developed for multiple-choice tests may not be appropriate for performance assessments. The first is that performance assessments result, typically, in polytomously scored assessment data which require different types of judgments to be made by panelists than when scores are dichotomous. Second, performance assessments may be designed to assess multiple attributes, skills, and knowledge, and the judgments involved in standard setting need to take these aspects into account. Third, the smaller number of tasks used in performance assessments, in comparison with multiple-choice tests, may make it possible to make judgments about student performance at the overall test level instead of at the item level. In addition, the smaller number of tasks on a performance assessment has implications for the generalizability of performance on one task to other tasks and may put additional requirements on the panelists when making judgments and setting standards at the task level.

Hambleton, Jaeger, Plake, and Mills (2000) presented a comprehensive review of standard setting procedures developed for performance assessments. These authors focused on one of the key dimensions of standard setting, that is, panelists' judgments. Panelists' judgments involve consideration of the tasks or items presented to examinees, the classification of examinees based on evidence outside the test or assessment for which performance standards are to be set, the classification of responses of examinees to stimulus material presented in the test or assessment, and the scored performance of examinees. These authors described 10 standard setting methods and discussed their advantages and disadvantages. Their review of these standard setting procedures is summarized in Table 40.2.

The extensive list of available methods highlights the wide use of the standard setting procedures and, the high activity level in this area of research, as well as the ongoing search for methods that produce reliable and meaningful performance level scores. It is clear from this review that different methods may work best for certain assessments. For example, Holistic or Direct Judgment methods that require review of examinee performance on all items, may be most applicable when there are a small number of test items and the Contrasting Groups method may be most applicable when teacher judgments or classroom assessment results are available. Whatever standard setting method is used, it is important to keep in mind that these are score creation mechanisms. As a result, it is necessary to demonstrate the accuracy and meaningfulness of performance level scores. In order to do this, standard setting procedures need to have data collection designs in place that provide evidence of such accuracy and meaningfulness. The following section summarizes a framework for a comprehensive way of validating performance level scores that includes standard setting procedures as one of the components of the validation framework.

Validating Performance-level Score Interpretations

Haertel and Lorié (2004) developed a conceptual framework for validity arguments supporting performance level score interpretations. These authors emphasized that validity arguments and interpretations must address the adequacy and appropriateness of performance standards as well as the accuracy of examinee classifications based on the corresponding cut-scores. They identified a set of validity arguments and their implied propositions and discussed the types of evidence that would support such propositions. An example they presented provides an opportunity to consider the validation of performance-level scores and the validity research design implications of these types of score interpretations. In this example, the testing context was a district-wide fourth-grade reading test where student performance was classified into one of two groups, pass or fail. The implied interpretation of the two classifications was that if the student passed, she/he had met the district's minimum expectations for end of grade 4 reading proficiency. On the other hand, if the student's performance was classified as a fail, the resulting interpretation was that the student had not met the district's minimum requirement for end of grade 4 reading proficiency (see Table 40.3).

Haertel and Lorié (2004) presented five propositions related to these interpretations (see Table 40.4). The propositions highlight the key implications of the two score interpretations as well as the requirements needed to make the two interpretations. These requirements include the link between instruction and district curricula, the availability of the district curricula in a curricular framework, the alignment of the test with a set of content standards identified in the framework, the reliability of the test and the minimization of construct-irrelevant variance, a clear and agreed upon performance standard, and a cut-score accurately aligned with the performance standard. A set of validity evidence that can be used to support these propositions is presented in Table 40.4. Obtaining and providing evidence related to each of these requirements implies that a validity research design needs to be in place that will address the following:

1. *Evidence of the link between instruction and curricula:* This requires that data collection efforts (from a representative sample of schools within a district) address the link between the implemented curricula, instructional methods and the district curricula.

2. *Evidence of teacher and school knowledge about district curricula:* This requires that a district actively communicate the curricular framework to schools and teachers and ensure that there is evidence of the existence and adequacy of such communication.

3. *Evidence of the alignment of the test with a set of content standards identified in the district curricular framework:* Typical evidence of test content alignment with district curricula needs to be supplemented with other validity evidence that includes information about the cognitive demands and complexity of assessment tasks as well as about the alignment of such aspects of assessment tasks with district curricular goals.

TABLE 40.2. Standard Setting Procedures for Performance Assessments

Method	Advantages/Disadvantages
Extended Angoff (Hambleton & Plake, 1995; Loomis & Bourque, 2001): Panelists make judgments about expected score on an item for a borderline examinee. For each item an average of the panelists' performance estimates are calculated. The cut-score is the aggregation of these per item averages. These averages can be simple averages or can be weighted by item according to a weighting function that can be determined by the panelists.	**Advantages**: Its simplicity and its allowance for differential weighting of items depending on judges' item importance ratings. **Disadvantages:** The performance on the test is viewed as compartmentalized at the item level.
Estimated Mean, Expected Score Distribution (Loomis & Bourque, 2001): It is similar to the Extended Angoff method but requires the judges to estimate the distribution of borderline examinees at each of the performance levels.	**Advantages:** It can potentially provide information about the performance of borderline examinees. **Disadvantage:** Estimation of the distribution of borderline examinees can be complicated for the panelists.
Item-Mapping (Bookmark)(Mitzel et al., 2001): It is based on an IRT-based scaling of items or tasks. The panelists are asked to decide the expected performance level of the examinees in each of the performance levels.	**Advantages:** Simplifies the panelists' tasks by presenting the items ordered according to difficulty based on the IRT scaling. **Disadvantages:** The role of displaying performance data in determining the performance standards is unknown.
Contrasting Groups (Cohen, Kane & Crooks, 1999): This method utilizes test performance information for the same set of examinees based on two tests or two sets of performance information. The two score distributions for examinees who are classified in each performance level score category are compared and score points that optimally distinguish between performance level scores are selected as performance standards.	**Advantages:** One set of performance information is typically teachers' judgment of students' expected performance. As a result, teachers tend to view this procedure positively. **Disadvantages:** First, in setting standards there is reliance on performance information without a consideration of test characteristics. Second, the degree to which performances on two tests (or judgments) are comparable is questionable, especially when tests are administered for different purposes and/or in different formats (e.g., classroom assessment and large-scale assessment).
Examinee Paper Selection: Panelists select actual examinee papers that demonstrate the expected level of performance of borderline examinees for each item. The scores on the selected papers are averaged and are used as the minimum passing value for each performance level for each item. The minimum values are then summed to determine each cut-score.	**Advantages:** Focusing on actual examinee products is appealing to panelists. **Disadvantages:** One of the challenges of this method is having the range of examinee papers that are illustrative of all performance levels.
Holistic (Booklet) (Jaeger & Mills, 2001; Kingston, Kahl, Sweeney, & Bay, 2001): The focus is the examinee's performance on all of the test items rather than a single test item; otherwise it is very similar to the Examinee Paper Selection method.	**Advantages:** The use of an examinee's actual papers is an advantage. In addition, an examinee's performance is observed on a set of items rather than on just a single item. **Disadvantages:** This method, which requires an evaluation of examinee performance over a large number of items, can be cognitively very challenging for the panelists.
Analytical Method (Plake & Hambleton, 2001): Performance on each section of the assessment is reviewed and classified into performance levels by the panelists. The ratings across the panelists are compared and discussed. The performance standards are calculated by using the average scores of papers assigned to the boundary categories.	**Advantages:** This method is appealing to panelists because it allows them to make judgments based on actual student responses or products. **Disadvantages:** The method is challenging in that assigning student papers to borderline categories requires fine judgments by the panelists.
Dominant Profile Method (Plake, Hambleton, & Jaeger, 1997): This method is based on a consensus-building approach and is typically applied to tests with a small number of items and two performance categories. The panelists' task is to generate the decision rule (pass/fail) that determines which scores across items are the minimum required for a pass decision. Panelists are asked to create their initial decision rules for passing independently. These decisions are then considered, modified, and discussed by the panelists until a consensus about the pass/fail decision criterion is reached.	**Advantage:** This method provides panelists flexibility in identifying the decision rule for passing. **Disadvantage:** The critical aspect of this method, achieving consensus among the panelists, is not always easy to achieve.
Judgmental Policy Capturing Method (Jaeger, 1995): Panelists examine the profiles of student performance scores across a set of items, typically no more than 10 because a consideration of students' performance across items to develop profiles is complex and demanding. Performance score profiles are rank-ordered from highest to lowest, and panelists specify the lowest overall performance score necessary to pass an assessment.	**Advantage:** This method is multidimensional in that panelists make judgments of performance on the basis of multiple criteria. **Disadvantages:** This method requires extensive training of panelists in order that they understand the scoring criteria for each item. Further, the criteria to set cut-scores or to assign performance profiles to categories may be multidimensional in nature.
Direct Judgment Method (Hambleton et al., 2001): This method is similar to the Judgmental Policy Capturing method in that it requires panelists to examine the profiles of student performance across a set of items. To determine the performance level deemed to be a pass, however, panelists must determine the weight that is to be assigned to each of the assessment tasks.	**Advantage:** Panelists express very high confidence in the performance standards produced using this method, in which weights define the relative importance of the assessment tasks. **Disadvantage:** Panelists require extensive training in order to complete the challenging task of identifying performance standards on the basis of profiles of examinees' performances.

TABLE 40.3. Interpretation of Performance on the Fourth-Grade Reading Test

Testing Context	Decision	Interpretation
Fourth-grade reading test	Pass	Met the district's minimum expectations for reading proficiency at the end of fourth grade
	Fail	Has not met the district's minimum expectations for reading proficiency at the end of fourth grade

4. *The reliability of the test and the minimization of the construct-irrelevant variance:* This evidence should include information about the generalizability of scores across tasks, raters, and item types (Brennan, 1983; Candell & Ercikan, 1994; Cronbach, Gleser, Nanda, & Rajaratnam, 1972). Such evidence, which requires an elaborate generalizability study, needs to be part of the initial assessment design rather than applied as an afterthought. Minimization of construct-irrelevant variance can include evidence from sensitivity reviews of test items and analyses of differential item functioning.

5. *A clear and agreed upon performance standard:* This requires documentation and analyses of the standard setting procedures, as well as evidence of meaningfulness and clarity of performance standards for educational practitioners.

6. *A cut-score that is accurately aligned with the performance standard:* This evidence is related to the degree to which student performance is accurately and meaningfully classified into performance levels as well as the degree to which these performance levels correspond to performance standards.

The example described by Haertel and Lorié (2004) and discussed earlier can be expanded easily to include larger numbers of performance score levels. The types of validity arguments and evidence that can be expected with larger numbers of performance score levels will be similar to those for fewer levels, but with appropriate modifications to include evidence to justify the finer distinctions among student performance levels.

TABLE 40.4. Propositions in Interpretations of Scores and Validity Evidence

Proposition	Validity Evidence
1. Content Standards—Elementary reading instruction in the district is guided by a clear description of the intended content of the reading curriculum. The description might be found in a state or local curriculum framework.	A clear description of the domain of reading skills the test was intended to measure Evidence that the domain matched the curriculum framework used by the district Documentation of a sound test development process
2. Alignment—The content of the reading test is well aligned with the content standards.	An evaluation that the development was successful
3. Accuracy and Precision—Reading test scores accurately reflect examinees' reading proficiency. The test is sufficiently reliable and scores are not unduly influenced by motivation, test wiseness, or other extraneous factors.	Evidence of test reliability Evidence of minimal construct-irrelevant variance 　Test is administered under standardized conditions 　Examinees are motivated to show their best work 　Examinees are not excessively anxious 　Test is not unduly speeded 　Item formats are familiar to examinees 　Items are not amenable to guessing 　Test vocabulary is at an appropriate level 　Performance is not unduly affected by students' background 　Test is free from bias
4. Performance Standard—There is an agreement with regard to the minimum acceptable level of reading proficiency for students at the end of fourth grade, which is described in terms of specific reading tasks within an outcome domain. The outcome domains are closely tied with content standards.	Evidence that the proficiencies are drawn from the content standards and are measured by the test Evidence that the standard setting was defensible as a legitimate exercise of authority The test score scale must be criterion referenced so that an examinee's capabilities are accurately identified There are low levels of false positives and false negatives
5. Cut Score—The cut score is established that accurately differentiates between students who have met the performance standard and those who have not.	The cut score is set at an appropriate level, which is neither too low or too high

Guidelines Regarding Accuracy of Classifying Student Performance to Performance Levels

Validity of performance level score reporting is closely tied to the accuracy of such scores. In performance level score reporting, student performance is classified into one of a number of performance levels. Previous research has shown that one of the factors that determine the accuracy of these classifications is a test's measurement accuracy (Hambleton & Slater, 1997; Livingston & Lewis, 1995; Traub & Rowley, 1980), particularly measurement accuracy at cut-score points. The closer scores are to cut-scores, the greater the likelihood that misclassification errors will take place. In most large-scale assessments, there are multiple performance levels and cut-scores, which means that a larger proportion of students have scores close to cut-scores than if there were only two proficiency levels. Therefore, with larger numbers of proficiency levels, lower classification accuracies should be expected. Ercikan and Julian (2002) provided information about the classification accuracies that can be expected from tests with certain measurement accuracies and numbers of performance levels; namely, that classification accuracy decreases on average by 0.1 points for an increase of one performance level, 0.2 for an increase of two performance levels, and 0.2 to 0.3 for an increase of three performance levels. These guidelines indicate that when the desired level of classification accuracy is 0.90 for two performance levels, a minimum reliability of 0.85 is needed. For higher numbers of performance levels, a reliability estimate of 0.95 or higher would be needed for the same classification accuracy level. Thus, a classification accuracy of 0.90 would be highly unlikely for four or more performance levels. The research conducted by Ercikan and Julian also demonstrated that classification accuracy can be dramatically different for examinees of different ability levels. Comparing classification accuracy across tests, therefore, could be deceptive, because classification accuracy may be higher for one test for certain score ranges and lower for others. This type of limitation of the accuracy of performance level scores has serious implications, especially when these scores are used for high-stakes decision making. These authors recommended that classification accuracy be reported separately for different score ranges, particularly for a set of critical score ranges where classification accuracy is deemed important.

CONCLUSIONS

This chapter has described developments in assessment design, practices, and models. The first three sections of the chapter focused on assessments that support learning.

These assessments are intended to assess constructs that are related directly to learning as well as to provide types of scores that are informative in different learning environments. Although considerable effort is being made to develop assessments for accountability purposes, these efforts are not necessarily moving assessment in a positive direction. Instead of focusing attention on such efforts, therefore, the first part of this chapter focused on the factors that are necessary for large-scale assessments and formative classroom assessments to support learning and to be effective. These types of assessments are expected to move assessment practice in classrooms as well as at large-scale levels closer to learning and instruction.

The section on evidence centered design was intended to describe and to model the design of assessments of constructs that are desirable instructional and curricular goals but are also complex in nature. These types of assessments have the potential of moving education forward in an important way in many curricular areas by not reducing these constructs into more easily assessed but less educationally desirable outcomes.

The psychometric models are integral components of assessment practices, and advances in assessment cannot be made without parallel developments in these models. Fortunately, with advances in statistical estimation and computer technologies over the past 10 years, there has been immense progress in the development and application of models that can be used to create scores that are informative in learning environments. Most of these models, however, need to be tested and examined for a wider array of assessment purposes. As a consequence, there is a tremendous amount of research needed in this area.

Research on validity has been one of the most influential forces in changing assessment practices. Since Messick's work on validity (Messick, 1989), which emphasized a unified notion of validity, it has been no longer appropriate to talk about assessments having high degrees of content validity and low degrees of construct validity. These aspects of validity are interrelated, and interpretations of scores are affected by all aspects of validity. Similarly, the developments in the area of validity that have been reviewed in this chapter are expected to affect the way tests are developed and scores are interpreted. Developments resulting from investigations of comparability of constructs assessed for groups have broadened the types of fairness and validity questions that are typically asked. The focus on identifying sources of DIF has made it explicit that there can be multiple sources of DIF, and therefore multiple sources of error and bias in assessments. Findings from research on comparability of constructs in multiple language versions of assessments have indicated that there are large differences in constructs assessed by different language versions of tests and have pointed to serious limitations in interpretability of scores from these assessments (Ercikan, 2002, 2003; Ercikan & Koh, 2005). All of these findings call into question current methodologies used in scaling international assessments and interpretations of scores from such assessments.

The methodologies used to examine student cognitive processes and to identify task cognitive complexity have the potential of moving our assessment practices forward in a way that goes beyond a focus on the surface features of tasks and tests. Baxter and Glaser's work (Baxter & Glaser, 1998, 2002) on the cognitive complexity of tasks showed how to target assessment tasks to assess certain content but be able to tap desired levels of cognitive complexity as well. This research has taught us that item formats (e.g., open-ended questions) do not necessarily tap higher levels of cognitive complexity and that we need to look more closely at characteristics of test items in order to examine the types of cognitive complexity being tapped. Ercikan's research (Ercikan, 1998, 2002, 2003) on comparability of test items in different languages has shown that the vocabulary, style, and format in which items are presented can affect what the items assess as well as its difficulty.

Student scores are one of the most important components of an assessment. The last section of the chapter deals with the types of scores that are used most commonly in present-day large-scale assessments. The methods used in creating these scores as well as issues regarding the validity and reliability of these scores were discussed. The use of appropriate standard setting procedures was shown to be key to creating accurate and meaningful performance level scores. The wide range of methods presented in this section should provide readers with guidance in identifying appropriate methodologies for their specific assessment contexts. Finally, validity and accuracy of performance level scores were emphasized and attention was drawn to two issues. One is that even the simplest interpretations of scores, such as pass/fail, have associated with them a wide range of validity arguments that require extensive research efforts to provide supporting evidence. The other is that notions of accuracy are different for performance level scores than for raw scores or IRT-based scale scores even though performance level scores may be based on such scores.

The developments in assessment of student learning during the past 10 years continued to be at the center of educational research, policy, and attention. In the next decade, some of these developments are expected to find further applications and refinements, and others will be replaced by issues, methods, and focus that will be determined by information needs of the day. In the past decade, two primary needs have driven the research and efforts in this area. One has been the accountability for schools, and the other has been desires to improve learning in substantive areas. In the next decade, neither of these needs is likely to go away; however, developments in other areas such as educational psychology, computer technology, and changes in views of successful schooling may lead to a different set of assessment efforts and research on assessment. To match such an expected development, assessments are expected to pay closer attention to cognitive requirements of test items, a closer attention to classroom processes beyond performance on a standardized achievement test, and production of immediate assessment information based on automated item and task development and scoring.

ACKNOWLEDGMENTS

Sections of this chapter were written while on leave at the Eastern Mediterranean University, Turkish Republic of Northern Cyprus. I thank Peter Seixas, who helped me develop the example on historical literacy assessments by providing me resources on historical thinking, having discussions about assessing historical thinking, and making comments and corrections on a draft version of this chapter. Similarly, I acknowledge Peter Lee for reviewing parts of the chapter and making comments and a correction. I also thank Phil Winne and the two external reviewers Mark Gierl and Barbara Plake for their wonderful, specific, and constructive comments.

References

Adams, R. J., Wilson, M., and Wang, W.-C. (1997). The multidimensional random coefficients multinomial logit model. *Applied Psychological Measurement, 21,* 1–23.

Allalouf, A., Hambleton, R., & Sireci, S. (1999). Identifying the causes of translation DIF on verbal items. *Journal of Educational Measurement, 36,* 185–198.

Baxter, G. P., and Glaser, R. (1998). Investigating the cognitive complexity of science assessments. *Educational Measurement: Issues and Practice, 17,* 37–45.

Bennett, R. E. (1999). Using new technology to improve assessment. *Educational Measurement: Issues and Practice, 18,* 5–12.

Black, P., & Wiliam, D. (1998). Inside the black box: Raising standards through classroom assessment. *Phi Delta Kappan, 80*, 139–148.

Brennan, R. L. (1983). *The elements of generalizability theory.* Iowa City, LA: American College Testing Program.

Brookhart, S. M., & DeVoge, J. G. Testing a theory about the role of classroom assessment in student motivation and achievement. *Applied Measurement in Education, 12*, 409–426.

Bryke, A. S., & Raudenbush, S. (1992). *Hierarchical linear models: Application and data analysis methods.* Newbury Park, England: Sage.

Candell, G., & Ercikan, K. (1994). On the generalizability of school-level performance assessment scores. *International Journal of Educational Research, 21*, 267–278.

Chappuis, S., & Stiggins, R. J. (2002). Classroom assessment for learning. *Educational Leadership, 60*, 1–5.

Chudowsky, N., & Pellegrino, J. W. (2003). Large-scale assessments that support learning: What will it take. *Theory Into Practice, 42*, 75–84.

Cizek, C. J. (2001). *Setting performance standards concepts, methods, and perspectives.* Mahwah, NJ: Lawrence Erlbaum Associates.

Cohen, A., Kane, M. T., & Crooks, T. J. (1999). A generalized examinee centered method for setting standards on achievement tests. *Applied Measurement in Education, 12*, 343–366.

Cronbach, L. J., Gleser, G. C., Nanda, H., & Rajaratnam, N. (1972). *The dependability of behavioural measurements: Theory of generalizability for scores and profiles.* New York: Wiley.

DiBello, L. V., Stout, W. F., & Roussos, L. A. (1995). Unified cognitive/psychometric diagnostic assessment likelihood-based classification techniques. In P. D. Nichols, S. F. Chipman, & R. L. Brennan (Eds.), *Cognitively diagnostic assessment.* Hillsdale, NJ: Lawrence Erlbaum Associates.

Douglas, J., Roussos, L., & Stout, W. (1996). Item-bundle DIF hypothesis testing: Identifying suspect bundles and assessing their differential functioning. *Journal of Educational Measurement, 33*, 465–484.

Embretson, S. E. (1985). Multicomponent latent trait models for test design. In Embretson, S. E. (Ed.), *Test design: Developments in psychology and psychometrics* (pp. 195–218). Hillsdale, NJ: Lawrence Erlbaum Associates.

Embretson, S. E. (1991). A multidimensional latent trait model for measuring learning and change. *Psychometrika, 56*, 495–515.

Embretson, S. E. (1995a). A measurement model for linking individual learning to process and knowledge: application to mathematical reasoning. *Journal of Educational Measurement, 32*, 277–294.

Embretson, S. E. (1995b). Developments toward a cognitive design system for psychological tests. In Lubinski, D. and Dawis, R. V. (Eds.), *Assessing individual differences in human behavior: New concepts, methods and findings.* Palo Alto CA: Davies-Black.

Embretson, S. E. (1999). *Generating items during testing: Psychometric issues and problems.* Presidential Address at the 1999 European Meeting of the Psychometric Society, Lüneburg, Germany.

Ercikan, K. (1998). Translation effects in international assessments. *International Journal of Educational Research, 29*, 543–553.

Ercikan, K. (2002). Disentangling sources of differential item functioning in multi-language assessments. *International Journal of Testing, 2*, 199–215.

Ercikan, K. (2003). Are the English and French versions of the Third International Mathematics and Science Study administered in Canada comparable? Effects of adaptations. *International Journal of Educational Policy, Research and Practice, 4*, 55–76.

Ercikan, K. & Mendes-Barnett, S. (2003, April). *Disentangling sources of DIF: Interpretation of results from SIBTEST.* Paper presented at the annual meeting of the National Council on Measurement in Education, Chicago, IL.

Ercikan, K., Domene, J. F., Law, D., Arim, R., Gagnon, F., & Lacroix, S. (2004, April). *Identifying sources of DIF using think-aloud protocols: Comparing thought processes of examinees taking tests in English versus in French.* Paper presented at the annual meeting of the National Council on Measurement in Education, San Diego, CA.

Ercikan, K., & Julian, M. (2002). Classification accuracy of assigning student performance to proficiency levels: Guidelines for assessment design. *Applied Measurement in Education, 15*, 269–294.

Ercikan, K., & Koh, K. (2005). Construct comparability of the English and French versions of TIMSS. *International Journal of Testing, 5*, 23–35.

Ercikan, K., Schwarz, R., Julian, M., Burket, G., Weber, M., & Link, V. (1998). Calibration and scoring of tests with multiple-choice and constructed-response item types. *Journal of Educational Measurement, 35*, 137–155.

Ericsson, K. A., & Simon, H. A. (1984). *Protocol analysis: Verbal reports as data.* Cambridge, MA: MIT Press.

Fischer, G. H. (1995). Linear logistic models for change. In G. H. Fisher and I. W. Molenaar (Eds.), *Rasch models: Foundation, recent development, and applications.* New York: Springer-Verlag.

Fitzpatrick, A. R., Ercikan, K., Yen, W., & Ferrara, S. (1998). The consistency between ratings collected in different test years. *Applied Measurement in Education, 11*, 195–208.

Fraser, C., & McDonald, R. P. (1988). NOHARM: Least squares in item factor analysis. *Multivariate Behavioral Research, 23*, 267–269.

Gierl, M., & Khaliq, S. (2001). Identifying sources of differential item and bundle functioning on translated achievement tests: A confirmatory analysis. *Journal of Educational Measurement, 38*, 164–187.

Gipps, C. (1999). Socio-cultural aspects of assessment. *Review of Research in Education, 24*, 355–392.

Glaser, R., & Baxter, G. P. (2002). Cognition and construct validity: Evidence for the nature of cognitive performance in assessment situations. In H. Braun, D. Jackson, & D. Wiley (Eds), *The Role of Constructs in Psychological and Educational Measurement* (pp. 179–191). Mahwah, NJ: Erlbaum.

Haertel, E., H., & Lorie, W. A. (2004). Validating standards-based test score interpretations. *Measurement: Interdisciplinary Research and Perspectives, 2*, 61-104.

Hambleton, R. K. (1996). Advances in assessment models, methods, and practices. In D. C. Berliner & R. C. Calfee, (Eds.), *Handbook of educational psychology* (pp. 889-925). New York: American Council on Education/Macmillan.

Hambleton, R. K., Jaeger, R. M., Mills, C. N., & Plake, B. S. (2001). *Handbook of methods for setting performance standards on complex performance assessments.* Washington DC: Chief Council on State School Officers.

Hambleton, R. K., Jaeger, R. M., Plake, B. S., & Mills, C. (2000). Setting performance standards on complex educational assessments. *Applied Psychological Measurement, 24*, 355-366.

Hambleton, R. K., & Plake, B. S. (1995). Using an extended Angoff procedure to set standards on complex performance assessments. *Applied Measurement in Education, 8*, 41-55.

Hambleton, R. K., & Slater, S. C. (1997). Reliability of credentialing examinations and the impact of scoring models and standard setting policies. *Applied Measurement in Education, 10*, 19-39.

Hamilton, L. S., Nussbaum, E. M., & Snow, R. E. (1997). Interveiw procedures for validating sience assessments. *Applied Measurement in Education, 10*, 181-200.

Holland, P. W., & Thayer, D. T. (1988). Differential item performance and Mantel-Haenszel. In H. Wainer & H. Braun (Eds.), *Test validity* (pp. 129-145). Hillsdale NJ: Lawrence Erlbaum Associates.

Jaeger, R. M. (1995). Setting performance standards through two-stage judgmental policy capturing. *Applied Measurement in Education, 8*, 15-40.

Jaeger, R. M., & Mills, C. N. (2001). An integrated judgment procedure for setting standards on complex large-scale assessments. In G. J. Cizek (Ed.), *Standard-setting: Concepts, methods, and perspectives.* Mahwah NJ: Lawrence Erlbaum Associates.

Janssen, R. and de Boeck, P. (1997). Psychometric modeling of componentially designed synonym tasks. *Applied Psychological Measurement, 21*, 37-50.

Jöreskog, K. G., & Sörbom, D. (1979). *Advances in factor analysis and structural equation models.* Cambridge, MA: Abt Books.

Junker, B. (1999). *Some statistical models and computational methods that may be useful for cognitively relevant assessment.* Paper prepared for the National Research Council Committee on the Foundations of Assessment. Retrieved August 2, 2004, from http://www.stat.cmu.edu/~brian/nrc/cfa/.

Kingston, N. M., Kahl, S. R., Sweney, K. P., & Bay, L. (2001). Setting performance standads using the body of work method. In G. J. Cizek (Ed.), *Standard-setting: Concepts, methods, and perspectives.* Mahwah, NJ: Lawrence Erlbaum Associates.

Lane, S. (2004, April). *Validity of high-stakes assessment: Are students engaged in complex thinking?* Presidential address at the annual meeting of the National Council on Measurement in Education, Chicago.

Lane, L., Wang, N., & Magone, M. (1996). Gender-related differential item functioning on a middle-school mathematics performance assessment. *Educational Measurement: Issues and Practice, 15*, 21-28.

Latham, A. S., Gitomer, D., & Ziomek, R. (1999). What the tests tell us about new teachers. *Educational Leadership, 56*, 23-26.

Lee, J. (2004). How feasible is Adequate Yearly Progress (AYP)? Simulations of school AYP "Uniform Averaging" and "Safe Harbor" under the No Child Left Behind Act. Education Policy Analysis Archives, 12. Retrieved August 6, 2004, from http://epaa.asu.edu/epaqa/ v12n14/

Lee, P. J., & Shemilt, D. (2003). Progression and progression models in history. *Teaching History, 113*, 13-23.

Lee, P. (2001). Learning history: Principles into practice. In *How students learn: History, math, and science in the classroom, National Research Council.* Washington, DC: National Academies Press.

Leucht, R. M. (2001, April). *Challenges of Web-based assessment.* Paper presented at the annual meeting of the National Council on Measurement in Education, Seattle, WA.

Linden, W. J. van der, & Glas, A. W. (2000). *Computerized adaptive testing: Theory and practice.* Dordrecht, The Netherlands: Kluwer-Nijhoff.

Linn, R. L. (2003). Accountability: Responsibility and reasonable expectations. *Educational Researcher, 32*, 3-13.

Linn, R. L., Baker, E. L., & Betebenner, D. W. (2002). Accountability systems: Implications of requirements of the No Child Left Behind Act 2001. *Educational Researcher, 31*, 3-16.

Linn, R. L., & Harnisch, D. L. (1981). Interactions between item content and group membership on achievement test items. *Journal of Educational Measurement, 18*, 109-118.

Linn, R. L., & Haug, C. (2002). Stability of school-building accountability scores and gains. *Educational Evaluation and Policy Analysis, 24*, 29-36.

Livingston, S. A., & Lewis, C. (1995). Estimating the consistency and accuracy of classifications based on test scores. *Journal of Educational Measurement, 32*, 179-198.

Loomis, S. C., & Bourque, M. L. (2001). From tradition to innovation: Standard setting on the National Assessment of Educational Progress. In G. J. Cizek (Ed.), *Standard-setting: Concepts, methods, and perspectives.* Mahwah, NJ: Lawrence Erlbaum Associates.

Lord, F. M. (1980). *Applications of item response theory to practical testing problems.* Hillsdale, NJ: Lawrence Erlbaum Associates.

Magone, M. E., Cai, J., Silver, E. A., & Wang, N. (1994). Validating the cognitive complexity and content validity of a mathematics performance assessment. *International Journal of Educational Research, 21*, 317-340.

Maryland State Board of Education (1995). *Maryland school performance report: State and school systems.* Baltimore, MD: Author.

Melnick, S. J., & Pullin, D. (2000). Can you take dictation? Prescribing teacher quality through testing. *Journal of Teacher Education, 51*, 262-275.

Memory, D. M., Antes, R. L., Corey, N. R., & Chaney, D. E. (2001). Should tougher basic skills requirements be viewed as a means of strengthening the teaching force? *Journal of Personnel Evaluation in Education, 15*, 181-191.

Messick, S. (1989). Validity. In R. L. Linn (Ed.), *Educational Measurement* (3rd) (pp. 13-103). New York: American Council on Education and Macmillan.

Mislevy, R. J., Steinberg, L. S., & Almond, R. G. (2002). On the structure of educational assessments. *Measurement: Interdisciplinary Research and Perspectives, 1*, 3-63.

Mitchell, R., & Barth, P. (1999). How teacher licensing tests fall short. *Thinking K-16, 3*, 3-23.

Mitzel, H. D., Lewis, D. M., Patz, R. J., & Green, D. R. (2001). The bookmark procedure: Cognitive perspectives on standard setting. In G. J. Cizek (Ed.), *Standard-setting: Concepts, methods, and perspectives*. Mahwah, NJ: Lawrence Erlbaum Associates.

Mislevy, R., Wilson, M., Ercikan, K., & Chudowski, N. (2002). Psychometric principles in student evaluation. In D. Nevo & D. Stufflebeam (Eds.), *International handbook of educational evaluation* (pp. 478-520). Dordrecht, The Netherlands: Kluwer Academic.

Muraki, E., & Carlson, J. E. (1995). Full-information factor analysis for polytomous item responses. *Applied Psychological Measurement, 19*, 73-90.

Muthen, B. O., & Khoo, S. T. (1998). Longitudinal studies of achievement growth using latent variable modeling. *Learning and Individual Differences, 10*, 73-101.

National Research Council. (2001). *Knowing what students know: The science and design of educational assessment*. J. W. Pellegrino, N. Chudowsky, & R. Glaser (Eds.). Washington, DC: National Academy Press.

O'Neill, K. A., & McPeek, W. M. (1993). Item and test characteristics that are associated with differential item functioning. In P. W. Holland & H. Wainer (Eds.), *Differential item functioning* (pp. 255-276). Hillsdale, NJ: Lawrence Erlbaum Associates.

Pearson, P. D., Calfee, R., Walker Webb, P. L., & Fleischer, S. (2002). *The role of performance-based assessments in large-scale accountability systems: Lessons learned from the inside*. Washington, DC: Council of Chief State School Officers.

Pellegrino, J. W., Baxter, G. P., & Glaser, R. (1999). Addressing the "two disciplines" problem: Linking theories of cognition and learning with assessment and instructional practice. *Review of Research in Education, 24*, 307-353.

Pirolli, P., & Wilson, M. (1998). A theory of the measurement of knowledge content, access, and learning. *Psychological Review, 105*, 58-82.

Plake, B. S., & Hambleton, R. K. (2000). A standard setting method designed for complex performance assessments: Categorical assignments of student work. *Educational Assessment, 6*, 197-215.

Plake, B. S., Hambleton, R. K., & Jaeger, R. M. (1997). A new standard setting method for performance assessments: The dominant profile judgment method and some field test results. *Educational and Psychological Measurement, 57*, 400-412.

Plake, B. S., & Hambleton, R. K. (2001). The analytic judgement method for setting standards on complex performance assessments. In G. J. Cizek (Ed.), Standard-setting: Concepts methods, and perspectives. Hillsdale NJ: Erlbaum, 283-312.

Popham, W. J. (2003). The seductive allure of data. *Educational Leadership, 60*, 48-52.

Raudenbush, S. W., Bryke, A. S., & Congdon, R. T. (1999). *Hierarchial linear modeling* 5 [computer program]. Lincolnwood, IL: Scientific Software.

Reckase, M. D. (1985). The difficulty of test items that measure more than one ability. *Applied Psychological Measurement, 9*, 401-412.

Roussos, L., & Stout, W. (1996). A multidimensionality based DIF analysis paradigm. *Applied Psychological Measurement, 20*, 355-371.

Scheuneman, J. D., & Geritz, K. (1990). Using differential item functioning procedures to explore sources of item difficulty and group performance characteristics. *Journal of Educational Measurement, 27*, 09-131.

Schmitt, A. P., & Dorans, N. J. (1990). Differential item functioning for minority examinees on the SAT. *Journal of Educational Measurement, 27*, 67-81.

Seixas, P., & Peck, C. (2004). Teaching historical thinking. In A. Sears and I. Wright (Eds.), *Challenges and prospects for Canadian social studies* (pp. 109-117). Vancouver: Pacific Educational Press.

Shealy, R., & Stout, W. (1993). An item response theory model for test bias. In P. Holland & H. Wainer (Eds.), *Differential item functioning* (pp. 197-239) Hillsdale, NJ: Lawrence Erlbaum Associates.

Shepard, L. A. (2000). The role of assessment in a learning culture. *Educational Researcher, 29*, 4-14.

Sireci, G. S., Fitzgerald, C., & Xing, D. (1998). *Adapting credentialing examinations for international uses*. Laboratory of Psychometric and Evaluative Research Report No. 329. Amherst, MA: University of Massachusetts, School of Education.

Smith, M., & O'Day, J. (1997). Systemic school reform. In S. Fuhrman & B. Malen (Eds.), *The politics of curriculum and testing*. London: Falmer.

Stegelmann, W. (1983). Expanding the Rasch model to a general model having more than one dimension. *Psychometrika, 48*, 259-267.

Stiggins, R. J. (1997). *Student-centered classroom assessment*. Old Tappan, NJ: Prentice-Hall.

Stout, W., & Roussos, L. (1995). *SIBTEST Manual*. Urbana, IL: University of Illinois, Department of Statistics, Statistical Laboratory for Educational and Psychological Measurement.

Swanson, D. B., Clauser, B. E., Case, S. M., Nungester, R. J., & Featherman, C. (2002). Analysis of Differential Item Functioning (DIF) using hierarchical logistic regression models. *Journal of Educational and Behavioral Statistics, 27,* 53–77.

Tatsuoka, K. K. (1990). Toward an integration of item response theory and cognitive error diagnosis. In N. Fredriksen, R. Glaser, A. Lesgold, & M. G. Shafto (Eds.), *Diagnostic monitoring of skill and knowledge acquisition.* Hillsdale, NJ: Lawrence Erlbaum Associates.

Traub, R. E., & Rowley, G. L. (1980). Reliability of test scores and decisions. *Applied Psychological Measurement, 4,* 517–545.

U.S. Department of Education (2002). No Child Left Behind Act of 2001, Public Law 107-110, 115 Stat. 1425 (2002).

Willet, J., & Sayer, A. (1994). Using covariance structure analysis to detect correlates and predictors of individual change over time. *Psychological Bulletin, 116,* 363–380.

Wilson, D., Wood, R. L., & Gibbons, R. (1983). TESTFACT: test scoring and item factor analysis. [Computer program] Chicago: Scientific Software.

Wilson, M., & Adams, R. J. (1996). Evaluating progress with alternative assessments: A model for Title I. In M. B. Kane (Ed.), *Implementing performance assessment: Promise, problems and challenges* (pp. 39–61). Hillsdale, NJ: Lawrence Erlbaum Associates.

Wilson, M., & Sloane, K. (2000). From principles to practice: An embedded assessment system. *Applied Measurement in Education, 13,* 181–208.

Wu, M., Adams, R. J., & Wilson, M. (1998). ACER *ConQuest* [computer program]. Hawthorn, Australia: Australian Council on Educational Research.

Zwick, R. (2000). The assessment of differential item functioning in computer-adaptive tests. In W. J. van der Linden & C. A. W. Glas (Eds.), *Computerized adaptive testing: Theory and practice* (pp. 221–244). Dordrecht, The Netherlands: Kluwer-Nijhoff.

Zwick, R., Donoghue, J. R., & Grima, A. (1993). Assessment of differential item functioning for performance tasks. *Journal of Educational Measurement, 30*(3), 233–251.

·41·

ASSESSMENT OF TEACHER LEARNING
AND DEVELOPMENT

Carol Kehr Tittle
City University of New York

This chapter considers assessment of teacher learning and development from a particular perspective: What assessment procedures have been used in research and development studies of classroom teachers working to change their practice? These studies may be: (a) reform-focused research and development projects, such as teaching mathematics; or (b) smaller-scale studies focused on particular aspects of teacher learning, such as knowledge of content. The purpose in examining these studies, and related studies within the expert/novice tradition, is to provide examples of methods and procedures used in the *context of assessing teacher learning and development*. The selected studies provide examples of assessments in areas that have developed in research on teaching within the subject matters (Berliner & Calfee, 1996; Richardson, 2001).

For the purposes of this chapter, assessment examples are grouped within two main areas of research: (a) teacher subject matter or content knowledge, and related topics, including pedagogical content knowledge (Shulman, 1986), that is, teacher content knowledge for teaching a subject (Hill, Schilling, & Ball, 2004); and (b) teacher development. A third section, "A Special Case: NBPTS," examines selected issues and emerging research related to the National Board for Professional Teaching Standards. These research and assessment examples are particularly relevant for educational psychologists, since they represent a coming together of research on teaching the subject matters, cognitive psychology, and sociocultural, interpretive perspectives. Further, examining the details of

how different researchers assess teacher knowledge, for example, provides a basis for selecting among alternative methods.

The use of research studies for this chapter also identifies what the chapter omits. The chapter does not describe teacher assessments that have been developed for licensure or certification purposes. Porter, Youngs, and Odden (2001) have a comprehensive, comparative and technical review of past, continuing, and new approaches to major assessment programs for teacher licensure and certification at the national, state and district levels. Included at the national level are the *Praxis Series* (Educational Testing Service), INTASC (Interstate New Teacher Assessment and Support Consortium), and the NBPTS (National Board for Professional Teaching Standards). The purpose of these programs is to ascertain teacher status on criteria or standards, rather than the learning and development of licensed and certified practicing teachers (as discussed later).

TEACHER ASSESSMENT AND VALIDITY

This section considers (a) purposes for teacher assessments; (b) teachers themselves as users of assessments; and (c) implications of purposes and teachers as users for collecting validity-related evidence in assessing the learning and development of teachers.

Purposes for Teacher Assessments

Broadly considered, there are three main purposes or categories of use of assessments with teachers: research (explanation/understanding, including evaluation research), instruction (development and changes in teacher knowledge, beliefs, and practice), and licensure and certification.

Research. The use of assessment processes for "research" requires attention to methodology, format, and technical requirements of assessments, including reliability and validity. However, requirements for informed consent before participation help to ensure that there will be no adverse consequences of research assessments for a teacher, personally or professionally. Whereas certification and licensure are intended to provide summative assessments describing attainment of standards or criteria, many of the assessments used in research can be formative in function. That is, in the context of research or evaluation projects for teacher learning and development, assessments can be used to provide feedback and information for the teacher participant to use in evaluating progress toward some desired goal, as well as providing information to researchers.

Assessments designed for use in research can be analyzed for their potential instructional value by examining their interpretations and use by teachers. Teachers can evaluate assessments for researchers on a criterion of usefulness. Further, teacher interpretations and uses of the assessments may be part of the line of evidence justifying the assessments as part of the research and become part of the process to develop validity-related evidence for the assessments themselves. (See "*Validation Processes*," later.)

Teacher Development. The use of assessment processes in the context of professional development suggests that the assessments can be woven into or emerge from a teacher's learning and development activities. In this case the purpose for assessment is primarily formative. This role of assessments is to provide both the teacher-learner and the instructor-program developers with information to adjust—modify and change—the instruction and learning processes. The contexts for these assessments may be formal or informal programs that are intended to support teacher learning and development.

Teachers in these contexts can be described as *in transition*, that is, they are moving along a "passage or evolution from one form, stage, or style to another . . ." (Fennema & Nelson, 1997, p. x). Teacher assessments have a role in this process, just as classroom student assessments play a role in supporting student learning in school. An educational psychology of teacher assessment will focus on teacher learning and the development of teaching practice. Formative assessments serve diagnostic purposes, identifying needed developments, and summative assessments indicate attainment of specific goals (and can be diagnostic as well).

Licensure and Certification. Licensing and certification are broadly defined here to include *selection* for teacher education programs or for teaching positions, and certification or recertification for job retention. These uses place different demands on the assessments of teachers, primarily to meet both psychometric and legal requirements much like those for student tests labeled as "high-stakes" tests (Dwyer & Stufflebeam, 1996; Porter et al., 2001, p. 260).

Whereas licensing is regulatory, certification may be undertaken voluntarily by teachers. Teachers identify themselves as candidates for board certification, to meet "high and rigorous standards for what accomplished teachers should know and be able to do" (National Board for Professional Teaching Standards [NBPTS], 2001, p. 10). Teachers voluntarily undertake a series of assessments in a process designed by and administered by the National Board for Professional Teaching Standards. Porter et al. (2001) provide a thorough review and discussion of assessments currently used for certification purposes. Vandevoort, Amrein-Beardsley, and Berliner (2004) provide a concise history of the NBPTS.

Teachers as Assessment Users

Several perspectives are useful when examining assessments and the characteristics of assessment processes. One framework that has been proposed (Tittle, 1994) takes into account (a) interpreters and users, (b) the epistemology and theories underlying the assessment, such as, on teaching (Donmoyer, 2001) and on teacher development (Richardson & Placier, 2001); and (c) the context of the assessment—in this chapter, teacher participants in a study, the setting of the program, and formats/processes of assessments.

The immediate focus here is on the interpreters and users of assessments of teachers. For each of the purposes of teacher assessments described earlier, the main users of the assessments can be identified. For the use of teacher assessments in *research and evaluation*, the primary users of the assessments are the researchers, those who supported the study, and those in the professional, teacher, or larger communities who access study reports. For the use of teacher assessments in *learning and development* activities, the primary users have been those who design and conduct the formal or informal teacher development programs. For the use of teacher assessments in *licensure and certification*, the primary users are the licensing agency and employers. Certification by the NBPTS may also be used by teachers for professional advancement, as an indicator of professional achievement and recognition, and to expand their expertise into mentoring, coaching other teachers, and leadership positions.

The distinctions between formative and summative uses of teacher assessments were mentioned earlier in the contexts of *research* and *teacher development* programs. The diagnostic use of teacher assessments can mean that the individual teacher participating in an assessment process is an important interpreter and user of teacher assessments, along with research and instruction staff. From the perspective of educational psychology, thinking about the teacher as interpreter and user draws attention to (a) the relevance of current cognitive, sociocultural, and interpretive perspectives for assessments of teachers; (b) the analysis of assessments from a system perspective, and (c) the need for studying the systemic validity of assessments for teacher learning and development (cf. Frederiksen & Collins, 1989). It also focuses attention on existing knowledge, beliefs, and practice, that is, the situated nature of teacher knowledge, as well as on future actions and intents of the teacher user (Goldsmith & Schifter, 1997; Shulman & Shulman, 2004). Professional activities and communities of teachers examining their practice may foster learning and development around the processes used in assessments (e.g., Frederiksen, Sipusic, Sherin, & Wolfe, 1998).

Implications for Validity

Validity-related evidence for tests and assessments is described in the *Standards for Educational and Psychological Testing* (AERA, APA, & NCME, 1999). Two aspects of assessments of teacher learning and development are considered here in relation to the *Standards*: (a) the proposed users of the assessments; and (b) the validation processes and validity-related evidence.

Test Takers and Test Users. The *Standards* (1999) are consistent in drawing distinctions between test takers and test users. Part I, "Test construction, evaluation and documentation," and Part II, "Fairness in testing," are the responsibility of those who develop, market, evaluate, or mandate the administration of tests and the rights and obligations of test takers. In Part III of the *Standards*, "The responsibilities of test users," attention is centered on the responsibilities of those who are considered the *users* of tests, and includes all participants who are involved

actively in interpretation and use of test results, other than the test takers themselves. In Chapters 13 and 14 of Part III, "Educational testing and assessment" and "Testing in employment and credentialing," the test (assessment) taker is distinguished from the test user.

The purposes of assessment in large-scale testing programs in education (for accountability and policy, less often for teacher use; Tittle, 1989) and the uses of standardized tests and assessments in employment settings have often defined the separation of information given to test takers and test users. "Supporting documentation for tests," Chapter 6 in the *Standards*, is concerned that test developers, publishers, and distributors communicate with test users, and, "In addition to technical documentation, descriptive materials are needed in some settings to inform examinees... about the nature and content of the test" (1999, p. 68). Standard 6.8 states that if a test is designed to be scored or interpreted by test takers, evidence should be provided to that effect. In this case, interpretive materials should also be given to the test taker.

In research and development projects for teacher learning and development, the teacher as learner and as transitioning in the development of practice is a different participant in the assessment or testing process than are students or potential employees. Teacher participants typically are voluntary, are motivated to learn, and may be part of teacher learning communities of practice, communities that have been described as part of the context of change (e.g., Franke, Carpenter, Levi, & Fennema, 2001; McLaughlin & Talbert, 2001). Under these conditions it is more accurate to view teachers both as participants (assessment takers) and as assessment users (Frederiksen et al., 1998).

In a different context, that of certification, the NBPTS is an assessment system for certifying accomplished teachers based on high standards. This large-scale assessment system relies partly on a process in which teachers develop samples of their teaching practice to meet NBPTS standards. As discussed later, the effects of this process are starting to be examined. From the view of systemic validity, feedback or interpretive aids that are included need to be expanded both conceptually and methodologically. The validity-related evidence for the assessment system needs to encompass the design and testing of how and what teachers learn from preparing their own materials for assessment evaluation by others, using the language of standards and of assessments.

Validation Processes and Influences on Assessments. "Validity refers to the degree to which evidence and theory support the interpretations of test scores entailed by proposed uses of tests" (1999, p. 9). And, "Validation can be viewed as developing a scientifically sound validity argument to support the intended interpretations of test scores and their relevance to the proposed use" (p. 9). Continuing changes in discussions about validity were reflected in the *Standards* (1999). The *Standards* described different *sources of validity evidence*, to continue the change *from labeling* distinct types of validity, such as content validity, *to emphasizing* a reduced reliance on a single source of validity evidence. Cognitive psychology has been an influence, and there is a broadening of sources of evidence, to include evidence based on (a) test content; (b) response processes—the analyses of individual responses, including questioning an individual or talk-alouds, both for examinees and observers or judges; (c) internal structure; (d) relations to other variables; and (e) consequences of testing. This last category would include evidence on teacher interpretation and use of assessments.

The *Standards* also emphasize that a sound validity argument integrates various strands of evidence into "...a coherent account of the degree to which existing evidence and theory support the intended interpretation of test scores for specific uses" (p. 17). The *Standards* stress that this validation argument ultimately relies on all evidence available—starting from the beginning of the development of a testing or assessment system. With regard to the distinction between tests and assessments, and the procedures to which the *Standards* apply, there are no distinctions when an evaluative device or procedure is used to sample an individual's behavior, and then evaluated and scored using a standardized process (p. 3). The *Standards* also use the term *construct* broadly to indicate "the concept or characteristic that a test is designed to measure" (p. 5). Throughout the discussions of test (assessment) validity there is a stress on theory, evidence, and processes of validation.

Influences on Assessments of Teachers. In studies of teacher learning and development the assessment methods and procedures are influenced by changes in validity theory and forms of assessments (Hambleton, 1996), and by current work and theories in educational psychology and educational research. These theories build on cognitive psychology and concepts of constructivism, as well as sociocultural and interpretive perspectives on learning and development for teachers and for students. Some research and assessment methods are evolving from: (a) work within the expert/novice paradigm; (b) research using cognitive and other analyses of protocols, texts, videotapes, and classroom discourse; and (c) research on discourse and participation in other teacher development interaction situations, such as, using analyses of content, speech, group processes, and professional activities.

The expansion of assessment methods and procedures is also a function of the shift to situate the understanding of teacher knowledge and practice within the subject matters (e.g., Mayer, 2004; Shulman, 1986), and to define constructs such as subject-matter knowledge, pedagogical content knowledge, and explanations. It is also related to the efforts to set higher standards for American schools and to use standards in the assessments of students and teachers. In the professional communities there has been a movement toward teaching and learning for understanding. Major disciplinary professional organizations developed standards, such as the National Council of Teachers of Mathematics (2000) and the National Science Education Standards (National Research Council, 1996). These are widely seen to have supported the efforts for reform and to help define what it means to teach for understanding.

The emphasis on defining constructs used in reform projects, such as teaching for understanding and teacher pedagogical content knowledge, is supported by the *Standards* (1999) discussions of validity-related evidence. The use of multiple strands of evidence and the development of a scientifically sound argument for interpretation of assessments are important to research on teacher learning. For the research and development examples in this chapter, the interpretation of assessments is strongest when there have been efforts (a) to define major constructs; (b) to use several sources of evidence; and (c) to use an evolving theory to support the arguments for interpretation.

The studies in this chapter provide examples of assessments used in research on and evaluations of teacher learning and development. These examples are selective, and many are from research on mathematics teaching and learning. Studies often use multiple assessments, focusing on more than one construct or category of teacher knowledge and practice.

The remainder of this chapter is organized primarily by the constructs that are the focus of assessments in teacher learning and development: (a) teacher knowledge, including teacher pedagogical content knowledge, aspects of classroom practice such as lesson structures and explanations, knowledge of student thinking, knowledge of procedures for evaluating students, and teachers participating/collaborating with researchers in design experiments and video clubs; and (b) teacher development. Teacher development includes (a) longitudinal studies that attempt to characterize the overall change in or state of teachers' practice and beliefs; and (b) teacher learning communities. The last section is "A Special Case: NBPTS." The conclusion identifies the importance of contexts of assessments, technology, and emerging challenges.

ASSESSING TEACHER KNOWLEDGE

Since Shulman published his landmark chapter, *"Paradigms and research programs in the study of teaching"* (Shulman, 1986), research on teaching has continued to expand in many of the theoretical perspectives and research paradigms he identified. Research and assessments of teacher learning and development reflect all the complexities that are inherent in teaching and in attempting to negotiate among different perspectives on teacher knowledge and practice. By 1992, the National Council of Teachers of Mathematics had published an entire volume devoted to mathematics, *Handbook of Research on Mathematics Teaching and Learning* (Grouws, 1992).

The *Handbook of Educational Psychology* (Berliner & Calfee, 1996) had a major section on the school curriculum and psychology, with chapters on a comparative psychology of school subjects, and on teaching and instruction in history, science, mathematics, and literacy, among others. Another major section was teaching and instruction, with chapters on learning to teach, teacher beliefs and knowledge, and teaching and learning in a classroom context. An extensive compendium of research is found in the *Handbook of Research on Teaching, fourth edition* (Richardson, 2001). In the volume there are 51 chapters, including one on teacher assessments, as well as 14 on teaching the subject matters, and five on teachers and teaching, including teacher knowledge of subject matter. Some of the chapters in the present *Handbook* extend those in earlier handbooks.

This section of the chapter includes examples intended to illustrate assessment methods and procedures that have been used in research on teacher knowledge, and often uses examples from research on teaching elementary school mathematics. The section begins with descriptions of the assessments used in three lines of research: (a) the work of Leinhardt and her colleagues using the expert/novice framework in cognitive psychology (e.g., Leinhardt & Smith, 1985) involving videotaping small numbers of classroom teachers identified as experts on the basis of consistently above-average mathematics achievement test scores of their students; (b) the work of Carpenter, Fennema, Peterson, and others on the Cognitively Guided Instruction (CGI) project (e.g., Carpenter, Fennema, Peterson, Chiang, & Loef, 1989), using an experimental design, paper-and-pencil belief and knowledge assessments, classroom observations, case studies, and student achievement measures, in a project to assist teachers to understand research-based knowledge of the development of student thinking in problem solving; and (c) the work building on the Teacher Education and

Learning to Teach (TELT) study (Kennedy, Ball, & McDiarmid, 1993), using structured interviews and paper-and-pencil measures to assess teacher knowledge of mathematics for teaching (Hill, Schilling & Ball, 2004; Ma, 1999) and the relationship of such knowledge to student achievement (Hill, Rowan, & Ball, 2004).

Each of these lines of research has assessments and procedures that are continued in other examples in this section on assessing teacher knowledge and thinking, defined here to include related studies on teachers learning formative assessment strategies, and procedures used by researchers working with teachers to change their classroom practice, whether in design-based research or in video clubs.

Assessments in Expert/Novice Research: Leinhardt and Colleagues

Leinhardt (1993) has described her methodology as a series of steps: (a) deciding on the subject matter (elementary mathematics with an emphasis on subtraction, fractions, and graphing); (b) identifying teachers to work with her for a period of 3 to 10 years—teachers who have had consistently had high student achievement over a period of several years; (c) using a part of the subject matter that is an important part of the curriculum; and (d) eventually observing and videotaping blocks of classroom lessons; (e) interviewing teachers pre- and post lesson; and (f) using other content-related assessment tasks. Several examples of these studies follow.

"Systems" of Teacher Knowledge. An early study (Leinhardt & Smith, 1985) focused on fractions since the subject matter involves complex relationships among the meaning and representations of fractions and basic arithmetic operations. Four expert fourth-grade teachers were identified; two of these experts seemed to have high knowledge of subject matter, one had moderate knowledge, and one had low knowledge. Novices were two student teachers. The data included observations for 3 months of the year; 10 hours of videotaping; interviews on several topics, including the taped lessons (stimulated recalls); planning and evaluation of their lessons; and fraction knowledge tasks. Card sort tasks on math topics were used: Teachers were asked to sort 40 math problems and give their rationales for sorting. One interview focused on fractions and asked teachers to identify fractions, terminology, representations, and equivalence. For each section, teachers were asked to define the construct (e.g., equivalence or reducing fractions), recognize cases and noncases, compute with the fraction, generate examples, and explain features.

Two types of analyses of these data were made. First, the fraction interview and mathematics card sort were examined for consistent patterns of knowledge and understanding. Second, three teachers, two teachers with high knowledge and one with middle-level knowledge, were closely examined. Videotapes of each teaching a lesson on reducing fractions that lasted one or two periods were examined in detail. The teachers had taught the lessons in the same progression, used the same texts, pages of text, and similar examples; they taught the topics in approximately the same order.

The purpose of these analyses was to examine differences in content used and communicated, because the teachers' performances were "superficially similar," that is, similar on the interview, student gains, and following of the text in the same way. However, their knowledge organization was different. The difference in organization of knowledge was identified in the analyses of the semantic nets (visual displays showing the number of concepts used and the relationships among the concepts; see Leinhardt and Smith, 1985, pp. 249–250) and teacher interviews (stimulated recalls). One expert teacher was unique. This teacher's lessons were "characterized as providing a richness of representation, systems, general heuristics for solutions, and linkages to basic math principles" (p. 263). The other two teachers' lessons were described as teaching explicit algorithms.

In this study Leinhardt and Smith described the cognitive system of a teacher as represented in two organized knowledge bases: (a) general teaching skills and strategies; and (b) domain-specific information necessary for the content presentation. "This second body of information . . . includes algorithmic competence, and at some level, implicit understanding of how procedures work, as well as the goals, subgoals and constraints of the tasks being taught" (p. 248). The declarative knowledge base (teacher-known facts about fractions) was analyzed by constructing semantic nets based on lesson videotapes and the parallel stimulated recalls (teachers talking about their lessons). Procedural knowledge here was represented by algorithms and heuristics operating on declarative knowledge. Another aspect of the data analysis was that "interviews and card sort data were used to confirm the presence of a particular hypothesized concept or relationship. . . this type of nonstatistical but formal analysis of qualitative data for a small number of cases . . . has become a confirmable methodology for psychology" (p. 251).

This study provides an example of the application of cognitive science methods to describe (assess) teacher knowledge and contrast differences among three teachers who varied in level of organization and understanding of conceptual knowledge of fractions and strategies for teaching for mathematical problem solving. The three "expert" teachers were apparently similar in student outcomes (as identified by consistency of student gains on standardized tests) and in interview protocols. The use of several assessment procedures enabled detailed analyses of teacher understanding, particularly in the differences among the experts in the semantic nets describing classroom lessons, that is, displaying the number of concepts and the relationships among concepts in a lesson. These detailed analyses of *systems* of knowledge "hold promise of identifying components of competency involving multiple representations, understanding of the function of basic arithmetic principles such as the identity function, and multiple linkages across concepts that are used in any one aspect of arithmetic" (p. 269). As they note, identifying such *systems* could help in diagnosis and support of teacher learning. Also, the semantic nets and related methods can be translated into text and other teacher learning supports (pp. 269–270).

Knowledge of Lesson Structures: Routines and Agendas. Teacher lesson structures, one form of some content-related teacher knowledge, are part of a sustained body of research on teacher knowledge and the subject matters by Leinhardt and others (Leinhardt, Putman, Stein, & Baxter, 1991). Leinhardt and Greeno (1986) conducted a study of skilled teachers' classroom lessons and drew on the fourth-grade teachers, procedures, and extensive data sets described earlier (Leinhardt, 1993; Leinhardt & Smith, 1985). They proposed that skill in teaching rests on two systems of knowledge, *lesson structure* and *subject matter*. And, "a skilled teacher has a complex knowledge structure composed of interrelated sets of organized actions . . . schemata" (p. 75). *Schemata* can be global activities, such as checking homework, and smaller activities, such as distributing papers to a class. Skilled teachers have *routines*, and a lesson is based on an *agenda*, an operational plan for the lesson. They detailed and defined these constructs, as well as others that fit with them, such as *activity structures*, the main segments of a lesson such as lesson presentation, guided practice, and homework correction. A planning net for an oral homework check was made. The figure (planning net) represented a set of goals, such as call out item content—obtain choral answer to item, and the set of actions necessary to arrive at the goal (a flowchart).

The study itself involved comparisons of eight expert teachers and four novices. Transcripts of two experts and one novice were selected for detailed interpretation of goals, activity structures, and routines. Data are presented for median duration of activities (in minutes) and range of activity structures (e.g., presentation and review, shared presentation, drill, homework, guided practice, tutoring, test). Detailed comparisons of experts and novices conducting *homework checks* and making a *presentation* are shown in flowcharts focused on goals and outcomes. In this study, the assessment of teacher knowledge is segmented and coded using the language of schemata, activities, agendas, and routines.

Highlighting how the teaching episodes function depends on contrasting the differences between teachers just completing teacher education programs and teachers with experience who have successfully taught students who succeed on standardized tests of mathematics. The current use of this methodology and assessments of teacher lessons would result, perhaps, in different outcomes. The use of groups and group problem solving, along with the goal of setting problems to challenge and engage students, may result in a different set of activities and times spent in them for teachers of mathematics in reform projects. The use of the combined methodology—extended videotaping of classrooms over time—along with teacher interviews (stimulated recall) and use of tasks specifically developed as assessments of mathematical knowledge, however, has supported the development of lines of evidence for constructs such as 'systems' of teacher knowledge and the use of cognitive methods such as semantic net diagrams for the assessment of teacher knowledge.

Teacher Explanations. Leinhardt (1989) looked more closely at the teaching and thinking of experts and novices, in terms of the nature of lessons and building *explanations* of mathematical material. She emphasized that the form and content of lesson segments is dependent on the mathematical topic taught, and also that the definitions of effective lessons are based on a model of teacher-based presentation and exploration of new content, followed by independent student practice. A less teacher-centered or inquiry-based approach was recognized as an alternative to their teaching model.

The study again used four expert teachers and two novices (from the sample and data described earlier). Another planning net, a model of an explanation, was given. The analyses of expert and novice *agendas* were based on preclass interviews, including the agenda question, What are you going to do today? One novice explanation and one expert explanation were used to construct semantic net diagrams displaying the content of the lessons. Nodes in the diagram show the concepts presented; lines between nodes indicate how concepts were connected and organized in relation to each other. An immediate, visible difference is that there are isolated, unconnected concepts in the novice diagram and everything is connected in the expert's diagram, and the net is visually denser. Leinhardt (2001) provides an integrative review of work

on teacher explanations, situating this "fine-grained" aspect of teaching as an activity, viewed from the sociocultural perspective. Although a core model of explanations is generic (p. 345), "in-class instructional explanations in mathematics and in history have fundamentally different core questions" (pp. 346–347). The importance of subject matter is fundamental to studies of teacher learning and development, with corresponding requirements for researchers and assessment developers to know the content in depth or to work as part of a team with subject matter specialists.

Summary. The importance of the assessment methods in these studies by Leinhardt and her colleagues is that they are focused tightly on the teacher in the classroom, teaching, and on teacher practice as talked about by the teacher (stimulated recall using the videotapes). A limitation of these studies is the method used to identify the expert teachers and the changing views of teaching mathematics (NCTM, 2000). Standardized achievement tests, in the 1970s and 1980s, may have been less oriented to assessing student conceptual understanding of mathematics and mathematical problem solving. Nonetheless, differences among the teachers were identified in what Leinhardt and Smith (1985) describe as "systems"—that is, *what* mathematical knowledge is held and *how* that knowledge is held (organized) in practice, here in lessons on fractions. Issues of generalizability of findings, to less teacher-centered classrooms or to expert teachers identified by different criteria, as well generalizability as to what other knowledge "*systems*" may be, are speculative (see Ma, 1999, for *knowledge packages*, and Sherin, 2002, for *content knowledge complexes*). The assessment methodology, in its procedures and analyses, are likely to be judged robust. The cognitive analysis of teacher classroom videotapes is also found in the work of Sherin and her colleagues (described later in this section).

Assessments in CGI: Teachers Using Knowledge About Children's Thinking

Cognitively Guided Instruction (CGI) is a study of teachers' use of (research-based) knowledge of children's mathematical thinking and the effects of this teacher knowledge on classroom practice and on student achievement (Carpenter et al., 1989). Forty first-grade teachers and their classrooms of students were randomly assigned (by school) to experimental or control groups. The initial workshop/treatment materials and videotapes elaborated a framework, a research-based analysis of children's development of problem-solving skills in addition and subtraction. Examples of word problem types were join or separate (result unknown, change unknown, and start unknown). Children's problem-solving strategies included directly representing actions or relationships in problems, counting strategies, and number facts.

Teacher Knowledge. Teacher knowledge of student mathematical thinking was assessed at the end of the school year by asking them (a) to predict the strategy each target student would use to answer five items on the student's number facts interview; (b) to predict the strategy the student would use on six word problems in a problem-solving interview; and (c) to predict whether the student would correctly answer eight specific problems on a written problem-solving test. Teacher predictions were matched with students' actual responses to obtain a score. CGI teachers differed from control group teachers in their knowledge of student strategies for both number facts and problem solving.

Classroom observations involved the use of two observation systems at the same time, one focused on the teacher and one focused on the student. The observation categories included setting (whole class, etc.); lesson phases (review, development, etc.); and mathematics content (number facts, represented problems, word problems, etc.). Teacher behavior subcategories were derived from CGI principles: feedback to process; feedback to answer; pose problems to students; and listen to student process of problem-solving aloud. Student problem solving strategies were coded in both teacher and student systems: direct modeling, advanced counting, derived facts, and recall. Teachers and students were observed for four separate week-long periods (minimum of 16 days), November through April.

Comparisons of mean proportions of time spent indicated that control teachers spent more time on number fact problems and CGI teachers spent more time on word problems, listening to student answers to problems, and expected students to use multiple strategies in problem solving. Similar results or trends appeared in the student observation data.

Teacher Pedagogical Content Beliefs. In the CGI study a 48-item measure of teacher pedagogical content beliefs was developed specifically in relation to teaching and learning addition and subtraction in first-grade mathematics (Carpenter, Fennema, Peterson, & Carey, 1988; Peterson, Fennema, Carpenter, & Loef, 1989). Four subscales were developed, 12 items each, with a five-point Likert scale for responses: (a) how children learn mathematics; (b) belief that skills should be taught in relation to understanding and problem solving; (c) belief that children's natural development of mathematical ideas provides the basis for sequencing topics for instruction; and (d) mathematics instruction should facilitate children's

construction of knowledge. A structured belief interview was also used, audiotaped and transcribed. After the interview, interviewers rated teachers on a 5-point scale for each construct. Trained coders also evaluated the interview protocols on the same 5-point scale. Teachers varied in beliefs and the four scales were positively intercorrelated (r values from .57 to .76); Cronbach's alphas ranged from .75 to .86. Seven teachers high on all four scales (cognitively based perspective, **CB**) and 7 consistently low (less cognitively based perspective, **LCB**) were compared (Peterson et al., 1989).

In terms of assessment methodology, a different approach to assessing teacher beliefs is found in the study on teaching reading by Richardson, Anders, Tidwell, and Lloyd (1991). Teacher beliefs about reading comprehension were assessed using a beliefs interview with open-ended questions. Glaser and Strauss's constant comparative method was used to develop coding categories for the interview. A continuum emerged for theoretical orientations—learning a set of skills versus reading and contact with literature; a second dimension of purpose of reading emerged—constructivist at one end versus meaning in the text.

Teacher Pedagogical Content Knowledge. Carpenter et al. (1988) reported on forty first-grade teachers' pedagogical content knowledge based on the CGI framework. The teachers' pedagogical content knowledge was assessed in spring 1986 for (a) distinctions between problem types; (b) general knowledge of strategies; and (c) knowledge of their own students. The two measures of *problem types* were writing word problems, writing six word problems that would be best represented by six number sentences (corresponding to the six join-and-separate problem types); and relative problem difficulty, judging or predicting which word problem would be most difficult for a first grader in each of 16 pairs of problems, based on the word problem type framework. *General knowledge of children's strategies* presented the teacher with videotapes of three children solving word problems, and for each (after two viewings) asked the teacher how the child would respond (strategy used) to additional problems. To assess teacher *knowledge of their own students*, teachers were asked to demonstrate how each of six students from the class (randomly selected) would solve six different addition and subtraction problems. These students had solved the same problems in individual interviews 1–2 days before.

Peterson et al. (1989) also reported on these tasks to assess teachers' pedagogical content knowledge in addition and subtraction (Carpenter et al., 1988). Peterson et al. provided detailed analyses and case examples from the protocols of the 7 **CB** and 7 **LCB** (see Beliefs) teachers' analyses of relative difficulty of word problems. More of the CB teachers knew and understood the complex distinctions between word problems, and they gave a child a problem and listened to the child work the problem; LCB teachers mentioned using tests, records, written seatwork, or other incidental information.

Summary. The assessments of teachers' knowledge in the CGI studies include paper-and-pencil and interview measures of knowledge of the framework and knowledge of their students' performances. Classroom observations and student achievement measures—both standardized tests and project-specific measures—are also included. The pedagogical content beliefs and the pedagogical content knowledge assessments, although not drawn from classroom records such as videotapes, have been analyzed in relation to each other and to student achievement. Technical data on reliability, rater training, and agreement data are given for these assessments. Included in the CGI training materials are examples showing classroom teachers working with groups of students. Analyses of CGI "expert" teachers would add to the understanding of the types of "systems" of knowledge held by these teachers in their classroom practice, particularly in working with small groups of students, in elementary school mathematics.

Assessing Mathematical Knowledge for Teaching: TELT Interviews and Other Survey Items

The *Teacher Education and Learning to Teach* study (TELT) of the National Center for Research on Teacher Education developed assessments of teacher knowledge. The line of work here is focused on what Ball, Lubienski, and Mewborn (2001) discuss as mathematical knowledge for teaching, including the ideas of pedagogical content knowledge (Shulman, 1986). Ball et al. argue for the importance of knowledge of mathematics in and for teaching (p. 449).

TELT Assessments. The study package for TELT (Kennedy et al. 1993) is extensive and includes an interview that provided teachers with hypothetical teaching situations and asked them how they would respond to them. The situations were standardized, and the responses open-ended. Seven teaching tasks were identified (e.g., generating representations of concepts, responding to student difficulties with a particular concept), and there was a corresponding mathematical or writing issue for each. The corresponding mathematical issue for generating representations of concepts was *division by fractions.* Several of the mathematics protocols have been used in other research assessing teacher knowledge of mathematics in the context of teaching tasks (Jones, 2005; Ma, 1999).

Ma compared elementary school teachers in China and the United States (TELT and other teachers) on their understanding of knowing and teaching of fundamental mathematics. For the Chinese teachers she used the TELT interview protocols on mathematics topics of place value—subtraction with regrouping; division of fractions; multidigit multiplication; and perimeter and area of a closed figure. The protocols included four of the common teaching tasks in TELT: teaching a topic; responding to a student's mistake; generating a representation of a certain topic; and responding to a novel idea raised by a student. Ma interviewed 72 Chinese teachers, eight of whom averaged 18 years experience. These eight were her "experts," that is, Chinese teachers with profound understanding of fundamental mathematics (PUFM). Ma identified what she describes as *knowledge packages*, reflecting the Chinese teacher's theories about learning mathematics, and compare the *systems* of Leinhardt and Smith (1985) from analyses based on an expert teacher's classroom videotapes, and the *content knowledge complex* of Sherin (2002) from analyses that include teacher classroom videotapes (described later).

Teachers' Mathematical Knowledge for Teaching. Work has continued on developing structured, multiple-choice, paper-and-pencil measures of teachers' mathematical knowledge for teaching (Hill, Schilling, & Ball, 2004) and content knowledge for teaching reading (Phelps & Schilling, 2004) in survey forms. Items for mathematics in each of two content areas—number concepts and operations—included two kinds of teacher knowledge—knowledge of content itself and combined knowledge of students and content. A third content area—patterns, functions, and algebra—included items written only for knowledge of content.

Items were pilot tested in California's Mathematics Professional Development Institutes (MPDIs). Several factor analytic methods were used and results were not clear cut in terms of the dimensionality of the items, but did support use of the data to select items for scales that combined numbers and operations within (a) knowledge of content (CK); Cronbach's alphas for each of three forms (A, B, C) are .719, .766, .784; and (b) knowledge of students and content, alphas .622, .657, .698. Number of items per scale ranged from 19 to 26, across the three forms. Content knowledge for teaching items for patterns, functions, and algebra were also kept in these analyses. Work assessed the content-related validity of the items for NCTM and California standards, and a talk-aloud on items and answers, a cognitive tracing study, was conducted.

Change in Teachers' Mathematical Knowledge for Teaching. Hill and Ball (2004) used only numbers and operations for analyses on three forms of content knowledge

(CK) for teaching elementary mathematics (with 26, 24, and 23 items and reliability estimates of .72, .78, and .71, respectively). These items were used before and after summer 2001 California's Mathematics Professional Development Institutes (MPDI) of 1 to 3 weeks' duration, taught by mathematicians and mathematics educators. Of an estimated 2,300 teachers served by the MPDIs, there are 398 teachers in the study. Pre-MPDI and post-MPDI scores were compared. Equated pretest scores (for the three forms) averaged .47 logits (one-parameter Rasch model) and 1.06 for the posttest (standard deviations of 1.05 and 1.29 logits, respectively). The effect size was between a third and half standard deviation and significant: (a) the gain was on the order of two to three item increases; and (b) MPDIs varied in effectiveness in increasing teacher knowledge. Limitations to this study include the sample, in terms of both teachers and the MPDIs, and the preliminary nature of the CK scales themselves.

Teachers' Mathematical Knowledge for Teaching and Effects on Students.

The effects of teachers' mathematical knowledge used in teaching on student achievement is one part of a large study of three programs of comprehensive school reform (CSR), *Accelerated Schools, Project America's Choice*, and *Success for All* (Hill, Rowan, & Ball, 2005). The Study of Instructional Improvement project (SCII) supported the writing, development, and analyses of the K-6 teacher survey items (described earlier; Hill, Schilling, & Ball, 2004). Content Knowledge for Teaching Mathematics (CKT-M) was included on teachers' surveys (about 30 items; reliability. 88). CKT-M includes both common mathematical content knowledge and specialized items engaging teachers, for example, in (a) appraising nonstandard solution methods; (b) showing or representing numbers or operations using manipulatives; and (c) providing explanations for common mathematical rules—for example, why any number can be divided by 4 if the last two digits are divisible by 4 (Hill et al., 2004, p. 19). There was also a measure of Content Knowledge for Teaching Reading (CKT-R) used in the analyses (alpha .92); it included knowledge of *word analysis* and *comprehension* in three areas: knowledge of content (KC); knowledge of students and content, and knowledge of content and teaching (KCT). Phelps and Schilling (2004) provide more detailed analyses of the CKT-R measure.

The overall SCII sample includes high-poverty elementary schools, about 89 CSR schools and 26 comparison schools. The teacher sample in Hill, Rowan, and Ball (2005) includes about 334 grade 1 and 365 grade 3 teachers, an average of 3.2 teachers per school. Student mobility resulted in complete data for an average of 3.9 students per classroom in the grade 1 sample and 6.6 students per classroom in the grade 3 sample. The analyses included correlations and regression models within grade. Results indicate that CKT-M and CKT-R are moderately correlated ($r = .39$ grade 1; $r = .37$ grade 3). CKT-M is not significantly correlated with teacher preparation or years of experience in grade 1; in grade 3 CKT-M was correlated .11 with certification.

A variance decomposition analysis indicates variance due to different sources was: students within classrooms, 85 percent grade 1 and 90 percent grade 3; teachers, 8 percent grade 1 and 2 percent grade 3 (both significant); and schools, 6 percent grade 1 and 7 percent grade 3. Regression models were used to examine predictors of student mathematics achievement test gain scores; using teacher variables, CKT-M is the strongest predictor at the teacher variable level. As Hill et al. (2005) recognize, these data are suggestive and the analyses are weakened by missing data, sample size, (modest) overlap of the student test (Terra Nova) with classroom curriculum (e.g., for grade 3, 54 percent of the items cover the SII main topics), and, in another instance, an inability to separate the effects of variables such as math methods and mathematics content courses. (Teacher logs were also used to sample variables such as mathematics curriculum and math lesson length; see Rowan, Harrison, & Hayes, 2004, for descriptions.)

Summary.

Methods of assessing mathematics knowledge for teaching have changed from the TELT individual interview procedures. Ball, Hill, and their colleagues have developed items that include stems (situations or problems) accompanied by one or more items. These items are written for distinct mathematical areas (e.g., number concepts) in the elementary school, or, as with Phelps and Schilling (2004), in reading comprehension and word analyses. The mathematics items have been piloted and used in two large studies, MPDI and SCII. Factor analyses, item response theory (IRT) analyses, pre–post MPDI score increases, and teacher-level predictors of student gain scores in mathematics achievement support the promise of these efforts to develop items that can be used as indictors of content knowledge for teaching (CKT-M) in large-scale evaluations or survey studies in the elementary grades.

These data also indicate the limitations of paper-and-pencil survey instruments for use other than as indicators, although this is an important role, as suggested by the study linking CKT-M with student achievement. The interpretations of these data as indicators of subject matter knowledge for teaching or teacher pedagogical content knowledge rest on the theoretical and empirical arguments for the construct itself. The argument and validity-related evidence start with the research literature on teaching, linking the literature and practice as sources for item construction, conducting a series of factor analyses and correlation analyses with other data, and testing hypotheses related to the construct. As an indicator, the data appear to support use of CKT-M in large-scale survey and evaluation work.

Criticisms of the concept of pedagogical content knowledge (PCK) have been summarized by Baxter and Lederman (1999); they reviewed many of the PCK assessments in science. As they note, PCK is a construct, and assessments in any particular form and with a particular teacher may not elicit PCK. These criticisms identify the need for validity evidence related to the use of an assessment for a particular purpose. These same criticisms apply to any assessment, such as student knowledge of a concept in science or mathematics. Assessments that take the form of eliciting teacher thinking through tasks (e.g., sorting examples of mathematical problems), interviews, or paper-and-paper pencil surveys, as with the content knowledge for teaching items, are subject to the same criticisms as student achievement tests. Baxter and Lederman make an important point: studies that use multiple assessments are more persuasive. The assessments and procedures used in the major studies of teacher knowledge described earlier, as well as other research reported hereafter, help to illustrate the point that multiple sources of evidence for a construct may be more persuasive to a potential user of an assessment or data. Interpretations of data as evidence of constructs such as CKT-M or PCK, content knowledge complex, or systems of mathematical knowledge are most persuasive in a context where there are efforts to carefully define the construct, use multiple sources (assessments) for evidence, and use an evolving theory to support interpretations.

Assessing Teacher Knowledge of Evaluating Students for Learning

This section includes studies that examine how teachers evaluate or assess students' knowledge and teachers learning how to evaluate student knowledge. These studies concern diagnostic or formative evaluation in which teachers use classroom assessments to support student learning. The first study (Langenthal, 2004) is an example of assessment procedures used to elicit teacher knowledge about the academic progress of their students in learning to read. The next series of studies are reports on researchers working with teachers in England to enhance their diagnostic or formative evaluation skills in early elementary school classrooms (Torrance & Pryor, 1998), and in secondary school mathematics and science classrooms (Black & Wiliam, 1998; Wiliam, Lee, Harrison, & Black, 2004). The latter study examines the effects on student achievement when teachers learn formative assessment strategies. The last example is the Classroom Assessment

Project to Improve Teaching and Learning (CAPITAL), again involving researchers working with teachers on their assessments (Coffey, Moorthy, Sato, Thibeault, & Atkin, in press).

Assessing Teacher Knowledge of Student Progress in Reading. Langenthal (2004) used a comparison of 10 novice and 10 experienced first-grade teachers to gain an understanding of reading teachers' knowledge of progress of their students. The relationships between teacher knowledge of beginning word-reading acquisition and teachers' assessment practices were examined using (a) a written questionnaire on teaching experience, course work, and knowledge about reading instruction and linguistics/structure of language; and (b) an audiotaped, detailed 2-hour teacher interview of structured tasks and questions. In a think-aloud task, teachers were asked to rank their students according to their reading skills, give the reasons for the placement, and give each child's reading strengths or weaknesses. Analyses of the think-aloud task focused on coding teacher statements that referred to alphabetic, word reading, language, and phonological processes; other coding categories were text reading and comprehension, motivational conditions affecting learning, home influences, and test scores.

Assessing Teacher Knowledge of Classroom Formative Assessment. Reviews and research in England have been concerned with how teachers assess children (Gipps, 1999) and with classroom learning when teachers have emphasized formative assessment (Black & Wiliam, 1998, 2003). Black and Wiliam (1998) define classroom formative assessments as "encompassing all those activities undertaken by teachers, and/or by their students, which provide information to be used as feedback to modify the teaching and learning activities in which they are engaged" (p. 8). In their 2003 review, Black and Wiliam locate the formative assessment emphasis on classroom *processes*. Torrance and Pryor (1998) examined classroom interactions and teacher language to describe and analyze teachers' informal assessment practices in infant classrooms (ages 5–7 years). Transcripts of whole-class lessons, teacher–individual student interviews (assessment interview) and observations are presented, along with interpretive comments on assessment-related text. Two general categories of teachers' classroom assessments were identified: convergent assessment and divergent assessment (p. 153). *Convergent assessment* aims to discover *whether* the learner knows or understands a predetermined thing, and *divergent assessment* aims to discover *what* the learner knows or understands.

This study was followed by work in a collaborative project with a team of five primary school teacher researchers (Torrance & Pryor, 2000). The teacher researchers conducted action research on their own classroom practices (reports and analyses of the data), including classroom audio and videotapes. A descriptive and analytic framework of processes of formative assessments included a description of teacher actions, and each action was examined for possible teacher intentions and possible positive effects for student. Part of the analyses suggest that identifying and assessing classroom social norms, as well as assessing norms related to specific classroom subject matter and practices, are important since they establish student expectations and discourse practices (related examples are the sociomathematical norms and classroom mathematical practices described by Cobb & Yackel, 1996, and the discussion by Lampert, 1990). The process of changing student and teacher roles and discourse is identified in the work of Black and his colleagues also.

Black and Wiliam (2003) and Black, Harrison, Lee, Marshall, & Wiliam (2003) describe a project to put findings on formative assessment into practice: That is, did teachers learn to change how they evaluate students? And, did teacher use of formative assessment affect student achievement (Wiliam et al., 2004)? They worked with six secondary schools, and their mathematics and science teachers (two mathematics and two science teachers from each school, 24 teachers). An initial 6 months was spent in which teachers were encouraged to experiment with some strategies and techniques suggested by research, such as rich questioning, comment-only marking, sharing criteria with learners, and student peer- and self-assessment. Four major types of teacher action evolved: questioning, feedback by marking, peer and self assessment, and the formative use of summative tests. Qualitative data were used to describe teacher change (Black et al., 2003), including: (a) transcripts of three interviews with individual teachers, from the beginning of the project, end of first year, and end of second year; (b) notes on lesson observations; (c) records, documents, and observation notes from project meetings with teachers; and (d) teacher action plans, journals, and reflections.

Four categories of ways in which teachers adopted formative assessment to evaluate students were developed, from: (a) experts who embedded formative strategies and integrated them in practice; to (d) teachers who had attempted strategies but had not embedded any strategies into their practice. In a study of teacher assessment effects on student achievement (Wiliam et al., 2004), a comparison class was identified for each project class. Local or national achievement measures were used to compare students in the two classes, and effect sizes were calculated for each of the paired classes in order to examine the effects of teachers' changing evaluation practice on student achievement. The mean effect size was .32, suggesting the gains possible when teachers undertake to implement formative assessment with their students.

In the CAPITAL project a team of researchers worked for 3 years with 25 science teachers, as teachers examined and changed their classroom assessment practices to assessments that foster learning (Coffey et al., in press). Researchers spent time in classrooms and talked extensively with students and teachers, writing detailed field notes and sometimes videotaping. Teachers were interviewed, and formal interviews were audiotaped and transcribed. Student and classroom work documents were collected. Researchers met monthly with the collaborative group of teachers; at times work from a teacher's classroom was presented. All meetings were videotaped and analyzed. Researchers facilitated weeklong summer institutes. Coffey et al. provide a series of case studies of individual teachers and focus on the individual teacher in demonstrating the differences among teachers in thinking and action in classroom assessment for learning.

Summary. Teacher knowledge of students gained through assessment is an important aspect of formative evaluation of students. This working knowledge may be aspects of what Shulman (1986) called *general pedagogical knowledge* and also part of pedagogical content knowledge. The assessments methods just described included talk aloud procedures on a cognitive task (in comparisons of experienced/novice teachers), case studies of individual teachers, effects on student test scores when teachers implement formative assessment strategies, and classroom observations, interviews, and documents. Teachers typically establish classroom discourse and subject matter norms around classroom activities, including marking or commenting on the quality of student work and providing feedback. As Coffey et al. note, assessment practices are often hard to distinguish from teaching. It can be argued that assessment occurs whenever teachers talk about the quality of student work. As their comments suggest, research on teacher learning about assessments for formative purposes requires going beyond instances of documenting formative assessments. Research on teachers changing their classroom discourse is needed, and frameworks examples such as the one of Cobb and Yackel (1996) may be useful models.

Assessments in Teacher/Researcher Collaborative Learning Projects

The assessment examples in this category arise when researchers and teachers are collaborating on a project to change teacher practice. The focus in these studies is often on student learning. Here the focus is on teacher learning. Teacher assessments in several different types of studies are examined here: (a) collaborative projects such as researchers working with teachers in design experiments, or, as Sandoval and Bell (2004) have labeled them, design-based research; and (b) video club projects, involving detailed analyses of teachers modifying practice (Sherin & Han, 2004).

Design-Experiment Projects. An example of a *design project* is one described by Lehrer and Schauble (2000). In this project teachers designed learning environments for developing student modeling thinking. An example of engaging children in model-based reasoning is an activity with the goal of symbolizing and measuring, such as data displays that describe a collection of mittens in a first-grade classroom. The project intention is to involve the researchers in active collaborative work with teachers, generating a knowledge base of student development of thinking in mathematics and science modeling, and simultaneously fostering teacher development and a community of colleagues within the school district.

Forty-five teachers and their classes (grades 1–5) in four elementary schools participated. The focus is on student thinking: "Teachers work individually or in teams to develop model-eliciting tasks and document major transitions in student thinking as students engage in cycles of modeling" (Lehrer & Schauble, 2000, p. 139). Teacher evidence of student thinking could be examples of student work, video clips, and transcriptions of audio recordings. In-depth long-term case studies of six teachers were in process. Observers recorded evidence about how teachers assist practices and create and sustain classroom norms related to use of inscriptions (deliberately selecting and amplifying particular attributes for further study) and notations. Individual, 3-hour interviews of 27 teachers were conducted at the end of the first two school years, on mathematics and science, and ways to teach them. Teachers were given examples of student work and asked questions about what each might indicate about the student.

Clark and Lesh (2003) provide an example of using *a model-eliciting problem for teachers*—asking teachers to create a concept map for each student model-eliciting problem they implemented in their classroom. The map focused teachers on student thinking in solving a specific mathematical problem, and revealed teaching thinking. Over time, in the assessment here, the teacher maps became more elaborated.

Cobb and his colleagues have focused on the development of student thinking using an interpretive framework in a classroom-based design research project, a classroom teaching experiment conducted with a practicing teacher who is a member of the research and development team (Cobb & Yackel, 1996). A case study reported in Wood, Cobb, and Yackel (1991) examined teacher reorganization of practice. They used selected daily video recordings of grade 2 mathematics lessons along with field notes, open-ended interviews, and notes from project meetings. Rethinking the next experiment, conducted with a group of 25 teachers, the process and outcomes suggested that the researchers needed to develop analytical approaches that located teachers' learning within the social context of both the professional teaching community and their classroom (Cobb & McLain, 2001). They suggested that it will be necessary to conduct ongoing analyses of the institutional settings in which teachers work in order to understand teacher learning and constraints on teacher learning.

Using Videotapes and Video Club Projects. Another model of working with teachers and assessing teacher learning occurs in studies using videotapes of teacher classroom practice. The work of Sherin is used here as an example. Teachers have engaged in viewing videotapes of their classrooms in a series of studies in which Sherin and her colleagues (e.g., Sherin & Han, 2004) have participated as facilitators. These studies vary in the number of times teachers' classrooms are video taped and in the lesson units involved.

Video club (Frederiksen et al., 1998) meetings typically involve two or more teachers, one or two researchers, and are usually videotaped. A facilitator (researcher or teacher) will select, with a teacher, a videotape excerpt to show at the meeting. In a video club meeting with other teachers, the excerpt is viewed and the events/issues in it are discussed. The goal is to question, reflect on, and learn about teaching (Sherin & Han, 2004). An instance of the learning of four middle-school mathematics teachers over a year-long series of 10 video club meetings is reported. The teachers were participating in the project *Fostering a Community of Teachers as Learners*.

Sherin and Han (2004) used Fredericksen's (1992) observation that teachers watching videotapes will notice particular events, labeled as "call-outs," as significant. They analyzed (a) the "call-out" events and issues; and (b) whether the teachers' attention could be drawn to call outs about student thinking in mathematics. The researcher (Sherin) participated in the video club by (a) making comments intended, "to elicit teacher ideas about what stood out to them in the video excerpts"; and (b) "focusing the teachers' attention on issues related to student conceptions" (p. 167). Analyses of the transcripts of the videotapes of the first seven meetings began with noting where there was a change in topic, and dividing each transcript into a set of individual segments. Five topics were identified: pedagogy, student conceptions, classroom discourse, mathematics, and other. (Coder agreement was 87 percent, and consensus was reached on all topics.) Time spent on each topic was calculated, and number of segments per topic initiated by teacher or researcher was obtained.

Several aspects of the analyses indicated changes in the discussions over time, e.g., change from discussions of alternative pedagogies to explanations of the teaching strategy used. Analyses also examined the types of changes in teachers' discussions of student conceptions. Three levels were identified: Level 1, quoted what student said; Level 2, explore meaning of student statement; and Level 3, involved generalization and synthesis of students' thinking

Two teachers' implementation of a reform-based linear-functions unit in their high school algebra classes were videotaped and analyzed by Sherin (2002). Data included three videotaped interviews with each teacher before starting the unit to assess teacher conceptions of linear functions as a mathematical domain and ideas about teaching linear functions. Each of five classes was videotaped daily, for the duration of the unit (March to May), with two cameras to capture the classroom interaction and the teacher. Written observations were made for over half of the classes. Weekly video club meetings of teachers and researchers were also videotaped. These meetings involved the two teachers and the two researchers discussing the classroom videotapes.

Sherin made fine-grained analyses of the videotapes of teachers in each situation—interviews, classroom, and weekly meetings. The iterative process of analysis identified three classes of interactions between teachers' content knowledge complexes (linked subject matter and pedagogical content knowledge) and the novel curriculum: *transform, adapt*, and *negotiate*. *Negotiate* involves a teacher developing new content knowledge and at the same time making changes as a lesson unfolds—and, "illustrates the active learning that is the essence of reform mathematics teaching" (Sherin, 2002, p. 130). This iterative process of analysis typically occurs over a series of lessons. The 6 weeks of the unit consisted of 17 lessons, each of which lasted from 1 to 3 days. Each lesson was examined for evidence of the three classes of interaction, with a set of observable criteria such that an episode could be as coded one of the three, transform, adapt, or negotiate. A single lesson could be coded as examples of one or more of the categories. Coding was independently verified for 70 percent of the instances identified.

The resulting process or cycle in which negotiation may occur is carefully shown in a case study, the *Real Staircases* lesson. Since the teacher taught the same lesson for several classes on the same day, cycles in the process of negotiating could be captured, and the teacher's

discussion in the video club provided evidence of her awareness of what she was working to change. The cycle of negotiations resulted in increased knowledge in both subject matter knowledge and pedagogical content knowledge, and also suggested that it results in new *content knowledge complexes*. The assessment of teacher learning here is based on extensive records of practice that include videotapes and observations, as well as researcher and teacher interactions (video club) centered on teacher practice.

Van Es and Sherin (2002) describe the use of a multimedia tool designed to help teachers view videotapes in a particular way, *learning to notice*. The Video Analysis Support Tool (VAST) was designed to support teacher ability to notice and interpret aspects of classroom practice important to reform pedagogy. Specific features of the software are intended to scaffold teachers to notice and interpret classroom interactions, and teachers view the video from their own classroom. Prompts focus teachers on three aspects of classroom interaction—student thinking, teacher's roles, and discourse. Teachers are scaffolded–What do you notice? to identify call-outs, to use evidence from the video to support call outs, and to interpret events noticed in the video (Frederiksen et al., 1998). Written essays from teaching interns were used to examine the effects of use. The results suggest that a brief use of VAST (three sessions) had some influence on the analyses of their practice by the teaching interns.

As these and other studies indicate, the use of video records in the assessment of teacher learning is increasing. Brophy (2004) includes chapters with examples of using video cases, online video, and documentary cases of NBPTS-certified teachers.

Summary. In this section on teacher assessments in teacher/researcher collaborative learning projects, two types of studies have been described—design-based research and video club projects. In the limited number of design-based research studies examined here, the assessments of teacher learning are limited. Teacher case studies and structured interviews were being developed in one study and changes in teacher concept maps described for another. Perhaps this is not surprising since the focus in most design-based research projects appears to be predominantly on assessing student learning, and there may be few collaborating teachers or collaborating researchers (see Sandoval & Bell, 2004).

The individual teacher video and video club studies by Sherin and her colleagues are focused on teacher learning. They use cognitive analyses and coding of discourse of individual teachers or small groups of teachers. The database typically consists of classroom videotapes and the videotapes of teacher/researcher video club discussions. These studies contribute assessments based on detailed documentation and descriptions of teacher learning, including documenting teacher learning in the process of teaching and then in talking about their own teaching. New constructs are proposed for investigation and assessment, such as *content knowledge complexes, negotiation,* and teacher *levels of analysis of student thinking.* Verification is provided by independent, trained coders and by carefully selected case examples of teacher practice. These studies extend the lines of research initiated by Leinhardt and her colleagues into reform-focused mathematics classrooms in which teachers are learning about their practice (a) using extensive videotape records of classroom teaching; and (b) talking about their (videotaped) teaching in the video clubs, in a social context.

ASSESSING TEACHER DEVELOPMENT AND CHANGE

Resources for understanding and locating research on teacher development include Wilson and Berne (1999) on research in professional development, Cochran-Smith and Lytle (1999) on teacher learning in communities, and Richardson and Placier (2001) on teacher change. Richardson and Placier identify teacher change as work described in terms such as *learning, development, improvement, implementation,* and *self-study*; these terms are often used interchangeably. They organize their review into two areas, examining (a) individual and small-group change processes; and (b) an organizational view. The teacher development focus in this chapter is on individual and group change.

The assessments used in research are presented in two sections, Longitudinal Studies and Teacher Learning Communities. The assessments in the *longitudinal studies* section characterize the outcomes of teacher development programs as an overall change for a teacher, encompassing major aspects of knowledge and beliefs about teaching and classroom practice. Assessments in the *teacher learning communities* section focus on teacher change when a teacher is participating in a group of teachers working to change their practice in larger social settings. These projects focus on the group or a department in a school as the unit within which teacher change is assessed.

Assessments in Longitudinal Studies

Reading Comprehension: Richardson and Colleagues. A study on teaching and staff development in reading comprehension using research-based practice was reported by Richardson (1994). Practice was defined to include

three elements: it is observable, it is describable (can be explained), and it is linked to a theoretical notion of the reading process. As a way to study teacher beliefs and practices, the idea of a line of inquiry, "practical arguments," was used that supported explaining the justifications or reasons for practice, to assist teachers to be reflective about practice (Fenstermacher, 1994). As part of a staff development process, practical argument sessions were held individually, with a teacher and researchers looking at videotapes of the teacher's practice; the sessions were audiotaped and transcribed. Group sessions with school faculty were also videotaped. Transcripts were analyzed by topic and process (Richardson & Hamilton, 1994).

The study examined teacher beliefs, practice, and change by using interviews, observers, and baseline videotaped observations. A handwritten timed narrative record described classroom events and was coded for lesson theme, focus, and practice. Observers completed a follow-up questionnaire. The videotaped observations in the second year were used to assess changes in practice in the categories: reading comprehension instruction, degree of teacher-directed instruction, choice of text/use of text, and student interactions. An example of a teacher's change is along a dimension or scale, from use of basal readers to use of literature.

Summer Math and Related Programs: The ACMI. Simon and Schifter (1991) describe the SummerMath program and a specific project within it, the Educational Leaders in Mathematics (ELM). Intensive summer courses and ongoing classroom support were to assist teachers' development of a constructivist view upon which to base instructional decisions. Data included writings, synthesis papers, and anonymous responses to open-ended questions. These writings were categorized independently by the researchers into themes indicative of program impact.

The Assessment of Constructivism in Mathematics Instruction (ACMI) was developed based on extensive classroom observation of teachers and their changes in thinking and practice (Schifter & Simon, 1992). The structure of the ACMI is based on an assessment tool for adoption of innovations, the Levels of Use (LoU; Hall et al., cited in Schifter & Simon, 1992). The ACMI consists of a structured interview and a procedure for rating the responses. The ACMI has the following levels: Level 0: does not hold a constructivist epistemology; Levels I and II: not applicable; Level III: holds a constructivist epistemology, but has difficulty implementing instruction in response to it; Level IVA: holds a constructivist epistemology, and is comfortable with instruction, focuses on teaching behaviors; Level IVB: focuses on student learning from a constructivist perspective.

Distinctions between teachers at different levels are shown by examples of teacher responses, interviewer follow-up questions, and analyses of why a teacher is placed at one developmental level versus another. Schifter and Fosnot (1993) developed case studies of teachers who participated in the SummerMath programs, and discuss some of them in relation to the ACMI levels. (The ACMI in Schifter and Fosnot is modified for Level III: has a rudimentary understanding of constructivism, but has difficulty basing instruction on this understanding.)

CGI: Changes in Teacher Beliefs and Practice. There have been several follow-up studies of the teachers who participated in the *Cognitively Guided Instruction* (CGI) project that was based on providing teachers a framework for understanding children's thinking, a developmental framework of children's strategies and order of difficulty of beginning word problems. (See also CGI teacher assessments in the earlier section on Teacher Knowledge.)

Fennema et al., (1996) reported changes in beliefs and practice of 21 first-, second-, and third-grade teachers over the 4-year period they were in a CGI teacher development program. Data on instruction and beliefs were available for 21 teachers, consisting of audiotape transcriptions of classroom observations, interviews, CGI Belief Scale scores, and field notes of informal observations. Fennema et al. built on and adapted the ACMI (Schifter & Fosnot, 1993), defining four instructional and four belief levels of Cognitively Guided Instruction. Five coders were trained using data from nonstudy teachers until there was agreement on definitions. Complete data sets, consisting of information from all years of teacher participation for each of the 21 teachers, were assigned to each of the five coders. Each rater studied all data on a teacher and assigned an instructional level and a belief level for each year for each teacher, giving written evidence directly from the various transcripts to support the level assigned. Results for the 21 teachers are given for beliefs and instructional levels, such as showing level of beliefs at initial and final years of CGI. Examples of teacher statements and evidence are given for teachers at each level of belief and similarly for instruction. For example, the highest levels (4B) for instruction and beliefs are defined as follow:

4B Instruction— Provides opportunities for children to be involved in a variety of problem-solving activities. Elicits children's thinking, attends to children sharing their thinking, and adapts instruction according to what is shared. Instruction is driven by teacher's knowledge about individual children in the classroom.

4B Beliefs—Believes that children can solve problems without instruction across mathematics content domains and that what he or she knows about children's thinking should inform his or her decision making, both regarding interactions with the students and curriculum design. (Fennema et al., 1996, pp. 412-413).

CGI and Teacher Self-sustaining Change. The ideas of self-sustaining generative change are explored in Franke, Carpenter, Levi, and Fennema (2001). Follow-up data collection in 1996–1997 included 22 first- through fifth-grade teachers in eight schools. Each teacher was interviewed and 20 teachers observed in classroom teaching. Observations focused on problems posed by the teacher, student solution strategies, teacher–student interactions, and student–student interactions about mathematical thinking. Detailed field notes, audio records, and teacher interviews were collected. The interview included assessing teacher perceptions of how and why she had changed since the teacher development program ended in 1993, with specific questions related to (a) mathematics instruction, (b) knowledge and use of children's mathematical thinking; (c) the type of support they currently had in their mathematics instruction; and (d) whether they talked regularly with other teachers about mathematics instruction.

In analyzing the data for levels of teacher development, the procedures used in Fennema et al. (1996) were adapted to combine the beliefs and instruction (practice) into one set of levels (see Franke, Fennema, & Carpenter, 1997). The levels are now identified as *Levels of Engagement with Children's Mathematical Thinking*. As an example, Level 4B is changed as follows:

Level 4B: The teacher knows how what an individual child knows fits in with how children's mathematical understanding develops.
Creates opportunities to build on children's mathematical thinking.
Describes in detail individual children's mathematical thinking. Uses what he or she learns about individual students' mathematical thinking to drive instruction. (Franke et al., 2001 p. 662)

Overall, this scheme is viewed as a series of graduated benchmarks. Holistic readings of the observation and interview data were made to code level of engagement. The readings involved (a) looking for evidence that would support each benchmark; and (b) reading for evidence indicating that a teacher did not reach a benchmark. Another set of readings was undertaken to characterize change, using four categories. Reliability of coding was checked, case exemplars were chosen, and analyses made of teachers' perceived support for CGI examined patterns, which were found within schools.

At the highest levels, the distinctions between teachers are based on how they view their knowledge of children's mathematical thinking. Level 4B teachers are described as viewing that knowledge as their own, to adapt and use creatively, constantly testing this knowledge against what they observe and revising their knowledge, learning from their students, engaging in practical inquiry, and viewing themselves as constantly learning, deepening their understanding about how children's thinking develops, and going beyond the initial CGI framework. These Level 4B teachers are described as becoming generative in their growth.

Ten teachers were at the 4B level at follow-up; one had been at Level 3 at the end of the original project. She was in one of two schools where teachers had formed collaborative groups and had daily ongoing support, talking about and sharing articles, all focused on learning more about children's mathematical thinking in their classrooms, and she had moved to Level 4B. For Level 4B teachers with little support within their schools, they looked outside the schools. Some were leading workshops for other teachers (Franke et al., 2001).

Summary. The set of longitudinal studies described here have focused on characterizing a set of teacher characteristics into broader constructs than those typically identified in the section on teacher knowledge. The Summer-Math programs and the CGI follow-up studies, in particular, have developed an integrative appraisal of teacher beliefs, knowledge and practice. Using qualitative data sets for each teacher, a group of trained and experienced CGI raters used 'holistic' readings to code CGI *Levels of engagement with Children's Mathematical Thinking.* The Levels, with case exemplar benchmarks, provide replicable, reliable assessment procedures (a) to describe teacher development, within the CGI framework; and (b) to identify the situations in which fully engaged teaching was being sustained. For several teachers, sustaining fully engaged teaching occurred in a school with colleagues at the same level.

Projects in *Teacher Learning Communities* attempt to create these situations or environments to support teacher learning and development. These examples may be accompanied by shifts in the focus of assessment procedures, from teacher in the activity of classroom practice to teacher in activities outside the classroom.

Teacher Learning Communities

Professional development, learning communities, teacher inquiry groups, collaborative groups—there are several terms used to identify teachers working to support each other in learning and changing classroom practice in projects aimed at teaching for understanding. The assessment processes vary depending on the goals of the projects, and the projects are designed in a variety of ways. Typically, the goals of projects here are similar to those in the longitudinal studies (above): teacher development and change in their world view, including their knowledge, beliefs, and practice. However, the

constructs are different: for example, *breadth* and *depth* of participation in *school-based activities*, as contrasted with *content knowledge complexes*. The context for assessment can include the teacher in classroom practice, and also shift to the individual in social activities in the school.

School Mathematics Communities: QUASAR. The *Quantitative Understanding: Amplifying Student Understanding and Reasoning* (QUASAR) project (Silver & Stein, 1996) was a 5-year national reform project to foster the development of enhanced mathematics instruction programs in six urban middle schools (grades 6–8). QUASAR served students from economically disadvantaged neighborhoods. The school mathematics program was to be the unit of change. The entire middle-school mathematics faculty, local mathematics educator consultants (referred to as resource partners), and building administrators were to work together, developing instructional materials and practice aligned with the NCTM standards.

Teachers' learning was viewed as taking place in workshops and other activities, such as developing curriculum materials and assessments. Viewing teaching as *chains of assistance* was useful both in examining teachers in classrooms with students, and teachers interacting with other teachers (Brown, Stein, & Forman, 1996). Brown, et al. examined data from one school: (a) classroom observations (videotapes and field notes); (b) artifacts such as lesson plans and handouts; and (c) interviews before and after observed lessons. Data also included (a) interviews with project participants about staff development sessions; (b) videotapes of staff development sessions and their related artifacts; and (c) teachers' journals and related artifacts. An example and analysis is given of a teacher providing assistance to students in a classroom lesson. The example was identified when two researchers independently viewed segments of videotapes and made judgments on the extent to which five characteristics of good assistance (Tharp & Gallimore, 1988) were present.

Stein and Brown (1997) note that use of sociocultural theory to understand change shifts the unit of analysis from the individual teacher to the social practice/ activities of teachers, and "learning is redefined as transformations in the ways in which teachers participate in these social practices" (p. 159). Analysis of one middle school indicated that teachers viewed themselves as a cohesive group, actively working together to create and sustain a reform-oriented mathematics program. As newcomers entered this community, most became practicing members. Interview transcripts and paper-and-pencil rankings of the importance of various forms of teacher assistance indicated that teachers perceived the value of interactions with colleagues. Further observations, site visits, and teacher journals confirmed the importance of communications and connections among teachers. An index of teachers' participation patterns was developed, in which the *breadth* of participation across school-based community activities was viewed as an index of teacher learning (pp. 168–169). Another index of a community of practice was the *depth* of activity over time, tracing teacher participation patterns with respect to one particular work practice, such as mathematics course teaching assignments, over a 5-year time period (Stein, Silver, & Smith, 1998).

Related work by McLaughlin and Talbert (2001) supports the importance of communities of teaching practice and provides a survey instrument, including scales of teacher perceptions of collegiality and community.

An Interdisciplinary Community. A different type of teacher community was the focus of a project in an urban high school with 22 English and social studies teachers, a special education teacher, an ESL teacher, and university facilitators (Grossman, Wineburg, & Woolworth, 1998, 2001). The group met at the school twice a month over a two-and-a-half-year period, to participate in joint readings and discussions of history and literature texts, and to plan an interdisciplinary curriculum. Some teachers were interested primarily in the curriculum development and others in the opportunity to read and discuss texts, and struggle with the differences in reading text in the two disciplines. By the fourth month, teachers had divided into multiple factions and alliances (Grossman et al., 2001). Work related to managing group interactions had not been part of the planning process, as the theoretical framework had largely drawn on cognitive psychology.

Grossman et al. (2001) use transcripts of the group's meetings to illustrate a framework that provides the markers of community formation, from beginning, to evolving, to mature, on four dimensions: (a) formation of group identity and norms of interaction; (b) navigating fault lines; (c) negotiating the essential tension; and (d) communal responsibility for individual growth. Data included transcripts of meetings and material resources participants brought to meetings (readings, videotapes, lesson plans, etc.), and other communications from teachers, such as e-mail.

Five semistructured interviews were conducted over the 2.5 years of the project with each individual participant, including a think-aloud task that used a set of readings in history and English, including a poem, an excerpt from a memoir, and a historical document. The purpose of using three different texts was to try to, "understand how teachers constructed interpretations from text and how their readings differed across disciplines" (Grossman

et al., 2001, p. 1006). Teachers were also asked to talk about how students might read these texts. Surveys and evaluations were also collected, as well as documents teachers shared with each other. Field notes and the use of postdiscussion analytic memos were described as useful in reconstructing the affective climate of discussions and aspects of interactions (Grossman et al., 1998).

All text-based discussions of the group were transcribed (Grossman et al., 1998). A four-tiered coding scheme was used: (a) discussion turn (responding to previous comment, asking a question, etc.); (b) each turn according to knowledge source of what was said (autobiographical information, teaching experience, present text, etc.); (c) each comment about texts according to a scheme of evaluating textual understanding (levels of reading)—reading, interpretation, criticism, and epistemological; and (d) code tags: teaching, revoicing, meta, etc. The data set was analyzed to answer questions such as, Are there changes in members participation in group discussions of text—e.g., roles and frequency of participation? Here the assessments describe group processes and individual participation in the group, in an activity outside of the classroom.

Fostering a Community of Teachers as Learners. Four *within* disciplinary perspectives are compared in a project that followed a model proposed for fostering a community of students as learners (FCL) by Brown and Campione (1996). Teacher learning of pedagogical reform was examined for different forms within the disciplines of English language arts, mathematics, science, and social studies (Shulman & Sherin, 2004). Four aspects of FCL were set as themes for the disciplines and the case studies: (a) searching for the big ideas; (b) an analytic challenge—when is a disciplinary topic 'jigsawable'? (c) curricular habits and impact on pedagogical changes; and (d) challenges of implementation of a community of learners.

For the discipline of mathematics, Sherin, Mendez, and Louis (2004) describe the work of two researchers with David, a middle school mathematics teacher, over a two-year period. Data collection the first year was videotaping one class daily during implementation of a 4-week probability unit. The second year his third-period class was videotaped two-to-three times per week for the entire year. Field notes were made each time the class was observed. The three authors met weekly to discuss the classroom experimentation and FCL pedagogy, including discussions of student work, curriculum materials, and videotape excerpts from David's class.

Fine-grained analyses of the videotapes used the techniques of Frederiksen et al. (1998) from the video portfolio project to analyze whole-class instruction and interactions between the teacher and a small numbers of students. The analyses focused on key processes during instruction when teacher knowledge is accessed, drawing on the work of Leinhardt et al. (1991) and using agendas, representations, explanations, and teacher response to student questions. Analyses suggest that trying to apply FCL pedagogy with mathematics was facilitated by development in three related areas of teacher knowledge: (a) understanding of mathematics, from a view of mathematics as a set of concepts to be learned, to a view of mathematics as being composed of important concepts and important processes; (b) implementing mathematics reform, from not just curriculum development and implementation to include redesigning the teacher's role in instruction; and (c) ideas about FCL pedagogy, that the basis for FCL in mathematics was the building of a discourse community.

In reassessing how and what teachers learn, Shulman and Shulman (2004) summarized their work from the FCL and other projects, stressing that, "An accomplished teacher is a member of a professional community, who is ready, willing, and able to teach and learn from his or her teaching experiences" (p. 259). They speculate that there are five clusters of attributes around which accomplished teaching develops—cognitive, dispositional, motivational, performance, and reflective. These clusters have much in common with characteristics of teachers assessed as evidencing self-sustaining, generative change (Franke et al., 2001), and with suggestions to consider individual motivational and dispositional factors, as well as developmental processes, in teacher professional development (Goldsmith and Schifter, 1997). The clusters provide additional areas for developing assessments when educational psychologists are assessing teacher learning and development.

Summary. In this section on teachers as learners in communities of practice, the assessment methods and processes rely heavily on videotapes and text. That is, assessments include analyses of actions and talk (discourse) occurring in settings in which teachers interact with students in classrooms, with other teachers, and with researchers. The activity settings and the context for assessments include individual teachers in classrooms (FCL, Sherin et al., 2004) and teacher chains of assistance in the classroom (QUASAR, Brown et al., 1996). There are also teacher activity settings outside of the classroom (Grossman et al, 2001; Sherin et al, 2004; Sherin & Han, 2004; Stein & Brown, 1997; Stein et al., 1998), and there the focus of assessments changes.

As the units of assessment and context shift, so do the methods and procedures of assessment. The fine-grained cognitive analyses useful for small numbers of individual teachers in videotapes of classroom practice (and interviews about practice) is replaced by content analyses of topics and call-outs in video clubs, and analyses of group processes and discussion content in an interdisciplinary, ongoing group of teachers and researchers. When the focus is the school or mathematics department, a larger shift occurs. Although individual teachers may be the unit of analysis, the number and complexity of activity settings increases, emphasizing activities outside the classroom. In some instances, activity settings are identified outside of the school, such as for teacher participation in activities in professional associations. In assessments for these different context and activity settings, researchers have created other indices or indicators to describe changes, such as the *breadth* and *depth* of teacher participation patterns.

A SPECIAL CASE: THE NBPTS

The National Board of Professional Teaching Standards (NBPTS) sets standards and conducts assessments in order to certify that teachers meet "high and rigorous standards for what accomplished teachers should know and be able to do" (NBPTS, 2001, p. 10). As described earlier, teachers voluntarily participate in the NBPTS process, and teachers typically report that the preparation for certification is valuable (Sato, 2004). As with other large-scale teacher assessments, the NBPTS started with the writing of standards (Porter et al., 2001). The scoring of each entry in a portfolio, such as a videotape, uses rubrics developed from standards. The standards and assessment rubrics provide a framework that is interpreted by teacher candidates in order to prepare their videotapes and portfolios for evaluation by NBPTS.

The work by Frederiksen (1992) and Frederiksen et al. (1998) is discussed first, providing a systemic validity approach to developing a prototype process of teachers developing videos for portfolios. Next two areas of emerging NB research and assessment are identified related to systemic validity of the NBPTS: (a) relationships of NB certification and student achievement; and (b) teacher learning during the NB certification process.

Systemic Validity in Teacher Assessments

Frederiksen et al. (1998) proposed to create and evaluate a prototype for a performance assessment of accomplished teaching that was "systemically valid." Systemic effects would come from three properties of their design: (a) *directness*, evaluating teaching goals and functions as realized in the classroom; (b) *transparency of values and criteria*, using the assessment would make teachers aware of characteristics of outstanding teaching valued in their profession; and (c) *reflective practice*, that is, participating in the assessment process should enable teachers to reflect on their own and others' teaching practice. Practices for viewing and interpreting teaching in the assessment process would contribute to learning and teacher development, and to systemic validity (Frederiksen & Collins, 1989). This contribution would depend on two factors: (a) teachers developing a *socially shared language of practice* for describing important functions of classroom teaching, and (b) teachers *using this language* in discussing videos of teaching covering a wide range of classroom situations.

An interpretive framework (and criteria) would serve as the language of practice. To make sense of classroom videos, teachers would need experience in learning and using a conceptual framework (or criteria) to observe and reflect on their experience. This framework, embedded in the assessment, would need to be useful to teachers talking about their practice and participating in the social activity of preparing or scoring a video portfolio. Criteria needed to, "characterize the functions served by particular teaching goals and processes as they play out in classroom conversations and interactions, rather than refer to particular teaching actions themselves" (Frederiksen et al., 1998, p. 227). Examples of *functional* criteria are, "mathematical thinking is going on" and "Participants in the class are showing mutual respect" and are not focused on the teacher per se.

Initially, a small set of high school mathematics teachers viewed videotapes and made "call-outs" of noteworthy teaching episodes or features of teaching. In an iterative process, sets of categories were developed, resulting in a hierarchical classification, first 18 aspects of teaching and then four general, top-level criteria: Pedagogy, Climate, Mathematical thinking, and Management. A video exemplar library was constructed: criteria and their subgroups or aspects were defined by reference to sets of call-outs, and video footage showing exemplars. Each exemplar included: video footage of a teaching episode, context for the episode, ratings of the quality of the exemplar, and a rationale for the ratings. The library was intended to help teachers learn to "see" (Frederiksen, 1992).

The main work of Frederiksen et al. (1998) consisted of a series of small-scale studies. The studies focused on methods for how to produce and score video portfolios. Fourteen participating teachers were recruited to prepare portfolios; in preparation they participated in video clubs (four to six teachers, plus teacher facilitators, in three high schools). They met six to seven times over the year, and developed three or four practice videos before doing the portfolios. Scorers were eight mathematics teachers; they worked in pairs, independently viewing the portfolio, integrating evidence for the criteria (based on call-outs they recorded), writing a rationale, and participating in social moderation. Scorers were trained on a series of exemplars from the Exemplar Library to 'see' teaching using the interpretive framework.

Studies and analyses examined: (a) whether scorers were influenced by class characteristics, teacher interactions, and student involvement; (b) scorers' classifications of individual teaching episodes and interrelations among the interpretive categories (multidimensional scaling); (c) semantic analysis of scorers' written rationales and scorers' internalization of the categories of the scoring framework; and (d) individual interviews and talk-alouds while scoring a video portfolio. Two approaches to scoring were identified—*top-down*, evidence confirmed the "theory" of the scorer, and *bottom-up*, the scorer recorded evidence (call-outs)—and combined the evidence into an overall evaluation. Effects of participation in the assessment of professional practice were identified in examples (self-reported) of self-assessment, reflective awareness, changes in teaching practices, and, stimulated by the video clubs, trying new forms of teaching. If assessment goals include the enhancement of professional practice, "The design must enable teachers to develop a 'working understanding' of teaching" (Frederiksen et al., 1998, p. 281).

The considerations of systemic validity led to the design properties here of *directness* and *transparency*: (a) identifying call-outs in teacher classroom videotapes; and (b) providing classroom exemplars (on a videotape library) for each of the four main areas of functional criteria identified in the study—Pedagogy, Climate, Mathematical thinking, and Management. The property of *reflective practice* was supported in the video clubs (and see studies by Sherin and colleagues described earlier).

Systemic Validity and the NBPTS

The development and technical qualities of the NBPTS assessments and procedures have been well summarized by Porter et al. (2001). Two areas of emerging research on the NBPTS are briefly identified here: (a) achievement of students of NB certified teachers and noncertified teachers; and (b) teacher learning during NB certification processes. In the first area, recent studies use large-scale existing databases for students and teachers. In the second area, research and assessment are focused on understanding what it is that teachers learn while preparing for NBPTS; these studies indicate a need to examine the contexts in which different aspects of teacher knowledge and practice may be expected to develop.

Student Achievement and NB Teachers. Recent research supported by the NPBTS has examined the relationships of NB teacher certification and gains in student achievement. Goldhaber and Anthony (2004) used 3 years of North Carolina statewide teacher and student data and educational production functions (regression models) to examine teacher effects on student growth on state test scores for grades 3, 4, and 5. Numbers of students for each year and for each subject area were about 200,000; for the total grades 3–5, numbers of students and NB teachers were about 230/11 in 1997, 1,500/77 in 1998, and 4,300/215 in 1999. Student-level value-added models were estimated, and NBCT teachers were compared to unsuccessful NBPTS applicants and to teachers who have not pursued NBPTS certification.

The results indicate that NBPTS clearly identifies the more effective teachers among NBPTS applicants. NB teachers, prior to becoming certified, were more effective at increasing student achievement than their non-certified counterparts. The statistical significance and magnitude of NB teacher effects on student achievement differs by grade level, subject (reading or mathematics), and student type (younger students and low-income students).

A study conducted in Arizona (Vandervoort et al.,2004) compared the achievement scores in reading, mathematics, and language arts for elementary school students of 35 NB certified teachers and noncertified peers in 14 school districts. Four years of results for grades 3–6 for the three tests yielded 48 comparisons. Gain scores were adjusted for student entering ability in this causal comparative design. Students of NB teachers did better on 35 of 48 comparisons, and 11 comparisons were statistically significant. Mean differences in effect sizes were about .12 over all years and subjects.

Cavalluzzo (2004) also examined student and teacher records, using a sample of ninth- and 10th-grade students from Miami–Dade County public schools. Production function models (regression analyses) were used, with the state end-of-grade examination in mathematics as the dependent variable. Characteristics of students (e.g., repeating a grade, gifted) and teacher characteristics (NB certified, failed NB, withdrew) and additional teacher variables (regular state certification in mathematics, teaching in license, etc.), and school variables (per pupil spending, student mobility, etc.) were entered in the set of regression models. The regression analyses indicated that the coefficient on NBC is positive, and significant; the effect size is about .12.

To date, these studies of the relationships between NB certification and student achievement find modest and significant effect sizes, and differences between NB certified teachers, those who fail or withdraw from the NB certification process, and other teachers.

Teacher Learning.. Several studies have emerged that begin to assess the effects of NBPTS certification processes on teachers. Lustick (2002) described a study using a quasi-experimental design, the Recurrent Institutional Cycle Design (RICD), to answer the question of what teachers may be learning from National Board certification, focusing on the Adolescent and Young Adult Science area. The design included cross-sectional and longitudinal data on 120 teacher candidates for certification. The design permits comparison of possible (differential) teacher learning effects for the 13 NBPTS standards, from the time a teacher initiates the assessment process to completion. Pre- and postgroup assessments were structured teacher interviews, transcribed and then scored by multiple assessors according to the NBPTS framework for accomplished science teaching.

Lustick and Sykes (2004) report findings (effect size of .47) suggesting that the intervention (preparation for the NBPTS certification process) has an effect on candidates' understanding of science teaching-related knowledge. This is based on comparing groups of teachers before (pre) undertaking certification and (different) groups upon (post) completion of the process. The biggest effect sizes (learning outcomes) were for two of the 13 standards—Science Inquiry (.61) and Assessment (.60). Analyses of qualitative data (open-ended interview questions) found three standards were most frequently mentioned by teachers—Scientific Inquiry, Assessment, and Reflection—and they may have been most productive in stimulating teacher learning. For example, the improvement in Scientific Inquiry supports the inference that teachers are learning to align their practice with NB's conception of scientific inquiry and teaching; similar comments apply to the Assessment standard, which emphasizes repeated use of focused, detailed and extensive evidence around student learning.

Another finding from the qualitative analyses suggested different orientations to learning from the NB certification process: (a) *dynamic learning*, self-reports of "immediate, meaningful change in a teacher's beliefs, understandings, and actions in the classroom" (p. 31); (b) *technical learning*, an emphasis on acquiring techniques useful in obtaining certification that do not carry over to teaching itself; and (c) *deferred learning*, that there might be influences on practice sometime in the future. Although there are limitations in this study, such as the fact that agreement among raters was modest (*r* about .46), the design is a valuable approach to the pre- and postintervention measurement problem in this certification context.

Lustic and Sykes provide one aspect of systemic validity-related evidence. As they point out, NBPTS was clearly intended to serve the purpose of professional development. The performance assessment processes include portfolios and assessment center measures, a long process of preparation, and the encouragement that teachers have mentors and coached performance and/or work with colleagues; all are designed to foster learning. One question is whether and to what extent the NBPTS process can be oriented to be analogous to a teacher's classroom or formative assessment of students (Black & Wiliam, 2003; Brookhart, 2003). That is, to what extent can the "system" serve more directly to support learning and provide information on the "way forward," as processes and assessments that can lead to learning for professional development. The Lustic and Sykes (2004) categories of teacher orientation to learning from the NB certification process (dynamic learning vs. technical learning) indicate the importance of trying to identify the systemic effects of NB assessment processes.

The NBPTS has taken steps to provide information, through written materials prepared for candidates, and a Web link to the *Digital Edge Learning Interchange*, an online library that includes examples of the teaching of national board-certified teachers. The library has lesson plans, video clips, student work samples, assessment tools, resources, research, and teacher reflections. Another NBPTS web feature on *Candidate Support and Higher Education Initiatives* assists teachers to access state and local information supporting teacher NBPTS certification, and to locate names of board-certified teachers. The use of written materials and Web examples of NBPST are a part of what teachers may find useful. However, if a teacher relies primarily on written materials there may be several consequences. One consequence is that teachers may focus narrowly on understanding and interpreting the NBPTS "discourse." The second consequence is that there is no direct or formative assessment of the teacher's own interpretations of these materials.

Surveys and individual interviews provide examples of teachers stating the value of preparing for certification. Lustic and Sykes provide more direct evidence of teacher learning in the area of science certification. And, studies are beginning to examine more closely what happens when teachers meet in groups to talk about the standards, teaching videos, and writing about practice. Burroughs, Schwartz, and Hendricks-Lee (2000) consider difficulties candidates report experiencing, and interpreted them as difficulties with the certification *discourse*. Four candidates participated in an NBPTS support group that met monthly, funded by a state department of education, and situated at a large university. Burroughs et al. observed and interviewed the four teachers: two were part of a group that met frequently, sharing and critiquing a particular portfolio entry; one met with a colleague and attended some monthly meetings; and the fourth worked with a colleague at a nearby school and went to few monthly meetings. Interviews were transcribed; field notes were made as candidates discussed entry requirements and standards, in working sessions with drafts of portfolio pieces.

The candidate difficulties that emerged from the qualitative data were classified into five categories: writing apprehension, representing tacit knowledge, understanding sampling logic, negotiating the standards, and providing evidence from teaching (role of evidence and artifacts). For example, in putting practice into words, a teacher also had to show that practice matched the standards, that is, negotiating the standards: "You're matching [narratives] up to the standards and you know, though, usually they do match up, it's just finding that exact place where they do match up and seeing how their wording is" (Burroughs et al., p. 360). Burroughs et al. are describing part of the nature of the task of becoming board certified—joining the NBPTS discourse community. In this case, the teacher's comment may have something in common with the teachers assessed for NB learning, and the Lustic and Sykes (2004) category of *technical learning*, where the techniques useful in certification may not carry over into teaching.

Burroughs et al. make several points about the NBPTS standards, suggesting that they are highly decontextualized and represented in written language, and teachers, in return, must represent their practice in the same form. Keiffer-Barone and Burroughs (2002) collected data over a 1-year period for a group of five teachers participating in a support group preparing for the Early Adolescence/English Language Arts certificate. Data were collected by participant observation, semistructured interviews, and document analysis. Teachers met biweekly, for discussion, drafting, and revision of portfolios. There were large-group meetings and small-group meetings with a board-certified teacher as mentor.

Difficult discussions were about describing their professional accomplishments: What "counts"? How did the standards define an accomplishment, and how did their involvement meet the standards of accomplished teaching? The mentor teacher guided discussions, about what activities "fit" the improvement of instructional programs, advancement of knowledge, practice of colleagues and community involvement of the standards. Work with the teaching videotapes was reported to be important and the discourse of the standards-assisted standards-based feedback.

Summary. Systemic validity (Frederiksen et al., 1998) places an emphasis on examining the structure and processes of the NBPTS certification from the perspectives of designing systems that have properties of directness, transparency of values and criteria, and reflective practice. The recent studies of student achievement and NB-certified teachers compared to other teachers show modest effect sizes. Vandervoort et al. (2004) raise the question of "false positives" among NB-certified teachers, citing a study by Pool, Ellett, Schiavone, and Carey-Lewis. The study by Lustic and Sykes (2004) also suggests variability among candidates and NB teachers in the type of learning that occurs during certification, and might contribute to greater variability among NB-certified teachers.

Research is needed to examine how representative the performance of knowledge and practice demonstrated for NB assessment certification is of sustained classroom practice, that is, for larger and more sustained samples of practice in school settings. The emerging assessments of teacher learning in preparation groups can be extended to other situations, such as teacher use of Web-based models of teaching, including use of NBPTS web site links. The teaching models available to NB candidates and the extent to which they implement NB standards can be assessed, as well as the transparency and values in criteria for rubrics and standards. Examining major aspects of NB processes for their support of teacher learning (that is, formative assessment properties) may yield results and suggestions that support both the consistency and depth of teacher development. In brief, the NBPTS offers a challenge to educational psychologists who study teacher learning and development, as well as assessment researchers. The assessment methods and procedures described in work on teacher knowledge and teacher learning communities have contributions to make in research and development of the NBPTS and to understanding teacher learning and professional development more generally.

CONCLUSIONS

Several lines of emphasis emerged from reviewing assessments of teacher learning and development. These are (a) the main contexts in which assessments of teacher learning and development are taking place; (b) the importance of technology to these assessments and teacher learning; (c) the challenges in emerging areas for assessment; and (d) revisiting validity.

Contexts of Assessment

Of the several contexts for assessment of teacher learning and development, two currently dominate in the studies reviewed here. These contexts for assessments are (a) teacher interactions with students in classroom practice; and (b) interactions with teacher colleagues, mentors, and researchers or assessors. These social contexts are seen as important for teacher learning and development, and hence for assessment. In order to document change in classroom practice and teacher talk about practice, records of practice and teacher talk about practice are the basic "data" for analyses.

Teacher talk or discourse can occur in many settings, including interviews, groups discussing practice, viewing videotapes, or other settings, such as tasks in which teacher explanations and representations of problems are elicited. These are settings in which explanations and justifications of subject matter knowledge, knowledge of students and student assessments, beliefs, pedagogy, and understandings about practice can emerge. Assessments in the context of practice and in teachers' talk about practice (including its conceptual and theoretical bases) underscore the importance of using multiple sources of data as evidence for inferences about teacher learning and development.

Use of Technology

Videotapes are often used in the assessments examined in this review. The use of videotapes in interviews, classrooms, and group discussions results in records that can be examined many times, as well as by different viewers. Videotapes are particularly important for teacher learning, as well as for assessment. This technology affords and encourages checking different interpretations against other videotape samples and transcripts, and data from other sources. A teacher can view classroom videotapes alone, with a mentor, or in small groups of teachers and researchers. Evaluations and assessments of teacher learning and development from use of other technology, such as Web-based resources of exemplars of teaching or online mentoring, were not readily available. These are also important areas for research and development of assessments of teacher learning.

Challenges in Emerging Areas for Assessments

The areas emerging as challenges for assessments include (a) constructs in the areas of teacher knowledge; (b) constructs in the areas of motivation and teachers sustaining their own learning and development, and related assessment constructs of teacher learning communities; and (c) teacher learning in the special case of the NBPTS.

Teacher Knowledge. Researchers have continued to define and assess constructs related to how and what specific content knowledge is used in teaching. Initial work from the TELT study was extended by development of survey or indicator items on mathematical knowledge for teaching (Hill, Schilling, & Ball, 2004) and knowledge for teaching reading (Phelps & Schilling, 2004). Examples of other constructs emerging from assessments of teacher learning are teacher knowledge of classroom formative assessment in the context of a subject matter (e.g., Black & Wiliam, 2003; Black, Harrison, Lee, Marshall, & Wiliam, 2003); and content knowledge complexes—linked subject matter and pedagogical content knowledge (Sherin, 2002). These areas pose major challenges in continuing to define the relevant processes and to develop replicable assessment procedures.

Teachers Sustaining Their Own Development. There are references to motivation and affective (or dispositional) characteristics as important in teacher learning. Few studies address these areas, areas that are likely to be important for assessments of long-term professional learning and development. However, some case studies and research are suggestive of their importance (Schifter & Fosnot, 1993; Shulman & Shulman, 2004). Goldsmith and Schifter (1997) suggested that descriptions of teacher development need to add accounts of individual motivational and dispositional factors. Franke et al. (2001) described teachers who *are* self-generating and continue to modify their practice. These are additional areas for developing assessments when educational psychologists are assessing teacher learning and development, particularly for long-term research and follow-up studies.

The work of Schifter and that of the CGI research team also suggest that assessments in long term follow-up studies need to include areas such as teachers' perceptions of influences on their continuing professional learning and development (see also McLaughlin & Talbert, 2001). These influences may include colleagues, professional development programs, and institutional supports.

Teacher Learning and NBPTS. The NBPTS is a special case of assessments and standards providing a structure and processes intended to stimulate teacher learning as well as assess attainment. The exact nature of what is learned in NBPTS preparation, and how it is learned, is just beginning to be examined. Researchers have started to describe some of the processes used and the difficulties that teachers encounter in preparing materials, videotapes, and so on for the NBPTS standards. The Lustic and Sykes (2004) study provides preliminary and important findings that suggest examining which standards teachers focus on, perceptions of what specifically is learned in the various parts of the assessment process, and orientations toward learning and professional development held by applicants.

The NBPTS has a community of NBPTS assessment developers, external users of the NBPTS, and internal users—teachers, their mentors, and colleagues. A systemic view of validity (Frederiksen & Collins, 1989) suggests the importance of the internal users of the NBPTS. In NBPTS a logic linking standards, assessment procedures, and consistent coding and reliability of assessor raters has been established. It is less clear what the NBPTS assessment system "means" for teacher development, from the interpretive and practice perspectives of teachers, their colleagues, and their mentors.

Revisiting Validity

This chapter began with, and now concludes with, a discussion of teacher assessment and validity. Donmoyer (2001) suggested that studies of teaching can be made for different purposes and can be examined using different methods and perspectives. The assessment examples in this chapter are with their exception of the NBPTS, set within particular research studies, many exploring aspects of teacher learning in reform projects.

Evaluating validity-related evidence for interpretations and use of assessment findings may be thought about as a process, a process of making a series of judgments. These judgments take into account the underlying theories, the details, and the explicitness of the entire set of methods and procedures of a study that yields assessments of teacher development. The reasoning and justifications that are intended to support interpretations of teacher learning and development are most persuasive when there is an integrated argument based on several lines of evidence. As with all arguments for validity, accepting validity-related evidence ultimately rests on the underlying theory and arguments for the assessments; these arguments are used in a web of meaning, and justified within a community—here a community of researchers, instructional and assessment developers, and teachers. More specifically, in the context of the NBPTS teachers *are* interpreters and users of teacher assessments: Teacher interpretations and uses provide necessary validity evidence and are integral to systemic validation arguments for teacher assessments.

References

American Educational Research Association, American Psychological Association, & National Council on Measurement in Education. (1999). *Standards for educational and psychological testing.* Washington, DC: American Educational Research Association.

Ball, D. L., Lubienski, S. T., & Mewborn, D. S. (2001). Research on teaching mathematics: The unsolved problem of teachers' mathematical knowledge. In V. Richardson (Ed.), *Handbook of research on teaching* (4th ed., pp. 433–456). Washington, DC: American Educational Research Association.

Baxter, J. A., & Lederman, N. G. (1999). Assessment and measurement of pedagogical content knowledge. In J. Gess-Newsome & N. G. Lederman (Eds.), *Examining pedagogical content knowledge: The construct and its implications for science education* (pp. 147–161). Norwell, MA: Kluwer Academic.

Berliner, D. C., & Calfee, R. C. (Eds.). (1996). *Handbook of educational psychology.* New York: Simon & Schuster Macmillan.

Black, P., Harrison, C., Lee, C., Marshall, B., & Wiliam, D. (2003). *Assessment for learning: Putting it in practice.* Maidenhead, England: Open University Press.

Black, P., & Wiliam, D. (1998). Assessment and classroom learning. *Assessment in Education: Principles, Policy & Practice, 5*(1), 7–74.

Black, P., & Wiliam, D. (2003). "In praise of educational research": Formative assessment. *British Educational Research Journal, 29,* 623–637.

Brookhart, S. M. (2003). Developing measurement theory for classroom assessment purposes and uses. *Educational Measurement: Issues and Practice, 22*(4), 5–12.

Brophy, J. (Ed.). (2004). *Using video in teacher education: Vol. 10. Advances in research on teaching.* San Diego, CA: Elsevier.

Brown, A. L., & Campione, J. C. (1996). Psychological theory and the design of innovative learning environments: On procedures, principles, and systems. In L. Schauble & R. Glaser (Eds.), *Innovations in learning: New environments for education* (pp. 289–325). Mahwah, NJ: Lawerence Erlbaum Associates.

Brown, C. A., Stein, M. K., & Forman, E. A. (1996). Assisting teachers and students to reform the mathematics classroom. *Educational Studies in Mathematics, 31,* 63–93.

Burroughs, R., Schwartz, T. A., & Hendricks-Lee, M. (2000). Communities of practice and discourse communities: Negotiating boundaries in NBPTS certification. *Teachers College Record, 102,* 344–374.

Carpenter, T. P., Fennema, E., Peterson, P. L., & Carey, D. A. (1988). Teachers' pedagogical content knowledge of students' problem solving in elementary arithmetic. *Journal for Research in Mathematics Education, 19,* 385–401.

Carpenter, T. P., Fennema, E., Peterson, P. L., Chiang, C-P., & Loef, M. (1989). Using knowledge of children's mathematics thinking in classroom teaching: An experimental study. *American Educational Research Journal, 26,* 499–531.

Cavalluzzo, L. C. (2004, November). *Is National Board Certification an effective signal of teacher quality?* Alexandria, VA: CNA Corporation.

Clark, K. K., & Lesh, R. (2003). A modeling approach to describe teacher knowledge. In R. Lesh & H. M. Doerr (Eds.), *Beyond constructivism: Models and modeling perspectives on mathematics problem solving, learning, and teaching* (pp. 159–173). Mahwah, NJ: Lawerence Erlbaum Associates.

Cobb, P., & McClain, K. (2001). An approach for supporting teachers' learning in social context. In F-L. Lin & T. J. Cooney (Eds.), *Making sense of mathematics teacher education* (pp. 207–231). Dordrecht, The Netherlands: Kluwer Academic.

Cobb, P., & Yackel, E. (1996). Constructivist, emergent, and sociocultural perspectives in the context of developmental research. *Educational Psychologist, 31,* 175–190.

Cochran-Smith, M., & Lytle, S. L. (1999). Relationships of knowledge and practice: Teacher learning in communities. In A. Iran-Nejad & P. D. Pearson (Eds.), *Review of research in education* (Vol. 24, pp. 249–305). Washington, DC: American Educational Research Association.

Coffey, J. E., Moorthy, S., Sato, M., Thibeault, M., & Atkin, J. M. (in press). *Changing everyday assessment in the classroom.* New York: Teachers College Press.

Donmoyer, R. (2001). Paradigm talk reconsidered. In V. Richardson (Ed.), *Handbook of research on teaching* (4th ed., pp. 174–197). Washington, DC: American Educational Research Association.

Dwyer, C. A., & Stufflebeam, D. (1996). Teacher evaluation. In D. C. Berliner & R. C. Calfee (Eds.), *Handbook of educational psychology* (pp. 765–786). New York: Simon & Schuster Macmillan.

Fennema, E., Carpenter, T. P., Franke, M. L., Levi, L., Jacobs, V. R., & Empson, S. B. (1996). A longitudinal study of learning to use children's thinking in mathematics instruction. *Journal for Research in Mathematics Education, 27,* 403–434.

Fennema, E., & Nelson, B. S. (Eds.). (1997). *Mathematics teachers in transition.* Mahwah, NJ: Lawerence Erlbaum Associates.

Fenstermacher, G. D. (1994). The place of practical argument in the education of teachers. In V. Richardson (Ed.), *Teacher change and the staff development process* (pp. 23–42). New York: Teachers College Press.

Franke, M. L., Carpenter, T. P., Levi, L., & Fennema, E. (2001). Capturing teachers' generative change: A follow-up study of professional development in mathematics. *American Educational Research Journal, 38,* 653–689.

Franke, M. L., Fennema, E., & Carpenter, T. (1997). Changing teachers: Interactions between beliefs and classroom practice. In E. Fennema & B. S. Nelson (Eds.), *Mathematics teachers in transition* (pp. 255–282). Mahwah, NJ: Lawerence Erlbaum Associates.

Frederiksen, J. R. (1992, April). *Learning to "see": Scoring video portfolios.* Paper presented at the annual meeting of the

American Educational Research Association, San Francisco, CA.

Frederiksen, J. R., & Collins, A. (1989). A systems approach to educational testing. *Educational Researcher, 18*(9), 27-32.

Frederiksen, J. R., Sipusic, M., Sherin, M., & Wolfe, E. W. (1998). Video portfolio assessment: Creating a framework for viewing the functions of teaching. *Educational Assessment, 5,* 225-297.

Gipps, C. (1999). Socio-cultural aspects of assessment. In A. Iran-Nejad & P. D. Pearson (Eds.), *Review of research in education* (Vol. 24, pp. 355-392). Washington, DC: American Educational Research Association.

Goldhaber, D., & Anthony, E. (2004). *Can teacher quality be effectively assessed?* Retrieved June 14, 2004, from Center for Reinventing Public Education Web site: http://www.crpe.org/workingpapers/pdf/NBPTSquality_report.pdf

Goldsmith, L., & Schifter, D. (1997). Understanding teachers in transition: Characteristics of a model for developing teachers. In E. Fennema & B. S. Nelson (Eds.), *Mathematics teachers in transition* (pp. 19-54). Mahwah, NJ: Lawerence Erlbaum Associates.

Grossman, P., Wineburg, S., & Woolworth, S. (1998, April). *But what did we learn? Understanding changes in a community of teacher learners.* Paper presented at the annual meeting of the American Educational Research Association, San Diego, CA.

Grossman, P., Wineburg, S., & Woolworth, S. (2001). Toward a theory of teacher community. *Teachers College Record, 103,* 942-1012.

Grouws, D. A. (Ed.). (1992). *Handbook of research on mathematics teaching and learning.* New York: Macmillan.

Hambleton, R. K. (1996). Advances in assessment models, methods, and practices. In D. C. Berliner & R. C. Calfee (Eds.), *Handbook of educational psychology* (pp. 899-925). New York: Macmillan.

Hill, H. C., & Ball, D. L. (2004). Learning mathematics for teaching: Results from California's Mathematics Professional Development Institutes. *Journal for Research in Mathematics Education, 35*(5), 330-351.

Hill, H. C., Rowan, B., & Ball, D. L. (2005). Effects of teachers' mathematical knowledge for teaching on student achievement. *American Educational Research Journal, 42*(2), 371-406.

Hill, H. C., Schilling, S. G., & Ball, D. L. (2004). Developing measures of teachers' mathematics knowledge for teaching. *Elementary School Journal, 105*(1), 11-30.

Jones, Y. (2005). *Knowing how and knowing why: Expert and in transition teacher understandings of representations, translations, and connections for dividing with fractions.* Unpublished doctoral dissertation, City University of New York.

Keiffer-Barrone, S. K., & Burroughs, R. (2002, April). *It's not about the test: The National Board for Professional Teaching Standards as a discourse community.* Paper presented at the annual meeting of the American Educational Research Association, New Orleans, LA.

Kennedy, M. M., Ball, D. L., & McDiarmid, G. W. (1993). *A study package for examining and tracking changes in teachers' knowledge* (Tech. Ser. 93-1). East Lansing, MI: National Center for Research on Teacher Education.

Lampert, M. (1990). When the problem is not the question and the solution is not the answer: Mathematical knowing and teaching. *American Educational Research Journal, 27,* 29-63.

Langenthal, A. (2004). *How do novice and experienced first-grade teachers evaluate reading progress in their students?* Unpublished doctoral dissertation, City University of New York.

Lehrer, R., & Schauble, L. (2000). Modeling in mathematics and science. In R. Glaser (Ed.), *Advances in instructional psychology: Vol. 5. Educational design and cognitive science* (pp. 101-159). Mahwah, NJ: Lawerence Erlbaum Asociates.

Leinhardt, G. (1989). Math lessons: A contrast of novice and expert competence. *Journal for Research in Mathematics Education, 20,* 52-75.

Leinhardt, G. (1993). On teaching. In R. Glaser (Ed.), *Advances in instructional psychology* Vol. 4 (pp. 1-54). Hillsdale, NJ: Lawerence Erlbaum Associates.

Leinhardt, G. (2001). Instructional explanations: A commonplace for teaching and location for contrast. In V. Richardson (Ed.), *Handbook of research on teaching* (4th ed., pp. 333-357). Washington, DC: American Educational Research Association.

Leinhardt, G., & Greeno, J. G. (1986). The cognitive skill of teaching. *Journal of Educational Psychology, 78,* 75-95.

Leinhardt, G., Putnam, R. T., Stein, M. K., & Baxter, J. (1991). Where subject knowledge matters. In J. Brophy (Ed.), *Advances in research on teaching: Vol. 2. Teacher's knowledge of subject matter as it relates to their teaching practice* (pp. 87-113). Greenwich, CT: JAI Press.

Leinhardt, G., & Smith, D. A. (1985). Expertise in mathematics instruction: Subject matter knowledge. *Journal of Educational Psychology, 77,* 247-271.

Lustick, D. S. (2002, April). *National board certification as professional development.* Paper presented at the annual meeting of the American Educational Research Association, New Orleans, LA.

Lustic, D., & Sykes, G. (2004, November). *National Board Certification as professional development: What are teachers learning? An investigation of learning from the NBPTS certification process.* East Lansing, MI: College of Education, Michigan State University.

Ma, L. (1999). *Knowing and teaching mathematics: Teachers' understanding of fundamental mathematics in China and the United States.* Mahwah, NJ: Lawerence Erlbaum Associates.

Mayer, R. E. (2004). Teaching of subject matter. *Annual Review of Psychology, 55,* 715-744.

McLaughlin, M. W., & Talbert, J. E. (2001). *Professional communities and the work of high school teaching.* Chicago: The University of Chicago Press.

Munby, H., Russell, T., & Martin, A. K. (2001). Teachers' knowledge and how it develops. In V. Richardson (Ed.), *Handbook of research on teaching* (4th ed., pp. 877-904). Washington, DC: American Educational Research Association.

National Board for Professional Teaching Standards. (2001). *The impact of National Board Certification on teachers: A survey of National Board certified teachers and assessors.* Retrieved June 1, 2004 from http://www.nbpts.org/pdf/ResRpt.pdf

National Council of Teachers of Mathematics. (2000). *Principles and standards for school mathematics.* Reston, VA: Author.

National Research Council. (1996). *National science education standards.* Washington, DC: National Academy Press.

Peterson, P. L., Fennema, A., Carpenter, T. P., & Loef, M. (1989). Teachers' pedagogical content beliefs in mathematics. *Cognition and Instruction, 6,* 1-40.

Phelps, G., & Schilling, S. (2004). Developing measures of content knowledge for teaching reading. *Elementary School Journal, 105*(1), 31-48.

Porter, A. C., Youngs, P., & Odden, A. (2001). Advances in teacher assessments and their uses. In V. Richardson (Ed.), *Handbook of research on teaching* (4th ed., pp. 259-297). Washington, DC: American Educational Research Association.

Richardson, V. (Ed.). (1994). *Teacher change and the staff development process.* New York: Teachers College Press.

Richardson, V. (Ed.). (2001). *Handbook of research on teaching* (4th ed.). Washington, DC: American Educational Research Association.

Richardson, V., Anders, P., Tidwell, D., & Lloyd, C. (1991). The relationship between teachers' beliefs and practices in reading comprehension instruction. *American Educational Research Journal, 28,* 559-586.

Richardson, V., & Hamilton, M. L. (1994). The practical-argument staff development process. In V. Richardson (Ed.), *Teacher change and the staff development process* (pp. 109-134). New York: Teachers College Press.

Richardson, V., & Placier, P. (2001). Teacher change. In V. Richardson (Ed.), *Handbook of research on teaching* (4th ed., pp. 905-947). Washington, DC: American Educational Research Association.

Rowan, B., Harrison, D. M., & Hayes, A. (2004). Using instructional logs to study mathematics curriculum and teaching in the early grades. *Elementary School Journal, 105*(1), 103-127.

Sandoval, W. A., & Bell, P. (2004). Design-based research methods for studying learning in context: Introduction. *Educational Psychologist, 39*(4), 199-201.

Sato, M. (2004, April). *Teacher learning through the National Board certification process.* Paper presented at the annual meeting of the American Educational Research Association, San Diego, CA.

Schifter, D, & Fosnot, C. T. (Eds.). (1993). *Reconstructing mathematics education: Stories of teachers meeting the challenge of reform.* New York: Teachers College Press.

Schifter, D., & Simon, M. A. (1992). Assessing teachers' development of a constructivist view of mathematics learning. *Teaching & Teacher Education, 8,* 187-197.

Sherin, M. G. (2002). When teaching becomes learning. *Cognition and Instruction, 20,* 119-150.

Sherin, M. G., & Han, S. Y. (2004). Teacher learning in the context of a video club. *Teacher and Teacher Education, 20,* 163-183.

Sherin, M. G., Mendez, E. P., & Louis, D. A. (2004). A discipline apart: The challenge of 'fostering a community of learners' in a mathematics classroom. *Journal of Curriculum Studies, 36*(2), 207-232.

Shulman, L. S. (1986). Paradigms and research programs in the study of teaching: A contemporary perspective. In. M. C. Wittrock (Ed.), *Handbook of research on teaching* (3rd ed., pp. 3-36). New York: Macmillan.

Shulman, L. S., & Sherin, M. G. (2004). Fostering communities of teachers as learners: Disciplinary perspectives. *Journal of Curriculum Studies, 36*(2), 135-140.

Shulman, L. S., & Shulman, J. H. (2004). How and what teachers learn: A shifting perspective. *Journal of Curriculum Studies, 36*(2), 257-271.

Silver, E. A., & Stein, M. K. (1996). The QUASAR project: The "revolution of the possible" in mathematics instructional reform in urban middle schools. *Urban Education, 30,* 476-522.

Simon, M. A., & Schifter, D. (1991). Towards a constructivist perspective: An intervention study of mathematics teacher development. *Educational Studies in Mathematics, 22,* 309-331.

Stein, M. K., & Brown, C. (1997). Teacher learning in a social context: Integrating collaborative and institutional processes with the study of teacher change. In E. Fennema & B. S. Nelson (Eds.), *Mathematics teachers in transition* (pp. 155-192). Mahwah, NJ: Lawrence Erlbaum Associates.

Stein, M. K., Silver, E. A., & Smith, M. S. (1998). Mathematics reform and teacher development: A community of practice perspective. In J. G. Greeno & S. V. Goldman (Eds.), *Thinking practices in mathematics and learning* (pp. 17-52). Mahwah, NJ: Lawrence Erlbaum Associates.

Tharp, R. G., & Gallimore, R. (1988). *Rousing minds to life: Teaching, learning, and schooling in social context.* New York: Cambridge University Press.

Tittle, C. K. (1989). Validity: Whose construction is it in the teaching and learning context? *Educational Measurement: Issues and Practice, 8,* 5-13, 24.

Tittle, C. K. (1994). Toward an educational psychology of assessment for teaching and learning: Theories, contexts, and validation arguments. *Educational Psychologist, 29,* 149-162.

Torrance, H., & Pryor, J. (1998). *Investigating formative assessment: Teaching, learning and assessment in the classroom.* Philadelphia: Open University Press.

Torrance, H., & Pryor, J. (2000, April). *Developing formative assessment in the classroom.* Paper presented at the annual meeting of the American Educational Research Association, New Orleans, LA.

Vandervoort, L. G., Amrein-Beardsley, A., & Berliner, D. C. (2004, September 8). National Board certified teachers and their students' achievement. *Education Policy*

Analysis Archives, 12(46). Retrieved December 13, 2004 from http://epaa.asu.edu/epaav12n46/

Van Es, E. A., & Sherin, M. G. (2002). Learning to notice: Scaffolding new teachers' interpretations of classroom interactions. *Journal of Technology and Teacher Education, 10*, 571–596.

Wiliam, D., Lee, C., Harrison, C., & Black, P. (2004). Teachers developing assessment for learning: Impact on student achievement. *Assessment in Education: Principles, Policy and Practice, 11*(1), 49–65.

Wilson, S. M., & Berne, J. (1999). Teacher learning and the acquisition of professional knowledge: An examination of research on contemporary professional development. In A. Iran-Nejad & P. D. Pearson (Eds.), *Review of research in education* (Vol. 24, pp. 173–209). Washington, DC: American Educational Research Association.

Wood, T., Cobb, P., & Yackel, E. (1991). Change in teaching mathematics: A case study. *American Educational Research Journal, 28*, 587–616.

AFTERWORD

Patricia A. Alexander
University of Maryland

Philip H. Winne
Simon Fraser University

In bringing this volume to a close, we reflect briefly on relations between its content and the educational and political context in which those ideas and perspectives have taken shape. Here we construe *context* in a broad manner: more accurately as a metacontext—a melding of educational psychology's past, present, and future. For us, there is no question that the collective wisdom represented in this Handbook can and should inform and enlighten those concerned and committed to learning and teaching in all its forms and settings. But some overarching aspects of this volume might not be highly salient even to those well versed in some of its individual topics or thematic areas. As editors, we believe we occupy a unique position to observe these overarching aspects, having shepherded the volume from inception to print.

For that reason, we take this occasion—this coda—to share realizations that arose during the editorial process in hope of stimulating further thought. Specifically, we ponder three final contrasts that, in our view, mark the field of educational psychology and forecast issues that will shape future research and educational relevance:

- Complexity versus certainty
- Reconceptualization or reiteration
- Interdisciplinarity and indistinguishability

Our discussion of these matters is punctuated by reflections of David Berliner and Robert Calfee, coeditors of the first edition of the Handbook, whose opening chapters capture the past and potential future of this field.

COMPLEXITY VERSUS CERTAINTY

Berliner observed that educational psychology "is complex enough an enterprise to make some educational psychologists and social scientists despair" (p. 6, this volume). Perusing this volume confirms Berliner's concern about the complexity of scholarship in educational psychology that must address myriad factors within a matrix of *person × content × context × time* (Alexander, 2005; Berliner, this volume). Indeed, each chapter in this Handbook has itself been the subject of scores of studies and extensive volumes over the past decade and into the distant past. Moreover, even the coverage in this large volume is but the tip of the proverbial iceberg; there are more topics, theories, models, and perspectives that could have been included.

This conceptual complexity is exacerbated by ontological and epistemological issues that may prove even more a barrier to achieving educational relevance. The ontological and epistemological stances within the community of educational psychologists are truly diverse. Theories and models of learning and teaching range from radical constructivism to situativity and from behaviorism to socioculturalism. There is no single-mindedness within our community. We view this as a strength and a challenge.

We concur with Berliner that relationships between educational psychologists and educational practitioners have been rocky. Some educational psychologists have perceived themselves as scientifically superior to educational practitioners; some educational practitioners have judged educational psychologists to be detached from or ignorant of everyday issues and concerns. Presently, as Calfee noted in his chapter, educational psychologists continue to seek appropriate relations with practice. The problem is made all the worse by the seemingly obsessive focus on test achievement within contemporary postindustrial societies, most notably the United States. In essence, whereas educational psychologists want to pursue research on learning and teaching, remaining cognizant of the complexity of *person × content × context × time* configurations, the public and policymakers seem much more narrowly focused on test achievement, especially in basicmakers reading and mathematics for underachieving students. Educational psychology and educational practice may find themselves at ontological loggerheads over the relevance of theory and research that ranges widely, relative to work that addresses just today's issue as framed by today's sociocultural context.

There are also nontrivial epistemological differences between educational psychologists and practitioners in education that warrant consideration. In recognition of their scientific roots, educational researchers speak and write conditionally. We are sensitive to limitations of our work, attentive to the conditions over which our findings generalize, and embrace variance as a source of information. This cautious, conditional stance of science fails to translate well outside our community and, if Cronbach (1975) was right, may be an intrinsic weakness in the joust of epistemology and practice. As Berliner and Calfee acknowledge, even as our science reveals and brings thoughtful order to this complexity, the public and the policymakers seek one-dimensional and near-certain resolutions to educational problems everyone recognizes as serious.

Is there a resolution to this contest between complexity versus certainty? If we look outside educational psychology to the domain of physics, one possibility arises. As Nobel Prize physicist Leon Lederman (1995) argued, the willingness of physicists to abandon the search for certainty was a breakthrough for that field. Scientists were free to explore the boundaries of possibilities in nature and, as possible, to bring current knowledge to bear on practical problems.

With that knowledge [that atoms produce light when electrons jump to a lower energy level] we have been able to fill the world with LASERs and television sets and fluorescent bulbs and everything that creates light. But even though we can make these things, physicists realized that we will never be able to know how an individual electron behaves. Complete certainty about such a simple and fundamental fact could never be known. Instead of certainty, we would have to live with uncertainty. And that, ironically, was what revolutionized physics—it was the "big" discovery.

We suggest it is worthwhile for educational psychologists to adopt this stance. Even if we cannot abandon our responsibility to ensure that practitioners realize our findings have variance (our confidence interval), we can communicate what we know with appropriate conviction and clarity to those who seek anchors in the turbulent waters of educational practice. In reading the contributions of this Handbook, we believe it is evident there are many such principles that merit communication. Although applications of principles do not have certain outcomes in the case of any particular individual, these guiding principles do have direct relevance to enhancing learning and teaching in schools and other venues.

RECONCEPTUALIZATION OR REITERATION

Handbooks, such as this one, have as one goal encapsulating complex domains and years of theory and research. In this Handbook, we expect readers will discern trends that currently dominate. As with all complex domains, ours can be perceived through a veil of "isms." As Berliner and Calfee discuss, our history is one of moves and shifts: from pragmatism to behaviorism and from information processing to constructivism, and more. For instance, when describing recurring tensions between the scientific and the functional, Berliner remarked, "The pendulum has swung: a hundred years earlier it was science that was struggling for legitimation against a discourse that was overwhelmingly philosophical and moral. Now it is the hegemony of that scientific approach that is under attack by others" (see current volume, p. 981).

This leads to a critical question about our field. Are we engaged in true paradigm shifts where one theoretical orientation to educational questions is supplanted with a more valid or developmentally more sophisticated orientation (Kuhn, 1996)? Or, is it more a case that perspectives or orientations move in and out of favor following various transformations and updates? From this latter viewpoint, educational psychology might be understood as the history of conceptual persuasion, if you will. Whose ideas and whose voices gain prominence? Whose voices are silenced or made barely audible?

If there were evidence of true paradigm shifts, then we would not expect prior theoretical perspectives such as behaviorism to reappear, even in modified form. This is clearly not the case. For instance, as Calfee observed, the cognitive orientation that predominated during the latter half of the 20th century "has not gone unchallenged": "Indeed, Roediger (2004) has claimed victory for Behaviorism, offering evidence that (a) all psychological researchers depend on observable behaviors as the source of data, and (b) behavioral methods have proven effective in dealing with a range of educational challenges, ranging from classroom management to the treatment of autism" (p. 32, this volume).

Others have remarked on the coming and goings of "new" educational orientations and perspectives that have had multiple lives within communities of educational research and educational practice (Alexander, Murphy, & Woods, 1996; Cuban, 1993). Consider debates mentioned by Calfee over sources of knowledge as being the "in the head" or "in the environment." These shifts have oscillated over centuries in attempts to explain human knowledge (Kant 1787/1963; Reynolds, Sinatra, & Jetton, 1996). We forecast it is not likely that such ontological and epistemological conundrums will find resolution in the near future.

So what does this contrast of reconceptualization versus reiteration imply for the next decade of educational psychology research? One clear message that we have espoused on prior occasions is the need for present and future generations of educational psychologists to ground themselves in their disciplinary histories (Alexander, 2003; Winne, 1999) The more we know about the history of the field and its cognate fields (e.g., developmental psychology, history, or mathematics), and the better we understand the roots of the specific arenas in which we immerse ourselves (e.g., motivation, technology, or assessment), then the less apt we are to reenact (unintentionally) that past. Again, we recognize that such reenactments, by virtue of the changing time and contexts, cannot be duplications of the past. But, unless we respect and critique what has come before, we risk reiterations that fail the test of historical analysis or that recoil in the harsh light of educational practice. As others have expressed (Berliner, 1993; Matthews, 1994; McDermott, 2003), we judge that researchers too often disassociated from the field's philosophical and psychological roots— the very roots that have given this field its character and direction.

We also do not want to be accused of wrongly glorifying our past. The field has unquestionably grown and developed as a community of practice. We do not advocate taking steps backward to contexts where the pure science of learning and teaching was held to be superior to the "messy" daily events in schools and out of school. We do not want to resurrect naïve beliefs that learning and teaching are context free and transpire outside the continuous presence of society or culture. We have matured beyond such simplistic notions. Nonetheless, the field risks too much if we do not comprehend how we have come to this position and do not at least attempt to unearth our pasts and trace our roots. We hold this especially critical for a community that does not abandon past theories or models but carries the ontological and epistemological beliefs of the past forward in forging contemporary theories and models.

INTERDISCIPLINARITY AND INDISTINGUISHABILITY

Berliner gallantly attempted to respond to a most perplexing question: With all the change in educational psychology over the centuries, and even in the decade from the first to second volumes of the Handbook, what has remained consistent about our field? How does that stable core help us understand what it means to be an educational psychologist? Berliner (this volume) explored that question through the following poignant example:

But if we look at our origins we see that the fundamental nature of our enterprise is about using psychological concepts and methods for understanding the four commonplaces of education that philosopher Joseph Schwab first made popular (1973): *someone* (a teacher, parent or a technological device) teaches *something* (how to fix a bicycle, two column addition with regrouping, the periodic table) to *someone else* (a student, novice, worker) in *some setting* (classroom, garden, assembly line). . . . Psychologizing the problems of practice, that is, making them more often the source of our inquiries, could eliminate the characteristic of irrelevance that history shows is as much essence in educational psychology as are our achievements in assessment or motivation.

When we combine Berliner's retrospective with Calfee's prospective on educational psychology, we can appreciate that this essence of educational psychology has recently stretched in many different directions in response to increasingly varied and complex questions, problems, and issues. What does this stretching and expansion bode for our field? Can the core of educational psychology hold with calls for even more diversification and metamorphosis?

The increasing influx into educational psychology of those rooted in alternative disciplines and apprenticed in diverse traditions, armed with new questions and methodologies, is simultaneously a source of strength and concern for the field. Those strengths include the potential for enhanced relevance and sustained presence about which Berliner and Calfee wrote in their opening chapters. But will it become even more difficult to perceive of educational psychology as an identifiable and distinguishable domain if interdisciplinarity grows unbounded? Will the four commonplaces that Schwab (1973) established as our core—someone teaching something to someone else in some setting—still be sufficient to anchor our identity? In the short run (i.e., the next decade or so), the outlook seems promising. But the picture becomes more difficult to discern when one peers deeper into the future. Will interdisciplinarity give way to indistinguishability?

As the editors of this report on the state of the art, we remain optimistic about the ability of educational psychology to embrace multiple perspectives, enfold diverse disciplinary orientations, and retain its core identify.

We have had the privilege of working closely with many renowned scholars, including those who contributed to this Handbook. We have also witnessed the vitality, intelligence, and creativity of the "up-and-coming generation" of educational psychologists. Who can doubt the future contributions of this community of practice when its members are so capable and committed?

We hypothesize the third edition of the *Handbook of Educational Psychology* will validate this prediction as it reinforces the past, current, and future contributions of educational psychology to questions of human learning and development. Taking our cue from Leon Lederman, we embrace uncertainty on this issue and anticipate with scientific curiosity the multitude of "discoveries" that await.

References

Alexander, P. A. (2003). Coming home: Educational psychology's philosophical pilgrimage [Special Issue on "Rediscovering the philosophical roots of educational psychology"]. *Educational Psychologist, 38*(3), 129–132.

Alexander, P. A., Murphy, P. K., & Woods, B. S. (1996). Of squalls and fathoms: Navigating the seas of educational innovation. *Educational Researcher, 25*(3), 31–36, 39.

Berliner, D. C. (1993). The 100-year journey of educational psychology: From interest, to disdain, to respect for practice. In T. K. Fagan & G. R. VandenBos (Eds.), *Exploring applied psychology: Origins and critical analysis*. Washington, DC: American Psychological Association.

Cronbach, L. J. (1975). Beyond the two disciplines of psychology. *American Psychologist, 30*, 116–127.

Cuban, L. (1993). *How teachers taught: Constancy and change in American classrooms, 1890–1980*. New York: Teachers College Press.

Kant, I. (1963). *Critique of pure reason* (N. Kemp Smith, trans.). London: Macmillan. (Original published in 1787).

Kuhn, T. S. (1996). *The structure of scientific revolutions* (3rd ed.). Chicago: University of Chicago Press.

Lederman, L. (1995). Why Bother? *The Nobel Legacy: 2 — PBS Video*. New York: Public Broadcasting Service.

Matthews, M. R. (1994). *Science teaching: The role of history and philosophy of science*. New York: Routledge.

McDermott, J. J. (2003). Hast any philosophy in thee, shepherd? *Educational Psychologist, 38*(3), 133–136.

Reynolds, R. E., Sinatra, G. M., & Jetton, T. L. (1996). Views of knowledge acquisition and representation: A continuum from experience centered to mind centered. *Educational Psychologist, 31*, 93–104.

Roediger, R. (2004, March). What happened to behaviorism? *Newspaper of the American Psychological Society, 17*(3), 5, 40-42.

Schwab, J. J. (1973). The practical 3: Translation into curriculum. *School Review, 81*, 501–522.

Winne, P. H. (1999). How to improve the credibility of research in education. *Issues in Education*, 5, 273–278.

AUTHOR INDEX

SUBJECT INDEX

Note *t* indicates tables, *f* indicates figures, *n* indicates notes

methodological issues, 227–229, 231–233, 826, 831–834, 919, 921
mindfulness and, 416
in mini-cultures of practice, 606
misconceptions and, 307, 309, 515
motivation and, 33, 335, 573, 782–783, 782*t*, 794, 976
multiple levels of, 231–232, 232*t*
of natural categories, 521–522
observational, 787–788
parental support for, 628–629
and participation, 332, 500
personality and, 174
perspectives on
adult learning, 127–128
andragogical model, 127
Carroll, John B., 19
cognitive, 812
conceptual change model, 308
conceptual collisions between, 229–231
constructivism, 246, 437
co-regulated learning models, 332–333
frames of inquiry, 915
individualism vs. collectivism, 676–677, 676*t*
learning by doing, 804
learning in context, 804–806
Select-Organize-Integrate (SOI) theory, 290–291, 291*f*, 295
situated learning theory, 21, 804
social cultural, 602–605, 605–608, 915
social learning theory, 805
synthesis of, 227–234
transformative, 127
portfolio evaluation, 832–834
poverty and, 221, 628
principles of, 229–231
Problem-Based Learning, 703–705, 828, 829*f*
problem solving and, 299
productive environments, 502
progress vs. long-term retention, 522
Project-Based Learning, 703, 705
race/ethnicity and, 628–629, 785–786
research on, 62, 909*t*, 919, 921
responsiveness-to-intervention and, 202
rote vs. meaningful, 289, 519
scaffolding and, 336–337, 520–521, 786–787, 813
schema and, 248
scientific reasoning, 811, 835–836
self-regulatory, 176–177, 750
situated, 332–333
social construction of, 603
social emotional, 171–172
social situations and, 226–228
spaced vs. massed practice, 519
specificity and schooling effect, 66–67
standards, 222, 797

strategies, 276–277, 572, 813
of teachers, 968–969
temperament and, 401
third spaces, 501
transfer, 214–215, 221, 221*n6*, 225, 230, 586–587, 698
zone of proximal development, 67, 518, 533, 786–787
Learning by Design, 702–703, 705
Learning disabilities
cooperative learning and, 189, 794–795
frames of inquiry and, 912
reading disabilities, 639
reading instruction and, 435, 448
self-regulated learning and, 907
strategy instruction with, 270, 274–275
tutoring, 790–791
visuospatial impairment and, 197–199
writing, 274–275
writing achievement and, 468
Learning Style Inventory (LSI), 841, 842*f*
Learning Together technique, 783
Learnlab, 228–229
Lesbian, gay, bisexual, transgendered (LGBT), 724
Lesson study in mathematics (Japan), 486–487
Letter knowledge, 69, 71
Lifelong learning, 116, 127–128, 132, 811, *see also* Adult education
LIFE project, 216–217, 231–233
Lifespan developmental perspective, 118–122
Life structure in age-based theory, 123
Linear functions, 869, 966
Linear logistic test model (LLTM), 938
Literacy, *see also* Reading; Writing
acquisition of, 67
adult, 116, 127–128, 130
among Hispanics, 616
children at risk, 430–431, 789
Chinese vs. U.S. emphasis on, 75
cross-language transfer, 580–581
learning specificity and, 67
media, 439, 446
National Reading Panel report, 67–68
No Child Left Behind (NCLB) Act of 2001 and, 68
parenting and, 66
Peer-Assisted Literacy Strategies, 430–431
preschool influence on, 64
vocabulary and, 69
Locus of control, 351–353
Log file analysis, 836–838
Logical positivism, *see* Positivism
Logics-in-use, *see* Frames of inquiry
Longitudinal studies
methodology, 827, 838, 867*f*, 868, 886–887
on patterns of activity, 837–838

on student learning, 940
on teacher learning, 967–970
Long-term memory
in Cattell-Horn-Carroll theory, 141, 148*t*
gender differences, 644
generation activities and, 519
knowledge models in, 251–255, 252*t*
learning and, 290–291, 291*f*
recall vs. transfer, 831
second language learning, 585–586
strategy use and, 266–267
writing and, 458, 460, 461
Low achievers, 334–335, 379, 430–431, 439–440, *see also* Children at risk

M

Machine cognitivist paradigm, 217*n2*
Mainstreaming, *see* Inclusion, research design on
Maintenance of strategies, 275, 280
Manipulatives and learning, 293
Map skills, 563–566, 910*t*
Maslow, Abraham, 351
Mastery goals
academic achievement and, 377
and affect, 382–383
approach/avoidance, 410*n*
competence beliefs and, 359
definition, 371
and fear of failure, 412
and need achievement, 412
performance goals vs., 176–177, 330, 334, 357–358, 371–372, 382, 410
school reform efforts and, 406
self-handicapping and, 377
utility of, 377
values and, 381
Mastery motivation theory, 359
Mathematics, *see also* Mathematics instruction
ability, 73, 649
accountability, 502–503
addition, 786
adolescent changes in valuing of, 94
African Americans and, 74, 497–498
American Indian/Alaskan Native and, 74, 497
American vs. East Asian children, 73, 486
assessment/accountability and, 77–79, 938
attachment and, 407
automaticity and, 292
avoidance and, 337–338
belongingness and, 657
calculator use, 292
career choice and ability in, 649
in China, 73–75, 480–481, 961
competence beliefs, 93
computer-based microworlds, 293